To our students, who give us hope that this work will make a difference

INTERNATIONAL AND TRANSNATIONAL CRIMINAL LAW

ASPEN PUBLISHERS

INTERNATIONAL AND TRANSNATIONAL CRIMINAL LAW

David Luban
University Professor
Georgetown University Law Center

Julie R. O'Sullivan
Professor of Law
Georgetown University Law Center

David P. Stewart
Visiting Professor of Law
Georgetown University Law Center

Wolters Kluwer
Law & Business

AUSTIN   BOSTON   CHICAGO   NEW YORK   THE NETHERLANDS

To contact Customer Care, e-mail customer.care@aspenpublishers.com, call 1-800-234-1660, fax 1-800-901-9075, or mail correspondence to:

Aspen Publishers
Attn: Order Department
PO Box 990
Frederick, MD 21705

Printed in the United States of America.

1 2 3 4 5 6 7 8 9 0

ISBN 978-0-7355-6214-1

Library of Congress Cataloging-in-Publication Data

Luban, David, 1949-
 International and transnational criminal law / David Luban, Julie R. O'Sullivan,
 David P. Stewart.
   p. cm.
 Includes index.
 ISBN 978-0-7355-6214-1
 1. Criminal law. 2. Criminal jurisdiction. 3. International offenses. 4. International criminal courts. I. O'Sullivan, Julie R., 1959- II. Stewart, David P. III. Title.

 K5015.4.L83 2010
 345 — dc22   2009040965

This book contains paper from well-managed forests to SFI standards.

About Wolters Kluwer Law & Business

Wolters Kluwer Law & Business is a leading provider of research information and workflow solutions in key specialty areas. The strengths of the individual brands of Aspen Publishers, CCH, Kluwer Law International and Loislaw are aligned within Wolters Kluwer Law & Business to provide comprehensive, in-depth solutions and expert-authored content for the legal, professional and education markets.

CCH was founded in 1913 and has served more than four generations of business professionals and their clients. The CCH products in the Wolters Kluwer Law & Business group are highly regarded electronic and print resources for legal, securities, antitrust and trade regulation, government contracting, banking, pension, payroll, employment and labor, and healthcare reimbursement and compliance professionals.

Aspen Publishers is a leading information provider for attorneys, business professionals and law students. Written by preeminent authorities, Aspen products offer analytical and practical information in a range of specialty practice areas from securities law and intellectual property to mergers and acquisitions and pension/benefits. Aspen's trusted legal education resources provide professors and students with high-quality, up-to-date and effective resources for successful instruction and study in all areas of the law.

Kluwer Law International supplies the global business community with comprehensive English-language international legal information. Legal practitioners, corporate counsel and business executives around the world rely on the Kluwer Law International journals, loose-leafs, books and electronic products for authoritative information in many areas of international legal practice.

Loislaw is a premier provider of digitized legal content to small law firm practitioners of various specializations. Loislaw provides attorneys with the ability to quickly and efficiently find the necessary legal information they need, when and where they need it, by facilitating access to primary law as well as state-specific law, records, forms and treatises.

Wolters Kluwer Law & Business, a unit of Wolters Kluwer, is headquartered in New York and Riverwoods, Illinois. Wolters Kluwer is a leading multinational publisher and information services company.

SUMMARY OF CONTENTS

CONTENTS

CHAPTER 2

| INTERNATIONAL LAW PRELIMINARIES | 27 |

CHAPTER 3

| INTERNATIONAL CRIMINAL TRIBUNALS: FROM NUREMBERG TO THE HAGUE — AND BEYOND | 71 |

PART II

PROCEDURAL ISSUES IN TRANSNATIONAL PRACTICE   133

CHAPTER 4

**COMPARATIVE CRIMINAL PROCEDURE AND
SENTENCING**   135

CHAPTER 5

JURISDICTION   169

CHAPTER 6

CHAPTER 7

U.S. CONSTITUTIONAL RIGHTS IN A TRANSNATIONAL CONTEXT

CHAPTER 8

OBTAINING EVIDENCE ABROAD

CHAPTER 9

INTERNATIONAL EXTRADITION AND ITS ALTERNATIVES   389

CHAPTER 10

THE EFFECT OF TREATY RIGHTS, AS CONSTRUED BY INTERNATIONAL TRIBUNALS, ON DOMESTIC CRIMINAL ENFORCEMENT: THE DEATH PENALTY   441

PART III

TRANSNATIONAL CRIME

CHAPTER 11

ORGANIZED CRIME

CHAPTER 12

TRAFFICKING IN PERSONS, DRUGS, AND ARMS   537

CHAPTER 13

MONEY LAUNDERING   579

CHAPTER 14

CORRUPTION   621

CHAPTER 15

TERRORISM   669

CHAPTER 18

DEFENSES TO INTERNATIONAL CRIMINAL PROSECUTIONS — 917

CHAPTER 21

| WAR CRIMES | **1037** |

CHAPTER 22

TORTURE AND CRUEL, INHUMAN, AND DEGRADING TREATMENT OR PUNISHMENT   1081

CHAPTER 23

SEXUAL VIOLENCE   1143

CHAPTER 24

ALTERNATIVES TO PROSECUTION AFTER ATROCITY: A SURVEY OF OTHER TRANSITIONAL JUSTICE MECHANISMS   1191

PREFACE

In the past two decades, few legal subjects have grown in importance more dramatically than *international criminal law*, which we define as crimes proscribed by international law, whether or not they are also criminalized in states' domestic laws, and which are often prosecuted in international or hybrid international-national tribunals. International criminal law represents one of humankind's boldest ambitions: to control large-scale violence through law. The principal origins of this discipline are found, of course, in the post-WWII Nuremberg and Tokyo Tribunals, but international criminal law lay largely dormant for decades. The creation of international tribunals in the early 1990s transformed the legal landscape. Responding to nightmarish atrocities in Rwanda and the former Yugoslavia, the United Nations created the ad hoc Tribunals, which expanded the scope of both criminal law and international law in ways that seemed like a pipe dream only a few years before. Soon other tribunals followed, including those addressing crimes committed in Sierra Leone, Cambodia, Timor Leste, and Lebanon. After hard negotiations, the International Criminal Court (ICC) began operating in 2002. Within the space of a few years, a large jurisprudence of accountability for mass atrocities sprang into existence, and the development of this body of law shows no sign of abating.

For centuries, states have cooperated in bringing individual perpetrators to justice, for example through bilateral extradition treaties and other mechanisms for promoting mutual assistance in criminal matters. Over the past two or three decades, however, globalization has expanded the importance of domestic criminal law applied to conduct across borders. We call this *transnational criminal law*. Transnational and international criminal law often overlap, and some domestic criminal statutes originated in international law. But transnational criminal jurisprudence is not the same as the jurisprudence of the international tribunals. Transnational criminal law includes states' extraterritorial use of their own laws — against, for example, money laundering, corruption, torture, terrorism, and trafficking — in their own courts. It presents some of the same practical challenges as international law enforcement — for example, securing the presence of a defendant for trial and obtaining extraterritorial evidence. But it sometimes raises unique challenges — for example, issues of immunity that do not arise under international criminal law. Our ambition in this book is to cover both the international and transnational aspects of this fascinating and sometimes heartbreaking field.

Perhaps because international and transnational criminal law enforcement is so dynamic and practically important, it greatly interests students. We offer this casebook in the belief that it provides (1) a unique range of coverage and (2) a mix of perspectives that students will appreciate.

First, in terms of scope, the book covers the central features of both international and transnational criminal law. In covering these subjects, we necessarily include extensive analysis of what could be conceived of as yet another category of cross-border criminal law—*treaty crimes*—that we treat essentially as a hybrid of the first two. In our view, treaty crimes consist of activity declared criminal by international law (like international criminal law), but enforced through the domestic criminal law of the treaty's states parties (like transnational criminal law). Although this book is designed primarily for U.S. classrooms, we believe it important, where possible, to draw on the laws and judicial decisions from countries other than the United States if for no other reason than to challenge U.S. students to re-examine familiar rules and cultural assumptions. Finally, our international, transnational, and comparative focus is applied not only to substantive crimes, but also to procedural issues of importance to this area of practice.

We recognize the ambition reflected in attempting to cover international and transnational substantive and procedural criminal law in a way that is comprehensive, accessible, and compelling. And we assume that no professor could cover all of these subjects in one course. Our hope is that the book will meet the needs of most students, while providing professors the flexibility to craft a curriculum that reflects their own interests. The coauthors have road-tested all of the chapters. Our teaching reviews indicate that various students prefer different portions of the class. They have, however, universally appreciated the melding of international, transnational, and comparative materials in one course.

Second, the different perspectives reflected throughout these pages derive principally from our own varied academic interests and professional experiences. David Luban, a legal theorist and ethicist, has written on war, terrorism, and international crime. His interests in history, and his work in professional responsibility, also permeate the book. Julie O'Sullivan is a former criminal defense lawyer and federal prosecutor; her academic focus has been on federal white-collar crime. Her practical perspectives find voice not only in the procedural and transnational portions of the book, but also in chapters that deal more generally with the application of theory to law on the ground. David Stewart practiced international law for three decades in the U.S. Department of State's Legal Adviser's Office with experience in the negotiation and drafting of international agreements, as well as policy issues in the international human rights and criminal law arenas (among others). His experience in diplomacy and international law outside the criminal sphere are reflected throughout these chapters.

We discovered that, despite our different backgrounds, we agreed on what the book should cover and on what basic approach to take in covering it. That approach is, of necessity, both practical and theoretical. We believe that students should be provided with a firm foundation in the law and practical realities of international and transnational criminal practice. At the same time, to equip them to respond effectively to further developments, students must be exposed to the history, policy, and theory of that law and practice. We should note that—as might be expected given the scope of this work and the varied experiences of its authors—we occasionally viewed the same issues very differently. Although each chapter has one and sometimes two principal authors, all of us have carefully reviewed each other's work, sometimes with spirited critiques and always with multiple revisions. We believe that ultimately these differences contribute to a challenging and balanced book that will appeal to a range of professors and students.

Some additional background regarding our choice of topics, and ordering of those topics, may be in order. To make the book self-contained and accessible to law students at all levels of preparation, we include introductory chapters on the nature of criminal law and the benefits and challenges of attempting cross-border criminal accountability (Chapter 1), the fundamentals of public international law (Chapter

2), and the historical development of international and hybrid criminal tribunals with some attention to domestic prosecutions (Chapter 3). We do not require, as a prerequisite for the course, that students have taken substantive criminal law, criminal procedure, or even international law. We have found that by covering these preliminary chapters, students are ready to tackle the more advanced topics that follow. Indeed, we have successfully taught this material as a first-year elective more than half a dozen times. We strongly encourage professors to start with Chapter 1, even if the students enrolled in a course have taken substantive criminal law, because it identifies themes and questions that will echo throughout the course and that are revisited in the concluding chapter.

The second part of the book focuses on topics — many of them, for lack of a better word, "procedural" in nature — that have particular relevance to transnational practice. These include comparative criminal procedure and sentencing (Chapter 4), jurisdiction (Chapter 5), immunities (Chapter 6), U.S. constitutional rights in a transnational context (Chapter 7), obtaining evidence abroad (Chapter 8), and international extradition and its alternatives (Chapter 9). We also include a discussion of the effect of treaty rights on domestic criminal enforcement — covering also the important subject of interpretation in international law — in the context of extradition to meet the death penalty and the international and U.S. litigation involving consular notification issues (Chapter 10).

Two notes are appropriate with respect to Part II of the book. First, we have found that a number of these chapters, though perhaps most pertinent to transnational practice, should find their way into a class that focuses on international (rather than only transnational) criminal law. Comparative criminal procedure and sentencing, jurisdiction, immunity, and extradition are four logical candidates. Second, our focus in some of these chapters is on U.S. law, while in others we include separate sections on U.S. law. We believe this approach is practical and natural given the focus of this part. Graduates who pursue careers in international criminal justice will often work for the U.S. government, agencies, or law firms that represent foreign clients in U.S. courts. Federal procedural rules and statutes, applied transnationally, will be their daily fare.

The third portion of the book focuses on substantive transnational crimes, including organized crime (Chapter 11); trafficking in persons, drugs, and arms (Chapter 12); money laundering (Chapter 13); corruption (Chapter 14); and terrorism (Chapter 15). We selected a variety of transnational crimes — all of which are also "treaty crimes" — to permit those who adopt our conception of the course to pick among these offerings according to their interests. Others who wish to focus only on transnational crime could create an entire course out of Chapters 1 through 13. The crimes we chose reflect varieties of criminal conduct that have serious implications for international stability, security, and development. Most of these chapters include substantial comparative and international elements, focusing not only on U.S. domestic law, but also on cognate offenses from at least one other country and applicable international treaty regimes.

Although those committed to a strictly international criminal law focus may be tempted to forgo assignments in Part III, we believe that it is very helpful to expose students to at least some of these transnational materials. First, it is likely that students, if they practice in this area, will practice in the transnational sphere. Second, students need a firm grounding in what interests can — as a legal, practical, or political matter — be effectively vindicated through domestic prosecutions before they can evaluate the necessity for, or efficacy of, an international criminal law regime. Finally, as we believe the materials will demonstrate, it is increasingly difficult to separate "domestic" from "international" criminal law and enforcement. The globalization of criminal activity, the multiplication of international agreements concerning criminal law and enforcement, and international tribunals' willingness to apply international human rights norms to domestic processes mean that the distinction between truly "international" law and municipal law is quickly blurring.

In Part IV we turn to international criminal law *stricto sensu,* commencing with a detailed examination of the structure and functioning of the International Criminal Court (Chapter 16), applicable modes of participation and *mens rea* (Chapter 17), and possible defenses (Chapter 18). Chapters focusing on the great international crimes follow: crimes against humanity (Chapter 19), genocide (Chapter 20), and war crimes (Chapter 21). (NB: The crime of aggression—not yet defined for purposes of the International Criminal Court—is treated in our discussion of Nuremberg in Chapter 3, the ICC in Chapter 16, and war crimes in Chapter 21; once the ICC's Assembly of States Parties reaches agreement on this subject for purposes of the Rome Statute, it may merit its own chapter.) We chose to include two chapters on particular types of major international crimes—torture (Chapter 22) and sexual violence (Chapter 23)—because of their current importance *and* because they provide effective platforms to explore other themes or legal issues. For example, the torture chapter provides an excellent vehicle for exploring lawyers' professional roles and responsibilities in advising on, as well as litigating, issues in international and transnational criminal law. The sexual violence chapter details the historical neglect of this horrific category of crime and illustrates how international criminal norms can evolve—being translated first into legal proscriptions and ultimately into accountability.

We conclude the book in Chapter 24 by exploring means other than criminal prosecutions that have been used to address the aftermath of societal conflict. We focus on truth and reconciliation commissions, but also talk about lustration, civil remedies, and their variations. This chapter recognizes that societies emerging from mass violence have a variety of aims—including rebuilding their social fabric—and may require remedies or mechanisms in addition to, or in lieu of, criminal proceedings. Special emphasis is given to the question of context, that is, to the truism that there is no one-size-fits-all means of restoring peace and achieving justice in the aftermath of atrocity. Attention must be devoted to the particular circumstances of the given society at issue—including that society's history, culture, resources, security and political situation, priorities, and needs. This chapter permits students to return to some of the fundamental issues posed in the first chapter, such as how can "justice" be achieved after atrocity? What communities or audiences are addressed through these prosecutions, and where the international community and the victimized society have different interests, which should prevail? What are the purposes of criminal trials in traumatized societies? Are those purposes practically achievable given the nature of criminal law and international politics? What crimes should be subject to international sanction; when should they be investigated and prosecuted in national, hybrid, or international tribunals; and why? Should "justice" achieved through criminal accountability ever be sacrificed to achieve societal peace and security?

We recognize that international and transnational criminal law raise many hot-button political issues. Given how closely the subject connects with international diplomacy and armed conflict, it could hardly be otherwise. Human rights groups contend with states over issues of international criminal accountability. But they also contend with each other, just as developing states contend with developed states, former colonies with former colonialists, internationalists with nationalists, peace groups with war fighters, lawyers with politicians, and defendants' rights advocates with champions of accountability. Our aim has been to present all points of view as fairly and objectively as possible.

Nearly every week brings new wrinkles and new developments in international and transnational criminal law. It is one of the fastest-evolving legal subjects, perhaps because it is still so young. Many of the cases and issues in this book are headline grabbers that students will instantly recognize. Some no doubt will be yesterday's news by the time the book is published. A Web site accompanies the book, www.internationalcriminallaw.com, and we will do our level best to keep it current.

The new and rapidly changing nature of this discipline also demands of authors a large measure of humility. As noted, we have taught this subject many times and have tried to include within this text all that we think is necessary and important. We invite readers to let us know if they think that the selection or ordering of subject matters is deficient. Also as noted, we have tried to be both accurate and evenhanded in our presentation of contested or controversial subjects. Here, too, we wish to hear from you if you have objections to our presentation. Finally, although this text is designed primarily for U.S. classrooms, we have taken pains to include non-U.S. materials and to introduce comparative elements wherever possible. We wish to avoid a U.S.-centered view of the world, and strongly believe that students will understand their own legal culture, and international law, best when they also understand alternative national approaches. Any and all suggestions about sources we have overlooked would be most gratefully received. We can be contacted by e-mail at david.luban@gmail.com, osullij1@law.georgetown.edu, and stewartd@ law.georgetown.edu.

ACKNOWLEDGMENTS

Producing this book has been immeasurably assisted by the hard work and moral support of our research assistants: Mark Aziz, Laura Brookover, Vernon Cassin, Devon Chaffee, Jennifer Clark, Catherine Foster, Sophia Heller, Daniel Hornal, Matthew King, Lorinda I. Laryea, Jason Manning, Anna Melamud, Justin Murray, Jennifer O'Connor, Ben Patton, Ned Sebelius, Rebecca Smallwood, Jonathan Stewart, Emily J. Sweeney-Samuelson, Pierre-thomas Taponier, Anne Taylor, Markus Wagner (now himself a law professor), and Yvette Wood. Georgetown's fabulous law librarians and their staff have been indispensible at every stage of the project.

We are also grateful to George Taft, Larry May, Mark Osiel, and Robert Sloane for their substantive and stylistic comments about several of our chapters. We owe a particular debt to Chimène Keitner, who has taught from our materials and given us careful detailed comments on much of the manuscript. Anonymous reviewers for Aspen Publishers provided helpful comments on early drafts of the chapters.

We are grateful as well to Barbara Roth, our excellent editor at Aspen Publishing; Lisa Wehrle, who meticulously copyedited the sprawling manuscript; and Peter Skagestad, who has patiently produced the book.

Above all, we thank our students, to whom this book is dedicated — our chief inspiration, and our reason for writing the book in the first place. Their enthusiasm for the subject, their comments on the many early drafts of chapters, and their informed and intelligent questions in class have shaped the chapters significantly. Many of our students have had extensive backgrounds in human rights and humanitarian organizations, intelligence work, the military, or international tribunals. Thus we have regularly been able to count on the fact that someone in the classroom knows more than we do on many topics. Needless to say, all errors in the book are our responsibility, although we each reserve the right to blame our co-authors.

Finally, we would like to thank the following authors, publishers, and copyright holders for their permission to reproduce excerpts from their works in this casebook, including:

Diane Marie Amann, Application of the Fifth Amendment to U.S. Constitution in International Context — Fear of Foreign Prosecution as Ground for Invoking Privilege Against Self-Incrimination — Relevance of Growing International Law Enforcement Cooperation — Role of U.S. Judiciary in Foreign Relations, 92 Am. J. Intl. L. 759, 763 (2004). Reprinted with the permission of the American Society of International Law and the author.

Kai Ambos, Article 25: Individual Criminal Responsibility, in Commentary on the Rome Statute of the International Criminal Court: Observers' Notes, Article by Article 438 (Otto Triffterer ed., 1999), copyright © by Nomos Verlagsgesellschaft mbH & Co., KG. Reprinted with the permission of the publisher.

From EICHMANN IN JERUSALEM by Hannah Arendt, copyright © 1963, 1964 by Hannah Arendt, copyright renewed © 1991, 1992 by Lotte Kohler. Used by permission of Viking Penguin, a division of Penguin Group (USA) Inc.

Miriam J. Aukerman, Extraordinary Evil, Ordinary Crime: A Framework for Understanding Transitional Justice, 15 Harv. Hum. Rts. J. 39 (2002). Reprinted with the permission of the publisher.

Orna Ben-Naftali & Keren Michaeli, Public Committee Against Torture in *Israel v. Government of Israel*, 101 Am. J. Intl. L. 459 (2007). Reprinted with the permission of the American Society of International Law.

Richard B. Bilder & Detlev F. Vagts, Editorial, Speaking Law to Power: Lawyers and Torture 98 Am. J. Intl. L. 689 (2004). Reprinted with the permission of the American Society of International Law and the authors.

Rosa Ehrenreich Brooks, Law in the Heart of Darkness: Atrocity & Duress, 43 Va. J. Intl. L. 861 (2003). Reprinted with the permission of the author.

Stefan D. Cassella, The Forfeiture of Property Involved in Money Laundering Offenses, 7 Buff. Crim. L. Rev. 583, 585-586 (2004), copyright © by University of California Press and Buffalo Criminal Law Review. Reprinted by permission of the author and the publisher.

Ann B. Ching, Comment, Evolution of the Command Responsibility Doctrine in Light of the *Celebici* Decision of the ICTY, 25 N.C. J. Intl. L. & Com. Reg. 167, 186-205 (1999). Reprinted with the permission of the author.

Roger S. Clark, Article 122: Amendments to Provisions of an Institutional Nature, in Commentary on the Rome Statute of the International Criminal Court: Observers' Notes, Article by Article 1275 (Otto Triffterer ed., 1999), copyright © by Nomos Verlagsgesellschaft mbH & Co., KG. Reprinted with the permission of the publisher.

Roger S. Clark, The United Nations Convention Against Transnational Organized Crime, 50 Wayne L. Rev. 161 (2004). Reprinted with the permission of The Wayne Law Review and the author.

Allison M. Danner & Jenny S. Martinez, Guilty Associations: Joint Criminal Enterprise, Command Responsibility, and the Development of International Criminal Law, 93 Cal. L. Rev. 75 (2005), copyright © 2005 by the California Law Review, Inc. Reprinted from California Law Review Vol. 93 No. 1, by permission of the California Law Review, Inc. and the authors.

Margaret McAuliffe deGuzman, Article 21: Applicable Law, in Commentary on the Rome Statute of the International Criminal Court: Observers' Notes, Article by Article 438 (Otto Triffterer ed., 1999), copyright © by Nomos Verlagsgesellschaft mbH & Co., KG. Reprinted with the permission of the publisher.

Richard Falk, Accountability for War Crimes and the Legacy of Nuremberg, in War Crimes and Collective Wrongdoing: A Reader (Aleksander Jókic ed., 2001). Reprinted with the permission of the publisher, Blackwell Publishing.

Glenn Frankel, Belgian War Crimes Law Undone by Its Global Reach; Cases Against Political Figures Sparked Crises. From The Washington Post, September 30, 2003, copyright © 2002 The Washington Post. All rights reserved. Used by permission and protected by the Copyright Laws of the United States. The printing, copying, redistribution, or retransmission of the Material without express written permission is prohibited.

Kenneth S. Gallant, Politics, Theory and Institutions: Three Reasons Why International Criminal Defence Is Hard, and What Might Be Done About One of Them, 14 Crim. L.F. 317 (2003), copyright © by Springer. Reprinted with kind permission of Springer Science and Business Media and the author.

Richard J. Goldstone & Janine Simpson, Evaluating the Role of the International Criminal Court as a Legal Response to Terrorism, 16 Harv. Hum. Rts. J. 13 (2003), copyright © 2003 The President and Fellows of Harvard College and the Harvard Human Rights Journal. Reprinted with the permission of the publisher.

Henry M. Hart, Jr., The Aims of the Criminal Law, 23 Law & Contemp. Probs. 401 (1958), copyright © 1958 by Duke University. Reprinted with the permission of Duke University School of Law.

John Hasnas, Once More unto the Breach: The Inherent Liberalism of the Criminal Law and Liability for Attempting the Impossible, 54 Hastings L.J. 1 (2002), copyright © 2002 by University of California, Hastings College of the Law. Reprinted from HASTINGS LAW JOURNAL, Volume 54, Number 1, November 2002, 1-77, by permission of the publisher and the author.

Priscilla B. Hayner, Unspeakable Truths: Confronting State Terror and Atrocity 14 (Routledge 2001). Reprinted with the permission of the author.

Michael Ignatieff, Lemkin's Word, The New Republic (Feb, 26, 2001). Reprinted with the permission of the author.

Michael Ignatieff, The Torture Wars, The New Republic (Apr. 20, 2002). Reprinted with the permission of the author.

Mark W. Janis, An Introduction to International Law. Reprinted/Adapted with the permission of Aspen Publishers, from Mark W. Janis, An Introduction to International Law, Third edition, pp. 80-81, copyright © 1999.

Donald Kommers, "Part III, 7: The Right to Personality," in *The Constitutional Jurisprudence of the Federal Republic of Germany* (2nd ed., 1997), pp. 314-319. Copyright, 1997, Duke University Press. All rights reserved. Used by permission of the publisher.

Martti Koskenniemi, Between Impunity and Show Trials, 6 Max Planck Yrbk. of U.N. Law 1 (2002), by permission of the Publisher, Koninklijke Brill NV, and the author.

Charles Krauthammer, It's Time to Be Honest About Doing Terrible Things, The Weekly Standard, Vol. 11, Issue 12 (Dec. 5, 2005). Reprinted with the permission of the author.

Sarel Kandell Kromer, The Rwandan Reconciliation, Wash. Post, Oct. 16, 2005, at B02. Reprinted with the permission of the author.

Chandran Kukathas, Genocide and Group Rights (unpublished manuscript 2006). Reprinted with the permission of the author.

Peggy Kuo, Esq., Prosecuting Crimes of Sexual Violence in an International Tribunal, 34 Case W. Res. J. Intl. L. 305, 308 (2002). Reprinted with the permission of the author and the publisher.

Peter Landesman, A Woman's Work, N.Y. Times Magazine (Sept. 15, 2002), copyright © 2002, Peter Landesman. Reprinted by permission.

Doug Linder, The Subsequent Nuremberg Trials: An Overview, *available at* http://www.law.umkc.edu/faculty/projects/ftrials/nuremberg/subsequenttrials.html. Reprinted with the permission of the author.

David Luban, The Legacies of Nuremberg, in Legal Modernism 336, 341-342 (1994), copyright © by the University of Michigan 1994. Originally published in 54 Social Research 779-829 (1987). Reprinted with the permission of the Journal of Social Research and The University of Michigan Press.

David Luban, Liberalism, Torture, and the Ticking Time Bomb, 91 Va. L. Rev. 1425 (2005), copyright © Virginia Law Review Association. Reprinted with the permission of the Virginia Law Review Association.

David Luban, A Theory of Crimes Against Humanity, 29 Yale J. Intl. L. 85, 86-91, 111-113, 117-119 (2004). Reprinted with the permission of The Yale Journal of International Law.

David Luban, The War on Terrorism and the End of Human Rights, 22 Phil. & Pub. Poly. Q., no. 3, Summer 2002, pp. 9-14. Reprinted with the permission of the author.

Jane Mayer, A Deadly Interrogation: Can the C.I.A. Legally Kill a Prisoner? The New Yorker 46 (Nov. 14, 2005). Reprinted with the permission of the author.

Jane Mayer, The Memo: How an Internal Effort to Ban Abuse and Torture of Detainees Was Thwarted, The New Yorker (Feb. 27, 2006). Reprinted with the permission of the author.

Jane Mayer, Outsourcing Torture: The Secret History of America's "Extraordinary Rendition" Program, The New Yorker (Feb. 14, 2005). Reprinted with the permission of the author.

Model Penal Code, copyright © 1962 by the American Law Institute. Reprinted with permission. All rights reserved.

Herbert V. Morais, Fighting International Crime and Its Financing: The Importance of Following a Coherent Global Strategy Based on the Rule of Law, 50 Vill. L. Rev. 583 (2005). Reprinted with the permission of Villanova Law Review.

Moises Naim, ILLICIT: How Smugglers, Traffickers and Copycats Are Hijacking the Global Economy (2006). Reprinted with the permission of the author.

Frank Neubacher, How Can It Happen That Horrendous State Crimes Are Perpetrated? Journal of International Criminal Justice, Volume 4 (2006), 787-799, by permission of Oxford University Press.

Jens David Ohlin, Applying the Death Penalty to Crimes of Genocide, 99 Am. J. Intl. L. 747 (2005). Reproduced with permission from The American Society of International Law and the author.

Mark Osiel, Mass Atrocity, Collective Memory, and the Law 1-2, 60-62, 65-67 (1997), copyright © 1997 by Transaction Publishers. Reprinted by permission of the publisher.

Photo Archive at the United States Holocaust Memorial Museum. The views or opinions expressed in this book, and the context in which the images are used, do not necessarily reflect the views or policy of, nor imply approval or endorsement by, the United States Holocaust Memorial Museum.

Donald K. Piragoff, Article 30: Mental Element, in Commentary on the Rome Statute of the International Criminal Court: Observers' Notes, Article by Article 438 (Otto Triffterer ed., 1999), copyright © by Nomos Verlagsgesellschaft mbH & Co., KG. Reprinted with the permission of the publisher.

Eric Posner & Adrian Vermeule, A "Torture" Memo and Its Tortuous Critics, Wall Street Journal, July 6, 2004. Copyright © Dow Jones & Co., Inc. Reprinted with permission.

Research in International Law Under the Auspices of the Faculty of the Harvard Law School—Jurisdiction with Respect to Crime, 29 Am. J. Intl. L. 435, 519-520 (Supp. 1935). Reprinted with the permission of the American Society of International Law.

Restatement (Third) of the Foreign Relations Law of the United States, copyright © 1987 by the American Law Institute. Reprinted with permission. All rights reserved.

Eric Rosand, Security Council Resolution 1373, the Counter-Terrorism Committee, and the Fight Against Terrorism 97 Am. J. Intl. L. 333, 333-336, 337-340 (2003). Reprinted with the permission of the American Society of International Law.

Tina Rosenberg, Overcoming the Legacies of Dictatorship. Reprinted by permission of FOREIGN AFFAIRS, (Volume 74, May/June 1995). Copyright © 1995 by the Council on Foreign Relations, Inc., www.ForeignAff.airs.org.

Boaz Sangero, Are All Forms of Joint Crime Really "Organized Crime"? On the New Israeli Combating Criminal Organizations Law and Parallel Legislation in the U.S. and Other Countries, 29 Loy. L.A. Intl. & Comp. L. Rev. 61 (2007). Reprinted with permission of the publisher.

David J. Scheffer, U.S. Sabotages International Court at Its Peril, Seattle Post-Intelligencer, Feb. 1, 2004. Reprinted with the permission of the author.

Kim Lane Scheppele, The International State of Emergency: Challenges to Constitutionalism After September 11 (unpublished manuscript 2008). Reprinted with the permission of the author.

Robert D. Sloane, The Expressive Capacity of International Punishment: The Limits of the National Law Analogy and the Potential of International Criminal Law, 43 Stan. J. Intl. L. 39 (2007), copyright © by Stanford University. Reprinted with the permission of the Stanford Journal of International Law and the author.

Abraham Sofaer, No Exceptions, Wall Street Journal, Nov. 26, 2005, at A11. Reprinted with the permission of the author.

Gary D. Solis, Abu Ghraib — Another Black Hole? Journal of International Criminal Justice, Volume 2 (2004), 988-998, by permission of Oxford University Press.

David P. Stewart, Internationalizing the War on Drugs: The UN Convention Against Illicit Traffic in Narcotic Drugs and Psychotropic Substances, 18 Denv. J. Intl. L. & Poly. 387 (1990). Reprinted with the permission of the Denver Journal of International Law and Policy and the author.

Robert Tarun, Basics of the Foreign Corrupt Practices Act, April 2006 Edition. Reprinted with the permission of the author.

From THE ANATOMY OF THE NUREMBERG TRIALS by Telford Taylor, copyright © 1992 by Telford Taylor. Used by permission of Alfred A. Knopf, a division of Random House, Inc.

Otto Triffterer, Article 10, in Commentary on the Rome Statute of the International Criminal Court: Observers' Notes, Article by Article 317 (Otto Triffterer ed., 1999), copyright © by Nomos Verlagsgesellschaft mbH & Co., KG. Reprinted with the permission of the publisher.

Richard Vernon, What Is Crime Against Humanity?, 10 J. Pol. Phil. 231, 241-246 (2002), copyright © 2002 by Blackwell Publishing Ltd. Reproduced with permission of Blackwell Publishing Ltd.

Patricia M. Wald, Accountability for War Crimes: What Roles for National, International, and Hybrid Tribunals?, 98 Am. Socy. Intl. L. Proc. 192 (2004), reprinted with permission of the publisher.

Patricia McGowan Wald, The Omarska Trial — A War Crimes Tribunal Close-Up, 57 SMU L. Rev. 271 (2004), copyright © by Southern Methodist University. Reprinted with the permission of SMU Law Review and the author.

Ruth Wedgwood, Slobodan Milosevic's Last Waltz, N.Y. Times, Mar. 12, 2007, reprinted with the permission of the New York Times.

Edward M. Wise, RICO and Its Analogues: Some Comparative Considerations, 27 Syracuse J. Intl. L. & Com. 303, 321 (2000). Reprinted with the permission of the Syracuse Journal of International Law and Commerce.

INTERNATIONAL AND TRANSNATIONAL
CRIMINAL LAW

PART
I

Introduction

CHAPTER
1

The Idea of International
Criminal Law

This chapter has a simple and straightforward goal: to introduce the subject of the book and to sketch the background you need to make sense of the materials that follow. First, we explain what the study of international criminal law encompasses. Second, we provide a preliminary sketch of what gives criminal law its unique characteristics. In the next chapter, we offer a second preliminary sketch, this one of the basics of international law.

Each of these subjects is a large one, and the materials in these two chapters offer no more than the ABCs of the subject. As the book proceeds, we will flesh out each of these sketches with more detail.

A. WHAT IS INTERNATIONAL CRIMINAL LAW?

At bottom, international criminal law is just what the name suggests: It consists of criminal law applied across national borders. But this encompasses several different legal regimes.

1. Transnational Criminal Law

The first, which we call *transnational criminal law*, consists of the part of any nation's domestic criminal law "which regulates actions or events that transcend national frontiers."[1] The concept is very simple. A state[2] such as the United States has laws against crimes such as bank fraud. If a U.S. national, in the United States, commits bank fraud against a U.S. bank, no transnational issue arises, and ordinary domestic criminal law applies. But what if a Canadian, in Canada, commits fraud against a U.S. bank, perhaps by hacking into its computers? In that case, the perpetrator has presumably violated Canadian law — but what of U.S. law? Can the U.S. legal system reach

---

1. Phillip C. Jessup, Transnational Law 2 (1956).
2. As explained in more detail in the next chapter, the word *state* in international law refers to nations or countries.

the Canadian's conduct in Canada? That is a question of transnational criminal law. We will study many such questions. For example:

1. Does the U.S. bank fraud statute regulate conduct committed in Canada?
2. Do U.S. courts have jurisdiction over such conduct?
3. What, if anything, can U.S. police do to arrest the Canadian suspect?
4. If Canadian police arrest the suspect, can he be extradited to the United States?
5. Do U.S. constitutional rights (such as the right against compelled self-incrimination) apply to the Canadian in Canada?
6. Does it matter whether his conduct is also a crime under Canadian law, and, if it does, which nation's legal system gets priority?
7. What are the mechanics of evidence gathering in a foreign country?
8. What should Canada do if the punishment the suspect faces in the United States would be grossly excessive (or, in the case of the death penalty, outlawed) under Canadian law?

These are only a few of the questions that arise.

In an era of globalization, transnational crimes—that is, crimes committed across borders—have proliferated. Organized crime operates with the sophistication and cosmopolitanism of vast multinational corporations—and some multinational corporations engage in crime. Vast underworld networks exist for trafficking in narcotics, prostitutes, slaves, weapons, stolen goods, diamonds, nuclear contraband, international terror, and laundered money. Identity theft, within a matter of minutes, can put your credit card information in the hands of a hacker half a world away. Much of transnational criminal law has evolved from the decades of efforts by national governments to secure international cooperation and assistance in law enforcement against crimes committed by foreigners. States are jealous of their own borders, prerogatives, and jurisdictions. But, step by step and agreement by agreement, an infrastructure of international legal assistance has developed, and these institutions have spurred states' efforts to "globalize" their own criminal law.

2. International Crimes

The second great division of international criminal law might be called *international criminal law in the strict sense*—henceforth, we will simply say "international criminal law" for short, as distinguished from transnational criminal law. This refers to wrongs that are criminalized under international law, whether or not they are also criminalized in states' domestic laws. This category of crimes is small and to date consists only of the "great crimes": crimes against humanity, genocide, war crimes, and, at least in principle, the crime of aggression. These are the great crimes because they generally consist of mass atrocities that show up, glowing in infamy, on the radar of world politics. Often, these crimes cannot effectively be prosecuted or repressed by the territorial state where they are committed, either because the state itself has perpetrated them or because its government has collapsed in civil war, in anarchy, or through foreign conquest. These crimes may be tried either by international tribunals or, under some jurisdictional theories, by hybrid (mixed international and domestic) or purely domestic tribunals.

3. Treaty-Based Domestic Crimes

A third category, overlapping with the first two, consists of activity declared criminal by international treaties, but enforced under the domestic law of states that join the treaties. Treaties sometimes criminalize conduct because states recognize that it is international in character and can be attacked only through international cooperation. Such conduct includes air piracy and hijacking, counterfeiting, terrorism, trafficking in women and children, and narcotics trafficking. We have already mentioned that many of these are transnational crimes: They violate some states' domestic criminal laws, but they must be enforced across borders. But others were criminalized domestically only after the international community agreed on treaties to suppress them.

Typically, these treaties require their parties to enact domestic criminal laws against the activities, to grant themselves jurisdiction to try such crimes even when they are committed abroad, and to participate in international enforcement by agreeing to either extradite or prosecute suspected criminals in their custody. As the name suggests, treaty-based domestic crimes blend properties of transnational and international crimes. Like the "great crimes," treaty-based crimes are objects of international concern, and law enforcement efforts are coordinated through international law and mechanisms. Like transnational crimes, statutory prohibitions of these acts are part of domestic law, and domestic rather than international tribunals enforce the laws. Although the distinction is somewhat artificial, we classify them separately from the other two categories because the treaties that drive the enforcement efforts are entirely international, but the enforcement efforts themselves are conducted under the auspices of national law.

According to one noted authority, "international crimes" — encompassing both the international and treaty-based domestic categories described here — consist of conduct prohibited by multilateral treaties covering 22 subjects: (1) aggression, (2) war crimes, (3) unlawful use or emplacement of weapons, (4) crimes against humanity, (5) genocide, (6) racial discrimination and apartheid, (7) slavery and related crimes, (8) torture, (9) unlawful human experimentation, (10) piracy, (11) aircraft hijacking, (12) threat and use of force against internationally protected persons (usually, these are government officials), (13) taking of civilian hostages, (14) drug offenses, (15) international traffic in obscene publications, (16) destruction or theft of national treasures, (17) environmental protection, (18) unlawful use of the mails, (19) interference with submarine cables, (20) falsification and counterfeiting, (21) bribery of foreign public officials, and (22) theft of nuclear materials.[3] Today, many would add international terrorism in its various manifestations to the list.

B. WHAT IS CRIMINAL LAW?

To understand what is distinctive in international criminal law, we must begin by understanding the nature of criminal law itself. The excerpt following is one of the best-known attempts to define the specific character of criminal law.[4]

---

3. M. Cherif Bassiouni, A Draft International Criminal Code and Draft Statute for an International Criminal Court 28-29 (1987).

4. Another valuable attempt to define the nature of criminal law and international criminal law is Edward M. Wise, International Crimes and Domestic Criminal Law, 38 DePaul L. Rev. 923 (1989).

HENRY M. HART, JR., THE AIMS OF THE CRIMINAL LAW
23 Law & Contemp. Probs. 401 (1958)

. . . What do we mean by "crime" and "criminal"? Or, put more accurately, what should we understand to be "the method of the criminal law," the use of which is in question? . . .

1. The method operates by means of directions, or commands, formulated in general terms, telling people what they must or must not do. Mostly, the commands of the criminal law are "must-nots," or prohibitions, which can be satisfied by inaction. "Do not murder, rape, or rob." But some of them are "musts," or affirmative requirements, which can be satisfied only by taking a specifically, or relatively specifically, described kind of action. "Support your . . . children," and "File your income tax return."

2. The commands are taken as valid and binding upon all those who fall within their terms when the time comes for complying with them, whether or not they have been formulated in advance in a single authoritative set of words. They speak to members of the community, in other words, in the community's behalf, with all the power and prestige of the community behind them.

3. The commands are subject to one or more sanctions for disobedience which the community is prepared to enforce.

Thus far, it will be noticed, nothing has been said about the criminal law which is not true also of a large part of the noncriminal, or civil, law. The law of torts, the law of contracts, and almost every other branch of private law that can be mentioned operate, too, with general directions prohibiting or requiring described types of conduct, and the community's tribunals enforce these commands. What, then, is distinctive about the method of the criminal law?

Can crimes be distinguished from civil wrongs on the ground that they constitute injuries to society generally which society is interested in preventing? The difficulty is that society is interested also in the due fulfillment of contracts and the avoidance of traffic accidents and most of the other stuff of civil litigation. . . . Does the distinction lie in the fact that proceedings to enforce the criminal law are instituted by public officials rather than private complainants? The difficulty is that public officers may also bring many kinds of "civil" enforcement actions — or an injunction, for the recovery of a "civil" penalty, or even for the detention of the defendant by public authority.[5] Is the distinction, then, in the peculiar character of what is done to people who are adjudged to be criminals? The difficulty is that, with the possible exception of death, exactly the same kinds of unpleasant consequences, objectively considered, can be and are visited upon unsuccessful defendants in civil proceedings.

If one were to judge from the notions apparently underlying many judicial opinions, and the overt language even of some of them, the solution of the puzzle is simply that a crime is anything which is called a crime, and a criminal penalty is simply the penalty provided for doing anything which has been given that name. So vacant a concept is a betrayal of intellectual bankruptcy. . . . Moreover, it is false to popular understanding, and false also to the understanding embodied in existing constitutions. By implicit assumptions that are more impressive than any explicit assertions, these constitutions proclaim that a conviction for crime is a distinctive and serious matter — something, and not a nothing. What is that something?

---

5. Moreover, in many countries, crime victims are permitted to initiate criminal prosecutions. — Eps.

4. What distinguishes a criminal from a civil sanction and all that distinguishes it, it is ventured, is the judgment of community condemnation which accompanies and justifies its imposition. As Professor Gardner wrote not long ago, in a distinct but cognate connection:

> The essence of punishment for moral delinquency is in the criminal conviction itself. One may lose more money on the stock market than in a court-room; a prisoner of war camp may well provide a harsher environment than a state prison; death on the field of battle has the same physical characteristics as death by sentence of law. It is the expression of the community's hatred, fear, or contempt for the convict which alone characterizes physical hardship as punishment.

If this is what a "criminal" penalty is, then we can say readily enough what a "crime" is. It is not simply anything which a legislature chooses to call a "crime." It is not simply antisocial conduct which public officers are given a responsibility to suppress. It is not simply any conduct to which a legislature chooses to attach a "criminal" penalty. It is conduct which, if duly shown to have taken place, will incur a formal and solemn pronouncement of the moral condemnation of the community.

5. The method of the criminal law, of course, involves something more than the threat (and, on due occasion, the expression) of community condemnation of antisocial conduct. It involves, in addition, the threat (and, on due occasion, the imposition) of unpleasant physical consequences, commonly called punishment. But if Professor Gardner is right, these added consequences take their character as punishment from the condemnation which precedes them and serves as the warrant for their infliction. Indeed, the condemnation plus the added consequences may well be considered, compendiously, as constituting the punishment. Otherwise, it would be necessary to think of a convicted criminal as going unpunished if the imposition or execution of his sentence is suspended. . . .

NOTES AND QUESTIONS

1. Throughout this excerpt, Hart refers to "the community": the community's sense of right and wrong, standards that speak to members of the community, the conditions of community life and the interdependencies of the people who are living in the community, duty to the community, community attitudes and needs, and so on. Is there a single, cohesive international "community" for these purposes? On what basis can one nation's criminal law be justly applied across borders, to foreigners living in a foreign country? That is, if the criminal law reflects a single community's moral sense and depends on shared knowledge of that moral sense and widespread knowledge of the law, how can "the method of criminal law" apply transnationally in very different communities?

2. Malum in se *and* malum prohibitum. Elsewhere in his essay, Hart emphasizes that if criminal law is to work, people must know of its existence and content:

> If the legislature does a sound job of reflecting community attitudes and needs, actual knowledge of the wrongfulness of the prohibited conduct will usually exist. Thus, almost everyone is aware that murder and forcible rape and the obvious forms of theft are wrong. But in any event, knowledge of wrongfulness can fairly be assumed. For any member of the community who does these things without knowing that they are criminal is blameworthy, as much for his lack of knowledge as for his actual conduct.

Henry M. Hart, Jr., The Aims of the Criminal Law, 23 Law & Contemp. Probs. 401, 413 (1958). Does this argument apply when a state's criminal laws are enforced transnationally? How can the national of one country be expected to know the "community attitudes and needs" of another?

One possible answer to this question is that all legal systems penalize serious crimes such as murder, rape, aggravated assault, and armed robbery—and even if they did not, we all recognize that these are wrongful acts. They are, in traditional criminal law terms, *malum in se*—Latin for "wrong in themselves."

However, other acts might be crimes only because a state has chosen to make them crimes. A state may declare it a crime to transport cigarettes across the border, or to fail to pay taxes, or to smoke hashish, or to dump effluent in excess of a specified amount in the river, or to have sex with an unmarried 16-year-old. Another state may attach no criminal penalties to these acts, and nothing in the act itself signals that it is intrinsically criminal or morally outrageous. Such acts are "criminal" simply because the criminal law prohibits them: They are, in the traditional language, *malum prohibitum*—"wrong because prohibited."

In these terms, we may rephrase the question: Doesn't Hart's worry about criminal sanctions applied to people who don't know the law always arise when a state's criminal laws against *malum prohibitum* conduct are enforced transnationally? Can the worry also be valid when the laws forbid *malum in se* conduct?

3. Actus reus *and* mens rea. One of the fundamental distinctions in criminal law flows naturally from Hart's emphasis on moral blameworthiness as the distinctive characteristic of crime. This is the distinction between *actus reus* and *mens rea*—bad acts and guilty mind. To prove a crime, a prosecutor must prove both elements, that is, both that the accused engaged in the forbidden conduct and that the accused had a guilty mental state. (In addition, if the statute specifies that an act is criminal only in some circumstances, the prosecutor must prove the circumstances. In general, the three elements of any crime are *actus reus, mens rea,* and attendant circumstances.)

U.S. law recognizes several guilty mental states: engaging in the conduct *purposely* or *willingly*, engaging in the conduct *knowingly*, engaging in the conduct *recklessly*, and engaging in the conduct *negligently*. These are listed here in order of decreasing blameworthiness. Doing a bad act purposely is worse than doing it merely knowingly, which is worse than doing it recklessly, which is worse than doing it negligently. Statutes specify which mental state is necessary to make the conduct criminal. Other countries' legal systems classify the mental states differently.

We examine the guilty mental states in greater detail in Chapter 17.

C. CRIME AND PUNISHMENT

Hart argues that moral condemnation, not punishment, is the defining feature of criminal law. That is because other areas of law also involve sanctions (for example, contract or tort damages). Only when the sanction is joined with moral condemnation does it become punishment. But Hart does not deny the obvious: that punishment is the salient feature of criminal law in most people's minds.

What is the purpose of criminal punishment and thus of the criminal justice system? Theorists differ. Punishment may well have originated as sheer revenge, "payback," and until the early nineteenth century European practices of punishment often included grisly and terrible tortures—the "cruel and unusual" punishments forbidden by the Eighth Amendment to the U.S. Constitution. But already in 1764, the influential Italian reformer Cesare Beccaria argued in his famous book *On Crimes and Punishments* that the only rationally acceptable basis for punishment is utilitarian:

> [T]he purpose of punishments is not to torment and afflict a sentient being or to undo a crime which has already been committed. Far from acting out of passion, can a political body, which is the calm agent that moderates the passions of private individuals, harbor useless cruelty, the tool of fury and fanaticism or weak tyrants? Can the cries of a poor wretch turn back time and undo actions which have already been done? The purpose of punishment, then, is nothing other than to dissuade the criminal from doing fresh harm to his compatriots and to keep other people from doing the same. Therefore, punishments and the method of inflicting them should be chosen that, mindful of the proportion between crime and punishment, will make the most effective and lasting impression on men's minds and inflict the least torment on the body of the criminal.[6]

The purpose of government, Beccaria argued, is to achieve the greatest good for the greatest number. That implies that the pain suffered by the criminal must be counted as a drawback to punishment, rather than a plus: Anyone's pain subtracts from the total social good. The criminal's pain must therefore be weighed against the benefit to society, and it follows that only the least severe punishment that can maintain good social order is justifiable. "Everything beyond that is an abuse and not justice, a fact but scarcely a right."[7] Beccaria opposed both torture and the death penalty. He argued that states are justified by a social contract, in which the people surrender to the government only enough of their natural liberty to make society secure; and, he thought, no rational person would surrender his right to life or her immunity from torture. Beccaria's theories were influential in the American colonies.

On the opposite side from Beccaria, the eighteenth-century German philosopher Immanuel Kant argued that the utilitarian theory of punishment is unjust and immoral because inflicting harm on the criminal to further the good of other people treats the criminal as a means, not as an end in himself. That, according to Kant, would violate the criminal's right to be treated as a person and not a mere tool of society. For Kant, retribution based on the criminal's guilt is the only legitimate basis for punishment; and Kant defended the so-called *lex talionis*—the biblical theory of an eye for an eye.

Kant's theory, which on a theoretical level exhibits greater respect for human rights than does utilitarianism, may in practice yield harsher consequences than Beccaria's utilitarianism because it insists on punishing wrongdoers in the name of justice, even if doing so has no practical purpose. Famously, Kant argued that even if a society on a remote island resolved to disband itself and scatter around the world, "the last murderer remaining in prison would first have to be executed."[8] Otherwise, Kant argued, the residents would be condoning murder and making themselves little better than accomplices to it. Where the great virtue of Beccaria's utilitarianism lies in its critique of needlessly cruel punishment, the great virtue of Kant's retributivism lies in its recognition that punishment is first and foremost a response to past wrongdoing, and that leaving crimes unpunished leaves the demands of justice unmet.

---

6. Cesare Beccaria, On Crimes and Punishments ch. 12 (David Young trans., Hackett Publishing Co. 1986) (1764).

7. Id. at 8-9.

8. Immanuel Kant, Metaphysical First Principles of the Doctrine of Right, in The Metaphysics of Morals 142 (Mary Gregor trans., Cambridge Univ. Press 1991) (1780).

Kant's theory is also important because it reminds us that criminal prosecution and conviction are unjust unless the defendant has actually done something wrong. Even if it would be socially useful to prosecute the innocent, doing so would be wrong. Personal guilt, and only personal guilt, matters. This is an especially important reminder in international criminal law, where it might be tempting to prosecute leaders of a dictatorial regime for crimes the regime committed, even though no evidence ties the leaders to any specific crime. Under Kant's retributive principles, that would be unjust, even if it was politically useful for the new, democratic regime. The prosecution would violate the notion that only personal guilt matters and substitute mere guilt by association.

Theorists continue to debate these issues today. Essentially, Beccaria and the utilitarians offer *forward-looking* theories of punishment, in which the argument for punishment is that it will lead to better future consequences for society. Kant and the retributivists offer *backward-looking* theories, in which the argument for punishment is ultimately grounded in the wrongfulness of the criminal's past deeds, rather than any future good that punishment could establish.

Among modern theorists, the aims of punishment are most commonly described as retribution, rehabilitation, incapacitation, and deterrence — both *special deterrence*, that is, deterring the offender from doing it again, and *general deterrence*, that is, deterring other people from committing the crime. Notice that deterrence, incapacitation, and rehabilitation are all forward-looking rationales for punishment. Only retribution is backward-looking, although in practice the other theories all presume that only convicted offenders may be punished. A fifth aim is preventing crime by promoting respect for the law's authority. This differs from deterrence because deterrence motivates people to lawful behavior out of fear of punishment, rather than out of respect for the law. This fourth theory has been developed elaborately by German penologists, who describe it as "positive general prevention" — "positive" because it prevents crime by cultivating a positive attitude toward the law, rather than the negative prevention offered by deterrent threats; and "general" because it is aimed at the general population, not the particular offender.[9]

In practice, modern legal systems seldom aim for theoretical purity by choosing one or the other basis for punishment. Instead, they take them all. U.S. federal law incorporates all these theories in its basic sentencing statute, 18 U.S.C. §3553. The statute requires punishment "sufficient, but not greater than necessary" to achieve multiple aims: to reflect the seriousness of the offense and provide just punishment (retribution), to protect the public from further crimes of the defendant (incapacitation), to provide adequate deterrence, and to promote respect for the law (positive general prevention).

What about rehabilitation and education of offenders? Prison employees are still called "corrections officers," and many prisons are administered by a Department of Corrections (or, in some U.S. states, a Department of Rehabilitation) — a linguistic residue of a rehabilitative vision of criminal punishment. So too, some criminologists believe that the most effective and morally legitimate criminal justice systems aim, after shaming the offender through punishment, to reintegrate offenders into society.[10] And 18 U.S.C. §3553 states that one aim of punishment is "to provide

---

9. For a useful English-language discussion, see Markus Dirk Dubber, Theories of Crime and Punishment in German Criminal Law, 53 Am. J. Comp. L. 679 (2005).

10. John Braithwaite, Crime, Shame, and Reintegration (1989); Jean Hampton, The Moral Education Theory of Punishment, 13 Phil. & Pub. Aff. 208 (1984).

the defendant with needed educational or vocational training, medical care, or other correctional treatment in the most effective manner."

But a later statute asserts "the inappropriateness of imposing a sentence to a term of imprisonment for the purpose of rehabilitating the defendant or providing the defendant with needed educational or vocational training, medical care, or other correctional treatment."[11] There is a story behind these choices. Traditionally, the federal sentencing system was characterized by vast judicial discretion—that is, once a conviction was obtained, sentencing judges had the discretion to choose a sentence within a broad penalty range set by statute. As long as the judge kept within the statutory range, there were virtually no rules about how he or she made the choice of sentence, and the sentence was effectively unreviewable by a court of appeals. Judicial discretion was viewed as necessary to serve the "medical" model of criminal justice that prevailed for many decades. That model contemplated that rehabilitation was the primary goal of criminal punishment, and that judges, in each case, could prescribe the punishment most likely to ensure that the individual prisoner was returned to society as a responsible and law-abiding citizen. The downside, however, was "severe disparities in sentences received and served by defendants committing the same offense and having similar criminal histories."[12] Furthermore, the rehabilitation rationale suffered as many observers concluded that prison terms had not, and were unlikely to, result in effective rehabilitation. Accordingly, in 1984 Congress created the U.S. Sentencing Commission and charged it with the task of overhauling federal criminal sentencing policy to constrain the discretion of sentencing judges so as to promote uniformity and proportionality in sentencing. In so doing, Congress instructed the Commission in the quoted statute that rehabilitation is no longer a valid aim of incarceration—although it is still relevant to criminal penalties other than jail terms (for example, fines, probation, or restitution).

How a state conceives the purpose of punishment can greatly influence the punishments it metes out. For example, the German Federal Constitutional Court reasoned from the goal of rehabilitation to the conclusion that a sentence of life without parole is unconstitutional:

> In enforcing this punishment [of life imprisonment] in the Federal Republic, state officials are under a duty not merely to incarcerate but also to rehabilitate the prisoner through appropriate treatment, a policy consistent with previous decisions of this court. The court on several occasions has maintained that rehabilitation is constitutionally required in any community that establishes human dignity as its centerpiece and commits itself to the principle of social justice. The [prisoner's] interest in rehabilitation flows from Article 2(1) in tandem with Article 1.[13] The condemned criminal must be given the chance, after atoning for his crime, to reenter society. . . . An assessment of the constitutionality of life imprisonment from the vantage point of Article 1(1) and the principle of the rule of law shows that a humane enforcement of life imprisonment is possible only when the prisoner is given a concrete and realistically attainable chance to regain his freedom at some later point in time; the state strikes at the very heart of human dignity if [it] treats the prisoner without regard to the development of his personality

---

11. 28 U.S.C. §994(k) (2006).

12. Blakely v. Washington, 542 U.S. 296, 315 (2004) (O'Connor, J., dissenting).

13. Article 1(1) of the German constitution (the "Basic Law," *Grundgesetz für die Bundesrepublik Deutschland*), states: "Human dignity shall be inviolable. To respect and protect it shall be the duty of all state authority." Article 2(1) states: "Every person shall have the right to free development of his personality insofar as he does not violate the rights of others or offend against the constitutional order or the moral law." —EDS.

and strips him of all hope of ever earning his freedom . . . , [a hope] which makes the sentence bearable in terms of human dignity.[14]

Readers familiar with contemporary U.S. debates over the death penalty will very likely find this conclusion surprising: In U.S. debates, life without parole is often regarded as the liberal alternative to capital punishment. Many states besides Germany have no such sentence as life without parole. In addition to reflecting different philosophies of punishment, this striking discrepancy between these approaches foreshadows some of the difficulties that international tribunals face in determining sentencing schemes that seem just to all the participating nations. We take up this subject in Chapter 4.

Do you see relevant differences between domestic criminal justice systems and the international legal community? Do the arguments for condemnation (not necessarily punishment) have more or less traction with regard to international crimes? What about Beccarian concerns about prevention and deterrence, or Kantian notions of retribution? Compare the U.S. sentencing statutes with the following excerpt from an opinion of the International Criminal Tribunal for the former Yugoslavia (ICTY).

PROSECUTOR v. BLASKIC
Case No. IT-95-14-A, Judgment (July 29, 2004)

678. . . . The Appeals Chamber recalls that Article 24(1) of the Statute [creating the ICTY] limits the penalty imposed by the Trial Chamber to imprisonment. In imposing a sentence, the International Tribunal has recognized the following purposes to be considered: (i) individual and general deterrence concerning the accused and, in particular, commanders in similar situations in the future; (ii) individual and general affirmative prevention aimed at influencing the legal awareness of the accused, the victims, their relatives, the witnesses, and the general public in order to reassure them that the legal system is being implemented and enforced; (iii) retribution; (iv) public reprobation and stigmatisation by the international community; and (v) rehabilitation.

NOTES AND QUESTIONS

1. The phrase "individual and general affirmative prevention" in *Blaskic* derives from the German theory of positive general prevention.

2. What, if anything, is the difference between retribution (aim (iii)) and "public reprobation and stigmatisation" (aim (iv))? Doesn't retribution always stigmatize the criminal? Are there forms of stigmatizing people that aren't retribution?

3. Is rehabilitation a legitimate goal of punishment for perpetrators of mass atrocities? Is it consistent with public reprobation and stigmatization?

---

14. Life Imprisonment Case (1977), 45 BverGE 187, in The Constitutional Jurisprudence of the Federal Republic of Germany 308-309 (Donald P. Kommers ed. & trans., 2d ed. 1997).

D. THE NEED FOR SAFEGUARDS IN THE CRIMINAL LAW

So far, we have introduced basic concepts of criminal law and punishment, linking both to the moral blameworthiness of wrongdoers. As the following excerpt indicates, however, this leaves out an equally important part of the picture: the need for safeguards against wrongful conviction and punishment.

1. The Risk of Overenforcement

JOHN HASNAS, ONCE MORE UNTO THE BREACH: THE INHERENT LIBERALISM OF THE CRIMINAL LAW AND LIABILITY FOR ATTEMPTING THE IMPOSSIBLE
54 Hastings L.J. 1, 49-51 (2002)

. . . There is a principled difference between moral and criminal responsibility. Moral responsibility indicates that one is deserving of punishment. Criminal responsibility authorizes some human beings to punish others. Criminal responsibility inherently involves an element of human agency that moral responsibility does not.

In making a determination of moral responsibility, we are concerned only with the actions of one party, the agent whose conduct is being evaluated. The only relevant issue is whether the agent has acted in a morally unacceptable way; whether he or she has violated a moral tenet or failed to fulfill a moral obligation. Determining that the agent has acted in a morally blameworthy manner does not in itself authorize anyone else to take action against him or her. The inquiry is an abstract one involving no practical enforcement issues.

The case is different when we make a determination of criminal responsibility. Such a determination requires not only a finding that the defendant has acted in a culpable manner that manifests his or her dangerousness or depravity, but also that it is proper for agents of the government to impose a criminal sanction on him or her. Here, we are necessarily concerned with the actions of two parties, the defendant and the government enforcement agents. Unless these agents are both omniscient and incorruptible, the class of cases in which the defendant has culpably manifested his or her dangerousness or depravity cannot be coextensive with the class of cases in which the imposition of the criminal sanction is justified. There will always be some cases in which the effort to impose punishment on a class of defendants who morally deserve it would subject the public to an unacceptable risk of harm from the errors or venality of the human beings charged with enforcing the law. If the criminal justice system were guaranteed to be administered with godlike perfection, then realms of criminal responsibility and moral responsibility would indeed be coextensive. But this is not the world in which we live. Thus determinations of criminal responsibility must always consider practical matters of administration that determinations of moral responsibility ignore.

. . . The purpose of the criminal law is to provide an orderly society in which citizens are secure in their persons and property; to protect citizens against harm from the other members of society. Obviously, to accomplish this end, it must protect citizens against threats to their persons and property from other members of society acting in their individual capacities; it must provide protection against "criminals." However, it would be pointless to do so in a way that left the citizens exposed to threats to their persons and property from the individuals acting as governmental enforcement agents. To serve its purpose, the criminal law must be structured to provide citizens with the optimal amount of protection to their persons and property against invasion from all other members of society, whether acting individually or officially.

... Because the criminal law is administered by human beings who are as error-prone and susceptible to temptation as anyone else, every gain in protection against criminal activity that comes from more effective enforcement produces a loss in protection against ill-considered or improper official action. Conversely, every enhancement in protection against the state hampers governmental agents' ability to provide protection against individual criminals. Theorists can and do argue about where the line should be drawn to realize the optimal level of protection, but the line must be drawn somewhere. Thus, judgments of criminal responsibility necessarily involve a weighing of competing interests that judgments of moral responsibility do not.

2. The Basic Protections in Criminal Law and Procedure

Whether the defining feature of criminal law is punishment or moral condemnation, everyone recognizes that criminal condemnation is perhaps the most serious action the law can take. As a result, in most nations, criminal law and procedure must conform to especially stringent requirements. Among those recognized in U.S. domestic law as well as in contemporary international criminal law are the following.

1. *Principle of Legality*: No one can be criminally convicted for conduct that is not unlawful; and no one can be punished except as the law specifies. The Principle of Legality actually contains two sub-principles, which are often stated in two Latin maxims:
    (A) *nulla crimen sine lege* (no crime without law) and
    (B) *nulla poena sine lege* (no punishment without law).
        These two principles, though similar, are not identical. The first principle has to do with what kind of conduct can result in criminal conviction. It insists that only conduct that the law says is criminal can result in criminal conviction. Typically, that means that conduct, no matter how heinous, cannot lead to criminal conviction unless a criminal statute, specifying both the *actus reus* and the *mens rea* of the offense, prohibits it. The second principle focuses on punishment, not on conduct. It says that no punishment can be inflicted unless the law provides for it. To see why the second principle differs from the first, imagine someone convicted of a crime for which the law provides punishment of up to a year in prison. If the judge sentences the offender to two years, the sentence violates *nulla poena sine lege* (because the punishment is greater than what the law provides) but not *nulla crimen sine lege* (because the conviction is lawful). Both principles are essential parts of the Principle of Legality.
2. *Principle of Fair Notice*: No one can be condemned for a crime without fair notice that the conduct is criminal.
3. *Principle of Nonretroactivity*: No criminal law can be applied retroactively.
        Nonretroactivity can be regarded as a corollary to the Principle of Legality and the Principle of Fair Notice. If the criminal statute is retroactive, then at the time the "crime" was committed there was no law against it and no notice that it was criminal. A conviction would therefore violate both the Principle of Legality and the Principle of Fair Notice. The Principle of Nonretroactivity is embodied in

the U.S. Constitution in the ban on *ex post facto* laws in Article I, Section 9, Clause 3.

4. *Principle of Lenity:* This principle is also known as strict construction of the criminal law. Criminal statutes must always be narrowly construed, and if a statute is ambiguous, it must be construed in the most lenient way, that is, in the way most favorable for the defendant.

5. The presumption of innocence.

6. The requirement that guilt must be established beyond a reasonable doubt.

7. The basic procedural rights:

(A) The right to a (i) speedy (ii) public trial before (iii) an impartial tribunal that (iv) bases its decision solely on the evidence offered at trial.

(B) The right to offer a defense.

(C) The right to be informed of the charges, in a language that the accused person understands, through a written indictment that specifies the charges and the conduct charged.

(D) The right of the accused to confront the witnesses against him.

(E) The right of the accused to have compulsory process for obtaining witnesses in his favor.

(F) The right to counsel and the privilege against self-incrimination.

(G) The ban on double jeopardy — that is, repeated prosecution for the same offense. In international legal standards, the ban on double jeopardy is called *ne bis in idem* (literally, "not twice for the same").

All of these are embodied in American constitutional law, mostly in the Fifth and Sixth Amendments. All are embodied explicitly in the Statute of the International Criminal Court. Furthermore, all these rights are guaranteed in Articles 14 and 15 of the International Covenant on Civil and Political Rights, one of the basic treaties concerning international human rights (which has 160 states parties, including the United States).

Also important are basic principles governing the prosecutor's role. However, unlike the other rights listed here, these are not firmly settled in international law:

8. (A) The prosecutor must (in the words of U.S. ethical standards), seek justice, not victory.

(B) The prosecutor must not initiate or continue proceedings against someone without probable cause.

Finally, as alluded to in our earlier discussion of Kant, criminal guilt must be *personal:*

9. *Principle of Personal Responsibility:* No one should be convicted of a crime unless he or she bears personal responsibility for that crime, either as a principal or as an accessory. Guilt by mere association is unjust.

Notice the Principle of Personal Responsibility does not require that the offender has committed the crime himself. He may have hired someone else to do it, or tricked someone into doing it, or assisted someone else in doing it, or even be responsible as a superior. What matters is that, directly or indirectly, he bears personal responsibility for the crime in some way.

It also deserves mention that personal responsibility may, but need not, include legal entities such as corporations. In U.S. law, for example, corporations may be convicted of crimes if their employees commit those crimes in the actual or apparent scope of their duties. Corporations act only through their agents, and so convicting the corporation for the crimes of its agents *is* a form of personal responsibility for the corporate "person." But it would violate the Principle of Personal Responsibility to convict one employee of the corporation for a crime with which she had no connection at all, merely because the perpetrator was also an employee. (Many legal systems, it should be noted, do not have the concept of corporate criminality.)

All of these principles and requirements have one basic purpose: to safeguard against the danger of wrongful criminal conviction.

E. IS INTERNATIONAL CRIMINAL LAW DIFFERENT? THE EICHMANN TRIAL

In our initial excerpt, Hart — like most criminal lawyers — is evidently thinking exclusively of *domestic* criminal law, that is, criminal law within a single national community. The questions following the excerpt suggested that standard theories of the aims of criminal law, such as Hart's, may have a tougher time accounting for transnational criminal law, that is, national law applied across borders in other countries. The same may be true of international criminal law, that is, the law governing the basic international crimes of genocide, crimes against humanity, and war crimes.

Here the difficulty is perhaps more fundamental than the questions of jurisdiction and fair notice across borders. It arises from the fact that the aims of trying perpetrators of the great crimes — notably, national leaders — are anything but routine. Such trials always follow moments of cataclysm: wars and civil wars, bloody ethnic or religious struggles, political upheavals, revolutions or other changes of basic political systems. Instead of being a normal part of the daily functioning of government, international criminal trials typically occur after governments have fallen or been radically altered.

Such trials, then, are part of *transitional justice* — the whole range of legal issues that arise when one form of government replaces another. Where ordinary criminal law is a product of continuity, international criminal law in the strict sense is a product of discontinuity, of upheaval and political rupture. Inevitably, then, the trials take on political overtones; and sometimes the requirements of politics and those of criminal law are in tension with each other. Politics is broad and partial; criminal law, as we have seen, is supposed to be narrow and impartial.

Furthermore, there is often a fundamental difference between the perpetrators of atrocity crimes and "ordinary" criminals. Ordinary crimes are deviations from the social order, but mass atrocities are often organized by the leaders of a regime, and the perpetrators are not deviants but conformists. The political philosopher Hannah Arendt — excerpted below — coined the phrase "banality of evil" to describe everyday, obedient conformists who commit horrible crimes without malicious motives beyond the desire to do what they are told. Mark Drumbl, in an important study of legal punishment for mass atrocities, emphasizes this difference and argues that it may remove one of the most important reasons for punishment: the incapacitation of wrongdoers.[15]

Finally, in the aftermath of a cataclysm, the desire to give victims a voice and allow them to seek whatever closure remains to them by condemning their persecutors, seems especially urgent, more so than in everyday domestic criminal enforcement (where it is also important, of course). This, too, can create tensions with the

---

15. Mark A. Drumbl, Atrocity, Punishment, and International Law (2007).

requirements of justice for the accused. As two commentators observe, this tension derives from the close connection between international criminal law and international human rights law. After all, the mass atrocities that form the subject matter of international criminal law are invariably major human rights violations. But, the two commentators note:

> In several fundamental ways, however, the working presumptions of human rights law and criminal law present mirror images of each other. In a criminal proceeding, the focus is on the defendant and the burden is on the prosecuting authority to prove that the individual before the court has committed a crime. Ambiguity about that assertion is to be construed in favor of the criminal defendant, and the trier of fact is charged with determining what the defendant did and what his mental state was toward the acts constituting the crime. In human rights proceedings, by contrast, the focus is on the harms that have befallen the victim and on the human rights norm that has been violated. One consequence of this focus is that the substantive norms of international human rights law are generally broadly interpreted to ensure that harms are recognized and remedied, and that, over time, there is progressively greater realization of respect for human dignity and freedom. The analogous rules of domestic criminal law, by contrast, are supposed to be strictly construed in favor of the defendant. And while criminal law tends toward the specific and the absolute, human rights law embraces some contingent, aspirational norms.
>
> The confluence in international criminal law between criminal law principles drawn from domestic criminal law and the philosophical commitments of international human rights law sets up two opposing optics with which to adjudicate a violation. Should it be in the defendant-centered mode of a criminal trial or the victim-oriented style of a human rights proceeding? Should it hew to the rule of lenity that protects defendants from unexpected expansions of the law, or should it reflect the aspirational character of international human rights law? . . . [T]hese conflicting tensions surface in important ways in the jurisprudence of international criminal law.[16]

The following excerpts explore these tensions through a case study — the trial of Adolf Eichmann. Along with the postwar Nuremberg trials, the trial of Eichmann was the most significant criminal case arising from the Holocaust.

Eichmann (1906-1962) was an SS lieutenant colonel who was in charge of rounding up Europe's Jews and transporting them to death camps. At the end of World War II he managed to escape to Argentina, where he lived incognito until 1960. At that time, Israeli agents kidnapped Eichmann on the streets of Buenos Aires and transported him to Israel to be put on trial. Although Eichmann was not one of the "top Nazis," he was the highest-ranking Nazi official whose sole responsibility was carrying out the Holocaust. Previous war-crimes trials at Nuremberg had focused principally on the "crimes against peace" — Germany's war of aggression that became World War II — rather than specifically focusing on the Holocaust, and the Eichmann trial was the first major trial of an individual emphasizing solely the mass murder of the European Jews. The trial received an enormous amount of publicity. Eichmann was convicted and executed in 1962.

David Ben-Gurion, who was prime minister of Israel at the time, was quite explicit about the aims of the Eichmann trial. Ben-Gurion's goals were openly political. He wanted to educate Israelis — many of them recent immigrants from non-European countries — about the Holocaust. He also wanted to remind the rest of the world of its

---

16. Allison Marston Danner & Jenny S. Martinez, Guilty Associations: Joint Criminal Enterprise, Command Responsibility, and the Development of International Criminal Law, 93 Cal. L. Rev. 75, 89-90 (2005).

horrors, in order to emphasize the importance and necessity of the state of Israel. Furthermore, although this was not one of Ben-Gurion's aims, the trial would prove to be a crucial therapeutic moment for Holocaust survivors in Israel. Many of them had kept their stories to themselves for years, and the Eichmann trial provided an opportunity for the survivors to bring their terrible stories out into the open.

The readings that follow use the Eichmann trial to raise crucial threshold questions about international criminal law. How does it differ from "everyday" domestic criminal law? Do trials of the major international crimes have different purposes from ordinary law enforcement? What are those differences, are they legitimate, and are they consistent with doing justice to the accused? Are these trials political trials, and if so, are they political in an objectionable way?

PROSECUTOR v. EICHMANN

Criminal Case No. 40/61, Judgment
Israel, District Court of Jerusalem (1961)

1. Adolf Eichmann has been brought to trial in this Court on charges of unsurpassed gravity — charges of crimes against the Jewish People, crimes against humanity, and war crimes. The period of the crimes ascribed to him, and their historical background, is that of the Hitler regime in Germany and in Europe, and the counts of the indictment encompass the catastrophe which befell the Jewish People during that period — a story of bloodshed and suffering which will be remembered to the end of time.

This is not the first time that the Holocaust has been discussed in court proceedings. It was dealt with extensively at the International Military Tribunal at Nuremberg during the Trial of the Major War Criminals, and also at several of the trials which followed; but this time it has occupied the central place in the Court proceedings, and it is this fact which has distinguished this trial from those which preceded it. Hence also the trend noticed during and around the trial, to widen its range. The desire was felt — understandable in itself — to give, within the trial, a comprehensive and exhaustive historical description of events which occurred during the Holocaust, and in so doing, to emphasize also the inconceivable feats of heroism performed by ghetto-fighters, by those who mutinied in the camps, and by Jewish partisans.

How could this happen in the light of day, and why was it just the German people from which this great evil sprang? Could the Nazis have carried out their evil designs without the help given them by other peoples in whose midst the Jews dwelt? Would it have been possible to avert the Holocaust, at least in part, if the Allies had displayed a greater will to assist the persecuted Jews? Did the Jewish People in the lands of freedom do all in its power to rally to the rescue of its brethren and to sound the alarm for help? What are the psychological and social causes of the group-hatred [sic] which is known as anti-Semitism? Can this ancient disease be cured, and by what means? What is the lesson which the Jews and other nations must draw from all this, as well as every person in his relationship to others? There are many other questions of various kinds which cannot even all be listed.

2. In this maze of insistent questions, the path of the Court was and remains clear. It cannot allow itself to be enticed into provinces which are outside its sphere. The judicial process has ways of its own, laid down by law, and which do not change, whatever the subject of the trial may be. Otherwise, the processes of law and of court procedure are bound to be impaired, whereas they must be adhered to punctiliously, since they are in themselves of considerable social and educational significance, and the trial would otherwise resemble a rudderless ship tossed about by the waves.

It is the purpose of every criminal trial to clarify whether the charges in the prosecution's indictment against the accused who is on trial are true, and if the accused is convicted, to mete out due punishment to him. Everything which requires clarification in order that these purposes may be achieved, must be determined at the trial, and everything which is foreign to these purposes must be entirely eliminated from the court procedure. Not only is any pretension to overstep these limits forbidden to the court — it would certainly end in complete failure. The court does not have at its disposal the tools required for the investigation of general questions of the kind referred to above. For example, in connection with the description of the historical background of the Holocaust, a great amount of material was brought before us in the form of documents and evidence, collected most painstakingly, and certainly in a genuine attempt to delineate as complete a picture as possible. Even so, all this material is but a tiny fraction of all that is extant on this subject. According to our legal system, the court is by its very nature "passive," for it does not itself initiate the bringing of proof before it, as is the custom with an enquiry commission. Accordingly, its ability to describe general events is inevitably limited. As for questions of principle which are outside the realm of law, no one has made us judges of them, and therefore no greater weight is to be attached to our opinion on them than to that of any person devoting study and thought to these questions. These prefatory remarks do not mean that we are unaware of the great educational value, implicit in the very holding of this trial, for those who live in Israel as well as for those beyond the confines of this state. To the extent that this result has been achieved in the course of the proceedings, it is to be welcomed. Without a doubt, the testimony given at this trial by survivors of the Holocaust, who poured out their hearts as they stood in the witness box, will provide valuable material for research workers and historians, but as far as this Court is concerned, they are to be regarded as by-products of the trial.

MARK OSIEL, MASS ATROCITY, COLLECTIVE MEMORY, AND THE LAW
1-2, 60-62, 65-67 (1997)

We ought to evaluate transitions to democracy with greater attention to the kind of public discussion they foster concerning the human rights abuse perpetrated by authoritarian rulers, recently deposed. We should evaluate the prosecution of these perpetrators in light of how it influences such public deliberations.

To that end, the law's conventional concerns with deterrence and retribution will receive lesser emphasis. The rules designed to keep these concerns at center stage will sometimes need to be compromised. Such compromises are necessary and appropriate, I suggest, in the aftermath of large-scale brutality sponsored by an authoritarian state [as in the Argentine Dirty War]. At such times, the need for public reckoning with the question of how such horrific events could have happened is more important to democratization than the criminal law's more traditional objectives. This is because such trials, when effective as public spectacle, stimulate public discussion in ways that foster the liberal virtues of toleration, moderation, and civil respect. Criminal trials must be conducted with this pedagogical purpose in mind. . . .

By highlighting official brutality and public complicity, these trials often make people willing to reassess their foundational beliefs and constitutive commitments, as few events in political life can do. In the lives of individuals, these trials thus often become, at very least, an occasion for personal stock-taking. They are "moments of truth," in several senses. Specifically, the present moments of transformative opportunity in the lives of individuals and societies, a potential not lost upon the litigants themselves. Prosecutors and judges in these cases thus rightly aim to shape collective memory of horrible events in ways that can be both successful as public spectacle and consistent with liberal legality. . . .

There is reason to wonder whether justice to the defendant, however heinous his wrongs, has been compromised when it can be said, as does one Israeli historian, that "the trial was only a medium, and Eichmann's role was simply to be there, in the glass booth; the real purpose of the trial was to give voice to the Jewish people, for whom Israel claimed to speak." Another Israeli scholar adds that "Eichmann rather swiftly became peripheral to his own trial, which was deliberately designed to focus more comprehensively on the Nazi crimes against the Jews." Those initially willing to testify in his defense were deterred from so doing by threat of prosecution for their own wartime activities. . . .

The primary limit that liberalism imposes on storytelling in criminal trials is the principle of personal culpability: the requirement that no defendant be held responsible for the wrongs of others beyond his contemplation or control. This entails a judicial duty to focus on a very small piece of what most observers will inevitably view as a much larger puzzle, to delimit judicial attention to that restricted place and period within which the defendant willfully acted.

Episodes of administrative massacre, however, generally involve many people acting in coordinated ways over considerable space and time, impeding adherence to this stricture. Moreover, to tell a compelling story, one that will persuade its intended audience that it is not unfairly singling out a serviceable scapegoat, the state (in the person of the prosecutor) must be able to paint the larger tableaux. Hence the recurrent tension, of which trial participants have often been well aware, between the needs of persuasive storytelling and the normative requirements of liberal judgment.

. . . In prosecuting Eichmann, Ben-Gurion wanted, above all else, to retell the story told at Nuremberg in an entirely different way. This retelling would conceive the offense as a "crime against the Jewish people," rather than against "humanity"— the latter concept an invention of the secular Enlightenment. . . . It was designed to reflect the Zionist view that liberalism, with its aim of moral universalism, had misled the Jews into seeking assimilation within gentile societies, rather than reestablishing their own. . . . Ben-Gurion sought to frame the courtroom narrative . . . as a tale about the Jewish community's collective victimization, suffering, resistance, resurrection (from the ashes of failed assimilation), and, finally, redemption as a powerful nation-state.

. . . The orchestration of criminal trials for pedagogic purposes—such as the transformation of a society's collective memory—is not inherently misguided or morally indefensible. The defensibility of the practice depends on the defensibility of the lessons being taught. . . .

. . . [A] liberal state may employ a "show trial" for administrative massacre to display the horrific consequences of the illiberal vices and so to foster among its citizens the liberal values (including respect for basic individual rights . . .). . . . The law accomplishes this only when courts and juries themselves respect the law, that is, when they adhere to legal rules reflecting liberal principles of procedural fairness and personal culpability as conditions of criminal liability. The most gripping of legal yarns must hence be classified as a failure if its capacity for public enthrallment is purchased at the price of violating such strictures.

HANNAH ARENDT, EICHMANN IN JERUSALEM: A REPORT ON THE BANALITY OF EVIL

5, 286 (rev. ed. 1964)

There is no doubt from the very beginning that it is Judge Landau who sets the tone, and that he is doing his best, his very best, to prevent this trial from becoming a show trial under the influence of the prosecutor's love of showmanship. . . . Clearly, this courtroom is not a bad place for the show trial David Ben-Gurion, Prime Minister of Israel, had in mind when he decided to have Eichmann kidnapped in Argentina and brought to the District Court of Jerusalem to stand trial for his role in the "final solution of the Jewish question." . . . [I]n the courtroom [Ben-Gurion] speaks with the voice of Gideon Hausner, the Attorney General, who, representing the government, does his best, his very best, to obey his master. And if, fortunately, his best often turns out not to be good enough, the reason is that the trial is presided over by someone who serves Justice as faithfully as Mr. Hausner serves the State of Israel. . . . Justice insists on the importance of Adolf Eichmann, son of Karl Adolf Eichmann, the man in the glass booth built for his protection: medium-sized, slender, middle-aged, with receding hair, ill-fitting teeth, and nearsighted eyes, who throughout the trial keeps craning his scraggy neck toward the bench (not once does he face the audience), and who desperately and for the most part successfully maintains his self-control despite the nervous tic to which his mouth must have become subject long before this trial started. On trial are his deeds, not the sufferings of the Jews, not the German people or mankind, not even anti-Semitism and racism. . . .

It may be argued that all the general questions we involuntarily raise as soon as we begin to speak of these matters — why did it have to be the Germans? why did it have to be the Jews? what is the nature of totalitarian rule? — are far more important than the question of the kind of crime for which a man is being tried, and the nature of the defendant upon whom justice must be pronounced; more important, too, than the question of how well our present system of justice is capable of dealing with this special type of crime and criminal. . . . It can be held that the issue is no longer a particular human being, a single distinct individual in the dock. . . . All this has often been argued. . . . If the defendant is taken as a symbol and the trial as a pretext to bring up matters which are apparently more interesting than the guilt or innocence of one person, then consistency demands that we bow to the assertion made by Eichmann and his lawyer: that he was brought to book because a scapegoat was needed. . . .

I need hardly say that I would never have gone to Jerusalem if I had shared these views. I held and hold the opinion that this trial had to take place in the interests of justice and nothing else.

NOTES AND QUESTIONS

1. The Jerusalem court and Hannah Arendt both argue that the sole legitimate aim of a criminal trial is to determine the guilt or innocence of the defendant. In contrast, Mark Osiel contends that determining guilt or innocence after mass atrocities, where many people participate, requires examining a context that is far wider than the defendant's own actions. Osiel also defends the legitimacy of framing trials with political goals in mind. Who is right? Or is there some way to reconcile the two positions?

2. Osiel highlights a recurrent dilemma facing prosecutors in cases of state-sponsored or organization-sponsored atrocities. The prosecutor may focus solely and narrowly on the deeds of the accused and not on other atrocities in which the accused played no direct role — but at the cost of misunderstanding the humanitarian catastrophe in which the accused played a part. Alternatively, the prosecutor can try to "paint with a broad brush" to make the entire situation comprehensible — but at the cost of introducing legal irrelevancies. How should prosecutors resolve this dilemma?

In the United States, the Federal Rules of Evidence prohibit the introduction of irrelevant evidence, where Rule 401 defines relevant evidence as "evidence having any tendency to make the existence of any fact that is of consequence to the determination of the action more probable or less probable than it would be without the evidence." Furthermore, even relevant evidence "may be excluded if its probative value is substantially outweighed by the danger of unfair prejudice, confusion of the issues, or misleading the jury, or by considerations of undue delay, waste of time, or needless presentation of cumulative evidence." Fed. R. Evid. 403.

In the *Eichmann* trial, the prosecution introduced a great deal of testimony by Holocaust survivors that would have failed these tests, because the events to which they testified either had nothing directly to do with Eichmann, or could amply be proven without any recourse to their testimony. As Prosecutor Gideon Hausner explained, if convicting Eichmann had been his only goal, "it was obviously enough to let the archives speak; a fraction of them would have sufficed to get Eichmann sentenced ten times over. . . . I knew we needed more than a conviction; we needed a living record of a gigantic human and national disaster." Gideon Hausner, Justice in Jerusalem 291, 292 (1966). Hausner explained that the intended audience was both the younger generation of Israelis, with "no real knowledge, and therefore no appreciation, of the way in which their own flesh and blood had perished," and the world at large, "which had so lightly and happily forgotten the horrors that occurred before its eyes, to such a degree that it even begrudged us the trial of the perpetrator." Id.

Commentator Lawrence Douglas describes Hausner's goal as follows:

> The act of creating an opportunity for the public sharing of the narratives of the survivors, the proxies of the dead, was itself a way of doing justice. Hausner's reflections on the strategy of the prosecution thus reveal a remarkable reversal of legal priority: instead of the testimony serving as a means of proving the state's case, Hausner asks one to imagine the trial itself as a means of offering public testimonials. No doubt Hausner would vigorously resist the force of this observation, arguing that the individual testimonies served to clarify the nature and meaning of the defendant's actions. Still, the juridical value of the testimony can be understood as largely a by-product of a process prompted by a radical theory of the trial. The trial was a vehicle of the stories of survivors.

Lawrence Douglas, The Memory of Judgment: Making Law and History in the Trials of the Holocaust 106 (2001). Douglas adds:

> For Hausner, . . . the magnitude of the crimes, their unprecedented nature, the scars on the survivors created the need to reimagine the legal form; the court, by contrast, reached the opposite conclusion. It was the very magnitude of the horrors that framed the futility of attempting to comprehend them. . . . [T]he attempt to do so was an act of overreaching that, in the court's mind, would erode the legitimacy of the . . . institution making such pronouncements. To attempt fully to represent and explain the Holocaust is to exit the world of legitimate juridical function and to risk spectacular failure.

Id. at 144.

Two excerpts from the Eichmann trial illustrate the tension. Both involved the testimony of Holocaust survivors who were also literary figures. The first was the testimony of Abba Kovner, a celebrated resistance fighter and one of Israel's best-known poets. Although Kovner's testimony touched on Eichmann at a few points, most of it consisted of stories, some inspiring and some heartbreaking, of the resistance fighters of the Vilna ghetto and their fates. After Kovner concluded his testimony, the court admonished the prosecutor:

> *Presiding Judge.* Mr. Hausner, we have heard shocking things here, in the language of a poet, but I maintain that in many parts of this evidence we have strayed far from the subject of this trial. There is no possibility at all of interrupting evidence such as this, while it is being rendered, out of respect for the witness and out of respect for the matter he is relating. It is your task . . . to eliminate everything that is not relevant to the trial, so as not to place the Court once again — and this is not the first time — in such a situation. I regret that I have to make these remarks, after the conclusion of evidence such as this.

1 Eichmann Trial at 466, quoted in Douglas, supra, at 137-138, and available at http://www.nizkor.org/hweb/people/e/eichmann-adolf/transcripts/Sessions/Session-027-10.html (at session 27 part ten).

The most famous moment in the Eichmann trial occurred during the testimony of Yehiel Dinur, a death-camp survivor who had published several books on Auschwitz under the name "Katzetnik [concentration camp inmate] 135633"—the number tattooed on his arm in the camp.[17]

Presiding Judge: What is your full name?
Witness: Yehiel Dinur.
Attorney General: Mr. Dinur, you live in Tel Aviv, at 78 Rehov Meggido, and you are a writer?
Witness Dinur: Yes.
Q: You were born in Poland?
A: Yes.
Q: And you were the author of the books Salamandra, The House of Dolls, The Clock Above the Head, and They Called Him Piepel?
A: Yes.
Q: What was the reason that you hid your identity behind the pseudonym "K. Zetnik," Mr. Dinur?
A: It was not a pen name. I do not regard myself as a writer and a composer of literary material. This is a chronicle of the planet of Auschwitz. I was there for about two years. Time there was not like it is here on earth. Every fraction of a minute there passed on a different scale of time. And the inhabitants of this planet had no names, they had no parents nor did they have children. There they did not dress in the way we dress here; they were not born there and they did not give birth; they breathed according to different laws of nature; they did not live — nor did they die — according to the laws of this world. Their name was the number "Katzetnik." They were clad there, how would you call it. . . .
Q: Yes. Is this what you wore there? [Shows the witness the prison garb of Auschwitz.]
A: This is the garb of the planet called Auschwitz. And I believe with perfect faith that I have to continue to bear this name so long as the world has not been aroused after this crucifixion of a nation, to wipe out this evil, in the same way as humanity was aroused after the crucifixion of one man. I believe with perfect faith that, just as in astrology the stars influence our destiny, so does this planet of the ashes, Auschwitz, stand in opposition to our planet earth, and influences it. If I am able to stand before you today and relate the events within that

---

17. "KZ" — pronounced kah-tzet in German, hence the pen-name "Katzetnik" — stands for *Konzentrationslager*, that is, "concentration camp." — EDS.

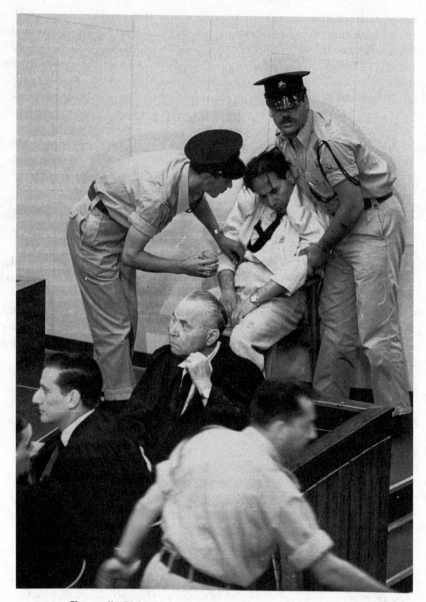

Katzetnik (Yehiel Dinur) collapses at the Eichmann trial.

planet, if I, a fall-out of that planet, am able to be here at this time, then I believe with perfect faith that this is due to the oath I swore to them there. They gave me this strength. This oath was the armour with which I acquired the supernatural power, so that I should be able, after time — the time of Auschwitz — the two years when I was a Musselman, to overcome it.

For they left me, they always left me, they were parted from me, and this oath always appeared in the look of their eyes. For close on two years they kept on taking leave of me and they always left me behind. I see them, they are staring at me, I see them, I saw them standing in the queue. . . .

Q: Perhaps you will allow me, Mr. Dinur, to put a number of questions to you, if you will agree?

A: [Tries to continue] I remember . . .

Presiding Judge: Mr. Dinur, kindly listen to what the Attorney General has to say.

[Witness Dinur rises from his place, descends from the witness stand, and collapses on the platform. The witness fainted.]

Presiding Judge: I think we shall have to adjourn the session. I do not think that we can continue.

Attorney General: I did not anticipate this.

Presiding Judge: [After some time] I do not think that it is possible to go on. We shall adjourn the Session now, and please, Mr. Hausner, inform us of the condition of the witness and whether he will at all be able to give his testimony today. And I would ask you to do so soon.

3 Eichmann Trial at 1237, available at http://www.nizkor.org/hweb/people/e/eichmann-adolf/transcripts/Sessions/Session-068-01.html (session 68 part 1).

Dinur did not return. In the Judgment, the court alluded to his abortive testimony only once:

> . . . Documents were submitted describing the Holocaust in the East, but the bulk of the evidence consisted of statements by witnesses, "brands plucked from the fire," who followed each other in the witness box for days and weeks on end. They spoke simply, and the seal of truth was on their words. But there is no doubt that even they themselves could not find the words to describe their suffering in all its depth. . . . [T]he sum total of the suffering of the millions—about a third of the Jewish people, tortured and slaughtered—is certainly beyond human understanding, and who are we to try to give it adequate expression? This is a task for the great writers and poets. Perhaps it is symbolic that even the author, who himself went through the hell named Auschwitz, could not stand the ordeal in the witness box and collapsed.
>
> Moreover, this part of the indictment is not in dispute in this case. The witnesses who gave evidence about this part were hardly questioned at all by Counsel for the Defence, and at a certain stage in the proceedings he even requested that the Court therefore waive the hearing of these witnesses. To this we could not agree because, since the Accused denied all the counts in the indictment, we had to hear also the evidence on the factual background of the Accused's responsibility, and could not break up the indictment according to a partial admission of facts by the Accused.

Eichmann judgment, ¶119.

Do you find persuasive the court's reason for permitting witnesses with no specific knowledge about Eichmann to testify about the horrors of the Holocaust "for days and weeks on end"? Is it true, as Judge Landau says of the testimony of Abba Kovner, that "[t]here is no possibility at all of interrupting evidence such as this, while it is being rendered, out of respect for the witness and out of respect for the matter he is relating"? The defense had offered to stipulate to the facts of the Holocaust. Did the court owe a duty to permit the survivors their days and weeks in court? Is this what a criminal trial is supposed to be?

CHAPTER
2

International Law Preliminaries

This chapter sets out some basics of international law—the minimum background necessary to understand the materials that follow. We begin by exploring the standard "classical" ideas underlying international law and how they have evolved since World War II (Section A). Then we introduce the basic sources of international law: treaties, custom, general principles, judicial decisions and writings of jurists, and so-called peremptory norms (Section B). After a brief discussion of the perennial question of whether international law is "real" law (Section C), we conclude by exploring the relationship between international law and the law of individual countries and, in particular, the United States (Section D).

Obviously, this chapter cannot substitute for a course in international law, and some of the most crucial topics in international law do not appear here. For one thing, we focus only on *public* international law—international law involving relations among states and international organizations (such as tribunals). We thus omit the elaborate body of doctrines and procedures that govern private law litigation concerning transnational legal issues. For another, we omit discussion of international economic law, including issues of trade law and international sanctions, which can sometimes have criminal aspects. Likewise, we omit crucial subjects like the law of the sea, international environmental law, and the law of international institutions such as the United Nations or the World Trade Organization. This chapter covers only some topics necessary to study international criminal law, which itself forms a relatively small part of international law as a whole.

A point about terminology: In international law—we sometimes call it *IL* for short—the word *state* always means an independent, sovereign country or nation such as Canada, China, or Côte d'Ivoire. This can be confusing for U.S. lawyers, who often use the word to refer to the 50 states of the United States. When we talk about the 50 U.S. states and the context might be unclear, we call them *U.S. states*. International lawyers call state law that applies within a state *municipal law* or *domestic law*. We use the phrase *domestic law*. International agreements and judicial opinions usually capitalize *State*; we generally do not do so except in quotations.

A. THE CLASSICAL PICTURE OF INTERNATIONAL LAW

In its classical formulation, international law governs the relations among sovereign states. As a kind of "public" law, it addresses relationships between states and individuals only incidentally or secondarily. Some international law scholars emphasize this difference by distinguishing between "horizontal" relations of one state to another and "vertical" relations between a state and its citizens or subjects. In the most restrictive view of IL, only horizontal relations count. This classical picture assumes the following:

1. International law governs the relations among states, not between states and their citizens or subjects. IL is to the "society of states" what domestic law is to the persons within a state. In other words, states, not people, business corporations, or international organizations, are the "citizens" of international legal society.
2. Each state has exclusive sovereign authority over its own territory and the persons within that territory.
3. No state has authority over another sovereign state. All states are equal, and no state has authority within the territory of another sovereign state.
4. There is no world government.
5. Therefore, rules of international law exist only when sovereign states consent to them. They can consent explicitly, by making treaties (also known as *conventions* or *international agreements*—for our purposes, the terms are interchangeable). Or states can consent implicitly, by coordinating their behavior through custom. As we will see, *treaty law* and *customary international law* are the two most important forms of IL.

   Because rules of IL require state consent, the classical picture of IL is sometimes called the *consensual model* of IL.
6. Individuals have no rights or obligations under IL unless states grant the rights or create the obligations, either through treaty or custom. International law in its most restrictive form does not "recognize" individuals, only states; and individuals often lack standing to raise claims before international bodies.

Reviewing these six principles, it becomes evident that the idea of international criminal law, which deals entirely with individuals and often crosses state boundaries, fits badly with the classical picture of IL. And indeed, prior to World War II, there was little international law, either conventional or customary, on the subject. As we will see, the rise of international human rights and international criminal law after World War II, as well as the creation of the United Nations (UN), added new principles to the corpus of international law to such an extent that the classical picture no longer accurately portrays IL today. This is especially true of human rights law and international economic law: In both these subjects, many argue that the six classical assumptions no longer accurately describe the law.

1. Historical Overview

The term *international law* is more or less interchangeable with the older term *law of nations*. The newer term was coined in 1780 by the English jurist and philosopher Jeremy Bentham, who thought that it is less likely than *law of nations* to be confused with domestic law. *Law of nations* translates the Latin phrase *jus gentium*, a Roman law concept that referred to the body of law common to all the peoples in the Roman Empire.

The classical picture of international law is the product of a specific time and place: Europe in the age of the nation-state, which began roughly in the seventeenth century. The European origin of international law turns out to be crucial if we wish to understand political debates about IL today. Among other things, it helps explain the resentment that former European colonies occasionally express toward international criminal enforcement. We offer the following view to stimulate discussion and analysis.[1]

a. Westphalian Sovereignty

The classical picture of a world with sovereign states as the primary legal actors began to emerge at the end of the Thirty Years' War (1618-1648), the bloodiest and most catastrophic war in European history before the twentieth century. European society before the Thirty Years' War was not organized into national states as we know them now. Rather, Europe was a political hodgepodge of overlapping dukedoms and principalities, organized loosely into larger political units with crisscrossing loyalties and uncertain jurisdictional boundaries. The war began as a civil war between Protestants and Catholics in Germany, but eventually it embroiled most European powers in a complex struggle for power, territory, and influence. It ended with the Peace of Westphalia, an elaborate treaty that settled the remaining territorial claims. Crucially, the parties to the treaty realized that their only hope for peace lay in an agreement that rulers would not interfere with each other's government of their own territory. Thus was born the modern legal doctrine of sovereignty.

For our purposes, the crucial clauses of the Peace of Westphalia are Articles 64 and 65, which granted sovereign rights to the 300 small principalities that made up the Holy Roman Empire. According to Article 64,

> to prevent for the future any Differences arising in the Politick State, all and every one of the Electors, Princes and States of the Roman Empire, are so establish'd and confirm'd in their antient Rights, Prerogatives, Libertys, Privileges, free exercise of Territorial Right, as well Ecclesiastick, . . . that they never can or ought to be molested therein by any whomsoever upon any manner of pretence.[2]

Article 65 permitted the principalities to "make Alliances with Strangers for their Preservation and Safety," notwithstanding their allegiance to the emperor. These clauses are, symbolically at least, the origin of the doctrine of sovereignty spelled out in the second and third principles of the classical doctrine of IL. Each state is sovereign over its own territory, no state can exercise sovereignty within another state's territory, and states have the right to form their own foreign policies, including decisions about which treaties to enter into with other states. For this reason, the classical picture is often called *Westphalian sovereignty*.

Decades before the Thirty Years' War, the French jurist Jean Bodin developed a theory of absolute royal sovereignty in his famous work *Six Books on the*

---

1. A rich literature is emerging on the history of international law, reflecting diverse perspectives. For several recent examples, see Anthony Anghie, Imperialism, Sovereignty, and the Making of International Law (2005); Wilhelm Grewe & Michael Byers, The Epochs of International Law (2000); Martti Koskenniemi, The Gentle Civilizer of Nations: The Rise and Fall of International Law, 1870-1960 (2002); Stéphane Beaulac, The Westphalian Legal Orthodoxy—Myth or Reality?, 2 J. Hist. Intl. L. 148 (2000); Brett Bowden, The Colonial Origins of International Law: European Expansion and the Classical Standard of Civilisation, 7 J. Hist. Intl. L. 1 (2005); Alexander Orakhelashvili, The Idea of European International Law, 17 Eur. J. Intl. L. 315 (2006).

2. The Treaty of Münster (a city in Westphalia) may be found at the Web site of the Avalon Project of Yale Law School, http://avalon.law.yale.edu/17th_century/westphal.asp.

Commonwealth (1576).[3] Bodin hoped that a strong, centralized monarch whose sovereignty was indivisible would cure the religious wars that wracked France at the time. So too, the English philosopher Thomas Hobbes defended absolute sovereignty in *Leviathan* (1651), a book composed against the background of the religiously inspired English civil war. It is striking that in theory as well as practice, sovereignty was seen primarily as the cure for the evils of civil war and ideological strife. Even in the twentieth century, sovereignty received its strongest defense by the German jurist Carl Schmitt, who grew alarmed over the rebellions and uprisings that tormented the German Republic of the 1920s.[4] (Unfortunately, Schmitt thought that the cure was not merely a sovereign but a dictator, and he eventually became a leading lawyer under Adolf Hitler.) All these theorists insisted that the only cure for disorder is a sovereign with near-absolute powers. As we shall see, one of the obstacles to the development of international legal accountability of political leaders has been their claim to a sovereign right over their own people — a claim, in effect, that their conduct is above the law.

Of course, few if any modern sovereigns are absolute monarchs or führers. Modern sovereignty is divided between different branches of government and many officials; and in many states elections vest sovereignty in the many hands of "the people" rather than concentrating it in a single hand. Nevertheless, from the point of view of classical international law, how sovereignty gets parceled up within a state is irrelevant from the point of view of other states: the basic legal fiction is that every state confronts every other state as a single, undivided sovereign entity. The inner workings of each state remain a "black box" to every other state.

b.   Other Historical Sources of International Law

Along with the wars of religion that gave birth to the theory of Westphalian sovereignty, European international law received a boost from expanding commerce and navigation that began even before the Age of Exploration. Out of practical necessity, maritime codes evolved among the chief seafaring states — England, France, Spain, the Netherlands, and the Baltic states. So too, international merchants developed their own customary norms of fair dealing (called the *law merchant* or *lex mercatoria*), which were precursors of modern international commercial law.

Furthermore, within the Catholic Church — often charged with negotiating peace among warring princes — theories of international law were worked out in considerable detail by canon lawyers of enormous talent. Often, these were natural law theories, which assumed that relations among states are governed by a universal law of nature ordained by God and discoverable by human reason.[5] Natural law is diametrically opposed to the consensual theory of classical IL: The former finds the source of law in "nature and nature's God," the latter in the "positive law," consent, and free will of states. Nevertheless, many of the doctrines of the natural lawyers would be reworked and adopted by later international lawyers, even when their basic philosophy rejected natural law. The natural lawyers brought rigor and system to the law of

---

3. The chapters on sovereignty are available in English in Jean Bodin, On Sovereignty (Julian H. Franklin ed. & trans., 1992).

4. Carl Schmitt, Political Theology: Four Chapters on the Concept of Sovereignty (George Schwab trans., MIT Press 1985) (1922).

5. Among the greatest of the natural lawyers was Hugo Grotius, a Dutch lawyer and diplomat known as the "father of international law." His masterpiece, *The Laws of War and Peace, Including the Law of Nature and of Nations* (1625), proved enormously influential and still attracts readers today.

nations, even if many later lawyers abandoned the philosophical and religious under-pinnings of their work.

It is important to realize that in its formative centuries, the law of nations—genuine public international law, not the law merchant or canon law—did not include very much. Essentially, it consisted of rules concerning the acquisition of territory and recognition of states, rules about diplomatic immunity, and the law governing the high seas. The only international crimes recognized in the early law of nations were piracy and violation of the laws of war: piracy, because it was committed on the high seas rather than in any state's territory, and war crimes, because chivalric codes governed knights who formed an international warrior elite. (However, these codes offered little protection for noncombatants or even for foot soldiers. They were mostly concerned with ensuring that noble knights were not killed by commoners or done in before their families could ransom them back—the ransom of captives being one of the chief sources of income for professional soldiers.) The minimalist content of the law of nations should not surprise us. Commerce across the seas, diplomacy, and war were pretty much the only interactions states had with each other.

c. The Age of Imperialism

One of the basic facts of modern history is the military and political dominance of the European West over the rest of the world, beginning with the discovery of the Americas. Europeans conquered and—through disease as well as design—exterminated most inhabitants of the Americas. Europeans subjugated India, and eventually China as well (though without dethroning the emperors); they occupied Australia, New Zealand, and other Pacific Islands; they colonized Africa; and they chipped away at the Ottoman Empire, eventually reducing it to a second-rate power until they dismantled it at the end of World War I. Historians disagree about the root cause of European dominance, but no one denies the effect—and the outcome totally reshaped the global community.

Not surprisingly, European dominance also dictated the future of international law. It guaranteed that the European conception of IL—the apparatus of Westphalian sovereignty and the consensual theory—would dominate the rest of the world. European dominance had another effect as well, which was anything but benign. Europeans regarded their civilization as plainly superior to that of the rest of the world. Theirs were the "civilized" states, and in the European view Westphalian sovereignty and state consent applied only to civilized states. The society of states meant the society of *civilized* states, and that meant primarily the society of Christian states. The United States and Latin American states eventually joined the club, but until the twentieth century the center of gravity remained in Europe. Christian sovereigns could enter into legal relations with each other. They also recognized—grudgingly—that ancient empires such as China and Japan were proper subjects of international law. But they could hardly bring themselves to view African monarchs and Cherokee chiefs as the legal equals of European kings. When they pretended to, it was often for the deeply cynical purpose of signing treaties with tribal "sovereigns" who could not read them, in which they deeded to the Europeans all rights to their realms in return for small gifts.[6]

---

6. Adam Hochschild, King Leopold's Ghost 70-72 (1998); Koskenniemi, supra note 1, at 136-143.

In European eyes, colonialism was a benign enterprise that would bring the benefits of Christianity and "civilization" to savages and inferior races. Colonialism doubtless conferred some tangible benefits on some subject peoples, in the form of new technologies, economic development, or education. But the process of European colonization was often savagely brutal, especially in Africa, where racist ideology combined with sheer greed to produce treatment of native peoples that was nothing short of atrocious. In the four decades that Belgium's King Leopold personally owned the Congo, for example, the population dropped by an estimated 10 million people — 50 percent. Many were literally enslaved by the Belgians, held in submission with guns and whips, and worked to death extracting rubber and ivory.[7] Congo was perhaps the worst example, but grave abuses and exploitation were far from unusual among European colonizers. The twentieth century's first genocide was committed by Germany against the rebellious Herero people in German Southwest Africa (modern-day Namibia). The German general von Trotha ordered all the Hereros killed, and within three years, three-fourths of them were dead.

The result of European expansion was a world in which international law had spread over the entire face of the globe, but with a double standard: sovereign equality among "civilized" states and subjugation for the rest.

In the nineteenth century natural law doctrines declined, and the idea that sovereigns can do anything not explicitly prohibited by their own consent — including the legal right to engage in war as a legitimate instrument of national policy — reached its high-water mark.

d.   The Consequences of World War II

For the purposes of this book, five important developments affecting the scope and content of international law came in the wake of World War II.

i.   The End of European Dominance

First, the war (so soon after World War I) ended more than three centuries of European dominance, including dominance over international law. Much of Europe lay in ruins. Total war dead have been estimated at 65 to 75 million people, on top of the 13 to 15 million killed in World War I; and in Germany, the Soviet Union, China, and Japan, major cities were obliterated.[8]

ii.   Decolonization

Second, weakened European states could no longer hang on to their colonies, and over the next two decades nearly all former colonies became independent states. Moreover, ideology changed, and even former colonial powers came to reject colonialism as politically immoral — a change comparable to the rejection of human slavery in the nineteenth century. Together, the end of European dominance and

---

7. Hochschild, supra note 6, at 233. For many years, King Leopold literally owned the Congo — it was his own personal land. Only later did he transfer it to the Belgian state.

8. Milton Leitenberg, Deaths in Wars and Conflicts Between 1945 and 2000, Cornell University Peace Studies Program, Occasional Paper #29 (July 2003).

the decolonization process meant that henceforth other cultures and other ways of understanding the world informed the process of international lawmaking. Ironically, however, decolonization probably strengthened rather than weakened the classical Westphalian picture of sovereignty. Former colonies, now independent states, were understandably proud to attain self-determining sovereign status. Suggestions by well-meaning jurists that Westphalian sovereignty has outlived its usefulness have often met strong resistance from former colonies, which regard criticisms of sovereignty as a veiled form of neocolonialism. We shall see this dynamic at work in the *Arrest Warrant Case (Congo v. Belgium)*, the leading case on criminal immunity of foreign officials, in Chapter 6.

iii.   The Trials of Major War Criminals

The third major development lay in the postwar trials of German and Japanese leaders before international military tribunals at Nuremberg and Tokyo. We examine these in detail later in the next chapter. Here, we simply note that at Nuremberg, a body of law developed under which the international community could hold individuals liable for crimes, even if the crimes were committed with the blessing of the perpetrators' own governments.

The Nuremberg and Tokyo trials influenced the development of modern international law in at least three ways:

1. they were conducted by the first modern international criminal tribunals;
2. they established the idea of personal responsibility and accountability as a matter of international law, stripping immunity from heads of state and removing defenses of superior orders and legality under domestic law; and
3. they created many specific legal doctrines that have been incorporated into international criminal law by subsequent tribunals and national courts.

iv.   Human Rights Law

The fourth crucial postwar development is the emergence of international human rights law. The level of atrocity in World War II — most notoriously, the Holocaust — sounded an alarm throughout the world that special protection is necessary for individual human rights and human dignity. After the war, Eleanor Roosevelt became head of a UN committee charged with producing a human rights document. In 1948, the General Assembly adopted the Universal Declaration of Human Rights (UDHR).

Deliberations over the UDHR were marked by deep philosophical and political disagreements. For example, Western capitalist states argued that political rights such as freedom of speech and freedom to organize political parties are the most important human rights, whereas socialist and communist countries focused on economic rights such as the right to a job. Women's rights, along with freedom of religion, also proved controversial. Fundamental questions arose over whether the document should refer to God or discuss the divine origin of human dignity. (The delegates decided to omit reference to God.) Furthermore, many countries harbored suspicions that a binding human rights treaty might erode their sovereignty. To quiet the latter suspicion, the UDHR was specifically cast as a declaration and *not* a treaty, and it created no binding legal obligations. (However, as we shall see, portions of the UDHR are now accepted by many as reflecting customary international law.) Under the skillful leadership of Eleanor Roosevelt and a remarkable group of four statesmen from China, France, Lebanon, and Canada, the delegates hammered out a workable document that was adopted by the General Assembly without a single "no" vote (although eight states abstained).[9]

Nearly two decades later, the UDHR received an important supplement when the UN General Assembly adopted two binding human rights treaties. The International Covenant on Civil and Political Rights (ICCPR) was favored by Western capitalist countries and focused on civil rights, civil liberties, and rights to political participation. The International Covenant on Economic, Social, and Cultural Rights (ICESCR) received its impetus from the socialist world and focused on economic rights (such as the right to fair wages and freedom from hunger) and social rights (such as the right to education). The General Assembly proposed these two treaties in 1966, and they entered into force (that is, became legally operative when a specified minimum number of states became parties to the treaties through ratification under domestic law) a decade later. About three-fourths of all states are parties to each of them. (The United States is party to ICCPR but not ICESCR.)

Together, the UDHR, ICCPR, and ICESCR are often referred to as the *International Bill of Rights*. The ICCPR also contains an Optional Protocol permitting individuals to file human rights complaints with the UN's Human Rights Committee, and a Second Optional Protocol abolishing the death penalty. The United States is not a party to either protocol.

In addition to these basic documents, states have adopted other treaties to protect human rights. Crucial among them for purposes of this book are

- the Convention on the Prevention and Punishment of the Crime of Genocide (Genocide Convention), adopted in 1948 and entered in force two years later;
- the Convention Against Torture (CAT), adopted in 1984 and entered into force in 1987; and
- the four Geneva Conventions (1949), which govern the treatment of wartime captives, together with two supplementary protocols adopted in 1977.

Others include treaties to combat racial discrimination and discrimination against women; treaties to protect children and to combat human trafficking; and important regional human rights treaties open to states in geographic regions such as the Americas, Africa, or Europe. The most powerful of these is the 1950 European Convention for the Protection of Human Rights and Fundamental Freedoms (the European Convention). The European Court of Human Rights (ECHR), created by the European Convention to adjudicate complaints lodged under the Convention, is considered to be the foremost court of human rights in the world. Other regional treaties include the African [Banjul] Charter on Human and People's Rights and the American Convention on Human Rights.

Some human rights treaties contain criminal enforcement provisions, but most do not. None of the three documents in the International Bill of Rights contains criminal enforcement provisions. Nevertheless, the growth of human rights law changed the paradigm of IL, and this paradigm shift paved the way for the growth of international criminal law. Under the classical view, IL primarily concerns the mutual relations of states. With the emergence of the international law of human rights, it is now recognized that how a state deals with its own citizens and subjects is also a legitimate focus

---

9. A highly readable account is Mary Ann Glendon, A World Made New: Eleanor Roosevelt and the Universal Declaration of Human Rights (2001).

of international law. In much the same way, the emergence of international criminal law reflects acceptance by the international community that it is a legitimate function of international law to impose criminal liability upon individuals for gross violations of human rights (such as genocide, crimes against humanity, or trafficking in children). In other words, the development of international criminal law has been closely connected to, and a real beneficiary of, the human rights revolution.

It is important to recognize that by themselves, human rights treaties do not necessarily protect human rights in fact. Nor is it sufficient merely for states to become parties to those treaties. Indeed, one well-known study found that many states' human rights records got worse rather than better after they ratified human rights treaties.[10] What matters is whether and how states live up to their commitments by respecting human rights in practice — in other words, how they actually implement their treaty obligations at the domestic level. The same can be said, of course, about international criminal law treaties. For our purposes, however, the significance of human rights treaties lies in their vast effect on the structure of IL, regardless of how well they have succeeded in their goals of protecting human rights.

v. The United Nations

The fifth crucial consequence of World War II is the birth of the United Nations, perhaps the most important of the five changes in international law we have examined. Like the other topics we survey here, this is a very large subject, and we mention only a few features of the UN system that are important for international criminal law.

(1) Basic Structure: General Assembly, Security Council, and Secretariat

The United Nations is not a world government. It is, fundamentally, an organization of states designed in part to head off major world conflicts before they happen. The UN Charter, adopted in 1945, is a multilateral treaty. This treaty currently boasts 192 states parties. (A *state party* is a country that has formally accepted, and thus is legally bound by, the treaty as a result of its ratification of the treaty pursuant to the requirements of its domestic law.) The Charter is a treaty with special "constitutional" status: It creates the institutions of the UN and defines their powers, and Article 103 of the Charter specifies that if the Charter conflicts with any other treaty to which a UN member state is a state party, the Charter prevails.

The UN has a complex organizational structure. The most pertinent components of the UN system for our purposes are the General Assembly, the Security Council, the Secretariat, and the International Court of Justice (ICJ).

The General Assembly is an assembly of all the member states, each of which gets a single vote. The General Assembly is *not* a global legislature, however: With minor exceptions, its powers are limited to discussion, recommendation, and choosing members of other UN bodies. It cannot enact "world laws." The real decision-making power in the UN in the 15-member Security Council, which, under Article 24 of the Charter, has "primary responsibility for the maintenance of international peace and security." The Security Council has 5 permanent members — the United States, Russia, China, the United Kingdom, and France — each of which has the power to

---

10. Oona A. Hathaway, Do Human Rights Treaties Make a Difference?, 111 Yale L.J. 1935 (2002).

veto any Security Council resolution. The other 10 members are elected for two-year terms by the General Assembly.

Article 39 of the Charter indicates the wide-ranging power of the Security Council:

> The Security Council shall determine the existence of any threat to the peace, breach of the peace, or act of aggression and shall make recommendations, or decide what measures shall be taken . . . to maintain or restore international peace and security.

This Article belongs to Chapter VII of the Charter—hence the often-heard reference to the Council's "Chapter VII powers." These include the power to impose compulsory sanctions and the power to send armed peacekeepers, drawn from the armies of member states, to international trouble spots. As we shall see, several international criminal tribunals were created under the Security Council's Chapter VII powers.

The Secretariat, working under the Secretary General, is roughly analogous to the executive branch of a national government. Its almost 9,000 employees carry out functions that, in the words of the UN's Web site, "range from administering peace-keeping operations to mediating international disputes, from surveying economic and social trends and problems to preparing studies on human rights and sustainable development. Secretariat staff also inform the world's communications media about the work of the UN; organize international conferences on issues of worldwide concern; and interpret speeches and translate documents into the Organization's official languages."[11] From an IL perspective, reports to and by the Secretary General can serve as important interpretive authorities and help define the contours of states' obligations under relevant texts.

(2) The International Court of Justice

The ICJ (sometimes called the World Court) is the judicial arm of the UN. It has jurisdiction to hear certain disputes between states—not individual litigants—over questions of international law when the parties to the dispute have so agreed. By virtue of Article 96 of the Charter, it can also render advisory opinions when requested by the General Assembly, Security Council, or (in some circumstances) other UN organs.

To U.S. students, the name *World Court* may suggest a court of vast powers—something akin to a Supreme Court of international law, proclaiming universally binding interpretations of international law. This is far from the case, however, as Article 59 from the Statute of the International Court of Justice makes clear: "The decision of the Court has no binding force except between the parties and in respect of that particular case." In other words, the ICJ's decisions bind only the states litigating in the case at hand; they do not bind even those states in similar disputes arising between them. In some respects, therefore, the ICJ is more like an arbitrator than a Supreme Court. In theory at least, its decisions are not binding precedents, and there is no principle of *stare decisis*. That is, the ICJ does *not* issue opinions that definitively resolve international law questions for all time and all purposes. One of the difficulties of studying international law is that there *is* no such body. The ICJ is actually very limited in its jurisdiction and powers, consistent with traditional notions of sovereignty. However, even though ICJ opinions are not binding precedents, they can

---

11. United Nations, Secretariat Home Page, http://www.un.org/documents/st.htm.

be extremely influential persuasive authority on international law and are often cited for that purpose.

The ICJ consists of 15 judges, no two of whom can be from the same state. States nominate candidates, and the UN General Assembly and Security Council vote on them. Judges serve renewable nine-year terms, and they are typically drawn from the upper echelon of international lawyers in their home states.

Who can litigate before the ICJ? The answer is, states, and states alone. No individuals, corporations, organizations of states (such as the Organization of American States or the North Atlantic Treaty Organization), or nongovernmental organizations such as Amnesty International can appear as parties before the ICJ. Often, however, states bring cases before the ICJ because of injuries done by other states to their own nationals or corporations.

When can the ICJ take jurisdiction over a dispute among states? The ICJ Statute defines two forms of jurisdiction: optional and compulsory.

STATUTE OF THE INTERNATIONAL COURT OF JUSTICE
Article 36

1. The jurisdiction of the Court comprises all cases which the parties refer to it and all matters specially provided for in the Charter of the United Nations or in treaties and conventions in force.

2. The states parties to the present Statute may at any time declare that they recognize as compulsory ipso facto and without special agreement, in relation to any other state accepting the same obligation, the jurisdiction of the Court in all legal disputes concerning:

    a. the interpretation of a treaty;

    b. any question of international law;

    c. the existence of any fact which, if established, would constitute a breach of an international obligation;

    d. the nature or extent of the reparation to be made for the breach of an international obligation.

3. The declarations referred to above may be made unconditionally or on condition of reciprocity on the part of several or certain states, or for a certain time. . . .

Thus, states can be sued in the ICJ only if they consent. Even the ICJ's so-called compulsory jurisdiction is compulsory only if a nation has agreed to be subject to the ICJ's jurisdiction, and states can withdraw their consent (as the United States did in 1986 when it did not like an ICJ ruling against it).

Finally, the ICJ has no power to enforce its judgments through sanctions. The only effective remedy for a state's noncompliance with an ICJ order is a political appeal to the member nations and the Security Council.

In addition to litigation between states — so-called contentious cases — the ICJ "may give an advisory opinion on any legal question at the request of whatever body may be authorized by or in accordance with the Charter of the United Nations to make such a request" (Article 65). Some of these advisory opinions are extraordinarily interesting and important. In 1996, at the request of the UN General Assembly, the ICJ issued an advisory opinion on the legality of nuclear weapons; and in 2004 — again at the request of the General Assembly — it rendered an advisory opinion on the legality of Israel's security fence.[12] These opinions result in no "order," but they are important authority on international law. The ICJ has issued only 24 advisory opinions since its founding.

Historically, the ICJ (like its League of Nations predecessor, the Permanent Court of International Justice — which, despite its name, lasted only a few years) has never been enormously active. This is hardly surprising, given that only states can litigate in these courts. In effect, the ICJ is the court of a community with 192 residents, all of whom prefer to settle most of their grievances through negotiation rather than litigation. In its 80-year history, the ICJ and its predecessor have rendered fewer than 200 decisions, most of them concerning boundary disputes.

However, in recent years the ICJ's docket has been filled with high-profile cases, including some important international criminal law cases concerning jurisdiction, allegations of genocide filed by Bosnia against Serbia and by the Democratic Republic of Congo against Rwanda, and some actions by Serbia against other countries growing out of the Balkan wars of the 1990s.[13]

It is difficult to judge the full effect of the United Nations on the classical Westphalian picture of IL. The UN was founded by states that jealously guarded their own sovereignty, as states continue to do today. Among the most important provisions of the Charter are Article 2(1), which enshrines "the principle of the sovereign equality of all its Members"; Article 2(4), which forbids states from using force or the threat of force against the territorial integrity or political independence of any state; and Article 51, which preserves each state's inherent right of self-defense.

At the same time, however, the veto power of the Security Council's permanent members ensures that in a world of "sovereign equality," some states are more equal than others. More important, it seems clear that the UN has profoundly altered the structure of international decision making and made unilateralism less legitimate. In this way, it indirectly limits states' sovereign powers. Finally, as we shall see, the UN has become an important source of customary international law.

2. The Modified Classical Picture of International Law

Where have these changes in the international legal order left us? The easiest way to see the changes is by reviewing the elements of the classical picture, noting the exceptions along the way.

1. Public international law still governs the relations among states but increasingly addresses questions about how states deal with individuals — notably including environmental law, laws of war and humanitarian law, human rights law, and international criminal law, all of which do protect rights and impose obligations on persons.
2. Each state has exclusive sovereign authority over its own territory and citizens — except that states have no authority to launch aggressive wars, nor to violate basic human rights, nor to sponsor actions that constitute international crimes (among other exceptions).

---

12. Legality of the Threat or Use of Nuclear Weapons, Advisory Opinion, 1996 I.C.J. 226 (July 8); Legal Consequences of the Construction of a Wall in the Occupied Palestinian Territory, Advisory Opinion, 2004 I.C.J. 136 (July 9).

13. Students should consult the ICJ's Web site, http://www.icj-cij.org/. Examine the home page and the "Cases" section for an overview of the court's activities.

3. No state has authority over another sovereign state — except that the UN Security Council can authorize action on the territory of states against threats to international peace and security.
4. There is no world government — but there are numerous regional and worldwide organizations that sometimes assume limited governmental functions.
5. Therefore, rules of international law exist only when sovereign states consent to them — except, as we shall see, that agreements to violate basics of the international order (such as the prohibition on genocide or on aggressive war) have no legal force even if states consent to them.
6. Individuals do have rights and obligations under IL insofar as states have recognized such rights and obligations through treaties or customary international law. It is still true, however, that normally individuals lack standing to raise claims of IL before international bodies — except bodies such as the European Court of Human Rights.

We should emphasize that this modified classical picture of international law holds to a greater extent in some areas of law than others. In international trade law, for example, states have accepted a greater role for individuals and individual participation than in international criminal law; and European Union members have likewise ceded more sovereignty than the classical picture (even the modified classical picture) may suggest.[14]

B. THE SOURCES OF INTERNATIONAL LAW

We turn next to the sources of international law, in order to understand what IL consists of. The following documents are two of the most influential statements of the sources of international law.

STATUTE OF THE INTERNATIONAL COURT OF JUSTICE
Article 38

1. The Court, whose function is to decide in accordance with international law such disputes as are submitted to it, shall apply:
    a. international conventions, whether general or particular, establishing rules expressly recognized by the contesting states;
    b. international custom, as evidence of a general practice accepted as law;
    c. the general principles of law recognized by civilized nations;
    d. subject to the provisions of Article 59, judicial decisions and the teachings of the most highly qualified publicists of the various nations, as subsidiary means for the determination of rules of law.

---

14. For recent scholarly discussion of the uncertain hold of Westphalian sovereignty, see Stephen D. Krasner, Sovereignty: Organized Hypocrisy (1999); John H. Jackson, Sovereignty-Modern: A New Approach to an Outdated Concept, 97 Am. J. Intl. L. 783 (2003).

RESTATEMENT (THIRD) OF THE FOREIGN RELATIONS
LAW OF THE UNITED STATES

(1987)

§102 SOURCES OF INTERNATIONAL LAW

(1) A rule of international law is one that has been accepted as such by the international community of states
  (a) in the form of customary law;
  (b) by international agreement; or
  (c) by derivation from general principles common to the major legal systems of the world.

(2) Customary international law results from a general and consistent practice of states followed by them from a sense of legal obligation.

(3) International agreements create law for the states parties thereto and may lead to the creation of customary international law when such agreements are intended for adherence by states generally and are in fact widely accepted.

(4) General principles common to the major legal systems, even if not incorporated or reflected in customary law or international agreement, may be invoked as supplementary rules of international law where appropriate.

COMMENTS & ILLUSTRATIONS:

Comment:

. . . *b. Practice as customary law.* "Practice of states," Subsection (2), includes diplomatic acts and instructions as well as public measures and other governmental acts and official statements of policy, whether they are unilateral or undertaken in cooperation with other states (for example in organizations such as the Organization for Economic Cooperation and Development). Inaction may constitute state practice, as when a state acquiesces in acts of another state that affect its legal rights. The practice necessary to create customary law may be of comparatively short duration, but under Subsection (2) it must be "general and consistent." A practice can be general even if it is not universally followed; there is no precise formula to indicate how widespread a practice must be, but it should reflect wide acceptance among the states particularly involved in the relevant activity. . . . A principle of customary law is not binding on a state that declares its dissent from the principle during its development. See Comment d.

c. Opinio juris. For a practice of states to become a rule of customary international law it must appear that the states follow the practice from a sense of legal obligation (*opinio juris sive necessitatis*); a practice that is generally followed but which states feel legally free to disregard does not contribute to customary law. A practice initially followed by states as a matter of courtesy or habit may become law when states generally come to believe that they are under a legal obligation to comply with it. It is often difficult to determine when that transformation into law has taken place.

d. Dissenting views and new states. Although customary law may be built by the acquiescence as well as by the actions of states (Comment b) and become generally binding on all states, in principle a state that indicates its dissent from a practice while the law is still in the process of development is not bound by that rule even after it matures. Historically, such dissent and consequent exemption from a principle that became general customary law has been rare. A state that enters the international system after a practice has ripened into a rule of international law is bound by that rule.

e. General and special custom. The practice of states in a regional or other special grouping may create "regional," "special," or "particular" customary law for those states *inter se.*

f. International agreement as source of law. An international agreement creates obligations binding between the parties under international law. International agreements may contribute to customary law. See Comment i.

g. Binding resolutions of international organizations. Some international agreements that are constitutions or charters of international organizations confer power on those organizations to impose binding obligations on their members by resolution, usually by qualified majorities. Such obligations derive their authority from the international agreement constituting the organization, and resolutions so adopted by the organization can be seen as "secondary sources" of international law for its members. For example, the International Monetary Fund may prescribe rules concerning maintenance or change of exchange rates or depreciation of currencies.

h. The United Nations Charter. The Charter of the United Nations has been adhered to by virtually all states. Even the few remaining non-member states have acquiesced in the principles it established. The Charter provisions prohibiting the use of force have become rules of international law binding on all states. . . .

i. International agreements codifying or contributing to customary law. International agreements constitute practice of states and as such can contribute to the growth of customary law under Subsection (2). Some multilateral agreements may come to be law for non-parties that do not actively dissent. That may be the effect where a multilateral agreement is designed for adherence by states generally, is widely accepted, and is not rejected by a significant number of important states. A wide network of similar bilateral arrangements on a subject may constitute practice and also result in customary law. If an international agreement is declaratory of, or contributes to, customary law, its termination by the parties does not of itself affect the continuing force of those rules as international law. However, the widespread repudiation of the obligations of an international agreement may be seen as state practice adverse to the continuing force of the obligations. See Comment j.

j. Conflict between international agreement and customary law. Customary law and law made by international agreement have equal authority as international law. Unless the parties evince a contrary intention, a rule established by agreement supersedes for them a prior inconsistent rule of customary international law. However, an agreement will not supersede a prior rule of customary law that is a peremptory norm of international law. . . .

k. Peremptory norms of international law (jus cogens). Some rules of international law are recognized by the international community of states as peremptory, permitting no derogation. These rules prevail over and invalidate international agreements and other rules of international law in conflict with them. Such a peremptory norm is subject to modification only by a subsequent norm of international law having the same character. It is generally accepted that the principles of the United Nations Charter prohibiting the use of force (Comment h) have the character of *jus cogens.*

l. General principles as secondary source of law. Much of international law, whether customary or constituted by agreement, reflects principles analogous to those found in the major legal systems of the world, and historically may derive from them or from a more remote common origin. General principles common to systems of national law may be resorted to as an independent source of law. That source of law may be important when there has not been practice by states sufficient to give the particular principle status as customary law and the principle has not been legislated by general international agreement.

General principles are a secondary source of international law, resorted to for developing international law interstitially in special circumstances. For example, the passage of time as a defense to an international claim by a state on behalf of a national may not have had sufficient application in practice to be accepted as a rule of customary law. Nonetheless, it may be invoked as a rule of international law, at least in claims based on injury to persons, because it is a general principle common to the major legal systems of the world and is not inappropriate for international claims. Other rules that have been drawn from general principles include rules relating to the administration of justice, such as the rule that no one may be judge in his own cause; res judicata; and rules of fair procedure generally. General principles may also provide "rules of reason" of a general character, such as acquiescence and estoppel, the principle that rights must not be abused, and the obligation to repair a wrong. International practice may sometimes convert such a principle into a rule of customary law. . . .

NOTES AND QUESTIONS

1. Article 38 of the ICJ Statute sets out the sources of law that the ICJ will use in resolving disputes brought before it. Strictly speaking, it binds only the ICJ and does not purport to set out a universal system of international law. Nevertheless, because the ICJ settles disputes about international law among consenting UN members, its statute has had great persuasive power in the delineation of the sources of IL. The Restatement (Third) of the Foreign Relations Law of the United States, composed by the influential American Law Institute, represents a dominant mainstream view of IL in the postwar world. Do the ICJ Statute and the Restatement identify the same sources of IL? Do they accord different weights to different sources?

2. Both documents single out two fundamental sources of IL: treaties (agreements) and custom. Both acknowledge the role of so-called general principles — the ICJ Statute regarding them as a primary source of IL, the Restatement regarding them as a supplementary, interpretive source. The ICJ Statute also recognizes the opinions of highly qualified commentators as a supplemental source. A few comments are in order about each of these.

1. International Agreements (Treaties)

An international agreement, also known as a treaty or convention (the words *treaty* and *convention* are synonyms in IL; *covenant*, *protocol*, and *pact* are also synonyms for *treaty*), is an explicit agreement among its states parties. The IL rules about treaties are themselves codified in a treaty, the Vienna Convention on the Law of Treaties (VCLT), which was adopted in 1969 and entered into force in 1980. The United States has not ratified the VCLT but generally accepts that many of its provisions represent a codification of binding customary international law.

The two most basic principles in the VCLT are simple: First, under Article 6, "[e]very State possesses capacity to conclude treaties"; and second, under Article 26, "[e]very treaty in force is binding upon the parties to it and must be performed by them in good faith." This latter principle is often referred to by the Roman law maxim *pacta sunt servanda* (agreements must be kept).

Treaties are negotiated and signed by representatives of the states parties' governments. To become binding, the states must then formally accept or ratify a treaty, although treaties themselves can stipulate alternative means of acceptance. What constitutes ratification in a given state depends on the state's domestic law. Thus, for example, in the United States, a treaty signed by the executive does not take effect until after two-thirds of the Senate gives its advice and consent to the treaty and the president then formally ratifies it.

A treaty normally does not come into force — that is, bind the parties as a matter of IL to all the treaty's particulars — until a certain number of states have signed and ratified it, thus becoming parties to it. The number of states that must join prior to the treaty "entering into force" is generally spelled out in the treaty itself. Students may encounter another word — *accession* — in connection with treaty membership. Accession, which has the same effect as ratification, simply means that a state has agreed to be bound by the treaty after the treaty has come into force. According to Article 18 of the VCLT, signing a treaty obligates states not to take actions that would "defeat the object and purpose" of the treaty, even if the treaty has not yet been accepted or entered into force.

States need not accept treaties in an all-or-nothing manner (unless the treaty provides otherwise). Thus, states are permitted to enter "reservations" to portions of a treaty, provided that the reservation is not "incompatible with the object and purpose" of the treaty and that reservations are not precluded by the terms of the treaty. They may also accompany their acceptance of a treaty with "understandings" about how they interpret the meaning of phrases and concepts in the treaty, or "declarations" of actions the state will or will not take in complying with the treaty. In the United States, these three types of qualifications to a treaty are often referred to collectively as RUDs.

2. *Customary International Law*

As the ICJ Statute and the Restatement indicate, customary international law (CIL) consists of widespread state practice (sometimes designated by the Latin word *usus*) undertaken out of a sense of legal obligation (usually referred to as *opinio juris*). Both elements are required. A sense of legal obligation with no state practice could hardly count as customary law because the custom is missing. Conversely, states might engage in a customary practice for reasons of political expediency rather than a belief that the practice is legally required. In that case, the practice is not CIL. It is important to bear in mind this difference between nonbinding custom and customary international law.

One particular category of political expediency can be especially difficult to distinguish from CIL. This consists of rules of *comity*. Comity generally means something akin to courtesy or mutual respect — a willingness to accommodate other states out of goodwill (and, usually, the hope that the other state will reciprocate), rather than legal obligation. To illustrate with a trivial example, states customarily treat visiting presidents and prime ministers with courtesy and decorum. The host state does not put them up in cheesy strip-mall motels or serve them instant coffee in Styrofoam cups. But the pomp and circumstance of state visits is a matter of comity, not a rule of international law. There is no legal obligation to roll out the red carpet and use the fancy china. By contrast, that visiting heads of state or heads of government will typically enjoy immunity from suit in the courts of the host country is a matter of CIL, a binding rule widely recognized and accepted by the international community.

(On rare occasions, U.S. courts have treated rules of comity as legally binding, but in contexts far removed from international criminal law.[15])

As comment b to Restatement §102 indicates, "state practice" need not consist solely of state behavior "on the ground." Instead, it can be evidenced by official governmental acts such as the passage of laws. Because of the difficulty of determining state practice, today many look to supplemental indicators. For example, when a duly authorized foreign minister says "we accept X or don't accept Y," that can be authoritative. When the UN General Assembly unanimously adopts a resolution specifically endorsing a statement of CIL, that too can provide some authoritative evidence.

The fact that state practice can be evidenced by such acts of national governments as passing laws or ratifying treaties is very important. For example, it is universally agreed that CIL prohibits states from engaging in torture. But a glance through the annual reports of Amnesty International or U.S. State Department country reports on human rights shows that a great many states persist in the practice of torture. How, then, could the rule of CIL exist, if state practice consists of torture rather than its absence? The answer is that states can violate legal obligations that they themselves have helped create, engaging in torture even though they officially condemn it. Virtually all states have enacted laws criminalizing torture or ratified the UN Convention Against Torture, or both. In international law, their domestic laws and treaty ratifications *are* state practice that contributes to the formation of CIL. Hence, it is no contradiction to announce that a CIL rule against torture exists in a world where torture continues to be practiced or condoned by many states. It means only that those states (and their officials) violate the law.

The fact that state practice can include state acts that are symbolic rather than tangible — the enactment of laws or the ratification of a treaty — does have one curious implication. It means that sometimes the identical state behavior — for example, the enactment of a criminal law against torture in order to comply with treaty obligations — gets "double counted" as both state practice and *opinio juris*. There is nothing untoward about this: If a state criminalizes torture out of respect for what it takes to be international legal obligation, then enacting the anti-torture statute is at once state practice and evidence of *opinio juris*.

Official state pronouncements and declarations, General Assembly resolutions, and the like are sometimes referred to as "soft law." Unlike treaty ratifications, they do not themselves impose legal obligations, and so they are not "hard law." However, they can contribute to the formation of CIL by providing evidence of states' *opinio juris*, and jurists have sometimes claimed that over time and repetition, soft law pronouncements have hardened into CIL.

Other commentators object to the proposition that nonbinding soft law can transmute into binding hard law through widespread repetition — or that there is such a thing as soft or nonbinding law. As one author warns, "the accumulation of nonlaw or prelaw is no more sufficient to create law than is thrice nothing to make something."[16] This is particularly important in the area of human rights, where, according to critics, states frequently issue pious declarations in favor of human rights

---

15. See, e.g., F. Hoffmann-La Roche Ltd. v. Empagran S.A., 542 U.S. 155 (2004); Hartford Fire Ins. Co. v. California, 509 U.S. 764 (1993); Hilton v. Guyot, 159 U.S. 113 (1895). The doctrine of comity appears to have originated in seventeenth-century Holland. See Hessel E. Yntema, The Comity Doctrine, 65 Mich. L. Rev. 9, 25-28 (1966).

16. Prosper Weil, Towards Relative Normativity in International Law?, 77 Am. J. Intl. L. 413, 417 (1983).

while continuing to ignore those rights both in their own domestic law and in their behavior on the ground. The declarations may lead human rights–oriented jurists to announce new customary rules of human rights law that seem to be purchased through talk alone (and talk is cheap). Thus, two respected jurists criticize such rules as "a cultured pearl version of customary international law" that operates "through proclamation, exhortation, repetition, incantation, lament."[17] Two other scholars, labeling such rules "the new customary international law," denounce them as "incoherent and illegitimate."[18] As we will see in this book, similar criticisms have been raised against expansive new rules of international criminal law.

Do you agree with the criticism? How could a defender of the "new customary international law" respond? If all states denounce human slavery and label it "criminal," even in nonbinding "soft" government statements, isn't that a basis for stating that human slavery violates CIL, even if the practice persists in some countries?

According to comment b to Restatement §102, "a practice can be general even if it is not universally followed." In other words, a rule of CIL can exist even if some states do not participate in the custom — and the rule may bind those states as well. How is this consistent with the consensual model of IL, according to which states can be bound by rules only if they consent to them?

Perhaps it is not. One way that IL accommodates the tension between consensualism and the binding force of customary rules is by creating an important exception. A state that persistently objects to a rule of CIL throughout the period in which the rule is being formed will not be bound by the rule. However, if the state has not persistently objected, it may be bound by the rule whether it likes it or not. To take an important example: Over the past 60 years, the majority of states have abolished capital punishment in their domestic law or practice, and several multilateral treaties (including the Second Protocol to the ICCPR) have also abolished it among their states parties. However, even if an anti-death-penalty rule of CIL is emerging, it would not bind any state that has persistently objected.

How are rules of CIL determined? Unfortunately, there are few shortcuts to the painstaking process of examining treaties together with the laws, judicial decisions, official acts, and actual practice of many states, state by state, to determine that a state practice backed by *opinio juris* exists. International judicial decisions and scholarly treatises on CIL sometimes make for mind-numbingly tedious reading as, for paragraph after paragraph and page after page, they review the minutiae of documents from many states. Tedious or not, however, this is the only responsible way to determine CIL. Even then, controversies can emerge. For example, in 2005 the International Committee on the Red Cross (ICRC) published a handbook on the CIL governing armed conflicts, the product of a ten-year research effort by a large team. A first volume that enumerates and explains the CIL rules is 676 pages long. Two additional volumes canvass worldwide state practice and *opinio juris* for each of these rules — and these volumes weigh in at 4,449 pages.[19] Nevertheless, the U.S. State and Defense Departments have issued a detailed criticism of the ICRC's handbook, arguing that its authors and editors relied on some sources that are not

17. Bruno Simma & Philip Alston, The Sources of Human Rights Law: Custom, *Jus Cogens*, and General Principles, 12 Austl. Y.B. Intl. L. 82, 89 (1992).

18. Jack L. Goldsmith & Eric A. Posner, Understanding the Resemblance Between Modern and Traditional Customary International Law, 40 Va. J. Intl. L. 639, 640 (2000).

19. Customary International Humanitarian Law (Jean-Marie Henckaerts & Louise Doswald-Beck eds., 2005): volume 1, Rules; volume 2, Practice, Parts I and II.

legitimate state practice or *opinio juris* and overread other sources.[20] (In its turn, the ICRC has defended its work against the U.S. criticisms.[21])

3. General Principles

As both the ICJ Statute and the Restatement indicate, general principles common to most domestic legal systems are also a source of international law. Comment *l* to Restatement §102 cites as examples "the rule that no one may be judge in his own cause; res judicata; and rules of fair procedure generally." Within international criminal law, important general principles include the principle of legality and the rule against double jeopardy (referred to in international practice by the Latin phrase *ne bis in idem*).

Notice that in Article 38 of the ICJ statute, general principles are a source of law on the same footing as treaty and custom; but in Restatement §102, they are only a secondary source of law. What might account for that difference? How well do general principles fit with the consensual model of IL? Have states that adopted the ban on double jeopardy in their domestic criminal justice systems really consented to having it become a rule of international law?

As a practical matter, the determination of "general principles" may invest judges with a great deal of discretion. An ICJ judge has opined that "the true view of the duty of international tribunals [in applying 'general principles'] is to regard any features or terminology which are reminiscent of the rules and institutions of private law as an indication of policy and practices rather than as directly importing these rules and institutions."[22] Similarly, two judges of the International Tribunal for the Former Yugoslavia (ICTY) explained in *Prosecutor v. Erdemovic*:

> [O]ur approach will necessarily not involve a direct comparison of the specific rules of each of the world's legal systems, but will instead involve a survey of those jurisdictions whose jurisprudence is, as a practical matter, accessible to us in an effort to discern a general trend, policy or principle underlying the concrete rules of that jurisdiction which comports with the object and purpose of the establishment of the International Tribunal.[23]

4. "Judicial Decisions and Teachings of the Most Highly Qualified Publicists"

Notice that Article 38 of the ICJ Statute makes "judicial decisions and teachings of the most highly qualified publicists" subsidiary sources of law, while Restatement §102

---

20. Letter from John B. Bellinger III, State Department Legal Advisor, and William B. Haynes II, General Counsel of Dept. of Defense, to Jakob Kellenberger, President, ICRC, Nov. 3, 2006, available at http://www.defenselink.mil/home/pdf/Customary_International_Humanitiarian_Law.pdf; reprinted as John B. Bellinger III & William B. Haynes II, A US Government Response to the International Committee of the Red Cross Study *Customary International Humanitarian Law*, 89 Intl. Rev. Red Cross 433 (June 2007). For additional criticisms, see Perspectives on the ICRC Study on Customary International Humanitarian Law (Elizabeth Wilmshurst and Susan Breau eds., 2007).

21. Jean-Marie Henckaerts, *Customary International Humanitarian Law: A Response to U.S. Comments*, 89 Intl. Rev. Red Cross 473 (June 2007).

22. South West Africa Case, Advisory Opinion, 1950 I.C.J. 28, 148 (July 11) (separate opinion of Judge McNair).

23. Case No. IT-96-22-A, Judgment, ¶57 (Oct. 7, 1997) (joint opinion of Judges McDonald and Vohrah).

does not include them as sources of law at all. What might account for this difference? One factor may be a difference between the United States and most European and Latin American legal systems. In the latter, academic experts play a much more prominent role in the legal system than in the United States. Their opinions and commentaries are often relied on by judges and legislators, in much the same way that U.S. judges may rely on decisions by important judges in other jurisdictions as persuasive authority. For better or for worse, academics have no such authority in the legal system of the United States. Should "the most highly qualified publicists" count as a source of law?

Among "the most highly qualified publicists," one that deserves special mention is the International Law Commission (ILC). The ILC was established in 1947 by the UN General Assembly to prepare drafts on various subjects in international law. It consists of 34 IL experts, elected by the General Assembly to five-year terms, and it meets annually. Its drafts carry considerable authority.

5.   *"Peremptory Norms"* (Jus Cogens)

Comment k of the Restatement excerpt discusses special norms of international law that "prevail over and invalidate international agreements and other rules of international law in conflict with them." The terminology comes from Article 53 of the VCLT:

> A treaty is void if, at the time of its conclusion, it conflicts with a peremptory norm of general international law. For the purposes of the present Convention, a peremptory norm of general international law is a norm accepted and recognized by the international community of States as a whole as a norm from which no derogation is permitted and which can be modified only by a subsequent norm of general international law having the same character.

A more common name for such peremptory norms is *jus cogens* (pronounced "yoos kogenz," with a hard *g*).[24] In theory, at least, the *jus cogens* norms are the most fundamental norms of international law — its (almost) immovable bedrock. Most scholars would include among the *jus cogens* norms: *pacta sunt servanda* (treaties are to be kept), the rule against launching aggressive war, and fundamental human rights norms such as the prohibitions on genocide and slavery.

A *jus cogens* norm is, in other words, a norm of international law that is so basic and important that (1) it invalidates treaties that violate it; (2) it cannot be changed the way that lesser norms of CIL are, namely through state practice and *opinio juris* changes; and (3) there is no "opting out" by claiming to be a persistent objector. In theory, a norm of *jus cogens* can change if another norm of *jus cogens* displaces it, but there are no undisputed cases where that has happened. (Some commentators argue that the widespread acceptance of NATO's attack on Serbia in the Kosovo war indicates that the *jus cogens* norm against military interventions has been displaced by a permission to engage in humanitarian intervention, but this view is quite controversial.)

Strictly speaking, the only legal force of *jus cogens* norms the VCLT recognizes is that states cannot adopt treaties that violate them. But in practice, jurists have sometimes

---

24. The word *jus* means "law," while *cogens* is a form of the Latin verb *coacto*, "to compel." *Jus cogens* is "compulsory law." In legal terminology, the opposite of *jus cogens* is *jus dispositiva*, which refers to law that parties can change at will.

given *jus cogens* norms—especially fundamental human rights norms—an almost natural law status. In the words of the International Law Commission, "[i]t is not the form of a general rule of international law but the particular nature of the subject matter with which it deals that may . . . give it the character of *jus cogens*."[25] When we study the *Pinochet* case in Chapter 6, we will see that the British judges in the case frequently refer to torture as a "*jus cogens* crime."

Lawyers and judges have sometimes drawn wide-ranging conclusions about *jus cogens* norms. They have argued, for example, that every state has a legal interest in ensuring that *jus cogens* norms are not violated. Lawyers refer to obligations that fall on all states as *erga omnes* (toward all) obligations, and in one often-quoted dictum, the ICJ stated that "the principles and rules concerning the basic rights of the human person" give rise to obligations *erga omnes*.[26] And sometimes it is said that any state can assert "universal jurisdiction" over crimes that violate *jus cogens* norms—an issue we shall study in detail in Chapter 5. Other jurists disagree that *jus cogens* norms create universal obligations or universal jurisdiction.

Finally, we should note a certain air of mystery about where *jus cogens* norms come from. There is no settled list of *jus cogens* norms, and states seldom issue public proclamations about *jus cogens*. Although the Latin name might suggest that thousands of years of legal tradition underwrite *jus cogens*, this is simply not true. Current doctrines asserting that aggressive war and atrocious human rights abuses violate *jus cogens* date back only as far as the end of World War II. Indeed, the entire jurisprudence of *jus cogens* is a postwar creation.[27] Labeling a deed such as torture a "*jus cogens* crime" has great rhetorical force, but it is not easy to show how or when the prohibition against torture became a *jus cogens* norm. "*Jus cogens* crime" is a claim that the international community regards torture as a bedrock violation of international law—and that is something that needs to be demonstrated by citing widespread state *opinio juris* to that effect. In practice, lawyers and courts seldom undertake this demonstration. Instead, "*jus cogens* crime" simply becomes a label equivalent in meaning to "particularly grave international crime."

C. IS INTERNATIONAL LAW REAL LAW?

What happens if a state violates international law? The short answer is: often very little. When Israel kidnapped Adolf Eichmann from the streets of Buenos Aires and brought him to trial in Israel for his role in the Holocaust, Israel's actions clearly violated Argentina's sovereignty. But the only consequence was a protest from Argentina, resulting in an agreement whereby Israel apologized and Argentina dropped its demand that Eichmann be returned. More dramatically, when Nicaragua's Sandinista government brought legal action against the United States for supporting anti-Sandinista rebels and mining Nicaraguan territorial waters, the United States simply pulled out of the litigation and withdrew from the ICJ's mandatory jurisdiction over

---

25. Report of the International Law Commission on the Work of Its Eighteenth Session, [1966] 2 Y.B. Int'l L. Comm'n 173, 248, U.N. Doc. A/6309/Rev.1 (1966).

26. Barcelona Traction, Light & Power Co., Ltd. (New Application) (Belg. v. Spain), 1970 I.C.J. Rep. 4, ¶¶32-34 (Judgment of Feb. 5).

27. See Lauri Hannikainen, Peremptory Norms (*Jus Cogens*) in International Law: Historical Development, Criteria, Present Status (1988).

future cases (something that other states have done as well). After the ICJ ruled in Nicaragua's favor, there were no sanctions against the United States.[28]

Of course, sometimes violations of international law do have dramatic consequences. When Iraq invaded Kuwait in 1991, the response was a UN-sanctioned war. But Iraq's seizure of Kuwait was an exception that proves the rule: It was a major, not minor, breach of IL; it threatened security interests of major powers including the United States, which led the war; and Iraq was militarily far weaker than the United States and its allies.[29]

Given that there are often no coercive sanctions for violations of IL, many lawyers and students wonder whether IL is really "law." How can it be law if, in many cases, the only sanction for violating it is political or diplomatic, and subject therefore to states' calculations about whether it is worth it to fuss about another state's violation of IL — which, for all but the largest infractions, it seldom is?

The nineteenth-century jurist John Austin famously defined law as commands of a sovereign, backed by threats.[30] If Austin is right, then IL — with no sovereign (no world government) and no guarantee of real threats — surely cannot be law. But Austin's definition is not the only one, and it has often been criticized. The British philosopher H. L. A. Hart pointed out that much of law consists of the creation of powers — for example, the power to make a will, the power to get married, the power to form a corporation — and not commands. Such laws are not backed by threats, other than the threat of nullity. If a valid will requires two witnesses and you have only one, the only consequence is that your will fails; but you won't be punished for the lack of a witness.[31] This sounds very much like the "sanction" of nullity for treaty breach in Article 60 of the VCLT. Another prominent legal theorist, John Finnis, argues that the primary function of laws is to coordinate activities for the common good — think of traffic laws — and thus that nothing in the concept of law requires external sanctions.[32] This, too, closely describes the evolution of international law. Most international rules aim at coordinating activities such as shipping on the high seas, exchanges of diplomats and ambassadors, and mundane but vital activities like linking national postal systems into an effective international system or maintaining transnational airline security. Postal treaties hardly require punitive sanctions: No state has an interest in permitting international delivery of the mails to collapse.

But do states comply with international law when they have an interest in violating it? One influential school of international relations scholars — the "realists" — holds that states (or, in some versions, national leaders) act only in their self-interest, regardless of law. Weak states may comply with international law, but strong states will do so only when their leaders think it is in their self-interest to do so. Realists tend to be skeptical about the normative force of international law. One recent study of the way that sovereignty claims actually work in the real world concludes that states honor each other's sovereignty verbally, but in actual practice violate it whenever national leaders think it is in their interest to do so. The author dismisses sovereignty talk as "organized hypocrisy."[33]

However, other scholars who accept the basic realist contention that states (or their leaders) are motivated largely by self-interest point out that having a system of

---

28. Military and Paramilitary Activities in and Against Nicaragua (Nicar. v. United States), 1986 I.C.J. Rep. 14 (Judgment of June 27).
29. See Paul W. Kahn, Lessons for International Law from the Gulf War, 45 Stan. L. Rev. 425 (1993).
30. John Austin, The Province of Jurisprudence Determined (1832).
31. H.L.A. Hart, The Concept of Law 27-28 (2d ed. 1994) (1961).
32. John Finnis, Natural Law and Natural Rights (1979).
33. Krasner, supra note 14.

international norms in place may turn out to be in the interest of states and leaders. In prisoners' dilemmas and similar collective action problems, self-interested strategies lead parties to inferior outcomes, and the most plausible way out is for parties to create norms of cooperation and bind themselves to obey these norms.[34]

One way to think about the matter is this: If (a) it is in most states' interests to have some rule of IL in place (for example, a rule of diplomatic immunity); and (b) the only way to maintain the rule is to abide by it most of the time; then (c) it will be in most states' interest to abide by the rule most of the time, even if they could achieve short-term gains by cheating. Louis Henkin, one of the greatest of international law scholars, famously asserted that "[a]lmost all nations observe almost all principles of international law and almost all of their obligations almost all of the time."[35] The argument above suggests why. (Is this theory persuasive in the context of human rights treaties? That is, are states likely to care enough about how other states treat their own citizenry to induce reciprocal compliance?) Some scholars of international relations point out that realism neglects domestic politics, where even very hard-nosed leaders may face influential constituencies at home that value international legal compliance; this might provide another explanation of why states so often comply with international law even when doing so is contrary to short-term self-interest.

Even if Henkin overstates his case (it is hard to know), his view, like those of Hart and Finnis, provides a useful alternative perspective to Austin and the realists. As you consider the various rules and doctrines of international criminal law set out in this book, it will always be useful to keep these two perspectives in mind. For every doctrine, an important question will be "Why should states and leaders comply?" And for every judicial decision, it will be helpful to ask whether the result follows from legal reasoning or simply from those in positions of power throwing their weight around.[36]

D. INTERNATIONAL LAW IN DOMESTIC LEGAL SYSTEMS

What role does international law play in domestic legal systems? The answer depends on each domestic legal system. States retain sovereign authority over their own legal systems, and it is therefore up to them to decide the role that IL plays in their own law.

Some states give IL pride of place in their own legal systems, to the extent of subordinating their own law to international norms. Thus, for example, Article 25 of the German Basic Law (the constitution of Germany) states:

> The general rules of public international law constitute an integral part of federal law. They take precedence over statutes and directly create rights and duties for the inhabitants of the federal territory.[37]

---

34. For an application of these ideas to customary international law, see Jack L. Goldsmith & Eric A. Posner, A Theory of Customary International Law, 66 U. Chi. L. Rev. 1113 (1999). And for a more general explanation of how norms evolve from coordination problems, see Edna Ullman-Margalit, The Emergence of Norms (1977).

35. Louis Henkin, How Nations Behave 42 (1968).

36. For a survey of theories about why states comply with IL, see Harold Hongju Koh, Why Do Nations Obey International Law?, 106 Yale L.J. 2599 (1997). In The Limits of International Law (2005), Jack Goldsmith and Eric Posner articulate a "rational choice" approach, contending that "international law emerges from states acting rationally to maximize their interests, given their perceptions of the interests of other states and the distribution of state power" (p. 3).

37. Art. 25 GG [Grundgesetz] (2003). By "general rules of public international law," the German constitution has been held to mean only rules of customary international law, not treaty law.

The Greek constitution of 1975 contains a similar provision; and several other European states, either through their constitutions or the practice of their courts, apply international law directly as if it were their own law.[38]

Matters are different in the United States. Under Article VI of the Constitution (the Supremacy Clause), duly ratified treaties are considered part of the "supreme Law of the Land," but there is no mention of customary international law. The details of how international law relates to U.S. law will play a prominent role in the materials on jurisdiction in Chapter 5. We will postpone a detailed treatment until then. Here, we simply summarize a few basic principles.

1. Constitutional Division of Authority

The U.S. Constitution only sketches out the powers of the three branches with respect to international affairs, war, and other matters that pertain to international law. Article I, Section 8 of the Constitution invests Congress with the following explicit foreign affairs–related powers:

> Clause 1: The Congress shall have Power To lay and collect Taxes, Duties, Imposts and Excises, to pay the Debts and provide for the common Defence and general Welfare of the United States; but all Duties, Imposts and Excises shall be uniform throughout the United States; . . .
> Clause 3: To regulate Commerce with foreign Nations, and among the several States, and with the Indian Tribes;
> Clause 4: To establish an uniform Rule of Naturalization, and uniform Laws on the subject of Bankruptcies throughout the United States; . . .
> Clause 10: To define and punish Piracies and Felonies committed on the high Seas, and Offences against the Law of Nations;
> Clause 11: To declare War, grant Letters of Marque and Reprisal, and make Rules concerning Captures on Land and Water;
> Clause 12: To raise and support Armies, but no Appropriation of Money to that Use shall be for a longer Term than two Years;
> Clause 13: To provide and maintain a Navy;
> Clause 14: To make Rules for the Government and Regulation of the land and naval Forces; . . .
> Clause 18: To make all Laws which shall be necessary and proper for carrying into Execution the foregoing Powers, and all other Powers vested by this Constitution in the Government of the United States, or in any Department or Officer thereof.[39]

---

38. For a survey, see Luzius Wildhaber & Stephan Breitenmoser, The Relationship Between Customary International Law and Municipal Law in Western European Countries, 48 Zeitschrift für ausländisches öffentliches Recht und Völkerrecht 163 (1988).

39. With respect to the division of foreign affairs powers between the U.S. state and the U.S. federal governments, the Constitution, Article I, Section 10 provides:

> Clause 1: No State shall enter into any Treaty, Alliance, or Confederation; [or] grant Letters of Marque and Reprisal; . . .
> Clause 2: No State shall, without the Consent of the Congress, lay any Imposts or Duties on Imports or Exports, except what may be absolutely necessary for executing its inspection Laws: and the net Produce of all Duties and Imposts, laid by any State on Imports or Exports, shall be for the Use of the Treasury of the United States; and all such Laws shall be subject to the Revision and Controul of the Congress.
> Clause 3: No State shall, without the Consent of Congress, lay any Duty of Tonnage, keep Troops, or Ships of War in time of Peace, enter into any Agreement or Compact with another State, or with a foreign Power, or engage in War, unless actually invaded, or in such imminent Danger as will not admit of delay.

With respect to presidential powers, the Constitution is terser still. Thus, Article II, Section 1, Clause 1 states that the "executive Power shall be vested in a President of the United States of America." Section 2 then provides:

Clause 1: The President shall be Commander in Chief of the Army and Navy of the United States, and of the Militia of the several States, when called into the actual Service of the United States; . . .

Clause 2: He shall have Power, by and with the Advice and Consent of the Senate, to make Treaties, provided two thirds of the Senators present concur; and he shall nominate, and by and with the Advice and Consent of the Senate, shall appoint Ambassadors, [and] other public Ministers and Consuls. . . .

Finally, Article III, Section 1 of the Constitution vests in the U.S. Supreme Court (and such inferior courts as Congress may establish) the "judicial Power of the United States." Section 2 then sets forth the jurisdiction of the Court:

Clause 1: The judicial Power shall extend to all Cases, in Law and Equity, arising under this Constitution, the Laws of the United States, and Treaties made, or which shall be made, under their Authority; — to all Cases affecting Ambassadors, other public Ministers and Consuls; — to all Cases of admiralty and maritime Jurisdiction; — to Controversies to which the United States shall be a Party; — to Controversies between . . . a State, or the Citizens thereof, and foreign States, Citizens or Subjects.

Clause 2: In all Cases affecting Ambassadors, other public Ministers and Consuls, and those in which a State shall be Party, the supreme Court shall have original Jurisdiction. In all the other Cases before mentioned, the supreme Court shall have appellate Jurisdiction. . . .

As we shall see in future chapters, these provisions often cannot be taken literally. For example, the Constitution provides only Congress with the power to declare war, but most of the wars conducted by the United States in its history have been pursued without a declaration of war and have been initiated through presidential action, followed by a congressional resolution supporting the executive's action. The Constitution also specifies a procedure for the conclusion of treaties with foreign nations, which requires supermajority approval by the Senate (and no involvement by the House). Yet the Supreme Court has upheld the president's power to enter into binding agreements with other nations without the procedures contemplated in the Treaty Clause. Students may not be surprised to learn that the Supreme Court's gloss is critical to understanding the content of these powers. What students may find unexpected, however, is how many unanswered questions there are in this area and how spotty and vague are the precedents that allocate power among the branches in critical areas of war, foreign affairs, and international law creation and enforcement.

2. Treaty Law in U.S. Law

The distinction between conventional (treaty) law and customary law plays a large role in the American treatment of IL. The Supremacy Clause in Article VI, Clause 2 of the Constitution provides:

This Constitution, and the Laws of the United States which shall be made in Pursuance thereof; *and all Treaties made, or which shall be made, under the Authority of the United States, shall be the supreme Law of the Land;* and the Judges in every State shall be bound thereby, any Thing in the Constitution or Laws of any State to the Contrary notwithstanding. (Emphasis added.)

As between treaties and federal statutes, the Supreme Court explained a long time ago that "[b]y the Constitution a treaty is placed on the same footing, and made of like obligation, with an act of legislation. Both are declared by that instrument to be the supreme law of the land, and no superior efficacy is given to either over the other."[40] Given that treaties and statutes have equal legal force, if there is a conflict between a treaty provision and an act of Congress (and courts cannot reconcile the two, as they will try hard to do), a rule of "*last in time*" prevails. Conversely, "[a] provision of a treaty of the United States that becomes effective as law of the United States supersedes as domestic law any inconsistent preexisting provision of a law or treaty of the United States."[41]

As with federal statutes, the judiciary provides the ultimate authoritative interpretation of treaties within U.S. law. However, treaties are negotiated by the executive branch, and "the Executive Branch's interpretation of treaty provisions is entitled to 'great weight' "[42] in judicial interpretation of treaties. This presumption in favor of executive branch interpretations of treaties marks a difference between treaties and federal statutes.

a. Self-Executing and Non-Self-Executing Treaties

One more doctrinal point about treaties in U.S. law is very important. In *Whitney v. Robertson*,[43] the Supreme Court stated that a conflict between a treaty and a statute can arise only if the treaty is "self-executing." The distinction between self-executing and non-self-executing treaty provisions is among the most significant—and, for most mortals, among the most confusing—in U.S. treaty law. It dates from Chief Justice Marshall's opinion in *Foster v. Neilson*,[44] which concerned a treaty with Spain. The crucial language is this:

> A treaty is in its nature a contract between two nations, not a legislative act. It does not generally effect, of itself, the object to be accomplished, especially so far as its operation is infra-territorial; but is carried into execution by the sovereign power of the respective parties to the instrument.
>
> In the United States a different principle is established. Our constitution declares a treaty to be the law of the land. It is, consequently, to be regarded in courts of justice as equivalent to an act of the legislature, whenever it operates of itself without the aid of any legislative provision. But when the terms of the stipulation import a contract, when either of the parties engages to perform a particular act, the treaty addresses itself to the political, not the judicial department; and the legislature must execute the contract before it can become a rule for the Court.[45]

---

40. Whitney v. Robertson, 124 U.S. 190, 194 (1888).
41. Restatement (Third) of the Foreign Relations Law of the United States §115(1)(2) (1987). The issue of treaties superseding statutes seldom arises, however. For an example, see Cook v. United States, 288 U.S. 102 (1933) (treaty limiting searches of British ships overrides a prior statute authorizing such searches).
42. Sanchez-Llamas v. Oregon, 548 U.S. 331, 378 (2006) (Breyer, J., dissenting) (citing Sumitomo Shoji America, Inc. v. Avagliano, 457 U.S. 176, 184-185 (1982)).
43. 124 U.S. at 194.
44. 27 U.S. (2 Pet.) 253 (1829).
45. Id. at 314.

This passage, and the doctrines that flow from it, are somewhat confusing, and the terminology of "self-executing" and "non-self-executing" treaties has led to extensive debate among courts and commentators about how to tell when treaty provisions are self-executing and what legal force they have when they are not self-executing.

In 2008, the Supreme Court decided *Medellín v. Texas*,[46] an important case that appears to resolve several unsettled questions about self-executing treaties. The specific issue concerned an ICJ decision ordering the United States to reopen the cases of Mexican nationals facing U.S. death sentences, who had been denied treaty-based rights to be told when they were arrested that they could contact the Mexican consulate. We examine this issue at greater length in Chapter 10; here, our concern is solely with the way the Court deals with treaties and the nature of self-execution.

Three treaties were at issue in *Medellín*. First is the Vienna Convention on Consular Relations (VCCR), to which the United States is a party and which grants Mexican nationals certain rights if they are arrested in the United States. Second is an Optional Protocol to the VCCR — to which the United States was also a party — specifying that the parties will settle disputes over the treaty by going to the ICJ. And third is Article 94 of the UN Charter, according to which " [e]ach Member of the United Nations undertakes to comply with the decision of the [ICJ] in any case to which it is a party."

Mexico litigated against the United States in the ICJ on behalf of 51 Mexican nationals on U.S. death rows who had not been told in a timely way that they could contact the Mexican consulate, which sometimes provides assistance to Mexicans in legal trouble in the United States, for example by hiring good defense lawyers. The failure to notify the nationals of their rights to consular access violated the VCCR. Some of them appealed, but their appeals were denied on the ground that they had raised the VCCR issue too late and procedurally defaulted. In a decision called *Avena*,[47] the ICJ found in Mexico's favor and ordered the United States to review and reconsider the Mexicans' state court convictions "by means of its own choosing."[48] President George W. Bush ordered the state of Texas to comply with the ICJ order; simultaneously, however, he withdrew the United States from the Optional Protocol, so that the United States would no longer be obligated to resolve future disputes over the VCCR in the ICJ. The case came to the Supreme Court after Texas refused to comply with the president's order.

For our present purposes, the key portions of the decision concern the question of whether the treaties are self-executing. (The Court addressed a second question as well, namely whether the president has the constitutional power to order Texas to comply with the ICJ judgment; the Court held against the president.)

MEDELLÍN v. TEXAS
128 S. Ct. 1346 (2008)

Chief Justice ROBERTS delivered the opinion of the Court. . . .

No one disputes that the *Avena* decision — a decision that flows from the treaties through which the United States submitted to ICJ jurisdiction with respect to Vienna Convention disputes — constitutes an *international* law obligation on the part of the United States. But not all international law obligations automatically constitute binding federal law enforceable in United States courts. The question we confront

---

46. 128 S. Ct. 1346 (2008).
47. Avena & Other Mexican Nationals (Mex. v. U.S.), 2004 I.C.J. 12 (Judgment of Mar. 31).
48. Id. at 72.

here is whether the *Avena* judgment has automatic *domestic* legal effect such that the judgment of its own force applies in state and federal courts.

This Court has long recognized the distinction between treaties that automatically have effect as domestic law, and those that — while they constitute international law commitments — do not by themselves function as binding federal law. The distinction was well explained by Chief Justice Marshall's opinion in Foster v. Neilson, 27 U.S. 253 (1829), which held that a treaty is "equivalent to an act of the legislature," and hence self-executing, when it "operates of itself without the aid of any legislative provision." When, in contrast, "[treaty] stipulations are not self-executing they can only be enforced pursuant to legislation to carry them into effect." Whitney v. Robertson, 124 U.S. 190, 194 (1888). In sum, while treaties "may comprise international commitments . . . they are not domestic law unless Congress has either enacted implementing statutes or the treaty itself conveys an intention that it be 'self-executing' and is ratified on these terms." Igartua-De La Rosa v. United States, 417 F.3d 145, 150 (CA1 2005) (en banc) (Boudin, C.J.).[49]

A treaty is, of course, "primarily a compact between independent nations." It ordinarily "depends for the enforcement of its provisions on the interest and the honor of the governments which are parties to it." . . . "If these [interests] fail, its infraction becomes the subject of international negotiations and reclamations. . . . It is obvious that with all this the judicial courts have nothing to do and can give no redress." Only "[i]f the treaty contains stipulations which are self-executing, that is, require no legislation to make them operative, [will] they have the force and effect of a legislative enactment."[50]

Medellín and his amici nonetheless contend that the Optional Protocol, United Nations Charter, and ICJ Statute supply the "relevant obligation" to give the *Avena* judgment binding effect in the domestic courts of the United States. Because none of these treaty sources creates binding federal law in the absence of implementing legislation, and because it is uncontested that no such legislation exists, we conclude that the *Avena* judgment is not automatically binding domestic law.

A

The interpretation of a treaty, like the interpretation of a statute, begins with its text. Because a treaty ratified by the United States is "an agreement among sovereign powers," we have also considered as "aids to its interpretation" the negotiation and drafting history of the treaty as well as "the postratification understanding" of signatory nations.

As a signatory to the Optional Protocol, the United States agreed to submit disputes arising out of the Vienna Convention to the ICJ. The Protocol provides: "Disputes arising out of the interpretation or application of the [Vienna] Convention shall lie within the compulsory jurisdiction of the International Court of Justice." Of course, submitting to jurisdiction and agreeing to be bound are two different things. . . .

---

49. [Court's footnote 2:] The label "self-executing" has on occasion been used to convey different meanings. What we mean by "self-executing" is that the treaty has automatic domestic effect as federal law upon ratification. Conversely, a "non-self-executing" treaty does not by itself give rise to domestically enforceable federal law. Whether such a treaty has domestic effect depends upon implementing legislation passed by Congress.

50. [Court's footnote 3:] Even when treaties are self-executing in the sense that they create federal law, the background presumption is that "[i]nternational agreements, even those directly benefiting private persons, generally do not create private rights or provide for a private cause of action in domestic courts." Accordingly, a number of the Courts of Appeals have presumed that treaties do not create privately enforceable rights in the absence of express language to the contrary. . . .

The most natural reading of the Optional Protocol is as a bare grant of jurisdiction. It provides only that "[d]isputes arising out of the interpretation or application of the [Vienna] Convention shall lie within the compulsory jurisdiction of the International Court of Justice" and "may accordingly be brought before the [ICJ] . . . by any party to the dispute being a Party to the present Protocol." The Protocol says nothing about the effect of an ICJ decision and does not itself commit signatories to comply with an ICJ judgment. The Protocol is similarly silent as to any enforcement mechanism.

The obligation on the part of signatory nations to comply with ICJ judgments derives not from the Optional Protocol, but rather from Article 94 of the United Nations Charter — the provision that specifically addresses the effect of ICJ decisions. Article 94(1) provides that "[e]ach Member of the United Nations *undertakes to comply* with the decision of the [ICJ] in any case to which it is a party." (emphasis added). The Executive Branch contends that the phrase "undertakes to comply" is not "an acknowledgement that an ICJ decision will have immediate legal effect in the courts of UN members," but rather "a *commitment* on the part of UN Members to take *future* action through their political branches to comply with an ICJ decision."

We agree with this construction of Article 94. . . .

The remainder of Article 94 confirms that the U.N. Charter does not contemplate the automatic enforceability of ICJ decisions in domestic courts. Article 94(2) — the enforcement provision — provides the sole remedy for noncompliance: referral to the United Nations Security Council by an aggrieved state.

The U.N. Charter's provision of an express diplomatic — that is, nonjudicial — remedy is itself evidence that ICJ judgments were not meant to be enforceable in domestic courts. . . .

If ICJ judgments were instead regarded as automatically enforceable domestic law, they would be immediately and directly binding on state and federal courts pursuant to the Supremacy Clause. Mexico or the ICJ would have no need to proceed to the Security Council to enforce the judgment in this case. . . .

The ICJ Statute, incorporated into the U.N. Charter, provides further evidence that the ICJ's judgment in *Avena* does not automatically constitute federal law judicially enforceable in United States courts. To begin with, the ICJ's "principal purpose" is said to be to "arbitrate particular disputes between national governments." Accordingly, the ICJ can hear disputes only between nations, not individuals. More important, Article 59 of the statute provides that "[t]he decision of the [ICJ] has *no binding force* except between the parties and in respect of that particular case." (emphasis added). The dissent does not explain how Medellín, an individual, can be a party to the ICJ proceeding. . . .

The pertinent international agreements, therefore, do not provide for implementation of ICJ judgments through direct enforcement in domestic courts. . . .

B

The dissent faults our analysis because it "looks for the wrong thing (explicit textual expression about self-execution) using the wrong standard (clarity) in the wrong place (the treaty language)." Given our obligation to interpret treaty provisions to determine whether they are self-executing, we have to confess that we do think it rather important to look to the treaty language to see what it has to say about the issue. That is after all what the Senate looks to in deciding whether to approve the treaty. . . .

As against this time-honored textual approach, the dissent proposes a multifactor, judgment-by-judgment analysis that would "jettiso[n] relative predictability for the open-ended rough-and-tumble of factors." The dissent's novel approach to deciding which (or, more accurately, when) treaties give rise to directly enforceable federal law is arrestingly indeterminate. . . .

Our Framers established a careful set of procedures that must be followed before federal law can be created under the Constitution — vesting that decision in the political branches, subject to checks and balances. They also recognized that treaties could create federal law, but again through the political branches, with the President making the treaty and the Senate approving it. The dissent's understanding of the treaty route, depending on an ad hoc judgment of the judiciary without looking to the treaty language — the very language negotiated by the President and approved by the Senate — cannot readily be ascribed to those same Framers.

The dissent's approach risks the United States' involvement in international agreements. It is hard to believe that the United States would enter into treaties that are sometimes enforceable and sometimes not. Such a treaty would be the equivalent of writing a blank check to the judiciary. Senators could never be quite sure what the treaties on which they were voting meant. Only a judge could say for sure and only at some future date. This uncertainty could hobble the United States' efforts to negotiate and sign international agreements. . . .

C

Our conclusion that *Avena* does not by itself constitute binding federal law is confirmed by the "postratification understanding" of signatory nations. There are currently 47 nations that are parties to the Optional Protocol and 171 nations that are parties to the Vienna Convention. Yet neither Medellín nor his amici have identified a single nation that treats ICJ judgments as binding in domestic courts. . . .

Our conclusion is further supported by general principles of interpretation. To begin with, we reiterated in *Sanchez-Llamas* what we held in *Breard*, that " 'absent a clear and express statement to the contrary, the procedural rules of the forum State govern the implementation of the treaty in that State.' " Given that ICJ judgments may interfere with state procedural rules, one would expect the ratifying parties to the relevant treaties to have clearly stated their intent to give those judgments domestic effect, if they had so intended. Here there is no statement in the Optional Protocol, the U.N. Charter, or the ICJ Statute that supports the notion that ICJ judgments displace state procedural rules. . . .

Our prior decisions identified by the dissent as holding a number of treaties to be self-executing, stand only for the unremarkable proposition that some international agreements are self-executing and others are not. It is well settled that the "[i]nterpretation of [a treaty] . . . must, of course, begin with the language of the Treaty itself." As a result, we have held treaties to be self-executing when the textual provisions indicate that the President and Senate intended for the agreement to have domestic effect. . . .

D

Our holding does not call into question the ordinary enforcement of foreign judgments or international arbitral agreements. Indeed, we agree with Medellín that, as a general matter, "an agreement to abide by the result" of an international adjudication — or what he really means, an agreement to give the result of such adjudication domestic legal effect — can be a treaty obligation like any other, so long as the agreement is consistent with the Constitution. The point is that the particular treaty obligations on which Medellín relies do not of their own force create domestic law.

The dissent worries that our decision casts doubt on some 70-odd treaties under which the United States has agreed to submit disputes to the ICJ according to "roughly similar" provisions. Again, under our established precedent, some treaties are self-executing and some are not, depending on the treaty. That the judgment of an international tribunal might not automatically become domestic law hardly means the underlying treaty is "useless." Such judgments would still constitute international obligations, the proper subject of political and diplomatic negotiations. And Congress could elect to give them wholesale effect . . . through implementing legislation, as it regularly has. . . .

Further, that an ICJ judgment may not be automatically enforceable in domestic courts does not mean the particular underlying treaty is not. Indeed, we have held that a number of the "Friendship, Commerce, and Navigation" Treaties cited by the dissent are self-executing—based on "the language of the[se] Treat[ies]." . . . Contrary to the dissent's suggestion, . . . neither our approach nor our cases require that a treaty provide for self-execution in so many talismanic words; that is a caricature of the Court's opinion. Our cases simply require courts to decide whether a treaty's terms reflect a determination by the President who negotiated it and the Senate that confirmed it that the treaty has domestic effect. . . .

III

[The Court rejects Medellín's argument that the President's order to U.S. states to comply with *Avena* suffices to make it binding on state courts. It holds that only Congress, not the President, has the authority to make a non-self-executing treaty self-executing.]

The requirement that Congress, rather than the President, implement a non-self-executing treaty derives from the text of the Constitution, which divides the treaty-making power between the President and the Senate. The Constitution vests the President with the authority to "make" a treaty. If the Executive determines that a treaty should have domestic effect of its own force, that determination may be implemented "in mak[ing]" the treaty, by ensuring that it contains language plainly providing for domestic enforceability. If the treaty is to be self-executing in this respect, the Senate must consent to the treaty by the requisite two-thirds vote, consistent with all other constitutional restraints.

Once a treaty is ratified without provisions clearly according it domestic effect, however, whether the treaty will ever have such effect is governed by the fundamental constitutional principle that " '[t]he power to make the necessary laws is in Congress; the power to execute in the President.' " As already noted, the terms of a non-self-executing treaty can become domestic law only in the same way as any other law— through passage of legislation by both Houses of Congress, combined with either the President's signature or a congressional override of a Presidential veto. . . .

Justice STEVENS, concurring in the judgment.

There is a great deal of wisdom in Justice Breyer's dissent. I agree that the text and history of the Supremacy Clause, as well as this Court's treaty-related cases, do not support a presumption against self-execution. . . . In the end, however, I am persuaded that the relevant treaties do not authorize this Court to enforce the judgment of the International Court of Justice (ICJ) in [*Avena*].

The source of the United States' obligation to comply with judgments of the ICJ is found in Article 94(1) of the United Nations Charter, which was ratified in 1945.

Article 94(1) provides that "[e]ach Member of the United Nations *undertakes to comply* with the decision of the [ICJ] in any case to which it is a party." (emphasis added). In my view, the words "undertakes to comply" — while not the model of either a self-executing or a non-self-executing commitment — are most naturally read as a promise to take additional steps to enforce ICJ judgments. . . .

On the other hand Article 94(1) does not contain the kind of unambiguous language foreclosing self-execution that is found in other treaties. The obligation to undertake to comply with ICJ decisions is more consistent with self-execution than, for example, an obligation to enact legislation. . . . Furthermore, whereas the Senate has issued declarations of non-self-execution when ratifying some treaties, it did not do so with respect to the United Nations Charter.

Absent a presumption one way or the other, the best reading of the words "undertakes to comply" is, in my judgment, one that contemplates future action by the political branches. . . .

Justice BREYER, with whom Justice SOUTER and Justice GINSBURG join, dissenting.

The Constitution's Supremacy Clause provides that "all Treaties . . . which shall be made . . . under the Authority of the United States, shall be the supreme Law of the Land; and the Judges in every State shall be bound thereby." The Clause means that the "courts" must regard "a treaty . . . as equivalent to an act of the legislature, whenever it operates of itself without the aid of any legislative provision." . . .

The United States has signed and ratified a series of treaties obliging it to comply with ICJ judgments in cases in which it has given its consent to the exercise of the ICJ's adjudicatory authority. Specifically, the United States has agreed to submit, in this kind of case, to the ICJ's "compulsory jurisdiction" for purposes of "compulsory settlement." And it agreed that the ICJ's judgments would have "binding force . . . between the parties and in respect of [a] particular case." President Bush has determined that domestic courts should enforce this particular ICJ judgment. And Congress has done nothing to suggest the contrary. Under these circumstances, I believe the treaty obligations, and hence the judgment, resting as it does upon the consent of the United States to the ICJ's jurisdiction, bind the courts no less than would "an act of the [federal] legislature."

I . . .

The critical question here is whether the Supremacy Clause requires Texas to follow, i.e., to enforce, this ICJ judgment. The Court says "no." And it reaches its negative answer by interpreting the labyrinth of treaty provisions as creating a legal obligation that binds the United States internationally, but which, for Supremacy Clause purposes, is not automatically enforceable as domestic law. . . .

In my view, the President has correctly determined that Congress need not enact additional legislation. The majority places too much weight upon treaty language that says little about the matter. The words "undertak[e] to comply," for example, do not tell us whether an ICJ judgment rendered pursuant to the parties' consent to compulsory ICJ jurisdiction does, or does not, automatically become part of our domestic law. To answer that question we must look instead to our own domestic law, in particular, to the many treaty-related cases interpreting the Supremacy Clause. Those cases, including some written by Justices well aware of the Founders' original intent, lead to the conclusion that the ICJ judgment before us is enforceable as a matter of domestic law without further legislation.

A

Supreme Court case law stretching back more than 200 years helps explain what, for present purposes, the Founders meant when they wrote that "all Treaties . . . shall be the supreme Law of the Land." [Justice Breyer reviews early Supreme Court cases distinguishing self-executing from non-self-executing treaty provisions.] . . .

Since *Foster* and *Pollard*, this Court has frequently held or assumed that particular treaty provisions are self-executing, automatically binding the States without more. See Appendix A, infra (listing, as examples, 29 such cases, including 12 concluding that the treaty provision invalidates state or territorial law or policy as a consequence). . . . As far as I can tell, the Court has held to the contrary only in two cases. . . . The Court has found "self-executing" provisions in multilateral treaties as well as bilateral treaties. And the subject matter of such provisions has varied widely, from extradition, to criminal trial jurisdiction, to civil liability, to trademark infringement, to an alien's freedom to engage in trade, to immunity from state taxation, to land ownership, and to inheritance.

Of particular relevance to the present case, the Court has held that the United States may be obligated by treaty to comply with the judgment of an international tribunal interpreting that treaty, despite the absence of any congressional enactment specifically requiring such compliance. . . .

All of these cases make clear that self-executing treaty provisions are not uncommon or peculiar creatures of our domestic law; that they cover a wide range of subjects; that the Supremacy Clause itself answers the self-execution question by applying many, but not all, treaty provisions directly to the States; and that the Clause answers the self-execution question differently than does the law in many other nations. The cases also provide criteria that help determine *which* provisions automatically so apply—a matter to which I now turn.

B . . .

1

The case law provides no simple magic answer to the question whether a particular treaty provision is self-executing. But the case law does make clear that, insofar as today's majority looks for language about "self-execution" in the treaty itself and insofar as it erects "clear statement" presumptions designed to help find an answer, it is misguided. See, e.g., ante (expecting "clea[r] state[ment]" of parties' intent where treaty obligation "may interfere with state procedural rules"); ante (for treaty to be self-executing, Executive should at drafting "ensur[e] that it contains language plainly providing for domestic enforceability").

The many treaty provisions that this Court has found self-executing contain no textual language on the point. Few, if any, of these provisions are clear. Those that displace state law in respect to such quintessential state matters as, say, property, inheritance, or debt repayment, lack the "clea[r] state[ment]" that the Court today apparently requires. . . . This is also true of those cases that deal with state rules roughly comparable to the sort that the majority suggests require special accommodation. . . . These many Supreme Court cases finding treaty provisions to be self-executing cannot be reconciled with the majority's demand for textual clarity.

Indeed, the majority does not point to a single ratified United States treaty that contains the kind of "clea[r]" or "plai[n]" textual indication for which the majority searches. . . . And that is not because the United States never, or hardly ever, has entered into a treaty with self-executing provisions. The case law belies any such conclusion. Rather, it is because the issue whether further legislative action is required before a treaty provision takes domestic effect in a signatory nation is often a matter of how that Nation's domestic law regards the provision's legal status. And that domestic status-determining law differs markedly from one nation to another. . . . As Justice Iredell pointed out 200 years ago, Britain, for example, taking the view that the British Crown makes treaties but Parliament makes domestic law, virtually always requires parliamentary legislation. And the law of other nations, the Netherlands for example, directly incorporates many treaties concluded by the executive into its domestic law even without explicit parliamentary approval of the treaty.

The majority correctly notes that the treaties do not explicitly state that the relevant obligations are self-executing. But given the differences among nations, why would drafters write treaty language stating that a provision about, say, alien property inheritance, is self-executing? How could those drafters achieve agreement when one signatory nation follows one tradition and a second follows another? Why would such a difference matter sufficiently for drafters to try to secure language that would prevent, for example, Britain's following treaty ratification with a further law while (perhaps unnecessarily) insisting that the United States apply a treaty provision without further domestic legislation? Above all, what does the absence of specific language about "self-execution" prove? It may reflect the drafters' awareness of national differences. It may reflect the practical fact that drafters, favoring speedy, effective implementation, conclude they should best leave national legal practices alone. It may reflect the fact that achieving international agreement on *this* point is simply a game not worth the candle.

In a word, for present purposes, the absence or presence of language in a treaty about a provision's self-execution proves nothing at all. At best the Court is hunting the snark. At worst it erects legalistic hurdles that can threaten the application of provisions in many existing commercial and other treaties and make it more difficult to negotiate new ones.

2

The case law also suggests practical, context-specific criteria that this Court has previously used to help determine whether, for Supremacy Clause purposes, a treaty provision is self-executing. The provision's text matters very much. But that is not because it contains language that explicitly refers to self-execution. For reasons I have already explained, one should not expect *that* kind of textual statement. Drafting history is also relevant. But, again, that is not because it will explicitly address the relevant question. Instead text and history, along with subject matter and related characteristics will help our courts determine whether, as Chief Justice Marshall put it, the treaty provision "addresses itself to the political . . . department[s]" for further action or to "the judicial department" for direct enforcement. . . .

In making this determination, this Court has found the provision's subject matter of particular importance. Does the treaty provision declare peace? Does it promise not to engage in hostilities? If so, it addresses itself to the political branches. Alternatively, does it concern the adjudication of traditional private legal rights such as rights to own property, to conduct a business, or to obtain civil tort recovery? If so, it may well address itself to the Judiciary. Enforcing such rights and setting their boundaries is the bread-and-butter work of the courts.

One might also ask whether the treaty provision confers specific, detailed individual legal rights. Does it set forth definite standards that judges can readily enforce? Other things being equal, where rights are specific and readily enforceable, the treaty provision more likely "addresses" the judiciary.

Alternatively, would direct enforcement require the courts to create a new cause of action? Would such enforcement engender constitutional controversy? Would it create constitutionally undesirable conflict with the other branches? In such circumstances, it is not likely that the provision contemplates direct judicial enforcement.

Such questions, drawn from case law stretching back 200 years, do not create a simple test, let alone a magic formula. But they do help to constitute a practical, context-specific judicial approach, seeking to separate run-of-the-mill judicial matters from other matters, sometimes more politically charged, sometimes more clearly the responsibility of other branches, sometimes lacking those attributes that would permit courts to act on their own without more ado. And such an approach is all that we need to find an answer to the legal question now before us.

c

Applying the approach just described, I would find the relevant treaty provisions self-executing as applied to the ICJ judgment before us (giving that judgment domestic legal effect) for the following reasons, taken together.

First, the language of the relevant treaties strongly supports direct judicial enforceability, at least of judgments of the kind at issue here. . . . [Justice Breyer points to language in the Optional Protocol, and argues that the language in Article 94(1) of the U.N. Charter stating that "[e]ach Member . . . undertakes to comply with the decision" of the ICJ indicates legal obligation, because "undertake" is standard terminology for promise or agreement.] . . .

Second, the Optional Protocol here applies to a dispute about the meaning of a Vienna Convention provision that is itself self-executing and judicially enforceable. The Convention provision is about an individual's "rights," namely, his right upon being arrested to be informed of his separate right to contact his nation's consul. The provision language is precise. The dispute arises at the intersection of an individual right with ordinary rules of criminal procedure; it consequently concerns the kind of matter with which judges are familiar. The provisions contain judicially enforceable standards. . . .

This Court has found similar treaty provisions self-executing. . . . It is consequently not surprising that, when Congress ratified the Convention, the State Department reported that the "Convention is considered entirely self-executive and does not require any implementing or complementing legislation." . . .

Third, logic suggests that a treaty provision providing for "final" and "binding" judgments that "settl[e]" treaty-based disputes is self-executing insofar as the judgment in question concerns the meaning of an underlying treaty provision that is itself self-executing. . . .

Fourth, the majority's very different approach has seriously negative practical implications. The United States has entered into at least 70 treaties that contain provisions for ICJ dispute settlement similar to the Protocol before us. Many of these treaties contain provisions similar to those this Court has previously found self-executing — provisions that involve, for example, property rights, contract and commercial rights, trademarks, civil liability for personal injury, rights of foreign diplomats, taxation, domestic-court jurisdiction, and so forth. If the Optional Protocol here, taken together with the U.N. Charter and its annexed ICJ Statute, is insufficient to warrant enforcement of the ICJ judgment before us, it is difficult to see how one could reach a different conclusion in any of these other instances. And the consequence is to undermine longstanding efforts in those treaties to create an effective international system for interpreting and applying many, often commercial, self-executing treaty provisions. . . .

Nor can the majority look to congressional legislation for a quick fix. Congress is unlikely to authorize automatic judicial enforceability of *all* ICJ judgments, for that could include some politically sensitive judgments and others better suited for enforcement by other branches: for example, those touching upon military hostilities, naval activity, handling of nuclear material, and so forth. Nor is Congress likely to have the time available, let alone the will, to legislate judgment-by-judgment enforcement of, say, the ICJ's (or other international tribunals') resolution of non-politically-sensitive commercial disputes. . . .

Fifth, other factors, related to the particular judgment here at issue, make that judgment well suited to direct judicial enforcement. The specific issue before the ICJ concerned " 'review and reconsideration' " of the "possible prejudice" caused in each of the 51 affected cases by an arresting State's failure to provide the defendant with rights guaranteed by the Vienna Convention. . . . As the ICJ itself recognized, "it is the judicial process that is suited to this task." . . .

Sixth, to find the United States' treaty obligations self-executing as applied to the ICJ judgment (and consequently to find that judgment enforceable) does not threaten constitutional conflict with other branches; it does not require us to engage in nonjudicial activity; and it does not require us to create a new cause of action. . . .

Seventh, neither the President nor Congress has expressed concern about direct judicial enforcement of the ICJ decision. . . .

For these seven reasons, I would find that the United States' treaty obligation to comply with the ICJ judgment in *Avena* is enforceable in court in this case without further congressional action beyond Senate ratification of the relevant treaties. The majority reaches a different conclusion because it looks for the wrong thing (explicit textual expression about self-execution) using the wrong standard (clarity) in the wrong place (the treaty language). Hunting for what the text cannot contain, it takes a wrong turn. It threatens to deprive individuals, including businesses, property owners, testamentary beneficiaries, consular officials, and others, of the workable dispute resolution procedures that many treaties, including commercially oriented treaties, provide. In a world where commerce, trade, and travel have become ever more international, that is a step in the wrong direction. . . .

NOTES AND QUESTIONS

1. Prior to *Medellín*, lower courts and scholars disagreed about whether non-self-execution meant primarily that a treaty creates no cause of action in federal court until it is implemented or whether, more broadly, non-self-execution meant that the treaty has no effect as federal law. On the broader reading, the president's (and executive agencies') constitutional obligation to "faithfully execute" the laws would not cover non-self-executing treaties until Congress implements them. In note 2 of *Medellín*, the Court defines a non-self-executing treaty as one that "does not by itself give rise to domestically enforceable federal law." Does this definition settle the issue? Is the Court saying that a non-self-executing treaty provision is one with no domestic legal effect whatsoever before implementation, or only one that U.S. courts cannot enforce until implementation? Under the former, broader, interpretation, in what sense are non-self-executing treaties "supreme law of the land"? Does this interpretation read the Supremacy Clause out of the Constitution for non-self-executing treaties?

2. In note 3, the Court clarifies that even self-executing treaties do not necessarily create individual causes of action in court. This occasionally has been a contested

issue in transnational criminal cases when persons arrested abroad and tried in U.S. courts attempt to raise treaty violations by U.S. officials as grounds for dismissing their cases. Courts sometimes reject these defenses on the ground that the treaty is non-self-executing and therefore cannot be raised by the defendant. See, e.g., United States v. Postal, 589 F.2d 862, 878 (5th Cir. 1979).

3. One persistent question has been how to tell when a treaty provision is self-executing. Sometimes, the U.S. Senate attaches RUDs to treaties declaring that the United States considers the treaty (or portions of it) non-self-executing. Thus, for example, when the Senate ratified the Convention Against Torture (CAT), it attached a declaration that the Convention's substantive articles are not self-executing. (Several of these articles were subsequently implemented through federal legislation.)

What if the treaty or its ratification instrument contains no explicit statement about whether it is self-executing? Before *Medellín*, scholars debated whether, absent a Senate RUD or clear treaty language, one should presume that treaty provisions are self-executing or presume that they are not. *Medellín* appears to settle this question by finding that a self-executing treaty is one that "contains language plainly providing for domestic enforceability." This "clear and express statement" rule suggests a presumption of non-self-execution. (The rejected alternative would have been for the Court to conclude that, given the text of the Supremacy Clause, treaties are self-executing unless they clearly indicate that they are not.) However, the Court also states that there are no "talismanic words" necessary for a treaty's language to show that it is self-executing. In other words, the treaty provision need not contain a provision expressly stating that it is self-executing. In that case, how different is the majority's approach to determining whether a treaty is self-executing from the dissenters' multifactor test?

For further discussion of self-executing treaties, see Restatement (Third) of the Foreign Relations Law of the United States §111 cmt. i (1987); Valerie Clare Epps, The *Medellín v. Texas* Symposium: A Case Worthy of Comment, 31 Suffolk Transnatl. L. Rev. 209 (2008); John H. Jackson, Status of Treaties in Domestic Legal Systems: A Policy Analysis, 86 Am. J. Intl. L. 310 (1992); Edward T. Swaine, Taking Care of Treaties, 108 Colum. L. Rev. 331 (2008); Carlos Manuel Vázquez, Treaties as the Law of the Land: The Supremacy Clause and the Judicial Enforcement of Treaties, 122 Harv. L. Rev. 599 (2008).

4. The dissent worries that the *Medellín* holding may invalidate many other treaties that use the same language of "undertaking" to indicate treaty obligations. In the wake of *Medellín*, the Department of State began reviewing U.S. treaties to determine the effect that *Medellín* may have on their domestic enforceability.

5. It is important to remember that some provisions of a treaty may be self-executing while some may not. Although courts and commentators occasionally ask whether treaties are or are not self-executing, this is an imprecise way of phrasing the question. Because some portions of a treaty may be self-executing while others are not, the question should really be framed only about specific treaty provisions, not about entire treaties (unless, of course, explicit language states that an entire treaty is or is not non-self-executing).

6. The *Medellín* Court observes that even if a treaty provision cannot be enforced as domestic law, it still remains an international obligation of the United States. So too, if a later-in-time statute supersedes a ratified treaty, the treaty will lack force in the domestic legal system of the United States, to the extent that they are clearly inconsistent. But unless the United States withdraws from the treaty, the treaty remains in

force and the *international* legal obligation remains unchanged. In either case, conflicts may arise between domestic law and international law.

The result is that domestic U.S. law may place the United States in violation of international law. The self-same act—in the *Avena/Medellín* issue, denial of defendants' VCCR claims—may be *required* by U.S. law and *forbidden* by international law. As we shall see in Chapter 5, U.S. courts are required to interpret federal statutes to minimize such clashes. Murray v. The Schooner Charming Betsy, 6 U.S. (2 Cranch) 64, 118 (1804). But when the clash is unavoidable, then *as a matter of U.S. law*, U.S. law prevails over international law. This poses a stark contrast with the German constitutional provision with which we began this section.

b. U.S. Treaty Law: Summary

We may summarize this discussion of treaty law in the law of the United States:

A. The Constitution's Supremacy Clause declares that the Constitution itself, treaties of the United States, and federal laws enacted by Congress are all "the supreme Law of the Land" (Art. VI). In terms of the legal hierarchy of sources made "supreme Law" in the Supremacy Clause, the Constitution always takes precedence, and treaties are treated on a par with federal statutes.

B. Accordingly, "a provision of an international agreement of the United States will not be given effect as law in the United States if it is inconsistent with the United States Constitution."[51]

C. Given that treaties and federal statutes have the same legal force, if a conflict arises between a treaty provision and an act of Congress, the "last in time" prevails. "An act of Congress supersedes an earlier rule of international law or a provision of an international agreement if the purpose of the act to supersede the earlier rule or provision is clear or if the act and the earlier rule or provision cannot be fairly reconciled."[52] Conversely, "[a] provision of a treaty of the United States that becomes effective as law of the United States supersedes as domestic law any inconsistent preexisting provision of a law or treaty of the United States."[53]

D. However, it is important to note that the fact that "a rule of international law or a provision of an international agreement is superseded as domestic law does not relieve the United States of its international obligation or of the consequences of a violation of that obligation."[54]

E. Treaties, under the Supremacy Clause, are "supreme over the law of the several States."[55] A ratified self-executing treaty, then, will nullify an inconsistent state law.

F. Article III, Section 2 of the U.S. Constitution states that cases arising under treaties are within the judicial power of the United States "and, subject to Constitutional and statutory limitations and requirements of justiciability, are within the jurisdiction of the federal courts."[56]

G. Because of a treaty's status as "supreme Law," *all* courts in the United States, including U.S. state courts, "are bound to give effect to international law and to international agreements of the United States, except that a 'non-self-executing' agreement will not be given effect as law in the absence of necessary implementation."[57]

---

51. Restatement (Third) of the Foreign Relations Law of the United States §115(3).
52. Id. §115(1)(a).
53. Id. §115(1)-(2).
54. Id. §115(1)(b); see also id. ch. 2, introductory note; §111 cmt. a; §115 cmt. b.
55. Id. §111(1).
56. Id. §111(2).
57. Id. §111(3).

H. A treaty's text, or an RUD attached by the Senate at ratification, may expressly declare which provisions of the treaty are or are not self-executing. In the absence of such express declaration, treaty provisions are only self-executing if treaty language plainly provides for domestic enforceability.[58]

I. "The determination and interpretation of international law presents federal questions and their disposition by the United States Supreme Court is conclusive for other courts in the United States."[59]

3. *Customary International Law in U.S. Law*

The Supremacy Clause of the Constitution does not mention customary international law; by its terms, only the Constitution, statutes, and treaties are "supreme Law of the Land." Indeed, the only mention of CIL in the Constitution is a clause in Article I, Section 8 empowering Congress "to define and punish . . . Offences against the Law of Nations." Nevertheless, the U.S. courts have adhered to the rule that prevailed in England before independence (and continues to prevail there today): that, in some respects at least, customary international law *is* part of "the Law of the Land." As stated by the U.S. Supreme Court in its canonical form in the 1900 decision *The Paquete Habana*:

> International law is part of our law, and must be ascertained and administered by the courts of justice of appropriate jurisdiction, as often as questions of right depending upon it are duly presented for their determination. For this purpose, where there is no treaty, and no controlling executive or legislative act or judicial decision, resort must be had to the customs and usages of civilized nations; and, as evidence of these, to the works of jurists and commentators, who by years of labor, research and experience, have made themselves peculiarly well acquainted with the subjects of which they treat. Such works are resorted to by judicial tribunals, not for the speculations of their authors concerning what the law ought to be, but for trustworthy evidence of what the law really is.[60]

This view from *The Paquete Habana* restates what had generally been Supreme Court doctrine in the nineteenth century, particularly in respect of maritime and admiralty questions. For example, Chief Justice Marshall wrote: "The Court is bound by the law of nations, which is a part of the law of the land."[61] The Supreme Court's early embrace of customary international law should not surprise us, given that in the founding era there were several reasons the United States would wish to be bound by the law of nations, especially in the context of maritime trading relations. One of the major defects of the Articles of Confederation was the inability of the national government to conduct a coherent foreign policy; and, as John Jay wrote in Federalist No. 3, "[i]t is of high importance to the peace of America that she observe the laws of nations towards all, and to me it appears evident that this will be more perfectly and punctually done by one national government than it could be either by thirteen separate States or by three or four distinct confederacies. . . ." In the words of one scholar, "[t]he framers of the Constitution were preoccupied with enforcing the new

---

58. *Medellín*, 128 S. Ct. at 1369.
59. Restatement (Third) of the Foreign Relations Law of the United States §112(2).
60. The Paquete Habana, 175 U.S. 677, 700 (1900).
61. The Nereide, 13 U.S. (9 Cranch) 388 (1815).

nation's obligations, fearful that violations of international law would drag the country into war with one of the more powerful European nations."[62]

In addition to pragmatic concerns, considerations of national dignity played a role. Being subject to the law of nations meant that the United States had entered as a full-fledged citizen into the community of nations. Rather than simply being an external source of burdensome obligations, being obligated by the law of nations was, in effect, a status symbol. Indeed, Alexander Hamilton had complained in Federalist No. 15 that, under the Articles of Confederation,

> [w]e may indeed with propriety be said to have reached almost the last stage of national humiliation. There is scarcely any thing that can wound the pride or degrade the character of an independent nation which we do not experience. Are there engagements to the performance of which we are held by every tie respectable among men? These are the subjects of constant and unblushing violation. . . . Is respectability in the eyes of foreign powers a safeguard against foreign encroachments? The imbecility of our government even forbids them to treat with us. Our ambassadors abroad are the mere pageants of mimic sovereignty.

As Chief Justice John Jay wrote, "The United States, by taking a place among the nations of the earth, had become amenable to the law of nations."[63]

The Paquete Habana instructed the courts to enforce CIL "when there is no controlling executive or legislative act."[64] Is the act of an executive official that violates CIL a controlling executive act? An affirmative answer would mean that CIL is "part of our law" only insofar as it addresses the conduct of state and local officials and private parties, yet the Court in *The Paquete Habana* itself enforced CIL against federal officials—naval officers who captured Cuban fishing vessels in violation of CIL. Some lower courts have concluded that CIL may not be enforced in the face of conflicting decisions of the president and other high-level officials. Important questions left open by *The Paquete Habana* concern the extent to which U.S. courts may enforce CIL against officials of the federal executive branch and which officials they can enforce CIL against.

The proposition that CIL is "part of our law" has received significant scholarly criticism of late, especially as applied to the "new" CIL that addresses a state's treatment of its own citizens, such as customary human rights law. Critics of the "new" CIL object that absorbing CIL into U.S. law is undemocratic because, in their view, it means that the obligations of Americans will be determined by the practice of foreigners or the symbolic statements of foreign officials in the UN General Assembly, rather than by U.S. political institutions responding to the will of the American people. In the words of two leading critics,

> [w]hen a federal court applies CIL as federal common law, it is not applying law generated by U.S. lawmaking processes. Rather, it is applying law derived from the views and practices of the international community. The foreign governments and other non-U.S. participants in this process "are neither representative of the American political community nor responsive to it." Indeed, under modern conceptions of CIL, CIL rules may be created and bind the United States without any express support for the rules from the

---

62. Beth Stephens, The Law of Our Land: Customary International Law as Federal Law After *Erie*, 66 Fordham L. Rev. 393, 402 (1997).

63. Chisholm v. Georgia, 2 U.S. (2 Dall.) 419, 474 (1793).

64. 175 U.S. at 700.

U.S. political branches. Nonetheless, as federal law, such CIL would preempt state law and, under certain formulations of the modern position, might bind the President and supersede prior inconsistent federal legislation.[65]

To this argument, defenders of CIL respond that customary rules represent the state practice and *opinio juris* of the U.S. government as well as foreign states, and therefore are not undemocratic; and rules to which the United States is a persistent objector do not bind it. The traditional position that CIL is "part of our law" has many scholarly defenders, and in 2004 the Supreme Court reaffirmed this proposition: "For two centuries we have affirmed that the domestic law of the United States recognizes the law of nations. . . . It would take some explaining to say now that federal courts must avert their gaze entirely from any international norm intended to protect individuals."[66] The case from which this language is quoted concerned a 1789 statute giving federal courts jurisdiction over "a tort committed in violation of the law of nations." The so-called Alien Tort Statute, long unused, had been revived beginning in the 1980s as a way of suing foreign human rights violators in U.S. courts. Turning back challenges to the statute, the Court permitted such lawsuits for a limited number of customary human rights violations, equivalent in their definiteness and universal recognition to those recognized in the eighteenth century.

The role of CIL and the extent to which it has effect as part of domestic law remains controversial. Objections to the "new" CIL form part of a larger debate about the place of international and foreign legal sources in the legal system of the United States. The issue has surfaced in a number of decisions about the death penalty and gay rights. When considering whether executing minors or the mentally retarded violates "evolving standards of decency," the majority of the Supreme Court has occasionally made reference to the way in which the courts or legislatures of other countries have treated the issue. In each case, Justice Antonin Scalia has strongly objected. In his dissenting opinion in *Atkins v. Virginia*,[67] Justice Scalia wrote: "Equally irrelevant are the practices of the 'world community,' whose notions of justice are (thankfully) not always those of our people." So too, in *Lawrence v. Texas*,[68] the Court struck down a statute criminalizing homosexual sodomy. The Court's majority cited European sources to refute an assertion in a prior Supreme Court opinion that gay rights claims are "insubstantial in our Western civilization."[69] Justice Scalia objected that "[c]onstitutional entitlements do not spring into existence . . . because *foreign nations* decriminalize conduct."[70]

These cases do not concern international criminal law. However, questions about whether certain crimes are part of the customary "law of war" have arisen in U.S. military commissions in Guantánamo, and these raise the issue of what force customary law has in the U.S. domestic law that establishes these commissions.

The issue of the role of foreign law in U.S. domestic law has generated passionate controversy. The following resolution was introduced into the House of Representatives in 2004 by Rep. Thomas Feeney (R-Fla.) and 59 other representatives.

---

65. Curtis A. Bradley & Jack L. Goldsmith, Customary International Law as Federal Common Law: A Critique of the Modern Position, 110 Harv. L. Rev. 815, 857 (1997). See also Anthony J. Bellia Jr. & Bradford R. Clark, The Federal Common Law of Nations, 109 Colum. L. Rev. 1 (2009).
66. Sosa v. Alvarez-Machain, 542 U.S. 692, 752 (2004).
67. 536 U.S. 304, 347-348 (2002).
68. 539 U.S. 558 (2003).
69. Id. at 573.
70. Id. at 598 (Scalia, J., dissenting; emphasis in original).

H. RES. 568

**Introduced in the 108th Congress, Second Session
March 17, 2004**

RESOLUTION

Expressing the sense of the House of Representatives that judicial determinations regarding the meaning of the laws of the United States should not be based on judgments, laws, or pronouncements of foreign institutions unless such foreign judgments, laws, or pronouncements inform an understanding of the original meaning of the laws of the United States.

Whereas the Declaration of Independence announced that one of the chief causes of the American Revolution was that King George had "combined to subject us to a jurisdiction foreign to our constitution and unacknowledged by our laws";

Whereas the Supreme Court has recently relied on the judgments, laws, or pronouncements of foreign institutions to support its interpretations of the laws of the United States, most recently in Lawrence v. Texas, 123 S. Ct. 2472, 2474 (2003);

Whereas the Supreme Court has stated previously in Printz v. United States, 521 U.S. 898, 921 n.11 (1997), that "We think such comparative analysis inappropriate to the task of interpreting a constitution . . .";

Whereas Americans' ability to live their lives within clear legal boundaries is the foundation of the rule of law, and essential to freedom;

Whereas it is the appropriate judicial role to faithfully interpret the expression of the popular will through laws enacted by duly elected representatives of the American people and our system of checks and balances;

Whereas Americans should not have to look for guidance on how to live their lives from the often contradictory decisions of any of hundreds of other foreign organizations;

And

Whereas inappropriate judicial reliance on foreign judgments, laws, or pronouncements threatens the sovereignty of the United States, the separation of powers and the President's and the Senate's treaty-making authority: Now, therefore, be it

Resolved, That it is the sense of the House of Representatives that judicial determinations regarding the meaning of the laws of the United States should not be based in whole or in part on judgments, laws, or pronouncements of foreign institutions unless such foreign judgments, laws, or pronouncements are incorporated into the legislative history of laws passed by the elected legislative branches of the United States or otherwise inform an understanding of the original meaning of the laws of the United States.

NOTES AND QUESTIONS

1. The House did not act on this resolution, but it articulates an important strand of U.S. sentiment. Clearly, it concerns far more than customary international law—indeed, its primary target is not international law but judicial appeals to laws of other countries in interpreting U.S. law. But Resolution 568's considerations undoubtedly apply to customary international law as well.

2. Do you agree with Resolution 568? What would be an appropriate democratic case for the rule that "international law is part of our law," given that CIL is subject to

the vagaries of decisions by other governments? Or is CIL less subject to the vagaries of other governments than its critics believe? Is Resolution 568 excessively isolationist and xenophobic?

3. Opponents of Resolution 568 quickly pointed out that U.S. courts routinely cite foreign legal sources in uncontroversial ways. For example, in international commercial litigation a U.S. court may have to determine whether a contract is valid under the law of the country in which it was made. In analyzing that country's contract law, U.S. courts will look to the judgments and other authorities of that country. To give another example, before granting an extradition request by a foreign state, U.S. courts must determine that the conduct alleged in the request actually constitutes a crime under that state's laws—another context in which a U.S. court must treat foreign legal authorities as binding. Finally, in some cases choice-of-law rules require U.S. courts to adjudicate a case under foreign law, and here too U.S. courts treat the other state's legal authorities as binding. If U.S. courts gave heed to Resolution 568, they could not adjudicate any of these cases in a sane manner.

Responding to this objection, supporters of Resolution 568 clarified that cases like these are not their target. They introduced a different version of Resolution 568 in the following session. House Resolution 97 and Senate Resolution 92 (introduced in the First Session of the 109th Congress) express "the sense . . . that judicial determinations *regarding the meaning of the Constitution of the United States* should not be based on judgments, laws, or pronouncements of foreign institutions unless such foreign judgments, laws, or pronouncements inform an understanding of the original meaning of the Constitution of the United States" (emphasis added). This is narrower than Resolution 568, because it concerns only the interpretation of the U.S. Constitution, not of "the laws of the United States." How much of a difference does this make?

4. Is the citation of foreign legal sources less democratic than courts' citation of dictionaries, legal treatises, or scientific studies? Nobody elected the authors of these works. How about the use in judicial opinions of quotations from Shakespeare or the Bible?

CHAPTER
3

International Criminal Tribunals: From Nuremberg to The Hague — and Beyond

In the materials that follow, we examine the background of modern international criminal law in the strict sense (as we labeled it in Chapter 1): law establishing international crimes and international institutions for trying them.

We begin by examining in detail the prototype of all subsequent international tribunals. This was the military tribunal set up by the victorious World War II Allies at Nuremberg, Germany, to try Germans and their allies accused of war crimes, aggression, and crimes against humanity. We then briefly examine the parallel Tokyo Tribunal, which tried Japanese leaders facing similar charges. There were no further international criminal tribunals for nearly half a century, until the United Nations established the International Criminal Tribunal for the Former Yugoslavia (ICTY) in 1993 and the International Criminal Tribunal for Rwanda (ICTR) in 1994. In the remainder of the chapter, we briefly survey the range of post-ICTR tribunals — in East Timor, in Sierra Leone, in Cambodia, and elsewhere. The International Criminal Court (ICC) is treated in a separate chapter.

A. THE NUREMBERG TRIBUNAL

In his anguished poem *September 1, 1939*, W.H. Auden lamented, "the unmentionable odour of death/Offends the September night." September 1, 1939, was the date that Nazi Germany launched World War II by invading Poland. By the time the war ended on August 16, 1945, an estimated 50 to 60 million people had perished as a result of the fighting. The Soviet Union alone lost almost 25 million, more than half of them civilians. Germany suffered 7.5 million war dead, amounting to more than 10 percent of its population. Germany's beautiful ancient cities had been reduced to rubble, and Nuremberg prosecutor Robert Jackson did not exaggerate when he referred to "the ruin that lies from the Rhine to the Danube." Tens of millions of people wandered the European countryside as refugees or displaced persons. The utter devastation not only inspired the creation of the UN, it also provided impetus to create a legal category of "crimes against peace," essentially the planning and launching of wars of aggression.

The war dead included more than 12 million civilian victims of Nazi mass murder, about half of them Jews annihilated in the "Final Solution to the Jewish Problem" — a Nazi code phrase for genocide. Other groups targeted for total eradication included

Jehovah's Witnesses, Roma and Sinti people (gypsies), and homosexuals; in addition, the Nazis murdered an estimated 200,000 mentally and physically handicapped persons in a eugenics-inspired, pseudoscientific program of "mercy killings." Millions of people, mostly Jews, perished in industrialized death camps whose names have attained iconic significance: Belzec, Chelmno, Majdanek, Sobibor, Treblinka, and, above all, Auschwitz, where between 1 and 2 million Jews were murdered, sometimes at a rate of 12,000 to 15,000 in a single day. Another 800,000 Jews were shot or gassed by "special action groups" (*Einsatzgruppen*) in eastern Europe, including 35,000 machine-gunned at Babi Yar ravine, near Kiev, in just two days in 1941. In addition to groups targeted for total destruction, the Germans killed approximately 2 million non-Jewish Poles, especially targeting intelligentsia, political leaders, and clergy.

Other German atrocities with significance for the future development of international criminal law include (1) the brutal mistreatment of Soviet prisoners of war — approximately 3 million perished in German POW camps — who suffered far worse treatment than POWs from France, Great Britain, or the United States because of Nazi theories of Slavic racial inferiority, coupled with fear and hatred of "international Bolshevism"; (2) extensive use of slave labor, as major German corporations set up factories next to concentration camps to exploit inmates not targeted for immediate death, many of whom were literally worked to death, while other civilians were forcibly transported to Germany as workers; (3) horrifying medical experiments performed on conscious human beings in the camps; (4) widespread torture; (5) looting; (6) rape; and (7) "disappearances" of political prisoners in the "Night and Fog" (*Nacht und Nebel*) program.

In September 1944, U.S. Secretary of State Henry Stimson wrote to President Franklin D. Roosevelt, "It is primarily by the thorough apprehension, investigation and trial of all the Nazi leaders and instruments of the Nazi system of terrorism such as the Gestapo, with punishment delivered as promptly, swiftly and severely as possible, that we can demonstrate the abhorrence which the world has for such a system and bring home to the German people our determination to extirpate it and its fruits forever."[1] Stimson's memorandum contains the root idea of the Nuremberg trial of the German leadership, which was created at U.S. insistence, over the objections of Great Britain.

Not that Great Britain disagreed with the need to respond to Nazi crimes. Confronting evidence of the Holocaust, Winston Churchill wrote on July 11, 1944, to Anthony Eden, "There is no doubt that this is probably the greatest and most horrible crime ever committed in the whole history of the world. . . . It is quite clear that all concerned who may fall into our hands, including the people who only obeyed orders by carrying out the butcheries, should be put to death after their association with the murders has been proved."[2]

But the British did not want to put the top Nazis on trial — they wanted to round them up and shoot them. The British feared that Adolf Hitler and other German leaders "would use the courtroom as a forum for accusing the British and French of having grievously injured Germany after World War I by the terms of the Versailles Treaty, the French occupation of the Ruhr in 1923, the failure of the victorious powers to disarm, and other political and economic sins."[3] In the British view, war-crimes trials should be reserved for low-ranking accused; the higher-ups should face summary execution on the basis of purely political decisions. The Soviet government had a third view: The guilt of the German leadership should be determined by

---

1. Ann Tusa & John Tusa, The Nuremberg Trial 52 (1984).
2. Robert E. Conot, Justice at Nuremberg 11 (1983).
3. Telford Taylor, The Anatomy of the Nuremberg Trials 51 (1992).

political decision with no trials—the same as the British idea—but international trials should nevertheless be held to determine degree of guilt and sentences.[4] In effect, the trials would merely ratify prior political decisions—a version of the rule of law that Joseph Stalin had perfected at the so-called Moscow Witch Trials of 1936-1938, in which he liquidated all his potential rivals in the Central Committee and military command. (Ironically, the Soviet prosecutor in the Moscow trials, Andrei Vishinsky, eventually became the USSR's delegate to the UN conference that produced the Universal Declaration of Human Rights.) At one meeting, Stalin appalled Churchill and Roosevelt by raising a toast to the execution of 50,000 German officers.

The U.S. view prevailed. The Allies met in London to discuss and draft the charter of the future tribunal, which set up shop in the southwest German city of Nuremberg—a symbolically important location because Nuremberg had been the site of Nazi Party rallies in the 1930s, and it was at Nuremberg that Hitler announced major anti-Jewish legislation in 1935. Heading the U.S. delegation was Supreme Court Justice Robert Jackson, who took a leave of absence from the Court and afterward served as lead U.S. prosecutor at Nuremberg.

The Allies hoped to try the top Nazis in the first round of trials; but most of the Nazi leadership had committed suicide or fled. The suicides included Hitler, propaganda minister Joseph Goebbels, and SS chief Heinrich Himmler. Out of the top echelon, only Hermann Göring, the head of the air force, was in Allied hands—but after his conviction, he too managed to kill himself before the Allies could hang him. Reinhard Heydrich, the original architect of the Holocaust, had been assassinated by Czech partisans; and Adolf Eichmann, who organized the roundup and transport of the Jews, fled to Argentina until his capture by Israeli agents in 1960. Martin Bormann, the secretary of the Nazi Party, also vanished, never to be seen again. He was tried *in absentia* at Nuremberg and sentenced to death. The Allies held Rudolf Hess, the Party secretary whom Bormann had replaced, and tried him at Nuremberg. But Hess—who was captured when he parachuted into England in 1941 on an unauthorized solo mission to propose a truce—was insane.[5] Defendant Robert Ley, the head of the German Labor Front, hanged himself in Allied captivity before the trial. The Allies also hoped to try Gustav Krupp, the leading arms manufacturer of the Third Reich, as a representative of the regime's industrial elite. But Krupp turned out to be a feeble, senile man in diapers and was dropped from the list of defendants.

Eventually, the Allies tried 22 members of the remaining political, economic, and military leadership of the Third Reich. Three were acquitted; the remainder received terms of years or death sentences.

The following excerpt sets out the substantive criminal law of the Charter.

CHARTER OF THE INTERNATIONAL MILITARY TRIBUNAL (THE "LONDON AGREEMENT" OR "NUREMBERG CHARTER")

Aug. 8, 1945, 59 Stat. 1544, 82 U.N.T.S. 279, 284

... ARTICLE 6

The Tribunal established by the Agreement referred to in Article 1 hereof for the trial and punishment of the major war criminals of the European Axis countries shall have

---

4. Id. at 59.

5. Hess nevertheless received a life sentence. Ironically, after all the other prisoners had died or been released, Hess alone remained in Spandau Prison, where he was the only inmate in the building. He committed suicide in 1987 at the age of 93.

the power to try and punish persons who, acting in the interests of the European Axis countries, whether as individuals or as members of organizations, committed any of the following crimes.

The following acts, or any of them, are crimes coming within the jurisdiction of the Tribunal for which there shall be individual responsibility:

(a) CRIMES AGAINST PEACE: namely, planning, preparation, initiation or waging of a war of aggression, or a war in violation of international treaties, agreements or assurances, or participation in a common plan or conspiracy for the accomplishment of any of the foregoing;

(b) WAR CRIMES: namely, violations of the laws or customs of war. Such violations shall include, but not be limited to, murder, ill-treatment or deportation to slave labor or for any other purpose of civilian population of or in occupied territory, murder or ill-treatment of prisoners of war or persons on the seas, killing of hostages, plunder of public or private property, wanton destruction of cities, towns or villages, or devastation not justified by military necessity;

(c) CRIMES AGAINST HUMANITY: namely, murder, extermination, enslavement, deportation, and other inhumane acts committed against any civilian population, before or during the war; or persecutions on political, racial or religious grounds in execution of or in connection with any crime within the jurisdiction of the Tribunal, whether or not in violation of the domestic law of the country where perpetrated.

Leaders, organizers, instigators and accomplices participating in the formulation or execution of a common plan or conspiracy to commit any of the foregoing crimes are responsible for all acts performed by any persons in execution of such plan.

ARTICLE 7

The official position of defendants, whether as Heads of State or responsible officials in Government Departments, shall not be considered as freeing them from responsibility or mitigating punishment.

ARTICLE 8

The fact that the Defendant acted pursuant to order of his Government or of a superior shall not free him from responsibility, but may be considered in mitigation of punishment if the Tribunal determines that justice so requires.

ARTICLE 9

At the trial of any individual member of any group or organization the Tribunal may declare (in connection with any act of which the individual may be convicted) that the group or organization of which the individual was a member was a criminal organization.

ARTICLE 10

In cases where a group or organization is declared criminal by the Tribunal, the competent national authority of any Signatory shall have the right to bring individuals to trial for membership therein before national, military or occupation courts. In any such case the criminal nature of the group or organization is considered proved and shall not be questioned.

NOTES AND QUESTIONS

1. Notice from Article 6 that the jurisdiction of the Tribunal reaches only "persons . . . acting in the interests of the European Axis countries. . . ." No provision permitted the trial of Allied perpetrators of similar crimes. Yet Jackson wrote to Truman that the Allies "have done or are doing some of the very things we are prosecuting Germans for. The French are so violating the Geneva Convention in the treatment of prisoners of war that our command is taking back prisoners sent to them. . . . We are prosecuting plunder and our Allies are practicing it. We say aggressive war is a crime and one of our allies asserts sovereignty over the Baltic States based on no title except conquest." Robert E. Conot, Justice at Nuremberg 68 (1983). Churchill ordered the bombing of civilian neighborhoods in German cities, and Truman himself ordered the atomic bombing of Hiroshima and Nagasaki; U.S. Admiral Chester Nimitz admitted that he conducted unrestricted submarine warfare (a war crime charged against German Admiral Dönitz); and the Soviet Union massacred between 15,000 and 20,000 Polish officers in Katyn Forest in anticipation of a postwar conquest of Poland. Does the Charter's limited jurisdiction reduce the Tribunal to mere hypocrisy or "victor's justice"? Should the Tribunal have extended its jurisdiction to the Allies? What would the likely response have been to such a proposal?

One consequence of restricting Article 6 to Axis defendants was that aggressive war, war crimes, and crimes against humanity were not turned into genuine international crimes at Nuremberg: They were crimes only when committed by the Axis countries. In the case of aggression, this was a deliberate choice of two of the Allies, France and the Soviet Union, whose representatives argued in London that aggressive war is *not* a crime. Telford Taylor, The Anatomy of the Nuremberg Trials 65-66 (1992). Not until 1950 did the UN General Assembly declare that the substantive law of the Nuremberg Charter constitutes universal principles of international law. Principles of International Law Recognized in the Charter of the Nuremberg Tribunal and Judgment of the Tribunal, U.N. GAOR, 5th Sess., Supp. No. 12, U.N. Doc. A/1316 (July 29, 1950).

2. Notice also that "[l]eaders, organizers, instigators and accomplices participating in the formulation or execution of a common plan or conspiracy to commit any of the foregoing crimes are responsible for all acts performed by any persons in execution of such plan." The purpose of this clause was to enable the Tribunal to "reach back" to the years between Hitler's 1933 ascendancy to power and September 1, 1939, and criminalize atrocities committed against German Jews. The legal predicate for this strategy (devised by U.S. lawyer Murray Bernays) was the crime of conspiracy. Bernays believed that it would be a mistake to try individuals without putting the Nazi movement itself on trial. His distinctive idea was to liken the Nazi movement to a conspiracy by a gang of criminals who seized the German government and used it as a tool to carry out the gang's criminal aims.

One difficulty with Bernays's idea was that the crime of conspiracy is unknown in civil law countries, including France and Russia. As one historian reported the London debates:

During much of the discussion, the Russians and French seemed unable to grasp all the implications of the concept; when they finally did grasp it, they were genuinely shocked.

The French viewed it entirely as a barbarous legal mechanism unworthy of modern law, while the Soviets seemed to have shaken their head in wonderment — a reaction, some cynics may believe, prompted by envy.

Bradley F. Smith, Reaching Judgment at Nuremberg 51 (1977). One reason for this shocked response was the proposition that each and every conspirator is "responsible for all acts performed by any persons in execution of such plan" — in this case, for literally tens of millions of murders. Is this extended theory of liability a good way to treat participation in a conspiracy? A few months after the adoption of the Nuremberg Charter, the U.S. Supreme Court incorporated this extended notion of liability into federal criminal law. Pinkerton v. United States, 328 U.S. 640, 647 (1946), holds that each conspirator is responsible for all reasonably foreseeable offenses committed by other conspirators in furtherance of the conspiracy, a concept known in U.S. law as "*Pinkerton* liability." As we shall see in Chapter 17, subsequent international tribunals more influenced by civil law concepts than the Nuremberg Tribunal have dropped the crime of conspiracy from those enumerated in international criminal law. The conspiracy crime does not appear in the UN's 1950 Nuremberg Principles.

Some commentators have argued that another problem with Bernays's idea is that, by treating the Hitler regime as a gang of criminals who somehow managed to take over Germany, Bernays trivialized history and in effect exonerated the German people from any moral responsibility for the crimes of their government. David Luban, The Legacies of Nuremberg, in Legal Modernism 367-368 (1994); Ann Tusa & John Tusa, The Nuremberg Trial 54-57 (1984). Of course, doing so may have had the useful effect of reminding the German people, digging out from the devastation of the war, that they too were victims of the Hitler regime. In this way, the trial may have helped in the postwar reconstruction of Germany as a democratic state, perhaps more than recriminations against the German people would have. In your view, are such political considerations appropriate in devising a legal theory for an international tribunal? What, if not a step in reconstructing Germany as a democratic state, *was* the point of the Nuremberg Tribunal?

3. Another of Bernays's ideas for putting the Nazi movement as well as individuals on trial is embodied in Articles 9 and 10 of the Charter. Article 9 enables the Tribunal to declare entire organizations to be criminal organizations. The Indictment asked for such declarations of criminality against the Leadership Corps of the Nazi Party, the Gestapo (secret police) and Security Service, the SS, the Storm Troopers, the Reich Cabinet, the General Staff, and the High Command. According to Article 10, after such a finding, any member of the organization could be found guilty of its crimes simply by proving that he was a member of the organization. It is a concept of collective guilt; Bernays thought it essential because it would facilitate the otherwise impossible task of trying hundreds of thousands of individual perpetrators. As we shall see below, the Tribunal found Articles 9 and 10 hard to stomach and drastically limited their applicability. These articles also do not appear in the UN's Nuremberg Principles.

4. One persistent challenge facing international tribunals lies in the fact that their procedural rules must meld the widely varying procedures of different legal systems. As Telford Taylor explains, this was true at Nuremberg:

Under the Continental system (known to lawyers as the "inquisitorial" system), most of the documentary and testimonial evidence is presented to an examining magistrate, who assembles all of it in a dossier. If this process establishes a sufficient basis for prosecution, copies of the dossier and the indictment based on it are given to the defendant and to the court which is to try the case, and the trial then proceeds with both the court and the concerned parties fully informed in advance of the evidence for and against the defendant. If the court, on its own motion or at the request of one of the parties, decides to take further testimony, the witnesses are usually questioned by the judges, rather than the lawyers, so that cross-examinations by opposing counsel, which play so large a part in Anglo-American trials, do not often occur. The defendant is not allowed to testify under oath, but may make an unsworn statement to the court. . . .

Naturally, the limited role of lawyers in Continental criminal trials had little appeal for British barristers or American advocates. The French and Russians went a long way to meet their allies' psychological needs for the adversarial process, even though they understood it very imperfectly; at the very last meeting Nikitchenko had to ask: "What is meant in the English by 'cross-examine'?" Falco found "a little shocking" the idea that the defense would not, prior to trial, be informed of "the whole case against them" and complained: "It seems there is a possibility under this draft that the defense could be faced during the trial with the opening of a Pandora's box of unhappy surprises, inasmuch as during the trial there is liberty to the prosecution to produce something new." Jackson was driven close to distraction:

> . . . I would not know how to proceed with a trial in which all the evidence had been included in the indictment. I would not see anything left for a trial and, for myself, I would not know what to do in open court.

The differences were resolved by compromises which were crude but proved workable. For example, the Charter would require, contrary to Anglo-American practice, that the indictment "shall include full particulars specifying in detail the charges against the defendants" and that there would be "documents" submitted with the indictment, but, contrary to Continental practice, it did not require that the prosecution present *all* of its evidence with the indictment. Contrary to Continental practice the defendants could testify as witnesses in their own behalf, but contrary to Anglo-American practice, defendants could also make an unsworn statement at the end of the trial.

Taylor, supra, at 63-64. The four victorious powers (France, Great Britain, the Soviet Union, and the United States) divided the judicial and prosecutorial responsibilities among them. All four had judges on the tribunal, and all four shared in prosecuting the case: There were four chief prosecutors, each focusing on one aspect of the cases. U.S. Supreme Court Justice Robert Jackson opened for the prosecution, in a lengthy speech famous for its eloquence. We quote two excerpts from the speech — Jackson's initial presentation of the case and part of his argument that the trial was not illegitimately *ex post facto*.

OPENING STATEMENT OF ROBERT JACKSON

2 The Trial of German Major War Criminals by the International Military Tribunal Sitting at Nuremberg, Germany, Nov. 21, 1945 (1946)

May it please Your Honour,

The privilege of opening the first trial in history for crimes against the peace of the world imposes a grave responsibility. The wrongs which we seek to condemn and punish have been so calculated, so malignant and so devastating, that civilisation cannot tolerate their being ignored, because it cannot survive their being repeated. That four great nations, flushed with victory and stung with injury, stay the hands of vengeance and voluntarily submit their captive enemies to the judgment of the law, is one of the most significant tributes that Power ever has paid to Reason.

This Tribunal, while it is novel and experimental, is not the product of abstract speculations nor is it created to vindicate legalistic theories. This inquest represents the practical effort of four of the most mighty of nations, with the support of seventeen more, to utilise International Law to meet the greatest menace of our times — aggressive war. The common sense of mankind demands that law shall not stop with the punishment of petty crimes by little people. It must also reach men who possess themselves of great power and make deliberate and concerted use of it to set in motion evils which leave no home in the world untouched. It is a cause of that magnitude that the United Nations will lay before Your Honour.

In the prisoners' dock sit twenty-odd broken men. Reproached by the humiliation of those they have led, almost as bitterly as by the desolation of those they have attacked, their personal capacity for evil is forever past. It is hard now to perceive in these miserable men as captives the power by which as Nazi leaders they once dominated much of the world and terrified most of it. Merely as individuals their fate is of little consequence to the world.

What makes this inquest significant is that these prisoners represent sinister influences that will lurk in the world long after their bodies have returned to dust. We will show them to be living symbols of racial hatreds, of terrorism and violence, and of the arrogance and cruelty of power. They are symbols of fierce nationalism and of militarism, of intrigue and war-making which embroiled Europe generation after generation, crushing its manhood, destroying its homes, and impoverishing its life. They have so identified themselves with the philosophies they conceived, and with the forces they have directed, that tenderness to them is a victory and an encouragement to all the evils which attached to their names. Civilisation can afford no compromise with the forces which would gain renewed strength if we deal ambiguously or indecisively with the men in whom those forces now precariously survive.

What these men stand for we will patiently and temperately disclose. We will give you undeniable proofs of incredible events. The catalogue of crimes will omit nothing that could be conceived by a pathological pride, cruelty, and lust for power. These men created in Germany, under the "Führerprinzip," a National Socialist despotism equalled only by the dynasties of the ancient East. They took from the German people all those dignities and freedoms that we hold natural and inalienable rights in every human being. The people were compensated by inflaming and gratifying hatreds toward those who were marked as "scapegoats." Against their opponents, including Jews, Catholics, and free labour, the Nazis directed such a campaign of arrogance, brutality, and annihilation as the world has not witnessed since the pre-Christian ages. They excited the German ambition to be a "master race," which of course implies serfdom for others. They led their people on a mad gamble for domination. They diverted social energies and resources to the creation of what they thought to be an invincible war machine. They overran their neighbours. To sustain the "master race" in its war-making, they enslaved millions of human beings and brought them into Germany, where these hapless creatures now wander as "displaced persons." At length, bestiality and bad faith reached such excess that they aroused the sleeping strength of imperilled Civilisation. Its united efforts have ground the German war machine to fragments. But the struggle has left Europe a liberated yet prostrate land where a demoralised society struggles to survive. These are the fruits of the sinister forces that sit with these defendants in the prisoners' dock.

In justice to the nations and the men associated in this prosecution, I must remind you of certain difficulties which may leave their mark on this case. Never before in legal history has an effort been made to bring within the scope of a single litigation the developments of a decade, covering a whole continent, and involving a score of nations, countless individuals, and innumerable events. Despite the magnitude of the task, the world has demanded immediate action. This demand has had to be met, though perhaps at the cost of finished craftsmanship. In my country, established courts, following familiar procedures, applying well-thumbed precedents, and dealing with the legal consequences of local and limited events, seldom commence a trial within a year of the event in litigation. Yet less than eight months ago today the courtroom in which you sit was an enemy fortress in the hands of German S.S. troops. Less than eight months ago nearly all our witnesses and documents were in enemy hands. The law had not been codified, no procedures had been established, no tribunal was in existence, no usable courthouse stood here, none of the hundreds of tons of official German documents had been examined, no prosecuting staff had been assembled, nearly all of the present defendants were at large, and the four prosecuting powers had not yet joined in common cause to try them. I should be the last to deny that the case may well suffer from incomplete researches, and quite likely will not be the example of professional work which any of the prosecuting nations would normally wish to sponsor. It is, however, a completely adequate case to the judgment we shall ask you to render, and its full development we shall be obliged to leave to historians.

Before I discuss particulars of evidence, some general considerations which may affect the credit of this trial in the eyes of the world should be candidly faced. There is a dramatic disparity between the circumstances of the accusers and of the accused that might discredit our work if we should falter, in even minor matters, in being fair and temperate.

Unfortunately, the nature of these crimes is such that both prosecution and judgment must be by victor nations over vanquished foes. The world-wide scope of the aggressions carried out by these men has left but few real neutrals. Either the victors must judge the vanquished or we must leave the defeated to judge themselves. After the First World War we learned the futility of the latter course. The former high station of these defendants, the notoriety of their acts, and the adaptability of their conduct to provoke retaliation, make it hard to distinguish between the demand for a just and measured retribution, and the unthinking cry for vengeance which arises from the anguish of war. It is our task, so far as is humanly possible, to draw the line between the two. We must never forget that the record on which we judge these defendants today is the record on which history will judge us tomorrow. To pass these defendants a poisoned chalice is to put it to our lips as well. We must summon such detachment and intellectual integrity to our task that this trial will commend itself to posterity as fulfilling humanity's aspirations to do justice. At the very outset, let us dispose of the contention that to put these men to trial is to do them an injustice entitling them to some special consideration. These defendants may be hard pressed but they are not ill used. . . .

If these men are the first war leaders of a defeated nation to be prosecuted in the name of the law, they are also the first to be given a chance to plead for their lives in the name of the law. Realistically, the Charter of this Tribunal, which gives them a hearing, is also the source of their only hope. It may be that these men of troubled conscience, whose only wish is that the world forget them, do not regard a trial as a favour. But they do have a fair opportunity to defend themselves—a favour which, when in power, they rarely extended even to their fellow countrymen. Despite the fact that public opinion already condemns their acts, we agree that here they must be given a presumption of innocence, and we accept the burden of proving criminal acts and the responsibility of these defendants for their commission. . . .

We would also make clear that we have no purpose to incriminate the whole German people. We know that the Nazi Party was not put in power by a majority of the German vote. We know it came to power by an evil alliance between the most extreme of the Nazi revolutionists, the most unrestrained of the German reactionaries, and the most aggressive of the German militarists. If the German populace had willingly accepted the Nazi programme, no Storm-troopers would have been needed in the early days of the Party, and there would have been no need for concentration camps or the Gestapo, both of which institutions were inaugurated as soon as the Nazis gained control of the German state. Only after these lawless innovations proved successful at home were they taken abroad.

The German people should know by now that the people of the United States hold them in no fear, and in no hate. It is true that the Germans have taught us the horrors of modern warfare, but the ruin that lies from the Rhine to the Danube shows that we, like our Allies, have not been dull pupils. If we are not awed by German fortitude and proficiency in war, and if we are not persuaded of their political maturity, we do respect their skill in the arts of peace, their technical competence, and the sober, industrious and self-disciplined character of the masses of the German people. In 1933, we saw the German people recovering prestige in the commercial, industrial and artistic world after the set-back of the last war. We beheld their progress neither with envy nor malice. The Nazi regime interrupted this advance. The recoil of the Nazi aggression has left Germany in ruins. The Nazi readiness to pledge the German word without hesitation, and to break it without shame, has fastened upon German diplomacy a reputation for duplicity that will handicap it for years. Nazi arrogance has made the boast of the "master race" a taunt that will be thrown at Germans the world over for generations. The Nazi nightmare has given the German name a new and sinister significance throughout the world, which will retard Germany a century. The German, no less than the non-German world, has accounts to settle with these defendants. . . .

While this declaration of the law by the Charter is final, it may be contended that the prisoners on trial are entitled to have it applied to their conduct only most charitably if at all. It may be said that this is new law, not authoritatively declared at the time they did the acts it condemns, and that this declaration of the law has taken them by surprise.

I cannot, of course, deny that these men are surprised that this is the law; they really are surprised that there is any such thing as law. These defendants did not rely on any law at all. Their programme ignored and defied all law. . . . International Law, Natural Law, German Law, any law at all, was to these men simply a propaganda device to be invoked when it helped and to be ignored when it would condemn what they wanted to do. That men may be protected in relying upon the law at the time they act, is the reason we find laws of retrospective operation unjust. But these men cannot bring themselves within the reason of the rule which in some systems of jurisprudence prohibits *ex post facto* laws. They cannot show that they ever relied upon International Law in any state or paid it the slightest regard. . . .

The re-establishment of the principle that there are unjust wars and that unjust wars are illegal is traceable in many steps. One of the most significant is the Briand-Kellogg Pact of 1928, by which Germany, Italy and Japan, in common with practically all nations of the world, renounced war as an instrument of national policy, bound themselves to seek the settlement of disputes only by pacific means, and condemned recourse to war for the solution of international controversies. This pact altered the legal status of a war of aggression. . . .

A failure of these Nazis to heed, or to understand the force and meaning of this evolution in the legal thought of the world, is not a defence or a mitigation. If anything, it aggravates their offence and makes it the more mandatory that the law they have flouted be vindicated by juridical application to their lawless conduct. . . .

Any resort to war — to any kind of a war — is a resort to means that are inherently criminal. War inevitably is a course of killings, assaults, deprivations of liberty, and destruction of property. An honestly defensive war is, of course, legal and saves those lawfully conducting it from criminality. But inherently criminal acts cannot be defended by showing that those who committed them were engaged in a war, when war itself is illegal. The very minimum legal consequence of the treaties making aggressive wars illegal is to strip those who incite or wage them of every defence the law ever gave, and to leave war-makers subject to judgment by the usually accepted principles of the law of crimes.

But if it be thought that the Charter, whose declarations concededly bind us all, does contain new law, I still do not shrink from demanding its strict application by this Tribunal. The rule of law in the world, flouted by the lawlessness incited by these defendants, had to be restored at the cost to my country of over a million casualties, not to mention those of other nations. I cannot subscribe to the perverted reasoning that society may advance and strengthen the rule of law by the expenditure of morally innocent lives, but that progress in the law may never be made at the price of morally guilty lives.

It is true, of course, that we have no judicial precedent for the Charter. But International Law is more than a scholarly collection of abstract and immutable principles. It is an outgrowth of treaties and agreements between nations, and of accepted customs. Yet every custom has its origin in some single act, and every agreement has to be initiated by the action of some State. Unless we are prepared to abandon every principle of growth for International Law, we cannot deny that our own day has the right to institute customs and to conclude agreements that will themselves become sources of a newer and strengthened International Law. International Law is not capable of development by the normal processes of legislation, for there is no continuing international legislative authority. Innovations and revisions in International Law are brought about by the action of governments such as those I have cited, designed to meet a change in circumstances. It grows, as did the Common Law, through decisions reached from time to time in adapting settled principles to new situations. The fact is that when the law evolves by the case method, as did the Common Law and as International Law must do if it is to advance at all, it advances at the expense of those who wrongly guessed the law and learned too late their error. The law, as far as International Law can be decreed, had been clearly pronounced when these acts took place. Hence we are not disturbed by the lack of judicial precedent for the inquiry it is proposed to conduct.

JUDGMENT OF THE INTERNATIONAL MILITARY TRIBUNAL FOR THE TRIAL OF GERMAN MAJOR WAR CRIMINALS

Nuremberg, Sept. 30 and Oct. 1, 1946

. . . In Berlin, on the 18th October, 1945, in accordance with Article 14 of the Charter, an Indictment was lodged against the defendants named in the caption above, who had been designated by the Committee of the Chief Prosecutors of the signatory Powers as major war criminals. . . .

This Indictment charges the defendants with Crimes against Peace by the planning, preparation, initiation and waging of wars of aggression, which were also wars in violation of international treaties, agreements, and assurances; with War crimes; and with Crimes against Humanity. The defendants are also charged with participating in the formulation or execution of a common plan or conspiracy to commit all these crimes. The Tribunal was further asked by the Prosecution to declare all the named groups or organisations to be criminal within the meaning of the Charter. . . .

Four hundred and three open sessions of the Tribunal have been held. Thirty-three witnesses gave evidence orally for the Prosecution against the individual defendants, and 61 witnesses, in addition to 19 of the defendants, gave evidence for the Defence.

A further 143 witnesses gave evidence for the Defence by means of written answers to interrogatories.

The Tribunal appointed Commissioners to hear evidence relating to the organisations, and 101 witnesses were heard for the Defence before the Commissioners, and 1,809 affidavits from other witnesses were submitted. Six reports were also submitted, summarising the contents of a great number of further affidavits.

Thirty-eight thousand affidavits, signed by 155,000 people, were submitted on behalf of the Political Leaders, 136,213 on behalf of the SS, 10,000 on behalf of the SA, 7,000 on behalf of the SD, 3,000 on behalf of the General Staff and OKW, and 2,000 on behalf of the Gestapo.

The Tribunal itself heard 22 witnesses for the organisations. The documents tendered in evidence for the prosecution of the individual defendants and the organisations numbered several thousands. A complete stenographic record of everything said in Court has been made, as well as an electrical recording of all the proceedings. . . .

THE COMMON PLAN OR CONSPIRACY AND AGGRESSIVE WAR

The Tribunal now turns to the consideration of the Crimes against peace charged in the Indictment. Count One of the Indictment charges the defendants with conspiring or having a common plan to commit crimes against peace.

Count Two of the Indictment charges the defendants with committing specific crimes against peace by planning, preparing, initiating, and waging wars of aggression against a number of other States. It will be convenient to consider the question of the existence of a common plan and the question of aggressive war together, and to deal later in this Judgment with the question of the individual responsibility of the defendants.

The charges in the Indictment that the defendants planned and waged aggressive wars are charges of the utmost gravity. War is essentially an evil thing. Its consequences are not confined to the belligerent States alone, but affect the whole world.

To initiate a war of aggression, therefore, is not only an international crime; it is the supreme international crime differing only from other war crimes in that it contains within itself the accumulated evil of the whole.

The first acts of aggression referred to in the Indictment are the seizure of Austria and Czechoslovakia and the first war of aggression charged in the Indictment is the war against Poland begun on the 1st September, 1939.

Before examining that charge it is necessary to look more closely at some of the events which preceded these acts of aggression. The war against Poland did not come suddenly out of an otherwise clear sky; the evidence has made it plain that this war of aggression, as well as the seizure of Austria and Czechoslovakia, was pre-meditated and carefully prepared, and was not undertaken until the moment was thought opportune for it to be carried through as a definite part of the pre-ordained scheme and plan.

For the aggressive designs of the Nazi Government were not accidents arising out of the immediate political situation in Europe and the world; they were a deliberate and essential part of Nazi foreign policy. . . .

THE LAW OF THE CHARTER

The jurisdiction of the Tribunal is defined in the Agreement and Charter, and the crimes coming within the jurisdiction of the Tribunal, for which there shall be individual responsibility, are set out in Article 6. The law of the Charter is decisive, and binding upon the Tribunal.

The making of the Charter was the exercise of the sovereign legislative power by the countries to which the German Reich unconditionally surrendered; and the undoubted right of these countries to legislate for the occupied territories has been recognized by the civilised world. The Charter is not an arbitrary exercise of power on the part of the victorious nations, but in the view of the Tribunal, as will be shown, it is the expression of international law existing at the time of its creation; and to that extent is itself a contribution to international law.

The Signatory Powers created this Tribunal, defined the law it was to administer, and made regulations for the proper conduct of the Trial. In doing so, they have done together what any one of them might have done singly; for it is not to be doubted that any nation has the right thus to set up special courts to administer law. With regard to the constitution of the court, all that the defendants are entitled to ask is to receive a fair trial on the facts and law.

The Charter makes the planning or waging of a war of aggression or a war in violation of international treaties a crime; and it is therefore not strictly necessary to consider whether and to what extent aggressive war was a crime before the execution of the London Agreement. But in view of the great importance of the questions of law involved, the Tribunal has heard full argument from the Prosecution and the Defence, and will express its view on the matter.

It was urged on behalf of the defendants that a fundamental principle of all law — international and domestic — is that there can be no punishment of crime without a pre-existing law. "*Nullum crimen sine lege, nulla poena sine lege.*" It was submitted that *ex post facto* punishment is abhorrent to the law of all civilised nations, that no sovereign power had made aggressive war a crime at the time that the alleged criminal acts were committed, that no statute had defined aggressive war, that no penalty had been fixed for its commission, and no court had been created to try and punish offenders.

In the first place, it is to be observed that the maxim *nullum crimen sine lege* is not a limitation of sovereignty, but is in general a principle of justice. To assert that it is unjust to punish those who in defiance of treaties and assurances have attacked neighboring states without warning is obviously untrue, for in such circumstances the attacker must know that he is doing wrong, and so far from it being unjust to punish him, it would be unjust if his wrong were allowed to go unpunished. Occupying the positions they did in the government of Germany, the defendants, or at least some of them must have known of the treaties signed by Germany, outlawing recourse to war for the settlement of international disputes; they must have known that they were acting in defiance of all international law when in complete deliberation they carried out their designs of invasion and aggression. On this view of the case alone, it would appear that the maxim has no application to the present facts.

This view is strongly reinforced by a consideration of the state of international law in 1939, so far as aggressive war is concerned. The General Treaty for the Renunciation of War of 27th August, 1928, more generally known as the Pact of Paris or the Kellogg-Briand Pact, was binding on sixty-three nations, including Germany, Italy and Japan at the outbreak of war in 1939. . . .

The question is, what was the legal effect of this Pact? The nations who signed the Pact or adhered to it unconditionally condemned recourse to war for the future as an instrument of policy, and expressly renounced it. After the signing of the Pact, any nation resorting to war as an instrument of national policy breaks the Pact. In the opinion of the Tribunal, the solemn renunciation of war as an instrument of national policy necessarily involves the proposition that such a war is illegal in international law; and that those who plan and wage such a war, with its inevitable and terrible consequences, are committing a crime in so doing. . . .

But it is argued that the Pact does not expressly enact that such wars are crimes, or set up courts to try those who make such wars. To that extent the same is true with regard to the laws of war contained in the Hague Convention. The Hague Convention of 1907 prohibited resort to certain methods of waging war. These included the inhumane treatment of prisoners, the employment of poisoned weapons, the improper use of flags of truce, and similar matters. Many of these prohibitions had been enforced long before the date of the Convention; but since 1907 they have certainly been crimes, punishable as offences against the laws of war; yet the Hague Convention nowhere designates such practices as criminal, nor is any sentence prescribed, nor any mention made of a court to try and punish offenders. For many years past, however, military tribunals have tried and punished individuals guilty of violating the rules of land warfare laid down by this Convention. In the opinion of the Tribunal, those who wage aggressive war are doing that which is equally illegal, and of much greater moment than a breach of one of the rules of the Hague Convention. In interpreting the words of the Pact, it must be remembered that international law is not the product of an international legislature, and that such international agreements as the Pact of Paris have to deal with general principles of law, and not with administrative matters of procedure. The law of war is to be found not only in treaties, but in the customs and practices of states which gradually obtained universal recognition, and from the general principles of justice applied by jurists and practised by military courts. This law is not static, but by continual adaptation follows the needs of a changing world. Indeed, in many cases treaties do no more than express and define for more accurate reference the principles of law already existing. . . .

THE LAW RELATING TO WAR CRIMES AND CRIMES AGAINST HUMANITY . . .

With regard to crimes against humanity, there is no doubt whatever that political opponents were murdered in Germany before the war, and that many of them were kept in concentration camps in circumstances of great horror and cruelty. The policy of terror was certainly carried out on a vast scale, and in many cases was organised and systematic. The policy of persecution, repression and murder of civilians in Germany before the war of 1939, who were likely to be hostile to the Government, was most ruthlessly carried out. The persecution of Jews during the same period is established beyond all doubt. To constitute crimes against humanity, the acts relied on before the outbreak of war must have been in execution of, or in connection with, any crime within the jurisdiction of the Tribunal. The Tribunal is of the opinion that revolting and horrible as many of these crimes were, it has not been satisfactorily proved that they were done in execution of, or in connection with, any such crime. The Tribunal therefore cannot make a general declaration that the acts before 1939 were crimes against humanity within the meaning of the Charter, but from the beginning of the war in 1939 war crimes were committed on a vast scale, which were also crimes against humanity; and insofar as the inhumane acts charged in the Indictment, and committed after the beginning of the war, did not constitute war crimes, they were all committed in execution of, or in connection with, the aggressive war, and therefore constituted crimes against humanity. . . .

THE ACCUSED ORGANISATIONS

[Under Article 9 of the Charter, entire organisations could be declared criminal. Under Article 10,] . . . the declaration of criminality against an accused organisation is final, and cannot be challenged in any subsequent criminal proceeding against a member of that organisation. Article 10 is as follows:

> "In cases where a group or organisation is declared criminal by the Tribunal, the competent national authority of any Signatory shall have the right to bring individuals to trial for membership therein before national, military or occupation courts. In any such case the criminal nature of the group or organisation is considered proved and shall not be questioned."

The effect of the declaration of criminality by the Tribunal is well illustrated by Law Number 10 of the Control Council of Germany passed on 20th day of December, 1945, which provides:

> ". . . (3) Any person found guilty of any of the crimes above mentioned may upon conviction be punished as shall be determined by the Tribunal to be just. Such punishment may consist of one or more of the following:
> *(a)* Death.
> *(b)* Imprisonment for life or a term of years, with or without hard labour.
> *(c)* Fine, and imprisonment with or without hard labour, in lieu thereof."

In effect, therefore, a member of an organisation which the Tribunal has declared to be criminal may be subsequently convicted of the crime of membership and be punished for that crime by death. This is not to assume that international or military courts which will try these individuals will not exercise appropriate standards of justice. This is a far-reaching and novel procedure. Its application, unless properly safeguarded, may produce great injustice.

Article 9, it should be noted, uses the words "The Tribunal may declare" so that the Tribunal is vested with discretion as to whether it will declare any organisation criminal. This discretion is a judicial one and does not permit arbitrary action, but should be exercised in accordance with well settled legal principles, one of the most important of which is that criminal guilt is personal, and that mass punishments should be avoided. If satisfied of the criminal guilt of any organisation or group, this Tribunal should not hesitate to declare it to be criminal because the theory of "group criminality" is new, or because it might be unjustly applied by some subsequent tribunals. On the other hand, the Tribunal should make such declaration of criminality so far as possible in a manner to insure that innocent persons will not be punished.

A criminal organisation is analogous to a criminal conspiracy in that the essence of both is cooperation for criminal purposes. There must be a group bound together and organised for a common purpose. The group must be formed or used in connection with the commission of crimes denounced by the Charter. Since the declaration with respect to the organisations and groups will, as has been pointed out, fix the criminality of its members, that definition should exclude persons who had no knowledge of the criminal purposes or acts of the organisation and those who were drafted by the State for membership, unless they were personally implicated in the commission of acts declared criminal by Article 6 of the Charter as members of the organisation. Membership alone is not enough to come within the scope of these declarations.

NOTES AND QUESTIONS

1. What are Jackson's and the Tribunal's arguments that the trial was not illegitimately based on retroactive law? Are these arguments convincing?

2. What was the purpose of the Nuremberg trials? Deterrence? Retribution? Rehabilitation?

3. Article 6(c) defines crimes against humanity as "murder, extermination, enslavement, deportation, and other inhumane acts committed against any civilian population, *before or during the war* . . ." (emphasis added). How faithful is the Tribunal's judgment to the language indicating that atrocious conduct occurring before the war can constitute crimes against humanity?

4. Under the Tribunal's analysis of Articles 9 and 10, what must prosecutors prove to convict a member of a criminal organization such as the SS of crimes committed by the SS? Is this a concept of collective guilt or individual guilt? Could an SS member who never killed anyone be convicted of the war crime of murder?

5. The Allies greatly feared the revival of Nazism in Germany. Those Nuremberg defendants sentenced to death were hanged, and their corpses were photographed with their names pinned to their shirt-fronts, out of fear that neo-Nazis might whisper that they were still alive. Then their bodies were cremated in the ovens of the Dachau concentration camp, and the ashes scattered on a river—as a symbolic gesture, but also to ensure that the graves would not become neo-Nazi shrines.

6. Do you agree with the Tribunal that "[t]o initiate a war of aggression . . . is not only an international crime; it is the supreme international crime"? Is it worse than genocide? Why might the Tribunal have thought the answer is yes? Consider the following reading.

DAVID LUBAN, THE LEGACIES OF NUREMBERG

in Legal Modernism 336, 341-342 (1994)

It is impossible for us to read accounts of the Nuremberg trial without realizing that it signifies something much different to us than it did to those who conceived it. For us, Nuremberg is a judicial footnote to the Holocaust; it stands for the condemnation and punishment of genocide, and its central achievement lies in recognizing the category of *crimes against humanity*. . . .

For those who conceived of the trial, on the other hand, its great accomplishment was to be the criminalization of aggressive war, inaugurating an age of world order. . . .

For the trial's framers, then, its decisive legal achievement lay in recognizing the category of *crimes against peace*— "planning, preparation, initiation or waging of a war of aggression. . . ."

The idea that Nuremberg was to be the Trial to End All Wars seems fantastic and naive forty years (and 150 wars) later. It has also done much to vitiate the real achievements of the trial, in particular the condemnation of crimes against humanity. To end all war, the authors of the Nuremberg Charter were led to incorporate an intellectual confusion into it. The Charter criminalized aggression; and by criminalizing aggression, the Charter erected a wall around state sovereignty and committed itself to an old-European model of unbreachable nation-states.

But crimes against humanity are often, even characteristically, carried out by states against their own subjects. The effect . . . of criminalizing such acts (Article 6(c)) and assigning personal liability to those who order them and carry them out (Articles 7 and 8) is to pierce the veil of sovereignty. As a result, Article 6(a) pulls in the opposite direction from Articles 6(c), 7, and 8, leaving us, as we shall see, with a legacy that is at best equivocal. . . .

[Article 6(a) has] been a major moral enemy of the human rights movement, inasmuch as attempts at sanctions or interventions against human rights offenders are invariably denounced as violations of their sovereignty. It is the tension between statism and human rights that renders the legacy of Nuremberg equivocal; the human rights movement and human rights violators are vying for the contested legacy of Nuremberg.

Jackson saw this point all too clearly. When Gros, the French representative at the conference establishing the Nuremberg trial, argued that humanitarian intervention in a country's internal affairs was a traditional legal principle that would be contravened by Article 6(a), Jackson countered that nonintervention was sacred to Americans, who had no intention of letting other countries interfere in our own policies of racial discrimination.[6] . . . By contrast, the other horn of the Article 6 dilemma was seized by Thurgood Marshall and his colleagues in the NAACP in their brief in *Morgan v. Virginia*, a transportation-desegregation case: they argued that Americans had not spilled their blood in a war against "the apostles of racism" abroad only to permit its flourishing at home. . . . The Supreme Court gave them a seven-to-one victory, striking down racial segregation on interstate buses; Justice Jackson, ironically, could not participate because he was in Nuremberg prosecuting the Nazis.

B.   THE SUBSEQUENT NAZI TRIALS

The four Allied powers that occupied Germany at the end of the Second World War together enacted a statute, Allied Control Council Law No. 10, which formed the basis for additional trials at Nuremberg and elsewhere. CCL 10, like the Nuremberg Charter, criminalized crimes against peace, war crimes, crimes against humanity, and membership in a criminal organization. It defined some of the offenses slightly

---

6. Robert H. Jackson, International Conference on Military Trials, London, 1945, Dept. of State Publication No. 3080, at 331, 333 (1945): "It has been a general principle of foreign policy of our Government from time immemorial that the internal affairs of another government are not ordinarily our business; that is to say, the way Germany treats its inhabitants, or any other country treats its inhabitants, is not our affair any more than it is the affair of some other government to interpose itself in our problems. . . . We have some regrettable circumstances at times in our own country in which minorities are unfairly treated."

differently than the Nuremberg Charter, however. For example, under CCL 10 crimes against peace included "initiation of invasions" of other countries even when the invasions were not resisted — specifically, the German annexation of Austria and part of Czechoslovakia before World War II. Its definition of crimes against humanity included actions performed before the war; and it added imprisonment, torture, and rape to the list of enumerated offenses that would count as crimes against humanity. Although these were implicit in the Nuremberg Charter's catch-all category of "other inhumane acts," CCL 10 was the first modern statute to declare that torture and rape during organized attacks on civilian populations are international crimes.

More controversial was CCL 10's declaration that mere membership in a criminal organization was a crime — indeed, a death penalty crime. Following the Nuremberg Tribunal's judgment, courts softened this provision and held that membership in a criminal organization was a crime only if the member had at least personal knowledge of its criminal acts or purposes.

Thousands of Germans were tried under CCL 10, by courts convened by one or another of the Allies. Among the most interesting were the trials held by the Americans in the second round at Nuremberg. Where the first Nuremberg trials aimed at the leadership of the Third Reich, the second round singled out representative categories of German society who had colluded with Nazi atrocities: industrialists, doctors, lawyers, judges, and others (see Table 3-1). Thus, the defendants in the "Doctors Trial" were physicians and medical administrators involved in one of the Third Reich's most chilling criminal enterprises: performing atrocious medical experiments on living, conscious concentration camp inmates.

Table 3-1
The Second Round of Nuremberg Trials

Case name	Defendants and charges	Verdict
#1 The Doctors (or Medical) Case	Twenty-three Nazi physicians charged with conducting inhuman experiments on German civilians and nationals of other countries. The experiments ranged from studying the effects of high altitude and malaria to sterilization.	Sixteen defendants convicted (including seven sentenced to death), seven acquitted.
#2 Milch Case	Former German Field Marshall Erhard Milch charged with murder and cruel treatment of POWs, and with participation in experiments dealing with effects of high altitude and freezing.	Convicted and sentenced to life in prison.
#3 The Justice (or Judges) Case	Nine members of the Reich Ministry of Justice and seven members of the People's and Special Courts charged with using their power as prosecutors and judges to commit war crimes and crimes against humanity.	Ten defendants convicted, four acquitted (one defendant died before verdict, and a mistrial was declared in one case).

Table 3-1 Continued

Case name	Defendants and charges	Verdict
	(This trial inspired the movie *Judgment at Nuremberg*.)	
#4 The Pohl/WVHA Case	Oswald Pohl and seventeen other members of WVHA (Economic and Administrative Office) charged with war crimes against POWs in concentration camps which WVHA controlled after spring of 1942.	Fifteen defendants convicted, three acquitted. Three defendants were sentenced to death, the rest to prison terms.
#5 The Flick Case	Six members of the Flick Concern, a group of industrial enterprises (including coal mines and steel plants) charged with using slave labor and POWs, deporting persons for labor in German-occupied territories, and plundering private property—the "Aryanization" of Jewish properties.	Three defendants (including Friedrich Flick) convicted and sentenced to prison, three acquitted.
#6 The I.G. Farben Case	Twenty-four defendants, all in the IG Farben industrial concern, charged with plunder and spoliation of private property in German-occupied territories and other war crimes.	Thirteen defendants found guilty on one or more charges and sentenced to prison.
#7 The Hostage Case	Twelve defendants, officers in the German Armed Forces, charged with murdering thousands of civilians in Greece, Yugoslavia, and Albania; committing acts of devastation in Norway and other countries; drafting orders denying POWs rights; and ordering the slaughter of surrendered troops.	Eight defendants found guilty and sentenced to prison, two acquitted. Two other defendants committed suicide before the verdict.
#8 The R.U.S.H.A. Case	Fourteen defendants, officials in the Race and Settlement Office and the Office for the Strengthening of Germandom, charged with crimes against humanity relating to murder, deportation, and torture on political, racial, and religious grounds.	Thirteen defendants found guilty on one or more charge, one defendant acquitted.

Continued

Table 3-1 Continued

Case name	Defendants and charges	Verdict
#9 The Einsatzgruppen Case	Twenty-four defendants, all members of German mobile killing units, the Einsatz-gruppen, charged with the murder and ill treatment of POWs and civilians in occupied countries, and with wanton destruction not justified by military necessity.	All twenty-four defendants were found guilty on one or more charge. Fourteen defendants were sentenced to die, but ten later had their sentences reduced.
#10 The Krupp Case	Alfred Krupp and eleven other defendants, all members of the Krupp industrial concern, charged with enslavement and other war crimes, including the plunder of public and private property.	Eleven defendants were found guilty on one or more charge and sentenced to jail terms, one defendant acquitted.
#11 The Ministries Case	Twenty-one defendants, including three Reich Ministers, as well as other members of the Nazi Party hierarchy, charged with waging wars of aggression, violating international treaties, and committing various crimes of war and crimes against humanity.	Nineteen defendants found guilty on at least one charge and sentenced to terms ranging from 4 to 25 years.

Source: Adapted from Doug Linder, The Subsequent Nuremberg Trials: An Overview (2000), available at http://www.law.umkc.edu/faculty/projects/ftrials/nuremberg/subsequenttrials .html.

Doctors. Although some of these trials are now of merely historical interest, others had a more lasting impact. Particularly influential was the Doctors Trial because in its judgment the court articulated a set of principles — the Nuremberg Code — that became the foundation for modern medical and experimental ethics. The Nuremberg Code marks the first authoritative statement of the principle that medical experiments require the informed, voluntary consent of the subject.

Industrialists. Equally interesting (though less influential) were the trials of industrialists who used slave labor. The idea that businessmen who are complicit in atrocious crimes may themselves be criminally liable is an important one. These cases raise the difficult question of how active complicity must be to rise from the level of moral responsibility to that of criminal guilt. We shall study this question in greater detail in Chapter 17.

Along the same lines, the British tried three men involved in the manufacture of Zyklon B, the gas used in the death camps, which was originally devised and manufactured as a pesticide. The defendants were the company's CEO, his second in command, and the gassing technician. They were charged with the war crime of supplying poison gas knowing that it would be used in the murder of Allied nationals. The technician was acquitted after persuading the court that he did not know Zyklon

B would be used on human beings; the other defendants were convicted and hanged.[7] The issue was revived in 2005 when a Dutch businessman, Franz van Anraat, was convicted by a Dutch court of complicity in war crimes for selling Saddam Hussein's government chemicals used to make poison gas that Saddam used against Kurds in Iraq.[8]

Lawyers and judges. Particularly poignant for lawyers was the *Justice Case*, which tried leading judges and jurists from the Third Reich who had enforced discriminatory or politicized Nazi law, or otherwise perverted the legal process to commit war crimes or crimes against humanity. This included, for example, judges in the infamous People's Court, which handed out death sentences to political opponents of the Hitler regime. Others were lawyers who wrote memos justifying the mistreatment of Soviet prisoners and the executions of captured commissars and captured Allied commandos. On the basis of Articles 6(c) and 7 (or rather, their counterparts in CCL 10), the tribunal found it irrelevant that all these actions accorded with German law; it likewise brushed aside the defense of judicial immunity, arguing that the defense would be available only to a genuinely impartial judge. The *Justice Case* became the model for the Academy Award–winning film *Judgment at Nuremberg.*

Radbruch's Formula. One of the lasting legacies of the perversion of justice by German lawyers and judges was the so-called Radbruch Formula. Gustav Radbruch was a prominent German jurist and legal theorist. After the war, Radbruch wrote several famous essays criticizing German judges for enforcing evil law and analyzing the question of when a judge enforcing the law thereby becomes guilty if the law itself is evil. Radbruch concluded that judges are guilty only if the law is so evil that it cannot be regarded as law at all. In that case, he argued, a judge handing down a death sentence becomes indistinguishable from a murderer. According to Radbruch, we sometimes find a conflict between two basic values of the legal system: justice and predictability (what Radbruch called "legal certainty"). Strictly adhering to the law as it is written creates predictability, but it may lead to substantively unjust outcomes; trying to do justice in each individual case may undermine predictability. In Radbruch's view, "The conflict between justice and legal certainty may well be resolved in this way: The positive law . . . takes precedence even when its content is unjust and fails to benefit the people, unless the conflict between statute and justice reaches such an intolerable degree that the statute, as 'flawed law,' must yield to justice."[9] This would happen, according to Radbruch, where the statute aimed to destroy "equality, the core of justice" (as in the Nazi anti-Jewish legislation). Under Radbruch's Formula, therefore, judges must enforce the law even if it leads to an unjust outcome unless the unfairness of the law becomes "intolerable." Radbruch's Formula has become an established part of German jurisprudence, and it was used after the fall of the Berlin Wall, in the trials of the East German border guards who shot people attempting to escape to the West.[10]

---

7. The Zyklon B Case (Trial of Bruno Tesch and Two Others), British Military Court, Hamburg, 1st-8th March 1946, in 1 Law-Reports of Trials of War Criminals, The United Nations War Crimes Commission, London, HMSO, 1947.

8. Van Anraat narrowly escaped a genocide conviction because the court concluded that his intention was merely to make money, not to destroy the Kurds. See Harmen G. Van der Wilt, Genocide, Complicity in Genocide and International v. Domestic Jurisdiction: Reflections on the *van Anraat* Case, 4 J. Intl. Crim. Just. 239 (2006).

9. Gustav Radbruch, Gesetzliches Unrecht und Übergesetzliches Recht [Statutory Lawlessness and Supra-Statutory Law], 1 Süddeutschen Juristen-Zeitung 105 (1946), translated in 26 Oxford J. Legal Studies 1, 7 (2006) (U.K.).

10. For discussion, see Peter E. Quint, The Border Guard Trials and the East German Past—Seven Arguments, 48 Am. J. Comp. L. 541 (2000).

C. THE TOKYO TRIBUNAL

In addition to the Nuremberg trials, the end of World War II also saw an international military tribunal for the Japanese leadership, held at Tokyo. Japan, like Germany, had committed large- and small-scale atrocities, including mistreatment and murder of captives, sexual enslavement of Korean "comfort women," and massacres of civilians, including the 1938 Rape of Nanking, in which up to 300,000 Chinese civilians were killed.

Although it was nominally conducted by all the Allies, the International Military Tribunal for the Far East (IMTFE) was dominated by the United States. U.S. General Douglas MacArthur established its Charter (based on the Nuremberg Charter with a few small modifications and written by U.S. officials), chose the judges, and made the important decision not to try the Japanese emperor or crown prince. The 11 judges came from the 9 nations that were party to the Japanese surrender agreement, plus India and the Philippines, who were added to have an Asian presence on the court. Although all 11 nations were represented on the prosecution team, there was only a single chief prosecutor, Joseph Keenan, an American. At Nuremberg, recall, each of the four principal Allies provided its own chief prosecutor, and the four teams divided responsibilities among themselves.

Due in large part to lack of understanding of Japanese governmental decision-making processes, the selection of defendants at Tokyo was somewhat haphazard. Twenty-eight military and governmental officials were eventually tried, including Prime Minister Tojo. Two defendants died of natural causes, and one was removed during the trial because of a mental breakdown. Far more than at Nuremberg, the IMTFE involved a clash of cultures, including tensions between colonial powers like Great Britain and colonies such as India. Indeed, the Indian judge, Radhabinod Pal, issued a 700-page dissent from the IMTFE's judgment, and in one frequently quoted passage Justice Pal argued passionately that the ban on aggressive war represented an effort by colonial powers to freeze the international status quo to their own advantage. In addition to Justice Pal, one other judge dissented, and three wrote separate opinions. A particularly telling example of the clash of cultures occurred when, in open court, the U.S. official in charge of all translations of documents and testimony testified that "it is an established fact that an Oriental, when pressed, will dodge the issue."[11] The Tribunal was also marred by serious failures by the chief prosecutor, who lacked organizational skills, was frequently absent, and had a history of serious drinking problems.

Seven of the defendants were sentenced to death, 16 to life imprisonment, and 2 to terms of years. There were no acquittals. The rules of the tribunal permitted a death penalty by simple majority vote of the judges, and one defendant was hanged on a 6-5 vote.[12] When the defendants appealed their convictions to the U.S. Supreme Court, MacArthur announced that if the Court granted habeas corpus, he would ignore it.[13] Instead, the Court concluded that it had no jurisdiction in Hirota v. MacArthur, 338 U.S. 197 (1949). In 1955, the 13 convicts who remained alive were paroled.

The Tokyo trials exerted far less influence than Nuremberg. In part, this was because the Japanese crimes were less extensive than those of the Germans; in

---

11. Arnold C. Brackman, The Other Nuremberg: The Untold Story of the Tokyo War Crimes Trials 161-162 (1987).
12. Richard H. Minear, Victors' Justice: The Tokyo War Crimes Trial 91 (1977).
13. Herbert P. Bix, Hirohito and the Making of Modern Japan 609 (2000).

part, because the Tribunal's domination by Americans made it appear less genuinely international. More important, to many observers it seemed less fair and more like victors' justice — indeed, one major book about the IMFTE is titled *Victors' Justice.*[14] So it appeared to Justice Pal, who wrote in his dissenting opinion, "If Japan is judged, the Allies should also be judged equally."

As a side note, the Tokyo Tribunal included the first female prosecutor at a major war crimes trial, Grace Llewellyn Kanode.[15]

In the following sections, we examine the international criminal tribunals that emerged in the 1990s to deal with the Balkan Wars, the Rwandan genocide, and other high-profile cases of mass atrocity. Before leaving the World War II trials, however, it is worthwhile to consider why they came about and whether the political motivations of the Allies in creating them continue to be pertinent in the contemporary world. Richard Falk, a distinguished commentator and international lawyer, offers the following pessimistic view. It forms a counterpoint to the idealism reflected in Robert Jackson's Nuremberg oration. While you read, reflect on which viewpoint seems most accurate.

RICHARD FALK, ACCOUNTABILITY FOR WAR CRIMES AND THE LEGACY OF NUREMBERG

in War Crimes and Collective Wrongdoing: A Reader 114, 120-123, 130-131 (Aleksandar Jókic ed., 2001)

. . . It has been natural until quite recently to view the narrative of international law as one expression of the optimistic western idea of linear history. In this sense, Nuremberg is both an event and a process. This process is often interpreted teleologically as containing an assured promise of future justice, one dimension of which will be a reliable framework within which to establish the accountability of leaders for severe violations of international law. According to such thinking, it is merely a matter of patience, allowing political evolution to run its course, until a fully articulated international legal order emerges that is global in scope, evenhanded in application, and effective in operation. . . .

In a fundamental sense, as with human rights, it is difficult to comprehend why sovereign states should have been ever willing to validate such a subversive idea as that of international criminal accountability of leaders for war crimes. It goes directly against the spirit and ideology of sovereignty. It only makes sense from a statist perspective if the imposition of accountability is understood to be a *particular* advantageous response to a given geopolitical challenge, whose wider implications can be avoided. . . .

. . . Nuremberg was an exceptional circumstance that allowed geopolitical forces to coalesce around the idea of a criminal prosecution of surviving leaders. Among the

---

14. Minear, supra note 12. See generally Allison Marston Danner, Beyond the Geneva Conventions: Lesson from the Tokyo Tribunal in Prosecuting War and Terrorism, 46 Va. J. Intl. L. 83 (2005). A comprehensive recent study, which incorporates documentary evidence unavailable to Minear, summarizes the "victors' justice" debate and sheds significant new light on the significance of the Tokyo trials. Yuma Totani, The Tokyo War Crimes Trial: The Pursuit of Justice in the Wake of World War II (2008).

15. Neil Boiser & Robert Cryer, The Tokyo International Military Tribunal: A Reappraisal 78 (2008).

factors that can be mentioned are the following: the claim of the victorious powers that the losing side embodied an evil ideology; the public pressure for some sort of punitive action against those believed responsible for waging such a devastating war; the consensus among leaders that Germany (and Japan) must not be held collectively responsible in the manner of the peace settlement after the First World War (what might be called "the lesson of Versailles"); the closely related geopolitical idea in the West that the defeated enemy states might soon become valued allies in the next phase of geopolitical rivalry; the guilty conscience in the West that not enough had been done to protect the victims of Nazi persecution before and during the war itself (for example, the refusal of liberal democracies to accept Jewish refugees; the failure to bomb the railroad tracks leading to Auschwitz), and the overall sense that the reconstruction of world order around moderate lines would be helped by a dignified trial of German defendants as opposed to the impression created by a vengeful process of summary execution. In addition, there were those, such as Jackson and [Telford] Taylor, who believed that Nuremberg represented a solemn commitment by the convening governments to submit to the rule of law in their international activities, and that such submission might help to prevent the recurrence of major wars in the future.[16] And there were those who went further, viewing Nuremberg as a desirable and necessary step toward realizing a far wider program of global reform. In this latter view only some form of world government, accompanied by disarmament at the level of the state, could save the human species from extinction given the prospect of the next world war being fought with nuclear weaponry. . . .

My point here is that Nuremberg occurred only for opportunistic reasons within the specific historical setting of the ending of the Second World War, and that far deeper than the normative impulses associated with imposing criminal liability on the individuals responsible were the currents of opinion that stressed the vital importance of moving toward unabashed realism in terms of American participation in the world. This outlook included warnings to avoid taking the UN too seriously as a basis for collective security, and the corresponding importance of peacetime military vigilance at the level of the state. The main realist contention being that countervailing power, and the credibility associated with its potential use, could both keep the peace and avoid aggressive attacks on the established territorial and political order. . . .

If such a "reading" of Nuremberg is made, how then can one explain its resurfacing in the 1990s? There are at least four lines of explanation. First of all, the end of the cold war meant that allegations of criminality would not be perceived as mainly an exercise in hostile propaganda that dangerously inflamed efforts to sustain what had come to be called "peaceful coexistence." Secondly, . . . that to an extent not even imagined at Nuremberg, the Nuremberg Promise was taken seriously by morally engaged sectors of civil society. Thirdly, the war in Bosnia with its genocidal features, especially "ethnic cleansing," again challenged the liberal democracies to show that they cared about the victims, a pressure intensified by "the CNN factor." And fourthly, there was a geopolitical incentive to create some sort of international criminal tribunal to cope with the security threats to the established order posed by international terrorism, the drug trade, and the revival of piracy at sea.

---

16. Brig. Gen. Telford Taylor (1908-1998) was one of Jackson's assistant prosecutors at Nuremberg and eventually became the head prosecutor of the second round of Nuremberg trials. Later he became a Columbia University law professor. Taylor reemerged into prominence during the Vietnam War, when he accused the U.S. government of war crimes. Among his many books is *Anatomy of the Nuremberg Trials* (1992). — Eds.

These international factors led to the reemergence of a circumstance where the revival of Nuremberg was again, almost 50 years later, a matter of "geopolitical convenience." . . .

The legacy of Nuremberg remains complex and controversial, but the 1990s saw the revival of a serious effort on several fronts to push forward with the central effort to hold perpetrators of crimes of state individually accountable. In this respect, also, Telford Taylor's underlying commitment to treat the Nuremberg Judgment as the foundation for future accountability seems somewhat closer to realization than during the cold war, but with still a long path ahead littered with obstacles. One of the most formidable of these obstacles is the reluctance of major states, especially the United States and China, to participate in this process if it includes the risk that their leaders might stand accused at some future point. . . . International experience to date suggests that an international tribunal of the Nuremberg type will only be brought into being if it is geopolitically convenient for the governments of the leading states, an observation that casts some shadows across the current efforts at The Hague and in Arusha. . . .

It seems evident that individual accountability for crimes of state is an integral part of any adequate conception of a *just* world order. But it seems equally evident that the realist gatekeepers of the international legal order will not accept comprehensive legal and moral restraints on the exercise of force as an instrument of foreign policy. In this regard, Taylor's notion that America made "a tragic mistake" in Vietnam by contradicting the standards it had established at Nuremberg missed the central point that American leadership was never prepared to accept such a framework of restraint as seriously applicable to *its* future diplomacy. In fact, the country was all along mainly led by realists in the Machiavellian tradition that believed that the security interests of the state were paramount, especially in light of "the lessons of Munich," and found discussions of limits imposed by international law diversionary unless used as propaganda tools for castigating enemies or rationalizing contested moves in foreign policy.

D.   THE INTERNATIONAL CRIMINAL TRIBUNAL FOR FORMER YUGOSLAVIA

It would be more than 40 years until the next international tribunal, which was established by the United Nations in the wake of the brutal civil war (the "Balkan Wars") following the breakup of Yugoslavia in the early 1990s.

In 1993, after a UN investigation of crimes committed in the Balkan Wars, the UN Security Council adopted Resolutions 808 and 827, creating the International Criminal Tribunal for the Former Yugoslavia (ICTY). The Tribunal, sitting at The Hague in the Netherlands, is divided into three Trial Chambers of three judges each and one Appellate Chamber of five judges. Its statute grants it jurisdiction over the crimes of genocide, crimes against humanity, "violations of the laws and customs of war," and grave breaches of the Geneva Conventions, committed in the territory of former Yugoslavia after January 1, 1991. The UN has now endorsed the Tribunal's completion strategy to finish all trials and appeals by 2010; however, the arrest in 2008 of Radovan Karadžić, one of the two most wanted suspects, is likely to prolong the ICTY until his trial is completed.

1. Background: The Balkan Wars

Yugoslavia (the name means "state of the south Slavs") came into existence in 1918, pieced together out of smaller ethnic provinces after the Austro-Hungarian and Ottoman Empires collapsed at the end of World War I. Occupied by Germany in World War II, it became a non-Soviet communist country after the war. From 1945 until 1990, the Socialist Federal Republic of Yugoslavia (FRY) consisted of six republics — Bosnia and Herzegovina ("Bosnia"), Croatia, Macedonia, Montenegro, Serbia, and Slovenia — and two autonomous regions that were effectively incorporated into Serbia in 1990. Some republics were populated predominantly by one ethnic group (for example, the Serbs in Serbia and the Croats in Croatia). Bosnia, however, was multiethnic, with a population of approximately 44 percent Muslim, 31 percent Serb, and 17 percent Croat as of 1991. It became the setting for some of the most brutal crimes of the Balkan Wars.

Serbs are predominantly Eastern Orthodox in religion, while Croats are Roman Catholic. Muslims originally came to Yugoslavia in the Ottoman invasions, historically a source of resentment by Christians in the region. In addition to religion-based tension, some bitterness between the Serbs and Croats dates from World War II, when Croatia temporarily became a fascist state while Serbian royalists resisted the Nazis. The persecution that Serbia endured during the war generated a lasting desire among Serbs not to become victims again and fueled a militant nationalism.

Despite these historical sources of tension, the various ethnicities share a language and, to a large degree, a culture. As in many other multiethnic societies, Yugoslavia represented an uneasy mix of animosity and coexistence. Marshal Josip Broz Tito, the communist strongman who ruled postwar Yugoslavia, was able to suppress ethnic nationalism. Tito died in 1980, however, and economic difficulties in the decade following his death set the stage for rising nationalism and ethnic friction. Yugoslavia finally broke apart in 1991 and 1992.

In June 1991, Slovenia and Croatia declared their independence from the FRY. Their decision to leave the Republic was immediately challenged militarily by Serbia, which wished to retain the Yugoslav Republic. Slovenia secured its independence after only a few weeks of fighting with the predominantly Serb forces of the People's Army of the former Yugoslavia (JNA). The armed conflict in Croatia, however, stretched on for years, and ultimately ended only in 1995. This conflict between Serbia and Croatia was replete with brutality and war crimes on both sides, and it played a significant part in dividing Bosnia along ethnic lines.

Late 1991 brought increased fragmentation of the FRY. Macedonia successfully broke off in September 1991. Non-Serbs largely abandoned the JNA, which became, in effect, the Serbian army. Meanwhile, the two autonomous Serb regions within Croatia proclaimed themselves to be the Serbian Republic of Krajina in December 1991, and a Serbian nationalist party in Bosnia announced a separate independent Serb republic within Bosnia — which later became "Republika Srpska" — to become effective upon international recognition of Bosnia. The Serbs claimed approximately 70 percent of Bosnian lands, leaving 30 percent to be divided between Bosnia's Muslims and Croats.

In March 1992, Bosnia declared independence following a referendum. In the referendum balloting, Muslims and Croats overwhelmingly voted in favor of independence but most Serbs boycotted the referendum and declared it invalid. Violence escalated and broke into full-fledged war in early April 1992 when the Republic of Bosnia and Herzegovina was recognized by the European Community and the United States. A fierce struggle for territorial control ensued among the three major groups in Bosnia: Muslim, Serb, and Croat.

In eastern Bosnia, which is close to Serbia, the conflict was particularly fierce between the Bosnian Serbs and the Bosnian Muslims. UN peacekeepers proved unable to stop the fighting. In the war's most notorious incident, Bosnian Serb units sidelined the outnumbered and outgunned Dutch peacekeepers at the town of Srebrenica, which the UN had declared a safe zone for civilians. They then separated Muslim men and older boys from women and children, expelled the women and children, and slaughtered more than 7,000 men and boys.

In April 1992, Serbia and Montenegro established a Serb-dominated federal state called the Federal Republic of Yugoslavia, under the leadership of an ultra-nationalist president, Slobodan Milošević. The former Yugoslav army, the JNA, became the army of this Federal Republic of Yugoslavia, although many Bosnian Serbs were effectively transferred to the Bosnian Serb army. The objective of Serbia, its army, and the Serbian nationalist party in Bosnia at this stage was to create a Serb-dominated western extension of Serbia, taking in Serb-dominated portions of Croatia and Bosnia. This would then, together with Serbia, its two autonomous provinces, and Montenegro, form a new and smaller Yugoslavia with a substantially Serb population.

However, the large Muslim and Croat populations native to and living in Bosnia and Herzegovina posed an obstacle to "Greater Serbia." To deal with that problem, the practice of ethnic cleansing was adopted: murdering, driving away, or expelling other ethnicities. *Ethnic cleansing* was a new phrase but hardly a new concept: It dates back at least to biblical times. In Yugoslavia, ethnic cleansing had been employed in the Croatian conflict, and all participants in the Bosnian struggle apparently used it to some degree. The Serbs seemed to do so more comprehensively, perhaps because it was a concept that was endorsed by some Serb writers who had long envisaged the redistribution of populations, by force if necessary, in the course of achieving a Greater Serbia.

Serb units set up concentration camps reminiscent of those of the Nazis, in which acts of singular atrocity were performed. Among other tactics, the Serb militia units committed widespread rapes, in "rape motels" and camps, for the purpose of impregnating Muslim women with Serbian babies, as an attack on the Muslim communities.

In Bosnia, the Serbs formed a new Serbian Army of Bosnia (VRS). Technically, it was not part of the JNA and had no formal connection with Serbia (facts that had legal significance when the ICTY later tried to connect atrocities committed by the VRS to Serbian politicians). An overwhelming majority of the VRS was composed of former JNA soldiers and officers who remained in Bosnia to fight on the Serbs' behalf after the JNA was ostensibly withdrawn. Paramilitary groups from Serbia also operated in Bosnia. Nominally Bosnian, the VRS and the Bosnian Serb militias were supported by, and allegedly under the control of, Serbia. (When Milošević was finally tried before the ICTY, one of the contested issues was whether he had actually directed Bosnian Serb forces that committed atrocities.) The Bosnian government fielded Bosnian territorial defense units, which, although predominantly Muslim, also included Croats and Serbs. Finally, the Bosnian Croatian armed forces included the Bosnian-based Croatian Defense Council and members of the Republic of Croatia's armed forces. Generally (but not always) Muslims and Croats were aligned in the war against Serbian forces, and those opposing the Serbian military received various types of support from the Republic of Croatia.

In August 1992, Helsinki Watch issued a report on War Crimes in Bosnia, which concluded that "[t]o varying degrees, all parties to the conflict in Bosnia-Herzegovina have violated international humanitarian law, or the laws of war. Croatian and Muslim forces have taken hostages, mistreated persons in their custody and harassed Serbs in areas in which they control. Serbian forces have committed the same abuses but on broader scale." Two months later, the UN Security Council adopted Resolution 780, which created a Commission of Experts to investigate serious violations of international humanitarian law in former Yugoslavia. The Commission, directed by law professor M. Cherif Bassiouni, made 35 field missions to the war zone over the next two years and assembled 65,000 pages of documents and 300 hours of videotapes. The subsequent work of the ICTY rested substantially on these documents, videotapes, and the Commission's 3,500-page final report.

The Bosnian War came to an end in 1995, after NATO bombed Serb forces in Bosnia to protect the UN safe zones and Croatian forces inflicted a decisive defeat on the JNA, recapturing central Croatia (and, in an act of ethnic cleansing, expelling tens of thousands of Serbs from Krajina). At that point, Milošević became receptive to peace talks, which occurred in Dayton, Ohio, and resulted in a treaty signed on December 14.

Conflict erupted again in 1999, when the province of Kosovo attempted to secede from Yugoslavia. Kosovo is inhabited by a Serb minority and an Albanian Muslim majority. Escalating combat between Serb forces and the Muslim "Kosovo Liberation

Army" raised international fears of a second Bosnia. When peace talks, aimed at installing NATO peacekeepers, failed, NATO, spearheaded by the United States, began bombing Serb units. NATO planners wrongly assumed that Milošević would fold in a few days, as he had in 1995. Instead, Serb militias and security units attacked, killing several thousand Muslims and driving hundreds of thousands of other Muslims out of the country. NATO eventually expanded its air war from Kosovo to Belgrade, Serbia's capital city, and Milošević surrendered in June 1999, three months after the bombing began. The Kosovo events became part of ICTY's docket: While the Kosovo war was going on, ICTY issued an indictment against Milošević for war crimes and crimes against humanity.

Two years later, a popular uprising overthrew Milošević, and the successor Yugoslav government eventually turned him over to the ICTY, where he was tried for numerous crimes, including genocide. The Milošević trial was notorious and controversial. Milošević never acknowledged the legitimacy of the Tribunal, charging that it represented nothing more than a Western plot against Serbia. At first he refused legal counsel and insisted on representing himself. The result was delay and disruption, as Milošević delivered lengthy speeches and diatribes. He proved to be a fierce cross-examiner and lost no opportunity to abuse and humiliate prosecution witnesses. The trial was also repeatedly delayed because of Milošević's ill health (he had a heart condition). Eventually, the Tribunal responded to these health-related delays by compelling Milošević to work in conjunction with counsel rather than representing himself. In 2006, complaining again about his health, Milošević demanded to be sent to Russia for treatment, which the Tribunal refused (in part out of concern that Russia would shelter Milošević and refuse to return him to The Hague). Mere weeks before the four-year-long trial was due to end, Milošević was found dead in his cell. His supporters charged that ICTY had, in effect, killed Milošević by refusing his requests to go to Russia for treatment; ICTY investigators claimed that Milošević had secretly stopped taking his medications, in the hope that his symptoms would compel his release to Russia. Regardless of whether either account is correct, the death of Milošević before the trial's completion meant that the Tribunal could issue no judgment. It was a colossal setback for the ICTY.

As mentioned above, in 2008 the Serbian government arrested Radovan Karadžić, the former president of the Bosnian Serb republic, and one of the two most wanted fugitives of the Balkan Wars. (The other is General Ratko Mladić, who remains at large.) As of mid-2009, the Karadžić case remains at the pretrial stage; the actual trial, when it occurs, is likely to take center stage at ICTY, as the Milošević trial had earlier.

2.   The Tribunal

a.   The ICTY Statute

Article 1 of ICTY's Statute grants it "the power to prosecute persons responsible for serious violations of international humanitarian law committed in the territory of the former Yugoslavia since 1991." The substantive criminal law differs in some respects from the law at Nuremberg. It does not include crimes against peace. War crimes are specified in greater detail and are divided into two categories: grave breaches of the Geneva Conventions (that is, crimes of violence against prisoners and detainees) and war crimes involving excessive destruction or banned weapons. The list of crimes against humanity derives from Allied Control Council Law No. 10, the statute used in Germany in the second round of Nuremberg trials. Along with murder, deportation, extermination, enslavement, persecution, and "other inhumane acts"—the crimes against humanity enumerated in the Nuremberg Charter—it adds imprisonment, rape, and torture, "when committed in armed conflict, whether international or internal in character, and directed against any civilian population." In addition, the ICTY statute adds genocide to the list of crimes, alongside war crimes and crimes against humanity. Only natural persons (not corporations, organizations, or governments) can be defendants; and, following the Nuremberg model, the head-of-state and superior-orders defenses are abolished.

The ICTY established an organizational structure followed subsequently by the ICTR and ICC. Sitting in The Hague, it consists of three Trial Chambers, an Appellate Chamber, an independent Prosecutors' Office, and a Registry that administers the Tribunal. Judges come from many nations and sit in three-judge panels (in the Trial Chambers) and five-judge panels (in the Appellate Chamber). No two judges can be nationals of the same state. Rules of procedure and evidence draw on both the common law and civil law traditions.

ICTY can impose sentences of imprisonment, but not the death penalty.

b. Jurisdiction

The Tribunal has *concurrent* jurisdiction with national tribunals of the various Yugoslav states: Cases can be tried either before the Tribunal or a national court. But ICTY has *primacy* over national courts; it was feared that if the national tribunals had primacy they might insist on trying their own perpetrators in order to shield them. In this respect, the ICTY differs radically from the International Criminal Court, which gives national tribunals primacy and can admit only cases that states are unwilling or unable to investigate and try. The ICTY has transferred a few cases to national courts involving lower-level figures, whom the Tribunal generally does not indict.

The jurisdiction of ICTY is broad, perhaps broader than the drafters of the Statute had contemplated. As indicated above, it possesses "the power to prosecute persons responsible for serious violations of international humanitarian law committed in the territory of the former Yugoslavia since 1991 in accordance with the provisions of the present Statute." (The final clause, "in accordance with the provisions of the present Statute," means simply that the Tribunal can try only the crimes enumerated in the Statute.) The jurisdiction was framed broadly in order to encompass all the varying ethnic groups involved in the violence, but it had at least one unexpected consequence. When NATO forces began bombing in the 1998 Kosovo war, then-ICTY prosecutor Louise Arbour personally visited all the NATO capitals to warn member states that any serious war crimes their forces committed fell under ICTY's jurisdiction and could be prosecuted. Reportedly, her visits caused considerable astonishment. (There were, however, no prosecutions of NATO forces, despite Serbian allegations of NATO war crimes.)

c. The Work of the Tribunal

As of mid-2009, ICTY has tried almost 100 cases, resulting in some 53 Trial Chamber judgments and 36 Appeals Chamber judgments (along with hundreds of decisions and orders). Its docket (including both completed and uncompleted cases) involves more than 160 defendants, and two indictees (including major suspect Ratko Mladić) remain at large. Defendants include all the ethnic groups in former Yugoslavia and all levels of the command structure: grunt-level perpetrators of atrocities, local and larger-scale military commanders, and major political leaders.

The best way to obtain a quick overview of ICTY's work is by examining its Web site, http://www.icty.org/. Click on "The Cases." Cases are indexed by defendants' names and also the names of geographic regions where the crimes took place — thus, for example, the *Čelebići* case, also known as *Mucic et al.*, concerns several defendants occupying positions of authority at the Čelebići prison camp in Bosnia, where inmates were tortured, raped, beaten, killed, or otherwise abused. Clicking on the blue-and-white "i" icon next to each case name brings up a short summary of the case, including information about defendants, brief narrative descriptions of the events the case concerns, and judgments and sentences. Half an hour spent skimming these summaries will provide a measure of the Tribunal's work and also of the range of atrocities and depth of tragedy in the Balkan Wars. The full opinions are also available. However, they are very lengthy, running to hundreds of pages, because — in the civil law tradition — they include detailed descriptions of the evidence and fully reasoned factual findings as well as legal findings. The Tribunal also aims to establish a historical record and therefore includes very full factual findings.

At first ICTY's work was hampered by the difficulty of capturing defendants, who were often protected by political sympathizers. UN and NATO troops, who might have helped capture suspects, reportedly were reluctant to do so because they believed it would undermine their basic peacemaking mission by making them appear to be taking sides in the ethnic conflict. The Tribunal's first case arose because the defendant, Dražen Erdemović — a soldier who participated in the Srebrenica massacre — turned himself in and pled guilty. ICTY's first contested trial came about only because the defendant, Duško Tadić, made the mistake of visiting Germany, where he was arrested and turned over to ICTY. Tadić, a Bosnian Serb café owner and karate instructor, had repeatedly visited a prison camp, where he participated in brutal beatings and tortures of prisoners. (By some accounts, Tadić took vengeance on men who had defeated him in prewar karate tournaments.) He was convicted and sentenced to 20 years.

After Milošević fell from power in 1999, the new government of Serbia began to cooperate with ICTY to a far greater extent. Nevertheless, one major suspect still remains at large, Ratko Mladić, the commander of the Bosnian Serb army.

Other practical issues confronting ICTY — as well as ICTR, the Rwanda tribunal — include the difficulty of gathering evidence in communities that are often quite hostile to the enterprise, and the difficulty and expense of protecting witnesses, who may be subject to vengeance and retribution if they testify before the Tribunal and then return to their own communities. This is particularly difficult for victims of sexual violence. Relocating a Yugoslav family in a witness protection program costs hundreds of thousands of dollars a year, and although the tribunals have large budgets (ICTY's 2008-2009 budget is almost $350 million, while ICTR's is $250 million), extensive witness relocation is impracticable.

Some critics wonder whether hundreds of millions of dollars prosecuting a small number of offenders is money well spent. Do the tribunals cost too much? One noted expert defends the tribunal: "To put the costs of international justice in perspective, one must recall that the ICTY was seeking to prosecute political and military leaders responsible for the murder and torture of hundreds of thousands of victims. The closest domestic analogue is the trial of major mob figures or terrorists, which in the United States have cost as much as $70 million for a single trial."[17] The current ICTY

---

17. Michael P. Scharf, The Tools for Enforcing International Criminal Justice in the New Millennium: Lessons from the Yugoslavia Tribunal, 49 DePaul L. Rev. 925, 934 (2000).

budget includes almost $4 million for what promises to be a major but vital expense: archiving the extensive evidence the Tribunal has gathered. Because electronic files can be altered, the primary documents (which may be necessary for future trials of perpetrators still at large) must be securely preserved. Even after the Tribunal has concluded its work, the evidence remains crucial to maintaining the archives in a way that is immune from the efforts of potential historical revisionists to doctor the record.

The ICTY jurisprudence is extensive (the judgments of the Tribunal amount to thousands of pages) and remarkably interesting; the Tribunal has innovated in many areas of both substantive international criminal law and procedure. Arguably, its jurisprudence has "moved the ball" in international criminal law more than any other development since Nuremberg, and possibly more than the Nuremberg Tribunal itself. Rather than discussing the ICTY's jurisprudence here, we will refer to it repeatedly in other chapters as topics arise.

d. The Legality of the Tribunal

A major question is on what basis the Security Council has the authority to establish an international tribunal. This was answered in ICTY's first tried case, *Prosecutor v. Tadić*. The excerpt below refers to several crucial Articles from Chapter VII of the UN Charter:

> **Article 39.** The Security Council shall determine the existence of any threat to the peace, breach of the peace, or act of aggression and shall make recommendations, or decide what measures shall be taken in accordance with Articles 41 and 42, to maintain or restore international peace and security.
>
> **Article 41.** The Security Council may decide what measures not involving the use of armed force are to be employed to give effect to its decisions, and it may call upon the Members of the United Nations to apply such measures. These may include complete or partial interruption of economic relations and of rail, sea, air, postal, telegraphic, radio, and other means of communication, and the severance of diplomatic relations.
>
> **Article 42.** Should the Security Council consider that measures provided for in Article 41 would be inadequate or have proved to be inadequate, it may take such action by air, sea, or land forces as may be necessary to maintain or restore international peace and security. Such action may include demonstrations, blockade, and other operations by air, sea, or land forces by Members of the United Nations.

PROSECUTOR v. TADIĆ

Case No. IT-94-1, Decision on the Defence Motion for Interlocutory Appeal on Jurisdiction (Oct. 2, 1995)

. . . 26. Many arguments have been put forward by Appellant in support of the contention that the establishment of the International Tribunal is invalid under the Charter of the United Nations or that it was not duly established by law. . . .

27. These arguments raise a series of constitutional issues which all turn on the limits of the power of the Security Council under Chapter VII of the Charter of the United Nations and determining what action or measures can be taken under this

Chapter, particularly the establishment of an international criminal tribunal. Put in the interrogative, they can be formulated as follows:

1. was there really a threat to the peace justifying the invocation of Chapter VII as a legal basis for the establishment of the International Tribunal?
2. assuming such a threat existed, was the Security Council authorized, with a view to restoring or maintaining peace, to take any measures at its own discretion, or was it bound to choose among those expressly provided for in Articles 41 and 42 (and possibly Article 40 as well)?
3. in the latter case, how can the establishment of an international criminal tribunal be justified, as it does not figure among the ones mentioned in those Articles, and is of a different nature?

1. THE POWER OF THE SECURITY COUNCIL TO INVOKE CHAPTER VII

28. Article 39 opens Chapter VII of the Charter of the United Nations and determines the conditions of application of this Chapter. It provides:

"The Security Council shall determine the existence of any threat to the peace, breach of the peace, or act of aggression and shall make recommendations, or decide what measures shall be taken in accordance with Articles 41 and 42, to maintain or restore international peace and security." (United Nations Charter, 26 June 1945, Art. 39.)

It is clear from this text that the Security Council plays a pivotal role and exercises a very wide discretion under this Article. But this does not mean that its powers are unlimited. The Security Council is an organ of an international organization, established by a treaty which serves as a constitutional framework for that organization. The Security Council is thus subjected to certain constitutional limitations, however broad its powers under the constitution may be. Those powers cannot, in any case, go beyond the limits of the jurisdiction of the Organization at large, not to mention other specific limitations or those which may derive from the internal division of power within the Organization. In any case, neither the text nor the spirit of the Charter conceives of the Security Council as *legibus solutus* (unbound by law). . . .

29. What is the extent of the powers of the Security Council under Article 39 and the limits thereon, if any?

The Security Council plays the central role in the application of both parts of the Article. It is the Security Council that makes the *determination* that there exists one of the situations justifying the use of the "exceptional powers" of Chapter VII. And it is also the Security Council that chooses the reaction to such a situation: it either makes *recommendations* (i.e., opts not to use the exceptional powers but to continue to operate under Chapter VI) or decides to use the exceptional powers by ordering measures to be taken in accordance with Articles 41 and 42 with a view to maintaining or restoring international peace and security.

The situations justifying resort to the powers provided for in Chapter VII are a "threat to the peace," a "breach of the peace" or an "act of aggression." While the "act of aggression" is more amenable to a legal determination, the "threat to the peace" is more of a political concept. But the determination that there exists such a threat is not a totally unfettered discretion, as it has to remain, at the very least, within the limits of the Purposes and Principles of the Charter.

30. It is not necessary for the purposes of the present decision to examine any further the question of the limits of the discretion of the Security Council in determining the existence of a "threat to the peace," for two reasons.

The first is that an armed conflict (or a series of armed conflicts) has been taking place in the territory of the former Yugoslavia since long before the decision of the Security Council to establish this International Tribunal. If it is considered an international armed conflict, there is no doubt that it falls within the literal sense of the words "breach of the peace" (between the parties or, at the very least, would be [seen] as a "threat to the peace" of others).

But even if it were considered merely as an "internal armed conflict," it would still constitute a "threat to the peace" according to the settled practice of the Security Council and the common understanding of the United Nations membership in general. . . .

2. The Range of Measures Envisaged Under Chapter VII

31. Once the Security Council determines that a particular situation poses a threat to the peace or that there exists a breach of the peace or an act of aggression. . . . the Security Council has a broad discretion in deciding on the course of action and evaluating the appropriateness of the measures to be taken. The language of Article 39 is quite clear as to the channelling of the very broad and exceptional powers of the Security Council under Chapter VII through Articles 41 and 42. These two Articles leave to the Security Council such a wide choice as not to warrant searching, on functional or other grounds, for even wider and more general powers than those already expressly provided for in the Charter. . . .

3. The Establishment of the International Tribunal as a Measure Under Chapter VII

32. . . . In its resolution 827, the Security Council considers that "in the particular circumstances of the former Yugoslavia," the establishment of the International Tribunal "would contribute to the restoration and maintenance of peace" and indicates that, in establishing it, the Security Council was acting under Chapter VII. . . . However, it did not specify a particular Article as a basis for this action. . . .

(A) What Article of Chapter VII Serves as a Basis for the Establishment of a Tribunal?

34. . . . *Prima facie*, the International Tribunal matches perfectly the description in Article 41 of "measures not involving the use of force." . . .

35. . . . Article 41 reads as follows:

> "The Security Council may decide what measures not involving the use of armed force are to be employed to give effect to its decisions, and it may call upon the Members of the United Nations to apply such measures. These may include complete or partial interruption of economic relations and of rail, sea, air, postal, telegraphic, radio, and other means of communication, and the severance of diplomatic relations." (United Nations Charter, art. 41.)

It is evident that the measures set out in Article 41 are merely illustrative *examples* which obviously do not exclude other measures. All the Article requires is that they do not involve "the use of force." It is a negative definition.

That the examples do not suggest judicial measures goes some way toward the other argument that the Article does not contemplate institutional measures implemented directly by the United Nations through one of its organs but, as the given examples suggest, only action by Member States, such as economic sanctions (though possibly coordinated through an organ of the Organization). However, as mentioned above, nothing in the Article suggests the limitation of the measures to those implemented by States. The Article only prescribes what these measures cannot be. Beyond that it does not say or suggest what they have to be.

Moreover, even a simple literal analysis of the Article shows that the first phrase of the first sentence carries a very general prescription which can accommodate both institutional and Member State action. The second phrase can be read as referring particularly to one species of this very large category of measures referred to in the first phrase, but not necessarily the only one, namely, measures undertaken directly by States. It is also clear that the second sentence, starting with "These [measures]" not "Those [measures]," refers to the species mentioned in the second phrase rather than to the "genus" referred to in the first phrase of this sentence.

36. . . . In sum, the establishment of the International Tribunal falls squarely within the powers of the Security Council under Article 41.

(B) CAN THE SECURITY COUNCIL ESTABLISH A SUBSIDIARY ORGAN WITH JUDICIAL POWERS?

37. The argument that the Security Council, not being endowed with judicial powers, cannot establish a subsidiary organ possessed of such powers is untenable: it results from a fundamental misunderstanding of the constitutional set-up of the Charter.

Plainly, the Security Council is not a judicial organ and is not provided with judicial powers (though it may incidentally perform certain quasi-judicial activities such as effecting determinations or findings). The principal function of the Security Council is the maintenance of international peace and security, in the discharge of which the Security Council exercises both decision-making and executive powers.

38. The establishment of the International Tribunal by the Security Council does not signify, however, that the Security Council has delegated to it some of its own functions or the exercise of some of its own powers. Nor does it mean, in reverse, that the Security Council was usurping for itself part of a judicial function which does not belong to it but to other organs of the United Nations according to the Charter. The Security Council has resorted to the establishment of a judicial organ in the form of an international criminal tribunal as an instrument for the exercise of its own principal function of maintenance of peace and security, i.e., as a measure contributing to the restoration and maintenance of peace in the former Yugoslavia. . . .

40. For the aforementioned reasons, the Appeals Chamber considers that the International Tribunal has been lawfully established as a measure under Chapter VII of the Charter.

NOTES AND QUESTIONS

1. Is it reasonable to suppose that the work of the Tribunal would help lead to a reestablishment of peace and security in former Yugoslavia? How would the Tribunal do so?

2. A major issue confronting ICTY, as well as other international tribunals, is whether it should direct its attention entirely at the "big fish" defendants — organizers and planners — or should it include prosecutions of low-level perpetrators. ICTY has prosecuted both. Erdemović and Tadić were both low-level perpetrators, and perhaps they were prosecuted only because at that time they were the only defendants ICTY had in its custody. The general rule has been to target only the most senior officials. It is also arguable that the colossal expense of trial before an international tribunal can be justified only if the defendants are important figures. For one thing, important figures are arguably the only ones likely to be deterred by the prospect of prosecution in an international tribunal, which will seem quite remote to foot soldiers and other "little" defendants. On the other hand, if one purpose of the tribunals is to give victims justice, it may be important to try at least some of the actual rapists and triggermen. That may, of course, give rise to the sense of selective prosecution — the sense that one triggerman is singled out almost at random while his comrades go on their way. What is your view?

3. Early in its existence, the ICTY confronted an ethical problem among defense lawyers: It was discovered that some defense counsel were paying their clients kickbacks to ensure that they could keep their lucrative assignments. The practice, which was also prevalent in the ICTR, was quickly stamped out.

4. The ICTY, like subsequent international tribunals, has no death penalty.

5. For rather obvious reasons, the ICTY made efforts to ensure that it tried defendants from all major ethnic groups and places within former Yugoslavia. Some believe that this policy has led to disparities in the strength or seriousness of some cases.

e. Plea Bargaining

One of the most controversial issues facing the ICTY, as well as the other international tribunals, is the practice of plea bargaining. The purposes of plea bargaining are essentially two: first, to clear the docket by obtaining convictions without the difficulty and uncertainty of a trial; and second, to get defendants to cooperate by offering information needed to investigate other cases. (In U.S. jargon, this is nicknamed "flipping" defendants or "getting them to flip.")

Plea bargaining takes two forms: sentence bargaining, in which defendants are offered a reduced sentence in return for a guilty plea, and charge bargaining, in which defendants are offered the chance to plead guilty to lesser charges (which often guarantees a reduced sentence). In international tribunals, where all the available charges are very serious, charge bargaining is rare (although we will see that it has played a role in the ICTR). Sentence bargaining works only if the judges are likely to accept prosecutors' sentencing recommendations. Otherwise, of course, prosecutors have nothing to offer.

At first, the ICTY frowned on plea bargaining. For one thing, plea bargaining is mainly practiced in common law states; civil law systems do not use it much. Second, with very few cases in its early years, ICTY's need to clear the dockets quickly did not exist. Third, the crimes seemed too grisly to try to flip defendants by cutting them a deal; in the words of then-ICTY President Antonio Cassese, "The persons appearing before us will be charged with genocide, torture, murder, sexual assault, wanton destruction, persecution and other inhuman acts. After due reflection, we have decided that *no one* should be immune from prosecution for crimes such as these, no matter how useful their testimony may otherwise be."[18] Tribunal rules do not require judges to accept prosecutors' sentencing recommendations; and, during ICTY's first nine years, only seven defendants pleaded guilty, two without bargaining for better sentences.

In recent years, however, the Security Council has pressured ICTY to wind up its (extremely expensive) operations sooner rather than later. In 2002-2003, prosecutors offered defendants substantial sentencing discounts and obtained ten guilty pleas in quick succession. By the end of the year, however, the ICTY Trial Chambers became disenchanted with the prosecutors' recommendations for relatively lenient sentences and began sentencing defendants who pleaded guilty to more years than the prosecutors recommended. As a result, defendants who realize that they cannot rely on the judges to uphold plea agreements no longer plead guilty, and the rate of guilty pleas has fallen off dramatically since the high-water mark of 2003.[19]

NOTES AND QUESTIONS

1. Do you agree with the practice of plea bargaining in cases of serious war crimes, crimes against humanity, or genocide? Without a trial, which aims of the criminal process can be fulfilled? For a sophisticated effort to answer these questions, see Ralph Henham & Mark Drumbl, Plea Bargaining at the International Criminal Tribunal for the Former Yugoslavia, 16 Crim. L.F. 49, 56-59, 74-87 (2005).

2. There has been some criticism of plea bargaining at ICTY based on inadequate process: Judges sometimes read extremely lengthy plea agreements before eliciting the defendant's assent, rather than doing so after each admission the defendant is making; defendants sometimes have inadequate understanding of the consequences of a guilty plea because judges have not adequately explained them; some defendants' counsel, coming from the civil law system of Yugoslavia, do not fully understand plea bargaining themselves. Julian A. Cook III, Plea Bargaining at The Hague, 30 Yale J. Intl. L. 473 (2005). Under civil law procedure, there must be a trial even after a guilty plea, and it has been reported that some ICTY defendants who pled guilty were stunned to learn that their plea was the end of the proceeding.

3. ICTY prosecutors who favor plea bargaining emphasize that the practice helps them overcome the grave difficulties of proving their cases. At Nuremberg, the cases were easy to prove because the meticulous German bureaucracy had documented everything. The prosecution had little need for eyewitness accounts, except to add "color" and to relieve the excruciating boredom of prosecutors reading document after document aloud. Matters are far different in former Yugoslavia and Rwanda. Two ICTY prosecutors write that their cases

> most closely resemble domestic organized crime investigations, but with significantly heightened complexity. . . . The usual difficulties of obtaining . . . information in domestic jurisdictions are greatly exacerbated in the post-war Balkans, where

---

18. Quoted in Nancy Amoury Combs, Procuring Guilty Pleas for International Crimes: The Limited Influence of Sentencing Discounts, 59 Vand. L. Rev. 69, 84 (2006).
19. Id. at 92-100.

ethnic loyalties are reinforced by threats of ostracism and physical violence that continue to this day. Plea agreements provide a mechanism for surmounting these obstacles — and ultimately a chance to alter those very aspects of the political and social environment.

Albert Tieger & Milbert Shin, Plea Agreements in the ICTY: Purposes, Effects and Propriety, 3 J. Intl. Crim. Just. 666, 669 (2005). Tieger and Shin also believe that plea agreements can contribute to forming a historical record. They point to the guilty plea of Biljana Plavšić, the former president of Republika Srpska, who admitted to an "organized effort to remove Bosnian Muslims and Bosnian Croats from territory claimed by Serbs . . . an effort which victimized countless innocent people. . . . In this obsession of ours to never again become victims, we had allowed ourselves to become victimizers." Id. at 671-672.

4. On the other hand, the Tribunal Chambers have expressed some concern that plea bargaining to obtain evidence introduces inequality among defendants: Those with valuable information can get more lenient sentences than defendants who have committed equivalent crimes but have no evidence to give. To this concern, Tieger and Shin reply that cooperation is much more difficult for defendants with evidence to give because they will be implicating others; their cooperation also "shatters the myth that crimes did not occur." Id. at 677-678. How important do you believe that equality among defendants is, in comparison with the prosecutors' need for cooperation and information?

3. The Bosnian War Crimes Chamber

Supplementing the ICTY is the Bosnian War Crimes Chamber (WCC). (We use the shortened name *Bosnia* for Bosnia-Herzegovina.) Bosnia established the WCC in 2002. Unlike other international criminal tribunals, the Sarajevo-based WCC is not a stand-alone institution for the prosecution of war crimes but belongs to the domestic court system of postwar Bosnia.

WCC began hearings in September 2005, and December 2005 marked the opening of the first trial, involving two former Bosnian soldiers accused of running a concentration camp for nearly 300 Croats. The WCC has reached verdicts on a range of crimes and defendants, and as of early 2009 has completed 22 cases with another 53 in process.

In the "most important group trial for genocide currently being held in the world,"[20] the WCC reached a verdict in July 2008. In the first case before the court relating to the Srebrenica massacre (and the first involving genocide charges), it found seven defendants guilty and acquitted four others for lack of evidence.[21]

The WCC is one important example of a so-called hybrid tribunal that blends domestic and international elements and structures. Other hybrid tribunals discussed later in this chapter are the Special Court for Sierra Leone and the Cambodian Extraordinary Chamber. Hybrids are meant to solve some of the persistent problems

---

20. Emmanuel Chicon, Bosnia, the Overachieving Student, Intl. Just. Trib., Dec. 17, 2007, available at http://www.justicetribune.com/index.php?page=v2_article&id=3993.

21. Aida Cerkez-Robinson, 7 Bosnian Serbs Guilty of Genocide in Srebrenica, A.P. News, July 29, 2008, available at http://news.findlaw.com/ap_stories/i/1103/07-29-2008/20080729105006_20.html.

facing international criminal tribunals: They are remote from the countries where the atrocities took place, they often seem like a foreign imposition, they do nothing to build rule of law capacity in those (often devastated) countries, they are slow and expensive, and they usually focus only on major perpetrators. On the other hand, purely national courts typically suffer from lack of resources and unenthusiastic support from international donors. They may have insufficient doctrinal and procedural guidance on how to apply international legal standards; and they may suffer from local (and ethnic) biases and the perception of victor's justice. Hybrid courts, by blending domestic and international elements, hope to overcome both sets of weaknesses.[22] (For further discussion of hybrid tribunals, see Section F.1 below on the Special Court for Sierra Leone.)

One other factor went into the creation of the Bosnian WCC: The ICTY's mandate is running out, leaving it in need of a legitimate exit strategy, even though numerous cases remain to be prosecuted and new criminals from the war will be found and identified for years to come.[23] The ICTY has begun referring cases to the WCC as part of its goal of transferring "lower-level and intermediate accused" for prosecution by willing and able domestic courts.[24]

The WCC is best described as a domestic court with substantial international personnel, designed to evolve over time "from a hybrid to a purely domestic structure."[25] Several unique features stand out. First, the lawyers and judges initially formed a largely international staff, but they are set to be gradually replaced by national staff over the course of five years. Accordingly, the remaining international judges are scheduled for departure at the end of 2009, a fact which has given rise to some concerns.[26]

Second, the Bosnian court has jurisdiction not only over international crimes, but also over domestic organized and economic crimes, along with various administrative matters.[27]

Third, the penal procedures for the Tribunal bear international markings that fit awkwardly in the Bosnian judicial tradition. The current rules, which blend the prosecutorial and inquisitorial models in a way that is largely foreign to Bosnia, may represent an instance where international expertise complicates rather than aids the national judicial system's development.[28]

---

22. For detailed discussion of the strengths and weaknesses of various kinds of tribunals, and the potentially creative solutions offered by hybrid tribunals, see Laura A. Dickinson, The Promise of Hybrid Courts, 97 Am. J. Intl. L. 295 (2003); Estelle R. Higonnet, Restructuring Hybrid Courts: Local Empowerment and National Criminal Justice Reform, 23 Ariz. J. Intl. & Comp. L. 347 (2006). But see Chandra Lekha Sriram, Wrong-Sizing International Justice? The Hybrid Tribunal in Sierra Leone, 29 Fordham Intl. L.J. 472 (2006).

23. The crucial pressure for adopting this streamlined exit strategy comes from the UN Security Council, which has announced resolutions directing the ICTY to concentrate on the prosecution of senior leaders, S.C. Res. 1503, ¶7, U.N. Doc. S/RES/1503 (Aug. 28, 2003), and to refer the indictments of lower- and intermediate-level accused to national courts. S.C. Res. 1534, ¶6, U.N. Doc. S/RES/1534 (Mar. 26, 2004).

24. Daryl A. Mundis, The Judicial Effects of the "Completion Strategies" on the International Criminal Tribunals, 99 Am. J. Intl. L. 142, 150, 152 (2005).

25. Higonnet, supra note 22, at 408.

26. Chicon, supra note 20.

27. Court of Bosnia and Herzegovina, Public Information and Outreach Section, http://www.sudbih.gov.ba/?id=1150&jezik=e.

28. Massimo Moratti & Berber Hettinga, Bosnia Opens Third Generation of Justice, Intl. Just. Trib., Sept. 12, 2005, available at http://www.justicetribune.com/index.php?page=v2_article&id=3145.

Fourth, and perhaps most important, the WCC shares prosecutorial responsibility with lower "cantonal" courts (analogous to district courts). Much like the ICTY screens and defers lower- and intermediate-level cases to the WCC, the WCC has a screening process to determine whether to defer cases to the cantonal courts; it retains "highly sensitive" cases for prosecution in Sarajevo and sends others down the ladder. The pressures in favor of, and problems arising from, deferring cases to the lower courts parallel in some respects those favoring and opposing the transfer of cases from the international level to the state court: The centralized court is resource taxed and ill equipped to handle its excessive caseload, but the district courts are sometimes accused of local bias and lack of uniformity, especially on procedural matters.[29] All these factors make the WCC different from the other hybrid tribunals, and some have called it a "third generation of international justice" with its own innovative structure.[30]

The ICTY has a separate panel of judges, called the Referral Bench, which decides whether to grant requests to transfer defendants from the ICTY to various national jurisdictions (including the WCC, but also other national courts in the region that meet the criteria).[31] The guiding factors are the gravity of the offense, the level of responsibility of the perpetrator, and the probability of a fair trial in the court of referral.[32] The rule provides for referral to the authorities of a state (1) in whose territory the crime was committed, (2) in which the accused was arrested, or (3) which has jurisdiction and is willing and adequately prepared to accept such a case.[33] Citizenship is not a significant factor.[34] Referral is prohibited if the receiving state might impose the death penalty.[35]

One final noteworthy feature of the WCC is that it requires that trials be completed within one year of the indictment. The decision arose out of frustration with the snail's pace of ICTY proceedings. Still, it has been widely criticized, and there is pressure to repeal it; but meanwhile, it has kept numerous trials moving along efficiently toward judgment.[36]

---

29. See Chicon, supra note 20; Erna Mackic, Courts Need Clearer Rules on War Crime Trials, BIRN Just. Rep., June 5, 2008, available at http://www.publicinternationallaw.org/warcrimeswatch/ (follow these hyperlinks: Archives, then 3.21—June 9, 2008).

30. Moratti and Hettinga, supra note 28.

31. Such transfers are authorized under Rule 11 *bis*, Rules of Procedure and Evidence, at 8, ICTY Doc. IT/32/Rev. 39 (Sept. 22, 2006).

32. Susan Somers, Rule 11 *Bis* of the International Criminal Tribunal for the Former Yugoslavia: Referral of Indictments to National Courts, 30 B.C. Intl. & Comp. L. Rev. 175, 180 (2007). The Referral Bench has interpreted "level of responsibility" to include "both the *military rank* of the Accused and their *actual role* in the commission of the crimes." Prosecutor v. Ademi & Norac, Case No. IT-04-78-PT, Decision for Referral to the Authorities of the Republic of Croatia Pursuant to Rule 11 *bis*, ¶29 (Sept. 14, 2005).

33. Rule 11 *bis*, Rules of Procedure and Evidence, at 8, ICTY Doc. IT/32/Rev. 39 (Sept. 22, 2006).

34. Prosecutor v. Mejakic et al., Case No. IT-02-65-PT, Decision on Prosecutor's Motion for Referral of Case Pursuant to Rule 11 *Bis*, ¶38 (July 20, 2005).

35. Somers, supra note 32, at 182.

36. See Thierry Cruvellier & Berber Hettinga, The "Bosnian Model" Takes Its First Steps, Intl. Just. Trib., Feb. 6, 2006, available at http://www.justicetribune.com/index.php?page=v2_article&id=3335.

E. THE INTERNATIONAL CRIMINAL TRIBUNAL FOR RWANDA

1. Background on the Rwandan Genocide

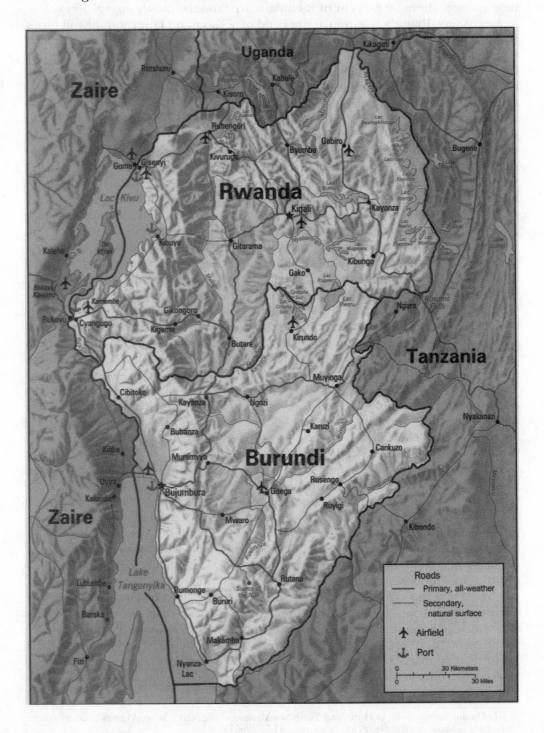

Rwanda is a small country in the Great Lakes region of East-Central Africa. Approximately the size of Maryland and with a population approaching 9 million people, Rwanda is the most densely populated nation in Africa. It is a beautiful hilly country, with volcanic mountains in its northwest and excellent soil and climate for agriculture; indeed, about 90 percent of Rwandans are farmers, mostly engaged in subsistence farming. Rwanda is known as the Land of a Thousand Hills, and the hill forms the basic unit of political organization.

Rwanda's population consists of three major ethnic groups: the Hutu majority (about 85 percent), the Tutsi minority (about 14 percent), and a tiny population (1 percent) of Twa pygmies. The majority of Rwandans are Roman Catholics, with an additional quarter of the country Protestant.

Because the Rwandan genocide took place mostly along ethnic lines, with Hutus slaughtering Tutsis (along with some Hutus who were perceived to be genocide opponents), it is important to understand the Hutu-Tutsi divide. To do so is fraught with peril, however, because virtually every historical account is wrapped in uncertainty and myth, and the various myths took on deadly political spin during the period leading up to the genocide. The two groups have lived together throughout Rwanda since at least the fifteenth century, and half a millennium of intermarriage has blurred whatever historical or other differences might have existed between the two groups.[37] In the common stereotype, Tutsis are taller, with thinner faces, than Hutus, who are stereotypically short, stocky, and round-faced; but countless Hutus and Tutsis do not look like the stereotype. Stereotypically, the Hutus were farmers, the Tutsis were pastoralists. In a country that measured wealth in cattle, this implied that the Tutsis were wealthier, although poor Tutsis and wealthy Hutus existed.

During the centuries following the arrival of pastoralists in the fifteenth century, a Rwandan state gradually developed under Tutsi kings, although with an important presence of Hutus at the royal court. By the eighteenth century, the state was more or less centralized. Political governance ran from royal court to province to district to hill, with positions of greatest power occupied by Tutsis, but with many important administrative positions held by Hutus. Political conflict at that time did not run along ethnic lines: In the words of political scientist Gérard Prunier, "at the time [of precolonial political consolidation] *it was a center versus periphery affair and not one of Tutsi versus Hutu.*"[38]

Europeans first visited Rwanda in the nineteenth century—first Germans, then Belgians, who colonized the country. Ironically, the rigid and racist Hutu-Tutsi split was more a product of Belgian colonialism and its racial theories than an "age-old" ethnic hatred, as the media sometimes portrayed it. The Belgians believed that the tall, thin-faced Tutsi came from racially superior stock. Drawing on the Bible for their history, missionary "anthropologists" decided that the Tutsi were descendants of Noah's son Ham, who had come from Ethiopia and conquered the "native" Hutus. The Hutus were supposedly of Bantu stock, which the Belgians regarded as inferior. As the Belgians saw matters, the reason that the king was Tutsi and that chiefs were mostly Tutsi was that the Tutsis were natural aristocrats and conquistadores. The Belgians legally reinforced the political and economic dominance of Tutsis over Hutus, using the Tutsi ruling class to administer their colony. The Hutus became a subjugated people, heavily taxed, excluded from higher education, and often compelled to do forced labor. In 1933-1934, the Belgians conducted a census, classifying

---

37. On the anthropology of Hutus and Tutsis, see Mahmood Mamdani, When Victims Become Killers: Colonialism, Nativism, and Genocide in Rwanda 41-59 (2001).
38. Gérard Prunier, The Rwanda Crisis: History of a Genocide 21 (1995) (emphasis in original).

every Rwandan by ethnicity, and instituted a system of ethnic identity cards. That was the fatal point at which *Hutu* and *Tutsi* became rigid, destiny-like identities, regardless of whether a Rwandan was the product of generations of ethnic intermarriage.

After the Second World War, an anticolonial reaction set in among Belgian priests and administrators, who attempted to undermine the dominance of the Tutsi minority over the Hutu majority. Although their motives were well-meaning and egalitarian, these anticolonialist Belgians helped sow the seeds of the poisonous "Hutu Power" ideology that eventually fueled the genocide. According to this ideology, Hutus were the "original" Rwandans, and Rwanda belonged to them, not the Tutsi "outsiders." Many Hutus embraced this ideology, regardless of the facts that no one really knew who the original Rwandans were and that Tutsis had lived side by side with Hutus for 500 years. In the so-called revolution of 1959-1961, which involved widespread violence and harassment by Hutus against Tutsis, Belgian colonialism began to dissolve; and in 1962 Rwanda became officially independent. The first postcolonial government was a Hutu-run authoritarian state, in which the formerly oppressed became the new oppressors. Thousands of Tutsis fled the country, particularly when President Grégoire Kayabanda used ethnic scapegoating and hate-mongering against Tutsis to help solve political problems by inciting massacres of Tutsis. Hutus expropriated Tutsi land (which they regarded, not without reason, as land unjustly appropriated by Tutsis during the years of colonialism).

In 1973, an army officer, Juvénal Habyarimana, overthrew Kayabanda and created the second Rwandan republic. For a number of years, the Habyarimana regime maintained stability, and conditions became more bearable for the Tutsis, who continued to experience discrimination and harassment, but not widespread violence. Eventually, however, Habyarimana and his powerful wife Agathe set up a near-totalitarian dictatorship similar to Kayabanda's and fomented anti-Tutsi riots and pogroms that drove more Tutsis from the country.

Many of these Tutsi refugees wound up in neighboring, English-speaking, Uganda. In 1990, an army of Rwandan refugees, many of whom had received military training in the Ugandan army, formed the Rwandan Patriotic Front (RPF) and invaded Rwanda from Uganda. Unsuccessful at first, by 1992 the RPF began defeating the Rwandan army and took over northeast Rwanda. The war caused a major flight of internal refugees, displaced from their homes. At the same time, a fall in world coffee prices caused an economic crisis because coffee is Rwanda's principal cash crop. In this period of crisis, Hutu Power ideologues began preaching violence against Tutsi "cockroaches," charging them with being traitors who supported the RPF invaders. Militias of unemployed Hutu youths, known as *interahamwe*, began military drills with guns and machetes, and the Rwandan government began importing weapons. Observers in Rwanda in the early 1990s reported a menacing, poisonous atmosphere throughout the country.

Compounding the problem were catastrophic events in Burundi, Rwanda's neighbor to the south. Like Rwanda, Burundi has a Hutu majority and Tutsi minority. But unlike Rwanda, Burundi has a history of the Tutsi government massacring Hutus; Burundi was like Rwanda in reverse. In 1993, the Burundian government launched a large-scale attack against Hutus, killing an estimated hundreds of thousands, and driving tens of thousands of Hutus northward into Rwanda.

Meanwhile, RPF successes brought President Habyarimana to the negotiating table, and a peace accord was hammered out in Arusha, Tanzania, which would have created multiparty democracy in Rwanda—an outcome despised by Hutu Power advocates and also by the powerful clique surrounding Lady Agathe Habyarimana. Hutu Power extremists painted the RPF invasion and the Arusha Accord as an attempt to install Tutsi Power, undo the revolution of 1959, and take back the land Hutus had expropriated from Tutsis during the revolution. In an overcrowded country where peasants struggled to grow subsistence crops, this was a terrifying threat to the Hutu peasantry. With one out of seven Hutus driven from their homes by the civil war, and tens of thousands of traumatized, vengeful Hutu refugees from the Burundian massacres lodged in southern Rwanda, the fuse was lit for genocide.[39]

The explosion began on April 6, 1994, when a plane carrying President Habyarimana and the president of Burundi was shot down by a missile over Rwanda's capital. No one has ever conclusively determined who shot down the presidential plane, but the assassination sprung the trap of genocide, in a manner so organized that many believe it must have been preplanned. Within hours, the Rwandan army and the *interahamwe* began systematically slaughtering Tutsis, as well as moderate Hutus. Hundreds of thousands of Hutus joined in the mass killings. Not all of the killers were Hutu Power extremists: As one Hutu explained, "If you stayed at home, you risked being labeled an accomplice and suffering death yourself."[40] For the next hundred days, Rwanda became a scene of unparalleled horror. Killers used guns, clubs, and machetes; they raped their victims and subjected them to unspeakable tortures. (For grim details, see the article by Peter Landesman, A Woman's Work, in Chapter 23.) Teachers killed their pupils, and nurses murdered their patients; some of the génocidaires were human rights activists and Catholic nuns. The rate of killing exceeded that of the Holocaust, and by the time the genocide ended, between 500,000 and a million Tutsis (and their Hutu sympathizers) were dead.

Rwanda's highly centralized political organization, and the often-noted habit of obedience on the part of Rwandan peasants, facilitated the genocide. It was largely orchestrated from above, although it took on a life of its own from below. Also noteworthy was the role played by Rwanda's radio station, the Radio-Television Milles Collines (RTMC). Hutu Power broadcasters incited the génocidaires and at times gave them specific information about carloads of fleeing Tutsis, allowing the *interahamwe* to intercept and massacre them.

(One caution about the history given here: Although we draw it from reputable scholarly sources, defendants before the ICTR and their supporters vehemently deny that the 1994 killings were an organized genocide. They insist that the anti-Tutsi attacks began as a legitimate self-defense effort against the RPF invasion, which spiraled out of control.)

Only military victory by the RPF ended the genocide. The RPF drove back the Rwandan army and advanced rapidly on Kigali, Rwanda's capital city. The army, the génocidaires, and hundreds of thousands of terrified Hutus (who feared that the Tutsis would now take vengeance) fled westward before the advancing RPF. In the aftermath of the genocide, a French intervention force arrived in Rwanda — but the French government had been a longtime supporter of the Habyarimana regime, and the French troops protected the fleeing Hutus and, perhaps unwittingly, allowed the génocidaires to escape to eastern Congo (formerly Zaire). Eventually, most of the Hutu refugees returned to Rwanda after the victorious RPF reassured them that they would be safe; but many génocidaires remained in Congo, and for years launched cross-border attacks into Rwanda. They remain a source of violence and instability in eastern Congo today.

One more part of the background story needs to be told, and that is the inaction of the international community. Rwanda is a nation of little strategic or economic

---

39. Mamdani, note 37, at 203-205.
40. Id. at 195.

significance to the great powers; and the genocide came at a particularly awkward time, when diplomatic and humanitarian efforts were focused on the former Yugoslavia. In addition, the U.S. government was leery of African interventions after its humanitarian efforts in Somalia in the early 1990s had ended in a debacle, with 18 U.S. troops killed and their bodies paraded around Mogadishu. The UN had installed a small peacekeeping force, UNAMIR, in Rwanda. But despite urgent warnings of the coming genocide from UNAMIR's commander, Canadian general Roméo Dallaire, the UN's central peacekeeping office repeatedly denied him permission to take steps such as seizing arms caches. After the genocide began, Dallaire requested reinforcements and rules of engagement that would have allowed him to stop the genocide; but again New York denied him permission. Throughout the period of the genocide, the U.S. mission at the UN actively lobbied to shrink rather than expand UNAMIR, and (as we shall see in the genocide chapter) the U.S. government fought hard to prevent the Rwandan events from being labeled a genocide, for fear that would generate pressure to intervene. U.S. officials insist that the information available to them made it unclear initially that genocide was going on, although they knew that widespread ethnic atrocities were in progress. When African countries offered to send an intervention force if the United States would provide air transport, the United States responded by offering to rent the aircraft at a steep fee. The United States sent troops and aid only after the genocide was over, and much of it went to Hutu refugee camps in the Congo that were under the control of the génocidaires. Years later, in March 1998, President Bill Clinton went to Rwanda and publicly apologized for U.S. inaction.

But the United States by no means bears sole responsibility for world inaction. UN Secretary General Boutros Boutros-Ghali was absent from New York for much of the period of the genocide. And France, with deep connections to the Rwandan government and mistrust of the RPF (which came out of Anglophone Uganda) was hostile to intervention on behalf of the Tutsis. Indeed, French media and government sources misrepresented the Rwandan events as a Tutsi genocide against the Hutus. Western media were largely absent from Rwanda, and the world press repeatedly distorted what was going on as a civil war rather than a genocide, with equal atrocities on "both sides," the whole thing resulting from age-old tribal hatreds incomprehensible to outsiders.

Toward the end of the genocide, the chairmanship of the Security Council rotated to pro-interventionist New Zealand, which fought off great-power efforts to keep Rwanda off the agenda and intended to force a vote. At that point, France offered to send an intervention force to Rwanda. But, as explained above, the French force — "Operation Turquoise" — arrived only when the RPF had already halted most of the genocide, and French troops protected the génocidaires as they fled to the Congo.[41]

After the genocide, General Dallaire, haunted by the atrocities he witnessed but was powerless to stop, suffered a breakdown. He has subsequently recovered and become a renowned speaker on the issue of genocide.

It is in this context that we turn to the ICTR.

---

41. See Philip Gourevitch, We Wish to Inform You That Tomorrow We Will Be Killed with Our Families: Stories from Rwanda 154-161 (1998); Prunier, supra note 38, at 277-298. Prunier was a consultant to the French government on Operation Turquoise. For accounts of the world response, or rather lack of response, see Samantha Power, "A Problem from Hell": America and the Age of Genocide 329-389 (2002) (detailing the U.S. response); Linda Melvern, A People Betrayed (2000) (focusing on the UN response); and Roméo Dallaire's memoir, Shake Hands with the Devil: The Failure of Humanity in Rwanda (2003).

2. *The Tribunal*

a. Founding

Like the ICTY, the Rwanda Tribunal was created by the UN Security Council under its Chapter VII powers, after a finding that the Rwandan genocide had created a threat to international peace and security, and that the Tribunal "would contribute to the process of national reconciliation and to the restoration and maintenance of peace." Although the Tribunal's legitimacy was not questioned by defendants as Tadić had questioned the legitimacy of the ICTY, the creation of the ICTR represented a further evolution of the power of the Security Council to establish tribunals. The Balkan Wars occurred between several states (Serbia, Croatia, Bosnia, Slovenia) and therefore represented a genuinely international situation. But the Rwanda genocide was internal to Rwanda. Consider whether "the process of national reconciliation" in Rwanda is a legitimate basis for Security Council action under Article 39, which requires a threat to *international* peace and security. Was the Tribunal a genuine effort to respond to an ongoing threat, or was it rather a belated response to international outrage at what transpired in Rwanda during the "hundred days of genocide" in which the UN took no constructive action? Or finally, was it an essential means by which the international community showed that it treats mass killings in Africa and Europe in similar ways?

At the time of the resolution creating the Tribunal, Rwanda itself happened to have a seat on the Security Council. When it came time to vote on the resolution, Rwanda cast the only "no" vote. Why? Rwanda had several objections to the Tribunal. First, it would be located outside Rwanda. The Security Council placed the Tribunal in Arusha, Tanzania. Symbolically, Arusha was significant because it was the site of the peace accord shortly before the genocide. It also seemed essential that the ICTR not be located in Rwanda itself, where there would be great security problems and where, it was feared, the Tribunal would itself become a provocation. Nevertheless, Rwanda believed that it was essential for trials to occur where the Rwandan people could see them. Second, Rwanda objected because ICTR would not be able to impose the death penalty, and the Rwandan government believed that genocide should be punishable by death. One Rwandan official complained that the major perpetrators would live out their lives in comfort in a "full-service Swedish prison." (Most of those convicted, however, are imprisoned in Mali, Benin, or Swaziland under conditions that are hardly luxurious. However, some have indeed been imprisoned in France, Italy, or Sweden, where confinement conditions are better.[42]) Rwanda preferred that the international community assist it by capturing and extraditing alleged perpetrators, to face trial in Rwandan courts.

On the other hand, Rwanda itself was lamentably unable to take on the burden of trying its own. By the end of the genocide, Rwanda's legal system was in ruins; and the number of suspects in Rwandan prisons exceeded 100,000. This itself created a major humanitarian crisis because genocide suspects were literally rotting away in overcrowded, disease-ridden prisons. In the words of one visitor to the Gitarama prison,

> [t]here were three layers of prisoners: at the bottom, lying on the ground, there were the dead, rotting on the muddy floor of the prison. Just above them, crouched down, there were the sick, the wounded, those whose strength had drained away. They were waiting to die. Their bodies had begun to rot and their hope of survival was reduced to a matter of

---

42. Combs, supra note 18, at 116.

days or even hours. Finally at the top, standing up, there were those who were still healthy. They were standing straight and moving from one foot to the other, half asleep. Why? Simply because that's where they happened to be living. Whenever a man fell over, it was a gift to the survivors: a few extra centimetres of space. I remember a man who was standing on his shins: his feet had rotted away.[43]

In another chapter, we discuss the Rwandan response to this crisis, especially its innovative creation of informal traditional courts called *gacaca* to deal with the innumerable cases.[44]

Interestingly, in 2007 Rwanda's parliament abolished the death penalty, specifically to enable the transfer of genocide suspects from the ICTR back to Rwanda. As the ICTR reaches the end of its mandate and seeks to wrap up business, it has sometimes attempted to transfer cases to other countries (a procedure that its rules permit under some circumstances); abolishing the death penalty allows Rwanda itself to take these cases.

b. The Statute

Article 1 of the ICTR Statute grants the Tribunal "the power to prosecute persons responsible for serious violations of international humanitarian law committed in the territory of Rwanda and Rwandan citizens responsible for such violations committed in the territory of neighbouring States between 1 January 1994 and 31 December 1994." Notice both the limited time duration and the extended territorial jurisdiction of ICTR.

In most other respects, the Statute follows the ICTY model. ICTR is structured similarly to the ICTY, with Trial Chambers, an Appellate Chamber, a Registry, and an independent prosecutors' office.

Among the crimes, the ICTR Statute lists genocide first (it was listed last in the ICTY Statute). Given the character of the Rwandan events, this seems appropriate. The Statute also alters the definition of crimes against humanity. Where the ICTY Statute requires that the crimes be committed during an armed conflict, the ICTR Statute requires that they be "committed as part of a widespread or systematic attack against any civilian population on national, political, ethnic, racial or religious grounds." Here, for the first time, a tribunal statute severs the link between crimes against humanity and war (what scholars call "the war nexus") and acknowledges that crimes against humanity can be committed independently of an armed conflict. The ICTR definition also incorporates a discrimination requirement ("committed . . . on national, political, ethnic, racial or religious grounds") that has not appeared in any other definition of crimes against humanity.

c. Jurisdiction

As we have seen, the Yugoslav Tribunal has very broad jurisdiction, encompassing persons who commit any statute crimes in the territory of former Yugoslavia

---

43. André Sibomana, Hope for Rwanda 108-109 (Carina Tertsakian trans. 1997). For similar accounts, see Gourevitch, supra note 41, at 246-248 (1998); Scott Peterson, Me Against My Brother: At War in Somalia, Sudan, and Rwanda 318 (2000).

44. For a detailed description of the legal response within Rwanda to the genocide, see Mark A. Drumbl, Atrocity, Punishment, and International Law 71-99 (2007).

since 1991. By contrast, the UN Security Council granted the ICTR a far narrower temporal jurisdiction but somewhat wider spatial jurisdiction. It has jurisdiction over "persons responsible for serious violations of international humanitarian law committed in the territory of Rwanda and Rwandan citizens responsible for such violations committed in the territory of neighbouring States between 1 January 1994 and 31 December 1994." The final date was uncontroversial: by December 31, 1994, the genocide in Rwanda was over, and the RPF government was in place. But the initial date, January 1, 1994, aroused more controversy. The time period was extended backward from April 6, 1994 — the date of President Habyarimana's assassination — to include the planning stage of the crimes.[45] But the question is whether going back three months was long enough.

The Rwandan government did not think so, and the Tribunal's limited temporal jurisdiction was the first of seven reasons given by Rwanda for voting against ICTR's establishment.[46] Rwanda regarded the temporal jurisdiction as "inadequate" because it would prevent the Tribunal from addressing acts committed in 1992 and 1993 to prepare for genocide as well as four specific massacres of Tutsis carried out from 1990 through 1993. Rwanda concluded that "[a]n international tribunal which refuses to consider the causes of the genocide in Rwanda and its planning, and that refuses to consider the pilot projects that preceded the major genocide of April 1994, cannot be of any use to Rwanda, because it will not contribute to eradicating the culture of impunity or creating a climate conducive to national reconciliation."[47]

Some scholars speculated that certain criminal acts (planning, conspiring, etc.) that occurred before January 1, 1994, could still be punishable if there were a nexus between those acts and the genocide committed in 1994.[48] This theory was tested dramatically in a case involving three journalists charged with direct and public incitement to genocide and conspiracy to commit genocide.

In 2003, the Trial Chamber convicted two journalists for anti-Tutsi broadcasting by Radio Television Libre des Mille Collines (RTLM), and a third for his role as editor-in-chief of the anti-Tutsi newspaper *Kangura*. The conviction was partly based on articles or broadcasts from before 1994. The Trial Chamber reasoned that both conspiracy and incitement were continuing crimes, so that the pre-1994 journalism fell within the ICTY's temporal jurisdiction. However, in 2007 the Appeals Chamber held that

> the Tribunal should have jurisdiction to convict an accused only where all of the elements required to be shown in order to establish his guilt were present in 1994. . . . The existence of continuing conduct is no exception to this rule. . . . [E]ven where such conduct commenced before 1994 and continued during that year, a conviction may be based only on that part of such conduct having occurred in 1994.[49]

---

45. 1 Virginia Morris & Michael Scharf, The International Criminal Tribunal for Rwanda 297-299 (1998).

46. Id. at 301.

47. U.N. SCOR, 49th Sess., 3453rd mtg. at 14-15, U.N. Doc. S/PV.3453 (Nov. 8, 1994), reprinted in Virginia Morris & Michael Scharf, The International Criminal Tribunal for Rwanda (1999). See also Raymond Bonner, Top Rwandan Criticizes U.N. Envoy, N.Y. Times, Nov. 8. 1994, at A11.

48. Payam Akhavan, The International Criminal Tribunal for Rwanda: The Politics and Pragmatics of Punishment, 90 Am. J. Intl. L. 501, 506 (1996); Morris & Scharf, supra note 45, at 302-303.

49. Prosecutor v. Nahimana, Barayagwiza, & Ngeze, Case No. ICTR-99-52-A, Appeals Chamber Judgment, ¶¶313, 317 (Nov. 28, 2007).

For this reason, it reversed the convictions for incitement to genocide based on pre-1994 journalism. (The Appeals Chamber did permit pre-1994 conduct to be admitted as evidence that might indicate the motive and meaning of conduct in 1994.) Two judges dissented. Judge Pocar stated: "Insofar as offences are repeated over time and are linked by a common intent or purpose, they must be considered as a continuing offence, that is a single crime," while Judge Shahabudeen argued that an incitement operates gradually on its listeners as they process and assimilate its meaning, so that even if the inciting speech occurred before 1994, its inciting effect continued into the year of the genocide.[50]

All three defendants were also convicted of conspiracy to commit genocide.[51] Here the analysis was slightly different than in the incitement charge. The Trial Chamber stated:

> [C]onspiracy is an inchoate offence, and as such has a continuing nature that culminates in the commission of the acts contemplated by the conspiracy. For this reason, acts of conspiracy prior to 1994 that resulted in the commission of genocide in 1994 fall within the temporal jurisdiction of the Tribunal.[52]

The theory that conspiracy is a continuing crime rests on a traditional view that the conspiracy is renewed each day the conspirators maintain it. On appeal, the journalists' conspiracy convictions were reversed on the facts, without reaching this issue. While Judge Shahabudeen concludes from this that the Appeals Chamber left the Trial Chamber's conspiracy analysis intact,[53] the earlier-quoted dictum that all the elements of the crime must have taken place in 1994 casts doubt on whether the temporal jurisdiction issue for conspiracy has truly been resolved.

d.   The Work of the Tribunal

As in the case of ICTY, the best way to understand the work of the Rwandan Tribunal is by navigating its Web site, http://ictr.org. Perhaps the most obvious difference between the ICTR and ICTY is that the Rwandan Tribunal has completed far fewer cases. As of early 2009, it has completed only 29 cases, with 7 on appeal. Twenty-three more cases were on trial in 2008, and another 8 await trial. This actually represents a significant speed-up: Five years earlier, only 9 cases had been decided.

Why has the Rwanda Tribunal proceeded so slowly? There are several reasons. First, Rwanda's own disaffection with the ICTR has hampered cooperation in evidence gathering. Defense lawyers have complained that Rwanda will provide only pro-prosecution evidence. Second, the Tribunal has suffered from repeated administrative failures. Third, proceedings involve translations back and forth between three languages, English, French, and Kinyarwanda, Rwanda's native tongue. Fourth, some observers have alleged that Tribunal lawyers from the developing world have

---

50. Id., Partly Dissenting Opinion of Judge Pocar, ¶2; Partly Dissenting Opinion of Judge Shahabudeen, ¶¶24-26.

51. Prosecutor v. Nahimana, Barayagwize, & Ngeze, Case No. ICTR 99-52-T, Judgment and Sentence, ¶1055 (Dec. 3. 2003).

52. Id. at ¶1044.

53. Prosecutor v. Nahimana, Appeals Chamber Judgment, Partly Dissenting Opinion of Judge Shahabudeen, ¶31.

deliberately prolonged proceedings because the UN salaries are so much higher than they can earn at home.[54]

A final reason arises from a deliberate strategic choice by the Tribunal prosecutors. Believing that the trials will function best by creating a detailed historical record, they have elected to call very large numbers of witnesses. In addition, following the model of the two rounds of Nuremberg trials, many of the cases involve multiple defendants, representing major sectors of Rwandan society (military, government, media). Mounting such complex cases has slowed down the trial process; many cases involve hundreds of trial days.[55]

Jurisprudentially, the Rwanda Tribunal has made notable contributions. The crime of genocide figured only rarely in the ICTY cases, in large part because it is far more difficult to prove than war crimes or crimes against humanity. In Rwanda, unsurprisingly, genocide has frequently been the key issue, and we owe much of contemporary genocide jurisprudence to the ICTR. To take one notable example, the ICTR's *Akayesu* decision found that rape can be a form of genocide when it aims to impregnate a woman with a baby whose father comes from another ethnic group or when rape traumatizes the victim so that she loses the wish to procreate.[56] The ICTR has also broken new ground by finding that media figures can be complicit in genocide through their publications and broadcasts.

Moreover, the Rwanda Tribunal secured an early guilty plea from Rwanda's prime minister, Jean Kambanda; Théoneste Bagosora, who many believe to be the principal architect of the genocide, was convicted in December 2008 and sentenced to life. Kambanda was the first head of government convicted for international crimes.

e.   Plea Bargaining

Unlike the ICTY, the practice of plea bargaining has been largely nonexistent at the ICTR. This is for several reasons. One of ICTR's first cases involved Prime Minister Jean Kambanda. Kambanda pleaded guilty, under the belief (encouraged by prosecutors) that he would receive a short sentence. Instead, prosecutors recommended a life sentence. Needless to say, this outcome did not encourage other defendants to plead guilty. A second reason that there have been few guilty pleas is that defendants believe that their conditions of confinement are better in Arusha than in the Malian prisons where most have been sent; as a result, they prefer to prolong their stay in Arusha by going to trial. Furthermore, some of the defendants are infected with HIV and believe that their lives will be so short that sentencing discounts do not matter; they prefer to roll the dice at trial and hope for acquittal.[57]

Most interesting, however, is a fourth reason. It is conventional wisdom that most criminal defendants have only one interest, reducing their sentences. How the law characterizes their actions does not interest them unless a lesser offense means a lesser sentence. According to Nancy Amoury Combs, matters are very different at

---

54. See, e.g., Helena Cobban, Healing Rwanda, Boston Rev. Dec. 2003/Jan. 2004, available at http://bostonreview.net/BR28.6/cobban.html; Combs, supra note 17, at 121; UN Office of Internal Oversight Services, Report of the Office of Internal Oversight Services on the Investigation into Possible Fee-splitting Arrangements . . . at ICTR and ICTY, Feb. 1, 2001 (U.N. Doc. A/55/759) at 2, 3 (finding "frivolous motions and other delaying tactics before the Trial Chambers").

55. Cobban, supra note 54.

56. Prosecutor v. Akayesu, Case No. ICTR-96-4-T, Judgment, ¶¶507-508 (Sept. 2, 1998).

57. Combs, supra note 18, at 118.

ICTR. Most defendants were prominent Hutus, and it matters greatly to them how the trial characterizes them:

> The great majority of ICTR defendants . . . steadfastly deny that genocide occurred in Rwanda, maintaining instead that the 1994 violence took place in the context of the long-running war between the Rwandan government and the RPF. ICTR defendants do not dispute that events spiraled out of control and that unfortunate and unnecessary violence was targeted against Tutsi civilians. But they maintain that this violence constituted the excesses of a legitimate and spontaneous national defense effort, not a genocidal plan to eliminate the Tutsi.[58]

As a result, as long as the charge against them is genocide, they reject sentencing discounts. Apparently, these defendants are willing to sacrifice years in prison to avoid being labeled génocidaires.

NOTES AND QUESTIONS

1. The ICTR has experienced other problems. One is the same problem of "victor's justice" that dogged the Nuremberg trials. Hutus charge that many Tutsis in the RPF committed war crimes and crimes against humanity, and believe that unless Tutsis are tried, the ICTR is unfair and partial. However, efforts by the ICTR to investigate alleged crimes by Tutsis were rebuffed by the Rwandan government, and prosecutor Carla del Ponte claims that political pressure from Rwanda led to her removal as prosecutor for ICTR (she remained ICTY prosecutor). Helena Cobban, Healing Rwanda, Boston Rev. Dec. 2003/Jan. 2004, available at http://bostonreview.net/ BR28.6/cobban.html. Some observers believe that the lack of Tutsi defendants delegitimizes the ICTR in the eyes of Hutus, and reinforces their ideological view that no genocide took place and that genocide charges are simply a conspiracy against them.

Do you believe it is essential for the ICTR to bring cases against Tutsis? How can it do so without Rwandan cooperation? Or is it sufficient to try only génocidaires, given that the alleged crimes of the RPF are orders of magnitude smaller than the genocide?

2. A second problem has been the difficulty of making the Tribunal's work available to Rwandans in Rwanda. For several years after the ICTR's creation, its Web site was only in French and English; although it now includes Kinyarwanda, document translation has proceeded at a glacial pace. (Students who visit the Kinyarwanda portion of the Web site and click on "Imanza" (cases) will discover that as of early 2009 only four decisions have been translated.) The Tribunal does, however, send videotapes of its proceedings to Rwanda, with simultaneous translation into Kinyarwanda.

Some observers, both in and out of Rwanda, have charged that the real audience of ICTR is the international community, not Rwanda. If so, is that a major objection? If the aims of an international tribunal include general deterrence, making a historical record, and reinforcing the importance of international norms, why isn't the international audience as important as the Rwandan audience? Or is this line of thought simply another manifestation of the same "who cares about Rwanda?" mentality that led the international community to ignore the genocide while it was happening?

3. Critics have also charged that the ICTR has done an inadequate job of witness protection, so that vulnerable witnesses such as rape victims, who had been promised

---

58. Id. at 118.

confidentiality, returned to Rwanda to discover that their identities had been revealed. Even more problematic, rape victim witnesses who had been infected with HIV by defendants found that the Tribunal was providing free medication to their rapists but would not pay for medication for them.[59] The ICTR does, however, run a medical clinic for witnesses, which has provided anti-retroviral treatment for those who need it.

F. OTHER INTERNATIONAL TRIBUNALS

Several other international tribunals have also come into existence in recent years. These include those in Sierra Leone, East Timor, Cambodia, and Lebanon.

1. Sierra Leone

The Special Court for Sierra Leone (SCSL) was established "to prosecute persons who bear the greatest responsibility for serious violations of international humanitarian law and Sierra Leonean law committed in the territory of Sierra Leone since 30 November 1996, including those leaders who, in committing such crimes, have threatened the establishment of and implementation of the peace process in Sierra Leone."[60] For almost ten years, the small West African country was ravaged by an exceptionally brutal civil war involving pro-government forces (the Civilian Defense Force, or CDF) and two rebel groups (the RUF and AFRC), all of which were implicated in atrocities. The conflict was not so much about politics as about control of Sierra Leone's diamond mines, and the war was partly funded through the sale of "conflict diamonds" or "blood diamonds." All the factions recruited child soldiers — many through kidnapping or the threat of death — who were often kept in a state of perpetual intoxication on palm wine or drugs. Girls were sexually enslaved or forced into "bush marriages." The forces of one faction, the RUF, were notorious for amputating limbs of civilians as a terror tactic. Liberian President Charles Taylor allegedly sponsored and funded the RUF; he is the best-known defendant before the Special Court. The war ended as UN peacekeepers gradually succeeded in disarming the factions.

Created by a treaty between the UN and Sierra Leone, the Special Court is a hybrid tribunal that shares features of national and international courts (for example, it includes Sierra Leonean domestic crimes among those over which it has jurisdiction, and it shares jurisdiction with Sierra Leone's national courts). However, in determining that Charles Taylor cannot receive head-of-state immunity, the SCSL has held that it is fundamentally an international tribunal. (The decision is excerpted in Chapter 6 on immunities.) Unlike ICTY and ICTR, no state other than Sierra Leone itself is obligated to cooperate with the Special Court. International judges outnumber Sierra Leonean national judges two to one in the Trial Chamber and three to two in the Appeals Chamber. The SCSL is located in the territory of Sierra Leone, which enables the prosecutor and other officials to conduct extensive domestic outreach to inform

---

59. Samantha Power, Rwanda: The Two Faces of Justice, New York Review of Books, Jan. 16, 2003.
60. Statute of the SCSL, Article 1.

and involve Sierra Leoneans in the judicial process—a high priority of the Special Court.

One additional novelty of the Special Court is that it operates concurrently with a Truth and Reconciliation Commission (TRC). Some observers report that there has been occasional rivalry between the two institutions, which are claimed to have fundamentally inconsistent missions (reconciliation versus retribution).

The prosecutor indicted 12 persons in four major cases: one trial each for defendants from the three major armed factions, and the case against former Liberian President Charles Taylor. Two major RUF defendants died, and their indictments were therefore dismissed in 2003. In a setback to the court, a third, CDF leader Sam Hinga Norman, died just weeks before the court was prepared to issue a verdict. Indictments remain in force against AFRC leader Johnny Paul Koroma, whose whereabouts are unknown. Two of the trials—those involving members of the CDF and the AFRC—have been completed, including appeals. All defendants were convicted on multiple charges.

Notably, in a civil war in which some of the most appalling atrocities were committed by child soldiers, the SCSL's statute exempts anyone under the age of 15 from prosecution. For individuals between 15 and 18 years old, the SCSL has jurisdiction, but the prosecutor is obliged to take into consideration the age of the offender, alternatives such as the truth and reconciliation process, and the desirability of rehabilitation.[61] In practice, prosecution of children under 18 years old is unlikely, in light of the statute's provision in Article 1 that the court has power to prosecute only those "who bear the greatest responsibility for serious violations of international law and Sierra Leonean law." Children, while widely used as combatants, were not likely in leadership positions where they would bear "the greatest responsibility" for offenses. In 2002, the prosecutor announced that he would not prosecute children, although his statement did not specify what ages this decision covered.[62]

Separate from the issue of prosecuting juveniles themselves is the question of criminal responsibility for recruiting children, a widespread practice in the Sierra Leone conflict. The SCSL trials are the first to prosecute this offense under international law.[63] The Appeals Chamber ruled in 2004 that the prohibition against child recruitment had crystallized as customary international law by 1996, thus eliminating any problem of retroactivity for this issue.[64] This ruling came in the case against the pro-government militia (the CDF), but the charge of child recruitment was also brought against the other defendants. Ultimately, three AFRC defendants were convicted of recruiting and enlisting child soldiers, while the two CDF defendants were acquitted (one on appeal). Noteworthy in these cases was the Trial Chamber's reliance on legal materials from the International Criminal Court to help define the scope and elements of the crime, even though the ICC had not yet tried its first case.[65]

61. Suzannah Linton, Cambodia, East Timor and Sierra Leone: Experiments in International Justice, 12 Crim. L.F. 185, 237 (2001).

62. Press Release, Special Court for Sierra Leone, Special Court Prosecutor Says He Will Not Prosecute Children, Nov. 2, 2002, available at http://www.sc-sl.org/press-2002.html (follow hyperlink to Nov. 2, 2002 press release).

63. Noah B. Novogrodsky, Litigating Child Recruitment Before the Special Court for Sierra Leone, 7 San Diego Intl. L.J. 421 (2006).

64. Prosecutor v. Norman, Case No. SCSL-2004-14-AR72(E), Decision on Preliminary Motion Based on Lack of Jurisdiction (Child Recruitment), ¶53 (May 31, 2004), available at http://www.sc-sl.org/CDF-decisions.html (follow hyperlink to Appeals Chamber Decisions, SCSL-2004-14-AR72(E)-7398).

65. Prosecutor v. Brima ("AFRC"), Case No. SCSL-04-16-T, Judgment, ¶¶734-735 (June 20, 2007), available at http://www.sc-sl.org/AFRC.html.

In addition to child soldiers, the SCSL confronted several other novel and important legal issues. One concerned the status of a provision in the ceasefire agreement ending the civil war — the Lomé Accord — which granted amnesty for crimes committed by the RUF in the course of the violence. The RUF defendants challenged their indictment based on the amnesty. The Appeals Chamber rejected the challenge on the ground that the RUF had no capacity under international law to enter into enforceable treaties. While it affirmed the right of states to grant amnesties even for serious international crimes, the Chamber also cautioned that "where jurisdiction is universal, a State cannot deprive another State of its jurisdiction to prosecute the offender by the grant of amnesty."[66] In effect, this argument reaffirms the international status of the SCSL by emphasizing that the treaty establishing it involves the international community, whereas the Lomé Accord's parties were the warring factions and the Sierra Leonean government.

The SCSL has also made significant decisions on crimes of sexual violence, discussed in greater detail in Chapter 23; see also Section G below.

As the first hybrid tribunal, the SCSL has been a focal point of discussion of hybrids' plusses and minuses. Proponents point to the defects of purely domestic and purely international models, including problems of legitimacy (the illegitimacy of distance and foreignness for international tribunals, and the illegitimacy of bias and victor's justice for purely domestic tribunals); problems of longer-term capacity building (international tribunals have considerable institutional resources, but institutional capacity leaves with the tribunal when proceedings are over); and problems of norm penetration (without a mixture of domestic and international elements, international legal norms do not get communicated to domestic leaders, lawyers, and citizens). On the other hand, whereas supporters argue that hybrids capture the best of both international and local approaches to justice, detractors object that they capture the worst of both: They are vulnerable to local bias, political manipulation, insecurity, selective prosecution, and victor's justice, on the one hand, but are nonetheless viewed as foreign impositions, on the other.

One legal issue vividly illustrates some of the tensions that the hybrid tribunals bring to the fore. The Trial Chamber convicted the two CDF leaders of war crimes, but then mitigated their sentence because they were "defending a cause that is palpably just and defendable."[67] Reportedly, this accorded with the overwhelming sentiment "on the street" in Sierra Leone. However, factoring in the justness of the cause in war crimes proceedings departs significantly from the reigning conception of the law of war, according to which war crimes are equally grave no matter which side commits them. Mitigating the sentence on the basis of "just cause" was widely criticized, particularly by international human rights groups.[68] Some critics believed that the mitigation grew out of the hybrid character of the court, which made it more responsive to local Sierra Leonean sentiment. Eventually, however, the Appeals Chamber reversed, holding that "just cause" is not a legitimate basis for reduction of sentence.[69]

---

66. Prosecutor v. Kallon & Kamara, Case No. SCSL-2004-16-AR72(E), Decision on Challenge to Jurisdiction: Lomé Accord Amnesty, ¶67 (Mar. 13, 2007). For discussion of the amnesty issue, see Charles P. Trumbull IV, Giving Amnesties a Second Chance, 25 Berkeley J. Intl. L. 283 (2007).

67. Prosecutor v. Fofana, Case No. SCSL-04-14-T, Judgment, ¶86 (Oct. 9, 2007).

68. See, e.g., Human Rights Watch, Political Considerations in Sentence Mitigation for Serious Violations of the Laws of War Before International Criminal Tribunals (Mar. 2008), http://www.hrw.org/backgrounder/ij/sierraleone0308.

69. Prosecutor v. Fofana, Case No. SCSL-04-14-A, Judgment, ¶¶529-535 (May 28, 2008).

NOTES AND QUESTIONS

1. Observers note that Sierra Leone's situation after the war exemplified many of the problems that hybrid tribunals seek to address. The domestic justice system was strained to the breaking point and was rife with corruption. It was unable to provide trials — much less fair ones — for leading war criminals. The lack of judges, magistrates, prosecutors, and courtrooms led to a huge backlog of cases. Human Rights Watch, World Report 2003, Sierra Leone, available at http://www.hrw.org/wr2k3/africa10.html. Although the incoming Sierra Leonean President Kabbah opposed a purely international solution because he considered local participation important, he knew that a purely local solution was impossible due to the likelihood of retaliation against judges and other governmental officials involved in the prosecution. Laura A. Dickinson, The Promise of Hybrid Courts, 97 Am. J. Intl. L. 295, 299 (2003).

2. At least one commentator has lauded the SCSL as "the standard for future war crimes tribunals." Nancy Kaymar Stafford, A Model War Crimes Court: Sierra Leone, 10 ILSA J. Intl. & Comp. L. 117, 142 (2003). Another concurs: "Thus far the Special Court for Sierra Leone is arguably proving to be more efficient, less costly, more accessible to local populations, and less politically inflammatory with groups of former low-level perpetrators than either ad hoc tribunal or the other two hybrids." Etelle R. Higonnet, Restructuring Hybrid Courts: Local Empowerment and National Criminal Justice Reform, 23 Ariz. J. Intl. & Comp. L. 347, 385-386 (2006). The SCSL was reportedly better received by the local population than either the ICTY or ICTR, and its outreach programs include town-hall meetings, consultation with locals, and well-constructed booklets. Donna E. Arzt, International Processes: Views on the Ground: The Local Perception of International Criminal Tribunals in the Former Yugoslavia and Sierra Leone, 603 Annals 226 (2006); Michael Scharf & Ahran Kang, Milosevic & Hussein on Trial: PANEL 3: The Trial Process: Prosecution, Defense and Investigation: Errors and Missteps: Key Lessons the Iraqi Special Tribunal Can Learn from the ICTY, ICTR, and SCSL, 38 Cornell Intl. L.J. 911, 917-918 (2005).

3. The one instance in which the hybrid model proved inadequate is the trial of former Liberian president Charles Taylor, who allegedly instigated the civil war by backing the RUF. Although the Sierra Leonean government was eager to see Taylor tried, it concluded that his presence in Sierra Leone would be too dangerous, possibly tempting his followers to violence. The Sierra Leone government asked the Netherlands to host the trial in The Hague, which the Dutch refused to do until some other state volunteered to imprison Taylor if convicted. Eventually the United Kingdom agreed to jail Taylor. Some proponents of international tribunals rather than hybrids point out that holding trials within a recently traumatized country creates enormous security risks: Witnesses are harder to protect and easier to intimidate or murder, court personnel can become targets of vindictive faction members, and the possibility that trial events might unravel a fragile peace cannot be discounted. How would you assess the costs and benefits of hybrid tribunals?

2. East Timor (Timor-Leste)

In 1975, Indonesia invaded and incorporated the Portuguese colony of East Timor (now Timor-Leste). Forces within East Timor launched an armed insurgency that over years attracted brutal counterinsurgency methods and led to a large number of deaths and other human rights violations. In 1999, the UN sponsored an independence referendum in which most East Timorese supported independence.

Pro-Indonesian militias, backed by the Indonesian army, launched an armed campaign of arson and murder, killing about 2,000 people and driving half a million from their homes. A UN-sponsored military intervention by Australia put an end to the campaign, and the UN established the United Nations Transitional Authority for East Timor (UNTAET) to govern during the passage to independence.

Part of UNTAET was the Serious Crimes Unit (SCU), which was to investigate and prosecute war crimes and crimes against humanity before a hybrid tribunal, the Special Panels. The SCU ran into numerous problems, however, and has largely been a failure. Investigating up to 1,400 homicides, it succeeded in convicting only 84 low-level perpetrators out of 391 indicted — in part because 309 of those indicted "were presumed to be outside the jurisdiction of East Timor. . . . [T]he vast majority of those indicted are residing in Indonesia."[70] Its arrest warrants for 300 Indonesians have been ignored by Indonesia, which does not recognize the tribunal. These include Indonesian General Wiranto, accused of allowing his men to commit at least a thousand murders. Wiranto is a popular political figure in Indonesia and became a major party's presidential candidate in the 2004 elections. The Special Panels for Serious Crimes and the SCU closed down in May 2005, as required by Security Council Resolution 1543.

Indonesia set up its own human rights tribunal to deal with cases from Timor-Leste. It acquitted 17 out of 18 of those who appeared before it.

In 2005, the UN Secretary-General presented recommendations from a Committee of Experts to the Security Council. These included a six-month time frame for Indonesia to accept international support for prosecutions, and that an ongoing international component be retained for Timor-Leste to enable continuation of the work of the Special Panels. Failing these steps, the report recommended that the Security Council create an ad hoc international tribunal for Timor-Leste in a third state. To date, none of these recommendations have been enacted.

In a separate development related to the outbreak of violence in April-May 2006, at the request of Timor-Leste, the UN established an Independent Commission of Special Inquiry. The Secretary-General announced the appointed commissioners in June 2006. Among their tasks is to "[recommend] measures to ensure account-ability for crimes and serious violations of human rights allegedly committed during the [above-mentioned] period."[71]

Timor-Leste, like Sierra Leone, also had a truth and reconciliation commission. Anita Roberts contrasts the parallel criminal prosecution and truth and reconciliation processes in Sierra Leone and Timor-Leste. In Timor-Leste, the Commission on Truth and Friendship was permitted to share certain information with the Special Panels:

> This approach is in contrast to the two-track model adopted in Sierra Leone where the Special Court and the Truth and Reconciliation Commission adopted a "firewall model" that permitted no information-sharing between the two institutions. The Sierra Leone Truth and Reconciliation Commission considered uncovering the "truth" and acknowl-edging the suffering of victims as objectives of greater importance than the facilitation of prosecution. As such, witnesses in Sierra Leone could testify before the Sierra Leone Truth and Reconciliation Commission without fear of having their statements subpoenaed by the prosecutor's office. In Timor-Leste, however, in line with the framing

---

70. David Cohen, Indifference and Accountability: The United Nations and the Politics of International Justice in East Timor, East-West Center Spec. Rep. No. 9 (East-West Center) (2006).

71. The Secretary-General, Secretary-General Names Members of Independent Commission of Inquiry for Timor-Leste, U.N. Doc. SG/A/1011 (June 29, 2006), available at http://www.un.org/News/Press/docs/2006/sga1011.doc.htm.

of the justice debate with its emphasis on justice as a precondition of reconciliation, a variant on the free access information-sharing model was employed.[72]

The issue of plea bargaining arose in Timor-Leste in a particularly interesting way, which highlights the importance of cultural beliefs in what many criminologists consider a process dominated by rational calculation of self-interest:

> The majority of East Timorese survive by means of subsistence farming and believe that, to ensure appropriate weather conditions, soil fertility, and the like, they must maintain excellent relations with their ancestors. Maintaining these relations requires East Timorese to perform certain rituals, adhere to certain taboos, and maintain hierarchical social relationships. . . .
>
> The need to appease powerful ancestral spirits also informs the East Timorese understanding of crime and its appropriate punishment. The East Timorese view crimes and other transgressions of the social order as disruptions of the cosmic flow of values. Because crime creates an imbalance of values, the appropriate response to crime must aim to restore that balance. . . . Such a restoration requires reconciliation between affected individuals and their communities, and to achieve that reconciliation, offenders are typically required to acknowledge their wrongdoing publicly, to apologize, and to obtain the victim's forgiveness. . . . The desirability — indeed, the compelling need — in the East Timorese belief system for reconciliation motivated most Special Panels defendants to confess their wrongdoing regardless of whether sentencing concessions were promised them in return for their confessions. Special Panels defendants wanted to return to their original communities after suffering whatever punishment the Special Panels chose to mete out, but they knew that they would not be welcomed back unless they had reconciled with their victims.[73]

This was particularly true in early cases, when defense counsel was not doing a particularly zealous job of representing their clients. When the quality of defense counsel improved in later cases, defense lawyers insisted on sentencing discounts in return for guilty pleas, even though their clients' attitudes were no different than those of earlier defendants. Prosecutors, laboring under tight time constraints, had little alternative to negotiation. Reflect on whether the work of the defense lawyers marks an improvement over the prior situation, or whether the choice of defendants to accept punishment for the transgressions is a moral choice worthy of praise and respect.

3. Cambodia

From 1975 to 1979, the Khmer Rouge regime in Cambodia perpetrated an "auto-genocide" in which 2 million people died. (The term *auto-genocide* refers to the fact that both the perpetrators and most of the victims belong to the same ethnic group, the Khmer.) The basis for the genocide was ideological and was based on a peculiar utopian vision of Cambodia — or, as the Khmer Rouge called it, Kampuchea — as an agrarian society. This led the Khmer Rouge to target urban elements, such as educated people, as class enemies. (*Genocide*, however, might not be the legally correct

---

72. Anita Roberts, The Two-Track Model of Transitional Justice in Timor-Leste: Is it Working?, 5 Austl. J. Asian L. 260, 272 (2003).
73. Combs, supra note 18, at 129-132.

term because, as we will see in the materials on genocide, the crime of genocide must be directed at a specific racial, religious, national, or ethnic group. That definition may exclude extermination of people on grounds of class membership.) The Khmer Rouge was ousted in 1979 by Vietnamese-backed forces, but remained as an active insurgency. Starting in 1998, the UN negotiated with the government of Cambodia to establish a hybrid national/international tribunal. Finally, in October 2004, the Cambodian parliament approved the treaty, clearing the way for the Extraordinary Chambers in the Courts of Cambodia (ECCC). The tribunal has jurisdiction to prosecute those "most responsible for the crimes and serious violations of Cambodian penal law, international humanitarian law and custom, and international conventions recognized by Cambodia, that were committed during the period from 17 April 1975 to 6 January 1979." By July 2006, the tribunal's prosecutors had begun to collect evidence.

In contrast with the Sierra Leone and Timor-Leste tribunals, the ECCC is composed of a majority of national judges. The trial chamber has three Cambodian and two international judges, and the Supreme Court Chamber has four Cambodian judges and three international judges. However, decisions of the court must command a "supermajority" (majority plus one vote), meaning that at least one international judge must sign on to any decision.

These provisions are a compromise born of years of difficult negotiations. "The negotiations had been conducted in an atmosphere of suspicion and mistrust which the conclusion of the agreement did not end. Article 28 [which provides that the UN can withdraw financial and other assistance if Cambodia improperly implements the agreement] reflects a queasy lack of confidence with which the Agreement is viewed by the UN. Doubts as to whether these trials will really produce any measure of justice are widespread."[74]

The Extraordinary Chamber has had a rocky beginning, plagued with controversies and accusations of corruption, charging that Cambodians were being compelled to pay large kickbacks to officials if they wanted jobs at the Chamber. At one point, the international judges threatened to boycott because of a Cambodian proposal to charge foreign lawyers a $5,000 registration fee; eventually, the judges agreed on a compromise of $500. And, when one of the Cambodian judges was replaced by the government, critics accused Cambodia of interference with judicial impartiality. The Cambodian government has denied all allegations of wrongdoing, claiming that they are politically motivated. In 2008, the trials came near to unraveling as the Extraordinary Chamber ran out of money; it was rescued by a contribution from Japan.

Khmer Rouge supreme leader Pol Pot had died in 1998. In 2006, less than three weeks after judges and prosecutors were sworn in, Ta Mok, one of the two senior Khmer Rouge officials in custody, also died. Nevertheless, by mid-2008, five defendants were in custody, charged with crimes against humanity and war crimes, and investigations and preliminary hearings were under way. In March 2009, the first trial began. The defendant, Kaing Guek Eav (nicknamed "Duch" — pronounced 'doik') was the commander of a notorious torture and execution camp.

One issue that may arise before the court is the amnesty question. The government issued informal amnesties to members of the Khmer Rouge who defected to the government side. The government also issued one formal amnesty to a senior official,

---

74. Sylvia de Bertodano, Problems Arising from the Mixed Composition and Structure of the Cambodian Extraordinary Chambers, 4 J. Intl. Crim. Just. 285, 289 (2006).

Ieng Sary. As we have seen, similar amnesties had been granted in Sierra Leone, but the SCSL did not recognize them on the ground that its character is largely international. However, this argument is weaker in the case of the ECCC, which of all the hybrid courts has the least international character.[75]

Criticisms of the court include its basis on a weak national judicial system, the potential for corruption, and the supermajority formula, which may make it difficult to reach decisions.[76] Another challenge is the lapse of time since the events under investigation occurred, which, in addition to the potential for perpetrators to die before their cases come to trial, complicates evidence gathering and the reliability of testimony.[77]

4.   Lebanon

The most unusual of the international criminal tribunals was established by the UN Security Council Resolution 1664 in 2006. It was established to prosecute the suspected assassins of Rafik Hariri, a prominent political figure and former prime minister of Lebanon. The case could hardly be more politically sensitive: Many observers believe that the Syrian government, which controlled Lebanon for years and still exerts enormous influence there, orchestrated the hit. Lebanon's government is weak, and the country continues to be fraught with tension; it seemed clear that only an international court would be capable of trying the case. The Special Tribunal sits in Leidschendam, Netherlands, and as of 2009 is still investigating the crime.

What makes the Special Tribunal unusual is not only that it exists solely to try a single crime, but also that the Tribunal will use Lebanese domestic law.

G.   THE EVOLVING TREATMENT OF SEXUAL VIOLENCE

One noteworthy feature of the international tribunals' statutes and jurisprudence has been increasing awareness of sexualized violence as an international crime. This is a relatively recent development in humanitarian law. That is not because anyone doubts that rape is a serious crime, nor that it all too often accompanies the kind of situations that international tribunals address. Rather, until recently rape was thought to be just one war crime among many, along with looting or murder — condemnable, of course, but unsurprising and perhaps inevitable in war. The attitude of many was like that of Shakespeare's Henry V, threatening

---

75. Sarah Williams, The Cambodian Extraordinary Chambers—A Dangerous Precedent for International Justice?, 53 Intl. Comp. L.Q. 227, 239 (2004). For further reading on the Cambodian tribunal, see Bringing the Khmer Rouge to Justice: Prosecuting Mass Violence Before the Cambodian Courts (Jaya Ramji & Beth Van Schaack eds., 2005). The Web site Cambodia Tribunal Monitor (http://www.cambodiatribunal.org/) provides documents and up-to-date analysis.

76. See de Bertodano, supra note 74, at 286, 289-293.

77. See Mohamed Ali Lejmi, Prosecuting Cambodian Genocide: Problems Caused by the Passage of Time Since the Alleged Commission of Crimes, 4 J. Intl. Crim. Just. 300 (2006).

the rulers of a French city with the fate that will befall them if they don't surrender to him:

> *What is't to me, when you yourselves are cause,*
> *If your pure maidens fall into the hand*
> *Of hot and forcing violation?*
> *What rein can hold licentious wickedness*
> *When down the hill he holds his fierce career?*[78]

Thus, in the original definition at the Nuremberg Tribunal, rape was not listed as a separate crime against humanity. Its first separate mention was in a crimes against humanity statute enacted by the Allied Control Council, which governed Germany in the occupation. Among the most shocking crimes in the Balkan Wars were systematic rapes and sexual enslavements at so-called rape motels, intended to turn Muslim women into outcasts in their own communities and impregnate them with Serb babies. Rape is a separately enumerated crime against humanity in the ICTY and ICTR Statutes; and Article 4(e) of the ICTR Statute lists among its war crimes "rape, enforced prostitution, and any form of indecent assault." As we shall see, the ICTR's significant decision in *Prosecutor v. Akayesu* held that under certain circumstances rape can be a form of genocide, when its aim was to traumatize Tutsi women into not wishing to have children or, alternatively, to impregnate them with Hutu babies.

Sierra Leone was the site of horrific mass rapes. The Statute of the Special Court lists "sexual slavery, enforced prostitution, forced pregnancy, and any other form of sexual violence" among its offenses, as well as rape. Articles 2(g) and 3(e). Moreover, in 2004 the Special Court permitted the prosecutor to amend indictments, adding forced marriage as a crime against humanity. Reversing the Trial Chamber in the AFRC trial, the Appeals Chamber agreed that forced marriage is a distinct crime against humanity; on the other, the SCSL excluded evidence of gender-based violence entirely from the CDF trial. The East Timor regulations itemize "sexual slavery, . . . forced pregnancy, [and] enforced sterilization" alongside rape and other forms of sexual violence.[79] And the Rome Statute of the ICC lists, among crimes against humanity, "[r]ape, sexual slavery, enforced prostitution, forced pregnancy, enforced sterilization, or any other form of sexual violence of comparable gravity."[80]

We treat the subject of sexual violence in greater detail in Chapter 23.

H. CRIMINAL RESPONSIBILITY AND ORGANIZATIONS

Recall the "criminal organizations" doctrine in Articles 9 and 10 of the Nuremberg Charter. Its hallmark was that a declaration of criminality of the organization was intended to translate into criminality of its members. This is very different from the idea of corporate crime as it exists in U.S. domestic law and the domestic law of some other states. Under U.S. law, a corporation is a legal person, as established in the

---

78. Henry V act 3, sc. 3.
79. §§6.1(b) (xxii), 6.1(e) (vi), 5.1(g).
80. Rome Statute of the ICC, Article 7(1) (g).

landmark case *New York Central & Hudson River Railroad v. United States.*[81] It acts, of course, through its agents, and in federal law the basic doctrine is *respondeat superior.* Any crime committed by an employee in the actual or apparent course of his or her duties is a crime of the organization. In effect, U.S. prosecutors have the discretionary choice of indicting the employee, indicting the corporation, or both. In theory, those choices are made based on whether the evidence shows that the corporation as a whole has a "rotten" or criminal culture, in which case the corporation can rightfully be indicted. Corporations cannot be jailed, of course (although in a few oddball cases judges have sentenced corporations to jail time and suspended the sentence).[82] Their punishments can consist of fines or of "corporate capital punishment," which can mean revoking the corporation's charter or setting the level of fine to remove all its assets.

It is an important feature of all the international tribunals after Nuremberg that they have jurisdiction only over natural persons — not corporations, not organizations, and not states. This represents an important policy choice, based on the elementary idea that it is people, not intangible legal persons, who commit crimes, and those people should not be able to screen themselves from accountability behind the organizational veil. Corporations, in an often-quoted adage by the British jurist Baron Thurlow, have "no soul to damn and no body to kick."[83] Furthermore, some states have no domestic doctrine of corporate criminal liability and would likely reject an international doctrine; in any event, the differences among states' corporate laws would complicate any efforts to define a satisfactory international doctrine. Finally, investigating corporate policies would greatly depend on the cooperation of the corporation's home state, and it might be anticipated that states will not be enthusiastic about harming their own industries.

Yet there are arguments on the other side. One is that a corrupt organization should not be able to scapegoat individuals while continuing to go about its business as usual. One sometimes hears about officials or executives "taking the bullet" of criminal conviction for the team; criminologist John Braithwaite reports on executives who described their job to him as "Vice-President in Charge of Going to Jail."[84] By explicitly indicting and convicting a "rogue" organization, the machinery of public disapproval can be directed at its proper target. Moreover, if international punishments, presumably financial, could be visited on corporate bad actors, goals of deterrence might be achievable. Thus, for example, some multinational corporations have become defendants in civil suits charging that they colluded with governments committing international crimes or that they instigated those crimes.[85] Such conduct might be deterred by the prospect of criminal conviction resulting in fines, loss of capacity to do business in important markets, or confiscations. Luis Moreno-Ocampo,

---

81. 212 U.S. 481 (1909).

82. See, e.g., United States v. Allegheny Bottling Co., 695 F. Supp. 856 (E.D. Va. 1988) (sentencing a Pepsi-Cola bottling plant to three years' imprisonment); State v. Shepherd Constr. Co., 281 S.E.2d 151 (Ga. 1981) (finding applicable to corporations a penal provision providing jail time, with a fine as alternative sentence).

83. See John C. Coffee, Jr., No Soul to Damn: No Body to Kick: An Unscandalized Inquiry into the Problem of Corporate Punishment, 79 Mich. L. Rev. 386 (1980).

84. John Braithwaite, Passing the Buck for Corporate Crime, Austl. Socy., Apr. 1991, at 3. See also Robert Jackall, Moral Mazes: The World of Corporate Managers 85 (1988).

85. See, e.g., John Doe I v. Unocal, 395 F.3d 932 (9th Cir. 2002) (allegations of corporate collusion with forced labor in Myanmar); Wiwa v. Royal Dutch Petroleum Co., 226 F.3d 88 (2d Cir. 2000) (allegations that petroleum company instigated Nigerian government's execution of indigenous rights activists).

the first chief prosecutor of the ICC, stated early in his tenure that he intended to investigate corporate involvement in international crimes.[86]

Holding states criminally responsible is even more problematic. In 2001 the International Law Commission adopted Draft Articles on State Responsibility for Internationally Wrongful Acts, which sets out basic principles of state responsibility. But this draft nowhere suggests that "state responsibility" might include criminal culpability. While no one doubts that states can and do sponsor crime — the term *state-sponsored terrorism* is now a familiar one in the everyday lexicon — that does not mean that a coherent doctrine of state criminality exists.

In 2007 the International Court of Justice (ICJ) decided an important case on whether Serbia bears responsibility for genocide in Bosnia — more precisely, whether Serbia breached its international obligations under the Genocide Convention.[87] On factual and evidentiary grounds, the ICJ found that the Srebrenica massacre was the only proven genocidal event from the Bosnian war; and it found that Serbia was neither responsible nor complicit in the massacre. But the ICJ held that states can indeed bear responsibility for genocide. It is important to realize that this is not criminal responsibility: The case was a "civil" one, in which Bosnia was asking for reparations. The court did find Serbia in breach of its treaty obligation to prevent and punish genocide in Bosnia, but it did not order reparations.

---

86. For further reading, see Brent Fisse & John Braithwaite, Corporations, Crime and Accountability (1993); Steven R. Ratner, Corporations and Human Rights: A Theory of Legal Responsibility, 111 Yale L.J. 443 (2001).

87. Case Concerning the Application of the Convention on the Prevention and Punishment of the Crime of Genocide (Bosnia and Herzergovina v. Serbia and Montenegro), I.C.J. General List No. 91 (Judgment of February 26, 2007).

PART II

Procedural Issues in Transnational Practice

CHAPTER
4

Comparative Criminal Procedure and Sentencing

While the domestic legal systems of the world share many fundamental concepts, they also vary widely in procedure and substance, especially with regard to criminal prosecutions. An appreciation of the main differences will help students, particularly those trained or studying in the United States, to put much of the following discussion in this book into its proper perspective. For that purpose and because the various international, ad hoc, and hybrid courts and tribunals draw their procedures from various legal systems, and not least because the practice of criminal law is increasingly "transnational," we offer here an admittedly generalized overview of comparative criminal procedure and some questions for consideration.[1]

By way of background, many scholars tend to consign contemporary legal systems into one of five or six broad categories. The main distinction is sometimes made between those following the common law tradition (for example, the United States, the United Kingdom, and most of the Commonwealth countries), and those rooted in the civil law or civilian tradition (for example, most of Western Europe and Central and South America). In the former, constitutional doctrines of separation of powers, the independence of the judiciary, the principle of judicial review, and the role of judge-made law (including *stare decisis* or judicial precedent) are prominent, while civil law systems are frequently described as being based on a more unitary (or even bureaucratic) view of state authority, resting primarily on comprehensive legal codes reflecting the will of the legislator and permitting a relatively circumscribed role for the courts.

For most of the twentieth century, one could also identify a socialist law tradition (for example, in the former Soviet Union and much of Eastern Europe), which combined features of a code-based system, a judiciary with a sharply limited scope, and a system of political supervision ensuring decisional fidelity to the governing principles of Marxism-Leninism. Islamic states and peoples generally combine systems. Within some subjects, notably family law, they follow *shari'a* law reflecting the divinely revealed principles and requirements of the Koran (*Qur'an*). In other substantive areas, such as commercial law, they use civil codes modeled closely on those of European countries. In Africa and elsewhere, the role of custom or indigenous law

---

1. A more detailed comparative discussion can be found in Criminal Procedure: A Worldwide Study (Craig M. Bradley ed., 2d ed. 2007) and European Criminal Procedures (Mireille Delmas-Marty & J.R. Spencer eds., 2002). For a fascinating discussion of the impact of different legal cultures and approaches in the procedural context of the International Criminal Tribunal for the Former Yugoslavia, see Vladimir Tochilovsky, International Criminal Justice: "Strangers in the Foreign System," 15 Crim. L.F. 319 (2004).

still exerts a profound influence, and local communal values and procedures continue to play an important role in informal systems of justice and accountability. Finally, the legal systems of the People's Republic of China (PRC) and other Asian countries can be said to share certain common elements reflecting the unique historical, cultural, religious, and political traditions of that region. However, in Asia, as in the Islamic world, traditional elements combine with law based on Western models: for example, in 1896 Japan adopted a civil code based on that of Germany, while postwar Japanese antitrust law draws directly on U.S. models.

Although useful on one level, these broad distinctions can be misleading. Many legal systems do not fit neatly into the categories described above, nor are the categories themselves entirely accurate descriptors. Codification of both substantive and procedural law is increasingly prevalent in the common law countries, for example, and in many civil law systems, decisional law (known in French as *jurisprudence* or in Spanish as *jurisprudencia*) actually plays a significant if not necessarily binding role. Even within the Romano-Germanic civil law tradition, marked differences have long existed between the French approach (which has heavily influenced the legal systems of Italy, Portugal, and Spain) and the German (followed by the Nordic countries, South Korea, and Greece). At the same time, both approaches have long incorporated procedural elements associated with the common law (for example, public trials and oral testimony).

More important, many domestic systems embrace or even combine elements of the different approaches. In Canada, for example, where the common law tradition has long dominated, Quebec remains a stalwart civil law jurisdiction (far more so than the U.S. state of Louisiana, where civil law traditions continue to influence the law, or the Commonwealth of Puerto Rico, where local law is decidedly civil in nature). Because of its historical ties to France as well as England, Scotland is often proudly described as an "uncodified" civil law country with many common law traditions. Typically, the former socialist or communist countries boasted (at least superficially) strong constitutions and sophisticated legal codes. The still-evolving Russian legal system reflects efforts to graft both civil and common law procedures onto a Soviet-era structure. Some Islamic states (for example, Turkey) pursue a secularist approach based on civil law concepts. For historical reasons, the legal system in Japan incorporates many features of Western constitutionalism and the civil law tradition, while the former British colonies of Sri Lanka, Brunei, and Pakistan all use essentially common law systems. Customary law and procedure prevails in much of Afghanistan and parts of South Asia. Contemporary Chinese law combines elements of civil, socialist, and communal law, where minor crimes are often dealt with by reeducation through labor laws or by mediation committees made up of informed citizens.

One result of an increasingly interconnected world (one hesitates to use the all-purpose label *globalization* in this context) is a clear trend toward harmonization, if not actual convergence, among the various legal systems around the world. For a variety of reasons, the traditional boundaries between different legal "systems" or "traditions" are eroding. Obviously, every domestic legal system in the world is subject as never before to the pressures of transnational trade and investment, the cross-border flow of people and information, and the internationalization of crime. The influence of regional integration — for example within the European Union or the Organization of American States or as a result of the harmonization efforts of the Council of Europe, the African Union, and the Organization of Economic Cooperation and Development (OECD) — and the efforts of such UN bodies as the United Nations Commission on International Trade Law (UNCITRAL) unquestionably force states to adjust their laws and institutions in the direction of effective interoperability if not actual harmonization.

International human rights law exerts an increasingly powerful and pervasive force on domestic criminal procedure. Decisions by the European Court of Human Rights, the Inter-American Human Rights Commission and Court, and the UN Human Rights Committee (established to oversee the implementation of the International Covenant on Civil and Political Rights) all push states in the direction of procedural fairness and recognition of defendants' rights, in some cases actually forcing modifications in national rules to conform to regional and universal norms.[2] Most countries today value fair trials conducted by an independent judiciary. Rights-oriented approaches are increasingly common in all systems, including recognition of the presumption of innocence, protections against self-incrimination, and evidentiary rules excluding coerced confessions.

Finally, the emergence of international criminal tribunals (and such hybrids as the trial in Scotland of Libyan agents who blew up a U.S. airliner over Lockerbie, Scotland, in 1988) has required states to come to agreement not only on the substantive principles of international criminal law but also on the rules of procedure and evidence. While it may still be too early to proclaim the existence of a universally accepted body of procedural rules, the decisions of these human rights bodies and supranational criminal courts provide a growing source of analysis and guidance from which a universal code of criminal procedure may one day emerge.[3]

Despite possible convergence, differences between the common law and civilian approaches can be startling to lawyers from the other system. As we noted in the preceding chapter, the lawyers who negotiated the procedural rules at the Nuremberg trial found some practices in each others' systems baffling and objectionable: The French delegate, used to a largely documentary case seen in advance by both sides, was shocked by the Anglo-American "trial by surprise," while the Russian delegate never quite grasped what a cross-examination is. On the other side, U.S. delegate Robert Jackson complained that if all the prosecution's evidence was included in the indictment, he could see no point to having a trial and would have no idea what to do in court.[4]

Legal systems are dynamic and constantly changing. For the student of international criminal law, however, an understanding of some of the specific variations in criminal procedure that still exist among and between legal systems will be essential. Therefore, we will sketch these in broad outline, readily acknowledging that many distinctions lie in the details.

---

2. Stefan Trechsel, Human Rights in Criminal Proceedings (2005); Mitchel de S.-O.-l'E. Lasser, The European Pasteurization of French Law, 90 Cornell L. Rev. 995 (2005) (discussing decisions by the European Court of Human Rights ordering Belgium and France to modify their appellate procedures on due process grounds).

3. Some commentators suggest that legal systems are slowly converging as a result of pressure on adversarial systems to equalize the disparity in parties' resources and a complementary pressure on inquisitorial systems for closer scrutiny of police practices and trial protection for defendants. See, e.g., Nico Jörg, Stewart Field, & Chrisje Brants, Are Inquisitorial and Adversarial Systems Converging? Criminal Justice in Europe: A Comparative Study (1995). They also note that "[e]ach depends on its own historically developed institutions and the faith that different societies place in them. Continental systems function by virtue of society's faith in the fundamental commitment of state institutions to act in the interests of justice (in all senses of the word); they will continue to function legitimately only for so long as that trust is not abused and the safeguards provided by the division of power and subsequent hierarchical control continue to work." Id. at 55.

4. Telford Taylor, The Anatomy of the Nuremberg Trials: A Personal Memoir 63-64 (1992).

A. DIFFERENCES IN THE CRIMINAL PROCESS

1. *The Common Law and Civil Law Systems: An Overview*

In the United States, criminal charges can be brought by a variety of actors ranging from local officials to federal prosecutors, but not by victims or private individuals in their own right. Generally, law enforcement is thought of as primarily the responsibility of the individual states within the U.S. federal system; only 5 percent of criminal cases are in fact prosecuted at the federal level, although many of those cases are high-profile and involve transnational features. Whether in federal or state courts, a criminal proceeding can be described essentially as an adversarial process, a contest pitting the prosecutor against the accused and his defense counsel. The prosecutor is most often an elected official or an appointee working for an elected official, acting on behalf of "the people." With considerable independence of action, the prosecutor controls the bringing of charges (subject, on the federal level although not in many states, to approval by a grand jury in the case of the most serious charges) and retains considerable discretion to engage in plea bargaining. Pretrial investigations are conducted independently by the prosecution and the defense, and the system imposes some checks on the conduct of the prosecution's investigations (requiring, for example, the disclosure of potentially exculpatory evidence to the accused prior to the trial).

In the United States, the paradigmatic main event is a trial in open court, with live witness testimony, frequently (but not always) in front of a jury of "peers" (private citizens) whose job is to decide whether the prosecutor has proved the charges. The rules require the prosecution to prove its case beyond a reasonable doubt. Emphasis is placed on direct questioning and cross-examination, subject to rules of evidentiary admissibility. Real or tangible evidence needs to be spoken for by witnesses with direct knowledge (for example, to demonstrate a "chain of custody" for critical items in the government's possession). The trial judge sits as an impartial governor of the trial process whose main job is to ensure that the rules are adhered to and the law is properly applied. (In nonjury trials, of course, the judge also serves as the trier of fact.) Note, however, that the paradigm is misleading. For example, over the last decade the guilty plea rate in federal criminal cases has hovered around 95 percent; slightly higher rates prevail in the individual states. Thus, the overwhelming majority of criminal cases in the U.S. system are resolved without any trial. To be sure, taking a guilty plea generally involves a brief hearing at which the judge advises the defendant of his rights and tries to ensure, through a short colloquy, that the plea tendered is knowing, intelligent, and voluntary. However, the government normally is not required to discuss its evidence, let alone make any showing of guilt.

By contrast, traditional or classical civil law systems of criminal justice are commonly said to employ an inquisitorial approach in which the goal is to establish the fact of the defendant's guilt or innocence by means of an official (and, in theory at least, objective or impartial) fact-finding inquest in which judges play an active role in posing questions and directing the inquiry. The prosecutor is a professional governmental official and may in fact have judicial status (both judges and prosecutors are often called *magistrates*). The defendant enjoys fewer rights to resist or object to the process than in the United States. Once it has been determined that a crime has been committed, a preliminary investigation is undertaken to determine the facts of the situation, typically under the direction of an investigating magistrate or a public prosecutor.[5] The emphasis is on a thorough pretrial investigation rather than on the trial itself. Relevant evidence is gathered and compiled before trial, and the principal basis of the court's deliberation is a complete case file or *dossier* containing all relevant information, including the personality and circumstances of the defendant. Pretrial "discovery" of evidence is far less common (for example, in the exculpatory sense of Brady v. Maryland, 373 U.S. 83 (1963)), and pretrial motions (that is, challenging the legality of searches and seizures or seeking suppression of evidence) are relatively unknown. On the other hand, the written indictment typically contains a rather full statement of evidence against the defendant, and the "trial by surprise" familiar in the courtroom dramas beloved by U.S. television audiences does not exist in civil law systems.

Civil law investigating magistrates and procurators are career civil servants, not political appointees like U.S. attorneys or elected officials like district attorneys in the United States. In comparison to their U.S. counterparts, they enjoy remarkable independence. Italian prosecutors have relentlessly pursued high officials of their own government, including a dozen prosecutions of Prime Minister Silvio Berlusconi, who was acquitted in 11 separate trials and amnestied after a perjury conviction. (The colorful Berlusconi once said, "I'm the universal record-holder for the number of trials in the entire history of man — and also of other creatures who live on other planets.") The independence of the civil law investigating magistrate has played a significant role in transnational criminal law. In the 1990s, Spanish investigating magistrate Baltasar Garzón launched an inquest into crimes committed against Spanish nationals during Argentina's so-called "dirty war." Eventually, the trail led from Argentina to Chile, and Garzón initiated a famous effort to extradite the former Chilean dictator Augusto Pinochet to Spain — to the dismay of the Spanish government, which found itself embroiled in diplomatic backlash from Chile as well as other countries. Notably, Garzón expanded his investigation to include crimes committed by Pinochet against non-Spaniards. Garzón also went after leaders of the Argentine junta (but was rebuffed by the Spanish court), and secured convictions against lower-ranked Argentinians for international crimes committed in the dirty war. So too, a Belgian investigating magistrate, Damien Vandermeersch, approved investigations of numerous world leaders under Belgium's war crimes statute (subsequently repealed). Both the Pinochet case and Belgium's efforts are treated in more detail in Chapter 6 on immunity from prosecution. To the great displeasure of the Italian government, Italian prosecutor Armando Spataro continues to pursue a controversial case against 26 CIA officers and 7 Italians for their alleged involvement in the kidnapping of a radical Islamic cleric in Milan as part of the "extraordinary rendition" program pursued by the United States in its "global war on terror."[6]

---

5. The investigating magistrate — or investigating judge — is called *juge d'instruction* in French, *juez instructor* in Spanish, and *Untersuchungsrichter* (literally, "investigation judge") in German. The most familiar term for the prosecutor in civil law systems is *procurator* or its French equivalent *procureur*. The German equivalent is *state's attorney* (*Staatsanwalt*). Some care must be exercised with the terms *procurator* and *procureur* since the position entails different functions depending on the legal system in question. In some countries, especially within the civil law tradition, procurators are (like magistrates) powerful civil servants within or affiliated with the Ministry of Justice who direct the police and supervise preliminary investigations up until the time formal charges are brought. In others, they serve as local prosecutors responsible for initiating and pursuing criminal charges throughout the process.

6. The trial was suspended in December 2008 after the Italian government authorized witnesses to invoke state secret privileges and moved to dismiss the case. Despite a subsequent decision by the Italian Constitutional Court excluding classified information from the proceedings, Judge Ocar Magi ruled in May 2009 that the trial could continue. See http://www.nytimes.com/2009/05/21/world/europe/21italy.html.

The civil law trial proceeding itself may be relatively brief and informal by common law standards. The duty of the court is to seek the truth, and the principal examination of the defendant (and witnesses, if any) is conducted primarily by the presiding judge. Jury trials are rare in French-influenced systems, although in Germany, lay jurors deliberate side by side with the judges. Depending on the particular national system, defense counsel may not be permitted to question the accused or witnesses directly, but must instead submit questions to the presiding judge, who will in turn ask them. Generally speaking, there are few exclusionary rules, and any relevant evidence is admissible, including hearsay. Trials tend to be much shorter, and in some cases no provision is made for closing statements or summations. Often, written statements by absent witnesses will be readily acceptable, and in certain situations, trials in absentia are possible.

Here again, the labels can be deceptive. As one of this book's authors has written, "The label 'inquisitorial' is quite misleading. . . . It evokes images of the auto-da-fé and the Iron Maiden, the Pit and the Pendulum. In fact, the term refers simply to the much greater role played by the court. . . ."[7] Furthermore, few countries today fall neatly into the accusatorial or inquisitorial camps, and many observers believe that the systems are gradually converging. In Brazil, for example, a civil law system predominates, yet the criminal procedure code encompasses prosecutorial discretion, a recently introduced plea bargaining system (*delação premiada*), and compulsory trial by jury for the most serious murders, as well as a form of habeas corpus. As a practical matter, the distinction between inquisitorial and accusatorial modes is often more theoretical than actual since the trial of a major crime in any developed legal system tends to be an intense and combative experience.

Different legal systems provide different judicial structures, pathways, and procedures for various types of criminal prosecutions. Unified trial courts such as those found in the United States are not replicated in many countries. Instead, the criminal courts may be entirely separate from the civil, commercial, or labor courts, and in fact different courts may have jurisdiction, and different procedures may apply, depending on the severity of the crimes charged. French law, for example, distinguishes among three levels of crimes: the most serious *crimes*, the less significant *delits* (misdemeanors), and minor offenses known as *contraventions*. Summary procedures are often provided for lesser offenses (for example, the *Strafbefehlsverfahren* in Germany). A few countries still use police courts to dispose of lesser criminal offenses. Separate military courts may have jurisdiction over crimes affecting security and military matters, even when committed by civilians, and in some countries specialized courts exist for the prosecution of criminal offenses involving drugs, guns, and tax or customs rules. France has separate courts for those accused of terrorist offenses as well as for offenses committed by governmental officials in the conduct of their duties.

Which system is likely to produce more accurate results? According to John Merryman, an eminent comparativist:

> For those who are concerned about the relative justice of the two systems, a statement made by an eminent scholar after long and careful study is instructive: he said that if he were innocent, he would prefer to be tried by a civil law court, but that if he were guilty, he would prefer to be tried by a common law court. This is, in effect, a judgment that criminal proceedings in the civil law world are more likely to distinguish accurately between the guilty and the innocent.[8]

---

7. David Luban, Lawyers and Justice: An Ethical Study 93-94 (1988).
8. John Henry Merryman, The Civil Law Tradition 139 (1969).

However, critics have complained about a pro-prosecution slant in civil law systems.[9] One recent commentator remarks that

> it is not surprising that many *avocats* [French courtroom lawyers] feel that the system is stacked against them. Recently, one *avocat*, checking the court file several days before the argument of a criminal appeal, discovered the court's judgment against his client already prepared and postdated. Another *avocat* recalls having been told in private by a judge not to worry about a case because "what you can say for your client isn't very important. Our role is to punish him. Your role is not so much to defend as to console him."[10]

On the other hand, the French acquittal rate — 4 percent of adjudicated cases — is higher than the 1 percent rate in the United States.[11] Moreover, the turnstile-like U.S. plea bargaining system — where the defense counsel's role has been described as "meet 'em, greet 'em, plead 'em" — is largely unknown in the civil law world. In 2004, 97 percent of U.S. convictions were secured through guilty pleas, and plea bargaining makes many of the defendant's trial rights irrelevant.[12] For example, under the U.S. *Brady* rule, prosecutors must make timely disclosure of exculpatory facts to the defense. But does *timely* mean "in time for the trial" or "in time for the plea bargain"? In a 2002 case, the Supreme Court held that prosecutors have no constitutional obligation to disclose evidence before plea bargaining that the defense could use to impeach prosecution witnesses — even though such evidence would have to be turned over to the defense before trial.[13]

In *The Faces of Justice: A Traveller's Report* (1961), journalist Sybille Bedford reports on trials in five European countries. Although nearly half a century old, her description of a German criminal trial remains largely accurate and will help convey some of the differences (and similarities) between criminal trials in the civil law and common law systems.

Dr. Ulrich Brach was a physician in the (peacetime) German army. While home for a visit, he shot to death a man who had exposed himself to Dr. Brach's 12-year-old daughter. The daughter had told her parents on several occasions that a man had exposed himself as she walked to and from school through a park. On the last occasion, the doctor took a revolver, found the man in the park, and arrested him. The man tried to escape over a wall out of the park, and Dr. Brach began shooting, trying to hit the escapee's foot. One of the doctor's three shots killed the man.

A chief judge and two assistant judges presided over the trial. This court also included six lay jurors, who deliberated together with the judges. In German trials, the judges perform the bulk of witness examination; after they finish, the state's attorney and defense counsel can pose additional questions, but usually have little to add. The defendant himself also may directly question witnesses. As is typical in civil law procedure, the defendant has no privilege against self-incrimination, but is not put under oath and therefore cannot be caught in a "perjury trap."

---

9. See, e.g., Nikos Patouris, Partisan Justice and Party-Dominated Justice, 57 NYU L. Rev. 203, 209-211 (1982); Edward A. Tomlinson, Nonadversarial Justice: The French Experience, 42 Md. L. Rev. 131 (1983).

10. John Leubsdorf, Man in His Original Dignity: Legal Ethics in France 83 (2001).

11. For the French acquittal rate in 2005, see Annuaire statistique de la justice, série 2001-2005, L'activité pénale de 2001 à 2005, available at http://www.stats.justice.gouv.fr/pdf/2005/dlactp/p5pentc.pdf (last visited Apr. 9, 2009) (21,368 acquittals out of 493,915); for the U.S. acquittal rate in large urban counties in 2004, see U.S. Dept. of Justice Bureau of Justice Statistics, Felony Defendants in Large Urban Counties, 2004, Table 19, available at http://www.ojp.usdoj.gov/bjs/pub/html/fdluc/2004/tables/fdluc04st19.htm (last visited Apr. 9, 2009).

12. U.S. Dept. of Justice Bureau of Justice Statistics, supra note 11.

13. United States v. Ruiz, 536 U.S. 622 (2002).

The judges are well prepared for the trial, as Bedford explains:

Continental judges have it all in front of them. . . . They sit by no means every day, and the best of their working time is spent on paperwork. The accused may have been questioned — by another judge, the Untersuchungsrichter [investigation judge] in the German-speaking countries, the Juge d'instruction in France. . . . Everything he said has been taken down in writing, and this evidence, in a fat dossier, lies open now at the relevant page before the presiding judge.

All the same, here too the evidence must be heard again at the trial, must be, as in English courts, oral and direct. . . . It all has to be said again for the last and final time that counts and, as in England, it will often turn out to be rather different from the original deposition.[14]

Either side may appeal the verdict, and the appellate court engages in *de novo* review of the evidence.

SYBILLE BEDFORD, THE FACES OF JUSTICE:
A TRAVELLER'S REPORT
117-119 (1961)

It was a strange experience to hear this presentation of a case by both sides, as it were, in one; not a prosecution case followed by a defence case, but an attempt to build the whole case, the case as it might be presented in a summing-up, as it went. A strange experience to hear the (attenuated) inquisitorial procedure at work, to hear all questions, probing questions and soothing questions, accusatory and absolving questions, questions throwing a favourable light and questions having the opposite effect, flow from one and the same source, the bench, and only from the bench, while public prosecutor and counsel for the defence sat mute, taking notes.

"Dr. Brach, were you accustomed to handling a revolver?"

"No. It was a new weapon. I had never used it before."

"You must have had some instruction or practice in the Army?"

"None at all. As a medical officer I had nothing to do with such things."

"You told us earlier today that you were called up and served during the war — before you were even a medical student — you must have had small-arms instruction then? Didn't you know that a revolver is a most unreliable weapon — ?"

"Yes, but — "

"Well, in heaven's name, man, didn't you know that it is about *the* most *uncertain, unsafe* weapon there is?" This was said with considerable severity, although not so much in the manner of a judge addressing an exhortation to the dock, as in the tone of man to man.

"When it comes to one's child being indecently molested twice a week — "

"Twice a week? This is the first time you told this court anything of the kind!"

"It happened all the time."

"You did not give that figure, or anything like it, to the examining judge?"

[It had already come out that the doctor had said very little during the preliminary investigation; instead he had given a detailed interview to an illustrated weekly. "Why did you do that?" "I don't know." "Don't you know the motives for your actions, Dr. Brach?" "Well, the editor had asked me to."]

"My wife went to the police," said Dr. Brach.

---

14. Sybille Bedford, The Faces of Justice: A Traveller's Report 110-111 (1961).

"How often? Twice a week?"

"Again and again. It didn't do any good."

"Herr Oberstaatsanwalt, have you any information about complaints to the police?" The prosecutor answered that his department knew only of the one that had been lodged in the spring of 1958.

"My wife went at least a dozen times," said Dr. Brach, "and she didn't go every time it happened."

"And these alleged visitations always took place in the park?"

"Yes, on the girl's way to school."

"Couldn't she have taken another way?" asked the younger judge.

"She could have gone through the town," said the judge president, "by making a slight detour she need not have gone through the park at all."

"Yes, she could have."

"Did you not tell her?"

"I think I did. I know my wife told her."

The younger judge, the one who spoke with the Baden accent, said, "You *think* you told her? Didn't you say, Look here you mustn't go to school through the park, I forbid you to go to school through the park?"

"I did speak to her," Dr. Brach said, deadpan and helpless.

"One or two more points. Can you tell us something more about your state of mind on that Saturday noon, Doctor? You hadn't slept, luncheon was late, you were pretty irritable? When your girl came in with the news, did you feel annoyed at your weekend being spoilt?"

"That didn't occur to me," said Dr. Brach. [This question of the judge was later harshly criticized in the press.] . . .

"To wind up, we should like to know something about your general attitude. . . . How do you personally feel about the phenomenon of exhibitionism? Do you think exhibitionists are people who act under a pathological compulsion? Do you think they are sick people? Or perverts? Are they particularly repulsive to you?"

"I think an adult who exposes himself indecently to a child is a criminal."

[Dr. Brach was convicted but received a lenient sentence.]

NOTES AND QUESTIONS

1. One important difference between the common law and civil law systems is the greater role assumed by judges and the diminished role played by advocates. This corresponds with far different demographics. "In the civil law, judges are active front-line workers. The civil law, with its judicial workforce, requires a vastly larger judicial plant and relatively fewer lawyers. . . . Comprehensive figures on the number of judges and lawyers are hard to come by, but civil law countries tend to have one judge for every three to four lawyers, whereas the ratio in common law countries is typically one judge for every 25 to 50 attorneys." Marc Galanter, Dining at the Ritz: Visions of Justice for the Individual in the Changing Adversarial System, in Beyond the Adversarial System 126 (Helen Stacy & Michael Lavarch eds., 1999).

2. Defense counsel plays a smaller role in a civil law trial than in a common law trial. In Germany, in the words of two experts:

> Attorneys have no expertise in developing their case through questioning witnesses, and are even less knowledgeable in the art of cross-examination. Judges regard motions under section 239 [which permits defense counsel to ask questions after judicial questioning is completed] as expressions of criticism of their own interrogation methods.

In addition, aggressive partisan "distortions" of a witness' recollection are seen as irreconcilable with the overall stress on inquisitorial methods of finding the truth.

Richard S. Frase & Thomas Weigend, German Criminal Justice as a Guide to American Law Reform: Similar Problems, Better Solutions?, 18 B.C. Intl. & Comp. L. Rev. 317, 357-358 (1995). Similarly in France,

> a defense *avocat* can do little. His main act is to present an oral argument. His goal is to bring before the tribunal the human reality of his client, usually in the hope of securing a lenient sentence. The Goncourt brothers are probably not the only defendants to have been warned against retaining a brilliant *avocat* whose talent might irritate the judges and counseled to choose a mediocrity whose vacuity might draw their pity.

John Leubsdorf, Man in His Original Dignity: Legal Ethics in France 83 (2001).

In both France and Germany, advocates regard themselves as independent from their clients — a very different conception of lawyerly independence than in the United States, where the ideal of "independent professional judgment" means independence from anyone other than the client. See, e.g., ABA Model Rules Prof'l Conduct 1.8(f)(2) (2008) (prohibiting lawyers from accepting compensation from someone other than the client if doing so will interfere with independent professional judgment) and 5.4(c) (prohibiting lawyers from permitting third parties to "direct or regulate the lawyer's professional judgment . . ."). Both the statute regulating the German legal profession and the code of professional ethics define the lawyer as an "independent organ of the administration of justice," and leading commentators make clear that this means not only independence from the state, but also independence from the client. David Luban, The Sources of Legal Ethics: A German-American Comparison of Lawyers' Professional Duties, 48 Rabels Zeitschrift für ausländisches und internationales Privatrecht 245, 266-267 (1984). In France, lawyers "continue to refer to clients and other nonlawyers as *les profanes*, the uninitiated. Clients address an *avocat* as *Maître* (master), while *avocats* write to each other as *Monsieur* or *Madame* (Mr. or Mrs.)." Leubsdorf, supra, at 13; see generally id. at 13-28 (independence of lawyers from clients). Both France and Germany prohibit courtroom lawyers from becoming in-house counsel to corporations because of the threat that being tied to a single client might pose to lawyerly independence. Although German commentaries and ethics rules require loyalty to clients and zeal on their behalf, they also emphasize limits on advocacy. Luban, supra, at 267-268.

U.S.-trained lawyers are likely to blanch at such attitudes; they frequently quote the famous speech of the nineteenth-century British barrister Lord Brougham:

> [A]n advocate, in the discharge of his duty, knows but one person in all the world, and that person is his client. To save that client by all means and expedients, and at all hazards and costs to other persons, and, among them, to himself, is his first and only duty; and in performing this duty he must not regard the alarm, the torments, the destruction which he may bring upon others.

The Trial of Queen Caroline 8 (J. Nightingale ed., London 1820-1821). But their civil law colleagues respond that the excesses of partisan zeal in U.S. litigation distort the search for truth, encourage unethical hardball behavior, and defeat justice. In your view, what are the relative advantages and disadvantages of the common law and civil law conceptions of the advocate's role?

3. One notable difference between U.S. lawyers and those in the civil law world concerns the pretrial preparation of witnesses — a practice also known as "witness

proofing" and "witness familiarization." A U.S. lawyer who fails to interview witnesses carefully and prepare them for the rigors of trial, perhaps even rehearsing ("mooting") them, has done an inadequate job, verging on malpractice. Of course, lawyers may not suborn perjury or knowingly put on false testimony. But so long as a witness testifies truthfully, there are few, if any, limits on coaching the witness before the trial. Lawyers can tell witnesses how to dress and how to carry themselves; they can remind witnesses to maintain eye contact with jurors and keep their tempers in check. Witness preparation might include telling scientific experts to reduce their pomposity, simplify their language, and avoid "on the one hand, on the other hand" answers; in fact, no rule prohibits lawyers from proposing specific alternative wording to a witness so long as the witness agrees that it represents her truthful opinion. In Germany, by contrast, the ethics rule on interviewing witnesses provides that "in all cases even the appearance of impermissible influence is prohibited." Grundsätzen des anwaltlichen Standesrechts §6(5). According to the Pre-Trial Chamber of the International Criminal Court (ICC), witness proofing would be "either unethical or unlawful in jurisdictions as different as Brazil, Spain, France, Belgium, Germany, Scotland, Ghana, England and Wales and Australia, to give just a few examples." Prosecutor v. Lubanga, Case No. ICC-01/04-01/06, Decision on the Practices of Witness Familiarisation and Witness Proofing, Pre-Trial Chamber I, ¶37 (Nov. 8, 2006). Interestingly, among these are several common law jurisdictions; indeed, the Code of Conduct of the Bar Council of England and Wales does not permit barristers to "rehearse, practice, or coach a witness in relation to his evidence" (§705), although it does permit them to discuss evidence with witnesses.

The permissibility of witness preparation remains unsettled in international criminal tribunals. Several decisions by the International Criminal Tribunal for Former Yugoslavia (ICTY) expressly permit witness preparation, whereas the ICC has forbidden it. Ruben Karemaker, B. Don Taylor III, & Thomas Wayde Pittman, Witness Proofing in International Criminal Tribunals: A Critical Analysis of Widening Procedural Divergence, 21 Leiden J. Intl. L. 683, 689 (2008). One ICTY decision explicitly notes that the practice is common in adversarial procedural systems. Prosecutor v. Limaj, Bala, and Musliu, Case No. IT-03-66-T, Decision on Defence Motion on Prosecution Practice of "Proofing" Witnesses, at 2 (Dec. 10, 2004).

U.S. lawyers defend witness preparation and rehearsal by noting that without it, juries may devalue truthful testimony because of irrelevancies: the fact that the witness seems pompous, or doesn't make eye contact, or loses her temper when the adversary badgers and baits her. Witnesses also must be prepared, for example, to recognize when an answer to a question might cause an inadvertent waiver of important common law or constitutional privileges. Most important, witness preparation is deemed necessary to ensure accurate and truthful testimony; if done correctly, it is a service to the witness. When trial approaches—perhaps long after the operative events at issue—witnesses' recollections of important facts may be hazy or incorrect. Refreshing witnesses' recollections by reference to their prior, contemporaneous accounts furthers the search for the truth. Note, too, that defense counsel are aware that their testifying clients often try to shade or change their stories in order to avoid liability, thus exposing themselves to additional peril in the form of perjury or obstruction charges. If a defendant is taking the stand, then, defense counsel will invest substantial time toward ensuring that her client's testimony is truthful. Prosecutors in the United States have an obligation not to put on perjured testimony; they, too, then, will want to work with their witnesses—particularly cooperators who themselves must admit some level of culpability but may have an incentive to shade or shift blame—are telling the truth, and witness preparation is one means of doing so.

Critics respond that witness preparation decreases the authenticity of witnesses' testimony, smears cosmetics on demeanor evidence (that is, evidence based on witnesses' behavior, which jurors use to assess credibility), and—by putting words in witnesses' mouths and putting them on guard about what not to say—is indistinguishable from suborning perjury. In your view, is U.S.-style witness preparation essential to zealous advocacy, or is it an affront to justice?

Having presented an overview of the similarities and differences between adversarial and inquisitorial processes, we now turn to a more detailed examination of variations in criminal procedure under the different systems.

2. Arrest and Detention

Virtually all countries today prohibit arbitrary arrest and detention (arbitrariness in this context meaning, at a minimum, that the arrest was not carried out pursuant to law and the person arrested was not seized *in flagrante* or while committing the crime). However, in many foreign legal systems, the police are authorized to conduct warrantless arrests for relatively minor offenses. In the United Kingdom, the power to arrest without a warrant extends to all "arrestable" offenses, which are defined by statute to include those for which a sentence of five years or more imprisonment may be imposed. By contrast, in Japan most arrests require a judicially issued warrant. Canadian practice relies primarily on the issuance of summonses requiring the accused to appear in court, and arrest warrants are infrequently used.

In many civil law systems, the police are authorized to detain individuals for investigative purposes for a certain period of time even without a judicial determination of reasonable grounds to suspect that the detainees did in fact commit a crime. Sometimes referred to as *provisional arrest* or *preventive detention*, this power is intended to preserve the authorities' ability to conduct an appropriate investigation rather than to prevent a crime from occurring or to ensure the safety of the individual in question. In France the applicable term is *garde à vue* (or detention pending initial investigative inquiries), and the law generally permits such detention for 24 hours, extendable to 48 hours. Generally, the approval of a supervising magistrate or procurator is required for lengthier detentions. Considerable controversy surrounds legislative provisions permitting substantially lengthier periods of investigative detention in terrorist cases (for example, in the United Kingdom).

Generally speaking, during this period the police are free to conduct their investigation largely on their own, although some systems provide that in serious cases an examining magistrate will supervise the proceeding. The detainee may not be entitled to legal advice or representation, and counsel (even if available) is generally not permitted to attend the actual police interrogations. As a matter of law, the detainee may not enjoy a legally cognizable right to silence or protection against self-incrimination at this stage of the proceedings. In Japan, however, the right to counsel attaches at the time of arrest and the police must inform the detainee of the reasons for the arrest and of his right to counsel.

Within the United States the authority to arrest and detain depends on probable cause and is subject to active judicial scrutiny. Suspects are protected against coercive interrogation by their anti-self-incrimination and due process rights, backed by the requirement of *Miranda* warnings and provision of a right to counsel during interrogation. Not all domestic systems accord similar rights for detainees.

The vast majority of the world's legal systems recognize no right to bail, and provisional detention or "remand" is the norm. There are, of course, wide variations among legal systems in entitlement to release from custody pending formal charging and prosecution. In the United States, release on bail prior to trial generally depends on the perceived danger the defendant may pose to the community and the risk that the defendant will flee to avoid trial. In the United Kingdom, the presumption is that an accused is entitled to bail, subject to statutory exceptions. Bail is technically authorized in France but not often granted. Swedish law does not provide for release on bail. Italian law provides for house arrest (*arresti domiciliari*). Both house arrest and entitlement to bail are increasingly recognized in Latin America.

3.   *Habeas Corpus v.* Recurso de Amparo

Virtually all legal systems today provide, in one fashion or another, a mechanism by which the legality of an individual's pretrial detention can be scrutinized by a judicial authority. Certainly the underlying right of an individual to be free from arbitrary or unlawful arrest, and to be able to bring a challenge, is enshrined in the major human rights treaties, including the International Covenant on Civil and Political Rights (Article 9), the African Charter on Human and Peoples' Rights (Article 6), the American Convention on Human Rights (Article 7), and the European Convention for the Protection of Human Rights and Fundamental Freedoms (Article 5). The specific domestic procedures vary, of course, but students of international criminal law should be familiar with two of the best known: habeas and *amparo*.

The common law concept of habeas corpus (historically known in the Anglo-Saxon tradition as *The Great Writ*) contemplates a relatively narrow and expedited procedure intended to protect against illegal detention and imprisonment. The writ itself commands the custodian of the detainee to bring the individual in question before the court for that purpose, not for a determination of guilt or innocence. Many lawyers consider that simple procedure one of the fundamental guarantees against governmental abuse.[15] By statute (see 28 U.S.C. §§2241, 2254, 2255), Congress has given federal courts habeas corpus jurisdiction to consider constitutional challenges to state as well as federal convictions. In addition to habeas rights granted by statute, the Supreme Court has held that habeas corpus is a constitutional right, and rebuffed a law extinguishing statutory habeas for detainees at Guantánamo Bay.[16]

By comparison, the term *recurso de amparo* (prevalent in many Central and Latin American countries) refers to a specialized form of litigation that permits individuals and legal entities to challenge a range of government acts allegedly infringing on their fundamental rights. It can be used to determine the legality of a criminal detention but is more broadly employed in civil and administrative contexts as a protective mechanism to avert anticipated harmful action (in fact, in Chile, the writ is called *recurso de protección*).[17] The specific procedure varies from jurisdiction to jurisdiction, but in general, where the claim is based on constitutional rights, it must be addressed

---

15. The U.S. Constitution explicitly provides that the "privilege of the writ . . . shall not be suspended, unless when in cases of rebellion or invasion the public safety may require it" (Art. I, §9). As students of history know, the writ has in fact been suspended on occasion (during the Civil War by both sides and by President Grant during Reconstruction). More recently, Congress has circumscribed its availability in the Antiterrorism and Effective Death Penalty Act of 1996, 8 U.S.C. §1535, and the Prison Litigation Reform Act of 1995, 18 U.S.C. §3626.

16. Boumediene v. Bush, 128 S. Ct. 2229 (2008).

17. "If the two remedies are examined together, it is possible to conclude that *amparo* comprises a whole series of remedies and that habeas corpus is but one of its components." Inter-American Court of Human Rights, Habeas Corpus in Emergency Situations (Arts. 27.2, 25.1, and 7.6 of the American Convention on Human Rights), Advisory Opinion OC-8/87, ¶34 (Jan. 30, 1987).

to the Supreme Court of the country in question, sometimes under the name *accion de tutela.* A related but distinct procedure in some Latin American civil law systems is the *actio popularis,* or "popular complaint," by which any individual can challenge the constitutionality of a governmental act in the "public interest," whether or not he is personally affected by it.

With respect to challenges to criminal detentions, what varies considerably is the period of time within which, by law, a detainee must be brought before a court for a determination of the legality of her continued detention. This period may vary from as little as two days to as long as a month (for example, in the case of people detained as "terrorists"). In the Netherlands, for example, every detained person must be interviewed by an examining magistrate within three days of arrest. Similarly, Japanese law requires that a judge must authorize continued detention within 72 hours of an arrest.

4. *Pretrial Investigation*

As indicated above, in many legal systems a procurator or examining magistrate plays the central role in directing the course of the pretrial criminal process, receiving and deciding whether to act on complaints, directing (to a greater or lesser extent) the conduct of the police investigation, authorizing searches and seizures, and compiling the case file or dossier.

Under U.S. law, a search or seizure must meet the reasonableness requirement of the Fourth Amendment, which generally means that, at a minimum, the search or seizure was supported by some level of individualized suspicion (generally probable cause) and was reasonable in its execution. Some situations—notably the arrests of persons or searches of places within a home—require a warrant issued by the judiciary. Even where no warrant is required, law enforcement often must be prepared to demonstrate before a judge that the search or seizure was supported by probable cause. Nearly all legal systems have similarly protective requirements and exceptions, although few address the issues on the basis of constitutional provisions such as those in the U.S. Bill of Rights. In many cases, the procedural law requires a search warrant issued by a judge; in others, the police or prosecutors can act on their own authority. Of course, where the warrants are issued by the same magistrate who is supervising the pretrial investigation, the requirement may seem to lack much of its potency and prophylactic power.

Very few legal systems apply the same type of blanket exclusionary rules to evidence obtained by unlawful searches and coerced confessions as the United States does for violations of constitutional protections.[18] In addition, rules vary on *accès au dossier* and whether evidence must be turned over to the opposing party and at which stage of the proceedings. In Japan, for example, prosecutors are not affirmatively required to turn over exculpatory evidence to a defendant, although they do have an obligation to disclose such evidence to the court when it is material to the proceeding.

5. *The Decision to Prosecute*

In the United States, it is generally up to the prosecutor to decide whether a criminal case should proceed, either charging a suspect with an information (the procedure

---

18. The Japanese Adversary System in Context: Controversies and Comparisons (Malcolm M. Feeley & Setsuo Miyazawa eds., 2002).

authorized in most individual states) or seeking an indictment by presenting evidence before a grand jury or to a judge in a preliminary examination (the procedure that prevails in some states and in the federal system). The prosecutor may decide not to pursue the case at all or may engage in negotiations with the suspect for information or a guilty plea in return for a lesser charge or requested sentence. Although these decisions, like the prosecutor's overall conduct, are reviewable by the court, the system is characterized by a substantial measure of prosecutorial discretion, powers that are magnified by the plea rates.

The principle of prosecutorial discretion (like the institution of the grand jury) is unknown in the vast majority of criminal justice systems around the world. Instead, the procurator or investigating magistrate has a mandatory duty to bring charges against anyone whose guilt has been substantially established as a result of the relevant investigation. The notion of compulsory prosecution of all offenses for which there is sufficient evidence, sometimes referred to under the rubric of the "principle of legality," is perhaps strictest in systems based on the Romano-Germanic tradition. Under French law, if the *juge d'instruction* decides there is a valid case against a suspect, he must refer the suspect to a tribunal or court, at which point his investigative mandate will have been discharged.

In many civil law systems, once this point has been reached, defendants are not allowed by law to plead guilty. The case must be tried before the court. In practice, however, there appear to be divergent national approaches. For example, Italy accepted the practice of guilty pleas in 1988, and French law now permits them for *délits* punishable by less than five years' imprisonment. By contrast, in the United Kingdom, plea bargaining is often said not to occur. Where guilty pleas are excluded, a defendant's confession will generally be treated as merely one more fact to be entered into evidence and will not remove the requirement that the prosecution present a full case.

6. Conduct of the Trial

In the United States, once adversarial proceedings have begun, the case is brought before a petit jury of between 6 and 12 private citizens or may alternatively be tried by a judge sitting alone if the defense requests it (and, in some jurisdictions, where the prosecution agrees to this procedure). The jury is selected from a pool typically drawn from the register of voters, and individual jurors are subject to challenge and rejection by the prosecution and defense alike. Reliance on the jury system is a well-known hallmark of the U.S. legal system, guaranteed by the Sixth Amendment to the U.S. Constitution.

While jury trials in criminal cases are far from the norm in most other legal systems, they do exist outside of the United States, even in such civil law countries as Austria, Belgium, Denmark, and Italy. Many Latin American countries provide for a *jurado de consiencia* or equivalent. In England the right to trial by jury is provided only as a matter of statute, and the law provides that certain felonies known as "either-way" offenses can be tried in the Magistrates' Court without a jury and are subject to lesser maximum punishments. In Ireland and Australia, the use of a jury system has been circumscribed,[19] and in Mexico, although they are mentioned in the Constitution, jury trials have not in fact been used. No such right exists in Israel, Lithuania, Luxembourg, the Philippines, or Sweden, to name only a few. Spain added the

---

19. In Ireland's Special Criminal Courts, created by the Offenses Against the State Act 1939, cases are decided by three judges sitting without a jury. In their current form, they deal with Irish Republican Army and organized crime cases, and the number of such courts was expanded by legislation in 2004. See generally http://www.courts.ie.

possibility of juries during the 1990s, and Japan has recently introduced the jury system for the most serious crimes. Russia, which adopted jury trials for certain offenses in 1993, has recently abolished them in cases involving terrorism and treason. In Greece, felonies are judged, with some exceptions, by a "mixed" court of four jurors and three professional judges who may advise the jury on complex legal questions. As we saw in the trial of Dr. Brach, many civil law systems include *lay judges* or *people's assessors*, nonlawyers who hear and vote on the evidence along with the presiding judge in the most serious cases. In systems based on *shari'a* law, criminal trials tend to be much shorter and less formal, with no right to a jury trial (although lay judges are frequently used), and the accused must defend himself with little or no right to legal representation.

A typical criminal trial in the United States begins with opening statements in which the prosecutor describes for the judge and jury the nature of the charges and the evidence to be presented establishing the defendant's guilt, and defense counsel outlines the reasons for believing that reasonable doubt exists about that proposition. The prosecution then presents its case, calling witnesses and presenting documentary, physical, and other evidence against the defendant. After the prosecution rests, the defense may move to dismiss the case if it believes there is insufficient evidence to sustain a conviction. Given the presumption of innocence, the burden is always on the prosecution, and the defense has no obligation to put on a case. Alternatively, the defense may proceed to present its case and call further witnesses; all witnesses are sworn to tell the truth and may be cross-examined by the opposing side. The rules of evidence function as a system of objections by adversaries, and evidence may be excluded if it violates the rules or is considered likely to prejudice the trier of fact. For example, hearsay evidence is disallowed for its biasing effect without substantiation. After all witnesses have been examined and all evidence presented, the opposing sides make their summations and the case is submitted for decision.

As described above, a criminal trial in a civil law country centers on direct examination of the accused by the presiding judge (and sometimes by the prosecutor), based largely on the *dossier* containing the written results of the pretrial investigation. Because the defendant is typically represented by counsel and because counsel is permitted to participate in the process, it is misleading to assert that inquisitorial civil law systems are inherently or entirely nonadversarial. Still, the criminal procedure in civil law systems does not embrace the right of confrontation as that concept is known in U.S. constitutional law, and defense counsel may not be permitted to examine or cross-examine witnesses directly. There are, of course, variations: In Japan, for example, witnesses can be cross-examined, and the defendant has the right to introduce rebuttal evidence and to make closing arguments.

One consequence of this difference in trial procedure is the relative absence of objections to admissibility of evidence, and of claims of prejudice, in non-common law courts. Nearly all jurisdictions around the world, regardless of legal tradition or orientation, afford the defendant some protection against compelled self-incrimination; indeed, the defendant's right not to be compelled to testify against herself or to confess guilt is recognized in Article 14(3)(g) of the International Covenant on Civil and Political Rights (ICCPR). However, the extent of this protection varies among systems, as does the right to remain silent in the face of custodial interrogation. Few countries have rules as stringent as those required by the Fifth Amendment to the U.S. Constitution. An important distinction in Canadian law, for example, is that this right does not apply to a person who is not charged in the case in question. Thus, a person subject to a subpoena, who is not charged in connection with the offense being considered, must give testimony even if it is incriminating.

In the United States, after both sides have presented their cases and made closing arguments, the judge gives the jury detailed legal instructions as to what elements of proof they must find to exist in order to return a guilty verdict on the various specific counts. The members of the jury then adjourn to deliberate in private, electing a foreperson from among their number. In relatively rare situations the jury may be sequestered to insulate it from press coverage of the trial proceedings and from attempts to subvert or intimidate jury members. The jury generally must agree unanimously on its verdict. As a matter of due process, the jury may convict only when it determines that the defendant's guilt has been established beyond a reasonable doubt. An inability of the jurors to agree will result in a hung jury, opening the way for a retrial or dismissal of the charges. By contrast, in most civil law systems, the presiding judge is required to explain the basis for the court's verdict in a "reasoned judgment."

7. Rights of Appeal

The right to appeal from a criminal conviction is universally recognized and is protected by the major human rights treaties. Domestic procedures vary significantly, however. In the United States and most other jurisdictions, after conviction and sentencing for a criminal offense, defendants may appeal a guilty verdict and/or sentence to the next higher court. U.S. appellate courts do not retry the case or review the merits of the verdict. Instead, they only examine the record of the proceedings in the lower court to determine if errors were made that require a new trial, resentencing, or a complete discharge of the defendant, depending on the circumstances. The prosecution may not appeal after an acquittal. Under limited circumstances the prosecution may appeal from certain rulings by the court before the verdict is given and may also appeal from the sentence itself (for example, if it believes the sentence is too lenient). In all Anglo-American common law courts, appellate review of lower court decisions may also be obtained on specific issues by filing a petition for discretionary review by prerogative writ in certain cases.

In civil law systems, by contrast, review of the factual basis underlying a criminal conviction is normal. (It is called *de novo review.*) Appellate rules and procedures are complex and vary greatly among national legal systems. In general, however, both defendant and prosecution have an affirmative right to at least one level of review on the merits (in French, this is known as *appel*). However, the ability of either prosecutor or defendant to challenge the conduct of the trial or its outcome on the basis of procedural fault or errors of substantive law (*cassation*) is relatively circumscribed. In Japan, for example, appeal to the Supreme Court is limited to constitutional questions. Uniquely, many civil law systems also provide an extraordinary procedure for reconsideration of a judgment of conviction on the grounds of factual error (*revision*), and where trials *in absentia* are permitted, a special procedure (*opposition*) permits the nonappearing party to have the same case reheard by the same court.

8. Victims' Rights

Many developed legal systems make special provision for assistance to victims of violent crimes. For example, all U.S. states today operate violent crime compensation programs. In the United Kingdom, violent crime victims are able to claim compensation from the Criminal Injuries Compensation Authority (CICA), a government-funded body, for personal injuries sustained as a result of a wide variety of attacks. The injury does not have to be physical; claims are cognizable for nervous shock from witnessing or seeing the results of an attack on a loved one, and for emotional trauma from sexual assault or rape or from any other violent crime, such as a racially motivated attack. The CICA actually publicizes a "tariff" indicating how much a particular injury is worth (for example, dislocated jaw, £2,000; fractured skull without an operation, £2,500; loss of leg above the knee, £40,000).

Within the Council of Europe (COE), a multilateral treaty (the 1983 European Convention on the Compensation of Victims of Violent Crimes) obligates states parties to provide compensation to "those who have sustained serious bodily injury or impairment of health directly attributable to an intentional crime of violence [and] the dependents of persons who have died as a result of such crime . . . even if the offender cannot be prosecuted or punished." (Art. 2). In June 2006, the COE's Committee of Ministers called upon COE member states to improve implementation of this Convention by providing increased assistance to victims, including, inter alia, state-funded compensation to victims of serious, intentional, violent crimes, including sexual violence.[20]

Many legal systems pay particular attention to vindicating the rights and interests of crime victims as part of the criminal process itself. It is not uncommon, for example, for courts to order a criminal defendant, upon conviction, to pay compensation to a victim for damages to or loss of property, with the same effect as an independent civil judgment (sometimes, but not always, with preclusive effect). A unique feature in European (including Russian) procedure entitles victims themselves (as well as their heirs or assignees such as insurance companies) to pursue a right of recovery of civil damages from the accused as an integral part of the criminal proceeding. In such situations, the claimant actually participates in the criminal proceeding (as a *partie civile*, *Nebenkläger*, or *acusador privado*), with standing to offer evidence and examine witnesses. The PRC's criminal procedure code permits victims of material losses to file "incidental civil actions" to be heard together with the relevant criminal proceeding.

9.   Efforts to Establish Institutional Bridges

As divergent as the world's criminal procedural systems are, several notable attempts have been undertaken to bridge these differences for a more fluid system of justice, largely in Europe. One of these is the creation of the European Arrest Warrant (EAW), a judicial judgment by the court of a member state of the European Union (EU) for the arrest or surrender of a specified person in another member state. Use of the EAW applies in conducting criminal investigations or the carrying out of a custodial sentence or detention order, and is limited by the length of any applicable sentence. The effort to implement it throughout Europe represents an attempt to speed up the process of extradition and move some of the authority in seizing criminals abroad from the political to the judicial branch.[21] Still, the process is not without problems; in Germany, the Federal Constitutional Court declared the

---

20. See Recommendation Rec(2006)8 adopted on 14 June 2006, http://www.coe.int/t/cm/adoptedTexts_en.asp.
21. See generally http://ec.europa.eu/justice_home/fsj/criminal/extradition/fsj_criminal_extradition_en.htm (last visited Apr. 9, 2009).

EAW void in July 2005, finding that it encroached disproportionately on the freedom from extradition and the right of recourse to judicial review.[22]

The EU's effort at integrating its collective judicial process is further illustrated by the creation of EUROJUST, an EU body made up of prosecutors, magistrates, and police officers of roughly equal competence from each of the member states. Created in 1999, the organization's purpose is to increase the effectiveness of each state's domestic authorities when they are dealing with the investigation and prosecution of cross-border and organized crime.[23]

B. PERSPECTIVES

We have seen wide variation among systems of criminal justice. The natural question that arises is, what makes a criminal justice system fair and acceptable? One answer is given in two articles of the ICCPR, one of the central multilateral human rights treaties, with more than 160 states parties (not including, however, such major states as China and Pakistan).

INTERNATIONAL COVENANT ON CIVIL AND POLITICAL RIGHTS
999 U.N.T.S. 171 (1966, entered into force 1976)

ARTICLE 14

1. All persons shall be equal before the courts and tribunals. In the determination of any criminal charge against him, or of his rights and obligations in a suit at law, everyone shall be entitled to a fair and public hearing by a competent, independent and impartial tribunal established by law. The press and the public may be excluded from all or part of a trial for reasons of morals, public order (ordre public) or national security in a democratic society, or when the interest of the private lives of the parties so requires, or to the extent strictly necessary in the opinion of the court in special circumstances where publicity would prejudice the interests of justice; but any judgement rendered in a criminal case or in a suit at law shall be made public except where the interest of juvenile persons otherwise requires or the proceedings concern matrimonial disputes or the guardianship of children.

2. Everyone charged with a criminal offence shall have the right to be presumed innocent until proved guilty according to law.

3. In the determination of any criminal charge against him, everyone shall be entitled to the following minimum guarantees, in full equality:

(a) To be informed promptly and in detail in a language which he understands of the nature and cause of the charge against him;

(b) To have adequate time and facilities for the preparation of his defence and to communicate with counsel of his own choosing;

(c) To be tried without undue delay;

---

22. See http://www.bundesverfassungsgericht.de/en/press/bvg05-064en.html (last visited Apr. 9, 2009).

23. See http://www.eurojust.europa.eu.

(d) To be tried in his presence, and to defend himself in person or through legal assistance of his own choosing; to be informed, if he does not have legal assistance, of this right; and to have legal assistance assigned to him, in any case where the interests of justice so require, and without payment by him in any such case if he does not have sufficient means to pay for it;

(e) To examine, or have examined, the witnesses against him and to obtain the attendance and examination of witnesses on his behalf under the same conditions as witnesses against him;

(f) To have the free assistance of an interpreter if he cannot understand or speak the language used in court;

(g) Not to be compelled to testify against himself or to confess guilt.

4. In the case of juvenile persons, the procedure shall be such as will take account of their age and the desirability of promoting their rehabilitation.

5. Everyone convicted of a crime shall have the right to his conviction and sentence being reviewed by a higher tribunal according to law.

6. When a person has by a final decision been convicted of a criminal offence and when subsequently his conviction has been reversed or he has been pardoned on the ground that a new or newly discovered fact shows conclusively that there has been a miscarriage of justice, the person who has suffered punishment as a result of such conviction shall be compensated according to law, unless it is proved that the non-disclosure of the unknown fact in time is wholly or partly attributable to him.

7. No one shall be liable to be tried or punished again for an offence for which he has already been finally convicted or acquitted in accordance with the law and penal procedure of each country.

Article 15

1. No one shall be held guilty of any criminal offence on account of any act or omission which did not constitute a criminal offence, under national or international law, at the time when it was committed. Nor shall a heavier penalty be imposed than the one that was applicable at the time when the criminal offence was committed. If, subsequent to the commission of the offence, provision is made by law for the imposition of the lighter penalty, the offender shall benefit thereby.

2. Nothing in this article shall prejudice the trial and punishment of any person for any act or omission which, at the time when it was committed, was criminal according to the general principles of law recognized by the community of nations.

In interpreting these provisions, the Human Rights Committee (which supervises implementation of the Covenant) has stressed the need to ensure equal access to courts, to provide fair and public hearings, and to guarantee the competence, impartiality, and independence of the judiciary, both in law and practice.[24] Do the guarantees enshrined in Articles 14 and 15 of the ICCPR represent the bare minimum a legal system must meet to be legitimate?

---

24. See General Comment No. 13 ("Equality before the courts and the right to a fair and public hearing by an independent court established by law"), adopted April 13, 1984, available at http://www.unhchr.ch/tbs/doc.nsf/0/bb722416a295f264c12563ed0049dfbd?Opendocument.

Consider this question in connection with the following excerpt describing the Rwandan response to the tens of thousands of prisoners suspected (in some cases falsely) of participating in the 1994 genocide.

SAREL KANDELL KROMER, THE RWANDAN RECONCILIATION
Wash. Post, Oct. 16, 2005

The nine Rwandan judges filed into a grassy enclosure shaded by tarps to keep out the equatorial sun. Each wore a blue, green and yellow sash that said "inyangamugayo" — trusted person. Two prisoners were summoned from the rear. Fifty or 60 people sitting on benches facing the court stood up. The chief judge said, "We are going to remember." Then, a long silence.

They were there not only to remember, but to be able to stop remembering, to find truth and maybe justice, and to rebuild their lives. This is the gacaca court (pronounced ga-cha-cha). The name means "on the grass." Throughout Rwanda's history, neighbors have settled disputes by adjourning to the gacaca to sit, discuss and mediate personal and community problems.

But now these Rwandan courts are faced with trying more than 40,000 prisoners implicated in the genocide of 1994, when the members of the country's Hutu ethnic majority killed nearly 1 million minority Tutsis in a 100-day rampage. Most of the accused have been in jail for more than 10 years without trial. While the masterminds of the genocide — those who planned, organized and incited it — will be tried by the International Criminal Tribunal for Rwanda operating in Tanzania, and others charged with murder will be tried in regular criminal courts, the many more who abetted the slaughter will go before the gacaca courts. The gacaca judges are not lawyers, but respected persons selected by the community.

This is a strangely inspiring process to witness, especially for me, a retired lawyer used to the often acrimonious U.S. system. While the crimes in Rwanda are deeply disturbing, the gacaca courts, which generally meet once a week, emphasize reconciliation and deemphasize retribution — though further punishment for those accused is still possible. There are approximately 10,000 gacaca courts, each with nine elected judges. They are how most ordinary people here are coming to terms with the past.

Rwandans want, above all, to find out exactly where and how those close to them died. Without this knowledge, it is hard to move on. Genocide memorials have been erected throughout the country in the solemn style of our Vietnam Veterans Memorial, only the slates are largely blank, listing hundreds of names of the known dead but leaving space for tens of thousands of others who perished and whose names are unknown. The need to learn the names of the dead is greater than the need to punish.

I was in Rwanda with my son over the summer to visit American friends. One conducts anti-violence workshops for gacaca judges for the African Great Lakes Initiative, a Quaker group. Her husband is a health adviser for the U.S. Agency for International Development. Given my experience as a public interest lawyer, I wanted to attend a gacaca, even if I had to absorb the proceedings through someone translating Kinyarwanda in a low voice.

During the session I attended one day in early August, one of the accused, a man named Nicodemus, was summoned before the bench. His accuser rose, took an oath and stated: "Nicodemus was persecuting Tutsis, hunting them. I am not sure if he killed them." He then asked the tribunal to forgive Nicodemus, as though charging him in public were its own form of revenge.

A second accuser, named Bimenyimana, rose and accused Nicodemus of killing someone named Concord. A judge asked, "How do you know Concord died?" Bimenyimana answered, "I had lunch with people who said he died." The judge: "How did he die?" Accuser: "I don't know. I didn't see him again, and we were neighbors." At this point the judge read out an article of the laws of gacaca, informing the accuser that he was in danger if he was perjuring himself. At the earlier information stage of the court process, he had stated that he didn't know how certain people had died; now the judges wanted to ascertain whether he was bringing false testimony.

An imposing woman in a striking brown dress with a blue and white pattern and matching headdress rose from the audience and advised the accuser Bimenyimana to tell the truth. "Other people here are neighbors of Nicodemus," she said. Although Kigali is a populous city, the neighborhood where Nicodemus lived is a small, tightly knit community within the city where everyone seems to know everyone else.

To a foreigner like me, the ethnic lines that once meant life or death appeared blurred. Nicodemus was Hutu; the accuser who asked the tribunal to forgive him appeared to be Tutsi, but it wasn't obvious. Both Hutus and Tutsis sat on the tribunal; I could not tell the difference. Still other Rwandans are part Hutu and part Tutsi.

To many, the Hutu/Tutsi distinction is a matter of economic or social standing rather than ethnic origins. A display in the Kigali Memorial Centre says that if a Hutu acquired 10 cows or more, he was considered a Tutsi. The Tutsi guide who took us to the Kigali memorial had invited his Hutu friend along. We stood in the peace garden of roses overlooking the city's hills. Smiling, the guide said: "I'm Tutsi. He's Hutu. Why aren't we fighting?" Both young men had been children when the genocide occurred and have grown up together.

The first day my son and I spent in the country was a Saturday set aside for community service. We could have stayed inside, but we decided to join in. We were handed machetes, and walked down the dirt road to the center of Kicukiro, a sector of Kigali, together with hundreds of other people to clear land for a community center. It was surreal, given that machetes were the weapons used in much of the killing. Yet perhaps it was a metaphor — as though ploughshares had turned to swords and back again.

After two hours of clearing brush, digging boulders from the earth and, to everyone's delight, finding a stolen television hidden in the tall grasses, the community gathered under a shelter at the soccer field to discuss an important piece of news: One thousand prisoners who had been jailed without trial for 10 years were about to be returned to this community of about 8,000 people for trial before the gacaca courts. Many were already in the neighborhood, recognizable by the pink outfits prisoners must wear, working on public service projects by day and returning to prison at night.

Two years earlier, during a similar program, released prisoners had attacked people who had turned them in and community members had avenged murders allegedly committed by those who had been released. How to reintegrate the prisoners more successfully was now a major concern. Moreover, many prisoners' wives had remarried and established new lives during the decade their men were jailed. The prisoners would need food, shelter and jobs.

. . . At the gacaca another accuser was sworn in. He was the brother of Concord, who died. He said that Bimenyimana was telling the truth and that another prisoner, Ntabakunzi, was with Nicodemus when the killings occurred. A woman in a yellow outfit and headdress rose to suggest that the tribunal wait for Ntabakunzi's testimony. Another woman rose and said, "Ntabakunzi is the man who raped me." The chief judge of the tribunal asked her to return the following week to give sworn testimony.

A man in the back row talked directly to Nicodemus: "If given time to speak, tell the truth. Even if Ntabakunzi is not here to testify, please tell us the truth. What happened?"

That is the question that this green, hilly country is facing. Once the story has been told, the dead can rest and the survivors can get on with life.

It seemed as though every family included a victim, a perpetrator or a collaborator — sometimes all three. My friend told me that a Rwandan colleague of hers at the Friends Peace House described this scene: " 'People killed and saved people at the same time. Twelve people broke in through the roof of my home and started killing. They hacked my parents with machetes before my eyes. When someone attacked me, the person killing my parents stopped, said "no children" and got everyone to leave.' "

The application form for attending gacaca asks people to explain the benefit to them and to Rwanda of their attendance. My son and I felt we had an obligation to bear witness so we could tell others about this place. In the children's room of the Kigali genocide memorial there are pictures: "David: loved football, made people laugh, wanted to be a doctor, killed by machete." Or, "Lisa, infant: favorite food: mother's milk, favorite person, mom, thrown against wall."

Last week I learned from my translator that the gacaca court, after hearing further evidence, found Nicodemus guilty and sent him back to prison.

Despite the stain of violence, Rwandan society appears to have strengths that could help it heal. The young woman who translated the gacaca hearings has adopted three genocide orphans and taken in a close friend who had been unfairly jailed and lost his job. And people conduct themselves with dignity. In day-to-day life, I saw no littering, no begging, no eating in public and a pride in personal appearance that defies the omnipresent dust. And in the gacaca, where it would have been understandable for anger to burst forth, there was restraint and decorum.

Rwandans have a saying: "God does his work throughout the world by day, and comes home to Rwanda to sleep at night." If so, maybe Rwandans will one day be able to sleep more peacefully.

NOTES AND QUESTIONS

1. The gacaca genocide courts were created legislatively by Rwanda in 2004. The legislation divided offenders into three categories. Category 1 offenders, the most serious, include "planners, leaders, notorious murderers, torturers . . . , rapists and sexual torturers, and those who committed dehumanizing acts against a dead body." Mark A. Drumbl, Atrocity, Punishment, and International Law at 86 (2007) (summarizing Article 51 of the Rwandan legislation). These offenders are not eligible for gacaca trials and are bound over to the criminal justice system. Category 2 offenders include murderers and those who committed other acts against the person; Category 3 offenders committed crimes against property.

Traditional gacaca courts were used principally for property, inheritance, and family law matters, and only occasionally for crimes of violence. Traditionally, they aimed at reconciliation, and their remedies heavily featured the payment of compensation, rather than punishment; prolonged incarceration was never part of the traditional gacaca scheme. The post-genocide gacacas retain some aspects of the traditional gacaca: among the remedies included in the legislation are community service and victim compensation. But they also include imprisonment for up to thirty years. Professor Drumbl observes that the post-genocide gacacas are really a blend of the traditional informal gacaca with the more formal and legalistic procedures of Western-style criminal courts—partly as a result of pressure by the international community. With the possibility of harsh sentences, the need for greater due process than in traditional gacacas seems evident; but in Professor Drumbl's opinion, there is a loss in traditional restoration and reintegration of offenders, which is troubling because it appears that perhaps as many as a million Rwandans may ultimately be implicated in the genocide. For detailed discussion of the gacaca mechanism, see Drumbl, Atrocity, Punishment, and International Law (2007) at 85-99.

2. Can justice be administered by informal methods like gacaca? Or is it necessary to have a formal, rule-based process with fully trained counsel, professional prosecutors, independent judges, and the possibility of effective appeals? Is outside oversight and supervision required, for example, by the legislature, nongovernmental organizations, or the international community? What guarantees the impartiality of gacaca? What protects defendants from witnesses who testify against them for motives of personal grudge, vendetta, or perhaps even a desire to take the accused person's property? For a recent discussion of the continuing attempts to reintegrate the Hutus, see "The genocide in Rwanda: The difficulty of trying to stop it happening ever again," The Economist (Apr. 8, 2009), available at http://www.economist.com/world/mideast-africa/displaystory.cfm?story_id = 13447279 (last visited May 27, 2009).

3. Recall from Chapter 3 that after the genocide more than 100,000 suspects were in custody, many quite literally rotting away in appalling conditions. Rwanda had no judicial capacity to try them all. Consider that after the genocide some observers estimated that fewer than two dozen trained lawyers remained in the entire country. Does it make sense to insist on trial processes approximating the ICCPR standards? Or is this a case of "the best is the enemy of the good"?

4. What are the most important safeguards of the rights of the individual defendant? The right to counsel? The presumption of innocence? Protection against self-incrimination? A speedy trial? A right to appeal? Must criminal trials be open to the public? Are juries required? Are trials *in absentia* inherently unjust?

5. What special considerations, if any, are raised by pursuing criminal prosecutions in the context of ongoing civil disorder or in a postconflict situation? Consider the example above from the perspective of the issues raised in Chapter 1 about the overall purpose and objectives of international criminal justice.

C.   SENTENCING NORMS AND PROCEDURES

1.   National Sentencing Regimes

Domestic procedures regarding the sentencing of convicted criminals, as well as punishment policies, vary widely throughout the world, with little correlation to the type of legal system in question.

In the United States, a guilty verdict (whether by judge or jury) is followed by sentencing, often at a separate hearing once the prosecution, defense, and court develop information based on which the judge may craft a sentence. (Capital cases always require a separate penalty phase in which the jury determines whether to recommend the death penalty.) In some state systems in the United States, juries make recommendations on punishments under the guidance of the court; in others, sentencing is a purely judicial function. In England, by contrast, when a jury is employed, its only job is to determine guilt or innocence, and it has no role in sentencing and punishment.

Although it is common in the United States for judges to receive sentencing reports and recommendations, most civil systems by comparison employ more extensive procedures to aid the court in its understanding of the convicted individuals in determining an appropriate penalty. The French version is the best known of these, requiring an investigation into the defendant's personality.

In traditional civil law systems, the convicting court also determines the punishment, with strict regard to the penalties prescribed by the relevant code. Verdicts are typically far more detailed, sentencing is not generally a separate phase, and in many situations, sentencing directly follows conviction. In France, for example, conviction of the most serious offenses (*crimes*) by the *cour d'assise* leads directly to a vote on punishment by secret ballot, with the decision requiring a simple majority, unless the maximum penalty is sought, in which case there must be a majority of at least eight votes against four. If the required majority is not reached, then a second vote is taken on a less severe punishment than the previous one, and this is repeated until a penalty gains majority vote. In the Italian *corte di assise* juries play a similar role, casting votes on a sentence, but in this case before a panel of judges, providing some transparency. In Germany, there is no separation of sentencing from the determination of guilt or innocence; the judgment and, in the event of a conviction, sentence are issued by the court in one pronouncement with a required majority of two-thirds.

The sentencing policies and practices of each state reflect the purposes for punishment described in Chapter 1. For example, Italian law requires that a judge bear in mind any possibility for reformation of the accused in imposing a sentence. Similarly, the German Constitution's emphasis on human dignity requires that the primary aim of punishment be to help offenders readapt to civil society, with the judge taking into account "the potential effect of the measure on his future life."[25] Further, in cases where the sentence is less than six months, suspension is automatic if there are guarantees of reform (these may be based generally on the defendant's personality).

The United States continues to boast the highest incarceration rate of any nation. According to the Department of Justice's Bureau of Justice Statistics, at midyear 2005, the nation's total prison and jail population stood at over 2.1 million persons, or 738 per 100,000 residents (approximately 1 in every 136), well ahead of the closest competitors (Russia, the United Kingdom, South Africa, Israel, and Mexico). A substantial number of the prisoners were serving relatively short sentences; the rate of state and federal prisoners sentenced to more than one year was 488 per 100,000. Over the preceding decade, the incarcerated population grew an average of 3.4 percent annually. Some attribute this continuing growth to the success of policies responding to violent crime, others to disproportionate mandatory sentencing of people convicted of relatively minor drug offenses (by some estimates, roughly one in four inmates was in jail for a drug offense). The disparate impact of incarceration on various ethnic and racial groups is well documented. According to the DOJ report, an estimated 12 percent of black males, 3.7 percent of Hispanic males, and 1.7 percent of white males in their late 20s were in prison or jail. Only 6.4 percent of state and federal inmates were not U.S. citizens.[26]

---

25. §46(1), StGB.

26. See DOJ/BJS Bulletin 213133, Prison and Jail Inmates at Midyear 2005 (May 2006), available at http://www.ojp.usdoj.gov/bjs/abstract/pjim05.htm. For additional information, see http://www .sentencingproject.org and http://www.kcl.ac.uk/schools/law/research/icps (last visited Apr. 9, 2009).

The severity of punishments also varies by country. In many legal systems, the maximum penalty is life in prison. In a number of jurisdictions (Germany and Mexico, for example) constitutional law does not permit life sentences without possibility of parole; in others, the law provides for release, or at least automatic review and the strong possibility of parole or pardon, after 20 or 25 years (30 years in Belgium, 14 in India, 10 in Japan). In practice, in the continental European systems, 20 years' imprisonment is a severe sentence. U.S. sentencing policies and practices result in longer prison sentences than in most other countries. Where the United States has been widely criticized for its harsh sentencing regimes, other states have been accused of excess lenience for certain crimes.

Capital punishment is an especially troubling subject, with wide variations among countries and passionate disagreements. For information about national practices, see Chapter 10.

2. Sentencing in International Tribunals

Not surprisingly, national differences in sentencing philosophy and severity have been transposed to the international arena. When dealing with international crimes, often involving the most egregious crimes known to man, how should the international community forge a consensus on appropriate criminal sanctions?

JENS DAVID OHLIN, APPLYING THE DEATH PENALTY TO CRIMES OF GENOCIDE

99 Am. J. Intl. L. 747 (2005)[27]

After the Rwandan genocide of 1994, the United Nations Security Council moved quickly to establish an international tribunal to indict the architects of the slaughter. . . . [However, w]hereas the Nuremberg Tribunal imposed death sentences for the most culpable instigators of the Holocaust, there would be no death sentences for the architects of the Hutu genocidal campaign against the Tutsi. Over the course of forty years, there was a sea shift in attitudes about the legality of the death penalty. When the Allies announced their decision to apply the death penalty at Nuremberg, few objected or suggested that executions would violate international human rights law. . . .

But just four decades later when the Security Council authorized the creation of the International Criminal Tribunal for Rwanda (ICTR), few states championed the death penalty. Indeed, many human rights lawyers took for granted that an emerging norm of international law forbade the use of the death penalty in all circumstances, even for the extreme crime of genocide. This view prevailed among the European powers on the Security Council, any one of which could exercise its veto to block empowering a tribunal to impose capital punishment. Just as the permissibility of the death penalty was considered so obvious at Nuremberg that no serious discussion of the matter was required, so its *impermissibility* was now considered so obvious that once again no serious debate ensued. . . .

But this was certainly not the conventional wisdom among the Rwandan delegation to the United Nations. The death penalty remain[ed] a part of the Rwandan judicial

---

27. Reproduced with permission from The American Society of International Law.

system and Rwandan diplomats were incensed because the West's failure to prevent the genocide was now being compounded by a judicial system that would allow the perpetrators to escape with their lives. For the Rwandans, true national reconciliation would be possible only if there was justice for the genocide, and justice by their terms meant execution for the guilty. Indeed, prosecutions for genocide in Rwanda's domestic judicial system ended in death sentences, producing the paradoxical result that the worst offenders — the architects who were tried at the international tribunal — received lighter sentences than those who were convicted by Rwandan courts for mere participation in the genocide. Although European countries considered Rwanda at fault for this paradox (for engaging in executions in the first place), the Rwandans blamed them for imposing their standards of criminal justice on a sovereign nation with distinct cultural norms. Indeed, it was not the West that had suffered the genocide, and it was not the West that must forge a new way of life from the ashes of the genocide.

Part of the disconnect between the Rwandans and the West stemmed from different attitudes about the death penalty and the underlying rationale for criminal punishment. But the rift exposed a deeper trouble with the international jurisprudence of genocide. It is often remarked that the legal prohibition against the death penalty represents an emerging norm of customary international law. But while there is a growing literature on the death penalty in general, as well as a sizable literature on the international law of genocide, the intersection of the two issues has largely been ignored.

The issue is of more than just historical concern. Iraqi government officials [executed] Saddam Hussein [after convicting him of crimes against humanity]. Indeed, the establishment of an international tribunal to prosecute Hussein was never fully considered because both the U.S. and the Iraqi governments favored keeping the death penalty on the table — an unlikely prospect for an international tribunal. (Similarly, there was never any serious discussion of an international tribunal for [al] Qaeda terrorists.) The abolitionist commitments of many human rights activists and their government supporters have effectively prevented the internationalization of the Iraqi proceedings. . . .

. . . For purposes of this analysis, it is assumed that there is an emerging norm of customary international law that generally prohibits the death penalty. The question . . . is the content of the norm. Does it or should it apply to genocide?

NOTES AND QUESTIONS

1. *Capital punishment.* In June 2007, the Rwandan legislature abolished the death penalty. It appears that this was a pragmatic reaction to the fact that, absent such a move, the ICTR would not transfer cases back to Rwandan courts as it winds up its business.

2. *Sentencing at the ad hoc tribunals.* "Although international criminal law punishes a select few of those who commit the most egregious crimes of concern to the international community at large, its sanctions tend to range from less severe to as severe as the punishments for ordinary murder in many countries. . . . There is something puzzling about this." Mark A. Drumbl, Collective Violence and Individual Punishment: The Criminality of Mass Atrocity, 99 Nw. U. L. Rev. 539, 578 (2004-2005).

Consider the sentence handed down in the case of Dragan Nikolic, a commander in the Susica detention camp in Bosnia. Nikolic admitted to persecuting "Muslim and other non-Serb detainees by subjecting them to murders, rapes and torture. . . . In addition, Dragan Nikolic participated in creating and maintaining an atmosphere of terror in the camp through murders, beatings, sexual violence and other physical and mental abuse. [He] persecuted Muslim and other non-Serb detainees by participating in sexual violence directed at the female detainees." Prosecutor v. Dragan Nikolic, Case No. IT-94-2-S, Sentencing Judgment, ¶¶66-68 (Dec. 18, 2003). Among Nikolic's crimes were nine murders, the repeated torture of five individuals, and delivering many women to be raped and sexually assaulted by "camp guards, special forces, local soldiers and other men." Id. ¶87. Nikolic pleaded guilty, and the prosecutor recommended a single sentence of 15 years' imprisonment.

The ICTY Trial Chambers considered several aggravating factors, including Nikolic's position of authority and the vulnerability of his victims. In addition, the Chambers considered the depravity of the crimes: "[It is] hard to imagine how murder, torture and sexual violence could be committed in a harsher and more brutal way than employed by the Accused, assisted by others. Not one single day and night at the camp passed by without Dragan Nikolic and other co-perpetrators committing barbarous acts. . . . The Accused brutally and sadistically beat the detainees. He would kick and punch detainees and use weapons such as iron bars, axe handles, rifle butts, metal 'knuckles,' truncheons, rubber tubing with lead inside, lengths of wood and wooden bats to beat the detainees. . . . One of the most chilling aspects of the Accused's behaviour was the enjoyment he derived from his acts. . . . When detainees who were being beaten begged to be shot, the Accused would reply: '*A bullet is too expensive to be spent on a Muslim.*'" Id. ¶¶186-187, 189, 192. The court stated that the aggravating factors standing alone would warrant a life sentence, but then considered mitigating factors including Nikolic's "guilty plea, remorse, reconciliation and substantial co-operation with the Prosecution." Id. ¶¶214, 217.

In conclusion, the court rejected the prosecution's sentencing recommendation, stating: "The brutality, the number of crimes committed and the underlying intention to humiliate and degrade would render a sentence such as that recommended unjust. The Trial Chamber believes that it is not only reasonable and responsible, but also necessary in the interests of the victims, their relatives and the international community, to impose a higher sentence than the one recommended by the Parties." Id. ¶281. Instead of the 15 years recommended by the prosecutor, the court sentenced Nikolic to 23 years. The sentence was subsequently reduced on appeal to 20 years. How does the prosecutor's recommended sentence compare to the sentencing practices for murder, torture, and sexual assault with which you are familiar?

At the lengthy end, the ICTY initially sentenced Serbian militia General Radislav Krstić to 46 years for genocide, and Croat officer Tihomir Blaškić to 45 years for failure to prevent or punish atrocities committed by his troops. However, both sentences were greatly reduced when convictions of the two men on several of the charges were reversed on appeal. Krstić, now convicted of aiding and abetting genocide, had his sentence reduced to 35 years, while Blaškić, introducing 8,000 pages of new evidence at his appeal, got 9 years (and early release).

To provide a frame of reference, a study done by the Max Planck Institute at the request of the ICTY is helpful. The researchers did not study actual results in specific criminal cases. Rather, they sent out sample cases framed as crimes against humanity to experts in various countries. They asked the experts to respond with the national norms on sentencing for the crimes (1) under general criminal law in that jurisdiction, and (2) as crimes against humanity if the domestic legislation specifically addressed crimes against humanity. The following summarizes the study's findings with respect to the *maximum* penalties in 2003 for the offense as a general criminal offense (as opposed to a crime against humanity):

Murder carried out by means of participation in shooting:

25 yrs:	Spain (10-25 yrs)
30 yrs:	Belgium (20-30 yrs), Brazil (6-30 yrs)
50 yrs:	Mexico (fine-50 yrs)
Life:	Austria (10 yrs-life), Chile (5 yrs, 1d-life), France (2 yrs-life), Germany (3 yrs-life), Italy (21 yrs-life), Ivory Coast (10 yrs-life), Poland (12 yrs-life), Sweden (10 yrs-life)
Life (mandatory):	Argentina, Canada, England and Wales, Finland, Greece, South Africa, Turkey
Death:	China (10 yrs-death), Russia (8.5 yrs-death), USA (life-death)

Torture carried out by means of sustained and/or repeated beatings:

57 months:	USA
10 yrs:	Austria, Finland, Germany, Sweden
15 yrs:	Chile, Poland
16 yrs:	Brazil, Italy
20 yrs:	France, Greece
24 yrs:	Russia
Life:	Argentina, England, Ivory Coast
Death penalty:	China

Facilitating sexual violence/rape by personally removing or facilitating the removal of female detainees:

2 yrs:	England
9 yrs:	USA
10 yrs:	France, Poland, Sweden
20 yrs:	Brazil, Greece, Ivory Coast
22 yrs:	Belgium
25 yrs:	Argentina
Life:	Austria, Canada, Chile, France, South Africa
Death:	China

Bear in mind as well that those convicted by the Ad Hoc Tribunals may not serve their entire sentence. "The possibility of a defendant's pardon or commutation of a defendant's sentence will depend, in part, on the laws of the State where the defendant is ultimately imprisoned." Allison Marston Danner, Constructing a Hierarchy of Crimes in International Criminal Law Sentencing, 87 Va. L. Rev. 415, 500-501 (2001). "[D]efendants imprisoned in Europe are typically eligible for release after they have served one-half to two-thirds of their sentences." Nancy Amoury Combs, Procuring Guilty Pleas for International Crimes: The Limited Influence of Sentence Discounts, 59 Vand. L. Rev. 69, 116 (2006). For example, the ICTY sentenced Anto Furundžija to 10 years' imprisonment for co-perpetrating torture and to eight years for aiding and abetting in outrages upon personal dignity, including rape. Prosecutor v. Anto Furundžija, Case No. IT-95-17/1-T, Judgment (Dec. 10, 1998). The two sentences were to be served concurrently in Finland. Furundžija was released after six years and eight months.

3. *Differences in sentencing practices between ICTY and ICTR.* While the ICTY and the ICTR both have recourse to a maximum penalty of life imprisonment, there is a "marked disparity between the sentences handed down by the ICTY Trial Chambers and those pronounced by the ICTR Trial Chambers." Stuart Beresford, Unshackling the Paper Tiger — the Sentencing Practices of the Ad Hoc International Criminal Tribunals for the Former Yugoslavia and Rwanda, 1 Intl. Crim. L. Rev. 33, 49 (2001); see also Mark A. Drumbl, Collective Violence and Individual Punishment, 99 Nw. U. L. Rev. 539 (2005). The ICTY almost never issues life sentences and seldom issues sentences of more than 20 years. ICTR, by contrast, has issued more than a dozen life sentences, and most of its sentences have been for 20 years or more. In December 2008, ICTR imposed a life sentence on Col. Théonaste Bagosora, considered by many to be the architect of the Rwandan genocide. The relative predominance of life sentences and longer prison terms by the ICTR may in fact be related to the number of convictions for genocide. Beresford, supra, at 50. In the ICTR, the prosecution has successfully won 16 genocide convictions. By contrast, although the ICTY has found defendants guilty of various types of complicity in genocide, not one defendant has been successfully prosecuted in that tribunal for his own perpetration of genocide.

Another factor may be the somewhat greater prevalence of plea bargaining at the ICTY than at the ICTR. To date, 20 ICTY defendants (34.5 percent) have entered guilty pleas, compared to 6 ICTR defendants (21.7 percent of total convicted). Finally, the statutes of both the ICTY and the ICTR state that the Tribunals "shall have recourse to the general practice regarding prison sentences in the courts of" the former Yugoslavia and Rwanda, respectively. Statute of the Intl. Criminal Tribunal for the Former Yugoslavia art. 24(1); Statute of the Intl. Criminal Tribunal for Rwanda art. 23(1). The Tribunals have held that they are not bound by local practice. See, e.g., Prosecutor v. Dragan Nikolic, Case No. IT-94-2-S, Sentencing Judgment, ¶148 (Dec. 18, 2003); Robert D. Sloane, Sentencing for the "Crime of Crimes": Appraising the Penal Jurisprudence of the International Criminal Tribunal for Rwanda, 5 J. Intl. Crim. Just. 713 (2007). Yet some commentators attribute the more lenient ICTY sentences to a reluctance to depart from the sentencing practice of the former Yugoslavia, where the maximum prison sentence for a capital offense was 20 years. Mary Margaret Penrose, Lest We Fail: The Importance of Enforcement in International Criminal Law, 15 Am. U. Intl. L. Rev. 321, 376 (1999); see also Beresford, supra, at 47-48, 51. In domestic Rwandan courts, by contrast, the most serious offenders were, until recently, subject to a mandatory death sentence, and life sentences are authorized for serious crimes such as murder. Sloane, supra, at 721.

Recall, also, the Rwandan objections to the rejection of the death penalty as a possible sanction under the ICTR. Could this provide a partial explanation for the ICTR's relative willingness to impose life imprisonment, the maximum sentence available?

4. *Sentencing disparities.* Should we be troubled by these sentencing disparities between the ICTY and the ICTR? Assume for the moment that two offenders, one in the former Yugoslavia and one in Rwanda, commit the same crimes against humanity but, upon conviction, the first defendant serves 5 years and the second 25 years in prison. Is there one "correct" sentence for crimes against humanity, regardless of the locality of conviction or the tribunal before which the case is tried? In the United States, a revolution in federal sentencing practices began in the 1980s, in major part due to congressional discomfort with the disparate sentences imposed by various judges in cases involving similar crimes and similarly situated defendants. Congress created the U.S. Sentencing Commission and charged it with articulating rules to constrain the discretion of federal judges in sentencing. (The U.S. Sentencing

Guidelines were considered mandatory until the U.S. Supreme Court found mandatory guidelines to be unconstitutional; accordingly, the guidelines are now advisory only, but are still commonly employed as a benchmark in federal sentencing proceedings.)

In essence, the U.S. Sentencing Commission isolated (and assigned weights to) the various factors that judges had long considered relevant to crafting a sentence. For example, in drug trafficking cases, the principal determinants were the type and amount of drugs at issue; in fraud cases, such factors as the amount of loss involved, whether the fraud targeted vulnerable individuals, whether the defendant abused a position of trust in perpetrating her crime, and the like. Would creating such guidelines for international tribunals make sense? Among the factors cited by the Ad Hoc Tribunals in sentencing are

- the perpetrator's position of authority and abuse of trust (Kambanda),
- participation in planning the crimes (Kambanda, Serushago),
- number of victims (Kambanda),
- sadism or zeal in committing the crimes (Kayishema, Nikolic),
- behavior of the defendant at trial (Kayishema, where one defendant laughed while victims testified),
- cooperation with the prosecutor (Kambanda, Serushago),
- guilty plea including the timing of such a plea (Ruggio, Plavsic),
- voluntary surrender (Serushago),
- family situation of the perpetrator including whether he has children (Serushago),
- age of perpetrator (Erdemović, Serushago),
- expression of remorse (Serushago, Erdemović), and
- duress (Erdemović).

See Andrew N. Keller, Punishment for Violations of International Criminal Law: An Analysis of Sentencing at the ICTY and ICTR, 12 Ind. Intl. & Comp. L. Rev. 53 (2001); Drumbl, Collective Violence and Individual Punishment, supra, at 554, 555, 558-559, 561-565. Can you think of additional factors that ought to be considered? How would you prioritize or weigh these factors?

One of the perceived problems with sentencing proceedings before the Ad Hoc Tribunals is a lack of transparency, and thus accountability for and review of sentencing choices. See, e.g., Jennifer J. Clark, Zero to Life: Sentencing Appeals at the International Criminal Tribunals for the Former Yugoslavia and Rwanda, 96 Geo. L.J. 1685 (2008). Thus, for example, commentators have cited the statutory provision on sentencing that leaves much to the discretion of judges; the judges' general failure to conduct separate sentencing hearings; the judges' habit of setting one overall sentence for multiple crimes, making appellate review of individual sentences for individual crimes difficult; and the failure of Trial Chambers to provide, in writing, sufficient reasons for their sentencing decisions. See, e.g., Sloane, supra, at 4; Keller, supra, at 66-69.

5. *Sentencing rationales.* What purposes do the sanctions handed down by the Ad Hoc Tribunals serve? Mark Drumbl notes that "many different rationales for sentencing — deterrence (whether general or specific), retribution, incapacitation, and rehabilitation — are evoked in different cases." Mark A. Drumbl, Sentencing Policies and Practices in the International Criminal Tribunals, 15 Fed. Sent. R. 140, 143 (2002). How well do you think the sentences handed down by the Tribunals fulfill the most prominent functions, retribution and deterrence? Would a more lenient or

more severe sentencing scheme serve any of the goals of punishment more effectively? What impact could sentencing decisions have on the overarching need for reconciliation in war-torn societies? See generally Stuart Beresford, Unshackling the Paper Tiger—the Sentencing Practices of the Ad Hoc International Criminal Tribunals for the Former Yugoslavia and Rwanda, 1 Intl. Crim. L. Rev. 33 (2001); William A. Schabas, Sentencing by International Tribunals: A Human Rights Approach, 7 Duke J. Comp. & Intl. L. 461, 502 (1997). Is this impact an appropriate consideration in determining sentences for perpetrators of atrocities?

The most detailed and complete study of sentencing practices for atrocity crimes—both by international tribunals and domestic courts—is Mark A. Drumbl, Atrocity, Punishment, and International Law (2007). Not only does Drumbl provide a wealth of useful data, he offers an important analysis of the theories of criminal punishment for atrocity crimes. Drumbl criticizes international tribunals for imposing a single model of legal accountability—Western-style trials followed by lengthy imprisonment for those convicted—on cultures where this model seems like an alien imposition. In Drumbl's view, that model is designed for situations in which criminals are deviant from prevailing social norms. In mass atrocities, however, the norms themselves may be the problem, as was true for example in Nazi Germany and Rwanda. When a murderer is not a deviant but a conformist, what purpose is served by locking him away for decades? That kind of punishment should be reserved for the "conflict entrepreneurs" who instigate the murder programs. Drumbl argues that rather than imposing a one-size-fits-all model of liberal trials and imprisonment, international law should defer to local practices that may instead focus on apology, the payment of compensation, the return of property stolen from the victim, community service, and eventual reintegration of the lower-level criminals into society. Does this seem like a good enough response?

Professor Robert D. Sloane takes a slightly different tack, arguing that the "expressive" capacity of punishment should be the primary justification for international criminal law (ICL) sentencing and that such conventional goals of punishment as deterrence (crime control) and retribution make much less sense in the ICL context. Robert D. Sloane, The Expressive Capacity of International Punishment: The Limits of the National Law Analogy and the Potential of International Criminal Law, 43 Stan. J. Intl. L. 39 (2007). Professor Sloane notes first that ICL differs from national criminal law in at least three significant ways that the national law analogy can obscure:

> First, unlike national criminal law, ICL purports to serve multiple communities, including both literal ones—for example, ethnic or national communities—and the figurative "international community," which, needless to say, is not monolithic; it consists of multiple, often competing, constituencies and interests. . . . At sentencing, arrayed against these diverse communal interests and objectives is the convicted's core liberty interest.
>
> Second, the national law analogy can obscure the collective character of ICL crimes . . . , a feature that distinguishes them from most similar crimes of violence in the national sphere. Arguably, the collective nature of the victim of international crimes . . . aggravates the culpability of the perpetrator, just as the prejudicial motive and harm of a bias crime render an assault or murder, for example, more blameworthy because of secondary harms. At the same time, the collective nature of the perpetrator—his role and status relative to the nation-state, military organization, or other collective entity implicated by ICL crimes—arguably mitigates culpability in some circumstances insofar as collectivity might be thought to diffuse moral responsibility, mitigating each perpetrator's guilt in some proportion to that of the collective.

Third, perpetrators of ICL crimes often act in a normative universe that differs dramatically from the relatively stable, well-ordered society that most national criminal justice systems take as their baseline. ICL crimes typically occur during periods of war, ethnic conflict, or other societal breakdown characterized by the erosion, if not inversion, of basic social norms against violence, either generally or relative to certain demonized and dehumanized ethnic, political, religious, national, or racial groups. Conceptualizing war criminals and *génocidaires* as deviants from fundamental societal norms may make less sense where their criminal conduct, while deviant by reference to international norms and general principles of law common to civilized nations, nonetheless becomes in some sense *normative* within the criminal's community, be it national, ethnic, racial, or martial.

Id. at 41-42. Professor Sloane questions whether deterrence is a realistic goal of ICL sentencing, arguing, inter alia, that deterrence

requires the credible and authoritative communication of a threatened sanction. . . . It is one thing for a criminal justice system clearly to communicate a threat within a literal community. . . . It is quite another for a culturally foreign and geographically distant tribunal, which lacks its own police force and enforces the law sporadically and inconsistently at best, to communicate a credible threat authoritatively. . . . [Further,] if the rational-actor model of deterrence is suspect in the national context, it is exponentially so in the international, where war, large-scale violence, and collective pathologies, as well as the institutional and resource limitations of ICL, can be expected to distort the viability of the familiar cost-benefit calculus on which that model depends. It is doubtful that the average war criminal . . . weighs the risk of prosecution, discounted by the likelihood of apprehension, against the perceived benefits of his crimes.

Id. at 72. Professor Sloane also contends that

despite the prevalence of secular philosophical versions, retributivism — with its characteristic discourse of "just deserts," blameworthiness, and the restoration of some moral balance — remains strongly redolent of religious notions of justice ill-suited to a diverse international community of states and peoples. And secular justifications for retributivism transposed to the ICL context make little sense largely because they presuppose a more coherent, univocal, and stable community than international law offers.

Id. at 77-78. Professor Sloane argues that

the expressive dimensions of punishment best capture both the nature of international sentencing and its realistic institutional capacity to make a difference given the legal, political, and resource constraints that will continue, for the foreseeable future, to afflict international criminal tribunals. . . . ICL's ability to contribute to the lofty objectives ascribed to it depends far more on enhancing its value as authoritative expression than on ill-fated efforts to identity the "right" punishment, whatever that could mean, for often unconscionable crimes.

Id. at 42-43. This expressive rationale counsels, he argues, for "first, the institutionalization of sentencing hearings as a vital component of ICL trials; [and] second, greater attention to context and the role of the defendant vis-à-vis any implicated collective entities (states, armies, tribes, and so forth) as relevant aggravating or mitigating circumstances and a jurisprudence that distinguishes rank-and-file perpetrators from the architects and orchestrators of ICL crimes." Id. at 44.

What do you think?

CHAPTER
5

Jurisdiction

What gives anyone authority to make and enforce criminal law across borders? Criminal law border-crossing defines the entire subject of international criminal law, so no question is more basic. Not only is it basic, it is also difficult. On the classical Westphalian conception of state sovereignty, a state exerts sovereign power over its own territory, but not over the territory of any other state. How, then, can states exercise criminal jurisdiction over conduct in another sovereign state? For that matter, how can an international body like the United Nations or the International Criminal Court do so? Created by multilateral treaties, these bodies can exercise power only if their states parties have the power themselves.

For lawyers, these are questions about *jurisdiction*, and we will explore the principles governing transnational jurisdiction in the present chapter. We begin by studying the international law principles governing states' assertion of extraterritorial criminal jurisdiction. As always, these may or may not play a significant role in states' domestic law. Some states' domestic law gives international law pride of place; other states absorb international law but give it a subsidiary role. We will study this issue by looking at one particular domestic legal system, that of the United States. Parallel issues, of course, arise for other states. As we will see, U.S. domestic law includes international law principles in the tests it has evolved of whether a criminal statute applies extraterritorially, but international law is only a subsidiary factor in answering the question.

A. PRINCIPLES OF TRANSNATIONAL JURISDICTION IN INTERNATIONAL LAW

International law does not leave the issue of jurisdiction entirely to states' domestic law, which, in a worst-case scenario, might expand jurisdiction at the whims of an overreaching legislature or prosecutor. Such expansion might be proper under domestic law but nevertheless breach international legal principles by infringing on other states' sovereignty. We begin by examining the international law principles governing jurisdiction.

1.   Three Forms of Jurisdiction

International lawyers generally distinguish three separate issues of international jurisdiction:

RESTATEMENT (THIRD) OF THE FOREIGN RELATIONS LAW OF THE UNITED STATES

(1987)

§401 CATEGORIES OF JURISDICTION

Under international law, a state is subject to limitations on

(a) jurisdiction to prescribe, i.e., to make its law applicable to the activities, relations, or status of persons, or the interests of persons in things, whether by legislation, by executive act or order, by administrative rule or regulation, or by determination of a court;

(b) jurisdiction to adjudicate, i.e., to subject persons or things to the process of its courts or administrative tribunals, whether in civil or in criminal proceedings, whether or not the state is a party to the proceedings;

(c) jurisdiction to enforce, i.e., to induce or compel compliance or to punish noncompliance with its laws or regulations, whether through the courts or by use of executive, administrative, police, or other nonjudicial action.

NOTES AND QUESTIONS

Jurisdiction to prescribe raises the basic question of international criminal law: Does state A have the authority to extend the reach of its criminal law to conduct committed in state B?

Jurisdiction to adjudicate concerns a different issue. Even if state A has jurisdiction to prescribe certain conduct committed in state B, A's courts may lack jurisdiction to decide cases involving conduct committed in B. To take a prominent recent example, the U.S. government argued that U.S. courts lack jurisdiction over Guantánamo Naval Base in Cuba, so that U.S. courts could not hear habeas corpus motions filed on behalf of foreigners detained at Guantánamo. The district court agreed, but a divided Supreme Court eventually reversed.[1] The government did not dispute that the United States has jurisdiction to prescribe in Guantánamo; but jurisdiction to prescribe does not necessarily imply jurisdiction to adjudicate.

Jurisdiction to enforce raises issues distinct from both of these. Here, the principal question is a practical one: When (or how) can a state conduct a criminal investigation, or make an arrest, in another country? In practice, states cooperate with each other in law enforcement efforts but thorny issues arise when cooperation fails. Sometimes, states will conduct their own investigations in other countries without the permission of local authorities, or even make arrests in other countries that — because the other country is not cooperating — may amount to kidnappings under the domestic law of the country where the arrest is made. What are the legal

---

1. Rasul v. Bush, 215 F. Supp. 2d 55 (D.D.C. 2002); Rasul v. United States, 542 U.S. 466 (2004).

consequences in such cases? We will explore some of these issues in Chapter 8 on transnational evidence gathering and again in Chapter 9 on extradition.

Although the three categories of jurisdiction raise distinct issues, jurisdiction to prescribe is by far the most important in practice, and it is the one we shall focus on in the materials that follow.

2. *Jurisdiction to Prescribe: Basic Principles*

Ultimately, the question of what kinds of jurisdiction states can assert boils down to what the legitimate functions of states are. States consist, at bottom, of territory and people; and so it will come as no surprise that the two fundamental bases for jurisdiction are territorial and personal. In addition, international law recognizes that states have a legitimate interest in the security of their own basic interests, including their borders and their currency, and so protection of these interests creates another basis for jurisdiction. Finally, international law recognizes a handful of crimes as so heinous or so difficult for a single state to police that any state should be able to assert jurisdiction over alleged perpetrators if the state has them in its custody.

For this reason, authorities (including section 402 of the *Restatement*) recognize five jurisdictional principles in international law, including international criminal law:

1. Territorial principle. This is jurisdiction over crimes committed within the state's territory (including by extension "territories" such as ships at sea flying the state's flag).

But what does it mean for a crime to be committed within the state's territory? If Jones stands on the Canadian side of the border and shoots Smith, who is standing on the U.S. side, has the crime been committed in U.S. territory or in Canadian territory?

The law answers "both." The shooting is a single, unitary act, one part of which occurs in Canada and one in the United States. We can analogize the shooting to a punch in the nose. If someone asks, "Where is the punch? In the fist or in the nose?" the only plausible answer is "in both." In our shooting example, Jones is the *subject* who performs the shooting (in Canada), and Smith (in the United States) is the *object* of the shooting. The action includes both subject and object, and therefore the shooting takes place in both territories.

Lawyers therefore distinguish two kinds of territorial jurisdiction:

- *Subjective territorial jurisdiction* exists when the perpetrator's conduct occurs in the state's territory.
- *Objective territorial jurisdiction* — known more simply as *effects jurisdiction* — exists when the effect of the criminal action is located in the state's territory.

In our trans-border shooting example, then, international law permits Canada to take jurisdiction over Jones's misdeed based on the subjective territorial principle, while the United States can take jurisdiction under the effects (objective territorial) principle.

2. Nationality principle. This is jurisdiction over crimes committed by a state's nationals (sometimes including permanently resident aliens). It is sometimes called "active personality" jurisdiction.

3. Passive personality principle. This is jurisdiction over crimes committed against a state's nationals. The perpetrator of a crime is the "active" personality, and the victim is the "passive" personality.

Nationality (active personality) jurisdiction and passive personality jurisdiction are the two forms of personal jurisdiction.

4. Protective principle. This is jurisdiction over a limited set of crimes committed against a state's most vital interests.

5. Universality principle, giving rise to "universal jurisdiction." This is jurisdiction that a state takes regardless of where the crime was committed, or whether it damages that state's vital interests, or what the nationality of the perpetrator or victim might be. Historically, universal jurisdiction was based on nothing more than having custody of the accused person; hence the older authorities defined universal jurisdiction principally "by reference to the custody of the person committing the offence."[2]

Today, lawyers are more apt to think about universal jurisdiction as a special case reserved for a small set of the most troubling crimes, rather than defining it in terms of custody. (Indeed, as we shall see, some states have asserted universal jurisdiction even without having custody of the accused offender.) The chief point, however, is that universal jurisdiction unmoors states from the limits of territory, nationality of perpetrator or victim, and vital interests in the other principles.

It will readily be seen that these five principles will often allow more than one state to assert jurisdiction. Jurisdiction may be exclusive in some instances, permissive in others, or even concurrent (overlapping). Thus, conflicts can easily arise. Suppose that a U.S. national, living in Paris, swindles a Russian national living in Buenos Aires. Under the IL jurisdictional principles, four different states could assert jurisdiction over this crime. (Which principle goes with which state?) The following principle is intended to help states resolve jurisdictional conflicts:

RESTATEMENT (THIRD) OF THE FOREIGN RELATIONS LAW OF THE UNITED STATES

(1987)

§403. LIMITATIONS ON JURISDICTION TO PRESCRIBE

(1) Even when one of the bases for jurisdiction under §402 is present, a state may not exercise jurisdiction to prescribe law with respect to a person or activity having connections with another state when the exercise of such jurisdiction is unreasonable.

Subsection (2) of §403 goes on to itemize eight factors for determining when the exercise of jurisdiction is unreasonable: territorial links; other connections between the state and the person responsible for the conduct; the kind of activity to be regulated; justified expectations; the importance of the regulation to the international political, legal, or economic system; tradition; other states' interests in regulating the activity; and the likelihood of conflict with regulation by another state. See §403(2)(a)-(h). And subsection (3) cautions that when it would not be unreasonable for two or more states to assert jurisdiction, "each state has an obligation to evaluate

---

2. Research in International Law under the Auspices of the Faculty of the Harvard Law School — Jurisdiction with Respect to Crime, 29 Am. J. Intl. L. 435, 519-520 (Supp. 1935).

its own as well as the other state's interest in exercising jurisdiction . . . ; a state should defer to the other state if that state's interest is clearly greater."

No internationally agreed rule or mechanism exists for resolving competing jurisdictional claims. Conflicts over jurisdiction can be intensely political. Although §403 lays out an eight-factor legal test that courts can use to sort out competing jurisdictional claims, jurisdictional conflicts are often worked out through diplomatic channels, with one state abandoning its jurisdictional claims to accommodate political requests or pressure from another.

3. The Territorial Principle

Territoriality is the most important jurisdictional principle. It is hardly controversial that when a perpetrator commits a crime in a state's territory, the state can exert jurisdiction over the crime. In our earlier terminology, *subjective territorial jurisdiction* is pretty straightforward. When we turn to *objective territorial* or *effects* jurisdiction, however, vexing questions can arise. What effects are we talking about, how directly must the perpetrator cause them, and how far do states get to reach?

The cases and materials in this section illustrate evolving thought, both in and out of the United States, about extraterritorial assertions of jurisdiction and the limits of the territorial principle.

REPORT ON EXTRATERRITORIAL CRIME AND THE CUTTING CASE

in Papers Relating to the Foreign Relations of the United States for the Year 1887, at 757, 761-766, 771, 778-779, 813, 839-840 (1888)

[EDS. NOTE: In 1886, A.K. Cutting, a U.S. national who edited a newspaper in Paso del Norte, Mexico, published insults in it against Emiglio Medina, a Mexican who proposed to open a rival newspaper. Medina filed a criminal complaint against Cutting in Mexico for defamation, which was discharged after Cutting agreed to publish a retraction (in the case, this was called a conciliation). Cutting then crossed the Rio Grande to El Paso, Texas, where — in a U.S. newspaper — he repeated the insults and indeed heaped additional insults on Medina. On returning to Mexico Cutting was arrested and imprisoned in a "loathesome and filthy" cell, "locked up with eight or ten other prisoners . . . in one room, 18 by 40 feet, with only one door, which is locked at night, making it a close room in every respect, there being no other means of ventilation." Report, at 758. The U.S. government protested, and an exchange of diplomatic and legal arguments ensued. Mexico refused to release Cutting. The Mexican ambassador explained that Article 186 of the Mexican penal code granted extraterritorial jurisdiction over crimes such as Cutting's defamation of Medina, while the principle of judicial independence prevented the Mexican government from interfering with the legal process. However, in response to the U.S. protests, Mexico brought Cutting to trial. Judge Zubia found Cutting guilty of violating Article 646 of the Mexican penal code, a criminal defamation statute. Cutting was sentenced to a year at hard labor, a $600 fine, and payment of civil damages to Medina.

The case then went to the supreme court of Chihuahua. Cutting refused to choose a lawyer, so the court appointed a public defender. Medina, however, withdrew his complaint, apparently for "the quieting of the alarm consequent upon his complaint." Report, at 767. (One may read between the lines that U.S. protests led the Mexican government to pressure Medina to drop the complaint.) The court nevertheless affirmed Cutting's conviction, but, because Medina had withdrawn the complaint, the court reduced Cutting's sentence to time served.

The materials that follow are drawn from a lengthy State Department report on the Cutting affair. Included is the opinion by Judge Zubia; a critique of the opinion by John B. Moore, Third Assistant Secretary of State (a legal advisor); and a small portion of Moore's vast analysis of the international law issues raised by the case.]

JUDGE ZUBIA'S OPINION

It appears, 3. That the parties being present before the mediating judge, agreed on the publication ... of a retraction which was written by Medina and corrected by Cutting, the publication to be made four times in English, and ... also in Spanish.

It appears, 4. That Cutting, instead of complying with the agreement as stipulated in the conciliation, published on the 20th of the same month of June a retraction only in English ... , in small type and with material errors that rendered it almost unintelligible, and published ... against Medina, and denounced as contemptible the agreement of conciliation. ...

Considering, 2. That although it is true that there was in regard to this matter an act of conciliation, which would have satisfied the plaintiff if it had been carried out, it is also true that the terms of this act were not complied with, and that, for this reason, the responsibility of the penal offense remains the same.

Considering, 3. That the proof of the lack of fulfillment of the compromise entered into in the judgment of conciliation is actually in the communication published by Cutting in the El Paso Sunday Herald, in which he ratified the original assertion that Emigdio Medina was a fraud and a swindler, and at the same time in the article published in El Centinela of the same date, leaving out all the capital letters and putting the name of Medina in microscopic type in order to make the reading of it difficult.

Considering, 4. That ratification, according to the dictionary of Escriche, is the confirmation and sanction of what has been said or done, it is retroactive, and by consequence does not constitute an act different from that to which it refers: "*Ratihabitio retrotrahitur ad initium,*" [ratification returns back to the beginning] nor does new responsibility, distinct from that which originally existed, arise therefrom.

Considering, 5. That this being so, the criminal responsibility of Cutting arose from the article published in El Centinela, issued in this town, which article was ratified in the Texas newspaper, which ratification, however, did not constitute a new penal offense to be punished with a different penalty from that which was applicable to the first publication.

Considering, 6. That even on the supposition, not admitted, that the defamation arose from the communication published on the 20th of June in the El Paso Sunday Herald, Article 186 of the Mexican penal code provides that—

"Penal offenses committed in a foreign country by a Mexican against Mexicans or foreigners, or by a foreigner against Mexicans," may be punished in the Republic and according to its laws, subject to the following conditions:

1. That the accused be in the Republic, whether he came voluntarily or has been brought by extradition proceedings; ... 4. That the breach of law of which he is accused shall have the character of a penal offense both in the country in which it was committed and in the Republic; .... —requisites which have been fully met in the present case, for ... the penal offense of which Cutting is accused has that character in the country in which it was committed and in the Republic, as can be

seen in the penal code in force in the State of Texas, Articles 616, 617, 618, and 619, and in the penal code of the State of Chihuahua, Articles 642 and 646....

Considering, 7. That according to the rule of law *Judex non de legibus, sed secundum leges debet judicare* [a judge is not a legislator, but is required to follow the law], it does not belong to the judge who decides to examine the principle laid down in said Article 186, but to apply it fully, it being the law in force in the State.

Considering, 8. That this general rule has no other limitation than that expressed in Article 126 of the general constitution, which says "This constitution, the laws of the Congress of the Union passed in pursuance thereof, and all the treaties made or to be made by the President of the Republic with the approval of the Congress, shall be the supreme law of the whole Union. The judges of each State shall act according to said constitution, laws, and treaties, notwithstanding the existence of contrary provisions in the constitutions or laws of the States."

Considering, 9. That the said Article 186 of the penal code, far from being contrary to the supreme law or to the treaties made by the President of the Republic, has for its object, as is seen in the expository part of the same code, page 38, "the free operation of the principle on which the right to punish is founded, to wit, justice united to utility."

Considering, 10. That even supposing, without conceding it, that the penal offense of defamation was committed in the territory of Texas the circumstance that the newspaper El Paso Sunday Herald was circulated in this town, of which circumstance Medina complained, and which was the ground of ordering the seizure of the copies which might be found in the office of Cutting, in this same town, properly constituted the consummation of the crime....

Considering, 15. That the responsibility of Cutting is fully proved, since it appears in credible documents which have in nowise been contradicted by their author; and if any doubt should exist respecting the malicious intent with which the first publication was made, it would disappear in view of the subsequent ratifications made in the El Paso Sunday Herald and in the Evening Tribune, in which Cutting expressly says that Emigdio Medina is a fraud, swindler, coward, and thief.[3] ...

THE SENTENCE

In view of the foregoing ..., it is ordered and adjudged as follows:

First. For the penal offense of defamation committed against the person of Emigdio Medina, A.K. Cutting is sentenced to serve a year at hard labor and pay a fine of $600, or, in default thereof, endure additional imprisonment of a hundred days.

Second. He is also sentenced to pay the civil indemnity, to be fixed according to the provisions of Article 313 of the penal code....

MOORE'S REJOINDER

From this decision the following facts appear: 1. Premise 6 ["Considering, 6"] discloses that the original ground on which Mr. Cutting was held to answer the charge of defamation was the publication of the card in the El Paso (Texas) Herald.

---

3. [Judge Zubia's note 1:] The epithets applied by Cutting to Medina in the card published in Texas, as appears from a copy of the card now before the writer, were "fraud" and "dead beat."

2. Consideration 3 ["Considering, 3"] discloses that the publication of the card in the Texas newspaper was treated as a breach of the "conciliation," which, having once been entered into, must have been violated by Cutting before Medina could have maintained a criminal suit for the defamation in El Centinela of June 6. It thus appears that the "conciliation" was held to be binding on Cutting in Texas, and consequently to have extraterritorial effect.

3. Consideration 6 discloses that Mr. Cutting was also held on the ground that the publication in Texas constituted of itself a distinct and complete offense, punishable under Article 186 of the penal code.

4. Consideration 6 also discloses that in order to bring the case within the provisions of Article 186, the Texas code was introduced to show that the publication in the Texas newspaper constituted a penal offense in that State. Thus Judge Zubia became the vicarious interpreter of the Texas criminal law, and substituting himself, by authority of Article 186, for the judge and jury required for the trial in that State of the alleged violation of its laws, decided that such violation had been committed.

The importance of this observation can be appreciated only when we take into account that under section 2291 of the Texas code, "*it is no offense to publish true statements of fact* as to the qualification of any person for any occupation, profession, or trade;" and that, under the constitution of Texas (Art. 1, sec. 6), "in all indictments for libels, the jury shall have the right *to determine the law and the facts,* under the direction of the court, as in other cases." Under these legislative and constitutional provisions it would be impossible for any judge, domestic or foreign, to say, or for any expert to prove before a foreign tribunal, that the publication of the statement in question was a criminal libel in Texas. Yet, notwithstanding the rule that no penal law is extraterritorial, and in spite of the consideration that for a foreign tribunal to undertake to execute penally a law of the United States against a citizen of the United States may justly be, and in the case in question actually was, regarded as an offense against the United States, the Mexican judge not only undertook to interpret and apply the Texas law of criminal libel against a citizen of the United States, but interpreted and applied it in a manner flagrantly at variance with the methods and guarantees of the fundamental law of the State that enacted it.

It has sometimes been argued that the publication in the Texas newspaper of the card in relation to Medina gave the Mexican court unquestionable jurisdiction in the premises, because it was a violation of the "conciliation," which, being in the nature of a contract, was binding on the parties everywhere; and that, had the court proceeded on this ground alone, the United States would have had no cause for complaint. The fallacy of this argument should seem apparent.

It is true that the proceeding defined in Mexican law as a "conciliation" imports an agreement between parties, and thus bears some formal analogy to a private contract; but it also imports a compromise of a pre-existing criminal liability, which revives if the defendant violate the terms of the "conciliation." To argue, therefore, that the fact of publication in the Texas newspaper was properly held to be a violation of the "conciliation," and to be attended with all the consequences of such violation, is merely to concede, in another form, but to the full extent, the claim asserted in Article 186, and enforced in the present case, that foreigners may incur liability to criminal prosecution in Mexico for acts wholly committed and consummated in a foreign country.

This conclusion is not affected by the fact stated in Judge Zubia's decision that where the terms of a conciliation have been violated, the prosecution relates back to the original offense; nor mitigated by the argument sometimes advanced, that the "act of conciliation" is purely voluntary. To the first suggestion it is sufficient to reply that the question whether the breach of a "conciliation" revives or creates liability to criminal prosecution is not material. It is enough that the breach restores that liability which the "conciliation" had removed. As to the second point, it is only necessary to advert to the fact that, while a defendant is not legally compelled to sign a "conciliation," it may afford the means, and the only means, of escape from the uncertainties and tribulations of criminal prosecution and its possibly grave consequences.

To concede that a "conciliation" may have extraterritorial force would be to permit Mexico to impose upon citizens of the United States while in Mexico the burden of continued obedience to Mexican penal law, even after their return to their own country. From this burden their only escape would be to renounce the benefits of the provisions of Mexican law relating to the "act of conciliation" and undergo criminal prosecution. . . .

Moore's Analysis of the IL Jurisdictional Issue

[Moore's examination of the issue of territorial jurisdiction runs to 70 pages of small print, exhaustively canvassing British and U.S. case law; jurisdictional legislation from 22 European and Latin American countries; scholarly opinion ("the opinion of the publicists"); and international precedents — all of this, one might add, from apparently untranslated sources, long before the existence of databases or digests. This is the hardcore, old-school method of ascertaining customary international law through the sweat of one's brow.

Moore concedes that the effects principle applies. "The principle that a man who outside of a country willfully puts in motion a force to take effect in it is answerable at the place where the evil is done, is recognized in the criminal jurisprudence of all countries." Report, at 771. Nevertheless, he concludes "that in no case has an English or an American court assumed jurisdiction, even under statutes couched in the most general language, to try and sentence a foreigner for acts done by him abroad, unless they were brought, either by an immediate effect or by direct and continuous causal relationship, within the territorial jurisdiction of the court." Id. at 778-779. He finds, further, that "among all the countries whose legislation has been examined Russia and Greece are the only ones whose assertion of extraterritorial jurisdiction is as extensive and absolute in form as that of Mexico." Id. at 791. He continues:

> There being no principle of international law that permits the tribunals of a nation to try and punish foreigners for acts done by them outside of the national territory or jurisdiction, *it necessarily follows that any assumption to do so, in respect to particular crimes, must rest, as an exception to the rule, either upon the general concurrence of nations, in respect to the crimes in question, or upon an express convention. . . . It must be shown that Article 186 is sustained both in amplitude of extent and in form by a general concurrence of positive legislation.* This, as we have seen, can not be done.

Id. at 813. Emphasis in original. He then concludes:]

Three causes have operated during the present century to diminish extraterritorial pretensions in criminal matters: (1) The growth of the idea of nationality and of national equality; (2) the development and extension of commercial intercourse; (3) the more general recognition and performance by independent states of their rights and duties under international law.

The first cause has operated to produce a clearer apprehension of the objects of national existence and of the bounds of national authority; the second has rendered more apparent the necessity of personal immunity from vexatious and unjust prose-cutions under foreign and unknown laws; the third has made governments more ready to abandon assumptions of authority which infringe the rights of other sovereign powers.

The infliction of punishment involves an exercise of power, and power implies subjection. . . . For a nation to hold its penal laws to be binding on all persons within the territory of another state, is to assert a right of sovereignty over the latter, and impair its independence. . . .

NOTES AND QUESTIONS: THE CUTTING CASE

1. Cutting made a contract—the "conciliation" with Medina—in which the criminal complaint against him was dropped in return for his retraction. He then breached the contract in Texas—or at least that is what Judge Zubia's opinion finds. Why shouldn't the criminal complaint be reinstated?

2. Moore complains that the Mexican jurisdiction statute, which requires "that the breach of law of which he is accused shall have the character of a penal offense both in the country in which it was committed and in the Republic," makes a Mexican judge "the vicarious interpreter of the Texas criminal law, . . . substituting himself . . . for the judge and jury required for the trial in that State of the alleged violation of its laws." Is this fair? Doesn't the Mexican statute merely require the judge to determine that defamation is a crime both in Mexico and the United States? That is apparently how Judge Zubia reads it: He proves that the requirement is satisfied simply by listing the antidefamation statutes in Chihuahua and Texas.

As we will see when we turn to the topic of extradition, judges routinely make judgments that alleged behavior is criminal both in their own state and in the foreign state that has made an extradition request. That is because the so-called dual crim-inality rule is built into most extradition treaties: A person can be extradited only when the alleged conduct is criminal in both the state requesting extradition and the state that receives the request. Is Judge Zubia doing anything more than verifying dual criminality for defamation?

3. Suppose that Medina, as a newspaper publisher, would count as a "public figure" under U.S. law. In that case, under today's law, Cutting's criticisms of Medina would be protected under the First Amendment. (Not so in 1887, before the First Amend-ment protections of freedom of speech and of the press had been incorporated into the Fourteenth Amendment and applied to the U.S. states.) Should Mexico be able to exert jurisdiction over constitutionally protected conduct in El Paso? Suppose that tomorrow a dictatorship makes it a crime to criticize the Great Leader and arrests a U.S. journalist who has done so in a U.S. publication. Can this be a legitimate exercise of jurisdiction under the objective territorial principle? What if the dictator can demonstrate that the journalist's writings had stimulated political unrest in his country?

The basic puzzle of jurisdiction to prescribe in a world of sovereign states may be explained quite simply. On the one hand, a sovereign state should have the right to enact any laws it wishes, including criminal statutes with extraterritorial application. On the other hand, a sovereign state should have the sole power to legislate conduct in its own territory. Which of these rights is more basic—the right of every sovereign state to define the jurisdiction of its own criminal laws or the right of every sovereign state to exercise sole legislative power over its own territory? The following is the best-known international case on this question.

THE CASE OF THE S.S. LOTUS
(FRANCE v. TURKEY)

Permanent Court of International Justice
1927 P.C.I.J. (ser. A) No. 10 (Sept. 7)

... On August 2nd, 1926, just before midnight, a collision occurred between the French mail steamer *Lotus*, proceeding to Constantinople, and the Turkish collier *Boz-Kourt*, between five and six nautical miles to the north of Cape Sigri (Mitylene). The *Boz-Kourt*, which was cut in two, sank, and eight Turkish nationals who were on board perished. After having done everything possible to succour the shipwrecked persons, of whom ten were able to be saved, the *Lotus* continued on its course to Constantinople, where it arrived on August 3rd.

At the time of the collision, the officer of the watch on board the *Lotus* was Monsieur Demons, a French citizen, lieutenant in the merchant service and first officer of the ship, whilst the movements of the *Boz-Kourt* were directed by its captain, Hassan Bey, who was one of those saved from the wreck. ...

On August 5th, Lieutenant Demons was requested by the Turkish authorities to go ashore to give evidence. The examination, the length of which incidentally resulted in delaying the departure of the *Lotus*, led to the placing under arrest of Lieutenant Demons — without previous notice being given to the French Consul-General — and Hassan Bey, amongst others. This arrest, which has been characterized by the Turkish Agent as arrest pending trial (*arrestation preventive*), was effected in order to ensure that the criminal prosecution instituted against the two officers, on a charge of manslaughter, by the Public Prosecutor of Stamboul, on the complaint of the families of the victims of the collision, should follow its normal course.

The case was first heard by the Criminal Court of Stamboul on August 28th. On that occasion, Lieutenant Demons submitted that the Turkish Courts had no jurisdiction; the Court, however, overruled his objection. When the proceedings were resumed on September 11th, Lieutenant Demons demanded his release on bail: this request was complied with on September 13th, the bail being fixed at 6,000 Turkish pounds.

On September 15th, the Criminal Court delivered its judgment, the terms of which have not been communicated to the Court by the Parties. It is, however, common ground, that it sentenced Lieutenant Demons to eighty days' imprisonment and a fine of twenty-two pounds, Hassan Bey being sentenced to a slightly more severe penalty. ...

The prosecution was instituted in pursuance of Turkish legislation. ...

Article 6 of the Turkish Penal Code ... runs as follows:

> "Any foreigner who, apart from the cases contemplated by Article 4, commits an offence abroad to the prejudice of Turkey or of a Turkish subject, for which offence Turkish law prescribes a penalty involving loss of freedom for a minimum period of not less than one year, shall be punished in accordance with the Turkish Penal Code provided that he is arrested in Turkey. The penalty shall however be reduced by one third and instead of the death penalty, twenty years of penal servitude shall be awarded. ..."

... The Court is asked to state whether or not the principles of international law prevent Turkey from instituting criminal proceedings against Lieutenant Demons under Turkish law. ...

... [T]he Court must now ascertain which were the principles of international law that the prosecution of Lieutenant Demons could conceivably be said to contravene.

It is Article 15 of the Convention of Lausanne of July 24th, 1923, respecting conditions of residence and business and jurisdiction, which refers the contracting Parties to the principles of international law as regards the delimitation of their respective jurisdiction.

This clause is as follows:

"Subject to the provisions of Article 16, all questions of jurisdiction shall, as between Turkey and the other contracting Powers, be decided in accordance with the principles of international law." . . .

The Court, having to consider whether there are any rules of international law which may have been violated by the prosecution in pursuance of Turkish law of Lieutenant Demons, is confronted in the first place by a question of principle which, in the written and oral arguments of the two Parties, has proved to be a fundamental one. The French Government contends that the Turkish Courts, in order to have jurisdiction, should be able to point to some title to jurisdiction recognized by international law in favour of Turkey. On the other hand, the Turkish Government takes the view that Article 15 allows Turkey jurisdiction whenever such jurisdiction does not come into conflict with a principle of international law.

The latter view seems to be in conformity with the special agreement itself, No. 1 of which asks the Court to say whether Turkey has acted contrary to the principles of international law and, if so, what principles. According to the special agreement, therefore, it is not a question of stating principles which would permit Turkey to take criminal proceedings, but of formulating the principles, if any, which might have been violated by such proceedings.

This way of stating the question is also dictated by the very nature and existing conditions of international law.

International law governs relations between independent States. The rules of law binding upon States therefore emanate from their own free will as expressed in conventions or by usages generally accepted as expressing principles of law and established in order to regulate the relations between these co-existing independent communities or with a view to the achievement of common aims. Restrictions upon the independence of States cannot therefore be presumed.

Now the first and foremost restriction imposed by international law upon a State is that—failing the existence of a permissive rule to the contrary—it may not exercise its power in any form in the territory of another State. In this sense jurisdiction is certainly territorial; it cannot be exercised by a State outside its territory except by virtue of a permissive rule derived from international custom or from a convention.

It does not, however, follow that international law prohibits a State from exercising jurisdiction in its own territory, in respect of any case which relates to acts which have taken place abroad, and in which it cannot rely on some permissive rule of international law. Such a view would only be tenable if international law contained a general prohibition to States to extend the application of their laws and the jurisdiction of their courts to persons, property and acts outside their territory, and if, as an exception to this general prohibition, it allowed States to do so in certain specific cases. But this is certainly not the case under international law as it stands at present. Far from laying down a general prohibition to the effect that States may not extend the application of their laws and the jurisdiction of their courts to persons, property and acts outside their territory, it leaves them in this respect a wide measure of discretion which is only limited in certain cases by prohibitive rules; as regards other cases, every State remains free to adopt the principles which it regards as best and most suitable. . . .

In these circumstances all that can be required of a State is that it should not overstep the limits which international law places upon its jurisdiction; within these limits, its title to exercise jurisdiction rests in its sovereignty.

It follows from the foregoing that the contention of the French Government to the effect that Turkey must in each case be able to cite a rule of international law authorizing her to exercise jurisdiction, is opposed to the generally accepted international law to which Article 13 of the Convention of Lausanne refers. . . .

Though it is true that in all systems of law the principle of the territorial character of criminal law is fundamental, it is equally true that all or nearly all these systems of law extend their action to offences committed outside the territory of the State which adopts them, and they do so in ways which vary from State to State. The territoriality of criminal law, therefore, is not an absolute principle of international law and by no means coincides with territorial sovereignty.

This situation may be considered from two different standpoints corresponding to the points of view respectively taken up by the Parties. According to one of these standpoints, the principle of freedom, in virtue of which each State may regulate its legislation at its discretion, provided that in so doing it does not come in conflict with a restriction imposed by international law, would also apply as regards law governing the scope of jurisdiction in criminal cases. According to the other standpoint, the exclusively territorial character of law relating to this domain constitutes a principle which, except as otherwise expressly provided, would, *ipso facto*, prevent States from extending the criminal jurisdiction of their courts beyond their frontiers; the exceptions in question, which include for instance extraterritorial jurisdiction over nationals and over crimes directed against public safety, would therefore rest on special permissive rules forming part of international law.

Adopting, for the purposes of the argument, the standpoint of the latter of these two systems, it must be recognized that, in the absence of a treaty provision, its correctness depends upon whether there is a custom having the force of law establishing it. The same is true as regards the applicability of this system — assuming it to have been recognized as sound — in the particular case. It follows that, even from this point of view, before ascertaining whether there may be a rule of international law expressly allowing Turkey to prosecute a foreigner for an offence committed by him outside Turkey, it is necessary to begin by establishing both that the system is well-founded and that it is applicable in the particular case. Now, in order to establish the first of these points, one must, as has just been seen, prove the existence of a principle of international law restricting the discretion of States as regards criminal legislation.

Consequently, whichever of the two systems described above be adopted, the same result will be arrived at in this particular case: the necessity of ascertaining whether or not under international law there is a principle which would have prohibited Turkey, in the circumstances of the case before the Court, from prosecuting Lieutenant Demons. . . .

As has already been observed, the characteristic features of the situation of fact are as follows: there has been a collision on the high seas between two vessels flying different flags, on one of which was one of the persons alleged to be guilty of the offence, whilst the victims were on board the other.

. . . No argument has come to the knowledge of the Court from which it could be deduced that States recognize themselves to be under an obligation towards each other only to have regard to the place where the author of the offence happens to be at the time of the offence. On the contrary, it is certain that the courts of many countries, even of countries which have given their criminal legislation a strictly territorial character, interpret criminal law in the sense that offences, the authors of which at the moment of commission are in the territory of another State, are nevertheless to be regarded as having been committed in the national territory, if one of the constituent elements of the offence, and more especially its effects, have taken place there. . . . Consequently, once it is admitted that the effects of the offence were produced on the Turkish vessel, it becomes impossible to hold that there is a rule of international law which prohibits Turkey from prosecuting Lieutenant Demons because of the fact that the author of the offence was on board the French ship. Since, as has already been observed, the special agreement does not deal with the provision of Turkish law under which the prosecution was instituted, but only with the question whether the prosecution should be regarded as contrary to the principles of international law, there is no reason preventing the Court from confining itself to observing that, in this case, a prosecution may also be justified from the point of view of the so-called territorial principle. . . .

The conclusion at which the Court has therefore arrived is that there is no rule of international law in regard to collision cases to the effect that criminal proceedings are exclusively within the jurisdiction of the State whose flag is flown.

This conclusion moreover is easily explained if the manner in which the collision brings the jurisdiction of two different countries into play be considered.

The offence for which Lieutenant Demons appears to have been prosecuted was an act — of negligence or imprudence — having its origin on board the *Lotus*, whilst its effects made themselves felt on board the *Boz-Kourt*. These two elements are, legally, entirely inseparable, so much so that their separation renders the offence non-existent. Neither the exclusive jurisdiction of either State, nor the limitations of the jurisdiction of each to the occurrences which took place on the respective ships would appear calculated to satisfy the requirements of justice and effectively to protect the interests of the two States. It is only natural that each should be able to exercise jurisdiction and to do so in respect of the incident as a whole. It is therefore a case of concurrent jurisdiction. . . .

FOR THESE REASONS,
The Court,
having heard both Parties,
gives, by the President's casting vote — the votes being equally divided — , judgment to the effect

(1) That . . . Turkey, by instituting criminal proceedings in pursuance of Turkish law against Lieutenant Demons, . . . has not acted in conflict with the principles of international law. . . .

NOTES AND QUESTIONS

1. The *Lotus* case was heard before the Permanent Court of International Justice (PCIJ) — the predecessor of the current International Court of Justice. Just as the ICJ is an organ of the United Nations, the PCIJ was an organ of the League of Nations. Notwithstanding its optimistic name — *Permanent* Court of International Justice — the PCIJ lasted just 24 years, from 1922-1946. But its decisions retain contemporary relevance because the jurisprudence of the PCIJ was "folded into" the ICJ's, as though they were a single court. *Lotus* stands among the most influential and frequently cited PCIJ and ICJ cases.

2. The *Lotus* court divided evenly, 6-6. By the rules of the PCIJ, the court's president was authorized to resolve ties with a second vote. However, one of the dissenting judges based his dissent on a matter unrelated to the main issue of the case. He stated in his dissent that he concurred with the court's opinion that international law did not prohibit Turkey from exercising jurisdiction, so on the key issue the vote was 7-5.

3. How important to the decision of the case were the following facts: (a) that Lieutenant Demons was in Turkey, of his own free will, when he was arrested and tried; (b) that Turkish nationals were killed in the accident; and (c) that the Turkish victims were aboard a Turkish vessel — hence, within Turkish territory according to an established rule of international law?

4. Given these facts, why does France object to Turkey's exercise of jurisdiction? After all, France would have no objection to Turkey prosecuting Demons if, while vacationing in Turkey, he had killed Turkish nationals through drunk driving.

5. How broad is the holding in *Lotus*? In his dissenting opinion, Judge Loder paraphrases the court's opinion as saying that "under international law everything which is not prohibited is permitted. . . . Every door is open unless it is closed by treaty or by established Custom."

Notice that the *Lotus* court's opinion describes "the very nature . . . of international law" along the lines of the consensualist model described in Chapter 2: "The rules of law binding upon States . . . emanate from their own free will as expressed in conventions or by usages generally accepted as expressing principles of law." From this, the court concludes: "Restrictions upon the independence of States cannot therefore be presumed."

However, in the next paragraph, the court mentions "the first and foremost restriction imposed by international law," namely that a state "may not exercise its power in any form in the territory of another state." Thus, a state may exercise jurisdiction transnationally only "by virtue of a permissive rule derived from international custom or from a convention." How different is this principle from "the contention of the French Government to the effect that Turkey must in each case be able to cite a rule of international law authorizing her to exercise jurisdiction"?

Has Turkey exercised its jurisdiction outside its own territory? If so, then under what "permissive rule" may Turkey do so? If not, then what is France complaining about?

6. The court states that this "is a case of concurrent jurisdiction" — both Turkey and France may exercise jurisdiction over Lieutenant Demons for the collision. In such cases, states usually decide through diplomatic channels who "gets to go first" in trying a defendant. Are there considerations of justice that would favor Turkish jurisdiction in this case? French jurisdiction? Using the reasonableness factors in Restatement §403 (see Section A.2 above), which state has a better claim to jurisdiction over Lieutenant Demons? As we shall see in Section A. below, France asserts criminal jurisdiction over French nationals regardless of where they committed the crime. Should that matter?

7. Thirty years after *Lotus*, the Convention on the High Seas adopted a rule of law that is the opposite of *Lotus*:

> In the event of a collision or of any other incident of navigation concerning a ship on the high seas, involving the penal or disciplinary responsibility of the master or of any other person in the service of the ship, no penal or disciplinary proceedings may be instituted against such persons except before the judicial or administrative authorities either of the flag State or of the State of which such person is a national.

Convention on the High Seas art. 11(1), Apr. 29, 1958, 450 U.N.T.S. 82. The same rule was incorporated into the Law of the Sea Convention, art. 97, reprinted in 21 I.L.M. 1261 (1982).

8. *Lotus* is one of the most famous of all international opinions, and lawyers ever since have used the expression "*Lotus* principle" or "freedom principle" as shorthand for the proposition that states have the right to do anything not explicitly prohibited by customary international law or convention. Three eminent judges have described the *Lotus* approach as "the high water mark of laissez-faire in international relations." Arrest Warrant of Apr. 11, 2000 (Dem. Rep. Congo v. Belg.) (joint separate opinion of Judges Higgins, Buergenthal, and Kooijmans, ¶51), reprinted at 41 I.L.M. 536, 585 (2002). *Lotus*, as we have seen, permits states complete latitude unless their action is prohibited by a rule of international law — and such rules must themselves be the products of state consent.

As we indicated in the last chapter, however, modern international law no longer grants states complete laissez-faire in as many matters as it did in 1927, when *Lotus* was decided. International human rights standards limit what states can do within their own borders; and, after Nuremberg, defendants accused of genocide, crimes against humanity, crimes against peace, and war crimes can no longer offer in defense that these actions were permitted or required under domestic law. Even outside the arena of international human rights, some international lawyers believe that the laissez-faire approach in *Lotus* is no longer tenable in the modern world. A powerful statement of the problem appears in Judge Shahabudeen's dissenting opinion from the ICJ's Advisory Opinion on the Legality of the Threat or Use of Nuclear Weapons:

> The General Assembly's question [about the legality of nuclear use] presents the Court, as a World Court, with a dilemma: to hold that States have a right to use nuclear weapons is to affirm that they have a right to embark on a course of conduct which could result in the extinction of civilization, and indeed in the dissolution of all forms of life on the planet, both flora and fauna. On the other hand, to deny the existence of that right may seem to contradict the "Lotus" principle, relied on by some States, to the effect that States have a sovereign right to do whatever is not prohibited under international law, in this respect it being said that there is no principle of international law which prohibits the use of such weapons.

35 I.L.M. 809, 867 (1996) (dissenting opinion of Judge Shahabudeen), pt. II. In Judge Shahabudeen's view, the *Lotus* principle is untenable because it leads to a conclusion inconsistent with the very foundation of legality, namely that a course of action that might lead to the extinction of humanity is legally permissible: "[I]f mankind in the broad is annihilated, States disappear and, with them, the basis on which rights and obligations exist within the international community." Id. pt. I.2.

9. Contemporary international human rights standards include minimum standards of due process. See ICCPR, Articles 9, 14, and 15. Should a state whose domestic criminal procedures fall below these standards be able to exercise criminal jurisdiction over extraterritorial conduct? For example, under contemporary standards, should Turkey be able to exercise jurisdiction over Lieutenant Demons if it turned out that Turkey did not provide him with "free assistance of an interpreter" at his initial hearing, as required by ICCPR Article 14(3)(f)?

10. Compare the *Lotus* principle (that states enjoy "a wide measure of discretion which is only limited in certain cases by prohibitive rules; as regards other cases, every state remains free to adopt the principles which it regards as best and most suitable") with Moore's conclusion in *Cutting*:

There being no principle of international law that permits the tribunals of a nation to try and punish foreigners for acts done by them outside of the national territory or jurisdiction, it necessarily follows that any assumption to do so, in respect to particular crimes, must rest, as an exception to the rule, either upon the general concurrence of nations, in respect to the crimes in question, or upon an express convention.

Which is right?

11. The fact remains, however, that contemporary international law provides no agreed rule or mechanism for resolving competing jurisdictional claims, whether in the criminal arena or other fields. Various alternative approaches have been proposed for dealing with overlapping claims. For a discussion, see the Report of the International Bar Association's Task Force on Extraterritorial Jurisdiction (2009).

UNITED STATES v. RICARDO
619 F.2d 1124 (5th Cir. 1980)

THOMAS, Circuit Judge:

Appellants were convicted of two marijuana counts,[4] stemming from the seizure of a shrimp boat, the *Sincere Progress I*, in the Gulf of Mexico, on the late evening and early morning of November 4-5, 1978. Following their convictions, appellants Ricardo, Torres, Garcia, and Rodriquez-Marino were sentenced to three and one-half (3½) years imprisonment with a special parole term of five (5) years on each of Counts I and II, to run concurrently. Due to their increased involvement in the drug transaction, appellants Conrado, Durrange, and Neuman received ten (10) years. In addition, Durrange and Neuman received $15,000 consecutive fines on Counts I and II. All of the appellants are Colombian, with the exception of Durrange and Neuman, who are American. In order to understand the nature of appellants' arguments, a recital of the factual setting is necessary.

I. FACTS

On November 4, 1978, a Coast Guard cutter, the *Point Hope*, was instructed to proceed southeast from Galveston, Texas, to a point approximately 125-150 miles from the American coast, in order to search for a fishing boat of unknown nationality. The vessel was reported to be without power and was drifting in a northerly direction with the assistance of a makeshift sail. Several hours later, a vessel was sighted which fit the radio description. Approaching the vessel from the stern, the crew from the cutter noticed tobacco-like sweepings 50-100 yards astern. The cutter then proceeded to circle the vessel in order to determine the vessel's nationality and rating. There was [*sic*] no visible markings, either on the stern or the bow of the vessel, and no flag was being flown. It was determined from the side of the deckhouse that the vessel's name was the *Sincere Progress I*.

Radio contact could not be established with the *Sincere Progress* but shortly after the initial approach, one of the defendants (Neuman) appeared on deck. From an

---

4. [Court's footnote 1:] All defendants were charged with and convicted of: Count I, conspiracy to import marijuana, pursuant to 21 U.S.C. §963, and Count II, conspiracy to possess marijuana with intent to distribute it, pursuant to 21 U.S.C. §846.

account of the subsequent conversation with Coast Guard officers, the following facts were ascertained: There were two Americans on board (Neuman and Durrange), and five Colombians (Ricardo, Torres, Garcia, Rodriquez-Marino, and Conrado), none of whom could speak English. The Americans were allegedly on board because their sailboat had sunk off the coast of Florida and they had been rescued by the Colombians. However, when asked about specifics, neither American could remember the name or registration number of their "lost" sailboat.

While Neuman and Lieutenant Veselka were conversing, objects were thrown overboard from the *Sincere Progress*. The cutter retrieved the objects, which were later examined and determined to be nautical charts. These charts had markings on them, indicating that the *Sincere Progress*'s probable destination was a point approximately sixty miles off the coast of Matagorda, Texas. The charts also indicated that the *Sincere Progress* began its journey in Colombia and proceeded through the Caribbean Sea and Yucatan Channel into the Gulf of Mexico.

Without the assistance of an interpreter, communication with the Colombians was difficult. The *Point Hope*, which had been maintaining radio contact with the New Orleans headquarters, received instructions to board the *Sincere Progress*, ostensibly for the purpose of determining nationality and registry. A boarding party of three crew members was dispatched to retrieve this information. Once on board, papers reflecting registry of the vessel were requested, but none could be produced. Appellant Neuman stated that all the vessel's papers and logs were washed overboard in a storm. The engine room main beam was then examined for registry information, but none could be found. A nameplate on the wheelhouse gave the manufacturer's insignia, "Atlantic Marine, 1969." Finally the hold of the ship was examined, and it was here that the marijuana was discovered.

The two Americans requested that they be allowed to return to port on board the *Point Hope*. This request was granted upon the condition that they be placed under arrest and read their Miranda rights. The other defendants remained on the *Progress*, and, due to high seas, were given towing assistance into the Galveston port. The two vessels arrived in Galveston on the night of November 5, 1978. At that time, the Americans were again read their Miranda rights and then questioned by a Federal agent with the Drug Enforcement Agency (DEA). Appellant Neuman said that he built a sailboat in Florida which later sunk off the coast in a trial run. This allegation ties in with his story about being rescued by the *Sincere Progress* and explains why he could not remember the sailboat's name or registration number. Appellant Durrange told a similar story. In addition, both appellants stated that they knew marijuana was on board the *Progress*.

The Colombians were not placed under arrest until November 7, 1978. At that time . . . [Conrado] stated that the crew of the *Sincere Progress* was hired by two unknown Cubans who gave them coordinates to follow through the Yucatan Channel and into the Gulf of Mexico. There, the *Sincere Progress* was to rendezvous about sixty miles off the Texas coast with another vessel for the purpose of transferring the marijuana cargo. In order to corroborate his story, he produced a chart indicating similar coordinates to the charts previously thrown overboard and retrieved by the Coast Guard cutter. . . .

II.   EXTRATERRITORIAL JURISDICTION

Appellants' initial challenge concerns the district court's jurisdiction over the case. Their argument is based in part on the premise that in order for extraterritorial acts to be in violation of the laws of the United States, there must be some nexus to the United States. The argument follows that there were no acts committed within the territorial jurisdiction of the United States and that, as a result, jurisdiction is improper.

The circumstances of the case reveal that the plan commenced outside the United States. Charts confiscated during the investigation indicate that the voyage originated in Colombia. According to the Americans, they left in their sailboat from Miami, Florida. Assuming their version is correct, the only nexus to the United States is indirect because they were not the masterminds behind the scheme. When the *Progress* was intercepted, it was approximately 125-150 miles from the Texas Coast. From these facts alone, it is apparent that the Government failed to prove the existence of an overt act committed within the United States. The Government did prove, however, that the *Progress* intended to rendezvous with another vessel off the coast of Texas, in order to unload their cargo. Given this proof, along with the proximity to the United States coast and the general heading of the ship, we are convinced that the object of appellants' plan had consequences within the United States. Under these circumstances, the question we now address is whether, pursuant to either conspiracy statute, a territorial act must be committed within the United States and in furtherance of the conspiracy before jurisdiction attaches.

Under the conspiracy statutes in question, §§846 and 963, it is not incumbent upon the Government to allege or prove an overt act in order to obtain a conviction. While it is now settled law that proof of an overt act is not required under the conspiracy statutes, the jurisdictional requisites are not settled. The United States and this Circuit have traditionally adhered to the objective principle of territorial jurisdiction, which attaches criminal consequences to extraterritorial acts that are intended to have effect in the sovereign territory, at least where overt acts within the territory can be proved. United States v. Postal, 589 F.2d 862, 885 (5th Cir.) and cases cited therein. Implicit in these statutes is the notion that the prescribed prohibitions apply extraterritorially. It seems somewhat anomalous, however, that Congress intended these statutes to apply extraterritorially, but that jurisdiction attaches only after an act occurred within the sovereign boundaries. Thus, even though the statutes were designed to prevent one type of wrong *ab initio*, under the traditional approach, the courts were without power to act. This dichotomy directly contravenes the purpose of the enabling legislation.

As a result, it is now settled in this Circuit that when the statute itself does not require proof of an overt act, jurisdiction attaches upon a mere showing of intended territorial effects. *Postal*, 589 F.2d at 886, n. 39. The fact that appellants intended the conspiracy to be consummated within the territorial boundaries satisfies jurisdictional requisites. Under the most recent holding in this Circuit, we conclude that, ". . . the district court had jurisdiction to try the defendants for a conspiracy aimed at violating United States law and intending effects in its territory even in the absence of proof of an overt act committed within this country." . . .

Affirmed.

NOTES AND QUESTIONS

1. The defendants in *Ricardo* were convicted under two conspiracy statutes. We take this opportunity to introduce the concept of conspiracy, which we first encountered in Chapter 3. Conspiracy receives additional discussion in Chapter 17.

Conspiracy is what criminal lawyers call an "inchoate" (incomplete) crime. Inchoate crimes are undertaken in the course of planning and committing another crime: the "object offense." Attempts are likewise inchoate crimes. The theory behind criminalizing what might be otherwise-innocent actions as conspiracies or attempts is straightforward: They aren't really innocent. They are steps the criminal takes on the path to wrongdoing; in a sense, they are components of the wrongdoing. The fact that the perpetrator got caught before completing the crime seems irrelevant to the ultimate question of culpability. As a matter of crime control, the public interest lies in stopping crime early, and it would frustrate the purposes of law enforcement if efficient policing simply resulted in releasing those bent on crime. Hence, criminalizing early-stage crimes seems clearly in the public interest.

For a sophisticated discussion of the crime-fighting virtues of conspiracy law, see Neal Kumar Katyal, Conspiracy Theory, 112 Yale L.J. 1307 (2003); and for a classic critique of conspiracy law, Philip E. Johnson, The Unnecessary Crime of Conspiracy, 61 Cal. L. Rev. 1137 (1973).

2. The basic federal conspiracy statute, 18 U.S.C. §371, contains three simple elements: "(1) the existence of an agreement to achieve an unlawful objective; (2) the defendant's knowing and voluntary participation in the conspiracy; and (3) the commission of an overt act in furtherance of the conspiracy." United States v. Cure, 804 F.2d 625, 628 (11th Cir. 1986). The first element — a group plan involving two or more persons — is usually called the *plurality requirement*; the third element, the *overt act requirement*. Section 371 distinguishes two separate categories of conspiracy: conspiracies to defraud the United States and conspiracies to commit an offense against the United States (that is, a federal crime). But there are many other federal conspiracy statutes in addition to §371.

The overt act requirement helps distinguish genuine conspiracies from mere discussion. With the first overt act, the conspirators have crossed the fatal threshold from talk to action. And, once the threshold is past, the consequences are grave. Under U.S. doctrine, even if one of the conspirators gets cold feet and does nothing further to assist the conspirators, she is still liable unless she takes active steps to withdraw from the conspiracy. Merely staying home on the day of the crime won't do it. And, under so-called *Pinkerton* liability, each conspirator is liable for every reasonably foreseeable crime committed by every co-conspirator in furtherance of the object offense, even if she did not know about the co-conspirator's crime. Pinkerton v. United States, 328 U.S. 640 (1946). In very large conspiracies — drug cartel activity, for example — the number of crimes that each of the dozens of co-conspirators can be liable for is truly staggering. As a practical matter, *Pinkerton* liability gives prosecutors enormous leverage to "flip" conspirators and get them to testify against higher-ups. See Katyal, supra, at 1339-1340, 1356-1367.

Conspiracy doctrine is a creature of the common law. Civil law systems such as those of Western Europe and Latin America have no counterpart crime. As we saw in Chapter 3, the Anglo-American law of conspiracy crossed the oceans when the leaders of the Axis countries were tried in Nuremberg and Tokyo after World War II. When the international tribunals of the 1990s were created (the Yugoslav and Rwandan tribunals), Anglo-American conspiracy concepts and civilian concepts of accomplice liability were blended to create a complex doctrine of "joint criminal enterprise" to ensnare the remote planners of genocides and crimes against humanity. See Chapter 17.

3. The basic jurisdictional puzzle in *Ricardo* may be simply stated: How can the defendants' actions be said to have an "effect" in the United States if they were nabbed before they ever got within a hundred miles of U.S. territorial waters? For

that matter, what exactly is the "effect" of an inchoate crime like conspiracy? International law, which does not contain general principles of conspiracy law, does not answer this question. But U.S. courts have addressed the question as a matter of domestic law.

In Ford v. United States, 273 U.S. 593, 624 (1927), the Supreme Court found that a "conspiracy charged, although some of the conspirators were corporally on the high seas, had for its object crime in the United States, and was carried on partly in and partly out of this country, and so was within its jurisdiction under the principles above settled." The Ninth Circuit Court of Appeals relied on *Ford* to find jurisdiction over a Malaysian who participated in a heroin-smuggling scheme, because one of his co-conspirators committed an overt act in the United States. Chua Han Mow v. United States, 730 F.2d 1308, 1312 (9th Cir. 1984).

4. In *Ricardo*, was there an overt act in the United States? The court avoids this issue by observing that the conspiracy statutes in this case contain no overt act requirement. The two statutes under which the *Ricardo* defendants were charged (21 U.S.C. §§846 and 963) have identical wording:

> Any person who attempts or conspires to commit any offense defined in this subchapter shall be subject to the same penalties as those prescribed for the offense, the commission of which was the object of the attempt or conspiracy.

As the opinion indicates, one statute accompanies prohibitions on importing marijuana; the other accompanies prohibitions on possessing marijuana with intent to distribute.

What follows from the finding that these statutes contain no overt act requirement? Is the court saying that without an overt act element, effects jurisdiction exists without any part of the conspiracy occurring in the United States? *Ricardo* asserts that "it is now settled in this Circuit that when the statute itself does not require proof of an overt act, jurisdiction attaches upon a mere showing of intended territorial effects. *Postal*, 589 F.2d 862 at 886, n.39." However, the passage referred to in *United States v. Postal* says nothing of the kind:

> This result may well lead to the conclusion that the proof of an overt act within the United States is no longer required for jurisdictional purposes and that mere proof of intended territorial effects is sufficient. We need not, however, resolve this issue because we find that an overt act was proved to have occurred in the United States.

Postal, 589 F.2d at 886 n.39. What *Ricardo* describes as "settled law" is in reality an unresolved issue that the court declined to reach.

Does it follow from *Ricardo* that two people, anywhere in the world, who conspire to smuggle marijuana into the United States fall under U.S. criminal jurisdiction? Would that be a bad result?

5. Try putting the shoe on the other foot. Suppose that a group of U.S. nationals — just for fun, suppose that they are prominent business executives — agree in New York City to commit a crime in Mexico, say bribing a Mexican official to look the other way at regulatory violations in a factory they own in Mexico. Mexican officials learn of the conspiracy from an informant present at the meeting. As the business executives are yachting on the high seas, but before they have carried out their plan, Mexican agents arrest them and take them to Mexico City, proposing to put them on trial for conspiracy. How likely is it that the United States would agree that Mexico has objective territorial jurisdiction? Recall the U.S. position in *Cutting*.

6. One of the highest profile drug conspiracy cases involved Panamanian strong-man (and de facto ruler) General Manuel Noriega. In 1988, a Miami grand jury indicted Noriega for participating in a major international conspiracy to distribute cocaine in the United States. Two years later, escalating incidents between Panama and the United States culminated in a U.S. invasion of Panama. General Noriega fled. He sought asylum in the Vatican embassy in Panama, but after U.S. forces bombarded the embassy with ultra-loud rock music for three days, the papal nuncio persuaded Noriega to surrender to U.S. authorities. Noriega was brought to the United States for trial. Noriega argued that his prosecution violated international law in several respects, one of them being lack of jurisdiction. (Noriega also claimed diplomatic and head-of-state immunity, but the court rejected his claims.) Rejecting Noriega's argument, Judge Hoeveler wrote:

. . . As Noriega concedes, the United States has long possessed the ability to attach criminal consequences to acts occurring outside this country which produce effects within the United States. For example, the United States would unquestionably have authority to prosecute a person standing in Canada who fires a bullet across the border which strikes a second person standing in the United States. The objective territorial theory of jurisdiction, which focuses on the effects or intended effects of conduct, can be traced to Justice Holmes' statement that "[a]cts done outside a jurisdiction, but intended to produce or producing effects within it, justify a State in punishing the cause of the harm as if he had been present at the effect, if the State should succeed in getting him within its power." Strassheim v. Daily, 221 U.S. at 285. Even if the extra-territorial conduct produces no effect within the United States, a defendant may still be reached if he was part of a conspiracy in which some co-conspirator's activities took place within United States territory. The former Fifth Circuit, whose decisions establish prec-edent for this Court, has on numerous occasions upheld jurisdiction over foreigners who conspired to import narcotics into the United States but never entered this country nor personally performed any acts within its territorial limits, as long as there was proof of an overt act committed within the United States by a co-conspirator.

More recently, international law principles have expanded to permit jurisdiction upon a mere showing of *intent* to produce effects in this country, without requiring proof of an overt act or effect within the United States. According to the Restatement (Third):

Cases involving intended but unrealized effect are rare, but international law does not preclude jurisdiction in such instances, subject to the principle of reasonable-ness. When the intent to commit the proscribed act is clear and demonstrated by some activity, and the effect to be produced by the activity is substantial and fore-seeable, the fact that a plan or conspiracy was thwarted does not deprive the target state of jurisdiction to make its law applicable.

§402 comment d.

In the drug smuggling context, the "intent doctrine" has resulted in jurisdiction over persons who attempted to import narcotics into the United States but never actually succeeded in entering the United States or delivering drugs within its borders. The fact that no act was committed and no repercussions were felt within the United States did not preclude jurisdiction over conduct that was clearly directed at the United States.

These principles unequivocally support jurisdiction in this case. The indictment charges Noriega with conspiracy to import cocaine into the United States and alleges several overt acts performed within the United States in furtherance of the conspiracy. Specifically, the indictment alleges that co-conspirators of Noriega purchased a Lear jet in Miami, which was then used to transport drug proceeds from Miami to Panama.

Moreover, Noriega's activities in Panama, if true, undoubtedly produced effects within this country as deleterious as the hypothetical bullet fired across the border. The indictment alleges that, as a result of Noriega's facilitation of narcotics activity in Panama, 2,141 pounds of cocaine were illegally brought into Miami from Panama. While the ability of the United States to reach and proscribe extraterritorial conduct having effects in this country does not depend on the amount of narcotics imported into the United States or the magnitude of the consequences, the importation of over 2,000 pounds of cocaine clearly has a harmful impact and merits jurisdiction. Finally, even if no overt acts or effects occurred within the territorial borders, the object of the alleged conspiracy was to import cocaine into the United States and therefore an intent to produce effects is present.

... Noriega ... cites the principle of reasonableness recently articulated in the Restatement (Third) §403, but fails to say how extending jurisdiction over his conduct would be unreasonable. ... Given the serious nature of the drug epidemic in this country, certainly the efforts of the United States to combat the problem by prosecuting conduct directed against itself cannot be subject to the protests of a foreign government profiting at its expense. ...

United States v. Noriega, 746 F. Supp. 1506, 1512-1515 (S.D. Fla. 1990).

Judge Hoeveler quotes Justice Holmes's opinion in *Strassheim v. Daily* as follows: "acts done outside a jurisdiction, but intended to produce *or* producing effects within it, justify a State in punishing the cause of the harm as if he had been present at the effect, if the State should succeed in getting him within its power" (emphasis added). However, this is a misquotation. Holmes's opinion uses the word *and*, not *or*: "acts done outside a jurisdiction, but intended to produce *and* producing effects within it. ..." *Noriega* is not the only reported opinion to misquote *Strassheim* in this way: The same misquotation appears in United States v. Rodriguez, 182 F. Supp. 479, 488 (S.D. Cal. 1960). Does this misquotation affect the analysis?

7. In practice, the "intent doctrine" has achieved traction within U.S. law only in the relatively narrow area of drug smuggling and importation. Should a concept as intangible as intent be the basis for extraterritorial criminal jurisdiction? In at least one case, a court has found the lack of the requisite intent if the defendant was merely sending the drugs through the United States on their way elsewhere. Republic of Fr. v. Moghadam, 617 F. Supp. 777, 787 (N.D. Cal. 1985).

8. Do the conspiracy statutes cited in *Ricardo* apply extraterritorially? U.S. courts have found no difficulty in answering yes. The basic rule is that conspiracy statutes have extraterritorial reach provided that the object crime is prohibited by a statute with extraterritorial reach. See, e.g., *Chua Han Mow*, 730 F.2d at 1311; *Noriega*, 746 F. Supp. at 1516.

9. *Ricardo* is one of many cases arising from the United States' "War on Drugs" that pose jurisdictional questions because the U.S. Coast Guard intercepted a drug shipment on the high seas. Other cases also employ expansive legal theories to find objective territorial jurisdiction. In *Postal*, for example, U.S. enforcement personnel boarded a ship registered in the Grand Cayman Islands, outside U.S. territorial waters. Finding marijuana, they arrested the defendants, who were convicted for drug conspiracies. On appeal the defendants argued that boarding the vessel violated the Convention on the High Seas (to which the United States is a party). Article 6 of that Convention vests exclusive jurisdiction over a ship to its flag state — here, the Grand Cayman Islands. A 1933 Supreme Court case holds that when the United States "had imposed a territorial limitation upon its own

authority" by entering a treaty, then "[o]ur government, lacking power to seize, lacked power, because of the Treaty, to subject the vessel to our laws." Cook v. United States, 288 U.S. 102, 121 (1933).

Postal replied that *Cook* applies only when the treaty in question is self-executing. (Recall from Chapter 2 that a self-executing treaty is one that has domestic effect without the need for implementing legislation.) Even though the language of Article 6 of the Convention on the High Seas "[o]n its face . . . would bear a self-executing construction," *Postal* reasons that it actually is non-self-executing. "The Convention on the High Seas is a multilateral treaty which has been ratified by over fifty nations, some of which do not recognize treaties as self-executing. It is difficult therefore to ascribe to the language of the treaty any common intent that the treaty should of its own force operate as the domestic law of the ratifying nations." *Postal*, 589 F.2d at 877-878. Does this imply that no multilateral treaties are self-executing if any of the parties' legal systems do not recognize self-execution? In that case, very few multilateral treaties are self-executing because many states (for example, the United Kingdom) do not recognize self-execution.

10. In United States v. Robinson, 843 F.2d 1 (1st Cir. 1988), the Coast Guard searched a Panamanian ship 500 miles from the United States and found 20 tons of marijuana. The defendants appealed their drug possession conviction on jurisdictional grounds. The statute under which they were convicted, 46 U.S.C. §70503 (at the time numbered 21 U.S.C. §955a(c)) applies only within U.S. "customs waters" (the 12-mile-limit). However, "customs waters" also includes foreign ships whose government has agreed to permit boarding and searching. Here, the court found that after stopping the ship, the Coast Guard obtained Panama's permission to board and search. It also found that the prosecution did not violate the *ex post facto* clause, even though "[i]n light of our concession that Panama's consent was necessary to apply American law, that law did not apply until sometime . . . after the appellants' acts of possessing the marijuana were complete." Id. at 4. The Eleventh Circuit Court of Appeals used a similar argument that "customs waters" includes a Panamanian ship boarded on the high seas, when Panama granted its consent only after the ship was boarded. United States v. Romero-Galue, 757 F.2d 1147 (11th Cir. 1985).

11. In other cases as well, current U.S. practice makes ambitious use of the objective territoriality principle. Thus, in two cases — peculiarly similar in their facts — cruise ship personnel, citizens of St. Vincent and the Grenadines, were prosecuted in the United States for sexually molesting underage U.S. girls while the ships were on the high seas. The ships themselves were of foreign registration, but in both cases, the U.S. courts held that they had jurisdiction under the objective territorial principle (among other principles). United States v. Niel, 312 F.3d 419 (9th Cir. 2002); United States v. Roberts, 1 F. Supp. 2d 601, 607-608 (E.D. La. 1998). In the words of *Niel,*

> [u]nder the territorial principle, the United States may assert jurisdiction when acts performed outside of its borders have detrimental effects within the United States. . . . The victim was an American citizen who lives and goes to school in the United States, and who sought counseling in this country after the attack. These facts are enough to support jurisdiction under the territorial principle.

312 F.3d at 422. Are they?

12. Can current U.S. treatment of the objective territorial principle be squared with the U.S. position in *Cutting?*

4. The Nationality Principle

RESTATEMENT (THIRD) OF THE FOREIGN RELATIONS LAW OF THE UNITED STATES

(1987)

§402(2) BASES OF JURISDICTION TO PRESCRIBE

... [A] state has jurisdiction to prescribe law with respect to the activities, interests, status, or relations of its nationals outside as well as within its territory. ...

PROBLEM 1

Suppose that the United States enacts the Defense of Life Act, which criminalizes euthanasia and physician-assisted suicide as violations of federal civil rights law. Dr. K. is a U.S. national who is a physician and pro-euthanasia activist. In protest of U.S. policies against physician-assisted suicide, Dr. K. has moved her practice to the European country of Lowlandia.

Lowlandia has tolerated physician-assisted suicide for a number of years. Although it is still prohibited under Lowlandia's criminal code, the Lowlandian Justice Ministry has entered into an agreement with the Lowlandian Medical Association not to prosecute cases of physician-assisted suicide if certain carefully defined conditions are met. These are designed to ensure that the patient's decision is voluntary and that the patient is enduring great suffering with no realistic chance of improvement. Dr. K. has assisted several patients, including patients from the United States who followed her to Lowlandia, in terminating their own lives; she has also written op-eds about her practice, which she publishes in U.S. news media. She has become a well-known — some would say notorious — figure. Dr. K. frequently visits the United States, where she owns a summer home. She maintains U.S. bank accounts, into which she has occasionally deposited income gained in Lowlandia.

The Justice Department announces that it will use the Defense of Life Act's criminal provisions to prosecute Dr. K. for homicides committed in Lowlandia. After charges are filed, Dr. K. files a motion to dismiss, arguing that international law does not permit extraterritorial jurisdiction in this case. The act does not explicitly state that it applies extraterritorially. How should the judge rule on the international law issue?[5]

RESEARCH IN INTERNATIONAL LAW UNDER THE AUSPICES OF THE FACULTY OF THE HARVARD LAW SCHOOL: II. JURISDICTION WITH RESPECT TO CRIME

29 Am. J. Intl. L. 435, 519-520 (Supp. 1935)

The competence of the State to prosecute and punish its nationals on the sole basis of their nationality is universally conceded. Such jurisdiction is based upon the

---

5. "Lowlandia" is a thinly disguised Netherlands. The legal situation described in the problem was that of the Netherlands until 2002, when the legislature officially decriminalized physician-assisted suicide under certain conditions.

allegiance which the person charged with crime owes to the State of which he is a national. . . . Under existing international practice, a State is assumed to have practically unlimited legal control over its nationals. This competence is justified on the ground that a State's treatment of its nationals is not ordinarily a matter of concern to other States or to international law.

Jurists have advanced an interesting variety of reasons for the State's control over its nationals. It has been said (1) that since the State is composed of nationals, who are its members, the State's law should apply to them wherever they may be; (2) that the State is primarily interested in and affected by the conduct of its nationals; (3) that penal laws are of a personal character, like those governing civil status, and that, while only reasons *d'ordre public* [of public order] justify their application to aliens within the territory, they apply normally to nationals of the State everywhere; (4) that the protection of nationals abroad gives rise to a reciprocal duty of obedience; (5) that any offence committed by a national abroad causes a disturbance of the social and moral order in the State of his allegiance; (6) that the national knows best his own State's penal law, that he is more likely to be fairly and effectively tried under his own State's law and by his own State's courts, and that the most appropriate jurisdiction from the point of view of the accused should be considered rather than a jurisdiction determined by reference to the offence; (7) that without the exercise of such jurisdiction many crimes would go unpunished, especially where States refuse to extradite their nationals.

NOTES AND QUESTIONS

1. How good are these arguments? A critic might complain that nationality jurisdiction treats nationals as little more than property of the state; it is moralistic, paternalistic, and illiberal. Is it really true "that any offence committed by a national abroad causes a disturbance of the social and moral order" of his home state (argument 5)? Or that "the state is primarily interested in and affected by the conduct of its nationals" abroad (argument 2)? Wouldn't that make it a Nanny State?

2. Consider, for example, Singapore's Misuse of Drugs Act (Chapter 185). Section 8(b) of the act criminalizes drug possession and drug use, and contains the following:

CONSUMPTION OF DRUG OUTSIDE SINGAPORE BY CITIZEN OR PERMANENT RESIDENT

8A. — (1) Section 8(b) shall have effect in relation to a person who is a citizen or a permanent resident of Singapore outside as well as within Singapore where he is found as a result of urine tests conducted under section 31(4)(b) to have smoked, administered to himself or otherwise consumed a controlled drug or a specified drug.

(2) Where an offense under section 8(b) is committed by a person referred to in subsection (1) in any place outside Singapore, he may be dealt with as if that offense had been committed within Singapore.

Does it really cause "a disturbance of the social and moral order" of Singapore if one of its permanent residents smokes marijuana on a Caribbean holiday? Why is Singapore "primarily interested in and affected by" this conduct? Singapore's broadly worded anticorruption statute, which forbids all forms of public, private, or commercial bribery, contains a similar jurisdictional clause stating that if a Singaporean national or permanent resident engages in corruption outside Singapore "he may be dealt with in respect of that offense as if it had been committed within Singapore." Singapore

Prevention of Corruption Act (Chapter 241), §37(1). Why should it matter to Singapore if a Singaporean national, living in Russia and working for a Russian employer, greases a business transaction on behalf of that employer with a bribe ("gratification," in the terminology of the Singapore statute) paid in St. Petersburg to other Russians?

Is it a better organizing principle for the international community to base jurisdictional presumptions on nationality or on territory? Within the United States, should a California citizen (a resident of San Francisco, for example) be subject to California law in Arkansas? And vice versa? How should jurisdictional conflicts be resolved?

3. Both practical and theoretical limitations exist to the prosecution of extraterritorial crimes by a state's nationals. On the practical level, the obvious problem lies in evidence gathering abroad, coupled with related issues of fairness to the defendant, who may not have the ability to gather exculpatory evidence abroad or to confront witnesses whose affidavits or depositions the prosecution enters into evidence. On the theoretical level, the assertion of nationality jurisdiction may impinge on the territorial jurisdiction of the state where the crime is committed. If a U.S. national robs a bank in France, it seems clear that France has the primary claim to prosecute the case. Recall that §403 of the Restatement forbids "unreasonable" exercises of jurisdiction — and there is little doubt that it would be unreasonable for the United States to prosecute the French bank robbery if France wished to do so.

4. Why, then, would a state exercise nationality jurisdiction rather than permitting the territorial state to prosecute a crime? One obvious reason is fear that the defendant would not receive fair trial or punishment in the territorial state. Another reason is that the national has fled back to her home state and that the law of the home state forbids extradition to the territorial state where the crime was committed.

5. One example illustrating this phenomenon appeared in a notorious case from 1997. Two teenagers, Aaron Needle and Samuel Sheinbein, murdered another teen in a Maryland suburb, then burned and dismembered his body. Needle committed suicide in jail; but Sheinbein, with the aid of his father, fled to Israel. Sheinbein's father held Israeli citizenship, and — under Israeli law — that made Samuel Sheinbein an Israeli citizen as well. Israeli law forbids the extradition of an Israeli citizen to face trial in another state. A deeply divided Israeli Supreme Court upheld Sheinbein's claim that he could not be extradited. Israel substitutes nationality jurisdiction for extradition:

> The courts in Israel are competent to try under Israeli law an Israeli national or resident of Israel who committed abroad an act which had it been committed in Israel, would be one of the offences included in the Schedule to the Extradition Law, 5714-1954. . . . An Israeli national shall not be extradited save for an offence committed before he became an Israeli national.

Offenses Committed Abroad Law, 1978, 32 L.S.I. 63, 1(1)4A, 2(1)1A (1977-1978). Samuel Sheinbein preferred to be tried under Israeli law rather than Maryland law because Israel has no death penalty. He entered a guilty plea to murder under Israeli law and was sentenced to 24 years — a lengthy sentence by Israeli standards, but widely denounced in the United States as a travesty of justice, given the atrocious character of his crime. In the aftermath of the Sheinbein case, Israel amended its extradition law to avoid becoming a haven for fugitives. For accounts of the case, see Abraham Abramovsky & Jonathan I. Edelstein, The Sheinbein Case and the Israeli-American Extradition Experience: A Need for Compromise, 32 Vand. J. Transnatl. L. 305 (1999); Dina Maslow, Note: Extradition from Israel: The Samuel Sheinbein Case, 7 Cardozo J. Intl. & Comp. L. 387 (1999).

As we will see in Chapter 10, some states refuse to extradite fugitives to the United States because of their opposition to the death penalty. When the fugitive has dual nationality, prosecution under nationality jurisdiction, as in the Sheinbein case, becomes a live possibility. For an interesting account of such a case involving a French American dual national, see Renee Lettow Lerner, The Intersection of Two Systems: An American on Trial for an American Murder in the French Cour d'Assises, 2001 U. Ill. L. Rev. 791.

6. The United States has traditionally made little use of nationality jurisdiction. However, the Supreme Court has authorized nationality jurisdiction in two criminal cases. Blackmer v. United States, 284 U.S. 421 (1932), affirmed a criminal contempt conviction against an American in Paris who ignored subpoenas to testify in the District of Columbia. According to the Court, Blackmer "continued to owe allegiance to the United States. By virtue of the obligations of citizenship, the United States retained its authority over him, and he was bound by its laws made applicable to him in a foreign country." Id. at 436. And in Skiriotes v. United States, 313 U.S. 69 (1941), the Court affirmed the conviction of a U.S. national who violated a law against sponge diving, even though he was outside U.S. territorial waters at the time. In both *Blackmer* and *Skiriotes*, the Court stated that no principle of international law was at issue, but both represent nationality-based criminal jurisdiction.

Among U.S. statutes that explicitly apply to conduct by U.S. nationals outside U.S. territory are 18 U.S.C. §953 (unauthorized attempts to influence a foreign government in its relations with the United States); §2381 (treason); §2340A (torture outside U.S. territory); §2423 (sex tourism and transportation of minors); §2441 (war crimes); and 50 U.S.C. Appx. §§453, 462 (mandatory draft registration).

7. Other states make vigorous use of nationality jurisdiction. In civil law nations, nationality, perhaps even more than territoriality, serves as the basic organizing principle of international jurisdiction. France, for example, asserts extraterritorial jurisdiction over French nationals in all felony cases. France, Code de Procedure Pénale, Article 689. The most extensive reach of nationality jurisdiction is in India. Chapter 1, §4 of the Indian Penal Code states: "The provisions of this Code apply also to any offence committed by (1) any citizen of India in any place without and beyond India. . . . In this section the word 'offence' includes every act committed outside India which, if committed in India, would be punishable under this Code." One scholar has proposed that the United States make more extensive use of nationality jurisdiction over offenses committed by civilian employees of the U.S. military overseas. Geoffrey R. Watson, Offenders Abroad: The Case for Nationality-Based Criminal Jurisdiction, 17 Yale J. Intl. L. 41 (1992).

UNITED STATES v. CLARK
435 F.3d 1100 (9th Cir. 2006)

. . . BACKGROUND

Michael Lewis Clark, a seventy-one year old U.S. citizen and military veteran, primarily resided in Cambodia from 1998 until his extradition in 2003. He typically took annual trips back to the United States and he also maintained real estate, bank accounts, investment accounts, a driver's license, and a mailing address in this country. Following a family visit in May 2003, Clark left Seattle and flew to Cambodia via Japan, Thailand, and Malaysia. He was traveling on a business visa that he renewed on an annual basis.

While in Cambodia, Clark came to the attention of Action Pour Les Enfants, a non-governmental organization whose mission is to rescue minor boys who have been sexually molested by non-Cambodians. Clark came under suspicion when street kids reported to social workers that he was molesting young boys on a regular basis. The organization in turn reported him to the Cambodian National Police. In late June 2003, the Cambodian police arrested Clark after discovering him in a Phnom Penh guesthouse engaging in sex acts with two boys who were approximately ten and thirteen years old. He was charged with debauchery. The United States government received permission from the Cambodian government to take jurisdiction over Clark.

U.S. officials—assisted by the Cambodian National Police and the Australian Federal Police—conducted an investigation that led to Clark's confession and extradition to the United States. As part of the investigation, the younger boy told authorities that he had engaged in sex acts with Clark because he needed money to buy food for his brother and sister. The older boy stated that Clark had hired him in the past to perform sex acts, on one occasion paying five dollars. Other young boys whom Clark had molested reported that they were paid about two dollars, and Clark stated that he routinely paid this amount. Clark acknowledged that he had been a pedophile since at least 1996, "maybe longer," and had been involved in sexual activity with approximately 40-50 children since he began traveling in 1996.

Upon his return to the United States, Clark was indicted under the provisions of the newly-enacted Prosecutorial Remedies and Other Tools to End the Exploitation of Children Today Act of 2003 ("PROTECT Act"). He pled guilty to two counts under 18 U.S.C. §2423(c) and (e) but reserved the right to appeal his pre-trial motion to dismiss based on constitutional, jurisdictional, and statutory construction grounds.

On appeal, Clark's challenge centers on the constitutionality of §2423(c). Adopted in 2003 as part of the PROTECT Act, §2423(c) provides as follows:

> (c) Engaging in illicit sexual conduct in foreign places. Any United States citizen or alien admitted for permanent residence who travels in foreign commerce, and engages in any illicit sexual conduct with another person shall be fined under this title or imprisoned not more than 30 years, or both.

... The statute defines "illicit sexual conduct" in two ways: First, the definition includes "a sexual act ... with a person under 18 years of age that would be in violation of [several sex abuse statutes]." ... These violations share the common characteristic that there is no economic component to the crime. In other words, they are non-commercial sex acts.

In contrast, the second prong of the definition covers "any commercial sex act (as defined in section 1591 [18 U.S.C. §1591]) with a person under 18 years of age." ... Clark acknowledges that his conduct qualifies as illicit sexual conduct, and he admitted in his plea agreement that he "intended to pay each of the boys and each of the boys expected such payment in exchange for the sexual encounter." Accordingly, it is this second "commercial sex act" prong that is at issue in Clark's appeal.

ANALYSIS

Clark does not dispute that he traveled in "foreign commerce," nor does he dispute that he engaged in illicit commercial sexual conduct. The challenge he raises is to congressional authority to regulate this conduct. In addition to his Commerce Clause challenge, Clark attacks his conviction on international law, statutory construction, and Due Process grounds. . . . [W]e begin our analysis with Clark's non-constitutional claims. . . .

We start with Clark's argument that extraterritorial application of §2423(c) violates principles of international law. On *de novo* review, we hold that extraterritorial application is proper based on the nationality principle.

The legal presumption that Congress ordinarily intends federal statutes to have only domestic application is easily overcome in Clark's case because the text of §2423(c) is explicit as to its application outside the United States. By its terms, the provision is exclusively targeted at extraterritorial conduct.

Having addressed this threshold issue, we ask whether the exercise of extraterritorial jurisdiction in this case comports with principles of international law. . . . Of the five general principles that permit extraterritorial criminal jurisdiction, the nationality principle most clearly applies to Clark's case. The nationality principle "permits a country to apply its statutes to extraterritorial acts of its own nationals." Jurisdiction based solely on the defendant's status as a U.S. citizen is firmly established by our precedent. Clark's U.S. citizenship is uncontested. Accordingly, extraterritorial application of §2423(c) to Clark's conduct is proper based on the nationality principle.[6]

Clark also seeks to invalidate the statute because, in his view, extraterritorial application is unreasonable. The record provides no support for this argument. . . . Cambodia consented to the United States taking jurisdiction and nothing suggests that Cambodia objected in any way to Clark's extradition and trial under U.S. law. Clark himself stated to a U.S. official in Cambodia that he "wanted to return to the United States" because he saw people dying in the Cambodian prison "and was very much afraid that if [he] stayed in that prison, [he] would not survive." Having been saved from immediate prosecution in Cambodia, it is somewhat ironic that he now challenges the law in a United States court. . . .

The next question is whether extraterritorial application of §2423(c) violates the Due Process Clause of the Fifth Amendment because there is an insufficient nexus between Clark's conduct and the United States. We hold that, based on Clark's U.S. citizenship, application of §2423(c) to his extraterritorial conduct is neither "arbitrary nor fundamentally unfair."

Clark is correct that to comply with the Due Process Clause of the Fifth Amendment, extraterritorial application of federal criminal statutes requires the government to demonstrate a sufficient nexus between the defendant and the United States "so that such application would not be arbitrary or fundamentally unfair." . . .

In Blackmer v. United States, 284 U.S. 421 (1932), the Supreme Court explained that the extraterritorial application of U.S. law to its citizens abroad did not violate the Fifth Amendment. The Court declared that despite moving his residence to France, the U.S.-citizen defendant "continued to owe allegiance to the United States. By virtue of the obligations of citizenship, the United States retained its authority over him, and he was bound by its laws made applicable to him in a foreign country." This longstanding principle that citizenship alone is sufficient to satisfy Due Process concerns still has force.

Clark offers no authority that calls into question this principle. Instead, he relies on cases that involved *foreign* nationals, which meant that the courts had no choice but to look beyond nationality to establish the defendants' ties with the United States.

---

6. [Court's footnote: 10] Although the district court found that extraterritorial jurisdiction was proper under both the nationality principle and universality principle, we decline to address whether the universality principle also applies in Clark's case because extraterritorial application of a criminal law need be justified by only one of the five principles of extraterritorial authority.

Clark is a U.S. citizen, a bond that "implies a duty of allegiance on the part of the member and a duty of protection on the part of the society. These are reciprocal obligations, one being a compensation for the other." Predicated on this imputed allegiance, application of §2423(c) to Clark's extraterritorial conduct does not violate the Due Process Clause. . . .

[The court next considers the issue of whether Congress exceeded its constitutional authority in enacting the sex tourism statute. This is principally an issue of domestic rather than international law. We return to it, and the court's analysis of it, later in this chapter, when we examine the principles of extraterritorial jurisdiction in U.S. law. See Section B.2 below — EDS.]

NOTES AND QUESTIONS

1. Do you agree that a "duty of allegiance," predicated on the fact of nationality, provides "a sufficient nexus" for the application of domestic law to extraterritorial activities? If not for all activities, then which ones?

2. The phenomenon of "sex tourism" rose to prominence after the Vietnam War, during which a large and notorious sex industry grew up in Thailand, where U.S. troops went on leave. Disturbingly, the industry included a large number of child prostitutes. After the war, the red light districts in Bangkok and beach resorts such as Pattaya continued to thrive, with patronage by sex tourists from Japan, Australia, Europe, and the United States. In addition to Thailand, the Asian sex industry includes the Philippines, Sri Lanka, and Cambodia; and human rights groups estimate that more than a million underage prostitutes work in the Asian sex trade. See, e.g., Abigail Schwartz, Sex Trafficking in Cambodia, 17 Colum. J. Asian L. 371 (2004); Sara K. Andrews, Comment: U.S. Domestic Prosecution of the American International Sex Tourist: Efforts to Protect Children from Sexual Exploitation, 94 J. Crim. L. & Criminology 415 (2004); Eric Thomas Berkman, Note: Responses to the International Child Sex Tourism Trade, 19 B.C. Intl. & Comp. L. Rev. 397 (1996). But sex tourism is not only an Asian problem; sex trades with foreign customers and underage prostitutes have expanded in Latin America and Africa as well. Nancy Beyer, Note: The Sex Tourism Industry Spreads to Costa Rica and Honduras: Are These Countries Doing Enough to Protect Their Children from Sexual Exploitation?, 29 Ga. J. Intl. & Comp. L. 301 (2001); Gregory S. Loyd, Note: Child Sexual Exploitation in Costa Rica, 12 Ind. Intl. & Comp. L. Rev. 157 (2001).

Children wind up in the sex trade for economic reasons: In some cases their impoverished parents sell them into it (an all-too-common modern form of slavery); in others, sex entrepreneurs dupe parents into believing that they will provide legitimate jobs or schooling for their daughters. Once in the trade, pimps and madams keep prostitutes in the brothels by threats, force, and, often, drugs. Indeed, coercion sometimes proves unnecessary because the sex trade is more lucrative than any of the limited number of alternatives available for poor children, such as begging. For a dollars-and-cents discussion of the economics of the sex trade, see Suwanna Satha-Anand, Looking to Buddhism to Turn Back Prostitution in Thailand, in The East Asian Challenge for Human Rights 193 (Joanne R. Bauer & Daniel A. Bell eds., 1999). The preference of men for child prostitutes is often based on the belief that they are less likely to carry HIV (pimps market children as virgins), along with the widespread superstition that sex with a virgin can cure AIDS. Home states generally have laws against child prostitution on the books but lack the means and often the will to enforce these laws, particularly given the income that the sex industry brings into national economies. For a clear explanation of the dynamics of the sex trade and sex trafficking in Asia, see Schwartz, supra, at 381-391. As in the Vietnam War, a military presence can exacerbate the problem. After the arrival of UN peacekeepers in Cambodia—with active libidos and full wallets—the number of prostitutes in Phnom Penh grew from 1,500 to 20,000 in just two years. Id. at 407; see also Jennifer Murray, Note: Who Will Police the Peace-Builders? The Failure to Establish Accountability for the Participation of United Nations Civilian Police in the Trafficking of Women in Post-Conflict Bosnia and Herzegovina, 34 Colum. Hum. Rts. L. Rev. 475 (2003); Marc Lacey, In Congo War, Even Peacekeepers Add to Horror, N.Y. Times, Dec. 18, 2004, at A1.

The 1990s saw substantial progress in legal efforts to crack down on sex tourism. Sweden, Germany, Australia, and the United States enacted anti-sex-tourism legislation; currently, over 30 countries have criminalized sex tourism. See Online CSEC [Commercial Sexual Exploitation of Children] Database: http://www.ecpat.net/EI/CSEC_onlineDatabase.asp (last visited June 10, 2009). For details of the foreign legislation, see Berkman, supra. The UN Convention on the Rights of the Child (UNCRC) entered into force in 1990. It has been ratified by every state except Somalia and the United States—Somalia because it lacks a government, and the United States because of concerns that implementation of certain of its provisions would infringe on established tenets of federalism (such as local control of education) as well as family rights. Article 19 of UNCRC requires states parties to "take all appropriate legislative, administrative, social and educational measures to protect the child from all forms of physical or mental violence, injury or abuse, neglect or negligent treatment, maltreatment or exploitation including sexual abuse"; and, in the wake of UNCRC, sex tourism centers have beefed up legislation and protective measures.

The George W. Bush administration made the protection of children from exploitation and trafficking one of its human rights priorities, and under President Bush the U.S. Senate ratified an Optional Protocol to UNCRC targeting child prostitution and child pornography. The Optional Protocol requires states to criminalize "offering, obtaining, procuring or providing a child for child prostitution" as well as "an attempt to commit any of the said acts and to complicity or participation in any of the said acts." Articles 3(1)(b) & 3(2). It also permits states to establish whatever criminal jurisdiction is necessary to punish such acts when committed by a national of the state. Article 4(2)(a). It was in response to the Optional Protocol that the United States enacted the PROTECT Act—beefing up earlier anti-sex-tourism legislation passed by the Clinton administration in 1994.

3. The enhanced sex tourism statute, 18 U.S.C. §2423 (2003), under which Clark was convicted, reads as follows.

§2423. Transportation of Minors . . .

   (b) Travel with intent to engage in illicit sexual conduct.—A person who travels in interstate commerce or travels into the United States, or a United States citizen or an alien admitted for permanent residence in the United States who travels in foreign commerce, for the purpose of engaging in any illicit sexual conduct with another person shall be fined under this title or imprisoned not more than 30 years, or both.
   (c) Engaging in illicit sexual conduct in foreign places. — Any United States citizen or alien admitted for permanent residence who travels in foreign commerce, and engages

in any illicit sexual conduct with another person shall be fined under this title or imprisoned not more than 30 years, or both.

    (d) Ancillary offenses.—Whoever, for the purpose of commercial advantage or private financial gain, arranges, induces, procures, or facilitates the travel of a person knowing that such a person is traveling in interstate commerce or foreign commerce for the purpose of engaging in illicit sexual conduct shall be fined under this title, imprisoned not more than 30 years, or both.

    (e) Attempt and conspiracy.—Whoever attempts or conspires to violate subsection (a), (b), (c), or (d) shall be punishable in the same manner as a completed violation of that subsection.

    (f) Definition.—As used in this section, the term "illicit sexual conduct" means (1) a sexual act (as defined in section 2246) with a person under 18 years of age that would be in violation of chapter 109A [a group of sexual abuse statutes] if the sexual act occurred in the special maritime and territorial jurisdiction of the United States; or (2) any commercial sex act (as defined in section 1591) with a person under 18 years of age.

    (g) Defense.—In a prosecution under this section based on illicit sexual conduct as defined in subsection (f)(2), it is a defense, which the defendant must establish by a preponderance of the evidence, that the defendant reasonably believed that the person with whom the defendant engaged in the commercial sex act had attained the age of 18 years.

As of January 2008, Immigration and Customs Enforcement (ICE) agents "have made more than 67 arrests under the child sex tourism provisions of the PROTECT Act. Of those, 47 have been convicted and others are still being prosecuted." ICE Fact Sheet: Operation Predator: Child Exploitation and Sexual Crimes (Jan. 25, 2008), available at http://www.ice.gov/pi/news/factsheets/070607operationpredator.htm (last visited June 10, 2009).

4. Section (b) of the statute, it is important to note, criminalizes the mere act of travel for the purpose of engaging in illicit sexual conduct—whether or not the perpetrator has actually engaged in the conduct. The criminal act has been completed the moment the perpetrator touches down at the destination. United States v. Bredimus, 234 F. Supp. 2d 639 (N.D. Tex. 2002). Prosecutors nevertheless found §2423(b) difficult to use because of the difficulty of proving the intention with which the perpetrator travels.

5. *The Passive Personality Principle*

RESTATEMENT (THIRD) OF THE FOREIGN RELATIONS LAW OF THE UNITED STATES

(1987)

§402 JURISDICTION TO PRESCRIBE

COMMENT:

. . . *g. The passive personality principle.* The passive personality principle asserts that a state may apply law—particularly criminal law—to an act committed outside its territory by a person not its national where the victim of the act was its national. The principle has not been generally accepted for ordinary torts or crimes, but it is increasingly accepted as applied to terrorist or other organized attacks on a state's nationals by reason of their nationality, or to assassination of a state's diplomatic representatives or other officials.

PROBLEM 2

A. In 1986, Congress enacted the following statute in response to a terrorist attack on an Italian cruise ship in which a U.S. passenger was murdered:

18 U.S.C. §2332. CRIMINAL PENALTIES

(a) Homicide. Whoever kills a national of the United States, while such national is outside the United States, shall,—

(1) if the killing is murder . . . , be fined under this title, punished by death or imprisonment for any term of years or for life, or both. . . .

(d) Limitation on prosecution. No prosecution for any offense described in this section shall be undertaken by the United States except on written certification of the Attorney General or the highest ranking subordinate of the Attorney General with responsibility for criminal prosecutions that, in the judgment of the certifying official, such offense was intended to coerce, intimidate, or retaliate against a government or a civilian population.

Consider the following hypothetical, based on an actual 2004 event: Chechen rebels fighting against Russia launch a terrorist attack against a Russian school, killing many parents and children. Unbeknownst to the rebels, one of the children is a U.S. national who is an exchange student. The planner of the attack escapes. A year later he is captured by U.S. forces in Afghanistan and brought to the United States. The United States has no extradition treaty with Russia.

1. Should the planner be tried for homicide under §2332?
2. Would it make a difference if there was an extradition treaty with Russia and Russia requested that he be extradited to stand trial for the mass murder?
3. Would it make a difference if the defendant had come to the United States voluntarily, rather than being captured abroad and brought to the United States against his will?
4. What if, instead of an exchange student killed in a terrorist attack on a school, the U.S. national was a war correspondent traveling with Russian army units in Chechnya and killed by rebel fire during a nighttime battle? Has the Chechen planner had fair notice that he is liable to felony prosecution in the United States for violence committed—against Russians, he thought—in his rebellion against Russia?

B. Article 113-7 of the French Penal Code provides: "French criminal law is applicable to any felony, as well as to any misdemeanor punishable by imprisonment, committed by a French or foreign national outside the territory of the French Republic, where the victim is a French national at the time of the offense." French courts have construed Article 113-7 broadly, to include crimes such as defamation and trademark infringement. Furthermore, "Article 113-7 is not qualified by a 'dual criminality' requirement. Hence, a foreign national can be prosecuted in France for an action considered legal where it took place."[7] In addition, many French regulations have criminal penalties attached to them. These include, for example, violation of labor regulations requiring any manager who lays off a worker to provide the worker access to an employee-counselor.[8]

Suppose that a U.S. manager lays off a French national from a business in the United States. The worker receives no access to an employee-counselor; indeed, she is summarily fired and, as is common practice in many U.S. businesses, escorted from the building by security guards without being permitted to return to her desk. The despondent worker commits suicide, and the incident receives wide publicity in French newspapers. On vacation in Paris, the U.S. manager is arrested and charged with criminal violation of the French labor code. Is this a legitimate prosecution?

NOTES AND QUESTIONS

1. Comment *g* in the Restatement, quoted above, suggests that the passive personality principle will be used only in crimes, such as terrorist attacks, in which a state's nationals are attacked because of their nationality. However, the U.S. homicide statute in Part A of Problem 2 includes no such requirement: The murder must take place during a terrorist attack on some government or civilian population — but it need not be the U.S. government or a U.S. population.

2. Likewise, we have earlier mentioned cases in which cruise ship personnel have been prosecuted for sexually molesting underage Americans on the high seas, with the effects principle providing one predicate for extraterritorial application of U.S. laws. As it happens, the courts in both these cases also asserted that the passive personality principle would permit extraterritorial application of sex abuse statutes. United States v. Neil, 312 F.3d 419, 422 (9th Cir. 2002); United States v. Roberts, 1 F. Supp. 2d 601 (E.D. La. 1998). So too, in United States v. Hill, 279 F.3d 731 (9th Cir. 2002), the court invoked the passive personality principle to justify prosecuting a woman who harbored her husband in Mexico to help him flee child support payments from a previous marriage:

> Finally, the passive personality theory, which bases jurisdiction on the nationality of the victim, sanctions extraterritorial application of the harboring statute in the instant case. The victims here — Charlie's ex-wife, Victoria, and their children — are all United States citizens. Not surprisingly, the record shows that Charlie's failure to pay child support for twenty years had a significant negative impact on the victims' financial condition. Hill's harboring conduct prolonged their situation. Therefore, extraterritorial jurisdiction is appropriate under this theory. . . .

Id. at 740. In none of these cases did the victim's nationality play a role in the crime. Do they represent legitimate uses of the passive personality principle?

3. United States v. Yunis, 924 F.2d 1086 (D.C. Cir. 1991), involved a Lebanese national who hijacked a Royal Jordanian airliner in Beirut, to protest the presence of Palestinians in Lebanon. After a circuit around the Mediterranean, with refueling stops in Cyprus and Sicily as well as unsuccessful attempts to fly to Tunis and Syria, the plane landed in Beirut, where Yunis and his confederates released the passengers and

---

7. Eric Cafritz & Omer Tene, Article 113-7 of the French Penal Code: The Passive Personality Principle, 41 Colum. J. Transnatl. L. 585, 588 (2003).
8. Id. at 591.

blew up the plane. Two U.S. nationals had been on board. The FBI planned an elaborate scheme to capture Yunis. Two years after the hijacking, they lured him onto a yacht in international waters (supposedly to do a drug deal), arrested him, and brought him to the United States for trial on charges of conspiracy, aircraft piracy, and hostage taking. His motions to dismiss for lack of jurisdiction were denied, and the district court cited the passive personality principle (as well as universality) as providing "ample grounds for this Court to assert jurisdiction over Yunis." United States v. Yunis, 681 F. Supp. 896, 903 (D.D.C. 1988). The court of appeals affirmed.

4. Although U.S. courts have used the passive personality principle in a handful of cases, by and large the principle has not found favor in the United States. In *Cutting*, the United States firmly rejected Mexico's use of the passive personality principle. So too, the 1935 Harvard Research on International Law jurisdiction project described the principle as "more strongly contested than any other type of competence" and "the most difficult to justify in theory." Harvard Research on International Law, Jurisdiction with Respect to Crime, 29 Am J. Intl. L. 435, 579 (Supp. 1935). Not only does it intrude on other states' sovereignty, it also raises questions of fair notice and legality — how is a foreigner, acting outside of a country, supposed to be on notice that his action is criminal within that country? Furthermore, the deterrent power of criminal law given effect through passive personality is surely quite weak. For a discussion of these policy arguments, see Geoffrey R. Watson, The Passive Personality Principle, 28 Texas Intl. L.J. 1, 14-22 (1993). Do states' interests in protecting their own citizens abroad sufficiently justify passive personality jurisdiction?

6. *The Protective Principle*

RESTATEMENT (THIRD) OF THE FOREIGN RELATIONS LAW OF THE UNITED STATES

(1987)

§402(3) BASES OF JURISDICTION TO PRESCRIBE

Subject to §403, a state has jurisdiction to prescribe law with respect to . . .

(3) certain conduct outside its territory by persons not its nationals that is directed against the security of the state or against a limited class of other state interests.

COMMENT:

. . . *f. The protective principle.* Subsection (3) restates the protective principle of jurisdiction. International law recognizes the right of a state to punish a limited class of offenses committed outside its territory by persons who are not its nationals — offenses directed against the security of the state or other offenses threatening the integrity of governmental functions that are generally recognized as crimes by developed legal systems, e.g., espionage, counterfeiting of the state's seal or currency, falsification of official documents, as well as perjury before consular officials, and conspiracy to violate the immigration or customs laws. The protective principle may be seen as a special application of the effects principle, but it has been treated as an independent basis of jurisdiction. The protective principle does not support application to foreign nationals of laws against political expression, such as libel of the state or of the chief of state.

PROBLEM 3

Assume that for several years, the West African state of Atlantia has been wracked by civil war. Rebel groups, financed by gems and minerals from territory under their control, purchase their arms from U.S. and European suppliers. Atlantia enacts legislation making it a crime to traffic arms to the rebel groups or to conspire to do so. Executives from weapons-exporting companies located in Hartford, Connecticut, and Cologne, Germany, visit Atlantia. They are arrested and charged with conspiracy to traffic, based on business conversations with rebel leaders in Hartford and Cologne. Does the protective principle permit their prosecution?

PROSECUTOR v. ADOLF EICHMANN

Criminal Case No. 40/61, Judgment
Israel, District Court of Jerusalem
(1961)

30. . . . The State of Israel's "right to punish" the Accused derives, in our view, from two cumulative sources: a universal source (pertaining to the whole of mankind) which vests the right to prosecute and punish crimes of this order in every state within the family of nations; and a specific or national source which gives the victim nation the right to try any who assault its existence.

This second foundation of penal jurisdiction conforms, according to the acknowledged terminology, to the protective principle (the *competence réelle*). . . . Oppenheim-Lauterpacht I para. 147, p. 333, says that the penal jurisdiction of the state includes "crimes injuring its subjects or serious crimes against its own safety." . . .

34. The connection between the State of Israel and the Jewish People needs no explanation. The State of Israel was established and recognized as the State of the Jews. . . . It would appear that there is no need for any further proof of the obvious connection between the Jewish People and the State of Israel: This is the sovereign state of the Jewish People. . . .

In the light of the recognition by the United Nations of the right of the Jewish People to establish their State, and in the light of the recognition of the established Jewish State by the family of nations, the connection between the Jewish People and the State of Israel constitutes an integral part of the law of nations.

The massacre of millions of Jews by the Nazi criminals that very nearly led to the extinction of the Jewish People in Europe, was one of the tremendous causes for the establishment of the State of the survivors. The State cannot be cut off from its roots which also lie deep within the Holocaust of European Jewry.

Half of the citizens of the State have immigrated from Europe in recent years, some before and some after the Nazi massacre. There is hardly one of them who has not lost parents, brothers and sisters, and many lost their spouses and their offspring in the Nazi hell. Under these circumstances, which are without precedent in the annals of any other nation, can there be any one who would contend that there is no sufficient "linking point" between the crime of the extermination of the Jews of Europe and the State of Israel?

35. . . . [T]he people is one and the crime is one. . . . To argue that there is no connection, is like cutting away the roots and branches of a tree and saying to its trunk: I have not hurt you.

Indeed, this crime very deeply concerns the vital interests of the State of Israel, and pursuant to the "protective principle," this State has the right to punish the criminals. . . .

The very existence of a people who can be murdered with impunity is in danger, to say nothing of the danger to its "honour and authority" (Grotius). This has been the curse of the diaspora and the want of sovereignty of the Jewish People, upon whom any criminal could commit his outrages without fear of being punished by the people outraged. Hitler and his associates exploited the defenceless position of the Jewish People in its dispersion, in order to perpetrate the total murder of that People in cold blood. It was also in order to provide some measure of redress for the terrible injustice of the Holocaust that the sovereign state of the Jews, which enables the survivors of the Holocaust to defend its existence by the means at the disposal of a state, was established on the recommendation of the United Nations. One of the means therefor is the punishment of the murderers who did Hitler's contemptible work. It is for this reason that the Law in question has been enacted.

36. Counsel contended that the protective principle cannot apply to this case because that principle is designed to protect only an existing state, its security and its interests, while the State of Israel had not existed at the time of the commission of the crime. . . .

In our view, learned Counsel errs when he examines the protective principle in this retroactive Law according to the time of the commission of the crimes, as is the case in an ordinary law. . . . The protected interest of the State recognized by the protective principle is, in this case, the interest existing at the time of the enactment of the Law, and we have already dwelt on the importance of the moral and protective task which this Law is designed to achieve in the State of Israel.

38. [B]ut may a new state try crimes at all that were committed before it was established? . . .

During the period preceding the establishment of the sovereign State, the Jewish National Home may be seen as reflecting the rule *nasciturus pro jam nato habetur* [an unborn child is considered born]. The Jewish "Yishuv" [community] in Palestine constituted during that period a "state-on-the-way," which in due time reached a sovereign status. The lack of sovereignty made it impossible for the Jewish "Yishuv" in the country to enact a criminal law against the Nazi crimes at the time of their commission, but these crimes were also directed against that "Yishuv" which constituted an integral part of the Jewish People, and the enactment with retroactive application of the Law in question by the State of Israel answered the need which had already existed previously.

The historical facts explain the background of the legislation in question; but it seems to us that, from a legal point of view, the power of the new State to enact retroactive legislation does not depend on that background alone, and is not conditioned by the continuity of law between Palestine and the State of Israel. Let us take an extreme example and assume that the Gypsy survivors — an ethnic group or a nation who were also, like the Jewish People, victims of the "crime of genocide" — would have gathered after the War and established a sovereign state in any part of the world. It seems to us that no principle of international law could have denied the new state the natural power to put on trial all those killers of their people who fell into their hands. The right of the injured group to punish offenders derives directly, as Grotius explained from the crime committed against them by the offender, and it was only want of sovereignty that denied them the power to try and punish the offender. If the injured group or people thereafter reaches political sovereignty in any territory, it may make use of such sovereignty for the enforcement of its natural right to punish the offender who injured it.

NOTES AND QUESTIONS

1. According to the *Eichmann* court, what is the state interest that Eichmann's prosecution protects? Is this a legitimate use of the protective principle? How much latitude should states have to define their own vital interests? In the Kosovo War, crimes were committed by Kosovar Serbs against Kosovar Albanians. Should Albania be able to enact a criminal statute with extraterritorial reach to punish the perpetrators? Should Pakistan be able to criminalize anti-Muslim ethnic violence in India?

2. In §34, the *Eichmann* court refers to "the recognition by the United Nations of the right of the Jewish People to establish their State." This refers to the creation of the state of Israel in 1948. Palestine (including Israel and Jordan) had previously been under the control or "mandate" of Great Britain. In 1947, the UN General Assembly approved a plan to end the British mandate in 1948 and divide Palestine into an Arab state (the future Jordan) and a Jewish state (the future Israel). UN General Assembly Resolution 181 (Nov. 29, 1947). The court argues that this, together with international recognition of the State of Israel, demonstrates that "the connection between the Jewish People and the State of Israel constitutes an integral part of the law of nations." Does it follow that international law recognizes a connection between Israel and non-Israeli Jews?

3. In U.S. practice, the protective principle has been invoked in order to justify drug arrests on the high seas. Does mere possession of narcotics offend a vital sovereign interest or the integrity of essential governmental operations? How should the state interest be defined for purposes of the protective principle? Does it encompass a generalized interest in protecting the integrity of national borders against smuggling? Consider an argument of the Eleventh Circuit Court of Appeals:

> Even absent a treaty or arrangement, the United States could, under the "protective principle" of international law, prosecute foreign nationals on foreign vessels on the high seas for possession of narcotics. The protective principle permits a nation to assert jurisdiction over a person whose conduct outside the nation's territory threatens the nation's security or could potentially interfere with the operation of its governmental functions.

United States v. Romero-Galue, 757 F.2d 1147, 1154 (11th Cir. 1985). The statute in question in *Romero-Galue*, 21 U.S.C. §955a(c) (subsequently transferred to as 46 U.S.C. §70503), criminalizes possession with intent to distribute regardless of which state is the intended place of distribution. Suppose that the ship is transporting marijuana from a state where it is lawful to grow it to a state where it is lawful to smoke it. Why should the United States be permitted to seize the ship's crew and prosecute them for a major felony? Is it entirely up to the United States to decide whether their activity threatens the nation's security? Who else could make that decision?

4. Counterfeiting is one paradigm crime under the protective principle. A state's currency can be dramatically undermined by counterfeiting abroad, even if none of the counterfeit money ever circulates within the state. Along the same lines, the Ninth Circuit Court of Appeals has held that a statute banning fraudulent concealment of assets during a bankruptcy has extraterritorial reach because of the important governmental interest in maintaining public confidence in the bankruptcy system. Stegeman v. United States, 425 F.2d 984, 985 (9th Cir. 1970).

5. A second paradigm crime that the protective principle reaches is espionage. In United States v. Zehe, 601 F. Supp. 196 (D. Mass. 1985), an East German national was indicted for acts of espionage against the United States committed in Mexico and East Germany. Zehe moved to dismiss for lack of jurisdiction. The court rejected Zehe's argument, asserting that

> Congress has the power to prosecute both citizens and noncitizens for espionage com-mitted outside of this country's territorial limits. The defendant concedes that under principles of international law recognized by United States courts, Congress is compe-tent to punish criminal acts, wherever and by whomever committed, that threaten national security or directly obstruct governmental functions. Espionage against the United States, because it is a crime that by definition threatens this country's security, can therefore be punished by Congress even if committed by a noncitizen outside the United States.

Id. at 198. The court also found congressional intent to apply the Espionage Act extraterritorially.

6. The comment from the Restatement quoted above argues that the protective principle can be seen as a version of the effects principle (objective territorial principle). There is a difference, however. What makes the effects principle a version of territorial jurisdiction is that the effect of conduct "belongs" to the conduct just as much as the cause. A shooting involves both a marksman and a target, and the bullet striking the target is no less an element of the shooting than the pulling of the trigger is. The same cannot obviously be said about remote effects. Thus, counterfeiting a few thousand Mexican pesos will not necessarily cause instability in Mexico's currency, and it might therefore be difficult for Mexico to claim effects jurisdiction over foreign counterfeiters. So too, acts of (or attempts at) espionage might conceivably cause no demonstrable damage to U.S. security. Should they therefore fall beyond the reach of national jurisdiction? The First Circuit Court of Appeals draws the distinction between the two principles as follows:

> The objective territorial principle is distinct from the protective theory in that in the latter all the elements of the crimes occur in the foreign country, and jurisdiction exists because these actions have a potentially adverse effect upon security or governmental function, with no actual effect taking place in the country.

United States v. Smith, 680 F.2d 255, 258 (1st Cir. 1982).

For further reading, see Iain Cameron, The Protective Principle of International Criminal Jurisdiction (1994).

7. *The Universality Principle and Universal Jurisdiction*

RESTATEMENT (THIRD) OF THE FOREIGN RELATIONS LAW OF THE UNITED STATES

(1987)

§404 Universal Jurisdiction to Define and Punish Certain Offenses

A state has jurisdiction to define and prescribe punishment for certain offenses recognized by the community of nations as of universal concern, such as piracy, slave trade, attacks on or hijacking of aircraft, genocide, war crimes, and perhaps certain acts of terrorism, even where none of the bases of jurisdiction indicated in §402 is present.

COMMENTS & ILLUSTRATIONS:

Comment:

a. *Expanding class of universal offenses.* This section, and the corresponding section concerning jurisdiction to adjudicate, §423, recognize that international law permits any state to apply its laws to punish certain offenses although the state has no links of territory with the offense, or of nationality with the offender (or even the victim). Universal jurisdiction over the specified offenses is a result of universal condemnation of those activities and general interest in cooperating to suppress them, as reflected in widely accepted international agreements and resolutions of international organizations. These offenses are subject to universal jurisdiction as a matter of customary law. Universal jurisdiction for additional offenses is provided by international agreements, but it remains to be determined whether universal jurisdiction over a particular offense has become customary law for states not party to such an agreement. A universal offense is generally not subject to limitations of time.

. . . Universal jurisdiction is increasingly accepted for certain acts of terrorism, such as assaults on the life or physical integrity of diplomatic personnel, kidnapping, and indiscriminate violent assaults on people at large.

b. *Universal jurisdiction not limited to criminal law.* In general, jurisdiction on the basis of universal interests has been exercised in the form of criminal law, but international law does not preclude the application of non-criminal law on this basis, for example, by providing a remedy in tort or restitution for victims of piracy.

NOTES AND QUESTIONS

1. The concept of universal jurisdiction reaches far back into the history of international law. Medieval law in the Italian city-states allowed any state that had custody to prosecute *vagabundi*—vagabonds, persons with no permanent place of residence — for serious offenses if it was impractical to return them to the *locus delicti*, the place the crime was committed. The sixteenth-century Spaniard Covarruvias argued that the same principle should apply to any serious crime, whether or not the offender was a vagabond. Covarruvias proposed that the state having custody— the *locus deprehensionis*—had a duty either to extradite serious offenders or to punish them. In order to punish them, the state would have to establish jurisdiction. This was the first form of universal jurisdiction. It was "subsidiary" to the jurisdiction of the *locus delicti* because extraditing the offender was preferable to trying the offender in courts of a state that had no connection with the crime beyond the fact of having the defendant in custody.

As we shall see, Covarruvias's proposal — either extradite or prosecute — has been embodied in many twentieth-century treaties. It is usually referred to by the Latin phrases *aut dedere, aut prosequi* (either extradite or prosecute) or *aut dedere, aut judicare* (either extradite or try). An equivalent to the term *subsidiary universal jurisdiction* is *extradite or prosecute jurisdiction*.

2. In the seventeenth century, Grotius, one of the founders of international law, argued that states should have universal jurisdiction over crimes that "excessively

violate the law of nature or of nations. . . ." Hugo Grotius, The Law of War and Peace bk. II, ch. 20, §49 (1625). Another founding figure of international law, the Swiss jurist Vattel, proposed in 1758 that this includes "poisoners, assassins, and incendiaries by profession," who "may be exterminated wherever they are seized; for they attack and injure all nations, by trampling underfoot the foundations of their common safety. Thus, pirates are sent to the gibbet by the first into whose hands they fall." Emmerich Vattel, The Law of Nations or Principles of Natural Law Applied to the Conduct and Affairs of Sovereigns, bk. I, ch. 19, ¶233 (J. Chitty trans. 1839). Although nowadays Vattel's list of universal jurisdiction crimes may strike us as quaint, the idea that certain crimes make the criminal an "enemy of the human race" — *hostis generis humani*, in the usual phrase used by international lawyers — is not quaint at all. Substitute "skyjackers, war criminals, and torturers" — or, for that matter, Somali pirates — for Vattel's enumeration and you get a familiar list of universal jurisdiction offenses. Multilateral treaties require states parties to establish extradite or prosecute jurisdiction at least over skyjacking and torture, while the Geneva Conventions against war crimes go even further: They define a category of "grave breaches" and obligate states parties "to search for persons alleged to have committed, or to have ordered to be committed, such grave breaches, and . . . bring such persons, regardless of their nationality, before its own courts." (This language appears in differently numbered articles in the four Geneva Conventions: GC 1, art. 49; GC 2, art. 50; GC 3, art. 129; GC 4, art. 146.) Fulfilling this obligation would apparently require states to establish universal jurisdiction. (However, the Geneva Conventions do not say so explicitly.)

3. As Vattel's reference to pirates makes clear, piracy was the first widely recognized universal jurisdiction offense. Pirates committed their robberies on the high seas, outside the territorial jurisdiction of any state, and pirate crews might include men of many nations. Often, no state had a better territorial or nationality-based claim to try pirates than did any other state. It proved most convenient to permit whoever captured the pirates to try them. Although many contemporary writers point to piracy as the leading precedent for modern uses of universal jurisdiction, modern uses focus on the peculiarly heinous character of the offenses, rather than the practicalities of trial. For a spirited argument that piracy does not provide a good analogy to modern universal jurisdiction, see Eugene Kontorovich, The Piracy Analogy: Modern Universal Jurisdiction's Hollow Foundation, 45 Harv. Intl. L.J. 183 (2004); see also Alfred P. Rubin, The Law of Piracy (2d ed. 1998).

Recently, piracy has emerged as a headline-grabbing issue. In the first half of 2009, over 20 countries had sent warships to patrol for pirates off the coast of Somalia. The UN Security Council has called upon all nations with the capacity to deploy naval vessels to seize pirate ships and equipment, and, with notification to the Somali government, to pursue and apprehend pirates taking refuge in Somalia. S.C. Res. 1816, U.N. Doc. S/RES/1816 (June 2, 2008); S.C. Res. 1851, U.N. Doc. S/RES/ 1851 (Dec. 16, 2008). In early 2009, the U.S.-flagged *Maersk Alabama* container ship was seized by pirates off the coast of Somalia. Because the *Maersk Alabama* is a U.S.-flagged ship, the U.S. navy responded and freed the ship and crew, killing several of the pirates and bringing one captured pirate to stand trial in New York.

While a country clearly has jurisdiction over pirates captured in the act of attacking vessels flying its own flag, things can be more complicated in other situations. What happens, for example, when the Canadian navy apprehends pirates attacking a Liberian-flagged ship? Canada was roundly criticized for releasing, without prosecution, a boatload of pirates in April 2009. Although there is no question that international law permits Canada to try the pirates under universal jurisdiction, Canada has no universal jurisdiction statute in its domestic law. Canadian officials claimed they had no choice but to release the pirates for want of jurisdiction. Katie Derosa, Canada Extends Anti-Pirate Mission, Natl. Post, May 4, 2009, available at http://www.nationalpost.com/story.html?id=1561517; Canada Seeks to Change Policy on Pirate Prosecution: MacKay, CBC News, May 21, 2009, available at http://www.cbc.ca/world/story/2009/05/21/canada-piracy-kenya894.html.

In practice, prosecuting states may also face the problem of what to do with convicted pirates after their sentences have been served, since their countries of origin may not be enthusiastic about taking them back. For discussion of these issues, see Eugene Kontorovich, "A Guantánamo on the Sea": The Difficulties of Prosecuting Pirates and Terrorists, 98 Cal. L. Rev. (forthcoming 2010).

4. The most common basis for modern universal jurisdiction lies in twentieth-century multilateral treaties for the suppression of various crimes. (The discussion that follows is drawn from Luc Reydams, Universal Jurisdiction: International and Municipal Legal Perspectives (2003).) Before World War II, these included international conventions for suppressing counterfeiting, narcotics trafficking, and terrorism. All these conventions created "subsidiary" universal jurisdiction, along the lines proposed three centuries earlier by Covarruvias: They specify that the custodial state should prosecute the crimes, but only if extradition to states with a connection to the crime proves impossible. Soon after the war came the Geneva Conventions, which create a basis for prosecuting war crimes regardless of the offender's nationality or the location of the crime. See Chapter 21. Later, states included criminal provisions in treaties to protect cultural property in wartime and in the Law of the Sea. A treaty declared apartheid an international crime. There are many others. See M. Cherif Bassiouni, International Criminal Law Conventions and Their Penal Provisions (1997). For a history of universal jurisdiction, and a summary of the relevant treaties, see Reydams, supra, at 28-80. Lawyers often refer to such jurisdiction as "universal," although in fact it arises only pursuant to the treaty and is "universal" only among the parties to the treaty.

The Hague Hijacking Convention of 1970 created a model of subsidiary universal jurisdiction that more than 20 treaties have since copied. These treaties follow a characteristic pattern:

1. They require states parties to criminalize the conduct in their domestic codes, if they haven't already done so.
2. They typically set out agreed grounds for states to assert primary jurisdiction, for example, over crimes committed in their territory, on board their vessels or aircraft, sometimes by their nationals, less often against their nationals, or where the enforcing state was the "target" of the crime.
3. Even when they have no such ground to prosecute, states are obliged either to extradite the accused to a requesting state or, if extradition is denied, to submit for prosecution domestically. For a summary of the *aut dedere aut prosequi* clauses in numerous multilateral conventions, see M. Cherif Bassiouni, Universal Jurisdiction for International Crimes: Historical Perspectives and Contemporary Practice, 42 Va. J. Intl. L. 81, 122-134 (2001).
4. They require the states parties to establish jurisdiction that will enable them to prosecute those offenders they do not extradite. This means that states parties are required to establish universal jurisdiction over the offense, at least for cases where they do not extradite the offender.

5. It is important to understand the difference between "pure" universal jurisdiction and subsidiary universal jurisdiction. (And both are different from the
jurisdiction exercised by the ICC and other international tribunals, which is
sometimes, misleadingly, labeled *universal.*) Universal jurisdiction strictly considered permits any state to try an offense under its domestic law regardless of
that state's lack of connection to the offense, the offender, or the victim — and
without regard to any international agreement. By contrast, subsidiary
universal jurisdiction allows states with no connection to the offense to try it
only if they find the offender in their territory and cannot extradite the suspect
to a state that does have connection with the offense. Some lawyers and scholars reserve the term *universal jurisdiction* for the first situation and distinguish
it from extradite or prosecute jurisdiction, which typically arises under a treaty
regime.

Some object to universal jurisdiction on the ground that it represents a unilateral
assertion of domestic jurisdiction subject to no established rules or principles (including the particular offenses to which it can be applied). By comparison, extradite or
prosecute jurisdiction typically does reflect an accepted international regime regarding a specific crime (or set of crimes) denominated as being of genuine international
concern, and that regime applies among consenting treaty partners. Cf. United
States v. Yousef, 327 F.3d 56, 96 n.29 (2d Cir. 2003). Other lawyers, however, regard
subsidiary universal jurisdiction as simply one species of universal jurisdiction. This
issue arises in the following important case.

CASE CONCERNING THE ARREST WARRANT OF 11 APRIL 2000 (DEMOCRATIC REPUBLIC OF THE CONGO v. BELGIUM)

2002 I.C.J. Rep. 3 (Feb. 14), reprinted in 41 ILM 536 (2002)

[In 1999, Belgium enacted a law "concerning the Punishment of Serious Violations
of International Humanitarian Law." Article 7 of the Belgian Law provided: "The
Belgian courts shall have jurisdiction in respect of the offences provided for in the
present Law, wheresoever they may have been committed." As detailed in the next
reading, this law was repealed in August 2003.

On April 11, 2000, a Belgian investigating judge in a Brussels trial court issued an
international warrant against the Congolese Minister of Foreign Affairs, Abdulaye
Yerodia Ndombasi, requesting his detention pending a request for extradition.
The warrant stated that Yerodia was being charged as perpetrator or co-perpetrator
of grave breaches of the Geneva Conventions and crimes against humanity. The
charges were based on "various speeches inciting racial hatred" and "particularly
virulent remarks" Yerodia allegedly made in the Congo in August 1998 (before he
was foreign minister). These remarks allegedly incited the population to attack Tutsi
residents of Kinshasa, leading to manhunts, lynchings, summary executions, arbitrary
arrests, and unfair trials, with several hundred deaths resulting. Although the opinion
does not quote Yerodia's remarks, at oral argument Jacques Vergès, representing
Congo, stated:

In the first place, he is alleged to have made a televised statement on 4 August 1998, in
which "speaking in Kilongo, the language of the Bas Congo [*sic*]," he called on "his
brothers" to "rise up as one to throw the common enemy out of the country" using all

possible weapons available, "including shotguns, machetes, pickaxes, arrows, sticks and stones." The author of the document finds the terms thus employed "clear enough to call on the inhabitants of that region to attack the Tutsis," a word not actually uttered in the speech which he quotes.

It is further alleged that on 27 August 1998 H.E. Mr. Yerodia Ndombasi said of the enemy: "They are scum, germs that must be methodically eradicated. We are determined to utilize the most effective remedy."[9]

By way of further background, Yerodia was part of Laurent Kabila's government. In 1998, when Yerodia allegedly made his inflammatory speeches, a full-fledged war between Congo and Rwanda had broken out, and Congo had been invaded by the Rwandese army. In the wake of the 1994 Rwandan genocide, tens of thousands of the militiamen who had perpetrated that genocide fled to eastern Congo, where they continued armed forays into Rwanda. This led to the Rwandan offensive against Congo. The Rwandan leadership was primarily Tutsi.

In October 2000, Congo instituted proceedings against Belgium in the ICJ to attack the warrant against Yerodia. Congo complained that Belgium had violated the "principle that a state may not exercise its authority on the territory of another state," the "principle of sovereign equality among all Members of the United Nations," and the diplomatic immunity of the minister for foreign affairs of a sovereign state. Congo requested that the Belgian warrant be canceled as remedy for the "moral injury" done to Congolese sovereignty.

In a cabinet shakeup a month later, Yerodia moved from the foreign minister's portfolio to that of minister of education, and in April 2001 he left the government. Belgium argued that this mooted the Congo's Application, which Belgium claimed had been based solely on "moral injury" of an arrest warrant for an incumbent foreign minister. Congo countered that the moral injury would continue to exist until Belgium retracted the warrant, and the Court agreed with Congo that it still had jurisdiction over the case.

However, both parties narrowed the grounds of dispute. Originally, Congo argued both that Belgium's exercise of universal jurisdiction violates international law and that foreign ministers enjoy immunity. In the actual case, the parties litigated only the immunity issue. As a result, the Court's opinion did not address the validity under international law of Belgium's universal jurisdiction statute. It held by a vote of 13-3 that Belgium had violated international legal obligations toward Congo by failing to respect the immunity of its foreign minister and voted 10-6 that, as remedy, Belgium must cancel the warrant.

Because of this procedural history, the Court's Judgment does not address the universal jurisdiction issue, only the issues of jurisdiction and foreign ministerial immunity. We will study the Court's Judgment in Chapter 6 on immunity. However, several of the judges wrote separate opinions that treated the universal jurisdiction issue. We present excerpts from the separate opinions of Judge Guillaume (France; president of the ICJ); Judges Buergenthal (USA), Higgins (UK), and Kooijmans (Netherlands), writing jointly; Judge Bula-Bula (Democratic Republic of Congo); and Judge Van den Wyngaert (Belgium). Judges Bula-Bula and Van den Wyngaert are not regular members of the Court, but rather ad hoc judges, appointed in accordance with ICJ rules, which entitle the litigant states to representation on the Court. Both ad hoc judges are law professors; in addition, Christine Van den Wyngaert had drafted the Belgian universal jurisdiction statute.]

---

9. Testimony, Nov. 20, 2000, available at http://www.icj-cij.org/docket/files/121/4231.pdf.

SEPARATE OPINION OF PRESIDENT GUILLAUME

1. I fully subscribe to the Judgment rendered by the Court. I believe it useful however to set out my position on one question which the Judgment has not addressed: whether the Belgian judge had jurisdiction to issue an international arrest warrant against Mr. Yerodia Ndombasi on 11 April 2000. . . .

4. . . . The primary aim of the criminal law is to enable punishment in each country of offences committed in the national territory. That territory is where evidence of the offence can most often be gathered. That is where the offence generally produces its effects. Finally, that is where the punishment imposed can most naturally serve as an example. . . .

The question has, however, always remained open whether States other than the territorial State have concurrent jurisdiction to prosecute offenders. A wide debate on this subject began as early as the foundation in Europe of the major modern States. Some writers, like Covarruvias and Grotius, pointed out that the presence on the territory of a State of a foreign criminal peacefully enjoying the fruits of his crimes was intolerable. They therefore maintained that it should be possible to prosecute perpetrators of certain particularly serious crimes not only in the State on whose territory the crime was committed but also in the country where they sought refuge. In their view, that country was under an obligation to arrest, followed by extradition or prosecution, in accordance with the maxim *aut dedere, aut judicare.*

Beginning in the eighteenth century however, this school of thought favoring universal punishment was challenged by another body of opinion, one opposed to such punishment and exemplified notably by Montesquieu, Voltaire and Jean-Jacques Rousseau. Their views found expression in terms of criminal law in the works of Beccaria, who stated in 1764 that "judges are not the avengers of humankind in general. A crime is punishable only in the country where it was committed." . . .

In practice, the principle of territorial sovereignty did not permit of any exception in respect of coercive action, but that was not the case in regard to legislative and judicial jurisdiction. In particular, classic international law does not exclude a State's power in some cases to exercise its judicial jurisdiction over offences committed abroad. But as the Permanent Court stated, once again in the "Lotus" case, the exercise of that jurisdiction is not without its limits. Under the law as classically formulated, a State normally has jurisdiction over an offence committed abroad only if the offender, or at the very least the victim, has the nationality of that State or if the crime threatens its internal or external security. Ordinarily, States are without jurisdiction over crimes committed abroad as between foreigners.

5. Traditionally, customary international law did, however, recognize one case of universal jurisdiction, that of piracy. . . . [U]niversal jurisdiction is accepted in cases of piracy because piracy is carried out on the high seas, outside all State territory. However, even on the high seas, classic international law is highly restrictive, for it recognizes universal jurisdiction only in cases of piracy and not of other comparable crimes which might also be committed outside the jurisdiction of coastal States, such as trafficking in slaves or in narcotic drugs or psychotropic substance.

6. The drawbacks of this approach became clear at the beginning of the twentieth century in respect of currency counterfeiting, and the Convention of 20 April 1929, prepared within the League of Nations, marked a certain development in this regard. That Convention enabled States to extend their criminal legislation to counterfeiting crimes involving foreign currency. . . .

A similar approach was taken by the Single Convention on Narcotic Drugs of 30 March 1961 and by the United Nations Convention on Psychotropic Substances of 21 February 1971, both of which make certain provisions subject to "the constitutional limitations of a Party, its legal system and domestic law." There is no provision governing the jurisdiction of national courts in any of these conventions, or for that matter in the Geneva Conventions of 1949.

7. A further step was taken in this direction beginning in 1970 in connection with the fight against international terrorism. To that end, States established a novel mechanism: compulsory, albeit subsidiary, universal jurisdiction. This fundamental innovation was effected by The Hague Convention for the Suppression of Unlawful Seizure of Aircraft of 16 December 1970. The Convention places an obligation on the State in whose territory the perpetrator of the crime takes refuge to extradite or prosecute him. But this would have been insufficient if the Convention had not at the same time placed the States parties under an obligation to establish their jurisdiction for that purpose. Thus, Article 4, paragraph 2, of the Convention provides:

> "Each Contracting State shall . . . take such measures as may be necessary to establish its jurisdiction over the offence in the case where the alleged offender is present in its territory and it does not extradite him pursuant to [the Convention]."

This provision marked a turning point, of which The Hague Conference was moreover conscious. From then on, the obligation to prosecute was no longer conditional on the existence of jurisdiction, but rather jurisdiction itself had to be established in order to make prosecution possible.

8. The system as thus adopted was repeated with some minor variations in a large number of conventions. . . .

9. Thus, a system corresponding to the doctrines espoused long ago by Grotius was set up by treaty. Whenever the perpetrator of any of the offences covered by these conventions is found in the territory of a State, that State is under an obligation to arrest him, and then extradite or prosecute. It must have first conferred jurisdiction on its courts to try him if he is not extradited. Thus, universal punishment of the offences in question is assured, as the perpetrators are denied refuge in all States.

By contrast, none of these texts has contemplated establishing jurisdiction over offences committed abroad by foreigners against foreigners when the perpetrator is not present in the territory of the State in question. Universal jurisdiction in absentia is unknown to international conventional law.

10. Thus, in the absence of conventional provisions, Belgium, both in its written Memorial and in oral argument, relies essentially on this point on international customary law. [Judge Guillaume proceeds to criticize the evidence Belgium cites to show the emergence of a customary rule permitting universal jurisdiction. He examines legislation and case law from France, Germany, and the Netherlands, none of which, on his analysis, provides for universal jurisdiction over defendants who are not present in the territory of the state asserting jurisdiction.] . . .

13. Having found that neither treaty law nor international customary law provide a State with the possibility of conferring universal jurisdiction on its courts where the author of the offence is not present on its territory, Belgium contends lastly that, even in the absence of any treaty or custom to this effect, it enjoyed total freedom of action. To this end it cites from the Judgment of the Permanent Court of International Justice in the "Lotus" case:

> "Far from laying down a general prohibition to the effect that States may not extend the application of their laws and the jurisdiction of their courts to persons, property and acts

outside their territory, [international law] leaves them in this respect a wide measure of discretion which is only limited in certain cases by prohibitive rules."

Hence, so Belgium claimed, in the absence of any prohibitive rule it was entitled to confer upon itself a universal jurisdiction in absentia.

14. This argument is hardly persuasive. Indeed the Permanent Court itself, having laid down the general principle cited by Belgium, then asked itself "whether the foregoing considerations really apply as regards criminal jurisdiction." It held that either this might be the case, or alternatively, that: "the exclusively territorial character of law relating to this domain constitutes a principle which, except as otherwise expressly provided, would, *ipso facto*, prevent States from extending the criminal jurisdiction of their courts beyond their frontiers." In the particular case before it, the Permanent Court took the view that it was unnecessary to decide the point. Given that the case involved the collision of a French vessel with a Turkish vessel, the Court confined itself to noting that the effects of the offence in question had made themselves felt on Turkish territory, and that consequently a criminal prosecution might "be justified from the point of view of this so-called territorial principle."

15. The absence of a decision by the Permanent Court on the point was understandable in 1927, given the sparse treaty law at that time. The situation is different today, it seems to me — totally different. The adoption of the United Nations Charter proclaiming the sovereign equality of States, and the appearance on the international scene of new States, born of decolonization, have strengthened the territorial principle. International criminal law has itself undergone considerable development and constitutes today an impressive legal corpus. It recognizes in many situations the possibility, or indeed the obligation, for a State other than that on whose territory the offence was committed to confer jurisdiction on its courts to prosecute the authors of certain crimes where they are present on its territory. International criminal courts have been created. But at no time has it been envisaged that jurisdiction should be conferred upon the courts of every State in the world to prosecute such crimes, whoever their authors and victims and irrespective of the place where the offender is to be found. To do this would, moreover, risk creating total judicial chaos. It would also be to encourage the arbitrary for the benefit of the powerful, purportedly acting as agent for an ill-defined "international community." Contrary to what is advocated by certain publicists, such a development would represent not an advance in the law but a step backward. . . .

Joint Separate Opinion of Judges Higgins, Kooijmans and Buergenthal

[In the opening paragraphs, omitted here, the three judges argue that the Court should have reached the issue of universal jurisdiction and explain why it was within the Court's powers to do so.]

19. We therefore turn to the question whether States are entitled to exercise jurisdiction over persons having no connection with the forum State when the accused is not present in the State's territory. The necessary point of departure must be the sources of international law identified in Article 38, paragraph 1(c), of the Statute of the Court, together with obligations imposed upon all United Nations Members by Security Council resolutions, or by such General Assembly resolutions as meet the criteria enunciated by the Court in the case concerning Legality of the Threat or Use of Nuclear Weapons, Advisory Opinion (I.C.J. Reports 1996, p. 226, para. 70).

[The three judges analyze war crimes legislation from Australia, the United Kingdom, France, Germany, the Netherlands, and Canada; case law from the UK, Australia, Austria, France, the Netherlands, Germany, and the United States; and treaties, including the Genocide Convention, the Geneva Conventions, the Single Convention on Narcotics and Drugs, the Hague Convention for the Unlawful Seizure of Aircraft, the International Convention Against the Taking of Hostages, and the Convention Against Torture.]

44. If a dispassionate analysis of State practice and Court decisions suggests that no such [universal] jurisdiction is presently being exercised, the writings of eminent jurists are much more mixed. The large literature contains vigorous exchanges of views (which have been duly studied by the Court) suggesting profound differences of opinion. But these writings, important and stimulating as they may be, cannot of themselves and without reference to the other sources of international law, evidence the existence of a jurisdictional norm. The assertion that certain treaties and court decisions rely on universal jurisdiction, which in fact they do not, does not evidence an international practice recognized as custom. And the policy arguments advanced in some of the writings can certainly suggest why a practice or a court decision should be regarded as desirable, or indeed lawful; but contrary arguments are advanced, too, and in any event these also cannot serve to substantiate an international practice where virtually none exists.

45. That there is no established practice in which States exercise universal jurisdiction, properly so called, is undeniable. As we have seen, virtually all national legislation envisages links of some sort to the forum State; and no case law exists in which pure universal jurisdiction has formed the basis of jurisdiction. This does not necessarily indicate, however, that such an exercise would be unlawful. In the first place, national legislation reflects the circumstances in which a State provides in its own law the ability to exercise jurisdiction. But a State is not required to legislate up to the full scope of the jurisdiction allowed by international law. The war crimes legislation of Australia and the United Kingdom afford examples of countries making more confined choices for the exercise of jurisdiction. Further, many countries have no national legislation for the exercise of well recognized forms of extraterritorial jurisdiction, sometimes notwithstanding treaty obligations to enable themselves so to act. National legislation may be illuminating as to the issue of universal jurisdiction, but not conclusive as to its legality. Moreover, while none of the national case law to which we have referred happens to be based on the exercise of a universal jurisdiction properly so called, there is equally nothing in this case law which evidences an *opinio juris* on the illegality of such a jurisdiction. In short, national legislation and case law, — that is, State practice — is neutral as to exercise of universal jurisdiction.

46. There are, moreover, certain indications that a universal criminal jurisdiction for certain international crimes is clearly not regarded as unlawful. The duty to prosecute under those treaties which contain the *aut dedere aut prosequi* provisions opens the door to a jurisdiction based on the heinous nature of the crime rather than on links of territoriality or nationality (whether as perpetrator or victim). The 1949 Geneva Conventions lend support to this possibility, and are widely regarded as today reflecting customary international law.

47. The contemporary trends, reflecting international relations as they stand at the beginning of the new century, are striking. The movement is towards bases of jurisdiction other than territoriality. "Effects" or "impact" jurisdiction is embraced both by the United States and, with certain qualifications, by the European Union. Passive personality jurisdiction, for so long regarded as controversial, is now reflected not only in the legislation of various countries (the United States, Ch. 113A, 1986

Omnibus Diplomatic and Antiterrorism Act; France, Art. 689, Code of Criminal Procedure, 1975), and today meets with relatively little opposition, at least so far as a particular category of offences is concerned.

48. In civil matters we already see the beginnings of a very broad form of extraterritorial jurisdiction. Under the Alien Torts Claim Act, the United States, basing itself on a law of 1789, has asserted a jurisdiction both over human rights violations and over major violations of international law, perpetrated by non-nationals overseas. Such jurisdiction, with the possibility of ordering payment of damages, has been exercised with respect to torture committed in a variety of countries (Paraguay, Chile, Argentina, Guatemala), and with respect to other major human rights violations in yet other countries. While this unilateral exercise of the function of guardian of international values has been much commented on, it has not attracted the approbation of States generally.

49. Belgium — and also many writers on this subject — find support for the exercise of a universal criminal jurisdiction in absentia in the "Lotus" case. . . . [T]he Court finally concluded that for an exercise of extraterritorial criminal jurisdiction (other than within the territory of another State) it was equally necessary to "prove the existence of a principle of international law restricting the discretion of States as regards criminal legislation."

50. The application of this celebrated dictum would have clear attendant dangers in some fields of international law. (See, on this point, Judge Shahabudeen's dissenting opinion in the case concerning Legality of the Threat or Use of Nuclear Weapons Advisory Opinion, I.C.J. Reports 1996, pp. 394-396.) Nevertheless, it represents a continuing potential in the context of jurisdiction over international crimes.

51. That being said, the dictum represents the high water mark of laissez-faire in international relations, and an era that has been significantly overtaken by other tendencies. The underlying idea of universal jurisdiction properly so-called (as in the case of piracy, and possibly in the Geneva Conventions of 1949), as well as the *aut dedere aut prosequi* variation, is a common endeavour in the face of atrocities. The series of multilateral treaties with their special jurisdictional provisions reflect a determination by the international community that those engaged in war crimes, hijacking, hostage taking, torture should not go unpunished. Although crimes against humanity are not yet the object of a distinct convention, a comparable international indignation at such acts is not to be doubted. And those States and academic writers who claim the right to act unilaterally to assert a universal criminal jurisdiction over persons committing such acts, invoke the concept of acting as "agents for the international community." This vertical notion of the authority of action is significantly different from the horizontal system of international law envisaged in the "Lotus" case.

At the same time, the international consensus that the perpetrators of international crimes should not go unpunished is being advanced by a flexible strategy, in which newly-established international criminal tribunals, treaty obligations and national courts all have their part to play. We reject the suggestion that the battle against impunity is "made over" to international treaties and tribunals, with national courts having no competence in such matters. Great care has been taken when formulating the relevant treaty provisions not to exclude other grounds of jurisdiction that may be exercised on a voluntary basis. . . .

52. We may thus agree with the authors of Oppenheim's International Law (9th Ed., p. 998), that:

> "While no general rule of positive international law can as yet be asserted which gives to states the right to punish foreign nationals for crimes against humanity in the same way

as they are, for instance, entitled to punish acts of piracy, there are clear indications pointing to the gradual evolution of a significant principle of international law to that effect."

[The remainder of the opinion, which deals with the issue of whether the Belgian court can exercise its jurisdiction in absentia, is omitted. The three judges conclude that if universal jurisdiction can be exercised, it can be exercised in absentia, but only (a) if due process safeguards are put in place and (b) over the most serious international crimes. The judges also take issue with the Court's remedy of ordering Belgium to cancel the warrant.]

SEPARATE OPINION OF JUDGE BULA-BULA

. . . 6. Covering a great deal of ground, and out of regard for the Court and its working methods, I will confine myself to recalling very concisely, from Belgian, Congolese, transnational and international sources, certain factual data, of both indirect and direct relevance, which make up the background to the case concerning the Arrest Warrant of 11 April 2000. Through these brief references, I seek both to exorcize the past and to foster between the Applicant and the Respondent, States intimately linked by history, effective implementation of the principle of *sovereign equality between States*. . . .

8. Rereading the account of the decolonization of the Congo prepared by one of the 40 or so political reconciliation conferences, we learn the following:

> "Following his victory in the legislative elections, Patrice Emery Lumumba, after consulting the main parties and political personalities at that time, formed a Government.
> On 23 June 1960, he obtained the confidence of Parliament, even before the latter's election of Kasavubu as Head of State, thanks to the Lumumba Party's majority.
> Less than a week on from 30 June 1960, on 4 July, the army and police mutinied. Following the provocative statement by [Belgian] General Janssens to the military—"after independence equals before independence"—the disturbances worsened. Katanga proclaimed its secession on 11 July 1960 and South Kasai its autonomy on 8 August 1960. Territorial and military administration collapsed and financial resources dried up. The people's sovereignty was under threat.
> Despite the co-operation agreements signed between the Kingdom of Belgium and the young Republic on 29 June 1960, the crisis was aggravated by the untimely intervention of Belgian troops. . . . [A]s a result of Belgian diplomatic manoeuvres, the United Nations hesitated to intervene. . . ."

9. Rightly or wrongly, the report also cites Belgium for its responsibility in the removal from office of Prime Minister Lumumba:

> "After our country had achieved independence . . . President Kasavubu and Prime Minister Lumumba worked harmoniously together. They had even toured Elisabethville together. I believe that the Belgians were against this harmony. So they provoked this divisive tension. . . . I telephoned Lumumba to tell him about it. He then contacted President Kasavubu. I thought they had taken precautions against those manoeuvres. I was surprised to hear on the radio around 5 September 1960 of the dismissal of Lumumba and on the same day of that of Kasavubu by Lumumba.

10. According to the report: "The Belgian ambassador in Leopoldville was behind the creation of the autonomous State of South Kasai. By 8 August 1960, it was a *fait*

accompli." In regard to the murder of Prime Minister Lumumba and his companions, . . . [a] witness, Mr. Gabriel Kitenge, stated the following:

> "When the aircraft arrived, he recognized only one of the three packages, Mr. Lumumba, who was covered in bruises and trying to cling to a wall. All three were unloaded alive at Elisabethville. Soon afterwards they were taken to the villa Brouwez a few kilometres from the airport. . . .
> They were executed in the bush a kilometre from the villa. Under the command of a white officer, the black soldiers shot Okito first and finished off with Lumumba.
> . . . On the orders of a senior Belgian police officer, the three prisoners were shot one after the other and thrown into a common grave which had already been dug."

11. The conference report concluded with a proposal for "the opening of proceedings." It stated:

> "The murders of Lumumba, Mpolo and Okito, although not falling within the categories currently defined by the United Nations, should be assimilated to *crimes against humanity*, for these were acts of persecution and murder for political reasons."

This proposal may thus stimulate reflection on the part of writers who note uncertainties in the notion of crime against humanity. . . .

13. More recently, the United Nations Commission responsible for investigating the illegal exploitation of the natural resources of the Congo cited, among others, Belgian companies in occupied territories. Could it not be that the purported "neutrality" of the local Belgian authorities in the face of the armed aggression suffered by the Congo since 2 August 1998 is being undermined by the participation of private groups or Belgian parastatal entities in the looting of the natural resources of the Congo, as established by a United Nations investigation? All the more so in that the investigation has established a link between that illegal exploitation and the continuation of the war.

14. The immediate circumstances which gave rise to the issue of the warrant were amply debated by the Parties. It would be pointless to go over them again. Nonetheless, there are pertinent questions raised by this case. Why is it that virtually all of those charged before the Belgian courts, including Mr. Abdulaye Yerodia Ndombasi, belong essentially to a political tendency that was ousted in 1960 and, thanks to a variety of circumstances, regained power in 1997? Why does the respondent State not exercise its territorial jurisdiction by prosecuting Belgian companies established on its territory suspected of illegal activities in areas of foreign occupation within the Congo?

15. These are some of the facts emerging from a rapid survey covering more than four decades whereby the respective conducts of the Parties to the dispute before us may be judged. They should be compared with Belgium's closing speech. Even as the respondent State brings its peroration to a glowing close with an invocation of the democracy and human rights which purportedly guided its conduct, at the same time it reopens one of the most shameful pages in the history of decolonization. In the 1960s, it appeared to grant the Congo its independence while, with the right hand, it was at the same time virtually ensuring the destabilization of that sovereignty and of the new-born Congolese democracy. The author Joseph Ki-Zerbo was able to write that, in the Congo, "independence was thrown like a bone to the natives in order the better to exploit their divisions, . . . the model for poisoned grants of independence." . . .

23. The relevance of Mr. Ndombasi's loss of governmental responsibilities lies in the glaring light it throws on Belgium's flagrant meddling in the Congo's internal affairs. Further evidence of this can be found in the identity of certain Congolese complainants, members of a Congolese opposition political party, whose names the Respondent obstinately refused to reveal to the Court for so-called "security" reasons. Whichever way you look at it, this case clearly demonstrates the Respondent's interference in the Applicant's internal affairs. . . .

24. So long as there shall exist the authentic, independent State of the Congo, born of decolonization . . . that debt will continue to exist. This is not a debt due to one specific incumbent Government—a government bound, moreover, to pass on one day like every government. What is at stake here is a debt owed to the Congolese people, freely organized in a sovereign State calling for its dignity to be respected.

25. But dignity has no price. It is one of those intangible assets, on which it is impossible to put a price in money terms. When a person, whether legal or natural, gives up his dignity, he loses the essence of his natural or legal personality. The dignity of the Congolese people, victim of the neocolonial chaos imposed upon it on the morrow of decolonization, of which the current tragic events largely represent the continued expression, is a dignity of this kind. . . .

71. The exercise of "universal" jurisdiction thus presupposes the existence of "adequate charges," under the terms of the humanitarian convention. Are there any in this case? The Applicant has rejected them. Presidents of the Congolese Bar asserted before local media, the day after notification of the warrant on 12 July 2000, that "the case-file was empty." In its warrant, the Respondent failed to specify adequate charges, apart from an unproven assertion that the accused "actively and directly" participated in committing serious offences under international humanitarian law. . . .

74. Should the former model colony of the Belgian Congo, without any *proof*, prosecute one of the Congolese leaders, who, like his fellow countrymen, rose up against the foreign invaders and their Congolese henchmen? The idea that a State could have the legal power to try offences committed abroad, by foreigners against foreigners, while the suspect himself is on foreign territory, runs counter to the very notion of international law. . . .

79. In providing, in Article 7 of the Law of 16 June 1993, as amended on 10 February 1999, that "Belgian courts have jurisdiction to try the offences provided for in the present Law, irrespective of *where such offences have been committed*," Belgium adopted legislation that was totally unprecedented. It set itself up, if not as the prosecutor for the human race in the trans-temporal and trans-spatial sense attributed to this term by R. J. Dupuy, then at least as arbiter of transnational justice, in accordance with the doctrine of "law without frontiers." This approach could even be said to transcend international law itself, since the latter deals essentially with relations between structures with defined borders, namely States. Yet even a cursory assessment shows that the Respondent is violating international law. It is not entitled, as the law currently stands, disdainfully to transcend it. Thus, Heads of States in office Laurent Gbagbo (Côte d'Ivoire) on 26 June 2001, Saddam Hussein on 29 June 2001, Fidel Castro (Cuba) on 4 October 2001, Denis Sassou Nguesso (Congo-Brazzaville) on 4 October 2001, Yasser Arafat on 27 November 2001, a Prime Minister, Ariel Sharon (Israel) on 1 July 2001, an incumbent Minister for Foreign Affairs, Abdulaye Yerodia Ndombasi on 11 April 2000, are the subject of complaints or prosecutions before the Belgian courts for various "international crimes." The list is still far from exhaustive, the name of President Paul Biya (Cameroon) having been added in December 2001. Joe Verhoeven rightly feared that the result would be chaos, by definition the

opposite of an order already precarious in the international arena. The Court must necessarily be called upon to intervene.

80. It should be strongly emphasized that Mr. A. Yerodia Ndombasi would appear to be the only person to have been served with an "international arrest warrant." Most singular. It should also be emphasized that the proceedings against Mr. Ariel Sharon, closely watched all over the world, have apparently been quietly put on hold while Belgium seeks an honourable way out for him through a form of a legal technicality; that since then the highest political authorities in the land have been queuing up at the universities (ULB) to give lectures abruptly denouncing the absurdities of this law, and that, since the close of the oral argument in November 2001, one of Belgium's counsel has altered his teaching in favour of a *sine qua non* territorial connection. Such is the showing of the Belgian Law when put to the test of international *Realpolitik.* The chances are that the proceedings instituted following a complaint by "unrepentant subjects of law" against Mr. A. Sharon will be a dead letter.

81. Belgium has neither any obligation — as discussed above — or any entitlement under international law to pose as prosecutor for all mankind, in other words, to claim the right to redeem human suffering across national borders and over generations. The State practice referred to above also applies to my comments here. In no sense, however, is this to argue the case for impunity, whether geographical or temporal, including in wars of colonial conquest and neo-colonial reconquest in Africa, America, Asia, Europe and Oceania.

82. As victims of the violence of the aggressors and the series of grave breaches of international humanitarian law, such as the occupation of the Inga Dam and the severing of power and water supplies, particularly in Kinshasa, a city of over five million people, resulting in numerous deaths, the Congolese people have consistently called for the withdrawal of the regular occupying forces from Uganda, Rwanda and Burundi. They have also called for the setting up of an international criminal tribunal on the Congo. This tribunal would try all persons, whether perpetrators, co-perpetrators or accomplices, whether African or non-African, having committed war crimes and crimes against humanity, such as the extermination of over two-and-a-half million Congolese in the regions under foreign occupation since 2 August 1998. It would seem that those victims are (as yet) of no concern to Belgium, sadly notorious rightly or wrongly for its colonial and neo-colonial past in the field of human rights in the Congo, where a situation of grave, systematic and massive human rights violations persists which requires a response from international opinion. To echo the very fitting words of the French Ambassador to Kinshasa: "on such an issue, there must be no beating about the bush. Endless semantics are not an option when an entire people is dying." For "it is war . . . the occupying armies are on Congolese soil despite the injunctions of the international community."

DISSENTING OPINION OF JUDGE VAN DEN WYNGAERT

35. . . . This . . . is the core of the problem of impunity: where national authorities are not willing or able to investigate or prosecute, the crime goes unpunished. And this is precisely what happened in the case of Mr. Yerodia. The Congo accused Belgium of exercising universal jurisdiction in absentia against an incumbent Foreign Minister, but it had itself omitted to exercise its jurisdiction in presentia in the case of Mr. Yerodia, thus infringing the Geneva Conventions and not complying with a host of United Nations resolutions to this effect. . . .

46. Despite uncertainties that may exist concerning the definition of universal jurisdiction, one thing is very clear: the ratio legis of universal jurisdiction is based on the international reprobation for certain very serious crimes such as war crimes and crimes against humanity. Its raison d'être is to avoid impunity, to prevent suspects of such crimes finding a safe haven in third countries. . . .

51. It follows from the "Lotus" case that a State has the right to provide extraterritorial jurisdiction on its territory unless there is a prohibition under international law. I believe that there is no prohibition under international law to enact legislation allowing it to investigate and prosecute war crimes and crimes against humanity committed abroad.

It has often been argued, not without reason, that the "Lotus" test is too liberal and that, given the growing complexity of contemporary international intercourse, a more restrictive approach should be adopted today. In the Nuclear Weapons case, there were two groups of States each giving a different interpretation of "Lotus" on this point and President Bedjaoui, in his separate opinion, expressed hesitations about "Lotus." Even under the more restrictive view, Belgian legislation stands. There is ample evidence in support of the proposition that international law clearly permits States to provide extraterritorial jurisdiction for such crimes. . . .

56. The "Lotus" case is not only an authority on jurisdiction, but also on the formation of customary international law. . . . A "negative practice" of States, consisting in their abstaining from instituting criminal proceedings, cannot, in itself, be seen as evidence of an *opinio juris*. Only if this abstinence was based on a conscious decision of the States in question can this practice generate customary international law. As in the case of immunities, such abstinence may be attributed to other factors than the existence of an *opinio juris*. There may be good political or practical reasons for a State not to assert jurisdiction in the absence of the offender.

It may be politically inconvenient to have such a wide jurisdiction because it is not conducive to international relations and national public opinion may not approve of trials against foreigners for crimes committed abroad. This does not, however, make such trials illegal under international law.

A practical consideration may be the difficulty in obtaining the evidence in trials of extraterritorial crimes. Another practical reason may be that States are afraid of overburdening their court system. . . . The concern for a linkage with the national order thus seems to be more of a pragmatic than of a juridical nature. It is not, therefore, necessarily the expression of an *opinio juris* to the effect that this form of universal jurisdiction is contrary to international law. . . .

NOTES AND QUESTIONS

1. As noted earlier, the ICJ never actually reached the universal jurisdiction issue discussed in these separate opinions. The Court decided the case on grounds of ministerial immunity from prosecution; we will study this aspect of the case in Chapter 6 on immunity.

Currently (June 2009), another case about universal jurisdiction is pending before the ICJ. This case involves France and the Republic of Congo (the "other" Congo — Congo-Brazzaville):

The Congo's Application accuses France of violating the rule that a state may not, in breach of the principle of sovereign equality among all member states of the United Nations, exercise its authority on the territory of another state (here, the Congo) by allowing the French judicial authorities to take investigation and prosecution measures based on a complaint for crimes against humanity and torture filed by various plaintiffs against, inter alia, Congolese President Denis Sassou Nguesso and Congolese Minister of the Interior Pierra Oba. In connection with these proceedings, a local French court has issued a warrant for the Congolese president to be examined as a witness.

Pieter H.F. Bekker, Prorogated and Universal Jurisdiction in the International Court: *The Congo v. France*, ASIL Insights, April 2003, available at http://www.asil.org/insigh103.htm.

2. In *Arrest Warrant*, there were nine separate opinions, and eight of them—representing 10 of the 16 judges—had something to say about universal jurisdiction. President Guillaume opposed Belgium's assertion of universal jurisdiction, and Judges Higgins, Kooijmans, and Buergenthal's separate opinion favored permitting it. In addition, Judge Koroma (Sierra Leone) favored universal jurisdiction, and Judges Ranjeva (Madagascar) and Rezek (Brazil) opposed it. The two ad hoc judges split on national lines (Judge Van den Wyngaert for universal jurisdiction, Judge Bula-Bula opposed). And Judge Oda (Japan) concluded that international law is in too much flux to tell whether it now permits universal jurisdiction or not. Thus, the judges split 5-4 in favor of universal jurisdiction, with one "abstention." None of the remaining 6 judges addressed the universal jurisdiction issue.

3. As discussed earlier, more than 20 international treaties have established *aut dedere aut judicare* jurisdiction over crimes such as aerial hijacking. Typically, such conventions add explicit language that the treaty "does not exclude any criminal jurisdiction exercised in accordance with national law." This raises an important question: Is the universal jurisdiction established under the convention "subsidiary," as President Guillaume asserts in paragraph 7 of his opinion in *Arrest Warrant*? That is, do the conventions require extradition to the *locus delicti* as option A, with prosecution only as option B? Or do these treaties permit states to establish pure, nonsubsidiary universal jurisdiction under their own national laws, as Judge van den Wyngaert argues is permissible under the *Lotus* principle?

At any rate, two postwar international conventions seemingly presuppose a form of nonsubsidiary universal jurisdiction. These are the Geneva Conventions and the Convention on Apartheid, both of which permit states to try offenders of any nationality, without requiring extradition as option A. For discussion of these conventions, see Luc Reydams, Universal Jurisdiction: International and Municipal Legal Perspectives 53-56, 59-61 (2003).

4. Prior to the establishment of the ICC, many commentators favored universal jurisdiction for international crimes, believing that this might be the only way in which high officials who perpetrate crimes against their own people could be held accountable. See, e.g., Kenneth C. Randall, Universal Jurisdiction Under International Law, 66 Tex. L. Rev. 785 (1988). Proponents of universal jurisdiction argue that it extends to so-called *jus cogens* crimes. Even after the creation of the ICC, some commentators believe that universal jurisdiction remains important because the ICC faces both political and logistic problems that may prevent it from addressing more than a handful of cases.

Others, however, strongly oppose universal jurisdiction, on grounds similar to those President Guillaume sets forth in his opinion. These commentators argue that broad use of universal jurisdiction really amounts to one state infringing on the sovereignty of another, and that international tribunals are the proper response when states will not or cannot punish their own international criminals.

An intermediate position holds that universal jurisdiction is appropriate, but only for "core" crimes when the territorial state is unwilling or unable to prosecute.

5. Judge Bula-Bula's opinion raises an uncomfortable, even explosive issue in the background of this case: Belgium was Congo's colonial master, and in its decades of rule it was responsible for unspeakable atrocities that reduced Congo's population by an estimated 50 percent— 10 million people. The history of Belgian rule is described in horrifying detail in Adam Hochschild's remarkable book, *King Leopold's Ghost: A Story of Greed, Terror, and Heroism in Colonial Africa* (1998); and Joseph Conrad— who worked on ships on the Congo River—captured some of the infamy in his novella *Heart of Darkness*. This made Belgium's efforts to try Yerodia for crimes against humanity a particularly bitter pill for many Congolese to swallow.

Judge Bula-Bula also reminds readers that Belgium played a role in assassinating the Congolese nationalist leader Patrice Lumumba shortly after decolonization. Lumumba became Congo's prime minister in 1960, during a period of crisis. At this time, Katanga, the country's richest province, seceded. Lumumba agitated first to have Belgians leave the country—which the UN arranged—then, eventually to have the UN pull out, because Lumumba didn't trust them. Lumumba then began to court Soviet help. At that point, as U.S. Senate documents later showed, the U.S. government authorized the CIA to murder Lumumba; the plan was frustrated by UN troops and the CIA's lack of interest in the project. Even so, Lumumba did not last long. President Kasa Vubu forced him out of the government. Kasa Vubu captured Lumumba, had him savagely beaten and flown to Elisabethville (now Lubumbashi). There, Lumumba was placed in the hands of a Belgian officer, Captain Julien Gat. Gat and police commissioner Franz Verscheure drove Lumumba into the bush and had him killed and buried. Later, Belgian officers dismembered Lumumba's body with a hacksaw and dissolved it in a vat of sulfuric acid. These events are detailed in Ludo De Witte, *The Assassination of Lumumba* (2001), and summarized in Brian Urquhart, The Tragedy of Lumumba, N.Y. Rev. Books, Oct. 4, 2001.

Lumumba's followers went into exile—and among them was Laurent Kabila, the president of the Congo in whose cabinet Yerodia (also a Lumumbist) served.

Quite apart from the legal question, should a former colonial master attempt to exercise universal criminal jurisdiction over human rights abusers in its former colony? Note that Belgium's prosecution of Yerodia is not the only case: Spain has attempted to prosecute gross human rights violations in its former colonies— Argentina, Chile (the Pinochet case), and Mexico. See Francisco Valdes, Postcolonial Encounters in the Post-Pinochet Era: A Lat-Crit Perspective on Spain, Latinas/os and "Hispanismo" in the Development of International Human Rights, 9 U. Miami Intl. & Comp. L. Rev. 189, 208-211 (2000-2001). One author pointedly observes that there is a certain hypocrisy in Spain prosecuting officials of former colonies while failing to prosecute members of its own Franco dictatorship. Reydams, Universal Jurisdiction: International and Municipal Legal Perspectives, at 92. More recently, many African countries opposed Belgium's efforts to prosecute Chad's former dictator Hissène Habré under universal jurisdiction, believing that this is properly a matter for Africans, not former colonial powers, to deal with.

Not all universal jurisdiction prosecutions have involved former colonial states trying suspects from their own former colonies. In the wake of the Balkans Wars, several individuals were tried under universal jurisdiction statutes by German and Danish courts after they had fled to those countries. Mark A. Drumbl, Atrocity, Punishment, and International Law 109-110 (2007).

6. As Judge Bula-Bula's opinion notes, Belgium used its universal jurisdiction statute to launch numerous investigations of world leaders. But the prosecutions of world

leaders were not initiated by the Belgian government. Article 9(3) of the Belgian statute established the right of "any person who claims to be the victim" of a universal jurisdiction crime to initiate a criminal investigation — a procedural device known as *constitution de partie civile* (which, in Belgian and French criminal procedure, exists for all crimes and misdemeanors).

However, as the following reading indicates, Belgium's ambitious experiment in universal jurisdiction came crashing down in 2003. For a clear description of the Belgian events leading up to 2003, see Reydams, Universal Jurisdiction: International and Municipal Legal Perspectives, at 106-118. Reydams is highly critical of the Belgian experiment in universal jurisdiction.

GLENN FRANKEL, BELGIAN WAR CRIMES LAW UNDONE BY ITS GLOBAL REACH; CASES AGAINST POLITICAL FIGURES SPARKED CRISES

Wash. Post, Sept. 30, 2003*

... When it was passed unanimously by Parliament in 1993, Belgium's war crimes law seemed anything but controversial, a mere legislative implementation of the 1949 Geneva Conventions protecting civilians in time of war.

Under the principle of universal jurisdiction, neither the complainants nor the accused needed to be Belgian for a case to go forward. And because Belgium follows continental European legal systems, any private person can bring a criminal complaint, which a magistrate is required to investigate and then determine whether further action is warranted.

But no one attempted to use the new law until the slaughter in Rwanda, a former Belgian colony. Then Eric Gillet, one of Belgium's most prominent human rights lawyers, decided to take up ... [cases] of about 30 Rwandans living in Belgium. ...

It took more than six years of investigation and legal maneuvering, but in 2001, four Rwandans went on trial: two Roman Catholic nuns, accused of encouraging Hutu thugs to butcher several thousand Tutsis who had sought shelter at the nuns' convent, and a government minister and a university professor, both alleged to have incited other killers. ...

It took the jury 11 hours to find the four defendants guilty on most of the 55 counts, including murder and incitement to genocide. They were sentenced to between 12 and 20 years. Human rights advocates hailed the verdict, predicting it would be a springboard for other cases.

Their prediction was all too accurate. One week later, a group of Palestinians living in Lebanon filed a complaint against Sharon for his alleged role, when he was the Israeli defense minister, in the 1982 massacre of hundreds of refugees by Christian militiamen in the Sabra and Shatila camps outside Beirut.

... [T]he case plunged Belgium into a diplomatic crisis when then-Israeli Foreign Minister Binyamin Netanyahu denounced the complaint as an anti-Semitic "blood libel" and recalled Israel's new ambassador before he could take up his post. Sharon canceled an official trip to Brussels to visit the European Union headquarters.

The case against Sharon was suspended after the International Court of Justice in The Hague ruled in a separate case that leaders of foreign governments had temporary immunity while in office. But the complainants continued to pursue others allegedly involved in the camp massacre, including former Israeli general Amos Yaron.

And the cases kept coming. Though several other countries had war crimes laws based on universal jurisdiction, only Belgium seemed prepared to follow up when accusations were made.

Complaints were filed against then-Iraqi President Saddam Hussein; the late Congolese ruler Laurent Kabila and his foreign minister, Abdoulaye Yerodia Ndombasi; Maj. Gen. Paul Kagame, the Rwandan president; former Iranian president Ali Akbar Hashemi Rafsanjani; the former ruling generals of Guatemala; and a group of international oil companies accused of collaborating with the military rulers of Burma. . . .

Then the United States became involved. In March [2003], a group of Iraqis, sponsored by an organization reported to have links to Hussein's government, brought a complaint against former president Bush, Vice President Cheney, Secretary of State Colin L. Powell and retired Gen. Norman Schwarzkopf for their alleged roles in the U.S. missile attack on the Amiriya bunker in Baghdad, where at least 200 Iraqi civilians were killed on Feb. 12, 1991. Cheney was then secretary of defense and Powell was chairman of the Joint Chiefs of Staff.

Belgian Foreign Minister Louis Michel immediately denounced the complaint, declaring that the law was "being abused by opportunists." . . .

In April, the government rushed through Parliament a modified statute stipulating that a mandatory investigation could take place only if the complaint had a direct link to Belgium. Otherwise, the justice minister could intervene and order the case sent to the country of origin.

That didn't solve the problem. Four days before Belgium's national elections in May, another group of Iraqi plaintiffs filed a complaint against U.S. Gen. Tommy R. Franks, commander of forces in the Iraq war. In addition, a small Flemish nationalist party filed a complaint against Michel for approving arms sales to Nepal. . . .

Belgian Prime Minister Guy Verhofstadt, who had defended the law until then, pledged rapid action to repeal it.

But the time frame was not fast enough for Donald H. Rumsfeld. When the U.S. defense secretary visited Brussels a month later, he told reporters that he feared U.S. officials would not be able to visit the country for fear of being prosecuted and that the United States would withhold further funding for construction of a new NATO headquarters. This wasn't a threat, he added. "Belgium needs to recognize that there are consequences for its actions," he said. "It's perfectly possible to meet elsewhere."

Rumsfeld's remarks left Belgians feeling "a kind of vertigo," said Destexhe, the Belgian senator and human rights activist. "Suddenly, the law became very unpopular. People like me were saying, 'We've got to get out of this.' " . . .

In revising the law, the Belgian government sought to ensure this time that there would be no loopholes. The new act repealed the 1993 law and established a formal procedure for nullifying pending complaints. It also limited jurisdiction to complaints in which either the victim or defendant was a Belgian national or resident. Even then, the federal prosecutor could reject a complaint without investigation or the possibility of appeal if he deemed it "manifestly without grounds" or determined that it should be brought in another country. Any official of a NATO or European Union nation gets automatic immunity.

The government rushed through the new law on Aug. 1. It took effect six days later, and was upheld by Wednesday's ruling of the Belgian Supreme Court. . . .

NOTES AND QUESTIONS

1. The U.S. response to Belgium's universal jurisdiction law was, to say the least, far from enthusiastic. Indeed, in May 2003, three congressmen introduced a Universal Jurisdiction Rejection Act of 2003 (H.R. 2050) into the House of Representatives, designed "[t]o prohibit cooperation with or assistance to any investigation or prosecution under a universal jurisdiction statute." After Belgium repealed its statute, the bill died.

A century ago, the U.S. government was equally unenthusiastic about universal jurisdiction. In the *Cutting* analysis, State Department legal advisor John B. Moore swiftly dismissed "the punishment by each state of all offenses, wherever and by whomsoever committed. It is unnecessary to discuss this theory specifically, because . . . it is so rhapsodical and cosmopolitan in its character, and, while intended to be benevolent, is so impracticable and intrusive, that it has never assumed a legislative guise. . . ." Report on Extraterritorial Crime and the Cutting Case, in Papers Relating to the Foreign Relations of the United States for the Year 1887, at 781 (1888).

2. Surprisingly, perhaps, twentieth-century U.S. courts have occasionally been receptive to jurisdiction based on the presence of the offender. Recall a case discussed earlier in this chapter, United States v. Yunis, 924 F.2d 1086 (D.C. Cir. 1991). The statutes under which Yunis was prosecuted grant U.S. jurisdiction over foreign offenders "afterwards found in the United States." The court of appeals held that it was irrelevant that Yunis was "found" in the United States only after having been seized on the high seas and brought there.

Yunis set a precedent for two subsequent cases involving skyjacker terrorists. United States v. Yousef, 927 F. Supp. 673 (S.D.N.Y. 1996), concerned terrorists who were charged with conspiring to blow up U.S. airliners, in the course of which conspiracy they blew up a movie theater in the Philippines and a Philippine airliner bound for Tokyo. Yousef was captured in Pakistan and turned over to U.S. officials, who brought him to the United States for prosecution. (Yousef alleged that Pakistani officials tortured him for two months first, with an FBI agent present at one session, but the court did not find his accusations credible.) Like Yunis, Yousef's motion to dismiss on jurisdictional grounds was denied because the statute created universal jurisdiction. However, the Second Circuit Court of Appeals rejected this rationale, instead grounding jurisdiction in U.S. statutes implementing a treaty. United States v. Yousef, 327 F.3d 56, 91 (2d Cir. 2003). In a third case, United States v. Rezaq, 134 F.3d 1121 (D.C. Cir. 1998), terrorists hijacked an Egyptair flight from Athens to Cairo, landed in Malta, and executed U.S. and Israeli passengers. Rezaq was sentenced to 25 years under Maltese law, but was released after 7 years. He went to Nigeria, where he was seized and turned over to waiting U.S. officials, who brought him to the United States for prosecution. The court rejected his double jeopardy claim, as well as his jurisdictional claim, under the *Yunis* argument of universal jurisdiction.

Can U.S. hostility to Belgium's universal jurisdiction statute be reconciled with *Yunis*?

3. In addition to these examples of universal criminal jurisdiction, the so-called Alien Tort Statute, 28 U.S.C. §1350, gives federal courts civil jurisdiction over torts "committed in violation of the law of nations" — a statute used by victims of human rights violations outside the United States to sue perpetrators, with no necessary territorial or nationality connection with the United States.

4. Belgium's universal jurisdiction statute was not completely gutted by the 2003 amendment. An exception permits prosecutions if an investigating judge had already initiated proceedings and at least one plaintiff was Belgian (or the defendant

maintained a primary residence in Belgium). Loi relative aux violations grave du droit international humanitaire, Aug. 5, 2003, M.B., Aug. 7, 2003, art. 29, §3. Under this exception, in September 2005 Belgium issued an arrest warrant for the former Chadian dictator Hissène Habré (nicknamed "the African Pinochet"), who was living in Senegal. In November 2005, Senegal's High Court declared that it lacked jurisdiction to extradite Habré, and Senegal's president referred the matter to the African Union. In July 2006, the African Union called on Senegal to try Habré, and in 2008 Senegal amended its constitution and enacted legislation permitting it to do so. Meanwhile, in August 2008, a Chadian court sentenced Habré to death in absentia for crimes against humanity and war crimes. Habré remains in Senegal.

For analysis of Belgium's amended statute, see Steven R. Ratner, Belgium's War Crimes Statute: A Postmortem, 97 Am. J. Intl. L. 888 (2003); Luc Reydams, Belgium Reneges on Universality: The 5 August 2003 Act on Grave Breaches of International Humanitarian Law, 1 J. Intl. Crim. Just. 679 (2003). And, for further reading on universal jurisdiction, see Luc Reydams, Universal Jurisdiction: International and Municipal Legal Perspectives (2003); Princeton Principles on Universal Jurisdiction (2001), available at http://lapa.princeton.edu/hosteddocs/unive_jur.pdf.

5. A significant attempt to exercise universal jurisdiction in order to help out an international tribunal occurred in 2005-2006. As discussed in Chapter 3, the International Criminal Tribunal for Rwanda (ICTR) tries cases arising out of the 1994 genocide. One genocide suspect, Michel Bagaragaza, agreed to surrender provided he could be tried by a national court rather than the ICTR. ICTR rules permit such transfer of cases to national courts that have jurisdiction. Norway agreed to try Bagaragaza, who then surrendered. Both parties moved that the ICTR permit Norway to try Bagaragaza.

However, Norway has no domestic criminal statute against genocide. Instead, Norway proposed to try Bagaragaza under its domestic murder statute. This raises a question: How would Norway have jurisdiction over murders committed by Rwandans against other Rwandans in Rwanda, with no connection to Norway? The answer is that Norway has a universal jurisdiction statute of truly cosmic scope, according to which "Norwegian criminal law shall be applicable to acts committed abroad by a foreigner when the act is one dealt with in [enumerated sections of the criminal code, including §233, the prohibition on murder]. . . ." Norwegian Criminal Code §12(4)(a), available at http://www.ub.uio.no/ujur/ulovdata/lov-19020522-010-eng.pdf. Section 13 specifies that such jurisdiction may be exercised only "when the King so decides."

In 2006, the ICTR's Trial Chamber denied the motion to permit Norway to take jurisdiction. The Trial Chamber ruled that genocide, not murder, is the crime specified in the ICTR indictment of Bagaragaza, and trying him for murder is not an adequate substitute for trying him for genocide. Prosecutor v. Bagaragaza, Case No. ICTR-2005-86-R11 bis, Decision on the Prosecution Motion for Referral to the Kingdom of Norway (May 19, 2006). The Appeals Chamber upheld the Trial Chamber's decision, and in 2007 the Trial Chamber agreed to refer Bagaragaza's case to the Netherlands rather than Norway. This plan was defeated when a Dutch court ruled in a different case arising out of the Rwandan genocide that it does not have universal jurisdiction over crimes committed before 2003, when the Netherlands revised its law against genocide. Eventually, Bagaragaza was transferred back to the ICTR in Arusha, where in 2008 he signed a confidential plea agreement with the prosecutor.

6. What substantive criminal law should define universal jurisdiction offenses? One scholar has argued that the substantive definitions of crimes should come from international law, rather than the forum state's domestic law. This would preclude forum states from writing their own broad definitions of international crimes and

using those definitions to try foreigners under universal jurisdiction. Anthony J. Colangelo, The Legal Limits of Universal Jurisdiction, 47 Va. J. Intl. L. 149 (2006). The author uses this principle to criticize Spain's attempted prosecution of Chilean dictator Augusto Pinochet for genocide.

7. In an important 2007 decision, the Spanish Supreme Court agreed. The case concerned the prosecution of an Argentinian naval officer, Adolfo Scilingo, for crimes committed during the Argentinian "dirty war" of 1976-1983, in which thousands of Argentinians disappeared, were tortured, or were murdered by the ruling junta. Spain prosecuted Scilingo under universal jurisdiction. The Supreme Court dismissed genocide charges against Scilingo because the Spanish anti-genocide statute defines the crime more broadly than international law. However, the argument proved to be a two-edged sword: The court convicted Scilingo of crimes against humanity, even though Spain passed its crimes against humanity statute only in 2004, long after Scinlingo's crimes. The court argued that the definition of crimes against humanity had belonged to customary international law at the time of Scilingo's crimes, and the Spanish constitution of 1978 requires that domestic law be interpreted in light of international human rights law. Scilingo was sentenced to 25 years. Richard J. Wilson, Spanish Supreme Court Affirms Conviction of Argentine Former Naval Officer for Crimes Against Humanity, ASIL Insight, Jan. 30, 2008, available at http://www.asil.org/insights080130.cfm.

8. As of 2009, Spain has replaced Belgium as the most active practitioner of universal jurisdiction prosecutions of foreigners' human rights abuses outside Spanish territory. Even before the Scilingo case, a landmark decision by Spain's Constitutional Court allowed a genocide investigation concerning Guatemala to go forward, even without any connection to Spain (such as Spanish victims). Guatemala Genocide, Judgment No. STC 237/2005 (Tribunal Constitucional Sept. 26, 2005); for an English-language summary, see Naomi Roht-Arriaza, International Decision: Spanish Constitutional Tribunal Decision on Universal Jurisdiction over Genocide Claims, 100 Am. J. Intl. L. 207 (2006). In the words of the constitutional court, the penal interest in such crimes "transcend the harm to the specific victims and affect the international community as a whole. Therefore, prosecution and punishment are not only a shared commitment, but a shared interest of all states. . . ." Roht-Arriaza translation, International Decision, at 211. The tribunal reaffirmed this broad use of universal jurisdiction in a case involving Chinese persecution of members of the Falun Gong religious group and permitted investigation to continue of China's ex-president Jiang Zemin and the head of China's Falun Gong Unit.

9. In the wake of the Abu Ghraib prison abuses, human rights activists in the United States, Germany, and elsewhere have made several efforts to institute the foreign prosecution for torture of senior U.S. officials, including former defense secretary Donald Rumsfeld, in countries with universal jurisdiction statutes. One such effort, launched in France, was dismissed on the basis of official immunity in 2007. For further discussion, see Chapter 6 on immunity of government officials. Another, launched in Germany, was dismissed in 2005 on the ground that the United States has primary responsibility for investigating and prosecuting charges involving Americans that have no nexus with Germany. After the United States enacted the Military Commissions Act in 2006, which retroactively decriminalized humiliating and degrading treatment of detainees, the activists refiled their complaint, arguing that the Act demonstrates U.S. unwillingness to investigate and prosecute its own officials. In 2007, the German prosecutor once again dismissed the complaint on the grounds of lack of a German nexus. Germany's Code of Crimes Against International Law, §1,

states: "This Act shall apply to all crimes against international law designated under this Act, to serious criminal offenses designated therein, even when the offense was committed abroad and bears no relation to Germany." Should the German prosecutor have dismissed the case?

The human rights activists continue to press their case against the U.S. officials in Spain. Prosecuting the US for War Crimes: Case Against Rumsfeld Heads for Spain, Spiegel Online, Apr. 30, 2007, http://www.spiegel.de/international/europe/0,1518,480215,00.html. See also Marjorie Cohn, Spain Leads the Way, Apr. 7, 2009, http://www.counterpunch.org/cohn04072009.html. Do these prosecutions demonstrate the potential for abusing universal jurisdiction or the need for universal jurisdiction?

B.   EXTRATERRITORIAL APPLICATION OF U.S. CRIMINAL STATUTES

We next turn to the question of how U.S. domestic law answers the question of whether a U.S. criminal statute applies outside the territory of the United States. As we will see, whether a U.S. criminal statute applies to conduct outside U.S. borders depends on three factors:

1.   whether the Constitution grants Congress the power to legislate extraterritorially on the subject matter of the statute;
2.   whether Congress intended the statute to reach outside U.S. territory; and
3.   whether international law permits the United States to assert jurisdiction over conduct outside U.S. borders.

PROBLEM 4

Consider that the FBI is conducting a money laundering investigation against Dr. Fixer, an important businessman in the country of Angora. They suspect Fixer is on the payroll of a drug cartel, and they are following a stream of money (well, actually, a mighty river of money) he has caused to be sent from Angora to banks in many other countries. From these banks, the money eventually makes its way to confidential bank accounts in Switzerland and the Cayman Islands.

One country along Fixer's money trail is the Republic of Macadamia. U.S. authorities subpoena records from the Macadamian Bank of Commerce (MBC), which complies with the subpoena.[10] However, federal agents subsequently learn from an informant that a senior officer at MBC, Mr. Banker, has altered some bank records submitted to the U.S. government. He did this in order to conceal deposits and transactions involving his secretive wealthy clients. The MBC was not party to his alteration of bank records and did not know about it.

---

10. The United States has no direct subpoena authority over banks in other countries. However, a provision in the USA Patriot Act empowers the U.S. government to prevent foreign banks that refuse to comply with U.S. subpoenas from doing business in the United States, a threat that generally works wonders in getting foreign banks to comply with U.S. subpoenas. See 31 U.S.C. §5318(k)(3)(A)(i).

Mr. Banker visits the United States, and federal agents arrest him when he lands. He is charged with violating the obstruction of justice statute, 18 U.S.C. §1503, which reads in relevant part:

> Whoever . . . corruptly . . . influences, obstructs, or impedes, or endeavors to influence, obstruct, or impede, the due administration of justice, shall be punished. . . .

Within U.S. domestic law, tampering with subpoenaed documents to impede a federal investigation clearly violates this statute. However, Mr. Banker moves to dismiss for lack of jurisdiction, arguing:

1. that §1503 does not apply outside the territory of the United States;
2. that Congress lacks constitutional authority to criminalize obstruction of federal investigations outside of the United States;
3. that extraterritorial application of §1503 violates international law; and
4. that the prosecution violates the principle of legality as embodied in the Due Process Clause of the U.S. Constitution because Mr. Banker lacked fair notice that the statute applies to him in Macadamia.

How should the court rule on this motion? Analyze the problem using the materials that follow.

1. Constitutional Authority

The U.S. Constitution plainly contemplates that some criminal statutes will have extraterritorial reach. The Venue Clause of Article 3 includes crimes "not committed within any [U.S.] State" and specifies that for such crimes "the Trial shall be at such Place or Places as the Congress may by Law have directed." Art. 3, §2, cl. 3. Some U.S. criminal statutes state explicitly that they govern conduct committed outside U.S. borders as well as conduct within. For example, an important antiterrorism statute, which forbids providing material support or resources to foreign terrorist organizations, includes a clause that reads:

> **(d) Extraterritorial jurisdiction** — There is extraterritorial Federal jurisdiction over an offense under this section.

18 U.S.C. §2339B(d).

Other federal statutes include no such clause, but their subject matter makes it plausible that Congress intended them to apply extraterritorially. Consider, for example, the federal statute making it a crime to suborn perjury, that is, to induce someone else to commit perjury. Perjury is defined as lying under oath about material facts "before a competent tribunal, officer, or person, in any case in which a law of the United States authorizes an oath to be administered," or the equivalent in written declarations. The perjury statute explicitly applies "whether the statement or subscription is made within or without the United States." 18 U.S.C. §1621. However, the subornation statute states only that "[w]hoever procures another to commit any perjury is guilty of subornation of perjury. . . ." 18 U.S.C. §1622. Nowhere does §1622 state that it criminalizes foreign as well as domestic subornings of perjury. But it would be illogical for Congress to make subornation a crime without intending the statute to apply wherever the perjury statute itself applies. After all, the most likely place for someone to "procure another to commit perjury" is the locale where the perjury itself occurs. It is much more likely that Congress intended this statute, just as much as the perjury statute, to apply extraterritorially. As we shall see shortly, reasoning in this way from the purpose of the law to congressional intent is precisely the analytic framework for determining extraterritoriality adopted by the U.S. Supreme Court in United States v. Bowman, 260 U.S. 94 (1922).

Nevertheless, it is important to realize that at the time of the founding of the United States, and for the better part of subsequent U.S. history, the United States was clearly, even emphatically, a nation focused on territorial jurisdiction. The rebellious colonists bristled at the notion that the king's justice followed his subjects wherever they went. Their view was straightforward: Commit a crime in England, get English law; commit a crime in Virginia, get Virginia law. As a common law country, the United States largely rejected nationality-based jurisdiction, in contrast to post-Revolutionary France and her civil law cohorts, which freely asserted it and still do. (Today, however, the United States has adopted a few nationality-based extraterritorial criminal statutes. See Section A.4 above.)

The rapid embrace by the United States of extraterritoriality is a product of mid- to late-twentieth-century developments, beginning with commerce (in the form of antitrust statutes with extraterritorial reach), then narcotics, then corruption, then terrorism. Some observers note that the United States vaulted from being in the back of the pack to being way out front when it comes to extraterritorial criminal jurisdiction.

But that jumps the gun. As a matter of domestic law, Congress cannot legislate extraterritorially unless it has the constitutional authority to do so. Notice that this raises a different question than whether international law permits the United States to apply its laws extraterritorially. The present question has nothing to do with international law. It is the question of whether, as a matter of domestic constitutional law, Congress can extend the reach of its criminal statutes beyond the borders of the United States.

The Constitution defines Congress's legislative authority in the 18 clauses of Article 1, Section 8. Of these clauses, two explicitly grant Congress authority to enact criminal laws. These are the Counterfeiting Clause and the Define and Punish Clause:

> The Congress shall have Power . . .
>   To provide for the Punishment of counterfeiting the Securities and current Coin of the United States [cl. 6 — the Counterfeiting Clause];
>   To define and punish Piracies and Felonies committed on the high Seas, and Offences against the Law of Nations [cl. 10 — the Define and Punish Clause].[11]

The Define and Punish Clause explicitly grants Congress the power to criminalize extraterritorial conduct, but that power is also implicit in the Counterfeiting Clause. Foreign counterfeiting carries the same dangers to the U.S. currency system as domestic counterfeiting, and there can be no doubt that the Counterfeiting Clause empowers Congress to punish foreign counterfeiting.

In addition, Clause 14 of Article 8 confers on Congress the power "[t]o make Rules for the Government and Regulation of the land and naval Forces." That includes the power to enact a military criminal code. This, too, will have extraterritorial reach because U.S. armed forces operate outside the United States as well as inside.

But all three of these clauses concern specialized situations. What about a more general authority for extraterritorial jurisdiction in criminal law? To the extent it

---

11. U.S. Const. art. 1, §8.

exists, this derives from the Foreign Commerce Clause and the Necessary and Proper Clause:

> To regulate Commerce *with foreign Nations*, and among the several States, and with the Indian tribes [cl. 3—the Foreign Commerce Clause; emphasis added];
>
> To make all Laws which shall be necessary and proper for carrying into Execution the foregoing Powers, and all other Powers vested by this Constitution in the Government of the United States, or in any Department or Officer thereof[12] [cl. 18—the Necessary and Proper Clause].

PROBLEM 5

What is the constitutional basis, if any, for extraterritorial application of the following real and imaginary federal statutes?

1. The obstruction of justice statute in Problem 4 above, 18 U.S.C. §1503.

2. A homicide statute that makes it a federal crime to kill, attempt to kill, conspire to kill, or engage in serious physical violence against a U.S. national "while such national is outside the United States," if the crime is "intended to coerce, intimidate, or retaliate against a government or a civilian population." 18 U.S.C. §2332. The statute was enacted in response to a notorious 1986 incident in which terrorists captured an Italian cruise ship, the *Achille Lauro*, and brutally murdered a wheelchair-bound U.S. tourist. The "intended to coerce" language was added to ensure that the statute did not reach "[s]imple barroom brawls or normal street crime,"[13] but rather crimes of political violence—terrorism, in short, although the statute does not use the word. Note that the "government or civilian population" need have no connection with the United States.

3. An aircraft sabotage statute that makes it a federal crime to commit violence on "any civil aircraft registered in a country other than the United States," to destroy such an aircraft, or to plant a bomb on such an aircraft, regardless of where the offense occurs and regardless of whether any U.S. nationals are on board. 18 U.S.C. §32(b). The statute in question was enacted to implement a multilateral treaty to which the United States is a party, which declares these deeds to be international crimes.

4. The same statute if there were no such treaty.

The aircraft sabotage example in note 3 above is an example of a criminal statute of extraterritorial reach that Congress enacted to implement an international treaty. There are several such treaties, governing crimes of international concern such as aircraft hijacking, hostage taking, drug trafficking, and torture. Typically, such treaties require the states parties to take steps including: (1) criminalizing the activity if it is not already a domestic crime; (2) either extraditing or prosecuting suspects in their custody; and (3) creating the necessary criminal jurisdiction to prosecute them, if it does not already exist.

The question is, where does Congress get the authority to legislate as the treaties require? One answer is that it derives from the Necessary and Proper Clause, as explained in the 1920 Supreme Court decision Missouri v. Holland, 252 U.S. 416 (1920): "If the treaty is valid there can be no dispute about the validity of the [implementing] statute under Article 1, Section 8, as a necessary and proper means to execute the powers of the Government." Id. at 432. *Missouri v. Holland* was a controversial decision because it seems to imply that the federal government can make an

---

12. Id.
13. H.R. Conf. Rep. No. 783, 99th Cong., 2d Sess. 87 (1986).

end run around Congress's limited constitutional powers by negotiating a treaty that requires implementing legislation outside those powers.[14] In other words, it appears to empower the Congress to adopt legislation pursuant to the Treaty Power which it could not enact under its other enumerated powers. The only constraint might be the "validity" of the treaty in question. Advocates of states' rights objected to the potential *Holland* created for expanding the power of the federal government at the expense of the U.S. states; and in the 1950s, unsuccessful efforts were made to undo *Holland* through a constitutional amendment.

However, when a treaty establishes aerial hijacking or torture as an international crime, there is an alternative route to congressional authority. The treaty, by internationalizing the crime, arguably makes it an "offense against the law of nations," and thus Congress is empowered to legislate by the Define and Punish Clause.[15]

Outside of such treaties, the principal constitutional basis for extraterritorial criminal jurisdiction lies in the Foreign Commerce Clause.

UNITED STATES v. CLARK

435 F.3d 1100 (9th Cir. 2006), *cert. denied*, 549 U.S. 1343 (2007)

[Another excerpt from this significant decision appears in Section A.4 above on nationality jurisdiction. The case, you will recall, concerned a U.S. national prosecuted under the federal sex tourism statute, 18 U.S.C. §2423, for having travelled abroad for paid sex with children in Cambodia. The earlier excerpt included the court's discussion of international law jurisdiction, and whether the lack of nexus between the acts and the United States renders the statute unconstitutional under the Due Process Clause. The following excerpt addresses Congress's constitutional authority to regulate extraterritorial commercial sex acts.]

. . . In considering whether Congress exceeded its power under the Foreign Commerce Clause in enacting §2423(c), we ground our analysis in the fundamental principle that "[i]t is an essential attribute of [Congress's power over foreign commerce] that it is exclusive and plenary." . . . In light of Congress's sweeping powers over foreign commerce, we conclude that Congress acted within its constitutional bounds in criminalizing commercial sex acts committed by U.S. citizens who travel abroad in foreign commerce.

At the outset, we highlight that §2423(c) contemplates two types of "illicit sexual conduct": non-commercial and commercial. Clark's conduct falls squarely under the second prong of the definition, which criminalizes "any commercial sex act . . . with a person under 18 years of age." 18 U.S.C. §2423(f)(2). In view of this factual posture, we . . . limit our holding to §2423(c)'s regulation of commercial sex acts.

A. THE COMMERCE CLAUSE: STRUCTURE AND HISTORY

Chief Justice Marshall observed long ago that "[t]he objects, to which the power of regulating commerce might be directed, are divided into three distinct classes — foreign

---

14. See Nicholas Quinn Rosenkranz, Executing the Treaty Power, 118 Harv. L. Rev. 1867 (2005) (criticizing *Holland*).

15. For further reading, see Andreas F. Lowenfeld, U.S. Law Enforcement Abroad: The Constitution and International Law, 83 Am. J. Intl. L. 880 (1989).

nations, the several states, and Indian Tribes. When forming this article, the convention considered them as entirely distinct." Looking to the text, the single clause indeed embodies three subclauses for which distinct prepositional language is used: "To regulate Commerce with foreign Nations, and among the several States, and with the Indian Tribes." U.S. Const. art. I, §8, cl. 3.

Among legal scholars there has been considerable debate over the intrasentence unity—or disunity, as the case may be—of the three subclauses, considering that they share the common language "[t]o regulate Commerce." Some commentators take the view that Congress's powers over commerce with foreign nations and Indian tribes are broader than over interstate commerce. . . .

Other scholars maintain that Congress has coextensive powers under the Commerce Clause's subdivisions. . . . Despite the long-running lively debate among scholars, no definitive view emerges regarding the relationship among the three subclauses. Nonetheless, Supreme Court precedent points to the conclusion that the Foreign Commerce Clause *is* different than the Interstate Commerce Clause. . . .

Regardless of how separate the three subclauses may be in theory, the reality is that they have been subject to markedly divergent treatment by the courts. . . . Most notably, regardless of whether the subject matter is drugs, gender-motivated violence, or gun possession, a prominent theme runs throughout the interstate commerce cases: concern for state sovereignty and federalism. On the other hand, "[t]he principle of duality in our system of government does not touch the authority of the Congress in the regulation of foreign commerce." This distinction provides a crucial touchstone in applying the Foreign Commerce Clause, for which Congress's authority to regulate has not been defined with the precision set forth by [United States v. Morrison, 529 U.S. 598 (2000) and United States v. Lopez, 514 U.S. 549 (1995)] in the interstate context.

We start with the component that has dominated judicial consideration of the Commerce Clause: "among the several States." After decades of expansive reading by the courts, the mid-1990s saw a retrenchment in Commerce Clause jurisprudence beginning with the watershed case of *Lopez*. In *Lopez*, the Court held that a statute which criminalized possession of a firearm in a school zone was beyond Congress's Commerce Clause authority. In so holding, the Court stressed its concern that an overly expansive view of the Interstate Commerce Clause "would effectually obliterate the distinction between what is national and what is local and create a completely centralized government." The Court reiterated these concerns five years later in *Morrison* in striking down a provision under the Violence Against Women Act. . . .

In addition to announcing a shift to a more constrained view of Congress's power over interstate commerce, *Lopez* and *Morrison* ossified the three-category framework that the Court had long applied to interstate commerce cases. [T]hese three familiar categories are (1) the use of the channels of interstate commerce; (2) the instrumentalities of interstate commerce, or persons or things in interstate commerce; and (3) activities that substantially affect interstate commerce. Within the interstate commerce arena, the guiding force of *Lopez* and *Morrison* quickly took firm hold, and lower courts have adhered closely to the three-prong structure.

This past term the Court introduced a new wrinkle in interstate commerce's jurisprudential fabric when it held that the Controlled Substances Act was a valid exercise of Congress's powers under the Commerce Clause. See [Gonzalez v. Raich, 545 U.S. 1 (2005)]. *Raich* . . . took a more generous view of Congress's power over interstate commerce than seen in *Lopez* and *Morrison*. Over the dissent's pointed objections, the majority concluded that "Congress had a rational basis for concluding that leaving home-consumed marijuana outside federal control would similarly affect price and market conditions." This "rational basis" for finding a nexus between home-consumed marijuana and the interstate market put the regulation "squarely within Congress' commerce power." . . .

. . . In contrast to the federal government's relationship with the states, its relationship with Indian tribes is "based on a history of treaties and the assumption of a 'guardian-ward' status." The Commerce Clause stands as one of the main textual grants of Congress's plenary power to regulate this special relationship between the federal government and Indian tribes. In this context, the Court has defined Congress's authority under the Indian Commerce Clause without reference to the rigid categories of *Lopez* and *Morrison*.

As with the Indian Commerce Clause, the Foreign Commerce Clause has followed its own distinct evolutionary path. Born largely from a desire for uniform rules governing commercial relations with foreign countries, the Supreme Court has read the Foreign Commerce Clause as granting Congress sweeping powers. This view was laid down nearly two centuries ago when Chief Justice Marshall stated that "[i]t has, we believe, been universally admitted, that [the words of the Commerce Clause] comprehend every species of commercial intercourse between the United States and foreign nations."

The Court has been unwavering in reading Congress's power over foreign commerce broadly. . . . There is no counterpart to *Lopez* or *Morrison* in the foreign commerce realm that would signal a retreat from the Court's expansive reading of the Foreign Commerce Clause. In fact, the Supreme Court has never struck down an act of Congress as exceeding its powers to regulate foreign commerce.

Federalism and state sovereignty concerns do not restrict Congress's power over foreign commerce and the need for federal uniformity "is no less paramount" in assessing the so-called "dormant" implications of congressional power under the Foreign Commerce Clause. By contrast, under the dormant Interstate Commerce Clause, "reconciliation of the conflicting claims of state and national power is to be attained only by some appraisal and accommodation of the competing demands of the state and national interests involved." . . .

B. SECTION 2423(C)'S REGULATION OF COMMERCIAL SEX ACTS IS A VALID EXERCISE OF CONGRESS'S FOREIGN COMMERCE CLAUSE POWERS

Taking a page from *Raich*, we review the statute under the traditional rational basis standard. The question we pose is whether the statute bears a rational relationship to Congress's authority under the Foreign Commerce Clause.

Although it is important to view the statute as a whole, parsing its elements illustrates why the statute fairly relates to foreign commerce. The elements that the government must prove under §2423(c)'s commercial sex acts prong are straightforward. First, the defendant must "travel[ ] in foreign commerce." Second, the defendant must "engage[ ] in any illicit sexual conduct with another person," which in this case contemplates "any commercial sex act . . . with a person under 18 years of age." We hold that §2423(c)'s combination of requiring travel in foreign commerce, coupled with engagement in a commercial transaction while abroad, implicates foreign commerce to a constitutionally adequate degree.

Beginning with the first element, the phrase "travels in foreign commerce" unequivocally establishes that Congress specifically invoked the Foreign Commerce Clause. The defendant must therefore have moved in foreign commerce at some point to trigger the statute. In Clark's case, he traveled from the United States to Cambodia.

"Foreign commerce" has been defined broadly for purposes of Title 18 of the U.S. Code, with the statutory definition reading, in full: "The term 'foreign commerce', as used in this title, includes commerce with a foreign country." 18 U.S.C. §10. Admittedly, this definition is not particularly helpful given its rearrangement of the words being defined in the definition itself. Courts have understandably taken the broad wording to have an expansive reach. . . . Clark got on a plane in the United States and journeyed to Cambodia. This act is sufficient to satisfy the "travels in foreign commerce" element of §2423(c).

Once in Cambodia, the second element of §2423(c) was also met, namely, "engage[ment] in any illicit sexual conduct with another person," which in this case was commercial sex under §2423(f)(2). As the Supreme Court recognized centuries ago, the Commerce Clause "comprehend[s] every species of commercial intercourse between the United States and foreign nations." Section 2423(c) regulates a pernicious "species of commercial intercourse": commercial sex acts with minors. . . .

The essential economic character of the commercial sex acts regulated by §2423(c) stands in contrast to the non-economic activities regulated by the statutes at issue in *Lopez* and *Morrison*. In both *Lopez* and *Morrison*, the Supreme Court voiced strong concerns over Congress's use of the Commerce Clause to enact "a criminal statute that by its terms has nothing to do with 'commerce' or any sort of economic enterprise, however broadly one might define those terms." Like the statute regulating illicit drugs at issue in *Raich*, the activity regulated by the commercial sex prong of §2423(c) is "quintessentially economic," and thus falls within foreign trade and commerce. . . .

The combination of Clark's travel in foreign commerce and his conduct of an illicit commercial sex act in Cambodia shortly thereafter puts the statute squarely within Congress's Foreign Commerce Clause authority. In reaching this conclusion, we view the Foreign Commerce Clause independently from its domestic brethren. . . .

At times, forcing foreign commerce cases into the domestic commerce rubric is a bit like one of the stepsisters trying to don Cinderella's glass slipper; nonetheless, there is a good argument that, as found by the district court, §2423(c) can also be viewed as a valid regulation of the "channels of commerce." Our previous decisions have recognized that Congress legitimately exercises its authority to regulate the channels of commerce where a crime committed on foreign soil is necessarily tied to travel in foreign commerce, even where the actual use of the channels has ceased. . . .

FERGUSON, Circuit Judge, dissenting:

The Constitution cannot be interpreted according to the principle that the end justifies the means. The sexual abuse of children abroad is despicable, but we should not, and need not, refashion our Constitution to address it. The majority holds that "travel in foreign commerce, coupled with engagement in a commercial transaction while abroad, implicates foreign commerce to a constitutionally adequate degree." I respectfully disagree.

. . . The activity regulated by 18 U.S.C. §2423(c), illicit sexual conduct, does not in any sense of the phrase relate to commerce *with foreign nations*. Rather, §2423(c) is a criminal statute that punishes private conduct fundamentally divorced from foreign commerce. Article I, section 8, clause 3, while giving Congress broad authority over our commercial relations with other nations, is not a grant of international police power. I respectfully dissent from the majority's assertion that the Commerce Clause authorizes Congress to regulate an activity with a bare economic component, as long as that activity occurs subsequent to some form of international travel. I also note that the conduct in this case will not go unpunished, as the reasonable course of action remains of recognizing Cambodia's authority to prosecute Clark under its own criminal laws. . . .

Our national government is a government of "enumerated powers," which presupposes powers that are not enumerated, and therefore not accorded to Congress. As such, the Commerce Clause is "subject to outer limits." Through a long line of cases, the Supreme Court has developed a tri-category framework that helps courts ascertain these outer limits, and whether a particular enactment exceeds them. In the foreign commerce context, the majority would replace this time-tested framework with its own broad standard: whether a statute "has a constitutionally tenable nexus with foreign commerce." The majority views the foreign commerce prong of the Commerce Clause "independently from its domestic brethren," though Congress's authority in both spheres is governed by the same constitutional language: "[t]o regulate Commerce," art. I, §8, cl. 3. In so doing, the majority goes farther than our precedent counsels and dispenses with the tri-category framework that has grounded Commerce Clause analysis in the modern era.

The majority portrays the raison d'etre of the tri-category framework as addressing "unique federalism concerns that define congressional authority in the *interstate* context." It is thus able to conclude that this framework is generally inapplicable to foreign commerce cases. A fairer understanding of the tri-category framework is that it has evolved not only in response to federalism concerns that courts have read into Congress's Interstate Commerce power, but also to give content to what it means generally "[t]o regulate Commerce." . . . While Congress's authority to regulate foreign commerce may well be broader than its authority to regulate interstate commerce, its authority in the foreign sphere is not different in kind. In both spheres, Congress is only authorized "[t]o regulate Commerce," art. I, §8, cl. 3, and not those activities that are fundamentally divorced from commerce. . . .

Under the tri-category framework, . . . §2423(c) is not a regulation of the channels of foreign commerce. Section 2423(c) lacks any of the tangible links to the channels of commerce that would justify upholding it under Congress's Foreign Commerce power.

The Supreme Court has held that Congress's authority to regulate the channels of commerce encompasses keeping those channels "free from immoral and injurious uses." . . .

Under this rubric, the current 18 U.S.C. §2423(b) contains a defensible link to the channels of foreign commerce, as it covers people who "[t]ravel with intent to engage in illicit sexual conduct." . . . The activity regulated by §2423(b), intention to engage in illicit sexual conduct, is at least tenably related to the channels of commerce in that the defendant engages in travel *with illegitimate ends*. The person indicted under §2423(b) has a plane ticket in hand, has paid a travel agent to set up the trip, or has otherwise committed an act that is both wrongful (because of the criminal intent) and tangibly related to the channels of commerce.

By contrast, §2423(c) neither punishes the act of traveling in foreign commerce, or the wrongful use or impediment of use of the channels of foreign commerce. Rather, it punishes future conduct in a foreign country entirely divorced from the act of traveling except for the fact that the travel occurs at some point prior to the regulated conduct. The statute does not require any wrongful intent at the time the channel is being used, nor does it require a temporal link between the "travel[ ] in foreign commerce," and the underlying regulated activity. . . .

The mere act of boarding an international flight, without more, is insufficient to bring all of Clark's downstream activities that involve an exchange of value within the ambit of Congress's Foreign Commerce power. On some level, every act by a U.S. citizen abroad takes place subsequent to an international flight or some form of "travel[ ] in foreign commerce." This cannot mean that every act with a bare economic component that occurs downstream from that travel is subject to regulation by the United States under its Foreign Commerce power, or the Commerce Clause will have been converted into a general grant of police power. It is telling to note that, theoretically, the only U.S. citizens who could fall outside the reach of §2423(c) if they engage in illicit sexual conduct abroad are those who never set foot in the United States (i.e., U.S. citizens by virtue of their parent's citizenship), and thus never travel in "Commerce with foreign Nations." In short, §2423(c) is divorced from its asserted Commerce Clause underpinnings. The statute does not set another "guidepost" regarding Congress's Foreign Commerce power — it exceeds it. . . .

Further, the underlying act, even if considered economic or commercial, is certainly not a presence of commerce *with foreign nations.* In the most sterile terms, an act of paid sex with a minor that takes place overseas is not an act of commerce with other nations. Under the interpretation of the majority, the purchase of a lunch in France by an American citizen who traveled there by airplane would constitute a constitutional act of engaging in foreign commerce. . . .

. . . Sexual exploitation of children by foreigners is thoroughly condemnable, but the question before us is whether Congress properly invoked its power "[t]o regulate Commerce with foreign Nations" in enacting §2423(c) to address this problem. It did not. I therefore respectfully dissent.

NOTES AND QUESTIONS

1. Which approach do you find more persuasive, the majority's or the dissent's? Does nationality alone provide a sufficient nexus for regulation of personal conduct (sexual or other) in foreign places? Note that §2423(c) applies to lawful permanent residents as well as citizens. What are the limits, if any, of this authority? In rejecting a jurisdictional challenge to a subsequent prosecution under §2423(c), one court relied in part on *Clark* for the proposition that "citizenship alone grants Congress the right to enact laws with extraterritorial application, thus authorizing jurisdiction under the 'national' principle." U.S. v. Martinez, 599 F. Supp. 2d 784, 800 (W.D. Tex. 2009).

2. The majority rests its analysis on a very broad reading of the Foreign Commerce Clause, unrestricted by federalism or state sovereignty concerns. Since the act in question was in its view unquestionably "commercial" and followed Clark's travel in foreign commerce, it concluded, the statute meets the "traditional rational basis" standard required by the Constitution. Judge Ferguson's dissent challenges that conclusion on the grounds that "[t]he mere act of boarding an international flight, without more, is insufficient to bring all of Clark's downstream activities that involve an exchange of value within the ambit of Congress's Foreign Commerce power." Do you see problems with using foreign travel as a predicate for criminalizing an act abroad, when the travel itself is not part of the illegal act in question?

3. Judge Ferguson also notes that Cambodia could prosecute Clark under its domestic laws. How important is that to his analysis? Recalling our discussion of the *Cutting* case earlier in this chapter, what if the act in question was not a criminal

offense where it occurred? Should that be a relevant factor in assessing the legitimacy of the U.S. statute?

4. To illustrate, what if a foreign country exercised "nationality" jurisdiction to make it a criminal offense for any of its citizens, or any noncitizens resident in its territories (including U.S. students studying at its universities), to purchase "immoral" books or movies while traveling in other countries? How would you defend such a statute in argument before the International Court of Justice?

2.   *Determining Extraterritorial Applicability of a Criminal Statute*

After determining that Congress has the authority to enact a criminal statute with extraterritorial reach, the logical next question is how to determine whether a statute that does not explicitly state that it applies extraterritorially actually does.

UNITED STATES v. BOWMAN
260 U.S. 94 (1922)

Mr. Chief Justice TAFT delivered the opinion of the Court.

[The *Dio* was a U.S. ship sailing to Rio de Janeiro, owned by a company in which the United States was the sole shareholder. Two of the *Dio*'s crew members conspired with a Standard Oil employee and a ship repairer in Rio to defraud the company by ordering more fuel in Rio than was actually purchased and pocketing the profits. Three of the defendants were U.S. nationals, while the fourth, a British subject, was still at large. The defendants were charged under §35 of the Criminal Code with three counts of fraud against the government and three counts of conspiracy to commit fraud. The counts all concerned extraterritorial conduct: on the high seas, in the port of Rio, and in the city of Rio. The district court dismissed the charges based on the lack of extraterritorial jurisdiction of §35.]

The court in its opinion conceded that under many authorities the United States as a sovereign may regulate the ships under its flag and the conduct of its citizens while on those ships. . . . The court said, however, that while private and public ships of the United States on the high seas were constructively a part of the territory of the United States, indeed peculiarly so as distinguished from that of the States, Congress had always expressly indicated it when it intended that its laws should be operative on the high seas. The court concluded that because jurisdiction of criminal offenses must be conferred upon United States courts and could not be inferred, and because §35, like all the other sections of c. 4, contains no reference to the high seas as a part of the locus of the offenses defined by it, as the sections in cc. 11 and 12 of the Criminal Code do, §35 must be construed not to extend to acts committed on the high seas. It confirmed its conclusion by the statement that §35 had never been invoked to punish offenses denounced if committed on the high seas or in a foreign country.

We have in this case a question of statutory construction. The necessary locus, when not specially defined, depends upon the purpose of Congress as evidenced by the description and nature of the crime and upon the territorial limitations upon the power and jurisdiction of a government to punish crime under the law of nations. Crimes against private individuals or their property, like assaults, murder, burglary, larceny, robbery, arson, embezzlement and fraud of all kinds, which affect the peace and good order of the community, must of course be committed within the territorial jurisdiction of the government where it may properly exercise it. If punishment of them is to be extended to include those committed outside of the strict territorial jurisdiction, it is natural for Congress to say so in the statute, and failure to do so will negative the purpose of Congress in this regard. . . .

But the same rule of interpretation should not be applied to criminal statutes which are, as a class, not logically dependent on their locality for the Government's jurisdiction, but are enacted because of the right of the Government to defend itself against obstruction, or fraud wherever perpetrated, especially if committed by its own citizens, officers or agents. Some such offenses can only be committed within the territorial jurisdiction of the Government because of the local acts required to constitute them. Others are such that to limit their locus to the strictly territorial jurisdiction would be greatly to curtail the scope and usefulness of the statute and leave open a large immunity for frauds as easily committed by citizens on the high seas and in foreign countries as at home. In such cases, Congress has not thought it necessary to make specific provision in the law that the locus shall include the high seas and foreign countries, but allows it to be inferred from the nature of the offense. Many of these occur in c. 4, which bears the title "Offenses against the operations of the Government." Section 70 of that chapter punishes whoever as consul knowingly certifies a false invoice. Clearly the locus of this crime as intended by Congress is in a foreign country and certainly the foreign country in which he discharges his official duty could not object to the trial in a United States court of a United States consul for crime of this sort committed within its borders. Forging or altering ship's papers is made a crime by §72 of c. 4. It would be going too far to say that because Congress does not fix any locus it intended to exclude the high seas in respect of this crime. The natural inference from the character of the offense is that the sea would be a probable place for its commission. Section 42 of c. 4 punishes enticing desertions from the naval service. Is it possible that Congress did not intend by this to include such enticing done aboard ship on the high seas or in a foreign port, where it would be most likely to be done? Section 39 punishes bribing a United States officer of the civil, military or naval service to violate his duty or to aid in committing a fraud on the United States. It is hardly reasonable to construe this not to include such offenses when the bribe is offered to a consul, ambassador, an army or a naval officer in a foreign country or on the high seas, whose duties are being performed there and when his connivance at such fraud must occur there. So, too, §38 of c. 4 punishes the willfully doing or aiding to do any act relating to the bringing in, custody, sale or other disposition of property captured as prize, with intent to defraud, delay or injure the United States or any captor or claimant of such property. This would naturally often occur at sea, and Congress could not have meant to confine it to the land of the United States. Again, in §36 of c. 4, it is made a crime to steal, embezzle, or knowingly apply to his own use ordnance, arms, ammunition, clothing, subsistence, stores, money or other property of the United States furnished or to be used for military or naval service. It would hardly be reasonable to hold that if any one, certainly if a citizen of the United States, were to steal or embezzle such property which may properly and lawfully be in the custody of army or naval officers either in foreign countries, in foreign ports or on the high seas, it would not be in such places an offense which Congress intended to punish by this section.

What is true of these sections in this regard is true of §35, under which this indictment was drawn. . . .

It is directed generally against whoever presents a false claim against the United States, knowing it to be such, to any officer of the civil, military or naval service or to any department thereof, or any corporation in which the United States is a stockholder, or whoever connives at the same by the use of any cheating device, or whoever enters a conspiracy to do these things. The section was amended in 1918 to include a corporation in which the United States owns stock. This was evidently intended to protect the Emergency Fleet Corporation in which the United States was the sole stockholder, from fraud of this character. That Corporation was expected to engage in, and did engage in, a most extensive ocean transportation business and its ships were seen in every great port of the world open during the war. The same section of the statute protects the arms, ammunition, stores and property of the army and navy from fraudulent devices of a similar character. We can not suppose that when Congress enacted the statute or amended it, it did not have in mind that a wide field for such frauds upon the Government was in private and public vessels of the United States on the high seas and in foreign ports and beyond the land jurisdiction of the United States, and therefore intend to include them in the section.

Nor can the much quoted rule that criminal statutes are to be strictly construed avail. As said in [United States v. Lacher, 134 U.S. 624, 629 (1890)]: "penal provisions, like all others, are to be fairly construed according to the legislative intent as expressed in the enactment." They are not to be strained either way. It needs no forced construction to interpret §35 as we have done.

. . . The three defendants who were found in New York were citizens of the United States and were certainly subject to such laws as it might pass to protect itself and its property. Clearly it is no offense to the dignity or right of sovereignty of Brazil to hold them for this crime against the government to which they owe allegiance. The other defendant is a subject of Great Britain. He has never been apprehended, and it will be time enough to consider what, if any, jurisdiction the District Court below has to punish him when he is brought to trial.

The judgment of the District Court is reversed, with directions to overrule the demurrer and for further proceedings.

NOTES AND QUESTIONS

1. Bowman's *application. Bowman* sets out the basic analytical framework for determining whether a federal criminal statute that does not explicitly state whether it applies extraterritorially does so. The starting point, of course, is a presumption of nonextraterritoriality. Notice that *Bowman* includes important limitations:

   (a) It applies only to criminal statutes.
   (b) It applies only to criminal statutes that do not state explicitly whether or not they apply extraterritorially.
   (c) It applies only to "criminal statutes which are, as a class, not logically dependent on their locality for the Government's jurisdiction, but are enacted because of the right of the Government to defend itself against obstruction, or fraud wherever perpetrated, especially if committed by its own citizens, officers or agents."

This final limitation leaves open several questions:

   (i) Does the *Bowman* analysis apply to *all* criminal statutes that are "not logically dependent on their locality for the Government's jurisdiction," or only to those "enacted because of the right of the Government to defend itself against obstruction, or fraud . . ."?

(ii) Thus, does it apply only to crimes against the U.S. government, or also to some crimes against private individuals, if the crimes are not logically dependent on their locality for the government's jurisdiction?

(iii) Finally, does the analysis apply only to U.S. citizens, officers, and agents, or also to foreign nationals who aren't officers and agents of the U.S. government?

The answers U.S. courts have given to these questions point in the direction of more expansive rather than more limited extraterritorial jurisdiction:

(i) Crimes against the government other than obstruction or fraud. Courts have cited *Bowman* as authority for extraterritorial application of U.S. criminal statutes dealing with crimes other than obstruction and fraud against the U.S. government. Thus, a statute against theft of government property was applied to actions of U.S. nationals in Vietnam. United States v. Cotten, 471 F.2d 744 (9th Cir. 1973). A statute penalizing violent racketeering crimes was applied to the murder in Mexico of tourists mistaken for Drug Enforcement Agency operatives. United States v. Vasquez-Velasco, 15 F.3d 833, 839 (9th Cir. 1994). Likewise, a drug conspiracy statute was applied to acts committed in Canada, citing *Bowman* to gain extraterritorial application of the statute. United States v. McAllister, 160 F.3d 1304, 1307 (11th Cir. 1998). The general rule, as articulated in 1941 by the Supreme Court, is that "a criminal statute dealing with acts that are directly injurious to the government, and are capable of perpetration without regard to particular locality, is to be construed as applicable to citizens of the United States upon the high seas or in a foreign country though there be no express declaration to that effect." Skiriotes v. Florida, 313 U.S. 69, 73-74 (1941).

These and other courts read *Bowman* to stand for "the rule that Congress need not expressly provide for extraterritorial application of a criminal statute if the nature of the offense is such that it may be inferred." *Skiriotes*, 313 U.S. at 74. They derive this reading from *Bowman*'s reliance on "the purpose of Congress as evidenced by the description and nature of the crime." Congressional purpose to apply statutes extraterritorially will be inferred if (in *Bowman*'s words) "to limit their locus to the strictly territorial jurisdiction would be greatly to curtail the scope and usefulness of the statute." In other words, the operative principle in *Bowman* is statutory interpretation based on congressional intent, where the intent is inferred because the statute would be less effective without extraterritorial jurisdiction.

(ii) Crimes against private victims. What if the victim is not the government of the United States? Language in *Bowman* suggests that it would be inappropriate for the United States to assert jurisdiction over "crimes against private individuals or their property" that are committed in another state, presumably because that state has jurisdiction over them. Only if Congress explicitly states that such a statute is to apply extraterritorially should a court grant extraterritorial jurisdiction. However, in United States v. Baker, 609 F.2d 134, 136 (5th Cir. 1980), the court found that *Bowman* permits courts to infer extraterritorial jurisdiction "from the nature of the offenses and Congress's other legislative efforts to eliminate the type of crime involved," regardless of whether the crime victimizes the government. On this basis, the *Baker* court gave extraterritorial application to a drug possession statute that did not state that it applied extraterritorially. Similarly, in United States v. Ivanov, 175 F. Supp. 2d 367 (D. Conn. 2001), a court found that several computer crime statutes applied to a hacker in Russia who defrauded a Connecticut company, even though the statutes do not say explicitly that they apply extraterritorially. *Ivanov* does not cite *Bowman*, but it follows a similar methodology, inferring from the language and aim of the statute what Congress must have intended and employing congressional intent to construe the statute. In Stegeman v. United States, 425

F.2d 984 (9th Cir. 1970), the court used *Bowman* to apply a bankruptcy fraud statute extraterritorially; however, perhaps to square its decision with the language of *Bowman*, it insisted that the statute "was enacted to serve important interests of government, not merely to protect individuals who might be harmed by the prohibited conduct." Id. at 986.

(iii) Crimes committed by foreign nationals abroad. Finally, subsequent decisions have applied *Bowman* when the alleged perpetrator of the crime was a foreign national abroad. In United States v. Pizzarusso, 388 F.2d 8 (2d Cir. 1968), the Second Circuit Court of Appeals upheld the conviction of a Canadian national who lied on her visa application in Montreal, violating a federal statute, 18 U.S.C. §1546, which forbids a "false statement with respect to a material fact" on an immigration document. Although the statute makes no mention of extraterritorial jurisdiction, and the court notes that *Bowman* does not reach the issue, it had little difficulty in concluding that Congress intended §1546 to apply extraterritorially. "In the ordinary course of events we would naturally expect false statements in visa applications to be made outside the territorial limits of the United States." Id. at 9. The court found constitutional authority for applying the statute extraterritorially because it "represents a law which is 'necessary and proper for carrying into Execution' . . . the Congressional power over the conduct of foreign relations." Id. at 10. More directly, Judge Sand's opinion in United States v. Usama bin Laden states that

> [a]lthough *Bowman* "is expressly limited by its *facts* to prosecutions of United States citizens," (emphasis added) its underlying rationale is not dependant on the nationality of the offender. Rather, *Bowman* rests on two factors: (1) the right of the United States to protect itself from harmful conduct—irrespective of the locus of the conduct, and (2) the presumption that Congress would not both (a) enact a statute designed to serve this protective function, and—where the statute proscribes acts that could just as readily be performed outside the United States as within it—(b) undermine this protective intention by limiting the statute's application to United States territory. Given that foreign nationals are in at least as good a position to perform extraterritorial conduct as are United States nationals, it would make little sense to restrict such statutes to United States nationals.

92 F. Supp. 2d 189, 194 (S.D.N.Y. 2000).

2. *The territorial presumption and the* Charming Betsy *canon.* The *Bowman* Court states: "The necessary locus, when not specially defined, depends upon the purpose of Congress as evidenced by the description and nature of the crime *and upon the territorial limitations upon the power and jurisdiction of a government to punish crime under the law of nations*" (emphasis added). So far we have focused on the first element of the *Bowman* test: the purpose of Congress. What about the second element, the "territorial limitations upon the power and jurisdiction of a government to punish crime under the law of nations"?

Is the Court saying that, as a matter of U.S. law, Congress cannot exert its criminal jurisdiction outside the United States unless international law permits it to do so? Surely not, because that would mean international law has the same status in the United States as the Constitution itself. That is plainly wrong. As we saw in Chapter 2, Section D, treaties (at least those considered to be self-executing) have the same status as federal statutes under the Supremacy Clause, and whichever is later in time will control; and customary international law has no greater status than treaties. Nothing in the constitutional text suggests that a treaty (much less a rule of CIL) limits Congress's Article I, Section 8 authority to legislate. Thus, if Congress chooses to give a criminal statute extraterritorial reach, and it has a constitutional basis for doing so, then the statute will have extraterritorial reach whether or not that violates international law.

But remember that the *Bowman* Court is analyzing only statutes that do not specify whether they have extraterritorial reach. The passage just quoted says, "The necessary locus, *when not specially defined,* depends upon [etc.] . . ." Apparently, the Court means only that when the statute is silent on the question of extraterritoriality, international law plays a role alongside "purpose . . . as evidenced by the description and nature of the crime" in interpreting the statute.

In this regard, two long-standing canons of statutory interpretation prove vital. One is the *territorial presumption*: "the legislation of the Congress, unless the contrary intent appears, is construed to apply only within the territorial jurisdiction of the United States." Blackmer v. United States, 284 U.S. 421, 437 (1932); see also EEOC v. Arabian Am. Oil Co., 499 U.S. 244, 248 (1991) ("It is a longstanding principle of American law 'that legislation of Congress, unless a contrary intent appears, is meant to apply only within the territorial jurisdiction of the United States.' *Foley Bros. . . .* This 'canon of construction . . .' serves to protect against unintended clashes between our laws and those of other nations which could result in international discord."); Foley Bros. v. Filardo, 336 U.S. 281, 285 (1949) ("The canon of construction which teaches that legislation of Congress, unless a contrary intent appears, is meant to apply only within the territorial jurisdiction of the United States, *Blackmer v. United States,* . . . is a valid approach whereby unexpressed congressional intent may be ascertained. It is based on the assumption that Congress is primarily concerned with domestic conditions."); Am. Banana Co. v. United Fruit Co., 213 U.S. 347, 357 (1909) ("in case of doubt" there is "a construction of any statute as intended to be confined in its operation and effect to the territorial limits over which the lawmaker has general and legitimate power").

For detailed discussion of the territorial presumption and an argument that globalization has made it obsolete, see Gary B. Born, A Reappraisal of the Extraterritorial Reach of U.S. Law, 24 Law & Poly. in Intl. Bus. 1 (1992).

The second relevant rule of statutory interpretation is the so-called *Charming Betsy* canon, named after the 1804 Supreme Court decision Murray v. The Schooner *Charming Betsy*, 6 U.S. (2 Cranch) 64: "an act of Congress ought never to be construed to violate the law of nations if any other possible construction remains." Born, supra, at 118. (Although named after the *Charming Betsy* case, the canon really originated three years earlier, in Talbot v. Seeman, 5 U.S. (1 Cranch) 1, 43 (1801): "the laws of the United States ought not, if it be avoidable, so to be construed as to infract the common principles and usages of nations, or the general doctrines of national law.")

Or, as the Restatement (Third) of the Foreign Relations Law of the United States phrases it: "Where fairly possible, a United States statute is to be construed so as not to conflict with international law or with an international agreement of the United States." Restatement §114. Notice the difference in phrasing: In the original decision, the question is whether a statutory interpretation consistent with IL is "possible," whereas the Restatement replaces "possible" with "fairly possible," that is, reasonable. What, if any, difference does this make, and which version of the canon makes more sense? For a helpful examination of the *Charming Betsy* canon, see Curtis A. Bradley, The *Charming Betsy* Canon and Separation of Powers: Rethinking the Interpretive Role of International Law, 86 Geo. L.J. 479 (1998).

How do these canons apply to *Bowman* analysis and the question of whether a criminal statute applies extraterritorially? The territorial presumption means that unless Congress explicitly states that a statute is to apply extraterritorially, we must presume that it does not. What will it take to overcome this presumption? Here, *Bowman* tells us that if "strictly territorial jurisdiction would . . . greatly . . . curtail the scope and usefulness of the statute," we are entitled to infer congressional intent to apply it extraterritorially, unless extraterritorial application would violate international law. Then, the *Charming Betsy* canon urges us to interpret the statute to remove the conflict. Because the statute does not say that it applies extraterritorially, that suggests reading it to have only territorial application.

3. *Reasonableness.* Is it fair to nationals of another country to hold them criminally liable in a U.S. court for actions in their own country? In Problem 4, does Mr. Banker have fair notice that lying to U.S. investigators when they ask him questions in his own country is a U.S. felony for which he can do five years? Put the shoe on the other foot. Suppose that, in your home town, a foreign official asks you a question that you are disinclined to answer truthfully, and you lie in response. Would it be fair if, when you visit that country some day, you found yourself on trial for having told that lie, facing five years in a foreign prison? In the real-life *Pizzarusso* case, discussed in Note 1 above, Jean Philomena Pizzarusso received "only" a one-year suspended sentence and two years of probation — but the question remains whether she had fair notice that lying in Montreal on a U.S. visa application would subject her to a U.S. felony prosecution. (Again, put the shoe on the other foot.)

Recall the distinction drawn in Chapter 1 between *malum in se* and *malum prohibitum* offenses: those in which the underlying act is in itself wrong, such as rape or embezzling, and those in which the underlying act is wrong only if the law prohibits it, like smuggling or nonpayment of tax. Henry Hart writes:

> When a criminal enactment proscribes conduct which is *malum in se*, such as murder or manslaughter . . . the moral standards of the community are available always as a guide in the resolution of its indeterminacies, and there is a minimum of unfairness when doubt is resolved against a particular defendant. This guidance is missing when the proscribed conduct is merely *malum prohibitum.*

Henry M. Hart, Jr., The Aims of the Criminal Law, 23 Law & Contemp. Probs. 401, 420 (1958). Indeed, it is a violation of due process to criminalize conduct that a reasonable person would not anticipate is criminal. Lambert v. California, 355 U.S. 225 (1957) (finding a due process violation in a Los Angeles municipal statute requiring convicted criminals visiting Los Angeles to register with the police, on the ground that defendant could not be expected to know about the statute).

What follows from this argument? Does extraterritorial application of a U.S. criminal statute violate the Principle of Fair Notice if it concerns *malum prohibitum* conduct? Many, perhaps most, inmates of federal prisons who are not U.S. nationals and who were convicted for extraterritorial conduct got there by drug smuggling and were arrested on the high seas. Didn't they have fair notice? Shouldn't they have anticipated criminal penalties for running boatloads of marijuana and cocaine to the United States? Is drug smuggling *malum in se* or *malum prohibitum?*

4. *Effects in other countries.* Sometimes domestic criminal statutes can criminalize domestic conduct that concerns extraterritorial events. For example, in 2005 the Supreme Court upheld the wire fraud conviction of three U.S. nationals who, within the United States, devised a scheme to smuggle liquor into Canada in order to avoid paying Canadian excise taxes. Pasquantino v. United States, 544 U.S. 349 (2005). But the Court overturned the conviction of a man for violating a federal statute that prohibits convicted felons from purchasing firearms. The man had been convicted and imprisoned in Japan for smuggling firearms into that country, and after his release he purchased a handgun in Pennsylvania. Small v. United States, 544 U.S. 385 (2005).

Neither case directly raises the issue of extraterritorial application of U.S. criminal statutes because in both cases the criminal conduct occurred within U.S. territory. Thus, the *Bowman* analysis is not relevant. But both cases raise related interpretive issues of whether terms in a criminal statute have extraterritorial reach. In *Small*, the Court invoked the territorial presumption to conclude that the statute forbidding firearms purchases by those convicted in "any court" was referring only to "any U.S. court." Although the territorial presumption does not directly apply to the case because Small had purchased his gun within the United States, "a similar assumption is appropriate when we consider the scope of the phrase 'convicted in any court' here." *Small*, 544 U.S. at 389. Four dissenting Justices criticized this assumption because Congress's safety-based concern to keep weapons out of the hands of felons in the United States would logically apply regardless of where they had committed their felonies. Id. at 399-403 (Thomas, J., dissenting). Without citing *Bowman*, the dissenters engaged in *Bowman*-like reasoning: In their view, the statutory purpose requires a broad, extraterritorial reading of "any court," and therefore one must assume that was Congress's intent.

The wire fraud statute, 18 U.S.C. §1343, prohibits using "wire, radio, or television communication in interstate or foreign commerce" for a "scheme or artifice to defraud, or for obtaining money or property by means of false or fraudulent pretenses." In *Pasquantino*, the question was whether prosecutors were using the statute merely to enforce Canadian tax law. A long-standing common law rule — the "revenue rule" — prohibits using domestic courts to enforce foreign tax judgments because doing so would require inappropriate judicial scrutiny of other states' tax policy decisions. But the Court noted that the defendants' fraud was planned and executed within U.S. territory. It concluded that the prosecution was enforcing only the domestic wire fraud statute, not Canadian tax law. Justice Ginsburg, joined by three other Justices, disagreed: "[T]he defendants' conduct arguably fell within the scope of §1343 only because of their purpose to evade Canadian customs and tax laws; shorn of that purpose, no other aspect of their conduct was criminal in this country." *Pasquantino*, 544 U.S. at 381-382 (Ginsburg, J., dissenting). In her view, the Court's decision gives the wire fraud statute "an extraordinary extraterritorial effect" that Congress gave no indication it intended. Id. at 378.

Are these two decisions consistent?

NOTES: THE BOWMAN FLOWCHART

We may summarize the *Bowman* inquiry into whether a U.S. criminal statute applies extraterritorially by constructing a flowchart directing the inquiry.

Figure 5-1 divides the inquiry into five sequenced questions:

1. the inquiry into whether Congress has constitutional authority to legislate extraterritorially on the subject of the statute;
2. whether Congress explicitly declared that it was doing so;
3. if Congress said nothing explicitly, whether the statute is one that Congress would reasonably have intended to apply extraterritorially because lack of extraterritorial application would "greatly curtail" its usefulness in fulfilling its purpose;
4. whether international law permits the United States to exercise extraterritorial jurisdiction; and, if not,

Figure 5-1 The Extraterritorial Application of U.S. Criminal Law — a Flowchart

1. **Does Congress have the constitutional authority to enact a statute on this subject with extraterritorial application?**

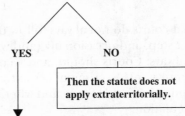

YES   NO

> Then the statute does not apply extraterritorially.

2. **Does the statute explicitly state that it applies extraterritorially?**

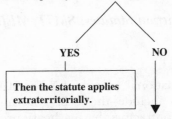

YES   NO

> Then the statute applies extraterritorially.

3. **Does the first *Bowman* factor apply? That is: Would Congress reasonably have intended the statute to apply extraterritorially?**

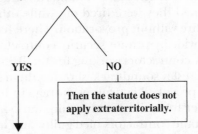

YES   NO

> Then the statute does not apply extraterritorially.

4. **Does the second *Bowman* factor apply? That is: Is there a principle of jurisdiction in international law that grants the U.S. jurisdiction to prescribe this statute?**

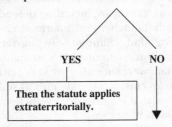

YES   NO

> Then the statute applies extraterritorially.

5. **Is there a "fairly possible" interpretation of the statute under which it does not contradict international law?**

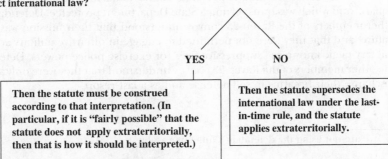

YES   NO

> Then the statute must be construed according to that interpretation. (In particular, if it is "fairly possible" that the statute does not apply extraterritorially, then that is how it should be interpreted.)

> Then the statute supersedes the international law under the last-in-time rule, and the statute applies extraterritorially.

5. whether there is some "fairly possible" reading of the statute that does not violate international law (including, specifically, reading the statute to apply only within U.S. territory).

We note that courts do not always follow this chart in the order given. Often, courts skip the first step, and occasionally (and wrongly) they overlook the fourth and fifth steps. Not always: Courts should, and frequently do, consider the international law aspects of applying U.S. criminal law extraterritorially, asking whether this is a "reasonable application" of U.S. law and whether it passes the outer limits of permissible criminal regulation.

3.   Special Jurisdiction Statutes: SMTJ, MEJA, Special Aircraft Jurisdiction

PROBLEM 6

Blackwater International (renamed Xe as of February 2009) is a private security firm whose clients include the U.S. government. Private military contractors, like other private contractors, have a heavy presence in Iraq. In September 2007, Blackwater employees guarding U.S. State Department personnel were involved in a Baghdad firefight that left numerous Iraqi civilians dead or wounded. The contractors claimed they were fired on, while other witnesses claimed that the contractors opened fire without provocation. There had been previous instances of ultra-aggressive behavior by private security contractors, including a widely publicized "trophy video" by contractors working for the British firm Aegis (posted on YouTube), set to an Elvis Presley soundtrack, showing them shooting up Iraqi civilians. The Blackwater incident provoked enormous outrage in Iraq and led the Iraqi government to expel Blackwater from the country temporarily.

One of the contractors pled guilty, and his plea agreement sets out the factual basis for prosecuting five others. It states in part:

> The government's evidence would prove that on September 16, 2007, at least six members of the Raven 23 convoy, including defendant R,[16] opened fire with automatic weapons and grenade launchers on unarmed civilians located in and around Nisur Square in central Baghdad, killing at least fourteen people, wounding at least twenty people, and assaulting but not injuring at least eighteen others. None of these victims was an insurgent, and many were shot while inside of civilian vehicles that were attempting to flee from the Raven 23 convoy. One victim was shot in his chest, while standing in the street with his hands up. At least eighteen vehicles were damaged, some substantially, by gunfire from the Raven 23 convoy.
>
> On September 16, 2007, the Raven 23 convoy was responding to the detonation of a vehicle-born improvised explosive device (VBIED) that had been just exploded in the vicinity of a different Blackwater personal security detail located about a mile from Nisur Square, and which was transporting a State Department protectee. Defendant R and the other members of the Raven 23 convoy understood that their mission was defensive in nature, and that they were not permitted to engage in offensive military action, use the military tactic known as "suppressive fire," or exercise police powers. Defendant R and the other members of the Raven 23 convoy understood that they were only authorized to discharge their firearms in self-defense and as a last resort.

---

16. We are not using the defendant's full name. — Eds.

U.S. contractors could not be prosecuted by Iraq because of an order issued by the Coalition Provisional Authority immunizing them. There is also significant doubt that U.S. military law can be used to prosecute civilians who are not working directly with the military. The Blackwater incident occurred at a Baghdad intersection outside any U.S. base or facility. Use the statutes discussed in the materials that follow to answer these questions:

(a) In December 2008 the Blackwater guards were indicted for manslaughter and weapons offenses. They have moved to dismiss for lack of jurisdiction on the ground that the relevant U.S. statutes do not apply to offenses committed by civilians in a foreign country against foreign nationals. The government asserts that the Military Extraterritorial Jurisdiction Act (MEJA), in conjunction with the Special Military Territorial Jurisdiction (SMTJ) statute, discussed below, grants jurisdiction.

The indictment states that the five defendants "were employed by the Armed Forces outside the United States, as defined in 18 U.S.C. §3267(1), that is: the defendants were employees and subcontractors of Blackwater Worldwide, a company contracting with the United States Department of State, who were employed to provide personal security services in the Republic of Iraq, which employment related to supporting the mission of the United States Department of Defense in the Republic of Iraq." How would you rule?

(b) What if, instead of the State Department, the contractors were providing security for a private corporation under contract with the U.S. government to rebuild the Iraqi power grid?

(c) What if the contractors in part (b) were not U.S. or Iraqi nationals? (Many private security firms employ ex-military or security personnel from other countries, such as Nepal, South Africa, and Israel.)

Complicating the issue of extraterritorial jurisdiction is the question of how far territorial jurisdiction extends. In addition to the actual territory of the 50 U.S. states, plus the Commonwealth of Puerto Rico and territories such as Guam and the U.S. Virgin Islands, time-honored legal custom holds that ships flying the U.S. flag count as U.S. territory. But these are not the only special cases because Congress has extended U.S. territorial jurisdiction by statute. The following statute sets out other locales that fall within the "special maritime and territorial jurisdiction" (SMTJ) of the United States.

18 U.S.C. §7. SPECIAL MARITIME AND TERRITORIAL JURISDICTION OF THE UNITED STATES DEFINED

The term "special maritime and territorial jurisdiction of the United States," as used in this title, includes: . . .

(3) Any lands reserved or acquired for the use of the United States, and under the exclusive or concurrent jurisdiction thereof, or any place purchased or otherwise acquired by the United States by consent of the legislature of the State in which the same shall be, for the erection of a fort, magazine, arsenal, dockyard, or other needful building. . . .

(7) Any place outside the jurisdiction of any nation with respect to an offense by or against a national of the United States.

(8) To the extent permitted by international law, any foreign vessel during a voyage having a scheduled departure from or arrival in the United States

with respect to an offense committed by or against a national of the United States.

(9) With respect to offenses committed by or against a national of the United States . . .

(A) the premises of United States diplomatic, consular, military or other United States Government missions or entities in foreign States, including the buildings, parts of buildings, and land appurtenant or ancillary thereto or used for purposes of those missions or entities, irrespective of ownership; and

(B) residences in foreign States and the land appurtenant or ancillary thereto, irrespective of ownership, used for purposes of those missions or entities or used by United States personnel assigned to those missions or entities. . . .

Other clauses, omitted from this excerpt, create SMTJ over the high seas; "any other waters within the admiralty and maritime jurisdiction of the United States and out of the jurisdiction of any particular State"; U.S. vessels within such waters, and U.S. aircraft flying over such waters or over the high seas; U.S. vessels in the Great Lakes; certain guano islands; and U.S. spacecraft in flight. The statute also specifies that it does not supersede treaties or international agreements with which it conflicts and does not apply to persons covered by MEJA, discussed in Note 3 immediately following.

NOTES AND QUESTIONS

1. One principal aim of the SMTJ statute has nothing to do with extraterritoriality: It is to establish federal jurisdiction over federal facilities, such as military bases, within U.S. territory. That is the principal meaning of §7(3), reproduced above. Doing so enables federal authorities to assume primary law enforcement responsibilities over federal facilities. This is done in two ways. First, any conduct that is a crime under the law of the U.S. state where the federal facility is located will be punished as such under federal law. 18 U.S.C. §13. Second, the federal criminal code includes approximately 30 provisions that specifically criminalize conduct committed in the SMTJ, even if that conduct would be a U.S. state rather than a federal crime if committed on U.S. territory outside the SMTJ. These include arson (18 U.S.C. §81), assault (18 U.S.C. §113), maiming (18 U.S.C. §114), murder (18 U.S.C. §1111), robbery (18 U.S.C. §2111), sexual abuse (18 U.S.C. §§2242-2244), and others. Notice that these are counterparts to typical crimes under U.S. states' laws.

However, the SMTJ also includes locales in foreign countries, such as overseas military bases. The aim of the special jurisdiction statute is, self-evidently, to expand U.S. territorial jurisdiction to cover ambiguous cases. Is it legitimate for a state to unilaterally declare foreign territory part of its "territorial jurisdiction"? Doing so, it should be noted, does not extinguish the foreign country's territorial jurisdiction. Potential jurisdictional conflicts are limited because, when the U.S. sites military bases in foreign countries or acquires foreign facilities for its use, the two governments negotiate a Status of Forces Agreement (SOFA). A typical SOFA will stipulate that if, for example, a U.S. service member commits a crime against other U.S. nationals on a U.S. base in a foreign country, the host country will allow the United States to prosecute the crime. The SMTJ provides the legal authority under U.S. domestic law for courts to assert territorial jurisdiction in such cases.

2. Section 7(9) of the statute fills in certain jurisdictional gaps to allow the United States to prosecute crimes committed on its facilities abroad, when the territorial state may have no interest in prosecuting them or when the United States does not wish the

territorial state to prosecute them. It was added to the statute in October 2001 as part of the USA Patriot Act.

The jurisdictional gap that §7(9) now fills came to light spectacularly in a well-publicized case decided a year before §7(9) was added: United States v. Gatlin, 216 F.3d 207 (2d Cir. 2000). Gatlin was a civilian employee at a U.S. military base in Germany who, while his wife was on duty in Bosnia, began sexual relations with his 13-year-old stepdaughter. She became pregnant and had his baby. Gatlin was convicted of sexual abuse and appealed on jurisdictional grounds. The Second Circuit Court of Appeals reversed Gatlin's conviction. Based on its reading of the legislative history of §7(3) of the SMTJ statute, it concluded that Congress did not intend it to apply criminal statutes outside of U.S. territory.

3. Soon after *Gatlin*, the Ninth Circuit Court of Appeals considered a distressingly similar case, United States v. Corey, 232 F.3d 1166 (9th Cir. 2000). Corey, a civilian postmaster who had worked on U.S. military bases in Japan and the Philippines, was convicted of forcing his stepdaughter to have sex with him for five years, beginning when she was 15. Unlike the Second Circuit, the Ninth Circuit held that Corey's crimes fell within §7(3) of the special maritime and territorial jurisdiction. (However, the court reversed Corey's conviction because of unrelated trial errors.) The Ninth Circuit opinion scathingly criticized *Gatlin*'s analysis. However, *Corey* itself was not uncontroversial, and Judge McKeown wrote a strong dissent.

Complicating *Corey* was the fact that the sexual abuse in the Philippines occurred off the premises of the military base, in a private apartment leased by the U.S. embassy. The Ninth Circuit held that the apartment fell within §7(3)'s language of "lands reserved or acquired for the use of the United States, and under the exclusive or concurrent jurisdiction thereof." This was a questionable conclusion because it is far from obvious why a private apartment in a foreign country should fall under the concurrent jurisdiction of the United States; and it certainly does not fall under the exclusive jurisdiction of the United States. Section 7(9) fills in the possible jurisdictional gap in §7 and makes it clear that both Gatlin's and Corey's conduct will unambiguously fall within the special territorial jurisdiction of the United States.

4. *MEJA.* Section 7(9) was not Congress's only response to these cases. (Indeed, §7(9) was not added to the SMTJ statute because of *Corey* and *Gatlin*, but to expand U.S. territorial jurisdiction in the wake of 9/11.) The *Gatlin* panel was disturbed by the result it reached, and Judge Cabranes ordered its opinion sent to the chairmen of both the House and Senate Judiciary Committees, where an expanded jurisdictional statute had been stalled for years because of Defense Department objections. The prospect that defendants like Gatlin might escape punishment worked wonders in the U.S. Congress, and MEJA was soon enacted. It facilitates the prosecution of civilians accompanying U.S. military personnel for crimes committed on foreign soil. MEJA defines jurisdiction as follows:

18 U.S.C. §3261. (MILITARY EXTRATERRITORIAL JURISDICTION ACT)

Criminal Offenses Committed by Certain Members of the Armed Forces and by Persons Employed by or Accompanying the Armed Forces Outside the United States

(a) Whoever engages in conduct outside the United States that would constitute an offense punishable by imprisonment for more than 1 year if the conduct had been engaged in within the special maritime and territorial jurisdiction of the United States —

    (1) while employed by or accompanying the Armed Forces outside the United States; or

    (2) while a member of the Armed Forces subject to [the Uniform Code of Military Justice],

shall be punished as provided for that offense. . . .

Other subsections specify that MEJA may not be used to prosecute anyone if a foreign government is prosecuting the person for the same conduct; that MEJA does not prevent military tribunals or courts-martial from exercising jurisdiction; and that members of the armed forces subject to military law may not be tried under MEJA until they are out of the military.

Both MEJA and the SMTJ statute may prove important for the prosecution of crimes committed by civilian contractors working for the U.S. military. Until late 2004, MEJA contained a large loophole: Only civilian contractors employed by the Department of Defense (DOD) were subject to it. Many private military contractors, including those implicated in the Abu Ghraib abuses, were employed by the Department of the Interior rather than DOD, and thus not subject to MEJA. However, in late 2004 Congress amended the Act to plug this loophole. Now, the statutory phrase "employed by the Armed Forces outside the United States" includes not only DOD contractors but also employees of contractors of "any other Federal agency, or any provisional authority, to the extent such employment relates to supporting the mission of the Department of Defense overseas." 18 U.S.C. §3267.

Even this extension of MEJA may not cover cases such as that described in Problem 6. Because the Blackwater contractors were tasked with defending State Department personnel, some military law experts argued they were not "supporting the mission of the Department of Defense overseas" as §3267 requires. On the other hand, it could be argued that the contractors' job does indeed support the DOD mission overseas by freeing up military personnel for other tasks. But this issue remains unsettled.

5. In the wake of the Blackwater incident, legislation was introduced to expand MEJA so that it explicitly covers persons "employed under a contract (or subcontract at any tier) awarded by any department or agency of the United States, where the work under such contract is carried out in an area, or in close proximity to an area (as designated by the Department of Defense), where the Armed Forces is conducting a contingency operation." MEJA Expansion and Enforcement Act of 2007, H.R. 2740, 110th Cong. (2007), passed the House of Representatives in October 2007. See http://www.govtrack.us/congress/billtext.xpd?bill = h110-2740. As of mid-2009, the legislation has not been passed.

6. Only a handful of cases have been brought under MEJA. The first occurred in 2005, when a civilian was convicted of stabbing her husband to death at a U.S. base in Turkey. United States v. Arnt, 474 F.3d 1159 (9th Cir. 2007). Two years later, a civilian contractor in Baghdad was convicted of child pornography offenses. Other cases involve former military members, who can no longer be prosecuted within the military justice system for crimes committed while in the military. One such case involved sexual assault of a fellow soldier in Iraq. United States v. Maldonado, No. 06-12232, 2007 U.S. App. LEXIS 2129 (11th Cir. Jan. 31, 2007) (unpublished). Others have involved alleged war crimes. In 2008, a former Marine sergeant charged with ordering the execution of four Iraqi prisoners was acquitted by a jury in Riverside, California (despite a taped phone conversation in which he appeared to

admit ordering the killings); another former soldier, charged with raping and murdering an Iraqi family, awaits trial as of mid-2009. His motion to dismiss—based on arguments that prosecuting him under MEJA is unconstitutional—was denied. United States v. Green, Memorandum on Motion to Dismiss, 2008 WL 4000868 (Aug. 26, 2008).

7. Before *Gatlin* and *Corey*, the leading case on the special maritime and territorial jurisdiction for criminal matters was a Fourth Circuit decision, United States v. Erdos, 474 F.2d 157 (4th Cir. 1973). *Erdos* concerned a U.S. diplomat who murdered another U.S. national on the grounds of the U.S. embassy in Equatorial Guinea. It found that the killing fell under the special maritime and territorial jurisdiction of the United States.

8. *Corey, Gatlin,* and *Erdos* are representative of one major category of crimes committed by nationals outside U.S. territory that the United States has a special interest in pursuing: heinous or sensational crimes by U.S. civilians against other U.S. civilians, when the defendants are U.S. government employees and the crimes are committed on U.S. foreign bases or embassies. A natural question is why the state in which the crime occurs does not prosecute. In Erdos's case, the answer is straightforward: He had diplomatic immunity, and the U.S. government apparently preferred bringing him home for trial rather than waiving immunity. In Gatlin's case, the family had returned to the United States before his stepdaughter gave birth and revealed that Gatlin was the father. If Germany wished to prosecute Gatlin, it would have had to seek his extradition, and Germany had no compelling reason to do so. The record does not indicate whether the Philippines attempted to prosecute Corey, but Japan would presumably have little interest in doing so years after he had left the country. Foreign governments may have no reason to pursue crimes committed by Americans against other Americans on American bases or embassies, and indeed, in some situations, the United States may request the foreign government not to do so.

9. Note that 18 U.S.C. §7 and MEJA are not the only special jurisdiction statutes. In addition, the title on transportation in the United States Code defines a "special aircraft jurisdiction" in 49 U.S.C. §46501, and it extends the reach of some criminal statutes to aircraft within the special aircraft jurisdiction in 49 U.S.C. §46506. In United States v. Georgescu, 723 F. Supp. 912 (E.D.N.Y. 1989), a Romanian national was prosecuted for fondling a nine-year-old Norwegian girl on a Scandinavian Airlines flight from Copenhagen, Denmark, to New York. The incident occurred over the high seas, and Georgescu was arrested when the airplane landed for violating a U.S. sexual abuse statute. Even though the airplane had Swedish registration, and the only connection between the incident and the United States was the aircraft's destination, Judge Jack Weinstein found U.S. jurisdiction under the special aircraft jurisdiction. He wrote:

> Even if Congress's criminalization of defendant's alleged acts and its exercise of jurisdiction were counter to international law, this fact does not lessen the validity of the statutes as superseding domestic legislation. International law is "subject to the Constitution, and is also subject to 'repeal' by other law of the United States." Restatement, supra ch. 2, Introductory Note, at 40; *id.* §111 (2), at 42. While the courts must make a fair effort to interpret domestic law in a way consistent with international obligations, see e.g., . . . *Murray v. Schooner Charming Betsy,* . . . in the event of irreconcilable conflict, the courts are bound to apply domestic law if it was passed more recently. . . . The statutory provisions under which defendant is being prosecuted were passed subsequent to the development of the traditional notions of international law jurisdiction to which defendant argues this court is confined. . . . The domestic statutes are controlling.

723 F. Supp. at 921. Judge Weinstein argued that the initial exercise of jurisdiction in arresting Georgescu made sense for purposes of detention and evidence gathering. He acknowledged that pursuing the prosecution further than that "may create logistical problems involving the location of witnesses, and evidentiary obstacles involving the testimony of the alleged victim." Nevertheless, "[d]espite this court's reservations about the wisdom of further prosecution in this country, it lacks the power to refuse jurisdiction on equitable grounds." Id. at 922. Assuming that international law would not permit the United States to assert territorial jurisdiction over Sweden, does the special aircraft jurisdiction statute violate IL? Why does it matter which came first, the special aircraft jurisdiction statute or the international law principles of jurisdiction?

Judge Weinstein replies that a U.S. court, confronted with an "irreconcilable conflict" between U.S. law and international law, must follow U.S. law. Is this a desirable outcome in *Georgescu*?

CHAPTER

6

Immunities

Our discussion of the subject of universal criminal jurisdiction in Chapter 5 raised the important question of when, under international law, states are competent to investigate and prosecute foreigners who have been accused of committing international crimes, either in their own countries or elsewhere. When such prosecutions involve senior officials of foreign governments, issues of immunity under international law may arise.

The question of immunity arises in the narrow context of domestic prosecution of foreign government officials, in other words, one state prosecuting officials of another state. Whether and when those government officials can be prosecuted by the responsible authorities of their *own* governments and under their *own* law is, of course, a question of domestic law, and one not dependent on internationally recognized principles of jurisdiction (even if the particular substantive crimes at issue might be defined by international law). The competence of international courts and tribunals to try such individuals is still a different question. In general, international criminal tribunals do not grant immunity based on official status, not even to heads of state. The prototype of this stripping-away of immunity appears in the Charter of the Nuremberg Tribunal, in Article 7: "The official position of defendants, whether as Heads of State or responsible officials in Government Departments, shall not be considered as freeing them from responsibility or mitigating punishment." Almost identical language appears in Article 7(2) of the Statute of the ICTY, Article 6(2) of the Statute of the ICTR, and Article 27 of the Rome Statute of the ICC.

The issue we address here concerns only the prosecution of officials of state A in the courts of state B, and in particular the extent to which international law may accord state A's officials a measure of immunity from the criminal jurisdiction of state B. Because it is easy to confuse the two issues, we repeat: This chapter concerns only the immunity of state officials from prosecution in the domestic courts of another state, not in an international tribunal; generally, international law provides no immunity before international tribunals.

When domestic criminal prosecutions involve foreign officials, the legal issues can be complicated. Several different types of immunity are recognized by international law: diplomatic and consular immunities, the immunities enjoyed by representatives to and officials and staff of public international organizations, those accorded to visiting foreign officials on "special missions," and head-of-state immunity. Generally speaking, the immunities provided by these principles apply only to certain governmental officials and only in foreign courts; not every visiting official is entitled to immunity, regardless of rank. Since international law does not, at least at this juncture, recognize the possibility of criminal proceedings against "states" qua "states," there is no need here to address concepts of sovereign immunity. In any event, neither the pertinent U.S. statute (the Foreign Sovereign Immunities Act) nor the recently adopted UN Convention on the Jurisdictional Immunities of States and Their Properties applies to criminal proceedings.[1]

In the first two sections of this chapter, we examine diplomatic and consular immunity. The difference between diplomats and consular officials is this: The main function of a diplomatic mission (that is, an embassy) is to represent the government of the sending state to the government of the receiving state and to conduct bilateral relations across the entire spectrum of governmental interaction — political, economic, commerce and trade, military, science, labor, and so on. Diplomats are thus generally located in the receiving state's capital and are normally involved in formal representational and reporting interactions with the host government. By contrast, consular functions primarily involve the interests and problems of private individuals and entities, such as issuing visas to non-nationals for travel to the sending state; providing assistance to sending state nationals while in the receiving country (for example, issuing replacement passports or helping those who have been arrested or imprisoned); promoting bilateral commercial, economic, educational, and cultural relations; transmitting judicial documents; and so on. Consulates are thus frequently found outside the capital, in major cities or tourist areas where nationals of the sending state are likely to be found or do business.

The line between diplomats and consular officials is sometimes indistinct. Diplomats, for example, often protect or promote the interests of individuals or private entities, embassies often have consular sections, and both may legitimately gather information and report on developments in the receiving country. However, as a matter of international law, the two are governed by different legal regimes: the 1961 Vienna Convention on Diplomatic Relations and the 1963 Vienna Convention on Consular Relations. In addition, states often conclude bilateral arrangements governing such matters between themselves. As we shall see, diplomats generally have greater (although not absolute) immunity while consular officers have more limited (functional or "official acts") immunity.

A.   DIPLOMATIC IMMUNITY

The Vienna Convention on Diplomatic Relations[2] provides "diplomatic agents" (that is, the head of the mission or a member of the mission's diplomatic staff) with immunity against all criminal prosecutions (and most civil actions) in the courts of the countries to which they have been accredited. Specifically, Article 31(1) provides that "[a] diplomatic agent shall enjoy immunity from the criminal jurisdiction of the

---

1. Foreign Sovereign Immunities Act of 1976, codified as amended at 28 U.S.C. §§1330, 1332, 1391(f), 1441(d), 1602-1611; UN Convention on Jurisdictional Immunities of States and Their Property, adopted by G.A. Res. A/59/508 (Dec. 2, 2004), reprinted in 44 I.L.M. 803.

2. The relevant text is the Vienna Convention on Diplomatic Relations, Apr. 18, 1961, 23 U.S.T. 3227, T.I.A.S. No. 7502, 500 U.N.T.S. 96 (entered into force with respect to the United States on December 13, 1972), a self-executing treaty applied as a matter of federal law. See also the Diplomatic Relations Act of 1978, 22 U.S.C. §§254a-254e.

receiving State."[3] In addition, Article 29 states that "[t]he person of a diplomatic agent shall be inviolable. He shall not be liable to any form of arrest or detention. The receiving State shall treat him with due respect and shall take all appropriate steps to prevent any attack on his person, freedom or dignity."[4] Under Article 30, the diplomatic private residence, papers, correspondence, and (subject to certain limitations) personal property also enjoy inviolability.[5] The diplomat's immunity and inviolability also extend to members of his or her family who form "part of the household," as well as to members of the mission's "administrative and technical staff" as long as they are not nationals of the receiving state.[6]

Several points bear emphasis. Immunity is accorded to diplomats and other members of a foreign embassy in the host (or receiving) state in order to facilitate their functions as emissaries and representatives of the sending state. Since the assignment of ambassadors and other mission members depends on the consent of the receiving state (in diplomatic practice called *agrément* with respect to the ambassador), it follows that an individual's entitlement to immunity under the Convention is premised upon acceptance as a diplomatic agent by the receiving state. No one is able to assert diplomatic immunity unilaterally. In U.S. practice, that means entitlement to immunity from the jurisdiction of U.S. courts depends on certification by the Department of State that the individual in question has been accredited as a diplomat or other member of a mission (the particular passport or visa issued to the individual is not determinative). With few exceptions, the courts have accepted such certifications as determinative of entitlement to immunity.[7]

Moreover, the immunity and inviolability provided under the Convention are not "personal" rights of the individual in question but belong to the sending state. They must be raised by the sending state and (as Article 32 of the Convention expressly recognizes) they can be waived only by the sending state. A diplomatic officer may not, of his own accord, waive his immunity.[8]

The remedy for abuse of diplomatic privileges is for the receiving state to declare the individual in question *persona non grata* and to require him or her to leave the country within a reasonable time. Should the individual not depart within the stated period, the receiving state may, at its option, consider that his diplomatic functions have ended and decline to recognize his privileges and immunities any longer.

While (in the case of criminal jurisdiction) immunity is absolute, it is temporally limited. Under Article 39 of the Convention, entitlement to privileges and immunities generally begins when the diplomat enters the territory of the receiving state to take up his or her post and ends when he or she leaves the country after his assignment has come to an end (or after a "reasonable period" in which to do so). Immunity persists even after her departure, however, with respect to "acts performed by such a person in the exercise of his functions as a member of the mission."[9]

3. Vienna Convention, supra note 2, art. 31(1).
4. Id. art. 29.
5. Id. art. 30.
6. Id. art. 37(1), (2).
7. See, e.g., United States v. Al-Hamdi, 356 F.3d 564 (4th Cir. 2004); United States v. Kostadinov, 734 F.2d 905 (2d Cir. 1984).
8. See, e.g., Knab v. Republic of Georgia, 1998 WL 34067108 (D.D.C. May 29, 1998).
9. Vienna Convention, supra note 2, art. 39.

UNITED STATES v. GUINAND

688 F. Supp. 774 (D.D.C. 1988)

GASCH, Senior District Judge.

Defendant is charged with distribution of cocaine in violation of 21 U.S.C. §841(a) at a time when he enjoyed diplomatic immunity as a member of the administrative staff of the Embassy of Peru. He has moved to dismiss the indictment under the provisions of 22 U.S.C. §254d, which reads as follows:

> Any action or proceeding brought against an individual who is entitled to immunity with respect to such action or proceeding under the Vienna Convention on Diplomatic Relations, under section 3(b) or 4 of this Act [i.e., 22 U.S.C. §§254b or 254c], or under any other laws extending diplomatic privileges and immunities, shall be dismissed. Such immunity may be established upon motion or suggestion by or on behalf of the individual, or as otherwise permitted by law or applicable rules of procedure.

It appears from the submissions of the parties that defendant entered into a narcotic [sic] transaction with an undercover agent of the Metropolitan Police Department. Thereafter Sergeant Gonzalez of the Metropolitan Police Department, with the knowledge and approval of an Assistant United States Attorney, spoke with defendant and advised him that he would be subject to immediate deportation from this country under the circumstances unless he agreed to cooperate with the police and the Drug Enforcement Administration. It was represented to defendant that, if he did this, his departure from the country could be delayed until his cooperation had been completed and a reasonable time thereafter. A reasonable time is usually interpreted as thirty days.

It further appears from the pleadings that, following defendant's cooperation with the authorities, the Embassy of Peru terminated his employment and he was given the usual period within which to depart the country. In the interim, he married an American citizen and has been accorded permanent resident alien status by the Immigration and Naturalization Service.

The issue before the Court is whether the immunity with which defendant was cloaked at the time these acts allegedly were committed continues indefinitely or whether that immunity ceases at the time his duties at the Embassy were terminated and he was given a reasonable time within which to depart.

The government, among other exhibits, has filed the declaration of the legal adviser of the Department of State, Judge Abraham Sofaer. The Court notes that the Supreme Court has stated in Sumitomo Shoji America, Inc. v. Avagliano, 457 U.S. 176, 184-85 (1982): "Although not conclusive, the meaning attributed to treaty provisions by the Government agencies charged with their negotiation and enforcement is entitled to great weight." Accordingly, the Court notes from the declaration of Judge Sofaer:

> The United States Government has consistently interpreted Article 39 of the VCDR to permit the exercise of U.S. jurisdiction over persons whose status as members of the diplomatic mission has been terminated for acts they committed during the period in which they enjoyed privileges and immunities, except for acts performed in the exercise of the functions as a member of the mission. (Article 3 of the VCDR lists the permissible functions of a diplomatic mission.)
>
> The Department of State has publicly stated this interpretation to U.S. law enforcement authorities, to Congress, and to members of foreign diplomatic missions in the United States.

An official State Department publication intended to provide guidelines to law enforcement authorities on various categories of foreign missions personnel and the privileges and immunities to which they are entitled, states, in pertinent part, as follows:

> . . . criminal immunity expires upon the termination of the diplomatic or consular tour of the individual enjoying such immunity, including a reasonable period of time for such person to depart the U.S. territory. Thereafter, if the law enforcement authorities of the United States can obtain personal jurisdiction over a person alleged to have committed criminal acts in the United States, normal prosecution may go forward.

The declaration of Judge Sofaer also states that this official interpretation of the pertinent sections of the Vienna Convention on Diplomatic Relations,[10] of which the United States is a signatory, has been communicated to all diplomatic missions.

On March 21, 1984, the Secretary of State declared:

> On the termination of criminal immunity, the bar to prosecution in the United States would be removed and any serious crime would remain as a matter of record. If a person formerly entitled to privileges and immunities returned to this country and continued to be suspected of a crime, no bar would exist to arresting and prosecuting him or her in the normal manner for a serious crime allegedly committed during the period in which he or she enjoyed immunity. This would be the case unless the crime related to the exercise of official functions, or the statute of limitations for that crime had not imposed a permanent bar to prosecution.

The Court, though not bound by the State Department's interpretation of the Vienna Convention, finds that it is entitled to great weight and that it is supported by such authorities as have been brought to the attention of the Court. The fact that there is little judicial authority on the precise point with which the Court is confronted is indicative of the fact that when one who enjoys diplomatic status and immunity is faced with the alternative of departing from the country or going to trial on criminal charges, he elects departure. . . .

In view of the foregoing and since it clearly appears that defendant is no longer clothed with diplomatic immunity and that he has failed to depart from the United States within a reasonable time after his cooperation with the police and since, although he presently has the status of permanent resident alien, that status affords him no immunity from prosecution, the motion to dismiss is denied.

B.   CONSULAR IMMUNITY

By comparison to diplomats, consular officers have only limited protections under their separate Vienna Convention.[11] Under Article 43(1), consular officers and

---

10. [Court's footnote 1:] The pertinent article of that Convention is Section 2 of Article 39: "When the functions of a person enjoying privileges and immunities have come to an end, such privileges and immunities shall normally cease at the moment when he leaves the country, or on expiry of a reasonable period in which to do so, but shall subsist until that time even in case of armed conflict. However, with respect to acts performed by such a person in the exercise of his functions as a member of the mission, immunity shall continue to subsist."

11. Vienna Convention on Consular Relations, Apr. 24, 1963, 21 U.S.T. 77, T.I.A.S. No. 6820, 596 U.N.T.S. 261.

employees are not "amenable to the jurisdiction of the judicial or administrative authorities of the receiving State in respect of acts performed in the exercise of consular functions."[12] Article 41(1) provides that "[c]onsular officers shall not be liable to arrest or detention pending trial, except in the case of a grave crime and pursuant to a decision by a competent judicial authority."[13] Similar provisions are found in many bilateral consular treaties between the United States and other countries, although a few (dating mostly from the Cold War era) provide enhanced immunities on a reciprocal basis.

Again, only individuals who have been duly accredited as consular officials are entitled to the benefit of these provisions. Honorary consular officers, who in many instances may be nationals of the receiving state, are also entitled to the protections of Article 43(1).

STATE v. KILLEEN
592 P.2d 268 (Or. Ct. App. 1979)

GILLETTE, Judge.

Defendant appeals his conviction of a traffic infraction. [The conviction was for disobeying a traffic control device, for which defendant was fined $10.] He advances two arguments: first, that because of his status as honorary consul for the nation of Malaysia, the state courts have no jurisdiction over him and, second, that the infraction was committed in the course of his consular duties and that he is consequently immune from prosecution under the terms of the treaty governing consular relationships between the United States and Malaysia.

Defendant's contention that the state court lacked jurisdiction is predicated on 28 U.S.C. §1351, which provides:

> The (United States) district courts shall have original jurisdiction, exclusive of the courts of the States, of all actions and proceedings against consuls or vice consuls of foreign states.

Section 1351 and its predecessors have been construed as precluding state court jurisdiction only in those instances where the federal courts have jurisdiction over the subject matter of the proceeding. Thus, in Ohio ex rel. Popovici v. Agler, 280 U.S. 379 (1930), the United States Supreme Court held that the courts of Ohio had jurisdiction over a divorce proceeding involving a Romanian vice consul. The court reasoned that the United States courts have no jurisdiction over divorce cases, that "the whole subject of the domestic relations of husband and wife ... belongs to the laws of the states" (280 U.S. at 383), and that it was not the intent of Congress to deny American citizens, whether the consular officials themselves or their spouses, access to any court with the power to grant a divorce.

The reasoning of *Popovici* was applied by the California District Court of Appeal in Silva v. Superior Court, 52 Cal. App. 3d 269, 125 Cal. Rptr. 78 (2nd Dist. 1975), in which the court held that the California state courts had jurisdiction to try a Mexican

---

12. Id. art 43(1).
13. Id. art. 41(1).

consul for a state offense. After an extensive analysis of the legislative history of Section 1351 and of prior judicial interpretations, the court stated:

> As the federal court has no jurisdiction to try consuls for violation of state criminal statutes, jurisdiction over this type of action like the divorce proceedings in *Popovici* rests exclusively in the state court. . . . [I]t is reasonable not to construe section 1351 as divesting state courts of jurisdiction over actions against consuls arising under local criminal statutes for acts outside the scope of consular duties.

We conclude that Section 1351 does not divest the courts of Oregon of jurisdiction over consular officials charged with violations of state law at least when the violations are not committed in the performance of official consular duties.

The defendant further argues, however, that the infraction of which he was convicted was committed in connection with his consular duties, in that the infraction occurred while he was driving to the Portland airport for the purpose of delivering documents to a Malaysian national. The scope of the official duties of Malaysian consuls is defined by the Consular Convention between the United States and the United Kingdom, 3 UST 3434.[14] Defendant relies on two provisions of that treaty, the first of which provides:

> A consular officer or employee shall not be liable, in proceedings in the courts of the receiving state, in respect of acts performed in his official capacity, falling within the functions of a consular officer under this Convention unless the sending state requests or assents to the proceedings through its diplomatic representative.

The second relevant provision states:

> A consular officer shall be entitled within his district to (a) interview, communicate with and advise any national of the sending state. . . .

In construing the privileges and immunities of consuls under treaties such as the one we consider here, certain basic propositions must be borne in mind. Absent an express treaty provision to the contrary, consuls do not enjoy the plenary insulation from the judicial procedures of the receiving state (i.e., country) which ambassadors or ministers enjoy; they are subject to the jurisdiction of the receiving state except "in respect of acts performed in the exercise of consular functions." 1963 Vienna Convention, 21 UST 103, Articles 41, 43. Moreover, the privileges and immunities of honorary consuls, who, unlike career consuls, are generally citizens of the United States and are designated by the sending state for the conduct of commercial or other limited functions, have been frequently held to be even more circumscribed than the immunities of career consuls.

In summary, whatever the outer limits of the immunity of consuls from prosecution may be, the weight of authority is that that immunity does not extend to acts which are not performed in the exercise of official consular duties, as defined in applicable treaties and by reference to general law regarding consular functions and privileges.

The state argues in this case that, although the defendant's meeting with a Malaysian national at Portland International Airport was an exercise of his consular duties, the act of driving to the airport was not a consular activity.

---

14. [Court's footnote 2:] The treaty between the United States and the United Kingdom applies because Malaysia was a colony of the latter at the time the treaty was consummated. . . .

It is unnecessary, however, for us to decide in this case whether getting to and from the place where the actual consular business is conducted is a consular function. The United States Department of State has concluded that traffic offenses, even if committed by persons of ambassadorial rank in the exercise of their official duties, are not beyond the purview of the state courts. In 1965, Assistant Secretary of State Douglas MacArthur II, in responding to a question from Senator Case of New Jersey, wrote:

> . . . the Department of State has concluded that a traffic ticket or summons does not constitute legal process within the meaning of Sections 252 and 253 of Title 22 in the United States Code (relating to the immunity of ambassadors and ministers). Thus, the issuance of such tickets or summonses would not violate the immunity provision set forth in those two statutory sections. We would, therefore, take the view that authorities in all jurisdictions in the United States would be free to issue regular traffic tickets or summonses to any driver with diplomatic or consular status who fails to observe traffic laws and regulations. . . .

The Department of State's interpretations of the existence and scope of diplomatic privileges and immunities are to be accorded great weight by the courts. Although the State Department's letter from which we have quoted purported to construe two sections of the United States Code rather than the specific consular treaty upon which defendant relies, those statutory provisions confer absolute immunity upon ambassadors and ministers, while the treaty provisions accord a much more limited scope of immunity to this defendant. In light of the State Department's interpretation, we conclude that, even if the act of driving to the airport were a consular function, the defendant would not be relieved of responsibility for the traffic infraction he committed while performing that function.

Affirmed.

See also United States v. Cole, 717 F. Supp. 309 (E.D. Pa. 1989) (consul general not entitled to immunity from prosecution for participating in a conspiracy to launder illegal proceeds of drug trafficking; conspiracy to distribute drugs is not a consular function, and an act in furtherance of a conspiracy by a consular officer which takes advantage of the privileges of that position does not suddenly make it a consular function).

C.   INTERNATIONAL ORGANIZATIONS

A much more complicated legal scheme elaborates the privileges and immunities of public international organizations, their staff, and the representatives of member states. In general, the inquiry must start with an examination of the basic constitutive document establishing the organization in question (that is, its charter or articles of agreement). In particular situations, there may also be a specific treaty regime regarding the status of the organization and its staff in each of its member states. Moreover, the organization will typically have entered into a headquarters agreement with the governments of the countries in which it has its principal offices. Finally, individual countries may have provided separately under their domestic laws for the status, privileges, and immunities of international organizations that exist or function within their territories. Determining the applicable rules in a given case may require reference to each of these texts.

As a general matter of law and practice, however, only "functional" or "official acts" immunity (even more limited than consular immunity) is accorded to the officials and staff members of such organizations. The principal representatives of member states (that is, their ambassadors) may, depending on the specific situation, be accorded diplomatic privileges and immunities, while lesser ranking mission members may not.

In the United States, which is host to several public international organizations (for example, the United Nations, the World Bank, the Organization of American States) and various entities associated with them, the basic rules are provided by the respective headquarters agreement and/or separate instrument governing the privileges and immunities of the organization, as well as the International Organizations Immunities Act, 22 U.S.C. §288 et seq. The IOIA applies only to those organizations which have been formally designated by executive order as entitled to benefit from its provisions. It provides, inter alia, that

> [r]epresentatives of foreign governments in or to international organizations and officers and employees of such organizations shall be immune from suit and legal process relating to acts performed by them in their official capacity and falling within their functions as such representatives, officers, or employees except insofar as such immunity may be waived by the foreign government or international organization concerned.

Note that not all international organizations with a presence in the United States have been designated under the IOIA.

In the case of the UN, the status of representatives of member states (that is, their ambassadors) is governed principally by the Charter of the United Nations. Article 105, paragraph 2 provides that such representatives in the territory of other member nations are to enjoy "such privileges and immunities as are necessary for the independent exercise of their functions in connection with the Organization." In addition, section 15 of the Headquarters Agreement between the United States and the United Nations, 22 U.S.C. §287, specifically requires the United States to accord to resident representatives of member states "the same privileges and immunities, subject to corresponding conditions and obligations, as it accords to diplomatic envoys accredited to it." Thus, members of UN Missions who possess diplomatic ranks are afforded the same privileges and immunities as bilaterally accredited diplomats under the Vienna Convention on Diplomatic Relations.

D. CURRENT AND FORMER HEADS OF STATE AND OTHER OFFICIALS

As a matter of customary international law, sitting heads of state and government are absolutely immune from criminal prosecution (and have broad immunity from civil suit) in the courts of foreign states. The doctrine is typically interpreted to encompass members of the family and personal staff who are traveling with the head of state or government (the "entourage"). Such immunity ensures that the most senior government leaders, who play a uniquely preeminent role in international diplomacy, can exercise their functions without interference from foreign courts. It also ensures respect for the dignity of their office and acknowledges the coequal status of states in the international system. Private legal disputes with a foreign head of state are expected to be resolved through that official's own courts, state-to-state mechanisms, or recourse after the official has left office (subject to any residual immunities that may apply for official acts). Obviously, there's an element of reciprocal self-interest at work here as well.

In U.S. practice, determinations concerning visiting heads of state and government are made by the executive branch pursuant to the president's constitutional authority over foreign relations, in particular his authority under Article II, Section 3, to "receive Ambassadors and other public Ministers." In specific cases, these determinations are submitted by the Department of Justice in the form of "suggestions of immunity" and have traditionally been accepted as determinative by the courts. *Saltany et al. v. Reagan et al.*,[15] for example, arose from a 1986 U.S. bombing in Libya, in response to which several residents of Libya sued U.S. officials along with foreign officials who supposedly colluded with the United States. These included British Prime Minister Margaret Thatcher. Dismissing the case, the district court found: "Pursuant to 28 U.S.C. §517 the United States has suggested to the Court the immunity from its jurisdiction of Prime Minister Thatcher as the sitting head of the government of a friendly foreign state. The Department of State has made the requisite certification and determination to allow the immunity. The Court must accept them as conclusive."[16]

Head-of-state immunity also extends to *former* incumbents, although — as the readings in this section demonstrate — the scope of immunity in such situations is unclear, especially when the case concerns international crimes. Generally speaking, former heads of state and government have "residual immunity" for official acts taken while in office, but none for purely private conduct. As the following section illustrates, what counts as an official act can pose complex legal issues.

1. Pinochet

a. Background

The 1999 UK House of Lords' decision regarding Chilean General (and former president) Augusto Pinochet upheld the customary international law principle of residual head-of-state immunity from criminal prosecution for official acts. However, it denied Pinochet's entitlement to that immunity from torture charges because of the application of the UN Convention Against Torture. The highly publicized case arose in the context of a provisional arrest warrant pursuant to a Spanish request for extradition; it turned on the UK's obligation, as a party to the 1984 UN Convention Against Torture, to extradite or prosecute any person facing torture charges found within its territory.

General Pinochet seized power in Chile in a 1973 military coup against the elected president, Salvator Allende. Allende enjoyed considerable support in Chile, and to secure power, Pinochet's military government severely repressed opponents and suspected opponents. Thousands of Chileans were driven into exile, arrested, tortured, killed, or "disappeared" in Operation Condor, Pinochet's campaign to consolidate power and break the opposition. Pinochet remained in power until 1990, when — after he had permitted and lost a referendum on whether he should remain Chile's

---

15. 702 F. Supp. 319 (D.D.C. 1988).

16. Id. at 320, citing Ex Parte Republic of Peru, 318 U.S. 578 (1943), and Republic of Mexico v. Hoffman, 324 U.S. 30 (1945).

leader — he stepped down. Before relinquishing power, the Pinochet government passed an amnesty law for crimes committed in the "Dirty War" against its opponents. Pinochet was also made senator for life, which gave him parliamentary immunity from Chilean prosecution. (The law was revoked in 2000.) Chile's post-Pinochet government acquiesced in these measures, reportedly out of concern that an attempt to repeal them and prosecute the dirty warriors might provoke another military coup against the still-fragile democracy. Chile's government sided with Pinochet in the British litigation, arguing that whether Pinochet should be held accountable for his regime's crimes was an internal political and legal question for Chile — and warning that other states' actions against Pinochet might destabilize the Chilean government.

b.   Legal Chronology

The legal chronology of the Pinochet case contains several steps. The investigation of Pinochet was undertaken by a Spanish investigating magistrate, Baltazar Garzón. Judge Garzón had begun investigating the murder and disappearance of Spanish nationals in Argentina during its "Dirty War," and this led to an investigation of similar operations in Chile.

In 1998, ex-president Pinochet traveled to London for medical treatment, where he was arrested on an extradition warrant issued by Judge Garzón under the Torture Convention. Spain had ratified the Convention in October 1987, and the United Kingdom did so on December 8, 1988, after its implementing legislation (Section 134 of the Criminal Justice Act 1988) had come into force on September 29, 1988. These dates matter because one important legal question concerned the date on which the UK's obligations became effective. The Divisional Court held, however, that Pinochet was immune from prosecution (and therefore extradition) as a former head of state. On appeal, a panel of the House of Lords reversed that decision and found him extraditable by a 3-2 vote (*Pinochet I*).[17] The reasoning of the panel in *Pinochet I* was quite broad, and the opinion was viewed as a resounding victory for the international human rights movement.

However, it transpired that one of the panel judges in the majority, Lord Hoffman, had failed to disclose his participation in the fund-raising arm of Amnesty International (AI), which had been an intervener in the litigation. The House of Lords vacated *Pinochet I* because that failure to disclose created an apparent conflict of interest.[18] A new panel reheard the extradition issue, and on March 24, 1999, it found Pinochet extraditable but on narrower grounds and for a smaller set of crimes than in *Pinochet I*. That decision (*Pinochet II*) is excerpted below.

After Pinochet was found extraditable, the British Home Secretary, Jack Straw, had to decide whether to permit the extradition to go forward. Political pressure on both sides was intense. Straw decided to let the extradition proceed, but soon afterward, in what many observers saw as a diplomatic solution to what had become a sticky political wicket, he found that Pinochet was medically and mentally unfit to stand trial in Spain. Released from house arrest in 2000, Pinochet returned to Chile, where he subsequently faced a number of criminal charges (including torture, disappearances,

---

17. Regina v. Bow St. Metro. Stipendiary Magistrate, Ex parte Pinochet Ugarte (No. 1) [2000] 1 A.C. 61 (H.L. 1998), reprinted in 37 I.L.M. 1302 (1998).

18. Regina v. Bow St. Metro. Stipendiary Magistrate, Ex parte Pinochet Ugarte (No. 2), [2000] 1 A.C. 119 (H.L. 1999), reprinted in 38 I.L.M. 430 (1999).

kidnappings, murders, and even fraud and tax evasion). In several of these cases, he was found fit to stand trial, stripped of his immunity under Chilean law, and placed under house arrest. However, General Pinochet died in Chile in December 2006, before any trials took place.

One bit of terminology will be necessary to understand the following opinions. The various judges speak of immunity *ratione personae* and immunity *ratione materiae*. Literally, the term *ratione personae* means "by reason of person," while *ratione materiae* means "by reason of subject matter." In U.S. terminology, one might say *personal immunity* and *subject matter immunity*, although the parallel is not exact. As used here, the distinction is between immunity that adheres by virtue of the position held by the individual (immunity *ratione personae*) and the immunity that adheres by virtue of the functions of that position (immunity *ratione materiae*). Thus, a sitting head of state enjoys the former, while a former head of state enjoys only the latter (immunity with respect to official acts).

REGINA v. BOW STREET METROPOLITAN STIPENDIARY MAGISTRATE, EX PARTE PINOCHET UGARTE (NO. 3)

United Kingdom House of Lords [2000] 1 A.C. 147 (1999), 2 W.L.R. 827 (H.L.), reprinted in 38 I.L.M. 581 (1999)

LORD BROWNE-WILKINSON

My Lords,

As is well known, this case concerns an attempt by the Government of Spain to extradite Senator Pinochet from this country to stand trial in Spain for crimes committed (primarily in Chile) during the period when Senator Pinochet was head of state in Chile. The interaction between the various legal issues which arise is complex. I will therefore seek, first, to give a short account of the legal principles which are in play in order that my exposition of the facts will be more intelligible.

OUTLINE OF THE LAW

In general, a state only exercises criminal jurisdiction over offences which occur within its geographical boundaries. If a person who is alleged to have committed a crime in Spain is found in the United Kingdom, Spain can apply to the United Kingdom to extradite him to Spain. The power to extradite from the United Kingdom for an "extradition crime" is now contained in the Extradition Act 1989. That Act defines what constitutes an "extradition crime." For the purposes of the present case, the most important requirement is that the conduct complained of must constitute a crime under the law both of Spain and of the United Kingdom. This is known as the double criminality rule.

Since the Nazi atrocities and the Nuremberg trials, international law has recognised a number of offences as being international crimes. Individual states have taken jurisdiction to try some international crimes even in cases where such crimes were not committed within the geographical boundaries of such states. The most important of such international crimes for present purposes is torture which is regulated by the International Convention Against Torture and other Cruel, Inhuman or Degrading Treatment or Punishment, 1984. The obligations placed on the United Kingdom by that Convention (and on the other 110 or more signatory states who have adopted the Convention) were incorporated into the law of the United Kingdom by section 134 of the Criminal Justice Act 1988. That Act came into force on 29 September 1988. Section 134 created a new crime under United Kingdom law, the crime of torture. As required by the Torture Convention "all" torture wherever committed world-wide was made criminal under United Kingdom law and triable in the United Kingdom. No one has suggested that before section 134 came into effect torture committed outside the United Kingdom was a crime under United Kingdom law. Nor is it suggested that section 134 was retrospective so as to make torture committed outside the United Kingdom before 29 September 1988 a United Kingdom crime. Since torture outside the United Kingdom was not a crime under U.K. law until 29 September 1988, the principle of double criminality which requires an Act to be a crime under both the law of Spain and of the United Kingdom cannot be satisfied in relation to conduct before that date if the principle of double criminality requires the conduct to be criminal under United Kingdom law *at the date it was committed.* If, on the other hand, the double criminality rule only requires the conduct to be criminal under U.K. law *at the date of extradition* the rule was satisfied in relation to all torture alleged against Senator Pinochet whether it took place before or after 1988. . . .

[Construing the United Kingdom's extradition statute, Lord Browne-Wilkinson concludes that it requires the conduct to be criminal under U.K. law at the time it was committed, not the date of extradition. The *Pinochet I* panel had supposed otherwise. Therefore, Lord Browne-Wilkinson concludes that only tortures committed under Pinochet after September 1988 are extraditable offenses. Most of the Pinochet regime's tortures occurred in the 1970s, so the result was that only a handful of alleged tortures would be extraditable. This is because of the UK's domestic law governing extradition, not because of international law.]

 . . . It follows that the main question discussed at the earlier stages of this case — is a former head of state entitled to sovereign immunity from arrest or prosecution in the U.K. for acts of torture — applies to far fewer charges. But the question of state immunity remains a point of crucial importance since, in my view, there is certain conduct of Senator Pinochet (albeit a small amount) which does constitute an extradition crime and would enable the Home Secretary (if he thought fit) to extradite Senator Pinochet to Spain unless he is entitled to state immunity. . . .

TORTURE

Apart from the law of piracy, the concept of personal liability under international law for international crimes is of comparatively modern growth. The traditional subjects of international law are states not human beings. But consequent upon the war crime trials after the 1939-45 World War, the international community came to recognise that there could be criminal liability under international law for a class of crimes such as war crimes and crimes against humanity. . . . At least from that date onwards the concept of personal liability for a crime in international law must have been part of international law. In the early years state torture was one of the elements of a war crime. In consequence torture, and various other crimes against humanity, were linked to war or at least to hostilities of some kind. But in the course of time this linkage with war fell away and torture, divorced from war or hostilities, became an international crime on its own. . . .

Moreover, the Republic of Chile accepted before your Lordships that the international law prohibiting torture has the character of *jus cogens* or a peremptory norm, i.e. one of those rules of international law which have a particular status. . . . The *jus cogens* nature of the international crime of torture justifies states in taking universal jurisdiction over torture wherever committed. International law provides that offences *jus cogens* may be punished by any state because the offenders are "common enemies of all mankind and all nations have an equal interest in their apprehension and prosecution." . . .

But there was no tribunal or court to punish international crimes of torture. Local courts could take jurisdiction. . . . But the objective was to ensure a general jurisdiction so that the torturer was not safe wherever he went. For example, in this case it is alleged that during the Pinochet regime torture was an official, although unacknowledged, weapon of government and that, when the regime was about to end, it passed legislation designed to afford an amnesty to those who had engaged in institutionalised torture. If these allegations are true, the fact that the local court had jurisdiction to deal with the international crime of torture was nothing to the point so long as the totalitarian regime remained in power: a totalitarian regime will not permit adjudication by its own courts on its own shortcomings. Hence the demand for some international machinery to repress state torture which is not dependent upon the local courts where the torture was committed. In the event, over 110 states (including Chile, Spain and the United Kingdom) became state parties to the Torture Convention. But it is far from clear that none of them practised state torture. What was needed therefore was an international system which could punish those who were guilty of torture and which did not permit the evasion of punishment by the torturer moving from one state to another. The Torture Convention was agreed not in order to create an international crime which had not previously existed but to provide an international system under which the international criminal — the torturer — could find no safe haven. . . .

THE TORTURE CONVENTION

Article 1 of the Convention defines torture as the intentional infliction of severe pain and of suffering with a view to achieving a wide range of purposes "when such pain or suffering is inflicted by or at the instigation of or with the consent or acquiesence of a public official or other person acting in an official capacity." . . .

Who Is an "Official" for the Purposes of the Torture Convention?

The first question on the Convention is to decide whether acts done by a head of state are done by "a public official or a person acting in an official capacity" within the meaning of Article 1. The same question arises under section 134 of the Criminal Justice Act 1988. The answer to both questions must be the same. . . .

It became clear during the argument that both the Republic of Chile and Senator Pinochet accepted that the acts alleged against Senator Pinochet, if proved, were acts done by a public official or person acting in an official capacity within the meaning of Article 1. . . . The crucial question is not whether Senator Pinochet falls within the definition in Article 1: he plainly does. The question is whether, even so, he is procedurally immune from process. To my mind the fact that a head of state can be guilty of the crime casts little, if any, light on the question whether he is immune from prosecution for that crime in a foreign state. . . .

Universal Jurisdiction

. . . Since Chile, Spain and the United Kingdom are all parties to the Convention, they are bound under treaty by its provisions whether or not such provisions would apply in the absence of treaty obligation. Chile ratified the Convention with effect from 30 October 1988 and the United Kingdom with effect from 8 December 1988.

STATE IMMUNITY

This is the point around which most of the argument turned. It is of considerable general importance internationally since, if Senator Pinochet is not entitled to immunity in relation to the acts of torture alleged to have occurred after 29 September 1988, it will be the first time so far as counsel have discovered when a local domestic court has refused to afford immunity to a head of state or former head of state on the grounds that there can be no immunity against prosecution for certain international crimes.

... The issue is whether international law grants state immunity in relation to the international crime of torture and, if so, whether the Republic of Chile is entitled to claim such immunity even though Chile, Spain and the United Kingdom are all parties to the Torture Convention and therefore "contractually" bound to give effect to its provisions from 8 December 1988 at the latest.

It is a basic principle of international law that one sovereign state (the forum state) does not adjudicate on the conduct of a foreign state. The foreign state is entitled to procedural immunity from the processes of the forum state. This immunity extends to both criminal and civil liability. State immunity probably grew from the historical immunity of the person of the monarch. In any event, such personal immunity of the head of state persists to the present day: the head of state is entitled to the same immunity as the state itself. The diplomatic representative of the foreign state in the forum state is also afforded the same immunity in recognition of the dignity of the state which he represents. This immunity enjoyed by a head of state in power and an ambassador in post is a complete immunity attaching to the person of the head of state or ambassador and rendering him immune from all actions or prosecutions whether or not they relate to matters done for the benefit of the state. Such immunity is said to be granted *ratione personae*.

What then when the ambassador leaves his post or the head of state is deposed?...

The continuing partial immunity of the ambassador after leaving post is of a different kind from that enjoyed *ratione personae* while he was in post. Since he is no longer the representative of the foreign state he merits no particular privileges or immunities as a person. However in order to preserve the integrity of the activities of the foreign state during the period when he was ambassador, it is necessary to provide that immunity is afforded to his official acts during his tenure in post. If this were not done the sovereign immunity of the state could be evaded by calling in question acts done during the previous ambassador's time. Accordingly under Article 39(2) the ambassador, like any other official of the state, enjoys immunity in relation to his official acts done while he was an official. This limited immunity, *ratione materiae*, is to be contrasted with the former immunity *ratione personae* which gave complete immunity to all activities whether public or private.

In my judgment at common law a former head of state enjoys similar immunities, *ratione materiae*, once he ceases to be head of state. He too loses immunity *ratione personae* on ceasing to be head of state.... As ex-head of state he cannot be sued in respect of acts performed whilst head of state in his public capacity. Thus, at common law, the position of the former ambassador and the former head of state appears to be much the same: both enjoy immunity for acts done in performance of their respective functions whilst in office....

... Accordingly, in my judgment, Senator Pinochet as former head of state enjoys immunity *ratione materiae* in relation to acts done by him as head of state as part of his official functions as head of state.

The question then which has to be answered is whether the alleged organisation of state torture by Senator Pinochet (if proved) would constitute an act committed by

Senator Pinochet as part of his official functions as head of state. It is not enough to say that it cannot be part of the functions of the head of state to commit a crime. Actions which are criminal under the local law can still have been done officially and therefore give rise to immunity *ratione materiae*. The case needs to be analysed more closely.

Can it be said that the commission of a crime which is an international crime against humanity and *jus cogens* is an act done in an official capacity on behalf of the state? I believe there to be strong ground for saying that the implementation of torture as defined by the Torture Convention cannot be a state function. . . .

I have doubts whether, before the coming into force of the Torture Convention, the existence of the international crime of torture as *jus cogens* was enough to justify the conclusion that the organisation of state torture could not rank for immunity purposes as performance of an official function. At that stage there was no international tribunal to punish torture and no general jurisdiction to permit or require its punishment in domestic courts. Not until there was some form of universal jurisdiction for the punishment of the crime of torture could it really be talked about as a fully constituted international crime. But in my judgment the Torture Convention did provide what was missing: a worldwide universal jurisdiction. Further, it required all member states to ban and outlaw torture: Article 2. How can it be for international law purposes an official function to do something which international law itself prohibits and criminalises? Thirdly, an essential feature of the international crime of torture is that it must be committed "by or with the acquiesence of a public official or other person acting in an official capacity." As a result all defendants in torture cases will be state officials. Yet, if the former head of state has immunity, the man most responsible will escape liability while his inferiors (the chiefs of police, junior army officers) who carried out his orders will be liable. I find it impossible to accept that this was the intention.

Finally, and to my mind decisively, if the implementation of a torture regime is a public function giving rise to immunity *ratione materiae*, this produces bizarre results. Immunity *ratione materiae* applies not only to ex-heads of state and ex-ambassadors but to all state officials who have been involved in carrying out the functions of the state. . . . Under the Convention the international crime of torture can only be committed by an official or someone in an official capacity. They would all be entitled to immunity. It would follow that there can be no case outside Chile in which a successful prosecution for torture can be brought unless the State of Chile is prepared to waive its right to its officials' immunity. Therefore the whole elaborate structure of universal jurisdiction over torture committed by officials is rendered abortive and one of the main objectives of the Torture Convention — to provide a system under which there is no safe haven for torturers — will have been frustrated. In my judgment all these factors together demonstrate that the notion of continued immunity for ex-heads of state is inconsistent with the provisions of the Torture Convention.

For these reasons in my judgment if, as alleged, Senator Pinochet organised and authorised torture after 8 December 1988, he was not acting in any capacity which gives rise to immunity *ratione materiae* because such actions were contrary to international law, Chile had agreed to outlaw such conduct and Chile had agreed with the other parties to the Torture Convention that all signatory states should have jurisdiction to try official torture (as defined in the Convention) even if such torture were committed in Chile.

As to the charges of murder and conspiracy to murder, no one has advanced any reason why the ordinary rules of immunity should not apply and Senator Pinochet is entitled to such immunity.

For these reasons, I would allow the appeal so as to permit the extradition proceedings to proceed on the allegation that torture in pursuance of a conspiracy to commit torture, including the single act of torture which is alleged in charge 30, was being committed by Senator Pinochet after 8 December 1988 when he lost his immunity. . . .

LORD GOFF OF CHIEVELEY

My Lords,

. . . The central question in the appeal is whether Senator Pinochet is entitled as former head of state to the benefit of state immunity *ratione materiae* in respect of the charges advanced against him. . . .

There can be no doubt that the immunity of a head of state, whether *ratione personae* or *ratione materiae*, applies to both civil and criminal proceedings. This is because the immunity applies to any form of legal process. The principle of state immunity is expressed in the Latin maxim *par in parem non habet imperium* [an equal has no dominion over an equal], the effect of which is that one sovereign state does not adjudicate on the conduct of another. This principle applies as between states, and the head of a state is entitled to the same immunity as the state itself, as are the diplomatic representatives of the state. . . .

[Lord Goff argues that international law prior to adoption of the 1984 Torture Convention did not remove state immunity from the crime of torture.]

It follows that, if state immunity in respect of crimes of torture has been excluded at all in the present case, this can only have been done by the Torture Convention itself. . . .

It is to be observed that no mention is made of state immunity in the Convention. Had it been intended to exclude state immunity, it is reasonable to assume that this would have been the subject either of a separate article, or of a separate paragraph in Article 7, introduced to provide for that particular matter. This would have been consistent with the logical framework of the Convention, under which separate provision is made for each topic, introduced in logical order. . . .

[I]t appears to me to be clear that, in accordance both with international law, and with the law of this country which on this point reflects international law, a state's waiver of its immunity by treaty must, as Dr. Collins submitted, always be express. Indeed, if this was not so, there could well be international chaos as the courts of different state parties to a treaty reach different conclusions on the question whether a waiver of immunity was to be implied.

However it is, as I understand it, suggested that this well-established principle can be circumvented in the present case on the basis that . . . such torture does not form part of the functions of public officials or others acting in an official capacity including, in particular, a head of state. Moreover since state immunity *ratione materiae* can only be claimed in respect of acts done by an official in the exercise of his functions as such, it would follow, for example, that the effect is that a former head of state does not enjoy the benefit of immunity *ratione materiae* in respect of such torture after he has ceased to hold office.

In my opinion, the principle which I have described cannot be circumvented in this way. I observe first that the meaning of the word "functions" as used in this context is well established. The functions of, for example, a head of state are governmental functions, as opposed to private acts; and the fact that the head of state performs an act, other than a private act, which is criminal does not deprive it of its governmental character. This is as true of a serious crime, such as murder or torture, as it is of a lesser crime. . . .

. . . In this connection it must not be overlooked that there are many reasons why states, although recognising that in certain circumstances jurisdiction should be vested in another national court in respect of acts of torture committed by public officials within their own jurisdiction, may nevertheless have considered it imperative that they should be able, if necessary, to assert state immunity. The Torture Convention applies not only to a series of acts of systematic torture, but to the commission of, even acquiescence in, a single act of physical or mental torture. Extradition can nowadays be sought, in some parts of the world, on the basis of a simple allegation unsupported by prima facie evidence. In certain circumstances torture may, for compelling political reasons, be the subject of an amnesty, or some other form of settlement, in the state where it has been, or is alleged to have been, committed.

Furthermore, if immunity *ratione materiae* was excluded, former heads of state and senior public officials would have to think twice about travelling abroad, for fear of being the subject of unfounded allegations emanating from states of a different political persuasion. In this connection, it is a mistake to assume that state parties to the Convention would only wish to preserve state immunity in cases of torture in order to shield public officials guilty of torture from prosecution elsewhere in the world. Such an assumption is based on a misunderstanding of the nature and function of state immunity, which is a rule of international law restraining one sovereign state from sitting in judgment on the sovereign behaviour of another. . . . Preservation of state immunity is therefore a matter of particular importance to powerful countries whose heads of state perform an executive role, and who may therefore be regarded as possible targets by governments of states which, for deeply felt political reasons, deplore their actions while in office. But, to bring the matter nearer home, we must not overlook the fact that it is not only in the United States of America that a substantial body of opinion supports the campaign of the I.R.A. to overthrow the democratic government of Northern Ireland. It is not beyond the bounds of possibility that a state whose government is imbued with this opinion might seek to extradite from a third country, where he or she happens to be, a responsible Minister of the Crown, or even a more humble public official such as a police inspector, on the ground that he or she has acquiesced in a single act of physical or mental torture in Northern Ireland. The well-known case of The Republic of Ireland v. The United Kingdom (1978) 2 E.H.R.R. 25 provides an indication of circumstances in which this might come about.

Reasons such as these may well have persuaded possible state parties to the Torture Convention that it would be unwise to give up the valuable protection afforded by state immunity. . . .

The cumulative effect of all these considerations is, in my opinion, to demonstrate the grave difficulty of recognising an implied term, whatever its form, on the basis that it must have been agreed by all the state parties to the Convention that state immunity should be excluded. . . .

For these reasons I am of the opinion that the proposed implication must be rejected not only as contrary to principle and authority, but also as contrary to common sense. . . .

I would therefore dismiss the appeal of the Government of Spain from the decision of the Divisional Court.

LORD HOPE OF CRAIGHEAD

My Lords,

. . . The sovereign or governmental acts of one state are not matters upon which the courts of other states will adjudicate. . . . The conduct does not have to be lawful to attract the immunity.

. . . There are only two exceptions to this approach which customary international law has recognised. The first relates to criminal acts which the head of state did under the colour of his authority as head of state but which were in reality for his own pleasure or benefit. The examples which Lord Steyn gave [in *Pinochet I*] of the head of state who kills his gardener in a fit of rage or who orders victims to be tortured so that he may observe them in agony seem to me plainly to fall into this category and, for this reason, to lie outside the scope of the immunity. The second relates to acts the prohibition of which has acquired the status under international law of *jus cogens*. This compels all states to refrain from such conduct under any circumstances and imposes an obligation *erga omnes* to punish such conduct. . . .

But even in the field of such high crimes as have achieved the status of *jus cogens* under customary international law there is as yet no general agreement that they are outside the immunity to which former heads of state are entitled from the jurisdiction of foreign national courts. . . .

. . . [I]t would be wrong to regard the Torture Convention as having by necessary implication removed the immunity *ratione materiae* from former heads of state in regard to every act of torture of any kind which might be alleged against him falling within the scope of Article 1. . . . [T]he definition in Article 1 is so wide that any act of official torture, so long as it involved "severe" pain or suffering, would be covered by it.

. . . There is no requirement that it should have been perpetrated on such a scale as to constitute an international crime in the sense described by Sir Arthur Watts in his Hague Lectures at p. 82, that is to say a crime which offends against the public order of the international community. A single act of torture by an official against a national of his state within that state's borders will do. The risks to which former heads of state would be exposed on leaving office of being detained in foreign states upon an allegation that they had acquiesced in an act of official torture would have been so obvious to governments that it is hard to believe that they would ever have agreed to this. . . .

Nevertheless there remains the question whether the immunity can survive Chile's agreement to the Torture Convention if the torture which is alleged was of such a kind or on such a scale as to amount to an international crime. . . .

The allegations which the Spanish judicial authorities have made against Senator Pinochet fall into that category. . . . [W]e are not dealing in this case — even upon the restricted basis of those charges on which Senator Pinochet could lawfully be extradited if he has no immunity — with isolated acts of official torture. We are dealing with the remnants of an allegation that he is guilty of what would now, without doubt, be regarded by customary international law as an international crime. This is because he is said to have been involved in acts of torture which were committed in pursuance of a policy to commit systematic torture within Chile and elsewhere as an instrument of government. . . .

. . . In my opinion, once the machinery which . . . [the Torture Convention] provides was put in place to enable jurisdiction over such crimes to be exercised in the courts of a foreign state, it was no longer open to any state which was a signatory to the Convention to invoke the immunity *ratione materiae* in the event of allegations of systematic or widespread torture committed after that date being made in the courts of that state against its officials or any other person acting in an official capacity. . . .

I would not regard this as a case of waiver. Nor would I accept that it was an implied term of the Torture Convention that former heads of state were to be deprived of their immunity *ratione materiae* with respect to all acts of official torture as defined in article 1. It is just that the obligations which were recognised by customary international law in the case of such serious international crimes by the date when Chile ratified the

Convention are so strong as to override any objection by it on the ground of immunity *ratione materiae* to the exercise of the jurisdiction over crimes committed after that date which the United Kingdom had made available.

I consider that the date as from which the immunity *ratione materiae* was lost was 30 October 1988, which was the date when Chile's ratification of the Torture Convention on 30 September 1988 took effect. . . . But I am content to accept the view of my noble and learned friend Lord Saville of Newdigate that Senator Pinochet continued to have immunity until 8 December 1988 when the United Kingdom ratified the Convention.

It follows that I . . . too would allow the appeal, to the extent necessary to permit the extradition to proceed on the charges of torture and conspiracy to torture relating to the period after 8 December 1988. . . .

LORD HUTTON

My Lords,

[Lord Hutton began by agreeing that for extradition purposes, the conduct in question had to be criminal under UK law at the date of commission.] . . .

But the issue in the present case is whether Senator Pinochet, as a former head of state, can claim immunity (*ratione materiae*) on the grounds that acts of torture committed by him when he was head of state were done by him in exercise of his functions as head of state. In my opinion he is not entitled to claim such immunity. The Torture Convention makes it clear that no state is to tolerate torture by its public officials or by persons acting in an official capacity. . . .

Therefore having regard to the provisions of the Torture Convention, I do not consider that Senator Pinochet or Chile can claim that the commission of acts of torture after 29 September 1988 were functions of the head of state. The alleged acts of torture by Senator Pinochet were carried out under colour of his position as head of state, but they cannot be regarded as functions of a head of state under international law when international law expressly prohibits torture as a measure which a state can employ in any circumstances whatsoever and has made it an international crime. . . .

A number of international instruments define a crime against humanity as one which is committed on a large scale. . . . However, article 4 of the Torture Convention provides that:

> Each state party shall ensure that *all* acts of torture are offences under its criminal law. (Emphasis added.)

Therefore I consider that a single act of torture carried out or instigated by a public official or other person acting in an official capacity constitutes a crime against international law, and that torture does not become an international crime only when it is committed or instigated on a large scale. Accordingly I am of opinion that Senator Pinochet cannot claim that a single act of torture or a small number of acts of torture carried out by him did not constitute international crimes and did not constitute acts committed outside the ambit of his functions as head of state. . . .

Therefore for the reasons which I have given I am of opinion that Senator Pinochet is not entitled to claim immunity in the extradition proceedings in respect of conspiracy to torture and acts of torture alleged to have been committed by him after 29 September 1988 and to that extent I would allow the appeal. . . .

LORD SAVILLE OF NEWDIGATE

My Lords,

... Since 8 December 1988 Chile, Spain and this country have all been parties to the Torture Convention. So far as these countries at least are concerned it seems to me that from that date these state parties are in agreement with each other that the immunity *ratione materiae* of their former heads of state cannot be claimed in cases of alleged official torture. In other words, so far as the allegations of official torture against Senator Pinochet are concerned, there is now by this agreement an exception or qualification to the general rule of immunity *ratione materiae.*

I do not reach this conclusion by implying terms into the Torture Convention, but simply by applying its express terms. A former head of state who it is alleged resorted to torture for state purposes falls in my view fairly and squarely within those terms and on the face of it should be dealt with in accordance with them. Indeed it seems to me that it is those who would seek to remove such alleged official torturers from the machinery of the Convention who in truth have to assert that by some process of implication or otherwise the clear words of the Convention should be treated as inapplicable to a former head of state, notwithstanding he is properly described as a person who was "acting in an official capacity."

I can see no valid basis for such an assertion. It is said that if it had been intended to remove immunity for alleged official torture from former heads of state there would inevitably have been some discussion of the point in the negotiations leading to the treaty. I am not persuaded that the apparent absence of any such discussions takes the matter any further. If there were states that wished to preserve such immunity in the face of universal condemnation of official torture, it is perhaps not surprising that they kept quiet about it.

It is also said that any waiver by states of immunities must be express, or at least unequivocal. I would not dissent from this as a general proposition, but it seems to me that the express and unequivocal terms of the Torture Convention fulfil any such requirement. To my mind these terms demonstrate that the states who have become parties have clearly and unambiguously agreed that official torture should now be dealt with in a way which would otherwise amount to an interference in their sovereignty. ...

I would accordingly allow this appeal to the extent necessary to permit the extradition proceedings to continue in respect of the crimes of torture and (where it is alleged that torture resulted) of conspiracy to torture, allegedly committed by Senator Pinochet after 8 December 1988. ...

LORD MILLETT

My Lords,

... The doctrine of state immunity is the product of the classical theory of international law. This taught that states were the only actors on the international plane; the rights of individuals were not the subject of international law. States were sovereign and equal: it followed that one state could not be impleaded in the national courts of another; *par in parem non habet imperium.* States were obliged to abstain from interfering in the internal affairs of one another. International law was not concerned with the way in which a sovereign state treated its own nationals in its own territory. It is a cliche of modern international law that the classical theory no longer prevails in its unadulterated form. The idea that individuals who commit crimes recognised as such by international law may be held internationally accountable for their actions is now an accepted doctrine of international law. . . .

Two overlapping immunities are recognised by international law; immunity *ratione personae* and immunity *ratione materiae*. They are quite different and have different rationales.

Immunity *ratione personae* is a status immunity. An individual who enjoys its protection does so because of his official status. It enures for his benefit only so long as he holds office. While he does so he enjoys absolute immunity from the civil and criminal jurisdiction of the national courts of foreign states. But it is only narrowly available. It is confined to serving heads of state and heads of diplomatic missions, their families and servants. It is not available to serving heads of government who are not also heads of state, military commanders and those in charge of the security forces, or their subordinates. It would have been available to Hitler but not to Mussolini or Tojo. . . .

The immunity of a serving head of state is enjoyed by reason of his special status as the holder of his state's highest office. He is regarded as the personal embodiment of the state itself. It would be an affront to the dignity and sovereignty of the state which he personifies and a denial of the equality of sovereign states to subject him to the jurisdiction of the municipal courts of another state, whether in respect of his public acts or private affairs. His person is inviolable; he is not liable to be arrested or detained on any ground whatever. The head of a diplomatic mission represents his head of state and thus embodies the sending state in the territory of the receiving state. While he remains in office he is entitled to the same absolute immunity as his head of state in relation both to his public and private acts.

This immunity is not in issue in the present case. Senator Pinochet is not a serving head of state. If he were, he could not be extradited. It would be an intolerable affront to the Republic of Chile to arrest him or detain him.

Immunity *ratione materiae* is very different. This is a subject-matter immunity. It operates to prevent the official and governmental acts of one state from being called into question in proceedings before the courts of another, and only incidentally confers immunity on the individual. It is therefore a narrower immunity but it is more widely available. It is available to former heads of state and heads of diplomatic missions, and any one whose conduct in the exercise of the authority of the state is afterwards called into question, whether he acted as head of government, government minister, military commander or chief of police, or subordinate public official. The immunity is the same whatever the rank of the office-holder. . . . The immunity finds its rationale in the equality of sovereign states and the doctrine of non-interference in the internal affairs of other states. . . . The immunity is sometimes also justified by the need to prevent the serving head of state or diplomat from being inhibited in the performance of his official duties by fear of the consequences after he has ceased to hold office. This last basis can hardly be prayed in aid to support the availability of the immunity in respect of criminal activities prohibited by international law. . . .

The charges brought against Senator Pinochet are concerned with his public and official acts, first as Commander-in-Chief of the Chilean army and later as head of state. He is accused of having embarked on a widespread and systematic reign of terror in order to obtain power and then to maintain it. If the allegations against him are true, he deliberately employed torture as an instrument of state policy. As international law stood on the eve of the Second World War, his conduct as head of state after he seized power would probably have attracted immunity *ratione materiae*. If so, I am of opinion that it would have been equally true of his conduct during the period before the coup was successful. He was not then, of course, head of state. But he took advantage of his position as Commander-in-Chief of the army and made use of the existing military chain of command to deploy the armed forces of the state against its constitutional government. These were not private acts. They were official and governmental or sovereign acts by any standard.

The immunity is available whether the acts in question are illegal or unconstitutional or otherwise unauthorised under the internal law of the state, since the whole purpose of state immunity is to prevent the legality of such acts from being adjudicated upon in the municipal courts of a foreign state. A sovereign state has the exclusive right to determine what is and is not illegal or unconstitutional under its own domestic law. Even before the end of the Second World War, however, it was questionable whether the doctrine of state immunity accorded protection in respect of conduct which was prohibited by international law. . . .

. . . By the time Senator Pinochet seized power, the international community had renounced the use of torture as an instrument of state policy. The Republic of Chile accepts that by 1973 the use of torture by state authorities was prohibited by international law, and that the prohibition had the character of *jus cogens* or obligation *erga omnes*. But it insists that this does not confer universal jurisdiction or affect the immunity of a former head of state *ratione materiae* from the jurisdiction of foreign national courts.

In my opinion, crimes prohibited by international law attract universal jurisdiction under customary international law if two criteria are satisfied. First, they must be contrary to a peremptory norm of international law so as to infringe a *jus cogens*. Secondly, they must be so serious and on such a scale that they can justly be regarded as an attack on the international legal order. Isolated offences, even if committed by public officials, would not satisfy these criteria. . . .

In my opinion, the systematic use of torture on a large scale and as an instrument of state policy had joined piracy, war crimes and crimes against peace as an international crime of universal jurisdiction well before 1984. I consider that it had done so by 1973 [when Pinochet seized power]. For my own part, therefore, I would hold that the courts of this country already possessed extra-territorial jurisdiction in respect of torture and conspiracy to torture on the scale of the charges in the present case and did not require the authority of statute to exercise it. . . .

For my own part, I would allow the appeal in respect of the charges relating to the offences in Spain and to torture and conspiracy to torture wherever and whenever carried out. But the majority of your Lordships think otherwise, and consider that Senator Pinochet can be extradited only in respect of a very limited number of charges. This will transform the position from that which the Secretary of State considered last December. I agree with my noble and learned friend Lord Browne-Wilkinson that it will be incumbent on the Secretary of State to reconsider the matter in the light of the very different circumstances which now prevail.

LORD PHILLIPS OF WORTH MATRAVERS

My Lords,
. . . In the latter part of this century there has been developing a recognition among states that some types of criminal conduct cannot be treated as a matter for the exclusive competence of the state in which they occur. . . . Since the Second World War states have recognised that not all criminal conduct can be left to be dealt with as a domestic matter by the laws and the courts of the territories in which such conduct occurs. There are some categories of crime of such gravity that they shock the consciousness of mankind and cannot be tolerated by the international community.

Any individual who commits such a crime offends against international law. The nature of these crimes is such that they are likely to involve the concerted conduct of many and liable to involve the complicity of the officials of the state in which they occur, if not of the state itself. In these circumstances it is desirable that jurisdiction should exist to prosecute individuals for such conduct outside the territory in which such conduct occurs.

I believe that it is still an open question whether international law recognises universal jurisdiction in respect of international crimes — that is the right, under international law, of the courts of any state to prosecute for such crimes wherever they occur. . . . Rather, states have tended to agree, or to attempt to agree, on the creation of international tribunals to try international crimes. They have however, on occasion, agreed by conventions, that their national courts should enjoy jurisdiction to prosecute for a particular category of international crime wherever occurring.

. . . [N]o established rule of international law requires state immunity *ratione materiae* to be accorded in respect of prosecution for an international crime. International crimes and extra-territorial jurisdiction in relation to them are both new arrivals in the field of public international law. I do not believe that state immunity *ratione materiae* can co-exist with them. The exercise of extra-territorial jurisdiction overrides the principle that one state will not intervene in the internal affairs of another. It does so because, where international crime is concerned, that principle cannot prevail. An international crime is as offensive, if not more offensive, to the international community when committed under colour of office. Once extra-territorial jurisdiction is established, it makes no sense to exclude from it acts done in an official capacity.

There can be no doubt that the conduct of which Senator Pinochet stands accused by Spain is criminal under international law. The Republic of Chile has accepted that torture is prohibited by international law and that the prohibition of torture has the character of *jus cogens* and or obligation *erga omnes*. It is further accepted that officially sanctioned torture is forbidden by international law. The information provided by Spain accuses Senator Pinochet not merely of having abused his powers as head of state by committing torture, but of subduing political opposition by a campaign of abduction, torture and murder that extended beyond the boundaries of Chile. When considering what is alleged, I do not believe that it is correct to attempt to analyse individual elements of this campaign and to identify some as being criminal under international law and others as not constituting international crimes. If Senator Pinochet behaved as Spain alleged, then the entirety of his conduct was a violation of the norms of international law. He can have no immunity against prosecution for any crime that formed part of that campaign. . . .

For these reasons, I would allow the appeal in respect of so much of the conduct alleged against Senator Pinochet as constitutes extradition crimes. I agree with Lord Hope as to the consequences which will follow as a result of the change in the scope of the case.

NOTES AND QUESTIONS

1. Lord Browne-Wilkinson summarized the speeches as follows in his "Report of the Appellate Committee to the House" (March 24, 1999):

In today's judgement, six members of the Committee hold that, under the ordinary law of extradition, Senator Pinochet cannot be extradited to face charges in relation to torture occurring before 29th September 1988 because until that date the double criminality principle was not satisfied. The result of this decision is to eliminate the majority of the charges levelled against Senator Pinochet. . . . Most of the allegations against Senator Pinochet relate to the period of the coup in Chile in 1973 and the years immediately thereafter. The only charges left which are extradition crimes comprise one isolated charge of torture after the 29th September 1988, certain conspiracies to torture relating to the period from 29th September 1988 to January 1990 and certain charges of conspiracy in Spain to commit murder in Spain. As to these very limited charges the question of immunity remains relevant. . . .

Although six members of the Appellate Committee hold that he is not entitled to immunity on torture charges, our reasons vary somewhat. Three of us (my noble and learned friends Lord Hope of Craighead, Lord Saville of Newdigate, and myself) consider that Senator Pinochet only lost his immunity when the Torture Convention became binding on Spain, United Kingdom and Chile. This occurred on 8th December 1988 when the United Kingdom ratified the Convention. Lord Hutton holds that Senator Pinochet's immunity ended on 29th September 1988 (when the Criminal Justice Act 1988, section 134 came into force). Lord Millett and Lord Phillips of Worth Matravers hold that Senator Pinochet was never at any stage entitled to immunity. Although the reasoning varies in detail, the basic proposition common to all, save Lord Goff of Chieveley, is that torture is an international crime over which international law and the parties to the Torture Convention have given universal jurisdiction to all courts wherever the torture occurs. A former head of state cannot show that to commit an international crime is to perform a function which international law protects by giving immunity. Lord Goff is of the view that neither in international law nor by virtue of the Torture Convention has Senator Pinochet been deprived of the benefit of immunity as a former head of state.

The majority therefore considers that Senator Pinochet can be extradited only for the extradition crimes of torture and conspiracy to torture alleged to have been committed after 8th December 1988.

2. The following excerpts from *Pinochet I* address the question of whether torture can be an official act:

LORD STEYN:

If a head of state orders victims to be tortured in his presence for the sole purpose of enjoying the spectacle of the pitiful twitchings of victims dying in agony (what Montaigne described as the farthest point that cruelty can reach) that could not be described as acts undertaken by him in the exercise of his functions as a head of state.

LORD LLOYD OF BERWICK:

Of course it is strange to think of murder or torture as "official" acts or as part of the head of state's "public functions." But if for "official" one substitutes "governmental" then the true nature of the distinction between private acts and official acts becomes apparent. . . . It is a regrettable fact that almost all leaders of revolutionary movements are guilty of killing their political opponents in the course of coming to power, and many are guilty of murdering their political opponents thereafter in order to secure their power. Yet it is not suggested (I think) that the crime of murder puts the successful revolutionary beyond the pale of immunity in customary international law.

3. Some years after *Pinochet*, the UK House of Lords confronted the separate but related question whether foreign government officials were entitled to immunity in UK courts from *civil* liability in respect of claims of torture committed abroad. In Jones v. Ministry of the Interior Al-Mamlaka Al-Arabiya AS Saudiya (The Kingdom of Saudi Arabia) and Others, [2006] U.K.H.L. 26, four British citizens sought damages from both the Kingdom of Saudi Arabia and several of its police officials for personal

injuries arising out of assault and battery, trespass to the person, torture and false imprisonment allegedly committed within Saudi Arabia. The Court of Appeal had dismissed the claims brought against the Saudi Kingdom itself on grounds of state (or sovereign) immunity, but allowed the torture claims to proceed against various individual defendants. [2005] Q.B. 699. The House of Lords reversed, finding no basis in international law or practice for that distinction or for a general exception to immunity in civil suits for damages arising from grave abuses such as torture.

As framed by Lord Bingham, the case posed the need to balance "the condemnation of torture as an international crime against humanity and the principle that states must treat each other as equals not to be subjected to each other's jurisdiction." *Jones*, [2006] U.K.H.L. 26, ¶1. Under UK law, the sovereign immunity of the Saudi Kingdom in this circumstance was clear. But what about the individual defendants? Lord Bingham found that they had at all material times acted as servants or agents of the Saudi Kingdom, so that their acts were attributable to the Kingdom. "A state can only act through servants and agents; their official acts are the acts of the state; and the state's immunity in respect of them is fundamental to the principle of state immunity." Id. ¶30.

Lord Hoffmann agreed with Lord Bingham that, although torture cannot be justified by any rule of domestic or international law, it is a different question "whether such a norm conflicts with a rule which accords state immunity." Id. ¶43. "There is nothing in the Torture Convention which creates an exception to state immunity in civil proceedings." Id. ¶46. He observed that "[t]he notion that acts contrary to *jus cogens* cannot be official acts has not been well received by eminent writers on international law. . . . I would reject the argument that torture or some other contravention of a *jus cogens* [principle] cannot attract immunity *ratione materiae* because it cannot be an official act." Id. ¶¶84, 85.

Is this last statement of Lord Hoffman's consistent with *Pinochet*? The majority in *Pinochet* held that because the Convention criminalizes such acts and expressly requires states parties to take and (in some circumstances) exercise criminal jurisdiction over offenses of torture committed outside its territory, torture could not be "official." As Lord Brown-Wilkinson asked (rhetorically), "How can it be for international law purposes an official function to do something which international law itself prohibits and criminalises?" Saudi Arabia is party to the Torture Convention, so presumably *Pinochet*'s reasoning would apply to torture committed by Saudi officials just as much as to General Pinochet.

In *Jones*, however, the Law Lords reached a very different conclusion: that the immunity of the state itself in civil cases necessarily applies to officials of the state acting in their official capacities, since a state can act only through its officials. This appears to be true, in the *Jones* rationale, for illegal acts as well as those that are legal, and Lord Hoffmann noted that there had been "no suggestion" in the case that the conduct of the individual defendants "was not in discharge or purported discharge of their public duties." Id. ¶11. Neither Lord Hoffmann nor Lord Bingham found any basis for concluding that allegations of torture fall outside the scope of immunity because such acts cannot constitute part of the functions of a state.

A similar view appears in the ICTY Appeals Chamber's decision in Prosecutor v. Blaskic, 110 I.L.R. 607 (ICTY 1997). According to the ICTY, state officials

are mere instruments of a State and their official action can only be attributed to the State. They cannot be the subject of sanctions or penalties for conduct that is not private but undertaken on behalf of a State. In other words, State officials cannot suffer the consequences of wrongful acts which are not attributable to them personally but to the State on whose behalf they act: they enjoy so-called "functional immunity." This is a well-established rule of customary international law going back to the eighteenth and nineteenth centuries, restated many times since. More recently, France adopted a position based on that rule in the *Rainbow Warrior* case. The rule was also clearly set out by the Supreme Court of Israel in the *Eichmann* case.

Id. at 707, ¶38. However, the Tribunal offers these remarks to explain why it lacks power to issue subpoenas to state officials. The "functional immunity" does not apply to ICTY's criminal jurisdiction over state officials, and the Tribunal goes on to point out that the Israeli Supreme Court set out the rule of immunity in *Eichmann* but then found that it does not apply to war crimes or crimes against humanity.

Following this line of thought, can the two House of Lords decisions be reconciled on the basis that *Pinochet* concerned the exercise of criminal jurisdiction while *Jones* involved claims for civil damages? Lord Hoffman evidently thought so, observing that *Pinochet* was "categorically different from the present, since it concerned criminal proceedings falling squarely within the universal criminal jurisdiction mandated by the Torture Convention" (referring to the "extradite or prosecute" obligation). *Jones*, [2006] U.K.H.L. 26, ¶19. By comparison, Article 14 of the Convention obligates states parties to provide a civil remedy for torture only when it occurs within its own territory. Moreover, nothing in the Torture Convention creates an exception to state immunity in civil proceedings. Id. ¶46. In ¶68, Lord Hoffman concluded that "the Torture Convention withdrew the immunity against criminal prosecution but did not affect the immunity for civil liability."

Does *Jones* suggest that civil immunity might not have been available if the Torture Convention *had* required states parties to open their courts to civil claims involving torture committed abroad (that is, to establish "universal civil jurisdiction")? Lord Hoffmann noted that in his opinion the exercise of universal civil jurisdiction under the U.S. Alien Tort Statute is "not required and perhaps not permitted by customary international law" and not part of the law of England. Id. ¶58.

2. The ICJ's Arrest Warrant Decision

Besides heads of state and government, what other state officials are immune from criminal prosecution in another state's courts? That is the question addressed in the following excerpts from the 2002 judgment of the International Court of Justice in the *Case Concerning the Arrest Warrant of 11 April 2000 (Democratic Republic of the Congo v. Belgium)*. The ICJ addresses the question for foreign ministers.

The underlying facts of this case were summarized in Chapter 5's discussion of universal jurisdiction, where we included excerpts from the decision's separate opinions; you may wish to review this summary. In brief, Belgium issued an arrest warrant against Congo's foreign minister Yerodia, based on charges that he had committed international crimes through an inflammatory speech in the Congo's capital city that allegedly incited violent mass attacks against Congolese Tutsis.

CASE CONCERNING THE ARREST WARRANT OF 11 APRIL 2000 (DEMOCRATIC REPUBLIC OF THE CONGO v. BELGIUM)

2002 I.C.J. 3 (Feb. 14), reprinted in 41 I.L.M. 536 (2002)

. . . 13. On 11 April 2000 an investigating judge of the Brussels tribunal de première instance issued "an international arrest warrant in absentia" against Mr. Abdulaye

Yerodia Ndombasi, charging him, as perpetrator or co-perpetrator, with offences constituting grave breaches of the Geneva Conventions of 1949 and of the Additional Protocols thereto, and with crimes against humanity.

At the time when the arrest warrant was issued Mr. Yerodia was the Minister for Foreign Affairs of the Congo.

14. The arrest warrant was transmitted to the Congo on 7 June 2000, being received by the Congolese authorities on 12 July 2000. According to Belgium, the warrant was at the same time transmitted to the International Criminal Police Organization (Interpol), an organization whose function is to enhance and facilitate cross-border criminal police co-operation worldwide; through the latter, it was circulated internationally.

15. In the arrest warrant, Mr. Yerodia is accused of having made various speeches inciting racial hatred during the month of August 1998. The crimes with which Mr. Yerodia was charged were punishable in Belgium under the Law of 16 June 1993 "concerning the Punishment of Grave Breaches of the International Geneva Conventions of 12 August 1949 and of Protocols I and II of 8 June 1977 Additional Thereto," as amended by the Law of 19 February 1999 "concerning the Punishment of Serious Violations of International Humanitarian Law" (hereinafter referred to as the "Belgian Law"). . . .

17. On 17 October 2000, the Congo filed in the Registry an Application instituting the present proceedings . . . , in which the Court was requested "to declare that the Kingdom of Belgium shall annul the international arrest warrant issued on 11 April 2000." The Congo . . . claimed that "[t]he non-recognition, on the basis of Article 5 . . . of the Belgian Law, of the immunity of a Minister for Foreign Affairs in office" constituted a "[v]iolation of the diplomatic immunity of the Minister for Foreign Affairs of a sovereign State, as recognized by the jurisprudence of the Court and following from Article 41, paragraph 2, of the Vienna Convention of 18 April 1961 on Diplomatic Relations." . . .

51. The Court would observe at the outset that in international law it is firmly established that, as also diplomatic and consular agents, certain holders of high-ranking office in a State, such as the Head of State, Head of Government and Minister for Foreign Affairs, enjoy immunities from jurisdiction in other States, both civil and criminal. For the purposes of the present case, it is only the immunity from criminal jurisdiction and the inviolability of an incumbent Minister for Foreign Affairs that fall for the Court to consider.

52. A certain number of treaty instruments were cited by the Parties in this regard. . . .

These conventions provide useful guidance on certain aspects of the question of immunities. They do not, however, contain any provision specifically defining the immunities enjoyed by Ministers for Foreign Affairs. It is consequently on the basis of customary international law that the Court must decide the questions relating to the immunities of such Ministers raised in the present case.

53. In customary international law, the immunities accorded to Ministers for Foreign Affairs are not granted for their personal benefit, but to ensure the effective performance of their functions on behalf of their respective States. In order to determine the extent of these immunities, the Court must therefore first consider the nature of the functions exercised by a Minister for Foreign Affairs. He or she is in charge of his or her Government's diplomatic activities and generally acts as its representative in international negotiations and intergovernmental meetings. Ambassadors and other diplomatic agents carry out their duties under his or her

authority. His or her acts may bind the State represented, and there is a presumption that a Minister for Foreign Affairs, simply by virtue of that office, has full powers to act on behalf of the State (see, e.g., Art. 7, para. 2(a), of the 1969 Vienna Convention on the Law of Treaties). In the performance of these functions, he or she is frequently required to travel internationally, and thus must be in a position freely to do so whenever the need should arise. He or she must also be in constant communication with the Government, and with its diplomatic missions around the world, and be capable at any time of communicating with representatives of other States. The Court further observes that a Minister for Foreign Affairs, responsible for the conduct of his or her State's relations with all other States, occupies a position such that, like the Head of State or the Head of Government, he or she is recognized under international law as representative of the State solely by virtue of his or her office. He or she does not have to present letters of credence: to the contrary, it is generally the Minister who determines the authority to be conferred upon diplomatic agents and countersigns their letters of credence. Finally, it is to the Minister for Foreign Affairs that chargés d'affaires are accredited.

54. The Court accordingly concludes that the functions of a Minister for Foreign Affairs are such that, throughout the duration of his or her office, he or she when abroad enjoys full immunity from criminal jurisdiction and inviolability. That immunity and that inviolability protect the individual concerned against any act of authority of another State which would hinder him or her in the performance of his or her duties.

55. In this respect, no distinction can be drawn between acts performed by a Minister for Foreign Affairs in an "official" capacity, and those claimed to have been performed in a "private capacity," or, for that matter, between acts performed before the person concerned assumed office as Minister for Foreign Affairs and acts committed during the period of office. Thus, if a Minister for Foreign Affairs is arrested in another State on a criminal charge, he or she is clearly thereby prevented from exercising the functions of his or her office. The consequences of such impediment to the exercise of those official functions are equally serious, regardless of whether the Minister for Foreign Affairs was, at the time of arrest, present in the territory of the arresting State on an "official" visit or a "private" visit, regardless of whether the arrest relates to acts allegedly performed before the person became the Minister for Foreign Affairs or to acts performed while in office, and regardless of whether the arrest relates to alleged acts performed in an "official" capacity or a "private" capacity. Furthermore, even the mere risk that, by traveling to or transiting another State a Minister for Foreign Affairs might be exposing himself or herself to legal proceedings could deter the Minister from traveling internationally when required to do so for the purposes of the performance of his or her official functions. . . .

56. The Court will now address Belgium's argument that immunities accorded to incumbent Ministers for Foreign Affairs can in no case protect them where they are suspected of having committed war crimes or crimes against humanity. In support of this position, Belgium refers in its Counter-Memorial to various legal instruments creating international criminal tribunals, to examples from national legislation, and to the jurisprudence of national and international courts. . . .

58. The Court has carefully examined State practice, including national legislation and those few decisions of national higher courts, such as the House of Lords or the French Court of Cassation. It has been unable to deduce from this practice that there exists under customary international law any form of exception to the rule according immunity from criminal jurisdiction and inviolability to incumbent Ministers for

Foreign Affairs, where they are suspected of having committed war crimes or crimes against humanity.

The Court has also examined the rules concerning the immunity or criminal responsibility of persons having an official capacity contained in the legal instruments creating international criminal tribunals, and which are specifically applicable to the latter. . . . It finds that these rules likewise do not enable it to conclude that any such an exception exists in customary international law in regard to national courts.

Finally, none of the decisions of the Nuremberg and Tokyo international military tribunals, or of the International Criminal Tribunal for the former Yugoslavia, cited by Belgium deal with the question of the immunities of incumbent Ministers for Foreign Affairs before national courts where they are accused of having committed war crimes or crimes against humanity. The Court accordingly notes that those decisions are in no way at variance with the findings it has reached above.

In view of the foregoing, the Court accordingly cannot accept Belgium's argument in this regard.

59. It should further be noted that the rules governing the jurisdiction of national courts must be carefully distinguished from those governing jurisdictional immunities: jurisdiction does not imply absence of immunity, while absence of immunity does not imply jurisdiction. Thus, although various international conventions on the prevention and punishment of certain serious crimes impose on States obligations of prosecution or extradition, thereby requiring them to extend their criminal jurisdiction, such extension of jurisdiction in no way affects immunities under customary international law, including those of Ministers for Foreign Affairs. These remain opposable before the courts of a foreign State, even where those courts exercise such a jurisdiction under these conventions.

60. The Court emphasizes, however, that the immunity from jurisdiction enjoyed by incumbent Ministers for Foreign Affairs does not mean that they enjoy impunity in respect of any crimes they might have committed, irrespective of their gravity. Immunity from criminal jurisdiction and individual criminal responsibility are quite separate concepts. While jurisdictional immunity is procedural in nature, criminal responsibility is a question of substantive law. Jurisdictional immunity may well bar prosecution for a certain period or for certain offences; it cannot exonerate the person to whom it applies from all criminal responsibility.

61. Accordingly, the immunities enjoyed under international law by an incumbent or former Minister for Foreign Affairs do not represent a bar to criminal prosecution in certain circumstances.

First, such persons enjoy no criminal immunity under international law in their own countries, and may thus be tried by those countries' courts in accordance with the relevant rules of domestic law.

Secondly, they will cease to enjoy immunity from foreign jurisdiction if the State which they represent or have represented decides to waive that immunity.

Thirdly, after a person ceases to hold the office of Minister for Foreign Affairs, he or she will no longer enjoy all of the immunities accorded by international law in other States. Provided that it has jurisdiction under international law, a court of one State may try a former Minister for Foreign Affairs of another State in respect of acts committed prior or subsequent to his or her period of office, as well as in respect of acts committed during that period of office in a private capacity.

Fourthly, an incumbent or former Minister for Foreign Affairs may be subject to criminal proceedings before certain international criminal courts, where they have jurisdiction. Examples include the International Criminal Tribunal for the former Yugoslavia, and the International Criminal Tribunal for Rwanda. . . .

62. Given the conclusions it has reached above concerning the nature and scope of the rules governing the immunity from criminal jurisdiction enjoyed by incumbent Ministers for Foreign Affairs, the Court must now consider whether in the present case the issue of the arrest warrant of 11 April 2000 and its international circulation violated those rules. . . .

70. The Court notes that the issuance, as such, of the disputed arrest warrant represents an act by the Belgian judicial authorities intended to enable the arrest on Belgian territory of an incumbent Minister for Foreign Affairs on charges of war crimes and crimes against humanity. The fact that the warrant is enforceable is clearly apparent from the order given to "all bailiffs and agents of public authority . . . to execute this arrest warrant" . . . and from the assertion in the warrant that "the position of Minister for Foreign Affairs currently held by the accused does not entail immunity from jurisdiction and enforcement." The Court notes that the warrant did admittedly make an exception for the case of an official visit by Mr. Yerodia to Belgium, and that Mr. Yerodia never suffered arrest in Belgium. The Court is bound, however, to find that, given the nature and purpose of the warrant, its mere issue violated the immunity which Mr. Yerodia enjoyed as the Congo's incumbent Minister for Foreign Affairs. The Court accordingly concludes that the issue of the warrant constituted a violation of an obligation of Belgium towards the Congo, in that it failed to respect the immunity of that Minister and, more particularly, infringed the immunity from criminal jurisdiction and the inviolability then enjoyed by him under international law.

78. For these reasons,
THE COURT, . . .
(2) By thirteen votes to three,

> Finds that the issue against Mr. Abdulaye Yerodia Ndombasi of the arrest warrant of 11 April 2000, and its international circulation, constituted violations of a legal obligation of the Kingdom of Belgium towards the Democratic Republic of the Congo, in that they failed to respect the immunity from criminal jurisdiction and the inviolability which the incumbent Minister for Foreign Affairs of the Democratic Republic of the Congo enjoyed under international law. . . .

(3) By ten votes to six,

> Finds that the Kingdom of Belgium must, by means of its own choosing, cancel the arrest warrant of 11 April 2000 and so inform the authorities to whom that warrant was circulated. . . .

DISSENTING OPINION OF JUDGE VAN DEN WYNGAERT

1. I have voted against paragraphs (2) and (3) of the *dispositif* of this Judgment. International law grants no immunity from criminal process to incumbent Foreign Ministers suspected of war crimes and crimes against humanity. There is no evidence for the proposition that a State is under an obligation to grant immunity from criminal process to an incumbent Foreign Minister under customary international law. By issuing and circulating the warrant, Belgium may have acted contrary to international comity. It has not, however, acted in violation of an international legal obligation. . . .

10. I disagree with the reasoning of the Court, which can be summarized as follows: (a) there is a rule of customary international law granting "full" immunity to

incumbent Foreign Ministers (Judgment, para. 54), and (b) there is no rule of customary international law departing from this rule in the case of war crimes and crimes against humanity (Judgment, para. 58). Both propositions are wrong. . . .

11. I disagree with the proposition that incumbent Foreign Ministers enjoy immunities on the basis of customary international law for the simple reason that there is no evidence in support of this proposition. Before reaching this conclusion, the Court should have examined whether there is a rule of customary international law to this effect. It is not sufficient to compare the rationale for the protection from suit in the case of diplomats, Heads of State and Foreign Ministers to draw the conclusion that there is a rule of customary international law protecting Foreign Ministers: identifying a common raison d'être for a protective rule is one thing, elevating this protective rule to the status of customary international law is quite another thing. The Court should have first examined whether the conditions for the formation of a rule of customary law were fulfilled in the case of incumbent Foreign Ministers. In a surprisingly short decision, the Court immediately reaches the conclusion that such a rule exists. A more rigorous approach would have been highly desirable.

12. In the brevity of its reasoning, the Court disregards its own case law on the subject on the formation of customary international law. In order to constitute a rule of customary international law, there must be evidence of State practice (*usus*) and *opinio juris* to the effect that this rule exists. . . .

13. In the present case, there is no settled practice (*usus*) about the postulated "full" immunity of Foreign Ministers to which the International Court of Justice refers in paragraph 54 of its present Judgment. There may be limited State practice about immunities for current or former Heads of State in national courts, but there is no such practice about Foreign Ministers. On the contrary, the practice rather seems to be that there are hardly any examples of Foreign Ministers being granted immunity in foreign jurisdictions. . . .

A "negative practice" of States, consisting in their abstaining from instituting criminal proceedings, cannot, in itself, be seen as evidence of an *opinio juris*. Abstinence may be explained by many other reasons, including courtesy, political considerations, practical concerns and lack of extraterritorial criminal jurisdiction. Only if this abstention was based on a conscious decision of the States in question can this practice generate customary international law. . . .

15. There are fundamental differences between the circumstances of diplomatic agents, Heads of State and Foreign Ministers. The circumstances of diplomatic agents are comparable, but not the same as those of Foreign Ministers. Under the 1961 Vienna Convention on Diplomatic Relations, diplomatic agents enjoy immunity from the criminal jurisdiction of the receiving State. However, diplomats reside and exercise their functions on the territory of the receiving States whereas Ministers normally reside in the State where they exercise their functions. Receiving States may decide whether or not to accredit foreign diplomats and may always declare them *persona non grata*. Consequently, they have a "say" in what persons they accept as a representative of the other State. They do not have the same opportunity vis-à-vis Cabinet Ministers, who are appointed by their governments as part of their sovereign prerogatives.

16. Likewise, there may be an analogy between Heads of State, who probably enjoy immunity under customary international law, and Foreign Ministers. But the two cannot be assimilated for the only reason that their functions may be compared. Both represent the State, but Foreign Ministers do not "impersonate" the State in the same way as Heads of State, who are the State's alter ego. State practice concerning immunities of (incumbent and former) Heads of State does not, per se, apply to

Foreign Ministers. There is no State practice evidencing an *opinio juris* on this point. . . .

21. . . . Proceeding to assimilations of [this] kind . . . would dramatically increase the number of persons that enjoy international immunity from jurisdiction. There would be a potential for abuse. *Male fide* [bad faith] Governments could appoint suspects of serious human rights violations to cabinet posts in order to shelter them from prosecution in third States. . . .

27. Apart from being wrong in law, the Court is wrong for another reason. The more fundamental problem lies in its general approach, that disregards the whole recent movement in modern international criminal law towards recognition of the principle of individual accountability for international core crimes. The Court does not completely ignore this, but it takes an extremely minimalist approach by adopting a very narrow interpretation of the "no immunity clauses" in international instruments. . . .

28. The Court fails to acknowledge this development, and does not discuss the relevant sources. Instead, it adopts a formalistic reasoning, examining whether there is, under customary international law, an international crimes exception to the — wrongly postulated — rule of immunity for incumbent Ministers under customary international law. By adopting this approach, the Court implicitly establishes a hierarchy between the rules on immunity (protecting incumbent Foreign Ministers) and the rules on international accountability (calling for the investigation of charges against incumbent Foreign Ministers charged with war crimes and crimes against humanity).

By elevating the former rules to the level of customary international law in the first part of its reasoning, and finding that the latter have failed to reach the same status in the second part of its reasoning, the Court does not need to give further consideration to the status of the principle of international accountability under international law. As a result, the Court does not further examine the status of the principle of international accountability. Other courts, for example the House of Lords in the *Pinochet* case and the European Court of Human Rights in the *Al-Adsani* case, have given more thought and consideration to the balancing of the relative normative status of international *jus cogens* crimes and immunities. . . .

34. I now turn to the Court's proposition that immunities protecting an incumbent Foreign Minister under international law are not a bar to criminal prosecution in certain circumstances, which the Court enumerates. . . . (Judgment, para. 61).

In theory, the Court may be right: immunity and impunity are not synonymous and the two concepts should therefore not be conflated. In practice, however, immunity leads to *de facto* impunity. All four cases mentioned by the Court are highly hypothetical.

35. Prosecution in the first two cases presupposes a willingness of the State which appointed the person as a Foreign Minister to investigate and prosecute allegations against him domestically or to lift immunity in order to allow another State to do the same.

This, however, is the core of the problem of impunity: where national authorities are not willing or able to investigate or prosecute, the crime goes unpunished. And this is precisely what happened in the case of Mr. Yerodia. The Congo accused Belgium of exercising universal jurisdiction *in absentia* against an incumbent Foreign Minister, but it had itself omitted to exercise its jurisdiction *in presentia* in the case of Mr. Yerodia, thus infringing the Geneva Conventions and not complying with a host of United Nations resolutions to this effect.

The Congo was ill placed when accusing Belgium of exercising universal jurisdiction in the case of Mr. Yerodia. If the Congo had acted appropriately, by investigating charges of war crimes and crimes against humanity allegedly committed by Mr. Yerodia in the Congo, there would have been no need for Belgium to proceed with the case. . . .

The Congo did not come to the Court with clean hands. In blaming Belgium for investigating and prosecuting allegations of international crimes that it was obliged to investigate and prosecute itself, the Congo acts in bad faith. It pretends to be offended and morally injured by Belgium by suggesting that Belgium's exercise of "excessive universal jurisdiction" was incompatible with its dignity. However, as Sir Hersch Lauterpacht observed in 1951, "the dignity of a foreign state may suffer more from an appeal to immunity than from a denial of it." . . .

36. The third case mentioned by the Court in support of its proposition that immunity does not necessarily lead to impunity is where the person has ceased to be a Foreign Minister. In that case, he or she will no longer enjoy all of the immunities accorded by international law in other States. The Court adds that the lifting of full immunity, in this case, is only for "acts committed prior or subsequent to his or her period of office." For acts committed during that period of office, immunity is only lifted "for acts committed during that period of office in a private capacity." Whether war crimes and crimes against humanity fall into this category the Court does not say.

It is highly regrettable that the International Court of Justice has not, like the House of Lords in the *Pinochet* case, qualified this statement. It could and indeed should have added that war crimes and crimes against humanity can never fall into this category. Some crimes under international law (e.g., certain acts of genocide and of aggression) can, for practical purposes, only be committed with the means and mechanisms of a State and as part of a State policy. They cannot, from that perspective, be anything other than "official" acts. Immunity should never apply to crimes under international law, neither before international courts nor national courts. . . .

The International Court of Justice should have made it clearer that its Judgment can never lead to this conclusion and that such acts can never be covered by immunity.

37. The fourth case of "non-impunity" envisaged by the Court is that incumbent or former Foreign Ministers can be prosecuted before "certain international criminal courts, where they have jurisdiction."

The Court grossly overestimates the role an international criminal court can play in cases where the State on whose territory the crimes were committed or whose national is suspected of the crime are not willing to prosecute. The current *ad hoc* international criminal tribunals would only have jurisdiction over incumbent Foreign Ministers accused of war crimes and crimes against humanity in so far as the charges would emerge from a situation for which they are competent, i.e., the conflict in the former Yugoslavia and the conflict in Rwanda. . . .

. . . [T]he International Criminal Court, like the *ad hoc* international tribunals, will not be able to deal with all crimes that come under its jurisdiction. The International Criminal Court will not have the capacity for that, and there will always be a need for States to investigate and prosecute core crimes. These States include, but are not limited to, national and territorial States. Especially in the case of sham trials, there will still be a need for third States to investigate and prosecute. . . .

38. My conclusion on this point is the following: the Court's arguments in support of its proposition that immunity does not, in fact, amount to impunity, are very unconvincing.

39. My general conclusion on the question of immunity is as follows: the immunity of an incumbent Minister for Foreign Affairs, if any, is not based on customary international law but at most on international comity. It certainly is not "full" or absolute and does not apply to war crimes and crimes against humanity. . . .

87. . . . [G]ranting immunities to incumbent Foreign Ministers may open the door to other sorts of abuse. It dramatically increases the number of persons that enjoy international immunity from jurisdiction. Recognizing immunities for other members of government is just one step further: in present-day society, all Cabinet members represent their countries in various meetings. If Foreign Ministers need immunities to perform their functions, why not grant immunities to other cabinet members as well? The International Court of Justice does not state this, but doesn't this flow from its reasoning leading to the conclusion that Foreign Ministers are immune? The rationale for assimilating Foreign Ministers with diplomatic agents and Heads of State, which is at the centre of the Court's reasoning, also exists for other Ministers who represent the State officially, for example, Ministers of Education who have to attend UNESCO conferences in New York or other Ministers receiving honorary doctorates abroad. *Male fide* governments may appoint persons to Cabinet posts in order to shelter them from prosecutions on charges of international crimes. Perhaps the International Court of Justice, in its effort to close one Pandora's box for fear of chaos and abuse, has opened another one: that of granting immunity and thus *de facto* impunity to an increasing number of government officials.

NOTES AND QUESTIONS

1. See also *Ghaddafi*, reprinted at 125 I.L.R. 490 (French Cour de Cassation 2000) ("international custom precludes Heads of State in office from being the subject of proceedings before the criminal courts of a foreign State, in the absence of specific provisions to the contrary binding on the parties concerned"); H.S.A. et al. v. S.A. et al., reprinted at 42 I.L.M. 596 (Belgian Cour de Cassation 2003) ("customary international law opposes the idea that heads of State and heads of government may be the subject of prosecutions before criminal tribunals in a foreign State, in the absence of contrary provisions of international law obliging the States concerned").

2. In paragraph 36 of her dissent in *Arrest Warrant*, Judge van den Wyngaert raises the question of which acts of a foreign minister are immune from prosecution after the minister leaves office. She argues that the *Pinochet* court found that certain official acts, such as genocide and aggression, create no subject matter immunity. Is this a correct reading of *Pinochet*? Genocide is prohibited under the Convention Against Genocide, which requires states parties to criminalize genocide; but the Convention does not make genocide a universal jurisdiction crime. Rather, it requires only that states parties try cases of genocide occurring in their own territory. The Rome Statute of the International Criminal Court criminalizes both genocide and aggression but it, too, does not suggest that they are universal jurisdiction crimes. How central to *Pinochet*'s reasoning is the requirement that torture is a universal jurisdiction crime?

3. The *Arrest Warrant* judgment addressed the issue of immunity only in the context of head-of-state immunity (as extended to the foreign minister acting as the government's international representative), and only in the context of a current (rather than former) official. As Lord Hoffmann noted in *Jones*, "the *Arrest Warrant* case confirms the opinion of the judges in the *Pinochet* case that General Pinochet

would have enjoyed immunity, on a different basis, if he had still been Head of State." *Jones v. Ministry of the Interior Al-Mamlaka Al-Arabiya AS Saudiya (The Kingdom of Saudi Arabia) and Others*, [2006] U.K.H.L. 26, ¶49. Moreover, it did not address the issue that *Pinochet* turned on: Whether the crimes of which Yerodia was accused could not be regarded as official acts because they are international crimes. Does the judgment in *Jones* shed light on that issue?

4. Since the Abu Ghraib prison abuse revelations in 2004, a coalition of human rights and public interest lawyers have filed complaints with national prosecutors in at least five countries against high U.S. officials, including Donald Rumsfeld, the U.S. secretary of defense at the time of the Abu Ghraib abuses. The complaints alleged that Rumsfeld "personally crafted and ordered the use of 'harsh' interrogation techniques constituting torture." Germany dismissed the complaints twice on the basis that the United States, not Germany, is the proper state to investigate and, if necessary, prosecute alleged crimes by U.S. officials. France rejected the complaint on the basis of immunity, in the following letter:

Paris, 27 February 2008

Public Prosecutor (*Procureur général*) to the
Paris Court of Appeal
to
Mr. Patrick Baudouin
39, avenue Rapp
75007 Paris

Subject: Case of Donald Rumsfeld — triggering contesting the decision of the Paris District Prosecutor (*Procureur de la République*) to dismiss the case, 16 November 2007.

Dear Sir,

I read your letter dated 20 December 2007 contesting the 16 November 2007 decision taken by the Paris District Prosecutor (*Procureur de la République*) to dismiss the case mentioned in the reference.

After examining the case file again, I think the following points should be borne in mind:

The International Court of Justice, in its 14 February 2002 Judgment in "Democratic Republic of Congo v. Belgium," notes that: "*certain holders of high-ranking office in a State, such as the Head of State, Head of Government and Minister for Foreign Affairs, enjoy immunities from jurisdiction in other States, both civil and criminal*" in the exercise of their functions. Upon termination of their functions, the Judgment states that immunity for high-ranking officers shall cease, but only for acts performed prior or subsequent to his or her period in office, or acts committed during the period in office which are unrelated to their duties on behalf of their respective States.

The charges against Mr. Rumsfeld cannot be dissociated from his functions since, in the complaint, he is accused of having initiated or at least tolerated practices which, if confirmed, could fall under the New York Convention on Torture of 10 December 1984, and were carried out while he was US Secretary of Defence, between 20 January 2001 and 8 November 2006. The situation, thus, is different from that, for instance of Augusto Pinochet Ugarte, who was accused of acts (kidnapping, sequestration, assassinations) that did not fall under the exercise of his functions as President but were marginal to them.

The functions of a Secretary of Defence clearly fall within the framework defined by the International Court of Justice, which considers that immunity depends on the essentially diplomatic nature of the functions exercised, requiring numerous travels abroad, under the same conditions as the Head of State and the Minister for Foreign Affairs. . . .

> This explains why the decision taken on 16 November by the Paris District Prosecutor (*Procureur de la République*) to the *Tribunal de Grande Instance* of Paris to dismiss the case does not call for any remarks from my side.
>
> Sincerely yours,
>
> The Public Prosecutor
> (*Procureur Général*)

The complaint was filed after Rumsfeld left office, so the proper immunity test is that of immunity for former officials, not incumbent officials. How does the public prosecutor distinguish the Rumsfeld case from *Pinochet*? Is the prosecutor saying that initiating or tolerating torture is one of the functions of a defense secretary, whereas murder and kidnapping are not a function of a head of state? Does this make sense? Notice that the public prosecutor also finds that the office of a defense secretary is an inherently diplomatic office, like that of foreign minister. Do you agree? Judge van den Wyngaert asks in paragraph 87 of her *Arrest Warrant* dissent what other officials, besides foreign ministers, would receive immunity under the ICJ's opinion. How would you answer that question?

5. U.S. courts have had few opportunities to explore head-of-state immunity from criminal prosecution. The most significant instance occurred in the prosecution of General Manuel Noriega, the commander in chief of Panama's armed forces and de facto ruler of Panama from 1983-1989. Noriega was captured when U.S. troops invaded Panama in 1989. Shortly before, a U.S. grand jury had indicted Noriega for a massive drug trafficking conspiracy, and in response Noriega had declared that a state of war existed between Panama and the United States. The U.S. invasion took place a few days after Noriega's declaration of war. He was convicted of cocaine trafficking. Noriega asserted head-of-state immunity, but the U.S. government had never recognized him as Panama's legitimate ruler because the country had a president, Eric Arturo Delvalle. The district court denied Noriega's immunity claim because he was never the de jure head of state of Panama; the Eleventh Circuit Court of Appeals affirmed, arguing that it should defer to the executive branch's determination of who is and is not a head of state. United States v. Noriega, 117 F.3d 1206, 1209-1212 (11th Cir. 1997). Noriega has been in U.S. prison since his conviction. He has prisoner of war status. As he nears release, both Panama and France wish to extradite him — the former to serve a murder sentence based on an in absentia conviction, the latter to serve a ten-year sentence for money laundering.

3. Immunity Before Hybrid Courts: The Charles Taylor Case

In 2002, a treaty between the UN and the government of Sierra Leone established a court in that country to try the leaders of the three warring factions who since 1996 had nearly destroyed the country, performing acts of unspeakable atrocity. "Specifically, the charges include murder, rape, extermination, acts of terror, enslavement, looting and burning, sexual slavery, conscription of children into an armed force, and attacks on United Nations peacekeepers and humanitarian workers, among others."[19] The court is a novel hybrid having both national and international features:

---

19. Sierra Leone Tribunal, http://www.sc-sl.org/CASES/tabid/71/Default.aspx (last visited Jun. 12, 2009).

It applies international criminal law against war crimes and crimes against humanity, but also Sierra Leonean law.[20] Furthermore, the court has concurrent jurisdiction with Sierra Leonean national courts (Article 8(1)), but takes primacy over the national courts (Article 8(2)). And, like ICTY, ICTR, and the Nuremberg Tribunal, its statute states that "[t]he official position of any accused persons, whether as Head of State or Government or as a responsible government official, shall not relieve such person of criminal responsibility nor mitigate punishment" (Article 6(2)).

Also indicted was Liberian president Charles Taylor, who allegedly sponsored a faction in the civil war, largely to obtain control of Sierra Leone's diamond mines. Taylor responded with a motion claiming head-of-state immunity, based on *Arrest Warrant*. Taylor argued that, just as Belgium's arrest warrant for Yerodia violated Congolese sovereignty, the Sierra Leonean Special Court would be violating Liberia's sovereignty by indicting its president for acts performed while in office.

In a decision of May 31, 2004, the Special Court denied his motion. It argued that even though the Special Court was created through a different mechanism than ICTY and ICTR—a treaty rather than a Security Council resolution—it still has a fundamentally international rather than national status. "We reaffirm . . . that the Special Court is not a national court of Sierra Leone and is not part of the judicial system of Sierra Leone exercising judicial powers of Sierra Leone. . . . We come to the conclusion that the Special Court is an international criminal court."[21]

With this conclusion in hand, the Special Court cites language from *Arrest Warrant* emphasizing that the immunity the ICJ recognizes does not apply "to criminal proceedings before *certain international criminal courts, where they have jurisdiction. Examples include the International Criminal tribunal for the former Yugoslavia, and the International Criminal tribunal for Rwanda.* . . ."[22] The Special Court continues:

51. A reason for the distinction, in this regard, between national courts and international courts, though not immediately evident, would appear due to the fact that the principle that one sovereign state does not adjudicate on the conduct of another state; the principle of state immunity derives from the equality of sovereign states and therefore has no relevance to international criminal tribunals which are not organs of a state but derive their mandate from the international community. Another reason is as put by Professor Orentlicher in her *amicus* brief that:

states have considered the collective judgment of the international community to provide a vital safeguard against the potential destabilizing effect of unilateral judgment in this area.

52. Be that as it may, the principle seems now established that the sovereign equality of states does not prevent a Head of State from being prosecuted before an international criminal tribunal or court. . . .

53. In this result the Appeals Chamber finds that Article 6(2) of the Statute [denying head-of-state immunity] is not in conflict with any peremptory norm of general international law and its provisions must be given effect by this court. We hold that the official position of the Applicant as an incumbent Head of State at the time when these criminal proceedings were initiated against him is not a bar to his prosecution by this court. The Applicant was and is subject to criminal proceedings before the Special Court for Sierra Leone.

---

20. Statute for the Special Court of Sierra Leone, Arts. 2-5, available at http://www.specialcourt.org/documents/SpecialCourtStatuteFinal.pdf).
21. Immunity Decision of the Special Court, May 31, 2004, ¶¶40, 42.
22. Id. ¶51, quoting *Arrest Warrant*, ¶61 (emphasis added by the Special Court).

Taylor was forced into exile and found political asylum in Nigeria. Eventually, however, Nigeria withdrew his asylum, and he was captured and turned over to the Sierra Leonean government for trial before the Special Court. In an unusual move, the governments of Liberia and Sierra Leone — nervous that the trial on its territory might destabilize the region — requested that the trial take place in The Hague, at the facilities of the International Criminal Court. The Dutch government was willing to permit this only if some other state promised to incarcerate Taylor in case of conviction. After the UK agreed to do so in June 2006, Taylor was transferred to The Hague, where, in early 2009, his trial is ongoing.

CHAPTER
7

U.S. Constitutional Rights in a Transnational Context

As the jurisdiction chapter made evident, crime and law enforcement have gone transnational. This chapter explores the further question whether the protections afforded criminal suspects and defendants in the U.S. Constitution follow U.S. law enforcement agents across borders, require exclusion of evidence seized from non-U.S. nationals or evidence secured abroad, or may subject U.S. agents to damages awards in civil suits founded on constitutional violations. In short, here we concentrate on the many issues that arise when the procedural protections included in the U.S. Bill of Rights are sought to be applied in a transnational context.

These questions are increasingly important as the United States pursues its "war on terror." The Bill of Rights applies to federal and state governmental agents of all types, soldiers in the field as well as law enforcement personnel. Can the hundreds of persons seized in Afghanistan and detained without prior judicial process in Guantánamo Bay claim that "their" Fourth Amendment right against unreasonable seizures was violated? If so, what remedy is available? What if an individual is abducted by U.S. agents, tortured outside U.S. territory, but never prosecuted in the United States? Does the Due Process Clause mandate that money damages be available to him? Must U.S. agents or service personnel interrogating foreign nationals accused of terrorist attacks against U.S. targets abroad provide counsel to those who request it during interrogation? Should the exclusionary remedy be available to foreign nationals captured abroad but tried under U.S. law in U.S. courts?

The U.S. Supreme Court has yet to resolve many of these questions. Indeed, its precedents regarding the transnational application of the Constitution are not only scarce, but also doctrinally incoherent. The Court's difficulties appear to stem in part from the fact that various Justices over the last century endorsed different conceptions of just who is entitled to claim the Constitution's protections against U.S. government action. As might be expected given the prevailing theory of international law at the time, the early cases reflect a strict territorial focus. In more recent cases, however, some Justices have departed from the traditional model to focus on "membership" rather than "territory." Under this view, the Constitution is a social compact whose protections may be claimed only by those who have voluntarily agreed to be subject to the reciprocal burdens imposed by U.S. law. A competing "universalist" theory posits that the Constitution is designed essentially to circumscribe the powers of the government the better to protect inalienable or "natural" rights against governmental interference. This theory mandates that the U.S. government may act only in conformance with its authorizing charter, whether its actions are foreign or domestic.

Finally, some Justices have advocated a "global due process" approach, which recognizes that the Constitution has some purchase overseas, but its protections vary based on their importance and the circumstances of the case. This debate, although theoretical, is far from "academic"; whether U.S. citizens and others can claim the benefit of fundamental procedural safeguards in criminal investigations conducted by U.S. authorities in a transnational context hinges in no small part on its resolution.

A. FOURTH AMENDMENT

UNITED STATES v. VERDUGO-URQUIDEZ
494 U.S. 259 (1990)

[REHNQUIST, C.J., delivered the opinion of the Court, in which WHITE, O'CONNOR, SCALIA, and KENNEDY, JJ., joined. KENNEDY, J., filed a concurring opinion. STEVENS, J., filed an opinion concurring in the judgment. BRENNAN, J., filed a dissenting opinion, in which MARSHALL, J., joined. BLACKMUN, J., filed a dissenting opinion.]

Chief Justice REHNQUIST delivered the opinion of the Court.

The question presented by this case is whether the Fourth Amendment applies to the search and seizure by United States agents of property that is owned by a nonresident alien and located in a foreign country. We hold that it does not.

Respondent Rene Martin Verdugo-Urquidez is a citizen and resident of Mexico. He is believed by the United States Drug Enforcement Agency (DEA) to be one of the leaders of a large and violent organization in Mexico that smuggles narcotics into the United States. . . .

. . . Terry Bowen, a DEA agent assigned to the Calexico DEA office, decided to arrange for searches of Verdugo-Urquidez's Mexican residences located in Mexicali and San Felipe. Bowen believed that the searches would reveal evidence related to respondent's alleged narcotics trafficking activities and his involvement in the kidnaping and torture-murder of DEA Special Agent Enrique Camarena Salazar (for which respondent subsequently has been convicted in a separate prosecution). Bowen telephoned Walter White, the Assistant Special Agent in charge of the DEA office in Mexico City, and asked him to seek authorization for the search from the Director General of the Mexican Federal Judicial Police (MFJP). After several attempts to reach high ranking Mexican officials, White eventually contacted the Director General, who authorized the searches and promised the cooperation of Mexican authorities. Thereafter, DEA agents working in concert with officers of the MFJP searched respondent's properties in Mexicali and San Felipe and seized certain documents. In particular, the search of the Mexicali residence uncovered a tally sheet, which the Government believes reflects the quantities of marijuana smuggled by Verdugo-Urquidez into the United States.

The District Court granted respondent's motion to suppress evidence seized during the searches, concluding that the Fourth Amendment applied to the searches and that the DEA agents had failed to justify searching respondent's premises without a warrant. A divided panel of the Court of Appeals for the Ninth Circuit affirmed. It cited this Court's decision in Reid v. Covert, 354 U.S. 1 (1957), which held that American citizens tried by United States military authorities in a foreign country were entitled to the protections of the Fifth and Sixth Amendments, and concluded that "[t]he Constitution imposes substantive constraints on the federal government, even when it operates abroad." Relying on our decision in INS v. Lopez-Mendoza, 468 U.S. 1032 (1984), where a majority of Justices assumed that illegal aliens in the United States have Fourth Amendment rights, the Ninth Circuit majority found it "difficult to conclude that Verdugo-Urquidez lacks these same protections." It also observed that persons in respondent's position enjoy certain trial-related rights, and reasoned that "[i]t would be odd indeed to acknowledge that Verdugo-Urquidez is entitled to due process under the fifth amendment, and to a fair trial under the sixth amendment, . . . and deny him the protection from unreasonable searches and seizures afforded under the fourth amendment." Having concluded that the Fourth Amendment applied to the searches of respondent's properties, the court went on to decide that the searches violated the Constitution because the DEA agents failed to procure a search warrant. Although recognizing that "an American search warrant would be of no legal validity in Mexico," the majority deemed it sufficient that a warrant would have "substantial constitutional value in this country," because it would reflect a magistrate's determination that there existed probable cause to search and would define the scope of the search.

The dissenting judge argued that this Court's statement in United States v. Curtiss-Wright Export Corp., 299 U.S. 304, 318 (1936), that "[n]either the Constitution nor the laws passed in pursuance of it have any force in foreign territory unless in respect of our own citizens," foreclosed any claim by respondent to Fourth Amendment rights. More broadly, he viewed the Constitution as a "compact" among the people of the United States, and the protections of the Fourth Amendment were expressly limited to "the people." We granted certiorari.

Before analyzing the scope of the Fourth Amendment, we think it significant to note that it operates in a different manner than the Fifth Amendment, which is not at issue in this case. The privilege against self-incrimination guaranteed by the Fifth Amendment is a fundamental trial right of criminal defendants. Although conduct by law enforcement officials prior to trial may ultimately impair that right, a constitutional violation occurs only at trial. The Fourth Amendment functions differently. It prohibits "unreasonable searches and seizures" whether or not the evidence is sought to be used in a criminal trial, and a violation of the Amendment is "fully accomplished" at the time of an unreasonable governmental intrusion. For purposes of this case, therefore, if there were a constitutional violation, it occurred solely in Mexico. Whether evidence obtained from respondent's Mexican residences should be excluded at trial in the United States is a remedial question separate from the existence *vel non* of the constitutional violation.

The Fourth Amendment provides:

> The right of the people to be secure in their persons, houses, papers, and effects, against unreasonable searches and seizures, shall not be violated, and no Warrants shall issue, but upon probable cause, supported by Oath or affirmation, and particularly describing the place to be searched, and the persons or things to be seized.

That text, by contrast with the Fifth and Sixth Amendments, extends its reach only to "the people." Contrary to the suggestion of amici curiae that the Framers used this phrase "simply to avoid [an] awkward rhetorical redundancy," "the people" seems to have been a term of art employed in select parts of the Constitution. The Preamble declares that the Constitution is ordained and established by "the People of the United States." The Second Amendment protects "the right of the people to keep and bear Arms," and the Ninth and Tenth Amendments provide that certain rights and powers are retained by and reserved to "the people." See also U.S. Const., Amdt. 1 ("Congress shall make no law . . . abridging . . . *the right of the people* peaceably to assemble") (emphasis added); Art. I, §2, cl. 1 ("The House of Representatives shall be composed of Members chosen every second Year *by the People of the several States*") (emphasis added). While this textual exegesis is by no means conclusive, it suggests that "the people" protected by the Fourth Amendment, and by the First and Second Amendments, and to whom rights and powers are reserved in the Ninth and Tenth Amendments, refers to a class of persons who are part of a national community or who have otherwise developed sufficient connection with this country to be considered part of that community. See United States ex rel. Turner v. Williams, 194 U.S. 279, 292 (1904) (Excludable alien is not entitled to First Amendment rights, because "[h]e does not become one of the people to whom these things are secured by our Constitution by an attempt to enter forbidden by law"). The language of these Amendments contrasts with the words "person" and "accused" used in the Fifth and Sixth Amendments regulating procedure in criminal cases.

What we know of the history of the drafting of the Fourth Amendment also suggests that its purpose was to restrict searches and seizures which might be conducted by the United States in domestic matters. . . . The driving force behind the adoption of the Amendment, as suggested by Madison's advocacy, was widespread hostility among the former colonists to the issuance of writs of assistance empowering revenue officers to search suspected places for smuggled goods, and general search warrants permitting the search of private houses, often to uncover papers that might be used to convict persons of libel. The available historical data show, therefore, that the purpose of the Fourth Amendment was to protect the people of the United States against arbitrary action by their own Government; it was never suggested that the provision was intended to restrain the actions of the Federal Government against aliens outside of the United States territory.

The global view taken by the Court of Appeals of the application of the Constitution is also contrary to this Court's decisions in the *Insular Cases*, which held that not every constitutional provision applies to governmental activity even where the United States has sovereign power. See, e.g., Balzac v. Porto Rico, 258 U.S. 298 (1922) (Sixth Amendment right to jury trial inapplicable in Puerto Rico); Ocampo v. United States, 234 U.S. 91 (1914) (Fifth Amendment grand jury provision inapplicable in Philippines); Dorr v. United States, 195 U.S. 138 (1904) (jury trial provision inapplicable in Philippines); Hawaii v. Mankichi, 190 U.S. 197 (1903) (provisions on indictment by grand jury and jury trial inapplicable in Hawaii); Downes v. Bidwell, 182 U.S. 244 (1901) (Revenue Clauses of Constitution inapplicable to Puerto Rico). In *Dorr*, we declared the general rule that in an unincorporated territory, one not clearly destined for statehood, Congress was not required to adopt "a system of laws which shall include the right of trial by jury, and that *the Constitution does not, without legislation and of its own force, carry such right to territory so situated.*" (Emphasis added). Only "fundamental" constitutional rights are guaranteed to inhabitants of those territories. If that is true with respect to territories ultimately governed by Congress, respondent's claim that the protections of the Fourth Amendment extend to aliens in foreign nations is even weaker. And certainly, it is not open to us in light of the *Insular Cases* to endorse the view that every constitutional provision applies wherever the United States Government exercises its power.

Indeed, we have rejected the claim that aliens are entitled to Fifth Amendment rights outside the sovereign territory of the United States. In Johnson v. Eisentrager, 339 U.S. 763 (1950), the Court held that enemy aliens arrested in China and imprisoned in Germany after World War II could not obtain writs of habeas corpus in our federal courts on the ground that their convictions for war crimes had violated the Fifth Amendment and other constitutional provisions. The *Eisentrager* opinion acknowledged that in some cases constitutional provisions extend beyond the citizenry; "[t]he alien . . . has been accorded a generous and ascending scale of rights as he increases his identity with our society." But our rejection of extraterritorial application of the Fifth Amendment was emphatic:

> Such extraterritorial application of organic law would have been so significant an inno-vation in the practice of governments that, if intended or apprehended, it could scarcely have failed to excite contemporary comment. Not one word can be cited. No decision of this Court supports such a view. None of the learned commentators on our Constitution has even hinted at it. The practice of every modern government is opposed to it.

If such is true of the Fifth Amendment, which speaks in the relatively universal term of "person," it would seem even more true with respect to the Fourth Amendment, which applies only to "the people."

To support his all-encompassing view of the Fourth Amendment, respondent points to language from the plurality opinion in Reid v. Covert, 354 U.S. 1 (1957). *Reid* involved an attempt by Congress to subject the wives of American servicemen to trial by military tribunals without the protection of the Fifth and Sixth Amendments. The Court held that it was unconstitutional to apply the Uniform Code of Military Justice to the trials of the American women for capital crimes. Four Justices "reject[ed] the idea that when the United States acts *against citizens* abroad it can do so free of the Bill of Rights." (Emphasis added). The plurality went on to say:

> The United States is entirely a creature of the Constitution. Its power and authority have no other source. It can only act in accordance with all the limitations imposed by the Constitution. When the Government reaches out to punish *a citizen* who is abroad, the shield which the Bill of Rights and other parts of the Constitution provide to protect his life and liberty should not be stripped away just because he happens to be in another land. (Emphasis added.)

Respondent urges that we interpret this discussion to mean that federal officials are constrained by the Fourth Amendment wherever and against whomever they act. But the holding of *Reid* stands for no such sweeping proposition: it decided that United States citizens stationed abroad could invoke the protection of the Fifth and Sixth Amendments. The concurrences by Justices Frankfurter and Harlan in *Reid* resolved the case on much narrower grounds than the plurality and declined even to hold that United States citizens were entitled to the full range of constitutional protections in all overseas criminal prosecutions. See id., at 75 (Harlan, J., concurring in result) ("I agree with my brother Frankfurter that . . . we have before us a question analo-gous, ultimately, to issues of due process; one can say, in fact, that the question of which specific safeguards of the Constitution are appropriately to be applied in a particular context overseas can be reduced to the issue of what process is 'due' a defendant in the particular circumstances of a particular case"). Since respondent is not a United States citizen, he can derive no comfort from the *Reid* holding.

Verdugo-Urquidez also relies on a series of cases in which we have held that aliens enjoy certain constitutional rights. See, e.g., Plyler v. Doe, 457 U.S. 202, 211-212 (1982) (illegal aliens protected by Equal Protection Clause); Kwong Hai Chew v. Colding, 344 U.S. 590, 596 (1953) (resident alien is a "person" within the meaning of the Fifth Amendment); Bridges v. Wixon, 326 U.S. 135, 148 (1945) (resident aliens have First Amendment rights); Russian Volunteer Fleet v. United States, 282 U.S. 481 (1931) (Just Compensation Clause of Fifth Amendment); Wong Wing v. United States, 163 U.S. 228, 238 (1896) (resident aliens entitled to Fifth and Sixth Amendment rights); Yick Wo v. Hopkins, 118 U.S. 356, 369 (1886) (Fourteenth Amendment protects resident aliens). These cases, however, establish only that aliens receive constitutional protections when they have come within the territory of the United States and developed substantial connections with this country. See, e.g., *Plyler*, 457 U.S., at 212 (The provisions of the Fourteenth Amendment "'are universal in their application, *to all persons within the territorial jurisdiction . . .*'"); *Kwong Hai Chew*, 344 U.S., at 596, n. 5 ("The Bill of Rights is a futile authority for the alien seeking admission for the first time to these shores. But *once an alien lawfully enters and resides in this country* he becomes invested with the rights guaranteed by the Constitution to all people within our borders") (emphasis added). Respondent is an alien who has had no previous significant voluntary connection with the United States, so these cases avail him not.

Justice Stevens' concurrence in the judgment takes the view that even though the search took place in Mexico, it is nonetheless governed by the requirements of the Fourth Amendment because respondent was "lawfully present in the United States . . . even though he was brought and held here against his will." But this sort of presence, lawful but involuntary, is not of the sort to indicate any substantial connection with our country. The extent to which respondent might claim the protection of the Fourth Amendment if the duration of his stay in the United States were to be prolonged, by a prison sentence, for example, we need not decide. When the search of his house in Mexico took place, he had been present in the United States for only a matter of days. We do not think the applicability of the Fourth Amendment to the search of premises in Mexico should turn on the fortuitous circumstance of whether the custodian of its nonresident alien owner had or had not transported him to the United States at the time the search was made.

The Court of Appeals found some support for its holding in our decision in INS v. Lopez-Mendoza, 468 U.S. 1032 (1984), where a majority of Justices assumed that the Fourth Amendment applied to illegal aliens in the United States. We cannot fault the Court of Appeals for placing some reliance on the case, but our decision did not expressly address the proposition gleaned by the court below. The question presented for decision in *Lopez-Mendoza* was limited to whether the Fourth Amendment's exclusionary rule should be extended to civil deportation proceedings; it did not encompass whether the protections of the Fourth Amendment extend to illegal aliens in this country. The Court often grants certiorari to decide particular legal issues while assuming without deciding the validity of antecedent propositions, and such assumptions, even on jurisdictional issues — are not binding in future cases that directly raise the questions. Our statements in *Lopez-Mendoza* are therefore not dispositive of how the Court would rule on a Fourth Amendment claim by illegal aliens in the United States if such a claim were squarely before us. Even assuming such aliens would be entitled to Fourth Amendment protections, their situation is different from respondent's. The illegal aliens in *Lopez-Mendoza* were in the United States voluntarily and presumably had accepted some societal obligations; but respondent had no voluntary connection with this country that might place him among "the people" of the United States. . . .

Not only are history and case law against respondent, but as pointed out in Johnson v. Eisentrager, 339 U.S. 763 (1950), the result of accepting his claim would have significant and deleterious consequences for the United States in conducting activities beyond its boundaries. The rule adopted by the Court of Appeals would apply not only to law enforcement operations abroad, but also to other foreign policy operations which might result in "searches or seizures." The United States frequently employs Armed Forces outside this country, over 200 times in our history, for the protection of American citizens or national security. Application of the Fourth Amendment to those circumstances could significantly disrupt the ability of the political branches to respond to foreign situations involving our national interest. Were respondent to prevail, aliens with no attachment to this country might well bring actions for damages to remedy claimed violations of the Fourth Amendment in foreign countries or in international waters. See Bivens v. Six Unknown Federal Narcotics Agents, 403 U.S. 388 (1971). Perhaps a *Bivens* action might be unavailable in some or all of these situations due to "'special factors counselling hesitation,'" but the Government would still be faced with case-by-case adjudications concerning the availability of such an action. And even were *Bivens* deemed wholly inapplicable in cases of foreign activity, that would not obviate the problems attending the application of the Fourth Amendment abroad to aliens. The Members of the Executive and Legislative Branches are sworn to uphold the Constitution, and they presumably desire to follow its commands. But the Court of Appeals' global view of its applicability would plunge them into a sea of uncertainty as to what might be reasonable in the way of searches and seizures conducted abroad. Indeed, the Court of Appeals held that absent exigent circumstances, United States agents could not effect a "search or seizure" for law enforcement purposes in a foreign country without first obtaining a warrant, which would be a dead letter outside the United States, from a magistrate in this country. Even if no warrant were required, American agents would have to articulate specific facts giving them probable cause to undertake a search or seizure if they wished to comply with the Fourth Amendment as conceived by the Court of Appeals.

We think that the text of the Fourth Amendment, its history, and our cases discussing the application of the Constitution to aliens and extraterritorially require rejection of respondent's claim. At the time of the search, he was a citizen and resident of Mexico with no voluntary attachment to the United States, and the place searched was located in Mexico. Under these circumstances, the Fourth Amendment has no application.

For better or for worse, we live in a world of nation-states in which our Government must be able to "functio[n] effectively in the company of sovereign nations." Some who violate our laws may live outside our borders under a regime quite different from that which obtains in this country. Situations threatening to important American interests may arise half-way around the globe, situations which in the view of the political branches of our Government require an American response with armed force. If there are to be restrictions on searches and seizures which occur incident to such American action, they must be imposed by the political branches through diplomatic understanding, treaty, or legislation. . . .

Justice KENNEDY, concurring.

I agree that no violation of the Fourth Amendment has occurred and that we must reverse the judgment of the Court of Appeals. Although some explanation of my views is appropriate given the difficulties of this case, I do not believe they depart in fundamental respects from the opinion of the Court, which I join.

In cases involving the extraterritorial application of the Constitution, we have taken care to state whether the person claiming its protection is a citizen, see, e.g., Reid v. Covert, 354 U.S. 1 (1957), or an alien, see, e.g., Johnson v. Eisentrager, 339 U.S. 763 (1950). The distinction between citizens and aliens follows from the undoubted proposition that the Constitution does not create, nor do general principles of law create, any juridical relation between our country and some undefined, limitless class of noncitizens who are beyond our territory. We should note, however, that the absence of this relation does not depend on the idea that only a limited class of persons ratified the instrument that formed our Government. Though it must be beyond dispute that persons outside the United States did not and could not assent to the Constitution, that is quite irrelevant to any construction of the powers conferred or the limitations imposed by it. As Justice Story explained in his Commentaries:

> A government may originate in the voluntary compact or assent of the people of several states, or of a people never before united, and yet when adopted and ratified by them, be no longer a matter resting in compact; but become an executed government or constitution, a fundamental law, and not a mere league. But the difficulty in asserting it to be a compact between the people of each state, and all the people of the other states is, that the constitution itself contains no such expression, and no such designation of parties.

The force of the Constitution is not confined because it was brought into being by certain persons who gave their immediate assent to its terms.

For somewhat similar reasons, I cannot place any weight on the reference to "the people" in the Fourth Amendment as a source of restricting its protections. With respect, I submit these words do not detract from its force or its reach. Given the history of our Nation's concern over warrantless and unreasonable searches, explicit recognition of "the right of the people" to Fourth Amendment protection may be interpreted to underscore the importance of the right, rather than to restrict the category of persons who may assert it. The restrictions that the United States must observe with reference to aliens beyond its territory or jurisdiction depend, as a consequence, on general principles of interpretation, not on an inquiry as to who formed the Constitution or a construction that some rights are mentioned as being those of "the people."

I take it to be correct, as the plurality opinion in Reid v. Covert sets forth, that the Government may act only as the Constitution authorizes, whether the actions in question are foreign or domestic. But this principle is only a first step in resolving this case. The question before us then becomes what constitutional standards apply when the Government acts, in reference to an alien, within its sphere of foreign operations. We have not overruled either In re Ross, 140 U.S. 453 (1891), or the so-called *Insular Cases*. These authorities, as well as United States v. Curtiss-Wright Export Corp., 299 U.S. 304, 318 (1936), stand for the proposition that we must interpret constitutional protections in light of the undoubted power of the United States to take actions to assert its legitimate power and authority abroad. Justice Harlan made this observation in his opinion concurring in the judgment in Reid v. Covert:

> I cannot agree with the suggestion that every provision of the Constitution must always be deemed automatically applicable to American citizens in every part of the world. For *Ross* and the *Insular Cases* do stand for an important proposition, one which seems to me a wise and necessary gloss on our Constitution. The proposition is, of course, not that the Constitution "does not apply" overseas, but that there are provisions in the Constitution which do not *necessarily* apply in all circumstances in every foreign place. In other words, it seems to me that the basic teaching of *Ross* and the *Insular Cases* is that there is no rigid and abstract rule that Congress, as a condition precedent to exercising power over Americans overseas, must exercise it subject to all the guarantees of the Constitution, no matter what the conditions and considerations are that would make adherence to a specific guarantee altogether impracticable and anomalous.

The conditions and considerations of this case would make adherence to the Fourth Amendment's warrant requirement impracticable and anomalous. Just as the Constitution in the *Insular Cases* did not require Congress to implement all constitutional guarantees in its territories because of their "wholly dissimilar traditions and institutions," the Constitution does not require United States agents to obtain a warrant when searching the foreign home of a nonresident alien. If the search had occurred in a residence within the United States, I have little doubt that the full protections of the Fourth Amendment would apply. But that is not this case. The absence of local judges or magistrates available to issue warrants, the differing and perhaps unascertainable conceptions of reasonableness and privacy that prevail abroad, and the need to cooperate with foreign officials all indicate that the Fourth Amendment's warrant requirement should not apply in Mexico as it does in this country. For this reason, in addition to the other persuasive justifications stated by the Court, I agree that no violation of the Fourth Amendment has occurred in the case before us. The rights of a citizen, as to whom the United States has continuing obligations, are not presented by this case.

I do not mean to imply, and the Court has not decided, that persons in the position of the respondent have no constitutional protection. The United States is prosecuting a foreign national in a court established under Article III, and all of the trial proceedings are governed by the Constitution. All would agree, for instance, that the dictates of the Due Process Clause of the Fifth Amendment protect the defendant. Indeed, as Justice Harlan put it, "the question of which specific safeguards . . . are appropriately to be applied in a particular context . . . can be reduced to the issue of what process is 'due' a defendant in the particular circumstances of a particular case." *Reid*, 354 U.S., at 75. Nothing approaching a violation of due process has occurred in this case.

Justice STEVENS, concurring in the judgment.

In my opinion aliens who are lawfully present in the United States are among those "people" who are entitled to the protection of the Bill of Rights, including the Fourth Amendment. Respondent is surely such a person even though he was brought and held here against his will. I therefore cannot join the Court's sweeping opinion. I do agree, however, with the Government's submission that the search conducted by the United States agents with the approval and cooperation of the Mexican authorities was not "unreasonable" as that term is used in the first Clause of the Amendment. I do not believe the Warrant Clause has any application to searches of noncitizens' homes in foreign jurisdictions because American magistrates have no power to authorize such searches. I therefore concur in the Court's judgment.

Justice BRENNAN, with whom Justice MARSHALL joins, dissenting. . . .

The Constitution is the source of Congress' authority to criminalize conduct, whether here or abroad, and of the Executive's authority to investigate and prosecute such conduct. But the same Constitution also prescribes limits on our Government's authority to investigate, prosecute, and punish criminal conduct, whether foreign or domestic. As a plurality of the Court noted in Reid v. Covert, 354 U.S. 1, 5-6 (1957): "The United States is entirely a creature of the Constitution. Its power and authority have no other source. It can only act in accordance with all the limitations imposed by the Constitution." See also *ante* (Kennedy, J., concurring) ("[T]he Government may act only as the Constitution authorizes, whether the actions in question are foreign or domestic"). . . . The Court today creates an antilogy: the Constitution authorizes our Government to enforce our criminal laws abroad, but when Government agents exercise this authority, the Fourth Amendment does not travel with them.

This cannot be. At the very least, the Fourth Amendment is an unavoidable correlative of the Government's power to enforce the criminal law.

. . . According to the majority, the term "the people" [within the meaning of the Fourth Amendment] refers to "a class of persons who are part of a national community or who have otherwise developed sufficient connection with this country to be considered part of that community." The Court admits that "the people" extends beyond the citizenry, but leaves the precise contours of its "sufficient connection" test unclear. At one point the majority hints that aliens are protected by the Fourth Amendment only when they come within the United States and develop "substantial connections" with our country. At other junctures, the Court suggests that an alien's presence in the United States must be voluntary and that the alien must have "accepted some societal obligations."[1] At yet other points, the majority implies that respondent would be protected by the Fourth Amendment if the place searched were in the United States.[2]

What the majority ignores, however, is the most obvious connection between Verdugo-Urquidez and the United States: he was investigated and is being prosecuted for violations of United States law and may well spend the rest of his life in a United States prison. The "sufficient connection" is supplied not by Verdugo-Urquidez, but by the Government. Respondent is entitled to the protections of the Fourth Amendment because our Government, by investigating him and attempting to hold him accountable under United States criminal laws, has treated him as a member of our community for purposes of enforcing our laws. He has become, quite literally, one of the governed. Fundamental fairness and the ideals underlying our Bill of Rights compel the conclusion that when we impose "societal obligations," such as the obligation to comply with our criminal laws, on foreign nationals, we in turn are obliged to respect certain correlative rights, among them the Fourth Amendment. . . .

Mutuality is essential to ensure the fundamental fairness that underlies our Bill of Rights. Foreign nationals investigated and prosecuted for alleged violations of United States criminal laws are just as vulnerable to oppressive Government behavior as are United States citizens investigated and prosecuted for the same alleged violations. . . .

Mutuality also serves to inculcate the values of law and order. By respecting the rights of foreign nationals, we encourage other nations to respect the rights of our citizens. Moreover, as our Nation becomes increasingly concerned about the domestic effects of international crime, we cannot forget that the behavior of our law enforcement agents abroad sends a powerful message about the rule of law to

---

1. [Court's footnote 6:] In this discussion, the Court implicitly suggests that the Fourth Amendment may not protect illegal aliens in the United States. Numerous lower courts, however, have held that illegal aliens in the United States are protected by the Fourth Amendment, and not a single lower court has held to the contrary.

2. [Court's footnote 7:] The Fourth Amendment contains no express or implied territorial limitations, and the majority does not hold that the Fourth Amendment is inapplicable to searches outside the United States and its territories. It holds that respondent is not protected by the Fourth Amendment because he is not one of "the people." Indeed, the majority's analysis implies that a foreign national who had "developed sufficient connection with this country to be considered part of [our] community" would be protected by the Fourth Amendment regardless of the location of the search. Certainly nothing in the Court's opinion questions the validity of the rule, accepted by every Court of Appeals to have considered the question, that the Fourth Amendment applies to searches conducted by the United States Government against United States citizens abroad. A warrantless, unreasonable search and seizure is no less a violation of the Fourth Amendment because it occurs in Mexicali, Mexico, rather than Calexico, California.

individuals everywhere. As Justice Brandeis warned in Olmstead v. United States, 277 U.S. 438 (1928):

> If the Government becomes a lawbreaker, it breeds contempt for law; it invites every man to become a law unto himself; it invites anarchy. To declare that in the administration of the criminal law the end justifies the means . . . would bring terrible retribution. Against that pernicious doctrine, this Court should resolutely set its face. Id., at 485 (dissenting opinion).

This principle is no different when the United States applies its rules of conduct to foreign nationals. If we seek respect for law and order, we must observe these principles ourselves. Lawlessness breeds lawlessness.

Finally, when United States agents conduct unreasonable searches, whether at home or abroad, they disregard our Nation's values. For over 200 years, our country has considered itself the world's foremost protector of liberties. . . .

. . . [T]he Framers of the Bill of Rights did not purport to "create" rights. Rather, they designed the Bill of Rights to prohibit our Government from infringing rights and liberties presumed to be pre-existing. The Fourth Amendment, for example, does not create a new right of security against unreasonable searches and seizures. . . . The focus of the Fourth Amendment is on *what* the Government can and cannot do, and *how* it may act, not on *against whom* these actions may be taken. Bestowing rights and delineating protected groups would have been inconsistent with the Drafters' fundamental conception of a Bill of Rights as a limitation on the Government's conduct with respect to all whom it seeks to govern. It is thus extremely unlikely that the Framers intended the narrow construction of the term "the people" presented today by the majority. . . .

The majority's rejection of respondent's claim to Fourth Amendment protection is apparently motivated by its fear that application of the Amendment to law enforcement searches against foreign nationals overseas "could significantly disrupt the ability of the political branches to respond to foreign situations involving our national interest." The majority's doomsday scenario — that American Armed Forces conducting a mission to protect our national security with no law enforcement objective "would have to articulate specific facts giving them probable cause to undertake a search or seizure" — is fanciful. Verdugo-Urquidez is protected by the Fourth Amendment because our Government, by investigating and prosecuting him, has made him one of "the governed." Accepting respondent as one of "the governed," however, hardly requires the Court to accept enemy aliens in wartime as among "the governed" entitled to invoke the protection of the Fourth Amendment. See Johnson v. Eisentrager, supra.

Moreover, with respect to non-law-enforcement activities not directed against enemy aliens in wartime but nevertheless implicating national security, doctrinal exceptions to the general requirements of a warrant and probable cause likely would be applicable more frequently abroad, thus lessening the purported tension between the Fourth Amendment's strictures and the Executive's foreign affairs power. Many situations involving sensitive operations abroad likely would involve exigent circumstances such that the warrant requirement would be excused. Therefore, the Government's conduct would be assessed only under the reasonableness standard, the application of which depends on context. . . .

Because the Fourth Amendment governs the search of respondent's Mexican residences, the District Court properly suppressed the evidence found in that search because the officers conducting the search did not obtain a warrant. I cannot agree with Justice Blackmun and Justice Stevens that the Warrant Clause has no application to searches of noncitizens' homes in foreign jurisdictions because American magistrates lack the power to authorize such searches.[3] The Warrant Clause would serve the same primary functions abroad as it does domestically, and I see no reason to distinguish between foreign and domestic searches.

The primary purpose of the warrant requirement is its assurance of neutrality. As Justice Jackson stated for the Court in Johnson v. United States, 333 U.S. 10, 13-14 (1948):

> The point of the Fourth Amendment, which often is not grasped by zealous officers, is not that it denies law enforcement the support of the usual inferences which reasonable men draw from evidence. Its protection consists in requiring that those inferences be drawn by a neutral and detached magistrate instead of being judged by the officer engaged in the often competitive enterprise of ferreting out crime. . . .

A warrant also defines the scope of a search and limits the discretion of the inspecting officers. These purposes would be served no less in the foreign than in the domestic context.

The Warrant Clause cannot be ignored simply because Congress has not given any United States magistrate authority to issue search warrants for foreign searches. Congress cannot define the contours of the Constitution. If the Warrant Clause applies, Congress cannot excise the Clause from the Constitution by failing to provide a means for United States agents to obtain a warrant.

Nor is the Warrant Clause inapplicable merely because a warrant from a United States magistrate could not "authorize" a search in a foreign country. Although this may be true as a matter of international law, it is irrelevant to our interpretation of the Fourth Amendment. As a matter of United States constitutional law, a warrant serves the same primary function overseas as it does domestically: it assures that a neutral magistrate has authorized the search and limited its scope. The need to protect those suspected of criminal activity from the unbridled discretion of investigating officers is no less important abroad than at home. . . .

Justice BLACKMUN, dissenting.

I cannot accept the Court of Appeals' conclusion, echoed in some portions of Justice Brennan's dissent, that the Fourth Amendment governs every action by an American official that can be characterized as a search or seizure. American agents acting abroad generally do not purport to exercise *sovereign* authority over the foreign nationals with whom they come in contact. The relationship between these agents and foreign nationals is therefore fundamentally different from the relationship between United States officials and individuals residing within this country.

I am inclined to agree with Justice Brennan, however, that when a foreign national is held accountable for purported violations of United States criminal laws, he has effectively been treated as one of "the governed" and therefore is entitled to

---

3. [Court's footnote 13:] Justice Stevens concurs in the judgment because he believes that the search in this case "was not 'unreasonable' as that term is used in the first Clause of the Amendment." I do not understand why Justice Stevens reaches the reasonableness question in the first instance rather than remanding that issue to the Court of Appeals. Justice Kennedy rejects application of the Warrant Clause not because of the identity of the individual seeking protection, but because of the location of the search. *Ante* (concurring opinion) ("[T]he Fourth Amendment's warrant requirement should not apply in Mexico as it does in this country"). Justice Kennedy, however, never explains why the Reasonableness Clause, as opposed to the Warrant Clause, would not apply to searches abroad.

Fourth Amendment protections. Although the Government's exercise of *power* abroad does not ordinarily implicate the Fourth Amendment, the enforcement of domestic criminal law seems to me to be the paradigmatic exercise of sovereignty over those who are compelled to obey. In any event, as Justice Stevens notes, respondent was lawfully (though involuntarily) within this country at the time the search occurred. Under these circumstances I believe that respondent is entitled to invoke protections of the Fourth Amendment. I agree with the Government, however, that an American magistrate's lack of power to authorize a search abroad renders the Warrant Clause inapplicable to the search of a noncitizen's residence outside this country.

The Fourth Amendment nevertheless requires that the search be "reasonable." And when the purpose of a search is the procurement of evidence for a criminal prosecution, we have consistently held that the search, to be reasonable, must be based upon probable cause. Neither the District Court nor the Court of Appeals addressed the issue of probable cause, and I do not believe that a reliable determination could be made on the basis of the record before us. I therefore would vacate the judgment of the Court of Appeals and remand the case for further proceedings.

NOTES AND QUESTIONS

1. The Supreme Court states that the question presented is "whether the Fourth Amendment *applies* to the search and seizure by United States agents of property that is owned by a nonresident alien and located in a foreign country" (emphasis added). Most courts and commentators read *Verdugo-Urquidez* to answer the question with a firm "no." But if one looks more closely at the reasoning employed by the majority as well as the concurring and dissenting opinions, the holding is not as clear-cut as many assume. Indeed, one could make a good argument that five Justices actually believed that the Fourth Amendment *applied* to the search and seizure in this case (that is, that Verdugo-Urquidez *could* claim some Fourth Amendment right) but that it was not *violated* on the merits. To parse the positions of the various members of the Court, one needs to understand how Fourth Amendment questions are analyzed in the general run of cases — that is, to understand the Justices' analysis of whether there was a *violation* under the Fourth Amendment in the case. The order in which the following questions are presented is not invariable; our discussion is organized to lay out the doctrine in a way that will help readers sort out the opinions in *Verdugo-Urquidez.*

A. *Does the Fourth Amendment apply?* The first question is whether the Fourth Amendment applies at all in a given context. The "majority" opinion in *Verdugo-Urquidez* argues that the Fourth Amendment cannot be claimed by a nonresident alien who is not voluntarily residing in the United States and has no substantial connection with the country, where the property searched is overseas.

The question of the applicability of the Fourth Amendment does not arise in the overwhelming majority of cases, which generally deal with the search or seizure of the persons, papers, or effects of U.S. citizens within the borders of the United States. What makes this case different, of course, are (1) the person seeking to claim the benefit of the Fourth Amendment is an alien without substantial and voluntary connections to the United States, and (2) the property searched lies outside the United States. Are both of these conditions necessary to the majority opinion's conclusion? Or is each alone sufficient to warrant that holding? That is, does the Fourth Amendment protect aliens whose persons or property is searched or seized within the United States? Does it protect the persons or property of U.S. nationals when they are outside the United States but are searched or seized by U.S. governmental personnel?

Note that the search of Verdugo-Urquidez's residence may have violated the Mexican Constitution's search and seizure provision. See Eric Bentley, Jr., Toward an International Fourth Amendment: Rethinking Searches and Seizures Abroad After *Verdugo-Urquidez*, 27 Vand. J. Transnatl. L. 329, 351 (1994). Assuming that to be true, if the United States will not apply the Fourth Amendment to foreign officials' searches and seizures, and it will not comply with foreign search and seizure laws, what protection do defendants like Verdugo-Urquidez have? Here, a search "that apparently violated the domestic search-and-seizure standards of both the United States and Mexico was held to neither standard. Essentially, the Court concluded, no law applied." Id. at 352.

Keep in mind that constitutional search and seizure protections are designed to protect the innocent, even though they necessarily are most often claimed by the guilty. The Supreme Court instituted the exclusionary rule as a remedy for unconstitutional searches and seizures because it concluded that where innocent persons are subject to such abuses and no contraband is found, there is no effective remedy and thus no deterrent against future abuses. The exclusionary rule, then, embodies the Supreme Court's belief that it is only by applying the exclusionary rule in cases where rights are violated and contraband *is* found that a deterrent for such abuses is created and the innocent are ultimately protected. In light of this, does it make sense that, where the U.S. seeks to conduct investigative activity abroad against foreign nationals, those foreign nationals are "essentially international outcasts" in terms of search and seizure rights? Id. at 351.

B. *Was this a search by a U.S. government actor?* To find a violation of the guarantees of the Bill of Rights, one must generally demonstrate "state action" — that is, that the constitutional violation was perpetrated by the United States or a U.S. state government, not private actors. "State action," however, is not restricted to actions taken by law enforcement. It applies to any state or federal agents, including, for example, public school officials as well as police officers. Obviously, the majority opinion in *Verdugo-Urquidez* is concerned that, were the Fourth Amendment to apply to extraterritorial searches of non-U.S. nationals' property, it would limit the activities of U.S. soldiers during wartime. If the applicability of Fourth Amendment concepts in wartime is troubling, should the answer be to hold the Fourth Amendment *not applicable,* or to formulate exceptions to the doctrines that control the determination of whether a *violation* has occurred?

The U.S. circuit courts agree that the substantive prohibitions in the Fourth Amendment, as well as the exclusionary rule that is applied to deter future abuses, are *not* applicable to the actions of the foreign law enforcement officers. This rule, often called the international "silver platter" rule, means that evidence collected by foreign officials on their own territory under their own law and turned over to U.S. officials is admissible in U.S. courts, even though it was gathered in a manner that would not have been permissible on U.S. soil.

There are a couple of narrowly drawn exceptions to the international silver platter rule. First, if the circumstances of the foreign search and seizure "shock the conscience," the federal courts may exercise their supervisory authority to exclude the fruits *in federal court.* See, e.g., United States v. Barona, 56 F.3d 1087, 1091 (9th Cir. 1995). (One might also argue that due process provides a basis for excluding such evidence in state trials.) Second, evidence illegally seized by foreign agents may be excluded in U.S. courts where the cooperation between U.S. and foreign law enforcement agencies is designed to evade constitutional requirements applicable to officials. See United States v. Maturo, 982 F.2d 57, 61 (2d Cir. 1992).

Finally, and most importantly, evidence seized by non-U.S. agents may still be excluded if the "[f]ederal agents so substantially participate in the raids so as to convert them into joint ventures between the United States and the foreign officials." Stonehill v. United States, 405 F.2d 738, 743 (9th Cir. 1968). It is very difficult to prevail on this ground: The federal courts engage in a "virtually unanimous" practice of denying claims to this exception. Bentley, supra, 27 Vand. J. Transnatl. L. at 377. For example, the Fifth Circuit holds that the Fourth Amendment is "inapplicable to an action by a foreign sovereign in its own territory in enforcing its own laws, even though officials were present and cooperated in some degree." Birdsell v. United States, 346 F.2d 775, 782 (5th Cir. 1965). Several courts have also ruled that communication between U.S. and foreign officials leading to the seizure of evidence that is subsequently turned over to U.S. authorities is insufficient to convert the search into a joint venture. See, e.g., United States v. Hawkins, 661 F.2d 436, 455-456 (5th Cir. 1981) (DEA's notification of Panamanian authorities regarding suspected crash of plane carrying cocaine insufficient to trigger Fourth Amendment protections); United States v. Heller, 625 F.2d 594, 599-600 (5th Cir. 1980) (tip from U.S. officials to British police regarding defendant insufficient to trigger Fourth Amendment).

Even if a joint venture is found, however, "the law of the foreign country must be consulted at the outset as part of the determination whether or not the search was reasonable." *Barona*, 56 F.3d at 1091. If foreign law was complied with, then the search is considered "reasonable" within the meaning of the Fourth Amendment and the exclusionary rule cannot be invoked in U.S. courts. Even if the foreign law was *not* complied with, however, "the good faith exception to the exclusionary rule becomes part of the analysis." Thus, if the defendant shows that the United States and foreign officials were engaged in a joint venture *and* that a violation of foreign law occurred making the search unreasonable, the evidence may still be admissible if the United States demonstrates that its agents relied in good faith upon the foreign officials' representations that their law was being complied with. *Barona*, 56 F.3d at 1092. Recall the controversy touched upon in Chapter 2 regarding the appropriate place of foreign law in U.S. law. How would the sponsors of H. Res. 568 (reprinted in Chapter 2) react to this use of foreign law to evaluate the constitutional reasonableness of a search or seizure? More important, does this use of foreign law make sense?

Note that this rule applies not only in prosecutions against non-U.S. nationals who have a sufficient connection to the United States to claim the protection of the Fourth Amendment, but also where U.S. citizens' property is searched or seized abroad. For example, in *United States v. Barona*, U.S. and Danish officials conducted a joint investigation of a U.S. citizen in Denmark. The Ninth Circuit held that the evidence seized abroad in this investigation did not have to be excluded unless the search violated Danish law (thus rendering it "unreasonable" under the United States' Fourth Amendment) and U.S. officials did not rely in good faith on Danish assertions that the search comported with foreign law. There has been an explosion in cooperation in international law enforcement, through informal contacts as well as through the agency of bilateral or multinational cooperation agreements. See, e.g., Bentley, supra, 27 Vand. J. Transnatl. L. at 365-370. Given the increasing extent of joint law enforcement investigations, does this stringent test constitute, as Judge Reinhardt argued in dissent, a "substantial step toward the elimination of what was once a firmly established constitutional right, the right of American citizens to be free from unreasonable searches and seizures conducted by their own government"? *Barona*, 56 F.3d at 1099 (Reinhardt, J., dissenting).

C. *Was this a "search" or "seizure" within the meaning of the Fourth Amendment?* What constitutes a "search" or "seizure" within the meaning of the Fourth Amendment cannot be determined by reference to the dictionary definition of those terms. A Fourth Amendment *seizure* takes place with respect to *property* when the governmental action interferes with the suspect's property or possessory interests in a meaningful way. See, e.g., United States v. Karo, 468 U.S. 705, 712 (1984). With respect to *seizures* of *persons*, "[i]t is quite plain that the Fourth Amendment governs 'seizures' of the person which do not eventuate in a trip to the station house and prosecution for crime, 'arrests' in traditional terminology. It must be recognized that whenever a police officer accosts an individual and restrains his freedom to walk away, he has 'seized' that person." Terry v. Ohio, 392 U.S. 1, 16 (1968).

At one time, the concept of a Fourth Amendment *search* was defined largely by reference to property rights. Thus, for example, were the police to put a wiretap on a telephone line *outside* a suspect's home, that was *not* deemed to be a search for constitutional purposes because the official action did not constitute a trespass on the suspect's property. In 1967, however, in response to developments in surveillance technology, the U.S. Supreme Court revolutionized the concept of Fourth Amendment searches by adopting a test that relies principally on *privacy*, not *property*. See Katz v. United States, 389 U.S. 347 (1967). In *Katz*, the Court found that federal agents had conducted an unconstitutional search when they attached an electronic listening device to the *outside* of a *public* telephone booth from which the defendant was conducting his bookie operations. The definition of a Fourth Amendment search that flowed from *Katz* has two components: (1) the government action must invade a defendant's subjective expectation of privacy, and (2) that expectation of privacy must be one that society is willing to accept as reasonable. (This formula also determines whether the defendant has the standing to claim that his rights were violated and thus claim the exclusionary remedy. See Rakas v. Illinois, 439 U.S. 128 (1978).)

Privacy interests arise in response to legal entitlements and societal expectations and customs. See, e.g., Minnesota v. Olson, 495 U.S. 91 (1990). If the Fourth Amendment applies extraterritorially, in respect to U.S. citizens or other persons with substantial and voluntary connections to the United States, *by whose privacy expectations is the search definition to be governed?* U.S. notions of privacy may be both over- and under-inclusive when measured by the mores of other societies. If courts are charged with determining whether given U.S. governmental conduct abroad constitutes a search, should it look to the understandings prevailing in the foreign society? What are the difficulties with this approach?

D. *Does the Warrant Clause apply or does an exception exist in this context?* Once all the preliminaries are satisfied — that is, the Fourth Amendment applies, the action challenged was undertaken by U.S. state or federal agents, and the activity involved is a Fourth Amendment search or seizure — the fundamental question left to be resolved is whether the Fourth Amendment was *violated*.

The Fourth Amendment is composed of two clauses, the Reasonableness Clause ("The right of the people to be secure in their persons, houses, papers, and effects, against unreasonable searches and seizures, shall not be violated") and the Warrant Clause ("and no Warrants shall issue, but upon probable cause, supported by Oath or affirmation, and particularly describing the place to be searched, and the persons or things to be seized"). The two clauses are read separately. That is, the reasonableness of a search or seizure does not necessarily depend on the existence of a valid warrant.

Accordingly, when analyzing a Fourth Amendment question, one generally first asks whether a warrant was required. If the Warrant Clause applies, the text of the Amendment itself requires (a) probable cause, (b) supported by oath or affirmation, and (c) a particular description of the person to be arrested or the place to be searched and the items therein to be seized. The Supreme Court generally says that exceptions to the warrant "requirement" are few and far between, but actually the reverse is true: Except in the context of a home search or arrest in a home, a warrant is generally *not* required. The Court has achieved this result by creating very broad exceptions to the warrant requirement in different contexts, for example, in vehicle searches, public arrests, and the like. These exceptions are generally based on (1) the lesser expectations of privacy the public can claim in given places, (2) historical practice, and/or (3) practical problems or exigencies.

In its decision in In re Terrorist Bombings of U.S. Embassies in East Africa (Fourth Amendment Challenges), 552 F.3d 157 (2d Cir. 2008), the Second Circuit recently decided, as a matter of first impression, that "the Fourth Amendment's Warrant Clause has no extraterritorial application and that foreign searches of U.S. citizens conducted by U.S. agents are subject only to the Fourth Amendment's requirement of reasonableness." Id. at 171. In so doing, the court relied heavily on the various Justices' *Verdugo-Urquidez* opinions. Should the question be resolved differently when the target is a U.S. citizen, as in the bombings case, as opposed to a foreign national with no substantial connection with the United States, as in *Verdugo-Urquidez*?

E. *Is the search or seizure reasonable?* If a warrant is *not* required under the Warrant Clause, that is not the end of the inquiry. One must then turn to the Reasonableness Clause to determine whether the search or seizure is constitutionally reasonable. (Even if a warrant *is* required, one must still examine the reasonableness of official conduct in some cases because the *execution* of warrants must also be reasonable.)

As the Second Circuit recently explained in holding the search of a U.S. citizen's home and telephone records overseas reasonable for Fourth Amendment purposes, "[t]o determine whether a search is reasonable under the Fourth Amendment, we examine the 'totality of the circumstances' to balance 'on the one hand, the degree to which it intrudes upon an individual's privacy and, on the other, the degree to which it is needed for the promotion of legitimate governmental interests.'" Id. at 172 (quoting Samson v. California, 547 U.S. 843, 848 (2006)). Generally (but certainly not invariably, especially in the context of administrative searches), the reasonableness inquiry means that some level of individualized suspicion (for example, probable cause or reasonable suspicion) is required and that the scope, nature, and duration of a search or seizure is limited to that which is reasonable.

F. *Application.* In *Verdugo-Urquidez*, it was clear that U.S. agents initiated and were involved in a qualifying Fourth Amendment search and that no valid warrant was secured prior to the search. Accordingly, the analysis here would proceed as follows: (1) Does the Fourth Amendment *apply* in this situation? (2) If it does apply, was the Fourth Amendment *violated*, that is, was a warrant required, and, if not, was this search reasonable?

On what ground does the Chief Justice resolve the case? What about Justice Kennedy, the crucial fifth vote? Does he claim that the Fourth Amendment does *not* apply here? Note that he consistently states that "*no violation* of the Fourth Amendment occurred" (emphasis added). He also takes pains to disagree with the majority opinion's discussion of the scope of the word "people" in the Fourth Amendment and he says that the government "may act only as the Constitution authorizes, whether the actions in question are foreign or domestic." Finally, he, unlike others who joined the Chief Justice's opinion, felt it necessary to discuss why he thought that "the Constitution does not require United States agents to obtain a warrant when searching a foreign home of a nonresident alien." Given this, doesn't Justice Kennedy in fact "depart in fundamental respects from the opinion of the Court"? How could he join it?

What about Justice Stevens, who concurs in the judgment? He argues that aliens who are "lawfully" even if involuntarily present in the United States, are "people" protected by the Fourth Amendment. Justice Stevens, then, would appear to believe that the Fourth Amendment could be claimed by Verdugo-Urquidez. Why was it not "violated" in his mind? One could argue that Justices Stevens and Kennedy agree that the Fourth Amendment does apply and that the warrant requirement does not. Why are they not writing together? Why does Kennedy join the opinion and Stevens does not? How about Justices Brennan and Marshall? Finally, where does Justice Blackmun come out? Counting heads, could one argue that a majority of the Justices believed that the Fourth Amendment *does apply* in these circumstances, but that it was not *violated*?

Given this analysis, what are the implications of this decision for other cases involving (i) searches or seizures within the United States of (legal or illegal) aliens' property? (ii) searches or seizures abroad of aliens' property when the (legal or illegal) aliens reside in the United States or have other voluntary and substantial connections with the United States? (iii) searches or seizures abroad of U.S. citizens' property or persons?

2. Perhaps more important than a head count in predicting how these questions will be answered is the conceptual basis on which the various opinions justify the applicability or nonapplicability of the Fourth Amendment. That is, who can claim the benefits of the Fourth Amendment and under what circumstances? It would seem that there could be a number of ways one could determine the applicability of the Fourth Amendment:

A. *Territorial.* Consistent with traditional notions of sovereignty that prevailed at the time of the framing, one could argue that the Constitution should apply only within the territorial bounds of the United States. Indeed, although the majority opinion does not stress this fact in discussing the *Insular Cases*, those seeking application of the U.S. Constitution in some of the *Insular Cases* were U.S. citizens — but the Supreme Court denied them the protection of the U.S. Constitution even when their cases were tried in territories over which the U.S. had sovereign control. See, e.g., David J. Bederman, Extraterritorial Domicile and the Constitution, 28 Va. J. Intl. L. 451, 473 (1987-1988) (under the *Insular Cases*, "the rule became that Americans in unincorporated territories were entitled only to fundamental rights; those residing elsewhere out of the United States received no protections at all"). Wouldn't a territorial approach be the cleanest way to decide this case? Does strict reference to territory make sense today? The Court did not even seem to consider this approach (nor did the government apparently push it). Why?

B. *Nationality.* Is the *Verdugo-Urquidez* majority saying that aliens (outside and perhaps inside the United States) may not claim the benefit of the Fourth Amendment? What portions of the majority opinion are susceptible to such a reading? Prior to *Verdugo-Urquidez*, it was not contested that the Fourth Amendment applied to all persons within the borders of the United States when the searches were conducted by U.S. authorities on U.S. territory. Since the Supreme Court's decision, however, a number of courts have questioned whether undocumented aliens who were found on U.S. territory and whose property was searched by U.S. authorities in the United States could claim Fourth Amendment protection. See, e.g., Torres v. Texas, 818 S.W.2d 141, 143-144 n.1 (Tex. App. 1991) ("We do not believe that the protection of the Fourth Amendment to the United States Constitution nor Article I, Section 9 of the Texas Constitution apply to . . . illegal aliens, unless they have developed sufficient connection with this country to be considered a part of the community."). What parts of even the majority opinion argue *against* the view that only U.S. citizens have a sufficient "juridical" relation to the U.S. government and Constitution to claim the benefit of the Bill of Rights? What Supreme Court precedents may foreclose a determination that rests solely on nationality?

C. *"Natural rights" (or "universalism") theory.* One could argue that the Constitution is a document intended to constitute and bind a sovereign, the federal government, wherever it may act. This view of the Constitution focuses on the identity of the alleged infringer of the right, rather than the relationship of the victim to the infringer. Under this theory, then, the emphasis is not on *where* the search occurred (territoriality) or the *connection* (or lack thereof) between the defendant and the United States (nationality/community). Rather, this conception sees the Constitution as a pact designed to restrain governmental action and power in order to protect the preexisting "natural" or "inalienable" rights of those subject to its powers, *not* a document that "grants" rights to certain persons in certain locations. What are the problems with this approach? See, e.g., Gerald L. Neuman, Whose Constitution?, 100 Yale L.J. 909, 916-917 (1990-1991); Note, The Extraterritorial Applicability of the Fourth Amendment, 102 Harv. L. Rev. 1672, 1676 (1989). Which Justices in *Verdugo-Urquidez*, if any, seem to adopt this view? On what authority?

D. *"Membership" or "social compact" model.* The Supreme Court's majority opinion in *Verdugo-Urquidez* seems to rest on the proposition that only U.S. citizens or aliens who have a voluntary and significant connection or attachment to the United States can claim the protections of the Fourth Amendment, at least where the search or seizure occurs overseas. The Chief Justice's opinion makes reference to the dissenting opinion in the Ninth Circuit below, authored by Judge Wallace, and in particular his theory that the Constitution's reach ought to be determined by reference to a "social compact" theory. In his *Verdugo-Urquidez* dissent below, Judge Wallace argued:

> My conclusion that the fourth amendment protects only the people of the United States is supported by an examination of our constitutional history, which indicates that the Constitution was conceived as a "compact" or "social contract" among the people of the United States. In our pre-constitutional era, the "compact" or "social contract" concept of government pervaded American political philosophy, both in theory and in practice. . . .
>
> Prevalent during the period leading to the American Revolution was the recurrent notion that a government was created by a compact among those governed and that the government could not infringe certain rights of those empowering it. John Locke, one of the most influential political philosophers of the time, conceived of government as a social compact in which formerly free individuals voluntarily united to establish communities. In order to protect what he considered to be a person's most essential liberties, Locke believed it was necessary that each person surrender some part of his or her natural independence. Of particular relevance to the revolutionary sentiment that was mounting at the time was Locke's vision of revolution as an act that undid all existing political compacts, thereby leaving the people free to enter willingly into a new political compact. . . .
>
> Examining the Constitutional Convention against this background, it is not surprising that when the Framers set about the task of drafting the Constitution of the United States, they conceived of it as a "compact" or "social contract." Moreover, implicit in their understanding that the Constitution would be a compact was the realization that correlative rights and obligations would govern relations between the people and their newly-created national government. In return for certain guarantees restricting the scope of government, the people of the states ceded to a central authority limited powers of government. . . . [I]t appears that the Framers understood that the social compact embodied in the Constitution necessarily required that the people give up some degree of liberty in order for them to secure others in return.

Because the social compact theory of the Constitution contemplates that each individual will give up a share of liberty to preserve the rest, I believe that . . . the compact theory is [not] undermined by the presence of the theory which emphasizes the "natural rights" of men. Viewing the compact and natural rights paradigms as mutually exclusive misperceives the interrelationship between these two. . . . While the Framers may have understood the liberties enumerated in the Bill of Rights to reflect man's "natural rights," they also recognized that the Constitution embodies a compact among the People of the United States to sacrifice some modicum of these "natural rights" in order to create a central government capable of preserving the rest. Thus, rather than coexisting in tension with the compact theory, the "natural rights" theory fits comfortably into its central tenet.

A number of fundamental axioms can be deduced from the Constitution's regime of reciprocal rights and obligations. Chief among these is that one can make no claim of entitlement to rights without also assuming corresponding obligations. No one can seriously doubt that the compact applies only to the people who empowered the government of the United States for the benefit of themselves and their posterity, not to other peoples of the world who neither ceded authority to it in exchange for certain guarantees of liberty nor otherwise consented to its rule.

These axioms find support in an unbroken line of Supreme Court cases reflecting the understanding of the Constitution as a compact between the people of the United States and its government. . . .

United States v. Verdugo-Urquidez, 856 F.2d 1214, 1231-1233 (9th Cir. 1988) (Wallace, J., dissenting).

The *Verdugo-Urquidez* Ninth Circuit majority opinion rejected Judge Wallace's approach, relying on historical records explaining that the Constitution's primary role was to protect the "natural" or "inalienable" rights of man against encroachment by the government, wherever it might act. The Ninth Circuit also argued that Justice Story, in his Commentaries on the Constitution of the United States, cast "considerable doubt on the validity of the compact theory":

> . . . For instance, Justice Story found it peculiar to think of the Constitution as a contract because constitutions "are not only not founded upon the assent of all the people within the territorial jurisdiction, but that assent is expressly excluded by . . . [restricting] ratification . . . to those, who are qualified voters." Thus the Constitution may not be treated as a contract because it purports to bind those who did not assent to it, were not permitted to assent to it and, as well, those born after its ratification. Justice Story concluded that if the Constitution protects all "The People" of the United States, as it surely does, the protection it gives them cannot derive solely from a contract theory.
>
> It would, indeed, be an extraordinary use of language to consider a declaration of rights in a constitution, and especially of rights, which it proclaims to be "unalienable and indefeasible," to be a matter of *contract*, and resting on such a basis, rather than a solemn recognition and admission of those rights, arising from the law of nature, and the gift of Providence, and incapable of being transferred or surrendered.

Id. at 1220. The Ninth Circuit majority contended that *all* of the "unbroken" line of cases cited by Judge Wallace to support the "Constitution as compact" theory involved some conflict between the state and federal governments; the "social compact" theory was used in those cases to explain that in ratifying the Constitution, the states surrendered some of their authority to the federal government. Finally, the majority below pointed out that the Supreme Court "has extended significant constitutional protections to aliens within the United States, without distinguishing between those who are here legally or illegally, or between residents and visitors.

From these cases, we learn that aliens within the United States enjoy the benefits of the first, fifth, sixth and fourteenth amendments." Id. at 1222. The majority below argued that these precedents, benefitting illegal aliens within U.S. territory, cannot be squared with the "social compact" theory. Who has the better of this argument?

Does Justice Kennedy agree with this theory? What of Justice Stevens's emphasis on the fact that the defendant was within the territory of the United States, regardless of where the objectionable search took place? Is he arguing that this creates a "contractual" relationship? What of Justices Brennan, Marshall, and Blackmun? These three Justices make policy arguments for why their proposed ruling would make sense (for example, it would inculcate the values of law and order, it adheres to our Nation's values, and so on). But what constitutional theory supports their view? Are they arguing that a contract was essentially foisted on the defendant by the U.S. government's election to enforce its laws abroad?

E. *"Global due process" or balancing approach.* Another approach recognizes that the Constitution binds the government abroad as well as at home but takes on one of the difficulties of a universalist or natural rights approach: its lack of limits. Surely, critics argue, every person on the planet may not claim the protections of the Bill of Rights against actions by the U.S. government. The global due process model, then, takes a little from both the natural rights and the social compact theories. The basic assumption is that the U.S. government must abide by the restrictions imposed on it in its charter, but some consideration is given to the fact that because aliens outside the United States have few obligations under U.S. law, they also have a lesser claim to the rights embodied in U.S. municipal law. See, e.g., Neuman, supra, 100 Yale L.J. at 919-920. The nature of an alien's claim thus depends to some extent on the reciprocity of obligation and protection, as well as the perceived importance of the right involved. The concurrences of Justices Frankfurter and Harlan in *Reid v. Covert* offer an example of this approach. Does Justice Kennedy adopt this conception of the operation of the U.S. Constitution? What are the difficulties, both theoretical and practical, with this approach? Could one argue that Justice Brennan's emphasis on reciprocity means that he ultimately relies on this theory, rather than on the universalism or social contract theories?

3. Given that both the majority opinion and Justice Brennan's dissent touch on the practical and policy implications of the Court's ruling, it may be appropriate to examine how workable the majority opinion is. Justice Brennan points out the inconsistencies in the majority opinion's statements regarding just who can claim membership in the social compact. The majority opinion's ambiguity has spawned uncertainty in the lower courts. See Douglas I. Koff, Note, Post-*Verdugo-Urquidez*: The Sufficient Connection Test — Substantially Ambiguous, Substantially Unworkable, 25 Colum. Hum. Rts. L. Rev. 435, 484-485 (1993-1994) (examining the majority opinion and cases attempting to apply *Verdugo-Urquidez*'s "substantial and voluntary" connection test and concluding that the test is confusing and difficult to apply consistently). If the courts faced with the question *ex post* are confused, how can army personnel on the ground be expected to determine *ex ante* what connections a suspect has with the United States and whether those connections are sufficient to require that U.S. agents adhere to Fourth Amendment standards? Would it have made more sense for the Court to have ruled that the Fourth Amendment applies only within the United States or may be claimed only by U.S. citizens abroad? Or should the Court have found the Fourth Amendment applicable but come up with some blanket national security exception to the warrant requirement and some per se reasonableness rule in times of war?

Where the military searches or seizes non-U.S. nationals abroad, it may well be that the evidence secured or the person seized will never see the inside of a U.S. courtroom. But the issue of whether aliens abroad may claim the protection of the Bill of Rights has arisen in the context of suits for money damages as well as in criminal prosecutions. Can the majority's blanket rule that persons such as Verdugo-Urquidez have no Fourth Amendment claims be explained as the most effective means to avoid a deluge of damages suits, particularly in times of war? Should the prospect of damages liability be a consideration in the Court's determination of the scope of the Fourth Amendment?

4. Is *Verdugo-Urquidez* ultimately a separation of powers case? Is this again an instance where the Court is implicitly if not explicitly deferring to the executive and legislative powers over foreign affairs? Why is the articulated rule of the Court responsive to this concern?

B.   CONSTITUTIONAL HABEAS WRIT AND SUSPENSION CLAUSE

Application of the U.S. Constitution to non-U.S. persons or in non-U.S. territory raises (at least) three questions: (1) Is there a substantive constitutional right prohibiting the governmental conduct alleged to have been inflicted on the persons seeking relief? (2) Can the persons seeking relief claim the benefits of that "right" under the U.S. Constitution? (3) Have the persons seeking relief pursued the appropriate legal means for relief? (That is, for example, are they entitled to pursue a habeas remedy? Could they seek civil damages for violation of their rights?) Our discussion in Part A focuses on the first two questions because, as was suggested in the notes that followed the *Verdugo-Urquidez* case, understanding Justice Kennedy's opinion requires an understanding of the distinction between saying that there was no constitutional violation and saying that the defendant had no rights to violate. In the Supreme Court's latest effort to determine the scope of constitutional guarantees, reproduced in heavily redacted part below, the second and third questions are inextricably intertwined because the appropriate legal means for relief (the habeas writ) is also the constitutional right claimed by non-U.S. persons held outside the territory over which the United States is legally sovereign.

BOUMEDIENE v. BUSH
128 S. Ct. 2229 (2008)

Justice KENNEDY delivered the opinion of the Court.

Petitioners are aliens designated as enemy combatants and detained at the United States Naval Station at Guantanamo Bay, Cuba. There are others detained there, also aliens, who are not parties to this suit.

Petitioners present a question not resolved by our earlier cases relating to the detention of aliens at Guantanamo: whether they have the constitutional privilege of habeas corpus, a privilege not to be withdrawn except in conformance with the Suspension Clause, Art. I, §9, cl. 2. We hold these petitioners do have the habeas corpus privilege. Congress has enacted a statute, the Detainee Treatment Act of 2005

(DTA), 119 Stat. 2739, that provides certain procedures for review of the detainees' status. We hold that those procedures are not an adequate and effective substitute for habeas corpus. Therefore §7 of the Military Commissions Act of 2006 (MCA), 28 U.S.C.A. §2241(e) (Supp. 2007), operates as an unconstitutional suspension of the writ. We do not address whether the President has authority to detain these petitioners nor do we hold that the writ must issue. These and other questions regarding the legality of the detention are to be resolved in the first instance by the District Court. . . .

III

In deciding the constitutional questions now presented we must determine whether petitioners are barred from seeking the writ or invoking the protections of the Suspension Clause either because of their status, i.e., petitioners' designation by the Executive Branch as enemy combatants, or their physical location, i.e., their presence at Guantanamo Bay. The Government contends that noncitizens designated as enemy combatants and detained in territory located outside our Nation's borders have no constitutional rights and no privilege of habeas corpus. Petitioners contend they do have cognizable constitutional rights and that Congress, in seeking to eliminate recourse to habeas corpus as a means to assert those rights, acted in violation of the Suspension Clause.

We begin with a brief account of the history and origins of the writ. Our account proceeds from two propositions. First, protection for the privilege of habeas corpus was one of the few safeguards of liberty specified in a Constitution that, at the outset, had no Bill of Rights. In the system conceived by the Framers the writ had a centrality that must inform proper interpretation of the Suspension Clause. Second, to the extent there were settled precedents or legal commentaries in 1789 regarding the extraterritorial scope of the writ or its application to enemy aliens, those authorities can be instructive for the present cases.

A

The Framers viewed freedom from unlawful restraint as a fundamental precept of liberty, and they understood the writ of habeas corpus as a vital instrument to secure that freedom. Experience taught, however, that the common-law writ all too often had been insufficient to guard against the abuse of monarchial power. That history counseled the necessity for specific language in the Constitution to secure the writ and ensure its place in our legal system. . . .

Th[e] history [of the habeas writ in England] was known to the Framers. It no doubt confirmed their view that pendular swings to and away from individual liberty were endemic to undivided, uncontrolled power. The Framers' inherent distrust of governmental power was the driving force behind the constitutional plan that allocated powers among three independent branches. This design serves not only to make Government accountable but also to secure individual liberty. Because the Constitution's separation-of-powers structure, like the substantive guarantees of the Fifth and Fourteenth Amendments, see Yick Wo v. Hopkins, 118 U.S. 356, 374 (1886), protects persons as well as citizens, foreign nationals who have the privilege of litigating in our courts can seek to enforce separation-of-powers principles.

That the Framers considered the writ a vital instrument for the protection of individual liberty is evident from the care taken to specify the limited grounds for its suspension: "The Privilege of the Writ of Habeas Corpus shall not be suspended, unless when in Cases of Rebellion or Invasion the public Safety may require it." Art. I, §9, cl. 2. . . . Surviving accounts of the ratification debates provide additional evidence that the Framers deemed the writ to be an essential mechanism in the separation-of-powers scheme. . . .

In our . . . system the Suspension Clause is designed to protect against . . . cyclical abuses. The Clause protects the rights of the detained by a means consistent with the essential design of the Constitution. It ensures that, except during periods of formal suspension, the Judiciary will have a time-tested device, the writ, to maintain the "delicate balance of governance" that is itself the surest safeguard of liberty. The Clause protects the rights of the detained by affirming the duty and authority of the Judiciary to call the jailer to account. The separation-of-powers doctrine, and the history that influenced its design, therefore must inform the reach and purpose of the Suspension Clause.

B

The broad historical narrative of the writ and its function is central to our analysis, but we seek guidance as well from founding-era authorities addressing the specific question before us: whether foreign nationals, apprehended and detained in distant countries during a time of serious threats to our Nation's security, may assert the privilege of the writ and seek its protection. . . . [The Court concludes that neither side has been able to find on-point precedents relating to the common law writ as it existed in 1789 and declines to infer that such a lack of precedent advantages either side.]

IV

Drawing from its position that at common law the writ ran only to territories over which the Crown was sovereign, the Government says the Suspension Clause affords petitioners no rights because the United States does not claim sovereignty over the place of detention. . . .

We . . . do not question the Government's position that Cuba, not the United States, maintains sovereignty, in the legal and technical sense of the term, over Guantanamo Bay. But this does not end the analysis. Our cases do not hold it is improper for us to inquire into the objective degree of control the Nation asserts over foreign territory. As commentators have noted, "'[s]overeignty' is a term used in many senses and is much abused." See 1 Restatement (Third) of Foreign Relations Law of the United States §206, Comment b, p. 94 (1986). . . . Indeed, it is not altogether uncommon for a territory to be under the de jure sovereignty of one nation, while under the plenary control, or practical sovereignty, of another. This condition can occur when the territory is seized during war, as Guantanamo was during the Spanish-American War. Accordingly, for purposes of our analysis, we accept the Government's position that Cuba, and not the United States, retains de jure sovereignty over Guantanamo Bay. As we did in [Rasul v. Bush, 542 U.S. 466 (2004)], however, we take notice of the obvious and uncontested fact that the United States, by virtue of its complete jurisdiction and control over the base, maintains de facto sovereignty over this territory.

. . . For the reasons indicated above, the history of common-law habeas corpus provides scant support for th[e] proposition [that de jure sovereignty is the touchstone of habeas corpus jurisdiction]; and, for the reasons indicated below, that position would be inconsistent with our precedents and contrary to fundamental separation-of-powers principles.

A

The Court has discussed the issue of the Constitution's extraterritorial application on many occasions. These decisions undermine the Government's argument that, at least as applied to noncitizens, the Constitution necessarily stops where de jure sovereignty ends.

The Framers foresaw that the United States would expand and acquire new territories. Article IV, §3, cl. 1, grants Congress the power to admit new States. Clause 2 of the same section grants Congress the "Power to dispose of and make all needful Rules and Regulations respecting the Territory or other Property belonging to the United States." Save for a few notable (and notorious) exceptions, e.g., Dred Scott v. Sandford, 19 How. 393, 15 L. Ed. 691 (1857), throughout most of our history there was little need to explore the outer boundaries of the Constitution's geographic reach. When Congress exercised its power to create new territories, it guaranteed constitutional protections to the inhabitants by statute. In particular, there was no need to test the limits of the Suspension Clause because, as early as 1789, Congress extended the writ to the Territories.

Fundamental questions regarding the Constitution's geographic scope first arose at the dawn of the 20th century when the Nation acquired noncontiguous Territories: Puerto Rico, Guam, and the Philippines — ceded to the United States by Spain at the conclusion of the Spanish-American War — and Hawaii — annexed by the United States in 1898. At this point Congress chose to discontinue its previous practice of extending constitutional rights to the territories by statute.

In a series of opinions later known as the *Insular Cases*, the Court addressed whether the Constitution, by its own force, applies in any territory that is not a State. The Court held that the Constitution has independent force in these territories, a force not contingent upon acts of legislative grace. Yet it took note of the difficulties inherent in that position.

Prior to their cession to the United States, the former Spanish colonies operated under a civil-law system, without experience in the various aspects of the Anglo-American legal tradition, for instance the use of grand and petit juries. At least with regard to the Philippines, a complete transformation of the prevailing legal culture would have been not only disruptive but also unnecessary, as the United States intended to grant independence to that Territory. The Court thus was reluctant to risk the uncertainty and instability that could result from a rule that displaced altogether the existing legal systems in these newly acquired Territories.

These considerations resulted in the doctrine of territorial incorporation, under which the Constitution applies in full in incorporated Territories surely destined for statehood but only in part in unincorporated Territories. As the Court later made clear, "the real issue in the *Insular Cases* was not whether the Constitution extended to the Philippines or Porto Rico when we went there, but which of its provisions were applicable by way of limitation upon the exercise of executive and legislative power in dealing with new conditions and requirements." It may well be that over time the ties between the United States and any of its unincorporated Territories strengthen in ways that are of constitutional significance. But, as early as . . . 1922, the Court took for granted that even in unincorporated Territories the Government of the United States was bound to provide to noncitizen inhabitants "guaranties of certain fundamental personal rights declared in the Constitution." Yet noting the inherent practical difficulties of enforcing all constitutional provisions "always and everywhere," the Court devised in the *Insular Cases* a doctrine that allowed it to use its power sparingly and where it would be most needed. This century-old doctrine informs our analysis in the present matter.

Practical considerations likewise influenced the Court's analysis a half-century later in *Reid*, 354 U.S. 1. The petitioners there, spouses of American servicemen, lived on American military bases in England and Japan. They were charged with crimes committed in those countries and tried before military courts, consistent with executive agreements the United States had entered into with the British and Japanese governments. Because the petitioners were not themselves military personnel, they argued they were entitled to trial by jury.

Justice Black, writing for the plurality, contrasted the cases before him with the *Insular Cases*, which involved territories "with wholly dissimilar traditions and institutions" that Congress intended to govern only "temporarily." Justice Frankfurter[, in his opinion concurring in the result,] argued that the "specific circumstances of each particular case" are relevant in determining the geographic scope of the Constitution. And Justice Harlan[, also concurring in the result,] . . . was most explicit in rejecting a "rigid and abstract rule" for determining where constitutional guarantees extend. He read the *Insular Cases* to teach that whether a constitutional provision has extraterritorial effect depends upon the "particular circumstances, the practical necessities, and the possible alternatives which Congress had before it" and, in particular, whether judicial enforcement of the provision would be "impracticable and anomalous."

That the petitioners in *Reid* were American citizens was a key factor in the case and was central to the plurality's conclusion that the Fifth and Sixth Amendments apply to American civilians tried outside the United States. But practical considerations, related not to the petitioners' citizenship but to the place of their confinement and trial, were relevant to each Member of the *Reid* majority. And to Justices Harlan and Frankfurter (whose votes were necessary to the Court's disposition) these considerations were the decisive factors in the case.

Indeed the majority splintered on this very point. The key disagreement between the plurality and the concurring Justices in *Reid* was over the continued precedential value of the Court's previous opinion in In re Ross, 140 U.S. 453 (1891), which the *Reid* Court understood as holding that under some circumstances Americans abroad have no right to indictment and trial by jury. The petitioner in *Ross* was a sailor serving on an American merchant vessel in Japanese waters who was tried before an American consular tribunal for the murder of a fellow crewman. The *Ross* Court held that the petitioner, who was a British subject, had no rights under the Fifth and Sixth Amendments. The petitioner's citizenship played no role in the disposition of the case, however. The Court assumed (consistent with the maritime custom of the time) that Ross had all the rights of a similarly situated American citizen. Id., at 479 (noting that Ross was "under the protection and subject to the laws of the United States equally with the seaman who was native born"). The Justices in *Reid* therefore properly understood *Ross* as standing for the proposition that, at least in some circumstances, the jury provisions of the Fifth and Sixth Amendments have no application to American citizens tried by American authorities abroad.

The *Reid* plurality doubted that *Ross* was rightly decided, precisely because it believed the opinion was insufficiently protective of the rights of American citizens. But Justices Harlan and Frankfurter, while willing to hold that the American citizen petitioners in the cases before them were entitled to the protections of Fifth and Sixth Amendments, were unwilling to overturn *Ross*. Instead, the two concurring Justices distinguished *Ross* from the cases before them, not on the basis of the citizenship of the petitioners, but on practical considerations that made jury trial a more feasible option for them than it was for the petitioner in *Ross*. If citizenship had been the only relevant factor in the case, it would have been necessary for the Court to overturn *Ross*, something Justices Harlan and Frankfurter were unwilling to do.

Practical considerations weighed heavily as well in Johnson v. Eisentrager, 339 U.S. 763 (1950), where the Court addressed whether habeas corpus jurisdiction extended to enemy aliens who had been convicted of violating the laws of war. The prisoners were detained at Landsberg Prison in Germany during the Allied Powers' postwar occupation. The Court stressed the difficulties of ordering the Government to produce the prisoners in a habeas corpus proceeding. It "would require allocation of shipping space, guarding personnel, billeting and rations" and would damage the prestige of military commanders at a sensitive time. In considering these factors the Court sought to balance the constraints of military occupation with constitutional necessities.

True, the Court in *Eisentrager* denied access to the writ, and it noted the prisoners "at no relevant time were within any territory over which the United States is sovereign, and [that] the scenes of their offense, their capture, their trial and their punishment were all beyond the territorial jurisdiction of any court of the United States." The Government seizes upon this language as proof positive that the *Eisentrager* Court adopted a formalistic, sovereignty-based test for determining the reach of the Suspension Clause. We reject this reading for three reasons.

First, we do not accept the idea that the above-quoted passage from *Eisentrager* is the only authoritative language in the opinion and that all the rest is dicta. The Court's further determinations, based on practical considerations, were integral to . . . its opinion and came before the decision announced its holding.

Second, because the United States lacked both de jure sovereignty and plenary control over Landsberg Prison, it is far from clear that the *Eisentrager* Court used the term *sovereignty* only in the narrow technical sense and not to connote the degree of control the military asserted over the facility. The Justices who decided *Eisentrager* would have understood sovereignty as a multifaceted concept. In its principal brief in *Eisentrager*, the Government advocated a bright-line test for determining the scope of the writ, similar to the one it advocates in these cases. Yet the Court mentioned the concept of territorial sovereignty only twice in its opinion. That the Court devoted a significant portion of [its opinion] . . . to a discussion of practical barriers to the running of the writ suggests that the Court was not concerned exclusively with the formal legal status of Landsberg Prison but also with the objective degree of control the United States asserted over it. Even if we assume the *Eisentrager* Court considered the United States' lack of formal legal sovereignty over Landsberg Prison as the decisive factor in that case, its holding is not inconsistent with a functional approach to questions of extraterritoriality. The formal legal status of a given territory affects, at least to some extent, the political branches' control over that territory. De jure sovereignty is a factor that bears upon which constitutional guarantees apply there.

Third, if the Government's reading of *Eisentrager* were correct, the opinion would have marked not only a change in, but a complete repudiation of, the *Insular Cases*' (and later *Reid*'s) functional approach to questions of extraterritoriality. We cannot accept the Government's view. Nothing in *Eisentrager* says that de jure sovereignty is or has ever been the only relevant consideration in determining the geographic reach of the Constitution or of habeas corpus. Were that the case, there would be considerable tension between *Eisentrager*, on the one hand, and the *Insular Cases* and *Reid*, on the other. Our cases need not be read to conflict in this manner. A constricted reading of *Eisentrager* overlooks what we see as a common thread uniting the *Insular Cases*,

Eisentrager, and *Reid*: the idea that questions of extraterritoriality turn on objective factors and practical concerns, not formalism.

B

The Government's formal sovereignty-based test raises troubling separation-of-powers concerns as well. The political history of Guantanamo illustrates the deficiencies of this approach. The United States has maintained complete and uninterrupted control of the bay for over 100 years. At the close of the Spanish-American War, Spain ceded control over the entire island of Cuba to the United States and specifically "relinquishe[d] all claim[s] of sovereignty . . . and title." From the date the treaty with Spain was signed until the Cuban Republic was established on May 20, 1902, the United States governed the territory "in trust" for the benefit of the Cuban people. And although it recognized, by entering into the 1903 Lease Agreement, that Cuba retained "ultimate sovereignty" over Guantanamo, the United States continued to maintain the same plenary control it had enjoyed since 1898. Yet the Government's view is that the Constitution had no effect there, at least as to noncitizens, because the United States disclaimed sovereignty in the formal sense of the term. The necessary implication of the argument is that by surrendering formal sovereignty over any unincorporated territory to a third party, while at the same time entering into a lease that grants total control over the territory back to the United States, it would be possible for the political branches to govern without legal constraint.

Our basic charter cannot be contracted away like this. The Constitution grants Congress and the President the power to acquire, dispose of, and govern territory, not the power to decide when and where its terms apply. Even when the United States acts outside its borders, its powers are not "absolute and unlimited" but are subject "to such restrictions as are expressed in the Constitution." Abstaining from questions involving formal sovereignty and territorial governance is one thing. To hold the political branches have the power to switch the Constitution on or off at will is quite another. The former position reflects this Court's recognition that certain matters requiring political judgments are best left to the political branches. The latter would permit a striking anomaly in our tripartite system of government, leading to a regime in which Congress and the President, not this Court, say "what the law is." Marbury v. Madison, 1 Cranch 137, 177, 2 L. Ed. 60 (1803).

These concerns have particular bearing upon the Suspension Clause question in the cases now before us, for the writ of habeas corpus is itself an indispensable mechanism for monitoring the separation of powers. The test for determining the scope of this provision must not be subject to manipulation by those whose power it is designed to restrain.

C

As we recognized in *Rasul*, the outlines of a framework for determining the reach of the Suspension Clause are suggested by the factors the Court relied upon in *Eisentrager*. In addition to the practical concerns discussed above, the *Eisentrager* Court found relevant that each petitioner:

(a) is an enemy alien; (b) has never been or resided in the United States; (c) was captured outside of our territory and there held in military custody as a prisoner of war; (d) was tried and convicted by a Military Commission sitting outside the United States; (e) for offenses against laws of war committed outside the United States; (f) and is at all times imprisoned outside the United States.

Based on this language from *Eisentrager*, and the reasoning in our other extraterritoriality opinions, we conclude that at least three factors are relevant in determining the reach of the Suspension Clause: (1) the citizenship and status of the detainee and the adequacy of the process through which that status determination was made; (2) the nature of the sites where apprehension and then detention took place; and (3) the practical obstacles inherent in resolving the prisoner's entitlement to the writ.

Applying this framework, we note at the onset that the status of these detainees is a matter of dispute. The petitioners, like those in *Eisentrager*, are not American citizens. But the petitioners in *Eisentrager* did not contest, it seems, the Court's assertion that they were "enemy alien[s]." In the instant cases, by contrast, the detainees deny they are enemy combatants. They have been afforded some process in CSRT proceedings to determine their status; but, unlike in *Eisentrager*, there has been no trial by military commission for violations of the laws of war. The difference is not trivial. The records from the *Eisentrager* trials suggest that, well before the petitioners brought their case to this Court, there had been a rigorous adversarial process to test the legality of their detention. The *Eisentrager* petitioners were charged by a bill of particulars that made detailed factual allegations against them. To rebut the accusations, they were entitled to representation by counsel, allowed to introduce evidence on their own behalf, and permitted to cross-examine the prosecution's witnesses.

In comparison the procedural protections afforded to the detainees in the CSRT hearings are far more limited, and, we conclude, fall well short of the procedures and adversarial mechanisms that would eliminate the need for habeas corpus review. Although the detainee is assigned a "Personal Representative" to assist him during CSRT proceedings, the Secretary of the Navy's memorandum makes clear that person is not the detainee's lawyer or even his "advocate." The Government's evidence is accorded a presumption of validity. The detainee is allowed to present "reasonably available" evidence, but his ability to rebut the Government's evidence against him is limited by the circumstances of his confinement and his lack of counsel at this stage. And although the detainee can seek review of his status determination in the Court of Appeals, that review process cannot cure all defects in the earlier proceedings.

As to the second factor relevant to this analysis, the detainees here are similarly situated to the *Eisentrager* petitioners in that the sites of their apprehension and detention are technically outside the sovereign territory of the United States. As noted earlier, this is a factor that weighs against finding they have rights under the Suspension Clause. But there are critical differences between Landsberg Prison, circa 1950, and the United States Naval Station at Guantanamo Bay in 2008. Unlike its present control over the naval station, the United States' control over the prison in Germany was neither absolute nor indefinite. Like all parts of occupied Germany, the prison was under the jurisdiction of the combined Allied Forces. The United States was therefore answerable to its Allies for all activities occurring there. The Allies had not planned a long-term occupation of Germany, nor did they intend to displace all German institutions even during the period of occupation. The Court's holding in *Eisentrager* was thus consistent with the *Insular Cases*, where it had held there was no need to extend full constitutional protections to territories the United States did not intend to govern indefinitely. Guantanamo Bay, on the other hand, is no transient possession. In every practical sense Guantanamo is not abroad; it is within the constant jurisdiction of the United States.

As to the third factor, we recognize, as the Court did in *Eisentrager*, that there are costs to holding the Suspension Clause applicable in a case of military detention abroad. Habeas corpus proceedings may require expenditure of funds by the Government and may divert the attention of military personnel from other pressing tasks.

While we are sensitive to these concerns, we do not find them dispositive. Compliance with any judicial process requires some incremental expenditure of resources. Yet civilian courts and the Armed Forces have functioned along side each other at various points in our history. See, e.g., Duncan v. Kahanamoku, 327 U.S. 304 (1946); Ex parte Milligan, 4 Wall. 2, 18 L. Ed. 281 (1866). The Government presents no credible arguments that the military mission at Guantanamo would be compromised if habeas corpus courts had jurisdiction to hear the detainees' claims. And in light of the plenary control the United States asserts over the base, none are apparent to us.

The situation in *Eisentrager* was far different, given the historical context and nature of the military's mission in post-War Germany. When hostilities in the European Theater came to an end, the United States became responsible for an occupation zone encompassing over 57,000 square miles with a population of 18 million. In addition to supervising massive reconstruction and aid efforts the American forces stationed in Germany faced potential security threats from a defeated enemy. In retrospect the post-War occupation may seem uneventful. But at the time *Eisentrager* was decided, the Court was right to be concerned about judicial interference with the military's efforts to contain "enemy elements, guerilla fighters, and 'were-wolves.'"

Similar threats are not apparent here; nor does the Government argue that they are. The United States Naval Station at Guantanamo Bay consists of 45 square miles of land and water. The base has been used, at various points, to house migrants and refugees temporarily. At present, however, other than the detainees themselves, the only long-term residents are American military personnel, their families, and a small number of workers. The detainees have been deemed enemies of the United States. At present, dangerous as they may be if released, they are contained in a secure prison facility located on an isolated and heavily fortified military base.

There is no indication, furthermore, that adjudicating a habeas corpus petition would cause friction with the host government. No Cuban court has jurisdiction over American military personnel at Guantanamo or the enemy combatants detained there. While obligated to abide by the terms of the lease, the United States is, for all practical purposes, answerable to no other sovereign for its acts on the base. Were that not the case, or if the detention facility were located in an active theater of war, arguments that issuing the writ would be "impracticable or anomalous" would have more weight. Under the facts presented here, however, there are few practical barriers to the running of the writ. To the extent barriers arise, habeas corpus procedures likely can be modified to address them.

It is true that before today the Court has never held that noncitizens detained by our Government in territory over which another country maintains de jure sovereignty have any rights under our Constitution. But the cases before us lack any precise historical parallel. They involve individuals detained by executive order for the duration of a conflict that, if measured from September 11, 2001, to the present, is already among the longest wars in American history. The detainees, moreover, are held in a territory that, while technically not part of the United States, is under the complete and total control of our Government. Under these circumstances the lack of a precedent on point is no barrier to our holding.

We hold that Art. I, §9, cl. 2, of the Constitution has full effect at Guantanamo Bay. If the privilege of habeas corpus is to be denied to the detainees now before us, Congress must act in accordance with the requirements of the Suspension Clause. This Court may not impose a de facto suspension by abstaining from these controversies. The MCA does not purport to be a formal suspension of the writ; and the Government, in its submissions to us, has not argued that it is. Petitioners, therefore, are entitled to the privilege of habeas corpus to challenge the legality of their detention. . . .

Justice SCALIA, with whom THE CHIEF JUSTICE, Justice THOMAS, and Justice ALITO join, dissenting.

Today, for the first time in our Nation's history, the Court confers a constitutional right to habeas corpus on alien enemies detained abroad by our military forces in the course of an ongoing war. . . . My problem with today's opinion is . . . fundamental . . . : The writ of habeas corpus does not, and never has, run in favor of aliens abroad; the Suspension Clause thus has no application, and the Court's intervention in this military matter is entirely ultra vires. . . .

The Suspension Clause of the Constitution provides: "The Privilege of the Writ of Habeas Corpus shall not be suspended, unless when in Cases of Rebellion or Invasion the public Safety may require it." Art. I, §9, cl. 2. As a court of law operating under a written Constitution, our role is to determine whether there is a conflict between that Clause and the Military Commissions Act. A conflict arises only if the Suspension Clause preserves the privilege of the writ for aliens held by the United States military as enemy combatants at the base in Guantanamo Bay, located within the sovereign territory of Cuba. . . .

. . . The Court resorts to "fundamental separation-of-powers principles" to interpret the Suspension Clause. According to the Court, because "the writ of habeas corpus is itself an indispensable mechanism for monitoring the separation of powers," the test of its extraterritorial reach "must not be subject to manipulation by those whose power it is designed to restrain."

That approach distorts the nature of the separation of powers and its role in the constitutional structure. The "fundamental separation-of-powers principles" that the Constitution embodies are to be derived not from some judicially imagined matrix, but from the sum total of the individual separation-of-powers provisions that the Constitution sets forth. Only by considering them one-by-one does the full shape of the Constitution's separation-of-powers principles emerge. It is nonsensical to interpret those provisions themselves in light of some general "separation-of-powers principles" dreamed up by the Court. Rather, they must be interpreted to mean what they were understood to mean when the people ratified them. And if the understood scope of the writ of habeas corpus was "designed to restrain" (as the Court says) the actions of the Executive, the understood limits upon that scope were (as the Court seems not to grasp) just as much "designed to restrain" the incursions of the Third Branch. "Manipulation" of the territorial reach of the writ by the Judiciary poses just as much a threat to the proper separation of powers as "manipulation" by the Executive. As I will show below, manipulation is what is afoot here. The understood limits upon the writ deny our jurisdiction over the habeas petitions brought by these enemy aliens, and entrust the President with the crucial wartime determinations about their status and continued confinement.

The Court purports to derive from our precedents a "functional" test for the extraterritorial reach of the writ, which shows that the Military Commissions Act unconstitutionally restricts the scope of habeas. That is remarkable because the most pertinent of those precedents, Johnson v. Eisentrager, 339 U.S. 763, conclusively establishes the opposite. There we were confronted with the claims of 21 Germans held at Landsberg Prison, an American military facility located in the American Zone of occupation in postwar Germany. They had been captured in China, and an

American military commission sitting there had convicted them of war crimes — collaborating with the Japanese after Germany's surrender. Like the petitioners here, the Germans claimed that their detentions violated the Constitution and international law, and sought a writ of habeas corpus. Writing for the Court, Justice Jackson held that American courts lacked habeas jurisdiction:

> We are cited to [*sic*] no instance where a court, in this or any other country where the writ is known, has issued it on behalf of an alien enemy who, at no relevant time and in no stage of his captivity, has been within its territorial jurisdiction. Nothing in the text of the Constitution extends such a right, nor does anything in our statutes.

Justice Jackson then elaborated on the historical scope of the writ:

> The alien, to whom the United States has been traditionally hospitable, has been accorded a generous and ascending scale of rights as he increases his identity with our society. . . .
> But, in extending constitutional protections beyond the citizenry, the Court has been at pains to point out that it was the alien's presence within its territorial jurisdiction that gave the Judiciary power to act.

Lest there be any doubt about the primacy of territorial sovereignty in determining the jurisdiction of a habeas court over an alien, Justice Jackson distinguished two cases in which aliens had been permitted to seek habeas relief, on the ground that the prisoners in those cases were in custody within the sovereign territory of the United States. Id., at 779-780 (discussing Ex parte Quirin, 317 U.S. 1 (1942), and In re Yamashita, 327 U.S. 1 (1946)). "By reason of our sovereignty at that time over [the Philippines]," Jackson wrote, "Yamashita stood much as did Quirin before American courts."

Eisentrager thus held — held beyond any doubt — that the Constitution does not ensure habeas for aliens held by the United States in areas over which our Government is not sovereign.[4] . . .

There is simply no support for the Court's assertion that constitutional rights extend to aliens held outside U.S. sovereign territory, see *Verdugo-Urquidez*, 494 U.S., at 271, and *Eisentrager* could not be clearer that the privilege of habeas corpus does not extend to aliens abroad. By blatantly distorting *Eisentrager*, the Court avoids the difficulty of explaining why it should be overruled. The rule that aliens abroad are not constitutionally entitled to habeas corpus has not proved unworkable in practice; if anything, it is the Court's "functional" test that does not (and never will) provide clear guidance for the future. *Eisentrager* forms a coherent whole with the accepted proposition that aliens abroad have no substantive rights under our Constitution. Since it was announced, no relevant factual premises have changed. It has engendered considerable reliance on the part of our military. And, as the Court acknowledges, text and history do not clearly compel a contrary ruling. It is a sad day for the

---

4. [Scalia's footnote 3:] In its failed attempt to distinguish *Eisentrager*, the Court comes up with the notion that "de jure sovereignty" is simply an additional factor that can be added to (presumably) "de facto sovereignty" (i.e., practical control) to determine the availability of habeas for aliens, but that it is not a necessary factor, whereas de facto sovereignty is. It is perhaps in this de facto sense, the Court speculates, that *Eisentrager* found "sovereignty" lacking. If that were so, one would have expected *Eisentrager* to explain in some detail why the United States did not have practical control over the American zone of occupation. It did not (and probably could not).

rule of law when such an important constitutional precedent is discarded without an apologia, much less an apology.

What drives today's decision is neither the meaning of the Suspension Clause, nor the principles of our precedents, but rather an inflated notion of judicial supremacy. The Court says that if the extraterritorial applicability of the Suspension Clause turned on formal notions of sovereignty, "it would be possible for the political branches to govern without legal constraint" in areas beyond the sovereign territory of the United States. That cannot be, the Court says, because it is the duty of this Court to say what the law is. It would be difficult to imagine a more question-begging analysis. "The very foundation of the power of the federal courts to declare Acts of Congress unconstitutional lies in the power and duty of those courts to decide cases and controversies properly before them." Our power "to say what the law is" is circumscribed by the limits of our statutorily and constitutionally conferred jurisdiction. And that is precisely the question in these cases: whether the Constitution confers habeas jurisdiction on federal courts to decide petitioners' claims. It is both irrational and arrogant to say that the answer must be yes, because otherwise we would not be supreme.

But so long as there are some places to which habeas does not run — so long as the Court's new "functional" test will not be satisfied in every case — then there will be circumstances in which "it would be possible for the political branches to govern without legal constraint." Or, to put it more impartially, areas in which the legal determinations of the other branches will be (shudder!) supreme. In other words, judicial supremacy is not really assured by the constitutional rule that the Court creates. The gap between rationale and rule leads me to conclude that the Court's ultimate, unexpressed goal is to preserve the power to review the confinement of enemy prisoners held by the Executive anywhere in the world. The "functional" test usefully evades the precedential landmine of *Eisentrager* but is so inherently subjective that it clears a wide path for the Court to traverse in the years to come. . . .

Today the Court warps our Constitution in a way that goes beyond the narrow issue of the reach of the Suspension Clause, invoking judicially brainstormed separation-of-powers principles to establish a manipulable "functional" test for the extraterritorial reach of habeas corpus (and, no doubt, for the extraterritorial reach of other constitutional protections as well). It blatantly misdescribes important precedents, most conspicuously Justice Jackson's opinion for the Court in *Johnson v. Eisentrager*. It breaks a chain of precedent as old as the common law that prohibits judicial inquiry into detentions of aliens abroad absent statutory authorization. And, most tragically, it sets our military commanders the impossible task of proving to a civilian court, under whatever standards this Court devises in the future, that evidence supports the confinement of each and every enemy prisoner.

The Nation will live to regret what the Court has done today. I dissent.

NOTES AND QUESTIONS

1. In deciding whether these individuals — non-U.S. nationals captured abroad and held outside the de jure sovereign territory of the United States — could claim the constitutional habeas writ, why did the Justices all but ignore the Court's most recent precedent — *Verdugo-Urquidez*? The Court obviously did not echo the *Verdugo-Urquidez* opinion's central emphasis on whether the non-U.S. person seeking to claim a constitutional right has a substantial and voluntary connection with the United States,

but neither did Justice Scalia's dissent. Should the relevant analysis regarding extra-territorial applications of the Constitution be right-specific?

Note that the *Boumediene* decision means that non-U.S. nationals captured abroad and held at Guantánamo (and perhaps other places under de facto U.S. control) can proceed with habeas claims in U.S. courts. The prisoners will be asserting there, as well as in military commission hearings, that they have a variety of constitutional "rights," including a right to equal legal treatment, a right against compelled self-incrimination, a due process right against use of coerced testimony, a right to compulsory process and to the effective assistance of counsel, a right to confront and cross-examine witnesses, a right to a speedy and public trial, a right to grand jury indictment, and a right against ex post facto charges. To keep up with the litigation as it proceeds, see http://www.scotusblog.com/wp/ and http://balkin.blogspot.com/.

2. What is the test one should take away from this case, at least as to who can seek to challenge their detention under the constitutional habeas writ? What part in the analysis does de facto sovereignty play — that is, is it a necessary even if not a sufficient condition where a non-U.S. person seeks to rely on the constitutional habeas writ? So could those detained by U.S. soldiers in Afghanistan and Iraq claim a habeas remedy? What more would one need to know to answer that question? Can you discern any theory of the Constitution underlying the majority's approach (that is, territorial, nationality, social compact, natural rights, due process)?

3. On the same date that *Boumediene* was decided, the Court also decided on the scope of the habeas statute when two U.S. citizens captured abroad sought its protection in Munaf v. Geren, 128 S. Ct. 2207 (2008). In *Munaf,* two American citizens voluntarily traveled to Iraq, allegedly committed crimes while there, and were apprehended in Iraq by U.S. forces acting as a part of the multinational coalition force operating under the unified authority of U.S. military officers (the Multinational Force-Iraq or MNF-I). The arrested Americans sought in habeas petitions filed in U.S. district court to enjoin their transfer from a detainee camp operated by the MNF-I to the custody of the Central Criminal Court for Iraq for trial and, if convicted, punishment by Iraq authorities under Iraqi law.

The Supreme Court held in *Munaf* that the habeas statute *does* extend to American citizens held overseas by American forces operating subject to an American chain of command, even if, as a formal matter, they are held by the multinational MNF-I. However, the Court ultimately held that the petitioners had no legally enforceable right not to be transferred to Iraqi authorities for criminal proceedings. It noted that Iraq has a sovereign right to prosecute the petitioners for crimes committed on its soil. The Court stated that it has twice rejected claims that the Constitution prohibits the executive from transferring prisoners to a foreign country for prosecution in an allegedly unconstitutional trial. Concerns about potential torture do not change the analysis; the decision to transfer prisoners lies with the political branches, not the judiciary. This is not an extradition case but rather one involving the transfer to a sovereign's authority of an individual captured and already detained in that sovereign's territory. Therefore, the government does not need specific statutory or treaty authority to detain and transfer the petitioners. Additionally, the United States, as part of MNF-I, is acting at the behest of the Iraqi government. It follows, the Court ruled, that the United States has the authority to transfer to Iraq those being detained for violations of Iraqi law in Iraqi territory.

C. INTERROGATIONS AND THE FIFTH/FOURTEENTH AMENDMENT DUE PROCESS CLAUSE

The Fifth Amendment's and Fourteenth Amendment's Due Process Clauses protect against violations of constitutional procedural standards *and* safeguard certain substantive rights. The irreducible minimum *procedural* guarantee inherent in the term "due process" generally requires that, before a defendant is subjected to more than a temporary deprivation of her liberty, she must be provided (1) notice and (2) an opportunity to be heard (3) before a neutral decision maker. In this section, we are less concerned with procedural due process rights and more concerned with what limits the Supreme Court has imposed under *substantive* due process on the conduct of interrogations and other means of securing information from a suspect or prisoner. In two lines of substantive due process cases, the Court has been willing to address the *means* used by police to extract information or obtain custody of the defendant rather than just the fairness of the *processes* used to try her.

In the first line of "substantive due process" cases, courts have (although infrequently) relied on due process to dismiss cases or suppress evidence where the governmental action involved "shocked the conscience" of the court, even if the actions did not undermine the likely accuracy or reliability of the verdict. It was in the foundational case, *Rochin v. California*,[5] that the Court articulated a "shock the conscience" standard for testing substantive due process claims in at least some circumstances. In so doing, it asserted that "[i]t has long since ceased to be true that due process of law is heedless of the means by which otherwise relevant and credible evidence is obtained" and that there is a "general requirement that States in their prosecutions respect certain decencies of civilized conduct."[6]

In *Rochin*, three law enforcement officers, acting on the suspicion that Rochin was selling drugs:

> forced open the door of [his] room. . . . Inside they found [Rochin] sitting partly dressed on the side of the bed, upon which his wife was lying. On a "night stand" beside the bed the deputies spied two capsules. When asked "Whose stuff is this?" Rochin seized the capsules and put them in his mouth. A struggle ensued, in the course of which the three officers "jumped upon him" and attempted to extract the capsules. The force they applied proved unavailing against Rochin's resistance. He was handcuffed and taken to a hospital. At the direction of one of the officers a doctor forced an emetic solution through a tube into Rochin's stomach against his will. This "stomach pumping" produced vomiting. In the vomited matter were found two capsules which proved to contain morphine.[7]

Without considering the state's interest in the evidence so seized, the Court concluded that these "brutal" tactics violated due process, reasoning as follows:

> [W]e are compelled to conclude that the proceedings by which this conviction was obtained do more than offend some fastidious squeamishness or private sentimentalism about combating crime too energetically. This is conduct that shocks the conscience. Illegally breaking into the privacy of the petitioner, the struggle to open his mouth and remove what was there, the forcible extraction of his stomach's contents — this course of

---

5. 342 U.S. 165 (1952).
6. Id. at 172-173.
7. Id. at 166.

proceeding by agents of government to obtain evidence is bound to offend even hardened sensibilities. They are methods too close to the rack and the screw to permit of constitutional differentiation.[8]

The *Rochin* "shocks the conscience" test seems to apply when the Court cannot find a specific constitutional guarantee on point. The most frequently cited recent use of this test was in *County of Sacramento v. Lewis*,[9] a case involving a *civil* suit. In *Lewis*, the Court rejected a proposed negligence standard where the parents of a motorcycle passenger killed in a high speed chase with police sought damages based on an alleged deprivation of the passenger's substantive due process right to life. The Court held that a *deliberate* act was required before damages could be claimed. In so doing, it reasoned:

> We have . . . rejected the lowest common denominator of customary tort liability as a mark of sufficiently shocking conduct, and have held that the Constitution does not guarantee due care on the part of state officials; liability for negligently inflicted harm is categorically beneath the threshold of constitutional due process. It is, on the contrary, behavior at the other end of the culpability spectrum that would most probably support a due process claim; *conduct intended to injure in some way unjustifiable by any government interest is the sort of official action most likely to rise to the conscience-shocking level.*[10]

A second set of "substantive due process" cases — those raising "due process voluntariness" claims — require a little background information to assist students accustomed to dealing with such questions under the rubric of the Fifth Amendment right against compelled self-incrimination and *Miranda v. Arizona*.[11] Early on, the Supreme Court held that the first eight amendments to the U.S. Constitution operate only to limit the actions of the federal government. Thus, the Fifth Amendment itself does not require the U.S. states to honor a defendant's right against compelled self-incrimination. Over time, however, the Supreme Court has held almost all of the "fundamental rights" reflected in the Bill of Rights to be applicable to the U.S. states through the Due Process Clause of the Fourteenth Amendment. Because the Supreme Court did not rule that the Fifth Amendment right against compelled self-incrimination was applicable to the U.S. states through the Fourteenth Amendment's Due Process Clause until 1964, it faced a problem prior to 1964 in dealing with U.S. state cases in which confessions had been coerced from defendants and used against them in state trials. The Fifth Amendment right against self-incrimination being unavailable at the time, the Supreme Court responded to the problem of compelled confessions by reading into the Fourteenth Amendment's Due Process Clause a bar on the admission of "involuntary" confessions in state criminal trials.

The first such "due process voluntariness" case, *Brown v. Mississippi*,[12] dealt with a confession obtained through physical violence, but later cases accepted the idea that other forms of abuse, including sleep deprivation, psychological coercion, and the like, could render a confession inadmissible in U.S. state criminal trials. Initially the focus was on excluding confessions that had been rendered untrustworthy by the use of coercion. Over time, however, the Supreme Court's cases reflected another focus: Even where confessions might be trustworthy, the Court excluded those that had

---

8. Id. at 172.
9. 523 U.S. 833 (1998).
10. Id. at 848-849 (emphasis added).
11. 384 U.S. 436 (1966).
12. 297 U.S. 278 (1936).

been obtained through police methods that the Court found intolerable.[13] The "test" employed in these cases was whether, in the totality of the circumstances, the police "broke the will" of the defendant so as to render his subsequent statement "involuntary" or "coerced." But often the results in the cases reflected the Justices' belief that a certain type of interrogation technique was out of bounds in a modern criminal justice system, even if it had resulted in a perfectly valid confession.

The subjectiveness of the Court's "due process voluntariness" standard made it difficult to apply with any consistency and, faced with innumerable cases raising due process voluntariness claims, the Supreme Court cast about for a more manageable approach. Having determined that the Fifth Amendment right against compelled self-incrimination applied to the U.S. states through the Due Process Clause of the Fourteenth Amendment in 1964, the Court turned away from the totality-of-the-circumstances test found wanting in the due process voluntariness cases, and set about creating "bright-line rules" to govern Fifth Amendment confession law in *Miranda v. Arizona*.[14] It is important to note that *Miranda* and subsequent Fifth Amendment rights against compelled self-incrimination cases did not overrule the earlier due process voluntariness precedents. One can raise both due process "voluntariness" and Fifth Amendment/*Miranda* objections to the admission of "coerced" confessions. However, "giving the [*Miranda*] warnings and getting a waiver has generally produced a virtual ticket of admissibility; maintaining that a statement is involuntary even though given after warnings and voluntary waiver of rights requires unusual stamina, and litigation over voluntariness tends to end with the finding of a valid waiver."[15] We will examine the scope of the Fifth Amendment's right against compelled self-incrimination and its applicability to overseas interrogations in Part D below. For now, our focus is on what substantive due process rights are embodied in the Due Process Clauses.

Why are these two different lines of due process precedents important? Because each potentially has some application to the legal regulation of attempts to interrogate or otherwise extract information from suspects. And the choice of the pertinent line of cases can have important consequences. For example, the "due process voluntariness" cases do not permit balancing; if a defendant's statement is deemed "coerced" or "involuntary" because the police "broke his will," the Fifth or Fourteenth Amendment has been violated, and suppression of any statement and derivative evidence is ordinarily required. The "shocks the conscience" test used in *Rochin* and as applied in later cases, by contrast, appears to permit some balancing between the governmental interest at stake and the degree of intentional pain inflicted on the defendant when determining whether a constitutional line has been crossed.

The Supreme Court's latest word on this subject can be found in *Chavez v. Martinez*,[16] which involved a civil rights suit founded on an abusive interrogation. After an altercation with police, Oliverio Martinez was shot several times by one of the officers, causing severe injuries that left Martinez permanently blinded and paralyzed from the waist down. Martinez was arrested and transported to the emergency room. It is the interrogation by Officer Chavez that took place at that point that was the reason for the civil suit. As Justice Kennedy related the facts:

---

13. See, e.g., Ashcraft v. Tennessee, 322 U.S. 143 (1944).
14. 384 U.S. 436 (1966).
15. Missouri v. Seibert, 542 U.S. 600, 608-609 (2004) (plurality opinion).
16. 538 U.S. 760 (2003).

The District Court found that Martinez "had been shot in the face, both eyes were injured; he was screaming in pain, and coming in and out of consciousness while being repeatedly questioned about details of the encounter with the police." His blinding facial wounds made it impossible for him visually to distinguish the interrogating officer from the attending medical personnel. The officer made no effort to dispel the perception that medical treatment was being withheld until Martinez answered the questions put to him. There was no attempt through *Miranda* warnings or other assurances to advise the suspect that his cooperation should be voluntary. Martinez begged the officer to desist and provide treatment for his wounds, but the questioning persisted despite these pleas and despite Martinez's unequivocal refusal to answer questions.[17]

Justice Stevens quotes at length the recorded interrogation,[18] during which it was clear that Martinez thought that he was dying and was crying out in agony.[19] As Justice Ginsburg noted, "'[i]n this debilitated and helpless condition, [Martinez] clearly expressed his wish not to be interrogated.' Chavez nonetheless continued to question him, 'ceas[ing] the interrogation only during intervals when [Martinez] lost consciousness or received medical treatment.' Martinez was 'weakened by pain and shock'; 'barely conscious, . . . his will was simply overborne.'"[20]

Martinez sued for civil damages for violation of his constitutional rights under 42 U.S.C. §1983. He alleged that Chavez's actions violated his Fifth Amendment right against compelled self-incrimination as well as his Fourteenth Amendment substantive due process right to be free from coercive questioning. The Ninth Circuit held that Chavez had violated Martinez's Fifth and Fourteenth Amendment rights, and that Chavez was not entitled to a defense of qualified immunity because a reasonable officer would have known that persistent interrogation of the suspect despite repeated requests to stop violated Martinez's "clearly established" constitutional rights.

The Supreme Court reversed and remanded for further consideration of the Fourteenth Amendment claim, with six Justices writing separate opinions. A divided majority of the Court held that the Due Process Clauses of the Fifth and Fourteenth Amendments, rather than the Fifth Amendment's privilege against compelled self-incrimination, govern a civil rights suit alleging that a state officer used coercive interrogation tactics to elicit an involuntary confession *when the confession was never used in court.* (We shall study *Chavez*'s treatment of the Fifth Amendment right against compelled self-incrimination in Part D below. For now, our focus is on the standard applied to test whether Martinez's substantive due process rights were violated in this interrogation.)

A number of the Justices seemed to believe that the *Rochin* "shocks the conscience" precedent, not the long line of "due process voluntariness" cases, supplied the appropriate test. In a passage joined by the Chief Justice and Justice Scalia, Justice Thomas conceded that police torture or other abuse, while not actionable under the Fifth Amendment's right against compelled self-incrimination if not admitted at trial, is actionable under the Fourteenth Amendment's Due Process Clause.[21] The Chief Justice and Justices Scalia and Thomas stated the due process test to be:

---

17. Id. at 798.
18. Id. at 784-786.
19. See id. at 784.
20. Id. at 800.
21. Id. at 773.

Convictions based on evidence obtained by methods that are "so brutal and so offensive to human dignity" that they "shoc[k] the conscience" violate the Due Process Clause. Rochin v. California, 342 U.S. 165, 172, 174 (1952). Although *Rochin* did not establish a civil remedy for abusive police behavior, we recognized in County of Sacramento v. Lewis, 523 U.S. 833, 846 (1998), that deprivations of liberty caused by "the most egregious official conduct" may violate the Due Process Clause. While we rejected, in *Lewis*, a §1983 plaintiff's contention that a police officer's deliberate indifference during a high-speed chase that caused the death of a motorcyclist violated due process, we left open the possibility that unauthorized police behavior in other contexts might "shock the conscience" and give rise to §1983 liability.[22]

The Chief Justice and Justices Thomas and Scalia concluded, however, that "Chavez's questioning did not violate Martinez's due process rights" under this test.[23] They ruled that the interrogation in *Chavez* did not "shock" their collective consciences, reasoning:

Even assuming, *arguendo*, that the persistent questioning of Martinez somehow deprived him of a liberty interest, we cannot agree with Martinez's characterization of Chavez's behavior as "egregious" or "conscience shocking." As we noted in *Lewis*, the official conduct "most likely to rise to the conscience-shocking level" is the "conduct intended to injure in some way unjustifiable by any government interest." Here, there is no evidence that Chavez acted with a purpose to harm Martinez by intentionally interfering with his medical treatment. Medical personnel were able to treat Martinez throughout the interview and Chavez ceased his questioning to allow tests and other procedures to be performed. Nor is there evidence that Chavez's conduct exacerbated Martinez's injuries or prolonged his stay in the hospital. Moreover, the need to investigate whether there had been police misconduct constituted a justifiable government interest given the risk that key evidence would have been lost if Martinez had died without the authorities ever hearing his side of the story.[24]

"Significantly, Justice Thomas failed to consider whether Martinez's statements were voluntary, even though that issue had been central to the lower courts' analysis. . . . Whether Justice Thomas simply chose not to consider the voluntariness issue, whether he thought it was irrelevant to the substantive due process claim, or whether he thought it was subsumed within the shocks the conscience inquiry is unclear."[25]

Justice Kennedy also reasoned that the officer's intent and the government interest at stake should be considered, apparently signaling that he, too, believed that the *Rochin* test controlled, but he concluded on these facts that the requisite showing had been made. First, Justice Kennedy said that since Martinez had not been shot for the purpose of extracting a statement, the case could be analyzed as if the wounds had been inflicted by a third person.[26] He then argued that "[t]here is no rule against interrogating suspects who are in anguish and pain. The police may have legitimate reasons, borne of exigency, to question a person who is suffering or in distress."[27] Justice Kennedy went on to explain:

---

22. Id. at 774.
23. Id.
24. Id. at 774-775.
25. John T. Parry, Constitutional Interpretation, Coercive Interrogation, and Civil Rights Litigation After *Chavez v. Martinez*, 39 Ga. L. Rev. 733, 748-749 (2005).
26. 538 U.S. at 796.
27. Id.

There are, however, actions police may not take if the prohibition against the use of coercion to elicit a statement is to be respected. The police may not prolong or increase a suspect's suffering against the suspect's will. That conduct would render government officials accountable for the increased pain. The officers must not give the impression that severe pain will be alleviated only if the declarant cooperates, for that, too, uses pain to extract a statement. In a case like this one, recovery should be available under §1983 if a complainant can demonstrate that an officer exploited his pain and suffering with the purpose and intent of securing an incriminating statement.[28]

The remaining opinions, although not crystal clear, seem to rely mainly on due process voluntariness language or precedents rather than the *Rochin* "shock the conscience" test. Thus, Justice Ginsburg wrote separately to state her view "that even if no finding were made concerning Martinez's belief that refusal to answer would delay his treatment, or Chavez's intent to create such an impression, the interrogation in this case would remain a clear instance of the kind of compulsion no reasonable officer would have thought constitutionally permissible."[29] Justice Stevens, too, harbored no doubt that the conduct involved violated constitutional standards, concluding that, as a matter of fact, the interrogation employed "torturous methods" and that, as a matter of law, "that type of brutal police conduct constitutes an immediate deprivation of the prisoner's constitutionally protected interest in liberty."[30] (Justice Souter, joined by Justice Breyer, concluded, with respect to the merits, that "it is enough to say that Justice Stevens shows that Martinez has a serious argument in support of" a substantive due process claim.)[31]

Should a due process claim rest in part on the police officer's intent? What if the police officer was not acting with the "purpose" of securing an incriminating statement but rather was acting out of anger, vengeance, or sadism? Should the government's interest in the information be relevant to this analysis? Under the analysis of the Chief Justice and Justices Thomas and Scalia, would the government be able to torture a suspect without violating due process norms in the interest of cracking a terrorist cell?

If Fifth (and Fourteenth) Amendment due process *does* provide some protection against torture, does that protection apply to protect U.S. citizens or aliens abroad from misconduct by U.S. agents or others acting under their direction or control? In *Harbury v. Deutch*,[32] Jennifer Harbury, the widow of a murdered Guatemalan citizen, Efrain Bamaca-Velasquez, brought an action for damages under *Bivens v. Six Unknown Federal Narcotics Agents*,[33] claiming, inter alia, that CIA agents participated in the torture and murder of her husband in Guatemala. She sought damages for deprivation of her husband's due process rights. Harbury first argued that, because many of the U.S. government officials she alleged to have conspired to torture her husband did so within the United States, her case did not require extraterritorial application of the Fifth Amendment. The D.C. Circuit rebuffed this theory citing *Verdugo-Urquidez* and explaining that the Supreme Court in that case had treated the alleged Fourth Amendment violation as having occurred entirely in Mexico even though the search had been conceived, planned, and ordered by DEA agents in the United States.

---

28. Id. at 797.
29. Id. at 799.
30. Id. at 783-784.
31. Id. at 779.
32. 233 F.3d 596 (D.C. Cir. 2000), *rev'd on other grounds*, 536 U.S. 403 (2002), *aff'g dismissal after remand on other grounds*, 522 F.3d 413 (D.C. 2008).
33. 403 U.S. 388 (1971).

The D.C. Circuit then held that the Fifth Amendment's Due Process Clause does not apply to foreign nationals overseas. In so doing, it relied on *Johnson v. Eisentrager* (discussed at length in *Verdugo-Urquidez*) and on the *Verdugo-Urquidez* Court's characterization of *Eisentrager*: "[W]e have rejected the claim that aliens are entitled to Fifth Amendment rights outside the sovereign territory of the U.S."[34] The D.C. Circuit therefore determined that foreign nationals have no U.S. due process right against official torture overseas. Do you think this is a fair use of *Eisentrager* and *Verdugo-Urquidez*? Is *Harbury* still good law after *Boumediene*?

D.   FIFTH AMENDMENT RIGHT AGAINST SELF-INCRIMINATION

IN RE TERRORIST BOMBINGS OF U.S. EMBASSIES IN EAST AFRICA (FIFTH AMENDMENT CHALLENGES) UNITED STATES OF AMERICA v. ODEH ET AL.

552 F.3d 177 (2d Cir. 2008)

José A. CABRANES, Circuit Judge:

Defendants-appellants Mohamed Rashed Daoud Al-'Owhali and Mohamed Sadeek Odeh challenge their convictions in the United States District Court for the Southern District of New York (Leonard B. Sand, Judge) on numerous charges arising from their involvement in the August 7, 1998 bombings of the American Embassies in Nairobi, Kenya and Dar es Salaam, Tanzania (the "August 7 bombings"). In this opinion we consider their challenges to the District Court's rulings that denied, for the most part, their respective motions to suppress statements each of them made overseas to U.S. and non-U.S. officials. . . .

Al-'Owhali . . . contend[s] that . . . the "Advice of Rights" form ("AOR") that he received [did not] satisf[y] Miranda v. Arizona, 384 U.S. 436 (1966). . . . As explained in greater detail below, [this claim lacks] merit. The . . . AOR substantially complied with the government's obligations, insofar as it had any, under *Miranda*, and the admission of Al-'Owhali's . . . statements did not otherwise run afoul of the Fifth Amendment. . . .

Al-'Owhali was detained on August 12, 1998 by Kenyan authorities in "an arrest [that] was valid under Kenyan law." Within one hour of his arrest, Al-'Owhali was transported to Kenyan police headquarters in Nairobi and interrogated by two members of the Joint Terrorist Task Force—an FBI Special Agent and a New York City police detective—operating out of New York City and two officers of Kenya's national police. The New York police detective presented Al-'Owhali with an Advice of Rights form often used by U.S. law enforcement when operating overseas. The AOR, written in English, read in its entirety as follows:

> We are representatives of the United States Government. Under our laws, you have certain rights. Before we ask you any questions, we want to be sure that you understand those rights.

---

34. *Verdugo-Urquidez*, 494 U.S. at 269.

You do not have to speak to us or answer any questions. Even if you have already spoken to the Kenyan authorities, you do not have to speak to us now.

If you do speak with us, anything that you say may be used against you in a court in the United States or elsewhere.

In the United States, you would have the right to talk to a lawyer to get advice before we ask you any questions and you could have a lawyer with you during questioning. In the United States, if you could not afford a lawyer, one would be appointed for you, if you wish, before any questioning.

Because we are not in the United States, we cannot ensure that you will have a lawyer appointed for you before any questioning.

If you decide to speak with us now, without a lawyer present, you will still have the right to stop answering questions at any time.

You should also understand that if you decide not to speak with us, that fact cannot be used as evidence against you in a court in the United States.

I have read this statement of my rights and I understand what my rights are. I am willing to make a statement and answer questions. I do not want a lawyer at this time. I understand and know what I am doing. No promises or threats have been made to me and no pressure or coercion of any kind has been used against me. . . .

2. The Applicability of the Fifth Amendment and *Miranda* to the Admission at Trial of Inculpatory Statements Made in Foreign Custody to U.S. Agents. . . .

A. THE FIFTH AMENDMENT RIGHT AGAINST SELF-INCRIMINATION IN DOMESTIC TRIALS

We note at the outset that our analysis of the applicability of the Fifth Amendment to this prosecution differs from our analysis of the Fourth Amendment's applicability. While a violation of the Fourth Amendment's prohibition of unreasonable searches and seizures occurs at the time of the search or seizure, regardless of whether unlawfully obtained evidence is ever offered at trial, a violation of the Fifth Amendment's right against self-incrimination occurs only when a compelled statement is offered at trial against the defendant. In United States v. Verdugo-Urquidez, the Supreme Court explained that "[t]he privilege against self-incrimination guaranteed by the Fifth Amendment is a fundamental trial right of criminal defendants. Although conduct by law enforcement officials prior to trial may ultimately impair that right, a constitutional violation occurs only at trial." The Fourth Amendment "functions differently"; it is violated "at the time of an unreasonable governmental intrusion." Accordingly, the Fourth Amendment's prohibition of unreasonable searches and seizures regulates the activities of the government when investigating crimes, while the Fifth Amendment's privilege against self-incrimination regulates the admissibility of a defendant's statements at trial.

Because a putative violation of the Fourth Amendment is "fully accomplished" at the place and time of the alleged intrusion, a claimed violation occurring overseas entails an analysis of the extraterritorial application of the Fourth Amendment. No such analysis is necessary with respect to the Fifth Amendment's privilege against self-incrimination because that provision governs the admissibility of evidence at U.S. trials, not the conduct of U.S. agents investigating criminal activity. For this reason, it naturally follows that, regardless of the origin — i.e., domestic or foreign — of a statement, it cannot be admitted at trial in the United States if the statement was "compelled." U.S. Const. amend. V. Similarly, it does not matter whether the defendant is a U.S. citizen or a foreign national: "no person" tried in the civilian courts of the United States can be compelled "to be a witness against himself." Id.

While the Supreme Court has not been called upon to state this latter principle explicitly,[35] it has held that the Fifth Amendment's right to due process of law applies equally to U.S. citizens and foreign nationals present in the United States, even those here unlawfully.[36] We see no basis to consign the "fundamental trial right" of a defendant to be free of compelled self-incrimination to lesser status. Indeed, the principles animating the privilege against self-incrimination apply with equal force to both citizens and foreigners who are haled into our courts to answer criminal charges. As described by the Supreme Court:

> [The privilege against self-incrimination] reflects many of our fundamental values and most noble aspirations: our unwillingness to subject those suspected of crime to the cruel trilemma of self-accusation, perjury or contempt; our preference for an accusatorial rather than an inquisitorial system of criminal justice; our fear that self-incriminating statements will be elicited by inhumane treatment and abuses; our sense of fair play which dictates a fair state-individual balance by requiring the government to leave the individual alone until good cause is shown for disturbing him and by requiring the government in its contest with the individual to shoulder the entire load; our respect for the inviolability of the human personality and of the right of each individual to a private enclave where he may lead a private life[;] our distrust of self-deprecatory statements; and our realization that the privilege, while sometimes a shelter to the guilty, is often a protection to the innocent.

United States v. Balsys, 524 U.S. 666, 690 (1998). For these reasons, we have previously required that, in order to be admitted in our courts, inculpatory statements obtained overseas by foreign officials must have been made voluntarily. See [United States v. Yousef, 327 F.3d 56, 145 (2d Cir. 2003)] ("[S]tatements taken by foreign police in the absence of *Miranda* warnings are admissible if voluntary.").

We do not read the Supreme Court's holding in Johnson v. Eisentrager, 339 U.S. 763 (1950), as evidence to the contrary. In *Eisentrager,* twenty-one Germans convicted of war crimes by a U.S. military court located in China petitioned the U.S. District Court for the District of Columbia for a writ of habeas corpus because, inter alia, their trials entailed the use of testimony allegedly compelled in violation of the Fifth Amendment. At the outset, the Court emphasized the "inherent distinctions recognized throughout the civilized world between . . . resident enemy aliens who have submitted themselves to our laws and nonresident enemy aliens who at all times have remained with, and adhered to, enemy governments." With respect to extending constitutional protections to aliens within the borders of the United States, the Court explained "the alien's presence within its territorial jurisdiction . . . gave the Judiciary power to act." The petitioners in *Eisentrager,* however, were not within the territorial jurisdiction of the United States; they were captured and tried in China and imprisoned in Germany. The Court explained that "the nonresident enemy alien, especially one who has remained in the service of the enemy, does not have even th[e] qualified access [of a resident enemy alien] to our courts, for he neither has comparable claims upon our institutions nor could his use of them fail to be helpful to the enemy." Most significantly, the Court viewed the availability of habeas corpus to non-resident enemy aliens as a mechanism

---

35. [Court's footnote 15:] This may be so because, as here, the government has previously taken the position that it does not dispute the applicability of the self-incrimination clause to non-U.S. citizens.

36. [Court's footnote 16:] The Supreme Court has held that resident aliens are protected by the Fifth Amendment's privilege against self-incrimination. See United States v. Balsys, 524 U.S. 666, 671 (1998) ("Resident aliens . . . are considered 'persons' for purposes of the Fifth Amendment and are entitled to the same protections under the [Self-Incrimination] Clause as citizens.").

for undermining American military efforts. Part and parcel of waging war, the Court observed, is "[t]he jurisdiction of military authorities, during or following hostilities, to punish those guilty of offenses against the laws of war." For these reasons, the Court's rejection of the Fifth Amendment claim in *Eisentrager* cannot be unmoored from the salient facts of the case: an overseas conviction of "nonresident enemy aliens," following the cessation of hostilities, by a duly-constituted military court. Cf. Boumediene v. Bush, 128 S.Ct. 2229, 2261 (2008) (explaining that "at the time *Eisentrager* was decided, the Court was right to be concerned about judicial interference with the military's efforts to contain enemy elements, guerilla fighters, and 'were-wolves'" in light of the "historical context and nature of the military's mission in post-War Germany" (internal quotation marks omitted)). The *Eisentrager* holding is inapposite, therefore, to the facts before us: a domestic prosecution of nonresident aliens brought to this country specifically to be prosecuted by our civilian criminal courts.

Accordingly, we hold that foreign nationals interrogated overseas but tried in the civilian courts of the United States are protected by the Fifth Amendment's self-incrimination clause.

B. THE APPLICATION OF *MIRANDA* TO U.S. INTERROGATIONS CONDUCTED OVERSEAS

Having determined that the Fifth Amendment right against self-incrimination governs the admissibility at trial of statements made overseas, we turn to the related question of *Miranda*'s applicability to overseas interrogations conducted by U.S. agents. The Supreme Court has not ruled on this particular question, but it has held that the framework established by "*Miranda* . . . govern[s] the admissibility of statements made during custodial interrogation in both state and federal courts." Dickerson v. United States, 530 U.S. 428, 432 (2000). Proceeding on the assumption that the *Miranda* framework generally governs the admissibility of statements obtained overseas by U.S. agents, we conclude that the application of that framework to overseas interrogations may differ from its domestic application, depending on local circumstances, in keeping with the context-specific nature of the *Miranda* rule.

In *Dickerson*, the Supreme Court explained that the *Miranda* "warning/waiver" framework arose from the risk "that the coercion inherent in custodial interrogation blurs the line between voluntary and involuntary statements, and thus heightens the risk that an individual will not be 'accorded his privilege under the Fifth Amendment . . . not to be compelled to incriminate himself.'" 530 U.S. at 435 (quoting *Miranda*, 384 U.S. at 439) (alterations in original). In response, the Court set forth "constitutional guidelines" conditioning the admissibility of statements obtained in custodial interrogations on whether a suspect had been warned that he:

> has the right to remain silent, that anything he says can be used against him in a court of law, that he has the right to the presence of an attorney, and that if he cannot afford an attorney one will be appointed for him prior to any questioning if he so desires.

Undergirding these guidelines are two objectives: "trustworthiness and deterrence." Oregon v. Elstad, 470 U.S. 298, 308 (1985). By "adequately and effectively appris[ing] [a suspect] of his rights" and reassuring the suspect that "the exercise of those rights must be fully honored," the *Miranda* warnings "combat the[] pressures" inherent in custodial interrogations. In so doing, they enhance the trustworthiness of any statements that may be elicited during an interrogation. With respect to deterrence, the Court has explained that, "[b]y refusing to admit evidence gained as a result of [willful or negligent] conduct [depriving the defendant of a right], the courts hope to instill in those particular investigating officers, or in their future counterparts, a greater degree of care toward the rights of an accused." Thus, courts suppress un-warned statements, even those that may otherwise be voluntary and trustworthy, in order to deter future misconduct by law enforcement agents.

Recognizing that the threat of suppression in U.S. courts for failure to comply with *Miranda* holds little sway over foreign authorities, we have declined to suppress un-warned statements obtained overseas by foreign officials. In United States v. Welch, we recognized, in line with the approach of the Ninth Circuit, that "the *Miranda* requirements were primarily designed to prevent United States police officers from relying upon improper interrogation techniques and as the requirements have little, if any, deterrent effect upon foreign police officers, the *Miranda* warnings should not serve as the sine qua non of admissibility." 455 F.2d 211, 213 (2d Cir. 1972); see Kilday v. United States, 481 F.2d 655, 656 (5th Cir. 1973) ("[T]he United States Constitution cannot compel such specific, affirmative action [i.e., providing *Miranda* warnings] by foreign sovereigns, so the policy of deterring so-called 'third degree' police tactics, which underlies the *Miranda* exclusionary rule, is inapposite to this case."). Instead of applying *Miranda* in such cases, we have required that "[w]henever a court is asked to rule upon the admissibility of a statement made to a foreign police officer, the court must consider the totality of the circumstances to determine whether the statement was voluntary. If the court finds the statement involuntary, it must exclude this because of its inherent unreliability."

When U.S. law enforcement agents or officials are involved in overseas interrogation, however, the deterrence rationale retains its force. In such circumstances, the twin goals of ensuring trustworthiness and deterring misconduct might compel the application of *Miranda*. We suggested as much in Yousef, 327 F.3d at 56. In *Yousef*, we observed that "statements taken by foreign police in the absence of *Miranda* warnings are admissible if voluntary," subject to two exceptions. One of these exceptions — the so-called "joint venture doctrine" — appears to have been "implicitly adopted" by our Court, even though we have "failed to define its precise contours."[37] Pursuant to this exception, "statements elicited during overseas interrogation by foreign police in the absence of *Miranda* warnings must be suppressed whenever United States law enforcement agents actively participate in questioning conducted by foreign authorities." Other circuits have explicitly recognized the applicability of *Miranda* to custodial statements elicited overseas through the active participation of U.S. agents. See United States v. Heller, 625 F.2d 594, 599 (5th Cir. 1980) ("[I]f American officials participated in the foreign search or interrogation, or if the foreign authorities were acting as agents for their American counterparts, the exclusionary rule should be invoked."); Pfeifer v. U.S. Bureau of Prisons, 615 F.2d 873, 877 (9th Cir. 1980) ("Under the joint venture doctrine, evidence obtained through activities of foreign officials, in which federal agents substantially participated and which violated the accused's Fifth Amendment or *Miranda* rights, must be suppressed in a subsequent trial in the United States."). In light of these precedents, we proceed on the assumption that the *Miranda* "warning/waiver" framework generally governs the admissibility in our domestic courts of custodial statements obtained by U.S. officials from individuals during their detention under the authority of foreign governments.[38]

---

37. [Court's footnote 18:] The other exception noted by the *Yousef* Court pertains to "statements obtained under circumstances that 'shock the conscience.'"

38. [Court's footnote 19:] Our recognition that *Miranda* might apply to foreign detainees held overseas should in no way impair the ability of the U.S. government to gather foreign intelligence. First, *Miranda*'s "public safety" exception, see New York v. Quarles, 467 U.S. 649 (1984), would likely apply overseas with no less force than it does domestically. When exigent circumstances compel an un-warned interrogation in order to protect the public, *Miranda* would not impair the government's ability to obtain that information. Second, we emphasize that the *Miranda* framework governs only the admission of

Even if we were to conclude, rather than assume, that *Miranda* applies to overseas interrogations involving U.S. agents that would not mean that U.S. agents must recite verbatim the familiar *Miranda* warnings to those detained in foreign lands. As the Supreme Court explained in Duckworth v. Eagan, the "*Miranda* warnings [need not] be given in the exact form described in that decision." 492 U.S. 195, 202 (1989). In fact, the Supreme Court decried a reviewing court's "rigidity . . . [in requiring a] precise formulation of the warnings given a criminal defendant" in California v. Prysock, holding that "no talismanic incantation [i]s required to satisfy [*Miranda*'s] strictures." 453 U.S. 355, 359 (1981). Indeed, the *Miranda* Court itself stated that its "decision in no way creates a constitutional straitjacket" and that "other procedures which are at least as effective in apprising accused persons of their right of silence and in assuring a continuous opportunity to exercise it" could pass constitutional muster. The *Dickerson* Court observed that "no constitutional rule is immutable," citing exceptions to the *Miranda* rule — such as the "public safety" exception, see New York v. Quarles, 467 U.S. 649, 657 (1984) (concluding that "the need for answers to questions in a situation posing a threat to the public safety outweighs the need for the [*Miranda*] rule protecting the Fifth Amendment's privilege against self-incrimination"), and the exception for prior inconsistent statements, see Harris v. New York, 401 U.S. 222, 226 (1971) (holding that "[t]he shield provided by *Miranda* cannot be perverted into a license to use perjury by way of a defense, free from the risk of confrontation with prior inconsistent utterances"). The Court explained: "No court laying down a general rule can possibly foresee the various circumstances in which counsel will seek to apply it, and the sort of modifications represented by these cases are as much a normal part of constitutional law as the original decision."

The federal appellate decisions applying *Miranda*'s "warning/waiver" framework to overseas interrogations demonstrate the flexibility and adaptability of the rule. In Cranford v. Rodriguez, 512 F.2d 860 (10th Cir. 1975), the Tenth Circuit considered a challenge to a waiver form brought by a defendant initially detained in Mexico by Mexican authorities and subsequently questioned there by U.S. agents. After rejecting the argument that *Miranda* did not apply outside the United States, the Tenth Circuit considered the sufficiency of a standard waiver form modified to omit "the line respecting appointment of a lawyer and inserting instead that if [the suspect] wished to consult the American Consulate the latter would be advised of his detention and '[the suspect] will be given the opportunity to talk to a Consulate representative.'" The Tenth Circuit considered this "variation" of the standard *Miranda* warnings to be "unavoidable [due to the lack of availability of a U.S. lawyer in Mexico] and not prejudicial." It stated that "[t]he petitioner was admonished that he need not speak; that he was [informed that he was] entitled to talk to a Consulate official; that anything he said could be used against him in court; and that if he decided to answer questions without a lawyer he could stop at any time." The Tenth Circuit held that this "good faith effort" to inform a suspect of his rights complied with the *Miranda* framework.

The Fifth Circuit reached a similar conclusion in United States v. Dopf, a case considering the admissibility of statements obtained in a custodial interview held in Mexico by a U.S. agent in light of a warning that omitted reference to the appointment of counsel. 434 F.2d 205 (5th Cir. 1970). Specifically, the U.S. agent warned the suspects that "anything they said could be used against them when and if they were returned to the United States; that he could not furnish them with a lawyer in Mexico but offered to contact the American Consul on their behalf." Even though the agent

---

custodial statements at U.S. trials. Insofar as U.S. agents do not seek to introduce statements obtained through overseas custodial interrogations at U.S. trials, *Miranda*'s strictures would not apply.

had neither informed the suspects of their right to appointed counsel nor obtained written waivers from them, the Fifth Circuit concluded:

> [The agent] did everything that he reasonably could have done to protect the rights of appellants by advising them of their right to remain silent, of the possible use against them of incriminatory statements, of the reason why they could not be furnished counsel by the U.S. Government while they were in Mexico and of the availability of the American Consul for their assistance.

As these decisions demonstrate, where *Miranda* has been applied to overseas interrogations by U.S. agents, it has been so applied in a flexible fashion to accommodate the exigencies of local conditions. This context-specific approach is wholly consistent with our reading of the Supreme Court decisions construing the *Miranda* framework, and we now apply that approach to the facts of this case.[39]

3. APPLICATION OF THE FIFTH AMENDMENT AND *MIRANDA* TO DEFENDANTS' STATEMENTS

Turning . . . to the AOR, we observe that it provided five notices to Al-'Owhali [and his co-defendant]. . . . It warned them that under U.S. law: (1) they had the right to remain silent; (2) if they chose to speak, anything they said could be used against them in court; (3) in the United States, they would have had the right to consult with a lawyer and to have a lawyer present during questioning; (4) in the United States, a lawyer would have been appointed for them if they could not afford one; and (5) if they chose not to speak, that fact could not be used against them in a U.S. court. It further advised them that "[b]ecause we are not in the United States, we cannot ensure that you will have a lawyer appointed for you before any questioning." The District Court held that the AOR ran afoul of *Miranda* because it suggested that defendants lacked the right to the presence and appointment of counsel because they were held outside of the United States. We do not believe that the AOR was as deficient as the District Court believed it to be, but, as explained below, we also think that the advice as to the right to counsel could have been made clearer. . . .

The AOR presented defendants with a factually accurate statement of their rights under the U.S. Constitution and how those rights might be limited by the governing non-U.S. criminal procedures. In addition, it advised defendants of a right normally not contained in *Miranda* warnings — that the defendants' silence could not be used against them at an American trial. This additional warning amplified the AOR's cautionary message and thus reinforces the warning's adequacy under *Miranda*.

Like the District Court, we consider the first two warnings in the AOR — the right to remain silent and the introduction at trial of any statements made thereafter — to be entirely consistent with the text and teaching of *Miranda*.

With respect to the rights to presence and appointment of counsel, however, we disagree with the District Court's conclusion that the AOR "wrongly convey[ed] to a suspect that, due to his custodial situs outside the United States, he currently possesse[d] no opportunity to avail himself of the services of an attorney before or during questioning by U.S. officials." The AOR, in the District Court's view, "prematurely

---

39. [Court's footnote 20:] Because we conclude that, assuming they apply, the strictures of *Miranda* were satisfied in this case . . . we leave for another day the question of whether the *Miranda* "warning/ waiver" framework governs the admissibility of statements obtained in the course of custodial interrogations conducted overseas.

foreclose[d] the significant possibility that the foreign authorities themselves may, if asked, either supply counsel at public expense or permit retained counsel inside the stationhouse." The District Court held that U.S. agents participating in overseas investigations must "[t]o the maximum extent reasonably possible, [make] efforts . . . to replicate what rights would be present if the interrogation were being conducted in America." They must also "be clear and candid as to both the existence of the right to counsel and the possible impediments to its exercise." To explain and illustrate its holding, the District Court suggested that an acceptable *Miranda* warning would include the offer to "ask the foreign authorities to permit access to a lawyer or to appoint one for [the suspect]." Because the AOR read to Al-'Owhali . . . did not include such an offer, and because it suggested that "[t]he right to counsel . . . depend[ed] on geography, when instead it actually hinged on foreign law," the District Court held that the "AOR, on its face, [was] inadequate under *Miranda* and its progeny."

In our view, the AOR presented defendants with a factually accurate statement of their right to counsel under the U.S. Constitution; it also explained that the effectuation of that right might be limited by the strictures of criminal procedure in a foreign land. We do not agree with the District Court's view that the relevant section of the AOR amounts to a suggestion that counsel is not available. The AOR informed defendants that "in the United States" they would be entitled to the presence and appointment of defense counsel, but because they were not in the United States, U.S. agents could not ensure that counsel would, in fact, be appointed. This is so because the law of Kenya, as the detaining authority—and not U.S. law—governed whether defendants were entitled to (a) the appointment of publicly financed counsel and (b) the presence of counsel during interrogations. In that sense, the right to counsel did indeed "depend on geography." In cases where a suspect has no entitlement to counsel under the law of the foreign land, it would be misleading to inform him falsely that he was guaranteed the presence or appointment of an attorney—and *Miranda* does not require the provision of false assurances.

The warning at issue here was candid: It explained the rights provided by the U.S. Constitution, while recognizing that, because defendants were detained outside the United States, U.S. law did not govern the terms of their detention or interrogation. Rather than indicating that defendants had no right to appointed counsel, the AOR stated that defendants may have to look to local law for the effectuation of those rights. . . . [W]e do not equate the language of the AOR with a statement that counsel was unavailable. Instead, we read that language as a candid acknowledgment of the possible disparity between rights established by the U.S. Constitution, on the one hand, and the availability of counsel and entitlement to the assistance of counsel under the law of the detaining authority, on the other.

The District Court compensated for this potential disparity between U.S. constitutional rights and the rights that obtain overseas by requiring U.S. agents to study local criminal procedure and urge local officials to provide suspects with counsel, if requested, so as to "replicate" the rights that they would have in the United States. We do not agree that *Miranda* requires such efforts.

As the Supreme Court set forth in *Duckworth*, "*Miranda* does not require that attorneys be producible on call, but only that the suspect be *informed* . . . that he has the right to an attorney before and during questioning, and that an attorney would be appointed for him if he could not afford one" (emphasis added). . . . *Miranda* requires government agents to be the conduits of *information* to detained suspects — both as to (1) their rights under the U.S. Constitution to the presence and appointment of counsel at custodial interrogations and (2) the procedures through which they might be able to vindicate those rights under local law. It does not compel the police to serve as *advocates* for detainees before local authorities, endeavoring to expand the rights and privileges available under local law. This is not to say that if, after being informed of his *Miranda* rights, a detainee insists on the immediate appointment of counsel as a condition of making a statement, the U.S. officials are barred from attempting to expedite the provision of counsel. Quite the contrary; doing so is perfectly consistent with *Miranda*, but it is not required.

Because compliance with *Miranda* does not require law enforcement to advocate on behalf of suspects detained in the United States, we see no basis for adopting a different rule for detainees held overseas by foreign powers. It is true that the rights of foreign detainees to the presence and appointment of counsel will depend on foreign law, but, as noted above, *Miranda* does not require the provision of legal services. It requires only that, until legal services are either provided or waived, no interrogation take place. At the request of foreign detainees or on their own initiative, U.S. agents are free to describe the procedures by which attorneys are made available in foreign countries, so long as they make an honest, good faith effort to provide accurate information. Foreign detainees may, of course, insist that they receive local counsel or U.S. counsel as a condition of making a statement. In response, U.S. agents may, in their discretion, appeal to local authorities to appoint counsel or even obtain U.S. counsel for them. Alternatively, foreign detainees may determine that, in light of the difficulty of obtaining or unavailability of counsel under local law, it is in their best interests to waive their right to counsel and make a statement to U.S. agents. We see nothing contrary to the spirit or letter of *Miranda*, particularly as construed in *Duckworth*, in either of these results.

We are aware that, as defendants urge, foreign detainees may run the risk of refusing to speak to U.S. officials only to find themselves forced to speak to their foreign jailors. This would be so, however, even if U.S. agents made efforts to secure counsel on their behalf and those efforts proved fruitless. The risk of being forced to speak to their foreign jailor would also exist, moreover, if U.S. agents were not involved at all. Of course, statements obtained under these circumstances could not be admitted in a U.S. trial if the situation indicated that the statements were made involuntarily.[40]

Our decision not to impose additional duties on U.S. agents operating overseas is animated, in part, by our recognition that it is only through the cooperation of local authorities that U.S. agents obtain access to foreign detainees. We have no desire to strain that spirit of cooperation by compelling U.S. agents to press foreign governments for the provision of legal rights not recognized by their criminal justice systems. "For better or for worse, we live in a world of nation-states in which our Government must be able to 'function effectively in the company of sovereign nations.' Some who violate our laws may live outside our borders under a regime quite different from that which obtains in this country." *Verdugo-Urquidez*, 494 U.S. at 275. The rule of *Miranda* does not require conscripting our agents to be legal advocates for foreign detainees thereby disrupting the delicate relations between our government and a foreign power.

Although we do not find the advice of rights concerning counsel as deficient as did the District Court, we think the wording that was used created a needless risk of misunderstanding by stating, albeit accurately, what the right to counsel would have been had the interrogation occurred in the United States. An advice of rights should state only what rights are available, not what rights would be available if

---

40. [Court's footnote 22:] . . . We are satisfied that the statements at issue here were given voluntarily.

circumstances were different. This does not mean that U.S. agents need to determine what rights are in fact available under local law. All they need to say is that counsel rights depend on local law, and that the U.S. agents will afford the accused whatever rights are available under local law. Thus, an AOR used hereafter might usefully advise as to counsel rights in the following language:

> Whether you can retain a lawyer, or have a lawyer appointed for you, and whether you can consult with a lawyer and have a lawyer present during questioning are matters that depend on local law, and we cannot advise you on such matters. If local authorities permit you to obtain counsel (retained or appointed) and to consult with a lawyer at this time, you may attempt to obtain and consult with an attorney before speaking with us. Similarly, if local authorities permit you to have a lawyer present during questioning by local authorities, your lawyer may attend any questioning by us.

For these reasons, we conclude that the AOR substantially complied with whatever *Miranda* requirements were applicable. . . .

NOTES AND QUESTIONS

1. In brief, as regards oral testimony, the Fifth Amendment right against compelled self-incrimination "'can be asserted in any proceeding, civil or criminal, administrative or judicial, investigatory or adjudicatory,' in which the witness reasonably believes that the information sought, or discoverable as a result of his testimony, could be used in a subsequent state or federal criminal proceeding." United States v. Balsys, 524 U.S. 666, 672 (1998); cf. also Julie R. O'Sullivan, Federal White Collar Crime 1117-1157 (2d ed. 2004) (Fifth Amendment rules regarding the compelled production of documents and other tangible items). The witness need only demonstrate "reasonable cause to apprehend danger from a direct answer" to claim the Fifth Amendment privilege. Ohio v. Reiner, 532 U.S. 17, 21 (2001) (per curiam). Finally, the privilege against compelled self-incrimination "not only extends to answers that would in themselves support a conviction under a . . . criminal statute but likewise embraces those which would furnish a link in the chain of evidence needed to prosecute the claimant for a . . . crime." Hoffman v. United States, 341 U.S. 479, 486 (1951).

However, the Supreme Court has held that the privilege is designed only to shield a defendant from self-accusation in *criminal* proceedings. If the defendant's statement cannot be received in evidence in a criminal proceeding — for example, because the defendant has received immunity or the statute of limitations has run on the crime under investigation — then the defendant has no right to assert. He can be forced to testify, under pain of contempt and jail, even if his answers would subject him to embarrassment, civil liability, professional sanctions, or the like.

How should the protection summarized above be applied when a defendant seeks to exclude from a U.S. criminal trial evidence coerced from him in an overseas interrogation? Does the "membership" of the defendant matter? Should it matter where the interrogation took place? Is a majority of the Supreme Court likely to agree with the Second Circuit's Fifth Amendment analysis?

That analysis finds support in an earlier — and oft-ignored — precedent of the Supreme Court, Bram v. United States, 168 U.S. 532 (1897). In *Bram*, the defendant allegedly killed three people while on an American ship (which haled from Boston) on the high seas. The Court did not mention the nationality of Bram or his victims; one assumes that all were Americans. After the murders were discovered, the ship docked in Fairfax, Nova Scotia, whereupon Bram was taken into custody. While he was in the Canadian jail, he was brought before an officer of the Halifax police, strip searched, and subjected to fairly mild questioning. The statements Bram made during the course of this interrogation were admitted into evidence against him in his homicide trial in U.S. federal court in Boston. In hearing Bram's challenge to the admission of his statement, the Supreme Court examined the foreign official's conduct on foreign soil and determined that that official's conduct violated Bram's Fifth Amendment right against compelled self-incrimination because it rendered his confession involuntary. Id. at 565; see also United States v. Yunis, 859 F.2d 953, 970-971 (D.C. Cir. 1988) (Mikva, J., concurring specially). It should be noted, however, that the question whether the Fifth Amendment could be claimed at all in the circumstances does not appear to have been litigated. Instead, the Court's lengthy opinion dwelt on the question whether the factual circumstances were such as to compel Bram to speak involuntarily during the interrogation.

2. Most courts have assumed that aliens, once in the United States, can claim a Fifth Amendment right against compelled self-incrimination. See, e.g., United States v. Balsys, 524 U.S. 666, 671 (1998) ("Resident aliens . . . are considered 'persons' for purposes of the Fifth Amendment and are entitled to the same protections under the [Compelled Self-Incrimination] Clause as citizens."); Yunis, 859 F.2d at 971 (Mikva, J., concurring specially) ("Nor can there be any doubt that, once Yunis is in an American courtroom, he is protected by the privilege against self-incrimination despite his alien status"); see also Wong Wing v. United States, 163 U.S. 228, 238 (1896) ("it must be concluded that all persons within the territory of the United States are entitled to the protection guaranteed by th[e fifth and sixth] amendments").

In United States v. Balsys, 524 U.S. 666 (1998), the Supreme Court addressed a related question: whether a resident alien could assert a Fifth Amendment right against compelled self-incrimination to resist an American subpoena based on his fear of *foreign* prosecutions. Balsys was a resident alien living in New York. He was being investigated by the Department of Justice's Office of Special Investigations ("OSI") for allegedly participating in Nazi persecution during World War II. The Court did not question that Balsys could have asserted a Fifth Amendment right against compelled self-incrimination in the face of a federal prosecution, but any possible American criminal charges for participation in the Nazi genocide or for lying on his visa application were barred by the applicable statute of limitations. As noted above, Balsys would normally be unable to resist official demands for his testimony in such circumstances because the Fifth Amendment right ceases with the cessation of a realistic threat of criminal sanctions.

When OSI issued a subpoena requiring Balsys to testify at a deposition, however, he refused to answer on the ground that his answers would subject him to a real and substantial fear of prosecution in Lithuania or Israel. The Supreme Court held that he had no Fifth Amendment right to assert where his exposure arose from possible criminal prosecution by countries other than the United States. This decision was founded in part on the determination that a potential foreign criminal case does not qualify as "any criminal case" in the language of the Fifth Amendment. The Supreme Court rejected a plain language approach, arguing that "any" must be read in context:

> In the Fifth Amendment context, the Clause in question occurs in the company of guarantees of grand jury proceedings, defense against double jeopardy, due process, and compensation for property taking. Because none of these provisions is implicated

except by action of the government that it binds, it would have been strange to choose such associates for a Clause meant to take a broader view, and it would be strange to find such a sweep in the Clause now. . . . Because the Fifth Amendment opens by requiring a grand jury indictment or presentment "for a capital, or otherwise infamous crime," the phrase beginning "any" in the subsequent Self-Incrimination Clause may sensibly be read as making it clear that the privilege it provides is not so categorically limited. We therefore take this to be the fair reading of the adjective "any," and we read the Clause contextually as apparently providing a witness with the right against self-incrimination when reasonably fearing prosecution by the government whose power the Clause limits, but not otherwise.

Id. at 673-674. Does this reasoning have any bearing on the conceptual basis for extraterritorial constitutional application (for example, the universalist theory)?

The *Balsys* Court added one caveat to its holding: If "the United States and its allies had enacted substantially similar criminal codes aimed at prosecuting offenses of international character, and if it could be shown that the United States was granting immunity from domestic prosecution for the purpose of obtaining evidence to be delivered to other nations as prosecutors of a crime common to both countries, then an argument could be made that the Fifth Amendment should apply based on fear of foreign prosecution simply because that prosecution was not fairly characterized as distinctly 'foreign.'" Id. at 698. In *Balsys*, however, the Court concluded that "[t]here is no system of complementary substantive offenses at issue here, and the mere support of one nation for the prosecutorial efforts of another does not transform the prosecution of the one into the prosecution of the other." Id. at 699-700.

Justices Breyer and Ginsberg dissented, arguing that the "basic values that this Court has said underlie the Fifth Amendment's protection are each diminished if the privilege may not be claimed here." Id. at 720 (Breyer, J., dissenting). Justice Ginsberg wrote a short, separate dissent to state:

> The privilege against self-incrimination, "closely linked historically with the abolition of torture," is properly regarded as a "landmar[k] in man's struggle to make himself civilized." In my view, the Fifth Amendment privilege against self-incrimination prescribes a rule of conduct generally to be followed by our Nation's officialdom. It counsels officers of the United States (and of any State of the United States) against extracting testimony when the person examined reasonably fears that his words would be used against him in a later criminal prosecution. As a restraint on compelling a person to bear witness against himself, the Amendment ordinarily should command the respect of United States interrogators, whether the prosecution reasonably feared by the examinee is domestic or foreign. On this understanding of the "fundamental decenc[y]" the Fifth Amendment embodies, "its expression of our view of civilized governmental conduct," I join Justice Breyer's dissenting opinion.

Id. at 701-702 (Ginsburg, J., dissenting). Do their dissents give you any insight into how Justices Ginsburg and Breyer would have voted in *Verdugo-Urquidez* had they been on the Court at that time?

Professor Diane Marie Amann has criticized the Court's holding, arguing that the Court's reading of precedent was obviously in error. She further notes:

> Although the privilege against self-incrimination, in all its contours, may not yet be described as customary international law, an international right to silence is emerging among those "generally recognized international standards which lie at the heart of the notion of fair procedure." Furthermore, the rapid increase in global law-enforcement

efforts, through extradition and mutual legal assistance treaties, international police forces, and other means, has created an international system of law enforcement that rivals the intrafederal system prevailing in the United States. . . . Finally, the historical purposes of the privilege require that courts concern themselves with the harm that compelling testimony will wreak on the individual. That the final harm — the use of compelled testimony in a manner that might secure conviction and, perhaps, the ultimate punishment — would occur abroad ought not to end the matter. This final harm could not be achieved without the participation of U.S. interrogators, investigators, prosecutors and judges, all of whom ordinarily must obey the strictures of the Constitution. The majority's articulation of an exception to its general rule against extension of the privilege offers little solace, given that it found no cause to apply the exception in this case.

Diane Marie Amann, Application of the Fifth Amendment to U.S. Constitution in International Context — Fear of Foreign Prosecution as Ground for Invoking Privilege Against Self-Incrimination — Relevance of Growing International Law Enforcement Cooperation — Role of U.S. Judiciary in Foreign Relations, 92 Am. J. Intl. L. 759, 763 (2004).

3. What is the Second Circuit's holding with respect to aliens' "rights" under *Miranda* when questioned by American agents abroad? This is actually a very complex issue, which breaks down into two questions: (A) whether the Fifth Amendment *requires* the provision of *Miranda*'s various protections (because if *Miranda* is not a "constitutional" rule, the Supreme Court is exceedingly unlikely to extend its reach overseas); and (B) whether there should be an exception to the *Miranda* rules in cases of overseas interrogations.

A. *Does the Fifth Amendment require the provision of* Miranda's *protections?* The constitutional status of *Miranda* is still in question given recent Supreme Court precedents. A detailed review of the relevant precedents is beyond the scope of this chapter, but the following summary may suffice to give some sense of how difficult this question is.

Recall our discussion in Part C above of the Supreme Court's historical treatment of coerced confession cases under the Due Process Clause of the Fourteenth Amendment and its unhappiness with the subjectivity of its voluntariness "totality of the circumstances" test. We noted that the Supreme Court held in 1964 that the Fifth Amendment's right against compelled self-incrimination was applicable to the U.S. states through the Due Process Clause of the Fourteenth Amendment. See Malloy v. Hogan, 378 U.S. 1 (1964). Once the Fifth Amendment right against compelled self-incrimination was isolated as the primary operative provision applicable to coerced confession cases, the Court set about creating "bright-line rules" to govern this Fifth Amendment confession law in Miranda v. Arizona, 384 U.S. 436 (1966). (Recall, however, that the Supreme Court did not overrule its prior due process voluntariness cases; it simply augmented them with a Fifth Amendment right against compelled self-incrimination/*Miranda* objection to the admission of "coerced" confessions.)

The entire basis on which *Miranda* rests is the Court's conclusion that custodial interrogations by known government agents are inherently coercive. Absent the construction of procedural rules to safeguard the effective exercise of a defendant's Fifth Amendment right against compelled self-incrimination, any statement flowing from a custodial interrogation must be deemed compelled within the meaning of the Fifth Amendment. Where a defendant is subjected to a custodial interrogation, then, *Miranda* requires the provision of the now-familiar warnings, creates a preindictment right to counsel that would not otherwise exist under the Sixth Amendment, and imposes a stringent waiver standard before confessions secured in the course of a custodial interrogation may be admitted into evidence. If the government does not comply with these safeguards, the presumption is that the inherently coercive nature of the encounter has in fact resulted in an involuntary confession.

Miranda was decided in the heyday of the "liberal" Warren Court. Over time, the Court attempted to cut back on *Miranda,* calling it a "prophylactic" rule subject to exceptions, rather than a constitutional imperative. By classing *Miranda* as "merely" prophylactic, the Court sought to justify making exceptions to its application that were inconsistent with its stated rationale. For example, in New York v. Quarles, 467 U.S. 649 (1984), police captured a man whom they had been told had committed a crime with a gun and then fled into a grocery store. After a number of officers surrounded the suspect, frisked him (discovering an empty holster), and handcuffed him, one of the officers asked the suspect where the gun was. The question presented to the Supreme Court was whether the suspect's statement, "the gun is over there," could be admitted into evidence, even though it was made during a custodial interrogation and without *Miranda* warnings. The Court held that "on these facts there is a 'public safety' exception to the requirement that *Miranda* warnings be given before a suspect's answers may be admitted into evidence." Id. at 655. Moreover, the Court ruled that, even though the officers in *Quarles* had testified that they did not feel threatened by the suspect and did not ask the question out of a concern for their or the public's safety, the exception applied because the public safety exception is an objective test and does not depend on the actual motivation of the officers involved. Id. at 656.

Justice Marshall argued in dissent that *Miranda* "created a constitutional presumption that statements made during custodial interrogations are compelled in violation of the Fifth Amendment and are thus inadmissible in criminal prosecutions." Id. at 683 (Marshall, J., dissenting). He then noted the inconsistency between a "public safety" exception and this constitutional presumption:

> In fashioning its "public-safety" exception to *Miranda,* the majority makes no attempt to deal with the constitutional presumption established by that case. The majority does not argue that police questioning about issues of public safety is any less coercive than custodial interrogation into other matters. The majority's only contention is that police officers could more easily protect the public if *Miranda* did not apply to custodial interrogations concerning the public's safety. But *Miranda* was not a decision about public safety; it was a decision about coerced confessions. Without establishing that interrogations concerning the public's safety are less likely to be coercive than other interrogations, the majority cannot endorse the "public-safety" exception and remain faithful to the logic of Miranda v. Arizona.

Id. at 684. The Court's characterization of *Miranda* as a "non-constitutional" prophylactic rule also allowed it to exempt *Miranda* from doctrines that apply to "constitutional" rules. Thus, the Supreme Court determined that the "fruit of the poisonous tree" doctrine — which decrees that derivative evidence seized through exploitation of a constitutional violation must be excluded from evidence — does not apply to *Miranda* violations. See Oregon v. Elstad, 470 U.S. 298 (1985).

The problem with treating *Miranda* as a "non-constitutional" prophylaxis was that the Supreme Court regularly, over more than 40 years, overturned U.S. state convictions based on state officials' violation of the *Miranda* rules. The question then arose: If *Miranda* is *not* a *constitutional* rule, how does the Supreme Court get off imposing it on the U.S. states? For example, in *Elstad*, Justice Stevens took issue with the Court's assumption that violating *Miranda* was not tantamount to violating the Fifth Amendment itself:

> . . . This Court's power to require state courts to exclude probative self-incriminatory statements rests entirely on the premise that the use of such evidence violates the Federal Constitution. The same constitutional analysis applies whether the custodial interrogation is actually coercive [for Fifth Amendment purposes] or irrebuttably presumed to be coercive [under *Miranda*]. If the Court does not accept that premise, it must regard the holding in the *Miranda* case itself, as well as all of the federal jurisprudence that has evolved from that decision, as nothing more than an illegitimate exercise of raw judicial power.

Id. at 371-372 (Stevens, J., dissenting).

This question came to a head in Dickerson v. United States, 530 U.S. 428 (2000). *Dickerson* concerned a federal statute, 18 U.S.C. §3501, that had been passed shortly after *Miranda* was decided and that purported to "overrule" *Miranda*. In essence, §3501 provided that confessions would be admissible if they passed the due process voluntariness test — whether or not the police had abided by *Miranda*'s strictures. Curiously, over 40 years, successive Democratic and Republican administrations had refused to enforce or press the applicability of the statute, and thus the issue whether the statute in fact overruled *Miranda* — that is, whether *Miranda* was a constitutional rule — was not litigated until 2000. In *Dickerson*, the Supreme Court held (over the emphatic dissent of Justices Scalia and Thomas) that "*Miranda*, being a constitutional decision of this Court, may not be in effect overruled by an Act of Congress, and we decline to overrule *Miranda* ourselves. We therefore hold that *Miranda* and its progeny in this Court govern the admissibility of statements made during custodial interrogations in both state and federal courts." 530 U.S. at 432.

Unfortunately, *Dickerson* was not the end of the story. A number of subsequent Supreme Court decisions indicate that the Court remains deeply divided on the question of *Miranda*'s constitutional status. See, e.g., United States v. Patane, 542 U.S. 630 (2004); Missouri v. Seibert, 542 U.S. 600 (2004); Chavez v. Martinez, 538 U.S. 768 (2003). The reasoning expressed by various Justices in these very splintered opinions also is relevant to the question of the extraterritorial reach of the Constitution. For example, at least three of the Justices have indicated their belief that a "violation" of the Fifth Amendment does not necessarily occur at the time the compelled statement is introduced in a U.S. trial, but rather occurs "the moment torture or its close equivalents are brought to bear." *Chavez*, 538 U.S. at 789 (Kennedy, J., concurring and dissenting). Would the Second Circuit's analysis be affected were a majority of the Court to conclude, as does Justice Kennedy, that "[c]onstitutional protection for a tortured suspect is not held in abeyance until some later criminal proceeding takes place"? Id. at 789-790.

To return to *Chavez*, discussed in Part C above, recall that *Chavez* involved a civil rights suit founded on an abusive interrogation. The deeply divided Supreme Court held that the Due Process Clauses of the Fifth and Fourteenth Amendments, rather than the Fifth Amendment's privilege against compelled self-incrimination, govern a civil rights suit alleging that a state officer used coercive interrogation tactics to elicit an involuntary confession *when the confession was never used in court*. The reason the case attracted a lot of attention was the potential that state and federal actors would be held civilly liable for damages for violations of *Miranda*, regardless of whether the evidence was ever used at trial. Six Justices, in various opinions, opined in *Chavez* that a violation of *Miranda* rights does not provide a basis for a federal civil rights action for damages.

Six Justices wrote opinions in *Chavez*. Reference to those opinions sheds light on the extent to which the Justices believe *Miranda* to be constitutionally required; their reasoning also implicates the question of just *where* a violation of the Fifth Amendment occurs when a confession is coerced or tortured from a suspect outside the territory of the United States. Justice Thomas, writing a plurality opinion joined by the Chief Justice, Justice O'Connor (in relevant part), and Justice Scalia, reasoned as follows:

> We have . . . established the *Miranda* exclusionary rule as a prophylactic measure to prevent violations of the right protected by the text of the Self-Incrimination Clause — the admission into evidence in a criminal case of confessions obtained through coercive custodial questioning. Accordingly, Chavez's failure to read *Miranda* warnings to Martinez did not violate Martinez's constitutional rights and cannot be grounds for a §1983 action. And the absence of a "criminal case" in which Martinez was compelled to be a "witness" against himself defeats his core Fifth Amendment claim. The Ninth Circuit's view that mere compulsion violates the Self-Incrimination Clause, finds no support in the text of the Fifth Amendment and is irreconcilable with our case law. Because we find that Chavez's alleged conduct did not violate the Self-Incrimination Clause, we reverse the Ninth Circuit's denial of qualified immunity as to Martinez's Fifth Amendment claim.

Id. at 766-773. How can this be squared with *Dickerson*?

Justice Souter, joined by Justice Breyer, concurred in the judgment, agreeing with the Thomas plurality that Martinez's claim under §1983 for violation of his privilege against compelled self-incrimination had to be rejected. Justice Souter explained, however, that:

> . . . I believe that our decision requires a degree of discretionary judgment greater than Justice Thomas acknowledges. As he points out, the text of the Fifth Amendment (applied here under the doctrine of Fourteenth Amendment incorporation) focuses on courtroom use of a criminal defendant's compelled, self-incriminating testimony, and the core of the guarantee against compelled self-incrimination is the exclusion of any such evidence. . . . Martinez's testimony would clearly be inadmissible if offered in evidence against him. But Martinez claims more than evidentiary protection in asking this Court to hold that the questioning alone was a completed violation of the Fifth and Fourteenth Amendments subject to redress by an action for damages under §1983.
>
> To recognize such a constitutional cause of action for compensation would, of course, be well outside the core of Fifth Amendment protection, but that alone is not a sufficient reason to reject Martinez's claim. . . .
>
> I do not, however, believe that Martinez can make the "powerful showing," subject to a realistic assessment of costs and risks, necessary to expand protection of the privilege against compelled self-incrimination to the point of the civil liability he asks us to recognize here. The most obvious drawback inherent in Martinez's purely Fifth Amendment claim to damages is its risk of global application in every instance of interrogation producing a statement inadmissible under Fifth and Fourteenth Amendment principles, or violating one of the complementary rules we have accepted in aid of the privilege against evidentiary use. If obtaining Martinez's statement is to be treated as a stand-alone violation of the privilege subject to compensation, why should the same not be true whenever the police obtain any involuntary self-incriminating statement, or whenever the government so much as threatens a penalty in derogation of the right to immunity,

or whenever the police fail to honor *Miranda*? Martinez offers no limiting principle or
reason to foresee a stopping place short of liability in all such cases.

Id. at 777-779. In a footnote, Justice Souter noted that "[t]he question whether the
absence of *Miranda* warnings may be a basis for a §1983 action under any circumstance is not before the Court." Id. at 779. Finally, in a sentence joined by Justices
Breyer, Stevens, Kennedy, and Ginsburg, Justice Souter uttered the one statement in
the case to command a majority of the Court: "Whether Martinez may pursue a claim
of liability for a substantive due process violation is thus an issue that should be
addressed on remand, along with the scope and merits of any such action that may
be found open to him." Id. at 779-780.

In his separate opinion, Justice Kennedy, joined by Justice Stevens, agreed with the
Thomas plurality that failure to give a *Miranda* warning does not, without more,
establish a completed constitutional violation actionable under 42 U.S.C. §1983
when an unwarned interrogation ensures. Id. at 789. However, Justice Kennedy,
joined by Justices Stevens *and* Ginsburg, argued that "Justice Souter and Justice
Thomas are wrong . . . to maintain that in all instances a violation of the Self-
Incrimination Clause simply does not occur unless and until a statement is introduced at trial, no matter how severe the pain or how direct and commanding the
official compulsion used to extract it." Id. at 790.

> The conclusion that the Self-Incrimination Clause is not violated until the govern-
> ment seeks to use a statement in some later criminal proceeding strips the Clause of an
> essential part of its force and meaning. This is no small matter. It should come as an
> unwelcome surprise to judges, attorneys, and the citizenry as a whole that if a legislative
> committee or a judge in a civil case demands incriminating testimony without offering
> immunity, and even imposes sanctions for failure to comply, that the witness and
> counsel cannot insist the right against compelled self-incrimination is applicable then
> and there. Justice Souter and Justice Thomas, I submit, should be more respectful of the
> understanding that has prevailed for generations now. To tell our whole legal system that
> when conducting a criminal investigation police officials can use severe compulsion or
> even torture with no present violation of the right against compelled self-incrimination
> can only diminish a celebrated provision in the Bill of Rights. A Constitution survives
> over time because the people share a common, historic commitment to certain simple
> but fundamental principles which preserve their freedom. Today's decision undermines
> one of those respected precepts. . . .
>
> In my view the Self-Incrimination Clause is applicable at the time and place police use
> compulsion to extract a statement from a suspect. The Clause forbids that conduct.
> A majority of the Court has now concluded otherwise, but that should not end this
> case. It simply implicates the larger definition of liberty under the Due Process Clause
> of the Fourteenth Amendment. Turning to this essential, but less specific, guarantee, it
> seems to me a simple enough matter to say that use of torture or its equivalent in an
> attempt to induce a statement violates an individual's fundamental right to liberty of the
> person. The Constitution does not countenance the official imposition of severe
> pain or pressure for purposes of interrogation. This is true whether the protection is
> found in the Self-Incrimination Clause, the broader guarantees of the Due Process
> Clause, or both.

Id. at 791-796. After examining the facts of the case, Justice Kennedy stated that he
would affirm the Ninth Circuit's holding that a Fifth Amendment cause of action
under §1983 had been stated. He noted, however, that if he and Justices Stevens and
Ginsburg were to adhere to this position, there would be no controlling judgment of
the Court. "In these circumstances, and because a ruling on substantive due process

in this case could provide much of the essential protection the Self-Incrimination Clause secures," Justices Kennedy, Stevens, and Ginsburg joined that part of Justice Souter's opinion remanding the Due Process claim for further consideration. Id. at 799.

Justice Ginsburg, in another separate opinion, explained that, for the reasons well stated in Justice Kennedy's opinion, "I would hold that the Self-Incrimination Clause applies at the time and place police use severe compulsion to extract a statement from a suspect." Id. at 799. She, like Justice Kennedy, thought that the interrogation was a clear constitutional violation—in her mind, "a clear instance of the kind of compulsion no reasonable officer would have thought constitutionally permissible." Id.

Given the various Justices' opinions in *Chavez*, is it clear that the Fifth Amendment violation in the context of a coerced confession occurs only at trial and thus only in the territorial United States? Why does the *location* of the violation matter?

B. Should there be an exception to the *Miranda* rules in cases of overseas interrogations? Even if *Miranda* is a constitutional rule, the Supreme Court has carved out exceptions to its applicability in certain circumstances—essentially where the costs of the rule outweigh its benefits. What is the cost/benefit likely to be where non-U.S. nationals claim the benefits of *Miranda* during custodial interrogations abroad by U.S. agents? Is the Court likely to hold that *Quarles*'s "public safety" exception survived *Dickerson*? If so, might the Court use it to craft a wartime exception? See Mark A. Godsey, Miranda's Final Frontier—The International Arena: A Critical Analysis of *United States v. Bin Laden*, and a Proposal for a New Miranda Exception Abroad, 51 Duke L.J. 1703 (2001-2002).

E. SIXTH AMENDMENT RIGHT TO COUNSEL

The Sixth Amendment guarantees that "[i]n all criminal prosecutions, the accused shall enjoy the right . . . to have the Assistance of Counsel for his defence." In *United States v. Balsys*, discussed in Part D above, the Supreme Court stated during the course of its textual analysis of the Fifth Amendment that the Sixth Amendment "clearly applies only to domestic criminal proceedings."[41] If one sees the Sixth Amendment right to counsel as a right confined to having counsel stand up and defend one in a court of law, it is easy to see why the Court characterized it as a purely domestic right. The potential for transnational applications of the Sixth Amendment are raised, however, by the fact that the Sixth Amendment right to counsel has force before any trial begins.

The Sixth Amendment right is triggered by the commencement of adversary proceedings against the defendant. This right entitles a person "to the help of a lawyer at or after the time that judicial proceedings have been initiated against him 'whether by way of formal charge, preliminary hearing, indictment, information or arraignment.'"[42] In *Brewer v. Williams*,[43] the Court affirmed the "vital need" for the Sixth Amendment counsel right at the pretrial stage: "'perhaps the most critical period of the proceedings [is] . . . from the time of [defendants'] arraignment

---

41. United States v. Balsys, 524 U.S. 666, 672 (1998).
42. Brewer v. Williams, 430 U.S. 387, 398 (1977).
43. Id.

until the beginning of trial, when consultation, thorough-going investigations and preparation'" is "'vitally important.'"[44]

Perhaps more important for purposes of assessing the extraterritorial reach of the Sixth Amendment counsel right is the fact that, in some circumstances, that right will limit contacts between the defendant and the government and, specifically, circumscribes *postindictment* interrogations. The Supreme Court has held that "once formal criminal proceedings begin, the Sixth Amendment renders inadmissible in the prosecution's case in chief statements 'deliberately elicited' from a defendant without an express waiver of the right to counsel."[45] The fruits of postindictment questioning are only admissible in a prosecution's case in chief if the government can prove a knowing, voluntary, and intelligent waiver of the Sixth Amendment counsel right. "[W]hen a suspect waives his right to counsel after receiving warnings equivalent to those prescribed by Miranda v. Arizona, that will generally suffice to establish a knowing and intelligent waiver of the Sixth Amendment right to counsel for purposes of postindictment questioning."[46] In the absence of such warnings and a qualifying waiver, however, counsel must be present for any postindictment "deliberate elicitation" by government agents.

To determine whether the Court would be willing to acknowledge an extraterritorial right to counsel under the Sixth Amendment during foreign interrogations, one needs to understand the expressed object of this right. Recall that the *Miranda* right to counsel is designed to alleviate "the compulsion inherent in custodial surroundings."[47] The Sixth Amendment is not concerned with compulsion. First, and very generally, "[t]he State's interest in truth seeking is congruent with the defendant's interest in representation by counsel, for it is an elementary premise of our system of criminal justice that partisan advocacy on both sides of a case will best promote the ultimate objective that the guilty be convicted and the innocent go free."[48] Additionally, the "Sixth Amendment right to counsel is much more pervasive [than the *Miranda* right to counsel] because it affects the ability of the accused to assert any other rights he may have."[49] The Sixth Amendment's counsel right is viewed as the "lynchpin" on which the effective exercise of the defendant's other trial rights — to cross-examine, call witnesses, and the like — depends.

The bar on deliberate elicitation of information from an indicted defendant in absence of counsel or a qualifying waiver is based on a number of related ideas. "The Sixth Amendment guarantees the accused, at least after the initiation of formal charges, the right to rely on counsel as a 'medium' between him and the State."[50] This rule, then, "serves the salutary purpose of preventing police interference with the relationship between a suspect and his counsel once formal proceedings have been initiated."[51] Many of the opinions recognize that, after the initiation of formal proceedings, the prosecution and defense have squared off; basic fairness requires that the government avoid interference with the counsel relationship where the government's role has shifted from investigation to accusation and the "defendant finds himself faced with the prosecutorial forces of organized society."[52]

---

44. Id. at 398 (quoting Powell v. Alabama, 287 U.S. 45, 57 (1932)).
45. Michigan v. Harvey, 494 U.S. 344, 348 (1990).
46. Id. at 349.
47. *Miranda*, 384 U.S. at 458.
48. *Harvey*, 494 U.S. at 357 (Stevens, J., dissenting).
49. Id.
50. Maine v. Molton, 474 U.S. 159, 176 (1985).
51. United States v. Henry, 447 U.S. 264, 276 (1980) (Powell, J., concurring).
52. Kirby v. Illinois, 406 U.S. 682, 689 (1972).

This rationale reflects a fundamental ethical principle: Once the adversary process has begun, a party (particularly the government) may not contact his adversary (particularly an individual defendant unschooled in the law) in the absence of counsel. By seeking information in the absence of counsel, state agents effectively interpose themselves between client and counsel, rendering counsel's advice meaningless and impairing her effectiveness at trial. Without the rules governing postindictment questioning in absence of counsel, then, there would be "insufficient protection against any attempt by the State to supplant 'the public trial guaranteed by the Bill of Rights' with a 'secret trial in the police precincts.'"[53] There is also a sense that, once the state has indicted, it is acting unethically in seeking pretrial discovery beyond that provided for in the discovery rules.

Given the above, should the postindictment Sixth Amendment counsel right extend to persons interrogated abroad? When (and thus where) is the Sixth Amendment "violated" in a case where the defendant is questioned postindictment in the absence of his counsel or a valid waiver? Consider the following case.

UNITED STATES v. RAVEN
103 F. Supp. 2d 38 (D. Mass. 2000)

[Raven, a citizen of the Netherlands, had been indicted in the United States. Had Raven been a U.S. citizen, he unquestionably would have had a right to counsel during the course of any questioning by U.S. agents, and statements secured without a knowing, intelligent, and voluntary waiver of that right would normally be inadmissible in U.S. courts — at least where the interrogation occurred in the United States. Raven had engaged counsel to represent him in a Belgian case concerning allegations similar to those raised in the U.S. case. His counsel was not present, however, when Raven was interrogated after his U.S. indictment by Belgian and U.S. law enforcement representatives while he was in custody in Belgium. Nor, apparently, was a valid waiver found. The district court in Massachusetts denied Raven's motion to suppress based on alleged violations of Raven's Fifth and Sixth Amendment rights, reasoning as follows.]

Raven is correct that, even as an alien, he would have been entitled to some constitutional protections if he had been in the United States at the time of the questioning. The Supreme Court has extended certain constitutional rights to foreign nationals when they reside or are being held in the United States. See, e.g., Yick Wo v. Hopkins, 118 U.S. 356, 369 (1886); Wong Wing v. United States, 163 U.S. 228, 236 (1896).

When the questioning takes place overseas, however, foreign nationals do not benefit from the protections of the United States Constitution. Although the Supreme Court has not specifically addressed the question of whether the Sixth Amendment applies extraterritorially, it has held that the protections of the Fourth and Fifth Amendments do not apply to foreign nationals outside of the United States. Johnson v. Eisentrager, 339 U.S. 763, 784 (1950) (Fifth Amendment not applicable to aliens outside of the United States); United States v. Verdugo-Urquidez, 494 U.S. 259, 269 (1990) (Fourth Amendment not applicable to alien when search conducted by United States law enforcement agents in foreign country). This Court is persuaded that, having rejected the extraterritorial application of the Fourth and Fifth

---

53. *Harvey*, 494 U.S. at 358 (Stevens, J., dissenting).

Amendments to aliens, the Supreme Court would do likewise if requested to enforce the Sixth Amendment under similar circumstances.

Moreover, the United States law enforcement representatives who questioned Raven in Belgium complied with all applicable laws of their host country. After receiving a Letter Rogatory issued by this Court, the Belgian government instructed the American law enforcement representatives that they could go forward with questioning Raven only without his counsel present. Further, those representatives obtained the approval of a Belgian Magistrate Judge before proceeding to question Raven without counsel present. Only after confirming that Belgian law does not allow a defendant's counsel to be present during questioning did the American law enforcement representatives proceed with the interview. This Court finds that comity compels such action and that Raven's statements to those representatives should not be suppressed.

QUESTION

Is this a fair application of the Supreme Court's precedent?

CHAPTER
8

Obtaining Evidence Abroad

The vast expansion in transnational crime increasingly requires the acquisition of evidence located in one country for use in criminal proceedings in another. But prosecutors and defense attorneys alike face significant obstacles in obtaining what they need. This chapter focuses on the question: What "discovery" tools are available to prosecutors and defense lawyers when the alleged crimes span national borders?

The domestic rules on collecting evidence in criminal proceedings vary widely from country to country. To be effective at trial, evidence abroad needs to be acquired quickly and in an admissible form according to the rules of the forum state. But evidence that might be readily admissible in one jurisdiction is often barred in another. For instance, U.S. "chain of custody" requirements rarely find parallels in foreign law, and hearsay—whose admissibility is restricted in U.S. criminal proceedings—is, by contrast, a perfectly acceptable form of evidence in many other countries (particularly those in the civil law tradition). The scope and application of privileges also differ markedly. In the United States, corporations and other impersonal entities may claim the protections of the attorney-client privilege, but in other countries that privilege may be invoked only by natural persons. Many countries have privacy and secrecy laws that protect bank records, official government records, and personal information far more broadly than U.S. law.[1]

Investigative practices that seem routine to U.S. prosecutors or defense counsel may in fact be criminal offenses elsewhere. In many countries, investigating crimes and gathering evidence are functions reserved solely to the domestic judicial authorities or police. Even when permissible, sending law enforcement officials to a foreign nation to gather evidence can be slow, expensive, and potentially inefficient. Yet relying on foreign authorities to provide the needed evidence may present its own difficulties. For example, many countries are reluctant to cooperate at the early stages of a criminal investigation before formal charges have been brought, and some are not likely to cooperate in cases in which the forum country's assertion of extraterritorial criminal jurisdiction is considered excessive. What constitutes a crime in one jurisdiction may not be one in another; conflicts in law and government policy can also hinder the process.

---

1. The Cayman Islands, Panama, Singapore, and Switzerland, among others, have long been known for their strict bank secrecy provisions. The emergence of much broader data protection and privacy laws in recent years, particularly within the European Union, has had a substantial impact on evidence collection in criminal cases.

In practice, the barriers to securing admissible evidence are often higher for government prosecutors, not only because they bear the burden of proving the defendant's guilt, but also because traditionally governments have not been enthusiastic about enforcing, or appearing to enforce, the criminal laws and processes of other countries.

A.   HYPOTHETICAL

You are an assistant U.S. attorney overseeing the federal investigation of Jessica Robinson, a citizen of the State of Paradox and the suspected leader of an international drug cartel that for many years has succeeded in importing large quantities of cocaine into the United States via Central America and the Caribbean. Informants and undercover agents have learned through their dealings with members of Robinson's cartel that she has deposited millions of dollars in proceeds from drug trafficking at branches of the Commercial Bank of Sweetland (CBS), a large multinational bank headquartered in Europe with branches in the United States and abroad. If you can get the records of those transactions, you may have enough evidence to charge Robinson with drug trafficking and money laundering. You might also be able to use those records to trace suspected bribery payments to state and local officials in the United States.

But Paradox has strict bank secrecy laws that permit disclosure of those records only if a Paradox judge issues an order finding that the evidence is sufficient to prosecute a crime under Paradoxian law or with the consent of the account holder. Failure to comply with those laws is a criminal offense, although the laws are not consistently enforced. Paradoxian law currently does not make it a crime for a citizen of that country to export drugs into other countries.

How might you try to get the bank records located in Paradox? In what ways could you seek the cooperation of the relevant authorities in Paradox, formally or informally? Can you compel CBS to produce the records? Would your analysis be different if the law in Paradox permitted no exceptions? Or if Paradox did not recognize any protection against self-incrimination? What if Robinson had U.S. citizenship or traveled to the United States? Could you compel her consent to release of the records? Would you be prepared to authorize your investigators to go to Paradox in an effort to obtain the records themselves, by whatever means might be available? How could you be certain that the records would be admissible before the grand jury or at trial?

B.   LETTERS ROGATORY

The traditional means of obtaining evidence from other countries has been by *Letters Rogatory*, which are requests issued by the courts in one country to the courts in another. Letters rogatory are "the medium, in effect, whereby one country, speaking through one of its courts, requests another country acting through its own courts and by methods of court procedure peculiar thereto and entirely within the latter's control, to assist the administration of justice in the former country; such requests being made, and being usually granted, by reason of the comity existing between nations in ordinary peaceful times."[2] Compliance with letter rogatory requests is discretionary because international law imposes no obligation on states to respond. Cooperation is thus based on considerations of comity.

Once issued, letters rogatory are typically transmitted through governmental channels (that is, from the requesting court to the ministry of justice, then from one foreign ministry to another, and through the ministry of justice to the court in the requested country). That journey may take a considerable amount of time. The specific procedures for responding to letters rogatory are left to the domestic law of the requested state, and there is no guarantee that the information or evidence, if ultimately provided, will be complete or in an acceptable (admissible) form.

In the United States, the Department of State has long been empowered by statute, 28 U.S.C. §1781, to process letters rogatory issued by courts in the United States, to transmit them to the appropriate foreign or international tribunals, officers, or agencies, and to receive and return them after execution. The same statute authorizes the Department to receive letters rogatory issued by a foreign or international tribunal, to transmit them to the tribunal, officer, or agency in the United States to whom it is addressed, and to receive and return the responses.

Under 28 U.S.C. §1782, federal district courts are authorized to require the giving of testimony and the production of documents or other evidence "for use in a proceeding in a foreign or international tribunal, including criminal investigations conducted before formal accusation." The court may do so in response to a letter rogatory issued, or request made, by a foreign or international tribunal or upon application by "any interested person." The court "may direct that the testimony or statement be given, or the document or other thing be produced, before a person appointed by the court," and the court also "may prescribe the practice and procedure, which may be in whole or part the practice and procedure of the foreign country or the international tribunal, for taking the testimony or statement or producing the document or other thing." The statute notes, however, that "[t]o the extent that the order does not prescribe otherwise, the testimony or statement shall be taken, and the document or other thing produced, in accordance with the Federal Rules of Civil Procedure." It also expressly provides that "[a] person may not be compelled to give his testimony or statement or to produce a document or other thing in violation of any legally applicable privilege."

IN RE CLERICI
481 F.3d 1324 (11th Cir. 2007)

[Clerici, a Panamanian citizen and merchant who also resided in Miami, brought a civil lawsuit against a Panamanian business, NoName Corporation, and others in the courts of Panama and obtained a judicial seizure of NoName's property. Clerici's lawsuit was subsequently dismissed for lack of prosecution, and the Panamanian Court vacated the attachment of NoName's property. NoName then sued Clerici in Panamanian court claiming damages arising from the dismissed civil suit and the attachment of its property. At the conclusion of NoName's suit, it won a sizable damages judgment against Clerici. In support of its efforts to enforce that judgment, NoName sought information about Clerici's assets and other financial matters in Panama and elsewhere. The Panamanian Court issued a letter rogatory to the

---

2. The Signe, 37 F. Supp. 819, 820 (E.D. La. 1941).

"Judicial Authorities of the City of Miami" requesting assistance in obtaining answers from Clerici, noting that the evidence obtained "will be used in the civil process before this court." The U.S. attorney filed an *ex parte* application pursuant to 28 U.S.C. §1782 for an order appointing an assistant U.S. attorney as a commissioner for the purpose of obtaining the evidence requested by the Panamanian court.]

HULL, Circuit Judge:

This case involves the authority of federal district courts to assist in the production of evidence — here, sworn answers to written questions — for use in a foreign court. . . .

Beginning in 1948, "Congress substantially broadened the scope of assistance federal courts could provide for foreign proceedings," pursuant to 28 U.S.C. §1782. Intel Corp. v. Advanced Micro Devices, Inc., 542 U.S. 241 (2004) (reviewing at length the 150-year history of congressional efforts to provide judicial assistance to foreign tribunals and amendments designed to broaden the scope of §1782). "The history of Section 1782 reveals Congress' wish to strengthen the power of district courts to respond to requests for international assistance."

Because "Congress has given the district courts such broad discretion in granting judicial assistance to foreign countries, this court may overturn the district court's decision only for abuse of discretion." This review is "extremely limited and highly deferential." Further, "[t]his deferential standard is identical to that used in reviewing the district court's ordinary discovery rulings." . . .

A district court has the authority to grant an application for judicial assistance if the following statutory requirements in §1782(a) are met: (1) the request must be made "by a foreign or international tribunal," or by "any interested person"; (2) the request must seek evidence, whether it be the "testimony or statement" of a person or the production of "a document or other thing"; (3) the evidence must be "for use in a proceeding in a foreign or international tribunal"; and (4) the person from whom discovery is sought must reside or be found in the district of the district court ruling on the application for assistance. 28 U.S.C. §1782(a). If these requirements are met, then §1782 "authorizes, but does not require, a federal district court to provide assistance. . . ."

As to the third statutory requirement, we reject Clerici's contention that the requested evidence was not "for use in a proceeding" before the Panamanian Court. Here, there is a proceeding currently pending before the Panamanian Court that allows NoName or the Panamanian Court to question Clerici under oath about his properties, rights, credits, sustenance means, and other sources of income from the date of his court-ordered obligation. . . . Because Clerici was residing in Florida, however, the Panamanian Court issued a letter rogatory seeking international assistance in order to obtain this evidence. The Panamanian Court's letter rogatory itself stated that this evidence "will be used in the civil process before this court." Such a request is clearly within the range of discovery authorized under §1782 and comports with the purpose of the statute to provide assistance to foreign tribunals.

Given the pending proceeding before the Panamanian Court, Clerici is reduced to arguing that a "proceeding" means an adjudicative proceeding, and thus, NoName's post-judgment petition regarding a judgment that already has been rendered is not a "proceeding" within the meaning of the statute. This argument is also without merit for several reasons. First, §1782 only states that the evidence must be "for use in a proceeding," and nothing in the plain language of §1782 requires that the proceeding be adjudicative in nature. In fact, the statute specifically provides that the evidence obtained through §1782 can be used in "criminal investigations conducted *before* formal accusation," even though such investigations are not adjudicative proceedings.

Second, the Supreme Court has recognized the "broad range of discovery" authorized under §1782 and has held that §1782 is not limited to proceedings that are pending or imminent. Rather, the proceeding for which discovery is sought need only be "within reasonable contemplation." Here, the proceeding actually was filed before the letter rogatory was even issued, and the third statutory requirement for a proper request under §1782 is satisfied.

Because all four statutory requirements are met, the Panamanian Court's request for assistance in obtaining Clerici's sworn answers for use in the proceeding in Panama was proper under §1782. Accordingly, the district court had authority to grant the §1782 discovery application.

Even so, "a district court is not required to grant a §1782(a) discovery application simply because it has the authority to do so." Once the prima facie requirements are satisfied, the Supreme Court in *Intel* noted these factors to be considered in exercising the discretion granted under §1782(a): (1) whether "the person from whom discovery is sought is a participant in the foreign proceeding," because "the need for §1782(a) aid generally is not as apparent as it ordinarily is when evidence is sought from a nonparticipant"; (2) "the nature of the foreign tribunal, the character of the proceedings underway abroad, and the receptivity of the foreign government or the court or agency abroad to U.S. federal-court judicial assistance"; (3) "whether the §1782(a) request conceals an attempt to circumvent foreign proof-gathering restrictions or other policies of a foreign country or the United States"; and (4) whether the request is otherwise "unduly intrusive or burdensome." The Supreme Court in *Intel* added that "unduly intrusive or burdensome requests may be rejected or trimmed."

Our review of the *Intel* factors reveals that none of the factors favors Clerici, and that the district court did not abuse its discretion in granting the §1782 application. . . .

NOTES AND QUESTIONS

1. Over the years, there has been considerable debate about the precise scope of §1782, including who is "an interested person," what qualifies as a "foreign or international tribunal," and what exactly is encompassed by the term "proceeding." As indicated in the excerpt above, the U.S. Supreme Court addressed these questions in Intel Corp. v. Advanced Micro Devices, Inc., 542 U.S. 241 (2004). AMD had filed an antitrust complaint against its competitor Intel before the Directorate of Competition of the Commission of the European Communities in Brussels; AMD sought an order under §1782 requiring Intel to produce potentially relevant documents for use in that case. Intel resisted on the grounds that the statutory requirements had not been met. Noting that the statute is permissive (that is, authorizes but does not require federal courts to provide judicial assistance), the Court held that (i) the Commission is a "tribunal" when it acts "as a first-instance decision maker," (ii) a complainant before the Commission qualifies as an "interested person," and (iii) the proceeding for which discovery is sought need not actually be pending or imminent, and a dispositive ruling need only be "in reasonable contemplation." Resolving a long-standing difference among appellate circuits about "dual discoverability" — that is, a potential requirement that the information sought must be discoverable in the requested state as well as the requesting state — the Court also held that the statute contains no "threshold requirement" that the evidence sought would have been discoverable under the law governing the foreign proceeding in question, nor does it require

that U.S. law would allow discovery in domestic proceedings analogous to those before the foreign tribunal.

2. Like *In re Clerici*, the *Intel* case involved a civil proceeding. The statute, of course, applies to criminal as well as civil cases, including "criminal investigations conducted before formal accusation" (added in 1996). Assuming that the Court's interpretation of §1782 would not differ in a criminal context, what kinds of foreign criminal proceedings could be covered? The lack of an "imminence requirement" has been challenged on the ground that it would permit foreign investigators too much latitude. That argument was rejected, however, in United States v. Sealed 1, Letter of Request for Legal Assistance from the Deputy Prosecutor General of the Russian Federation, 235 F.3d 1200 (9th Cir. 2000). In rejecting such a requirement, the Ninth Circuit reasoned: "Appellant's insistence on 'imminence' would create an untenable Catch-22 for foreign law-enforcement authorities seeking U.S. aid: investigators would be unable to receive such help before proceedings actually became imminent, and yet the proceedings might never become imminent because the investigators would be stymied in collecting evidence necessary to justify the filing of criminal charges." Id. at 1205. What about proceedings before international criminal tribunals, such as the ICTR or ICTY? Should §1782 be interpreted to have extraterritorial reach — in other words, to permit a court to compel production of evidence from a third country for use in a foreign criminal proceeding? See Norex Petroleum Ltd. v. Chubb Ins. Co. of Can., 384 F. Supp. 2d 45 (D.D.C. 2005). Can it include requests for materials covered by grand jury secrecy rules? See United Kingdom v. United States, 238 F.3d 1312 (11th Cir. 2001).

3. Because compliance with letters rogatory is completely discretionary, governments (as well as courts) can refuse to fulfill them or simply not act upon a request, without stating reasons. The statute imposes no dual criminality requirement — that is, a rule that would prevent the provision of assistance except when the offense in question is recognized under the requested state's laws. But would it be proper to decline to process a request if the underlying conduct being criminally investigated was, or might be, constitutionally protected under U.S. law? Where an "analogous" prosecution might otherwise violate U.S. law, for example, because of double jeopardy or statute of limitations reasons? Because the foreign proceeding was politically motivated or threatened to involve politically sensitive questions?

4. Many foreign criminal systems do not permit assistance at the investigatory (preindictment) stage of proceedings. Accordingly, federal prosecutors cannot rely on letters rogatory to secure pertinent evidence from such countries, even though a formal grand jury investigation is underway.

5. Under 18 U.S.C. §3292, a court must suspend the running of a statute of limitations for an offense, prior to the return of an indictment, if the court finds by a preponderance of the evidence that an official request has been made for evidence of that offense in a foreign country and that "it reasonably appears, or reasonably appeared at the time the request was made, that such evidence is, or was, in such foreign country." A suspension under this provision ends when the relevant foreign court or authority takes "final action" on the request. In United States v. Bischel, 61 F.3d 1429, 1433 (9th Cir. 1995), *final action* was interpreted to mean "a dispositive response." According to United States v. Kozeny, 541 F.3d 166 (2d Cir. 2008), the application to suspend must be filed before the limitations period has expired.

6. Within the United States, service of documents issued in connection with foreign or international proceedings (including criminal proceedings) is authorized by 28 U.S.C. §1696. That statute provides that "the district court of the district in which a person resides or is found may order service upon him of any document issued in

connection with a proceeding in a foreign or international tribunal." A district court may issue such an order based either on a letter rogatory issued by a foreign or international tribunal or upon application of "any interested person." The statute further provides, however, that "[s]ervice pursuant to this subsection does not, of itself, require the recognition or enforcement in the United States of a judgment, decree, or order rendered by a foreign or international tribunal."

7. By statute, any U.S. national or resident who submits papers to a foreign court or other authority "in opposition to an official request for evidence of an offense" must also serve such pleading or other document on the attorney general (or on the appropriate attorney for the government). 18 U.S.C. §3506. Special requirements apply to persons who are "party to a criminal proceeding in a court of the United States." Id. The term *official request* includes letters rogatory, requests under a treaty or convention, or "any other request for evidence made by a court of the United States or an authority of the United States having criminal law enforcement responsibility, to a court or other authority of a foreign country." Id.

C. COMPULSORY PROCESS UNDER DOMESTIC LAW

As an alternative to requesting the assistance of foreign authorities through a letter rogatory, those seeking evidence abroad may try to force the production of evidence through domestic compulsory process. This option may be available to a U.S. prosecutor, for example, with respect to a foreign defendant or witness over whom the court has personal jurisdiction. As a general matter, courts in the United States may order any individual over whom they have jurisdiction to disclose or produce evidence within that person's control or authority, even if the evidence lies outside the territorial jurisdiction of the particular court in question. Special provision is often made in domestic law for asserting such authority on the basis of nationality or citizenship. This is far more common in civil law countries than in those that follow the common law tradition, but even in the United States, federal courts are authorized, under 28 U.S.C. §1783, to order the issuance of subpoenas to nationals or residents of the United States who are in a foreign country requiring their appearance as witnesses or the production of documents or other evidence if the court finds it necessary in the interest of justice. The provision applies in criminal proceedings under Federal Rule of Criminal Procedure 17(e)(2). Under §1784, courts may punish noncompliance by imposing sanctions for contempt.

Resort to compulsory measures in such situations often raises questions of due process, conflicts of law, foreign sovereign compulsion, and even Fifth Amendment issues concerning self-incrimination. Such methods can be effective when directed to U.S. nationals or residents abroad, especially if the requested evidence is deemed to be within their possession, custody, or control even if located abroad. It is more difficult to compel third parties to produce documents located abroad or to enforce a subpoena directing witness testimony from foreign persons or the production of documents from foreign entities. This issue arises most frequently when a foreign business concern is subject to personal jurisdiction in U.S. courts by virtue of its business activities in the United States, but the relevant evidence sought is located abroad. But what happens when a grand jury subpoenas business and bank records located abroad even though disclosure might be restricted or forbidden by foreign law?

IN RE GRAND JURY SUBPOENA DATED AUGUST 9, 2000

218 F. Supp. 2d 544 (S.D.N.Y. 2002)

CHIN, District Judge.

A grand jury in this district is investigating allegations that a New York corporation (the "Corporation") bribed senior officials in a foreign country (the "Republic") to help American companies secure the rights to the vast natural resources of that country. In particular, the grand jury is investigating whether the Corporation and its principal paid millions of dollars to high-ranking governmental officials of the Republic [in violation of the Foreign Corrupt Practices Act (FCPA), 15 U.S.C. §§78m(b), (d)(1), (g)-(h), 78dd-2, 78ff (1997), amended by the International Anti-bribery and Fair Competition Act of 1998, 15 U.S.C. §§78dd-1 to 78dd-3, 78ff].

On August 9, 2000, the grand jury issued a subpoena directing the Corporation to produce virtually all of its business records dating from 1991. Over time, the Corporation has produced a number of documents — some 300,000 pages — but has refused to comply fully. The Corporation argues that it need not produce the withheld documents because 1) approximately 1,100 responsive documents located in New York are protected by the Republic's executive privilege, and 2) none of the documents located in its offices in the Republic may be produced without violating Republic law. . . .

This case of first impression presents the question whether a grand jury investigating suspicions that an American citizen and corporation have bribed senior foreign officials may subpoena documents that (1) the subject nation asserts are within its executive privilege, and (2) are located, in part, abroad where production is prohibited — not just by local law, but by specific opinions rendered by high legal officials of the foreign country.

After weighing the conflicting interests at stake, I conclude that the grand jury is entitled to documents from all three of the Corporation's offices, including those located in the Republic, because the Government has overcome the asserted privilege, and the interest of the United States in enforcing its criminal laws outweighs any difficulties that the Corporation may face in complying with the subpoena in contravention of Republic law. . . .

Doe, an American citizen, is the president and principal owner of the Corporation. He is a close advisor to senior officials in the Republic and has been appointed by the Republic as a special consultant to advise on commercial and economic affairs.

The Corporation is a merchant banking firm, incorporated in New York, with its principal office in New York City. The Corporation also has offices in the Republic, and most of its employees there are citizens of the Republic. The Corporation has been appointed by the Republic to provide consultant services on strategic planning and attracting foreign investment.

The Republic is recognized by the United States and is considered to be an important ally of this country. The Republic is home to vast natural resources that have been the subject of a number of large investments by American companies in joint ventures with Republic-owned companies. . . .

The Corporation asserts that it first learned of the investigation beginning in June 2000. The Corporation applied to the Ministry of Justice and the Supreme Court of the Republic "for formal clarification of the legal status of [Doe and the Corporation]" "with respect to anticipated efforts by U.S. authorities to obtain records." Shortly thereafter, two of the highest ranking legal officials of the Republic issued a joint statement concerning the relationship among the Republic, Doe, and the Corporation. The joint statement recounts the various appointments granted to

Doe and the Corporation, and summarizes that Doe "provided and continues to provide" "advice and counsel" to high officials on "issues pertaining to the development of trade" between the Republic and the United States. It states that "[a]ny communication between the Republic and Mr. Doe with respect to matters of State is part of the executive deliberative process of the executive power of the Republic." It further states that any such information is considered "highly confidential and under the protection of executive privilege."

Following the subpoena issued in August 2000, the Corporation again petitioned the Ministry of Justice for direction. On December 15, 2000, Doe wrote to the Minister of Justice. Doe asked whether responsive documents in the Corporation's offices in the Republic "can, or should be submitted in response to the subpoena." The letter asks for a determination whether the documents belong to the Corporation or to the Republic under Republic law, what jurisdiction the Republic maintains over them, and what "limitations" exist under Republic law that would prohibit transmission of the documents out of the country.

The Minister of Justice responded on January 25, 2001, opining that any information Doe possessed was considered "strictly confidential," "protected by the sovereign rights of the Republic," and "not subject to transfer to any third parties." The letter sets out seven paragraphs that describe Republic law forming the basis for the Minister's opinion. That law essentially forbids disclosure of information "connected with the interests of the State" or the "national interests" of the Republic in the development of its natural resources. The letter also points out that, under the agreement between the Corporation and the Republic, any transfer of information "is possible only with the agreement of the executive branch of the Republic." The Minister also notes that information concerning "official or commercial secrets" is protected "when this information has real or potential commercial value because it is not known by third parties." Finally, the Minister warns that no documents may be removed that contain "information of State importance," especially information "connected with the national interests," "without observing the procedures established" by Republic law.

Following a demand by the Government in March 2002 that the Corporation comply with the August 2000 subpoena, the Corporation petitioned the Ministry of Justice a third time. The Minister's response refers to Doe's letter of April 12, 2002 asking for clarification regarding civil and criminal penalties that may be imposed "in the event that documents were released from the Corporation's offices" in the Republic and what "defense and/or exceptions exist." The letter, which attaches the relevant statutes from the January 2001 letter, instructs that criminal disclosures of state secrets may be punished by incarceration of up to three years, and generally that "information given to any party by the [Republic] that relates to the national interests of [the Republic] . . . cannot be removed from the territory . . . without the permission of the [Republic]."

In addition to these responses to the Corporation, the Republic made efforts to persuade the United States Government to stop the investigation, including a personal appeal from high officials of the Republic to the United States Department of State. The Corporation and the Republic also sought, and were denied permission, to disclose the Government's motion papers in this case as part of an existing effort to lobby other executive agencies to halt the investigation. These efforts have not been successful. . . .

When a subpoena is directed at information abroad that is protected against disclosure by foreign law, a court must examine the conflicting interests to determine whether to order compliance or excuse it. Like courts in other circuits, the Second

Circuit applies a balancing test distilled from the Restatements of the Foreign Relations Law of the United States, and has endorsed consideration of the following factors: (1) the competing interests of the nations whose laws are in conflict, (2) the hardship of compliance on the party or witness from whom discovery is sought, (3) the importance to the litigation of the information and documents requested, and (4) the good faith of the party resisting discovery. Minpeco, S.A. v. Conticommodity Servs., Inc., 116 F.R.D. 517, 523 (S.D.N.Y. 1987); see First Am. Corp. v. Price Waterhouse LLP, 154 F.3d 16, 22 (2d Cir. 1998) (citing *Minpeco* with approval).

The analysis is broad, and it may encompass additional considerations—whether they are enumerated separately or considered as part of the four *Minpeco* factors. This circuit employs the same analysis to decide whether to compel discovery and whether to impose sanctions for noncompliance.

The possibility of civil or criminal sanction will not necessarily prevent enforcement of a subpoena. See Restatement (Second) of the Foreign Relations Law of the United States, §§39-40 (1965). When the laws of two jurisdictions conflict, the court must balance the interests, including the respective interests of the states involved and the hardship that would be imposed upon the person or entity subject to compliance. The Restatement (Third) of the Foreign Relations Law of the United States, section 442(1)(c), further directs courts to consider the importance of the documents requested to the underlying litigation, the availability of alternative means of disclosure, and the degree of specificity of the request.

Most of the authority in the criminal context concerns subpoenas for records protected by foreign bank secrecy laws. Courts consistently hold that the United States['] interest in law enforcement outweighs the interests of the foreign states in bank secrecy and the hardships imposed on the entity subject to compliance. See, e.g., United States v. Davis, 767 F.2d 1025 (2d Cir. 1985) (finding interest in enforcing criminal laws against fraud overcame Cayman Islands' interest in bank secrecy). But see In re Sealed Case, 825 F.2d 494, 499 (D.C. Cir. 1987) (reversing contempt sanction against bank, stating "we should say it causes us considerable discomfort to think that a court of law should order a violation of law, particularly on the territory of the sovereign whose law is in question"). . . .

Maintaining the secrecy of the grand jury's investigation is important, and I perceive no corresponding need to allow respondents access to information. It is fundamental that the grand jury's "task is to conduct an *ex parte* investigation to determine whether or not there is probable cause to prosecute a particular defendant." . . .

The documents in New York and the Republic are subject to the jurisdiction of the Court. "The grand jury is an appendage or agency of the court," and "may investigate any crime that is within the jurisdiction of the court," not "limited to conduct occurring in the district." A witness summoned by the grand jury cannot "resist the production of documents on the ground that the documents are located abroad." The test for production is "control, not location."

Although the Corporation has insisted production is prohibited by Republic law—and has stated that its employees might have to spirit the documents out of a Republic government building with armed guards—there is no serious question at this time that the documents remain within their control. The documents are located in the private offices of an American corporation. . . .

[After determining that the "act of state" doctrine did not apply in this case and that the documents in question did not fall within the "state secrets" or "deliberative process" privileges, the court addressed the competing interests of the United States and the Republic in requiring the requested disclosure.]

After consideration of relevant factors to be applied in cases of jurisdictional conflict, I conclude that the Corporation must produce the records in question, notwithstanding a risk that doing so will subject it to criminal or civil penalties in the Republic.

The first step in the analysis is to examine the competing interests of the United States and the Republic, and the extent that these interests will be furthered or impaired by an order compelling production.

The United States interest in enforcing its criminal laws is unquestionably strong. In a criminal case brought by the Government, the Court owes "some deference to the determination by the Executive Branch — the arm of the government charged with primary responsibility for formulating and effectuating foreign policy — that the adverse diplomatic consequences of the discovery request would be outweighed by the benefits of disclosure."

Specifically, the United States has a strong national interest in combating international bribery. The United States has been a leader in the international effort against it; Congress passed amendments strengthening the FCPA in 1998. Indeed, the resolution of this high profile investigation — which involves large suspected payments to the leaders of a foreign government — is important to both countries. American companies are among the largest investors in the Republic. At the same time, the Republic is widely perceived to suffer from corruption. Whether these perceptions are true, the Republic at least arguably shares the United States['] interest in combating bribery, especially as its economic growth depends upon international partnerships and trade in its developing natural resources. This alignment of interests distinguishes an FCPA investigation from other crimes where international discovery is sought.[3]

I accept that the Republic asserts a "fundamental national interest in protecting the confidentiality of . . . issues of state importance." The Minister of Justice has examined the relationship among Doe, the Corporation, and the Republic, and concluded that the records the Corporation possesses in that country that concern matters of state importance must not be disclosed. As discussed above, I defer to this opinion, and I give considerable weight to the Republic's interest in protecting the records of its consultants from disclosure, especially as those records concern matters of vital economic importance. In addition, I give substantial weight to the Republic's intervention in this matter, as contrasted to cases where "a foreign government's failure to express a view in such a context militates against a finding that strong national interests of the foreign country are at stake." Nonetheless, these interests must be considered in the context of all the circumstances.

I am not persuaded that Doe or any Corporation employee is likely to be prosecuted. Notwithstanding the opinions of the Ministry of Justice, neither the

---

3. [Court's footnote 7:] There appear to be just two cases where such discovery was denied in the criminal context. Discovery was denied to a criminal defendant in United States v. Rubin, 836 F.2d 1096, 1102 (8th Cir. 1988), which affirmed a district court quashing of a criminal defendant's subpoena for Cayman Islands banking records of a third party. The records sought were not in the control of a target of the proceeding, and were sought for a criminal trial, unlike the weight of the authority which concerns grand jury proceedings, which "maintain the secrecy of their proceedings, and therefore the foreign interest in protecting the privacy of bank customers is diminished."

At the contempt stage, in In re Sealed Case, 825 F.2d 494 (D.C. Cir. 1987), the court reversed a contempt order against a foreign bank that refused to comply with a grand jury subpoena. While expressing doubts about ordering the violation of foreign law on foreign soil, the court pointed out its holding was limited to the "peculiar" facts of the case, noting that "the bank, against whom the order is directed, is not itself the focus of the criminal investigation in this case but is a third party that has not been accused of any wrongdoing."

Corporation nor the Republic has presented any evidence that the confidentiality asserted by the Republic is enforced by any active prosecution. For this reason, the law cited by Ministry of Justice "cannot be construed as a law intended to universally govern the conduct of litigation" in a foreign court. Bodner v. Banque Paribas, 202 F.R.D. 370, 376 (S.D.N.Y. 2000) (declining to enforce French blocking statute); cf. Reinsurance Co. of Am., Inc. v. Administratia Asigurarilor de Stat., 902 F.2d 1275, 1281 (7th Cir. 1990) (noting, in evaluating hardship, evidence that the Romanian State Secrecy law is directed at domestic affairs and is vigorously enforced).

The Corporation may face some hardship. Many of the employees that would actually perform the production are Republic citizens, although Doe is an American and the Corporation is a New York corporation. Production of the documents will take place in the Republic, and this factor also weighs against ordering compliance. Courts have found this hardship mitigated, however, by noting that to some extent businesses that "serve two sovereigns" assume the risk of conflicting legal imperatives. In addition, production of the documents is relatively straightforward, as the documents can be copied and shipped to the Corporation's New York offices, and thus there is "no need for a long and continuing course of conduct that the foreign jurisdiction might find offensive." [United States v. Chase Manhattan Bank, N.A., 584 F. Supp. 1080, 1086 (S.D.N.Y. 1984).]

An affirmative showing of good faith is required at the order stage. I find that the Corporation has "courted legal impediments" and does not appear to have genuinely attempted to comply. Rather than use his significant influence to gain cooperation of Republic officials, Doe has sought advice from the Ministry of Justice intended to elicit support for resisting anticipated subpoenas from the grand jury. In three letters to the Ministry of Justice, Doe asked whether responsive documents in the Corporation's offices in the Republic "can, or should be submitted in response to the subpoena" and suggests bases for non-compliance, including whether the documents belong to the Corporation or the Republic under the Republic's law, what jurisdiction the government maintains over them, and what "limitations" exist under the Republic's law that would prohibit transmission of the documents out of the country.

I conclude that, on balance, these factors favor ordering the Corporation to comply with the grand jury's subpoena. The Republic's interest in protecting governmental confidentiality is strong, and the interest cannot be more strongly asserted than by the appearance in this action by the Republic itself and several legal opinions by the Minister of Justice. I find, however, that the United States['] interest in investigating suspected violations of its criminal laws outweighs the Republic's interest. This calculus is especially important in an investigation of violations of the FCPA, as enforcement would be eviscerated if a foreign sovereign could intervene and thwart an investigation merely by asserting local secrecy law or executive privilege. A foreign government that is alleged to be a recipient of bribes from an American corporation cannot be permitted to bring a grand jury investigation to a halt, thereby undermining the FCPA, merely by declaring the American corporation's files off-limits.

For the reasons set forth above, the Government's motion to compel is granted.

NOTES AND QUESTIONS

1. Note the court's discussion of the "balancing factors" relevant to assessing the competing interests of the Republic and the United States. Do you agree with the court's analysis of the weight to be given to the various factors in this situation? Would you have evaluated the factors differently? Did it make a difference that the

information was sought pursuant to a grand jury subpoena? Should it? Under what circumstances would a foreign state's interests outweigh the law enforcement purposes of the United States?

2. In the current Restatement (Third) of the Foreign Relations Law of the United States (1987), this issue is addressed as follows:

§442. REQUESTS FOR DISCLOSURE: LAW OF THE UNITED STATES

(1) (a) A court or agency in the United States, when authorized by statute or rule of court, may order a person subject to its jurisdiction to produce documents, objects, or other information relevant to an action or investigation, even if the information or the person in possession of the information is outside the United States.

(b) Failure to comply with an order to produce information may subject the person to whom the order is directed to sanctions, including finding of contempt, dismissal of a claim or defense, or default judgment, or may lead to a determination that the facts to which the order was addressed are as asserted by the opposing party.

(c) In deciding whether to issue an order directing production of information located abroad, and in framing such an order, a court or agency in the United States should take into account the importance to the investigation or litigation of the documents or other information requested; the degree of specificity of the request; whether the information originated in the United States; the availability of alternative means of securing the information; and the extent to which noncompliance with the request would undermine important interests of the United States, or compliance with the request would undermine important interests of the state where the information is located.

(2) If disclosure of information located outside the United States is prohibited by a law, regulation, or order of a court or other authority of the state in which the information or prospective witness is located, or of the state of which a prospective witness is a national,

(a) a court or agency in the United States may require the person to whom the order is directed to make a good faith effort to secure permission from the foreign authorities to make the information available;

(b) a court or agency should not ordinarily impose sanctions of contempt, dismissal, or default on a party that has failed to comply with the order for production, except in cases of deliberate concealment or removal of information or of failure to make a good faith effort in accordance with paragraph (a);

(c) a court or agency may, in appropriate cases, make findings of fact adverse to a party that has failed to comply with the order for production, even if that party has made a good faith effort to secure permission from the foreign authorities to make the information available and that effort has been unsuccessful.

Comment c to this section, discussing "relevant foreign and United States interests," states the following:

In making the necessary determination of foreign interests under Subsection (1)(c), a court or agency in the United States should take into account not merely a general policy of the foreign state to resist "intrusion upon its sovereign interests," or to prefer its own system of litigation, but whether producing the requested information would affect important substantive policies or interests of the foreign state. In making this determination, the court or agency will look, inter alia, to expressions of interest by the foreign state, as contrasted with expressions by the parties; to the significance of disclosure in the regulation by the foreign state of the activity in question; and to indications of the foreign state's concern for confidentiality prior to the controversy in connection with which the information is sought.

In making the necessary determination of the interests of the United States under Subsection (1)(c), the court or agency should take into account not merely the interest of the prosecuting or investigating agency in the particular case, but the long-term interests of the United States generally in international cooperation in law enforcement and judicial assistance, in joint approach to problems of common concern, in giving effect to formal or informal international agreements, and in orderly international relations. In private actions, it is open to a court in the United States to invite the United States attorney or other appropriate official to advise it of the interests of the United States government.

For a recent discussion of the §442(1)(c) factors in a civil context, see Strauss v. Credit Lyonnais, S.A., 249 F.R.D. 429 (E.D.N.Y. 2008).

3. What is the role of good faith in this balancing process? In United States v. First National Bank of Chicago, 699 F.2d 341 (7th Cir. 1983), the IRS issued a summons for records located in the First National Bank's branch in Athens, Greece. Greek law exposed bank employees to criminal sanctions for revealing depositor information, including not less than six months' imprisonment, and the bank declined to comply with the summons. In reversing the district court's order to enforce the summons, the Seventh Circuit determined that the bank had adequately demonstrated that compliance would in fact subject its employees to the risk of substantial criminal penalties under Greek law and that "a balancing of relevant competing interests weighs against compelling disclosure at this time." Id. at 342. It noted, however, that the fact that foreign law could subject a person to criminal sanctions in the foreign country if he produces certain information does not automatically bar a domestic court from compelling production. Applying the factors set forth in §40 of the Restatement (Second), the court of appeals acknowledged the interests of the United States in collecting taxes but noted that the interests of Greece served by its bank secrecy law were also important. Id. at 346. The court remanded the case with directions to the lower court to consider whether to issue an order requiring First Chicago to make a good-faith effort to receive permission from the Greek authorities to produce the information specified in the summons. It also acknowledged that the Eleventh Circuit had reached a different result in In re Grand Jury Proceedings, 691 F.2d 1384 (11th Cir. 1982), a case involving a bank that also was apparently "a neutral source of information" but that had not made a good-faith effort to comply with the subpoena.

4. In In re Grand Jury Proceedings Bank of Nova Scotia, 740 F.2d 817 (11th Cir. 1984), the U.S. branch of a Canadian bank was held in contempt for failing to produce records in the Bahamas and the Cayman Islands, where (the bank contended) the records were protected by bank secrecy laws. The bank tried but failed to obtain permission to disclose the records from Cayman courts; it also sought unsuccessfully to quash the subpoena in the issuing U.S. court. When the governor of the Cayman Islands used his statutory authority to permit disclosure, the bank produced all the documents from its Cayman branch. Why then did the U.S. courts find that the bank had not acted in good faith? Had you been counsel to the bank, what would you have advised it to do differently?

5. As noted in the *Clerici* decision, a different analysis was applied in In re Sealed Case, 825 F.2d 494 (D.C. Cir. 1987), when the appeals court reversed a district court's imposition of a $50,000 a day fine for contempt. In that case, a bank owned by the government of X, with branches in both the U.S. and the country of Y, refused to cooperate with a grand jury subpoena of records. The bank secrecy laws of country Y made it a criminal offense for a bank or a person to reveal to anyone, other than the customer, information about banking transactions or bank documents created in country Y that relate to the customer and her transactions. A U.S. grand jury opened

an investigation into money laundering charges against U.S. citizens and businesses. A subpoena duces tecum was issued to both the manager and the bank for records created in Y while the manager was working there. The bank obtained releases from some customers but otherwise refused to testify, citing Y's bank secrecy laws, and argued that compliance with the subpoena would subject both the manager and the bank to criminal prosecution in Y.

> A decision whether to enter a contempt order in cases like this one raises grave difficulties for courts. We have little doubt, for example, that our government and our people would be affronted if a foreign court tried to compel someone to violate our laws within our borders. The legal expression of this widespread sentiment is found in basic principles of international comity. But unless we are willing simply to enter contempt orders in all such cases, no matter how extreme, in utter disregard of comity principles, we are obliged to undertake the unseemly task of picking and choosing when to order parties to violate foreign laws.

825 F.2d at 498-499.

6. *Compelled consent.* Can the Fifth Amendment privilege against self-incrimination play a role here? United States v. Ghidoni, 732 F.2d 814 (11th Cir. 1984), involved an indictment for tax evasion handed down after the Bank of Nova Scotia investigation and turned on the question whether Ghidoni could invoke the privilege to protect against sanctions resulting from his refusal to sign a consent for the government to obtain records from the bank's branch in the Cayman Islands. During the discovery phase of his trial, a subpoena was served upon the bank's Miami branch for Ghidoni's bank records. The government sought, through subpoena, to force Ghidoni to sign a "form of consent" to production of his records. Ghidoni refused to comply, arguing that signing the consent would be tantamount to self-incrimination. His argument was rejected by the court, which held that the act of signing this consent form — which was written entirely in the hypothetical and did not state that Ghidoni had an account or records at the bank and said only that the form could be *construed* as consent — was not "testimonial" and therefore not incriminating, although the documents ultimately released pursuant to the consent might be. In 1988, the U.S. Supreme Court upheld *Ghidoni,* ruling that such compelled consents do not violate the Fifth Amendment where they do not communicate any information to the recipient of the information. "[T]o be testimonial, an accused's communication must itself, explicitly or implicitly, relate a factual assertion or disclose information." Doe v. United States, 487 U.S. 201, 210 (1988).

7. *Fear of foreign prosecution.* In United States v. Balsys, 524 U.S. 666 (1998), the U.S. Supreme Court held that a valid Fifth Amendment claim could not be founded on fear of foreign prosecution. Balsys, a resident alien, was under investigation by the Department of Justice's Office of Special Investigations for having misrepresented his participation in Nazi atrocities in Lithuania during World War II — a fact that, if proved, would subject him to deportation. He declined to respond to OSI's questions at a deposition, claiming that his answers could subject him to foreign criminal prosecution by Lithuania, Israel, and Germany. Overturning the Second Circuit's decision that a real and substantial fear of foreign prosecution was sufficient to justify invoking the privilege, the Court held that concern with foreign prosecution is beyond the scope of the Fifth Amendment. The accepted interpretation of the Self-Incrimination Clause limits it to fear of prosecution by the same government whose power it limits (that is, federal and state authorities). It is possible, the Court said, that cooperative conduct between the United States and foreign governments

might develop to a point at which fear of foreign prosecution could be "tantamount to a fear of a criminal case brought by the [U.S.] Government itself," but the case at hand did not support such an argument. Applying the *Balsys* rationale, the Seventh Circuit has held that First Amendment claims based on fear of foreign prosecution are no defense to contempt charges. In re Grand Jury Proceeding of the Special April 2002 Grand Jury, 347 F.3d 197 (7th Cir. 2003).

8. *Other evidentiary issues.* When evidence is gathered abroad by foreign officials, pursuant to foreign law, for use in criminal proceedings in the United States, do other U.S. constitutional proscriptions or requirements apply, for example, under the Fourth Amendment? Courts have formulated several approaches to resolving these issues, in particular the "silver platter" and "joint venture" doctrines. These doctrines have already been explored in the preceding chapter on constitutional rights.

9. *Documentary records.* U.S. law makes special provision for the introduction of documentary evidence obtained abroad. For example, 18 U.S.C. §3491 states that foreign documents and written materials obtained outside the United States may be deemed admissible when appropriately authenticated. In some instances, U.S. consular officers are empowered to take testimony abroad and to authenticate foreign documents under 18 U.S.C. §§3492 and 3493. An important exception to the hearsay rule is provided by 18 U.S.C. §3505, which states that foreign records of "regularly conducted activity" shall not be excluded as evidence if a foreign certification attests that the record was made at or near the time of the occurrence of the matters set forth by (or from information transmitted by) a person with knowledge of those matters, and the record was kept in the course of a regularly conducted business activity and as a matter of regular practice.

D. MUTUAL LEGAL ASSISTANCE

To overcome the shortcomings associated with letters rogatory as well as the difficulties encountered with attempts to use compulsory process under domestic law, states have increasingly sought to establish new forms of cooperative working relationships between their law enforcement communities. These mechanisms are often referred to under the rubric of "mutual legal assistance." Note that, as discussed below, this form of evidence gathering is generally available only to states and their authorized agents, and *not* to the defense in criminal cases.

1. Direct Cooperation

The term *mutual legal assistance* encompasses cooperation not only between foreign courts in respect of criminal proceedings, but also directly between law enforcement organizations, agencies, and officials. One type of voluntary (and typically highly effective) cooperation exists directly between law enforcement bodies in different countries (sometimes called *cop-to-cop assistance*). In fact, probably the largest volume of information (often in the form of investigative leads) is handled at the police or investigative agency level. Throughout the world, an informal network operates through long-established relationships between national law enforcement bodies. Governments frequently foster such relationships. For example, at many U.S. embassies abroad, experienced agents of the Federal Bureau of Investigation are assigned as legal attachés to serve as points of contact with host country investigative and enforcement agencies. In various countries, agents of the Drug Enforcement Agency, the U.S. Secret Service, and the Bureau of Immigration and Customs Enforcement may have similar roles. The agencies handle most of the work themselves, including transmitting requests for assistance, processing responses, passing on foreign requests to authorities in the United States, or serving as a conduit for others pursuing evidence. Most requests pertain to obtaining public records, locating persons, serving documents, executing investigative requests, setting up interviews, conducting joint investigations, and assisting in ongoing investigations. While methods and subject matter differ, this type of mutual legal assistance is characterized by voluntary participation by all parties.

INTERPOL and Europol. On the international level, INTERPOL has also become an important conduit for U.S. evidentiary requests and is used frequently by U.S. law enforcement agencies to gather investigative information from foreign agencies and records. INTERPOL also assists in humanitarian requests like locating land records or missing persons. An international organization of 187 country members, INTERPOL depends on voluntary cooperation and does not have authority to issue subpoenas or to enforce compulsory process.[4] The European Law Enforcement Organization, or Europol, an analogous organization within the European Union, is aimed at improving effective cooperation between law enforcement authorities in EU member countries in combating international organized crime and terrorism.[5]

Eurojust. Within the European Union, a new organization entitled Eurojust was created in December 2001 to help national authorities coordinate the investigation and prosecution of serious cross-border crime. Eurojust consists of experienced senior magistrates, prosecutors, judges, and other legal experts seconded (or assigned) from every EU country, working as a team to provide immediate legal advice and assistance to the investigators, prosecutors, and judges in EU member states. It also handles letters rogatory, directing them to the appropriate national authorities. At least in theory, Eurojust has the advantage of an overall view of criminal patterns or trends within the EU, and can make recommendations to national authorities. However, Eurojust has no authority to launch or carry out investigations itself.[6]

OAS Hemispheric Information Exchange Network. Within the Organization of American States, the Hemispheric Information Exchange Network for Mutual Assistance in Criminal Matters and Extradition operates within the framework of the Meeting of Ministers of Justice or of Ministers or Attorneys General of the Americas (REMJA). It includes (i) a free "virtual library" that contains information about the legal system in, and treaty relations between, the 34 member states; and (ii) a secure electronic communication system that facilitates direct contact between Central Authorities in member states.[7]

Other Mechanisms. Still other forms of evidence and information sharing have been developed over time. In 1987, for example, the Commonwealth Law Ministers adopted a nonbinding set of recommendations "to increase the level and scope of assistance rendered between Commonwealth Governments in criminal matters." Entitled "a Scheme Relating to Mutual Assistance (the 'Harare Scheme')," these

---

4. See generally http://www.interpol.int.
5. See http://www.europol.europa.eu.
6. More information on Eurojust is found at http://www.eurojust.europa.eu.
7. The virtual library is available at http://www.oas.org/juridico/mla.

undertakings cover much of the same ground as a mutual legal assistance treaty, including, for example, identifying and locating persons, serving documents, examining witnesses, obtaining evidence, effecting searches and seizures, facilitating the appearance of witnesses (including persons in custody), and tracing, seizing, and confiscating the proceeds and instrumentalities of crime.[8]

2. *Mutual Legal Assistance Treaties*

Other arrangements for interstate cooperation in the criminal field are more formal — specifically, the bilateral and multilateral agreements known as *mutual legal assistance treaties* (MLATs). These treaties provide a mutually agreed-upon framework for the exchange of evidence and information relating to a broad range of criminal activity between prosecutorial (rather than judicial) authorities. Because the procedures are standardized between states parties, requests can be processed far more quickly, and because the treaties typically provide only limited grounds for declining to act on requests, evidence can be obtained much more quickly and efficiently. Further, evidence obtained pursuant to an MLAT is more likely to arrive in the receiving jurisdiction in an admissible form. Importantly, MLATs represent legally binding commitments between states parties to cooperate in sharing evidence. As a result, most nations around the world now have entered into such arrangements in one form or another.

MLATs are specific to the criminal process and typically include provisions governing various forms of assistance from the beginning of an investigation through trial and postconviction procedures. Unlike letters rogatory, for example, MLATs allow not only for the collection of testimony and statements, documents, and other physical evidence, but also for the execution of search and seizures, the freezing or forfeiture of assets, the location and identification of persons or things, the sharing of the proceeds or instrumentalities of offenses, and the transfer of prisoners in custody to testify as witnesses. Most MLATs also have a catch-all article that allows for the transfer of any evidence not prohibited by the sending state's laws. MLATs do not usually require "dual criminality" but allow for assistance in any situation that does not directly violate the requested country's laws and constitution.

Perhaps the greatest advantage of an MLAT is the establishment of a direct, expedited channel of communication through "Central Authorities." For the United States, this function is performed by the Office of International Affairs (OIA) in the Criminal Division of the U.S. Department of Justice. This feature is particularly helpful in encouraging cooperation with civil law countries, which traditionally have been willing to provide legal assistance only when requested by official judicial authorities. The process of negotiating an agreement on mutual legal assistance is itself an important means for improving bilateral understanding and appreciation of the legal systems and procedures in other countries, especially those with different legal traditions.

The United States' first bilateral MLAT was signed with Switzerland in 1977.[9] Since then, the United States has signed over 50 bilateral MLATs and similar agreements,

---

8. The most recent text of the "Harare Scheme," as amended in October 2005, is found at http://www.thecommonwealth.org/shared_asp_files/uploadedfiles/2C167ECF-0FDE-481B-B552-E9BA23857CE3_HARARESCHEMERELATINGTOMUTUALASSISTANCE2005.pdf.

9. See Treaty between the United States and Switzerland on Mutual Assistance in Criminal Matters, May 25, 1973, 27 U.S.T. 2019, T.I.A.S. No. 8302.

and others are in various stages of negotiation and approval.[10] In 2003, an innovative umbrella MLAT was concluded with the EU (discussed below). An illustrative bilateral MLAT with a civil law jurisdiction is the treaty with Japan, signed August 5, 2003, and reproduced in selected part below.[11]

TREATY BETWEEN JAPAN AND THE UNITED STATES OF AMERICA ON MUTUAL LEGAL ASSISTANCE IN CRIMINAL MATTERS

Japan and the United States of America,

Desiring to establish more effective cooperation between both countries in the area of mutual legal assistance in criminal matters,

Desiring that such cooperation will contribute to combating crime in both countries,

Have agreed as follows:

ARTICLE 1

1. Each Contracting Party shall, upon request by the other Contracting Party, provide mutual legal assistance (hereinafter referred to as "assistance") in connection with investigations, prosecutions and other proceedings in criminal matters in accordance with the provisions of this Treaty.

2. The assistance shall include the following:

(1) taking testimony, statements or items;

(2) examining persons, items or places;

(3) locating or identifying persons, items or places;

(4) providing items in the possession of governmental departments or agencies;

(5) presenting an invitation to a person whose appearance in the requesting Party is sought;

(6) transfer of a person in custody for testimony or other purposes;

(7) assisting in proceedings related to forfeiture and immobilization of proceeds or instrumentalities of criminal offenses; and

(8) any other assistance permitted under the laws of the requested Party and agreed upon between the Central Authorities of the Contracting Parties.

---

10. A nonexhaustive list of current U.S. MLATs (and similar agreements) includes Antigua & Barbuda (entered into force 1999), Argentina (1993), Australia (1999), Austria (amended 2005), Bahamas (1987), Barbados (2000), Belgium (amended 2004), Belize (2003), Brazil (2001), Bulgaria (signed 2007), Canada (1990), Cayman Islands (1986), China (2000), Cyprus (2002), Czech Republic (2000), Denmark (signed 2005), Dominica (2000), Egypt (2001), Estonia (2000), Finland (signed 2004), France (amended 2004), Germany (signed 2003), Greece (2001), Grenada (1999), Hungary (amended 2005), Hong Kong (2000), India (2005), Ireland (amended 2005), Israel (1999), Japan (2006), Latvia (amended 2005), Liechtenstein (2003), Lithuania (amended 2005), Luxembourg (amended 2005), Malaysia (signed 2006), Malta (signed 2006), Mexico (1987), Netherlands (amended 2004), Nigeria (2003), Panama (1991), Poland (1999), Portugal (signed 2005), Romania (amended 2007), Russia (2002), St. Kitts & Nevis (2000), St. Lucia (2000), St. Vincent & the Grenadines (1999), Slovenia (signed 2005), South Africa (2001), Spain (amended 2004), Sweden (amended 2004), Switzerland (1977), Trinidad & Tobago (1999), Ukraine (2001), United Kingdom (amended 2004), Uruguay (1991), Venezuela (2004). Generally, see http://travel.state.gov/law/info/judicial/judicial_690.html.

11. See Treaty Doc. 108-12, Nov. 24, 2003; Sen. Ex. Rept. 109-14 (Apr. 6, 2006). The U.S.-Japan MLAT entered into force in July 2006.

The term "items" as used in this Treaty means documents, records and articles of evidence.

3. Each Contracting Party shall, upon request by the other Contracting Party, provide assistance in accordance with the provisions of this Treaty in connection with an administrative investigation of suspected criminal conduct, in such cases and upon such conditions as the Central Authority of the requested Party deems appropriate, if the Central Authority of the requesting Party certifies that:

(1) the authority conducting the administrative investigation has statutory or regulatory authority for the administrative investigation of facts that could constitute criminal offenses, including referring matters to prosecutors for criminal prosecution or providing testimony, statements or items obtained during administrative investigations to prosecutors in accordance with specific procedures; and

(2) the testimony, statements or items to be obtained will be used in the requesting Party in an investigation, prosecution or other proceeding in criminal matters, including the decision whether to prosecute.

4. Except as otherwise provided for in this Treaty, assistance shall be provided without regard to whether the conduct that is the subject of the investigation, prosecution or other proceeding in the requesting Party would constitute a criminal offense under the laws of the requested Party.

5. This Treaty is intended solely for assistance between the Contracting Parties. The provisions of this Treaty neither create a new right nor affect a pre-existing right on the part of a private person to impede the execution of a request or to suppress or exclude any evidence. . . .

ARTICLE 3

1. The Central Authority of the requested Party may deny assistance if the requested party considers that:

(1) a request relates to a political offense;

(2) the execution of a request would impair its security or other essential interests;

(3) a request does not conform to the requirements of this Treaty; or

(4) the conduct that is the subject of the investigation, prosecution or other proceeding in the requesting Party would not constitute a criminal offense under the laws of the requested Party and the execution of a request requires a court warrant or other compulsory measures under the laws of the requested Party.

2. Before denying assistance pursuant to paragraph 1, the Central Authority of the requested Party shall consult with the Central Authority of the requesting Party to consider whether assistance can be provided subject to such conditions as the requested Party may deem necessary. If the requesting Party accepts such conditions, the requesting Party shall comply with them.

3. If assistance is denied, the Central Authority of the requested Party shall inform the Central Authority of the requesting Party of the reasons for the denial.

ARTICLE 4

1. The Central Authority of the requesting Party shall make a request in writing. However, the Central Authority of the requesting Party may make a request by any

other reliable means of communication if the Central Authority of the requested Party considers it appropriate to receive a request by that means. In such cases, the Central Authority of the requested Party may require the Central Authority of the requesting Party to provide supplementary confirmation of the request in writing. A request shall be made in the language of the requested Party unless otherwise agreed between the Central Authorities of the Contracting Parties.

2. A request shall include the following:

(1) the name of the authority conducting the investigation, prosecution or other proceeding;

(2) the facts pertaining to the subject of the investigation, prosecution or other proceeding; the nature and the stage of the investigation, prosecution or other proceeding; and the text of the relevant laws of the requesting Party;

(3) a description of the assistance requested; and

(4) a description of the purpose of the assistance requested.

3. To the extent necessary and possible, a request shall also include the following:

(1) information on the identity and whereabouts of any person from whom testimony, statements or items are sought;

(2) a description of the manner in which testimony, statements or items are to be taken or recorded;

(3) a list of questions to be asked of the person from whom testimony, statements or items are sought;

(4) a precise description of persons or places to be searched and of items to be sought;

(5) information regarding persons, items or places to be examined;

(6) a description of the manner in which an examination of persons, items or places is to be conducted and recorded, including the format of any written record to be made concerning the examination;

(7) information regarding persons, items or places to be located or identified;

(8) a description of any particular procedure to be followed in executing the request;

(9) information on the allowances and expenses to which a person whose appearance is sought before the appropriate authority in the requesting Party will be entitled; and

(10) any other information that should be brought to the attention of the requested Party to facilitate the execution of the request.

ARTICLE 5

1. The Central Authority of the requested Party shall promptly execute a request in accordance with the relevant provisions of this Treaty or transmit it to the authority having jurisdiction to do so. The competent authorities of the requested Party shall do everything in their power to ensure the execution of a request.

2. The Central Authority of the requested Party shall make all necessary arrangements for the execution of a request in the requested Party.

3. A request shall be executed in accordance with the provisions of this Treaty and the laws of the requested Party. The manner or particular procedure described in a request referred to in paragraph 3(2), 3(6) or 3(8) of Article 4 shall be followed to the extent it is in accordance with the laws of the requested Party, and where it is possible.

4. In order to execute a request pursuant to paragraph 1,

(1) with respect to the United States of America, the courts shall have the authority to issue subpoenas, search warrants or other orders necessary to execute a request; and

(2) with respect to Japan, the judge will have the authority to issue warrants or orders necessary to execute a request.

5. If the execution of a request is deemed to interfere with an ongoing investigation, prosecution or other proceeding in the requested Party, the Central Authority of the requested Party may postpone the execution or make the execution subject to conditions deemed necessary after consultations between the Central Authorities of the Contracting Parties. If the requesting Party accepts such conditions, the requesting Party shall comply with them.

6. The requested Party shall make its best efforts to keep confidential the fact that a request has been made, the contents of a request, the outcome of the execution of a request and other relevant information concerning the execution of a request if such confidentiality is requested by the Central Authority of the requesting Party. If a request cannot be executed without disclosure of such information, the Central Authority of the requested Party shall so inform the Central Authority of the requesting Party, which shall then determine whether the request should nevertheless be executed.

7. The Central Authority of the requested Party shall respond to reasonable inquiries by the Central Authority of the requesting Party concerning the status of the execution of a request.

8. Upon request by the Central Authority of the requesting Party, the Central Authority of the requested Party shall inform in advance the Central Authority of the requesting Party of the date and place of the execution of a request.

9. The Central Authority of the requested Party shall promptly inform the Central Authority of the requesting Party of the result of the execution of a request, and shall provide the Central Authority of the requesting Party with the testimony, statements or items obtained as a result. If a request cannot be executed in whole or in part, the Central Authority of the requested Party shall inform the Central Authority of the requesting Party of the reasons therefore.

ARTICLE 6

1. Unless otherwise agreed between the Central Authorities of the Contracting Parties, the requested Party shall pay all costs related to the execution of a request, except for the fees of an expert witness, the costs of translation, interpretation and transcription, and the allowances and expenses related to travel of persons pursuant to Articles 14 and 15. Such fees, costs, allowances and expenses shall be paid by the requesting Party.

2. If it becomes apparent that expenses of an extraordinary nature are required to execute a request, the Central Authorities of the Contracting Parties shall consult to determine the conditions under which a request will be executed.

ARTICLE 7

1. The Central Authority of the requested Party may request that the requesting Party not use any testimony, statements or items provided under this Treaty other

than in the investigation, prosecution or other proceeding described in a request without prior consent of the Central Authority of the requested Party. In such cases, the requesting Party shall comply with such a request.

2. The Central Authority of the requested Party may request that testimony, statements or items provided under this Treaty be kept confidential or be used only subject to other conditions it may specify. If the requesting Party agrees to such confidentiality or accepts such conditions, it shall comply with them.

3. Nothing in this Article shall preclude the use or disclosure of testimony, statements or items provided under this Treaty to the extent that there is an obligation under the Constitution of the requesting Party to do so in a criminal prosecution. The Central Authority of the requesting Party shall inform the Central Authority of the requested Party in advance of any such proposed use or disclosure.

4. Testimony, statements or items provided under this Treaty that have been made public in the requesting Party consistent with the provisions of this Article may thereafter be used for any purpose. . . .

ARTICLE 9

1. The requested Party shall take testimony, statements or items, and shall employ, if necessary, compulsory measures in order to do so.

2. The requested Party shall make its best efforts to make possible the presence of such persons as specified in a request for taking testimony, statements or items during the execution of the request, and to allow such persons to question the person from whom testimony, statements or items are sought. In the event that such direct questioning is not permitted, such persons shall be allowed to submit questions to be posed to the person from whom testimony, statements or items are sought.

3. The requested Party shall execute a request for the search and seizure of any item for the requesting Party, if such measures are necessary and the request includes information justifying those measures under the laws of the requested Party.

4. (1) If a person, from whom testimony, statements or items are sought pursuant to this Article, asserts a claim of immunity, incapacity or privilege under the laws of the requesting Party, testimony, statements or items shall nevertheless be taken.

(2) In cases where testimony, statements or items are taken in accordance with subparagraph (1), they shall be provided, together with the claim referred to in that subparagraph, to the Central Authority of the requesting Party for resolution of the claim by the competent authorities of the requesting Party.

ARTICLE 10

1. The requested Party shall examine persons, items or places, and shall employ, if necessary, compulsory measures in order to do so. Such measures may include the destruction of items, in whole or in part, and the entry into places.

2. Examinations pursuant to this Article may include taking of photographs or creation of video records of persons, items or places, and may involve the participation of expert witnesses.

3. The requested Party shall make its best efforts to make possible the presence of such persons as specified in a request for examining persons, items or places during the execution of a request. . . .

ARTICLE 13

1. Testimony, statements or items provided under this Treaty may be authenticated by the requested Party by use of a form in the Attachment, which is an integral part of this Treaty. Testimony, statements or items authenticated in such manner shall be admissible in evidence in proceedings in the requesting Party in accordance with the relevant provisions of the Attachment.

2. The continuity of custody of items seized by the requested Party, the identity of the items and the integrity of their condition may be certified by the requested Party by use of a form in the Attachment. Such certification shall be admissible in evidence in proceedings in the requesting Party in accordance with the relevant provisions of the Attachment. . . .

ARTICLE 15

1. A person in the custody of one Contracting Party whose presence in the territory of the other Contracting Party is necessary for testimony or other purposes shall be transferred for those purposes to that other Contracting Party, if the person consents and if the Central Authorities of the Contracting Parties agree, when permitted under the laws of the requested Party.

2. (1) The receiving Party shall have the authority and the obligation to keep the person transferred pursuant to paragraph 1 in the custody of the receiving Party, unless permitted by the sending Party to do otherwise.

(2) The receiving Party shall immediately return the person transferred to the custody of the sending Party as agreed beforehand, or as otherwise agreed between the Central Authorities of the Contracting Parties.

(3) The receiving Party shall not require the sending Party to initiate extradition proceedings for the return of the person transferred.

(4) The person transferred shall receive credit for service of the sentence imposed in the sending Party for the time served in the custody of the receiving Party.

3. The person transferred to the receiving Party pursuant to this Article shall enjoy the safe conduct provided for in Article 14 in the receiving Party until the return to the sending Party, unless the person consents and the Central Authorities of the Contracting Parties agree otherwise. In implementing this paragraph, "the requesting Party" and "the requested Party" referred to in Article 14 shall be read as "the receiving Party" and "the sending Party" respectively.

ARTICLE 16

1. The requested Party shall assist, to the extent permitted by its laws, in proceedings related to the forfeiture of the proceeds or instrumentalities of criminal offenses. Such assistance may include action to temporarily immobilize the proceeds or instrumentalities pending further proceedings.

2. If the Central Authority of one Contracting Party becomes aware of proceeds or instrumentalities of criminal offenses that are located in the territory of the other Contracting Party and may be forfeitable or otherwise subject to seizure under the laws of that other Contracting Party, the Central Authority of the first Contracting Party may so inform the Central Authority of that other Contracting

Party. If that other Contracting Party has jurisdiction in this regard, its Central Authority may present the information to its relevant authorities for a determination whether any action is appropriate. The Central Authority of that other Contracting Party shall report to the Central Authority of the first Contracting Party on the action taken by the relevant authorities.

3. A Contracting Party that has custody over such proceeds or instrumentalities of criminal offenses shall retain or dispose of them in accordance with its laws. That Contracting Party may transfer such proceeds or instrumentalities, in whole or in part, to the other Contracting Party, to the extent permitted by the laws of the first Contracting Party and upon such conditions as it deems appropriate. . . .

NOTES AND QUESTIONS

1. *Scope.* One of the main benefits of an MLAT is that it establishes legally binding treaty commitments to provide the specified assistance (in distinction to the discretionary mechanism of a letter rogatory). For that reason, however, governments take great care in negotiating their obligations in the treaties and specifying when and how they are to be carried out. What is the permissible scope of requests to which the United States and Japan have agreed under Article 1 of this treaty? Is the list exhaustive? Note in particular that under Article 1(1), assistance is available for "investigations, prosecutions and other proceedings in criminal matters," and under Article 1(3) the treaty covers assistance not just for criminal prosecutions but also for "administrative investigation[s] of suspected criminal conduct" upon certain conditions. To what does the latter language refer?

2. *Central authorities.* What are the responsibilities of the respective Central Authorities in making and executing requests under Articles 4 and 5? How much discretion do they have in carrying out requests? Under Article 6, who pays for the costs of executing requests? Japan has designated two Central Authorities. Why would it do so?

3. *Dual criminality.* Unlike extradition treaties, most MLATs contain a provision similar to Article 1(4), which provides that "except as otherwise provided for in this Treaty, assistance shall be provided without regard to whether the conduct that is the subject of the investigation, prosecution or other proceeding in the requesting Party would constitute a criminal offense under the laws of the requested Party." But note the further provision in Article 3(4), permitting refusal of a request when "the conduct that is the subject of the investigation, prosecution or other proceeding in the requesting Party would not constitute a criminal offense under the laws of the requested Party and the execution of a request requires a court warrant or other compulsory measures under the laws of the requested Party." Some treaties contain similar conditions regarding transfer of persons, searches and seizures, and assistance in forfeiture proceedings. For example, Article 1(3) of the 2001 bilateral MLAT with Sweden provides that before executing a request for the transfer of a person, the requesting state may require that the subject offense be punishable under its law. Treaty Doc. 107-12 (2002), Sen. Ex. Rept. 110-13 (2008).

In the relatively rare situations where the domestic law of a foreign state generally requires "dual criminality" (that is, prevents the provision of any form of assistance except when the offense in question is recognized under that country's law), it may be necessary to include a nonexclusive list of covered offenses. See, e.g., art. 1(2) of the 2006 U.S.-Malaysia MLAT, Treaty Doc. 109-22 (2006), Sen. Ex. Rept. 110-14 (2008).

4. *Refusals.* On what grounds may a request be denied under Article 3? Do you think that refusals based on the fact that a request relates to "a political offense" or that its execution "would impair [national] security or other essential interests" give too much discretion to a state party? Some treaties exclude requests in connection with offenses under military law that would not be prosecutable under ordinary criminal law.

Generally, under MLAT arrangements, governments may deny requests either on purely technical grounds (failure to provide the specified information in the request itself) or when the request is "contrary to its public interest, as determined by its Central Authority." Requests may also be postponed, sometimes indefinitely, if granting the request would interfere with an ongoing investigation or prosecution. See art. 5(5). In some treaties, additional grounds for refusal are specified, for example, where there are substantial grounds for believing the request was made for the purpose of investigating, prosecuting, or punishing a person on account of that person's race, religion, sex, ethnic origin, nationality, or political opinion; where the person has already been convicted or acquitted of the same offense; or where the request relates to an act that, in the requested state, would not have been punishable by deprivation of liberty for a year or more. See, e.g., art. 3(1) of the U.S.-Malaysia MLAT, supra.

5. *Bank secrecy.* In some MLATs, a specific provision prohibits the refusal of a request solely on the ground of bank secrecy or because the offense involves fiscal matters. See, e.g., art. 3(3) of the U.S.-Malaysia MLAT, supra: "Assistance shall not be refused solely on the ground of secrecy of banks and similar financial institutions or that the offense is also considered to involve fiscal matters."

One of the main innovations of the 2003 U.S.-EU MLAT is the requirement that a requested state must provide certain information on bank accounts and financial transactions. While such assistance may not be refused on grounds of bank secrecy, a requested state may limit its obligations to offenses punishable under the laws of both the requested and requesting states or to "designated serious offenses." Arts. 4(4) and (5).

6. *Transfer of persons in custody.* Note that Article 15 authorizes the temporary transfer of persons in custody from one state party to the other for the purpose of giving testimony. It obligates the requesting state to return those persons without using extradition procedures. Such provisions are increasingly common in MLAT agreements. In the United States, the necessary authority to comply is provided to the U.S. attorney general under 18 U.S.C. §3508(b):

> Where the transfer to the United States of a person in custody for the purposes of giving testimony is provided for by treaty or convention, by this section, or both, that person shall be returned to the foreign country from which he is transferred. In no event shall the return of such person require any request for extradition or extradition proceedings, or proceedings under the immigration laws.

7. *Search, seizure, forfeiture.* Articles 9 and 10 contemplate the use of compulsory measures to carry out treaty requests, including conducting searches and seizures in accordance with the law of the requested party. Note the provisions in Article 9(4) regarding claims of immunity, incapacity, and privilege. Article 16 addresses the possibility of seizure and forfeiture of the proceeds and instrumentalities of crime. How effective do you think these provisions might be in practice?

8. *Authentication and admissibility.* One of the principal purposes of an MLAT is to assure that the requested testimony, statements, documents, and other evidentiary

materials are provided to the requesting state in a manner so that it will be admissible in court. Note the provisions in Article 13 regarding authentication, and in particular the provision in Article 13(1) that "testimony, statements or items authenticated in such manner shall be admissible in evidence in proceedings in the requesting Party in accordance with the relevant provisions of the Attachment." The attachment contains agreed forms designed specifically to address the problem of admissibility in this bilateral context. To the extent that the treaty makes evidence "admissible" when submitted under cover of these forms, has it effectively amended or supplanted the otherwise applicable rules of evidence?

9. *Confidentiality and limitations on use.* Article 7 addresses certain limitations on the possible use of testimony and evidence furnished pursuant to the treaty, including the imposition of confidentiality requirements. Why would governments want or accept such conditions? Are they problematic from the point of view of criminal suspects or defendants? MLATs generally make provision for confidential treatment of requests and information at the request of either state party, even concerning whether or not a request has been made. Such provisions increase the likelihood that nations will cooperate on issues concerning international terrorism and transnational organized crime where the threat of retaliation or compromise of sensitive operations is a risk.

10. *Exclusivity.* Article 1(5) states that the treaty is intended "solely for assistance between the Contracting Parties" and that its provisions "neither create a new right nor affect a pre-existing right on the part of a private person to impede the execution of a request or to suppress or exclude any evidence." Because the treaties are designed as mechanisms for government-to-government cooperation and are not intended to provide defendants or others a means of evidence gathering, these are standard provisions in U.S. MLATs. See, for example, art. 1(4) of the U.S.-India MLAT, Treaty Doc. 107-3 (2002). Indeed, foreign states will frequently insist on some protection against far-reaching discovery requests by the suspects in an investigation or the defendants in a prosecution. Attempts to challenge this aspect of MLAT practice have generally been unavailing. See, e.g., United States v. Rommy, 506 F.3d 108 (2d Cir. 2007) (rejecting claim that evidence allegedly obtained in violation of an MLAT should be excluded); United States v. Davis, 767 F.2d 1025 (2d Cir. 1985) (defendant lacked standing to move to exclude or suppress records on the basis of a purported violation of the treaty); United States v. Rosen, 240 F.R.D. 204 (E.D. Va. 2007) (MLAT treaty process is exclusively for signatory governments, and denial of motion to compel the executive branch to invoke the treaty for the benefit of a defendant does not implicate a constitutional right to due process); Robert Neale Lyman, Compulsory Process in a Globalized Era: Defendant Access to Mutual Legal Assistance Treaties, 47 Va. J. Intl. L. 261 (2006).

Although some bilateral treaties, such as the one between the United States and the United Kingdom, are intended to serve as a "first resort" (in that the states parties will look first to the treaty mechanism before resorting to unilateral compulsory measures), most MLATs are not considered the exclusive means for obtaining evidence and other material.

11. *Implementation in U.S. law.* In the United States, MLATs are generally considered to be self-executing, meaning that once the Senate has given its advice and consent and the president has ratified it, the treaty operates with the force of domestic law without the need for specific implementing legislation. Authority to carry out treaty obligations is found, at least in part, in the provisions of existing law, in particular 28 U.S.C. §§1781 and 1782. See In re Request from the Czech Republic Pursuant to the Treaty Between the United States and the Czech Republic on Mutual Assistance in Criminal Matters in the Matter of Jiri Koblizek, 2008 WL 179263 (M.D. Fla. 2008)

(applying the *Clerici* factors). Can you think of any reason why there should not be a general implementing statute for these treaties?

In a case of first impression, In re Commissioner's Subpoenas, 325 F.3d 1287 (11th Cir. 2003), the court of appeals held that the bilateral MLAT between the United States and Canada obligated the United States, at the request of Canada, to issue subpoenas to compel the testimony of witnesses in a criminal investigation prior to the filing of formal charges. As a self-executing treaty, the court said, the MLAT provided "slightly broader authority" than 28 U.S.C. §1782 for U.S. federal courts to use their power to issue subpoenas to compel testimony in aid of pre-charge criminal investigations. A liberal interpretation of the MLAT, it concluded, was consistent with the treaty's intended goal of improving the effectiveness of both countries' ability to investigate, prosecute, and suppress crime.

Requests for assistance pursuant to an MLAT may be granted under §1782 when a foreign criminal proceeding lies "within reasonable contemplation." See In re Wilhelm, 470 F. Supp. 2d 409 (S.D.N.Y. 2007).

12. *Multilateral treaties.* The UN has also endorsed a Model Treaty on Mutual Assistance in Criminal Matters, G.A. Res. 45/117, 45 U.N. GAOR Supp. No. 49A, U.N. Doc. A/45/49 (Dec. 14, 1990). Several regional MLATs are also in effect. A European Union Convention on Mutual Assistance in Criminal Matters (see http://eur-lex.europa.eu/LexUriServ/LexUriServ.do?uri = celex:42000A0712(01):en:html) was adopted in May 2000 to supplement and improve the mechanisms established in the groundbreaking 1959 Council of Europe Mutual Legal Assistance Treaty and its 1978 and 2001 Protocols (see http://conventions.coe.int). The Organization of American States has also adopted an MLAT promoting assistance in "investigations, prosecutions, and proceedings that pertain to crimes over which the requesting state has jurisdiction at the time the assistance is requested." See Inter-American Convention on Mutual Assistance in Criminal Matters., May 23, 1992, O.A.S.T.S. No. 75, available at http://www.oas.org/juridico/english/treaties/a-55.html. There is an optional protocol on taxes. See Optional Protocol Related to the Inter-American Convention on Mutual Assistance in Criminal Matters, OAS, June 11, 1993, O.A.S.T.S. No. 77, available at http://www.oas.org/juridico/english/treaties/a-59.html. Currently, the OAU and UNAFRI are drafting conventions on mutual legal assistance.

13. *U.S.-EU MLAT.* The United States has traditionally been reluctant to enter into multilateral treaty obligations regarding mutual legal assistance, preferring bilateral agreements instead. Can you identify a reason why this might be so? In 2003, however, the United States signed an MLAT with the EU and subsequently negotiated some 25 implementing bilaterals with EU member states (see Treaty Doc. 109-13, Sept. 28, 2006). This rather complex arrangement is intended to modernize and supplement existing bilateral treaties with EU members and, for the eight EU members with which the United States does not have bilateral treaties, to establish new arrangements. Because the EU is a "contracting party" in its own right, it will bear responsibility for implementation and oversight of the operation of the treaty. Among the main innovations of the U.S.-EU agreement are provisions relating to bank secrecy, the formation of joint investigative teams, mechanisms for using video-conferencing technology in criminal investigations and proceedings, and provision of assistance to certain administrative authorities (such as the Federal Trade Commission, the Securities and Exchange Commission, and the Commodity Futures Trading Commission).

14. *Mini-MLATs.* Many of the recent international criminal law conventions contain detailed provisions obligating states parties to provide specific forms of assistance to other states parties in support of the goals of the convention. Among the most fully developed of these "mini-MLATs" are those found in the 1988 U.N. Convention

Against Illicit Trafficking in Narcotic Drugs and Psychotropic Substances (U.N. Doc. E/CONF.82/15 (Dec. 19, 1988), reprinted in 28 I.L.M. 493 (1983)), and the 2000 U.N. Convention Against Transnational Organized Crime. See G.A. Res. 55/25, 55 U.N. GAOR Supp. 49, U.N. Doc. A/55/49 (Jan. 8, 2001), reprinted in 40 I.L.M. 335 (2001); see also the 1996 Inter-American Convention Against Corruption, reprinted in 35 I.L.M. 724 (1996), available at http://www.oas.org/juridico/english/Treaties/b-58.html. Why might it be more acceptable to undertake such obligations in the context of a convention focused on a specific criminal phenomenon than in a generic multilateral treaty on mutual legal assistance?

15. *Executive agreements.* Over time, the United States has also engaged in a series of executive agreements allowing for the sharing of information in specific investigations. Some 30 of these agreements were negotiated during the 1970s in the context of the investigations into the activities of the Boeing and McDonnell Douglas companies. The SEC has also entered into numerous memoranda of understanding with its foreign counterparts which are used in securities fraud investigations.

CHAPTER
9

International Extradition
and Its Alternatives

A criminal defendant must personally appear in a U.S. courtroom in order to be tried and convicted of a criminal offense, at least at the outset of the process. (The same is true of most other countries, although some civil law systems permit trials and convictions in absentia.) How, then, can U.S. authorities secure custody of a suspect or indicted defendant who resides in, or is present on, the territory of another state? Under what circumstances can an individual in the United States be transferred to a foreign jurisdiction for prosecution?

The traditional mechanism involves extradition, which refers to the formal procedure by which one state transfers custody of a fugitive or an accused person (sometimes referred to as the "relator") to another state for purposes of criminal prosecution. Although criminal suspects may consent to a request for extradition, or even "waive" the extradition process entirely, they need not do so; the return of the accused can be effected regardless of consent.

International extradition is generally regulated by treaty. In most circumstances, bilateral treaties between the two countries will set forth the rules governing the extradition of individuals. For the surrendering state, however, the process is always grounded in domestic law and legal requirements because it involves the surrender of jurisdiction over the individual in question. Most states have specific statutory schemes designed to provide procedural safeguards as well as a measure of political involvement in the process.

Extradition decisions may also be affected by nonextradition treaties or (where there is no applicable treaty) by customary international law. Especially where extradition is sought to face a capital charge, the requested state will have to consider whether extradition in the circumstances of a particular case may violate its obligations under human rights treaties. The application of human rights treaties to extradition decisions will be discussed in Chapter 10.

Extradition is not the only legal mechanism by which individuals may be transferred to another country. It may be distinguished from other procedures available under the immigration laws of the custodial state for delivering the fugitive into foreign custody, such as transfer of prisoners, deportation, and exclusion. Other methods exist by which a state can seek to obtain custody of a wanted person from outside its jurisdiction, including luring and abduction. Each of these options has controversial aspects, as discussed below.

No rule of customary international law requires a state to surrender its own nationals or other fugitives to countries where they have been accused or convicted of a crime. But states have long recognized that reciprocal arrangements promote important law enforcement interests. In fact, bilateral treaties containing extradition provisions between the ancient Egyptians and the Hittites were among the first recorded agreements in international practice, and today extradition remains largely, although not exclusively, a matter of treaty obligation.

The current global network of bilateral extradition treaties is vast and reflects differences in national laws and policies.[1] A number of multilateral treaties and agreements contain extradition procedures, particularly under the auspices of regional organizations. Within the Organization of American States (OAS), for example, six member states have ratified the 1981 Inter-American Convention on Extradition.[2] Likewise, both the Council of Europe (COE) and the European Union (EU) have adopted extradition conventions. The first COE treaty was approved in 1957, and was supplemented by protocols in 1975 and 1978.[3] In 1995 the EU adopted a Convention on Simplified Extradition Procedure, and a more extensive extradition treaty was agreed to in 1996.[4] Many modern criminal law treaties (the UN counterterrorism treaties, for example) also contain "extradite or prosecute" provisions.

Some states, however, the United States among them, require or rely primarily on bilateral treaties in order to effect extradition. The United States is currently a party to more than 100 such treaties.[5] In addition, many states are able to transfer fugitives in the absence of a treaty. The Commonwealth Countries, for example, have adopted the so-called London Scheme for Extradition within the Commonwealth, an arrangement that governs the extradition of persons from one to another if the person is accused of an offense. Although not in the form of a legally binding treaty, it functions in practice much like a treaty regime.[6]

Extradition law can be complicated (and occasionally politically sensitive), and the details vary from country to country. In this chapter, we focus only on the major issues in U.S. law and practice.

---

1. To suggest a standard global approach, the UN General Assembly adopted a Model Extradition Treaty, G.A. Res. 45/116 (annex) (Dec. 14, 1990), as amended, U.N. Doc. A/RES/52/88, annex I (Dec. 12, 1997), available at http://www.unodc.org/pdf/model_treaty_extradition.pdf.

2. Inter-American Convention on Extradition, Feb. 25, 1981, O.A.S.T.S. No. 60, 1752 U.N.T.S. 177.

3. European Convention on Extradition, Dec. 13, 1957, E.T.S. 24; see also the 1962 "Benelux" Extradition and Mutual Legal Assistance Treaty Between Belgium, Luxembourg, and the Netherlands, June 27, 1962, 616 U.N.T.S. 79.

4. 1995 Convention, OJ C 78 (Mar. 30, 1995); EU Council Act of Sept. 27, 1996, OJ C 313 (Oct. 23, 1996), available at http://eur-lex.europa.eu/en/index.htm (select "Search" and then search legislation for OJ C numbers).

5. The bilateral treaties are listed in 18 U.S.C. §3181 note. The United States remains a party to the 1933 Montevideo Convention on Extradition, 49 Stat. 311, and has on rare occasions invoked its provisions. More recently, the Senate gave its advice and consent to ratification of an Agreement on Extradition Between the United States and the European Union (EU), together with 27 bilateral instruments with EU member states to implement the main Agreement. See Cong. Rec. S9238 (daily ed., Sept. 23, 2008); see also Sen. Ex. Rept. 110-12 and 110-13 (Sept. 11, 2008). This treaty is intended to modernize and expand existing extradition relationships with EU member states. It does so in several ways, for example, by replacing outdated lists of extraditable offenses with the "dual criminality" approach and by providing more expeditious procedures for preparing and transmitting extradition requests.

6. Adopted at the Law Ministers' Meeting in Kingstown in 2002, updating an earlier (1990) version. See generally http://thecommonwealth.org (click "Law" and then "Criminal Law").

A. HYPOTHETICAL

As an assistant U.S. attorney, you have been investigating the activities of a child pornography ring which operates in the territory of the Republic of Bellehaven but markets its movies and videos in the United States by Internet. Although it appears that all participants in the ring's productions are citizens of Bellehaven, customers in the United States are able to purchase videos and movies by credit card for delivery by regular mail. In addition, your investigators have documented control of this activity by an organized crime syndicate known as "the Cartel." Most of the Cartel's operatives are also citizens of, and reside in, Bellehaven, but the person in charge of its pornography business, Lola La Rue, is a national of the neighboring country of Verdant. It is believed that Lola siphons most of the profits from the business for her personal benefit, laundering the money through various offshore bank accounts before investing it in otherwise legitimate real estate ventures, cattle ranches, and art works in her home country.

You have sufficient information to obtain a federal arrest warrant for Lola, and you have determined that she frequently travels outside Bellehaven, but never to the United States. What are your options for gaining lawful custody over Lola?

Would it matter that Bellehaven has strong laws against child pornography but treats them as minor offenses (for which the penalty never exceeds six months imprisonment) and never applies those laws to activities taking place outside its own national territory? That Verdant has no laws prohibiting child pornography and never extradites its own citizens? Assuming you did obtain a warrant for Lola's arrest, would it have any validity outside the United States? Under what circumstances? Can you imagine any situation in which U.S. law enforcement authorities might be authorized to detain or otherwise get custody of Lola in another country? On what grounds could Lola challenge her arrest, once she is brought before a U.S. court?

B. THE EXTRADITION PROCESS

1. Extradition Requirements and Procedures

While the content and formalities of an actual request for international extradition are typically governed by the relevant treaty or international agreement, the procedural aspects of extradition are largely a matter of internal or domestic law.

Extradition requests *by* the United States to obtain custody of an individual *from* foreign countries originate with the prosecutor with jurisdiction in the case. At the federal level, an application will be transmitted by the appropriate U.S. or assistant U.S. attorney directly to the Office of International Affairs (OIA) at the Department of Justice. Although no uniform procedure exists at the U.S. state level, most states require a local prosecutor to forward the application to the governor's office, which in turn transmits it to OIA.

Following a determination that extradition would be authorized under the relevant treaty and the applicable provisions of U.S. law, the attorneys at OIA work with the prosecuting authority to prepare the supporting documentation. Such documentation often includes an affidavit in which the prosecutor summarizes the facts, states the offense charged, and relates these charges to the relevant treaty; a copy of the applicable criminal code violation and the statute of limitations; a copy of the arrest warrant and the indictment; and other supporting affidavits. The Justice Department reviews this documentation for compliance with the relevant treaty and any requirements under the laws of the requested state before forwarding it to the Department of State.[7] In turn, the State Department examines the request against the treaty provisions and prepares the formal request to be signed by the secretary of state. That request is transmitted in diplomatic channels to the foreign ministry of the state concerned.

The procedure for extraditing an individual *from* the United States *to* a foreign country where he has been charged with committing a crime is governed by 18 U.S.C. §§3181-3195. Even though extradition treaties are considered self-executing, they operate in conjunction with these statutory provisions. Requests from foreign countries are transmitted, in accordance with the provisions of the relevant treaty, through diplomatic channels (typically via the requesting state's embassy in Washington) to the Department of State and then to OIA, which reviews them for consistency with the relevant treaty. Application is then made to the appropriate federal court.[8] The U.S. attorney's office for that district argues the case on behalf of the requesting country.

Section 3184 establishes a two-part process. First, a judicial officer, upon a complaint made under oath charging any person found within the officer's jurisdiction with having committed within the jurisdiction of the foreign government any of the crimes provided for by treaty, issues an arrest warrant for the individual sought for extradition upon a determination that (1) a treaty exists between the requesting country and the United States, and (2) the crime charged is covered by the treaty. When the individual has been apprehended, the judicial officer then conducts a hearing to determine if the officer "deems the evidence sufficient to sustain the charge under the provisions of the proper treaty."[9] If the judicial officer makes such a determination, the officer "shall certify the same, together with a copy of all the testimony taken before him, to the Secretary of State, that a warrant may issue upon the requisition of the proper authorities of such foreign government, for the surrender of such person."[10]

Once the judge certifies that extradition is appropriate, it is then within the secretary of state's sole discretion to determine whether the relator should actually be extradited. The secretary (not the court) may also attach conditions to the order of extradition or use diplomatic methods to ensure fair treatment for the relator.[11] The following case demonstrates the mechanics of the extradition process.

IN RE BILANOVIC

2008 U.S. Dist. LEXIS 97893 (W.D. Mich. 2008)

SCOVILLE, J.

This is an extradition proceeding brought under 18 U.S.C. §3184 by the United States of America at the request of the government of Bosnia and Herzegovina (BiH), seeking the extradition of Eset Bilanovic. The United States filed its complaint on

---

7. See generally the U.S. Attys.' Manual, §§9-15.200–9-15.250, available at http://www.usdoj.gov/usao/eousa/foia_reading_room/usam/.

8. Id. §9-15.700.

9. 18 U.S.C. §3184.

10. Id.

11. United States v. Kin-Hong, 110 F.3d 103 (1st Cir. 1997).

August 14, 2008, for extradition pursuant to the Treaty Concerning Mutual Extradition of Law Breakers Between the United States and the Kingdom of Servia, effective June 12, 1902 ("the Extradition Treaty"). Attached to the complaint, among other items, was a request for extradition from the Ministry of Justice of BiH and a ten-page criminal judgment ("Verdict") of the Municipal Court of Bugojno, dated June 24, 1999, finding Eset Bilanovic guilty of murder.

FINDINGS OF FACT . . .

The verdict of the Municipal Court contained detailed factual findings to support the conviction. In summary, the court found that on February 9, 1995, around 7:40 p.m., in front of Bilanovic's coffee bar in the City of Bugojno, Eset Bilanovic had a verbal altercation with Muharem Corhusic and several of his friends. Corhusic was a rowdy and sometimes violent patron of the coffee shop. This particular argument involved the purchase of a piece of plexiglass from Corhusic. During the argument, Mr. Corhusic threw the plexiglass in the direction of Eset Bilanovic, and the plexiglass broke. Bilanovic then pulled a 7.65 mm pistol out of his belt and fired two shots at Corhusic, hitting him in the region of the neck and head. He approached Corhusic and from a distance of one meter fired another shot into his head, inflicting a fatal injury. The factual findings contained in the court's verdict detailed the events leading up to the crime and an analysis of the evidence in light of the elements of the offense under the law of BiH. The court also considered and rejected the defenses of diminished capacity and self-defense. The court analyzed and rejected the argument that the only crime committed was manslaughter, because of the period of delay between any act of legal provocation and the shooting. The court sentenced Eset Bilanovic to a period of imprisonment for nine years, finding that this sentence "is adequate to the severity of the criminal offense committed and to the personality of the accused, and that the sentence shall have enough influence on him not to commit such or other criminal offenses."

On February 27, 2006, the Minister of Justice of BiH, Slobodan Kovac, issued a diplomatic note requesting the extradition of Eset Bilanovic from the United States to BiH. Attached to the request were the verdict of the Municipal Court of Bugojno, the birth certificate and certificate of citizenship of Eset Bilanovic, a copy of Article 171 of the Criminal Code of BiH, and other supporting documents. The United States Attorney for this District filed a complaint on August 14, 2008, and Magistrate Judge Hugh W. Brenneman, Jr. issued a warrant of arrest. On October 30, 2008, Deputy United States Marshal Joseph Guzman, assisted by the Kentwood Police Department, arrested Eset Bilanovic without incident in a parking lot at 44th Street and Breton Road in Kentwood, Michigan. . . .

The person who is wanted by BiH for extradition and the person who appeared before the court have identical names, dates of birth, places of birth, father's name and mother's name. On this basis, the court finds as a fact that the Eset Bilanovic who is in custody and appeared before this court is the same Eset Bilanovic who is wanted for extradition to BiH.

EXTRADITION TREATY

The treaty upon which the United States relies is the Treaty Concerning Mutual Extradition of Law Breakers Between the United States and the Kingdom of Servia (then the common spelling of Serbia) signed October 25, 1901, in Belgrade. The United States Senate gave advice and consent to ratification on January 27, 1902, and President Theodore Roosevelt ratified the treaty on March 7, 1902. Servia ratified the treaty on March 17, 1902, and the treaty entered into force on June 12, 1902, thirty days after the parties exchanged instruments of ratification.

The Extradition Treaty requires the contracting parties to deliver up persons "charged with or convicted of any of the crimes and offenses specified [in Article II] committed within the jurisdiction of one of the high contracting parties." (Art. I). Extradition is conditioned upon the production of "such evidence of criminality as, according to the laws of the place where the fugitive or person so charged shall be found, would justify his or her apprehension and committal for trial if the crime or offense had been committed there." (Art. I). The extradition treaty contains a list of extraditable offenses, including the following:

1.   Murder, comprehending assassination, parricide, infanticide, and poisoning; attempt to commit murder; manslaughter, when voluntary.

(Art. II). If the person whose extradition is sought has been convicted of a crime, the treaty requires production of a duly authenticated copy of the sentence of the court in which the person has been convicted. (Art. III). The extradition treaty excludes from extradition political offenses (Art. XI) and charges barred by the statute of limitations of the rendering country. (Art. VII).

The Kingdom of Servia, one of the contracting parties, became a part of the Kingdom of Serbs, Croats and Slovenes in 1918, as a consequence of World War I. The country was renamed Yugoslavia in 1929 and was subsequently renamed the Federal People's Republic of Yugoslavia in 1946, when a communist government took power. In 1963, the country was again renamed, calling itself the Socialist Federal Republic of Yugoslavia (SFRY). The SFRY consisted of six constituent republics: SR [socialist republics] Slovinia, SR Croatia, SR Serbia, SR Bosnia-Herzegovina, SR Montenegro, and SR Macedonia. Beginning in 1991, the SFRY began to disintegrate as the result of the civil wars which followed the secession of most of the country's constituent entities. The Republic of Bosnia-Herzegovina declared its independence from Yugoslavia in 1992. The United States recognized BiH as an independent state and established diplomatic relations the same year. In connection with the recognition of BiH, its President, Alija Izetbegovic, informed the United States Secretary of State by letter dated April 19, 1992, that "Bosnia is ready to fulfill the treaty and other obligations of the former SFRY." Since that time, BiH has requested the extradition of at least three other persons pursuant to the 1902 extradition treaty, and the Executive Branch of the United States government has continued to honor the extradition treaty. There is no evidence that either the United States or the government of BiH has ever repudiated the extradition treaty.

Conclusions of Law

A. REQUIREMENTS FOR EXTRADITION

Under 18 U.S.C. §3184, a person facing possible extradition to a foreign country is entitled to a hearing before a United States judge or magistrate judge. To justify extradition, the United States must establish that (1) a valid extradition treaty exists between the United States and the country requesting extradition; (2) the treaty provides for extradition for the crime charged; (3) the evidence supporting the extradition complaint conforms to the applicable standards established by the treaty and the laws of the United States; and (4) the evidence supports a finding of probable cause to believe that the charged crime has been committed and that the person to be extradited is the person who committed it. 18 U.S.C. §§3184, 3190. The government must also show that the fugitive has not established, by a preponderance of the evidence, any valid defense to the extradition (as opposed to a defense to the crime). Such defenses to extradition include the assertion that the crime for which the person is accused is political in nature, see, e.g., Barapind v. Enomoto, 360 F.3d 1061, 1073 (9th Cir. 2004), or that extradition would violate the applicable statute of limitations. . . .

If all requirements for extradition, including the existence of probable cause, are satisfied, the judge then makes a finding of extraditability, and the case is certified to the Secretary of State for further action. After the court has completed its limited inquiry, the Secretary of State conducts an independent review of the case to determine whether to issue a warrant of surrender. "The Secretary exercises broad discretion that may properly consider myriad factors affecting both the individual defendant as well as foreign relations, which the extradition court may not." . . .

B. CONCLUSIONS OF LAW

2. Existence of Extradition Treaty

With one narrow exception not applicable here, the Extradition Act requires the existence of a "treaty or convention for extradition" between the United States and a foreign country as a prerequisite to extradition. 18 U.S.C. §3184. Mr. Bilanovic strenuously asserts that no valid treaty exists between the United States and BiH. The court rejects this argument and concludes that the 1902 Extradition Treaty remains in effect. . . .

A court's role in reviewing this issue is severely circumscribed by concepts of separation of powers. The determination whether a treaty applies by the doctrine of state succession is essentially an Executive Branch decision. This authority derives from Article II, §2 of the United States Constitution, which confers the treaty-making power on the President, with the advice and consent of the Senate. See Valentine v. United States ex rel. Neidecker, 299 U.S. 5 (1936). The scope of judicial inquiry is therefore limited to the position of the Executive Branch on the question of state succession, but also may include evidence of the foreign government's position on the same issue. In other words, the court is to examine conduct indicating an intent to be bound by the Executive Branches of each nation. The fact that a country has invoked an extradition treaty in the case at bar is evidence of its implied adoption of the treaty.

Because extradition is essentially a political question, the position of the Executive Branch is entitled to considerable deference, if not dispositive weight. Therefore, in determining whether a treaty is still in existence, the federal courts generally "defer to the intentions of the State Departments of the two countries." One court of appeals has remarked that every circuit court reviewing an extradition decision has deferred to the opinion of the United States Department of State in determining whether a treaty remained binding under the State Succession Doctrine. [See Kastnerova v. United States, 365 F.3d 980, 986 (11th Cir. 2004) (collecting cases).]

The evidence before the court . . . clearly demonstrates that both the United States and BiH continue to honor the 1902 Extradition Treaty, at least by implication. . . .

The facts set forth in the affidavit of Avril D. Haines, Assistant Legal Advisor for Treaty Affairs of the United States . . . are more than sufficient to support a finding that the 1902 Extradition Treaty remains in effect between the United States and BiH. . . .

3. Treaty Authorization of Extradition for Crime Charged

The next prerequisite to extradition is a finding that the treaty authorizes extradition for the crime charged. In the present case, the 1902 Extradition Treaty specifically identifies murder as an offense for which extradition shall be granted. (Art. II(1)). Further, the treaty applies both to persons who have been charged with an enumerated offense and those persons who have been "convicted" of any such crime. (Art. I).

Included within this inquiry is the requirement of "dual criminality." That is, a fugitive is subject to extradition only if the acts charged are criminal under the laws of both countries. This rule does not require that the name by which the crime is described in the two countries must be the same, or that the scope of liability must be coextensive in each country. "It is enough if the particular act charged is criminal in both jurisdictions." The 1902 Extradition Treaty specifically embodies the concept of dual criminality in the last sentence of Article II. This requirement is easily satisfied in the present case. "Murder is a crime in every state of the United States." Certain murders are also proscribed by federal law. 18 U.S.C. §1111. Furthermore, the killing for which Mr. Bilanovic was convicted cannot possibly be deemed a "political offense," nor has he raised this defense to extradition.

The court therefore concludes that the provisions of the 1902 Extradition Treaty provide for extradition for the crime charged.

4. Authenticated Evidence

To justify extradition, the government must support the extradition complaint with evidence conforming to the applicable standards declared by law. Those standards are supplied by the Extradition Act, 18 U.S.C. §3190, which establishes the criteria for authenticating depositions, warrants, and other papers offered in evidence in an extradition hearing. . . . In the present case, the Verdict and other documents supporting the extradition request of BiH are accompanied by a certificate from Douglas L. McElhaney, then the Ambassador of the United States of America in Sarajevo, Bosnia and Herzegovina. Ambassador McElhaney's certificate avers that the attached documents "are properly and legally authenticated so as to entitle them to be received in evidence for similar purposes of the Tribunals of Bosnia and Herzegovina, as required by Title 18, United States Code, §3190." The Ambassador's certification satisfies the requirements of the Extradition Act.

In addition to satisfying the requirements of statute, the government is obliged to comply with any requirements of the treaty. Article III of the 1902 Extradition Treaty requires, in the case of a person convicted of a crime or offense, presentation of "a duly authenticated copy of the sentence of the Court in which he has been convicted." The United States has satisfied this requirement of the Treaty by presenting to this court an authenticated copy of the Verdict of the Municipal Court in Bugojno, as well as a certified translation of the Verdict.

5. Probable Cause Determination

The paramount issue of every extradition proceeding is the existence of probable cause. "The function of the committing magistrate is to determine whether there is competent evidence to justify holding the accused to await trial, and not to determine whether the evidence is sufficient to justify a conviction." "The probable cause standard applicable to an extradition hearing is the same as the standard used in federal preliminary hearings." The government must satisfy the probable cause standard on the question of identity as well as the sufficiency of the evidence.

(a) Identity

The documentary evidence before the court establishes probable cause that the Eset Bilanovic now in this court's custody is the same Eset Bilanovic wanted for extradition to BiH. . . .

(b) Evidence of Criminality

The evidence before the court is sufficient to establish probable cause to support the charge of murder. The evidence of probable cause is contained completely in the Verdict of the Municipal Court of Bugojno, appended to the extradition complaint. For the reasons set forth below, the Municipal Court's summary of evidence is more than sufficient to establish probable cause. . . .

NOTES AND QUESTIONS

1. *Treaty requirement.* The main purpose of an extradition treaty is to establish a legal obligation to extradite and to specify the circumstances under which extradition must be accomplished or may be declined. Absent a treaty, no obligation exists under international law to extradite individuals to other countries. As indicated above, some states may, under their domestic law, extradite in the absence of a treaty. By contrast, U.S. law has long required a treaty basis for extradition. See 18 U.S.C. §3181(a). Can you identify any reasons for such a long-standing position? Note, however, that §3181(b), added in 1996, permits

> the surrender of persons, other than citizens, nationals, or permanent residents of the United States, who have committed crimes of violence against nationals of the United States in foreign countries without regard to the existence of any treaty of extradition with such foreign government if the Attorney General certifies, in writing, that (1) evidence has been presented by the foreign government that indicates that had the offenses been committed in the United States, they would constitute crimes of violence as defined under section 16 of this title; and (2) the offenses charged are not of a political nature.

For a discussion of the history of U.S. extradition practice and a critique of the requirement for a bilateral treaty, see M. Cherif Bassiouni, Reforming International Extradition: Lessons of the Past for a Radical New Approach, 25 Loy. L.A. Intl. & Comp. L. Rev. 389 (2003).

Note that courts generally defer to the executive branch's determination that a treaty remains valid and in force. Where older treaties are involved, such as in the *Bilanovic* case, questions of "state succession" occasionally arise. Here too, deference is paid to the views of the government. See, e.g., In re Extradition of Coe, 261 F. Supp. 2d 1203 (C.D. Cal. 2003) (recognition of foreign government is a political question on which the court must defer to the political branches). Courts also typically give "great weight" to the executive branch's construction of a treaty. United States v. Kin-Hong, 110 F.3d 103 (1st Cir. 1997) (citing Factor v. Laubenheimer, 290 U.S. 276 (1933), and United States v. Howard, 996 F.2d 1320 (1st Cir. 1993) (deference to executive in extradition context stems, at least in part, from fact that the executive wrote and negotiated the operative documents)).

2. *International tribunals.* The advent of new international criminal tribunals and courts created some novel problems in respect of the treaty requirement. In Ntakirutimana v. Reno, 184 F.3d 419 (5th Cir. 1999), the U.S. government sought to extradite Rwandan Bishop Elizaphan Ntakirutimana to the International Criminal Tribunal for Rwanda (ICTR) to answer charges of genocide, complicity in genocide, conspiracy to commit genocide, crimes against humanity, and serious violations of Common Article 3 to the Geneva Conventions. The Fifth Circuit held that it was not unconstitutional to surrender Ntakirutimana to the ICTR, even in absence of an Article II treaty, if the extradition was authorized by statute, in that case a congressional-executive agreement specifically negotiated and enacted for that purpose (Pub. L. No. 104-106, §1342 (1996)). Are there special considerations in considering extradition for purposes of prosecution before an international tribunal?

Regarding the International Criminal Court (ICC), current U.S. law provides: "Notwithstanding any other provision of law, no agency or entity of the United States Government or of any State or local government may extradite any person from the United States to the International Criminal Court, nor support the transfer of any United States citizen or permanent resident alien to the International Criminal Court." 22 U.S.C. §7423(d).

3. *Who is extraditable?* A primary function of the extradition hearing is to establish that the person in custody is in fact the person whose extradition is sought.

In many states, particularly those in the civil law tradition, extradition of citizens is forbidden, either as a matter of constitutional law or by long-standing practice. Typically, such states are at the same time able to prosecute their own citizens for criminal activity wherever committed, on the basis of nationality jurisdiction. By contrast, common law jurisdictions (such as the United States, the United Kingdom, Canada, and most other Commonwealth countries) will typically extradite their own nationals, on the basis that crimes should be prosecuted where committed. In such jurisdictions, the use of nationality jurisdiction has traditionally been circumscribed. Which of the two approaches seems more appropriate? In modern practice, the United States seeks to include a provision in its bilateral treaties with civil law countries that extradition shall not be refused on the ground that the person sought is a national of the requested state. See, e.g., Article 3(1) of the new U.S.-Bulgarian Extradition Treaty, which provides that "[a] Party shall not refuse extradition based solely on the nationality of the person sought with respect to offenses falling within" a specific list of 30 offenses. Treaty Doc. 110-12 (Jan. 22, 2008).

The United States does not exclude its nationals from extradition. However, in Valentine v. United States ex rel. Neidecker, 299 U.S. 5 (1936), the Supreme Court considered the effect of a clause in the extradition treaty between the United States and France, stating that neither state "shall be bound to deliver up its own citizens or subjects." The question was whether this provision implicitly granted to the U.S. executive the discretionary power to surrender U.S. citizens. The *Valentine* Court said no, reasoning that since neither statute nor treaty conferred upon the executive the specific authority to extradite a citizen, "the President is without power to surrender the respondents." Id. at 18.

For years, the *Valentine* problem required U.S. negotiators to take considerable care in crafting the provisions of bilateral extradition treaties to ensure that U.S. citizens and nationals could be surrendered to foreign countries. Still, a number of older treaties lacked the necessary permissive language. In 1990, the issue was resolved by the enactment of 18 U.S.C. §3196, which provides: "If the applicable treaty or convention does not obligate the United States to extradite its citizens to a foreign country, the Secretary of State may, nevertheless, order the surrender to that country of a United States citizen whose extradition has been requested by that country if the other requirements of that treaty or convention are met." The constitutionality of this provision was upheld in Hilario v. United States, 854 F. Supp. 165 (E.D.N.Y. 1994); see also In re Extradition of Sacirbegovic, 280 F. Supp. 2d 81 (S.D.N.Y. 2003).

By contrast, Israel amended its extradition law in 1978 to preclude the extradition of nationals. In September 1997, Samuel Sheinbein, a 19 year-old U.S. citizen, fled to Israel to avoid standing trial for the murder of his former friend, Alfred Tello, whose dismembered body had been found in a house in a Maryland suburb. Sheinbein successfully claimed the benefit of the 1978 law on the basis that his father, born in prestate Israel, was an Israeli citizen. The Israeli Supreme Court sustained that contention; Sheinbein subsequently pled guilty to murder in a Jerusalem district court and was sentenced to 24 years imprisonment. In April 1999, Israel amended its statute to permit the extradition of nationals who are residents of Israel at the time an extradition request is made, on condition that, if convicted, they must be returned to Israel to serve any prison sentence. See Abraham Abramovsky & Jonathan I. Edelstein, The Post-Sheinbein Israeli Extradition Law: Has It Solved the Extradition Problems Between Israel and the United States or Has It Merely Shifted the Battleground? 35 Vand. J. Transnatl. L. 1 (2002). See also the discussion of the Sheinbein case in Chapter 5, Section A.4.

Most multilateral counterterrorism treaties include an explicit undertaking, when extradition is refused on the basis of nationality, to submit the case for prosecution in lieu of extradition (the so-called *aut dedere aut judicare* provision). The International Law Commission (part of the UN) is currently considering whether the *aut dedere aut judicare* rule has been incorporated into customary international law. See http://untreaty.un.org/ilc/guide/gfra.htm. Does such a provision make sense? Why (or why not)?

4. *Extraditable offenses.* The extradition court must also establish that the offense for which extradition is sought falls within the terms of the treaty. Typically, this means the offense must satisfy the requirement of "dual criminality" and be punishable by at least one year of imprisonment. (In U.S. practice, the one-year threshold generally marks the difference between a misdemeanor and a felony.) Embodied in most extradition treaties, the dual criminality principle requires that the crime for which the suspect or defendant is requested constitute an offense under the laws of both the requesting and the requested state. See for example art. 2(1) of the new Extradition Treaty Between the United States and Malta: "An offense shall be an extraditable offense if it is punishable under the laws of the Requesting and Requested States by deprivation of liberty for a maximum period of more than one year or by a more severe penalty." Treaty Doc. 109-17 (Sept. 6, 2006). What function does this rule serve?

Older treaties (such as the one at issue in *Bilanovic*) typically listed the specific offenses for which extradition could be obtained. Note the quoted provision from Article I(1) on "murder" in the opinion above. Is that definition sufficiently precise? By contrast, most newer treaties follow the "no list" approach, which provides simply that the offenses for which a person can be extradited must be criminal offenses in both jurisdictions and satisfy the formula provided in the treaty (that is, a minimum of a year's imprisonment). Which approach — "list" or "no list" — makes more sense?

In the "no list" situation, the inquiry into dual criminality can be difficult. In United States v. Saccoccia, 58 F.3d 754 (1st Cir. 1995), the court of appeals observed that

> [t]he principle of dual criminality does not demand that the laws of the surrendering and requesting states be carbon copies of one another. Thus, dual criminality will not be defeated by differences in the instrumentalities or in the stated purposes of the two nations' laws. By the same token, the counterpart crimes need not have identical elements. Instead, dual criminality is deemed to be satisfied when the two countries' laws are substantially analogous. . . . If the same conduct is subject to criminal sanctions in both jurisdictions, no more is exigible.

Id. at 766. For a recent discussion of the "substantially analogous" test, see Man-Seok Choe v. Torres, 525 F.3d 733 (9th Cir. 2008).

Still, the dual criminality requirement can create difficulties because of differing concepts, terminology, and jurisdictional premises in various legal systems. In determining whether the requirement is satisfied, U.S. courts will generally look at the operative facts underlying the charged offense and determine whether these facts would constitute a crime under applicable U.S. state or federal law. The issue is often not straightforward. For example, U.S. criminal law contains a variety of complex crimes, such as the Racketeer Influenced and Corrupt Organizations Act (RICO), the money laundering statutes, and Continuing Criminal Enterprise (CCE) liability, which are defined in terms of other crimes ("predicate offenses") and contain complex proof requirements. Problems can arise when trying to determine whether these statutes have counterparts in foreign legal systems. See, e.g., United States v. Saccoccia, 58 F.3d 754 (1st Cir. 1995); In re Extradition of Chan Hon-Ming, 2006 WL 3518239 (E.D.N.Y. 2006). Most modern U.S. bilateral treaties provide that an offense will be extraditable "whether the laws in the Contracting States place the offense within a different category of offenses or describe the offense by different terminology, so long as the underlying conduct is criminal in both States." See., e.g., Art. II(3)(a) of the 2001 U.S.-Peru Extradition Treaty.

Defendants already extradited to the United States and seeking to overturn their criminal convictions based on challenges to their extradition may have difficulty raising dual criminality objections. Some courts have held that U.S. courts are obliged to defer to the sending state's determination of whether dual criminality is satisfied in any particular case. See, e.g., United States v. Campbell, 300 F.3d 202 (2d Cir. 2002); United States v. Salinas Doria, 2008 WL 4684229 (S.D.N.Y. 2008).

5. *Exclusions.* Extradition treaties frequently contain exclusions for offenses of a fiscal or economic nature (not, however, in contemporary U.S. practice). Why would this be so? The United States has frequently included offenses such as tax evasion, organized crime, drug trafficking, and money laundering in its treaties. See Bruce Zagaris, U.S. Efforts to Extradite Persons for Tax Offenses, 25 Loy. L.A. Intl. & Comp. L. Rev. 653 (2003). Can you identify reasons why many states might not share a mutual interest in enforcing those laws? Also typically excluded are offenses under military law or against military personnel or property if they are not otherwise offenses under ordinary law. Why would states be reluctant to extradite for such offenses?

6. *Other grounds for refusal.* The political offense/motivation exclusion, mentioned in the *Bilanovic* decision, is discussed below in Section B.3. A universally accepted ground for declining extradition is double jeopardy (sometimes referred to as *ne bis in idem,* or *autrefois acquit, autrefois convict*) to cover the situation when a final judgment has been entered against the person for the same crime in the requested state. For a recent U.S.

decision on double jeopardy in the extradition context, see In re Coleman, 473 F. Supp. 2d 713 (N.D. W. Va. 2007). Most treaties also authorize refusal of an extradition request when the requested state has already determined not to prosecute the individual in question for the charged offense, or when the individual in question is under active investigation or is being prosecuted by the requested state for the same offense.

Undue delay or lapse of time (sometimes referred to as "prescription") can also provide justified grounds for refusal. Treaties often provide a defense to extradition where the prosecution of the individual sought is barred by the statute of limitations of either the requested or the requesting state. In the United States, this defense is available only if based in treaty. The individual's status as a fugitive will usually toll the statute. However, the statute of limitations is no defense to charges of war crimes, crimes against humanity, or genocide. See 1968 UN Convention on the Non-Applicability of Statutes of Limitations to War Crimes and Crimes Against Humanity, G.A. Res. 2391 (XXIII), 754 U.N.T.S. 73 (45 states parties); European Convention on Non-Application of Statute of Limitations, E.T.S. No. 82; ICC Statute, art. 29.

When an otherwise extraditable offense potentially entails a death sentence, countries in which capital punishment has been abolished may decline the request in the absence of sufficient assurances that such a sentence would not be imposed or, if imposed, would not be carried out. Provisions to that effect have been incorporated in a number of modern bilateral treaties between the United States and other countries (e.g., Argentina, France, India, Peru, Poland, the Republic of Korea, and the United Kingdom).

Article 7 of the new U.S.-Romania Extradition Treaty provides, for example:

> When the offense for which extradition is sought is punishable by death under the laws in the Requesting State and is not punishable by death under the laws in the Requested State, the Requested State may grant extradition on the condition that the death penalty shall not be imposed on the person sought, or, if for procedural reasons such condition cannot be complied with by the Requesting State, on condition that the death penalty, if imposed, shall not be carried out. If the Requesting State accepts extradition subject to the condition attached pursuant to this Article, it shall comply with the condition.

Treaty Doc. 110-11 (Jan. 22, 2008).

For some countries, the possibility of a life sentence can also constitute a barrier to extradition. See Matthew Bloom, Note, A Comparative Analysis of the United States's Response to Extradition Requests from China, 33 Yale J. Intl. L. 177 (2008); Vanessa Maaskamp, Note, Extradition and Life Imprisonment, 25 Loy. L.A. Intl. & Comp. L. Rev. 741 (2003).

7. *Lack of jurisdiction.* A related ground for declining an extradition request may arise when the charges brought by the requesting state rest on a jurisdictional assertion not recognized by the requested state. This may occur even where the crime itself satisfies the dual criminality requirement, if, for example, the charges rest on extraterritorial application of the requesting state's law. In a federal system, some crimes rest on unique jurisdictional premises (such as interstate transportation of underage women or wire fraud) that are unknown to the juridical systems of unitary (that is, nonfederal) states. In some bilateral treaties, this jurisdictional issue is specifically addressed. See, for example, Article II(4) of the Extradition Treaty with Italy, which provides that "[t]he provisions of this Article apply whether or not the offense is one for which United States federal law requires proof of an element, such as interstate transportation, the use of the facilities of interstate commerce, or the effects upon such commerce, since such an element is required for the sole purpose of establishing the jurisdiction of United States federal courts."

8. *Rule of specialty.* The "rule of specialty" requires that the extradited individual may be tried only for the specific crime for which she was surrendered unless the surrendering country consents. The doctrine also prohibits the requesting state from reextraditing the individual in question to a third state for crimes committed before extradition unless it first obtains the permission of the original requested state. U.S. law recognized this rule as long ago as United States v. Rauscher, 119 U.S. 407 (1886), and it is specifically articulated in virtually all U.S. extradition treaties. The First Circuit has explained the application of this doctrine as follows:

> The principle of specialty—a corollary to the principle of dual criminality—generally requires that an extradited defendant be tried for the crimes on which extradition has been granted, and none other. . . . Enforcement of the principle of specialty is founded primarily on international comity. The requesting state must "live up to whatever promises it made in order to obtain extradition" because preservation of the institution of extradition requires the continuing cooperation of the surrendering state. Since the doctrine is grounded in international comity rather than in some right of the defendant, the principle of specialty may be waived by the asylum state. . . . In the last analysis, then, the inquiry into specialty boils down to whether, under the totality of the circumstances, the court in the requesting state reasonably believes that prosecuting the defendant on particular charges contradicts the surrendering state's manifested intentions, or, phrased another way, whether the surrendering state would deem the conduct for which the requesting state actually prosecutes the defendant as interconnected with (as opposed to independent from) the acts for which he was extradited.

United States v. Saccoccia, 58 F.3d 754, 766-767 (1st Cir. 1995); see also United States v. Cuevas, 496 F.3d 256 (2d Cir. 2007). On whether the extraditing state's unilaterally imposed sentencing limits (that is, other than those expressly authorized under the treaty) are binding on the United States under the specialty doctrine, see Rodriguez Benitez v. Garcia, 495 F.3d 640 (9th Cir. 2007).

9. *Standing relating to "specialty" claims.* Although the Supreme Court in *Rauscher* found that the relator was entitled to raise and seek relief for alleged treaty violations, without reference to any protest by the requested state, the federal circuits have since split on this issue. Several have suggested that the rule of specialty is intended only to protect the interests of the requested state and, therefore, "[t]he right to insist on application of the principle of specialty belongs to the requested state, not to the individual whose extradition is requested." Demjanjuk v. Petrovsky, 776 F.2d 571, 584 (6th Cir. 1985); see also United States v. Kaufman, 874 F.2d 242, 243 (5th Cir. 1989). Others have adopted the position that the relator has standing to raise any objections that the original requested state would be entitled to raise. See, e.g., United States v. Garrido-Sanatan, 360 F.3d 565, 579 n.10 (6th Cir. 2004) (collecting cases); United States v. Puentes, 50 F.3d 1567, 1572 & n.2 (11th Cir. 1995). In *Puentes*, the court of appeals permitted an individual who had been extradited from Uruguay and tried for conspiracy to import cocaine into the United States to challenge his conviction under the rule of specialty, ruling that

> an individual extradited pursuant to an extradition treaty has standing under the doctrine of specialty to raise any objections which the requested nation might have asserted. The extradited individual, however, enjoys this right at the sufferance of the requested nation. As a sovereign, the requested nation may waive its right to object to a treaty violation and thereby deny the defendant standing to object to such an action.

Which approach do you think has the most merit?

10. *Provisional arrest and bail.* As indicated in the *Bilanovic* decision, the first conse-quence of a valid extradition request is normally the "provisional" arrest of the individual whose extradition is sought. U.S. courts may issue such a warrant upon appli-cation by the government containing sufficient information to inform the fugitive of the charges against him. The information contained in the complaint usually includes a summary of the factual circumstances of the alleged offense and a showing that "probable cause" exists that the accused is the person charged or convicted and has committed the crime charged or for which he was convicted. See the U.S. Attys.' Manual, *supra* note 7, §9-15.230. At the request of a member state, INTERPOL can issue a "Red Notice" informing other members about the issuance of an arrest warrant for an iden-tified fugitive (or a court decision about a person wanted to serve a sentence). In many countries, the Red Notice can serve as the basis for provisional arrest with a view to extradition. (All told, INTERPOL publishes seven different kinds of color-coded notices.) See http://www.interpol.int/Public/Notices/default.asp.

In the ordinary case, there is a strong presumption against bail in such situations. See Wright v. Henkel, 190 U.S. 40 (1903). The extradition statute does not provide for bail, and since an extradition proceeding is not considered a criminal case, the Bail Reform Act, 18 U.S.C. §3141 et seq., does not apply. However, bail may be granted on a showing of "special circumstances." See, e.g., United States v. Wroclawski, 574 F. Supp. 2d 1040 (D. Ariz. 2008); United States v. Ramnath, 533 F. Supp. 2d 662 (E.D. Tex. 2008); United States v. Zarate, 492 F. Supp. 2d 514 (D. Md. 2007); In re Extra-dition of Sacirbegovic, 280 F. Supp. 2d 81 (S.D.N.Y. 2003).

Most bilateral extradition treaties require the release of provisionally arrested per-sons within a stated period (usually 45 or 60 days) if a formal extradition request complying with other treaty requirements has not been received. Under 18 U.S.C. §3188, a court may order the discharge of any person committed for rendition to a foreign government if, within two months of commitment, that person is not "deliv-ered up and conveyed out of the United States."

2. *Judicial Role*

The final decision in an international extradition is an executive rather than a judicial function. For this reason, the extradition court may conduct only a limited inquiry. "An extradition proceeding is not a forum in which to establish the guilt or innocence of the accused; rather, the sole inquiry is into probable cause."[12] Depositions, warrants, or other papers upon which the extradition court relies must be properly authenticated by a diplomatic official of the State Department resident in the requesting country, as required by 18 U.S.C. §3190. If properly authenticated, evidence may be received in an extradition proceeding that would be inadmissible in a preliminary examination.

HOXHA v. LEVI
371 F. Supp. 2d 651 (E.D. Pa. 2005)

[The Republic of Albania sought the extradition of Krenar Hoxha, a naturalized citizen living in the United States, on charges of murdering three Albanian citizens in Albania. Hoxha had been tried and convicted in absentia by the Court of First

---

12. In re Extradition of Drayer, 190 F.3d 410, 415 (6th Cir. 1999).

Instance of the Judicial Circle for Fier for the "honor" killing of Ilmi and Roza Kasemi, and their son, Eltion Kasemi, allegedly because Ilmi had been involved in an illicit relationship with Hoxha's married sister, Mimoza. Hoxha was initially sentenced to life in prison, but his conviction was overturned by the Appeal Tribunal of Vlore on procedural grounds. In subsequent proceedings, he was again convicted, but his sentence was reduced to 22 years and later to 14 years and 8 months. Eventually, the same Appeal Tribunal overturned his conviction on the ground that he had been denied the constitutional right "to be called and to attend the proceedings."

Albania subsequently submitted an extradition request pursuant to the 1935 bilateral treaty, which obliged the United States, "upon requisition duly made as herein provided, [to] deliver up to justice any person who may be charged with, or may have been convicted of, any of the crimes or offenses specified in Article II of the present treaty." Murder was explicitly listed in that article. The district court issued a warrant for Hoxha's arrest. Following a finding of extraditability by a magistrate judge, Hoxha filed a petition for habeas corpus under 28 U.S.C. §2241, arguing inter alia that certain of the evidentiary allegations underlying the Albanian request had been extracted under threat of torture and had later been recanted. At least one declarant, he contended, was prepared to testify to that effect by telephone. Conceding that the evidentiary case was "riddled with holes," the district court nonetheless rejected the petition.]

SCHILLER, J. . . .

B. HABEAS REVIEW OF AN EXTRADITION ORDER

An extradition order is not a final order of a district court and therefore may not be appealed under 28 U.S.C. §1291. Although an extradition order may be challenged via a habeas corpus petition, the scope of review is extremely limited. "Habeas corpus is available only to inquire whether the magistrate [judge] had jurisdiction, whether the offense charged is within the treaty and, by a somewhat liberal extension, whether there was any evidence warranting the finding that there was reasonable ground to believe the accused guilty." It is within this framework that this Court shall consider Hoxha's habeas petition.

Wisely, Hoxha does not attack the jurisdiction of the magistrate judge. A magistrate judge may conduct extradition proceedings if authorized to do so by a court of the United States. 18 U.S.C. §3184. . . . Nevertheless, Hoxha . . . claims that probable cause did not exist. Second, Hoxha . . . claims that if extradited, he will face reprisals and death at the hands of Albanian authorities. He claims that his extradition should therefore be barred by Article III of the Convention Against Torture and Other Cruel, Inhuman or Degrading Treatment of Punishment, of which the United States is a party.

1. Probable Cause

When determining whether probable cause exists in the context of an extradition proceeding, courts apply the identical standard used in federal preliminary hearings. Under that standard, the burden rests with the government to present "evidence sufficient to cause a person of ordinary prudence and caution to conscientiously entertain a reasonable belief of the accused's guilt." In making this determination, the sufficiency of the evidence for conviction purposes is not to be examined; the Government has met its burden if the evidence is sufficient to warrant a finding that there are reasonable grounds to believe the fugitive is guilty and thus hold him for trial. The habeas court does not sit to superimpose its view of the record on that of the extradition magistrate. Therefore, the writ will not issue if the magistrate relied on competent evidence sufficient to support the conclusion that a reasonable person would believe the petitioner guilty.

Hoxha's argument on the issue of probable cause relies on the purportedly recanted statement of Daut Hoxha, Hoxha's cousin. According to that statement, Hoxha arrived at Daut's home immediately after committing the killings. Hoxha was holding a plastic bag that contained a gun. Daut took the bag with the gun and Hoxha headed back toward his house. Several hours later, Hoxha returned to Daut's home and asked for the gun so that he could throw it in the Gjanica River. Hoxha and Daut then headed to a nearby village where Daut's cousin, Fetah, lived. When they arrived at Fetah's home, Daut hid the gun in a sofa. Daut's statement goes on to recount the bitter family history that led to the killings and also states that Hoxha informed Daut, "you will hear later what I have done." Hoxha argues that any evidence tying him to the killings flows from the statements of Daut, his sister, and his wife, which were the product of torture and have since been recanted.

In finding probable cause existed, however, Judge Hart assumed that Daut's statements implicating Hoxha were untrue. In other words, sufficient evidence existed aside from Daut's statements to justify holding Krenar for trial.[13] The affidavit of Ardian Visha, Prosecutor at the General Prosecutor's Office in Albania, sets forth the evidence supporting a finding of probable cause. Among this evidence is a gun seized from the home of Fetah Hoxha, which ballistics confirmed was the weapon used to kill the victims; the statement of Fetah that Daut came to his house with another individual; the declaration of Rahman Sheqeri, who states that he saw Hoxha with a gun a couple weeks prior to the killings near the victims' home, and the statement of Murat Kasemi, the victim's brother, who claims to have heard gun shots on the night of the murder.[14] Furthermore, Matilda Kasemi, the couple's surviving daughter, witnessed the killings and would be able to identify the killer if provided an opportunity. All of this evidence, properly considered by Judge Hart and this Court, is more than sufficient to constitute probable cause. Although the statement of Daut Hoxha provides additional support for a finding of probable cause, particularly insofar as Daut led the police to the exact location of the gun, his words are not necessary to sustain this finding.

---

13. [Court's footnote 1:] It is for this reason that Hoxha's argument that the Magistrate Judge incorrectly refused to allow live testimony from witnesses in Albania is both unpersuasive and irrelevant. The credibility of witnesses and relevant facts are matters to be determined by an Albanian court. See In re Sindona, 450 F. Supp. 672, 685 (S.D.N.Y. 1978) ("The rule is that the accused has no right to introduce evidence which merely contradicts the demanding country's proof, or which only poses conflicts of credibility."). Rather than permissibly seeking to explain the evidence put forth by the Albanian authorities, Hoxha seeks to try this matter in the United States by contradicting the evidence against him. This he may not do. Id. (noting it would contradict purpose of extradition treaties if requesting country were required to conduct a full trial in United States and could only obtain extradition after a full trial in this country). Furthermore, even accepting certain testimony as recanted, probable cause exists to certify Hoxha as extraditable.

14. [Court's footnote 2:] Also challenged are the declarations of Bajame Hoxha and Adriana Hoxha. Bajame, Daut's wife, asserts that after she heard Daut and Hoxha enter her home in the early morning hours of the night of the killings, she returned to the house a few hours later to find a plastic bag in the corridor of her home. Adriana Hoxha, Daut's sister, claims that the morning after the killings, she heard a conversation between Daut and Hoxha in which Hoxha told Daut that he would later learn what Hoxha has done. Even discounting all three declarations, however, probable cause exists. Furthermore, the recantations raise credibility issues best left to the Albanian judicial system. Whether to believe all, any, or none of the witnesses who have now apparently changed their stories is simply not a matter properly decided by this Court.

The Court observes that the case against Krenar appears riddled with holes, especially if one discounts the allegedly recanted statements. In fact, Judge Hart stressed that were he presented with the evidence before him at a trial conducted in the United States, the Government would not even be able to present its case to the jury, because "[t]here's absolutely no basis to find guilt beyond a reasonable doubt [based on the evidence the Government presented]." But that was not the question posed in the extradition hearing nor is it the question posed by the instant habeas petition. The Government need not put on evidence sufficient to convict Hoxha based on a reasonable doubt standard. Probable cause is all that is required, and probable cause is what the Government has provided. . . .

3. Humanitarian Exception to Extradition Laws

Finally, Hoxha argues that he should not be extradited because he would face torture and possible death should he be returned to Albania. Article III of the UN Convention Against Torture and Other Cruel, Inhuman or Degrading Treatment ("Convention Against Torture") forbids the extradition of a person to a country if there are substantial grounds to believe that the person will be tortured upon return. According to Hoxha, this provision has been both ratified and codified into law by the United States. Hoxha further argues that this Court should create a "humanitarian exception" that would allow the Court to ignore the extradition order because the actions to which Hoxha might be subjected in Albania would greatly offend the Court's sense of decency.

Hoxha's argument, while appealing on a certain level, fails to square with the law, and is a matter clearly committed to the discretion of the Secretary of State. The State Department has enacted regulations, pursuant to the Foreign Affairs Reform and Restructuring Act, 8 U.S.C. §1231 (2005), aimed at implementing the Convention Against Torture. The clear policy of the United States is "not to expel, extradite, or otherwise effect the involuntary return of any person to a country in which there are substantial grounds for believing the person would be in danger of being subject to torture, regardless of whether the person is physically present in the United States." Act of Oct. 21, 1998, Pub. L. No. 105-277, 112 Stat. 2681. The regulations, however, mandate that "the Secretary is the U.S. official responsible for determining whether to surrender a fugitive to a foreign country by means of extradition." 22 C.F.R. §95.2(b) (2005). In other words, while the judicial branch is charged with deciding whether an individual is extraditable, the decision to extradite the individual rests with the executive branch. It is within the sole discretion of the Secretary of State to refuse to extradite an individual on humanitarian grounds in light of the treatment and consequences that await that individual. Indeed, regulations are in place for situations when allegations of torture are asserted. In such cases, "appropriate policy and legal offices review and analyze information relevant to the case in preparing a recommendation to the Secretary as to whether or not to sign the surrender warrant." 22 C.F.R. §95.3(a). Then, the Secretary is charged with surrendering the individual, denying surrender of the individual, or surrendering the individual subject to conditions. 22 C.F.R. §95.3(b). The Secretary's decision, in this regard, is not subject to judicial review. 22 C.F.R. §95.4 ("Decisions of the Secretary concerning surrender of fugitives for extradition are matters of executive discretion not subject to judicial review.").

In sum, the separate branches of government each have clearly defined roles in the extradition process. It is the duty of the judicial branch to ensure that the individual sought is subject to extradition, while it is the duty of the executive branch, which possesses great power in the realm of foreign affairs, to ensure that extradition is not sought for political reasons and that no individual will be subject to torture if extradited. Accordingly, this Court rejects Hoxha's invitation to create a judicial humanitarian grounds exception to the laws of extradition.[15]

III. CONCLUSION

Jurisdiction of the Magistrate Judge in this case was clearly proper, the crime of murder falls within the terms of the Extradition Treaty, and probable cause exists that Krenar Hoxha is responsible for the three murders for which Albania seeks his extradition. This Court's scope of review limited to those issues, the Court must therefore deny Hoxha's habeas petition. An appropriate Order follows.

NOTES AND QUESTIONS

1. On appeal, the Third Circuit affirmed this decision, rejecting, inter alia, Hoxha's arguments that (i) the magistrate judge should have allowed the testimony of the recanting witnesses, and (ii) the doctrine of non-inquiry was not a bar to consideration of humanitarian concerns. Hoxha v. Levi, 465 F.3d 554 (3d Cir. 2006). We discuss the doctrine of non-inquiry (which prevents U.S. courts from passing judgment on other states' legal systems) in Note 5, infra.

2. *Review of extraditability decisions.* Decisions by federal magistrates or judges finding an individual extraditable are not final decisions and thus may not be appealed directly. Instead, review is by means of habeas corpus under 28 U.S.C. §2241. The scope of the habeas inquiry is limited to determining whether (1) the extradition judge had jurisdiction over the matter, (2) the extradition judge had jurisdiction over the person sought to be extradited, (3) the extradition treaty was in full force and effect, (4) the crime fell within its terms, and (5) there was competent legal evidence to support a finding of extraditability. This inquiry may also concern any contested defenses, exceptions, or exclusions under the relevant treaty, but does not concern guilt or innocence. The relator may appeal a denial of habeas under 28 U.S.C. §2253, whereas the government may not seek judicial review of a refusal to certify a case for extradition at any level. Instead, the government may file a new complaint as often as it wishes, unhindered by any analogue to double jeopardy.

---

15. [Court's footnote 3:] The U.S. State Department is aware that Albanian police have beaten and tortured suspects and that prison conditions in Albania are poor. See U.S. Dep't of State, Country Report on Human Rights Practices in Albania 2004 (Feb. 28, 2005), available at http://www.state.gov/g/drl/rls/hrrpt/2004/41666.htm. Sending any individual to a country where he or she faces even the prospect of cruel or inhumane treatment cannot be squared with the ideals of freedom and respect for the individual embodied by our laws and cherished by our citizens. As President Bush has declared, "torture is never acceptable, nor we do hand over people to countries that do torture." See Jane Mayer, Outsourcing Torture, The New Yorker, Feb. 14, 2005, available at [http://www.newyorker.com/archive/2005/02/14/050214fa_fact6]. Nevertheless, it has been alleged that U.S. and Albanian agents have collaborated to further the U.S. policy whereby persons suspected of terrorism are sent to countries that engage in deplorable and illegal interrogation practices. See id.; see also Megan K. Stack & Bob Drogin, Detainee Says U.S. Handed Him Over for Torture, L.A. Times, Jan. 13, 2005, at A1. Accordingly, this Court trusts that the State Department will seriously examine the charges of torture that Hoxha has levied against Albanian authorities and faithfully uphold this Government's clear policy of refusing to extradite a person when there are substantial grounds for believing that person would be subjected to torture.

The ultimate decision on whether to issue an extradition warrant lies within the U.S. secretary of state's discretion. Under 18 U.S.C. §3186,

> [t]he Secretary of State may order the person committed . . . to be delivered to any authorized agent of such foreign government, to be tried for the offense of which charged. Such agent may hold such person in custody, and take him to the territory of such foreign government, pursuant to such treaty. A person so accused who escapes may be retaken in the same manner as any person accused of any offense.

The possibility that the secretary could decline to order extradition (in effect, overruling a judicial finding) without being subject to further judicial review has been challenged (unsuccessfully) on separation of powers arguments. In Lobue v. Christopher, 893 F. Supp. 65 (D.D.C. 1995), Judge Royce Lamberth found that the statute unconstitutionally confers upon the secretary of state the authority to review the legal determinations of Article III judges. However, his decision was vacated on jurisdictional grounds, LoBue v. Christopher, 82 F.3d 1081 (D.C. Cir. 1996), and has not been followed by other courts. See, e.g., In re Extradition of Chan Seong-I, 346 F. Supp. 2d 1149 (D.N.M. 2004). For a discussion, see Christopher Man, Extradition and Article III: A Historical Examination of the "Judicial Power of the United States," 10 Tul. J. Intl. & Comp. L. 37 (2002).

3. *Probable cause.* As Judge Schiller noted, in the U.S. system the extradition hearing has a distinctly limited purpose. It is not a trial on the merits to determine guilt or innocence but a means of determining whether probable cause exists to hold the relator for trial in the requesting state. "The probable cause standard applicable in extradition proceedings is defined in accordance with federal law and has been described as 'evidence sufficient to cause a person of ordinary prudence and caution to conscientiously entertain a reasonable belief of the accused's guilt.'" United States v. Wiebe, 733 F.2d 549, 553 (8th Cir. 1984). As another court put it, "[s]ection 3184 therefore requires the extradition court to conduct essentially the same preliminary inquiry typically required for issuance of a search warrant or an arrest warrant for crimes committed in this country — a familiar task for any magistrate judge." Haxhiaj v. Hackman, 528 F.3d 282, 287 (4th Cir. 2008); Eain v. Wilkes, 641 F.2d 504, 508-509 (7th Cir. 1981) (explaining that an extradition request must "'be supported by sufficient evidence to show . . . that there is sufficient justification for the individual's arrest had the charged crime been committed in the United States'").

A foreign conviction entered after a trial at which the defendant was present will generally suffice, in and of itself, to establish probable cause. In such cases, the extradition court may rely solely on a certified copy of the foreign conviction. This rule applies even when the person was present at the commencement of criminal proceedings but fled before the proceedings concluded. However, when the foreign conviction was rendered in absentia, the fact of the judgment, standing alone, is insufficient to establish probable cause. The government is then required to present proofs from which the extradition court can make an independent assessment of whether probable cause exists. *Haxhiaj*, 528 F.3d 282.

In civil law jurisdictions, as well as in some other common law systems, the relevant standard is "prima facie case," that is, whether such evidence would justify committal for trial if the offense had been committed in that jurisdiction.

In the extradition hearing, the relator may not offer substantive defenses to the charges but may present evidence that rebuts ("explains away or completely obliterates") the government's evidence of probable cause. In re Extradition of Singh, 2005 WL 3030819, at *20 (E.D. Cal. Nov. 9, 2005). "Whatever the precise boundary between admissible 'explanatory' evidence and inadmissible 'contradictory' evidence, evidence that would completely negate probable cause is admissible in an extradition hearing." Sandhu v. Burke, 2000 WL 191707, at *5 (S.D.N.Y. Feb. 10, 2000). The courts are divided over whether recantation evidence is admissible. See In re Extradition of Berri, 2008 WL 4239170 (E.D.N.Y. Sept. 11, 2008); United States v. Hunte, 2006 WL 20773 (E.D.N.Y. Jan. 4, 2006).

4. *Evidentiary rules.* In U.S. law, international extradition proceedings are, in some respects, *sui generis*—neither criminal nor entirely civil in nature. They are not governed by the Federal Rules of Evidence or the Rules of Criminal Procedure. Fed. R. Crim. P. 1(a)(5); Fed. R. Evid. 1101(d)(3); Martin v. Warden, Atlanta Penitentiary, 993 F.2d 824 (11th Cir. 1993). "[D]iscovery in an international extradition hearing is limited and lies within the discretion of the magistrate." United States v. Kraiselburd, 786 F.2d 1395, 1399 (9th Cir. 1986); see also Koskotas v. Roche, 931 F.2d 169, 175 (1st Cir. 1992) (stating that, "in an extradition proceeding, discovery is not only discretionary with the court, it is narrow in scope").

Admissibility of depositions, warrants, or other papers in support of or in opposition to extradition is governed by 18 U.S.C. §3190. During the hearing itself, hearsay and otherwise excludable evidence is admissible. In re Extradition of Moreno-Vazquez, 2008 WL 3926427 (M.D. Ala. Nov. 17, 2008); Afanasjev v. Hurlburt, 418 F.3d 1159 (11th Cir. 2005); Mainero v. Gregg, 164 F.3d 1199 (9th Cir. 1999). The court's determination may rest on hearsay in whole or in part. See Collins v. Loisel, 259 U.S. 309 (1922); O'Brien v. Rozman, 554 F.2d 780 (6th Cir. 1977). Therefore, the court's findings may be made completely on documentary evidence. See, e.g., Bingham v. Bradley, 241 U.S. 511 (1916); *O'Brien*, 554 F.2d at 783.

In part because extradition proceedings are not "criminal proceedings" within the meaning of the Bill of Rights, the exclusionary rule is not applicable in extradition proceedings, even where the evidence sought to be excluded was alleged to have been obtained by torture. Atuar v. United States, 156 Fed. Appx. 555 (4th Cir. 2005). The accused's due process rights appear to be fairly limited, although courts have held that the accused has a due process right to enforce the terms of a plea bargain in the context of extradition. Plaster v. United States, 720 F.2d 340 (4th Cir. 1983) (promise not to extradite); Geisser v. United States, 513 F.2d 862 (5th Cir. 1975) (promise to use best efforts to avoid extradition).

5. *The rule of non-inquiry.* The limited nature of habeas review stems in part from what is known as the "rule of non-inquiry." Under this rule, extradition courts refrain from investigating the fairness of the requesting state's justice system, as well as from inquiring into the procedures or treatment that await a surrendered fugitive in the requesting country. Basso v. U.S. Marshal, 278 Fed. Appx. 886, 887 (11th Cir. 2008); *Haxhiaj*, 528 F.3d 282. Consideration of these issues rests within the exclusive prerogative of the executive branch in its discretionary power to issue the extradition warrant. As stated by the First Circuit in United States v. Kin-Hong, 110 F.3d 103, 110-111 (1st Cir. 1997): "The rule of non-inquiry, like extradition procedures generally, is shaped by concerns about institutional competence and by notions of separation of powers. It is not that questions about what awaits the relator in the requesting country are irrelevant to extradition; it is that there is another branch of government, which has both final say and greater discretion in these proceedings, to whom these questions are more properly addressed."

6. *Torture Convention.* However, as suggested by the *Hoxha* decision, U.S. ratification of the U.N. Convention Against Torture introduced a new element into application of the rule of non-inquiry. United Nations Convention Against Torture and Other Cruel, Inhuman or Degrading Treatment or Punishment, Dec. 10, 1984, 1465

U.N.T.S. 85, 114, reprinted in 23 I.L.M. 1027 (1984). The United States ratified the Convention on October 21, 2004. Article 3 of the Convention provides that "[n]o State Party shall expel, return ("refouler") or extradite a person to another State where there are substantial grounds for believing that he would be in danger of being subjected to torture." To implement this provision (among others), Congress enacted the Foreign Affairs Reform and Restructuring Act of 1998 (the FARR Act), Pub. L. No. 105-277, div. G, 112 Stat. 2681-2682, codified at 8 U.S.C. §1231 note. Section 2242(a) of that act provides that "[i]t shall be the policy of the United States not to expel, extradite, or otherwise effect the involuntary return of any person to a country in which there are substantial grounds for believing the person would be in danger of being subjected to torture, regardless of whether the person is physically present in the United States."

The applicable State Department regulations identify the secretary of state as "the U.S. official responsible for determining whether to surrender a fugitive to a foreign country by means of extradition." 22 C.F.R. §95.2(b) (2006). They provide that "to implement the obligation assumed by the United States pursuant to Article 3 of the Convention, the Department considers the question of whether a person facing extradition from the U.S. 'is more likely than not' to be tortured in the State requesting extradition when appropriate in making this determination." Id. They further state that in each case in which there is an allegation relating to torture, "appropriate policy and legal offices [shall] review and analyze information relevant to the case in preparing a recommendation to the Secretary as to whether or not to sign the surrender warrant." Id. §95.3(a). Importantly, they provide that "[d]ecisions of the Secretary concerning surrender of fugitives for extradition are matters of executive discretion not subject to judicial review." Id. §95.4.

In view of this regulatory structure, the court in *Hoxha* declined to create a new "humanitarian exception" to extradition based on the rule of non-inquiry. It was not the first court to wrestle with this issue. See, e.g., Prasoprat v. Benov, 421 F.3d 1009, 1016 n.5 (9th Cir. 2005); Cornejo-Barreto v. Siefert, 379 F.3d 1075 (9th Cir. 2004); Cornejo-Barreto v. Seifert, 218 F.3d 1004 (9th Cir. 2000). Nor was it the last.

In Mironescu v. Costner, 480 F.3d 664 (4th Cir. 2007), *cert. dismissed*, 128 S. Ct. 976 (2008), the Fourth Circuit confronted the issue head on. Mironescu had been convicted in absentia in Romania for various crimes relating to automobile theft and sentenced to four years imprisonment. After an extradition warrant had been signed, he filed a habeas corpus petition under 28 U.S.C. §2241 challenging the secretary of state's decision on the ground that he was likely to be tortured upon his return to Romania. He argued that under the Convention Against Torture (CAT) and the FARR Act, the secretary has a mandatory duty not to extradite a fugitive who is likely to be tortured after his surrender, and that the secretary's decision to extradite him in the face of evidence to that effect was arbitrary and capricious. The district court enjoined his extradition, and the government appealed.

Specifically, the government argued that the scope of habeas review in extradition cases is limited and the rule of non-inquiry bars such claims. After reviewing the history of the rule, the court of appeals concluded that "in light of the Secretary's conceded obligation under the FARR Act not to extradite Mironescu if he is likely to face torture, the rule of non-inquiry does not bar habeas review of the Secretary's extradition decision." 480 F.3d at 675. Relying on its decision in Plaster v. United States, 720 F.2d 340 (4th Cir. 1983), it reasoned that while the executive branch has unlimited discretion to *refuse* to extradite a fugitive, it lacks the discretion to extradite a fugitive when extradition would violate his federal rights. (Nonetheless, it also concluded that the district court had erred in denying the government's motion to dismiss on procedural grounds.)

The *Mironescu* decision is unlikely to be the last word on this issue. See, e.g., Khouzam v. Attorney General, 549 F.3d 235 (3d Cir. 2008); see generally Matthew Murchison, Note: Extradition's Paradox: Duty, Discretion, and Rights in the World of Non-Inquiry, 43 Stanford J. Intl. L. 295 (2007); Andrew J. Parmenter, Comment, Death by Non-Inquiry: The Ninth Circuit Permits the Extradition of a U.S. Citizen Facing the Death Penalty for a Nonviolent Drug Offense, 45 Washburn L.J. 657 (2006).

3. The "Political Offense" Exception

Most modern extradition treaties permit the requested state to deny the request for extradition on the grounds that the charged offense is political or "of a political nature." This exception has long been accepted as a means to preserve political asylum, but its operation has been fraught with controversy. Originally devised in the Age of Revolution to allow states to give sanctuary to political opponents of other states, its application is far more problematic in the context of modern-day terrorism, particularly in light of the various antiterrorism conventions aimed at preventing fugitives from escaping justice.

ORDINOLA v. HACKMAN
478 F.3d 588 (4th Cir. 2007)

WILLIAMS, Circuit Judge.

[In order to combat violent left-wing rebels — the "Shining Path" movement — Peruvian President Alberto Fujimori responded "with tactics that nearly matched the Shining Path's brutality." Wilmer Yarleque Ordinola became a group chief in the Colina Group, a paramilitary organization created by the government to fight the Shining Path. "Peru's extradition request alleges that Ordinola, while serving in the Colina Group, kidnapped and murdered noncombatant civilians on four separate occasions in 1991 and 1992." Ordinola sought political asylum in the United States in 2001, but in 2003 Peru requested his extradition "for the alleged crimes of aggravated homicide, aggravated kidnapping, forced disappearance of persons, inflicting major intentional injuries, and delinquent association." Peru and the United States have a bilateral extradition treaty. Ordinola, however, claimed that under the political offense exception he could not be extradited. The magistrate judge rejected his claim, concluding "that although Ordinola's alleged crimes occurred during a severe political uprising, the crimes were not sufficiently incidental to the uprising and thus did not fall within the exception. He reasoned that any political intentions Ordinola had in committing the alleged crimes were not enough to render the acts political offenses in light of the fact that Ordinola committed the crimes against noncombatant civilians and engaged in acts that violated the laws of armed conflict and international standards of civilized conduct." The district judge reversed and granted Ordinola's petition for a writ of habeas corpus. "The court concluded that Ordinola's crimes were sufficiently incidental to the political uprising because the Peruvian government led Ordinola to believe that the victims of Ordinola's crimes were terrorists. As such, the court reasoned that Ordinola did not knowingly kill innocent civilians." The government appealed.]

II

The political offense exception to extradition forbids countries from extraditing people who are accused of offenses that are "political" in nature. Like the vast majority of modern-day extradition treaties, the extradition Treaty between the United States and Peru provides a political offense exception: "Extradition shall not be granted if the offense for which extradition is requested constitutes a political offense." Extradition Treaty, art. IV, sec. 2. Unfortunately, however, these treaties do not define "political offense." Accordingly, we are forced to rely on judicial constructions, history, purpose, and State Department interpretations to determine the phrase's meaning. . . .

Extradition requests are of ancient origin. Extradition was the process by which states requested the surrender of "pure" political offenders, i.e., those accused of treason and contemptuous behavior toward the monarch. The first known extradition treaty — representing "one of the oldest documents in diplomatic history" — was entered into by the Egyptians and Hittites circa 1280 B.C. The political offense exception to extradition, however, is a far more recent development, tracing its beginnings to the Enlightenment ideals encapsulated in the French and American revolutions.

These ideals supported a belief that people possessed an inalienable right to resist and abolish tyrannical governments. See, e.g., The Declaration of Independence para. 1 (U.S. 1776) ("We hold these truths to be self-evident. . . . That whenever any Form of Government becomes destructive of these ends, it is the Right of the People to alter or to abolish it. . . ."). It was with these ideals in mind that Thomas Jefferson, as Secretary of State in 1792, recommended against entering into an extradition treaty with Spain . . .

The theory underpinning the political offense exception, then, is as old as our country.[16] The exception was deemed necessary to protect those people who justly fought back against their government oppressors to secure political change. In 1843, a decade after nations such as Belgium, France, and Switzerland included the political offense exception in their extradition treaties, the United States followed suit.

Traditionally, there have been two categories of political offenses: "pure" and "relative." The core "pure" political offenses are treason, sedition, and espionage. "Pure" political offenses do not have any of the elements of a common crime because "[s]uch laws exist solely because the very political entity, the state, has criminalized such conduct for its self-preservation." Such crimes are perpetrated directly against the state and do not intend to cause private injury. Most extradition treaties preclude extradition for "pure" political offenses. "Relative" political offenses, on the other hand, are common crimes that are so intertwined with a political act that the offense itself becomes a political one. As evidenced by this discussion, while "pure" political offenses are easy to identify, determining whether a common offense is "relatively" political requires close attention to the specific facts at issue.

---

16. [Court's footnote 9:] Arguments sounding in the exception were made in the famous extradition case of Jonathan Robbins at the turn of the Nineteenth Century. The British requested Robbins's extradition for his role in a mutiny aboard a British ship. Although Robbins claimed he was an American impressed into service by the British and was seeking to restore his liberty, President Adams came to the unpopular conclusion that Robbins should be extradited. See United States v. Robins, 27 F. Cas. 825, F. Cas. No. 16175 (D.S.C. 1799) ("[Robbins] was warranted by the most sacred rights of nature, and the laws of nations, to have recourse to violence in the recovery of that liberty, of which he had been unjustly deprived."); see also Ex Parte Kain, 14 F. Cas. 78, 81, F. Cas. No. 7597 (S.D.N.Y. 1853) ("It was the apprehension of the people of this country, at the time, that the offence of Jonathan Robbins . . . was a political offense. . . . Assuming such apprehension to have been well founded, the intense public indignation that followed was creditable to the nation.").

Most American courts addressing "relative" political offenses have developed a two-prong test to determine whether an offense is sufficiently political to fall within the exception. Known as "the incidence test," it asks whether (1) there was a violent political disturbance or uprising in the requesting country at the time of the alleged offense, and if so, (2) whether the alleged offense was incidental to or in the further-ance of the uprising. We, too, adopt the incidence test as our lodestar. . . .

IV

The Government argues that the district court failed to afford the magistrate judge's opinion proper deference and that it misapplied the political offense exception because Ordinola's offenses were not incident to the political uprising in Peru.[17] It contends that if allowed to stand, the opinion would extend the narrow doctrine "to virtually every misdeed, no matter how heinous, committed by a person purporting to act under a political cloak." Ordinola, on the other hand, argues that the district court did not err and that there exists a close nexus between Ordinola's alleged actions and his political objective. We agree in principle with the Government. . . .

B

To fall within the political offense exception, Ordinola's alleged actions must have been incidental to or in furtherance of a violent political uprising in Peru. Although Ordinola's actions occurred in the course of a violent political uprising, he cannot show that the magistrate judge erred in finding that those actions were not in fur-therance of quelling the uprising.

As an initial matter, we — like the magistrate judge and district court — have little trouble in agreeing that the alleged actions here occurred during the course of a violent political uprising. The Peruvian government and the Shining Path were engaged in a violent struggle for control of the country. According to one expert's opinion of the situation in 1992, "[a]pproximately 50 percent of Peruvian territory and approximately 65 percent of the country's population [was] under a state of national emergency." Clearly, then, it is appropriate to describe the situation in Peru at the time of Ordinola's alleged actions as "a political revolt, an insurrection, or a civil war."

The more difficult question is whether Ordinola's alleged offenses were incident to the political uprising. First, we recognize that it makes little sense to ask whether his actions were in furtherance of or "in aid" of the uprising. Ordinola, acting on behalf of the Peruvian government, was attempting to defeat, not aid, the uprising. Accord-ingly, we must slightly alter the question and instead ask whether Ordinola's actions were incident to or in furtherance of quelling the violent uprising.

The parties disagree over the extent to which this test is subjective or objective. The district court, for example, focused in part on its independent factual finding that Ordinola had no "knowledge regarding the innocence of the civilians" at the time of

---

17. [Court's footnote: 12] There also exists a colorable argument that the exception applies only to those fighting government oppression, and therefore not to government actors. The Government expressly declined to make this argument, and we will not do so *sua sponte* in the absence of full argument by the parties. We note, however, that although such a limitation finds strong support in the history and original purpose of the rule, no such limitation can be inferred from the plain language of the Treaty. We further note that in this age of guerrilla warfare, where different factions often control individual pockets of a country in the midst of a civil war, it might be beyond the judiciary's competency to determine whether the nominal government party is in fact the ruling party in any particular situs.

the attacks and thus intended to quell the uprising via his actions. The Government contends that it is a mistake to focus on the intentions, or motives, of the accused. Instead, the Government argues, courts must concentrate on the act itself, as the Treaty exempts political *offenses*, not politically motivated *offenders*.

We conclude that courts must look at the question both subjectively and objectively, although the objective view must usually carry more weight. Courts have long recognized the relevancy of subjective motives in the political offense context. We read these cases to mean that for a claimant to come within the protections of the political offense exception, it is necessary, but not sufficient, for the claimant to show that he was politically motivated. In other words, a claimant whose common crime was not subjectively politically motivated cannot come within the exception regardless of whether the offense itself could be described as an objectively "political" one.[18]

Aside from the subjective component, a claimant must also show that the offense was objectively political. This is because the Treaty itself exempts political *offenses*, and a political motivation does not turn every illegal action into a political offense. The Treaty, then, cannot be read to protect every act — no matter how unjustifiable and no matter the victim — simply because the suspect can proffer a political rationale for the action.

Here, we assume without deciding that Ordinola's actions were politically motivated. . . . We see no reason to delve into this inquiry because, as explained below, we conclude that Ordinola is charged with offenses that are not political under the Treaty.

To determine whether a particular offense is political under the Treaty, we must look to the totality of the circumstances, focusing on such particulars as the mode of the attack and the identity of the victims, for example. In *Ornelas*, the Supreme Court examined Mexico's extradition request for a member of a band of armed men who attacked and killed a group of Mexican soldiers and civilians. Ornelas claimed that he was part of a border revolutionary movement and that his actions were in furtherance of that movement. [Ornelas v. Ruiz, 161 U.S. 502, 510-511 (1896)]. In a similar procedural posture to this case, the magistrate determined that the acts were not of a political character, but the district court disagreed on habeas review. In reviewing the Government's appeal, the Supreme Court queried whether the magistrate had "no choice, on the evidence, but to hold, in view of the character of the foray, the mode of attack, the persons killed or captured, and the kind of property taken or destroyed," that Ornelas's offenses were political. In answering that question in the negative, the Supreme Court found it relevant that, inter alia, "private citizens" were the victims of some of the assaults, private property was taken, and Ornelas was part of a bandit group, acting without "uniforms or flag."

In examining the Colina Group's modes of attack, the magistrate judge noted that Ordinola was being charged for his role in killing fifteen people when the Colina Group "opened fire on [a] crowd of men, women, and children." He also noted that Ordinola and other Colina Group agents made a group of students "dig trenches, forced them into the holes, killed them with gunfire, and buried them." Likewise,

---

18. [Court's footnote: 13] By way of example, consider a hostage situation where the hostage takers demand the release from prison of their revolutionary leader as the condition for the release of the hostages. But this demand is in fact a ruse to distract the government and its hostage negotiators. The true interest of the hostage takers is in buying time so that they can break into a large vault containing valuables housed in the same building as the hostages. Thus, although the offense could be viewed as objectively political, the offenders have only a monetary motive and therefore could not take advantage of the political offense exception. For a cinematic variation of this example, see Die Hard (20th Century Fox 1988).

masked agents kidnapped a director of a news program, forced him to dig his grave, and killed him by shooting him in his head. Finally, the magistrate judge found that the agents acted on behalf of a friend of the military—who was perturbed by his workers' demands for higher wages—by kidnapping and murdering the men and then decorating the scene with Shining Path symbols to make it appear that the men had fallen victim to the Shining Path. The mode of these attacks does not favor Ordinola. They suggest a level of indiscriminate, clandestine killing based on suspect intelligence and political favors, as well as subsequent cover-ups that attempted to conceal the murders and destroy evidence.

Ordinola fares no better when looking to "the persons killed." None of the victims at issue here were armed at the time of attack or engaging in any overt hostility toward the Peruvian government. The magistrate judge . . . noted, inter alia, that the little boy who was killed while running to aid his dying father "was almost certainly not a terrorist, and the same can most likely be said for the other partygoers." The magistrate judge also found that the factory workers were targeted not because they were terrorists, but "because their boss wanted to retaliate against them for demanding better working conditions."

. . . Ordinola . . . contends that the civilian status of the victims is not especially relevant in this instance. We disagree.

Ordinola relies on language from *Quinn v. Robinson*,[19] where the Ninth Circuit concluded that "there is no justification for distinguishing . . . between attacks on military and civilian targets." In support of this "non-judgmental" contention, the court noted its view that "[i]t is for the revolutionaries, not the courts, to determine what tactics may help further their chances of bringing down or changing the government."

We respectfully disagree with this conclusion and hold that there are in fact sound justifications for distinguishing between civilian and governmental—or in this case, revolutionary—targets. The first justification, of course, is that the Supreme Court has held that the civilian status of the "persons killed" *is* relevant. Moreover, both the Second and Seventh Circuits have addressed the question and have concluded, like we do, that the status of the victims is relevant.

Second, it must be remembered that we are interpreting the Treaty to define the term "political offense." In doing so, we must afford "great weight" to the meaning attributed to the provision by the State Department, as it is charged with enforcing the Treaty. The State Department has previously expressed the view that "the political offense exception is not applicable to violent attacks on civilians," and at oral argument, Government counsel informed us that the department continues to generally adhere to that view.

Third, the status of the victims has been an important factor since the inception of the political offense exception. In fact, aside from Ninth Circuit caselaw, we can find no other American authority stating that the civilian status of victims is irrelevant. Rather, the precedents and authorities stand firmly on the opposite front.

Fourth, by refusing to examine the scope of the attack, the mode of the attack, and the victims of the attack, the Ninth Circuit's approach results in defining a political offense as any common crime that occurs during a political uprising so long as the

---

19. [Court's footnote: 15] Quinn was a member of the Irish Republican Army whom Great Britain sought to extradite for murder and bombings. Quinn v. Robinson, 783 F.2d 776, 781 (9th Cir. 1986). The Ninth Circuit, in a splintered opinion with all three members of the panel writing, concluded that the political offense exception did not apply. Judge Reinhardt's lead opinion ultimately concluded that London (the site of the crimes) was not the situs of an ongoing rebellion. . . .

accused claims a political motive connected to the uprising. As explained above, we must reject such a subjective test.

Accordingly, the magistrate judge's reasonable finding that Ordinola's alleged offenses were carried out against innocent civilians largely dooms Ordinola's argument. Because that finding was legitimately made, it simply cannot be said that the magistrate judge had no choice but to define Ordinola's alleged actions as political offenses. To have been considered political offenses, Ordinola's actions would had to have been in some way proportional to or in furtherance of quelling the Shining Path's rebellion. The magistrate judge did not err in recognizing that terror, for terror's sake, was not a sufficient method of quelling the Shining Path's uprising.

C

Finally, both parties suggest that we make inferences based on the motives of the requesting government. For example, Ordinola contends that "a new government seeks to punish [him as a] member[] of a former government for [his] conduct in suppressing a violent uprising." The Government, for its part, points out that this is not a "new government" comprised of the revolutionaries Ordinola once fought; rather, it is the same democratically elected government — albeit a different administration — that requests Ordinola's extradition. Although the Government's interpretation is correct on the facts, the motives of the requesting government are irrelevant to our decision. The Treaty states that extradition will be denied "if the *executive authority* of the Requested State determines that the request was politically motivated." Extradition Treaty, art. IV, sec. 3 (emphasis added). Any question into the Peruvian government's motivations is therefore well beyond this Court's legitimate realm of authority under the Treaty and must be addressed solely to the Secretary of State.

V

For the reasons outlined above, the district court erred in granting Ordinola's petition for a writ of habeas corpus. In affording proper deference under habeas review to the magistrate's decision, we simply cannot say that the magistrate judge had "no choice" but to find that the common crimes Ordinola is alleged to have committed against noncombatant civilians were political offenses under the Treaty with Peru. We therefore must vacate the district court's grant of the writ, and remand for reentry of a Certification of Extraditability. We note, however, that judicial review is not the only recourse available to Ordinola, as he is free to contest his extradition before the United States Secretary of State.

NOTES AND QUESTIONS

1. Do you agree with the Fourth Circuit's analysis? What are the proper tests to determine the applicability of the political question exception? Are special rules warranted in respect of contemporary manifestations of terrorism? See generally Christine van den Wyngaert, Political Offence Exception to Extradition: The Delicate Problem of Balancing the Rights of the Individual and the International Public Order (1980); David M. Lieberman, Note, Sorting the Revolutionary from the Terrorist: The Delicate Application of the "Political Offense" Exception in U.S. Extradition Cases, 59 Stan. L. Rev. 181 (2006); Rachael Mackenzie, Comment, Limiting the Political

Offense Exception to Extradition Treaties to Crimes Objectively Criminal, 31 Suffolk Transnatl. L. Rev. 711 (2008).

2. In a concurring opinion, Circuit Judge Traxler observed that Ordinola claimed he had committed the acts in question in the course of his duties as a Colina Group member to fight the terrorist threat posed by the Shining Path and that he was merely carrying out his duty to preserve the government in the midst of political upheaval. This defense, Judge Traxler noted, "raises an interesting theoretical issue about the application of the political offense exception to former government agents charged with crimes committed while there is an ongoing political uprising against the government" because on one view everything they do is arguably political. 478 F.3d at 612. Judge Traxler quoted the following excerpt from Comment, Offending Officials: Former Government Actors and the Political Offense Exception to Extradition, 94 Cal. L. Rev. 423, 423-424 (2006):

> The original purpose of the political offense exception to extradition was to protect revolutionaries from being returned to . . . face prosecution for crimes committed against their governments. . . . Arguably, everything a government actor does is "political" . . . [and therefore] the exception theoretically protects former government officials from facing their accusers merely because they used to govern them.

Although the issue was not technically before the court (since the government had elected not to pursue the argument), Judge Traxler made the following observations:

> [I]n Ordinola's mind, he was fighting an insurgency. . . . But, if we are going to permit a former government actor to avail himself of the political offense exception, the offender's subjective motivation cannot serve as the sole determinate [*sic*] of whether an offense is a political one. . . .

478 F.3d at 612-613. He concluded:

> [W]hen the magistrate judge viewed the evidence objectively, he found it insufficient to show that the killings and kidnappings were to suppress the Shining Path revolution. Men, women, and children had been killed indiscriminately. Shining Path slogans had been painted on the walls after the fact. Bodies were hidden or incinerated. Not one shred of objective evidence showed any of the victims to have been members or supporters of the Shining Path. Evidence that Ordinola was told by informants or superiors that the persons to be killed were insurgents or their supporters is not objective proof that they were. Instead, that evidence goes to what Ordinola subjectively believed and may be of relevance by way of defense to the charges if he is ultimately returned to Peru for trial. Here, however, it cannot avail him.

Id. at 616. Do you find Judge Traxler's analysis persuasive?

3. The seminal political offense decision of Quinn v. Robinson, 783 F.2d 776 (9th Cir. 1986), with which the *Ordinola* court disagreed, was only one in a series of cases addressing this issue in the context of IRA activities in Northern Ireland. In addition to those cited in the opinion, see In re Extradition of Smyth, 61 F.3d 711 (9th Cir. 1995), *amended*, 73 F.3d 887, *cert. denied*, 581 U.S. 1022 (1996); In re Extradition of Howard, 996 F.2d 1320 (1st Cir. 1993); McMullen v. United States, 953 F.2d 761 (2d Cir. 1992); In re Mackin, 668 F.2d 122 (2d Cir. 1981). Why do you suppose the Northern Ireland situation gave rise to such contentious cases?

4. *The New U.S.-U.K. Extradition Treaty.* The 1972 U.S.-U.K. Extradition Treaty and its 1985 Supplementary Treaty, 28 U.S.T. 227 and T.I.A.S. No. 12,050 respectively,

expressly gave to the judiciary the authority to consider whether an extradition request was motivated by a desire to punish the person sought on account of race, religion, nationality, or political opinion, or if that person would be subject to unfair treatment in the requesting state. In 2006 the U.S. Senate gave its advice and consent to ratification of a new bilateral treaty to replace those earlier agreements.

The new Extradition Treaty narrows the scope of the political offense exception. Article 4 lists specific offenses that are excluded from the political offense exception, including the following: (a) an offense for which both parties have the obligation pursuant to a multilateral international agreement to extradite the person sought or to submit the case to their competent authorities for decision as to prosecution; (b) a murder or other violent crime against the person of a head of state of one of the parties, or of a member of the head of state's family; (c) murder, manslaughter, malicious wounding, or inflicting grievous bodily harm; (d) an offense involving kidnapping, abduction, or any form of unlawful detention, including the taking of a hostage; (e) placing or using, or threatening the placement or use of, an explosive, incendiary, or destructive device or firearm capable of endangering life, or of causing grievous bodily harm, or of causing substantial property damage; (f) possession of an explosive, incendiary, or destructive device capable of endangering life, of causing grievous bodily harm, or of causing substantial property damage; (g) an attempt or conspiracy to commit, participation in the commission of, aiding and abetting, counseling or procuring the commission of, or being an accessory before or after the fact to any of the foregoing offenses.

Notwithstanding these exceptions, Article 4(3) of the new treaty provides that "extradition shall not be granted if the competent authority of the Requested State determines that the request was politically motivated." Importantly, the same provision states that "[i]n the United States, the executive branch is the competent authority for the purposes of this Article," thus reversing the rule in the Supplementary Treaty and clarifying that the responsibility for decisions relating to political offenses and "political motivation" is vested in the executive rather than the judiciary. A similar statement is included in Article 4(4), which provides that "the competent authority of the Requested State may refuse extradition for offenses under military law that are not offenses under ordinary criminal law."

Before the Senate Foreign Relations Committee, the administration described the new treaty as a "vital tool" in counterterrorism efforts. Are the listed exclusions from the political offense exception justified by the threats of international terrorism? Are they too broad or too narrow? Do you see any problems with Article 4? Consider that, in its resolution of advice and consent, the Senate included the following understanding:

> Under United States law, a United States judge makes a certification of extraditability of a fugitive to the Secretary of State. In the process of making such certification, a United States judge also makes determinations regarding the application of the political offense exception. Accordingly, the United States of America understands that the statement in paragraphs 3 and 4 of Article 4 that "in the United States, the executive branch is the competent authority for the purposes of this Article" applies only to those specific paragraphs of Article 4, and does not alter or affect the role of the United States judiciary in making certifications of extraditability or determinations of the application of the political offense exception.

Cong. Rec. S9786 (Sept. 20, 2006).

5. In Vo v. Benov, 447 F.3d 1235 (9th Cir. 2006), a naturalized U.S. citizen contested his extradition to Thailand to stand trial for the attempted bombing of the

Vietnamese Embassy in Bangkok on the grounds that the alleged plot constituted a political offense. Applying the "incidence" test as articulated in *Quinn,* the court of appeals rejected that argument, holding that both the "uprising" and the charged offense must occur within the country or territory in which those "rising up" reside. An attack on a country's embassy in a foreign country could not meet this criterion. "This limitation ensures that the political offense exception will not serve to protect international terrorism." Id. at 1241.

C. ALTERNATIVES TO EXTRADITION

International extradition can sometimes be slow, complicated, and even cumbersome, especially when the requesting state does not provide the necessary documentation in proper or timely fashion, or when the relator challenges the process and its underlying fairness. In some circumstances, more expeditious alternatives are available to government authorities, including the use of provisions for the removal of noncitizens under the relevant immigration laws (for example, visa revocation). In some countries, noncitizens can simply be expelled without recourse to formal judicial or administrative procedures. This section examines several of these alternatives.

On relatively rare occasions, governments resort to extralegal steps, including what has somewhat euphemistically been called *extraordinary rendition,* meaning use of forcible measures of self-help to obtain custody over an accused in another country (with or even without the tacit consent of that country's government).

1. *Expedited Procedures*

a. European Arrest Warrant

Over the years, various treaties have been adopted within the European Community to simplify and harmonize extradition relationships between member countries, including a 1987 agreement on double jeopardy, one in 1989 on the simplification and modernization of methods of transmitting extradition requests, a 1990 agreement on the transfer of proceedings in criminal matters, and a convention in 1991 on the enforcement of foreign criminal sentences. The adoption of the European Arrest Warrant (EAW) and Surrender Procedures has effectively replaced extradition in covered situations.[20]

The EAW can be issued by a national court for offenses carrying a penalty of more than a year in prison (or for individuals already sentenced to a prison term of at least four months). The state in which the person is arrested is obliged to return the individual to the issuing state within a maximum period of 90 days of the arrest. Since execution of these warrants is simply a judicial process, the procedure takes place without political involvement. Moreover, EU countries can no longer refuse to surrender their own nationals subject to the procedure, and the principle of dual criminality has been abolished for 32 specific categories of offenses. These include

---

20. European Council Framework Decision 2002/584/JHA, June 13, 2002, OJ L 190 of 18.07.2002. Member states were required to introduce legislation to bring the European Arrest Warrant (EAW) into force by January 1, 2004.

participation in a criminal organization; terrorism; trafficking in human beings; sexual exploitation of children and child pornography; illicit trafficking in arms, ammunition, and explosives; corruption; fraud, including fraud pertaining to the financial interest of the European Union; money laundering; and counterfeiting of money including the euro.[21]

b.   Transfer of Prisoners

Some modern extradition treaties specifically authorize the "temporary transfer" of individuals who have been tried, sentenced, and are serving their time in one state to another state for purposes of criminal prosecution on other charges. Once the trial in the requesting state is completed, the person will be returned to complete the original sentence. If that person is convicted and a period of incarceration is imposed in relation to the offense for which she was temporarily surrendered, she will serve that additional sentence in the original country.

This procedure is to be distinguished from arrangements in specialized "prisoner transfer treaties" providing that persons convicted of a crime in a foreign country can be returned to their country of nationality to complete their sentences. U.S. law expressly provides for such arrangements pursuant to 18 U.S.C. §4100 et seq.[22] The United States is a party to the widely ratified 1983 Council of Europe's Convention on the Transfer of Sentenced Persons,[23] the 1993 Inter-American Convention on Serving Criminal Sentences Abroad,[24] and 12 bilateral treaties (all told, prisoner transfer arrangements are in effect with more than 65 countries). In general, such transfers are discretionary and require the consent of both governments as well as the individual concerned. Transfer is possible only after final sentence has been rendered and no further appeals are possible, and when any minimum periods of incarceration specified by the law of the custodial state have been met. In the United States, prisoners in U.S. state (as opposed to federal) custody often face difficulties in obtaining the necessary consent.[25]

c.   Recognition of Penal Judgments and Transfer of Proceedings

Within the Council of Europe (COE) and the European Community, still other mechanisms have been devised to facilitate mutual cooperation and enforcement of criminal penalties. In 1970, the COE adopted the European Convention on the International Validity of Criminal Judgments (E.T.S. No. 70), which provides in essence that contracting states are authorized to enforce "criminal sanctions" resulting from any final decision delivered by a criminal court of other contracting states under certain conditions (for example, when the sentenced person is "ordinarily

---

21. See http://ec.europa.eu/justice_home/fsj/criminal/extradition/fsj_criminal_extradition_en.htm and http://www.ecba-eaw.org/cms. The validity of the EAW has been challenged in Germany and Spain. See Gregory J. Mann, Note, The European Arrest Warrant: A Short-Lived Mechanism for Extradition?, 34 Syracuse J. Intl. L. & Com. 715 (2007).

22. See also 28 C.F.R. §2.68.

23. The COE treaty is also known as the Strasbourg Convention, 35 U.S.T. 2867, T.I.A.S. No. 10,824.

24. See Sen. Treaty Doc. 104-35 (Sept. 30, 1996).

25. For more information on the U.S. International Prisoner Transfer Program, see http://www.usdoj.gov/criminal/oeo/links/intlprisoner/intlprisoner.html. See also David S. Finkelstein, Note, "Ever Been in a [Foreign] Prison?": The Implementation of Transfer of Penal Sanctions Treaties by U.S. States, 66 Fordham L. Rev. 125 (1997).

resident" in the enforcing state, the sentence is "likely to improve the prospects for [that person's] social rehabilitation," and enforcement would not "run counter to the fundamental principles of the legal system of the requested State"). In effect, this treaty avoids the need for extradition of persons already convicted and sentenced.

To much the same effect is the Convention on the Transfer of Proceedings in Criminal Matters adopted by the COE two years later (E.T.C. No. 73). This treaty contemplates a request from one state party to another for prosecution (rather than enforcement of a sentence already rendered). Such a request may be made if the act in question is a punishable offense in both the requesting and the requested states, if the accused is normally resident in the requested state or is a national of that state, if he is to serve a prison sentence or face other proceedings in that state, and if the transfer of proceedings is warranted in the interests of a fair trial or if the enforcement in the requested state of a sentence (following conviction) would likely improve the prospects for his social rehabilitation. The requested state may not refuse the request unless it considers that the offense is of a political nature or that the request is based on considerations of race, religion, or nationality. Proceedings might be "transferred" for practical reasons, for example, if the accused is being held (or is subject to prosecution) in the requested state or when extradition is not possible — for example, because the custodial state cannot extradite its own nationals. For some European states, such transfers are possible even in the absence of a treaty basis. In 1990, the UN adopted a Model Treaty on the Transfer of Proceedings in Criminal Matters (see G.A. Res. 45/118 (Dec. 14, 1990)).

2. Exclusion and Removal

Of particular importance — at least where the person sought is not a citizen — is the option of using available authority under immigration laws to exclude or remove the individual in question. (*Removal* is sometimes called *deportation*.) Statistically, removal occurs far more frequently than extradition (for the simple reason that most removals are based on violations of immigration law, rather than requests from foreign law enforcement personnel). For example, in fiscal year 2004, 202,842 foreign nationals were formally removed from the United States; 1,035,477 more foreign nationals accepted offers of voluntary departure; and 88,897 criminal aliens were removed from the United States. By contrast, in 2004, the State Department reported only approximately 940 completed extraditions (no specific information was available regarding the number of surrenders pursuant to waivers of extradition).

Where the individual is wanted by the law enforcement authorities in her country of nationality, arrangements are often made for an arrest immediately upon arrival. In effect, then, deportations and exclusions can function as de facto extraditions, but under different standards and restrictions than those that accompany the formal extradition process.

Certain classes of aliens are inadmissible under the Immigration and Nationality Act (INA), including, for example, terrorists; members of the Communist or any other totalitarian party; persons who have engaged in Nazi persecution, genocide, or extrajudicial killing; participants in the recruitment of child soldiers; individuals likely to become a "public charge"; and those whose entry or proposed activities in the United States are reasonably likely to have "potentially serious adverse foreign policy consequences for the United States."[26]

---

26. See 8 U.S.C. §1182(a).

NOTES AND QUESTIONS

1. *Foreign policy exclusion.* The last category can raise difficult questions of due process and fairness. The Immigration and Nationality Act, at 8 U.S.C. §1227(a)(4)(C)(i), provides that an "alien whose presence or activities in the United States the Secretary of State has reasonable ground to believe would have potentially serious adverse foreign policy consequences for the United States is deportable." In Massieu v. Reno, 915 F. Supp. 681, 686 (D.N.J. 1996), the district court held that statute unconstitutional because it gave the secretary of state "unfettered and unreviewable discretion to deport any alien lawfully within the United States, *not* for identified reasons relating to his or conduct in the United States or elsewhere but, rather, because that person's mere presence here would impact in some unexplained way on the foreign policy interests of the United States." Not only was the statute void for vagueness, the court said, it failed to give Mario Ruiz Massieu, a Mexican national, due process of law and constituted an unconstitutional delegation of legislative power to the executive. On appeal, that decision was reversed on the limited ground that Ruiz Massieu had failed to exhaust his administrative remedies before petitioning the court for review. The court of appeals did not address the constitutional questions. Massieu v. Reno, 91 F.3d 416 (3d Cir. 1996).

The case had extraordinary facts. Ruiz Massieu was a prominent figure in the PRI, Mexico's then-ruling party, and had twice been deputy attorney general. His brother, an even more prominent political figure, was assassinated in 1994. Ruiz Massieu launched an investigation of his brother's murder and identified a PRI official as the organizer of the hit. That official was protected by government immunity and eventually vanished without a trace. Ruiz Massieu angrily resigned from his office and the PRI, then published a book alleging that highly placed PRI members had ordered the murder of his brother, who was a critic of the government. Soon Ruiz Massieu began receiving death threats and was interrogated by authorities for alleged criminal activity.

Ruiz Massieu fled Mexico in 1995. He lawfully entered the United States (where he owned a home) and boarded a flight to Spain. At the Newark Airport, however, he was arrested by U.S. Customs officials, and two days later Mexico requested his extradition. The New Jersey magistrate judge turned down the request, finding no probable cause, and noting not only that the Mexican evidence was "incredible and unreliable," but that some affidavits had been obtained by torture. Over the next four months, the government attempted three more times, before two different magistrates, to have Ruiz Massieu declared extraditable, for embezzlement and an obstruction offense. Each time, the magistrates refused the request, finding insufficient evidence of probable cause. Finally, Mexico abandoned the extradition attempts.

In the words of U.S. District Judge Maryanne Barry,

> It was then, however, that this case took a turn toward the truly Kafkaesque. On December 22, 1995, immediately after Magistrate Judge Chesler issued his opinion, Mr. Ruiz Massieu was taken into custody by the Immigration and Naturalization Service ("the INS") pursuant to a previously unserved and unannounced detainer dated September 29, 1995. In addition, he was served with an INS Order to Show Cause and Notice of Hearing. The notice advised Mr. Ruiz Massieu that he was ordered to show cause as to why he should not be deported because,
>
> > the Secretary of State has made a determination that, pursuant to Section 241(a)(4)(C) of the Immigration and Nationality [*sic*] Act, 8 U.S.C. §1251(a)(4)(C), there is reasonable ground to believe your presence or activities in the United States would have potentially serious adverse foreign policy consequences for the United States. . . .

Massieu, 915 F. Supp. at 689. The INS produced a letter from Secretary of State Warren Christopher to Attorney General Janet Reno asking that Ruiz Massieu be deported to Mexico. The letter said that "our inability to return to Mexico Mr. Ruiz Massieu — a case the Mexican Presidency has told us is of the highest importance — would jeopardize our ability to work with Mexico on law enforcement matters. It might also cast a potentially chilling effect on other issues our two governments are addressing." Id. at 689.

Judge Barry held that the statute was void for vagueness because it "provides absolutely no notice to aliens as to what is required of them under the statute" to avoid detention. Id. at 699.

In subsequent administrative proceedings, an immigration judge held that the government had introduced insufficient evidence to support the charge that Ruiz Massieu's presence in the country would have potentially serious adverse foreign policy consequences and, accordingly, held him not deportable. The INS, however, prevailed in its appeal to the Board of Immigration Appeals (BIA). The BIA held that the secretary of state's letter stating his determination on this issue, and providing facially reasonable and bona fide reasons for that determination, was sufficient evidence. In re Ruiz Massieu, 22 I. & N. Dec. 833 (BIA June 10, 1999). Two months later, Ruiz Massieu was indicted in Houston on narcotics and money laundering charges. Two days before arraignment on these charges, Ruiz Massieu committed suicide. At that point, he had been living under house arrest for four years.

Does Judge Barry's holding (that the statute is void for vagueness) overlook the fact that the statute is not about the alien's conduct but about the foreign policy interests of the United States? Ruiz Massieu had entered the United States legally and was merely trying to leave for Spain. Even if his "presence or activities in the United States would have potentially adverse foreign policy consequences for the United States," why should he be sent back to Mexico rather than be allowed to proceed on his way to Spain? For a discussion of this case in the context of bilateral U.S.-Mexican extradition relations, see Rodrigo Labardini, Deportation in Lieu of Extradition from Mexico, 20 (No. 6) Intl. Enforcement L. Rep. 239 (2004).

2. *Terrorists.* A related provision, 8 U.S.C. §1533(a)(1)(D), governs the removal of alien terrorists. To secure such a removal order, the Department of Justice must prove to an immigration judge (1) that the targeted alien is a terrorist and (2) that removal of the alien under the normal procedures "would pose a risk to the national security of the United States." The statute provides that alien terrorists who are ordered removed "shall be [removed] to any country which the alien shall designate." 8 U.S.C. §1537(b)(2)(A). The alien need not be removed to the country selected by the alien, however, "if the Attorney General, in consultation with the Secretary of State, determines that removal of the alien to the country so designated would impair a treaty obligation or adversely affect United States foreign policy." In such a situation, the alien can be sent to any country willing to receive her. 8 U.S.C. §1537(b)(2)(B). Thus, so long as a legitimate foreign policy interest supports the attorney general's refusal to remove an alien to the country of his designation, the alien can legally be removed to any country of the attorney general's choice. Some view these provisions as inadequate. See John Yoo, Transferring Terrorists, 79 Notre Dame L. Rev. 1183, 1191-1193 (2004).

3. *Nazi persecutors and human rights violators.* U.S. immigration law provides that participants in Nazi-sponsored acts of persecution during the period March 23, 1933, to May 8, 1945, and aliens who have engaged in genocide, are both inadmissible to, and deportable from, the United States. See 8 U.S.C. §§1182(a)(3)(E), 1227(a)(4)(D). The Department of Justice's Office of Special Investigations (OSI) brings denaturalization proceedings against suspected Nazi war criminals who immigrated to the

United States after World War II. The government must present clear, convincing, and unequivocal evidence that the individuals in question engaged in, or assisted in, Nazi persecution or lied on their applications for entry and/or citizenship about having "assisted in Nazi persecution or engaged in genocide." The World War II cases are civil proceedings, and the individuals in question are not subject to prosecution under U.S. law. Since 1979, when OSI was established, over 1,500 investigations have been conducted, and nearly 110 individuals have been denaturalized or removed under this authority. For recent cases, see United States v. Kalymon, 541 F.3d 624 (6th Cir. 2008); Demjanjuk v. Mukasey, 514 F.3d 616 (6th Cir. 2008); United States v. Mandycz, 359 F. Supp. 2d 601 (E.D. Mich. 2005), *aff'd*, 447 F.3d 951 (6th Cir.).

Some of those removed are subsequently prosecuted in their countries of origin. For example, following his deportation to Lithuania in 1996, Kazys Gimzaukas was convicted of participating in genocide. In United States v. Balsys, 524 U.S. 666 (1998), the Supreme Court held that an alien in denaturalization or removal proceedings could not invoke a Fifth Amendment privilege against self-incrimination, even based upon a real and substantial likelihood of prosecution and conviction in the countries to which he might be deported.

In 2004, the statutory authority for OSI's activities was broadened to encompass criminal and civil denaturalization proceedings for severe human rights violations, in particular by aliens who "ordered, incited, assisted, or otherwise participated in conduct outside the United States that would, if committed in the United States or by a United States national, be genocide." Congress also authorized the denaturalization of those who, while serving as foreign government officials, were responsible for or directly carried out "particularly severe violations of religious freedom" as defined by the International Religious Freedom Act of 1998, 22 U.S.C. §6402. See the Intelligence Reform and Terrorism Prevention Act of 2004, Pub. L. No. 108-458, Title V, Subtitle E (Dec. 17, 2004).

By contrast, consider the "Holocaust denial" case of Germar Rudolf, also known as Germar Scheerer, a German citizen who fled his homeland in 1995 following his conviction for inciting racial hatred in violation of the German Penal Code. The relevant provision (StGB art. 130, §§3-5, entitled *Volksverhetzung* or "incitement of the masses") criminalizes publicly approving of, denying, or otherwise trivializing an act committed under the rule of National Socialism in a manner capable of disturbing the public order. On the basis of soil samples taken from the site of the Auschwitz concentration camp, Sheerer alleged that the gas and delousing chambers in which mass killings occurred showed no residual chemical signs of Zyklon B use. He published a report arguing that the mass killings could not have occurred as commonly believed. The highest court in Germany upheld his conviction and the sentence of 14 months' imprisonment.

Scheerer fled to avoid his sentence and eventually entered the United States as a "conditional parolee." His application for asylum was rejected because he had presented "no cognizable claim of past persecution or well-founded fear of future persecution" as required by the Immigration and Nationality Act. His petitions for withholding of removal and adjustment of status to lawful permanent resident alien were also denied. In November 2005, he was removed to Germany to begin serving his sentence. In due course, the Eleventh Circuit upheld the government's actions. See Scheerer v. U.S. Atty. Gen., 445 F.3d 1311 (11th Cir. 2006).

Are such provisions justified? Absent requests for extradition, should individuals who commit serious crimes abroad be permitted to remain in the United States? Because the initial decisions in the process of removal are made in administrative rather than judicial proceedings, do such provisions give too much authority to the government? Are such provisions inherently subject to political considerations?

4. *Torture claims.* In accordance with the Torture Convention, as implemented by the FARR, the INA and its implementing regulations specifically provide for withholding of removal for aliens who are more likely than not to face torture upon their return. See INA §241(b)(3), and 8 C.F.R. §§1208.16(c) and 1208.17(a). A substantial body of case law has arisen in respect of these provisions; for two recent illustrative decisions, see Pierre v. Atty. Gen., 528 F.3d 180 (3d Cir. 2008) (deportation of Haitian ex-convict in the context of allegations that he would face indefinite detention and lack of appropriate medical care upon his return); Alhaddad v. Mukasey, 2008 WL 5160149 (6th Cir. Dec. 9, 2008) (Israeli citizen's fear of persecution and torture if returned to Gaza).

Where there are reasonable grounds to regard the alien in question "as a danger to national security," however, that alien is statutorily ineligible for asylum, withholding from removal, or protection under CAT. See INA §208(b)(2)(A)(iv), 8 U.S.C. §1158(b)(2)(A)(iv) (exception to grant of asylum); INA §241(b)(3)(B)(iv), 8 U.S.C. §1231(b)(3)(B)(iv) (exception to withholding from removal).

For recent discussions of the interplay between these provisions, see Malkandi v. Mukasey, 544 F.3d 1029 (9th Cir. 2008); Yusupov v. Atty. Gen., 518 F.3d 185 (3d Cir. 2008).

5. *Diplomatic assurances.* As indicated above, in some situations it is possible for the executive branch to seek appropriate guarantees from the authorities of the destination country that the individual will not be tortured following her return. For an extensive discussion of the role of assurances in different contexts, see Ashley Deeks, Promises Not to Torture: Diplomatic Assurances in U.S. Courts, ASIL Discussion Paper (Dec. 2008), available at http://www.asil.org/files/ASIL-08-DiscussionPaper.pdf. See also Khouzam v. Atty. Gen., 549 F.3d 235 (3d Cir. 2008) (assessing the effect of government assurances that the individual would not be tortured upon his return); Saadi v. Italy, App. No. 37201/06, Judgment and Satisfaction (Feb. 28, 2008) (court must determine in each case the weight to be given to the receiving state's diplomatic assurances in determining whether transfer would violate Article 3 of the European Convention on Human Rights), available at http://www.echr.coe.int.

Does an individual have a cause of action against U.S. officials who violate the prohibition against removal to another country with the knowledge or intention that the individual would be detained and tortured? See Arar v. Ashcroft, 532 F.3d 157 (2d Cir. 2008) (rehearing en banc granted Aug. 12, 2008) (holding that plaintiff could not maintain a *Bivens* action based on alleged constitutional violations that arose out of his removal to a foreign country where, he alleges, he was tortured). The *Arar* case bears some similarity to *Ruiz Massieu*, in that Arar (a Canadian national) was present in the United States only as a stopover on his way to another country. In this case, U.S. authorities suspected him of terrorist-related actions and sent him to Syria. They were acting in part on information about Arar supplied by the Canadian government, which eventually conducted a formal inquiry into its own behavior and concluded that its information was erroneous. The Canadian prime minister formally apologized to Arar, and Canada paid him a $10.5 million settlement. Neither Syria nor the United States has admitted error or conceded that Arar was tortured.

3. Abduction

In some circumstances, neither extradition nor any of the alternative mechanisms discussed above might be available to bring about the apprehension and transfer of a fugitive or wanted person. The reasons could include the lack of applicable bilateral or multilateral treaties, an ineffective or corrupt legal system in the country where the fugitive is found, potential threats against the host government (for example, from terrorist groups or drug cartels) if the individual is turned over, or even poor or hostile political relationships between the two countries. The dilemma can also arise in the case of "failed" states, which lack a viable central government capable of making a decision. In such situations, can nothing be done?

NOTES

1. *Legality.* As the foregoing indicates, as a matter of national law extradition is generally not an exclusive procedure, and individuals may be delivered (or "rendered") to other countries by various means. Virtually every state, however, would consider it a violation of its territorial sovereignty if foreign law enforcement agents carried out an arrest on its territory and removed the detained individuals extralegally. Nonetheless, such practices (forcible abductions, sometimes euphemistically called *irregular renditions*) do occur, if infrequently. In most countries, they likely constitute a criminal offense, exposing the foreign officials to prosecution and possibly giving rise to liability of the foreign state under international law. As noted in Reporters' Comment c to §432 of the Restatement (Third) of the Foreign Relations Law of the United States (1987):

> *Consequences of violation of territorial limits of law enforcement.* If a state's law enforcement officials exercise their functions in the territory of another state without the latter's consent, that state is entitled to protest and, in appropriate cases, to receive reparation from the offending state. If the unauthorized action includes abduction of a person, the state from which the person was abducted may demand return of the person, and international law requires that he be returned. If the state from which the person was abducted does not demand his return, under the prevailing view the abducting state may proceed to prosecute him under its laws.

As we saw in Chapter 1, in 1960, the Nazi war criminal Adolf Eichmann was abducted from Argentina by agents of the State of Israel and taken to Israel for trial on charges stemming from Eichmann's role in the Holocaust. The UN Security Council adopted a resolution declaring that such acts, "which affect the sovereignty of a Member State and therefore cause international friction, may, if repeated, endanger international peace and security." S.C. Res. 138, at 4, U.N. Doc. S/RES/4349 (June 23, 1960). Thereafter, Argentina and Israel reached a settlement that did not call for Eichmann's return. When the defense of forcible abduction was raised during the trial of Eichmann, the Israeli district court ruled, "In view of the settlement of the incident between the two countries before trial brought, judgment may without hesitation be based on the continuous line of British, Palestinian and American case law, beginning with *Ex parte Scott* and going on to *Frisbie v. Collins* and after." Atty. Gen. v. Eichmann, 36 I.L.R. 18, 70-71 (Dist. Ct. Isr. 1961), *aff'd*, 36 I.L.R. 277 (Sup. Ct. Isr. 1962).

2. *Male captus, bene detentus.* At the same time, nearly all states have followed the rule that, absent protest from other states, they may exercise jurisdiction over persons brought before their courts through "irregular" means, even through an abduction from another state in violation of international law. The Latin phrase *male captus, bene detentus* — "bad capture, good detention" — succinctly names this doctrine. English cases going back to the early nineteenth century have followed the *male captus, bene detentus* rule. See, e.g., Ex parte Scott, 9 B. & C. 446, 109 Eng. Rep. 166 (K.B. 1829); Ex parte Elliott, [1949] 1 All E.R. 373 (K.B.). In the United States, the Supreme Court so

held in the leading cases of Ker v. Illinois, 119 U.S. 436 (1886), and Frisbie v. Collins, 342 U.S. 519 (1952) (hence it is known as the *Ker-Frisbie* doctrine). U.S. courts consistently apply the doctrine. For example, see United States v. Amawi, 2008 WL 820157 (N.D. Ohio Mar. 24, 2008). Over time, however, a few limited exceptions to the doctrine have emerged. See United States v. Salinas Doria, 2008 WL 4684229 (S.D.N.Y. Oct. 21, 2008).

3. *Relationship to extradition treaties.* The Supreme Court addressed the issue in the context of an argument that jurisdiction over an individual brought to the United States by irregular methods is improper when a valid extradition treaty is in place.

UNITED STATES v. ALVAREZ-MACHAIN
504 U.S. 655 (1992)

Chief Justice REHNQUIST delivered the opinion of the Court.

The issue in this case is whether a criminal defendant, abducted to the United States from a nation with which it has an extradition treaty, thereby acquires a defense to the jurisdiction of this country's courts. We hold that he does not, and that he may be tried in federal district court for violations of the criminal law of the United States.

Respondent, Humberto Alvarez-Machain, is a citizen and resident of Mexico. He was indicted for participating in the kidnap and murder of United States Drug Enforcement Administration (DEA) special agent Enrique Camarena-Salazar and a Mexican pilot working with Camarena, Alfredo Zavala-Avelar. The DEA believes that respondent, a medical doctor, participated in the murder by prolonging Agent Camarena's life so that others could further torture and interrogate him. On April 2, 1990, respondent was forcibly kidnapped from his medical office in Guadalajara, Mexico, to be flown by private plane to El Paso, Texas, where he was arrested by DEA officials. The District Court concluded that DEA agents were responsible for respondent's abduction, although they were not personally involved in it.[27]

Respondent moved to dismiss the indictment, claiming that his abduction constituted outrageous governmental conduct, and that the District Court lacked jurisdiction to try him because he was abducted in violation of the extradition treaty between the United States and Mexico. Extradition Treaty, May 4, 1978, [1979] United States-United Mexican States, 31 U.S.T. 5059, T.I.A.S. No. 9656 (Extradition Treaty or Treaty). The District Court rejected the outrageous governmental conduct claim, but held that it lacked jurisdiction to try respondent because his abduction violated the Extradition Treaty. The District Court discharged respondent and ordered that he be repatriated to Mexico.

The Court of Appeals affirmed the dismissal of the indictment and the repatriation of respondent, [holding that the forcible abduction of a Mexican national with the authorization or participation of the United States violated the Extradition Treaty between the United States and Mexico]. . . . We granted certiorari, and now reverse.

Although we have never before addressed the precise issue raised in the present case, we have previously considered proceedings in claimed violation of an extradition treaty and proceedings against a defendant brought before a court by means of a

---

27. [Court's footnote 2:] Apparently, DEA officials had attempted to gain respondent's presence in the United States through informal negotiations with Mexican officials, but were unsuccessful. DEA officials then, through a contact in Mexico, offered to pay a reward and expenses in return for the delivery of respondent to the United States.

forcible abduction. We addressed the former issue in United States v. Rauscher, 119 U.S. 407 (1886); more precisely, the issue whether the Webster-Ashburton Treaty of 1842, 8 Stat. 572, 576, which governed extraditions between England and the United States, prohibited the prosecution of defendant Rauscher for a crime other than the crime for which he had been extradited. Whether this prohibition, known as the doctrine of specialty, was an intended part of the treaty had been disputed between the two nations for some time. Justice Miller delivered the opinion of the Court, which carefully examined the terms and history of the treaty; the practice of nations in regards to extradition treaties; the case law from the States; and the writings of commentators, and reached the following conclusion:

> [A] person who has been brought within the jurisdiction of the court *by virtue of proceedings under an extradition treaty*, can only be tried for one of the offences described in that treaty, and for the offence with which he is charged in the proceedings for his extradition, until a reasonable time and opportunity have been given him, after his release or trial upon such charge, to return to the country from whose asylum he had been forcibly taken under those proceedings. (Emphasis added.)

In addition, Justice Miller's opinion noted that any doubt as to this interpretation was put to rest by two federal statutes which imposed the doctrine of specialty upon extradition treaties to which the United States was a party. Unlike the case before us today, the defendant in *Rauscher* had been brought to the United States by way of an extradition treaty; there was no issue of a forcible abduction.

In Ker v. Illinois, 119 U.S. 436 (1886), also written by Justice Miller and decided the same day as *Rauscher*, we addressed the issue of a defendant brought before the court by way of a forcible abduction. Frederick Ker had been tried and convicted in an Illinois court for larceny; his presence before the court was procured by means of forcible abduction from Peru. A messenger was sent to Lima with the proper warrant to demand Ker by virtue of the extradition treaty between Peru and the United States. The messenger, however, disdained reliance on the treaty processes, and instead forcibly kidnapped Ker and brought him to the United States. We distinguished Ker's case from *Rauscher*, on the basis that Ker was not brought into the United States by virtue of the extradition treaty between the United States and Peru, and rejected Ker's argument that he had a right under the extradition treaty to be returned to this country only in accordance with its terms. We rejected Ker's due process argument more broadly, holding in line with "the highest authorities" that "such forcible abduction is no sufficient reason why the party should not answer when brought within the jurisdiction of the court which has the right to try him for such an offence, and presents no valid objection to his trial in such court."

In Frisbie v. Collins, 342 U.S. 519 (1952), we applied the rule in *Ker* to a case in which the defendant had been kidnapped in Chicago by Michigan officers and brought to trial in Michigan. We upheld the conviction over objections based on the Due Process Clause and the federal Kidnapping Act and stated:

> This Court has never departed from the rule announced in [*Ker*] that the power of a court to try a person for crime is not impaired by the fact that he had been brought within the court's jurisdiction by reason of a "forcible abduction." No persuasive reasons are now presented to justify overruling this line of cases. They rest on the sound basis that due process of law is satisfied when one present in court is convicted of crime after having been fairly apprized of the charges against him and after a fair trial in accordance with constitutional procedural safeguards. There is nothing in the Constitution that requires

a court to permit a guilty person rightfully convicted to escape justice because he was brought to trial against his will.

Frisbie, supra, at 522 (citation and footnote omitted).

The only differences between *Ker* and the present case are that *Ker* was decided on the premise that there was no governmental involvement in the abduction; and Peru, from which Ker was abducted, did not object to his prosecution.[28] Respondent finds these differences to be dispositive, . . . contending that they show that respondent's prosecution, like the prosecution of Rauscher, violates the implied terms of a valid extradition treaty. The Government, on the other hand, argues that *Rauscher* stands as an "exception" to the rule in *Ker* only when an extradition treaty is invoked, and the terms of the treaty provide that its breach will limit the jurisdiction of a court. Therefore, our first inquiry must be whether the abduction of respondent from Mexico violated the Extradition Treaty between the United States and Mexico. If we conclude that the Treaty does not prohibit respondent's abduction, the rule in *Ker* applies, and the court need not inquire as to how respondent came before it.

In construing a treaty, as in construing a statute, we first look to its terms to determine its meaning. The Treaty says nothing about the obligations of the United States and Mexico to refrain from forcible abductions of people from the territory of the other nation, or the consequences under the Treaty if such an abduction occurs. Respondent submits that Article 22(1) of the Treaty, which states that it "shall apply to offenses specified in Article 2 [including murder] committed before and after this Treaty enters into force," evidences an intent to make application of the Treaty mandatory for those offenses. However, the more natural conclusion is that Article 22 was included to ensure that the Treaty was applied to extraditions requested after the Treaty went into force, regardless of when the crime of extradition occurred.

More critical to respondent's argument is Article 9 of the Treaty, which provides:

> 1. Neither Contracting Party shall be bound to deliver up its own nationals, but the executive authority of the requested Party shall, if not prevented by the laws of that Party, have the power to deliver them up if, in its discretion, it be deemed proper to do so.
> 2. If extradition is not granted pursuant to paragraph 1 of this Article, the requested Party shall submit the case to its competent authorities for the purpose of prosecution, provided that Party has jurisdiction over the offense.

According to respondent, Article 9 embodies the terms of the bargain which the United States struck: If the United States wishes to prosecute a Mexican national, it may request that individual's extradition. Upon a request from the United States, Mexico may either extradite the individual or submit the case to the proper authorities for prosecution in Mexico. In this way, respondent reasons, each nation preserved its right to choose whether its nationals would be tried in its own courts or by the courts of the other nation. This preservation of rights would be frustrated if either nation were free to abduct nationals of the other nation for the purposes of prosecution. More broadly, respondent reasons, as did the Court of Appeals, that all the processes and restrictions on the obligation to extradite established by the Treaty would make no sense if either nation were free to resort to forcible kidnapping to

---

28. [Court's footnote 9:] Ker also was not a national of Peru, whereas respondent is a national of the country from which he was abducted. Respondent finds this difference to be immaterial.

gain the presence of an individual for prosecution in a manner not contemplated by the Treaty.

We do not read the Treaty in such a fashion. Article 9 does not purport to specify the only way in which one country may gain custody of a national of the other country for the purposes of prosecution. In the absence of an extradition treaty, nations are under no obligation to surrender those in their country to foreign authorities for prosecution. Extradition treaties exist so as to impose mutual obligations to surrender individuals in certain defined sets of circumstances, following established procedures. The Treaty thus provides a mechanism which would not otherwise exist, requiring, under certain circumstances, the United States and Mexico to extradite individuals to the other country, and establishing the procedures to be followed when the Treaty is invoked.

The history of negotiation and practice under the Treaty also fails to show that abductions outside of the Treaty constitute a violation of the Treaty. As the Solicitor General notes, the Mexican Government was made aware, as early as 1906, of the *Ker* doctrine, and the United States' position that it applied to forcible abductions made outside of the terms of the United States-Mexico Extradition Treaty. Nonetheless, the current version of the Treaty, signed in 1978, does not attempt to establish a rule that would in any way curtail the effect of *Ker*. . . .[29]

Thus, the language of the Treaty, in the context of its history, does not support the proposition that the Treaty prohibits abductions outside of its terms. The remaining question, therefore, is whether the Treaty should be interpreted so as to include an implied term prohibiting prosecution where the defendant's presence is obtained by means other than those established by the Treaty.

Respondent contends that the Treaty must be interpreted against the backdrop of customary international law, and that international abductions are "so clearly prohibited in international law" that there was no reason to include such a clause in the Treaty itself. The international censure of international abductions is further evidenced, according to respondent, by the United Nations Charter and the Charter of the Organization of American States. Respondent does not argue that these sources of international law provide an independent basis for the right respondent asserts not to be tried in the United States, but rather that they should inform the interpretation of the Treaty terms.

The Court of Appeals deemed it essential, in order for the individual defendant to assert a right under the Treaty, that the affected foreign government had registered a protest. Respondent agrees that the right exercised by the individual is derivative of the nation's right under the Treaty, since nations are authorized, notwithstanding the terms of an extradition treaty, to voluntarily render an individual to the other country on terms completely outside of those provided in the treaty. The formal protest, therefore, ensures that the "offended" nation actually objects to the abduction and has not in some way voluntarily rendered the individual for prosecution. Thus the Extradition Treaty only prohibits gaining the defendant's presence by means other than those set forth in the Treaty when the nation from which the defendant was abducted objects.

This argument seems to us inconsistent with the remainder of respondent's argument. The Extradition Treaty has the force of law, and if, as respondent asserts, it is self-executing, it would appear that a court must enforce it on behalf of an individual regardless of the offensiveness of the practice of one nation to the other nation. In

---

29. [Court's footnote 12:] The parties did expressly include the doctrine of specialty in Article 17 of the Treaty, notwithstanding the judicial recognition of it in United States v. Rauscher, 119 U.S. 407 (1886).

Rauscher, the Court noted that Great Britain had taken the position in other cases that the Webster-Ashburton Treaty included the doctrine of specialty, but no importance was attached to whether or not Great Britain had protested the prosecution of Rauscher for the crime of cruel and unusual punishment as opposed to murder.

More fundamentally, the difficulty with the support respondent garners from international law is that none of it relates to the practice of nations in relation to extradition treaties. In *Rauscher*, we implied a term in the Webster-Ashburton Treaty because of the practice of nations with regard to extradition treaties. In the instant case, respondent would imply terms in the Extradition Treaty from the practice of nations with regards to international law more generally.[30] Respondent would have us find that the Treaty acts as a prohibition against a violation of the general principle of international law that one government may not "exercise its police power in the territory of another state." There are many actions which could be taken by a nation that would violate this principle, including waging war, but it cannot seriously be contended that an invasion of the United States by Mexico would violate the terms of the Extradition Treaty between the two nations.[31]

In sum, to infer from this Treaty and its terms that it prohibits all means of gaining the presence of an individual outside of its terms goes beyond established precedent and practice. In *Rauscher*, the implication of a doctrine of specialty into the terms of the Webster-Ashburton Treaty, which, by its terms, required the presentation of evidence establishing probable cause of the crime of extradition before extradition was required, was a small step to take. By contrast, to imply from the terms of this Treaty that it prohibits obtaining the presence of an individual by means outside of the procedures the Treaty establishes requires a much larger inferential leap, with only the most general of international law principles to support it. The general principles cited by respondent simply fail to persuade us that we should imply in the United States-Mexico Extradition Treaty a term prohibiting international abductions.

Respondent and his *amici* may be correct that respondent's abduction was "shocking," and that it may be in violation of general international law principles. Mexico has protested the abduction of respondent through diplomatic notes and the decision of whether respondent should be returned to Mexico, as a matter outside of the Treaty, is a matter for the Executive Branch.[32] We conclude, however, that respondent's abduction was not in violation of the Extradition Treaty between the United States and Mexico, and therefore the rule of *Ker v. Illinois* is fully applicable to this case. The fact of respondent's forcible abduction does not therefore prohibit his trial in a court in the United States for violations of the criminal laws of the United States.

---

30. [Court's footnote 14:] Similarly, the Court of Appeals . . . reasoned that international abductions violate the "purpose" of the Treaty, stating that "[t]he requirements extradition treaties impose constitute a means of safeguarding the sovereignty of the signatory nations, as well as ensuring the fair treatment of individuals." The ambitious purpose ascribed to the Treaty by the Court of Appeals, we believe, places a greater burden on its language and history than they can logically bear. In a broad sense, most international agreements have the common purpose of safeguarding the sovereignty of signatory nations, in that they seek to further peaceful relations between nations. This, however, does not mean that the violation of any principle of international law constitutes a violation of this particular treaty.

31. [Court's footnote 15:] In the same category are the examples posited by respondent in which, after a forcible international abduction, the offended nation protested the abduction and the abducting nation then returned the individual to the protesting nation. These may show the practice of nations under customary international law, but they are of little aid in construing the terms of an extradition treaty, or the authority of a court to later try an individual who has been so abducted. . . .

32. [Court's footnote 16:] The Mexican Government has also requested from the United States the extradition of two individuals it suspects of having abducted respondent in Mexico, on charges of kidnapping. . . .

NOTES AND QUESTIONS

1. Does the *Alvarez-Machain* Court hold that the abduction of the defendant was *legal* as a matter of domestic and international law? That it was not forbidden by the extradition treaty? Or is its holding limited to an assessment of what remedies are available to abducted defendants? In United States v. Gardiner, 279 Fed. Appx. 848, 850 (11th Cir. 2008), the court relied on *Alvarez-Machain* and *Ker* for the proposition that "[a]bsent an express prohibition, even if a formal extradition has been initiated, a government may obtain custody of a defendant by other methods, including abduction, expulsion, or surrender by the host country." Claims that abduction is unlawful in the face of a valid treaty are unlikely to be successful. See, e.g., Reyes-Vasquez v. Atty. Gen., 304 Fed. Appx. 33 (3d Cir. 2008).

2. Under what circumstances might one argue that forcible abduction should be permitted—or at least that no remedy should be available for the individual defendant? Should the nature of the crime, the necessity and proportionality of abduction, or evidence of complicity by the state in which the defendant found refuge be relevant? See, e.g., Douglas Kash, Abducting Terrorists Under PDD-39: Much Ado About Nothing New, 13 Am. U. Intl. L. Rev. 139 (1997); Gregory S. McNeal & Brian J. Field, Snatch-and-Grab Ops: Justifying Extraterritorial Abduction, 16 Transnatl. L. & Contemp. Probs. 491 (2007); Andrew J. Calica, Note, Self-Help Is the Best Kind: The Efficient Breach Justification for Forcible Abduction of Terrorists, 37 Cornell Intl. L.J. 389, 394 (2004) ("the theory of efficient breach justifies forcible abduction as a method of combating terrorism when existing methods of international resolution have failed").

3. The *Alvarez-Machain* Court views the question presented through the lens of the classical picture of international law, where the only cognizable parties are states. How, if at all, could you recast the defendant's arguments to force the Court to abandon the classical view of international law and focus on the "human rights" of the defendant? None of the international human rights conventions, for example, explicitly provides that forcible abduction or irregular extradition violates international human rights law. However, the irregularity of the procedure might be held to deprive the "rendered" individual of her human rights. In 1981 the Human Rights Committee (established pursuant to Article 28 of the International Covenant on Civil and Political Rights) decided that the abduction of a Uruguayan refugee from Argentina by Uruguayan security officers constituted arbitrary arrest and detention in violation of Article 9(1) of the Covenant. 36 U.N. GAOR, Supp. No. 40, at 176-189 (July 29, 1981).

4. Recall the difference between a claim under a treaty and a claim under customary international law. The legal advisor to the secretary of state at the time *Alvarez-Machain* was litigated, former federal judge Abraham Sofaer, testified before Congress that such abductions violate customary international law. FBI Authority to Seize Suspects Abroad: Hearing Before the Subcomm. on Civil and Constitutional Rights, Comm. on the Judiciary, 100th Cong. 35 (1989). If customary international law is "part of our law," as the Court held in *The Paquete Habana*, 175 U.S. 677, 700 (1900), why did the Court in *Alvarez-Machain* focus exclusively on whether the abduction violated the U.S.-Mexico extradition treaty? Why did it not uphold the dismissal of the charges as a remedy for the executive's violation of CIL?

In *Alvarez-Machain*, the U.S. Supreme Court noted that "[r]espondent does not argue that [principles of customary] international law provide an independent basis for the right respondent asserts not to be tried in the United States." Did the respondent's failure to rely independently on CIL reflect his recognition that CIL would not have provided an independent basis for relief? Professor Vázquez provides another explanation:

> [At oral argument,] Justice Sandra Day O'Connor asked Alvarez's lawyer whether the Court should consider customary international law as an alternative ground for repatriation if the Court should conclude that the treaty does not prohibit foreign kidnapping. He responded that customary international law was among a number of grounds relied on by Alvarez in the lower courts but not addressed by those courts. Because the issue had not been fully considered by the lower courts or by the parties in their written submissions, he indicated that it would be more appropriate for the Court to leave that issue open for initial consideration by the lower courts on remand.

Carlos Manuel Vázquez, Misreading High Court's Alvarez Ruling, Legal Times, Oct. 5, 1992, at 30. On remand, the Ninth Circuit dealt with the argument that a violation of CIL deprived the court of jurisdiction as follows:

> The principal . . . issue is whether customary international law alone, absent reliance on a formal treaty, may justify the district court's order that Alvarez-Machain be repatriated to Mexico. We have carefully reviewed the Supreme Court's opinion and the district court's findings. If the Supreme Court's opinion does not preclude us from applying general principles of international law in support of the district court's repatriation order, then the district court's findings and conclusions do preclude that result. To the extent that customary international law may arguably provide a basis for an exception to the *KerrFrisbie* Doctrine, the exception has been recognized only in a situation in which the government's conduct was outrageous. The district court found that situation did not occur here.

United States v. Alvarez-Machain, 971 F.2d 310, 311 (9th Cir. 1992).

5. In 1980, the Office of Legal Counsel (OLC) for the U.S. Justice Department rendered an opinion that the FBI had no authority to abduct a fugitive residing in a foreign state when those actions were contrary to CIL. Extraterritorial Apprehension by the Federal Bureau of Investigation, 4B Op. Off. Legal Counsel 543 (1980). Relying on the maxim that statutes are to be construed where possible to be consistent with international law, the OLC concluded that the general statute authorizing the FBI to investigate and arrest individuals for violations of U.S. law does not confer authority to arrest individuals in contravention of CIL.

In 1989, the OLC withdrew the 1980 opinion and issued in its place one entitled "Authority of the Federal Bureau of Investigation to Override International Law in Extraterritorial Law Enforcement Activities," 13 Op. Off. Legal Counsel 163 (1989). The new opinion noted that the president does not need statutory authority to conduct law enforcement activities because he possesses such authority by virtue of the Constitution itself. The opinion further concluded that "[b]oth the Congress and the President, acting within their respective spheres, retain the authority to override" customary international law:

> . . . [T]he sovereign's authority to override customary international law necessarily follows from the nature of international law itself. Customary international law is not static: it evolves through a dynamic process of state custom and practice. States ultimately adhere to a norm of practice because they determine that upholding the norm best serves their long-run interests and because violation of the norm may subject the nation to public obloquy or expose it to retaliatory violations. States necessarily must have the authority to contravene international norms, however, for it is the process of changing

state practice that allows customary international law to evolve. . . . If the United States is to participate in the evolution of international law, the Executive must have the power to act inconsistently with international law where necessary. "It is principally the President, 'sole organ' of the United States in its international relations, who is responsible for the behavior of the United States in regard to international law, and who participates on her behalf in the indefinable process by which customary international law is made, unmade, remade." Louis Henkin, Foreign Affairs and the Constitution 188 (1972). Thus, the power in the Executive to override international law is a necessary attribute of sovereignty and an integral part of the President's foreign affairs power. Indeed, the absence of such authority in the Executive would profoundly and uniquely disable the United States — rendering the nation a passive bystander, bound to follow practices dictated by other nations, yet powerless to play a role in shaping those practices.

Id. at 170-171. The 1989 opinion asserted that the president could delegate his authority to contravene CIL to the attorney general, but it recommended that such authority not be delegated further, stating that the legal argument would be weaker if the decision were made by officials below cabinet rank. Why is it important that the decision to contravene CIL be made by the president or a cabinet-level officer? What concerns would you expect the president and attorney general to have in deciding whether to exercise this authority? There is no evidence that the abduction of Alvarez-Machain was authorized by the president or attorney general. Should that have mattered in determining whether the court on remand should have dismissed the indictment for lack of jurisdiction?

6. Alvarez-Machain was tried in 1992 for the torture and murder of DEA Agent Enrique Camarena-Salazar. At the close of the government's case, the district court granted Alvarez-Machain's motion for a judgment of acquittal, meaning that, even viewing the evidence in the light most favorable to the government, no reasonable jury could conclude that Alvarez-Machain was guilty beyond a reasonable doubt. After returning to Mexico, Alvarez-Machain sued the United States, the U.S. officials who arranged his abduction, and Mexican nationals who carried out the abduction, seeking damages. After a great deal of litigation, the Supreme Court held that Alvarez-Machain could not recover. The suit against the United States and the U.S. officials was dismissed on grounds of sovereign immunity. With respect to the Mexican nationals, the Court ruled that damages were not available under federal law, but it left open the possibility of recovery under the tort law of California or Mexico. See Sosa v. Alvarez-Machain, 542 U.S. 692 (2004).

7. If what was done to Alvarez-Machain was a clear breach of IL, and that breach did not deprive the U.S. courts of jurisdiction or require the remedy of dismissal, as the *Alvarez-Machain* decision has been read by some to hold, what other arguments may the defendants make here? Consider the possible arguments raised in *Nikolic*, which follows.

PROSECUTOR v. NIKOLIC

Case No. IT-94-2-AR73, Interlocutory Appeal Concerning Legality of Arrest (June 5, 2003)

[The UN Security Council, responding to the atrocities perpetrated during the break-up of the former Yugoslavia, created the International Criminal Tribunal for the Former Yugoslavia (ICTY) in 1993. In an ICTY prosecution of Dragan Nikolic for international crimes, Nikolic challenged the legality of his arrest and detention, claiming to have been kidnapped in Serbia and delivered into the hands of the ICTY "special police force" (SFOR). The case raised the question whether the ICTY would accept the doctrine of *male captus, bene detentus* or would, instead, decline jurisdiction based on the alleged abduction. The Trial Chamber refused to terminate the proceedings on the basis of its factual determination that the Tribunal and its SFOR had not been involved in the abduction and that the manner in which the accused was taken did not amount to serious mistreatment. On appeal, the ICTY Appeals Chamber reasoned as follows.]

17. The essence of the Defence's position is that SFOR, and by extension [the Office of the ICTY Prosecutor (OTP)], acted in collusion with the individuals who took the Accused from Serbia and Montenegro to SFOR in Bosnia and Herzegovina. SFOR knew that the accused had been kidnapped. By taking the Accused into its custody, SFOR effectively accepted that kidnapping in breach of Serbia and Montenegro's sovereignty and the Accused's human rights. Therefore, jurisdiction must be set aside.

18. . . . [T]he first issue to be addressed is in what circumstances, if any, the International Tribunal should decline to exercise its jurisdiction because an accused has been brought before it through conduct violating State sovereignty or human rights. Once the standard warranting the declining of the exercise of jurisdiction has been identified, the Appeals Chamber will have to determine whether the facts of this case are ones that, if proven, would warrant such a remedy. If yes, then the Appeals Chamber must determine whether the underlying violations are attributable to SFOR and by extension to the OTP. . . .

20. The impact of a breach of a State's sovereignty on the exercise of jurisdiction is a novel issue for this Tribunal. There is no case law directly on the point, and the [ICTY's] Statute and the Rules provide little guidance. Article 29 of the Statute, inter alia, places upon all States the duty to cooperate with the International Tribunal in the investigation and prosecution of persons accused of committing serious violations of international humanitarian law. It also requires States to comply without undue delay with requests for assistance or orders issued by Trial Chambers, including the arrest or detention of persons. The Statute, however, does not provide a remedy for breaches of these obligations. In the absence of clarity in the Statute, Rules, and jurisprudence of the International Tribunal, the Appeals Chamber will seek guidance from national case law, where the issue at hand has often arisen, in order to determine State practice on the matter.

21. In several national cases, courts have held that jurisdiction should not be set aside, even though there might have been irregularities in the manner in which the accused was brought before them. In the *Argoud* case [1964], the French Court of Cassation (Criminal Chamber) held that the alleged violation of German sovereignty by French citizens in the operation leading to the arrest of the accused did not impede the exercise of jurisdiction over the accused. . . . The *Cour de Sûreté*, the lower court, had actually noted that the State concerned (Germany) had not lodged any formal complaint and that ultimately, the issue was dealt with through diplomatic means. In *Stocke* [1984], the German Federal Constitutional Court (Bundesverfassungsgericht) endorsed a ruling by the Federal Court of Justice (Bundesgerichtshof) rejecting the appeal of the accused, a German national residing in France, claiming that he was the victim of an unlawful collusion between the German authorities and an informant who had deceptively brought him to German territory. The Court found that, even though there existed some decisions taking the opposite approach, according to international practice, courts would in general only refuse to assume jurisdiction in a case of a kidnapped accused if another State had protested against the kidnapping and had requested the return of the accused. In *United States v. Alvarez-Machain* [1992], the

Supreme Court of the United States held that the abduction of an accused who was a Mexican citizen, though it may have been in violation of general international law, did not require the setting aside of jurisdiction even though Mexico had requested the return of the accused.

22. On the other hand, there have been cases in which the exercise of jurisdiction has been declined. In *Jacob-Salomon* [1936], an ex-German citizen was abducted on Swiss territory, taken to Germany, and held for trial on a charge of treason. The Swiss Government protested vigorously, claiming that German secret agents had been involved in the kidnapping, and sought the return of Jacob-Salomon. Though it denied any involvement of German agents in Swiss territory, the German government agreed (without arbitration) to return Jacob-Salomon to the Swiss Government. More recently, in *State v. Ebrahim* [1991], the Supreme Count of South Africa had no hesitation in setting aside jurisdiction over an accused kidnapped from Swaziland by the security services. Similarly, in the *Bennet* case [1993], the House of Lords granted the appeal of a New Zealand citizen, who was arrested in South Africa by the police and forcibly returned to the United Kingdom under the pretext of deporting him to New Zealand. It found that if the methods through which an accused is brought before the court were in disregard of extradition procedure, the court may stay the prosecution and order the release of the accused.

23. With regard to cases concerning the same kinds of crimes as those falling within the jurisdiction of the International Tribunal, reference may be made to *Eichmann* and *Barbie*. In *Eichmann* [1962], the Supreme Court of Israel decided to exercise jurisdiction over the accused, notwithstanding the apparent breach of Argentina's sovereignty involved in his abduction. It did so mainly for two reasons. First, the accused was "a fugitive from justice" charged with "crimes of an universal character ... condemned publicly by the civilized world." Second, Argentina had "condoned the violation of her sovereignty and has waived her claims, including that for the return of the appellant. Any violation therefore of international law that may have been involved in this incident ha[d] thus been removed." In *Barbie* [1983], the French Court of Cassation (Criminal Chamber) asserted its jurisdiction over the accused, despite the claim that he was a victim of a disguised extradition, on the basis, inter alia, of the special nature of the crimes ascribed to the accused, namely, crimes against humanity.

24. Although it is difficult to identify a clear pattern in this case law, and caution is needed when generalising, two principles seem to have support in State practice as evidenced by the practice of their courts. First, in cases of crimes such as genocide, crimes against humanity and war crimes which are universally recognised and condemned as such ("Universally Condemned Offences"), courts seem to find in the special character of these offences and, arguably, in their seriousness, a good reason for not setting aside jurisdiction. Second, absent a complaint by the State whose sovereignty has been breached or in the event of a diplomatic resolution of the breach, it is easier for courts to assert their jurisdiction. The initial *iniuria* has in a way been cured and the risk of having to return the accused to the country of origin is no longer present. Drawing on these indications from national practice, the Appeals Chamber adds the following observations.

25. Universally condemned offences are a matter of concern to the international community as a whole. There is a legitimate expectation that those accused of these crimes will be brought to justice swiftly. Accountability for these crimes is a necessary condition for the achievement of international justice, which plays a critical role in the reconciliation and rebuilding based on the rule of law of countries and societies torn apart by international and internecine conflicts.

26. This legitimate expectation needs to be weighed against the principle of State sovereignty and the fundamental human rights of the accused. The latter point will be addressed . . . below. In the opinion of the Appeals Chamber, the damage caused to international justice by not apprehending fugitives accused of serious violations of international humanitarian law is comparatively higher than the injury, if any, caused to the sovereignty of a State by a limited intrusion on its territory, particularly when the intrusion occurs in default of the State's cooperation. Therefore, the Appeals Chamber does not consider that in cases of universally condemned offences, jurisdiction should be set aside on the ground that there was a violation of the sovereignty of a State, when the violation is brought about by the apprehension of fugitives from international justice, whatever the consequences for the international responsibility of the State or organisation involved. This is all the more so in cases such as this one, in which the State whose sovereignty has allegedly been breached has not lodged any complaint and thus has acquiesced in the International Tribunal's exercise of jurisdiction. *A fortiori*, and leaving aside for the moment human rights considerations, the exercise of jurisdiction should not be declined in cases of abductions carried out by private individuals whose actions, unless instigated, acknowledged or condoned by a State, or an international organisation, or other entity, do not necessarily in themselves violate State sovereignty.

27. Therefore, even assuming that the conduct of the Accused's captors should be attributed to SFOR and that the latter is responsible for a violation of Serbia and Montenegro's sovereignty, the Appeals Chamber finds no basis, in the present case, upon which jurisdiction should not be exercised.

28. Turning now to the issue of whether the violation of the human rights of an accused requires the setting aside of jurisdiction by the International Tribunal, the Appeals Chamber recalls first the analysis of the Trial Chamber. The Trial Chamber found that the treatment of the Appellant was not of such an egregious nature as to impede the exercise of jurisdiction. The Trial Chamber, however, did not exclude that jurisdiction should not be exercised in certain cases. It held that:

> in circumstances where an accused is very seriously mistreated, maybe even subject to inhuman, cruel or degrading treatment, or torture, before being handed over to the Tribunal, this may constitute a legal impediment to the exercise of jurisdiction over such an accused. This would certainly be the case where persons acting for SFOR or the Prosecution were involved in such very serious mistreatment.

29. This approach, the Appeals Chamber observes, is consistent with the dictum of the U.S. Federal Court of Appeals in *Toscanino* [2d Cir. 1974]. In that case, the Court held that "[we] view due process as now requiring a court to divest itself of jurisdiction over the person of a defendant where it has been acquired as the result of the Government's deliberate, unnecessary and unreasonable invasion of the accused's constitutional rights." A Trial Chamber of the International Tribunal in *Dokmanovic* [1997] also relied on this approach. Along the same lines, the [UN's International Criminal Tribunal for Rwanda (ICTR)] Appeals Chamber in *Barayagwiza* [1999] held that a court may decline to exercise jurisdiction in cases "where to exercise that jurisdiction in light of serious and egregious violations of the accused's rights would prove detrimental to the court's integrity."

30. The Appeals Chamber agrees with these views. Although the assessment of the seriousness of the human rights violations depends on the circumstances of each case and cannot be made *in abstracto*, certain human rights violations are of such a serious

nature that they require that the exercise of jurisdiction be declined. It would be inappropriate for a court of law to try the victims of these abuses. Apart from such exceptional cases, however, the remedy of setting aside jurisdiction will, in the Appeals Chamber's view, usually be disproportionate. The correct balance must therefore be maintained between the fundamental rights of the accused and the essential interests of the international community in the prosecution of persons charged with serious violations of international humanitarian law.

31. In the present case, the Trial Chamber examined the facts agreed to by the parties. . . . Upon this review, the Appeals Chamber concurs with the Trial Chamber that the circumstances of this case do not warrant, under the standard defined above, the setting aside of jurisdiction.

NOTES AND QUESTIONS

1. Do you agree with the Appeals Chamber that special considerations apply in the case of "universally condemned offences"? Is the logic that offenses which have been proscribed by treaty and/or are considered *jus cogens* violations will, by their very gravity, justify the assertion of "universal jurisdiction" and the application of the *male captus, bene detentus* rule? Generally, see Aparna Sridhar, Note, The International Criminal Tribunal for the Former Yugoslavia's Response to the Problem of Transnational Abduction, 42 Stan. J. Intl. L. 343 (2006).

2. Most domestic courts that have considered the issue do not limit the application of *male captus, bene detentus* in such a fashion. As the Appeals Chamber noted, in Atty. Gen. of Israel v. Eichmann, 36 I.L.R 5 (Dist. Ct. Jer. 1961), *aff'd*, 36 I.L.R 277 (Sup. Ct. Isr. 1962), discussed in Chapter 5, the Israeli Supreme Court rejected a challenge to its jurisdiction and denied Eichmann's objections to his arrest. However, its holding rested on the more general proposition that "it is an established rule of law that a person being tried for an offense against the law of a State may not oppose his trial by reason of the illegality of his arrest or of the means whereby he was brought within the jurisdiction of that State." Id.

4. Luring

The apprehension of a suspect or fugitive on the high seas or elsewhere outside of any territorial jurisdiction clearly does not violate the sovereignty of any state, including that of the individual's nationality. A somewhat more difficult question may arise when the law enforcement authorities of the apprehending state use a form of ruse or trickery to "lure" the individual to leave one state so they can obtain custody for purposes of criminal prosecution.

One example occurred in the aftermath of the hijacking and eventual destruction of Royal Jordanian Airlines Flight 402 in Beirut, Lebanon, in 1985. Following intensive investigation, the alleged leader of the plot, Fawaz Yunis, was located in Cyprus. After obtaining an arrest warrant, the FBI enticed Yunis onto a yacht with promises of a drug deal, and once the vessel entered international waters, they arrested him. Yunis was transferred to a U.S. navy munitions ship, where he was interrogated for several days; he was then transferred to a navy aircraft carrier and eventually was flown to Washington, D.C., for arraignment on charges of conspiracy, hostage taking, and aircraft damage. A charge of aircraft piracy was added later. Yunis challenged his arrest on a number of grounds, including the manner in which he was apprehended.[33] In *United States v. Yunis*, the court of appeals affirmed his conviction. On the jurisdictional issue, it said there was "nothing in the record suggesting the sort of intentional, outrageous government conduct" necessary to sustain Yunis' argument that jurisdiction was improper under *United States v. Toscanino*,[34] which held that due process requires courts to divest themselves of personal jurisdiction acquired through "the government's deliberate, unnecessary and unreasonable invasion of the accused's constitutional rights."[35] More recently a Chamber of the ICTY rejected the argument that "luring" for purposes of apprehension and prosecution violates principles of international law or the sovereignty of the country from which the individual was enticed to leave.[36]

---

33. 924 F.2d 1086 (D.C. Cir. 1991). We examine Yunis's challenges to U.S. jurisdiction in Chapter 5, Sections A.5 and A.7.

34. 500 F. 2d 267 (2d Cir. 1974).

35. Id. at 275.

36. Prosecutor v. Dokmanovic, Case No. IT-95-13a-PT, T. Ch. 11 (Oct. 22, 1997).

CHAPTER
10

The Effect of Treaty Rights, as Construed by International Tribunals, on Domestic Criminal Enforcement: The Death Penalty

As was discussed in Chapter 2, the emergence since World War II of international human rights law has modified the "Westphalian" concept of sovereignty, in the sense of "a nation-state's 'right' to monopolize certain exercises of power with respect to its territory and citizens."[1] Thus, international law now regulates not only the relations among states, but also certain aspects of the relations between states and individuals, including a state's own citizens. What previously was considered a purely internal matter, beyond the reach of international debate and regulation, is now a proper subject of international law. Human rights conventions reach into the territory of a state party and oblige governments to respect, protect, and promote certain rights for all within their territory and subject to their jurisdiction. The legitimacy of human rights norms is no longer the principal issue; the challenge now lies in their effective enforcement.

One of the challenges of enforcement is arriving at an authoritative interpretation of the content or application of the "human right" at issue. "Sovereignty" concepts again play a role in this regard. "Westphalian" sovereignty "has been discredited in many ways . . . , but it is still prized and harbored by those who maintain certain 'realist' views or who otherwise wish to prevent (sometimes with justification) foreign or international powers and authorities from interfering in a national government's decisions and activities."[2] "If sovereignty implies that there is 'no higher power' than the nation-state, then it is argued that no international law norm is valid unless the state has somehow 'consented' to it."[3] A treaty, of course, is deemed a consensual source of international law. "However, important questions arise in connection with many treaty details, such as when a treaty-based international institution sees its practice and 'jurisprudence' evolve over time and purports to obligate its members even though they opposed that evolution."[4]

---

1. John H. Jackson, Sovereignty-Modern: A New Approach to an Outdated Concept, 97 Am. J. Intl. L. 782, 782 (2003).
2. Id.
3. Id.
4. Id. at 783.

The terms of many of the human rights conventions are, like many constitutional guarantees, expressed generally. To take the example presented in the first set of materials within, the European Convention for the Protection of Human Rights and Fundamental Freedoms (European Convention) states in Article 3 that "[n]o one shall be subjected to torture or to inhuman or degrading treatment or punishment." A state might readily agree to this fine-sounding norm, yet have no idea what an international tribunal might determine to be its meaning in 50 years' time. Would the United Kingdom have known, at the time it entered into this treaty in 1950, that the court charged with enforcement of the European Convention would in 1989 determine that the United Kingdom would violate this provision by *extraditing* a criminal suspect to the United States, where he *could, if convicted and sentenced to death*, face "inhuman or degrading treatment" by virtue of the agony of *waiting* on death row for execution pursuant to a capital sentence? Would the European Court of Human Rights (ECHR), in arriving at such a conclusion, be "making" law, and thus invading the sovereign prerogatives of states parties beyond that to which they agreed by embracing the Convention's generalized norms? The ECHR cases discussed within raise these and other fundamental questions: What methods of interpretation are appropriate for treaties? What is the proper role of courts or other adjudicatory bodies in the development of international law? Note that these important questions demand answers well beyond the discrete context of capital sentencing. Many of the human rights norms whose definition and application is entrusted to international tribunals relate to criminal law and procedure applicable in a variety of cases.

A second enforcement challenge lies in convincing states to comply with the interpretations arrived at by international tribunals. This task may involve layers of difficulty: What if the domestic courts in the state party whose conduct is found wanting do not agree with the international tribunal's reading of the applicable treaty? What if domestic law does not permit the kind of remedies the international tribunal says are necessary to vindicate that right? What if the state party determines that its relations with subnational governmental units (for example, the U.S. states in America) counsel against effectuating the decisions of international tribunals? What if the state party at issue simply refuses to accede to the international tribunal's judgment? The "consular notification" cases in Section B below address these questions. The materials also allow readers to think about these issues in the particular context of the U.S. structure of government. Thus, the "consular notification" cases explore (1) the place of international law in U.S. law and in the U.S. federal system, and (2) the ability of states parties to international agreements, and their individual citizens, to enforce treaty rights in U.S. courts.

This last subject is of great importance because, as Dr. Matthew C.R. Craven has argued, "[t]he presumption is that even though States draft and ratify treaties binding themselves, as a matter of international law, to the protection and promotion of human rights, there are no real reciprocal benefits to be derived from compliance such that it is unrealistic to expect States to carry out those obligations in good faith."[5] The treaty bodies that oversee compliance with human rights treaty obligations can exert some influence over states that fail to meet their obligations primarily through "shaming." Viewed from the wronged individual's point of view, however, the most effective means of enforcement is through remedies provided under national law. It is of considerable importance to the efficacy of these human rights regimes that

---

5. Matthew C.R. Craven, The Domestic Application of the International Covenant on Economic, Social and Cultural Rights, 40 Netherlands Intl. L. Rev. 367, 567-568 (1993).

"international treaty standards should operate directly and immediately within the domestic legal system, and should be enforceable through judicial remedies."[6]

Finally, these cases permit students to explore the difficulties that may arise when nations and international tribunals are faced with evolving human rights norms. In the first set of cases (Section A below), the human rights at issue are the prohibition on torture or inhuman or degrading punishment and the "inherent right to life." These rights are being invoked to prevent the extradition of persons who may, if extradited and convicted, be subjected to the "death row phenomenon" (the agony of awaiting execution) and, ultimately, capital punishment. The second set of cases (Section B below) concern a treaty right—an alien's right to be advised "without delay" upon the alien's arrest in a foreign country of the alien's right to have her consulate notified of her detention. The reason that these cases have taken on the urgency they have, however, is the fact that many of the persons claiming violations of this right have been convicted and sentenced to death in the United States. In short, either explicitly or implicitly, these materials reflect a profound disagreement over whether capital punishment is a human rights issue.

In conjunction with the readings in this chapter, students ought to read the following primary materials, all of which are available on our Web site: Articles 1-3, 15, 32, and 46 of the European Convention; Protocol Nos. 6 and 13 to that Convention; Articles 27-28, 31-35, 39-40 of the Vienna Convention on the Law of Treaties; and §§325-326 and 334 of the Restatement (Third) of the Foreign Relations Law of the United States.

A. THE DEATH PENALTY AND EXTRADITION

1. Background

Is there an emerging global consensus that the death penalty is cruel and unusual except, perhaps, in wartime? Those who would answer in the affirmative may point to the fact that various international conventions have limited the application of capital punishment to the most serious offenses, have restricted eligible offenders (excluding, for instance, juvenile offenders, pregnant women, new mothers, persons over 70, and persons suffering from mental retardation), and have instituted procedural safeguards.

At present, protocols to three treaties, two regional and one open to the world, provide for the abolition of the death penalty. For our purposes, only one treaty regime—the European Convention—need be highlighted. In 1982, the Council of Europe adopted Protocol No. 6 to the European Convention. Protocol No. 6 seeks to abolish the death penalty in peacetime. As of 2008, 46 of the 47 countries that are party to the European Convention had ratified or acceded to Protocol No. 6 as well.[7] The sole holdout to Protocol No. 6 is Russia, which has signed but not ratified it. In March 2002, the Council of Europe adopted Protocol No. 13 to the European Convention. This Protocol seeks the abolition of the death penalty in times of

---

6. Id.
7. See Council of Europe, Protocol No. 6 to the Convention for the Protection of Human Rights and Fundamental Freedoms Concerning the Abolition of the Death Penalty (Aug. 18, 2008).

peace *and* war. As of July 2008, 40 member states had ratified or acceded to Protocol No. 13.[8]

According to Amnesty International, over half the countries of the world have abolished in law (de jure) or in practice (de facto) use of the death penalty. As of August 2009, Amnesty reports, 58 jurisdictions, including the United States, China, and India, are "retentionist" in that they authorize and carry out capital sentences. Amnesty counts 139 countries as "abolitionist" in law or practice: 94 countries have abolished the death penalty for all crimes, 10 have abolished it for ordinary crimes, and 35 countries are treated as abolitionist in practice, because, although their laws authorize the death penalty for ordinary crimes, they have not carried out an execution for at least ten years and are believed to have a policy or established practice of not carrying out executions.[9] This represents a dramatic shift. At the beginning of the twentieth century, only 3 states had permanently abolished the death penalty for all crimes, Costa Rica, San Marino, and Venezuela.

That 58 jurisdictions are presently "retentionist" may potentially overstate the extent of support for the death penalty worldwide. Thus, for example, in 2007, a minimum of 1,252 persons were executed in 24 countries around the world. And 5 countries, China, Iran, Saudi Arabia, Pakistan, and the United States, were responsible for 88 percent of the executions.[10] The abolitionist trend is especially marked in Europe, where the Parliamentary Assembly of the Council of Europe requires a commitment to abolition as a condition of entry into the organization, and where the European Union has a policy for promotion of abolition in nonmember states.[11] It is also notable that the UN Security Council excluded the death penalty in establishing the International Criminal Tribunal for Former Yugoslavia (ICTY) in 1993 and the International Criminal Tribunal for Rwanda (ICTR) in 1994, and that the Statute of the International Criminal Court does not permit capital punishment for the most heinous crimes known to man, including genocide and crimes against humanity. Some argue that, according to traditional methods of international law analysis, the growing trend toward abolition reflects a "general principle" of law, or even an

---

8. See Council of Europe, Protocol No. 13 to the Convention for the Protection of Human Rights and Fundamental Freedoms, Concerning the Abolition of the Death Penalty in All Circumstances (July 12, 2008) (referencing Protocol No. 6 as CETS No. 114 and Protocol No. 13 as CETS No. 187). The two other treaties that provide for abolition of capital punishment are the Second Optional Protocol to the International Covenant on Civil and Political Rights (ICCPR) and the Protocol to the American Convention on Human Rights to Abolish the Death Penalty adopted in 1990 by the General Assembly of the Organization of American States (OAS).

In 1989, the UN General Assembly adopted the Second Optional Protocol to the ICCPR. The ICCPR's Second Optional Protocol provides for the total abolition of the death penalty but permits states parties to retain capital punishment in wartime if they make a declaration to that effect at the time of ratification or accession. The ICCPR's Second Optional Protocol has been ratified or acceded to by 66 states as of April 2008.

Like the ICCPR's Protocol, the OAS Protocol contemplates the total elimination of the death penalty but permits states to retain capital punishment in wartime. As of October 2006, this Protocol had been ratified by 8 states. See Organization of American States, Department of International Law, A-53: Protocol to the American Convention on Human Rights to Abolish the Death Penalty (June 8, 1990).

9. See Amnesty International, The Death Penalty: Abolitionist and Retentionist Countries, http://www.amnesty.org/en/death-penalty/abolitionist-and-retentionist-countries.

10. See Amnesty International, The Death Penalty: An International Perspective (2008); see also U.S. Department of Justice, Bureau of Justice Statistics, Capital Punishment Statistics, http://www.ojp.usdoj.gov/bjs/cp.htm (last visited Apr. 29, 2009) (documenting 42 executions in the United States in 2007).

11. See, e.g., European Union Guidelines to EU Policy Towards Third Countries on the Death Penalty (1998).

emergent rule of customary international law, against the application of the death penalty (subject to some major persistent objectors such as the United States).[12]

But does "bean-counting" de jure and de facto abolitionist states provide a misleading picture of the state of custom with relation to the death penalty? China, India, and the United States — the three most populous nations in the world — are among the "retentionist" jurisdictions described by Amnesty International. Of the ten largest countries measured in terms of population, all but Brazil and Russia are "retentionist" on Amnesty's list; according to Amnesty, the Russian Federation introduced a moratorium on executions in August 1996 but "executions were carried out between 1996 and 1999 in the Chechen Republic." The eight retentionist countries account for somewhat more than half the total world population. Consider for a moment the importance of national state practices in influencing the content of customary international law. Should the size of the populations of the different states matter in defining customary international law? Should the way in which their governments are organized matter, that is, the extent to which their policies regarding capital punishment are or are not determined by popular vote? Can a "general principle" or a rule of CIL derived from the practices of abolitionist *or* retentionist countries around the globe somehow legally bind representative democracies whose laws and practices reflect the freely expressed (contrary) views of their people?

Note the continuing influence of the "Westphalian" model of state sovereignty and equality in excluding the size of the country, or the nature of its internal decision-making processes, from the effect given its practice in defining the content of customary international law.[13] Recall our definition of CIL in Chapter 2. Is there a sufficient general state practice and *opinio juris* to constitute a norm of CIL banning the death penalty?

2. ECHR: *Soering (1989)*

The issues discussed above have been brought into sharp focus in the context of extradition, when a state seeks to obtain custody of an accused on capital charges from a country that has abolished the death penalty. When one country seeks the extradition of an individual from another country to face criminal proceedings, several kinds of legal authority may come into play. National law will usually prescribe the authority and procedures for international extradition and may require reference to treaty obligations. That is, bilateral extradition treaties may exist that set forth the rules governing the extradition of individuals between two countries. Whether an extradition treaty is required, and how the treaty should be interpreted and applied (and by whom), is a question left to national law. For present purposes, we wish to focus on the extent to which extradition decisions may be affected by (nonextradition) treaties or by customary international law. Especially where extradition is sought to face a capital charge, countries will have to consider whether extradition in the circumstances of a particular case may violate CIL or any human rights treaties to which the countries are party. A number of treaties could be relevant to this

---

12. But see Laurence E. Rothenberg, International Law, U.S. Sovereignty, and the Death Penalty, 35 Geo. J. Intl. L. 547, 555-561 (2004) (arguing that the number of abolitionist states is not sufficient to establish consistent and uniform custom, and that "states that have eliminated capital punishment may have done so out of moral, ethical, or even religious concerns rather than out of *opinio juris*").

13. See generally Rex D. Glensy, Which Countries Count? *Lawrence v. Texas* and the Selection of Foreign Persuasive Authority, 45 Va. J. Intl. L. 357 (2005).

discussion, but we will focus on the European Convention, which has been interpreted to constrain extraditions. In this section, we reference the case law of the
tribunal entrusted with enforcing the European Convention, the ECHR.

Some additional background is in order regarding the European Convention. In
1949, the leaders of postwar Europe met to create a new regional international
organization, the Council of Europe.[14] The Council had many aims, including
rebuilding Europe after World War II; holding firm against Soviet aggression,
which had consumed much of Eastern Europe; and creating the groundwork for
a European political union. One of the greatest achievements of the Council of
Europe's founders was the establishment of "the foremost international legal system
for the protection of human rights," the European Convention and its enforcement
mechanism.[15] The European Convention was signed in 1950 and came into force in
1953. As of 2008, 47 European countries have ratified or subsequently acceded to the
Convention.

The European Convention and its protocols provide for a long list of substantive
individual rights, but "what makes the European Convention on Human Rights truly
a distinctive contribution to modern international law is not its enumeration of substantive rights, but its establishment of an effective form of international legal
machinery to enforce those rights."[16] Initially, that machinery included two institutions, a commission and a court. In Protocol 11, however, the Convention merged
these two institutions into one court: the ECHR.

The ECHR's docket has grown rapidly in the past decade as its role as a kind of
human rights constitutional court expands. In all of the 1960s, the ECHR issued only
10 judgments and decisions; in 1981, 404 applications were registered; by 1997 the
number had ballooned to 4,750. In response to the increasing caseload, Protocol No. 11
was adopted, establishing a permanent court in 1998. By 2001, 13,858 applications
were submitted to the ECHR, a 130 percent increase from 1998. In 2004, Protocol No. 14
was introduced in an effort to further streamline the system, but the caseload
continues to increase. In 2005, the ECHR disposed of 27,600 applications, handing
down more than 900 judgments in the process. Still, by the end of 2005, more than
81,000 cases remained pending.[17] In contrast, the International Court of Justice (ICJ)
in 2007 maintained 12 cases on its docket.

The complainants who may bring cases before the ECHR have evolved, but at
present the ECHR's busy docket is explained in part by the fact that, unlike the
ICJ, private parties can complain to the ECHR about the alleged breach of the Convention by any state party. Litigants may also have been encouraged by the effectiveness of the ECHR in securing execution of the ECHR's judgments, including
damages awards.[18] Finally, the ECHR's popularity among individual litigants has

---

14. Note that the Council of Europe is an organization distinct from the European Union (EU). The
principal difference between the Council of Europe and the EU is that while the Council focuses on
human rights protection and rule of law, the EU's primary purpose is to promote economic and political
partnership and integration in Europe. More specifically, the Council, founded in 1949, has 47 member
countries and 5 observer countries, and aims to develop democratic principles based on the European
Convention on Human Rights and other reference texts on the protection of individuals throughout
Europe. Meanwhile, the EU is an economic and political partnership among 27 European countries that
seeks to achieve peace, prosperity, and freedom for its citizens.

15. Mark W. Janis, An Introduction to International Law 257-258 (3d ed. 1999).

16. Id. at 260-261.

17. See Council of Europe, European Court of Human Rights, Information Document on the Court
(Sept. 2006), http://www.echr.coe.int/NR/rdonlyres/981B9082-45A4-44C6-829A-202A51B94A85/0/
ENG_Infodoc.pdf.

18. See Council of Europe, Human Rights and Legal Affairs, http://www.coe.int/t/e/human_rights/
execution/01_introduction/01_Introduction.asp#TopOfPage (last visited Apr. 29, 2009).

probably been heightened in recent years, as the ECHR has demonstrated an increasing willingness to rule against states parties in favor of individual petitioners.

A final note is appropriate to underscore the practical consequences of the application of human rights norms to extradition decisions. Obviously, the question of whether the death penalty is a human rights issue subject to international law regulation is critical for the individuals involved. It also presents important consequences for law enforcement within and among states. Because the ECHR decided that the European Convention limits the extent to which member states could extradite persons to face the death penalty in nonmember countries in *Soering v. United Kingdom* (reproduced below),

> Member States of the Council of Europe no longer extradite to states where it is likely that capital punishment will be imposed. . . . Inevitably, most extradition practice involves those states with which there is a land border. As a general rule, neither Mexico nor Canada will extradite to the United States in capital cases. . . . The vast majority of U.S. extradition practices must now involve assurances that capital punishment will not be imposed.[19]

It is also important to note that the deep European antipathy to the death penalty is beginning to have even broader consequences. Thus, the "refusal of abolitionist states to cooperate in imposing capital punishment is increasingly manifesting itself in another related manner, namely, in denying other forms of mutual legal assistance."[20] In short, the stakes in the debate traced in this section are high.

SOERING v. UNITED KINGDOM
161 Eur. Ct. H.R. (ser. A) (1989)

[The applicant, Jens Soering, was a German national, detained in England pending extradition to the United States to face murder charges in Virginia. Soering was an 18-year-old student at the University of Virginia at the time of the murders. He was charged, with his 20-year-old girlfriend and fellow student, Elizabeth Haysom, with murdering Haysom's parents in Virginia. Soering and Haysom fled to the United Kingdom. When interviewed in the United Kingdom by a Virginia sheriff in the presence of UK police officers, Soering recounted the couple's efforts to overcome Haysom's parents' opposition to their relationship and the subsequent murders. Soering was indicted in Virginia for capital and noncapital murder, and extradition was sought from the United Kingdom to the United States.

The British Embassy in Washington made the following request to United States authorities:

> Because the death penalty has been abolished in Great Britain, the Embassy has been instructed to seek an assurance, in accordance with the terms of . . . the Extradition Treaty, that, in the event of Mr Soering being surrendered and being convicted of the crimes for which he has been indicted . . . , the death penalty, if imposed, will not be carried out.

---

19. William A. Schabas, Indirect Abolition: Capital Punishment's Role in Extradition Law and Practice, 25 Loy. L.A. Intl. & Comp. L. Rev. 581, 590, 604 (2003).

20. Id. at 603; see also generally Kathryn F. King, The Death Penalty, Extradition, and the War Against Terrorism: U.S. Responses to European Opinion About Capital Punishment, 9 Buff. Hum. Rts. L. Rev. 161 (2003); James Finstein, Note, Extradition or Execution? Policy Constraints in the United States' War on Terror, 77 S. Cal. L. Rev. 835 (2004); Murali Jasti, Note, Extraditing Terrorists Hits a Death Penalty Kibosh, 22 Wis. Intl. L.J. 163 (2004).

Should it not be possible on constitutional grounds for the United States Government to give such an assurance, the United Kingdom authorities ask that the United States Government undertake to recommend to the appropriate authorities that the death penalty should not be imposed or, if imposed, should not be executed.

In apparent response to this request, the Virginia prosecutor certified as follows:

I hereby certify that should Jens Soering be convicted of the offence of capital murder as charged in Bedford County, Virginia . . . a representation will be made in the name of the United Kingdom to the judge at the time of sentencing that it is the wish of the United Kingdom that the death penalty should not be imposed or carried out.

In transmitting this assurance to British authorities, the federal government of the United States "undertook to ensure that the commitment of the appropriate authorities of the Commonwealth of Virginia to make representations on behalf of the U.K. would be honoured." The Virginia authorities informed the United Kingdom that no further assurances would be offered because the county attorney intended to seek the death penalty in Soering's case. (Around this time, Haysom, Soering's girlfriend, was extradited to the United States and pled guilty as an accessory to the murder of her parents; she was sentenced to 90 years' imprisonment.)

At the extradition hearing the U.S. government introduced evidence that Soering had killed Haysom's parents. On Soering's behalf, a psychiatric report was introduced concluding that Soering "was immature and inexperienced and had lost his personal identity in a symbiotic relationship with his girlfriend — a powerful, persuasive and disturbed young woman." The report described the relationship as a " '*folie a deux*,' in which the most disturbed partner was Miss Haysom." It stated that this relationship at the time of the offense led to Soering's "suffering from an abnormality of mind due to inherent causes as substantially impaired his mental responsibility for his acts. . . ." The report continued:

The degree of disturbance of Miss Haysom borders on the psychotic and, over the course of many months, she was able to persuade Soering that he might have to kill her parents for she and him to survive as a couple. . . . Miss Haysom had a stupefying and mesmeric effect on Soering which led to an abnormal psychological state in which he became unable to think rationally or question the absurdities in Miss Haysom's view of her life and . . . her parents. . . . In conclusion, it is my opinion that, at the time of the offences, Soering was suffering from an abnormality of mind which, in this country, would constitute a defence of "not guilty to murder but guilty of manslaughter."

The hearing magistrate found the psychiatric evidence irrelevant to the issue before him and concluded that Soering was subject to extradition. After further efforts for discretionary refusal of extradition in England failed, Soering filed an application in the ECHR, which granted "interim relief to keep him in Britain pending decision." Soering's application to the ECHR indicated that Soering would consent to deportation to his native Germany. Excerpts from the Court's opinion appear below.]

II. RELEVANT DOMESTIC LAW AND PRACTICE IN THE UNITED KINGDOM . . .

30. The extradition arrangements between the United Kingdom and the United States of America are governed by the Extradition Treaty signed by the two Governments. . . .

By virtue of Article I of the Extradition Treaty, "each Contracting Party undertakes to extradite to the other, in the circumstances and subject to the conditions specified in this Treaty, any person found in its territory who has been accused or convicted of any offence [specified in the Treaty and including murder], committed within the jurisdiction of the other Party." . . .

36. There is no provision in the Extradition Acts relating to the death penalty, but Article IV of the United Kingdom-United States Treaty provides:

> If the offence for which extradition is requested is punishable by death under the relevant law of the requesting Party, but the relevant law of the requested Party does not provide for the death penalty in a similar case, extradition may be refused unless the requesting Party gives assurances satisfactory to the requested Party that the death penalty will not be carried out.

37. In the case of a fugitive requested by the United States who faces a charge carrying the death penalty, it is the Secretary of State's practice, pursuant to Article IV of the United Kingdom-United States Extradition Treaty, to accept an assurance from the prosecuting authorities of the relevant State that a representation will be made to the judge at the time of sentencing that it is the wish of the United Kingdom that the death penalty should be neither imposed nor carried out. This practice has been described by Mr. David Mellor, then Minister of State at the Home Office, in the following terms:

> The written undertakings about the death penalty that the Secretary of State obtains from the federal authorities amount to an undertaking that the views of the United Kingdom will be represented to the judge. At the time of sentencing he will be informed that the United Kingdom does not wish the death penalty to be imposed or carried out. That means that the United Kingdom authorities render up a fugitive or are prepared to send a citizen to face an American court on the clear understanding that the death penalty will not be carried out — it has never been carried out in such cases. It would be a fundamental blow to the extradition arrangements between our two countries if the death penalty were carried out on an individual who had been returned under those circumstances.

There has, however, never been a case in which the effectiveness of such an understanding has been tested. . . .

G. PRISON CONDITIONS IN MECKLENBURG CORRECTIONAL CENTER . . .

64. The applicant adduced much evidence of extreme stress, psychological deterioration and risk of homosexual abuse and physical attack undergone by prisoners on death row, including Mecklenburg Correctional Center. This evidence was strongly contested by the United Kingdom Government on the basis of affidavits sworn by administrators from the Virginia Department of Corrections. . . .

68. A death row prisoner is moved to the death house 15 days before he is due to be executed. The death house is next to the death chamber where the electric chair is situated. Whilst a prisoner is in the death house he is watched 24 hours a day. He is isolated and has no light in his cell. The lights outside are permanently lit. A prisoner who utilises the appeals process can be placed in the death house several times.

H. THE GIVING AND EFFECT OF ASSURANCES IN RELATION TO THE DEATH PENALTY

69. Relations between the United Kingdom and the United States of America on matters concerning extradition are conducted by and with the Federal and not the

State authorities. However, in respect of offences against State laws the Federal authorities have no legally binding power to provide, in an appropriate extradition case, an assurance that the death penalty will not be imposed or carried out. In such cases the power rests with the State. . . .

According to evidence from the Virginia authorities, Virginia's capital sentencing procedure and notably the provision on post-sentencing reports would allow the sentencing judge to consider the representation to be made on behalf of the United Kingdom Government pursuant to the assurance given by the Attorney for Bedford County. In addition, it would be open to the Governor to take into account the wishes of the United Kingdom Government in any application for clemency. . . .

JUDGMENT (OF THE COURT)

I. ALLEGED BREACH OF ARTICLE 3

80. The applicant alleged that the decision by the Secretary of State for the Home Department to surrender him to the authorities of the United States of America would, if implemented, give rise to a breach by the United Kingdom of Article 3 of the Convention, which provides:

> No one shall be subjected to torture or to inhuman or degrading treatment or punishment.

A. APPLICABILITY OF ARTICLE 3 IN CASES OF EXTRADITION

81. The alleged breach derives from the applicant's exposure to the so-called "death row phenomenon." This phenomenon may be described as consisting in a combination of circumstances to which the applicant would be exposed if, after having been extradited to Virginia to face a capital murder charge, he were sentenced to death.

82. . . . The applicant . . . submitted that Article 3 not only prohibits the Contracting States from causing inhuman or degrading treatment or punishment to occur within their jurisdiction but also embodies an associated obligation not to put a person in a position where he will or may suffer such treatment or punishment at the hands of other States. For the applicant, at least as far as Article 3 is concerned, an individual may not be surrendered out of the protective zone of the Convention without the certainty that the safeguards which he would enjoy are as effective as the Convention standard.

83. The United Kingdom Government, on the other hand, contended that Article 3 should not be interpreted so as to impose responsibility on a Contracting State for acts which occur outside its jurisdiction. In particular, in its submission, extradition does not involve the responsibility of the extraditing State for inhuman or degrading treatment or punishment which the extradited person may suffer outside the State's jurisdiction. To begin with, it maintained, it would be straining the language of Article 3 intolerably to hold that by surrendering a fugitive criminal the extraditing State has "subjected" him to any treatment or punishment that he will receive following conviction and sentence in the receiving State. Further arguments advanced against the approach of the Commission were that it interferes with international treaty rights; it leads to a conflict with the norms of international judicial process, in that it in effect involves adjudication on the internal affairs of foreign States not Parties to the Convention or to the proceedings before the Convention institutions; it entails grave difficulties of evaluation and proof in requiring

the examination of alien systems of law and of conditions in foreign States; the practice of national courts and the international community cannot reasonably be invoked to support it; it causes a serious risk of harm in the Contracting State which is obliged to harbour the protected person, and leaves criminals untried, at large and unpunished.

In the alternative, the United Kingdom Government submitted that the application of Article 3 in extradition cases should be limited to those occasions in which the treatment or punishment abroad is certain, imminent and serious. In its view, the fact that by definition the matters complained of are only anticipated, together with the common and legitimate interest of all States in bringing fugitive criminals to justice, requires a very high degree of risk, proved beyond reasonable doubt, that ill-treatment will actually occur. . . .

85. As results from Article 5(1)(f), which permits "the lawful . . . detention of a person against whom action is being taken with a view to . . . extradition," no right not to be extradited is as such protected by the Convention. Nevertheless, in so far as a measure of extradition has consequences adversely affecting the enjoyment of a Convention right, it may, assuming that the consequences are not too remote, attract the obligations of a Contracting State under the relevant Convention guarantee. What is at issue in the present case is whether Article 3 can be applicable when the adverse consequences of extradition are, or may be, suffered outside the jurisdiction of the extraditing State as a result of treatment or punishment administered in the receiving State.

86. Article 1 of the Convention, which provides that "the High Contracting Parties shall secure to everyone within their jurisdiction the rights and freedoms defined in Section I," sets a limit, notably territorial, on the reach of the Convention. In particular, the engagement undertaken by a Contracting State is confined to "securing" . . . the listed rights and freedoms to persons within its own "jurisdiction." Further, the Convention does not govern the actions of States not Parties to it, nor does it purport to be a means of requiring the Contracting States to impose Convention standards on other States. Article 1 cannot be read as justifying a general principle to the effect that, notwithstanding its extradition obligations, a Contracting State may not surrender an individual unless satisfied that the conditions awaiting him in the country of destination are in full accord with each of the safeguards of the Convention. Indeed, as the United Kingdom Government stressed, the beneficial purpose of extradition in preventing fugitive offenders from evading justice cannot be ignored in determining the scope of application of the Convention and of Article 3 in particular.

In the instant case it is common ground that the United Kingdom has no power over the practices and arrangements of the Virginia authorities which are the subject of the applicant's complaints. It is also true that in other international instruments cited by the United Kingdom Government—for example the 1951 United Nations Convention relating to the Status of Refugees, the 1957 European Convention on Extradition and the 1984 United Nations Convention against Torture and Other Cruel, Inhuman and Degrading Treatment or Punishment—the problems of removing a person to another jurisdiction where unwanted consequences may follow are addressed expressly and specifically.

These considerations cannot, however, absolve the Contracting Parties from responsibility under Article 3 for all and any foreseeable consequences of extradition suffered outside their jurisdiction.

87. In interpreting the Convention regard must be had to its special character as a treaty for the collective enforcement of human rights and fundamental freedoms.

Thus, the object and purpose of the Convention as an instrument for the protection of individual human beings require that its provisions be interpreted and applied so as to make its safeguards practical and effective. In addition, any interpretation of the rights and freedoms guaranteed has to be consistent with "the general spirit of the Convention, an instrument designed to maintain and promote the ideals and values of a democratic society."

88. Article 3 makes no provision for exceptions and no derogation from it is permissible under Article 15 in time of war or other national emergency. This absolute prohibition on torture and on inhuman or degrading treatment or punishment under the terms of the Convention shows that Article 3 enshrines one of the fundamental values of the democratic societies making up the Council of Europe. It is also to be found in similar terms in other international instruments such as the 1966 International Covenant on Civil and Political Rights and the 1969 American Convention on Human Rights and is generally recognised as an internationally accepted standard.

The question remains whether the extradition of a fugitive to another State where he would be subjected or be likely to be subjected to torture or to inhuman or degrading treatment or punishment would itself engage the responsibility of a Contracting State under Article 3. That the abhorrence of torture has such implications is recognised in Article 3 of the United Nations Convention Against Torture and Other Cruel, Inhuman or Degrading Treatment or Punishment, which provides that "no State Party shall . . . extradite a person where there are substantial grounds for believing that he would be in danger of being subjected to torture." The fact that a specialised treaty should spell out in detail a specific obligation attaching to the prohibition of torture does not mean that an essentially similar obligation is not already inherent in the general terms of Article 3 of the European Convention. It would hardly be compatible with the underlying values of the Convention, that "common heritage of political traditions, ideals, freedom and the rule of law" to which the Preamble refers, were a Contracting State knowingly to surrender a fugitive to another State where there were substantial grounds for believing that he would be in danger of being subjected to torture, however heinous the crime allegedly committed. Extradition in such circumstances, while not explicitly referred to in the brief and general wording of Article 3, would plainly be contrary to the spirit and intendment of the Article, and in the Court's view this inherent obligation not to extradite also extends to cases in which the fugitive would be faced in the receiving State by a real risk of exposure to inhuman or degrading treatment or punishment proscribed by that Article.

89. What amounts to "inhuman or degrading treatment or punishment" depends on all the circumstances of the case. Furthermore, inherent in the whole of the Convention is a search for a fair balance between the demands of the general interest of the community and the requirements of the protection of the individual's fundamental rights. As movement about the world becomes easier and crime takes on a larger international dimension, it is increasingly in the interest of all nations that suspected offenders who flee abroad should be brought to justice. Conversely, the establishment of safe havens for fugitives would not only result in danger for the State obliged to harbour the protected person but also tend to undermine the foundations of extradition. These considerations must also be included among the factors to be taken into account in the interpretation and application of the notions of inhuman and degrading treatment or punishment in extradition cases.

90. It is not normally for the Convention institutions to pronounce on the existence or otherwise of potential violations of the Convention. However, where an applicant

claims that a decision to extradite him would, if implemented, be contrary to Article 3 by reason of its foreseeable consequences in the requesting country, a departure from this principle is necessary, in view of the serious and irreparable nature of the alleged suffering risked, in order to ensure the effectiveness of the safeguard provided by that Article.

91. In sum, the decision by a Contracting State to extradite a fugitive may give rise to an issue under Article 3, and hence engage the responsibility of that State under the Convention, where substantial grounds have been shown for believing that the person concerned, if extradited, faces a real risk of being subjected to torture or to inhuman or degrading treatment or punishment in the requesting country. The establishment of such responsibility inevitably involves an assessment of conditions in the requesting country against the standards of Article 3 of the Convention. Nonetheless, there is no question of adjudicating on or establishing the responsibility of the receiving country, whether under general international law, under the Convention or otherwise. In so far as any liability under the Convention is or may be incurred, it is liability incurred by the extraditing Contracting State by reason of its having taken action which has as a direct consequence the exposure of an individual to proscribed ill-treatment.

B. APPLICATION OF ARTICLE 3 IN THE PARTICULAR CIRCUMSTANCES OF THE PRESENT CASE
92. The extradition procedure against the applicant in the United Kingdom has been completed, the Secretary of State having signed a warrant ordering his surrender to the United States' authorities, this decision, albeit as yet not implemented, directly affects him. It therefore has to be determined on the above principles whether the foreseeable consequences of Mr. Soering's return to the United States are such as to attract the application of Article 3. This inquiry must concentrate firstly on whether Mr. Soering runs a real risk of being sentenced to death in Virginia, since the source of the alleged inhuman and degrading treatment or punishment, namely the "death row phenomenon," lies in the imposition of the death penalty. Only in the event of an affirmative answer to this question need the court examine whether exposure to the "death row phenomenon" in the circumstances of the applicant's case would involve treatment or punishment incompatible with Article 3.

1. Whether the Applicant Runs a Real Risk of a Death Sentence and Hence of Exposure to the "Death Row Phenomenon"

93. The United Kingdom Government . . . did not accept that the risk of a death sentence attains a sufficient level of likelihood to bring Article 3 into play. Their reasons were fourfold.

Firstly, . . . the applicant has not acknowledged his guilt of capital murder as such.

Secondly, only a *prima facie* case has so far been made out against him. In particular, in the United Kingdom Government's view the psychiatric evidence is equivocal as to whether Mr. Soering was suffering from a disease of the mind sufficient to amount to a defence of insanity under Virginia law.

Thirdly, even if Mr. Soering is convicted of capital murder, it cannot be assumed that in the general exercise of their discretion the jury will recommend, the judge will confirm and the Supreme Court of Virginia will uphold the imposition of the death penalty. The United Kingdom Government referred to the presence of important mitigating factors, such as the applicant's age and mental condition at the time of commission of the offence and his lack of previous criminal activity, which would have to be taken into account by the jury and then by the judge in the separate sentencing proceedings.

Fourthly, the assurance received from the United States must at the very least significantly reduce the risk of a capital sentence either being imposed or carried out.

At the public hearing the Attorney General nevertheless made clear his Government's understanding that if Mr. Soering were extradited to the United States there was "some risk," which was "more than merely negligible," that the death penalty would be imposed.

94. As the applicant himself pointed out, he has made to American and British police officers and to two psychiatrists admissions of his participation in the killings of the Haysom parents. . . . It is not for the European Court to usurp the function of the Virginia courts by ruling that a defence of insanity would or would not be available on the psychiatric evidence as it stands. The United Kingdom Government is justified in its assertion that no assumption can be made that Mr. Soering would certainly or even probably be convicted of capital murder as charged. Nevertheless, as the Attorney General conceded on its behalf at the public hearing, there is "a significant risk" that the applicant would be so convicted. . . .

97. The Commonwealth's Attorney for Bedford County, Mr. Updike, who is responsible for conducting the prosecution against the applicant, has certified that "should Jens Soering be convicted of the offence of capital murder as charged . . . a representation will be made in the name of the United Kingdom to the judge at the time of sentencing that it is the wish of the United Kingdom that the death penalty should not be imposed or carried out." The Court notes . . . that this undertaking is far from reflecting the wording of Article IV of the 1972 Extradition Treaty between the United Kingdom and the United States, which speaks of "assurances satisfactory to the requested Party that the death penalty will not be carried out." However, the offence charged, being a State and not a Federal offence, comes within the jurisdiction of the Commonwealth of Virginia; it appears as a consequence that no direction could or can be given to the Commonwealth's Attorney by any State or Federal authority to promise more; the Virginia courts as judicial bodies cannot bind themselves in advance as to what decisions they may arrive at on the evidence; and the Governor of Virginia does not, as a matter of policy, promise that he will later exercise his executive power to commute a death penalty.

This being so, Mr. Updike's undertaking may well have been the best "assurance" that the United Kingdom could have obtained from the United States Federal Government in the particular circumstances. According to the statement made to Parliament in 1987 by a Home Office Minister, acceptance of undertakings in such terms "means that the United Kingdom authorities render up a fugitive or are prepared to send a citizen to face an American court on the clear understanding that the death penalty will not be carried out. . . . It would be a fundamental blow to the extradition arrangements between our two countries if the death penalty were carried out on an individual who had been returned under those circumstances." Nonetheless, the effectiveness of such an undertaking has not yet been put to the test.

98. The applicant contended that representations concerning the wishes of a foreign government would not be admissible as a matter of law under the Virginia Code or, if admissible, of any influence on the sentencing judge.

Whatever the position under Virginia law and practice, and notwithstanding the diplomatic context of the extradition relations between the United Kingdom and the United States, objectively it cannot be said that the undertaking to inform the judge at the sentencing stage of the wishes of the United Kingdom eliminates the risk of the death penalty being imposed. In the independent exercise of his discretion the Commonwealth's Attorney has himself decided to seek and to persist in seeking the death penalty because the evidence, in his determination, supports such action.

If the national authority with responsibility for prosecuting the offence takes such a firm stance, it is hardly open to the Court to hold that there are no substantial grounds for believing that the applicant faces a real risk of being sentenced to death and hence experiencing the "death row phenomenon."

99. The Court's conclusion is therefore that the likelihood of the feared exposure of the applicant to the "death row phenomenon" has been shown to be such as to bring Article 3 into play.

2. Whether in the Circumstances the Risk of Exposure to the "Death Row Phenomenon" Would Make Extradition a Breach of Article 3

(a) General Considerations

100. As is established in the Court's case law, ill-treatment, including punishment, must attain a minimum level of severity if it is to fall within the scope of Article 3. The assessment of this minimum is, in the nature of things, relative; it depends on all the circumstances of the case, such as the nature and context of the treatment or punishment, the manner and method of its execution, its duration, its physical or mental effects and, in some instances, the sex, age and state of health of the victim.

Treatment has been held by the Court to be both "inhuman" because it was premeditated, was applied for hours at a stretch and "caused, if not actual bodily injury, at least intense physical and mental suffering," and also "degrading" because it was "such as to arouse in [its] victims feelings of fear, anguish and inferiority capable of humiliating and debasing them and possibly breaking their physical or moral resistance." In order for a punishment or treatment associated with it to be "inhuman" or "degrading," the suffering or humiliation involved must in any event go beyond that inevitable element of suffering or humiliation connected with a given form of legitimate punishment. In this connection, account is to be taken not only of the physical pain experienced but also, where there is a considerable delay before execution of the punishment, of the sentenced person's mental anguish of anticipating the violence he is to have inflicted on him.

101. Capital punishment is permitted under certain conditions by Article 2(1) of the Convention, which reads:

> Everyone's right to life shall be protected by law. No one shall be deprived of his life intentionally save in the execution of a sentence of a court following his conviction of a crime for which this penalty is provided by law.

In view of this wording, the applicant did not suggest that the death penalty per se violated Article 3. He, like the two Government Parties, agreed with the Commission that the extradition of a person to a country where he risks the death penalty does not in itself raise an issue under either Article 2 or Article 3. On the other hand, Amnesty International in their written comments argued that the evolving standards in Western Europe regarding the existence and use of the death penalty required that the death penalty should now be considered as an inhuman and degrading punishment within the meaning of Article 3.

102. Certainly, "the Convention is a living instrument which . . . must be interpreted in the light of present-day conditions"; and, in assessing whether a given treatment or punishment is to be regarded as inhuman or degrading for the purposes of Article 3, "the Court cannot but be influenced by the developments and commonly accepted standards in the penal policy of the member States of the Council of Europe in this field." De facto the death penalty no longer exists in time of peace in the

Contracting States to the Convention. In the few Contracting States which retain the death penalty in law for some peacetime offences, death sentences, if ever imposed, are nowadays not carried out. This "virtual consensus in Western European legal systems that the death penalty is, under current circumstances, no longer consistent with regional standards of justice," to use the words of Amnesty International, is reflected in Protocol No. 6 to the Convention, which provides for the abolition of the death penalty in time of peace. Protocol No. 6 was opened for signature in April 1983, which in the practice of the Council of Europe indicates the absence of objection on the part of any of the Member States of the Organisation; it came into force in March 1985 and to date has been ratified by 13 Contracting States to the Convention, not however including the United Kingdom.

Whether these marked changes have the effect of bringing the death penalty per se within the prohibition of ill-treatment under Article 3 must be determined on the principles governing the interpretation of the Convention.

103. The Convention is to be read as a whole and Article 3 should therefore be construed in harmony with the provisions of Article 2. On this basis Article 3 evidently cannot have been intended by the drafters of the Convention to include a general prohibition of the death penalty since that would nullify the clear wording of Article 2(1).

Subsequent practice in national penal policy, in the form of a generalised abolition of capital punishment, could be taken as establishing the agreement of the Contracting States to abrogate the exception provided for under Article 2(1) and hence to remove a textual limit on the scope for evolutive interpretation of Article 3. However, Protocol No. 6, as a subsequent written agreement, shows that the intention of the Contracting Parties as recently as 1983 was to adopt the normal method of amendment of the text in order to introduce a new obligation to abolish capital punishment in time of peace and, what is more, to do so by an optional instrument allowing each State to choose the moment when to undertake such an engagement. In these conditions, notwithstanding the special character of the Convention, Article 3 cannot be interpreted as generally prohibiting the death penalty.

104. That does not mean however that circumstances relating to a death sentence can never give rise to an issue under Article 3. The manner in which it is imposed or executed, the personal circumstances of the condemned person and a disproportionality to the gravity of the crime committed, as well as the conditions of detention awaiting execution, are examples of factors capable of bringing the treatment or punishment received by the condemned person within the proscription under Article 3. Present-day attitudes in the Contracting States to capital punishment are relevant for the assessment whether the acceptable threshold of suffering or degradation has been exceeded.

(b) The Particular Circumstances

105. The applicant submitted that the circumstances to which he would be exposed as a consequence of the implementation of the Secretary of State's decision to return him to the United States, namely the "death row phenomenon," cumulatively constitute such serious treatment that his extradition would be contrary to Article 3. He cited in particular the delays in the appeal and review procedures following a death sentence, during which time he would be subject to increasing tension and psychological trauma; the fact, so he said, that the judge or jury in determining sentence is not obliged to take into account the defendant's age and mental state at the time of the offence; the extreme conditions of his future detention in "death row" in Mecklenburg Correctional Center, where he expects to be the victim of violence and sexual

abuse because of his age, colour and nationality; and the constant spectre of the execution itself, including the ritual of execution. . . .

(i) Length of Detention Prior to Execution

106. The period that a condemned prisoner can expect to spend on death row in Virginia before being executed is on average six to eight years. This length of time awaiting death is . . . in a sense largely of the prisoner's own making in that he takes advantage of all avenues of appeal which are offered to him by Virginia law. The automatic appeal to the Supreme Court of Virginia normally takes no more than six months. The remaining time is accounted for by collateral attacks mounted by the prisoner himself in habeas corpus proceedings before both the State and Federal courts and in applications to the Supreme Court of the United States for certiorari review, the prisoner at each stage being able to seek a stay of execution. The remedies available under Virginia law serve the purpose of ensuring that the ultimate sanction of death is not unlawfully or arbitrarily imposed.

Nevertheless, just as some lapse of time between sentence and execution is inevitable if appeal safeguards are to be provided to the condemned person, so it is equally part of human nature that the person will cling to life by exploiting those safeguards to the full. However well-intentioned and even potentially beneficial is the provision of the complex of post-sentence procedures in Virginia, the consequence is that the condemned prisoner has to endure for many years the conditions on death row and the anguish and mounting tension of living in the ever-present shadow of death.

(ii) Conditions on Death Row

107. As to conditions in Mecklenburg Correctional Center, where the applicant could expect to be held if sentenced to death, the Court bases itself on the facts which were uncontested by the United Kingdom Government, without finding it necessary to determine the reliability of the additional evidence adduced by the applicant, notably as to the risk of homosexual abuse and physical attack undergone by prisoners on death row.

[In connection with the] stringency of the custodial régime in Mecklenburg, . . . the United Kingdom Government drew attention to the necessary requirement of extra security for the safe custody of prisoners condemned to death for murder. Whilst it might thus well be justifiable in principle, the severity of a special régime such as that operated on death row in Mecklenburg is compounded by the fact of inmates being subject to it for a protracted period lasting on average six to eight years.

(iii) The Applicant's Age and Mental State

108. At the time of the killings, the applicant was only 18 years old and there is some psychiatric evidence, which was not contested as such, that he "was suffering from [such] an abnormality of mind . . . as substantially impaired his mental responsibility for his acts."

Unlike Article 2 of the Convention, Article 6 of the 1966 International Covenant on Civil and Political Rights and Article 4 of the 1969 American Convention on Human Rights expressly prohibit the death penalty from being imposed on persons aged less than 18 at the time of commission of the offence. Whether or not such a prohibition be inherent in the brief and general language of Article 2 of the European Convention, its explicit enunciation in other, later international instruments, the former of which has been ratified by a large number of States Parties to the European Convention, at the very least indicates that as a general principle the youth of the person concerned is a circumstance which is liable, with others, to put in question the compatibility with Article 3 of measures connected with a death sentence.

It is in line with the Court's case law to treat disturbed mental health as having the same effect for the application of Article 3.

109. Virginia law, as the United Kingdom Government and the Commission emphasised, certainly does not ignore these two factors. Under the Virginia Code account has to be taken of mental disturbance in a defendant, either as an absolute bar to conviction if it is judged to be sufficient to amount to insanity or, like age, as a fact in mitigation at the sentencing stage. Additionally, indigent capital murder defendants are entitled to the appointment of a qualified mental health expert to assist in the preparation of their submissions at the separate sentencing proceedings. These provisions in the Virginia Code undoubtedly serve, as the American courts have stated, to prevent the arbitrary or capricious imposition of the death penalty and narrowly to channel the sentencer's discretion. They do not however remove the relevance of age and mental condition in relation to the acceptability, under Article 3, of the "death row phenomenon" for a given individual once condemned to death.

Although it is not for this Court to prejudge issues of criminal responsibility and appropriate sentence, the applicant's youth at the time of the offence and his then mental state, on the psychiatric evidence as it stands, are therefore to be taken into consideration as contributory factors tending, in his case, to bring the treatment on death row within the terms of Article 3. . . .

(c) Conclusion

111. For any prisoner condemned to death, some element of delay between imposition and execution of the sentence and the experience of severe stress in conditions necessary for strict incarceration are inevitable. The democratic character of the Virginia legal system in general and the positive features of Virginia trial, sentencing and appeal procedures in particular are beyond doubt. The Court agrees with the Commission that the machinery of justice to which the applicant would be subject in the United States is in itself neither arbitrary nor unreasonable, but, rather, respects the rule of law and affords not inconsiderable procedural safeguards to the defendant in a capital trial. Facilities are available on death row for the assistance of inmates, notably through provision of psychological and psychiatric services.

However, in the Court's view, having regard to the very long period of time spent on death row in such extreme conditions, with the ever-present and mounting anguish of awaiting execution of the death penalty, and to the personal circumstances of the applicant, especially his age and mental state at the time of the offence, the applicant's extradition to the United States would expose him to a real risk of treatment going beyond the threshold set by Article 3. A further consideration of relevance is that in the particular instance the legitimate purpose of extradition could be achieved by another means which would not involve suffering of such exceptional intensity or duration.

Accordingly, the Secretary of State's decision to extradite the applicant to the United States would, if implemented, give rise to a breach of Article 3.

This finding in no way puts in question the good faith of the United Kingdom Government, which has from the outset of the present proceedings demonstrated its desire to abide by its Convention obligations, firstly by staying the applicant's surrender to the United States authorities in accord with the interim measures indicated by the Convention institutions and secondly by itself referring the case to the Court for a judicial ruling. . . .

CONCURRING OPINION OF JUDGE DE MEYER

The applicant's extradition to the United States of America would not only expose him to inhuman or degrading treatment or punishment. It would also, and above all, violate his right to life.

Indeed, the most important issue in this case is not "the likelihood of the feared exposure of the applicant to the 'death row phenomenon,'" but the very simple fact that his life would be put in jeopardy by the extradition.

The second sentence of Article 2(1) of the Convention, as it was drafted in 1950, states that "no one shall be deprived of his life intentionally save in the execution of a sentence of a court following his conviction of a crime for which this penalty is provided by law." . . .

When a person's right to life is involved, no requested State can be entitled to allow a requesting State to do what the requested State is not itself allowed to do.

If, as in the present case, the domestic law of a State does not provide the death penalty for the crime concerned, that State is not permitted to put the person concerned in a position where he may be deprived of his life for that crime at the hands of another State.

That consideration may already suffice to preclude the United Kingdom from surrendering the applicant to the United States.

There is also something more fundamental.

The second sentence of Article 2(1) of the Convention was adopted, nearly forty years ago, in particular historical circumstances, shortly after the Second World War. In so far as it still may seem to permit, under certain conditions, capital punishment in time of peace, it does not reflect the contemporary situation, and is now overridden by the development of legal conscience and practice.

Such punishment is not consistent with the present state of European civilisation.

De facto, it no longer exists in any State Party to the Convention.

Its unlawfulness was recognised by the Committee of Ministers of the Council of Europe when it adopted in December 1982, and opened for signature in April 1983, the Sixth Protocol to the Convention, which to date has been signed by 16, and ratified by 13, Contracting States.

No State Party to the Convention can in that context, even if it has not yet ratified the Sixth Protocol, be allowed to extradite any person if that person thereby incurs the risk of being put to death in the requesting State.

Extraditing somebody in such circumstances would be repugnant to European standards of justice, and contrary to the public order of Europe.

The applicant's surrender by the United Kingdom to the United States could only be lawful if the United States were to give absolute assurances that he will not be put to death if convicted of the crime he is charged with.

No such assurances were, or can be, obtained. . . .

In fact, the Commonwealth's Attorney dealing with the case intends to seek the death penalty and the Commonwealth's Governor has never commuted a death sentence since the imposition of the death penalty was resumed in 1977.

In these circumstances there can be no doubt whatsoever that the applicant's extradition to the United States would violate his right to life.

NOTES AND QUESTIONS

1. The United Kingdom argued to the ECHR, as a threshold matter, that Article 3 of the European Convention had no application to the United Kingdom's decision to

extradite someone to a nonsignatory country. The United Kingdom's position is (in essence) that the European Convention should not apply to its extradition decision because the United Kingdom would not be imposing or administering this penalty on its territory and under its laws. Under the ECHR's logic, does an extraditing state party to the European Convention have to satisfy itself that the non-state party to which it proposes to extradite an individual meets *all* the human rights standards set by the European Convention, or is the ECHR's analysis confined to Article 3's ban on torture? See *Soering* ¶¶86-87. For example, Article 10(1) of the European Convention provides that "[e]veryone has the right to freedom of expression," and Article 11(1) states that "[e]veryone has the right to freedom of peaceful assembly and to freedom of association with others." Would the UK also be required to ensure that the United States and Virginia respect these rights, as interpreted by the ECHR, before it is permitted to extradite a defendant to the United States for prosecution in Virginia? These rights, unlike the prohibition on torture contained in Article 3, are derogable in time of war or other public emergency under Article 15 of the European Convention. Under ECHR's analysis in *Soering*, does the derogable nature of these obligations matter in determining whether they apply to states parties' decisions to extradite to a non-state party that may not comply with Articles 10 and 11 as interpreted by the ECHR? See *Soering* ¶88.

The Canadian Supreme Court rejected a similar argument tendered in United States v. Burns, [2001] 1 S.C.R. 283 (Can). The extradition treaty between Canada and the United States provides that the requested state may refuse extradition unless the requesting state provides assurances that the death penalty will not be imposed. A U.S. state (Washington) requested extradition of the defendant to meet capital murder charges. The Canadian government had a policy that it would not seek assurances except in extraordinary circumstances, and it did not in Burns's case. The Canadian Supreme Court had previously held that the minister of justice had not abused his discretion in extraditing death-eligible persons to the United States without seeking assurances and that the extraditions did not violate the Canadian Charter of Rights. Kindler v. Canada, [1991] 2 S.C.R. 779 (Can); Reference re Ng Extradition [1991] 2 S.C.R. 858 (Can). In *Burns*, the Canadian Supreme Court revisited these decisions to decide anew whether the Canadian government's practice could be reconciled with the Canadian Charter of Rights and Freedoms, which guarantees "[e]veryone . . . the right to life, liberty and security of the person and the right not to be deprived thereof except in accordance with the principles of fundamental justice."

The Canadian Supreme Court in *Burns* first noted that the Charter only guarantees rights from infringement by the Canadian Parliament and the government of each province, but, relying on *Soering*, the Court held that the decision to extradite without assurances would be a "necessary link in the chain of causation leading to the death penalty." The Court then applied a balancing test — in which the Canadian opposition to capital punishment was a predominant factor — and held that the Canadian government *is* constitutionally bound to ask for and obtain an assurance that the death penalty will not be imposed as a condition of extradition in all but exceptional circumstances. See also Venezia v. Ministero Di Grazia E Giustizia, Corte cost., 27 June 1996, n.223, Racc. uff. corte cost. 61 (Italian Constitutional Court held that extradition of a fugitive indicted for a crime for which capital punishment is provided by the law of the requesting state would violate the Italian Constitution, regardless of the sufficiency of the assurances provided by the requesting state that the death penalty would not be imposed or, if imposed, would not be executed); Mohamed & Another v. President of the RSA & Others, 2001(7) B.C.L.R. 685 (CC) (S. Afr.)

(South African Constitutional Court adopted a per se rule against either extradition or deportation in lieu of extradition to state where the death penalty is threatened).

2. On the merits, Soering's nominal claim is not that capital punishment constitutes the treatment proscribed by Article 3, but rather, that the "death row phenomenon" is "torture or inhumane or degrading treatment or punishment." See *Soering* ¶81. Is the ECHR's decision in *Soering* founded only on the "death row phenomenon" in general — the anguish any defendant might feel attendant to lengthy delays in the administration of the capital sentence — or is it dependent on the circumstances of this particular case given Soering's age and mental situation? See John Dugard & Christine Van den Wyngaert, Reconciling Extradition with Human Rights, 92 Am. J. Intl. L. 187, 198-199 (1998) ("There is a difference of opinion among writers and judges over whether *Soering* is authority for the proposition that the death row phenomenon per se will bar extradition or whether it was too firmly premised on the personal circumstances of Soering to permit such a conclusion."). What circumstances does the ECHR look to in finding a violation of Article 3 in this case?

U.S. courts do not recognize the "death row phenomenon" as a valid claim under the Eighth Amendment. See, e.g., Knight v. Florida, 528 U.S. 990 (1999) (sources cited by Thomas, J., concurring in the denial of certiorari); see also Lackey v. Texas, 514 U.S. 1045 (1995) (Stevens, J., respecting the denial of certiorari). The United States has also excluded the *Soering* interpretation of "cruel, inhuman or degrading treatment or punishment" in its reservations to both the International Covenant on Civil and Political Rights (ICCPR) and the UN Convention Against Torture and Other Cruel, Inhuman and Degrading Treatment or Punishment. See Dugard & Wyngaert, supra, 92 Am. J. Intl. L. at 198. Courts in other countries, however, have found that "it is an inhuman act to keep a man facing the agony of execution over a long, extended period of time." Pratt v. Atty. Gen. of Jam., [1994] 2 A.C. 1, 4 All. E.R. 769 (P.C. 1993) (en banc); see also id. at 32-33, 4 All E.R., at 785-786 (collecting cases).

3. The ECHR believes that it is foreclosed from holding that capital punishment is forbidden by Article 3 as a matter of treaty interpretation. What interpretive aids does the ECHR use in reaching this determination? Amnesty International, and concurring Judge De Meyer, believe that "the evolving standards in Western Europe regarding the existence and use of the death penalty required that the death penalty should now be considered as an inhuman and degrading punishment within the meaning of Article 3" despite the plain language of Article 2(1) recognizing the continued validity of the death penalty. *Soering* ¶101. What is the legal basis for their argument? Is Judge De Meyer using "evolving standards" for treaty *interpretation*, or is he contending that these evolving standards have now hardened into *customary international law*? Can customary international law supersede a treaty? See Restatement (Third) of the Foreign Relations Law of the United States §102 cmt. j (1986) ("A new rule of customary law will supersede inconsistent obligations created by an earlier agreement if the parties so intend and the intention is clearly manifested"). Can a treaty be *amended* based on the "evolving standards" (as expressed, perhaps, in party practices) as determined by a court? What does the Vienna Convention on the Law of Treaties (VCLT) say about how multilateral treaties such as the Vienna Convention on Consular Relations (VCCR) may be amended? See VCLT arts. 39, 40. Although the ECHR does not use "evolving standards" to abrogate Article 2(1) of the Convention, it does use such standards in its interpretation of the Convention's dictates. How? See, e.g., *Soering* ¶¶102, 104.

4. Did the ECHR's interpretive approach comport with the VCLT, to which the United Kingdom and Germany are parties and which the ICJ regards as expressing the customary law of treaties even in cases involving non-states parties? See VCLT arts.

31-33. The first rule of treaty interpretation is embodied in Article 31 of the VCLT: A "treaty should be interpreted in good faith in accordance with the ordinary meaning to be given the terms of the treaty in their context and in the light of its object and purpose." The "ordinary meaning" of the text of the treaty is at the top of the interpretive hierarchy. The VCLT limits the use of supplementary means of interpretation to instances in which they "confirm the meaning resulting from the application of Article 31" or when the means used in Article 31 yield an ambiguous or obscure meaning or "a result which is manifestly absurd or unreasonable." Id. art. 32. As Professor Bederman has explained:

> The chief division [between U.S. practice and international approaches to treaty interpretation] concerns American courts' willingness to deviate from the text of a treaty in search of intent, and to embrace a meaning advanced by the executive branch that may not accord with international expectations or the canon of liberal interpretation and good faith. This schism in method has been well-documented, and judges in the United States are increasingly realizing that the approach taken by the [VCLT] may lead to interpretative outcomes very different from those suggested by some of the litigants.
>
> The [VCLT] focuses primarily on the text of an international agreement, seen through its "context and in light of its object and purpose." Resort to extrinsic evidence of the parties' intent, including *travaux [préparatoires]*, is meant to be only an exceptional occurrence. The use of peculiarly national materials for interpretive purposes is manifestly disapproved of by the Vienna Convention. . . .

David J. Bederman, Revivalist Canons and Treaty Interpretation, 41 UCLA L. Rev. 953, 972-973 (1993-1994) ("*travaux préparatoires*," meaning "preliminary works," are the record of negotiations preceding the conclusion of a treaty; at times, they are referenced as a means of determining the "intention" of the states that drafted the convention sought to be interpreted). Did the ECHR in *Soering* follow the approach of the VCLT? Did it employ an "American" method of analysis, or did it forge its own interpretive approach?

5. Should the interpretive methods employed in a given case depend on the *type* of treaty at issue? In *Soering*, the European Court notes that "[i]n interpreting the Convention regard must be had to its special character as a treaty for the collective enforcement of human rights and fundamental freedoms." *Soering* ¶87. This passage may echo for American law students the U.S. Supreme Court's famous expression in McCulloch v. Maryland, 17 U.S. (4 Wheat) 316, 322 (1819): "[W]e must never forget, that it is a Constitution we are expounding." But what does this *mean*? Professor Bederman argues that

> [s]ome treaties clearly have the flavor of legislation; indeed, some rise to the level of organic, "constitutional" texts. For these charters, rules of interpretation approximating those for statutory construction would seem to be the most appropriate. Other agreements clearly evidence contractual features. Interpreting courts in this country have thus sought to apply basic contractual methods to these texts. . . . Finally, there is an argument that treaties are special and that they should not be interpreted in the same way as either contracts or statutes. After all, in the United States, treaties are not concluded by a legislative body. And, a treaty is a contract in only the most generic sense. Many established norms of contract law are simply inapplicable to treaties.

Bederman, supra, 41 UCLA L. Rev. at 963-964. Professor Vagts describes treaties like the European Convention as "quasi-constitutional," thus requiring "special treatment in light of the necessity of adaptation over a longer period of time to the necessities of the age." Detlev F. Vagts, Treaty Interpretation and the New American Ways of Law Reading, 4 Eur. J. Intl. L. 472, 475, 494 (1993). Would the view that the European Convention is a quasi-constitutional document, as opposed to a contract or other type of agreement, influence the degree to which state practice, and in particular evolving ideas regarding the morality of capital punishment, should be considered?

6. At the time *Soering* was decided, the United Kingdom had not yet ratified Protocol No. 6 to the European Convention, prohibiting the carrying out of the death penalty in times of peace. If the United States had sought Soering's extradition from a European state that *had* ratified Protocol No. 6, would the ECHR have based its holding on Protocol No. 6 rather than Article 3? Or is there a reason why the ECHR would be willing to attribute to a state party a non-state party's actions contravening Article 3 but not its actions that contravene Protocol No. 6? See supra Note 1 following *Soering*. If there is no difference, then does the "death row phenomenon" claim hold any relevance for extradition requests from states that have ratified Protocol No. 6 (that is, all European states except Russia)?

7. Consider, in this regard, Öcalan v. Turkey, 2005-IV Eur. Ct. H.R. 282, which involved a Turkish national, Abdullah Öcalan, who was the founder and, at the time of his arrest, leader of the Workers' Party of Kurdistan (PKK). Since approximately 1984, the PKK had carried out an armed struggle within Turkey involving much violence and loss of life. After his arrest, Öcalan admitted to the public prosecutor and the Ankara State Security Court (Security Court) that his and the PKK's initial aim had been to found an independent Kurdish State. He asserted, however, that with the passage of time they had changed their objective and sought to secure a share of power for the Kurds as a free people within the Turkish Republic. Öcalan was indicted in April 1999 and charged with activities carried out for the purpose of bringing about the secession of part of the national territory. The Turkish government sought the death penalty.

When the criminal proceedings against Öcalan began, the Turkish Constitution provided that state security courts were to be composed of a president, two other full members, and two substitute members. The president of the State Security Court, one of the full members, and one of the substitute members were to be civilian judges, and the other full member and substitute member were to be military judges. In June 1999, Turkey's Grand National Assembly amended Turkey's Constitution and laws to exclude military judges from state security courts. This amendment took effect while the criminal proceedings against Öcalan were already underway. At a hearing on June 23, 1999 the judge who had been appointed to replace the military judge sat as a member of Öcalan's trial court for the first time. The Security Court noted that the new judge had already read the file and the transcripts, in accordance with the Turkish Code of Criminal Procedure, and had followed the proceedings from the outset and attended the hearings.

On June 29, 1999, the Security Court found Öcalan guilty of carrying out acts designed to bring about the secession of part of Turkey's territory and of training and leading a gang of armed terrorists for that purpose. It sentenced Öcalan to death, finding that he was the founder and principal leader of an organization, the PKK, whose aim was to detach a part of the territory of the Republic of Turkey so as to form a Kurdish State with a political regime based on Marxist-Leninist ideology.

In February 1999, Öcalan filed a complaint (application) against the Republic of Turkey before the ECHR alleging that Turkey had violated a variety of European Convention provisions in the course of arresting him, detaining him, trying him, and sentencing him to death. For present purposes, the most pertinent claims were that Turkey had violated Articles 2 (right to life), 3 (prohibition of ill treatment), 6 (right to a fair trial), and 14 (prohibition of discrimination).

Two years later, in October 2001, the Turkish Constitution was amended so that the death penalty could no longer be ordered or implemented other than in time of war, in time of imminent threat of war, or for acts of terrorism. As a result of the amendment, a prisoner whose death sentence for an act of terrorism had been commuted to life imprisonment was required to spend the rest of his life in prison. In October 2002, the Security Court commuted Öcalan's death sentence to life imprisonment.

Öcalan's application was first heard by an ECHR Chambers consisting of seven judges. See European Convention art. 27(1). That Chambers issued its judgment on March 12, 2003, holding, inter alia, that Turkey had violated various provisions of the European Convention, including:

(1) Article 6, §1 because Öcalan had not been tried by an independent and impartial tribunal by virtue of the participation of a military judge in part of the proceedings against him;
(2) Article 6, §1, taken together with Article 6, §3(b) and (c), in that Öcalan had not had a fair trial due to restrictions on his ability to communicate with his lawyers outside of the hearing of third parties, restrictions on access to counsel and counsel visits, and improper restrictions on counsel's timely access to the case file; and
(3) Article 3 on account of the imposition of the death penalty following an unfair trial.

The Chambers also ruled, however, that Turkey had not violated Article 2, or Article 14 taken together with Article 2, as regards the implementation of the death penalty and that there had been no violation of Article 3 as regards the implementation of the death penalty.

At the government's request and pursuant to a chamber's referral, the case was then heard by the ECHR's Grand Chambers — the rough equivalent to a U.S. federal appellate court's grant of a rehearing en banc. See European Convention arts. 27 and 43. The Grand Chambers issued its judgment on May 12, 2005, ruling for Öcalan on the ground that Turkey violated Article 2 of the European Convention by imposing the death penalty following an unfair trial.

The following language is the important part of the opinion for our purposes:

> 162. The Court must first address the applicant's submission that the practice of the Contracting States in this area can be taken as establishing an agreement to abrogate the exception provided for in the second sentence of Article 2 §1, which explicitly permits capital punishment under certain conditions. In practice, if Article 2 is to be read as permitting capital punishment, notwithstanding the almost universal abolition of the death penalty in Europe, Article 3 cannot be interpreted as prohibiting the death penalty since that would nullify the clear wording of Article 2 §1 (see Soering v. the United Kingdom, judgment of 7 July 1989, Series A no. 161, §103).
>
> 163. The Grand Chamber agrees with the following conclusions of the Chamber on this point (see paragraphs 189-196 of the Chamber judgment):
>
>> . . . the Court must first address the applicant's submission that the practice of the Contracting States in this area can be taken as establishing an agreement to abrogate the exception provided for in the second sentence of Article 2 §1, which explicitly permits capital punishment under certain conditions.
>>
>> . . . The Court reiterates that it must be mindful of the Convention's special character as a human-rights treaty and that the Convention cannot be interpreted in a vacuum. It should so far as possible be interpreted in harmony with other rules of public international law of which it forms part. It must, however, confine its

primary attention to the issues of interpretation and application of the provisions of the Convention which arise in the present case.

. . . It is recalled that the Court accepted in its *Soering v. the United Kingdom* judgment that an established practice within the Member States could give rise to an amendment of the Convention. In that case the Court accepted that subsequent practice in national penal policy, in the form of a generalised abolition of capital punishment, could be taken as establishing the agreement of the Contracting States to abrogate the exception provided for under Article 2 §1 and hence remove a textual limit on the scope for evolutive interpretation of Article 3 (see the above-cited judgment, §103). It was found, however, that Protocol No. 6 showed that the intention of the States was to adopt the normal method of amendment of the text in order to introduce a new obligation to abolish capital punishment in time of peace and to do so by an optional instrument allowing each State to choose the moment when to undertake such an engagement. The Court accordingly concluded that Article 3 could not be interpreted as generally prohibiting the death penalty (ibid. §§103-104).

. . . The applicant takes issue with the Court's approach in the *Soering* judgment. His principal submission was that the reasoning is flawed since Protocol No. 6 represents merely one yardstick by which the practice of the States may be measured and that the evidence shows that all members of the Council of Europe have, either de facto or de jure, effected total abolition of the death penalty for all crimes and in all circumstances. He contended that as a matter of legal theory there was no reason why the States should not be capable of abolishing the death penalty both by abrogating the right to rely on the second sentence of Article 2 §1 through their practice and by formal recognition of that process in the ratification of Protocol No. 6.

. . . The Court reiterates that the Convention is a living instrument which must be interpreted in the light of present-day conditions and that the increasingly high standard being required in the area of the protection of human rights and fundamental liberties correspondingly and inevitably requires greater firmness in assessing breaches of the fundamental values of democratic societies.

. . . It reiterates that in assessing whether a given treatment or punishment is to be regarded as inhuman or degrading for the purposes of Article 3 it cannot but be influenced by the developments and commonly accepted standards in the penal policy of the member States of the Council of Europe in this field (see *Soering*, judgment cited above, §102). Moreover, the concepts of inhuman and degrading treatment and punishment have evolved considerably since the Convention came into force in 1950 and indeed since the Court's *Soering v. the United Kingdom* judgment in 1989.

. . . Equally the Court observes that the legal position as regards the death penalty has undergone a considerable evolution since the *Soering* case was decided. The de facto abolition noted in that case in respect of twenty-two Contracting States in 1989 has developed into a de jure abolition in forty-three of the forty-four Contracting States and a moratorium in the remaining State which has not yet abolished the penalty, namely Russia. This almost complete abandonment of the death penalty in times of peace in Europe is reflected in the fact that all the Contracting States have signed Protocol No. 6 and forty-one States have ratified it, that is to say, all except Turkey, Armenia and Russia. It is further reflected in the policy of the Council of Europe which requires that new member States undertake to abolish capital punishment as a condition of their admission into the organisation. As a result of these developments the territories encompassed by the member States of the Council of Europe have become a zone free of capital punishment.

. . . Such a marked development could now be taken as signalling the agreement of the Contracting States to abrogate, or at the very least to modify, the second sentence of Article 2 §1, particularly when regard is had to the fact that all

Contracting States have now signed Protocol No. 6 and that it has been ratified by forty-one States. It may be questioned whether it is necessary to await ratification of Protocol No. 6 by the three remaining States before concluding that the death penalty exception in Article 2 has been significantly modified. Against such a consistent background, it can be said that capital punishment in peacetime has come to be regarded as an unacceptable . . . form of punishment which is no longer permissible under Article 2.

164. The Court notes that by opening for signature Protocol No. 13 concerning the abolition of the death penalty in all circumstances the Contracting States have chosen the traditional method of amendment of the text of the Convention in pursuit of their policy of abolition. At the date of this judgment, three member States have not signed this Protocol and sixteen have yet to ratify it. However, this final step toward complete abolition of the death penalty—that is to say both in times of peace and in times of war—can be seen as confirmation of the abolitionist trend in the practice of the Contracting States. It does not necessarily run counter to the view that Article 2 has been amended in so far as it permits the death penalty in times of peace.

165. For the time being, the fact that there are still a large number of States who have yet to sign or ratify Protocol No. 13 may prevent the Court from finding that it is the established practice of the Contracting States to regard the implementation of the death penalty as inhuman and degrading treatment contrary to Article 3 of the Convention, since no derogation may be made from that provision, even in times of war. However, the Grand Chamber agrees with the Chamber that it is not necessary for the Court to reach any firm conclusion on these points since, for the following reasons, it would be contrary to the Convention, even if Article 2 were to be construed as still permitting the death penalty, to implement a death sentence following an unfair trial.

Note that, at the time of the events being reviewed in *Öcalan*, Turkey had not yet ratified Protocol No. 6. Turkey has subsequently ratified that Protocol. Would the ECHR's analysis have differed had Turkey been a party to the Protocol at the time of the relevant events?

8. The ECHR explained the status quo in Case of Bader and Others v. Sweden, no. 13284/04, 2005-XI Eur. Ct. H.R., §42, in which the Court characterized its reasoning in *Öcalan* as follows:

The Grand Chamber abstained from reaching any firm conclusion as to whether Article 2 of the Convention could be considered to have been amended so as to prohibit the death penalty in all circumstances (ibid. §165). Meanwhile, it considered that it would be contrary to the Convention, even if Article 2 were to be construed as still permitting the death penalty, to implement a death sentence following an unfair trial as an arbitrary deprivation of life was prohibited (ibid. §165).

a.   Comparing U.S. Constitutional "Evolving Norms" Jurisprudence

If the European Convention is treated as having "quasi-constitutional" status for interpretive purposes, is what the ECHR does in *Soering* akin to the type of interpretation used by the U.S. Supreme Court in interpreting the U.S. Constitution? The U.S. Supreme Court focuses on "evolving" norms when determining the content of the prohibition on "cruel and unusual" punishment contained in the Eighth Amendment to the U.S. Constitution. For example, in *Atkins v. Virginia*,[21] the Court held that

---

21. 536 U.S. 304 (2002).

the Eighth Amendment barred executions of "mentally retarded" criminals. In so doing, the Court emphasized that "[t]he basic concept underlying the Eighth Amendment is nothing less than the dignity of man. . . . The Amendment must draw its meaning from the evolving standards of decency that mark the progress of a maturing society."[22] But how are such "evolving standards" determined as a practical matter? The *Atkins* Court explained:

> Proportionality review under those evolving standards should be informed by "objective factors to the maximum possible extent." We have pinpointed that the "clearest and most reliable objective evidence of contemporary values is the legislation enacted by the country's legislatures." . . . [O]bjective evidence, though of great importance, [does] not "wholly determine" the controversy, "for the Constitution contemplates that in the end our own judgment will be brought to bear on the question of the acceptability of the death penalty under the Eighth Amendment."[23]

Chief Justice Rehnquist dissented, and in so doing took the *Atkins* majority to task for what he found to be their reliance on insufficiently "objective" sources in conducting their proportionality review:

> In my view, . . . two sources — the work product of legislatures and sentencing jury determinations — ought to be the sole indicators by which courts ascertain the contemporary American conceptions of decency for purposes of the Eighth Amendment. They are the only objective indicia of contemporary values firmly supported by our precedents. More importantly, however, they can be reconciled with the undeniable precepts that the democratic branches of government and individual sentencing juries are, by design, better suited than courts to evaluating and giving effect to the complex societal and moral considerations that inform the publicly acceptable criminal punishments.
>
> In reaching its conclusion today, the Court does not take notice of the fact that neither petitioner nor his amici have adduced any comprehensive statistics that would conclusively prove (or disprove) whether juries routinely consider death a disproportionate punishment for mentally retarded offenders like petitioner. Instead, it adverts to the fact that other countries have disapproved the imposition of the death penalty for crimes committed by mentally retarded offenders. I fail to see, however, how the views of other countries regarding the punishment of their citizens provide any support for the Court's ultimate determination. While it is true that some of our prior opinions looked to "the climate of international opinion" to reinforce a conclusion regarding evolving standards of decency, we have since explicitly rejected the idea that the sentencing practices of other countries could "serve to establish the first Eighth Amendment prerequisite, that [a] practice is accepted among our people."[24]

Justice Scalia also penned a scathing dissent, in which he awarded the "Prize for the Court's Most Feeble Effort to fabricate 'national consensus' " to the majority's reliance, inter alia, on the views of "members of the so-called 'world community.' "[25] He asserted that the "practices of the 'world community,' whose notions of justice are (thankfully) not always those of our people," were "irrelevant."[26]

---

22. Id. at 311-312 (quoting Trop v. Dulles, 356 U.S. 86 (1958)).
23. Id. at 312-313.
24. Id. at 324-325 (Rehnquist, J., dissenting).
25. Id. at 347 (Scalia, J., dissenting).
26. Id.

Similarly, in *Roper v. Simmons*,[27] the U.S. Supreme Court held that the death penalty could no longer be imposed for crimes committed when the defendant was under the age of 18. In *Atkins*, the Court had referred to the views of the world community only in a sentence in a footnote. The *Roper* Court, by contrast, devoted a short section of its opinion to the question:

Our determination that the death penalty is disproportionate punishment for offenders under 18 finds confirmation in the stark reality that the United States is the only country in the world that continues to give official sanction to the juvenile death penalty. This reality does not become controlling, for the task of interpreting the Eighth Amendment remains our responsibility. Yet at least from the time of the Court's decision in [Trop v. Dulles, 356 U.S. 86 (1958)], the Court has referred to the laws of other countries and to international authorities as instructive for its interpretation of the Eighth Amendment's prohibition of "cruel and unusual punishments."

As respondent and a number of amici emphasize, Article 37 of the United Nations Convention on the Rights of the Child, which every country in the world has ratified save for the United States and Somalia, contains an express prohibition on capital punishment for crimes committed by juveniles under 18. United Nations Convention on the Rights of the Child, art. 37, Nov. 20, 1989, 1577 U.N.T.S. 3 (entered into force Sept. 2, 1990). No ratifying country has entered a reservation to the provision prohibiting the execution of juvenile offenders. Parallel prohibitions are contained in other significant international covenants. See ICCPR, art. 6(5), Dec. 16, 1966, 999 U.N.T.S., at 175 (prohibiting capital punishment for anyone under 18 at the time of offense) (signed and ratified by the United States subject to a reservation regarding Article 6(5)); American Convention on Human Rights: Pact of San Jose, Costa Rica, art. 4(5), Nov. 22, 1969, 1144 U.N.T.S. 146 (entered into force July 19, 1978) (same); African Charter on the Rights and Welfare of the Child, art. 5(3), OAU Doc. CAB/LEG/24.9/49 (1990) (entered into force Nov. 29, 1999) (same).

Respondent and his amici have submitted, and petitioner does not contest, that only seven countries other than the United States have executed juvenile offenders since 1990: Iran, Pakistan, Saudi Arabia, Yemen, Nigeria, the Democratic Republic of Congo, and China. Since then each of these countries has either abolished capital punishment for juveniles or made public disavowal of the practice. In sum, it is fair to say that the United States now stands alone in a world that has turned its face against the juvenile death penalty.

Though the international covenants prohibiting the juvenile death penalty are of more recent date, it is instructive to note that the United Kingdom abolished the juvenile death penalty before these covenants came into being. The United Kingdom's experience bears particular relevance here in light of the historic ties between our countries and in light of the Eighth Amendment's own origins. The Amendment was modeled on a parallel provision in the English Declaration of Rights of 1689, which provided: "[E]xcessive Bail ought not to be required nor excessive Fines imposed; nor cruel and unusual Punishments inflicted." As of now, the United Kingdom has abolished the death penalty in its entirety; but, decades before it took this step, it recognized the disproportionate nature of the juvenile death penalty; and it abolished that penalty as a separate matter. In 1930 an official committee recommended that the minimum age for execution be raised to 21. Parliament then enacted the Children and Young Person's Act of 1933, which prevented execution of those aged 18 at the date of the sentence. And in 1948, Parliament enacted the Criminal Justice Act, prohibiting the execution of any person under 18 at the time of the offense. In the 56 years that have passed since the United Kingdom abolished the juvenile death penalty, the weight of authority against it there, and in the international community, has become well established.

---

27. 543 U.S. 551 (2005).

It is proper that we acknowledge the overwhelming weight of international opinion against the juvenile death penalty, resting in large part on the understanding that the instability and emotional imbalance of young people may often be a factor in the crime. The opinion of the world community, while not controlling our outcome, does provide respected and significant confirmation for our own conclusions.[28]

Justice O'Connor, who dissented on the constitutionality of the death penalty, defended the Court's use of comparative and international legal materials:

Over the course of nearly half a century, the Court has consistently referred to foreign and international law as relevant to its assessment of evolving standards of decency. This inquiry reflects the special character of the Eighth Amendment, which, as the Court has long held, draws its meaning directly from the maturing values of civilized society. Obviously, American law is distinctive in many respects, not least where the specific provisions of our Constitution and the history of its exposition so dictate. But this Nation's evolving understanding of human dignity certainly is neither wholly isolated from, nor inherently at odds with, the values prevailing in other countries. On the contrary, we should not be surprised to find congruence between domestic and international values, especially where the international community has reached clear agreement—expressed in international law or in the domestic laws of individual countries—that a particular form of punishment is inconsistent with fundamental human rights. At least, the existence of an international consensus of this nature can serve to confirm the reasonableness of a consonant and genuine American consensus.[29]

Justice Scalia, also in dissent in *Roper*, once again argued that such uses were illegitimate:

Because I do not believe that the meaning of our Eighth Amendment, any more than the meaning of other provisions of our Constitution, should be determined by the subjective views of five Members of this Court and like-minded foreigners, I dissent. . . .

The Court begins by noting that "Article 37 of the United Nations Convention on the Rights of the Child, which every country in the world has ratified *save for the United States* and Somalia, contains an express prohibition on capital punishment for crimes committed by juveniles under 18." Ante (emphasis added). The Court also discusses the [ICCPR], which the Senate ratified only subject to a reservation that reads:

The United States reserves the right, subject to its Constitutional restraints, to impose capital punishment on any person (other than a pregnant woman) duly convicted under existing or future laws permitting the imposition of capital punishment, including such punishment for crime committed by persons below eighteen years of age.

Unless the Court has added to its arsenal the power to join and ratify treaties on behalf of the United States, I cannot see how this evidence favors, rather than refutes, its position. That the Senate and the President—those actors our Constitution empowers to enter into treaties—have declined to join and ratify treaties prohibiting execution of under-18 offenders can only suggest that *our country* has either not reached a national consensus on the question, or has reached a national consensus contrary to what the Court announces. . . .

More fundamentally, however, the basic premise of the Court's argument—that American law should conform to the laws of the rest of the world—ought to be rejected out of hand. In fact the Court itself does not believe it. In many significant respects the

---

28. *Roper*, 543 U.S. at 575-578.
29. Id. at 604-605 (O'Connor, J., dissenting).

laws of most other countries differ from our law—including not only such explicit provisions of our Constitution as the right to jury trial and grand jury indictment, but even many interpretations of the Constitution prescribed by this Court itself. The Court-pronounced exclusionary rule, for example, is distinctively American. When we adopted that rule in Mapp v. Ohio, 367 U.S. 643, 655 (1961), it was "unique to American Jurisprudence." Since then a categorical exclusionary rule has been "universally rejected" by other countries [citing English, Canadian and ECHR sources].

The Court has been oblivious to the views of other countries when deciding how to interpret our Constitution's requirement that "Congress shall make no law respecting an establishment of religion. . . ." Amdt. 1. Most other countries—including those committed to religious neutrality—do not insist on the degree of separation between church and state that this Court requires. . . .

And let us not forget the Court's abortion jurisprudence, which makes us one of only six countries that allow abortion on demand until the point of viability. . . .

The Court's special reliance on the laws of the United Kingdom is perhaps the most indefensible part of its opinion. . . . It is beyond comprehension why we should look . . . to a country that has developed, in the centuries since the Revolutionary War—and with increasing speed since the United Kingdom's recent submission to the jurisprudence of European courts dominated by continental jurists—a legal, political, and social culture quite different from our own. If we took the Court's directive seriously, we would also consider relaxing our double jeopardy prohibition, since the British Law Commission recently published a report that would significantly extend the rights of the prosecution to appeal cases where an acquittal was the result of a judge's ruling that was legally incorrect. . . .

The Court should either profess its willingness to reconsider all these matters in light of the views of foreigners, or else it should cease putting forth foreigners' views as part of the *reasoned* basis of its decisions. To invoke alien law when it agrees with one's own thinking, and ignore it otherwise, is not reasoned decisionmaking, but sophistry.[30]

Note, finally, that in the U.S. Supreme Court's latest relevant case, *Kennedy v. Louisiana*,[31] the Court held that the Eighth Amendment prohibits the death penalty for the rape of a child where the crime did not result, and was not intended to result, in death. In so holding, the Court relied on a "national consensus" (revealed, inter alia, in a survey of U.S. state statutes and practices) and its own "independent judgment" about the consistency of that punishment with "evolving standards of decency." The Court did not refer to international sources or practices at all in its opinion, although international law standards had been briefed.

In light of the opinions in *Roper*, would you expect the United States Supreme Court to follow ECHR decisions on the legality of the death penalty? If not, why is the dissent so concerned about reference to "foreign" law? Should the views of the "world community" be excluded from the determination of "evolving standards," as Justice Scalia argues? Does the *Soering* opinion address the question? How does the ECHR go about isolating "evolving standards"? Does it rely on "objective" evidence?

b. The Role of Judges

Justice Scalia charged in his dissent in *Atkins*: "Seldom has an opinion of this Court rested so obviously upon nothing but the personal views of its Members."[32]

---

30. Id. at 608, 622-627 (Scalia, J., dissenting).
31. 128 S. Ct. 2641 (2008).
32. 536 U.S. at 338 (Scalia, J., dissenting).

Justice Scalia's objection to his colleagues' reliance on their "personal views" is founded in the nature of the U.S. Constitution and the U.S. democratic system. U.S. law students will recall the debate about the "countermajoritarian difficulty" presented by U.S. Supreme Court review of decisions of the political branches. In a nutshell, "[o]ne of the most important dilemmas in American constitutional law arises from the tension between the basic principle that the Constitution reposes sovereign authority in the people, who elect their representatives, and the (perhaps) competing principle that the Constitution itself defeats democratic efforts by the public to proceed in one or another direction" by investing the Supreme Court with the power to invalidate as unconstitutional state and federal legislative efforts.[33] Does the ECHR face a similar "difficulty"? Consider the following notes.

NOTES

1. Under Articles 20-23 of Protocol 11 to the European Convention, there is one judge for (and usually from) each of the Convention's states parties. The judges are elected by the Parliamentary Assembly of the Council of Europe, sit for six-year terms, and may be reelected. The ECHR is clearly meant to be representative of states parties, but is it meant to be "politically accountable"?

2. When the United Kingdom signed on to the European Convention, was it foreseeable, especially in light of Article 2, that Article 3's prohibition would be interpreted to prohibit extradition to a state that might impose the death penalty? Note that before the application of human rights conventions such as the European Convention in the extradition context, criminal suspects had very few rights with which to challenge their extradition. Many states, moreover, still apply the doctrine of non-inquiry in extradition cases; this doctrine (embraced, among others, by the U.S. courts) dictates that the courts of the requested state cannot review the judicial and penal circumstances of the requesting state at the suspect's request. Any inquiry into such circumstances is viewed as the job of the executive branch, which is entrusted with the final discretionary decision regarding extradition after courts have determined that a suspect is legally extraditable. *Soering*, then, must be considered against this long-standing judicial practice of refusing to second-guess the extradition judgments of the executive, particularly at the behest of a defendant seeking to challenge the fairness of the process or punishment likely to be given him in the requesting state.

3. In this context, might a decision by a *court*, here the ECHR, that countermands sovereign choices — reflected in treaty language and settled extradition practice — in aid of "evolving norms" among the states parties raise the hackles of those committed to the Westphalian model? One could argue that the ECHR's "difficulty," if it has one, then, should be characterized as a "sovereignty difficulty" — that is, some might argue that relying on subjective norms constitutes "rulemaking" that impinges on the sovereign choices of the states parties. Does the ECHR in fact face such a "sovereignty difficulty"? Consider Professor Janis's explanation of the perceived role of judges in international tribunals:

> . . . Article 38(1)(d) of the Statute of the International Court of Justice lists "judicial decisions and the teachings of the most highly qualified publicists of the various nations,

---

33. Geoffrey R. Stone, Louis M. Seidman, Cass R. Sunstein, & Mark V. Tushnet, Constitutional Law 35-36, 39 (4th ed. 2001).

as subsidiary means for the determination of rules of law." Given their classification as "subsidiary means" and because Article 38 lists international conventions, international custom, and the general principles of law ahead of judicial decisions and the opinion of publicists, it is often suggested that the most important modern role for judges and scholars is collecting the data necessary to establish or explicate rules drawn from the other three (and implicitly higher) sources of international law. . . . Only somewhat less generally accepted than the judges' and scholars' role as a cumulator is their role as evaluator [of the state of the law at any given time.] . . . A third role for decisions and doctrine is what one might call aspirational. Here the judge or scholar frames a rule or some principle of international law in the belief that it ought to be adopted. . . . Probably the judge's and scholar's most controversial function in international law has to do with rule formation, the role that most impinges upon the power of sovereign states. For those positivists who believe that only states create international legal rules, the very idea that individuals may contribute to the making of an international law may be heresy. . . .

Reprinted/adapted with the permission of Aspen Publishers from Mark W. Janis, An Introduction to International Law, Third edition, pp. 80-81, copyright ©1999. Although the idea of judges as makers of law may seem familiar in common law countries, in the countries operating under civil law "there has been much more suspicion of the powers of judges. Based, in part, on the role of judges in the ancien regime in France, civil lawyers assign formal rulemaking powers only to the legislature." Id. at 82. At least in theory, then, civil lawyers "look askance at the notion that a judge can make rules of law." Id.

4. In the United States, there has been an outpouring of scholarship on the question of how constitutional text ought to be interpreted—in part in reaction to the "countermajoritarian difficulty." For example, "[i]t is sometimes suggested that the meaning of a constitutional provision should be ascertained by reference to its original meaning, or the intent of the framers and ratifiers. Perhaps the original understanding can discipline the judges and diminish the democratic problems posed by judicial review; perhaps the original understanding can make interpretation more mechanical and rule-like, and also minimize judicial discretion." Geoffrey R. Stone, Louis M. Seidman, Cass R. Sunstein, & Mark V. Tushnet, Constitutional Law 38 (4th ed. 2001). If the ECHR has its own "countermajoritarian difficulty," might this type of interpretive approach satisfy its critics?

3.   The Next Frontier? Life Without Parole

A number of countries, such as Venezuela and Costa Rica, have prohibited life imprisonment in their constitutions, and in other countries, such as Peru, courts have found that provisions for life imprisonment without possibility of parole were unconstitutional.[34] Other constitutions, including those of Ecuador and Uruguay, do not expressly address life imprisonment but provide that the purpose of the penitentiary system is education or rehabilitation, which is believed by some scholars to form a basis to invalidate a life sentence without possibility of parole. In Canada, where only the national government has jurisdiction over serious crime, by statute sentences for life imprisonment authorize consideration for parole release after 25 years.[35]

---

34. This paragraph is based on Dirk Van Zyl Smit, Life Imprisonment as the Ultimate Penalty in International Law: A Human Rights Perspective, 9 Crim. L.F. 5, 26-45 (1999), and Rodrigo Labardini, Life Imprisonment and Extradition, Historical Development, International Context and the Current Situation in Mexico and the United States, 11 Sw. J.L. & Trade Am. 1, 2-3, 27-34 (2005).

35. See Labardini, supra note 34, at 24.

In Europe, many countries simply do not authorize a sentence of life in prison without parole. Norway abolished life imprisonment in 1981; Portugal also abolished life without parole.[36]

Restrictions on sentences of life imprisonment have the potential to seriously disrupt extradition relationships. For example, several of Venezuela's bilateral treaties deny extradition unless assurances are provided that life imprisonment will not be sought or imposed; Costa Rica will not extradite without assurances that neither the death penalty nor life imprisonment will be sought. Spain has prohibited life imprisonment since the 1980s but will extradite to other countries that impose life in prison, provided the sentence is reviewable after some time.

Viewed from the perspective of the U.S. government, the most serious situation was presented by Mexico. The Mexican Supreme Court in 2001 ruled that life in prison is unconstitutional and held further that a state requesting extradition would need to provide assurances that life in prison (without parole) would not be imposed. This ruling proved a major concern affecting many requests for extradition from the United States.[37] In 2005, however, the Mexican Court upheld the constitutionality of what were, in effect, life sentences (a term of 105 years before eligibility for parole).[38]

Finally, consider the case of Germany. At the center of German Basic Law's constitutional scheme of values is human dignity: Article I(1) states: "The dignity of man is inviolable. To respect and protect it is the duty of all state authority." The German Constitutional Court, in 1977, held that life in prison could be compatible with human dignity only if the prisoner retained a concrete expectation of eventually being released. Consider the following excerpted (and translated) version of its reasoning.

DONALD P. KOMMERS, THE CONSTITUTIONAL JURISPRUDENCE OF THE FEDERAL REPUBLIC OF GERMANY
314-319 (2d ed. 1997)
(translation of the Life Imprisonment Case (1977), 45 BVerfGE 187)

Life imprisonment has for ages been at the core of criminal sanctions. Its significance in modern times has decreased because the death penalty is now the harshest penalty. The dispute over the death penalty has made life imprisonment an alternative the constitutionality of which has not generally been questioned. A substantial amount of older literature has examined in depth the effect and consequences of life imprisonment on the human personality. Advocates of the death penalty advance the argument that life imprisonment is a more cruel and inhuman punishment than the death penalty. . . .

. . . [Although the framers of the Basic Law may have contemplated that, in abolishing the death penalty, life imprisonment would serve as a substitute penalty,] [t]his determination . . . does not clearly decide the constitutional issue before use. Neither the original history nor the ideas and intentions of the framers are of decisive importance in interpreting particular provisions of the Basic Law. Since the adoption of the Basic Law, our understanding of the content, function and effect of basic rights has

---

36. See id. at 33.
37. See id. at 48-58.
38. See Francisco J. Ortega, Note, De Facto Life Imprisonment in Mexico and the U.S.-Mexico Extradition Treaty of 1978, 24 Wis. Intl. L.J. 1017 (2007).

deepened. Additionally, the medical, psychological and sociological effects of life imprisonment have become better known. Current attitudes are important in assessing the constitutionality of life imprisonment. New insights can influence and even change the evaluation of this punishment in terms of human dignity and the principles of a constitutional state.

. . . The constitutional principles of the Basic Law embrace the respect and protection of human dignity. The free human person and his dignity are the highest values of the constitutional order. The state in all its forms is obliged to respect and defend it. This is based on the conception of man as a spiritual-moral being endowed with the freedom to determine and develop himself. . . . The individual must allow those limits on his freedom of action that the legislature deems necessary in the interests of the community's social life; yet the autonomy of the individual has to be protected. This means that [the state] must regard every individual within society with equal worth. It is contrary to human dignity to make persons the mere tools of the state. The principle that "each person must shape his own life" applies unreservedly to all areas of law; the intrinsic dignity of each person depends on his status as an independent personality. . . . Every [criminal] punishment must justly relate to the severity of the offense and the guilt of the offender. Respect for human dignity especially requires the prohibition of cruel, inhuman and degrading punishments. [The state] cannot turn the offender into an object of crime prevention to the detriment of his constitutionally protected right to social worth and respect. [It] must preserve the underlying assumptions governing the individual and the social existence of the human person. Thus Article 1 (1) [human dignity] considered in tandem with the principle of the state based on social justice requires the state to guarantee that minimal existence — especially in the execution of criminal penalties — necessary for a life worthy of a human being. If human dignity is understood in this way, it would be intolerable for the state forcefully to deprive a person of his freedom without at least providing him with the chance to ever again regain this freedom. . . .

. . . [A] humane enforcement of life imprisonment is possible only when the prisoner is given a concrete and realistically attainable chance to regain his freedom at some later point in time; the state strikes at the very heart of human dignity if [it] treats the prisoner without regard to the development of his personality and strips him of all hope of ever earning his freedom. . . .

NOTES AND QUESTIONS

1. The German Court went on to uphold a sentence of life imprisonment for "wanton" murder, provided that there was an individualized consideration of the particular prisoner's situation in terms of his capacity for rehabilitation and a concrete and regularized possibility of regaining freedom. Subsequent legislation establishing 15-year minimum terms before a life sentence could be considered for parole was upheld by the German Constitutional Court. But its later case law made clear that even those sentenced for the most heinous of crimes (sending 50 persons, including children and pregnant women, to death in the gas chambers of Auschwitz, for example) must not be denied all hope of release, and the decision whether they should be released cannot depend only on the gravity of the crime but must also consider the "personality, age and prison record of the offender." Kommers, supra, at 321.

2. What effect are such domestic rulings likely to have in any future litigation before the ECHR? Is life imprisonment — and particularly life without possibility

of parole — "torture or . . . inhuman or degrading treatment or punishment" within the meaning of Article 3 of the European Convention? Could it be said to deprive the prisoner of his "right to life" under Article 2?

B. CONSULAR NOTIFICATION AND THE DEATH PENALTY: THE EFFECT OF TREATY RIGHTS ON DOMESTIC CRIMINAL PROCESSES IN THE UNITED STATES

In *Soering*, one sees not only the influence of individual human rights on the transnational administration of criminal law, but also a willingness by those charged with enforcing international rights covenants to give such rights precedence over the traditional authority of states to make extradition decisions. While *Soering* limits a core state function — extradition — it does not involve the application of human rights obligations to domestic processes of criminal law enforcement. That is, although it inherently involves a decision that the U.S. states' penal regime would impose "degrading" or "inhuman" treatment on those sought to be extradited, it does not purport to directly tell the U.S. states how they *must* as a matter of international law process their cases.

The "consular notification" cases that follow do not involve a human rights treaty per se, but they do involve international efforts to enforce international individual rights, derived again from treaty obligations, to domestic processes of criminal prosecution. For example, in one of these cases, the ICJ found the United States in violation of an ICJ order by virtue of the defaults of the U.S. Supreme Court, the U.S. solicitor general, and the governor of Arizona — all of whom contended that they were acting consistently with what they determined to be the United States' international obligations as well as the U.S. Constitution and applicable federal and U.S. state statutes. Accordingly, one could say that these cases cut even closer to the sovereignty bone. They also raise important questions regarding the place of international law in U.S. law and in the U.S. federal system, and the ability of states parties to international agreements, and their individual citizens, to enforce treaty rights in U.S. courts.

The Vienna Convention on Consular Relations (VCCR) is a multilateral treaty that has been ratified by 172 states. Unlike the European Convention at issue in the above cases, the VCCR is not primarily a human rights treaty. Rather, it is generally concerned with defining the role, powers, rights, privileges, and duties of consular officers representing one state party in the territory of another. The cases discussed within, however, are generally ones in which asserted VCCR "rights" are relied upon by foreign nationals who have been sentenced to death after a conviction in U.S. courts. The not-so-subtle subtext in much of this litigation, then, is that the VCCR claims are being used as a means of halting or postponing the execution of foreign nationals whose countries have abolished the death penalty and view capital punishment as a violation of basic human rights. The VCCR and its two protocols were ratified and entered into force for the United States in 1969.

The operative provision of the VCCR is Article 36 ("Communication and Contact with Nationals of the Sending State"). Article 36(1)(b) gives foreign nationals the right to request that consular officials of their home states be notified, without delay, whenever they are arrested or detained. Presumably to make meaningful this provision, Article 36(1)(b) also provides that, upon arrest, a foreign national must be informed of these rights, also without delay. Article 36(1)(c) provides that consular officers have the freedom to visit, correspond with, and arrange legal representation for their detained nationals. Finally, Article 36(2) provides that the "rights" provided for in Article 36 "shall be exercised in conformity with the laws and regulations of the receiving State, subject to the proviso, however, that the laws and regulations must enable full effect to be given to the purposes for which the rights accorded under this article are intended."

The United States proposed and subsequently ratified an Optional Protocol Concerning the Compulsory Settlement of Disputes. Article 1 of the Optional Protocol provides:

> Disputes arising out of the interpretation or application of the [Vienna] Convention shall lie within the compulsory jurisdiction of the International Court of Justice and may accordingly be brought before the Court by a written application made by any party to the dispute being a Party to the present Protocol.

Although this Optional Protocol was in effect during almost all the litigation involving the consular litigation issue examined within, U.S. Secretary of State Condoleezza Rice sent a letter to UN Secretary-General Kofi Annan on March 7, 2005, in which Secretary Rice advised the Secretary-General that the United States had decided to withdraw from the Optional Protocol giving the International Court of Justice (ICJ) jurisdiction to adjudicate disputes arising under the VCCR.

The VCCR protections may not seem so fundamental as to provoke the struggle between ICJ and the United States revealed in the following pages, but one can see why the Article 36 rights have substance. Posit a citizen of country A taken into custody in another state not renowned for its commitment to due process or fair treatment of country A's nationals; in such circumstances, the incarcerated citizen, and presumably her government, would place a premium on consular notification rights. Not surprisingly, then, the U.S. State Department has expressed the view that "Article 36 of the Vienna Convention contains obligations of the highest order and should not be dealt with lightly."[39]

Despite the United States' assurances of reciprocal treatment and professed interest in promoting compliance with Article 36, there have been many, *many* instances in which U.S. law enforcement authorities have failed to notify foreign nationals of their rights.[40] This default has occurred in U.S. federal and state cases of all types, and, as Professor John Quigley has explained,

> [a] failure to inform a foreign national of the right of consular access has been raised at different stages of the criminal process, and for different reasons. Foreign nationals who have made incriminating statements upon arrest have sought to suppress such statements for failure of the authorities to tell them, prior to interrogation, of the right of consular access. Some foreign nationals have raised a failure of notification as a reason to dismiss an indictment. Others have raised the issue at trial, as a bar to

---

39. Valerie Epps, Violations of the Vienna Convention on Consular Relations: Time for Remedies, 11 Williamette J. Intl L. & Dispute Res. 1, 11 (2004).

40. See, e.g., DPIC, Foreign Nationals and the Death Penalty in the United States, http://www .deathpenaltyinfo.org/foreign-nationals-and-death-penalty-us ("There is overwhelming evidence that prompt notification of these rights across the United States remains highly sporadic. . . . [For example,] official records produced by the plaintiff [in recent noncapital litigation] revealed that over 53,000 foreign nationals were arrested in New York City during 1997, but that the NYPD Alien Notification Log registered only 4 cases in which consulates were notified of those arrests — a failure rate well in excess of 99 per cent (even presuming that a majority of the detainees might have declined consular notification.)").

conviction. Still others have raised it on appeal or in [collateral attacks on a conviction after that conviction has become final due to the exhaustion of appellate remedies on direct review (habeas corpus proceedings)], as a reason to reverse a conviction. Many of the cases have involved capital sentences, and the foreign national seeks remission of the death sentence.[41]

The VCCR litigation raises at least two questions relevant to this chapter whose importance extends far beyond the VCCR: (1) Who can claim treaty "rights," and how can such rights be enforced in U.S. courts? (2) What effect does the decision of an international tribunal in litigation to which the United States is a party have in U.S. courts and U.S. state courts?

1.   Background on Federalism Issues Raised by Habeas Review

The subject matter of this chapter might not seem an obvious candidate for raising federalism issues. These materials, however, raise many interesting issues relating to the relationship between federal and U.S. state interests and powers, and the appropriate place of international law in the United States' federal system. A little background is in order, both to explain the genesis of the federalism problems and to prepare you for the issues discussed within.

Probably the most important reason that these "vertical" separation of powers issues arise in this context stems from the fact that criminal law enforcement is a function that traditionally was left to the U.S. states. Even though there has been an increasing "federalization" of crime, it is still true that approximately 95 percent of all U.S. criminal prosecutions take place in U.S. state courts, and the overwhelming number of death sentences imposed are the result of U.S. state prosecutions. Federal courts may, however, become involved in state criminal matters by virtue of their jurisdiction to hear the petitions of state prisoners for postconviction relief, commonly known as petitions for a writ of habeas corpus.

On habeas review, state prisoners may attack their state law convictions and/or sentences by asserting that they are in custody "in violation of the Constitution or laws or treaties of the United States."[42] Because such cases involve federal judges reviewing state judges' compliance with federal law, including federal trial court judges reviewing the decisions of the highest courts of the U.S. states, it is an area where federal-state tensions are inevitable. The U.S. Supreme Court, and the U.S. Congress in the Antiterrorism and Effective Death Penalty Act (AEDPA), have sought to abate these federalism tensions by restricting the availability of the habeas writ. One of the doctrines employed to do so is that of the "procedural default." A state prisoner seeking to litigate a claim on habeas before a federal court must have given the state courts a fair shot at remedying any alleged breach of federal law; accordingly, he must first raise and litigate the issue in state court. If he raises it for the first time on federal habeas review, he is deemed to have "procedurally defaulted" the claim unless he can excuse his default by showing "cause" (for his inability to raise the claim previously) and "prejudice." (Many states provide their own postconviction habeas-type remedies and apply the same types of procedural default bars in that forum as well.)

---

41. John Quigley, The Law of State Responsibility and the Right to Consular Access, 11 Willamette J. Intl. L. & Dispute Res. 39, 40 (2004).
42. 28 U.S.C. §§2241(c)(3), 2254.

2.   Enforcing Treaty "Rights" in U.S. Courts and the Force of ICJ Judgments

Under what circumstances can a treaty be said to create substantive "rights," flowing either to states parties or to individuals, enforceable in international fora or U.S. courts? The following notes explore these important questions, but first recognize that:

(1) We are potentially talking about (at least) two different types of "rights": the primary, *substantive* "right" (such as defendants' claimed "right" to VCCR notification) and a secondary "right" to *enforce* the primary right.
(2) Both rights (substantive and enforcement) might be claimed to exist — and to be enforceable — under either international or domestic law.
(3) There may be (at least) two categories of claimants to treaty rights — the states parties to the international agreement and their individual nationals.

With respect to states parties, there is usually no question that the states parties have primary, substantive rights under the international agreement vis-à-vis other states parties — the question is generally one of the appropriate forum for enforcement. The treaty with which we are presently concerned has an optional protocol providing for adjudication of controversies among states parties who join that protocol before the ICJ. The question raised for present purposes is whether the states parties can also pursue relief under domestic law.

As we know, individuals traditionally were not the "holders" of treaty rights. With the advent of, inter alia, the human rights movement, this has changed — and the change extends beyond classic human rights treaties to other types of treaties (like the VCCR) that arguably create primary, substantive rights flowing to individuals under international or domestic law. The question becomes, then, which treaties make individuals "the direct and intended beneficiaries of obligations imposed on states by international law."[43] Even if individuals are, as a matter of international or domestic law, deemed to have such primary rights, however, they are not necessarily guaranteed secondary enforcement rights under international or domestic law. Thus, as is true even under certain human rights regimes that do not provide for a forum for enforcement of claims, individuals may "lack the power to set in motion the machinery of international law for sanctioning violations of the obligations international law imposes."[44]

A good example is that posed in these cases. Article 34(1) of the ICJ Statute provides that "[o]nly states may be parties in cases before the Court." Thus, although the ICJ believes that individuals have "rights" under the VCCR, such persons are precluded by the ICJ's constituting statute from suing in the ICJ to enforce whatever rights they may claim under international law. Accordingly, while the ICJ may recognize individuals' primary rights under the VCCR, it is unable to provide secondary enforcement rights in its court to those individuals. The relative dearth of international enforcement mechanisms available to individuals (the notable exception being the ECHR), makes the availability of domestic law enforcement mechanisms even more critical.

The questions we will be pursuing in these materials deal with states parties' and individuals' primary substantive and secondary enforcement rights as a matter of U.S. law, in U.S. courts. That is, we will be evaluating whether states parties and individuals

---

43. Carlos Manuel Vázquez, Treaty-Based Rights and Remedies of Individuals, 92 Colum. L. Rev. 1082, 1087 (1992).
44. Id.

have "primary" rights created by the VCCR *under U.S. law* and whether the fact that a state party or individual has a "primary" right under international law guarantees that that person has, as a matter of *U.S. law,* a secondary right of enforcement *in U.S. courts.*

a.   U.S. Supreme Court: *Breard*

The U.S. Supreme Court first addressed VCCR Article 36 claims in *Breard v. Greene.*[45] Breard was a Paraguayan national who had been convicted and sentenced to death in Virginia state court. Breard raised his claim that his conviction and sentence should be overturned because of violations of VCCR Article 36 on federal habeas corpus review. The federal courts held that Breard had procedurally defaulted his Article 36 claim when he failed to raise it in state court, and that he could not demonstrate the cause and prejudice necessary to excuse his default. Accordingly, the federal courts rejected his habeas claim. Breard then petitioned the U.S. Supreme Court for certiorari.

The Republic of Paraguay, the Paraguayan ambassador to the United States, and the Paraguayan consul general to the United States also brought suit in federal court alleging that their rights under the VCCR had been violated. The Consul General added a claim under the civil rights statute, 42 U.S.C. §1983, alleging a denial of his rights under the VCCR. On April 3, 1998, the Republic of Paraguay also instituted proceedings against the United States in another forum — the ICJ — alleging that the United States violated the VCCR at the time of Breard's arrest.

Article 41 of the ICJ Statute authorizes the ICJ to "*indicate,* if it considers that circumstances so require, any provisional measures which ought to be taken to preserve the respective rights of either party" (emphasis added). It goes on to state that, pending the ICJ's final decision in a case in which measures have been "indicated," "notice of the measures suggested shall forthwith be given to the parties and to the Security Council."

On April 9, 1998, the ICJ noted jurisdiction in *Breard* and issued "provisional measures" requesting that the United States "take all measures at its disposal to ensure that Angel Francisco Breard is not executed pending the final decision in these proceedings. . . ." At that point, there was a significant question whether the ICJ's "provisional orders" were binding or simply advisory, and even whether the ICJ had the jurisdiction to issue them. The United States took the position that the "better argument" was that the order was not binding. Without hearing oral argument, the Supreme Court issued a brief per curiam decision denying any relief in *Breard,* reasoning, in part, as follows:

> It is clear that Breard procedurally defaulted his claim, if any, under the Vienna Convention by failing to raise that claim in the state courts. Nevertheless, in their petitions for certiorari, both Breard and Paraguay contend that Breard's Vienna Convention claim may be heard in federal court because the Convention is the "supreme law of the land" and thus trumps the procedural default doctrine. This argument is plainly incorrect. . . .
>
> . . . [W]hile we should give respectful consideration to the interpretation of an international treaty rendered by an international court with jurisdiction to interpret such, it has been recognized in international law that, absent a clear and express statement to the contrary, the procedural rules of the forum State govern the implementation

---

45. 523 U.S. 371 (1998) (per curiam).

of the treaty in that State. This proposition is embodied in the Vienna Convention itself, which provides that the rights expressed in the Convention "shall be exercised in conformity with the laws and regulations of the receiving State," provided that "said laws and regulations must enable full effect to be given to the purposes for which the rights accorded under this Article are intended." Article 36(2). It is the rule in this country that assertions of error in criminal proceedings must first be raised in state court in order to form the basis for relief in habeas. Claims not so raised are considered defaulted. By not asserting his Vienna Convention claim in state court, Breard failed to exercise his rights under the Vienna Convention in conformity with the laws of the United States and the Commonwealth of Virginia. Having failed to do so, he cannot raise a claim of violation of those rights now on federal habeas review. . . .

As for Paraguay's suits (both the original action and the case coming to us on petition for certiorari), neither the text nor the history of the Vienna Convention clearly provides a foreign nation a private right of action in United States' courts to set aside a criminal conviction and sentence for violation of consular notification provisions. The Eleventh Amendment provides a separate reason why Paraguay's suit might not succeed. That Amendment's "fundamental principle" that "the States, in the absence of consent, are immune from suits brought against them . . . by a foreign State" was enunciated in Principality of Monaco v. Mississippi, 292 U.S. 313, 329-330 (1934). Though Paraguay claims that its suit is within an exemption dealing with continuing consequences of past violations of federal rights, we do not agree. The failure to notify the Paraguayan Consul occurred long ago and has no continuing effect. . . .

Insofar as the Consul General seeks to base his claims on §1983, his suit is not cognizable. Section 1983 provides a cause of action to any "person within the jurisdiction" of the United States for the deprivation "of any rights, privileges, or immunities secured by the Constitution and laws." As an initial matter, it is clear that Paraguay is not authorized to bring suit under §1983. Paraguay is not a "person" as that term is used in §1983. Nor is Paraguay "within the jurisdiction" of the United States. And since the Consul General is acting only in his official capacity, he has no greater ability to proceed under §1983 than does the country he represents. Any rights that the Consul General might have by virtue of the Vienna Convention exist for the benefit of Paraguay, not for him as an individual. . . .

For the foregoing reasons, we deny the petition for an original writ of habeas corpus, the motion for leave to file a bill of complaint, the petitions for certiorari, and the accompanying stay applications filed by Breard and Paraguay.[46]

After the Supreme Court denied relief, Breard was executed. The United States apologized to Paraguay for its failure to abide by Article 36 in Breard's case, and Paraguay dismissed its ICJ action. Accordingly, the ICJ's take on the U.S. Supreme Court's interpretation of the VCCR awaited further litigation, this time between the United States and Germany.

b.   U.S. Supreme Court: *LaGrand*

Two German nationals — Karl and Walter LaGrand — were convicted and sentenced to death in Arizona. The LaGrand brothers had been raised almost entirely in the United States, and there was a real question just when the state authorities became aware that they were German nationals. In any case, they were not told of their Article 36 rights. The German government, once advised of the case after

---

46. Id. at 375-379.

conviction, made requests for clemency, which were denied as to Karl LaGrand, who was executed. The requests were not grounded on the consular notification violation.

On March 2, 1999 — the day before the scheduled execution of Walter LaGrand on March 3, 1999 — Germany filed an action in the ICJ. The ICJ issued *ex parte* provisional measures on the execution date, March 3, 1999. The first "provisional measure" issued by the ICJ read:

> The United States of America should take all measures at its disposal to ensure that Walter LaGrand is not executed pending the final decision in these proceedings, and should inform the Court of all the measures which it has taken in implementation of this Order.

The second measure required the government of the United States to "transmit this Order to the Governor of the State of Arizona." The U.S. solicitor general, in response, argued in the U.S. Supreme Court that the Vienna Convention "does not furnish a basis for this Court to grant a stay of execution," and "an order of the ICJ indicating provisional measures is not binding and does not furnish a basis for judicial relief."

In an order issued the same day, the U.S. Supreme Court declined to exercise its original jurisdiction in a suit filed by Germany against both the United States and the governor of Arizona. The Supreme Court, over the dissents of Justices Breyer and Stevens, declined to exercise jurisdiction to hear the case "[g]iven the tardiness of the pleas and the jurisdictional barriers they implicate."[47] In explaining these "imposing threshold barriers," the Supreme Court stated:

> First, it appears that the United States has not waived its sovereign immunity. Second, it is doubtful that Art. III, §2, cl. 2, provides an anchor for an action to prevent execution of a German citizen who is not an ambassador or consul. With respect to the action against the State of Arizona, as in Breard v. Greene, 523 U.S. 371, 377 (1998) (per curiam), a foreign government's ability here to assert a claim against a State is without evident support in the Vienna Convention and in probable contravention of Eleventh Amendment principles. This action was filed within only two hours of a scheduled execution that was ordered on January 15, 1999, based upon a sentence imposed by Arizona in 1984, about which the Federal Republic of Germany learned in 1992. . . .[48]

Walter LaGrand was executed two and one-half hours after the Supreme Court issued its decision.[49]

c. ICJ: *LaGrand*

Germany pursued the LaGrands' case before the ICJ, seeking, among other things, a determination that the United States violated the Geneva Convention by failing to notify the defendant and requesting further relief. The ICJ ruled as follows:

(1) The ICJ held the United States had "depriv[ed] Germany of the rights accorded it under Article 36, paragraph 1(a) and 1(c), and thus violated these provisions of the Convention."[50]

---

47. Federal Republic of Germany v. United States, 526 U.S. 111, 112 (1999) (per curiam).
48. Id. at 112.
49. Carlos Manuel Vázquez, Night and Day: *Coeur D'Alene, Breard,* and the Unraveling of the Prospective-Retrospective Distinction in Eleventh Amendment Doctrine, 87 Geo. L.J. 1, 6 & n.42 (1998).
50. The LaGrand Case (F.R.G. v. U.S.), 2001 I.C.J. 466, ¶73 (June 27).

(2) The ICJ then also held that *individuals*, as well as states parties such as Germany, may claim rights under the VCCR, reasoning:

> The Court notes that Article 36, paragraph 1(b), spells out the obligations the receiving State has towards the detained person and the sending State. It provides that, at the request of the detained person, the receiving State must inform the consular post of the sending State of the individual's detention "without delay." It provides further that any communication by the detained person addressed to the consular post of the sending State must be forwarded to it by authorities of the receiving State "without delay." Significantly, this subparagraph ends with the following language: "The said authorities shall inform the person concerned without delay of *his rights* under this subparagraph" (emphasis added). Moreover, under Article 36, paragraph 1 (c), the sending State's right to provide consular assistance to the detained person may not be exercised "if he expressly opposes such action." The clarity of these provisions, viewed in their context, admits of no doubt. . . . Based on the text of these provisions, the Court concludes that Article 36, paragraph 1, creates individual rights, which, by virtue of Article I of the Optional Protocol, may be invoked in this Court by the national State of the detained person. These rights were violated in the present case. . . .[51]

(3) Germany argued that the "procedural default" rule, as applied in this case to preclude habeas review of the LaGrand brother's VCCR claims, itself violated Article 36(2). The ICJ was careful to emphasize

> that a distinction must be drawn between that rule as such and its specific application in the present case. In itself, the rule does not violate Article 36 of the Vienna Convention. The problem arises when the procedural default rule does not allow the detained individual to challenge a conviction and sentence by claiming, in reliance on Article 36, paragraph 1, of the Convention, that the competent national authorities failed to comply with their obligation to provide the requisite consular information "without delay," thus preventing the person from seeking and obtaining consular assistance from the sending State.[52]

The ICJ then accepted Germany's contention, arguing as follows:

> In this case, Germany had the right at the request of the LaGrands "to arrange for [their] legal representation" and was eventually able to provide some assistance to that effect. By that time, however, because of the failure of the American authorities to comply with their obligation under Article 36, paragraph 1(b), the procedural default rule prevented counsel for the LaGrands to effectively challenge their convictions and sentences other than on United States constitutional grounds. As a result, although United States courts could and did examine the professional competence of counsel assigned to the indigent LaGrands by reference to United States constitutional standards, the procedural default rule prevented them from attaching any legal significance to the fact, inter alia, that the violation of the rights set forth in Article 36, paragraph 1, prevented Germany, in a timely fashion, from retaining private counsel for them and otherwise assisting in their defence as provided for by the Convention. Under these circumstances, the procedural default rule had the effect of preventing "full effect [from being] given to the purposes for which the rights accorded under this article are intended," and thus violated paragraph 2 of Article 36.[53]

---

51. Id. ¶¶77, 89.
52. Id. ¶90.
53. Id. ¶91.

(4) As far as remedy is concerned, the ICJ ruled as follows:

> The Court observes . . . that it can determine the existence of a violation of an international obligation. If necessary, it can also hold that a domestic law has been the cause of this violation. In the present case the Court has made its findings of violations of the obligations under Article 36 of the Vienna Convention. . . . But it has not found that a United States law, whether substantive or procedural in character, is inherently inconsistent with the obligations undertaken by the United States in the Vienna Convention. In the present case the violation of Article 36, paragraph 2, was caused by the circumstances in which the procedural default rule was applied, and not by the rule as such.
>
> In the present proceedings the United States has apologized to Germany for the breach of Article 36, paragraph 1, and Germany has not requested material reparation for this injury to itself and to the LaGrand brothers. It does, however, seek assurances. . . . The Court considers in this respect that if the United States . . . should fail in its obligation of consular notification to the detriment of German nationals, an apology would not suffice in cases where the individuals concerned have been subjected to prolonged detention or convicted and sentenced to severe penalties. In the case of such a conviction and sentence, it would be incumbent upon the United States to allow the review and reconsideration of the conviction and sentence by taking account of the violation of the rights set forth in the Convention. This obligation can be carried out in various ways. The choice of means must be left to the United States. . . .[54]

The Court, in setting forth its judgment, concluded "for these reasons, the Court . . . [f]inds that should nationals of the Federal Republic of Germany nonetheless be sentenced to severe penalties, without their rights under Article 36, paragraph 1(b), of the Convention having been respected, the United States of America, by means of its own choosing, shall allow the review and reconsideration of the conviction and sentence by taking account of the violation of the rights set forth in that Convention."[55]

(5) Finally, the ICJ held that the United States had violated its international legal obligation to comply with the provisional measures issued by the Court under Article 41 of the ICJ statute on March 3, 1999. Germany had claimed that the United States committed a threefold violation of the Court's Order of 3 March 1999: (1) "In the course of these proceedings—and in full knowledge of the Order of the International Court—the Office of the Solicitor General, a section of the U.S. Department of Justice—in a letter to the Supreme Court argued once again that: 'an order of the International Court of Justice indicating provisional measures is not binding and does not furnish a basis for judicial relief.'"; (2) "the U.S. Supreme Court—an agency of the United States—refused by a majority vote to order that the execution be stayed"; and (3) the governor of Arizona did not order a stay of the execution of Walter LaGrand although she was vested with the right to do so by the laws of the state of Arizona.[56]

In response, the United States argued that it "did what was called for by the Court's 3 March Order, given the extraordinary and unprecedented circumstances in which it was forced to act." The United States argued that the U.S. government "immediately transmitt[ed] the Order to the Governor of Arizona" and that "the United States placed the Order in the hands of the one official who, at that stage, might have had

---

54. Id. ¶125.
55. Id. ¶128.
56. Id. ¶94.

legal authority to stop the execution."[57] The United States further contended that "[t]wo central factors constrained the United States' ability to act. The first was the extraordinarily short time between issuance of the Court's Order and the time set for the execution of Walter LaGrand. . . . The second constraining factor was the character of the United States of America as a federal republic of divided powers."[58]

The ICJ made short work of the United States' argument that the terms of the provisional measures did not "create legal obligations binding on [it]."[59] Conceding that "[n]either the Permanent Court of International Justice, nor the present Court to date, has been called upon to determine the legal effects of orders made under Article 41 of the Statute," the ICJ nevertheless held that the provisional measures were binding on the United States, that the United States' actions fell short of those required by the provisional measures, and that the United States was therefore in breach of its obligations under Article 41 of the ICJ statute.[60]

While acknowledging that, "due to the extremely late presentation of the request for provisional measures, there was certainly very little time for the United States authorities to act,"[61] the Court observed

> . . . nevertheless, that the mere transmission of its Order to the Governor of Arizona without any comment, particularly without even so much as a plea for a temporary stay and an explanation that there is no general agreement on the position of the United States that orders of the International Court of Justice on provisional measures are non-binding, was certainly less than could have been done even in the short time available. The same is true of the United States Solicitor General's categorical statement in his brief letter to the United States Supreme Court that "an order of the International Court of Justice indicating provisional measures is not binding and does not furnish a basis for judicial relief." . . .
>
> It is also noteworthy that the Governor of Arizona, to whom the Court's Order had been transmitted, decided not to give effect to it, even though the Arizona Clemency Board had recommended a stay of execution for Walter LaGrand.
>
> Finally, the United States Supreme Court rejected a separate application by Germany for a stay of execution, "[g]iven the tardiness of the pleas and the jurisdictional barriers they implicate." Yet it would have been open to the Supreme Court, as one of its members urged, to grant a preliminary stay, which would have given it "time to consider, after briefing from all interested parties, the jurisdictional and international legal issues involved . . ." (Federal Republic of Germany et al. v. United States et al., United States Supreme Court, 3 March 1999).
>
> The review of the above steps taken by the authorities of the United States with regard to the Order of the International Court of Justice of 3 March 1999 indicates that the various competent United States authorities failed to take all the steps they could have taken to give effect to the Court's Order. The Order did not require the United States to exercise powers it did not have; but it did impose the obligation to "take all measures at its disposal to ensure that Walter LaGrand is not executed pending the final decision in these proceedings. . . ." The Court finds that the United States did not discharge this obligation.
>
> Under these circumstances the Court concludes that the United States has not complied with the Order of 3 March 1999. . . .[62]

---

57. Id. ¶95.
58. Id.
59. Id. ¶96.
60. Id. ¶98; see also id. ¶¶109-112.
61. Id. ¶111.
62. Id. ¶¶112-115.

NOTES AND QUESTIONS

1. The traditional view is that a treaty creates substantive rights only as between the states parties to the convention. Not surprisingly, then, the ICJ had no difficulty determining that the United States' noncompliance with the VCCR violated Germany's "rights." The next question, then, is assuming Germany has a primary, substantive right under international law, can it enforce that right in U.S. courts? The Paraguayan and German governments obviously believed that they should have had recourse, on behalf of their nationals, to U.S. courts to enforce the strictures of the VCCR on U.S. law enforcement authorities.

In the Supreme Court's decision denying Germany any relief in *LaGrand*, Federal Republic of Germany v. United States, 526 U.S. 111, 112 (1999), and in the Court's earlier denial of relief in *Breard*, the Court contended that a foreign nation's suit against a U.S. state official to vindicate the foreign citizen's rights under Article 36 in U.S. courts would probably be barred by the Eleventh Amendment to the U.S. Constitution. The Supreme Court's Eleventh Amendment jurisprudence is both notoriously difficult and consistently criticized. It is worth, however, taking a brief look at this Eleventh Amendment question because it is so central to whether a state party to the VCCR can vindicate its treaty rights in U.S. courts when the state party's national has been convicted in U.S. state court (as are the overwhelming majority of defendants in U.S. criminal cases). Professor Carlos Vázquez has criticized the Court's "probable" Eleventh Amendment result as follows:

> The Supreme Court has long interpreted the Eleventh Amendment to protect the states from private lawsuits based on federal law. At the same time, it has alleviated the rule-of-law problems with this immunity by holding that, at least in certain circumstances, a suit against a state official challenging the official's violation of federal law is not a suit against the state and thus is not barred. This principle, which the Supreme Court has said "gives life to the Supremacy Clause," has become known as the Ex parte Young[, 209 U.S. 123 (1908)] "exception" to the Eleventh Amendment. . . . The limits of this exception were elaborated in Edelman v. Jordan, [415 U.S. 651 (1974),] in which the Court held that the exception does not extend to suits seeking "retroactive" relief "which requires the payment of funds from the state treasury." Later cases have read *Edelman* as establishing that suits seeking "prospective" relief from a state official's violation of federal law are not barred by the Eleventh Amendment, while suits seeking "retrospective" or "retroactive" relief are barred.
>
> The inadequacies of the prospective-retrospective distinction have long been noted by scholars and lower courts. . . . The difficulty of explaining the Court's results as applications of a rule turning on prospectivity has led the lower courts to assimilate the prospective-retrospective terminology as short-hand for a rule barring suits seeking damages and damage-like monetary remedies from the state treasury. . . . Insofar as the distinction operates merely to bar suits for damages and similar monetary relief, the rule is relatively straightforward. . . .
>
> . . . [The Fourth Circuit's decision in *Breard*] led to [a] recent Supreme Court decision that necessitates a re-examination of the prospective-retrospective distinction. . . . The [Fourth Circuit] came to the startling and counterintuitive conclusion that the Eleventh Amendment bars a suit seeking to halt an execution because such relief is retroactive, not prospective. The Court of Appeals affirmed the dismissal of . . . Paraguay's claims. It concluded that Paraguay was seeking retrospective relief because Virginia's violation of the treaty took place in the past. Since Virginia was no longer hindering Breard's right to consult with his consul, there was no ongoing violation of the treaty; hence, Paraguay was not seeking prospective relief from an ongoing violation of federal law. In a

similar case, United Mexican States v. Woods, [126 F.3d 1220, 1223 (9th Cir. 1998),] the Ninth Circuit reached the same conclusion.

Paraguay and Breard both sought relief in the United States Supreme Court, as did Mexico. . . . The per curiam opinion in Breard v. Greene[, 523 U.S. 371 (1998),] devotes only five sentences to the Eleventh Amendment issue. In those sentences the Court expressed agreement with the Fourth Circuit's conclusion that Paraguay's suit was barred by the Eleventh Amendment.

When two courts of appeals conclude that a court order halting an execution scheduled to take place in the future is retrospective relief barred by the Eleventh Amendment, and the Supreme Court finds nothing wrong with that conclusion, something is awry. The error becomes evident when one compares the form of relief sought in these cases to the forms of relief sought in a typical habeas corpus petition. Indeed, in both the Fourth Circuit and Ninth Circuit cases, the prisoner himself sought the very same relief in a habeas proceeding, and in neither habeas proceeding was an Eleventh Amendment problem even suggested. As Justice Souter observed in [Seminole Tribe v. Florida, 517 U.S. 44, 178 (1996) (Souter, J., dissenting)], the reason federal habeas relief for state prisoners does not raise Eleventh Amendment problems is that such petitions fall within the *Ex parte Young* exception. If the applicability of the *Ex parte Young* exception turns on whether the relief sought is prospective or retrospective, and if a habeas petition seeking to halt the execution of a state prisoner because of a violation of federal law falls within that exception, then the lawsuits brought by Paraguay and Mexico seeking the very same relief must fall within it too.

Carlos Manuel Vázquez, Night and Day: *Coeur D'Alene, Breard,* and the Unraveling of the Prospective-Retrospective Distinction in Eleventh Amendment Doctrine, 87 Geo. L.J. 1, 2-7 (1998).

2. Suppose, despite the above critique, that the U.S. Supreme Court were correct that the Eleventh Amendment bars suits by foreign states against U.S. state officials in U.S. courts based on Article 36 violations against the foreign states' citizens. Would the fact that U.S. law does not allow foreign nations to *enforce* the "primary" treaty rights of the state party or its nationals against the U.S. states in federal court *itself* constitute a violation of the VCCR? If the U.S. Supreme Court were faced with a situation in which the ICJ required the United States to provide a remedy effectuating treaty rights to foreign states, but U.S. law (that is, the Eleventh Amendment) forbade the provision of that remedy, what would be the result? Can the United States be sanctioned under international law for abiding by otherwise valid domestic law?

3. In *LaGrand*, the ICJ resolved an open question — that is, whether it had jurisdiction to issue binding "provisional measures" to safeguard the status quo pending resolution of a case — with a resounding "yes." The ICJ then found that the U.S. government had not done enough to satisfy the order, and in particular cited the Solicitor General's position that the ICJ order was nonbinding; the U.S. Supreme Court's failure to grant a stay; and the Governor of Arizona's disregard of the ICJ order. Can a *court* violate a treaty? See, e.g., John Quigley, The Law of State Responsibility and the Right to Consular Access, 11 Willamette J. Intl. L. & Dispute Res. 50 (2004); see also Islamic Republic of Iran v. United States, Dec. No. 586-A-27-FT (June 5, 1998) (Iran-U.S. Claims Tribunal held that U.S. courts' failure to enforce a Tribunal award constituted a violation by the United States of its obligation under the U.S.-Iran agreement and awarded damages against the United States). What of the actions of the Arizona governor? Can the United States be internationally responsible for the acts or omissions of U.S. states or U.S. state officials?

4. Turning to the question whether *individuals* have substantive "primary" rights under the VCCR, the ICJ ruled that, by not informing the LaGrand brothers of their rights, and thereby depriving Germany of the possibility of rendering assistance contemplated in the Convention, the U.S. breached its obligations to Germany *and to the LaGrands*. In other words, the ICJ found that Article 36 "creates individual rights, which, by virtue of Article I of the Optional Protocol, may be invoked in this Court by the national State of the detained person." *LaGrand*, 2001 I.C.J. 466, at ¶77. The Inter-American Court of Human Rights also reads Article 36 to provide individuals with rights. The Right to Information on Consular Assistance in the Framework of the Guarantees of the Due Process of Law, Advisory Opinion OC-16/99, Inter-Am. Ct. H.R. (ser. A), ¶84 (1999).

The U.S. State Department, however, took the position—pressed without success before the ICJ and the Inter-American Court of Human Rights—that Article 36 does not create individual rights under international law. The United States based its argument primarily on a statement made in the preamble to the Convention, which reads: "[t]he purpose of [consular] privileges and immunities is not to benefit individuals but to ensure the efficient performance of functions by consular posts on behalf of their respective States." Do you find this argument persuasive? Note that the U.S. Department of State had, in the Tehran Hostages case before the ICJ in 1979-1980, taken the position that "Article 36 establishes rights not only for the consular officer but, perhaps even more importantly, for the nationals of the sending State who are assured access to consular officers." Quigley, supra, 11 Willamette J. Intl. L. & Dispute Res. at 45-46. Professor Quigley notes that "[t]his contradiction in the U.S. position on the issue of rights under Article 36 called into question its bona fides and rendered its stance, already based on an implausible reading of the preamble, even less tenable. [B]oth the Inter-American Court of Human Rights and the International Court of Justice have rejected the U.S. analysis and found that Article 36 creates rights for individuals." Id.

5. The above discussion concerns whether individuals can claim (in Professor Vázquez's terms) "primary" rights under the treaty—that is, whether they are the direct and intended beneficiaries of the treaty's terms. Did the ICJ go even further, holding that U.S. courts must provide *individual defendants* a "secondary right" to *enforce* their "primary treaty rights" *in U.S. courts*? Isn't this the import of the ICJ's discussion of the procedural rules that have operated to bar individual litigants from seeking relief on habeas?

6. In terms of prospective relief, the ICJ ruled that, should German nationals nonetheless be sentenced to severe penalties without their rights under the Vienna Convention having been respected, the United States "by means of its own choosing, *shall allow the review and reconsideration of the convention and sentence by taking account of the violation of the rights set forth in that Convention.*" *LaGrand*, 2001 I.C.J. 466, at ¶128 (emphasis added); see also id. ¶125. Once again, the ICJ decision appears to be at odds with the Supreme Court's views. Is the ICJ's *LaGrand* decision binding on federal courts? Does the *LaGrand* court require U.S. state and federal courts, or legislatures, to amend their rules so as to avoid finding Article 36 claims procedurally defaulted?

d. ICJ: *Avena*

In January 2003, the Mexican government filed suit in the ICJ against the United States, alleging violations of the VCCR in the cases of 54 Mexican nationals who had been sentenced to death in U.S. state criminal proceedings. The ICJ issued its opinion in *Avena and Other Mexican Nationals (Mexico v. United States),*[63] holding, inter alia, that:

(1) the U.S. had breached Article 36(1)(b) in the case of 51 of the Mexican nationals by failing "to inform detained Mexican nationals of their rights under that paragraph" and "to notify the Mexican consular post of the[ir] detention";[64]

(2) in 49 cases, the U.S. had violated its obligations under Article 36(1)(a) "to enable Mexican consular officers to communicate with and have access to their nationals, as well as its obligation under paragraph 1(c) of that Article regarding the right of consular officers to visit their detained nationals";[65] and

(3) in 34 cases, the breaches of Article 36(1)(b) also violated the United States' obligation under paragraph 1(c) "to enable Mexican consular officers to arrange for legal representation of their nationals."[66]

In terms of remedies, the ICJ:

(1) denied Mexico's request for annulment of its nationals' convictions and sentences;[67]

(2) ordered the United States to "permit review and reconsideration" of the Mexican nationals' cases by the United States courts "with a view to ascertaining whether in each case the violation of Article 36 committed by the competent authorities caused actual prejudice to the defendants in the process of administration of criminal justice," that is, "whether the violations of Article 36, paragraph 1, are to be regarded as having, in the causal sequence of events, ultimately led to convictions and severe penalties";[68]

(3) ordered that "this question is to be examined under the concrete circumstances of each case," and a uniform remedy of application of an exclusionary rule or reversal of a conviction is not invariably required;[69]

(4) ruled that the review and reconsideration of the conviction *and* sentence[70] contemplated in each case must be carried out "by taking account of the violation of the rights set forth in the Convention,"[71] and it is not sufficient that the courts will hear instead a due process argument;[72]

(5) held that this review and reconsideration of the violation and the possible prejudice from the violation must be done pursuant to a "judicial process," and hearings during the course of a clemency proceeding are insufficient;[73] and

---

63. 2004 I.C.J. 1 (Mar. 31).

64. Id. ¶¶106(1)-(2), 153(4).

65. Id. ¶¶106(3), 153(5)-(6).

66. Id. ¶¶106(4), 153(4), 153(7). The ICJ clarified that the phrase "without delay" in Article 36 means that the duty to provide consular information exists once it is realized that the person is a foreign national, or once there are grounds to think so, but does not necessarily mean "immediately after arrest." Id. ¶¶63, 85-88.

67. Id. ¶123.

68. Id. ¶¶121-122.

69. Id. ¶127.

70. Id. ¶138.

71. Id. ¶131.

72. Id. ¶¶134, 138, 139.

73. Id. ¶¶140-141, 143.

(6) ruled that the procedural default doctrines could not bar the required review and reconsideration.[74]

The ICJ reached each of these holdings by a vote of 14-1, with the U.S. judge voting with the majority.

e.   U.S. Supreme Court: *Sanchez-Llamas*

SANCHEZ-LLAMAS v. OREGON
548 U.S. 331 (2006)

Chief Justice ROBERTS delivered the opinion of the Court.

[Moises Sanchez-Llamas, a Mexican national, was convicted of, inter alia, aggravated murder and sentenced to over 20 years in prison. Before his trial, Sanchez-Llamas had moved to suppress statements he made to the police, arguing that suppression was warranted because the authorities had failed to comply with VCCR Article 36 after his arrest. Mario Bustillo, a Honduran national convicted of murder and sentenced to 30 years in prison, did not raise his VCCR claim until his direct appeal under state law.]

II

We granted certiorari as to three questions presented in these cases: (1) whether Article 36 of the Vienna Convention grants rights that may be invoked by individuals in a judicial proceeding; (2) whether suppression of evidence is a proper remedy for a violation of Article 36; and (3) whether an Article 36 claim may be deemed forfeited under state procedural rules because a defendant failed to raise the claim at trial.

As a predicate to their claims for relief, Sanchez-Llamas and Bustillo each argue that Article 36 grants them an individually enforceable right to request that their consular officers be notified of their detention, and an accompanying right to be informed by authorities of the availability of consular notification. Respondents and the United States, as amicus curiae, strongly dispute this contention. They argue that "there is a presumption that a treaty will be enforced through political and diplomatic channels, rather than through the courts." Brief for United States (quoting Head Money Cases, 112 U.S. 580, 598 (1884) (a treaty " 'is primarily a compact between independent nations,' " and " 'depends for the enforcement of its provisions on the interest and the honor of the governments which are parties to it' ")). Because we conclude that Sanchez-Llamas and Bustillo are not in any event entitled to relief on their claims, we find it unnecessary to resolve the question whether the Vienna Convention grants individuals enforceable rights. Therefore, for purposes of addressing petitioners' claims, we assume, without deciding, that Article 36 does grant Bustillo and Sanchez-Llamas such rights.

---

74. Id. ¶¶112-113, 133-134.

A

Sanchez-Llamas argues that the trial court was required to suppress his statements to police because authorities never told him of his rights under Article 36. He refrains, however, from arguing that the Vienna Convention itself mandates suppression. We think this a wise concession. The Convention does not prescribe specific remedies for violations of Article 36. Rather, it expressly leaves the implementation of Article 36 to domestic law: Rights under Article 36 are to "be exercised in conformity with the laws and regulations of the receiving State." Art. 36(2). As far as the text of the Convention is concerned, the question of the availability of the exclusionary rule for Article 36 violations is a matter of domestic law.

It would be startling if the Convention were read to require suppression. The exclusionary rule as we know it is an entirely American legal creation. More than 40 years after the drafting of the Convention, the automatic exclusionary rule applied in our courts is still "universally rejected" by other countries. It is implausible that other signatories to the Convention thought it to require a remedy that nearly all refuse to recognize as a matter of domestic law. There is no reason to suppose that Sanchez-Llamas would be afforded the relief he seeks here in any of the other 169 countries party to the Vienna Convention.

For good reason then, Sanchez-Llamas argues only that suppression is required because it is the appropriate remedy for an Article 36 violation under United States law, and urges us to require suppression for Article 36 violations as a matter of our "authority to develop remedies for the enforcement of federal law in state-court criminal proceedings." . . .

To the extent Sanchez-Llamas argues that we should invoke our supervisory authority, the law is clear: "It is beyond dispute that we do not hold a supervisory power over the courts of the several States." . . .

We also agree with the State of Oregon and the United States that our authority to create a judicial remedy applicable in state court must lie, if anywhere, in the treaty itself. Under the Constitution, the President has the power, "by and with the Advice and Consent of the Senate, to make Treaties." Art. II, §2, cl. 2. The United States ratified the Convention with the expectation that it would be interpreted according to its terms. See Restatement (Third) of Foreign Relations Law of the United States §325(1) (1986) ("An international agreement is to be interpreted in good faith in accordance with the ordinary meaning to be given to its terms in their context and in the light of its object and purpose"). If we were to require suppression for Article 36 violations without some authority in the Convention, we would in effect be supplementing those terms by enlarging the obligations of the United States under the Convention. This is entirely inconsistent with the judicial function.

Of course, it is well established that a self-executing treaty binds the States pursuant to the Supremacy Clause, and that the States therefore must recognize the force of the treaty in the course of adjudicating the rights of litigants. And where a treaty provides for a particular judicial remedy, there is no issue of intruding on the constitutional prerogatives of the States or the other federal branches. Courts must apply the remedy as a requirement of federal law. But where a treaty does not provide a particular remedy, either expressly or implicitly, it is not for the federal courts to impose one on the States through lawmaking of their own.

Sanchez-Llamas argues that the language of the Convention implicitly requires a judicial remedy because it states that the laws and regulations governing the exercise of Article 36 rights "must enable *full effect* to be given to the purposes for which the rights . . . are intended," Art. 36(2) (emphasis added). In his view, although "full effect" may not automatically require an exclusionary rule, it does require an appropriate judicial remedy of *some* kind. There is reason to doubt this interpretation. In particular, there is little indication that other parties to the Convention have interpreted Article 36 to require a judicial remedy in the context of criminal prosecutions.

Nevertheless, even if Sanchez-Llamas is correct that Article 36 implicitly requires a judicial remedy, the Convention equally states that Article 36 rights "shall be exercised in conformity with the laws and regulations of the receiving State." Art. 36(2). Under our domestic law, the exclusionary rule is not a remedy we apply lightly. "[O]ur cases have repeatedly emphasized that the rule's 'costly toll' upon truth-seeking and law enforcement objectives presents a high obstacle for those urging application of the rule." Because the rule's social costs are considerable, suppression is warranted only where the rule's "'remedial objectives are thought most efficaciously served.'" . . .

In sum, neither the Vienna Convention itself nor our precedents applying the exclusionary rule support suppression of Sanchez-Llamas' statements to police.

B

The Virginia courts denied petitioner Bustillo's Article 36 claim on the ground that he failed to raise it at trial or on direct appeal. The general rule in federal habeas cases is that a defendant who fails to raise a claim on direct appeal is barred from raising the claim on collateral review. There is an exception if a defendant can demonstrate both "cause" for not raising the claim at trial, and "prejudice" from not having done so. Like many States, Virginia applies a similar rule in state postconviction proceedings, and did so here to bar Bustillo's Vienna Convention claim. Normally, in our review of state-court judgments, such rules constitute an adequate and independent state-law ground preventing us from reviewing the federal claim. Bustillo contends, however, that state procedural default rules cannot apply to Article 36 claims. He argues that the Convention requires that Article 36 rights be given "'full effect'" and that Virginia's procedural default rules "prevented any effect (much less 'full effect') from being given to" those rights.

This is not the first time we have been asked to set aside procedural default rules for a Vienna Convention claim. Respondent Johnson and the United States persuasively argue that this question is controlled by our decision in Breard v. Greene, 523 U.S. 371 (1998) (per curiam). In *Breard*, the petitioner failed to raise an Article 36 claim in state court—at trial or on collateral review—and then sought to have the claim heard in a subsequent federal habeas proceeding. He argued that "the Convention is the 'supreme law of the land' and thus trumps the procedural default doctrine." We rejected this argument as "plainly incorrect," for two reasons. First, we observed, "it has been recognized in international law that, absent a clear and express statement to the contrary, the procedural rules of the forum State govern the implementation of the treaty in that State." Furthermore, we reasoned that while treaty protections such as Article 36 may constitute supreme federal law, this is "no less true of provisions of the Constitution itself, to which rules of procedural default apply." In light of *Breard*'s holding, Bustillo faces an uphill task in arguing that the Convention requires States to set aside their procedural default rules for Article 36 claims. . . .

Bustillo[] . . . argues that since *Breard*, the ICJ has interpreted the Vienna Convention to preclude the application of procedural default rules to Article 36 claims. The LaGrand Case (F.R.G. v. U.S.), 2001 I.C.J. 466 (Judgment of June 27) (*LaGrand*), and the Case Concerning Avena and other Mexican Nationals (Mex. v. U.S.), 2004 I.C.J. No. 128 (Judgment of Mar. 31) (*Avena*), were brought before the ICJ by the governments of Germany and Mexico, respectively, on behalf of several of their nationals facing death sentences in the United States. The foreign governments claimed that their nationals had not been informed of their right to consular notification. They further argued that application of the procedural default rule to their nationals' Vienna Convention claims failed to give "full effect" to the purposes of the Convention, as required by Article 36. The ICJ agreed, explaining that the defendants had procedurally defaulted their claims "because of the failure of the American authorities to comply with their obligation under Article 36." Application of the procedural default rule in such circumstances, the ICJ reasoned, "prevented [courts] from attaching any legal significance" to the fact that the violation of Article 36 kept the foreign governments from assisting in their nationals' defense.

Bustillo argues that *LaGrand* and *Avena* warrant revisiting the procedural default holding of *Breard*. . . . We disagree. Although the ICJ's interpretation deserves "respectful consideration," we conclude that it does not compel us to reconsider our understanding of the Convention in *Breard*.

Under our Constitution, "[t]he judicial Power of the United States" is "vested in one supreme Court, and in such inferior Courts as the Congress may from time to time ordain and establish." Art. III, §1. That "judicial Power . . . extend[s] to . . . Treaties." Id., §2. And, as Chief Justice Marshall famously explained, that judicial power includes the duty "to say what the law is." Marbury v. Madison, 1 Cranch 137, 177, 2 L. Ed. 60 (1803). If treaties are to be given effect as federal law under our legal system, determining their meaning as a matter of federal law "is emphatically the province and duty of the judicial department," headed by the "one supreme Court" established by the Constitution. It is against this background that the United States ratified, and the Senate gave its advice and consent to, the various agreements that govern referral of Vienna Convention disputes to the ICJ.

Nothing in the structure or purpose of the ICJ suggests that its interpretations were intended to be conclusive on our courts. The ICJ's decisions have "*no binding force* except between the parties and in respect of that particular case," Statute of the International Court of Justice, Art. 59 (emphasis added). Any interpretation of law the ICJ renders in the course of resolving particular disputes is thus not binding precedent *even as to the ICJ itself*; there is accordingly little reason to think that such interpretations were intended to be controlling on our courts. The ICJ's principal purpose is to arbitrate particular disputes between national governments. While each member of the United Nations has agreed to comply with decisions of the ICJ "in any case to which it is a party," United Nations Charter, Art. 94(1), the Charter's procedure for noncompliance — referral to the Security Council by the aggrieved state — contemplates quintessentially *international* remedies, Art. 94(2).

In addition, "[w]hile courts interpret treaties for themselves, the meaning given them by the departments of government particularly charged with their negotiation and enforcement is given great weight." Although the United States has agreed to "discharge its international obligations" in having state courts give effect to the decision in *Avena*, it has not taken the view that the ICJ's interpretation of Article 36 is binding on our courts. Moreover, shortly after *Avena*, the United States withdrew from the Optional Protocol concerning Vienna Convention disputes. Whatever the effect of *Avena* and *LaGrand* before this withdrawal, it is doubtful that our courts should give decisive weight to the interpretation of a tribunal whose jurisdiction in this area is no longer recognized by the United States.

LaGrand and *Avena* are therefore entitled only to the "respectful consideration" due an interpretation of an international agreement by an international court. Even according such consideration, the ICJ's interpretation cannot overcome the plain import of Article 36. As we explained in *Breard*, the procedural rules of domestic law generally govern the implementation of an international treaty. In addition, Article 36 makes clear that the rights it provides "shall be exercised in conformity with the laws and regulations of the receiving State" provided that "full effect . . . be given to the purposes for which the rights accorded under this Article are intended." Art. 36(2). In the United States, this means that the rule of procedural default—which applies even to claimed violations of our Constitution—applies also to Vienna Convention claims. Bustillo points to nothing in the drafting history of Article 36 or in the contemporary practice of other signatories that undermines this conclusion.

The ICJ concluded that where a defendant was not notified of his rights under Article 36, application of the procedural default rule failed to give "full effect" to the purposes of Article 36 because it prevented courts from attaching "legal significance" to the Article 36 violation. This reasoning overlooks the importance of procedural default rules in an adversary system, which relies chiefly on the parties to raise significant issues and present them to the courts in the appropriate manner at the appropriate time for adjudication. Procedural default rules are designed to encourage parties to raise their claims promptly and to vindicate "the law's important interest in the finality of judgments." The consequence of failing to raise a claim for adjudication at the proper time is generally forfeiture of that claim. As a result, rules such as procedural default routinely deny "legal significance"—in the *Avena* and *LaGrand* sense—to otherwise viable legal claims.

Procedural default rules generally take on greater importance in an adversary system such as ours than in the sort of magistrate-directed, inquisitorial legal system characteristic of many of the other countries that are signatories to the Vienna Convention. "What makes a system adversarial rather than inquisitorial is . . . the presence of a judge who does not (as an inquisitor does) conduct the factual and legal investigation himself, but instead decides on the basis of facts and arguments pro and con adduced by the parties." In an inquisitorial system, the failure to raise a legal error can in part be attributed to the magistrate, and thus to the state itself. In our system, however, the responsibility for failing to raise an issue generally rests with the parties themselves.

The ICJ's interpretation of Article 36 is inconsistent with the basic framework of an adversary system. Under the ICJ's reading of "full effect," Article 36 claims could trump not only procedural default rules, but any number of other rules requiring parties to present their legal claims at the appropriate time for adjudication. If the State's failure to inform the defendant of his Article 36 rights generally excuses the defendant's failure to comply with relevant procedural rules, then presumably rules such as statutes of limitations and prohibitions against filing successive habeas petitions must also yield in the face of Article 36 claims. This sweeps too broadly, for it reads the "full effect" proviso in a way that leaves little room for Article 36's clear instruction that Article 36 rights "shall be exercised in conformity with the laws and regulations of the receiving State." Art. 36(2).

Much as Sanchez-Llamas cannot show that suppression is an appropriate remedy for Article 36 violations under domestic law principles, so too Bustillo cannot show that normally applicable procedural default rules should be suspended in light of the type of right he claims. In this regard, a comparison of Article 36 and a suspect's rights under *Miranda* disposes of Bustillo's claim. Bustillo contends that applying procedural default rules to Article 36 rights denies such rights "full effect" because the violation itself—i.e., the failure to inform defendants of their right to consular notification—prevents them from becoming aware of their Article 36 rights and asserting them at trial. Of course, precisely the same thing is true of rights under *Miranda.* Police are required to advise suspects that they have a right to remain silent and a right to an attorney. If police do not give such warnings, and counsel fails to object, it is equally true that a suspect may not be "aware he even *had* such rights until well after his trial had concluded." Nevertheless, it is well established that where a defendant fails to raise a *Miranda* claim at trial, procedural default rules may bar him from raising the claim in a subsequent postconviction proceeding.

Bustillo responds that an Article 36 claim more closely resembles a claim, under Brady v. Maryland, 373 U.S. 83 (1963), that the prosecution failed to disclose exculpatory evidence — a type of claim that often can be asserted for the first time only in postconviction proceedings. The analogy is inapt. In the case of a *Brady* claim, it is impossible for the defendant to know as a *factual* matter that a violation has occurred before the exculpatory evidence is disclosed. By contrast, a defendant is well aware of the fact that he was not informed of his Article 36 rights, even if the *legal* significance of that fact eludes him. . . .

We therefore conclude, as we did in *Breard*, that claims under Article 36 of the Vienna Convention may be subjected to the same procedural default rules that apply generally to other federal-law claims. . . .

Although these cases involve the delicate question of the application of an international treaty, the issues in many ways turn on established principles of domestic law. Our holding in no way disparages the importance of the Vienna Convention. The relief petitioners request is, by any measure, extraordinary. Sanchez-Llamas seeks a suppression remedy for an asserted right with little if any connection to the gathering of evidence; Bustillo requests an exception to procedural rules that is accorded to almost no other right, including many of our most fundamental constitutional protections. It is no slight to the Convention to deny petitioners' claims under the same principles we would apply to an Act of Congress, or to the Constitution itself.

Justice BREYER, with whom Justice STEVENS and Justice SOUTER join, and with whom Justice GINSBURG joins [in relevant part], dissenting. . . .

The first question presented is whether a criminal defendant may raise a claim (at trial or in a postconviction proceeding) that state officials violated Article 36 of the Convention. The Court assumes that the answer to this question is "yes," but it does not decide the matter because it concludes in any event that the petitioners are not entitled to the remedies they seek. . . .

. . . [T]he first question raises an important issue of federal law that has arisen hundreds of times in the lower federal and state courts. Those courts have divided as to the proper answer. And the issue often arises in a legal context where statutes or procedural requirements arguably block this Court's speedy review. We granted the petitions for certiorari in significant part in order to decide this question. And, given its importance, we should do so.

In answering the question it is common ground that the Convention is "self-executi[ng]." See S. Exec. Rep. No. 91-9, p. 5 (1969). That is to say, the Convention "operates of itself without the aid of any legislative provision." Foster v. Neilson, 2 Pet. 253, 314 (1829). The parties also agree that we need not decide whether the Convention creates a "private right of action," i.e., a private right that would allow an individual to bring a lawsuit for enforcement of the Convention or for damages based on its violation. Rather, the question here is whether the Convention provides, in these cases, law applicable in legal proceedings that might have been brought irrespective of the Vienna Convention claim, here an ordinary criminal appeal and an ordinary postconviction proceeding.

Bustillo, for example, has brought an action under a Virginia statute that allows any convicted person to seek release from custody on the ground that "he is detained without lawful authority." Sanchez-Llamas has challenged his state criminal conviction on direct appeal, and in that proceeding he is entitled to claim that his conviction violates state or federal law. In both cases the petitioners argue that a court decision favoring the prosecution would violate the Convention (as properly interpreted), and therefore the Constitution forbids any such decision. See U.S. Const., Art. VI, cl. 2. This argument in effect claims that the Convention itself provides applicable law that here would favor the petitioners if, but only if, they are correct as to their interpretation of the Convention (which is, of course, a different matter).

The petitioners must be right in respect to their claim that the Convention provides law that here courts could apply in their respective proceedings. The Convention is a treaty. And "all Treaties made . . . under the Authority of the United States, shall be the supreme Law of the Land; and the Judges in every State shall be bound thereby." U.S. Const., Art. VI, cl. 2. As Chief Justice Marshall long ago explained, under the Supremacy Clause a treaty is "to be regarded in courts of justice as equivalent to an act of the legislature, whenever it operates of itself without the aid of any legislative provision."

Directly to the point, this Court stated long ago that a treaty "is a law of the land as an act of Congress is, whenever its provisions prescribe a rule by which the rights of the private citizen or subject may be determined. And when such rights are of a nature to be enforced in a court of justice," in such a case the court is to "resor[t] to the treaty for a rule of decision for the case before it as it would to a statute." Head Money Cases, 112 U.S. 580, 598-599 (1884).

As noted above, the parties agree that the Convention "operates of itself without the aid of any legislative provision." The question, then, is the one this Court set forth in the *Head Money Cases*: Does the Convention set forth a "law" with the legal stature of an Act of Congress? And as the Court explained, we are to answer that question by asking, does the Convention "prescribe a rule by which the rights of the private citizen . . . may be determined"? Are the obligations set forth in Article 36(1)(b) "of a nature to be enforced in a court of justice"?

The "nature" of the Convention provisions raised by the petitioners indicates that they are intended to set forth standards that are judicially enforceable. Those provisions consist of the rights of a foreign national "arrested" or "detained in any other manner" (1) to have, on his "reques[t]," the "consular post" "inform[ed]" of that arrest or detention; (2) to have forwarded "without delay" any "communication addressed to the consular post"; and (3) to be "inform[ed] . . . without delay" of those two "rights." Art. 36(1)(b). These rights do not differ in their "nature" from other procedural rights that courts commonly enforce.

Moreover, the language of Article 36 speaks directly of the "rights" of the individual foreign national. See Art. 36(1)(b) ("The said authorities shall inform the person concerned without delay of *his rights* under this sub-paragraph" (emphasis added)). Article 36 thus stands in stark contrast to other provisions of the Convention, which speak in terms of the rights of the member nations or consular officials.

Suppose that a pre-*Miranda* federal statute had said that arresting authorities "shall inform a detained person without delay of his right to counsel." Would courts not have automatically assumed that this statute created applicable law that a criminal defendant could invoke at trial? What more would the statute have to say?

Further, this Court has routinely permitted individuals to enforce treaty provisions similar to Article 36 in domestic judicial proceedings. In United States v. Rauscher, 119 U.S. 407, 410-411 (1886), for example, this Court concluded that the defendant could raise as a defense in his federal criminal trial the violation of an extradition treaty that said, " 'It is agreed that the United States and Her Britannic Majesty shall, upon mutual requisitions by them . . . deliver up to justice all persons' " charged with certain crimes in the other country. Similarly, in Kolovrat v. Oregon, 366 U.S. 187, 191, n. 6 (1961), the Court held that foreign nationals could challenge a state law limiting their right to recover an inheritance based on a treaty providing that " '[i]n all that concerns the right of acquiring, possessing or disposing of every kind of property . . . citizens of [each country who reside in the other] shall enjoy the rights which the respective laws grant . . . in each of these states to the subjects of the most favored nation.' " And in Asakura v. Seattle, 265 U.S. 332, 340 (1924), the Court allowed a foreign national to challenge a city ordinance forbidding noncitizens from working as pawnbrokers under a treaty stating that " 'citizens or subjects of each of the High Contracting Parties shall have liberty . . . to carry on trade' " and " 'generally to do anything incident to or necessary for trade upon the same terms as native citizens or subjects.' "

In all these cases, the Court recognized that (1) a treaty obligated the United States to treat foreign nationals in a certain manner; (2) the obligation had been breached by the Government's conduct; and (3) the foreign national could therefore seek redress for that breach in a judicial proceeding, even though the treaty did not specifically mention judicial enforcement of its guarantees or even expressly state that its provisions were intended to confer rights on the foreign national. Language and context argue yet more strongly here in favor of permitting a criminal defendant in an appropriate case to find in the Convention a law to apply in the proceeding against him.

In addition, the Government concedes that individual consular officials may enforce *other* provisions of the Convention in American courts. For example, Article 43(1) grants consular officials immunity from "the jurisdiction of the" host country's "judicial or administrative authorities" for "acts performed in the exercise of consular functions." The federal courts have held that a consular official may raise Article 43(1) in a judicial proceeding, even though that provision does not expressly mention a judicial remedy. What in Article 36 warrants treating it differently in this respect?

Finally, the international tribunal that the United States agreed would resolve disputes about the interpretation of the Convention, the ICJ, has twice ruled that an arrested foreign national may raise a violation of the arresting authorities' obligation to "inform [him] without delay of his rights under" Article 36(1) in an American judicial proceeding. See *Avena*, 2004 I.C.J. No. 128; *LaGrand*, 2001 I.C.J. 466. That conclusion, as an "interpretation of an international agreement by an international court" deserves our " 'respectful consideration.' " That "respectful consideration," for reasons I shall explain, counsels in favor of an interpretation that is consistent with the ICJ's reading of the Convention here.

The Government says to the contrary that Article 36 is "addressed solely to the rights of States and not private individuals"; hence, a foreign national may not claim in an American court that a State has convicted him without the consular notification that Article 36 requires. But its arguments are not persuasive. The Government rests this conclusion primarily upon its claim that there is a "long-established presumption that treaties and other international agreements do not create judicially enforceable individual rights."

The problem with that argument is that no such presumption exists. . . .

. . . [T]he *Head Money Cases* make clear that a treaty may confer certain enforceable "rights upon the citizens or subjects of one of the nations residing in the territorial limits of the other." See also 2 Restatement (Third) on Foreign Relations Law of the United States §907 (1986) ("A private person having rights against the United States under an international agreement may assert those rights in courts in the United States").

And the language of the Convention makes clear that it is such a treaty. Indeed, to my knowledge no other nation's courts (or perhaps no more than one) have held to the contrary. The cases cited by the respondents and the Government do not say otherwise.

The Government also points out that the Executive Branch's interpretation of treaty provisions is entitled to "great weight." I agree with this presumption. But the Executive's views on our treaty obligations are "not conclusive." Where language, the nature of the right, and the ICJ's interpretation of the treaty taken separately or together so strongly point to an intent to confer enforceable rights upon an individual, I cannot find in the simple fact of the Executive Branch's contrary view sufficient reason to adopt the Government's interpretation of the Convention.

Accordingly, I would allow the petitioners to raise their claims based on violations of the Convention in their respective state-court proceedings. . . .

NOTES AND QUESTIONS

1. The Supreme Court did not resolve the first issue presented — that is, whether the individual defendants had "rights" under the VCCR — but the dissent did. Were you persuaded by the dissent's position?

Assuming that U.S. courts were to credit the ICJ's judgment that the VCCR creates primary "rights" in individuals under international law, do U.S. courts necessarily have to recognize those "rights" as a matter of U.S. law or to grant individuals secondary enforcement rights in U.S. courts? The Sixth Circuit's explanation (below) of the U.S. law regarding the potential for individuals' secondary enforcement rights in U.S. courts is fairly typical of judicial expositions on the subject.

> . . . Under federal law treaties have the same legal effect as statutes. As a general rule, however, international treaties do not create rights that are privately enforceable in the federal courts.
>
>> A treaty is primarily a compact between independent nations. It depends for the enforcement of its provisions on the interest and honor of the governments which are parties to it. If these fail, its infraction becomes the subject of international negotiations and reclamation, so far as the injured parties choose to seek redress, which may in the end be enforced by actual war. It is obvious that with all this the judicial courts have nothing to do and can give no redress.
>
> Head Money Cases, 112 U.S. 580, 598 (1884). "International agreements, even those directly benefitting private persons, generally do not create private rights or provide for a private cause of action in domestic courts. . . ." Restatement (Third) of the Foreign Relations Law of the United States §907, cmt. a (1987). In fact, courts presume that the rights created by an international treaty belong to a state and that a private individual cannot enforce them.
>
> Nonetheless, the Supreme Court has recognized that treaties can create individually enforceable rights in some circumstances. See, e.g., United States v. Alvarez-Machain, 504 U.S. 655, 667-68 (1992) (citing United States v. Rauscher, 119 U.S. 407 (1886)). "Whether or not treaty violations can provide the basis for particular claims or defenses thus appears to depend upon the particular treaty and claim involved." Absent express language in a treaty providing for particular judicial remedies, the federal courts will not vindicate private rights unless a treaty creates fundamental rights on a par with those protected by the Constitution. Acknowledging that the Vienna Convention "arguably confers on an individual the right to consular assistance following arrest," the Supreme

> Court has left open the question of whether the Vienna Convention creates an individual right enforceable by the federal courts. *Breard*, 523 U.S. at 376.

United States v. Emuegbunam, 268 F.3d 377, 389-390 (6th Cir. 2001). To assess the Sixth Circuit's analysis, one must first recognize that treaties are hybrid creatures in U.S. law.

First, "[t]reaties are frequently described as contracts between nations. As instruments of international law, they establish obligations with which international law requires the parties to comply. . . . [I]t is widely held that treaties, as international instruments, establish legal obligations and correlative legal rights only of the nations that are parties to them, not of individuals." Carlos Manuel Vázquez, Treaty-Based Rights and Remedies of Individuals, 92 Colum. L. Rev. 1082, 1082 (1992). This is the quality of treaties emphasized by the Sixth Circuit above. But in the United States, treaties also have a second quality: They are "supreme Law of the Land" under the Supremacy Clause. As a type of "law" equal to federal legislation, shouldn't self-executing treaties be enforceable in U.S. courts by individuals just as those "laws" are? See, e.g., id. at 1097, 1101, 1108-1110, 1113.

Consider in this regard Professor Carlos Vázquez's take on the question of individual rights under treaties in U.S. courts:

> It is true that treaties are contracts between nations. It is also true that, as a matter of international law, the breach of a treaty by one party is generally a matter to be pursued by the other parties. At the time of the Framing of the Constitution, the mechanisms for enforcing treaties were primarily diplomacy and, as a last resort, war. Under traditional international law, individuals generally lacked standing to complain of a nation's treaty violation or to seek any remedy on the international plane. Moreover, treaties were not enforceable in domestic courts solely by virtue of the treaty itself. Under international law and domestic laws of the countries then in existence, judges could enforce treaties only if authorized to do so by domestic law.
>
> The Framers of the Constitution were acutely aware of these characteristics of treaties, which had led to significant problems for the United States under the Articles of Confederation. In order to avoid the foreign relations difficulties that would result from treaty violations, and to capture the benefits of a reputation for treaty compliance, the Founders gave treaties the force of domestic law enforceable in domestic courts. The Supremacy Clause thus *supplements* international law mechanisms for enforcing treaties by adding domestic mechanisms. It assimilates treaties to federal statutes and the Constitution, thus obviating the differences in enforcement mechanisms that would otherwise exist between these forms of law. Among other things, the Supremacy Clause makes treaties enforceable in court at the behest of individuals.
>
> The one exception the Supreme Court has recognized to the rule of equivalent treatment comes from its holding in *Foster v. Neilson* that some treaties are non-self-executing because of what they have to say on the need for legislative implementation. . . . [N]on-self-executing treaties are sometimes described as treaties that lack the domestic force of law. Of course, the plain text of the Supremacy Clause rules out the possibility that a treaty might be valid and in force yet lack the force of domestic law. *Foster* itself offers a basis for reconciling the concept with the constitutional text: a non-self-executing treaty has the force of domestic law, but it is a law "addressed to" Congress. Such a treaty is not judicially enforceable because, in our constitutional system, the courts lack power to order the legislature to legislate.

Carlos Manuel Vázquez, Treaties as Law of the Land: The Supremacy Clause and the Judicial Enforcement of Treaties, 122 Harv. L. Rev. 599, 605-607 (2008).

2. Assuming that American law does not recognize individual, primary treaty rights under the VCCR or provide secondary enforcement rights, is Article 36 a dead letter for practical purposes? If even states parties to the VCCR cannot seek relief on behalf of their nationals in U.S. courts, are the "rights" embodied in the Convention meaningless? See, e.g., Chapter 2; Marbury v. Madison, 5 U.S. (1 Cranch) 137 (1803) ("The government of the United States has been emphatically termed a government of laws, and not of men. It will certainly cease to deserve this high appellation, if the laws furnish no remedy for the violation of a vested legal right."). As *LaGrand* demonstrates, states parties can seek a judgment against another state party before the ICJ (although individuals such as Breard cannot), but what relief can the ICJ provide as a practical matter, and how can it enforce its judgment? Might resort to the ICJ actually prove counterproductive? What of diplomatic and political appeals?

f. U.S. Supreme Court: *Medellín*

Jose Ernesto Medellín Rojas, a Mexican national who had lived in the United States since preschool, had been one of the persons whose rights had been litigated by the Mexican government in *Avena*. He had been convicted of capital murder in Texas courts and sentenced to death for "the gang rape and brutal murders of two Houston teenagers."[75] At the time of his arrest, Medellín was 18; he was not advised of his "rights" under Article 36. According to his petition for certiorari, Medellín's lead counsel was suspended from the practice of law for ethics violations during the investigation and prosecution of Medellín's case, and counsel did very little, during either the guilt or penalty phase, to assist Medellín. By contrast, Medellín's habeas lawyers later argued, even

> [t]he United States recognizes that the consular assistance Mexico provides its nationals in capital cases is "extraordinary." At the time Mr. Medellín was arrested and tried, Mexican consular officers routinely assisted capital defendants by providing funding for experts and investigators, gathering mitigating evidence, acting as a liaison with Spanish-speaking family members, and most importantly, ensuring that Mexican nationals were represented by competent and experienced defense counsel. As a result of the Article 36 violation in his case, however, Mr. Medellín had no opportunity to receive the assistance of Mexican consular officers either before or during his trial.[76]

One year after Mexican consular authorities learned of Medellín's detention and began assisting him, Medellín filed an application for a writ of habeas corpus in Texas court arguing, among other things, that his conviction and sentence should be vacated as a remedy for the violation of his Article 36 rights. The trial court denied relief, holding, inter alia, that Medellín's claim had been procedurally defaulted; the Texas Court of Criminal Appeals affirmed. Medellín then filed a petition for a writ of habeas corpus in federal court raising an Article 36 claim. The district court denied relief, ruling the VCCR claim procedurally defaulted. In the alternative, the district court concluded that it was compelled to deny relief by Fifth Circuit precedent holding that the VCCR does not create individually enforceable rights, that no judicial remedy is available for its violation, and that Medellín could not show prejudice unless the VCCR violation also qualified as a violation of a constitutional right.

---

75. Medellín v. Texas, 128 S. Ct. 1346 (2008).
76. Petition for a Writ of Certiorari at 8-10, Medellín v. Dretke, No. 04-5928 (U.S. Aug. 18, 2004).

The Fifth Circuit then denied relief. In so doing, it acknowledged that *Avena*, which had issued after the district court's ruling, had been brought on behalf of Medellín, among others. It also recognized that the ICJ had held in *LaGrand* and reiterated in *Avena* that the application of procedural default rules to bar review of the VCCR claims violated VCCR Article 36, and that Article 36 conferred individually enforceable rights. The Fifth Circuit ruled, however, that the first holding contradicted the Supreme Court's decision in *Breard v. Greene* and that the second contravened its own circuit precedent. Accordingly, the court held that it was bound to disregard *LaGrand* and *Avena* unless and until the Supreme Court or, in terms of the second holding, the en banc court of appeals, decided otherwise.

The Supreme Court granted certiorari and issued its decision in *Medellín v. Texas* in March 2008. We read excerpts of that decision in the course of Chapter 2's discussion of self-executing and non-self-executing treaties. You will recall, then, that the Supreme Court, per Chief Justice Roberts, held in *Medellín* that the ICJ's *Avena* decision was not directly enforceable domestic federal law that preempted state procedural bars. In so doing, the Court acknowledged that the *Avena* judgment *did* create an international obligation on the part of the United States. Nonetheless, the Court held that the treaty obligation was not automatically binding as domestic law because the relevant treaty sources — the Optional Protocol, the UN Charter, and the ICJ Statute — were non-self-executing and had not been implemented by Congress in a binding federal statute. The Court also held that the president's memorandum to the attorney general, which stated that the United States would discharge its international obligations under *Avena* by having state courts give effect to that decision, did not independently require states to provide reconsideration and review of Medellín's claim without regard to state procedural default rules. The Court found in this regard that the president's foreign affairs authority — and in particular his power to resolve international claims disputes — cannot stretch so far as to permit him to force state courts to reopen final criminal judgments to conform to the demands of a non-self-executing treaty as interpreted by an international tribunal.

PART

III

Transnational Crime

In the following chapters, we will study a number of "transnational crimes," a term defined in Chapter 1 to include those crimes in a nation's domestic criminal law "which regulate[] actions or events that transcend national frontiers."[1] Given the increasingly transnational nature of criminal activities, many crimes fit within this category, but no one volume could cover them all. Accordingly, many candidate crimes could not be explored here, including, for example, antitrust offenses and cybercrimes. Instead, we decided to focus on organized crime; trafficking in drugs, persons, and weapons; money laundering; corruption; and terrorism. These crimes are ones of particular concern to the world community, as demonstrated by the fact that all of them are both transnational crimes *and* "treaty crimes" in our taxonomy—meaning that the cross-border activity under consideration has been declared criminal by international treaties, but the criminal prohibitions are enforced under domestic laws of states that join the treaties, rather than by international tribunals.

Exposure to these transnational materials is critical to an understanding of the field of international criminal law. First, it is highly likely that you, if you practice in this area at all, will encounter and deal with "transnational crimes" under domestic law rather than cases within the jurisdiction of any international tribunal. Second, you need a firm grounding in what interests can—as a legal, practical, or political matter—be effectively vindicated through domestic prosecutions before you can evaluate the necessity for, or efficacy of, a criminal law regime enforced in international tribunals. Finally, as we believe the materials will demonstrate, it is increasingly difficult to separate "domestic" from "international" criminal law and enforcement. The globalization of criminal activity, the multiplication of international agreements concerning criminal law and enforcement, and the willingness of international tribunals to apply international human rights norms to domestic processes, mean that the distinction between truly "international" law and municipal law is quickly blurring.

Recognizing that these materials will most often be used in U.S. law school classes, we believe students should be exposed to non-U.S. responses to the problems posed by these transnational crimes. After all, multilateral criminal law treaties, by definition, must take into account differing approaches to criminal law and procedure in various national legal systems and cultures. Thus, the chapter on organized crime contains an extensive discussion of comparative national responses to group criminality, and the chapter on money laundering compares the Swiss answer to such activity with its U.S. counterpart. The following brief discussion by Professor Edward

---

1. Phillip C. Jessup, Transnational Law 2 (1956).

Wise regarding the nature of comparative criminal analysis and its value may be of assistance as an introduction to these comparative materials.

EDWARD M. WISE, RICO AND ITS ANALOGUES: SOME COMPARATIVE CONSIDERATIONS

27 Syracuse J. Intl. L. & Com. 303 (2000)

. . . Comparative law involves determining, and trying to understand or explain, the relationships, the similarities and the differences, between legal systems. Some comparatists prefer to focus on sameness, similarities, and universals; others on disparities, differences, and particularities. Comparativism does not necessarily imply universalism: it can take particularist forms in which sensitivity to the local specificity of legal culture is central. At various times, one or the other of these two tendencies — the universalist and the particularist — predominates, although not exclusively so. There is always a healthy tension between them, and movement back and forth. Both kinds of approach are needed to throw full light on the objects of comparative study, on the relationships between legal systems, which include patterns both of similarity and of difference. It is not particularly helpful to regard comparative law simply as a matter of looking for clones of our own institutions in the practices of others, or of looking abroad for models that we can imitate. The driving force behind comparative study should be the desire to avoid provincialism, to open our eyes to what goes on elsewhere, to see that other people share our concerns and, although they may reach different results, are engaged in debates that parallel and that can, if we allow them to, enrich our own. What is required, above all, is openness, not necessarily to foreign models, to plans for building better mousetraps; but to the sharing of ideas, and to seeing how they play out in different contexts.

In looking at foreign practices and institutions, it is important to keep in mind that they are not monoliths, any more than our own are. Law is not merely a body of uncontested rules; it is a social activity, and the people engaged in that activity may differ among themselves as to what the legal rule is and should be. A legal culture, like any other culture, "is not a flow, nor even a confluence; the form of its existence is a struggle, or at least a debate — it is nothing if not a dialectic." This is a central point in Rodolfo Sacco's theory of "legal formants":[2]

> Professor Sacco has shown that there often is not, in a given legal system, a single unvarying rule on a particular point, but rather a series of different (sometimes conflicting) formulations of the applicable rule, depending on the kind of source consulted. The code may say one thing, the courts another; scholars may state the rule differently; the tacit rule actually followed may again be different from what anyone says it is. These different possible formulations are "formants" of the rule as it obtains in that particular jurisdiction. Understanding a legal system requires attention to the different incidences of its rules at various levels of practice and layers of discourse."[3] . . .

---

2. [Wise's footnote 90:] See Rodolfo Sacco, Legal Formants: A Dynamic Approach to Comparative Law (pts. 1 & 2), 39 Am. J. Comp. L. 1, 343 (1991).

3. [Wise's footnote 91:] Rudolf B. Schlesinger et al., Comparative Law: Case-Text-Materials 288 (6th ed. 1998).

In all legal systems criminal law in particular takes the form of an ongoing debate, a continuing dialectic, in which jurists grapple with much the same tensions. The terms of the dialectic are similar everywhere. As a result, diverse systems of criminal law have greater unity than is commonly realized, not necessarily on the surface, but in their underlying principles; not necessarily in their results, but in the perennial problems they generate. . . . In this respect, theorizing about criminal law throughout much of the world takes place within a single circle of legal culture, a common global tradition of criminal law scholarship. This makes conversation between scholars in different countries possible and potentially fruitful. But to engage in conversation, one has to listen as well as speak.

CHAPTER
11

Organized Crime

The term *organized crime* is used, in the vernacular, to describe the unlawful activities of highly organized, disciplined associations (gangs, mafias, triads, cartels, syndicates, tongs, etc.) engaged in illegal ventures for profit. Such ventures include, but are not limited to, gambling, prostitution, money laundering and loan sharking, narcotics trafficking, alien smuggling, and labor racketeering.[4] Obviously, a great deal of activity is covered by the term *organized crime*, making difficult the translation of that term into a sufficiently particular legal definition to sustain criminal sanctions. Criminologists, law enforcement personnel, and academics have, for example, come up with a number of attributes of "organized crime":

1. Traditionally, an "organized crime" group is motivated by money or power, not by ideology; the *nonideological* nature of such groups means that any political activity (generally corrupt) is an instrument for achieving their criminal aims or shielding them from law enforcement, not a goal in itself.
2. An organized crime group is *ongoing in nature* and is designed to continue over time and beyond the participation (or even lifetimes) of current members.
3. An organized crime syndicate typically has a *limited membership which is bound by understood rules.* The selection criteria may vary — with qualifications being based, inter alia, on ethnicity, family, race, criminal record, or other factors. Members may require sponsorship and may be tested or serve an apprenticeship during which the candidates demonstrate a commitment to the goals and rules of the organization, as well as a willingness to follow orders and maintain secrecy.
4. The power structure within an organized criminal organization is *hierarchical.* Some generalize that this hierarchy is characterized by three enduring "ranks." Those who occupy these positions may change with time, but the organizational structure remains, as does the authority inherent in the positions.
5. Organized criminal groups attempt to promote *specialization* in their functioning. Thus, for example, these groups may have enforcers, charged with using violence to achieve group ends, as well as "fixers" (dispensing bribes) and money launders. The efficiencies and economies of scale such specialization permits increase profits; the compartmentalization of knowledge that flows from specialization limits all participants' exposure to discovery or prosecution.
6. In an organized criminal organization, *violence and bribery are routinely used* as a means to achieve the organization's ends.

---

4. See, e.g., the Omnibus Crime Control and Safe Streets Act of 1968, tit. I, pt. F(b), Pub. L. No. 90-351, 82 Stat. 197 (1968).

7. One of the goals of an organized criminal group is *a monopolistic position* either within its spheres of business or in the geographical areas in which it operates. Such a monopoly position, often achieved through violence and corrupt relations with law enforcement, is a means to increase profits and power.[5]

How would one translate these attributes into the elements necessary to criminal liability for organized criminal activity? Countries around the world, as well as the United Nations in its Convention Against Transnational Organized Crime (UNTOC), have struggled with this question.

One might legitimately ask if such a definitional exercise is even necessary — that is, why the international community should concentrate on organized crime as a distinct type of criminal wrong, as opposed to focusing on the underlying criminal acts undertaken by the group. The answer may be derived from some of the attributes identified above.

First, criminals operating in a group are likely to be more successful in achieving their objectives, more dangerous in doing so, and less likely to deviate from the criminal path. Specialization and divisions of labor permit criminal groups to operate more efficiently and effectively. For example, "snakeheads" and "coyotes" who traffic in persons are more likely to succeed when the "talents" of different persons are brought to bear on the enterprise (drivers, lookouts, etc.) than when one trafficker attempts to go it alone. Such economies of scale also help the group to avoid detection. "Although large drug gangs may be more visible than solo operators, they are also more likely to have the money to be successful bribers."[6] Similarly, members of a group of criminals can assist each other in evading detection, overwhelm enforcement resources through multiple concerted criminal acts, and shield members from criminal liability by compartmentalizing knowledge of the total range of gang activities.[7] Psychological research also demonstrates that individuals act differently when operating in a group; they are more apt to act against their own self-interest, to take bigger risks, and to engage in more extreme behavior than they might as individuals. Also, groups "are more likely than individuals to have committed or to go on to commit other crimes."[8]

Second, transnational organized crime has a corrosive effect on civil society the world over. The scope of organized criminality is not restricted to the groups of criminals organized solely for the purpose of committing crimes; rather, organized crime invades and taints legitimate enterprises as well. Thus, organized criminal groups may take over legitimate entities such as businesses and even governments, through wrongful means such as extortion or bribery. They may also use legitimate enterprises as a front for, or an instrument through which they carry on, illicit activities such as laundering money. As highlighted above, violence is a tool of the trade for organized gangs, and, by virtue of their enormous resources, criminal groups often wield considerable power and are able to corrupt political institutions and undermine democratic accountability in the various states in which they operate. In the words of the UN's Office on Drugs and Crime, a concerted international legal effort to address transnational organized crime was imperative because such crime constitutes "one of the major threats to human security, impeding the social, economic, political, and

---

5. See Howard Abadinsky, Organized Crime 1-3 (Sabra Horne et al. eds., 6th ed. 2000).

6. Neal Kumar Katyal, Danger in Numbers: Why It Makes Sense to Have Harsh Punishments for Conspiracy, Legal Aff., Mar./Apr. 2003, at 44.

7. Id.

8. Id. at 45.

cultural development of societies worldwide."[9] Combating these threats requires innovative legal mechanisms, training, and technical assistance programs to enhance the capacities of criminal justice systems and law enforcement agencies.

Although individual countries have struggled with how to address the discrete problem of group criminality for many years, the international community focused its energies on the problem relatively recently. This focus became imperative with the accelerating pace of "globalization." Not only do organized groups of criminals now have a variety of means of moving persons, arms, drugs, and other contraband over borders, but also advances in technology mean that they can communicate with greater speed and secrecy. Perhaps most important, they can send, receive, and launder the proceeds of their illicit activity with a keystroke; financial transactions that take seconds to complete by computer may take investigators years to unravel. In short, all the technological advances that have made the world more interdependent have also created unprecedented opportunities for organized criminal groups successfully to operate across national borders.

Respect for state sovereignty and the legal constraints that flow from it mean that law enforcement cannot operate as effectively across borders as criminal gangs do. Criminal groups have exploited the difficulties domestic authorities have encountered in pursuing transnational crimes. They have benefited, for example, from cumbersome extradition procedures and legal constraints on evidence gathering abroad. Because of criminal syndicates' transborder reach and the special challenges they pose to the law enforcement efforts of individual states in the international system, the international community has come to realize that closer and more effective coordination between national investigators and prosecutors is required.

Before attempting to forge new avenues of international enforcement cooperation and other mechanisms to address the problem of organized criminality, however, those charged with drafting a convention had to define *organized crime*. In the United States and some other common law countries, the offense of conspiracy has often been used for this purpose. As Professor Neal Katyal summarized the U.S. conspiracy law:

> Imagine that Joe and Sandra agree to rob a bank. From the moment of agreement, they can be found guilty of conspiracy even if they never commit the robbery (it's called "inchoate liability"). Even if the bank goes out of business, they can still be liable for the conspiracy ("impossibility" is not a defense). Joe can be liable for other crimes that Sandra commits to further the conspiracy's objective, like hot-wiring a getaway car (that's called *Pinkerton* liability, after a 1946 Supreme Court case involving tax offenses). He can't evade liability by staying home on the day of the robbery (a conspirator has to take an affirmative act to "withdraw"). And if the bank heist takes place, both Joe and Sandra can be charged with bank robbery and with the separate crime of conspiracy, each of which carries its own punishment (the crime of conspiracy doesn't "merge" with the underlying crime).[10]

Federal authorities determined that even conspiracy law was insufficient to the task of dealing with organized crime in the United States. Accordingly, they enacted the Racketeer Influenced and Corrupt Organizations (RICO) statute, 18 U.S.C. §1961 et seq., which is examined in greater depth within. RICO was designed to aid in the eradication of organized crime by establishing new crimes *and* by providing

---

9. UN Office on Drugs and Crime, Organized Crime, http://www.unodc.org/unodc/en/organized-crime/index.html (last visited July 15, 2009).
10. Katyal, supra note 6, at 44.

enhanced sanctions (such as forfeiture) and remedies (such as treble damages civil liability) to deal with the unlawful activities of criminal syndicates.[11]

RICO spells out four distinct offenses in §1962. Oddly, the least-used offenses, violations of §§1962(a) and 1962(b), are those that address the primary evil that RICO was designed to attack: the infiltration of legitimate enterprises by organized crime groups. Section 1962(a) proscribes the use of the proceeds of racketeering activity to acquire an "enterprise." A violation of this section might be proved, for example, were a narcotics trafficker to purchase a legitimate business with the proceeds of multiple drug transactions. Similarly, §1962(b) bars the use of a pattern of racketeering to acquire an enterprise. It would be violated, for example, where a mobster takes over a legitimate business through a series of extortionate acts or arsons designed to intimidate the legitimate owners into selling out.

The most often-employed substantive prohibitions are §1962(d), which simply proscribes conspiracies to violate the other subsections, and §1962(c). Section 1962(c) makes it "unlawful for any person employed by or associated with any enterprise . . . to conduct or participate . . . in the conduct of such enterprise's affairs through a pattern of racketeering activity." Section 1962(c), for example, would apply to an auto dealer who uses his dealership to operate a stolen car ring.

A "pattern of racketeering activity" is defined in §1961(1) as the commission of two or more statutorily defined crimes (often called RICO "predicates") within a span of ten years. Literally hundreds of state, federal, and even foreign law crimes can serve as RICO predicates and thus as the outlawed "racketeering activity." For example, RICO charges can be built upon two or more instances of sports bribery, credit card fraud, passport forgery, criminal copyright infringement, and embezzlement from labor unions, as well as (the perhaps more predictable) offenses of murder, extortion, gambling, kidnapping, arson, robbery, bribery, and distribution of controlled substances.

One of the issues to arise in the application of RICO (and to challenge those drafting an internationally acceptable definition of "organized crime") is whether simple conspiracies should be subject to the enhanced penalties meant to be reserved for gangsters — and if not, how such a distinction can be drawn in defining the crime. In other words, how does one draft a definition of a forbidden joint enterprise that effectively distinguishes between two individuals who conspire over the course of ten years to rob two convenience stores and an organized crime family prosecutable under RICO? In answer to this question, U.S. courts have grafted onto RICO a gloss that requires proof of an ongoing, truly organized criminal group. Thus, the Supreme Court noted in *United States v. Turkette*[12] that an "enterprise" is something more than simply a pattern of racketeering acts: "The enterprise is an entity, for present purposes a group of persons associated together for a common purpose of engaging in a course of conduct. . . . [Proof of an enterprise requires] evidence of an ongoing organization, formal or informal, and . . . evidence that the various associates function as a continuing unit."[13] Further, a couple of random crimes planned by two or more persons does not constitute a "pattern of racketeering activity." In *H.J. Inc. v. Northwestern Bell Telephone Co.*,[14] the Supreme Court held that a "pattern" requires proof of "*continuity plus relationship*."[15] The predicate crimes must be related, in the sense that they "have the same or similar purposes, results, participants, victims,

---

11. United States v. Turkette, 452 U.S. 576, 589 (1981).
12. Id.
13. Id. at 583.
14. 492 U.S. 229 (1989).
15. Id. at 239 (emphasis original) (citation omitted).

or methods of commission, or otherwise are interrelated by distinguishing character-istics and are not isolated events."[16] "Continuity," the Court explained, "is both a closed- and open-ended concept, referring either to a closed period of repeated conduct, or to past conduct that by its nature projects into the future with a threat of repetition."[17]

Most civil law countries do not accept "conspiracy" as a separate, stand-alone crime, and international tribunals, save in the case of genocide, have also been reluctant to use it. Nor has RICO in all its particulars proved to be an attractive template for other countries' legal efforts to prosecute organized crime. In Section A, we reproduce a portion of Professor Edward Wise's comparative analysis of national responses to the problem of defining "organized crime." As he notes, other means of addressing these problems have evolved, one of which is to criminalize *membership* in a group that commits crimes, an option rejected by U.S. legislators concerned that such an approach would create constitutional problems. All countries, however, have faced similar concerns in crafting their solutions. We use an excerpt of Dr. Boaz Sangero's analysis of Israeli legislation to illustrate some of the factors considered in arriving at these solutions.

The international community, then, faced a dual definitional challenge in drafting a legal convention requiring the criminalization of transnational organized crime. First, the convention had to reconcile, or at least take account of, the different solu-tions countries had come up with to deal with the problem of organized criminality. Second, it had to ensure that the solution it arrived at took account of the concerns that have complicated national debates: How to accommodate "organized crime" prohibitions with principles of freedom of association and the requisite in criminal law of personal culpability. For example, most criminal enterprises do not have "membership lists" or notarized "agreements" listing their criminal ends; if "mem-bership" or a conspiratorial "agreement," not a particular act, is the determinant of criminal liability, might not mistakes be easy to make? The drafters' challenge, then, was to come up with a convention that permitted fact finders to meaningfully distin-guish between dangerous organized criminal organizations—and criminals—and those who simply have unfortunate taste in friends. In Section B, we rely upon Professor Roger Clark's analysis of the result of the international community's efforts: the UN Convention Against Transnational Organized Crime. In reviewing these materials, consider how well the international community has responded to the practical and definitional challenges discussed above.

A. COMPARATIVE ANALYSIS OF NATIONAL EFFORTS TO CRIMINALIZE "ORGANIZED CRIME"

EDWARD M. WISE, RICO AND ITS ANALOGUES: SOME COMPARATIVE CONSIDERATIONS

27 Syracuse J. Intl. L. & Com. 303 (2000)

. . . RICO has been characterized as "the most important substantive and procedural law tool in the history of organized-crime control." It is particularly important

---

16. Id. at 240.
17. Id. at 241.

because it changed the way in which cases involving organized crime are investigated and prosecuted: it encourages investigators "to think in terms of gathering evidence and obtaining indictments against entire 'enterprises' like each organized crime family," and it allows prosecutors to present at trial "a complete picture of what the defendant was doing and why, instead of the artificially fragmented picture that traditional criminal law demands."

RICO is not, however, the only piece of "legal weaponry" that has been deployed against organized crime in the United States. It is part of a larger arsenal. That arsenal includes as well the provisions for electronic eavesdropping contained in Title III of the Omnibus Crime Control and Safe Streets Act of 1968[, codified at 18 U.S.C. §§2510-2520]; other parts of the Organized Crime Control Act of 1970, especially the title that first authorized the federal witness protection program; the Continuing Criminal Enterprise statute enacted as part of the Comprehensive Drug Abuse Prevention and Control Act of 1970[, codified at 21 U.S.C. §848]; the expanded forfeiture provisions contained in the Comprehensive Forfeiture Act of 1984; and the Money Laundering Control Act of 1986[, codified at 18 U.S.C. §§1956-1957]. All of these fall outside the four corners of RICO proper. Calling for other countries to build similarly comprehensive arsenals is not the same as saying that they ought to replicate the RICO statute verbatim. Indeed, for another country to reproduce the whole of RICO exactly would be (to borrow a phrase used by Lawrence Friedman in a different context) "both miraculous and insane." It may be instructive to consider why this should be so.

One possible explanation for the dearth of exact copies of RICO abroad may be that other countries have not had exactly the same problems with organized crime as those that led to enactment of RICO in the United States. Law, after all, is supposed to respond to social needs, or at least to perceived social needs. If law really were, as it sometimes is asserted to be, a "mirror of society," countries with similar social problems would tend to enact similar laws; and, conversely, countries with different social problems would be unlikely to enact the same or similar laws. It has been suggested that different countries, indeed, have responded to the problem of organized crime "according to the specific local threats raised by the criminal groups they have to deal with" and "according to their own particular perception of the problem." Thus, while Italy, as we shall see, has enacted an anti-mafia statute that, although not precisely a clone, bears some resemblance to RICO, "[o]ther countries without experience of the extensive organized crime groups active in Italy and the USA for so many years" are said to "have hesitated to follow the Italian and American example, convinced that the category of 'conspiracy crime' suffices to deal with the new types of organized crime."[18]

It is possible, however, that hesitation about following the American example may, in this instance, have other roots as well. The law's responsiveness to immediate social needs is often exaggerated. Law, as Alan Watson argues, can be and has been, over long stretches of time, extremely dysfunctional; at any rate, there is no "close, inherent, necessary relationship between existing rules of law and the society in which they operate." . . . [Al]though "[t]he life of the law . . . has been experience," an important part of that experience is a country's particular legal culture; lawyers' habits of mind may have as much, if not more, to do than social, economic, and political

---

18. [Wise's footnote 20:] [Sabrina Adamoli et al., Organized Crime Around the World 136 (HEUNI Publication Series No. 31, 1998).] "Conspiracy crime," as the term is used in this statement, includes the crime of forming or participating in a criminal association, which in many countries is the closest equivalent there is to the common-law crime of conspiracy. See id. at 132.

circumstances in determining the form the law takes. Organized crime is supposed to be a world-wide problem. Racketeer influenced and corrupt organizations surely are not unique to the United States. If other countries have hesitated to replicate all the details of RICO exactly, it may not only be because they have had a different and less extensive experience of organized crime than the United States; it may also have to do with certain features of the RICO statute itself that make it practically inimitable.

In the first place, RICO is a very complex statute. . . . [Its] provisions are complex in part because they are concerned with multifarious harms. Two of RICO's substantive subsections[, 18 U.S.C. §1962(a) and (b),] are clearly concerned with the infiltration of legitimate businesses by organized crime: they prohibit both (a) using income derived from racketeering activity (defined in terms of a long litany of state and federal crimes [in 18 U.S.C. §1961(1)]) to acquire an interest in an enterprise; and (b) acquiring or maintaining control of the enterprise through a pattern of racketeering activity. According to one view, the take-over of legitimate enterprises by organized crime was the specific evil, the principal harm, against which RICO was directed.

A further subsection[, §1962(c),] makes it a crime for anyone employed by or associated with an enterprise to conduct or participate in the affairs of the enterprise through a pattern of racketeering activity. Arguably, this provision was aimed at racketeers who use a business to commit crimes once they have taken it over. But, read literally, it applies to anyone who commits a series of predicate crimes while conducting a business enterprise. The enterprise does not necessarily have to be a legal entity. [The definition of "enterprise" in §1961(4) specifies that it] can be a "group of individuals associated in fact." Thus, subsection (c) can be read to apply to anyone who engages in a pattern of racketeering activity as a member of a group. Read this way, RICO reaches, in effect, the operations of organized crime itself.

According to another view, RICO was intended, from the beginning, to have this effect: it was meant to cover all forms of criminality involving "enterprises," no matter whether the crimes in question are committed against, through, or by an enterprise. This view has prevailed. *United States v. Turkette*[19] is the crucial case. [In it, the Supreme Court held that a group of criminals "associated in fact" to pursue entirely illegitimate ends could constitute a RICO enterprise.] RICO, as interpreted, has not been limited to cases involving the infiltration of a legitimate business by organized crime. It has not even been limited to cases involving organized crime. It can be invoked whenever predicate crimes are committed by someone associated with an "enterprise," in the loosest possible sense of the term. . . .

. . . [A] hypothetical foreign legislator, even though minded to reproduce as much of RICO as possible, would find that it hardly makes sense to enact a word-for-word copy. . . . [C]ertain aspects of RICO depend so closely on distinctive peculiarities of United States law that it would be more than usually obtuse to try to transpose them into other legal systems. For instance, the enterprise against, by, or through which a RICO violation is committed must be one "which is engaged in, or the activities of which affect, interstate or foreign commerce" [under each substantive prohibition, 18 U.S.C. §1962(a), (b), and (c)]. This requirement of an interstate or foreign commerce nexus is necessary only because of our own particular federal arrangements which limit the power of Congress to legislate with respect to criminal law. Likewise, the definition of "racketeering activity" in terms of a list of predicate offenses that includes both state and federal crimes presupposes a federal system in which there are

---

19. [Wise's footnote 21:] United States v. Turkette, 452 U.S. 576 (1981).

both state and federal crimes. The provision allowing the government to obtain injunctive relief to prevent continuing RICO violations, [18 U.S.C. §1964(a),] presupposes a legal system that permits courts to issue injunctions — and, ultimately, the whole history of Anglo-American equity. The provision for private civil enforcement, allowing "any person injured in his business or property" by a RICO violation to sue for treble damages,[20] . . . is distinctively American — more distinctively American than apple pie or the death penalty. It would be regarded elsewhere as a fundamental category mistake. In the field of antitrust law itself, from which the RICO provision for treble damages derives, the most important single difference between the United States and Europe lies in our heavy reliance on private enforcement through suits for treble damages. The prospect of recovering such damages (coupled with an equally distinctive "American rule" as to costs, so that a losing plaintiff will not be saddled with paying the defendant's attorney's fees) provides a crucial incentive for private enforcement.

In other countries, the award of treble or any kind of punitive damages to a private party would be regarded as indicative of a failure to draw a proper distinction between criminal and private law. Other countries are far more willing than we are, as a procedural matter, to allow a private party — the so-called *partie civile* — to pursue civil claims and to participate along with the prosecution in a criminal trial. But, so far as remedies go, "civil law systems are virtually unanimous in rejecting the notion of punitive damages recoverable by the victim (as distinguished from fines paid to the state as punishment)." . . .

Other features of the RICO statute are perhaps more readily adaptable for use in foreign countries. Apart from its provisions for private enforcement, the two leading innovations found within the RICO statute are (a) the idea of asset forfeiture and (b) the idea of criminalizing participation in the activities of a criminal organization. Not coincidentally, in recent decades throughout the world, "the main innovations in criminal legislation against organized crime" also "have concerned participation in the activities of criminal organizations and the confiscation of assets acquired by means of criminal activity."

. . . [T]he idea of asset forfeiture has been remarkably influential abroad. It is fair to say that, in this regard, RICO started a world-wide trend that can be traced to the example set by the United States in 1970. . . . [A]t least the idea of forfeiture itself seems to be one that can be transposed readily into other systems. Indeed, as a general proposition, innovations with respect to sanctions may be more readily exportable than offense definitions which tend to be tied to the technical peculiarities of a particular legal culture.

The idea of criminalizing participation in the activities of a criminal organization is realized in RICO[, in §1962(c),] through language that makes it "unlawful for any person employed by or associated with any enterprise engaged in, or the activities of which affect, interstate or foreign commerce, to conduct or participate, directly or indirectly, in the conduct of such enterprise's affairs through a pattern of racketeering activity or collection of unlawful debt." This language does more, of course, than penalize participation in a criminal organization; it makes it unlawful for anyone connected with any kind of "enterprise" to engage in a series of predicate crimes on its behalf. In this regard, the statutory language is polysemous: it has multiple

---

20. [Wise's footnote 34:] 18 U.S.C. §1964 (b) ("Any person injured in his business or property by reason of a violation of section 1962 of this chapter may sue therefor in any appropriate United States district court and shall recover threefold the damages he sustains and the cost of the suit, including a reasonable attorney's fee").

significations. But a central function of this language, at least as it has been inter-preted, is that "it criminalizes membership in a group bent on crime." It thereby does indirectly what in 1970 was assumed could not be done directly: it makes active Mafia membership a crime. . . .

The drafters of RICO took it for granted that they could not directly proscribe the status of being a member of a criminal organization. Instead, they listed the crimes in which organized crime groups typically are supposed to engage, and then made it criminal to participate in a group that commits such crimes. RICO, in this respect, is not unlike conspiracy, which technically is defined in terms of an act — the act of agreeing to commit a crime — but which courts treat "as though it were a group rather than an act." RICO has been used to greatest effect, like conspiracy, to prosecute those who commit crimes as part of a group. It goes beyond conspiracy, however, in that it permits the joinder of members of a group who are too loosely connected with each other to be considered parties to a single conspiratorial agreement. It allows the pros-ecution to reach all members of the group in one trial, to expose the full scope of the organization, to "present a complete picture of a large-scale, ongoing, organized-crime group engaged in diverse rackets and episodic explosions of violence."

The language used in RICO to criminalize participation in a criminal organization has not commended itself to law-makers in other countries. The main reason may be that other countries have long done directly what RICO does only by indirection: they already have laws proscribing membership in criminal associations. They also have a long history of ambivalence about such laws.

To some extent, laws proscribing criminal associations are a surrogate for the doctrine of conspiracy, which does not exist as such outside of the common law world. The fact that a defendant acted with others is often treated as an aggravating circumstance when it comes to sentencing: crimes committed in concert are regarded as posing a greater social danger than crimes committed alone, and therefore as warranting enhanced punishment. But it is a different question whether participation in a group bent on crime should be treated as an independent offense, punishable in itself. Common law countries do treat conspiracy as a separate offense. Other legal systems do not. The notion that agreement to commit a crime constitutes a crime in itself does not exist in civil law countries. Article 115 of the Italian Penal Code explic-itly rejects the common law position: "Except as the law provides otherwise, whenever two or more persons agree to commit an offense, and it is not committed, none of them shall be punishable for the mere fact of agreement . . ." Nor do civil law countries accept the *Pinkerton* rule, by which, in the United States, conspiracy can function as a mode of accessorial liability, making all parties to the conspiracy liable for all crimes committed by their confederates, regardless of whether the ordinary requirements for complicity have been satisfied.[21] . . .

Although conspiracy as an autonomous crime is unknown in civil law countries, those countries do have a number of doctrines that can be used to perform the same functions as the common law concept of conspiracy. This is a familiar phenomenon in comparative law. The technical constructs of one legal system rarely coincide precisely with those of another. A body of law, criminal law included, is not only a set of rules directed to officials or to the public telling them how they are supposed to behave; it is also a language, a way of framing experience, a scheme by which reality is shaped and defined. Different languages, different legal systems, carve up reality in different ways — just as beef is cut up differently in different countries. . . .

---

21. [Wise's footnote 53:] Pinkerton v. United States, 328 U.S. 640 (1946).

The standard recipe in comparative law for dealing with such conceptual disparities is to look for functional equivalents and to use them as a basis for comparison. Applying this kind of functional approach, ... Italian law, for instance, achieves many of the same practical results as Anglo-American doctrines of conspiracy: in part by stretching the law of attempt to cover cases of inchoate criminality that we would treat as cases of conspiracy; in part by extending the concept of complicity to include cases of "moral complicity," which can have the same effect as the *Pinkerton* rule; in part by employing the provisions of the Italian Penal Code that proscribe membership in a criminal association.[22]

... [Consider] Italian Penal Code (art. 416), [which] criminaliz[es] *associazion[i] per delinquere* (association[s] for delinquency) ... as follows:

> When three or more persons associate for the purpose of committing more than one crime, those who promote or constitute or organize the association shall be punished, for that alone, by imprisonment for from three to seven years.
>
> For the act of participating in the association alone, the punishment shall be imprisonment for from one to five years.
>
> The leaders shall be subject to the same punishment prescribed for the promoters.
>
> If the associates roam the countryside or public roads in arms, the term of imprisonment shall be for from five to fifteen years.
>
> The punishment shall be increased if the number of associates is ten or more.[23]

Under this provision, agreement to commit a crime is not in itself punishable. Article 115 of the Italian Penal Code bars that. Article 416 requires an association. The association need not have a specific structure, but it must be a more or less permanent group of at least three persons, committed not to perpetrating a single crime, but to an open-ended course of criminal conduct.

In 1982, the Italian Penal Code was amended to add a new offense of "mafia-type association" (*associazione di tipo mafioso*). The new article 416 *bis* reads as follows:

> Whoever belongs to a mafia-type association composed of three or more persons shall be punished by imprisonment of from three to six years.
>
> Those who promote, direct, or organize the association shall be punished, for that alone, by imprisonment of from four to nine years.
>
> An association is a mafia-type association when those who belong to it rely on the intimidative force of associative ties, and on the discipline and code of silence resulting therefrom, in order to commit crimes, to acquire directly or indirectly the management or control of economic activities, of concessions, permits, public contracts and services, or to obtain unjust profits or benefits for themselves or others, or for the purpose of impeding or obstructing the free exercise of the vote or of procuring votes for themselves or others on the occasion of an election. . . .

---

22. [Wise's footnote 59:] See Elisabetta Grande, Accordo Criminoso e Conspiracy: Tipicità e Stretta Legalità nell' Analisi Comparata (1993).

23. [Wise's footnote 72:] C.P. art. 416, in The Italian Penal Code 145-46. There ... is an interesting comment on [this provision] in a note contributed by Nino Levi to the Michael & Wechsler casebook: "The crime of association for delinquency in Italian law is, within its scope, the analogue of criminal conspiracy in Anglo-American law and raises similar problems. Moreover, it stands in no better repute among those who value individual liberty highly. It was employed at the end of the 19th century as a means of persecuting labor and hounding socialist organizations. Under fascism it has been unnecessary to resort to it in political matters but in the field of ordinary crimes it is associated with summary repression, as, for example, in the repression of the Mafia." Jerome Michael & Herbert Wechsler, Criminal Law and Its Administration: Cases, Statutes and Commentaries 639 n.4 (1940).

If the economic activities over which the associates aim to assume or maintain control are financed in whole or in part with the proceeds, products, or profits of crime, the punishment prescribed in the foregoing paragraphs shall be increased by from one-third to one-half.

Upon conviction, confiscation of things that were used or destined for use in committing a crime and things that are the proceeds, products, or profits or that constitute an instrumentality thereof shall always be mandatory.

The provisions of the present article shall also apply to the Camorra and to other associations, whatever their local designation, that rely on the intimidative force of associative ties in order to pursue aims corresponding to those of mafia-type associations.

This anti-mafia law incorporates several features borrowed from RICO, including the idea of asset forfeiture. But insofar as it can be considered a clone of RICO, it seems, at least in length, a somewhat stunted clone. . . . Article 416 proper (association for delinquency) already had been used against the Mafia. By directing itself specifically against "mafia-type associations," article 416 *bis* mainly has a "high symbolic value." Like RICO, it provides a basis on which all of the members of a large crime syndicate can be tried together, and all of its ramifications and radiations exposed. Unlike RICO, it comes right out and says that the gravamen of the offense consists of belonging to a certain type of association.

BOAZ SANGERO, ARE ALL FORMS OF JOINT CRIME REALLY "ORGANIZED CRIME"? ON THE NEW ISRAELI COMBATING CRIMINAL ORGANIZATIONS LAW AND PARALLEL LEGISLATION IN THE U.S. AND OTHER COUNTRIES

29 Loy. L.A. Intl. & Comp. L. Rev. 61 (2007)

[In 2003, Israel enacted a new statute targeted at organized crime. In addition to creating new criminal offenses, the statute doubled the penalty for existing offenses committed in the context of a criminal organization and created mechanisms for forfeiture of property. In light of these provisions, consider the substance of the statute, discussed below.]

. . . The new offenses are set forth in sections 2 and 4 of the Combating Criminal Organizations Law, as follows:

2. (a) A person who heads a criminal organization or a person who does one of the following acts in a manner that could promote the criminal activity of a criminal organization shall be liable to imprisonment for 10 years:

(1) he directly or indirectly manages, organizes, directs or supervises activities in a criminal organization;

(2) he directly or indirectly finances activities of a criminal organization or receives financing for the purpose of operating the organization or decides with respect to the distribution of monies in a criminal organization.

(b) A person providing a consulting service to a criminal organization with the object of promoting the criminal activities of the criminal organization shall be liable to imprisonment for ten years.

(c) Where an offense as stated in subsections (a) and (b) has been committed with respect to a criminal organization whose activities also include an offense for which the penalty prescribed exceeds imprisonment for 20 years, the person committing such an offense shall be liable to imprisonment for 20 years. . . .

4. A public servant who abuses his office or powers in a manner that could promote the criminal activity of a criminal organization shall be liable to imprisonment for ten years.

The need for these new offenses was explained in the draft bill as follows:

> Section 2 — it is proposed to establish that holding significant positions in a criminal organization shall, in and of itself, constitute a criminal offense carrying a prison term of ten or twenty years, in accordance with the severity of the organization's activity; this provision is designed to cope with the difficulty in proving the link between those holding positions in criminal organizations and the offenses actually committed, and it states that it is enough to head, manage, finance the organization, and so forth, in order for this to be considered an offense. . . .
>
> Section 4 — one of the gravest dangers of organized crime is the corruption of the public system; therefore, it is proposed that an offense be established for the use by a public servant of his office or powers in order to promote the activity of a criminal organization. . . .

. . . [W]hen characterizing organized crime in the explanatory notes of the draft bill, its authors wrote of an organization with a hierarchical structure, distance between "commanders" and "soldiers," a mechanism for discipline and harsh sanctions for its breach, and the resulting evidentiary difficulties. They also wrote about infiltration into the corridors of power, violence, and corruption.

[T]hese are all typical attributes of organized crime. Based on these frightening characteristics, the statute's proponents demanded of the legislature, and received, very severe tools of law enforcement. . . .

The problem is that not a single one of these major attributes of organized crime found its way into the definition of a criminal organization established in the new statute. In comparison to many laws from other countries, the Israeli definition is the broadest to be found:

> "[C]riminal organization" means an incorporated or unincorporated body of persons acting in an organized, systematic and continuous format for the commission of offenses which, under the laws of Israel, fall within the category of a felony or the offenses enumerated within the First Schedule, except offenses falling within the category of a felony enumerated within the Second Schedule; for this purpose, it is irrelevant—
>
> (1) whether or not the members of the organization know the identity of the other members;
> (2) whether the composition of the members of the group is fixed or changing;
> (3) whether the aforesaid offenses . . . are committed or intended to be committed in Israel or abroad . . . ;
> (4) whether the organization also commits lawful acts and whether it also acts for lawful purposes.

In effect, the definition encompasses nearly all forms of joint crime, whether it entails complicity in a felony . . . or whether it only entails the formation of a conspiracy. Most offenses are not committed by only one person, but rather, in unison, by two or more persons and many offenders are habitual criminals. Therefore, a very significant number of crimes actually committed is liable to fall within the purview of this drastic statute, which is designed to deal with the special phenomenon of organized crime.

How did this come about? Why has Israeli law taken matters even further than Italy, where the dimensions of the Mafia phenomenon — and its inherent violence and corruption — have reached epidemic proportions? . . .

Before the discussion of possible narrower definitions of a criminal organization, which may be observed through a comparative study of other legal systems, it should be noted that the broad Israeli definition was not established because of a lack of familiarity with alternative definitions. The rejection of . . . narrower definitions in their entirety has resulted in a definition so broad that, in effect, it no longer characterizes a criminal organization. Following is a survey of the proposals to restrict the definition of a criminal organization:

1. For the Purpose of Financial or Material Benefit

The United Nations Palermo Treaty of 2000 refers to an "organized criminal group" whose aim is to commit serious crimes for the purpose of obtaining financial or material benefit. A similarly narrow definition may be found in the penal law of New Zealand.

In the explanatory notes of the Israeli draft bill, the rejection of this narrower definition was explained as follows:

> [The definition] was adapted to the needs of the State of Israel; thus, in some models, an emphasis was placed on the financial objectives of the organization, whereas the proposed definition does not limit the objectives of the organization, so that it may also include other objectives, such as ideological objectives. . . .

One of the authors of the draft bill has given a further explanation for rejecting this narrower definition:

> For if this is an organization that commits serious crimes, there is no reason why it should not be considered a criminal organization, whether or not its objectives are financial.

However, as we shall see below, the new statute does not even require that this be "an organization that commits serious crimes."

2. An Organization the Main Objective of Which Is the Commission of Crimes

Such a restriction in the definition of a criminal organization may be found in statutes in Canada, Austria, and Germany. The drafters of the Israeli statute rejected this narrower definition, as well, "because there may be organizations operating in a legal disguise, whereby it is difficult to define the criminal objective as the main objective." Furthermore, in the definition of a "criminal organization" in the new Israeli statute, it was expressly established that "it is irrelevant . . . whether the organization also commits lawful acts and whether it also acts for lawful purposes."

3. Secrecy

Reference to a criminal organization in the Swiss Criminal Code is limited to an organization that keeps its structure and membership secret, the objective of which is to conduct violent criminal activity or to obtain benefit through criminal means. The element of secrecy was rejected in Israel, "since even if this element often characterizes criminal organizations, there is no reason that an organization not be classified as a criminal organization simply because it operates openly."

4. THE HIERARCHICAL STRUCTURE OF AN ORGANIZATION

Israel rejected a narrower definition entailing the hierarchical nature of an organization, found in several legal systems, with the following argument:

> Even a hierarchical structure, which characterizes many of the criminal organizations that the statute is meant to deal with, has not been established as part of the definition, since, if an organization possesses the remaining elements (an organized, systematic and continuous format for the commission of crime), its existence is dangerous even without proof of a defined hierarchical structure.

The rejection took place despite the fact that, in the draft bill, the hierarchical structure of a criminal organization served as one of the attributes of an organization justifying the enactment of the statute.

5. INFILTRATING THE CORRIDORS OF POWER

A narrower definition of a criminal organization, entailing infiltration into the corridors of power, was also rejected in Israel "for reasons similar" to those for rejecting the requirement regarding the hierarchical structure of the organization. This is despite the fact that, in the draft bill, "infiltrating government in order to ensure protection for continued activity" served as an attribute of criminal organizations justifying a new statute designed to fight them.

6. USE OF MEASURES OF INTIMIDATION (A MAFIA-TYPE ORGANIZATION)

The Italian Criminal Code refers to a Mafia-type criminal organization as one in which members use measures of intimidation deriving from a bond of membership and a vow of silence to commit crimes and acquire gains and advantages.

This narrower definition was also presented before the members of the Knesset Law Committee, but was not included in the new statute.

7. AN ATTEMPT TO CORRUPT OR INTIMIDATE

[According to criminologists,] the two key elements of organized crime are violence and corruption. In the statutory definition of a criminal organization, both of these elements may be required together; a specific one of the two may be required on its own (. . . infiltrating the corridors of power; use of measures of intimidation); or either one of them may be required, on its own, without specifying which one (thus, according to the definition of a criminal organization contained in the Austrian Criminal Code, it is required to show an attempt to corrupt or intimidate others). The new Israeli statute did not even contain this basic and minor restriction. . . .

NOTES AND QUESTIONS

1. Which statute — the United States' RICO, the Italian cognates, or the Israeli legislation — best captures the attributes of organized crime as described in our

introduction? Would the Italian or the Israeli prohibitions likely survive attack under the First Amendment to the U.S. Constitution? For additional comparative analyses, see Alexandra V. Orlova, Missing the Mark: The Russian Experience with Defining "Organized Crime," 1 Colum. J. E. Eur. L. 207 (2007); Chris Coulson, Note, Criminal Conspiracy Law in Japan, 28 Mich. J. Intl. L. 863 (2007).

2. In the United States, conspiracy is regarded as the prosecutors' "darling" because it is a powerful weapon. First, under U.S. law, conspiracy is a separate offense from the criminal objects of the conspiracy. Thus, assuming that a criminal agreement has been reached (and, under some statutes, an overt act in furtherance of the conspiracy has been taken), the government can secure a conspiracy conviction whether or not the conspiracy has been successful in its criminal objectives. If the conspiracy has been successful, the government can charge both the conspiracy and its criminal ends as separate counts, which may result in longer sentences upon conviction.

Second, conspiracy provides many practical advantages. In federal court, conspiracy means that (1) certain statements of co-conspirators may avoid the evidentiary bar against the admissibility at trial of hearsay statements (Fed. R. Evid. 801(D)(2)(E)); (2) different offenses, which normally could not be joined in one indictment or trial, may be charged and tried together (Fed. R. Crim. P. 8); (3) the government may choose to locate the trial in any venue in which one or more overt acts were taken pursuant to the conspiracy, regardless of where the co-conspirators live or work; and (4) the general five-year statute of limitations applicable in federal criminal cases does not begin to run until the last overt act is committed. Finally, many defense lawyers argue that the biggest advantage to the government of a conspiracy charge is the "spillover" effect that evidence about a wide-ranging conspiracy may have on the individual defendants—many of whom may not even have known the identity, let alone been aware of the activities, of those persons with whom they are standing trial.

3. In light of all that conspiracy provides prosecutors in attacking organized criminality, why is RICO necessary? It turns out that RICO gives federal prosecutors still more advantages. Consider the following summary from former prosecutor (and current U.S. District Court Judge) Gerard E. Lynch:

> . . . Since section 1962(c) defines participating in the affairs of an enterprise through a pattern of racketeering as a crime separate and apart from the predicate acts, it does not merely enhance the statutory penalty for the predicate acts, but rather permits the imposition of consecutive sentences for the RICO offense and the predicates. Because the RICO offense is a separate crime, the statute of limitations runs only from its completion; thus, every additional racketeering offense committed in furtherance of the enterprise's affairs within ten years of a previous one extends the statute of limitations for another five years for prosecution of the entire pattern. A RICO indictment thus may hold a defendant accountable for acts that took place twenty or more years before the date of the indictment—not for the penalty attached to the predicate crime, but for the separately defined RICO offense.
>
> Even within the ordinary limits of the double jeopardy principle and the statute of limitations, a prosecutor can use section 1962(c) to place before a single jury in a single trial offenses that could not otherwise be included in the same indictment or admitted into evidence at the same trial. Suppose, for example, the authorities develop evidence that the same defendant from whom they have recently made an undercover purchase of narcotics is a member of an organized crime family who committed a contract killing three years earlier. Under our ordinary, transaction-bound rules of procedure and evidence, the defendant would have to be tried separately for each offense. Since the earlier crime is plainly not part of the same course of events as the later, joinder of the

two crimes would not be possible; if the homicide had taken place in another state, jurisdictional or venue problems would also prevent joinder.

In a trial on the narcotics charge alone, moreover, the evidence of a prior homicide committed by the defendant would likely be excluded as irrelevant and highly prejudicial. Evidence that the defendant in a narcotics trial was part of the "Mafia" would surely be excluded as merely prejudicial evidence of the defendant's character and associations. And the prosecutor presumably would not even think about trying to elicit evidence of crimes that some other member of the same crime family had committed, in which this particular defendant was not personally involved. Evidence of the defendant's involvement in organized crime or of the murder he may have committed might finally surface after the defendant's conviction, as part of an argument for a severe sentence.

If the case could be indicted and tried under RICO, however, all of the evidence regarding this defendant's activities could easily be presented in the same trial. Since the government would have to allege and prove a pattern of racketeering activity, the murder and the narcotics offense could be alleged as elements of the same crime, the violation of section 1962(c). The rules precluding admission of evidence of other crimes, consequently, would simply have no application — evidence of the homicide would not be evidence of a prior crime, but evidence of the very offense charged in the indictment.

Jurisdictional and venue problems disappear, as well. It is irrelevant that the federal government lacks jurisdiction to prosecute ordinary homicides; the crime charged here is racketeering that affects interstate commerce, not murder. The single crime of racketeering, like any other crime, can be prosecuted in any district where a portion of the crime was committed, so any venue problem with combining crimes committed in different districts disappears.

The government would also have to allege and prove that the crimes were committed in furtherance of the affairs of an enterprise, so the prosecution would be permitted to show the existence, purposes and structure of the organized crime family, and the defendant's membership in it. Even if no other defendant were on trial, this may necessitate reference to criminal activities committed by other members of the organization, as examples of its continuing nature, hierarchical structure, or purposes as an entity; if the defendant were indicted along with several other alleged members of the same organized crime family, as is commonly done in RICO prosecutions, their crimes would of course have to be proved too. Joining those defendants in the same indictment would automatically be proper, of course; since the defendants were all jointly charged with the same crime — the RICO violation — we are faced not with the joinder of several separate offenses by different actors, but with a single offense all the defendants are alleged to have committed together.

Hon. Gerard E. Lynch, RICO: The Crime of Being a Criminal, Parts III & IV, 87 Colum. L. Rev. 920, 940-941 (1987) (footnotes omitted).

B. THE UN CONVENTION AGAINST TRANSNATIONAL ORGANIZED CRIME

On November 15, 2000, the UN General Assembly adopted the UN Convention Against Transnational Organized Crime (Organized Crime Convention) supplementary protocols (trafficking in persons, smuggling of migrants, and trafficking in firearms, which are discussed in Chapter 12) in order to promote more effective cooperation in preventing and combating transnational organized crime. It is not an exaggeration to say that the Convention (sometimes referred to as the UNTOC or the Palermo Convention) represents the single most ambitious international response to the challenges of international criminal activity ever undertaken by the international community. The Convention itself entered into force in September 2003; the United States' ratification became effective in December 2005.[24]

The scope of the Convention is broad. By its terms, it applies to the prevention, investigation, and prosecution of "transnational offences" by organized crime groups, specifically including four categories of crimes (participation in an organized criminal group, laundering of criminal proceeds, corruption, and obstruction of justice) as well as "serious crime" (meaning conduct constituting an offence punishable by either a maximum deprivation of liberty of at least four years, or a more serious penalty). States parties are obliged to criminalize the offenses of participation in an organized criminal group, laundering of criminal proceeds, corruption, and obstruction of justice under their domestic laws.

The Convention and its Protocols establish global standards that all states parties must meet while providing for flexibility in the manner in which national systems meet them. For example, the Convention and Protocols define — for the first time in binding international instruments — organized crime, migrant smuggling, and trafficking in persons, and they require all parties to criminalize this defined conduct under their domestic law. But they permit individual countries to tailor implementation of these obligations to their particular needs. For example, the Convention recognizes that different countries have different approaches to the crime that in the United States is labeled as conspiracy.

The international norms established by the Convention and its Protocols reflect a common recognition of the imperative to facilitate increased cooperation among governments in combating new forms of transborder criminal activity. They help to accomplish this by including accepted definitions of the most important crimes, by providing specific obligations for international assistance (including through extradition and mutual legal assistance), and by establishing far-reaching provisions for services and protections for victims of crimes, including in appropriate cases shelter, medical, and legal assistance.

The complete text of the Convention is available on our Web site; concentrate in particular on Articles 2-8, 10-18, 23, and 34.[25] Despite a growing number of ratifications (150 as of August 2009), it is difficult to determine how many states have adopted effective implementing legislation, and references to the Convention in reported judicial decisions are virtually nonexistent.

Questions concerning specific provisions are posed in the Notes and Questions that follow. As you read the Convention and review the following analysis of its provisions, ask yourself: If you had been one of the negotiators, would you have advocated different wording for any provisions? How would you advise a national legislature with respect to its implementation?

---

24. UNTOC G.A. Res. 55/25, annex I, U.N. GAOR, 55th Sess., Supp. No. 49, at 44, U.N. Doc. A/45/49 (vol. I) (2001); Convention and Protocols available at http://www.unodc.org/unodc/en/treaties/CTOC/index.html#Fulltext. The United States ratified the Convention in 2005, see Treaty Doc. 108-16 (2004) and Sen. Exec. Rep. 109-4 (2005). See generally David McLean, Transnational Organized Crime: A Commentary on the United Nations Convention and Its Protocols (Oxford Commentaries on International Law) (2007).

25. See http://www.internationalcriminallaw.org (last visited July 8, 2009).

ROGER S. CLARK, THE UNITED NATIONS CONVENTION AGAINST TRANSNATIONAL ORGANIZED CRIME

50 Wayne L. Rev. 161 (2004)

... Article 5, paragraph 1 of the Convention requires State Parties to "adopt such legislative and other measures as may be necessary to establish as criminal offences, when committed intentionally":

(a) Either or both of the following as criminal offences distinct from those involving the attempt or completion of the criminal activity:

(i) Agreeing with one or more other persons to commit a serious crime for a purpose relating directly or indirectly to the obtaining of a financial or other material benefit and, where required by domestic law, involving an act undertaken by one of the participants in furtherance of the agreement or involving an organized criminal group;

(ii) Conduct by a person who, with knowledge of either the aim and general criminal activity of an organized criminal group or its intention to commit the crimes in question, takes an active part in:

a. Criminal activities of the organized criminal group;

b. Other activities of the organized criminal group in the knowledge that his or her participation will contribute to the achievement of the above-described criminal aim;

(b) Organizing, directing, aiding, abetting, facilitating or counseling the commission of serious crime involving an organized criminal group.[26]

The opening words of the chapeau in subsection (a) are crucial: a new substantive offense is to be created, involving participation in a criminal group; it is to be additional to ("distinct from") any other specific offense (or attempted offense) committed by one or more of the participants. Some Convention definitions need mention. Article 2 defines an "organized criminal group," for the purposes of the Convention, as "a structured group of three or more persons, existing for a period of time and acting in concert with the aim of committing one or more serious crimes or offences established in accordance with this Convention, in order to obtain, directly or indirectly, a financial or other material benefit." "Structured group" means "a group that is not randomly formed for the immediate commission of an offence and that does not need to have formally defined roles for its members, continuity of its membership or a developed structure." "Serious crime," in turn, means "conduct constituting an offence punishable by a maximum deprivation of liberty of at least four years or a more serious penalty." This specific-content-free definition of serious crime is fundamental to the way the Convention itself operates. The scope of the Convention's application turns ultimately on the seriousness of the particular activities (judged in a rough and ready way by the penalty) rather than on substantive content. It is left to its Protocols to spell out some particular substantive areas (obviously not all) to which

---

26. [Clark's footnote 27:] Art. 34 (1) of the Convention requires States Parties to "take the necessary measures, including legislative and administrative measures, in accordance with fundamental principles of [their] domestic law, to ensure the implementation of [their] obligations under this Convention." Art. 34 (2) insists that "[t]he offences established in accordance with articles 5, 6, 8 and 23 of this Convention shall be established in the domestic law of each State Party independently of the transnational nature or the involvement of an organized criminal group as described in article 3, paragraph 1, of this Convention, except to the extent that article 5 of this Convention would require the involvement of an organized criminal group." This is rather a remarkable de-coupling of the obligations of a Party from the "Transnational" basis of the Convention. Art. 34 (3) permits a Party to adopt "more strict or severe measures than those provided for by this Convention for preventing and combating transnational organized crime."

the basic obligations of the Convention are to be applied, namely the Protocol to Prevent, Suppress and Punish Trafficking in Persons, Especially Women and Children, the Protocol against the Smuggling of Migrants by Land, Sea and Air and the Protocol Against the Illicit Manufacturing of and Trafficking in Firearms, Their Parts and Components and Ammunition. States becoming Parties to one or more of the Protocols in addition to the framework Convention itself undertake an obligation to criminalize the particular activities defined in the appropriate Protocol or Protocols. The Protocols are thus suppression conventions of a more traditional kind, criminalizing the substantive activities that are proscribed by the particular instrument.

. . . Article 5 is very much the result of a negotiation in which the ways in which different legal systems approach group criminality were brought together, at the same time with the appreciation that it was not a question of choosing one over the others, but of attaining a functional synthesis. It provides various options for various mindsets.

Thus, subparagraph (a) (i) of article 5, paragraph 1, while it avoids the word "conspiracy," is speaking essentially of that institution as understood in the Anglo-American common law. It is clearly an inchoate, preparation-type offense which could catch participants in the criminal net before a substantive crime (or even an attempt) has occurred. In both English and American law, conspiracy is well-established as an inchoate offense. By and large, conspiracy as an inchoate offense has not found its way into international criminal law treaties[, with the exception of the Genocide Convention]. In the present Convention, a specific reference to "conspiracy to commit" (apparently as an inchoate offense) appears (randomly?) only in respect of the crime of money laundering, the criminalization of which is required by article 6.[27] The "no-name conspiracy" contemplated by article 5(1)(a)(i) is thus relatively novel.

In addition, the Convention appears to follow the American common law position that punishment for the group criminality and any completed offenses may be cumulative.

The material following the words "where required by domestic law" in article 5, para. 1(a)(i) inject some flexibility into the requirement to criminalize. A State may add a requirement that there be "an act undertaken by one of the participants in furtherance of the agreement. . . ." This is a close relative of the common law "overt act" requirement, introduced statutorily in many jurisdictions. Like its common law counterpart, it appears to be a minimal requirement; there is no suggestion that the "act" need be criminal in itself or that it amount to an attempt. A State can also be in compliance with its rock-bottom obligations under the Convention if it limits group membership liability to situations where the enterprise involves an "organized criminal group" as defined in the Convention.[28] There is much give and take here, in deference to the way different legal systems cope with the basic problem, but an irreducible minimum of criminalization is reached.

---

27. [Clark's footnote 39:] Art. 6 of the Convention requires the criminalization of laundering proceeds of crime and, "subject to the basic concepts of its legal system . . . [p]articipation in, *association with or conspiracy to commit*, attempts to commit and aiding, abetting, facilitating and counseling the commission of any of the offences established in accordance with this article." Transnational Crime Convention, art. 6, para. 1(b)(ii) (author's emphasis added).

28. [Clark's footnote 42:] Both the requirement of an aim to commit "serious crime" (with potential of at least four years deprivation of liberty according to article 2(b)) and the requirement that the group be "organized" and thus "structured" according to article 2(a) and (c) respectively narrow the types of conspiracy that must be criminalized. States requiring involvement of an organized group for the purposes of subpara. (a)(i) must "ensure that their domestic law covers all serious crimes [as defined] involving organized criminal groups." Transnational Crime Convention, art. 5, para. 3. Parties limiting their legislation either by the "act" requirement or that of an "organized criminal group" must notify the United Nations Secretary-General, the depositary of the Convention. Id.

Subparagraph (a) (ii) of article 5, paragraph 1, on the other hand, is designed to be more congenial to civil law systems with which conspiracy has not found favor. It penalizes those who knowingly associate themselves with and take an "active part" in an organized criminal group. To come within the ambit of the subparagraph, the perpetrator must either be active in the criminal activities of the group, or active in its other activities with the appropriate knowledge, namely that the participation will contribute to the achievement of the criminal aim. It is pretty clear that a perpetrator may contravene this standard without doing acts that make him or her complicit under traditional principles for a serious crime as defined in the Convention. The conduct may, in itself, be a "non-serious" crime or even lawful. As is common in the area of individual criminal responsibility, there is overlap both among these various verbs and between what is caught by subparagraph (a)'s variants (i) and (ii).[29]

So far, we have been discussing situations where there is no need for proof of connection to a particular completed (or attempted) offense. One who goes as far as complicity in a serious crime involving an organized criminal group is, however, caught by [Article 5(1)(b)] for "[o]rganizing, directing, aiding, abetting, facilitating or counseling the commission of serious crime involving an organized criminal group." Unfortunately, the article does not expand further on the mens rea and actus reus of these forms of participation or complicity. The Prosecutor would probably need to show an intent that the particular crime occur and that the accomplice made some, at least minimal, contribution towards its occurrence.[30]

In many American jurisdictions, conspiracy is also used as an alternative to complicity theories such as aiding and abetting. Typically it imposes liability for substantive offenses (including attempts) on people at the periphery of the criminality who could not be convicted on standard complicity theories. This is often achieved by basing liability on a showing of what amounts to negligent connection with the criminal activity, rather than an intentional or knowing one. This version of conspiracy as a theory of secondary responsibility is not found in the Transnational Crime Convention, nor in the international criminal law treaties in general. Something close to it, under the guise of contributing to crime by a group of persons acting with a "common purpose" has, however, been appearing in international case-law and in some recent treaties.

. . . The Obligation to Criminalize Laundering

Article 6 of the Transnational Crime Convention deals with criminalization of the laundering of proceeds of crime. Parties are to seek to apply this principle to "the widest range of predicate offences."[31] At the least, it must include all "serious" crime

---

29. [Clark footnote 44:] Transnational Crime Convention art. 5(1)(a). A member of the U.N. Secretariat who was close to the drafting describes art. 5(1)(a)(ii) as a form of "enterprise liability." "The provision allows the prosecution of suspects even if a single common criminal enterprise or single common agreement cannot be proven. It is enough to prove that a crime has been committed on behalf or in the interest of a boss of an organized crime group without his/her knowledge of the particular crime." Slawomir Redo, New United Nations provisions against economic crime, in Przestepczosc Gospodarcza perspektywy Polski I Unii Eurpoejskiej (Economic Crime in Polish and European Union Perspective) (Andrzej Adamski ed., 2003).

30. [Clark's footnote 46:] The words "when committed intentionally" in the chapeau to art. 5, para. 1 must travel right through the paragraph, including the complicity provisions. The need for some actual or potential contribution is hornbook law.

31. [Clark's footnote 50:] The definition of "predicate offence" is a little circular: ". . . any offence as a result of which proceeds have been generated that may become the subject of an offence as defined in article 6 of this Convention." Convention art. 2(h). "Predicate" to describe the underlying substantive activities seems to be RICO usage. I am not familiar with the use of the term in other legal systems.

as defined and the offences established in accordance with articles 5 (already discussed), 8 (corruption), and 23 (requires criminalization of obstruction of justice). [Under Article 6(2)(c),] subject to a double criminality requirement, predicate offences must include "offences committed both within and outside the jurisdiction of the State Party in question." In what appears to be a recognition of the potential double jeopardy or merger problems under some legal systems, the Transnational Crime Convention provides that: "If required by fundamental principles of the domestic law of a State Party, it may be provided that the [laundering offences] do not apply to the persons who committed the predicate offence." A State Party is required, "subject to the basic concepts of its legal system," to criminalize, "[p]articipation in, association with or conspiracy to commit, attempts to commit and aiding and abetting, facilitating and counseling the commission of any of the offences established in accordance with this article."

In a striking example of a programmatic provision, the criminalization obligations for money laundering are backed up by a requirement in article 7 of the Transnational Crime Convention that States Parties institute a comprehensive domestic regulatory and supervisory regime for banks and non-bank financial institutions, and where appropriate, other bodies particularly susceptible to money laundering.[32]

. . . THE CRIMINALIZATION OF CORRUPTION

Article 8 is another criminalization provision, in this case dealing with corruption. Parties are required to establish as criminal both the promise, offering or giving to a public official[33] and the solicitation or acceptance by such an official "of an undue advantage, for the official himself or herself or another person or entity, in order that the official act or refrain from acting in the exercise of his or her official duties."[34] "Participation as an accomplice" in corruption is also to be made criminal. States Parties must take legislative, administrative and prosecutorial measures to promote integrity and to prevent, detect and punish the corruption of public officials.

. . . CRIMINAL RESPONSIBILITY OF LEGAL PERSONS

Some legal systems still find it difficult to conceptualize the criminal responsibility of legal persons. Article 10 of the Transnational Crime Convention encourages Parties to shed such hangups but leaves some room for maneuver on the details:

> 1. Each State Party shall adopt such measures as may be necessary, consistent with its legal principles, to establish the liability of legal persons for participation in serious

---

32. [Clark's footnote 56:] [Transnational Crime Convention] at art. 7(1)(b). The article also encourages exchanges of information at the national and international levels (subpara. (1)(b)); and consideration of measures to monitor movement of cash and negotiable instruments across borders (para. 2). It calls upon states to "use as a guideline the relevant initiatives of regional, interregional and multilateral organizations against money laundering (para. 3)" and encourages them to "develop and promote global, regional, subregional and bilateral cooperation among judicial, law enforcement and financial regulatory authorities in order to combat money laundering (para. 4)." Id.

33. [Clark's footnote 58:] "Public official," for these purposes, means a public official or a person who provides a public service as defined in the domestic law and as applied in the criminal law of the State Party in which the person in question performs that function. Transnational Crime Convention, art. 8, para. 4.

34. [Clark's footnote 59:] Id. at art. 8(1). Parties are also required to consider criminalizing corruption involving a foreign public official or international civil servant. Id., para. 2.

crimes involving an organized criminal group and for offences established in accordance with articles 5, 6 and 23 of this Convention.

2. Subject to the legal principles of the State Party, the liability of legal persons may be criminal, civil or administrative.

3. Such liability shall be without prejudice to the criminal liability of the natural persons who have committed the offences.

4. Each State Party shall, in particular, ensure that legal persons held liable in accordance with this article are subject to effective, proportionate and dissuasive criminal or non-criminal sanctions, including monetary sanctions.

Corporate criminal responsibility was controversial during the drafting of the Rome Statute of the International Criminal Court. France and Solomon Islands led an unsuccessful effort to include such responsibility in the Statute. A more modest effort has succeeded here. The proposed I.C.C. provision would have been obligatory on all parties, whereas that in the Convention on Transnational Organized Crime allows some wiggle room by deferring some to the "legal principles" of individual States Parties.

. . . Gravity of Penalties

As is now typical in international criminal law treaties, the Parties are required to make the offences established in accordance with the treaty "liable to sanctions that take into account the gravity of that offence." They are similarly required to establish a long statute of limitations period [under Article 11(5)]. Nonetheless, there are some constraints on how far homogenization of the domestic systems will go. A matter implied in previous international criminal law treaties is spelled out in this one [in Article 11(6)]:

Nothing contained in this Convention shall affect the principle that the description of the offences established in accordance with this Convention and of the applicable legal defences or other legal principles controlling the lawfulness of conduct is reserved to the domestic law of a State Party and that such offences shall be prosecuted and punished in accordance with that law.

. . . Forfeiture (Alias Confiscation)

[Forfeiture] is the subject of two articles in the Convention against Transnational Organized Crime, article 12, headed "Confiscation and seizure" and article 13 on "International cooperation for purposes of confiscation." Article 12 requires that State Parties adopt, to the greatest extent possible within their domestic legal systems, measures to enable confiscation of proceeds derived from the Transnational Crime Convention offences, property, equipment or other instrumentalities used in or destined for use in offences covered by the Transnational Crime Convention, property into which proceeds have been transferred, proceeds intermingled with property derived from legitimate sources, and income or other benefits derived from the proceeds. Moreover, the confiscation provision encourages the stripping of bank secrecy. It provides that for the purposes of article 12 and of article 13 (on international cooperation), "each State Party shall empower its courts or other competent authorities to order that bank, financial or commercial records be made available." States may not decline to act under this obligation on the ground of bank secrecy. Following the unfortunate precedent of the 1988 Drug Convention, the article also provides that States Parties may consider the possibility of requiring that an offender demonstrate the lawful origin of alleged proceeds of crime or other property liable to confiscation, to the extent that such a requirement is consistent with the principles of their domestic law and with the nature of the judicial and other proceedings. Burden-shifting provisions such as this are open to serious abuse, and should not be encouraged, even if hedged around with references to "principles of domestic law."

Article 13, on international cooperation for purposes of confiscation, is a kind of miniature Mutual Legal Assistance Treaty. Parties are to assist one another to the greatest extent possible within their legal systems, especially to identify, trace and freeze or seize assets subject to the regime of the Organized Crime Convention. They are encouraged to enter into further bilateral and multilateral arrangements to enhance the effectiveness of this provision.

Article 14 of the Transnational Crime Convention, which deals with the disposal of proceeds of crime or confiscated property, has some interesting echoes of comparable earlier provisions in international criminal law. When a request to confiscate has been made by another State Party, for example, States are required, to the extent permitted by domestic law and if so requested, to give careful consideration to returning the property to the state of origin so that there may be compensation to victims or a return of property to their legitimate owners. States are encouraged to enter into arrangements to make some of the proceeds available for technical assistance or to assist intergovernmental bodies engaged in the fight against organized crime. They are also to consider "[s]haring with other States Parties, on a regular or case-by-case basis, such proceeds of crime or property, or funds derived from the sale of such proceeds of crime or property, in accordance with its domestic law or administrative procedures." Such arrangements, a type of contingency fee deal, are a feature of drug conventions, Mutual Legal Assistance Treaties, and even some of the early slave trade treaties.

. . . JURISDICTION

Article 15 is the fundamental jurisdictional provision that goes with the suppression obligation. It requires that each State Party adopt such measures as may be necessary to establish its jurisdiction over the Transnational Crime Convention offenses when, (a) the offense is committed in the territory of that Party, or (b) when it is committed on board a vessel that is flying the flag of that Party or an aircraft that is registered under the laws of the Party at the time that the offense is committed. In addition, [and subject to Article 4, which protects the principle of nonintervention in the domestic affairs of other states,] there is also permissive jurisdiction where the offense is committed against a national of the party (passive personality jurisdiction) and where it is committed by a national of the Party or a stateless person who has his or her habitual residence there. There is also permissive jurisdiction in respect of certain of the organized criminal group situations[35] and laundering[36] that might not literally fit

---

35. [Clark's footnote 85:] [Transnational Crime Convention] at art. 15, para. 2(c)(i) (stating where the offense is one of those established in accordance with article 5, para. 1 "and is committed outside its territory with a view to the commission of a serious crime within its territory."). This is an expanded "effects" theory of jurisdiction, or perhaps a "protective" one.

36. [Clark's footnote 86:] Id. at art. 15, para. 2(c)(ii) (stating where the offense is established in accordance with art. 6, para. 1(b)(ii) "and is committed outside its territory with a view to the commission of an offense established in accordance with article 6, paragraph 1(a)(i) or (ii) or (b)(i) of this Convention within its territory."). This is another expansive "effects" or "protective" theory.

within a territorial theory. In what has now become a boilerplate provision in extradition treaty practice, States that do not extradite their nationals must adopt the
measures necessary to establish their jurisdiction over offences covered by the Transnational Crime Convention when they do not extradite on this basis. There is an even
broader permissive provision in the Transnational Crime Convention empowering a
State Party to "adopt such measures as may be necessary to establish its jurisdiction
over the offences covered by the Convention when the alleged offender is present in
its territory and it does not extradite him or her." This appears to be a universal
jurisdiction provision, or at least the modest (permissive) version of it, "custodial"
or subsidiary jurisdiction.

The article also includes an interesting coordination provision to the effect that if a
State Party exercising jurisdiction under either the mandatory or the permissive theories of the Convention has been notified, or has otherwise learned, that one or more
other States Parties are conducting an investigation, prosecution or judicial proceeding in respect of the same conduct, the competent authorities of those States Parties
shall, as appropriate, consult with one another with a view to coordinating their
actions. As is the case with the various terrorism treaties, one of the objects of the
Convention against Transnational Organized Crime is to make sure that there are no
safe havens. Potential costs of this cause lie in the possibility of clashes of jurisdiction
where two or more States may act concurrently, and the chance of double jeopardy.
International law in both these areas is a work in progress. Since general international
law has not established a priority system among various jurisdictional theories, the
solution is negotiation, especially on the basis of where the strongest case may be
mounted. The danger of the "risks of concurrent jurisdiction" was downplayed at an
early stage of the drafting, when it was "pointed out, however, that concurrent jurisdiction might not be a negative development, as it would indicate the interest of
numerous States to deal with specific problems. In addition, conflicts of jurisdiction
were rather rare and were invariably resolved at the practical level by an eventual
determination of which jurisdiction would be ultimately exercised on the basis of the
chances for successful prosecution and adjudication of the particular case."

. . . MACHINERY: EXTRADITION, MUTUAL LEGAL ASSISTANCE, TRANSFER AND ALL THAT

There follow a number of machinery provisions that represent the state of the art in
international criminal law treaties, based on work done earlier in the terrorism and
drug treaties. Article 16 deals with extradition, article 17 with the transfer of sentenced persons, article 18 with mutual legal assistance,[37] article 19 with joint investigations, article 20 with special investigative techniques, such as controlled delivery
and electronic or other forms of surveillance. Article 21 invites States to explore the
possibility of transferring proceedings to one another, in particular in cases where
several jurisdictions are involved, with a view to concentrating the prosecution. Article
22 permits a State Party to adopt such legislative or other measures as may
be necessary to take into consideration [a] . . . previous conviction in another state

---

37. [Clark's footnote 95:] A somewhat innovative provision is art. 18, para. 9 which makes the absence
of dual criminality only an optional ground for refusing a request for mutual legal assistance, rather than a
mandatory one. The idea is to free up the possibilities of obtaining assistance. Currently, in respect of both
extradition and mutual legal assistance, there are problems with dual criminality in bilateral relations
where one party does not have legislation dealing with group criminality. For parties to the Transnational
Crime Convention, compliance with the criminalization obligations will narrow the range of difficulties
that remain.

of an alleged offender for the purpose of using such information in criminal proceedings relating to offences covered by the Convention. Article 23 requires Parties to criminalize the use of physical force, threats or intimidation, or the promise of giving an undue advantage in certain cases to obstruct justice in respect of offenses under the Convention. Article 24 deals with the protection of witnesses and Article 25 with assistance to and protection of victims. Article 26 is aimed at enhancing cooperation with law enforcement authorities on the part of those who participate or have participated in organized criminal groups. In particular, it contemplates the possibility of mitigating punishment and even granting immunity for an accused who provides substantial cooperation in the investigation or prosecution of an offence. Article 27 deals with law enforcement cooperation and article 28 with collection, exchange and analysis of information on the nature of organized crime. Articles 29 and 30 speak quite comprehensively to training and bilateral and multilateral technical assistance, particularly to developing countries and countries in transition. Finally, at the national level, article 31 requires States to endeavor to develop and evaluate projects and to establish and promote best practices and policies aimed at the prevention of transnational organized crime. A particular feature of this involves strategies for dealing with governmental corruption.

All in all, these machinery provisions represent a good example of the detailed ways in which multilateral treaties are used to encourage States to move in particular directions under their domestic law in order to approach a problem that has been perceived and conceptualized on the global level.

. . . REVIEW BY THE CONFERENCE OF THE PARTIES

Article 32 of the Transnational Crime Convention is innovative procedurally in the international criminal law area. It provides for the establishment of a Conference of the Parties to the Convention to "improve the capacity of States Parties to combat transnational organized crime and to promote and review the implementation of this Convention." The Conference is to agree upon mechanisms for achieving these objectives, including: facilitating activities under articles 29 (training and technical assistance), 30 (economic development and technical assistance) and 31 (prevention), including by encouraging the mobilization of voluntary contributions; facilitating the exchange of information on patterns and trends in transnational organized crime and successful practices for combating it; cooperating with relevant international and regional organizations and nongovernmental organizations; reviewing periodically the implementation of the Convention; making recommendations to improve it. Parties are to supply information as required by the Conference and to such supplemental review mechanisms as the Conference may create. It remains to be seen how this will play out. Efforts in the past to monitor implementation of United Nations Standards and Norms in Criminal Justice have been frustrating, particularly because there was no clear treaty obligation on States to provide relevant information. There are continuing efforts to breathe life into the process. We have, however, seen vigorous efforts in monitoring legislative and executive compliance in the terrorism area under the aegis of Security Council Resolution 1373. The informal organization support[ed] by thirty-one countries known as the "Financial Action Task Force" (FATF) and others provide potential models. With Article 32 of the Convention on Transnational Organized Crime giving some teeth to the obligation to cooperate in implementation in its sphere of application, one can expect further creativity across the whole area of dissemination and implementation of international standards.

NOTES AND QUESTIONS

1. *Definitions.* How does the Convention define *organized crime*? How does its definition comport with the various national approaches outlined in the articles excerpted in Section A above? Is the Convention's approach a satisfactory one? Some commentators believe that the definition is potentially both overinclusive and underinclusive, and that its ultimate form owed more to the need to compromise than to legal precision. See, e.g., Alexandra V. Orlova & James W. Moore, "Umbrellas" or "Building Blocks"? Defining International Terrorism and Transnational Organized Crime in International Law, 27 Hous. J. Intl. L. 267 (2004-2005). Further, according to the chief Canadian negotiator of the Palermo Convention, Keith Morrill:

> The primary concentration was on working out the "co-operation provisions" of the Convention (that is, extradition, mutual legal assistance and police co-operation). In other words, what was hoped would be accomplished was not a convention that provides a comprehensive definition of organized crime, but rather a convention that serves as a "tool box" to enable the functioning of various "co-operation provisions." Thus, the definition of an organized criminal group, contained in Article 2, alongside other provisions of the Convention, serves the utilitarian purpose of accommodating the provisions dealing with extradition, mutual legal assistance and police co-operation.

Id. at 285.

2. *Obligations of states parties.* Generally, Article 34(1) obligates each state party to "take the necessary measures, including legislative and administrative measures, in accordance with fundamental principles of its domestic law, to ensure the implementation of its obligations under this Convention." Articles 5, 6, 8, and 23 require states parties to criminalize the conduct described in those articles (participation in an organized criminal group, laundering the proceeds of crime, corruption, and obstruction of justice), and Article 11 provides that each state party shall make their commission "liable to sanctions that take into account the gravity" of those offenses. To what extent are these obligations, or the overall purpose of the Convention, limited by Article 4(1), which says explicitly that "States Parties shall carry out their obligations under this Convention in a manner consistent with the principles of sovereign equality and territorial integrity of States and that of non-intervention in the domestic affairs of other States"? Or Article 4(2), which provides that "[n]othing in this Convention entitles a State Party to undertake in the territory of another State the exercise of jurisdiction and performance of functions that are reserved exclusively for the authorities of that other State by its domestic law"?

Article 11(6) can be read to subject the description of covered offenses, and the lawfulness of their prosecution and punishment, to the domestic law of each state party. In light of this provision, what normative effect can the Convention have in changing the laws and practices of states parties?

3. *Federalism.* In transmitting the Organized Crime Convention to the U.S. Senate for its advice and consent to ratification, the president recommended conditioning U.S. adherence, inter alia, on a reservation reserving "the right to assume obligations under this convention in a manner consistent with its fundamental principles of

federalism." Treaty Doc. 108-16, at vii (Feb. 23, 2004). By way of explanation, the proposed reservation noted that:

> U.S. federal criminal law, which regulates conduct based on its effect on interstate or foreign commerce, or other federal interest, serves as the principal legal regime in the United States for combating organized crime, and is broadly effective for that purpose. Federal criminal law does not apply in the rare case where such criminal conduct does not so involve interstate or foreign commerce, or another federal interest. There are a number of conceivable situations involving such rare offenses of a purely local character where U.S federal and state criminal law may not be entirely adequate to satisfy an obligation under the Convention. The Government of the United States of America therefore reserves to the obligations set forth in the Convention to the extent they address conduct which would fall within this narrow category of highly localized activity.

The Senate agreed, including that reservation in its resolution of advice and consent. See 151 Cong. Rec. S11335 (2005). Can you conceive of activities within the scope of Articles 5, 6, 8, or 23 that might fall outside the reach of federal criminal laws based on the Interstate or Foreign Commerce Clause? If they did, would they nonetheless be subject to investigation and prosecution under U.S. state or local law? Even in such situations, would the Offenses Clause of the U.S. Constitution provide Congress authority to enact laws to "fill in the gaps" required to implement the Convention? Why do you suppose the administration felt such a reservation was necessary despite the language in Article 34 conditioning the obligation of every state party to implement the Convention "in accordance with fundamental principles of its domestic law"?

The administration also proposed a further caveat to its obligations, stating that in view of its federalism reservation, no implementing legislation was needed or intended. The Senate concurred, adopting the following "declaration":

> [I]n view of its federalism reservation, current United States law, including the laws of the States of the United States, fulfills the obligations of the Convention for the United States. Accordingly, the United States of America does not intend to enact new legislation to fulfill its obligations under the Convention.

If existing U.S. law (state and federal) is in fact adequate to implement fully the obligations undertaken in this Convention, what is the effect of the "federalism" reservation?

4. *Jurisdictional provisions.* Article 3(2) defines "transnational offenses" as those committed: (a) in more than one state; (b) in one state but with a substantial part of its preparation, planning, direction, or control taking place in another state; (c) in one state but involving an organized criminal group that engages in criminal activities in more than one state; or (d) in one state, but having "substantial effects" in another state. How does this Article relate to the mandatory and permissive jurisdictional provisions of Article 15, which provides:

> 1. Each State Party shall adopt such measures as may be necessary to establish its jurisdiction over the offences established in accordance with articles 5, 6, 8 and 23 of this Convention when:
> (a) The offence is committed in the territory of that State Party; or
> (b) The offence is committed on board a vessel that is flying the flag of that State Party or an aircraft that is registered under the laws of that State Party at the time that the offence is committed.

2. Subject to article 4 of this Convention, a State Party may also establish its jurisdiction over any such offence when:

(a) The offence is committed against a national of that State Party;

(b) The offence is committed by a national of that State Party or a stateless person who has his or her habitual residence in its territory; or

(c) The offence is:

(i) One of those established in accordance with article 5, paragraph 1, of this Convention and is committed outside its territory with a view to the commission of a serious crime within its territory;

(ii) One of those established in accordance with article 6, paragraph 1 (b) (ii), of this Convention and is committed outside its territory with a view to the commission of an offence established in accordance with article 6, paragraph 1 (a) (i) or (ii) or (b) (i), of this Convention within its territory.

3. For the purposes of article 16, paragraph 10, of this Convention, each State Party shall adopt such measures as may be necessary to establish its jurisdiction over the offences covered by this Convention when the alleged offender is present in its territory and it does not extradite such person solely on the ground that he or she is one of its nationals.

4. Each State Party may also adopt such measures as may be necessary to establish its jurisdiction over the offences covered by this Convention when the alleged offender is present in its territory and it does not extradite him or her.

5. If a State Party exercising its jurisdiction under paragraph 1 or 2 of this article has been notified, or has otherwise learned, that one or more other States Parties are conducting an investigation, prosecution or judicial proceeding in respect of the same conduct, the competent authorities of those States Parties shall, as appropriate, consult one another with a view to coordinating their actions.

6. Without prejudice to norms of general international law, this Convention does not exclude the exercise of any criminal jurisdiction established by a State Party in accordance with its domestic law.

Under Article 15(1), states parties are obliged to establish their jurisdiction over the offenses described in Articles 5, 6, 8, and 23 when committed in their territory or on board their vessels or aircraft. By comparison to this mandatory provision of "territorial" jurisdiction, Article 15(2) permits states parties to establish jurisdiction on several other grounds. What are they? Are these provisions consonant with established principles of international law? Or are they novel in any respect?

Because current U.S. law does not always extend criminal jurisdiction over covered offenses when they take place outside U.S. territory on board vessels flying the U.S. flag or aircraft registered under U.S. law, the administration proposed (and the Senate accepted) a reservation to Article 15(1)(b) reserving the right to apply the obligations thereunder except "to the extent provided for under its federal law." Do you think that reservation was necessary?

5. *Extraterritorial application of RICO.* The extraterritorial reach of the federal RICO statute appears to be a matter of case-by-case interpretation. For example, in North South Finance Corp. v. Al-Turki, 100 F.3d 1046 (2d Cir. 1996), the court of appeals addressed the application of RICO to a dispute among groups of foreign companies and foreign nationals arising out of the 1989 sale and reorganization of a French bank named Saudi European Bank (SEB). Neither the purchasers nor the sellers were U.S. entities. The district court held that whether RICO applied in a given case depends on whether the conduct of the defendants in the United States was "material to the completion of a racketeering act." Considering the particular circumstances, the district court dismissed for lack of subject matter jurisdiction.

The Second Circuit affirmed, noting that since the statute is silent as to its extraterritorial application, the issue must turn on congressional intent, that is, "whether Congress would have intended that federal courts should be concerned with specific international controversies." Id. at 1051. Looking to precedents in the areas of international securities transactions and antitrust matters, the Second Circuit identified two possible tests for ascertaining the answer: The "conduct" test applied by the lower court and the "effects" test. Under the former, mere preparatory activities or conduct far removed from the consummation of the fraud could not suffice to establish jurisdiction. Under the latter, a criminal statute can be given extraterritorial reach whenever a predominantly foreign transaction has substantial effects within the United States, and transactions with only remote and indirect effects in the United States do not qualify.

The Second Circuit noted that there was no indication that Congress intended the "effects" test to apply to RICO, and in any event plaintiffs in this proceeding evidently could not demonstrate "substantial effects." See also Doe I v. State of Israel, 400 F. Supp. 2d 86, 115-116 (D.D.C. 2005) ("the activity at issue must, at minimum, produce or be intended to produce effects in this country. . . . [Congress did not intend] an extraterritorial application of RICO to solely personal harms suffered overseas that only marginally—and tangentially—impact American commerce").

Under either the "effects" or "conduct" tests, would RICO satisfy the requirements of Article 3(2) of the UN Convention?

6. In July 2008, a novel issue was raised in the Federation of Russia: Can the civil RICO statute be properly applied in a foreign court? The Federal Customs Service of the Russian Federation (FCS) brought suit in the Arbitrazh Court of the City of Moscow against the Bank of New York-Mellon (BNY) to recover treble damages arising from a money laundering offense committed by two BNY employees. In the ongoing litigation, the central issue is whether a foreign court is properly equipped to interpret and apply such a complex body of U.S. law. The defendants have argued that the RICO statute, despite any civil remedies, is a criminal statute at its core and the only proper court to hear a suit brought under any RICO section is the United States. The plaintiffs have responded that the civil cause of action in §1964, which is the basis of their claim for treble damages in this case (alleged to total $22.5 *billion*), can be applied by a foreign court as easily as in any other choice-of-law situations—and that application of foreign law is common in contract litigation.

Why didn't the FCS file suit in U.S. district court? Should it be forced to? If the suit is allowed to move forward in Russia, what further transnational litigation issues could arise if BNY loses?

7. *Extradition.* In the same fashion as several other international criminal law treaties, Article 16 elaborates a comprehensive extradition regime for states parties to the Convention. It applies to the core offenses under Articles 5, 6, 8, and 23, and to "serious crimes" under Article 2(b) so long as the offenses in question are criminal under the laws of both the requesting and requested states. By virtue of Article 16(3), these offenses will be included as an extraditable offense in any existing extradition treaties between states parties to the Convention. Where no such treaty exists, states that make extradition conditional on a treaty may rely on the Convention as the legal basis for extradition.

Article 16(8) requires states parties to expedite extradition procedures and simplify extradition requirements in respect of covered offenses, and authorizes them to request provisional arrests and "other appropriate measures" to ensure the presence of a fugitive or accused at extradition proceedings. What measures might those be?

Importantly, Article 16(9) of the Convention follows the familiar pattern of other modern international criminal law treaties in obligating states parties to establish *aut dedere aut judicare* ("extradite or prosecute") jurisdiction. Note, however, that the obligation is limited to circumstances in which the state party declines to extradite the alleged offender "solely on the ground that he or she is one of its nationals." In your view, is this a sufficient undertaking?

Extradition may not be refused "on the sole ground that the offence is also considered to involve fiscal matters." Which of the covered offenses is likely to raise this issue?

8. *Mutual legal assistance.* Article 18(1) obligates states parties to afford each other the "widest measure" of mutual legal assistance in investigations, prosecutions, and judicial proceedings relating to Convention offenses. However, under Article 18(6), this undertaking does not affect the obligations between states parties under "any other treaty, bilateral or multilateral, that governs or will govern, in whole or in part, mutual legal assistance." In effect, the latter provision limits the application of mutual legal assistance provisions to situations where states parties do not have other applicable arrangements. Paragraphs 9 through 29 set forth the procedures that will govern requests for assistance in such situations.

Uniquely, Article 18(9) permits states parties to decline to render assistance because of lack of dual criminality. Why do you suppose the negotiators included such a provision? By contrast, a state party may not decline to render mutual legal assistance on the basis of bank secrecy or because the request is considered to involve "fiscal matters," see Articles 18(8) and (22), but may refuse if "execution of the request is likely to prejudice its sovereignty, security, *ordre public* or other essential interests," see Article 18(21)(b). Is this a significant loophole?

Note the unusual provisions in Article 18(18) providing for the use of video conferencing "where an individual has to be heard as a witness or expert by the judicial authorities of another State Party." What problems could you anticipate in conducting such a hearing? Also uniquely, Article 18(27) makes it possible to grant a period of "safe conduct" to a witness, expert, or other person who consents to give evidence or otherwise assist in an investigation, prosecution, or judicial proceeding in a state party where he or she might otherwise be subject to detention, prosecution, or punishment. Do you think this provision is likely to be effective in practice?

9. *Special investigative techniques.* Under Article 20, and "where permitted by the basic principles of its domestic legal system," each state party must make provision for the use of "controlled delivery" and other special investigative techniques "such as electronic or other forms of surveillance and undercover operations." (The term "controlled delivery" is defined by Article 2(i).) The Convention contemplates that states parties will conclude appropriate bilateral or multilateral agreements for this purpose. If you were negotiating such an agreement with another country, what specific methods would you propose to include to combat organized crime?

10. *Witnesses and victims.* In the United States, witness protection has frequently been considered essential in the effective investigation and prosecution of organized crime. Article 24 obligates states parties to take appropriate measures, within their means, to provide witnesses and, as appropriate, their relatives and other persons close to them "effective protection from potential retaliation or intimidation" when they testify in relevant proceedings. What are some of the specific measures contemplated by this article? Are they likely to be sufficient?

Similarly, under Article 25, states parties must take "appropriate measures" to protect and assist victims of covered offenses, "in particular in cases of threat of retaliation or intimidation," and to establish procedures for access to compensation and restitution. In addition, they must enable their views to be considered during criminal proceedings, subject to domestic law and in a manner not prejudicial to the rights of the defense.

11. *International cooperation.* In addition to mutual legal assistance in specific cases, the Convention imposes several more general requirements on states parties to cooperate in the prevention, investigation, and prosecution of organized crime. Consider, for example, the detailed provisions of Articles 26 (measures to enhance cooperation with law enforcement authorities), 27 (law enforcement cooperation), 28 (collection, exchange, and analysis of information), and 29 (training and technical assistance). Under Article 30(2), states parties are required to "make concrete efforts" to enhance cooperation as well as financial and material assistance to developing countries "to fight transnational organized crime effectively and to help implement this Convention successfully." What kinds of "concrete efforts" would you propose, if you were asked to design a program to implement these provisions?

In this regard, consider in particular the scope of Article 31, which encourages states parties to develop policies and "best practices" aimed at the prevention of transnational organized crime. With regard to paragraph 3 of that article, in what way do you consider that the goals of the Convention are promoted by "the reintegration into society" of individuals who have been convicted of covered offenses?

12. *Regional initiatives.* The European Commission has taken a number of steps to prepare for the effective implementation of the Convention and to improve law enforcement cooperation in combating organized crime within the European Union, including through EUROPOL (European Law Enforcement Organisation), EUROJUST (European Union's Judicial Cooperation Unit), and the European Forum on Organized Crime Prevention. See http://ec.europa.eu/justice_home/fsj/crime/fsj_crime_intro_en.htm (last visited July 7, 2009).

Within the Organization of American States, a Special Committee on Transnational Organized Crime has been established to prepare a draft hemispheric plan of action against transnational organized crime, based on the UN Convention and its Protocols. See AG/RES. 2116 (XXXV-O/05) (Fighting Transnational Organized Crime in the Hemisphere) (June 7, 2005). The proposed work plan of this Special Committee contemplated coordinated approaches to a wide range of issues, including drugs and money laundering, corruption, illicit arms trafficking, kidnapping, cyber crime, alien smuggling and trafficking in persons, gang activity, and mutual legal assistance in criminal matters.

13. *Terrorism.* During the negotiation of the Convention, the Turkish delegation tried, without success, to include various formulations linking "terrorist crimes" to "organized crimes." Similarly, the Egyptian delegation sought clear and express references to the "growing relationship between transnational organized crimes and terrorist crimes." See Report of the Ad Hoc Committee on the Elaboration of a Convention Against Transnational Organized Crime on the Work of Its First to Eleventh Sessions, ¶¶82, 89, U.N. Doc. A/53/383 (Nov. 2, 2000). Why do you suppose these efforts found little sympathy with other delegations? Is the Convention properly focused on "profit-driven" crime?

CHAPTER
12

Trafficking in Persons, Drugs, and Arms

Perhaps the fastest growing category of transnational crime is "trafficking." In its most general sense, the term describes the illicit movement of contraband across national boundaries. The contraband can be drugs, weapons, money, exotic or endangered animals, stolen automobiles, cigarettes, counterfeit watches or compact discs, purloined art or antiquities, ivory, "blood diamonds," nuclear and other radioactive material, and even human beings or body organs. Although the substance of what is moved differs, all trafficking crimes share similar traits and tend to be interconnected.[1] The violent drug trade depends upon trafficking in money, which invariably involves money laundering (often by converting the proceeds into other trafficked goods) and corruption of officials, and frequently leads to the clandestine movement of people and weapons as well. Crime syndicates that become proficient in conducting one type of illicit trafficking frequently use the same methods to move other goods or material.[2]

The primary aim of this chapter is to explore various approaches taken by international criminal law instruments and by U.S. domestic law to curb these practices. We focus on trafficking in persons, drugs, and small arms, for three reasons: The volume and value of activity in those areas make them particularly important,[3] the effects on society are especially acute, and they have recently been addressed in several multilateral treaties adopted by the United Nations.[4]

---

1. We focus here on large-scale crimes, typically committed by organized groups for profit, in contrast to offenses committed by individuals for personal reasons. To illustrate the distinction, consider the Christmas Eve 2008 arrest of an Australian teacher by Egyptian authorities for allegedly trying to leave the country with 2,000-year-old mummified animals (two cats and an ibis) in his suitcase. Authorities also confiscated 19 figurines of the revered ancient Egyptian gods Horus and Thoth. See http://allaboutegypt .org/tag/horus. While initial reports gave no reason to think this incident was part of an organized for-profit operation, Egypt has long battled sophisticated smuggling rings that send pirated antiquities to Western Europe and elsewhere for sale to private collectors.

2. See generally Transnational Threats: Smuggling and Trafficking in Arms, Drugs and Human Life (Kimberely L. Thachuk ed., 2007); Melvyn Levitsky, Transnational Criminal Networks and International Security, 30 Syracuse J. Intl. L. & Com. 227 (2003).

3. By some estimates, trafficking in drugs generates nearly $400 billion a year, trafficking in arms about half that amount, and trafficking in people between $7 billion and $12 billion annually. See generally Scott Ehlers, Drug Trafficking and Money Laundering, Foreign Policy in Focus, June 1998, http:// www.fpif.org/briefs/vol3/v3n16lau.html, and Primer on the Anti-Trafficking in Persons Act of 2003 (2d ed. 2004), http://www.trafficking.org.ph/papers/ra9208primereng.pdf. By comparison, illegal trafficking in wildlife is estimated to be worth $5 billion to $20 billion annually. See Open CRS, Center for Democracy and Technology, International Illegal Trade in Wildlife: Threats and U.S. Policy, Feb. 2, 2009, http://opencrs.com/document/RL34395.

4. The Protocol to Prevent, Suppress and Punish Trafficking in Persons, Especially Women and Children (Trafficking Protocol) and the Protocol against the Smuggling of Migrants by Land, Sea and Air

To be sure, the contemporary phenomena of trafficking in each of these areas raise significant policy issues. Is human trafficking, for example, best understood as a function of globalization and increased freedom of movement around the world, as a consequence of economic disparity or simple poverty, as an immigration problem, or as a law enforcement challenge? What in fact is the link between human trafficking, prostitution, and pornography? Should a clearer distinction be made between consensual and nonconsensual activities (smuggling versus trafficking)? In the field of drug trafficking, can criminalization ever produce significant reductions as long as demand remains strong? Or is a noncriminal approach to the consumption or "demand side" of the equation the necessary prerequisite to reducing the "supply side" inflow of illicit substances? Does the so-called war on drugs actually make trafficking more lucrative and thus invite the involvement of organized criminal groups and increase drug-related violence? Is it possible to regulate the illicit trade in small arms effectively when so many governments engage in large (and "licit") sales of guns and ammunition as instruments of their foreign policies? Can international trafficking in arms ever be effectively regulated as long as possession and use of such weapons is lawful (even protected) under the national laws of the major states involved in manufacture of arms?

These are only some of the questions that generate vigorous debate among policy-makers, criminologists, sociologists, social scientists, and others. In the discussion that follows, we note a few references to which students can turn to pursue these broader issues. At the heart of our current discussion, however, is the narrower question of which legal doctrines and institutional strategies are likely to be most effective at controlling international trafficking in its various forms.

Currently, one of the leading strategies involves the adoption of treaties requiring states parties to criminalize specified activities within their own territories. Given divergent national approaches to many issues that relate to trafficking (for example, the laws of some countries tolerate prostitution or the personal use of certain drugs or individual possession of firearms), such instruments require states parties to change their national laws and enact implementing legislation, making domestic enforcement of these international prohibitions one of their own national priorities. On the other hand, the cross-border nature of trafficking may require internationally coordinated solutions, such as permitting (or requiring) individual states to exercise extraterritorial jurisdiction to prosecute specified offenses that occur elsewhere, with the obligatory assistance of other states regarding extradition, information sharing, and other forms of cooperation.

A third approach would be full "internationalization" — either by creating some form of super-national regulatory mechanisms (aimed at real harmonization of domestic policies and procedures) or by including trafficking crimes within the jurisdiction of international tribunals (such as the International Criminal Court) so that violators could be criminally prosecuted at the global level. To date, the international community has generally pursued a combination of the first and second options, as

---

(Smuggling Protocol), more commonly known as the Palermo Protocols, were adopted by G.A. Res. 55/25 (Nov. 15, 2000) along with the Convention Against Transnational Organized Crime (TOC Convention). They came into force on December 25, 2003, and January 28, 2004, respectively. The Protocol against the Illicit Manufacturing of and Trafficking in Firearms, their Parts and Components and Ammunition (Firearms Protocol), also attached to the TOC Convention, was adopted separately by G.A. Res. 55/255 (May 31, 2001) and entered into force on July 3, 2005. The 1988 UN Convention Against Illicit Traffic in Narcotic Drugs and Psychotropic Substances came into force on November 11, 1990 (the United States ratified in February 1990). The texts are available on our Web site. See generally United Nations Office on Drugs and Crime, http://www.unodc.org/unodc/en/treaties/index.html (last visited July 8, 2009).

reflected in the various international conventions discussed below. Although international regulatory mechanisms exist in both the arms and drugs areas, trafficking crimes are not (yet) addressed by the various international criminal courts or tribunals.

Still another approach involves the imposition of sanctions on countries that fail to live up to internationally approved standards for the prevention and prosecution of trafficking. This approach is illustrated by the provisions in the U.S. Trafficking Victims Protection Act that authorize the unilateral withholding of "nonhumanitarian, non-trade-related foreign assistance" to countries that fail to make "significant efforts" to comply with the specified "minimum standards for the elimination of trafficking" in persons outlined in the statute.[5] Countries are assessed, annually, in the Department of State's Trafficking in Persons Report (discussed below). Those receiving the worst ("Tier 3") assessment are eligible for such withholding of assistance.[6]

Despite intense international interest and the recent adoption of several anti-trafficking treaties, case law and concrete evidentiary material is in short supply. We include the topic because it will certainly become one of the most important areas of international criminal law in the future. Familiarity with the various approaches taken in different instruments provides useful background and perspective.

By way of introduction, consider the following excerpt from Moisés Naím's book *Illicit* (2006), in which he describes "three grand illusions [that] persist in the way we — the public and the politicians in whom we place our trust — address global illicit trade."

> First is the illusion that there is nothing new. Illicit trade is age-old, a continuous facet and side effect of market economies or of commerce in general. Illicit trade's ancestor, smuggling, traces back to ancient times, and many a "thieves' market" survives in the world's commercial hubs. Therefore, skeptics would argue that since smuggling has always been more a nuisance than a scourge, it is a threat we can learn to live with as we have always done.
>
> But this skepticism ignores the important transformations of the 1990s. Changes in political and economic life, along with revolutionary technologies in the hands of civilians, have dissolved the sealants that governments traditionally relied on to secure their national borders. At the same time, the market-oriented economic reforms that swept the world in the 1990s boosted incentives to break through these sealants — legally or otherwise. Not only did the hold of governments on borders weaken, but the reforms amplified the rewards awaiting those who were prepared to break the rules.
>
> Technology enlarged the market, not just geographically by lowering transport costs but also by making possible the trade in a whole range of goods that didn't exist before, such as pirated software or genetically modified marijuana. New technologies also made it possible to trade internationally products that in the past were hard or impossible to transport or hold in "inventory" — human kidneys, for instance. Markets, of course, were also enlarged when governments deregulated previously closed or tightly controlled economies and allowed foreigners to visit, trade, and invest more freely.

---

5. 22 U.S.C. §7107(a).

6. The 2008 Report placed the following countries in the "Tier 3" category: Algeria, Burma, Cuba, Fiji, Iran, Kuwait, Moldova, North Korea, Oman, Papua New Guinea, Qatar, Saudi Arabia, Sudan, and Syria. See U.S. Dept. of State, Office to Monitor and Combat Trafficking in Persons, Trafficking in Persons Report (2008), available at http://www.state.gov/g/tip/rls/tiprpt/2008/105383.htm.

The massive transfer of goods and equipment once under the exclusive control of national armies into private hands released into the market products ranging from rocket launchers to SCUD missiles and nuclear designs and machinery. Moreover, governments also boosted illicit trade by criminalizing new activities. File sharing through the internet, for example, is a newly illegal activity that has added millions to the ranks of illicit traders.

A clue to the explosion of illicit trade is the relentless rise of money laundering. Eventually, every illicit line of business generates money that needs to be laundered. And there is ample evidence that despite all the precautions and enforcement measures now in place, there is more and more dirty money floating in the international financial system now than ever before.

Yet until now, with the exception of narcotics, illicit trade has simply not been a priority in international law and treaty making, or in international police work and cooperative law enforcement. The United Nations devised common language to describe it only in the year 2000, and most countries have a long way to go in adapting their laws to international standards, let alone enforcing them. It took the advent of software piracy and the birth of "intellectual property crime" to add a fillip to international efforts against counterfeiting. And trafficking in persons — the most morally outrageous of all the forms of illicit trade — was defined in the 1990s only by academics and activists, and made the subject of a specific, comprehensive law in the United States in 2000. (Only seventeen other countries have done the same.)

The second illusion is that illicit trade is just about crime. It is true that criminal activities surged and became global in the 1990s. But thinking about international illicit trade as just another manifestation of criminal behavior misses a larger, more consequential point. Global criminal activities are *transforming the international system,* upending the rules, creating new players, and reconfiguring power in international politics and economics. The United States attacked Iraq because it feared that Saddam Hussein had acquired weapons of mass destruction. But during the same time a stealthy network led by A. Q. Khan, a Pakistani engineer, was profiting by selling nuclear bomb-making technology to whoever could pay for it.

Throughout the twentieth century, to the extent that governments paid attention to illicit trade at all, they framed it — to their public, and to themselves — as the work of criminal organizations. Consciously or not, investigators around the world took the model of the American and Sicilian Mafia as their blueprint. Propelled by this mindset, the search for traffickers — almost always in drugs — led to what investigators thought could be only corporate-like organizations: structured, disciplined, and hierarchical. The Colombian cartels, Chinese tongs, Hong Kong triads, Japanese yakuza, and eventually after 1989 the Russian mafiya were all approached this way: first as criminal organizations, only later as traders. In most countries, the laws employed to prosecute illicit traders remain those born of the fight against organized crime, like the racketeering and corrupt organizations (RICO) statutes in the United States.

Only recently has this mind-set begun to shift. Thanks to al-Qaeda the world now knows what a network of highly motivated individuals owing allegiance to no nation and empowered by globalization can do. The problem is that the world still thinks of these networks mostly in terms of terrorism. Yet, as the pages ahead show, profit can be as powerful a motivator as God. Networks of stateless traders in illicit goods are changing the world as much as terrorists are — probably more. But a world obsessed with terrorists has not yet taken notice.

The third illusion is the idea that illicit trade is an "underground" phenomenon. Even accepting that trafficking has grown in volume and complexity, many — not least politicians — seek to relegate it to a different world than that of ordinary, honest citizens and constituents. The language we use to describe illicit trade and to frame our efforts to contain it betrays the enduring power of this illusion. The word *offshore* — as in *offshore finance* — vividly captures this sense that illicit trade takes place somewhere else. So does *black market*, or the supposedly clearly distinct *clean* and *dirty money.* All signify a clarity, an ability to draw moral and economic lines and patrol their boundaries that is confounded in practice. This is the most dangerous of all these illusions, because it treads on moral grounds and arguably lulls citizens — and hence public opinion — into a sense of heightened righteousness and false security.

This point is not about moral relativism. A thief is a thief. But how do you describe a woman who manages to provide some material well-being to her destitute family in Albania or Nigeria by entering another country illegally and working the streets as a prostitute or as a peddler of counterfeited goods? What about bankers in Manhattan or London who take home big year-end bonuses as a reward for having stocked their bank's vaults with the deposits of "high-net worth individuals" whose only known job has been with a government in another country? Many American high-schoolers can procure a joint of marijuana more easily than they can purchase a bottle of vodka or a pack of cigarettes, and they know they don't really run any major risk in doing so. Meanwhile honest Colombian judges or police officers are routinely gunned down in a war on drugs that the U.S. government funds to the tune of $40 billion a year. These are not just infuriating contradictions, unfair double standards, or interesting paradoxes. They are powerful clues about how age-old human mores have acquired new hues.

Since the early 1990s, global illicit trade has embarked on a great mutation. It is the same mutation as that of international terrorist organizations like al-Qaeda or Islamic Jihad — or for that matter, of activists for the global good like the environmental movement or the World Social Forum. All have moved away from fixed hierarchies and toward decentralized networks; away from controlling leaders and toward multiple, loosely linked, dispersed agents and cells; away from rigid lines of control and exchange and toward constantly shifting transactions as opportunities dictate. It is a mutation that governments in the 1990s barely recognized and could not, in any case, hope to emulate.

The world's first unmistakable glimpse of this transformation came on September 11, 2001. Politicians would later say that on that day "the world changed." It might be more apt to say that on that day something about the world was revealed — at the very least, the incredible power now residing in the hands of an entirely new kind of international entity, inherently stateless and deeply elusive. As subsequent events demonstrated, even experts disagreed as to what they were observing, and what it might have to do with specific states and regimes.

Left unchecked, illicit trade can only pursue its already well advanced mutation. There is ample evidence that it offers terrorists and other miscreants means of survival and methods of financial transfer and exchange. Its effect on geopolitics will go further. In developing countries and those in transition from communism, criminal networks often constitute the most powerful vested interests confronting the government. In some countries, their resources and capabilities even surpass those of their governments. These capabilities often translate into political clout. Traffickers and their associates control political parties, own significant media operations, or are the major philanthropists behind nongovernmental organizations. This is a natural outcome in countries where no economic activity can match illicit trade in size or profits and therefore traffickers become the nation's "big business." And once their business becomes large and stable, trafficking networks do as big businesses are prone to do everywhere else: diversify into other businesses and invest in politics. After all, gaining access and influence and seeking government protection has always been part and parcel of big business.

Therefore not only are illicit networks tightly intertwined with licit private sector activities, but they are also deeply embedded within the public sector and the political system. And once they have spread into licit private corporations, political parties, parliaments, local governments, media groups, the courts, the military, and the nonprofit sector, trafficking networks assume a powerful — and in some countries unrivalled — influence on matters of state.

Perversely, the awareness of the ravaging effects of illicit trade often sparks nationalistic impulses and insular responses. Ironically, these reactions end up working in favor of the traffickers — for the more states seek to raise barriers against the flow of illicit goods, services, and labor, the more the traffickers stand to profit from their trade. National borders are a boon to criminals and a block to law enforcement agencies. Borders create profit opportunities for smuggling networks and weaken nation-states by limiting their ability to curb the onslaughts of the global networks that hurt their economies, corrupt their politics, and undermine their institutions.

This story is no longer just about crime. It is also about a new form of politics in the twenty-first century. And about the new economic realities that have brought to the fore a whole new set of political actors whose values may collide with yours and mine, and whose intentions threaten us all.[7]

Taking into account the "great mutation" in illicit trade described by Moisés Naím and its "transformative effect" on the existing international system, what changes should be made in the ways in which international criminal law addresses the phenomenon of trafficking? What strategies are likely to be the most effective?

A.   TRAFFICKING IN PERSONS

Human trafficking is the modern evolution of one of the oldest crimes: Slavery. In some respects, contemporary trafficking in persons is every bit as pernicious as (and larger in scale than) the slave trade was at its height during the eighteenth century. In its modern manifestations, it takes a variety of forms, including the exploitation of people for prostitution and other sex trade purposes, forced labor, sweat shops and domestic servitude, forced marriages, debt bondage, child labor, and other practices.[8]

One of the fullest pictures of the phenomenon is provided by the U.S. Department of State, which is required by law to submit a report each year to the U.S. Congress on the steps taken by foreign governments to eliminate severe forms of trafficking in persons. These Trafficking in Persons (TIP) Reports are intended to highlight the magnitude of the problem, the efforts of the international community to combat it, and the steps taken by the United States to encourage foreign governments to take effective action. As the 2008 Report notes:

> Annually, according to U.S. Government-sponsored research completed in 2006, approximately 800,000 people are trafficked across national borders, which does not include millions trafficked within their own countries. Approximately 80 percent of transnational victims are women and girls and up to 50 percent are minors. The majority of transnational victims are females trafficked into commercial sexual exploitation. These numbers do not include millions of female and male victims around the world

---

7. Moisés Naím, Illicit: How Smugglers, Traffickers, and Copycats Are Hijacking the Global Economy 3-9 (2006).

8. A vast body of information and literature exists on this topic. See generally Anthony M. DeStefano, The War on Human Trafficking: U.S. Policy Assessed (2008); Silvia Scarpa, Trafficking in Human Beings: Modern Slavery (2008); James C. Hathaway, The Human Rights Quagmire of "Human Trafficking," 49 Va. J. Intl. L. 1 (2008); David A. Feingold, Human Trafficking, Foreign Policy, Sept.-Oct. 2005, at 26, 26-32; Claire Ribando Seelke & Alison Siskin, Trafficking in Persons: U.S. Policy and Issues for Congress (Congressional Research Service Report for Congress, RL34317, 2008), available at http://assets.opencrs.com/rpts/RL34317_20080814.pdf.

who are trafficked within their own national borders—the majority for forced or bonded labor.

Human traffickers prey on the vulnerable. Their targets are often children and young women, and their ploys are creative and ruthless, designed to trick, coerce, and win the confidence of potential victims. Very often these ruses involve promises of a better life through employment, educational opportunities, or marriage.

The nationalities of trafficked people are as diverse as the world's cultures. Some leave developing countries, seeking to improve their lives through low-skilled jobs in more prosperous countries. Others fall victim to forced or bonded labor in their own countries. Women, eager for a better future, are susceptible to promises of jobs abroad as babysitters, housekeepers, waitresses, or models—jobs that traffickers turn into the nightmare of forced prostitution without exit. Some families give children to adults, often relatives, who promise education and opportunity—but sell the children into exploitative situations for money. But poverty alone does not explain this tragedy, which is driven by fraudulent recruiters, employers, and corrupt officials who seek to reap unlawful profits from others' desperation.[9]

The cost of trafficking in human terms is staggering. As the 2006 TIP Report noted,

> Victims of human trafficking pay a horrible price. Psychological and physical harm, including disease and stunted growth, often have permanent effects. In many cases the exploitation of trafficking victims is progressive: a child trafficked into one form of labor may be further abused in another. It is a brutal reality of the modern-day slave trade that its victims are frequently bought and sold many times over — often sold initially by family members. Victims forced into sex slavery are often subdued with drugs and subjected to extreme violence. Victims trafficked for sexual exploitation face physical and emotional damage from violent sexual activity, forced substance abuse, exposure to sexually transmitted diseases including HIV/AIDS, food deprivation, and psychological torture. Some victims suffer permanent damage to their reproductive organs. Many victims die as a result of being trafficked. When the victim is trafficked to a location where he or she cannot speak or understand the language, this compounds the psychological damage caused by isolation and domination by traffickers.[10]

The international community has recognized that all states have an obligation to prevent trafficking in persons and to punish the perpetrators.[11] The principal global instrument in this area is the UN Protocol to Prevent, Suppress and Punish Trafficking in Persons, Especially Women and Children (Trafficking Protocol), discussed in Section A.3 below.[12] To understand its significance, we provide a brief summary of prior international efforts to address the phenomenon.

---

9. See U.S. Dept. of State, Office to Monitor and Combat Trafficking in Persons, Trafficking in Persons Report (2008), available at http://www.state.gov/g/tip/rls/tiprpt/2008.

10. See U.S. Dept. of State, Office to Monitor and Combat Trafficking in Persons, Trafficking in Persons Report (2006), available at http://www.state.gov/g/tip/rls/tiprpt/2006. The United Nations' Office on Drugs and Crime (UNODC) publishes detailed analyses and reports on human trafficking, see http://www.unodc.org/unodc/en/human-trafficking/index.html. Various nongovernmental organizations also monitor and report on the phenomenon; see, e.g., Humantrafficking.org, http://www.humantrafficking.org (last visited July 8, 2009) and Coalition Against Trafficking in Women, http://www.catwinternational.org (last visited July 8, 2009).

11. See, e.g., G.A. Res. 63/156, U.N. Doc. A/RES/63/156 (Dec. 18, 2008) on Trafficking in Women and Girls (adopted Jan. 30, 2009).

12. Another major instrument is the 2000 Optional Protocol to the Convention on the Rights of the Child, on the Sale of Children, Child Prostitution and Child Pornography, G.A. Res. 54/263, U.N. Doc. A/RES/54/263, 2171 U.N.T.S. 27531 (May 25, 2000), reprinted in 39 I.L.M. 1285 (2000), discussed infra at Section A.4.

1. *Historical Antecedents*

The international community struggled throughout the nineteenth and early twentieth centuries to establish effective mechanisms to curb the international slave trade, concluding some 30 separate agreements between 1815 and 1957. Of these early efforts, perhaps the most significant from the perspective of international criminal law is the 1890 General Act Relative to the African Slave Trade, which sought (unsuccessfully as it turned out) to establish an international tribunal for the suppression of the slave trade.

It quickly became apparent that an exclusive focus on traditional slave trading was inadequate. Modern slavery takes many different forms, including forced or compulsory labor (especially involving children), debt bondage, forced marriage, serfdom, and prostitution. During the first half of the twentieth century, the international community devised numerous instruments to counter various aspects of the newly emergent practices.[13] Following World War I, the League of Nations adopted the Slavery Convention of 1926, which represented a general commitment to prevent and suppress the slave trade and to bring about the abolition of slavery in all its forms.[14] A more "criminal law" approach was taken by the 1956 UN Supplementary Convention on the Abolition of Slavery, the Slave Trade and Institutions and Practices Similar to Slavery, which required states parties to criminalize "[t]he act of conveying or attempting to convey slaves from one country to another by whatever means of transport, or being accessory thereto," as well as the "act of enslaving another person or of inducing another person to give himself or a person dependent upon him into slavery, or of attempting these acts, or being accessory thereto, or being a party to a conspiracy to accomplish any such acts."[15]

The 1982 UN Convention on the Law of the Sea also addressed the issue, requiring every state party to "take effective measures to prevent and punish the transport of slaves in ships authorized to fly its flag" and granting warships of all countries the right of visit to board vessels on the high seas when reasonable grounds exist for suspecting that the vessel is participating in the slave trade. However, the Convention did not grant states the right to seize foreign vessels or arrest foreign crews engaged in slave trading.[16]

---

13. These agreements include, inter alia, (i) the International Agreement of 18 May 1904 for the Suppression of the White Slave Traffic, 3 L.N.T.S. 278, as amended by the Protocol approved by the General Assembly of the United Nations on 3 December 1948, 39 U.N.T.S. 23; (ii) the International Convention of 4 May 1910 for the Suppression of the White Slave Traffic, as amended by the above-mentioned Protocol; (iii) the International Convention of 30 September 1921 for the Suppression of the Traffic in Women and Children, as amended by the Protocol approved by the General Assembly of the United Nations on 20 October 1947, and (iv) the International Convention of 11 October 1933 for the Suppression of the Traffic in Women of Full Age, as amended by the aforesaid Protocol.

14. Slavery, Servitude, Forced Labour, and Similar Institutions and Practices Convention of 1926, Sept. 26, 1926, 60 L.N.T.S. 253, 60 U.N.T.S. 253, amended with the approval of the UN General Assembly in 1953 by a Protocol, 7 U.S.T. 479, 182 U.N.T.S. 51, T.I.A.S. 3532 (Dec. 7, 1953).

15. Arts. 3, 6; 266 U.N.T.S. 3, 18 U.S.T. 3201, T.I.A.S. 6418 (June 10, 1958).

16. U.N. Convention on the Law of the Sea, Dec. 10, 1982, 1833 U.N.T.S. 3, arts. 99, 110(1)(b). For additional background on the issue of slavery, see the Web sites for the Special Rapporteur on Contemporary Forms of Slavery, http://www2.ohchr.org/english/issues/slavery/rapporteur/index.htm (last visited July 8, 2009); U.N. Econ. & Soc. Council [ECOSOC], Sub-Commission on Prevention of Discrimination & Protection of Minorities, Final Report on Systematic Rape, Sexual Slavery and Slavery-like Practices During Armed Conflict, U.N. Doc. E/CN.4/Sub.2/1998/13 (June 22, 1998) (prepared by Gay J. McDougall), available at http://www.unhchr.ch/Huridocda/Huridoca.nsf/(Symbol)/E.CN.4 .Sub.2.1998.13.En?Opendocument.

2. 1949 Prostitution Convention

One important conceptual antecedent to the Trafficking Protocol was the 1949 UN Convention for the Suppression of the Traffic in Persons and of the Exploitation of the Prostitution of Others (Prostitution Convention).[17] This treaty, which entered into force in July 1951, was intended to unify four prior international agreements for the suppression of trafficking in women and children. Substantively it was directed at the procurer and required states parties to take measures to prevent prostitution, to rehabilitate prostitutes, and to control the traffic in persons of either gender for purposes of prostitution. As indicated by the excerpts below, it broadened the definition of slavery from the 1926 Convention to include practices and institutions of debt bondage, servile forms of marriage, and the exploitation of children and adolescents.

Article 1 of the 1949 Convention requires states parties to prosecute anyone "who to gratify the passions of another: procures, entices or leads away, for purposes of prostitution, another person, even with the consent of that person" or "exploits the prostitution of another person, even with the consent of that person." Article 2 requires punishment of anyone who "keeps or manages, or knowingly finances or takes part in the financing of a brothel" or "knowingly lets or rents a building or other place or any part thereof for the purpose of the prostitution of others." The Convention also requires states parties to criminalize "attempts to commit" any of the offenses referred to in Articles 1 and 2, "acts preparatory to the commission thereof," and "intentional participation" in those acts "[t]o the extent permitted by domestic law" under Articles 3 and 4.

Finally, the Convention provided that listed offenses "shall be regarded as extraditable offences in any extradition treaty which has been or may hereafter be concluded between any of the Parties to this Convention" (Art. 8) and requires that states "shall be bound to execute letters of request relating to offences referred to in the Convention in accordance with their domestic law and practice" (Art. 13).

NOTES AND QUESTIONS

1. As of mid-2009, 81 states had become parties to the 1949 Prostitution Convention (most recently Kazakhstan, Montenegro, and Guatemala). While that is a substantial number in terms of overall treaty practice, it is still considerably fewer than half of all states in today's international community.

2. The United States has neither signed nor acceded to the 1949 Convention. Note that the Convention does not criminalize the act of prostitution itself but only requires states parties to punish people who facilitate the prostitution of another person, regardless of the consent of that person and without reference to purpose of commercial gain. In the United States, regulation of prostitution, including facilitation and procurement, is primarily a function of state law, and while "facilitation" of prostitution is unlawful everywhere, prostitution itself is not per se illegal in at least one U.S. state (Nevada), although it is regulated there. The reach of existing federal law is limited, resting primarily on Congress's constitutional authorization to regulate interstate or foreign commerce, and does not extend to prostitution, which remains a matter for regulation under the police power of the individual states.

---

17. 96 U.N.T.S. 271 (Mar. 21, 1950).

3. This poses a familiar but troublesome question of federalism when it comes to U.S. treaty implementation. On the one hand, if full compliance with the treaty would require action arguably beyond the reach of Congress's powers to regulate commerce under Article I, Section 8 of the U.S. Constitution, would it be sufficient for the federal government to rely on the criminal laws of the 50 states and subordinate jurisdictions to guarantee compliance with the Convention? What if a particular state refused to implement the obligations of the Convention or change its laws? What remedy would the federal government have? On the other hand, would ratification of the Convention give the federal government broader authority than it might otherwise have, for example to enact legislation that would not otherwise be sustainable under the Commerce Clause? What about Article VI of the Constitution, which provides that treaties are part of the "supreme Law of the Land"? See Missouri v. Holland, 252 U.S. 416 (1920) (upholding federal legislation to implement a duly ratified treaty that could not be sustained solely on Commerce Clause authority).

4. During the negotiation of the 1949 Convention, the U.S. delegation proposed adding a "federal clause" limiting the obligation of federal (or "non-unitary") states parties in respect of those "articles which are determined in accordance with the constitutional processes of that State to be appropriate in whole or in part for action by the constituent states, provinces, or cantons or territories." In such cases, the only obligation of the federal government would have been to "bring such articles, with favorable recommendation, to the notice of the appropriate authorities of the states, provinces, or cantons at the earliest possible moment." In your view, would this be an acceptable approach to treaty implementation or consistent with the object and purpose of this particular Convention? Note that neither the clause proposed by the United States nor any other clause providing special consideration to countries with federal forms of government was ultimately included in the Convention.

5. Under the Vienna Convention on the Law of Treaties, a reservation is permissible unless specifically prohibited by the terms of the treaty in question or if the reservation would be "incompatible with the object and purpose of the treaty." In your view, would it be permissible for a state party to condition its obligations under the Convention to the extent they could be carried out only by the central government? For example, the United States took the following reservation to the UN Convention Against Transnational Organized Crime:

> The Government of the United States of America reserves the right to assume obligations under this convention in a manner consistent with its fundamental principles of federalism, pursuant to which both federal and state criminal laws must be considered in relation to the conduct addressed in the Convention. U.S. federal criminal law, which regulates conduct based on its effect on interstate or foreign commerce, or another federal interest, serves as the principal legal regime within the United States for combating organized crime, and is broadly effective for this purpose. Federal criminal law does not apply in the rare case where such criminal conduct does not so involve interstate or foreign commerce, or another federal interest. There are a small number of conceivable situations involving such rare offenses of a purely local character where U.S. federal and state criminal law may not be entirely adequate to satisfy an obligation under the Convention. The Government of the United States of America therefore reserves to the obligations set forth in the Convention to the extent they address conduct that would fall within this narrow category of highly localized activity. . . .

The reservation applied to only a "small number of conceivable situations" because federal law provided the principal legal regime for combating organized crime.

The analogous reservation for the 1949 Convention would cover a wider scope because state law provides the principal legal regime for regulating prostitution.

6. For general background on the 1949 Convention, see Stephanie Farrior, The International Law on Trafficking in Women and Children for Prostitution: Making It Live Up to Its Potential, 10 Harv. Hum. Rts. J. 213 (1997).

3. The UN Trafficking Protocol

In 2000, the UN General Assembly adopted the Protocol to Prevent, Suppress and Punish Trafficking in Persons, Especially Women and Children (Trafficking Protocol), supplementing the UN Convention Against Transnational Organized Crime (discussed in Chapter 11).[18] The Protocol came into force for the United States in December 2005.

The Protocol now provides the basis for renewed global efforts to combat trafficking in persons. The full text is available on our Web site, and you should take the opportunity to review it carefully. We emphasize here only a few key provisions.

(i) *Definitions.* Article 3 of the Trafficking Protocol provides:

(a) "Trafficking in persons" shall mean the recruitment, transportation, transfer, harbouring or receipt of persons, by means of the threat or use of force or other forms of coercion, of abduction, of fraud, of deception, of the abuse of power or of a position of vulnerability or of the giving or receiving of payments or benefits to achieve the consent of a person having control over another person, for the purpose of exploitation. Exploitation shall include, at a minimum, the exploitation of the prostitution of others or other forms of sexual exploitation, forced labour or services, slavery or practices similar to slavery, servitude or the removal of organs;
(b) The consent of a victim of trafficking in persons to the intended exploitation set forth in subparagraph (a) of this article shall be irrelevant where any of the means set forth in subparagraph (a) have been used;
(c) The recruitment, transportation, transfer, harbouring or receipt of a child for the purpose of exploitation shall be considered "trafficking in persons" even if this does not involve any of the means set forth in subparagraph (a) of this article;
(d) "Child" shall mean any person under eighteen years of age.

Under Article 4, the Protocol is deemed to apply to the prevention, investigation, and prosecution of "offences [that] are transnational in nature and involve an organized criminal group, as well as to the protection of victims of such offences." Article 5 requires states parties to establish these offense as crimes "when committed intentionally," and in addition to criminalize "trafficking" as defined above, including attempts, participation as an accomplice, and "organizing or directing other persons to commit" a covered offense.

(ii) *Prevention.* Importantly, Article 9 of the Protocol requires states parties to establish policies and programs "to prevent and combat trafficking in persons" and "to protect victims of trafficking in persons, especially women and children, from revictimization." They must take measures "to alleviate the factors that make persons,

---

18. G.A. Res. 55/25, Annex II, U.N. Doc. A/55/383 (Nov. 15, 2000), reprinted in 40 I.L.M. 335 (2001). The full text of the Protocol is available on our Web site. See also the Coalition Against Trafficking in Women, http://www.catwinternational.org (last visited July 8, 2009), and the Web site of the U.N. High Commissioner for Human Rights, http://www2.ohchr.org/english/law/protocoltraffic.htm (last visited July 8, 2009).

especially women and children, vulnerable to trafficking, such as poverty, underdevelopment and lack of equal opportunity" and "to discourage the demand that fosters all forms of exploitation of persons, especially women and children, that leads to trafficking."

(iii). *Border measures.* Article 11 requires measures to strengthen border controls "to prevent and detect trafficking in persons," including by preventing "means of transport operated by commercial carriers" from being used in the commission of covered offenses.

NOTES AND QUESTIONS

1. Consider the definition of "trafficking in persons" in Article 3 of the Protocol. Compare it to the definitions and criteria in the 1949 Convention. As discussed above, the 1949 Convention focuses on the trafficker's intent to "gratify the passions of another" and covers even fully consensual acts. In contrast, the 2000 Protocol is keyed to concepts of exploitation, coercion, and abuse of power, and extends far beyond the notion of "trade," reflecting the realities of contemporary practices. Note in particular the inclusion of the notion of "coercion" as well as "the abuse of a position of vulnerability." The latter could encompass a broad range of situations, including poverty, hunger, illness, ethnic or racial discrimination, lack of education, and lack of access to the protective mechanisms of society (such as police and the courts). Note also that Article 3's definition is keyed to the "purpose of exploitation." The provision gives several examples of circumstances that ("at a minimum") qualify as "exploitation" — prostitution of others or other forms of sexual exploitation, forced labor or services, slavery or practices similar to slavery, servitude, or the removal of organs. Are these definitional differences significant? Which more fully address the realities of human trafficking?

2. Interestingly, transport of the trafficked person across national boundaries is not specifically required by the definition set forth in Article 3 of the Trafficking Protocol. However, Article 4 states that the Protocol applies to offenses that are "transnational in nature and involve an organized criminal group, as well as to the protection of victims of such offences." The obvious intent of the "transnational" element was to exclude acts and practices that are solely domestic and therefore inappropriate for international regulation (from the point of view of national sovereignty). But how clear is the distinction in practice? For example, would the Protocol support prosecution for an act of trafficking that took place entirely within the borders of a given state? What if that act involves persons who have traveled from another country or funding from abroad? What criteria would you propose for determining whether a given instance of "trafficking" was "transnational in nature"?

3. Article 5 introduces the requirement of intentionality in the context of the obligation of states parties to criminalize covered offenses under their domestic laws. Do you read that requirement as an addition to the "purpose of exploitation" element in the Article 3 definition itself? Or are the two equivalent? What kind of proof of intention would be sufficient to demonstrate a "purpose of exploitation"? Why do you suppose the international community did not simply make trafficking a *malum in se* crime?

4. Beyond its strictly criminal aspects, the Protocol contemplates broad cooperative efforts by the international community to combat trafficking. What specific measures of interstate cooperation would be most effective? In this context, consider the following excerpt from Mohamed Mattar, Incorporating the Five Basic Elements of

a Model Antitrafficking in Persons Legislation in Domestic Laws: From the United Nations Protocol to the European Convention, 14 Tul. J. Intl. & Comp. L. 357, 413-418 (2006) (footnotes omitted):

> Trafficking in persons is a transnational crime. In fact, the UN Protocol applies only to the offenses of trafficking in persons "where those offenses are transnational in nature." [Art. 4.] Trafficking is considered transnational in nature, not only if it is committed in more than one state, but if a "substantial part of its preparation, planning, direction, or control takes place in another state," if it "involves an organized criminal group that engages in criminal activities in more than one state," or if it "has substantial effect in another state." [UN Convention on Transnational Organized Crime, Art. 3(2).] Thus, the transnational nature of the crime warrants transnational policies.
>
> Transnational policies should cover what I call the Three X's of transnational trafficking: extradition, extraterritoriality, and exchange of information.
>
> First, trafficking in persons must be recognized as an extraditable offense. It is interesting to note that under article 16(4) of the Transnational Crime Convention, if "a State Party that makes extradition conditional on the existence of a treaty receives a request for extradition from another State Party with which it has no extradition treaty, it may consider the Convention the legal basis for extradition in respect of any offence to which this article applies."
>
> Second, antitrafficking legislation should also have extraterritorial jurisdiction; this means the application of domestic laws regardless of the place where the act was committed. Both the Council of Europe and United Nations have addressed these issues with regard to peacekeeping missions. There are currently fifteen UN peacekeeping missions operating around the world. Rule 4 of the UN peacekeeper Code of Conduct says that UN peacekeepers should "not indulge in immoral acts of sexual, physical, or psychological abuse or exploitation of the local population or United Nations staff, especially women and children." At the same time, UN peacekeepers fall under the exclusive criminal jurisdiction of their own national authorities and have immunity from local prosecution. It is up to the UN Board of Inquiry to find reasonable grounds for a charge of serious misconduct with a recommendation that the peacekeeper be repatriated for subsequent disciplinary action in his country. However, as I testified before Congress in 2003, of only twenty-four officers repatriated to their countries for misconduct, none has been prosecuted for violating Rule 4 of the Code of Conduct. . . .
>
> Today, we may argue for the universality principle. According to the universality principle, certain offenses are recognized by the community of nations as of universal concern so as to establish a universal jurisdiction. These offenses include crimes against humanity, which are defined under article 7 of the International Criminal Court (ICC) statute to include: "enslavement, sexual slavery, enforced prostitution, and any other form of sexual violence of comparable gravity." The ICC defines enslavement to mean "the exercise of any or all of the powers attaching to the right of ownership over a person and includes the exercise of such power in the course of trafficking in persons in particular women and children."
>
> Third, exchange of information between countries of origin and countries of destination must take place. Bilateral treaties on mutual assistance in criminal matters must be a part of any transnational legal response because apprehension of traffickers, investigation of cases of trafficking, and prosecution of the traffickers sometimes require cooperation between countries of origin and countries of destination in matters including request for assistance, search, seizure, attachment and surrender of property, measures for securing assets, service of judicial decision, judgments and verdicts, appearance of witness and expert witnesses, and transmittal of information of records.

Do you agree with Mattar that trafficking in persons should be considered a "universal" crime, that is, one that can be prosecuted and punished by any state even in the absence of any connection between it and the perpetrator or victim, and even where no relevant act had been taken in or effect manifested on the territory of the forum state?

5. In addition to the initiatives taken at the global level, concerted programs to combat trafficking are also sponsored regionally. Consider, for example, the Council of Europe's Convention on Action Against Trafficking in Human Beings, available at http://conventions.coe.int (last visited July 8, 2009). See Anke Sembacher, The Council of Europe Convention on Action Against Trafficking in Human Beings, 14 Tul. J. Intl. & Comp. L. 435 (2006). For information on efforts to eliminate trafficking in persons within the OAS, see http://www.oas.org/atip/default1.asp (last visited July 8, 2009). See generally Jennifer M. Chacón, Misery and Myopia, Understanding the Failures of U.S. Efforts to Stop Human Trafficking, 74 Fordham L. Rev. 2977 (2006).

4.   The UN Protocol on the Sale of Children

Still another recent multilateral instrument addressed to trafficking in persons is the 2000 Optional Protocol to the Convention on the Rights of the Child, on the Sale of Children, Child Prostitution and Child Pornography.[19] Although contemporaneous with the Trafficking Protocol, it is focused specifically on practices involving the most powerless and innocent of all humans because, as its preamble notes, children are among the most vulnerable groups and "girl children are disproportionately represented among the sexually exploited."

In distinction to the Trafficking Protocol, this treaty follows the traditional "criminalization" approach typical of most other international criminal law treaties. Article 3 requires states parties to criminalize a set of covered crimes whether (i) committed domestically or transnationally or (ii) on an individual or organized basis. They include offering, delivering, or accepting, by whatever means, a child for the purpose of sexual exploitation of the child; transfer of organs of the child for profit; engagement of the child in forced labor; improperly inducing consent, as an intermediary, for the adoption of a child in violation of applicable international legal instruments on adoption; offering, obtaining, procuring, or providing a child for child prostitution; and producing, distributing, disseminating, importing, exporting, offering, selling, or possessing for the above purposes, child pornography.

The Protocol specifies that states must exercise their criminal jurisdiction over these crimes on the basis of "active" as well as "passive" nationality jurisdiction, i.e., when the alleged offender is a national of that state or a person who has his habitual residence in its territory as well as when the victim is a national of that state. Moreover, the Protocol explicitly provides for "extradite or prosecute" jurisdiction and requires each state party to establish its jurisdiction to prosecute "when the alleged offender is present in its territory and it does not extradite him or her to another State Party on the ground that the offense has been committed by one of its

---

19. G.A. Res. 54/263, Annex II, U.N. Doc. A/RES/54/263, 2171 U.N.T.S. 27531 (May 25, 2000), reprinted in 39 I.L.M. 1285 (2000), available at http://www.unhchr.ch/html/menu2/6/protocolchild .htm. As of the end of 2008, the Protocol had 130 parties (including the United States). See also ILO Convention No. 182 Concerning the Prohibition and Immediate Action for the Elimination of the Worst Forms of Child Labour (June 17, 1999), available at http://www.ilo.org/public/english/standards/relm/ ilc/ilc87/com-chic.htm.

nationals." Covered offenses are deemed to fall within any existing extradition treaty between states parties (Art. 4).

The Protocol sets forth a requirement of "mutual legal assistance" in connection with relevant investigations or criminal or extradition proceedings as well as an obligation to take measures for the seizure and confiscation of materials, assets, and other instrumentalities used to commit or facilitate covered offenses and the proceeds derived from such offenses (Art. 6(2)).

Finally, states parties are obliged to strengthen their efforts at international cooperation for the prevention, detection, investigation, prosecution, and punishment of offenses and to address "the root causes, such as poverty and underdevelopment, contributing to the vulnerability of children to the sale of children, child prostitution, child pornography and child sex tourism" (Art. 10(3)).

Is the "criminalization" approach reflected in this Protocol the more appropriate or effective way to address this particular phenomenon? In considering this issue, take into account the U.S. domestic approach, discussed in the following section.

5. Trafficking Victims Protection Act

The principal anti-trafficking provisions in U.S. domestic law are set forth in the Trafficking Victims Protection Act (TVPA).[20] Adopted independently of the Trafficking Protocol but intended to achieve the same goals, the TVPA is aimed at punishing and prosecuting traffickers, preventing trafficking, and protecting victims of trafficking. It created new crimes covering trafficking with respect to slavery, involuntary servitude, and forced labor. It also required courts to order restitution and forfeiture of assets upon conviction of these crimes, and enabled victims to seek witness protection and other types of assistance.

In its statement of statutory purpose, Congress articulated a broad U.S. policy in the following terms:

> Trafficking in persons is a transnational crime with national implications. To deter international trafficking and bring its perpetrators to justice, nations including the United States must recognize that trafficking is a serious offense. This is done by prescribing appropriate punishment, giving priority to the prosecution of trafficking offenses, and protecting rather than punishing the victims of such offenses. The United States must work bilaterally and multilaterally to abolish the trafficking industry by taking steps to promote cooperation among countries linked together by international trafficking routes. The United States must also urge the international community to take strong action in multilateral fora to engage recalcitrant countries in serious and sustained efforts to eliminate trafficking and protect trafficking victims.[21]

The TVPA reflects three complementary strategies to combat trafficking: prevention of the crime, protection of and assistance to the victims, and prosecution of the

---

20. The TVPA was enacted as a subsection of the Victims of Trafficking and Violence Protection Act, Pub. L. No. 106-386, 114 Stat. 1464 (2000), and subsequently amended by the Trafficking Victims Protection Reauthorization Act of 2003, Pub. L. No. 108-193, 117 Stat. 2875 (2003), and the Trafficking Victims Protection Reauthorization Act of 2005, Pub. L. No. 109-164, 119 Stat. 3558 (2005), codified at 18 U.S.C. §§1589-1595 and 22 U.S.C. §§7101-7110.

21. 22 U.S.C. §7101(b)(24). For additional information on the situation within the United States, see the Attorney General's Annual Report to Congress on U.S. Government Activities to Combat Trafficking in Persons Fiscal Year 2007 (May 2008), available at http://www.usdoj.gov/olp/human_trafficking.htm.

perpetrators. Notably, the statute expanded the crimes and enhanced the penalties available to federal prosecutors pursuing traffickers (for example, forfeiture of the proceeds and instrumentalities of trafficking) and created new mechanisms for assistance and compensation to victims, including, for example, the victim's right to pursue civil damages.[22]

In addition to establishing new interagency coordinating mechanisms to combat trafficking to or in the United States, the TVPA established a national policy not to provide "nonhumanitarian, nontrade-related foreign assistance to any government that does not comply with minimum standards for the elimination of trafficking and is not making significant efforts to bring itself into compliance with such standards." It also provided authority for economic sanctions against any foreign person playing "a significant role in a severe form of trafficking in persons, directly or indirectly in the United States," or materially assisting or supporting such activities.[23]

The term "severe forms of trafficking in persons" is defined to include (a) "sex trafficking in which a commercial sex act is induced by force, fraud, or coercion, or in which the person induced to perform such act has not attained 18 years of age"; and (b) "the recruitment, harboring, transportation, provision, or obtaining of a person for labor or services, through the use of force, fraud, or coercion for the purpose of subjection to involuntary servitude, peonage, debt bondage, or slavery."[24] "Sex trafficking" means "the recruitment, harboring, transportation, provision, or obtaining of a person for the purpose of a commercial sex act."[25]

NOTES AND QUESTIONS

1. Compare the statutory definitions of "severe forms of trafficking" with the definition of "trafficking" in the Trafficking Protocol. As a prosecutor, which would you find more difficult to prove in a given case of trafficking for purposes of sexual exploitation?

2. Now consider the "sex trafficking" provisions of the TVPA, codified at 18 U.S.C. §1591 (as amended at the end of 2008):

> (a) Whoever knowingly—
>   (1) in or affecting interstate or foreign commerce, or within the special maritime and territorial jurisdiction of the United States, recruits, entices, harbors, transports, provides, obtains, or maintains by any means a person; or
>   (2) benefits, financially or by receiving anything of value, from participation in a venture which has engaged in an act described in violation of paragraph (1),
>   knowing, or in reckless disregard of the fact, that means of force, threats of force, fraud, coercion described in subsection (e)(2), or any combination of such means will be used to cause the person to engage in a commercial sex act, or that the person has not attained the age of 18 years and will be caused to engage in a commercial sex act, shall be punished as provided in subsection (b).

---

22. 18 U.S.C. §§1591-1595.
23. 22 U.S.C. §§7103, 1707-1708.
24. Id. §7102(8)(a) and (b).
25. Id. §7102(9).

(b) The punishment for an offense under subsection (a) is—

(1) if the offense was effected by means of force, threats of force, fraud, or coercion described in subsection (e)(2), or by any combination of such means, or if the person recruited, enticed, harbored, transported, provided, or obtained had not attained the age of 14 years at the time of such offense, by a fine under this title and imprisonment for any term of years not less than 15 or for life; or

(2) if the offense was not so effected, and the person recruited, enticed, harbored, transported, provided, or obtained had attained the age of 14 years but had not attained the age of 18 years at the time of such offense, by a fine under this title and imprisonment for not less than 10 years or for life.

(c) In a prosecution under subsection (a)(1) in which the defendant had a reasonable opportunity to observe the person so recruited, enticed, harbored, transported, provided, obtained or maintained, the Government need not prove that the defendant knew that the person had not attained the age of 18 years. . . .

(e) In this section:

(1) The term "abuse or threatened abuse of law or legal process" means the use or threatened use of a law or legal process, whether administrative, civil, or criminal, in any manner or for any purpose for which the law was not designed, in order to exert pressure on another person to cause that person to take some action or refrain from taking some action.

(2) The term "coercion" means—

(A) threats of serious harm to or physical restraint against any person;

(B) any scheme, plan, or pattern intended to cause a person to believe that failure to perform an act would result in serious harm to or physical restraint against any person; or

(C) the abuse or threatened abuse of law or the legal process.

(3) The term "commercial sex act" means any sex act, on account of which anything of value is given to or received by any person.

(4) The term "serious harm" means any harm, whether physical or nonphysical, including psychological, financial, or reputational harm, that is sufficiently serious, under all the surrounding circumstances, to compel a reasonable person of the same background and in the same circumstances to perform or to continue performing commercial sexual activity in order to avoid incurring that harm.

(5) The term "venture" means any group of two or more individuals associated in fact, whether or not a legal entity.

3. As a prosecutor, would you rather pursue a criminal case on the basis of the definitions contained in the Trafficking Convention or under the statute quoted above?

4. The following excerpted decision, while dealing with the application of the TVPA in a domestic rather than transnational setting, discusses some of the congressional purposes behind the statute and illustrates some of the potential difficulties that will arise in applying the law to specific circumstances, including those of a transnational nature.

UNITED STATES v. MARCUS
487 F. Supp. 2d 289 (E.D.N.Y. 2007)

[Defendant Marcus was convicted, after a jury trial, of sex trafficking in violation of a prior version of 18 U.S.C. §1591 (as well as forced labor under 18 U.S.C. §1589 and dissemination of obscene materials through an interactive computer service under 18 U.S.C. §1462). The prosecution centered on conduct related to his alternative sexual lifestyle, described by the court as "bondage, dominance/discipline, submission/sadism, and masochism" or "BDSM." The complaining witness (Jodi) testified that initially she entered into a consensual BDSM relationship with Marcus, who subsequently used force and coercion to prevent her from leaving when she sought to do so. Among other things, she testified that she was beaten, whipped, choked, and forced to have sexual intercourse, for example, while tied to a wall. At various times, she was not allowed to wear clothing; could not eat, drink, or speak without permission; was allowed to sleep for only a couple of hours at a time; and was expected to follow the defendant's instructions. Defendant considered her to be his "property" and at one point shaved her head and branded a "G" into her buttocks with a coat hanger. When she indicated a desire to leave, the defendant threatened to send photographs of her activities to her family and the media. She testified that she remained with the defendant against her will for nearly two years, during which time she engaged in BDSM conduct with the defendant and others, which was photographed and placed on his Web site.

The defendant moved under Federal Rule of Criminal Procedure 29 to set aside the jury verdict on three grounds. First, he argued that the TVPA does not apply to conduct that took place as part of an "intimate, domestic relationship" or to consensual BDSM activities. Second, he claimed that the term "commercial sex act" in 18 U.S.C. §1591 did not apply when the defendant received revenue for photographic depictions of sex acts as opposed to the acts themselves. Third, he contended that the government had failed to present sufficient evidence of a "nexus" between the force or coercion employed by the defendant and the commercial sex act element of his sex trafficking conviction or the labor or services element of his forced labor conviction. The court rejected all three arguments.]

District Judge Ross:

. . . 1. APPLICABILITY OF THE TVPA TO DOMESTIC, INTIMATE RELATIONSHIPS

The defendant relies primarily on the legislative history of the TVPA to make the case that the charged statutes are inapplicable to intimate relationships. According to the defendant, the legislative history demonstrates that these statutes were intended to respond to the "problem of international slave trafficking," which is "a far cry from acts of violence and abuse that take place in the context of an intimate personal relationship." On this basis, he claims that his intimate relationship with [the complainant] renders inapplicable (a) the "labor or services" element of the forced labor statute and (b) the "commercial sex act" element of the sex trafficking statute. The court is not persuaded that the statutory language of either statute is ambiguous such that a resort to the legislative history is appropriate and, moreover, finds that the legislative history fails to support the defendant's reading of the statutory language. Finally, to the extent that there are any ambiguities in the statutory language, the court finds that they are hypothetical only and inapplicable to the instant case.

(a) Meaning of "Labor or Services" in the Forced Labor Statute . . .

The defendant argues that the legislative history of the TVPA shows that the statute was only meant to proscribe conduct that compels the victim to provide labor or services "for a business purpose." However, the court finds no justification for this contention. While the legislative history of the TVPA undoubtedly focuses primarily on the need to combat international sex trafficking, the Congressional purpose and findings of the TVPA make clear the intended broad scope of the legislation. The stated purpose of the TVPA is "to combat trafficking in persons, a contemporary manifestation of slavery whose victims are predominantly women and children, to ensure just and effective punishment of traffickers, and to protect their victims." See §102(a), 114 Stat. at 1466. Among the Congressional findings are the following:

(3) Trafficking in persons is not limited to the sex industry. This growing transnational crime also includes forced labor and involves significant violations of labor, public health, and human rights standards worldwide.

(4) . . . Traffickers lure women and girls into their networks through false promises of decent working conditions at relatively good pay as nannies, maids, dancers, factory workers, restaurant workers, sales clerks, or models. Traffickers also buy children from poor families and sell them into prostitution or into various types of forced or bonded labor. . . .

(6) Victims are often forced through physical violence to engage in sex acts or perform slavery-like labor. Such force includes rape and other forms of sexual abuse, torture, starvation, imprisonment, threats, psychological abuse, and coercion.

§102(b), 114 Stat. at 1466-67. While the court observes that Congress did not expressly indicate its desire to regulate labor or services performed within the household, the legislative history provides no cause to believe that Congress intended that type of labor to be excluded from the legislation's reach. In fact, the conference report on the TVPA expressly indicates the intention of Congress that §1589 be used to regulate such conduct, emphasizing that:

it is intended that prosecutors will be able to bring more cases in which individuals have been trafficked into domestic service, an increasingly common occurrence, not only where such victims are kept in service through overt beatings, but also where the traffickers use more subtle means designed to cause their victims to believe that serious harm will result to themselves or others if they leave, as when a nanny is led to believe that children in her care will be harmed if she leaves the home.

H.R. Conf. Rep. 106-939, 106th Cong. (Oct. 5, 2000). Moreover, while the legislative history does not address situations where traffickers have intimate relationships with their victims, the court's survey of the TVPA's legislative history reveals no expressed intention to preclude criminal liability in those contexts. Accordingly, the court . . . concludes that, "[h]ad Congress intended the narrow construction [the defendant] urges, it could have so indicated. It did not, and we decline to introduce that additional requirement on our own." . . .

(b) Meaning of "Commercial Sex Act" in the Sex Trafficking Statute

The defendant additionally contends that the meaning of the term "commercial sex act" in 18 U.S.C. §1591 is ambiguous because it "may be deemed to include all sexual behavior provided that the defendant somehow profits from it; or, it may be limited to sexual conduct which falls outside the scope of the intimate relationship between the defendant and the complainant." The court finds this argument nonsensical, as the statute's plain language refutes the former interpretation. Section 1591 proscribes trafficking a person knowing that "force, fraud, or coercion . . . will be used to cause the person to engage in a commercial sex act." 18 U.S.C. §1591(a). The statute defines a commercial sex act as "any sex act, on account of which anything of value is given to or received by any person." Id. §1591(c)(1). So, while a commercial sex act is quite broadly defined in the statute, the requirement that it be a product of force, fraud or coercion precludes the potential broad sweep about which the defendant expresses concern. As will be discussed below, the government has presented sufficient evidence to show that the commercial sex acts at issue here were not a product of an intimate relationship but, rather, were obtained through force, fraud or coercion. . . .

2. APPLICABILITY OF THE TVPA TO BDSM CONDUCT

The defendant argues that various aspects of the statutes at issue become ambiguous when applied to a BDSM relationship. The court finds that any ambiguities in the statutes were already resolved in the defendant's favor at trial and, therefore, a judgment of acquittal on these grounds is unwarranted. . . .

D. SUFFICIENCY OF THE EVIDENCE WITH REGARD TO THE NEXUS BETWEEN THE DEFENDANT'S ABUSE OF THE VICTIM AND A COMMERCIAL SEX ACT OR LABOR AND SERVICES

The defendant makes two additional arguments as to why the evidence is insufficient to support his conviction: (1) the government failed to establish a sufficient nexus between the defendant's conduct and the commercial sex acts at issue; and (2) the evidence does not show a link between the defendant's abuse of [the complainant] and the labor and services provided by [the complainant]. . . .

1. NEXUS BETWEEN THE DEFENDANT'S CONDUCT AND A "COMMERCIAL SEX ACT" UNDER THE SEX TRAFFICKING STATUTE

As the court instructed the jury, the government was required to prove three elements beyond a reasonable doubt in order for the jury to find the defendant guilty of sex trafficking in violation of 18 U.S.C. §1591. The government had to prove that: (1) the defendant engaged in a prohibited trafficking activity; (2) the defendant's trafficking activity affected interstate commerce; and (3) the defendant knowingly used force, fraud or coercion to cause the trafficked individual to engage in a commercial sex act. (Jury Chg. 13-14.) The defendant submits that the government failed to establish the third element of this offense, because the evidence is insufficient to show a relationship between the force, fraud, or coercion employed by the defendant and the commercial sex acts at issue. The court finds the defendant's argument in this regard unpersuasive. . . .

[The court found "at least two instances in which a reasonable jury could have found, based on the evidence presented at trial, that the defendant's non-consensual application of force directly caused [the complainant] to engage in a commercial sex act" as well as sufficient evidence "to support the inference that the defendant's use of force, fraud and coercion to prevent Jodi from leaving were not only aimed at preserving their sexual relationship but also intended to maintain her services as a model for his commercial website."]

The defendant argues that the existence of a prior consensual relationship between the defendant and [the complainant] in which the infliction of punishment and pain was part of their mutual sexual gratification makes it impossible to determine whether the defendant abused Jodi to compel the performance of a commercial sex act. He argues that the violence inflicted could also have been for purely sexual pleasure or as a means to reinforce their previously agreed-upon roles in the relationship. The court acknowledges that the issue of whether the government proved beyond a reasonable doubt that the defendant used non-consensual force, fraud or coercion to cause [the complainant] to engage in a commercial sex act is difficult and complicated. However, this was precisely the question that the jury was charged with resolving, and the evidence was adequate to support its conclusion. The existence of other potential motivations for the defendant's behavior does not alter the court's determination in this regard.

NOTES AND QUESTIONS

1. The sex trafficking statute (18 U.S.C. §1591) has been held applicable to intrastate as well as interstate activity. See, e.g., United States v. Paris, No. 03:06-CR-64 (CFD), 2007 WL 3124724 (D. Conn. Oct. 24, 2007). The district court in *Paris* noted that, in enacting the TVPA, Congress specifically determined that trafficking in persons "substantially affects interstate and foreign commerce" and that a clear nexus existed between the defendant's intrastate recruiting of women to commit commercial sex acts and the interstate market for commercial sex. It was thus "within Congress's power to regulate [the defendant's] intrastate recruiting and obtaining of women to perform commercial sex acts." Compare United States v. Morrison, 529 U.S. 598 (2000), and United States v. Lopez, 514 U.S. 549 (1995), where the Supreme Court refused to validate two statutes (the Violence Against Women Act, 42 U.S.C. §13981, and the Gun-Free School Zones Act, 18 U.S.C. §922(q)(1)(A) respectively), because Congress lacks authority under the Commerce Clause to regulate noneconomic, violent criminal conduct based solely on that conduct's aggregate effect on interstate commerce.

2. The *Marcus* opinion devotes substantial attention to various legal distinctions (for example, between domestic and commercial relationships, coercive as opposed to consensual situations, prostitution versus "commercial sex acts"). If the statute in fact were interpreted to reach "noncommercial" or "noneconomic" acts, would it be unconstitutional? Had the TVPA been enacted to implement the Trafficking Protocol, would this issue still arise?

3. Federal criminal law has long prohibited involuntary servitude and slavery, see 18 U.S.C. §1581. Similarly, immigration law prohibits harboring aliens for purposes of prostitution, 8 U.S.C. §1328. Cf. United States v. Gasanova, 332 F.3d 297 (5th Cir. 2003) (affirming conviction for bringing Uzbekistani women illegally into the United States to dance in a topless bar in Texas).

4. Prosecutorial efforts to deal with trafficking within the United States often rely on preexisting statutes, for example, the venerable Mann Act, which in its current formulation makes it illegal to transport any individual in interstate or foreign commerce "with intent that such individual engage in prostitution, or in any sexual activity for which any person can be charged with a criminal offense." 18 U.S.C. §2421. It also provides that "whoever knowingly persuades, induces, entices, or coerces any individual to travel in interstate or foreign commerce, or in any Territory or Possession of the United States, to engage in prostitution, or in any sexual activity for which any person can be charged with a criminal offense, or attempts to do so, shall be fined under this title or imprisoned not more than 20 years, or both." 18 U.S.C. §2422. A related provision, 18 U.S.C. §2423, makes it illegal to transport minors (below the age of 18) in interstate or foreign commerce for illegal sexual activity.

5. These provisions were revised and strengthened by the Prosecutorial Remedies and Other Tools to End the Exploitation of Children Today Act (PROTECT Act, Pub. L. No. 108-21, 117 Stat. 650 (2003)), which includes provisions concerning child trafficking, sex tourism, and other forms of exploitation of minors and, importantly, extended U.S. criminal jurisdiction to cover illicit sexual conduct abroad by U.S. citizens. See 18 U.S.C. §2423. The constitutionality of these provisions was upheld in United States v. Clark, 435 F.3d 1100 (9th Cir. 2006), discussed at the end of Chapter 5.

6. In a particularly notable assertion of extraterritorial criminal jurisdiction, the Trafficking Victims Protection Reauthorization Act of 2005 extended the TVPA's reach to offenses committed by persons "employed by or accompanying the Federal Government outside the United States." See Pub. L. No. 109-164, §103(a)(1), 119 Stat. 3558, codified at 18 U.S.C. §§3271-3272. The statute applies if the conduct in question would have been a crime if committed within the United States or the "special maritime and territorial jurisdiction" under 18 U.S.C. §7. However, no prosecution is permitted "if a foreign government, in accordance with jurisdiction recognized by the United States, has prosecuted or is prosecuting such person for the conduct constituting such offense, except upon the approval of the Attorney General or the Deputy Attorney General (or a person acting in either such capacity), which function of approval may not be delegated."

The statute applies to anyone (including a non-U.S. citizen) employed as a federal civilian employee, as a federal contractor or subcontractor at any tier, or as an employee of a federal contractor (including a subcontractor at any tier) who is present or residing outside the United States in connection with such employment and is not a national of or ordinarily resident in the host nation. The term "accompanying the Federal Government outside the United States" is defined to include dependants of persons within the foregoing group. Id. Referring back to our discussion in Chapter 3 of the international law bases for extraterritorial jurisdiction, on which basis can this jurisdictional assertion be justified?

7. Is a law enforcement approach the most effective way to address trafficking in persons for purposes of sexual exploitation? See Jayashri Srikantiah, Perfect Victims and Real Survivors: The Iconic Victim in Domestic Human Trafficking Law, 87 B.U. L. Rev. 157 (2007); Susan W. Tiefenbrun, Updating the Domestic and International Impact of the U.S. Victims of Trafficking Protection Act of 2000: Does Law Deter Crime?, 38 Case W. Res. J. Intl. L. 249 (2006/2007); Iris Yen, Of Vice and Men: A New Approach to Eradicating Sex Trafficking by Reducing Male Demand Through Educational Programs and Abolitionist Legislation, 98 J. Crim. L. & Criminology 653 (2008).

8. For additional background on these issues, see generally Siddarth Kara, Sex Trafficking: Inside the Business of Modern Slavery (2008); Janie Chuang, The United States as Global Sheriff: Using Unilateral Sanctions to Combat Human Trafficking, 27 Mich. J. Intl. L. 437 (2007); Rosy Kandathil, Global Sex Trafficking and the Trafficking Victims Protection Act of 2000: Legislative Responses to the Problem of Modern Slavery, 12 Mich. J. Gender & L. 87 (2005); Martti Lehti & Kauko Aromaa, Trafficking for Sexual Exploitation, 34 Crime & Just. 133 (2006); Cynthia Shepherd Torg, Human Trafficking Enforcement in the United States, 14 Tul. J. Intl. & Comp. L. 503 (2006). See also Catharine A. MacKinnon, Pornography as Trafficking, 26 Mich. J. Intl. L. 993 (2005) ("In material reality, pornography is one way women and children are trafficked for sex.").

6.   Smuggling of Migrants

In addition to the Trafficking Protocol, a separate supplementary protocol to the UN Transnational Organized Crime Convention on migrant smuggling was adopted at the same time.[26] As indicated below, the Smuggling Protocol requires states parties to adopt specified criminal offenses in their domestic laws.

---

26. Protocol Against the Smuggling of Migrants by Land, Sea and Air, supplementing the UN Convention Against Transnational Organized Crime, G.A. Res. 55/25, Annex III, U.N. Doc. A/55/383 (Nov. 15, 2000), reprinted in 40 I.L.M. 335 (2001).

The two protocols—smuggling and trafficking—cover conceptually distinct but related crimes. Although both involve "irregular" or illegal migration, the protocols differ on the element of coercion. Individuals who are "trafficked" are typically victims, exploited without their consent for purposes of forced labor and prostitution, and the trafficker frequently retains control over the migrant through fraud, coercion, or circumstances. By contrast, people who are smuggled are generally considered to have willingly engaged the "services" of the smuggler to procure their illegal entry into another state, usually to pursue economic opportunities (although many seek political refuge or are trying to flee violence and conflict of various kinds). This is not to say, of course, that willing illegal migrants are free from the risk of exploitation. In many cases, they are equally in danger.

Despite those differences, both phenomena are increasingly controlled by transnational organized crime syndicates and place the individuals concerned at great risk. The media often report incidents of migrants drowning in unsafe vessels or suffocating in overcrowded compartments on ships or in trucks. Many of those who do reach their destinations find themselves locked in cycles of violence, exploitation, and abuse. Because the illegal migrants fear arrest and deportation, on one hand, and retribution by their criminal sponsors, on the other, the crimes tend to be underreported; the true extent of the phenomenon, therefore, is unknown.

The text of the Smuggling Protocol is available on our Web site. For present purposes, the most relevant provisions can be summarized briefly.

(i) *Definition*: The term "smuggling of migrants" means "the procurement, in order to obtain, directly or indirectly, a financial or other material benefit, of the illegal entry of a person into a State Party of which the person is not a national or a permanent resident."

(ii) *Criminalization*: Each state party is required to criminalize the smuggling of migrants "when committed intentionally and in order to obtain, directly or indirectly, a financial or other material benefit." In addition, it must be an offense to produce a fraudulent travel or identity document, or to procure, provide, or possess such a document, for the purpose of enabling the smuggling of migrants. Also covered are attempts, participation as an accomplice, and "organizing or directing other persons to commit" a covered offense.

NOTES AND QUESTIONS

1. Both Protocols (Trafficking and Smuggling) contain provisions common to many international criminal law instruments, for example, requiring states parties to establish and implement domestic law enforcement mechanisms and to cooperate with other states parties to strengthen international prevention and punishment of the covered activities. However, the two differ in several key respects, particularly in the protections afforded to migrants. The Trafficking Protocol provides for a broad range of protective and rehabilitative measures for the victims of trafficking, including protecting their identity and privacy, providing for their "physical, psychological, and social recovery," and taking steps to ensure housing, medical care, training, and repatriation. Trafficking Protocol, art. 6. The Smuggling Protocol, by contrast, contains rather minimal reference to the protection needs of smuggled persons. It does, however, stipulate that the migrants themselves should not be subject to criminal prosecution because of their illegal entry into the territory of the state party, and requires states to "ensure the safety and humane treatment of the persons on board" vessels that are searched, and to implement their preexisting, absolute obligations

under international law to protect the right to life and the right not to be subjected to torture or to cruel, inhuman, or degrading treatment or punishment. Smuggling Protocol, arts. 5, 9, & 16(1). Do trafficked persons merit more protection and assistance than those who have been "smuggled"? Why should smuggled persons be exempt from criminal prosecution for having entered the territory illegally?

2. The Smuggling Protocol does impose specific obligations on states to cooperate in the suppression of smuggling of migrants by sea. Arts. 8 and 9. Still other provisions impose obligations regarding the exchange of information between states sharing common borders, the strengthening of border control, the validity and control of travel documents, training and technical cooperation, and the return of smuggled migrants. Arts. 10-15, 18.

3. The principal "alien smuggling" statute in the United States is codified at 8 U.S.C. §1324, which makes it a crime to bring an alien into the United States (for the purpose of financial gain) without prior official authorization, to transport or move an illegal alien within the United States, to harbor or conceal an illegal alien within the United States, and to encourage or induce an illegal alien to enter the United States. In United States v. Delgado-Garcia, 374 F.3d 1337 (D.C. Cir. 2004), the court of appeals held that those subsections of §1324(a) prohibiting conspiring to induce aliens illegally to enter the United States, and the statute prohibiting attempting to bring illegal aliens into the United States, apply extraterritorially. See also United States v. Villaneuva, 408 F.3d 193 (5th Cir. 2005).

B. TRAFFICKING IN DRUGS

For obvious reasons, the precise extent of global trafficking in illicit drugs is difficult to calculate. The United Nations has estimated the commercial value of drug consumption worldwide at approximately $300-400 billion, although that figure is open to some debate.[27] What is abundantly clear, however, is that the forces of illegal narcotics production, distribution, and consumption fuel a worldwide trade of vast proportions with clear connections to transnational organized crime, arms trafficking, and terrorism. The recent surge in violence by Mexico's powerful drug cartels is ample testament to that sad fact.

Some illegal substances are manufactured (for example, amphetamines and methamphetamines), others are farmed (for example, cannabis), and others are grown and processed (for example, coca/cocaine, opium/heroin). Regardless of their origins, there is no doubt that production of these substances is a worldwide phenomenon. According to the UN's 2008 World Drug Report,[28] over 90 percent of the world's heroin comes from poppies grown in Afghanistan; most cocaine is processed from leaf cultivated in Colombia, Peru, and Bolivia; most amphetamines are produced in Europe; and most methamphetamines are produced in North America and Southeast Asia.

---

27. UN World Drug Report for 2005, available at http://www.unodc.org/pdf/WDR_2005/volume_1_chap2.pdf. See generally Peter Reuter & Victoria Greenfield, Measuring Global Drug Markets: How Good Are the Numbers and Why Should We Care About Them?, 2 World Econ. 159 (2001).

28. See UN World Drug Report for 2008, available at www.unodc.org/documents/wdr/WDR_2008/WDR_2008_eng_web.pdf.

Consumption is also global. According to the same UN Report, based on treatment demand, opiates remain the primary problem in Europe and Asia; in South America, cocaine use predominates; and in Africa, cannabis abuse is the main problem. In North America, opiates, cocaine, and cannabis together account for roughly three-quarters of overall use. The UN estimates that overall there are now some 208 million drug users, equivalent to about 5 percent of the global population aged 15 to 64. Cannabis remains by far the most widely used drug (by 165.5 million people), followed by amphetamine-type stimulants (some 34 million people). The number of opiate abusers is estimated at some 16.5 million, of which 12 million are heroin abusers. Some 16 million people are cocaine users.[29]

The public health effects of drug trafficking and use are devastating. They include the adverse impact that drug abuse inflicts on the health of the individual user and that user's family, as well as broader health consequences, such as HIV infections attributable to use of contaminated needles. The social consequences of widespread drug abuse are also well documented. Traffickers, sellers, and users frequently resort to violent criminal activity to protect their investments, to launder their profits, and to finance their habits. Organized criminal gangs that deal in illicit drugs corrupt all facets of the societies in which they operate and threaten the rule of law. In some cases, autocratic regimes and other human rights abusers are sustained by their tolerance of, or involvement in, illicit drug trafficking. The nexus between illegal drug revenues and terrorism has been clearly established, and evidence demonstrates that terrorists benefit from drug trafficking proceeds to finance their trafficking in small arms and light weapons.

At the same time, law enforcement measures to counter and regulate drug trafficking and usage are controversial, and some argue that current regulatory approaches ("the war on drugs") may exacerbate many of the problems that they seek to eliminate (drug-related violence, corruption, and so on). Some critics contend that the most effective way to combat drug trafficking may be a market-based mechanism based on decriminalization of drug use and distribution. That approach would arguably remove the distribution and sale of drugs from the black market, depriving the criminal organizations of the profits of their trade.[30]

1. International Cooperation

International cooperative efforts to contain and disrupt international drug trafficking activities have taken various forms. The U.S. Department of State's 2008 International Narcotics Control Strategy Report (the INCSR)[31] describes the efforts of key countries to attack all aspects of the international drug trade during the previous year. The following excerpt describes relevant U.S. policies and efforts.

---

29. Id.

30. A vast and contentious literature on this topic is readily available. For one view, see James Gray, Why Our Drug Laws Have Failed: A Judicial Indictment of War on Drugs (2001). See generally Kal Raustiala, Law, Liberalization and International Narcotics Trafficking, 32 N.Y.U. J. Intl. L. & Pol. 89 (1999).

31. The INCSR is available at http://www.state.gov/p/inl/rls/nrcrpt/2008. Reporting, in and of itself, may also be an effective tool in combating trafficking. For example, see Mohamed Y. Mattar, Comparative Models of Reporting Mechanisms on the Status of Trafficking in Human Beings, 41 Vand. J. Transnatl. L. 1355 (2008).

U.S. DEPARTMENT OF STATE, INTERNATIONAL
NARCOTICS CONTROL STRATEGY REPORT

(2008)

ATTACKING TRAFFICKING ORGANIZATIONS

Law enforcement tactics have grown more sophisticated over the past two decades to counter the sophisticated trafficking networks that transport large volumes of drugs internationally. Rather than measuring progress purely by seizures and numbers of arrests, international law enforcement authorities have increasingly targeted resources against the highest levels of drug trafficking organizations (DTOs). Increasingly, international law enforcement authorities are learning the art of conspiracy investigations, using mutual legal assistance mechanisms and other advanced investigative techniques to follow the evidence to higher and higher levels of leadership within the syndicates, and cooperating on extradition so that the kingpins have no place to hide. These sophisticated law enforcement and legal tools are endorsed as recommended practices within both the 1988 UN Drug Control Convention and the UN Convention against Transnational Organized Crime. This increasingly mainstream approach towards targeting the organizational leadership of drug syndicates and disrupting their lines of control and command is paying great dividends.

The drug trade depends upon reliable and efficient distribution systems to get its product to market. While most illicit distribution systems have short-term back-up channels to compensate for temporary law enforcement disruptions, a network under intense enforcement pressure cannot function for long. In cooperation with law enforcement officials in other nations, our goal is to disrupt and dismantle these organizations, to remove the leadership and the facilitators who launder money and provide the chemicals needed for the production of illicit drugs, and to destroy their networks. By capturing the leaders of trafficking organizations, we demonstrate both to the criminals and to the governments fighting them that even the most powerful drug syndicates are vulnerable to concerted action by international law enforcement authorities.

Mexican drug syndicates continue to oversee much of the drug trafficking in the United States, with a strong presence in most of the primary U.S. distribution centers. The Calderon Administration's courage, initiative and success have exceeded all expectations of cooperation in facing this threat. President Calderon has addressed some of the most basic institutional issues that have traditionally confounded Mexico's success against the cartels, using the military to reestablish sovereign authority and counter the cartels' firepower, moving to establish integrity within the ranks of the police, and pursuing concrete actions that promise to give law enforcement officials and judicial authorities the resources and the legal underpinning they need to succeed. . . . [Discussion of the bilateral "Merida Initiative" has been omitted — EDS.]

EXTRADITION

There are few legal sanctions that international criminals fear as much as extradition to the United States, where they can no longer use bribes and intimidation to manipulate the local judicial process. Governments willing to risk domestic political repercussions to extradite drug kingpins to the United States are finding that public acceptance of this measure has steadily increased.

Mexican authorities extradited a record 83 fugitives to the United States in 2007, including prominent members of the Gulf Cartel, the sixth consecutive year this number has increased. Colombia has an outstanding record of extradition of drug criminals to the United States, and the numbers have increased even more in recent years. The Government of Colombia extradited a record 135 defendants in 2007, including priority targets Degaberto Florez, Aldemar Rendon Ramirez, the Bernal-Palacios brothers, and Luis Gomez-Bustamante; and AUC paramilitary associate Hector Rodriguez. Overall, 618 individuals have been extradited to the U.S. since December 1997.

Also in 2007, two Afghan drug traffickers with links to the insurgency volunteered to be transported from Afghanistan to stand trial in the United States. The first, Mohammad Essa, was a key heroin distributor for the Haji Baz Mohammad network in the United States. He fled the United States when Baz Mohammad was sent to stand trial in New York. In December 2006, he was apprehended in Kandahar Province by the United States military during a battle with insurgents, and he was voluntarily transferred back to the United States in April 2007. The second was Khan Moham-mad, who was a supporter of the insurgency and arrested in Nangarhar Province in October 2006. He was indicted for selling opium and heroin to Afghan law enforce-ment informants with the understanding that the drugs were destined for the United States. He was voluntarily transferred to the United States in November 2007 and will stand trial in Washington, D.C. Afghanistan and the United States do not yet have a formal bilateral agreement on extradition, but U.S. justice mentors are working with the Afghan Government to draft a broad extradition law.

INSTITUTIONAL REFORM

FIGHTING CORRUPTION

Among all criminal enterprises, the drug trade is best positioned to spread corruption and undermine the integrity and effectiveness of legitimate governments. Drugs generate illegal revenues on a scale without historical precedent. No commodity is so widely available, so cheap to produce, and as easily renewable as illegal drugs. A kilogram of cocaine can be sold in the United States for more than 15 times its value in Colombia, a return which dwarfs regular commodities and distorts the licit economy.

No government is completely safe from the threat of drug-related corruption, but young democracies are especially vulnerable — particularly fragile democracies in post-conflict situations. The weakening of government institutions through bribery and intimidation ultimately poses just as great a danger to democratic governments as the challenge of armed insurgents. Drug syndicates seek to subvert governments in order to guarantee themselves a secure operating environment. Unchecked, the drug cartels have the wherewithal to buy their way into power. By keeping a focus on eliminating corruption, we can prevent the nightmare of a government entirely manipulated by drug lords from becoming a reality.

IMPROVING CRIMINAL JUSTICE SYSTEMS

A pivotal element of USG international drug control policy is to help strengthen enforcement, judicial, and financial institutions worldwide to narrow the opportuni-ties for infiltration and corruption by the drug trade. Corruption within a criminal justice system has enormously detrimental impact; law enforcement agencies in drug source and transit countries may arrest influential drug criminals only to see them released following a questionable or inexplicable decision by a single judge, or a prosecutor may obtain an arrest warrant but be unable to find police who will execute it. As governments work for basic reforms involving transparency, efficiency, and better pay for police and judges, we see systemic improvements.

The USG is continuing its support to Afghanistan to counter the drug trade that threatens stability and economic development as the country emerges from decades of war. Efforts to improve the capability of Afghanistan to investigate, arrest, prose-cute, and incarcerate those guilty of narcotics violations are integrated into the overall justice sector strategy that the United States pursues jointly with the Afghan Govern-ment and international partners. Together with our international partners, we are training and mentoring Afghanistan's Counternarcotics Criminal Justice Task Force and Central Narcotics Tribunal in Kabul. These efforts are tied into other USG justice assistance programs to build and reform the criminal, commercial, and civil justice systems to establish the rule of law.

Next Steps

The drug trade is fundamentally an illicit business. It enters the legitimate commercial world through its dependence on raw materials, processing chemicals, transportation networks, and its need to launder its profits through legitimate commercial and financial channels. We must intensify our efforts to block the drug business in all these areas, in particular focusing on the financial end because this black market can easily be diverted to fund insurgencies and terrorism, and to undermine the institutions of government. Since governments individually control domestic access to the global financial system, they have the potential, by working together, to make it difficult for drug profits to enter the legitimate international financial system.

However, the international narcotics trade has long demonstrated its ability to adapt to law enforcement constraints, and the drug trade itself also evolves, with the increasing use of synthetic drugs, Internet sales and distribution, state-of-the-art communications and technical and financial expertise. Even the best alternative livelihoods cannot compete with the financial pressures on, and armed threats to, those who grow illicit crops.[32]

2.   *Prior Conventions*

Because of its adverse impacts on people and societies, narcotics trafficking was one of the first areas in which the international community sought to agree on collective mechanisms to control and then to criminalize transborder activity. Those responses included a series of conventions spanning much of the past hundred years.[33]

---

32. The 2008 INCSR is available at http://www.state.gov/p/inl/rls/nrcrpt/2008.

33. Among the earliest attempts to control drug trafficking were those focused on the opium trade under the direction of the International Opium Commission of 1909. The International Opium Con-vention of 1912, 38 Stat. 1912, 8 L.N.T.S. 187 (Jan. 23, 1912), established a form of international regu-latory control over the trade. Additional efforts under the League of Nations resulted in the 1931 Convention for Limiting the Manufacture and Regulating the Distribution of Narcotic Drugs, 48 Stat. 1543, T.S. No. 863, 139 L.N.T.S. 301 (July 13, 1931), and the 1936 Convention for the Suppression of Illicit Traffic in Dangerous Drugs, 198 L.N.T.S. 299 (June 26, 1936). Subsequently, under the auspices first of the League of Nations and then of the United Nations, a series of multilateral conventions was developed in order to supervise and regulate the production, control, and shipment of narcotic drugs for

The 1961 Single Convention on Narcotic Drugs[34] consolidated the earlier international instruments into a simpler, more streamlined regime. The most important substantive provisions of the earlier treaties were integrated into a single treaty, and their various oversight mechanisms were merged into a unified body, the International Narcotics Control Board. The Single Convention extended international control to the cultivation of plants grown as the raw material of natural narcotic drugs, putting cannabis plant and coca bush under the same international control system as that applied to opium. Subject to certain grace periods, it prohibited the practices of opium smoking, opium eating, coca leaf chewing, hashish smoking, and the use of the cannabis plant for any nonmedical purposes. Article 36 requires states parties to criminalize the intentional "cultivation, production, manufacture, extraction, preparation, possession, offering, offering for sale, distribution, purchase, sale, delivery on any terms whatsoever, brokerage, dispatch, dispatch in transit, transport, importation and exportation of drugs contrary to the provisions of this Convention."

In 1972, the Single Convention was amended by a protocol,[35] which strengthened its provisions related to preventing the illicit production of, traffic in, and use of narcotics. It also highlighted the need to provide treatment and rehabilitation services to drug abusers by stressing that treatment, education, aftercare, rehabilitation and social reintegration should be considered as alternatives to, or in addition to, imprisonment for abusers who commit drug offenses.

The 1971 Psychotropic Substances Convention extended international control beyond narcotic drugs to manmade hallucinogens, stimulants, and sedatives.[36] Based largely on the control system of the 1961 Single Convention, the 1971 Convention distinguished between those substances that are completely prohibited except for limited scientific and medical purposes, and those whose manufacture, distribution, trade, and use is merely curtailed. The World Health Organization (WHO) is designated to make recommendations about which substances should be on which list to the UN Commission on Narcotic Drugs, which serves as the central policymaking body within the UN system on questions of drug abuse control. The Commission has various oversight functions, including those under the 1961 and 1971 Conventions, and it decides which substances should be placed under international control and to what degree.

Together, the amended Single Convention and the Psychotropic Substances Convention regulate the legal production and distribution of controlled substances for medical and scientific purposes and make all other production illegal. They also provide the international basis for domestic legislation such as the Comprehensive Drug Abuse Prevention Act of 1970.[37]

3.   The 1988 Illicit Trafficking Convention

Adopted by consensus at an international conference of 106 states in Vienna in December 1988, the UN Convention Against Illicit Traffic in Narcotic Drugs and

---

licit (that is, medical and scientific) purposes. These conventions created a complex and to some degree overlapping system of regulations as well as international oversight bodies to monitor and enforce their provisions.

34. 18 U.S.T. 1407, T.I.A.S. 6398, 520 U.N.T.S. 204 (Mar. 30, 1961), reprinted in 10 I.L.M. 261 (1971).
35. 26 U.S.T. 1439, T.I.A.S. 8118, 976 U.N.T.S. 3 (Mar. 25, 1972).
36. 32 U.S.T. 543, T.I.A.S. 9725, 1019 U.N.T.S. 175 (Feb. 21, 1971).
37. Pub. L. No. 91-513, 84 Stat. 1236 (1970), codified as amended at 21 U.S.C. §§810-966.

Psychotropic Substances (Illicit Trafficking Convention)[38] aimed to establish a new international legal regime for combating international drug trafficking. Reflecting general agreement that the existing treaty-based mechanisms had proved ineffective in containing and suppressing the increasing volume of illicit trafficking across national boundaries, the UN General Assembly had unanimously tasked the UN Commission on Narcotic Drugs to prepare a new convention to complement the 1961 Single and 1971 Psychotropic Substances Conventions. The resulting 1988 Convention explicitly recognized that illicit trafficking constitutes "an international criminal activity" and requires that each state party establish as criminal offenses under its domestic law a comprehensive list of activities involved in or related to international drug trafficking (Illicit Trafficking Convention, preamble and art. 3). It obligates states parties to cooperate in taking broad measures to suppress illicit trafficking across national boundaries and, within their own jurisdictions, to enact and enforce specific domestic laws aimed at suppressing the drug trade. These laws include those related to money laundering, confiscation of assets, extradition, mutual legal assistance and trade in chemicals, materials, and equipment used in the manufacture of controlled substances. The Convention is one of the most detailed and far-reaching instruments ever adopted in the field of international criminal law.

The United States participated actively in the negotiation of the Convention, and many of its provisions reflect legal approaches and devices already found in U.S. law. At the same time, for many other countries lacking the modern legal tools for effective counternarcotics enforcement, the Convention broke new ground; achieving consensus among states with widely varied domestic systems of criminal law was a substantial achievement requiring innovation and a certain degree of compromise.

Consider the following overview of the Convention's main provisions.

DAVID P. STEWART, INTERNATIONALIZING THE WAR ON DRUGS: THE UN CONVENTION AGAINST ILLICIT TRAFFIC IN NARCOTIC DRUGS AND PSYCHOTROPIC SUBSTANCES

18 Denv. J. Intl. L. & Poly. 387 (1990)

SUMMARY OF PROVISIONS

As adopted, the Convention calls upon party states to take specific law enforcement measures to improve their ability to identify, arrest, prosecute and convict those who traffic in drugs across national boundaries. Such measures include the establishment of drug-related criminal offenses and sanctions under domestic law, making such offenses the basis for international extradition between party states, and providing for mutual legal assistance in the investigation and prosecution of covered offenses, as well as the seizure and confiscation of proceeds from and instrumentalities used in illicit trafficking activities.

In addition, the Convention imposes new and more stringent controls on the international trade of previously unmonitored chemicals, equipment and other materials used in the clandestine manufacture of drugs, and obliges party states to cooperate among themselves in suppressing illicit traffic by sea or through the mails. Party states must take appropriate measures to ensure that private means of transport

---

38. UN Convention Against Illicit Traffic in Narcotic Drugs and Psychotropic Substances, Dec. 20, 1988, U.N. Doc. E/CONF.82/15, 1990 U.N.T.S. 165, reprinted in 28 I.L.M. 493 (1989), entered into force Nov. 11, 1990.

operated by commercial carriers are not used for illicit trafficking and must apply measures to suppress illicit trafficking in free trade zones and free ports that are no less stringent than those applied in other parts of their territories. Party states are also required to take effective action to prevent illicit cultivation of plants containing narcotic or psychotropic substances, to cooperate in eradicating illicitly cultivated crops, and to adopt measures aimed at eliminating or reducing illicit demand.

Finally, the UN Commission on Narcotic Drugs and the UN International Narcotics Control Board are empowered with administrative and oversight responsibilities concerning the operation of the Convention and the responsibilities of the party states.

OFFENSES AND SANCTIONS

Article 3 of the Illicit Trafficking Convention requires that each party state establish as criminal offenses under its domestic law a comprehensive list of activities involved in or related to international drug trafficking. These offenses largely track existing provisions of U.S. law, but are currently not covered in the criminal law of many other nations; in the latter, their adoption will extend and substantially strengthen criminal regulation of international drug trafficking.

Specifically, the mandatory offenses covered by Article 3(1) of the Convention include:

- the production, manufacture, distribution or sale of any narcotic drug or psychotropic substance contrary to the provisions of the 1961 Single Convention or the 1971 Psychotropic Substances Convention;
- the cultivation of opium poppy, coca bush or cannabis plant contrary to those earlier Conventions;
- the possession or purchase of any narcotic drug or psychotropic substance for the purpose of illicit trafficking;
- the manufacture, transport or distribution of materials, equipment and substances for the purpose of illicit cultivation, production or manufacture of narcotic drugs or psychotropic substances;
- the organization, management or financing of any of the foregoing offenses.

The last provision, which criminalizes the financing, organizing or managing of any of the acts listed above, should be a significant tool in reaching the highest levels of the trafficking organizations, or cartels. In addition, the Convention specifically criminalizes drug-related money laundering, including the conversion or transfer of property derived from the offense, as well as the concealment or disguise of its true nature and source.

Also under Article 3(1), party states are required, subject to their constitutional principles and basic concepts of their legal systems, to establish as criminal offenses:

- the acquisition, possession or use of property knowingly derived from the above offenses;
- possession of equipment, materials and substances knowingly used or to be used in the illicit cultivation, production or manufacture of narcotic drugs or psychotropic substances;
- publicly inciting or inducing others to commit the above-listed offenses;
- related offenses of conspiracy, participation, aiding and abetting, etc.

The obligation of a party state to establish this group of offenses is made "subject to its constitutional principles and the basic concepts of its legal system," because of the difficulties encountered by the negotiators in formulating precise definitions acceptable to differing legal systems. For example, in systems where prosecutorial discretion is limited or nonexistent, there was concern that innocent conduct not be covered inadvertently; concepts of "conspiracy" and "criminal association" differ significantly from country to country; and for some, including the United States, a literal reading of the provisions concerning incitement and inducement could have created constitutional difficulties.

These "core" or "covered" offenses under Article 3(1) constitute the cornerstone of the Convention, and are specifically focused on those drug trafficking and money laundering activities which have the greatest international impact. Many of the other provisions in the Convention, for example those relating to confiscation, extradition and mutual legal assistance, are keyed to these particular offenses.

[Article 3 of the] Convention treats "personal use" offenses separately, requiring party states to adopt such measures, subject to constitutional principles and basic concepts of their legal systems, as may be necessary to criminalize the intentional possession, purchase and cultivation of illicit narcotic drugs and psychotropic substances for personal consumption contrary to the 1961 Single Convention, as amended, or the 1971 Psychotropic Substances Convention. This distinction was intended to differentiate those offenses from the relatively more serious offenses defined in paragraph 1 of Article 3, which are directly related to international trafficking. This distinction thereby limits the obligations imposed upon party states with respect to extradition and mutual legal assistance and permits party states to fashion alternative remedies such as treatment and rehabilitation, rather than incarceration, in appropriate cases.

Each party state is obliged to make these covered acts punishable by sanctions which take into account the grave nature of the offenses, such as imprisonment, fines and confiscation. The Convention requires competent authorities to take into account factual circumstances making the commission of the offenses particularly serious, such as the involvement of organized criminal groups, use of violence, victimization of minors, and the fact that the offender holds public office.

Importantly, the Convention provides that the covered offenses shall not be considered "fiscal offenses," "political offenses" or "regarded as politically motivated" for purposes of its confiscation, extradition and mutual legal assistance provisions.

JURISDICTION

For the most part, the offenses covered by the Convention are international offenses, involving acts which occur in, or have an effect on, more than one state. To give effect to these offenses, each party state is required under Article 4 of the Convention to establish jurisdiction when the offenses are committed in its territory or on board its vessels or aircraft. A state may, but is not required to, establish jurisdiction over offenses: (a) committed anywhere by its nationals or habitual residents; (b) on board vessels outside its territorial sea which it is properly boarding and searching; and (c) with respect to conspiratorial actions committed outside its territory with a view to commission of a covered offense within its territory. The Convention thus recognizes a number of conceptual bases for the exercise of prosecutorial jurisdiction but does not assign a priority in the case of overlapping or competing jurisdiction.

The Convention also requires the establishment of jurisdiction to prosecute when the party state refuses to extradite an alleged offender on the ground that the offense was committed in its territory or on board its aircraft or vessel, or that the offender is its national. Concomitantly, when a party state does not extradite an alleged offender for those reasons, it is obliged [under Article 6] to submit the case to its competent authorities for the purpose of prosecution, unless otherwise agreed with the party requesting extradition. This is a somewhat more limited form of "general jurisdiction" than found in other international criminal law treaties, in that jurisdiction to prosecute is permitted but not required when extradition is refused for any reason other than those given above.

NOTES AND QUESTIONS

1. *Assessing effectiveness.* As of mid-2009, 184 states had ratified or acceded to the Illicit Narcotics Trafficking Convention (most recently, Namibia, the Democratic People's Republic of Korea, and Lichtenstein). How does one evaluate the effectiveness or success of a treaty regime? Consider the following possible criteria. Does widespread ratification alone provide a reliable measurement? Or is enactment of appropriate implementing legislation a better indicator? Does one also have to evaluate the extent to which the relevant domestic laws are actively and effectively enforced? The number of prosecutions and convictions? The degree to which states parties are meeting their obligations to extradite and provide mutual legal assistance? Or should the evaluation ultimately turn only on a documented decline in the volume of drugs produced, distributed, or consumed worldwide?

2. *Jurisdictional questions.* States willing to prosecute persons engaged in transborder traffic in drugs may have difficulty securing the attendance of defendants at trial through extradition and may be reluctant (for political or policy reasons) to resort to extraordinary methods such as abduction. Some countries, including many "producer" countries, are unable to extradite their nationals, and may at the same time be unable to prosecute because of grudging provision in local law for prosecutions of persons for extraterritorial activities. In short, there remain significant barriers to the use of national prosecutions to address the drug trafficking problem. Do these factors argue in favor of adopting a "universal jurisdiction" regime (in which any state can prosecute any trafficker for any covered offense)? See Anne H. Geraghty, Universal Jurisdiction and Drug Trafficking: A Tool for Fighting One of the World's Most Pervasive Problems, 16 Fla. J. Intl. L. 371 (2004); Jimmy Gurulé, The 1988 UN Convention Against Illicit Traffic in Narcotic Drugs and Psychotropic Substances — A Ten Year Perspective: Is International Cooperation Merely Illusory?, 22 Fordham Intl. L.J. 74 (1998).

3. *International tribunals?* Are international prosecutions a promising avenue? Interestingly, the International Criminal Court grew out of a suggestion initially lodged by Trinidad and Tobago to create a permanent international criminal court to address drug trafficking. The initial draft of the ICC statute contemplated giving that institution jurisdiction over these offenders and other persons who commit "treaty crimes." That proposal was rejected. Was that a mistake? If domestic prosecutions have not succeeded in dampening the growth of drug use and trafficking, and if international conventions requiring states to prosecute offenders under their domestic law have not worked, is it time to consider making drug trafficking a true "international" crime that can be prosecuted in international tribunals? What factors ought to determine whether a specific criminal activity warrants treatment as an international crime?

4. *Sovereignty concerns.* Aggressive unilateral counternarcotics policies by consumer countries can provoke resistance and reaction in producer countries (recall Moisés Naím's reference to "nationalistic impulses and insular responses"). Given the agreed aims of the Convention, are these concerns legitimate? Consider the

implications, for example, of the first operative paragraph of the most recent UN General Assembly resolution on "international cooperation against the world drug problem."

> *Reaffirms* that countering the world drug problem is a common and shared responsibility that must be addressed in a multilateral setting, requires an integrated and balanced approach and must be carried out in full conformity with the purposes and principles of the Charter of the United Nations and other provisions of international law, and in particular with full respect for the sovereignty and territorial integrity of States, for the principle of non-intervention in the internal affairs of States and for all human rights and fundamental freedoms, and on the basis of equal rights and mutual respect.

G.A. Res. 63/197, ¶1, U.N. Doc. A/RES/63/197 (Dec. 18, 2008).

5. *Domestic cultivation.* Although the main thrust of the Convention is aimed at the suppression of trafficking across borders, Article 14 obliges each state party to take appropriate internal measures to prevent the illicit cultivation of, as well as to promote the eradication of, plants containing narcotic or psychotropic substances (such as opium poppy, coca bush, and cannabis plants) cultivated illicitly in its territory.

6. *Demand reduction, treatment, and rehabilitation.* Under Article 14(4) of the Illicit Trafficking Convention, states parties must also take "appropriate measures aimed at eliminating or reducing illicit demand for narcotic drugs and psychotropic substances, with a view to reducing human suffering and eliminating financial incentives for illicit traffic." In addition, in conjunction with (or as an alternative to) criminal prosecution, states parties are encouraged to provide measures such as treatment, education, aftercare, rehabilitation, or social reintegration for offenders. Illicit Trafficking Convention, art. 3 (4)(b). G.A. Res. 63/197, ¶¶8(b) and 9, also encourages states to emphasize demand reduction and the prevention, treatment, and rehabilitation of "drug use disorders."

7. *Law enforcement techniques.* Significantly, the Illicit Trafficking Convention endorsed specific law enforcement measures tailored to illicit trafficking across national boundaries. For example, under Article 11, states are required to take the necessary measures to allow for the use of "controlled deliveries" at the international level to the extent permitted by the basic principles of their respective domestic legal systems and on the basis of mutual agreements or arrangements. The technique of "controlled delivery" contemplates the known passage of an illicit consignment through a territory in which the authorities elect not to effect an arrest or seizure immediately, in order to trace the further movement of the consignment and to identify higher levels of the trafficking organization. Widely used by U.S. law enforcement authorities, the technique had not been universally adopted, and in some states it actually contravenes the obligation of authorities not to condone or tolerate known illegal behavior. Its inclusion in the Convention not only reflects the endorsement of the technique by the international community, but also provides a specific basis in international law for its adoption and use at the domestic level. Reflecting the fact that the technique can be expensive in terms of manpower and resources, the Convention provides that the decision to employ it shall be made on a case-by-case basis, when necessary, taking into consideration financial arrangements and understandings.

8. *Extradition and mutual legal assistance.* Following the pattern of many international criminal law treaties, the 1988 Convention contains extradite-or-prosecute obligations and provides that extradition requests may not be refused on the grounds that they involve "fiscal," "political," or "politically motivated" offenses. Art. 6. It also imposes broad mutual legal assistance requirements and states that "[a] Party

shall not decline to render mutual legal assistance under this article on the ground of bank secrecy." Art. 7(5). Thus, bank secrecy laws cannot be used to justify refusal of a request for mutual legal assistance under this Convention or under any of the bilateral treaties affected by its provisions.

9. *Forfeiture.* Article 5 requires states parties to enact far-reaching domestic laws providing for the "confiscation" (that is, freezing, seizing, and forfeiting) of all forms of property, proceeds, or instrumentalities used in or derived from covered offenses. It also emphasizes the importance of international cooperation in forfeiture proceedings by requiring states parties, upon request of another, to assist in taking measures to identify, trace, and freeze or seize proceeds, property, instrumentalities, or any other objects for the purposes of eventual confiscation either by the requesting party or its own authorities.

10. *Border searches.* As with the Trafficking in Persons and Smuggling Protocols, the 1988 Convention specifically addresses steps to be taken to interdict trafficking offenses at the borders. In this connection, note the long-recognized authority of U.S. law enforcement agencies to perform warrantless searches and inspections at the country's international borders. See, e.g., 19 U.S.C. §§1581-1582; 31 U.S.C. §5317. In United States v. Flores-Montano, 541 U.S. 149, 152-153 (2004), the U.S. Supreme Court upheld a warrantless border search of an automobile that included the removal and disassembly of the car's gas tank despite the lack of reasonable suspicion. In so doing, it explained that

> [t]he Government's interest in preventing the entry of unwanted persons and effects is at its zenith at the international border. Time and again, we have stated that "searches made at the border, pursuant to the longstanding right of the sovereign to protect itself by stopping and examining persons and property crossing into this country, are reasonable simply by virtue of the fact that they occur at the border." . . . It is axiomatic that the United States, as sovereign, has the inherent authority to protect, and a paramount interest in protecting, its territorial integrity.

Id. (citing United States v. Ramsey, 431 U.S. 606, 616 (1977)). The Ninth Circuit has noted, however, that in some circumstances it might be appropriate to require some level of suspicion in the case of highly intrusive searches in order to protect the dignity and privacy interests of the person being searched. ("We decline the government's invitation to decide this case by holding that, at the border, anything goes."). United States. v. Seljan, 547 F.3d 993, 1000 (9th Cir. 2008).

The search need not take place at the actual border but can be conducted at its "functional equivalent" (or even, in the case of what has been called an "extended border search," at "a greater spatial and temporal distance" from the actual border than searches at the functional equivalent). See United States v. Abbouchi, 502 F.3d 850 (9th Cir. 2007) (search of outbound package at UPS's Louisville "hub").

11. *Interdiction on the high seas.* Efforts to suppress narcotics trafficking often raise issues of extraterritorial jurisdiction, especially when the law enforcement activities of the United States are aimed at interdicting drug smugglers on the high seas. Consider the situation in United States v. Bravo, 489 F.3d 1 (1st Cir. 2007), where the U.S. Coast Guard interdicted an apparently "stateless" vessel in international waters 180 nautical miles south of Santo Domingo, Dominican Republic. The Maritime Drug Law Enforcement Act (MDLEA) allows the United States to conduct drug law enforcement activities outside of the United States, and more specifically, exercise jurisdiction over stateless vessels. 46 U.S.C. App. §1903(c). On board was approximately 5,000 pounds of marijuana with a street value of $7.5 million. The vessel was taken to San

Juan, Puerto Rico, and its crew turned over to U.S. Immigration and Customs Enforcement (ICE). They were eventually convicted of possession with intent to distribute, aiding and abetting, and conspiracy to possess with intent to distribute.

On appeal, the defendants argued that they were neither citizens nor residents of the United States, their vessel was not registered in the United States, they had not been apprehended in U.S. waters, and the government had not demonstrated that the marijuana transported in the vessel would affect the United States. Absent a "nexus" to the United States, they contended, it was a violation, inter alia, of due process to apply the MDLEA, 46 App. U.S.C.A. §1903(c)(1)(A), to this situation. The First Circuit rejected that argument, noting that since Congress had not enacted the statute under its Commerce Clause authority, no nexus was required, and that the exercise of jurisdiction was justified under the so-called protective principle and in light of relevant international treaties, including the 1988 Illicit Trafficking Convention.

C. TRAFFICKING IN ARMS

"Small arms" are weapons intended for personal use such as revolvers, self-loading pistols, submachine guns, assault rifles, and even shoulder-fired missiles. By contrast, "light weapons" are those intended to be used by crews of a few persons, including heavy machine guns, recoilless rifles, anti-tank and anti-aircraft missiles and rockets, and low caliber mortars. According to some estimates, over 500 million small arms and light weapons (SALW) currently exist, and the magnitude of the annual transnational trade is calculated in the billions of dollars. (The trade in larger conventional weapons and in biological, chemical, and nuclear weapons is generally referred to as "proliferation" and occurs between small numbers of largely state actors.)

Regulation of the burgeoning global SALW market is made difficult by several factors, most importantly the ready availability of the weapons themselves. Small arms and light weapons are manufactured by over 1,000 companies in nearly 100 countries, most of which permit their export. The major exporting countries are generally said to include Brazil, China, Germany, Italy, the Russian Federation, and the United States. Small arms are particularly suited to illegal trafficking because they are readily portable, easily concealed, relatively inexpensive, highly durable, and, in less developed economies, can often be bartered for food, livestock, diamonds, or other commodities. Indeed, in some conflictive areas, SALW are said to have become a kind of currency.

Control is also difficult because SALW do have legitimate uses, for example, by law enforcement and the military, making categorical prohibitions problematic. The right to own and trade in arms is protected in many legal systems (including in the United States), making regulation difficult. The line between licit trade and illicit trafficking is often blurred by the lack of strict international criteria and controls. However fuzzy the line, it is frequently crossed. Lawfully produced arms can be diverted and sold illegally to criminal organizations because domestic rules and regulations are frequently ineffective and their enforcement lax.

Because SALW frequently find their way to criminal organizations, terrorists, and subversives, such weapons are a major destabilizing phenomenon in much of the world. In many local or regional conflicts, SALW are the predominant weapons. Easy to use, they have the capacity to cause widespread death and injury. Their availability thus can have profound civil and political consequences. In fact, it was through international involvement in peacekeeping operations in the mid-90s, following the end of the Cold War, that the extent of the problem became known.

The UN General Assembly has emphasized that the illicit SALW trade "poses a serious threat to peace, reconciliation, safety, security, stability and sustainable development at the individual, local, national, regional and international levels."[39] As noted in the Secretary General's Report on Small Arms:[40]

> Small arms are cheap, light and easy to handle, transport and conceal. While a build-up of small arms alone may not create the conflicts in which they are used, their excessive accumulation and universal availability tends to aggravate conflicts by increasing the lethality and duration of violence and by increasing the sense of insecurity which leads to a greater demand for weapons. Most present-day conflicts are fought mainly with small arms and light weapons. They are broadly used in inter-State conflict and they are the weapons of choice in civil wars and for terrorism, organized crime and gang warfare.

> The vast majority of direct conflict deaths are attributable to the use of small arms, and . . . civilian populations—increasingly also children—bear the brunt of armed conflict more than ever. . . . Similarly, small arms are the dominant tools of criminal violence in ostensibly non-conflict societies, and the rate of firearms-related homicides in post-conflict societies frequently outnumbers battlefield deaths. . . .

> Small arms facilitate a vast spectrum of human rights violations, including killing and maiming, rape and other forms of sexual violence, enforced disappearance, torture and forced recruitment of children by armed groups or forces. More human rights abuses are committed with them than with any other weapon.

Despite recognition of the scope of the problem and its adverse effects, the international community has only recently begun to take steps to deal with the global trade in small arms. In July 2001 the United Nations convened a global Conference on the Illicit Trade in Small Arms and Light Weapons in All Its Aspects. The Conference produced an agreed "Program of Action" calling on states to take measures to prevent, combat, and eradicate the illicit trade in small arms and light weapons.[41] Among others, these steps include adopting and implementing adequate laws, regulations, and administrative procedures to control the production of small arms and light weapons; their export, import, transit, or retransfer, including through use of authenticated end-user certificates; and their illegal manufacture, possession, stockpiling and trade, export, and transit in or through their territories. The Conference also called upon all states voluntarily to submit national reports on implementation of the program.[42]

Two multilateral instruments reflect these first efforts to come to grips with this aspect of trafficking.[43]

---

39. G.A. Res. 63/72, ¶1, U.N. Doc. A/RES/63/72 (Dec. 2, 2008).

40. UN Doc. S/2008/258, ¶¶3-5 (Apr. 17, 2008).

41. The Program of Action is contained in the Report of the United Nations Conference on the Illicit Trade in Small Arms and Light Weapons in All Its Aspects, July 9-20, 2001, U.N. Doc. A/CONF.192/15, available at http://disarmament.un.org/cab/poa.html. A follow-up review conference was held in 2006. See http://www.un.org/events/smallarms2006/.

42. For a description of these and related efforts, see http://disarmament.un.org/cab/salw.html (last visited July 8, 2009).

43. See generally Harold Hongju Koh, A World Drowning in Guns, 71 Fordham L. Rev. 2333 (2003).

1. *UN Firearms Protocol*

The Protocol Against the Illicit Manufacturing of and Trafficking in Firearms, Their Parts and Components and Ammunition was adopted in 2001 to supplement the UN Convention against Transnational Organized Crime. As of mid-2009, 79 states have become parties to the Protocol, most recently the Dominican Republic, Bahamas, Kazakhstan, and Mongolia, but not including the United States.[44] The purpose of the Protocol is to promote, facilitate, and strengthen cooperation among states in preventing, combating, and eradicating the illicit manufacturing of and trafficking in firearms, their parts and components, and ammunition. It combines measures to control the manufacture and traffic of firearms, inter alia through government licensing procedures for marking and tracing firearms, with criminal penalties for violations.

PROTOCOL AGAINST THE ILLICIT MANUFACTURING OF AND TRAFFICKING IN FIREARMS, THEIR PARTS AND COMPONENTS AND AMMUNITION

Article — Use of Terms

For the purposes of this Protocol:

(a) "Firearm" shall mean any portable barrelled weapon that expels, is designed to expel or may be readily converted to expel a shot, bullet or projectile by the action of an explosive, excluding antique firearms or their replicas. Antique firearms and their replicas shall be defined in accordance with domestic law. In no case, however, shall antique firearms include firearms manufactured after 1899;

(b) "Parts and components" shall mean any element or replacement element specifically designed for a firearm and essential to its operation, including a barrel, frame or receiver, slide or cylinder, bolt or breech block, and any device designed or adapted to diminish the sound caused by firing a firearm;

(c) "Ammunition" shall mean the complete round or its components, including cartridge cases, primers, propellant powder, bullets or projectiles, that are used in a firearm, provided that those components are themselves subject to authorization in the respective State Party;

(d) "Illicit manufacturing" shall mean the manufacturing or assembly of firearms, their parts and components or ammunition:

(i) From parts and components illicitly trafficked;

(ii) Without a licence or authorization from a competent authority of the State Party where the manufacture or assembly takes place; or

(iii) Without marking the firearms at the time of manufacture, in accordance with article 8 of this Protocol;

Licensing or authorization of the manufacture of parts and components shall be in accordance with domestic law;

(e) "Illicit trafficking" shall mean the import, export, acquisition, sale, delivery, movement or transfer of firearms, their parts and components and ammunition from or across the territory of one State Party to that of another State Party if any

---

44. G.A. Res. 55/255, U.N. Doc. A/RES/55/255 (May 31, 2001), entered into force on July 3, 2005. See generally http://www.unodc.org/unodc/en/treaties/CTOC/index.html (last visited July 8, 2009).

one of the States Parties concerned does not authorize it in accordance with the terms of this Protocol or if the firearms are not marked in accordance with article 8 of this Protocol;

(f) "Tracing" shall mean the systematic tracking of firearms and, where possible, their parts and components and ammunition from manufacturer to purchaser for the purpose of assisting the competent authorities of States Parties in detecting, investigating and analysing illicit manufacturing and illicit trafficking. . . .

Article 5 — Criminalization

1. Each State Party shall adopt such legislative and other measures as may be necessary to establish as criminal offences the following conduct, when committed intentionally:

(a) Illicit manufacturing of firearms, their parts and components and ammunition;

(b) Illicit trafficking in firearms, their parts and components and ammunition;

(c) Falsifying or illicitly obliterating, removing or altering the marking(s) on firearms required by article 8 of this Protocol.

2. Each State Party shall also adopt such legislative and other measures as may be necessary to establish as criminal offences the following conduct:

(a) Subject to the basic concepts of its legal system, attempting to commit or participating as an accomplice in an offence established in accordance with paragraph 1 of this article; and

(b) Organizing, directing, aiding, abetting, facilitating or counselling the commission of an offence established in accordance with paragraph 1 of this article.

Article 6 — Confiscation, Seizure and Disposal

1. Without prejudice to article 12 of the Convention, States Parties shall adopt, to the greatest extent possible within their domestic legal systems, such measures as may be necessary to enable confiscation of firearms, their parts and components and ammunition that have been illicitly manufactured or trafficked.

2. States Parties shall adopt, within their domestic legal systems, such measures as may be necessary to prevent illicitly manufactured and trafficked firearms, parts and components and ammunition from falling into the hands of unauthorized persons by seizing and destroying such firearms, their parts and components and ammunition unless other disposal has been officially authorized, provided that the firearms have been marked and the methods of disposal of those firearms and ammunition have been recorded.

2.   OAS Firearms Convention

Some years before the UN acted, the Organization of American States had adopted a similar treaty, the Inter-American Convention Against the Illicit Manufacturing of and Trafficking in Firearms, Ammunition, Explosives, and Other Related Materials, adopted by the OAS General Assembly on November 13, 1997.[45]

---

45. The text of the Convention is available at http://www.oas.org/juridico/English/treaties/a-63.html. As of mid-2009, 30 of 34 OAS member states had formally ratified or acceded to the Convention. The United States has signed but not ratified. See Treaty Doc. 105-49 (June 9, 1998).

The stated purpose of the Convention (sometimes referred to by its Spanish acronym "CIFTA") is "to prevent, combat, and eradicate the illicit manufacturing of and trafficking in firearms, ammunition, explosives, and other related materials" (Art. II). Its approach is partly criminal. Each state party is obliged to establish as criminal offenses the illicit manufacturing of and trafficking in those items when those offenses are committed within its territory, by its nationals or habitual residents, and "when the alleged criminal is present in its territory and it does not extradite such person to another country on the ground of the nationality of the alleged criminal" (Art. V(3)). Other provisions address extradition, mutual legal assistance, and training of law enforcement personnel, and provide for exchanges of information needed by law enforcement officials who are investigating arms trafficking offenses.

Interestingly, and in keeping with the 1988 Illicit Trafficking Convention, the OAS Convention specifically endorses "controlled deliveries," which it defines as "allowing illicit or suspect consignments of firearms, ammunition, explosives, and other related materials to pass out of, through, or into the territory of one or more states, with the knowledge and under the supervision of their competent authorities, with a view to identifying persons involved in the commission of [covered] offenses" (Art. I (7)). Article XVIII (1) provides that "[s]hould their domestic legal systems so permit, States Parties shall take the necessary measures, within their possibilities, to allow for the appropriate use of controlled delivery at the international level, on the basis of agreements or arrangements mutually consented to, with a view to identifying persons involved in the offenses referred to in Article IV and to taking legal action against them."

States parties must require "appropriate markings" of firearms at the time of manufacture, and when they are imported (Art. VI). Under Article VII, states parties "undertake to confiscate or forfeit firearms, ammunition, explosives, and other related materials that have been illicitly manufactured or trafficked," and to "adopt the necessary measures to ensure that all firearms, ammunition, explosives, and other related materials seized, confiscated, or forfeited as the result of illicit manufacturing or trafficking do not fall into the hands of private individuals or businesses through auction, sale, or other disposal."

Beyond that, the Convention requires each state party to establish or maintain an "effective system of export, import, and international transit licenses or authorizations for transfers of firearms, ammunition, explosives, and other related materials" (Art. IX(1)). States parties must also adopt such measures as may be necessary to detect and prevent illicit trafficking in firearms, ammunition, explosives, and other related materials between their respective territories, by strengthening controls at export points (Art. X).

For purposes of oversight, the Convention established a Consultative Committee, consisting of one representative of each state party, to promote and facilitate the exchange of information, training and technical assistance, to encourage cooperation between national authorities, and generally to "facilitate the application of this Convention" (Art. XX(1)). Decisions of this body are only "recommendatory in nature" (Art. XX(2)).

NOTES AND QUESTIONS

1. In mid-April 2009, President Obama announced his intention to submit the OAS Firearms Convention to the U.S. Senate for advice and consent to ratification.

See Joint Press Conference with President Felipe Calderon of Mexico, Apr. 16, 2009, available at http://www.whitehouse.gov/the_press_office/Joint-Press-Conference-With-President-Barack-Obama-And-President-Felipe-Calderon-Of-Mexico-4/16/2009.

2. Both the UN and the OAS instruments prohibit the unauthorized or unlicensed manufacture or assembly of firearms, or the manufacture of unmarked firearms. "Illicit trafficking" consists of the "unauthorized" import, export, acquisition, sale, delivery, movement, or transfer of firearms across national boundaries (or, in the case of the UN Protocol, if the firearms are not properly marked). Why would the international community have opted for such a regulatory approach? Is such an approach likely to be effective, given the vested interests of some states to engage in arms transfers? Can you suggest other possible approaches to be taken at the international level?

3. Is a focus on controlling the manufacture of firearms likely to be more productive than the less-than-successful efforts of the international community to regulate the growth and production of illicit narcotics, or the chemicals and equipment used in their cultivation and refinement?

4. Should there be a more comprehensive international convention establishing common standards for the import, export, and transfer of convention weapons? In 2006, the UN General Assembly called for the creation of an intergovernmental group of experts to examine that question. See G.A. Res. 61/89 (Dec. 8, 2006). Its recent report stopped well short of an enthusiastic embrace of the idea. See U.N. Doc. A/63/334 (Aug. 26, 2008).

5. Are illicit arms trafficking offenses well suited to prosecution before international tribunals? Given the central role of SALW in fueling and facilitating conflict situations, where great loss of life and the most serious human rights violations are likely to occur, why shouldn't such offenses be included within the jurisdiction of such tribunals? Cf. Claudette Torbey, The Most Egregious Arms Broker: Prosecuting Arms Embargo Violators in the International Criminal Court, 25 Wis. Intl. L.J. 335 (2007).

6. In the United States, several statutes are relevant to arms trafficking and its regulation, in particular the Arms Export Control Act, 22 U.S.C. §2751 et seq.; the Export Administration Act of 1979, 50 U.S.C. App. §2401 et seq., as continued under Executive Order No. 12924; and the International Economic Emergency Powers Act, 50 U.S.C. §1701 et seq. (as amended). The Arms Export Control Act requires all SALW manufacturers, exporters, and importers to register and obtain licenses; stipulates the purposes for which weapons may lawfully be exported; and requires foreign governments or entities to obtain approval from the U.S. government before selling or transferring arms to a third country. See 22 U.S.C. §2278. A complicated regulatory regime exists to implement these statutes: The main components are the International Traffic in Arms Regulations (ITAR), 22 C.F.R. pt. 120 et seq.; the Export Administration Regulations (EAR), 15 C.F.R. §730 et seq.; and the Foreign Assets Control Regulations, 31 C.F.R. §500 et seq. Domestically, the main federal statute is the Gun Control Act of 1968, 18 U.S.C. §§921-924. Anyone engaged in the business of dealing in the commercial manufacturing or importing of firearms must be licensed under that statute, which also requires recordkeeping and imposes restrictions on which items can be exported. Section 922(a)(3) makes it illegal for a person, other than a licensed importer, dealer, or manufacturer, to transport into or receive in the U.S. state where he resides firearms purchased or otherwise obtained by that person outside of his state of residence.

7. For a recent review of efforts within the European Union to control trafficking in small arms, see Zeray Yihdego, The EU's Role in Restraining the Unrestrained Trade in Conventional Weapons, 10 German L.J. 281 (2009).

CHAPTER
13

Money Laundering

What *is* money laundering? Under the most commonly accepted definition, it is the process through which criminals hide, disguise, and legitimize the financial proceeds of their crimes.[1] This conception of money laundering focuses on the *concealment* of the source, location, or ownership of criminally tainted money. A slight variant of this definition — again focusing on concealment — is that money laundering includes advising or assisting persons to structure transactions so as to avoid applicable reporting, recordkeeping, or tax laws. The genesis of this definition lies in the mechanics of the drug trade.

Experts estimate that the weight of the cash flowing from the illegal drug trade is ten times the weight of the drugs purchased; thus, for example, "22 pounds of heroin generates 256 pounds of street cash, based on the weight of $5's, $10's, and $20's."[2] Assume for the moment that drug dealers on the street garner approximately $57 billion in annual cash sales in the United States.[3] These sales leave them with an estimated 13 to 15 *million pounds* of cocaine-crusted small bills. Were a dealer, with no visible means of (legitimate) support, to buy homes, cars, or other big-ticket items with bags filled with crumpled $20 bills, he would attract the attention of law enforcement officials and may witness the seizure and forfeiture of his criminally derived cash. Those seeking to enjoy their ill-gotten gains, then, must "launder" the cash proceeds of their crimes without attracting the notice of enforcement authorities.

Such laundering can take an infinite number of forms. It can be very simple — for example, a drug dealer may simply swap small bills for large ones to decrease the bulk of his proceeds and to rid the dealer of money potentially "marked" by law enforcement. However, the type of laundering with which the international community was most concerned until recently — that conducted by high-level drug traffickers — generally involves moving the cash through a complex series of transactions or accounts, often involving legitimate financial institutions and transborder transfers, before the proceeds are then invested in assets or made available in seemingly legitimate bank accounts, investments, and currency.

Although drug traffickers may face the biggest challenge by virtue of the fact that street sales yield large volumes of small bills, many if not all of those committing

---

1. See, e.g., Financial Action Task Force, http://www.fatfgafi.org/document/29/0,3343,en_32250379_32235720_33659613_1_1_1_1,00.html (last visited July 15, 2009).

2. Drug Money Weighs 10 Times More Than Drugs Sold, Money Laundering Monitor, July-Dec. 1998, at 10.

3. David Marshall Nissman, The Colombia Black Market Peso Exchange, U.S. Attys.' Bull., June 1999, at 34, quoted in Rebecca Gregory, The Lawyer's Role: Will Uncle Sam Want You in the Fight Against Money Laundering and Terrorism?, 72 UMKC L. Rev. 23 (2003).

crimes for profit must attempt to conceal the fruit of their crimes and "cleanse" its provenance sufficiently to enjoy it without peril. The range of those committing crimes for profit—and thus potential launderers—is vast. Thus, for example, those who engage in arms smuggling and human trafficking presumably are able and willing to continue their activities only if they can successfully legitimate and thus enjoy the proceeds of their crimes. Government officials who accept bribes and "kleptocrats" who loot national treasuries must launder the proceeds of their corruption. The success of such persons in doing so has resulted in financial catastrophes in which billions of dollars have "gone missing" and governments have fallen in the ensuing corruption scandals.[4] "The laundering of the proceeds of crime is a necessary means to carry out the trade in diamonds that has fuelled armed conflict in Liberia, Angola and Sierra Leone, together with their accompanying arms deals and payoffs."[5] Even those committing environmental crimes—such as the illegal trading in ozone-depleting chlorofluorocarbons (CFCs) or engaging in illegal logging or toxic waste dumping—must launder their tainted proceeds.[6]

Another definition of money laundering is dealing in funds to facilitate criminal activity (sometimes also referred to as "criminal financing"). This may involve reinvesting tainted funds in criminal enterprises. For example, a drug dealer may take the proceeds of his crime and buy guns or other tools of the drug trade to support his ongoing enterprise. However, the term *money laundering* can also refer to the use of *un*tainted funds to further criminal endeavors. Thus, for example, if an individual sends his legitimately earned money to finance terrorist activities, this can be conceived of as money laundering. The U.S. money laundering statute does not view this as concealment; it describes it instead as the use of tainted or untainted money to *promote* further crimes, and the object of law enforcement in addressing this activity is generally said to be to disrupt criminal financing. It can, however, be explained as a form of concealment: "A person financing a crime such as terrorism with clean money might still be engaged in some sort of laundering (or obscuring of the source of funds) in order to achieve anonymity or at least pseudonymity, but the soil being washed away is not the crime that produced the money, but the person who finances it."[7]

Finally, the term *money laundering* can describe the use of the proceeds of criminal activity when one knows or should know of the criminal origins of the proceeds. Defined in such a way, this type of money laundering offense is essentially a tainted money possession or spending prohibition rather than an effort to prevent the concealment of past crimes and proceeds or the promotion of further crimes.

Money laundering is not a new phenomenon; some date this practice to 2000 B.C., when Chinese merchants sought to hide money from greedy rulers, to medieval pirates' and merchants' attempts to conceal their assets, or to the Prohibition era in the United States, when Al Capone and Bugs Moran used Laundromats as fronts to hide revenue from their illegal gambling, prostitution, and liquor trafficking businesses.[8] Yet as far as we know, the first effort to subject this practice to criminal

---

4. See, e.g., Jonathan M. Winer, Illicit Finance and Global Conflict, Economies of Conflict: Private Sector Activity in Armed Conflict (Programme for Intl. Co-op. & Conflict Resol./Fafo Report 380) (2002), available at http://www.fafo.no/pub/rapp/380/index.htm.

5. Id.

6. See id.

7. Mariano-Florentino Cuellar, The Tenuous Relationship Between the Fight Against Money Laundering and the Disruption of Criminal Finance, 93 J. Crim. L. & Criminology 311, 337 (2003).

8. See, e.g., A Brief History of Money Laundering, Countermoneylaundering.com, http://www.countermoneylaundering.com/public/?q=node/6 (last visited July 12, 2009); UN Office on Drugs and Crime, International Money Laundering Information Network (IMoLIN), Financial Havens, Banking Secrecy and Money Laundering (1998), available at http://www.imolin.org/imolin/finhaeng.html.

regulation and traffickers to criminal penalty was in 1970, when the U.S. Congress enacted the Bank Secrecy Act. That Act was *not* about secrecy; rather, as amended, it requires various institutions and businesses (including, for example, banks, car dealerships, casinos, auctioneers, and accountants and lawyers) to file Currency Transaction Reports (CTRs) with the Treasury Department documenting cash transactions of more than $10,000. It is a crime to neglect to file a CTR when required, to falsify reports, or to "structure" transactions so as to avoid reporting requirements.[9] In 1996 Congress further amended the Bank Secrecy Act to require depositary institutions to file Suspicious Activity Reports (SARs) when they detect certain suspicious or unusual transactions.[10]

Not content with merely tracing cash or suspicious transactions, Congress was determined to outlaw money laundering as a criminal wrong distinct from the criminal activity that gave rise to the tainted proceeds laundered. Thus, Congress augmented its reporting regime in 1986 by enacting one of the world's first money laundering statutes,[11] codified as amended in 18 U.S.C. §§1956 and 1957, and by authorizing forfeiture of tainted funds under 18 U.S.C. §981.

The international community joined the anti-money laundering effort in 1988 by drafting the Convention Against Illicit Traffic in Narcotic Drugs and Psychotropic Substances (the 1988 Illicit Trafficking Convention). This Convention, which has been signed and ratified by 184 nations (as of July 2009),[12] requires that states parties put in place legislation to make money laundering of drug trafficking proceeds a criminal offense. The treaty also obligated states parties to facilitate cooperative investigations and international assistance in prosecution and extradition. Subsequently, many nations around the globe did put into place criminal money laundering prohibitions and provided for forfeiture of tainted funds.[13] Additional conventional obligations with respect to money laundering have come into effect, most notably in the UN Convention Against Transnational Crime, discussed in Chapter 11, supra, and the UN Convention Against Corruption, examined in Chapter 14, infra.

Below, in Section A, we examine the evolving conventional, or "hard," law that has developed to address money laundering. This introductory section also outlines some of the "soft" law put in place through less formal initiatives, as well as private sector measures taken by financial actors. Given that the focus of money laundering traditionally has been on making sure that legitimate enterprises are not abused for criminal ends, it is perhaps not surprising that the "victims" (financial institutions, for example) and their regulators have an investment in the prevention and detection of laundering. Thus, this enforcement area may be unique in the diversity of means — private, regulatory, and criminal — taken to address criminal conduct. Although our focus is the criminal prohibitions brought to bear on money laundering, consider the degree to which, in this area at least, noncriminal preventative measures are likely to be more effective than criminal enforcement in rooting out laundering.

In Section B, we compare the domestic criminal prohibitions against money laundering in two states that are sophisticated and important banking centers: Switzerland and the United States. This comparison illustrates the differing ways in which these two nations have chosen to conceptualize, define, and enforce

---

9. See 31 U.S.C. §§5311-5326; see also 31 C.F.R. §103.

10. 31 U.S.C. §§5311-5355.

11. See, e.g., Jeffrey Robinson, The Laundrymen 24 (Arcade Publishing 1997) (1996).

12. See UN Office on Drugs and Crime, Status of Treaty Adherence, http://www.unodc.org/unodc/en/treaties/illicit-trafficking.html (last visited July 15, 2009).

13. See, e.g., Elwood E. Sanders, Jr. & George E. Sanders, The Effect of the USA Patriot Act on the Money Laundering and Currency Transaction Laws, 4 Rich. J. Global L. & Bus. 47, 64-71 (2004) (discussing a variety of states' money laundering statutes).

prohibitions against money laundering. Note that the legal *concept* of a crime of money laundering is only about 20 years old, and both Switzerland and the United States initially passed their money laundering statutes in response to domestic imperatives; neither country, in other words, designed their statutes to implement international conventional requirements. Consider, then, whether these statutes meet the developing international standards discussed in Section A.

Finally, because money laundering is a new criminal norm, the international community is constantly learning and reacting to evolving challenges — just as wrongdoers will continue to adapt to the international community's defenses. As we discuss in Section B, the international community put greater emphasis after September 11 on addressing the question of criminal financing and, specifically, the financing of terrorism. In Section C, we examine one of the challenges facing the international community in the future: A system of nonbanking financial transfers called Hawala.

A. INTERNATIONAL REGIMES RELATING TO MONEY LAUNDERING

HERBERT V. MORAIS, FIGHTING INTERNATIONAL CRIME AND ITS FINANCING: THE IMPORTANCE OF FOLLOWING A COHERENT GLOBAL STRATEGY BASED ON THE RULE OF LAW
50 Vill. L. Rev. 583, 591-603 (2005)

. . . At the international level, several legal measures have been developed over the last sixteen years to fight money laundering. These measures consist of a mixture of "hard law" and "soft law." The "hard law" consists of international treaty obligations or international decisions, usually adopted under the aegis of the United Nations or regional organizations that are legally binding on sovereign member States. The "soft law" consists of various recommendations, guidelines, codes and best practices issued by different international organizations and financial supervisory bodies. These latter prescriptions are not legally binding but have strong persuasive effect.

The first shots in the war against money laundering were fired in 1988 when — in the specific context of the war against drug trafficking — the United Nations sponsored the adoption of the [UN Convention Against Illicit Traffic in Narcotic Drugs and Psychotopic Substances of 1988 (the 1988 Illicit Trafficking Convention)[14]]. This was the first international treaty to call on States to criminalize the laundering of the proceeds of crimes. . . .

The provisions of the Convention deal primarily with measures to combat illicit traffic in narcotic drugs and psychotropic substances and related law enforcement issues. There is, however, one provision that deals directly with the laundering of the proceeds derived from the offences established by the Convention. Article 3, Section 1 "Offences and Sanctions" of the Convention sets out a number of provisions calling on States Parties to adopt such measures as may be necessary to establish certain acts, including money laundering, as criminal offences under their national laws.

---

14. 1582 U.N.T.S. 164 (Dec. 19, 1988). The Convention entered into force on November 11, 1990. — EDS.

Article 3 . . . of the Convention defines the crime of money laundering as follows:

> [(b)] (i) The conversion or transfer of property, knowing that such property is derived from any offence or offences established in accordance with subparagraph (a) of this paragraph, or from an act of participation in such offence or offences, for the purpose of concealing or disguising the illicit origin of the property or of assisting any person who is involved in the commission of such an offence or offences to evade the legal consequences of his actions;
>
> (ii) The concealment or disguise of the true nature, source, location, disposition, movement, rights with respect to, or ownership of property, knowing that such property is derived from an offence or offences established in accordance with subparagraph (a) of this paragraph or from an act of participation in such an offence or offences;
>
> [(c) Subject to its constitutional principles and the basic concepts of its legal system:
>
> (i) The acquisition, possession or use of property, knowing, at the time of the receipt, that such property was derived from an offence or offences established in accordance with subparagraph (a) of this paragraph or from an act of participation in such an offence or offences.]

Section 4 of the Convention then requires State Parties to establish sanctions for the offences set forth in Section 1 taking into account "the grave nature of these offences." Accordingly, punishment through "imprisonment or other forms of deprivation of liberty, pecuniary sanctions and confiscation" was stipulated as the appropriate sanction. The other provisions of the Convention deal with jurisdiction over the offences [Art. 4], confiscation [Art. 5], extradition [Art. 6], mutual legal assistance [Art. 7], and other measures for international cooperation [Arts. 8-20].

In June 1998, the United Nations General Assembly adopted a Political Declaration and Action Plan Against Money Laundering at its Twentieth Special Session devoted to "countering the world drug problem together."[15] The General Assembly Resolution urged all states to implement the provisions of the [1988 Illicit Trafficking] Convention and "other relevant international instruments on money laundering" and then set out a list of guiding principles for national action.

In August 2000, the [UN Convention Against Transnational Crime (the Palermo Convention)] was adopted in Palermo, Italy.[16] Recognizing that, in the post–Cold War era, various forms of transnational organized crime posed a serious threat to security, democracy, the rule of law and political and financial stability, the Convention requires State Parties to outlaw some of the most common offences, such as involvement or participation in organized criminal groups, money laundering and corruption of public officials. It is particularly noteworthy that this Convention includes two articles dealing with the criminalization of the laundering of the proceeds of serious crimes and two other articles dealing with the criminalization of corruption. The definition of the money laundering offence incorporated in this Convention[, in Art. 6, §1(a),] is substantially identical to that included in the Vienna Convention and other international conventions and regulations.

---

15. [Morais's footnote 37:] G.A. Res. S20/4D, U.N. GAOR, 20th Special Sess., U.N. Doc. A/S-20/AC.1/L.1 (1998). This declaration was adopted by the United Nations General Assembly on June 10, 1998.

16. [Morais's footnote 39:] U.N. Convention Against Transnational Organized Crime, G.A. Res. 55/25, U.N. GAOR, 55th Sess., U.N. Doc. A/55/383 (2000). The Convention was adopted by the U.N. General Assembly on November 15, 2000. The Convention entered into force on September 29, 2003. . . .

Finally, it should be noted that the [UN Convention Against Corruption (Corruption Convention)][17] includes two comprehensive provisions calling on State Parties to criminalize all forms of money laundering under their national laws. In addition, it is particularly noteworthy that money laundering has been included as one of the major targets in the war against corruption.

The United Nations' efforts to combat money laundering are coordinated by the United Nations Office on Drugs and Crime (UNODC), by way of its Global Program Against Money Laundering (GPML). Through the GPML, the UNODC assists member countries with policy development, legislation, technical assistance, problem solving and training in combating money laundering.

A number of key regional organizations have also adopted legal measures to combat money laundering. The Council of Europe adopted the Convention on Laundering, Search, Seizure and Confiscation of the Proceeds from Crime in 1990 in Strasbourg.[18] This Convention contains both substantive law provisions to combat money laundering, as well as mechanisms for international cooperation and mutual assistance in criminal matters. An interesting feature of this Convention is that the Council may invite any non-member state to accede to the Convention. In 1991, the Council of the European Communities issued Council Directive 91/308/EEC on "Prevention of the Use of the Financial System for the Purpose of Money Laundering" ("Council Directive"). This Directive is legally binding on member States and deals largely with the prevention of money laundering through the abuse of the financial system. Finally, in 1999, the Organization of American States (OAS) adopted the Model Regulations Concerning Laundering Offences Connected to Illicit Drug Trafficking and Related Offences, prepared by the Inter-American Drug Abuse Control Commission (CICAD).[19] These CICAD Model Regulations are intended to serve as a guide to OAS member countries in the adoption of national laws against money laundering.

Outside the framework of the United Nations and the regional organizations, the Financial Action Task Force (FATF), an intergovernmental group established by the Group of Seven (G-7) in Paris in 1989, has the primary responsibility for coordinating global efforts to combat money laundering. The FATF consists of thirty-one member jurisdictions and two international organizations, the European Commission and the Gulf Cooperation Council. The FATF maintains a small Secretariat at the offices of the Organization for Economic Cooperation and Development (OECD) and is assisted in its work by a number of regional FATF-style bodies such as: the Asia/Pacific Group on Money Laundering (APG), the Caribbean Financial Action Task Force (CFATF), the Council of Europe Select Committee of Experts on the Evaluation of Anti-Money Laundering Measures (MONEYVAL, formerly PC-R-EV), the Eurasian Group (EAG), the Financial Action Task Force of South America Against Money Laundering (GAFISUD), the Eastern and Southern Africa Anti-Money Laundering Group (ESAAMLG) and the Middle East and North Africa FATF (MENAFATF).

---

17. Convention Against Corruption, G.A. Res. 58/4, U.N. GAOR, 58th Sess., U.N. Doc. A/58/422 (2003). The Convention was adopted by the U.N. General Assembly on October 31, 2003. — Eds.

18. [Morais's footnote 47:] Convention on Laundering, Search, Seizure and Confiscation of the Proceeds from Crime, Nov. 8, 1990, Europ. T.S. No. 141. . . .

19. [Morais' footnote 49:] See CICAD, Inter-American Drug Abuse Control Commission, Model Regulations Concerning Laundering Offenses Connected with Illicit Drug Trafficking and Other Serious Offences, available at http://www.imolin.org/imolin/en/cicadml.html.

In 1990, the FATF published the Forty Recommendations on Money Laundering ("FATF Forty") to provide detailed recommendations and guidelines to member and non-member countries and financial institutions on how to formulate and implement measures to combat money laundering. The FATF Forty were revised and reissued in 1996. In June 2003, the FATF Forty were substantially revised and reissued to reflect the accumulated experience, to take account of the new typologies of money laundering identified by the FATF's annual typologies exercises, and finally to cover the financing of terrorism. The FATF Forty has been aptly described as "the crown jewel of soft law" against money laundering. The recommendations set out in the FATF Forty, as revised, are divided into four major categories.

1. RECOMMENDATIONS TO STRENGTHEN NATIONAL LEGAL SYSTEMS

These recommendations, addressed to countries, set out various legislative measures that should be taken to prevent, detect and punish money laundering. The most important of these measures is the criminalization of money laundering. Going well beyond the 1996 Recommendations, the latest FATF Forty calls on countries to "apply the crime of money laundering to all serious offences, with a view to including the widest range of predicate offences." To this end, each country "should at a minimum include a range of offences within each of the designated categories of offences." The term "designated categories of offences" is defined as twenty categories of crimes.

In addition, the FATF Forty includes a number of other recommendations calling on countries to ensure that predicate offences for money laundering "extend to conduct that occurred in another country, which constitutes an offence in that country, and which would have constituted a predicate offence had it occurred domestically." Countries are also asked to apply criminal liability and, where that is not possible, civil or administrative liability, to legal persons; adopt provisions for the freezing, seizure and confiscation of criminal assets; ensure that financial institution secrecy laws do not inhibit the implementation of FATF Forty; adopt "safe harbour" rules to protect financial institutions, their directors, officers and employees from criminal and civil liability if they report suspicious transactions; and to establish effective, proportionate and dissuasive sanctions (criminal, civil or administrative) for both natural and legal persons.

2. RECOMMENDATIONS TO STRENGTHEN CUSTOMER DUE DILIGENCE, REPORTING OF SUSPICIOUS TRANSACTIONS, REGULATION AND SUPERVISION

This second set of recommendations, previously limited in their application to banks and non-bank financial institutions, seeks to strengthen and broaden the standards for exercising customer due diligence, verifying the identity of customers and reporting suspicious transactions to the authorities. Most importantly, the definition of "financial institutions" was broadened to cover any person or entity who conducts, as a business, one or more of thirteen separate activities or operations for or on behalf of a customer. Particularly noteworthy is the inclusion of a new recommendation calling on countries to stipulate, at a minimum, that "businesses providing a service of money or value transfer should be licensed or registered, and subject to effective systems for monitoring and ensuring compliance with national requirements to combat money laundering and terrorist financing."

Next, two new recommendations were introduced to extend the application of these standards to certain "designated non-financial businesses and professions," which has been defined to mean casinos, real estate agents, dealers in precious metals and stones, lawyers, notaries and other independent legal professionals and accountants and trust and company service providers when they are involved with their clients or customers in preparing or executing financial or similar transactions. Countries are also urged to consider applying FATF Forty to businesses and professions other than designated non-financial businesses and professions that pose a money laundering or terrorist financing risk.

In addition, more elaborate standards have been specified for the verification of customer identity, particularly with respect to the identity of beneficial owners and the nature of intended business relationships and transactions. Of particular significance are the new recommendations calling on financial institutions to implement enhanced customer diligence measures in relation to "politically exposed persons" (PEPs) with a view to targeting corruption, one of the major sources of money laundering, and cross-border correspondent banking relationships. The recommendations also call on financial institutions to maintain records for at least five years and to establish appropriate training, compliance management and audit systems.

Finally, the recommendations call on countries to strengthen the regulation and supervision of financial institutions. Of particular significance are those calling on competent authorities to "take the necessary legal or regulatory measures to prevent criminals or their associates from holding or being the beneficial owner of a significant or controlling interest or holding a management function in a financial institution," sometimes referred to as the application of "fit and proper tests" or "integrity standards" for financial institution officials.

3. Recommendations to Strengthen Institutional and Other Measures

The third set of recommendations, addressed to countries, deals with strengthening institutional and other measures for the enforcement of laws to combat money laundering and the financing of terrorism. The first of these recommendations calls on countries to establish a Financial Intelligence Unit (FIU) to serve as a national center for receiving, requesting, analyzing and disseminating suspicious transaction reports for law enforcement purposes. The task of financial intelligence is a highly specialized one. It requires high technical and forensic skills as the typical money laundering case is complex, cross-border in nature and difficult to unravel. The FIU also serves as a focal point for coordination and cooperation with FIUs in other jurisdictions in the investigation of money laundering and financing of terrorism cases. The second series of recommendations calls on countries to properly equip their law enforcement authorities with the necessary powers of investigation, including the ability to obtain documents and information for their investigations and to furnish adequate financial, human and technical resources and effective mechanisms to these authorities to enable them to carry out their responsibilities effectively.

The next set of recommendations under this heading calls on countries to prevent the unlawful use of legal persons by money launderers, particularly by ensuring that there is adequate, accurate and timely information on the beneficial ownership and control of legal persons and to prevent the unlawful use of legal arrangements (such as express trusts) by money launderers, through information requirements similar to those set forth in Recommendation 5.

4. RECOMMENDATIONS TO STRENGTHEN INTERNATIONAL COOPERATION AND MUTUAL ASSISTANCE MEASURES

The final set of recommendations asks countries to cooperate closely and effectively with, and extend mutual legal assistance to, other foreign judicial and law enforcement authorities in money laundering and terrorist financing investigations. Specifically, countries are asked to rapidly, constructively and effectively provide the widest possible range of mutual legal assistance and cooperation in investigations, prosecutions and related proceedings. Such cooperation and assistance should also extend to requests by foreign countries to identify, freeze, seize and confiscate property laundered, proceeds from money laundering or predicate offences, instrumentalities used in or intended for use in the commission of these offences or property of corresponding value. Countries are encouraged to enter into arrangements for coordinating seizure and confiscation proceedings, which may include the sharing of confiscated assets. Finally, the recommendations call for cooperation in the extradition (or, where that is not possible, the prosecution) of criminals involved. . . .

As the FATF Forty belongs to the realm of recommendations, it represents the "soft law" against money laundering and the financing of terrorism. This raises an interesting issue as to its legal status or effect. In and of themselves, these recommendations are persuasive in nature and do not impose legal obligations on FATF members or non-member jurisdictions. On the other hand, I would strongly argue that, to the extent that these recommendations amplify or elaborate on general principles of law or legal obligations already set out in several international treaties, conventions and numerous national laws, they carry a strong expectation of adherence if not compliance. Furthermore, to the extent that these recommendations seek to proscribe an international crime, it could be argued that there should be little or no disagreement within the community of States as to the achievement of the objectives of these recommendations notwithstanding differences of opinion on the means to achieve them.

A number of other international financial supervisory bodies have also been active in combating money laundering through the adoption and issuance of recommendations, directives, guidelines and best practices. Notable among these is the Basel Committee on Banking Supervision (previously called the Basel Committee on Banking Regulation and Supervisory Practices), established by the central bank governors of the Group of Ten (G-10) countries in 1974. This Committee issued a Statement on Prevention of Criminal Use of the Banking System for the Purpose of Money Laundering in 1988. In 1997, the Basel Committee issued the Core Principles of Banking Supervision. The Committee also issued detailed guidelines on Customer Due Diligence for Banks in October 2001. All of these prescriptions call on banking supervisors to ensure that banks have internal policies, practices and procedures, including "know your customer" procedures. These procedures are designed to prevent banks from being used, intentionally or unintentionally, by criminal elements. It is important to note that, while the Basel Committee essentially represents the G-10 industrial countries and its principles and recommendations are advisory in character, its recommendations are given great weight by national bank supervisory bodies throughout the world.

In 1992, the International Organization of Securities Commissions (IOSCO), whose members are national securities commissions, stock exchanges and regional and international organizations, adopted a Resolution on Money Laundering, which sets out anti-money laundering guidelines for its members. In 1998, it issued the IOSCO Objectives and Principles, which outlines key measures for national securities supervisors to take to counter fraud and money laundering.

Similarly, in 2003, the International Association of Insurance Supervisors (IAIS), an association of national insurance supervisors established in 1994, issued the Insurance Core Principles and Methodology to guide insurance supervisors in countering fraud and money laundering. In 2004, the IAIS issued a very comprehensive Guidance Paper on Anti-Money Laundering and Combating the Financing of Terrorism.

At the private sector level, eleven major international private banks known as the Wolfsberg Group, in cooperation with Transparency International, adopted the Global Anti-Money Laundering Guidelines for Private Banking ("Wolfsberg AML Principles") in October 2000. In January 2002, the Wolfsberg Group issued the Statement on the Suppression of the Financing of Terrorism. The statement sets forth a number of guidelines for financial institutions to follow in order to prevent the flow of terrorist funds through the financial system. The International Federation of Accountants (IFAC), established in 1977, has issued guidance on the role of auditors in detecting fraud and errors in financial statements, in particular ISA 240.

To sum up the discussion of international legal measures adopted to combat money laundering, it is clear that there is currently a formidable body of international treaty law that criminalizes money laundering. This body of "hard law" is supported by a second hierarchy of "soft law" — recommendations, guidelines and international best practices — that have served to put flesh and bones on the general principles set out in the international treaties and conventions. It is left to individual countries to implement this body of law through the adoption and enforcement of national laws and regulations, the establishment of effective institutional arrangements and the extension of cooperation and mutual assistance to other jurisdictions. Likewise, financial institutions and other entities and persons involved are expected to implement such rules through their internal policies, operations and systems.

B. COMPARATIVE MONEY LAUNDERING STATUTES: SWITZERLAND AND THE UNITED STATES

1. Swiss Law

LOI FEDERALE DU 3 OCTOBRE 1951 SUR LES STUPEFIANTS ET LES SUBSTANCES PSYCHOTROPES [LSTUP] [FEDERAL LAW ON NARCOTICS AND PSYCHOTROPIC SUBSTANCES]

Oct. 3, 1961, RS 812.121 (Switz.)

ARTICLE 19

1. Whoever, without the right, cultivates alkaloid plants or hemp for the purpose of producing drugs,

Whoever, without the right, manufactures, extracts, modifies or prepares drugs,

Whoever, without the right, stores, sends, transports, imports, exports or carries in transit,

Whoever, without the right, offers, distributes, sells, brokers, procures, prescribes, places into the market or disposes of,

Whoever, without the right, possesses, holds, buys or acquires in another manner,

Whoever takes steps to these ends,

Whoever finances an illegal drug trade or serves as an intermediary for such financing,

Whoever publicly incites others to consume drugs or reveals the means to obtain or consume them,

Is punishable, if he acted intentionally, by deprivation of liberty for at most three years or a monetary penalty. In serious cases, the penalty will be deprivation of liberty for at least one year which can be combined with a monetary penalty.

2. Serious cases occur when the offender

    a. knows or must be aware that the infraction involves a quantity of drugs that could endanger the health of a large number of people

    b. acts in association with a group organized to carry out the illegal drug trade

    c. deals drugs professionally and makes thereby a significant turnover or profit

3. If the offender acts negligently in committing the acts covered in 1 above, he is punishable by deprivation of liberty of at most one year or a monetary penalty.

4. If the offense takes place abroad and the offender is arrested in Switzerland and not extradited, the offender is subject to the sanctions provided for in 1) and 2) if the act is prohibited in the country in which it was carried out.

CODE PÉNAL SUISSE [PENAL CODE]

Dec. 21, 1937, RS 311 (Switz.).[20]

ARTICLE 305*BIS*: MONEY LAUNDERING

1. Whoever carries out an act that is aimed at frustrating[21] the identification of the origin, the tracing or the confiscation of assets which he knows or must assume originate from a felony

is liable to a custodial sentence of up to three years or to a monetary penalty.

2. In serious cases, the penalty is a custodial sentence of up to five years or a monetary penalty. A custodial sentence shall be combined with a monetary penalty of up to 500 daily penalty units.[22]

A serious case is constituted, in particular, where the offender:

    a. acts as a member of a criminal organisation;

---

20. We have translated the Swiss statutes into English, with the exception of Article 305*bis*, because translations of this provision vary in their choice of terms in potentially important ways. The above translation is available at a Swiss government link found at http://www.gwg.admin.ch/e/themen/pdf/StGBArt305bis.pdf. See also http://www.gwg.admin.ch/e/themen/bekaempfung/index.php. The Swiss Embassy cautions, however, that the law is official only in its original German, French, and Italian language versions. — EDS.

21. This phrase, describing the requisite impact of the transaction on the ability of authorities to discover the criminal origin of the money, is a particular sticking point in translating the statute into English from the French ("*un acte propre a entraver*") and the German ("*eine Handlung . . . die geeignet ist . . . zu vereiteln*"). Among the translations of this term into English are an act that "is likely to obstruct," "inherently impedes," "may prevent," "is suited to thwart," "could frustrate," and "hinders." — EDS.

22. The monetary penalties available under the Swiss Penal Code were amended as of January 1, 2007, so that judges now assess the amount of the penalty based on "daily penalty units" (also called "fine-units," "*jours-amende*," or "fine-days"). Before this change, serious money laundering under Article 305*bis* required, if a penal sentence was imposed, that a fine of up to 1 million francs also be imposed. Under the new "fine-units" structure, serious money laundering (up to 500 daily penalty units) could carry with it a fine from 500 francs to 1.5 million francs. — EDS.

b. acts as a member of a group that has been formed for the purpose of the continued conduct of money laundering activities; or,

c. achieves a large turnover or substantial profit through commercial money laundering

3. The offender shall also be liable to the foregoing penalties where the principal offence was committed abroad within a jurisdiction provided such an act is an offence at the place of commission.

ARTICLE 305*TER*: LACK OF DUE DILIGENCE IN FINANCIAL TRANSACTIONS AND RIGHT OF NOTIFICATION

1. Whoever in a professional capacity accepts, deposits, helps to invest or to transfer the assets of a third party and fails to verify the identity of the beneficial owner with the diligence that can reasonably be expected under the circumstances
   shall be sentenced to deprivation of liberty for at most one year or by a monetary penalty.

2. The persons referred to in paragraph 1 have the right to notify the Swiss criminal prosecution authorities, and the Federal authorities designated by law, about evidence leading to the conclusion that assets represent the proceeds of a criminal activity.

R. v. PUBLIC PROSECUTOR OF THE CANTON OF VAUD
Tribunal Fédéral [Federal Court], June 6, 2003, No. 6S.59/2003/svc (Switz.)

FACTS

A. On December 21, 2001, the magistrate's court of the district of Lausanne convicted R. of a serious violation of the federal drug law (art. 9(2)(a) Drug Law) and money laundering (art. 305*bis*(1) Penal Code) and sentenced him to two years imprisonment, minus 27 days time served, and to expulsion for a period of ten years, with suspension for five years. The court moreover ordered the seizure and relinquishment to the state of the sums of 2,520 francs, 4,398.85 francs and 5,142 francs seized from the accused and compelled him to pay compensation of 2,500 francs. The court also convicted several codefendants, including T.

B. R.'s conviction rests on the following summarized facts.

B.a R., a Chilean national born in 1965, arrived in Switzerland in 1981 with his parents. After completing school, he held various jobs, which he fulfilled to his employers' satisfaction. He holds a residence permit type C, is single and is the father of a child for whom he pays monthly support. On August 5, 1996, he was convicted by the Lausanne magistrate's court of violation of the Drug Law and sentenced to ten months imprisonment, with suspension for two years. According to several medical reports, he is currently drug-free.

B.b Starting in 1997, T., a Chilean national born in 1962, established a major drug operation in Switzerland and abroad. To accomplish this, he relied on the knowing assistance of several compatriots living in Switzerland who he knew were drug users.

Between March 1998 and September 1999, T. visited Switzerland, with the intent to increase cocaine imports from Latin America. The drugs were to be packaged in CD cases and video boxes, and placed in postal packages to be addressed to various individuals, who may or may not have been aware of the operation, residing in francophone Switzerland. In this context, several cocaine users, including R., gave T. the names of individuals who could receive the packages. This system allowed T., as head of the operation, to import in all 1.5 kgs of cocaine, the sale of which to various drug addicts brought him a profit of at least 20,000 francs. A non-negligible amount of cocaine was also provided for free to these individuals or to third parties in payment for their services or as a friendly gesture. The analysis of the seized cocaine showed a level of purity around 50% for one sample and 68% for the other.

To finance his drug imports and pay his suppliers, usually in advance, T. transferred proceeds of his drug deals to Chile or Argentina via Western Union. Because he was in Switzerland illegally, he could not carry out the transfers himself, so he asked his codefendants to do it.

B.c Starting in April 1999, R. helped collect 12 packages with 480 g of cocaine. Of these, one was seized by the police, two others were kept by R. and the remainder had been delivered to T. R. personally sold 90 g of cocaine, making a profit of 2,025 francs.

Regarding the money transfers to Chile intended to finance the drug imports, R. also made four payments of 1,000-3,000 francs. It was noted that he had no doubt that the money came from the cocaine sales.

B.d Based on these facts, R. was found guilty of a serious violation of the Drug Law under Art. 19(1)(2)-(7) and 19(2)(a), as well as money laundering under Art 305*bis*(1) of the Criminal Code.

At sentencing, the extent of the accused's guilt was taken into account, given that he had participated over a relatively long period of time in a major drug operation. It was also noted that, even if at the time of the events he was seriously addicted to cocaine, his criminal liability was complete. In light of these elements, and in fairness to his codefendants, it was decided that a penalty whose length would allow a granting of suspension could not be considered, even though the accused seemed to have made a break from his past of drug addiction and had demonstrated exemplary behavior since his release on probation; a relatively severe sanction must be imposed even more so because the accused did not heed the warning provided by his conviction three years earlier for which he received a moderate sentence accompanied by suspension. It was also noted that the serious infraction against the public order that the accused had caused by his drug dealing justified his expulsion from Switzerland for a period of ten years in light of his guilt. This measure however was accompanied by a suspension of five years, in light of the extent of the roots established by the accused in Switzerland.

Finally, in light of the profit that the defendant received through his dealing, it was decided that there were grounds to oblige him to pay compensation of approximately 2,500 francs.

C. In its decision of July 12, 2002, the Superior penal court of the Vaud Cantonal court set aside the appeal filed by R. and affirmed the lower court's judgment.

The accused transferred to Chile money from cocaine dealing intended to finance further cocaine imports. The cantonal court deemed in particular that these actions fell under Articles 19(1)(7) of the Drug Law and 305*bis* of the Penal Code which are concurrently applicable. In addition, the accused contested the sentence applied by the lower court—both the length of the period of expulsion and the compensatory damages of 2,500 francs. The cantonal court held that the grievances raised by the accused to contest his sentence, the duration of his expulsion and the required compensatory payment were unfounded. . . .

2. The appellant contests that a money laundering violation occurred and asserts that in the case in point this violation cannot be retained together with a violation of

Art. 19(1) of the Drug Law. He notes that the fact of having transferred money to Chile on behalf of T. is completely covered by the latter provision.

2.1 Art. 19(1)(7) of the Drug Law prohibits intentionally financing the illegal drug trade or acting as an intermediary for such financing. This provision establishes a separate offence for complicity in putting drugs in the market in so far as this takes the form of financing. One who provides the financial means allowing the procurement, transport or distribution of drugs commits the act of financing the illegal drug trade. The offender need not be directly involved with the risks of the drug operation. One who provides money knowing and desiring or at least considering and accepting that the money will be used for the illegal drug trade, commits the drug financing offense. The concept of trafficking includes the acts described in lines 1 through 6 of Article 19(1) of the Drug Law. The offense must involve a future, not yet completed, drug deal.

An individual is guilty of money laundering if he commits an act likely to obstruct the establishment of the source, the discovery, or the confiscation of assets which he knows or must assume represent the proceeds of a criminal activity. (Art. 305*bis*(1) Penal Code.) This is an offense against the administration of justice. The criminal act consists of preventing access by the criminal authorities to the proceeds of a crime, by making it more difficult to establish the link between the assets and the crime. This can consist of any act designed to prevent the identification of the origin of assets, or their discovery or seizure. Transferring the proceeds of crime from one country to another is such an act. All assets resulting from a crime, as defined in Art. 9 of the Penal Code [subject to more than one year imprisonment], can be involved in money laundering. It is not necessary that they contribute to the commission of a new crime. As to the subjective element, the offender must ha[ve] acted intentionally, or with willful blindness, and that he knew or must have assumed at the moment of the act that the assets were proceeds of a crime. In this respect, it is sufficient if he was aware of circumstances creating a suspicion that the assets were proceeds of a crime and that he accepted that possibility.

According to the existing jurisprudence, money laundering can be charged in addition to financing the drug trade under Art. 19(1)(7) of the Drug Law. Indeed, the two offenses infringe on different protected interests — administration of justice for money laundering and public health for drug crimes. They also occur in different situations: Art. 19 prohibits providing the financial means for future drug deals while Art. 305*bis* sanctions the act of impeding the search for a link between a crime (in general one that has already been committed) and the assets that result from the crime.

Therefore, it has been held that one who changes money in small bills coming from a completed drug deal to hide their origin commits laundering, which is distinct from the dealing itself, and that if he then invests the money in new drug acquisition he commits the act of financing the drug trade.

2.2 The decision under appeal accepted that the appellant repeatedly transferred money to Chile to allow T. to import cocaine for his drug operation in Switzerland and that he did so with full knowledge of the facts, at the request of T. who could not carry out these transactions himself because he was staying in Switzerland illegally. It also accepted that the money thus transferred was the proceeds of a major cocaine operation run by T. and that the appellant had no doubt as to the origins of the funds. Based on these facts, it held that R. transferred from Switzerland to another country money that he knew was intended to finance future cocaine deals and that he did so knowingly and at least accepting to support such deals. In this way he served as an intermediary for the financing of the drug trade and his actions fall under Art. 19(1)(7) of the Drug Law, which is not in dispute.

The result of these facts, however, is also that the transferred funds came from T.'s major cocaine operation, thus from a crime [as defined in Art. 9], which was likely to obstruct the confiscation, the establishment of the source and the discovery of these funds, and that the appellant knew this and accepted it. Indeed, it was noted that the appellant had no doubt as to the criminal origin of the funds and he nonetheless transferred them, such that he must have known that his actions were likely to obstruct their confiscation, the establishment of their source and their discovery. In this regard, his acts are not covered by Art. 19(1)(7) of the Drug Law, but by Art 305*bis* of the Penal Code. His acts thus constitute a money laundering offense. In contesting this, the appellant asserts that he never intended to distribute the proceeds of the drug trade nor therefore to commit an act of obstruction, but rather only agreed to serve as an intermediary in the financing of future drug deals. However this assertion departs from the findings of fact on the cantonal level regarding his state of mind and willingness, which cannot be reviewed in an appeal. . . .

The appellant's acts therefore meet the elements of the money laundering offense under Art 305*bis* of the Penal Code as well as the offense of financing the drug trade under Art. 19(1)(7) of the Drug Law such that both charges can be brought without violating federal law according to the existing jurisprudence which is not contested by the appellant.

3. The appellant urges that he received an excessive sentence in light of the elements to be taken into consideration under the framework of Article 63 of the Penal Code.

The judge has broad discretion in sentencing. An appeal . . . based on the length of the sentence therefore can only be admitted if the sanction exceeded the legal framework, if it was based on criteria outside of Art. 63 of the Penal Code, if the elements of discretion envisioned by that provision were not taken into account or if the sentence seems so severe or so lenient that one must consider an abuse of discretionary power. . . .

3.3 The quantity of drugs, and their level of purity, does not carry much weight in determining the sentence. For violations of the Drug Law, as in other areas, the sentence must be determined in light of the seriousness of the act attributed to the offender. The danger posed by the drug involved in these dealings is certainly one of the relevant elements to determine the seriousness of the offense, but it must be viewed together with other elements; it is therefore only a factor among others that does not carry a preponderance of weight in the considerations.

. . . [T]he sentence of 2 years of imprisonment in light of the appellant's guilt, in no way allows a conclusion that excessive significance was attributed to the quantity of drugs involved in the offense.

3.4 The appellant and his codefendants received different sentences, which necessarily considers the seriousness of the offense committed by each individual and in particular their respective roles. . . .

3.5 As noted in the decision under appeal, it is clear that the original judges took into account the motives of the appellant, even if they did not expressly refer to them at the sentencing stage. The court in particular took into account the fact that the appellant was seriously addicted to cocaine and agreed to participate in T.'s drug operation in order to obtain cocaine more easily or for free. . . .

3.9 The sentence of 2 years imprisonment was set based on relevant criteria without evidence that major elements were omitted or wrongly considered. And taking into account the guilt of the appellant, the sentence is certainly not of a severity that would indicate an abuse of discretionary power. There is therefore no violation of federal law. . . .

NOTES AND QUESTIONS

1. After a number of widely publicized scandals involving the use of Swiss banks to launder crime proceeds in the late 1970s and 1980s, Switzerland became an active participant in the international fight against money laundering. See, e.g., Nadja Capus, Country Report: Combating Money Laundering in Switzerland, in A Comparative Guide to Anti-money Laundering 123-125 (Mark Pieth & Gemma Aiolfi eds., 2004). Switzerland is a member of the Basel Committee and joined FATF in 1990. Switzerland has also ratified the 1988 UN Convention Against Illicit Traffic in Narcotic Drugs and Psychotropic Substances (1988 Illicit Trafficking Convention); the Council of Europe's 1990 Convention on Laundering, Search, Seizure and Confiscation of the Proceeds from Crime (CE Convention); and the UN Convention Against Transnational Organized Crime (Palermo Convention). It has signed, but not yet ratified, the UN Convention Against Corruption (Corruption Convention).

In terms of domestic activity, the first Swiss reaction to the problem of money laundering was to rely on private and administrative means to prevent such activities. Thus, for example, in 1977 the Swiss banking community created a Code of Conduct governing the acceptance of funds and the use of banking secrecy (CDB), which established, inter alia, "a duty of due care for signatory banks in the identification of would-be account holders and depositors." Rebecca G. Peters, Money Laundering and Its Current Status in Switzerland: New Disincentives for Financial Tourism, 11 Nw. J. Intl. L. & Bus. 104 (1990). "Some of the requirements laid down in the private code of conduct (CDB) of the Swiss bankers have, albeit indirectly, been elevated into a form of binding Swiss law by the supervisory practice of the Swiss Banking Commission." Guy Stessens, Money Laundering: A New International Law Enforcement Model (2000).

The Swiss emphasis on private initiatives and administrative sanctions continues. Switzerland's most comprehensive legislation dealing with money laundering, its 1997 Fight against Money Laundering Act, primarily contemplates administrative enforcement or the supervision of self-regulated bodies. The principal innovations of the 1997 Act are two: (1) codification of the Know Your Customer rules and (2) the creation of a duty to report suspicions of criminal activity and freeze assets related to that activity. See Shelby R. du Pasquier, The Swiss Anti-money Laundering Legislation, 13 J. Intl. Banking L. 160, 163 (1998). The imposition of the second duty "constitutes a real novelty in the Swiss legal system" and was "incorporated into the Act in spite of fierce opposition from Swiss financial circles" in order to bring Switzerland into line with FATF recommendations. Id.

Given the subject matter of this text, we will not delve into the administrative regulations governing money laundering in either the United States or Switzerland. It is worth noting, for the relevance it may have to our comparison of the relevant criminal prohibitions, that the Swiss money laundering regime "marshals the private self-enforcement policies and behavior of the banking industry without great recourse to public agencies" and relies on the industry to employ "broad and subjective analysis of potential customers and transactions." Thomas D. Grant, Toward a Swiss Solution for an American Problem: An Alternative Approach for Banks in the War on Drugs, 14 Ann. Rev. Banking L. 225, 231 (1995). The U.S. regime, by contrast, "relies almost exclusively upon the authority of federal agencies" such as the Internal Revenue Service (IRS), the Customs Service, the Office of the Comptroller of the Currency (OCC), the Office of Thrift Supervision (OTS), and the Federal Reserve Board to create and oversee the use of "minute and exhaustive checklists and rules." Id.

As Professor Stessens notes, the Swiss approach is primarily preventative — that is, banking law is used to prevent laundering. He argues that the United States uses primarily a "repressive approach founded in criminal law." Stessens, supra, at 108-109. He posits that part of the explanation for this disparate approach is to be found in the origin of the funds sought to be laundered:

> Most of the proceeds of crime that are laundered in the United States probably stem from offenses committed within the United States, even though the money laundering operations involved may have international ramifications. On the other hand, most of the funds that are deposited in Switzerland, including criminally derived proceeds, are derived from foreign activities. . . . Swiss authorities and Swiss banks were therefore more interested in safeguarding their own interests, the reputation of the Swiss financial industry, than in preventing the financial spin-off of criminal activities that occurred outside Switzerland. Criminal law and . . . enforcement are looked upon as tools for defending society — tools of last resort even: the criminal law . . . is therefore primarily used by the Swiss in defence of their own nation, rather than others. The criminalisation of money laundering, including the proceeds derived from a foreign offence, is an important deviation from this traditional approach to the criminal law.

Id. at 110.

2. *Compliance with Article 3 of the 1988 Illicit Trafficking Convention.* Consider Article 305*bis*. It obviously encompasses concealment of criminal proceeds, but what of the other definitions posited in the introduction to this chapter? Does this statute effectively implement Switzerland's obligations under Article 3 of the 1988 Illicit Trafficking Convention, quoted in the reading in Section A above? See FATF-GAFI, Third Mutual Evaluation Report on Anti-money Laundering and Combating the Financing of Terrorism-Switzerland, Summary, at 3 (Oct. 14, 2005) (finding that Article 305*bis* does not formally include all required elements (conversion or transfer) but noting that the case law under that article appears to show that it encompasses elements of conversion and transfers, and that possession is covered by the Swiss notion of obstruction); cf. Lore Rutz-Burri, "Beefing Up" the Federal Government: Switzerland's Response to Complex National and International Crime, 42 Crim. L. Bull. 3 (2006) (reviewing "watershed" reforms in the administration of Swiss criminal law and providing overview of Swiss government and criminal process).

3. Actus reus. What showing will suffice to demonstrate that the defendant has committed an "act likely to obstruct the establishment of the source, the discovery, or the confiscation of assets which he knows or must assume represent the proceeds of a criminal activity"? This very broad description of the *actus reus* of the crime has been criticized in the literature because of the felt "lack of criteria regarding how abstract or specific the possible obstruction has to be for the offence to be regarded as committed." Capus, supra, at 140. Under the case law, however, some "clear" cases of money laundering may include the physical movement of criminal assets overseas, payments in cash, transferring assets from a Swiss to a foreign account, any transformation of criminally derived proceeds from cash into any form of investment, and the use of intermediaries. Id.

4. Mens rea. Two issues are presented by the statute: (1) the *mens rea* that must be demonstrated with respect to the defendant's awareness that the assets at issue are the proceeds of criminal activity, and (2) the *mens rea* attending the defendant's obstructive act.

With respect to the first issue, the statute states that the defendant must "know[] or must assume" that the assets at issue are the proceeds of a criminal activity. This does not permit liability based on negligence or even gross negligence, but it does permit a defendant to be convicted based on her willful blindness. Stessens, supra, at 125. As expressed in S. v. Public Prosecutor of the Canton of Bern, 119 IV 242, Judgment of the Court of Cassation (22 Sept. 1993):

> According to jurisprudence, . . . it is enough when reasons for suspicion give rise to the possibility of a criminal act. It is not necessary for the recipient [to] know the exact nature of the money. . . . It is sufficient and necessary that the money launderer know the circumstances that raise the suspicion that the money comes from a crime. . . . It suffices that he reckoned with the possibility that the money came from a qualified drug deal or, if applicable, other crimes like theft or fraud and took this into account; in other words that he reckoned with a fact pattern that is qualified as a drug crime or other crime. . . . Based on the appellant's knowledge of the objective professional and financial situation as well as the large sum involved, the lower court rejected the argument that the appellant could have assumed the money came from a lesser crime not subject to the money laundering offense. He therefore had to have assumed that the money was of criminal origin. . . . Based on the described circumstances, the appellant at any rate saw the possibility that the money came from offenses that, like drug dealing, are classified as crimes [as opposed to lesser offenses that are not predicate offenses for money laundering]. The lower court did not err in finding that he acted recklessly (*dol eventuel*) with regard to the criminal nature of the predicate offense.

The civil law concept of *dol eventuel*—which is one of three subcategories of intention—is often equated (as it was in the above opinion) to common law notions of recklessness, but it is slightly different. For example, under German law *dolus eventualis* "is constituted by knowledge of a possible (as distinct from inevitable) outcome of one's actions combined with a positive mental or emotional disposition toward it, which [German courts have] expressed as approval of or reconciling oneself to the possible outcome." Greg Taylor, Concepts of Intention in German Criminal Law, 24 Oxford J. Legal Stud. 99, 102 (2004). Although the first part of this concept—the knowledge of a possible or probable risk—comports with the common law concept of recklessness, that portion of *dolus eventualis* that requires that the defendant approved of or reconciled himself to the possible risk as a means of attaining his goal is foreign to most common lawyers. See Chapter 17 ("Modes of Participation and *Mens Rea*"). The *dol eventuel* required in Switzerland would seem to create a difficult burden for the prosecution because it must prove that the defendant either subjectively knew or "consider[ed] and accept[ed] the possibility that the assets in question have a criminal source." du Pasquier, supra, at 161 n.7.

With respect to the second question, the requisite *mens rea* may depend upon how the language of the statute is understood in its official French and German. Part of the difficulty of translation into English is the fact that the critical phrase has been read in different ways, some of which imply a *mens rea* and others of which do not: an act that "is likely to obstruct," "inherently impedes," "may prevent," "is suited to thwart," "could frustrate," and "hinders." What does the court in R.'s case require? Does it indicate that the *dol eventuel* standard will apply here as well? See also Capus, supra, at 141 (noting that the defendant "must have known about the criminal origins of the money *and must have accepted that confiscation would be obstructed through his actions*") (emphasis added).

5. *Predicate offenses.* The statute requires that the property laundered have a criminal source. Consistent with a trend to broaden the predicate offenses for money laundering beyond proceeds only of drug crimes, the Swiss statute applies to proceeds from all types of crimes, including theft, breach of fiduciary duty,

receiving stolen goods, robbery, fraud, extortion and blackmail, usury, fraudulent bankruptcy, unlawful imprisonment and kidnapping, participating in a criminal organization, and acceptance of bribes by public officials. See du Pasquier, supra, at 161; Shelby R. du Pasquier & Dr. Andreas von Planta, Money Laundering in Switzerland, 18 Intl. Bus. Law. 394, 394 (1990). Difficulties arose because under Swiss law, crimes are restricted to what are believed to be serious offenses and do not include lesser offenses (*délits*) and misdemeanors (*contraventions*). Thus, for example, although insider trading, price manipulation, and tax fraud are illegal, they were not crimes under Swiss law. Switzerland has responded to FATF's recommendations in its mutual evaluation of Swiss money laundering efforts by expanding the list of predicate crimes to include insider trading and price manipulation, as well as smuggling committed by criminal organizations, counterfeiting of goods, and product piracy. See Press Release, Federal Authorities of the Swiss Confederation, Tailored Revision of Money Laundering Legislation and Speedy Partial Revision of Insider Criminal Law Provisions (Sept. 29, 2006), available at http://www.news.admin.ch/dokumentation/00002/00015/index.html?lang = en&msg-id = 7541.

Note that the scope of qualifying predicate "crimes" will affect the ability of Swiss prosecutors to pursue cases where the monies are generated through criminal conduct outside Switzerland, which, as was discussed above, seems to be the usual situation they face. To be actionable under the statute, "it is understood that the tainted funds [must] have their source in (i) an offence committed in Switzerland which constitutes a crime according to the definition given by Swiss criminal law . . . , or (ii) an offence committed outside of Switzerland but which is considered in Switzerland to be a crime." du Pasquier & Planta, supra, at 394. Until recently, then, if the tainted funds were the product of (for example) insider trading in the United States, the laundering of those funds would not be proscribed in Switzerland.

Perhaps more notably, if U.S. prosecutors sought to pursue those who laundered the insider trading funds under the U.S. statute, and requested the assistance of the Swiss in gathering the relevant evidence in Switzerland, might the Swiss law definition of qualifying predicate "crimes" create problems? An important side effect of the definition of money laundering is its effect on Switzerland's obligations under existing mutual legal assistance treaties. Thus, "[u]nder Swiss federal law and various treaties entered into by Switzerland concerning mutual assistance in criminal matters, Swiss authorities may grant judicial assistance to a requesting country only with respect to acts which constitute a crime not only under the laws of the requesting country, but also under the laws of Switzerland." Peters, supra, at 137-138.

6. *Criminal financing.* As the case of R. makes clear, the Swiss money laundering statute does not on its face prohibit criminal financing; rather, if criminal financing is to be targeted, criminalization of the financing must be authorized in another subject-specific statute, such as that prohibiting drug financing. In addition to Article 19(1) of the Drug Law, reproduced above, the Swiss penal code contains separate provisions proscribing support for organized crime, Swiss Penal Code, Art. 260*ter*, and the financing of terrorism, Swiss Penal Code, Art. 260*quinquies*:

ARTICLE 260*TER*

Criminal Organizations
    1. Whoever participates in an organization that keeps its structure and its size secret and who pursues the goal of committing violent criminal acts or of obtaining

funds by criminal means, whoever supports such an organization in its criminal activity, will be punished by imprisonment of at most five years or by a monetary penalty.

2. The judge can liberally reduce the penalty for individuals who tried to prevent the pursuit of the organization's criminal activity.

3. An individual is also liable if he committed the act in another country if the organization carries out or must carry out its criminal activity in whole or in part in Switzerland.

ARTICLE 260*QUINQUIES*

Financing Terrorism

1. Whoever gathers or makes available funds planning to finance an act of criminal violence aimed at intimidating a population or at forcing a State or an international organization to take or omit to take any act, will be punished by imprisonment of five years at most or by a monetary penalty.

2. If the perpetrator only accepted the possibility that the funds in question would go toward financing a terrorist act, he is not liable under the meaning of this section.

3. The act is not considered financing terrorism when it is aimed at installing or re-establishing a democratic regime in a legal state or at protecting or permitting the exercise of human rights.

4. Paragraph 1 does not apply if the financing is intended to support acts which are not in conflict with the rules of international law applicable in armed conflict.

Finally, Swiss Penal Code Art. 260*bis*, although it does not specifically mention financing, criminalizes "taking concrete steps of a technical or organizational nature whose nature and scope indicate they were directed at leading to the carrying out of murder, assassination, severe bodily injury, robbery, kidnapping, hostage taking, arson or genocide." Swiss Penal Code, Art. 260*bis*.

However, the Swiss penal law does not, at present, have explicit criminal financing prohibitions that relate to the promotion of such offenses as fraud. Why might this be important? Might this affect the ability of the Swiss to render legal assistance to other nations if they were to pursue these activities under their domestic law?

7. *Article 305*ter. Refer back to Article 305*ter*. Its first paragraph was enacted in 1990:

[This provision] punishes the act of accepting, keeping on deposit, helping to invest, or transferring assets of a third party without verifying the beneficial ownership of these assets with the vigilance required by the circumstances of the particular case. . . . In practice, [the provision is] aimed at enforcing a minimum standard of Know Your Customer rules for financial transactions.

du Pasquier, supra, at 160-161. Article 305*ter* was amended in 1994 to add paragraph 2, which gives financial sector actors the *right* to report suspicious transactions to criminal authorities. Until the second paragraph was added to Article 305*ter*, the right to report suspicious conduct was the subject of substantial legal question in light of the Swiss bank secrecy laws. Id. at 162. Note well, however, that Article 305*ter* creates only a *right* to report, not a legal duty to do so; it was only in the generally noncriminal money laundering statute of 1997 that the Swiss imposed reporting requirements by law on its banks and other financial institutions.

2.   *U.S. Law*

Before reading *Piervinanzi*, below, review the U.S. money laundering statutes, 18 U.S.C. §§1956 and 1957, reproduced on our Web site.

UNITED STATES v. PIERVINANZI
23 F.3d 670 (2d Cir. 1994)

MAHONEY, Circuit Judge:

Michael Piervinanzi and Daniel Tichio appeal from judgments of conviction entered July 31, 1992 in the United States District Court for the Southern District of New York, Peter K. Leisure, Judge, after an eleven-day jury trial. The jury found Piervinanzi and Tichio guilty of conspiracy, attempted bank fraud, and attempted money laundering charges arising from a scheme to fraudulently transfer funds overseas from an account at Irving Trust Company ("Irving Trust"). The jury also convicted Piervinanzi of wire fraud, attempted bank fraud, attempted money laundering, and money laundering charges stemming from a separate but related scheme targeting an account at Morgan Guaranty Trust Company ("Morgan Guaranty"). The district court sentenced Piervinanzi to concurrent terms of 210 months imprisonment on each of seven counts of conviction, imposed a five-year term of supervised release for one attempted money laundering count and concurrent three-year terms of supervised release on the six other counts, and fined him $10,000. The court sentenced Tichio to concurrent terms of 135 months imprisonment on each of his three counts of conviction, and to concurrent three-year terms of supervised release.

We vacate Piervinanzi's conviction for money laundering under 18 U.S.C. §1957, and remand both cases to the district court for resentencing. We affirm the convictions in all other respects.

BACKGROUND

This case involves two separate but related schemes to transfer funds electronically out of banks and overseas. The basic facts are not in dispute.

A. THE IRVING TRUST SCHEME

From 1982 to 1988, Lorenzo DelGiudice was an auditor and computer operations specialist for Irving Trust. DelGiudice was responsible for monitoring and improving the security of the bank's wire transfer procedures to prevent unauthorized transfers. In March 1988, Anthony Marchese told DelGiudice that he and Piervinanzi were planning to rob an armored car. DelGiudice suggested a less violent alternative — an unauthorized wire transfer of funds from Irving Trust into an overseas account. DelGiudice explained that he could use his position at Irving Trust to obtain the information necessary to execute such a transfer. DelGiudice also explained that it would be necessary to obtain an overseas bank account for the scheme to succeed, because (1) United States banking regulations made the rapid movement of proceeds difficult, and (2) a domestic fraudulent transfer could, if detected, be readily reversed.

Marchese then introduced DelGiudice to Tichio. After DelGiudice explained the wire transfer scheme to Tichio, Tichio said that he could provide a foreign account to receive the stolen funds. Tichio made arrangements with Dhaniram Rambali, a business associate, to use Rambali's personal account at First Home Bank in the Cayman Islands to receive the stolen funds. Tichio then told DelGiudice that he would be able to provide access to accounts in the Cayman Islands, and emphasized that the strong bank secrecy laws there would prevent tracing of the purloined funds. Tichio told DelGiudice that the $10 million they were then planning to steal could be repatriated in monthly amounts of $200,000.

DelGiudice and Marchese distrusted Tichio's commitment to repatriate the money to them and feared for their safety, especially in view of the protracted payout schedule that Tichio had proposed. Marchese suggested that Piervinanzi be recruited to provide security for the operation; Piervinanzi's reputed ties to organized crime, he suggested, would deter Tichio from treachery or violence. Marchese and Tichio then met with Piervinanzi, who agreed to participate in the scheme and ensure that no one would "be hurt." Piervinanzi thereafter asked his brother, Robin Piervinanzi ("Robin"), to make the telephone call to Irving Trust that would initiate the transfer of funds to the Cayman Islands. Primarily in order to compensate Piervinanzi for his efforts, the conspirators increased the amount they planned to steal from $10 million to $14 million, of which DelGiudice and Marchese would receive $4 million each, and Tichio and Piervinanzi would receive $3 million each.

Despite Piervinanzi's participation, DelGiudice remained concerned about his safety, and decided to "sabotage [the] deal." However, DelGiudice did not want his coconspirators to know that he was intentionally frustrating their efforts. Accordingly, when he created the script that Robin would read when calling Irving Trust, DelGiudice left one necessary piece of information out of it: the name of a bank in the United States that would serve as the correspondent bank of First Home Bank in the Cayman Islands.[23] DelGiudice knew that if this information was not provided by the caller, it was likely that the transaction would not be consummated.

On July 6, 1988, Robin called Irving Trust and identified himself as "Joseph Herhal," an officer at Beneficial Corporation ("Beneficial"), whose Irving Trust account had been selected by DelGiudice for the transfer. Robin instructed a clerk to wire $14.2 million from the Beneficial account to Rambali's account at First Home Bank in the Cayman Islands. Reading from the script provided by DelGiudice, Robin supplied all required information except the identity of the correspondent bank. In the course of processing the transaction, the clerk contacted Beneficial to ask the identity of the American correspondent bank for First Home Bank. The clerk then learned that Beneficial had not requested the wire transfer, and halted the transaction. To deflect suspicion from himself, DelGiudice told Marchese that Irving Trust had stopped the transfer because First Home Bank was a "fly by night" operation.

B. THE MORGAN GUARANTY SCHEME

In July 1988, in a move unrelated to the attempted bank fraud, DelGiudice left his job at Irving Trust and accepted a "better position" at Morgan Guaranty as audit manager. His first assignment at Morgan Guaranty was to perform an audit of the bank's wire transfer department. During the autumn of 1988, DelGiudice, Marchese, and Piervinanzi began planning a fraudulent wire transfer from Morgan Guaranty. DelGiudice agreed to acquire the necessary information for the transfer; Marchese and Piervinanzi took responsibility for arranging other aspects of the scheme, such as locating an overseas bank account to receive the stolen funds, recruiting a "caller"

---

23. [Court's footnote 2:] Under banking practice, money cannot be transferred overseas directly, but must instead go through a correspondent bank where the recipient offshore bank has an account.

to initiate the wire transfer, and arranging for the distribution of the proceeds. They agreed that Tichio would not be involved in the Morgan Guaranty scheme.

Marchese and Piervinanzi contacted Philip Wesoke, a self-styled "financial consultant" who had previously invested (and lost) money for Piervinanzi. Marchese and Piervinanzi told Wesoke that they represented individuals who wanted to invest $14 to $20 million discreetly in a liquid, unregistered asset. Marchese and Piervinanzi told Wesoke that the investment could be "settled" overseas, and Piervinanzi mentioned the Cayman Islands, saying that he and Marchese had recently completed a transaction there. Having learned from the aborted Irving Trust scheme that correspondent bank information was necessary to transfer funds out of the country, Piervinanzi told Wesoke to provide the identity of a correspondent bank.

Wesoke recommended, and Piervinanzi and Marchese agreed, that they invest in diamonds. Wesoke accordingly arranged for a syndicate of Israeli diamond dealers to assemble a portfolio of diamonds for the conspirators. Wesoke also provided Piervinanzi with the necessary account and correspondent bank information for the planned recipient bank.

DelGiudice had selected an account of Shearson Lehman Hutton, Inc. ("Shearson") at Morgan Guaranty as his target, and compiled the necessary information for the transfer. Piervinanzi gave DelGiudice the information that Wesoke had provided concerning the recipient bank and its American correspondent bank. DelGiudice then met with Robin, who again was chosen to make the call that would trigger the fraudulent transfer. DelGiudice provided Robin with the appropriate Morgan Guaranty telephone number, dictated a script for him to use, and told him when to make the call.

On February 23, 1989, Robin telephoned Morgan Guaranty and, purporting to be Shearson employee William Cicio, directed a wire transfer of $24 million to the selected account in London, with Bankers Trust Company in New York ("Bankers Trust") serving as the correspondent bank. Although Robin supplied all the information needed to complete the transfer, Morgan Guaranty's clerk became suspicious because she had spoken with Cicio previously, and discerned that the voice on the telephone was not Cicio's. The clerk processed the transfer, but reported her suspicions to a supervisor. Either the supervisor or the clerk then contacted Shearson and learned that the transaction had not been authorized. Although the $24 million had already reached Bankers Trust, the wire transfer was stopped and reversed.

C. THE PROCEEDINGS BELOW

1. Indictment and Trial

The FBI arrested Piervinanzi on March 2, 1989 for his participation in the Morgan Guaranty scheme. On March 20, 1989, the original indictment was filed in this case, charging Piervinanzi alone with one count of wire fraud in violation of 18 U.S.C. §§1343 and 2. A twenty-three count superseding indictment was filed on December 18, 1990. This indictment was redacted to seven counts at trial. Counts one through three involved the Irving Trust scheme, while counts four through seven involved the Morgan Guaranty scheme. Count one charged Piervinanzi and Tichio with conspiracy to commit wire fraud, bank fraud, and money laundering in violation of 18 U.S.C. §371. Count two charged Piervinanzi and Tichio with attempted bank fraud in violation of 18 U.S.C. §§1344 and 2. Count three charged Piervinanzi and Tichio with attempted money laundering in violation of 18 U.S.C. §1956(a)(2) and 2. Count four charged Piervinanzi with wire fraud in violation of 18 U.S.C. §§1343 and 2. Count five charged Piervinanzi with attempted bank fraud in violation of 18 U.S.C. §§1344 and 2. Count six charged Piervinanzi with attempted money laundering in violation of 18 U.S.C. §§1956(a)(2) and 2. Count seven charged Piervinanzi with money laundering in violation of 18 U.S.C. §§1957(a) and 2. Trial commenced on May 1, 1991 and concluded on May 17, 1991, when the jury returned a verdict convicting Piervinanzi and Tichio on all counts. . . .

DISCUSSION . . .

A. MONEY LAUNDERING CONVICTION OF PIERVINANZI UNDER §1957(a)

Piervinanzi was convicted on count seven of the indictment of violating 18 U.S.C. §1957(a) for his participation in the Morgan Guaranty scheme. This statute provides in relevant part:

> (a) Whoever . . . knowingly engages or attempts to engage in a monetary transaction in criminally derived property that is of a value greater than $10,000 and is derived from specified unlawful activity, shall be punished as provided in subsection (b). . . .
> (f) As used in this section — . . .
> (2) the term "criminally derived property" means any property constituting, or derived from, proceeds obtained from a criminal offense; and
> (3) the term "specified unlawful activity" has the meaning given that term in section 1956 of this title.

As defined in §1956, "specified unlawful activity" includes bank fraud. See §1956(c)(7)(D).

Count seven charged that Piervinanzi violated §1957 by fraudulently causing the transfer of approximately $24 million from Morgan Guaranty. Piervinanzi argues that the language of the statute only encompasses transactions in which a defendant first obtains "criminally derived property," and then engages in a monetary transaction with that property. Because the funds transferred from Morgan Guaranty were not yet property derived from the wire fraud and bank fraud scheme, Piervinanzi contends, his actions did not come within the purview of §1957. The government does not dispute this reading of the statute, and joins Piervinanzi's request to vacate his conviction on this count. . . .

The language of §1957 supports Piervinanzi's interpretation of that statute. The ordinary meaning of the word "obtained" entails possession of a thing. See Webster's Third New International Dictionary 1559 (1986). Similarly, the word "property" implies ownership, or the "exclusive right to possess, enjoy, and dispose of a thing." Id. at 1818. The use of such language demonstrates a congressional intent that the proceeds of a crime be in the defendant's possession before he can attempt to transfer those proceeds in violation of §1957. See United States v. Johnson, 971 F.2d 562, 569 (10th Cir. 1992) ("both the plain language of §1957 and the legislative history behind it suggest that Congress targeted only those transactions occurring after proceeds have been obtained from the underlying unlawful activity"); United States v. Lovett, 964 F.2d 1029, 1042 (10th Cir. 1992) ("Congress intended [§1957] to separately punish a defendant for monetary transactions that follow in time the underlying specified unlawful activity that generated the criminally derived property in the first place.") (citing H.R. Rep. No. 855, 99th Cong., 2d Sess., pt. 1, at 7 (1986) (the "House Report")).

Piervinanzi and his colleagues succeeded in transferring $24 million from Morgan Guaranty to Bankers Trust, but these funds never came into the possession or under the control of the conspirators. Thus, Piervinanzi was improperly convicted of money laundering in violation of §1957, and we reverse his conviction on count seven.

B. MONEY LAUNDERING CONVICTIONS UNDER §1956(a)(2)

Piervinanzi contends that the proof at trial did not establish the elements of money laundering or attempted money laundering under 18 U.S.C. §1956(a)(2), and therefore that his convictions under counts three and six of the indictment must be reversed. He argues that §1956(a)(2) is not violated unless there is some "secondary laundering activity not previously made criminal by pre-existing criminal statutes." Accordingly, he contends, because the asserted criminal laundering activity, the overseas transfer of the bank funds, was simply a component of the bank frauds that the conspirators attempted to perpetrate against Irving Trust and Morgan Guaranty, there was no analytically distinct "secondary" activity, and thus no criminal laundering violative of §1956(a)(2)....

... 2. Scope of Section 1956(a)(2)

Piervinanzi contends that the language of §1956(a)(2) (1988), its legislative history, pertinent case law, ... and relevant Sentencing Guidelines commentary all support the conclusion that this provision proscribes only "laundering" activity that is analytically distinct from the underlying criminal activity that it promotes, and that the overseas fund transfers intended in this case do not satisfy this statutory requirement. For the reasons that follow, we reject his reading of §1956(a)(2).

a. Statutory Language

The statutory language at issue requires that there be a transmission of funds "with the intent to promote the carrying on of specified unlawful activity." §1956(a)(2)(A). As previously noted, "specified unlawful activity" includes bank fraud. The counts (three and six) of the indictment that charge violations of §1956(a)(2) both specify that the overseas fund transfers were designed to further "a fraudulent scheme in violation of 18 U.S.C. §1344 [i.e., bank fraud]."

Piervinanzi contends that in this case, the overseas transmission of funds "merges" with the underlying bank fraud, precluding independent liability under §1956(a)(2). In our view, however, the conduct at issue in this case falls within the prohibition of the statute. The conspirators understood the use of overseas accounts to be integral to the success of both the Irving Trust and Morgan Guaranty schemes. DelGiudice explained to the other conspirators that use of foreign accounts would make the fraudulently obtained funds more difficult to trace. Tichio obtained access to Rambali's Cayman Islands bank account because he understood that bank secrecy laws there would hamper official efforts to recover the stolen funds. Similarly, Piervinanzi and Marchese told Wesoke that they wished to "settle[]" their transaction overseas. Because transferring the funds overseas (and beyond the perceived reach of U.S. officials) was integral to the success of both fraudulent schemes, it is undeniable that the attempted transfers were designed to "promote" the underlying crime of bank fraud. Contrary to Piervinanzi's assertion, this reading of the statute does not "merge" the underlying criminal activity and promotion through laundering into one. The act of attempting to fraudulently transfer funds out of the banks was analytically distinct from the attempted transmission of those funds overseas, and was itself independently illegal. See 18 U.S.C. §1344.

Analysis of the overall structure of §1956 confirms this interpretation. Section 1956(a)(1),[24] the domestic money laundering statute, penalizes financial transactions that "involv[e] . . . the proceeds of specified unlawful activity." The provision requires first that the proceeds of specified unlawful activity be generated, and second that the defendant, knowing the proceeds to be tainted, conduct or attempt to conduct a financial transaction with these proceeds with the intent to promote specified unlawful activity.[25] By contrast, §1956(a)(2) contains no requirement that "proceeds" first be generated by unlawful activity, followed by a financial transaction with those proceeds, for criminal liability to attach. Instead, it penalizes an overseas transfer "with the intent to promote the carrying on of specified unlawful activity." §1956(a)(2)(A).

The fact that Congress uses different language in defining violations in a statute indicates that Congress intentionally sought to create distinct offenses. The clearly demarcated two-step requirement which Piervinanzi advocates in the construction of §1956(a)(2) is apparent in other provisions of the federal money laundering statutes, but not in §1956(a)(2). We have no authority to supply the omission.

Piervinanzi also contends that the prohibition in §1956(a)(2)(A) of "carrying on" underlying criminal activity would be meaningless, and the phrase rendered superfluous, unless it connotes continuous criminal activity that is not presented by the discrete bank frauds in this case. (This argument could be presented even more strongly by Tichio, who engaged in only one of the attempted frauds.) The "specified unlawful activity" that must be "carried on" to result in a §1956(a)(2) violation, however, is consistently defined in each paragraph of §1956(c)(7) as including discrete, singular offenses, as follows: "*any act* or activity constituting an offense" (paragraph (A), emphasis added); "*an offense*" (paragraph (B), emphasis added); "*any act* or acts constituting a continuing criminal enterprise" (paragraph (C), emphasis added); and "*an offense*" (paragraph (D), emphasis added). Thus, we conclude, §1956(a)(2) can be satisfied by the "carrying on" of a single offense of "bank fraud," and "carrying on" in §1956(a)(2), rather than connoting continuous criminal activity, has essentially the same meaning as "conducts" in §1956(a)(1). Indeed, this is the primary meaning of "carry on." See Webster's Third New International Dictionary 344.

b. Legislative History

The relatively scanty legislative history of §1956(a)(2) supports this analysis. The Senate report on the version of the bill reported to the Senate explains that §1956(a)(2) is "designed to illegalize international money laundering transactions," and "covers situations in which money is being laundered . . . by transferring it out of the United States." S. Rep. No. 433, 99th Cong., 2d Sess. 11 (1986) (the "Senate Report"). The Senate Report's discussion of §1956(a)(2) is conspicuously silent

---

24. [Court's footnote 7:] Section 1956(a)(1) provides in relevant part:

> Whoever, knowing that the property involved in a financial transaction *represents the proceeds of some form of unlawful activity*, conducts or attempts to conduct such a financial transaction which in fact involves the proceeds of specified unlawful activity—
> (A)(i) with the intent to promote the carrying on of specified unlawful activity, . . . shall be sentenced to a fine . . . or imprisonment for not more than twenty years, or both.

[Emphasis added.]

25. [Court's footnote 8:] In this respect, §1956(a)(1) is similar to §1957(a), which requires the separate obtention of "criminally derived property" followed by a monetary transaction with that property. See supra part A of this Discussion.

about any requirement that the funds be proceeds of some distinct activity, merely stating that the statute is violated when a defendant "engage[s] in an act of transporting or attempted transporting and either intend[s] to facilitate a crime or know[s] that the transaction was designed to facilitate a crime."[26] By contrast, the Senate Report explains that §1956(a)(1) "requires that the property involved in a transaction must in fact be proceeds of 'specified unlawful activity' ..." ...

c. Case Law

Nor do the precedents invoked by Piervinanzi sustain his position. He points, for example, to the following statement in [*United States v. Stavroulakis*]:

> Section 1956 creates the crime of money laundering, and it takes dead aim at the attempt to launder dirty money. Why and how that money got dirty is defined in other statutes. *Section 1956 does not penalize the underlying unlawful activity from which the tainted money is derived.*

[952 F.2d 686, 691 (2d Cir. 1992) (emphasis added).] In the context of this case, the emphasized language is a truism that begs the question whether the intended overseas transfers should be considered as separate secondary "laundering" or a component of the underlying bank fraud.

Our opinion in United States v. Skinner, 946 F.2d 176 (2d Cir. 1991), is considerably more relevant. Concededly, in that case we construed §1956(a)(1), which requires that separate proceeds be utilized in a financial transaction. See supra note 7. Our focus in *Skinner*, however, was upon the statutory requirement, identical in this respect to §1956(a)(2)(A), that a financial transaction be undertaken "with the intent to promote the carrying on of specified unlawful activity." §1956(a)(1)(A)(i). We concluded that this language applied to the transportation of money orders to pay for purchases of cocaine. Although the transactions "in reality represented only the completion of the sale" of cocaine, we concluded that they were made to facilitate the sale of cocaine and thus were made "with the intent to promote the carrying on of specified unlawful activity."

A number of cases from other circuits support this view. [For example,] ... the Third Circuit held that the cashing of government checks to complete mail frauds perpetrated against the Internal Revenue Service constituted a §1956(a)(1) violation, although the proceeds of the fraud were concededly spent for personal purposes and not "plowed back" into the criminal venture. See United States v. Paramo, 998 F.2d 1212, 1216-18 (3d Cir. 1993).

Similarly, we are not persuaded by Piervinanzi's references to United States v. Jackson, 935 F.2d 832 (7th Cir.1991), and United States v. Hamilton, 931 F.2d 1046 (5th Cir. 1991). *Jackson* comments that §1956(a)(1)(A)(i) is "aimed at ... the practice of plowing back proceeds of 'specified unlawful activity' to promote that activity." *Hamilton* states that §1956(a)(2) is meant to criminalize the transfer of funds "that would contribute to the growth and capitalization of the drug trade or other unlawful activities." In both cases, the same statutory language ("promote the carrying on of specified unlawful activity," §1956(a)(1)(A)(i) and (a)(2)(A)) is construed.

The *Jackson* comment faithfully reflects the facts of that case, in which a violation of §1956(a)(1) was premised upon the use of proceeds from drug sales to purchase

---

26. [Court's footnote 9:] As Piervinanzi points out, the language of §1956(a)(2) was subsequently amended prior to its enactment to substitute "promotes" for "facilitates." We do not regard this amendment as altering the outcome in this case. The overseas transfers contemplated by the conspirators would clearly have both facilitated and promoted the underlying bank fraud that they hoped to achieve.

beepers for use by participants in the criminal drug enterprise. We agree with *Paramo*, however, that *Jackson* did not intend "either to delineate the universe of conduct prohibited under section 1956(a)(1)(A)(i), or to decide whether a defendant could violate that section other than by plowing back the proceeds of unlawful activity." The focus in *Hamilton* was upon the violation of §1956(a)(2) involved in a hypothetical transfer of legitimately derived funds from a foreign source to the United States to capitalize a domestic drug enterprise.

Neither case establishes that a defendant may be deemed to "promote the carrying on of specified unlawful activity" *only* when the laundering would promote subsequent criminal activity. As previously discussed, such a reading would not accord with the plain meaning of the statute. Further, *Hamilton* involved a scheme similar to that in *Skinner*, in which the proceeds of drug sales were sent through the mails to pay for a drug purchase. As in *Skinner*, the defendant was convicted of violating §1956(a)(1), although there was no indication that the transferred proceeds were to be invested in subsequent illegal activities. . . .

NOTES AND QUESTIONS

1. The U.S. money laundering statutes (18 U.S.C. §§1956 and 1957) are obviously much more complex than their Swiss counterpart. Is the degree of detail necessary?

Review the definitions of money laundering that are discussed at the beginning of this chapter. What types of money laundering do §§1956 and 1957 cover that Article 305*bis* of the Swiss Penal Code does not? *Should* "criminal finance" be included in a general money laundering prohibition, or should a bar on the financing of criminal activity be crime-specific (for example, as reflected in Article 19(1)(7) of the Swiss Drug Law with respect to the "act of financing the illegal drug trade")?

Note that the Swiss court describes money laundering as an "offense against the administration of justice" in that the "criminal act consists of preventing access by the criminal authorities to the proceeds of a crime, making it more difficult to establish the link between the assets and the crime" (§2.1). By contrast, the U.S. money laundering statute is found in Chapter 95 of the U.S. criminal code, which is entitled "Racketeering" and contains other offenses that deal with, for example, interference with commerce by threats or violence (§1951), use of interstate commerce to engage in murder-for-hire (§1958), and violent crime in aid of racketeering activity (§1959). Is this difference in conceptualization reflected in the definitions of money laundering?

2. Section 1956 is structured to identify two different types of culpable acts in its principal prohibitions: "transactions" (1956(a)(1)) and "transportations" (1956(a)(2)). The culpable acts are criminal where those acts are accompanied (inter alia) with the requisite knowledge or intent. To summarize very generally (the specifics are provided below), defendants are criminally culpable if they conduct a qualifying transaction or transport monies *either* "with the *intent to promote* the carrying on of specified unlawful activity" *or knowing* that the transaction or transportation was "designed in whole or in part . . . to conceal or disguise" the nature, location, source, ownership, or control of the dirty money.

3. *Transaction offenses.* The elements of a "transaction" offense are that the defendant:

(a) conducted or attempted to conduct a financial transaction;

The *actus reus* under 1956(a)(1) is a prohibited "financial transaction," which is defined very broadly to extend far beyond transactions with banks or other financial institutions. See 18 U.S.C. §1956(c)(3), (4). "Virtually any exchange of money between two parties constitutes a financial transaction subject to criminal prosecution under §1956, provided that the transaction has at least a minimal effect on interstate commerce [see §1956(c)(4)] and satisfies at least one of the four intent requirements" (described below). Twenty-Third Survey of White Collar Crime, Money Laundering, 45 Am. Crim. L. Rev. 741, 755-756 (2008).

      (b) knowing that the property involved in the transaction represented the proceeds of unlawful activity;

Under §1956(c)(1), the element of "knowing that the property involved in a financial transaction represents the proceeds of some form of unlawful activity" means only that "the person knew the property involved in the transaction represented proceeds from *some form, though not necessarily which form,* of activity that constitutes a felony under State, Federal, or foreign law, *regardless of whether or not such activity is [specified unlawful activity].*" 18 U.S.C. §1956(c)(1) (emphasis added).

      (c) the transaction in fact "involv[ed]" the proceeds of "specified unlawful activity"; and

The financial transaction must "in fact involve[]" the proceeds of specified unlawful activity in a §1956(a)(1) "transaction" prosecution. The requirement that the transaction involve the proceeds of "specified unlawful activity" (and, under §1956(a)(1)(A)(i), be intended to promote the carrying on of "specified unlawful activity") is not terribly limiting, however. "Specified unlawful activity" covers a very broad array of crimes, including drug-related activity, racketeering, and white collar crimes (e.g., 18 U.S.C. §§201 (federal public corruption), 666 (federal program theft, fraud, or bribery), 1341 (mail fraud), 1343 (wire fraud), 1344 (bank fraud), 1503 (obstruction of justice), 1512 (witness tampering), 1951 (Hobbs Act), 1952 (Travel Act), 2314-2315 (interstate transportation of stolen property), certain environmental violations, fraud in the sale of securities, "any felony violation of the Foreign Corrupt Practices Act," and "[a]ny act or activity constituting an offense involving a Federal health care offense" 18 U.S.C. §1956(c)(7)). In the USA PATRIOT Act, Congress added offenses relating to the provision of material support to terrorists (18 U.S.C. §§2339, 2339A, 2339B) and computer fraud and abuse violations (18 U.S.C. §1030) to the list of "specified unlawful activities." §1956(c)(7)(D).

      For our purposes, it is important to note that §1956(c)(7)(B) includes in the list of specified unlawful activities certain offenses against *foreign* states. "Thus, proceeds of certain crimes committed in another country may constitute proceeds of a specified unlawful activity for purposes of the money laundering statutes." U.S. Dept. of Justice, Criminal Resource Manual No. 2101. The statute states that, "*with respect to financial transactions occurring in whole or in part in the United States,*" an offense against a foreign nation involving controlled substances violations, certain serious crimes (e.g., murder, kidnapping, arson, and extortion), and bank fraud perpetrated against a foreign bank constitute "specified unlawful activity." §1956(c)(7)(B)(i)-(iii) (emphasis added). In the USA PATRIOT Act, Congress added "bribery of a public official, or the misappropriation, theft, or embezzlement of public funds by or for the benefit of a public official," §1956(c)(7)(B)(iv), "smuggling or export control violations" involving certain controlled materials, §1956(c)(7)(B)(v), and "an offense with respect to which the United States would be obligated by a multilateral treaty, either to extradite the alleged offender or to submit the case for prosecution, if the offender were found within the territory of the United States." §1956(c)(7)(B)(vi).

      (d) the defendant acted with the requisite knowledge or purpose.

We will focus on two of the four *alternative* means under §1956(a)(1) that the government may use to demonstrate that the defendant acted with the requisite knowledge or purpose: (i) cases in which the government charges that the defendant conducted the financial transaction "with the *intent to promote* the carrying on of specified unlawful activity" (a "promotion" transaction offense under §1956(a)(1)(A)(i)); and (ii) cases in which the government alleges that the defendant *knew* that the transaction was "designed in whole or in part . . . to conceal or disguise" the nature, location, source, ownership, or control of the proceeds of "specified unlawful activity" (a "concealment" transaction offense under §1956(a)(1)(B)(i)). (The other two alternatives are (iii) cases in which the government contends that the defendant conducted the financial transaction with the intent to engage in tax fraud (§1956(a)(1)(A)(ii)); and (iv) cases in which the government alleges that the defendant knew that the transaction was designed to avoid a transaction reporting requirement under state or federal law (§1956(a)(1)(B)(ii)).)

Note that a "promotion" offense requires that the defendant acted with the "*intent* to promote the carrying on of specified unlawful activity" while the "concealment" offense requires only that the defendant "*knew*" that the transaction was designed, at least in part, to conceal.

4. *Transportation offenses.* The elements of a "transportation" offense are that the defendant:

(a) transported, transmitted, or transferred (or attempted to do so);

While the culpable act at the heart of a §1956(a)(1) case is conducting a "financial transaction" (or an attempt to conduct a qualifying transaction), the *actus reus* of a §1956(a)(2) case is the transport, transmission, or transfer (or attempt to do so) of a "monetary instrument or funds from a place in the United States to or through a place outside the United States or to a place in the United States from or through a place outside the United States." Note that §1956(a)(2) prohibits international wire transfers as well as the physical transportation of monetary instruments or funds.

(b) monetary instruments or funds;

Under §1956(c)(5), "monetary instruments" include coin and currency (of any country), traveler's checks, personal checks, bank checks, money orders, and investment securities or negotiable instruments.

(c) across the border of the United States; and

Section 1956(a)(2) requires that the funds or monetary instruments cross a U.S. border—"either originating or terminating in the United States." U.S. Dept. of Justice, Criminal Resource Manual No. 2101, supra. If the funds are transferred between two countries outside the United States and never cross the U.S. border, the launderers may not be convicted under §1956(a)(2). See United States v. Kramer, 73 F.3d 1067, 1072-1073 (11th Cir. 1996). However, the nominally domestic "transaction" money laundering provision of §1956(a)(1) *may* be used where the laundering transaction occurs entirely abroad, assuming the other elements of the offense are proved. See, e.g., United States v. Tarkoff, 242 F.3d 991 (11th Cir. 2001) (holding that transfers from Curacao to Israel and between accounts in Israel constitute "financial transactions" under §1956(c)(4) and were within the reach of §1956(a)(1)(B)(i)).

(d) acted with the requisite knowledge or purpose.

We will again focus on only two of the three *alternative* means by which the government can demonstrate that the defendant acted with the requisite knowledge or purpose under §1956(a)(2): (i) cases charging that the defendant transported the funds "with the intent to promote the carrying on of specified unlawful activity" (a "promotion" transaction offense under §1956(a)(2)(A)); and (ii) cases charging that the defendant transported funds knowing that the funds involved in the transportation represent the proceeds of some form of unlawful activity and knowing that such transfer is designed in whole or in part to conceal or disguise the nature, location, source, ownership, or control of the proceeds of specified unlawful activity (a "concealment" transaction offense under §1956(a)(2)(B)(i)). (The last alternative is

(iii) cases charging that the defendant knew that the transaction was designed to avoid a transaction reporting requirement under state or federal law (§1956(a)(2)(B)(ii)). Unlike §1956(a)(1)(A)(ii), a transportation case under §1956(a)(2) cannot be made based upon a transportation of funds with the intent to engage in tax fraud.)

5. *Concealment.* Do the U.S. statute's concealment provisions satisfy Article 3 of the 1988 Illicit Trafficking Convention?

For purposes of both "transaction" (§1956(a)(1)(B)(i)) and "transportation" (1956(a)(2)(B)(i)) cases, the government must show that "proceeds" of one of the predicate crimes was sought to be laundered. The prosecution must prove that the defendant *knew* both that the transaction or transportation represented the "proceeds of some form of unlawful activity" *and* that the culpable act was designed in whole or in part to conceal or disguise the nature, location, source, or ownership of the "proceeds" of specified unlawful activity. It is critical to note, however, that the defendant need not him- or herself be acting with the *intent* to conceal. Thus, for example, a real estate broker who helps a drug dealer consummate a real estate transaction knowing that it involves the proceeds of some sort of illegal activity and knowing that the dealer intends to conceal his proceeds can be convicted under this section even if she herself does not intend to conceal the ill-gotten proceeds. See United States v. Campbell, 977 F.2d 854 (4th Cir. 1992).

In the United States, as in Switzerland, a defendant's "knowledge" can be proved by evidence of his or her "willful blindness." See id. But there is a great deal of confusion as to what "willful" blindness means in U.S. federal courts. Some courts argue that it is in essence the defendant's failure, in the face of evidence of wrongdoing, to investigate sufficiently; this conception targets the "ostrich" defendant. This approach is one that sounds in recklessness — the defendant is culpable for his conscious failure to satisfy his duty to learn the facts and thus avoid criminality. As the Seventh Circuit has reasoned,

> When a mistaken assertion is very likely to mislead and to cause damage, and the defendant knows of this risk yet could have avoided the harm at no (or trivial) cost by checking up on facts within his reach, we call the omission to investigate criminal recklessness. An ostrich instruction points the jury in the right direction without dwelling on the fine details of recklessness.

United States v. Ramsey, 785 F.2d 184, 189 (7th Cir. 1986). Given the difference between U.S. concepts of recklessness and the Swiss conception of *dol eventuel* (explored above), it seems that U.S. prosecutors have a lighter burden of proof.

In the past, a number of U.S. courts, led by the Ninth Circuit, rejected any attempt to found willful blindness culpability on a recklessness theory. They appeared to believe that the defendant should be held liable under a willful blindness charge only when he is less "ostrich" than "fox" — that is, when he *chooses* to remain ignorant of facts "so he can plead lack of positive knowledge in the event he should be caught." "The grand-scheming Fox, who aims to do wrong and structures his own ignorance merely to prepare a defense, has the same level of culpability as any other willful wrongdoer — the highest level, in the Model Penal Code schema." David Luban, Contrived Ignorance, 87 Geo. L.J. 957, 969 (1999). In jurisdictions where willful blindness instructions are aimed at running foxes to ground, the purpose of the instruction is said to be to inform the jury that it may consider evidence of the defendant's *charade* of ignorance as circumstantial proof of guilty knowledge.

The Ninth Circuit recently overruled decisions that had been read to require that the government prove the defendant's *motive* in avoiding knowledge — that is, that the defendant was remaining ignorant in order to avoid criminal liability. In United States v. Heredia, 483 F.3d 913, 920 (9th Cir. 2007), the en banc court approved a willful blindness charge that permitted a finding of "knowledge" based on the fact that (1) the "defendant was aware of a 'high probability' that he [was] in the possession of contraband," and (2) he " 'deliberately avoided learning the truth.' " The court made clear, however, that "the *reason* the individual fails to take that final step[that is, whether the aim was to provide him- or herself with a defense in the event of prosecution] has no bearing on whether he has sufficient information so he can properly be deemed to 'know' the fact." Id. at 920 n.10.

As far as what suffices to demonstrate a design to "conceal" by the drug dealer, "using a third party, for example, a business entity or a relative, to purchase goods on one's behalf or from which one will benefit usually constitutes sufficient proof of a design to conceal." United States v. Willey, 57 F.3d 1374, 1385 (5th Cir. 1995). "Evidence that the defendant commingled illegal proceeds with legitimate business funds has been held to be sufficient to support the design element." Id. at 1386. "Moving money through a large number of accounts has, in the light of other evidence, also been found to support the design element of this offense, even when all the accounts to which the defendant transferred the money and from which he withdrew it were in his name." Id. Thus, the cases "demonstrate that in order to establish the design element of money laundering, it is not necessary to prove with regard to any single transaction that the defendant removed all traces of his involvement with the money or that the particular transaction charged is itself highly unusual, although either of these elements might be sufficient to support a money laundering conviction." Id.

Some courts, however, have reversed convictions where the government's theory would convert the money laundering statute into a "money spending" statute. For example, in United States v. Rockelman, 49 F.3d 418, 422 (8th Cir. 1995), the Eighth Circuit reversed a money laundering conviction for lack of concealment because the defendant purchased a home with illegal cash proceeds and placed the title in the name of his business, making no attempt to conceal his own identity or the source of the funds.

The Supreme Court recently addressed the design-to-conceal element in Cuellar v. United States, 128 S. Ct. 1994 (2008). In that case, the defendant took substantial trouble to conceal $81,000 in a car that he planned to drive over the United States-Mexico border. The Supreme Court reversed his conviction under §1956(a)(2)(B)(i), ruling that a concealment money laundering conviction required proof that the transportation's *purpose*—not merely its effect—was to conceal or disguise one of the listed attributes. In other words, the defendant had to transport in order to conceal; it was not sufficient to show simply that he concealed in the course of transporting.

Where the government has had difficulty identifying any actionable "concealment," it has come up with novel—and highly contestable—theories of "promotion," discussed below.

6. *Promotion*. The Swiss money laundering statute does not cover the "promotion" offenses provided for in U.S. law under §1956(a)(1)(A)(i) or §1956(a)(2)(A), although such activity may be covered in discrete, offense-specific criminal financing provisions of the Swiss Code. Under the U.S. conception of money laundering, however, under either the "transaction" or "transportation" sections, the government may pursue a defendant for promoting criminal activity. The government must show that the defendant conducted a financial transaction or transported monetary instruments or funds with the intent to promote the carrying on of specified

unlawful activity. Is this portion of the U.S. law required under existing international conventions?

One issue raised in *Piervinanzi* that has appeared with some frequency due to prosecutors' novel theories of "promotion" is whether a defendant can be convicted for "promoting" an *ongoing* crime or a *completed* crime, or whether she can be convicted only where there is proof that she is seeking to "promote" the commission of a *future* "specified unlawful activity." How would a Swiss court resolve this under the Swiss Drug Law?

The U.S. circuit courts are split on this question under both the "transaction" and the "transportation" offenses. The *Piervinanzi* court cites in support of its resolution the case of United States v. Paramo, 998 F.2d 1212 (3d Cir. 1993). In *Paramo*, a conspirator employed by the IRS sent tax refund checks through the mail to fictitious payees in New York. Paramo retrieved the checks and sent them to his brother, who then deposited them in his bank account in anticipation of sharing the proceeds of the fraud with Paramo and the bent IRS employee. Paramo was convicted of transaction "promotion" money laundering founded on the deposit of the embezzled checks. On appeal, Paramo contended that the underlying offense that generated the proceeds—the mail fraud—was complete as of the mailing of the checks and thus that he could not be convicted of money laundering for "promoting" a completed crime. The Third Circuit disagreed, ruling that Paramo had "promoted" the carrying on of the completed crime of mail fraud when he cashed the checks, reasoning that "because Paramo believed cashing the checks was necessary to realize any benefit from the mail fraud, the jury could infer he cashed each check to promote the carrying on of the antecedent fraud." Id. at 1217 (characterizing government's argument, which the court accepted).

Under *Paramo*, is there any real distinction between the money laundering and the underlying predicate fraud? Is there anything troubling about holding that the underlying crime is sufficiently complete to generate the necessary "proceeds" while at the same time sufficiently incomplete so that the distribution of proceeds actually "promotes" it?

As *Piervinanzi* illustrates, the same question arises under §1956(a)(2)(A). The Second Circuit finds in *Piervinanzi* that, as a *factual* matter, there is no merger because the bank fraud charge focused on the defendants' efforts to get the money (improperly) out of the bank while the money laundering concerned their efforts to send the money overseas. If the bank fraud is accomplished when the money is improperly transferred out of a client's account, how can the overseas transfer of the funds "promote" this completed fraud?

The Second Circuit reasons that the use of the foreign accounts was designed in part to "hamper official efforts to recover the stolen funds" and thus served to "promote" the underlying (completed) bank fraud. Does this sound like "promotion" or "concealment"? Is this an inference that could credibly be drawn in any case where international transfers of stolen or embezzled funds occur? Does this holding effectively remove crime "promotion" as an element of the crime?

Recently, the Supreme Court provided some definition of the term "proceeds" and, in so doing, relied on the argument that absent a restricted reading of the term, "merger" issues would mean that every gambling case would also constitute a money laundering case. See United States v. Santos, 128 S. Ct. 2020 (2008). In *Santos*, the defendant was convicted of money laundering based on his acceptance of a salary paid from the commission generated by an illegal lottery. A plurality of the Supreme Court reversed his conviction, holding that, at least in the circumstances of an illegal gambling business, "proceeds" under 1956(a)(1)(A)(i) of the money laundering statute meant "profits" and not simply "receipts." Justice Stevens provided the fifth vote necessary for the judgment, but he opined that "proceeds" might mean "receipts," and not solely "profits," in cases involving offenses that Congress was targeting in the money laundering statute, *viz.* organized crime syndicates or the sale of contraband.

7. *Using "clean" funds to promote specified unlawful activity.* The Second Circuit in *Piervinanzi* identifies a very important difference between a "transaction" promotion offense under §1956(a)(1)(A)(i) and a "transportation" promotion offense under §1956(a)(2)(A): The "transaction" offense requires that *dirty money* ("proceeds") be used to promote the specified unlawful activity but the "transportation" offense does not.

The *Piervinanzi* court ruled that, unlike other portions of the statute, including §1956(a)(1)(A)(i) (and, for that matter, §1957), §1956(a)(2)(A) "contains no requirement that 'proceeds' first be generated by unlawful activity, followed by a financial transaction with those proceeds." Does this mean that a defendant can be prosecuted for "laundering" money that is not derived from criminal activity if he sends the money over a U.S. border intending to promote specified unlawful activity? The Department of Justice believes that the answer is "yes." Money Laundering, U.S. Attys.' Bull., June 1999, http://www.usdoj.gov/usao/eousa/foia_reading_room/usab4703.pdf.

What are the implications of a holding that a defendant can be convicted of "promoting" a specified unlawful activity through transfers of innocent funds abroad or the repatriation of innocent funds from abroad? In such cases, is any dirty money being laundered? Or is the focus of the criminality the aiding and abetting of the specified unlawful activity? Why not charge it as such? Might jurisdictional concerns force prosecutors to seek a money laundering charge rather than a charge founded on the illegal conduct sought to be promoted? Is this an appropriate exercise of prosecutorial discretion?

8. *Section 1957.* The elements of a §1957 prosecution are that the defendant:

(a) knowingly engaged or attempted to engage;
(b) in a monetary transaction;
(c) in criminally derived property (i.e., "proceeds") with a value of more than $10,000;
(d) knowing that the property was derived from unlawful activity; and
(e) the property was, in fact, derived from "specified unlawful activity."

Notably, §1957 does *not* require proof that the defendant actually laundered the funds or intended to promote unlawful activity or to conceal the provenance of dirty money. It does not require that the defendant even know that others are engaging in the transaction to promote or conceal unlawful activity. Thus, "[t]he most significant difference [between §1957 cases and] §1956 prosecutions is the intent requirement. Under §1957, the four intents have been replaced with a $10,000 threshold amount for each . . . transaction and the requirement that a financial institution be involved in the transaction. . . . [T]he prosecutor need not prove any intent to promote, conceal or avoid the reporting requirements. . . ." U.S. Dept. of Justice, Criminal Resource Manual No. 2101, supra.

What is the purpose of this prohibition? "In enacting §1957, Congress intended to dissuade people from engaging in even ordinary commercial transactions with people suspected to be involved in criminal activity." Twenty-Third Survey of White Collar Crime, Money Laundering, 45 Am. Crim. L. Rev. 741, 747 (2008). Further, the act "makes the subsequent use of criminal proceeds in any transaction illegal in perpetuity, extending well beyond the statute of limitations for the original conduct." Id. at 744.

[Section 1957] is a powerful tool because it makes any dealing with a bank potentially a trap for the drug dealer or any other defendant who has a hoard of criminal cash derived from the specified crimes. If he makes a "deposit, withdrawal, transfer or exchange" with this cash, he commits the crime; he's forced to commit another felony if he wants to use a bank. This draconian law, so powerful by its elimination of criminal intent, freezes the proceeds of specific crimes out of the banking system.

United States v. Rutgard, 116 F.3d 1270, 1291-1292 (9th Cir. 1997). The Swiss do not have a comparable criminal prohibition. See Guy Stessens, Money Laundering: A New International Law Enforcement Model 115-116 (2000). Should they? What obligations might they have in this regard under Article 3 of the 1988 Illicit Trafficking Convention?

9. *Extraterritorial reach.* Sections 1956 and 1957 both provide for extraterritorial jurisdiction. Section 1956(f) states:

> There is extraterritorial jurisdiction over the conduct prohibited by this section if—
> (1) the conduct is by a United States citizen or, in the case of a non-United States citizen, the conduct occurs in part in the United States; and
> (2) the transaction or series of related transactions involves funds or monetary instruments of a value exceeding $10,000.

Congress sought to limit extraterritorial jurisdiction "to situations in which the interests of the United States are involved, either because the defendant is a U.S. citizen or because the transaction occurred in whole or in part in the United States." S. Rep. No. 99-433, at 14 (1986). The $10,000 jurisdictional limit was intended to ensure that extraterritorial jurisdiction "is confined to significant cases." Id. If it wished to do so, could Congress expand the scope of extraterritorial jurisdiction? If so, on what basis?

Section 1957(a) states that an offense has been proved if the elements of the crime are met in certain circumstances, and those circumstances are set forth in §1957(d):

> (1) that the offense under this section takes place in the United States or in the special maritime and territorial jurisdiction of the United States; or
> (2) that the offense under this section takes place outside the United States and such special jurisdiction, but the defendant is a United States person. . . .

The Department of Justice requires its prosecutors to secure prior approval from the Asset Forfeiture and Money Laundering Section of the Criminal Division prior to commencing an investigation based solely on the extraterritorial jurisdiction provisions of §§1956 and 1957. See U.S. Dept. of Justice, U.S. Attorneys' Manual §9-105.300. Why might this requirement be imposed in extraterritorial but not domestic cases? Where the illegal conduct charged is clearly within the statutorily prescribed extraterritorial jurisdiction, what considerations, if any, might counsel the Department of Justice to withhold approval of a prosecution?

10. *Comparative penalties.* Violations of §§1956(a)(1) and 1956(a)(2) are felonies punishable by a fine of not more than $500,000 or twice the value of the property involved in the transaction, whichever is greater, and up to 20 years' imprisonment. Violations of §1957 are felonies punishable by a fine and up to 10 years' imprisonment.

Compare these penalties to those authorized under the Swiss statute. Can these differences be justified? Note that Paragraph 4 of Article 3 of the 1988 Illicit Trafficking Convention requires states parties to establish sanctions for the offences set forth in Paragraph 1 taking into account "the grave nature of these offences." Do the Swiss sanctions meet this mandate? Might one look to the maximum penalties provided under Swiss law for other serious crimes to make this determination? Note, for example, that in Switzerland theft carries a maximum sentence of 5 years unless the case involves professional thieves or other aggravating circumstances, in which case the maximum penalty is 10 years; extortion and bribery have a 5-year statutory maximum in the ordinary case; counterfeiting money requires imprisonment of at least 1 year but, at least in minor cases, no more than 3 years; domestic and foreign bribery carry a maximum sentence of 5 years.

Recall the case excerpted earlier in this chapter, *R. v. Public Prosecutor of the Canton of Vaud.* How much time would R. actually receive in Switzerland versus the United States? Note that the advisory U.S. Federal Sentencing Guidelines provide a more accurate picture of what the actual sentence is likely to be than the statutory maximums described above. Although the guidelines are periodically amended, and we do not have sufficient facts about R.'s case to do a thorough analysis in any case, the authors' estimate is that R.'s advisory guidelines sentence, for both the money laundering and the drug offense, and taking into account R.'s criminal history, would be approximately 7 to 9 years (with no provision for parole). In Swiss court, the defendant received 2 years.

11. *Forfeiture.* As the discussion of international efforts to combat money laundering in Section A illustrates, one vital element of the battle is the identification, seizure, and forfeiture of laundered funds. "Switzerland has a sophisticated and comprehensive confiscation regime," as does the United States. FATF-GAFI, Third Mutual Evaluation Report on Anti-money Laundering and Combating the Financing of Terrorism-Switzerland, Summary, at 3 (Oct. 14, 2005). Forfeiture is, however, an exceedingly complex subject, and it cannot be treated in any depth in this volume. We provide the following brief synopsis of the power of the U.S. money laundering forfeiture provisions to explain, in part, the dynamic discussed in the notes above — that is, federal prosecutors' enthusiasm for coming up with novel theories to justify charging money laundering.

In brief, U.S. money laundering charges permit the government to seek civil or criminal forfeiture under 18 U.S.C. §§981 and 982. In criminal cases, §982 provides that "[t]he court in imposing sentence on a person convicted of an offense in violation of section 1956, 1957, or 1960 of this title, *shall* order that the person forfeit to the United States any property, real or personal, involved in such offense, or any property traceable to such property." (Emphasis added.) The United States' money laundering forfeiture provisions are broader than the provisions available to claim the proceeds of most other types of wrongdoing. As Stefan D. Cassella explains:

> Most federal criminal statutes now authorize the forfeiture of assets as part of the punishment that may be imposed when a defendant is convicted of a criminal offense. But not all forfeiture provisions are created equal. Most statutes authorizing forfeiture are narrow provisions that allow the government to confiscate the proceeds of the crime giving rise to the forfeiture, and the property that is directly traceable to it, but nothing more. A person who engages in corporate fraud or makes off with public funds may have to forfeit the ill-gotten gains, but in most cases, he cannot be made to part with the untainted property that he used to commit the crime. Other statutes go a step further,

permitting the forfeiture of "facilitating property," like the drug smuggler's car or the counterfeiter's computer, that made the crime easier to commit or harder to detect.

In money laundering cases, however, the statutes are broader still, authorizing the forfeiture of any "property involved" in the money laundering offense. . . . [T]hat means that in the appropriate circumstances the government can recover the money being laundered, the money or other property that is commingled with it or obtained in exchange for it when the money laundering transaction takes place, and other property that facilitates the money laundering offense. Examples include clean money the defendant used to conceal or disguise laundered funds, the legitimate business he used as a front for his money laundering operations, and real property, securities, and luxury items in which he invested the laundered funds to keep them hidden from view. Only the forfeiture statutes for RICO and terrorism offenses provide the government with a law enforcement tool that is so sweeping in scope or so powerful in application.

Stefan D. Cassella, The Forfeiture of Property Involved in Money Laundering Offenses, 7 Buff. Crim. L. Rev. 583, 585-586 (2004).

C. CHALLENGES FOR THE FUTURE

As noted in the introduction to this chapter, one area that has received increased interest after September 11 has been "criminal financing." Another is what the FATF refers to as "Alternative Remittance Systems," the United States terms "Informal Value Transfer Systems," and Hong Kong calls "Unregulated Remittance Centers."[27] These systems operate on every continent, in different variations. What they have in common is that they are alternatives to formal banking; they are often preferred "over formal money transfer systems because they are cheaper and more pleasant, have lower transaction costs and increased confidentiality."[28] In some parts of the world, these informal systems are virtually the only means of money transfers due to inadequate banking facilities. Described below is one variant of these systems.

HEARING ON HAWALA AND UNDERGROUND TERRORIST FINANCING MECHANISMS, PREPARED STATEMENT OF MR. PATRICK JOST, SRA INTERNATIONAL

Before the Subcomm. on Intl. Trade & Fin. of the S. Comm. on Banking, Hous., and Urb. Aff., 107th Cong. (Nov. 14, 2001)

. . . [T]here are two essential characteristics of hawala — the first is a network of hawala brokers or dealers, called hawaladars in Hindi and Urdu and often referred to as "hawala operators" in the English language South Asian press, and the second is the trust that exists not only between hawaladars but between hawaladars and their clients.

With this context, let me proceed with an example of a typical hawala transaction. Suppose an individual in a large US city wishes to remit the sum of $5,000 to a relative

---

27. S. Selena Nelson, Note, Regulating Money Laundering in the United States and Hong Kong: A Post 9-11 Comparison, 6 Wash. U. Global Stud. L. Rev. 723, 724 (2007).
28. Id. at 729.

living in South Asia. This individual contacts a hawaladar, and they negotiate terms. These terms often include the rate of exchange and the manner of delivery of the money. The hawaladar will take the money, and make contact with an associate in or near the place where the money is to be delivered. This second hawaladar will make the necessary delivery arrangements. This can be done by sending a courier to the person with the money, or by providing a phone number to be called to arrange delivery.

It is useful to think of the above example as a hawala "theme"; and what actually happens, is, as in improvised music the "variations" on the theme. The hawala system is very flexible, so many variations occur. This can be seen in the ways hawaladars settle their debts. Sometimes, the flow between two hawaladars is balanced, so, in a reasonable amount of time, debts are settled automatically.

Another possibility is that the hawaladar has money in a country and cannot remove it due to measures designed to counter capital flight. These measures can be circumvented via hawala. The hawaladar accepts money in his current country of residence, and has an associate "drain" the supply of money in the other country until it is gone.

Some hawaladars utilize invoice manipulation schemes to settle their debts. These schemes are often necessary because of remittance controls. For example, a hawaladar operating in the United States could send an associate $100,000 by purchasing $200,000 worth of goods that his associate wants. He ships the merchandise with an invoice for $100,000. The associate receives the merchandise and pays the first hawaladar $100,000. This payment appears to be legitimate because of the shipment and the invoice. The associate has $200,000 worth of merchandise for which only $100,000 was paid. This technique, known as "under invoicing" is one way of circumventing remittance controls as well as settling debts between hawaladars.

The inverse of this, "over invoicing," also exists. It would, for example, be used to transfer money to the United States. A hawaladar operating in the United States would purchase $100,000 worth of goods that his associate wants. He would ship the goods with an invoice for $300,000. Payment of this amount would allow the associate to move $200,000 to the United States. Like "under invoicing" this technique can be used to circumvent remittance controls and settle debts between hawaladars.

What might be termed "debt assignment" also takes place. If hawaladar A owes money to hawaladar B, and hawaladar B owes money to hawaladars C and D, hawaladar B might ask A to settle the debts with C and D, settling his debt with B. As with other aspects of hawala transactions, there is a great deal of flexibility. Hawaladars will use these settlement methods — or variations on theme — as needed and dictated by circumstances.

The majority of hawala transfers out of the United States are remittances by South Asians living and working here to friends or relatives still in South Asia. There are several reasons for this. The first is a cultural preference for hawala. Hawala was developed as a remittance mechanism in South Asia before the appearance of "western" style banking, and continues to be used. The second is cost effectiveness. Since hawaladars do not necessarily respect official exchange rates, they can often deliver more rupees per dollar than an institution that respects official exchange rates. This is an important part of hawala; hawaladars make a certain amount of their profit off of exchange rate speculation, and much "colorful language" is often used while bargaining over very small differences in exchange rates! A third is speed — many hawaladars offer service "in two hours" even though 24 hours is more realistic, given time differences, but is, in any case, almost always faster than bank transfers. The final consideration is reliability, closely related to the trust component of hawala—transfers are not "lost in the mail" or "held up at the bank"; when someone places an order with a hawaladar, there is little if any doubt that the money will be delivered.

In some respects, the hawala system is self-regulating. Hawaladars form an extended community, and it is rare for them to defraud one another or their clients. In the rare cases where this has happened, other hawaladars have been known to make good on the debts of their colleague. While it is possible that some sort of "disciplinary action" will be taken, a hawaladar who commits fraud is one who cannot be trusted. Without the trust of other hawaladars, he can no longer function effectively.

To summarize, hawala is a system that is cost effective, quick, reliable and secure. These characteristics of hawala account, in large part, for its use instead of other remittance systems. There are also places, like Afghanistan, where hawala is the only viable remittance system. These factors also account for the use of hawala by certain terrorist organizations. Osama bin Ladin is a Saudi with connections to Afghanistan and Somalia. All of these are countries where hawala is the preferred means of remitting money.

Terrorists, drug traffickers and other criminals also exploit another characteristic of hawala. This is its frequent lack of a complete paper trail documenting all parties to a transaction. It is not uncommon for hawaladars to maintain only logs of debts with other hawaladars. Records of remittance clients and beneficiaries are kept only long enough to facilitate the transaction, and the debt logs are often kept until the debts have been settled.

The lack of a paper trail is but one of several difficulties in investigating the criminal use of hawala. Even when records are available, they are rarely in English, necessitating translation. Even though the records may contain names of other hawaladars, the names are rarely, if ever complete enough to facilitate proper identification—references to "Ali Hussein" or "Shahbhai" are typical.

The most significant investigative barrier is probably the fact that "hawala behavior" lies well outside the cultural experience of most US investigators. Hawala is a system where large amounts of money are handed over without receipts, confirmation numbers, or identification. Hawala transactions take place in the context of a large network unlike a "traditional" corporate structure. The business of hawala is conducted informally, with little in the way of overhead and almost nothing in the way of a regulatory infrastructure, making it, in this respect, nearly the antithesis of banking.

I would like to devote the remainder of my remarks to possible solutions to the problems posed by hawala.

Recent legislative changes calling for the registration and supervision of hawaladars, as well as for identifying hawala transactions as potentially suspicious are commendable first steps, but I do believe that much remains to be done.

There are two areas that I believe need to be addressed. First, I believe that it is essential for banks and other financial institutions already required to file Suspicious Activity Reports (SARs) to develop an understanding of "what hawala looks like" and act accordingly. This will help in the identification of hawaladars. If a bank has a client who is conducting hawala transactions, and this client is identified as doing so, and a SAR is filed, this can be used by the authorities to determine whether or not the hawaladar is licensed appropriately. . . .

Even though it is certainly possible for terrorists and other criminals to move vast amounts of money into the United States via hawala with little or no trace, some of this money is useless unless it can be converted into an acceptable form. This necessitates a relationship between banks and hawala. This relationship is a potential vulnerability in a hawala money laundering or terrorist financing scheme, and this vulnerability should be exploited. . . .

The second area deals with the difference between money laundering and terrorist financing. In brief, money laundering is the process of taking money from "dirty" sources and making it "clean" so that it can be used for what are often legitimate purposes.

This is not always the case with terrorist financing. In many cases, terrorist money has a "clean" origin and a "dirty" purpose. Some terrorists . . . are wealthy, and use their own funds — often derived from legitimate sources — to finance acts of terror. Other terrorists make use of funds received from charities; some of these organizations appear to have been established solely for the purpose of raising money for terrorists, others are possible unwitting participants in terrorism.

In both of these cases, the money comes from legitimate sources — business dealings or charitable contributions — so what happens with it is not money laundering. What happens in many instances of terrorist financing can almost be seen as the inverse of money laundering. "Clean money" becomes "dirty money" — money used to finance acts of terror.

So, from one perspective, and with a certain amount of simplification, money laundering and terrorist financing are opposites. In money laundering, dirty money becomes clean; in terrorist financing, clean money becomes dirty. From another perspective, however, the processes have much in common. . . . I believe that it is essential that what is known about terrorist financing be made available to financial institutions to assist them not only in complying with reporting requirements but to aid them in developing new information about methods. Even though a certain amount of what has been learned about money laundering can be used, terrorist financing is not always the same, so new indicators will have to be developed.

NOTES AND QUESTIONS

At least since 1992, Congress has prohibited illegal money transmitting businesses in 18 U.S.C. §1960. This section was generally aimed at money transmitters who failed to secure the requisite state licenses for their businesses. See Money Laundering: Panelists Explore USA PATRIOT Act's Effects on Anti-money Laundering Laws, 70 Crim. L. Rep. (BNA) 536 (2002). In the USA PATRIOT Act, however, Congress made a number of changes to the statute that earned §1960 at least one commentator's vote for the measure that would emerge out of the Act as the new "prosecutor's darling." Id.

Section 1960 now provides that whoever knowingly conducts, controls, manages, supervises, directs, or owns all or part of an unlicensed money transmitting business is guilty of a felony punishable by fine and up to 5 years' imprisonment. This section (both before the USA PATRIOT Act and after) includes within the definition of "money transmitting" a wealth of activity. Thus, the term "money transmitting" includes "transferring funds on behalf of the public by any and all means including but not limited to transfers within this country or to locations abroad by wire, check, draft, facsimile, or courier." §1960(b)(2). Further, in the USA PATRIOT Act, Congress expanded the definition of the proscribed "unlicensed money transmitting business" to include

a money transmitting business which affects interstate or foreign commerce in any manner or degree and . . . involves the transportation or transmission of funds that are known to the defendant to have been derived from a criminal offense or are intended to be used to promote or support unlawful activity.

§1960(b)(1)(C). Unlike §§1956 and 1957, §1960 is not tied to a list of "specified unlawful activities" and thus potentially applies to defendants who transmit funds derived from, or in support of, *all* types of federal (and perhaps state or foreign) crimes. Would the hawala system be considered a network of "money transmitting" businesses?

CHAPTER
14

Corruption

As UN Secretary-General Kofi Annan explained in lauding the conclusion of the U.N. Convention Against Corruption:

> Corruption is an insidious plague that has a wide range of corrosive effects on societies. It undermines democracy and the rule of law, leads to violations of human rights, distorts markets, erodes the quality of life, and allows organized crime, terrorism and other threats to human security to flourish.
>
> This evil phenomenon is found in all countries—big and small, rich and poor—but it is in the developing world that its effects are most destructive. Corruption hurts the poor disproportionately—by diverting funds intended for development, undermining government's ability to provide basic services, feeding inequality and injustice, and discouraging foreign aid and investment. Corruption is a key element in economic underperformance, and a major obstacle to poverty alleviation and development.[1]

"Corruption" encompasses a wide variety of behavior by public and private actors who misuse their positions of trust for personal gain. Our principal focus, like that of the international community at present, is on bribery of public officials by those seeking to obtain or retain business. The World Bank has "conservative[ly] estimate[d]" that the value of bribes paid by the private sector to the public sector annually is US $1 trillion.[2] This figure does not include the embezzlement of public funds, the theft or misuse of public assets, or the dollars lost to nepotism and other such misuses of office. Thus, for example, it does not include what Transparency International has estimated as the between US $15 and $35 billion President Suharto embezzled in Indonesia and the US $5 billion each that Presidents Marcos, Mobutu, and Abacha stole from the Philippines, Zaire, and Nigeria, respectively.[3]

Moreover, Transparency International makes a good case that these numbers can never completely capture the political, economic, social, and environmental costs of corruption:

> The following example illustrates the dilemma of pressing the issue into facts and figures: A power plant is being built somewhere in the world, at a cost of US $100 million. It could be argued that—were it not for corruption—the cost could have been as low as US $80 million. The financial damage to the public would then be US $20 million.

---

1. Kofi Annan, Statement on the Adoption by the General Assembly of the United Nations Convention Against Corruption (Oct. 31, 2003), http://www.un.org/News/Press/docs/2003/sgsm8977.doc.htm.
2. Daniel Kaufmann, Six Questions on the Cost of Corruption, http://www.worldbank.org (search for "Six Questions on the Cost of Corruption") (last visited July 13, 2009).
3. Id.

In practice, quite often projects are planned simply so that those involved can make huge private profits. Assuming that the power plant was superfluous, the financial damage would have to be assessed at US $100 million. Yet no major construction project leaves the environment untouched. The results may be: increased pollution, a lowering of land prices, resettlement of local residents, an increased debt burden for the country, etc. This calculation — probably closest to reality — is immensely complex. On a global scale, it seems almost impossible. But even if one were to calculate the environmental damage, the increase of the debt burden and other factors, how would one measure the erosion of public confidence and the deterioration of a government's legitimacy, which are the direct result of corruption?[4]

Oftentimes, the corrupt payments to government officials are made by juridical and natural persons who are nationals of other countries. Such transnational corrupt payments constitute a threat to the international community as a whole: "Transnational bribery damages the quality of [states'] relationship[s] and contributes to global instability. Bribery debilitates governments, and cripples a channel critical to transnational relations."[5] Although many nations have outlawed bribery of their own government officials under national law (what we refer to as "domestic bribery"), for many years the United States was alone in prohibiting corrupt payments to *foreign* officials (what we call "transnational bribery"). The United States' decision to criminalize such conduct resulted from the disclosure in the 1970s that hundreds of U.S. corporations had been involved in over $300 million in illegal payments to domestic and foreign officials. Congress determined that such bribes were "counter to the moral expectations and values of the American public," "erode[d] public confidence in the integrity of the free market system," "embarrass[ed] friendly governments, lower[ed] the esteem for the United States among the citizens of foreign nations, and len[t] credence to the suspicions sown by foreign opponents of the United States that American enterprises exert a corrupting influence on the political processes of their nations."[6] Accordingly, in 1977 Congress enacted the Foreign Corrupt Practices Act (FCPA), codified as amended at 15 U.S.C. §78dd-1 et seq. Congress's object in passing the FCPA was to establish ethical business practices and standards for U.S. companies that operate in foreign countries, without regard for the customs and practices of those countries.

Over time, the international community has come to recognize the dangers that corruption poses to development, stability, and peace and, since 1996, many significant anticorruption regional conventions have come into effect: the Organization for Economic Cooperation and Development's (OECD's) Convention on Combating Bribery of Foreign Public Officials in International Business Transactions (OECD Convention), the Inter-American Convention Against Corruption (IACAC) negotiated in the Organization of American States (OAS), the African Union Convention on Preventing and Combating Corruption, and the Criminal and Civil Law Conventions on Corruption in the Council of Europe. The jurisdiction of international

---

4. Transparency International, Frequently Asked Questions About Corruption, http://www.transparency.org/news_room/faq/corruption_faq (follow "Can the costs of corruption be quantified?" hyperlink) (last visited July 13, 2009).

5. Philip Nichols, Are Extraterritorial Restrictions on Bribery a Viable and Desirable International Policy Goal Under the Global Conditions of the Late Twentieth Century? Increasing Global Security by Controlling Transnational Bribery, 20 Mich. J. Intl. L. 451, 476 (1999); see also Alejandro Posadas, Combating Corruption Under International Law, 10 Duke J. Comp. & Intl. L. 345 (2000).

6. H.R. Rep. No. 95-640, at 4-5 (1977); see also S. Rep. No. 95-114, at 3-4 (1977), reprinted in 1977 U.S.C.C.A.N. 4098, 4100-4101.

criminal tribunals does not extend to corruption.[7] The international community has come together, however, to craft the United Nations Convention Against Corruption (UNCAC), which entered into force on December 14, 2005, and as of mid-2009 claims 136 states parties.

The United States' FCPA regime is complex, and many U.S. companies operating overseas rely heavily on expert counsel to ensure that they are compliant. Furthermore, to implement its obligations under the OECD Convention, the United States expanded the reach of the FCPA to include non-U.S. companies and actors previously not regulated; the amended FCPA, then, significantly increases the peril of foreign businesses and their agents. Enforcement of the FCPA is also booming. In 2003, there were 8 reported FCPA enforcement actions; in 2008, there were 37 reported FCPA actions, including a "blockbuster" settlement in which Siemens AG pled guilty to violating the FCPA and agreed to pay a record-breaking $800 million fine ($350 million in civil disgorgement paid to the Securities and Exchange Commission and a $450 million criminal fine paid to the Department of Justice).[8]

The materials that follow begin with a set of problems. Use these problems to frame your reading in the rest of this chapter. They will help you to conquer the complexities of the FCPA statute (discussed in Section B) and to better understand and assess the legal regime constructed by the international community in response to the growing problem of transborder corruption (discussed in Section C).

A. PROBLEMS

Even in a federal criminal code brimming with examples of vague and poorly worded statutes, the FCPA is notable for its amazingly convoluted drafting. Never a beauty to begin with, the FCPA has been made uglier still by a congressional predisposition to slap amendments onto the statute with no apparent regard for the integrity or coherence of its prohibitions. For these reasons, you will need to navigate this statute with great care. In getting your bearings, pay particular attention to *who* is covered by the anti-bribery provisions (that is, who the potential defendants are) and *in what circumstances* such persons are covered.

In aid of that effort, work through the following hypotheticals.[9] You should also return to these problems when studying the international materials in

---

7. Some argue, however, that corruption should be treated as an international crime. See, e.g., Ilias Bantekas, Corruption as an International Crime and Crime Against Humanity, 4 J. Intl. Crim. J. 466 (2006); Sonja Starr, Extraordinary Crimes at Ordinary Times: International Justice Beyond Crisis Situations, 101 Nw. U. L. Rev. 1257 (2007).

8. See, e.g., Arnold & Porter LLP, Client Advisory: Survey of Recent FCPA Developments (Feb. 2009), http://arnoldandporterllp.com/resources/documents/CA_SurveyofRecentFCPADevelopments_15-page_012209.pdf. The previous record FCPA fine was $44 million. In addition, "Siemens announced that it was settling a parallel corruption probe that German authorities were conducting for about US$815 million, bringing Siemens' total settlement bill to US$1.6 billion." Id. at 2. The United States alleged that the German company paid 4,200 bribes totaling more than $1 billion to government officials in 10 countries. Id.

9. Many of the countries chosen for the hypotheticals were drawn from among those perceived to be most corrupt according to Transparency International's Corruption Perceptions Index 2007, available at http://www.transparency.org/policy_research/surveys_indices/cpi (last visited July 13, 2009).

Section C of this chapter, and ask whether the results reached would be different were the various international conventions discussed to be implemented in full as domestic law.

A. Bolox is a Pakistani company that has its principal place of business in Pakistan. It is trying to sell airplane parts to the Indonesian government. One of its employees, Petty Bone, a U.S. citizen resident in Indonesia, gives an official in the Indonesian government $20,000 in cash to secure three work visas for Bolox employees. The employee also gives a candidate for the Indonesian legislature first class plane tickets to Pakistan for the legislator and his extended family. The purported object of the candidate's trip is to allow him to visit Bolox's manufacturing facility. With Bone's knowledge, the candidate cashes in the tickets and keeps the money. Could Bolox be prosecuted under the FCPA? Could Bolox's employee? The candidate? What if the employee who made the payment and provided the tickets was Indonesian but Bolox was listed on the New York Stock Exchange? If the payment for work visas was only $1,000, would any of the participants be liable under the FCPA? Under the UN Convention Against Corruption (UNCAC)?

B. Marcus Blotonk is a citizen of Chad residing in New York. He is a consultant who advises businesses that wish to invest in Chad and surrounding countries. He arranges for a company, Cauliflower Inc., that is chartered in Chad but is a wholly owned subsidiary of a U.S. company, to pay a "consulting fee" to his cousin, a poor yet deserving student resident in Chad. Blotonk's cousin is married to a woman whose uncle is a senior official in the government of Chad. Could Blotonk, his cousin, his cousin's wife, her uncle, and the U.S. company be prosecuted under the FCPA for this payment? Would the exposure of these persons change if the uncle mailed a note to Blotonk, thanking him for his "contribution" and promising to keep an "eye out" for Cauliflower's interests? What would be their potential exposure under the UNCAC?

C. Reginald Potty is a French national residing in France and working for a French company that is organized under French law and has its principal place of business in France. Potty gives an official in the government of Turkmenistan $40,000 in exchange for the official's "yes" vote on pending legislation that would ease the French company's entry into the market for widgets in Turkmenistan. Potty's French bank e-mails confirmation of the wire transfer to Potty's AOL e-mail account. Can Potty, the French company, and the legislator be prosecuted under the FCPA? Could Potty and the French company be prosecuted under the FCPA if Potty had instead given the $40,000 to the director of a private company in Turkmenistan to obtain an exclusive subcontract for widgets for the French company? Would their exposure change under the UNCAC?

D. Retrograde, a company that is organized under the laws of the Cayman Islands but has its principal place of business in Texas, enters into a joint venture with Likely, a company chartered and resident in Bangladesh, for the sale of dredging equipment to the government of Bangladesh. Retrograde has agreed to provide the financing and technical expertise for the venture, while Likely will provide the facilities, labor, material, and other resources necessary to the project in Bangladesh. In the joint venture agreement, Likely represents that it will comply with the FCPA. Likely advises Retrograde executives in Texas that the procurement process has been held up because government officials are worried about the quality of the equipment; Likely requests an additional $50,000 in financing to "iron out" these difficulties. Retrograde instructs a German bank with which it has a line of credit to release the funds to Likely. Can Retrograde, Likely, and their agents be prosecuted?

B.   ELEMENTS OF AN FCPA ANTI-BRIBERY OFFENSE

UNITED STATES v. KAY
359 F.3d 738 (5th Cir. 2004)

WIENER, Circuit Judge:

Plaintiff-appellant, the United States of America ("government") appeals the district court's grant of the motion of defendants-appellees David Kay and Douglas Murphy ("defendants") to dismiss the Superseding Indictment ("indictment") that charged them with bribery of foreign officials in violation of the Foreign Corrupt Practices Act ("FCPA")[, 15 U.S.C. §78dd-1 et seq. (2000).] In their dismissal motion, defendants contended that the indictment failed to state an offense against them. The principal dispute in this case is whether, if proved beyond a reasonable doubt, the conduct that the indictment ascribed to defendants in connection with the alleged bribery of Haitian officials to understate customs duties and sales taxes on rice shipped to Haiti to assist American Rice, Inc. in obtaining or retaining business was sufficient to constitute an offense under the FCPA. Underlying this question of sufficiency of the contents of the indictment is the preliminary task of ascertaining the scope of the FCPA, which in turn requires us to construe the statute. . . .

American Rice, Inc. ("ARI") is a Houston-based company that exports rice to foreign countries, including Haiti. Rice Corporation of Haiti ("RCH"), a wholly owned subsidiary of ARI, was incorporated in Haiti to represent ARI's interests and deal with third parties there. As an aspect of Haiti's standard importation procedure, its customs officials assess duties based on the quantity and value of rice imported into the country. Haiti also requires businesses that deliver rice there to remit an advance deposit against Haitian sales taxes, based on the value of that rice, for which deposit a credit is eventually allowed on Haitian sales tax returns when filed.

In 2001, a grand jury charged Kay with violating the FCPA and subsequently returned the indictment, which charges both Kay and Murphy with 12 counts of FCPA violations. As is readily apparent on its face, the indictment contains detailed factual allegations about (1) the timing and purposes of Congress's enactment of the FCPA, (2) ARI and its status as an "issuer" under the FCPA, (3) RCH and its status as a wholly owned subsidiary and "service corporation" of ARI, representing ARI's interest in Haiti, and (4) defendants' citizenship, their positions as officers of ARI, and their status as "issuers" and "domestic concerns" under the FCPA. The indictment also spells out in detail how Kay and Murphy allegedly orchestrated the bribing of Haitian customs officials to accept false bills of lading and other documentation that intentionally understated by one-third the quantity of rice shipped to Haiti, thereby significantly reducing ARI's customs duties and sales taxes. In this regard, the indictment alleges the details of the bribery scheme's machinations, including the preparation of duplicate documentation, the calculation of bribes as a percentage of the value of the rice not reported, the surreptitious payment of monthly retainers to Haitian officials, and the defendants' purported authorization of withdrawals of funds from ARI's bank accounts with which to pay the Haitian officials, either directly or through intermediaries—all to produce substantially reduced Haitian customs and tax costs to ARI. Further, the indictment alleges discrete facts regarding ARI's domestic incorporation and place of business, as well as the particular instrumentalities of interstate and foreign commerce that defendants used or caused to be used in carrying out the purported bribery.

In contrast, without any factual allegations, the indictment merely paraphrases the one element of the statute that is central to this appeal, only conclusionally accusing defendants of causing payments to be made to Haitian customs officials:

> for purposes of influencing acts and decisions of such foreign officials in their official capacities, inducing such foreign officials to do and omit to do acts in violation of their lawful duty, and to obtain an improper advantage, in order to *assist* American Rice, Inc. in *obtaining and retaining business* for, and directing business to American Rice, Inc. and Rice Corporation of Haiti. (Emphasis added.)

Although it recites in great detail the discrete facts that the government intends to prove to satisfy each other element of an FCPA violation, the indictment recites no particularized facts that, if proved, would satisfy the "assist" aspect of the business nexus element of the statute, i.e., the nexus between the illicit tax savings produced by the bribery and the assistance such savings provided or were intended to provide in *obtaining or retaining business* for ARI and RCH. Neither does the indictment contain any factual allegations whatsoever to identify just *what* business in Haiti (presumably some rice-related commercial activity) the illicit customs and tax savings assisted (or were intended to assist) in obtaining or retaining, or just *how* these savings were supposed to assist in such efforts. In other words, the indictment recites no facts that could demonstrate an actual or intended cause-and-effect nexus between reduced taxes and obtaining identified business or retaining identified business opportunities. . . .

Because an offense under the FCPA requires that the alleged bribery be committed for the purpose of inducing foreign officials to commit unlawful acts, the results of which will assist in obtaining or retaining business in their country, the questions before us in this appeal are (1) whether bribes to obtain illegal but favorable tax and customs treatment can ever come within the scope of the statute, and (2) if so, whether, in combination, there are minimally sufficient facts alleged in the indictment to inform the defendants regarding the nexus between, on the one hand, Haitian taxes avoided through bribery, and, on the other hand, assistance in getting or keeping some business or business opportunity in Haiti.

B. Words of the FCPA . . .

The FCPA prohibits payments to foreign officials for purposes of:

> (i) influencing any act or decision of such foreign official in his official capacity, (ii) inducing such foreign official to do or omit to do any act in violation of the lawful duty of such official, or (iii) securing any improper advantage . . . in order to assist [the company making the payment] in obtaining or retaining business for or with, or directing business to, any person. [15 U.S.C. §78dd-1(a)(1).]

None contend that the FCPA criminalizes every payment to a foreign official: It criminalizes only those payments that are intended to (1) influence a foreign official to act or make a decision in his official capacity, or (2) induce such an official to perform or refrain from performing some act in violation of his duty, or (3) secure some wrongful advantage to the payor. And even then, the FCPA criminalizes these kinds of payments only if the result they are intended to produce — their *quid pro quo* — will *assist* (or is intended to assist) the payor in efforts to get or keep some *business* for or with "any person." Thus, the first question of statutory interpretation presented in this appeal is whether payments made to foreign officials to obtain unlawfully reduced customs duties or sales tax liabilities can ever fall within the scope of the FCPA, i.e., whether the illicit payments made to obtain a reduction of revenue liabilities can *ever* constitute the kind of bribery that is proscribed by the FCPA. The district court answered this question in the negative; only if we answer it in the affirmative will we need to analyze the sufficiency of the factual allegations of the indictment as to the one element of the crime contested here.

The principal thrust of the defendants' argument is that the business nexus element, i.e., the "assist . . . in obtaining or retaining business" element, narrowly limits the statute's applicability to those payments that are intended to obtain a foreign official's approval of a bid for a new government contract or the renewal of an existing government contract. In contrast, the government insists that, in addition to payments to officials that lead directly to getting or renewing business contracts, the statute covers payments that indirectly advance ("assist") the payor's goal of obtaining or retaining foreign business with or for some person. The government reasons that paying reduced customs duties and sales taxes on imports, as is purported to have occurred in this case, is the type of "improper advantage" that *always* will assist in obtaining or retaining business in a foreign country, and thus is always covered by the FCPA.

In approaching this issue, the district court concluded that the FCPA's language is ambiguous, and proceeded to review the statute's legislative history. We agree with the court's finding of ambiguity for several reasons. Perhaps our most significant statutory construction problem results from the failure of the language of the FCPA to give a clear indication of the exact scope of the business nexus element; that is, the proximity of the required nexus between, on the one hand, the anticipated results of the foreign official's bargained-for action or inaction, and, on the other hand, the assistance provided by or expected from those results in helping the briber to obtain or retain business. . . .

Second, the parties' diametrically opposed but reasonable contentions demonstrate that the ordinary and natural meaning of the statutory language *is* genuinely debatable and thus ambiguous. For instance, the word "business" can be defined at any point along a continuum from "a volume of trade," to "the purchase and sale of goods in an attempt to make a profit," to "an assignment" or a "project." Thus, dictionary definitions can support both (1) the government's broader interpretation of the business nexus language as encompassing any type of commercial activity, and (2) defendants' argument that "obtain or retain business" connotes a more pedestrian understanding of establishing or renewing a particular commercial arrangement. Similarly, although the word "assist" suggests a somewhat broader statutory scope,[10] it does not connote specificity or define either how proximate or how remote the foreign official's anticipated actions that constitute assistance must or may be to the business obtained or retained. . . .

Neither does the remainder of the statutory language clearly express an exclusively broad or exclusively narrow understanding of the business nexus element. The extent to which the exception for routine governmental action ("facilitating payments" or "grease") is narrowly drawn reasonably suggests that Congress was carving out very

---

10. [Court's footnote 18:] Invoking basic economic principles, the SEC reasoned in its amicus brief that securing reduced taxes and duties on imports through bribery enables ARI to reduce its cost of doing business, thereby giving it an "improper advantage" over actual or potential competitors, and enabling it to do more business, or remain in a market it might otherwise leave.

limited categories of permissible payments from an otherwise broad statutory prohibition.[11] As defendants suggest, however, another plausible implication for including
an express statutory explanation that routine governmental action does not include
decisions "to award new business to or to continue business with a particular party,"
[15 U.S.C. §78dd-1(f)(3)(B),] is that Congress was focusing entirely on identifiable
decisions made by foreign officials in granting or renewing specific business arrangements in foreign countries, and not on a more general panoply of competitive business advantages. . . .

C. FCPA Legislative History

As the statutory language itself is amenable to more than one reasonable interpretation, it is ambiguous as a matter of law. We turn therefore to legislative history in our
effort to ascertain Congress's true intentions.

1. 1977 Legislative History

Congress enacted the FCPA in 1977, in response to recently discovered but widespread bribery of foreign officials by United States business interests. Congress
resolved to interdict such bribery, not just because it is morally and economically
suspect, but also because it was causing foreign policy problems for the United States.
In particular, these concerns arose from revelations that United States defense contractors and oil companies had made large payments to high government officials in
Japan, the Netherlands, and Italy. Congress also discovered that more than 400 corporations had made questionable or illegal payments in excess of $300 million to
foreign officials for a wide range of favorable actions on behalf of the companies.

In deciding to criminalize this type of commercial bribery, the House and Senate
each proposed similarly far-reaching, but non-identical, legislation. In its bill, the
House intended "broadly [to] prohibit[ ] transactions that are *corruptly* intended
to induce the recipient to use his or her influence to affect *any* act or decision of a
foreign official. . . ." Thus, the House bill contained no limiting "business nexus"
element. Reflecting a somewhat narrower purpose, the Senate expressed its desire to
ban payments made for the purpose of inducing foreign officials to act "so as to direct
business to any person, maintain an established business opportunity with any person,
divert any business opportunity from any person or influence the enactment or promulgation of legislation or regulations of that government or instrumentality."

---

11. [Court's footnote 19:] Section 78dd-1(b) excepts from the statutory scope "any facilitating or
expediting payment to a foreign official . . . the purpose of which is to expedite or to service the performance of a routine governmental action by a foreign official. . . ." 15 U.S.C. §78dd-1(b). Section 78dd-
1(f)(3)(A), in turn, provides that:

> [T]he term "routine governmental action" means only an action which is ordinarily and
> commonly performed by a foreign official in —
> (i) obtaining permits, licenses, or other official documents to qualify a person to do busi-
> ness in a foreign country;
> (ii) processing governmental papers, such as visas and work orders;
> (iii) providing police protection, mail pick-up and delivery, or scheduling inspections
> associated with contract performance or inspections related to transit of goods across
> country;
> (iv) providing phone service, power and water supply, loading and unloading cargo, or
> protecting perishable products or commodities from deterioration; or
> (v) actions of a similar nature.

15 U.S.C. §78dd-1(f)(3)(A).

At conference, compromise language "clarified the scope of the prohibition by requiring that the purpose of the payment must be to influence any act or decision of a foreign official . . . so as to assist an issuer in obtaining, retaining or directing business to any person." In the end, then, Congress adopted the Senate's proposal to prohibit only those payments designed to induce a foreign official to act in a way that is intended to facilitate ("assist") in obtaining or retaining of business.

Congress expressly emphasized that it did not intend to prohibit "so-called grease or facilitating payments," such as "payments for expediting shipments through customs or placing a transatlantic telephone call, securing required permits, or obtaining adequate police protection, transactions which may involve even the proper performance of duties." Instead of making an express textual exception for these types of non-covered payments, the respective committees of the two chambers sought to distinguish permissible grease payments from prohibited bribery by only prohibiting payments that induce an official to act "corruptly," i.e., actions requiring him "to misuse his official position" and his discretionary authority, not those "essentially ministerial" actions that "merely move a particular matter toward an eventual act or decision or which do not involve any discretionary action."

In short, Congress sought to prohibit the type of bribery that (1) prompts officials to misuse their discretionary authority and (2) disrupts market efficiency and United States foreign relations, at the same time recognizing that smaller payments intended to expedite ministerial actions should remain outside of the scope of the statute. . . .

To divine the categories of bribery Congress did and did not intend to prohibit, we must look to the Senate's proposal, because the final statutory language was drawn from it, and from the SEC Report on which the Senate's legislative proposal was based. In distinguishing among the types of illegal payments that United States entities were making at the time, the SEC Report identified four principal categories: (1) payments "made in an effort to procure special and unjustified favors or advantages in the enactment or *administration of the tax* or other *laws*" of a foreign country; (2) payments "made with the intent to assist the company in obtaining or retaining government contracts"; (3) payments "to persuade low-level government officials to perform functions or services which they are obliged to perform as part of their governmental responsibilities, but which they may refuse or delay unless compensated" ("grease"), and (4) political contributions. The SEC thus exhibited concern about a wide range of questionable payments (explicitly including the kind at issue here) that were resulting in millions of dollars being recorded falsely in corporate books and records.

As noted, the Senate Report explained that the statute should apply to payments intended "to *direct business* to any person, *maintain an established business opportunity* with any person, divert any business opportunity from any person or *influence the enactment or promulgation of legislation or regulations* of that government or instrumentality." We observe initially that the Senate only loosely addressed the categories of conduct highlighted by the SEC Report. Although the Senate's proposal picked up the SEC's concern with a business nexus, it did not expressly cover bribery influencing the administration of tax laws or seeking favorable tax treatment. It is clear, however, that even though the Senate was particularly concerned with bribery intended to secure new business, it was also mindful of bribes that influence legislative or regulatory actions, and those that maintain established business opportunities, a category of economic activity separate from, and much more capacious than, simply "directing business" to someone.

The statute's ultimate language of "obtaining or retaining" mirrors identical language in the SEC Report. But, whereas the SEC Report highlights payments that go toward "obtaining or retaining *government contracts*," the FCPA, incorporating the Senate Report's language, prohibits payments that assist in obtaining or retaining *business*, not just government contracts. Had the Senate and ultimately Congress wanted to carry over the exact, narrower scope of the SEC Report, they would have adopted the same language. We surmise that, in using the word "business" when it easily could have used the phraseology of SEC Report, Congress intended for the statute to apply to bribes beyond the narrow band of payments sufficient only to "obtain or retain government contracts." The Senate's express intention that the statute apply to corrupt payments that *maintain* business opportunities also supports this conclusion.

For purposes of deciding the instant appeal, the question nevertheless remains whether the Senate, and concomitantly Congress, intended this broader statutory scope to encompass the administration of tax, customs, and other laws and regulations affecting the revenue of foreign states. To reach this conclusion, we must ask whether Congress's remaining expressed desire to prohibit bribery aimed at getting assistance in retaining business or maintaining business opportunities was sufficiently broad to include bribes meant to affect the administration of revenue laws. When we do so, we conclude that the legislative intent was so broad.

Congress was obviously distraught not only about high profile bribes to high-ranking foreign officials, but also by the pervasiveness of foreign bribery by United States businesses and businessmen. Congress thus made the decision to clamp down on bribes intended to prompt foreign officials to misuse their discretionary authority for the benefit of a domestic entity's business in that country. This observation is not diminished by Congress's understanding and accepting that relatively small facilitating payments were, at the time, among the accepted costs of doing business in many foreign countries.

In addition, the concern of Congress with the immorality, inefficiency, and unethical character of bribery presumably does not vanish simply because the tainted payments are intended to secure a favorable decision less significant than winning a contract bid. Obviously, a commercial concern that bribes a foreign government official to award a construction, supply, or services contract violates the statute. Yet, there is little difference between this example and that of a corporation's lawfully obtaining a contract from an honest official or agency by submitting the lowest bid, and — either before or after doing so — bribing a different government official to reduce taxes and thereby ensure that the under-bid venture is nevertheless profitable. Avoiding or lowering taxes reduces operating costs and thus increases profit margins, thereby freeing up funds that the business is otherwise legally obligated to expend. And this, in turn, enables it to take any number of actions to the disadvantage of competitors. Bribing foreign officials to lower taxes and customs duties certainly *can* provide an unfair advantage over competitors and thereby be of assistance to the payor in obtaining or retaining business. This demonstrates that the question whether the defendants' alleged payments constitute a violation of the FCPA truly turns on whether these bribes were intended to lower ARI's cost of doing business in Haiti enough to have a sufficient nexus to garnering business there or to maintaining or increasing business operations that ARI already had there, so as to come within the scope of the business nexus element as Congress used it in the FCPA. Answering this fact question, then, implicates a matter of proof and thus evidence.

In short, the 1977 legislative history, particularly the Senate's proposal and the SEC Report on which it relied, convinces us that Congress meant to prohibit a range of payments wider than only those that directly influence the acquisition or retention of government contracts or similar commercial or industrial arrangements. . . .

The congressional target was bribery paid to engender assistance in improving the business opportunities of the payor or his beneficiary, irrespective of whether that assistance be direct or indirect, and irrespective of whether it be related to administering the law, awarding, extending, or renewing a contract, or executing or preserving an agreement. In light of our reading of the 1977 legislative history, the subsequent 1988 and 1998 legislative history is only important to our analysis to the extent it confirms or conflicts with our initial conclusions about the scope of the statute.

2. 1988 LEGISLATIVE HISTORY

After the FCPA's enactment, United States business entities and executives experienced difficulty in discerning a clear line between prohibited bribes and permissible facilitating payments. As a result, Congress amended the FCPA in 1988, expressly to clarify its original intent in enacting the statute. Both houses insisted that their proposed amendments only clarified ambiguities "without changing the basic intent or effectiveness of the law."

In this effort to crystallize the scope of the FCPA's prohibitions on bribery, Congress chose to identify carefully two types of payments that are not proscribed by the statute. It expressly excepted . . . grease [payments in 15 U.S.C. §78dd-1(b) & (f)(3)(A), reproduced supra Court's note 19]), and it incorporated an affirmative defense for payments that are legal in the country in which they are offered or that constitute bona fide expenditures directly relating to promotion of products or services, or to the execution or performance of a contract with a foreign government or agency.[12] We agree with the position of the government that these 1988 amendments illustrate an intention by Congress to identify very limited exceptions to the kinds of bribes to which the FCPA does not apply. . . . [R]outine governmental action does not include the issuance of *every* official document or *every* inspection, but only (1) documentation that qualifies a party to do business and (2) scheduling an inspection—very narrow categories of largely non-discretionary, ministerial activities performed by mid- or low-level foreign functionaries. In contrast, the FCPA uses broad, general language in prohibiting payments to procure assistance for the payor in obtaining or retaining business, instead of employing similarly detailed language, such as applying the statute only to payments that attempt to secure or renew particular government contracts. . . .[13]

---

12. [Court's footnote 44:] 15 U.S.C. §78dd-1(c). The subsection provides in full:

> It shall be an affirmative defense to actions under subsections (a) or (g) of this section that—
> (1) the payment, gift, offer, or promise of anything of value that was made, was lawful under the written laws and regulations of the foreign official's, political party's, party official's, or candidate's country; or
> (2) the payment, gift, offer, or promise of anything of value that was made, was a reasonable and bona fide expenditure, such as travel and lodging expenses, incurred by or on behalf of a foreign official, party, party official, or candidate and was directly related to—
> (A) the promotion, demonstration, or explanation of products or services; or
> (B) the execution or performance of a contract with a foreign government or agency thereof.

Id.

13. [Court's footnote 46:] Defendants argue that Congress intended to maintain the statute's narrow scope by excluding from the routine governmental action exception "any decision by a foreign official whether, or on what terms, to award new business to or to continue business with a particular party. . . ." 15 U.S.C. §78dd-1(f)(3)(B). We disagree with defendants' contention that the language [of] these amendments indicates a narrow statutory scope. Read in light of Congress's original desire to stamp out foreign bribery run amok, we find that its intention in 1988 to exclude from the grease exception "decision[s] by a foreign official whether, or on what terms . . . to continue business with a particular party" replicates the equally capacious language of prohibition in the 1977 legislative history.

Defendants argue, nevertheless, that Congress's decision to reject House-proposed amendments to the business nexus element constituted its implicit rejection of such a broad reading of the statute. The House bill proposed new language to explain that payments for "obtaining or retaining business" also includes payments made for the "procurement of legislative, judicial, regulatory, or other action in seeking more favorable treatment by a foreign government." Indeed, defendants assert, the proposed amendment itself shows that Congress understood the business nexus provision to have narrow application; otherwise, there would have been no need to propose amending it.

Contrary to defendants' contention, the decision of Congress to reject this language has no bearing on whether "obtaining or retaining business" includes the conduct at issue here. In explaining Congress's decision not to include this proposed amendment in the business nexus requirement, the Conference Report stated that the "retaining business" language was

> not limited to the renewal of contracts or other business, but also includes a prohibition against corrupt payments related to the execution or performance of contracts or the carrying out of existing business, *such as a payment to a foreign official for the purpose of obtaining more favorable tax treatment.* . . . The term should not, however, be construed so broadly as to include lobbying or other normal representations to government officials. . . .

. . . [A]s a general matter, subsequent legislative history about unchanged statutory language would deserve little or no weight in our analysis. . . . [However,] . . . the legislative history . . . explains how the 1988 amendments relate to the original scope of the statute and concomitantly to the business nexus element.

First, the Conference Report expresses what is implied by the new affirmative defense for bona fide expenditures for the execution or performance of a contract. The creation of a defense for *bona fide* payments strongly implies that *corrupt*, non-bona-fide payments related to contract execution and performance have always been and remain prohibited. Instead of leaving this prohibition implicit, though, the Conference Report's description of "retaining business" explained that this phrase, and thus the statutory ambit, includes "a prohibition against *corrupt* payments related to the execution or performance of contracts. . . ."

Similarly, in its 1988 statutory description of routine governmental action, Congress stated that this exception *does not* include decisions about "whether, or on what terms . . . to continue business with a particular party," [15 U.S.C. §78dd-1(f)(3)(B),] which must mean, conversely, that decisions that do relate to "continu[ing] business with a particular party" *are* covered by, i.e., are not excepted from, the scope of the statute. . . .

Third, the Conference Report states that "retaining business" should not be construed so broadly as to include lobbying or "other normal representations to government officials." This statement directly reflects the Conference Committee's decision not to include language from the House bill focusing on legislature and regulatory activity so as to avoid any interpretation that might curb legitimate lobbying or representations intended to influence legislative, judicial, regulatory, or other such action. Thus, like other language of the report, far from being irrelevant to Congress's intentions in 1988, this provides a direct explanation of why Congress elected not to include the newly proposed language.

The remaining contested language in the 1988 Conference Report states that "retaining business" includes — covers — payments such as those made "to a foreign official *for the purpose of obtaining more favorable tax treatment.*" We know that the SEC was concerned specifically with these types of untoward payments in 1977, and that Congress ultimately adopted the more generally-worded prohibition against payments designed to *assist* in obtaining or retaining business. This specific reference in the Conference Report therefore appears to reflect the concerns that initially motivated Congress to enact the FCPA. But even if this language is not dispositive of the question, the rest of the passage does reflect Congress's purpose in passing the 1988 amendments, and therefore deserves weight in our analysis.

Finally, it is inaccurate to suggest, as defendants do, that this report language constituted an attempt to insert by subterfuge a meaning for "retaining business" that Congress had expressly rejected in conference. The only language that Congress chose not to adopt regarding the business nexus requirement concerned payments for primarily legislative, judicial, and regulatory advantages. Corrupt payments "related to the execution or performance of contracts or the carrying out of existing business" have no direct connection with the proposed language on legislative, judicial, and regulatory action, and thus were not part of the proposed amendment.

3. 1998 LEGISLATIVE HISTORY

In 1998, Congress made its most recent adjustments to the FCPA when the Senate ratified and Congress implemented the Organization of Economic Cooperation and Development's Convention on Combating Bribery of Foreign Public Officials in International Business Transactions (the "Convention"). Article 1.1 of the Convention prohibits payments to a foreign public official to induce him to "act or refrain from acting in relation to the performance of official duties, in order to obtain or retain business *or other improper advantage* in the conduct of international business." When Congress amended the language of the FCPA, however, rather than inserting "any improper advantage" immediately following "obtaining or retaining business" within the business nexus requirement (as does the Convention), it chose to add the "improper advantage" provision to the original list of abuses of discretion in consideration for bribes that the statute proscribes. Thus, as amended, the statute now prohibits payments to foreign officials not just to buy any act or decision, and not just to induce the doing or omitting of an official function "to assist . . . in obtaining or retaining business for or with, or directing business to, any person," but also the making of a payment to such a foreign official to secure an "improper advantage" that will assist in obtaining or retaining business.

The district court concluded, and defendants argue on appeal, that merely by adding the "improper advantage" language to the two existing kinds of prohibited acts acquired in consideration for bribes paid, Congress "again declined to amend the "'obtain or retain' business language in the FCPA." In contrast, the government responds that Congress's choice to place the Convention language elsewhere merely shows that Congress already intended for the business nexus requirement to apply broadly, and thus declined to be redundant.

The Convention's broad prohibition of bribery of foreign officials likely includes the types of payments that comprise defendants' alleged conduct. The commentaries to the Convention explain that "'[o]ther improper advantage' refers to something to which the company concerned was not clearly entitled, for example, an operating permit for a factory which fails to meet the statutory requirements." Unlawfully reducing the taxes and customs duties at issue here to a level substantially below that which ARI was legally obligated to pay surely constitutes "something [ARI] was not clearly entitled to," and was thus potentially an "improper advantage" under the Convention.

As we have demonstrated, the 1977 and 1988 legislative history already make clear that the business nexus requirement is not to be interpreted unduly narrowly. We therefore agree with the government that there really was no need for Congress to add "or other improper advantage" to the requirement.[14] In fact, such an amendment might have inadvertently swept grease payments into the statutory ambit—or at least created new confusion as to whether these types of payments were prohibited—even though this category of payments was excluded by Congress in 1977 and remained excluded in 1988; and even though Congress showed no intention of adding this category when adopting its 1998 amendments. That the Convention, which the Senate ratified without reservation and Congress implemented, would also appear to prohibit the types of payments at issue in this case only bolsters our conclusion that the kind of conduct allegedly engaged in by defendants can be violative of the statute.[15]

4. SUMMARY

. . . [W]e hold that Congress intended for the FCPA to apply broadly to payments intended to assist the payor, either directly or indirectly, in obtaining or retaining business for some person, and that bribes paid to foreign tax officials to secure illegally reduced customs and tax liability constitute a type of payment that can fall within this broad coverage. . . .

. . . We hasten to add, however, that this conduct does not automatically constitute a violation of the FCPA: It still must be shown that the bribery was intended to produce an effect—here, through tax savings—that would "assist in obtaining or retaining business."

D. SUFFICIENCY OF THE INDICTMENT

. . . We observe as a preliminary matter that this is the kind of case that a relatively few reported opinions have analyzed to determine whether an indictment that sets out the elements of the offense charged *merely by tracking the words of the statute itself,* is insufficient. Most reported opinions that have addressed this issue appear to approve the practice of tracking the statute as long as the words used expressly set out all of the elements necessary to constitute the offense. The cases in which an indictment that parrots the statute is held to be insufficient turn on a determination that the factual information that is *not* alleged in the indictment goes to the very *core of criminality* under the statute. . . .

---

14. [Court's footnote 66:] Although Congress intended to expand the scope of the FCPA in its implementation of the Convention, such expansion did not clearly implicate the business nexus element. Obviously, Congress added "any improper advantage" to the *quid pro quo* requirement. Other ways in which Congress intended to expand FCPA coverage included: (1) amending the statute to apply to "any person," instead of the more limited category of issuers registered under the 1934 Act and domestic concerns; (2) expanding the definition of "foreign official" to include officials of public international organizations; and (3) extending the FCPA to cover "acts of U.S. businesses and nationals in furtherance of unlawful payments that take place wholly outside the United States." S. Rep. No. 105-277, at 2-3 [1998].

15. [Court's footnote 68:] . . . We recognize that there may be some variation in scope between the Convention and the FCPA. The FCPA prohibits payments inducing official action that "assist[s] . . . in obtaining or retaining business"; the Convention prohibits payments that induce official action "to obtain or retain business or other improper advantage in the conduct of international business." Potential variation exists because it is unclear whether the Convention's "other improper advantage in the conduct of international business" language requires a business nexus to the same extent as does the FCPA. This case, however, does not require us to address potential discrepancies (including whether they exist) between the scope of the Convention and the scope of the statute, i.e., payments that clearly fall outside of the FCPA but clearly fall within the Convention's prohibition or vice versa, because we have already concluded that the type of bribery engaged in by defendants has the potential of violating the statute.

. . . As explained *ad nauseam* in the foregoing analysis of the legislative history of the FCPA, the "assist" nexus is indisputably the element of the crime that distinguishes it from garden-variety bribery on the broad end of the spectrum and bribery to obtain or retain a particular government contract on the narrow end. In terms of the sufficiency of the indictment, however, the question is whether the business nexus element — which in the instant indictment is merely a paraphrase of that part of the statute — goes to the "core of criminality" under the statute and contains generic terms, requiring more particularity. Stated differently, the question is whether the lack of detail in that part of the indictment that deals with this one element is more like an absence of detail as to how the crime was committed than a failure to specify what the crime was. . . .

Although we recognize that lowering tax and customs payments presumptively increases a company's profit margin by reducing its cost of doing business, it does not follow, *ipso facto*, — as the government contends — that such a result satisfies the statutory business nexus element. Even a modest imagination can hypothesize myriad ways that an unwarranted reduction in duties and taxes in a large-volume rice import operation could *assist* in obtaining or retaining business. For example, it could, as already indicated, so reduce the beneficiary's cost of doing business as to allow the beneficiary to underbid competitors for private commercial contracts, government allocations, and the like; or it could provide the margin of profit needed to fend off potential competition seeking to take business away from the beneficiary; or, it could make the difference between an operating loss and an operating profit, without which the beneficiary could not even stay in business; or it could free up funds to expend on legitimate lobbying or other influence-currying activities to favor the beneficiary's efforts to get, keep, or expand its share of the foreign business. Presumably, there are innumerable other hypothetical examples of how a significant diminution in duties and taxes could assist in getting or keeping particular business in Haiti; but that is not to say that such a diminution *always* assists in obtaining or retaining business. There are bound to be circumstances in which such a cost reduction does nothing other than increase the profitability of an already-profitable venture or ensure profitability of some start-up venture. Indeed, if the government is correct that anytime operating costs are reduced the beneficiary of such advantage is assisted in getting or keeping business, the FCPA's language that expresses the necessary element of assisting is obtaining or retaining business would be unnecessary, and thus surplusage — a conclusion that we are forbidden to reach.

. . . If business nexus is core, then in addition to alleging at least minimally sufficient facts that, if proved, will meet the other elements of a violation of the FCPA (such as the citizenship of the briber, the identity of the qualified business entity, the particular instrumentalities of foreign and interstate commerce employed, the identity of the foreign country and of the officials to whom the suspect payments are made, and the sought-after unlawful actions taken or not taken by the foreign official in consideration of the bribes), a sufficient FCPA indictment would also have to allege facts that at least minimally put the defense on notice of *what* business transactions or opportunities were purportedly sought to be obtained or retained, and *how* the results of the foreign official's unlawful acts were meant to "assist" in getting or keeping such business. . . .[16]

---

16. [Court's footnote 96:] On appeal, as in the district court, defendants advance alternative bases for holding the indictment insufficient. One such defense was grounded in the rule of lenity in the face of the statute's ambiguity, and another was grounded in the fair-warning requirement of the Due Process Clause in the face of the dearth of case law on the subject. As today we reverse the district court's dismissal of the indictment as insufficient and remand for further proceedings which might include a requirement that the government be more specific regarding the business nexus element, we do not address these alternative propositions. They can, however, be addressed for the first time by the district court on remand.

We conclude that, as important to the statute as the business nexus element is, it does not go to the FCPA's core of criminality. When the FCPA is read as a whole, its core of criminality is seen to be bribery of a foreign official to induce him to perform an official duty in a corrupt manner. The business nexus element serves to delimit the scope of the FCPA by eschewing applicability to those bribes of foreign officials that are not intended to assist in getting or keeping business, just as the "grease" provisions eschew applicability of the FCPA to payments to foreign officials to cut through bureaucratic red tape and thereby facilitate matters. Therefore, the indictment's paraphrasing of the FCPA's business nexus element passes the test for sufficiency, despite alleging no details regarding what business is sought or how the results of the bribery are meant to assist. . . .

NOTES AND QUESTIONS

1. *Elements.* The following are the elements that the government must prove beyond a reasonable doubt to secure an FCPA bribery conviction; subsequent Notes will explore the more complicated elements further.

> a. The defendant falls within one of three categories of persons covered by the FCPA (see also Note 3 below).
> b. The defendant made a payment of, or an offer, an authorization, or a promise to pay, money or anything of value, directly or indirectly through a third party.
> c. The defendant made the payment or promise to pay to a covered recipient, meaning:
> > (i) any foreign official;
> > (ii) any foreign political party or party official;
> > (iii) any candidate for foreign political office; or
> > (iv) any other person while "knowing" that the payment or promise to pay will be passed on to one of the above.
> d. In furtherance of the bribe or offer to bribe, "corruptly" committed the *actus reus* of the crime (see also Note 4 below);
> e. For the purpose of influencing an official act or decision of that person to do or omit to do any act in violation of his or her lawful duty, securing any improper advantage, or inducing that person to use his or her influence with a foreign government to affect or influence any government act or decision; and
> f. In order to assist in obtaining or retaining business for, with, or to any person.

2. *Nexus between bribe and maintaining or obtaining business.* In *Kay*, the Fifth Circuit struggled to identify the nexus that must exist between elements (e) and (f) described above. The district court in *Kay* had held that the payments in that case — bribes to secure undeserved breaks on customs duties and sales taxes — could not qualify as covered payments under the FCPA because they were not sufficiently closely related to obtaining or retaining business. The Fifth Circuit reversed, ruling that although the language of the statute is "ambiguous," such payments may in fact be covered in some circumstances. Shouldn't the rule of lenity have compelled a contrary result? Do you find the court's discussion in its footnote 96 satisfying?

This was a very important case given that many payments may be made to covered persons that do not directly relate to securing or retaining a particular business opportunity, but rather simply permit the company to operate more efficiently or cost-effectively than its competitors. The Fifth Circuit's opinion was awaited eagerly by

FCPA practitioners and businesspeople, who hoped that the opinion would clarify just how direct a relationship must exist between the payment and the business sought to be secured or maintained. Does the opinion provide this hoped-for guidance? Does the court's discussion suggest that the FCPA covers anything of value offered in exchange for any official action that may improve the business opportunities of the briber or its bottom line (as long as it is not a "grease" payment and meets the other requisites of the statute)? Some in the practice community have sharply criticized the *Kay* decision because it "leaves American companies and their counsel at sea as to whether or not certain types of payments to foreign officials violate the statute. . . . Unless [a proposed] payment is designed to secure or retain a contract, no brightline guidance can be given in the wake of the *Kay* decision." Irvin B. Nathan, Is Bribing Foreign Tax Collectors a Federal Crime? The Fifth Circuit Says Maybe Yes, Maybe No, Bus. Crimes Bull., June 2004, at 1, 4.

3. *Three categories of covered persons.* A preliminary definitional note may assist readers in understanding the following materials: throughout, "U.S. companies" refers to companies that are organized under the laws of the United States.

The anti-bribery provisions of the FCPA apply to three categories of covered persons (that is, potential defendants). Under which of these categories did the defendants in *Kay* fall?

A. Section 78dd-1 covers "issuers" and "any officer, director, employee, or agent of such issuer[s] or any stockholder thereof acting on behalf of such issuer[s]." 15 U.S.C. §78dd-1. An issuer is an entity whose securities are registered in the United States or that is required to file periodic reports with the SEC. Id. Note that under §78dd-1, companies that are issuers may be prosecuted even if they are not U.S. companies and are not "resident" in the United States. Further, the agents acting on behalf of an issuer need not be nationals of, or resident in, the United States to be themselves covered. And, although the nomenclature is awkward, issuers can be natural persons as well as companies.

B. Section 78dd-2 covers "domestic concerns" and "any officer, director, employee, or agent of such domestic concern or any stockholder thereof acting on behalf of such domestic concern." 15 U.S.C. §78dd-2. A "domestic concern" means "(A) any individual who is a citizen, national, or resident of the United States; and (B) any corporation, partnership, association, joint stock company, business trust, unincorporated organization, or sole proprietorship which has its principal place of business in the United States. . . ." Id. §78dd-2(h)(1). Companies having their principal place of business in the United States are considered "domestic concerns" even if they are not U.S. companies or agents of U.S. companies. Individuals who are not U.S. nationals are nonetheless "domestic concerns" if they are resident in the United States. Note also that non-U.S. companies not having their principal place of business in the United States and foreign nationals who are not resident in the United States may be prosecuted under this provision if they are acting as agents of a "domestic concern."

C. Section 78dd-3 covers foreign nationals or businesses that are neither "issuers" nor "domestic concerns" but that perform a qualifying act in furtherance of the illicit bribe in U.S. territory (or an agent of such national or business). 15 U.S.C. §78dd-3. This provision was added to the statute in 1998 to implement the Convention on Combating Bribery of Foreign Officials in International Business Transactions adopted by the OECD (the OECD Convention), to which the U.S. Senate gave its advice and consent in 1998. The OECD Convention requires all states parties to make it a criminal offense for "any person" to bribe a foreign official and requires signatories "to take such measures as may be necessary to establish its jurisdiction over the bribery of a foreign public official when the offense is committed in whole or in part in its territory." As a result, Congress acted in 1998 to extend the FCPA's coverage to persons who are not issuers or domestic concerns but who commit an offense, at least in part, in the United States.

This last provision significantly increases the jeopardy of non-U.S. companies and their agents because it reaches individuals who are not U.S. nationals or residents, and companies that are not regulated by the SEC, whose securities are not registered in the United States, and that are neither U.S. companies nor businesses having their principal place of business in the United States. See, e.g., id. §78dd-3(f)(1). These persons may be prosecuted under the FCPA's anti-bribery provisions if, "while in the territory of the United States," they "corruptly . . . make use of the mails or any other means or instrumentality of interstate commerce or . . . *do any act in furtherance*" *of the offer to bribe or illicit payment* (emphasis added). In short, any person (natural or juridical) who is not an "issuer" or a "domestic concern" but who takes any act in furtherance of a corrupt offer or payment in the territory of the United States is subject to U.S. prosecution — whether or not that "person" has any other connection to the United States. The Senate Report accompanying this amendment provided that "the territorial basis of jurisdiction should be broadly interpreted so that an extensive physical connection to the bribery act is not required." S. Rep. No. 105-277, at 6 (1998).

4. *Actus reus.* The guilty act necessary to an FCPA prosecution depends on who the defendant is. What *actus reus* was the government required to prove in *Kay* given the status of the defendants? There are three categories of such persons. Unfortunately, however, this breakdown of who must do what to be liable under the FCPA does not correspond neatly to the categories of covered persons described in Note 3 above.

A. "United States persons," defined as the subset of "issuers" and "domestic concerns" (and their agents) who are U.S. nationals or U.S. companies, will be liable if they make use of the mails or any means or instrumentalities of interstate commerce corruptly in furtherance of the corrupt payment *or take any act outside the United States in furtherance of a corrupt payment.*

Liability for use of the mails or any means or instrumentalities of interstate commerce corruptly in furtherance of the corrupt payment applies to all issuers and domestic concerns, regardless of their nationality. 15 U.S.C. §§78dd-1(a), 78dd-2(a). The "alternative jurisdiction" provisions tucked onto the end of §§78dd-1 and 78dd-2, however, further provide that where "issuers" and "domestic concerns" that are U.S. nationals or U.S. companies are implicated in the scheme, they need take no action within the United States in furtherance of the scheme, and indeed need not use the mails or other instrumentalities of interstate commerce, because *any act in furtherance of the bribery scheme overseas* will suffice to satisfy the *actus reus* requirement. Assuming that some act accompanied the alleged offer to pay, or the payment to, a foreign official overseas, it seems difficult to imagine that the *actus reus* requirement will not be met in any case involving a United States person.

B. "Issuers" and "domestic concerns" (and their agents) who are not U.S. nationals or U.S. companies will be liable if they "make use of the mails or any means or instrumentalities of interstate commerce corruptly in furtherance" of the corrupt payment to a foreign official. 15 U.S.C. §§78dd-1(a), 78dd-2(a).

This subsection would apply, in particular, to non-U.S. nationals resident in the United States and non-U.S. companies that have listed securities or SEC filing obligations under U.S. law, as well as non-U.S. companies resident in, or having their principal place of business in, the United States. Note that the *actus reus* is restricted to using the mails or means or instrumentalities of "interstate commerce." By omitting reference to "foreign commerce," is Congress requiring that the *actus reus* must take place in the United States?

C. Persons who are neither "issuers" nor "domestic concerns" (and their agents) can be prosecuted if "while in the territory of the United States," they corruptly "make use of the mails or any means or instrumentality of interstate commerce or . . . do *any other act in furtherance of*' the illicit payment (emphasis added). 15 U.S.C. §78dd-3.

It is worth stressing this point: Section 78dd-3, which applies to foreign nationals and foreign companies that are not "issuers" or "domestic concerns," provides that such persons may be liable if they take *any* act in furtherance of the corrupt payment within the territory of the United States. Moreover, the Justice Department explains this provision as follows:

> A foreign company or person is now subject to the FCPA if it takes any act in furtherance of the corrupt payment while within the territory of the United States. There is, however, no requirement that such act make use of the U.S. mails or other means or instrumentalities of interstate commerce. See §78dd-3(a), (f)(1). Although this section has not yet been interpreted by any court, the Department interprets it as conferring jurisdiction whenever a foreign company or national causes an act to be done within the territory of the United States by any person acting as that company's or national's agent.

U.S. Dept. of Justice, U.S. Attys.' Manual, Criminal Resource Manual §9-1018; see also Daniel P. Ashe, Comment, The Lengthening Anti-Bribery Lasso of the United States: The Recent Extraterritorial Application of the U.S. Foreign Corrupt Practices Act, 73 Fordham L. Rev. 2897, 2921-2925 (2005). In precedents decided under the fraud sections of the United States Code, the Supreme Court has held that "causing" something to be done does not mean "ordering" it to be done or even "assisting" or "instigating" the action. Instead, the Court has ruled in the fraud context that a defendant "causes" a jurisdictional element (a mailing or interstate wiring) "[w]here one does an act with knowledge that the [jurisdictional act] . . . will follow in the ordinary course of business, or where such [act] can reasonably be foreseen, even though not actually intended." Pereira v. United States, 347 U.S. 1, 8-9 (1954).

Compare the *actus reus* as defined for foreign "issuers" or "domestic concerns" (category B) with that applied to foreign companies with no ties to the United States (category C). Does the FCPA allow for more expansive jurisdiction over companies with fewer connections to the United States?

5. *Sanctions.* Under the FCPA and the alternative minimum fine statute, juridical "persons" who violate the anti-bribery provisions of the FCPA are subject to a fine of the greater of $2 million or twice the gross gain or loss flowing from the offense. 15 U.S.C. §§78ff(c)(1)(A), 78dd-2(g)(1)(A), 78dd-3(e)(1)(A); 18 U.S.C. §3571(d). Natural persons who willfully violate the anti-bribery provisions are subject to a criminal fine of not more than the greater of $250,000 or twice the gross gain or loss flowing from the offense, and imprisonment of not more than 5 years. 15 U.S.C. §§78ff(c)(2)(A), 78dd-2(g)(2)(A), 78dd-3(e)(2)(A); 18 U.S.C. §3571(b)(3), (d). Criminal fines imposed on individuals may not be paid by their employers or principals. See 15 U.S.C. §§78dd-2(g)(3), 78dd-3(e)(3), 78ff(c)(3). Any property, real or personal, "which constitutes or is derived from proceeds traceable to a violation of the FCPA, or a conspiracy to violate the FCPA, may be forfeited." Criminal Resource Manual, supra, §1019; see 18 U.S.C. §§981(a)(1)(C), 1956(c)(7). It is important to recognize that these are the statutory *maximums* applicable. Judges have the discretion to choose an appropriate sentence within that statutory maximum. 18 U.S.C. §3553.

In so doing, judges must consider the sentence yielded by application of the U.S. Sentencing Guidelines, but they are no longer bound by these sentencing guidelines. See United States v. Booker, 543 U.S. 220 (2005).

6. *Actionable corruption limited to bribery.* "Corruption" is not restricted to out-and-out bribery, which, in the *Kay* court's words, involves "seeking to induce a foreign official to act in consideration of a bribe (*quid pro quo*)." United States v. Kay, 359 F.3d 738, 744 (5th Cir. 2004). For example, the federal statute outlawing federal domestic public corruption, 18 U.S.C. §201, treats "bribery" and "gratuities" as separate offenses. As the Supreme Court explained in United States v. Sun-Diamond Growers of California, 526 U.S. 398 (1999):

> The distinguishing feature of each crime is its intent element. Bribery requires intent "to influence" an official act or "to be influenced" in an official act, while illegal gratuity requires only that the gratuity be given or accepted "for or because of" an official act. In other words, for bribery there must be a quid pro quo — a specific intent to give or receive something of value *in exchange* for an official act. An illegal gratuity, on the other hand, may constitute merely a reward for some future act that the public official will take (and may already have determined to take), or for a past act that he has already taken.

Id. at 404-405. The *Kay* court talks about a "quid pro quo" element. Does that mean that the FCPA only proscribes "bribes" and does not cover "gratuities"?

What about other types of "corrupt" activities? Joseph Nye provides the following definition of corruption: "behavior which deviates from the formal duties of a public role because of private-regarding (personal, close family, private clique) pecuniary or status gains; or violates rules against the exercise of certain types of private-regarding influence." J.S. Nye, Corruption and Political Development: A Cost-Benefit Analysis, 61 Am. Pol. Sci. Rev. 417, 419 (1967); see also Saladin Al-Jurf, Good Governance and Transparency: Their Impact on Development, 9 Transnatl. L. & Contemp. Probs. 193, 196 (1999) (citing the World Bank's definition of corruption as "[t]he abuse of public office for private gain"); cf. Philip B. Heymann, Democracy and Corruption, 20 Fordham Intl. L.J. 323, 325 (1996) (describing corruption "as secretly receiving private benefits to affect a decision that is supposed to be made in the interests of others and uninfluenced by private gain"). In short, corruption encompasses theft, nepotism, and misappropriation as well as bribery.

Why doesn't the FCPA focus on these other types of corruption? Might its focus on bribery be traceable to concerns regarding "cultural imperialism"? Steven Salbu cautions, for example, that extraterritorial application of anticorruption laws can be seen as an imposition of "discretionary values" in light of wide-ranging cultural perceptions of bribery and corruption worldwide. Steven R. Salbu, Extraterritorial Restriction of Bribery: A Premature Evocation of the Normative Global Village, 24 Yale J. Intl. L. 223, 226-227 (1999); see also Marie M. Dalton, Note, Efficiency v. Morality: The Codification of Cultural Norms in the Foreign Corrupt Practices Act, 2 N.Y.U. L. & Bus. 583 (2006).

In reviewing the international materials that follow, ask whether there is an evolving international consensus on actionable corruption and the extent to which international law, and perhaps the law in countries other than the United States, provide a *more* comprehensive anticorruption regime than the FCPA. See also Philip M. Nichols, George J. Siedel, & Matthew Kasdin, Corruption as a Pan-Cultural Phenomenon: An Empirical Study in Countries at Opposite Ends of the Former Soviet Empire, 39 Tex. Intl. L.J. 215, 243 (2004).

7. *Qualifying recipients of a bribe.* The recipient of the corrupt payment or offer to pay must be a "foreign official," a "foreign political party or official thereof or any candidate for foreign political office," or any other "person, while knowing that all or a portion of such money . . . will be offered . . . directly or indirectly, to any foreign official, to any foreign political party or official thereof, or to any candidate for foreign political office." 15 U.S.C. §§78dd-1(a), 78dd-2(a), 78dd-3(a). It is important to note that "foreign officials" include employees of state-owned enterprises (SOE). Thus, for example, prosecutions have been based on payments made to officials of the Iraqi Trading Company, which was a state-owned enterprise at the time, and to employees of Petroleous Mexicanos (PEMEX), an oil company owned by the Mexican government. United States v. Goodyear Intl. Corp., CR No. 89-0156 (D.D.C. 1989); United States v. Crawford Enter., Inc., CR No. 82-224 (S.D. Tex. 1982). Some have argued that FCPA compliance poses unique risks in countries such as China, "given the prevalence of state-owned or state-controlled enterprises." Mike Koehler, The Unique FCPA Compliance Challenges of Doing Business in China, 25 Wis. Intl. L.J. 397, 397 (2007). This has resulted in a comparatively large number of recent cases alleging FCPA violations based on payments made in China on this theory, including payments to physicians and lab personnel employed by Chinese government-owned or -operated hospitals, managers of government-controlled steel mills, and employees at government-owned airports. Id. at 406-410.

In 1998, Congress expanded the definition of "foreign official" to include officers, employees, or those acting on behalf of public international organizations. 15 U.S.C. §§78dd-1(f)(1), 78dd-2(h)(2), 78dd-3(f)(2). A "public international organization" is, in essence, an international organization whose officers and employees enjoy diplomatic immunity under the International Organizations Immunity Act, 22 U.S.C. §288, or organizations designated as "public international organizations" by executive order. Id. Among the organizations whose employees qualify for diplomatic immunity are the International Monetary Fund, the Organization of American States, the United Nations, the World Trade Organization, and the Organization for Economic Cooperation and Development.

8. *Prosecuting the recipient of bribes?* As a definitional matter, the term *active bribery* is used to describe offenses that target the persons who *make* the corrupt payment or offer to pay. The term *passive bribery* describes offenses outlawing the *receipt* of bribes. The FCPA has long been read to cover only active bribery—that is, it has been interpreted to preclude prosecutions of the foreign official, foreign political party or party official, or candidate for foreign office who was the *recipient* of the bribe. See, e.g., United States v. Castle, 925 F.2d 831, 834 (5th Cir. 1991) (noting the "overwhelming evidence of a Congressional intent to exempt foreign officials from prosecution for receiving bribes"). In 1991—notably, seven years *before* §78dd-3 was added to the FCPA scheme—the Fifth Circuit explained:

> The drafters of the statute knew that they could, consistently with international law, reach foreign officials in certain circumstances. But they were equally well aware of, and actively considered, the "inherent jurisdictional, enforcement, and diplomatic" difficulties raised by application of the bill to non-citizens of the United States. In the conference report, the conferees indicated that the bill would reach as far as possible, and listed all the persons or entities who could be prosecuted. The list includes virtually every person or entity involved, including foreign nationals who participated in the payment of the bribe when the U.S. courts have jurisdiction over them. But foreign officials were not included. . . .
>
> Most likely Congress made this choice because U.S. businesses were perceived to be the aggressors, and the efforts expended in resolving the diplomatic, jurisdictional, and

enforcement difficulties that would arise upon the prosecution of foreign officials was not worth the minimal deterrent value of such prosecutions. Further minimizing the deterrent value of a U.S. prosecution was the fact that many foreign nations already prohibited the receipt of a bribe by an official. In fact, whenever a nation permitted such payments, Congress allowed them as well. See 15 U.S.C. §78dd-2(c)(1).

Castle, 925 F.2d at 835. Do you think that the enactment of §78dd-3 changes this analysis? Could foreign officials who do, or conspire to do, any act within the territory of the United States to further the corrupt scheme be prosecuted under §78dd-3? Do the international anticorruption conventions examined in Section C below also regulate only passive bribery? Why might nations and the international community generally draw a distinction for purposes of criminal prosecution between those who offer or pay bribes to foreign officials and those foreign public officials who accept the bribes? Wouldn't deterrent considerations demand that criminal sanctions be applied to the "demand" side of these corrupt transactions as well as the "supply" side?

9. *Due process objection.* In its footnote 96, the *Kay* court does not respond to the defendants' due process objection. Where a foreign businessperson pays a foreign official a bribe on behalf of a foreign company, never sets foot in the United States, but could be deemed to have "caused" (that is, "foreseen") some competent act in U.S. territory (fax, telephone call, e-mail communication, or mailing), should that defendant have a due process objection to being hauled into court for an FCPA violation?

10. *Mens rea.* The government must prove that the defendant had a "corrupt" motive in acting in furtherance of the bribery scheme. The term *corruptly* appears in a number of important federal statutes, notably provisions dealing with federal public corruption, 18 U.S.C. §201(b), (c), and obstruction of justice, 18 U.S.C. §§1503, 1505, 1512. Yet it has proved difficult to define, and the meaning of the term shifts depending upon the statute at issue (and the circuit in which one finds oneself). The Eighth Circuit upheld a conviction obtained based on the following jury instruction for the word *corruptly* in the FCPA context:

> [T]he offer, promise to pay, payment or authorization of payment, must be intended to induce the recipient to misuse his official position or to influence someone else to do so. . . . [A]n act is "corruptly" done if done voluntarily [a]nd intentionally, and with a bad purpose of accomplishing either an unlawful end or result, or a lawful end or result by some unlawful method or means.

United States v. Liebo, 923 F.2d 1308, 1312 (8th Cir. 1991). The *Kay* court believes that Congress included the requirement of a "corrupt" intent to separate actionable bribes from "grease" payments, which originally were intended to be exempted from the 1977 FCPA's coverage but were not explicitly exempted until the 1988 amendments. In other words, the *Kay* court thought that the legislative history established that a "corrupt" intent required proof that the payments are designed to prompt an official to deviate from his official duty; payments that simply ensure that an official properly performs his ministerial duties would not be "corrupt." Does the above jury instruction capture this meaning of *corrupt*? Has this element, at least as explained by the *Kay* court, essentially been rendered superfluous by the addition in 1988 of an express exemption of "grease" payments?

Although the term does not appear in the substantive anti-bribery prohibition, the penalty provisions of the FCPA require that, to receive a criminal sentence, natural persons must be convicted of "willful" violations of the anti-bribery provisions. 15 U.S.C. §§78ff(c)(2)(A), 78dd-2(g)(2)(A), 78dd-3(e)(2)(A). The word *willfully* is "'a word of many meanings'" whose construction is "often dependent on the context in which it appears." Bryan v. United States, 524 U.S. 184, 191 (1998) (quoting Spies v. United States, 317 U.S. 492, 497 (1943)). "Most obviously it differentiates between deliberate and unwitting conduct, but in the criminal law it also typically refers to a culpable state of mind. . . . As a general matter, when used in the criminal context, a 'willful' act is one undertaken with a 'bad purpose.' In other words, in order to establish a 'willful' violation of a statute, 'the Government must prove that the defendant acted with knowledge that his conduct was unlawful.'" Id. at 191-192 (quoting Ratzlaf v. United States, 510 U.S. 135, 137 (1994)). However, in certain cases involving "willful" violations of the tax laws and the currency reporting requirements — that is, in cases involving "highly technical statutes that presented the danger of ensnaring individuals engaged in apparently innocent conduct" — the Supreme Court has read the word *willful* to require the government to prove that the defendant knew that her conduct violated a specific legal duty imposed by statute or regulation. Id. at 194. Might FCPA defendants make a valid claim to this heightened (and very difficult to prove) level of *mens rea*?

11. *Use of third parties and willful blindness.* A company or its agents may be criminally liable for payments actually made by another agent or intermediary if the company authorized the payment or "knew" that it would be offered or made. The FCPA prohibits such indirect payments by stating that it is unlawful for covered persons to offer or give a thing of value to "any person, while knowing that all or a portion of such . . . thing of value will be offered, given, or promised, directly or indirectly, to any foreign official, to any foreign political party or official thereof, or to any candidate for foreign political office" for purposes of obtaining or retaining business. 15 U.S.C. §§78dd-1(a)(3), 78dd-2(a)(3), 78dd-3(a)(3).

Notably, the FCPA specifically provides that the government need *not* prove that the covered person had actual knowledge that a payment or promise to pay an intermediary would be passed on to a foreign official. Rather, the FCPA defines a "knowing" state of mind to include willful blindness as well as actual subjective knowledge. It reads:

> (A) A person's state of such mind is "knowing" with respect to conduct, a circumstance, or a result if—
>> (i) such person is aware that such person is engaging in such conduct, that such circumstance exists, or that such result is substantially certain to occur; or
>> (ii) such person has firm belief that such circumstance exists or that such result is substantially certain to occur.
>
> (B) when knowledge of the existence of a particular circumstance is required for an offense, such knowledge is established if a person is aware of a high probability of the existence of such circumstance, unless the person actually believes that such circumstance does not exist.

Id. §§78dd-1(f)(2), 78dd-2(h)(3), 78dd-3(f)(3).

12. *Permissible payments and affirmative defenses.* As is discussed at length in *Kay,* the FCPA does not criminalize "facilitating" or "grease" payments to foreign officials who perform "routine governmental actions." Id. §§78dd-1(b), 78dd-2(b), 78dd-3(b); see also *Kay,* supra court's note 19 (reproducing text). The FCPA also provides for two affirmative defenses. See *Kay,* supra court's note 44. First, a defendant may assert that the payment was lawful "under the written laws and regulations" of the state at issue.

15 U.S.C. §§78dd-1(c), 78dd-2(c), 78dd-3(c). Why do you suppose that this defense is rarely successful?

Second, the FCPA permits a defendant to assert as an affirmative defense that the payment was a reasonable and bona fide expenditure (such as travel and lodging expenses) incurred by or on behalf of a foreign official, party official, or candidate, and was made in connection with the promotion, demonstration, or explanation of the defendant's products or services, or the execution or performance of a contract with a foreign government (or agency). Id. Note that this exception will not support payments disproportionate to what are legitimate, reasonable business or promotion expenses. Thus, for example, a U.S. company, Metcalf & Eddy, Inc., settled an enforcement action (without admitting liability) by agreeing to pay a $400,000 civil fine and $50,000 costs of investigation. The Department of Justice alleged in that case (among other things) that Metcalf & Eddy violated the FCPA by providing an Egyptian official and his family excessive amounts in connection with his travel to the United States, including, for example, paying him 150 percent of the estimated per diem for expenses in a lump sum payment while covering his and his family's actual expenses in the United States. See Robert W. Tarun, The Foreign Corrupt Practices Act: A Primer for Multinational General Counsel 16 (July 2008 ed.) (also available on our Web site).

13. *Recordkeeping and internal control violations.* The FCPA imposes certain record-keeping and internal control requirements on issuers (but not domestic concerns or other persons), which essentially require that publicly traded companies maintain accurate books and records. 15 U.S.C. §78m(b)(2). To facilitate discovery of improper transactions, the recordkeeping provisions target failures to record improper transactions, falsification of records to hide improper transactions, and omission from otherwise correct records of qualitative information indicating a transaction's impropriety. Marika Maris, Foreign Corrupt Practices Act, 43 Am. Crim. L. Rev. 575, 580 (2006). The internal control measures require reasonable assurances that transactions are properly authorized, recorded, and audited. Tarun, supra, at 10. Although these accounting provisions generally fall within the civil enforcement authority of the SEC, the Justice Department may bring criminal charges where the defendant willfully circumvented or failed to implement a system of internal accounting controls or willfully falsified an issuer's books and records. These violations carry the potential for hefty criminal penalties: for individuals, fines of up to the greater of $5 million or twice the gross gain or loss flowing from the offense and imprisonment up to 20 years; for corporations, fines of up to the greater of $25 million or twice the gross gain or loss flowing from the offense. 15 U.S.C. §78ff(a); 18 U.S.C. §3571(d).

14. *Use of foreign subsidiaries.* The version of the FCPA first passed in the House in 1977 defined "domestic concerns" to include foreign subsidiaries of U.S. companies "both because of the extensive use of subsidiaries as conduits for improper payments and because the extension of U.S. jurisdiction [to] foreign subsidiaries was necessary in order to avoid 'a massive loophole . . . through which millions of bribery dollars will continue to flow.'" H. Lowell Brown, Parent-Subsidiary Liability Under the Foreign Corrupt Practices Act, 50 Baylor L. Rev. 1, 29 (1998). The Senate's more restrictive definition did not include foreign subsidiaries, and, at conference, the House acceded to the Senate on this issue in recognition of "'the inherent jurisdictional, enforcement, and diplomatic difficulties raised by inclusion of foreign subsidiaries of U.S. companies in the direct prohibitions of the bill.'" Id. at 33. However, subsequent amendments to the FCPA, as well as the availability of a number of common law doctrines, have drastically increased the potential that a U.S. company

will be liable for the misconduct of its subsidiaries organized under the laws of foreign countries.

First, if the foreign subsidiary acted as an agent of the U.S. company, and the U.S. company had knowledge of, or was willfully blind to, the offending conduct, the U.S. company may be liable. See Note 11 above. Second, "U.S. parent corporations may be held liable for the acts of their foreign subsidiaries where they authorized, directed, or controlled the activity in question, as can U.S. citizens or residents, themselves 'domestic concerns,' who are employed by or acting on behalf of such foreign-incorporated subsidiaries." Criminal Resource Manual, supra, No. 1018; see 15 U.S.C. §78t(a), (b), (e) (liability as a controlling person, as a perpetrator through means, and as an aider and abettor under the securities laws). Third, FCPA liability may be grounded in common law doctrines. One such doctrine permits the piercing of the corporate veil in certain circumstances. Another uses *respondeat superior* principles to render a corporate parent liable for the activities of its subsidiary alter ego or agent. Brown, supra, 50 Baylor L. Rev. at 38. Generally under U.S. law, an organization (such as a corporation or partnership) can be held criminally liable for the misconduct of its employees and agents if such persons commit the criminal act within the scope of their actual or apparent authority and with the intention to benefit, at least in part, their organization; express organizational orders prohibiting employees or agents from engaging in such conduct generally does *not* suffice to relieve the organization of liability.

Fourth, the addition of the alternative jurisdiction provisions of §§78dd-1 and 78dd-2 means that a U.S. parent company will be liable under the FCPA if it takes any action abroad in furtherance of the bribery scheme. Finally, whereas before 1998 foreign subsidiaries were used precisely to avoid their being deemed "issuers" or "domestic concerns" under the FCPA, the addition of §78dd-3 means that foreign subsidiaries may themselves be held liable under the FCPA if any act in furtherance of the illicit bribe takes place in U.S. territory. Companies also have significant exposure for the books and records violations of subsidiaries if the parent owns or controls more than 50 percent of the subsidary's voting securities. See Brown, supra, 50 Baylor L. Rev. at 29-39; see generally Keith Loken, The OECD Anti-Bribery Convention: Coverage of Foreign Subsidiaries, 33 Geo. Wash. Intl. L. Rev. 325 (2001).

Under what theory or theories could the foreign subsidiary in *Kay* have been prosecuted?

15. *Opinion letters.* The FCPA provides issuers and domestic concerns with a process through which they can obtain Department of Justice review and an opinion regarding proposed, specific, and nonhypothetical business activities that raise FCPA concerns. See 15 U.S.C. §§78dd-1(d), (e); 78dd-2(e), (f); see also 28 C.F.R. §80.1 et seq. (DOJ Opinion Procedure). "The Opinion Procedure provides a mechanism by which any U.S. company or national may request a statement of the Justice Department's present enforcement intentions, under the antibribery provisions of the FCPA, regarding any proposed business conduct." Criminal Resource Manual, supra, No. 1016. "A favorable opinion from the Department of Justice creates a rebuttable presumption, applicable in any subsequent enforcement action, that the conduct described in the request conformed with the FCPA." Id. Despite this lure, the opinion procedure is rarely used: since 1980, the DOJ has rendered only 44 opinions pursuant to these regulations; only 14 opinions were issued between the enactment of the 1998 amendments and 2007. See Tarun, supra, at 11. "The reluctance of corporations to use the opinion procedure has been attributed to the risk of the loss of confidentiality, the possibility of negative results, and the risk of instigating further government investigation." Id. However, the Department of Justice, in

recognition of past criticism of its delays in issuing government opinions, improved its turnaround time.

16. *Alternative statutory means of prosecuting corruption.* In Gebardi v. United States, 287 U.S. 112 (1932), the Supreme Court held that where Congress enacts a substantive criminal statute that excludes a class of individuals from liability, prosecutors cannot evade congressional intent by charging those same individuals with conspiring to violate the statute. The Fifth Circuit applied this principle to the FCPA in United States v. Castle, 925 F.2d 831 (5th Cir. 1991). In *Castle*, the court determined that Congress intended to exempt foreign officials from the coverage of the FCPA, and thus, under *Gebardi*, such officials could not be charged with conspiracy to violate the FCPA. Id. at 836.

Where the elements of money laundering are met, however, those who may not be reachable under the FCPA may still find themselves subject to U.S. criminal prosecution. See 18 U.S.C. §§1956(c)(7)(B)(iv), 1957(f)(3). In United States v. Bodmer, 342 F. Supp. 2d 176 (S.D.N.Y. 2004), a Swiss national was arrested while in South Korea on business pursuant to a U.S. indictment charging him with conspiracy to violate the FCPA. Bodmer was a lawyer with a Swiss firm that represented certain "domestic concerns." The indictment alleged that Bodmer paid bribes and authorized the payment of bribes, on behalf of the domestic concerns, to Azeri officials to permit his clients' continued participation in the privatization of the State Oil Company of the Azerbaijan Republic. The district court ultimately held that although the 1998 amendments "made clear that foreign nationals acting as agents of domestic concerns are subject to the FCPA's criminal liability provisions," id. at 181, it was not clear that such persons were covered by the criminal anti-bribery provisions under the pre-1998 statute, which applied to Bodmer's activities. Accordingly, the court held that the portion of the indictment charging Bodmer with conspiracy to violate the FCPA contravened the constitutional fair notice requirement and the rule of lenity. Id. at 189. The court went on to hold, however, that the *Gebardi* principle did not demand dismissal of the charge of conspiracy to launder money. It reasoned that the language of the money laundering provision at issue, 18 U.S.C. §1956(a)(2)(A), "clearly penalizes the *transportation of monetary instruments in promotion* of unlawful activity, not the underlying unlawful activity." Id. at 191. The court concluded that "[w]hether Bodmer violated the FCPA, and the fact that he cannot be criminally sanctioned for that conduct, is irrelevant to proving that he transported money in furtherance of FCPA violations. Thus, the Government is not circumventing the FCPA's limitation on penalizing non-resident foreign nationals by charging Bodmer with money laundering." Id.

Violation of the FCPA may also qualify as "racketeering activity" upon which a prosecution (or treble damages civil liability) under the Racketeering Influenced and Corrupt Organizations (RICO) statute can be built. See 18 U.S.C. §1961(1); see also Envtl. Tectronics v. W.S. Kirkpatrick, 847 F.2d 1052, 1063 (3d Cir. 1988), *aff'd on other grounds*, 493 U.S. 400 (1990); but see Rotec Indus., Inc. v. Mitsubishi Corp., 163 F. Supp. 2d 1268, 1278 (D. Or. 2001).

However, one of the federal government's principal weapons in the fight against public corruption — the "honest services" theory of fraud under 18 U.S.C. §§1341 (mail fraud), 1343 (wire fraud), 1346 (definition of honest services fraud) — may not be available. Public corruption of *federal* officials may be pursued under 18 U.S.C. §201. There is no generally applicable federal statute that permits federal prosecutors to prosecute U.S. state and local corruption. As a consequence, creative federal prosecutors began using (and federal courts began approving) the use of the federal mail and wire fraud statutes to address this problem. Basically, the theory of such cases is that a public official commits actionable fraud by depriving the public of its right to his honest services. When a public official is bribed, he has essentially "sold" his disinterested decision making, to which the public has a "right," for personal gain. The *fraud*, however, inheres not in the bribe, but rather in the public official's failure to *disclose* to his constituency the material fact of the bribe. The Supreme Court found this theory unsupported by the mail and wire fraud statutes in McNally v. United States, 483 U.S. 350 (1987), but Congress overruled the Court's statutory interpretation by enacting 18 U.S.C. §1346. Section 1346 provides that, for purposes of the mail and wire fraud statutes, an actionable scheme to defraud includes a scheme "to deprive another of the intangible right of honest services." Should federal prosecutors be able to pursue *foreign officials* for "honest services" fraud under §1346?

The district court rejected such a prosecution in United States v. Giffen, 326 F. Supp. 2d 497 (S.D.N.Y. 2004). In *Giffen*, the defendant was charged with making unlawful payments totaling more than $78 million to Nurlan Balgimaev, the former prime minister and oil minister of the Republic of Kazakhstan, and Nursultan Nazarbaev, the president of Kazakhstan, in violation of the FCPA, 15 U.S.C. §78dd-2; the mail and wire fraud statutes, 18 U.S.C. §§1341, 1343, 1346; money laundering statutes, 18 U.S.C. §§1956, 1957; and the federal income tax laws, 26 U.S.C. §§7206, 7212. Giffen was the principal shareholder, board chairman, and chief executive officer of a New York–headquartered company called Mercator Corporation. The Kazakh government hired Mercator to advise it regarding its sales of oil and gas reserves to international oil companies. Giffen was named as counselor to the president, a semi-official title that permitted him to effect numerous oil and gas transactions. Mercator received substantial fees from the Kazakh government. In addition, Giffen deposited approximately $70 million in Swiss escrow accounts and diverted these escrow monies to different offshore entities to conceal the fact that he was funneling over $78 million to the senior Kazakh officials for their personal benefit. 326 F. Supp. 2d at 500. The indictment alleged that the illegal payments ensured that Giffen and Mercator "remained in a position from which they could divert large sums from oil transactions into accounts for the benefit of senior Kazakh officials and Giffen personally." Id.

Giffen did not challenge the indictment's reliance on the mail and wire fraud statute to the extent that the indictment charged a scheme to deprive Kazakhstan of property (that is, "tens of millions of dollars"). He did seek dismissal of those counts of the indictment that charged mail and wire fraud based on Giffen's alleged scheme to defraud the citizens of Kazakhstan of the honest services of their government officials. The district court accepted Giffen's argument that Congress did not intend the "honest services" definition of §1346 to apply to schemes to defraud *foreign* citizens of their right to the honest services of *foreign* officials. Id. at 504-506. The court also held that any such application would be unconstitutionally vague, as the statute did not provide sufficient notice that such schemes would be covered by §1346. Id. at 506-507. Finally, the district court considered Giffen's argument that the application of the "honest services" theory to prosecute him was "non-justiciable" and violated considerations of "international comity." The following is the district court's discussion:

> The concept of the Kazakh people's intangible right to honest services by their government officials requires definition. The indictment does not allege any facts or law regarding the meaning of honest services by Kazakh officials to the Kazakh people. The Government's argument that "[t]he notion that government officials owe a duty to provide honest services to the public is not so idiosyncratically American as to have no

application at all to Kazakhstan" is inapposite and begs the question. In a jarring disconnect, the Government acknowledges that "Kazakhstan has sought to derail the investigation and eventual prosecution of this matter by numerous appeals to officials . . . in the executive branch including . . . [the] Departments of State and Justice." Implicit in the Government's observation is the suggestion that Kazakhstan itself is unable to define "honest services" within its own polity.

In effect, the Government urges that American notions of honesty in public service developed over two centuries be engrafted on Kazakh jurisprudence. "While admittedly some . . . countries do not take their [anticorruption] responsibilities seriously, the correct answer to such a situation is not the extraterritorial application of United States law but rather cooperation between [the appropriate] home and host country . . . authorities." "An argument in favor of the export of United States law represents not only a form of legal imperialism but also embodies the essence of sanctimonious chauvinism." Rose Hall, Ltd. v. Chase Manhattan Overseas Banking Corp., 576 F. Supp. 107, 163 (D. Del. 1983), aff'd, Appeal of Chase Manhattan Overseas Banking Corp., 740 F.2d 956 (3d Cir. 1984). While well intentioned, the Government's suggestion that American legal standards be exported to Kazakhstan is simply a bridge too far.

"Because the principle of comity does not limit the legislature's power and is, in the final analysis, simply a rule of construction, it has no application where Congress has indicated otherwise." Until Congress authorizes an expansion of Section 1346 beyond pre-*McNally* precedent, this Court may not consider such an extraterritorial enlargement. . . .

Id. at 507-508; see also United States v. Lazarenko, No. CR 00-0284 MJJ, 2004 U.S. Dist. LEXIS 19660 (N.D. Cal. May 7, 2004) (dismissing honest services prosecution of the former prime minister of the Republic of Ukraine because the government failed to prove that the defendant violated any provision of Ukrainian law analogous to §1346). After reviewing the international materials in Section C below, do you think that it *is* "legal imperialism" to expect foreign officials to adhere to norms prohibiting bribery? For the United States to prosecute its own national for transnational bribery?

17. The priority the Department of Justice has given to criminal prosecution of FCPA cases has ebbed and flowed over the years. Traditionally, the number of prosecutions actually brought under the FCPA has not been great even in those periods when the Justice Department is relatively aggressive in pursuing these cases. See Philip Segal, Coming Clean on Dirty Dealing: Time for a Fact-Based Evaluation of the Foreign Corrupt Practices Act, 18 Fla. J. Intl. L. 169 (2006) (concluding after empirical study that the FCPA is underenforced). Just as there have not been many FCPA opinion letters issued by the Justice Department over the years, there also have not been a great many published court opinions clarifying the terms or application of the FCPA.

That said, this field appears to be one that is claiming a great deal of federal attention of late. The SEC and Justice Department, between 1978 and 2000, averaged only about 3 FCPA prosecutions a year. By contrast, there were 38 reported FCPA enforcement actions in 2007 and 37 in 2008. It was reported in early 2009 that "DOJ has stated publicly that it has between 80 and 100 ongoing FCPA investigations." Arnold & Porter LLP, Client Advisory: Survey of Recent FCPA Developments (Feb. 2009), available at http://arnoldandporterllp.com (search for "Survey of Recent FCPA Developments); see also Priya Cherian Huskins, FCPA Prosecutions: Liability Trend to Watch, 60 Stan. L. Rev. 1447, 1449 (2008); for updates, see White Collar Crime Prof Blog: FCPA, http://lawprofessors.typepad.com/whitecollarcrime_blog/fcpa/index.html (last visited July 12, 2009). At the end of 2008, the U.S. government concluded a settlement with a German engineering conglomerate, Siemens AG, in which Siemens agreed to pay an

$800 million fine to resolve civil and criminal actions—a fine that dwarfed the previous record fine of $44 million.

"Among the forces fueling the trend are the increasingly global reach of business and reforms ushered in after the last round of U.S. corporate scandals, which are prompting executives to dig deeper into their operations to find wrongdoing and turn themselves in, hoping for leniency. U.S. law enforcement, meanwhile, is marshaling more resources in a bid to level the playing field for companies competing against foreign rivals." Carrie Johnson, U.S. Targets Bribery Overseas: Globalization, Reforms Give Rise to Spike in Prosecutions, Wash. Post, Dec. 5, 2007, at D1.

The importance of the FCPA cannot be judged solely by tallying the number of investigations brought or prosecutions concluded. FCPA work is a vital area of white collar criminal practice because lawyers are consulted not just when a potentially corrupt payment is uncovered by the government, but also at every stage leading up to that point. Thus, FCPA practitioners consult with companies, among other things, on how to put in place systems to prevent such violations; on companies' potential exposure under the FCPA were they to engage in proposed mergers, acquisitions, joint ventures, contracts, consulting arrangements, and the like; on structuring transactions and contracts to avoid FCPA problems; on whether and how to conduct a corporate investigation of allegations of wrongdoing; on how to avoid an enforcement action by the SEC or a criminal prosecution by the Justice Department; and on how to settle or litigate such cases if they are brought.

The challenge of this FCPA practice lies in part in the fact that there is little in the way of public precedents on the subject and the FCPA itself is complex and, in many areas, vague. Much of this practice is conducted under the legal waterline: "Success" means that counsel has put in place an effective system to avoid FCPA problems or, if such problems arise, has dealt with the matter in such a way as to avoid any governmental interest or enforcement. Thus, FCPA practitioners' expertise depends more on experience in similar cases and consultations among lawyers who do FCPA work than on reading law reports. The practice is also extremely challenging for many of the reasons that white collar practice in general is challenging, including the potential that a client will be facing potential liability on a number of fronts simultaneously (civil enforcement action, criminal prosecution, private or shareholder ligation, etc.). For an excellent treatment of the nature and substance of FCPA practice in the United States, see Tarun, supra.

C. GLOBAL ANTICORRUPTION LAWS AND INITIATIVES

As noted in the introduction to this chapter, the international community has increasingly focused over the past two decades on the phenomenon of cross-border corruption. This international attention stemmed in part from the strong U.S. interest in establishing an international anti-bribery regime to level the playing field for U.S. companies, subject to the FCPA, vis-à-vis companies from countries with no such legislation. In addition, domestic corruption scandals in several European nations heightened public awareness of the problem and increased the pressure to address overseas bribery.[17]

---

17. See, e.g., Daniel K. Tarullo, The Limits of Institutional Design: Implementing the OECD Anti-Bribery Convention, 44 Va. J. Intl. L. 665, 679-680 (2004).

Among the concrete results of this focus has been the adoption of a number of multilateral treaties addressing the topic. The Organization for Economic Cooperation and Development (OECD) adopted a convention focused specifically on bribery. Three regional conventions focus on corruption more broadly: the Organization of American States' (OAS's) Inter-American Convention Against Corruption (IACAC), the Council of Europe's Criminal Law Convention on Corruption (COE Convention), and the African Union Convention on Preventing and Combating Corruption. The United States has ratified the IACAC and OECD Convention and participates as an observer in the COE, including in the body that oversees and monitors the COE Convention.

Although these regional efforts are important steps in combating corruption, many believe that corruption is a global problem that requires a worldwide solution. The newest and most comprehensive treaty, the UN Convention Against Corruption (UNCAC), is intended to provide that global approach. It is long and complex, and necessarily builds on the provisions of its predecessors. We begin, therefore, with a chronological examination of some of the treaties leading up to the UNCAC: the OAS, OECD, and COE Conventions.

In reviewing these materials, note the important ways in which the conventions differ with respect to what corrupt practices are prohibited, what constitutes a bribe, and what actions states parties must undertake in terms of criminalization, prevention, international cooperation, and participation in monitoring mechanisms. There are also important differences in the scope of the prohibitions and, in particular, in the potential offenders targeted: Some target only corruption of public officials, while others also address the corruption of private sector actors; some deal with bribery of domestic officials by persons within the same country (what we refer to as "domestic" bribery or corruption) while others focus only on corruption of foreign officials (what we refer to as "transnational" bribery or corruption); all the conventions cover the persons offering or paying the bribe ("active" corruption), but fewer also require the criminalization of the solicitation or receipt of transnational bribes ("passive" corruption). One question that you ought to consider in reviewing these materials is whether these various instruments demonstrate a trend toward broader prohibitions on corruption.

American businesspeople and lawyers are beginning to recognize that this international movement signals a "sea change in the way business will have to be conducted around the world."[18] The international conventions studied in this section have very practical implications for international businesses and their legal counsel. For example, whereas before companies had to worry only about the United States' FCPA, they will increasingly have to deal with similar measures instituted in countries around the globe, some of which may include more constrictive prohibitions than does the FCPA. Additionally, "these new conventions and the domestic laws they will foster dramatically strengthen international law enforcement by facilitating cross-border evidence gathering, asset seizures, extradition and other cooperation. The legal hurdles encountered in the past by the Department of Justice and the Securities and Exchange Commission will be greatly diminished. Accordingly, the business community can expect to see substantial heightened and successful international enforcement."[19]

---

18. Michael F. Zeldin & Carlo V. Di Floro, Effective Corporate Governance Under Emerging Global Anti-Corruption Laws, Bus. Crimes Bull., June 1999, at 1.

19. Id. at 8.

1.   The Inter-American Convention

The Inter-American Convention Against Corruption[20] (IACAC), adopted by the Organization of American States (OAS) in 1996, was the first multilateral treaty to address corruption.[21] The IACAC entered into force in March 1997, and has been ratified by all OAS member states (including the United States) except for Barbados.

Like the FCPA, the IACAC addresses corruption in the public sector only. However, it requires states parties to criminalize a list of "acts of corruption" that extend well beyond the passive, transnational bribery covered by the FCPA. Thus, the "acts of corruption" to which the Convention applies include both active *and* passive *domestic* bribery. The proscribed acts extend well beyond quid pro quo bribery. Also covered are acts or omissions by a public official in discharging her duties for the purpose of illicitly obtaining benefits; fraudulent use or concealment of property derived from covered corrupt practices; participating as a principal or accomplice or "in any other manner" in the corrupt acts; and conspiracy to commit the covered offenses (Art. VI).

The IACAC requires states parties to criminalize two further offenses — "illicit enrichment" (Art. IX) and transnational bribery (Art. VIII). "Illicit enrichment" is defined as a "significant increase in the assets of a government official that he cannot reasonably explain in relation to his lawful earnings during the performance of his functions." Transnational bribery focuses only on active bribery (that is, on those who offer illicit payments), not on passive bribery (that is, on those who accept or solicit bribes). No specific mention is made regarding bribery of international organization officials.

Under Article VIII's transnational bribery provision, a bribe involves "any article of monetary value, or other benefit, such as a gift, favor, promise or advantage." The bribe must be offered "in connection with any economic or commercial transaction." The required nexus to business is therefore broader than that envisioned in the FCPA and the OECD Convention (discussed below). Given this broad nexus language, grease or facilitation payments may well be prohibited, particularly since the IACAC includes no explicit exemption for such payments.[22]

Beyond these offenses, the IACAC contains an aspirational list of additional offenses for progressive development by states parties (Art. XI). These include improper use of official confidential information, improper use or diversion of state property, and seeking to obtain a decision from an official for illicit gain or benefit.

The IACAC requires states parties to establish jurisdiction over covered offenses committed in their territory and permits them also to establish nationality jurisdiction (Art. V(1) & (2)). If a state party declines to extradite offenders based on their nationality, the state party must establish the jurisdiction necessary to try such persons (Art. V(3)).

One notable feature the IACAC shares with the UNCAC treaty but not with the OECD and COE anticorruption instruments deserves mention: the broad range of domestic measures states parties must consider taking to prevent public corruption (Art. III). These include steps to create, maintain, and strengthen "standards of

---

20. Inter-American Convention Against Corruption, Mar. 29, 1996, 35 I.L.M. 724 (entered into force Mar. 6, 1997), available at http://www.oas.org/juridico/english/cordocs.htm; see generally Lucinda Low et al., The Inter-American Convention Against Corruption: A Comparison with the United States Foreign Corrupt Practices Act, 38 Va. J. Intl. L. 243 (1998).

21. Alejandro Posadas, Combating Corruption Under International Law, 10 Duke J. Comp. & Intl. L. 345, 383 (2000).

22. Id. at 388.

conduct for the correct, honorable, and proper fulfillment of public functions" and "mechanisms to enforce these standards of conduct" including, inter alia, training government personnel in the ethical rules governing their activities as well as "systems for registering the income, assets and liabilities of persons who perform public functions in certain posts" and "systems of government hiring and procurement of goods and services that assure the openness, equity and efficiency of such systems." Other measures include protections for whistle-blowers and denying "favorable tax treatment" for expenditures that violate anticorruption laws.

The IACAC requires states parties to make offenses established by the states parties in accordance with the convention extraditable offenses (Art. XIII) and to afford one another the "widest measure of mutual assistance" in the criminal investigation and prosecution of the acts of corruption described in the treaty (Art. XIV). States parties cannot invoke bank secrecy as a basis for refusing to assist another state, but the requesting state cannot use the information secured for any purpose other than the proceeding for which the information was requested absent the permission of the requested state (Art. XVI). The IACAC also requires mutual assistance in tracing and seizing proceeds of corruption (Art. XV). Notably, it provides that prosecuting states may share seized property or proceeds with states that assist in the investigation. Commentators note that this could provide "a significant incentive for developing countries to actively cooperate in prosecuting transnational bribery cases."[23]

2.   *The OECD Convention*

The OECD[24] Convention on Combating Bribery of Foreign Public Officials in International Business Transactions[25] (OECD Convention) is the narrowest of the multilateral treaties, focusing uniquely (like the FCPA) on transnational, active bribery.[26] It was adopted on November 21, 1997, and entered into force on February 15, 1999; it has since been ratified by all 30 OECD members as well as 7 nonmembers (Argentina, Brazil, Bulgaria, Chile, Estonia, Slovenia, and South Africa).

The treaty requires all states parties to take steps to criminalize the payment of bribes to foreign public officials (Art. 1). Specifically, the obligation is to make it an offense "for any person intentionally to offer, promise or give any undue pecuniary or other advantage, whether directly or through intermediaries, to a foreign public official, for that official or for a third party, in order that the official act or refrain from acting in relation to the performance of official duties, in order to obtain or retain business or other improper advantage in the conduct of international business." Passive bribery — the act of soliciting or accepting a bribe — is not covered. States parties must establish that complicity in active bribery (including incitement,

---

23. Id. at 390.

24. The Organization for Economic Cooperation and Development (OECD) provides a forum for member states to address economic, social, and governance issues. The OECD Secretariat provides research, data, and analysis to help countries develop and coordinate domestic and international policies. Membership in the OECD currently stands at 30 countries and is limited to countries committed to democratic government and a market-based economy. See http://www.oecd.org (last visited July 13, 2009).

25. Convention on Combating Bribery of Foreign Public Officials in International Business Transactions, Dec. 17, 1997, 37 I.L.M. 1 (entered into force Feb. 15, 1999).

26. Note, however, that the OECD Convention also has a narrow obligation with respect to money laundering. Article 7 provides that each state party that has made domestic bribery a predicate offense for the purposes of applying money laundering legislation must do so on the same terms for the bribery of a foreign public official.

aiding and abetting, or authorization of an act of bribery of a foreign public official) is criminalized. Attempt and conspiracy to bribe a foreign public official must be proscribed to the same extent as they are in the context of domestic corruption (Art. 1(2)). Although there is no explicit exception in the Convention for "facilitation payments," it appears to be understood that "grease" payments do not constitute actionable bribery.[27]

The Convention defines "foreign public officials" to include "any person holding a legislative, administrative or judicial office of a foreign country, whether appointed or elected; any person exercising a public function for a foreign country, including for a public agency or public enterprise; and any official or agent of a public international organisation" (Art. 1(4)(a)). The Convention thus does not appear to extend to purely private sector corruption.

The Convention calls for "effective, proportionate, and dissuasive criminal penalties" against those who commit the crime of bribing a foreign official (Art. 3). In addition to criminal penalties, the Convention requires states parties to consider "the imposition of additional civil or administrative sanctions." In some legal systems, legal persons (i.e., corporate entities) cannot be held criminally liable. The Convention deals with this possibility by requiring states parties "to establish the liability of legal persons for the bribery of a foreign public official" and to ensure that, if such entities are not amenable to criminal penalties, they will be subject to "effective, proportionate, and dissuasive non-criminal sanctions, including monetary sanctions" (Arts. 2 and 3(2)). Each state party is required to establish jurisdiction over bribery "when the offence is committed in whole or in part in its territory" and (if domestic law allows it to do so) when the offense is committed by one of its own nationals (Art. 4).

States parties must cooperate by providing mutual legal assistance in respect of criminal (and noncriminal) investigations. Bribery of a foreign public official is declared an extraditable offense, and if a state party declines to extradite its own nationals to face corruption charges, it must prosecute such persons itself (Arts. 9 and 10).

The Convention also provides for systematic monitoring of compliance through the OECD Working Group on Bribery (Art. 12). The Working Group conducts a comprehensive assessment of the conformity of the country's anti-bribery laws with the OECD Convention ("Phase 1") followed by in-country meetings with key actors from government, business, trade unions, and civil society to assess how effective that country's anti–foreign bribery laws are in practice ("Phase 2").[28]

3.   *The COE Convention*

The third multilateral anticorruption treaty is the Council of Europe's Criminal Law Convention on Corruption (COE Convention).[29] Adopted in November 1998 by the COE's Council of Ministers, the Convention entered into force in July 2002 and has been ratified by 42 member states. Like the IACAC, it represents a regional

---

27. Commentaries on the Convention on Combating Bribery of Foreign Public Officials in International Business Transactions ¶9, at 13, available at http://www.oecd.org/dataoecd/4/18/38028044.pdf; see also United States v. Kay, 359 F.3d 738, 755 n.67 (5th Cir. 2004).

28. Country Reports on the Implementation of the OECD Anti-Bribery Convention, http://www.oecd.org/document/24/0,3343,en_2649_34859_1933144_1_1_1_1,00.html (last visited July 16, 2009).

29. Criminal Law Convention on Corruption, Jan. 27, 1999, ETS No. 173 (entered into force July 1, 2002), available at http://www.conventions.coe.int/Treaty/Commun/QueVoulezVous.asp?NT=173&CM=8&DF=15/07/2009&CL=ENG.

consensus on how to respond to the criminal dimension of transborder corruption and the emergent requirements of international cooperation with respect to corruption. The United States signed the Convention (as an observer state of the COE) in October 2000. Note that a separate COE Convention, the Civil Law Convention on Corruption,[30] addresses the provision of effective remedies for persons who have suffered damage as a result of acts of corruption, including the possibility of obtaining compensation.

The COE Convention is more comprehensive than either the OECD Convention or the IACAC, seemingly requiring criminalization of a wide variety of corrupt activities: bribery of domestic public officials, both active (Art. 2) and passive (Art. 3); active and passive bribery of foreign public officials (Art. 5); active and passive bribery of members of domestic public assemblies (Art. 4) and foreign public assemblies (Art. 6); bribery in the private sector, both active (Art. 7) and passive (Art. 8); active and passive bribery of officials of international organizations (Art. 9) and members of international parliamentary assemblies (Art. 10); active and passive bribery of judges and officials of international courts (Art. 11).[31] Bribery is defined as giving "any undue advantage" for an official "to act or refrain from acting in the exercise of his or her functions" (Art. 2). Notably, in contrast to the other multilateral treaties, there is no requirement of a nexus between the bribe and business or commercial transactions.[32] The treaty makes no explicit exemption for "grease" payments. In addition to the above proscriptions on various forms of bribery, states parties must also criminalize trading in influence (Art. 12), the laundering of the proceeds of the criminal offenses covered by the treaty (Art. 13), and fraudulent accounting offenses (Art. 14). Under Article 15, states parties must establish criminal aiding and abetting liability.

It is critical to note, however, that Article 37 of the COE Convention allows states parties to enter reservations (which are valid for three years, but are renewable) that essentially gut many of these seemingly mandatory obligations to criminalize certain types of corruption. Thus, Article 37 states that a state party may reserve its "right not to establish as a criminal offense under its domestic law, in part or in whole, the conduct referred to" in all of six articles (Arts. 4, 6-8, 10, 12) and parts of another (Art. 5). States parties entering such reservations, then, may elect *not* to criminalize passive bribery of foreign public officials, active and passive bribery in the private sector, active and passive bribery of members of domestic and foreign public assemblies, active and passive bribery of members of parliamentary assemblies of international or supranational organizations, and trading in influence. A number of states parties have availed themselves of Article 37: Some countries have reserved the right not to criminalize an offense in its entirety (for example, Azerbaijan (Arts. 6, 10, 12, and passive bribery under Art. 5), Denmark (Art. 12), the Netherlands

---

30. Civil Law Convention on Corruption, Nov. 4, 1999, ETS No. 174 (entered into force Nov. 1, 2003), available at http://www.conventions.coe.int/Treaty/Commun/QueVoulezVous.asp?NT=174&CM=8&DF=18/08/2009&CL=ENG.

31. See also Additional Protocol to the Criminal Law Convention on Corruption, CETS No. 191 (entered into force Feb. 1, 2005), available at http://conventions.coe.int/Treaty/en/Treaties/Html/191.htm (adding active and passive bribery of domestic and foreign arbitrators and active and passive bribery of domestic and foreign jurors).

32. See Explanatory Report to the Criminal Law Convention on Corruption, explaining that the COE Convention "goes beyond the OECD provision" restricting bribery to payments "in order to obtain or retain business or other improper advantage" in that the COE Convention "contains no restriction as to the context in which the bribery of the foreign official occurs. Again, the aim is not only to protect free competition but the confidence of citizens in democratic institutions and the rule of law" Id. ch. 2, ¶49, available at http://conventions.coe.int/Treaty/en/Reports/Html/173.htm (last visited July 13, 2009).

(Art. 12), and Sweden (Art. 12)), while others have reserved the right to criminalize the described conduct only in certain circumstances (for example, Belgium, Czech Republic, Finland, Hungary, Poland, Portugal, Switzerland, and the United Kingdom).[33] What remains truly mandatory are active and passive domestic bribery of public officials (Arts. 2 and 3); active transnational bribery of foreign public officials (Art. 5); passive and active bribery of international organizations' officials (Art. 9); passive and active bribery of judges and officials of international courts (Art. 11); laundering of the proceeds of corruption offenses (Art. 13); and accounting offenses (Art. 14).

The Convention requires states parties to establish jurisdiction over criminal offenses established in accordance with the above-described articles where the offense is committed in their territory; the offender is one of their nationals, public officials, or a member of their domestic public assembly; or the offense involves one of their public officials or public assembly members or any official of an international organization, member of an international parliamentary assembly, or judge on an international court that is one of their nationals (Art. 17(1)). The COE Convention once again permits its states parties to reserve the right not to apply, or to attach conditions to, these jurisdictional rules (Art. 17(2)).

The COE Convention addresses the issue of liability of juridical persons by requiring states parties to ensure that legal persons can be held liable "for the criminal offences of active bribery, trading in influence and money laundering . . . committed for their benefit by any natural person, acting either individually or as part of an organ of the legal person, who has a leading position within the legal person" based on certain stated criteria (Art. 18). The Convention requires states parties to provide for "effective, proportionate and dissuasive sanctions and measures," with natural persons being subject to "deprivation of liberty which can give rise to extradition" (Art. 19(1)) and legal persons being subject to criminal or non-criminal sanctions, including monetary sanctions (Art. 19(2)).

Under the treaty, states parties are obliged to participate in a comprehensive regional cooperation framework aimed at improved mutual law enforcement assistance (Art. 26) and extradition (Art. 27). States parties are required to designate "central authorities" responsible for sending and answering requests for assistance; those authorities are empowered to communicate directly with each other as well as through Interpol (Arts. 29 and 30). Specific measures must be adopted to permit the use of "special investigative techniques" to facilitate evidence gathering, including the identification, tracing, freezing, and seizing of the "instrumentalities and proceeds of corruption" (Art. 23). Bank secrecy cannot be used as an obstacle to the measures described in Article 23. The Convention requires states parties to adopt measures to provide effective and appropriate protection for whistle-blowers and witnesses (Art. 22).

One unique feature of the COE Convention is the provision for an institutional monitoring mechanism known as the "Group of States Against Corruption" (GRECO) (Arts. 24 and 32). Membership in the GRECO overlaps, but is not identical to, membership in the COE Criminal Law Convention. According to its Statute, the aim of the GRECO is to improve its members' capacity to fight corruption by monitoring the compliance of states with their undertakings in this field. This mechanism, developed simultaneously with the COE Convention, relies on a process of mutual evaluation and peer pressure and includes the use of detailed questionnaires, country

---

33. See Council of Europe, Criminal Law Convention on Corruption, Explanatory Report, available at http://www.conventions.coe.int/Treaty/en/Treaties/Html/173-1.htm (last visited July 13, 2009).

visits by designated evaluation teams, and evaluation reports. Its sanctions include the possibility of publicly disclosing inadequate national anticorruption measures. It began functioning in May 1999.[34]

4.   The UN Convention

Building on the three previous treaties, as well as the provisions of Articles 8 and 9 of the UN Convention on Transnational Organized Crime (see Chapter 11), the United Nations Convention Against Corruption (UNCAC) was adopted by the UN General Assembly on October 31, 2003, and entered into force on December 14, 2005.[35] It is the broadest and most comprehensive of all the multilateral corruption conventions, open for ratification by all states. The United States ratified the treaty on October 30, 2006.[36]

a.   Criminalization Provisions

The UNCAC requires states parties to adopt legislation outlawing a range of corrupt activities and providing that committing these offenses or participating in them "in any capacity, such as an accomplice, assistant or instigator" gives rise to liability.[37] States parties are permitted but not required to criminalize attempts or preparations to commit the offenses (Art. 27). The UNCAC provides that corporate entities ("legal persons") must also be liable for the offenses, be it through criminal, civil, or administrative processes depending on the legal principles of each state party, and must receive "effective, proportionate and dissuasive" sanctions (Art. 26).

The UNCAC requires states parties to establish jurisdiction over offenses committed in their territory or onboard a flagship or registered aircraft of the states parties. States may, but are not required to, establish jurisdiction in a number of situations, including where the offense is committed by or against a national of a state party or against the state party itself (Art. 42).

In reviewing the covered offenses below, consider how the defined offenses relate to earlier anticorruption efforts and, in particular, whether the allocation between mandatory and permissive offenses reflects the division in the COE Convention between provisions as to which reservations are permitted and those as to which reservations cannot be made. We deal first with those acts that states parties are required to criminalize and then turn to the conduct that states parties need only consider making criminal.

---

34. See Council of Europe, Group of States Against Corruption, News Flash, Outcome of GRECO's 43rd Plenary Meeting (GRECO 43, Strasbourg, 29 June–2 July 2009), http://www.coe.int/t/dghl/monitoring/greco/default_en.asp (last visited July 13, 2009).

35. United Nations Convention Against Corruption, G.A. Res. 58/4, U.N. GAOR, 58th Sess., U.N. Doc. A/RES/58/4 (Oct. 31, 2003), available at http://www.unodc.org/unodc/en/treaties/CAC/index.html.

36. For list of signatories and parties to the treaty, see http://www.unodc.org/unodc/en/treaties/CAC/signatories.html (last visited July 13, 2009).

37. Note also that UNCAC Article 35 requires states parties "to ensure that entities or persons who have suffered damage as a result of an act of corruption have the right to initiate legal proceedings against those responsible for that damage in order to obtain compensation." Under U.S. law, at present, the FCPA does not provide for a private right of action, but in some situations activities related to corruption have been acknowledged as "predicate acts" for purposes of civil RICO claims. There has been some concern about whether Article 35 might serve as a basis for instituting a private lawsuit for damages, for example under the Alien Tort Statute (ATS), 28 U.S.C. §1350, on the theory that "acts of corruption" might be considered a violation of the Convention or of customary international law. That may be unlikely, in light of the Supreme Court's decision in Sosa v. Alvarez-Machain, 542 U.S. 692, 727 (2004) (stating that "a decision to create a private right of action is one better left to legislative judgment in the great majority of cases."). Should U.S. law be amended to provide for such a right of action?

1. *Bribery.* For *domestic* bribery, the UNCAC requires states parties to criminalize both passive and active bribery (Art. 15). For *transnational* bribery, however, the UNCAC, like the OECD Convention and the IACAC, provides that states parties *must* criminalize the promise, offering, or giving of bribes to foreign public officials or officials of public international organizations, but need only "consider" criminalizing solicitation or acceptance of bribes (Art. 16). The term "foreign public official" means "any person holding a legislative, executive, administrative or judicial office of a foreign country, whether appointed or elected; and any person exercising a public function for a foreign country, including for a public agency or public enterprise" (Art. 2).

The UNCAC does not contain an explicit exemption for small facilitation payments. It is worth noting, however, that the UNCAC adopts the same definition of what constitutes a bribe as that used in the OECD Convention: "an undue advantage, for the official himself or herself or another person or entity, in order that the official act or refrain from acting in the exercise of his or her official duties, in order to obtain or retain business or other undue advantage in relation to the conduct of international business" (Art. 16(1)). This definition is understood in the OECD Convention context to exclude facilitation payments.[38]

All the offenses covered under the UNCAC, including bribery, are to be considered criminal offenses "when committed intentionally" (Arts. 15-25). Article 28 seems to contemplate that states parties will add to this minimal *mens rea* when implementing the Convention; it provides that "[k]nowledge, intent or purpose required as an element of an offence established in accordance with this Convention may be inferred from objective factual circumstances." How does the *mens rea* contemplated under the UNCAC compare to the FCPA requirement that a criminal bribery offense, to be punishable, must be committed "corruptly" and "willfully"?

2. *Money laundering.* States parties must criminalize a variety of acts related to laundering the proceeds of covered crimes and should seek to apply the provision to "the widest range of predicate offenses" (Art. 23).

3. *Tax and accounting offenses.* States parties must disallow tax deductability for bribe payments (Art. 12(4)), and must prohibit the use of false or incomplete accounting documents and the failure to record payments in order to commit or conceal bribery or trading in influence (Art. 12(3)).

4. *Embezzlement, misappropriation, or diversion of property.* States parties must criminalize intentional "embezzlement, misappropriation or other diversion by a public official for his or her benefit or for the benefit of another person or entity, of any property, public or private funds or securities or any other thing of value entrusted to the public official by virtue of his or her position" (Art. 17).

5. *Obstruction of justice.* States parties must criminalize "the use of physical force, threats or intimidation," or bribery to interfere with testimony, evidence production, or judicial or law enforcement officials in the exercise of their duties related to the covered corruption offenses (Art. 25).

6. *Private sector bribery and embezzlement.* In contrast to the FCPA, the OECD Convention, and the IACAC, the UNCAC addresses corruption in the private sector, providing

---

38. See supra note 27, ¶1, text accompanying footnote.

that states parties "shall consider" criminalizing bribery of "any person who directs or works, in any capacity, for a private sector entity" (Art. 21). Such consideration must extend to both active and passive bribery. Bribery entails giving or accepting "an undue advantage" in order that the person "in breach of his or her duties, act or refrain from acting" (Art. 21). Article 22 further requires states parties to consider criminalizing embezzlement by private sector actors.

7. *Active or passive trading in influence, abuse of functions, illicit enrichment, and conceal-ment.* The Convention requires only that states parties "consider" criminalizing these acts. "Trading in influence" is defined to mean the offering of an "undue advantage" to a public official or any other person (or that person's solicitation of such advantage) "in order that the public official or the person abuse his or her real or supposed influence with a view to obtaining from an administration or public author-ity of the State Party an undue advantage" (Art. 18). "Abuse of functions" is defined as "the performance of or failure to perform an act, in violation of laws, by a public official in the discharge of his or her functions, for the purpose of obtaining an undue advantage for himself or herself or for another person or entity" (Art. 19). "Illicit enrichment" is defined as "a significant increase in the assets of a public official that he or she cannot reasonably explain in relation to his or her lawful income" (Art. 20). Finally, states parties must adopt measures to outlaw the laundering of proceeds of crimes covered by the Convention (Arts. 23-24). Note that these offenses are targeted at abuses that concern "public officials," rather than "foreign public officials."

b.   Seizure and Confiscation of Assets

A key aspect of the UNCAC, not addressed to the same extent in earlier anti-corruption conventions, concerns the recovery of assets, whether taken from the state or someone else, as well as the proceeds or instrumentalities of the corruption offenses (Arts. 31 and 51-59).

Each state party must take measures, "to the greatest extent possible within its domestic legal system," to enable confiscation of proceeds of crime derived from covered offenses or equivalently valued property, and the property, equipment, or other "instrumentalities used in or destined for use" in defined offenses. States parties must also take measures to identify, trace, freeze, and seize those assets for the purpose of eventual confiscation or release. Subsequent paragraphs address transformed, converted, and comingled assets, as well as the income or other ben-efits derived from the proceeds of crime. Under Article 31(7), each state party must accord its courts or other competent authorities the power to order the seizure of bank, financial, and commercial records; "bank secrecy" cannot be a reason for failing to do so. Article 40 also requires states parties to ensure that, "in the case of domestic criminal investigations of offences established in accordance with this Convention, there are appropriate mechanisms available within [the] domestic legal system to overcome obstacles that may arise out of the application of bank secrecy laws."

Article 51 declares that "the return of assets" is "a fundamental principle of this Convention" and calls upon states parties to "afford one another the widest measure of cooperation and assistance in this regard." Specific measures for international cooperation in the prevention and detection of transfers of criminal proceeds are set forth in Article 52. Article 52(1) requires states, inter alia, to "con-duct enhanced scrutiny of accounts sought or maintained by or on behalf of indi-viduals who are, or have been, entrusted with prominent public functions and their family members and close associates." Article 52(2)(b) further mandates that states parties notify financial institutions "of the identity of particular natural or legal persons to whose accounts such institutions will be expected to apply enhanced scrutiny." Do you see any issues related to possible U.S. implementation of these provisions?

Article 53 provides for the "direct recovery of property" acquired through the commission of a covered offense, including through civil litigation for the payment of compensation and through judicial recognition of a claim by another state party to be the "legitimate owner" of such property. Does U.S. law permit such actions by a foreign government in U.S. courts? If not, what kind of legislation would be required to give effect to this provision?

Each state party must take measures to permit its competent authorities to give effect to confiscation orders issued by the courts of another state party (Art. 54(1)(a)) and to order confiscation of property of foreign origin "by adjudication of an offence of money-laundering or such offense as may be within its jurisdiction" (Art. 54(1)(b)). Each state party must also consider other measures "to allow confiscation of such property without a criminal conviction in cases in which the offender cannot be prosecuted, by reason of death, flight or absence or in other appropriate cases" (Art. 54(1)(c)). In many countries, forfeiture of proceeds and instrumentalities is permissible only in conjunction with a criminal conviction for the offense that generated the original proceeds. In the United States, civil forfeiture is possible even if the owner of the property has not been convicted of a connected criminal offense. Should confiscation of illicit proceeds depend on a criminal conviction?

Article 54(2) requires measures of mutual legal assistance between states parties to freeze or seize criminal proceeds or instrumentalities. A requested state must take measures to freeze or seize the property in question when a court or other competent authority of the requesting state has issued an order to that effect, or when it otherwise has "a reasonable basis . . . to believe that there are sufficient grounds for taking such actions" (Art. 54(2)). Additional specific procedures for international cooperation for the purposes of confiscation include guidelines for recognizing and giving effect to requests from other states. For example, a state party receiving such a request from another state party must submit it to the competent authorities for them to issue an order of confiscation (Arts. 55-56).

Confiscated property must be disposed of (including by return to its prior legitimate owners) in accordance with the Convention and the domestic laws of the state party (Art. 57). Countries are required to enact legislation to permit such return, based on a request from another country, taking into account the rights of bona fide third parties (Art. 57(2)).

c.   Prevention

States parties must take or endeavor to take a variety of specific measures to prevent corruption in both the public and private sectors, including by establishing national anticorruption policies, practices, and bodies (Arts. 5-14). Specific steps concern creation and implementation of appropriate systems for hiring and training civil servants and other "nonelected" officials, mechanisms to ensure fair elections and transparency in funding electoral campaigns and political parties, and systems that regulate public procurement and management of public finances and generally promote "transparency" in public administration. Measures to strengthen the integrity of the judiciary are also required. With respect to the private sector, enhanced accounting and auditing standards are specified, as are "effective, proportionate and dissuasive civil, administrative or criminal penalties for failure to comply with such measures" (Art. 12(1)). Additional measures are required under Article 14 to prevent money laundering, including by instituting a "comprehensive domestic regulatory and supervisory regime for banks and . . . [other] financial institutions" and other persons or bodies "particularly susceptible to money-laundering." The Convention's intent is to strengthen the ability of states to detect and monitor the flow of cash across borders without impeding the movement of legitimate capital.

d. International Law Enforcement Cooperation

The UNCAC contains detailed requirements for cooperation and assistance between the law enforcement authorities of states parties through extradition, mutual legal assistance, informal law enforcement cooperation, technical assistance, information exchange, and other mechanisms.

Extradition. Article 44 establishes a more far-reaching regime than many of its predecessors. For example, it requires that covered offenses be deemed extraditable when dual criminality exists but also allows for extradition when it does not. As with other modern multilateral law enforcement treaties, the UNCAC can serve as the basis for extradition when a treaty is required but none is in force between the states concerned. States parties that decline to extradite their own nationals must refer those cases for prosecution; when extradition is sought solely for the service of a sentence, the requested country must incarcerate the fugitive if its domestic law permits. Conditional surrender, expedited extradition, and detention prior to extradition proceedings are all provided for.

Mutual legal assistance. States parties are required to afford each other the widest measure of mutual legal assistance "to the fullest extent possible under relevant laws" of the requested state (Art. 46(2)). This article functions essentially as a self-contained Mutual Legal Assistance Treaty (MLAT), establishing "central authorities" and providing authority for making and acting on requests for the taking of evidence, service of process, searches and seizures, examination of objects and sites, expert evaluations, procurement of originals and certified copies, identification and tracing of proceeds and instrumentalities for evidentiary purposes, and asset recovery, among other things. Dual criminality is not required, except in the case of requests that would involve coercive assistance (that is, search and seizure). Requests may be refused if deemed prejudicial to the sovereignty, security, *ordre public,* or other essential interests of the requested state, if prohibited under that state's domestic law, or otherwise contrary to its legal system (Art. 46(21)). States may not decline to render mutual legal assistance pursuant to Article 46 on the ground of bank secrecy.

Transfer. States parties are encouraged to enter into agreements or arrangements for the transfer of persons already sentenced for covered offenses, and for the transfer of criminal proceedings (Arts. 45 and 47).

Investigations. Article 49 encourages bilateral and multilateral arrangements for joint investigative bodies, and Article 50 mandates the use of special investigative techniques (including controlled deliveries and, where appropriate, other methods such as electronic surveillance and undercover operations) where permitted by domestic law. It allows for "case-by-case" arrangements for such use in the absence of agreement.

e. Technical Assistance and Information Exchange

States parties must develop or improve training for their personnel involved in preventing and combating corruption and consider affording ("according to their capacity") technical assistance for such training to developing countries (Art. 60(2)). States parties must consider sharing analytical expertise concerning corruption with a view to developing common definitions, standards, and methodologies (Art. 61(2)). States parties must make efforts to enhance cooperation with developing countries, including through financial and material assistance and technical assistance to support those countries' efforts to fight corruption (Arts. 60 and 62).

f. Monitoring Arrangements

In contrast to other corruption treaties, the UNCAC does not establish a clear monitoring or evaluation mechanism for reviewing and commenting upon implementation by states parties. Article 63 does provide for a Conference of States Parties to the Convention to be convened within a year of the UNCAC entering into force (that is, by December 14, 2006) to "promote and review its implementation" (Art. 63(1)). Article 63(7) authorizes the Conference of States Parties to establish, "if it deems it necessary, any appropriate mechanism or body to assist in the effective implementation of the Convention." However, the UNCAC provides no specific rules or framework for how that task is to be accomplished. What would be your suggestions for an effective mechanism?

5. Implementation

The proliferation of multilateral anticorruption conventions will have little effect on the primary conduct of corrupt officials absent effective implementation of the convention provisions in domestic law and the initiation of bribery investigations and prosecutions around the globe. Consider the following case brought under the Canadian statute passed to satisfy Canada's obligations under the OECD Convention. In relevant part, Section 3 of the Canadian Corruption of Foreign Public Officials Act of 1999 provides:

> 3.(1) Every person commits an offence who, in order to obtain or retain an advantage in the course of business, directly or indirectly gives, offers or agrees to give or offer a loan, reward, advantage or benefit of any kind to a foreign public official or to any person for the benefit of a foreign public official.
>
> (a) as consideration for an act or omission by the official in connection with the performance of the official's duties or functions; or
>
> (b) to induce the official to use his or her position to influence any acts or decisions of the foreign state or public international organization for which the official performs duties or functions.

The Canadian Act, in subsections 3.(4) and 3.(5), allows for "facilitation payments," which are made to expedite or secure the performance by a public official of any "act

of a routine nature" that is part of the foreign public official's duties or functions.[39]
Consider the following Canadian case.

R. v. WATTS

[2005] A.J. 568, QUICKLAW (A.C.Q.B. Jan. 10, 2005) (Oral Judgment)

THE COURT CLERK: Hydro Kleen Systems . . . stands charged that it, [b]etween the
1st day of August, 2000, and the 1st day of December, 2001, at or near Red Deer and
elsewhere in the Province of Alberta, in order to obtain or retain an advantage in the
course of business directly or indirectly gave, offered, or agreed to give or offer a loan,
reward, advantage or benefit, to wit: the sum of $28,299.88 more or less to a foreign
public official, to wit: Hector Ramirez Garcia[40] for the benefit of Hector Ramirez Garcia
as consideration for an act or omission by Hector Ramirez Garcia in connection with the
performance of his duties or functions on behalf of the United States of America,
United States Department of Justice, Immigration and Naturalization Service, contrary
to section 3(1)(a) of the Corruption of Foreign Public Officials Act SC 1998, C34.[41]

How say you to this charge? Do you plead guilty or not guilty on behalf of the
accused corporation?

MR. WILSON [representing Hydro Kleen Systems, Inc.]: The plea is guilty,
My Lord.

THE COURT: Exhibit 1 in the sentencing hearing then will be the agreed statement of facts filed by the Crown. . . .

EXHIBIT S-1—AGREED STATEMENT OF FACTS: Hydro Kleen Systems Inc.
[HKS] . . . is a company incorporated pursuant to the laws of Alberta and carries on
business in Red Deer and throughout North America. The business, which is referred
to as pigging, involves removing coke and other byproducts of the oil refining process.
[In pigging operations, inspection and cleaning devices called pigs are sent through
pipelines to check the condition of pipelines and clean them.] . . . Hydro Kleen Systems
Inc. and its competitors conduct a substantial portion of this business in the United
States of America by sending Canadian employees to the United States. . . . Robert C.
Watts was the president and majority shareholder of Hydro Kleen Systems Inc. Paulette
Francis Bakke was an employee of Hydro Kleen Systems Inc., holding the position of
operations coordinator. Don Forsey (phonetic) was an employee of Hydro Kleen Sys-
tems Inc., holding the position of worldwide sales and export manager.

Hector Ramirez Garcia was . . . a foreign public official holding the position of
senior immigration inspector with the United States Department of Justice, Immigration and Naturalization Service, stationed at the . . . Calgary International Airport.
Garcia and other INS officials were assigned to process and approve or refuse applications for . . . visas, a non-immigrant work permit available to Canadian citizens who
are employed by companies that have offices in both Canada and the United
States. . . . A fee of $110 is collected at the time of application. No additional fee
can be paid to expedite the process. . . .

---

39. See Dept. of Justice, Canada, The Corruption of Foreign Public Officials Act: A Guide (May 1999),
http://www.justice.gc.ca/eng/dept-min/pub/cfpoa-lcape/index.html. For the statute's text, see Canadian Legal Information Institute, Corruption of Foreign Public Officials Act (Feb. 1, 2002), http://
www.canlii.org/ca/sta/c-45.2/whole.html.

40. In a separate proceeding, Hector Garcia pled guilty to two counts of corruptly accepting secret
commissions under §426(1)(a)(ii) of the Criminal Code of Canada. Only one of the counts related to the
Hydro Kleen case. He received six-month jail sentences for each count, served concurrently. —EDS.

41. The Corruption of Foreign Public Officials Act was enacted to implement the OECD Convention. —EDS.

Mr. Forsey and Garcia were acquainted through a church connection. After Forsey told Garcia that Hydro Kleen Systems Inc. was periodically having problems in getting its employees over the border, Garcia approached Forsey and offered his services as an immigration consultant. . . . Garcia was hired in the name of Genesis Solutions 2000 by Hydro Kleen Systems Inc. as an immigration consultant on or about August, 2000. Garcia's services were retained by Hydro Kleen Systems Inc. in order to reduce legal fees paid to immigration lawyers and also because he knew all of the subtleties of the United States law, particularly as they vary over time. Garcia's services would better ensure that fewer, if any, difficulties would confront Hydro Kleen Systems Inc. or its employees in attempting to enter the United States.

Forsey introduced Garcia to Hydro Kleen Systems Inc. and participated in meetings which Garcia had with the company. Paulette Bakke made arrangements for Genesis Solutions 2000 to be added to the Hydro Kleen Systems Inc. payroll, and Robert Watts was aware that Hydro Kleen Systems Inc. had hired Garcia in the name of Genesis Solutions 2000 as an immigration consultant as set out above.

Between September 8th, 2000, and November 30th, 2001, both dates inclusive, Hydro Kleen Systems Inc. directly deposited $28,299.88 to the Genesis Solutions 2000 account with the Royal Bank of Canada. . . . These payments were made from the Hydro Kleen Systems Inc. payroll account. Garcia used all funds for his own personal purposes.

In return for these payments, as an immigration consultant, Garcia . . . advised Hydro Kleen Systems Inc. employees on what to say when crossing the border. . . . Garcia also assisted Hydro Kleen Systems Inc. officials and employees in drafting letters and documents that the Hydro Kleen Systems employees would use to apply for visas and/or to gain entry at United States port of entry. Under the terms of his employment with the Immigration and Naturalization Services, Garcia was prohibited from taking on outside work without permission from his superiors. At no time did he advise his superiors of his work for Hydro Kleen Systems, nor did he have permission to do this work. . . .

Without the knowledge of Hydro Kleen Systems Inc. and without instructions from Hydro Kleen Systems Inc., Garcia undertook an investigation of a number of persons employed by firms in competition with Hydro Kleen Systems Inc. It was his opinion that these persons were illegally gaining entry into the United States. In particular, his investigation focused on employees of Hydro Kleen Systems Inc.'s competitors, namely Innovative Coke Expulsion Inc. [ICE]. Garcia entered comments concerning these employees into a United States computer system named the national automated immigration lookout system. . . . As a result of Garcia's actions, these individuals were denied entry into the United States, in some cases after further questioning by Immigration and Naturalization Services' officers.

On or about September 27th, 2001, Garcia, on his own initiative, without the knowledge of Hydro Kleen Systems Inc., denied [an ICE employee] entry into the United States. He also required [the employee] to return on the following Monday and provide him with various application related documents which Garcia took and improperly photocopied. On or about October 4th, 2001, Garcia, on his own initiative and without Hydro Kleen Systems Inc.'s request, improperly provided copies of the confidential documents which he had seized from [the ICE employee] to Ms. Bakke and requested that Hydro Kleen Systems Inc. assist him with his investigation. . . .

[A]n undated email from Garcia to Ms. Bakke [advised] that he was working on petitions for Hydro Kleen Systems Inc. employees. By reply email, Bakke provided the names of seven persons for which she required . . . visas. . . .

On October 19th, 2001, Mr. Justice John D. Rooke of the Court of Queen's Bench granted an . . . order permitting representatives of ICE to conduct a search on the Hydro Kleen Systems Inc. premises. The order was executed on October 24th, 2001.

During that search, copies of the documents which Garcia had seized from [the ICE employee] were located and seized from a briefcase in the office of Robert C. Watts. Watts confirmed that the briefcase was his and stated that he got the . . . documents from his lawyer. . . . Watts had, in fact, received the documents from Ms. Bakke or another HKS employee one or two days before the execution of the . . . order.

And those are the facts that the Crown alleges and seeks to be admitted.

MR. WILSON: For the record, I formally admit those facts, My Lord.

THE COURT: On the basis of those facts, the court is therefore prepared to accept the guilty plea.

THE COURT: [P]ursuant to section 722 of the Criminal Code, . . . one of the individuals wishes to read his victim impact statement to the court. . . .

MR. SULLIVAN [President of Innovative Coke Expulsion, Inc.]: Innovative Coke Expulsion Inc., an Alberta company, was a competitor of Hydro Kleen Systems, an Alberta company doing business in Canada and the United States.

. . . Hector Ramirez Garcia, a citizen of the United States of America, . . . was convicted of accepting secret commissions under section 426(1)(a)(ii) of the Criminal Code of Canada. . . . Garcia's assistance in the preparation of visas conferred an improper benefit in a competitive environment. Our employees' economic prospects were harmed. Were our shareholders not of some financial strength, our company would have gone out of business.

To corruptly give a reward or benefit to a government employee who has the power to influence normal commercial acts is reprehensible and against any system of morality and law. Corruption distorts markets and harms overall economic, social, and political development. It is a pernicious disease and needs to be resisted by all citizens. This is the first case in Canada under Corruption of Foreign Public Officials Act 1998. To comply with regulations and the law has an economic cost. Unless all corporations comply and bear that cost, there can be no equal competition. The process is flawed. A lower cost structure as a result of non-compliance with the law is not acceptable.

In our case, this damage — the damage inflicted went beyond the monetary value of the corrupt payment to Garcia by Hydro Kleen Group. Our own employees questioned the point in maintaining our own ethical values. What's the use, was the most asked question. With this conviction and guilty plea under the Corruption of Foreign Public Official Act, I feel we can say that most assuredly the system works. Thank you.

MR. BEATTIE: With respect to the sentence, . . . the Corruption of Foreign Public Officials Act, section 3 subsection (2) provides [for a sentence not to exceed five years. The applicable sentencing principles emphasize specific and general deterrence.]

In this case, since there is a corporate accused involved, the most appropriate way to express this would be the imposition of a high fine, and it is the submission of the Crown, and I understand that the defence is in agreement with this recommendation, that a fine of $25,000, payable forthwith, would be an appropriate way of dealing with this matter. . . .

MR. WILSON: [Intervenes to emphasize that while Hydro Kleen hired Garcia to face fewer difficulties for its employees in attempting to enter the United States,] there is nothing to indicate that as a result of the contract with Garcia that my client's employees were improperly admitted into the U.S., and there's nothing to indicate that at any time my client instructed Garcia or paid Garcia to frustrate or impede the entry of competitor employees into the U.S.

THE COURT: . . . Where someone is dealing in international trade, especially with the United States, who is our closest and most important trading partner, matters that involve corruption that might interfere with trade are of much importance to Alberta. . . .

Mr. Sullivan has suggested, as has the Crown, that deterrence of individuals is of the utmost importance in these types of cases. Whether a $25,000 fine is significant or not, I can only determine that Mr. Beattie must have canvassed the significance and the amount of the fine and what effect it might have on Hydro Kleen as being a significant amount.

It bothers the court that these people are able to plea from a corporation to protect the operating minds of the company from the stigma attached to a criminal record. However, the court does take into consideration that the operating minds of this corporation do not escape with their integrity intact.

Mr. Sullivan, you have indicated in your statement that your employees have asked themselves, What is the use of being honest, being proper, in your business, activities? All I can say to you is, as a citizen, you have to appreciate there are many more important things than profit. Maybe there is no financial value, but I think our society still places a large value on the loss of one's soul, loss of one's integrity, a loss of one's good reputation, all for the sake of more profit.

I do not think your employees want to be seen as slippery, slimy snakes that slither on their bellies in order to win business advantage. That is, in my opinion, most people will conduct themselves in their business affairs in a high ethical standard because they want to be thought well of. And in many ways, that is the more important deterrent when people conduct their business practices.

In this case, I take into consideration Mr. Wilson's statements that a guilty plea has been entered. In these types of charges, especially the *mens rea* elements are difficult for the Crown to prove. A guilty plea means that a three-week trial was avoided, that the individual has accepted responsibility. A significant fine has been agreed to, and on those factors, I am not able to determine that the sentence is unfit and would thus justify my interference with the penalty arrangements that counsel have worked out amongst themselves.

For those reasons, thus I am prepared to accept the recommendation of the Crown as agreed to by the defence, and Hydro Kleen Systems Inc. will be fined $25,000, the fine to be paid forthwith.

NOTES AND QUESTIONS

1. Does Canada's statute effectively implement the OECD Convention? Canada ratified the UNCAC on October 2, 2007. (For the reservations it entered in doing so, see http://www.unodc.org/documents/treaties/UNCAC/ReservationsDeclarations/DeclarationsandReservations14Aug2008.pdf.) Does Canada need to amend its statute to comply with the UNCAC? Would the conduct described in this case subject the individuals and company to liability under the FCPA?

2. *Prosecutions under anticorruption conventions.* A number of states have brought national prosecutions under domestic laws enacted pursuant to the OECD Convention's provisions. See OECD, Country Reports on the Implementation of the OECD Anti-Bribery Convention Compilation of the Recommendations Made in the Phase 2 Reports (Feb. 2009), available at http://www.oecd.org/document/24/0,2340,en_2649_37447_1933144_1_1_1_37447,00.html; see also Margaret Ayres et al., Developments in U.S. and International Efforts to Prevent Corruption, 41 Intl.

Law. 597, 604-608 (2007). Sweden reported two convictions for bribery of foreign public officials in a case involving a World Bank project. Korea reported two convictions, both involving bribery of U.S. officials, and Switzerland reported one conviction. A number of states parties to the OECD Convention — notably Belgium, Brazil, Czech Republic, Finland, France, Ireland, Italy, New Zealand, Portugal, and the United Kingdom — have reported ongoing investigations or prosecutions under the Convention. It is difficult to identify prosecutions under the broader anticorruption conventions because the evaluation and monitoring processes for the IACAC and the COE Convention thus far have focused on preventive measures, investigation, and related issues. An evaluation of the implementation of criminalization provisions began in April 2006 for the IACAC and in January 2007 for the COE Convention. The details of the UNCAC evaluation mechanism have yet to be established.

3. *Domestic legislation.* One hindrance to prosecutions could be a lack of appropriate domestic legislation criminalizing the targeted practices. As of 2008, however, all 37 states parties to the OECD Convention, the narrowest in scope of all the multilateral conventions, had passed domestic implementing legislation, such as the Corruption of Foreign Public Officials Act relied on by Canada in *R. v. Watts*. The status of domestic criminal legislation for the broader anticorruption treaties, however, is difficult to evaluate given the absence of a focused evaluation of states parties' implementation of the criminalization provisions.

4. *Effect on corruption.* Some commentators contend that "[d]espite this impressive institutionalization of anti-corruption obligations and programs, . . . there is little evidence of any diminution in the incidence of corruption in, and by nationals of, the participating countries." Daniel K. Tarullo, The Limits of Institutional Design: Implementing the OECD Anti-Bribery Convention, 44 Va. J. Intl. L. 665, 666 (2004). The incidence of corruption — and thus the effectiveness of this international movement — is very difficult to assess empirically. One effort to test the impact of the Inter-American Convention Against Corruption (IACAC) demonstrates that the ratification and even the implementation into domestic law of this anticorruption treaty did not effect significant positive changes in corruption perception in the countries and time period (1996-2002) studied. Giorleny D. Altamirano, The Impact of the Inter-American Convention Against Corruption, 38 U. Miami Inter-Am. L. Rev. 487, 490-492, 537 (2006-2007). The author of this study concluded that, to make a difference, the legal threat of accountability must be credible. Further, "[t]he success of anti-corruption strategies depends on a number of factors including political will and commitment of national leaders, transparency and access to information, and an independent judicial system." Id. at 547. International assistance in monitoring anticorruption efforts, promoting a negative perception of corruption, and supporting states parties in their efforts to strengthen enforcement institutions is also required to make a real difference. Id. In short, as Giorleny Altamirano concludes, "[t]he fact that corruption perception has increased [in some countries after the IACAC] does not necessarily mean that the IACAC is failing to influence changes in behavior within the countries. Corruption is a pandemic, deeply rooted in a country's historical, social, economic, and institutional situation. The IACAC constitutes an important step in the fight against corruption, but it is only part of a systematic approach against the problem." Id. at 539.

Ndiva Kofele-Kale has reached a similar conclusion regarding the effect of anti-corruption initiatives in Africa, arguing that despite the many legal and rhetorical commitments made, "Africa has made little progress on this front." Ndiva Kofele-Kale, Change or the Illusion of Change: The War Against Official Corruption in Africa, 38 Geo. Wash. Intl. L. Rev. 697, 697 (2006). Kofele-Kale also cautions that treaty commitments will not do the entire job:

> Corruption flourishes in countries where a culture of transparency and accountability is lacking; where democratic institutions have been compromised; where market participants do not operate under an internationally-accepted set of standards; and where the rule of law ceases to exist. Since the majority of African states exist under these conditions, it is not surprising to encounter the abuse of public office for private gain. Consequently elaborate measures need to be taken in order to both establish an environment free of corruption and foster the goal of spurring economic development.

Id. at 697-698.

5. *U.S. implementation.* As discussed above, the United States amended the FCPA in 1998 to implement the OECD Convention. In addition to the FCPA, numerous U.S. federal statutes address a broader range of corrupt practices. These include 18 U.S.C. §201 (bribery of domestic federal public officials and accepting/soliciting such bribes); id. §§642-666 (embezzlement of public funds); id. §§1956-1957 (laundering the proceeds of crime); id. §§1341, 1343, 1346 (mail and wire fraud); id. §§1501-1520 (obstruction of justice); and 31 U.S.C. §§5311-5330 (Bank Secrecy Act). In light of this legislative framework, the United States adopted the following "understanding" upon ratification of the IACAC in 2000:

> . . . There is an extensive network of laws already in place in the United States that criminalize a wide range of corrupt acts. Although United States laws may not in all cases be defined in terms or elements identical to those used in the Convention, it is the understanding of the United States . . . that the kinds of official corruption which are intended under the Convention to be criminalized would in fact be criminal offenses under U.S. law. Accordingly, the United States does not intend to enact new legislation to implement Article VII of the Convention.

OAS, Dept. of Intl. Law, United States' Reservations, http://www.oas.org/juridico/english/Sigs/b-58.html (last visited July 13, 2009).

Additional understandings reflected the United States' view that, in light of existing law, no new federal offenses of "transnational bribery" or "illicit enrichment" would be required in order to comply with the obligations imposed by the Convention. Id.

When the United States ratified the UNCAC, it included a declaration stating that the provisions of the Convention (with the exception of Articles 44 (Extradition) and 46 (Mutual Legal Assistance)) are "non-self-executing." It also included a reservation based on federalism concerns:

> . . . U.S. federal criminal law, which regulates conduct based on its effect on interstate or foreign commerce, or another federal interest, serves as an important component of the legal regime within the United States for combating corruption and is broadly effective for this purpose. . . . There are conceivable situations involving offenses of a purely local character where U.S. federal and state criminal law may not be entirely adequate to satisfy an obligation under the Convention. Similarly, in the U.S. system, the states are responsible for preventive measures governing their own officials. . . . Accordingly, there may be situations where state and federal law will not be entirely adequate to satisfy an obligation in . . . the Convention. The United States . . . therefore reserves to the

obligations set forth in the Convention to the extent they (1) address conduct that would fall within this narrow category of highly localized activity or (2) involve preventive measures not covered by federal law governing state and local officials. . . .

UNODC, UN Convention Against Corruption, http://www.unodc.org/unodc/en/treaties/CAC/signatories.html (last visited July 13, 2009). Are these conditions to ratification necessary? Why?

CHAPTER
15

Terrorism

Terrorism and counterterrorism are vast legal topics, themselves the subjects of entire casebooks. The present chapter does not pretend to cover all the crucial areas in the legal treatment of terrorism. Attempts to bring individual terrorists to justice for specific acts frequently implicate many of the issues addressed elsewhere in this book: international cooperation in obtaining evidence, the use of extraordinary rendition or abduction, the reach of extraterritorial (or even universal) jurisdiction, the "extradite or prosecute" obligation, the applicability of constitutional rights to noncitizens, and so on. We focus here, however, on the international and transnational criminal law of terrorism: the efforts of states and the UN to define and repress a crime of terrorism through international law; the efforts of one government, that of the United States, to use its own domestic criminal law transnationally as a weapon against terrorism; and—just as important—the controversial efforts by the U.S. government to treat terrorists as "enemy combatants" who are not entitled to the rights granted by the justice system in criminal cases.

A. WHAT IS TERRORISM?

1. Terrorism: An Essentially Contested Concept

Terrorism is hardly a new phenomenon, and many governments have struggled over the years to combat it within their own borders. But, since September 11, 2001, no form of violence has consumed the world's attention more than terrorism, and specifically international terrorism. Yet states, political movements, and individuals scarcely agree on the definition of terrorism, or even its broadest contours. Richard Baxter, former professor of law at Harvard and judge on the International Court of Justice, once sardonically noted: "We have cause to regret that a legal concept of 'terrorism' was ever inflicted upon us. The term is imprecise; it is ambiguous; and above all, it serves no operative legal purpose."[1] One study counted 109 different definitions advanced between 1936 and 1981, including half a dozen by the U.S. government alone.[2] Both the UN General Assembly (UNGA) and the UN Security

---

1. Richard R. Baxter, A Skeptical Look at the Concept of Terrorism, 7 Akron L. Rev. 380, 380 (1974).
2. Walter Laqueur, Reflections on Terrorism, 64 For. Aff. 86, 88 (1986). See the extended discussion of definitional controversies in Political Terrorism (Alex P. Schmid & Albert J. Jongman eds., 1988).

Council (UNSC) have proposed definitions of terrorism, but the two definitions differ from each other.[3]

Theorists sometimes distinguish between *tactical* and *political* definitions of terrorism — that is, definitions that focus on terrorism's typical tactic of murderous attacks on the innocent, versus definitions that focus on terrorism's political goals, or the political status of the actors.[4] Many definitions combine both. Thus, the British scholar Sir Adam Roberts defines terrorism as

> the use of violence, often against people not directly involved in a conflict, by groups operating clandestinely, which generally claim to have high political or religious purposes, and believe that creating a climate of terror will assist attainment of their objectives. Terrorism of this kind almost always appears to be non-governmental, but in particular cases movements engaging in terrorism may have a degree of clandestine support from governments.[5]

A purely tactical definition might allow that states can themselves count as terrorist organizations, if they use violence to terrorize their opponents.[6] A political definition, on the other hand, might distinguish state violence from violence by non-state actors and insist that only the latter is terrorism, because only the latter is illegitimate. Yet militant groups often regard themselves as righteous warriors whose clandestine tactics are a necessity of asymmetric combat against enemies with trained armies and advanced military technology. It has become almost a cliché that one person's terrorist is another's freedom fighter.

Some definitions use political criteria to exempt certain organizations that would be included as terrorists under a tactical definition. For example, the Arab Convention on the Suppression of Terrorism defines terrorism broadly, but adds: "All cases of struggle by whatever means, including armed struggle, against foreign occupation and aggression for liberation and self-determination, in accordance with the principles of international law, shall not be regarded as an offence. This provision shall not apply to any act prejudicing the territorial integrity of any Arab State."[7] These provisions seem tailored so that antiforeign liberation groups do not count as terrorists, while antigovernment separatist groups within Arab states do count.

Virtually nobody disputes that the 9/11 attack on the World Trade Center was a paradigmatic case of international terrorism. In the vast literature aiming to define terrorism, several factors recur frequently, and all were present in the 9/11 attacks. These include violence or the threat of violence;[8] stealth rather than open conflict;[9] political or other ideological motivation;[10] intent to frighten a wider audience

---

3. International Convention for the Suppression of the Financing of Terrorism, G.A. Res. 54/109, ¶2(1)(b), U.N. GAOR, 54th Sess., U.N. Doc. A/RES/54/49 (Dec. 9, 1999); Threats to International Peace and Security Caused by Terrorist Acts, S.C. Res. 1566, ¶3, U.N. Doc. S/RES/1566 (Oct. 8, 2004).

4. C. A. J. Coady, Terrorism and Innocence, 8 J. Ethics 37, 40 (2004).

5. Adam Roberts, Defining Terrorism: Focusing on the Targets, International Institute for Strategic Studies, 7 (9) Strategic Comments (Nov. 2001), at 6.

6. Coady, supra note 4, at 40.

7. Arab Convention on the Suppression of Terrorism, art. 2(a) (Apr. 22, 1998) (adopted in Cairo), available at http://www.al-bab.com/arab/docs/league/terrorism98.htm.

8. James M. Lutz & Brenda J. Lutz, Terrorism: Origins and Evolution 7 (2005).

9. Ted Robert Gurr, Some Characteristics of Political Terrorism in the 1960s; In the Politics of Terrorism 31, 33 (Michael Stohl ed., 3d ed. 1988).

10. William G. O'Neill, Concept Paper: Beyond the Slogans: How Can the UN Respond to Terrorism? International Peace Academy, Conference on Responding to Terrorism: What Role for the United Nations?, at 6 (Oct. 25-26, 2002) (stating that "[t]errorism is not common crime or random violence that harms civilians; it is premeditated and has a political or religious purpose: regime change, ending an

(leading to selection of symbolic or high-visibility targets);[11] and targeting of civilians.[12] In addition, al Qaeda acted on its own rather than at the behest of any state, and the organization has no peaceful purposes. The 9/11 attacks were widely denounced as evil even by enemies of the United States and ideological soulmates of al Qaeda.

But what about actions that share only a few of these characteristics of the attacks on the World Trade Center? Are they terrorism? Are they ever legitimate? Here, consensus begins to unravel. Consider a few examples:

- The 9/11 attack on the Pentagon and the earlier al Qaeda attack on the U.S.S. *Cole*, a naval destroyer docked in Yemen. In a genuine international armed conflict—paradigmatically, a war between two states—both the Pentagon and the Navy destroyer would be legitimate military targets, unlike the "civilian" World Trade Center. So, too, groups such as Hamas and Hezbollah have launched attacks against Israeli military units. Likewise, Iraqi insurgents have carried out suicide bombings and planted improvised explosive devices (IEDs), targeting U.S. forces occupying Iraq. Are attacks on purely military targets terrorism? What if they are attacks against a foreign occupying army?

- In 1995, members of a Japanese religious cult, Aum Shinrikyo, released poison gas on a Tokyo subway, killing and injuring more than 50 people. Aum Shinrikyo had no political aims, although the subway attacks may have been a misguided attempt to deflect the government's investigation of the cult for other crimes, including the murder of dissident members. Must terrorist attacks be politically motivated? Should religiously motivated abortion clinic bombers and assassins of abortion doctors be regarded as ordinary criminals or as terrorists?

- Does terrorism include attacks against property rather than people? What about vandalism, such as protestors throwing rocks through windows or nonviolent demonstrators tearing down a security fence to gain access to official buildings to stage a sit-in? What about cyberterrorism, for example, hackers intentionally causing major computer networks to crash? Or ecoterrorism, such as burning down new housing developments of McMansions while they are being built? Consider the Boston Tea Party. In 1773, militant American colonists, angry about a tea tax imposed by the British king, boarded a merchant ship in Boston harbor late at night and threw the tea overboard, destroying the shipment. Was this an act of international terrorism?

- Among the most prominent crimes associated with terrorism is aircraft hijackings. Until 9/11, the intention of organized hijackers was almost never to harm the passengers—it was to publicize a political cause. The typical hijacking involved seizing an aircraft and ordering it to land in a country whose rulers were in ideological sympathy with the hijackers. Then the hijackers would negotiate the release of the hostages, sometimes obtaining amnesty for themselves and occasionally gaining the release of imprisoned colleagues. Groups engaged in hijackings have included Palestinian and Sikh independence groups, Japanese

occupation, promoting a world view based on a specific interpretation of theology, resisting influence from external political, cultural or religious sources"); Kevin Jack Riley & Bruce Hoffman, RAND Monograph Report, Domestic Terrorism: A National Assessment of State and Local Preparedness 2-3 (1995); Bruce Hoffman, Inside Terrorism 43 (1998) (noting that the terrorist "is fundamentally an altruist: he believes that he is serving a 'good' cause designed to achieve a greater good for a wider constituency").

11. See Audrey Kurth Cronin, Rethinking Sovereignty: American Strategy in the Age of Terrorism, 44 Survival 119, 121 (2002); Lutz & Lutz, supra note 8, at 8.

12. Riley & Hoffman, supra note 10, at 3.

radicals, Croatian and Kashmiri separatists, and opponents of dictatorships in Portugal, the Philippines, and Pakistan. If hijackers do not intend to harm people or damage property, are they nonetheless terrorists?

- There have been notorious incidents of state-supported terrorism or state terrorism. As we use the terms, *state-supported terrorism* refers to terrorism carried out by non-state organizations receiving support from a state; *state terrorism* refers to state agents themselves carrying out a terrorist attack. In 1988, agents of the government of Libya blew up a civilian airliner over Lockerbie, Scotland, and two years earlier bombed a disco frequented by U.S. troops stationed in Germany. The Taliban government willingly hosted al Qaeda training camps in Afghanistan. The Libyan actions are state terrorism, while the Taliban's are state support for terrorism. But the United States has also sponsored attacks and groups that some label terrorist: during the Cold War, the U.S. government armed mujahedin (militant Islamic fighters) in their ongoing conflict against the USSR in Afghanistan. Some mujahedin veterans, notably Osama bin Laden, later turned against the United States and formed the nucleus of al Qaeda. The U.S. government also armed the *contras*: Nicaraguan rebels trying to overthrow the Sandinista government. In 1986, the United States launched a bombing attack against Libyan leader Muammar al-Qaddafi (missing him but killing his 15-month old adopted daughter). Similarly, in 1998 the U.S. government launched a missile attack against a pharmaceutical factory in Sudan believed to be used by al Qaeda to manufacture chemical weapons. Some have claimed that the factory was nothing more than a pharmaceutical plant, with no al Qaeda connection (the matter remains disputed). Critics denounced these attacks as state terrorism; but some authorities have asserted that if a state does it, then by definition it cannot be terrorism.[13] Should peacetime attacks that would be terrorism if done by non-state groups also count as terrorism if states carry them out or sponsor them?

As mentioned earlier, some definitions categorically reject the possibility of state terrorism,[14] while others leave the possibility open. The term *terrorism* originated during the Reign of Terror in revolutionary France, and thus its origin points to the existence of "state terrorism."[15] The International Law Commission's 1954 Draft Code of Offenses Against the Peace and Security of Mankind recognized the possibility of state terrorism and state-supported terrorism: "the undertaking or encouragement by the authorities of a State of terrorist activities in another State, or the toleration by the authorities of a State of organized activities calculated to carry out terrorist acts in another State" is an offense against the "peace and security of mankind."[16] Additionally, vague language in some definitions condemns certain acts without specifying whether an actor need be public or private, thus leaving open the possibility of state terrorism.[17]

---

13. See Georges Abi-Saab, There Is No Need to Reinvent the Law, Crimes of War: International Law Since September 11 (Sept. 2002), available at http://www.crimesofwar.org/sept-mag/sept-abi.html (noting that larger states are generally opposed to a definition of terrorism that extends to state actors, while small states support such an extension).

14. See, e.g., Boaz Ganor, The Counter-Terrorism Puzzle: A Guide for Decision Makers 19 (2005); Hoffman, supra note 10, at 43 (1998).

15. John F. Murphy, State Support of International Terrorism: Legal, Political, and Economic Dimensions 4 (1989).

16. International Law Commission, Draft Code of Offenses Against the Peace and Security of Mankind art. 1(5) (1951); see also Frederick H. Gareau, State Terrorism and the United States: From Counterinsurgency to the War on Terrorism 15 (2004) (advocating a definition of terrorism that includes the possibility of state terrorism).

17. See, e.g., G.A. Res. 40/61, pmbl. ¶4, U.N. GAOR, 40th Sess., Supp. No. 53, U.N. Doc. A/40/53 (1985).

- It is often thought that political assassinations are terrorist tactics. Historians sometimes describe the nineteenth-century Russian anarchists who assassinated Czar Alexander II as the first terrorist group. If so, what about assassinations and targeted killings carried out clandestinely by (or on behalf of) government agencies? Are these state terrorism, and if so, does that make the governments that carry them out international terrorist organizations?

- Must terrorism be intended to terrorize a population? What if it has a more limited political aim — for example, what if a non-state group kidnaps a soldier as a hostage, in order to trade him or her for imprisoned group members? What if militants destroy property as a one-time political protest of some specific event? What if they narrowly target enemy leaders, rather than random victims? Is it still terrorism?

- Consider the militant groups Hamas and Hezbollah. Both of them commit terrorist acts. But both of them also provide indispensible social services to civilian communities in territory they control. Other groups as well combine violence with provision of civic services and philanthropic activities. Are members of the philanthropic "wing" of such hybrid organizations terrorists? Should financial contributors to the philanthropies be regarded as accomplices to terrorism?

- Are guerrilla fighters, who carry out attacks and then melt back into the surrounding population, terrorists? Were "irregular" American revolutionaries who murdered Tories therefore terrorists? What about Nelson Mandela and the African National Congress, which struggled violently against apartheid in South Africa? What about the Irgun, a Jewish militant group whose bombing of the King David Hotel in Jerusalem helped prompt the end of the British mandate in Palestine and the formation of the State of Israel? Irgun leader Menachem Begin later became Israel's prime minister. Additional Protocol I to the Geneva Conventions includes guerrilla fighters among those who qualify for prisoner of war status, so long as they display their arms openly during military operations (Article 44); and the Protocol gives "armed conflicts in which peoples are fighting against colonial domination and alien occupation and against racist regimes in the exercise of their right of self-determination" (Article 1(4)) equivalent legal status to wars between states. This Protocol currently has 168 states parties. (For further discussion, see Chapter 21, Section A.2.b.ii.)

Theorists sometimes use the term *essentially contested concept* to describe words for which every definition is so loaded with disputed theoretical or political assumptions that it seems impossible to arrive at a neutral, value-free, nonpartisan definition. The examples above, and others that readers can readily call to mind, illustrate that the word *terrorism* is almost certainly an essentially contested concept. As terrorism expert Bruce Hoffman somewhat cynically observes: "If one identifies with the victim of the violence . . . then the act is terrorism. If, however, one identifies with the perpetrator . . . it is not terrorism."[18] Is it that simple?

2.   *Definitions of Terrorism in U.S. Law*

At least four statutory definitions of terrorism appear in current U.S. law: one in an immigration law that prohibits granting visas to known terrorists or potential terrorists, one in a foreign relations law requiring the secretary of state to provide Congress

---

18. Hoffman, supra note 10, at 31.

with an annual report about terrorist organizations, one in general criminal law, and one defining a crime of terrorism by enemy combatants triable before military commissions.

8 U.S.C. §1182 [immigration law]

§1182.   Inadmissible Aliens . . .

(a)(3)(B)(iii) **"Terrorist activity" defined.** As used in this chapter, the term "terrorist activity" means any activity which is unlawful under the laws of the place where it is committed (or which, if it had been committed in the United States, would be unlawful under the laws of the United States or any State) and which involves any of the following:

(I) The highjacking or sabotage of any conveyance (including an aircraft, vessel, or vehicle).

(II) The seizing or detaining, and threatening to kill, injure, or continue to detain, another individual in order to compel a third person (including a governmental organization) to do or abstain from doing any act as an explicit or implicit condition for the release of the individual seized or detained.

(III) A violent attack upon an internationally protected person (as defined in section 1116(b)(4) of Title 18) or upon the liberty of such a person.

(IV) An assassination.

(V) The use of any—

(a) biological agent, chemical agent, or nuclear weapon or device, or

(b) explosive, firearm, or other weapon or dangerous device (other than for mere personal monetary gain),

with intent to endanger, directly or indirectly, the safety of one or more individuals or to cause substantial damage to property.

(VI) A threat, attempt, or conspiracy to do any of the foregoing.

(iv) Engage in terrorist activity defined. As used in this chapter, the term "engage in terrorist activity" means, in an individual capacity or as a member of an organization—

(I) to commit or to incite to commit, under circumstances indicating an intention to cause death or serious bodily injury, a terrorist activity;

(II) to prepare or plan a terrorist activity;

(III) to gather information on potential targets for terrorist activity;

(IV) to solicit funds or other things of value for—

(aa) a terrorist activity;

(bb) a terrorist organization described in clause (vi)(I) or (vi)(II); or

(cc) a terrorist organization described in clause (vi)(III), unless the solicitor can demonstrate that he did not know, and should not reasonably have known, that the solicitation would further the organization's terrorist activity; . . .

(VI) to commit an act that the actor knows, or reasonably should know, affords material support, including a safe house, transportation, communications, funds, transfer of funds or other material financial benefit, false documentation or identification, weapons (including chemical, biological, or radiological weapons), explosives, or training—

(aa) for the commission of a terrorist activity;

(bb) to any individual who the actor knows, or reasonably should know, has committed or plans to commit a terrorist activity;

(cc) to a terrorist organization described in subclause (I) or (II) of clause (vi) or to any member of such an organization; or

(dd) to a terrorist organization described in clause (vi)(III), or to any member of such an organization, unless the actor can demonstrate by clear and convincing evidence that the actor did not know, and should not reasonably have known, that the organization was a terrorist organization. . . .

(vi) Terrorist organization defined. As used in this section, the term "terrorist organization" means an organization —

(I) designated under [8 U.S.C. §1189];

(II) otherwise designated, upon publication in the Federal Register, by the Secretary of State in consultation with or upon the request of the Attorney General, as a terrorist organization, after finding that the organization engages in the activities described in subclause (I), (II), or (III) of clause (iv), or that the organization provides material support to further terrorist activity; or

(III) that is a group of two or more individuals, whether organized or not, which engages in the activities described in subclause (I), (II), or (III) of clause (iv).

22 U.S.C. §2656F [foreign relations law]

§2656f.   Annual Country Reports on Terrorism . . .

(d) Definitions. As used in this section —

(1) the term "international terrorism" means terrorism involving citizens or the territory of more than 1 country;

(2) the term "terrorism" means premeditated, politically motivated violence perpetrated against noncombatant targets by subnational groups or clandestine agents;

(3) the term "terrorist group" means any group practicing, or which has significant subgroups which practice, international terrorism; . . .

18 U.S.C. §2331 [criminal law][19]

§2331.   Definitions

As used in this chapter [18 U.S.C. §2331 et seq.] —

(1) the term "international terrorism" means activities that —

(A) involve violent acts or acts dangerous to human life that are a violation of the criminal laws of the United States or of any State, or that would be a criminal violation if committed within the jurisdiction of the United States or of any State;

(B) appear to be intended —

(i) to intimidate or coerce a civilian population;

(ii) to influence the policy of a government by intimidation or coercion; or

(iii) to affect the conduct of a government by mass destruction, assassination, or kidnapping; and

---

19. A similar definition appears in the Foreign Intelligence Surveillance Act (FISA), 50 U.S.C. §1801(c) and in 18 U.S.C. §3077, setting forth conditions under which someone will receive a reward for offering information regarding "terrorists."

(C) occur primarily outside the territorial jurisdiction of the United States, or transcend national boundaries in terms of the means by which they are accomplished, the persons they appear intended to intimidate or coerce, or the locale in which their perpetrators operate or seek asylum; . . .

(5) the term "domestic terrorism" means activities that—

(A) involve acts dangerous to human life that are a violation of the criminal laws of the United States or of any State;

(B) appear to be intended—

(i) to intimidate or coerce a civilian population;

(ii) to influence the policy of a government by intimidation or coercion; or

(iii) to affect the conduct of a government by mass destruction, assassination, or kidnapping; and

(C) occur primarily within the territorial jurisdiction of the United States.

10 U.S.C. §950v(24) [crimes triable by military commission]

§950v(24). Terrorism. Any person subject to this chapter [establishing military commissions] who intentionally kills or inflicts great bodily harm on one or more protected persons, or intentionally engages in an act that evinces a wanton disregard for human life, in a manner calculated to influence or affect the conduct of government or civilian population by intimidation or coercion, or to retaliate against government conduct, shall be punished. . . .

NOTES AND QUESTIONS

1. These four definitions are very different from one another. Compare them along the following dimensions:

a. Which of them rules out the possibility of state terrorism by definition?
b. Which of them requires that an act be illegal to count as terrorism?
c. Which of them specifies political motivation in order to classify an act as terrorism?
d. Which of them counts attacks on property as terrorism?

2. The definitions are used in laws serving different purposes: One aims to prevent terrorists or potential terrorists from entering the United States, one concerns the kind of terrorist activity that the secretary of state must report about to Congress, and two concern activities that can be punished under criminal law. Do these different policy objectives adequately explain the differences among the four definitions of terrorism?

3. The immigration statute is very broad-ranging in its definition of terrorist organizations and terrorist activity. Notice that "a group of two or more individuals, whether organized or not" that engages in, plans, or gathers information on targets for terrorist activity is a terrorist organization; and anyone who uses a firearm to cause substantial damage to property has engaged in terrorist activity. This includes rebel groups fighting against dictators in their own countries, including rebel groups that the United States supports. Anyone who contributes money to an organization that he or she "knows or should know" is planning terrorist activity has engaged in material

support of terrorism and cannot be admitted to the United States. Thus, individuals who contribute money to dual-purpose organizations like Hamas, which engages in the provision of social services as well as terrorism, are themselves engaging in terrorist activity. Spouses and children of terrorists are excluded from admission to the United States. There is no exception for material support given under duress, and Colombians who have been threatened into making payments to FARC rebels or have ransomed kidnapped relatives from them have been excluded from the United States. Melanie Nezer, The "Material Support" Problem: An Uncertain Future for Thousands of Refugees and Asylum Seekers, 10 Bender's Immigr. Bull. 1849, 1850 (2005). So too, members of Burmese religious minorities who "have contributed to ethnic and religious organizations that are associated with subgroups that oppose the repressive Burmese government" were denied protection because the subgroups are deemed to engage in terrorist activity. Id. (However, in 2006 Secretary of State Condoleezza Rice waived the legal barrier to admission in the case of Burmese refugees.) Are these definitions too broad?

4. Under the general criminal law definition, violent acts that "appear to be intended" to intimidate or coerce a population or influence a government policy through intimidation or coercion are terrorist acts. How broad is the "appear to be intended" clause? Suppose that someone plants a bomb in a mailbox in a misguided attempt to call attention to the lack of security in mailboxes. Should that count as terrorism? Could this definition include activities of criminal gangs with no political agendas?

3. Is Terrorism a Crime or an Act of War — or Both?

Terrorism is usually defined as political violence, but it does not automatically follow that terrorist acts are necessarily crimes. Acts of war are also political violence, as exemplified in General Carl Clausewitz's famous definition of war as politics by other means. In wartime, some violent acts are war crimes, but soldiers who adhere to the laws of war are not regarded as criminals, and the laws of war classify them as privileged belligerents whose lawful acts of combat cannot be prosecuted.[20] Terrorists may well regard themselves as soldiers in a war against imperialists or colonialists. Criminalizing terrorism supposes, on the contrary, that terrorism is not legitimate war making; it is merely murder or another crime.

When an act is both a crime and arguably an act of war, which paradigm ought to prevail? For example, compare the U.S. government's responses to the Oklahoma City bombing with its response to the attacks of 9/11. Timothy McVeigh, the Oklahoma City bomber, detonated a seven-ton truck bomb outside the Alfred P. Murrah Federal Building that killed 168 people, including 19 children — the deadliest act of terrorism committed on U.S. soil before 9/11. According to many, McVeigh, a follower of the radical right, believed himself "at war" with the U.S. government and acted in retaliation for the government's siege and attack in 1993 on the Branch Davidian complex in Waco, Texas, during which 80 cult members, including 27 children, were killed. McVeigh was treated as a criminal — indicted, tried, and ultimately executed pursuant to standard criminal processes. By contrast, from the very outset, the U.S. government chose to treat 9/11 as an act of war, rather than a heinous criminal offense. The term *global war on terror* — often abbreviated GWOT (pronounced "jee-wot") — became a familiar part of the world's vocabulary.

---

20. See Chapter 21 for extensive analysis of war crimes and the legal basis of the belligerent privilege.

A week after 9/11, the U.S. Congress passed an Authorization for the Use of Military Force (AUMF), which declares that "the President is authorized to use all necessary and appropriate force against those nations, organizations, or persons he determines planned, authorized, committed, or aided the terrorist attacks that occurred on September 11, 2001, or harbored such organizations or persons. . . ."[21] In *Hamdi v. Rumsfeld*[22] the Supreme Court held that the AUMF authorizes the detention of "enemy combatants" captured on the battlefield fighting against the United States or its coalition partners; *Hamdi* thus ratifies the conclusion that under the AUMF the struggle against al Qaeda is indeed a "war on terror."[23] But terrorists have also been convicted in civilian U.S. courts for crimes. These observations raise the question of whether terrorism should be classified as war, or crime, or war crime. The following reading analyzes this question.

DAVID LUBAN, THE WAR ON TERRORISM AND THE END OF HUMAN RIGHTS

22 Phil. & Pub. Poly. Q. 9 (2002)

In the immediate aftermath of September 11, President Bush stated that the perpetrators of the deed would be brought to justice. Soon afterwards, the President announced that the United States would engage in a war on terrorism. The first of these statements adopts the familiar language of criminal law and criminal justice. It treats the September 11 attacks as horrific crimes — mass murders — and the government's mission as apprehending and punishing the surviving planners and conspirators for their roles in the crimes. The War on Terrorism is a different proposition, however, and a different model of governmental action — not law but war. Most obviously, it dramatically broadens the scope of action, because now terrorists who knew nothing about September 11 have been earmarked as enemies. But that is only the beginning.

The model of war offers much freer rein than that of law, and therein lies its appeal in the wake of 9/11. First, in war but not in law it is permissible to use lethal force on enemy troops regardless of their degree of personal involvement with the adversary. The conscripted cook is as legitimate a target as the enemy general. Second, in war but not in law "collateral damage," that is, foreseen but unintended killing of noncombatants, is permissible. (Police cannot blow up an apartment building full of people because a murderer is inside, but an air force can bomb the building if it contains a military target.) Third, the requirements of evidence and proof are drastically weaker in war than in criminal justice. Soldiers do not need proof beyond a reasonable doubt, or even proof by a preponderance of evidence, that someone is an enemy soldier before firing on him or capturing and imprisoning him. They don't need proof at all, merely plausible intelligence. Thus, the U.S. military remains regretful but unapologetic about its January 2002 attack on the Afghani town of Uruzgan, in which 21 innocent civilians were killed, based on faulty intelligence that they were al Qaeda fighters. Fourth, in war one can attack an enemy without concern over whether he has done anything. Legitimate targets are those who in the course of combat *might* harm us, not those who *have* harmed us. No doubt there are other significant differences as well. But the basic point should be clear: given Washington's mandate to eliminate

---

21. Pub. L. No. 107-40, 115 Stat. 224 (2001).
22. 542 U.S. 547 (2004).
23. Id. at 520.

the danger of future 9/11s, so far as humanly possible, the model of war offers important advantages over the model of law.

There are disadvantages as well. Most obviously, in war but not in law, fighting back is a *legitimate* response of the enemy. Second, when nations fight a war, other nations may opt for neutrality. Third, because fighting back is legitimate, in war the enemy soldier deserves special regard once he is rendered harmless through injury or surrender. It is impermissible to punish him for his role in fighting the war. Nor can he be harshly interrogated after he is captured. The Third Geneva Convention provides: "Prisoners of war who refuse to answer [questions] may not be threatened, insulted, or exposed to unpleasant or disadvantageous treatment of any kind." And, when the war concludes, the enemy soldier must be repatriated.

Here, however, Washington has different ideas, designed to eliminate these tactical disadvantages in the traditional war model. Washington regards international terrorism not only as a military adversary, but also as a criminal activity and criminal conspiracy. In the law model, criminals don't get to shoot back, and their acts of violence subject them to legitimate punishment. That is what we see in Washington's prosecution of the War on Terrorism. Captured terrorists may be tried before military or civilian tribunals, and shooting back at Americans, including American troops, is a federal crime (for a statute under which John Walker Lindh was indicted criminalizes anyone regardless of nationality, who "outside the United States attempts to kill, or engages in a conspiracy to kill, a national of the United States" or "engages in physical violence with intent to cause serious bodily injury to a national of the United States; or with the result that serious bodily injury is caused to a national of the United States").[24]

Furthermore, the U.S. may rightly demand that other countries not be neutral about murder and terrorism. Unlike the war model, a nation may insist that those who are not with us in fighting murder and terror are against us, because by not joining our operations they are providing a safe haven for terrorists or their bank accounts. By selectively combining elements of the war model and elements of the law model, Washington is able to maximize its own ability to mobilize lethal force against terrorists while eliminating most traditional rights of a military adversary, as well as the rights of innocent bystanders caught in the crossfire.

The legal status of al Qaeda suspects imprisoned at the Guantánamo Bay Naval Base in Cuba is emblematic of this hybrid war-law approach to the threat of terrorism. In line with the war model, they lack the usual rights of criminal suspects—the presumption of innocence, the right to a hearing to determine guilt, the opportunity to prove that the authorities have grabbed the wrong man. But, in line with the law model, they are considered *unlawful* combatants. Because they are not uniformed forces, they lack the rights of prisoners of war and are liable to criminal punishment. Initially, the American government declared that the Guantánamo Bay prisoners have no rights under the Geneva Conventions. In the face of international protests, Washington quickly backpedaled and announced that the Guantánamo Bay prisoners would indeed be treated as decently as POWs—but it also made clear that the prisoners have no right to such treatment. Neither criminal suspects nor POWs, neither fish nor fowl, they inhabit a limbo of rightlessness. Secretary of Defense Rumsfeld's assertion that the U.S. may continue to detain them even if they are acquitted by a military tribunal dramatizes the point.

To understand how extraordinary their status is, consider an analogy. Suppose that Washington declares a War on Organized Crime. Troops are dispatched to Sicily, and a

---

24. Count One of the Lindh indictment charges him with violating 18 U.S.C. §2332(b), the statute quoted in the text. Lindh pled guilty to other offenses—EDS.

number of Mafiosi are seized, brought to Guantánamo Bay, and imprisoned without a hearing for the indefinite future, maybe the rest of their lives. They are accused of no crimes, because their capture is based not on what they have done but on what they might do. After all, to become "made" they took oaths of obedience to the bad guys. Seizing them accords with the war model: they are enemy foot soldiers. But they are foot soldiers out of uniform; they lack a "fixed distinctive emblem," in the words of The Hague Convention. That makes them unlawful combatants, so they lack the rights of POWs. They may object that it is only a unilateral declaration by the American President that has turned them into combatants in the first place—he called it a war, they didn't—and that, since they do not regard themselves as literal foot soldiers it never occurred to them to wear a fixed distinctive emblem. They have a point. It seems too easy for the President to divest anyone in the world of rights and liberty simply by announcing that the U.S. is at war with them and then declaring them unlawful combatants if they resist. But, in the hybrid war-law model, they protest in vain.

Consider another example. In January 2002, U.S. forces in Bosnia seized five Algerians and a Yemeni suspected of al Qaeda connections and took them to Guantánamo Bay. The six had been jailed in Bosnia, but a Bosnian court released them for lack of evidence, and the Bosnian Human Rights Chamber issued an injunction that four of them be allowed to remain in the country pending further legal proceedings. The Human Rights Chamber, ironically, was created under U.S. auspices in the Dayton peace accords, and it was designed specifically to protect against treatment like this. Ruth Wedgwood, a well-known international law scholar at Yale and a member of the Council on Foreign Relations, defended the Bosnian seizure in war-model terms. "I think we would simply argue this was a matter of self-defense. One of the fundamental rules of military law is that you have a right ultimately to act in self-defense. And if these folks were actively plotting to blow up the U.S. embassy, they should be considered combatants and captured as combatants in a war." Notice that Professor Wedgwood argues in terms of what the men seized in Bosnia were *planning to do*, not what they *did*; notice as well that the decision of the Bosnian court that there was insufficient evidence does not matter. These are characteristics of the war model. . . .

Is there any justification for the hybrid war-law model, which so drastically diminishes the rights of the enemy? An argument can be offered along the following lines. In ordinary cases of war among states, enemy soldiers may well be morally and politically innocent. Many of them are conscripts, and those who aren't do not necessarily endorse the state policies they are fighting to defend. But enemy soldiers in the War on Terrorism are, by definition, those who have embarked on a path of terrorism. They are neither morally nor politically innocent. Their sworn aim—"Death to America!"—is to create more 9/11s. In this respect, they are much more akin to criminal conspirators than to conscript soldiers. Terrorists will fight as soldiers when they must, and metamorphose into mass murderers when they can. Furthermore, suicide terrorists pose a special, unique danger. Ordinary criminals do not target innocent bystanders. They may be willing to kill them if necessary, but bystanders enjoy at least some measure of security because they are not primary targets. Not so with terrorists, who aim to kill as many innocent people as possible. Likewise, innocent bystanders are protected from ordinary criminals by whatever deterrent force the threat of punishment and the risk of getting killed in the act of committing a crime offer. For a suicide bomber, neither of these threats is a deterrent at all—after all, for the suicide bomber one of the hallmarks of a *successful* operation is that he winds up dead at day's end. Given the unique and heightened danger that suicide terrorists pose, a stronger response that grants potential terrorists fewer rights may be justified. Add to this the danger that terrorists may come to possess weapons of mass destruction, including nuclear devices in suitcases. Under circumstances of such dire menace, it is appropriate to treat terrorists as though they embody the most dangerous aspects of both warriors and criminals. That is the basis of the hybrid war-law model.

The argument against the hybrid war-law model is equally clear. The U.S. has simply chosen the bits of the law model and the bits of the war model that are most convenient for American interests, and ignored the rest. The model abolishes the rights of potential enemies (and their innocent shields) by fiat — not for reasons of moral or legal principle, but solely because the U.S. does not want them to have rights. The more rights they have, the more risk they pose. But Americans' urgent desire to minimize our risks doesn't make other people's rights disappear. Calling our policy a War on Terrorism obscures this point.

The theoretical basis of the objection is that the law model and the war model each comes as a package, with a kind of intellectual integrity. The law model grows out of relationships within states, while the war model arises from relationships between states. The law model imputes a ground-level community of values to those subject to the law — paradigmatically, citizens of a state, but also visitors and foreigners who choose to engage in conduct that affects a state. Only because law imputes shared basic values to the community can a state condemn the conduct of criminals and inflict punishment on them. Criminals deserve condemnation and punishment because their conduct violates norms that we are entitled to count on their sharing. But, for the same reason — the imputed community of values — those subject to the law ordinarily enjoy a presumption of innocence and an expectation of safety. The government cannot simply grab them and confine them without making sure they have broken the law, nor can it condemn them without due process for ensuring that it has the right person, nor can it knowingly place bystanders in mortal peril in the course of fighting crime. They are our fellows, and the community should protect them just as it protects us. The same imputed community of values that justifies condemnation and punishment creates rights to due care and due process.

War is different. War is the ultimate acknowledgment that human beings do not live in a single community with shared norms. If their norms conflict enough, communities pose a physical danger to each other, and nothing can safeguard a community against its enemies except force of arms. That makes enemy soldiers legitimate targets; but it makes our soldiers legitimate targets as well, and, once the enemy no longer poses a danger, he should be immune from punishment, because if he has fought cleanly he has violated no norms that we are entitled to presume he honors. Our norms are, after all, *our* norms, not his. Because the law model and war model come as conceptual packages, it is unprincipled to wrench them apart and recombine them simply because it is in America's interest to do so. To declare that Americans can fight enemies with the latitude of warriors, but if the enemies fight back they are not warriors but criminals, amounts to a kind of heads-I-win-tails-you-lose international morality in which whatever it takes to reduce American risk, no matter what the cost to others, turns out to be justified. This, in brief, is the criticism of the hybrid war-law model. . . .

NOTES AND QUESTIONS

1. The excerpt presents arguments both for and against the hybrid war-law model. Which arguments are stronger?

2. The article excerpted above was written in 2002, two years before the U.S. Supreme Court began to address issues of the status of detainees. At that time, the

U.S. government was holding many detainees incommunicado, some at Guantánamo Bay Naval Base, others in military brigs, and still others in secret CIA prisons (as was reported at the time and confirmed by President Bush in 2006). As indicated in the excerpt, President George W. Bush declared in February 2002 that the detainees do not qualify for Geneva Convention protections because they are unlawful enemy combatants. The government did not release the names of the Guantánamo prisoners and asserted that detainees had no rights to any form of legal process, including the right to consult counsel or the right to a hearing to determine whether they are in fact enemies rather than cases of mistaken identity. Because Guantánamo is located in Cuba, the government also asserted that no federal court has jurisdiction over the base, thereby, according to the Bush administration, making legal challenges to detention impossible.

At least two prisoners (Yaser Hamdi and Jose Padilla) were U.S. citizens held in military brigs within the United States. Hamdi had been captured in Afghanistan, while Padilla was arrested in Chicago based on intelligence that he was an al Qaeda operative. At first, the government took a very hard line about Hamdi and Padilla. Citing, among other things, the need to isolate them completely in order to interrogate them, the government denied them access to counsel; asserted that since they were enemy combatants they could be held without criminal charges until the end of the "war on terror"; asserted that the president, as commander in chief, has the sole constitutional discretion to designate persons, including U.S. citizens, as unlawful enemy combatants; asserted that courts have no authority even to hear challenges on these matters; and — after lower courts rebuffed this latter claim — asserted that a brief declaration by a civilian employee of the Pentagon, summarizing hearsay evidence, provided a sufficient factual basis to support the confinement of Hamdi and Padilla without charges because courts must defer to the executive on military matters.

Starting in 2004, the Supreme Court rebuffed many of these claims and reaffirmed the basic procedural rights of detainees. In *Hamdi*, the Court held that Hamdi, a Saudi who was born in the United States and therefore was a U.S. citizen, was entitled to some form of due process to determine if the factual basis for detaining him was true. After Hamdi prevailed in the Supreme Court, the government decided not to press its case against him: It sent Hamdi home to Saudi Arabia in return for him renouncing his U.S. citizenship. Padilla was eventually prosecuted in federal court, convicted of material support for terrorism and conspiracy, and sentenced to 17 years.

The same day the Court decided *Hamdi*, it held in Rasul v. Bush, 542 U.S. 466 (2004), that the habeas corpus statute gives U.S. courts jurisdiction to consider habeas petitions from detainees at Guantánamo. According to the *Rasul* Court, U.S. courts have jurisdiction over Guantánamo because the United States' indefinitely renewable lease with Cuba makes the U.S. naval base the equivalent of U.S. territory for purposes of habeas jurisdiction. In the wake of these decisions, detainees gained access to attorneys to represent them. In 2005 a JAG officer at Guantánamo, outraged that the prisoners were being held incommunicado, sent the prisoner list to a public interest law firm, for which he was court-martialed and imprisoned. Brooks Egerton, "Moral Decision" Jeopardizes Navy Lawyer's Career, Dallas Morning News, May 17, 2007. With the cat out of the bag, the government reversed policy and made the list public. Lawyers soon began obtaining "next friend" authorization from the detainees' families and challenging their detention in court. Meanwhile, following the Court's directive in *Hamdi*, the Pentagon established Combatant Status Review Tribunals (CSRTs) to examine the factual basis of Guantánamo detentions. The CSRTs provided minimal process to detainees (for example, their attorneys could not be present at the CSRT hearings, and the detainees themselves could not see the classified evidence against them). The CSRTs found most but not all the detainees to be enemy combatants, but many critics — including a military lawyer involved in the CSRT process — claimed that the hearings largely rubber-stamped such conclusions based on shaky evidence that the CSRTs uncritically accepted. Declaration of Lt. Col. Stephen Abraham, Reply to Opposition for Petition to Rehearing, Al-Odah v. United States, June 22, 2007, *available at* http://www.scotusblog.com/movabletype/archives/Al%20Odah%20reply%206-22-07.pdf.

Then, in Hamdan v. Rumsfeld, 548 U.S. 557 (2006), the Court held that Taliban and al Qaeda captives qualify for rights under common Article 3 of the Geneva Conventions. (Part of *Hamdan* is excerpted and discussed in Section C.2 below and part in Chapter 21.) *Hamdan* also declared that the military commissions set up by President Bush to try accused terrorists violate minimum trial standards under common Article 3. Finally, in Boumediene v. Bush, 128 S. Ct. 2229 (2008), the Court held that Guantánamo detainees have constitutional habeas corpus rights to challenge their detention in federal court — even in the absence of statutory habeas coverage. At that point, U.S. district courts began holding habeas hearings on detainees; as of August 2009, district courts have found six prisoners properly detained and 29 improperly detained. In February 2009, however, the Court of Appeals for the D.C. Circuit held that although *Boumediene* grants courts the authority to hold habeas hearings and order the release of detainees who prevail, courts lack the authority to order their release into the United States, because the political branches have plenary authority over immigration. Kiyemba v. Obama, 555 F.3d 1022 (D.C. Cir. 2009). (On October 20, 2009 the Supreme Court granted certiorari in *Kiyemba*.) One writer has observed that the grant of procedural rights to detainees by courts has not been accompanied by findings on the merits, and has not led to the release of detainees when the government opposes it. Jenny S. Martinez, Process and Substance in the "War on Terror," 108 Colum. L. Rev. 1013 (2008).

Part of the difficulty of returning detainees to their home states inheres in the United States' human rights commitments. Thus, under the Convention Against Torture, the United States has undertaken not to expel, return, or extradite a person to another state where there are substantial grounds for believing that he or she would be in danger of being tortured in the state. Those detainees who cannot be returned to their home countries for fear of torture must remain in Guantánamo (because of U.S. domestic political resistance to releasing them into the United States) unless some third country agrees to accept them, despite the finding that no basis exists for their detention.

In January 2009, President Barack Obama was inaugurated, and some expected that the government position in these cases might change. One of President Obama's first acts in office was to order the closure of Guantánamo by January 2010. Some progress has been made in finding jurisdictions willing to accept "cleared" detainees, including four Muslim Uighurs who could not be returned to China for fear of mistreatment and who have been resettled in Bermuda. As this book goes to press in fall 2009, however, some of the "cleared" detainees continue to be held at Guantánamo after nearly eight years. Moreover, the Obama administration has declared that *Boumediene*'s habeas rights do not extend to other foreign locations in which prisoners are held — notably, the Bagram detention facility in Afghanistan, where the United States has transported terror suspects captured outside Afghanistan as well as within it. And the U.S. Congress has repeatedly refused to permit detainees to be released — or, for that matter, brought to face trial — within the United States.

In light of these decisions and policies, to what extent can it be said that the United States continues to be committed to a hybrid war-law model in its response to terrorism?

3. The law recognizes one traditional category of acts that falls both under the law model and the war model: war crimes, that is, acts of war that violate the laws of war. See Chapter 21, infra, for analysis of war crimes. Under the laws of war, fighters who are not

part of a state's regular army, and who fight out of uniform or belong to irregular organizations lacking a command structure, are not privileged belligerents. In this sense, they are "unlawful combatants." However, being an unprivileged belligerent is not itself a war crime. Only if the combatant violates the law of war — for example, by deliberately attacking civilians — has he or she committed a war crime.

4. For discussion of the human rights aspect of the "war on terror," see David P. Stewart, Human Rights, Terrorism, and International Law, 50 Villa. L. Rev. 685 (2005); for discussion of the war and criminal-justice models, George P. Fletcher, Romantics at War: Glory and Guilt in the Age of Terrorism (2002); and, for discussion of trade-offs between security and civil liberties, see Laura K. Donohue, The Costs of Counterterrorism (2008); Eric A. Posner & Adrian Vermeule, Terror in the Balance: Security, Liberty, and the Courts (2007); Michael Ignatieff, The Lesser Evil: Political Ethics in the Age of Terror; David Luban, Eight Fallacies on Liberty and Security, in Human Rights in the War on Terror 242 (Richard Ashby Wilson, ed., 2005).

B. THE INTERNATIONAL LAW OF TERRORISM

In this section, we briefly address the efforts by states to combat terrorism through international law. Sections 1 and 2 review international treaties, section 3 summarizes regional treaties, and section 4 discusses UN Security Council resolutions and their implementation.

1. Efforts to Draft a Comprehensive Antiterrorism Treaty

Both the United Nations, and the League of Nations before it, have attempted to craft a general antiterrorism treaty, but with little success to date. Unsurprisingly, the main stumbling block has been the inability of the international community to agree on a definition of terrorism.

The League of Nations drafted the first international agreement regarding terrorism in 1937: the Convention for the Prevention and Punishment of Terrorism.[25] Article 1(2) defined terrorism as "criminal acts directed against a State and intended or calculated to create a state of terror in the minds of particular persons, or a group of persons or the general public." Article 2 detailed the specific acts that states parties were obliged to criminalize under the Convention, including, for example, willfully causing "death or grievous bodily harm or loss of liberty" to Heads of State or persons "exercising the prerogatives" of a Head of State, committing a "wilful act calculated to endanger the lives of members of the public," or manufacturing, obtaining, possessing or supplying arms, ammunition, explosive or "harmful substances with a view to the commission" of one of the enumerated acts.[26] The Convention obligated states party to make such acts criminal when committed on their own territory if those acts were directed at another state party.[27] However, only India ratified the Convention, and it never entered into force.[28]

---

25. League of Nations Convention for the Prevention and Punishment of Terrorism, Nov. 16, 1937, 16 L.N.T.S. 23 (1938) [hereinafter Convention], cited in Christopher L. Blakesley, Terrorism and Antiterrorism: A Normative and Practical Assessment 30 (2006). See Ben Saul, The Legal Response of the League of Nations to Terrorism, 4 J. Intl. Crim. Just. 78 (2006).
26. Convention, supra note 25, arts. 2(1)(a), 2(3), and 2(5).
27. Id. art. 3.
28. Saul, supra note 25, at 82.

For the next 60 years, the principal efforts of the international community focused instead on crafting responses to specific categories of terrorist acts. In practice, it proved far easier and perhaps more practical to reach agreement on criminalizing the specific acts committed by "terrorists" than to define the concept of "terrorism" itself.[29] The result was more than a dozen antiterrorism treaties, dealing inter alia with aerial hijackings and bombings, hostage taking, protection of nuclear materials, terrorist bombings and financing, and assassinations. These conventions are discussed in Section B.2 below.

Over the past decade, however, the UN has been engaged in another attempt to draft a general terrorism treaty, building on the foundations of the 1937 Convention and the series of specific antiterrorism treaties. In 1996, the General Assembly created an ad hoc committee, open to all UN member states, to elaborate an international convention for the suppression of terrorist bombings and, subsequently, an international convention for the suppression of acts of nuclear terrorism.[30] The committee completed the first of those conventions in 1997 and the second in 2005.[31]

The ad hoc committee was also directed to "supplement related existing international instruments, and thereafter to address means of further developing a comprehensive legal framework of conventions dealing with international terrorism."[32] Under that mandate, it has been working to prepare a Comprehensive Convention on International Terrorism (CCIT). This effort is ongoing, and the committee held its thirteenth session in mid-2009. Among the more significant provisions of the latest consolidated draft, from 2005, are the following (the full text is available on our Web site).

DRAFT COMPREHENSIVE CONVENTION AGAINST INTERNATIONAL TERRORISM

UN Doc. A/59/894

Consolidated text prepared by the coordinator for discussion

ARTICLE 2

1. Any person commits an offence within the meaning of the present Convention if that person, by any means, unlawfully and intentionally, causes:

(a) Death or serious bodily injury to any person; or

(b) Serious damage to public or private property, including a place of public use, a State or government facility, a public transportation system, an infrastructure facility or to the environment; or

---

29. Additionally, there have been efforts in a political context to achieve definitional consensus. See, for example, the Declaration on Measures to Eliminate International Terrorism, annexed to G.A. Res. 49/60, ¶3 (Dec. 9, 1994) ("Criminal acts intended or calculated to provoke a state of terror in the general public, a group of persons or particular persons for political purposes are in any circumstance unjustifiable, whatever the considerations of a political, philosophical, ideological, racial, ethnic, religious or any other nature that may be invoked to justify them"); see also the Declaration to Supplement the 1994 Declaration, annexed to G.A. Res. 51/210 (Dec. 17, 1996).

30. G.A. Res. 51/210, ¶9 (Dec. 17, 1996).

31. International Convention for the Suppression of Terrorist Bombings, G.A. Res. 52/164 (Dec. 15, 1997); International Convention for the Suppression of Acts of Nuclear Terrorism, G.A. Res. 59/290 (Apr. 13, 2005).

32. G.A. Res. 51/210, ¶9 (Dec. 17, 1996).

(c) Damage to property, places, facilities or systems referred to in paragraph 1(b) of the present article resulting or likely to result in major economic loss; when the purpose of the conduct, by its nature or context, is to intimidate a population, or to compel a Government or an international organization to do or to abstain from doing any act.

2. Any person also commits an offence if that person makes a credible and serious threat to commit an offence as set forth in paragraph 1 of the present article.

3. Any person also commits an offence if that person attempts to commit an offence as set forth in paragraph 1 of the present article.

4. Any person also commits an offence if that person:

(a) Participates as an accomplice in an offence as set forth in paragraph 1, 2 or 3 of the present article; or

(b) Organizes or directs others to commit an offence as set forth in paragraph 1, 2 or 3 of the present article; or

(c) Contributes to the commission of one or more offences as set forth in paragraph 1, 2 or 3 of the present article by a group of persons acting with a common purpose. Such contribution shall be intentional and shall either:

(i) Be made with the aim of furthering the criminal activity or criminal purpose of the group, where such activity or purpose involves the commission of an offence as set forth in paragraph 1 of the present article; or

(ii) Be made in the knowledge of the intention of the group to commit an offence as set forth in paragraph 1 of the present article. . . .

ARTICLE 4

The Present Convention shall not apply where the offence is committed within a single State, the alleged offender and the victims are nationals of that State, the alleged offender is found in the territory of that State and no other State has a basis under article 7, paragraph 1 or 2, of the present Convention to exercise jurisdiction. . . .

ARTICLE 6

Each State Party shall adopt such measures as may be necessary, including, where appropriate, domestic legislation, to ensure that criminal acts within the scope of the present Convention are under no circumstances justifiable by considerations of a political, philosophical, ideological, racial, ethnic, religious or other similar nature.

ARTICLE 7

1. Each State Party shall take such measures as may be necessary to establish its jurisdiction over the offences set forth in article 2 of the present Convention when:

(a) The offence is committed in the territory of that State; or

(b) The offence is committed on board a vessel flying the flag of that State or an aircraft which is registered under the laws of that State at the time the offense is committed; or

(c) The offence is committed by a national of that State.

2. A State Party may also establish its jurisdiction over any such offence when:

(a) The offence is committed by a stateless person who has his or her habitual residence in the territory of that State; or

(b) The offence is committed wholly or partially outside its territory, if the effects of the conduct or its intended effects constitute or result in, within its territory, the commission of an offence set forth in article 2; or

(c) The offence is committed against a national of that State; or

(d) The offence is committed against a State or government facility of that State abroad, including an embassy or other diplomatic or consular premises of that State; or

(e) The offence is committed in an attempt to compel that State to do or to abstain from doing any act; or

(f) The offence is committed on board an aircraft which is operated by the government of that State. . . .

ARTICLE 15

None of the offences set forth in article 2 . . . shall be regarded, for the purposes of extradition or mutual legal assistance, as a political offence or as an offence connected with a political offence or as an offence inspired by political motives. . . .

ARTICLE 20

1. Nothing in the present Convention shall affect other rights, obligations and responsibilities of States, peoples and individuals under international law, in particular the purposes and principles of the Charter of the United Nations, and international humanitarian law.

2. The activities of armed forces during an armed conflict, as those terms are understood under international humanitarian law, which are governed by that law, are not governed by the present Convention.

3. The activities undertaken by the military forces of a State in the exercise of their official duties, inasmuch as they are governed by other rules of international law, are not governed by the present Convention.

4. Nothing in the present article condones or makes lawful otherwise unlawful acts, nor precludes prosecution under other laws.

NOTES AND QUESTIONS

1. Compare the definition of terrorism in the above draft Convention to the one articulated by the 1937 League of Nations Convention: "[C]riminal acts directed against a State and intended or calculated to create a state of terror in the minds of particular persons, or a group of persons or the general public." Is the proposed CCIT definition an improvement over the League's definition, which one scholar has described as "remarkably durable"? Ben Saul, The Legal Response of the League of Nations to Terrorism, 4 J. Intl. Crim. Just. 78, 79 (2006).

2. Consider also the definitions adopted at various times by the UN General Assembly and the UN Security Council. For example, in 1999, the General

Assembly's International Convention for the Suppression of the Financing of Terrorism defined terrorism as any act

> intended to cause death or serious bodily injury to a civilian, or to any other person not taking an active part in the hostilities in a situation of armed conflict, when the purpose of such act, by its nature or context, is to intimidate a population, or to compel a Government or an international organization to do or to abstain from doing any act.

G.A. Res. 54/109, ¶2(1)(b), U.N. Doc. A/Res/54/109, (Dec. 9, 1999) (to which, as of mid-2009, 139 states were party). Five years later, the Security Council defined terrorism as

> criminal acts, including against civilians, committed with the intent to cause death or serious bodily injury, or taking of hostages, with the purpose to provoke a state of terror in the general public or in a group or persons or particular persons, intimidate a population or compel a government or an international organization to do or to abstain from doing any act, which constitute offenses within the scope of and as defined in the international conventions and protocols relating to terrorism.

S.C. Res. 1566, U.N. Doc. S/Res/1566, "Threats to International Peace and Security Caused by Terrorist Acts," ¶3 (October 8, 2004). Although Resolution 1566 calls on states to join antiterrorism treaties and improve cooperation in the struggle against terrorism, it does not require states to take any specific steps. Do you suppose it is easier for states to agree to formulations in nonbinding resolutions as opposed to legally binding treaties?

3. Consider the list of mandatory and permissive jurisdictional bases set forth in Article 7(1) and (2). They represent a considerable broadening of jurisdictional concepts in comparison to the territorial orientation of the 1937 Convention. Why would states resist making the optional bases mandatory?

4. Article 6 would require states parties to ensure that acts falling with the Convention's definitional and jurisdictional scope could "under no circumstances" be justified "by considerations of a political, philosophical, ideological, racial, ethnic, religious or other similar nature." Article 15 would exclude covered acts from the "political offense" exceptions to requests for extradition and mutual legal assistance. (These exceptions are discussed in Chapters 8 and 9.) Are these provisions too broad or not inclusive enough?

5. Note the scope of the "carve out" in Article 20 of the 2005 draft, particularly as it relates to military actions. Among other issues, the negotiators of the CCIT have disagreed over whether to include state acts, in addition to acts committed by individual and non-state groups, in the scope of the Convention. State acts of violence are arguably acts of war falling under the international laws of war. (See Chapter 21.A.2 for further discussion.) Some argue that exempting official acts would do little to undermine the comprehensive nature of the treaty because many such acts would be considered war crimes and could therefore be prosecuted internationally under international humanitarian law.

However, reliance on the laws of war to fill this gap creates its own problems: Not every member state of the United Nations has ratified the two Additional Protocols to the Geneva Conventions, which set out the detailed rules of war including the prohibition on attacking noncombatants. The lack of universal acceptance of these protocols raises concerns about including a broad definition of terrorism that would effectively duplicate the protocols. The laws of war also apply only during armed conflict, and some acts of state terrorism may not fulfill this requirement.

Those who wish to include states in the terrorism definition stress the need for a simple and authoritative convention, reflecting the General Assembly's unified voice, to prompt state action and interstate cooperation against terrorism. They make a plausible argument as well that it is unethical to exempt governments from blame because terrorist acts are condemnable regardless of who perpetrates them.

6. Some delegations have also been concerned with distinguishing legitimate resistance movements (for instance, civilian resistance to foreign occupation) from terrorist activity under the Convention. This issue can be difficult to separate from the issue of state terrorism, as in the Middle East where many acts of violence against civilians are performed by non-state actors but are allegedly supported, and in some cases controlled, by state governments. See generally Tal Becker, Terrorism and the State: Rethinking the Rules of State Responsibility (2006). For further discussion of the points of contention in the current negotiations, see Mahmoud Hmoud, Negotiating the Draft Comprehensive Convention on International Terrorism: Major Bones of Contention, 4 J. Intl. Crim. Just. 1031 (2006); Jean-Paul Laborde & Michael DeFeo, Problems and Prospects of Implementing UN Action Against Terrorism, 4 J. Intl. Crim. Just. 1087 (2006); and, more generally, the entire Journal of International Criminal Justice November 2006 special issue containing these articles, entitled Criminal Law Responses to Terrorism After September 11.

7. In 2007 the coordinator of the CCIT drafting efforts proposed amendments in response to an impasse over the issues presented by Article 20 (numbered Article 18 at the time), based on language contained in the Terrorist Bombings and Nuclear Terrorism Conventions. Consider the following proposal related to the "carve out" issue.

TEXT RELATING TO ARTICLE 18 OF THE DRAFT COMPREHENSIVE CONVENTION

1. Nothing in this Convention shall affect other rights, obligations and responsibilities of States, peoples and individuals under international law, in particular the purposes and principles of the Charter of the United Nations, and international humanitarian law.

2. The activities of armed forces during an armed conflict, as those terms are understood under international humanitarian law, which are governed by that law, are not governed by this Convention.

3. The activities undertaken by the military forces of a State in the exercise of their official duties, inasmuch as they are governed by other rules of international law, are not governed by this Convention.

4. Nothing in this article condones or makes lawful otherwise unlawful acts, nor precludes prosecution under other laws; acts which would amount to an offence as defined in article 2 of this Convention remain punishable under such laws.

5. This Convention is without prejudice to the rules of international law applicable in armed conflict, in particular those rules applicable to acts lawful under international humanitarian law.

Report of the Ad Hoc Committee (11th Sess. Feb. 5, 6, and 15, 2007), Annex, U.N. Doc. A/62/37, at 6. Which states would you expect to support this amendment, and which states would you expect to oppose it? Why?

8. For further reading on terrorism and one conception of how the international community should respond, see Philip Bobbitt's major work on the topic, Terror and Consent: The Wars for the Twenty-First Century (2008).

2. Specific Antiterrorism Treaties

As noted above, the difficulties that have been encountered in attempting to agree on a concrete definition of terrorism and to establish terrorism as a separate, discrete crime inspired the international community to try a "sectoral" approach. Rather than condemning the phenomenon of "terrorism" as such, the focus has instead been on criminalizing the particular acts that are often associated with terrorism. Not infrequently, these efforts have arisen in response to specific, high-visibility incidents that have engaged public attention and focused the world community on the need to take action. Thus, a spate of aircraft hijackings in the 1960s and 1970s spawned the Tokyo, Hague, and Montreal Conventions, all dealing with aspects of aerial hijacking;[33] and in reaction to the 1985 seizure of the cruise ship *Achille Lauro* off the coast of Egypt (during which U.S. citizen Leon Klinghoffer was murdered by members of the Palestine Liberation Front), the International Maritime Organization prepared a new Maritime Terrorism Convention in 1988.[34]

Of the 12 multilateral treaties done under UN auspices that are normally counted as counterterrorism conventions, most criminalize specific acts associated with terrorism.[35] These treaties generally adopt the same overall structural approach.

First, they define the specific crime in question. For example, the 1970 Hague Convention for the Suppression of Unlawful Seizure of Aircraft explains:

> Any person who on board an aircraft in flight:
>   (a) unlawfully, by force or threat thereof, or by any other form of intimidation, seizes, or exercises control of, that aircraft, or attempts to perform any such act, or
>   (b) is an accomplice of a person who performs or attempts to perform any such act commits an offence.

Any additional related offenses, such as conspiracy, are also explained and criminalized. For example, the 1997 New York Convention for the Suppression of Terrorist

---

33. Convention on Offenses and Certain Other Acts Committed on Board Aircraft, signed at Tokyo Sept. 14, 1963; Convention for the Suppression of Unlawful Seizure of Aircraft, signed at The Hague Dec. 16, 1970; Convention for the Suppression of Unlawful Acts Against the Safety of Civil Aviation, signed at Montreal Sept. 23, 1971; Protocol on the Suppression of Unlawful Acts of Violence at Airports Serving International Civil Aviation, signed at Montreal Feb. 24, 1988.

34. Convention for the Suppression of Unlawful Acts Against the Safety of Maritime Navigation, done at Rome Mar. 10, 1988.

35. The "core" multilateral treaties are normally thought to include the Convention on Offences and Certain Other Acts Committed on Board Aircraft, signed at Tokyo on September 14, 1963 ("Toyko"); the Convention for the Suppression of Unlawful Seizure of Aircraft, signed at The Hague on December 16, 1970 ("Hague"); the Convention for the Suppression of Unlawful Acts Against the Safety of Civil Aviation, concluded at Montreal on September 23, 1971 ("Montreal"); the Convention on the Prevention and Punishment of Crimes Against Internationally Protected Persons, including Diplomatic Agents, adopted in New York on December 14, 1973 ("IPP"), 1035 U.N.T.S. 167; the International Convention Against the Taking of Hostages, adopted in New York on December 17, 1979 ("Hostages"), T.I.A.S. 11081; the Protocol for the Suppression of Unlawful Acts of Violence at Airports Serving International Civil Aviation, supplementary to the Convention for the Suppression of Unlawful Acts Against the Safety of Civil Aviation, done at Montreal on February 24, 1988 ("Airport Protocol"); the Convention for the Suppression of Unlawful Acts Against the Safety of Maritime Navigation, done at Rome on March 10, 1988 ("Maritime Terrorism"); the Protocol for the Suppression of Unlawful Acts Against the Safety of Fixed Platforms Located on the Continental Shelf, done at Rome on March 10, 1988 ("Fixed Platforms Protocol"); the International Convention for the Suppression of Terrorist Bombings, adopted in New York on December 15, 1997 ("Terrorism Bombings"); and the International Convention for the Suppression of the Financing of Terrorism, adopted on December 9, 1999) ("Terrorist Financing"). The other two are more general in character: the Convention on the Marking of Plastic Explosives for the Purpose of Detection, signed at Montreal March 1, 1991 ("plastic explosives"), and the International Convention for the Suppression of Acts of Nuclear Terrorism, done at New York on April 13, 2005 ("nuclear terrorism").

Bombings makes it a crime to participate as an accomplice, to organize or direct others to commit, or to contribute to the commission by a group, of terrorist bombings.[36]

Next, each treaty requires states parties to establish the offense as a crime under their own domestic law. For example, according to the 1973 New York Convention on the Prevention and Punishment of Crimes Against Internationally Protected Persons, Including Diplomatic Agents, "[e]ach State Party shall make these crimes punishable by appropriate penalties which take into account their grave nature."[37]

Importantly, each state must establish jurisdiction over the offense. "Even where all elements of the criminal conduct are purely domestic, it is sufficient that the perpetrator has escaped from the country where the conduct took place and is located in another Contracting Party in order to trigger the application of these conventions."[38] Thus, the 1979 New York Convention Against the Taking of Hostages explains when jurisdiction is to be established:

> Each State Party shall take such measures as may be necessary to establish its jurisdiction over any of the offences set forth in article 1 which are committed:
>   (a) In its territory or on board a ship or aircraft registered in that State;
>   (b) By any of its nationals, or if that State considers it appropriate, by those stateless persons who have their habitual residence in its territory;
>   (c) In order to compel that State to do or abstain from doing any act; or
>   (d) With respect to a hostage who is a national of that State, if that State considers it appropriate.[39]

By comparison, the 1988 IMO Maritime Terrorism Convention requires states parties to establish jurisdiction over covered acts committed within their territory, on board a ship flying their flag, or by their nationals. It permits, but does not require, jurisdiction to be established over acts committed by stateless persons whose habitual residence is in the state party, or when during the commission of the acts in question a national of that state is seized, threatened, injured, or killed, or when the act is committed in an attempt to compel that state to do or abstain from doing a certain act.

All the major antiterrorism treaties contain an "extradite or prosecute" provision. For example, the 1988 Rome Convention for the Suppression of Unlawful Acts Against the Safety of International Maritime Navigation emphasizes that

> [t]he State Party in the territory of which the offender or the alleged offender is found shall . . . if it does not extradite him, be obliged, without exception whatsoever and whether or not the offence was committed in its territory, to submit the case without delay to its competent authorities for the purpose of prosecution, through proceedings in accordance with the laws of that State. Those authorities shall take their decision in the same manner as in the case of any other offence of a grave nature under the law of that State.[40]

---

36. Convention for the Suppression of Terrorist Bombings. U.N. Doc. A/RES/52/164, art. 2 (Dec. 15, 1997).

37. Convention on the Prevention and Punishment of Crimes Against Internationally Protected Persons, Including Diplomatic Agents, 28 U.S.T. 1975, T.I.A.S. No. 8632.

38. International Cooperation in Counter-Terrorism: The United Nations and Regional Organizations in the Fight Against Terror 9 (Guiseppi Nesi ed., 2006).

39. International Convention Against the Taking of Hostages, Dec. 17, 1979, T.I.A.S. No. 11,081, 1316 U.N.T.S. 204.

40. Convention for the Suppression of Unlawful Acts Against the Safety of International Maritime Navigation, Mar. 10, 1988, 1678 U.N.T.S. 222.

In almost all cases, the conventions provide for mutual legal assistance to prevent incidents and to bring the perpetrators to justice. For example, Article 6 of the 1971 Convention for the Suppression of Unlawful Acts Against the Safety of Civil Aviation provides that:

1. Upon being satisfied that the circumstances so warrant, any Contracting State in the territory of which the offender or the alleged offender is present, shall take into custody or take other measures to ensure his presence. The custody and other measures shall be as provided in the law of that State but may only be continued for such time as is necessary to enable any criminal or extradition proceedings to be instituted.
2. Such State shall immediately make a preliminary enquiry into the facts.
3. Any person in custody pursuant to paragraph 1 of this Article shall be assisted in communicating immediately with the nearest appropriate representative of the State of which he is a national.
4. When a State, pursuant to this Article, has taken a person into custody, it shall immediately notify the States mentioned in Article 5, paragraph 1, the State of nationality of the detained person and, if it considers it advisable, any other interested State of the fact that such person is in custody and of the circumstances which warrant his detention. . . . [41]

NOTES AND QUESTIONS

1. In addition to these treaties, the UN General Assembly adopted the International Convention for the Suppression of the Financing of Terrorism in New York on December 9, 1999. This Convention does not follow the sectoral approach because it attempts to suppress terrorism financing in general, rather than financing associated with only one particular criminal act. Other significant antiterrorism treaties that do not follow the sectoral approach include the Convention on the Physical Protection of Nuclear Material, adopted in Vienna on October 26, 1979; the Convention on the Marking of Plastic Explosives for the Purpose of Detection, done at Montreal on March 1, 1991; and the International Convention for the Suppression of Acts of Nuclear Terrorism, adopted in New York on April 13, 2005.

2. What are the advantages and disadvantages of the sectoral approach compared with efforts to create a comprehensive antiterrorism convention?

3.   Regional Counterterrorism Conventions

An increasing number of regional agreements are aimed at criminalizing terrorist acts and facilitating mutual legal assistance among states parties for the prevention and punishment of terrorist acts. Such treaties have been adopted, for example, within the European Union, the Organization of American States (OAS), the Organization of African Unity (OAU), the League of Arab States, the South Asian Association for Regional Cooperation, and the Commonwealth of Independent States. [42]

---

41. Convention for the Suppression of Unlawful Acts Against the Safety of Civil Aviation, Sept. 23, 1971, 24 U.S.T. 564, T.I.A.S. No. 7570.

42. Generally, see the UNDOC Web site, https://www.unodc.org/tldb/en/regional_instruments.html (last visited Oct. 5, 2009).

Predictably, these treaties vary significantly in substance and approach. For example, the 1977 Council of Europe (COE) Convention on the Suppression of Terrorism was intended as a supplement to the various extradition treaties in force among COE member states. It provides in Article 1 that listed offenses (including particularly those established by major multilateral treaties) shall not be regarded as "a political offence or as an offence connected with a political offence or as an offence inspired by political motives." Article 8(1) obligates states parties to "afford one another the widest measure of mutual assistance in criminal matters in connection with proceedings brought in respect of the offences mentioned. . . ."[43]

By comparison, the 1971 OAS Convention to Prevent and Punish the Acts of Terrorism Taking the Form of Crimes Against Persons and Related Extortion That Are of International Significance[44] anticipated the approach of the 1973 UN "IPP" Convention by obligating states parties to take "all the measures that they may consider to be effective, under their own laws, . . . to prevent and punish acts of terrorism, especially kidnapping, murder, and other assaults against the life or physical integrity of those persons to whom the state has the duty according to international law to give special protection, as well as extortion in connection with those crimes."[45]

The 1999 OAU Convention on the Prevention and Combating of Terrorism is substantively a criminal law treaty: It defines a set of "terrorist acts" and requires states parties to make those acts criminal offenses under their domestic laws, to extradite or prosecute offenders, and to extend to each other "the best possible mutual police and judicial assistance for any investigation, criminal prosecution or extradition proceedings related to the terrorist acts set forth in this Convention."[46] Although (like the draft CCIT) it provides that "[p]olitical, philosophical, ideological, racial, ethnic, religious or other motives shall not be a justifiable defense against a terrorist act," it also states that "the struggle waged by peoples in accordance with the principles of international law for their liberation or self-determination, including armed struggle against colonialism, occupation, aggression and domination by foreign forces shall not be considered as terrorist acts."[47] In addition, it requires states parties to "refrain from any acts aimed at organizing, supporting, financing, committing or inciting to commit terrorist acts, or providing havens for terrorists, directly or indirectly, including the provision of weapons and their stockpiling in their countries and the issuing of visas and travel documents."[48]

For its part, the 1999 Commonwealth of Independent States Treaty on Cooperation in Combating Terrorism is aimed at international assistance and rests primarily on the obligation of states parties to "cooperate in preventing, uncovering, halting and investigating acts of terrorism. . . ." Art. 2.[49] It lists a range of specific forms of cooperation, including inter alia implementing measures to improve "the system for physical protection of facilities," sending "special anti-terrorist units to render practical assistance in halting acts of terrorism," and "exchanging experience on the prevention and combating of terrorist acts."

---

43. European Convention on the Suppression of Terrorism, E.T.S. No. 90 (1970).
44. 27 U.S.T. 3929, T.I.A.S. 8413, done at Washington Feb. 2, 1971; text available at http://www
.oas.org/juridico/English/treaties/a-49.html.
45. Art. 1.
46. Arts. 1, 2, and 17 (text available at http://www.africa-union.org/root/AU/Documents/Treaties/
Text/Algiers_convention%20on%20Terrorism.pdf (last visited Oct. 5, 2009)).
47. Art. 3.
48. Art 4(1).
49. Text available at https://www.unodc.org/tldb/pdf/conv_cis_1999.pdf (last visited Oct. 5, 2009).

NOTES AND QUESTIONS

1. Do you see any advantages, or disadvantages, in addressing the phenomenon of terrorism on a regional as opposed to global level? Are there significant differences in the types of terrorist threats faced in various regions of the world?

2. Of the disparate approaches reflected in the regional conventions described above, do any seem more likely to be effective? Can you see reasons why some approaches might be acceptable regionally but not globally?

4. *UN Security Council Resolutions*

Among the most significant and controversial international efforts to bring law to bear on terrorism is a series of UNSC resolutions requiring member states to adopt tough antiterrorist measures.[50] Chapter VII of the UN Charter empowers the Security Council to determine the existence of threats to peace and breaches of the peace as well as acts of aggression, and to make recommendations or decide on measures to maintain or restore international peace and security. When it acts under the authority of Chapter VII, the Council's decisions are binding on member states, which have obligations under Articles 25 and 48(1) to accept and carry them out. Not all Security Council resolutions are decisions meant to bind member states, and even resolutions adopted under Chapter VII often include both binding and nonbinding elements. The intention to impose binding obligations is generally indicated by the formulaic language "The Security Council decides . . ." together with an invocation of the Security Council's Chapter VII authority. Other formulas, such as "calls upon" or "requests," are precatory, not mandatory, and do not create binding legal obligations.

Because Security Council resolutions have the potential to bind all states under Chapter VII, they can have a more immediate and global impact in comparison to multilateral conventions, which — even when completed — can take many years to garner ratifications and achieve effective implementation. At the same time, use of Chapter VII as an alternative to the process of negotiating and ratifying treaties can raise questions about diminishing the role of state consent in the formulation of new rules and obligations within the international community.

a. Resolution 1373: The UN as Legislator?

Soon after 9/11, the UNSC adopted Resolution 1373, a broad-ranging set of antiterrorism measures, including some intended to bind all member states.

UN SECURITY COUNCIL RESOLUTION 1373 (2001)
U.N. Doc. S/RES/1373 (2001), adopted September 28, 2001

The Security Council, . . .

Reaffirming . . . its unequivocal condemnation of the terrorist attacks which took place in New York, Washington, D.C. and Pennsylvania on 11 September 2001, and expressing its determination to prevent all such acts,

---

50. A full list of UNSC resolutions to counterterrorism is found at http://www.un.org/terrorism/sc-res.shtml (last visited Sept. 10, 2009).

Reaffirming further that such acts, like any act of international terrorism, constitute a threat to international peace and security,

Reaffirming the inherent right of individual or collective self-defence as recognized by the Charter of the United Nations as reiterated in resolution 1368 (2001),

Reaffirming the need to combat by all means, in accordance with the Charter of the United Nations, threats to international peace and security caused by terrorist acts, . . .

Acting under Chapter VII of the Charter of the United Nations,

1. *Decides* that all States shall:
(a) Prevent and suppress the financing of terrorist acts;
(b) Criminalize the wilful provision or collection, by any means, directly or indirectly, of funds by their nationals or in their territories with the intention that the funds should be used, or in the knowledge that they are to be used, in order to carry out terrorist acts;
(c) Freeze without delay funds and other financial assets or economic resources of persons who commit, or attempt to commit, terrorist acts or participate in or facilitate the commission of terrorist acts; of entities owned or controlled directly or indirectly by such persons; and of persons and entities acting on behalf of, or at the direction of such persons and entities, including funds derived or generated from property owned or controlled directly or indirectly by such persons and associated persons and entities;
(d) Prohibit their nationals or any persons and entities within their territories from making any funds, financial assets or economic resources or financial or other related services available, directly or indirectly, for the benefit of persons who commit or attempt to commit or facilitate or participate in the commission of terrorist acts, of entities owned or controlled, directly or indirectly, by such persons and of persons and entities acting on behalf of or at the direction of such persons;
2. *Decides also* that all States shall:
(a) Refrain from providing any form of support, active or passive, to entities or persons involved in terrorist acts, including by suppressing recruitment of members of terrorist groups and eliminating the supply of weapons to terrorists;
(b) Take the necessary steps to prevent the commission of terrorist acts, including by provision of early warning to other States by exchange of information;
(c) Deny safe haven to those who finance, plan, support, or commit terrorist acts, or provide safe havens;
(d) Prevent those who finance, plan, facilitate or commit terrorist acts from using their respective territories for those purposes against other States or their citizens;
(e) Ensure that any person who participates in the financing, planning, preparation or perpetration of terrorist acts or in supporting terrorist acts is brought to justice and ensure that, in addition to any other measures against them, such terrorist acts are established as serious criminal offences in domestic laws and regulations and that the punishment duly reflects the seriousness of such terrorist acts;
(f) Afford one another the greatest measure of assistance in connection with criminal investigations or criminal proceedings relating to the financing or support of terrorist acts, including assistance in obtaining evidence in their possession necessary for the proceedings;
(g) Prevent the movement of terrorists or terrorist groups by effective border controls and controls on issuance of identity papers and travel documents, and through measures for preventing counterfeiting, forgery or fraudulent use of identity papers and travel documents;

3. *Calls* upon all States to:

(a) Find ways of intensifying and accelerating the exchange of operational information, especially regarding actions or movements of terrorist persons or networks; forged or falsified travel documents; traffic in arms, explosives or sensitive materials; use of communications technologies by terrorist groups; and the threat posed by the possession of weapons of mass destruction by terrorist groups;

(b) Exchange information in accordance with international and domestic law and cooperate on administrative and judicial matters to prevent the commission of terrorist acts;

(c) Cooperate, particularly through bilateral and multilateral arrangements and agreements, to prevent and suppress terrorist attacks and take action against perpetrators of such acts;

(d) Become parties as soon as possible to the relevant international conventions and protocols relating to terrorism, including the International Convention for the Suppression of the Financing of Terrorism of 9 December 1999;

(e) Increase cooperation and fully implement the relevant international conventions and protocols relating to terrorism and Security Council resolutions 1269 (1999) and 1368 (2001);

(f) Take appropriate measures in conformity with the relevant provisions of national and international law, including international standards of human rights, before granting refugee status, for the purpose of ensuring that the asylum-seeker has not planned, facilitated or participated in the commission of terrorist acts;

(g) Ensure, in conformity with international law, that refugee status is not abused by the perpetrators, organizers or facilitators of terrorist acts, and that claims of political motivation are not recognized as grounds for refusing requests for the extradition of alleged terrorists; . . .

5. *Declares* that acts, methods, and practices of terrorism are contrary to the purposes and principles of the United Nations and that knowingly financing, planning and inciting terrorist acts are also contrary to the purposes and principles of the United Nations;

6. *Decides* to establish, in accordance with rule 28 of its provisional rules of procedure, a Committee of the Security Council, consisting of all the members of the Council, to monitor implementation of this resolution, with the assistance of appropriate expertise, and *calls upon* all States to report to the Committee, no later than 90 days from the date of adoption of this resolution and thereafter according to a timetable to be proposed by the Committee, on the steps they have taken to implement this resolution; . . .

9. *Decides* to remain seized of this matter.

ERIC ROSAND, SECURITY COUNCIL RESOLUTION 1373, THE COUNTER-TERRORISM COMMITTEE, AND THE FIGHT AGAINST TERRORISM

97 Am. J. Intl. L. 333 (2003)

Following September 11, 2001, the Security Council took a number of important steps in the fight against terrorism. It condemned global terror and recognized the right to self-defense under Article 51 of the UN Charter in responding forcefully to those horrific attacks. Perhaps its most significant action in this area, however, was the adoption of Resolution 1373 which established the Counter-Terrorism Committee (the CTC). . . .

Adopted on September 28, 2001, Resolution 1373 is the cornerstone of the United Nations' counterterrorism effort. It also represents a departure for the institution. Adopted under Chapter VII, it declares international terrorism a threat to "international peace and security" and imposes binding obligations on all UN member states. The Security Council's deep involvement in the United Nation's counterterrorism effort represents a new development. Hitherto, the general topic of international terrorism was largely considered a General Assembly issue. The General Assembly's Sixth (Legal) Committee had worked on several conventions on terrorism, including recently adopted conventions on terrorist bombings and terrorism financing. Since the fall of 2000, this group has continued its efforts to conclude a Comprehensive Convention on International Terrorism. Negotiators are grappling with the difficult issue of defining terrorism. Some states still want their friends to be able to use terrorism to advance their favorite causes. The oft-repeated phrase, "one's man terrorist is another man's freedom fighter," unfortunately remains relevant.

Resolution 1373 does not attempt to define terrorism. Nor does it, like Resolution 1390, seek to identify specific terrorists. In fact, the goal of the CTC, and of Resolution 1373 as a whole, is perhaps more ambitious: to raise the average level of government performance against terrorism across the globe. This means upgrading the capacity of each nation's legislation and executive machinery to fight terrorism.

Resolution 1373 requires all states to take steps to combat terrorism; it creates uniform obligations for all [192] member states to the United Nations, thus going beyond the existing international counterterrorism conventions and protocols binding only those that have become parties to them. This is an unprecedented step for the Security Council to take. The Council has taken provisions from a variety of international legal instruments that do not yet have universal support, such as the Terrorism Financing Convention, and incorporated them into a resolution that is binding on all UN member states. Some mistakenly think Resolution 1373 is directed mainly at terrorist financing. It does address this crucial area, but it also requires or urges other steps by states against terrorists, their organizations, and supporters — for example, to update laws and to bring terrorists to justice, improve border security and control traffic in arms, cooperate and exchange information with other states concerning terrorists, and provide judicial assistance to other states in criminal proceedings related to terrorism. More generally, it requires all member states to review their domestic laws and practices to ensure that terrorists cannot finance themselves or find safe havens for their adherents or their operations on these states' territory. . . .

Resolution 1373 established a committee of the Security Council (the CTC) consisting of all members of the Council, to monitor implementation of the resolution; and it calls upon all states to report to the CTC on the steps taken to implement Resolution 1373. . . .

Although Resolution 1373 established the CTC, the resolution did not provide guidance on how the committee should operate and what role it should play in combating terrorism. The way the CTC operates (transparently, through dialogue and by consensus), the role it plays (seeking to establish a dialogue between the Security Council and member states on how best to build global capacity against terrorism), and its focus on developing relationships with international, regional, and subregional organizations have largely been shaped by its first chairman, British Ambassador to the United Nations, Sir Jeremy Greenstock.

Chairman Greenstock's view, which was endorsed by the CTC, was that the CTC is not a sanctions committee, nor is its task to prosecute or condemn states. Although Resolution 1373 imposes uniform requirements on all member states, the CTC decided to work with each state to implement the resolution at its fastest capable speed, since states have varying levels of capacity in this regard. Thus, a degree of relativity has been injected into the process. Careful attention was paid to avoid making member states feel threatened by Resolution 1373: given its imposing requirements, the potential for certain states to feel threatened was and remains significant. By not targeting individual states, not condemning states, and focusing instead on technical capacity building, Greenstock was thus able to garner the support from virtually all [192] UN members.

. . . The resolution provides no end-date, and how long this process could take is manifestly uncertain. The first step in this dialogue was for each member state to submit a report to the CTC detailing the steps it has taken to implement Resolution 1373. The CTC has received reports from . . . 191 member states. The reports have varied in both quality and length, largely reflecting the different levels of capacity among states to implement Resolution 1373 and different levels of resources states have to prepare a report under Resolution 1373.

Following this submission, the relevant CTC subcommittee, along with its two experts, reviewed the report and drafted a letter from the CTC to the relevant state asking a series of follow-up questions, which were to be answered in the state's subsequent report. . . .

Recognizing just how broad the scope of Resolution 1373 is — it covers everything from border controls and terrorist financing to weapons transfers — the CTC decided to break down its assessments of member states' capacity into three stages. For the first, Stage A, the CTC agreed that states should have legislation in place covering all aspects of the resolution and should begin the process of becoming party to the twelve international terrorism conventions and protocols as soon as possible. In addition, the CTC agreed that states should establish effective executive machinery for preventing and suppressing terrorist financing. The CTC's review of the second set of reports, continued through early 2003, monitors all states regarding these two priorities.

. . . The CTC then will begin to focus on the Stage B priorities that the CTC also agreed to in July, namely: (1) having executive machinery in place covering all aspects of Resolution 1373, (2) having an effective government-wide coordination mechanism for counterterrorism activity, and (3) cooperating on bilateral, regional, and international levels, including exchange of information. Looking further ahead, the CTC envisions that in Stage C it will focus on the implementation of the above legislation and executive machinery to bring terrorists and their supporters to justice.

[D]uring its first year of operation, the CTC's accomplishments were significant and served those interested in enhancing multilateral counterterrorism efforts. . . . First, the cooperation the CTC has received from member states has been unprecedented. The CTC established a transparent and consensus-based working method and launched an open-ended dialogue with individual member states on each state's implementation of Resolution 1373. As already noted, all . . . states submitted first round reports called for by the resolution, self-assessments on implementation of Resolution 1373. So far, more than 140 have submitted second round reports, responding to CTC questions based on the first reports. . . . [T]hese reports show that a large number of states have been revising their laws in an effort to comply with Resolution 1373 and that the pace at which states have become party to the twelve international terrorism conventions and protocols has significantly increased since the CTC's establishment, especially with respect to the Terrorist Bombings and Terrorism Financing Conventions. . . .

As the above indicates, the CTC has gotten off to a good start, largely exceeding expectations. There are a number of challenges it will face and questions it must answer in the coming years, however. How the CTC handles them ultimately will help determine its success.

First is the issue of resources. The events of September 11, 2001, which led to the establishment of the CTC, have placed an enormous and unexpected financial burden on the United Nations Secretariat. . . .

The second challenge concerns assistance. . . . [T]he CTC does not itself possess the resources to provide assistance. . . . Unless the CTC is able to mobilize and coordinate assistance efforts to ensure comprehensive implementation of Resolution 1373, its efficacy will be questioned. . . .

The fourth challenge concerns the absence of an agreed definition of terrorism among UN member states. One of the reasons the CTC has maintained such broad support from member states is that it has been able to avoid dealing with the divisive issue of the definition of "terrorism." Resolution 1373 does not include a single definition; rather, it allows each member state to define terrorism under its domestic system. Thus, for example, when the Security Council, under Resolution 1373, "*decided* . . . that all States shall deny safe haven to those who finance, plan, support, or commit terrorist acts, or provide safe havens," it has allowed each state to determine against whom this provision is applied. . . .

The fifth challenge concerns the interplay between efforts to combat terrorism and the protection of human rights. There is a concern that implementation of Resolution 1373 not be used as an excuse to infringe on human rights. Sergio Vieira de Mello, the UN High Commissioner for Human Rights, and his predecessor, Mary Robinson, have urged the CTC to appoint an expert on human rights and assume responsibility for monitoring states' compliance with human rights norms in the area of counterterrorism. Vieira de Mello has even offered to provide the CTC with such an expert. The CTC has so far not taken up his offer. Rather, its position has been that while it does take human rights seriously and has engaged in a dialogue with the Office of the UN High Commissioner for Human Rights, the task of monitoring adherence to human rights obligations in the fight against terrorism falls outside of the CTC's mandate. This work should be left to human rights bodies and institutions, e.g., the Office of the High Commissioner for Human Rights, the UN Human Rights Committee, or the Council of Europe. . . .

KIM LANE SCHEPPELE, THE INTERNATIONAL STATE OF EMERGENCY: CHALLENGES TO CONSTITUTIONALISM AFTER SEPTEMBER 11

(2008) (unpublished manuscript)[51]

. . . The fundamental changes that have occurred since September 11 both articulate a new relationship between international and domestic law and also mark the declining hegemony of constitutionalist ideas among political elites. The primary marker of

---

51. This excerpt comes from a book currently under preparation. The longer excerpt from which it is drawn is available at http://publicpolicy.umd.edu/prospective/specialization/cp4/scheppele%20ISOE%20fall2006.rtf (last visited Sept. 22, 2009). See also Kim Lane Scheppele, Other People's Patriot Acts: Europe's Response to September 11, 50 Loy. L. Rev. 89 (2004); Scheppele, Law in a Time of Emergency: States of Exception and the Temptations of 9/11, 6 U. Pa. J. Const. L. 1001 (2004).

these changes is the increased abilities of national executives to use the cover of international law to undermine domestic constitutions at home. While this has not happened in every country, it has happened in a surprising range of states after September 11, including many states that have little or nothing to do with the front lines of the GWOT. From once-again-powerful Russia to tiny Vanuatu, from constitutionalist Britain to anti-constitutionalist Vietnam, countries around the world have been changing their laws and practices since September 11 to fight terrorism, using a template that has been internationally forged, transnationally transmitted through international and regional associations, and locally adjusted to produce results that challenge basic constitutionalist principles at home.

While the substance of these changes is new, the use of international law as a basis for promoting domestic legal change is not. Public international law, especially since World War II, has had an immense influence on the development of domestic constitutionalism around the world. The development and spread of international human rights law is part of what we might call the "first wave of public law globalization," and it has had a substantial effect on constitutional drafters, newly empowered constitutional courts and elite opinion, particularly in the 1980s and 1990s as first Southern Europe and then Latin America and then post-communist Europe entered the field of constitutional democratic states. Political coalitions in these places rallied around principles proclaiming the importance of parliamentary power, judicial independence and respect for human rights, principles articulated through international law debates and carried through transnational networks.

Since September 11, however, we have been witnessing the development of international security law, which constitutes a *second* wave of public law globalization, modeled on the first in the way it harnesses transnational organizations as a vector of change in diverse local settings. In this new wave, national executives are empowered relative to local parliaments and courts; security services and police are linked across countries more tightly than they are linked to bodies that might supervise them within their own states; and surveillance and control of local populations are elevated above legal transparency and the individuation of suspicion as principles organizing the relationship of the state to the individual. The development of this international security law after September 11 follows a pattern of adoption we already know well from the first wave of public law globalization even though its substance is quite different.

How does this influence of international law on domestic law take place? In the *first* wave of public law globalization, starting with World War II and continuing up through September 11, international human rights law provided a major support system for the development of constitutionalism around the world. . . . This is a model animated by respect for human dignity, filled in by a dense set of rights guarantees, and presided over by an active judiciary that ensures that states do not stray from the path of effective rights protection. . . .

The international struggle against terrorism, given additional power after September 11, has launched a *second* wave of public law globalization that pushes, substantively speaking, in the opposite direction from the first wave. The *anti-terrorism campaign* (for this is a better metaphor than war) is led from the security side of public international law through the United Nations Security Council and is potentially backed with sanctions in a way that the human rights framework has not been. Since September 11, the UN Security Council has adopted a series of resolutions that have been far more legislative in character than anything the Security Council had previously passed. Operating under Chapter VII of the UN Charter, which makes resolutions binding on all member states and therefore makes noncompliance at least theoretically subject to sanctions, the UN Security Council has required states:

- to create a separate crime of terrorism in their national laws (along with the crimes of conspiracy to commit terrorism, aiding and abetting terrorism, providing material support for terrorism and other ancillary offenses),
- to monitor terrorist finances and to halt transfers of money to and from named parties as soon as they appear on Security Council terrorism watch lists,
- to act affirmatively to prevent terrorist plots from hatching on their territory and therefore to increase the surveillance of and ability to gather information from domestic populations, and
- to monitor the system of transnational travel, refugee claims and asylum applications to make sure that terrorists are not moving around under cover of human-rights protections.

Following this program has meant that states have created new, vague and politically defined crimes, found ways around warrant-and-notice requirements before seizing property, launched massive new domestic surveillance programs, moved toward preventive detention and aggressive interrogation, and put up new barriers in the system of international migration. . . .

How has this happened? Obviously, the passage of resolutions by the Security Council, even under its Chapter VII powers, cannot bring such a security regime into being by itself. International law famously has compliance problems. The human rights field has certainly been plagued by uneven compliance, which is spotty at best among states prone toward mass violation and even weak in some areas among constitutionalist states. But with international security law, states have rushed to adopt new anti-terrorism laws with compliance levels that are extraordinary. Virtually all countries in the UN system have responded to the Security Council's anti-terrorism resolutions by changing their domestic laws. Kofi Annan himself is quoted on the UN Security Council's Counter-Terrorism Committee's website: "The work of the Counter-Terrorism Committee and the cooperation it has received from Member States have been unprecedented and exemplary."

Why has there been such a rush to comply with international security law? I will argue that it is because international security law has a different domestic constituency than the constituency for human-rights-based laws characteristic of the first wave of public law globalization. This time it is national executives (sometimes with and sometimes without legislative approval) who have moved swiftly to put the new international security law into practice. Moreover, national executives adopt such policies *despite* the effects that the new policies have on domestic constitutional structures and on the realization of rights, precisely because these policies tend to bolster the power of national executives relative to everyone else in their domestic political space. In fact, in countries where national executives were chafing at the constraints imposed on their use of state power by the new human-rights-infused constitutions and by new devices for sharing power adopted in the first wave of public law globalization, the anti-terrorism campaign has been the device through which national executives have attempted to loosen such constraints. . . .

The post-September-11 world, then, has provided these national executives with a way to empower themselves relative to the judges, non-governmental organizations advocating human rights, and disadvantaged constituencies who pushed along the last wave of public law globalization. But given that judges and human rights activists in particular used the high-minded rhetoric of "following international law" as one of the bases for their prior success, it is difficult for them to challenge the same rhetoric used now toward different ends. Countries that have altered their laws and legal frameworks after September 11 have often justified the changes by pointing to the wisdom and even necessity of following international law. But the international law invoked in the post-September-11 world has entirely different content than that invoked by international human rights supporters in the period of post-World-War-II constitution building. . . . In the anti-terrorism campaign, the new international public law seems primarily to provide the conditions for *undermining* domestic constitutional law, particularly its concern for balanced and checked constitutional powers, for human rights and for due process. . . .

In the international arena, the effect has been to bring a variety of purely local struggles into the purview of international anti-terrorism policy, with a subsequent enlargement of the anti-terrorism policy to terrorist and even merely dissident groups of far less than "global reach." To get China on board, many states (the U.S. lead among them) dutifully classified the formerly "freedom-fighting" Muslim Uighurs as terrorists, and Russia was able to get Chechen nationalists (including some who had been duly elected by the population of Chechnya) into that category as well. These previously local fights have, as a result, become part of the global anti-terrorism campaign. The anti-terrorism campaign is now a comprehensive international frame, much as the Cold War was, through which virtually all local disputes become linked in a broader calculus of interest that implicates the international community.

UN Security Council Resolution 1373 provided the framework for much post-September-11 legal activity. . . .

Most UN Security Council resolutions before 1373 had not looked like general laws, but instead like one-shot orders of some specificity. For example, a Security Council resolution might forbid all UN member states from selling weapons to a particular country, or might caution a particular state not to take certain steps. A Security Council resolution might condemn a particular course of action by a member state and require that state to reverse it, or it might establish trade embargoes against particular states for particular reasons. Resolution 1373 was different. . . .

Resolution 1373 required *all states to change their domestic laws* in very particular ways. As a result, it looked more like general legislation than like a typical Security Council resolution. . . .

a) Defining Terrorism

Despite initial resistance on the part of a number of countries to making terrorism a separate offense in domestic criminal law, most countries have now amended their criminal codes to single out terrorism for special treatment. But such criminalization requires that the crime be defined, and this is where the UN guidance ran out and domestic discretion began. In the absence of an agreed-upon definition of terrorism, not surprisingly, states defined terrorism in ways that suited them.

Some states without substantial constitutional traditions defined terrorism to be virtually any politically motivated challenge to the state, which almost entirely overlapped the field of political dissent. For example, Vietnam defined a terrorist as anyone who "oppose(s) the people's administration and infringe(s) upon the lives of officials, public employees or citizens." In Brunei, a terrorist is "any person who . . . by the use of any firearm, explosive, or ammunition acts in a manner prejudicial to public safety or to the maintenance of public order or incites to violence or counsels disobedience to the law or to any lawful order." Clearly, these definitions sweep quite broadly over activities of which the state may not approve, and so the anti-terrorism campaign has the potential to sweep up local political disagreement under the guise of fighting international terrorists. . . .

So far as anyone can tell from the CTC's reaction, it has not condemned any of these definitions. But it has tried to push countries that have not criminalized terrorism into doing so, even over resistance. Mexico, for example, indicated in its first report to the CTC in 2001 that it could clearly handle all crimes that might amount to terrorism within its current criminal code without explicitly calling terrorism a crime as such, especially if one took into account the provisions for conspiracy, aiding and abetting, and criminal association. But since Mexico was one of those few countries that reported the CTC questions along with its answers in its later reports, we can see that the CTC specifically pressed Mexico to criminalize "recruitment for the purposes of carrying out terrorist acts regardless of whether such acts have actually been committed or attempted." Mexico responded that such people could be punished as accomplices under the current penal code. By the time of the 2003 CTC report, however, Mexico reports having criminalized the recruitment of members to terrorist groups. It also added the new offenses of threats to commit terrorism, conspiracy to commit terrorism, and the concealment of terrorist activities. This appears to be as clear an indication as any that Mexico was pressured by the CTC to do this. We can also see in the CTC reports from Mexico that, in direct response to CTC request, Mexico changed the minimum sentence for a terrorism-related offense from 2 years to 18 years.

The worry here is that vague and politically calculated definitions of terrorism endanger ordinary political dissenters and allow the state to use the anti-terrorism campaign to go after domestic enemies who may not be connected to the transnational anti-terror plots. . . . And so far, the Counter-Terrorism Committee has seen no problems with overly zealous criminal anti-terrorism laws.

b) Disrupting Terrorism Financing

Perhaps the largest number of changes in the post-9/11, post-Resolution-1373 world have implicated procedures that countries have in place for being able to freeze or seize terrorist assets. Resolution 1373 requires states be able to "immediately" freeze the assets of those on the UN sanctions committee list. If there is a lengthy court process that must take place before assets can be frozen, then such processes cannot operate "immediately." As a result, there has been a press from the CTC out to the UN member states to find ways to freeze and even seize assets bypassing domestic judicial intervention. This pressure implicates two sorts of constitutional safeguards — protection for private property and the basic principle that no one shall be deprived of their rights without an opportunity to confront the evidence that is the basis for the deprivation.

How can the CTC demand that states freeze the assets of individuals immediately and without prior review by a court? The UN Security Council Sanctions Committee (another committee of the UN Security Council) creates lists of terrorist groups or individuals without disclosing the evidence on which the listing is based or even the process through which evidence is assessed. The CTC has been asking states to take these lists and immediately freeze the assets of all those on the lists anywhere in the world. The problem, of course, is that neither the Sanctions Committee nor the CTC has anything like a procedure for individualized hearings to determine that those placed on the UN lists are in fact who the Sanctions Committee believes them to be or that the assets so frozen would actually have been available to assist any terrorist plot. There is also no process at all through which an individual or group can contest this designation and the states asked to freeze assets are not given any evidence to assess whether the request is justified.

The demand that states freeze assets immediately has been complied with (at least as noted in the CTC reports) quite widely. Most states have found a way to freeze assets of individuals while bypassing their domestic courts. Sometimes, the freezing is done through an executive order (which means that the executive is able to suspend the right of property without any semblance of judicial process) or pursuant to a statute that delegates to the executive the power to enforce Security Council resolutions. Often, there is a standing order in place for banks to "automatically" freeze assets of anyone on the Security Council lists. [The author discusses examples of such automatic freezes in France, Spain, and Bulgaria.] . . .

The demand for immediate freezes of assets of individuals and groups has produced some push-back from states like Venezuela and Mexico which claimed at first that they could not freeze assets without a judicial order and that they could not get a judicial order without evidence that could be presented to a domestic judge that the person or group whose assets are frozen had violated a law. Mexico, in particular, was pressed though direct questions from the CTC on their policy of not allowing assets of suspected terrorists to be frozen if the suspected terrorist could prove the assets were legally acquired. But, after several reports attempting resistance to the CTC, both Venezuela and Mexico found a way to freeze assets without having to show any individualized proof to a domestic judge. . . .

c) Tracking Terrorists through Increased Surveillance

Security Council Resolution 1373 required states to increase their abilities to track and apprehend terrorists within their borders, and to share information across national borders relevant to this goal. This has given new license to states to loosen the legal requirements that have to be met before surveillance can be begun and to increase the length of time that surveillance of individuals and groups can be maintained. In addition, states have used this opportunity to rearrange their internal and external security agencies, often merging the institutions of the ordinary police with intelligence agencies that once reported only through the military. . . . [The author discusses examples from Argentina, Yemen, and Spain.]

Some states have openly changed their laws permitting increased surveillance and allowing new methods of terrorism detection in their domestic populations. . . . [The author discusses such legislation in New Zealand, Canada, and Kyrgyzstan.]

Information gathered by the security services about potential terrorists is now generally shared, both within and between governments. But what is not shared along with this information are the methods through which the information was initially acquired. Governments suspected of using coercion, torture and other illegal means acquire their tainted information and pass it on to other states, of course without disclosing that compromised methods have been used to acquire it. . . . Of course, the UN Security Council has not publicly condoned torture, but the framework of Resolution 1373 encourages information acquired through whatever methods a state feels entitled to use to be passed on to others and to be used in making judgments about individuals even within states that foreswear the practice of torture.

States are now encouraged to make use of this transnational blizzard of information obtained from other states in tracking terrorists even if the methods that were used to acquire such intelligence might not be acceptable in the receiving state. It is already well-documented that people have been put into indefinite detention in constitutional democracies without charges or trial, based on information gained from detainees who have almost surely been tortured, even though these constitutional democracies' own security services would not be able to conduct such interrogations (at least not officially). For example, the recent arrests of suspected terrorists in Britain who were said to have plotted to bomb several trans-Atlantic airliners headed to the US are now thought to have been spurred by an interrogation under torture of one of their number in Pakistan. The new forms of information gathering, surveillance and information sharing since September 11 have created an international soup of information, the precise reliability of which is very difficult to assess. The fact that countries that feel no limitations on using torture and other forms of coercion are urged to share information with countries that would not engage in such practices means that the anti-terrorism campaign is full of such tainted information. Moreover, the ability of security services around the world to use this information encourages a division of labor in which some states torture on behalf of other governments who want to keep their own hands clean.

d) DISRUPTING TRANSNATIONAL FLOWS OF PEOPLE

The refugee and asylum system was singled out for special attention in the UN resolution because the Security Council seems to have believed that terrorists are abusing this system for their own advantage. But the result has been a crackdown at the borders of many states, prejudicing the claims of legitimate refugees and asylum-seekers.

One particularly pernicious device for denying what may be legitimate asylum claims comes as countries (and the UN Security Council's Sanctions Committee itself) add new groups and individuals to the lists of banned terrorist organizations that most states keep these days. Countries often insist on having their own domestic oppositional groups listed as international terrorist organizations by other states as the price they charge for their participation in the anti-terrorism campaign. This is how the Muslim Uighurs, Chechen nationalists and Palestinian activists (among others) have come to be added to the lists of many countries that used to think of these groups as freedom fighters. Sometimes a country will attempt to list its own violent domestic opposition as a terrorist group. Once a group is listed as a terrorist organization, then other countries are not supposed to allow in members of that group. Unfortunately, once a country succeeds in listing its own domestic opposition as international terrorists, then these "terrorists" cannot escape the country where they are being hunted because the international community has now been called upon to refuse entry to anyone in these listed categories. . . .

Before going further, I should say that I don't think that most of these horrific consequences have been the Security Council's intention. Nonetheless, when the international terrorism fight takes priority over all other international considerations (like promoting constitutionalism and respecting human rights), the results are predictable. . . .

Many other critics argued that Resolution 1373, and the Counter-Terrorism Committee (CTC) it created, underemphasized respect for human rights in the fight against terrorism. Perhaps in response to such criticisms, the Security Council adopted Resolution 1456.

UN SECURITY COUNCIL RESOLUTION 1456 (2003)

U.N. Doc. S/RES/1456 (2003), adopted January 20, 2003

The Security Council,
  Decides to adopt the attached declaration on the issue of combating terrorism: . . .

6. States must ensure that any measures taken to combat terrorism comply with all their obligations under international law, and should adopt such measures in accordance with international law, in particular international human rights, refugee, and humanitarian law. . . .

b.   Other Significant Resolutions[52]

In 2004, the Security Council adopted Resolution 1535, which reorganizes the Counter-Terrorism Committee and establishes an Executive Directorate as a special political mission [which] will be responsible for the tasks [of the Committee]."[53]

Then, in 2005, it adopted Resolution 1624, which expresses deep concern about "incitement of terrorist acts motivated by extremism and intolerance" and calls upon states to make such incitement illegal, prevent it, and deny safe haven to inciters.[54] Although "calls upon" is less stringent than "decides," some might fear that Resolution 1624 authorizes states to suppress free speech and deny asylum to foreigners with militant opinions, and the Resolution takes care to emphasize rights to freedom of expression embodied in the Universal Declaration of Human Rights and the International Covenant on Civil and Political Rights, as well as rights to asylum under the Refugee Convention.

Along with Resolution 1373 and its progeny, the Security Council has taken significant measures to disrupt terrorist financing and sanction individuals and organizations that support terrorism. The first of these was the 1999 Resolution 1267, imposing sanctions on the Taliban for its support of Osama bin Laden, and establishing a committee in the Security Council (the "1267 Committee" or "Al-Qaida-Taliban Sanctions Committee") to monitor compliance. Subsequent resolutions expanded the scope of sanctions and refined the procedures for listing and de-listing sanctions targets in an effort to improve their fairness and transparency.[55] The most recent effort, Resolution 1822, was issued against a background of successful legal challenges to the 1267 regime in the European Court of Justice and the United Kingdom.[56]

---

52. A full list of UNSC antiterrorism resolutions is found at http://www.un.org/terrorism/sc-res.shtml (last visited Sept. 22, 2009).

53. S.C. Res. 1535, ¶¶2-3, U.N. Doc. S/RES/1535 (Mar. 26, 2004).

54. S.C. Res. 1624, U.N. Doc. S/RES/1624 (Sept. 14, 2005).

55. For details, see David P. Stewart, Introductory Note to UN Security Council Resolution 1822, 47 I.L.M. 1814 (2008).

56. Kadi v. Council, Judgment of Sept. 3, 2008 in Joined Cases C-402/05 P and C-415/05 P, available at http://curia.europa.eu/jurisp/cgi-bin/form.pl?lang=EN&Submit=Rechercher&numaff=C-402/05 (finding lack of fundamental fairness "[b]ecause the [European] Council neither communicated to the appellants the evidence used against them to justify the restrictive measures imposed on them nor afforded them the right to be informed of that evidence within a reasonable period after those measures were enacted"); Judgment of April 24, 2008 in A, K, M, Q & G v. H.M. Treasury, [2008] EWHC 869 (Admin.), ¶46, available at http://www.bailii.org/ew/cases/EWHC/Admin/2008/869.html (finding UK Orders implementing through criminal sanctions the assets freezes required under S.C. Res. 1267 must be quashed because they go beyond what would be "necessary and expedient" in order to implement the Security Council regime).

A brief examination of the UK case will illustrate some of the delicate problems that arise in the UN's effort to disrupt terrorist finance.[57] Four London residents received letters from the government stating that the Treasury "has reasonable grounds for suspecting that you are, or may be, a person who facilitates the commission of acts of terrorism. . . . In light of the sensitive nature of the information on which this decision was taken we are unable to give you further details."[58] As a result, their bank accounts were frozen, "although they have been granted licences to be paid social security benefits. In the case of A and K such benefits are to be paid only to their wives, who are permitted only to provide food and accommodation and no more than ten pounds a week in cash."[59] It "is not in dispute that G has been subject to the [freeze order] solely because he has been listed by the UN Sanctions Committee."[60] The freeze orders are enforced by criminal penalties.

The lower court held that the freeze orders and criminal sanctions go beyond the authority conferred by the UN resolutions and the UK's domestic law incorporating SC resolutions into British law. Reversing, the appellate panel concluded that the freeze orders are lawful provided that the words "or may be" are removed from the phrase "you are, or may be, a person who facilitates the commission of acts of terrorism." The propriety of the broad freeze order rests simply on the power and breadth of the UN resolutions:

> The UK Government is obliged to carry out the decisions of the UN Security Council: article 25 of the Charter. In order to combat terrorism the Security Council has passed a series of fierce resolutions. By such of the resolutions, . . . the council, seeking to respond to the threat in a manner probably far from the contemplation of the founders of the UN in 1946, has set up a system for a committee of its own to designate, by list, a person as being a member of Al-Qaida or an associate thereof, whom all member states are thereupon at once obliged to deprive of access to finance. The understandable objective is immediate disabling action against a person at [a] global level. But the way in which the Sanctions Committee operates in reaching a conclusion that a person be so designated is opaque and it is not amenable to review by the courts of the member states.[61]

Harsh or not, the court concluded, the UK government's implementation goes no further than the law itself authorizes. Thus, questions still remain about human rights under the UN resolutions. In the following excerpt, the CTC addresses them.

UN SECURITY COUNCIL COUNTER-TERRORISM COMMITTEE, HUMAN RIGHTS

http://www.un.org/sc/ctc/rights.html (2009)

The subject of counter-terrorism and human rights has attracted considerable interest since the establishment of the Counter-Terrorism Committee (CTC) in 2001. In Security Council resolution 1456 (2003) and later resolutions, the Council

---

57. Judgment of June 16, 18, Oct. 30 in A & Others v. H.M. Treasury, [2008] EWCA Civ. 1187.
58. Id. ¶26.
59. Id. ¶27.
60. Id. ¶30.
61. Id. ¶152 (speech of Wilson, LJ).

has said that States must ensure that any measures taken to combat terrorism comply with all their obligations under international law, and should adopt such measures in accordance with international law, in particular international human rights, refugee, and humanitarian law.

Security Council resolution 1373 (2001), which established the CTC, makes one reference to human rights, calling upon States to "take appropriate measures in conformity with the relevant provisions of national and international law, including international standards of human rights, before granting refugee status, for the purpose of ensuring that the asylum seeker has not planned, facilitated or participated in the commission of terrorist acts." The resolution's preamble also reaffirms the need to combat by all means, "in accordance with the Charter of the United Nations," threats to international peace and security caused by terrorist acts.

The Committee's initial policy on human rights was expressed by its first Chairman in a briefing to the Security Council on 18 January 2002: "The Counter-Terrorism Committee is mandated to monitor the implementation of resolution 1373 (2001). Monitoring performance against other international conventions, including human rights law, is outside the scope of the Counter-Terrorism Committee's mandate. But we will remain aware of the interaction with human rights concerns, and we will keep ourselves briefed as appropriate. It is, of course, open to other organizations to study States' reports and take up their content in other forums."

With the establishment of the Counter-Terrorism Committee Executive Directorate (CTED) by Security Council resolution 1535 (2004), the Committee began moving toward a more pro-active policy on human rights. . . .

In May 2006 the Committee adopted policy guidance for CTED in the area of human rights, saying that CTED should:

- Provide advice to the Committee, including for its ongoing dialogue with States on their implementation of resolution 1373 (2001), on international human rights, refugee and humanitarian law, in connection with identification and implementation of effective measures to implement resolution 1373 (2001);
- Advise the Committee on how to ensure that any measures States take to implement the provisions of resolution 1624 (2005) comply with their obligations under international law, in particular international human rights law, refugee law, and humanitarian law; and
- Liaise with the Office of the High Commissioner for Human Rights and, as appropriate, with other human rights organizations in matters related to counter-terrorism. . . .

The Committee and CTED now routinely take account of relevant human rights concerns in all their activities, including the preparation of preliminary implementation assessments (PIAs) relating to resolution 1373 (2001), country visits and other interactions with Member States. . . .

Most recently, as recommended by the CTED Executive Director and endorsed by Security Council resolution 1805 (2008), a working group on issues raised by resolution 1624 (2005) and human rights aspects of counter-terrorism in the context of resolution 1373 (2001) was established in CTED. The working group's main objectives are to enhance expertise and develop common approaches by CTED staff on these issues, as well as to consider ways in which the Committee might more effectively encourage Member States to comply with their international obligations in this area. . . .

NOTES AND QUESTIONS

1. Do you believe that the measures adopted by the Security Council and the Counter-Terrorism Committee adequately address the concerns raised by Professor Scheppele?

2. As noted by both Rosand and Scheppele, the Security Council does not attempt to define terrorism. Scheppele worries that this permits states to define their enemies, including domestic dissidents, as terrorists. Other writers have complained that some states err in the opposite direction. Stefan Talmon specifically cites Syria for exempting from its definition of terrorism "legitimate struggle against foreign occupation," thereby excluding attacks on Israeli civilians by Hamas, the Al Aqsa Martyrs Brigades, and Islamic Jihad. Talmon, Note and Comment: The Security Council as World Legislature, 99 Am J. Intl. L. 175, 189 (2005). Syria adopted language drawn from the Arab Convention on the Suppression of Terrorism, quoted earlier in this chapter.

3. In addition to Professor Scheppele, several commentators have argued that the quasi-legislative nature of Resolution 1373 represents a novelty in international law, whereby the Security Council asserts the power to create binding law, specifically criminal law. See Eric Rosand, The Security Council as "Global Legislator": Ultra Vires or Ultra Innovative?, 28 Fordham Intl. L.J. 542 (2005); Talmon, supra; Jose E. Alvarez, Hegemonic International Law Revisited, 97 Am. J. Intl. L. 873 (2003); Jane E. Stromseth, An Imperial Security Council? Implementing Security Council Resolution 1373 and 1390, 97 ASIL Proc. 41 (2003); Paul C. Szasz, The Security Council Starts Legislating, 96 Am. J. Intl. L. 901 (2002).

Should the Security Council be assuming the role of "global legislator" against terrorism in the absence of an antiterrorism convention? Is this overreaching? Or is it a necessity, given the threat posed by terrorist groups and the political gridlock that has delayed the adoption of an antiterrorism convention?

4. For more detailed discussion of other states' antiterrorism measures, see Anil Kalhan et al., Colonial Continuities: Human Rights, Terrorism, and Security Laws in India, 20 Colum. J. Asian L. 93 (2006)(discussing India); Reuven Young, Defining Terrorism: The Evolution of Terrorism as a Legal Concept in International Law and Its Influence on Definitions in Domestic Legislation, 29 B.C. Intl. & Comp. L. Rev. 23, 80-84 (2006)(discussing responses of New Zealand and India to Resolution 1373); Human Rights Watch, Hear No Evil, See No Evil: The UN Security Council's Approach to Human Rights Violations in the Global Counter-Terrorism Effort (2004), *available at* http://www.hrw.org/legacy/backgrounder/un/2004/un0804/index.htm (discussing Egypt, Uzbekistan, Malaysia, Morocco, and Sweden).

C. CRIMINAL PROSECUTION OF TERRORISM IN U.S. LAW

Having examined the international criminal law of terrorism, we turn to the domestic criminal law of terrorism, which can be applied transnationally if the domestic and international laws of jurisdiction permit. As in other chapters, we focus on the United States as an example of particular interest.

1. *Material Support for Terrorism and Terrorist Organizations*

As might be expected, the United States has numerous statutes criminalizing particular terrorist crimes, and many general-purpose criminal statutes also apply in terrorism cases. Norman Abrams gives some sense of the range of statutes in his summary of several prominent pre-9/11 terrorism cases:

> [Timothy] McVeigh, for example, was convicted of charges involving use of a weapon of mass destruction, 18 U.S.C. §2332a, destruction by explosives, 18 U.S.C. §844, and homicide offenses, 18 U.S.C. §§1111 and 1114. The convictions in the Salameh case[62] similarly were based on 18 U.S.C. §844 as well as using explosives to bomb automobiles used in interstate commerce, with reckless disregard for human life, 18 U.S.C. §33, assaulting federal officers, §111, using a destructive device in a crime of violence, 18 U.S.C. §924, and traveling in interstate commerce with intent to commit certain crimes, 18 U.S.C. §1952. In the Bin Laden prosecution [for the 1998 bombing of U.S. embassies in Kenya and Tanzania], the charged offenses involved conspiring to kill U.S. nationals under 18 U.S.C. §2332 and destruction of national defense facilities, 18 U.S.C. §2155 as well as offenses that had been used in the earlier cases. . . .[63]

All of these, however, were completed offenses. Post-9/11, where the major policy goal is preventing terrorist crimes rather than punishing them after they are committed, emphasis has shifted to criminal statutes designed to undermine support for terrorists. The two most important are the following.

18 U.S.C. §§2339A and 2339B

§2339A. Providing Material Support to Terrorists

(a) **Offense**. — Whoever provides material support or resources or conceals or disguises the nature, location, source, or ownership of material support or resources, knowing or intending that they are to be used in preparation for, or in carrying out, a violation of [35 enumerated criminal statutes] or in preparation for, or in carrying out, the concealment of an escape from the commission of any such violation, or attempts or conspires to do such an act, shall be fined under this title, imprisoned not more than 15 years, or both, and, if the death of any person results, shall be imprisoned for any term of years or for life. A violation of this section may be prosecuted in any Federal judicial district in which the underlying offense was committed, or in any other Federal judicial district as provided by law.

(b) **Definitions**. — As used in this section —

(1) the term "material support or resources" means any property, tangible or intangible, or service, including currency or monetary instruments or financial securities, financial services, lodging, training, expert advice or assistance, safehouses, false documentation or identification, communications equipment, facilities, weapons, lethal substances, explosives, personnel (1 or more individuals who may be or include oneself), and transportation, except medicine or religious materials;

---

62. This refers to the 1993 World Trade Center bombing. — Eds.
63. Norman Abrams, Anti-terrorism and Criminal Enforcement 121 (2d ed. 2005).

(2) the term "training" means instruction or teaching designed to impart a specific skill, as opposed to general knowledge; and

(3) the term "expert advice or assistance" means advice or assistance derived from scientific, technical or other specialized knowledge.

§2339B.   Providing Material Support or Resources to Designated Foreign Terrorist Organizations

(a) Prohibited Activities. —

(1) Unlawful conduct. — Whoever knowingly provides material support or resources to a foreign terrorist organization, or attempts or conspires to do so, shall be fined under this title or imprisoned not more than 15 years, or both, and, if the death of any person results, shall be imprisoned for any term of years or for life. To violate this paragraph, a person must have knowledge that the organization is a designated terrorist organization (as defined in subsection (g)(6)), that the organization has engaged or engages in terrorist activity (as defined in [immigration law], or that the organization has engaged or engages in terrorism (as defined in [foreign relations law]). . . .

(d) Extraterritorial Jurisdiction. —

(1) In general. — There is jurisdiction over an offense under subsection (a) if —

(A) an offender is a national of the United States . . . or an alien lawfully admitted for permanent residence in the United States . . . ;

(B) an offender is a stateless person whose habitual residence is in the United States;

(C) after the conduct required for the offense occurs an offender is brought into or found in the United States, even if the conduct required for the offense occurs outside the United States;

(D) the offense occurs in whole or in part within the United States;

(E) the offense occurs in or affects interstate or foreign commerce; or

(F) an offender aids or abets any person over whom jurisdiction exists under this paragraph in committing an offense under subsection (a) or conspires with any person over whom jurisdiction exists under this paragraph to commit an offense under subsection (a).

(2) Extraterritorial jurisdiction. — There is extraterritorial Federal jurisdiction over an offense under this section. . . .

(g) Definitions. — As used in this section — . . .

(4) the term "material support or resources" has the same meaning given that term in section 2339A (including the definitions of "training" and "expert advice or assistance" in that section); . . .

(6) the term "terrorist organization" means an organization designated as a terrorist organization under [immigration law].

(h) Provision of Personnel. — No person may be prosecuted under this section in connection with the term "personnel" unless that person has knowingly provided, attempted to provide, or conspired to provide a foreign terrorist organization with 1 or more individuals (who may be or include himself) to work under that terrorist organization's direction or control or to organize, manage, supervise, or otherwise direct the operation of that organization. Individuals who act entirely independently of the foreign terrorist organization to advance its goals or objectives shall not be considered to be working under the foreign terrorist organization's direction and control.

(i) **Rule of Construction**. — Nothing in this section shall be construed or applied so as to abridge the exercise of rights guaranteed under the First Amendment to the Constitution of the United States.

(j) **Exception**. — No person may be prosecuted under this section in connection with the term "personnel," "training," or "expert advice or assistance" if the provision of that material support or resources to a foreign terrorist organization was approved by the Secretary of State with the concurrence of the Attorney General. The Secretary of State may not approve the provision of any material support that may be used to carry out terrorist activity (as defined in section 212(a)(3)(B)(iii) of the Immigration and Nationality Act).

NOTES AND QUESTIONS

1. Note that whereas §2339B specifies that it has extraterritorial jurisdiction, §2339A does not. On ordinary principles of statutory construction, this difference between the two companion statutes — one mentions extraterritorial jurisdiction where its companion is silent — would lead us to conclude that §2339A does not apply transnationally. However, the current language resulted from a 1996 amendment in which Congress *deleted* a restriction of §2339A to material support "within the territory of the United States," which strongly suggests that §2339A no longer has any territorial restriction. Which reading makes the most sense?

Even if it applied only within U.S. territory, §2339A would nevertheless remain important transnationally because §2339B incorporates the definition of material support from §2339A. Furthermore, recall from Chapter 5.A.3 that a conspiracy to commit a federal crime within the United States may be prosecuted no matter where the conspiracy takes place, so long as at least one overt act occurs within the United States. Ford v. United States, 273 U.S. 593, 624 (1927); Chua Han Mow v. United States, 730 F.2d 1308, 1312 (9th Cir. 1984). Thus, a conspiracy to give material support to terrorist activity in the United States can be prosecuted no matter where it takes place.

2. A third antiterrorism statute, 18 U.S.C. §2339C, prohibits terrorist financing, and in 2004 Congress enacted 18 U.S.C. §2339D, which prohibits receiving "military-type training from or on behalf of" a foreign terrorist organization; both of these have extraterritorial jurisdictional clauses similar to §2339B. Additionally, as discussed in Chapter 13, the U.S. money laundering statutes can sometimes be used to address not only the laundering of "dirty" money but also the transfer of "clean" money to promote criminal activity, including terrorist acts.

3. The material support statutes have been frequently invoked by federal prosecutors in terrorism cases, often in conjunction with conspiracy charges. According to the Center on Law and Security at New York University Law School, between September 2001 and September 2008 there were 228 prosecutions under terrorism statutes, with 63 percent of convictions in those trials coming from plea arrangements. Center on Law and Security, New York University School of Law, Terrorist Trial Report Card: September 11, 2008, at 2, *available at* http://www.lawandsecurity.org/publications/Sept08TTRCFinal.pdf. The material support provisions make up the lion's share of the convictions under the terrorism statutes. "Overall, the two material support charges account for 71% of all convictions under the core terrorism statutes, while terrorist acts or conspiracy to commit terrorist acts (18 U.S.C. [§]2332) account for only 10% of those convictions." Id. at 6. A total of 81 defendants were charged with violating §2339A from September 11, 2001 through September 2008; 39 of the cases

are still pending, but of the 42 that have been resolved, 71 percent resulted in a conviction. Id. Of the 98 cases indicted under §2339B from September 11, 2001 through September 2008, 36 are still pending; of the 62 cases resolved, only 56 percent resulted in a conviction. Id. Most have been domestic cases, but a few— for example, the bombers of the U.S.S. *Cole*—have involved transnational application of §2339B. The more recently enacted §2339C has been used only twice, resulting in one conviction.

4. Some of the prosecutions have aroused controversy because the defendants have lacked any obvious means or skills to carry out terrorist attacks and have received harsh sentences even though they appeared to be little more than jihadi "wannabes," in the phrase of Wayne McCormick, Legal Responses to Terrorism, 2009 Supplement 4. These include:

- A group of young men who trained for jihad in Afghanistan by playing paintball in the Virginia hills. One, who traveled to Pakistan and trained with the terrorist group Lashkar-e-Taiba, was sentenced to life plus 45 years. Another, who denied having any terrorist intentions, nevertheless received a 65-year sentence. United States v. Khan, 309 F. Supp. 2d 789 (E.D. Va. 2004).

- The "Lackawanna Six" trained in an al Qaeda camp in Afghanistan and stayed in an al Qaeda safe house, both before 9/11. The government did not allege that they planned future criminal acts. They pled guilty to material support under §2339B, reportedly because they feared that if they did not plead they would be designated "enemy combatants" and detained indefinitely. Michael Powell, No Choice but Guilty; Lackawanna Case Highlights Legal Tilt, Wash. Post, July 29, 2003, at A1. They pled guilty before *Hamdi* established that U.S. nationals can challenge their designations as enemy combatants.

- Rafiq Sabir, a Florida physician, received a 25-year sentence for conspiracy to provide material support, based on his offer to an undercover agent to provide martial arts training to al Qaeda operatives. Press Release, U.S. Dept. of Justice, Florida Physician Sentenced to 25 Years for Conspiring and Attempting to Support Al Qaeda, Nov. 28, 2007, *available at* http://www.usdoj.gov/usao/nys/pressreleases/November07/sabirsentencingpr.pdf.

- Zubair Ahmed and Khalil Ahmed, two cousins hailing from Chicago, wished to become jihadis. They traveled to Egypt, hoping to receive training—from whom was never clear. After returning to the United States a month later, they planned to learn the use of firearms, discussed the possibility of taking an online course in gun-smithing, and researched the purchase of weapons. They had no concrete terrorist plans, however, and according to the indictment, Zubair told an unnamed person that they "needed five more years to complete their preparations for violent jihad." United States v. Ahmed, Indictment, at 9, *available at* http://www.usdoj.gov/usao/ohn/news/Ahmed_Indictment.pdf (last visited Sept. 22, 2009). The indictment does not allege that they ever met with any terrorist group anywhere. They pled guilty to conspiring to provide material support for terrorism. Press Release, U.S. Dept. of Justice, Chicago Cousins Plead Guilty to Conspiracy to Provide Material Support for Terrorism, Jan. 15, 2009, *available at* http://www.usdoj.gov/opa/pr/2009/January/09-nsd-041.html.

5. In one unusual case, a multinational corporation, Chiquita Banana, pled guilty to making payments to a right-wing paramilitary organization in Colombia, the AUC, which had been designated a foreign terrorist organization. The company paid a $25 million fine. Press Release, U.S. Dept. of Justice, Chiquita Brands International

Pleads Guilty to Making Payments to a Designated Terrorist Organization and Agrees to Pay $25 Million Fine, Mar. 19, 2007, *available at* http://www.usdoj.gov/opa/pr/2007/March/07_nsd_161.html.

6. The United States is by no means the only country to enact wide-reaching criminal statutes targeting otherwise-innocent behavior if it is done in support of terrorism. France criminalizes "[b]eing unable to account for resources corresponding to one's lifestyle when habitually in close contact with a person or persons who engage in [terrorism or terrorist financing]." Code Pénal, art. 421-2-3. In its report to the Security Council's Counter-Terrorism Committee, France refers to this novel crime as "pimping for terrorism." France, Fourth Supplementary Report Submitted by France to the Counter-Terrorism Committee Pursuant to ¶6 of Security Council Resolution 1373 (2001), in Letter Dated 19 March 2004 from the Chairman of the Security Council Committee to the President of the Security Council, S/2004/226, at 16.

The most fundamental questions about the material support statutes are whether they reach too broadly, in particular by interfering with constitutionally protected freedoms of expression and association, and whether they are defined in language that is too vague. A major issue — both for determining whether the statute infringes on First Amendment freedoms and for assessing vagueness challenges to criminal prosecutions or other uses of the statute — is what *mens rea* need be proved. Does the statute require only that one knowingly provide material support to a foreign terrorist organization (FTO), which, as noted, can simultaneously pursue both charitable and terrorist functions? Or does the statute further require that one provide material support knowing of the FTO's illegal activities — or even that one must do so with the specific intent of furthering the FTO's terrorist activity? A second major question concerns, in essence, the *actus reus* of the statute — that is, what constitutes "material support." In particular, courts have struggled with whether the provision of material support in the form of the statutorily identified "personnel" and "training" is sufficiently definite to pass constitutional muster. The cases that follow address these difficult questions.

UNITED STATES v. AL-ARIAN

308 F. Supp. 2d 1322 (M.D. Fla. 2004)

Moody, J.

This is a criminal action against alleged members of the Palestinian Islamic Jihad-Shiqaqi Faction (the "PIJ") who purportedly operated and directed fundraising and other organizational activities in the United States for almost twenty years. The PIJ is a foreign organization that uses violence, principally suicide bombings, and threats of violence to pressure Israel to cede territory to the Palestinian people. On February 19, 2003, the government indicted the Defendants in a 50 count indictment that included counts for: (1) conspiracy to commit racketeering (Count 1); (2) conspiracy to commit murder, maim, or injure persons outside the United States (Count 2); (3) conspiracy to provide material support to or for the benefit of foreign terrorists (Counts 3 and 4); (4) violations of the Travel Act (Counts 5 through 44); (5) violation of the immigration laws of the United States (Counts 45 and 46); (6) obstruction of justice (Count 47); and (7) perjury (Counts 48 through 50). . . .

Before reaching the statutory construction issues, it is helpful, if not necessary, to understand certain constitutional arguments raised by the parties that affect this Court's construction of [relevant statutes]. Defendants have moved to dismiss Counts 1 through 4 of the Indictment, arguing that the Indictment attempts to criminalize their First Amendment rights of speech in support of and association with the PIJ. . . .

The government responds that the Indictment alleges that Defendants engaged in criminal conduct and activities, not protected speech or association. . . .

While it may not be apparent from either parties' arguments, the dispute between the parties on what analysis applies and the constitutionality of Counts 3 and 4 of the Indictment actually turns on how this Court interprets [the Antiterrorism and Effective Death Penalty Act of 1996, Pub. L. No. 104-132, 110 Stat. 1214 (AEDPA)] and [the International Emergency Economic Powers Act of 1977, 50 U.S.C. §1701, et seq. (IEEPA)]. [These laws codify the material support statutes and the government's power to designate an organization as a FTO.]

The broader this Court interprets AEDPA and IEEPA, the more likely that the statutes receive a higher standard of review and are unconstitutional. For example, if this Court interprets AEDPA and IEEPA as requiring a specific intent to further the illegal activities of the FTO or SDT, then no constitutional problems exist. Similarly, if this Court interprets AEDPA's and IEEPA's prohibitions broadly and does not impose a specific intent *mens rea* requirement, it will likely be forced to perform a vagueness analysis and find portions of AEDPA and IEEPA unconstitutional, as did the Ninth Circuit in the *Humanitarian* cases. . . .

In *X-Citement Video*, the Supreme Court faced almost the same statutory interpretation issues faced in this case. There, the Supreme Court considered the Protection of Children Against Sexual Exploitation Act, 18 U.S.C. §2252. Section 2252 of that Act made it unlawful for any person to "knowingly" transport, ship, receive, distribute, or reproduce a visual depiction involving a "minor engaging in sexually explicit conduct." The Ninth Circuit had interpreted "knowingly" to only modify the surrounding verbs, like transport or ship. Under this construction, whether a defendant knew the minority of the performer(s) or even knew whether the material was sexually explicit was inconsequential. The Supreme Court reversed, concluding that, while the Ninth Circuit's construction of Section 2252 complied with the plain meaning rule, the construction caused absurd results. Under the Ninth Circuit's construction, the Court noted that a Federal Express courier who knew that there was film in a package could be convicted even though the courier had no knowledge that the film contained child pornography. To avoid such results, the Court utilized the cannons [*sic*] of statutory construction to imply a "knowing" requirement to each element, including the age of the performers and the sexually explicit nature of the material. The Court stated that in criminal statutes "the presumption in favor of a scienter requirement should apply to each of the statutory elements that criminalize otherwise innocent conduct."

Turning now to AEDPA, Section 2339B(a)(1) makes it unlawful for a person to "knowingly provide[] material support or resources[64] to a foreign terrorist organization, or attempts or conspires to do so. . . ." 18 U.S.C. §2339B(a)(1) (footnote added). The Ninth Circuit has twice in a single case interpreted Section

---

64. [Court's footnote 25:] The term "material support or resources" is defined in AEDPA to mean "currency or other financial securities, financial services, lodging, training, safehouses, false documentation or identification, communications equipment, facilities, weapons, lethal substances, explosives, personnel, transportation, and other physical assets, except medicine or religious materials." Id. §2339A(b); id. §2239B(g)(4).

2339B and found portions to be unconstitutionally vague as applied to the plaintiffs in that case. *See* [Humanitarian Law Project v. United States Dep't of Justice, 352 F.2d 382, 385 (9th Cir. 2003) (*Humanitarian II* or HLP II); Humanitarian Law Project v. Reno, 205 F.3d 1130, 1133-1136 (9th Cir. 2000) (*Humanitarian I* or HLP I)]. *Humanitarian* involved a civil action for declaratory and injunctive relief brought by six organizations and two United States citizens who wished to provide the Kurdistan Workers' Party (the "PKK") and the Liberation Tigers of Tamil Eelam (the "LTTE") with support for the political and nonviolent humanitarian activities of each organization.

In *Humanitarian I*, the Ninth Circuit faced head on a challenge to Section 2339B on freedom of association, freedom of speech, and vagueness grounds. The Ninth Circuit affirmed the district court's determination that AEDPA did not impinge upon the plaintiffs' associational or speech rights. However, the Ninth Circuit also affirmed the district court's determination that the terms "personnel" and "training" (specified elements of "material support") were unconstitutionally vague because those terms could impinge on a person's advocacy rights. The Ninth Circuit commented that:

> Someone who advocates the cause of PKK could be seen as supplying them with personnel; it even fits under the government's rubric of freeing up resources, since having an independent advocate frees up members to engage in terrorist activities instead of advocacy. But advocacy is pure speech protected by the First Amendment.

Id. at 1137.[65]

Similarly, the Ninth Circuit stated that training was also vague because it could include "a plaintiff who wishes to instruct members of a designated group on how to petition the United Nations to give aid to their group. . . ." The government "invite[d]" the Ninth Circuit to cure these vagueness problems by implying "knowingly," which occurs earlier in the statute, to the material support requirement. The Ninth Circuit rejected this construction, reasoning that such a construction would be judicially rewriting the statute. The Ninth Circuit construed "knowingly" as modifying only "provides," which meant that the scienter requirement was met when the accused had knowledge that he provided something, rather than "knowledge . . . that what is provided in fact constitutes material support."

On subsequent appeal in *Humanitarian II*, the Ninth Circuit reconsidered its interpretation of the *mens rea* requirement in *Humanitarian I*. Under its new interpretation, the Ninth Circuit concluded that Section 2339B also required proof that a person either knew: (a) that an organization was a FTO; or (b) of an organization's unlawful activities that caused it to be designated as a FTO. The Ninth Circuit then reaffirmed its prior holding on the vagueness of "personnel" and "training" without analyzing how the change in the *mens rea* requirement affected its prior vagueness analysis.

This Court agrees with the Ninth Circuit in *Humanitarian I* that a purely grammatical reading of the plain language of Section 2339B(a)(1) makes it unlawful for any person to knowingly furnish any item contained in the material support categories to an organization that has been designated a FTO. And like *Humanitarian II*, this Court agrees that this construction renders odd results and raises serious constitutional concerns. For example under *Humanitarian I*, a donor could be convicted for giving

---

65. [Court's footnote 27:] The *Humanitarian II* panel provided an illustration of how an advocate could free up members to engage in terrorism. The Ninth Circuit stated that "personnel" could include "efforts to urge members of Congress to support the release of Kurdish political prisoners in Turkey."

money to a FTO without knowledge that an organization was a FTO or that it committed unlawful activities, and without an intent that the money be used to commit future unlawful activities.[66]

Humanitarian II attempted to correct this odd result and accompanying constitutional concerns by interpreting "knowingly" to mean that a person knew: (a) an organization was a FTO; or (b) an organization committed unlawful activities, which caused it to be designated a FTO. But, *Humanitarian II*'s construction of Section 2339B only cures some of the Fifth Amendment concerns. First, *Humanitarian II* fails to comply with *X-Citement Video*'s holding that a *mens rea* requirement "should apply to each of the statutory elements that criminalize otherwise innocent conduct." *Humanitarian II* implies only a *mens rea* requirement to the FTO element of Section 2339B(a)(1) and not to the material support element. Under *Humanitarian II*'s construction, a cab driver could be guilty for giving a ride to a FTO member to the UN, if he knows that the person is a member of a FTO or the member or his organization at sometime conducted an unlawful activity in a foreign country. Similarly, a hotel clerk in New York could be committing a crime by providing lodging to that same FTO member under similar circumstances as the cab driver. Because the *Humanitarian II*'s construction fails to avoid potential Fifth Amendment concerns, this Court rejects its construction of Section 2339B.

Second, the *Humanitarian II* construction does not solve the constitutional vagueness concerns of Section 2339B(a)(1), which can be avoided by implying a *mens rea* requirement to the "material support or resources" element of Section 2339B(a)(1). If this Court accepted the *Humanitarian II* construction, it would likely have to declare many more categories of "material support" (in addition to "training" and "personnel" determined to be unconstitutionally vague in the *Humanitarian* cases) unconstitutionally vague for impinging on advocacy rights, including "financial services," "lodging," "safe houses," "communications equipment," "facilities," "transportation" and "other physical assets." Using the Ninth Circuit's vagueness example on "training,"[67] the statute could likewise punish other innocent conduct, such as where a person in New York City (where the United Nations is located) gave a FTO member a ride from the airport to the United Nations before the member petitioned the United Nations. Such conduct could be punished as providing "transportation" to a FTO under Section 2339B.[68] The end result of the Ninth Circuit's statutory construction in *Humanitarian II* is to render a substantial portion of Section 2339B unconstitutionally vague.

But, it is not necessary to do such serious damage to the statute if one follows the analysis used by the United States Supreme Court in *X-Citement Video*. This Court concludes that it is more consistent with Congress's intent, which was to prohibit material support from FTOs to the "fullest possible basis," to imply a *mens rea* requirement to the "material support" element of Section 2339B(a)(1). Therefore, this Court concludes that to convict a defendant under Section 2339B(a)(1) the government must prove beyond a reasonable doubt that the defendant knew that: (a) the organization was a FTO or had committed unlawful activities that caused it to be so

---

66. [Court's footnote 28:] Similarly, a bank teller who cashes the donor's check for a FTO could also be guilty despite a similar lack of knowledge.

67. [Court's footnote 30:] The Ninth Circuit utilized the example of "a plaintiff who wishes to instruct members of a designated group on how to petition the United Nations to give aid to their group. . . ."

68. [Court's footnote 31:] Other examples of innocent conduct that could be prohibited include the same person allowing the FTO member to spend the night at his house, cashing a check, loaning the member a cell phone for use during the stay, or allowing the member to use the fax machine or laptop computer in preparing the petition.

designated; and (b) what he was furnishing was "material support." To avoid Fifth Amendment personal guilt problems, this Court concludes that the government must show more than a defendant knew something was within a category of "material support" in order to meet (b). In order to meet (b), the government must show that the defendant knew (had a specific intent) that the support would further the illegal activities of a FTO.

This Court does not believe this burden is that great in the typical case. Often, such an intent will be easily inferred. For example, a jury could infer a specific intent to further the illegal activities of a FTO when a defendant knowingly provides weapons, explosives, or lethal substances to an organization that he knows is a FTO because of the nature of the support. Likewise, a jury could infer a specific intent when a defendant knows that the organization continues to commit illegal acts and the defendant provides funds to that organization knowing that money is fungible and, once received, the donee can use the funds for any purpose it chooses. That is, by its nature, money carries an inherent danger for furthering the illegal aims of an organization. Congress said as much when it found that FTOs were "so tainted by their criminal conduct that any contribution to such an organization facilitates that conduct."

This opinion in no way creates a safe harbor for terrorists or their supporters to try and avoid prosecution through utilization of shell "charitable organizations" or by directing money through the memo line of a check towards lawful activities.[69] This Court believes that a jury can quickly peer through such facades when appropriate. This is especially true if other facts indicate a defendant's true intent, like where defendants or conspirators utilize codes or unusual transaction practices to transfer funds. Instead, this Court's holding works to avoid potential constitutional problems and fully accomplish congressional intent.

NOTES AND QUESTIONS

1. The Court of Appeals for the Fourth Circuit addressed similar issues but reached the opposite result in United States v. Hammoud, 381 F.3d 316 (4th Cir. 2004). Mohammed Hammoud was a Lebanese national who solicited funds in Virginia for Hizballah, a designated FTO. He gave Hizballah $3,500 of his own money. Hammoud was convicted of material support and conspiracy to commit material support under §2339B, along with unrelated immigration and smuggling offenses. The court "notes the undisputed fact that Hizballah provides humanitarian aid to citizens of Lebanon. Hammoud argues that because Hizballah engages in both legal and illegal activities, he can be found criminally liable for providing material support to Hizballah only if he had a specific intent to further the organization's illegal aims. Because §2339B lacks such a specific intent requirement, Hammoud argues that it unconstitutionally restricts the freedom of association. . . ." 381 F.3d at 328. The court disagreed: "Hammoud's argument fails because §2339B does not prohibit mere association; it prohibits the *conduct* of providing material support to a designated FTO." Id. at 329. The court noted that even if Hammoud directed his funds solely to Hizballah's humanitarian activities, "money is fungible; giving support intended to

---

69. [Court's footnote 35:] For example, a donation to a suicide bomber's family given with the intent to encourage others to engage in such activities or support such activities would satisfy this specific intent requirement.

aid an organization's peaceful activities frees up resources that can be used for terrorist acts." Id. at 329 (quoting HLP I).

Judge Gregory dissented, stating that he follows the reasoning of *Al-Arian* and would reach the same conclusion. Id. at 371 (Gregory, J., dissenting). He rejects the sharp distinction drawn by the majority between criminalizing conduct (which is constitutionally permissible) and criminalizing mere association (which is unconstitutional):

> Every anti-Communist law struck down by the Supreme Court for imposing guilt by association could have simply been rewritten to penalize dues payments to the Party. It would also lead to the anomalous result that while leaders of the NAACP could not be held responsible for injuries sustained during an NAACP-led economic boycott absent proof of specific intent . . . the NAACP's thousands of individual *donors* could have been held liable without any showing of specific intent.

Id. at 377 (Gregory, J. dissenting) (quoting Hammoud and his amici). Is this argument persuasive? Courts have overwhelmingly followed the *Hammoud* majority view that criminalizing conduct is constitutionally different from criminalizing mere membership. See, for example, United States v. Taleb-Jedi, 566 F. Supp. 2d 157, 167 (E.D.N.Y. 2008).

2. The *Al-Arian* court relies extensively on the *Humanitarian* cases decided in the Ninth Circuit. Below we excerpt the latest opinion issued in the *Humanitarian* litigation saga — the fourth time in ten years that the circuit court has addressed the case. The *Al-Arian* opinion details the course of the first two rounds of litigation (through HLP II). The third round of Ninth Circuit review involved an aborted en banc rehearing of HLP II. In December 2004, shortly after oral argument in the en banc rehearing, Congress amended the material support statutes in the Intelligence Reform and Terrorism Prevention Act of 2004 (IRTPA), Pub. L. No. 108-458, 118 Stat. 3638. For purposes of our examination of *Al-Arian* and the *Humanitarian* cases, Congress made two important changes:

First, Congress amended the definition of "material support or resources" to define for the first time the terms "training" and "expert advice or assistance," 18 U.S.C. §2339(A)(b)(2)-(3), and clarified the prohibition against providing "personnel" to designated organizations, 18 U.S.C. §2339B(h).

Post-IRTPA, "training" refers to "instruction or teaching designed to impart a specific skill, as opposed to general knowledge." 18 U.S.C. §2339A(b)(2). "Expert advice or assistance" encompasses "advice or assistance derived from scientific, technical or other specialized knowledge." 18 U.S.C. §2339A(b)(3). "Personnel" includes "1 or more individuals" who "work under th[e] terrorist organization's direction or control or [who] organize, manage, supervise, or otherwise direct the operation of that organization." 18 U.S.C. §2339B(h). IRTPA narrowed the definition of "personnel" by providing that "[i]ndividuals who act entirely independently of the foreign terrorist organization to advance its goals or objectives shall not be considered to be working under the foreign terrorist organization's direction or control." Id.

Second, IRTPA expanded the definition of the *mens rea* applicable to §2339B's prohibition on providing "material support or resources" to a designated foreign terrorist organization. In addition to providing that "knowing[]" provision of material support is outlawed, the statute now provides that, to violate the statute, a person who provides "material support or resources" to a designated organization must know that (1) "the organization is a designated terrorist organization," (2) "the organization has engaged or engages in terrorist activity," or that (3) "the organization has engaged or engages in terrorism." 18 U.S.C. §2339B(a)(1). This language seemed to reflect the Ninth Circuit's holding in HLP II, where the circuit court held that "to sustain a conviction under

§2339B, the government must prove beyond a reasonable doubt that the donor had knowledge that the organization was designated by the Secretary as a foreign terrorist organization or that the donor had knowledge of the organization's unlawful activities that caused it to be so designated." HLP II, 352 F.3d at 403.

In the third round of *Humanitarian* litigation, then, the en banc court largely determined to let the district court take another crack at the contested — and now amended — statutory language. Thus, although the en banc Ninth Circuit affirmed the District Court's disposition of the appellants' First Amendment challenges, it vacated the relevant portion of HLP II dealing with the vagueness of the terms "personnel" and "training," and remanded to the district court. Humanitarian Law Project v. U.S. Dept. of State, 393 F.3d 902 (9th Cir. 2004) (HLP III).

The following case concerns the fourth round of the *Humanitarian* litigation: Once again, the district court found terms in the amended material support statute unconstitutionally vague, but rejected the plaintiffs' other challenges. Both parties appealed, and the opinion excerpted below (HLP IV) addresses those appeals.

HUMANITARIAN LAW PROJECT v. MUKASEY (HLP IV)

552 F.3d 916 (9th Cir. 2009) (Amended Opinion) *cert granted*, Nos. 08-1498, 09-89 (U.S. Sept. 30, 2009)

PREGERSON, Circuit Judge:

We are once again called upon to decide the constitutionality of sections 302 and 303 of the Antiterrorism and Effective Death Penalty Act ("AEDPA") and its 2004 amendment, the Intelligence Reform and Terrorism Prevention Act ("IRTPA").

I. OVERVIEW

Section 302(a) of AEDPA, . . . 8 U.S.C. §1189, authorizes the Secretary of State (the "Secretary") to designate a group as a "foreign terrorist organization." Section 303(a) makes it a crime for anyone to provide support to even the nonviolent activities of the designated organization. See 18 U.S.C. §2339B(a). Specifically, 8 U.S.C. §1189(a)(1) authorizes the Secretary of State

> to designate an organization as a foreign terrorist organization . . . if the Secretary finds that (A) the organization is a foreign organization; (B) the organization engages in terrorist activity . . . ; and (C) the terrorist activity or terrorism of the organization threatens the security of United States nationals or the national security of the United States.

8 U.S.C. §1189(a)(1). . . .

Plaintiffs are six organizations, a retired federal administrative law judge, and a surgeon. The Kurdistan Workers Party, a.k.a Partiya Karkeran Kurdistan ("PKK"), and the Liberation Tigers of Tamil Eelam ("LTTE") engage in a wide variety of unlawful and lawful activities. Plaintiffs seek to provide support only to nonviolent and lawful activities of PKK and LTTE. This support would help Kurds living in Turkey and Tamils living in Tamil Eelam in the Northern and Eastern provinces of Sri Lanka to achieve self-determination.[70]

---

70. [Court's footnote 1:] Plaintiffs who support PKK want: (1) to train members of PKK on how to use humanitarian and international law to peacefully resolve disputes, (2) to engage in political advocacy on

On October 8, 1997, the Secretary of State designated PKK, LTTE, and twenty-eight other foreign organizations as "foreign terrorist organizations." To this day, both PKK and LTTE remain on the designated foreign terrorist organization list. Plaintiffs, fearing that they would be criminally investigated, prosecuted, and convicted under section 2339B(a), have been withholding their support for the PKK and LTTE from the time they were designated as foreign terrorist organizations.

On March 19, 1998, Plaintiffs filed a complaint in the district court, alleging that AEDPA violated their First and Fifth Amendment rights. Plaintiffs sought a preliminary injunction to bar the government from enforcing against them AEDPA's prohibition against providing "material support or resources" to PKK and LTTE. . . .

III. DISCUSSION

A. SPECIFIC INTENT

In their prior appeals, Plaintiffs argued that AEDPA section 2339B(a) violates their Fifth Amendment due process rights because that section does not require proof of *mens rea* to convict a person for providing "material support or resources" to a designated foreign terrorist organization. In HLP-II, we read the statute to require that the donor of the "material support or resources" have knowledge "either of an organization's designation or of the unlawful activities that caused it to be so designated."

In December 2004, Congress passed IRTPA that revised AEDPA to essentially adopt our reading of AEDPA section 2339B to include a knowledge requirement. Thus, post-IRTPA, to convict a person for providing "material support or resources" to a designated foreign terrorist organization, the government must prove that the donor defendant "ha[d] knowledge that the organization is a designated terrorist organization, that the organization has engaged or engages in terrorist activity, or that the organization has engaged or engages in terrorism." 18 U.S.C. §2339B(a). . . .

Plaintiffs argue that IRTPA does not sufficiently cure AEDPA section 2339B's *mens rea* deficiency. They contend that section 2339B(a) continues to violate due process because it does not require the government to prove that the donor defendant acted with specific intent to further the terrorist activity of the designated organization. Plaintiffs urge us to invalidate the statute or, alternatively, to read a specific intent requirement into the statute. . . .

. . . They rely on Scales v. United States, 367 U.S. 203 (1961). In *Scales*, the Supreme Court held that it was wrong to impute criminal guilt based on membership in an organization without proof that the defendant acted with culpable intent. As amended, section 2339B(a) does not proscribe membership in or association with the terrorist organizations, but seeks to punish only those who have provided "material support or resources" to a foreign terrorist organization with knowledge that the organization was a designated foreign terrorist organization, or that it is or has engaged in terrorist activities or terrorism. Accordingly, unlike the statute in *Scales* which was silent with respect to requisite *mens rea*, section 2339B(a) exposes one to

---

behalf of Kurds who live in Turkey, and (3) to teach PKK members how to petition various representative bodies such as the United Nations for relief.

Plaintiffs who support LTTE want: (1) to train members of LTTE to present claims for tsunami-related aid to mediators and international bodies, (2) to offer their legal expertise in negotiating peace agreements between the LTTE and the Sri Lankan government, and (3) to engage in political advocacy on behalf of Tamils who live in Sri Lanka.

criminal liability only where the government proves that the donor defendant acted with culpable intent—knowledge.

. . . As the district court correctly observed, Congress could have, but chose not to, impose a requirement that the defendant act with the specific intent to further the terrorist activity of the organization, a requirement clearly set forth in sections 2339A and 2339C of the statute, but left out of section 2339B. . . .

Because there is no Fifth Amendment due process violation, we affirm the district court on this issue.

B. VAGUENESS . . .

Plaintiffs argue that [the amended definition of "material support or resources" in 18 U.S.C. §2339A(b)] . . . is impermissibly vague because the statute fails to notify a person of ordinary intelligence as to what conduct constitutes "material support or resources." Specifically, Plaintiffs argue that the prohibitions on providing "training," "expert advice or assistance," "service," and "personnel" to designated organizations are vague because they are unclear and could be interpreted to criminalize protected speech and expression.

The Due Process Clause of the Fifth Amendment requires that statutes clearly delineate the conduct they proscribe. While due process does not "require 'impossible standards' of clarity," the "requirement for clarity is enhanced when criminal sanctions are at issue or when the statute abut[s] upon sensitive areas of basic First Amendment freedoms." In such cases, the statute "must be sufficiently clear so as to allow persons of ordinary intelligence a reasonable opportunity to know what is prohibited." Moreover, "[b]ecause First Amendment freedoms need breathing space to survive, government may regulate in the area only with narrow specificity."

Vague statutes are invalidated for three reasons: "(1) to avoid punishing people for behavior that they could not have known was illegal; (2) to avoid subjective enforcement of laws based on 'arbitrary and discriminatory enforcement' by government officers; and (3) to avoid any chilling effect on the exercise of First Amendment freedoms."

1. "Training"

In *HLP I*, we held that the term "training" under AEDPA was unconstitutionally vague. At the time of Plaintiffs' initial challenge in 1998, AEDPA provided no definition of the term "training." After we issued our opinion in HLP I in 2000, Congress amended the statute and defined the term "training" as "instruction or teaching designed to impart a specific skill, as opposed to general knowledge." 18 U.S.C. §2339A(b)(2). On remand, Plaintiffs argued to the district court that the term "training" as defined by IRTPA remains unconstitutionally vague. Plaintiffs contended that persons of ordinary intelligence must discern whether the topic they wish to teach to members of designated organizations amounts to "teaching designed to impart a specific skill," which is criminalized, or "general knowledge," which is not. Specifically, Plaintiffs contended that they must guess whether training PKK members in how to use humanitarian and international human rights law to seek peaceful resolution of ongoing conflict amounts to teaching a "specific skill" or "general[ized] knowledge."

The district court again agreed with Plaintiffs. . . . We agree. . . .

To survive a vagueness challenge, the statute must be sufficiently clear to put a person of ordinary intelligence on notice that his or her contemplated conduct is unlawful. Because we find it highly unlikely that a person of ordinary intelligence would know whether, when teaching someone to petition international bodies for tsunami related aid, one is imparting a "specific skill" or "general knowledge," we find the statute's proscription on providing "training" void for vagueness. . . .

Even if persons of ordinary intelligence could discern between the instruction that imparts a "specific skill," as opposed to one that imparts "general knowledge," we hold that the term "training" would remain impermissibly vague. . . .

2. "Expert Advice or Assistance" . . .

IRTPA defines the term "expert advice or assistance" as imparting "scientific, technical, or other specialized knowledge." 18 U.S.C. §2339A(b)(3).

The government argues that the ban on "expert advice or assistance" is not vague. The government relies on the Federal Rules of Evidence's definition of expert testimony as testimony based on "scientific, technical, or other specialized knowledge." The government argues that this definition gives a person of ordinary intelligence reasonable notice of conduct prohibited under the statute. Plaintiffs contend that the definition of "expert advice or assistance" is vague as applied to them because they cannot determine what "other specialized knowledge" means.

We agree with the district court that "the Federal Rules of Evidence's inclusion of the phrase 'scientific, technical, or other specialized knowledge' does not clarify the term 'expert advice or assistance' for the average person with no background in law."

At oral argument, the government stated that filing an amicus brief in support of a foreign terrorist organization would violate AEDPA's prohibition against providing "expert advice or assistance." Because the "other specialized knowledge" portion of the ban on providing "expert advice or assistance" continues to cover constitutionally protected advocacy, we hold that it is void for vagueness.

The portion of the "expert advice or assistance" definition that refers to "scientific" and "technical" knowledge is not vague. Unlike "other specialized knowledge," which covers every conceivable subject, the meaning of "technical" and "scientific" is reasonably understandable to a person of ordinary intelligence. . . .

3. "Service"

IRTPA amended the definition of "material support or resources" to add the prohibition on rendering "service" to a designated foreign terrorist organization. There is no statutory definition of the term "service."

Plaintiffs argue that proscribing "service" is vague because each of the other challenged provisions could be construed as a provision of "service." The district court agreed.

We adopt the district court's holding and its reasoning. The term "service" presumably includes providing members of PKK and LTTE with "expert advice or assistance" on how to lobby or petition representative bodies such as the United Nations. "Service" would also include "training" members of PKK or LTTE on how to use humanitarian and international law to peacefully resolve ongoing disputes. Thus, we hold that the term "service" is impermissibly vague because "the statute defines 'service' to include 'training' or 'expert advice or assistance,'" and because "'it is easy to imagine protected expression that falls within the bounds' of the term 'service.'"

4. "Personnel"

In *HLP I*, we concluded that "personnel" was impermissibly vague because the term could be interpreted to encompass expressive activity protected by the First Amendment. . . . We observed that "[s]omeone who advocates the cause of the PKK could be seen as supplying them with personnel. . . . But advocacy is pure speech protected by the First Amendment."

As stated above, in 2004, Congress passed IRTPA which amended AEDPA. IRTPA added a limitation to the ban on providing "personnel." Section 2339B(h) clarifies that section 2339B(a) criminalizes providing "personnel" to a foreign terrorist organization only where a person, alone or with others, "[work]s under that terrorist organization's direction or control or . . . organize[s], manage[s], supervise[s], or otherwise direct[s] the operation of that organization." Section 2339B(h) also states that the ban on "personnel" does not criminalize the conduct of "[i]ndividuals who act entirely independently of the foreign terrorist organization to advance its goals or objectives."

. . . Unlike the version of the statute before it was amended by IRTPA, the prohibition on "personnel" no longer criminalizes pure speech protected by the First Amendment. Section 2339B(h) clarifies that Plaintiffs advocating lawful causes of PKK and LTTE cannot be held liable for providing these organizations with "personnel" as long as they engage in such advocacy "entirely independently of th[ose] foreign terrorist organization[s]."

Because IRTPA's definition of "personnel" provides fair notice of prohibited conduct to a person of ordinary intelligence and no longer punishes protected speech, we hold that the term "personnel" as defined in IRTPA is not vague.

C. OVERBREADTH

Plaintiffs argue that the terms "training," "personnel," "expert advice or assistance" and "service" are substantially overbroad. [The court rejects this argument "because AEDPA section 2339B is not aimed at expressive conduct and because it does not cover a substantial amount of protected speech."] . . .

D. LICENSING SCHEME

IRTPA added section 2339B(j), an entirely new section, to AEDPA. Section 2339B(j) allows the Secretary of State, with the concurrence of the Attorney General, to grant approval for individuals and organizations to carry out activities that would otherwise be considered providing "material support or resources" to designated foreign terrorist organizations. . . .

Plaintiffs argue that this provision constitutes an unconstitutional licensing scheme. We disagree. . . .

We recognize that it is possible for the Secretary to exercise his or her discretion in a way that discriminates against the donor of "material support or assistance." For example, the Secretary could conceivably exempt from prosecution a person who teaches peacemaking skills to members of Hezbollah, but deny Plaintiffs immunity from prosecution if they teach the same peacemaking skills to PKK. However, when evaluating the constitutionality of a licensing scheme, we look at how closely the prior restraint, on its face, regulates constitutionally protected activity. Here, even though it is possible for the Secretary to refuse to exercise his or her discretion to exempt from prosecution a disliked speaker, any such power is incidental. The statute does not give the Secretary "substantial power to discriminate based on the content or viewpoint of speech" or the identity of the speaker. . . .

Accordingly, we affirm the district court's holding that section 2339B(j) does not have a close enough nexus to protected speech to allow a facial challenge.

IV. CONCLUSION

For the foregoing reasons, the judgment of the district court is affirmed.

NOTES AND QUESTIONS

1. As we have seen, in the interval between *Al-Arian* and the 2009 HLP IV, Congress amended §2339B to expand on its scienter element: Thus, post-IRTPA, to convict a person for providing "material support or resources" to a designated foreign terrorist organization, the government must prove that the donor defendant "ha[d] knowledge that the organization is a designated terrorist organization, that the organization has engaged or engages in terrorist activity, or that the organization has engaged or engages in terrorism." 18 U.S.C. §2339B(a). Does this resolve all the problems raised in *Al-Arian* and Judge Gregory's *Hammoud* dissent? If the terms in the definition of material support are vague, how can a defendant know that he or she is providing material support unless he or she specifically intends to support the FTO? Is specific intent therefore necessary to avoid the problems of vagueness even in the amended statute?

2. The Ninth Circuit Court of Appeals finds the terms "training," "personnel," "expert advice and assistance," and "service" unconstitutionally vague. Judge Moody, in *Al-Arian*, suggests that other terms may also be vague: "financial services," "lodging," "safe houses," "communications equipment," "facilities," "transportation," and "other physical assets." Recall his example of a cab driver who takes a member of an FTO as a passenger, knowing that he is a member of an FTO. Can the cab driver be prosecuted for providing transportation to an FTO? Can the driver be reasonably expected to know that doing so is illegal? Do the definitions that Congress added in the IRTPA after *Al-Arian* was decided alleviate these concerns? Do you agree that terms of the statute are vague? Which ones?

3. In this connection, context may count:

> Thus, while a defendant's intent to further terrorist activities is not required under §2339B, the context and objectives of the defendant's conduct, as well as its proximity to "hard core" military activity, are relevant to a determination of whether the defendant would understand his conduct to be prohibited under the statute. . . . [T]he prosecution alleges that Warsame provided English lessons in an Al Qaeda clinic in Kandahar, Afghanistan, in part to assist nurses in reading English-language medicine labels. According to the prosecution, the nurses in the clinic attended to Al Qaeda members who were participating in nearby terrorist training camps. The alleged English-language training in this case has direct application to a FTO's terrorist activities, as it would likely speed the healing and eventual return of terrorist militants to Al Qaeda training camps. Further, the training was provided in an Al Qaeda clinic in Kandahar, in close proximity to terrorist training camps. As such, the Court finds that this alleged conduct is closely tied to terrorist activity, such that Warsame would likely understand his conduct to be criminalized as "training" under §2339B. . . . However, as with the definition of "personnel," the Court finds that mere allegations that Warsame taught English at an Al Qaeda clinic, without more specific allegations tying that conduct to terrorist activity, are not sufficient to survive a vagueness challenge with respect to the term "training."

United States v. Warsame, 537 F. Supp. 2d 1005, 1019-1020 (D. Minn. 2008). So too, Warsame should have understood that repaying a loan to an al Qaeda member is material support in the form of "currency." Id. at 1018.

4. What about giving medical treatment to wounded jihadis? Is that "expert advice or assistance" of the sort prohibited by the statute? Medical doctors traditionally have had a professional obligation to aid those in need of treatment, regardless of whom they are; and §2339B exempts the provision of "medicine" from the forbidden forms

of material support. Nevertheless, one district court found the term "expert advice or assistance" sufficiently clear that any reasonable doctor should understand that treating wounded terrorists is prohibited. United States v. Shah, 474 F. Supp. 2d 492, 494 (S.D.N.Y. 2007). (The fact that the doctor was also providing martial arts training to al Qaeda members presumably did not help his case.)

5. One important issue in material support cases under §2339B concerns the limited ability of an organization to challenge the secretary of state's designation of it as an FTO. Does this deny due process? The statute permits judicial review of such a designation, 8 U.S.C. §1189(b). But the review is severely truncated: It is based solely on an "administrative record." As explained by the D.C. Court of Appeals,

> At no point in the proceedings establishing the administrative record is the alleged terrorist organization afforded notice of the materials used against it, or a right to comment on such materials or the developing administrative record. Nothing in the statute forbids the use of "third hand accounts, press stories, material on the Internet or other hearsay regarding the organization's activities. . . ." The Secretary may base the findings on classified material, to which the organization has no access at any point during or after the proceeding to designate it as terrorist. . . . [At the review stage] the aggrieved party has had no opportunity to either add to or comment on the contents of that administrative record; and the record can, and in our experience generally does, encompass "classified information used in making the designation," as to which the alleged terrorist organization never has any access, and which the statute expressly provides the government may submit to the court *ex parte* and *in camera*.

Natl. Council of Resistance of Iran v. U.S. Dept. of State, 251 F.3d 192, 196-197 (D.C. Cir. 2001). The D.C. Circuit Court of Appeals held this to violate due process, and required that the secretary of state must provide organizations both timely notice of an impending designation and a hearing that provides "the opportunity to present, at least in written form, such evidence as those entities may be able to produce to rebut the administrative record or otherwise negate the proposition that they are foreign terrorist organizations." Id. at 209. However, in a follow-up case, the court rejected a due process challenge to the secretary's use of classified evidence in judicial review of a designation. People's Mojahedin Org. of Iran v. U.S. Dept. of State, 327 F.3d 1238 (D.C. Cir. 2003). Nor is it a violation of due process to forbid an organization from supplementing the administrative record during judicial review. Holy Land Found. v. Ashcroft, 333 F.3d 156 (D.C. Cir. 2003).

Significantly, in most of the United States a defendant in a §2339B case cannot collaterally challenge the FTO's designation as part of his or her defense because the designation statute permits challenges only in the Court of Appeals for the D.C. Circuit. United States v. Afshari, 392 F.3d 1031 (9th Cir. 2004). The *Afshari* decision drew a stinging rebuke from five Ninth Circuit judges who dissented from a petition for rehearing en banc. The case involved fundraising for an Iranian group, and the defendant argued that he had a First Amendment right to raise money for a political entity. Because it trenches on his First Amendment rights, §2339B is unconstitutional. Facing significant jail time, he should be able to challenge the designation as part of his argument that the statute is unconstitutional as applied to the organization for which he was raising funds. The dissenting judges agreed. They argued that the truncated review process for FTO designations denied the defendant an adversarial hearing for challenging the statute under which he was charged. United States v. Afshari, 446 F.3d 915 (9th Cir. 2006)(Kozinski, J., dissenting). How strong is this argument?

6. On September 30, 2009, the U.S. Supreme Court granted the government's petition for certiorari in HLP IV, and a conditional cross-appeal, and consolidated the two cases. See Nos. 08-1498, 09-89. In 2010, then, the Court will rule on whether

18 U.S.C. §2339B(a)(1), prohibiting the knowing provision of "personnel" or "any . . . service, . . . training, [or] expert advice or assistance" to a designated FTO, is unconstitutionally vague.

2. A Case Study of Material Support: Lawyers Representing Terrorists

How far can a lawyer go in representing accused terrorists or terrorist organizations? By representing such a client, is the lawyer providing "expert advice or assistance"? Is the lawyer providing "personnel" to the FTO? If so, the lawyer runs the risk of prosecution and imprisonment under the material support statutes.

One noteworthy case is that of lawyer Lynne Stewart. Stewart, a noted New York City defense lawyer and life-long supporter of leftist causes, represented the "blind sheik" Omar Abdul-Rahman, an Egyptian cleric serving a life-plus-65-years sentence in the United States for terrorism offenses that included assassinating Egyptian President Hosni Mubarak and bombing bridges and tunnels in the New York City region.[71] He was the spiritual leader of the "Islamic Group" (IG), the group that hoped to carry out these plans. Notoriously, the Egyptian branch of the IG, also under Sheik Rahman's leadership, had once murdered 62 tourists in Luxor, Egypt, in a terror campaign to destabilize the Egyptian government.

Fearing that Sheik Rahman would continue to direct the IG from prison, the attorney general ordered special administrative measures (SAMs) that limit his communications with the outside world. Before visiting her client in prison, Stewart was required to sign a pledge that she would abide by the SAMs. She was accused of violating the SAMs in two ways. First, she disguised the Sheik's IG-related conversations with the interpreter she used to communicate with her client "by making extraneous comments in English to mask the conversation in Arabic between [the interpreter] and Sheikh Abdel Rahman."[72] Second, "Stewart then released her client's statement to the press . . . 'withdrawing his support for the cease-fire [in Egypt] that currently exists.' "[73] Stewart was indicted for material support under §2339B. She was also indicted for making false statements to the government in violation of 18 U.S.C. §1001, by signing the statement that she would abide by the SAMs.

The judge dismissed the indictment on the ground that the material support statute was unconstitutionally vague. He wrote,

> the Government fails to explain how a lawyer, acting as an agent of her client, an alleged leader of an FTO, could avoid being subject to criminal prosecution as a "quasi-employee" allegedly covered by the statute. At the argument on the motions, the Government expressed some uncertainty as to whether a lawyer for an FTO would be providing personnel to the FTO before the Government suggested that the answer may depend on whether the lawyer was "house counsel" or an independent counsel — distinctions not found in the statute.[74]

The government re-indicted Stewart under §2339A, with its more demanding *mens rea* requirement. In the second round, the judge declined to find the statute void for vagueness,[75] and a jury convicted Stewart, who received a 28-month sentence. The

---

71. United States v. Rahman, 189 F.3d 88, 103-104 (2d Cir. 1999).
72. United States v. Sattar, 272 F. Supp. 2d 348, 370 (S.D.N.Y. 2003).
73. Id.
74. Id. at 359.
75. United States v. Sattar, 314 F. Supp. 2d 279 (S.D.N.Y. 2005).

jurors were persuaded by wiretap evidence that Stewart actually knew that her assistance was furthering crimes. Her supporters objected that the prosecution attempted to inflame the jury by trying Stewart together with the interpreter and by playing a tape of Osama bin Laden.

Stewart's supporters charged that the case was intended to intimidate defense lawyers and make them less zealous on behalf of accused terrorists. The case was controversial for several reasons: Stewart, a feminist and secularist, had no ideological sympathy with the Sheik or the IG; Stewart was a respected lawyer and a 62-year-old grandmother; and the draconian SAMs are themselves frequently criticized.

Most important, many lawyers saw little difference between what Stewart did and the kind of loyalty to their clients that criminal defense lawyers pride themselves on. In an interview, Stewart said, "There are a hundred lawyers who would do exactly what I did. There are a million lawyers who would do almost exactly what I did. Because this is the way you have to represent clients."[76] Law professor and criminal defender Abbe Smith expands on the point:

> Defense lawyers often become intensely identified with clients, perhaps especially so when the client is a social or political pariah. When everyone else is against the client, the lawyer "pumps up the volume" a bit. Add to this the criminal defender's tendency to flaunt authority, and you get defenders who are willing to break a rule here or there, especially when it comes to autocratic places like jails and prisons. . . .
>
> Lawyers are bound to become attached to clients out of a sense of shared humanity, because the lawyer-client relationship is a relationship after all. Attachment is not a bad thing. The best defenders are often the most attached, the most connected to clients. From the outside, it may seem obvious where natural and appropriate attachment ends and boundary violations begin. From the inside, it is not always so easy.
>
> The truth is zealous lawyers contemplate getting in a little trouble from time to time, though they do not expect to be criminally prosecuted. What defender has not on occasion violated a prison rule, passed on a communication they probably should not have passed on, attempted to soften an otherwise harsh criminal justice system? More importantly, what zealous, devoted defender refrains from speaking for clients simply because they are told not to?[77]

NOTES AND QUESTIONS

1. How persuasive do you find Professor Smith's defense of Stewart? Smith does not deny that Stewart crossed a boundary; rather, her argument seems to be that an anti-authoritarian, emotionally involved, client-centered personality, suspicious of red tape and feisty in opposing the government, may be a prerequisite for an effective criminal defender. Boundaries that may be clear to outsiders are less clear to a defender with the temperament Smith describes. Is that a good excuse?

2. In the Sheik's case, the SAMs specified that he would "not be permitted to talk with, meet with, correspond with, or otherwise communicate with any member, or representative, of the news media, in person, by telephone, by furnishing a recorded message, through the mails, through his attorney(s), or otherwise." United States v. Sattar, 272 F. Supp. 2d 348, 369 (S.D.N.Y. 2003). Stewart claimed that at the time she signed the pledge to abide by the SAMs, she had no intention to violate them, and thus she had not made a false statement to the government. The jury disbelieved her.

---

76. Susie Day Interview with Lynne Stewart (Nov. 25, 2002), http://www.frontpagemag.com/readArticle.aspx?ARTID=20988.

77. Abbe Smith, The Bounds of Zeal in Criminal Defense: Some Thoughts on Lynne Stewart, 44 S. Tex. L. Rev. 31, 45-50 (2002).

At least one federal judge thinks that attorneys should not be required to sign such a pledge as a precondition for meeting with their clients. William Young, the trial judge in the case of the "shoe bomber" Richard Reid — an al Qaeda operative who attempted to blow up an airliner with explosives packed in his shoes — refused to require Reid's counsel to sign a pledge that they would abide by the SAMs.

> The affirmation here unilaterally imposed by the Marshals Service as a condition of the free exercise of Reid's Sixth Amendment right to consult with his attorneys fundamentally and impermissibly intrudes on the proper role of defense counsel. They are zealously to defend Reid to the best of their professional skill without the necessity of affirming their bona fides to the government.
>
> Nor is this all. The Court takes judicial notice, pursuant to Federal Rule of Evidence 201, that the government has indicted attorney Lynne Stewart, Esq., inter alia, for violating 18 U.S.C. §1001, in that having signed the required affirmation, she violated the SAMs applicable to one Sheikh Abdel Rahman, and therefore knowingly made a false statement. Evidently, the government theorizes that the affirmation was knowingly false when made. Whatever the merits of the indictment, its chilling effect on those courageous attorneys who represent society's most despised outcasts cannot be gainsaid.

United States v. Reid, 214 F. Supp. 2d 84, 94-95 (D. Mass. 2002). The government agreed not to require Reid's counsel to sign a pledge to abide by the SAMs, so the judge never had to reach the issue of whether requiring such a pledge violates the Sixth Amendment. Should the Sixth Amendment impede the government from using SAMs to prevent terrorists from running their organizations from their prison cells?

3. What kind of activities on behalf of clients can be prosecuted as material support? May a lawyer represent an organization contesting its classification as an FTO? Defend an FTO in a civil suit? File a defamation claim on behalf of a member of an FTO? Take legal action to unfreeze funds belonging to a client FTO? Represent a Guantánamo detainee who belongs to an FTO in a habeas proceeding? Permit a client who is a member of an FTO to stay at the lawyer's home? Is there any way to tell which of these activities run the risk of prosecution? Should any of them be prosecuted?

D.   U.S. PROSECUTION OF TERRORISTS BY MILITARY COMMISSIONS

1.   Background

An alternative to prosecuting terrorists in federal court is prosecuting them in specially constituted military tribunals, known as "military commissions." As the name suggests, military commissions are criminal courts run by the military, with military officers as judges, jurors, and counsel (although defendants may retain civilian counsel as well). They are part of the Defense Department, and thus of the executive branch, rather than part of the judicial branch. They have their own rules of procedure and evidence; and they need not sit within the United States.

Before examining the military commission system, let us ask a fundamental question of principle: Why military commissions? What's the underlying idea behind prosecuting terrorists in military court rather than civilian court?

Earlier in this chapter we distinguished between a "crime model" and a "war model" for the campaign against terrorism. The crime model treats terrorist acts as crimes, and terrorist organizations as the equivalent of mafias. The war model treats terrorist organizations as irregular armies waging war on the United States, whose violence should be regarded as acts of war rather than civilian crimes. Trial by military commissions arises out of the war model.

Under the traditional laws of war between states, captured enemy soldiers who fought "cleanly" cannot be tried as criminals because they have done nothing wrong: It is not a crime to be a soldier and it is not a crime for a soldier to use deadly force against the enemy. In the language of the law of war, soldiers at war enjoy the *belligerent privilege* to use violence lawfully. Captured soldiers can be detained as POWs for the duration of the war, to keep them from returning to combat. But under the Geneva Conventions, detention as a POW is not "punishment," and captors must treat POWs as well as they treat their own troops.

However, if a soldier does not fight cleanly — that is, in accordance with the law of war — he or she can be tried as a war criminal. Soldiers who abuse enemy POWs, or who deliberately target civilians, or who use banned weapons, or who rape and pillage, are all war criminals, and they can be tried and punished for their war crimes. (For extended discussion of this legal framework, see Chapter 21, on war crimes.)

Traditionally, soldiers accused of war crimes are tried by military courts rather than civilian courts. The theory is that military judges and jurors are better equipped than civilians to understand which forms of wartime violence are criminal and which forms are lawful and therefore privileged. There is symmetry between "their" troops and "our" troops because soldiers are soldiers. Both do roughly the same things, and both are governed by the same laws of war. For a soldier, a "jury of one's peers" is therefore a jury of other soldiers. For similar reasons, soldiers of one's own who commit crimes while in military service are tried by a "court martial" — a military court — rather than a civilian court. This is simply a corollary of the underlying principle that enemy soldiers must be treated on a par with one's own soldiers. Both receive military justice rather than civilian justice.

The war model regards terrorists as enemy combatants rather than criminals. Or, more precisely, they are not only civilian criminals, but war criminals because the most typical form of terrorist violence — stealth attacks on civilians — targets civilians and therefore violates the laws of war. As enemy combatants accused of war crimes, they can face trial before a military tribunal. The civilian alternative remains open: John Walker Lindh, the "American Taliban," was charged and convicted in federal court.[78]

The U.S. government has several powerful reasons for seeking to try terrorist suspects in military tribunals rather than federal courts. First, in civilian criminal trials there may be security risks for court personnel and jurors, who might themselves become targets for terrorists. Second, trial in federal court could make it very difficult to protect classified information, including the identities of intelligence sources. Third, much of the intelligence would be based on hearsay — for obvious reasons, confidential sources could not be brought to the United States to testify — and some might come from sources who have been coerced or possibly tortured. Coupled with the problems generated by shaky chains of custody of physical evidence collected in war zones, there is a very real prospect that guilty terrorists would be acquitted because too little of the evidence against them is admissible in civilian criminal proceedings. Fourth, a civilian trial would provide terrorists with a highly visible soapbox to promote their cause or proclaim their "martyrdom" to sympathizers.

---

78. United States v. Lindh, 227 F. Supp. 2d 565 (E.D. Va. 2002).

The United States has a well-established system of military courts to conduct courts martial, staffed by military lawyers known as JAGs.[79] In the past, the military justice system came in for significant criticism, including a string of Supreme Court cases in the 1950s and 1960s prohibiting the trial of U.S. civilians in military courts because these trials lacked fundamental constitutional protections.[80] But subsequent changes in court martial law and practice have brought the military justice system into near parity with the civilian system. The U.S. military services are governed by their own body of law, the Uniform Code of Military Justice (UCMJ), which Congress enacted in 1950.[81] Alongside substantive criminal law, the UCMJ also sets out the procedural rules for courts martial.

Military commissions are specially constituted military tribunals, outside of the regular military justice system — and, in the post-9/11 commissions, with rules of procedure different from those the UCMJ sets out for courts martial.[82] They nevertheless have a long history: Military law expert David Glazier notes that "U.S. panels have tried more than 10,000 serious violations under the law of war since the military commissions' inception in 1847."[83] Thus, what makes the proposal to try terrorists before military commissions noteworthy is not that military commissions are unprecedented. Rather, they are controversial for two other reasons: First, as the materials that follow indicate, their structure and procedures deviate from court martial practice in ways that critics deem unfair. Second, terrorists are not uniformed soldiers who belong to a regular military organization. Arguably, they are civilians. Civilians, including terrorists, are a less obvious fit for military justice. The assumption of symmetry — that soldiers are the best judge of soldiers — seems doubtful when the enemy combatants are civilians engaging in completely irregular forms of violence. Historically, military commissions have been used to try foreign civilians in territories occupied by the U.S. military or within U.S. territory under martial law.[84] But the trial of terrorists does not fit either of these models. Viewed in this light, the practical arguments for military commissions may seem to spring from expediency, and the question remains whether they can be backed by firm legal principle.

Before 9/11, there were two chief Supreme Court precedents on military commissions. *Ex parte Milligan*[85] is a Civil War–era case involving an Indiana newspaper editor who was sentenced to death by a military commission for participating in a

---

79. *JAG* stands for "judge advocate general." Technically, only the commander of each service's Judge Advocate Corps is the judge advocate general, while other attorneys in the Corps are "judge advocates." But the practice of calling all lawyers in the Corps JAGs is well established, and the actual commander of the corps is distinguished by referring to him or her as *TJAG* — "the judge advocate general." In the United States, each armed service has its own JAG Corps with its own TJAG, who must be a three-star general or the naval equivalent. It is common, if grammatically illogical, to speak of "the TJAG" of each JAG Corps.

80. O'Callahan v. Parker, 395 U.S. 258 (1969) (forbidding military trial of soldier for a nonservice-connected crime), *overruled by* Solorio v. United States, 483 U.S. 435 (1987); McElroy v. United States ex rel. Guagliardo, 361 U.S. 281 (1960) (forbidding military trial of civilian employee for a capital crime); Kinsella v. United States ex rel. Singleton, 361 U.S. 234 (1960) (forbidding military trial of military spouse committing a noncapital crime); Reid v. Covert, 354 U.S. 1 (1957) (forbidding court martial of military spouses in capital crime).

81. 64 Stat. 109, 10 U.S.C. ch. 47.

82. For an analysis of the differences, see David Glazier, Note: Kangaroo Court or Competent Tribunal? Judging the 21st Century Military Commission, 89 Va. L. Rev. 2005 (2003); David Glazier, Full and Fair By What Measure? Identifying the International Law Governing Military Commission Procedure, 24 B.U. Intl. L.J. 55 (2006).

83. David Glazier, Precedents Lost: The Neglected History of the Military Commission, 46 Va. J. Intl. L. 5, 8 (2005).

84. Id. at 10.

85. 71 U.S. (4 Wall.) 2 (1866).

Confederate conspiracy. Rejecting the argument that the military commission had jurisdiction because of the "laws and usages of war," the Court stated:

> It can serve no useful purpose to inquire what those laws and usages are, whence they originated, where found, and on whom they operate; they can never be applied to citizens in states which have upheld the authority of the government, and where the courts are open and their process unobstructed.[86]

The Court concluded that as a civilian citizen of the United States, Milligan could not be denied his constitutional trial rights, including the right to trial before a duly constituted Article III court. The Court held that neither the president nor Congress could authorize trial by military commissions when trial in civilian court is possible; however, Chief Justice Chase and three other justices argued that Congress does indeed have the authority to establish military commissions and dissented from the majority's assertion to the contrary.

In 1942 the Court significantly limited *Milligan*. The World War II case *Ex parte Quirin*[87] involved eight German saboteurs who crossed the Atlantic by submarine and landed secretly on beaches in Long Island and Florida. They were captured, in civilian clothing, after two of them turned themselves in and informed on the others. President Roosevelt created a military commission to try them, and they were sentenced to death. Their military lawyers petitioned the Supreme Court for a writ of habeas corpus, but the Court unanimously denied the petition. Six of those seized were electrocuted, while the two who turned themselves in had their sentences commuted to life imprisonment. (They were released and deported in 1948.)

One of the saboteurs, Bruno Haupt, was a U.S. citizen. In his habeas petition he argued that *Milligan* meant he could not be tried by a military commission, only a civilian court. The *Quirin* Court disagreed and distinguished *Milligan* as follows:

> Milligan, a citizen twenty years resident in Indiana, who had never been a resident of any of the states in rebellion, was not an enemy belligerent either entitled to the status of a prisoner of war or subject to the penalties imposed upon unlawful belligerents. We construe the Court's statement as to the inapplicability of the law of war to Milligan's case as having particular reference to the facts before it.[88]

By contrast, the German saboteurs, including Haupt, were "unlawful belligerents" because they were "enemies who, with the purpose of destroying war materials and utilities, entered, or after entry remained in, our territory without uniform — an offense against the law of war."[89] The Court also noted that Congress had authorized the president to create military commissions.[90]

Quirin was a controversial case because of the highly irregular circumstances surrounding the decision. The military commission convened on July 2, 1942. President Roosevelt made it clear that he was in a hurry to execute the defendants, and the Supreme Court issued its decision before the trial was over, without an opinion; the Court said it would supply the opinion later. The timetable was remarkably compressed: The district court granted leave to the defendants to petition the Supreme Court on July 28; the Court convened on July 29, and denied habeas on July 31.

---

86. Id. at 45.
87. 317 U.S. 1 (1942).
88. Id. at 45.
89. Id. at 46.
90. Id. at 28.

The military commission convicted the men the following day, and they were executed a week later. By the time the Court wrote its opinion, the defendants had been dead and buried for more than two months. In Justice Antonin Scalia's dry understatement: "The case was not this Court's finest hour."[91]

Nevertheless, *Quirin* has been a highly influential case in the GWOT, in large part because of its use of the phrase "unlawful belligerent"; *Quirin* is the only Supreme Court case ever to use the term.[92] According to the George W. Bush administration, al Qaeda members are unlawful enemy combatants who can be tried by a military commission, and *Quirin* was the legal basis for this doctrine.

One additional World War II case has proven significant in the post-9/11 legal context: *Johnson v. Eisentrager*.[93] The case concerned German soldiers in China who continued fighting after Germany surrendered but before Japan did. They were tried before a U.S. military commission in China, convicted, and imprisoned in a U.S. military prison in Germany; they petitioned for habeas corpus on constitutional grounds. This opinion is subject to many different interpretations, but many argue that the Court held that enemy aliens abroad in the circumstances of those detained had no right to habeas corpus or to access to U.S. courts. In a footnote, *Eisentrager* also asserted that the Geneva Conventions of 1929 contemplated only diplomatic, not judicial, remedies for violation of prisoners' rights under the treaty.[94] *Eisentrager* was the Bush administration's leading authority in its efforts to deny habeas challenges and assertions of Geneva Convention and constitutional rights by detainees. *Rasul v. Bush*[95] held that the U.S. habeas statute applies in Guantánamo, distinguishing that case from *Eisentrager* because of factual differences and case law subsequent to *Eisentrager*. However, Justice Scalia, dissenting in *Rasul*, scathingly criticized the majority's effort to distinguish the cases, and concluded that "[t]oday's opinion . . . overrules *Eisentrager*."[96] The scope and continued viability of *Eisentrager* remain unclear. For more detailed discussion of constitutional rights abroad, see Chapter 7.

2. The Post-9/11 Military Commissions

President George W. Bush created the current military commissions by military order in November 2001, as the first captives from Afghanistan were being brought to Guantánamo.[97] Although the military order stipulated that the military commissions must provide a "full and fair trial,"[98] it was immediately subjected to criticism for some of its provisions: It relaxed evidentiary rules from those in civilian courts and courts martial to admit all "such evidence as would . . . have probative value to a reasonable person,"[99] with no exception for hearsay or coerced testimony; it permitted a death penalty conviction by a mere two-thirds majority of the jury;[100] it required

---

91. Hamdi v. Rumsfeld, 542 U.S. 507, 569 (Scalia, J., dissenting).
92. *Hamdi* subsequently mentioned the term by quoting *Quirin*.
93. 339 U.S. 763 (1950).
94. Id. at 789 n.14.
95. 542 U.S. 466 (2004).
96. Id. at 497 (Scalia, J. dissenting).
97. Detention, Treatment, and Trial of Certain Non-Citizens in the War Against Terrorism, Military Order of Nov. 16, 2001, 66 Fed. Reg. 57,831-36 (Nov. 16, 2001), Presidential Documents.
98. Id. §4(c)(2).
99. Id. §4(c)(3).
100. Id. §4(c)(6)-(7).

careful protection of classified information, raising the prospect of convictions based on evidence that the defense would not see;[101] it made the secretary of defense and president the ultimate court of appeal;[102] and it excluded all other courts, federal, state, or international, from the military commission process.[103] In the face of vigorous criticism, new rules were issued requiring a unanimous jury in death penalty cases and creating avenues for appellate review.

Nevertheless, nettlesome legal questions persisted on many issues: the fairness of the tribunals; possible violations of the Geneva Conventions because of process concerns; unclearness about which crimes constituted genuine violations of the laws of war; the possibility that evidence obtained under torture would be admitted; and even doubts about whether the president has the constitutional authority to create the commissions.[104]

Practical problems compounded the legal difficulties. The military commissions got off the ground slowly, with endless delays as the JAG defense lawyers — possibly to the surprise of the government — mounted challenge after challenge to commission procedures and criticized the tribunals vociferously in the press as unfair tribunals rigged for conviction.[105] To the government's embarrassment, three military prosecutors (two Air Force captains and an Air Force major) resigned to protest the military commissions' procedures.[106] In 2004, a veteran Marine Corps prosecutor, Colonel Stuart V. Crouch, quit the prosecution team because he became convinced that he would have to present evidence obtained through torture.[107] The Abu Ghraib scandal made the torture issue especially prominent. Defense lawyers challenged members of the initial panel of military commission judges for bias. Five years after President Bush's order creating the military commissions, they had yet to try their first case.[108] It was in this fraught context that the Supreme Court addressed their legitimacy.

HAMDAN v. RUMSFELD
548 U.S. 557 (2006)

[Salim Ahmed Hamdan, a Yemeni national captured in Afghanistan and sent to Guantánamo, was Osama bin Laden's driver. He was charged before a military commission with conspiracy "to commit . . . offenses triable by military commission," namely: "attacking civilians; attacking civilian objects; murder by an unprivileged belligerent; and terrorism." According to the Supreme Court, "There is no allegation that Hamdan had any command responsibilities, played a leadership role, or participated in the planning of any activity."]

---

101. Id. §4(c)(4).

102. Id. §4(c)(8).

103. Id. §7(b)(2).

104. Neal K. Katyal & Laurence H. Tribe, Waging War, Deciding Guilt: Trying the Military Tribunals, 111 Yale L.J. 1259 (2002).

105. See Commander Swift Objects, N.Y. Times Mag., June 13, 2004, available at http://www.nytimes.com/2004/06/13/magazine/commander-swift-objects.html?sec=&spon=&pagewanted=1.

106. Clive Stafford Smith, Eight O'Clock Ferry to the Windward Side: Seeking Justice in Guatánamo Bay 92 (2007).

107. Jess Bravin, The Conscience of the Colonel, Wall St. J., Mar. 31, 2007, at A1.

108. For a useful discussion of these and other problems, see David Glazier, A Self-Inflicted Wound: A Half-Dozen Years of Turmoil over the Guantánamo Military Commissions, 12 Lewis & Clark L. Rev. 231 (2008).

STEVENS, J. (plurality opinion in Parts V and VI-D-iv).

Hamdan filed petitions for writs of habeas corpus and mandamus to challenge the Executive Branch's intended means of prosecuting this charge. He concedes that a court-martial constituted in accordance with the Uniform Code of Military Justice (UCMJ), would have authority to try him. His objection is that the military commission the President has convened lacks such authority, for two principal reasons: First, neither congressional Act nor the common law of war supports trial by this commission for the crime of conspiracy—an offense that, Hamdan says, is not a violation of the law of war. Second, Hamdan contends, the procedures that the President has adopted to try him violate the most basic tenets of military and international law, including the principle that a defendant must be permitted to see and hear the evidence against him. . . .

[Hamdan prevailed in the district court but lost before the D.C. Court of Appeals.]

For the reasons that follow, we conclude that the military commission convened to try Hamdan lacks power to proceed because its structure and procedures violate both the UCMJ and the Geneva Conventions. Four of us also conclude that the offense with which Hamdan has been charged is not an "offens[e] that by . . . the law of war may be tried by military commissions."

IV

The military commission, a tribunal neither mentioned in the Constitution nor created by statute, was born of military necessity. Though foreshadowed in some respects by earlier tribunals like the Board of General Officers that General Washington convened to try British Major John Andre for spying during the Revolutionary War, the commission "as such" was inaugurated in 1847. As commander of occupied Mexican territory, and having available to him no other tribunal, General Winfield Scott that year ordered the establishment of both " '*military commissions*' " to try ordinary crimes committed in the occupied territory and a "*council of war*" to try offenses against the law of war. . . .

Exigency alone, of course, will not justify the establishment and use of penal tribunals not contemplated by Article I, §8, and Article III, §1, of the Constitution unless some other part of that document authorizes a response to the felt need. And that authority, if it exists, can derive only from the powers granted jointly to the President and Congress in time of war. . . .

Whether Chief Justice Chase [in his *Milligan* dissent] was correct in suggesting that the President may constitutionally convene military commissions "without the sanction of Congress" in cases of "controlling necessity" is a question this Court has not answered definitively, and need not answer today. For we held in *Quirin* that Congress had, through Article of War 15, sanctioned the use of military commissions in such circumstances. Article 21 of the UCMJ, the language of which is substantially identical to the old Article 15 and was preserved by Congress after World War II, reads as follows:

"Jurisdiction of courts-martial not exclusive.

"The provisions of this code conferring jurisdiction upon courts-martial shall not be construed as depriving military commissions, provost courts, or other military tribunals of concurrent jurisdiction in respect of offenders or offenses that by statute or by the law of war may be tried by such military commissions, provost courts, or other military tribunals."

We have no occasion to revisit *Quirin's* controversial characterization of Article of War 15 as congressional authorization for military commissions. Contrary to the Government's assertion, however, even *Quirin* did not view the authorization as a sweeping mandate for the President to "invoke military commissions when he deems them necessary." Rather, the *Quirin* Court recognized that Congress had simply preserved what power, under the Constitution and the common law of war, the President had had before 1916 to convene military commissions — with the express condition that the President and those under his command comply with the law of war. . . .

V

The common law governing military commissions may be gleaned from past practice and what sparse legal precedent exists. Commissions historically have been used in three situations. First, they have substituted for civilian courts at times and in places where martial law has been declared. . . . Second, commissions have been established to try civilians "as part of a temporary military government over occupied enemy territory or territory regained from an enemy where civilian government cannot and does not function." Illustrative of this second kind of commission is the one that was established, with jurisdiction to apply the German Criminal Code, in occupied Germany following the end of World War II.

The third type of commission, convened as an "incident to the conduct of war" when there is a need "to seize and subject to disciplinary measures those enemies who in their attempt to thwart or impede our military effort have violated the law of war," has been described as "utterly different" from the other two. Not only is its jurisdiction limited to offenses cognizable during time of war, but its role is primarily a factfinding one — to determine, typically on the battlefield itself, whether the defendant has violated the law of war. The last time the U.S. Armed Forces used the law-of-war military commission was during World War II. In *Quirin*, this Court sanctioned President Roosevelt's use of such a tribunal to try Nazi saboteurs captured on American soil during the War. And in *Yamashita*, we held that a military commission had jurisdiction to try a Japanese commander for failing to prevent troops under his command from committing atrocities in the Philippines.

Quirin is the model the Government invokes most frequently to defend the commission convened to try Hamdan. That is both appropriate and unsurprising. Since Guantánamo Bay is neither enemy-occupied territory nor under martial law, the law-of-war commission is the only model available. At the same time, no more robust model of executive power exists; *Quirin* represents the high-water mark of military power to try enemy combatants for war crimes.

The classic treatise penned by Colonel William Winthrop, whom we have called "the 'Blackstone of Military Law,'" describes at least four preconditions for exercise of jurisdiction by a tribunal of the type convened to try Hamdan. First, "[a] military commission, (except where otherwise authorized by statute), can legally assume jurisdiction only of offences committed within the field of the command of the convening commander." The "field of the command" in these circumstances means the "theatre of war." Second, the offense charged "must have been committed within the period of the war." No jurisdiction exists to try offenses "committed either before or after the war." Third, a military commission not established pursuant to martial law or an occupation may try only "[i]ndividuals of the enemy's army who have been guilty of illegitimate warfare or other offences in violation of the laws of war" and members of one's own army "who, in time of war, become chargeable with crimes or offences not cognizable, or triable, by the criminal courts or under the Articles of war." Finally, a law-of-war commission has jurisdiction to try only two kinds of offense: "Violations of the laws and usages of war cognizable by military tribunals only," and "[b]reaches of military orders or regulations for which offenders are not legally triable by court-martial under the Articles of war."

All parties agree that Colonel Winthrop's treatise accurately describes the common law governing military commissions, and that the jurisdictional limitations he identifies were incorporated in Article of War 15 and, later, Article 21 of the UCMJ. It also is undisputed that Hamdan's commission lacks jurisdiction to try him unless the charge "properly set[s] forth, not only the details of the act charged, but the circumstances conferring *jurisdiction*." The question is whether the preconditions designed to ensure that a military necessity exists to justify the use of this extraordinary tribunal have been satisfied here.

The charge against Hamdan . . . alleges a conspiracy extending over a number of years, from 1996 to November 2001. All but two months of that more than 5-year-long period preceded the attacks of September 11, 2001, and the enactment of the AUMF — the Act of Congress on which the Government relies for exercise of its war powers and thus for its authority to convene military commissions. Neither the purported agreement with Usama bin Laden and others to commit war crimes, nor a single overt act, is alleged to have occurred in a theater of war or on any specified date after September 11, 2001. None of the overt acts that Hamdan is alleged to have committed violates the law of war.

These facts alone cast doubt on the legality of the charge and, hence, the commission; as Winthrop makes plain, the offense alleged must have been committed both in a theater of war and *during*, not before, the relevant conflict. But the deficiencies in the time and place allegations also underscore — indeed are symptomatic of — the most serious defect of this charge: The offense it alleges is not triable by law-of-war military commission.

There is no suggestion that Congress has, in exercise of its constitutional authority to "define and punish . . . Offences against the Law of Nations," positively identified "conspiracy" as a war crime. As we explained in *Quirin*, that is not necessarily fatal to the Government's claim of authority to try the alleged offense by military commission; Congress, through Article 21 of the UCMJ, has "incorporated by reference" the common law of war, which may render triable by military commission certain offenses not defined by statute. When, however, neither the elements of the offense nor the range of permissible punishments is defined by statute or treaty, the precedent must be plain and unambiguous. . . .

This high standard was met in *Quirin*; the violation there alleged was, by "universal agreement and practice" both in this country and internationally, recognized as an offense against the law of war. . . .

That burden is far from satisfied here. The crime of "conspiracy" has rarely if ever been tried as such in this country by any law-of-war military commission not exercising some other form of jurisdiction, and does not appear in either the Geneva Conventions or the Hague Conventions — the major treaties on the law of war. . . .

[T]he only "conspiracy" crimes that have been recognized by international war crimes tribunals (whose jurisdiction often extends beyond war crimes proper to crimes against humanity and crimes against the peace) are conspiracy to commit genocide and common plan to wage aggressive war, which is a crime against the peace and requires for its commission actual participation in a "concrete plan to wage war." The International Military Tribunal at Nuremberg, over the prosecution's objections, pointedly refused to recognize as a violation of the law of war conspiracy to commit war crimes. . . .

VI

Whether or not the Government has charged Hamdan with an offense against the law of war cognizable by military commission, the commission lacks power to proceed. The UCMJ conditions the President's use of military commissions on compliance not only with the American common law of war, but also with the rest of the UCMJ itself, insofar as applicable, and with the "rules and precepts of the law of nations" — including, *inter alia*, the four Geneva Conventions signed in 1949. The procedures that the Government has decreed will govern Hamdan's trial by commission violate these laws.

A

The commission's procedures are set forth in Commission Order No. 1, which was amended most recently on August 31, 2005 — after Hamdan's trial had already begun. Every commission established pursuant to Commission Order No. 1 must have a presiding officer and at least three other members, all of whom must be commissioned officers. The presiding officer's job is to rule on questions of law and other evidentiary and interlocutory issues; the other members make findings and, if applicable, sentencing decisions. The accused is entitled to appointed military counsel and may hire civilian counsel at his own expense so long as such counsel is a U.S. citizen with security clearance "at the level SECRET or higher."

The accused also is entitled to a copy of the charge(s) against him, both in English and his own language (if different), to a presumption of innocence, and to certain other rights typically afforded criminal defendants in civilian courts and courts-martial. These rights are subject, however, to one glaring condition: The accused and his civilian counsel may be excluded from, and precluded from ever learning what evidence was presented during, any part of the proceeding that either the Appointing Authority or the presiding officer decides to "close." Grounds for such closure "include the protection of information classified or classifiable . . . ; information protected by law or rule from unauthorized disclosure; the physical safety of participants in Commission proceedings, including prospective witnesses; intelligence and law enforcement sources, methods, or activities; and other national security interests." Appointed military defense counsel must be privy to these closed sessions, but may, at the presiding officer's discretion, be forbidden to reveal to his or her client what took place therein.

Another striking feature of the rules governing Hamdan's commission is that they permit the admission of *any* evidence that, in the opinion of the presiding officer, "would have probative value to a reasonable person." Under this test, not only is testimonial hearsay and evidence obtained through coercion fully admissible, but neither live testimony nor witnesses' written statements need be sworn. Moreover, the accused and his civilian counsel may be denied access to evidence in the form of "protected information" (which includes classified information as well as "information protected by law or rule from unauthorized disclosure" and "information concerning other national security interests," so long as the presiding officer concludes that the evidence is "probative" . . . and that its admission without the accused's knowledge would not "result in the denial of a full and fair trial." Finally, a presiding officer's determination that evidence "would [not] have probative value to a reasonable person" may be overridden by a majority of the other commission members.

Once all the evidence is in, the commission members (not including the presiding officer) must vote on the accused's guilt. A two-thirds vote will suffice for both a verdict of guilty and for imposition of any sentence not including death (the imposition of which requires a unanimous vote). Any appeal is taken to a three-member review panel composed of military officers and designated by the Secretary of Defense, only one member of which need have experience as a judge. The review panel is directed to "disregard any variance from procedures specified in this Order or elsewhere that would not materially have affected the outcome of the trial before the Commission." Once the panel makes its recommendation to the Secretary of Defense, the Secretary can either remand for further proceedings or forward the record to the President with his recommendation as to final disposition. The President then, unless he has delegated the task to the Secretary, makes the "final decision." He may change the commission's findings or sentence only in a manner favorable to the accused.

B

Hamdan raises both general and particular objections to the procedures set forth in Commission Order No. 1. His general objection is that the procedures' admitted deviation from those governing courts-martial itself renders the commission illegal. Chief among his particular objections are that he may, under the Commission Order, be convicted based on evidence he has not seen or heard, and that any evidence admitted against him need not comply with the admissibility or relevance rules typically applicable in criminal trials and court-martial proceedings. . . .

C

In part because the difference between military commissions and courts-martial originally was a difference of jurisdiction alone, and in part to protect against abuse and ensure evenhandedness under the pressures of war, the procedures governing trials by military commission historically have been the same as those governing courts-martial. . . .

The uniformity principle is not an inflexible one; it does not preclude all departures from the procedures dictated for use by courts-martial. But any departure must be tailored to the exigency that necessitates it. That understanding is reflected in Article 36 of the UCMJ, which provides:

> "(a) The procedure, including modes of proof, in cases before courts-martial, courts of inquiry, military commissions, and other military tribunals may be prescribed by the President by regulations which shall, so far as he considers practicable, apply the principles of law and the rules of evidence generally recognized in the trial of criminal cases in the United States district courts, but which may not be contrary to or inconsistent with this chapter.
> "(b) All rules and regulations made under this article shall be uniform insofar as practicable and shall be reported to Congress."

. . . Without reaching the question whether any provision of Commission Order No. 1 is strictly "contrary to or inconsistent with" other provisions of the UCMJ, we conclude that the "practicability" determination the President has made is insufficient to justify variances from the procedures governing courts-martial. . . .

Nothing in the record before us demonstrates that it would be impracticable to apply court-martial rules in this case. . . . [T]he only reason offered in support of that determination is the danger posed by international terrorism. Without for one moment underestimating that danger, it is not evident to us why it should require, in the case of Hamdan's trial, any variance from the rules that govern courts-martial.

The absence of any showing of impracticability is particularly disturbing when considered in light of the clear and admitted failure to apply one of the most fundamental protections afforded not just by the Manual for Courts-Martial but also by the UCMJ itself: the right to be present. Whether or not that departure technically is "contrary to or inconsistent with" the terms of the UCMJ, the jettisoning of so basic a right cannot lightly be excused as "practicable." . . .

The Government's objection that requiring compliance with the court-martial rules imposes an undue burden both ignores the plain meaning of Article 36(b) and misunderstands the purpose and the history of military commissions. The military commission was not born of a desire to dispense a more summary form of justice than is afforded by courts-martial; it developed, rather, as a tribunal of necessity to be employed when courts-martial lacked jurisdiction over either the accused or the subject matter. Exigency lent the commission its legitimacy, but did not further justify the wholesale jettisoning of procedural protections. That history explains why the military commission's procedures typically have been the ones used by courts-martial. . . .

D

The procedures adopted to try Hamdan also violate the Geneva Conventions. . . .

i

The Court of Appeals relied on *Johnson v. Eisentrager*, 339 U.S. 763 (1950), to hold that Hamdan could not invoke the Geneva Conventions to challenge the Government's plan to prosecute him in accordance with Commission Order No. 1. *Eisentrager* involved a challenge by 21 German nationals to their 1945 convictions for war crimes by a military tribunal convened in Nanking, China, and to their subsequent imprisonment in occupied Germany. The petitioners argued, *inter alia*, that the 1929 Geneva Convention rendered illegal some of the procedures employed during their trials, which they said deviated impermissibly from the procedures used by courts-martial to try American soldiers. We rejected that claim on the merits because the petitioners (unlike Hamdan here) had failed to identify any prejudicial disparity "between the Commission that tried [them] and those that would try an offending soldier of the American forces of like rank," and in any event could claim no protection, under the 1929 Geneva Convention, during trials for crimes that occurred before their confinement as prisoners of war.

Buried in a footnote of the opinion, however, is this curious statement suggesting that the Court lacked power even to consider the merits of the Geneva Convention argument:

> "We are not holding that these prisoners have no right which the military authorities are bound to respect. The United States, by the Geneva Convention of July 27, 1929, 47 Stat. 2021, concluded with forty-six other countries, including the German Reich, an agreement upon the treatment to be accorded captives. These prisoners claim to be and are entitled to its protection. It is, however, the obvious scheme of the Agreement that responsibility for observance and enforcement of these rights is upon political and military authorities. Rights of alien enemies are vindicated under it only through protests and intervention of protecting powers as the rights of our citizens against foreign governments are vindicated only by Presidential intervention."

The Court of Appeals, on the strength of this footnote, held that "the 1949 Geneva Convention does not confer upon Hamdan a right to enforce its provisions in court."

Whatever else might be said about the *Eisentrager* footnote, it does not control this case. We may assume that "the obvious scheme" of the 1949 Conventions is identical in all relevant respects to that of the 1929 Geneva Convention, and even that that scheme would, absent some other provision of law, preclude Hamdan's invocation of the Convention's provisions as an independent source of law binding the Government's actions and furnishing petitioner with any enforceable right. For, regardless of the nature of the rights conferred on Hamdan, they are, as the Government does not dispute, part of the law of war. And compliance with the law of war is the condition upon which the authority set forth in Article 21 is granted.

ii

. . . [T]here is at least one provision of the Geneva Conventions that applies here even if the relevant conflict is not one between signatories. Article 3, often referred to as Common Article 3 because, like Article 2, it appears in all four Geneva Conventions, provides that in a "conflict not of an international character occurring in the territory of one of the High Contracting Parties, each Party to the conflict shall be bound to apply, as a minimum," certain provisions protecting "[p]ersons taking no active part in the hostilities, including members of armed forces who have laid down their arms and those placed *hors de combat* by . . . detention." One such provision prohibits "the passing of sentences and the carrying out of executions without previous judgment pronounced by a regularly constituted court affording all the judicial guarantees which are recognized as indispensable by civilized peoples." . . .

[The Court finds that Common Article 3 applies to the conflict with al Qaeda and the Taliban. This portion of the *Hamdan* opinion is reproduced in Chapter 21.]

iii

Common Article 3, then, is applicable here and, as indicated above, requires that Hamdan be tried by a "regularly constituted court affording all the judicial guarantees which are recognized as indispensable by civilized peoples." While the term "regularly constituted court" is not specifically defined in either Common Article 3 or its accompanying commentary, other sources disclose its core meaning. The commentary accompanying a provision of the Fourth Geneva Convention, for example, defines " 'regularly constituted' " tribunals to include "ordinary military courts" and "definitely exclud[e] all special tribunals." And one of the Red Cross' own treatises defines "regularly constituted court" as used in Common Article 3 to mean "established and organized in accordance with the laws and procedures already in force in a country."

. . . At a minimum, a military commission "can be 'regularly constituted' by the standards of our military justice system only if some practical need explains deviations from court-martial practice." As we have explained, see Part VI-C, *supra*, no such need has been demonstrated here.

iv

Inextricably intertwined with the question of regular constitution is the evaluation of the procedures governing the tribunal and whether they afford "all the judicial guarantees which are recognized as indispensable by civilized peoples." Like the phrase "regularly constituted court," this phrase is not defined in the text of the Geneva Conventions. But it must be understood to incorporate at least the barest of those trial protections that have been recognized by customary international law. Many of these are described in Article 75 of Protocol I to the Geneva Conventions of 1949, adopted in 1977 (Protocol I). Although the United States declined to ratify Protocol I, its objections were not to Article 75 thereof. Indeed, it appears that the

Government "regard[s] the provisions of Article 75 as an articulation of safeguards to which all persons in the hands of an enemy are entitled." Among the rights set forth in Article 75 is the "right to be tried in [one's] presence."

. . . [T]he procedures adopted to try Hamdan deviate from those governing courts-martial in ways not justified by any "evident practical need," and for that reason, at least, fail to afford the requisite guarantees. We add only that . . . various provisions of Commission Order No. 1 dispense with the principles, articulated in Article 75 [of Additional Protocol I of the Geneva Conventions] and indisputably part of the customary international law, that an accused must, absent disruptive conduct or consent, be present for his trial and must be privy to the evidence against him. That the Government has a compelling interest in denying Hamdan access to certain sensitive information is not doubted. But, at least absent express statutory provision to the contrary, information used to convict a person of a crime must be disclosed to him.

V

Common Article 3 obviously tolerates a great degree of flexibility in trying individuals captured during armed conflict; its requirements are general ones, crafted to accommodate a wide variety of legal systems. But *requirements* they are nonetheless. The commission that the President has convened to try Hamdan does not meet those requirements. . . .

The judgment of the Court of Appeals is reversed, and the case is remanded for further proceedings.

Justice BREYER, with whom Justice KENNEDY, Justice SOUTER, and Justice GINSBURG join, concurring.

. . . I join the Court's opinion, save Parts V and VI-D-iv. To state my reasons for this reservation, and to show my agreement with the remainder of the Court's analysis by identifying particular deficiencies in the military commissions at issue, this separate opinion seems appropriate.

I

Trial by military commission raises separation-of-powers concerns of the highest order. Located within a single branch, these courts carry the risk that offenses will be defined, prosecuted, and adjudicated by executive officials without independent review. . . . Concentration of power puts personal liberty in peril of arbitrary action by officials, an incursion the Constitution's three-part system is designed to avoid. It is imperative, then, that when military tribunals are established, full and proper authority exists for the Presidential directive. . . .

One limit on the President's authority is contained in Article 36 of the UCMJ. . . .

In this provision the statute allows the President to implement and build on the UCMJ's framework by adopting procedural regulations, subject to three requirements: (1) Procedures for military courts must conform to district-court rules insofar as the President "considers practicable"; (2) the procedures may not be contrary to or inconsistent with the provisions of the UCMJ; and (3) "insofar as practicable" all rules and regulations under §836 must be uniform, a requirement, as the Court points out, that indicates the rules must be the same for military commissions as for courts-martial unless such uniformity is impracticable. . . .

These principles provide the framework for an analysis of the specific military commission at issue here.

II

. . . To begin with, the structure and composition of the military commission deviate from conventional court-martial standards. Although these deviations raise questions about the fairness of the trial, no evident practical need explains them.

. . . [U]nder MCO [Military Commission Order] No. 1 an " 'Appointing Authority' " — either the Secretary of Defense or the Secretary's "designee" — establishes commissions subject to the order, approves and refers charges to be tried by those commissions, and appoints commission members who vote on the conviction and sentence. In addition the Appointing Authority determines the number of commission members (at least three), oversees the chief prosecutor, provides "investigative or other resources" to the defense insofar as he or she "deems necessary for a full and fair trial," approves or rejects plea agreements, approves or disapproves communications with news media by prosecution or defense counsel (a function shared by the General Counsel of the Department of Defense), and issues supplementary commission regulations (subject to approval by the General Counsel of the Department of Defense, unless the Appointing Authority is the Secretary of Defense).

. . . [T]he regulations governing the commissions at issue make several noteworthy departures [from court-martials]. At a general court-martial — the only type authorized to impose penalties of more than one year's incarceration or to adjudicate offenses against the law of war — the presiding officer who rules on legal issues must be a military judge. . . . To protect their independence, military judges at general courts-martial are "assigned and directly responsible to the Judge Advocate General or the Judge Advocate General's designee." . . . Here, by contrast, the Appointing Authority selects the presiding officer, and that officer need only be a judge advocate, that is, a military lawyer.

The Appointing Authority, moreover, exercises supervisory powers that continue during trial. Any interlocutory question "the disposition of which would effect a termination of proceedings with respect to a charge" is subject to decision not by the presiding officer, but by the Appointing Authority. Other interlocutory questions may be certified to the Appointing Authority as the presiding officer "deems appropriate." While in some circumstances the Government may appeal certain rulings at a court-martial — including "an order or ruling that terminates the proceedings with respect to a charge or specification" — the appeals go to a body called the Court of Criminal Appeals, not to the convening authority. The Court of Criminal Appeals functions as the military's intermediate appeals court; it is established by the Judge Advocate General for each Armed Service and composed of appellate military judges. This is another means in which, by structure and tradition, the court-martial process is insulated from those who have an interest in the outcome of the proceedings. . . .

As compared to the role of the convening authority in a court-martial, the greater powers of the Appointing Authority here — including even the resolution of dispositive issues in the middle of the trial — raise concerns that the commission's decision-making may not be neutral. If the differences are supported by some practical need beyond the goal of constant and ongoing supervision, that need is neither apparent from the record nor established by the Government's submissions.

These structural differences between the military commissions and courts-martial — the concentration of functions, including legal decisionmaking, in a single executive official; the less rigorous standards for composition of the tribunal; and the creation of special review procedures in place of institutions created and regulated by Congress — remove safeguards that are important to the fairness of the proceedings and the independence of the court. . . .

Apart from these structural issues, moreover, . . . the MCO abandons the detailed Military Rules of Evidence, which are modeled on the Federal Rules of Evidence in conformity with §836(a)'s requirement of presumptive compliance with district-court rules.

Instead, the order imposes just one evidentiary rule: "Evidence shall be admitted if . . . the evidence would have probative value to a reasonable person." . . .

The rule here could permit admission of multiple hearsay and other forms of evidence generally prohibited on grounds of unreliability. Indeed, the commission regulations specifically contemplate admission of unsworn written statements; and they make no provision for exclusion of coerced declarations save those "established to have been made as a result of torture." . . .

In sum, as presently structured, Hamdan's military commission exceeds the bounds Congress has placed on the President's authority. . . . Because Congress has prescribed these limits, Congress can change them, requiring a new analysis consistent with the Constitution and other governing laws. At this time, however, we must apply the standards Congress has provided. By those standards the military commission is deficient.

III

In light of the conclusion that the military commission here is unauthorized under the UCMJ, I see no need to consider several further issues addressed in the plurality opinion by Justice Stevens and the dissent by Justice Thomas. [These are "whether Common Article 3's standard . . . necessarily requires that the accused have the right to be present at all stages of a criminal trial"; and whether "Article 75 of Protocol I to the Geneva Conventions is binding law notwithstanding the earlier decision by our Government not to accede to the Protocol."] . . .

I likewise see no need to address the validity of the conspiracy charge against Hamdan. . . . In light of the conclusion that the military commissions at issue are unauthorized, Congress may choose to provide further guidance in this area. . . . With these observations I join the Court's opinion with the exception of Parts V and VI-D-iv.

Justice THOMAS, with whom Justice SCALIA joins, and with whom Justice ALITO joins in all but Parts I, II-C-1, and III-B-2, dissenting.

I

Our review of petitioner's claims arises in the context of the President's wartime exercise of his Commander in Chief authority in conjunction with the complete support of Congress. Accordingly, it is important to take measure of the respective roles the Constitution assigns to the three branches of our Government in the conduct of war.

[T]he structural advantages attendant to the Executive Branch — namely, the decisiveness, " 'activity, secrecy, and dispatch' " that flow from the Executive's " 'unity,' " — led the Founders to conclude that the "President ha[s] primary responsibility — along with the necessary power — to protect the national security and to conduct the Nation's foreign relations." . . . This Court has observed that these provisions confer upon the President broad constitutional authority to protect the Nation's security in the manner he deems fit.

Congress, to be sure, has a substantial and essential role in both foreign affairs and national security. But "Congress cannot anticipate and legislate with regard to every possible action the President may find it necessary to take or every possible situation in which he might act," and "[s]uch failure of Congress . . . does not, 'especially . . . in the areas of foreign policy and national security,' imply 'congressional disapproval' of action taken by the Executive." Rather, in these domains, the fact that Congress has provided the President with broad authorities does not imply — and the Judicial Branch should not infer — that Congress intended to deprive him of particular powers not specifically enumerated. . . .

Under this framework, the President's decision to try Hamdan before a military commission for his involvement with al Qaeda is entitled to a heavy measure of deference. In the present conflict, Congress has authorized the President "to use all necessary and appropriate force against those nations, organizations, or persons *he determines* planned, authorized, committed, or aided the terrorist attacks that occurred on September 11, 2001 . . . in order to prevent any future acts of international terrorism against the United States by such nations, organizations or persons." Authorization for Use of Military Force (AUMF) (emphasis added). . . . *Hamdi*'s observation that military commissions are included within the AUMF's authorization is supported by this Court's previous recognition that "[a]n important incident to the conduct of war is the adoption of measures by the military commander, not only to repel and defeat the enemy, but to seize and subject to disciplinary measures those enemies who, in their attempt to thwart or impede our military effort, have violated the law of war."

. . . In such circumstances . . . our duty to defer to the Executive's military and foreign policy judgment is at its zenith; it does not countenance the kind of second-guessing the Court repeatedly engages in today. . . .

II

The plurality accurately describes some aspects of the history of military commissions and the prerequisites for their use. . . . The Executive has easily satisfied these considerations here. The plurality's contrary conclusion rests upon an incomplete accounting and an unfaithful application of those considerations.

A

The first two considerations are that a law-of-war military commission may only assume jurisdiction of "offences committed within the field of the command of the convening commander," and that such offenses "must have been committed within the period of the war." Here, as evidenced by Hamdan's charging document, the Executive has determined that the theater of the present conflict includes "Afghanistan, Pakistan and other countries" where al Qaeda has established training camps, and that the duration of that conflict dates back (at least) to Usama bin Laden's August 1996 Declaration of Jihad Against the Americans. Under the Executive's description of the conflict, then, every aspect of the charge, which alleges overt acts in "Afghanistan, Pakistan, Yemen and other countries" taking place from 1996 to 2001, satisfies the temporal and geographic prerequisites for the exercise of law-of-war military commission jurisdiction. And these judgments pertaining to the scope of the theater and duration of the present conflict are committed solely to the President in the exercise of his Commander in Chief authority.

Nevertheless, the plurality concludes that the legality of the charge against Hamdan is doubtful because "Hamdan is charged not with an overt act for which he was caught redhanded in a theater of war . . . but with an *agreement* the inception of which long predated . . . the [relevant armed conflict]." The plurality's willingness to second-guess the Executive's judgments in this context, based upon little more than its unsupported assertions, constitutes an unprecedented departure from the tradition-ally limited role of the courts with respect to war and an unwarranted intrusion on executive authority. And even if such second-guessing were appropriate, the plural-ity's attempt to do so is unpersuasive.

As an initial matter, the plurality relies upon the date of the AUMF's enactment to determine the beginning point for the "period of the war," thereby suggesting that petitioner's commission does not have jurisdiction to try him for offenses committed prior to the AUMF's enactment. But this suggestion betrays the plurality's unfamiliarity with the realities of warfare and its willful blindness to our precedents. The starting point of the present conflict (or indeed any conflict) is not determined by congressional enactment, but rather by the initiation of hostilities. . . .

Moreover, the President's determination that the present conflict dates at least to 1996 is supported by overwhelming evidence. . . .

c

The fourth consideration relevant to the jurisdiction of law-of-war military commis-sions relates to the nature of the offense charged. As relevant here, such commissions have jurisdiction to try " '[v]iolations of the laws and usages of war cognizable by military tribunals only.' " . . .

The common law of war as it pertains to offenses triable by military commission is derived from the "experience of our wars" and our wartime tribunals, and "the laws and usages of war as understood and practiced by the civilized nations of the world." Moreover, the common law of war is marked by two important features. First, as with the common law generally, it is flexible and evolutionary in nature, building upon the experience of the past and taking account of the exigencies of the present. . . . Accordingly, this Court has recognized that the "jurisdiction" of "our common-law war courts" has not been "prescribed by statute," but rather "has been adapted in each instance to the need that called it forth." Second, the common law of war affords a measure of respect for the judgment of military commanders. . . . In recognition of these principles, Congress has generally " 'left it to the President, and the military commanders representing him, to employ the commission, *as occasion may require*, for the investigation and punishment of violations of the laws of war' " (quoting Win-throp 831; emphasis added).

In one key respect, the plurality departs from the proper framework for evaluating the adequacy of the charge against Hamdan under the laws of war. The plurality holds that where, as here, "neither the elements of the offense nor the range of permissible punishments is defined by statute or treaty, the precedent [establishing whether an offense is triable by military commission] must be plain and unambiguous." This is a pure contrivance, and a bad one at that. It is contrary to the presumption we acknowl-edged in *Quirin*, namely, that the actions of military commissions are "not to be set aside by the courts without the *clear conviction* that they are" unlawful. It is also contrary to *Yamashita*, which recognized the legitimacy of that military commission notwithstanding a substantial disagreement pertaining to whether Yamashita had been charged with a violation of the law of war. . . . Nor does it find support from the separation of powers authority cited by the plurality. Indeed, Madison's praise of the separation of powers in The Federalist No. 47, quoted *ante*, if it has any relevance at all, merely highlights the illegitimacy of today's judicial intrusion onto core executive prerogatives in the waging of war, where executive competence is at its zenith and judicial competence at its nadir.

The plurality's newly minted clear-statement rule is also fundamentally inconsistent with the nature of the common law which, by definition, evolves and develops over time and does not, in all cases, "say what may be done." Similarly, it is inconsistent with the nature of warfare, which also evolves and changes over time, and for which a flexible, evolutionary common-law system is uniquely appropriate. Though the charge against Hamdan easily satisfies even the plurality's manufactured rule, the plurality's inflexible approach has dangerous implications for the Executive's ability to discharge his duties as Commander in Chief in future cases. We should undertake to determine whether an unlawful combatant has been charged with an offense against the law of war with an understanding that the common law of war is flexible, responsive to the exigencies of the present conflict, and deferential to the judgment of military commanders.

1

Under either the correct, flexible approach to evaluating the adequacy of Hamdan's charge, or under the plurality's new, clear-statement approach, Hamdan has been charged with conduct constituting two distinct violations of the law of war cognizable before a military commission: membership in a war-criminal enterprise and conspiracy to commit war crimes. The charging section of the indictment alleges both that Hamdan "willfully and knowingly joined an enterprise of persons who shared a common criminal purpose," and that he "conspired and agreed with [al Qaeda] to commit . . . offenses triable by military commission."

The common law of war establishes that Hamdan's willful and knowing membership in al Qaeda is a war crime chargeable before a military commission. Hamdan, a confirmed enemy combatant and member or affiliate of al Qaeda, has been charged with willfully and knowingly joining a group (al Qaeda) whose purpose is "to support violent attacks against property and nationals (both military and civilian) of the United States." Moreover, the allegations specify that Hamdan joined and maintained his relationship with al Qaeda even though he "believed that Usama bin Laden and his associates were involved in the attacks on the U.S. Embassies in Kenya and Tanzania in August 1998, the attack on the USS *Cole* in October 2000, and the attacks on the United States on September 11, 2001." These allegations, against a confirmed unlawful combatant, are alone sufficient to sustain the jurisdiction of Hamdan's military commission.

For well over a century it has been established that "to unite with banditti, jayhawkers, guerillas, or any other unauthorized marauders is a high offence against the laws of war; *the offence is complete when the band is organized or joined. The atrocities committed by such a band do not constitute the offence, but make the reasons, and sufficient reasons they are, why such banditti are denounced by the laws of war.*" 11 Op. Att'y Gen., at 312 (emphasis added). In other words, unlawful combatants, such as Hamdan, violate the law of war merely by joining an organization, such as al Qaeda, whose principal purpose is the "killing [and] disabling . . . of peaceable citizens or soldiers." This conclusion is unsurprising, as it is a "cardinal principle of the law of war . . . that the civilian population must enjoy complete immunity." . . .

The conclusion that membership in an organization whose purpose is to violate the laws of war is an offense triable by military commission is confirmed by the experience of the military tribunals convened by the United States at Nuremberg. Pursuant to Article 10 of the Charter of the International Military Tribunal (IMT), the United States convened military tribunals "to bring individuals to trial for membership" in "a group or organization . . . declared criminal by the [IMT]." The IMT designated various components of four Nazi groups — the Leadership Corps, Gestapo, SD, and SS — as criminal organizations. "[A] member of [such] an organization [could] be . . . convicted of the crime of membership and be punished for that crime by death." Under this authority, the United States Military Tribunal at Nuremberg convicted numerous individuals for the act of knowing and voluntary membership in these organizations. . . .

3

Ultimately, the plurality's determination that Hamdan has not been charged with an offense triable before a military commission rests not upon any historical example or authority, but upon the plurality's raw judgment of the "inability on the Executive's part here to satisfy the most basic precondition . . . for establishment of military commissions: military necessity." This judgment starkly confirms that the plurality has appointed itself the ultimate arbiter of what is quintessentially a policy and military judgment, namely, the appropriate military measures to take against those who "aided the terrorist attacks that occurred on September 11, 2001." . . . Traditionally, retributive justice for heinous war crimes is as much a "military necessity" as the "demands" of "military efficiency" touted by the plurality, and swift military retribution is precisely what Congress authorized the President to impose on the September 11 attackers in the AUMF.

Today a plurality of this Court would hold that conspiracy to massacre innocent civilians does not violate the laws of war. This determination is unsustainable. . . . We are not engaged in a traditional battle with a nation-state, but with a worldwide, hydra-headed enemy, who lurks in the shadows conspiring to reproduce the atrocities of September 11, 2001, and who has boasted of sending suicide bombers into civilian gatherings, has proudly distributed videotapes of beheadings of civilian workers, and has tortured and dismembered captured American soldiers. But according to the plurality, when our Armed Forces capture those who are plotting terrorist atrocities like the bombing of the Khobar Towers, the bombing of the U.S.S. *Cole*, and the attacks of September 11 — even if their plots are advanced to the very brink of fulfillment — our military cannot charge those criminals with any offense against the laws of war. . . .

III

The Court holds that even if "the Government has charged Hamdan with an offense against the law of war cognizable by military commission, the commission lacks power to proceed" because of its failure "to comply with the terms of the UCMJ and the four Geneva Conventions signed in 1949. This position is untenable.

A

As with the jurisdiction of military commissions, the procedure of such commissions "has [not] been prescribed by statute," but "has been adapted in each instance to the need that called it forth." Indeed, this Court has concluded that "[i]n the absence of attempts by Congress to limit the President's power, it appears that, as Commander in Chief of the Army and Navy of the United States, he may, in time of war, establish and prescribe the jurisdiction and procedure of military commissions." . . .

The Court nevertheless concludes that at least one provision of the UCMJ amounts to an attempt by Congress to limit the President's power. This conclusion is not only contrary to the text and structure of the UCMJ, but it is also inconsistent with precedent of this Court. Consistent with *Madsen's*[109] conclusion pertaining to the common-law nature of military commissions and the President's discretion to prescribe their procedures, Article 36 of the UCMJ authorizes the President to establish procedures for military commissions "which shall, *so far as he considers practicable,* apply the principles of law and the rules of evidence generally recognized in the trial of criminal cases in the United States district courts, but which may not be contrary to or inconsistent with this chapter." (emphasis added). Far from constraining the President's authority, Article 36 recognizes the President's prerogative to depart from the procedures applicable in criminal cases whenever *he alone* does not deem such procedures "practicable." While the procedural regulations promulgated by the Executive must not be "contrary to" the UCMJ, only a few provisions of the UCMJ mention "military commissions," and there is no suggestion that the procedures to be employed by Hamdan's commission implicate any of those provisions. . . .

[T]his determination is precisely the kind for which the "Judiciary has neither aptitude, facilities nor responsibility and which has long been held to belong in the domain of political power not subject to judicial intrusion or inquiry." And, in the context of the present conflict, it is exactly the kind of determination Congress countenanced when it authorized the President to use all necessary and appropriate force against our enemies. Accordingly, the President's determination is sufficient to satisfy any practicability requirement imposed by Article 36(b). . . .

B

The Court contends that Hamdan's military commission is also unlawful because it violates Common Article 3 of the Geneva Conventions. Furthermore, Hamdan contends that his commission is unlawful because it violates various provisions of the Third Geneva Convention. These contentions are untenable.

1

As an initial matter, and as the Court of Appeals concluded, both of Hamdan's Geneva Convention claims are foreclosed by *Johnson* v. *Eisentrager*. . . . While this Court rejected the underlying merits of the respondents' Geneva Convention claims, it also held, in the alternative, that the respondents could "not assert . . . that anything in the Geneva Convention makes them immune from prosecution or punishment for war crimes." . . .

[T]he Court concludes that petitioner may seek judicial enforcement of the provisions of the Geneva Conventions because "they are . . . part of the law of war. And compliance with the law of war is the condition upon which the authority set forth in Article 21 is granted." . . .

[T]he Court's argument is too clever by half. The judicial non-enforceability of the Geneva Conventions derives from the fact that those Conventions have exclusive enforcement mechanisms, and this, too, is part of the law of war. . . .

3

. . . In any event, Hamdan's military commission complies with the requirements of Common Article 3. It is plainly "regularly constituted" because such commissions

---

109. Madsen v. Kinsella, 343 U.S. 341 (1952), upheld the jurisdiction of a military commission that tried a U.S. civilian for murdering her husband, a member of the U.S. armed forces, in occupied Germany — EDS.

have been employed throughout our history to try unlawful combatants for crimes against the law of war. . . .

The Court concludes Hamdan's commission fails to satisfy the requirements of Common Article 3 not because it differs from the practice of previous military commissions but because it "deviate[s] from [the procedures] governing courts-martial." But there is neither a statutory nor historical requirement that military commissions conform to the structure and practice of courts-martial. . . . The 150-year pedigree of the military commission is itself sufficient to establish that such tribunals are "regularly constituted court[s]."

Similarly, the procedures to be employed by Hamdan's commission afford "all the judicial guarantees which are recognized as indispensable by civilized peoples." . . .

[T]he plurality concludes that Hamdan's commission is unlawful because of the possibility that Hamdan will be barred from proceedings and denied access to evidence that may be used to convict him. But, under the commissions' rules, the Government may not impose such bar or denial on Hamdan if it would render his trial unfair, a question that is clearly within the scope of the appellate review contemplated by regulation and statute. . . .

In these circumstances, "civilized peoples" would take into account the context of military commission trials against unlawful combatants in the war on terrorism, including the need to keep certain information secret in the interest of preventing future attacks on our Nation and its foreign installations so long as it did not deprive the accused of a fair trial. . . .

Justice ALITO, dissenting, with whom Justice SCALIA and Justice THOMAS join. . . .

Common Article 3 . . . imposes three requirements. Sentences may be imposed only by (1) a "court" (2) that is "regularly constituted" and (3) that affords "all the judicial guarantees which are recognized as indispensable by civilized peoples." . . .

The second element ("regularly constituted") is the one on which the Court relies, and I interpret this element to require that the court be appointed or established in accordance with the appointing country's domestic law. . . .

I interpret Common Article 3 as looking to the domestic law of the appointing country because I am not aware of any international law standard regarding the way in which such a court must be appointed, set up, or established, and because different countries with different government structures handle this matter differently. Accordingly, "a regularly constituted court" is a court that has been appointed, set up, or established in accordance with the domestic law of the appointing country. . . .

I see no basis for the Court's holding that a military commission cannot be regarded as "a regularly constituted court" unless it is similar in structure and composition to a regular military court or unless there is an "evident practical need" for the divergence. There is no reason why a court that differs in structure or composition from an ordinary military court must be viewed as having been improperly constituted. Tribunals that vary significantly in structure, composition, and procedures may all be "regularly" or "properly" constituted. Consider, for example, a municipal court, a state trial court of general jurisdiction, an Article I federal trial court, a federal district court, and an international court, such as the International Criminal Tribunal for the former Yugoslavia. Although these courts are "differently constituted" and differ substantially in many other respects, they are all "regularly constituted."

If Common Article 3 had been meant to require trial before a country's military courts or courts that are similar in structure and composition, the drafters almost certainly would have used language that expresses that thought more directly. . . .

NOTES

1. In the Detainee Treatment Act of 2005 (DTA), 109 Pub. L. No. 148, 119 Stat. 2680, Congress amended the habeas statute to strip habeas jurisdiction over Guantánamo detainees from the federal courts. In portions of the opinion not included in this excerpt, the *Hamdan* Court held that the DTA's jurisdiction-stripping provisions did not apply to cases already in progress. It also rejected arguments that the Court should abstain from the case until final judgment was entered by Hamdan's military commission. Justice Scalia (joined by Justices Alito and Thomas) dissented on these issues.

2. As we shall see below, after *Hamdan* was decided Congress quickly reconstituted the military commissions, and Salim Hamdan eventually went to trial — the first case tried by a military commission. Defense counsel objected that Hamdan's mental condition had deteriorated from prolonged captivity and that he could not assist in his own defense; this, along with other objections, was rejected. A military jury convicted Hamdan in July 2008. Although the prosecutors asked for a 30-year sentence, the jury sentenced Hamdan to 66 months, of which he was credited (over prosecutors' objections) with 61 months for time served. In November 2008 he was sent back to Yemen to serve his remaining month.

3. As of October 2009, military commissions have convicted two additional defendants. David Hicks, an Australian national captured in Afghanistan, accepted a plea bargain in March 2007. His sentence for material support was 7 years, with all but 9 months suspended, and permission to serve his 9-month sentence in Australia. In November 2008, Ali al-Bahlul was convicted of doing media relations on behalf of al Qaeda and sentenced to life in prison. Bahlul had refused to participate in his defense or trial, and at his sentencing he declared that he was a member of al Qaeda and expressed defiance against the United States.

3. The Military Commissions Act of 2006

The *Hamdan* decision abruptly terminated military commission procedures. It did more than that, however. By finding that common Article 3 protects al Qaeda and Taliban prisoners, it created the possibility that U.S. personnel involved in detainee mistreatment might be prosecuted as war criminals. The federal war crimes act, 18 U.S.C. §2441, forbids violations of common Article 3, including torture and humiliating and degrading treatment of prisoners. More than that, common Article 3 forbids "the passing of sentences and the carrying out of executions without previous judgment pronounced by a regularly constituted court, affording all the judicial guarantees which are recognized as indispensable by civilized peoples." Because the *Hamdan* Court found that the military commissions violate this clause of common Article 3, participants in the military commissions process might also be liable to federal prosecution as war criminals. Congress quickly moved to change this situation and to regularize the military commissions. The result was the Military Commissions Act of 2006 (MCA), enacted in October 2006.[110]

The MCA did three things: First, it provided congressional authorization for the military commissions and enacted a substantial body of specific rules to govern them. Among these, it specified and defined a list of crimes triable by the military

---

110. Pub. L. No. 109-366, codified in 10 U.S.C. ch. 47A.

commissions. These include more than 20 internationally recognized war crimes;[111] hijacking, terrorism, and material support for terrorism, as defined in 18 U.S.C. §2339A;[112] wrongfully aiding the enemy and spying;[113] and conspiracy to commit any of the other crimes[114] (thereby settling the controversy in the *Hamdan* Court over whether conspiracy is a crime triable by a military commission).

Second, Congress moved energetically to strip away the power of courts over military commission cases:

> (b) ... Except as otherwise provided in this chapter and notwithstanding any other provision of law (including ... any ... habeas corpus provision), no court, justice, or judge shall have jurisdiction to hear or consider any claim or cause of action whatsoever ... relating to the prosecution, trial, or judgment of a military commission under this chapter, ... including challenges to the lawfulness of procedures of military commissions under this chapter.[115]

Only the D.C. Court of Appeals and Supreme Court have jurisdiction to hear appeals of final judgments of the military commissions, and only after all appeals within the commission system are exhausted.[116] Appeals are limited to matters of law; and "[t]he jurisdiction of the Court of Appeals on an appeal ... shall be limited to the consideration of (1) whether the final decision was consistent with the standards and procedures specified in this chapter; and (2) to the extent applicable, the Constitution and the laws of the United States."[117] To avoid future challenges under the Geneva Conventions, Congress specified: "No alien unlawful enemy combatant subject to trial by military commission under this chapter may invoke the Geneva Conventions as a source of rights."[118]

Third, in a separate portion of the act, it amended §2441 to decriminalize humiliating and degrading treatment and the violation of Article 3's "passing of sentences" clause. These were decriminalized retroactively to 1996, the date that the government determined was the beginning of the U.S. war with al Qaeda. In the face of widespread criticism that U.S. treatment of detainees violates international law, Congress specified that "no foreign or international sources of law shall supply a basis for a rule of decision in the courts of the United States interpreting the prohibitions enumerated in ... section 2441";[119] and it gave the president interpretive authority over the meaning and application of the Geneva Conventions.[120]

After the MCA, the military commissions resumed operation, leading to the conviction of Hamdan and Hicks.

NOTES AND QUESTIONS

1. The MCA was widely regarded as a triumph for the George W. Bush administration and a rebuke of the Supreme Court's *Hamdan* decision. Do you agree? Why or

---

111. 10 U.S.C. §948v(1)-(22).
112. Id. §948v(23)-(25).
113. Id. §948v(26)-(27).
114. Id. §948v(28).
115. Id. §950j(b).
116. Id. §950g(a)(1).
117. Id. §950g(c).
118. Id. §948b(g).
119. Military Commissions Act, Oct. 17, 2006, Pub. L. No. 109-366, §6(a), 120 Stat. 2632, ¶2.
120. Id. ¶3.

why not? Critics of the MCA charged that after the Supreme Court found improper behavior — possibly even war crimes — at Guantánamo, the government responded not by changing the behavior but by legalizing it. Is that a fair criticism?

Whether or not the criticisms were fair, they persisted, and in October 2009 Congress substantially revised the Military Commissions Act. H.R. 2647, National Defense Authorization Act for Fiscal Year 2010 [hereinafter: the 2010 NDAA]. As this book goes to press, both houses of Congress have passed the revision, and President Barack Obama is expected to sign the revision into law. The notes that follow will detail some of the criticisms and how Congress responded to them.

2. What does it mean to state that a military commission defendant cannot "invoke the Geneva Conventions as a source of rights"? Does it mean that defendant and his counsel are forbidden from raising arguments based on the Geneva Conventions? In that case, the provision could be unconstitutional under Legal Services Corp. v. Velazquez, 531 U.S. 533 (2001), which struck down a content-based restriction on what lawyers could argue in court. Or did the MCA mean that although defendants' counsel could raise Geneva-based arguments, the military commissions and courts were prohibited from considering them? Unless there is an alternative avenue for reviewing the claims, this may violate due process. See Carlos Manuel Vázquez, The Military Commissions Act, the Geneva Conventions, and the Courts: A Critical Guide, 101 Am. J. Intl. L. 73, 86-87 (2007). Perhaps for these reasons, in the 2010 NDAA, Congress eliminated this provision. In its place Congress substituted a more limited restriction: "No alien unprivileged enemy belligerent subject to trial by military commission under this chapter may invoke the Geneva Conventions as a basis for a private right of action." §948b(e).

3. In the 2006 MCA, Congress declared, "A military commission established under this chapter is a regularly constituted court, affording all the necessary 'judicial guarantees which are recognized as indispensable by civilized peoples' for purposes of common Article 3 of the Geneva Conventions." 18 U.S.C. §948b(f). Does Congress have the authority to declare this, or does the declaration trench on the constitutional authority of the courts as interpreters of the treaties of the United States? The 2010 NDAA eliminated this clause.

4. The MCA preserves some controversial features of the pre-*Hamdan* military commissions.

(a) One concerns classified information. The MCA provides that "[c]lassified information shall be protected and is privileged from disclosure if disclosure would be detrimental to the national security," 10 U.S.C. §949d(f)(1)(A), a determination "based on a finding by the head of that department or agency that (i) the information is properly classified; and (ii) disclosure of the information would be detrimental to the national security." 10 U.S.C. §949d(f)(1)(B). The MCA states that the military judge, "upon motion of trial counsel, shall permit trial counsel to introduce otherwise admissible evidence before the military commission, while protecting from disclosure the sources, methods, or activities by which the United States acquired the evidence if the military judge finds that (i) the sources, methods, or activities by which the United States acquired the evidence are classified, and (ii) the evidence is reliable." 10 U.S.C. §949d(f)(2)(B). A similar rule allows trial counsel to prevent disclosure of sources, methods, and activities during the discovery process. 10 U.S.C. §949j(c)(2). Critics point out that "methods . . . by which the United States acquired such evidence" might include torture or other forms of coercion, and thus that this provision permits prosecutors to cover up torture.

(b) Although the 2006 MCA provides a right against self-incrimination and excludes evidence obtained by torture, 10 U.S.C. §948r(a)-(b), it allows evidence "in which the degree of coercion is disputed"—meaning, for example, evidence obtained by harsh techniques that the defense calls torture but the government does not. This might include evidence obtained through waterboarding, prolonged sleep deprivation, "walling" (that is, slamming the detainee into a wall), and other methods that highly controversial Justice Department opinions declared not to be torture. (These methods and the "torture memos" are discussed in detail in Chapter 22.) Such evidence is admissible if "the military judge finds that (1) the totality of the circumstances renders the statement reliable and possessing sufficient probative value; and (2) the interests of justice would best be served by admission of the statement into evidence." 10 U.S.C. §948r(c).

The 2010 NDAA significantly amends these rules. It expands the ban on evidence obtained through torture to include a ban on evidence obtained through cruel, inhuman, or degrading treatment that does not rise to the level of torture. §948r(a). The 2010 NDAA eliminates the provision on evidence "in which the degree of coercion is disputed." Finally, it requires that statements by the accused may be admitted only if they are voluntary or, in the alternative, "made incident to lawful conduct during military operations at the point of capture or during closely related active combat engagement, and the interests of justice would best be served by admission of the statement into evidence." §948r(c)(2).

5. Controversies and embarrassments continued to dog the military commissions after they resumed following the enactment of the MCA. Colonel Morris Davis, the chief prosecutor, resigned in October 2007, alleging improper political pressure from higher-ups in the Pentagon to bring "sexy" cases in time for the 2008 election. Jess Bravin, Dispute Stymies Guantánamo Terror Trials, Wall St. J., Sept. 26, 2007; Josh White, Pressure Alleged in Detainees' Hearings: Ex-Prosecutor Says Pentagon Pushing "Sexy" Cases in 2008, Wash. Post, Oct. 21, 2007, at A15. In an op-ed, Davis wrote:

> I was the chief prosecutor for the military commissions at Guantánamo Bay, Cuba, until Oct. 4, the day I concluded that full, fair and open trials were not possible under the current system. I resigned on that day because I felt that the system had become deeply politicized and that I could no longer do my job effectively or responsibly.

Morris D. Davis, AWOL Military Justice, L.A. Times, Dec. 10, 2007, *available at* http://articles.latimes.com/2007/dec/10/news/OE-DAVIS10.

A year later, another military prosecutor resigned to protest the case he was asked to prosecute. Army Lt. Col. Darrell Vandeveld was assigned to prosecute Mohammed Jawad, a youthful defendant accused of attacking U.S. troops with a grenade in Afghanistan. In a declaration he filed in Jawad's habeas corpus case, Vandeveld asserted that Jawad had confessed only after having been subjected to the "frequent flier" program of intense sleep deprivation—he had been moved from cell to cell 112 times in two weeks. Declaration of Darrell Vandeveld, ¶14 (Jan. 12, 2009), *available at* http://www.aclu.org/pdfs/safefree/vandeveld_declaration.pdf.

Vandeveld's criticism was broader than Jawad's mistreatment, however:

> [T]o the shock of my professional sensibilities, I discovered that the evidence, such as it was, remained scattered throughout an incomprehensible labyrinth of databases primarily under the control of CITF,[121] or strewn throughout the prosecution offices in desk drawers, bookcases packed with vaguely-labeled plastic containers, or even simply piled

---

121. Criminal Investigations Task Force — EDS.

on the tops of desks vacated by prosecutors who had departed the Commissions for other assignments. I further discovered that most physical evidence that had been collected had either disappeared or had been stored in locations that no one with any tenure at, or institutional knowledge of, the Commissions could identify with any degree of specificity or certainty. The state of disarray was so extensive that I later learned, as described below, that crucial physical evidence and other documents relevant to both the prosecution and the defense had been tossed into a locker located at Guantánamo and promptly forgotten.

Id. ¶8. In July 2008, a federal judge in Jawad's habeas case found that the government did not have enough evidence to hold him. The Department of Justice announced that it would examine the possibility of prosecuting Jawad in civilian court.

7. Some defense lawyers, including military defenders, accused the government of interfering with their lawyer-client relationships and creating conflicts of interest. For details, see David Luban, Lawfare and Legal Ethics in Guantánamo, 60 Stan. L. Rev. 1981 (2008); for rebuttal, see Major General Charles J. Dunlap, Jr. & Major Linell A. Letendre, Military Lawyering and Professional Independence in the War on Terror: A Response to David Luban, 61 Stan. L. Rev. 417 (2008).

In May 2009, President Barack Obama issued the following statement.

STATEMENT OF PRESIDENT BARACK OBAMA ON MILITARY COMMISSIONS

Office of the Press Secretary, *available at* **http://www.whitehouse.gov/the_press_office/ Statement-of-President-Barack-Obama-on-Military-Commissions (May 15, 2009)**

Military commissions have a long tradition in the United States. They are appropriate for trying enemies who violate the laws of war, provided that they are properly structured and administered. In the past, I have supported the use of military commissions as one avenue to try detainees, in addition to prosecution in Article III courts. In 2006, I voted in favor of the use of military commissions. But I objected strongly to the Military Commissions Act that was drafted by the Bush Administration and passed by Congress because it failed to establish a legitimate legal framework and undermined our capability to ensure swift and certain justice against those detainees that we were holding at the time. Indeed, the system of Military Commissions at Guantánamo Bay had only succeeded in prosecuting three suspected terrorists in more than seven years.

Today, the Department of Defense will be seeking additional continuances in several pending military commission proceedings. We will seek more time to allow us time to reform the military commission process. The Secretary of Defense will notify the Congress of several changes to the rules governing the commissions. The rule changes will ensure that: First, statements that have been obtained from detainees using cruel, inhuman and degrading interrogation methods will no longer be admitted as evidence at trial. Second, the use of hearsay will be limited, so that the burden will no longer be on the party who objects to hearsay to disprove its reliability. Third, the accused will have greater latitude in selecting their counsel. Fourth, basic protections will be provided for those who refuse to testify. And fifth, military commission judges may establish the jurisdiction of their own courts.

These reforms will begin to restore the Commissions as a legitimate forum for prosecution, while bringing them in line with the rule of law. In addition, we will work with the Congress on additional reforms that will permit commissions to prosecute terrorists effectively and be an avenue, along with federal prosecutions in Article III courts, for administering justice. This is the best way to protect our country, while upholding our deeply held values.

NOTES AND QUESTIONS

1. It has been reported that President Obama plans to use the military commissions against high-value prisoners, such as 9/11 planner Khalid Sheikh Mohammed (KSM). Several of the prisoners, however, including KSM, have declared that they plan to boycott their own proceedings.

2. In light of the continuing difficulties faced by the military commissions, is it wise to continue them rather than trying the defendants in civilian court?

3. One problem with trying defendants in federal court is that many of them were denied their *Miranda* right to consult a lawyer for years, while they were isolated and intensively interrogated (some of them in secret CIA prisons). Reportedly, the FBI instituted "clean teams" to reinterview detainees in Guantánamo in order to obtain admissible evidence untainted by abuse or coercion. Josh White, Dan Eggen & Joby Warwick, U.S. to Try 6 on Capital Charges over 9/11 Attacks, Wash. Post, Feb. 12, 2008, at A1. Would such a procedure be sufficient in the case of defendants and witnesses who may have previously been tortured or otherwise abused?

4. Representative Jerry Nadler (D-NY) has said of President Obama's decision to restart the military commissions: "What bothers me is that they seem to be saying, 'Some people we have good enough evidence against, so we'll give them a fair trial. Some people the evidence is not so good, so we'll give them a less fair trial. We'll give them just enough due process to ensure a conviction because we know they're guilty.' That's not a fair trial, that's a show trial." Jess Bravin, Detainees, Even If Acquitted, Might Not Go Free, Wall St. J., July 8, 2009, at A4. Is this a fair criticism?

4.   Who Is an "Unlawful Combatant"?

Under the 2006 MCA, military commissions have jurisdiction only over "alien unlawful enemy combatants."[122] An "unlawful enemy combatant" is defined as:

> (i) a person who has engaged in hostilities or who has purposefully and materially supported hostilities against the United States or its co-belligerents who is not a lawful enemy combatant (including a person who is part of the Taliban, al Qaeda, or associated forces); or
> (ii) a person who, before, on, or after the date of the enactment of the Military Commissions Act of 2006 [enacted Oct. 17, 2006], has been determined to be an unlawful enemy combatant by a Combatant Status Review Tribunal or another competent tribunal established under the authority of the President or the Secretary of Defense.[123]

---

122. 10 U.S.C. §948d(a)-(b).
123. Id. §948a(1)(A)(i)-(ii).

Lawful enemy combatants, in turn, are defined in terms more or less equivalent to the Geneva Conventions' definition of privileged belligerents entitled to POW status: members of a state's regular armed forces, or militias belonging to states "which are under responsible command, wear a fixed distinctive sign recognizable at a distance, carry their arms openly, and abide by the law of war."[124] Other non-state actors fighting against the United States are, by definition, unlawful enemy combatants.

Two major issues arise under these definitions. First, the Geneva Conventions do not recognize categories of "lawful" or "unlawful" combatants. Instead, they recognize the categories of persons who qualify for POW status and civilians. If civilians directly engage in hostilities, they may be targeted by a state's military forces, but that does not make them "unlawful" combatants. The Geneva Conventions recognize a category of "grave breaches" — acts of violence contrary to the laws of war that count as war crimes, such as killing or torturing prisoners — and civilian fighters who commit grave breaches are not exempt from being categorized as war criminals. (For details of the Geneva Conventions' conception of grave breaches, see Chapter 21.A.2.b.) But the bare fact that civilians do not qualify for POW status does not make them "unlawful," and international law does not automatically classify their attacks on military targets as war crimes. The attacks are war crimes only if they violate the specific rules of combat that soldiers must follow. Thus, although the 2006 MCA labels civilians who fight the United States as unlawful enemy combatants, this is a domestic-law designation — they are not unlawful from the standpoint of the international law of war. To remove these confusions, the 2010 NDAA amends the terminology in the MCA. Now, instead of the phrase "unlawful enemy combatant," the amended MCA uses the Geneva terminology: "unprivileged enemy belligerent." §948a(7). However, the terms are nearly identical in definition, and the military commissions retain jurisdiction over "alien unprivileged enemy belligerents."

Second, there is a real, and hotly contested, question about how widely the net of unprivileged enemy belligerent status spreads. The U.S. government's definition of unprivileged enemy belligerent includes those who have "materially supported" hostilities against the United States. Recall the criminal law definition of "material support" from Section A.2 above:

> material support is "any property, tangible or intangible, or service, including currency or monetary instruments or financial securities, financial services, lodging, training, expert advice or assistance, safehouses, false documentation or identification, communications equipment, facilities, weapons, lethal substances, explosives, personnel (1 or more individuals who may be or include oneself), and transportation, except medicine or religious materials."[125]

This statutory definition would make people "unprivileged enemy belligerents" for conduct far removed from combat.

The question of who is an enemy combatant has arisen primarily in a different context from military commissions. The United States has repeatedly asserted that enemy combatants can be detained until the end of the war on terror, and the question of who is an enemy combatant arose repeatedly in detainee litigation.

---

124. Id. §948a(2).
125. 18 U.S.C. §2339A(b).

Perhaps the best known example is a colloquy between federal District Judge Joyce Hens Green and Brian Boyle, a U.S. government attorney:

THE COURT: I want to go back and give you some hypotheticals, . . . very quick hypotheticals about when an individual would be considered . . . an enemy combatant or supporting those forces, the Taliban, al-Qaeda and the like.

> A little old lady in Switzerland who writes checks to what she thinks is a charity that helps orphans in Afghanistan but really is a front to finance al-Qaeda activities. Would she be considered an enemy combatant or supporting? Now, these are real questions. I know you smile, but these are real questions.

MR. BOYLE: Let me answer it on two levels. First I would say that someone's intention or motivation for being a part of al-Qaeda forces or Taliban forces, for instance somebody who says well, I didn't really want to do this, but I was brought along unwillingly, this was never my gig, but I just got caught up in the moment, never my intention. But that, as I think is clearly defined by tradition, is not a factor that would disable the military from detaining the individual as an enemy combatant. . . .

THE COURT: So the person could be considered, hypothetically?

MR. BOYLE: In your precise hypothetical, I think the question — if in fact unwittingly this poor woman was financing al-Qaeda operations, but her story was, gosh, in fact I didn't know I was financing al-Qaeda operations. I thought it was a charity. I can tell you this much. It would be up to the military, and great deference would need to be paid to its judgment, as to what to believe in that scenario. I would think it would be up to the military to make that decision —

THE COURT: But she would be taken into custody?

MR. BOYLE: I think she could.

THE COURT: And denominated as an enemy combatant and then subsequently have a tribunal hearing.

MR. BOYLE: I think she could be subject to that process, and it would be up to the military to decide whom to believe.[126]

Judge Green offered several additional hypotheticals: "A resident of London who collects money from worshipers at mosques to support a hospital in Syria, but entrusts the money for that purpose to someone who is an al-Qaeda member";[127] "a resident of Dublin, England [*sic*] who teaches English to the son of a person the CIA knows to be a member of al-Qaeda";[128] "Mr. Smith [who] knows that his cousin has spoken favorably about a leader of al-Qaeda, and has reason to suspect that in fact his cousin is a member of al-Qaeda" and does not report the cousin to the authorities;[129] and "a Wall Street Journal reporter, working in Afghanistan, who knows the exact location of Osama bin Laden but does not reveal it to the United States Government in order to protect her source."[130] Mr. Boyle responded that while he finds it inconceivable that the U.S. government would detain either of the latter two, he would not rule out the possibility.

NOTES AND QUESTIONS

1. How would Judge Green's hypothetical cases fare under the MCA and the statutory definition of "material support"? Notice that the MCA definition includes a

---

126. Rasul v. Bush, Transcript of Motion to Dismiss Before the Honorable Joyce Hens Green District Judge (D.D.C., Dec. 1, 2004), at 25:3-26:18.
    127. Id. at 26:20-26:23.
    128. Id. at 27:4-27:5.
    129. Id. at 28:2-28:9.
    130. Id. at 29:7-29:10.

mental element, namely that the material support has been undertaken "purposefully."

2. Consider two additional cases: (1) the mother of an al Qaeda member or Taliban fighter in Afghanistan, who allows him to stay with her, knowing that he plans to rejoin the fight; (2) his sister, who sympathizes with him politically and gives him a cell phone for his birthday. Could either of them be prosecuted before a military commission? Should they be?

3. Before 9/11, the only mention of unlawful belligerent status in federal law appeared in *Quirin* and a handful of judicial opinions that quoted *Quirin*. Yet there is an important ambiguity in *Quirin*'s concept of an unlawful belligerent (or, in the 2006 MCA's terminology, "unlawful enemy combatant"). "Unlawful" may refer to the fact that the person does not satisfy the legal criteria to qualify as a privileged belligerent under the laws of war; or, alternatively, it may mean that the person has committed crimes. *Quirin* does not specify which it has in mind. According to the *Quirin* Court, the German saboteurs were "enemies who, with the purpose of destroying war materials and utilities, entered, or after entry remained in, our territory without uniform — an offense against the law of war."[131] This phrasing combines both understandings of "unlawful." The saboteurs "entered . . . our territory without uniform," which means that they lose the belligerent privilege. And the saboteurs did so "with the purpose of destroying war materials and utilities," which is a criminal act. The *Quirin* Court rolled the two aspects together into a single "offense against the law of war" without distinguishing them.

This distinction became important in debates about U.S. military commissions post-9/11. Did they intend to prosecute al Qaeda captives for being unlawful enemy combatants or for particular crimes they had committed? Recall that along with conspiracy, Hamdan was charged with having "willfully and knowingly joined an enterprise of persons who shared a common criminal purpose." In the excerpt from *Hamdan* above, Justice Thomas, dissenting, defended this charge as part of the common law of war. The MCA, on the other hand, does not explicitly include mere membership in al Qaeda as a crime. However, it includes material support of terrorism, and under 18 U.S.C. §2339A, this includes providing personnel, including oneself. Does this mean that the United States has criminalized membership in terrorist groups in and of itself?

4. Having considered the materials above, do you favor trying terrorist suspects before military commissions, federal courts, or whichever option the government chooses on a case-by-case basis?

---

131. *Quirin*, 317 U.S. at 46.

PART

IV

International Crime

In the chapters that follow, we explore in greater detail the "core" international crimes of genocide, crimes against humanity, and war crimes. In addition, two types of criminal conduct—torture and offenses involving sexual violence—that may fall within more than one of these overarching crime categories are the focus of separate treatment. We begin, however, with a close examination of the structure and functioning of the newest international forum in which these crimes may be prosecuted—the International Criminal Court (ICC). The different culpable roles—or modes of responsibility—that various persons may play in the course of an atrocity and the defenses that may be available to them under international criminal law receive treatment commensurate with their moral and legal importance. Finally, we conclude by exploring questions constantly confronted throughout these materials: When is criminal prosecution the best means to address or redress horrific international crimes? Should the "justice" meted out through criminal justice mechanisms ever take second seat to forging a "peace" through political accommodations or amnesties? Should truth and reconciliation be the goals rather than retribution? What alternative institutional structures or processes might we consider if criminal prosecution is either not optimal or not practically available?

The cases examined in this final part of the book are often bloody, harrowing, even positively obscene. One recurrent question flowing from this circumstance dogs all class discussions and ought, therefore, to be addressed at the outset: How can human beings *do* these things to each other? A horrifying lesson of the following chapters is that no cultures, societies, or people are immune, and none has a unique susceptibility to inhuman conduct. Does this bleak conclusion mean that future atrocities simply cannot be avoided and, more important for our purposes, that criminal prosecutions cannot deter future misconduct? Consider the following.

FRANK NEUBACHER, HOW CAN IT HAPPEN THAT HORRENDOUS STATE CRIMES ARE PERPETRATED?

4 J. Intl. Crim. Just. 787 (2006)

1. INTRODUCTION: EXPLAINING THE INCOMPREHENSIBLE

Most serious crimes committed by the state, such as genocide or systematic torture, leave observers with a sense of shock and bewilderment. As a first reaction, the origins of heinous crimes are sought in the pathological personality of the perpetrator or in the exceptional evil of a political system. At times, claims are even made that crimes like the holocaust are inherently unclassifiable, as they portray a unique, incomparable and incomprehensible incident. Hans Magnus Enzensberger argued that those who term Hitler a common criminal render him apparently harmless, mistransforming his crimes into something comprehensible. This perspective has merit, in particular if the dimensions of the crimes committed during the holocaust are considered. The genocide of the European Jews cannot simply be understood as a horrible accident of German or European history. Since it was planned and carried out in the centre of a modern, rational and enlightened society proud of its culture, it should rather be seen as a product and problem of this civilization and culture. And yet, in asking how we can explain state crime, we should not overlook lessons from the disciplines of social psychology and sociology regarding behaviour in decision-making situations. Not least because these disciplines may offer explanations based on the behaviour of normal people rather than monsters, demons or devils.

It is well known that most Nazis were very ordinary: many of them were loving husbands and caring family members, educated, generally law-abiding people — and yet they were also capable of horrendous criminal acts. In the course of the Jerusalem trial against Adolf Eichmann, head of department for Jews at the *Reichssicherheitshauptamt* (RSHA), a psychiatrist found Eichmann "in any case more normal than I am after having examined him." And philosopher Hannah Arendt pointed out that the commission of even such grievous crimes did not require human monsters. To her, Eichmann personified the "banality of evil" — a term that has come to be understood as a synonym for the thoughtlessness with which an individual in bureaucratic structures can participate in such criminality, unable or unwilling to confront the logical consequences of their own actions.

Confronted with the consequences of their deeds, even the perpetrators have difficulty in understanding those deeds and recognizing themselves therein. The excuses offered by Nazi criminals — for example, that they were compelled to obey orders — have provided nothing more than a legal defence strategy, albeit in vain. What then are the factors enabling people to display such cruel behaviour that they can hardly admit it to themselves, committing deeds that they themselves perceive as an attack on their self-image and pride, and which are consequently banished from memory or retrospectively falsified?

These questions are considered here from a criminological standpoint. Usually criminology deals with deviant behaviour. In this regard, however, state crime is special. The perpetrators of state crime are often not considered criminal by those in their own society, since their behaviour conforms with the expectations of others in that society. To call their behaviour deviant only makes sense with reference to some standard at a superior level (e.g. international law and universal norms). At the domestic level, a major part of the explanation has to deal with conformity or, as in Stanley Milgram's experiments, with obedience. Despite the focus on individual behaviour, it would be wrong to assume that the explanation is limited to the micro-level. The state is clearly implicated in the production of such behaviour through defining political aims, defining political in- and out-groups, disseminating propaganda and justifications for violence against the out-group, and signalling that it expects these aims, rules, views, and orders to be followed. After all, there are numerous links between the individual and the political level. . . . After exploring the implications of the Milgram experiments, the theory of "neutralization techniques" is presented. Originally developed in the context of individual crimes, it is here applied to the state level, offering an explanation of state crimes, wherein ordinary people commit extraordinary crimes. The theory is illustrated through analysis of the notorious secret speech by Heinrich Himmler advocating the extermination of Jews.

2. THE MILGRIM EXPERIMENTS AND BEYOND

The Milgram experiments — also known informally as the "Eichmann experiment" — were carried out at the . . . Yale at the beginning of the 1960s. Stanley Milgram's research work provided essential findings relating to the phenomenon of obedience and its destructive potential.[1] Its relevance is widely recognized in genocide studies. Milgram believed the essence of obedience to be a person coming to the point where he sees himself as a tool that carries out the will of others and is thus no longer responsible for his own actions. This reversal of self-image should be seen as the central issue in the complex problem of obedience. Once a person has completed this crucial transformation, all the essential traits of obedience appear. Adjustments within the thought process, willingness to participate in cruel deeds and the categories of self-justification built up by an obedient subject are generally similar. External circumstances do not make any difference — whether the subject is obeying in a psychological laboratory or the control station of a launch pad for inter-continental missiles.[2]

Psychologists concluded from Milgram's experiments that relatively ordinary people can be made to perform cruel acts on others. No deficits in their character are required, since they are simply fulfilling their duty, void of any personal animosity. The experiments suggested that the percentage of volunteers obeying a person in a position of authority could only be decreased by weakening the authority of that person. As if they acted in some kind of force field, the head of the experiment

---

1. [Neubacher's footnote 8:] S. Milgram, Obedience to Authority: An Experimental View (London: Harper Collins, 1974).

2. [Neubacher's footnote 11:] Milgram's experimental design that gave cause to his alarming observation presented itself as follows: Male volunteers received the order to subject other people to a number of painful electrical shocks under the pretext that the experiment was to analyse the effect of punishment on memory and learning. Each test person held the position of a "teacher" whose only task was to punish a "pupil" with supposed electrical shocks each time a mistake was made during a learning test with pair association. However, the pupil was actually a member of the research team who was simply play-acting, and there were no real shocks given. The test person was instructed to increase the voltage to the next highest level for each mistake made by the "pupil." The shock generator was clearly marked with 30 current levels, which appeared to be evidently connected to the "electrical chair" of the "pupil." The voltage ranged from "15 V: slight shock," over "195 V. very strong shock" and "375 V: danger, severe shock" up to "450 V." However, labelling from "435 V" onwards consisted of "XXX." The experiment began after the teacher/test person had himself been subjected to a real trial shock of 45 V and after the "pupil" had been tied down. Protest of the victim was coordinated to the supposed electrical shocks and was audible via a door being slightly ajar. At 75 V the "pupil" began to moan and grumble: at 150 V he demanded to be released from the experiment; at 180 V he yelled that he could not stand the pain any longer, and at 300 V he screamed with pain, insisted on his release and announced that he would refuse to answer any more questions. If the teacher/test person hesitated thereafter or protested against administering electrical shocks, the head of the experiment dressed in a grey coat would reply "You have no choice but to continue." In the absence of a reaction by the "pupil," the head of the experiment insisted on punishment nevertheless. The results showed that 62.5% of the test persons were obedient, i.e. two-thirds carried out the orders of the head of the experiment right up to the maximum shock of 450 V. A further 22.5% risked considerable physical injury despite protests of the "victim," while only 15% refused to carry out orders after the "victim" demanded breaking off the experiment for the first time. These results being virtually identical for men and women alike, caused a considerable shock in the scientific world and in the public. It was unequivocal that the phenomenon of obedience was due to authority. Upon changing the experiment so that the shock level was left to the test person's discretion, the majority used only minimum voltage on the "pupils," which was even below the level where first moans were uttered. Therefore, aggressive impulses of individuals as a cause for the behaviour in the experiment could be ruled out.

lost power over the volunteers to the same extent that the "victim/pupil" or two colluding, disobedient accomplices gained influence. In the "immediacy of the victim" condition, in which the volunteer was asked to force back the pupil's hand on the metal shock plate at the 150 V level, the percentage of obedient volunteers was considerably reduced to 30%. This was apparently because it is more difficult to harm a person who is concrete, visible, and able to observe our actions. In the "disobedient group" condition, in which two colluding accomplices who were, like the victim, members of the research team and were acting as co-teachers, refused to continue at different shock levels, obedience could be reduced as low as 10%. In this case, the volunteer was left alone with sole responsibility for carrying out the instructions, and typically did not want to appear callous in front of others. Moreover, both colluding accomplices had just demonstrated that disobedience was possible and how it could be done. Thus, they served as a model from which the volunteer could learn how to get out of the situation. Yet, Milgram concluded that the overall results raise the possibility that human nature cannot be counted on to insulate people from brutality and inhumane treatment. A substantial proportion of people do what they are told to do, irrespective of the content of the act and without limitations of conscience, so long as they perceive that the command comes from a legitimate authority.

Herbert Kelman built on Milgram's work by reflecting on the loss of moral restraint. He agreed with Milgram that "authorization" enhances the willingness of people to participate in massacres. According to Kelman, the situation becomes so defined that common moral principles are suspended. The perpetrators see themselves in a "no-choice situation" either because they feel their duty lies in obedience or because they feel involved in a "transcendent mission." In addition, Kelman identified two more significant processes: routinization and dehumanization.

The process of "routinization" minimizes the opportunities to question moral responsibility for repetitive actions. If others are also involved, nobody seems to be fully responsible; participants even mutually reinforce each other. Furthermore, moral reflection is limited by drill and numbing: the individual is gradually focused on the technical aspects of the routine job, e.g. how to arrange mass killings and make them more effective and less stressful for the executors. The greater the frequency of repetition of an action, the more the given definition of the situation becomes ingrained, including the techniques of justification. That is the reason why defiance becomes increasingly difficult after having made the first step ("passing the gate region"). Breaking off would be seen as admitting having repeatedly made the wrong decision. Psychologically, it is easier to continue and defend the given definition of the situation against reservations and doubts.

Through "dehumanization" the perpetrator excludes the victim from the community that is mutually bound by its morals, or as Helen Fein puts it, from "the universe of obligation." The victim is deprived of the protection generally granted to any human being, in that he or she is assigned degrading and subhuman characteristics. In effect, the people so characterized are removed from the in-group and relegated to the out-group. "Perceived as inferior, members of the out-group are easily stereotyped, scapegoated, and stigmatized, and the hostility toward them strengthens in-group solidarity."

3. Techniques of Neutralization

Taken together, these theories offer explanatory components ranging from Milgram's "obedience to authority" to Kelman's "process of dehumanization" and his "transcendent mission." Interestingly, there is a criminological theory that encompasses all these components: "denying the responsibility," "denying the victim" and "appeal to higher loyalties."

In their 1957 paper, Sykes and Matza presented a theory of delinquency based on the assumptions of learning theory that, first of all, provides an explanation of how ordinary citizens drift into criminality without rejecting the dominant social order. According to them, the delinquent generally accepts the legitimacy of this order including its basic norms (he is law-abiding). That is why he appears so ordinary and, in fact, is ordinary. However, he has learnt to neutralize these norms in specific situational contexts. The perpetrator claims an exceptional situation in which breaking the norm is justifiable without questioning the validity of the norm as such. Neutralization thus makes it possible for the violation to appear acceptable, if not legitimate. Moreover, the perpetrator protects his image and himself from self-blame and feelings of shame and guilt. In the words of Sykes and Matza, "he has his cake and eats it too."

Sykes and Matza divide neutralization into five different techniques:

(1) The Denial of Responsibility ("I did not mean it"):
   To minimize responsibility for the deed, it is transferred to external circumstances, e.g. an unlucky chain of events, legal incapacity or any other circumstances ("It was not my fault, I had no choice, I acted on superior orders").

(2) The Denial of Injury ("I didn't really hurt anybody"):
   Similarly, the wrongfulness of a deed can be denied by presenting theft as "borrowing" or brutal bodily harm as a "fair duel" with equal chances for the opponents.

(3) The Denial of the Victim ("They had it coming to them"):
   The status of victim can be denied in offences against property by referring to compensation at a later date, e.g. via insurance. For sexual offences the victim's consent can be claimed. Shedding a different light on the deed, the victim can also be presented as aggressor so that the delinquency appears to be an act of self-defence or a consequence of provocation. In extreme cases the perpetrator denies that there is a victim by denying that the victim is truly a "person." The rule "thou shalt not kill" does not apply as the victim is reduced to "enemy," "communist," "terrorist," "scum," "filth" or "bacillus," removing any human traits (dehumanization).

(4) The Condemnation of the Condemners ("Everybody is picking on me"):
   Furthermore, the delinquent can try to turn the tables by reasoning that the accusation against him is one-sided, hypocritical or a transparent political move. In this way, the accusers will be deprived of the moral right to accuse. For example, the police being involved in the arrest are called "brutal and corrupt henchmen," the prosecutor is termed "self-righteous," and the judges are described as the "tool of an unlawful system."

(5) The Appeal to Higher Loyalties ("I didn't do it for myself"):
   Finally, the delinquent seizes the opportunity to call upon a higher authority or rather upon higher values. The deed is then justified by stating that it was essential "for the rescue of one's own people" or "in the name of God" or "a higher justice." This last type of neutralization is characterized by presenting himself as an unselfish person driven by ethical motives. . . .

Another approach worth mentioning is Leon Festinger's theory of cognitive dissonance. His central statement is that cognitive dissonance arises when attitudes and behaviour patterns do not harmonize. Cognitive dissonance is always felt as something unpleasant, thus motivating the individual to its minimization. In order to regain balance within the cognitive system, i.e. to reduce dissonance, it is necessary to change individual cognitive elements. The most common way of reducing cognitive dissonance is by "spreading apart alternatives." After having chosen one of two alternatives, the desirability of the chosen one is increased and that of the non-chosen one is reduced. This process is often helped along by selecting information, i.e. dissonant information is avoided or suppressed. The fewer the opportunities to change the decision, the more pronounced these effects. Festinger himself did not apply his theory to delinquent behaviour. Nevertheless, his findings are applicable as the delinquent has feelings of dissonance because of the violation of the norm. In short, Festinger explains why a perpetrator neutralizes (motive) while Sykes and Matza . . . show how this goal is achieved (techniques).

4. Neutralization by the State: Labelling the Adversary a Political Enemy

History has shown that crimes committed or ordered by the state are particularly appalling. The scope for reinterpretation and neutralization grows within the political context. The extraordinary dimensions of genocide and state crime necessitate extremely intense neutralization in order for the crimes to become feasible. People or groups of people that have to be "combated," "killed" or "annihilated" are declared to be political enemies. Dehumanization is one of the most resolute forms of neutralization. Linguistically, this is enforced by euphemisms that disguise the fact that homicide or genocide is the final goal. Thus, terms such as "special treatment," "evacuation of Jews" or "ethnic cleansing" are used as synonyms for mass killings. Powerful "interpretation by the elite" legitimizes politically motivated violence by connecting it to the political order, its establishment and assertions. Carl Schmitt, for whom the essence of politics lay in the distinction between friend and foe, including the declaration of an internal enemy, represents a fatal school of thought that became totally dominant during the period of National Socialism through the dehumanization of political enemies. Deprived of all rights and of the status of a human being, the "enemy" was killed like an insect.

States violating human rights use the same neutralization techniques as individuals. State neutralization, however, is spread via the state's propaganda machine, thus having a far greater impact than individual neutralization. Collective awareness of right and wrong is synchronized, while neutralization techniques are offered to individuals to be taken into their repertoire of justification. In fact, this is a universal problem; techniques of neutralization and dehumanization can be observed in diverse societies. The genocides in Bosnia and Rwanda are no exceptions.

Neutralization by the state can equally be classified as belonging to one of the five techniques described by Sykes and Matza. Manners of speech and patterns of argumentation can deny unlawfulness as such ("the reports are false, made up, exaggerated," "we were at war," "times were like that," etc.); they can accuse the victim ("the others are the aggressors, we were just defending ourselves," "they have only got themselves to blame"); play down the state or society's own responsibility ("we had our orders," "otherwise others would have done it," "we had a blackout," "we couldn't know," "we were just small cogs," "we were in danger ourselves"); attack those who call a spade a spade ("elsewhere the situation is even worse," "for transparent reasons we are being scapegoated"); or appeal to higher loyalties ("it concerned our national security, our honour, a good cause, a higher form of justice," etc.: "the end justified the means"). The use of particular language or of official jargon is not necessarily based on a conscious decision of the individual. Analyses of decision-making processes in politics have shown the degree to which even political protagonists are subjected to the dynamics of social conformity. They consequently develop euphemisms to avoid any kind of direct reference to human suffering.

It is not far fetched to include Sykes and Matza's theory as a supporting pillar for a criminological theory of state crime. Subsequently, the application of the theory to the political level is tested through an analysis of Himmler's secret speech advocating the extermination of the Jews.

5. HEINRICH HIMMLER SPEAKING OF THE EXTERMINATION OF JEWS (4 OCTOBER 1943)

Himmler's speech in Posen (Poznan) on 4 October 1943 before the highest ranks of *SS-Gruppenführer* is both an eloquent and infamous example of state neutralization.[3] Infamous because Himmler termed the atrocity of the "extermination of the Jewish people" a "glorious chapter of our history, never having been written and never to be written," and described the participating officers as "decent." Infamous also for the way in which he seemed to anticipate the thoughts, anxieties and maybe even objections of his audience. Words of understanding are followed up by demands for even greater resolution and an appeal to an alleged historical necessity.

Himmler's words are an example for the horrifying re-evaluation and reinterpretation of state crimes: according to his perspective, the perpetrators of the holocaust are not criminals but decent men. Having set aside matters of personal interest, they

---

3. [Neubacher's footnote 32:] "I shall speak to you here with all frankness of a very serious subject. Among ourselves, it ought to be spoken of quite openly, although we shall never speak of it in public. Just as little as we hesitated to do our duty as ordered on 30 June 1934, and put comrades who had failed against the wall and shoot them, just as little did we ever speak of it, and shall never speak of it. It was a matter of course, of tact, which thank God lives within us that stopped us from conversing about it, talking about it. It made everybody shudder but at the same time everyone knew that he would do it again if ordered to do so, and if it was necessary.

I am now talking about the evacuation of Jews, the extermination of the Jewish people. It is one of those things which is easy to say. "The Jewish people are to be exterminated," says each party comrade, "this is clear, it is part of our party programme, elimination of the Jews, extermination, right, we'll do it." And then they all come along, these 80 million upright Germans, and each one of them has his decent Jew. Of course the others are swine, but this one is a first-class Jew. Of all those who talk like this, not one has watched, not one has ever lived through it. Most of you know what it means to see a hundred corpses lying together, five hundred, or a thousand. To have gone through this and yet — apart from a few exceptions, examples of human weakness — to have remained decent, this is what has made us hard. This is a glorious chapter in our history that has never been written and never shall be written. We know how difficult it would be for us if — with the air raids, the burdens and the deprivations of war — we still had the Jews, as secret saboteurs, agitators and trouble-mongers. We would now have probably reached the 1916/17 stage if Jews were still in the body of the German people.

The wealth they had we have taken from them. I have issued the strict order which SS-*Obergruppenführer* Pohl has carried out that this wealth is naturally to be passed to the Reich in its entirety. We have taken none of it. Individuals who have failed will be punished according to an order given by me at the beginning: he who takes even as much as one *Reichsmark* is condemned to death. A number of SS-men, although not many, have violated this order, and they will die without mercy. We had the moral right, we had the duty to our people to kill this people who wanted to kill us. However, we do not have the right to enrich ourselves by taking but one fur, one watch, one Mark, or one cigarette or anything else. In the end, we do not want, because we wiped out the bacillus, to become sick and die from the same bacillus. I shall never sit back and watch even the smallest spot of putrefaction develop or settle on this point. Wherever it grows we shall burn it out together. Altogether, we can say that we have fulfilled this most difficult duty for the love of our nation. And no harm has come to us in our innermost-self, in our soul, in our character." (Document 1919-PS. from: *Der Prozeß gegen die Hauptkriegsverbrecher vor dem Internationalen Militärgerichtshof*, vol. XXIX [Nuremberg: *Secretariate* of the IMT, 1947], 145-146.)

have coped with a difficult task expected to be carried out by them and thus deserve glory. The suffering of the victims is completely transformed into the suffering of the perpetrators. This shows that the National Socialist propaganda took great care not to give the impression of an amoral rule; on the contrary, old morals were transformed into new ones with different content. Propaganda did not just give crime the perfect appearance but also the perfect pomp of morals with duties and sanctions. One conclusion that can be drawn from Himmler's speech is this: only if it is perceived as a struggle for purity or as a war of life and death can mass murder be presented as heroic, or as a job to be done. Pity, pangs of conscience and symptoms of awareness of impropriety were labelled afresh within the framework of new "morals." For example, they were seen as false humanitarianism, left over from bourgeois morals, or signs of weakness. Nonetheless, the re-evaluation was not so comprehensive, the subconscience not so paralysed that the need to keep this work of annihilation secret was not felt. The mass killing of Jews, and the T4 euthanasia programme alike, violated normative standards even in Nazi Germany. That is why the importance of secrecy was repeatedly emphasized. At the beginning of his statement Himmler himself makes mention of this. As far as he is concerned, the "sacrifice" begins here: getting "one's hands dirty" without hope for public recognition.

Himmler's speech is peppered with neutralizations. Evidence of this can be found in (at least) 13 different passages in the text. Injury is being denied or rather minimized three times, when the "evacuation of Jews" is mentioned, or the "wealth" possessed by Jews from which "we did not take anything," at least not for the purpose of personal enrichment. Closely connected to this is the triple denial of the Jews' status as victims. Injustice is not just absent where no damage has been done but also where there is no victim. By presenting the Jews as "secret saboteurs, agitators, and trouble-mongers" or as "bacillus" endangering the "body of the German people," they are made to lose their status as victims and instead become aggressors. Consequently, killing them seems legitimate and even their due. Or, as Himmler put it: "We had the moral right, we had the duty to our people to kill the people who wanted to kill us." In this way Himmler claims the existence of an emergency, a conflict of life and death involving two people with mutually exclusive desires to live. Although this picture does not at all correspond to the facts, it does give the appearance of a legitimate fight for survival. The denial of the Jews' status as victims is reinforced by the degradation to a "bacillus," thereby completing the dehumanization process. A further denial of the victim, this time without reference to the Jews, is the passage on the *Röhm-Putsch* (30 June 1934). The politically motivated execution of "comrades" of the *Schutz-Abteilung* (SA) is passed off as just punishment for "failing themselves."

Himmler refers to a higher authority or higher values three times. Special emphasis is given to the "necessity" of annihilating the Jews and the "moral right" to commit this deed. The historic necessity of the mission is again shown by Himmler's reference to the years 1916/17. Furthermore, he stresses several times that the Jews were killed for reasons of honour and unselfishness, namely "love to our nation" and "duty towards our nation." Unselfish discharge of duties is connected twice to the reference of "duty ordered." One problem arises here: acting on superior orders can be seen as reducing personal responsibility (denial of responsibility), but the superior order can also be seen as a good reason for participating in a legitimate military/political campaign (appeal to higher loyalties). This demonstrates that the techniques of neutralization can be difficult to differentiate. In the end, even the fourth technique listed by Sykes and Matza (condemnation of the condemners) is represented in this speech. In order to immunize his followers against critique, Himmler portrays those of the "80 million upright Germans" opposing the deportation of Jews as naïve hypocrites who endorse the National Socialist party programme but are unwilling to get their hands dirty. Thus, the speech, that in which all five techniques are proven, culminates in this incomprehensible statement which is both the invocation of the "we feeling" and the assurance of a positive self-image: "And no harm has come to us in our innermost-self, in our soul, in our character."

6. Conclusion

The theory of neutralization techniques proves to be an important theoretical element in explaining macro-crimes, in particular linking the individual and the political level. It offers an explanation of how heinous crimes are possible as well as how ordinary citizens can get involved with them without feeling guilty. . . .

Neutralization does not just happen. It might be offered or ordered by the state but incorporating it into one's own justification repertoire is the active choice of each individual. Ordinary citizens, not monsters, drift into crime because they have decided to accept the given definition of a situation. In this sense, neutralization is no excuse in a legal sense — instead, it makes the contribution of the individual visible.

CHAPTER
16

The International Criminal Court

Nearly 60 years after the Nuremberg Tribunal pioneered the idea of individual accountability for international crimes, the International Criminal Court (ICC) came into being. It is the first permanent, rather than ad hoc, institution with jurisdiction over the core international crimes of genocide, aggression, crimes against humanity, and war crimes. The treaty that establishes the ICC, the Rome Statute of the International Criminal Court (the Rome Statute or the ICC Statute),[4] came into force on July 1, 2002, and as of July 2009 claimed 110 states parties. This unprecedented experiment in international justice is now a functioning reality. The Assembly of States Parties to the ICC Statute has adopted by consensus the ICC's Rules of Procedure and Evidence (RPE); Elements of Crimes; and Procedure for Nomination and Election of Judges, the Prosecutor, and Deputy Prosecutors. In 2003, the Assembly elected its first panel of judges and the ICC's first chief prosecutor, Luis Moreno-Ocampo.[5] In 2004, the ICC concluded an agreement with the United Nations that details the terms of the relationship between these independent international actors and contemplates close cooperation and consultation on matters of mutual interest.[6] The same year, the Regulations of the Court, setting forth the particulars of its routine functioning, became effective. Most important, the ICC's Office of the Prosecutor (OTP) has commenced substantive investigations into, and prosecutions of, crimes within the court's jurisdiction.

In its first five years of operation, the OTP received nearly 3,000 communications from groups or individuals in at least 107 countries involving alleged crimes in more than 150 countries in all regions of the world.[7] The vast majority were "manifestly outside [ICC] jurisdiction after initial review."[8] Ten "situations" were subjected to "intensive analysis"; of these, two (concerning Iraq and Venezuela) were declined, and at least six (apparently including Afghanistan, Chad, Colombia, Côte d'Ivoire,

---

4. U.N. Diplomatic Conference on Plenipotentiaries on the Establishment of an International Criminal Court, U.N. Doc. A/Conf. 183/9th (2002) [hereinafter Rome Statute or ICC Statute].

5. For information about ICC judges, see International Criminal Court, Biographical Notes: The Judges, http://www.icc-cpi.int/Menus/ICC/Structure+of+the+Court/Chambers/The+Judges (last visited July 13, 2009). For Mr. Luis Moreno-Ocampo's curriculum vitae, see http://www.icc-cpi.int/Menus/ICC/Structure+of+the+Court/Office+of+the+Prosecutor/Biographies/The+Prosecutor.htm (last visited July 13, 2009).

6. See Relationship Agreement Between the United Nations and the International Criminal Court, Oct. 4, 2004, U.N. Doc. A/58/874/Annex (2004) (entered into force Oct. 4, 2004).

7. ICC, Office of the Prosecutor, Report on the Activities Performed During the First Three Years, ¶6 (Sept. 12, 2006) [hereinafter ICC 2006 Report]; ICC Assembly of States Parties, Report on the Activities of the Court, ¶35 (Oct. 18, 2007). Both of these reports can be found at http://www.icc-cpi.int/ (last visited July 13, 2009).

8. ICC 2006 Report, supra note 7, ¶7.

Georgia, and Kenya) are currently ongoing.[9] Four situations referred to the ICC have progressed to full investigations. Of the four investigations, one, which the OTP formally commenced in 2005, resulted from a referral by the UN Security Council of the situation in Darfur, Sudan.[10] The remaining three investigations were all situations referred to the ICC by states parties alleging international crimes committed on their own territories—so-called self-referrals. These situations include Uganda (referred by the Ugandan president in December 2003), the Democratic Republic of Congo (DRC) (referred by the DRC president in April 2004), and the Central African Republic (CAR) (referred by the CAR government in December 2004).[11]

The ICC has made substantial progress, initiating cases and issuing arrest warrants in all four investigations. Because the investigations and cases are proceeding apace, any summary we attempt will be quickly outdated. Accordingly, we encourage readers to access the ICC's Web site for the status of outstanding matters and mention only certain of the proceedings to which further reference will be made in this chapter.[12]

Uganda. The prosecutor has initiated cases charging Lord's Resistance Army (LRA) commanders in the Ugandan matter. The LRA seeks to overthrow the government of President Yoweri Museveni due to claimed past abuses against Uganda's Acholi tribe—to which a majority in the LRA belong. The Ugandan government forces, the Ugandan People's Defence Forces (UPDF), have also been accused of committing atrocities against civilians. The violence has been ongoing for over 20 years and has resulted in tens of thousands of civilian deaths and the displacement of over 1.5 million people (90 percent of the population of northern Uganda).[13] In addition to harming adults, the LRA is alleged to have abducted, indoctrinated, and abused children; indeed, it has been estimated that 85 percent of the soldiers in the LRA are children between the ages of 11 and 15.[14] ICC arrest warrants were issued for crimes against humanity and war crimes against five LRA commanders—including LRA leader and self-styled New Testament prophet Joseph Kony—in July 2005. The warrants appear to have spurred the defendants to engage in talks with the government, and the government has, to date, therefore declined to arrest the LRA leadership in hopes that negotiations will yield peace, if not justice.

Democratic Republic of Congo. The prosecutor has also initiated three cases related to the DRC situation, and all three defendants are currently in custody at The Hague. One of the DRC cases—that against Thomas Lubanga Dyilo—is worth highlighting because it has generated substantial litigation. Lubanga is the alleged founder and former leader of the Union des Patriots Conglais (UPC) and served as the commander in chief of its armed military wing, the Forces Patriotiques pour la Libération du Congo (FPLC). This struggle is not as long-lived as that in Uganda, but it has a pronounced transborder element, pitting the DRC's government—supported by Angola, Namibia, and Zimbabwe—against the UPC/FPLC rebels—sometimes backed by Uganda and Rwanda—in the Ituri province of DRC. Much of the fighting has been driven by the DRC's vast mineral wealth, with other nations exploiting DRC's internal political instability to plunder the country's resources. The ICC charged

---

9. See id. ¶8.

10. U.N. S.C. Res. 1593 (June 13, 2005).

11. For a very brief summary of the situations, see Wasana Punyasena, Conflict Prevention and the International Criminal Court: Deterrence in a Changing World, 14 Mich. St. J. Intl. L. 39 (2006).

12. See International Criminal Court, http://www.icc-cpi.int (last visited July 13, 2009).

13. Eric Blumenson, The Challenge of a Global Standard of Justice: Peace, Pluralism, and Punishment at the International Criminal Court, 44 Colum. J. Transnatl. L. 801, 806 (2006).

14. Id.

Lubanga with the war crimes of enlisting, conscripting, and using children to participate in hostilities. He was arrested pursuant to an ICC arrest warrant in February 2006
and transferred to the ICC. His trial commenced in early 2009.

Darfur, Sudan. Since about 2003, the western Sudanese region of Darfur has been
the site of a massive humanitarian crisis. It began when rebel groups took up arms
against the Sudanese government in reaction to Darfur's political and economic
marginalization by the reigning regime. The rebels also fought to protect themselves
against the ethnic cleansing campaign conducted by government-backed militias,
recruited among groups in Darfur and Chad. The atrocities committed by these
government-supported *Janjaweed* fighters — and a scorched-earth government
offensive — have led to massive civilian deaths, displacement, and suffering. The
Pre-Trial Chamber, at the OTP's request, has issued three arrest warrants in the
Darfur situation calling for the apprehension of Sudanese President Omar al-
Bashir — the first sitting head of state charged by the ICC — Sudan's minister
of state for humanitarian affairs, Ahmad Harun, and militia/*Janjaweed* leader, Ali
Kushayb. They are charged with war crimes and crimes against humanity.

In short, the ICC is fully engaged in its mission. The question now is whether it will
fulfill the hopes of its champions: bringing to justice persons who have committed the
worst crimes known to humankind when individual states with jurisdiction over these
offenses are unable or unwilling to bring such persons to the dock. Will the ICC, in
such circumstances, prove to be an efficient and effective way to guarantee criminal
accountability and thus to create a deterrent to future crimes of aggression, war
crimes, crimes against humanity, and genocide?

Few nations voted against the ICC's formation (China, Iraq, Israel, Libya, Qatar, the
United States, and Yemen). And the ICC Statute has attracted an impressive number
of states parties — 110 at present — in a short period of time. One must also acknowledge, however, that many of the world's most populous and powerful countries either
have not signed the ICC Statute (for example, China, India, Indonesia, Pakistan, and
Turkey), have "unsigned" it after initially signing (for example, Israel and the United
States), or have signed but not ratified it (for example, Russia). Indeed, only 6 of the
20 most populous nations in the world are states parties to the ICC, and none of the
top four countries in terms of population — together accounting for almost half of
the world's population — have joined.[15] This situation reflects, to some extent, the
fact that in international practice, states can be cautious about making important,
potentially costly, and permanent commitments of this type. It is often the case that
new institutions gather support over years, not months. Some non-states parties have
claimed a need for time to consider the treaty or to reconcile their domestic law and
institutions to the ICC Statute. Certainly, the fact that a given state has not signed or
ratified the ICC Statute does not necessarily imply hostility toward the ICC, nor does it
signal a lack of enthusiasm about the goals of the institution.

Yet this circumstance creates both symbolic and practical problems. First, the
fundamental rationale of the Court is that there is a global consensus that the crimes
within the ICC's jurisdiction claim the condemnation of all of "humanity" and as
such it is appropriate that they be the subject of international prosecutions in the
event that states with jurisdiction over them fail to enforce international standards.

---

15. *Compare* International Criminal Court, The States Parties to the Rome Statute, http://www.icc
-cpi.int/Menus/ASP/states+parties/The+States+Parties+to+the+Rome+Statute.htm (last visited July
13, 2009), *with* GeoHive, Current World Population, http://www.geohive.com/earth/population1.aspx
(last visited July 13, 2009).

Yet, as the Indian Delegation noted when the ICC statute was adopted, "[w]e are reminded again and again that the ICC is being set up to try individuals who, on the grossest scale, violate the rights of individuals. It will act, in the name of humanity, to protect the interests of humanity. . . . And we are now about to adopt a Statute to which the Governments who represent two-thirds of humanity would not be a party."[16]

Second, the ICC's ultimate effectiveness will hinge in part on the degree to which it will be able to entice non-states parties to join the Court or at least to cooperate with it. At least in cases where a Security Council resolution has not referred the case to the Court, the ICC cannot claim a right to the cooperation of non-states parties in securing evidence, apprehending offenders, and funding the ICC's operations. And where non-states parties are truly concerned about possible abusive prosecutions and thus are reluctant to aid the fledgling institution, the Court may be stymied in its efforts to secure justice for the victims of horrific crimes.

Although critical to its ongoing success, inducing additional states to join the ICC regime may be challenging. A number of the holdouts object to important provisions of the Rome Statute that they claim render the ICC's functioning contrary to international law and subject to unchecked abuses of its broad powers for political purposes. Two institutional features that come in for the lion's share of criticism are (1) the prosecutor's power to initiate examinations of alleged crimes within the jurisdiction of the ICC without state party or UN Security Council referrals, and (2) the jurisdiction that the ICC Statute gives the Court over the nationals of non-states parties in certain circumstances.

The United States has been one such holdout. It is worth examining its position because it has been one of the most vigorous advocates for international criminal accountability, having spearheaded the Nuremberg and Tokyo trials and strongly supported the creation and functioning of the International Criminal Tribunal for Former Yugoslavia (ICTY) and the International Criminal Tribunal for Rwanda (ICTR) (together referred to within as the Ad Hoc Tribunals). Indeed, former ICTY and ICTR prosecutor, Richard Goldstone, has stated that one "cannot overemphasize the importance of the role played by the United States" in setting up and supporting the Ad Hoc Tribunals.[17] Fourteen years on, however, the ICC is a reality — but the United States has not joined it.[18]

---

16. Explanation of Vote by Mr. Dilip Lahiri, Head of Delegation of India, on the Adoption of the Statute of the International Court (July 17, 1998), http://www.un.org/icc/index.htm (select "Speeches/ Statements"; then "July 17"; then "Explanations of Vote by Mr. Dilip Lahiri, Head of Delegation of India") [hereinafter Indian Statement].

17. Hon. Richard Goldstone, Historical Evolution — From Nuremberg to the International Criminal Court, 25 Penn. St. Intl. L. Rev 763, 765 (2007).

18. On December 31, 2000, President Clinton signed the Rome Statute on behalf of the United States. He stated, however, that given U.S. concerns about "significant flaws" in the Treaty, "I will not, and do not recommend that my successor submit the Treaty to the Senate for advice and consent until our fundamental concerns are satisfied." Statement by the President, The White House, Office of the Press Secretary, Signature of the International Criminal Court Treaty (Dec. 31, 2000). The Clinton administration reasoned that, as a signatory of the treaty, the United States could attend the meetings of the Assembly of States Parties and attempt to continue to influence the structure and conduct of the ICC. However, Clinton's successor, George W. Bush, "unsigned" the treaty, informing the UN Secretary-General on May 6, 2002, that "the United States does not intend to become a party to the treaty" and, accordingly, that "the United States has no legal obligations arising from its signature." Press Statement, U.S. Dept. of State, International Criminal Court: Letter to UN Secretary-General Kofi Annan (May 6, 2002). In evaluating objections to the treaty, readers are encouraged to revisit this strategic choice, evaluating for themselves the (asserted) dangers the ICC poses to U.S. national interests and the likely efficacy of continuing engagement versus outright opposition in protecting those interests.

The George W. Bush administration was initially a vehement and vocal critic of the ICC Statute, but it softened its rhetoric over time and refrained from vetoing the Security Council Resolution referring the Darfur situation to the ICC.[19] It is too soon to tell what the Obama administration's position on the ICC will be. It is clear that the administration is, at the least, firmly committed to assisting the ICC in its Darfur cases.[20] The U.S. ambassador to the United Nations, Susan Rice, focused her remarks in her first appearance in the Security Council on "how the United Nations can better protect the millions of vulnerable civilians who are caught in the crossfire of conflicts worldwide."[21] She dwelt in particular on the horrors of the conflicts in three of the four areas in which the ICC has launched investigations and prosecutions — the Democratic Republic of Congo, Sudan, and Uganda. Finally, she had kind words for the ICC, stating that the ICC "looks to become an important and credible instrument for trying to hold accountable the senior leadership responsible for atrocities committed in the Congo, Uganda, and Darfur."[22]

That said, many believe that the United States, at present, is unlikely to join the ICC for a variety of reasons. The first is the traditional — and bipartisan — reluctance of the United States to embrace permanent supranational courts and institutions. Further, many U.S. objections to the treaty are fundamental. And, to the consternation of many U.S. senators, the ICC Statute does not permit states parties to make reservations to it (with one notable exception discussed within); thus, the treaty is largely a take-it-or-leave-it proposition.[23] The United States' nonparty status may be unfortunate circumstance for the Court because it must do without the United States' power, its financial and law enforcement resources, and the leadership role the country has often assumed in helping to craft and enforce international criminal law norms.

Because the ICC as an institution is taking its first steps, it remains to be seen whether the Court can, through able, politic, and important prosecutions and judicious declinations, win the trust, confidence, and ultimately the accession of non-states parties — particularly those wealthy and populous countries that could do much to support and promote the ICC's mission. Much would seem to depend upon whether the fears of those nations who believe that the ICC Statute is subject

---

19. See, e.g., Jess Bravin, U.S. Warms to Hague Tribunal: New Stance Reflects Desire to Use Court to Prosecute Darfur Crimes, Wall St. J., June 14, 2006, at A4.

20. Thus, candidate Obama, in April 2008, said that "the U.S. needs to work with the International Criminal Court (ICC) to ramp up the pace of indictments of those responsible for war crimes and crimes against humanity, while Khartoum must feel increased pressure to hand over those individuals already indicted by the Court." Questions for the Record, Sen. John Kerry, Nomination of Hillary Rodham Clinton, Dept. of State, Secretary of State, Question 117, at 65. Secretary of State Clinton, during her confirmation process, asserted that "the President-Elect believes, as do I, that we should support the ICC's investigations, including its pursuit of perpetrators of genocide in Darfur." Id. at 65 (Sec. Clinton response to Question 117). She further "commended" the Bush administration's indicated "willingness to cooperate with the ICC in the Darfur investigation," which she said "we also support." Id. Secretary Clinton concluded that "[w]e can provide assistance in the investigation; we can and should work with our allies in this effort. This is important because it would send a sign of seriousness about Darfur and our determination to end the killings and bring those responsible for war crimes to justice." Id.

21. Statement by Ambassador Susan E. Rice, U.S. Permanent Representative, on Respect for International Humanitarian Law, in the Security Council (Jan. 29, 2009).

22. Id.

23. Generally, in absence of any special rules in a treaty, state signatories may include "reservations" to a treaty upon ratification, providing that the "reservations" do not contravene the "object and purpose" of the treaty. See Vienna Convention on the Law of Treaties (VCLT) art. 20. Article 120 of the Rome Statute departs from this practice by (as is acceptable under the VCLT) providing that "[n]o reservations may be made to this Statute." Why did the delegates negotiating the Rome Treaty determine to insert this provision? Why does it so trouble the United States? See Leila Nadya Sadat & S. Richard Carden, The New International Criminal Court: An Uneasy Revolution, 88 Geo. L.J. 381, 451-452 (2000).

to grievous abuse are realized. Accordingly, in the following materials, we will explore the ICC Statute in some depth, mentioning also some of the principal objections lodged by non-states parties to the ICC. Because of the complexity of the Statute under which the ICC was created and functions, we will start with a case study (Part A) through which the workings of the ICC Statute can best be explored in the materials that follow. While the entire ICC Statute is a worthy read (and is posted on our Web site), be sure to read carefully Articles 1 through 24 before attempting to tackle the case study, and refer to other Articles as required in these materials.

A.   HYPOTHETICAL CASE STUDY

In 1947, two independent nations, Rancore and Vittima, were carved out of the former Duchy of Rancore-Vittima. Rancore and Vittima share a long border. Prior to separation, Rancoris dominated the government. There was a long history of conflict due to the historical political subjugation of Vittimes by Rancoris in the former Duchy — and that conflict continues despite the separation of the Duchy into independent states. Rancoris constitute 80 percent of the population of Rancore, and Vittimes constitute almost 80 percent of Vittima's population.

In January 2003, a transborder conflict erupted between the Rancoris and the Vittimes. The United Nations moved quickly to find a political solution. Finally, the leaders of Rancore and Vittima signed the Capital Peace Accord, which established a Truth and Reconciliation Commission (TRC). The TRC was empowered to "grant a full amnesty for all criminal charges . . . arising from conduct committed during and in furtherance of the armed conflict between the ethnic Rancoris and Vittimes, to any person who makes a full disclosure of all the relevant facts relating to such acts."

While this agreement settled the transborder dispute between the two nations, it did not resolve the ongoing, small-scale fighting between ethnic Rancoris and Vittimes *within* the Vittime province of Disputa. The small ethnic Rancori population of Vittima is concentrated in the Disputa province, which is located on the border of Rancore and Vittima. The Rancori population of Disputa province — and some Rancoris within Rancore — had created the Disputa Liberation Army (DLA), whose ultimate aim was to force the succession of the Disputa province from Vittima and its unification with Rancore.

Dr. Hate was a hero among Rancoris for his service, prior to the breakup of the Duchy of Rancore-Vittima, in maintaining the Rancori's political control of the Duchy. In April 2003, Dr. Hate, a citizen of Rancore and leader of the DLA, created a two-minute audiotape in his home in Rancore. In it, he urged:

> Rancori comrades, we must rid Disputa — a part of our homeland — of its Vittime occupiers. We must stamp them out — eliminate them all: men, women, and children. If Vittime women must have babies, ensure that they are Rancori babies — by force if necessary. It is only in this way that we can obliterate Vittime blood from Disputa province and achieve the unity of our land to the greater glory of our God.

It is important to understand why Dr. Hate was advocating rape. Because both Rancoris and Vittimes believe that a child's ethnic identity follows from that of his or her father, Dr. Hate and his cohorts in the DLA believed that forced impregnation of Vittime women by Rancori rebels in Disputa province would destroy Vittime family structures and dilute the Vittime population of Disputa province.

On May 1, 2003, the ICC Statute establishing the International Criminal Court entered into force for Vittima. Rancore is not a party to the ICC Statute, which its government has constantly contended is an illegitimate, unaccountable body that constitutes a dangerous invasion of state sovereignty.

Dr. Hate's tape was duplicated and repeatedly played in Disputa province between May 1 and May 15. Beginning on May 2, mobs of ethnic Rancoris began slaughtering Vittime citizens in Disputa. By the end of May, thousands of Vittimes were dead. On June 1, 2003, Dr. Hate was served with a subpoena from the TRC, requiring him to appear before that body in 30 days to explain his role in this slaughter.

Vittima's ambassador to the United Nations asked for immediate UN intervention to halt the killings. On July 1, 2003, acting under its Chapter VII peacekeeping authority, the UN Security Council passed Resolution 2241, which authorized a multilateral force (designated as the "Disputa Peacekeeping Force" (DPF)) to go into the Disputa province of Vittima and end the violence. At the insistence of the United States (which intended to contribute troops and other support to the DPF) but over the objection of other nations (including those that had no intention of participating in the DPF), the Resolution contained the following paragraph concerning the jurisdiction of the ICC:

> Current or former officials or personnel from a contributing State which is not a party to the Rome Statute of the International Criminal Court shall be subject to the exclusive jurisdiction of that contributing State for all alleged acts or omissions arising out of or related to . . . DPF, unless such exclusive jurisdiction has been expressly waived by that contributing State.

Captain Force is a U.S. citizen and member of the U.S. armed forces assigned to the DPF. On July 28, 2003, the day after the arrival of the first DPF troops in Disputa, DLA snipers attacked the peacekeeping force under Captain Force's command. Captain Force ordered his platoon to attack and destroy a nearby village, Gravesend, alleged in DPF intelligence reports to be a DLA stronghold. Captain Force ordered his troops to use every weapon at their disposal to eliminate the threat. The extraordinary artillery barrage that followed killed hundreds of noncombatants and destroyed every structure in the town.

It was later determined that the intelligence reports were mistaken. Gravesend was not a DLA stronghold and had, in fact, been undefended. All those killed were civilians. When this information was revealed, Captain Force was relieved of his command and dismissed from the DPF. The U.S. army conducted an inquiry but declined to court martial Captain Force under the U.S. Uniform Code of Military Justice. Captain Force was discharged from the army, however; he returned to the United States in disgrace and, finding no other employment, turned his hand to large-scale drug dealing.

Pursuant to a referral by France, the ICC prosecutor conducted an investigation into the allegations of criminal conduct lodged against Dr. Hate and Captain Force. Ultimately, Captain Force was charged with commission of war crimes under the following provisions of the ICC Statute:

> ICC Article 8(2)(b)(iv): "Intentionally launching an attack in the knowledge that such attack will cause incidental loss of life or injury to civilians or damage to civilian objects . . . which would be clearly excessive in relation to the concrete and direct overall military advantage anticipated."
>
> ICC Article 8(2)(b)(xiii): "Destroying or seizing the enemy's property unless such destruction or seizure be imperatively demanded by the necessities of war."

Dr. Hate was charged with war crimes and incitement to genocide under the following provisions of the ICC Statute:

> ICC Article 8(2)(b)(xxii): "Committing rape . . . [or] forced pregnancy . . . or any other form of sexual violence also constituting a grave breach of the Geneva Conventions."
>
> ICC Article 6: Genocide involving "the following acts committed with intent to destroy, in whole or in part, a national, ethnical, racial or religious group, as such: (a) Killing members of the group; . . . (d) Imposing measures intended to prevent births within the group."
>
> ICC Article 25: "Permitting, inter alia, imposition of individual criminal responsibility on: persons who solicit or induce others to commit the crime; persons who in any other way contribute to the commission of the crime by a group of persons acting with common purpose; and persons who directly and publicly incite others to commit genocide."

The Rancore legislature has never passed criminal statutes outlawing war crimes or genocide as such, but Rancore does have criminal statutes that provide for the punishment of rape and murder.

You will be asked to examine various issues raised by this hypothetical in the following readings.

B.   JURISDICTION, ADMISSIBILITY, AND OTHER ESSENTIALS

For the ICC to investigate or exercise jurisdiction over a case, a number of requisites must be met. As a preliminary matter, one must understand the terminology used to describe these requisites. The ICC Statute distinguishes between two concepts: jurisdiction and admissibility.

"Jurisdiction" refers to the legal limits of the Court's reach and is expressed in terms of jurisdiction over time (jurisdiction *ratione temporis*), subject matter (jurisdiction *ratione materiae*), space (jurisdiction *ratione loci*), as well as over particular persons (jurisdiction *ratione personae*). Generally, when issues of jurisdiction arise, the question relates to whether the ICC can delve into the investigation or prosecution of a given "situation" — where a crime may have been committed but a particular "case" has not yet been identified or made. The rules of jurisdiction are strict, and, under ICC Article 19(1), the Court *must* satisfy itself that it has jurisdiction, whether or not the issue is raised by the parties.

By contrast, ICC Article 19(1) provides that the Court "*may*, on its own motion, determine the admissibility of a case" (emphasis added). "Admissibility" relates to a foundational principle upon which the ICC is built: "complementarity." In short, the ICC is intended to "complement" the functioning of national justice systems, not to supplant them. The ICC will declare a case "inadmissible" if a state with jurisdiction over the case is, in good faith, investigating or has prosecuted or declined to prosecute the alleged miscreants. As this implies, the question of admissibility generally (but not always) arises later — when "situations" perhaps warranting the exercise of ICC jurisdiction have been winnowed down to a "case" relating to specific persons and events. The ICC may have jurisdiction over a "situation" by virtue of where it was perpetrated or by whom it was committed, yet the Court may decline to hear a case as "inadmissible" because the individual suspect is being prosecuted by a competent national legal system.

The following checklist, explored in more detail in the materials that follow, may be helpful. This checklist does not refer to the general objections available in criminal law, such as statute of limitations bars or the principle of legality, but those objections will also be discussed as appropriate in the following materials. One does not necessarily have to deal with these issues in this order; we have ordered them in the way that seems most logical to us.

1. *Temporal jurisdiction*: Was the crime "committed after the entry into force" of the ICC Statute on July 1, 2002? (ICC arts. 11, 24(1))
2. *Subject matter jurisdiction*: Is a qualifying crime alleged — that is, does the conduct constitute genocide, a war crime, a crime against humanity, or (once this offense is defined) the crime of aggression? (ICC art. 5)
3. *Territorial or personal jurisdiction*: Absent a Security Council referral, was the crime committed on the territory of a state, or by a national of a state, that is either (1) a state party to the ICC Statute or (2) a state that consented to jurisdiction of the ICC on an ad hoc basis? (ICC art. 12)
4. *Qualifying trigger for exercise of jurisdiction*: Was the "situation" at issue referred to the prosecutor by a state party or by the Security Council, or was the investigation initiated by the prosecution after approval by a Pre-Trial Chamber? (ICC arts. 13-15)
5. *Security Council "deferral" of jurisdiction*: Is the action barred by a competent Security Council resolution? (ICC art. 16)
6. *Admissibility/complementarity*: Is a state with jurisdiction over the crime investigating it, or has such a state prosecuted or declined prosecution? Is the state claiming primacy willing and able "genuinely" to carry out the investigation or prosecution, or has the state declining prosecution made that decision out of an unwillingness or inability of the state "genuinely" to prosecute? Is the crime "of sufficient gravity to justify further action by the Court"? (ICC art. 17)

1.   Temporal Jurisdiction

Under Article 11(1), the ICC has jurisdiction only with respect to *crimes committed after the entry into force of the statute on July 1, 2002.* It is worth stressing that ICC Article 11 is a jurisdictional requirement, not a statute of limitations. Indeed, ICC Article 29 expressly provides that "[t]he crimes within the jurisdiction of the Court shall not be subject to any statute of limitations."

NOTES AND QUESTIONS

1. *The strange case of ICC Article 11(2).* The ICC Statute entered into force on July 1, 2002, pursuant to ICC Article 126(1). The crimes in our case study all occurred after that date, and thus Article 11 is not a bar to jurisdiction. Note that, with respect to states that ratified the ICC Statute after July 1, 2002, the Statute enters into force on the first day of the month after the sixtieth day following the deposit of that state's instrument of ratification. See ICC art. 126(2). Under Article 126(2), the ICC Statute became operative as to Vittima on May 1, 2003. Need the crimes alleged also have occurred after *this* date?

Article 11(2) provides that, if a state becomes a party to the Statute "after its entry into force, the Court may exercise its jurisdiction only with respect to *crimes committed* after the entry into force of this Statute *for that State*, unless that State has [given its ad hoc consent through] . . . a declaration under article 12, paragraph 3." ICC art. 11(2) (emphasis added). Note that, as is discussed at greater length below, nationals of non-states parties can be subject in some circumstances to ICC jurisdiction — for example, where they commit atrocities on the soil of a state party or where the situation in which they are involved is referred to the ICC by the UN Security Council. Does Article 11(2) mean that crimes committed by nationals of the new state party, or events occurring in the territory of the new state party, *after* the entry into force of the Statute (July 1, 2002) but *before* 60 days after the deposit of the new state party's ratification instrument are outside the ICC's jurisdiction? That is, could states worried about prosecution of their nationals essentially immunize their nationals from ICC investigation of crimes committed during this period by *joining* the ICC?

One could perhaps extrapolate this from the meaning ascribed to the article by U.S. Ambassador David Scheffer, the leading U.S. diplomat in the negotiation of the Rome Treaty. He argues that Article 11(2) must mean that citizens of a state cannot fall under ICC jurisdiction for crimes they commit before the statute enters into force for *that country* because "otherwise one would have to argue that the requirement set out in Article 126(2) is meaningless with respect to the ratifying state's citizens, who, presumably, must have been subject to the jurisdiction of the ICC since 1 July 2002 (when the ICC became operational pursuant to Article 126(1))." David J. Scheffer, How to Turn the Tide Using the Rome Statute's Temporal Jurisdiction, 2 J. Intl. Crim. Just. 26, 29 (2004).

2. *Continuing or "straddle" crimes.* Returning to our case study, Captain Force's conduct occurred after the entry into force of the ICC Statute with respect to Vittima. How about Dr. Hate? If Dr. Hate's crime is deemed to have been committed when he taped his exhortation to genocide (April 2003), his crime would predate the entry into force of the Rome Treaty with respect to Vittima. Could the ICC prosecutor take the position that Dr. Hate's crime was not "committed" when he made the tape, but rather when it was disseminated? Could one argue that it was a "continuing" or "straddle" crime? This is a potentially important subcategory of cases, at least in the short term (before the ICC's temporal jurisdictional limitations become, through the inevitable passage of time, less important). Such continuing or straddle crimes might include, for example, forced "disappearances" or the forcible transfer or deportation of populations. These crimes might be initiated before the entry into force of the Statute, but may be said to "continue" after that date to the extent that the "disappearance" of persons continues or the displacement of populations persists. "[T]he issue of 'continuous crimes' remains undecided and it will be for the Court to determine how it should be handled." William A. Schabas, An Introduction to the International Criminal Court 72 (2d ed. 2004) (hereinafter, Schabas, Introduction to the ICC); see also Alan Nissel, Continuing Crimes in the ICC Statute, 25 Mich. J. Intl. L. 653 (2004).

3. *Seven-year war crimes opt-out.* The ICC Statute makes its own exception to ICC Article 120's bar on reservations by providing in ICC Article 124 that "a State, on becoming a party to this Statute, may declare that, for a period of seven years after the entry into force of this Statute for the State concerned, it does not accept the jurisdiction of the Court" with respect to the war crimes described in ICC Article 8 "when a crime is alleged to have been committed by its nationals or on its territory." Note that this war crime jurisdictional "opt-out" extends for seven years after the ICC Statute

enters into force for that joining state party. By its terms, this jurisdictional opt-out is not available to non-states parties.

Note that ICC Article 123(1) requires that the UN convene a Review Conference seven years after the entry into force of the statute (to be held in the first half of 2010). The only item required to be on the agenda is Article 124's war crimes opt-out. Only Colombia and France have entered Article 124 reservations to their ratifications, and France has since withdrawn its opt-out. Some believe that the lack of interest in this opt-out means that the Assembly of States Parties will eliminate it in 2010.

4. *Provisions that advantage states parties: Opt-outs for crimes added by amendment to ICC jurisdiction.* ICC Article 124 is not the only provision that potentially shields states parties while leaving the nationals of non-states parties at risk. ICC Article 121(5), which governs certain amendments to the ICC Statute, states:

> Any amendment to [the articles that provide what crimes fall within the subject-matter of the court (Art. 5) and define genocide (Art. 6), crimes against humanity (Art. 7), and war crimes (Art. 8)] shall enter into force for those States Parties which have accepted the amendment one year after the deposit of their instruments of ratification or acceptance. In respect of a State Party which has not accepted the amendment, the Court *shall not exercise its jurisdiction regarding a crime covered by the amendment when committed by that State Party's nationals or on its territory* (emphasis added).

States that *join* the treaty, then, can *shield* their citizens from jurisdiction over crimes not presently in the ICC Statute but later added through amendment to the Article specified. There is no similar "out," however, for non-state party nationals. In theory, at least, this means that the nationals of non-states parties could be prosecuted in the ICC for offenses — like drug trafficking or terrorism — that may be later added to the court's jurisdiction, while states parties could exempt their own citizens from liability for the same crimes.

Given the above, if a state is truly concerned with shielding its nationals from unwarranted ICC prosecution, shouldn't it *join* the Court? First, if Article 126(2) is read in the way suggested above, the nationals of newly joining states would seem to get an ICC pass for any alleged misconduct that occurred after July 1, 2002, but before the sixtieth day following the deposit of the state's instrument of ratification. The newly joining state could then opt out of the war crimes provision for seven years under ICC Article 124. Finally, it could shield its nationals (apparently indefinitely) from exposure to any crimes that the Assembly of States Parties decides to add to the ICC's jurisdiction under Article 121(5).

Presumably this scheme is designed to encourage states to ratify the ICC Statute. But does this make any sense when measured in terms of the purported object and purpose of the Statute? Is it fair to nonconsenting states? To illustrate, could two states enter into a treaty creating an international criminal tribunal with jurisdiction over every national in the world, except the citizens of the two states parties? Could they then offer to open the treaty court to other states and, as an incentive for membership, provide that joining states' nationals would also be exempt from the treaty court's jurisdiction?

2.   Subject Matter Jurisdiction

The ICC Statute states that the ICC "has jurisdiction in accordance with this Statute with respect to" the crime of genocide, crimes against humanity, war crimes, and the crime of aggression under ICC Articles 5(1), (2). ICC Article 70 also provides the ICC with jurisdiction over various "offences against [the] administration of justice." These offenses include perjury or presentation of false evidence, witness tampering, and corrupting, bribing, or retaliating against, court officials.

NOTES AND QUESTIONS

1. *The crime of aggression.* The inclusion of the crime of aggression within the ICC's jurisdiction was very controversial both because of the difficulty of arriving at a legal definition of the crime and because of a potential conflict between the ICC's jurisdiction and the role of the UN Security Council. China and the United States, both permanent members of the Security Council, were particularly concerned about the potential this grant of jurisdiction would have to undermine the authority of the Security Council under the UN Charter. See, e.g., Lu Jianping & Wang Zhixiang, China's Attitude Toward the ICC, 3 J. Intl. Crim. Just. 608, 612 (2005). These issues were not resolved at Rome; instead, the ICC Statute provides that the ICC "shall exercise jurisdiction over the crime of aggression once a provision is adopted . . . defining the crime and setting out the conditions under which the Court shall exercise jurisdiction with respect to this crime." ICC art. 5(2). ICC Article 123(1) states that the United Nations Review Conference, now scheduled for 2010, "may include, but is not limited to, the list of crimes contained in article 5." A special working group has been meeting annually since 2004 to come up with a draft definition of the crime of aggression for consideration at the Review Conference. See Noah Weisbord, Prosecuting Aggression, 49 Harv. Intl. L.J. 161, 161 (2008).

Why might states have difficulty arriving at a definition of aggression? Recall that the centerpiece of the Nuremberg trials was the charge of crimes against peace — the conduct of illegal war — in violation of applicable treaties, but the prosecution was not for aggression per se. And not every case in which aggression is claimed results from acts as blatant as Nazi Germany's attempts to conquer its neighbors. Part of the definitional difficulty stems from a concern that "many international rules on the legitimate use of force are disputed." Ruth Wedgwood, The Irresolution of Rome, 64 Law & Contemp. Probs. 193, 209-210 (2001). In particular, the debate over the appropriate contours of self-defense under customary international law (CIL) and the UN Charter continues. "The international legal community entertains a range of views about the limits of anticipatory self-defense, for example, when a hostile power acquires weapons of mass destruction with an apparent willingness to use them, or harbors a terrorist group with similar ambitions." Ruth Wedgwood, The United States and the International Criminal Court: Achieving a Wider Consensus Through the "Ithaca Package," 32 Cornell Intl. L.J. 535, 538 (1999). There is also disagreement over whether "humanitarian interventions" not authorized by the United Nations — like NATO's intervention in Kosovo — can be squared with the Charter's rules. Finally, some question whether the military forces of one country may pursue and attack terrorist groups who are retreating over a national border into the territory of another nation without that nation's consent; this is known as the "hot pursuit" question and it is one that has been highly relevant recently. See, e.g., Hot Pursuit: Legal or Illegal under International Law?, Intl. Rev., Spring 2009.

In the years after World War II, a number of attempts were made to define the crime of aggression, but none succeeded. Finally, in 1974, the UN General Assembly adopted Resolution 3314 (XXIX), U.N. Doc. A/RES/3314 (Dec. 14, 1974), which defined aggression but not for the purposes of criminal jurisdiction. Resolution 3314 stated that aggression is "the use of armed force by a State against the sovereignty, territorial integrity or political independence of another State, or in any other manner inconsistent with" the UN Charter. Id. art. 1. The General Assembly Resolution then listed seven illustrative, nonexclusive acts—such as the blockade of ports or invasion of another state's territory—that qualify as acts of aggression, subject to an important proviso. Id. art. 3. That proviso states that although the first use of armed force by a state in contravention of the Charter would constitute prima facie evidence of aggression, and although the seven listed actions facially qualify as acts of aggression, the Security Council may, "in conformity with the Charter, conclude that a determination that an act of aggression has been committed would not be justified in the light of other relevant circumstances, including the fact that the acts concerned or their consequences are not of sufficient gravity." Id. art. 2. In other words, G.A. Resolution 3314's "definition" of aggression is highly contextual and political in nature and identified the Security Council as the ultimate expert on the identification of true acts of aggression. While some viewed this as a breakthrough, others noted that "the definition was designed as guidance to the U.N. Security Council, not as a basis for prosecution." Weisbord, supra, 49 Harv. Intl. L.J. at 168.

The above illustrates that the definitional challenge is tied up in another issue: the question of institutional allocation of the responsibility for identifying aggression. Article 39 of the UN Charter states that "[t]he Security Council shall determine the existence of any threat to the peace, breach of the peace, or act of aggression and shall make recommendations, or decide what measures shall be taken in accordance with Articles 41 and 42, to maintain or restore international peace and security." Article 39 of the UN Charter says that identifying unlawful *acts* of aggression by *states* is the task primarily of the Security Council, but does this mean that the ICC can prosecute *individuals* for the *crime* of aggression only if the Security Council has referred the case to the ICC? The concluding sentence of ICC Article 5(2) states that the provision defining the crime of aggression and the conditions under which the ICC shall exercise jurisdiction over it "shall be consistent with the relevant provisions of the Charter of the United Nations." This was "a 'carefully constructed phrase' that was 'understood as a reference to the role the Council may or should play.'" Schabas, supra, Introduction to the ICC at 32 (citation omitted). What role *should* the Security Council play, and why? Consider the definition and triggering mechanism proposed by the special working group as of March 2009. Is this proposal workable?

Article 8*bis*

Crime of aggression

1. For the purpose of this Statute, "crime of aggression" means the planning, preparation, initiation or execution, by a person in a position effectively to exercise control over or to direct the political or military action of a State, of an act of aggression which, by its character, gravity and scale, constitutes a manifest violation of the Charter of the United Nations.

2. For the purpose of paragraph 1, "act of aggression" means the use of armed force by a State against the sovereignty, territorial integrity or political independence of another State, or in any other manner inconsistent with the Charter of the United Nations. Any of the following acts, regardless of a declaration of war, shall, in accordance with United Nations General Assembly resolution 3314 (XXIX) of 14 December 1974, qualify as an act of aggression:

(a) The invasion or attack by the armed forces of a State of the territory of another State, or any military occupation, however temporary, resulting from such invasion or attack, or any annexation by the use of force of the territory of another State or part thereof;

(b) Bombardment by the armed forces of a State against the territory of another State or the use of any weapons by a State against the territory of another State;

(c) The blockade of the ports or coasts of a State by the armed forces of another State;

(d) An attack by the armed forces of a State on the land, sea or air forces, or marine and air fleets of another State;

(e) The use of armed forces of one State which are within the territory of another State with the agreement of the receiving State, in contravention of the conditions provided for in the agreement or an extension of their presence in such territory beyond the termination of the agreement;

(f) The action of a State in allowing its territory, which it has placed at the disposal of another State, to be used by that State for perpetrating an act of aggression against a third State;

(g) The sending by or on behalf of a State of armed bands, groups, irregulars or mercenaries, which carry out acts of armed force against another State of such gravity as to amount to the acts listed above, or its substantial involvement therein.

ARTICLE 15*BIS*
EXERCISE OF JURISDICTION OVER THE CRIME OF AGGRESSION

1. The Court may exercise jurisdiction over the crime of aggression in accordance with article 13, subject to the provisions of this article.

2. Where the prosecutor concludes that there is a reasonable basis to proceed with an investigation in respect of a crime of aggression, he or she shall first ascertain whether the Security Council has made a determination of an act of aggression committed by the State concerned. The prosecutor shall notify the Secretary-General of the United Nations of the situation before the Court, including any relevant information and documents.

3. Where the Security Council has made such a determination, the Prosecutor may proceed with the investigation in respect of a crime of aggression,

4. **(Alternative 1)** In the absence of such a determination, the Prosecutor may not proceed with the investigation in respect of a crime of aggression,

Option 1 — end the paragraph here.

Option 2 — add: unless the Security Council has, in a resolution adopted under Chapter VII of the Charter of the United Nations, requested the Prosecutor to proceed with the investigation in respect of a crime of aggression.

4. **(Alternative 2)** Where no such determination is made within [6] months after the date of notification, the Prosecutor may proceed with the investigation in respect of a crime of aggression.

Option 1 — end the paragraph here.

Option 2 — add: provided that the Pre-Trial Chamber has authorized the commencement of the investigation in respect of a crime of aggression in accordance with the procedure contained in article 15;

Option 3 — add: provided that the General Assembly has determined that an act of aggression has been committed by the State referred to in article 8*bis*;

Option 4 — add: provided that the International Court of Justice has determined that an act of aggression has been committed by the State referred to in article 8*bis*.

5. A determination of an act of aggression by an organ outside the Court shall be without prejudice to the Court's determination of an act of aggression under this Statute.

6. This article is without prejudice to the provisions relating to the exercise of jurisdiction with respect to other crimes referred to in article 5.

Recall that under ICC Article 121(5), states parties can opt out where new crimes are added to the statute. May states parties opt out of ICC jurisdiction over aggression committed by its nationals if they do not like the definition ultimately adopted? (Note that non-states parties could not opt out.) Some argue that the above *additions* to the statute would not constitute "amendments to" Articles 5 through 8 and thus that the opt-out amendment procedure of Article 121(5) does not apply. If ICC Article 121(5) does not apply, then the other provision pertaining to substantive amendments to the statute — ICC Article 121(4) — would. Article 121 requires a two-thirds majority to "adopt" such amendments. See ICC art. 121(3). However, the amendment enters into force only when *seven-eighths* of states parties individually deposit instruments of ratification with the UN. See ICC art. 121(4). If a state party objects to the amendment, it has the right to withdraw from the treaty regime with "immediate effect." ICC art. 121(6). The question of which amendment procedure applies is receiving a great deal of attention from the states parties. Why?

2. *Genocide, crimes against humanity, and war crimes.* Our case study posits that Dr. Hate is charged with incitement to genocide and the war crimes of rape and forced pregnancy, and that Captain Force has been charged with war crimes. War crimes and genocide fit within the ICC's subject matter jurisdiction. What arguments can be made that the ICC does not have, or should not exercise, subject matter jurisdiction over these cases?

Note that Dr. Hate is charged with soliciting or inducing the war crime of rape under ICC Articles 8(2)(b)(xxii) and 25. Rape has long been expressly prohibited under international humanitarian law, but the relevant provisions of that law did not define rape. The definition of rape included in the ICC Statute and its Elements of Crimes was derived in large part from the case law generated by the Ad Hoc Tribunals. Similarly, the war crime charge of forced pregnancy under ICC Article 8(2)(b)(xxii) was defined for the first time in the ICC Statute. Finally, the Ad Hoc Tribunals broke new ground in recognizing that rape, in some circumstances, can constitute genocide.

As we explore at length below, one of the most controversial aspects of the ICC Statute is its assertion of jurisdiction over nationals of non-states parties in some circumstances. Some object, then, that the Statute exposes the citizens of non-states parties to "new" international criminal prohibitions not necessarily shared by the non-states parties' criminal codes. As Professor Marc Weller has explained:

> While the genuine universality of the crime of genocide, crimes against humanity and grave breaches of the Geneva law is not doubted, it is asserted that the ICC Statute expands upon the definitions of two out of these three crimes. Article 7 of the Statute offers an extensive definition of crimes against humanity. It includes, for instance, deportation or forcible transfer of populations, sexual slavery and other forms of sexual violence, enforced disappearance of persons and the crime of apartheid. Article 8 on war crimes goes beyond the crimes established as grave breaches of the Geneva law, offering "innovations" such as the intentional attacks on personnel or installations involved in international humanitarian operations or peace-keeping missions. The Statute is also quite liberal in ascribing universality to crimes committed in internal armed conflicts.

Marc Weller, Undoing the Global Constitution: U.N. Security Council Action on the International Criminal Court, 78 Intl. Aff. 693, 700 (2002); see also Guy Roberts, Assault on Sovereignty: The Clear and Present Danger of the New International Criminal Court, 17 Am. Univ. Intl. L. Rev. 35 (2001).

Further, some have objected to the vague and necessarily subjective nature of some of the ICC's proscriptions — and contend that many of these provisions require a second-guessing of military judgments by nonexpert civilians. Consider, for example, the case of Captain Force. Under ICC Article 8(2)(b)(iv), who determines whether the attack ordered "would be clearly excessive" in relation to the overall military advantage anticipated? Who determines whether Captain Force was entitled to rely on what turned out to be faulty intelligence? Under ICC Article 8(2)(b)(xiii), who determines whether the destruction of enemy property was "imperatively demanded by the necessities of war"? Presumably, these judgments are left in the first instance to the ICC prosecutor and, in the final analysis, to the ICC judges who adjudicate guilt or innocence. Can or should the ICC be charged with making these determinations? Are there any objective sources to which ICC actors may look in applying these provisions?

All of this leads to a number of important questions. Does the inclusion of these crimes in the ICC Statute mean that they have become part of CIL? What *is* the relationship between CIL and the ICC Statute? To the extent that the ICC Statute's definition of genocide does not expressly refer to rape, may the ICC Judges rely upon the case law developed by the ICTY and ICTR in interpreting their statute and the Elements of Crimes? What *are* the appropriate sources of law that ICC judges may look to in deciding the content of these crimes? Consider the following notes in attempting to answer these questions.

3. *The relationship between CIL and the ICC Statute.* What is the relation between how the ICC Statute defines the core crimes over which the ICC has jurisdiction and the state of CIL as developed in Nuremberg and subsequent tribunals? Certainly the Statute, as the product of a global diplomatic conference specifically called to define core crimes, can logically be taken — *in general* — as an authoritative expression of what states believe to be the current articulation of those crimes. However, the Statute does appear to expand the law developed in earlier tribunals in a number of areas, particularly coverage of internal armed conflicts and crimes of sexual violence. See, e.g., David J. Scheffer, U.S. Policy and the International Criminal Court, 32 Cornell Intl. L.J. 529, 530-531 (1999). Thus, Professor Schabas asserts that "while the correspondence with customary international law is close, it is far from perfect." Schabas, supra, Introduction to the ICC at 28.

ICC Article 10 declares that "[n]othing in this Part shall be interpreted as limiting or prejudicing in any way existing or developing rules of international law for purposes other than this Statute." "[T]his Part" means Part 2 of the ICC Statute, which includes Articles 5 through 21. Article 10 reflects the fact that the ICC Statute embodies a number of hard-fought compromises: "The purpose of article 10 is *first*, to avoid the impression that what has thus been codified is the only possible interpretation or a reflection of the minimum consent in the community of nations as a whole and *second*, to guard against these impressions being used to thwart the future development of international law outside the Statute." Otto Triffterer, Article 10, in Commentary on the Rome Statute of the International Criminal Court: Observers' Notes, Article by Article 317 (Otto Triffterer ed., 1999).

Some who argue that CIL goes *beyond* the prohibitions contained in the ICC Statute may wish to rely on this provision. This will become more important if CIL continues to evolve while the ICC Statute does not keep pace. For example, some countries wish CIL to evolve in particular directions not addressed in the ICC Statute. India explained that one of the three points of principle that prevented it from voting in favor of the ICC Statute was the fact that the Statute does not explicitly make first use of nuclear weapons a crime. See Indian Statement, supra note 13. If CIL were to develop such a norm, it may be that the ICC Statute will not keep pace because of its cumbersome amendment procedure (discussed within). Yet Article 10 can cut both ways. "To those who claim that the Statute sets a new minimum standard, for example in the field of gender crimes, conservative jurists will plead Article 10 and stress the differences between the texts in the Statute and their less prolix ancestors in the Geneva Conventions and related instruments." Schabas, supra, Introduction to the ICC, at 28.

4. *Interpretive principles and sources of law.* If a given prohibition in the ICC Statute is "new" to international tribunal charters, was apparently intended to reflect the case law developed in the Ad Hoc Tribunals, or is ambiguous in content or application, what rules and sources of law should guide ICC judges? The Court, in interpreting the ICC Statute, will necessarily be bound by the various provisions in the Statute that embody the legality principle. ICC Article 22(1) reflects the prohibition on retroactive *offenses* (*nulla crimen sine lege*), stating that a "person shall not be criminally responsible under this Statute unless the conduct in question constitutes, at the time it takes place, a crime within the jurisdiction of the Court." To make clear the interpretive approach necessary to this principle, the ICC Statute requires that "[t]he definition of a crime shall be strictly construed and shall not be extended by analogy. In case of ambiguity, the definition shall be interpreted in favour of the person being investigated, prosecuted or convicted." ICC art. 22(2). ICC Article 23, which embodies the prohibition on retroactive *penalties* (*nulla poena sine lege*) states that "[a] person convicted by the Court may be punished only in accordance with this Statute." Finally, ICC Article 24(2) requires that, "[i]n the event of a change in the law applicable to a given case prior to a final judgement, the law more favourable to the person being investigated, prosecuted or convicted shall apply."

Article 21 of the ICC Statute sets forth an explicit hierarchy of applicable law. "Article 21 constitutes the first codification of the sources of international *criminal* law. . . . The principal challenge faced in drafting article 21 was the need to adhere to the principle of *nullum crimen sine lege* in the context of the loosely structured international legal order, which lacks a sovereign legislature." Margaret McAuliffe deGuzman, Article 21: Applicable Law, in Commentary on the Rome Statute of the International Criminal Court: Observers' Notes, Article by Article 438 (Otto Triffterer ed., 1999) [hereinafter deGuzman, Observers' Notes]. Those drafting this article, then, wrestled with how much discretion to afford judges to "legislate" through interpretation.

Article 21(1)(a) provides that the ICC Statute itself, and the Elements of Crimes and Rules of Procedure and Evidence, are the primary sources of authority. In the event of an inconsistency between the Statutes and these Elements or Rules, the ICC Statute prevails. See ICC arts. 51(5), 9(3). In its first few opinions, the Appeals Chamber declined to venture further down the interpretive hierarchy, deciding that the Statute and Rules are sufficiently complete to answer questions at least of procedural concern. In particular, where the Statute and Rules do not expressly address a given issue, the Appeals Chamber has resisted invitations to fill the asserted "lacuna" by reference to other sources of law. See, e.g., Jason Manning, On Power, Participation and Authority: The International Criminal Court's Initial Appellate Jurisprudence, 38 Geo. J. Intl. L. 803, 832-839 (2007).

Second, the ICC Statute permits judges, "where appropriate," to consult conventional (treaty) law and "the principles and rules of international law, including established principles of the international law of armed conflict." ICC art. 21(1)(b). The reference to treaty law is clear. But what is meant by "the principles and rules of international law" in ICC Article 21(1)(b)? According to some commentators, the reference to "rules of international law" in ICC Article 21(1)(b) corresponds to CIL. deGuzman, supra, Observers' Notes, at 441-442. If ICC Article 21(1)(a) corresponds to the "international conventions" covered by ICJ Statute Article 38(1)(a), and ICC

Article 21(1)(b)'s reference to "rules of international law" translates into "international custom, as evidence of a general practice accepted as law" under ICJ Statute Article 38(1)(b), to what does Article 21(1)(b)'s reference to "principles . . . of international law" refer? A source of law in the ICJ statute as yet unaccounted for is "the general principles of law recognized by civilized nations." ICJ Statute art. 38(1)(c). But another subsection in this ICC article, Article 21(1)(c), concerns "general principles of law" derived from national systems. The fact that Article 21(1)(b)'s "principles . . . of international law" is included within a separate provision in the ICC Statute than Article 21(1)(c)'s "general principles of law" derived from national legal systems is, according to some observers, clear evidence that the drafters intended the two concepts to be distinct. See deGuzman, supra, Observers' Notes, at 441. If this is true, then to what does ICC Article 21(1)(b)'s "principles . . . of international law" refer? Such "principles" seem to have no corollary in the ICJ Statute or the sources of law found in the Restatement (Third) of Foreign Relations Law of the United States. What are they—natural law?

Article 21(1)(c) permits reference to "general principles of law" derived from national systems. Some states objected that Article 21 invests ICC judges with a great deal of discretion because it allows ICC judges to choose which jurisdictions they wish to consult, including whether or not to reference the laws of the states that would normally exercise jurisdiction over the crime.

ICC Article 21(2) *permits* but *does not require* the ICC to apply its own precedents to resolve a case; once again, then, it invests ICC judges with discretion in deciding the applicable law in a case. "This provision represents a compromise between the common law approach to judicial decisions as binding precedent, and the traditional civil law view that judicial pronouncements in specific cases bind only the parties before the court." deGuzman, supra, Observers' Notes, at 445. Recall that the ICJ Statute, in Article 38(1)(d), provides that "subject to the provisions of Article 59, judicial decisions and the teachings of the most highly qualified publicists of the various nations" may be consulted "as subsidiary means for the determination of rules of law." And ICJ Article 59 states that "the decision of the Court has no binding force except between the parties and in respect of that particular case." How does ICC Article 21(2) compare in its treatment of precedent and the teaching of "publicists"? In explaining the choices made in ICC Article 21(2), Margaret deGuzman notes:

> The inclusion of article 21 para. 2 in the ICC Statute points to an evolution in the attitude of the world community in this area. As an evolving body of law, without the benefits of legislative guidance, international criminal law requires a certain amount of judicial discretion. In enabling judges to take into account their prior holdings, article 21 para. 2 contributes to the development of a consistent and predictable body of international criminal law. This consistency and predictability, in turn, serves the principle of legality.

deGuzman, supra, Observers' Notes, at 445. Do you agree that there has been a meaningful "evolution" in the treatment of precedent from the ICJ to the ICC?

Finally, Article 21(3) provides, inter alia, that "[t]he application and interpretation of law pursuant to this article must be consistent with internationally recognized human rights." Does this mean that international human rights treaties will be relevant to interpretive questions? For example, a number of ICC decisions issued thus far rely on the case law of the European Court of Human Rights (ECHR), a non-criminal tribunal assessing the liability of states for asserted violations of the European Convention. Are the judges authorized to do so under Article 21?

5. *Treaty crimes.* Recall that Captain Force turned his hand to drug trafficking after his dismissal from the armed services. Why is this serious crime — which is of sufficient concern to the international community to be regulated through treaty — outside the jurisdiction of the ICC?

The initial impetus for the creation of the ICC was supplied by the prime minister of Trinidad and Tobago, who in 1989 proposed that the UN create an international court to prosecute international drug traffickers. In 1994, the UN's International Law Commission (ILC) adopted a Draft Statute for an International Criminal Court, which envisioned subject matter jurisdiction over genocide, aggression, war crimes, crimes against humanity, *and* "crimes, established under or pursuant to the treaty provisions listed in the Annex, which, having regard to the conduct alleged, constitute exceptionally serious crimes of international concern." Draft Statute for an International Criminal Court: Report of the International Law Commission on the Work of Its Forty-sixth Session, U.N. GAOR, 49th Sess., Supp. No. 10, U.N. Doc. A/49/10, art. 20(3) (1994). Such "treaty crimes" would have included terrorism and drug trafficking.

"The Rome Statute's Preparatory Committee, however, felt strongly that the Court's statute should define the crimes within its jurisdiction, rather than simply list them as the [ILC's] Draft had done. The failure to reach a consensus on the definition of treaty crimes prevented terrorism [and drug trafficking] from falling under the Court's jurisdiction." Richard J. Goldstone & Janine Simpson, Evaluating the Role of the International Criminal Court as a Legal Response to Terrorism, 16 Harv. Hum. Rts. J. 13, 14 (2003). It should be noted that although terrorism is not now part of the ICC's mandate, some acts of terrorism (and perhaps other treaty crimes) may be prosecutable as war crimes, crimes against humanity, or even genocide where the elements of those crimes are met. It is also likely that the Review Conference convened pursuant to ICC Article 123 in 2010 will revisit the question whether the ICC should be given jurisdiction over treaty crimes like certain acts of terrorism and drug trafficking.

3. Personal and Territorial Jurisdiction

a. Possible Defendants: Natural Persons

ICC Article 25 states that the ICC has "jurisdiction over natural persons pursuant to this Statute" and that "[a] person who commits a crime within the jurisdiction of the Court shall be individually responsible and liable for punishment in accordance with this Statute."

The ICC Statute does not provide for state responsibility for criminal acts — that is, states themselves cannot be charged with crimes. It does, however, add the caveat in Article 25(4) that "[n]o provision in this Statute relating to individual criminal responsibility shall affect the responsibility of States under international law." Further, the ICC Statute makes explicit that persons purporting to act on behalf of the state in committing their crimes will receive no consideration by virtue of their supposed "acts of State." ICC Article 27 provides that the Statute "shall apply equally to all persons without any distinction based on official capacity" and that "official capacity" shall "in no case exempt a person from criminal responsibility under this Statute."

Article 25 does not speak to the potential liability of legal "persons," such as governmental entities (for example, the SS or other Nazi organizations), or corporations or other business organizations. Commentators have concluded that "there can be no doubt that by limiting criminal responsibility to individual natural persons, the Rome Statute implicitly negates — at least for its own jurisdiction — the punishability of corporations and other legal entities."[24] Does this make sense given the nature of the atrocities with which international criminal law is concerned? As Professor Osiel queries,

> [c]ontrasted with conventional crimes, those conducted by a single person or small cabal, state atrocities are instead often "the product of collective, systematic, often-bureaucratic activity, made possible only by the collaboration of massive and complex organizations in the execution of criminal policies at the highest levels of government. How then, is individual responsibility to be located, limited, and defined within the vast bureaucratic apparatuses that make possible the pulling of a trigger or the dropping of a gas canister in some far-flung place?"[25]

Although early drafts contained provisions for the liability of legal entities — primarily to facilitate restitutionary and compensatory orders for victims — these proposals were rejected by the negotiators of the Rome Statute for a variety of reasons. First, it was thought that the Court's focus should be on individual, not collective, liability, on the theory that "[c]rimes against international law are committed by men, not by abstract entities, and only by punishing individuals who commit such crimes can the provisions of international law be enforced."[26] It was also believed that prosecuting legal entities would create serious practical problems. There is, as yet, no universally recognized standard for corporate liability, and the concept is in fact not even recognized in many criminal law systems. In such circumstances, the principle of complementarity (of ICC Article 17) would be rendered unworkable for at least some countries. Finally, "it was felt 'morally obtuse for States to insist on the criminal responsibility of all entities other than themselves.' "[27] What considerations might argue *for* provision of liability for legal "persons" such as corporations?[28]

b. Jurisdiction

We know from earlier readings that CIL recognizes the legitimacy of the exercise of a state's domestic criminal jurisdiction over potentially transborder criminality on four bases: territory (subjective or objective ("effects")), nationality (active and passive), protective, and universal jurisdiction. Under ICC Article 12, the ICC's jurisdiction over persons is defined by reference to territory and nationality, even though the ICC has neither (because it is an international court, not a sovereign state).

---

24. See, e.g., Albin Eser, Individual Criminal Responsibility, in I The Rome Statute of the International Criminal Court: A Commentary 767, 778 (A. Cassese, P. Gaeta, & J. Jones eds., 2002) [hereinafter Eser, Individual Responsibility]; Kai Ambos, Article 25: Individual Responsibility, Commentary on the Rome Statute of the International Criminal Court: Observers' Notes 475, 478 (Otto Triffterer ed., 1999) [hereinafter Ambos, Observers' Notes].

25. Mark Osiel, The Banality of Good: Aligning Incentives Against Mass Atrocity, 105 Colum. L. Rev. 1751, 1767 (2005) (quoting David Cohen, Beyond Nuremberg: Individual Responsibility for War Crimes, in Human Rights in Political Transitions: Gettysburg to Bosnia 53 (1999)).

26. I Trial of the Major War Criminals 223 (1947).

27. Eser, Individual Responsibility, supra note 24, at 779.

28. See also Diane Marie Amann, Capital Punishment: Corporate Criminal Liability for Gross Violations of Human Rights, 24 Hastings Intl. & Comp. L. Rev. 327 (2001); Andrew Clapham & Scott Jerbi, Categories of Corporate Complicity in Human Rights Abuses, 24 Hastings Intl. & Comp. L. Rev. 339 (2001); cf. Steven R. Ratner, Corporations and Human Rights: A Theory of Legal Responsibility, 111 Yale L.J. 443 (2001).

NOTES AND QUESTIONS

1. *The ICC's territorial and nationality jurisdiction.* With respect to jurisdiction over the person, the ICC Statute provides that the ICC has jurisdiction over crimes *committed by*:

> i. The national of a state party, wherever the crimes occurred; and
> ii. Nationals of *non*-states parties, wherever the crimes occurred, if the non-state party accepts the ad hoc jurisdiction of the ICC over such defendant nationals; and
> iii. Nationals of states parties or *non*-states parties, wherever the crimes occurred, in situations referred to the ICC by the U.N. Security Council.

See ICC arts. 12(2)(b) & (3), 13(b).

With respect to *territory*, the ICC has jurisdiction over:

> i. Crimes committed on the territory of states parties, whether or not the perpetrator is a national of a state party;
> ii. Crimes committed on the territory of a *non*-state party where that territorial state accepts the ad hoc jurisdiction of the ICC, whether or not the perpetrator is a national of a state party; and
> iii. Crimes committed on the territory of a state party or a non-state party in situations referred to the ICC by the Security Council, whether or not the perpetrator is a national of a state party.

See ICC arts. 12(2)(a) & (3), 13(b).

It is very important to note that ICC Article 12(2) limits ad hoc consents to non-states parties *on whose territory the crime occurred* or whose nationals *committed* the crimes. It would *not* permit, for example, (1) a state whose nationals were *victimized* in another country to confer jurisdiction by ad hoc consent, or (2) a state exercising universal jurisdiction to make an ad hoc "delegation" of the investigation or prosecution of that case to the ICC.

Returning to our case study, neither Dr. Hate (a Rancori citizen) nor Captain Force (a U.S. citizen) is a national of ICC states parties. Assume that neither the United States nor Rancore gives ad hoc consent to ICC jurisdiction over their nationals. In what circumstances would the ICC have jurisdiction over Dr. Hate and Captain Force?

2. *Jurisdiction over non-states parties' nationals.* Many non-states parties object to the ICC's jurisdiction over their nationals. The above-described scheme means that the ICC could exercise such jurisdiction in three situations.

First, if the UN Security Council refers a situation for investigation by the ICC, the court will have jurisdiction over qualifying crimes committed by anyone involved in the situation. Thus, for example, although Sudan is a non-state party to the ICC and the alleged crimes under investigation by the OTP took place on Sudanese territory and involve Sudanese nationals, the ICC has jurisdiction by virtue of the Security Council referral of the Darfur situation to the court.

Second, non-states parties' nationals fall within ICC's jurisdiction if they commit qualifying crimes on the territory of any of the 110 ICC states parties. ICC art. 12(2)(a). Russia—a non-state party to the ICC—is currently dealing with this reality because the ICC prosecutor is conducting a preliminary exploration of charges that Russian soldiers committed war crimes on the territory of an ICC state party, Georgia. The American Non-governmental Organizations Coalition for the International Criminal Court, Communications to the ICC and Other Actions Regarding the Situation in Georgia (Sept. 10, 2008), *available at* http://www.amicc.org/docs/

Georgia.pdf. As far as Captain Force is concerned, his crimes occurred in the territory of a state party (Vittima), and he is therefore subject to ICC jurisdiction, assuming the ICC can secure custody of him.

What about Dr. Hate? Where did he "commit" the alleged crime? He made the tape in Rancore, but it was distributed in Vittima. Is objective territorial, or "effects," jurisdiction encompassed within the ICC's Statute? Recall that a state is entitled to exercise jurisdiction over "conduct outside its territory that has or is intended to have substantial effect within its territory." Restatement (Third) of Foreign Relations Law of the United States §402 (1987). If the ICC were to construe its statute to include "effects" jurisdiction, it could exercise its jurisdiction, for example, over non-state party nationals who order an international crime on their own territory if that crime has or is intended to have a substantial effect within the territory of an ICC state party. "[G]iven the silence of the Statute about effects jurisdiction, there are compelling arguments in favour of a strict construction of Article 12 and the exclusion of such a concept." Schabas, supra, Introduction to the ICC at 79. What arguments can be made in favor of a broader construction?

Third, even if non-state party nationals commit qualifying crimes on the territory of non-states parties, those non-states parties can give ad hoc consent for the ICC to pursue cases against the perpetrators. ICC art. 12(3). To be clear, the non-states parties cannot trigger an ICC investigation, ICC art. 13, but were an ICC prosecutor to on his own initiate a preliminary examination based on information supplied to him by the non-state party or others, the non-state party could consent to full-fledged ICC jurisdiction over ensuring cases. ICC arts. 12(3), 13(c), 15(1). The Palestinian Authority has attempted to give the Office of the ICC Prosecutor ad hoc approval to investigate war crimes allegedly committed by Israel, a non-state party to the ICC, during its January 2009 incursion into Gaza. The question is not whether ad hoc consent can give the court jurisdiction, but rather whether the Palestinian Authority is a "state" authorized to provide such consent under the ICC Statute. See, e.g., "World Prosecutor" Renews Fight for Justice, Tell Me More, National Public Radio (Feb. 5, 2009) (interview with Mr. Moreno-Ocampo).

3. *Opportunistic and nonreciprocal referrals.* One of the reasons ICC Article 12 is controversial is the possibility of "opportunistic," and nonreciprocal, ad hoc consents to ICC jurisdiction by non-states parties. Under Article 12, non-states parties can consent to ICC jurisdiction for crimes committed by non-state party nationals on the territory of the consenting nation. Note, however, the language of Article 12(2), which speaks of non-state party consent to ICC jurisdiction over "*the conduct*" and "*the crime*," not the general "situation" (emphasis added). And Article 12(3) states that a non-state party may "accept the exercise of jurisdiction by the Court with respect to *the crime in question*" (emphasis added). Thus, this article is generally read as permitting ad hoc jurisdiction not of the general "situation" present in a certain armed conflict or territory, but rather only of particular cases. This reading gives rise to concerns about "nonreciprocal" ad hoc consents.

So, for example, assume that in our hypothetical neither Vittima *nor* Rancore were states parties to the ICC. If the above "plain language" reading of the statute were to prevail, Vittima could consent to ad hoc ICC jurisdiction over the alleged "crime[s]" of specific Rancori nationals on Vittima territory but the ICC would not have jurisdiction to investigate the entire "situation," including whatever crimes Vittima's citizens committed against Rancori nationals on Vittima territory. The only way that reciprocal jurisdiction over such crimes could be achieved is through Security Council referral of the entire situation to the ICC or through Vittima's (unlikely) ad hoc consent to ICC investigation of its nationals for particular crimes.

The potential for opportunistic nonreciprocal ad hoc consents is of concern to countries, like the United States, that have large forces overseas in peacekeeping missions and otherwise, although not necessarily to China and other non-states parties with fewer overseas military commitments. See Jianping & Zhixiang, supra, 3 J. Intl. Crim. Just. at 611. Some "have noted that this will permit any non-signatory nation that suffers an attack from the United States to invoke ICC jurisdiction opportunistically against the United States" and with no provision for reciprocity. Jack Goldsmith, The Self-Defeating International Criminal Court, 70 U. Chi. L. Rev. 89, 96 n.27 (2003).

The United States' opposition to this jurisdictional provision is said to be founded on the United States' unique exposure. As one member of the U.S. delegation to Rome has argued:

> The U.S. military has been much criticized for its stance on this critical aspect of the ICC Statute, but what the critics sometimes fail to recognize are the unique and vital national security responsibilities of the U.S. armed forces and the consequences of their front-line role in carrying out the nation's national security strategy. Though some bristle at a description of the United States as "the indispensable nation," it must be conceded that no other state regularly has nearly 200,000 troops outside its borders, either forward deployed or engaged in one of several operations designed to preserve international peace and security. To inhibit these forces as they seek to fill their crucial role is to take a step backwards in international peacemaking. "No peace without justice" was the mantra-like aphorism touted in Rome, but we must remember that likewise, there can be no justice without peace.

William K. Lietzau, International Criminal Law After Rome: Concerns from a U.S. Military Perspective, 64 Law & Contemp. Probs. 119, 126 (2001). Ambassador David Scheffer has further warned:

> The illogical consequence imposed by Article 12, particularly for nonparties to the Treaty, will be to limit severely those lawful, but highly controversial and inherently risky, interventions that the advocates of human rights and world peace so desperately seek from the United States and other military powers. There will be significant new legal and political risks in such interventions. . . .

David J. Scheffer, The United States and the International Criminal Court, 93 Am. J. Intl. L. 12, 19 (1999). Might one argue that some of these "highly controversial" incursions *should* be deterred? Might other nations take issue with what the intervening nation or group of nations deem "humanitarian" missions?

Finally, Professor Jack Goldsmith argues that the ICC's jurisdictional scheme may "do actual harm by discouraging the [nation being asked to intervene on humanitarian missions] from engaging in various human rights-protecting activities. And this, in turn, may increase rather than decrease the impunity of those who violate human rights." Goldsmith, supra, 70 U. Chi. L. Rev. at 89.

Is this reading of ICC Article 12 inevitable? Professor van der Vyver notes:

> It has been suggested that Article 12(3) should be interpreted subject to the principle of reciprocity that applies as a general rule of public international law: the complaining state cannot invoke the jurisdiction of the ICC for others without subjecting the conduct of its own forces to investigation with a view to possible prosecution in the ICC. This interpretation is admittedly not borne out by the actual wording of article 12(3) but would be in conformity with the principle that a state party (and the Security Council) only refers "a situation" to the prosecuting authorities of the ICC, leaving it up to the

prosecutor to decide, in full autonomy, whether to bring charges emanating from "the situation" under investigation, for what crimes, and against whom.

Johan D. van der Vyver, International Justice and the International Criminal Court: Between Sovereignty and the Rule of Law, 18 Emory Intl. L. Rev. 133, 139 (2004); see also Marcella David, Grotius Repudiated: The American Objections to the International Court and the Commitment to International Law, 20 Mich. J. Intl. L. 337, 370 (1999).

4. *Legal arguments regarding liability of nationals of non-states parties.* Various nations, including China, India, and the United States, contend that the ICC's purported jurisdiction over the nationals of non-states parties contravenes international law.

First, some rely on the Vienna Convention on the Law of Treaties (VCLT) and CIL, which they argue foreclose the exercise of jurisdiction over non-states parties' nationals absent those states' consent. VCLT Article 34 provides that "[a] treaty does not create either obligations or rights for a third State without its consent." VCLT Article 35 further provides that a treaty cannot impose an obligation on a third-party state unless that state "expressly accepts that obligation in writing." And "it is still axiomatic in international law that a state cannot be subjected to binding third-party dispute settlement unless it has consented in some way to such a process. Hence, it is asserted, the ICC cannot exercise powers over [non-state party] nationals unless the [state] becomes a party to the Statute." Weller, supra, 78 Intl. Aff. at 702. China, for example, asserts that the "jurisdiction of the ICC is not based on the principle of voluntary acceptance: the Rome Statute imposes obligations on non-States Parties without their consent, which violates the principle of state sovereignty and the [VCLT]." Jianping & Zhixiang, supra, 3 J. Intl. Crim. Just. at 611. Or, as the Indian government put it: "It is truly unfortunate that a Statute drafted for an institution to defend the law should start out straying so sharply from established international law. Before it tries its first criminal, the ICC would have claimed a victim of its own — the [VCLT]." Indian Statement, supra note 13.

One response to this legal argument is, in part, that the above-referenced VCLT provisions applicable to *state* responsibility do not apply equally to *individual nationals* under international law. "While compulsory jurisdiction over *states* has remained elusive, it is the very essence of the doctrine of universality that it can be applied by any state over the *national* of any other state without the need to obtain the consent from the latter state." Weller, supra, 78 Intl. Aff. at 702 (emphasis added). For nations that are not huge fans of universal jurisdiction, this may not persuade, but many of the states objecting to the legality of the ICC's jurisdiction have also entered into treaties that *require* their states parties to prosecute or extradite offenders in their custody — regardless of the nationality of the offenders — without any provision for consent by the states of which the defendants are nationals. And certainly criminal territorial jurisdiction has long been exercised by all states even where the offender is not a national of the territorial state, and no one would contend that the territorial state must secure the consent of the defendant's state of nationality. See, e.g., Michael P. Scharf, The ICC's Jurisdiction over the Nationals of Non-Party States: A Critique of the U.S. Position, 64 Law & Contemp. Probs. 67, 75 (2001). This seems like a straightforward and persuasive rebuttal of this legal objection. But could one make the argument that the ICC will necessarily pass — de facto if not de jure — on the legality of state conduct or policies? That is, could one contend that although the Statute authorizes only criminal responsibility for individual miscreants, if those defendants were acting only pursuant to state policy, any prosecution must inevitably adjudicate the legitimacy of their government's choices, as well as their own?

Those who object to the ICC's jurisdictional scheme make the further argument that, under international law, the ICC cannot exercise jurisdiction on the basis of the territoriality principle because a state cannot *delegate* its territorial jurisdiction to try an offender *to a treaty-based international court* without the consent of the state of nationality. That is, a non-state party may concede that individual states could exercise territorial jurisdiction over its nationals without its consent, but still contend that those states may not legally delegate that authority to the ICC. Defenders of the ICC point to the Nuremburg, Tokyo, and Ad Hoc Tribunals to show that it is not illegal under international law for states to delegate to the ICC some of their territorial jurisdiction. Objectors cite in response "the special circumstances of these cases, including the fact that the victorious allies could claim to act for Germany and Japan after their surrender, or the fact that the U.N. Security Council can act under Chapter VII, whereas a treaty-making conference such as the Rome Conference is lacking such powers." Weller, supra, 78 Intl. Aff. at 703. The Indian delegation went one further, contending that the decisions of the Security Council to create the Ad Hoc Tribunals were "of a dubious legality. The Charter did not give the Council the power to set up Courts, the Council did so in any case, and can do so again, only because its power cannot be challenged." Indian Statement, supra note 13. (This position was, as discussed in Chapter 3, rejected by the ICTY.)

Does the resolution of this legal question depend upon who bears the burden of proving, or disproving, the legality of this new practice? That is, states' delegation of territorial jurisdiction to a treaty-based international court is novel, but, under *The Case of the S.S. Lotus (France v. Turkey)*, 1927 P.C.I.J. (ser. A) No. 10 (Sept. 7) (excerpted and discussed in Chapter 5), could one argue that what is not proscribed is permitted? Could one argue in response that such a delegation is fundamentally inconsistent with the legal regime under which *Lotus* was decided? That is, as William K. Lietzau argues:

> Accepting, *arguendo*, the legality of [states' delegation of their jurisdiction to the ICC], it does not necessarily follow that the ICC can accept that delegation. International law surrounding jurisdiction is grounded in the framework of a Westphalian system of state responsibility. Traditionally, responsibility for the exercise of jurisdiction has rested on the states. Through the ICC's regime, a state may delegate jurisdictional "authority." That authority exists, however, within a paradigm in which the same state must accept responsibility for the exercise of jurisdiction, and may ultimately be held accountable for it. Responsibility and accountability cannot be delegated.

Lietzau, supra, 64 Law & Contemp. Probs. at 135.

5. *Democracy deficit?* Perhaps these legal arguments miss the point. Some argue that the ultimate problem with the ICC is that it suffers from a "democracy deficit" and thus is illegitimate. For example, Madeline Morris argues that by virtue of the Court's jurisdictional scheme, as well as its institutional structures, the ICC does not answer to any democratic political body. The ICC can, as presently constituted, conduct investigations and prosecutions that are contrary to the democratic will of some states.

> According to Morris, this means that in many cases, the Court will decide the fate of some individuals without being forced to answer to the people who are responsible for the well-being of the accused. Thus, given that all of the relevant human rights texts assert that there is a human right to democratic governance, the Rome Treaty, despite its undeniably noble intentions, violates human rights and thus is illegitimate.

Aaron Fichtelberg, Democratic Legitimacy and the International Criminal Court: A Liberal Defence, 4 J. Intl. Crim. Just. 765, 769 (2006) (summarizing, and disagreeing with, Professor Morris's arguments). Do you agree that "[w]hat is ultimately at stake, beneath the heated controversy concerning ICC jurisdiction over non-party nationals, is a tension embodied in the Rome Treaty between the human rights embodied in humanitarian law (rights to freedom from genocide, war crimes, and crimes against humanity) and the human right to democratic governance"? Madeline Morris, The Democratic Dilemma of the International Criminal Court, 5 Buff. Crim. L. Rev. 591, 593 (2002).

6. *Relevance of the legality principle?* As ICC Article 22 indicates, the legality inquiry is focused on whether the accused's conduct constitutes a crime "within the jurisdiction of the Court." Thus, the relevant reference to assess whether a defendant's conduct constitutes a crime at the time of its commission is the ICC Statute. Notably, the legality principle incorporated in ICC Article 22 *does not* require that the conduct in question be criminal under the law of the state from which the accused hales. Bruce Broomhall, Article 22: Nullum crimen sine lege, in Commentary on the Rome Statute of the International Criminal Court: Observers' Notes, Article by Article 456 (Otto Triffterer ed., 1999).

As we know from earlier readings, the legality principle has many purposes. Among them is the idea that conviction of a crime, where the law is not known or knowable, is both unfair and ineffectual in terms of serving the purposes of punishment. Is it "unfair" to charge persons the world over with (constructive) knowledge of just what the ICC Statute proscribes? Does it matter that the ICC Statute provides for the exercise of jurisdiction over the nationals of non-states parties? Former U.S. Ambassador at Large for War Crimes Issues David J. Scheffer queried: "Are we to assume now that all nationals of all non-Party States are on effective notice of the illegality of each and every ICC crime . . . even though their respective non-party governments may not have taken the actions (through treaty law or otherwise) internationally or domestically to confirm that illegality and put their nationals on notice of such criminal liability before the ICC?" Scheffer, supra, 2 J. Intl. Crim. Just. at 31. What did Justice Jackson say about this in his opening statement at Nuremberg? Finally, is there any legality objection to be founded on venue? That is, that a génocidaire, while knowing that he could be brought up on charges in a national system (for example, for murder), could not have anticipated that he would be tried for genocide before an international tribunal?

7. *The "traveling dictator" problem.* Another objection to the ICC's jurisdictional provisions concerns what is referred to as the "traveling dictator exception." Goldsmith, supra, 70 U. Chi. L. Rev. at 91. One consequence of the treaty's jurisdictional scheme is that officials from a non-state party who commit international crimes on their own territory (that is, on the territory of a non-state party) cannot be prosecuted, even if the perpetrators subsequently are found within the territory of a state party absent a UN Security Council referral.

For example, posit for the moment that the government of Rancore engages in a ruthless persecution of its own ethnic Vittime population in response to events in Vittima's Disputa province. Would those Rancoris who participate be subject to the jurisdiction of the ICC? Assuming that there is no ICC "effects" jurisdiction and in the absence of a Security Council referral, the answer is no. Where *non-state party nationals* commit international crimes against others *on the non-state party's territory*, there is no nationality or territorial basis for ICC jurisdiction absent the extremely unlikely consent of the *persecuting* state. "Leaders of non-signatory nations can commit crimes in their territories without fear of prosecution. Even if human rights abusers from non-signatory nations vacation in The Hague, they cannot be arrested and tried by the ICC." Goldsmith, supra, 70 U. Chi. L. Rev. at 91. This scheme was born of a compromise.

Germany initially proposed giving the ICC truly global jurisdiction, so that the Rome Treaty would have obligated states parties to arrest the traveling dictator and surrender him to the ICC if the dictator had been accused of a crime within the court's jurisdiction. Advocates of this approach argued that such jurisdiction was necessary to ensure that major violators were brought to justice and was legitimate because what they could do as individual nations they could do collectively through an international tribunal. But other nations objected to giving the ICC the practical equivalent of universal jurisdiction arguing, inter alia, that such jurisdiction had an uncertain basis in international law. As adopted, the statute represents a compromise: Citizens of non-states parties can be prosecuted for crimes committed in the territory of a state party or a state providing ad hoc consent, or where referred by the Security Council.

In the view of many critics, the problems of opportunistic and nonreciprocal referrals and the traveling dictator exception work together to create a wholly unsatisfactory result:

> Ironically, while on one hand the court's jurisdiction is too independent and robust, inserted limitations went in the wrong direction. Most atrocities — and certainly such is the case in recent years — are committed internally. And most internal conflicts are between warring parties of the same nationality. Such internal conflicts can easily escape the ICC's jurisdictional trigger of nationality *or* territory-based consent since the potentially relevant states are one and the same. Thus, the worst offenders of international humanitarian law can choose never to join the treaty and be fully insulated from its reach absent a Security Council referral. Recent events call our attention to Pol Pot and the vicious reign of the Khmer Rouge, the crimes of Saddam Hussein, and the Kosovo atrocities perpetrated by the regime of Slobodan Milosevic. To bring such rogue leaders or their mercenary consorts to justice often requires some form of intervention, perhaps based on Security Council authorization. However, any peacekeeper or peace enforcer sent to quash an ongoing humanitarian disaster, and perhaps to bring its perpetrators to justice, would not enjoy the same ICC immunity as the rogue state actors themselves. For instance, absent a Security Council referral, Milosevic would be immune from jurisdiction for any offense committed against his people, but NATO aircrews attempting to stop his forces from committing atrocities would not be.

Lietzau, supra, 64 Law & Contemp. Probs. at 129. To this should be added the concern that the questions of whether and when a military intervention is necessary or appropriate are almost always going to be highly contested internationally. Thus, it is feared, non-states parties that disagree with decisions to intervene may well press the ICC to prosecute nationals of the intervening power, and will provide ad hoc consents to ICC jurisdiction.

At the conclusion of the Rome negotiations, the United States tendered a provision that would exclude ICC jurisdiction over non-state party nationals when their conduct arose in the course of official acts of state. Ambassador Scheffer consistently argued that the official actions of a non-state party should not be subject to the ICC's jurisdiction except by Security Council action under the UN Charter. Scheffer's intent was to exclude, for example, ICC jurisdiction over U.S. soldiers ordered by their government to engage in a humanitarian intervention to prevent a threatened genocide without UN Security Council authorization. Would this provision adequately address U.S. legal objections to the ICC's treatment of non-state party nationals? What problems might such a provision create?

8. *Will the traveling dictator sign the Rome Treaty?* The traveling dictator problem was thought by some to constitute a grave threat to the efficacy of the ICC because, it was posited, only "angelic States — the Scandinavians, Canada, the Netherlands, and so on — would join the Court on such a basis." Editorial, International Criminal Court: The Secret of Its Success, 12 Crim. L.F. 415, 418 (2002). This concern rests, however, on an important assumption — that oppressive and abusive regimes will not subject themselves to ICC prosecution by joining the ICC. Consider the following:

> [A]s the pace of ratification accelerated in 2000 and 2001, an astonishing thing happened. The very States expected to steer clear of the Court because of their obvious vulnerability to prosecution started to produce instruments of ratification at United Nations headquarters. The first was Fiji, which had known severe civil conflict in the late 1900s. It was followed by Sierra Leone, where civil war had raged from 1991 until the Lome Peace Agreement of 1999, only to heat up once again in 2000. By the time the magic number of sixty ratifications was reached, several other countries that had known violent conflict and atrocity in recent years had joined the Court: Cambodia, Macedonia, Democratic Republic of Congo, Bosnia and Herzegovina, Yugoslavia, Croatia. Others in the same category are known to be preparing for ratification, such as Colombia and Burundi. [Colombia and Burundi have since joined the ICC.]
>
> These ratifications were totally unexpected. Obviously they disprove the arguments that were advanced at Rome by those who were critical of the compromise on jurisdiction in article 12. They suggest that States are ratifying the Statute precisely because they view the Court as a promising and realistic mechanism capable of addressing civil conflict, human rights abuses and war. This is entirely consistent, of course, with the logic of those who have argued over the years that international justice contributes to peace and security.

Id. Is this the only explanation that can be posited for the unexpected ratifications, or can a more cynical story be told? Note that all three state party referrals of cases to the ICC have been *self*-referrals in which the governments have asked the ICC to investigate rebels or others within their territory who are in conflict with the central authority. Does this raise a concern that governments may ratify the ICC to use it as a tool with which to deal with their internal political adversaries?

9. *Referral by the Security Council.* The last ground of jurisdiction — referral by the UN Security Council — is the way that reciprocity can be ensured in the context of ad hoc consents and the traveling dictator can be subjected to ICC jurisdiction. Under ICC Article 13(b), the ICC can exercise jurisdiction with respect to an Article 5 crime if "[a] situation in which one or more of such crimes appears to have been committed is referred to the Prosecutor by the Security Council acting under Chapter VII of the Charter of the United Nations."

If the Security Council triggers the involvement of the ICC, however, most commentators believe that it must be prepared to live with the parameters of the Statute. As Professor van der Vyver explains, the ICC "was not established by, and does not function as a subsidiary organ of, the Security Council, and owes its powers exclusively to the statute of its creation. The Security Council, in a word, cannot instruct the ICC to exercise powers not entrusted to the court by the ICC Statute." van der Vyver, supra, 18 Emory Intl. L. Rev. at 140. So, for example, the Security Council could not refer to the ICC alleged violations of treaty crimes where those crimes do not arguably fit within the specific subset of crimes over which the ICC Statute provides subject matter jurisdiction.

Is there any limitation here on the types of "situations" that may be referred, assuming that they concern qualifying crimes? Assume, for example, that the territorial jurisdiction of the ICC does not extend to "effects" jurisdiction and thus that Dr. Hate cannot be brought to justice under the ICC's provisions for nationality or territorial jurisdiction. Can the Security Council nevertheless confer jurisdiction on the ICC through referral? Note that Article 12(2)'s territorial and nationality limitations on the ICC's jurisdiction apply only "[i]n the case of article 13, paragraph (a) [referral by a state party] or (c) [initiation by the prosecutor]."

ICC Article 13(b), however, requires that the Security Council be acting pursuant to Chapter VII of the UN Charter, which means that the Council presumably must find the existence of a "threat to the peace," a "breach of the peace," or an "act of aggression." Let us assume that the Security Council makes such a referral. We know that the ICC is bound by statute to "satisfy itself that it has jurisdiction in any case brought before it." ICC art. 19(1). Does this mean that the ICC could, in examining its own jurisdiction, second-guess the Security Council about whether a qualifying "threat to the peace," a "breach of the peace," or an "act of aggression" exists to warrant a Security Council referral?

4.   Qualifying Trigger for Exercise of Jurisdiction

ICC Article 13 provides that the "[e]xercise of jurisdiction" depends on a qualifying trigger. That is, the initiative to look into a situation must come from one of the three following sources:

1.   the Security Council, whose role we have already examined;
2.   a state party; or
3.   the prosecutor, *proprio motu* (on his own motion).[29]

In the years since the ICC officially opened for business, the Court has agreed to investigate four cases, three of which were formally triggered by states parties (Uganda, CAR, and DRC) and concern alleged crimes committed on their own territory; the fourth investigation (Sudan) was triggered by a UN Security Council referral. Notably, the prosecutor has not yet elected to initiate a formal investigation of a situation relying on his *proprio motu* powers.

NOTES AND QUESTIONS

1. *State party referrals.* In our hypothetical case study, the situation was referred by France for investigation by the ICC. Does the referring state party have to have a relationship with the crime? That is, must the crime have occurred on its territory or have been perpetrated by its national? See ICC art. 14. Many commentators have assumed that, as a practical matter, referrals by states parties (for example, France) with respect to crimes occurring on the territory of *another* state (for example, Vittima and Rancore) will be rare — because of the potential adverse political, trade, or other ramifications of a referral. It is presumed that, in these circumstances, states will lobby the prosecutor to initiate the case, thus obtaining the same result but saving "the diplomatic discomforts that accompany public denunciation." Schabas, supra, Introduction to the ICC at 122.

---

29. ICC arts. 13(a), 14, 15.

2. *Non-states parties may give ad hoc consent but may not trigger investigations through referral.* Recall that Rancore is *not* a state party to the ICC Statute. Could it make a referral to the ICC regarding alleged crimes committed by Vittime citizens while on Rancore soil? One limitation on the "opportunistic" exercise of ad hoc jurisdiction, discussed above, is the fact that a non-state party *cannot* trigger proceedings under ICC Article 14. Thus, a non-state party that believes its nationals or interests were victimized through qualifying crimes *can* consent to the ICC's exercise of ad hoc jurisdiction under ICC Article 12, but it *cannot* trigger such jurisdiction through referral. Is this a meaningful restriction? As we shall see below, the ICC prosecutor may initiate inquiries on his own initiative (although not full-scale investigations absent judicial approval). Can non-states parties evade this Article 14 restriction, then, by asking the prosecutor to initiate a case *proprio motu*? Consider the case of Côte d'Ivoire, which is not a state party to the ICC. Apparently without being asked to do so, it accepted the jurisdiction of the ICC with respect to crimes committed on its territory since September 2002.

3. *Restraints on the OTP's* proprio motu *power: ICC Article 15.* One of the greatest concerns voiced by those who object to the structure of the ICC is the power of the prosecutor to delve into alleged crimes on her own initiative, including cases potentially concerning the nationals of non-state parties. The UN ILC's Draft Statute denied the prosecutor the power to initiate an investigation or prosecution. It contemplated that only the referrals of states parties and, in some cases, the Security Council could trigger the initiation of ICC proceedings. Allowing the ICC prosecutor, on her initiative, to trigger an investigation or prosecution was, and remains, highly controversial. The United States vigorously opposed the idea based on its domestic experience with "independent prosecutors" who, some believed, were dangerously (politically) unaccountable actors. Other non-states parties, such as China and India, have expressed similar fears. Thus, the Chinese government expressed concern that the "proprio motu power of the Prosecutor under Article 15 . . . may make it difficult for the ICC to concentrate on dealing with the most serious crimes, and may make the Court open to political influence so that it cannot act in a manner that is independent and fair." Jianping & Zhixiang, supra, 3 J. Intl. Crim. Just. at 612; see also Usha Ramanathan, India and the ICC, 3 J. Intl. Crim. Just. 627, 632-633 (2005). Many other countries and nongovernmental organizations (NGOs), in contrast, pushed hard for the idea of an independent prosecutor who could act *proprio motu*, and they ultimately prevailed.

In response to concerns about the *proprio motu* power, the ICC Statute contains a safeguard—in Article 15—designed to make the prosecutor accountable to the ICC judges in such circumstances. The ICC prosecutor can trigger examinations of situations, but his power to begin a case on his own initiative (*proprio motu*) is circumscribed by Article 15's Pre-Trial Chambers approval requirement. To be clear, this requirement does not apply in the event that investigation of a "situation" is "triggered" by states parties or the Security Council; *Article 15 applies only where the case was initiated by the prosecutor.*

Article 15 states that the "Prosecutor *may* initiate investigations *proprio motu* on the basis of information on crimes within the jurisdiction of the Court." ICC art. 15(1) (emphasis added). The use of the term *may* indicates that the initiation of such preliminary examinations is discretionary. The initiation must be based on "information," ICC art. 15(1), which can come from many sources—for example, states (including, apparently, non-states parties who are precluded from directly referring cases), the UN, intergovernmental or NGOs, or the victims themselves. See ICC art. 15(2).

The language of the Statute provides that the prosecutor may initiate an "investigation" *proprio motu*, but it is better termed a "preliminary examination," see ICC art. 15(6). If the prosecutor decides after her preliminary examination of the information provided that there is a "reasonable basis" for proceeding with an *investigation*, she must submit a request for authorization of an investigation, with documentation, to the Pre-Trial Chamber. ICC art. 15(3). In conducting its Article 15 review, the Pre-Trial Chamber panel of three judges must consider whether (1) there is a "reasonable basis to proceed," and (2) the Court appears to have jurisdiction. ICC art. 15(4). If the Pre-Trial Chamber is satisfied with the OTP's presentation, it "shall" authorize the "commencement of an investigation, without prejudice to subsequent determinations by the Court with regard to the jurisdiction and admissibility of a case." Id. If, however, the Pre-Trial Chamber rejects the prosecutor's request, the prosecutor can return with a new application for authorization based on new facts. ICC art. 15(5). But absent authorization, the prosecutor may not proceed with a formal investigation.

4. *Fear of the prosecutor's* proprio motu *powers, "invited" referrals, and the record to date.* Whether investing the ICC prosecutor with the power to commence preliminary examinations on his own initiative will prove to have been wise or foolish may well depend on how individual prosecutors conduct themselves during their tenures at the ICC. How does the record stand at present?

According to published sources, Mr. Moreno-Ocampo "has indicated a clear preference for initiating investigations of alleged core crimes, wherever possible, on the basis of a referral by a state party pursuant to Article 14 or by the Security Council pursuant to Article 13(b)." Hans-Peter Kaul, Construction Site for More Justice: The International Criminal Court After Two Years, 99 Am. J. Intl. L. 370, 374 (2005). Although one could argue that this policy is borne out by the facts to date — because there have been no formal "investigations" under Article 15 launched under the *proprio motu* power — one could also take issue with the characterization of some of the current cases before the ICC as pure state party referrals. The prosecutor reportedly played an aggressive behind-the-scenes role in "inviting" such referrals. Indeed, it has been suggested that the prosecutor threatened to use his own investigative powers were a "self-referral" by the territorial state party not forthcoming. Because the formal triggers for these cases were referrals by states parties, however, Article 15's limits on investigations initiated by the prosecutor *proprio motu* do not apply. Should they?

If one is to assess the entire record thus far, one must also consider the situations in which the prosecutor *declined* to initiate investigations using his *proprio motu* powers despite communications urging him to do so. Thus, the prosecutor received a number of communications urging him to look into the situation in Venezuela. He declined to initiate an investigation, however, because, among other things, some of the allegations concerned events outside the ICC's temporal jurisdiction and the information available did not provide "a reasonable basis" to believe that an essential element of crimes against humanity was met.

Mr. Moreno-Ocampo also reportedly received hundreds of communications urging him to investigate the situation in Iraq. In February 2006, he issued a letter explaining his determination that the situation in Iraq did not meet the statutory requirements for opening an investigation. He highlighted, among other things, (1) the requirement, not met in this situation, that, absent the ad hoc consent of Iraq, the crime be committed by a national of a state party or on the territory of a state party; (2) the crime of aggression lacks a definition; and (3) while many civilians were killed, there was insufficient evidence that attacks were intentional or clearly excessive and thus that the attacks constituted war crimes. Perhaps more notably, given concerns about his exercise of prosecutorial discretion, Mr. Moreno-Ocampo also found that although there was a reasonable basis to believe that some war crimes within the jurisdiction of the Court had been committed — namely willful killing and inhuman treatment — the information available did not rise to the required gravity for investigation. He concluded, inter alia, that the cases did not meet the gravity requirement of ICC Article 53 because of the relatively small number of victims (less than 20) identified.

5. *How to think about invited state party "self-referrals."* The three states parties "self-referrals" — by Uganda, DRC, and CAR — took most commentators by surprise. The negotiators of the ICC Statute reportedly assumed that state party referrals of *other* states for investigation would be rare and did not give any serious consideration to the possibility of states referring *themselves* for investigation. The advantages of such self-referrals to the OTP are clear (at least in cases where the self-referring state does not change its view of the wisdom of an ICC prosecution):

> [T]he Prosecutor has the advantage of knowing that that State has the political will to provide his Office with all the cooperation within the country that is required. . . . [T]he Prosecutor can be confident that the national authorities will assist the investigation, will accord the privileges and immunities necessary for the investigation, and will be anxious to provide if possible and appropriate the necessary level of protection to investigators and witnesses.

International Criminal Court, Office of the Prosecutor, Annex to the "Paper on Some Policy Issues Before the Office of the Prosecutor," §1.D, *available at* http://www .icc-cpi.int (follow the links for "Office of the Prosecutor" and "Policies and Strategies") (last visited July 13, 2009). The cooperation of the referring state may be critically important to an effective prosecution, particularly in situations where conflict is ongoing. Investigating crimes committed in noncooperating states has proved very difficult. For example, Mr. Moreno-Ocampo informed the Security Council in June 2006 that

> [t]he continuing insecurity in Darfur is prohibitive of effective investigations inside Darfur, particularly in light of the absence of a functioning and sustainable system for the protection of victims and witnesses. The investigative activities of the Office are therefore continuing outside Darfur. . . . [T]he ICC has established a temporary field presence in Chad in order to access the refugee population from Darfur currently situated in Eastern Chad. The activities of the Office were severely disrupted as a result of clashes between Chadian Government and rebel forces in April 2006. The field office was temporarily closed and staff withdrawn.

Third Report of the Prosecutor of the International Criminal Court to the U.N. Security Council Pursuant to UNSCR 1593 (2005), dated June 14, 2006, at 1.

Cases launched by self-referral may also benefit the referring states, especially those nations that lack the domestic capacity to pursue accountability and justice for prior atrocities. A self-referral that brings wrongdoers to justice may carry with it collateral benefits such as political stability, enhanced domestic criminal justice capabilities, and perhaps some measure of peace and reconciliation. Finally, self-referrals ought to reassure those in the international community who worry about the prosecutor's *proprio motu* power that he is not abusing his mandate.

Aside from the potential that invited self-referrals offer for evasion of the oversight mandated by Article 15, what are the downsides of this practice? Note in this regard that the three self-referrals tendered thus far all were made by the governments of countries that have been engaged in civil conflicts with rebel forces. One could argue that the self-referrals, alleging international crimes, may be political weapons used to discredit or incapacitate opponents of the referring regime. A number of concerns arise from this circumstance:

> First, [a practice of accepting such self-referrals] could encourage governments to externalize to the Court the domestic political problems they are unable or unwilling — because they do not wish to invest the necessary resources — to manage or resolve. Second it permits the referring government to co-opt the ICC in a confrontational criminal context for what — despite all the attendant violence — may essentially be political struggles, for which negotiation and settlement might be the only practicable mode of restoring minimum order.

Mahnoush H. Arsanjani & W. Michael Reisman, The Law-in-Action of the International Criminal Court, 99 Am. J. Intl. L. 385, 392 (2005).

Might an untoward reliance on self-referrals ultimately undermine the prosecutor's claim to political impartiality and independence — and thus the credibility of his office (and the ICC generally)? For example, Prosecutor Moreno-Ocampo held a joint press conference with Ugandan President Museveni in January 2004 to highlight the first state (self) referral to the ICC. Musevni's forces have been accused of perpetrating crimes within the court's jurisdiction. As one commentator noted, the joint appearance "was understandable because of the novelty, but may not have been the wisest course of action, since it immediately allowed the prosecutor to be accused of partiality in the case." Herbert Okun, The Role of International Criminal Justice in Peace Negotiations, 25 Penn. St. Intl. L. Rev. 779, 783 (2007).

Note, however, that the ICC Statute attempts to prevent "politically motivated" state referrals in Article 14, which specifies that when a state party makes a referral, it is of the "situation," not simply one or more cases or events. Thus, the OTP has in any state party self-referral the responsibility of looking at the situation as a whole — potentially including any crimes committed by the referring regime as well as rebel forces. In Uganda, for example, NGOs have accused the Ugandan national army, the UPDF, of crimes similar to those charged against the LRA. Although Mr. Moreno-Ocampo has stated that he is still seeking information regarding crimes allegedly committed by the UPDF, he has repeatedly explained his decision to date to proceed only against the LRA as a judgment on the relative "gravity" of the crimes committed on each side, stating that the LRA's crimes were more numerous and of a much higher level of gravity than those UPDF crimes thus far uncovered. Should the OTP bring charges relating to UPDF crimes, even if they are less grave on a relative scale, to prevent a perception that the ICC's even-handedness in looking into this situation has been compromised by the self-referral? Should the prosecutor be concerned about such perceptions?

Might the practice of self-referrals also create problems on a practical level, assuming that a state using this as a political weapon may revise its political calculus over time and fail to be as cooperative with the OTP as it should be?

Finally, might self-referrals — especially "invited" ones — allow the territorial government a tool that ultimately serves neither peace nor justice? Consider the following criticism voiced in 2005 regarding the Ugandan self-referral:

> [T]he Ugandan government had been unable to resolve the problem in the north for at least eighteen years. Whatever the reason for this failure and however hideous the crimes committed, one wonders what contribution to the settlement of the dispute accrues from

transferring the problem, at this juncture, to the International Criminal Court, a body that was neither intended nor equipped to resolve, through judicial means, a longstanding political problem of a government.

Arsanjani & Reisman, supra, 99 Am. J. Intl. L. at 393.

6. *Considerations relevant to commencement of a formal "investigation" regardless of the underlying "trigger."* ICC Article 53 identifies the standards by which the prosecutor must act in deciding to initiate an investigation or prosecution, as well as the powers of the Pre-Trial Chamber in reviewing such determinations. It is unclear what relation this article bears to Article 15, which governs the OTP's decision making only where a prosecutor has commenced a preliminary examination, or seeks to commence a full-scale investigation, *proprio motu*. Many, but not all, commentators believe that ICC Article 53 applies no matter how the case was "triggered" — that is, its standards control in situations triggered by the prosecutor *proprio motu* under Articles 13(c) and 15, as well those referred to the ICC by a state party or the Security Council under Article 13(a) and (b). See, e.g., Morten Bergsmo & Pieter Kruger, Article 53, in Commentary on the Rome Statute of the International Criminal Court: Observers' Notes, Article by Article 702 (Otto Triffterer ed., 1999).

Article 53 provides that the prosecutor "*shall* . . . initiate an investigation *unless* he or she determines that there is no reasonable basis to proceed under th[e] Statute." ICC art. 53(1)(emphasis added). In deciding whether to initiate an investigation in these circumstances, the prosecutor must consider three factors:

> (1) whether the "information available to him provides a reasonable basis to believe that a crime within the jurisdiction of the Court" has been committed or is continuing;
> (2) whether the case "is or would be admissible under Article 17"; and
> (3) taking "into account the gravity of the crime and the interests of victims, there are nonetheless substantial reasons to believe that an investigation would not serve the interests of justice."

ICC art. 53(1).

Gravity is not defined in the ICC Statute. Thus far, the OTP has considered the following factors in assessing gravity: "the scale of the crimes, the severity of the crimes, the systematic nature of the crimes, the manner in which they were committed, . . . the impact on victims," and the relative responsibility of the persons under consideration. Susana SaCouto & Katherine Cleary, The Gravity Threshold of the International Criminal Court, 23 Am. U. Intl. L. Rev. 807, 810 (2008); see also Margaret M. deGuzman, Gravity and the Legitimacy of the International Criminal Court, 32 Fordham Intl. L.J. 1400 (2009). What other factors should guide the prosecutor in deciding how to measure the gravity of a particular case? What ought to factor into the evaluation of "the interests of justice"?

7. *Moving from "investigation" to charging a crime under Article 53.* In considering whether her investigation should end in an actual prosecution, the prosecutor must evaluate: (1) whether there is a sufficient legal and factual basis for the case; (2) whether the case is admissible under ICC Article 17; and (3) whether a prosecution is "in the interests of justice, taking into account all the circumstances, including the gravity of the crime, the interests of victims and the age or infirmity of the alleged perpetrator, and his or her role in the alleged crime." ICC art. 53(2).

8. *Pre-Trial Chamber's review of prosecutorial declinations.* If the prosecutor decides, based on these factors, to *decline* to prosecute, he must inform the Pre-Trial Chamber and the referring state party or Security Council, providing them with his reasons as

well. ICC art. 53(2). In general, at the request of a referring state party or the Security Council under ICC Article 13(b), the Pre-Trial Chamber can review the prosecutor's decision to *decline* to launch an investigation or prosecution and "may request the Prosecutor to reconsider that decision." ICC art. 53(3)(a).

In addition, under ICC Article 53(3)(b), a Pre-Trial Chamber may, on its own initiative, review a prosecutor's decision to *decline* to initiate an investigation or prosecution *if the OTP's decision was based solely on the OTP's "interests of justice" determination* (under ICC art. 53(1)(c) or (2)(c)). "In such a case, the decision of the Prosecutor shall be effective *only if confirmed by the Pre-Trial Chamber.*" ICC art. 53(3)(b) (emphasis added).

In the United States, the decision whether *or not* to bring a case is left entirely to the executive branch, and this review power will strike U.S. prosecutors as very foreign; much of the power of U.S. prosecutors rests in their power to *decline* a case (in the United States, often without explanation). Prosecutors in civil law countries, however, are often required to bring every case for which they uncover sufficient evidence; in theory at least, they are not supposed to exercise discretion. Is this a compromise that will work?

9. *Other procedural checks on the ICC prosecutor: Confirmation hearings and other pretrial functions.* The Pre-Trial Chamber has other means of constraining the prosecutor's functioning. Thus, for example, prosecutors generally must seek the assistance of the Pre-Trial Chamber for the issuance of such orders and warrants as may be required for purposes of the investigation. See, e.g., ICC art. 57.

A potentially very important check on the OTP can be found in ICC Article 61, which requires that the ICC Pre-Trial Chamber "confirm" the charges on which the prosecutor intends to seek trial in an adversary process. The Article 61 procedure differs from the system used in the Ad Hoc Tribunals "where, more simply, the confirmation of indictment takes place in an ex parte hearing before a single judge, without any involvement of the Defence and is based only on the Prosecutor's allegations." Michela Miraglia, Admissibility of Evidence, Standard of Proof, and Nature of the Decision in the ICC Confirmation of Charges in *Lubanga*, 6 J. Intl. Crim. Just. 489, 490 (2008). The prosecutor is required at a confirmation hearing before the ICC Pre-Trial Chamber to support each charge "with sufficient evidence to establish substantial grounds to believe that the person committed the crime charged." ICC art. 61(5). Although the accused may object to the charges, challenge the prosecutor's evidence, and present evidence, ICC art. 61(6), the fact that this is supposed to be a screening mechanism rather than a full-blown trial is demonstrated by the provision allowing the prosecutor to "rely on documentary or summary evidence" and excusing her from calling the witnesses expected to testify at the trial. ICC art. 61(5).

At the confirmation hearing, the Pre-Trial Chamber must determine whether there is "sufficient evidence to establish substantial grounds to believe that the person committed each of the crimes charged." ICC art. 61(7). The Trial Chamber in the *Lubanga* case, relying upon "internationally recognized human rights jurisprudence" from the ECHR, explained its conception of this burden as follows:

37. In the opinion of the Chamber, the purpose of the confirmation hearing is limited to committing for trial only those persons against whom sufficiently compelling charges going beyond mere theory or suspicion have been brought. This mechanism is designed to protect the rights of the Defence against wrongful and wholly unfounded charges.

39. . . . [T]he Chamber considers that for the Prosecution to meet its evidentiary burden, it must offer concrete and tangible proof demonstrating a clear line of

reasoning underpinning its specific allegations. Furthermore, the "substantial grounds to believe" standard must enable all the evidence admitted for the purpose of the confirmation hearing to be assessed as a whole. After an exacting scrutiny of all the evidence, the Chamber will determine whether it is thoroughly satisfied that the Prosecution's allegations are sufficiently strong to commit [the defendant] for trial.

Prosecutor v. Lubanga, Case No. ICC-01/04-01/06, Decision on the Confirmation of Charges, Public Redacted Version with Annex I, at 13-14, ¶¶37-39 (Jan. 29, 2007). The Chamber by majority vote can confirm or decline to confirm the charges, or request further evidence or an amendment of the charge from the prosecutor. ICC art. 61(7). If the Pre-Trial Chamber declines to confirm charges, the prosecution is not precluded from subsequently requesting confirmation if that request is supported by additional evidence. ICC art. 61(8).

One Pre-Trial Chamber has read its role in confirming charges to include the power to amend the charges the prosecutor has proposed. In confirming the charges against Thomas Lubanga, the Pre-Trial Chamber classified the armed conflict identified for purposes of the war crimes charges as international, rather than noninternational, in scope. It therefore, *sua sponte*, amended the charges against Lubanga, substituting a charge of conscripting child soldiers in the context of an international conflict for the prosecutor's charge of child conscription in the context of a non-international conflict. See Jason Morgan-Foster, ASIL Insights, ICC Confirms Charges Against DRC Militia Leader, Mar. 9, 2007, http://www.asil.org/insights070309.cfm. The prosecutor sought leave to appeal, arguing that

> the clear language of the Statute . . . only allows the Chambers to adjourn the proceedings and request the Prosecution to consider amending a charge, if the Chamber is of the view that the evidence submitted appears to establish a different crime. As a result, the Prosecution is forced to proceed with a crime that it had already determined, after careful examination of the evidence in its possession, should not be charged, and to devote time and resources to supplement that evidence, if possible, in order to adequately substantiate that crime at trial.

Prosecutor v. Lubanga, Case No. ICC 01/04-01/06, Application for Leave to Appeal Pre-Trial Chamber I's Jan. 29, 2007 "Décision sur la confirmation des charges" (Feb. 5, 2007). Pre-Trial Chambers denied the prosecutor's request for leave to appeal. Prosecutor v. Lubanga, Case No. ICC 01/04-01/06, Decision on the Prosecution and Defense Applications for Leave to Appeal the Decision on the Confirmation of Charges (May 24, 2007).

10. *Victims.* Although one might assume that victims of international crimes would push the OTP consistently in the direction of prosecution, that has not yet proved to be the case; indeed victims' representatives have played an inhibiting role in the OTP's investigation of crimes committed by the LRA in Uganda. The primary victims in the conflict in northern Uganda are the Acholi people, who have been victimized by their own: Joseph Kony and his colleagues in the LRA. Many Acholis, however, reportedly believe that the leaders of the LRA should receive the same amnesty that the LRA rank and file have been given. As Professor Eric Blumenson explains:

> . . . Although vast numbers of Acholis have suffered death, dismemberment, rape and other atrocities at the hands of the rebels who comprise the Lord's Resistance Army, many leaders of this community are imploring the ICC to foreswear prosecution. They claim that the threat of international prosecution will deter the rebels from joining in a

peace agreement, and also argue that a combination of amnesty and restorative justice mechanisms will serve to promote justice and reconciliation better than prosecutions.

Eric Blumenson, National Amnesties and International Justice, 2 Eyes on the ICC 1, 1 & n.1 (2005); see also Pablo Castillo Diaz, The ICC in Northern Uganda: Peace First, Justice Later?, 2 Eyes on the ICC 17 (2005); Uganda's War Victims Prefer Peace over Punishment, Reuters, Apr. 30, 2007. The victims' views are reported to stem both from a "culture of forgiveness" and, more urgently, a belief that the atrocities will end only if prosecution is declined and amnesty awarded. The Ugandan government is, of course, in an awkward situation; Uganda is an ICC state party, and it referred the situation to the ICC prosecutor in the first instance. The status of the negotiations between the Ugandan government and the LRA changes frequently. At least at one time, however, prospects for peace appeared bright enough to prompt Ugandan President Yuweri Museveni to have said (reportedly) that if Kony accepted an amnesty, then Museveni would "fight tooth and nail" to protect Kony. Helena Cobban, Uganda: When International Justice and Internal Peace Are at Odds, Christian Sci. Monitor, Aug. 24, 2006.

The Uganda case certainly raises an important issue: Is a criminal prosecution always the best course? Many lawyers assume that use of judicial processes is indispensable in post-atrocity or civil war contexts. But may insisting on criminal investigations and prosecutions in some situations be actually counterproductive? What other paths are available to secure justice in these circumstances? If the victims in Uganda determine that ICC proceedings do not serve their interests, is it proper for human rights advocates, lawyers, or the international community to override their choice?

11. *Institutional checks on the ICC prosecutor.* Some non-states parties have expressed great concern that the OTP is not accountable. Some of the procedural checks — notably the requirement that the Pre-Trial Chamber approve investigations that the prosecutor wishes to initiate *proprio motu* — have been explored above. Is Article 15 enough? Or might invited referrals defeat this procedural control mechanism?

Some argue that political checks and balances built into many democratic criminal justice systems are both essential to the responsible conduct of any prosecutor's office *and* lacking in the ICC. It is worth exploring further the structure of the ICC in order to determine whether there are in fact institutional checks and balances available to meet objectors' concerns.

a. Relationship with United Nations

Although the ICC is formally distinct from the United Nations, that institution played an important role in the Court's creation and in funding the process of establishment. The precise nature of their relationship going forward is determined by an agreement. Under the ICC Statute itself, the UN is not given an oversight role. However, the Security Council does have the right to refer cases to the ICC, and in some instances to defer (perhaps indefinitely) prosecutions by affirmative resolution. See ICC arts. 13(b), 16. Are these powers likely to threaten a wayward prosecutor?

b. Assembly of States Parties

ICC Article 112 provides for an Assembly of States Parties. This body is responsible for a wide range of administrative matters, including providing the officers of the Court with general guidelines, adopting the budget, increasing the numbers of judges, and similar matters. The Assembly is also the forum for adoption of amendments to the ICC Statute. The Assembly was charged with completing the work of the

Rome Conference (adopting Elements of Crimes, Rules of Procedure and Evidence, and the like), which has largely been accomplished. Each state party has one representative to the Assembly, and signatories of the Rome Treaty that have not yet ratified it can send observers. The Assembly of States Parties also elects, and can remove, the ICC judges and prosecutor. See ICC arts. 36, 42, 46. To what extent could states use the Assembly to express concerns about what the OTP or ICC judges are doing? Can the Assembly be counted upon to "fire" a prosecutor who has run wild or pursued an obviously political agenda?

c. Complementarity

States may have other means of controlling the breadth of the prosecutor's agenda. The most obvious and important check exerted by states lies in the possibility that they will exercise preemptive jurisdiction under the complementarity regime. As is explored further below, if a state with jurisdiction over a matter undertakes genuinely to investigate and prosecute (or legitimately declines prosecution), the ICC is foreclosed from pursuing the case further.

d. Funding

"International criminal tribunals are proving to be immensely expensive. . . . [T]he UN secretary-general noted that the ad hoc tribunals for the former Yugoslavia and Rwanda, which were established at considerable cost, have expanded into large institutions, with more than two thousand positions altogether and 'a combined annual budget . . . equivalent to more than 15 per cent of the [UN] Organization's total regular budget.'" Arsanjani & Reisman, supra, 99 Am. J. Intl. L. at 402. The Ad Hoc Tribunals, which are supposed to be winding down their operations, are budgeted as follows: ICTR $286,687,300 for 2008-2009; the ICTY $347,566,900 for 2008-2009. See Secretary-General Report on ICTR Budget, delivered to G.A., U.N. Doc. A/62/468 (Oct. 5, 2007); Secretary-General Report on ICTY Budget, delivered to U.N. S.C. and G.A., U.N. Doc. A/63/210-S/2008/515 (Aug. 4, 2008).

The ICC is principally responsible for its own funding. It is financed by assessed contributions of the states parties, with a contribution from the UN based upon cases referred by the Security Council. See ICC arts. 115, 117. The ICC's financial status would certainly improve were it to win the support of more relatively rich nations such as Russia, China, and the United States, although the recent accession of Japan ought to improve the Court's financial prospects. To some extent, comparing the ICC budget with those of the ICTR and the ICTY is comparing apples and oranges because they currently all bear different burdens with respect to case investigations and prosecutions. That said, the magnitude of the difference in funding is sufficient to make a comparison at least interesting. The current ICC budget is less than half of that allocated to *each* of the ICTY and the ICTR as they wind up their business.

The ICC Assembly of States Parties approved a budget of €90,382,100 (approximately $116 million at a rate of 1 euro per 1.28 USD) for the year 2008. The proposed budget for 2009 totals €101,229,900 (approximately $130 million). See Assembly of States Parties to the Rome Statute of the International Criminal Court, Official Records, vol. 1, at 6 (7th sess. Nov. 14-22, 2008). Note, however, that because of the economic difficulties in which the states parties find themselves, the Assembly decided "on an exceptional and one-time basis" that the assessments would be based on a program budget of €96,299,900, with €5 million (approximately $6.4 million) coming from the court's working capital fund. Id.

The reason for international criminal justice's large price tag is that the tribunal must bear the costs of investigating large-scale and often distant atrocities, and it must also generally fund both the prosecution's and the defense's personnel and case preparation expenses. Add to these costs the costs of judges, courtrooms, administrative and infrastructure needs, jailing detainees, and the protection and care of witnesses and victims, and one has a very expensive undertaking. Might these funds be better directed to compensating victims, rebuilding war-torn societies, and the like?

Resources — or the lack thereof — may be one of the most important constraints on the ICC prosecutor. The tragic fact is that the ICC is likely to have more business than it can handle. During the prosecutor's tenure, he will consider many thousands of communications from all over the world encouraging him to investigate alleged international crimes. Ultimately, the prosecutor's decision about which cases should go forward will be influenced by the depth of the OTP's purse as much as anything else. The states parties to the ICC Statute likely will not wish to fund unlimited, expensive investigations. As Allison Danner argues, "[d]ue to the number of crimes potentially within the court's jurisdiction, [the ICC prosecutor] will not have the luxury of expending all his resources on one event. These constraints might limit the effectiveness of the ICC prosecutor, but they will also help ensure that he does not waste time pursuing trivial or groundless charges." Allison Marston Danner, Navigating Law and Politics: The Prosecutor of the International Criminal Court and the Independent Counsel, 55 Stan. L. Rev. 1633, 1652 (2003).

e. The Four "Organs": The Presidency

The ICC is composed of four "organs" in addition to the Assembly of States Parties. See ICC art. 34. The first "organ," the presidency, is comprised of three judges — a president and the first and second vice presidents. These officers are selected from, and elected by, a majority of the judges of the Court. ICC art. 38. The presidency decides on the appropriate workload of the other judges and proposes increases in the number of judges. ICC arts. 35(3), 36(2). The presidency is responsible for the administration of the Court and a variety of specialized functions set out in the Statute. See ICC art. 38(3).

f. The Four "Organs": The Judicial Divisions

The second "organ" consists of the judges, who are split into three "divisions": the Appeals Division, the Trial Division, and the Pre-Trial Division. See ICC arts. 34(b), 39. The judges who serve in these divisions are elected by a two-thirds majority on secret ballot of the Assembly of States Parties, and the judges must be nationals of a state party. See ICC art. 36(4)(b), (6). It has been argued that the requirement that judges be elected by two-thirds of the states parties in the Assembly "should ensure that they will be, and be perceived as being, impartial and reflective of the judicial community as it exists in most nations." Goldstone & Simpson, supra, 16 Harv. Hum. Rts. J. at 23.

Any state may propose one candidate for the Court in any given election, but only one judge of any particular nationality may serve at one time. ICC arts. 36(4)(b), 36(7). The ICC Statute further specifies the qualifications necessary to the job and allocates spots according to the judges' specialties. See ICC art. 36(3), (5) (criminalist judges v. internationalists). ICC Article 36(8) commits the states parties to "take into account" the need to ensure representation of the principal legal systems of the world, equitable geographic representation, "a fair representation of female and male judges," and legal expertise on specific issues such as violence against women or children.

The ICC Statute sets nine-year terms for the judges, and they are not eligible for reelection. See ICC art. 36(9). The Appeals Division is composed of the president and four other judges, all of whom serve their entire term in the Appeals Division. See ICC art. 39. The Trial and Pre-Trial Divisions are composed of not less than six judges, each of whom serves for at least three years within a division. Id. The Appeals Chamber is to sit as a full bench of the five judges, while the Trial Chambers sits in benches of three judges; the Pre-Trial Division can sit as three-judge or one-judge panels. Id.

g.   The Four "Organs": The Office of the Prosecutor

The third "organ" is the Office of the Prosecutor. ICC art. 42. This office is headed by the prosecutor, who is assisted by one or more deputy prosecutors, all of whom must be of different nationalities. The prosecutor and deputy prosecutors are elected by secret ballot of an absolute majority of the Assembly of States Parties. The maximum term of the prosecutor and the deputy prosecutors is nine years, and they may not be reelected. Id.

It is worth underscoring the OTP's mission, as defined by ICC Statute: The Office of the Prosecutor "shall be responsible for receiving referrals and any substantiated information on crimes within the jurisdiction of the Court, for examining them and for conducting investigations and prosecutions before the Court. A member of the Office shall not seek or act on instructions from any external source." ICC art. 42(1). As important, the prosecutor is required to "establish the truth" and to investigate "incriminating and exonerating circumstances equally." ICC art. 54(1).

h.   The Four "Organs": The Registry (and Defense Lawyers)

The fourth "organ" is the Registry, which is responsible for nonjudicial aspects of the administration and servicing of the Court. See ICC art. 43. The Registrar heads this organ and is elected by an absolute majority of the secret ballots of the judges for a five-year term. The only specific charge given to the Registry in the ICC Statute is that the registrar "shall set up a Victims and Witnesses Unit within the Registry," which must provide, in consultation with the OTP, "protective measures and security arrangements, counselling and other appropriate assistance for witnesses, victims who appear before the Court, and others who are at risk on account of testimony given by such witnesses." ICC art. 43(6). This unit must "include staff with expertise in trauma, including trauma related to crimes of sexual violence." Id.

Some have cited the ICC Statute's failure to create an independent defense organ analogous to the prosecutor's office as a deficiency in the statute. Kenneth S. Gallant, Politics, Theory and Institutions: Three Reasons Why International Criminal Defence Is Hard, and What Might Be Done About One of Them, 14 Crim. L.F. 317, 327 (2003). For example, Gallant has argued that a formal, truly independent institutional advocate for the defense is needed "for structural balance." He notes that while the prosecutor "may propose changes in the Rules of Procedure and Evidence, and has a voice when others suggest changes," and has a seat at the table in the budgetary process, there is no formal role in these areas for the defense built into the ICC Statute. Id. at 328. In response to concerns such as these, the regulations of the Court provided for the establishment of a permanent Office of Public Counsel for the Defence (OPCD), touted as "a significant innovation in the architecture of international criminal justice." International Criminal Court, Office of Public Counsel for the Defence, http://www.icc-cpi.int (follow the links for "The Registry," "Defence," and "Office of Public Counsel for the Defence") (last visited July 13, 2009). The credo of the OPCD is "to ensure 'equality of arms,' the rights of the defence and the right to a fair trial are safeguarded." Id. The OPCD is situated in the Registry, which will administer it; however, it "otherwise shall function as a wholly independent office." Id. The OPCD became operational with the appointment in January 2007 of its principal counsel, Mr. Xavier-Jean Keïta.

i. Assistance in Investigating and Securing Custody of Defendants

The states parties may also have more informal — but very important — methods of control. The ICC prosecutor, unlike municipal prosecutors, does not have a committed police force or guaranteed access to witnesses and evidentiary materials on the territory of sovereign states. The ICC Statute generally imposes on its states parties an obligation to "cooperate fully with the Court in its investigation and prosecution of crimes within the jurisdiction of the Court." ICC art. 86. ICC Article 93 requires states parties to comply with requests by the Court for, inter alia, assistance in ascertaining the identification and location of persons or items, taking evidence, questioning any person being investigated, serving documents, facilitating the voluntary appearance of witnesses or experts, examining places and sites, executing searches and seizures, providing records and documents, protecting victims and witnesses and preserving evidence, and identifying, tracing, and freezing or seizing proceeds, property, and assets and instrumentalities of crimes for the purpose of eventual forfeiture. Allison Danner argues that, "[i]n most cases, the prosecutor must submit his investigatory requests to states, which will then perform the investigations themselves. States that wish to obstruct an investigation may accomplish this objective relatively easily, and the ICC prosecutor will have little recourse. For these reasons, some scholars worry that the ICC prosecutor is actually so weak that he will be unable to function effectively." Danner, supra, 55 Stan. L. Rev. at 1648-1649.

States parties also undertake to comply with ICC requests for the arrest and surrender of wanted persons found on their territory — at least where compliance is in accord with the pertinent sections of the ICC Statute and procedures required by national law. See ICC art. 89. The prosecutor of necessity will be reliant on states' cooperation to secure the person of the defendant for trial as well as for her evidence. See, e.g., Jenia Iontcheva Turner, Nationalizing International Criminal Law, 41 Stan. J. Intl. L. 1, 11-12 (2005). One problem that has plagued the ICTY, the Special Court for Sierra Leone, and the Timor Leste Special Panels is their inability to secure the arrest of wanted defendants. The ICC's record in this regard is mixed. In the DRC prosecutions, three defendants have been turned over to the ICC pursuant to arrest warrants. But prospects in the Ugandan and Sudanese cases, at present, appear dimmer.

Although arrest warrants for five senior leaders of the LRA in Uganda were issued in July 2005, none of these individuals is yet in the custody of the ICC. (In the meantime, one defendant has been confirmed dead and another is suspected to have been killed.) Further, despite the outstanding warrants, Ugandan and UN officials have met with some of the defendants over the course of the multiyear peace negotiations. Rebels and Ugandan Government Agree to Terms of Prosecutions of War Crimes, N.Y. Times, Feb. 20, 2008, at A8; Barbara Among, Former Mozambican President Seeks to Rescue Peace Talks, East African (Kenya), Mar. 27, 2007, available at 2007 WLNR 5797532; Rob Crilly, UN Official Meets Ugandan Rebel Leader in Jungle

Outpost, Christian Sci. Monitor, Nov. 13, 2006, at 25. In 2008, the ICC registrar reported that regardless of peace negotiations or potential alternative judicial proceedings, the ICC would require the enforcement of its arrest warrants—but the question remains how it will do so. Simon Kasyate, Rebel Leader Will Be Arrested— Court, Monitor (Uganda), May 30, 2008, *available at* 2008 WLNR 10273782.

If this is the situation where the states parties on whose territory the atrocities occurred have themselves asked for the help of the ICC, how much more difficult will it be for the ICC effectively to investigate and secure the attendance of alleged international criminals after a UN Security Council referral of a situation transpiring on the territory of a hostile non-state party? Mr. Moreno-Ocampo reported to the UN Security Council that the government of Sudan is not cooperating with the ICC's efforts to arrest the first two defendants for whom the ICC issued arrest warrants; now that an arrest warrant has been issued for the Sudanese president, one can assume that the Sudanese government will do all it can to resist surrender of wanted persons to the ICC.

j. Dispute and Enforcement Mechanisms

At least where states parties are not giving the ICC the cooperation to which they have committed, what enforcement measures are available under the ICC Statute? The Assembly of States Parties is responsible for settling disputes between parties, although the Assembly may also choose to pursue alternative means of settlement, such as referral to the ICJ. If, despite its obligations to assist in ICC investigations, a state party chooses not to cooperate fully or at all, however, the prosecutor's options are limited. If the Security Council referred the case to the ICC, the ICC can ask the Security Council for assistance. ICC art. 87(7). Absent such a referral, ICC Article 87(7) provides that the Court would make a finding of noncompliance and then refer the matter to the Assembly of States Parties.

"As for the Assembly of States Parties, its powers, in the case of non-compliance, would seem to be limited to 'naming and shaming.' " Schabas, supra, Introduction to the ICC at 130; see Leila Nadya Sadat & S. Richard Carden, The New International Criminal Court: An Uneasy Revolution, 88 Geo. L.J. 381, 415-416 (2000). The exceptions to the requirement that states parties cooperate fully with the Court, as well as the lack of direct enforcement mechanisms available to that body, suggest to some the "unease of the States Parties to the Statute in Rome with the revolution they wrought." Id. at 416. Indeed, "it suggests that while States agreed to the establishment of the Court in principle, and even to its jurisdiction in theory, they are not willing to make the concessions to international cooperation that are needed to make the Court a success in practice." Id. at 445.

5. *Security Council "Deferral" of Jurisdiction*

In addition to the above-described power to refer "situations" for ICC investigation, the UN Security Council has the power, by resolution "adopted under Chapter VII of the Charter of the United Nations," to foreclose ICC investigation or prosecution for 12-month increments (ICC art. 16). Article 16 allows the Security Council to continue its efforts to resolve a threat to, or breach of, the peace, within its Charter mandate, and recognizes that in some situations the beginning of a criminal case may complicate or compromise those efforts. For example, some states have argued that the Article 16 power ought to be used in furtherance of a peaceful resolution to the horrors in Darfur. In July 2008, the UN Security Council adopted Resolution 1828, extending the mandate of the joint UN-African Union peacekeeping force in Darfur (UNAMID) for one year.[30] Russia, and others, supported the inclusion in the Resolution of an Article 16 deferral relating to the ICC prosecutor's then pending request for an arrest warrant for Sudanese President Omar Hassan Al-Bashir. The *Sudan Tribune* reported that "Libya and South Africa on behalf of the African Union (AU) lobbied other UNSC members to insert a paragraph in the resolution deciding to defer the indictment of the Sudanese president. . . . However the AU proposition was not included in the final draft, which instead included compromise language noting concern that any indictment of Beshir [*sic*] might jeopardize the Darfur peace process."[31] The United States has been one of the most vocal supporters of the ICC's Sudan investigation, thus far rebuffing suggestions that the Security Council ought to suspend the prosecutor's case under Article 16.[32]

Note here that the burden of political action lies on those wishing to secure a deferral. Further, on the face of ICC Article 16, the deferral expires after a year, thus requiring the states desiring a continuing deferral to summon the political capital necessary to secure a qualifying resolution on a yearly basis.

NOTES AND QUESTIONS

1. *Open questions.* This provision, like many others, is subject to important questions regarding its application. For example, does this provision permit the Security Council to grant blanket, prospective deferrals, or is it designed to be used only to bar ICC investigations and prosecutions with respect to past, individual instances of possible international criminal activity? If the Security Council acts under Chapter VII of the Charter, what restrictions might that provision impose on the substance of these deferrals?

2. *Objections to the role of the Security Council in the operation (referrals and deferrals) of the ICC.* India expressed objections to the ICC based on three "points of principle," two of which concerned the role of the Security Council first in being permitted to make referrals and second in being given the power to defer cases. In his July 17, 1998, explanation of the vote at the UN Conference on the Establishment of the International Criminal Court, the Head of India's delegation, Dilip Lahiri, explained as follows:

> [W]hat the [Security] Council seeks from the ICC through the Statute, and what the draft gives it, is . . . the power to refer, the power to block and the power to bind non-States Parties. All three are undesirable.
>
> The power to refer is now unnecessary. The Security Council set up the ad hoc tribunals because no judicial mechanism then existed to try the extraordinary crimes committed in the former Yugoslavia and in Rwanda. Now, however, the ICC would exist and States Parties would have the right to refer cases to it. The Security Council does not need to refer cases, unless the right given to it is predicated on two assumptions. First, that the Council's referral would be more binding on the Court than other referrals; this would

---

30. *Russia Concerned by UN Resolution on Sudan President Indictment*, Sudan Trib., Feb. 5, 2009.
31. Id.
32. Id.

clearly be an attempt to influence justice. Second, it would imply that some members of the Council do not plan to accede to the ICC, will not accept the obligations imposed by the Statute, but want the privilege to refer cases to it. This too is unacceptable.

The power to block is in some ways even harder to understand or to accept. On the one hand, it is argued that the ICC is being set up to try crimes of the gravest magnitude. On the other, it is argued that the maintenance of international peace and security might require that those who have committed these crimes should be permitted to escape justice, if the Council so decrees. The moment this argument is conceded, the Conference accepts the proposition that justice could undermine international peace and security.

The power to bind non-States Parties to any international treaty is not a power given to the Council by the Charter. Under the Law of Treaties, no state can be forced to accede to a treaty or be bound by the provisions of a treaty it has not accepted. The Statute violates this fundamental principle of international law by conferring on the Council a power which it does not have under the Charter, and which it cannot and should not be given by any other instrument. This is even more unacceptable, because the Council will almost certainly have on it some non-States Parties to this Statute. The Statute will, therefore, give non-States Parties, working through the Council, the power to bind other non-States Parties. If that is indeed the intention, why have we gone through this charade of a Conference of Plenipotentiaries, and the agonising over optional jurisdiction and State consent? Why wait now for signature and ratification? The permanent members of the Security Council could have got together with the like-minded and cobbled together a Statute with which the rest of the world in any case has no option but to comply if the Security Council, acting under Chapter VII, demands it. We believe, Mr. Chairman, that the role for the Security Council built into the Statute of the ICC sows the seeds of its destruction.

Indian Statement, supra note 13. What do you think of this critique?

3. *Article 16 "deferrals" at the behest of the United States.* The United States has often urged the Security Council to use its ICC Article 16 powers to foreclose the ICC's jurisdiction over the nationals of non-states parties involved in UN peacekeeping operations. Thus, in July 2002, the United States threatened to pull U.S. troops out of the Bosnian peacekeeping operations unless the Security Council adopted a resolution preventing the ICC from pursuing personnel from non-states parties participating in such operations. The Security Council, under heavy U.S. pressure, ultimately passed Resolution 1422, which stated that the Security Council, "*Acting* under Chapter VII of the U.N. Charter,"

> *Requests*, consistent with the provisions of Article 16 of the Rome Statute, that the ICC, if a case arises involving current or former officials or personnel from a contributing State not a Party to the Rome Statute over acts or omissions relating to a United Nations established or authorized operation, shall for a twelve-month period starting 1 July 2002 not commence or proceed with investigation or prosecution of any such case, unless the Security Council decides otherwise.

This measure was renewed for another year through UN Security Council Resolution 1487 on June 12, 2003. In 2004, the United States pressed for yet another renewal. UN Secretary-General Kofi Annan made a strong statement against the renewal, opining that "it would be unfortunate for one to press for such an exemption, given the prisoner abuse in Iraq [at Abu Ghraib prison] . . . and it would be even more unwise on the part of the Security Council to grant it. It would discredit the Council and the United Nations that stands for rule of law and the primacy of rule of law." American Immunity: The Unjustifiable Resolution, Intl. Just. Trib., June 21, 2004. After reports that China was considering abstaining (joining Benin, Brazil, Chile, France, Germany, Romania, and Spain on the list of reported prospective abstentions) and the failure of U.S. attempts to reach a compromise, the United States decided in late June 2004 to withdraw the resolution. Is the Security Council acting legitimately in invoking Chapter VII of the UN Charter as the basis for its action?

These resolutions were and are very controversial. Why? The U.S. government would query, in such circumstances, why it is not legitimate for it to ask, as a non-signatory to the ICC, that while its troops are participating in UN peacekeeping, they not be subject to the ICC's jurisdiction at the instigation of states hostile to U.S. policies or actions. The United States has one of the strongest systems of military justice in the world; why is it not legitimate for the United States to want to maintain the right to deal with its own miscreants? Is it legitimate for the U.S. government to say, essentially, that these issues are so important to U.S. interests that if they are not accommodated with Article 16 "deferrals," the United States will not contribute to peacekeeping missions in the future? How would you respond to these points?

Returning to our case study, note that the Security Council resolution posited there goes beyond the deferral contained in Resolution 1422. Can it be justified under Article 16? Is this provision contrary to the letter and spirit of the ICC Statute? Let us take the hypothetical one step further. The Vittima government might seek extradition of Captain Force if extraterritorial application of its drug laws was appropriate. Would the Security Council resolution prohibit that action? What if Captain Force returned to Vittima and was arrested for war crimes violations. Would the resolution be binding on Vittima's courts? What if he were arrested in France and subjected to prosecution on the basis of universal jurisdiction; would the resolution be binding on French courts? See generally Ademola Abass, The Competence of the Security Council to Terminate the Jurisdiction of the International Criminal Court, 40 Tex. Intl. L.J. 263 (2005); Roberto Lavalle, A Vicious Storm in a Teacup: The Action by the United Nations Security Council to Narrow the Jurisdiction of the International Criminal Court, 14 Crim. L.F. 195 (2003).

This hypothetical is drawn from an actual provision drafted by the United States. In July 2003, the United States introduced a provision in UN Security Council Resolution 1497, which was intended to authorize peacekeeping forces in Liberia and stated in relevant part:

> *The Security Council . . . Acting* under Chapter VII of the Charter of the United Nations . . .
>
> 7. *Decides* that current or former officials or personnel from a contributing State, which is not a party to the Rome Statute of the International Criminal Court, shall be subject to the exclusive jurisdiction of that contributing State for all alleged acts or omissions arising out of or related to the Multinational Force or United Nations stabilization force in Liberia, unless such exclusive jurisdiction has been expressly waived by that contributing State. . . .

According to Human Rights Watch, "[t]he United States took advantage of the dire circumstances in Liberia and the urgent need for international intervention to win inclusion of this text (paragraph 7) in the resolution, despite the serious misgivings of other Security Council member states. Three states (France, Germany, and Mexico) abstained from the vote in protest." Human Rights Watch, The Adoption of Security

Council Resolution 1497: A Setback for International Justice, *available at* http://
www.iccnow.org/documents/HRWPaperSCRes1497.pdf (last visited July 13, 2009).

The most recent of these resolutions was passed in connection with the March 24,
2005, UN Security Council Resolution 1590 establishing a UN Mission in Sudan.
Sudan is not a state party to the ICC Statute. On March 31, 2005, the UN Security
Council passed Resolution 1593, which referred the situation in Darfur, Sudan, to the
ICC and provides:

> *Acting* under Chapter VII of the Charter of the United Nations, . . .
>
> 6. *Decides* that nationals, current or former officials or personnel from a contributing
> State outside Sudan which is not a party to the Rome Statute of the International
> Criminal Court shall be subject to the exclusive jurisdiction of that contributing State
> for all alleged acts and omissions arising out of or related to operations in Sudan estab-
> lished or authorized by the Council or the African Union, unless such exclusive juris-
> diction has been expressly waived by that contributing State; . . .

Is this "deferral" even broader than those that preceded it? Given the political (and
public relations) ramifications of the United States' efforts to secure these blanket
exceptions, are its efforts too costly in view of the actual likelihood of ICC prosecutions of U.S. peacekeepers? Are these resolutions likely to be found effective by
the ICC?

For example, assume that a mercenary who participated in the slaughter of 1,000
men, women, and children at a Sudanese refugee camp is apprehended and sent to
The Hague for prosecution for crimes against humanity. Assume further that that
mercenary happens to be a U.S. citizen. May the ICC take jurisdiction over the case?
May Sudanese municipal courts? Is it likely that the United States will render the case
inadmissible through a municipal prosecution of the mercenary? In what jurisdiction
would prosecution of the mercenary most serve the interests of justice?

The United States has also taken domestic measures to blunt the ICC's ability, as a
practical matter, to proceed in cases against U.S. servicepersons or nationals: enacting
legislation (the ASPA) and undertaking Article 98 Agreements with other nations.
These will be explored further in the notes that follow.

4. *ASPA.* On August 2, 2002, President Bush signed into law the "American Service-
member's Protection Act" (ASPA), which includes (1) a prohibition on U.S. cooperation with (including extradition to) the ICC and a bar on provision of support to the
ICC; (2) a restriction on U.S. participation in UN peacekeeping operations absent an
exemption of U.S. personnel from ICC jurisdiction; (3) the prohibition of direct or
indirect transfer of classified military national security information (including law
enforcement intelligence) to the ICC; and (4) preauthorized executive authority to
free members of the armed forces of the United States and certain other persons
detained or imprisoned by or on behalf of the ICC (the so-called Hague Invasion
Clause). See 22 U.S.C. §§7423-7427. Originally, the ASPA contained a qualified prohibition of U.S. military assistance to states parties to the ICC who did not conclude
agreements shielding U.S. actors on their territories from ICC jurisdiction (see Article
98 Agreements, below); subsequent legislation threatened nonmilitary aid cutoffs as
well. The military aid cutoff was deemed counterproductive and was repealed.

The ASPA does give the president the power to waive its operative provisions. See,
e.g., id. §7422. And it states that nothing in its provisions would prohibit the United
States from "rendering assistance to international efforts to bring to justice Saddam
Hussein, Slobodan Milosevic, Osama bin Laden, other members of al Qaeda, leaders

of Islamic Jihad, and other foreign nationals accused of genocide, war crimes or crimes against humanity." Id. §7433.

5. *Article 98/BIA/BNA Agreements.* One of the most important steps the United States took to restrict the prosecution of U.S. nationals by the ICC was its attempt to conclude what are variously called "Article 98 Agreements," "Bilateral Immunity Agreements (BIAs)," or, our preferred usage, "Bilateral Non-surrender Agreements" (BNAs). BNAs purport to bar states parties to them from surrendering U.S. citizens to the ICC for prosecution, even if the nation at issue is also a party to the ICC Statute.

A little background regarding BNAs might be helpful in assessing the likely consequence of these agreements. As noted above, the ICC Statute generally imposes on its states parties an obligation to "cooperate fully with the Court in its investigation and prosecution of crimes within the jurisdiction of the Court," ICC art. 86, and, in particular, to comply with ICC requests for the arrest and surrender of wanted persons found on their territory—at least where compliance is in accord with the pertinent sections of the ICC Statute and procedures set by national law. See ICC art. 89. One limitation on these obligations is contained in ICC Article 98(2), which provides:

> The Court may not proceed with a request for surrender which would require the requested State to act inconsistently with its obligations under international agreements pursuant to which the consent of a *sending State* is required to surrender a person of that State to the Court, unless the Court can first obtain the cooperation of the sending State for the giving of consent for surrender (emphasis added).

This provision was included to deal with situations in which states' existing treaty obligations—such as Status of Force Agreements (SOFAs) and Status of Mission Agreements (SOMAs)—might conflict with the obligations they desired to undertake by becoming parties to the Rome Treaty. SOFAs and SOMAs are bilateral agreements that permit a state with troops or official personnel in the territory of another state (the "sending State") and the host state to sort out jurisdiction issues with respect to crimes the sending state's military and civilian personnel commit while on host state territory. Generally, in U.S. SOFAs, the "sending State" (the United States) retains primary jurisdiction over its soldiers unless it consents to prosecution by the host State. The fact that Article 98 was intended to deal with SOFA agreements is indicated by its use of the term "sending State," a term of art commonly used in such agreements. The Article 98 campaign, like the ASPA, had many critics, both as a matter of policy and as a matter of legal efficacy. With regard to the latter, some argued that Article 98 was intended to cover only SOFAs and SOMAs that existed at the time that the ICC state party ratified the treaty—and was not intended to allow countries hostile to the ICC a vehicle with which to secure impunity for its nationals. See, e.g., Amnesty Intl., International Criminal Court: US Efforts to Obtain Impunity for Genocide, Crimes Against Humanity and War Crime[s] passim (2002), *available at* http://www.amnesty.org/en/library/asset/IOR40/025/2002/en/dom-IOR400252002en.pdf. Others, such as Ambassador David J. Scheffer, explained that the Article 98 Agreements were flawed for other reasons:

> [w]e purposely negotiated the words "sending state" to ensure that Americans sent on official mission overseas—military, diplomatic, humanitarian—would retain this important protection. But Article 98 was never intended to protect unofficial actions, such as those taken by mercenaries or others acting without U.S. authority. Other countries agreed and gave us this well-defined protection. What has angered so many

overseas is that the Bush administration draws no distinction between official and unofficial actions — whatever an American does overseas must never reach the international court, regardless of whether he has authority to act. Nor will the administration compromise by pledging in the Article 98 agreements to ensure that any American charged with an atrocity crime indeed would be investigated and, if merited, prosecuted in U.S. courts and under U.S. law. There is also the substantial risk that ICC judges will interpret the American Article 98 agreements as covering only what was originally intended under the treaty, not what Washington wishes such agreements to protect.

David Scheffer, Unwilling Hands: U.S. Sabotages International Court at Its Peril, Seattle Post-Intelligencer, Feb. 1, 2004, at F1; see also Chimène Keitner, Crafting the International Criminal Court: Trials and Tribulations in Article 98(2), 6 UCLA J. Intl. L. & Foreign Aff. 215 (2001-2002); David A. Tallman, Note, Catch 98(2): Article 98 Agreements and the Dilemma of Treaty Conflict, 92 Geo. L.J. 1033 (2004).

Consider the following hypothetical. Assume that the ICC commences an investigation of atrocities committed in Colombia, which is a state party to the ICC but has also signed a BNA with the United States. In Colombia, U.S. mercenaries are fighting on all sides. Assume that one of the mercenaries commits a number of ICC crimes. The United States says it cannot and will not prosecute the mercenary domestically because he has no connection with the U.S. military or government and he has not violated any U.S. statute with extraterritorial reach. The ICC demands that Colombia turn the mercenary over for trial and Colombia demurs, citing its BNA with the United States. In what forum may Colombia's treaty obligations be adjudicated? If adjudication is in the ICC, how might ICC judges make the legal argument that BNAs concluded *after* the entry into force of the ICC Statute should not exempt ICC states parties from their obligation to surrender wanted persons to the ICC? See, e.g., van der Vyver, supra, 18 Emory Intl. L. Rev. at 144-147. *Is* Colombia in breach of its obligations under the ICC Statute? If so, what is the remedy for breach? In working through this problem, consult the VCLT Articles 6, 26, 30(4)(b), 31(1), and 60, as well as ICC Article 87(7), discussed above.

The United States threatened to cut off military and other types of aid to nations that refused to enter into Article 98 Agreements with it. By the end of the Bush administration, the U.S. government had reportedly concluded Article 98 Agreements with over 100 countries, the last being Montenegro on April 19, 2007, but some have not come into legal effect. Georgetown Law Library, International Criminal Court — Article 98 Agreements Research Guide (Apr. 2008), *available at* http://www.ll.georgetown.edu/guides/article_98.cfm [hereinafter GL Article 98 Guide]. The ICC Statute currently has 110 states parties and another 29 signatories. See http://www.iccnow.org/?mod=home. Of the ICC states parties, 46 have entered into Article 98 Agreements that have entered into force. See GL Article 98 Guide. An additional 49 non-states parties also have such Agreements in force with the United States. Id. However, many other states refused to sign an Article 98 Agreement either "because they valued the ICC highly, defending it on moral and normative grounds," or because they valued for its own sake the principle of keeping commitments. Judith Kelley, Who Keeps International Commitments and Why? The International Criminal Court and Bilateral Nonsurrender Agreements, 101 Am. Pol. Sci. Rev. 573 (Aug. 2007). Thus, 62 ICC states parties (and at least 20 non-states parties) have rejected U.S. pressure to conclude an Article 98 Agreement.

6. *Admissibility/Complementarity*

The ICC, like the Ad Hoc Tribunals before it, shares jurisdiction over international crimes with states that have jurisdiction over those crimes under international and domestic law. The ICC does not purport to "preempt" national jurisdiction; the unavoidable fact is that it would be impossible for the ICC to prosecute everyone who commits a crime within the jurisdiction of that entity. The world is simply too big, and the number of conflicts and atrocities too large, for any single court to handle more than a few such situations or cases. The interesting question is how the jurisdiction for such crimes is shared, or allocated.

The "most basic role that the ICC will have is the provision of an effective tribunal in which perpetrators of certain crimes can be prosecuted under international criminal law. In the light of this primary mission, it is interesting to note that the ICC Statute does not envisage the ICC as the primary tribunal for such prosecutions. Instead, the responsibility for investigating and prosecuting perpetrators of crimes within the ICC's jurisdiction remains first with domestic courts."[33] This scheme, embodied in ICC Article 17, reverses the jurisdictional allocation used in the Ad Hoc Tribunals, where the international forum could take jurisdiction even where domestic fora wished to proceed against the defendant.[34] This shift in primary responsibility is based on the so-called principle of complementarity, which renders an ICC prosecution "inadmissible" when a state with jurisdiction over the matter is willing and able genuinely to investigate or prosecute the crime at issue. The complementarity principle has been described as the bedrock principle upon which the ICC edifice was built. As the former chief prosecutor for the ICTY and ICTR, Richard Goldstone, has explained:

> Complementarity has various consequences. First, it allays fears that the ICC may encroach upon the sovereignty of nations. Second, the mere existence of the ICC's potential jurisdiction over certain crimes can act as an incentive for nations to incorporate those crimes into their domestic laws and so become vigilant in investigating alleged violations. Third, in the event that domestic courts do not adjudicate a matter within the ICC's jurisdiction, the ICC itself will be able to, thereby both ensuring that serious crimes do not go unpunished and that a measure of retribution sanctioned by the international community is meted out against the perpetrators of heinous acts.[35]

What, if any, are the potential downsides of complementarity?[36]

---

33. Richard J. Goldstone & Janine Simpson, Evaluating the Role of the International Criminal Court as a Legal Response to Terrorism, 16 Harv. Hum. Rts. J. 13, 21 (2003).

34. See Mohamed M. El Zeidy, The Principle of Complementarity: A New Machinery to Implement International Criminal Law, 23 Mich. J. Intl. L. 869, 882 (2002) (containing a comprehensive discussion of issues relating to complementarity).

35. Goldstone & Simpson, supra note 33, at 21.

36. See, e.g., Mark A. Summers, A Fresh Look at the Jurisdictional Provisions of the Statute of the International Criminal Court: The Case for Scrapping the Treaty, 20 Wis. Intl. L.J. 57 (2001).

NOTES AND QUESTIONS

1. *Open issues.* ICC Article 17, on its face, leaves many practical—and important—questions unanswered. For example, Article 17 provides that a case will be "inadmissible" where it is being investigated or prosecuted (or, after investigation, prosecution has been declined) "by a State which has jurisdiction over it." Does the exercise of "universal" jurisdiction by a state render a case "inadmissible"? Does "jurisdiction" in this sense mean formal criminal prosecution or can non-Western justice mechanisms or the "justice" achieved through Truth and Reconciliation Commissions (TRCs) also preempt ICC prosecutions? Consider the following notes.

2. *Non-Western adjudication methods.* How should the ICC treat for complementarity purposes means of conflict resolution that do not "look" like the type of criminal proceedings seen in Western civil or common law systems? For example, the Acholi in Uganda have a traditional system called *mat oput,* translated as "drinking the bitter root." Reportedly, this system "requires perpetrators to acknowledge their crimes, show remorse for them, and ask the community for forgiveness." Helena Cobban, Uganda: When International Justice and Internal Peace Are at Odds, Christian Sci. Monitor, Aug. 24, 2006. Those who object to the ICC's prosecution in Uganda "are working fast to have the main points of *mat oput* codified and incorporated into Ugandan law. . . . [They hope] that this will enable Uganda to tell the ICC that if the LRA leaders undergo *mat oput,* then they have been fully dealt with under Ugandan law, and therefore the ICC should withdraw its indictments." Id.

In early 2008, the Ugandan government and Joseph Kony agreed that "minor" crimes committed by the rebels during the war would be tried under *mat oput* and "serious crimes" by a special division of the Ugandan High Court. So far, the ICC has insisted that the arrest warrants are still valid despite this understanding. New Vision, Rebel Chief Refuses to Sign Peace Deal, Afr. News, Apr. 10, 2008.

3. *Truth and Reconciliation Commissions.* Our case study posits that the TRC is investigating Dr. Hate's conduct. Does the TRC proceeding foreclose ICC jurisdiction under Article 17? Does the possibility that Dr. Hate will receive amnesty in the course of the TRC show an unwillingness "genuinely to carry out the investigation or prosecution" functions? Should the ICC be able to override a state's decision to institute a TRC in lieu of criminal prosecutions? The South African TRC provided amnesty conditioned, inter alia, on a full confession. How should the ICC react in similar circumstances?

4. *Amnesty.* Note that the question of the effect of national proffers of amnesty is not restricted to the TRC context. The Ugandan government is reportedly considering granting immunity to the LRA commanders against whom the ICC has already initiated cases; some suggest that this amnesty is an essential bargaining chip in reaching a peace accord. Does the ICC Statute require, or permit, the prosecutor to bow to such amnesties? See, e.g., Eric Blumenson, National Amnesties and International Justice, 2 Eyes on the ICC 1 (2005). Would it matter how the amnesty came about—that is, by decree of the ruling party (for example, Chile's Pinochet), by a popular vote to grant amnesty to former leaders (for example, as in Uruguay), or as a part of a negotiated transfer of power (for example, as in South Africa)? Note that this is likely to be a recurring issue. As Professor Michael P. Scharf has explained:

> Notwithstanding the popular catch phrase of the 1990s—"no peace without justice"—achieving peace and obtaining justice are sometimes incompatible goals—at least in the short term. . . .

Reflecting this reality, during the past thirty years, Angola, Argentina, Brazil, Cambodia, Chile, El Salvador, Guatemala, Haiti, Honduras, Ivory Coast, Nicaragua, Peru, Sierra Leone, South Africa, Togo, and Uruguay have each, as part of a peace arrangement, granted amnesty to members of the former regime that committed international crimes within their respective borders. With respect to five of these countries—Cambodia, El Salvador, Haiti, Sierra Leone, and South Africa—the United Nations itself pushed for, helped negotiate, or endorsed the granting of amnesty as a means of restoring peace and democratic government.

In addition to amnesty (which immunizes the perpetrator from domestic prosecution), exile and asylum in a foreign country (which puts the perpetrator out of the jurisdictional reach of domestic prosecution) is often used to induce regime change, with the blessing and involvement of significant states and the United Nations. . . . Thus, for example, Ferdinand Marcos fled the Philippines for Hawaii; Baby Doc Duvalier fled Haiti for France; Mengisthu Haile Miriam fled Ethiopa for Zimbabwe; Idi Amin fled Uganda for Saudi Arabia; General Raoul Cedras fled Haiti for Panama; and Charles Taylor fled Liberia for exile in Nigeria—a deal negotiated by the United States and U.N. envoy Jacques Klein.

Michael P. Scharf, From the Exile Files: An Essay on Trading Justice for Peace, 63 Wash. & Lee L. Rev 339, 342-343 (2006). The amnesty issue raises, again, three "inescapable and extraordinarily difficult issues: (1) A question of justice: Does justice in the aftermath of crime always require prosecution? . . . (2) A question of impact: If justice does require prosecution, does this obligation outweigh all other considerations? . . . (3) A question of pluralism: As a global institution, how much deference should the ICC afford to diverse state approaches to the previous two questions?" Eric Blumenson, The Challenge of a Global Standard of Justice: Peace, Pluralism, and Punishment at the International Criminal Court, 44 Colum. J. Transnatl. L. 801, 804 (2006).

5. *Complementarity and Security Council referrals.* If the Security Council must live with the ICC Statute provisions even when it is referring a case under ICC Article 13(b), must it also bow to a state's assertion of primary jurisdiction? That is, does the Security Council have to live with the complementarity provisions of ICC Article 17? Although this issue appears to have been left unresolved in Rome and experts have expressed differing views on the question, the present ICC prosecutor appears to believe that complementarity limits apply regardless of how the case arrives at his office.

The issue arose for the first time in the Darfur situation, which was referred by the UN Security Council to the ICC. In response to this referral, the Sudanese government established the Darfur Special Court (in June 2005), two additional courts (in November 2005), and a number of ad hoc institutions to support the work of those courts, including investigatory commissions and committees. See Third Report of the Prosecutor of the International Criminal Court to the U.N. Security Council Pursuant to UNSCR 1593, at 3 (June 14, 2006). In a June 2006 report to the United Nations, Prosecutor Moreno-Ocampo noted that he was examining the admissibility issues in the case, emphasizing as he did so that "the admissibility assessment is a *case specific* assessment and not a judgment on the Sudan justice system as a whole." Id. at 6; see also Megan A. Fairlie, Establishing Admissibility at the International Criminal Court: Does the Buck Stop with the Prosecutor, Full Stop?, 39 Intl. Law. 817 (2005) (discussing admissibility challenges in the Darfur case).

It appears, then, that admissibility will not be a threshold inquiry based on state investigations or prosecutions falling within a general "situation," but rather will be made on a case-by-case basis using a variety of factors. For example, the prosecutor ultimately found the first two cases in the Darfur investigation admissible and the Pre-Trial Chamber agreed for the reasons summarized by the OTP as follows:

> The Prosecution's case is concerned with Ahmad Harun and Ali Kushayb joining together as part of a systematic and organized initiative to attack civilian populations in Darfur. There is no investigation in the Sudan into such criminal conduct. The Sudanese investigations do not encompass the same persons and the same conduct which are the subject of the case before the Court. To the extent that the investigations do involve one of the individuals named in the application, they do not relate to the same conduct which is the subject of the case before the Court. National proceedings are not in respect of the same incidents and address a significantly narrower range of conduct. . . .

Fifth Report of the Prosecutor of the International Criminal Court to the U.N. Security Council Pursuant to UNSCR 1593, at 3 (June 7, 2007).

Some contend that other parts of Article 17 raise as many concerns about ICC "encroachment" on sovereignty as that article is designed to answer. Article 17 gives the ICC potentially great discretion in determining its own reach, exacerbating the concerns of some states that the ICC may be used to pursue political ends. Consider, in this regard, the following two notes.

6. *ICC discretion in administration of Article 17: The gravity requirement.* Article 17(1) states that "the Court *shall* determine that a case is inadmissible," inter alia, when it is "not of sufficient gravity to justify further action by the Court." ICC art. 17(1)(d) (emphasis added). The ICC Statute does not, however, define what *gravity* means, thus potentially investing the ICC with a great deal of power to pick and choose its cases. In the DRC situation, the Pre-Trial Chamber attempted to set forth factors to use in evaluating gravity for admissibility purposes. Prosecutor v. Lubanga, Decision on the Prosecutor's Application for a Warrant of Arrest, Art. 58, ICC-01/04-01/06, at 27, ¶49 (Feb. 10, 2006):

> . . . [a]ny case arising from an investigation before the Court will meet the gravity threshold provided for in article 17(1)(d) of the Statute if the following three questions can be answered affirmatively:
>
> (i) Is the conduct which is the object of a case systematic or large-scale (due consideration should also be given to the social alarm caused to the international community by the relevant type of conduct)?;
>
> (ii) Considering the position of the relevant person in the State entity, organization or armed group to which he belongs, can it be considered that such person falls within the category of most senior leaders of the situation under investigation?; and
>
> (iii) Does the relevant person fall within the category of most senior leaders suspected of being most responsible, considering (1) the role played by the relevant person through acts and omissions when the State entities, organizations or armed groups to which he belongs commit systematic or large-scale crimes within the jurisdiction of the Court, and (2) the role played by State entities, organizations or armed groups in the overall commission of crimes within the jurisdiction of the Court in the relevant situation?

Id. ¶63. The ICC Appeals Chamber, however, rejected all the factors identified by the Pre-Trial Chamber. See Situation in the Democratic Republic of Congo, Case No. ICC-01/04, Judgment on the Prosecutor's Appeal Against the Decision of Pre-Trial Chamber I Entitled "Decision on the Prosecutor's Application for Warrants of Arrest, Article 58" (July 13, 2006) (unsealed Sept. 22, 2008).

In short, the Appeal Chamber reasoned that the first factor, requiring conduct that is either systematic or large-scale, "introduces at the admissibility stage of proceedings criteria that effectively blur the distinction between the jurisdictional requirements for war crimes and crimes against humanity that were adopted when defining the crimes that fall within the jurisdiction of the Court." Id. ¶70. Further, the "criterion of 'social alarm' depends upon subjective and contingent reactions to crimes rather than upon their objective gravity." Id. ¶72. The Appeals Chamber took issue with the Pre-Trial Chamber's reasoning — that "the deterrent effect would be greatest if the International Criminal Court only dealt with the highest ranking perpetrators" — in adopting the final two factors. Id. ¶73. The Appeals Chamber argued that "[t]he predictable exclusion of many perpetrators on the grounds proposed by the Pre-Trial Chamber could severely hamper the preventive, or deterrent, role of the Court which is a cornerstone of the creation of the International Criminal Court, by announcing that any perpetrators other than those at the very top are automatically excluded from the exercise of the jurisdiction of the Court." Id. ¶75.

Because the Pre-Trial Chamber and the Appeals Chamber adjudicated the gravity issue in *ex parte*, sealed hearings on OTP arrest warrant applications, and thus the defense had had no opportunity to participate, the Appeals Chamber declined to articulate what it believed the appropriate gravity factors to be, instead remanding to the Pre-Trial Chamber. Id. ¶¶89-92. What factors *should* be relevant to the "gravity" threshold for admissibility? See Margaret M. deGuzman, Gravity and the Legitimacy of the International Criminal Court, 32 Fordham Intl. L.J. 1400 (2009).

7. *ICC discretion in administration of Article 17: The "genuineness" requirement.* Perhaps more controversial are the provisions that permit the ICC to declare that a case is admissible despite the investigation and prosecution or declination by a state with jurisdiction over it because that state is unwilling or unable "*genuinely*" to address the case. ICC arts. 17(1)(a), (b), 2, 3 (emphasis added). This provision is obviously designed to prevent countries hostile to the ICC or bent on sheltering wrongdoers from preempting ICC prosecutions with sham investigations and proceedings of their own. But is it troubling that the ICC is charged with determining the "purpose" of the proceedings or decisions taken by the state asserting complementarity rights? ICC art. 17(2)(a). Or that the ICC will be judging whether there has been an "unjustified" delay in the state proceedings or whether the proceedings are "being conducted independently or impartially"? ICC art. 17(2)(b), (c). In considering these questions, one should note that these provisions do not apply only to states parties. *Any* state with jurisdiction over a crime, whether an ICC state party or not, can exercise this complementarity option. Accordingly, the ICC will be making these determinations about the bona fides of the criminal processes of nonsignatory states as well.

8. *Self-referrals and Article 17.* Three of the situations in which the OTP has made cases — involving crimes in Uganda, DRC, and CAR — were referred to that office by the territorial states concerned. One of the questions about the validity of self-referrals is whether the OTP can, for example, take a case in which the government of Uganda solicits the ICC prosecutor's help in prosecuting Ugandan rebels *without* showing that the Ugandan justice system is "unable" or "unwilling" to deal with the investigations and prosecutions within the meaning of Article 17. As Payam Akhavan notes:

> A negative interpretation of complementarity would maintain that Article 17 categorically limits ICC jurisdiction to those situations in which a state is unwilling or unable to exercise jurisdiction. That is, the ICC should be a substitute for national trials only when there is a failure to prosecute by the relevant national judicial system. This rule would

apply even in the case of states' voluntary relinquishment of jurisdiction to the ICC. . . . By contrast, a positive interpretation of complementarity would maintain that Article 17 limits ICC jurisdiction through the criterion of unwillingness or inability only when there is a conflict between the ICC and a national criminal jurisdiction. That is, when both the ICC and a state intend to prosecute, the ICC would be able to exercise jurisdiction only if it was established that the state's judicial system is either unwilling or unable genuinely to prosecute. . . . [O]n this interpretation, Article 17 presents no impediment to a state's voluntary deferral of investigation and prosecution to the ICC.

Payam Akhavan, The *Lord's Resistance Army* Case: Uganda's Submission of the First State Referral to the International Criminal Court, 99 Am. J. Intl. L. 403, 413 (2005). How *should* Article 17 be read?

The prosecutor has embraced a "positive" interpretation, indicating that in cases of self-referrals "there will be no question of 'unwillingness' or 'inability' under article 17" and that a self-referral in effect constitutes a waiver of complementarity protections. International Criminal Court, Office of the Prosecutor, Paper on Some Policy Issues Before the Office of the Prosecutor, at 5 (Sept. 2003), *available at* http://www.icc-cpi.int (follow the links for "Office of the Prosecutor" and "Policies and Strategies"). Might one argue, however, that complementarity protects not only the sovereignty of the referring state, but also the ICC itself by preventing states from off-loading politically risky cases onto the Court? Consider in this regard what some have identified as the classic moral hazard problem raised in Uganda, where "the national government could refer the situation to the foreign tribunal, rather than utilizing its own domestic institution . . . shift[ing] the financial and political costs of prosecution to the international institution . . . and effectively becoming a free rider." William Burke-White, Double Edged Tribunals: The Political Effects of International Criminal Tribunals, Address at Guest Lecture Series of the Office of the Prosecutor (July 28, 2006), http://www.icc-cpi.int (search for Burke-White).

9. *"Proactive" complementarity.* Some commentators have argued that in light of the overabundance of atrocity crimes, the resource constraints on the ICC, and that institution's commitment to allowing domestic criminal justice systems to take primacy, the ICC should negotiate the allocation of cases between local authorities and the ICC, foster domestic institutional capacity to pursue these cases, and otherwise devote substantial attention to making sure that the ICC *is* the last resort. Assuming that Article 17 even permits this kind of negotiated allocation of cases between state authorities and the ICC, is this conception of the ICC's role — referred to as "proactive" complementarity — consistent with its institutional structure and negotiating history? See, e.g., William W. Burke-White, Proactive Complementarity: The International Criminal Court and National Courts in the Rome System of International Justice, 49 Harv. Intl. L.J. 53 (2008).

10. *National legislation.* Recall that, in our case study, Rancore does not have statutes on the books prohibiting war crimes or genocide. Even if Dr. Hate were not given TRC amnesty, then, there would still be a question regarding Rancore's ability to exercise its "complementarity" option. That is, would Rancore's prosecution of Dr. Hate for "ordinary" crimes such as murder and rape, rather than for the precise crimes contained in the ICC Statute, suffice to render his case inadmissible under Article 17? Just how close need the statutory offenses be? What if the definition of war crimes differs between the two — need the constituent elements be identical? Cf. Prosecutor v. Bagaragaza, Case No. IC-2005-86-R11*bis*, Decision on the Prosecution Motion for Referral to the Kingdom of Norway (May 19, 2006) (holding that, because Norway does not have statutes barring genocide, and conspiracy to commit, and

complicity in, genocide, the defendant's alleged criminal acts "cannot be given their full legal qualifications under Norwegian criminal law" and therefore dismissing the motion for referral of the case from the ICTR to Norway for trial).

Some argue that "[i]f a State does not have penal legislation covering one or more of the crimes within the jurisdiction *ratione materiae* of the Court, it may well be relatively straightforward for the Court to determine that the State is 'unable genuinely' to proceed with the case." Katherine L. Doherty & Timothy L.H. McCormack, "Complementarity" as a Catalyst for Comprehensive Domestic Penal Legislation, 5 U.C. Davis J. Intl. L. & Poly. 147, 152 (1999). One important effect of the complementarity provisions, then, has been to spur states to enact domestic legislation that would permit them to render any ICC prosecution inadmissible; the adoption of new extraterritorially applicable criminal statutes, especially throughout Europe, has been essentially a "defensive measure." For discussion of the ways in which states have already moved to ensure that their criminal codes contain provisions necessary for exercise of a "complementarity" option, see, e.g., Michael P. Hatchell, Closing the Gaps in United States Law and Implementing the Rome Statute: A Comparative Approach, 12 ILSA J. Intl. & Comp. L. 183 (2005) (comparing implementing legislation of Canada, Australia, Germany, France, and the United Kingdom).

11. *Developed/developing world divide.* Former ICTY/ICTR prosecutor Louise Arbour has expressed a concern that "states with relatively developed legal systems will have a 'major trump card' to evade justice and will clash with developing countries that don't." Remigius Chibueze, United States Objection to the International Criminal Court: A Paradox of "Operation Enduring Freedom," 9 Ann. Surv. Intl. & Comp. L. 19, 41 (2003). Might this divide affect the election of judges and of the prosecutor? Might it also affect the decisions ICC officials make — perhaps creating irresistible impulses to guard the perceived viability and credibility of the ICC by caving to "political" pressures? See, e.g., Allison Marston Danner, Enhancing the Legitimacy and Accountability of Prosecutorial Discretion at the International Criminal Court, 97 Am. J. Intl. L. 510 (2003).

12. *The United States Code and complementarity.* Extending U.S. jurisdiction over covered international crimes would be the most potent and successful way to reduce or eliminate the possibility that any real violations involving U.S. citizens will end up before the ICC. Although some of the ICC crimes are presently reflected in the federal code, amendments may be required to achieve this end. Federal prosecutors may criminally prosecute those who commit torture outside the United States where the alleged offender is a U.S. national or is present in the United States. See 18 U.S.C. §2340A. Genocide may be charged under U.S. law where the crime happened in whole or in part in the United States, the offender is a national of, or a lawfully resident alien in, the United States, or the offender is present in the United States. See 18 U.S.C. §1091. However, the U.S. statute dealing with war crimes, 18 U.S.C. §2441, is more circumscribed. As will be discussed in future chapters, this section does not outlaw all that is forbidden by the ICC Statute. Further, §2441 allows U.S. courts to hear war crimes cases relating to offenses committed outside the United States only if the offense is committed by or against a member of the U.S. armed forces or a U.S. national. See 18 U.S.C. §2441(b). Is the United States ever likely to wish to exercise jurisdiction over war crimes committed by or against non-nationals to defeat ICC jurisdiction?

Finally, depending upon how great an identity the ICC requires between the offenses available under domestic law and the law applicable in the ICC, the United States may have difficulty exercising a "complementarity option" with respect to crimes against humanity because there is no federal statute explicitly addressed to this category of crimes. See generally Hatchell, supra, 12 ILSA J. Intl. & Comp. Law 183 (evaluating the U.S. Code in light of complementarity regime).

13. *Complementarity where nations disagree about the content of an IL crime.* Some are concerned that the complementarity regime is insufficient to guard nationals of non-states parties from "political" prosecutions by the ICC. The concern in these cases is the ineffectiveness of complementarity to deal with cases where there *is* no crime, rather than a crime unaddressed by national actors. In such cases, the prosecution would be "admissible" *not* because the non-state party with jurisdiction over a matter's legal system is, or will be adjudged by the ICC to be, deficient. Rather it is because the state party would not believe that these "politically" motivated charges have merit as a legal matter and so would not move to investigate or prosecute its own nationals.

This concern rests first on the argument that "the indeterminateness of international criminal law makes it easy to image the ICC and [states] having genuine, principled disagreements about whether a particular act is an international crime." Jack Goldsmith, The Self-Defeating International Criminal Court, 70 U. Chi. L. Rev. 89, 95 (2003).

> The most likely basis of disagreement . . . concerns war crimes arising from military strikes. The ICC has jurisdiction, for example, over a military strike that causes incidental civilian injury (or damage to civilian objects) "clearly excessive in relation to the concrete and direct overall military advantage anticipated." [ICC art. 8(2)(b)(iv).] Such proportionality judgments are almost always contested. The prosecutor for the NATO-dominated ICTY, for example, seriously considered prosecuting U.S. and NATO officials for (among other things) high-altitude bombings in Kosovo that accidentally killed civilians. The prosecutor's staff apparently advised her to pursue these charges, and her memorandum declining to do so seems tendentious because it takes all of NATO's factual assertions, in their best light, as true. Especially during a war in which irregular combatants hide among civilians, it is easy to imagine a prosecution on this basis. And who knows what might be included in the prohibitions on "severe deprivation of physical liberty in violation of fundamental rules of international law," [ICC art. 7(1)(e)] or on "[d]estroying or seizing the enemy's property unless . . . imperatively demanded by the necessities of war," [ICC art. 8(2)(b)(xiii)] or on "inhumane acts of a similar character [to crimes against humanity that] intentionally caus[e] great suffering, or serious injury to body or to mental or physical health." [ICC art. 7(1)(k)].

Id. at 95-96. Assume that an ICC state party objects to bombing conducted by another state during the course of a humanitarian intervention and refers the situation to the ICC, even though the bombing appears legal under the ICC war crimes provisions and certainly was thought to be so by the state that authorized its soldiers to conduct the bombing. In such circumstances, presumably these soldiers would not be investigated or prosecuted by their own government — they were, after all, following what they and their government thought were lawful orders. (And if the soldiers *are* investigated by their government and the state declines prosecution because it believes that the authorized actions are lawful, the state might be tagged by the ICC for engaging in sham proceedings to protect its own for their conduct of official state policy.) Is this likely to be a real concern?

14. *Politics and the ICC.* Throughout these materials, reference has been made to fears that the ICC institution, as presently structured, can be abused for political purposes. Some suggest, however, that the OTP prosecutor will not be doing his job if he does not consider in his decisionmaking political considerations. For example, Justice Richard Goldstone, formerly the chief prosecutor at the ICTY/ICTR, has stated that one of the primary lessons to be drawn from international justice

to date is that "it's all about politics." Richard Goldstone, Historical Evolution — From Nuremberg to the International Criminal Court, 25 Penn. St. Intl. L. Rev. 763, 766 (2007). First, he asserts that "[w]ithout politics you wouldn't have international criminal justice at all. Without politicians and without politics, these things don't happen and won't happen. . . . [P]olitics is the engine of international criminal courts. Money comes from countries, and it is politicians that have to vote it." Id. at 766, 773. Professor David Crane, formerly the chief prosecutor for the Special Court for Sierra Leone, agreed that while politics can be a "threat" to international justice, "[p]olitics . . . drives the international criminal justice train. The bottom line is that my experience in West Africa is that if the international community doesn't want to do it, it doesn't happen." Id. at 772. Second, without sustaining political support, the tribunals do not have the resources or cooperation without which they will not be able to function. As Justice Goldstone noted:

> Crucially, enforcement is political. There's no enforcement of any court order of an international court without political will on the governments from the countries [that] have to enforce the orders. I know that David Crane and I have probably spent well over 50 percent of our time in diplomacy, not sitting and drafting indictments. In the beginning in the ICTY, I spent 80 percent of my time on diplomacy. I would go to capitals and arrange for my investigators to travel in their countries. We had to get laws passed. We had to continue getting money from a cash-strapped United Nations. Had [David and I] not done it, neither of those institutions would have been viable.

Id. at 773; see also David Crane, Hybrid Tribunals — Internationalized National Prosecutions, 25 Penn. St. Intl. L. Rev. 803 (2007).

How can one reconcile the seeming mission of the ICC — that is, to ensure that an independent, nonpolitical OTP will bring cases against the worst offenders, even if countries with jurisdiction over the crimes lack the political will to do so — while also taking into account the apparent reality that politics *must* pervade prosecutorial decisionmaking for a tribunal to work? Is there a difference between a valid political consideration and an impermissible one?

C. PROCEDURAL RIGHTS

Fans of the ICC argue that the "highest standards of due process are guaranteed by the Rome Statute."[37] Going forward, the credibility of the ICC may depend upon the fairness with which its operations are perceived to be conducted.

1. Investigation and Exclusionary Rule

During an ICC investigation or prosecution, a person "[s]hall not be compelled to incriminate himself or herself" and "[s]hall not be subjected to arbitrary arrest or detention."[38] "Where there are grounds to believe that a person has committed a crime within the jurisdiction of the Court and that person is about to be questioned

---

37. Goldstone & Simpson, supra note 33, at 23.
38. ICC art. 55(1).

either by the Prosecutor, or by national authorities," the person has certain rights "of which he or she shall be informed prior to being questioned."[39] The person has the right "[t]o be informed, prior to being questioned, that there are grounds to believe that he or she committed a crime within the jurisdiction of the Court"; "[t]o remain silent, without such silence being a consideration in the determination of guilt or innocence"; to have the assistance of counsel of choice or, in cases where the "interests of justice so require" and the defendant is indigent, appointed counsel; "[t]o be questioned in the presence of counsel unless the person has voluntarily waived his or her right to counsel."[40] The defendant also has the right to apply for release pending trial.[41]

ICC critics often note that the ICC Statute does not contain a prohibition analogous to the U.S. Constitution's Fourth Amendment bar on unreasonable searches and seizures or other privacy invasions. Why might such a provision be unnecessary or at least not useful in the ICC context?

The ICC Statute also contains a form of exclusionary rule in Article 69(7); however, this article "does not provide for an absolute exclusionary rule regarding elements unlawfully collected, thus, placing itself at a distance from the common law models."[42] Evidence obtained by means of a violation of the ICC Statute "or internationally recognized human rights" shall not be admissible *if* the violation casts "substantial doubt on the reliability of the evidence" *or* the "admission of the evidence would be antithetical to and would seriously damage the integrity of the proceedings."[43] This means that even if evidence is obtained in contravention of the ICC Statute, or of national laws, this fact does not, without additional showings, necessarily result in exclusion.

In the confirmation hearing for the charges in the *Lubanga* case, for example, the Pre-Trial Chamber was confronted with the question of the admissibility of the fruit of a search and seizure found unlawful by a DRC court where the DRC court had ruled that the collected evidence had to be excluded from national proceedings. The Chamber determined, first, that it was not bound by the ruling of the DRC Court of Appeals. Second, it determined that the violation of the defendant's privacy interests occasioned by the challenged search and seizure was not a violation that could be "considered so serious as to amount to a violation of internationally recognized human rights."[44] In trying to determine whether the violation cast "substantial doubt on the reliability of the evidence" *or* the "admission of the evidence would be antithetical to and would seriously damage the integrity of the proceedings" within the meaning of Article 69, the Chamber stated that it had the "discretion to seek an appropriate balance between the Statute's fundamental values in each concrete case."[45] Ultimately, the Chamber concluded that the balancing weighed in the prosecutor's favor and admitted the evidence — at least for purposes of the confirmation proceedings.

In May 2006, the Pre-Trial Chambers, over the prosecutor's objection, adopted a presumption that the names and statements of witnesses upon whom the OTP

---

39. Id. art. 55(2).

40. Id.

41. Id. art. 60(2).

42. Michela Miraglia, Admissibility of Evidence, Standard of Proof, and Nature of the Decision in the ICC Confirmation of Charges in *Lubanga*, 6 J. Intl. Crim. Just. 489, 492 (2008).

43. ICC art. 69(7).

44. See Prosecutor v. Lubanga, Decision on the Confirmation of Charges, Public Redacted Version with Annex I ¶78 (Jan. 29, 2007).

45. Id. ¶84.

intends to rely at the confirmation hearing must be disclosed and that investigations must end when the confirmation hearing starts.[46]

2. *Evidence, Discovery, and Exculpatory Disclosure*

ICC Article 67(2) provides that a defendant has a right to disclosure by the prosecution of "evidence in the Prosecutor's possession or control which he or she believes shows or *tends to show* the innocence of the accused, or to mitigate the guilt of the accused, or which may affect the credibility of prosecution evidence" (emphasis added). The Trial Chamber in the *Lubanga* case has explained the requirement as follows: "Exculpatory material . . . includes material, first, that shows or *tends to show* the innocence of the accused; second, which mitigates the guilt of the accused; and, third, which may affect the credibility of prosecution evidence."[47]

Textually, at least, the ICC's exculpatory disclosure standard is broader than that constitutionally required of prosecutors in the United States under *Brady v. Maryland*.[48] As a matter of constitutional due process in U.S. courts, exculpatory material (so-called *Brady* material) need be disclosed only when it is "material," and that is defined to mean only when "there is a reasonable probability that, had the evidence been disclosed to the defense, the result of the proceeding would have been different."[49] Thus, rather than producing all materials that "tend" to exculpate as required by ICC Article 67(2), a U.S. prosecutor needs to assess only whether there is a reasonable probability — read as a "probability sufficient to undermine confidence in the outcome" — that its nondisclosure would change the court's ultimate determination.[50]

The Rules of Procedure and Evidence adopted by the Assembly of States Parties also provide for other types of pretrial discovery.[51] In particular, RPE 77 provides that the prosecutor shall permit the defense to inspect tangible objects in the possession or control of the OTP "which are material to the preparation of the defence or are intended for use by the Prosecutor as evidence for the purposes of the confirmation hearing or at trial, as the case may be, or were obtained from or belonged to the person." In construing this rule in the *Lubanga* case, the Appeals Chamber held that Rule 77's obligation to disclose items "material to the preparation of the defence" is not restricted only to material that relates to issues that "would either directly undermine the Prosecution case or support a line of arguments of the Defence."[52] "Rather, the term should be understood as referring to all objects that are relevant for the preparation of the defence."[53] In the *Lubanga* prosecution, the Appeals Chamber concluded, this required the prosecution to provide the defense with "material that relates to the general use of child soldiers in the DRC" because "it is needed before

---

46. See Prosecutor v. Lubanga, Case No. ICC-01/04-01/06, Decision Establishing General Principles Governing Applications to Restrict Disclosure Pursuant to Rule 81(2) and (4) of the Rules of Procedure and Evidence (May 19, 2006).

47. Prosecutor v. Lubanga, Case No. ICC-01/04-01/06, Decision on the Consequences of Non-disclosure of Exculpatory Materials Covered by Article 54(3)(e) Agreements and the Application to Stay the Prosecution of the Accused, Together with Certain Other Issues Raised at the Status Conference on 10 June 2008, at 26, ¶59 (June 13, 2008) (emphasis added) [hereinafter Trial Chamber Lubanga Disclosure Decision].

48. 373 U.S. 83 (1963).

49. United States v. Bagley, 473 U.S. 667, 682 (1985).

50. Id.

51. See RPE 76-80.

52. Prosecutor v. Lubanga, Case No. ICC-01/04-01/06, Transcript of Judgment, at 10 (July 11, 2008).

53. Id. at 10-11.

setting a line of defence to understand properly the situation in Ituri and generally the phenomenon of the use of child soldiers."[54]

In the *Lubanga* case, the Appeals Chamber interpreted the scope of the ICC discovery and exculpatory disclosure requirements in an important category of cases: where the OTP's evidence is derived from confidential materials received under ICC Article 54(3)(e). Before excerpting its decision, below, some background is necessary.

ICC Article 54(3)(e) specifies the powers and duties of the OTP, and it includes the following authorization: "The Prosecutor may . . . [a]gree not to disclose, at any stage of the proceedings, documents or information that the Prosecutor obtains on the condition of confidentiality and *solely for the purpose of generating new evidence*, unless the provider of the information consents" (emphasis added). Rule 82 of the RPE further provides that where material or information is in the possession or control of the prosecutor that is protected under Article 54(3)(e), the "Prosecutor may not subsequently introduce such material or information into evidence *without the prior consent* of the provider of the material or information and adequate prior disclosure to the accused" (emphasis added).

The UN, NGOs, and states have provided the OTP with information about past crimes under assurances of confidentiality pursuant to Article 54(3)(e). The confidentiality guarantee serves a number of purposes, some compelling. Thus, for example, aid agencies and other NGOs attempting to address humanitarian crises in war-torn states wish to avoid charges that they are taking sides (for example, in Sudan). Some states desire confidentiality because they want to avoid not only potential political ramifications, but also the possibility that their intelligence sources will be compromised. The difficulty is that the OTP apparently has come to rely heavily on such materials *for evidence as well as the purpose provided in Article 54(e)(3) — that is, as a lead or springboard to other sources of evidence —* because of the great difficulty it has encountered in investigating in war zones.

As the prosecutor explained to the Trial Chamber in *Lubanga*, the point of receiving these documents was "for the sake of the ongoing investigation and then to allow the Office of the Prosecutor to identify the materials it wishes to use as evidence and then seek permission."[55] In other words, the prosecutor accepted the materials deemed confidential, reviewed them, and then asked the information providers under RPE Rule 82 to waive confidentiality so that the prosecutor could use the information as evidence at trial.[56] The prosecutor asserted that Article 54(e)(3) did not limit confidentiality agreements to information obtained solely for the purpose of generating new evidence, again citing Rule 82, which anticipates that materials obtained under Article 54(e)(3) may later be introduced as evidence.

These circumstances prompted a sharp clash between the OTP and the Trial Chamber in the *Lubanga* prosecution centering on the conflict between the prosecutor's duty to abide by his confidentiality assurances under Article 54(e)(3) and his concurrent duties to provide exculpatory materials to the defense under Article 67 and other discovery under Rule 77. Despite the prosecutor's attempts to have the information providers waive confidentiality and thus permit disclosure of potentially exculpatory and discovery materials, some providers refused to do so — at least as of June 2008. The prosecutor asserted that he was not only unable to turn over these

---

54. Id. at 10, 11.
55. Prosecutor v. Lubanga, Case No. ICC-01/04-01/06, Decision on the Consequences of Nondisclosure of Exculpatory Materials Covered by Article 54(3)(e) Agreements and the Application to Stay the Prosecution of the Accused, Together with Certain Other Issues Raised at the Status Conference on 10 June 2008 ¶¶73-74 (June 13, 2008).
56. Id. ¶26.

confidential documents to the defense, but also unable to permit the Trial Chamber to view them by virtue of an agreement between the ICC and the United Nations and others regarding such evidence.[57] The OTP asserted that it had made disclosure of sufficient "similar materials" to permit a fair trial, but the Trial Chamber disagreed, suspending proceedings in the case after the prosecutor refused to turn over evidence obtained under Article 54(3)(e) and ruling that Lubanga's right to a fair trial was irreparably damaged by the OTP's refusal. After this ruling on July 2, 2008, the Trial Chamber ordered Lubanga's release. On the same date, the Trial Chamber granted the prosecutor's application for leave to appeal the substance of its decision. Lubanga's release was stayed pending the Appeals Chamber's judgment, reproduced below. The issue was ultimately resolved and Lubanga's trial commenced. Given the extent of the OTP's apparent reliance on Article 54(3)(e) in its evidence gathering, however, the question of the appropriate use of that article has continuing import.

PROSECUTOR v. LUBANGA

Case No. ICC-01/04-01/06 OA 13, Judgment on the Appeal of the Prosecutor Against the Decision of Trial Chamber I Entitled "Decision on the Consequences of Non-disclosure of Exculpatory Materials Covered by Article 54(3)(e) Agreements and the Application to Stay the Prosecution of the Accused, Together with Certain Other Issues Raised at the Status Conference on 10 June 2008"
(Oct. 21, 2008)

. . . I. Key Findings

1. The Prosecutor may only rely on article 54(3)(e) of the Statute for a specific purpose, namely in order to generate new evidence.

2. The use of article 54(3)(e) of the Statute by the Prosecutor must not lead to breaches of his obligations vis-à-vis the suspect or the accused person. Therefore, whenever the Prosecutor relies on article 54(3)(e) of the Statute he must bear in mind his obligations under the Statute and apply that provision in a manner that will allow the Court to resolve the potential tension between the confidentiality to which the Prosecutor has agreed and the requirements of a fair trial.

3. If the Prosecutor has obtained potentially exculpatory material on the condition of confidentiality pursuant to article 54(3)(e) of the Statute, the final assessment as to whether the material in the possession or control of the Prosecutor would have to be disclosed pursuant to article 67(2) of the Statute, had it not been obtained on the condition of confidentiality, will have to be carried out by the Trial Chamber and therefore the Chamber should receive the material. The Trial Chamber (as well as any other Chamber of this Court, including this Appeals Chamber) will have to respect the confidentiality agreement and cannot order the disclosure of the material to the defence without the prior consent of the information provider.

4. A conditional stay of the proceedings may be the appropriate remedy where a fair trial cannot be held at the time that the stay is imposed, but where the unfairness to the accused person is of such a nature that a fair trial might become possible at a later stage because of a change in the situation that led to the stay.

5. If the obstacles that led to the stay of the proceedings fall away, the Chamber that imposed the stay of the proceedings may decide to lift the stay of the proceedings in

---

57. Id. ¶¶64-66.

appropriate circumstances and if this would not occasion unfairness to the accused person for other reasons, in particular in light of his or her right to be tried without undue delay (see article 67(1)(c) of the Statute).

II. Procedural History

6. On 13 June 2008, Trial Chamber I rendered the "Decision on the consequences of non-disclosure of exculpatory materials covered by Article 54(3)(e) agreements and the application to stay the prosecution of the accused, together with certain other issues raised at the Status Conference on 10 June 2008" (ICC-01/04-01/06-1401; hereinafter: "Impugned Decision"), staying the proceedings before that Chamber in respect of Mr. Lubanga Dyilo and halting the trial process in all respects because in the view of the Trial Chamber, the non-disclosure of certain documents by the Prosecutor to the defence made a fair trial impossible. . . .

IV. Merits

. . . 1. relevant part of the impugned decision

21. The . . . Trial Chamber noted that in the case of Mr. Lubanga Dyilo, the Prosecutor was unable to disclose to the defence more than 200 documents that contain potentially exculpatory information or information that is potentially material to the preparation of the defence because the Prosecutor had obtained the documents on condition of confidentiality and the information providers had not subsequently given the consent to their disclosure to the defence and, in most cases, to the Trial Chamber. Thirty-two of these documents had been supplied to the Trial Chamber, albeit in a redacted form and from undisclosed providers. As regards documents obtained from the United Nations Organization (hereinafter: "United Nations" or "UN"), the information provider who had made available to the Prosecutor the majority of the documents in question, the Trial Chamber noted that in relation to 33 documents, the Chamber would not be able to see the documents themselves, but only "elements of information," and that in respect of the other documents, discussions between the Prosecutor and the UN were ongoing. The Trial Chamber explained that according to article 67(2) of the Statute it "is left to the Chamber to decide whenever there is a doubt as to the application of this provision." The Trial Chamber recalled article 18(3) of the Relationship Agreement between the International Criminal Court and the United Nations' (hereinafter: "ICC-UN Relationship Agreement"), which stipulates that the Prosecutor may agree that the United Nations provide him with documents and information on the condition of confidentiality, and that such documents and information may not, without the prior consent of the United Nations, be shared with third parties or with other organs of the Court, and referred in a footnote to the "Memorandum of Understanding between the United Nations and the International Criminal Court concerning Cooperation between the United Nations Organization Mission in the Democratic Republic of the Congo (MONUC) and the International Criminal Court" (ICC-01/04-01/06-1267-Anx2; hereinafter: "MONUC Memorandum of Understanding"). The Trial Chamber noted that it had not been furnished with the agreements concluded with other information providers.

22. The Trial Chamber analysed whether the Prosecutor had correctly applied article 54(3)(e) of the Statute to the agreements with the information providers

and concluded that he had given the provision a "broad and incorrect interpretation" because he had used the provision "routinely, in inappropriate circumstances, instead of resorting to it exceptionally, when particular, restrictive circumstances apply." The Trial Chamber found that the Prosecutor had used article 54(3)(e) of the Statute to obtain evidence to be used at trial, instead of using the material obtained to generate new evidence. According to the Trial Chamber, this constituted "a wholesale and serious abuse, and a violation of an important provision which was intended to allow the prosecution to receive evidence confidentially, in very restrictive circumstances." The Trial Chamber emphasised that the agreements between the Prosecutor and the information providers should not be allowed to "operate in a way that subverts the Statute" and that the Prosecutor has the choice between disclosing all potentially exculpatory material to the defence or not to do so in order to comply with the confidentiality agreements. The Trial Chamber noted furthermore that if the Prosecutor had applied article 54(3)(e) of the Statute appropriately, and limited its use to material that would lead to new evidence, the problem would not have arisen.

23. The Trial Chamber explained that in its view, the right to a fair trial included the right to disclosure of exculpatory evidence, relying inter alia on decisions of the International Criminal Tribunal for the former Yugoslavia (hereinafter: "ICTY") and of the European Court of Human Rights (hereinafter: "ECHR"). The Trial Chamber underlined that the jurisprudence of the ECHR and of this Appeals Chamber also indicated that any decisions as to whether information that normally would have to be disclosed may exceptionally be withheld from the defence must be made by a Chamber, and not by the Prosecutor.

2. ARGUMENTS OF THE PROSECUTOR

24. The Prosecutor submits that the Trial Chamber erred in the interpretation of the nature and scope of article 54(3)(e) of the Statute. In the view of the Prosecutor, the Trial Chamber created two categories of material, namely "lead" or "springboard" evidence on the one hand, which could be covered by article 54(3)(e) of the Statute, and incriminating or exculpatory evidence on the other hand, which could not be covered by this provision. The Prosecutor submits that this categorisation was erroneous, as article 54(3)(e) of the Statute does not establish to what uses "material *might* be put, but only the uses to which the material *can* be put without further consent from the provider." The Prosecutor emphasises that the providers, and not the Prosecutor, impose this restriction, and that the incriminating or exonerating character of the information provided may only become apparent at a later stage. Certain restrictions may only be necessary for a limited period of time, as is evidenced by rule 82 of the Rules of Procedure and Evidence.

25. The Prosecutor underlines that the ability to be provided with confidential information is "at the core of the Prosecution's ability to fulfil its mandate" and refers the Appeals Chamber to the Rules of Procedure and Evidence of the ICTY, which contain a similar provision, and which served as a basis for the drafting of article 54(3)(e) of the Statute. The Prosecutor submits that contrary to the findings of the Trial Chamber, article 54(3)(e) of the Statute is not numerically limited, nor only applicable in highly restricted or exceptional circumstances. Instead, in his submission, the realities of investigations in situations of ongoing conflict make it necessary that information may be provided on a confidential basis and that this ability "actually serves as a safeguard to the fairness and integrity of the proceedings."

26. The Prosecutor submits furthermore that the Trial Chamber erred when characterising his use of article 54(3)(e) of the Statute as being "a wholesale and serious abuse, and a violation of an important provision." The Prosecutor argues that this

finding of the Trial Chamber was based on a misinterpretation of the provision. The Prosecutor avers that when deciding to investigate the situation in the DRC, he required the material to focus his investigations. When receiving material on a confidential basis, it was always clear that the Prosecutor would only use this material for the purpose of gathering new evidence, but that the Prosecutor might later seek the consent of the providers that the material in question be used as evidence. Given that the material was collected before cases had been selected, he could not, at that point in time, assess the exculpatory nature of some of the material. In his view, such an approach is justified in situations of mass criminality. In light of the ongoing nature of the conflict in the DRC, it is, in the view of the Prosecutor, understandable that the providers would only give him access to the material on the condition of confidentiality, this being another indication that he did not abuse article 54(3)(e) of the Statute.

27. The Prosecutor maintains that "[i]n most instances" the Prosecutor had only relied on article 54(3)(e) of the Statute once it had become clear that the information provider would otherwise not make the material in question available to him, the only exception being material collected under the MONUC Memorandum of Understanding, which had been signed by the Registrar under the authority of the President of the Court. The Prosecutor notes furthermore that if he had not relied on article 54(3)(e) of the Statute, he would not have received the material in question. Thus, the assertion of the Trial Chamber that, but for the confidentiality agreements, the material would have been disclosed to the defence, is incorrect.

28. The Prosecutor states that in the event that potentially exculpatory information is covered by article 54(3)(e) of the Statute, he is under an obligation to request the information provider to consent to the lifting of the confidentiality; if such consent is not given, the Prosecutor will explore all other options, including the identification of new, similar exculpatory material, providing the material in summarised form, stipulating the relevant facts, or amending or withdrawing the charges.

3. ARGUMENTS OF MR. LUBANGA DYILO

29. Mr. Lubanga Dyilo refutes the arguments of the Prosecutor. He submits that the interpretation of article 54(3)(e) of the Statute in the Impugned Decision was correct and notes that article 54(1)(a) of the Statute obliges the Prosecutor to investigate incriminating and exonerating circumstances in order to establish the truth, with a view to submitting the results of his investigation to the defence and to the Judges. Thus, any restrictions to disclosure must be strictly construed, in particular if a third party is given the opportunity to determine whether or not material is disclosed to the defence and to the Judges. Confidentiality agreements inhibit the Prosecutor from publicly establishing the truth and therefore should only be relied upon if there is no other opportunity to obtain the material. Given that recourse to article 54(3)(e) of the Statute may also put in peril the right of the defence to disclosure of material pursuant to article 67(2) of the Statute and to rule 77 of the Rules of Procedure and Evidence, even more caution is necessary.

30. In the opinion of Mr. Lubanga Dyilo, the interpretation of article 54(3)(e) of the Statute proposed by the Prosecutor results in the Court and, in particular, its Prosecutor, being dependent on the information providers because it leaves it in their discretion to consent to the lifting of the confidentiality of the documents that they have supplied. This puts the independence of the Prosecutor at risk and results in the non-disclosure of exculpatory material to the defence, and in the inability of the Judges to ensure that the trial is fair and to order the production of additional evidence, should this become necessary. Therefore, it is submitted, the argument

of the Prosecutor that a broad interpretation of article 54(3)(e) of the Statute is appropriate in order to allow him to fulfil his mandate is misguided and leads to an abandonment of his functions. . . .

32. Mr. Lubanga Dyilo underlines that the Prosecutor does not contest that a large part of the evidence which he has collected is covered by article 54(3)(e) of the Statute, namely approximately 55% of the material relating to the investigation into the situation in the DRC, and about 8000 documents in the case of Mr. Lubanga Dyilo. He recalls that the Prosecutor informed the Trial Chamber in October 2007 that he would have to analyse more than 750 documents which he had received from the United Nations. In such circumstances, Mr. Lubanga Dyilo submits, it is appropriate to speak of an abuse of article 54(3)(e) of the Statute, in particular since none of the sources had specified the reasons for which it had requested that the material be treated confidentially. . . .

4. OBSERVATIONS OF THE VICTIMS AND RESPONSES THERETO

34. The victims agree with the arguments of the Prosecutor in relation to the first and second grounds of appeal, and repeat several of his arguments. Furthermore, they submit that material covered by article 54(3)(e) of the Statute does not have to be disclosed under article 67(2) of the Statute, even if such material contains exculpatory information. In their view, the disclosure obligation exists only in respect of "evidence." Material covered by article 54(3)(e) of the Statute cannot become evidence unless and until the information provider consents to the lifting of the confidentiality. The victims argue that in case of conflict between the rights of the accused person and the rights of the Prosecutor, the former do not necessarily have to prevail, in particular because the "right" of the Prosecutor to keep information confidential is but an obligation, which is meant to protect the rights of third parties such as victims, witnesses and other information providers. . . .

5. DETERMINATION BY THE APPEALS CHAMBER

37. For the reasons summarised below, the Appeals Chamber is not persuaded by the arguments raised by the Prosecutor under the first and second grounds of appeal.

38. The Appeals Chamber cannot identify an appealable error of law in the interpretation of article 54(3)(e) of the Statute by the Trial Chamber. In particular, the Appeals Chamber is not persuaded by the argument that the Trial Chamber misconceived the nature and operation of the provision. . . .

40. Pursuant to article 31 of the Vienna Convention on the Law of Treaties of 23 May 1969, article 54(3)(e) of the Statute must be interpreted in accordance with its ordinary meaning and in light of its object and purpose, as well as in the context of other provisions of the Statute regulating the functions and obligations of the Prosecutor.

41. A textual interpretation of article 54(3)(e) of the Statute indicates that the Prosecutor may only rely on the provision for a specific purpose, namely in order to generate new evidence. This interpretation is confirmed by the context of article 54(3)(e) of the Statute. It follows from article 54(1) of the Statute that the investigatory activities of the Prosecutor must be directed towards the identification of evidence that can eventually be presented in open court, in order to establish the truth and to assess whether there is criminal responsibility under the Statute.

42. The Appeals Chamber acknowledges the arguments of the Prosecutor as to the importance of article 54(3)(e) of the Statute, in particular in the early stages of an investigation. Undoubtedly, article 54(3)(e) of the Statute may be an important tool for the Prosecutor in the conduct of his investigations, which often will take place in

challenging circumstances. The Appeals Chamber accepts that the Prosecutor, when receiving material on the condition of confidentiality, may not be able to predict with certainty how this material can be used. Nevertheless, the use of article 54(3)(e) of the Statute must not lead to breaches of the obligations of the Prosecutor vis-à-vis the suspect or the accused person; article 54(1)(c) of the Statute expressly provides that the Prosecutor shall "[f]ully respect the rights of persons arising under this Statute." A fundamental right of the accused person in proceedings before the Court is the right to disclosure of "evidence in the Prosecutor's possession or control which he or she believes shows or tends to show the innocence of the accused, or to mitigate the guilt of the accused, or which may affect the credibility of prosecution evidence" (article 67 (2), first sentence, of the Statute) and the right "to inspect any book, documents, photographs and other tangible objects in the possession or control of the Prosecutor, which are material to the preparation of the defence" (rule 77 of the Rules of Procedure and Evidence).

43. As the present case demonstrates, the reliance by the Prosecutor on article 54(3)(e) of the Statute may lead to tensions with his disclosure obligations under article 67(2) of the Statute and rule 77 of the Rules of Procedure and Evidence: by accepting material on the condition of confidentiality, the Prosecutor potentially puts himself in a position where he either does not disclose material that he normally would have to disclose, or breaches a confidentiality agreement entered into with the provider of the material in question. The Appeals Chamber is not persuaded by the submission of the participating victims that article 67(2) of the Statute does not per se apply to material that is provided to the Prosecutor under article 54(3)(e) of the Statute. While it is true that article 67(2) of the Statute refers to "evidence" and material obtained under article 54(3)(e) of the Statute may only be introduced into evidence once the information provider has consented, the interpretation proposed by the participating victims would mean that the Prosecutor could withhold potentially large amounts of information he has collected on the basis of confidentiality agreements, without any control by the Chamber. This would be incompatible with the requirements of a fair trial, which must guide the interpretation and application of the Statute.

44. Therefore, whenever the Prosecutor relies on article 54(3)(e) of the Statute he must bear in mind his obligations under the Statute and apply that provision in a manner that will allow the Court to resolve the potential tension between the confidentiality to which the Prosecutor has agreed and the requirements of a fair trial. There might be circumstances in which this tension can be resolved by reverting to some or all of the measures referred to by the Prosecutor in his Document in Support of the Appeal and summarised at paragraph 28 above, in particular if only small numbers of documents are concerned. In the present case, however, material has been collected on a large scale, in particular on the basis of the ICC-UN Relationship Agreement and the MONUC Memorandum of Understanding. It appears from the record that when agreeing to receive the material on the condition of confidentiality the Prosecutor was aware that the material could contain exculpatory information. He relied on the expectation that the information providers would, at a later stage, agree to the lifting of the confidentiality, should this become necessary.

45. The Appeals Chamber is particularly concerned that when accepting large amounts of material from the United Nations, the relevance of which for future cases he could not appreciate at that time, the Prosecutor agreed that he would not disclose the material even to the Chambers of the Court without the consent of the information providers. By doing so, the Prosecutor effectively prevented the Chambers from assessing whether a fair trial could be held in spite of the

non-disclosure to the defence of certain documents, a role that the Chamber has to fulfil pursuant to the last sentence of article 67(2) of the Statute.

46. The last sentence of article 67(2) of the Statute provides that "[i]n case of doubt as to the application of [article 67(2) of the Statute], the Court shall decide." This indicates that the final assessment as to whether material in the possession or control of the Prosecutor has to be disclosed under that provision will have to be carried out by the Trial Chamber and that therefore the Chamber should receive the material. This understanding of the last sentence of article 67(2) of the Statute coincides with the overall role ascribed to the Trial Chamber in article 64(2) of the Statute to guarantee that the trial is fair and expeditious, and that the rights of the accused are fully respected. It is furthermore confirmed by the jurisprudence of the ECHR, to which the Trial Chamber referred at paragraphs 82 to 86 of the Impugned Decision. The Appeals Chamber recalls in this context that article 21(3) of the Statute stipulates that the Statute must be interpreted and applied consistently with internationally recognised human rights. The Appeals Chamber notes in particular that the Grand Chamber of the ECHR held at paragraph 60 of its judgment of 16 February 2000 in the case of *Rowe and Davis v. United Kingdom* (Application no. 28901/95; hereinafter: "Judgment in Rowe and Davis") that the right to a fair trial requires that "the prosecution authorities disclose to the defence all material evidence in their possession for or against the accused." While the ECHR accepted that the right to disclosure is not an absolute right, it emphasised at paragraph 63 of the Judgment in Rowe and Davis that:

> A procedure, whereby the prosecution itself attempts to assess the importance of con-
> cealed information to the defence and weigh it against the public interest in keeping the
> information secret, cannot comply with the above-mentioned requirements of Article 6
> §1 [right to a fair trial].

47. This approach has been confirmed in several subsequent decisions of the ECHR. At paragraph 56 of its judgment of 16 February 2000 in the case of *Jasper v. United Kingdom* (Application no. 27052/95), the ECHR noted that "[t]he fact that the need for disclosure was at all times under assessment by the trial judge provided a further, important, safeguard in that it was his duty to monitor throughout the trial the fairness or otherwise of the evidence being withheld," emphasising the need for judicial control of decisions restricting the disclosure of evidence.

48. In situations such as the present, where the material in question was obtained on the condition of confidentiality, the Trial Chamber (as well as any other Chamber of this Court, including this Appeals Chamber) will have to respect the confidentiality agreement concluded by the Prosecutor under article 54(3)(e) of the Statute and cannot order the disclosure of the material to the defence without the prior consent of the information provider (see article 64(6)(c) of the Statute and rule 81(3), first sentence, of the Rules of Procedure and Evidence). Instead, the Chamber will have to determine, in *ex parte* proceedings open only to the Prosecutor, whether the material would have had to be disclosed to the defence, had it not been obtained under article 54(3)(e) of the Statute. If the Chamber concludes that this is the case, the Prosecutor should seek the consent of the information provider, advising the provider of the ruling of the Chamber. If the provider of the material does not consent to the disclosure to the defence, the Chamber, while prohibited from ordering the disclosure of the material to the defence, will then have to determine whether and, if so, which counter-balancing measures can be taken to ensure that the rights of the accused are protected and that the trial is fair, in spite of the non-disclosure of the information.

49. In light of the above, the Appeals Chamber is not persuaded by the argument that the approach of the Prosecutor to article 54(3)(e) of the Statute was correct because he could rely on article 18(3) of the ICC-UN Relationship Agreement.

50. Article 18(3) of the ICC-UN Relationship Agreement reads as follows:

> The United Nations and the Prosecutor may agree that the United Nations provide documents or information to the Prosecutor on condition of confidentiality and solely for the purpose of generating new evidence and that such documents or information shall not be disclosed to other organs of the Court or to third parties, at any stage of the proceedings or thereafter, without the consent of the United Nations.

51. While article 18(3) provides that the Prosecutor may agree that material may not be disclosed to other organs of the Court, including to the Chambers, this does not mean that reliance by the Prosecutor on this provision would be appropriate in all circumstances. The wording of article 18(3) ("may agree") leaves room for other arrangements between the United Nations and the Prosecutor. Whenever material is offered to the Prosecutor on the condition of confidentiality, he will have to take into account the specific circumstances, including the expected content and nature of the documents, and its potential relevance to the defence. On that basis he will have to determine under what exact conditions he may accept the material in question, bearing in mind his obligations under the Statute, and in particular under its article 67(2). . . .

54. In light of the above, the Appeals Chamber is not persuaded by the submission of the Prosecutor that the Trial Chamber incorrectly created a category of "springboard" or "lead material," which it juxtaposed to evidence. The Trial Chamber accepted that material obtained under article 54(3)(e) of the Statute may potentially be used as evidence at a later stage — at paragraph 71 of the Impugned Decision the Trial Chamber expressly referred to rule 82(1) of the Rules of Procedure and Evidence.

55. Furthermore, the Appeals Chamber sees no error in the finding of the Trial Chamber that the reliance on article 54(3)(e) of the Statute should be "exceptional." The Chamber is not persuaded by the submission of the Prosecutor that the Trial Chamber incorrectly marginalised or numerically limited the potential use of article 54(3)(e) of the Statute. If read in context, it is evident that the references of the Trial Chamber to the "highly restricted circumstances" in which recourse to article 54(3)(e) of the Statute may be had and to the exceptional character of the provision was not meant to limit the number of documents that could be obtained on the condition of confidentiality, or otherwise to restrict inappropriately the use of the provision. Rather, the Trial Chamber recalled that the purpose for which material could be collected on the condition of confidentiality was limited to the generation of new evidence and that the provision must be applied in light of the other obligations of the Prosecutor. . . .

QUESTIONS

If, as the OTP has indicated in the course of this litigation, it has been heavily dependent upon its use of Rule 54(3)(e) for the evidence it has gathered to date, what are the implications of the Appeals Chamber ruling? Is the prosecutor barred from using Rule 54(3)(e) to obtain materials that he may eventually use at trial, assuming provider consent?

3. Trial, Sentencing, and Appeal

The parties may resolve the case by guilty plea,[58] and presumably through plea bargaining, which was a practice approved in the Ad Hoc Tribunals but which is largely unknown in civil law systems.

If the defendant elects to have his culpability tested through a trial, he generally has the right to be present, and the proceedings are, at least in theory, subject to limited exceptions, public.[59] The defendant is entitled to a presumption of innocence, and the burden of proof rests on the prosecutor to establish the defendant's guilt beyond a reasonable doubt.[60] The trial must be conducted fairly, impartially, and expeditiously,[61] with "full respect for the rights of the accused and due regard for the protection of victims and witnesses."[62] At trial, the defendant has the right: to be informed of the nature, cause and content of the charge in a language which he fully understands; to have "adequate time and facilities for the preparation of the defence and to communicate freely with counsel of the accused's choosing in confidence"; to be tried without "undue" delay; to conduct his defense in person or through his chosen representative or by appointed counsel; to examine witnesses against him and to obtain the attendance and examination of witnesses on his behalf; to raise defenses and present other evidence; to have the assistance of a competent interpreter; not to be compelled to testify or to confess guilt and to remain silent (without such silence being considered in the determination of guilt or innocence); to make an unsworn oral or written statement in his defense; and not to have imposed upon him a reversal of the burden of proof.[63]

NOTES AND QUESTIONS

1. *Adjudication: A common law/civil law hybrid?* Although the above carries with it much of the adversarial nature of common law criminal proceedings, the guilt or innocence of the accused is ultimately determined by a majority of the judges in the Trial Chamber, in keeping with the civil law tradition. A jury trial is not available. Although the judges' deliberations "shall remain secret," their decision "shall be in writing and shall contain a full and reasoned statement of the Trial Chamber's findings on the evidence and conclusions." ICC art. 74(4) & (5).

Note, too, that certain rulings by the ICC Trial Chamber in the *Lubanga* case indicate that ICC trials may have more than a slight civil law flavor. Thus, for example, as we shall see in the next section, victims may have the right to tender and examine or challenge evidence at trial (subject to judicial controls). Judges can questions witnesses. RPE Rule 140. Indeed, "the Court has the authority to request the submission of all evidence that it considers necessary for the determination of the truth" under ICC Article 69(3). The defendant can make an *unsworn* written or oral statement during trial. ICC art. 67(1)(h). And the Trial Chamber ruled in *Lubanga* that the parties must disclose the substance of their opening and closing statements to each

---

58. ICC arts. 64(8)(a), 65.
59. See id. art. 67(1).
60. See id. art. 66.
61. See id. arts. 64(2), 67(1).
62. Id. art. 64(2).
63. Id. art. 67(1).

other and to the Court a week in advance of delivering them orally. Prosecutor v. Lubanga, Case No. ICC-01/04-01/06, Decision on Opening and Closing Statements at 8, ¶19 (May 22, 2008). The ICC's Regulations of the Court, adopted by the judges in May 2004, contemplate that the Trial Chambers may take charge of the length and content of openings and closings, require that summaries of evidence and witness lists be produced, and exercise similar powers. ICC Regulation 54; see also ICC art. 64.

The Trial Chamber in the *Lubanga* case declined to permit counsel to prepare (or "proof") their witnesses; it ruled that while the Victim and Witnesses Unit of the Registry must give each witness a copy of his or her witness statements, the "party calling the witness is not to hold discussions with the [witnesses] about the topics that are to be dealt with in court during their evidence or exhibits which may be produced" until after the witnesses have given their evidence. Prosecutor v. Lubanga, Case No. ICC-01/04-01/06, Decision Regarding the Protocol on the Practices to be Used to Prepare Witnesses for Trial, at 16, 21 ¶¶28(c), 42 (May 23, 2008). Finally, it is unclear whether the more relaxed evidentiary standards of civil trials will control in the ICC. As the Trial Chamber asserted in *Lubanga*, the defense's suggestion that witnesses be warned against providing hearsay evidence was "inappropriate: exclusion of hearsay evidence is not expressly provided for in the Statute and the matter has not been the subject to a ruling by the Chamber." Id. at 21, ¶41.

2. *Sanctions.* If convicted, the defendant is sentenced by the Trial Chamber, subject to appeal. There is no provision for capital punishment in the ICC Statute. The Trial Chamber is authorized to impose a sentence of imprisonment for a specified number of years, generally not to exceed a maximum of 30 years. ICC art. 77(1)(a). "A term of life imprisonment" may be imposed only "when justified by the extreme gravity of the crime and the individual circumstances of the convicted person." ICC art. 77(1)(b).

3. *Appeals.* In the ICC, both the defendant and the prosecutor may appeal an adverse judgment for procedural error, error of fact, error of law, or (in the case of the defendant) any other ground "that affects the fairness or reliability of the proceedings or decision." ICC art. 81. A majority of judges in the Appeals Chamber may reverse or amend the decision or sentence appealed from, or may order a new trial before a different Trial Chamber. The Appeals Chamber may also remand a factual issue to the original Trial Chamber for it to determine and report back, or the Appeals Chamber may itself hear evidence. ICC art. 83.

Specified interlocutory decisions—such as decisions with respect to pretrial release, jurisdiction, or admissibility—may be appealed as of right. ICC art. 82(1). For other interlocutory decisions, the "lower" chamber controls the conduit to the Appeals Chamber. Article 82 provides the standard for such discretionary interlocutory appeals: A "decision [is appealable] that involves an issue that would significantly affect the fair and expeditious conduct of the proceedings or the outcome of the trial, and for which, *in the opinion of the Pre-Trial or Trial Chamber,* an immediate resolution by the Appeals Chamber may materially advance the proceedings." Id. art. 82(1)(d) (emphasis added). Pre-Trial Chambers have certified some questions for appeal and denied leave to appeal in other circumstances. See Jason Manning, On Power, Participation and Authority: The International Criminal Court's Initial Appellate Jurisprudence, 38 Geo. J. Intl. L. 803, 815 (2007).

It is too soon to draw any overarching conclusions from the few judgments issued as of this date by the ICC's Appeals Chamber. One note, however, may give a clue to the general orientation of that body. The judges constituting the Appeals Chamber are elected out of the same pool as the judges in the Pre-Trial and Trial Chambers. This has an important implication for the standard the Appeals Chamber applies because "there is no structural rationale for considering the Appeals Chamber superior in any sense other than its position on the hierarchy" and thus it appears that the Appeals Chamber approaches its task "in the spirit of reviewing a decision of a peer chamber rather than an inferior chamber." Id. at 808-809. Perhaps as a consequence, the Appeals Chamber has often declined to intervene when the prosecutor has sought to secure its review of important interlocutory rulings of the Pre-Trial Chambers without those Chambers' leave to appeal. Id. at 830-831.

D.   VICTIMS AND WITNESSES

One of the most important lessons the ICC learned from the missteps of prior tribunals is revealed in the Rome Treaty's provisions concerning the treatment of victims and witnesses. Victims' participation in the Ad Hoc Tribunals' work was restricted to help with the investigation, when asked, and taking the stand, when called. Many have faulted the Ad Hoc Tribunals for their exposure of witnesses to retaliation and their failure to address the suffering of victims.

In the ICC Statute and the Rules of Procedure and Evidence (RPE), the states parties attempted to address these concerns. "Victims" is defined in RPE Rule 85 as follows:

(a) "Victims" means natural persons who have suffered harm as a result of the commission of any crime within the jurisdiction of the Court;
(b) Victims may include organizations or institutions that have sustained direct harm to any of their property which is dedicated to religion, education, art or science or charitable purposes, and to their historic monuments, hospitals and other places and objects for humanitarian purposes.

Victims of crimes within the ICC's jurisdiction can provide information to the prosecutor to enable her to gather the evidence for an investigation. The ICC Statute and the RPE also grant unprecedented rights and services to the victims of atrocity. In particular, they contain express provision for victim participation, reparations, and protection.[64] Questions surrounding the definition of *victims,* and the appropriate extent of their participation in ICC investigations and proceedings, were some of the first questions of law litigated before the ICC. Consider the judgment of the Appeals Chamber, reproduced below, in the *Lubanga* case.

---

64. Victims may participate at various stages of the judicial proceedings, most often through a legal representative. Under RPE 89, victims must apply to the Registrar to participate, and their qualification as a "victim" may be tested by Chambers. Victims are free to choose legal representatives, but if they have not been able to do so, Chambers may ask the Registrar to choose a legal representative for them and the representatives' fees may be paid by the Registry for indigent victims under RPE 90. The Registry's Victim's Participation and Reparations Section (VPRS) is responsible for assisting victims in finding competent legal representation. The Office of Public Counsel for Victims provides support and assistance to the legal representatives of victims and to victims participating in the proceedings or asking for reparations. Under RPE 92, victims and their legal representatives are entitled to be notified of certain decisions (e.g., the prosecutor's decision not to initiate an investigation or not to prosecute) and proceedings (e.g., confirmation proceedings under art. 61).

PROSECUTOR v. LUBANGA

Case No. ICC-01/04-01/06, Transcript of Judgment in the Appeal of Decision on Victims' Participation of 18 January 2008 (July 11, 2008)

. . . III. MERITS OF THE APPEAL

A. THE FIRST ISSUE ON APPEAL: WHETHER THE NOTION OF VICTIM NECESSARILY IMPLIES THE EXISTENCE OF PERSONAL AND DIRECT HARM . . .

31. The word "harm" in its ordinary meaning denotes hurt, injury and damage. It carries the same meaning in legal texts, denoting injury, loss, or damage and the meaning of "harm" in rule 85(a) of the Rules.

32. The Appeals Chamber considers that the harm suffered by a natural person is harm to that person, i.e. personal harm. Material, physical, and psychological harm are all forms of harm that fall within the rule if they are suffered personally by the victim. Harm suffered by one victim as a result of the commission of a crime within the jurisdiction of the Court can give rise to harm suffered by other victims. This is evident for instance, when there is a close personal relationship between the victims such as the relationship between a child soldier and the parents of that child. The recruitment of a child soldier may result in personal suffering of both the child concerned and the parents of that child. It is in this sense that the Appeals Chamber understands the Trial Chamber's statement that "people can be the direct or indirect victims of a crime within the jurisdiction of the Court." The issue for determination is whether the harm suffered is personal to the individual. If it is, it can attach to both direct and indirect victims. Whether or not a person has suffered harm as the result of a crime within the jurisdiction of the Court and is therefore a victim before the Court would have to be determined in light of the particular circumstances. . . .

35. The Appeals Chamber considers that there may clearly be harm that could be both personal and collective in nature. The fact that harm is collective does not mandate either its inclusion or exclusion in the establishment of whether a person is a victim before the Court. The issue for determination is whether the harm is personal to the individual victim. The notion of harm suffered by a collective is not, as such, relevant or determinative. . . .

38. The Appeals Chamber determines the first issue on appeal as follows: the notion of victim necessarily implies the existence of personal harm but does not necessarily imply the existence of direct harm.

39. Accordingly, the Appeals Chamber confirms the finding of the Trial Chamber to the extent that the Trial Chamber determined that harm suffered by victims does not necessarily have to be direct and amends the decision to include that harm suffered by a victim applicant for the purposes of rule 85(a) must be personal harm.

B. THE SECOND ISSUE ON APPEAL: WHETHER THE HARM ALLEGED BY A VICTIM AND THE CONCEPT OF "PERSONAL INTERESTS" UNDER ARTICLE 68 OF THE STATUTE MUST BE LINKED WITH THE CHARGES AGAINST THE ACCUSED

53. . . . [T]he Trial Chamber stated that "Rule 85 does not have the effect of restricting the participation of victims to the crimes contained in the charges confirmed by Pre-Trial Chamber 1, and this restriction is not provided for in the Rome Statute framework."

54. The Appeals Chamber acknowledges that rule 85 does not have the effect of restricting the participation of victims to the crimes charged. However, the provision must be read in context and in accordance with its object and purpose. . . .

56. The Appeals Chamber recalls its judgment on the "Prosecutor's Application for Extraordinary Review of Pre-Trial Chamber I's 31 March 2006 Decision Denying Leave to Appeal" in which reference is made to article 31(1) of the Vienna Convention on the Law of Treaties as follows:

> The rule governing the interpretation of a section of the law is its wording read in context and in light of its object and purpose. The context of a given legislative provision is defined by the particular sub-section of the law read as a whole in conjunction with the section of an enactment in its entirety. Its objects may be gathered from the chapter of the law in which the particular section is included and its purposes from the wider aims of the law as may be gathered from its preamble and general tenor of the treaty.

57. On a contextual interpretation of rule 85, the Appeals Chamber notes that it is situated in Chapter 4 of the Rules: "Provisions relating to various stages of the proceedings," Section III: "Victims and witnesses," Subsection 1: "Definition and general principle relating to victims." The location of rule 85 in the Rules is indicative of a general provision relating to victims, applicable to various stages of proceedings.

58. In relation to the object and purpose of rule 85, the Appeals Chamber considers that the rule does not have the effect of mandating participation of victims instead the object and purpose of rule 85 is to define who are victims. Thus, whilst the ordinary meaning of rule 85 does not per se, limit the notion of victims to the victims of the crimes charged, the effect of article 68(3) of the Statute is that the participation of victims in the trial proceedings, pursuant to the procedure set out in rule 89(1) of the Rules, is limited to those victims who are linked to the charges. . . .

61. Participation of victims at trial will first and foremost, take place through the procedure of rule 89(1) of the Rules. By way of written applications, applicants will have to demonstrate, firstly, that they are victims within the meaning of rule 85 of the Rules. Secondly, pursuant to article 68(3) of the Statute, victims will first have to demonstrate that their personal interests are affected by the trial in order to be permitted to present their views and concerns at stages of the proceedings determined to be appropriate by the Court and in a manner which is not prejudicial to or inconsistent with the rights of the accused and a fair and impartial trial.

62. Given that the purpose of trial proceedings is the determination of the guilt or innocence of the accused person of the crimes charged, and that the application under rule 89(1) of the Rules in this context is for participation in the trial, only victims of these crimes will be able to demonstrate that the trial, as such, affects their personal interests. Therefore, only victims who are victims of the crimes charged may participate in the trial proceedings pursuant to article 68(3) of the Statute read with rule 85 and 89(1) of the Rules. Once the charges in a case against an accused have been confirmed in accordance with article 61 of the Statute, the subject matter of the proceedings in that case is defined by the crimes charged.

63. The Appeals Chamber agrees with the Prosecutor's contention that the parameters set forth in the charges define the issues to be determined at trial and limit the Trial Chamber's authority to the determination of those issues. Therefore, any determination of the Trial Chamber under article 68(3) of the Statute read with rules 85 and 89(1) of the Rules, in relation to a victim's status and/or participatory rights which is unrelated to the specific charges against the accused would fall outside this framework.

64. It is for the Trial Chamber to determine within this framework whether an applicant is a victim, because he or she suffered harm in connection with the particular crimes charged, and if so, whether the personal interests of the applicant are affected. If the applicant is unable to demonstrate a link between the harm suffered and the particular crimes charged, then even if his or her personal interests are affected by an issue in the trial, it would not be appropriate under article 68(3) read with rule 85 and 89(1) of the Rules for his or her views and concerns to be presented. . . .

C. THE THIRD ISSUE ON APPEAL: WHETHER IT IS POSSIBLE FOR VICTIMS PARTICIPATING AT TRIAL TO LEAD EVIDENCE PERTAINING TO THE GUILT OR INNOCENCE OF THE ACCUSED AND TO CHALLENGE THE ADMISSIBILITY OR RELEVANCE OF EVIDENCE

. . . 2. Arguments of the Prosecutor

69. The Prosecutor contends that the Trial Chamber "committed a legal error" when it held that victims may introduce evidence pertaining to the guilt or innocence of the accused, and to the extent that it permits victims to challenge the admissibility or relevance of evidence.

70. In relation to the first sub-issue, the Prosecutor advances four arguments each of which are set out separately below.

(a) The Presentation of Evidence Relating to Guilt or Innocence Rests with the Parties

71. Under this head, the Prosecutor argues that "[t]here does not appear to be any dispute that victims are not parties, nor that their role and rights differ from that of the Prosecution and the Defence. This reflects the balance of the Statute." He submits that the Rome Statute and the Rules establish a consistent system in relation to the submission of evidence by the parties. In this regard, only the parties have obligations of disclosure. The Prosecutor submits therefore, that to allow victims who have no disclosure obligations to present evidence relating to the guilt or innocence of the accused could have serious implications "both for proper trial management and for the rights of the defence." In addition, the Prosecutor argues that allowing victims to present evidence of guilt or innocence could lead to "shifting the burden of proof, which the Statute in Article 66(2), places clearly and exclusively upon the Prosecution." Finally, the Prosecutor submits that "the right of the parties to submit evidence carries a number of practical and logistical consequences" that the Statute accounts for by providing the Prosecution and the Defence "with means to collect such evidence, and in particular by providing at all times for the security of their personnel involved in such activities." The Prosecutor observes that there are no such provisions for victims and to allow them to collect and present evidence could affect their security and the security of persons at risk on account of the information collected.

(b) The Presentation of "Views and Concerns" Under Article 68(3) Does Not Include Introducing Evidence Relating to Guilt or Innocence

72. The Prosecutor argues that under article 68(3) of the Statute victims have the right to present their views and concerns. He submits that the "language of Article 68(3) thus provides that victims have been granted a right to present their personal perspective or opinion on an issue. 'Views and concerns' does not constitute the submission of evidence." The Prosecutor avers that the drafting history of article 68(3) confirms the interpretation that victims do not have the right to present evidence and points to early drafts of the Statute which included a provision granting legal representatives "the right to participate in the proceedings with a view to presenting additional evidence needed to establish the basis of criminal responsibility,"

which he submits "was removed from the Statute during the negotiations at Rome." The Prosecutor advances that "the Rules of Procedure and Evidence elaborate on the manner in which victims can participate, and comprehensively prescribe the system of victim participation." He argues that this comprehensive regime of victim participation makes no mention of victims having a right to present evidence during the trial. In fact, "the Rules covering the questioning of witnesses by victims and by the parties actually confirm that only the parties have the right to introduce evidence."

(c) The Trial Chamber's Powers Under Articles 64(6)(d) and 69(3) Do Not Provide a Basis for Victims or Other Participants to Submit Evidence Pursuant to a Request

73. Under this head, the Prosecutor submits that the provisions of Articles 64 and 69 cannot be interpreted to mean that victims could or should present evidence pertaining to the guilt or innocence of the accused. He argues that "the erroneous conflation of the interests of the victims and the role of the Prosecution" led to the Trial Chamber's ruling that victims will be allowed "to tender and examine evidence if in the view of the Chamber it will assist in the determination of the truth."

74. Moreover, he argues that "the Trial Chamber links the modalities of victims participation not to the autonomous and victims-specific provisions of Article 68 but to provisions regulating the functions and powers of the Chambers. This is not consistent with the specific participatory regime created by the Statute." In addition the Prosecutor submits that Article 69(3) and Article 64(6)(d) "provide the Chamber with an important, though residual, power to monitor and regulate the presentation of evidence by the parties, without affecting the rights of the victims." He argues that the language of these provisions do not create an independent basis for the submission of evidence by a participant. In the context of the drafting history of the Statute, the Prosecutor submits that "states moved away from a position where the Court had a duty to call evidence itself." Instead, he avers that the purpose of the provisions under consideration is "to ensure that the Chamber was not constrained by the evidence that the parties chose to provide and could ask the parties to present further evidence in their possession under certain circumstances."

(d) The Nature of Victim Participation in the Reparation Phase

75. The Prosecutor submits that "it is only during reparations proceedings that victims may submit material to the Chamber for the purposes of supporting a claim or influencing the determination of the ultimate issue."

76. In relation to the second sub-issue, the Prosecutor advances that "[a]rticle 64(9) refers to the Trial Chamber exercising its powers to rule on admissibility 'on application of *a party* or on its own motion.'" Thus the Prosecutor submits that the Trial Chamber erred to the extent that it granted the request of the legal representatives of victims to have the opportunity to challenge evidence.

3. Arguments of the Defence . . .

78. . . . [T]he Defence avers that the right to present evidence relating to guilt or innocence rests with the parties. The Defence submits that "[a]uthorising victims to submit evidence or to express their opinion on the evidence would mean forcing the defendant to confront more than one accuser, which would violate the principle of equality of arms, one of the necessary elements of a fair trial." In addition the Defence argue that "[t]he texts are clear in setting out the Prosecutor's disclosure obligations, as well as those of the Defence — in the rare cases that this applies. The total absence

of any provisions governing the disclosure of evidence by victims only serves to confirm that they may not lead evidence during the trial." . . .

7. Determination by the Appeals Chamber

86. In establishing a framework for the right of victims participating at trial to lead evidence and to challenge the admissibility or relevance of evidence the Trial Chamber stated . . . that "victims participating in the proceedings may be permitted to tender and examine evidence if in the view of the Chamber it will assist in the determination of the truth, and if in this sense the Court has 'requested' the evidence." [The Trial Chamber] stated further that "there is no provision within the Rome Statute framework which prohibits the Trial Chamber from ruling on the admissibility or relevance of evidence having taken into account the views and concerns of the victims, in accordance with Articles 68(3) and 69(4) of the Statute. In appropriate circumstances this will be allowed following an application." Earlier in [its opinion,] the Trial Chamber decided that "in order to participate at any specific stage in the proceedings, e.g. during the examination of a particular witness or the discussion of a particular legal issue or type of evidence, a victim will be required to show, in a discrete written application, the reasons why his or her interests are affected by the evidence or issue then arising in the case and the nature and extent of the participation they seek."

87. The Trial Chamber, in reaching these conclusions, relied on the following provisions of the Statute and the Rules:

88. Article 69(3) of the Statute, with emphasis on the second sentence, which provides:

> The parties may submit evidence relevant to the case, in accordance with Article 64. The Court shall have the authority to request the submission of all evidence that it considers necessary for the determination of the truth.

89. Rule 91(3) of the Rules provides:

> (a) When a legal representative attends and participates in accordance with this rule, and wishes to question a witness, including questioning under rules 67 and 68, an expert or the accused, the legal representative must make application to the Chamber. The Chamber may require the legal representative to provide a written note of the questions and in that case the questions shall be communicated to the Prosecutor and, if appropriate, the defence, who shall be allowed to make observations within a time limit set by the Chamber.
>
> (b) The Chamber shall then issue a ruling on the request, taking into account the stage of the proceedings, the rights of the accused, the interests of the witnesses, the need for a fair, impartial and expeditious trial and in order to give effect to article 68, paragraph 3. The ruling may include directions on the manner and order of the questions and the production of documents in accordance with the powers of the Chamber under article 64. The Chamber may, if it considers it appropriate, put the question to the witness, expert or accused on behalf of the victim's legal representative.

90. Article 68(3) of the Statute, in relevant part, provides:

> Where the personal interests of the victims are affected, the Court shall permit their views and concerns to be presented and considered at stages of the proceedings

determined to be appropriate by the Court and in a manner which is not prejudicial to or inconsistent with the rights of the accused and a fair and impartial trial. [. . .]

91. Article 69 (4), in relevant part, provides:

The Court may rule on the relevance or admissibility of any evidence, taking into account, inter alia, the probative value of the evidence and any prejudice that such evidence may cause to a fair trial [. . . .] . . .

93. The Appeals Chamber considers it important to underscore that the right to lead evidence pertaining to the guilt or innocence of the accused and the right to challenge the admissibility or relevance of evidence in trial proceedings lies primarily with the parties, namely, the Prosecutor and the Defence. The first sentence of article 69(3) is categorical: "[t]he parties may submit evidence relevant to the case, in accordance with article 64." It does not say "parties and victims may." The language of article 69(3) cited above, and article 64(6)(d) which provides that the Court shall have the authority to "[o]rder the production of evidence in addition to that already collected prior to the trial or presented during the trial by the parties" clearly envisions that evidence presented during the trial would be presented by the parties. The Rome Statute framework contains numerous provisions which support this interpretation such as those pertaining to the role assigned specifically to the Prosecutor in, inter alia, investigating the crimes, formulating the charges and determining what evidence should be brought in relation to the charges (articles 15, 53, 54, 58 and 61(5) of the Statute). Article 66(2) of the Statute provides: "[t]he onus is on the Prosecutor to prove the guilt of the accused." Presumptively, it is the Prosecutor's function to lead evidence of the guilt of the accused. In addition, the regime for disclosure contained in rules 76 to 84 of the Rules which sets out the specific obligations of the parties in this regard is a further indicator that the scheme is directed towards the parties and not victims.

94. However, the Appeals Chamber does not consider these provisions to preclude the possibility for victims to lead evidence pertaining to the guilt or innocence of the accused and to challenge the admissibility or relevance of evidence during the trial proceedings.

95. While mindful that the Prosecutor bears the onus of proving the guilt of the accused, it is nevertheless clear that "the Court has the authority to request the submission of all evidence that it considers necessary for the determination of the truth" (article 69(3) of the Statute). The fact that the onus lies on the Prosecutor cannot be read to exclude the statutory powers of the court, as it is the court that "must be convinced of the guilt of the accused beyond reasonable doubt" (article 66(3) of the Statute).

96. Indeed, the Statute by virtue of article 68(3) establishes the right for victim participation, for the first time, in international criminal proceedings. This right may be exercised where the personal interests of victims are affected at stages of the proceedings determined to be appropriate by the Court and in a manner which is not prejudicial to or inconsistent with the rights of the accused and a fair and impartial trial.

97. To give effect to the spirit and intention of article 68(3) of the Statute in the context of the trial proceedings it must be interpreted so as to make participation by victims meaningful. Evidence to be tendered at trial which does not pertain to the

guilt or innocence of the accused would most likely be considered inadmissible and irrelevant. If victims were generally and under all circumstances precluded from tendering evidence relating to the guilt or innocence of the accused and from challenging the admissibility or relevance of evidence, their right to participate in the trial would potentially become ineffectual.

98. The framework established by the Trial Chamber, as outlined in paragraph 86 above, is premised on an interpretation of article 69(3), second sentence, read with article 68(3) and rule 91(3) of the Rules, pursuant to which the Chamber, in exercising its competent powers, leaves open the possibility for victims to move the Chamber to request the submission of all evidence that it considers necessary for the determination of the truth.

99. In so doing the Trial Chamber did not create an unfettered right for victims to lead or challenge evidence, instead victims are required to demonstrate why their interests are affected by the evidence or issue, upon which the Chamber will decide, on a case-by-case basis whether or not to allow such participation. For example, should a victim demonstrate that his or her personal interests would be negatively affected if a particular witness (who could attest to the harm suffered by the victim) was not called to testify or if a piece of evidence (which would have ramifications on the safety and security of the victim) were to be declared admissible, then the victim would be able to move the Chamber to exercise its powers under article 69(3) to present the evidence or challenge the admissibility of the evidence respectively.

100. In deciding each application the Trial Chamber, being vigilant in safeguarding the rights of the accused could take into account, inter alia, whether the hearing of such evidence would be appropriate, timely or for other reasons should not be ordered. If the Trial Chamber decides that the evidence should be presented then it could rule on the modalities for the proper disclosure of such evidence before allowing it to be adduced and depending on the circumstances it could order one of the parties to present the evidence, call the evidence itself, or order the victims to present the evidence.

101. In relation to the right afforded to victims to challenge the admissibility or relevance of evidence, the Trial Chamber relied on its general powers under article 69(4) to declare any evidence admissible or relevant. The provision is silent as to who may challenge such evidence. Under article 64(9) of the Statute, the Trial Chamber has the power to rule on the admissibility or relevance of evidence on its own motion. These provisions must be seen in light of the provisions on victims' participation, in particular article 68(3) of the Statute and rules 89 and 91 of the Rules. In light of these provisions, nothing in articles 69(4) and 64(9) excludes the possibility of a Trial Chamber ruling on the admissibility or relevance of evidence after having received submissions by the victims on said evidence. The approach of the Trial Chamber in interpreting its powers, once again does not result in an unfettered right for victims but is subject to the application of article 68(3), which is the founding provision governing victim participation in the proceedings.

102. In addition the Trial Chamber finds support for this approach in the provision under rule 91(3) of the Rules. Under this rule the Trial Chamber may authorise, upon request, the legal representatives of victims to question witnesses or to produce documents in the restricted manner ordered. The Appeals Chamber considers that it cannot be ruled out that such questions or documents may pertain to the guilt or innocence of the accused and may go towards challenging the admissibility or relevance of evidence in so far as it may affect their interests earlier identified and subject to the confines of their right to participate. To exemplify this position one may envisage the adduction of evidence irrelevant to or inadmissible with regard to

identification of the harm suffered by the victim. The evidence may have a source lacking credibility or may not bear relevance to the identification of such harm. In some such situations, participating victims may challenge the admissibility or relevance of evidence to be adduced where its admission would affect their personal interests.

103. Other instances noted by the legal representatives of the victims merit consideration. In paragraph 29 of the Victims' Observations the legal representatives aver that:

> The personal interest of the victims may be affected by the presentation of a piece of evidence, and that they may have an interest in challenging its admissibility or relevance. That may even be one of the motivating factors for their participation in the proceedings. Such interest may result from the consequences which the evidence presented or proposed may have on their possible right to reparations, but also because the presentation of certain pieces of evidence may be directly prejudicial to them. By way of example, we can mention evidence:
>
> - which violates the rules of confidentiality, in particular, if the confidentiality affects victim protection (article 69(5))
> - which is obtained by a means which violates an internationally recognised human right of the victim or a family member (article 69(7))
> - whose presentation might be harmful to their security and safety or dignity
> - which would violate rules 70 and 71 in the case of sexual violence
> - which would violate an arrangement with the victim or a family member pursuant to article 54(d).

104. The Trial Chamber has correctly identified the procedure and confined limits within which it will exercise its powers to permit victims to tender and examine evidence: (i) a discrete application, (ii) notice to the parties, (iii) demonstration of personal interests that are affected by the specific proceedings, (iv) compliance with disclosure obligations and protection orders, (v) determination of appropriateness and (vi) consistency with the rights of the accused and a fair trial. With these safeguards in place, the Appeals Chamber does not consider that the grant of participatory rights to victims to lead evidence pertaining to the guilt or innocence of the accused and to challenge the admissibility or relevance of the evidence is inconsistent with the onus of the Prosecutor to prove the guilt of the accused nor is it inconsistent with the rights of the accused and a fair trial.

105. Accordingly, the Appeals Chamber confirms the decision of the Trial Chamber allowing participating victims the possibility to lead evidence pertaining to the guilt or innocence of the accused, and to challenge the admissibility or relevance of evidence in the trial proceedings. . . .

B. PARTLY DISSENTING OPINION OF JUDGE G.M. PIKIS

[Judge Pikis agreed with the Court's disposition of the first two issues, except to the extent that the Court held that harm need not be direct. The focus of the Judge's dissent, however, was on the third issue presented.]

4. I dissent from the majority judgment with regard to the resolution of [the third issue presented,] . . . namely whether it is possible for victims participating at the criminal trial a) to lead evidence pertaining to the guilt or innocence of the accused and b) to challenge the admissibility or relevance of evidence.

5. My answer to both questions is in the negative. Victims can neither adduce evidence on the guilt or innocence of the accused nor challenge the admissibility or relevance of evidence. My reasons for so holding are explained below.

6. The Statute does not permit the participation of anyone in the proof or disproof of the charges other than the Prosecutor and the accused. Exclusive responsibility is cast on the Prosecution for the investigation of a case, the collection of evidence, the arrest of the person, the substantiation of the charges at the confirmation hearing, and their proof at the trial.

7. The Prosecutor is the authority upon whom power is reposed to carry out investigations into a crime referred to him or coming to his notice. If he concludes that there is a reasonable basis for holding an investigation, he must seek authorisation from the Pre-Trial Chamber to hold an investigation. The initiation of an investigation is the prelude to any steps that may be taken thereafter for bringing a person to justice.

8. The investigatory and prosecutorial processes are entwined in the person of the Prosecutor. The Prosecutor is the organ of the Court to whom power is vested to apply for the issuance of a warrant of arrest or the issuance of a summons calling the person to appear. Article 54 of the Statute binds the Prosecutor to extend the investigation to all facts relevant to determining whether there appears to be criminal responsibility on the part of a person. In so doing, he is bound to investigate "incriminating and exonerating circumstances equally."

9. It is the duty of the Prosecutor to provide the person under investigation with a copy of the document containing the charges and the evidence on which the Prosecutor intends to rely at the confirmation hearing. Moreover, he is duty-bound to disclose to the person all evidence relevant to the cause, subject to any exceptions sanctioned under rule 81 of the Rules, and to make available for inspection to him/her material in his possession or control. The accused is not put on trial upon the charges preferred by the Prosecutor. The charges must be approved by the Pre-Trial Chamber upon the Prosecutor supporting "each charge with sufficient evidence to establish substantial grounds to believe that the person committed the crime charged." The confirmation of the charges depends on the discharge of this burden. No one other than the Prosecutor is vested with authority to adduce evidence at the confirmation hearing, evidence that may be challenged by the person who is also entitled to object to the charges, to challenge evidence presented by the Prosecutor, and to present evidence himself.

10. Rights comparable to those of the accused are assured to the person against whom the charges are directed at the confirmation hearing. Like the Pre-Trial Chamber, the Trial Chamber too must, prior to the commencement of the trial, make provision for the disclosure of documents or information not previously disclosed in order to afford an opportunity to the accused to prepare for the trial. Disclosure of evidence in the form of witness statements and material bearing on the charges is a prerequisite for the holding of a confirmation hearing and the trial. This is the norm laid down in the Statute, reflecting the norms of a fair trial.

11. It must be reminded that upon constitution of the Trial Chamber, the record of the proceedings before the Pre-Trial Chamber, that is, the record of the confirmation hearing, must be transmitted to the Trial Chamber.

12. The burden of proving the charges is on the Prosecutor. Article 66(2) of the Statute provides, "The onus is on the Prosecutor to prove the guilt of the accused." The Prosecutor is the only authority the accused has to confront in relation to the charges. The two sides are locked into a conflict upon the denial of the charges by

the accused. Neither the Trial Chamber nor the Pre-Trial Chamber is concerned with the collection of evidence. The Trial Chamber, as provided in article 69(3) of the Statute, may request either party to submit all evidence that it considers necessary for the determination of the truth; such evidence, no doubt, is the evidence of which it is apprised by the record of the confirmation hearing before it. The Trial Chamber is vested with a like power in the case of a plea of guilty, as it emerges from the provisions of article 65(3) of the Statute.

13. The Trial Chamber is bound to assure a fair and expeditious trial, with due regard to the rights of the accused and the protection of victims and witnesses, whose protection is envisaged by the provisions of article 68(1) of the Statute. The obligation to hold a trial in accordance with the norms of a fair trial is also imposed by the provisions of article 21(3) of the Statute. A fair trial entails an adversarial hearing, warranted, inter alia, by the rights of the accused, the sustenance of which is an inseverable element of a fair trial. Timely prior disclosure of the evidence that will be adduced at the trial, necessary for the preparation of the defence, is assured as a right of the accused by the provisions of article 67 of the Statute.

14. A series of decisions of the European Court of Human Rights identify the nature of a hearing conforming to the norms of a fair trial. An adversarial hearing casts the Prosecution and the defence in opposition, confronting one another in a process designed to determine whether the burden cast on the Prosecution is discharged at the end of the day. Fair trial imports equality of arms, as stressed in the case of *Brandstetter v. Austria*[, Judgement of 28 August 1991, Application No. 11170/84; 12876/87; 13468/87, ¶66.] Adversarial proceedings, it was said, entail the right, in a criminal case, "that both prosecution and defence must be given the opportunity to have knowledge of and comment on the observations filed and the evidence adduced by the other party." Adversarial proceedings are "intended above all to secure the interests of the parties and those of the proper administration of justice." It is worth mentioning that in *Dombo Beheer BV v. Netherlands*, [Judgment of 27 October 1993, Application No. 14448/88, ¶32,] the Chamber underlined that the requisites of an adversarial hearing must be strictly observed in criminal cases. In sum, in an adversarial hearing the two sides are cast in the position of adversaries, in connection with the determination of the only issue raised before the Chamber, the guilt or innocence of the accused. The adversary of the accused is the Prosecutor and none other. The defendant cannot have more than one accuser. It is not for the accused to prove his innocence. He is presumed to be innocent. The ultimate question is whether the Prosecution proved its case beyond reasonable doubt.

15. The participation of victims in the proceedings is confined to the expression of their views and concerns. As explained in my separate, concurring opinion in the decision of the Appeals Chamber of 13 June 2007, participation of victims is confined to the expression of their "views and concerns," whereafter I added, "It is a highly qualified participation limited to the voicing of their views and concerns. Victims are not made parties to the proceedings nor can they proffer or advance anything other than their 'views and concerns.'" In relation to what can victims express their views and concerns was the next subject I addressed in the above case. "Not in relation to the proof of the case or the advancement of the defence. The burden of proof of the guilt of the accused lies squarely with the Prosecutor (article 66(2) of the Statute). Provision is made in the Statute (article 54(1)) for the Prosecutor to seek and obtain information from victims about the facts surrounding the crime or crimes forming the subject-matter of the proceedings. That the judicial process should follow its

ordained course is a cause common to all; its sustenance is the responsibility of the Court, the guardian of the judicial process. It is not the victims' domain either to reinforce the prosecution or dispute the defence." The views and concerns of victims are, as indicated in the same opinion, ". . . referable to the cause that legitimizes their participation, the cause that distinguishes them from other victims, namely their personal interests to the extent they are affected by the proceedings."

16. The rights of the person under charge at the confirmation hearing and the accused assure them ". . . of prior knowledge of evidence and information founding the case against him/her. Such knowledge must be gained prior to the confirmation hearing or the trial in order to enable the person under charge or the accused to prepare the defence to the case against him/her."

17. Rule 91 of the Rules aims to elicit the parameters of participation. It is made clear that victims cannot question witnesses as of right. They may do so after the prior authorisation of the Chamber, and in a manner prescribed by the Chamber. Such questions must necessarily relate to the personal interests of the victims that legitimise their participation. Moreover, account must be taken of the rights of the accused, and in a manner that is neither prejudicial to nor inconsistent with the rights of the accused and a fair and impartial trial. It would not, for instance, be permissible for victims to raise questions relating to facts of which the accused was not forewarned by the disclosure of evidence on the subject. Under the Statute, the entire process, from investigation to trial, is fashioned on the principles of an adversarial hearing.

18. Victims may themselves be witnesses. Concerns about their safety and their right to reparations are no doubt subjects of concern to them. Participation of a victim at the trial, it must be clarified, is not a prerequisite for claiming reparations. Rule 94 of the Rules identifies the particulars to be provided by a victim claiming reparations. But reparations under the scheme of the Statute can only be claimed against a convicted person (article 77(2)).

19. Amenity on the part of victims to challenge the admissibility or relevance of evidence is the next issue to be addressed. The test for the reception of evidence is relevance to the subject-matter of the proceedings, that is, the charges. Relevant evidence is admissible unless the Court, for reasons laid down in the Statute, holds it to be inadmissible. Such reasons are identified in article 69(4) and (7) of the Statute. Evidence may be rejected on account of its probative value, or more accurately lack of it, and prejudice it may occasion to a fair trial or a fair evaluation of the testimony of a witness. Relevant evidence may also be rejected if obtained in breach of human rights if the violation casts doubts on the reliability of the evidence or where its admission would be antithetical or seriously damaging to the integrity of the proceedings. Logic is the guide to the determination of the relevance of evidence to the subject-matter of the proceedings, defined by the charges confronting the accused. The proof or disproof of the charges is a matter affecting the adversaries. The victims have no say in the matter. Their interest is that justice should be done, coinciding with the interest of the world at large that the criminal process should run its course according to law, according to the norms of a fair trial. Both the submission of evidence and its reception affect the parties to the adversity. It is not the victims' concern, a matter directly related to the reception of evidence, to either prove or disprove the charges. The interests of justice are safeguarded by the Chamber, trusted to ensure that only relevant and admissible evidence, in the context earlier defined, can be received in proceedings before it. The presumption of innocence leaves no room for anyone other than the Prosecutor to assert the contrary and seek to prove it by the adduction of relevant evidence, admissible in the criminal proceedings before the Chamber.

NOTES AND QUESTIONS

1. *Victim participation in the pretrial stages.* One issue that proved controversial early on was the degree to which victims could actively participate in the conduct of the OTP's *investigations.* Article 68(3) controls, and it provides:

> Where the personal interests of the victims are affected, the Court shall permit their views and concerns to be presented and considered at stages of the *proceedings* determined to be appropriate by the Court and in a manner which is not prejudicial to or inconsistent with the rights of the accused and a fair and impartial trial. Such views and concerns may be presented by the legal representatives of the victims where the Court considers it appropriate, in accordance with the Rules of Procedure and Evidence (emphasis added).

In the DRC case, the Pre-Trial Chamber granted victims participatory rights, "entitling them to express their views and concerns generally in respect of the Prosecutor's investigation" into the "situation." Situation in the Democratic Republic of the Congo, Case No. ICC-01/04 OA4 OA5 OA6, Judgment on Victim Participation in the Investigation Stage of the Proceedings in the Appeal of the OPCD Against the Decision of the Pre-Trial Chamber I of 7 December 2007 and in the Appeals of the OPCD and the Prosecutor Against the Decision of Pre-Trial Chamber I of 24 December 2007, ¶4 (Dec. 19, 2008). The Pre-Trial Chamber reasoned as follows:

> 63. The Chamber considers that the personal interests of victims are affected in general at the investigation stage, since the participation of victims at this stage can serve to clarify the facts, to punish the perpetrators of crimes and to request reparations for the harm suffered.
>
> 66. In light of this distinction, the Chamber considers that, during the stage of investigation of a situation, the status of victim will be accorded to applicants who seem to meet the definition of victims set out in rule 85 . . . in relation to the situation in question. At the case stage, the status of victim will be accorded only to applicants who seem to meet the definition of victims set out in rule 85 in relation to the relevant case.
>
> 72. The right to present their views and concerns and to file material pertaining to the ongoing investigation stems from the fact that the victims' personal interests are affected because it is at this stage that the persons allegedly responsible for the crimes from which they suffered must be identified as a first step towards their indictment. [. . .]

Id. (quoting Pre-Trial Chamber decision). The Appeals Chamber reversed, holding that "the decisions of the Pre-Trial Chamber acknowledging procedural status to victims, entitling them to participate generally in the investigation of a situation are ill-founded and must be set aside." Id. ¶59. The Appeals Chamber reasoned as follows:

> 45. The article of the Statute that confers power upon a victim to participate in any proceedings is article 68(3). What emerges from the case law of the Appeals Chamber is that participation can take place only within the context of judicial proceedings. Article 68(3) of the Statute correlates victim participation to "proceedings," a term denoting a judicial cause pending before a Chamber. In contrast, an investigation is not a judicial proceeding but an inquiry conducted by the Prosecutor into the commission of a crime with a view to bringing to justice those deemed responsible. . . .
>
> 51. The initial appraisal of a referral of a situation by a State Party, in which one or more crimes within the jurisdiction of the Court appear to have been committed as well

as the assessment of information reaching the Prosecutor and in relation to that the initiation by the Prosecutor of investigations *proprio motu* are the exclusive province of the Prosecutor (see, inter alia, articles 14, 15, 53, and 54 of the Statute).

52. The domain and powers of the Prosecutor are outlined in article 42 of the Statute, paragraph 1 of which reads:

> The Office of the Prosecutor shall act independently as a separate organ of the Court. It shall be responsible for receiving referrals and any substantiated information on crimes within the jurisdiction of the Court, for examining them and for conducting investigations and prosecutions before the Court. A member of the Office shall not see or act on instructions from any external source.

Manifestly, authority for the conduct of investigations vests in the Prosecutor. Acknowledgement by the Pre-Trial Chamber of a right to victims to participate in the investigation would necessarily contravene the Statute by reading into it a power outside its ambit and remit.

53. . . . [T]he victims argue that granting them victim status at the investigation stage would, inter alia, enable them to "clarify the facts," to make known "what was inflicted upon them" and that, following this information, the Prosecutor would investigate the events. In the view of the Appeals Chamber, there is ample scope within the statutory scheme . . . for victims and anyone else with relevant information to pass it on to the Prosecutor without first being formally accorded "a general right to participate." For example, under Article 15(2) the Prosecutor is authorised to receive information from, inter alia, any "reliable source" — including victims. He is similarly authorised under article 42(1) to receive and consider "any substantiated information on crimes within the jurisdiction of the Court." Victims may thus make representations to the Prosecutor on any matter pertaining to the investigations and to their interests. They are also specifically granted the right to make representations under articles 15(3) and 19(3) of the Statute.

2. *Victim participation at trial.* Obviously, the above-excerpted judgment of the Appeals Chambers demonstrates another civil law feature of ICC proceedings: victim participation at trial. The Appeals Chamber has made clear that victims will have a role not contemplated in most common law criminal proceedings. Did you find the majority's or the dissent's position on this issue more persuasive?

3. *The role of victims' views in prosecutorial decisionmaking.* As noted above, the Ugandan situation presents the prosecutor with a seeming dilemma: Vocal victims' advocates are urging the prosecutor *not* to proceed in the belief that LRA prosecutions may foreclose peace. How does one determine if these views are those of the majority of victims or only of a vocal few? If the majority of victims do share this view, should it be dispositive? What else must the OTP consider in making a decision whether to go forward in the LRA cases?

4. *Reparations to victims.* Another innovation in the ICC Statute is its provision for reparations. A victim may file a claim for reparations with the Registry. ICC art. 75; RPE 94. After appropriate notice and process, the Court may, "[t]aking into account the scope and extent of any damage, loss or injury," award reparations "on an individualized basis or, where it deems it appropriate, on a collective basis or both." RPE 97. Individual awards for reparation are made directly against the convicted person or, upon Court order, can be awarded through the Trust Fund set up under ICC Article 79 for the benefit of victims of crimes within the jurisdiction of the court and of the families of such victims. RPE 98. The Trust Fund is funded through collection of fines and orders of compensation issued against convicted persons, as well as voluntary contributions from governments, international organizations, corporations, and individuals. The OTP has moved to ensure that reparations are available

in the *Lubanga* case arising out of the DRC referral. Thus, the ICC requested states parties to trace, seize, and freeze any of Lubanga's assets to enable payment of reparations to victims in the event of his conviction. Prosecutor v. Lubanga, Case No. 01/04-01/06, Request to States Parties to the Rome Statute for the Identification, Tracing and Freezing or Seizure of the Property and Assets of Mr. Thomas Lubanga Dyilo (Mar. 31, 2006).

5. *Protection.* The ICC Statute pays considerable attention to the protection of the persons and privacy of victims, witnesses, and other persons put at risk by its operations. For example, the prosecutor is empowered to take measures to ensure "the confidentiality of information, the protection of any person or the preservation of evidence," ICC art. 54(3)(f); the Pre-Trial Chambers are authorized to provide for the "protection and privacy of victims and witnesses, [and] the preservation of evidence," ICC art. 57(3)(c); Trial Chambers are instructed to conduct trials with "due regard for the protection of victims and witnesses," ICC art. 64(2); and states parties undertake to comply with ICC requests for assistance in protecting victims and witnesses, ICC art. 93(1)(j). ICC Article 68(1) *requires* the Court and the prosecutor to "take appropriate measures to protect the safety, physical and psychological well-being, dignity and privacy of victims and witnesses." It also permits the Court to make arrangements, including conducting proceedings in camera, "to protect victims and witnesses." ICC art. 68(2), (3). Finally, ICC Article 68(5) states that where "the disclosure of evidence or information pursuant to this Statute may lead to the grave endangerment of the security of a witness or his or her family, the Prosecutor may," in pretrial proceedings, provide a summary of the information rather than the information itself.

The ICC Rules of Procedure and Evidence also provide for witness and victim protection. Upon the motion of the prosecution or the defense, or the request of a witness or victim, or upon its own motion, the Court may "order measures to protect a victim, a witness or another person at risk on account of testimony given by a witness," RPE 87, or "order special measures such as . . . measures to facilitate the testimony of a traumatized victim or witness, a child, an elderly person or a victim of sexual violence," RPE 88. ICC Article 43(6) requires that the Registry set up the victims and witnesses unit discussed above. That unit, in consultation with the OTP, provides medical, psychological, and other appropriate assistance for witnesses, victims, and other at-risk persons. The unit also plans protective measures and security arrangements for victims, witnesses, and others, and is charged with the negotiation of agreements with states concerning the resettlement of such persons. See, e.g., International Criminal Court, Victims and Witnesses Protection, http://www.icc-cpi.int/Menus/ICC/Structure+of+the+Court/Protection (last visited July 13, 2009).

CHAPTER
17

Modes of Participation and *Mens Rea*

During the course of a genocide or other atrocity, different people may play very different roles. Civilian leaders may instigate and encourage the slaughter, but never actually wield the machete that takes a life. Military commanders may discover that soldiers under their command have killed, tortured, or raped civilians in violation of the laws of war, but the commanders may take no action to punish such crimes or prevent further outrages. Civilians and soldiers may volunteer, or be pressed into service, in aid of international crimes: The cook in the concentration camp, the driver who takes prisoners to the site of their execution, and the grave digger may be marginal participants, yet without their assistance the crimes may not be possible. And those who play a role may not share the principals' evil design. Thus, for example, an industrialist who uses slave labor may be doing so purely to make a profit and not to further the genocidal plan of those who enslaved his workers. Certainly, the "[Jewish] kapos at Auschwitz who bullied and brutalized their fellow inmates"[1] did not share Hitler's genocidal intention; in fact, their motives varied widely: "'terror, ideological seduction, servile imitation of the victor, myopic desire for any power whatsoever, even though ridiculously circumscribed in space and time, cowardice, and, finally, lucid calculation.'"[2]

In all of these cases the question is whether the individuals involved should be found criminally liable for their actions or, in some cases, inaction. Because these are criminal cases, this question is couched in the legal language of the various "modes of participation" (such as aiding and abetting, incitement, and the like). This discussion, however, is ultimately a moral one: Just what level of participation, with what level of knowledge and intent and sometimes with what motive, makes one responsible in some degree for an atrocity? This moral question is at the heart of the following materials.

We will first turn to the cases that present some of the most difficult moral issues: those dealing with individuals at the lower levels of the military or civilian hierarchy. We will explore the legal means by which these individuals have been held liable, testing through a final section of case studies whether the results in cases decided after World War II reflect readers' moral intuitions. (We will turn in the next chapter to possible defenses to criminal charges under international law. In particular, that chapter will focus on the defenses of superior orders and duress that are often invoked by those at the bottom of the chain of command.)

---

1. David Luban, A Man Lost in the Gray Zone, 19 Law & Hist. Rev. 161, 162 (2001).
2. Id. (quoting Primo Levi); see also generally Orna Ben-Naftalis & Yogev Tuval, Punishing International Crimes Committed by the Persecuted, 4 J. Intl. Crim. Just. 128 (2006).

We will also focus on some of the cases that can be the most difficult as a legal or evidentiary matter: those concerning the criminal liability of individuals who hold high positions in a given regime or armed force and who may have blood on their hands figuratively but not literally. Among the modes of participation applicable in these cases is what is known as command or superior responsibility. According to this theory of liability, military commanders and civilian superiors may be held criminally responsible for their failure to prevent or punish crimes they knew or (sometimes) should have known were committed by those over whom they exercise effective control. (Our Web site contains a problem that permits students to test the various modes of participation relevant to such high-ranking persons by applying them to the case of General Radislav Krstić.)

Readers should be cautioned that these doctrines are complex and not entirely consistent. This is in large part due to the fact that the question of what degree of participation should render an individual liable to international criminal sanction arose for the first time only at Nuremburg. In a short space of time, and in a largely ad hoc manner without the benefit of a "world legislature," the international community has had to forge a substantive code of criminal responsibility that can be agreed upon by states throughout the world — including a wealth of states that harbor very different conceptions of how and when criminal liability ought to be imposed.

In reading these materials, remain sensitive to the fact that, as a practical matter, moral judgments may be impossible to vindicate in a court of law due to evidentiary and legal constraints. It is often difficult to pinpoint with precision what role a given person played when an international crime is committed in the heat of battle, in a crowded prison camp, or during the course of a chaotic civil war. The victims may be dead or grievously injured and, in any case, were very unlikely to have been taking contemporaneous notes. Witnesses may have a vested interest in keeping horrible truths concealed, and states may obstruct investigators because they would prefer to let sleeping dogs lie. "Difficulties inhere in establishing one individual's responsibility for crimes committed by many, especially given the vicissitudes of forensic evidence, the complexity of testimony, and the anonymity of mass graves."[3]

Even where the facts are reasonably clear regarding the acts attributable to an individual, it may not always be possible to prove the requisite mental elements of the crime at issue. The crucial distinctions between different modes of participation frequently boil down to what went on in the defendant's head — for example, whether he intended to kill civilians or "merely" acted negligently or recklessly with the result that innocents died. It is obviously difficult for the Trial Chambers to divine what a given defendant was thinking at the time of the operative events, and direct proof — in the form of the defendant's contemporaneous statements or the like — is often scarce on the ground. Prosecutors, then, frequently must rely upon circumstantial evidence to prove that, given the facts known to the defendant, he "must have known" or "must have intended" certain consequences. Courts, however, may require such inferences to be particularly compelling before adjudicating someone guilty of heinous international crimes lest they mistakenly render a defendant liable for negligence or stupidity.

One final aspect of the context against which these cases are tried ought to be emphasized: Mass atrocity generally occurs through the direct involvement and cooperation of thousands of individuals, often acting within the context of an organization or institution. For example, conservative estimates place the number of persons

---

3. Mark A. Drumbl, ASIL Insight: *ICTY Appeals Chamber Delivers Two Major Judgments: Blaškić and Krstić* (Aug. 2004), http://www.asil.org/insights.htm (click 2004 hyperlink).

participating in the Rwandan genocide at well over 200,000; some 100,000 Germans participated in the mass slaughters known as the Holocaust; 10,000 killers are estimated to have operated in the former Yugoslavian conflict.[4] More appalling still are the numbers of casualties caused by this concerted criminal activity. "Estimates for twentieth century *victims* of mass killings (including genocides), as distinguished from war deaths (other than through war crimes) range between 60 and 150 million."[5]

The sheer volume of victims and perpetrators presents a number of challenges. First, although the crimes of thousands may have been sponsored, encouraged, or condoned by entities—and those crimes either could not have been committed without institutional support or would not have been as widespread—international criminal law as presently constituted does not provide for the conviction of legal entities, such as states or corporations. Second, the complicit individuals at all levels in the applicable organization will have participated in different ways and with greater or lesser enthusiasm. International criminal law, however, presents fact finders with a binary alternative: Guilty or not guilty. The onus is on the prosecutor, then, to charge each defendant with that "mode of participation" that most closely approximates the defendant's role. Even where it is clear what the defendant actually did, and there is sufficient evidence to prove the defendant's state of mind while acting, the limited subset of "modes of participation" identified in criminal law may not capture the nuances of various individuals' participation.

In U.S. law, prosecutors generally turn to conspiracy law to deal with group criminality, but the crime of conspiracy is not recognized in most parts of the world and has never been popular in international criminal tribunals. The Ad Hoc Tribunals have responded to these difficulties by creating what is known as joint criminal enterprise (JCE) liability. Under the JCE concept, a defendant who intentionally participates in a joint criminal enterprise, often defined broadly such as "the ethnic cleansing of non-Serb populations in Bosnia," can be held liable for all foreseeable crimes committed in furtherance of that enterprise by others—even when the defendant did not intend those crimes or even know about them.

This type of JCE liability—as well as the command responsibility doctrine when applied to superiors who did not know, but *should* have known, of their subordinates' crimes—provide sobering examples of how the pressure to make cases influences the content of criminal law. As Professor Mark Drumbl has noted, application of the JCE theory and the command responsibility doctrine in such cases may "be controversial insofar as they can incorporate a level of vicariousness that obscures the actual degree of the defendant's personal culpability. This means that convictions based on these theories at times may be difficult to square with the premise that the criminal liability of principal perpetrators is to be individualized and clearly established."[6] And the individual defendants prosecuted under these theories should not be the only ones concerned about this dynamic. As Professor William Schabas argues, while proceeding under such theories may "facilitate the conviction of individual villains who have apparently participated in serious violations of human rights," it may also "result in discounted convictions that inevitably diminish the didactic significance of the Tribunal's judgements and that compromise its historical legacy."[7] In reviewing the

---

4. See Mark Osiel, The Banality of Good: Aligning Incentives Against Mass Atrocity, 105 Colum. L. Rev. 1751, 1752-1753 n.4 (2005).

5. Id.

6. Drumbl, supra note 3; see also David L. Nersessian, Whoops, I Committed Genocide! The Anomaly of Constructive Liability for Serious International Crimes, 30-SUM Fletcher F. World Aff. 81 (2006).

7. William A. Schabas, War Crimes and Human Rights: Essays on the Death Penalty, Justice and Accountability 485 (2008).

materials that follow, then, consider how the international community can respond to the difficulties presented in prosecuting mass crimes to ensure that the participants in such atrocities are brought to justice, while not abandoning the core commitment in criminal law to individual culpability.[8]

A. MODES OF PARTICIPATION GENERALLY

1. *Modes of Participation in the United States, the Ad Hoc Tribunals, and the ICC*

Having outlined all the difficulties prosecutors and judges have had in identifying legal modes of participation in terms that can be applied in a principled way in varied factual circumstances, one might ask: Why bother? In other words, why does this matter?

In some legal systems, such as in U.S. federal criminal law, the simple answer is that it generally doesn't. The United States Code recognizes three modes of generally applicable participation aside from liability as a principal or conspirator: aiding and abetting (18 U.S.C. §2), accessory after the fact (18 U.S.C. §3), and misprison of felony (18 U.S.C. §4). Although the latter two provide for lesser punishments than that which would apply to a principal, they are almost never used. Far and away the most frequently invoked alternative to liability as a "principal" is that of "aiding and abetting" liability. Section 2(a) provides that "[w]hoever commits an offense against the United States or aids, abets, counsels, commands, induces or procures its commission, is punishable as a principal." The U.S. Supreme Court reads this provision to mean that, in §2, Congress "abolishe[d] the distinction between principals and accessories and [made] them all principals."[9] Not only is an aider and abettor treated as legally equivalent to a principal for purposes of liability, the U.S. Sentencing Guidelines also draw no distinction for purposes of sentencing.

The constituting statutes of the Ad Hoc Tribunals did not create a hierarchy in various modes of participation, lumping them all into one provision. The Statutes of the ICTY (Article 7) and ICTR (Article 6) provide:

> A person who planned, instigated, ordered, committed or otherwise aided and abetted in the planning, preparation or execution of a crime [within the jurisdiction of the tribunal] . . . shall be individually responsible for the crime.

As one commentator explained, the Ad Hoc Tribunals' provisions represent an

> indiscriminate approach . . . toward participation in crime [that] accords with conventional Anglo-American criminal law doctrine and to an extent also with the law of a few countries, such as France, that belong to the continental legal tradition. However, a much larger group of national legal systems require that perpetration be sharply differentiated from complicity, and that the forms of complicity so identified be ranked in terms of their seriousness. Under the widely influential German law, for example,

---

8. See generally Osiel, supra note 4, at 1763-1767; Jenny S. Martinez, Understanding *Mens Rea* in Command Responsibility, 5 J. Intl. Crim. Just. 638, 639 (2007).

9. Standefer v. United States, 447 U.S. 10, 19 (1980).

"aiding" (rendering assistance to) a perpetrator is regarded as deserving a categorically milder punishment than "instigating" (or soliciting) the commission of crime.[10]

Although the ICTR and ICTY Statutes did not provide a hierarchy of modes, different levels of perceived culpability *were* reflected in sentencing at the Ad Hoc Tribunals. Thus, a defendant convicted of "committing" genocide received a harsher sentence than one who "merely" aided and abetted it.[11] Although this permitted the Ad Hoc Tribunals greater leeway in addressing the continuum of participation in atrocities — foreclosing a binary choice of "guilty" or "innocent" with respect to a single mode of participation — might this have some conceptual and practical downsides?[12]

ICC Article 25 (entitled "Individual Criminal Responsibility"), while not as precise as some would wish, represents a turn away from the "indiscriminate" approach of the Ad Hoc Tribunals' Statutes and toward a more finely calibrated, and explicitly hierarchical, articulation of culpable modes of participation.[13] It provides, in relevant part, as follows:

> 3. In accordance with this Statute, a person shall be criminally responsible and liable for punishment for a crime within the jurisdiction of the Court if that person:
>
> (a) Commits such a crime, whether as an individual, jointly with another or through another person, regardless of whether that other person is criminally responsible;
>
> (b) Orders, solicits or induces the commission of such a crime which in fact occurs or is attempted;
>
> (c) For the purpose of facilitating the commission of such a crime, aids, abets or otherwise assists in its commission or its attempted commission, including providing the means for its commission;
>
> (d) In any other way contributes to the commission or attempted commission of such a crime by a group of persons acting with a common purpose. Such contribution shall be intentional and shall either:
>
> (i) Be made with the aim of furthering the criminal activity or criminal purpose of the group, where such activity or purpose involves the commission of a crime within the jurisdiction of the Court; or
>
> (ii) Be made in the knowledge of the intention of the group to commit the crime;
>
> (e) In respect of the crime of genocide, directly and publicly incites others to commit genocide . . .

Article 25 obviously does not explicitly differentiate between the various subsections in terms of sentencing; it does not, for example, provide that those who "commit" a crime should be punished more harshly than those who "aid and abet" the offense. Yet it is likely that the ICC will use these distinctions in formulating appropriate sentences, given the effort made by the ICC Statute's drafters to more carefully

---

10. Mirjan Damaška, The Shadow Side of Command Responsibility, 49 Am. J. Comp. L. 455, 459 (2001).

11. See, e.g., Prosecutor v. Krstić, Case No. IT-98-33-T, Judgment (Aug. 2, 2001) (imposing a sentence of 46 years' imprisonment for conviction of war crimes, crimes against humanity, and genocide), *rev'd in part,* Case No. IT-98-33-A, Judgment (Apr. 19, 2004) (concluding that Krstić could be liable only for "aiding and abetting" genocide, rather than as a direct perpetrator of genocide in a joint criminal enterprise, and revising sentence downward to 35 years).

12. See, e.g., Osiel, supra note 4, at 1766-1773 (discussing the problem of allocating responsibility in crimes that are the product of massive government bureaucracies).

13. See generally Roger S. Clark, The Mental Element in International Criminal Law: The Rome Statute of the International Criminal Court and the Elements of Offenses, 12 Crim. L.F. 291, 321 (2001) (discussing Article 25 and his experiences while participating in its drafting).

distinguish between various modes of participation and to reflect these distinctions in the hierarchical structure of Article 25(3). The Court is given the authority to do this by ICC Article 78(1), which directs the Court to determine sentence by taking account of "the gravity of the crime and the individual circumstances of the convicted person."

Selecting the correct mode of participation is important quite apart from sentencing considerations, however. First, although at the inception of their operation, the Ad Hoc Tribunals were not terribly stringent in demanding that the prosecution identify in the indictment the mode of participation it was charging, over time the courts did impose more onerous pleading requirements. Thus, to do their jobs properly, both parties—the defense and the prosecution—must understand these concepts and be able to identify who is a "perpetrator" and who is only an "accomplice" (and what kind of accomplice) on a given set of facts. Second, if a defendant is a "perpetrator," and the crime occurs or is attempted, he can be held liable even if other alleged co-perpetrators are found not guilty (on the facts, or by reason of an excuse or justification). But if the defendant is charged as an accomplice or accessory, his liability is derivative of the principal's liability; if the principal is deemed not to have committed a crime, the defendant, too, will go free. Finally, the identification of the appropriate mode of participation is not "a mere shell game" for the individual defendant—the results of this categorization will have real effects for his reputation and the stigma he suffers.[14] And "[e]ach way of describing the relation among parties to mass atrocity also has implications for the story the trial will tell and the history to which it will contribute."[15]

2. *Principals/Perpetrators versus Accessories/Accomplices: An Introduction*

For purposes of this introduction, we can break culpable modes of participation into two categories: (1) liability as a principal or perpetrator—for present purposes defined as one who physically commits or is involved in the satisfaction of the elements of the crime; and (2) complicity in the principal's crime—which is variously expressed as accessorial or accomplice liability and which breaks down into a variety of subcategories (for example, aiding and abetting, inciting, soliciting, etc.).

It is worth repeating that this is a difficult area of study because domestic criminal systems around the globe differ substantially, both in their conceptualization of when persons should be liable as principals as opposed to accessories and in their implementation of these concepts in their national criminal codes. The vocabulary used to identify modes of participation—and the mental states that must attend them—vary within countries as well as among countries with different languages and legal traditions.

To the extent one can generalize, then, the law of complicity (also known as accomplice or accessorial liability) defines the circumstances in which one party (the secondary party, accomplice, or accessory) becomes liable for the crime of another (the primary actor, principal, or perpetrator).[16] Complicity liability is *derivative* because it depends on the commission of an unlawful act by the principal. If there is no primary violation of law by a principal or perpetrator, there can be no attendant accomplice or accessorial liability.

---

14. Osiel, supra note 4, at 1766.
15. Id.
16. Sanford H. Kadish, Complicity, Cause and Blame: A Study in the Interpretation of Doctrine, 73 Cal. L. Rev. 323, 336 (1985).

The accomplice generally is not directly responsible for the principal's act, however, because the law assumes that, where the principal's actions are fully voluntary, his unlawful conduct is the product of his own will and cannot be said to have been "caused" by the accomplice.[17] Thus, one who aids and abets the principal to commit the crime can be liable for doing so, but "not because he thereby caused the actions of the principal or because the actions of the principal are his acts."[18] To put it another way, the accomplice's liability is (generally) not vicarious in the sense that he is being held responsible for the actions of another, as in the case, for example, of a corporation being held responsible for the acts of its agents. The accomplice's liability is personal, if derivative; his liability "must rest on the violation of law by the principal, the legal consequences of which he incurs because of *his own actions*" in assisting or influencing the principal to commit a crime.[19]

3. *Analyzing Liability*

To sort out what "mode of participation," if any, might apply in a given case, one must begin with the basic principle that criminal liability is normally founded on the concurrence of two factors, "an evil meaning mind [and] an evil doing hand."[20] In common law systems, this is often expressed as a requirement that some degree of *mens rea* (guilty mind) must attend the *actus reus* (guilty act or nonaction where there is a duty to act) to warrant the imposition of a criminal stigma. Accordingly, when assessing whether an individual can be held liable as a principal/perpetrator or an accessory/accomplice, one must ask two fundamental questions — and perhaps three, depending on the answers given to the first two.[21] The first two concern *mens rea* and *actus reus*. If their answers add up to a crime committed as an accomplice, not a principal, the third question concerns what mode of accessorial liability best describes the defendant's participation.

a. *"Subjective" or "mental" element.* With respect to the guilty mind: Was the defendant's mental state at the time he acted (or failed to act) sufficient to make him liable as a principal or as an accomplice? The crime — and the modes of participation provided in the relevant tribunal — will decide whether, for example, knowledge is enough or whether some sort of intent or purpose must also be shown.

b. *"Objective" or "material" element.* With respect to the guilty act: Was what the defendant *did* (or failed to do in dereliction of a legal duty) sufficient to make him liable as a principal or as an accomplice? As we shall see, distinguishing between what constitutes principal versus accomplice liability can be very challenging because different legal systems draw the line in different places. Systems that emphasize the "objective" or "material" element of principal liability may decide that only those who actually perpetrate at least one element of the crime can be said to have "committed" it; no matter how much assistance others provided, no matter how invaluable that assistance was, and no matter the intent with which the assistance was offered, unless an individual actually participated in the satisfaction of the elements of the

---

17. Id. at 337.
18. Id.
19. Id. (emphasis added).
20. Morissette v. United States, 342 U.S. 246, 251 (1952).
21. Even the modes of analysis differ in common versus civil law traditions. For a discussion of the difference, and an argument regarding the advantages of the civil law viewpoint, see Kai Ambos, Remarks on the General Part of International Criminal Law, 4 J. Intl. Crim. Just. 660 (2006).

offense (for example, killed, raped, kidnapped, etc.), he cannot be deemed a principal perpetrator. Other systems (such as the ICTY in its JCE doctrine) emphasize the "subjective" or "mental" component; they may permit persons who had no part in the satisfaction of the physical elements of the crime to be deemed principal perpetrators when those persons had the intent to join with and further the actions of those who directly consummated the crime. Still other courts (such as the ICC's Pre-Trial Chambers I in *Lubanga*) may forge another path that contains both objective and subjective elements.

c. *If an accomplice, what kind?* If we decide — based on our analysis of the defendant's mental state and acts — that the defendant was complicit but did not act as a principal/perpetrator, we must then ask a third question: What *type* of accessorial liability is appropriate given the defendant's *actus reus* and *mens rea?* The types of actions that may render the accomplice liable bear many labels, but they can be said to boil down to two — *influencing* the decision of the principal to commit a crime and *helping* the principal commit the crime, where the helping actions themselves constitute no part of the actions prohibited by the definition of the crime.[22] The different types of accomplice or accessorial liability generally turn, again, on the degree of assistance or encouragement the defendant supplied, as well as the relative culpability inherent in his mental state.

Assessing the *type* of accessorial liability that may apply can be a complex undertaking because the lines between various legal categories are ones of degree. In the Ad Hoc Tribunals, for example, one must determine whether the defendant's assistance or influence was "substantial" to determine whether he qualifies as an aider and abettor. Further, the assessment of complicity liability is more complex than principal liability because it involves two dimensions of *mens rea* and *actus reus* problems — those associated with the accomplice and those associated with the principal.[23] For example, assume that a defendant either instigates a crime or lends assistance to the perpetrator. To determine whether he is complicit in the crime, we generally need to assess whether he had the requisite *mens rea* with respect to his own actions (for example, he acted "knowing" that he was lending assistance to the principal's endeavor or "intending" to facilitate the crime) *and* whether he had the requisite *mens rea* with respect to the principal's action (for example, he acted "knowing" of the principal's specific intent to commit genocide or "intending" that the principal's crime would succeed).

To flesh out the above analysis, we will begin with a tutorial on *mens rea* (Part B) and then explore the various ways in which courts have attempted to draw the line between principal and accessorial liability (Part C). This inquiry will require us to delve into JCE and conspiracy theories of liability. We will commence our discussion of accessorial liability with the important category of "aiders and abettors" (Part D). We will then turn to what, in the ICC at least, are deemed modes of accomplice participation, including ordering, soliciting, inducing, inciting genocide, and contributing to a criminal group's crime (Part E). We will conclude with analysis of command or superior responsibility liability (Part F). At chapter's end, we have included a number of cases drawn from the post–World War II trials (Part G). We encourage you to refer to these cases either at the beginning of your reading or at the end to test your knowledge of relevant concepts.

---

22. Kadish, supra note 16, at 342.
23. See, e.g., Sanford H. Kadish, Reckless Complicity, 87 J. Crim. L. & Criminology 369 (1996).

B.   "SUBJECTIVE" OR "MENTAL" ELEMENTS: *MENS REA*

To sort out the levels of individual culpability, one must focus on the defendants' mental state (what he knew, intended, etc.) as well as what the defendant actually did.

1.   *The United States' ALI Model Penal Code §2.02*

In U.S. law, crimes are often described by their elements — that is, those facts that must be charged and proven beyond a reasonable doubt to secure a conviction. An example can be derived from the case that spawned the opinions we will read within — the ICC prosecution of Thomas Lubanga Dyilo in the Democratic Republic of Congo situation under ICC Article 8(2)(b)(xxvi) for the war crimes of conscripting and enlisting children under the age of 15 years into an armed group (the *Forces Patriotiques pour la Libération du Congo* (FPLC), military wing of the *Union des Patriots Congolais* (UPC)) and using them to participate actively in hostilities. To obtain a conviction for this war crime, the ICC's Elements of Crimes requires that the following five elements be proved beyond a reasonable doubt:

1.   The perpetrator conscripted or enlisted one or more persons into the national armed forces or used one or more persons to participate actively in hostilities.
2.   Such person or persons were under the age of 15 years.
3.   The perpetrator knew or should have known that such person or persons were under the age of 15 years.
4.   The conduct took place in the context of and was associated with an international armed conflict.
5.   The perpetrator was aware of factual circumstances that established the existence of an armed conflict.

In U.S. law, as in the ICC Statute, different mental elements may apply to different material elements of a particular crime. For example, the above definition requires that the defendant "knew" of the existence of the armed conflict, but requires only negligence (the perpetrator "knew or *should have known*") with respect to the age of the persons he was enlisting or conscripting. To complicate matters further, the definition of what is necessary to prove, for example, that a defendant acted "knowingly" or "with intent" depends on which of three *types* of elements is at issue: the nature of the conduct (for example, the defendant conscripted persons into the national armed forces), the circumstances attending the conduct (for example, the conduct was associated with an international armed conflict), or the result or consequences of the conduct. Sometimes trying to force a given element into one of these categories to the exclusion of others may seem artificial because the crime alleged involves conduct that seems inextricably bound up in its consequences (for example, "killing"). However, matters may be clearer, for example, when one contrasts rape (a "conduct" prohibition) with "wilfully causing great suffering, or serious injury to body or health" (a "consequence" prohibition).

With this as background we can turn to the notoriously tricky — morally, conceptually, and as a matter of vocabulary — business of defining culpable mental states. A useful point of reference for U.S.-trained lawyers is the American Law Institute's

(ALI's) Model Penal Code (MPC) §2.02(2) ("Kinds of Culpability Defined"). The ALI identified four basic types of criminal *mens rea* for crimes that require proof of fault:

> (a) *Purposely.* A person acts purposely with respect to a material element of the offense when:
>
> (i) if the element involves the nature of his conduct or result thereof, it is his conscious object to engage in conduct of that nature or to cause such a result; and
>
> (ii) if the element involves attendant circumstances, he is aware of the existence of such circumstances or he believes or hopes that they exist.
>
> (b) *Knowingly.* A person acts knowingly with respect to a material element of an offense when:
>
> (i) if the element involves the nature of his conduct or the attendant circumstances, he is aware that his conduct is of that nature or that such circumstances exist; and
>
> (ii) if the element involves a result of his conduct, he is aware that it is practically certain that his conduct will cause such a result.
>
> (c) *Recklessly.* A person acts recklessly with respect to a material element of an offense when he consciously disregards a substantial and unjustifiable risk that the material element exists or will result from his conduct. The risk must be of such a nature and degree that, considering the nature and purpose of the actor's conduct and the circumstances known to him, its disregard involves a gross deviation from the standard of conduct that a law-abiding person would observe in the actor's situation.
>
> (d) *Negligently.* A person acts negligently with respect to a material element of an offense when he should be aware of a substantial unjustifiable risk that the material element exists or will result from his conduct. The risk must be of such a nature and degree that the actor's failure to perceive it, considering the nature and purpose of his conduct and the circumstances known to him, involves a gross deviation from the standard of care that a reasonable person would observe in the actor's situation.[24]

Recklessness under the MPC differs from negligence primarily because the former requires that the defendant subjectively recognize the risk he then unreasonably disregards, while the latter requires that the defendant's conduct be judged by an objective (reasonable person) standard. To complicate matters further, different legal systems employ the above terms "often with subtle differences in emphasis and meaning."[25] For example, "while both Britain and the United States employ the concept of recklessness, the US Model Penal Code focuses on *consciousness* of risk as the defining characteristic distinguishing recklessness from negligence, while British law (and some jurisdictions in the United States) apparently emphasizes the *degree* of risk."[26]

These distinctions can be fine ones — especially when what is at stake is the gray area between purpose and recklessness with respect to the *consequences* of one's action. The MPC definition of "knowing" is satisfied when, with respect to crimes addressed to the consequences of a defendant's conduct, the defendant "is aware that it is *practically certain* that his conduct will cause such a result." Further, many jurisdictions provide that a defendant "intentionally" causes a forbidden result if he "knows that his conduct is *substantially certain* to cause the result, whether or not he desires the result to occur."[27] "Recklessness" in causing a result, by contrast, exists when a defendant is "aware that his conduct *might* cause the result, though it is not substantially certain to happen."[28] In general, then, "while 'knowledge' and the knowing-type

---

24. ALI, Model Penal Code §2.02(2) (1962).
25. Martinez, supra note 8, at 644.
26. Id.
27. Wayne R. LaFave, Criminal Law 269 (4th ed. 2003).
28. Id.

of 'intention' require a consciousness of almost-certainty, recklessness requires a consciousness of something far less than certainty or even probability."[29]

These four forms of *mens rea* are not only different, they are rank-ordered in degree of guilt. In general, committing a bad act purposely is worse than doing it knowingly (but without purpose); committing it knowingly is worse than doing it recklessly; and reckless action is worse than merely negligent action.

2.   *Germany: Civil Law Concepts*

Other legal systems carve up the mental states differently than in the United States. In many civil law countries, notably Germany, the distinctions among, and definitions of, various levels of *mens rea* have been the subject of voluminous scholarship and commentary.[30] We will reference the German classifications because they have been very influential in the rest of Europe.[31] Although it would be impossible to summarize the literature in these pages, we will attempt a very brief and general vocabulary lesson. This tutorial is necessary not only for evaluating the meaning of the *mens rea* terms used in the ICC Statute, but also for reviewing more generally the literature on international criminal law, in which these terms frequently appear. Readers should keep in mind in reading the following materials, however, that various courts and commentators use these terms in slightly different ways and that the following is only an attempted and very abbreviated synthesis.

In the German criminal system, the "fault" that is a prerequisite to criminal liability inheres in either intention (*dolus*) or negligence (*culpa*). The German word *Vorsatz* captures the broad concept of intention.[32] Intention, in turn, is broken into three subcategories.[33] Thus, in the German system, there are three discrete categories of "intention," rather than, as in the United States, one word with many meanings depending on the context; and, in German law, there is no discrete concept of recklessness. As we shall see, the nearest German equivalent to recklessness is classified as a kind of intention. This matters for the student of international criminal law because when civilian jurists use the word *intention*, they may include crimes that U.S.-trained lawyers would regard as reckless rather than intentional.

Three Categories of Intention. The first category of intention is often referred to as *dolus directus* or *dolus directus in the first degree.*[34] These terms convey the concept of "purpose" or "desired outcome"; they signal that the outcome is what the defendant means to achieve.[35] Thus, the first category of intention can be analogized to "purpose" in the MPC system.

---

29. Id.

30. See, e.g., Greg Taylor, The Intention Debate in German Criminal Law, 17 Ratio Juris 346, 346-347 (2004).

31. See, e.g., Greg Taylor, Concepts of Intention in German Criminal Law, 24 Oxford J. Legal Stud. 99, 101 (2004).

32. Id. at 106.

33. Id. at 102.

34. Id. at 106.

35. Id.; see also Johan D. Van der Vyver, The International Criminal Court and the Concept of *Mens Rea* in International Criminal Law, 12 U. of Miami Intl. & Comp. L. Rev. 57, 62 (2004) (*dolus directus* indicates that the "illegality and/or harmful consequence of the act was foreseen and desired by the perpetrator").

The second category of "intention" is called "*dolus indirectus*" or "*dolus directus in the second degree*"; it is the analog to "knowledge" in the MPC scheme. Dr. Taylor explains:

> [This type of intention exists] when the actor knows that a consequence of her actions will almost certainly ensue, and includes the case in which the actor is uncertain whether his plan will in fact succeed, but knows that, *if* it does, a further consequence is almost certain to ensue. "Almost" is added here because it is generally recognized that nothing is absolutely certain in the world, and formulae such as "practically certain" are used to indicate that moral certainty is sufficient. It is also agreed that the actor does not have to desire the side-effect in question; knowledge is enough.[36]

Both of the first two categories of intention are uncontroversial in the courts or among commentators because there is thought to be "little difference in moral terms between intending a result . . . and knowing that it will occur."[37]

To illustrate the difference between these two mental states in practice, Professor Eser explains that *dolus directus* in the first degree is

> characterized by the perpetrator's full knowledge of all material elements of the crime and his purposeful will to bring about the prohibited result; in this so-called *dolus directus* in the first degree the volitional element is certainly predominant, as for instance in the case of genocide where the perpetrator plans on killing as many members of the protected ethnic group as possible. This final will to kill is less strong in terms of a *dolus directus* in the second degree when, as in the case of a war crime, the perpetrator aims at destroying a certain building, while not wishing, however certainly knowing, that he cannot reach his military aim without inevitably killing innocent civilians.[38]

The most controversial category of intention is the third, called "*dolus eventualis*" or conditional intention. It is the closest category to MPC recklessness, but we shall see that there are important differences. *Dolus eventualis* "is constituted by knowledge of a possible (as distinct from inevitable) outcome of one's actions combined with a positive mental or emotional disposition toward it, which [German courts have] expressed as approval of or reconciling oneself to the possible outcome."[39] Using the above example of a war crime, if the defendant is said to act with *dolus eventualis*, he would "not wish to kill civilians, but in being aware of this danger is prepared to approve of it if it should happen."[40]

Dolus eventualis can be divided into two components. First, the "cognitive" component requires that the defendant foresee the prohibited result as a possibility. (Scholars argue over how substantial or slight that possibility may be and still satisfy the standard.) Although the first part of this concept — the knowledge of a possible or probable risk — comports with the common law concept of recklessness, the second component does not. This second, "volitional" component requires that the defendant approved of or reconciled himself to the possible risk as a means of attaining his goal. It is this second element that is foreign to most common law lawyers. It is also this second aspect of the definition of *dolus eventualis* that is critical to distinguish it from the German concept of negligence, as well as the U.S. concept of recklessness.

---

36. Taylor, supra note 31, at 106.
37. Id.
38. Albin Eser, Mental Elements — Mistake of Fact and Mistake of Law, in 1 The Rome Statute of the International Criminal Court: A Commentary 899, 905-906 (A. Cassesse, P. Gaeta, & J. Jones eds., 2002) [hereinafter Eser, Mistake Commentary].
39. Taylor, supra note 31, at 102; see also Prosecutor v. Blaškić, Case No. IT-95-14-A, Judgment ¶39 (July 29, 2004).
40. Eser, Mistake Commentary, supra note 38, at 906.

Negligence. Only infrequently does the criminal law punish for negligence. In German criminal law, negligence requires that the defendant have some subjective awareness of risk. (In most common law systems, there is no distinction between conscious and unconscious negligence; criminal negligence is defined as conscious or unconscious deviation from the required standard of care, which causes a result prohibited by criminal law.) The distinction between *dolus eventualis* and negligence, then, is simply the defendant's disposition toward the possibility that the consequence feared will occur. A defendant accused of murder would be described as acting with (in translation of the German) "conscious negligence" or (in English-language terms) "advertent negligence" if he "earnestly (one might also translate: seriously) and not merely in a vague way relied on the non-occurrence of a fatal result."[41]

An example will illustrate the difference between *dolus eventualis* and conscious negligence as well as between *dolus eventualis* and recklessness as the Model Penal Code defines it. Consider a driver who seeks to pass on a road where he has not had the opportunity to check for oncoming traffic. "Such a driver, if competent, will realize the possibility that someone might be coming the other way, and thus will fulfill the first criterion of *dolus eventualis*. But, unless suicidal, he will not fulfill the second, for he will neither approve of the possibility of a car accident nor reconcile himself to it. Rather, he will trust in his luck and rely earnestly on the non-occurrence of an accident. Thus, our driver acts only with advertent negligence."[42] A U.S.-trained lawyer, by contrast, would have little difficulty classifying the case as one of reckless driving — and this illustrates the crucial difference between the U.S.-style recklessness and German-style *dolus eventualis*. Recklessness does not require mental acceptance or approval of the bad outcome, only conscious awareness of the risk that the outcome will eventuate. *Dolus eventualis* requires both. Returning again to our war crime example, a defendant would be said to be acting with advertent negligence, if he was "aware of the dangerousness of his bombing a building, but is not prepared to hit innocent civilians as well and therefore acts solely due to his relying on the absence of civilians at the scene."[43] He would not be acting with *dolus eventualis*, nor either of the other two categories of intent (*dolus directus* or *dolus indirectus*).

Why is this distinction important? In Germany the distinction between *dolus eventualis* and advertent negligence is important because negligence generally does not give rise to criminal liability unless the Criminal Code expressly provides otherwise.[44] For present purposes, the distinction may be important because, as noted, *dolus eventualis* is one subcategory of "intent" in many civil law countries. And the ICC Statute contains a default rule requiring a showing of "intent" for liability.

3. ICC: Article 30's "Mental Element"

ICC Article 30 ("Mental Element") contains a general definition of the mental states required for conviction under the Rome Treaty:

> 1. Unless otherwise provided, a person shall be criminally responsible and liable for punishment for a crime within the jurisdiction of the Court only if the material elements are committed with intent and knowledge.

---

41. Taylor, *supra* note 31, at 109. See above.
42. *Id.*
43. Eser, Mistake Commentary, *supra* note 38, at 906.
44. See Taylor, *supra* note 31, at 109.

2. For the purposes of this article, a person has intent where:
   (a) In relation to conduct, that person means to engage in the conduct;
   (b) In relation to a consequence, that person means to cause that consequence or is aware that it will occur in the ordinary course of events.

3. For the purposes of this article, "knowledge" means awareness that a circumstance exists or a consequence will occur in the ordinary course of events. "Know" and "knowingly" shall be construed accordingly.

ICC Article 30(1) begins by defining its scope: It applies to all crimes "unless otherwise provided" in the statutory definition.[45] If "otherwise provided" in other parts of the ICC Statute, the *mens rea* needed to prove a certain offense may be higher or lower than that specified in ICC Article 30.[46] For example, ICC Pre-Trial Chamber I confirmed the indictment of Thomas Lubanga Dyilo for the war crimes of conscripting and enlisting children under the age of 15 years and using them to participate actively in hostilities. In the course of so doing, the court noted that the third element listed in the Elements of Crimes for these offenses requires that, in relation to the age of the victims, "[t]he perpetrator knew or should have known that such person or persons were under the age of fifteen."[47] The Pre-Trial Chamber held that the "should have known" requirement "falls within the concept of negligence" (that is, "his or her lack of knowledge results from his or her failure to comply with his or her duty to act with due diligence").[48] The Chamber concluded:

> As a result, the "should have known" requirement as provided for in the Elements of Crimes in relation to articles 8(2)(b)(xxvi) and 8(2)(e)(vii) is an exception to the "intent and knowledge" requirement embodied in article 30 of the Statute. Accordingly, as provided for in article 30(1) of the Statute, it will apply in determining the age of the victims, whereas the general "intent and knowledge" requirement will apply to the other objective elements of the war crimes set forth in articles 8(2)(b)(xxvi) and 8(2)(e)(vii) of the Statute, including the existence of an armed conflict and the nexus between the acts charged and the armed conflict.[49]

Those who drafted ICC Article 30 intentionally phrased it in the conjunctive, thus making clear that both knowledge *and* intent are required to prove all crimes, unless another provision of the ICC Statute provides otherwise.[50]

Article 30's definitions, like those embodied in the ALI's §2.02, discussed above, depend to some extent on whether the crime at issue prohibits "conduct," attendant "circumstances," or "consequences."

- With respect to *conduct*, the ICC Statute provides only a definition of "intent," which is defined in volitional terms. Thus, a person acts with intent when he "means to engage in the conduct," ICC art. 30(2), and this "signifies, at a minimum, that conduct must be the result of a voluntary action on the part of the accused."[51] In addition to distinguishing between voluntary and involuntary

---

45. See also Finalized Draft Text of the Elements of Crimes, General Introduction ¶2; Clark, supra note 13, at 321.

46. See Prosecutor v. Lubanga, Case No. ICC-01/04-01/06, Decision on the Confirmation of Charges ¶356 (Jan. 29, 2007).

47. Id. ¶357.

48. Id. ¶358.

49. Id. ¶359.

50. See, e.g., Clark, supra note 13, at 301-303.

51. Donald K. Piragoff, Article 30: Mental Element, in Commentary on the Rome Statute of the International Criminal Court: Observers' Notes, Article by Article 533 (Otto Triffterer ed., 1999) [hereinafter Piragoff, Observers' Notes].

conduct, "[g]enerally, the term 'intent' also connotes some element, although even minimal, of desire or willingness to do the action, in light of an awareness of the relevant circumstances" but does not necessarily require proof that the defendant desired to bring about the consequences of the act.[52]

- With respect to *attendant circumstances*, the ICC provides only a definition of "knowledge." Thus, "knowledge" is defined in the ICC Statute as "awareness that a circumstance exists" under ICC Article 30(1).[53]

- With respect to a crime that focuses on *consequences*, the ICC Statute provides definitions of both "intent" and "knowledge." Thus, a person acts with "intent" with respect to a consequence if "that person means to cause that consequence or is aware that it *will occur* in the ordinary course of events" (emphasis added). A person acts "knowingly" with respect to a consequence if he is aware that the consequence "*will occur* in the ordinary course of events" (emphasis added). Students should focus on the requirement that the defendant must, at a minimum, act with an awareness that the forbidden consequence "*will* occur in the ordinary course of events." What does this mean?

Scholars debate whether ICC Article 30's default "intent and knowledge" requirement permits liability for persons who are reckless or act with only *dolus eventualis* with respect to "consequence" crimes. One certainly could argue that, even if "intent" in civil law systems might include *dolus eventualis*, that concept is not encompassed within Article 30's generally applicable *mens rea* because the ICC Statute requires intent *and knowledge*, and "knowledge" under the ICC Statute is restricted to just *dolus directus* and *dolus indirectus*.[54] Note that, to satisfy either requirement, the defendant would at the least have to be "aware" that a certain consequence "will occur," implying a level of awareness consistent with the MPC's definition of "knowledge" (that is, "aware of the existence of such circumstances or . . . believes or hopes that they exist") or German civil law conceptions of *dolus indirectus* (that is, knows that a consequence will almost certainly ensue) — not the lesser fault states of recklessness or *dolus eventualis*.

The ICTY Appeals Chamber, however, characterized its default *mens rea* as including recklessness and *dolus eventualis* (but not negligence).[55] How will the ICC read its Statute? The question is an important one because requiring at least proof of U.S. style "knowledge" or *dolus indirectus* for liability may be considerably more difficult than a minimum fault level of *dolus eventualis* or recklessness. Consider Pre-Trial Chamber I's discussion in the *Lubanga* case, below. Note that the Pre-Trial Chamber was discussing the war crime of conscripting or enlisting children under the age of 15 (ICC Article 8(2)(b)(xxvi)), the elements of which were discussed above.

PROSECUTOR v. LUBANGA

Case No. ICC-01/04-01/06, Decision on the Confirmation of Charges (Jan. 29, 2007)

. . . 350. Article 30 of the Statute sets out the general subjective element for all crimes within the jurisdiction of the Court . . .

---

52. Id. (emphasis added); see also Van der Vyver, supra note 35, at 61-62.
53. See Van der Vyver, supra note 35, at 66 (yes).
54. See id. at 66.
55. See Prosecutor v. Blaškić, Case No. IT-95-14-A, Judgment, ¶39 (July 29, 2004).

351. The cumulative reference to "intent" and "knowledge" requires the existence of a volitional element on the part of the suspect. This volitional element encompasses, first and foremost, those situations in which the suspect (i) knows that his or her actions or omissions will bring about the objective elements of the crime, and (ii) undertakes such actions or omissions with the concrete intent to bring about the objective elements of the crime (also known as *dolus directus* of the first degree).

352. The above-mentioned volitional element also encompasses other forms of the concept of *dolus* which have already been resorted to by the jurisprudence of the ad hoc tribunals, that is:

> i. situations in which the suspect, without having the concrete intent to bring about the objective elements of the crime, is aware that such elements will be the necessary outcome of his or her actions or omissions (also known as *dolus directus* of the second degree); and
> ii. situations in which the suspect (a) is aware of the risk that the objective elements of the crime may result from his or her actions or omissions, and (b) accepts such an outcome by reconciling himself or herself with it or consenting to it (also known as *dolus eventualis*).

353. The Chamber considers that in the latter type of situation, two kinds of scenarios are distinguishable. Firstly, if the risk of bringing about the objective elements of the crime is substantial (that is, there is a likelihood that it "will occur in the ordinary course of events"), the fact that the suspect accepts the idea of bringing about the objective elements of the crime can be inferred from:

> i. the awareness by the suspect of the substantial likelihood that his or her actions or omissions would result in the realisation of the objective elements of the crime; and
> ii. the decision by the suspect to carry out his or her actions or omissions despite such awareness.

354. Secondly, if the risk of bringing about the objective elements of the crime is low, the suspect must have clearly or expressly accepted the idea that such objective elements may result from his or her actions or omissions.

355. Where the state of mind of the suspect falls short of accepting that the objective elements of the crime may result from his or her actions or omissions, such a state of mind cannot qualify as a truly intentional realisation of the objective elements,[56] and hence would not meet the "intent and knowledge" requirement embodied in article 30 of the Statute.[57] . . .

---

56. [Court's footnote 437:] For instance, where the suspect is aware of the likelihood that the objective elements of the crime would occur as a result of his actions or omissions, and in spite of that, takes the risk in the belief that his or her expertise will suffice in preventing the realisation of the objective elements of the crime. This would be the case of a taxi driver taking the risk of driving at a very high speed on a local road trusting that nothing would happen on account of his or her driving expertise.

57. [Court's footnote 438:] The concept of recklessness requires only that the perpetrator be aware of the existence of a risk that the objective elements of the crime may result from his or her actions or omissions, but does not require that he or she reconcile himself or herself with the result. In so far as recklessness does not require the suspect to reconcile himself or herself with the causation of the objective elements of the crime as a result of his or her actions or omissions, it is not part of the concept of intention. According to Fletcher, "Recklessness is a form of *culpa*—equivalent to what German scholars call 'conscious negligence.' The problem of distinguishing 'intention' and 'recklessness' arises because in both cases the actor is aware that his conduct might generate a specific result." Fletcher, G.P., Rethinking Criminal Law, Oxford University Press, 2000, p. 443. Hence, recklessness does not meet the "intent and knowledge" requirement embodied in article 30 of the Statute. Negligence likewise does not meet the "intent and knowledge" requirement embodied in article 30 of the Statute.

NOTES AND QUESTIONS

1. Is the crime at issue one that prohibits consequences, attendant circumstances, and/or conduct? Should this matter to the Court's analysis?

2. Pre-Trial Chamber I clearly believes that it is appropriate to reference the civil law (rather than common law) concepts when interpreting ICC Article 30. It also seems to believe that Article 30's "intent and knowledge" default *mens rea* includes *dolus eventualis*. See Mohamed Elewa Badar, The Mental Element in the Rome Statute of the International Criminal Court: A Commentary from a Comparative Criminal Law Perspective, 19 Crim. L.F. 473, 487 (2008). Do you find the Court's analysis persuasive?

Professor Roger S. Clark, who was involved in the negotiation of the Rome Treaty, terms the Pre-Trial Chamber's conclusion regarding the content of Article 30 "thoughtful, but far from definitive." Roger S. Clark, Drafting a General Part to a Penal Code: Some Thoughts Inspired by the Negotiations on the Rome Statute of the International Criminal Court and by the Court's First Substantive Law Discussion in the *Lubanga Dyilo* Confirmation Proceedings, 19 Crim. L.F. 519, 527 (2008). Although he argues that the Chamber's reference to *dolus directus* of the second degree "comes close to knowledge as defined in Article 30 and may thus pass muster," "*dolus eventualis* and its common law cousin, recklessness, suffered banishment by consensus [during the negotiation of the ICC Statute]. If it is to be read into the Statute, it is in the teeth of the language and history." Id. at 529. For a detailed critique of the Chamber's analysis, and its application of the law to the facts, see Thomas Weigend, Intent, Mistake of Law, and Co-perpetration in the *Lubanga* Decision on Confirmation of Charges, 6 J. Intl. Crim. Just. 471 (2007).

C. "OBJECTIVE" OR "MATERIAL" ELEMENTS: "COMMITTING" A CRIME AS A PERPETRATOR

The crime alleged will define what constitutes the applicable *actus reus*. For example, the crime against humanity of murder contemplates that killing one or more persons is the *actus reus* of the crime. The liability of some of those who "commit" the crime, in the sense of those who act as a firing squad, may be straightforward. But what of people who do not pull the trigger, but instead provide invaluable assistance without which the crime would not have happened — are they principals or accomplices? Just how *much* assistance — with what *mens rea* — will take one over the line from accomplice to perpetrator? In these types of cases, courts have struggled to formulate an administrable test that will permit them to draw a distinction between those principals who "commit" the crime, and accessories, in circumstances where many people have contributed in some way to an international crime.

1. Joint Criminal Enterprise Liability in the ICTY

"Ironically, the most complex and conceptually challenging liability theory in international criminal law is the only one not mentioned explicitly in the statutes of the ICTY or ICTR: Joint criminal enterprise (which is also referred to by a variety of other terms, including 'common purpose,' and 'common plan,' liability) has largely been created by the judges and prosecutors of the Yugoslav Tribunal."[58] Through this theory of liability, persons who did not commit any of the elements of a crime — did not, for example, participate in the actual killing or rape that is the *actus reus* of the offense — may nonetheless be held liable as perpetrators or principals in the crime. The following is the explanation of the three forms of JCE liability from the foundational case, *Prosecutor v. Tadić.*

PROSECUTOR v. TADIĆ

Case No. IT-94-1-A, Judgment (July 15, 1999)

178. The Trial Chamber found, amongst other facts, that on 14 June 1992, the Appellant, with other armed men, participated in the removal of men, who had been separated from women and children, from the village of Sivci to the Keraterm camp, and also participated in the calling-out of residents, the separation of men from women and children, and the beating and taking away of men in the village of Jaskići.

181. . . . [F]ive men were found killed in Jaskići after the [Appellant's] armed group left; four of them were shot in the head. Nothing else as to who might have killed them or in what circumstances is known. . . .

183. . . . On the facts found, the only reasonable conclusion the Trial Chamber could have drawn is that the armed group to which the Appellant belonged killed the five men in Jaskići. . . .

185. The question therefore arises whether under international criminal law the Appellant can be held criminally responsible for the killing of the five men from Jaskići even though there is no evidence that he personally killed any of them. The two central issues are:

  (i) whether the acts of one person can give rise to the criminal culpability of another where both participate in the execution of a common criminal plan; and
 (ii) what degree of *mens rea* is required in such a case. . . .

190. . . . [The object and purpose of the ICTY statute command the conclusion that w]hoever contributes to the commission of crimes by the group of persons or some members of the group, in execution of a common criminal purpose, may be held to be criminally liable, subject to certain conditions, which are specified below.

191. The above interpretation [that responsibility under Article 7(1) is not limited to those who physically commit the crimes] is not only dictated by the object and purpose of the Statute but is also warranted by the very nature of many international crimes which are committed most commonly in wartime situations. Most of the time these crimes do not result from the criminal propensity of single individuals but constitute manifestations of collective criminality: the crimes are often carried out by groups of individuals acting in pursuance of a common criminal design. Although only some members of the group may physically perpetrate the criminal act (murder, extermination, wanton destruction of cities, towns or villages, etc.), the participation and contribution of the other members of the group is often vital in facilitating the commission of the offence in question. It follows that the moral gravity of such

---

58. Allison M. Danner & Jenny S. Martinez, Guilty Associations: Joint Criminal Enterprise, Command Responsibility, and the Development of International Criminal Law, 93 Cal. L. Rev. 75, 103-104 (2005).

participation is often no less — or indeed no different — from that of those actually carrying out the acts in question.

192. Under these circumstances, to hold criminally liable as a perpetrator only the person who materially performs the criminal act would disregard the role as co-perpetrators of all those who in some way made it possible for the perpetrator physically to carry out the criminal act. At the same time, depending upon the circumstances, to hold the latter liable only as aiders and abettors might understate the degree of their criminal responsibility. . . .

195. Many post–World War II cases concerning war crimes proceed upon the principle that when two or more persons act together to further a common criminal purpose, offences perpetrated by any of them may entail the criminal liability of all the members of the group. Close scrutiny of the relevant case law shows that broadly speaking, the notion of common purpose encompasses three distinct categories of collective criminality.

196. The first such category is represented by cases where all co-defendants, acting pursuant to a common design, possess the same criminal intention; for instance, the formulation of a plan among the co-perpetrators to kill, where, in effecting this common design (and even if one co-perpetrator carries out a different role within it), they nevertheless all possess the intent to kill. The objective and subjective prerequisites for imputing criminal responsibility to a participant who did not, or cannot be proven to have, effected the killing are as follows: (i) the accused must voluntarily participate in one aspect of the common design (for instance, by inflicting non-fatal violence upon the victim, or by providing material assistance to or facilitating the activities of his co-perpetrators); and (ii) the accused, even if not personally effecting the killing, must nevertheless intend this result.

197. With regard to this category, reference can be made to the . . . [*Almelo Trial.*][59] There a British court found that three Germans who had killed a British prisoner of war were guilty under the doctrine of "common enterprise." It was clear that they all had had the intention of killing the British soldier, although each of them played a different role. They therefore were all co-perpetrators of the crime of murder. . . .

202. The second distinct category of cases is in many respects similar to that set forth above, and embraces the so-called "concentration camp" cases. The notion of common purpose was applied to instances where the offences charged were alleged to have been committed by members of military or administrative units such as those running concentration camps; i.e., by groups of persons acting pursuant to a concerted plan. . . . In these cases the accused held some position of authority within the hierarchy of the concentration camps. Generally speaking, the charges against them were that they had acted in pursuance of a common design to kill or mistreat prisoners and hence to commit war crimes. . . . [In these cases, three requirements were identified:] (i) the existence of an organised system to ill-treat the detainees and commit the various crimes alleged; (ii) the accused's awareness of the nature of the system; and (iii) the fact that the accused in some way actively participated in the realisation of the common criminal design. . . .

203. . . . [In this category of cases, t]he *mens rea* element comprised: (i) knowledge of the nature of the system and (ii) the intent to further the common concerted design to ill-treat prisoners. It is important to note that, in these cases, the requisite intent could also be inferred from the position of authority held by the camp personnel. . . .

---

59. This case is summarized in Part G.3 below. — Eds.

204. The third category concerns cases involving a common design to pursue one course of conduct where one of the perpetrators commits an act which, while outside the common design, was nevertheless a natural and foreseeable consequence of the effecting of that common purpose. An example of this would be a common, shared intention on the part of a group to forcibly remove members of one ethnicity from their town . . . (to effect "ethnic cleansing") with the consequence that, in the course of doing so, one or more of the victims is shot and killed. . . . Criminal responsibility may be imputed to all participants within the common enterprise where the risk of death occurring was both a predictable consequence of the execution of the common design and the accused was either reckless or indifferent to that risk . . .

205. The case-law in this category has concerned first of all cases of mob violence, that is, situations of disorder where multiple offenders act out of a common purpose, where each of them commit offences against the victim, but where it is unknown or impossible to ascertain exactly which acts were carried out by which perpetrator, or when the causal link between each act and the eventual harm caused the victims is similarly indeterminate. [A case] illustrative of this category [is] . . . *Essen Lynching.* . . . [60]

220. . . . With regard to the third category of cases, it is appropriate to apply the notion of "common purpose" only where the following requirements concerning *mens rea* are fulfilled: (i) the intention to take part in a joint criminal enterprise and to further — individually and jointly — the criminal purposes of that enterprise; and (ii) the foreseeability of the possible commission by other members of the group of offences that do not constitute the object of the common criminal purpose. Hence, the participants must have had in mind the intent, for instance, to ill-treat prisoners of war (even if such a plan arose extemporaneously) and one or some members of the group must have actually killed them. In order for responsibility for the deaths to be imputable to the others, however, everyone in the group must have been able to *predict* this result. It should be noted that more than negligence is required. What is required is a state of mind in which a person, although he did not intend to bring about a certain result, was aware that the actions of the group were most likely to lead to that result but nevertheless willingly took that risk. In other words, the so-called *dolus eventualis* is required (also called "advertent recklessness" in some national legal systems). . . .

227. In sum, the objective elements (*actus reus*) of this mode of participation in one of the crimes provided for in the Statute (with regard to each of the three categories of cases) are as follows:

   i. *A plurality of persons.* They need not be organised in a military, political, or administrative structure, as is clearly shown by the *Essen Lynching* . . . case[].

  ii. *The existence of a common plan, design or purpose which amounts to or involves the commission of a crime provided for in the Statute.* There is no necessity for this plan, design or purpose to have been previously arranged or formulated. The common plan or purpose may materialise extemporaneously and be inferred from the fact that a plurality of persons acts in unison to put into effect a joint criminal enterprise.

 iii. *Participation of the accused in the common design* involving the perpetration of one of the crimes provided for in the Statute. This participation need not involve the commission of a specific crime under one of those provisions (for example,

---

60. This case is summarized in Part G.4 below. The case involved German soldiers who encouraged and then allowed a civilian mob to murder prisoners of war. — Eps.

murder, extermination, torture, rape, etc.), but may take the form of assistance in, or contribution to, the execution of the common plan or purpose.

228. By contrast, the *mens rea* element differs according to the category of common design under consideration. With regard to the first category, what is required is the intent to perpetrate a certain crime (this being the shared intent on the part of all co-perpetrators). With regard to the second category . . . , personal knowledge of the system of ill-treatment is required (whether proved by express testimony or a matter of reasonable inference from the accused's position of authority), as well at the intent to further this common concerted system of ill-treatment. With regard to the third category, what is required is the *intention* to participate in and further the criminal activity or the criminal purpose of the group and to contribute to the joint criminal enterprise or in any event to the commission of a crime by the group. In addition, responsibility for a crime other than the one agreed upon in the common plan arises only if, under the circumstances of the case, (i) it was *foreseeable* that such a crime might be perpetrated by one or other members of the group and (ii) the accused *willingly took that risk*.

NOTES AND QUESTIONS

1. As noted above, none of this is reflected in the ICTY's Statute. Does prosecution on this theory, then, offend the legality principle? Does JCE liability pose a risk that persons will be found guilty simply on the basis of association, rather than individual culpability?

2. Those who act with the knowledge and intent discussed above and who also fulfill the *actus reus* requirement of JCE liability are deemed liable as persons who "committed" the crime — that is, as *principals*, not aiders and abettors — even if they, like Tadić himself, were not proven to have physically participated in any of the operative events. If international law recognizes JCE liability, such as that discussed above, need we ever resort to other "modes of responsibility" such as aiding and abetting or the like — at least where a plurality of actors surround a criminal incident? Consider, when reading Part D below on aiding and abetting, how JCE differs from that type of accessorial liability. See also Prosecutor v. Tadić, Case No. IT-94-1-A, Judgment, ¶105 (July 15, 1999).

3. Much has been written about JCE liability, much of it critical. See, e.g., Symposium, Guilty by Association: Joint Criminal Enterprise on Trial, 5 J. Intl. Crim. Just. 67 (2007); Allison Marston Danner & Jenny S. Martinez, Guilty Associations: Joint Criminal Enterprise, Command Responsibility, and the Development of International Criminal Law, 93 Cal. L. Rev. 75 (2005). Some critics have said, only half in jest, that JCE really stands for "Just Convict Everyone." Is this criticism fair?

"Category three of JCE is particularly controversial because many national systems do not recognize the liability of participants in a common plan for crimes that fall outside the scope of the common objective." Danner & Martinez, supra, at 109. Some commentators also contend that, despite the extensive discussions in ICTY case law of international decisions, "the World War II cases provide almost no support for the most controversial aspects of contemporary joint criminal enterprise doctrine." Id. at 110. Finally, as Professors Danner and Martinez argue, under the third category of JCE:

[i]f the prosecution successfully demonstrates that the defendant intended to participate in a JCE, that defendant will be liable for crimes committed by others that he did not

intend, as long as those crimes were foreseeable. Category Three JCEs, therefore, lower the relevant mental state from intention or knowledge to recklessness. . . .

Depending on how broadly prosecutors describe the criminal goal of the enterprise in a JCE, or how loosely the judges construe foreseeability, an individual's liability can vary dramatically. What is the limit to intended or foreseeable wrongdoing in a country wracked by ethnic cleansing and armed conflict? As a practical matter, prosecutorial discretion appears to be the only meaningful limit on the extent of wrongdoing attributable to an individual defendant in JCE. . . .

Many JCEs, in fact, are described in expansive terms. The indictment of Milan Martic, for example, alleges that he was a participant in a JCE, the purpose of which was "the forcible removal of a majority of the Croat, Muslim and other non-Serb population from approximately one-third of the territory of the Republic of Croatia . . . and large parts of the Republic of Bosnia. . . ." Similarly, the indictments of several other individuals accuse them of participating in a JCE whose purpose was "the permanent forcible removal of Bosnian Muslims and Bosnian Croat inhabitants from the territory of the planned Serbian state." That these indictments have all been confirmed by a judge at the ICTY indicates that there is no systematic objection to allegations of JCEs of great breadth. . . .

Joint criminal enterprise raises the specter of guilt by association and provides ammunition to those who doubt the rigor and impartiality of the international forum. If conspiracy is the darling of the U.S. prosecutor's nursery, then it is difficult to see how JCE can amount to anything less than the nuclear bomb of the international prosecutor's arsenal.

Id. at 108-109, 135-137.

Some suggest that the best way to contain the reach of JCE liability is to give added emphasis to the "objective" element — that is, to require that the defendants' actions in furtherance of the common crime charged be proved indispensable or important to the success of the JCE. Thus, Professors Danner and Martinez recommend that "[i]nstead of seeking to restrict the scope of JCEs in an across-the-board fashion, the judges should require that prosecutors prove that the defendant has made a substantial contribution to the JCE charged. Such a requirement would both restrict the scope of the JCE the prosecution is able to charge and would help ensure that JCE is used primarily for senior leaders. At the very least, such a requirement will avoid the unsavory possibility of the prosecution proving a low-level defendant's contribution to a JCE defined as all the crimes occurring within a country over a multi-year period — a situation allowed under the current articulation of the rules." Id. at 150. In *Prosecutor v. Kvocka*, however, the ICTY Appeals Chamber ruled that the prosecutor need not prove that the defendants made a "substantial contribution" to a JCE in order to be held criminally liable. IT-98-30/1, Judgment, ¶97 (Feb. 28, 2005).

2.   *Contrasting Conspiracy Liability with JCE*

JCE liability looks a lot like conspiracy liability under U.S. law — for good reason. The JCE concept actually grew out of the application of conspiracy principles in the Nuremberg and other post–World War II trials. Although conspiracy was included in the Nuremberg Charter and was used as the basis for indictment, the IMT's lengthy judgment contains only a very abbreviated discussion of conspiracy liability. (For additional information on conspiracy in this context, refer to Chapter 3, Section A, in the Notes following the Nuremberg Charter, as well as the introduction to conspiracy law in the Notes following *United States v. Ricardo* in Chapter 5, Section A).

In the United States, different statutes define conspiracy in different terms, but the heart of most conspiracy cases is (1) an *agreement* between two or more persons to achieve an unlawful objective or to secure a lawful objective by unlawful means; and (2) the co-conspirators' knowing participation in the conspiracy with the intention of helping it succeed.[61] Some conspiracy statutes (including the most popular federal general conspiracy provision, 18 U.S.C. §371) require proof of an overt act in furtherance of the conspiracy, but overt acts can be entirely innocent ones and are therefore not difficult to make out. Many other state and federal statutes, and the common law version of conspiracy, do not even require proof of an overt act.[62] Conspiracy charges bring with them many procedural and evidentiary advantages for the government in U.S. prosecutions. As a practical matter, then, the government views the conspiracy statute as the "darling of the modern prosecutor's nursery,"[63] while most defense lawyers concur in Clarence Darrow's observation that "if there are still any citizens interested in protecting human liberty, let them study the conspiracy law of the United States."[64]

The most fundamental difference between conspiracy and JCE liability concerns their functions. JCE is (like aiding and abetting or inciting) a form of culpable participation — a theory of liability. It tells us when someone acting with others to commit a crime can be liable as a perpetrator for that crime when he did not actually commit the elements of the offense — but it is *not a separate substantive crime.* By contrast, conspiracy has two functions: (1) It is a *separate substantive crime for which one can be convicted on top of the crime that is the object of the conspiracy — whether or not that object is achieved* (e.g., 18 U.S.C. §371); *and* (2) it is, at least in some jurisdictions, a form of culpable participation.[65]

First Rationale for Conspiracy: Separate, Inchoate Crime. With respect to the first function, conspiracy is a stand-alone offense. Each co-conspirator is a principal perpetrator of the conspiracy; at least in U.S. law, there are no "degrees" of participation and no possibility of being an accomplice to a conspiracy. It is also an inchoate offense. A defendant can be convicted for the substantive crime of conspiracy, even if the crime that was the object of the conspiracy *was never committed, or even attempted,* so long as one overt act in furtherance of the conspiracy was performed. Note also, however, that even when the co-conspirators are able to complete the crime that they have conspired to achieve, the "conspiracy to commit an offense and the subsequent commission of that crime normally do not merge into a single punishable act."[66] "[I]t is well recognized that in most cases separate sentences can be imposed for conspiracy to do an act and for the subsequent accomplishment of that end."[67]

JCEs do not share this function under the Ad Hoc Tribunal case law. In these Tribunals, if a crime is not *committed* there can be no liability based on a criminal "agreement" combined with some overt action in furtherance of the agreement (except in genocide cases where a conspiracy charge is at least possible, if not often levied).

Second Rationale for Conspiracy: A Mode of Participation. This brings us to the second function of conspiracy: Conspiracy is, in some jurisdictions, a theory of liability

---

61. See, e.g., 18 U.S.C. §371; United States v. Cure, 804 F.2d 625, 628 (11th Cir. 1986).
62. See, e.g., 21 U.S.C. §§846, 963 (conspiracies to traffic in, or import, drugs).
63. Harrison v. United States, 7 F.2d 259, 263 (2d Cir. 1925) (per J. Learned Hand).
64. John R. Wing & Michael J. Bresnick, Curbing Conspiracy Charges: Effective Legal Arguments for White Collar Defendants, 7 Bus. Crimes Bull. 1 (Jan. 2001) (quoting Clarence Darrow's biography).
65. See Danner & Martinez, supra note 58, at 118-119.
66. Iannelli v. United States, 420 U.S. 770, 777 (1975).
67. Id. at 777-778.

through which a conspirator can be convicted for the *substantive crimes committed by his co-conspirators.* Under the common law and the U.S. Supreme Court's decision in *Pinkerton v. United States,*[68] co-conspirators are liable for all reasonably foreseeable substantive crimes committed by their co-conspirators in furtherance of the conspiracy. Although many U.S. states, the Model Penal Code, and civil law jurisdictions all reject this theory of liability, it is still used in U.S. federal courts and remains valid under U.S. Supreme Court case law. Thus, under *Pinkerton,* each member of a conspiracy is criminally liable for any substantive crimes committed by their co-conspirators (even though they neither participated in those substantive crimes nor actually knew about them) if the crimes were committed during the course and in furtherance of the conspiracy, occurred within the scope of the unlawful project, and were reasonably foreseeable. The third category of JCE bears a strong resemblance to *Pinkerton* liability.

The rationale behind the *Pinkerton* rule is that the co-conspirators are each others' agents as to acts that are reasonably foreseeable. The problem with this rationale is that, under U.S. conspiracy law (as well as under the Ad Hoc Tribunals' JCE law), the defendant need not know the other co-conspirators or what they are doing; thus, the agency rationale seems like a very punitive fiction. Further, under *Pinkerton,* the defendant is liable no matter how marginal his participation in the conspiratorial plan was; he may be liable for all that his far-flung co-conspirators do until the defendant withdraws from the conspiracy or the conspiracy ends. *Pinkerton* liability, like category three JCEs, has been criticized for being far too broad.

Should the ICC Add Conspiracy Liability? We have established that conspiracy is a separate, substantive offense under U.S. law, but it has not been a popular charge in the post-Nuremberg international tribunals to date and is not mentioned at all in the ICC Statute. Why not?

Under U.S. law, "[i]t is well settled that the law of conspiracy serves ends different from, and complementary to, those served by criminal prohibitions of the substantive offense."[69] The law of conspiracy serves two independent values: (1) It protects society from the dangers of concerted criminal activity, and (2) it serves a preventive function by stopping criminal conduct in its early stages of growth before it has a full opportunity to bloom.[70] With respect to the first value, courts reason:

> [C]ollective criminal agreement — partnership in crime — presents a greater potential threat to the public than individual delicts. Concerted action both increases the likelihood that the criminal object will be successfully attained and decreases the probability that the individuals involved will depart from their path of criminality. Group association for criminal purposes often, if not normally, makes possible the attainment of ends more complex than those which one criminal could accomplish. Nor is the danger of a conspiratorial group limited to the particular end toward which it has embarked. Combination in crime makes more likely the commission of crimes unrelated to the original purpose for which the group was formed. In sum, the danger which a conspiracy generates is not confined to the substantive offense which is the immediate aim of the enterprise.[71]

---

68. 328 U.S. 640 (1946).
69. United States v. Feola, 420 U.S. 671, 693 (1975).
70. Id. at 693-694.
71. Callanan v. United States, 364 U.S. 587, 593-594 (1961).

"The threat posed to society by these combinations arises from the creative interaction of two autonomous minds. It is for this reason that the essence of a conspiracy is an *agreement*."[72]

With respect to the second value:

> The law of conspiracy identifies the agreement to engage in a criminal venture as an event of sufficient threat to social order to permit the imposition of criminal sanctions for the agreement alone, plus an overt act in pursuit of it, regardless of whether the crime agreed upon actually is committed. Criminal intent has crystallized, and the likelihood of actual, fulfilled commission warrants preventive action.[73]

This latter rationale for conspiracy as a stand-alone substantive crime does not fit well with the law developed in the Ad Hoc Tribunals because, as discussed above, those Tribunals were not charged with nipping incipient international (nongenocide) crimes in the bud through conspiracy (or attempt) prosecutions. But some argue that the rationales underlying the proposed use of conspiracy at Nuremberg — principally the often overwhelming number of persons who must be tried after armed conflict leads to atrocity and the dearth of individualized evidence that may survive the conflict — continue to apply.[74] Further, the ICC Statute now recognizes attempt liability. In your view, should it also include conspiracy in the list of actionable crimes?

3. Attempts

Alongside conspiracy, common law systems recognize a second kind of inchoate crime: attempts. Like a conspiracy, an attempt is a self-standing crime that can be prosecuted, even if the attempted crime is never completed. The international tribunals prior to the ICC were not very receptive to prosecutions for criminal attempts, even attempts to commit atrocities. Attempt liability was not explicitly and autonomously recognized in the Nuremberg or Tokyo charters. The Ad Hoc Tribunals' statutes provide for attempt liability only in genocide cases. In all other instances, the ICTY and ICTR said that a crime had to be *committed* for liability to attach, even where the method of participation identified was the "preparation" or "planning" of a crime.[75]

The ICC Statute, in this respect, differs from the Nuremberg Charter and the Ad Hoc Tribunals' Statutes. Under Article 25(3)(f), a person shall be criminally responsible if that person "[a]ttempts to commit such a crime by taking action that commences its execution by means of a substantial step, but the crime does not occur because of circumstances independent of the person's intentions." The reason attempt liability makes sense has been explained as follows:

> First, a high degree of culpability attaches to an individual who attempts to commit a crime and is unsuccessful only because of circumstances beyond his control rather than his own decision to abandon the criminal endeavour. Secondly, the fact that an

---

72. United States v. Stevens, 909 F.2d 431, 433 (11th Cir. 1990).
73. *Feola*, 420 U.S. at 694.
74. See, e.g., Richard P. Barrett & Laura E. Little, Lessons of Yugoslav Rape Trials: A Role for Conspiracy Law in International Tribunals, 88 Minn. L. Rev. 30 (2003); Nina H.B. Jorgensen, A Reappraisal of the Abandoned Nuremberg Concept of Criminal Organisations in the Context of Justice in Rwanda, 12 Crim. L.F. 371 (2001).
75. See Prosecutor v. Akeyasu, Case No. 96-4-T, Judgment, ¶¶473, 480 (Sept. 2, 1998).

individual has taken a significant step towards the completion of one of the crimes . . . entails a threat to international peace and security because of the very serious nature of these crimes." . . . From a more social-psychological perspective, an essential detrimental effect can be seen in the impression of shattered confidence of the population in the stability of the legal order exerted by the attempt.[76]

With respect to the objective element of this mode of participation, ICC Article 25 states that a person must attempt the *commencement* of the execution of the crime by a *substantial step*. Professor Ambos notes this does not mean that "the crime in question [must] be partly executed, i.e., the person need not have realized one or more elements of the crime."[77] With respect to the mental element, it appears that attempt liability is founded on the same intent as is necessary for the completed crime.[78]

4.   The ICTR's "Integral Part" Test

Let us return from our brief foray into principal liability for the inchoate crimes of conspiracy and attempt, and focus anew on the question with which the ICTY struggled in creating JCE liability: When can a person such as Tadić, who is not accused of physically killing anyone, nonetheless be held responsible as a principal perpetrator for killings? Consider, in this regard, the "integral part" test formulated by the ICTR's Appeals Chamber in *Prosecutor v. Seromba*.[79]

In *Seromba*, the Appeals Chamber held that Athanase Seromba, a Roman Catholic priest in Rwanda, was guilty of "committing" genocide and the crime against humanity of extermination for his participation in the bulldozing of a Nyange church, which resulted in the deaths of at least 1,500 Tutsis who had taken refuge inside the church. In so doing, the Appeals Chamber reversed the Trial Chamber's judgment that Seromba was criminally responsible only as an aider and abettor and increased his sentence from 15 years to life imprisonment.[80]

The Trial Chamber found that Seromba discussed and "accepted" the local authorities' determination to bulldoze Seromba's own church with the Tutsi refugees inside.[81] Before beginning the bulldozing, the bulldozer driver "asked Seromba three times whether he should destroy the church."[82] Seromba responded in the affirmative and "said such words to [the] bulldozer driver . . . as would encourage him to destroy the church."[83] (According to the Appeals Chamber, these included the exhortation that "[d]emons ha[d] gotten in there [the church]" and that when "there are demons in the church, it should be destroyed.")[84] The Trial Chamber further found that Seromba told the driver where to begin, pointing out the church's

76. Albin Eser, Individual Criminal Responsibility, in 1 The Rome Statute of the International Criminal Court: A Commentary 767, 808-809 (A. Cassese, P. Gaeta, & J. Jones eds., 2002) [hereinafter Eser, Individual Responsibility Commentary].

77. Kai Ambos, Article 25: Individual Responsibility, Commentary on the Rome Statute of the International Criminal Court: Observers' Notes 475, 489 (Otto Triffterer ed., 1999) [hereinfter Ambos, Observers' Notes]; see also Eser, Individual Responsibility Commentary, supra note 76, at 811-814.

78. Eser, Individual Responsibility Commentary, supra note 76, at 811.

79. Case No. ICTR-2001-66-A, Judgment (March 12, 2008).

80. Id.

81. Id. ¶164.

82. Id. ¶165.

83. Id. ¶170.

84. Id. ¶165.

"fragile side."[85] Based on these findings, the Trial Chamber concluded that Seromba aided and abetted genocide.

The Appeals Chamber endorsed the Trial Chamber's findings of fact in this regard, but rejected its legal characterization of Seromba's conduct as "aiding and abetting" others' crime. The Trial Chamber had defined "committing" as meaning "the direct physical or personal participation of the accused in the perpetration of a crime or the culpable omission of an act that was mandated by a rule of criminal law."[86] The Appeals Chamber ruled, however, that "committing" genocide does *not* require "direct and physical perpetration"; instead, "committing" may occur where the actions of an accused are *"as much an integral part of the genocide as were the killings which [they] enabled."*[87]

Seromba, the Appeals Chamber concluded, was a "principal perpetrator of the crime itself by approving and embracing as his own the decision to commit the crime and thus should be convicted for committing genocide."[88] Seromba's actions, including his presence, utterances, approving and embracing the decision to bulldoze, and his giving of directions, amounted to an integral part of the genocidal destruction of the church. The court stressed the position of trust and authority Seromba held in the community in his position as priest. Under the court's "integral part" definition of "commission," it concluded that the fact "that Athanase Seromba did not personally drive the bulldozer that destroyed the church" was "irrelevant."[89] It continued: "What is important is that Athanase Seromba fully exercised his influence [as the parish priest] over the bulldozer driver who accepted Athanase Seromba as the only authority, and whose directions he followed."[90] The Appeals Chamber applied this expanded definition of "commission" to the crime against humanity of extermination as well as to genocide.[91]

Judge Liu, in dissent, argued that in the ICTY, "where there was no physical perpetration of the offence, commission has only ever been extended within the context of a JCE," which was not pleaded in Seromba's case.[92] The dissent further argued that the majority had blurred the line between "committing" and "aiding and abetting" with its new "integral part" test, opening the floodgates for finding individuals liable as perpetrators who did not directly participate in the crime.[93] Do you agree?

5.   ICC Article 25(3)(a): "Committing" a Crime

ICC Article 25(3)(a) provides that a natural person shall be criminally responsible as a perpetrator if he:

> (a) [c]ommits . . . a crime, whether as an individual, jointly with another or through another person, regardless of whether that other person is criminally responsible.

In the *Lubanga* case, the ICC prosecutor sought to hold the defendant liable for the war crime of conscripting and enlisting children under the age of 15 under ICC

---

85. Id. ¶170.
86. Id. ¶155.
87. Id. ¶161 (emphasis added).
88. Id.
89. Id. ¶171.
90. Id.
91. Id. ¶190.
92. Id. ¶6 (Liu, J., dissenting).
93. Id. ¶14.

Article 25(3)(a) as a co-perpetrator jointly with other FPLC officers, members, and supporters. Pre-Trial Chamber I, in confirming the charges, set forth its test for distinguishing between a perpetrator under ICC Article 25(3)(a) and accessorial liability under the remaining subsections of Article 25(3).

PROSECUTOR v. LUBANGA

Case No. ICC-01/04-01/06, Decision on the Confirmation of Charges (Jan. 29, 2007)

... 322. The concept of co-perpetration embodied in article 25(3)(a) of the Statute requires analysis. The Prosecution is of the opinion that article 25(3)(a) of the Statute adopts a concept of co-perpetration based on the notion of control of the crime in the sense that a person can become a co-perpetrator of a crime only if he or she has "joint control" over the crime as a result of the "essential contribution" ascribed to him or her.

323. The Prosecution acknowledges that the concept of co-perpetration pursuant to article 25(3)(a) of the Statute differs from that of co-perpetration based on the existence of a joint criminal enterprise or common purpose as reflected, in particular, in the jurisprudence of the ICTY. In this regard, the Prosecution submits that it is important to take into consideration the fundamental differences between the ad hoc tribunals and the Court, because the latter operates under a Statute which not only sets out modes of criminal liability in great detail, but also deliberately avoids the broader definitions found in, for example, article 7(1) of the ICTY Statute.

324. The Defence does not suggest any interpretation of the concept of co-perpetration, but it challenges the Prosecution's approach saying that it "goes beyond the clear terms of co-perpetration and indirect perpetration set out in the Statute, and is not supported by either customary international law, or general principles of law derived from legal systems of the world."[94]

325. The Legal Representatives of the Victims ... argue that the concept of co-perpetration set out in article 25(3)(a) of the Statute pertains to the concept of joint criminal enterprise or common purpose doctrine, the essential component of which is the sharing of a common criminal plan or purpose as opposed to retaining control over the crime.

326. The Chamber is of the view that the concept of co-perpetration is originally rooted in the idea that when the sum of co-ordinated individual contributions of a plurality of persons results in the realisation of all the objective elements of a crime, any person making a contribution can be held vicariously responsible for the contributions of all the others and, as a result, can be considered as a principal to the whole crime.

327. In this regard, the definitional criterion of the concept of co-perpetration is linked to the distinguishing criterion between principals and accessories to a crime where a criminal offence is committed by a plurality of persons.

328. The objective approach to such a distinction focuses on the realisation of one or more of the objective elements of the crime. From this perspective, only those who physically carry out one or more of the objective elements of the offence can be considered principals to the crime.

---

94. [Court's footnote 414:] The Defence alleges that the concept of joint control over the crime was developed primarily by German theorists, in particular Claus Roxin, and that such theories "are very much predicated on notions of hierarchy and obedience, and were formulated to address the type of systematic criminality which existed in Germany during World War II (as exemplified in the *Eichmann* case) and during the communist regime in the GDR."

329. The subjective approach — which is the approach adopted by the jurisprudence of the ICTY through the concept of joint criminal enterprise or the common purpose doctrine — moves the focus from the level of contribution to the commission of the offence as the distinguishing criterion between principals and accessories, and places it instead on the state of mind in which the contribution to the crime was made. As a result, only those who make their contribution with the shared intent to commit the offence can be considered principals to the crime, regardless of the level of their contribution to its commission.

330. The concept of control over the crime constitutes a third approach for distinguishing between principals and accessories which, contrary to the Defence claim, is applied in numerous legal systems. The notion underpinning this third approach is that principals to a crime are not limited to those who physically carry out the objective elements of the offence, but also include those who, in spite of being removed from the scene of the crime, control or mastermind its commission because they decide whether and how the offence will be committed.

331. This approach involves an objective element, consisting of the appropriate factual circumstances for exercising control over the crime, and a subjective element, consisting of the awareness of such circumstances.

332. According to this approach, only those who have control over the commission of the offence — and are aware of having such control — may be principals because:

i.   they physically carry out the objective elements of the offence (commission of the crime in person, or direct perpetration);
ii. they control the will of those who carry out the objective elements of the offence (commission of the crime through another person, or indirect penetration); or
iii. they have, along with others, control over the offence by reason of the essential tasks assigned to them (commission of the crime jointly with others, or co-perpetration).

333. Article 25(3)(a) of the Statute does not take into account the objective criterion for distinguishing between principals and accessories because the notion of committing an offence through another person — particularly where the latter is not criminally responsible — cannot be reconciled with the idea of limiting the class of principals to those who physically carry out one or more of the objective elements of the offence.

334. Article 25(3)(a) of the Statute, read in conjunction with article 25(3)(d), also does not take into account the subjective criteria for distinguishing between principals and accessories. In this regard, Chamber notes that, by moving away from the concept of co-perpetration embodied in article 25(3)(a), article 25(3)(d) defines the concept of (i) contribution to the commission or attempted commission of a crime by a group of persons acting with a common purpose, (ii) with the aim of furthering the criminal activity of the group or in the knowledge of the criminal purpose.

335. The Chamber considers that this latter concept — which is closely akin to the concept of joint criminal enterprise or the common purpose doctrine adopted by the jurisprudence of the ICTY — would have been the basis of the concept of co-perpetration within the meaning of article 25(3)(a), had the drafters of the Statute opted for a subjective approach for distinguishing between principals and accessories.

336. Moreover, the Chamber observes that the wording of article 25(3)(d) of the Statute begins with the words "[i]ny any other way contributes to the commission or attempted commission of such a crime."

337. Hence, in the view of the Chamber, article 25(3)(d) of the Statute provides for a residual form of accessory liability which makes it possible to criminalise those contributions to a crime which cannot be characterised as ordering, soliciting, inducing, aiding, abetting, or assisting within the meaning of article 25(3)(b) or article 25(3)(c) of the Statute, by reason of the state of mind in which the contributions were made.

338. Not having accepted the objective and subjective approaches for distinguishing between principals and accessories to a crime, the Chamber considers, as does the Prosecution and, unlike the jurisprudence of the ad hoc tribunals, that the Statute embraces the third approach, which is based on the concept of control over the crime.

339. In this regard, the Chamber notes that the most typical manifestation of the concept of control over the crime, which is the commission of a crime through another person, is expressly provided for in article 25(3)(a) of the Statute. In addition, the use of the phrase "regardless of whether that other person is criminally responsible" in article 25(3)(a) of the Statute militates in favour of the conclusion that this provision extends to the commission of a crime not only through an innocent agent (that is, through another person who is not criminally responsible), but also through another person who is fully criminally responsible.

340. The Chamber considers that the concept of co-perpetration embodied in article 25(3)(a) of the Statute by the reference to the commission of a crime "jointly with [. . .] another person" must cohere with the choice of the concept of control over the crime as a criterion for distinguishing between principals and accessories.

341. Hence, . . . the Chamber considers that the concept of co-perpetration embodied in article 25(3)(a) of the Statute coincides with that of joint control over the crime by reason of the essential nature of the various contributions to the commission of the crime.

3. Elements of Co-Perpetration Based on Joint Control over the Crime

342. The concept of co-perpetration based on joint control over the crime is rooted in the principle of the division of essential tasks for the purpose of committing a crime between two or more persons acting in a concerted manner. Hence, although none of the participants has overall control over the offence because they all depend on one another for its commission, they all share control because each of them could frustrate the commission of the crime by not carrying out his or her task.

A. Objective Elements

i) Existence of an Agreement or Common Plan Between Two or More Persons

343. In the view of the Chamber, the first objective requirement of co-perpetration based on joint control over the crime is the existence of an agreement or common plan between two or more persons. Accordingly, participation in the commission of a crime without co-ordination with one's co-perpetrators falls outside the scope of co-perpetration within the meaning of article 25(3)(a) of the Statute.

344. The common plan must include an element of criminality, although it does not need to be specifically directed at the commission of a crime. It suffices:

i. that the co-perpetrators have agreed (a) to start the implementation of the common plan to achieve a non-criminal goal, and (b) to only commit the crime if certain conditions are met; or

ii.   that the co-perpetrators (a) are aware of the risk that implementing the common plan (which is specifically directed at the achievement of a non-criminal goal) will result in the commission of the crime, and (b) accept such an outcome.

345. Furthermore, the Chamber considers that the agreement need not be explicit and that its existence can be inferred from the subsequent concerted action of the co-perpetrators.

ii) Co-Ordinated Essential Contribution by Each Co-Perpetrator Resulting in the Realisation of the Objective Elements of the Crime

346. The Chamber considers that the second objective requirement of co-perpetration based on joint control over the crime is the co-ordinated essential contribution made by each co-perpetrator resulting in the realisation of the objective elements of the crime.

347. In the view of the Chamber, when the objective elements of an offence are carried out by a plurality of persons acting within the framework of a common plan, only those to whom essential tasks have been assigned — and who, consequently, have the power to frustrate the commission of the crime by not performing their tasks — can be said to have joint control over the crime.

348. The Chamber observes that, although some authors have linked the essential character of a task — and hence the ability to exercise joint control over the crime — to its performance at the execution stage of the crime, the Statute does not contain any such restriction.

B. SUBJECTIVE ELEMENTS

i) The Suspect Must Fulfil the Subjective Elements of the Crime in Question

349. The Chamber considers that co-perpetration based on joint control over the crime requires above all that the suspect fulfil the subjective elements of the crime with which he or she is charged, including a requisite *dolus specialis*[95] or ulterior intent for the type of crime involved. . . .

ii) The Suspect and the Other Co-Perpetrators Must All Be Mutually Aware and Mutually Accept That Implementing Their Common Plan May Result in the Realisation of the Objective Elements of the Crime

361. The theory of co-perpetration based on joint control over the crime requires two additional subjective elements. The suspect and the other co-perpetrators (a) must all be mutually aware of the risk that implementing their common plan may result in the realisation of the objective elements of the crime, and (b) must all mutually accept such a result by reconciling themselves with it or consenting to it.

362. The Chamber considers that it is precisely the co-perpetrators' mutual awareness and acceptance of this result which justifies (a) that the contributions made by the others may be attributed to each of them, including the suspect, and (b) that they be held criminally responsible as principals to the whole crime.

363. . . . [T]wo scenarios must be distinguished. Firstly, if there is a substantial risk of bringing about the objective elements of the crime (that is, if it is likely that "it will occur in the ordinary course of events"), the mutual acceptance by the suspect and

---

95. In this context, the phrase *dolus specialis* refers to whatever *mens rea* the specific statutory provision requires. — Eds.

the other co-perpetrators of the idea of bringing about the objective elements of the crime can be inferred from:

i.   the awareness by the suspect and the other co-perpetrators of the substantial likelihood that implementing the common plan would result in the realisation of the objective elements of the crime; and

ii. the decision by the suspect and the other co-perpetrators to implement the common plan despite such awareness.

364. Secondly, if the risk of bringing about the objective elements of the crime is low, the suspect and the other co-perpetrators must have clearly or expressly accepted the idea that implementing the common plan would result in the realisation of the objective elements of the crime.

365. Consequently, although in principle, the war crime of enlisting or conscripting children under the age of fifteen years or using them to participate actively in hostilities requires only a showing that the suspect "should have known" that the victims were under the age of fifteen years, the Chamber considers that this subjective element is not applicable in the instant case. Indeed, the theory of co-perpetration based on joint control over the crime requires that all the co-perpetrators, including the suspect, be mutually aware of, and mutually accept, the likelihood that implementing the common plan would result in the realisation of the objective elements of the crime.[96]

iii) The Suspect Must Be Aware of the Factual Circumstances Enabling Him or Her to Jointly Control the Crime

366. The Chamber considers that the third and last subjective element of co-perpetration based on joint control of the crime is the awareness by the suspect of the factual circumstances enabling him or her to jointly control the crime.

367. In the view of the Chamber, this requires the suspect to be aware (i) that his or her role is essential to the implementation of the common plan, and hence in the commission of the crime, and (ii) that he or she can — by reason of the essential nature of his or her task — frustrate the implementation of the common plan, and hence the commission of the crime, by refusing to perform the task assigned to him or her.

NOTES AND QUESTIONS

1. Pre-Trial Chamber I calls its "objective" requirement as one of "joint control." Does this imply a superior-subordinate relationship, or is the court attempting instead to focus on how important the defendant's contribution was to the criminal plan? The court emphasizes, in discussing its "control" theory, that co-perpetrators are those "to whom essential tasks have been assigned" and thus who have the "power to frustrate the commission of the crime by not performing their tasks." Does this sound like the "substantial contribution" requirement for JCE liability suggested by some commentators but rejected by the ICTY Appeal Chamber? Or is this more stringent? How does

---

96. [Court's footnote 441:] Had the Prosecution alleged, for instance, that Thomas Lubanga Dyilo committed the above-mentioned crimes himself — as opposed to jointly with others — the "should have known" requirement would have been applicable in relation to determining the age of the victims.

it compare with the "integral part" test adopted by the ICTR Appeals Chamber in *Seromba?*

What of the subjective, or *mens rea*, element of co-perpetration liability where each defendant acts to further a common criminal plan?

2. Did Pre-Trial Chamber I reject JCE liability under the ICC Statute? Its conception of co-perpetration sounds like conspiracy-type liability, but is it? Can co-perpetrators under ICC Article 25(3)(a) be held responsible for acts beyond the common design, as in JCE Category Three or *Pinkerton* liability?

3. *Omissions.* Throughout its opinion, Pre-Trial Chamber I referred to acts or omissions because sometimes a crime is "committed" through "omission." This is consistent with the practice in the Ad Hoc Tribunals, where Trial Chambers have held that defendants can be liable through inaction, as well as affirmative action. See, e.g., Prosecutor v. Kvočka, Case No. IT-98-30/1-T, Judgment, ¶¶258-261 (Nov. 2, 2001); cf. Prosecutor v. Blaškić, Case No. IT-95-14-A, Judgment, ¶47 (July 29, 2004) ("The Appeals Chamber leaves open the possibility that in the circumstances of a given case, an omission may constitute the *actus reus* of aiding and abetting").

In U.S. criminal law, criminal liability for a *failure to act* — that is an omission — must be founded on a *duty to act* and that duty must arise from law. Generally, one has no legal duty to assist another person, even if that assistance will prevent great harm to another person and can be rendered with no danger or even inconvenience to the rescuer. In short, a moral duty does not necessarily translate in U.S. law into a legal duty. Legal duties to act can arise from official position, personal relationships, statute, contract, the voluntary assumption of care, or the creation of the risk in the first instance.

The ICC Statute does not clearly address the issue of whether liability generally can attach for omissions. Certainly, specific provisions in the Rome Treaty explicitly sanction such liability. Thus, for example, ICC Article 28 authorizes punishment in command responsibility cases for the failure of superiors to prevent or punish crimes by their subordinates. Yet the ICC's general part on *mens rea*, Article 30, is by its terms limited to "conduct." The Draft ICC Statute put forth by the Preparatory Commission recommended that the following provision be made: "Conduct . . . can constitute either an act or an omission, or a combination thereof" and individual criminal responsibility could flow from an omission to act only "if the person was under a legal obligation to avoid that [prohibited] result." Albin Eser, Individual Criminal Responsibility, in I The Rome Statute of the International Criminal Court: A Commentary 767, 819 (A. Cassese, P. Gaeta, & J. Jones eds., 2002). The drafters' attempt to craft a provision dealing with culpable omissions failed, primarily due to the difficulty of arriving at a consensus on the question of when omissions should be punishable. Id.

Some commentators, relying on the fact that these proposals were rejected, conclude that "abstinence from explicit regulation cannot be interpreted in any other way than the rejection of individual criminal responsibility for commission by omission, unless it has been specifically provided for as in the case of Article 28(a) of the ICC Statute." Id. Other commentators assert that while " 'conduct' denotes positive action," it "may possibly also include an intentional omission, where the causal result and moral culpability of the intentional omission is equivalent to the achievement of the same result caused by an intentional act." Donald K. Piragoff, Article 30: Mental Element, in Commentary on the Rome Statute of the International Criminal Court: Observers' Notes, Article by Article 532 (Otto Triffterer ed., 1999) (citing the war crime of causing starvation).

The Pre-Trial Chamber was not required to pass on this issue in *Lubanga*, so it would be a mistake to make too much of that court's repeated references to "omissions," but it may be an indication of the court's inclination were the question squarely presented.

D.   ACCOMPLICE LIABILITY: AIDING AND ABETTING

In the Ad Hoc Tribunals, the objective and subjective elements of aiding and abetting can be summarized as follows:

a.   The aider and abettor must have given the principal perpetrator practical assistance, encouragement, or moral support which has a *substantial effect* on the perpetration of the crime;

b.   The aider and abettor need *only* have knowledge that the acts performed by the aider and abettor assist in the commission of the specific crime of the principal;

c.   The aider and abettor need *not*, however, have intended to assist or facilitate the crime; and

d.   Where specific intent is required for commission of the ultimate crime, the aider and abettor must have knowledge that the principal has the requisite intent, but the aider and abettor need not necessarily share that intent (for example, to prove that a defendant aided and abetted a genocide, the prosecutor need only show that the defendant knew about the principal's genocidal intent, not that the defendant shared it).

According to the ICTY's Appeals Chamber, "[m]any domestic jurisdictions, both common and civil law, take the same approach with respect to the *mens rea* for aiding and abetting," that is, requiring only that an aider and abettor be "aware that he is aiding the principal perpetrator by his contribution," and, where specific intent (*dolus specialis*) is required, be aware of the principal perpetrator's specific intent.[97]

ICC Article 25(3)(c) renders liable an individual who "[f]or the purpose of facilitating the commission of such a crime," aids, abets or otherwise assists in its commission or its attempted commission, including providing the means for its commission. Aiding and abetting is a form of accomplice liability. Thus, unless the principal actually commits or attempts the crime, the accomplice will have no liability.[98] The Rome Statute's provision on aiding and abetting liability may constitute a significant — and potentially far-reaching — departure from the aiding and abetting jurisprudence of the Ad Hoc Tribunals because the *mens rea* required may be more stringent. Let us attempt to contrast the ICC and ICTY doctrines:

a.   Professor Ambos opines that the ICC Statute will share the objective element of aiding and abetting defined in the Ad Hoc Tribunals: "[A]iding and abetting encompasses *any assistance*, whether physical or psychological, which, however,

---

97. Prosecutor v. Krstić, Case No. IT-98-33-A, Judgment ¶141 (Apr. 19, 2004) (citing the law of France, Germany, Switzerland, the UK, Canada, Australia, and some jurisdictions in the United States).

98. Eser, Individual Responsibility Commentary, supra note 76, at 798.

had a *substantial effect* on the commission of the main crime. In other words, the limiting [objective] element is the 'substantial effect' requirement. Thus, the question arises when an effect is 'substantial.'"[99] But this reading is not inevitable. One could argue that the objective requirements of Article 25(3)(c) are actually low because the Article covers not only aiding and abetting but also *otherwise assisting*. Thus, even if "aiding and abetting" liability contains an unstated requirement of a substantial contribution, there is likely no such requirement modifying "otherwise" assisting.[100]

b. While the Ad Hoc Tribunals require only "knowledge," ICC Article 30 requires, in every case where not otherwise specified, proof of "knowledge" and "intent."

c. Article 30's *mens rea* is supplemented in the case of aiding and abetting by the express provisions of Article 25(3)(c), which require that the aiding and abetting (or otherwise assisting) be undertaken "*for the purpose of facilitating the commission of*" a qualifying crime. Professor Ambos concludes that "it is clear that purpose generally implies a specific subjective requirement stricter than mere knowledge."[101] Unlike the ICTY, then, the ICC implies that an intention to assist or facilitate the crime must be proved.

d. It is unclear whether the aider and abettor need only know of the principal's specific intent, as in the ICTY, or needs to share that intent.

In sum, it would seem that in the ICC, an aider and abettor must not only know that his acts assist in the commission of the principal's crime (and, where the crime requires specific intent, know that the principal will commit the crime with the requisite *mens rea*), *but also* "wish that his assistance shall facilitate the commission of the crime."[102] This could be an important change in international aiding and abetting standards, and one that may narrow the scope of liability for serious crimes. Which rule — that used by the Ad Hoc Tribunals or that adopted in the ICC Statute — *should* prevail?

Consider the rationales offered in U.S. jurisprudence. The federal courts and a majority of states in the United States require proof that an aider and abettor share the principal's intent. For example, the U.S. Supreme Court has held that, "[i]n order to aid and abet another to commit a crime it is necessary that a defendant 'in some sort associate himself with the venture, that he participate in it as something that he wishes to bring about, that he seek by his action to make it succeed.'"[103] Thus, the general U.S. rule is that the aider and abettor must *intend* that the principal commit the acts that give rise to the principal's liability.

Professor Kadish has posited a number of rationales for the U.S. "intention" requirement:

> The first is culpability, the second the policy safeguarding lawful conduct from risk, and the third an ethic of individualism and self-determination. The culpability consideration arises from the need that [the aider and abettor] satisfy the culpability requirement of

---

99. Ambos, Observers' Notes, supra note 77, at 482 (emphasis added).

100. Id. at 483 (noting that the term *facilitating* confirms "that a 'direct and substantial assistance is not necessary and that the act of assistance need not be the condition sine qua non of the crime.'"); see also Eser, Individual Responsibility Commentary, supra note 76, at 798-801.

101. Ambos, Observers' Notes, supra note 77, at 483.

102. Eser, Individual Responsibility Commentary, supra note 76, at 801; see also Eser, Mistake Commentary, supra note 38, at 901-902.

103. Nye & Nissen v. United States, 336 U.S. 613, 619 (1949); see also Kadish, supra note 16, at 346-347, 349; *Krstić*, Case No. IT-98-33-A, Judgment, ¶141 n.244.

[the principal's] crime in order that he may be found guilty of it. . . . The policy concern is that to burden peoples' actions with doubts and worries about what someone else might culpably do as a consequence of their own lawful actions would tend to create an undesirable insecurity in the conduct of ordinary affairs. It is true that the law commonly imposes on people the burden of avoiding unwarranted risks that their conduct will *cause* harm, at least when they are aware of the danger and the harm eventuates — manslaughter, for example. But it is apparently believed that a burden of avoiding unwarranted risks that their conduct will *help or encourage* another to commit crime is distinguishable in nature and degree. Finally, there is the ethic of individualism and self-determination reflected in traditional criminal law doctrine that except in limited specified circumstances neither what happens to another nor what another person does is one's responsibility. . . .[104]

Do these reasons persuade in this context?

E. ACCOMPLICE LIABILITY: INSTIGATING, INCITING, AND ACTING IN CONCERT IN THE ICC

"Committing" a crime (or "perpetration" under ICC Article 25(3)(a)) is covered in Part C above. Article 25(3)(b)-(e) provides various modes of accessorial liability, one of which — "aiding and abetting" under ICC Article 25(3)(c) — is discussed in Part D above. The following notes discuss the remaining modes of accomplice liability identified in ICC Article 25(3). One caveat may be appropriate before beginning: These categories are not without ambiguity and may not be, in fact, mutually exclusive. As one of those participating in the drafting of the Rome Statute noted, "codifying the general part of international criminal law was 'an arduous task of comparative criminal law synthesis.' Nothing of this nature is ever complete; there are gaps and deliberate (intentional and knowing) ambiguities."[105] No doubt, then, the ICC Chambers will add over time to our understanding of the requisites of accessorial responsibility under the Statute.

Instigating (that is, ordering, soliciting or inducing) the commission of crime. ICC Article 25(3)(b) renders an individual criminally liable if he "[o]rders, solicits, or induces the commission of a crime." These modes of participation are accessorial, so they are only actionable if the crime "*in fact occurs or is attempted.*" The consequence is that a superior is liable for ordering a war crime only if her subordinate attempts it or succeeds in carrying it out. If a soldier disobeys his superior's command to commit a crime without taking steps to execute that order which reach the level of an attempt, neither the commander nor the soldier will be liable.

"Ordering" could be considered either the action of a principal perpetrator under ICC Article 25(3)(a) — because the order constitutes "perpetration through means" — or the action of an accessory under Article 25(3)(b). Are those who "order" a crime sufficiently culpable that they should be considered "principals" who "commit" the crime under ICC Article 25(3)(a), rather than accomplices under ICC Article 25(3)(b)? Is this just a quibble?

---

104. Kadish, supra note 23, at 371-372.
105. Clark, supra note 13, at 334.

The requirements for "ordering" liability under 25(3)(b) echo (in part) the requirements of "command" or "superior" responsibility under ICC Article 28, examined in Part F below. It is important to recognize the relationship (at least in theory) between these two provisions. "Ordering" under ICC Article 25(3)(b) contemplates liability for an *affirmative* wrongful act—ordering the commission of the crime. The *actus reus* of the crime under ICC Article 28's "command" or "superior" responsibility, by contrast, is an *omission*—a failure to act to prevent or punish a crime committed by those over whom the superior exercises control.

The balance of ICC Article 25(3)(b) concerns "soliciting" or "inducing" a crime. These are classical modes of instigation for which persons may be liable as accomplices and do not require a relationship (e.g., superior-subordinate) for liability. In terms of the objective elements necessary to liability, soliciting generally encompasses encouraging or requesting another to commit the crime. Inducing means to influence the principal to commit the crime and can encompass the concept of "soliciting." This type of influence is normally psychological or financial, but it can also be of a physical nature.

Given the absence of a more specific *mens rea* in Article 25, the general "mental element" of ICC Article 30 applies. To be liable for soliciting or inducing a crime (that, again, must be committed or attempted), the defendant must have acted with knowledge and intent. The instigator must also know that the principal has the state of mind required for commission of the crime.[106]

Acting in concert for criminal purposes. ICC Article 25(3)(d) renders liable a defendant who "[i]n any other way contributes to the commission or attempted commission of a crime by a group of persons acting with a common purpose." Subparagraph (d) was lifted, almost verbatim, from the International Convention for the Suppression of Terrorist Bombings.[107] According to the ICTY Appeals Chambers, however, "[t]he negotiating process [leading up to the Convention] does not shed any light on the reasons behind the adoption of this text."[108]

In terms of the objective requirements of this subsection, complicity in group crimes is, like instigating or aiding and abetting, "accessorial in requiring the commission of the principal crime or at least the attempt thereof. . . . Unlike instigation and aiding and abetting, however, the contribution of the accomplice must be rendered to a 'crime by a group of persons acting with a common purpose.'"[109] This subsection states that a defendant can be liable if he contributes "in any other way" than the modes of participation already set forth in subsections (b) and (c) to this group crime. This means that the objective contribution made by the defendant need be very low indeed.

In terms of the subjective element of complicity in group crimes, ICC Article 25(3)(d)(i) and (ii) specifically require that the defendant's contribution to the group crime be "intentional" in one of two ways: (1) either the defendant must make his contribution with the aim of furthering the criminal activity of the group *or* (2) the defendant must act with knowledge of the intention of the group to commit the crime. Article 30's "intent" and "knowledge" requirement also applies, but Article 30's "intent" requirement must be defined by reference to the more specific—and potentially less demanding—provision in Article 25(3)(d)(ii) (requiring only knowledge of the intention of the group).

106. See Eser, Individual Responsibility Commentary, supra note 76, at 797.
107. U.N. Doc. A/RES/52/164 (Jan. 9, 1998).
108. Prosecutor v. Tadić, Case No. IT-94-1-A, Judgment ¶221 (July 15, 1999).
109. Eser, Individual Responsibility Commentary, supra note 76, at 802.

How does the provision for complicity in group crimes under ICC Article 25(3)(d) differ from JCE liability?

ICC Article 25(3)(d)'s complicity in group crimes provision is undoubtedly different from the substantive crime of conspiracy. The drafters of the Rome Treaty proposed inclusion of conspiracy to commit genocide in the ICC Statute, but they did not ultimately give the ICC *any* jurisdiction to hear conspiracy charges. Thus, ICC Article 25(3)(d)'s complicity in group crimes subsection provides one of several modes of responsibility for the substantive crime at issue. It does *not* permit separate convictions (as would a conspiracy charge) for both the substantive offense that is the object of group activity, and the group activity itself.

Further, ICC Article 25(3)(d) provides that complicity in group crimes will *only* be actionable where the crime is actually committed or attempted. By contrast, conspiracy may be an entirely inchoate offense, in that the crime upon which two or more persons agreed need not ever be attempted or committed. (ICC Article 25(3) obviates the requirement that the offense be committed or attempted only in cases of incitement to genocide, discussed below.) Another difference may be that conspiracy requires an agreement between two persons, while liability for complicity in "group" criminality may, according to some, require at least three participants in the common criminal design.[110]

Inciting the crime of genocide. ICC Article 25(3)(e) — providing criminal liability for incitement — is applicable only to the crime of genocide. This subsection, which provides that a person shall be criminally responsible if she "directly and publicly incites others to commit genocide," appears to have been lifted verbatim from Article III of the Genocide Convention of 1948 and its ICTY and ICTR analogues. The "use of the mass media to promote the commission of genocide in Rwanda" apparently influenced the decision to include a distinct provision on incitement to genocide in ICC Article 25.[111] An important difference between subparagraph (e) and subparagraphs (b), (c), and (d) of Article 25 is that incitement to genocide does *not* require the commission or even attempted commission of the actual crime. "Incitement to commit genocide" is a complete, actionable crime, whether or not genocide "in fact occurs or is attempted." For more detailed discussion of incitement to genocide, see Chapter 20, Section D.

F. COMMAND OR SUPERIOR RESPONSIBILITY

Military commanders and civilian superiors may be held criminally responsible for their failure to prevent or punish crimes committed by those over whom they exercise effective control under the command or superior responsibility doctrine (hereinafter referred to simply as the "command responsibility doctrine"). Although the command responsibility doctrine is well established in international law, the content of its constituent elements have shifted over time. This evolution in standards can be seen by comparing various instruments (found on our Web site): the Charter of the International Military Tribunal (Article 6), Protocol I to the Geneva Convention of 1949 (Article 86), the statutes governing the Ad Hoc Tribunals (ICTY Statute Article 7(3) and ICTR Statute Article 6(3)), and the ICC Statute's Article 28.

---

110. Id.
111. See Ambos, Observers' Notes, supra note 77, at 487.

Elements. The elements of command responsibility liability are generally expressed as that the defendant military commander or civilian superior

1.   had a superior-subordinate relationship with the lower-ranking perpetrator of the crime;
2.   knew, had reason to know, or should have known (the precise formulation is dependent on the jurisdiction) about his subordinate's criminal activity; and
3.   failed to take necessary and reasonable measures to prevent the criminal act or punish the perpetrator.

Some defendants have insisted that a fourth element be added — the requirement of a showing of some causal nexus between the subordinate's criminal acts and the superior's failure to take action — but the status of this element is (as is discussed below) questionable.

The content of these elements is influenced by how one conceptualizes this form of liability. As Professor Mark Osiel asks, "[w]hen prosecuting those at the highest echelons — a Slobodan Milošević, Saddam Hussein, or other chief of state — the foremost question becomes: On what basis may the acts of the lowliest subordinates be fairly ascribed to the most elevated superior, from whom they are so distant in space and time?"[112] Military codes and decisional law have understood command responsibility in three different ways. First, as discussed in the previous section, a commander can be understood as an accomplice (an abettor, instigator, or solicitor) of crimes committed by subordinates. Second, the commander can be held vicariously liable for the subordinates' crimes. And third, the commander's actions or omissions — for example, his failure to prevent or punish crimes his troops commit — can be regarded as a self-standing crime. (In the terminology of U.S. military law, for example, the feckless commander can be convicted of dereliction of duty or conduct unbecoming an officer.)

Conceptualized as vicarious liability for others' actions. One could argue that command responsibility should be viewed as a form of vicarious liability. Vicarious liability generally means that liability is founded not on the defendant's own actions, but rather is imposed on the defendant for the actions of others deemed attributable to him. It is among the oldest theories, found in the 1775 American Articles of War in George Washington's army: A commander "who shall refuse or omit to see justice done on the offender or offenders . . . shall upon due proof thereof, be punished as ordered by a general court-martial, in such manner as if he himself had committed the crimes or disorders complained of."[113]

The most obvious example of vicarious liability at work in criminal law is the imposition of a criminal sanction on a corporation. In U.S. law, corporations are held liable for the actions of their agents who commit crimes within the scope of their actual or apparent authority at least in part to benefit the corporation. The corporation will be held liable even if it, as an organization, did not condone or reward the misconduct; indeed, a corporation will be held criminally liable for the actions of its agents, even if the illegal conduct is contrary to express corporate policy or instructions. This rule demonstrates that corporate liability does not turn on the entity's perceived "blameworthiness" in the ordinary sense. Rather, the principal rationale for corporate criminal liability is that it is necessary for deterrence — in this context, more aptly

---

112. Osiel, supra note 4, at 1761-1762.
113. American Articles of War of 1775, Article 12, quoted in 2 William Winthrop, Military Law and Precedents 1480 (2d ed. 1896).

called "galvanizing deterrence." When dealing with corporations and other institutions or impersonal entities, it is not enough simply to deter individual actors from committing further crimes. Unless the institution in which they act reforms its policies and procedures (and the incentives they create for individuals), future wrongdoing cannot be avoided. Accordingly, "deterrence" in the institutional setting requires affirmative actions to reform the institutional culture (hence "galvanizing deterrence").

But a corporation is an artificial person with "no soul to damn, no body to kick." Criminal law generally frowns on the imposition of vicarious liability on flesh-and-blood individuals. Does the superior responsibility doctrine impose vicarious responsibility? Does it make individuals responsible for the actions of others in order to further instrumental goals — that is, to make sure that military and civilian institutions institute appropriate training, oversight, and disciplinary policies to guard against future wrongs? Or is the commander or other person deemed to be personally culpable?

Whether the command responsibility doctrine is vicarious will depend in major part on how the above elements are construed. Thus, if criminal responsibility is imposed on superiors as a matter of strict liability — that is, without regard to what the commander did or did not do, or did or did not know or think — this doctrine would be a species of vicarious liability. Given the types of atrocities sought to be deterred in these cases, *should* individual liability be threatened in order to galvanize military and civilian bureaucracies to do more to prevent crimes in the first instance?

Conceptualized as personal fault for omissions. The Ad Hoc Tribunals attempted to craft a doctrine founded on some degree of personal fault, not vicarious responsibility. As noted previously, at least in U.S. law, prosecutions for omissions must be founded on some law or relationship that creates a duty to act. Command responsibility liability is founded on a relationship — that is, the duty to act arises out of a superior's obligation to control the actions of his subordinates.

As the Trial Chamber in *Prosecutor v. Halilović*, explained:

> . . . Article 7(3) command responsibility is responsibility for an omission. The commander is responsible for the failure to perform an act required under international law. The omission is culpable because international law imposes an affirmative duty on superiors to prevent and punish crimes committed by their subordinates. Thus "for the acts of his subordinates" as generally referred to in the jurisprudence of the Tribunal does not mean that the commander shares the same responsibility as the subordinates who committed the crimes, but rather that because of the crimes committed by his subordinates, the commander should bear responsibility for his failure to act. . . . [A] commander is . . . [not responsible] as though he had committed the crime himself.[114]

Under this conceptualization of the doctrine, the goal of liability is to ensure that the criminal stigma is imposed on all persons in the chain of command who can be said to be individually culpable for violations of international criminal law. Where a senior military or governmental official formulated the policies that resulted in, for example, the targeting of civilians or ethnic cleansing, but did not personally get his hands bloody, he should be held to account for his role in the atrocities. How successful the doctrine is in identifying those individuals who should be deemed

---

114. Case No. IT-01-48, Judgment, ¶54 (Nov. 16, 2005). For a critique of *Halilović* and its successor cases, see Amy J. Sepinwall, Failure to Punish: Command Responsibility in Domestic and International Law, 30 Mich. J. Intl. L. 251 (2009) (defending vicarious liability theory and criticizing self-standing offense theory of command responsibility).

criminally culpable for their failures to act depends on the content of its elements. For example, in conflicts in which the warring sides are loosely constituted militias rather than armies of a traditional type, how does one prove the necessary "control" relationship? Can de facto control suffice or must lines of authority be formal?

A legal "duty" of commanders to control their subordinates has long been recognized in the military context. Expansion of the command responsibility doctrine to civilian authorities, however, has a less obvious basis in "duty." Just what type of relationship among civilians will render a superior criminally liable for his failure to control lower-ranking governmental personnel?

Notice as well the twofold content of all commanders' duty to control their subordinates. Commanders are obligated to prevent crimes by their subordinates, or, if they are unable to do so — perhaps because they learn of the crimes only after the fact — they must take steps to punish the crimes. Primary emphasis lies, of course, on the duty to prevent: In Benjamin Franklin's familiar words, an ounce of prevention is worth a pound of cure. But the duty to punish is extremely important because "punishment is an inherent part of prevention of future crimes."[115] "A military commander wields an instrument with the power of life and death. Covering up his troops' murders, rapes, or tortures fuzzies up rules that should be the brightest of bright lines. The troops quickly know when a cover-up has happened, and that knowledge 'undeters' violent young men, and risks turning an army into a gang of murderers, rapists, and torturers. . . ."[116] In some ways, the duty to punish is more difficult than the duty to prevent. Some commanders may be tempted to cover up their troops' war crimes: Such commanders may want to protect their troops, preserve morale, maintain their own reputations as leaders, and avoid giving enemies a propaganda tool. Several notorious war crimes cases have involved unsuccessful cover-ups.[117] As mentioned above, *Halilović* (the ICTY's leading case on the failure to punish) views it as a self-standing offense, rather than vicarious liability for the subordinates' crimes — although the Appeals Chamber acknowledges that the latter had hitherto been the more common interpretation in international law.[118] The ICTY's subsequent cases on failure to punish have followed *Halilović*.[119]

The content of the second, *mens rea*, element will also be critical in attempting to restrict liability to those who are individually culpable. The question is, once a relationship has been demonstrated, what level of mental culpability should render a commander or superior liable? Must she know about the crime committed or about to be committed, or can willful blindness, recklessness, or even negligence suffice?

Finally, when one is seeking to impose liability for criminal omissions, issues of causation often arise. What omission can be said to "cause" a crime about which the superior did not necessarily know? What if the enemy has targeted the commander's command and control capabilities — is it fair in such circumstances to hold that commander criminally culpable for failing to stop his subordinates' criminal activity? Should the operative failure to act be deemed the failure to train or put in place an effective reporting system rather than the failure to exercise control once atrocities are in progress?

---

115. *Halilović*, Case No. IT-01-48, Judgment, ¶96.

116. David Luban, War Crimes: The Law of Hell, in War and Political Philosophy 284 (Larry May ed., 2008).

117. Sepinwall, supra note 114, at 275-286 (discussing cover-ups in My Lai massacre and Haditha, as well as ICTY cases).

118. *Halilović*, Case No. IT-01-48, Judgment, ¶95.

119. Prosecutor v. Hadzihasanović, Case No. IT-01-47-T, ¶¶74-75 (Mar. 15, 2006); Prosecutor v. Orić, IT-03-68-T, ¶¶293, 724 (June 30, 2006).

In reviewing the following materials, students should consider whether command responsibility is best conceptualized as a form of vicarious liability or a penalty for personal wrongdoing or a combination of the two. If the goal is to hold wrongdoers-by-omission personally culpable for their own misconduct *and/or* to galvanize institutions and institutional actors to take positive steps to prevent future outrages, how might the elements of the command responsibility doctrine be articulated to further the goal(s) identified?

What alternative means are available for attributing the actions of the lowest ranks to the highest echelons of military and civilian authority? The ICTY often used JCE liability as an alternative to command responsibility. "In ascribing liability, superior responsibility looks at relationships vertically, while enterprise participation views them more horizontally and non-hierarchically."[120] JCE liability was generally believed to be easier to prove because, among other things, there is no need to prove a superior-subordinate "relationship." Category Three JCE liability permitted prosecutors to blame the defendant for all the foreseeable wrongs committed by other participants in the enterprise, and thus a harsher sentence was also likely to flow from a conviction founded on JCE as opposed to a command responsibility.[121] Does the ICC provide similar alternative theories of liability that could be used in lieu of or in addition to command responsibility?

1. *Relationship Element*

The ICTY's decision in the so-called *Čelebići* case[122] constituted the first instance since World War II in which a superior was found criminally liable under the command responsibility doctrine. It is often relied upon as evidence of the state of customary international law. The case concerned a prisoner of war camp at which atrocities were committed. With respect to the first, "relationship," element of superior liability, the issue was whether a position of de facto command may be enough to establish the requisite superior-subordinate relationship so long as the relevant degree of control over subordinates is established. The ICTY Appeals Chamber concluded that it was, reasoning:

> The power or authority to prevent or to punish does not solely arise from de jure authority conferred through official appointment. In many contemporary conflicts, there may be only de facto, self-proclaimed governments and therefore de facto armies and paramilitary groups subordinate thereto. Command structure, organised hastily, may well be in disorder and primitive. To enforce the law in these circumstances requires a determination of accountability not only of individual offenders but of their commanders or other superiors who were, based on evidence, in control of them without, however, a formal commission or appointment. A tribunal could find itself powerless to enforce humanitarian law against de facto superiors if it only accepted as proof of command authority a formal letter of authority, despite the fact that the superiors acted at the relevant time with all the powers that would attach to an officially appointed superior or commander.[123]

---

120. Osiel, supra note 4, at 1769.
121. Id. at 1766.
122. Prosecutor v. Delalić (Čelebići), Case No. IT-96-21-T (Nov. 16, 1998), on appeal, Case No. IT-96-21-A (Feb. 20, 2001).
123. See Prosecutor v. Delalić, Case No. IT-96-21-A, Judgment, ¶193 (Feb. 20, 2001).

Accordingly, the Appeals Chambers rejected the defendants' argument that command responsibility is limited to de jure commanders.[124] The Court went on to explain that the effective control necessary to a superior-subordinate relationship is demonstrated where a superior has "the material ability to prevent or punish criminal conduct, however that control is exercised."[125] Although indirect and direct relationships of subordination will suffice to show effective control, any forms of influence short of effective control over subordinates will not render an individual liable under command responsibility.[126] The ICTY ruled that it is not "controversial" that "civilian leaders may incur responsibility in relation to acts committed by their subordinates or other persons under their effective control."[127]

In applying the command responsibility doctrine to the facts of the case, the *Čelebići* court conducted a stringent review of the "relationship" element and found it lacking for two of three defendants, one of whom was Hazim Delić. Consider the following summary of his case and the ICTY's ruling in it:

The indictment charged Hazim Delić both with direct responsibility for crimes in which he was an alleged participant and with superior responsibility for crimes committed while he served as deputy commander and, later, as commander of Čelebići. To support these charges, the prosecution contended that Delić, in his role as deputy commander, had the authority of the full commander in the latter's absence. Furthermore, the prosecution argued that Delić had authority over the prison guards and the ability to punish or prevent their criminal acts and that he failed to do so because he also participated in these acts. As proof of his status as a superior within the camp hierarchy, the prosecution noted that Delić was responsible for administrative matters in the camp.

In response to these allegations, the defense contended that the prosecution failed to distinguish between the concepts of "command" and "rank." Namely, the defense asserted that superior responsibility attaches only by virtue of a position of command. Indeed, deputy commanders like Delić, while perhaps higher in "rank" than another soldier, was not in the actual chain of command. Thus, the defense argued Delić could only have been a conduit to transfer orders from the commander and lacked the true authority to have superior responsibility.

The tribunal recognized that the prosecution was not asserting that Delić could be held responsible even if he did not command anyone, but rather, that Delić could be responsible even while lacking formal command status. Therefore, the tribunal proceeded under the de facto command doctrine and inquired as to whether the prosecution had met its factual burden in proving that Delić exercised command authority over the Čelebići prison guards. First, the tribunal acknowledged the testimony of several eyewitnesses who stated that Delić appeared to be the "boss" of the guards. Nonetheless, the tribunal conceded that this alone was not sufficient evidence of Delić's authority. Second, the tribunal considered additional eyewitness testimony from former prisoners, who testified to seeing Delić give orders and exercise apparent influence, possibly through coercion and intimidation, over the prison guards. Still, the tribunal felt this evidence was not dispositive and went on to examine the acts and responsibilities of Delić in his role as deputy commander. The evidence tended to show that Delić was in charge of organizing the day to day affairs of the camp and assisting the commander in arranging for interrogation of prisoners. Still, the tribunal could not pin superior responsibility on these actions, emphasizing that his assistance in organizing daily activities did not "indicate that he had actual command authority in the sense that he could issue orders and punish and prevent the criminal acts of subordinates."

---

124. See id. ¶197.
125. Id. ¶¶197-198, 256, 266.
126. See id. ¶252.
127. Id. ¶196.

After examining all the evidence, the tribunal concluded that the prosecution had not met its burden in establishing Delić as a superior with the power to prevent or punish acts of his subordinates. Accordingly, Delić was not convicted of any war crimes in his capacity as deputy commander of Čelebići. Delić was found guilty, however, of several crimes in which he was allegedly a direct participant, including murder.[128]

One might argue that the "relationship" element was read too strictly in the ICTY, rendering the command responsibility doctrine all but useless given the difficulties of proof in situations where the crimes occur in the context of nontraditional warfare and over time. Is the standard for "effective" control unrealistic?

Some commentators posit that if the *Čelebići* camp case were brought today in the ICTY, it most likely would have been charged as a Category Two JCE.[129] *Should* a commander found not liable under the command responsibility doctrine be convicted under a JCE theory?

2.   Mens Rea *Element*

Modern discussions about the *mens rea* for command responsibility frequently reference a famous and controversial case from the end of World War II. It involved Japanese General Tomoyuki Yamashita, who commanded troops in the Philippines near the end of the war. Japanese troops carried out widespread atrocities in the Philippines, in which at least 25,000 civilians were killed. Women were raped, and resistance fighters were executed without trials. At Yamashita's trial before a U.S. military commission, his defense argued that U.S. forces had disrupted Japanese command and control to such an extent that the general had no capacity to learn what his troops were doing or to control them effectively. "How, it was asked [by Yamashita's defense], could he be held accountable for the actions of troops which had passed into his command only one month before, at a time when he was 150 miles away—troops whom he had never seen, trained or inspected, whose commanding officers he could not change or designate, and over whose actions he had only the most nominal control?"[130] The prosecution countered,

> Even if it were accepted that the accused did not know of what was going on in Batangas, the fact remained that he did not make an adequate effort to find out. It was his duty to know what was being done by his troops under his orders. The accused had pleaded that he was too hard pressed by the enemy to find out what was the state of discipline among his troops. The Prosecution claimed however that the performance of the responsibility of the commanding officer toward the civilian populations is as heavy a responsibility as the combating of the enemy. And if he chose to ignore one and devote all of his attention to the other he did so at his own risk.[131]

The prosecution labeled it "a clear case, in the international field, of criminal negligence."[132]

---

128. Ann B. Ching, Note, Evolution of the Command Responsibility Doctrine in Light of the *Čelebići* Decision of the ICTY, 25 N.C. J. Intl. L. & Com. Reg. 167, 186-205 (1999).

129. See Danner & Martinez, supra note 58, at 131.

130. Trial of Gen. Tomoyuki Yamashita, (8 Oct.-7 Dec. 1945), 4 L.R.T.W.C. 24 (1948).

131. Id. at 30.

132. Id. at 33.

The military commission convicted Yamashita, agreeing with the prosecutor "that the crimes were so extensive and widespread, both as to time and area, that they must either have been wilfully permitted by the accused, or secretly ordered by the accused. . . ."[133] This analysis suggests that the commission believed Yamashita knew or even intended that his troops commit the atrocities. Confusingly, however, the commission also held that "where murder and rape and vicious, revengeful actions are widespread offences, and there is no effective attempt by a commander to discover and control the criminal acts, such a commander may be held responsible, even criminally liable, for the lawless acts of his troops, depending upon their nature and the circumstances surrounding them."[134] This suggests that Yamashita could be convicted without intending or knowing his troops' war crimes, and indeed even if circumstances made an "effective attempt" to control his troops impossible.

The Supreme Court rejected Yamashita's habeas corpus petition, but Justice Murphy wrote a blistering dissent:

> In other words, read against the background of military events in the Philippines subsequent to October 9, 1944, these charges amount to this: "We, the victorious American forces, have done everything possible to destroy and disorganize your lines of communication, your effective control of your personnel, your ability to wage war. In those respects we have succeeded. We have defeated and crushed your forces. And now we charge and condemn you for having been inefficient in maintaining control of your troops during the period when we were so effectively besieging and eliminating your forces and blocking your ability to maintain effective control. Many terrible atrocities were committed by your disorganized troops. Because these atrocities were so widespread we will not bother to charge or prove that you committed, ordered or condoned any of them. We will assume that they must have resulted from your inefficiency and negligence as a commander. In short, we charge you with the crime of inefficiency in controlling your troops. We will judge the discharge of your duties by the disorganization which we ourselves created in large part. Our standards of judgment are whatever we wish to make them."
>
> Nothing in all history or in international law, at least as far as I am aware, justifies such a charge against a fallen commander of a defeated force. To use the very inefficiency and disorganization created by the victorious forces as the primary basis for condemning officers of the defeated armies bears no resemblance to justice or to military reality.[135]

Yamashita was hanged in 1946. To what extent Yamashita knew about or condoned his troops' atrocities remains a disputed matter of fact. However, the confusion the case generated — was his conviction based on a *mens rea* of knowledge (inferred from the wide extent of the crimes), negligence, or strict liability? — forms the background for the ICTY's efforts to create a far more precise definition of command responsibility.

There is a case to be made for imposing stringent duties on military commanders, as Professor Martinez indicates:

> Soldiers in battle do not exercise the full measure of free will attributed to private individuals in peacetime; the military hierarchy controls the soldier's actions, and a soldier obeys his (lawful) superior officers on pain of punishment or death. . . . By the internal logic of the laws of war, the soldier is not responsible for his actions, either in the sense of legal liability or in the sense of exercising agency in the moral decision to use lethal force against another human. But this belligerent's privilege is inextricably intertwined with the commander's responsibility for the soldier's actions, and a military

---

133. Id. at 34. The prosecutor's argument for this conclusion is in id., at 32.
134. Id. at 35.
135. In re Yamashita, 327 U.S. 1, 34-35 (1946) (Murphy, J. dissenting).

commander's duty to control his troops is the necessary corollary of his power. He is given license to turn ordinary men into lethally destructive, and legally privileged, soldiers; indeed, military training and command structures are expressly designed to dissolve the social inhibitions that normally prevent people from committing acts of extreme violence, and to remove their sense of moral agency when committing such acts. When these soldiers turn from their lawful military aims towards civilians or other targets protected by the laws of war, however, the commander is responsible for this misuse of the privilege of violence his orders have conferred on them. . . . The moral logic of the law of war breaks down if the commander has no duty to acquire knowledge of what the killing machines he has unleashed and whom he ostensibly controls are doing with the power he has conferred on them.[136]

Notwithstanding the logic of this argument—commanders bear heightened responsibility because of the lethality of the troops they command—the Ad Hoc Tribunals and ICC have not gone so far as to impose a negligence standard on commanders.

Thus, the *Čelebiči* Appeals Chamber was called upon to construe Article 7(3) of the ICTY Statute, which provided that command responsibility could appropriately be imposed where a superior "knew or had reason to know" that a subordinate is about to commit crimes or had done so. The Appeals Chamber stated that the phrase "reason to know" in Article 7(3) means that a superior will be charged with knowledge of subordinates' offences only if information of a general nature was available to him that would have put him on notice of those offenses.[137] In so holding, the *Čelebiči* Appeals Chamber expressly rejected the prosecution's argument for an alternative reading of the "had reason to know" standard:

> Article 7(3) of the Statute is concerned with superior liability arising from failure to act in spite of knowledge. Neglect of a duty to acquire such knowledge, however, does not feature in the provision as a separate offence, and a superior is not therefore liable under the provision for such failures but only for failing to take necessary and reasonable measures to prevent or to punish. The Appeals Chamber takes it that the Prosecution seeks a finding that "reason to know" exists on the part of a commander if the latter is seriously negligent in his duty to obtain the relevant information. The point here should not be that knowledge may be presumed if a person fails in his *duty* to obtain the relevant information of a crime, but that it may be presumed if he had the *means* to obtain the knowledge but deliberately refrained from doing so. The Prosecution's argument that a breach of the duty of a superior to remain constantly informed of his subordinates actions will necessarily result in *criminal* liability comes close to the imposition of criminal liability on a strict or negligence basis. It is however noted that although a commander's failure to remain apprised of his subordinates' action, or to set up a monitoring system may constitute a neglect of duty which results in liability within the military disciplinary framework, it will not necessarily result in criminal liability.[138]

The ICTY Appeals Chamber in *Prosecutor v. Blaškić* reaffirmed that a commander may not be convicted for negligent supervision or for a failure to put in place an effective reporting system, without more. Bosnian Croat military officer Tihomir Blaškić was the commander of the Croatian Defense Council (HVO) armed forces in Central Bosnia. The *Blaškić* case arose out of the conflict between the HVO and the Bosnian Muslim army in central Bosnia from May 1992 to January 1994. During this period, atrocities were committed in the region (in particular in the village of Ahmići)

---

136. Martinez, supra note 8, at 661-662.
137. See Prosecutor v. Čelebiči, Case No. IT-96-21-A, Judgment, ¶¶238, 241 (Feb. 20, 2001).
138. Id. ¶226.

by various military and paramilitary brigades. Blaškić was convicted before an ICTY Trial Chamber for ordering certain crimes against humanity and war crimes against Muslim civilians under ICTY Statute Article 7(1). The Trial Chambers also found him guilty under ICTY Statute Article 7(3) for his failure as a commander to prevent the commission of these crimes or otherwise punish the perpetrators.

The *Blaškić* Appeals Chambers overturned 16 of 19 convictions entered against Blaškić, reduced his sentence from 45 to 9 years (with credit for the 8 years he had already spent in prison), and then granted him early release. The Appeals Chamber found deficiencies in the case under both Article 7(1) and Article 7(3). As Professor Drumbl explains:

> Regarding art. 7(3), the Appeals Chamber criticized the understanding of command responsibility adopted by the Trial Chamber. It instead affirmed a different understanding, according to which "a superior will be criminally responsible through the principles of superior responsibility *only if information was available to him* which would have put him on notice of offenses committed by subordinates" (¶62). This suggests a tilt toward subjective knowledge as a basis for command responsibility for the acts of subordinates, instead of an objective standard. This would be a somewhat narrow reading of art. 7(3), which provides that a superior is not relieved of criminal responsibility if inter alia "he knew or had reason to know that the subordinate was about to commit [criminal] acts or had done so [. . .]." That said, the Appeals Chamber did say that "responsibility can be imposed for deliberately refraining from finding out [information]" (¶406). Recklessness or willful blindness therefore may suffice. . . .[139]

Does this make sense? Although this rule means liability will not be visited upon incompetent or stupid officers for failure to put in place an effective reporting system, does it also potentially exclude from liability those *most* culpable? That is, does this *mens rea* requirement let off the hook those who create the conditions for atrocities by not adequately training and disciplining their troops (and perhaps even encouraging them with winks and nods) but who create plausible deniability by avoiding any reports that might require their intervention? Does the doctrine of "willful blindness" apply to these persons?

What *is* willful blindness?

3. *Willful Blindness*

The above description of the *Blaškić* court's treatment of command responsibility implies that "willful blindness" may suffice to establish liability, even where information was *not* available to the commander that would have put him on notice of offenses committed by subordinates. The willful blindness (aka "conscious avoidance" or "ostrich") jury instruction is often used in U.S. white-collar crime cases as a way of easing prosecutors' burden of proving the *mens rea* of *knowledge*. These instructions vary in content, but the following language is frequently used (in different combinations):[140]

A. "The element of knowledge may be satisfied by inferences drawn from proof that a defendant deliberately closed his eyes to what would otherwise have been

---

139. Drumbl, supra note 3.

140. The following formulations are derived from a number of sources, including 1 Devitt & Blackmar, Federal Jury Practice and Instructions §17.09 (4th ed. 1992); United States v. St. Michael's Credit Union, 880 F.2d 579, 585 n.1 (1st Cir. 1989); United States v. Jewell, 532 F.2d 697, 704 n.21 (9th Cir. 1976).

obvious to him. A finding beyond a reasonable doubt of a conscious purpose to avoid enlightenment would permit an inference of knowledge. Stated another way, a defendant's knowledge of a fact may be inferred from willful blindness to the existence of the fact."

B. "Willful blindness may constitute knowledge of a fact only if you should find that the individual to whom knowledge is sought to be attributed was aware of a high probability that that fact existed."

C. "It is entirely up to you as to whether you find any deliberate closing of the eyes, and the inference to be drawn from any such evidence."

D. "A showing of negligence or mistake is not sufficient to support a finding of willfulness or knowledge."

E. Knowledge is not established by proof of a defendant's awareness of a high probability of the existence of the fact in question if the defendant "actually believes it does not exist."

Courts *say* that they are reluctant to give willful blindness instructions because of the danger such instructions may pose in allowing the jury to convict based on an *ex post facto* "he should have been more careful" theory or to convict on mere negligence. Unless carefully restricted, the instruction also carries the danger of shifting the burden to the defendant to prove her innocence. Nonetheless, willful blindness instructions are frequently used in federal criminal cases. What is the conceptual basis for equating "willful blindness" with "knowledge"? U.S. courts disagree.

Many courts assert that "[a]n ostrich instruction informs the jury that actual knowledge and deliberate avoidance of knowledge are the same thing."[141] As the Ninth Circuit stated in *United States v. Jewell*:

> The substantive justification for the rule is that deliberate ignorance and positive knowledge are equally culpable. The textual justification is that in common understanding one "knows" facts of which he is less than absolutely certain. To act "knowingly," therefore, is not necessarily to act only with positive knowledge, but also to act with an awareness of the high probability of the existence of the fact in question. When such awareness is present, "positive" knowledge is not required.[142]

Does this make sense? *Is* willful blindness tantamount in common understanding to positive knowledge, or is this doctrine better treated as an *exception* to the knowledge requirement, rather than a part of its definition? Are defendants who have remained willfully blind as culpable as those who actually knew?

Other courts contend that it is the defendant's failure, in the face of evidence of wrongdoing, to investigate sufficiently that is the basic problem with the "ostrich" defendant.[143] This approach is one that sounds in recklessness — the defendant is culpable for his conscious failure to satisfy his duty to learn the facts and thus avoid criminality.

Still other federal courts reject any attempt to found willful blindness culpability on a recklessness theory. Under one stricter formulation endorsed by a few courts, the defendant should be held liable under a willful blindness charge only when he is less

---

141. United States v. Ramsey, 785 F.2d 184, 189 (7th Cir. 1986).

142. 532 F.2d at 700.

143. United States v. Hiland, 909 F.2d 1114, 1130 (8th Cir. 1990) (" '[T]he purpose of a willful blindness theory is to impose criminal liability on people who, recognizing the likelihood of wrongdoing, nonetheless consciously refuse to take basic investigatory steps.'").

"ostrich" than "fox,"[144] that is, when the defendant *chooses* to remain ignorant of facts "so he can plead lack of positive knowledge in the event he should be caught."[145] "The grand scheming Fox, who aims to do wrong and structures his own ignorance merely to prepare a defense, has the same level of culpability as any other willful wrongdoer — the highest level, in the Model Penal Code schema."[146] In jurisdictions where willful blindness instructions are aimed at running foxes to ground, the purpose of the instruction is said to be to tell the jury that it may consider evidence of the defendant's *charade* of ignorance as circumstantial proof of guilty knowledge. In sum, as Glanville Williams explained:

> A court can properly find wilful blindness only where it can almost be said that the defendant actually knew. He suspected the fact; he realised its probability; but he refrained from obtaining the final confirmation because he wanted in the event to be able to deny knowledge. This, and this alone, is wilful blindness. It requires in effect a finding that the defendant intended to cheat the administration of justice. Any wider definition would make the doctrine of wilful blindness indistinguishable from the civil doctrine of negligence in not obtaining knowledge.[147]

This difference in conceptualization may have very practical consequences. For example, in the jurisdictions that view the fox, rather than the ostrich, as the appropriate focus of willful blindness liability, the courts before approving a willful blindness charge require that the prosecution show that the defendant deliberately avoided obtaining more knowledge *in order to provide herself with a defense in the event of prosecution.* Recently, an en banc Ninth Circuit Court of Appeals expressly overruled precedents in its jurisdiction that imposed this additional burden of proof.[148]

Is the Ad Hoc Tribunal anticipating convictions of the "ostriches" or the "foxes" under a willful blindness theory? In general, does ICC Article 30's requirement of knowledge — that is, some level of "awareness" — remove this theory of liability? It should be noted that Article 30 applies "[u]nless otherwise provided. . . ." Thus, at least as to ICC Article 28, "willful blindness" may be applicable regardless of whether it is an effective means of proving "knowledge" generally under Article 30.

4.   *Nexus Requirement*

Some defendants have argued that the prosecution must also demonstrate some nexus between the defendant commander's passivity and his subordinates' unlawful acts before command liability will attach. In *Prosecutor v. Blaškić,*[149] the ICTY Appeals Chambers purported to "clarif[y]" the law regarding the question of causation. First, the Appeals Chamber recognized that in the principal case on command responsibility, *Čelebići,* the Trial Chamber stated that "the superior may be considered to be

---

144. David Luban, Contrived Ignorance, 87 Geo. L.J. 957, 968-969 (1999).

145. United States v. Restrepo–Granda, 575 F.2d 524, 528 (5th Cir. 1978); see also United States v. de Francisco-Lopez, 939 F.2d 1405, 1409 (10th Cir. 1991) (" 'A deliberate ignorance instruction alerts the jury that the act of avoidance of knowledge of particular facts may itself circumstantially show that the avoidance was motivated by sufficient guilty knowledge to satisfy the . . . "knowing" element of the crime.' ").

146. Luban, supra note 144, at 969.

147. Glanville Williams, Criminal Law: The General Part 159 (2d ed. 1961).

148. See United States v. Heredia, 483 F.3d 913 (9th Cir. 2007) (en banc).

149. Case No. IT-95-14-A (July 29, 2004).

causally linked to the offences, in that, but for his failure to fulfil his duty to act, the acts of his subordinates would not have been committed." The Appeals Chamber further noted, however, that the *Čelebići* Trial Chamber did not cite authority for this view and that the *Čelebići* Trial Chamber subsequently argued as follows:

> Notwithstanding the central place assumed by the principle of causation in criminal law, causation has not traditionally been postulated as a *conditio sine qua non* for the imposition of criminal liability on superiors for their failure to prevent or punish offence committed by their subordinates. Accordingly, the Trial Chamber has found no support for the existence of a requirement of proof of causation as a separate element of superior responsibility, either in the existing body of case law, the formation of the principle in existing treaty law, or, with one exception, in the abundant literature on this subject.

The *Blaškić* Appeals Chamber finally concluded:

> [The *Čelebići*] Trial Chamber later concluded that the very existence of the principle of superior responsibility for the failure to punish, recognised under Article 7(3) of the Statute and in customary law, demonstrates the absence of a requirement of causality as a separate element of the doctrine of superior responsibility.
>
> The Appeals Chamber is therefore not persuaded by the Appellant's submission that the existence of causality between a commander's failure to prevent subordinates' crimes and the occurrence of these crimes, is an element of command responsibility that requires proof by the Prosecution in all circumstances of a case. . . . [I]t is more a question of fact to be established on a case by case basis, than a question of law in general.[150]

Does this discussion resolve the question of whether a causal nexus need be proved?

5. *ICC: Article 28*

ICC Article 28 provides:

> In addition to other grounds of criminal responsibility under this Statute for crimes within the jurisdiction of the Court:
>
> (a) A military commander or person effectively acting as a military commander shall be criminally responsible for crimes within the jurisdiction of the Court committed by forces under his or her effective command and control, or effective authority and control as the case may be, as a result of his or her failure to exercise control properly over such forces, where:
>
>   (i) That military commander or person either knew or, owing to the circumstances at the time, should have known that the forces were committing or about to commit such crimes; and
>
>   (ii) That military commander or person failed to take all necessary and reasonable measures within his or her power to prevent or repress their commission or to submit the matter to the competent authorities for investigation and prosecution.
>
> (b) With respect to superior and subordinate relationships not described in paragraph (a), a superior shall be criminally responsible for crimes within the jurisdiction of the Court committed by subordinates under his or her effective authority

---

150. Id. ¶¶75-77.

and control, as a result of his or her failure to exercise control properly over such subordinates, where:

> (i) The superior either knew, or consciously disregarded information which clearly indicated, that the subordinates were committing or about to commit such crimes;

> (ii) The crimes concerned activities that were within the effective responsibility and control of the superior; and

> (iii) The superior failed to take all necessary and reasonable measures within his or her power to prevent or repress their commission or to submit the matter to the competent authorities for investigation and prosecution.

What are the elements of command responsibility under ICC Article 28? How does ICC Article 28 differ from the Ad Hoc Tribunals' statutes and case law? Note in particular that ICC Article 28 articulates a different standard for civilian superiors than for military commanders. Why? Should the standards imposed differ, or might this differential treatment undermine the deterrent effect of this type of liability?[151]

What is the *mens rea* that is required to convict a commanding officer? A civilian? One of those participating in the negotiation of the Rome Statute has explained that the Statute generally does not sanction liability based on recklessness or negligence, Article 28 being the exception.[152] Does this make sense given the purposes of this type of liability?

What is the relationship between command responsibility and aiding and abetting? Can a commander be held liable for aiding and abetting *through omission* when he could not be held liable for his failure to prevent or punish under command responsibility? What is the difference between the requisites of the two types of liability?

G.   POST–WORLD WAR II CASE STUDIES

To illustrate the legal "modes of participation" employed in international tribunals, we provide synopses of cases prosecuted by the Allies after World War II and encourage you to read them with the above in mind. In so doing, ask yourself the following questions: How would you charge these defendants? What facts are significant, either in evaluating the guilt of those charged or the appropriate punishment they ought to receive? What arguments might you make if entrusted with the defense? What additional facts would you wish to know? Note that we will return to these case descriptions when exploring defenses to international criminal liability in Chapter 18.

1.   *The Jaluit Atoll Case*

Rear-Admiral Masuda of the Japanese navy ordered the execution, without trial, of three U.S. airmen who had been captured and were being held as prisoners of war. Pursuant to his command, Japanese Naval Lieutenant Yoshimura, Ensign Kawachi, and Warrant Officer Tanaka admitted to taking the three captives to a cemetery,

---

151. See generally Jamie A. Williamson, Command Responsibility in the Case Law of the International Criminal Tribunal for Rwanda, 13 Crim. L.F. 365 (2002); Greg R. Vetter, Command Responsibility of Non-military Superiors in the International Criminal Court (ICC), 25 Yale J. Intl. L. 89 (2000).

152. See Clark, supra note 13, at 300-303, 314-315 & n.80, 334.

secretly shooting them, and cremating their remains; one of the accused also used a sword during the executions. Ensign Tasaki admitted that, having been the jailer in charge of the prisoners, he had arranged their release to the executioners knowing that they were to be killed.[153]

2. *The Zyklon B Case*

Dr. Bruno Tesch was the sole owner of the firm of Tesch & Stabenow, a distributor of pesticides. Karl Weinbacher was Tesch's "Procurist or second-in-command." When Tesch was absent, Weinbacher was "fully empowered and authorized to do all acts on behalf of his principal which his principal could have done. His position was of great importance, since his principal would travel on the business of the firm for as many as 200 days in the year." The firm sold gas and gassing equipment for disinfecting public buildings, including Wehrmacht barracks and SS concentration camps. The chief gas involved was Zyklon B, a highly dangerous insecticide made primarily of prussic acid (cyanide). The company did not manufacture the gas; rather, it had an exclusive agency—a monopoly according to the prosecutor—for the supply of the gas east of the Elbe River. The gas was delivered from the manufacturer directly to the customer. Tesch & Stabenow also provided expert technicians to do the gassing. Dr. Joachim Drosihn, the company's "senior gassing technician," was invaluable in this respect. "The predominant importance of these gassing operations in war-time lay in their value in extermination of lice" and rodents.

The prosecution claimed:

> [F]rom 1941 to 1945 Zyklon B was being supplied as a direct result of orders accepted by the accused's firm. . . . On that basis, the Zyklon B was going in vast quantities to the largest concentration camps in Germany east of the Elbe. In these same camps the SS . . . were, from 1942 to 1945, systematically exterminating human beings to an estimated total of six million, of whom four and a half million were exterminated by the use of Zyklon B in one camp alone, known as Auschwitz/Birkenau. . . . [O]ver a period of time the three accused[, Tesch, Weinbacher, and Drosihn,] got to know of this wholesale extermination of human beings in the eastern concentration camps by the SS using Zyklon B gas, and that, having acquired this knowledge, they continued to arrange supplies of that gas to these customers in the SS in ever-increasing quantities, until in the early months of 1944 the consignment per month to Auschwitz concentration camp was nearly two tons. The case for the Prosecution was that knowingly to supply a commodity to a branch of the State which was using that commodity for the mass extermination of Allied civilian nationals was a war crime. . . .

A former bookkeeper and accountant employed by Tesch & Stabenow testified that he saw in the firm's files a report Tesch dictated accounting for a business trip. In this travel report, Tesch:

> recorded an interview with leading members of Wehrmacht, during which he was told that the burial, after shooting, of Jews in increasing numbers was proving more and more

---

153. Yoshimura, Kawachi, and Tanaka were convicted of the war crime of killing unarmed prisoners of war and sentenced to death by hanging, while Tasaki, after conviction, received 10 years' imprisonment. According to the case report, Tasaki's "punishment was lighter than that of the others because of the 'brief, passive and mechanical participation of the accused.'" The court rejected the defense of all but Masuda (who committed suicide before the trial) that they were acting "under orders of a superior authority, which they were bound to obey." [Trial of Rear-Admiral Nisuke Masuda and Four Others of the Imperial Japanese Navy (13 Dec. 1947), 1 L.R.T.W.C. 71 (The Jaluit Atoll Case).]

unhygienic, and that it is proposed to kill them with prussic acid. Dr. Tesch, when asked for his views, had proposed to use the same method, involving the release of prussic acid gas in an enclosed space, as was used in the extermination of vermin. He undertook to train the SS men in this new method of killing human beings.

Other witnesses from the firm testified that they had either seen the report or had been told by Dr. Tesch that Zyklon B could be, or was being, used to kill human beings. Weinbacher and Drosihn denied reading Tesch's travel report.

Evidence was adduced that Auschwitz received the largest shipments of Zyklon B of all the concentration camps. An ex-medical orderly at one of the other concentration camps testified that Dr. Tesch had conducted a prussic acid training course at an SS hospital — an allegation Tesch denied. The parties presented conflicting testimony regarding whether it was common knowledge in Germany during the relevant period that people were being gassed in the concentration camps. All of the defendants — Tesch, Weinbacher, and Drosihn — denied knowing that Zyklon B was used to kill human beings in the camps; they all denied ever having visited Auschwitz (although Drosihn did visit three "delousing facilities" at camps, including one where some gassing of human beings took place).

Dr. Tesch's counsel argued that Tesch believed the Zyklon B was being delivered only for purposes of disinfection. The amounts going to Auschwitz were not extraordinary given the number of inhabitants at that camp as well as its role, according to Tesch's understanding, as a transit point where much de-lousing was required. Counsel questioned whether the Zyklon B used at Auschwitz had even been supplied by Tesch & Stabenow, asserting that other firms had poached business opportunities in the firm's "exclusive" territory. Further, the SS had been active all over the occupied territories and had other means of securing the gas. Tesch noted that none of the firm's clerks recalled typing the infamous report about the proposed use of Zyklon B to kill Jews. Indeed, under "the existing war-time regulations of secrecy, it seemed impossible that a man as careful as Tesch should have dictated a report on an interview with the High Command on such a secret matter, placed the report where anyone in the office could have read it, . . . and then discussed it with his employees." Dr. Tesch was too busy to know how much gas went to Auschwitz, particularly since the supply of gas was not as important to the firm's business as the gassing activities.

Weinbacher (Tesch's second-in-command) testified that, when Tesch was traveling, Weinbacher looked after current business, saw to incoming and outgoing mail, answered inquiries, and confirmed orders received. In closing, Weinbacher's counsel correctly argued that there was no concrete proof that his client had seen the travel report or had been informed by anyone of the use being made of Zyklon B. He further noted that the accountants knew how much gas went to each customer, but his client did not. Further, far less gas was needed to kill people than was required to kill insects; accordingly the quantities of Zyklon B "needed for killing half a million or even a million human beings stood in such small proportion to the quantities needed for the killing of insects that it would not have been noticed at all."

Counsel for Dr. Drosihn argued that Drosihn, a zoologist, had nothing to do with the supply of gas and did not know the amounts of gas sold to different customers. Tesch testified that Drosihn was a technical expert and was not concerned with the business of the firm, a view that Weinbacher endorsed on the stand. Drosihn testified that he collaborated on scientific issues — for example, supervising the gassing of ships in the Hamburg docks and making sure that delousing chambers worked properly. Drosihn spend 150-200 days a year traveling on business.

The prosecution took the position that it was inconceivable that Dr. Tesch did not know of the amount of gas being supplied to the SS and to Auschwitz. The firm was wholly his property and Auschwitz was the firm's second-largest customer. With respect to Weinbacher, the prosecutor argued that he was in control of the firm for 200 days a year, with access to all the books and records. Finally, Drosihn "must to some extent have shared the confidence of Tesch and Weinbacher, even []though his activities were confined to the technical side of the firm as opposed to the sales and bookkeeping side."

The judge advocate, summing up, noted that "the real strength of the Prosecution in this case rests . . . upon the general proposition that, when you realize what kind of a man Dr. Tesch was, it inevitably follows that he must have known every little thing about this business." In Weinbacher's case, the judge advocate noted, "there was no direct evidence, either by way of conversation or of anything that he had written among the documents of the firm produced during the trial, which formed any kind of evidence specifically imputing knowledge to Weinbacher as to how Zyklon B was being used at Auschwitz." The judge advocate asked the court whether it was likely that "Weinbacher would constantly watch the figures relating to a less profitable activity of the firm, particularly since he received commission on profits as well as his salary." Finally, the judge advocate emphasized Drosihn's subordinate position and asked "whether there was any evidence that he was in a position either to influence the transfer of gas to Auschwitz or to prevent it. If he were not in such a position, no knowledge of the use to which the gas was being put could make him guilty."[154]

3.   The Almelo Case

A British pilot, Gerald Hood, bailed out of a burning plane over Holland and was hidden from the Germans for months by the Dutch underground. Ultimately, Hood—in civilian clothes—was concealed in the house of Mrs. van der Wal, a widow living with her son, Bote. Bote, a young Dutch citizen, was also hiding from the Germans in his mother's home to avoid compulsory labor service in Germany. Dutch Nazi police and the SS searched the van der Wal home for Bote and captured both him and Hood. They were taken to a prison where they were interrogated by Georg Sandrock, a German noncommissioned officer (NCO) serving in a special security detachment stationed in Ahnelo, Holland. The SS lieutenant who commanded the security detachment told Sandrock that the British airman and Dutch civilian had been condemned to death and that two men must be detailed to accompany Sandrock to a wood outside the town, where the prisoners were to be shot.

Hood was executed first; he was driven to the outskirts of town, told by Sandrock that he had been condemned to death, and shot from behind in the base of the neck by German NCO Ludwig Schweinberger on Sandrock's order. Joseph Hegemann stood by the car to ensure that people did not come near while the shooting took place. The next day, the same procedure was followed to kill van der Wal, except that Helmut Wiegner replaced Hegemann as the NCO ordered to remain by the car to

---

154. Tesch and Weinbacher were convicted of the war crime of supplying gas used to exterminate allied nationals interned in concentration camps "knowing that said gas was to be so used." They were both sentenced to death. Drosihn was acquitted. [Trial of Bruno Tesch and Two Others (8 March 1946), 1 L.R.T.W.C. 93 (The Zyklon B Case).]

prevent strangers from disturbing the other men during the execution. The prosecution, in describing the case, compared it to that of a crime committed by a criminal gang, every member of the gang being equally responsible for the fatal shot.[155]

4. *The Essen Lynching Case*

The German police handed three captured British airmen over to a military unit commanded by Germany Army Captain Erich Heyer. Heyer placed the airmen under the escort of two German soldiers, one of whom was Private Peter Koenen. Heyer, standing on the steps of the barracks in front of a crowd of German civilians, then instructed the escort to take the prisoners to the nearest Luftwaffe unit for interrogation. He did so in a loud voice so that the crowd could hear and would know exactly what would take place. Heyer also ordered the escort not to interfere in any way with the crowd if they should molest the prisoners, and remarked that the airmen ought to be shot or that they would be shot. It is unclear from the published account of the case whether Heyer made these last statements to the escort alone or whether he shouted these as well.

At the time, feelings against British airmen were running high in Germany because they were blamed for the aerial bombing that was devastating German cities. When the British prisoners of war were marched through one of Essen's main streets, the crowd assaulted them with fists and stones. An unidentified German corporal fired a revolver at one of the men and wounded him in the head. When the British airmen reached the bridge, they were thrown over the parapet and one died from the fall. The other two prisoners, not killed outright upon landing, were shot at from the bridge and were ultimately beaten and kicked to death by the crowd. Neither Heyer nor Koenen actually struck a physical blow against the prisoners. Koenen, though armed, did nothing to prevent the crowd's lynching.[156]

---

155. All four German NCOs were found guilty of the war crime of killing a British prisoner of war and/or a Dutch civilian. Sandrock and Schweinberger were sentenced to death by hanging, while Hegemann and Wiegner received sentences of 15 years' imprisonment. In so doing, the court rejected the defenses: (1) that the accused were forced to carry out their superior's orders; (2) that they did not know that it was an unlawful execution and thought that it was done after the individuals were tried by law; and (3) that they had acted under what they called "superior force," fearing the consequences for the accused themselves and for their families in case of disobedience. [Trial of Otto Sandrock and Three Others (26 Nov. 1945), 1 L.R.T.W.C. 35 (The Almelo case).]

A similar case involved eight members of a British Special Air Service Regiment captured after they had parachuted into France to aid the resistance. After being interrogated for several days, they were taken to a wood and shot. Participants of all military ranks involved in the killing were convicted. These included guards on the truck that conveyed the prisoners to the execution (all were corporals, and they received sentences of two, three, and eight years), as well as two who drove the executioners to the wood and helped fill the graves (eight-year sentences). Trial of Karl Adam Golkel and Thirteen Others (21 May 1946), 5 L.R.T.W.C. 45.

156. Heyer, Koenen, and five civilians were jointly charged with committing a war crime in that they were "concerned with" the killing of the British prisoners of war. Heyer, Koenen, and three of the civilians were convicted. Heyer was sentenced to death by hanging and Koenen to five years' imprisonment. Of the civilians, each of whom was proved to some part in the actual killings, one was sentenced to death by hanging, another to life imprisonment, and the final defendant to 10 years' imprisonment. The defense did not, in this case, plead superior orders. [Trial of Erich Heyer and Six Others (22 Dec. 1945), 1 L.R.T.W.C. 88 (The Essen Lynching Case).]

5.   *The Velpke Children's Home Case*

The Nazi Party was concerned that the productivity of female Polish farm workers was impaired by the fact that they were tending their infants. In an effort to "promote food production," a senior Nazi Party officer ordered Heinrich Gerike, the Nazi Party official for the Helmstedt district of Germany, to create an institution where the children could be kept after being taken away from their families. Gerike arranged for the establishment of a home for infant children forcibly separated from their Polish mothers in Velpke, Germany, in May 1944. Gerike chose for this purpose a fly-infested corrugated iron hut that lacked running water, light, and telephone services. The premises lacked facilities for dealing with illness, and the sick children could not be effectively separated from the healthy.

The German Labour Office ordered Valentina Bilien to assume the post of matron of the home, which she did against her will. Bilien, a German citizen who had recently returned from Russia where she had married and taught school, had no experience in running a home for infant children. She was at first given no staff, medical equipment, or records except for the register of incoming children. Gerike ordered Bilien not to return the children to their mothers or to send them to the hospital; she was instructed to "call in a doctor if necessary." Bilien later had the assistance of four helpers, Polish and Russian girls, but conditions were otherwise the same throughout the relevant period. Bilien went away for her meals and to shop and was never in the home at night, though her helpers stayed there. It was not alleged that Bilien (or any of the other accused) actually physically abused the children or wanted or intended the infants to die. Nonetheless, in six months, more than 80 Polish infants died, mostly from general weakness, dysentery, and catarrh of the intestines.

Gerike knew of the infants' death rate, but he never visited the home or talked to Bilien after the initial selection of the home's location. He appointed Georg Hessling—who also had no relevant experience—to administer the home. Hessling claimed that his only duty was to deal with the home's finances, a claim contested by Gerike. Bilien testified that she often complained to Hessling, but nothing was done other than to raise the entry age for the children from eight to ten days after a mother's confinement to four to six weeks after birth. One witness testified that Bilien sent some of the children back to their mothers after determining that they were dying for lack of their mothers' milk, but Hessling discovered what she had done and forbade her to return additional children.

Two doctors paid rare visits to the home before September 1944, when Dr. Richard Demmerich, though without official orders to do so, started to visit the home and tend the sick infants. Later, Demmerick accepted Bilien's suggestion that he tend only those children she brought to him; during this period, he visited the home only to sign death certificates. The case report notes that Demmerick "claimed that, due to his large practice, he could find no time to write any letters of protest to persons in authority, or, in the later period, to visit the babies."

Hermann Muller was the leading Nazi official in the village of Velpke. He had seen the home and disapproved of it, but Gerike told him that the home was not his responsibility. Muller did, however once telephone Gerike to tell him of the frequent deaths and received an assurance that something would be done to improve matters. Muller then appears to have dropped the matter.

Werner Noth was the mayor of Velpke. Although a member of the Nazi Party, he held no official position in it. He admitted that he had sent at least two children to the home against their parents' wishes, but it was not proved that he knew of the institution's neglect in caring for the infants.[157]

6. *The Hadamar Case*

As many as 10,000 Germans, alleged to be mentally ill, were admitted to a small state-run sanatorium in Hadamar, Germany. They were killed in basement gas chambers, disguised as shower rooms, by a staff of about 100. The gassings ended on Hitler's orders in 1941, and the killing rooms in the basement were dismantled and converted back to sickrooms. There was substantial evidence that those responsible believed that there was a German law authorizing or even directing "such disposition of the insane," but because these deaths were not the subject of the charges in the case, the existence of legal sanction for these killings was never decided.

The Hadamar facility, operating under the guise of a sanatorium, was reactivated as a killing center in August 1942. Polish and Russian men, women, and children — persons who were slated for forced labor but who were instead shipped to Hadamar between June 1944 and March 1945 — were the victims in the case actually tried. Approximately 476 such persons were killed within one or two days of their arrival at the Hadamar institution, either by injections of morphine or scopolamine, or by doses of veronal or chloral. The reason given by the officials and employees at Hadamar who directed and administered the fatal injections was that all the victims were incurably ill from tuberculosis. Some of the Hadamar staff assertedly were also told, and believed, that the Poles and Russians fell under the provision of German law that required the killing of the insane. None of those admitted was examined or treated by the institution's one doctor — a psychiatrist — prior to death. An exhumation and autopsy of the bodies of six Poles and Russians showed that at least one victim did not have tuberculosis and that the disease in the others was not in such an advanced state that death would follow in a short period of time. Upon arrival at the institution, records were properly made of the names of the patients and other data; the records of their deaths, however, were always falsified so that neither the real cause of death (fatal overdoses of narcotics) or the actual date of death (always occurring within an exceedingly short period of time after arrival) was shown.

Seven German civilians who worked at the institution were charged with war crimes in connection with the killing of the Polish and Russian civilians. Alfons Klein, the chief administrative officer of the institution, received the original orders for the killings, transmitted those orders to his staff, knew of the deaths, and was present when some of the fatal injections were given. He asserted that he protested the plan to send "incurable tubercular labourers" to Hadamar and to kill them, but that he had

---

157. The defense argued that the defendants "had done all that they could in the difficult position as regards accommodation, transport, suitable labour and medical services which resulted from the war." Noth also claimed that he had no power to alter the state of affairs at the home, which was under the control of the Nazi Party. Gerike, Hessling, Demmerick, and Bilien were found guilty of committing a war crime in that they "were concerned in the killing by willful neglect of a number of children, Polish Nationals." Gerike and Hessling were sentenced to death by hanging. Bilien was sentenced to 15 years' imprisonment and Demmerick to 10 years' imprisonment. Miller and Noth were acquitted. [Trial of Heinrich Gerike and Seven Others (3 Mar. 1946), 7 L.R.T.W.C. 76 (The Velpke Children's Home Case).]

no power to change the orders and, had he disobeyed them, he would have been sent to a concentration camp. Klein admitted that the killings were "wrong"; he rationalized, however, that because the patients were suffering and infecting others, it would have been cruel to let them live.

Dr. Adolf Wahlmann, a psychiatrist, was the institution's sole doctor. He knew of the order to kill the patients and determined the nature and the amount of the drugs to be used to achieve this end. Wahlmann also requisitioned the drugs necessary to his purpose, although he left the actual administration of drugs to his chief nurses.

Heinrich Ruoff and Karl Willig were nurses who administered the fatal doses and injections to hundreds of victims. Ruoff testified that he "made several efforts to leave Hadamar, but his requests were always refused." Both Ruoff and Willig were reportedly told that they would be sent to concentration camps if they complained. Willig testified that he believed that the patients were "incurably tubercular, [and he] had been told that there was a law which provided for their deaths and had attempted unsuccessfully to leave Hadamar." Most of the staff apparently did believe that the victims were ill because of "diagnoses of the doctors" and "because of their appearances."

Irmgard Huber was the chief female nurse and oversaw the seven other female nurses, some of whom also administered the fatal injections. She took part in morning conferences at which plans were made for the disposal of inmates and death certificates were signed. Huber was present on at least one occasion when a fatal injection or dosage was given to a patient and when false death certificates were filled out.

Adolf Merkle was the institution's bookkeeper, responsible both for registering the incoming patients and for recording dates and causes of death; in this latter role, he was responsible for the false entries on the death certificates. Although a nurse testified that Merkle knew what was going on, he "steadfastly denied that he knew the true state of affairs" or saw any dead bodies. Merkle testified that he believed that the victims died of tuberculosis or pneumonia.

Philipp Blum was a doorman and telephone switchboard operator at the hospital who, in January 1943, became the chief caretaker of the cemetery before being called to military service in August 1944. Accordingly, only the first batch of Poles and Russians arrived during his time at Hadamar, but he nonetheless supervised the burial in mass graves of at least 100 bodies, "more or less." Knowing he was responsible for their burial, Blum was in the ward when the patients received injections and he waited for them to die. Blum admitted to full knowledge of what was intended and what actually did take place.[158]

7. *The Rohde Case*

Two members of the Women's Auxiliary Air Force (WAAF) and two members of the First Aid Nursing Yeomanry (FANY) were sent to France in plain clothes to assist

---

158. All of the accused were found guilty of war crimes. Klein, Ruoff, and Willig were sentenced to be hanged. Wahlmann received life imprisonment, while Merkle, Blum, and Huber were sentenced to imprisonment for 35, 30, and 25 years, respectively. The defendants' claims that their conduct was legal under German law, that they operated pursuant to superior orders, and that they operated under coercion and necessity, were rejected as a matter of law and fact. [Trial of Alfons Klein and Six Others (15 Oct. 1945), 1 L.R.T.W.C. 46 (The Hadamar Trial).]

British Liaison officers charged with establishing communications between London and the Resistance Movement in France. The four women were captured and eventually were taken to Natzweiler camp. There, they were told that they were being inoculated against typhus but were instead injected with a lethal drug. Their remains were then immediately cremated.

Hartjenstein was Kommandant of the camp. Although he claimed to be absent from the camp on the date of the execution, and there was no definite evidence that he was actually present for the injections, the prosecution demonstrated that Hartjenstein attended a party at the camp on the date in question.

Magnus Wochner was the head of the camp's political department, and he operated under orders from the Security Police in Berlin rather than under Hartjenstein's command. Wochner testified that when the women were brought to his office from the prison in which they had been kept, and he was told that they were to be executed, he "sent them away, saying that the matter did not concern him." Wochner asserted that he learned of the killings only after his own capture. The prosecution had no proof that Wochner was present at the killings. There was testimony, however, that cremations could not be performed without Wochner's approval.

Werner Rohde was a medical officer and admitted to giving at least one injection, "intending to kill." He testified that he only performed this "distasteful task because he had orders to do so from one Otto." The prosecution showed, however, that "Otto" had no actual authority in the camp.

Peter Straub was in charge of the camp crematorium. He claimed that he was in Berlin on the date the women were killed, but another witness asserted that Straub had told the witness that he was present at the executions.

Staff-Sergeant Wolfgang Zeuss was seen "taking prisoners back and forth." Wochner testified that Zeuss was usually present at executions. Zeuss argued that he was on leave at the time, and this testimony was "to some extent supported by the other accused."

Franz Berg was a prisoner whose job it was to work the oven of the crematorium. He admitted that he lit the oven but without knowing that there was anything unusual in the circumstances. Berg was not alleged to have participated in the killings; he testified that he was locked in his room during the injection and that a fellow prisoner watched and related the events to him as they happened.

Emil Bruttel, a first aid NCO, admitted that he obeyed an order to bring the lethal drug and that he heard, in conversations between the doctors and other officers in the camp, references to "the four women spies," "we cannot escape the order," and "execution." Bruttel claimed that he initially did not understand that an execution was intended when he received his orders. He was outside the room where the executions took place. Bruttel testified that he would have preferred to have left the crematorium altogether but "could not do so without a lamp."

The prosecutor conceded that the women could possibly, under the least favorable construction, be classified as spies. He went on to argue that "[h]ad they had a trial by a competent court and subsequently been lawfully executed by shooting this case would never have been brought." Instead, he argued, there was no proof that the women had ever been to court or that any process at all was accorded them. Defense counsel retorted:

For us Germans the government in the last years have given us an enormous number of special courts amongst which I myself have found SS courts, SD courts, courts who everywhere decided the fate of a human being and normally passed sentences of death. . . . Quite a number of the accused in as much as they are only small men cannot be expected to know that perhaps there was no sentence, and finally it is my point of view that the sentence by a full court was not required in this case but a sentence by a single person may have sufficed.[159]

---

159. Zeuss was found not guilty. The court rejected the defendants' pleas of superior orders. It found the remaining accused guilty of committing a war crime by killing the four prisoners. Rohde was sentenced to death by hanging, Hartjenstein to life imprisonment, and Straub, Wochner, Berg, and Bruttel to imprisonment for 13, 10, 5, and 4 years, respectively. [Trial of Werner Rohde and Eight Others (1 June 1946), 5 L.R.T.W.C. 54.]

CHAPTER
18

Defenses to International
Criminal Prosecutions

A foot soldier is ordered to participate in the slaughter of unarmed civilians. He refuses, knowing that the order is both immoral and unlawful. His commanding officer does not wish to leave a witness to the crime who is not himself implicated in the atrocity, and so gives the soldier a choice: Either follow orders and participate in the killing of innocents, or join the civilians in the mass grave. What should the foot soldier do? How should the law treat him? In this chapter, we will explore what defenses (or, in ICC terms, grounds for excluding criminal responsibility) are recognized under international law. These questions raise important problems with which national legal systems have long struggled and as to which they have often reached disparate results, in part because of fundamental cultural differences.

For example, the question of how to treat intoxication as a potential ground for excluding criminal responsibility was highly controversial when the ICC Statute was negotiated. Those states committed to Islamic law "considered the excessive use of alcohol an aggravating circumstance, while delegations schooled in Western perceptions of accountability considered intoxication as a mitigating factor or even one that would exclude intent and knowledge."[1] As we shall see, a compromise was struck — in a footnote — that recognized that the defense of voluntary intoxication would generally only apply to isolated acts constituting war crimes, not to genocide or crimes against humanity.[2]

One important distinction must be drawn at the outset. Most legal systems distinguish between "justification" defenses and "excuse" defenses. Justification defenses make otherwise illegal acts lawful. The conception is that in certain circumstances society recognizes that the otherwise unlawful act is the lesser of two evils — as in the case of self-defense — or is actually required by law — in the case of an executioner "killing" a prisoner lawfully sentenced to death by a competent tribunal. Excuses, by contrast, do not render the defendant's action lawful. Rather, although the act will be deemed unlawful, the law concludes that it should not be punished. Thus, for example, where a defendant commits a murder acting under the influence of drugs involuntarily taken, a misapprehension of fact, or duress, his criminal action may be excused from punishment but will not be deemed justified or lawful.

---

1. Johan D. Van der Vyver, The International Criminal Court and the Concept of *Mens Rea* in International Criminal Law, 12 U. Miami Intl. & Comp. L. Rev. 59, 129 (2004).
2. Report of the Working Group on General Principles of Criminal Law, U.N. Doc. A/Conf. 183/C.1/WGGP/L.4/Add.1/Rev. 1, n.8 (July 2, 1993).

The distinction between excuse and justification defenses carries with it at least three practical consequences. First, where a defendant's action is excused, any of his accomplices who cannot claim the same excuse or another excuse or justification will remain liable. If the defendant's action is deemed justified, however, there is no accomplice liability because the primary conduct is, in the law's view, not unlawful. Thus, for example, if a defendant is found to have acted in legitimate self-defense—a justification defense—the killing will be deemed lawful. Any individuals who may have lent him assistance, then, would be as innocent as their principal.

Second, the victim of an excused crime could legitimately exercise his right to self-defense. Where conduct is justified, however, self-defense by the victim is not warranted because the conduct is lawful when initiated, and self-defense is only permissible where a person repels *unlawful* attacks by another. Finally, a person who is excused from liability may still be liable civilly for damages resulting from his crime. If the conduct is justified, however, civil recovery will be more difficult as the conduct is not deemed unlawful.[3]

The distinction between justification and excuse, although important (particularly in civil law countries), is not one that has been clearly drawn under international law. That said, Professor Antonio Cassese reasons that *excuses* under international law may be conceptualized as falling into two categories: (1) situations in which "on account of his (transient or permanent) psychological condition . . . , the person is not possessed of individual autonomy, that is, not endowed with the capacity and free will to decide upon his conduct";[4] and (2) situations in which the person is deemed not criminally culpable because, although he may have had the requisite "individual autonomy" and freely and competently chose to commit the crime, he is thought to lack "a criminal frame of mind on account of outside circumstances."[5] The first category of defenses would include insanity and intoxication, while the second would include duress and mistakes of fact and law.

Professor Cassese posits that at least three defenses may logically be classified as *justifications*.[6] First, an individual is justified in punishing enemy civilians or combatants guilty of international crimes after conviction for such offenses by a duly constituted tribunal. Second, self-defense is justified. Finally, Professor Cassese argues that lawful belligerent reprisals, including the use of prohibited weapons, may be deemed justified and thus not criminal. "Resort to those weapons is warranted by the need to stop gross breaches of international law by the adversary, or to respond to those breaches with a view to preventing their recurrence."[7]

International criminal law is, of course, in its infancy. The ICC Statute contains a number of provisions relevant to defenses, some of which codify the customary international law that has developed to date and some of which change customary rules. Some defenses that may be available in prosecutions under national law, such as

---

3. See Antonio Cassese, International Criminal Law 257 (2d ed. 2008).

4. Id. at 262 (emphasis omitted).

5. See id. at 263 (emphasis omitted).

6. Id. at 258. A fourth potential justification — consent of the victim — is a defense rarely discussed in the war crimes literature, even though it was raised with some frequency at Nuremberg in prosecutions for use of war prisoners in military operations or as a source of forced labor. "There is very little room indeed for consent as a defence in war crime trials, for when a victim cooperates in an attempt to avoid a worse fate, there can be no talk of volunteerism, which is the core element of consent." Albin Eser, "Defences" in War Crime Trials, in War Crimes in International Law 267 (Yoram Dinstein & Mala Tabory eds., 1996). Accordingly, a "consent" defense will not be further considered in these materials.

7. Cassese, supra note 3, at 255.

statutes of limitations bars and official immunity, are not available in the ICC.[8] In the following materials, we will focus on the most commonly asserted defenses under international law: duress, necessity, superior orders, and mistakes of fact and law. We will then briefly explore self-defense, insanity, and intoxication, as well as some defenses that are unlikely to fly in the ICC — reprisals, *tu quoque*, and conflict of interest. Defenses relating to asserted good-faith reliance on official interpretations of the law will be examined in Chapter 22's examination of torture and related subjects.

A. THE EXCUSE OF DURESS AND THE JUSTIFICATION OF NECESSITY

ROSA EHRENREICH BROOKS, LAW IN THE HEART OF DARKNESS: ATROCITY AND DURESS

43 Va. J. Intl. L. 861 (2003)

. . . [T]he first judgment handed down by the International Criminal Tribunal for the Former Yugoslavia (better know as "the Hague Tribunal") . . . [involved] an ordinary man who found one day that the moral terrain around him had changed beyond recognition. It is also, of course, a story about law. The case, *Prosecutor v. Erdemovic*,[9] was decided in 1997. . . .

. . . [I]t is a fascinating case. It addresses a particularly troublesome issue in criminal law: the scope of duress as a defense. This issue in turn leads to difficult questions about what law in general can offer us, what it is fair and reasonable to expect of ordinary human beings caught in terrible times, and whether it is wise to assume a sharp discontinuity between the ordinary and the extreme in life or in law. The *Erdemovic* case can be seen as a parable about the failure of law to live up to its optimistic promise (to protect humans from atrocity or provide guidance to those who wish to prevent atrocity). Alternatively, it can be seen as a parable about law's expressive and redemptive possibilities, even in the face of evil. . . .

II. ERDEMOVIĆ'S STORY

Dražen Erdemović was an ethnic Croat who lived in the Yugoslav republic of Bosnia-Herzegovina. In 1990, Erdemović, aged 18, began his mandatory military service in the Yugoslav National Army, which was at that time still more or less multi-ethnic in composition. . . . [When the] Republic of Bosnia and Herzegovina declared its independence from Yugoslavia . . . Erdemović, who had just finished his service with the Yugoslav National Army, was briefly mobilized into the new republic's army as civil war engulfed the region. In November 1992, however, Erdemović left the Bosnian army to

---

8. ICC Article 27 states that the Statute applies "equally to all persons without any distinction based on official capacity," including official capacities such as a head of state or government. ICC Article 29 provides that the "jurisdiction of the Court shall not be subject to any statute of limitations."

9. [Brooks's note 2:] Judgement, Prosecutor v. Erdemović, Case No. IT-96-22-A (I.C.T.Y. Appeals Chamber, Oct. 7, 1997).

serve with the Croatian Defense Council's police force. His tenure there was equally short.

By all accounts, Dražen Erdemović was an accidental and unwilling soldier, not a mercenary. He came from a pacifist, cosmopolitan background, and grew up with friends of many different ethnicities. He opposed the war, and did not wish to fight; when he left the Croatian Defense Force, he sought work as a locksmith. He eventually married a Serbian woman he had known since childhood, and the young couple drifted around Serbia for a time, trying to find work and a place where a multi-ethnic family could live unmolested. They considered leaving the Balkans altogether, and tried to get visas to Switzerland, but papers were difficult to obtain. Finally, with his wife pregnant and his savings almost gone, Erdemović turned to one of the few remaining sources of steady employment in the region, and in 1994 he enlisted once more, this time in the Bosnian Serb Army of Radovan Karadžić's self-proclaimed "Republica Srpska," the Serb enclave within Bosnia.

Although whispers of concentration camps, torture, and other atrocities had already reached well beyond the region, most of these rumored atrocities were attributed to vicious Serb paramilitaries and police, not to regular soldiers. When he joined up with the Bosnian Serb Army, Erdemović asked to serve in the 10th Sabotage Detachment because its members included Croats as well as Serbs, and because it was not a combat unit but dealt instead with specialized munitions tasks. For a time, all went well; Erdemović's wife bore a son, money came in, and Erdemović's military duties were not too onerous.

On July 16, 1995, however, the 10th Sabotage Detachment was ordered to the Branjevo collective farm in Pilica, not far from the city of Srebrenica, for a mission that was not disclosed to the soldiers until five buses pulled up and several hundred captive Muslim men and boys were let off, hands tied together. The Muslims — all in civilian clothes — were lined up with their backs to the soldiers, and Erdemović and his comrades were told that upon their commander's word, they were to shoot the civilians.

Dražen Erdemović was incredulous. As he later told the judges of the Hague Tribunal's Trial Chamber, "I said immediately that I did not want to take part in that and I said, 'Are you normal? Do you know what you are doing?' "[10] But Erdemović's commander told him bluntly that he had a choice: he could participate in the executions of the Muslim civilians, or, if he felt "sorry for them," he could "stand up, line up with them and we will kill you too."

Faced with such a choice, Dražen Erdemović reluctantly agreed to obey the order. He made one more effort to be merciful when he spotted an elderly man whom he recognized among the civilians. He told his commander that the man had helped save the lives of some Serbs on an earlier occasion, and suggested that at least his life might be spared. But his commander said that it was not possible to spare any of the civilians: none of them could be left alive as witnesses.

At this, Erdemović gave up his efforts to resist, and participated, however unwillingly, in the slaughter. He later told journalists that he tried to kill as few people as possible, and he made an effort not to shoot at the youngest victims. But the buses kept leaving and returning with more victims, and by the day's end, Erdemović estimated that his bullets might have killed as many as seventy or eighty people. Soldiers of the 10th Sabotage Unit killed some 1200 civilians that day, a goodly fraction of the

---

10. [Brooks's note 5:] Separate and Dissenting Opinion of Judge Stephen, Prosecutor v. Erdemović, Case No. IT-96-22-A (I.C.T.Y., Appeals Chamber, Oct. 7, 1997) at para. 11.

estimated seven thousand Srebrenica civilians slaughtered during the course of that week by the Bosnian Serb army.

Four months later, the Dayton Accords brought an ambiguous end to the war in Bosnia, and Dražen Erdemović, now 25 years old, again found himself demobilized. But his personal war was not quite over. Erdemović told his story to a journalist from the French newspaper *Le Figaro*, and informed her that he wanted to go to the Hague and tell his story there as well.

He did not have to wait long. The story in *Le Figaro* caused a sensation; it was the first acknowledgement by any of the perpetrators that Europe's worst massacre since the Holocaust had indeed occurred. . . . Shortly after the *Le Figaro* article was published, Erdemović was arrested by Yugoslav authorities,[11] and promptly transferred to the Hague.

. . . At the Hague, Erdemović repeated and amplified the confession he had made to *Le Figaro*. His own confession was the only incriminating evidence against him, and prosecutors were at first somewhat reluctant to charge him; the Hague Tribunal had been established in 1992 with much fanfare and with pledges to bring to justice the most high-ranking perpetrators, and a conscience-stricken 25-year-old Croatian foot soldier was no one's idea of a good start. In May 1996, however, Erdemović was charged with one count of crimes against humanity and one count of war crimes.

In November 1996 (after delays due partly to Erdemović's shaky mental and emotional state), he pled guilty to the first charge. But as he entered his plea, he reiterated to the trial court that he had participated in the massacre only because he would have been killed if he had not done so. "Your Honour, I had to do this. If I had refused, I would have been killed together with the victims. . . . I could not refuse because then they would have killed me."

After his guilty plea, Erdemović was sentenced by the trial court to ten years in prison. On appeal, his attorney argued that his guilty plea had been uninformed and equivocal, and that his statements should properly have been understood as a plea of not guilty because he had been under duress at the time he committed the acts charged.

This raised a novel question for the Tribunal: is duress (if proven) a complete defense to charges of crimes against humanity or war crimes, when the crimes at issue involve the killing of innocent people? The trial court had assumed that duress was not a complete defense, and could serve only as a mitigating factor in sentencing. The Appeals Chamber, however, acknowledged that the precise scope of the defense of duress was ambiguous. The Chamber declared it a case of first impression, and undertook to determine the appropriate international law rule relating to the scope of the duress defense.

There was no issue of fact at stake. . . . The prosecution stipulated that they accepted the truth of Erdemović's version of events, and agreed that he probably would have been shot by his commander had he refused to take part in the slaughter; indeed, his commander had shot another man in the unit for disobeying orders. Thus, the only question for the Appeals Chamber was whether duress should exonerate Erdemović altogether or merely reduce his sentence.

The judges of the Appeals Chamber agreed, after a survey of possible sources of international law on the issue — e.g., treaties, customary international law, decisions of previous tribunals of an international or transnational character such as the

---

11. [Brooks's note 10:] Ironically, he was arrested on suspicion of committing war crimes by the same regime complicit in ordering those crimes committed.

Nuremberg Tribunals — that there was no unambiguous international legal standard on the scope of the duress defense. The majority of the Appeals Chamber (Judges McDonald, Vohrah, and Li) then sought guidance from state practice, and concluded that while virtually all civil law jurisdictions surveyed permitted duress as a complete defense to all crimes, virtually all common law jurisdictions preclude the defense of duress to charges of murdering innocent people.[12]

The majority concluded that in light of the divide between common law and civil law jurisdictions, there was no useful "general principle of law recognized by civilized nations" that could be extrapolated from state practice. While they acknowledged a general principle that crimes committed under duress were less blameworthy than crimes committed without any duress or coercion, this did not resolve the question of whether an international criminal tribunal should properly treat duress as a complete defense or only as a mitigating factor.

Ultimately, by a vote of 3-2, the majority of the Appeals Chamber decided to adopt the general common law rule. The plurality opinion by Justices McDonald and Vohrah declared that while duress might be a mitigating factor that would affect sentencing, duress was *not* a defense to charges of crimes against humanity. Dražen Erdemović had properly entered a guilty plea; if duress existed, this might give rise to a lesser sentence, but no amount of duress could exonerate him altogether.

In some ways this seems like an astonishing conclusion. Dražen Erdemović had had no desire to kill innocent civilians, and he did so only when threatened with his own imminent death. In the context, his death would probably have served no purpose: the Muslim civilians would surely have been killed with or without Erdemović's participation, and refusal to participate in the massacre would merely have added Erdemović to the list of victims. In a sense, then, Erdemović's acquiescence in the massacre could even be said to have reduced the total amount of death and suffering that would take place, since at least it ensured that his own corpse would not be added to the pile at the end of the day. Had he persisted in his refusal to participate in the massacre, his refusal would have injured him irreparably and benefitted no one, but his participation in the massacre benefitted him — it kept him alive — while injuring no one who would not have been injured anyway.

Why then establish a legal standard disallowing the duress defense for Erdemović? By establishing this standard, the majority of the Appeals Chamber essentially declared that Erdemović's legal guilt was foreordained when he was ordered to Srebrenica. Erdemović could only have preserved his legal innocence by sacrificing his life. At Srebrenica, the only way to be innocent was to be dead. . . .

III. REASONABLENESS IN LAW . . .

We might distinguish between two somewhat different understandings of the term "reasonable." There is a weak sense of the word and a strong sense. First, much of the time, when we speak of the reasonable man (or reasonable woman, or reasonable poor person, etc.), we are speaking in fact of the "ordinary," normal or

---

12. [Brooks's note 19:] The U.S. was the sole exception, since a few U.S. states have adopted the Model Penal Code approach, which essentially mirrors the civil law approach. Nonetheless, most U.S. states adopt the traditional common law approach, and the U.S. military retains the common law approach. The Manual for Courts-Martial states that duress "is a defense to any offense except killing an innocent person." R.C.M. 916(h), Manual for Courts Martial, United States (2000 ed.).

typical man (or woman, or poor person, etc.); that is, someone who thinks, feels and behaves in an average sort of way. He or she may turn out not to be particularly "reasonable" in the sense of always reaching well-reasoned decisions, but even if his or her decisions are poorly reasoned, they are poorly reasoned in a way that is typical of the ordinary person. This first and weaker understanding of the "reasonable person" presumes a great bell curve applying to all realms of human behavior, and the reasonable person is the one we find at the bell curve's very middle. We may choose to imagine separate bell curves for men and for women, or for abused domestic partners, or for minorities, but on this conception of legal reasonableness, the reasonable person is always perched at the top of the bell curve. . . .

If we think this conception of reasonableness as ordinariness is too impoverished, we can turn to a second conception of reasonableness, one that is more substantive and robust. We could insist that a defendant's potential liability should be measured not by what an average or typical person with his characteristics *would* have done in a similar situation, but by what an average person *could* or *should* have done. As one scholar puts it, this stronger conception of reasonableness means that:

> The reasonable person has the virtue of *prudentia* and uses this in action. [Reasonableness] is a virtue that is incompatible with fanaticism or apathy, but holds a mean between these, as it does between excessive caution and excessive indifference to risk. Reasonable people take account of foreseeable risks, but with regard to serious possibilities and probabilities, not remote or fanciful chances. They do not jump to conclusions, but consider the evidence and take account of different points of view. They are aware that any practical dilemma may involve a meeting point of different values and interests, and they take the competing and converging values seriously. . . .

In this stronger conception of the reasonable, the reasonable person is inevitably some species of utilitarian; reasonableness depends precisely upon the capacity to balance harms. This second understanding of "reasonableness" as a standard for imposing liability is a great deal more demanding. It insists that to avoid liability, a person must be reasonable *not* in the sense of being ordinary, but in the sense of thinking through his actions and their consequences in a thoughtful, reasoned way, and behaving in ways that are sensible, careful, and prudent.

This conception of reasonableness is more nuanced and powerful, and consequently gives rise to new problems. How much care is enough? What reasons are good reasons? What risks are foreseeable? Which interests and values should come first? This understanding of reasonableness also seems to some critics to offer little when it comes to evaluating human emotions. In evaluating whether a defendant's use of force was legitimate in self-defense, for instance, the law may ask whether the defendant "reasonably feared" imminent bodily harm, or whether a woman's fear that she might be raped was a "reasonable fear." But what can it mean to ask whether someone's fear was "reasonable" when fear itself is an inherently "unreasonable" emotion? . . .

IV. THE ANOMALOUS ASPECTS OF THE DURESS DEFENSE

. . . [T]he drafters of the American Model Penal Code abandoned the traditional common law approach to duress, and proposed making duress available as a defense to all crimes, including homicide.[13] To do otherwise, they stated in the commentary, would be both imprudent and unfair:

> [L]aw is ineffective in the deepest sense, indeed . . . hypocritical, if it imposes on the actor who has the misfortune to confront a dilemmatic choice, a standard that his judges are not prepared to affirm that they should and could comply with if their turn to face the problem should arise. Condemnation in such a case is bound to be an ineffective threat; what is, however, more significant is that it is divorced from any moral base and is unjust. . . .

So: Erdemović was effectively faced with a choice.[14] He could participate in the massacre, and the civilians would die, but he would live, or he could refuse to participate and he would die right along with the civilian victims. Is it reasonable to expect Erdemović to have chosen other than as he did?

Under the weak conception of reasonableness — reasonableness as ordinariness — Erdemović was certainly reasonable. . . .

Erdemović's ultimate decision seems to hold up against the more rigorous understanding of reasonability, as well. Erdemović was prudent and thoughtful; he correctly assessed the risks and benefits of each course of action. Indeed, in a strict utilitarian sense, his participation in the massacre may well have minimized the number of deaths, by ensuring that at least he would not join the victims. On any reasonableness standard, Erdemović appears to have made a defensible choice. Asking him to make any other choice is akin to demanding that he make a martyr of himself, for no practical purpose. Who among us could meet that standard? . . .

No less a person than Judge Antonio Cassese (no slouch on human rights and humanitarian law) takes this view. Writing for the 2-judge dissent in *Erdemović*, Cassese first disputes the majority's assertion that there exists no clear general principle of law on the scope of the duress defense. He argues that a "correct" understanding of the case law would suggest that duress should be a defense even to charges of murder. Moreover, even if there was no clear principle, given the differing common law and civil law standards, Cassese insists that the Tribunal ought to have had recourse to the principle most favorable to the defendant.

More importantly, by declaring that duress cannot be a defense to charges of crimes against humanity or war crimes, Cassese suggests, in effect, that the majority has abandoned the most basic legal principles. Had Erdemović "compl[ied] with his legal duty not to shoot innocent persons," writes Cassese, "he would [have] forfeit[ed] his life for no benefit to anyone and to no effect whatsoever apart from setting a heroic example for mankind. . . ." Cassese believes that this sets the standard unacceptably high: "Law is based on what society can reasonably expect of its members. It should not set intractable standards of behaviour which require mankind to perform

---

13. [Brooks's note 34:] See MPC §2.09(1):

> It is an affirmative defense that the actor engaged in the conduct charged to constitute an offense because he was coerced to do so by the use of, or threat to use, unlawful force against his person or the person of another, which a person of reasonable firmness in his situation would have been unable to resist.

14. [Brooks's note 37:] . . . [O]lder analyses of duress tended to claim that duress was a defense because the existence of coercion made the act an involuntary act, or the coercion overbore the will. Most recent commentators have insisted that duress does not negate the voluntariness of the act in a strict sense: the duress actor consciously engages in the act. See generally id. Such commentators observe that the actor under duress does not lack a choice in the matter of his action; rather, he is faced with a difficult or unfair choice.

acts of martyrdom, and brand as criminal any behavior falling below those standards." . . .

The Appeals Chamber was ready enough to acknowledge the harshness of its rule, but viewed this harshness as no more than was necessary, citing [nineteenth-century English jurist Sir James Fitzjames] Stephen: "Surely it is at the moment when the temptation to crime is strongest that the law should speak most clearly and emphatically to the contrary."

I want to quote at length here from the plurality opinion:

> [T]he law should not be the product or slave of logic or intellectual hair-splitting, but must serve broader normative purposes in light of its social, political and economic role. It is noteworthy that the authorities we have just cited [e.g., Stephen] issued their cautionary words in respect of domestic society and in respect of a range of ordinary crimes including kidnapping, assault, robbery and murder.
>
> Whilst reserving our comments on the appropriate rule for domestic national contexts, we cannot but stress that we are not, in the International Tribunal, concerned with ordinary domestic crimes. The purview of the International Tribunal relates to war crimes and crimes against humanity committed in armed conflicts of extreme violence with egregious dimensions. . . . We are concerned that, in relation to the most heinous crimes known to humankind, the principles of law to which we give credence have the appropriate normative effect upon soldiers bearing weapons of destruction and upon the commanders who control them in armed conflict situations.
>
> The facts of this particular case, for example, involved the cold-blooded slaughter of 1200 men and boys by soldiers using automatic weapons. We must bear in mind that we are operating in the realm of international humanitarian law which has, as one of its prime objectives, the protection of the weak and vulnerable in such a situation where their lives and security are endangered. . . .
>
> If national law denies recognition of duress as a defense in respect of the killing of innocent persons, international criminal law can do no less than match that policy since it deals with murders often of far greater magnitude. If national law denies duress as a defense even in a case in which a single innocent life is extinguished due to action under duress, international law, in our view, cannot admit duress in cases which involve the slaughter of innocent human beings on a large scale. It must be our concern to facilitate the development and effectiveness of international humanitarian law and to promote its aims and application by recognising the normative effect which criminal law should have upon those subject to them.
>
> Indeed, Security Council Resolution 827, adopted in 1993, establishes the International Tribunal expressly as a measure to "halt and effectively redress" the widespread and flagrant violations of international humanitarian law occurring in the territory of the former Yugoslavia and to contribute thereby to the restoration and maintenance of peace.[15]

The plurality went on to cite a number of policy reasons for their decision,[16] insisting that "It would be naive to believe that international law operates and

---

15. [Brooks's note 47:] Cf. Regina v. Howe, 2 W.L.R. 568, 582 (1987) (opinion of Lord Hailsham). Responding to the argument that earlier prohibitions on the use of duress as a defense to homicide were antiquated and unfair in their insistence that it is better to die than take an innocent life, Hailsham wrote: "[It] ill becomes those of us who have participated in the cruel events of the 20th century to condemn as out of date those who wrote in defence of innocent lives in the 18th century."

16. [Brooks's note 48:] They reasoned, for instance, that permitting duress as a defense to homicide might permit leaders of gangs or terrorist organizations to effectively "immunize" their members from prosecution by threatening them with death if they failed to obey the leader's orders. Similarly, they asserted that precluding duress as a defense to murder might make individuals more willing to refuse to

develops wholly divorced from considerations of social and economic policy. . . . 'There is no avoiding the essential relationship between law and politics.' "

Cassese, in his dissent, calls this impermissible judicial law-making:

> In my view international law [on this issue] is not ambiguous or uncertain . . . [and] to uphold in this area of criminal law the concept of recourse to a policy-directed choice is tantamount to running foul of the customary principle *nullum crimen sine lege*. An international court must apply *lex lata*, that is to say, the existing rules of international law as they are created through the sources of the international legal system. If it has instead recourse to policy considerations . . . it acts *ultra vires*.

In the end, the plurality does not rest its decision upon any pragmatic or utilitarian calculus at all, but falls back on pure "moral principles." Ultimately, they find themselves relying on the arguments of canonical English legal scholars, and quoting from Hale's Pleas of the Crown: "If a man be desperately assaulted, and in peril of death, and cannot otherwise escape, unless to satisfy his assailant's fury he will kill an innocent person then present, the fear and actual force will not acquit him of the crime and punishment of murder, if he commit the fact for he ought rather to die himself, than kill an innocent." And again from Blackstone: A man under duress "ought rather to die himself, than escape by the murder of an innocent." . . .

. . . To Cassese's claim that this violates "basic principles of law," (i.e. law based on what society can reasonably expect of its members), the plurality opinion replies, essentially, "What of it?" The plurality's position is unyielding: "[O]ur rejection of duress as a defence to the killing of innocent human beings *does not depend upon what the reasonable person is expected to do*. We would assert an absolute moral postulate which is clear and unmistakable for the implementation of international humanitarian law."

Implicitly, we have here a statement about the acceptable moral contours of a human life, a statement about what it is that makes us human beings, without which we might as well be dead.

V. Assessing the Decision

How should we feel about this instance when the law seems to ask something unreasonable of us — this moment when the law seems to require heroism and martyrdom? . . .

Where we come out on this has a great deal to do with our conceptions of the appropriate temporal framework for understanding the events at issue. On the spot, it seems unfair to punish someone as a criminal just because he could not quite bring himself to die for the sake of a principle. But if we go back far enough — before the choices became so stark and unforgiving, before the threat of violence became so palpable and imminent — perhaps it is fair after all. Here, taking a different temporal view, the focus shifts to how the actor ended up in such a bad situation in the first place.[17]

Put another way: when we evaluate Dražen Erdemović's behavior on the farm outside Srebrenica, a lot depends on whether we see his story as a narrative about

---

kill, knowing they might be punished later. This seems a weak argument, however, for few people would likely see possible future prosecution as more worrisome than imminent death.

17. [Brooks's note 60:] Cf. MPC §209(2). The defense of duress is unavailable if "the actor recklessly placed himself in a situation in which it is probable that he would be subjected to duress." Id.

inevitability and determinism, or as a narrative about choice. To Antonio Cassese, Erdemović's story is a story about inevitability, and the very worst sort of moral luck. Erdemović was caught up in events beyond his control, and he had no more freedom than a pawn on chessboard: he was an ordinary man who one day simply found himself in an untenable situation. . . . We may assume that to Cassese, the true criminals were . . . the architects of Bosnia's ethnic cleansing.

To the majority, however, Erdemović's story is (implicitly) a narrative about choice. The majority treats Erdemović as a moral agent whose failure was only consummated at Srebrenica, but begun much earlier. Erdemović's crime, on this view, goes back some years; his crime was his repeated failure to take a real stand, to insist on loyalty to any one group or idea. . . .

. . . [D]espite his commander's insistence that there be no witnesses, Erdemović . . . survives to be a witness himself. And certainly this is one way to understand this case: as a story about the redemptive possibilities of witnessing. If Erdemović had not valued his own life a little bit more than a hero ought to value his own life, there might have been no one who was later willing and able to tell the tale of how the Bosnian Serb Army systematically slaughtered thousands of Srebrenica civilians. Erdemović's fellow soldiers were able, but unwilling to implicate themselves; the victims would have been willing, but, being dead, they were not able.

Erdemović's moral ambivalence proved crucial here: he was conscience-stricken enough to recognize the massacre as a terrible crime, and if he was not *quite* conscience-stricken enough to prefer death to the moral taint of participation, he was sufficiently conscience-stricken to confess to the first journalist he could find when the war ended, sufficiently conscience-stricken to confess once more at the Hague and plead guilty, and sufficiently conscience-stricken to provide critical information to Tribunal investigators that could help them prepare indictments against numerous more important suspects, such as General Ratko Mladić and Republica Srpska President Radovan Karadžić. As the prosecution team at the Hague Tribunal acknowledged, without Dražen Erdemović's eyewitness account of the massacre (later corroborated by forensic experts who examined the site) and his detailed description of the command structure of the Bosnian Serb Army, the Tribunal's efforts to build cases against the numerous much bigger fish would have been far more difficult. Perhaps, then, the very moral weakness that enabled Erdemović's survival also enabled him to do something morally good: bear witness to the crimes in which he had taken part, and honor the victims by acknowledging the horror of their deaths.

If the story of *Prosecutor v. Erdemović* is a story about one man's moral failure, partially redeemed by the process of bearing witness, it can also be read as a parable about the international community, its half-hearted institutional efforts to address and prevent atrocities, and the limits and possibilities of law. . . .

Recall that in 1995, unable to summon the political will to take sides in the Bosnian conflict or impose a peace, but dogged by media reports of atrocities against civilians, the UN Security Council came up with the idea of declaring certain areas within Bosnia UN "safe areas," to which civilians could go and be protected by UN peacekeeping troops. Srebrenica was one such "safe area," and in the summer of 1995 thousands of Bosnian Muslim civilians poured into Srebrenica to seek protection from the incursions of the Bosnian Serb army and paramilitaries. As the plurality opinion in the *Erdemović* case dryly notes, however, the Dutch UN troops protecting the "safe area" of Srebrenica (the judges had enough sense of shame to keep the term in quotation marks) surrendered their weapons to the Serbs and withdrew rather than risk a fight. It was their abandoned civilian charges who were brought by the busload for Erdemović and his fellow soldiers to slaughter.

Naturally, none of the Dutch UN peacekeepers were ever brought up on criminal charges for their failure to protect the civilians they were pledged to protect, and no high-ranking UN officials were charged as accomplices in the murder of the thousands who died, and none of the Security Council powers who gave the UN leaders their marching orders will ever truly be called to account. Peacekeeping soldiers and their political leaders are protected by a web of ad hoc and treaty-based immunities from prosecution, and for the most part this is probably as it should be. Nonetheless, it is worth noting that had these immunities been absent, and had ordinary common law principles of criminal liability applied, some or all of these actors might well be considered criminally liable for the deaths of the thousands of massacred Srebrenica civilians.[18] Certainly, the Srebrenica massacre could not have occurred without countless political and moral failures of the first order made by people and institutions with far more power and information than Private Dražen Erdemović.

. . . After the failure of the international community to prevent the Srebrenica massacre, and the embarrassing failure of the Tribunal to get its hands on any high-ranking suspects, how could the Tribunal permit the very first defendant brought before it — a man who *admitted* killing 70 to 100 innocent people — to walk free? Punishing Erdemović was the Tribunal's sole mechanism for honoring the pain of the victims at Srebrenica. Thus, the eloquent plurality opinion insisting on "absolute moral postulates" and declaring that not even the desire to avoid one's own death could justify atrocities. This allowed the majority on the Appeals Chamber to use law itself as a mechanism for bearing witness to the inexcusable moral failures of our collective institutions.

VI. Back to Erdemović

All very well, but despite the numerous and collective moral failures, only Dražen Erdemović went to prison. Someone had to be punished, and he was available, the sacrificial lamb. So, back to Erdemović: what did he make of the whole business?

. . . Erdemović himself seemed to have agreed with the majority's view of the issue. During his sentencing hearing in November 1996, he wept as he explained to the judges why he had decided to plead guilty, despite his conviction that he had acted under duress. At Srebrenica, he said,

> [My commander] said, "If you do not want to [participate in the executions], stand with them . . . so that we can kill you too. . . ." I was not afraid for myself at that point, not that much . . . but what would happen to my child and to my wife? So there was this enormous burden falling on my shoulders. . . . I knew that I would be killing people, that I could not hide this, that this would be burning at my conscience . . .
>
> [My attorney] told me, "Dražen, can you change your mind, your decision [to plead guilty]? . . . I do not know what will happen. . . ." [But] I told him because of those victims, because of my consciousness, because of my life, because of my child and my wife, I cannot change what I said . . . because of the peace of my mind, my soul, my honesty, because of the victims and war and because of everything.

---

18. [Brooks's note 65:] Although ordinarily omissions do not give rise to criminal liability, the peacekeepers stood in a special relationship to the civilians, arguably had something analogous to a contractual duty to protect them, and certainly promised to protect them, effectively dissuading the civilians from seeking to escape the region as they might have done had no claims about "safe areas" been made.

Although I knew that my family, my parents, my brother, my sister would have problems because of that, I did not want to change it. Because of everything that happened I feel terribly sorry, but I could not do anything. . . . Thank you. I have nothing else to say.

. . . Perhaps for Erdemović, pleading guilty — and accepting his sentence — was part of restoring his sense of himself as a moral person. Perhaps, from his own point of view, suffering his sentence (he ultimately served five years) was necessary to redemption. . . .

NOTES AND QUESTIONS

1. The defense of duress is often denominated as a "necessity" defense. Although very similar in terms of elements, the defenses of duress and necessity are actually different in a number of fundamental respects. First, a necessity defense is founded on threats to life or limb *caused by objective circumstances, not the action of a third party.* For example, this is the defense pleaded (without success) in the famous lifeboat case, in which the defendant sailors, adrift at sea and starving, killed and ate a dying cabin boy. Regina v. Dudley & Stephens, 14 Q.B.D. 273 (1884); see also United States v. Holmes, 26 F. Cas. 360 (C.C.E.D. Pa. 1842) (prosecuting sailors in a lifeboat for throwing passengers overboard to lighten the load). Duress, by contrast, relates to threats to life or limb *arising from the agency of another person.* Erdemović's situation was a classic situation of duress, not necessity, and was argued accordingly.

Second, at least in U.S. law, the rationale behind the two defenses, and thus their treatment, often differs in fundamental respects. (It must be remembered that all 50 U.S. states and the U.S. federal government have their own criminal codes, and thus there is no single source one can consult for the content of U.S. criminal law; accordingly, reference is made to generalizations about U.S. law in hornbooks in the course of this discussion.) "The rationale of the defense of duress is that the defendant ought to be *excused* when he is the victim of a threat that a person of reasonable moral strength could not fairly be expected to resist." Wayne R. LaFave, Criminal Law §9.7, at 491 (4th ed. 2003) (emphasis added). The generally stated rationale underlying the necessity defense is quite different:

The pressure of natural physical forces sometimes confronts a person in an emergency with a choice of two evils: either he may violate the literal terms of the criminal law and thus produce a harmful result, or he may comply with those terms and thus produce a greater or equal or lesser amount of harm. For reasons of social policy, if the harm which will result from compliance with the law is greater than that which will result from violation of it, he is by virtue of the defense of necessity *justified* in violating it. Necessity, then, . . . is a defense belonging in the *justification* category of defenses rather than the excuse category.

Id. §10.1 (emphasis added). Under the majority rule in the United States, necessity may be successfully asserted even when the harm done is intentional homicide, as long as that harm was reasonably thought to be less than the harm avoided (for example, one is killed to save two others). Id. §10.1(d). About half of U.S. jurisdictions, however, do not allow the defense of duress if the defendant has been charged with murder. Id. §9.7(b). Does this distinction make sense?

The differences between duress and necessity have blurred over time in U.S. law. Thus, "most but not all of the modern recodifications (following the Model Penal Code in this respect) contain a broader choice-of-evils defense that is not limited to any particular source of danger." Id. §10.1(a). International law appears to treat the two defenses alike, at least in terms of defining their elements. Thus, elements of both defenses under international law are: (1) The offensive act must have been done under an immediate threat of severe and irreparable harm to life or limb; (2) there is no adequate means of preventing the evil; (3) the act is proportionate to the harm threatened; (4) the situation leading to the application of duress or necessity must not have been the result of the defendant's volition. See Antonio Cassese, International Criminal Law 281 (2d ed. 2008). ICC Article 31(1)(d) also treats necessity and duress together, providing:

> (d) The conduct which is alleged to constitute a crime within the jurisdiction of the Court has been caused by duress resulting from a threat of imminent death or of continuing or imminent serious bodily harm against that person or another person, and the person acts necessarily and reasonably to avoid this threat, provided that the person does not intend to cause a greater harm than the one sought to be avoided. Such a threat may either be:
>   (i) Made by other persons; or
>   (ii) Constituted by other circumstances beyond that person's control.

Does this codify customary international law? Does it exclude the plea of duress in the situation of Erdemović?

2. Why else might we reject a duress defense where the crime involves the killing of innocents? Consider the argument that enforcement of international law helps create or reform moral norms. Might prosecution of even "duress" cases help eliminate future atrocities, not by deterring perpetrators, but by affirming a global condemnation of war crimes? If societal condemnation of war crimes is powerful enough, there might be fewer commanding officers willing to order the perpetration of atrocities. Or there might be enough resistance from the enlisted men that they could disobey an officer en masse without risking execution. If such signaling is effective at preventing war crimes, should we use it? Or is it nevertheless inappropriate to punish someone who committed such crimes under threat of death?

3. Might there be additional, practical reasons for rejecting a duress defense where the crime involves the killing of innocents? Recall the case studies with which we concluded Chapter 17; most of the defendants in these cases asserted a duress or superior orders defense (or both). Many defendants argued that it was fear for their own lives or the lives of family members that motivated their wrongful conduct. Can we expect courts and juries to decide, with any consistency and fairness, just how proximate, serious, and significant the threat must be to excuse the wrongful conduct as necessary or coerced? Should there be a requirement that the defense tender independent corroboration of the circumstances at issue and of the fact that duress was applied?

4. Can official actors argue, *ex ante*, that their proposed conduct is lawful because justified by possible necessity? Consider the following views expressed in the "Bybee Memo" (discussed at greater length in Chapter 22 on torture) and contrast them with the views of the Israeli Supreme Court.

BYBEE MEMO

Memorandum from Jay S. Bybee to Alberto Gonzalez
(Aug. 1, 2002)

[This memorandum was prepared by the Department of Justice's Office of Legal Counsel (OLC), was dated August 1, 2002, signed by former OLC head (now Ninth Circuit Judge) Jay S. Bybee, and addressed to the president's then counsel (and later attorney general) Alberto Gonzalez. The memo discussed whether harsh interrogation tactics violate U.S. obligations under the Convention Against Torture (CAT) and the U.S. statute prohibiting torture. This memo has become known variously as the "Bybee Memo," which is the usage employed in these materials, or simply the "Torture Memo." According to one of its principal authors, John Yoo, the Bybee Memo was prepared to give the CIA guidance on how far it could go in interrogating high-value al Qaeda detainees, including Abu Zubaydah and Khalid Sheikh Mohammed (KSM, the chief architect of 9/11). In addition to crafting a very narrow definition of torture, the Bybee Memo considered whether the defenses of necessity and self-defense could justify interrogation methods allegedly needed to elicit information to prevent a direct and imminent threat to the United States and its citizens.]

A. Necessity

We believe that a defense of necessity could be raised, under the current circumstances, to an allegation of [torture under] Section 2340A . . . Often referred to as the "choice of evils" defense, necessity has been defined as follows:

> Conduct that the actor believes to be necessary to avoid a harm or evil to himself or to another is justifiable, provided that:
> (a) the harm or evil sought to be avoided by such conduct is greater than that sought to be prevented by the law defining the offense charged; and
> (b) neither the Code nor other law defining the offense provides exceptions or defenses dealing with the specific situation involved; and
> (c) a legislative purpose to exclude the justification claimed does not otherwise plainly appear.

Model Penal Code §3.02; see also Wayne R. LaFave & Austin W. Scott, 1 Substantive Criminal Law §5.4 at 627 (1986 & 2002 supp.) [hereinafter LaFave & Scott]. Although there is no federal statute that generally establishes necessity or other justifications as defenses to federal criminal laws, the Supreme Court has recognized the defense. See United States v. Bailey, 444 U.S. 394, 410 (1980) (relying on LaFave & Scott and Model Penal Code definitions of necessity defense).

The necessity defense may prove especially relevant in the current circumstances. As it has been described in the case law and literature, the purpose behind necessity is one of public policy. According to LaFave and Scott, "the law ought to promote the achievement of higher values at the expense of lesser values, and sometimes the greater good for society will be accomplished by violating the literal language of the criminal law." LaFave & Scott, supra, at 629. In particular, the necessity defense can justify the intentional killing of one person to save two others because "it is better that two lives be saved and one lost than that two be lost and one saved." Id. Or, put in the language of a choice of evils, "the evil involved in violating the terms of the criminal law (. . . even taking another's life) may be less than that which would result from literal compliance with the law (. . . two lives lost)." Id.

Additional elements of the necessity defense are worth noting here. First, the defense is not limited to certain types of harms. Therefore, the harm inflicted by necessity may include intentional homicide, so long as the harm avoided is greater (i.e., preventing more deaths). Id. at 634. Second, it must actually be the defendant's intention to avoid the greater harm; intending to commit murder and then learning only later that the death had the fortuitous result of saving other lives will not support a necessity defense. Id. at 635. Third, if the defendant reasonably believed that the lesser harm was necessary, even if, unknown to him, it was not, he may still avail himself of the defense. As LaFave and Scott explain, "if A kills B reasonably believing it to be necessary to save C and D, he is not guilty of murder even though, unknown to A, C and D could have been rescued without the necessity of killing B." Id. Fourth, it is for the court, and not the defendant to judge whether the harm avoided outweighed the harm done. Id. at 636. Fifth, the defendant cannot rely upon the necessity defense if a third alternative is open and known to him that will cause less harm.

It appears to us that under the current circumstances the necessity defense could be successfully maintained in response to an allegation of a Section 2340A violation. On September 11, 2001, al Qaeda launched a surprise covert attack on civilian targets in the United States that led to the deaths of thousands and losses in the billions of dollars. According to public and governmental reports, al Qaeda has other sleeper cells within the United States and may be planning similar attacks. Indeed, al Qaeda plans apparently include efforts to develop and deploy chemical, biological and nuclear weapons of mass destruction. Under these circumstances, a detainee may possess information that could enable the United States to prevent attacks that potentially could equal or surpass the September 11 attacks in their magnitude. Clearly, any harm that might occur during an interrogation would pale to insignificance compared to the harm avoided by preventing such an attack, which could take hundreds of thousands of lives. . . .[19]

PUBLIC COMMITTEE AGAINST TORTURE IN ISRAEL v. ISRAEL
38 L.L.M. 147, HCJ 5100/94 (Sup. Ct. of Israel 1999)

PRESIDENT A. BARAK:

The General Security Service (hereinafter, the "GSS") investigates individuals suspected of committing crimes against Israel's security. . . . The interrogations are conducted on the basis of directives regulating interrogation methods. These directives

---

19. [Bybee's footnote 23:] In the CAT, torture is defined as the intentional infliction of severe pain or suffering "for such purpose[] as obtaining from him or a third person information or a confession." CAT art. 1.1. One could argue that such a definition represented an attempt to indicate that the good of obtaining information — no matter what the circumstances — could not justify an act of torture. In other words, necessity would not be a defense. In enacting Section 2340, however, Congress removed the purpose element in the definition of torture, evidencing an intention to remove any fixing of values by statute. By leaving Section 2340 silent as to the harm done by torture in comparison with other harms, Congress allowed the necessity defense to apply when appropriate.

Further, the CAT contains an additional provision that "no exceptional circumstances whatsoever, whether a state of war or threat of war, internal political instability or any other public emergency, may be invoked as a justification of torture." CAT art. 2.2. Aware of this provision of the treaty, and of the definition of the necessity defense that allows the legislature to provide for an exception to the defense, see Model Penal Code §3.02(b), Congress did not incorporate CAT article 2.2 into Section 2340. Given that Congress omitted CAT's effort to bar a necessity or wartime defense, we read Section 2340 as permitting the defense.

equally authorize investigators to apply physical means against those undergoing interrogation (for instance, shaking the suspect and the "Shabach" position [which involves placing a detainee in a low chair with a downward-tilting seat and his arms in an uncomfortable position]). The basis for permitting such methods is that they are deemed immediately necessary for saving human lives. Is the sanctioning of these interrogation practices legal? — These are the principal issues presented by the applicants before us.

BACKGROUND

1. The State of Israel has been engaged in an unceasing struggle for both its very existence and security, from the day of its founding. Terrorist organizations have established as their goal Israel's annihilation. Terrorist acts and the general disruption of order are their means of choice. In employing such methods, these groups do not distinguish between civilian and military targets. They carry out terrorist attacks in which scores are murdered in public areas, public transportation, city squares and centers, theaters and coffee shops. They do not distinguish between men, women and children. They act out of cruelty and without mercy. . . .

The facts presented before this Court reveal that one hundred and twenty one people died in terrorist attacks between 1.1.96 to 14.5.98. Seven hundred and seven people were injured. A large number of those killed and injured were victims of harrowing suicide bombings in the heart of Israel's cities. Many attacks — including suicide bombings, attempts to detonate car bombs, kidnappings of citizens and soldiers, attempts to highjack buses, murders, the placing of explosives, etc. — were prevented due to the measures taken by the authorities responsible for fighting the above described hostile terrorist activities on a daily basis. The main body responsible for fighting terrorism is the GSS.

In order to fulfill this function, the GSS also investigates those suspected of hostile terrorist activities. The purpose of these interrogations is, among others, to gather information regarding terrorists and their organizing methods for the purpose of thwarting and preventing them from carrying out these terrorist attacks. In the context of these interrogations, GSS investigators also make use of physical means. The legality of these practices is being examined before this Court in these applications.

[The Court examines the following practices used by the GSS: violent shaking, stress positions, hooding, loud music, excessive tightening of handcuffs, and sleep deprivation. The Court finds all of these practices to be violations of basic rights under Israeli and international law.]

PHYSICAL MEANS AND THE "NECESSITY" DEFENCE

33. . . . Can the authority to employ these interrogation methods be anchored in a legal source beyond the authority to conduct an interrogation? . . . An authorization of this nature can, in the State's opinion, be obtained in specific cases by virtue of the criminal law defense of "necessity", prescribed in the Penal Law. The language of the statute is as follows: (Article 34 (1)):

A person will not bear criminal liability for committing any act immediately necessary for the purpose of saving the life, liberty, body or property, of either himself or his fellow person, from substantial danger of serious harm, imminent from the particular state of things [circumstances], at the requisite timing, and absent alternative means for avoiding the harm.

The State's position is that by virtue of this "defence" to criminal liability, GSS investigators are also authorized to apply physical means, such as shaking, in the appropriate circumstances, in order to prevent serious harm to human life or body, in the absence of other alternatives. The State maintains that an act committed under conditions of "necessity" does not constitute a crime. Instead, it is deemed an act worth committing in such circumstances in order to prevent serious harm to a human life or body. We are therefore speaking of a deed that society has an interest in encouraging, as it is deemed proper in the circumstances. It is choosing the lesser evil. Not only is it legitimately permitted to engage in the fighting of terrorism, it is our moral duty to employ the necessary means for this purpose. This duty is particularly incumbent on the state authorities—and for our purposes, on the GSS investigators—who carry the burden of safeguarding the public peace. As this is the case, there is no obstacle preventing the investigators' superiors from instructing and guiding them with regard to when the conditions of the "necessity" defence are fulfilled and the proper boundaries in those circumstances. From this flows the legality of the directives with respect to the use of physical means in GSS interrogations. In the course of their argument, the State's attorneys submitted the "ticking time bomb" argument. A given suspect is arrested by the GSS. He holds information respecting the location of a bomb that was set and will imminently explode. There is no way to defuse the bomb without this information. If the information is obtained, however, the bomb may be defused. If the bomb is not defused, scores will be killed and maimed. Is a GSS investigator authorized to employ physical means in order to elicit information regarding the location of the bomb in such instances? The State's attorneys answers in the affirmative. The use of physical means shall not constitute a criminal offence, and their use is sanctioned, to the State's contention, by virtue of the "necessity" defence.

34. . . . [W]e are prepared to presume, as was held by the Inquiry Commission's Report, that if a GSS investigator—who applied physical interrogation methods for the purpose of saving human life—is criminally indicted, the "necessity" defence is likely to be open to him in the appropriate circumstances. A long list of arguments, from both the fields of Ethics and Political Science, may be raised for and against the use of the "necessity" defence. This matter, however, has already been decided under Israeli law. Israel's Penal Law recognizes the "necessity" defence.

35. Indeed, we are prepared to accept that in the appropriate circumstances, GSS investigators may avail themselves of the "necessity" defence, if criminally indicted. This however, is not the issue before this Court. We are not dealing with the potential criminal liability of a GSS investigator who employed physical interrogation methods in circumstances of "necessity." Moreover, we are not addressing the issue of admissibility or probative value of evidence obtained as a result of a GSS investigator's application of physical means against a suspect. We are dealing with a different question. The question before us is whether it is possible to infer the authority to, in advance, establish permanent directives setting out the physical interrogation means that may be used under conditions of "necessity." Moreover, we are asking whether the "necessity" defence constitutes a basis for the GSS investigator's authority to investigate, in the performance of his duty. According to the State, it is possible to imply from the "necessity" defence, available (post factum) to an investigator indicted of a criminal offence, an

advance legal authorization endowing the investigator with the capacity to use physical interrogation methods. Is this position correct?

36. In the Court's opinion, a general authority to establish directives respecting the use of physical means during the course of a GSS interrogation cannot be implied from the "necessity" defence. The "necessity" defence does not constitute a source of authority, allowing GSS investigators to make use physical means during the course of interrogations. The reasoning underlying our position is anchored in the nature of the "necessity" defence. This defence deals with deciding those cases involving an individual reacting to a given set of facts; it is an ad hoc endeavour, in reaction to an event. It is the result of an improvisation given the unpredictable character of the events. Thus, the very nature of the defence does not allow it to serve as the source of a general administrative power. The administrative power is based on establishing general, forward looking criteria. . . .

Moreover, the "necessity" defence has the effect of allowing one who acts under the circumstances of "necessity" to escape criminal liability. The "necessity" defence does not possess any additional normative value. In addition, it does not authorize the use of physical means for the purposes of allowing investigators to execute their duties in circumstances of necessity. The very fact that a particular act does not constitute a criminal act (due to the "necessity" defence) does not in itself authorize the administration to carry out this deed, and in doing so infringe upon human rights. The Rule of Law (both as a formal and substantive principle) requires that an infringement on a human right be prescribed by statute, authorizing the administration to this effect. The lifting of criminal responsibility does not imply authorization to infringe upon a human right. . . .

37. In other words, general directives governing the use of physical means during interrogations must be rooted in an authorization prescribed by law and not from defences to criminal liability. The principle of "necessity" cannot serve as a basis of authority. . . .

A FINAL WORD

39. This decision opens with a description of the difficult reality in which Israel finds herself security wise. We shall conclude this judgment by re-addressing that harsh reality. We are aware that this decision does not ease dealing with that reality. This is the destiny of democracy, as not all means are acceptable to it, and not all practices employed by its enemies are open before it. Although a democracy must often fight with one hand tied behind its back, it nonetheless has the upper hand. . . . This having been said, there are those who argue that Israel's security problems are too numerous, thereby requiring the authorization to use physical means. If it will nonetheless be decided that it is appropriate for Israel, in light of its security difficulties to sanction physical means in interrogations (and the scope of these means which deviate from the ordinary investigation rules), this is an issue that must be decided by the legislative branch which represents the people. . . .

40. Deciding these applications weighed heavy on this Court. True, from the legal perspective, the road before us is smooth. We are, however, part of Israeli society. Its problems are known to us and we live its history. . . . We are, however, judges. . . . When we sit to judge, we are being judged. Therefore, we must act according to our purest conscience when we decide the law. . . .

B.   SUPERIOR ORDERS AND MISTAKES OF LAW AND FACT

Could Erdemović have defended himself based on the fact that he was "merely" obeying orders? Under what circumstances should a subordinate be excused from criminal liability because he was acting under the direct command of a superior — either military or civilian?

A couple of preliminary points are worth making about the typical situations in which this defense is most often litigated before discussing the contours of the superior orders defense. First, this defense is usually asserted in the context of military orders, but it need not be so. A civilian may assert that she had no choice but to obey the commands of a state actor, at least where the necessary superior-subordinate relationship and command responsibility is established.[20] Second, the content of this defense is relatively recent in international law. It has almost always been litigated in connection with the trial of enemy personnel charged with war crimes. The victorious state's soldiers may well have committed war crimes, but history demonstrates that they are likely to be tried, if at all, under the local (or more probably military) law of their state of nationality.[21] Students should consider, then, whether the content or application of this defense smack of "victor's justice."

National legal systems have long struggled with the question whether obedience to superior orders shields those who *follow* an illegal order from criminal liability. (As we saw in Chapter 17, the liability of the superior issuing the illegal order is not in question; it may be premised on a variety of grounds, including liability for the affirmative act of "ordering" or responsibility under the superior or command responsibility doctrine.) Two competing values are said to be implicated.

On one hand, nations have a strong interest in maintaining strong, efficient, and successful armies. Discipline — meaning that subordinates will reliably carry out the orders of superior officers, especially in battle — is thought to be critical to achieving such an armed force. "Military discipline is designed, ultimately, to conduct men to battle, to lead them under fire to victory, and, if and when necessary, to impel them to sacrifice their lives for their country. In this aspect, military discipline entails a total reevaluation in the soul of the soldier: he must overcome his natural instinct to save his skin."[22] The success of the military venture, as well as the lives of many people, may well depend on the degree to which military discipline has inculcated in soldiers the instinct to follow orders without thought or hesitation. To further these interests, military law creates a legal duty for soldiers to obey orders, and soldiers who fail in this duty can be sentenced for their insubordination (at least in extreme cases) to death.

On the other hand, international law forbids certain acts such as genocide, crimes against humanity, and war crimes, and the "supremacy of the law" requires that such heinous acts — whether committed under orders or not — be punished.[23]

One could argue, of course, that because there is no "international army," the international legal system need not take account of the value of discipline in forging an effective fighting machine. Indeed, such discipline, especially enlisted in aid of

---

20. See, e.g., Yoram Dinstein, The Defence of "Obedience to Superior Orders" in International Law 1 (A.W. Sijthoff-Leyden 1965); see also Prosecutor v. Musema, Case No. ICTR-96-13-T, Judgment (Jan. 27, 2000) (command responsibility of a civilian); Prosecutor v. Kayishema & Ruzindana, Case No. ICTR-95-1-T, Judgment (May 21, 1999) (same); Alexander Zahar, Command Responsibility of Civilian Superiors for Genocide, 14 Leiden J. Intl. L. 591 (2001).

21. L.C. Green, Superior Orders in National and International Law 243 (A.W. Sijthoff-Leyden 1976).

22. Dinstein, supra note 20, at 5.

23. Id. at 6.

aggressive wars, might be said to be an affirmatively negative value in the international sphere. But the legitimacy of a superior orders defense does not rest on a balancing of *state* interests. Rather, it is the exceptional severity of the dilemma facing *individual* soldiers and other subordinates that must ultimately serve as the foundation of such a defense. Professor Dinstein summarized the dilemma best (although the penalties he identifies may no longer be applicable in many cases):

> The soldier finds himself in an intolerable position: if he obeys the order and infringes the provisions of international law, he might be sentenced to the gallows by an international tribunal or a national court of the enemy; if he disobeys it, and refrains from committing the crime, he is liable, in many cases, to face a firing-squad by decree of a court-martial of his own State.[24]

ICC Article 33 sets forth the requisites of the defense of "superior orders and prescription of law":

> 1. The fact that a crime within the jurisdiction of the Court has been committed by a person pursuant to an order of a Government or of a superior, whether military or civilian, shall not relieve that person of criminal responsibility unless:
>   (a) The person was under a legal obligation to obey orders of the Government or the superior in question;
>   (b) The person did not know that the order was unlawful; and
>   (c) The order was not manifestly unlawful.
> 2. For the purposes of this article, orders to commit genocide or crimes against humanity are manifestly unlawful.

Another defense that is often raised in conjunction with a claim of superior orders (but need not be) is mistake of law or fact. Consider, for example, whether a defense ought to be available to a soldier who is operating under a mistake of law or fact, such that he believes that the order is lawful and, indeed, the order would be lawful were the circumstances as the soldier believed them to be. For example, what if the defendant mistakenly believed that the law required him to follow an order to shoot a prisoner? What if the defendant instead made a mistake of fact—believing that the order he received lawfully required him to target an enemy's ammunition depot when in fact the building bombed was a civilian hospital? These types of claims arose with some frequency after World War II, particularly in the context of defendants tried for the war crime of illegally killing POWs. Defendants often asserted that they believed that the POWs had been lawfully tried and judicially condemned for war crimes or spying.

The line between mistakes of law and fact is difficult to draw, and the treatment of these mistakes differs between civil and common law systems—particularly where what is at issue are mistakes of law. "Civil law jurisdictions tend to be more generous with regard to mistakes of law, allowing for defences where there are reasonable mistakes relating to various aspects of crimes or defences. Although there may be a trend away from this, in common law systems mistakes generally only provide an excuse when they serve to undermine *mens rea*, making the plea one of failure of proof. Article 32 of the ICC Statute appears to adopt the common law approach."[25] It also covers the relationship between the defense of superior orders and mistakes of

---

24. Id. at 22.
25. Robert Cryer et al., An Introduction to International Criminal Law and Procedure 341 (2007).

law, precluding soldiers from succeeding on claims that they mistakenly thought orders to be lawful. Article 32 provides as follows:

> 1. A mistake of fact shall be a ground for excluding criminal responsibility only if it negates the mental element required by the crime.
> 2. A mistake of law as to whether a particular type of conduct is a crime within the jurisdiction of the Court shall not be a ground for excluding criminal responsibility. A mistake of law may, however, be a ground for excluding criminal responsibility if it negates the mental element required by such a crime, or as provided for in article 33.

Consider Professor Gary Solis's take on the application of the above-described defenses to those implicated in the abuses at Abu Ghraib.

GARY D. SOLIS, ABU GHRAIB — ANOTHER BLACK HOLE?
2 J. Intl. Crim. Just. 988 (2004)

In a bad movie script, the soldier's response to war crime charges is invariably: "I was only following orders." The very phrase brings a derisive moan. And yet . . .

The defence of several American soldiers charged with shameful criminal conduct involving Iraqi prisoners at Abu Ghraib prison appears to follow that familiar bad movie script. While it is foolhardy to predict trial tactics, one of the civilian Defence Counsel for Private First Class Lynndie R. England, the most notorious of the accused soldiers, has announced his intent to employ obedience to orders in response to the law of war charges that his client faces. England herself has said "that she was ordered to pose for photos showing her holding a leash around the neck of an Iraqi prisoner . . . she said her superiors praised the techniques she and other military police were using on prisoners. They just told us, 'Hey, you're doing great, keep it up.'" In a 5 May 2004 sworn written statement, as well, PFC England said she was following orders. Should they raise the defence of obedience to orders, those accused of Abu Ghraib offences will be the latest in a long line of accused who have sought to pass criminal responsibility to others who are more senior.

2. A BRIEF HISTORY OF OBEDIENCE TO ORDERS

In 1474, Peter von Hagenbach, Governor of Breisach, pleaded obedience to orders in defence of charges of murder, arson and rape. One hundred and thirty years later, the guard commander at the execution of Charles I, Captain Axtell, offered the same defence. Both von Hagenbach and Axtell were convicted and executed. Axtell's English court held:

> [The captain] justified all that he did was as a soldier, by the command of his superior officer, whom he must obey or die. It was . . . no excuse, for his superior was a traitor . . . and where the command is traitorous, there the obedience to that command is also traitorous.

In the seventeenth century, Grotius wrote, "[I]f the authorities issue any order that is contrary to the law of nature or to the commandments of God, the order should not be carried out."

. . . The first reported case of an American military person pleading the superior orders defence is that of Navy Captain George Little.[26] In 1799, Little seized a Danish ship during the American war with France. He conducted the seizure pursuant to, but without conforming to, the federal law on seizures. He was, however, complying with President John Adams's erroneous written instructions as to how naval commanders should carry out that law. The Danish owners sued for damages, lost at trial, but prevailed upon appeal. In the subsequent US Supreme Court opinion, Chief Justice John Marshall wrote that commanders, in obeying presidential instructions at variance with the underlying law, acted at their peril and were liable for damages. In other words, if the instruction is illegal, the subordinate must not obey it, and any subordinate who does obey is responsible for not recognizing its illegality.

This heavy burden of legal interpretation for the unsophisticated military officer of the period was even greater for the unschooled seaman or soldier, but the law's guidelines became clearer with time. In an 1813 federal case relevant to today's Abu Ghraib charges, one John Jones, the first lieutenant of an American privateer, pleaded his captain's orders in defence of charges of assault and theft aboard a captured ship.[27] In instructing the jury, the judge said:

> No military or civil officer can command an inferior to violate the laws of his country; nor will such command excuse, much less justify the act . . . the participation of the inferior officer, in an act he knows, or ought to know to be illegal, will not be excused by the order of his superior. . . .

America's Civil War-era Lieber Code did not address the question of superior orders. Lieber apparently presumed that soldiers would obey superiors and that domestic court opinions would control any issues that arose. . . .

The 1799 *Little* standard remained intact, clarified by *Jones*: a military individual is liable for those orders that he knows, or should know, to be unlawful. True, the idea that a soldier is liable for illegal acts carried out at the direction of a superior is complicated by the concept that soldiers may also be liable in military law if they do not carry out orders, and early American courts allowed little room for questioning orders, promoting an adherence to a doctrinal respondeat superior approach, [meaning a complete defense of superior orders,] regardless of the orders' legality.

In 1914, the US Army published The Rules of Land Warfare — its first manual relating to the law of war. Following the lead of Professor Lassa Oppenheim, author of Britain's 1912 revised handbook on the rules of land warfare, the new US manual declared superior orders a complete defence to law of war charges. This ignored American military and civilian case law of the previous 110 years. Through World War I and the period prior to World War II, obedience to orders remained a complete defence, largely because military and civilian courts failed to address it. In 1920, Army Colonel William Winthrop, the leading military legal scholar of the era, wrote, "[t]hat the act charged as an offence was done in obedience to the order — verbal or written — of a military superior, is, in general, a good defence at military law." A few lines later, he notably adds: "The order, to constitute a defence, must be a legal one. . . ." This caveat to the standard contained in the Rules of Land Warfare, as well as the then-current US Manual on Courts-Martial, was Winthrop's, based on common sense and historical practice.

---

26. [Solis's note 7:] Little v. Barreme, 6 U.S. (2 Cranch) 170 (1804).
27. [Solis's note 9:] U.S. v. Jones, 26 F. (CCD Pa. 1813) (No. 15494) 653.

As World War II raged, the United States, like the United Kingdom, continued to view superior orders as a complete defence to a subordinate's war crime charges. But, as early as 1942, the Allies anticipated the possibility of punishing the Axis, not only the leaders but also those who might have committed battlefield war crimes. Supported by the International Commission for Penal Reconstruction and Development, and the United Nations War Crimes Commission, the Allies announced that German and Japanese soldiers would be prosecuted for obeying improper orders and would not be allowed the defence of superior orders. The manifest illegality of an order would even preclude the defence in asserted cases of compulsion. That Allied position clearly required a swift re-evaluation of US policy, for America could hardly sponsor the defence that it intended to deny the enemy. In November 1944, the United States reversed and revised its field manual and, as before 1914, obedience to a superior's orders was no longer an automatic and complete defence. Great Britain, France and Canada made similar changes to their law-of-war manuals.

Article 8 of the Nuremberg International Military Tribunal (IMT) Charter reads: "[t]he fact that the defendant acted pursuant to an order of his Government or of a superior shall not free him from responsibility, but may be considered in mitigation of punishment. . . ." Yet it is not entirely correct to say that Nuremberg eliminated the defence of superior orders. In practice, the IMT injected a factor that effectively modified Article 8's blanket rejection of the defence: the IMT explained that the true test was not whether there was "the existence of the [manifestly illegal] order, but whether moral choice was in fact possible."[28]

Is there a loophole, however small, for today's Abu Ghraib accused? Will witnesses assert that PFC England, infamously pictured thumbs-up and pointing to prisoners' genitals, had no moral choice in her actions? Will Specialist Charles A. Graner Jr, seen grinning in Abu Ghraib photos with naked Iraqi prisoners, argue that he had no moral choice? It is unlikely that either England or Graner might simply say, as did SS General Otto Ohlendorf, on trial in the post-World War II General Staff prosecution, "*Befehlist befehl*" — orders are orders.

3. WHICH ORDERS ARE NOT TO BE OBEYED?

Presuming that an accused can demonstrate proof of having received an order upon which the charges rest, the question becomes whether the individual should have carried out the order.

In early twentieth-century America, case law began to define what orders were not to be obeyed. Two civilian opinions referred to illegal orders as those whose illegality was "apparent and palpable to the commonest understanding" and "so plain as to not admit of a reasonable doubt."

Case law and state practice make clear that manifestly illegal orders are not to be obeyed. But that term is rarely defined with any precision. The German Military Penal Code is one of the few that attempts a definition, saying that "illegality is manifest when it is contrary 'to what every man's conscience would tell him anyhow.'" Would a reasonable person recognize the wrongfulness of the act or order? "In short, where

---

28. [Solis's note 23:] UN War Crimes Commission, 4 Law Reports of Trials of War Criminals (1947-1949) 411. Some tribunals in effect held that if a subordinate did not know and could not be expected to know that the order he carried out was illegal, *mens rea* was lacking and the subordinate was not guilty. This reflection of today's US military standard is seen, for example, in the *Hostage* and *Einsatsgruppen* cases. . . .

wrongfulness [of an order] is clear, you must disobey, but you must resolve all genuine doubts about wrongfulness in favour of obedience." In an ambivalent situation, the court must resolve uncertainty as to whether the conduct or order was manifestly illegal in favour of the accused, for "the whole point of the rule is that no 'reasoning why' is necessary to discern the wrongfulness of an order immediately displaying its criminality on its face." An 1867 civilian case characterized such an order as "so palpably atrocious as well as illegal that one ought instinctively feel that it ought not to be obeyed. . . ." Examples are Lieutenant Calley's Vietnam War order to kill unarmed women and children, and a Korean War case involving an order to rape and steal. In a 1958 opinion, an Israeli court famously wrote:

> The distinguishing mark of a "manifestly unlawful order" should fly like a black flag. . . . Not formal unlawfulness, hidden or half-hidden, nor unlawfulness discernable only to the eyes of legal experts. . . . [The] unlawfulness piercing the eye and revolting the heart, be the eye not blind nor the heart stony and corrupt — that is the measure of "manifest unlawfulness" required to release a soldier from the duty of obedience.[29]

As Michael Walzer points out in *Just and Unjust Wars*:

> The right can in fact be recognized, since it often is, even in the chaos of combat. It is simply not true of soldiers, as one philosopher has recently written, that "war . . . in some important ways makes psychopaths of them all." . . . There is no general rule that requires us to make allowances.[30]

The Nuremberg IMT thought to drive a stake through the defence of superior orders. It did not. The perennial defence has been raised again and again, in Korea, in Vietnam, in the former Yugoslavia and now is anticipated in Iraq as well. . . .

5. Defence Issues

The Abu Ghraib accuseds' initial problem will be demonstrating that they actually received an order to perform the acts charged. What is an "order"? Simply a direction from a superior, usually a non-commissioned or commissioned officer, to do or refrain from doing a specified act or thing.

Does the defence have a written order to pile naked prisoners on top of each other in simulated sexual positions? To force nude prisoners to masturbate and photograph them while so engaged? To place women's underwear over the faces and heads of bound prisoners? And so on.

It is unlikely that such written orders exist. Instead, the defence is likely to present testimony from the accused and perhaps co-accused that they received verbal orders to "work 'em over" or "work 'em hard" or to "soften up" prisoners for later questioning by senior interrogators whose true names and civilian organizational affiliations were never revealed to the military underlings now standing accused of acts for which they were at the time congratulated.

What do terms like "work 'em hard" and "soften up" mean and how may they reasonably be interpreted? The defence is likely to argue that the orders allegedly

---

29. [Solis's note 33:] Chief Military Prosecutor v. Melinki and Others (13 Pesakim Mehozlim, 90), cited in A.G., Israel v. Eichmann, 36 International Law Reports (ILR), 277 (Sup. Ct. Israel 1962).

30. [Solis's note 34:] M. Walzer, Just and Unjust Wars (2nd edn. New York: Basic Books, 1992), 307.

received were subtle — but clear — in their direction to do whatever it took to prepare prisoners for subsequent interrogation. Will such arguments involving "orders" that cannot be verified by documentary proof and "orders" that cannot be ascribed to a specific individual who is subject to cross-examination be sufficient to initially raise the prosecution's burden of proving that the defence did not exist?

Is it reasonable that a soldier should view an individual who is not a member of the armed services as a superior? One of the Abu Ghraib accused, aged 26, is a sergeant. Another, aged 37, a staff sergeant. Three, aged 26, 29 and 35, are specialists (one grade junior to a non-commissioned officer) and 21-year-old Lynndie England's grade of private first class is junior to that of specialist. . . . Should individuals of such age, capacity and military experience appreciate that non-military persons, believed to be employees of US government agencies such as the Central Intelligence Agency, National Security Agency and Federal Bureau of Investigation, are not their "superiors"? Did they see their situation akin to a school student's whose homeroom teacher is their nominal superior but wherein all teachers in the school exercise some undefined but residual authority over them? Or should a soldier understand that only non-commissioned officers and officers of the armed services can issue orders to them?

Even presuming the military judge accepts the existence of such orders, the position of the accused remains perilous, for the defence of obedience to orders further requires that the accused "did not know and could not reasonably have been expected to know that the act ordered was unlawful."[31]

Might the accused argue that the encouragement and congratulations offered by senior interrogators were affirmation of the propriety of their conduct? Might the accused paraphrase the defence counsel in the trial of Adolf Eichmann?

> Where politics have failed, the order is considered as a crime in the eyes of the victor. He who has obeyed is unlucky: he has to pay for his loyalty. The gallows or a decoration? — that is the question; the deed which fails will be a common crime. If it succeeds, it will be sanctified.

Or will the military judge determine that the accused knew or reasonably should have been expected to know the unlawfulness of orders to leash a supine prisoner or orders to wire a prisoner's extremities, including his penis, and tell him that if he fell from the box atop which he stood, arms outstretched, he would be electrocuted? Will the court find that "no rational being of the accused's age, formal education, and military experience could have, under the circumstances, considered the order lawful?"[32] In this regard, a Vietnam-era appellate opinion involving US Marines seems applicable:

> A Marine is a reasoning agent, who is under a duty to exercise judgment in obeying orders to the extent that where such orders are manifestly beyond the scope of the authority of the one issuing the order, and are palpably illegal upon their face, then the act of obedience to such orders will not justify acts pursuant to such illegal orders.[33]

---

31. [Solis's note 50:] Department of the Army, Field Manual 27-10. The Law of Land Warfare, §509.a (1956), and Manual for Courts-Martial, Rule 916(d).

32. [Solis's note 52:] U.S. v. Kinder, 14 CMR (ACM 1954) 742, at 744.

33. [Solis's note 53:] U.S. v. Keenan, 39 CMR (USCMA 1969) 108, at 117, fn 3.

6. Mistake of Fact, Mistake of Law

The assertion that a soldier acted in obedience to superior orders is a defence only if the accused can show that he or she reasonably believed that the orders acted upon were lawful. But the soldier may assert that he or she carried out an unlawful order while mistaken as to a fact relevant to the order. For example, following a superior's order to fire on an escaping prisoner, a guard may shoot and kill the prisoner, knowing that customary international law allows deadly force as a final means of stopping escape. But the guard was mistaken in believing his or her superior's statement that an escape was in progress. In fact, the prisoner was on an authorized exercise run. The guard may successfully assert a defence of mistake of fact. His or her supervisor, of course, will have to contend with his or her own charges.

Similarly, a soldier may assert that he or she carried out an unlawful order while mistaken as to the law involved. For example, upon receiving orders to do so, a guard may imprison a local unlicensed arms dealer, not realizing that selling arms in Iraq requires no license. He or she may raise mistake of law as his or her defence, although it is most often not a defence to a criminal act.

Might an Abu Ghraib accused contend that he thought the law allowed the abuse of which he is charged? Or that some as yet unarticulated fact, some post-9/11 special Presidential allowance, perhaps, allowed such abuse? . . .

8. Conclusion

If the soldiers charged with abuses at Abu Ghraib prison defend on the basis of obedience to orders of superiors, the weight of history, US case law and the facts of their cases suggest that they will have a difficult time. . . .

Obedience to orders as a defence to war crime charges has a history of hundreds of years. But it has seldom been successful. We shall soon learn whether the tide has turned in the Abu Ghraib cases.

NOTES AND QUESTIONS

1. Private England was convicted in an army court-martial of one count of conspiracy, four counts of maltreating detainees, and one count of committing an indecent act. She was sentenced to three years in military prison and was released after serving 521 days with a dishonorable discharge. Specialist Graner was convicted of conspiracy to maltreat detainees, failing to protect detainees from abuse, cruelty, and maltreatment, as well as charges of assault, indecency, and dereliction of duty. He was sentenced to ten years in military prison, demotion to private, dishonorable discharge, and forfeiture of pay and allowances.

2. How does a plea of "superior orders" differ from the duress defense? They certainly may be raised together but need not be. Consider the following explanation:

> Superior orders may be issued without being accompanied by *any* threats to life or limb. In these circumstances, if the superior order involves the commission of an international crime (or . . . is manifestly illegal under international law), the subordinate is under a duty to refuse to obey the order. If, following such a refusal, the order is reiterated under a threat to life or limb, then the defence of duress may be raised, and the superior order loses any legal relevance. Equally, duress may be raised independently of superior

order[s], for example, where the threat issues from a fellow serviceman, or even a subordinate.

Antonio Cassese, International Criminal Law 284-285 (2d ed. 2008).

3. How does ICC Article 33's "superior orders" provision measure up to the standards discussed above? Can the defense of superior orders be invoked only in war crimes cases?

4. How does the mistake of law and fact provision in Article 32 correspond to the law that Gary Solis describes? Although Article 32 does not so state, most commentators believe that the erroneous belief "about factual circumstances must be based on reasonable grounds or in other words not be specious or far-fetched. More specifically, the mistake must not result from negligence." Cassese, supra, at 290.

5. With respect to mistakes of *fact*, one could argue that Article 31(1) does not add anything to the Statute because if the mistake negates the requisite *mens rea*— normally "knowledge" and "intent" under ICC Article 30 — then there has been a failure of proof and no defense is even required. Can the same be argued with respect to mistakes of *law*?

6. The rationale behind the general common law rule that "ignorance of the law is no excuse" is that society must encourage people to know the law so as to conform their conduct to accepted norms; if this excuse were recognized, it would create positive disincentives to learning the law. "In addition, (i) if ignorance of law were admitted as a defence, the applicability of international criminal law would differ from person to person, depending on their degree of knowledge of law; (ii) the admission of such a defence would eventually constitute an incentive for persons to break the law, by simply proving thereafter that in fact they were not aware of the existence of a legal ban." Cassese, supra, at 295. Could one argue that the new or imprecise character of international criminal prohibitions argue for giving this defense greater leeway?

7. One issue that may arise is whether these "defenses" can be involved where the "mistake" at issue relates not to an element of the crime, but rather to a fact that might permit the defendant to claim a defense (an excuse or a justification). For example, what if the defendant truly and reasonably believed that he was acting in self-defense, even if he was mistaken about the nature of the threat? Does this "mistake" negate the *mens rea* of the offense?

8. The following case involves one of the most notorious prosecutions in U.S. military history. Note that the defendant, First Lieutenant William Calley, was sentenced to 20 years' hard labor for what became known as the My Lai Massacre, in which 500 unarmed Vietnamese civilians were slaughtered. Calley eventually served approximately 3 years' house arrest for his crimes.

UNITED STATES v. CALLEY
22 U.S.C.M.A. 534 (U.S. Ct. Mil. App. 1973)

QUINN, Judge:

First Lieutenant [William] Calley stands convicted of the premeditated murder of 22 infants, children, women, and old men, and of assault with intent to murder a child of about 2 years of age. All the killings and the assault took place on March 16, 1968 in the area of the village of May Lai in the Republic of South Vietnam. The Army Court of Military Review affirmed the findings of guilty and the sentence, which, as reduced by the convening authority, includes dismissal and confinement at hard labor for 20 years. The accused petitioned this Court for further review, alleging 30 assignments of error. . . .

Lieutenant Calley was a platoon leader in C Company, a unit that was part of an organization known as Task Force Barker, whose mission was to subdue and drive out the enemy in an area in the Republic of Vietnam known popularly as Pinkville. Before March 16, 1968, this area, which included the village of My Lai 4, was a Viet Cong stronghold. C Company had operated in the area several times. Each time the unit had entered the area it suffered casualties by sniper fire, machine gun fire, mines, and other forms of attack. Lieutenant Calley had accompanied his platoon on some of the incursions.

On March 15, 1968, a memorial service for members of the company killed in the area during the preceding weeks was held. After the service Captain Ernest L. Medina, the commanding officer of C Company, briefed the company on a mission in the Pinkville area set for the next day. C Company was to serve as the main attack formation for Task Force Barker. In that role it would assault and neutralize May Lai 4, 5, and 6 and then mass for an assault on My Lai, 1. Intelligence reports indicated that the unit would be opposed by a veteran enemy battalion, and that all civilians would be absent from the area. The objective was to destroy the enemy. Disagreement exists as to the instructions on the specifics of destruction.

Captain Medina testified that he instructed his troops that they were to destroy My Lai 4 by "burning the hootches, to kill the livestock, to close the wells and to destroy the food crops." Asked if women and children were to be killed, Medina said he replied in the negative, adding that, "You must use common sense. If they have a weapon and are trying to engage you, then you can shoot back, but you must use common sense." However, Lieutenant Calley testified that Captain Medina informed the troops they were to kill every living thing — men, women, children, and animals — and under no circumstances were they to leave any Vietnamese behind them as they passed through the villages en route to their final objective. Other witnesses gave more or less support to both versions of the briefing.

On March 16, 1968, the operation began with interdicting fire. C Company was then brought to the area by helicopters. Lieutenant Calley's platoon was on the first lift. This platoon formed a defense perimeter until the remainder of the force was landed. The unit received no hostile fire from the village.

Calley's platoon passed the approaches to the village with his men firing heavily. Entering the village, the platoon encountered only unarmed, unresisting men, women, and children. The villagers, including infants held in their mothers' arms, were assembled and moved in separate groups to collection points. Calley testified that during this time he was radioed twice by Captain Medina, who demanded to know what was delaying the platoon. On being told that a large number of villagers had been detained, Calley said Medina ordered him to "waste them." Calley further testified that he obeyed the orders because he had been taught the doctrine of obedience throughout his military career. Medina denied that he gave any such order.

One of the collection points for the villagers was in the southern part of the village. There, Private First Class Paul D. Meadlo guarded a group of between 30 to 40 old men, women, and children. Lieutenant Calley approached Meadlo and told him, " 'You know what to do,' " and left. He returned shortly and asked Meadlo why the people were not yet dead. Meadlo replied he did not know that Calley had meant that they should be killed. Calley declared that he wanted them dead. He and Meadlo then opened fire on the group, until all but a few children fell. Calley then personally shot these children. He expended 4 or 5 magazines from his M-16 rifle in the incident.

Lieutenant Calley and Meadlo moved from this point to an irrigation ditch on the east side of My Lai 4. There, they encountered another group of civilians being held by several soldiers. Meadlo estimated that this group contained from 75 to 100 persons. Calley stated, " 'We got another job to do, Meadlo,' " and he ordered the group into the ditch. When all were in the ditch, Calley and Meadlo opened fire on them. Although ordered by Calley to shoot, Private First Class James J. Dursi refused to join in the killings, and Specialist Four Robert E. Maples refused to give his machine gun to Calley for use in the killings. Lieutenant Calley admitted that he fired into the ditch, with the muzzle of his weapon within 5 feet of people in it. He expended between 10 to 15 magazines of ammunition on this occasion.

With his radio operator, Private Charles Sledge, Calley moved to the north end of the ditch. There, he found an elderly Vietnamese monk, whom he interrogated. Calley struck the man with his rifle butt and then shot him in the head. Other testimony indicates that immediately afterwards a young child was observed running toward the village. Calley seized him by the arm, threw him into the ditch, and fired at him. Calley admitted interrogating and striking the monk, but denied shooting him. He also denied the incident involving the child. . . .

We turn to the contention that the judge erred in his submission of the defense of superior orders to the court. After fairly summarizing the evidence, the judge gave the following instructions pertinent to the issue:

> . . . Summary execution of detainees or prisoners is forbidden by law. . . . Thus, if you find that Lieutenant Calley received an order directing him to kill unresisting Vietnamese within his control or within the control of his troops, that order would be an illegal order.
>
> A determination that an order is illegal does not, of itself, assign criminal responsibility to the person following the order for acts done in compliance with it. Soldiers are taught to follow orders, and special attention is given to obedience of orders on the battlefield. Military effectiveness depends upon obedience to orders. On the other hand, the obedience of a soldier is not the obedience of an automaton. A soldier is a reasoning agent, obliged to respond, not as a machine, but as a person. The law takes these factors into account in assessing criminal responsibility for acts done in compliance with illegal orders.
>
> The acts of a subordinate done in compliance with an unlawful order given him by his superior are excused and impose no criminal liability upon him unless the superior's order is one which a man of ordinary sense and understanding would, under the circumstances, know to be unlawful, or if the order in question is actually known to the accused to be unlawful. . . .
>
> Unless you find beyond reasonable doubt that the accused acted with actual knowledge that the order was unlawful, you must proceed to determine whether, under the circumstances, *a man of ordinary sense and understanding would have known the order was unlawful. You [sic] deliberations on this question do not focus on Lieutenant Calley and the manner in which he perceived the legality of the order found to have been given him. The standard is that of a man of ordinary sense and understanding under the circumstances.* (Emphasis added.)

Appellate defense counsel contend that these instructions are prejudicially erroneous in that they require the court members to determine that Lieutenant Calley knew that an order to kill human beings in the circumstances under which he killed was illegal by the standard of whether "a man of ordinary sense and understanding" would know the order was illegal. They urge us to adopt as the governing test whether the order is so palpably or manifestly illegal that a person of "the commonest understanding" would be aware of its illegality. They maintain the standard stated by the judge is too strict and unjust; that it confronts members of the armed forces who are not persons of ordinary sense and understanding with the dilemma of choosing between the penalty of death for disobedience of an order in time of war on the one hand and the equally serious punishment for obedience on the other. Some thoughtful commentators on military law have presented much the same argument. . . .

In the stress of combat, a member of the armed forces cannot reasonably be expected to make a refined legal judgment and be held criminally responsible if he guesses wrong on a question as to which there may be considerable disagreement. But there is no disagreement as to the illegality of the order to kill in this case. For 100 years, it has been a settled rule of American law that even in war the summary killing of an enemy, who has submitted to, and is under, effective physical control, is murder. Appellate defense counsel acknowledge that rule of law and its continued viability, but they say that Lieutenant Calley should not be held accountable for the men, women and children he killed because the court-martial could have found that he was a person of "commonest understanding" and such a person might not know what our law provides; that his captain had ordered him to kill these unarmed and submissive people and he only carried out that order as a good disciplined soldier should.

Whether Lieutenant Calley was the most ignorant person in the United States Army in Vietnam, or the most intelligent, he must be presumed to know that he could not kill the people involved here. . . . An order to kill infants and unarmed civilians who were so demonstrably incapable of resistance to the armed might of a military force as were those killed by Lieutenant Calley is, in my opinion, so palpably illegal that whatever [conceptual] difference there may be between a person of "commonest understanding" and a person of "common understanding," that difference could not have had any "impact on a court of lay members receiving the respective wordings in instructions," as appellate defense counsel contend. . . .

Consequently, the decision of the Court of Military Review is affirmed. . . .

DARDEN, Chief Judge (dissenting):
Although the charge the military judge gave on the defense of superior orders was not inconsistent with the Manual treatment of this subject, I believe the Manual provision is too strict in a combat environment. Among other things, this standard permits serious punishment of persons whose training and attitude incline them either to be enthusiastic about compliance with orders or not to challenge the authority of their superiors. The standard also permits conviction of members who are not persons of ordinary sense and understanding.

. . . My impression is that the weight of authority . . . supports a more liberal approach to the defense of superior orders. Under this approach, superior orders should constitute a defense except "in a plain case of excess of authority, where at first blush it is apparent and palpable to the commonest understanding that the order is illegal."

. . . [T]his test . . . recognizes that the essential ingredient of discipline in any armed force is obedience to orders and that this obedience is so important it should not be penalized unless the order would be recognized as illegal, not by what some hypothetical reasonable soldier would have known, but also by "those persons at the lowest end of the scale of intelligence and experience in the services." . . .

The preservation of human life is, of course, or surpassing importance. To accomplish such preservation, members of the armed forces must be held to standards of conduct that will permit punishment of atrocities and enable this nation to follow civilized concepts of warfare. . . . But while humanitarian considerations compel us to consider the impact of actions by members of our armed forces on citizens of other nations, I am also convinced that the phrasing of the defense of superior orders should have as its principal objective fairness to the unsophisticated soldier and those of somewhat limited intellect who nonetheless are doing their best to perform their duty.

The test of palpable illegality to the commonest understanding properly balances punishment for the obedience of an obviously illegal order against protection to an accused for following his elementary duty of obeying his superiors. Such a test reinforces the need for obedience as an essential element of military discipline by broadly protecting the soldier who has been effectively trained to look to his superiors for direction. It also promotes fairness by permitting the military jury to consider the particular accused's intelligence, grade, training, and other elements directly related to the issue of whether he should have known an order was illegal. Finally, that test imputes such knowledge to an accused not as a result of simple negligence but on the much stronger circumstantial concept that almost anyone in the armed forces would have immediately recognized that the order was palpably illegal. I would adopt this standard as the correct instruction for the jury when the defense of superior orders is in issue. Because the original case language is archaic and somewhat ungrammatical, I would rephrase it to require that the military jury be instructed that, despite his asserted defense of superior orders, an accused may be held criminally accountable for his acts, allegedly committed pursuant to such orders, if the court members are convinced beyond a reasonable doubt (1) that almost every member of the armed forces would have immediately recognized that the order was unlawful, and (2) that the accused should have recognized the order's illegality as a consequence of his age, grade, intelligence, experience, and training. . . .

. . . Although crucial parts of his testimony were sharply contested, according to Lieutenant Calley, (1) he had received a briefing before the assault in which he was instructed that every living thing in the village was to be killed, including women and children; (2) he was informed that speed was important in securing the village and moving forward; (3) he was ordered that under no circumstances were any Vietnamese to be allowed to stay behind the lines of his forces; (4) the residents of the village who were taken into custody were hindering the progress of his platoon in taking up the position it was to occupy; and (5) when he informed Captain Medina of this hindrance, he was ordered to kill the villagers and to move his platoon to a proper position.

In addition to the briefing, Lieutenant Calley's experience in the Pinkville area caused him to know that, in the past, when villagers had been left behind his unit, the unit had immediately received sniper fire from the rear as it pressed forward. Faulty intelligence apparently led him also to believe that those persons in the village were not innocent civilians but were either enemies or enemy sympathizers. For a participant in the My Lai operation, the circumstances that could have obtained there may have caused the illegality of alleged orders to kill civilians to be much less clear than they are in a hindsight review.

Since the defense of superior orders was not submitted to the military jury under what I consider to be the proper standard, I would grant Lieutenant Calley a rehearing. . . .

C.   OTHER DEFENSES

1.   *Self-Defense*

Self-defense is lawful under customary international law provided that the following elements are met:

> (i) the action in self-defence is taken *in response to an imminent or actual unlawful attack* on the life of the person or of another person; (ii) there is *no other way of preventing or stopping the offence*; (iii) the unlawful conduct of the other *has not been caused by the person acting in self-defence*; and (iv) the conduct in self-defence is *proportionate* to the offence to which the person reacts.[34]

Could Erdemović have argued self-defense in addition to duress?

Article 31(1)(c) of the ICC Statute provides the following with respect to self-defense:

> [A] person shall not be criminally responsible if, at the time of that person's conduct: . . . The person acts reasonably to defend himself or herself or another person or, in the case of war crimes, property which is essential for the survival of the person or another person or property which is essential for accomplishing a military mission, against an imminent and unlawful use of force in a manner proportionate to the degree of danger to the person or the other person or property protected. The fact that the person was involved in a defensive operation conducted by forces shall not in itself constitute a ground for excluding criminal responsibility under this subparagraph.

Does this definition expand upon customary international law? The Bybee Memo, excerpted above, also argues that official torturers in the "Global War on Terror" may be able to claim the justification of "self-defense." Do you agree?

2.   *Insanity and Mental Disorders*

The insanity defense is one of the oldest in the criminal law. References to the diminished criminal responsibility of the insane date back to the sixth century, and the insanity defense has received support from such legal luminaries as Plato, Sir Edward Coke, and William Blackstone.[35] Unsurprisingly, the defense has been incorporated into international criminal law as well. Under Article 31(a) of the ICC Statute, a person

> shall not be criminally responsible if, at the time of that person's conduct . . . [t]he person suffers from a mental disease or defect that destroys that person's capacity to appreciate the unlawfulness or nature of his or her conduct, or capacity to control his or her conduct to conform to the requirements of law.

This standard allows two kinds of insanity defenses. First, a defendant can claim that, at the time of his conduct, he was unable to *understand* the nature of his actions.

---

34. See, e.g., Cassese, supra note 3, at 259.
35. See Susan D. Rozelle, Fear and Loathing in Insanity Law: Explaining the Otherwise Inexplicable *Clark v. Arizona*, 58 Case W. Res. L. Rev. 19, 23 (2007).

Second, he can claim that he was unable to *control* his actions—despite understanding what he was doing. Students of U.S. criminal law will recognize this latter option as the "irresistible impulse" defense—a defense disfavored in the majority of U.S. jurisdictions.

Note that to raise a complete defense in the ICC under Article 31(a), a defendant must show that his capacity to understand or control his conduct was *destroyed* by a mental disease or defect. Mere *impairment* of mental capacity is not a complete defense, but may be a mitigating factor under ICC Rules of Procedure and Evidence 145(2) in sentencing if the impairment was substantial. The ICTY has followed a similar approach.[36]

3. Intoxication

International criminals, not infrequently, are operating under the influence of drugs or drink when they commit their crimes. Thus,

> [i]n the Second World War the *Sonderkommandos*, who were forced to work in the concentration camps they were held in, were frequently given intoxicants. Many of the participants in Rwanda's genocide were drunk. Child soldiers are often given drugs or alcohol as a control mechanism, to loosen inhibitions and increase their ferocity.[37]

Might one make the argument that intoxication should *never* qualify as a defense to crimes within the jurisdiction of the ICC?

Under ICC Article 31(b), a person shall not be criminally responsible if, at the time of his conduct, he was in a state of intoxication that "destroy[ed]" either (1) his capacity to appreciate the unlawfulness or nature of his conduct, or (2) his capacity to control his conduct. The intoxication defense is thus very similar to the insanity defense. Unsurprisingly, there is an exception for voluntary intoxication where the person knew he was likely to engage in conduct constituting a crime under the ICC's jurisdiction—or where he disregarded the risk that he would do so. Effectively this means that voluntary intoxication by means of drugs or alcohol will rarely be a defense—because it is nearly impossible to establish that the defendant did not "disregard the risk" that, while intoxicated, he would take the actions he ended up taking. In addition, many of the crimes under the ICC's jurisdiction involve planning and preparation, which may be incompatible with an intoxication defense.

A more fertile ground for the intoxication defense is *involuntary* intoxication. This category might include unforeseen drug interactions, mistakes in medication, or forced consumption of drugs or alcohol. The last category may be especially relevant in crimes before international tribunals. There is a long history of forcing soldiers to take drugs before combat, ranging from the Hashishin of lore to Liberia's child soldiers. Offenses committed while under the influence of involuntary drug consumption might give rise to a successful intoxication defense.

---

36. See, e.g., Prosecutor v. Delalić, Case No. IT-96-21-A (Feb. 20, 2001).
37. Cryer, supra note 25, at 335.

4.   *Juvenile Status*

According to Amnesty International, approximately 250,000 children under the age of 18 are thought to be fighting in conflicts around the world.[38] Some of these children join armies "voluntarily," while others are conscripted. In Uganda, up to 85 percent of the Lord's Resistance Army may be children between the ages of 11 and 15.[39] In Sierra Leone, an estimated 5,000 juvenile combatants fought in the war.[40] Such children present a significant problem for international tribunals. On the one hand, many of these children have committed terrible crimes. On the other hand, the age of the perpetrators (and, often, the circumstances of their conscription) suggests a diminished moral blameworthiness.

The ICC Statute resolves this problem in the favor of juvenile defendants. Under Article 26 of the ICC Statute, "the court shall have no jurisdiction over any person who was under the age of 18 at the time of the alleged commission of a crime." Although framed as a jurisdictional prohibition, this is essentially a defense excusing crimes committed before the age of 18.

In addition, under Article 53(2), the ICC prosecutor, when deciding whether to investigate, must consider whether a prosecution is "not in the interests of justice" after considering factors including the age of the alleged perpetrator. Thus, the prosecutor might refrain from pursuing a case in which the perpetrator had been kidnapped as a child but had committed an international crime after turning 18.

The Special Court for Sierra Leone has followed a different approach. By statute, juveniles between the ages of 15 and 18 are diverted to a truth and reconciliation process, in which they are ultimately released back into their communities.[41]

Do these bright-line rules make sense? Consider whether a 17-year-old who voluntarily joins an army and commits terrible acts of genocide should be able to escape punishment and return home — perhaps to the same village he has victimized. Should the ICC and similar courts have discretion to punish more blameworthy minors? Some argue that the Special Court should punish certain juveniles — those who were at least 15 years old and voluntarily joined a warring faction — like their adult counterparts.[42] Is this a more appropriate solution?

5.   *Reprisals,* **Tu Quoque,** *and Conflict of Interest*

Article 31(3) empowers ICC judges to add grounds for excluding criminal responsibility not presently reflected in the ICC Statute where such grounds are "derived from applicable law as set forth in Article 21," that is, the ICC Statute, Elements of Crimes and Rules of Procedure and Evidence, applicable treaties, "principles and rules of international law," and general principles of law derived by the Court from national laws of legal systems of the world.[43] Article 31(3) "was a compromise to allay the concerns of those delegations at the Rome Conference, led by the US, who wanted

---

38. Amnesty International USA, Child Soldiers, http://www.amnestyusa.org/children/child -soldiers/page.do?id=1051047 (last visited May 2, 2009).

39. Eric Blumenson, The Challenge of a Global Standard of Justice: Peace, Pluralism, and Punishment at the International Criminal Court, 44 Colum. J. Transnatl. L. 801, 806 (2006).

40. See Joshua A. Romero, The Special Court for Sierra Leone and the Juvenile Soldier Dilemma, 2 Nw. U. J. Intl. Hum. Rts. 8 (2004).

41. See id. at 9.

42. See id. passim.

43. ICC Article 31 also provides that "[t]he procedure relating to the consideration of such a ground shall be provided for in the Rules of Procedure and Evidence." Rule 80 requires the defense to give notice

military necessity [and] reprisals . . . to be included as grounds to exclude criminal responsibility."[44] "Military necessity" is discussed in conjunction with war crimes in Chapter 21. We will consider only the possibility that a few defenses will be added by the ICC under Article 31(3): reprisals, "*tu quoque*," and conflict of interest.

The defense of "reprisals" is closely related to self-defense. In essence, it is self-defense applied to the *state*, rather than to the individual. Under this theory, a party to a conflict may violate international law to stop a violation of international law by another party. "[Reprisals] are a crude and dangerous form of law enforcement, but remain lawful in limited situations, and subject to a number of stringent requirements."[45] The ICTY Trial Chamber summarized these requirements in *Prosecutor v. Kupreškić* as follows:

> (a) the principle whereby they must be a last resort in attempts to impose compliance by the adversary with legal standards (which entails, amongst other things, that they may be exercised only after a prior warning that has been given which has failed to bring about the discontinuance of the adversary's crimes); (b) the obligation to take special precautions before implementing them (they may be taken only after a decision to this effect has been made at the highest political or military level; in other words they may not be decided by local commanders); (c) the principle of proportionality (which entails not only that the reprisals must not be excessive compared to the precedent unlawful act of warfare, but also that they must stop as soon as that unlawful act has been discontinued) and; (d) "elementary considerations of humanity."[46]

Reprisals may not be made against the sick, wounded, shipwrecked, prisoners of war, interned civilians, and those in occupied territories; others contest whether reprisals against all civilians and cultural property are also barred as a matter of customary international law.[47] Reprisals are not explicitly recognized in the ICC Statute; in evaluating whether it is likely that the ICC will read this defense into the statute under Article 31(3), consider the ICTY Trial Chamber's further commentary in *Prosecutor v. Kupreškić*:

> [W]hile reprisals could have had a modicum of justification in the past, when they constituted practically the only effective means of compelling the enemy to abandon unlawful acts of warfare and to comply in future with international law, at present they can no longer be justified in this manner. A means of inducing compliance with international law is at present more widely available and, more importantly, is beginning to prove fairly efficacious: the prosecution and punishment of war crimes and crimes against humanity by national or international courts. This means serves the purpose of bringing to justice those who are responsible for any such crime, as well as, albeit to a limited extent, the purpose of deterring at least the most blatant violations of international humanitarian law.[48]

---

to the prosecutor and Trial Chamber of its intent to raise a ground for excluding criminal responsibility under ICC Article 31(3) sufficiently in advance of trial to permit the prosecutor to prepare adequately for trial. It also requires the Trial Chamber to hear from the prosecutor and the defense before deciding whether to allow the defense to raise this ground. If the defense is permitted to raise it, the Trial Chamber "may" grant the prosecutor an adjournment to address the novel ground.

44. Kriangsak Kittichaisaree, International Criminal Law 269 (2001).
45. Cryer et al., supra note 25, at 347.
46. Prosecutor v. Kupreškić, Case No. IT-95-16, Judgment, ¶535 (Jan. 14, 2000).
47. See Cryer et al., supra note 25, at 347-348; but see Kittichaisaree, supra note 44, at 273.
48. *Kupreškić*, Case No. IT-95-16, Judgment, ¶530.

This position makes a fair amount of sense. After all, one of the primary roles of international criminal law is to provide a mechanism to deter and punish international crimes without resorting to further violence. To allow a reprisals defense would arguably undercut one of the central goals of the project. Nevertheless, might there be situations in which a rapid action in violation of international law is necessary to put an immediate end to a greater violation by another party? International tribunals, for all their virtues, are not known for their speed nor for their effectiveness at halting ongoing violations of international law.

A related defense is known as the "*tu quoque*" (as in "you, also" or "you, too") principle. The essence of this defense is that a defendant should not be held liable for international crimes that his opponents have also committed. This defense was raised at Nuremberg, with very limited success. Kriangsak Kittichaisaree explains:

> [The Nuremberg Tribunal] seemed to take this defence into account only in relation to the unrestricted submarine warfare under the command of Admiral Donitz. The Nuremberg Tribunal took note of the 8 May 1940 order of the British Admiralty to sink all vessels at sight in the Skagerrak as well as the view of Admiral Nimitz of the US Navy that unrestricted submarine warfare was carried out in the Pacific Ocean by the US from the first day the US entered WW II. The Nuremberg Tribunal then proceeded not to assess the sentence of Donitz on the ground of his breaches of the international law of submarine warfare.[49]

Is it likely that the ICC will read this defense into the Statute under Article 31(3)? Consider the ICTY Trial Chamber's discussion of this defense in *Kupreskic*:

> The *tu quoque* argument is flawed in principle. It envisages humanitarian law as based upon a narrow bilateral exchange of rights and obligations. Instead, the bulk of this body of law lays down absolute obligations, namely obligations that are unconditional or in other words not based on reciprocity. . . . After the First World War, the application of the laws of war moved away from a reliance on reciprocity between belligerents, with the consequence that, in general, rules came to be increasingly applied by each belligerent despite their possible disregard by the enemy. The underpinning of this shift was that it became clear to States that norms of international humanitarian law were not intended to protect State interests; they were primarily designed to benefit individuals *qua* human beings. Unlike other international norms, such as those of commercial treaties which can legitimately be based on the protection of reciprocal interests of States, compliance with humanitarian rules could not be made dependent on a reciprocal or corresponding performance of these obligations by other States. This trend marks the translation into legal norms of the "categorical imperative" formulated by Kant in the field of morals: one ought to fulfil an obligation regardless of whether others comply with it or disregard it.[50]

Do you agree that the laws of war are primarily intended to benefit individuals, rather than states? If so, are there exceptions? Might the *tu quoque* principle apply in those cases?

Another questionable defense that was asserted by military commanders at Nuremberg was a so-called conflict of interest defense: "Patriotic duty required them to stay at their posts, and in order to prevent the worst, they bowed to higher orders."[51] The basic idea is that the defendants actually took the moral high road by

---

49. Kittichaisaree, supra note 25, at 272.
50. *Kupreskic*, Case No. IT-95-16, Judgment, ¶¶517-518.
51. Eser, supra note 6, at 265.

staying on the job and mitigating the worst of the Nazi regime's criminal excesses, the assumption apparently being that had the "good guys" resigned or refused to serve, they would have been replaced by officers who were even worse. The Nuremberg judgments rejected this defense by reasoning, in essence, that the harm done by these officers remaining in office and thus conveying moral support for the Nazi regime was greater than whatever aid these officers were able, by virtue of remaining in positions of power, to lend to persecuted peoples.[52]

---

52. Id.

CHAPTER
19

Crimes Against Humanity

The modern notion of "crimes against humanity" originated with the drafting of the Nuremberg Charter in 1946. Early drafts of the Charter included only two categories of crimes: crimes against peace (that is, planning or launching aggressive war), and war crimes. However, the drafters soon realized that some of the most significant Nazi crimes did not seem to be traditional war crimes. Even before the war, the Hitler regime persecuted Jews and others within German territory; and, more basically, the Holocaust seemed to be a different kind of crime than other categories of war crimes. The lawyer Raphael Lemkin coined the word *genocide* in his 1944 book *Axis Rule in Europe*, and the first draft of the Nuremberg Charter listed genocide among the war crimes. But, perhaps because the word was novel and unfamiliar, it dropped out of subsequent drafts. "Crimes against humanity" took its place in the Charter.

In this chapter, we examine the law of crimes against humanity, and in the next we examine genocide, which has a different legal definition and a different underlying emphasis. But the two crimes are closely related, and both were in many ways a legal response to the Holocaust and other persecution of civilians.

Robert Jackson, the U.S. Supreme Court justice who took a leave of absence to negotiate the Nuremberg Charter and prosecute the top Nazis, apparently inserted the category of "crimes against humanity" after consulting with a famous international lawyer (Sir Hersch Lauterpacht); but neither of them ever disclosed the thinking behind their choice of terminology.[1] There was some background to the choice.

First, the 1899 Hague Convention—an important multilateral treaty establishing laws and regulations governing war—states in its preamble that both civilians and belligerents would remain protected by "the laws of humanity," even if no more specific regulation protects them. This is known as the Martens Clause of the Hague Convention (named after the Russian diplomat who proposed it), and the 1907 Hague Convention repeats it. But the Hague Conventions never state specifically what the "laws of humanity" include and do not define violations of those laws as a crime. (The vagueness was apparently deliberate: It turns out that Martens originally proposed the clause as a substitute for more specific rules that his government opposed.[2])

Second, in 1915, responding to reports of Turkish massacres of Armenians in Turkey, the Allied governments (France, Great Britain, and Russia) denounced

---

1. M. Cherif Bassiouni, Crimes Against Humanity in International Criminal Law 17-18 (2d ed. 1999).
2. Antonio Cassese, The Martens Clause: Half a Loaf or Simply Pie in the Sky?, 11 Eur. J. Intl. L. 187 (2000).

Turkey for "crimes against humanity and civilization," and four years later they proposed trying the Turkish leadership for these crimes. However, they dropped the proposal when the United States objected that there was no agreed-upon "law of humanity" on which criminal charges could be based. Given this slender authority regarding the origin of this crime category, and his own government's earlier skepticism, Jackson's reticence is understandable.

The Nuremberg Charter finally gave specificity to the nebulous concept of "crimes against humanity." Subsequent tribunals and statutes refined the concept and expanded the list of such crimes. The best way to understand what makes something a crime against humanity is simply to examine the ways in which the Nuremberg definition has evolved. We examine five definitions: those of the Nuremberg Tribunal and the Allied Control Council; those of the International Criminal Tribunal for Former Yugoslavia (ICTY) and International Criminal Tribunal for Rwanda (ICTR); and those of the International Criminal Court (ICC).

A. THE EVOLVING LAW OF CRIMES AGAINST HUMANITY

1. *The Nuremberg Charter and Control Council Law No. 10*

FIRST DEFINITION OF CRIMES AGAINST HUMANITY— NUREMBERG CHARTER, ARTICLE 6(C):

> *Crimes against humanity*: namely, murder, extermination, enslavement, deportation, and other inhumane acts committed against any civilian population, before or during the war, or persecutions on political, racial or religious grounds in execution of or in connection with any crime within the jurisdiction of the Tribunal, whether or not in violation of the domestic law of the country where perpetrated.[3]

The basic features of crimes against humanity as the Charter defined them are these:

(1) The crimes are committed against "any civilian population."
(2) There are two kinds of crimes against humanity:
  (A) crimes of the "murder type," which are listed in the opening clause of the definition (murder, extermination, enslavement, deportation, and "other inhumane acts"); and
  (B) crimes of the "persecution type," which consists of persecution on the basis of group membership. At Nuremberg, the relevant groups were racial, religious, and political.[4]

Notice that both types of crimes require that the victim be a member of a group. But for the crimes of the murder type, the group is any civilian population, whereas for crimes of the persecution type, the group must also be racial, religious, or political.

(3) The crimes are truly international because they are criminalized "whether or not in violation of the domestic law of the country where perpetrated."

---

3. 82 U.N.T.S. 280, 288.
4. The distinction between crimes of the murder type and crimes of the persecution type, and the terminology, comes from Egon Schwelb, Crimes Against Humanity, 23 Brit. Y.B. Intl. L. 178, 190 (1946).

As we will see, all subsequent statutory definitions of crimes against humanity share these three characteristics. A fourth element appears in some later statutes but not others:

(4) The crimes are connected with the war ("in execution of or in connection with any crime within the jurisdiction of the Tribunal," where the other crimes within the Tribunal's jurisdiction were crimes against peace and war crimes — hence, connected with the war). The requirement that crimes against humanity must have some connection to war is sometimes called the "war nexus."

Notice that the Charter definition also specifies that the crimes against humanity are punishable whether committed "before or during the war." However, as we saw in the Nuremberg judgment in Chapter 3, the Tribunal held that because of the war nexus, it had no jurisdiction over prewar crimes. In effect, this holding reads the "before the war" clause out of the Charter.

Why have a "war nexus"? Most commentators believe that the Nuremberg Tribunal was reluctant to broaden the definition of crimes against humanity beyond the "war nexus" because accepted principles of public international law recognized the exclusivity of a state's jurisdiction over actions vis-à-vis its own citizens within its own territory. In 1946, there was nothing like today's human rights law. The war nexus guaranteed that the international community cannot punish domestic crimes against humanity unless a state has violated the peace and therefore made its conduct a matter of international concern. As we shall see, it took nearly half a century before the legal definition of crimes against humanity eliminated the war nexus.

The Allied occupation government in Germany established a Control Council, which enacted a law covering the main offenses from the Nuremberg Charter. Control Council Law No. 10, usually abbreviated "CCL No. 10," was used in subsequent Nazi trials that the four Allies (Britain, France, the United States, and the Soviet Union) conducted in their occupation zones. CCL No. 10 defines crimes against humanity in Article II(c):

SECOND DEFINITION OF CRIMES AGAINST HUMANITY — CCL NO. 10 ARTICLE II(C):

Crimes against Humanity. Atrocities and offences, including but not limited to murder, extermination, enslavement, deportation, imprisonment, torture, rape, or other inhumane acts committed against any civilian population, or persecutions on political, racial or religious grounds whether or not in violation of the domestic laws of the country where perpetrated.[5]

Notice that CCL No. 10 differs from the Charter definition in three important ways. First, it adds imprisonment, torture, and rape to the list of crimes of the murder type — the first time that any of these was explicitly labeled an international crime. Second, it leaves out the "before or during the war" language. And third, it omits the war nexus.

The latter two changes raised the question of whether prewar Nazi misdeeds could be tried as crimes against humanity. The best-known postwar trials, conducted within the U.S. occupation zone, failed to resolve this question. In two cases, the occupation courts followed the lead of the Nuremberg Tribunal and refused to take jurisdiction

---

5. 15 Trials of War Criminals Before the Nuremberg Military Tribunals Under Control Council Law No. 10, Nuremberg, October 1946-April 1949, at 24 (U.S. Govt. Print. Off. 1949), available at http://avalon.law.yale.edu/imt/imt10.asp.

over pre-1939 crimes against humanity. But courts in two other cases stated in dicta that such jurisdiction would exist.[6]

2. *International Criminal Tribunals for Former Yugoslavia and Rwanda*

Article 5 of the ICTY's statute defines crimes against humanity as follows:

THIRD DEFINITION OF CRIMES AGAINST HUMANITY— ICTY STATUTE ARTICLE 5:

The International Tribunal shall have the power to prosecute persons responsible for the following crimes when committed in armed conflict, whether international or internal in character, and directed against any civilian population:

(a) murder;
(b) extermination;
(c) enslavement;
(d) deportation;
(e) imprisonment;
(f) torture;
(g) rape;
(h) persecutions on political, racial, and religious grounds;
(i) other inhumane acts.

Notice that the list of specific crimes is identical to that in CCL No. 10. The ICTY retains but modifies the war nexus: Now, the crimes against humanity are tied to the presence of "armed conflict, whether international or internal in character." At the time the Statute was written, it was unclear whether the Balkan wars would be legally classified as international or internal (civil) wars.

Many lawyers doubted that the war nexus should really be necessary for crimes against humanity. After all, one might suppose that large-scale murders and persecutions directed against civilian populations could be criminalized in times of peace as well as times of war. It seems likely that some states resisted dropping the war nexus out of fear that their own "peacetime" racial, ethnic, or religious discrimination could be labeled persecution and denounced as an international crime.

The ICTR Statute contains the identical list of specific crimes against humanity as the ICTY Statute and CCL No. 10. But there are two major differences between the ICTR and ICTY.

1.   The ICTR Statute was the first international instrument to drop the war nexus from its definition of crimes against humanity. (CCL No. 10 was the basis for national military trials, not international tribunals.) Even though there was an armed conflict going on in Rwanda between government troops and the Rwandan Patriotic Front (RPF), the massacres took place in noncombat zones and was not directly connected with the war. Furthermore, it was not an international armed conflict. For those reasons, Article 3 of the defining statute of the ICTR substitutes a new requirement for the war nexus: that the attack against a civilian population during which the crimes were committed is "widespread or systematic." As we shall see, the Rome Statute of the International Criminal Court adopts this language and abandons the war nexus.

---

6. Telford Taylor, The Nuremberg War Crimes Trials, 27 Intl. Conciliation 241, 342-344 (1949) (Document 450).

2. The Statute's chapeau adds one element to the definition that has not been used by any other tribunal, before or since:

FOURTH DEFINITION OF CRIMES AGAINST HUMANITY— ICTR STATUTE ARTICLE 3:

The International Tribunal for Rwanda shall have the power to prosecute persons responsible for the following crimes when committed as part of a widespread or systematic attack against any civilian population on national, political, ethnic, racial or religious grounds. . . .

Here, the attack on the civilian population must itself be based on "national, political, ethnic, racial or religious grounds." Under the circumstances of the Rwandan genocide, this requirement was understandable and created no confusion among lawyers or judges dealing with the cases. However, the definition is puzzling because the categories listed in the chapeau are not the same as the categories listed in the definition of the crime of persecution. The ICTR Statute's chapeau also suggests that even crimes of the murder type must be based on group discrimination.

NOTE: SHOULD THERE BE A GROUP DISCRIMINATION REQUIREMENT IN THE DEFINITION?

The question of whether some kind of group discrimination should be a required element for all crimes against humanity (and not just persecution) has been hotly debated and litigated. This is a question of considerable practical importance.

Suppose that a dictatorial government indiscriminately wipes out the entire population of a mixed-race, mixed-religion village. If there were a group discrimination requirement in the definition, this atrocity might not count as a crime against humanity, because it was not based on the racial, religious, or political identity of the victims. As we have just seen, the ICTR statute includes such a group discrimination requirement. The question whether there should always be a group discrimination requirement has divided courts as well as scholars:

1. In an early case, the ICTY Trial Chamber held that even though the statute does not require that crimes against humanity (other than persecution) be committed on discriminatory grounds, this requirement should be added because it was included in the original UN Secretary General's report that led to the creation of the Tribunal. Prosecutor v. Tadić, Case No. IT-94-1-T, Trial Chamber II, ¶¶644, 652 (May 7, 1997). But the Appeals Chamber reversed this finding two years later. On textual grounds, it held that discriminatory intent is an element of only one crime against humanity, that of persecution. Prosecutor v. Tadić, Case No. IT-94-1-A, Appeals Chamber, ¶¶281-305 (July 15, 1999).

2. France also read a discriminatory intent requirement into its domestic statutory definition of crimes against humanity, in the case of Paul Touvier, a French collaborator with the Nazis in World War II. The court identified "an essential element of a crime against humanity consisting in the fact that the alleged acts were performed *in a systematic manner in the name of a State practicing by such means a policy of ideological supremacy.*" Prosecutor v. Touvier, CA Paris 1e ch. Apr. 13, 1992, Gaz. Pal. 1992 I, 387, translated and reprinted in 100 Intl. L. Rep. 338, 351 (1995) (emphasis in original). The court referred to this "ideological supremacy" requirement as "an element of intention." Id.

This had the effect of exonerating French collaborators with the Nazis who did so out of opportunism or careerism rather than Nazi beliefs; their crimes could not be crimes against humanity unless they were motivated by governmental ideological convictions of supremacy over targeted groups. The *Touvier* ruling was controversial both in and out of France. Leila Sadat Wexler describes the holding as one of several "blatant attempts to exonerate, in advance, the Vichy government from wrong." Wexler notes some commentators' suspicions that the decision also may have aimed to release French officials from potential liability for atrocities they committed in Algeria. Leila Sadat Wexler, The Interpretation of the Nuremberg Principles by the French Court of Cassation: From Touvier to Barbie and Back Again, 32 Colum. J. Transnatl. L. 289, 355 (1994).

3. The Canadian Supreme Court at one point read a discriminatory intent requirement into Canada's crimes against humanity statute, in the trial of Imre Finta, a former Hungarian policeman who allegedly participated in anti-Jewish atrocities during World War II and later emigrated to Canada. "What distinguishes a crime against humanity from any other criminal offense under the Canadian Criminal Code is that the cruel and terrible actions which are essential elements of the offense were undertaken *in pursuance of a policy of discrimination or persecution of an identifiable group or race*." R. v. Finta, [1994] 1 S.C.R. 701, 814 (emphasis added). However, the court reversed itself in 2005, finding that the *Finta* court had misread the statute. Mugesera v. Canada (Minister of Citizenship & Immigration), 2005 S.C.C. 40, [2005] 2 S.C.R. 100, ¶¶173-174. Under the current reading, the statute does not require proof that the defendant had a discriminatory motivation.

4. The distinguished philosopher Larry May has argued (in his 2004 book *Crimes Against Humanity: A Normative Account*) that the intent to harm members of a group because of their group membership is the distinctive feature that turns domestic-law murders, rapes, and so on into crimes against humanity. Otherwise, May argues, there is nothing about these crimes that elevates them from objects of domestic concern to objects of international concern. For May, this follows from a view that he calls "moral minimalism": international law generally, and international criminal law in particular, will be most justified if it limits itself to maintaining peace among nations, with the least interference in states' internal affairs consistent with that goal. Only when states victimize entire groups is the international community entitled to intervene with criminal condemnation.

5. As we shall see in the next chapter, the crime of genocide *does* require proof of discriminatory intent, that is, intent to harm group members simply because of the group to which they belong. Thus, even though the law of crimes against humanity does not require discriminatory intent for crimes of the murder type, the law of genocide does.

6. And, of course, a discriminatory intent requirement does exist for crimes of the persecution type. Persecution is only a crime against humanity under the ICTR statute when it is done on political, racial, ethnic, or religious grounds.

3.   *Rome Statute of the International Criminal Court*

The biggest change in the law of crimes against humanity comes in the Rome Statute of the ICC. Because the ICTY and ICTR will end in a few years, the Rome Statute is likely to provide the standard definition of crimes against humanity for years to come. It therefore deserves close scrutiny.

FIFTH DEFINITION OF CRIMES AGAINST HUMANITY—ROME STATUTE OF THE ICC, ARTICLE 7:

1. For the purpose of this Statute, "crime against humanity" means any of the following acts when committed as part of a widespread or systematic attack directed against any civilian population, with knowledge of the attack:

(a) Murder;
(b) Extermination;
(c) Enslavement;
(d) Deportation or forcible transfer of population;
(e) Imprisonment or other severe deprivation of physical liberty in violation of fundamental rules of international law;
(f) Torture;
(g) Rape, sexual slavery, enforced prostitution, forced pregnancy, enforced sterilization, or any other form of sexual violence of comparable gravity;
(h) Persecution against any identifiable group or collectivity on political, racial, national, ethnic, cultural, religious, gender as defined in paragraph 3, or other grounds that are universally recognized as impermissible under international law, in connection with any act referred to in this paragraph or any crime within the jurisdiction of the Court;
(i) Enforced disappearance of persons;
(j) The crime of apartheid;
(k) Other inhumane acts of a similar character intentionally causing great suffering, or serious injury to body or to mental or physical health.[7]

Note several things about this definition. First, like the ICTR Statute, Article 7 abandons the war nexus and instead simply requires "a widespread or systematic attack directed against any civilian population," whether or not it occurs during armed conflict.

Second, the list of crimes of the murder type has expanded significantly. Now, in addition to murder, extermination, enslavement, deportation, torture, rape, and "other inhumane acts"—the crimes of the murder type in CCL No. 10 and the Statutes of ICTY and ICTR—the list includes forcible transfer of population (alongside deportation); other grave crimes of sexual violence such as sexual slavery, forced prostitution or pregnancy, and forced sterilization; enforced disappearances; and apartheid.

Third, the crime of persecution also has an expanded definition: Now it includes not only persecution on grounds of race, religion, ethnicity, or politics, but also persecution on grounds of nationality, culture, gender, or "other grounds that are universally recognized as impermissible under international law."

Fourth, the chapeau now specifies a *mens rea* for crimes against humanity: knowledge that the specific crime is part of the widespread or systematic attack against a civilian population.

Fifth, Article 7(2)(a) defines the phrase "attack directed against any civilian population" as "a course of conduct involving the multiple commission of acts referred to in paragraph 1 against any civilian population, pursuant to or in furtherance of a State or organizational policy to commit such attack."[8] This definition makes it clear that crimes against humanity require an organizational policy. It highlights an important

---

7. Rome Statute of the International Criminal Court, adopted by the U.N. Diplomatic Conference of Plenipotentiaries on the Establishment of an International Criminal Court on 12 July 1998, Art. 7, U.N. Doc. A/CONF. 183/9 (1998), 37 I.L.M. 999, *available at* http://www.icc-cpi.int/Menus/ICC/Legal+ Texts+and+Tools/.
8. Id.

idea that was latent in the concept of crimes against humanity from the beginning: that such crimes are perpetrated during attacks by organized groups.

Other portions of Article 7(2) and 7(3) define the specific crimes with greater precision than any of the previous statutes. The differing cultural standards of UN member states shaped some of these definitions. Thus, for example, Article 7(2)(f) clarifies that the term "forced pregnancy . . . shall not in any way be interpreted as affecting national laws relating to pregnancy" — an indirect way of saying that laws restricting abortion cannot be construed as the crime against humanity of forced pregnancy. So too, Article 7(3) states that in the prohibition of persecution on grounds of gender, "the term 'gender' refers to the two sexes, male and female, within the context of society. The term 'gender' does not indicate any meaning different from the above." This was added at the request of some states to make sure that failure to grant equal rights to gays, lesbians, bisexuals, and transgendered individuals could not be interpreted as the crime against humanity of persecution on grounds of gender.

B.   PROBLEMS ON CRIMES AGAINST HUMANITY

Consider the following fact patterns (some based on simplified versions of actual cases). Which of them constitute crimes against humanity under the ICC's Rome Statute, and which crimes against humanity do they constitute? (Even though these examples are drawn from pre-ICC incidents, which are not within its jurisdiction — and some of them *are* within the jurisdiction of ICTY or the Nuremberg Tribunals — the exercise here is to analyze them under the ICC statute.)

To address these problems, you will need to examine not only the Rome Statute, but also the Elements of Crimes that accompanies the Statute. These may be found on the Web site of the ICC.

1. During the Bosnian conflict, Muslim men were imprisoned by Serb troops in concentration camps. Defendant, a karate instructor, did not belong to the Serb military or paramilitary forces. But he had friends in the force, and they allegedly let him visit the camp to torture inmates who had at one time defeated him in karate tournaments. (Allegations in *Tadić*.)

2. Defendant joined with Rwandan *interahamwe* in attacks on Tutsis. He is accused of two counts of rape, both during the first day of the genocide. He claims that at the time of the alleged rapes he had no knowledge that the attack consisted of anything more than his own unit, with the unit commander acting on his own.

3. (a) Defendant was a Croatian officer engaged in ethnic cleansing in Eastern Croatia. He ordered his unit to burn down the houses of ethnic Serbs so that they would move out of the area, a common tactic of "ethnic cleansing."
   (b) What if the accusation was burning down the house of anyone who opposed the militia, regardless of ethnic identity?

4. (a) Defendant was a judge in a German trial court. From 1935 on, he enforced the Nuremberg Laws, which made it a crime for Jewish men to have sexual relations with Aryan women. On occasion he imposed extremely severe sentences.
   (b) Does it matter whether he imposed the sentences before or after the Nazi campaign against the Jews became systematically violent? (Historians generally date this to November 9, 1938, the date of *Kristallnacht*, the "Night of Broken

Glass," when the regime unleashed anti-Jewish riots throughout Germany, killed 91 Jews, and sent thousands more to concentration camps.) Before the campaign became systematically violent, was there an attack on a civilian population?

(c) Defendant was a judge in the special political court (the "People's Court") set up by Hitler for political cases, in order to bypass the ordinary judicial system. He sentenced a woman to death who had been caught helping Jews escape. Defendant had knowledge of the Holocaust.

5. Before East Timor became the independent nation of Timor-Leste, it belonged to Indonesia, which had occupied it in 1975. In 1999, the UN sponsored a self-determination referendum, and the island voted for independence. Violent conflict broke out, as small militia groups opposed to independence carried out small, uncoordinated missions against pro-independence civilians. Although no evidence indicates that the militia groups and attacks were coordinated with each other, together they killed many thousands of people. As a matter of policy, the Indonesian government ordered police not to stop the killings. Defendant belongs to one of the militias and is charged with multiple counts of murder.

(a) Is this an attack on a civilian population?

(b) Does it matter whether Defendant knew of the government's policy of noninterference?

6. Are terrorist attacks, such as September 11, the Madrid bombings of March 11, the pervasive violence by organized Sunni and Shi'ite groups in Iraq against each other, or the Mumbai attacks of 2008 crimes against humanity?

C. CASE LAW: APPLYING THE LAW

The following case arose out of a terrible event in the Bosnian war: on April 16, 1993, units of the HVO (the Croatian Defense Council, a military organization of Bosnian Croats) attacked the village of Ahmici, killed 100 Muslim residents, including women and children, and burned almost 170 Muslim houses along with two mosques. The six defendants all lived in and around Ahmići, and, as the courts noted, before the war, the Croatians and Muslims in Ahmići had lived together harmoniously. The case bears the name of three of the defendants: brothers Zoran and Mirjan Kupreškić, and their cousin Vlatko Kupreškić. Only one of the six defendants (not one of the Kupreškićs) held any military position. The opinion is noteworthy for its detailed analysis of the crime against humanity of persecution.

PROSECUTOR v. KUPREŠKIĆ

Case No. IT-95-16-T, Judgment, Trial Chamber (Jan. 14, 2000)

II. THE CHARGES AGAINST THE ACCUSED

31. . . . The Prosecutor alleged the following facts and charged the following counts:

32. The accused helped prepare the April 1993 attack on the Ahmići-Šantici civilians by: participating in military training and arming themselves; evacuating

Bosnian Croat civilians the night before the attack; organising HVO soldiers, weapons and ammunition in and around the village of Ahmići-Šantici; preparing their homes and the homes of their relatives as staging areas and firing locations for the attack, and by concealing from the other residents the fact that the attack was imminent.

33. Under COUNT 1 all six accused are charged with a CRIME AGAINST HUMANITY, punishable under Article 5(h) (persecution) of the Statute of the Tribunal, on the grounds that from October 1992 until April 1993 they persecuted the Bosnian Muslim inhabitants of Ahmići-Šantici and its environs on political, racial or religious grounds by planning, organising and implementing an attack which was designed to remove all Bosnian Muslims from the village and surrounding areas. As part of this persecution, the accused participated in or aided and abetted the deliberate and systematic killing of Bosnian Muslim civilians, the comprehensive destruction of their homes and property, and their organised detention and expulsion from Ahmići-Šantici and its environs.

34. Under COUNTS 2-9 the accused Mirjan and Zoran Kupreškić are charged with murder as a CRIME AGAINST HUMANITY, punishable under Article 5(a) (murder) of the Statute of the Tribunal, and a VIOLATION OF THE LAWS OR CUSTOMS OF WAR, punishable by Article 3 of the Statute of the Tribunal and recognised by Article 3(1)(a) (murder) of the Geneva Conventions. When the attack on Ahmići-Šantici commenced in the early morning of 16 April 1993, Witness KL was living with his son, Naser, Naser's wife, Zehrudina, and their two children, Elvis (aged 4) and Sejad (aged 3 months). Armed with an automatic weapon, Zoran and Mirjan Kupreškić entered Witness KL's house. Zoran Kupreškić shot and killed Naser. He then shot and wounded Zehrudina. Mirjan Kupreškić poured flammable liquid onto the furniture to set the house on fire. The accused then shot the two children, Elvis and Sejad. When Witness KL fled the burning house, Zehrudina, who was wounded, was still alive, but ultimately perished in the fire. Naser, Zehrudina, Elvis and Sejad all died and Witness KL received burns to his head, face and hands.

35. Under COUNTS 10 and 11 Zoran and Mirjan Kupreškić are charged with a CRIME AGAINST HUMANITY, punishable by Article 5(i) (inhumane acts) of the Statute of the Tribunal and a VIOLATION OF THE LAWS OR CUSTOMS OF WAR, punishable under Article 3 of the Statute of the Tribunal and recognised by Article 3(1)(a) (cruel treatment) of the Geneva Conventions, on the grounds of killing Witness KL's family before his eyes and causing him severe burns by burning down his home while he was still in it.

36. Under COUNTS 12-15 the accused Vlatko Kupreškić is charged with murder and inhumane and cruel treatment as CRIMES AGAINST HUMANITY, punishable under Article 5(a) (murder), and Article 5(i) (inhumane acts) of the Statute of the Tribunal, as well as VIOLATIONS OF THE LAWS OR CUSTOMS OF WAR, punishable by Article 3 of the Statute of the Tribunal and recognised by Article 3(1)(a) (murder and cruel treatment) of the Geneva Conventions. Before the 16 April 1993 attack, HVO soldiers armed with automatic rifles congregated at the residence of the accused in Ahmići. When the attack commenced, several HVO units used his residence as a staging area. Other HVO soldiers shot at Bosnian Muslim civilians from the accused's house throughout the attack. Members of the Pezer family, who were Bosnian Muslims, decided to escape through the forest. As they ran by the accused's house toward the forest, the accused and other HVO soldiers in front of his house, aiding and abetting each other, shot at the group, wounding D'enana [*sic*] Pezer, the daughter of Ismail and Fata Pezer, and another woman. Dzenana [*sic*] Pezer fell to the ground and Fata Pezer returned to assist her daughter. The accused and the HVO soldiers shot Fata Pezer and killed her.

37. Under COUNTS 16-19, Drago Josipovic and Vladimir Santic are charged with CRIMES AGAINST HUMANITY, punishable under Article 5(a) (murder) and 5(i) (inhumane acts) of the Statute of the Tribunal, as well as with VIOLATIONS OF THE LAWS OR CUSTOMS OF WAR, punishable by Article 3 of the Statute of the Tribunal and recognised by Article 3(1)(a) (murder and cruel treatment) of the Geneva Conventions. On 16 April 1993, numerous HVO soldiers, including the accused, attacked the home of Musafer and Suhreta Puščul, while the family, which included two young daughters, was sleeping. During the attack, the accused and other HVO soldiers, aiding and abetting one another, forcibly removed the family from their home and then killed Musafer Puščul whilst holding members of his family nearby. As part of the attack, the HVO soldiers, including the accused, vandalised the home and then burned it to the ground. . . .

V. THE APPLICABLE LAW . . .

B. CRIMES AGAINST HUMANITY

1. Objective and Subjective Elements of the Crimes Under Article 5

543. Article 5 of the Statute of the International Tribunal deals with crimes against humanity. The essence of these crimes is a systematic policy of a certain scale and gravity directed against a civilian population. In the *Nikolic* Rule 61 decision, the Trial Chamber set forth in broad terms three distinct components of crimes against humanity under the ICTY Statute:

> First, the crimes must be directed at a civilian population, specifically identified as a group by the perpetrators of those acts. Secondly, the crimes must, to a certain extent, be organised and systematic. Although they need not be related to a policy established at State level, in the conventional sense of the term, they cannot be the work of isolated individuals alone. Lastly, the crimes, considered as a whole, must be of a certain scale and gravity.

544. The following elements can be identified as comprising the core elements of crimes against humanity: first, the existence of an armed conflict; second, that the acts were part of a widespread or systematic occurrence of crimes directed against a civilian population (the requirement that the occurrence of crimes be widespread or systematic being a disjunctive one) and finally, that the perpetrator had knowledge of the wider context in which his act occurs.

2. The Requirement of an Armed Conflict

545. By requiring that crimes against humanity be committed in either internal or international armed conflict, the Security Council, in establishing the International Tribunal, may have defined the crime in Article 5 more narrowly than is necessary under customary international law.[9] . . .

546. The nature of the nexus required under Article 5 of the Statute is merely that the act be linked geographically as well as temporally with the armed conflict.

---

9. [Court's footnote 801:] See Prosecutor v. Tadić, (IT-94-1-AR72), Decision on Defence Motion for Interlocutory Appeal on Jurisdiction, Appeals Chamber, 2 Oct. 1995, at para. 141: "It is by now a settled rule of customary international law that crimes against humanity do not require a connection to international armed conflict. Indeed . . . customary international law may not require a connection between crimes against humanity and any conflict at all."

3. "Directed Against a Civilian Population"

547. It would seem that a wide definition of "civilian" and "population" is intended. This is warranted first of all by the object and purpose of the general principles and rules of humanitarian law, in particular by the rules prohibiting crimes against humanity. The latter are intended to safeguard basic human values by banning atrocities directed against human dignity. One fails to see why only civilians and not also combatants should be protected by these rules (in particular by the rule prohibiting persecution), given that these rules may be held to possess a broader humanitarian scope and purpose than those prohibiting war crimes. However, faced with the explicit limitation laid down in Article 5, the Trial Chamber holds that a broad interpretation should nevertheless be placed on the word "civilians," the more so because the limitation in Article 5 constitutes a departure from customary international law. . . .

549. Thus the presence of those actively involved in the conflict should not prevent the characterization of a population as civilian and those actively involved in a resistance movement can qualify as victims of crimes against humanity.

4. Can Crimes Against Humanity Comprise Isolated Acts?

550. In general terms, the very nature of the criminal acts over which the International Tribunal has jurisdiction under Article 5, in view of the fact that they must be "directed against any civilian population," ensures that what is to be alleged will not be one particular act but, instead, a course of conduct. Nevertheless, in certain circumstances, a single act has comprised a crime against humanity when it occurred within the necessary context.[10] For example, the act of denouncing a Jewish neighbour to the Nazi authorities—if committed against a background of widespread persecution—has been regarded as amounting to a crime against humanity. An isolated act, however—i.e. an atrocity which did not occur within such a context—cannot.

5. The Policy Element

551. With regard to the "form of governmental, organisational or group policy" which is to direct the acts in question, the Trial Chamber has noted that although the concept of crimes against humanity necessarily implies a policy element, there is some doubt as to whether it is strictly a requirement, as such, for crimes against humanity. In any case, it appears that such a policy need not be explicitly formulated, nor need it be the policy of a *State*.[11] . . .

---

10. [Court's footnote 809:] On this point, the Trial Chamber in *Tadić* has held that "[c]learly, a single act by a perpetrator taken within the context of a widespread or systematic attack against a civilian population entails individual criminal responsibility and an individual perpetrator need not commit numerous offences to be held liable. Although it is correct that isolated, random acts should not be included in the definition of crimes against humanity, that is the purpose of requiring that the acts be directed against a civilian population and thus "[e]ven an isolated act can constitute a crime against humanity if it is the product of a political system based on terror or persecution" (*Tadić*, Trial Chamber Judgement, 7 May 1997, para. 649, footnotes omitted).

11. [Court's footnote 811:] *Tadić*, Trial Chamber Judgement, 7 May 1997, at para. 653, where the Trial Chamber noted that "[t]he reason that crimes against humanity so shock the conscience of mankind and warrant intervention by the international community is because they are not isolated, random acts of individuals but rather result from a deliberate attempt to target a civilian population." It went on to explain that although traditionally this requirement was understood to mean that there must be some form of State policy to commit these acts occurred during this period, this was no longer the case (ibid., at para. 654). See also *Prosecutor v. Nikolic*, Rule 61 decision, at para. 26: "Although they [the crimes in question] need not be related to a policy established at State level, in the conventional sense of the term, they cannot be the work of isolated individuals alone."

6. Knowledge of the Context Within Which the Perpetrator's Actions Are Taken: The Mens Rea Requirement

556. The determination of the elements comprising the *mens rea* of crimes against humanity has proved particularly difficult and controversial. Nevertheless, the requisite *mens rea* for crimes against humanity appears to be comprised by (1) the *intent* to commit the underlying offence, combined with (2) *knowledge* of the broader context in which that offence occurs.

557. With regard to the latter requirement (knowledge), the ICTR in *Prosecutor v. Kayishema* noted as follows:

> [t]he perpetrator must knowingly commit crimes against humanity in the sense that he must understand the overall context of his act. [] Part of what transforms an individual's act(s) into a crime against humanity is the inclusion of the act within a greater dimension of criminal conduct; therefore an accused should be aware of this greater dimension in order to be culpable thereof. Accordingly, actual or constructive knowledge of the broader context of the attack, meaning that the accused must know that his act(s) is part of a widespread or systematic attack on a civilian population and pursuant to some sort of policy or plan, is necessary to satisfy the requisite *mens rea* element of the accused.

558. Two aspects of the subjective requirement of crimes against humanity are now free from dispute. Subsequent to the Appeals Chamber's decision in *Prosecutor v. Tadić*, crimes against humanity need be committed with a discriminatory intent only with regard to the category of "persecutions" under Article 5(h); i.e. the sole category in which discrimination comprises an integral element of the prohibited conduct. Otherwise, a discriminatory animus is not an essential ingredient of the *mens rea* of crimes against humanity. Nor are the *motives* (as distinct from the *intent*) of the accused, as such, of special pertinence. . . .

C. PERSECUTION AS A CRIME AGAINST HUMANITY . . .

2. The Actus Reus of Persecution . . .
(d) Can Persecution Cover Acts Not Envisaged in One of the Other Subheadings of Article 5?

608. The Prosecution argues that persecution can also involve acts other than those listed under Article 5. It is their submission that the meaning of "persecutory act" should be given a broad definition and includes a wide variety of acts not enumerated elsewhere in the Statute. By contrast, the Defence submits that the two basic elements of persecution are (a) the occurrence of a persecutory act or omission, and (b) a discriminatory basis for that act or omission on one of the listed grounds. As mentioned above, the Defence argues that persecution should be narrowly construed.

609. The Trial Chamber is thus called upon to examine what acts not covered by Article 5 of the Statute of the International Tribunal may be included in the notion of persecution. Plainly, the Trial Chamber must set out a clear-cut notion of persecution, in order to decide whether the crimes charged in this case fall within its ambit. In addition, this notion must be consistent with general principles of criminal law such as the principles of legality and specificity. First, the Trial Chamber will examine what types of acts, aside from the other categories of crimes against humanity have been deemed to constitute persecution. Secondly, it will examine whether there are elements underlying these acts which assist in defining persecution.

610. The Judgement of the IMT [the Nuremberg Tribunal] included in the notion of persecution a variety of acts which, at present, may not fall under the Statute of

the International Tribunal, such as the passing of discriminatory laws, the exclusion of members of an ethnic or religious group from aspects of social, political, and economic life, the imposition of a collective fine on them, the restriction of their movement and their seclusion in ghettos, and the requirement that they mark themselves out by wearing a yellow star. Moreover, and as mentioned above, several individual defendants were convicted of persecution in the form of discriminatory economic acts.

611. It is also clear that other courts have used the term *persecution* to describe acts other than those enumerated in Article 5. A prominent example is the trial of *Josef Altstötter et al.* (the *Justice* Trial). Altstötter and the other accused were former German Judges, Prosecutors or officials of the Reich Ministry of Justice. They were charged with a common design, conspiracy, plan and enterprise which "embraced the use of the judicial process as a powerful weapon for the persecution and extermination of all opponents of the Nazi regime regardless of nationality and for the persecution and extermination of races."

612. The U.S. Military Tribunal in the *Justice* case held that the national pattern or plan for racial persecution was one of actual extermination of Jewish and Polish people, but that "lesser forms of racial persecution were universally practiced by governmental authority and constituted an integral part in the general policy of the Reich." These lesser forms of persecution included the passing of a decree by which Jews were excluded from the legal profession; the prohibition of intermarriage between Jews and persons of German blood and the severe punishment of sexual intercourse between these groups; and decrees expelling Jews from public services, educational institutions, and from many business enterprises. Furthermore, upon the death of a Jew his property was confiscated, and under an amendment to the German Citizenship Law, the Security Police and the SD could also confiscate property of Jews who were alive. Jews were subject to more severe punishments than Germans; the rights of defendants in court were severely circumscribed; courts were empowered to impose death sentences on Poles and Jews even if not prescribed by law; and the police were given *carte blanche* in the punishment of Jews without resort to the judicial process. In summary, what was considered to be persecution in the *Justice* case was the use of a legal system to implement a discriminatory policy.

613. . . . Also, Artukovic was found guilty of acts such as the passing and implementation of discriminatory decrees ranging from Decrees on racial identity and the protection of Aryan blood or the honour of the Croatian people to the Decree on deporting unsuitable and dangerous individuals to internment and labour camps.

614. The Trial Chamber is thus bolstered in its conclusion that persecution can consist of the deprivation of a wide variety of rights. A persecutory act need not be prohibited explicitly either in Article 5 or elsewhere in the Statute. Similarly, whether or not such acts are legal under national laws is irrelevant. It is well-known that the Nazis passed many discriminatory laws through the available constitutional and legislative channels which were subsequently enforced by their judiciary. This does not detract from the fact that these laws were contrary to international legal standards. The Trial Chamber therefore rejects the Defence submission that persecution should not include acts which are legal under national laws.

615. In short, the Trial Chamber is able to conclude the following on the *actus reus* of persecution from the case-law above:

(a) A narrow definition of persecution is not supported in customary international law. Persecution has been described by courts as a wide and particularly serious *genus* of crimes committed against the Jewish people and other groups by the Nazi regime.

(b) In their interpretation of persecution courts have included acts such as murder, extermination, torture, and other serious acts on the person such as those presently enumerated in Article 5.

(c) Persecution can also involve a variety of other discriminatory acts, involving attacks on political, social, and economic rights. The scope of these acts will be defined more precisely by the Trial Chamber below.

(d) Persecution is commonly used to describe a series of acts rather than a single act. Acts of persecution will usually form part of a policy or at least of a patterned practice, and must be regarded in their context. In reality, persecutory acts are often committed pursuant to a discriminatory policy or a widespread discriminatory practice, as was found by the Zagreb District Court in *Artukovic*.

(e) As a corollary to (d), discriminatory acts charged as persecution must not be considered in isolation. Some of the acts mentioned above may not, in and of themselves, be so serious as to constitute a crime against humanity. For example, restrictions placed on a particular group to curtail their rights to participate in particular aspects of social life (such as visits to public parks, theatres or libraries) constitute discrimination, which is in itself a reprehensible act; however, they may not in and of themselves amount to persecution. These acts must not be considered in isolation but examined in their context and weighed for their cumulative effect.

3. The Definition of Persecution

616. In the Judgement of *Prosecutor v. Tadić*, Trial Chamber II held that persecution is a form of discrimination on grounds of race, religion or political opinion that is intended to be, and results in, an infringement of an individual's fundamental rights. It is not necessary to have a separate act of an inhumane nature to constitute persecution, but rather, the discrimination itself makes the act inhumane. The Trial Chamber held that the crime of persecution encompasses a wide variety of acts, including, inter alia, those of a physical, economic, or judicial nature that violate an individual's basic or fundamental rights. The discrimination must be on one of the listed grounds to constitute persecution.

617. As mentioned above, this is a broad definition which could include acts prohibited under other subheadings of Article 5, acts prohibited under other Articles of the Statute, and acts not covered by the Statute. The same approach has been taken in Article 7(2)(g) of the ICC Statute, which states that "[p]ersecution means the intentional and severe deprivation of *fundamental rights* contrary to international law by reason of the identity of the group or collectivity" (emphasis added).

618. However, this Trial Chamber holds the view that in order for persecution to amount to a crime against humanity it is not enough to define a core assortment of acts and to leave peripheral acts in a state of uncertainty. There must be *clearly defined limits* on the types of acts which qualify as persecution. Although the realm of human rights is dynamic and expansive, not every denial of a human right may constitute a crime against humanity.

619. Accordingly, it can be said that at a minimum, acts of persecution must be of an equal gravity or severity to the other acts enumerated under Article 5. This legal criterion has already been resorted to, for instance, in the *Flick* case.

620. It ought to be emphasised, however, that if the analysis based on this criterion relates only to the *level of seriousness* of the act, it does not provide guidance on *what types of acts* can constitute persecution. The *ejusdem generis* criterion can be used as a

supplementary tool, to establish whether certain acts which generally speaking fall under the proscriptions of Article 5(h), reach the *level of gravity* required by this provision. The only conclusion to be drawn from its application is that only *gross or blatant denials* of fundamental human rights can constitute crimes against humanity.

621. The Trial Chamber, drawing upon its earlier discussion of "other inhumane acts," holds that in order to identify those rights whose infringement may constitute persecution, more defined parameters for the definition of human dignity can be found in international standards on human rights such as those laid down in the Universal Declaration on Human Rights of 1948, the two United Nations Covenants on Human Rights of 1966 and other international instruments on human rights or on humanitarian law. Drawing upon the various provisions of these texts it proves possible to *identify a set of fundamental rights appertaining to any human being, the gross infringement of which may amount, depending on the surrounding circumstances, to a crime against humanity*. Persecution consists of a severe attack on those rights, and aims to exclude a person from society on discriminatory grounds. The Trial Chamber therefore defines persecution as *the gross or blatant denial, on discriminatory grounds, of a fundamental right, laid down in international customary or treaty law, reaching the same level of gravity as the other acts prohibited in Article 5*.

622. In determining whether particular acts constitute persecution, the Trial Chamber wishes to reiterate that acts of persecution must be evaluated not in isolation but in context, by looking at their cumulative effect. Although individual acts may not be inhumane, their overall consequences must offend humanity in such a way that they may be termed "inhumane." This delimitation also suffices to satisfy the principle of legality, as inhumane acts are clearly proscribed by the Statute.

623. The Trial Chamber does not see fit to identify which rights constitute fundamental rights for the purposes of persecution. The interests of justice would not be served by so doing, as the explicit inclusion of particular fundamental rights could be interpreted as the implicit exclusion of other rights (*expressio unius est exclusio alterius*). This is not the approach taken to crimes against humanity in customary international law, where the category of "other inhumane acts" also allows courts flexibility to determine the cases before them, depending on the forms which attacks on humanity may take, forms which are ever-changing and carried out with particular ingenuity. Each case must therefore be examined on its merits.

624. In its earlier conclusions the Trial Chamber noted that persecution was often used to describe a series of acts. However, the Trial Chamber does not exclude the possibility that a single act may constitute persecution. In such a case, there must be clear evidence of the discriminatory intent. For example, in the former Yugoslavia an individual may have participated in the single murder of a Muslim person. If his intent clearly was to kill him because he was a Muslim, and this occurred as part of a wide or systematic persecutory attack against a civilian population, this single murder may constitute persecution. But the discriminatory intent of the perpetrator must be proved for this crime to qualify as persecution.

625. Although acts of persecution are often part of a discriminatory policy, the Trial Chamber finds that it is not necessary to demonstrate that an accused has taken part in the formulation of a discriminatory policy or practice by a governmental authority. . . .

626. The Trial Chamber observes that in the light of its broad definition of persecution, the Prosecution cannot merely rely on a general charge of "persecution" in bringing its case. This would be inconsistent with the concept of legality. To observe the principle of legality, the Prosecution must charge particular acts (and this seems

to have been done in this case). These acts should be charged in sufficient detail for the accused to be able to fully prepare their defence.

627. In sum, a charge of persecution must contain the following elements:

(a) those elements required for all crimes against humanity under the Statute;
(b) a gross or blatant denial of a fundamental right reaching the same level of gravity as the other acts prohibited under Article 5;
(c) discriminatory grounds.

4. The Application of the Definition Set Out Above to the Instant Case

628. The Trial Chamber will now examine the specific allegations in this case, which are the "deliberate and systematic killing of Bosnian Muslim civilians," the "organised detention and expulsion of the Bosnian Muslims from Ahmići-Šantici and its environs," and the "comprehensive destruction of Bosnian homes and property." Can these acts constitute persecution?

629. In light of the conclusions above, the Trial Chamber finds that the "deliberate and systematic killing of Bosnian Muslim civilians" as well as their "organised detention and expulsion from Ahmići" can constitute persecution. This is because these acts qualify as murder, imprisonment, and deportation, which are explicitly mentioned in the Statute under Article 5.

630. The Trial Chamber next turns its attention to the alleged comprehensive destruction of Bosnian Muslim homes and property. The question here is whether certain property or economic rights can be considered so fundamental that their denial is capable of constituting persecution. The Trial Chamber notes that in the Judgement of the IMT, several defendants were convicted of economic discrimination. For example, Göring "persecuted the Jews . . . and not only in Germany where he raised the billion mark fine . . . this interest was primarily economic — how to get their property and how to force them out of economic life in Europe." Defendants Funk and Seyss-Inquart were also charged with acts of economic discrimination.

631. The Trial Chamber finds that attacks on property can constitute persecution. To some extent this may depend on the type of property involved: in the passage from *Flick* cited above the Tribunal held that the compulsory taking of industrial property could not be said to affect the life and liberty of oppressed peoples and therefore did not constitute persecution. There may be certain types of property whose destruction may not have a severe enough impact on the victim as to constitute a crime against humanity, even if such a destruction is perpetrated on discriminatory grounds: an example is the burning of someone's car (unless the car constitutes an indispensable and vital asset to the owner). However, the case at hand concerns the comprehensive destruction of homes and property. Such an attack on property in fact constitutes a destruction of the livelihood of a certain population. This may have the same inhumane consequences as a forced transfer or deportation. Moreover, the burning of a residential property may often be committed with a recklessness towards the lives of its inhabitants. The Trial Chamber therefore concludes that this act may constitute a gross or blatant denial of fundamental human rights, and, if committed on discriminatory grounds, it may constitute persecution.

5. The Mens Rea of Persecution

632. The Trial Chamber will now discuss the *mens rea* requirement of persecution as reflected in international case-law.

633. Both parties agree that the mental element of persecution consists of *discriminatory intent on the grounds provided in the Statute*. Nevertheless, the Trial Chamber will elaborate further on the discriminatory intent required.

634. When examining some of the examples of persecution mentioned above, one can discern a common element: those acts were all aimed at singling out and attacking certain individuals on discriminatory grounds, by depriving them of the political, social, or economic rights enjoyed by members of the wider society. The deprivation of these rights can be said to have as its aim the removal of those persons from the society in which they live alongside the perpetrators, or eventually even from humanity itself.

635. The grounds on which the perpetrator of persecution may discriminate are listed in Article 5(h) of the Statute as political, racial or religious grounds.

636. As set forth above, the *mens rea* requirement for persecution is higher than for ordinary crimes against humanity, although lower than for genocide. In this context the Trial Chamber wishes to stress that persecution as a crime against humanity is an offence belonging to the same *genus* as genocide. Both persecution and genocide are crimes perpetrated against persons that belong to a particular group and who are targeted because of such belonging. In both categories what matters is the intent to discriminate: to attack persons on account of their ethnic, racial, or religious characteristics (as well as, in the case of persecution, on account of their political affiliation). While in the case of persecution the discriminatory intent can take multifarious inhumane forms and manifest itself in a plurality of actions including murder, in the case of genocide that intent must be accompanied by the intention to destroy, in whole or in part, the group to which the victims of the genocide belong. Thus, it can be said that, from the viewpoint of *mens rea*, genocide is an extreme and most inhuman form of persecution. To put it differently, when persecution escalates to the extreme form of wilful and deliberate acts designed to destroy a group or part of a group, it can be held that such persecution amounts to genocide. . . .

NOTES AND QUESTIONS

1. The Trial Chamber acquitted the Kupreškić brothers and cousin on all counts except Count 1 because of insufficient evidence that they were present at the house of Witness KL. On Count 1, they were sentenced to terms ranging between six and ten years. The Appeals Chamber subsequently reversed their conviction on the remaining count because their identification was established solely on the basis of testimony by a single eyewitness, a 13-year-old girl, testifying five years later. The Appeals Chamber deemed her testimony insufficient because the attack took place in the middle of the night, she had been asleep when it began, the assailants had their faces heavily painted, and she had subsequently been exposed to a great deal of speculation in the family circle about the identities of the assailants that might have influenced her recollections. Given the conditions under which crimes against humanity are committed and the inevitable lengthy delays until they can be prosecuted, does this set the evidentiary bar too high? Or is a high bar crucial to prevent wrongful convictions?

2. In paragraph 543, the Trial Chamber quotes a previous decision establishing elements of crimes against humanity. How do these elements differ from those in the statute? The previous decision found that crimes against humanity consist of acts "directed at a civilian population, specifically identified as a group by the perpetrators of those acts." Did this formulation import an additional and burdensome *mens rea* element into the definition of the crimes?

3. In paragraph 618, the Trial Chamber cautions that "in order for persecution to amount to a crime against humanity it is not enough to define a core assortment of acts and to leave peripheral acts in a state of uncertainty. There must be *clearly defined limits* on the types of acts which qualify as persecution." Does the test the Chamber sets out in paragraph 621 meet this criterion?

PROSECUTOR v. MUSEMA

Case No. IT-96-13-A, Judgment and Sentence, Trial Chamber (Jan. 27, 2000)

... 1.4 THE ACCUSED ...

[At the time of the 1994 genocide, Alfred Musema-Uwimana was a 45-year-old, educated executive of the Gisovu tea factory as well as] a member of the "conseil préfectorial" in Byumba Préfecture and a member of the Technical Committee in the Butare Commune. Both positions of responsibility involved socio-economic and developmental matters and did not focus on préfectorial politics. . . .

3.3 CRIME AGAINST HUMANITY (ARTICLE 3 OF THE STATUTE) ...

(D) THE ENUMERATED ACTS ...

213. The Chamber notes that with respect to crimes against humanity, Musema is indicted for [the crimes against humanity of] murder, extermination, rape and other inhumane acts. . . .

Extermination

217. Pursuant to Article 3(c) of the Statute, extermination constitutes a crime against humanity. By its very nature, extermination is a crime which is directed against a group of individuals. Extermination differs from murder in that it requires an element of mass destruction, which is not a prerequisite for murder.

218. In both the *Akayesu* and *Rutaganda* Judgements, the elements of extermination were defined as follows:

(a) the Accused or his subordinate participated in the killing of certain named or described persons;
(b) the act or omission was unlawful and intentional;
(c) the unlawful act or omission must be part of a widespread or systematic attack;
(d) the attack must be against the civilian population;
(e) the attack must be on discriminatory grounds, namely: national, political, ethnic, racial, or religious grounds.[12]

219. The *Rutaganda* Judgement further held that the act or omission that constitutes extermination must be discriminatory in nature and directed against members of the civilian population. Further, this act or omission includes, but is not limited to, the direct act of killing. It can be any act or omission, or cumulative acts or omissions that cause the death of the targeted group of individuals.

---

12. Compare the ICTY and ICTR Statutes with respect to this element of a Crime Against Humanity. — EDS.

Rape

220. Rape may constitute a crime against humanity, pursuant to Article 3(g) of the Statute. In the *Akayesu* Judgement, rape as a crime against humanity was defined as:

> "[. . .] a physical invasion of a sexual nature, committed on a person under circumstances which are coercive. Sexual violence, which includes rape, is considered to be any act of a sexual nature which is committed on a person under circumstances which are coercive. This act must be committed:
>
>   (a) as part of a widespread or systematic attack;
>
>   (b) on a civilian population;
>
>   (c) on certain catalogued discriminatory grounds, namely: national, ethnic, political, racial, or religious grounds."

221. The Chamber notes that, while rape has been defined in certain national jurisdictions as non-consensual intercourse, variations on the acts of rape may include acts which involve the insertions of objects and/or the use of bodily orifices not considered to be intrinsically sexual.

222. The Chamber also observes that in defining rape, as a crime against humanity, the Trial Chamber in the *Akayesu* Judgement acknowledged:

> "that rape is a form of aggression and that the central elements of the crime of rape cannot be captured in a mechanical description of objects and body parts. The Convention against Torture and Other Cruel, Inhuman and Degrading Treatment or Punishment does not catalogue specific acts in its definition of torture, focussing rather on the conceptual framework of state sanctioned violence. This approach is more useful in international law. Like torture, rape is used for such purposes as intimidation, degradation, humiliation, discrimination, punishment, control or destruction of a person. Like torture, rape is a violation of personal dignity, and rape in fact constitutes torture when inflicted by or at the instigation of or with the consent or acquiescence of a public official or other person acting in an official capacity."

. . . 224. The Chamber has considered the alternative definition of rape set forth by Trial Chamber I of the ICTY in its *Furundžija* Judgement, which relies on a detailed description of objects and body parts. In this judgement the Trial Chamber looked to national legislation. . . .

225. The *Furundžija* Judgement further noted that "most legal systems in the common and civil law worlds consider rape to be the forcible sexual penetration of the human body by the penis or the forcible insertion of any other object into either the vagina or the anus." Nevertheless, after due consideration of the practice of forced oral penetration, which is treated as rape in some States and sexual assault in other States, the Trial Chamber in that case determined as follows:

> "183. The Trial Chamber holds that the forced penetration of the mouth by the male sexual organ constitutes a most humiliating and degrading attack upon human dignity. . . . It is consonant with this principle that such an extremely serious sexual outrage as forced oral penetration should be classified as rape."

226. The Chamber concurs with the conceptual approach set forth in the *Akayesu* Judgement for the definition of rape, which recognizes that the essence of rape is not the particular details of the body parts and objects involved, but rather the aggression that is expressed in a sexual manner under conditions of coercion.

227. The Chamber considers that the distinction between rape and other forms of sexual violence drawn by the *Akayesu* Judgement, that is "a physical invasion of a

sexual nature" as contrasted with "any act of a sexual nature" which is committed on a person under circumstances which are coercive is clear and establishes a framework for judicial consideration of individual incidents of sexual violence and a determination, on a case by case basis, of whether such incidents constitute rape. The definition of rape, as set forth in the *Akayesu* Judgement, clearly encompasses all the conduct described in the definition of rape set forth in *Furundžija*. . . .

229. For these reasons, the Chamber adopts the definition of rape and sexual violence set forth in the *Akayesu* Judgement.

Other Inhumane Acts

230. The Chamber notes that Article 3 of the Statute provides a list of eight enumerated acts that may constitute crimes against humanity. . . .

231. The Chamber notes that the ICC Statute provides that:

"Other inhumane acts [are acts] of a similar character [to the other specified enumerated acts] intentionally causing great suffering, or serious injury to body or to mental or physical health."

232. The Chamber finds that an act or omission will fall within the ambit of "Other inhumane Acts," as envisaged in Article 3(i) of the Statute, provided the nature and character of such act or omission is similar in nature, character, gravity and seriousness to the other acts, as enumerated in sub-articles (a) to (h) of Article 3. Further, the inhumane act or omission must:

(a) Be directed against member(s) of the civilian population;
(b) The perpetrator must have discriminated against the victim(s), on one or more of the enumerated discriminatory grounds;
(c) The perpetrator's act or omission must form part of a widespread or systematic attack and the perpetrator must have knowledge of this attack.

233. The Chamber agrees that the perpetrator's act(s) must be assessed "on a case-by-case basis," with a view to establishing whether such act(s) fall within the ambit of "Other inhumane Acts," as envisaged in Article 3 of the Statute. . . .

6.3 Legal Findings — Count 5: Crime Against Humanity (Extermination)

942. *Count 5* of the Indictment charges Musema with *crime against humanity (extermination)*, pursuant to Articles 3(b), 6(1) and 6(3) of the Statute. . . .

945. The Chamber has found, beyond a reasonable doubt that Musema:

- was armed with a rifle and that he ordered, aided and abetted and participated in the commission of attacks on Tutsi civilians who had sought refuge on Muyira hill on 13 and 14 May 1994, and in mid-May 1994. The Accused was one of the leaders of the attacks and some of the attackers were employees of the Gisovu Tea Factory who had traveled to Muyira hill in motor vehicles belonging to the Gisovu Tea Factory;
- participated in an attack on Tutsi civilians, who had sought refuge on Mumataba hill in mid-May 1994. Some of the attackers were tea factory employees who were transported to Mumataba hill in motor vehicles belonging to Gisovu Tea Factory. The Accused was present through out the attack and left with the attackers;

- participated in an attack on Tutsi civilians who had sought refuge in the Nyaka-vumu cave;
- participated in an attack on Tutsi civilians who had sought refuge on Gitwa hill on 26 April 1994; and
- participated in an attack on Tutsi civilians between 27 April and 3 May 1994 in Rwirambo.

946. The Chamber finds that in 1994, the Accused had knowledge of a widespread or systematic attack that was directed against the civilian population in Rwanda. This finding is supported by the presence of Musema at attacks in different locations in Kibuye *Préfecture*, as found above, by the testimony of the Accused, and by Defence exhibits. [The Chamber also cites several statements by Musema indicating knowledge of what was transpiring in Rwanda.]

948. The Chamber finds that, Musema's criminal conduct was consistent with the pattern of the then ongoing widespread or systematic attack on the civilian population and his conduct formed a part of this attack.

949. The Chamber finds, that Musema's conduct: in ordering and participating in the attacks on Tutsi civilians who had sought refuge on Muyira hill and on Mumataba hill; in aiding and abetting in the aforementioned attacks by providing motor vehicles belonging to Gisovu Tea Factory, for the transport of attackers to Muyira hill and Mumataba hill; and in his participation in attacks on Tutsi civilians who had sought refuge in Nyakavumu cave, Gitwa hill and Rwirambo, renders the Accused individually criminally responsible, pursuant to Article 6(1) of the Statute.

950. The Chamber has already found that there existed at the time of the events alleged in the indictment a *de jure* superior-subordinate relationship between Musema and the employees at the Gisovu Tea Factory. The Chamber also found that the Accused had the authority to take reasonable measures to prevent the use of Tea Factory vehicles, uniforms or other Tea Factory property in the commission of the attacks. The Chamber finds that the Accused, despite his knowledge of the participation of Gisovu Tea Factory employees in these attacks and their use of Tea Factory property in the commission of these attacks, failed to take any reasonable measures to prevent or punish such participation or such use of Tea Factory property.

951. The Chamber therefore finds beyond a reasonable doubt that Musema is individually criminally responsible for crime against humanity (extermination), pursuant to Articles 3(b), 6(1) and 6(3) of the Statute, as charged in Count 5 of the Indictment. . . .

6.6 COUNT 7: CRIME AGAINST HUMANITY (RAPE)

962. *Count 7* of the Indictment charges Musema with *crime against humanity (rape)*, pursuant to Articles 3(g), 6(1) and 6(3) of the Statute, for the acts alleged in paragraphs 4.1 to 4.11 of the Indictment.

963. In light of its factual findings with regard to the allegations in paragraph 4.10 of the Indictment, the Chamber considers the criminal responsibility of the Accused, pursuant to Articles 6(1) and 6(3) of the Statute. . . .

966. The Chamber has made the factual finding that on 13 May 1994 the Accused raped a Tutsi woman called Nyiramusugi. The Chamber recalls its finding in Section 6.3 supra, that the Accused had knowledge of a widespread or systematic attack on the

civilian population. The Chamber finds that the rape of Nyiramusugi by the Accused was consistent with the pattern of this attack and formed a part of this attack.

967. The Chamber therefore finds, that Musema is individually criminally responsible for crime against humanity (rape), pursuant to Articles 3(g) and (6)(1) of the Statute.

968. However, the Chamber finds, that the Prosecutor has failed to prove beyond a reasonable doubt any act of rape that had been committed by Musema's subordinates and that Musema knew or had reason to know of this act and he failed to take reasonable measures to prevent the said act or to punish the perpetrators thereof, following the commission of such act. The Prosecutor has therefore not proved beyond a reasonable the individual criminal responsibility of Musema, pursuant to Articles 3(g) and 6(3) of the Statute, as charged in Count 7 of the Indictment. . . .

NOTES AND QUESTIONS

1. The discussion of the crime of rape in international law arose because some states' domestic laws define rape narrowly, to include only penile penetration. For further discussion, see Chapter 23, on crimes of sexual violence.

2. Notice that paragraph 950 finds that Musema, a civilian executive of a tea company, had a *de jure* superior-subordinate relationship with his employees. Therefore, in paragraph 951, the Tribunal finds him individually culpable under, among other articles of the statute, Article 6(3): "The fact that any of the acts . . . was committed by a subordinate does not relieve his or her superior of criminal responsibility if he or she knew or had reason to know that the subordinate was about to commit such acts or had done so and the superior failed to take the necessary and reasonable measures to prevent such acts or to punish the perpetrators thereof." Is this correct? Suppose you know that one of your employees is about to commit a crime of violence, and you fail to take necessary and reasonable measures to stop the employee. Why, as a matter of law, should you be held individually liable for your employee's crime? Should it matter that the criminal act was neither actually nor apparently in the course of the employee's duty?

3. If the operative law were the Rome Statute, would Musema be guilty of crimes against humanity? How would the prosecutor demonstrate that the Rwandan genocide was "pursuant to or in furtherance of a State or organizational policy"? Would the conviction of high government officials be proof enough? Would it matter whether Musema knew that high government officials had formulated planned widespread attacks on the Tutsi population?

D.   CONCEPTUALIZING CRIMES AGAINST HUMANITY

We conclude this chapter with two theoretical excerpts aiming to explain what the "big idea" is behind the category of crimes against humanity: the specific evil against which this body of law is directed. These are not meant to be definitive, only suggestive. As you read, ask how well these theories fit the law and whether the theories seem to offer a satisfying way of tying together the various statutes we have studied.

RICHARD VERNON, WHAT IS CRIME AGAINST HUMANITY?

10 J. Pol. Phil. 231, 241-246 (2002)

Assuming that we take crimes against humanity to be evil, what is distinctive about the kind of evil they embody? In particular, how is the kind of evil that they embody different from other kinds of evil—such as abuses of human rights—that may also justify incursions into state sovereignty? What part is played by the "common plan" criterion (the requirement that abuse be systematic) and why does this magnify or else render unique the wrongness involved? What part, if any, is played by consideration about the scale of atrocity? . . . I want to argue . . . that we can give plausible answers to these questions if we think about crime against humanity as an abuse of state power involving a systematic inversion of the jurisdictional resources of the state.

It makes sense to begin with the lawyers' view, formalistic though it may seem, that the idea of crime against humanity involves a derogation from national sovereignty. States have, after all, claimed to be the unique definers and punishers of crime, and their power is based upon the extinction of local, communal, traditional, vigilante or vendetta modes of bringing justice and their replacement by the idea of "public wrongs." Consequently, it has become part of the very idea of crime that it is a three-party relation; while the victim suffers it, the relation between victim and offender is mediated by the "state" or "Crown" or "People," that is, a sovereign entity regarded as the author of law and against whom the crime is deemed to be an offense. A *crime* is something more than damage to a victim.

. . . Behind the very idea of a crime against humanity, therefore, there is an implied mental scheme of an abstract kind—a scheme implied by the belief that the sovereignty of states is morally conditional, and is suspended and superseded by events of a certain kind. . . .

. . . The crime against humanity model can move forward here by appealing, in the first instance, not to contestable normative theories about human rights, but to considerations about the nature of state power as an empirical matter. For there is a particular complex of events, reflecting three central features of state power, that undermines legitimacy in an especially radical way.

The first two of these features are large-scale administrative capacity and local authority. Both are features of the clearest cases of crime against humanity, which, at a minimum, require powerful mechanisms of collective action and the habits of obedience that sustain them, and an institution regarded as entitled to make binding declarations of rightness and wrongness. . . . To these two features we must add another, as their necessary precondition. State power is territorial, and so may be used to immobilize a group and also to deny it external help—to attack it while denying it hope of the desperate last recourse of either flight or protection, so that its resources can be brought to bear against it in an unimpeded way. Administrative capacity, local authority and territoriality come into being with the creation of states: when, therefore, they play an essential role in an attack on a group of a state's subjects, that group is absolutely worse off than it could be in the worst-case scenario of statelessness. This applies, it should be noted, only in the case of groups of a substantial size: what was done to the whole population of East Timor could not have been done if there were no Indonesian state, but individuals or smaller groups could be (and are) physically attacked, humiliated, and immobilized by informal structures of power. . . .

With this in mind, some of the questions noted at the beginning of this section can be approached. The idea of crime against humanity *does* have a distinct logic, based on an elaboration of the features of the modern state: it depends upon the model of a three-part relation which is characteristic of the rule of law, and draws upon the notions of territoriality, authority and monopoly of force. Out of these elements it constructs the outline of a particular kind of evil, one that consists in a systematic inversion: powers that justify the state are, perversely, instrumentalized by it, territoriality is transformed from a refuge to a trap, and the modalities of punishment are brought to bear upon the guiltless. When this complex is brought together, it is entirely natural to the moral imagination to suppose that the power to judge and to criminalize must migrate elsewhere.

The kind of evil in question is also distinguished, by this model, from violations of human rights. Human rights violations are individuated. What are termed "gross" human rights violations are additive; and they do pose the quantitative question of how many are acceptable before a response is called for. But crime against humanity is not an additive concept. It relates on the one hand to the necessary institutional prerequisites of an organized project, and on the other to damage suffered by individuals only by virtue of belonging to a group. Of course, from the victim's perspective neither of these considerations can be crucial; damage is damage, whatever its organizational prerequisites and whether or not it is group-based. But the whole argument developed above . . . requires a non-victim-based perspective in order to make sense of the three-party nature of crime.

Perhaps most clearly, the model makes sense of the "common plan" criterion. . . . In fact, the "common plan" requirement is virtually identical to the requirement of state initiative. . . .

But in particular, the model outlined here may help to deal with the troubling question of the scale of atrocity. Here intuitions tend, awkwardly, in different directions. On the one hand, we can hardly close our minds to questions of scale altogether . . . [:] the greatness of the evil owes something to its extent. So from this point of view numbers seem to count. . . . On the other hand, of course, moral sense rebels at the thought that numbers count in this way: that the Holocaust would have been *less of a crime* if only (say) three million had been killed, or that we might tell whether the Holocaust or Stalin's reign of terror was worse by simply counting bodies, or whether *enough* Kosovars were killed to make NATO's action against Serbia justifiable — inviting the cruel and absurd question, how many would have been enough? The view developed above suggests why numbers matter and also why they do not, as such, count. A crime against humanity is one that requires the application of a state's resources — the capacity to apply violence on a large scale, and the control of territory; and it also requires a target group substantial enough to have developed expectations of common survival. Numbers matter, then, as an indicator of something else, that is, of whether state power is essential, in these two ways, to the events in question. But above this (variable) threshold, questions of number (proportion, speed, etc.) have no weight at all, as far as the idea is concerned, given its non-additive nature. . . .

DAVID LUBAN, A THEORY OF CRIMES AGAINST HUMANITY
29 Yale J. Intl. L. 85, 86-91, 111-113, 117-119 (2004)

The phrase "crimes against humanity" has acquired enormous resonance in the legal and moral imaginations of the post-World War II world. It suggests, in at least two distinct ways, the enormity of these offenses. First, the phrase "crimes against humanity" suggests offenses that aggrieve not only the victims and their own communities, but all human beings, regardless of their community. Second, the phrase suggests that these offenses cut deep, violating the core humanity that we all share and that distinguishes us from other natural beings.

This double meaning gives the phrase potency, but also ambiguity — an ambiguity we may trace back to the double meaning of the word "humanity." "Humanity" means both the quality of being human — humanness — and the aggregation of all human beings — humankind. Taken in the former sense, "crimes against humanity" suggests that the defining feature of these offenses is the value they injure, namely humanness. The law traditionally distinguishes between crimes against persons, crimes against property, crimes against public order, crimes against morals, and the like. Here, the idea is to supplement the traditional taxonomy of legally protected values — property, persons, public order, morals — by adding that some offenses are crimes against humanness as such.

The terminology chosen by the framers of the Nuremberg Charter suggests that they were thinking of crimes against humanity in this sense. In Article 6, which enumerates the crimes under the Tribunal's jurisdiction, we find the traditional category of war crimes supplemented by two new categories: crimes against peace and crimes against humanity. The parallel wording suggests that crimes against humanity offend against humanity in the same way that crimes against peace offend against peace. If this parallelism holds, then "humanity" denotes the value that the crimes violate, just as "peace" denotes the value that wars of aggression and wars in violation of treaties assault. . . .

Taken in the latter sense, "humanity" refers to humankind — the set of individuals — not humanness. Under this interpretation, "crimes against humanity" suggests that the defining feature of these offenses is the party in interest. In law, some wrongs — chiefly civil wrongs, like torts — are thought to affect only the victims and their dependents. Other wrongs, inflicted on equally determinate victims, violate important community norms as well, and the community will seek to vindicate those norms independently of the victim. These wrongs are crimes, not torts or other civil breaches, and the community, not just the victims, has a distinct interest in punishment. . . . Viewed along these lines, the term "crimes against humanity" signifies that all humanity is the interested party and that humanity's interest may differ from the interests of the victims.

[For example, Hannah] Arendt quotes Telford Taylor's observation that "a crime is not committed only against the victim, but primarily against the community whose law is violated," a fact that she observes distinguishes crimes from civil wrongs. She then argues:

> The physical extermination of the Jewish people was a crime against humanity, perpetrated upon the body of the Jewish people. . . . Insofar as the victims were Jews, it was right and proper that a Jewish court should sit in judgment; but insofar as the crime was a crime against humanity, it needed an international tribunal to do justice to it.

. . . The central questions for any theory of crimes against humanity are how these deeds violate humanness, and why they offend against all humankind.

Labeling something a crime against humanity may well imply both conclusions, but it is important to realize that violating humanness and offending against humankind are not equivalent. Arguably, all human beings share an interest in suppressing grave acts of environmental destruction — an interest that may well justify making such acts international crimes; but the value that is harmed is not, strictly speaking, human at all. Conversely, an especially sadistic rape or murder might degrade the humanity of its victim without implicating the interests of the entire human race. Crimes against humanity are simultaneously offenses against humankind and injuries to humanness. They are so universally odious that they make the criminal *hostis humani generis* — an enemy of all humankind, like the pirate on the high seas under traditional international law — and they are universally odious because they injure something fundamental to being human in a way that municipal legal systems fail to address. But what is that something?

The answer I offer in this Article is that crimes against humanity assault one particular aspect of human being, namely our character as political animals. We are creatures whose nature compels us to live socially, but who cannot do so without artificial political organization that inevitably poses threats to our well-being, and, at the limit, to our very survival. Crimes against humanity represent the worst of those threats; they are the limiting case of politics gone cancerous. Precisely because we cannot live without politics, we exist under the permanent threat that politics will turn cancerous and the indispensable institutions of organized political life will destroy us. That is why all humankind shares an interest in repressing these crimes. The theory that I aim to defend here consists of two propositions: (i) that "humanity" in the label "crimes against humanity" refers to our nature as political animals, and (ii) that these crimes pose a universal threat that all humankind shares an interest in repressing. . . .

To declare that we are political animals is not meant as a metaphysical speculation. On the contrary, the observation that we are political animals is a wholly naturalistic one, anchored at bottom in common observation and common sense. It begins with the fact that we are just one kind of animal among many in the natural order. Some animals — tigers, bears, and butterflies, for example — lead an essentially solitary existence. They come together to mate, but they do not travel in packs or flocks, and outside the reproductive process they live alone. Others — the ants and the termites — are entirely social. Individual insects removed from the colony quickly die, and indeed they barely count as individuals, except in the arithmetic sense of being numerically distinct from one another. Human beings occupy a mid-point between these extremes. We live in groups, but we are not social animals in the selfless way that ants are social. . . . [U]nlike the bees and termites, human beings are individuals, and each of us recognizes himself or herself as an individual. This fact — call it self-awareness — lies at the basis of what the Universal Declaration of Human Rights calls "the inherent dignity" of each human being.

For us — self-aware individuals with interests of our own, who nevertheless have a natural need to live in groups — sociability has an ambiguous character. It is always at once a necessity and a threat. Kant speaks of mankind's "unsociable sociability," the "propensity to enter into society, bound together with a mutual opposition which constantly threatens to break up the society." "Unsociable sociability" seems like a happy phrase to describe why we are not so much *social* animals as *political* animals. For politics is the art of organizing society so that the "mutual opposition which constantly threatens to break up the society" does not turn our "propensity to enter into society" into a suicide pact. Politics is as much about individual self-assertion against groups as it is about group solidarity. Only individuals with unsociable natures *need* to be bound by political rather than natural bonds, but only individuals whose nature is sociable can be bound by political bonds. Human beings are both, and as I use it, the phrase "political animal" is nothing more than convenient shorthand for recognizing this double nature of ours. To call us political animals underlines a fundamental fact of life: we need to live in groups, but groups pose a perpetual threat to our individuality and individual interests. . . .

Crimes against humanity are committed against groups or populations; they are also committed by groups — by states or state-like organizations. This is another important way in which crimes against humanity may be understood as violations of our nature as political animals. Crimes against humanity are not just horrible crimes; they are horrible political crimes, crimes of politics gone cancerous. The legal category of "crimes against humanity" recognizes the special danger that governments, which are supposed to protect the people who live in their territory, will instead murder them, enslave them, and persecute them, transforming their homeland from a haven into a killing field. As political animals, we have no alternative to living in groups; and groups have no alternative to residing in territories under someone or another's political control. For a state to attack individuals and their groups solely because the groups exist and the individuals belong to them transforms politics from the art of managing our unsociable sociability into a lethal threat. Criminal politics bears the precise relationship to healthy politics that cancer bears to healthy tissue.

. . . To criminalize acts of a government toward groups in its own jurisdiction, and thus to pierce the veil of sovereignty through international criminal law, is tantamount to recognizing that the cancerous, autopolemic[13] character of crimes against humanity represents a perversion of politics, and thus a perversion of the political animal.

To describe autopolemic political violence as a perversion of politics is not uncontroversial; it represents a fundamentally liberal vision of politics. On one longstanding view of politics, violence, massacre, and persecution represent something close to the essence of politics, rather than a perversion of it. Machiavelli aimed to teach princes how not to be good and insisted that a prince is always better off being feared than loved. The historical examples Machiavelli used to illustrate his argument, drawn from classical antiquity as well as from the Italy of his own day, consist almost entirely of shocking treacheries, strangulations, and massacres. In the same vein, Shakespeare's histories, together with *Julius Caesar* and *Macbeth*, dramatize the most typical move in politics: the seizure of power through vile murder. The Greek city-states were perpetually riven by *stasis* (civil war); and even the Roman Republic, which hoped to pacify politics by forbidding active-duty military leaders from setting foot within the city, dissolved in a century of civil war and violence well before Caesar defied the ban and crossed the Rubicon. . . . All of this suggests that murderousness is not so much the occupational disease of princes as their occupation.

For liberals, the aim of government is advancing the interests of the governed rather than the power and glory of the rulers; the hallmark of liberalism lies in the protection of vital interests from encroachment by the state. Liberals are not so starry-eyed that they believe that politics is anything less than a bruising contact sport. Nevertheless, they draw the line at autopolemic violence. Theirs is a different vision of politics — a vision in which violence is counterposed to politics, rather than constituting it. To the claim that their vision is unrealistic and utopian, liberals can respond with important examples, of which the United States is one of the clearest because of its two centuries of peaceful presidential succession unmarred by coups d'etats.

The vision of human beings as political animals that I have presented here — and which, I am arguing, undergirds the legal conception of crimes against humanity — is liberal in the sense I have just described. It focuses on the natural need of human beings to dwell in society, the threat that social living inevitably poses to individual

---

13. The word *autopolemic* means "fighting a war against itself"; it refers to states violently attacking their own nationals. — EDS.

well-being, and the necessity of political organization to cabin that threat. Healthy politics is politics that succeeds in containing the threat. Perverted politics, or politics gone cancerous, intensifies the threat and in that respect truly counts as a crime against the human status.

NOTES AND QUESTIONS

1. Luban agrees with Vernon that the defining feature of crimes against humanity lies in what Vernon calls an "inversion" of politics and Luban calls "politics gone cancerous": Institutions fundamental to our survival instead turn on us and endanger us. Luban speaks of "the special danger that governments, which are supposed to protect the people who live in their territory, will instead murder them, enslave them, and persecute them, transforming their homeland from a haven into a killing field"; Vernon, in a similar vein, says that in crime against humanity "territoriality is transformed from a refuge to a trap." In your view, do these authors correctly identify the fundamental evil of crimes against humanity? What else could distinguish the evil of these crimes from that of other crimes?

The above analysis of crimes against humanity was adopted by the Argentinian Supreme Court in a 2007 case concerning a policeman who committed false imprisonment, battery, and deprivation of medicine in an attempt to garner a confession that could be used against a lawyer who had exposed crimes committed by the police department. The Supreme Court rejected the claim that these could be crimes against humanity. Referring to the Luban article excerpted above, the Supreme Court wrote:

> The purpose of crimes against humanity is to protect the uniquely human characteristic of being a "political animal," that is, to come together and form political organizations necessary to maintain social life. . . . The mere existence of this organization, however, implies a threat, at least an abstract threat, to individual wellbeing. Crimes against humanity represent the gravest threat: cases in which the political body has become cancerous or perverse. . . .
>
> This can then be used as a test. . . . Can the act be considered a product of a despotic or corrupt army or of a government power? The crimes committed by Derecho do not correspond to the fears recognized by the international community when they sought to define crimes against humanity. In Argentina, in 1988, there was not a state or organization dependent on the state that demonstrated any of the qualities common to a perverse machine practicing systematic and organized persecution of a group of citizens and therefore, deviating from its principal end of promoting the common good and the peaceful coexistence of society.

Corte Suprema de Justicia [CSJN], Decision of Nov. 7, 2007, "René Jésus Derecho/ recurso extraordinario," Fallos de la Corte Suprema de Justicia de la Nación [Fallos] (2007-330-3074) (Arg.), at 3083-3084.

Both authors treat the paradigm case of a crime against humanity to be a large-scale attack by a state against a subgroup on its own territory. As we have seen, the law provides a broader conception: The organized group need not be a state, and the attack need not be "widespread," as long as it is "systematic." Furthermore, the attack can be part of an effort to drive the group away—ethnic cleansing—rather than to trap and destroy it. Lastly, an organization or state can commit crimes against humanity against civilians in another state's territory. The Nazis did so in the territories they conquered. (In these cases, the crimes against humanity were also war crimes.) Do you think that the authors' model can be expanded to accommodate non-state-organized, non-large-scale ethnic cleansings as well as state-sanctioned extermination and persecution?

3. Additional important treatments of crimes against humanity include Larry May, Crimes Against Humanity: A Normative Account (2004) (a philosophical theory); Geoffrey Robertson, Crimes Against Humanity: The Struggle for Global Justice (2003) (a historical and legal account); M. Cherif Bassiouni, Crimes Against Humanity in International Criminal Law (2d ed. 1999) (the leading treatise); and Kai Ambos & Steffen Wirth, The Current Law of Crimes Against Humanity, 13 Crim. L.F. 1 (2002).

CHAPTER
20

Genocide

A. LEMKIN'S WORD

Genocide is sometimes called "the crime of crimes." Some jurists reject that label because they fear that singling out genocide might lead the world community to pay less attention to other mass atrocities, such as war crimes and crimes against humanity. This is an important caution. But the fact remains that within the public imagination, few words pack the emotional punch of "the G-word," and there can be little doubt that in most people's minds genocide is indeed the crime of crimes.

This is particularly remarkable because the word *genocide* did not exist until 1944. It was coined by a lawyer named Raphael Lemkin, a Polish Jew who fled the German invasion at the beginning of World War II and wound up in the United States. Lemkin knew nine languages, and he understood the power of words. As he struggled to alert the world to "the crime without a name," he knew he had to label it with a unique, unforgettable word. Earlier in his career, Lemkin had labeled the crime *barbarism*, and he urged the League of Nations to outlaw barbarism. But the name did not catch on, and his lobbying effort failed. Lemkin tried again.

This time he succeeded: It is hard to think of any other linguistic innovation in law that has become so familiar. *Genos* is the ancient Greek word for "tribe," while *-cide* is a suffix that means killing (it comes from the Latin *cidium*, "act of killing"). Lemkin formed the word *genocide* to indicate that this crime was not simply the destruction of human beings, even large numbers of human beings. It was the destruction of entire peoples.

Lemkin's word was new, but the crime it describes is not. In the Hebrew Bible, Saul and David receive divine commands to wipe out the Amalekites. "Now go and strike Amalek and devote to destruction all that they have. Do not spare them, but kill both man and woman, child and infant, ox and sheep, camel and donkey" (1 Samuel 15:2-3). At the end of the Third Punic War in 146 B.C., Rome completely razed the city of Carthage, and slaughtered or enslaved its entire people. How many lesser-known genocides or genocidal attacks have occurred is a matter for speculation, but they continued into the Middle Ages as Christians massacred Jews in several countries and Tamerlane killed hundreds of thousands of Hindus in Delhi. In the sixteenth century, French Catholics slaughtered an estimated 100,000 Protestant Huguenots.

The first twentieth-century genocide occurred in a colonial war between the Germans and the rebellious Herero people in German Southwest Africa (now Namibia). Under an "extermination order" from General Lothar von Trotha, German forces killed an estimated 65,000 Hereros, about three-fourths of the population, between 1904 and 1907. Von Trotha's order stated: "Within the German borders, every Herero, whether armed or unarmed, with or without cattle, will be shot."

Much better known is the Turkish destruction of the Ottoman Empire's Armenian minority during the First World War, with deaths estimated between 1 and 1.5 million. The Armenian Holocaust vividly illustrates the power of Lemkin's word *genocide*. To this day, Turkey strongly disputes that a genocide took place and has threatened criminal prosecution of Turks who admit the atrocities. By the same token, several countries, including the United States, have officially labeled it a genocide, and in 2005 the French National Assembly (the lower house of the French parliament) adopted a bill making it a crime to deny the Armenian genocide.

In 1921, a young Armenian, Soghoman Tehlirian, shot dead one of the chief organizers of the Armenian atrocities on a street in Berlin. Tehlirian was acquitted on the ground that the sufferings of the Armenian people had driven him temporarily insane. (A monument to Tehlirian stands in Fresno, California — home to a large Armenian American community — and reads: "This monument has been erected by the Armenian people in memory of Soghoman Tehlerian, the national hero who on March 15, 1921, brought justice upon Talaat Pasha, a principal Turkish perpetrator of the Armenian genocide of 1915, which claimed the lives of 1,500,000 Armenian martyrs.")

It was news of Talaat Pasha's assassination that launched Raphael Lemkin's decades-long campaign to have genocide declared a crime. Reportedly, Lemkin — then a law student — asked his professor why Talaat Pasha had never been prosecuted. Lemkin was told that no law forbade states from killing their own nationals. Lemkin replied, "It is a crime for Tehlirian to kill a man, but it is not a crime for his oppressor to kill more than a million men? That is most inconsistent."[1]

The following reading analyzes Lemkin's career and the significance of his work.

MICHAEL IGNATIEFF, LEMKIN'S WORD

New Republic, Feb. 26, 2001

When Claude Lanzmann was filming *Shoah*, he asked a Polish peasant whose fields abutted a death camp what he felt when he saw human ash from the crematoria chimneys raining down on his fields. The peasant replied: "When I cut my finger, I feel it. When you cut your finger, you feel it." The man's reply takes us to the heart of the problem of genocide. . . . Why is a crime committed against Jews or any other human group a crime against those who do not belong to that group?

The obvious answer seems obvious only if you assume what in fact requires demonstration, namely that we belong to the same species and owe each other the same duties of care. This concept came late to mankind, and to judge from the horrible century just past it is still struggling to make headway against the more evident idea that race, color, or creed mark impassable frontiers of moral concern. . . .

If all this is true, we need to force ourselves to think beyond the platitude that genocide is an abomination, and to understand the more difficult thought that it represents an unending moral temptation for mankind. The danger of genocide lies

---

1. Samantha Power, "A Problem from Hell": America and the Age of Genocide 17 (2002). Power's book contains a detailed account of Lemkin's career. On the history of genocide, see Ben Kiernan, Blood and Soil: A World History of Genocide and Extermination from Sparta to Darfur (2007). On Carthage, see id. at 50-51; on the Hereros, id. at 381-386; on the Armenians, id. at 395-415.

in its promise to create a world without enemies. Think of genocide as a crime in service of a utopia, a world without discord, enmity, suspicion, free of the enemy without or the enemy within. Once we understand that this utopia is the core of the genocidal intention, we have to realize that this utopia menaces us forever. Once we understand genocide as utopian, we understand also the vulnerability of universalism. The idea that there can be a "crime against humanity" is a counterintuitive one that has to make its way against the more alarming thought that what humans actually desire is not a world of brotherhood, but a world without enemies. . . .

The man who coined [the word "genocide"] was Raphael Lemkin, a lawyer born in Bialystok in Poland a hundred years ago. Cast ashore in America by the Holocaust, and acting as a private citizen, without state support or salary, he single-handedly drafted and lobbied for the passage of the Genocide Convention, approved by the U.N. General Assembly in December 1948. This would be achievement enough, but Lemkin died alone and remains almost forgotten. The word that he coined — "genocide" — is now so banalized and misused that there is a serious risk that commemoration of his work will become an act of forgetting, obliterating what was so singular about his achievement. . . .

Nobody before Lemkin had studied the German occupation from the standpoint of jurisprudence. His central insight was that the occupation, not just in Poland but all across Europe, had inverted the equality provisions of all the European legal traditions. Food in Poland was distributed on racial grounds, with Jews getting the least. Marriage in occupied Holland was organized entirely on racial lines: Germans responsible for getting Dutch women pregnant were not punished, as would be the case under normal military law; they were rewarded, because the resulting child would be a net addition to the Nordic race.

Lemkin was the first scholar to work out the logic of this jurisprudence. From its unremitting racial bias, he was able to understand, earlier than most, that the wholesale extermination of groups was not an accidental or incidental cruelty, nor an act of revenge. It was the very essence of the occupation. Lemkin published his findings, with the help of the Carnegie Endowment for International Peace, in 1944, in *Axis Rule in Occupied Europe.* This book is a rare example of scholarship as heroism: a patient, detailed, unprecedented, and unflagging demonstration, decree by decree, of modern despotism's infernal logic.

As Lemkin slowly worked out where this logic was headed, he was just as concerned about the fate of the Polish people as he was about the fate of his fellow Jews. In the decrees penalizing the use of the Polish language and promoting the destruction of Polish cultural monuments and treasures, the use of Poles for slave labor, the merciless repression of all resistance, and the settlement of Germans on Polish land — in all those awful edicts Lemkin could make out a concerted desire to subjugate, and if necessary to exterminate, the Polish people. The concept of genocide was invented, in other words, not only to describe the fate of his own people, but also to capture what was happening to the people to whom he would have belonged, had he been permitted. He was one of those Polish patriots never allowed membership in the nation that he claimed as his own. Lemkin's theoretical innovation taught a universalist lesson not least by example. . . .

Never secure in the Poland of his birth, he sought belonging in the law. He was not the only Jew from Bialystok to do so. Hersh Lauterpacht, later the Whewell Professor of Jurisprudence at Cambridge, was also from Bialystok, and made his escape to England in the 1920s. Like Lemkin, he became an international lawyer; and like Lemkin, he devoted his war work as a scholar to devising legal responses to barbarism.

In Lauterpacht's case, it was by drafting an international bill of rights that influenced both the Universal Declaration of Human Rights of 1948 and, more directly, the European Convention on Human Rights of 1950. Both men responded to barbarism in the same way: by seeking to draft international legal instruments that would ban it. In a deeper sense, both these men found a home in the law, and their passionate attachment to international law was a consequence of their homelessness anywhere else.

This ideal of a world made civilized by international convention drove Lemkin first to define genocide as a crime in international law, then to secure its inclusion in the Nuremberg indictments in 1945, and finally to secure a convention making [genocide an international crime] in 1948. When it was finally passed by the General Assembly in 1948, he was discovered weeping in a corridor of the United Nations. He wanted to be left alone, and in every sense he was alone. All of his family, except one brother, had perished in the Holocaust. . . .

Yet we cannot share the meaning that Lemkin gave to his concept. For if you were to ask Lemkin the question that I posed at the outset — why is a crime against Jews also a crime against Gentiles? — he would have replied that what human beings share is a common civilization, in which the achievements of one group are shared by all. Thus in a passage written in April 1945, at the very moment that the world was discovering what lay behind the barbed wire at Auschwitz and Belsen, he continued to write:

> Our whole heritage is a product of the contributions of all peoples. We can best under-stand this when we realize how impoverished our culture would be if the so-called inferior peoples doomed by Germany, such as the Jews, had not been permitted to create the Bible, or to give birth to an Einstein, a Spinoza; if the Poles had not had the oppor-tunity to give to the world a Copernicus, a Chopin, a Curie; the Czechs, a Huss, a Dvorak; the Greeks, a Plato and a Socrates; the Russians, a Tolstoy and a Shostakovich.

There is something affecting — and also something wrong — about this idea that what humanity holds in common is civilization. *Kultur* did not prevent Germans from massacring even their fellow citizens. Indeed, *Kultur* was Germanized in such a way as to deny Jews any right to belong to the civilization that they had made in common with Gentiles. Lemkin remained trapped by the hopeful optimism of a civilization in twilight, just as he was trapped by the illusion that what was Western was universal. But when Tutsis start massacring Hutus, when Khmers start killing fellow Cambodians, what shared civilization is supposed to mobilize Europeans to intervene?

This perplexity returns us to the Polish peasant and the mysterious question of why the fate of one group should concern the fate of another. What can we say that is truthful enough to acknowledge the ineluctable difference between human beings that saved Polish peasants from extermination and condemned their fellow beings to infamous death? What we can say — what Lemkin did not say — is that it is not civi-lization we share, but those very differences.

What it means to be a human being, what defines the very identity we share as a species, is the fact that we are differentiated by race, religion, ethnicity, and individual difference. These differentiations define our identity both as individuals and as a species. No other species differentiates itself in this individualized abundance. A sense of otherness, of distinctness, is the very basis of the consciousness of our individuality, and this consciousness, based in difference, is a constitutive element of what it is to be a human being. To attack any one of these differences — to round up women because they are women, Jews because they are Jews, whites because they are whites, blacks because they are blacks, gays because they are gay — is to attack the shared element that makes us what we are as a species. In this way of thinking, we understand humanity, our common flesh and blood, as valuable to the degree that it allows us to elaborate the dignity and the honor that we give to our differences — and that this reality of difference, both fated and created, is our common inheritance, the shared integument that we must fight to defend whenever any of us is attacked for manifesting it.

NOTES AND QUESTIONS

1. Samantha Power's book *"A Problem from Hell": America and the Age of Genocide* movingly describes Lemkin's tireless one-man lobbying campaign to have genocide declared an international crime. Lemkin lived by himself in a one-room New York apartment, barely supported by religious groups. Id. at 56, 77. After his lobbying succeeded in persuading the UN to pass a nonbinding anti-genocide resolution, he organized tirelessly on behalf of the binding Genocide Convention. And after the UN voted to approve the Genocide Convention and open it for ratification, he continued his Sisyphean efforts to persuade the United States to ratify it (which did not occur until nearly three decades after Lemkin's death). An admiring newspaper article referred to him as "that exceedingly patient and totally unofficial man." Id. at 76, quoting the *New York Times*. Lemkin died in 1959, completely penniless, but with his apartment "overflowing with memos prepared for foreign ministers and ambassadors, as well as some 500 books, each read, reread, and emphatically underlined." Id. at 78. An editorial about him in the *New York Times* recalled:

> Diplomats of this and other nations who used to feel a certain concern when they saw the slightly stooped figure of Dr. Raphael Lemkin approaching them in the corridors of the United Nations need not be uneasy anymore. They will not have to think up explanations for a failure to ratify the genocide convention for which Dr. Lemkin worked so patiently and so unselfishly for a decade and a half. . . . Death in action was his final argument — a final word to our own State Department, which has feared that an agreement not to kill would infringe upon our sovereignty.

Id. At the time of his death, Lemkin had authored nine books on international law, one on art criticism, and one on rose cultivation.

2. As the above quote indicates, the United States did not immediately embrace the Genocide Convention, for a number of reasons. These included concerns over infringement on national sovereignty, including Cold War suspicion by some senators of international institutions; objections to the vague wording of certain clauses; and concern that adversaries would exploit the Convention to target Americans because of lynchings and racial segregation in the South. The American Bar Association initially opposed it.

The Convention also had its champions, most notably Wisconsin Senator William Proxmire, who in 1967 promised to make a speech about it on the Senate floor every day until the Convention was ratified. Never missing a roll call in 22 years in the Senate, Proxmire delivered 3,211 speeches about the Genocide Convention. The Convention was finally ratified in 1986, after President Ronald Reagan's support overcame opposition in the Senate.

3. Strikingly, Michael Ignatieff describes the motive behind genocide as "utopian." What does Ignatieff mean by this unusual claim? In your view, is he correct?

B.   THE GENOCIDE CONVENTION

The foundation of today's legal conception of genocide is the Convention on the Prevention and Punishment of the Crimes of Genocide, often referred to simply as the Genocide Convention. It was drafted in the United Nations after intense negotiations. Approximately 140 states have joined the Genocide Convention, leaving about 50 states that are not parties.

CONVENTION ON THE PREVENTION AND PUNISHMENT OF THE CRIME OF GENOCIDE

78 U.N.T.S. 277 (entered into force Jan. 12, 1951)

Article I: The Contracting Parties confirm that genocide, whether committed in time of peace or in time of war, is a crime under international law which they undertake to prevent and to punish.

Article II: In the present Convention, genocide means any of the following acts committed with intent to destroy, in whole or in part, a national, ethnical, racial or religious group, as such:

(a) Killing members of the group;
(b) Causing serious bodily or mental harm to members of the group;
(c) Deliberately inflicting on the group conditions of life calculated to bring about its physical destruction in whole or in part;
(d) Imposing measures intended to prevent births within the group;
(e) Forcibly transferring children of the group to another group.

Article III: The following acts shall be punishable:

(a) Genocide;
(b) Conspiracy to commit genocide;
(c) Direct and public incitement to commit genocide;
(d) Attempt to commit genocide;
(e) Complicity in genocide.

Article IV: Persons committing genocide or any of the other acts enumerated in article III shall be punished, whether they are constitutionally responsible rulers, public officials or private individuals.

Article V: The Contracting Parties undertake to enact, in accordance with their respective Constitutions, the necessary legislation to give effect to the provisions of the present Convention, and, in particular, to provide effective penalties for persons guilty of genocide or any of the other acts enumerated in article III.

Article VI: Persons charged with genocide or any of the other acts enumerated in article III shall be tried by a competent tribunal of the State in the territory of which the act was committed, or by such international penal tribunal as may have jurisdiction with respect to those Contracting Parties which shall have accepted its jurisdiction.

Article VII: Genocide and the other acts enumerated in article III shall not be considered as political crimes for the purpose of extradition.

The Contracting Parties pledge themselves in such cases to grant extradition in accordance with their laws and treaties in force.

Article VIII: Any Contracting Party may call upon the competent organs of the United Nations to take such action under the Charter of the United Nations as they consider appropriate for the prevention and suppression of acts of genocide or any of the other acts enumerated in article III.

Article IX: Disputes between the Contracting Parties relating to the interpretation, application or fulfilment of the present Convention, including those relating to the responsibility of a State for genocide or for any of the other acts enumerated in article III, shall be submitted to the International Court of Justice at the request of any of the parties to the dispute. . . .

1.   Article 2: The Core Definition of the Crime

The most basic idea of the Genocide Convention lies in Article 1's assertion that genocide is a crime under international law. The insistence that it is a crime "whether committed in time of peace or in time of war" contrasts with the Nuremberg Charter's insistence that crimes against humanity require a "war nexus." (The requirement of a war nexus was dropped in the ICTR and ICC statutes. See the discussion of the war nexus in the preceding chapter.)

For the moment, we shall skip over all the other articles of the Genocide Convention except Article 2, which sets out the core definitions of the crime of genocide. We shall return to the other articles later.

a.   The Chapeau

The chapeau to Article 2 states that the five enumerated crimes are all genocide if committed "with intent to destroy, in whole or in part, a national, ethnical, racial or religious group, as such." Each part of the chapeau requires some preliminary explanation. Further explanation will emerge through the remaining readings in the chapter.

"*with intent to destroy . . . a . . . group . . .*" Genocide is what common lawyers call a "specific intent" crime. The Genocide Convention does not use this term, but the meaning is the same as the common law's specific intent (or its civil law equivalent, *dolus specialis*). For further elaboration, see the excerpt from *Akayesu*, reproduced below, ¶¶517-521. If the defendant participated in a murderous attack on a group, but with lesser intent — for example, intent to terrorize the group, or intent to harm them without destroying them — he or she may have committed a crime against humanity, but it is not genocide.

Thus, suppose that a militia decides to kill all the inhabitants of a certain region to steal their property and land. And suppose further that all those inhabitants belong to the same ethnic group, and the militiamen know it. Accused of genocide, a leader of the militia responds that if there was another way to get the land, he would not have killed them. The purpose was to steal the land, not to wipe out a particular group; killing the people was simply the easiest and safest way to steal the land. He would have done the same no matter what group it was. If the leader is telling the truth, then this is a crime against humanity (extermination), but it is *not* genocide because the intent to destroy the group was lacking. For further elaboration, see the excerpt from the UN's Darfur Report ¶¶513-518, reproduced below.

"*. . . to destroy . . . a . . . group, as such.*" What does "as such" add, and what does it mean? Early drafts of the Genocide Convention listed certain specified motives for the crime as a necessary element of the offense, in addition to the "intent to destroy." Lists of motives, as an element of genocide separate from intent, were deleted from the final draft and replaced with the phrase "as such."[2] It seems, then, that "to destroy . . . a . . . group, as such" means to destroy the group because of who they are — to destroy the Jews because they are Jews, to destroy the Tutsis because they are Tutsis, and so forth. Thus, the crime of genocide requires a complex intent: an intent to destroy a group on the basis of its group characteristic. This complex intent is not the same as a motive — for, as we have seen, the drafters decided against including motive among the elements of the crime. Whether the perpetrator acts out of vengefulness, or religious conviction, or political ideology, or military strategy, the *mens rea* is that of genocide if he or she aims to destroy a group because of who they are.

"*. . . in whole or in part . . .*" Destroying a group "as such" does not mean that an attack is genocide only if it aims to destroy the entire group. As paragraph 13 of the *Krstić* opinion, reproduced below, points out, even Hitler aimed to destroy only the European Jews, not all the Jews in the world. An attack aiming to destroy a significant part of the group can be genocide. The Genocide Convention has no "numbers requirement," in the sense of a minimum number of corpses needed to constitute genocide. But small-scale crimes directed at members of a particular group will not satisfy the "intent to destroy a group, as such" requirement. The "part" must be a meaningful or significant part.

The protected groups. The Genocide Convention specifies that genocide must be directed against national, ethnic, racial, or religious groups. Conspicuously missing are political groups. Whether political groups should be included in the definition was a matter of fierce debate during negotiations over the Genocide Convention.[3] Although some commentators have suggested that the chief opposition to including political groups was the Soviet bloc — the USSR had "liquidated" Russia's kulak (wealthy peasant) class in the 1930s on political grounds — other states and non-governmental organizations also opposed describing the destruction of political groups as genocide. These included the World Jewish Congress, which wanted to reserve the term "genocide" for the destruction of national and religious minorities.[4]

Under this definition, the murder of hundreds of thousands of Communists by Indonesia's government in 1965 (the so-called Year of Living Dangerously) would not qualify as genocide. And what about the Cambodian "auto-genocide" of 1975-1979, which killed an estimated 1-2 million people? After seizing power, the Khmer Rouge — an ideologically driven Communist revolutionary movement — launched a program to restructure Cambodia as a peasant society. City dwellers were forcibly evacuated to the countryside, and those unable to keep up with the march were killed. Once in the countryside, the "new people" — new, that is, to peasant life — were worked to death. The Khmer Rouge tortured and executed educated people, professionals, and other "bourgeois" or "reactionary" elements. They rounded up and executed wearers of eyeglasses. They also killed ethnic and religious minorities — which clearly fulfills the legal definition of groups protected under the Genocide

---

2. William A. Schabas, Genocide in International Law 245-253 (2000) (reviewing the drafting history).
3. Id. at 134-145.
4. Id. at 140. For further discussion, see Beth Van Schaack, The Crime of Political Genocide: Repairing the Genocide Convention's Blind Spot, 106 Yale L.J. 2259 (1997).

Convention. But these minorities represented only a small fraction of the targets. The vast majority of the victims belonged to the majority Khmer ethnic group — the same group that the Khmer Rouge belonged to.

It should be noted that several states have broadened the list of protected groups in their domestic anti-genocide laws. See Note 5 following the *Akayesu* case, below.

PROBLEM

Was the Khmer Rouge's reign of terror a genocide? What would the legal theory be?

b.   The Five Enumerated Crimes

Article 2 lists five crimes that count as genocide when the chapeau conditions are met: (a) killing members of the group, (b) causing serious bodily or mental harm to members of the group, (c) deliberately inflicting on the group conditions of life calculated to bring about its physical destruction in whole or in part, (d) imposing measures intended to prevent births within the group, and (e) forcibly transferring children of the group to another group.

Further discussion of the meaning of these particular crimes appears in the *Akayesu* opinion, excerpted below.

c.   Article 3: The Modes of Participation

Under Article 3, each of the five crimes can be committed in five ways, or "modes": (1) by committing the prohibited act directly, (2) by conspiring to commit it, (3) by attempting to commit it, (4) by being complicit in its commission, and (5) by directly and publicly inciting others to commit it.

The Rome Statute of the International Criminal Court (ICC) uses identical language to Article 2 when it defines the crime of genocide in its own Article 6. However, the Rome Statute does not include Article 3's catalog of modes of participation; it has its own definition of the modes of participation in crimes. See Chapter 17.

2.   Genocide in U.S. Criminal Law

The United States acceded to the Genocide Convention in 1986. The U.S. Senate attached several reservations and understandings to the Convention, and when Congress implemented the Convention through a criminal statute, it changed the language in several respects.

U.S. RUDs TO THE GENOCIDE CONVENTION

132 Cong. Rec. 2326, 2349 (1986) (U.S. adherence effective Feb. 23, 1988)

I. The Senate's advice and consent is subject to the following reservations:

(1) That with reference to Article IX of the Convention, before any dispute to which the United States is a party may be submitted to the jurisdiction of the

International Court of Justice under this article, the specific consent of the United States is required in each case.

(2) That nothing in the Convention requires or authorizes legislation or other action by the United States of America prohibited by the Constitution of the United States as interpreted by the United States.

II. The Senate's advice and consent is subject to the following understandings, which shall apply to the obligations of the United States under the Convention:

(1) That the term "intent to destroy, in whole or in part, a national, ethnical, racial, or religious group as such" appearing in Article II means the specific intent to destroy, in whole or in substantial part, a national, ethnical, racial or religious groups as such by the acts specified in Article II.

(2) That the term "mental harm" in Article II(b) means permanent impairment of mental faculties through drugs, torture or similar techniques.

(3) That the pledge to grant extradition in accordance with a state's laws and treaties in force found in Article VII extends only to acts which are criminal under the laws of both the requesting and the requested state and nothing in Article VI affects the right of any state to bring to trial before its own tribunals any of its nationals for acts committed outside a state.

(4) That acts in the course of armed conflicts committed without the specific intent required by Article II are not sufficient to constitute genocide as defined by this Convention.

(5) That with regard to the reference to an international penal tribunal in Article VI of the Convention, the United States declares that it reserves the right to effect its participation in any such tribunal only by a treaty entered into specifically for that purpose with the advice and consent of the Senate. . . .

18 UNITED STATES CODE §1091. GENOCIDE

(a) **Basic offense.** Whoever, whether in time of peace or in time of war, in a circumstance described in subsection (d) and with the specific intent to destroy, in whole or in substantial part, a national, ethnic, racial, or religious group as such —

(1) kills members of that group;

(2) causes serious bodily injury to members of that group;

(3) causes the permanent impairment of the mental faculties of members of the group through drugs, torture, or similar techniques;

(4) subjects the group to conditions of life that are intended to cause the physical destruction of the group in whole or in part;

(5) imposes measures intended to prevent births within the group; or

(6) transfers by force children of the group to another group;

or attempts to do so shall be punished. . . .

(c) **Incitement offense.** Whoever in a circumstance described in subsection (d) directly and publicly incites another to violate subsection (a) shall be fined not more than $500,000 or imprisoned not more than five years, or both.

(d) **Required circumstance for offenses.** The circumstance referred to in subsections (a) and (c) is that —

(1) the offense is committed in whole or in part within the United States;

(2) the alleged offender is a national of the United States . . . ;

(3) the alleged offender is an alien lawfully admitted for permanent residence in the United States . . . ;

(4) the alleged offender is a stateless person whose habitual residence is in the United States; or

(5) after the conduct required for the offense occurs, the alleged offender is brought into, or found in, the United States, even if that conduct occurred outside the United States.

§1093. DEFINITIONS

As used in this chapter—

(1) the term "children" means the plural and means individuals who have not attained the age of eighteen years;

(2) the term "ethnic group" means a set of individuals whose identity as such is distinctive in terms of common cultural traditions or heritage;

(3) the term "incites" means urges another to engage imminently in conduct in circumstances under which there is a substantial likelihood of imminently causing such conduct;

(4) the term "members" means the plural;

(5) the term "national group" means a set of individuals whose identity as such is distinctive in terms of nationality or national origins;

(6) the term "racial group" means a set of individuals whose identity as such is distinctive in terms of physical characteristics or biological descent;

(7) the term "religious group" means a set of individuals whose identity as such is distinctive in terms of common religious creed, beliefs, doctrines, practices, or rituals; and

(8) the term "substantial part" means a part of a group of such numerical significance that the destruction or loss of that part would cause the destruction of the group as a viable entity within the nation of which such group is a part.

QUESTIONS

1. The U.S. understandings of the Genocide Convention slightly narrow the notion of destroying a group "in part" by changing the phrase to "in substantial part"; the definition in §1093(8) further narrows or refines the concept of a "substantial part." Do these definitions comport with the language and spirit of the Genocide Convention?

2. Before 2007, the U.S. genocide statute restricted the crime to genocide committed within the United States or by a U.S. national. In 2007, Congress amended §1091 to include genocide committed abroad by non-U.S. nationals in its purview, as indicated in clauses (d)(3)-(5).

3. What is the point behind the narrow definition of "mental harm" in the Senate's RUD II(2), repeated in §1091(a)(3)? What possible abuses might result from leaving the term "mental harm" undefined or defining it broadly?

4. Senate RUD II(4) specifies that "acts in the course of armed conflicts committed without the specific intent required by Article II are not sufficient to constitute genocide as defined by this Convention." Why might the Senate think it important to clarify this point? Without this understanding, could the use of nuclear weapons qualify as genocide?

3.   The Theory Behind the Core Definition: The Value of Groups

Why does the Genocide Convention define the crime so differently from the crime against humanity of "extermination," which in practice obviously overlaps with genocide? Both crimes were originally defined at the end of World War II. As we saw in the preceding chapter, U.S. Supreme Court Justice Robert Jackson chose the label "crimes against humanity" in 1946, while Lemkin first published the word "genocide" in 1944. Interestingly, the very first American draft of the Nuremberg Charter included the word "genocide" among the crimes within the Tribunal's jurisdiction, but the word disappeared from subsequent drafts. There is no record explaining why; perhaps the term was too new and unfamiliar.

There are three large differences between the legal definitions of the two crimes. First, genocide is a specific intent offense while crimes against humanity require only knowledge and general intent as *mens rea*.

Second, genocide requires an attack on specific protected groups — racial, religious, national, or ethnic — while crimes against humanity require an attack against civilian populations, even if these are not protected groups.

Third, genocide involves the intent to destroy the protected group "as such," while crimes against humanity place no such emphasis on groups as such. As the following excerpt explains, the focus on groups as such was central to Lemkin's idea.

DAVID LUBAN, CALLING GENOCIDE BY ITS RIGHTFUL NAME: LEMKIN'S WORD, DARFUR, AND THE UN REPORT
7 Chi. Intl. L. Rev. 303, 309-310 (2006)

Lemkin defined "genocide" thoughtfully, and a deep philosophical point lay behind his definition. That point is that ethnic, racial, and religious groups possess value as groups — value over and above the value of the individuals who compose the groups. The individuals are valuable too, of course, and for those committed to human rights and human dignity, the value of those individuals is incalculable.

But humanity consists not only of many people — individualities in the plural. It consists as well of many peoples — a plurality of groups as well as individuals. Groups represent ways of life, imaginative visions of the good worked out collectively over the course of generations. . . . For that reason, to annihilate a group is a crime that diminishes humanity over and above the loss of the slaughtered individuals. In Lemkin's words:

> [N]ations are essential elements of the world community. The world represents only so much culture and intellectual vigor as are created by its component national groups. Essentially the idea of a nation signifies constructive cooperation and original contributions, based upon genuine traditions, genuine culture, and a well-developed national psychology. The destruction of a nation, therefore, results in the loss of its future contributions to the world.

Genocide impoverishes the world in the same way that losing an entire distinctive species—the pandas, the Siberian tigers, the rhinos—impoverishes the world over and above the loss of the individual pandas or tigers or rhinos.

––––––––––

In the following excerpt, philosopher Chandran Kukathas criticizes Lemkin's emphasis on groups over individuals. He begins his argument by observing that groups we belong to (such as our religious, national, ethnic, or racial groups) can matter to us for two different reasons. First, they matter to us because the group is useful to the individuals who belong to it, offering protection of their interests as well as a sense of identity. Kukathas labels this the "Collective Conception" of group value. He points out that on this Collective Conception, it is really individuals that matter, not groups: The groups matter only because they advance the interests of their members.

However, the Collective Conception of groups is not the only one. There is another conception that finds groups valuable as such—that is, over and above their usefulness to their members. Kukathas calls this the "Corporate Conception." The excerpt that follows argues that Lemkin adopted the Corporate Conception of groups. Kukathas then criticizes the group focus of the Genocide Convention.

CHANDRAN KUKATHAS, GENOCIDE AND GROUP RIGHTS
Closing Lecture at the Conference on Ethics in Africa (May 31, 2006)

In the Corporate Conception of groups and group rights . . . the group is more than the reflection of the interests of its members. The group itself is the bearer of value, and it is quite possible for the interests of the group to conflict with the interests of individual members. If, for example, the group is regarded as the carrier of a particular culture or tradition, on the Corporate Conception the group may have an interest in preserving that culture—and perhaps a right to do so—even if that conflicts with the self-declared interests of individual members who no longer wish to live by old traditions. The value of the group thus lies not merely—or perhaps, at all—in its value to its members but in its value to the world. At the extreme, this view suggests that the value of the group gives it rights that trump those of the individuals who comprise it—some of whom may want to dissent from its traditions. Protecting the group here would mean protecting it against anyone who might undermine it, including its own members. (This view is not as far-fetched as it might appear. Groups who, in the name of preserving the group's identity, deny their members freedom to dissent, or exit, from the group, and insist that outsiders have no right to intervene to uphold the rights of individual members, may be asserting a corporate conception of the group and its rights.) The Corporate Conception of groups and group rights asserts the equal worth of all groups, for no identity is worth more than any other. This holds whether the group in question is a religious sect or a nation-state.

Lemkin, in his critique of genocide, employed the Corporate Conception of groups or, more specifically, nations. His concern was the destruction of nations, which he saw as embodiments of particular traditions and cultures. The destruction of the nation was wrong because it resulted in the loss of its future contributions to the world. "The world," he wrote, "represents only so much culture and intellectual vigor as are created by its component national groups." He added: "Among the basic features which have marked progress in civilization are the respect for and appreciation of the national characteristics and qualities contributed to world culture by the different nations — characteristics and qualities which, as illustrated in the contributions made by nations weak in defense and poor in economic resources, are not to be measured in terms of national power and wealth."

According to the Collective Conception of the group, the value of the group lies in its capacity to serve the interests of its members. It serves those interests by providing goods, especially collective goods that it is particularly capable of producing, and which are of great importance to everyone. These goods might range from practical services, such as medical care, to less tangible — though no less important — goods such as a sense of identity. If for any reason the group were suddenly to cease providing these goods, whether because a lack of resources led to its no longer being able to supply particular benefits, or because the disintegration of the group led to its members having less and less with which to identify, the individual members would be harmed. Yet if, for any reason, the members of the group could obtain these goods elsewhere, securing practical necessities from other sources, and coming to identify with other groups for their sense of community and belonging, the loss of the group would be of no great moment on the Collective Conception. . . .

According to the Corporate Conception of groups, however, the value of groups persists independently of the interests of their members because the group itself, by its very existence, makes something else available to the world — something in its culture or traditions. There are two troubling features of this position. First, it presents a view of the value of groups that potentially elevates the group above the well-being or interests of its members, and in principle suggests it may be wrong for them to try to leave or even to reform the group if this would change or undermine its very character. This is undesirable to the extent that it requires that the lives of real persons would have to be subordinated to an abstraction: the character of the group. . . .

Second, if the value of groups lies in the benefit it brings to the world, it may turn out that some groups are less valuable than others, and even that some are not valuable at all. Some groups may not be valuable because they have little to offer: their traditions or cultural practices may have served their members well enough in their time, but are not likely to be of much use to anyone today. Others may not be valuable because what they have to offer has already been taken advantage of — perhaps their musical or technological contributions have already been absorbed by the cultures around them. . . . Finally some groups may not be valuable because their traditions are morally obnoxious. In some cases, even if the group has some admirable traditions these may not be enough to offset the despicable elements they harbor. The disappearance of traditions of slavery or female mutilation should be welcomed, even if the price is the loss of the less objectionable elements of a now derelict culture.

If we adopt the Corporate Conception of groups, then, it may well be that we must concede that *some* groups have value even if they offer little to their own members. But it seems unlikely that we must concede that *all* groups have value regardless of whether their members value them. The matter of the value of the group would become an empirical question, and it is perfectly possible that we would judge some groups to be of little worth.

If the foregoing analysis is sound, groups are much less important, morally speaking, than they seem. Yet in international law, and in the political theory that gave rise to this aspect of it, genocide is condemned largely because it involves the destruction of the group. It is time to ask whether the value of the group can really be what lies behind the judgment that genocide is a crime. . . .

If we adopt the Collective Conception of the group, the wrongness of genocide cannot lie in the harm it does to groups rather than individuals, since on this conception the group amounts to nothing more than an aggregation of individuals. If individuals are not harmed then no harm is done. Genocide, in this conception, is (criminally) wrong because it involves harm to individuals — to large numbers of individuals — who are harmed because of their group membership. If we adopt the Corporate Conception of the group, the wrongness of genocide would lie in the harm it does to groups regardless of its impact on individuals. At worst, to take that view would be to elevate the worth of an abstraction above the value of actual human lives. This would not only be perverse but also ironic in light of the fact that the numerous genocides have been carried out in the name of abstractions — ideology and racial purity among them. . . .

QUESTIONS

1. Is Kukathas correct that Lemkin's theory fails because it is too collectivist? That Lemkin's theory is objectionable because it assumes that groups making a contribution to world culture are more valuable than groups whose contribution to world culture is slight or even harmful?

2. How could there be a case where a group is destroyed "as such" but its members are not harmed? Would the forcible transfer of children out of the group (prohibited under the Genocide Convention) be such a case, if the children were placed with families who treated them well but raised them in a different culture? (For many years, Australia had such a policy toward aboriginals. Kukathas, who is Australian, may have had this case in mind.)

4.   The Meaning of "Ethnical"

One particularly difficult issue in interpreting Article 2 concerns what is meant by an "ethnical" group. Are there objective characteristics that make a group of people a single ethnic group? Or is ethnicity defined subjectively? If so, who defines it? Its own members? Or the group's enemies? The law has at various times endorsed all these conflicting answers.

Thus, for example, the U.S. genocide statute, 18 U.S.C. §1093(2), gives an objective definition to the term *ethnic group*:

> The term "ethnic group" means a set of individuals whose identity as such is distinctive in terms of common cultural traditions or heritage.

So did the ICTR in the 1988 *Akayesu* decision. In ¶513, the ICTR states that an ethnic group is a "group whose members share a common language or culture."

This objective definition faced significant criticism because it made it difficult to see why the Hutus and Tutsis were different ethnic groups: They have lived together for centuries, speak the same language, and share the same culture, including religion (mostly Roman Catholic). In a pair of 2001 decisions, the ICTY and the ICTR both moved to a more subjective identification. The ICTY argued that ethnic groups are defined principally by their enemies:

> Although the objective determination of a religious group still remains possible, to attempt to define a national, ethnic or racial group today using objective and scientifically irreproachable criteria would be a perilous exercise whose result would not necessarily correspond to the perception of the persons concerned by such categorisation. Therefore, it is more appropriate to evaluate the status of a national, ethnic or racial group from the point of view of those persons who wish to single that group out from the rest of the community. The Trial Chamber consequently elects to evaluate membership in a national, ethnic or racial group using a subjective criterion. It is the stigmatisation of a group as a distinct national, ethnic or racial unit by the community which allows it to be determined whether a targeted population constitutes a national, ethnic or racial group in the eyes of the alleged perpetrators. . . .
>
> A group may be stigmatised in this manner by way of positive or negative criteria. A "positive approach" would consist of the perpetrators of the crime distinguishing a group by the characteristics which they deem to be particular to a national, ethnic, racial or religious group. A "negative approach" would consist of identifying individuals as not being part of the group to which the perpetrators of the crime consider that they themselves belong and which to them displays specific national, ethnic, racial or religious characteristics. Thereby, all individuals thus rejected would, by exclusion, make up a distinct group.[5]

A month earlier, the ICTR's Trial Chamber offered a somewhat broader definition of an ethnic group, combining objective and subjective approaches: An ethnic group is "one whose members share a common language and culture; or, a group which distinguishes itself, as such (self identification); or, a group identified as such by others, including perpetrators of the crimes (identification by others)."[6]

NOTES AND QUESTIONS

1. What are the pluses and minuses of these definitions? Which do you favor?

2. Recall that Lemkin formulated his group-focused definition of genocide with national minorities — ethnic groups — in mind. As we saw, Lemkin believed strongly that different "nations" each make their own distinctive contributions to world culture. Can this be reconciled with the *Jelisić* definition of an ethnic group as a group identified as such by others? How can a "group" that exists only in the prejudices and fantasies of its persecutors make distinctive contributions to world culture? Does *Jelisić*'s "identification by others" theory of ethnicity undermine the theory behind criminalizing genocide?

3. For additional discussion of this issue, see ¶¶498-500 of the UN Commission's report on Darfur, excerpted below.

5. Other Clauses of the Genocide Convention

The notes and questions that follow deal with some of the other significant clauses of the Genocide Convention.

---

5. Prosecutor v. Jelisić, Case No. IT-95-10-T, Judgment, ¶¶70-71 (Dec. 14, 1999).
6. Prosecutor v. Kayishema & Ruzindana, Case No. ICTR-95-1-T, Judgment, ¶98 (May 21, 1999).

NOTES AND QUESTIONS

1. *Articles 5 and 7.* Article 5 requires states to enact criminal statutes against genocide "in accordance with their respective Constitutions." The quoted phrase permits states to tailor their genocide prohibitions to their own constitutional requirements. (Can you think of circumstances in which this might pose a problem? Consider, for example, whether the United States could constitutionally enact a law criminalizing hate-journalism as incitement to genocide.) And Article 7 requires states to extradite persons accused of genocide, but only "in accordance with their laws and treaties in force." It does not, therefore, require states to modify their extradition treaties and laws to incorporate the crime of genocide — only to grant extradition requests according to law. The first clause of Article 7 specifies that genocide does not fall under a common treaty exception to extradition, according to which political offenses are not extraditable. (See the discussion of the political offense exception in Chapter 9 on extradition.) Genocide goes beyond the tolerable limits of political crime.

2. *Article 6.* Article 6 authorizes jurisdictions to try genocide only in international tribunals and the territorial state in which the genocide was committed. Genocide as defined in the Genocide Convention is therefore *not* a "subsidiary" universal jurisdiction offense — contrary to some authorities. See Demjanjuk v. Petrovsky, 776 F.2d 571, 582 (6th Cir. 1985) (analyzing genocide as a universal jurisdiction offense). This may come as a surprise to those who assume that if anything should be a universal jurisdiction offense, it is genocide. In fact, efforts were made by several states during the negotiation of the Genocide Convention to make it a universal jurisdiction offense. Saudi Arabia, Lebanon, and Iran introduced pro-universal jurisdiction proposals, and received backing from Siam and Brazil. But the Soviet Union and the United States strongly opposed universal jurisdiction, and they were supported by France, the Netherlands, India, and Egypt. They objected to the infringement on state sovereignty involved in trying nationals, perhaps leaders, of another state for genocide; and Egypt expressed concern over the possibility of politicized prosecutions. The universal jurisdiction proposals met with decisive defeat. So did a Swedish proposal to add nationality jurisdiction to territorial jurisdiction as a basis for trying genocide suspects in national courts. William A. Schabas, Genocide in International Law 355-358 (2000).

Does that mean that any state that creates universal jurisdiction over genocide is in violation of the principles of jurisdiction in international law? Not according to the Israeli district court that tried Adolf Eichmann. The district court dismissed Eichmann's jurisdictional objections and concluded that Israel could exercise universal jurisdiction despite Article 6 of the Genocide Convention:

> [I]t cannot be assumed that Article 6 is designed to limit the jurisdiction of countries to try genocide crimes by the principle of territoriality. . . . [I]n the Convention for the Prevention and Punishment of Genocide, Member States of the United Nations . . . contented themselves with the determination of territorial jurisdiction as a compulsory minimum. . . . It is clear that the reference in Article 6 to territorial jurisdiction, apart from the jurisdiction of the non-existent international tribunal, is not exhaustive, and every sovereign state may exercise its existing powers within the limits of customary international law, and there is nothing in the adherence of a state to the Convention to waive powers which are not mentioned in Article 6.

Attorney General v. Eichmann, District Court of Jerusalem, Criminal Case No. 40/61, Judgment, ¶¶23-25 (1961), *available at* http://www.nizkor.org/ftp.cgi/people/e/eichmann.adolf/transcripts/ftp.py?people/e/eichmann.adolf/transcripts/Judgment/Judgment-004.

On this analysis, Article 6 requires states parties to establish territorial jurisdiction over genocide, but does not forbid them from establishing broader jurisdiction, up to the limits established by customary international law — presumably, the *Lotus* principle. Is this correct? What about the concerns over state sovereignty and politicized prosecutions that opponents of universal jurisdiction voiced during the drafting process of the Genocide Convention? If the Convention leaves it up to states to establish broader jurisdiction if they wish, won't those concerns still be there?

As we have seen, the United States originally went beyond the jurisdiction specified in Article 6, although not as far as universal jurisdiction: 18 U.S.C. §1091(d) created both territorial and nationality jurisdiction over genocide. The 2007 amendment broadened the statute even further, and it is now in effect a universal jurisdiction statute.

C. CASES

The following judicial decisions and international report explore subtleties in the legal definitions built into Articles 2 and 3 of the Genocide Convention. We begin with the ICTR Trial Chamber's *Akayesu* judgment, which represents the first genocide conviction in any international tribunal. This landmark decision provides important explanations of what the various crimes and modes of participation mean in practice.

Next comes the ICTY Appeals Chamber's decision in *Prosecutor v. Krstić.* Krstić was a Serbian general commanding part of the Drina Corps, which carried out the massacre of more than 7,000 Bosnian Muslim men at Srebrenica. This was the ICTY's first genocide conviction, although on appeal it was reduced to complicity in genocide. The excerpt presented below contains important discussion of the idea that genocide can include intentional destruction of part of a group rather than the whole group. It also discusses the kind of evidence needed to prove genocidal intent.

We then present an excerpt from the report of a UN Commission investigating whether events in Darfur, Sudan, constitute genocide. The Darfur Commission concluded that the evidence may sustain claims that war crimes and crimes against humanity are being committed in Darfur, but it does not sustain a claim of genocide. The analysis in this controversial report sheds light on whether tribal groups count as "ethnical" groups, as well as the distinction between genocide and crimes against humanity. While reading these excerpts, students should compare the way that the ICTY analyzed evidence in *Krstić* with the Darfur Commission's analysis of the evidence, and ask whether these are consistent with each other.

In 2009, the ICC's Pre-Trial Chamber confirmed charges against Sudan's president, Omar Al Bashir, and issued an arrest warrant. The prosecutor had asked for charges that included genocide, but the Pre-Trial Chamber rejected that request and confirmed only charges of crimes against humanity and war crimes. We include an excerpt from this decision rejecting genocide charges, a decision which at the time this book goes to press remains under appeal.

PROSECUTOR v. AKAYESU

Case No. ICTR-96-4-T, Judgment (Sept. 2, 1998)

[Jean Paul Akayesu was the bourgmestre (mayor) of Taba commune in Rwanda. He was accused of having done nothing to protect Tutsis in his commune from the genocide and of having participated in the genocide himself. He was convicted of genocide, direct and public incitement to genocide, and the crimes against humanity of murder, extermination, torture, and rape. He was acquitted of complicity in genocide. Akayesu was sentenced to life imprisonment. At his sentencing hearing, the tribunal summarized its factual findings as follows:

> . . . Trial Chamber 1 found that it was established beyond reasonable doubt that; . . .
>
> 2. Akayesu aided and abetted acts of sexual violence by allowing them to take place on or near the premises of the *bureau communal* while he was present on the premises and by facilitating the commission of these acts through his words of encouragement. [He also aided and abetted] other acts of sexual violence which by virtue of his authority sent a clear signal of official tolerance for sexual violence without which these acts of sexual violence would not have taken place.
>
> 3. On 19 April 1994, Akayesu addressed a meeting at Gisheshe and called on the population to fight against accomplices of the Inkotanye, knowing that his utterances would be understood by the people present to mean, kill the Tutsi, and as a result thereof widespread killing of Tutsi had commenced in Taba;
>
> 4. At this meeting in Gisheshe, Akayesu mentioned the name of Euphraim Karangwa. Later on, that same day, groups of people acting on the orders of Akayesu and in his presence, destroyed Karangwa's house and Karangwa's mother's house and killed Karangwa's three brothers.
>
> 5. Akayesu is individually, criminally responsible for the death of the eight refugees from Ruanda [*sic*] who were killed in his presence by the Interahamwe acting on his orders.
>
> 6. Akayesu is individually, criminally responsible for the killing of the five teachers who were killed by the Interahamwe and local population acting on his orders.
>
> Lastly, point 7, Akayesu is individually, criminally responsible for the torture of Victims, U, V, W, X, Y, and Z.

Prosecutor v. Akayesu, Case No. ICTR-96-4-T, Sentence (Oct. 2, 1998).]

. . . 492. Article 2 of the [ICTR's] Statute stipulates that the Tribunal shall have the power to prosecute persons responsible for genocide, complicity to commit genocide, direct and public incitement to commit genocide, attempt to commit genocide and complicity in genocide. . . .

Causing Serious Bodily or Mental Harm to Members of the Group (Paragraph B)

502. Causing serious bodily or mental harm to members of the group does not necessarily mean that the harm is permanent and irremediable.

503. In the Adolf Eichmann case, who was convicted of crimes against the Jewish people, genocide under another legal definition, the District Court of Jerusalem stated in its judgment of 12 December 1961, that serious bodily or mental harm of members of the group can be caused

> by the[ir] enslavement, starvation, deportation and persecution [. . .] and by their detention in ghettos, transit camps and concentration camps in conditions which were designed to cause their degradation, deprivation of their rights as human beings, and to suppress them and cause them inhumane suffering and torture.

504. For purposes of interpreting Article 2(2)(b) of the Statute, the Chamber takes serious bodily or mental harm, without limiting itself thereto, to mean acts of torture, be they bodily or mental, inhumane or degrading treatment, persecution.

Deliberately Inflicting on the Group Conditions of Life Calculated to Bring About Its Physical Destruction in Whole or in Part (Paragraph C)

505. The Chamber holds that the expression deliberately inflicting on the group conditions of life calculated to bring about its physical destruction in whole or in part, should be construed as the methods of destruction by which the perpetrator does not immediately kill the members of the group, but which, ultimately, seek their physical destruction.

506. For purposes of interpreting Article 2(2)(c) of the Statute, the Chamber is of the opinion that the means of deliberate inflicting on the group conditions of life calculated to bring about its physical destruction, in whole or part, include, inter alia, subjecting a group of people to a subsistence diet, systematic expulsion from homes and the reduction of essential medical services below minimum requirement.

Imposing Measures Intended to Prevent Births Within the Group (Paragraph D)

507. For purposes of interpreting Article 2(2)(d) of the Statute, the Chamber holds that the measures intended to prevent births within the group, should be construed as sexual mutilation, the practice of sterilization, forced birth control, separation of the sexes and prohibition of marriages. In patriarchal societies, where membership of a group is determined by the identity of the father, an example of a measure intended to prevent births within a group is the case where, during rape, a woman of the said group is deliberately impregnated by a man of another group, with the intent to have her give birth to a child who will consequently not belong to its mother's group.

508. Furthermore, the Chamber notes that measures intended to prevent births within the group may be physical, but can also be mental. For instance, rape can be a measure intended to prevent births when the person raped refuses subsequently to procreate, in the same way that members of a group can be led, through threats or trauma, not to procreate.

Forcibly Transferring Children of the Group to Another Group (Paragraph E)

509. With respect to forcibly transferring children of the group to another group, the Chamber is of the opinion that, as in the case of measures intended to prevent births, the objective is not only to sanction a direct act of forcible physical transfer, but also to sanction acts of threats or trauma which would lead to the forcible transfer of children from one group to another.

510. Since the special intent to commit genocide lies in the intent to "destroy, in whole or in part, a national, ethnical, racial or religious group, as such," it is necessary to consider a definition of the group as such. Article 2 of the Statute, just like the Genocide Convention, stipulates four types of victim groups, namely national, ethnical, racial or religious groups.

511. On reading through the *travaux préparatoires* of the Genocide Convention, it appears that the crime of genocide was allegedly perceived as targeting only "stable" groups, constituted in a permanent fashion and membership of which is determined by birth, with the exclusion of the more "mobile" groups which one joins through individual voluntary commitment, such as political and economic groups. Therefore, a common criterion in the four types of groups protected by the Genocide Convention is that membership in such groups would seem to be normally not challengeable

by its members, who belong to it automatically, by birth, in a continuous and often irremediable manner. . . .

516. Moreover, the Chamber considered whether the groups protected by the Genocide Convention, echoed in Article 2 of the Statute, should be limited to only the four groups expressly mentioned and whether they should not also include any group which is stable and permanent like the said four groups. In other words, the question that arises is whether it would be impossible to punish the physical destruction of a group as such under the Genocide Convention, if the said group, although stable and membership is by birth, does not meet the definition of any one of the four groups expressly protected by the Genocide Convention. In the opinion of the Chamber, it is particularly important to respect the intention of the drafters of the Genocide Convention, which according to the *travaux préparatoires*, was patently to ensure the protection of any stable and permanent group.

517. As stated above, the crime of genocide is characterized by its *dolus specialis*, or special intent, which lies in the fact that the acts charged, listed in Article 2 (2) of the Statute, must have been "committed with intent to destroy, in whole or in part, a national, ethnical, racial or religious group, as such."

518. Special intent is a well-known criminal law concept in the Roman-continental legal systems. It is required as a constituent element of certain offences and demands that the perpetrator have the clear intent to cause the offence charged. According to this meaning, special intent is the key element of an intentional offence, which offence is characterized by a psychological relationship between the physical result and the mental state of the perpetrator. . . .

520. With regard to the crime of genocide, the offender is culpable only when he has committed one of the offences charged under Article 2(2) of the Statute with the clear intent to destroy, in whole or in part, a particular group. The offender is culpable because he knew or should have known that the act committed would destroy, in whole or in part, a group.

521. In concrete terms, for any of the acts charged under Article 2 (2) of the Statute to be a constitutive element of genocide, the act must have been committed against one or several individuals, because such individual or individuals were members of a specific group, and specifically because they belonged to this group. Thus, the victim is chosen not because of his individual identity, but rather on account of his membership of a national, ethnical, racial or religious group. The victim of the act is therefore a member of a group, chosen as such, which, hence, means that the victim of the crime of genocide is the group itself and not only the individual. . . .

[The *Akayesu* judgment also includes important discussion of the crime of direct and public incitement to commit genocide. We treat this topic separately later in this chapter and include the relevant excerpt from *Akayesu* there.]

NOTES AND QUESTIONS

1. The ICTR Trial Chamber finds that "[c]ausing serious bodily or mental harm to members of the group does not necessarily mean that the harm is permanent and irremediable" (¶502). Compare this with the definition of mental harm in the U.S. genocide statute.

2. Of particular importance is the Chamber's holding in paragraphs 507 and 508 that rape can constitute the crime of genocide by imposing measures to prevent births. For further discussion of crimes of sexual violence, see Chapter 23.

3. In ¶509, the Chamber finds that "acts of threats or trauma which would lead to the forcible transfer of children from one group to another" can count as genocide. What kind of acts does this encompass? During World War II, many Jews gave their children to sympathetic Christian families to save them from deportation and death. Would this count as forcible transfer of children from one group to another by the Nazis?

4. Paragraph 511 argues that the Genocide Convention aimed to protect "stable" groups, that is, groups "constituted in a permanent fashion and membership of which is determined by birth." Is this accurate? Consider this objection from William Schabas, a leading expert on genocide:

> On closer scrutiny, three of the four categories in the Convention enumeration, national groups, ethnic groups, and religious groups[,] seem to be neither stable nor permanent. Only racial groups, when they are defined genetically, can lay claim to some relatively prolonged stability and permanence. The day after the General Assembly adopted the Genocide Convention it approved the Universal Declaration of Human Rights, which proclaims the fundamental right to change both nationality and religion, thereby recognizing that they are far from permanent and stable. National groups are modified dramatically as borders change and as individual and collective conceptions of identity evolve. Nationality may be changed, sometimes for large groups of individuals where, for example, two countries have joined or secession has occurred. Religious groups may come into existence and disappear within a single lifetime. As for ethnic groups, individual members may also come and go, although there will often be formal legal rules associated with this, determining ethnicity as a result of marriage or in the case of children whose parents belong to different ethnic groups.

William A. Schabas, Groups Protected by the Genocide Convention: Conflicting Interpretations from the International Criminal Tribunal for Rwanda, 6 ILSA J. Intl. & Comp. L. 375, 382 (2000).

5. Schabas also objects that *Akayesu*'s analysis "quite brazenly goes beyond the actual terms of the Convention definition" by expanding it to groups not included in Article 3's enumeration of protected groups. Id. at 380. However, other states have expanded the list of protected groups in their domestic genocide legislation beyond race, nationality, religion, and ethnicity. Thus, Colombia and Ethiopia include political groups, while Lithuania includes social and political groups; Costa Rica adds groups determined by age, political or sexual orientation, social position, economic situation, or civil status. The broadest definitions are those of France and Burkina Faso, which add to the Genocide Convention's list all groups determined by "any other arbitrary criterion." All these statutes may be found in Prevent Genocide International, The Crime of Genocide in Domestic Laws and Penal Codes, available at http://www.preventgenocide.org/law/domestic/ (last visited Aug. 16, 2009).

PROSECUTOR v. KRSTIĆ

Case No. IT-98-33-A, Judgment (Apr. 19, 2004)

I. INTRODUCTION

1. The Appeals Chamber . . . is seised of two appeals from the written Judgement rendered by the Trial Chamber on 2 August 2001 in the case of *Prosecutor* v. *Radislav*

Krstić, . . . ("Trial Judgement"). Having considered the written and oral submissions of the Prosecution and the Defence, the Appeals Chamber hereby renders its Judgement.

2. Srebrenica is located in eastern Bosnia and Herzegovina. It gave its name to a United Nations so-called safe area, which was intended as an enclave of safety set up to protect its civilian population from the surrounding war. Since July 1995, however, Srebrenica has also lent its name to an event the horrors of which form the background to this case. The depravity, brutality and cruelty with which the Bosnian Serb Army ("VRS") treated the innocent inhabitants of the safe area are now well known and documented. Bosnian women, children and elderly were removed from the enclave, and between 7,000–8,000 Bosnian Muslim men were systematically murdered.

3. Srebrenica is located in the area for which the Drina Corps of the VRS was responsible. Radislav Krstić was a General-Major in the VRS and Commander of the Drina Corps at the time the crimes at issue were committed. For his involvement in these events, the Trial Chamber found Radislav Krstić guilty of genocide; persecution through murders, cruel and inhumane treatment, terrorising the civilian population, forcible transfer and destruction of personal property; and murder as a violation of the laws or customs of war. Radislav Krstić was sentenced to forty-six years of imprisonment. . . .

II. THE TRIAL CHAMBER'S FINDING THAT GENOCIDE OCCURRED IN SREBRENICA . . .

5. The Defence appeals Radislav Krstić's conviction for genocide committed against Bosnian Muslims in Srebrenica. The Defence argues that the Trial Chamber both misconstrued the legal definition of genocide and erred in applying the definition to the circumstances of this case. With respect to the legal challenge, the Defence's argument is two-fold. First, Krstić contends that the Trial Chamber's definition of the part of the national group he was found to have intended to destroy was unacceptably narrow. Second, the Defence argues that the Trial Chamber erroneously enlarged the term "destroy" in the prohibition of genocide to include the geographical displacement of a community.

A. THE DEFINITION OF THE PART OF THE GROUP

6. Article 4 of the Tribunal's Statute, like the Genocide Convention, covers certain acts done with "intent to destroy, in whole or in part, a national, ethnical, racial or religious group, as such." The Indictment in this case alleged, with respect to the count of genocide, that Radislav Krstić "intend[ed] to destroy a part of the Bosnian Muslim people as a national, ethnical, or religious group." The targeted group identified in the Indictment, and accepted by the Trial Chamber, was that of the Bosnian Muslims. The Trial Chamber determined that the Bosnian Muslims were a specific, distinct national group, and therefore covered by Article 4. This conclusion is not challenged in this appeal.

7. As is evident from the Indictment, Krstić was not alleged to have intended to destroy the entire national group of Bosnian Muslims, but only a part of that group. The first question presented in this appeal is whether, in finding that Radislav Krstić had genocidal intent, the Trial Chamber defined the relevant part of the Bosnian Muslim group in a way which comports with the requirements of Article 4 and of the Genocide Convention.

8. It is well established that where a conviction for genocide relies on the intent to destroy a protected group "in part," the part must be a substantial part of that group. [The Appeals Chamber proceeds to quote multiple sources confirming that the "part" must be a substantial part: the ICTY Trial Chambers' decisions in *Jelisić* and *Sikirica*; the ICTR Trial Chambers' decisions in *Kayishema, Bagilishema,* and *Semanza*; comments by Lemkin and Nehemiah Robinson, another well-known early commentator; the International Law Commission; and Benjamin Whitaker, the Special Rapporteur to the United Nations Sub-Commission on Prevention of Discrimination and Protection of Minorities.] . . .

12. The intent requirement of genocide under Article 4 of the Statute is therefore satisfied where evidence shows that the alleged perpetrator intended to destroy at least a substantial part of the protected group. The determination of when the targeted part is substantial enough to meet this requirement may involve a number of considerations. The numeric size of the targeted part of the group is the necessary and important starting point, though not in all cases the ending point of the inquiry. The number of individuals targeted should be evaluated not only in absolute terms, but also in relation to the overall size of the entire group. In addition to the numeric size of the targeted portion, its prominence within the group can be a useful consideration. If a specific part of the group is emblematic of the overall group, or is essential to its survival, that may support a finding that the part qualifies as substantial within the meaning of Article 4.

13. The historical examples of genocide also suggest that the area of the perpetrators' activity and control, as well as the possible extent of their reach, should be considered. Nazi Germany may have intended only to eliminate Jews within Europe alone; that ambition probably did not extend, even at the height of its power, to an undertaking of that enterprise on a global scale. Similarly, the perpetrators of genocide in Rwanda did not seriously contemplate the elimination of the Tutsi population beyond the country's borders. The intent to destroy formed by a perpetrator of genocide will always be limited by the opportunity presented to him. While this factor alone will not indicate whether the targeted group is substantial, it can—in combination with other factors—inform the analysis.

14. These considerations, of course, are neither exhaustive nor dispositive. They are only useful guidelines. The applicability of these factors, as well as their relative weight, will vary depending on the circumstances of a particular case.

15. In this case, having identified the protected group as the national group of Bosnian Muslims, the Trial Chamber concluded that the part the VRS Main Staff and Radislav Krstić targeted was the Bosnian Muslims of Srebrenica, or the Bosnian Muslims of Eastern Bosnia. This conclusion comports with the guidelines outlined above. The size of the Bosnian Muslim population in Srebrenica prior to its capture by the VRS forces in 1995 amounted to approximately forty thousand people. This represented not only the Muslim inhabitants of the Srebrenica municipality but also many Muslim refugees from the surrounding region. Although this population constituted only a small percentage of the overall Muslim population of Bosnia and Herzegovina at the time, the importance of the Muslim community of Srebrenica is not captured solely by its size. As the Trial Chamber explained, Srebrenica (and the surrounding Central Podrinje region) were of immense strategic importance to the Bosnian Serb leadership. Without Srebrenica, the ethnically Serb state of Republika Srpska they sought to create would remain divided into two disconnected parts, and its access to Serbia proper would be disrupted. The capture and ethnic purification of Srebrenica

would therefore severely undermine the military efforts of the Bosnian Muslim state to ensure its viability, a consequence the Muslim leadership fully realized and strove to prevent. Control over the Srebrenica region was consequently essential to the goal of some Bosnian Serb leaders of forming a viable political entity in Bosnia, as well as to the continued survival of the Bosnian Muslim people. Because most of the Muslim inhabitants of the region had, by 1995, sought refuge within the Srebrenica enclave, the elimination of that enclave would have accomplished the goal of purifying the entire region of its Muslim population.

16. In addition, Srebrenica was important due to its prominence in the eyes of both the Bosnian Muslims and the international community. The town of Srebrenica was the most visible of the "safe areas" established by the UN Security Council in Bosnia. By 1995 it had received significant attention in the international media. In its resolution declaring Srebrenica a safe area, the Security Council announced that it "should be free from armed attack or any other hostile act." This guarantee of protection was re-affirmed by the commander of the UN Protection Force in Bosnia (UNPROFOR) and reinforced with the deployment of UN troops. The elimination of the Muslim population of Srebrenica, despite the assurances given by the international community, would serve as a potent example to all Bosnian Muslims of their vulnerability and defenselessness in the face of Serb military forces. The fate of the Bosnian Muslims of Srebrenica would be emblematic of that of all Bosnian Muslims.

17. Finally, the ambit of the genocidal enterprise in this case was limited to the area of Srebrenica. While the authority of the VRS Main Staff extended throughout Bosnia, the authority of the Bosnian Serb forces charged with the take-over of Srebrenica did not extend beyond the Central Podrinje region. From the perspective of the Bosnian Serb forces alleged to have had genocidal intent in this case, the Muslims of Srebrenica were the only part of the Bosnian Muslim group within their area of control.

18. In fact, the Defence does not argue that the Trial Chamber's characterization of the Bosnian Muslims of Srebrenica as a substantial part of the targeted group contravenes Article 4 of the Tribunal's Statute. Rather, the Defence contends that the Trial Chamber made a further finding, concluding that the part Krstić intended to destroy was the Bosnian Muslim men of military age of Srebrenica. In the Defence's view, the Trial Chamber then engaged in an impermissible sequential reasoning, measuring the latter part of the group against the larger part (the Bosnian Muslims of Srebrenica) to find the substantiality requirement satisfied. The Defence submits that if the correct approach is properly applied, and the military age men are measured against the entire group of Bosnian Muslims, the substantiality requirement would not be met.

19. The Defence misunderstands the Trial Chamber's analysis. The Trial Chamber stated that the part of the group Radislav Krstić intended to destroy was the Bosnian Muslim population of Srebrenica. The men of military age, who formed a further part of that group, were not viewed by the Trial Chamber as a separate, smaller part within the meaning of Article 4. Rather, the Trial Chamber treated the killing of the men of military age as evidence from which to infer that Radislav Krstić and some members of the VRS Main Staff had the requisite intent to destroy all the Bosnian Muslims of Srebrenica, the only part of the protected group relevant to the Article 4 analysis. . . .

23. The Trial Chamber's determination of the substantial part of the protected group was correct. The Defence's appeal on this issue is dismissed.

B. THE DETERMINATION OF THE INTENT TO DESTROY

24. The Defence also argues that the Trial Chamber erred in describing the conduct with which Radislav Krstić is charged as genocide. The Trial Chamber, the Defence submits, impermissibly broadened the definition of genocide by concluding that an effort to displace a community from its traditional residence is sufficient to show that the alleged perpetrator intended to destroy a protected group. By adopting this approach, the Defence argues, the Trial Chamber departed from the established meaning of the term genocide in the Genocide Convention — as applying only to instances of physical or biological destruction of a group — to include geographic displacement.

25. The Genocide Convention, and customary international law in general, prohibit only the physical or biological destruction of a human group. The Trial Chamber expressly acknowledged this limitation, and eschewed any broader definition. The Chamber stated: "[C]ustomary international law limits the definition of genocide to those acts seeking the physical or biological destruction of all or part of the group. [A]n enterprise attacking only the cultural or sociological characteristics of a human group in order to annihilate these elements which give to that group its own identity distinct from the rest of the community would not fall under the definition of genocide."

26. Given that the Trial Chamber correctly identified the governing legal principle, the Defence must discharge the burden of persuading the Appeals Chamber that, despite having correctly stated the law, the Trial Chamber erred in applying it. The main evidence underlying the Trial Chamber's conclusion that the VRS forces intended to eliminate all the Bosnian Muslims of Srebrenica was the massacre by the VRS of all men of military age from that community. The Trial Chamber rejected the Defence's argument that the killing of these men was motivated solely by the desire to eliminate them as a potential military threat. The Trial Chamber based this conclusion on a number of factual findings, which must be accepted as long as a reasonable Trial Chamber could have arrived at the same conclusions. . . .

27. Moreover, as the Trial Chamber emphasized, the term "men of military age" was itself a misnomer, for the group killed by the VRS included boys and elderly men normally considered to be outside that range. Although the younger and older men could still be capable of bearing arms, the Trial Chamber was entitled to conclude that they did not present a serious military threat, and to draw a further inference that the VRS decision to kill them did not stem solely from the intent to eliminate them as a threat. The killing of the military aged men was, assuredly, a physical destruction, and given the scope of the killings the Trial Chamber could legitimately draw the inference that their extermination was motivated by a genocidal intent.

28. The Trial Chamber was also entitled to consider the long-term impact that the elimination of seven to eight thousand men from Srebrenica would have on the survival of that community. In examining these consequences, the Trial Chamber properly focused on the likelihood of the community's physical survival. As the Trial Chamber found, the massacred men amounted to about one fifth of the overall Srebrenica community. The Trial Chamber found that, given the patriarchal character of the Bosnian Muslim society in Srebrenica, the destruction of such a sizeable number of men would "inevitably result in the physical disappearance of the Bosnian Muslim population at Srebrenica." Evidence introduced at trial supported this finding, by showing that, with the majority of the men killed officially listed as missing, their spouses are unable to remarry and, consequently, to have new children. The physical destruction of the men therefore had severe procreative

implications for the Srebrenica Muslim community, potentially consigning the community to extinction.

29. This is the type of physical destruction the Genocide Convention is designed to prevent. . . .

30. The Defence argues that the VRS decision to transfer, rather than to kill, the women and children of Srebrenica in their custody undermines the finding of genocidal intent. This conduct, the Defence submits, is inconsistent with the indiscriminate approach that has characterized all previously recognized instances of modern genocide.

31. The decision by Bosnian Serb forces to transfer the women, children and elderly within their control to other areas of Muslim-controlled Bosnia could be consistent with the Defence argument. This evidence, however, is also susceptible of an alternative interpretation. As the Trial Chamber explained, forcible transfer could be an additional means by which to ensure the physical destruction of the Bosnian Muslim community in Srebrenica. The transfer completed the removal of all Bosnian Muslims from Srebrenica, thereby eliminating even the residual possibility that the Muslim community in the area could reconstitute itself. The decision not to kill the women or children may be explained by the Bosnian Serbs' sensitivity to public opinion. In contrast to the killing of the captured military men, such an action could not easily be kept secret, or disguised as a military operation, and so carried an increased risk of attracting international censure.

32. In determining that genocide occurred at Srebrenica, the cardinal question is whether the intent to commit genocide existed. While this intent must be supported by the factual matrix, the offence of genocide does not require proof that the perpetrator chose the most efficient method to accomplish his objective of destroying the targeted part. Even where the method selected will not implement the perpetrator's intent to the fullest, leaving that destruction incomplete, this ineffectiveness alone does not preclude a finding of genocidal intent. The international attention focused on Srebrenica, combined with the presence of the UN troops in the area, prevented those members of the VRS Main Staff who devised the genocidal plan from putting it into action in the most direct and efficient way. Constrained by the circumstances, they adopted the method which would allow them to implement the genocidal design while minimizing the risk of retribution. . . .

34. The Defence also argues that the record contains no statements by members of the VRS Main Staff indicating that the killing of the Bosnian Muslim men was motivated by genocidal intent to destroy the Bosnian Muslims of Srebrenica. The absence of such statements is not determinative. Where direct evidence of genocidal intent is absent, the intent may still be inferred from the factual circumstances of the crime. The inference that a particular atrocity was motivated by genocidal intent may be drawn, moreover, even where the individuals to whom the intent is attributable are not precisely identified. If the crime committed satisfies the other requirements of genocide, and if the evidence supports the inference that the crime was motivated by the intent to destroy, in whole or in part, a protected group, a finding that genocide has occurred may be entered.

35. In this case, the factual circumstances, as found by the Trial Chamber, permit the inference that the killing of the Bosnian Muslim men was done with genocidal intent. As already explained, the scale of the killing, combined with the VRS Main Staff's awareness of the detrimental consequences it would have for the Bosnian Muslim community of Srebrenica and with the other actions the Main Staff took to ensure that community's physical demise, is a sufficient factual basis for the finding of specific intent. The Trial Chamber found, and the Appeals Chamber endorses this

finding, that the killing was engineered and supervised by some members of the Main Staff of the VRS. The fact that the Trial Chamber did not attribute genocidal intent to a particular official within the Main Staff may have been motivated by a desire not to assign individual culpability to persons not on trial here. This, however, does not undermine the conclusion that Bosnian Serb forces carried out genocide against the Bosnian Muslims. . . .

38. In concluding that some members of the VRS Main Staff intended to destroy the Bosnian Muslims of Srebrenica, the Trial Chamber did not depart from the legal requirements for genocide. The Defence appeal on this issue is dismissed.

REPORT OF THE INTERNATIONAL COMMISSION OF INQUIRY ON DARFUR TO THE UNITED NATIONS SECRETARY-GENERAL

Pursuant to Security Council Resolution 1564 of 18 September 2004
Geneva, 25 January 2005

[Darfur is a large, arid region in western Sudan, occupied by several tribal groups, including both farmers and herders. Although all the groups are Muslim, the herders identify themselves as Arabs, while the farmers are often identified as black Africans. (Like many such ethnic identifications, the Arab-African dichotomy is overly simple and highly politicized. See ¶510 of the excerpt that follows.) Chronic conflicts between farmers and herders over land use ensured tension between the groups.

In 2003, a long-running civil war between the north and south of Sudan was settled. Darfurian "African" groups feared that the peace deal would exclude them from political power and launched a rebellion against the government. In response, the government initiated a brutal counterinsurgency. The government encouraged and aided Arab raiders — the "janjaweed" militiamen — who launched violent attacks against "black" villages. Government forces often joined the janjaweed in these attacks. Thousands of people were killed and raped, and hundreds of thousands were displaced. Refugees teetered on the edge of survival in camps where they lacked food and water. To many observers, it appeared that a genocide was unfolding in Darfur. In 2004, U.S. Secretary of State Colin Powell declared the Darfur situation to be a genocide.

In September 2004, U.N. Security Council Resolution 1564 established a commission of inquiry into the Darfur crisis, in part to determine whether a genocide against the black tribes (or other international crimes) was occurring, and who was responsible. The Commission concluded that war crimes and crimes against humanity were occurring in Darfur, but found insufficient evidence of genocide.]

15. . . . The Commission discussed the question of the standard of proof that it would apply in its investigations. In view of the limitations inherent in its powers, the Commission decided that it could not comply with the standards normally adopted by criminal courts (proof of facts beyond a reasonable doubt), or with that used by international prosecutors and judges for the purpose of confirming indictments (that there must be a prima facie case). It concluded that the most appropriate standard was that requiring a reliable body of material consistent with other verified circumstances, which tends to show that a person may reasonably be suspected of being involved in the commission of a crime. The Commission would obviously not make final judgments as to criminal guilt; rather, it would make an assessment of possible suspects that would pave the way for future investigations, and possible indictments, by a prosecutor. . . .

SECTION II. HAVE ACTS OF GENOCIDE OCCURRED?

I. THE NOTION OF GENOCIDE

489. . . . [A] task assigned to the Commission is that of establishing whether the crimes allegedly perpetrated in Darfur may be characterized as acts of genocide, or whether they instead fall under other categories of international crimes. . . .

495. *Are tribal groups protected by international rules proscribing genocide?* In 1996 the United Nations International Law Commission in its report on the "Draft Code of Crimes Against Peace and Security of Mankind" stated that "The Commission was of the view that the present article [17 of the Draft Code] covered the prohibited acts when committed with the necessary intent against members of a *tribal group.*" According to anthropologists a "tribe" constitutes a territorial division of certain large populations, based on kinship or the belief that they descend from one ancestor: these aggregates have a chief and call themselves by one name and speak one language.

496. The aforementioned view about "tribal groups," which has remained isolated, may be accepted on condition that the "tribal group" should also constitute a distinct "racial, national, ethnical or religious" group. In other words, tribes as such do not constitute a protected group.

497. It is apparent that the international rules on genocide are intended to protect from obliteration groups targeted not on account of their constituting a territorial unit linked by some community bonds (such as kinship, language and lineage), but only those groups — whatever their magnitude — which show the particular hallmark of sharing a religion, or racial or ethnic features, and are targeted precisely on account of their distinctiveness. In sum, tribes may fall under the notion of genocide set out in international law only if, as stated above, they also exhibit the characteristics of one of the four categories of group protected by international law.

498. *The question of genocidal acts against groups that do not perfectly match the definitions of the four above mentioned groups.* The genocide perpetrated in 1994 in Rwanda vividly showed the limitations of current international rules on genocide and obliged the Judges of the ICTR to place an innovative interpretation on those rules. The fact is that the Tutsi and the Hutu do not constitute at first glance distinct ethnic, racial, religious or national groups. They have the same language, culture and religion, as well as basically the same physical traits. In *Akayesu* the ICTR Trial Chamber emphasized that the two groups were nevertheless distinct because (i) they had been made distinct by the Belgian colonizers when they established a system of identity cards differentiating between the two groups (§702), and (ii) the distinction was confirmed by the self-perception of the members of each group. As the Trials Chamber pointed out, "all the Rwandan witnesses who appeared before it invariably answered spontaneously and without hesitation the questions of the Prosecutor regarding their ethnic identity." The Trial Chamber also insisted on the fact that what was required by the international rules on genocide was that the targeted group be "a stable and permanent group," "constituted in a permanent fashion and membership of which is determined by birth," and be identifiable as such (§§511 and 702). The objective criterion of a "stable and permanent group," which, if considered per se, could be held to be rather questionable, was supplemented in the ICTR case law (and subsequently in that of the ICTY) by the subjective standard of perception and self-perception as a member of a group. According to this case law, in case of doubt one should also establish whether (i) a set of persons are perceived and in fact treated as belonging to one of the protected groups, and in addition (ii) they consider themselves as belonging to one of such groups.

499. In short, the approach taken to determine whether a group is a (fully) protected one has evolved from an objective to a subjective standard to take into account that "collective identities, and in particular ethnicity, are by their very nature social constructs, 'imagined' identities entirely dependent on variable and contingent perceptions, and *not* social facts, which are verifiable in the same manner as natural phenomena or physical facts." . . .

502. *Proof of genocidal intent.* Whenever direct evidence of genocidal intent is lacking, as is mostly the case, this intent can be inferred from many acts and manifestations or factual circumstances. In *Jelisić* the Appeals Chamber noted that "as to proof of specific intent, it may, in the absence of direct explicit evidence, be inferred from a number of facts and circumstances, such as the general context, the perpetration of other culpable acts systematically directed against the same group, the scale of atrocities committed, the systematic targeting of victims on account of their membership of a particular group, or the repetition of destructive and discriminatory acts" (§47).

503. Courts and other bodies charged with establishing whether genocide has occurred must however be very careful in the determination of the subjective intent. As the ICTY Appeals Chamber rightly put it in *Krstić (Appeal)*, "Genocide is one of the worst crimes known to humankind, and its gravity is reflected in the stringent requirements of specific intent. Convictions for genocide can be entered only where intent has been unequivocally established" (Judgment of 19 April 2004, at §134). On this ground the Appeals Chamber, finding that the Trial Chamber had erred in demonstrating that the accused possessed the genocidal intent, reversed the Trial Chamber's conviction of genocide and sentenced Krstić for complicity in genocide. . . .

505. *Is genocide graver than other international crimes?* It has widely been held that genocide is the most serious international crime. In *Kambanda* (§16) and *Serushago* (§15) the ICTR defined it as "the crime of crimes. . . ."

506. It is indisputable that genocide bears a special stigma, for it is aimed at the *physical obliteration* of human groups. However, one should not be blind to the fact that some categories of crimes against humanity may be similarly heinous and carry a similarly grave stigma. In fact, the Appeals Chamber of the ICTR reversed the view that genocide was the "crime of crimes." In *Kayishema and Ruyindana*, the accused alleged "that the Trial Chamber erred in finding that genocide is the 'crime of crimes' because there is no such hierarchical gradation of crimes." The Appeals Chamber agreed: "The Appeals Chamber remarks that there is no hierarchy of crimes under the Statute, and that all of the crimes specified therein are 'serious violations of international humanitarian law,' capable of attracting the same sentence." (§367).

II. DO THE CRIMES PERPETRATED IN DARFUR CONSTITUTE ACTS OF GENOCIDE?

507. *General.* There is no doubt that some of the objective elements of genocide materialized in Darfur. As discussed above, the Commission has collected substantial and reliable material which tends to show the occurrence of systematic killing of civilians belonging to particular tribes, of large-scale causing of serious bodily or mental harm to members of the population belonging to certain tribes, and of massive and deliberate infliction on those tribes of conditions of life bringing about their physical destruction in whole or in part (for example by systematically destroying their villages and crops, by expelling them from their homes, and by looting their cattle). However, two other constitutive elements of genocide require a more in depth analysis, namely whether (a) the target groups amount to one of the group[s] protected by international law, and if so (b) whether the crimes were committed with a genocidal intent. These elements are considered separately below.

508. *Do members of the tribes victims of attacks and killing make up objectively a protected group?* The various tribes that have been the object of attacks and killings (chiefly the Fur, Massalit and Zaghawa tribes) do not appear to make up ethnic groups distinct from the ethnic group to which persons or militias that attack them belong. They speak the same language (Arabic) and embrace the same religion (Muslim). In addition, also due to the high measure of intermarriage, they can hardly be distinguished in their outward physical appearance from the members of tribes that allegedly attacked them. Furthermore, inter-marriage and coexistence in both social and economic terms, have over the years tended to blur the distinction between the groups. Apparently, the sedentary and nomadic character of the groups constitutes one of the main distinctions between them. It is also notable that members of the African tribes speak their own dialect in addition to Arabic, while members of Arab tribes only speak Arabic.

509. *If not, may one hold that they subjectively make up distinct groups?* If objectively the two sets of persons at issue do not make up two distinct protected groups, the question arises as to whether they may nevertheless be regarded as such subjectively, in that they perceive each other and themselves as constituting distinct groups.

510. As noted above, in recent years the perception of differences has heightened and has extended to distinctions that were earlier not the predominant basis for identity. The rift between tribes, and the political polarization around the rebel opposition to the central authorities, has extended itself to issues of identity. Those tribes in Darfur who support rebels have increasingly come to be identified as "African" and those supporting the government as the "Arabs." . . . At least those most affected by the conditions explained above, including those directly affected by the conflict, have come to perceive themselves as either "African" or "Arab."

511. There are other elements that tend to show a self-perception of two distinct groups. In many cases militias attacking "African" villages tend to use derogatory epithets, such as "slaves," "blacks," "*Nuba*," or "*Zurga*" that might imply a perception of the victims as members of a distinct group. However, in numerous other instances they use derogatory language that is not linked to ethnicity or race.[7] As for the victims, they often refer to their attackers as *Janjaweed*, a derogatory term that normally designates "a man (a devil) with a gun on a horse." However, in this case the term Janjaweed clearly refers to "militias of *Arab* tribes on horseback or on camelback." In other words, the victims perceive the attackers as persons belonging to another and hostile group.

512. For these reasons it may be considered that the tribes who were victims of attacks and killings subjectively make up a protected group.

513. *Was there a genocidal intent?* Some elements emerging from the facts including the scale of atrocities and the systematic nature of the attacks, killing, displacement and rape, as well as racially motivated statements by perpetrators that have targeted members of the African tribes only, could be indicative of the genocidal intent.

---

7. [Report's footnote 189:] Epithets that eyewitnesses or victims reported to the Commission include the following: "This is your end. The Government armed me." "You are Massalit, why do you come here, why do you take our grass? You will not take anything today." "You will not stay in this country." "Destroy the *Torabora*." "You are Zaghawa tribes, you are slaves." "Where are your fathers, we would like to shoot and kill them." "Take your cattle, go away and leave the village." . . . During rape: "You are the mother of the people who are killing our people." "Do not cut the grass because the camels use it." "You sons of *Torabora* we are going to kill you." "You do not have the right to be educated and must be *Torabora*" (to an 18 year old student of a boarding school); "You are not allowed to take this money to fathers that are real *Torabora*" (to a girl from whom the soldier that raped her also took all her money); "You are very cheap people, you have to be killed."

However, there are other more indicative elements that show the lack of genocidal intent. The fact that in a number of villages attacked and burned by both militias and Government forces the attackers refrained from exterminating the whole population that had not fled, but instead selectively killed groups of young men, is an important element. A telling example is the attack of 22 January 2004 on Wadi Saleh, a group of 25 villages inhabited by about 11,000 Fur. According to credible accounts of eye witnesses questioned by the Commission, after occupying the villages the Government Commissioner and the leader of the Arab militias that had participated in the attack and burning, gathered all those who had survived or had not managed to escape into a large area. Using a microphone they selected 15 persons (whose name[s] they read from a written list), as well as 7 *omdas*, and executed them on the spot. They then sent all elderly men, all boys, many men and all women to a nearby village, where they held them for some time, whereas they executed 205 young villagers, who they asserted were rebels *(Torabora)*. According to male witnesses interviewed by the Commission and who were among the survivors, about 800 persons were not killed (most young men of those spared by the attackers were detained for some time in the Mukjar prison).

514. This case clearly shows that the intent of the attackers was not to destroy an ethnic group as such, or part of the group. Instead, the intention was to murder all those men they considered as rebels, as well as forcibly expel the whole population so as to vacate the villages and prevent rebels from hiding among, or getting support from, the local population.

515. Another element that tends to show the Sudanese Government's lack of genocidal intent can be seen in the fact that persons forcibly dislodged from their villages are collected in IDP camps. In other words, the populations surviving attacks on villages are not killed outright, so as to eradicate the group; they are rather forced to abandon their homes and live together in areas selected by the Government. . . . [T]he living conditions in those camps, although open to strong criticism on many grounds, do not seem to be calculated to bring about the extinction of the ethnic group to which the IDPs belong. Suffice it to note that the Government of Sudan generally allows humanitarian organizations to help the population in camps by providing food, clean water, medicines and logistical assistance (construction of hospitals, cooking facilities, latrines, etc.).

516. Another element that tends to show the lack of genocidal intent is the fact that in contrast with other instances described above, in a number of instances villages with a mixed composition (African and Arab tribes) have not been attacked. This for instance holds true for the village of Abaata (north-east of Zelingei, in Western Darfur), consisting of Zaghawa and members of Arab tribes.

517. Furthermore, it has been reported by a reliable source that one inhabitant of the Jabir Village (situated about 150 km from Abu Shouk Camp) was among the victims of an attack carried out by Janjaweed on 16 March 2004 on the village. He stated that he did not resist when the attackers took 200 camels from him, although they beat him up with the butt of their guns. Instead, prior to his beating, his young brother, who possessed only one camel, had resisted when the attackers had tried to take his camel, and had been shot dead. Clearly, in this instance the special intent to kill a member of a group to *destroy the group as such* was lacking, the murder being only motivated by the desire to appropriate cattle belonging to the inhabitants of the village. Irrespective of the motive, had the attackers' intent been to annihilate the group, they would not have spared one of the brothers.

518. *Conclusion.* On the basis of the above observations, the Commission concludes that the Government of Sudan has not pursued a policy of genocide. Arguably, two elements of genocide might be deduced from the gross violations of human rights perpetrated by Government forces and the militias under their control. These two elements are: first, the *actus reus* consisting of killing, or causing serious bodily or mental harm, or deliberately inflicting conditions of life likely to bring about physical destruction; and, second, on the basis of a subjective standard, the existence of a protected group being targeted by the authors of criminal conduct. Recent developments have led to the perception and self-perception of members of African tribes and members of Arab tribes as making up two distinct ethnic groups. However, one crucial element appears to be missing, at least as far as the central Government authorities are concerned: genocidal intent. Generally speaking the policy of attacking, killing and forcibly displacing members of some tribes does not evince a specific intent to annihilate, in whole or in part, a group distinguished on racial, ethnic, national or religious grounds. Rather, it would seem that those who planned and organized attacks on villages pursued the intent to drive the victims from their homes, primarily for purposes of counter-insurgency warfare. . . .

520. One should not rule out the possibility that in some instances *single individuals*, including Government officials, may entertain a genocidal intent, or in other words, attack the victims with the specific intent of annihilating, in part, a group perceived as a hostile ethnic group. If any single individual, including Governmental officials, has such intent, it would be for a competent court to make such a determination on a case by case basis. Should the competent court determine that in some instances certain individuals pursued the genocidal intent, the question would arise of establishing any possible criminal responsibility of senior officials either for complicity in genocide or for failure to investigate, or repress and punish such possible acts of genocide. . . .

522. The above conclusion that no genocidal policy has been pursued and implemented in Darfur by the Government authorities, directly or [through] the militias under their control, should not be taken as in any way detracting from, or belittling, the gravity of the crimes perpetrated in that region. As stated above genocide is not necessarily the most serious international crime. Depending upon the circumstances, *such international offences as crimes against humanity or large scale war crimes may be no less serious and heinous than genocide.* This is exactly what happened in Darfur, where massive atrocities were perpetrated on a very large scale, and have so far gone unpunished.

NOTES AND QUESTIONS

1. In a lengthy set of factual findings (omitted from this excerpt), the UN Commission found "mass killings of civilians by Government forces and militias" (¶273); that "almost all of the hundreds of attacks that were conducted in Darfur by Janjaweed and Government forces involved the killing of civilians" (¶276); the total destruction of more than 600 villages and hamlets (with another 100-200 partially destroyed) (¶301); the displacement of almost 2 million people (¶322); many cases of rape, gang-rape, and sexual enslavement—impossible to quantify because of victims' reluctance to talk—"used by the Janjaweed and Government soldiers (or at least with their complicity) as a deliberate strategy with a view to achieve certain objectives, including terrorizing the population, ensuring control over the movement of the

IDP population and perpetuating its displacement" (¶353). The majority of these attacks were launched against three "African" tribes in Darfur.

The Commission added that it "did not find any evidence of military activity by the rebels in the major areas of destruction that could in any way justify the attacks on military grounds" (¶313).

Given the standard of proof set out in ¶15 of the report, why aren't these facts sufficient to sustain a finding of genocide?

2. Compare the Commission's treatment of evidence with that of the *Krstić* tribunal. In particular, compare the two documents' treatment of the fact that military age men were killed but women spared, and the fact that much of the population was displaced from the area rather than killed. The report concludes that this is evidence of lack of genocidal intent; *Krstić* concludes the opposite. Which analysis makes the best sense?

3. Referring to the evidence in ¶¶516 and 517, one of the authors of this textbook has written that "the other pieces of no-genocide evidence cited in the U.N. Commission's report are . . . remarkably shabby." David Luban, Calling Genocide by Its Rightful Name: Lemkin's Word, Darfur, and the UN Report, 7 Chi. J. Intl. L. 303, 315 (2006). Do you agree?

4. Two months after the Commission's report, the UN Security Council, in Resolution 1593, referred the Darfur situation to the ICC. The United States abstained rather than vetoing the resolution. In return, the Resolution exempts nationals and officials of states that might contribute to any Darfur intervention from ICC jurisdiction. In February 2007, the ICC's prosecutor charged two Sudanese officials, including a minister of the interior, with crimes against humanity and war crimes. The Sudanese government responded defiantly: Instead of turning the accused officials over to the ICC, it appointed one of them minister of humanitarian affairs, placing him in charge of the very same refugees he was accused of attacking.

5. In 2009, the ICC prosecutor lodged charges against Sudan's president, Omar Al Bashir, and requested that the Pre-Trial Chamber issue an arrest warrant against him, on charges of war crimes, crimes against humanity, and genocide. The Pre-Trial Chamber's decision is excerpted below.

PROSECUTOR v. AL BASHIR

Case No. ICC-02/05-01/09, Decision on the Prosecution's Application for a Warrant of Arrest Against Omar Hassan Ahmad Al Bashir, Pre-Trial Chamber I (Mar. 4, 2009) (public redacted version)

1. On 31 March 2005, the United Nations Security Council, acting under Chapter VII of the Charter of the United Nations, adopted Resolution 1593 referring the situation in Darfur, Sudan since 1 July 2002 ("the Darfur situation") to the Prosecutor of the International Criminal Court, in accordance with article 13(b) of the Statute. . . .

3. On 1 June 2005, the Prosecution informed the Chamber of its decision to initiate an investigation into the Darfur situation. . . .

4. On 14 July 2008, the Prosecution filed an application under article 584 ("the Prosecution Application") requesting the issuance of a warrant of arrest against Omar Hassan Ahmad Al Bashir (hereinafter referred to as "Omar Al Bashir") for his alleged criminal responsibility in the commission of genocide, crimes against humanity and war crimes against members of the Fur, Masalit and Zaghawa groups in Darfur from 2003 to 14 July 2008. . . .

110. The Prosecution submits that there are reasonable grounds to believe that Omar Al Bashir bears criminal responsibility under article 25(3)(a) of the Statute for the crime of genocide as a result of:

i.   the killing of members of the Fur, Masalit and Zaghawa ethnic groups (article 6(a) — Count 1);
ii. causing serious bodily or mental harm to members of the Fur, Masalit and Zaghawa ethnic groups (article 6(b) — Count 2); and
iii. deliberately inflicting on the Fur, Masalit and Zaghawa ethnic groups conditions of life calculated to bring about the groups' physical destruction (article 6(c) — Count 3).

111. Nevertheless, the Prosecution acknowledges that (i) it does not have any direct evidence in relation to Omar Al Bashir's alleged responsibility for the crime of genocide; and that therefore (ii) its allegations concerning genocide are solely based on certain inferences that, according to the Prosecution, can be drawn from the facts of the case. . . .

113. The Majority also notes that the Elements of Crimes elaborate on the definition of genocide provided for in article 6 of the Statute, establishing that the three following elements must always be fulfilled for the existence of the crime of genocide:

i.   the victims must belong to the targeted group;
ii. the killings, the serious bodily harm, the serious mental harm, the conditions of life, the measures to prevent births or the forcible transfer of children must take place "in the context of a manifest pattern of similar conduct directed against that group or was conduct that could itself effect such destruction"; and
iii. the perpetrator must act with the intent to destroy in whole or in part the targeted group. . . .

117. The Majority observes that the definition of the crime of genocide in article II of the Convention on the Prevention and Punishment of the Crime of Genocide of 1948 ("the 1948 Genocide Convention") does not expressly require any contextual element. . . .

123. The Majority further observes that, according to this contextual element provided for in the Elements of Crimes, the conduct for which the suspect is allegedly responsible, must have taken place in the context of a manifest pattern of similar conduct directed against the targeted group or must have had such a nature so as to itself effect, the total or partial destruction of the targeted group. . . .

125. The Majority is aware that there is certain controversy as to whether this contextual element should be recognised. . . . [The Chamber nevertheless concludes that it is bound by the Elements of Crimes, and is empowered by the Rome Treaty to establish new interpretations of international law.] . . .

139. [T]he Majority considers that the crime of genocide is comprised of two subjective elements:

i.   a general subjective element that must cover any genocidal act provided for in article 6(a) to (e) of the Statute, and which consists of [the] article 30 intent and knowledge requirement; and
ii. an additional subjective element, normally referred to as "*dolus specialis*" or specific intent, according to which any genocidal acts must be carried out with the "intent to destroy in whole or in part" the targeted group. . . .

141. Given the factual allegations made by the Prosecution in the Prosecution Application, the Majority considers it to be of particular relevance for the purpose of the present case to distinguish between:

i.   the *dolus specialis*/specific intent required for the crime of genocide (genocidal intent consisting of the intent to destroy in whole or in part a national, ethnic, racial or religious group); and
ii. the *dolus specialis*/specific intent required for the crime against humanity of persecution (persecutory intent consisting of the intent to discriminate on political, racial, national, ethnic, cultural, religious, gender, or other grounds that are universally recognised as impermissible under international law, against the members of a group, by reason of the identity of the group). . . .

143. In the view of the Majority, the distinction between genocidal intent and persecutory intent is pivotal in cases of ethnic cleansing, a practice consisting of "rendering an area ethnically homogenous by using force or intimidation to remove persons of given groups from the area." This distinction is particularly relevant in cases such as the one at hand, in which allegations of forcible transfer and/or deportation of the members of the targeted group are a key component. . . .

145. Nevertheless, in the view of the Majority, this does not mean that the practice of ethnic cleansing—which usually amounts to the crime against humanity of persecution—can never result in the commission of the crime of genocide. In this regard, the Majority considers that such a practice may result in genocide if it brings about the commission of the objective elements of genocide provided for in article 6 of the Statute and the Elements of Crimes with the *dolus specialis*/specific intent to destroy in whole or in part the targeted group. . . .

147. The Prosecution highlights that it relies exclusively on proof by inference to substantiate its allegations concerning Omar Al Bashir's alleged responsibility for genocide. In particular, the Prosecution relies on inferences to prove the existence of Omar Al Bashir's *dolus specialis*/specific intent to destroy in whole or in part the Fur, Masalit and Zaghawa groups.

148. In this regard, the Majority observes that, according to the Prosecution, Omar Al Bashir was in full control of the "apparatus" of the State of Sudan, including the Sudanese Armed Forces and their allied Janjaweed Militia, the Sudanese Police Forces, the [National Intelligence and Security Service (NISS)] and the [Humanitarian Aid Commission (HAC)], and used such State apparatus to carry out a genocidal campaign against the Fur, Masalit and Zaghawa groups.

149. As a result, the Majority considers that if the materials provided by the Prosecution support the Prosecution's allegations in this regard, the existence of reasonable grounds to believe that Omar Al Bashir had a genocidal intent would automatically lead to the conclusion that there are also reasonable grounds to believe that a genocidal campaign against the Fur, Masalit and Zaghawa groups was a core component of the [Government of Sudan (GoS)] counter-insurgency campaign. . . .

151. It is for this reason that the Majority refers throughout the rest of the present decision to "the GoS's genocidal intent" as opposed to "Omar Al Bashir's genocidal intent."

152. Moreover, regardless of whether Omar Al Bashir had full control, or shared control with other high-ranking Sudanese political and military leaders, over the apparatus of the State of Sudan, the mental state of mid level superiors and low level physical perpetrators is irrelevant for the purpose of determining whether the materials provided by the Prosecution show reasonable grounds to believe that the

crime of genocide against the Fur, Masalit and Zaghawa groups was part of the GoS counter-insurgency campaign that started soon after the April 2003 attack on El Fasher airport and continued until the filing of the Prosecution Application on 14 July 2008.

153. The Majority observes that, according to the Prosecution, an inference of the GoS's genocidal intent "may properly be drawn from all evidence taken together, even where each factor on its own may not warrant such an inference."

154. Furthermore, the Prosecution submits that, in order for such an inference to be drawn, the existence of the GoS's genocidal intent "must be the only reasonable inference available on the evidence." . . .

158. In applying the law on the proof by inference to the article 58 evidentiary standard in relation to the existence of a GoS's genocidal intent, the Majority agrees with the Prosecution in that such a standard would be met only if the materials provided by the Prosecution in support of the Prosecution Application show that the only reasonable conclusion to be drawn therefrom is the existence of reasonable grounds to believe in the existence of a GoS's [*sic*] *dolus specialis*/specific intent to destroy in whole or in part the Fur, Masalit and Zaghawa groups.

159. As a result, the Majority considers that, if the existence of a GoS's genocidal intent is only one of several reasonable conclusions available on the materials provided by the Prosecution, the Prosecution Application in relation to genocide must be rejected as the evidentiary standard provided for in article 58 of the Statute would not have been met. . . .

163. The Majority observes that the Prosecution, at paragraphs 366 et seq of the Prosecution Application, provides for nine different factors from which to infer the existence of a GoS's genocidal intent.

164. In the Majority's view, they can be classified into the following categories:

i.   the alleged existence of a GoS strategy to deny and conceal the crimes allegedly committed in the Darfur region against the members of the Fur, Masalit and Zaghawa groups;

ii. some official statements and public documents, which, according to the Prosecution, provide reasonable grounds to believe in the (pre)existence of a GoS genocidal policy;

iii. the nature and extent of the acts of violence committed by GoS forces against the Fur, Masalit, and Zaghawa civilian population.

165. In relation to the alleged existence of a GoS strategy to deny and conceal the alleged commission of crimes in Darfur, the Majority considers that, even if the existence of such strategy was to be proven, there can be a variety of other plausible reasons for its adoption, such as the intention to conceal the commission of war crimes and crimes against humanity. . . .

167. In the Majority's view, the first three documents (the 1992 NIF Secret Bulletin, the 1994 Decree and 1995 Local Reform) do not provide, by themselves, any indicia of a GoS's [*sic*] genocidal intent. In this regard, the Majority considers that they provide, at best, indicia of the GoS's intent to discriminate against the members of the Fur, Masalit and Zaghawa groups by excluding them from federal government and implementing political arrangements aimed at limiting their power in their homeland (Darfur). Whether a different conclusion is merited when assessed in light of the rest of the materials provided by the Prosecution in support of the Prosecution Application is a question that shall be analysed below by the Majority.

168. In relation to the 1986 Armed Forces Memorandum and the 2003 West Darfur State Security minutes, the Majority considers that they are only evidence of the internal organisation and coordination among the three different levels of government in Sudan (Federal, State and Local), and among the different bodies within each of these levels of government. . . .

173. Finally, the Prosecution also relies on public speeches made by other members of the GoS, and in particular by Ahmad Muhammad Harun ("Ahmad Harun"), Deputy Minister for Internal Affairs from April 2003 until his appointment as Minister for Humanitarian Affairs in 2005:

i.   On or around 23 July 2003, at Khirwaa, Ahmad Harun is said to have addressed an audience that included two to three hundred conscripts who were wearing military uniforms, saying that there was a need to teach the rebels a lesson and that he had provided enough soap and that the conscripts had to do the remaining cleaning job.

ii. At a public meeting in Al Geneina in July 2003, where Ahmad Harun is said to have called on the people to go to their sons and ask them to lay down their firearms, he is also said to have stated that "the President had handed over to him the Darfur security file and given him all the power and authority to kill or forgive in Darfur for the sake of peace and security," and that "for the sake of Darfur, they were ready to kill 3/4 of the people in Darfur so that a 1/4 [*sic*] could live"; and

iii. At a public meeting in Mukjar on 7 August 2003, Ahmad Harun is said to have stated that there was a rebellion against the State in Darfur, and that, since the children of the Fur had become rebels, all the Fur and what they had, had become ["]booty for the Mujahidin"; . . .

175. Nevertheless, the Majority notes that there are reasonable grounds to believe that Ahmad Harun, who spent important amounts of time in Darfur, was not actually part of the highest level of the GoS in Khartoum and that his role was that of a link between the State Governors in the three Darfurian States and the said highest level of the GoS in Khartoum. . . .

192. . . . [T]he majority observes that there are reasonable grounds to believe that as part of the GoS counter-insurgency campaign, GoS forces:

i.   carried out numerous unlawful attacks, followed by systematic acts of pillage, on towns and villages, mainly inhabited by civilians belonging to the Fur, Masalit and Zaghawa groups;

ii. subjected thousands of civilians belonging primarily to the Fur, Masalit and Zaghawa groups to acts of murder, as well as to acts of extermination;

iii. subjected thousands of civilian women, belonging primarily to the said groups to acts of rape;

iv. subjected hundreds of thousands of civilians belonging primarily to the said groups to acts of forcible transfer; and

v.   subjected civilians belonging primarily to the said groups to acts of torture.

193. Nevertheless, the Majority considers that the existence of reasonable grounds to believe that GoS forces carried out such serious war crimes and crimes against humanity in a widespread and systematic manner does not automatically lead to the conclusion that there exist reasonable grounds to believe that the GoS

intended to destroy, in whole or in part, the Fur, Masalit and Zaghawa groups. . . .

201. As a result, the Majority considers that the existence of reasonable grounds to believe that the GoS acted with genocidal intent is not the only reasonable conclusion of the alleged commission by GoS forces, in a widespread and systematic manner, of the particularly serious war crimes and crimes against humanity mentioned above. . . .

204. In this regard, the Majority [makes] the following findings:

i. even if the existence of an alleged GoS strategy to deny and conceal the crimes committed in Darfur was to be proven, there can be a variety of plausible reasons for its adoption, including the intention to conceal the commission of war crimes and crimes against humanity;

ii. the Prosecution's allegations concerning the alleged insufficient resources allocated by the GoS to ensure adequate conditions of life in IDP Camps in Darfur are vague in light of the fact that, in addition to the Prosecution's failure to provide any specific information as to what possible additional resources could have been provided by the GoS, there existed an ongoing armed conflict at the relevant time and the number of IDPs, according to the United Nations, was as high as two million by mid 2004, and as high as 2.7 million today; . . .

v. despite the particular seriousness of those war crimes and crimes against humanity that appeared to have been committed by GoS forces in Darfur between 2003 and 2008, a number of materials provided by the Prosecution point to the existence of several factors indicating that the commission of such crimes can reasonably be explained by reasons other than the existence of a GoS's genocidal intent to destroy in whole or in part the Fur, Masalit and Zaghawa groups;

vi. the handful of GoS official statements (including three allegedly made by Omar Al Bashir himself) and public documents relied upon by the Prosecution provide only indicia of a GoS's persecutory intent (as opposed to a genocidal intent) against the members of the Fur, Masalit and Zaghawa groups; and

vii. as shown by the Prosecution's allegations in the case of *The Prosecutor v. Ahmad Harun and Ali Kushayb*, the Prosecution has not found any indicia of genocidal intent on the part of Ahmad Harun, in spite of the fact that the harsher language contained in the above-mentioned GoS official statements and documents comes allegedly from him.

205. In the view of the Majority, when all materials provided by the Prosecution in support of the Prosecution Application are analysed together, and consequently, the above-mentioned findings are jointly assessed, the Majority cannot but conclude that the existence of reasonable grounds to believe that the GoS acted with a *dolus specialis*/specific intent to destroy in whole or in part the Fur, Masalit and Zaghawa groups is not the only reasonable conclusion that can be drawn therefrom.

[The Court issues a warrant on two count of war crimes (intentionally directing attacks on civilians, and pillage) and five counts of crimes against humanity (murder, extermination, rape, torture, and forcible transfer of civilian populations). The warrant does not include counts of genocide.]

SEPARATE AND PARTLY DISSENTING OPINION OF JUDGE ANITA USACKA

1. I agree with my colleagues as to the outcome of the decision, as I am satisfied that there are reasonable grounds to believe that Omar Al Bashir is criminally responsible for war crimes and crimes against humanity, and that a warrant should be issued for his arrest. I disagree with the Majority, however, as I am satisfied that there are reasonable grounds to believe that Omar Al Bashir possessed genocidal intent and is criminally responsible for genocide.

2. This difference results from a divergence of opinion regarding

(i) whether the Prosecution must demonstrate, in order to establish reasonable grounds, that the only reasonable inference available on the evidence is that of genocidal intent, and;

(ii) the conclusions drawn from the analysis of the evidence presented. . . .

8. The Statute proscribes progressively higher evidentiary thresholds which must be met at each stage of the proceedings. At the arrest warrant/summons stage, the Pre-Trial Chamber need only be "satisfied that there are reasonable grounds to believe that the person has committed a crime within the jurisdiction of the Court." In contrast, when deciding whether or not to confirm the charges, the Chamber must determine whether there is "sufficient evidence to establish substantial grounds to believe that the person committed the crime charged." Finally, the Trial Chamber must "be convinced of the guilt of the accused beyond a reasonable doubt" in order to convict an accused. . . .

31. . . . [I]n my view, requiring the Prosecution to establish that genocidal intent is the only reasonable inference available on the evidence is tantamount to requiring the Prosecution to present sufficient evidence to allow the Chamber to be convinced of genocidal intent beyond a reasonable doubt, a threshold which is not applicable at this stage, according to article 58 of the Statute.

32. It is clear to me, however, that when the Prosecution alleges that the evidence submitted supports an inference of genocidal intent, in order for there to be reasonable grounds to believe that such an allegation is true, the inference must indeed be a reasonable one. Yet, in light of the differing evidentiary burdens at different phases of the proceedings, the Prosecution need not demonstrate that such an inference is the only reasonable one at the arrest warrant stage.

33. When several reasonable inferences may be drawn from the evidence, at the arrest warrant stage, the Prosecution need not prove whether there are substantial grounds, as would be necessary if the article 58 standard was equivalent to the standard of article 61(7) of the Statute. Nor must the Prosecution prove an allegation beyond a reasonable doubt, as would be required at trial under article 66(3) of the Statute. All that is required in order to obtain an arrest warrant is for the Prosecution to establish reasonable grounds to believe that an allegation is true.

[Judge Usacka analyzes the evidence and concludes that it meets this standard.]

NOTES AND QUESTIONS

1. The prosecution applied for leave to appeal the Pre-Trial Chamber's decision. (Under Article 82(1)(d) of the Rome Statute, a party may enter certain interlocutory appeals, but only if the Pre-Trial Chamber or Trial Chamber agrees that it

"would significantly affect the fair and expeditious conduct of the proceedings or the outcome of the trial.") The prosecution offered three grounds: (1) the Pre-Trial Chamber decision improperly raises the standard of proof for issuing an arrest warrant to what is, in effect, a "beyond a reasonable doubt" standard; (2) the Pre-Trial Chamber had based its factual conclusions on "extraneous factors": that the GoS's campaign had not killed or injured most villagers in its attacks, that the GoS had not set up the refugee camps, and that the prosecutor had not charged genocide against Ahmed Harun; and (3) the PTC did not take all the prosecution's evidence into account. Prosecutor v. Bashir, Case No. ICC-02/05-01/09, Prosecution's Application for Leave to Appeal the "Decision on the Prosecution's Application for a Warrant of Arrest Against Omar Hassan Ahmad Al Bashir," ¶¶13, 15, 18, 24 (Mar. 10, 2009). The Pre-Trial Chamber granted leave to appeal on the first issue, but denied permission to appeal on the latter two issues, on the ground that "the Second and Third Issues consist of a mere disagreement with the Majority's assessment of the evidence submitted by the Prosecutor to support his genocide-related allegations and, therefore, neither constitutes an 'issue' as defined by the Appeals Chamber." Id., Decision on the Prosecution's Application for Leave to Appeal the "Decision on the Prosecution's Application for a Warrant of Arrest Against Omar Hassan Ahmad Al Bashir," ¶8 (June 24, 2009). As this book goes to press, the Appeals Chamber has not decided the issue of what constitutes the proper evidentiary standard at the arrest-warrant stage for inferring genocidal intent.

2. In ¶158, the Pre-Trial Chamber describes its evidentiary standard as follows: "the only reasonable conclusion to be drawn [from the evidence] is the existence of reasonable grounds to believe in" the accused person's genocidal intent. What does "the only reasonable conclusion . . . is the existence of reasonable grounds" actually mean? Does it mean proof beyond reasonable doubt of genocidal intent? Or proof beyond reasonable doubt of reasonable grounds to believe in genocidal intent? What is that? Is there a practical difference between the two? In ¶159, the Pre-Trial Chamber paraphrases its test as follows: "if the existence of . . . genocidal intent is only one of several reasonable conclusions available . . . , the evidentiary standard . . . would not have been met." Is this the same as the test given in ¶158? Is it different from "beyond a reasonable doubt"?

3. The Pre-Trial Chamber distinguishes between genocidal intent and persecutory intent. Does this distinction make sense if the crimes against humanity of persecution and extermination are both charged? What is the difference between extermination accompanied by persecutory intent and genocide?

4. The arrest warrant against President Al Bashir precipitated a grave international crisis. Rejecting the accusations, Al Bashir has denounced the ICC as a neocolonialist organization. In retaliation against the warrant, Al Bashir expelled foreign humanitarian organizations from the Darfurian refugee camps, charging that they had assisted the ICC. The humanitarian organizations were responsible for keeping tens of thousands of people alive, and their expulsion almost immediately put those people at risk. Some humanitarian experts criticized the ICC for playing with fire. The African Union and the League of Arab States also denounced the ICC indictment, and some African states have threatened to quit the ICC unless the charges against Al Bashir are dropped. Defying the arrest warrant, Al Bashir visited several African and Arab countries, where he was warmly welcomed. China, a major trading partner and supporter of Sudan, has also denounced the arrest warrant and the ICC.

Other observers noted that by referring the Darfur situation to the ICC, the UN Security Council had placed the Office of the Prosecutor (OTP) in an untenable position: Either pursue charges against Al Bashir regardless of the political repercussions or ignore the overwhelming evidence of atrocity crimes in Sudan. Under Article 16 of the Rome Statute, the UN Security Council has the authority to defer the ICC case for a year or more in the interests of international peace and security. However, the Security Council has not exercised its Article 16 authority, in part because the United States supports the prosecution.

D. INCITEMENT TO GENOCIDE

PROSECUTOR v. AKAYESU

Case No. ICTR-96-4-T, Judgment (Sept. 2, 1998)

. . . 6.3.3. DIRECT AND PUBLIC INCITEMENT TO COMMIT GENOCIDE

THE CRIME OF DIRECT AND PUBLIC INCITEMENT TO COMMIT GENOCIDE, PUNISHABLE
UNDER ARTICLE 2(3)(C) OF THE STATUTE

549. Under count 4, the Prosecutor charges Akayesu with direct and public incitement to commit genocide, a crime punishable under Article 2(3)(c) of the Statute. . . .

554. Under the Statute, direct and public incitement is expressly defined as a specific crime, punishable as such, by virtue of Article 2(3)(c). With respect to such a crime, the Chamber deems it appropriate to first define the three terms: incitement, direct and public.

555. Incitement is defined in Common law systems as encouraging or persuading another to commit an offence. One line of authority in Common law would also view threats or other forms of pressure as a form of incitement. . . .

556. The public element of incitement to commit genocide may be better appreciated in light of two factors: the place where the incitement occurred and whether or not assistance was selective or limited. A line of authority commonly followed in civil law systems would regard words as being public where they were spoken aloud in a place that were public by definition. According to the International Law Commission, public incitement is characterized by a call for criminal action to a number of individuals in a public place or to members of the general public at large by such means as the mass media, for example, radio or television. It should be noted in this respect that at the time the Convention on Genocide was adopted, the delegates specifically agreed to rule out the possibility of including private incitement to commit genocide as a crime, thereby underscoring their commitment to set aside for punishment only the truly public forms of incitement.

557. The "direct" element of incitement implies that the incitement assume a direct form and specifically provoke another to engage in a criminal act, and that more than mere vague or indirect suggestion goes to constitute direct incitement. . . . The Chamber further recalls that incitement may be direct, and nonetheless implicit. Thus, at the time the Convention on Genocide was being drafted, the

Polish delegate observed that it was sufficient to play skillfully on mob psychology by casting suspicion on certain groups, by insinuating that they were responsible for economic or other difficulties in order to create an atmosphere favourable to the perpetration of the crime.

558. The Chamber will therefore consider on a case-by-case basis whether, in light of the culture of Rwanda and the specific circumstances of the instant case, acts of incitement can be viewed as direct or not, by focusing mainly on the issue of whether the persons for whom the message was intended immediately grasped the implication thereof.

559. In light of the foregoing, it can be noted in the final analysis that whatever the legal system, direct and public incitement must be defined for the purposes of interpreting Article 2(3)(c), as directly provoking the perpetrator(s) to commit genocide, whether through speeches, shouting or threats uttered in public places or at public gatherings, or through the sale or dissemination, offer for sale or display of written material or printed matter in public places or at public gatherings, or through the public display of placards or posters, or through any other means of audiovisual communication.

560. The *mens rea* required for the crime of direct and public incitement to commit genocide lies in the intent to directly prompt or provoke another to commit genocide. It implies a desire on the part of the perpetrator to create by his actions a particular state of mind necessary to commit such a crime in the minds of the person(s) he is so engaging. That is to say that the person who is inciting to commit genocide must have himself the specific intent to commit genocide, namely, to destroy, in whole or in part, a national, ethnical, racial or religious group, as such.

561. Therefore, the issue before the Chamber is whether the crime of direct and public incitement to commit genocide can be punished even where such incitement was unsuccessful. It appears from the *travaux préparatoires* of the Convention on Genocide that the drafters of the Convention considered stating explicitly that incitement to commit genocide could be punished, whether or not it was successful. In the end, a majority decided against such an approach. Nevertheless, the Chamber is of the opinion that it cannot thereby be inferred that the intent of the drafters was not to punish unsuccessful acts of incitement. In light of the overall *travaux*, the Chamber holds the view that the drafters of the Convention simply decided not to specifically mention that such a form of incitement could be punished.

562. . . . The Chamber holds that genocide clearly falls within the category of crimes so serious that direct and public incitement to commit such a crime must be punished as such, even where such incitement failed to produce the result expected by the perpetrator.

NOTES AND QUESTIONS

1. Consider the final two paragraphs of the excerpt. Does the Tribunal's conclusion that incitement to genocide can exist "even where such incitement failed to produce the result" violate the Principle of Lenity, according to which an ambiguous criminal statute must be read in the manner most favorable to the accused?

2. In December 2003, the ICTR convicted three journalists, Hassan Ngeze, Jean-Bosco Barayagwiza, and Ferdinand Nahimana, of genocide and incitement to

genocide. Ngeze edited *Kangura,* an anti-Tutsi "hate sheet," while the other two were founding members of Radio Television Milles Collines (RTLM), which broadcast anti-Tutsi propaganda and at times directed the génocidaires to their targets. The case raises important issues about the clash between freedom of political speech and the law against incitement to genocide. The clash perhaps reaches its highest level in the United States, where the First Amendment protects political speech and freedom of the press and where anti-hate-speech statutes such as exist in many nations would undoubtedly be found unconstitutional.

The Tribunal addresses this concern at great length in its judgment in the journalists' case. We quote just one paragraph from this compendious survey of many nations' jurisprudence on the issue:

> 1010. Counsel for Ngeze has argued that United States law, as the most speech-protective, should be used as a standard, to ensure the universal acceptance and legitimacy of the Tribunal's jurisprudence. The Chamber considers international law, which has been well developed in the areas of freedom from discrimination and freedom of expression, to be the point of reference for its consideration of these issues, noting that domestic law varies widely while international law codifies universal standards. The Chamber notes that the jurisprudence of the United States also accepts the fundamental principles set forth in international law and has recognized in its domestic law that incitement to violence, threats, libel, false advertising, obscenity, and child pornography are among those forms of expression that fall outside the scope of freedom of speech protection. In *Virginia v. Black,* the United States Supreme Court recently interpreted the free speech guarantee of the First Amendment of the Constitution to permit a ban on cross burning with intent to intimidate. The historical terrorization of African Americans by the Ku Klux Klan through cross burnings, in the Court's view, made the burning of a cross, as a recognized symbol of hate and a "true threat," unprotected as symbolic expression. Intimidation was held to be constitutionally proscribable "where a speaker directs a threat to a person or group of persons with the intent of placing the victim in fear of bodily harm or death." In the immigration context, adherents of National Socialism have been stripped of citizenship and deported from the United States on the basis of their anti-Semitic writings.

Prosecutor v. Nahimana, Barayawiza & Ngeze, Case No. ICTR-99-52-T, Judgment, ¶1010 (Dec. 3, 2003).

3. In December 2008, the ICTR convicted the Rwandan popular singer Simon Bikindi of direct and public incitement to genocide. The charge was based on three inflammatory Hutu-Power songs ("I hate these Hutus, these de-Hutuized Hutus, who have disowned their identity, dear comrades"). The Tribunal found that "none of these three songs constitute direct and public incitement to commit genocide per se." However, Bikindi had personally participated in at least one rally in which the songs were broadcast and in which Bikindi used the loudspeaker to call directly on Hutus to exterminate the Tutsi "snakes." Prosecutor v. Bikindi, Case No. ICTR-01-72-T, Judgment, ¶¶421-424 (Dec. 2, 2008). The Tribunal relied on Bikindi's speeches at this rally, not his songs, to convict him. He was sentenced to 15 years. The Tribunal did not discuss the question of how much Bikindi's status as a celebrity singer-songwriter gave added credibility to his speeches, and therefore constituted a background condition to finding direct and public incitement.

4. In 2005, the Canadian Supreme Court decided a case concerning the deportation of a Rwandan, Léon Mugesera. Mugesera v. Canada (Minister of Citizenship & Immigration), [2005] 2 S.C.R. 100, 2005 SCC 40. Mugesera, a prominent Hutu Power

activist, had made a notorious anti-Tutsi speech in November 1992, widely publicized in Rwanda. In one often-quoted passage, he said of the Tutsi, "your home is in Ethiopia, that we will send you by the Nyabarongo so you can get there quickly." The Nyabarongo is a river, and during the genocide many Tutsi corpses were indeed thrown into the Nyabarongo.

Mugesera's case was hotly contested. First, he claimed that his speech was misinterpreted. Just as important, he made the speech almost a year and a half before the genocide and had already emigrated from Rwanda when the genocide began.

The Canadian court nevertheless found that Mugesera was deportable on the ground of direct and public incitement of genocide. The court emphasized that although the genocide had not yet begun, ethnic massacres of Tutsis had been going on for two years when Mugesera made his speech, so that its murderous meaning would be clear to the audience. Nor did the time gap matter: The court closely followed the analysis of the crime in *Akayesu* and agreed with the ICTR that it was not necessary that an incitement have its intended effect to fulfill the definition of the crime. "In the case of the allegation of incitement to genocide, the Minister does not need to establish a direct causal link between the speech and any acts of murder or violence. Because of its inchoate nature, incitement is punishable by virtue of the criminal act alone irrespective of the result. It remains a crime regardless of whether it has the effect it is intended to have. . . . The Minister is not required, therefore, to prove that individuals who heard Mr. Mugesera's speech killed or attempted to kill any members of an identifiable group." Id. ¶85.

5. In one of the weirder developments, Mugesera's flamboyant lawyer Guy Bertrand moved to have the entire Canadian Supreme Court disqualify itself and permanently stay the proceedings, on the ground "that an extensive Jewish conspiracy was hatched to ensure that the Minister's appeal would succeed and that the respondent Mugesera and his family would be deported." Motion for a Permanent Stay of Proceedings Joint Reasons for Judgment, Mugesera v. Canada (Minister of Citizenship & Immigration), [2005] 2 S.C.R. 91, 2005 SCC 39, ¶9. According to Bertrand, the (Jewish) Canadian minister of justice had plotted to fill a court vacancy with a (Jewish) justice whose husband was the chair of the Canadian Jewish Congress, an intervening party in Mugesera's case. Although the justice recused herself from the case as soon as she joined the court, "All the members of this Court were said to be 'contaminated' by her appointment and incapable of being impartial toward the respondents." Id. ¶10. In rejecting the motion, the court strongly criticized Bertrand's lack of professionalism and "irresponsible innuendo," and concluded: "Regretfully, we must also mention that the motion and the documents filed in support of it include anti-Semitic sentiment and views that most might have thought had disappeared from Canadian society, and even more so from legal debate in Canada." Id. ¶¶16-17.

6. In an important article on incitement to genocide, Susan Benesch argues that speech should not count as incitement to genocide unless it is uttered in conditions where it has a realistic chance of producing genocide. A fanatic ranting to passersby on a soapbox in a remote country has not committed incitement to genocide no matter what he says. After analyzing the historical contexts in which speech really has incited genocide, Benesch proposes the following test:

1. Was the speech understood by the audience as a call to genocide? Did it use language, explicit or coded, to justify and promote violence?

2.   Did the speaker have authority or influence over the audience and did the audience have the capacity to commit genocide?
3.   Had the victims-to-be already suffered an outbreak of recent violence?
4.   Were contrasting views still available at the time of the speech? Was it still safe to express them publicly?
5.   Did the speaker describe the victims-to-be as subhuman, or accuse them of plotting genocide? Had the audience been conditioned by the use of these techniques in other, previous speech?
6.   Had the audience received similar messages before the speech?

Susan Benesch, Vile Crime or Inalienable Right: Defining Incitement to Genocide, 48 Va. J. Intl. L. 485, 498 (2008). Using this test, how would you evaluate genocidal political rhetoric by a political leader directed toward residents of a foreign country? To take a recent and well-publicized example, Iranian President Mahmoud Ahmadinejad is alleged to have called for Israel to be "wiped off the map," remarks that led a group of prominent Jews to call for his indictment for incitement to genocide. Gabrielle Birkner, Prominent Jews Urge Indictment of Iran President, N.Y. Sun, Dec. 15, 2006.

E.   STATE RESPONSIBILITY FOR GENOCIDE

As we know, international criminal responsibility is entirely individual. Only natural persons, not organizations, can be charged, tried, or punished for international crimes. The attempt at Nuremberg to try organizations such as the German General Staff or the SS was viewed skeptically by the Tribunal, and no court since then has made a similar attempt.

And yet there is an air of unreality about this because it is perfectly obvious that governments can plan criminal activities. But the closest the law can get to addressing governmental criminality is ascribing responsibility to states in noncriminal cases.

In 1993, shortly after it achieved independence, Bosnia filed a genocide action in the International Court of Justice (ICJ) against Serbia and Montenegro (we will say "Serbia" for short because Montenegro eventually became an independent state, and Serbia was more deeply implicated in the Bosnian war). Bosnia charged Serbia with planning, abetting, and committing genocide, and demanded financial compensation. The case lasted for 14 years and contained many legal twists and turns. Finally, in 2007, the ICJ decided the case.[8] In a controversial 170-page opinion, it dismissed most charges against Serbia. Although it was a civil case, the ICJ concluded that the standard of proof for a genocide accusation should be very high. It then argued that the only proven incident of genocide in the Bosnian war was the Srebrenica massacre — and that there was too little evidence to conclude that Serbia was complicit in Srebrenica. The only international obligation Serbia had breached was its obligation under Article 1 of the Genocide Convention to prevent and punish

---

8. Case Concerning the Application of the Convention for the Prevention and Punishment of the Crime of Genocide (Bosn. & Herz. v. Serb. & Mont.), 2007 I.C.J. General List No. 91 (Judgment of Feb. 26).

genocide; Serbia breached that obligation by not taking steps to stop the Srebrenica massacre and refusing to hand over Ratko Mladic and Radovan Karadzic (the two most wanted Bosnian Serb suspects) for trial. The ICJ did not award Bosnia any compensation.

Some critics argued that if the ICJ could not find genocide in this case, then the possibility of ever holding a state responsible for genocide is quite remote. The following article gives some sense of why the ICJ's decision was so controversial.

RUTH WEDGWOOD, SLOBODAN MILOSEVIC'S LAST WALTZ
N.Y. Times, Mar. 12, 2007

[The court's finding that the Srebrenica massacre is the only actionable instance of genocide] is a remarkable result. It's true that Srebrenica woke the West from its stupor and brought NATO military action. But the ethnic conflagration had already raged for three years, with countless acts of nationalist violence aimed at expelling Muslims from the north, south and east of Bosnia. Yet the International Court of Justice shrinks from recognition, failing to explain why the deliberate slaughter of civilians in the riverside town of Brcko in 1992, or the torture and execution of Muslim civilians in Foca, were legally different in kind from the Srebrenica murders.

The court does lay one misdemeanor at Serbia's doorstep: Belgrade failed to take steps to "prevent" the genocide at Srebrenica. For this, the court says, no damages are due. But that passive fault fails to account for Belgrade's robust program of financing, equipping and supporting criminal militias like Arkan's Tigers and the Gray Wolves, as well as the forces that specialized in leveling Muslim villages.

The court's judgment has broad implications. It amounts to a posthumous acquittal of Mr. Milosevic for genocide in Bosnia. Though he planned to divide the country in two, in a scheme devised with Croatia's president, Franjo Tudjman, and engineered the strategy of violent ethnic cleansing, the court concluded that this did not amount to a campaign to destroy the ethnic group of Bosnian Muslims in whole or in part, for he was just pushing their reduced numbers somewhere else. As a law student might suppose, it will take years of study to understand how that could be true.

Worse yet, by saying that only the Srebrenica massacre amounted to genocide, the International Court of Justice limits the charges that can be effectively brought against the Bosnian Serb leaders Radovan Karadzic and Ratko Mladic, if Belgrade at last allows them to be arrested.

It is hard to say why the court did not step back from these dire consequences. But there were both technical missteps and political snares in its judgment.

First, the World Court rejected the standard of vicarious liability used in the United Nations criminal tribunal for the former Yugoslavia. In applying the Geneva Conventions to the Bosnian fighting, the criminal court early concluded that Belgrade's support was enough to make major portions of the conflict into an international war.

But the International Court of Justice chides the United Nations criminal court for offering an opinion on an issue of "general" international law like state responsibility and, despite more than 10 years of settled criminal case law, rejects the criminal court's conclusion. This sibling rivalry between international courts has been gently called "fragmentation." It does not bode well for any coherent jurisprudence.

The World Court also insists that unless Belgrade gave "direct orders" for particular operations or the Bosnian Serbs were "completely dependent" on Belgrade, there is no liability at all. This will be a surprise to scholars of ordinary tort law, who are accustomed to supposing that responsibility for wrongdoing can be shared.

Though the court claims to be acting on the basis of a 1986 decision in a case pitting the United States against Nicaragua, the law has moved on since then. Indeed, the court's lackadaisical standard is at odds with United Nations Security Council Resolution 1373, passed in the wake of Sept. 11, which says that no state has a right to provide any intelligence, logistics or financing to terrorist activities.

Second, the International Court of Justice applies the demands of criminal proof to a civil case. The judges insist that even for civil liability, proof against Belgrade has to be "fully conclusive" and "incontrovertible," with a level of certainty "beyond any doubt." This standard is well known when the jail door will shut, but it exceeds the demands of civil liability. And in trying to meet this standard, the court declines to draw any adverse inference against Belgrade, even though the documents it turned over to the court were heavily redacted.

Third, the International Court of Justice has a small jurisdictional embarrassment. After the NATO military intervention in Kosovo, Serbia went to the United Nations war crimes prosecutor to complain about NATO's war fighting methods. The prosecutor concluded that there was no basis for a criminal investigation of NATO. Serbia then sued various NATO states in the International Court of Justice. These suits were dismissed on the ground that Yugoslavia was no longer a member of the United Nations and hence had no plaintiff's right of access to the court.

But reasons cut both ways, argued Belgrade, and disqualification as a plaintiff could also protect Serbia as a defendant in Bosnia's civil action. Lingering doubts about jurisdiction may have diminished the court's willingness to make more rigorous findings of liability in the Bosnian genocide case.

To be sure, the International Court of Justice has held that the Genocide Convention requires Serbia to surrender criminal suspects like Mr. Karadzic and General Mladic, who are wanted by the United Nations war crimes tribunal. But this is a redundant finding, for the legal authority of the Security Council already requires that surrender. It is not a substitute for clarity about Serbia's role. . . .

F.   ARE STATES OBLIGATED TO PREVENT GENOCIDE?

Article 1 of the Genocide Convention describes genocide as an international crime that states "undertake to prevent and punish." Does this establish a binding obligation on states-parties to take action against genocide? If so, important questions arise: (1) What kind of action? (2) Against genocide anywhere in the world, or only within one's own state? (3) Who is supposed to take the action? All states? Some states? The United Nations? These are deeply contested questions that do not have settled, universally accepted legal answers. Although these issues have no direct bearing on international criminal law, it is difficult to study the topic of genocide without wondering urgently whether states have an obligation to stop it.

What kind of action? Article 1 speaks of prevention and punishment—but a quick glance through the Genocide Convention's articles makes it clear that the main emphasis is on punishment rather than prevention. States must make genocide a domestic crime, prosecute it if they have jurisdiction, and, if not, extradite suspects to states that do have jurisdiction, as long as the extradition is legal. The Convention explicitly mentions only one preventive measure: According to Article 8, states may call upon the United Nations to take action against genocide. Consider whether this Article implies that states are not permitted to take any additional unilateral action against genocide in other countries (because of the interpretive rule *expressio unis est exclusio alterius*).

May states intervene militarily to prevent genocide in another state? In the public mind, humanitarian military intervention is probably the most salient preventive measure. But unilateral military intervention runs contrary to modern international law. On its face, it violates Article 2(4) of the United Nations Charter, which flat-out forbids member states from using force or the threat of force "against the territorial integrity or political independence of any state, or in any other manner inconsistent with the purposes of the United Nations." The only exception in the Charter is for self-defense.

However, the international community's lack of effective action in Rwanda in 1994 drew widespread outrage; and in 1999, NATO forces led by the United States intervened militarily in Kosovo in the face of a massive attack by Serbian forces against the Albanian Muslim minority. Although the NATO intervention was not unilateral, it was never authorized by the UN Security Council. A few months later, then Secretary-General Kofi Annan laid out the dilemma of humanitarian intervention in a much-publicized speech to the UN General Assembly:

> While the genocide in Rwanda will define for our generation the consequences of inaction in the face of mass murder, the more recent conflict in Kosovo has prompted important questions about the consequences of action in the absence of complete unity on the part of the international community.
>
> It has cast in stark relief the dilemma of what has been called humanitarian intervention: on one side, the question of the legitimacy of an action taken by a regional organization without a United Nations mandate; on the other, the universally recognized imperative of effectively halting gross and systematic violations of human rights with grave humanitarian consequences. . . .
>
> The Kosovo conflict and its outcome have prompted a wide debate of profound importance to the resolution of conflicts from the Balkans to Central Africa to East Asia. And to each side in this critical debate, difficult questions can be posed.
>
> To those for whom the greatest threat to the future of international order is the use of force in the absence of a Security Council mandate, one might ask — not in the context of Kosovo — but in the context of Rwanda: If, in those dark days and hours leading up to the genocide, a coalition of States had been prepared to act in defence of the Tutsi population, but did not receive prompt Council authorization, should such a coalition have stood aside and allowed the horror to unfold?
>
> To those for whom the Kosovo action heralded a new era when States and groups of States can take military action outside the established mechanisms for enforcing international law, one might ask: Is there not a danger of such interventions undermining the imperfect, yet resilient, security system created after the Second World War, and of setting dangerous precedents for future interventions without a clear criterion to decide who might invoke these precedents, and in what circumstances?[9]

---

9. Press Release, Secretary-General Presents His Annual Report to the General Assembly, U.N. Doc. SG/SM/7136, GA/9596 (Sept. 20, 1999), available at http://www.un.org/News/Press/docs/1999/19990920.sgsm7136.html.

Some scholars argue that the norm forbidding humanitarian military intervention is changing.[10] However, this remains a deeply contested proposition of international law.

Article 8 of the Genocide Convention permits states to refer genocides to competent organs of the United Nations. While various organs of the UN can enact resolutions or issue reports, only the Security Council has the power to impose sanctions, send in peacekeepers, or authorize interventions of any form. The Security Council was notoriously timid during the Rwanda genocide, and the veto power of members of the P-5 (the five permanent members of the Security Council) makes it difficult to authorize preventive action.

Against genocide anywhere in the world, or only within one's own state? Article 1 contains no explicit territorial limit on the obligation to prevent genocide. However, there is some basis in the text of the Convention for concluding that states are obligated to prevent genocide only within their own territory. As we have seen, Article 8 mentions only one permission (not an obligation) when states confront genocide: States may call upon the United Nations to take appropriate actions. If states are not even required to call on the United Nations to prevent genocide in other countries, how could they be obligated to take more drastic preventive measures? Note further that Article 6 of the Genocide Convention, concerning criminal trials for genocide, grants jurisdiction only to international tribunals or the state where the genocide took place. It might be argued that the Article 1 obligations to prevent and punish genocide go together and have the same territorial scope—so if a state is required to punish only genocide that occurs within its own territory, it follows that the obligation to prevent genocide must also apply only within a state's own territory.

However, this is not the way that the ICJ has interpreted the Article 1 obligation to prevent genocide. It found a wider scope of obligation in its *Bosnia v. Serbia* case. In 1996, rejecting Serbia's preliminary objections in that case, the court wrote: "[T]he rights and obligations enshrined by the Convention are rights and obligations *erga omnes*. The Court notes that the obligation each State thus has to prevent and to punish the crime of genocide is not territorially limited by the Convention."[11] Eleven years later, in the final judgment (discussed in Section E above), the court expanded on this holding:

> 183. The substantive obligations arising from Articles I and III are not on their face limited by territory. They apply to a State wherever it may be acting or may be able to act in ways appropriate to meeting the obligations in question. The extent of that ability in law and fact is considered, so far as the obligation to prevent the crime of genocide is concerned, in the section of the Judgement concerned with that obligation (cf. paragraph 430 below). . . .
>
> 430. Secondly, it is clear that the obligation in question is one of conduct and not one of result, in the sense that a State cannot be under the obligation to succeed, whatever the circumstances, in preventing the commission of genocide: the obligation

---

10. Jane Stromseth, Rethinking Humanitarian Intervention: The Case for Incremental Change, in Humanitarian Intervention: Ethical, Legal, and Political Dilemmas 232, 244-245 (J.L. Holzgrefe & Robert O. Keohane eds., 2003); Michael J. Glennon, Limits of Law, Prerogatives of Power: Interventionism After Kosovo (2001).

11. Application of the Convention on the Prevention and Punishment of the Crime of Genocide (Bosn. & Herz. v. Serb. & Mont.), Preliminary Objections, 1996 I.C.J. Reports 595, ¶31, (Judgment of July 11), available at http://www.icj-cij.org/docket/files/91/7349.pdf.

of States parties is rather to employ all means reasonably available to them, so as to prevent genocide so far as possible. A State does not incur responsibility simply because the desired result is not achieved; responsibility is however incurred if the State manifestly failed to take all measures to prevent genocide which were within its power, and which might have contributed to preventing the genocide. In this area the notion of "due diligence," which calls for an assessment *in concreto*, is of critical importance. Various parameters operate when assessing whether a State has duly discharged the obligation concerned. The first, which varies greatly from one State to another, is clearly the capacity to influence effectively the action of persons likely to commit, or already committing, genocide. This capacity itself depends, among other things, on the geographical distance of the State concerned from the scene of the events, and on the strength of the political links, as well as links of all other kinds, between the authorities of that State and the main actors in the events. The State's capacity to influence must also be assessed by legal criteria, since it is clear that every State may only act within the limits permitted by international law; seen thus, a State's capacity to influence may vary depending on its particular legal position vis-à-vis the situations and persons facing the danger, or the reality, of genocide. On the other hand, it is irrelevant whether the State whose responsibility is in issue claims, or even proves, that even if it had employed all means reasonably at its disposal, they would not have sufficed to prevent the commission of genocide. As well as being generally difficult to prove, this is irrelevant to the breach of the obligation of conduct in question, the more so since the possibility remains that the combined efforts of several States, each complying with its obligation to prevent, might have achieved the result — averting the commission of genocide — which the efforts of only one State were insufficient to produce.[12]

431. Thirdly, a State can be held responsible for breaching the obligation to prevent genocide only if genocide was actually committed. It is at the time when the commission of the prohibited act (genocide or any of the other acts listed in Article III of the Convention) begins that the breach of an obligation of prevention occurs. . . .

Who is supposed to take the action? Paragraph 430 of the *Bosnia v. Serbia* judgment suggests that any state that could, acting together with other states, do something to prevent genocide in another state, is obligated to do so, provided that the means are "reasonably available" and lawful. This analysis leaves many questions unanswered and unaddressed. Is the requirement realistic? What if other states are plainly not doing their part? Are states "jointly and severally" responsible for failures to take actions that might prevent genocide, so that even if no other states are acting, any state can be held responsible for not doing its share? Is there any state party to the Genocide Convention that is *not* responsible under this standard? Assuming that states responsible for violating the obligation to prevent genocide can be required to pay reparations to the victim state, who, if anyone, should pay?

The ICJ's analysis raises difficult questions for very powerful states — especially for the United States, which is often said to be the world's sole hyperpower, able to project its power worldwide to an extent far greater than that of other states. What, under the ICJ's standard, are the obligations of the United States to take steps to prevent genocide in remote parts of the world? Does the United States

---

12. Application of the Convention on the Prevention and Punishment of the Crime of Genocide (Bosn. & Herz. v. Serb. & Mont.), 2007 I.C.J. General List No. 91 (Judgment of Feb. 26), available at http://www.icj-cij.org/docket/files/91/13685.pdf?PHPSESSID = a43eeede4307abd6f1eb98ccb322305a.

bear a greater prevention responsibility than other states, simply by virtue of its powers? Is this reasonable or fair?

What about a member of the P-5 that vetoes a Security Council resolution to take preventive action against a genocide? Under the ICJ's standard, is that state in breach of its obligations under the Genocide Convention? (All members of the P-5 are parties to the Genocide Convention.)

CHAPTER
21

War Crimes

Along with crimes against humanity and genocide, the Rome Statute of the International Criminal Court (ICC) criminalizes two kinds of wrongdoing associated with war: aggression and war crimes.[1] The Nuremberg Charter had already defined a category of "crimes against peace," meaning the planning and launching of aggressive war; and all modern tribunals include war crimes in their roster of infamous deeds.

War crimes are unlawful acts committed in the course of conflict (in distinction from aggression, which is the crime of starting an unlawful war). They constitute the most traditional of the tribunal crimes, perhaps the only category that would have been familiar to jurists of earlier centuries. Indeed, the earliest recorded war-crimes trial occurred in 1474, when a coalition of states and cities tried and executed Peter von Hagenbach, the military governor of Breisach, Germany, who brutally tyrannized the population to subdue them.[2]

There were few war crimes trials in the ensuing centuries, although legal doctrines defining war crimes existed. In the nineteenth century, perhaps the best known example was the trial and execution of Confederate Colonel Henry Wirz, the commandant of the Andersonville prison camp, in which over 12,000 Union prisoners died of starvation and disease induced by the camp's brutal conditions. As we saw in Chapter 3, the victorious Allies in World War I insisted that Germany try its own war criminals. Approximately 800 defendants were tried in Leipzig, but Germans deeply resented the trials, and almost all the defendants were acquitted. It was this experience that led to the international military tribunal at Nuremberg and the era of modern war crimes prosecutions. Today, as we shall see, international law regards certain "grave breaches" of the most important treaties regulating the conduct of armed conflict as war crimes.

This chapter does not pretend to examine all war crimes; the subject is too large and specialized. Instead, the chapter explains the general principles underlying the law of war crimes, as well as the basic structure of the contemporary law of war (in Section A). In Section B, we examine the fundamental legal difference between international and noninternational armed conflicts. In Section C, we single out two

---

1. As noted in Chapter 16, the ICC will not prosecute the crime of aggression until the states parties agree on a legal definition of the crime, which will happen no sooner than 2010.

2. Edoardo Greppi, The Evolution of Individual Criminal Responsibility Under International Law, 835 Intl. Rev. of the Red Cross 531 (1999), available at http://www.icrc.org/Web/Eng/siteeng0.nsf/html/57JQ2X. Hagenbach's trial was not only the first international war crimes proceeding — it was also the first time that a commander was held criminally responsible for crimes committed by his troops, and the first time that an accused war criminal invoked the defense of superior orders. Hagenbach argued that he was acting on command of his sovereign, the Burgundian king Charles the Bold.

examples of war crimes for more detailed examination. These are so-called targeted killings of terrorists and the humiliating treatment of captives.

A. BACKGROUND

1. The Laws of War and Just War Theory

In many ways, the very idea of a "war crime" is puzzling. To suppose that war is a law-governed activity is by no means obvious, and eminent authorities have denied it. In Cicero's famous words, "laws are silent when arms are raised" (*silent enim leges inter arma*).[3] Even in peaceable civil society, according to Thomas Hobbes, "a man cannot lay down the right of resisting them, that assault him by force, to take away his life."[4] As for war, "The notions of right and wrong, justice and injustice have there no place. Where there is no common power, there is no law: where no law, no injustice. Force, and fraud, are in war the two cardinal virtues."[5] General Patton wrote, "War is not a contest with gloves. It is resorted to only when laws (which are rules) have failed."[6]

And yet most if not all known civilizations have distinguished between rightful and wrongful conduct, in war as in peace. Historian Steven Neff notes that ancient Greek myths distinguished between Ares, the god of mere violence, and Athena, the goddess of warfare understood "as an organised, disciplined, rationally conducted collective activity."[7] Other civilizations have drawn the same distinction in their own mythologies. The possibility that warriors can be disciplined and restrained distinguishes them from mere murderers.

The law of war evolved out of two preconditions, one social and one intellectual. The social condition is that professional warriors have often defined themselves by ideals of chivalry and honor. Chivalric ideals mean that warriors recognize the fighters on the other side as belonging to the same order of men (and, today, women) as themselves; indeed, in feudal Europe knights belonged to an international warrior class. In *The Iliad*, the oldest known war poem, the Greeks and the Trojans can seem almost interchangeable. We find the Greek warrior Diomedes and the Trojan Glaukos ritually exchanging insults and boasting of their lineage to each other before they fight. Doing so, they discover that their families are friends, so instead of slaughtering each other, they exchange armor as mutual gifts.[8] Lest this seem like a fairy tale from a remote age, something of the same order happened amidst the horrors of World War I, when German and British troops declared a Christmas truce, and came out of their trenches to celebrate together—after which they returned to the trenches and the worst carnage the world had ever seen. As we shall see, the Hague and Geneva Conventions (the foundation of the modern law of war) reflect the chivalric tradition. To take one notable example, modern treaty law recognizes "perfidy"—meaning deceptions such as pretending to be a civilian—as a crime "derived from the principle of

---

3. Marcus Tullius Cicero, Pro Milone 11.
4. Thomas Hobbes, Leviathan 86 (Thomas Oakeshott ed., 1957), ch. 14.
5. Id. at 83.
6. George S. Patton, The Effect of Weapons on War, Cavalry J., Nov. 1930, available at http://www.pattonhq.com/textfiles/effect.html.
7. Steven C. Neff, War and the Law of Nations: A General History 16 (2005).
8. Homer, The Iliad, bk. 6, ll. 140-280 (Robert Fitzgerald trans., 2004).

chivalry."[9] The chivalric notion that some weapons are too dishonorable to be used dates back at least to 1139, when the Second Lateran Council condemned the "murderous art of crossbowmen and archers, which is hateful to God, to be employed against Christians and Catholics."[10] Notably, the chivalric tradition emphasized restraint in war.

This is not to idealize chivalry. Medieval knights were often brutal men who, chivalry notwithstanding, had few compunctions about rape, pillage, or murder. Often they made their living by ransoming captives back to their families—so they had financial as well as honorable reasons for sparing captured knights, and they were perfectly content to kill prisoners if they were penniless foot soldiers rather than knights with money. The ban on crossbows and longbows probably originated because knights disliked weapons that allowed mere peasants to pick them off at a distance—and the ban conspicuously does not apply to using the weapons against non-Christians. Yet even acknowledging that "warriors' honor" has often been more myth than reality, it is an ideal that military professionals take very seriously, and it has deeply affected the law.

The intellectual background for laws of war lies in the so-called just war theory. Although many cultures have developed moral conceptions of war, the just war theory lying at the basis of the modern law of war was developed by Christian thinkers, beginning with Saint Augustine (354-430) and Saint Thomas Aquinas (1225-1274).[11] Just war theory is sophisticated and complex, but its basic doctrines can be summarized as follows.

a. *Jus ad bellum*

First, just war theory distinguishes between the justice *of* war and justice *in* war. To use the traditional Latin names, the former is "*jus ad bellum*," the latter "*jus in bello*"—JAB and JIB for short. JAB refers to principles determining when resort to war is just and when it is unjust. In traditional doctrine, a just war required several preconditions: The cause must be just, the war must be a last resort, it must be authorized by lawful government, the violence must be proportional to the cause, the war must be fought with rightful intention (in other words, the just cause cannot be a mere pretext), and the war must carry some possibility of success.

Within the just war paradigm, lawyers and theorists often disagreed sharply about what these conditions meant, and especially about what constitutes a "just cause" for going to war. Must all wars be defensive, or could a war be launched on grounds of vengeance, punishment, or—as Saint Augustine believed—because God has commanded it?[12] Can a state launch a war preemptively, to ward off a potential threat from another state that has not attacked it? What about a humanitarian military

---

9. Commentary on the Rome Statute of the International Criminal Court 218 (Otto Trifterer ed., 1999). Perfidy is criminalized in the Rome Statute art. 8(2)(b)(xi) and art. 23(b) of the regulations annexed to Hague Convention (IV) Respecting the Laws and Customs of War on Land, Oct. 18, 1907.

10. Second Lateran Council, 1139 A.D., Canon 29, *available at* http://www.dailycatholic.org/history/10ecumen.htm.

11. Augustine's writings on just war appear principally in three texts, the Letter to Marcellinus, Contra Faustus Manichaeus, and Qaestiones in Heptateuchem; Aquinas's views are in the Summa Theologica, esp. Question 40. The relevant passages are collected in Gregory M. Reichberg et al., The Ethics of War: Classic and Contemporary Readings (2006).

12. St. Augustine, Qaestiones in Heptateuchem, pt. 6, ¶10 ("But also this kind of war is without doubt just, which God commands.").

intervention? These questions received sophisticated treatment by canon lawyers in the Middle Ages and the early modern period.[13]

In the nineteenth century, the just war theory fell into temporary eclipse, as the major European states adopted the view that any use of force by a sovereign state is lawful. States launched wars to acquire colonies, to preserve the balance of power, or to snatch territory from weaker states.

Only in the wake of World War I, and more urgently after World War II, did states feel the need to return to something like a theory of *jus ad bellum*. They saw how disastrous free resort to war could be with modern weaponry, and the United Nations was founded "to save succeeding generations from the scourge of war, which twice in our lifetime has brought untold sorrow to mankind."[14] Under current international law, the JAB criteria are much simpler than traditional just war theory. Article 2(4) of the UN Charter bans all threats of force and use of force against another state's territorial integrity or political independence; under Article 51, the only exception is self-defense. Wars of aggression are therefore impermissible. As we saw in Chapter 3, the Nuremberg Charter declared aggressive war to be a "crime against peace" for which individual planners and perpetrators can be punished. The Rome Statute of the ICC likewise declares aggressive war to be a crime, but has delayed enforcement of this provision until the states parties arrive at a mutually acceptable legal definition of the crime of aggression.

Clearly, however, many traditional questions of JAB remain live issues. Scholars, diplomats, and lawyers continue to debate the legality of humanitarian intervention and preventive or preemptive war.

b.   *Jus in bello*

Jus in bello (JIB) refers to the rules of warfare. It assumes that warriors on either side of a war can fight either justly or unjustly; JIB and JAB are thus independent of each other. Contemporary just war theory recognizes four bedrock principles of JIB:

1.   *Noncombatant immunity*, also known as the Principle of Distinction: "The parties to the conflict must at all times distinguish between civilians and combatants. Attacks may only be directed against combatants. Attacks must not be directed against civilians."[15] "The parties to the conflict must at all times distinguish between civilian objects and military objectives. Attacks must not be directed against civilian objects."[16]

The Principle of Distinction covers not only civilians, but also enemy soldiers who have surrendered or become *hors de combat* (outside of combat) because of wounds or disease. Prisoners of war (POWs) may not be killed or mistreated. Violence must distinguish between combatants and noncombatants. There is one very important

---

13. Many of the classic texts of the medieval and early modern period are translated in Reichberg et al., *supra* note 11.

14. UN Charter pmbl.

15. 1 J.I. Henckaerts & L. Doswald-Beck, Customary International Law of War 3 (2005) (Rule 1). This comprehensive study by the International Committee of the Red Cross (ICRC) aims to restate customary international law, not the ethical theory of just war; but the quoted rule effectively restates the Principle of Distinction.

16. Id. at 25 (Rule 7).

exception to this assumed civilian immunity: "Civilians are protected against attack *unless and for such time as they take a direct part in hostilities.*"[17]

Just war theory recognizes that in war there will inevitably be innocent civilian casualties, even if warriors take great care to avoid them. Today, these are often referred to by the antiseptic phrase *collateral damage.* In less antiseptic terms, it means that all wars kill, maim, and ruin innocent civilians. Provided that this is unintentional, JIB permits collateral damage if it satisfies the following principle:

2. *Proportionality:* Collateral damage cannot be disproportionate to the military goals of the attack. Minor goals cannot justify major collateral damage.

Of course, proportionality calculations are inevitably imprecise. But that does not make the Principle of Proportionality empty. In contemporary military practice, the Principle of Proportionality often governs the choice of weapons: If a sniper shoots from the roof of an apartment building full of people, lawful militaries do not respond with high caliber weapons that will rip the building apart because they understand that doing so violates proportionality.

3. *Necessity.* No violence can be used that does not contribute to overcoming the enemy, whereas any act that helps overcome the enemy is permissible unless other *jus in bello* principles prohibit it.

"Military necessity" is often misunderstood to mean that regardless of the law, warriors can do whatever it takes to win. This latter doctrine is sometimes called by the German term "*Kriegsraison*" (reason of war), and if it were accepted, there could be no such thing as a law of war. *Kriegsraison* would trump any limits the law might impose. But this is not what the Principle of Necessity says. It permits only otherwise-lawful violence. Instead of providing an escape-hatch from legal obligation, the Principle of Necessity represents an outer limit, a prohibition rather than a permission: No violence is permitted unless it is militarily necessary and otherwise permitted by JIB. For example, even military necessity does not permit soldiers to kill prisoners, even if the "enemy combatants are captured by a small light unit (of, e.g., commandos or special forces), which can neither encumber itself with prisoners of war nor detach guards for their proper evacuation."[18]

A related fourth principle is this:

4. *No unnecessary suffering.* No violence can be used that inflicts unnecessary suffering.

Even though war often unleashes our most cruel and vengeful emotions, inflicting suffering purely for its own sake violates *jus in bello.* The prohibition on unnecessary suffering has generated treaties banning certain weapons, for example, blinding lasers and bullets that expand inside the human body or that are undetectable by X-rays.

Directly or indirectly, all modern laws of war follow from the principles of distinction, proportionality, necessity, and avoidance of unnecessary suffering. One legal consequence of JIB is of paramount importance: Warriors who comply with JIB have

---

17. Id. at 19 (Rule 6) (emphasis added).
18. Yoram Dinstein, The Conduct of Hostilities Under the Law of International Armed Conflict 19 (2004).

no criminal liability when they kill or injure the enemy or inflict proportionate collateral damage. They enjoy what is sometimes called the *belligerent privilege* or *belligerent immunity* from criminal prosecution — and, according to the just war theory, they have not committed a moral wrong.

A point of terminology. What we have called, generically, the "law of war" is often designated by two other names. Some call it the "law of armed conflict," or LOAC — the usual term employed by the U.S. military. Others refer to it as "international humanitarian law," or IHL. This is the preferred terminology of humanitarian organizations such as the International Committee of the Red Cross. The two do not totally coincide: *IHL* refers specifically to international law, while *LOAC* also includes states' domestic law. In the United States, for example, LOAC includes the Department of the Army's Law of Land Warfare, a manual codifying and operationalizing major treaty provisions.[19] But for most purposes, the terms LOAC and IHL may be used interchangeably. (It likely has not escaped your attention that the military term LOAC emphasizes armed conflict, while the Red Cross term IHL emphasizes humanitarianism.) We use IHL whenever we are referring specifically to the international law of war.

It is important not to confuse international *humanitarian* law with international *human rights* law. The former refers exclusively to laws of war; and it is a hotly debated legal question how much of human rights law applies at all during times of armed conflict — or in other words, how much is superseded in wartime by humanitarian law. Lawyers sometimes call the laws of war *lex specialis* — "special law" — to indicate its difference from the law prevailing in peaceable society, including human rights law. The difference can be striking, because the laws of war permit collateral damage that would amount to intolerable human rights violations in peacetime.

2. *The Geneva Conventions*

Modern IHL consists of both customary law and treaty law. In the law of war, these are very closely intertwined.[20] That is because states generally conform their own LOAC, military manuals, and the training of their forces to treaty provisions. By doing so, they engage in state practice backed by *opinio juris*, so that the treaty provisions become customary law as well, sometimes including treaty provisions from conventions to which states are not party. (As we will see, the United States has accepted as customary law of war several provisions of an Additional Protocol to the Geneva Conventions, even though the United States did not sign the Additional Protocol because it objected to other provisions.) In this area of law, the chief conventions have more or less defined customary IHL.

In 1859, a Swiss businessman named Henri Dunant visited the battlefield after the battle of Solferino, during the Second War of Italian Independence. Dunant was appalled by the piteous condition of the wounded and dying men who lay abandoned on the field, begging for water or simply moaning in pain, and founded the International Committee of the Red Cross (ICRC) to aid and succor the victims of war. As a result of years of ICRC lobbying, a number of states met at The Hague to negotiate treaties on wartime conduct. The result was a Hague Convention of 1899, and then another in 1907. These conventions drew on the first modern codification

---

19. Dept. of the Army, The Law of Land Warfare, FM 27-10 (1956).
20. See, e.g., Theodor Meron, The Geneva Conventions as Customary Law, 81 Am. J. Intl. L. 348 (1987).

of LOAC, the Lieber Code, drafted by Francis Lieber and adopted by the Union Army in the U.S. Civil War. Among other things, the Hague Conventions formulated specific rules of JIB, for example, prohibitions on poison weapons and bombardment of undefended cities.[21]

Another milestone in the evolution of IHL was the Geneva Convention of 1929, which created rules for the treatment of POWs. Despite the 1929 Convention, World War II was marked by horrific atrocities against POWs. After World War II, states convened again at Geneva and adopted the four Geneva Conventions of 1949, which replaced the 1929 version. The four GCs (as they are known) deal with the treatment of warriors who are hors de combat and civilians. The first two deal with sick and wounded soldiers, and the sick and wounded at sea. However, it is the third and fourth Geneva Conventions that are most important. GC III deals with prisoners of war, while GC IV deals with civilians who have been captured or interned; these two conventions are sometimes abbreviated GC-POW and GC-C.

In 1977, states negotiated two Additional Protocols to the Geneva Conventions, known as "AP I" and "AP II." The former deals with international armed conflict, while AP II deals with armed conflicts not of an international character (such as civil wars). The four 1949 GCs have 194 states parties, while 168 states have joined AP I and 164 have joined AP II. As mentioned above, the United States has not joined AP I or AP II. When the island republic of Nauru acceded to the GCs in 2006, they became "universal treaties" — all states now belong to them.

The unique role of the ICRC deserves note. Although it is a nongovernmental organization, the ICRC has become one of the major interpreters of the law of war; because of its acknowledged expertise, the ICRC commentaries on the Geneva Conventions (by Jean Pictet) have acquired semi-official standing. The Red Cross and Red Crescent organizations also play an official role, recognized in the major IHL treaties, in visiting prisoners to ascertain whether they are being well treated.[22] When Red Cross visitors find mistreatment, they make confidential reports to the detaining state. The Red Cross maintains strict neutrality, and in return for permission to visit prison camps, the organization keeps its findings confidential — a "devil's bargain" that human rights organizations sometimes find frustrating, but without which the Red Cross could not perform its mission. Often the unarmed Red Cross/Red Crescent teams exhibit stunning levels of personal courage, visiting murderous generals in combat zones to demand access to their prison camps, protected by nothing but their insignia. In the 1990s, ICRC personnel suffered more casualties than the entire U.S. army.

Together, "Hague law" and "Geneva law" form the core of modern IHL. In addition, states have negotiated numerous treaties on specific subjects (for example, attacks on cultural property and the environment) and weapons (for example, landmines). For a list of treaties, see the ICRC's Web site, http://www.icrc.org/ihl.

We turn now to an examination of the GCs and their Additional Protocols (APs). These form the foundation of current international war crimes doctrine.

---

21. Hague Convention Respecting the Laws and Customs of War on Land, Regulations Respecting the Laws and Customs of War on Land, Annex, arts. 23(a), 25, Oct. 18, 1907.

22. The Red Crescent is the Red Cross organization in Islamic countries, where the crescent emblem replaces the cross because of the religious significance of the cross. In 2005, states negotiated a third Additional Protocol to the Geneva Conventions, adding a religiously neutral symbol to be used by personnel from the Red Cross and Red Crescent. As of 2008, AP III has 36 states parties.

a.   The Structure of the GCs: Common Article 2

The Geneva Conventions provide separate rules for two kinds of armed conflicts: those between states ("international armed conflicts," or IACs) and armed conflicts "not of an international character" (NIACs). As the following Article explains, almost all the detailed GC rules apply only to IACs.

GENEVA CONVENTIONS OF AUGUST 12, 1949
75 U.N.T.S. 31, 85, 135, 287

ARTICLE 2

APPLICATION OF THE CONVENTION

In addition to the provisions which shall be implemented in peace time, the present Convention shall apply to all cases of declared war or of any other armed conflict which may arise between two or more of the High Contracting Parties, even if the state of war is not recognized by one of them.

The Convention shall also apply to all cases of partial or total occupation of the territory of a High Contracting Party, even if the said occupation meets with no armed resistance.

Although one of the Powers in conflict may not be a party to the present Convention, the Powers who are parties thereto shall remain bound by it in their mutual relations. They shall, furthermore, be bound by the Convention in relation to the said Power, if the latter accepts and applies the provisions thereof.

NOTES

1. Because this Article is identical in the four Geneva Conventions, it is sometimes called "common Article 2." Likewise, the one Geneva provision dealing with non-international armed conflicts is known as "common Article 3." (Common Article 3 is presented below.)

2. Notice that because at present all states are parties to the Geneva Conventions, the final paragraph of Article 2 has become moot.

3. Notice as well that under Article 2, the GCs apply both in cases of declared war and in other armed conflict between states. This is important, because the practice of formally declaring war for all practical purposes disappeared after World War II. The question then arises of what counts as an "armed conflict" between states. According to ICRC commentator Pictet, "Any difference arising between two States and leading to the intervention of members of the armed forces is an armed conflict within the meaning of Article 2, even if one of the Parties denies the existence of a state of war. It makes no difference how long the conflict lasts, how much slaughter takes place, or how numerous are the participating forces. . . ." 3 Jean Pictet, Commentary on the Geneva Conventions of 12 August 1949, at 23 (1952). As we shall see in Section B.2 below, the definition of "armed conflict" when one or more of the parties is a non-state actor is more complicated.

4. All the articles of the GCs except for common Article 3 apply only in an international armed conflict. Common Article 3, examined below in Section A.2.c., is the sole article of the GCs dealing with noninternational armed conflict. (However, Additional Protocol II deals entirely with noninternational armed conflicts.)

A quick glance through GC III reveals that POWs in international armed conflict enjoy a remarkably high level of protection. That is because POWs are the moral equals of the captors' own troops: Both are privileged belligerents. The fact that a POW may have killed the detaining power's troops in combat is irrelevant — he is morally and legally innocent of those killings, and from the moment he surrenders he must be treated on a par with the detaining powers' own troops, much as they might hate him for killing their buddies. POWs must be "quartered under conditions as favorable as those for the forces of the Detaining Power" (Article 25), treated with respect and honor, and indeed have their salaries paid by their captors (Article 60), to be repaid by the POWs' home states at war's end (Article 67). GC III even specifies which enemy officers POWs must salute (Article 39). POWs cannot be treated as criminals merely because they have fought; indeed, the only war crimes they can be punished for are those that their captors would punish if their own troops committed them (Arts. 87, 99, 102).

This does not mean that POWs cannot be tried and punished for war crimes, or, for that matter, for domestic crimes. But they must be crimes that the detaining power would try and punish their own forces and their own nationals for committing. To illustrate: In 1989, U.S. troops invaded Panama and captured Panama's military dictator Manuel Noriega, who was deeply implicated in the narcotics trade. Noriega was the head of Panama's defense forces, and held the rank of general. As a result, he received POW status. But that did not prevent his trial on narcotics charges, and he was convicted in federal court and sentenced to 25 years. United States v. Noriega, 808 F. Supp. 791 (S.D. Fla. 1992) (determining that Noriega enjoys POW status and that GC-POW is self-executing).

Just as GC III provides significant protections for POWs, GC IV provides a regime of protections for civilians in international armed conflict. These protections, spelled out in Articles 27-34 of GC IV, insist that civilians be treated "humanely" and protect civilians' basic human rights "against all acts of violence or threats thereof and against insults and public curiosity" (Article 27), as well as against "physical suffering or extermination" (Article 32). More elaborate rules govern the treatment of civilians who are interned, either for their own safety or because they pose a security risk.

5. The special status of POWs raises the important question of who counts as a legitimate prisoner of war. GC-POW answers this question in its Article 4.

GENEVA CONVENTION RELATIVE TO THE TREATMENT OF PRISONERS OF WAR, AUGUST 12, 1949

75 U.N.T.S. 972

ARTICLE 4

PRISONERS OF WAR

A. Prisoners of war, in the sense of the present Convention, are persons belonging to one of the following categories, who have fallen into the power of the enemy:

(1) Members of the armed forces of a Party to the conflict as well as members of militias or volunteer corps forming part of such armed forces.

(2) Members of other militias and members of other volunteer corps, including those of organized resistance movements, belonging to a Party to the conflict and operating in or outside their own territory, even if this territory is occupied,

provided that such militias or volunteer corps, including such organized resistance movements, fulfill the following conditions:

    (a) that of being commanded by a person responsible for his subordinates;

    (b) that of having a fixed distinctive sign recognizable at a distance;

    (c) that of carrying arms openly;

    (d) that of conducting their operations in accordance with the laws and customs of war.

(3) Members of regular armed forces who profess allegiance to a government or an authority not recognized by the Detaining Power.

(4) Persons who accompany the armed forces without actually being members thereof, such as civilian members of military aircraft crews, war correspondents, supply contractors, members of labour units or of services responsible for the welfare of the armed forces, provided that they have received authorization from the armed forces which they accompany, who shall provide them for that purpose with an identity card similar to the annexed model.

(5) Members of crews, including masters, pilots and apprentices, of the merchant marine and the crews of civil aircraft of the Parties to the conflict, who do not benefit by more favourable treatment under any other provisions of international law.

(6) Inhabitants of a non-occupied territory, who on the approach of the enemy spontaneously take up arms to resist the invading forces, without having had time to form themselves into regular armed units, provided they carry arms openly and respect the laws and customs of war.

NOTES

1. The question of who counts as a lawful prisoner of war has generated controversy in the "war on terror." To take one salient example, the question whether the Taliban satisfies the Article 4 criteria has generated extensive discussion within the United States. If they satisfy the Article 4 criteria, Taliban captives have POW status, and two important consequences follow: First, they enjoy the belligerent privilege and cannot be tried for fighting against U.S. forces; and second, they can be tried only before a court martial—a regularly constituted military court—because under U.S. law a court martial is the venue for trying members of the uniformed military. Conversely, if Taliban forces are not lawful combatants, they can be prosecuted for attempted or completed attacks on U.S. troops; and under U.S. domestic law they can be tried before specially constituted military commissions.

2. President George W. Bush determined that although the war with Afghanistan is an international armed conflict, members of the Taliban are unlawful combatants because the Taliban does not satisfy Article 4 of GC-POW. Memorandum from George W. Bush, Humane Treatment for Al Qaeda and Taliban Detainees, Feb. 7, 2002, reprinted in The Torture Papers 134, 135 (Karen J. Greenberg & Joshua L. Dratel eds., 2005). The president based his decision on an opinion of the Justice Department's Office of Legal Counsel, issued the same day as his finding. The OLC concluded that the Taliban lacks a centralized command structure, its members do not wear uniforms (the "fixed distinctive sign recognizable at a distance" required in Article 4(A)(2)(b)), and do not follow the laws of war. Thus, they are not a militia in the sense of Article 4(A)(2). Next, the OLC reasoned that the regular armed forces of a state must satisfy at least the same four criteria as a militia, and therefore the Taliban could not count as Afghanistan's regular army under Article 4(A)(1). Memorandum for Alberto R. Gonzales, OLC, Feb. 7, 2002, reprinted in The Torture Papers, at 137-142. Because the Taliban do not meet the Article 4 criteria, its fighters do not qualify for POW status. Soon after, a federal court supported this determination.

United States v. Lindh, 212 F. Supp. 2d 541, 557-558 (E.D. Va. 2002). This case concerned John Walker Lindh, the so-called "American Taliban" — a U.S. national who had joined the Taliban out of religious conviction. Lindh was indicted for, among other crimes, violating 18 U.S.C §2332b, which criminalizes violence or attempted violence against U.S. nationals outside the United States. Had Lindh been found to be a lawful combatant, such violence against U.S. forces would enjoy the belligerent immunity (although Lindh could possibly have been prosecuted for treason).

So too, several Taliban fighters have been indicted and bound over for trial in front of U.S. military commissions in Guantánamo. These include, for example, Omar Khadr, accused of throwing a grenade that killed a U.S. soldier. If Khadr (who was only 15 at the time of the alleged attack) were declared a POW, he could not be tried before a military commission, and indeed his alleged actions would not be criminal.

b.   War Crimes Under the Geneva Conventions: "Grave Breaches"

i.   What Are the Grave Breaches?

Each of the four GCs, and AP I, includes an article defining "grave breaches" of the Convention. These are the most serious war crimes; the drafters chose not to use the term *war crimes* only because different states' domestic legal systems differ over the definition of *crime,* and so it seemed better to choose a new term.

The grave breaches include core violations common to all four GCs:

> wilful killing, torture or inhuman treatment, including biological experiments, wilfully causing great suffering or serious injury to body or health. . . .[23]

Remember that the GCs concern the treatment of adversaries who are hors de combat and of civilians. Obviously, killing and injuring enemy forces in combat is not forbidden by the GCs — it's what combat is! — and lawful combat lethality is protected by the belligerent privilege.

In addition to the grave breaches common to all four GCs, the four Conventions include other grave breaches.

In GC I and GC II (dealing with sick, wounded, or shipwrecked forces on land and sea): "extensive destructions and appropriation of property, not justified by military necessity and carried out unlawfully and wantonly."[24] This provision was particularly intended to prohibit attacks on medical facilities or hospital ships.[25]

In GC III (dealing with prisoners of war): "compelling a prisoner of war to serve in the forces of the hostile Power, or wilfully depriving a prisoner of war of the rights of fair and regular trial prescribed in this Convention."[26]

In GC IV (dealing with civilian "protected persons"): "unlawful deportation or transfer or unlawful confinement of a protected person, compelling a protected person to serve in the forces of a hostile Power, or wilfully depriving a protected person of the rights of fair and regular trial prescribed in the present Convention, taking of hostages and extensive destruction and appropriation of property, not justified by military necessity and carried out unlawfully and wantonly."[27]

---

23. GC I, art. 50; GC II, art. 51; GC III, art. 130; GC IV, art. 147.
24. GC I, art. 50; GC II, art. 51.
25. 1 Jean Pictet, Commentary on the Geneva Conventions of August 12, 1949, at 372 (1952); 2 Pictet, supra, at 267.
26. GC III, art. 130.
27. GC IV, art. 147.

In AP I: "Any wilful act or omission which seriously endangers the physical or mental health or integrity of any person who is in the power of a Party other than the one on which he depends" is a grave breach (Article 11(4)). Article 85(3) of AP I broke new ground by making a large number of JIB violations grave breaches, including willful violations of the Principles of Distinction and Proportionality. Article 85(4)(d) makes attacks against cultural objects a grave breach, and also "unjustifiable delay in the repatriation of prisoners of war or civilians" (Article 85(4)(b)) and "practices of apartheid and other inhuman and degrading practices involving outrages upon personal dignity, based on racial discrimination" (Article 85(4)(c)). One of the grave breaches recognized by Article 85 was more controversial. Article 85(4)(a) makes "the transfer by the occupying Power of parts of its own civilian population into the territory it occupies" a grave breach — a provision that was widely understood to be directed against the Israeli settlements in Palestine.

ii. A Note on Additional Protocol 1

The 1977 Additional Protocols were negotiated beginning in 1974, at the end of the Vietnam War. This was a period of intense anticolonialist sentiment in the developing world, and AP I reflects this sentiment in several of its articles. Most notably, AP I expands the concept of international armed conflicts to include "armed conflicts in which peoples are fighting against colonial domination and alien occupation and against racist regimes in the exercise of their right of self-determination" (Article 1(4)). In line with this viewpoint, AP I extends POW protections to nonuniformed guerrilla fighters, so long as they display their arms openly during combat (Article 44). The United States, with the memory of Vietnam still fresh, rejected this proposal on the basis that legitimizing nonuniformed fighters who melt back into the surrounding population would lead to more civilian casualties. Article 44 was one reason that, in the end, the United States declined to join AP I.

Although AP I, unlike the GCs, has not been accepted by all states, many of its provisions are recognized as customary international law even by non-states parties. Notably, a U.S. State Department Deputy Legal Adviser published an article in 1988 announcing that the United States accepts 59 out of 91 of AP I's substantive articles as representing customary international law; he listed the Articles, which amount to 65 percent of AP I. Among them are Articles 11 and 85, the "grave breaches" provisions.[28]

iii. Repressing Grave Breaches

The GCs do not simply enumerate the grave breaches. They also require states parties to criminalize them. The following article is common to all four GCs, although it is numbered differently in each of them.

---

28. Mike Matheson, Additional Protocol I as Expressions of Customary International Law, 2 Am. U. J. Intl. L. & Poly. 428 (1988). Some commentators, however, have expressed doubt that Matheson's formulation remains correct. See 2005 Operational Law Handbook (Intl. & Operational Law Dept., 2005, errata sheet) ("overbroad"); W. Hays Parks, "Special Forces" Wear of Non-Standard Uniforms, 4 Chi. J. Intl. L. 519 n.55 (2003) ("personal opinion"); Charles Garraway, "England Does Not Love Coalitions." Does Anything Change?" in International Law Studies, vol. 82, The Law of War in the 21st Century: Weaponry and the Use of Force 238 (Anthony M. Helm ed., 2006) ("no longer authoritative"). For discussion, see Gary D. Solis, The Law of Armed Conflict: International Humanitarian Law in War (forthcoming). Solis accepts the Matheson formulation as a valid expression of the U.S. position.

GENEVA CONVENTIONS OF AUGUST 12, 1949
75 U.N.T.S. 31, 85, 135, 287

ARTICLES 49 (GC I); 50 (GC II); 129 (GC III); 146 (GC IV)

PENAL SANCTIONS: GENERAL OBSERVATIONS

The High Contracting Parties undertake to enact any legislation necessary to provide effective penal sanctions for persons committing, or ordering to be committed, any of the grave breaches of the present Convention. . . .

Each High Contracting Party shall be under the obligation to search for persons alleged to have committed, or to have ordered to be committed, such grave breaches, and shall bring such persons, regardless of their nationality, before its own courts. It may also, if it prefers, and in accordance with the provisions of its own legislation, hand such persons over for trial to another High Contracting Party concerned, provided such High Contracting Party has made out a "prima facie" case.

Each High Contracting Party shall take measures necessary for the suppression of all acts contrary to the provisions of the present Convention other than the grave breaches. . . .

In all circumstances, the accused persons shall benefit by safeguards of proper trial and defence, which shall not be less favourable than those provided by [GC articles defining minimum trial rights for war crimes].

NOTES

1. Of particular interest is the second paragraph of this Article, which in effect makes grave breaches of the GCs a universal jurisdiction offense.

2. As in the list of grave breaches, AP I breaks new ground in its Articles on repressing grave breaches. In Article 86, AP I introduces command responsibility for grave breaches committed by subordinates. See the discussion of command responsibility in Chapter 17.

c.   Common Article 3

Common Article 3 is the only Article in the GCs dealing with armed conflicts not of an international character, and it provides a lower level of protection than the remainder of the GCs.

GENEVA CONVENTIONS OF AUGUST 12, 1949
75 U.N.T.S. 31, 85, 135, 287

ARTICLE 3

CONFLICTS NOT OF AN INTERNATIONAL CHARACTER

In the case of armed conflict not of an international character occurring in the territory of one of the High Contracting Parties, each Party to the conflict shall be bound to apply, as a minimum, the following provisions:

(1) Persons taking no active part in the hostilities, including members of armed forces who have laid down their arms and those placed hors de combat by sickness, wounds, detention, or any other cause, shall in all circumstances be treated humanely,

without any adverse distinction founded on race, colour, religion or faith, sex, birth or wealth, or any other similar criteria. To this end the following acts are and shall remain prohibited at any time and in any place whatsoever with respect to the above-mentioned persons:

(a) violence to life and person, in particular murder of all kinds, mutilation, cruel treatment and torture;

(b) taking of hostages;

(c) outrages upon personal dignity, in particular, humiliating and degrading treatment;

(d) the passing of sentences and the carrying out of executions without previous judgment pronounced by a regularly constituted court affording all the judicial guarantees which are recognized as indispensable by civilized peoples.

(2) The wounded and sick shall be collected and cared for. . . .

NOTES AND QUESTIONS

1. Commentators often describe common Article 3 as a mini-convention embedded within the Geneva Conventions. It provides a minimum set of basic rights that captors must provide to their captives in civil wars or other noninternational armed conflicts. As mentioned, these afford a lower level of protection than the GCs provide in international armed conflicts. To take one notable example, CA 3 (as common Article 3 is typically known) forbids torture and outrages against personal dignity, but does not forbid the coercive interrogation of prisoners so long as the interrogations do not involve such violations. By contrast, POWs are protected from all forms of coercion:

> No physical or mental torture, nor any other form of coercion, may be inflicted on prisoners of war to secure from them information of any kind whatever. Prisoners of war who refuse to answer may not be threatened, insulted, or exposed to any unpleasant or disadvantageous treatment of any kind.

GC-POW, art. 17. POWs cannot be required to give any information except their name, rank, birthdate, and serial number. As for civilian captives, GC-C provides, quite simply, that "No physical or moral coercion shall be exercised against protected persons, in particular to obtain information from them or from third parties." GC-C, art. 31. Clearly, these provisions are far more protective than common Article 3.

2. Perhaps the most important respect in which CA 3 does not protect captives as thoroughly as in international armed conflicts is that it nowhere suggests that enemy fighters enjoy the belligerent privilege. (The same is true in AP II, which likewise pertains to noninternational armed conflicts.) Recall that GC-POW specifies that prisoners of war in international armed conflicts can be tried only for offenses that would also be criminal if the detaining power's forces committed them (Arts. 87, 99, 102). As long as the detaining power permits its troops to fight against the enemy, POWs cannot be tried for fighting against the enemy. This is not true in noninternational armed conflicts such as civil wars. There, nothing in the GCs prevents the state from declaring that all the enemy's activities are crimes under domestic law and punishing them for it after a fair trial. In the U.S. Civil War, this theory would have allowed the Union to declare the Confederate troops criminals.

To be sure, in civil wars AP II (dealing with noninternational armed conflicts) does require states to "endeavour to grant the broadest possible amnesty to persons who have participated in the armed conflict." AP II, art. 6(5). But this is a much weaker protection of rebel fighters than belligerent immunity: Endeavoring to grant amnesty is not the same as granting amnesty, and the broadest possible amnesty for rebels may in the state's opinion be quite narrow. In any event, the very use of the word *amnesty* implies that under AP II rebel fighters enjoy no belligerent immunity, else they would need no amnesty.

3. It is important to notice that nothing in the GCs requires states parties to criminalize violations of common Article 3 and thus to treat them as war crimes. Such violations are not grave breaches of the GCs. (Why?) To be sure, the previously quoted common Article on repressing grave breaches requires states parties to "take measures necessary for the suppression of all acts contrary to the provisions of the present Convention other than the grave breaches." Pictet's commentary strongly hints that such measures must include criminalizing violations that are not, technically speaking, grave breaches:

> In our opinion [the paragraph] covers everything a State can do to prevent the commission, or the repetition, of acts contrary to the Convention. . . . There can . . . be no doubt that the primary purpose of the paragraph is the "repression" of infractions other than "grave breaches," and that the administrative measures which may be taken to ensure respect for the provisions of the Convention on the part of the armed forces and the civilian population are only a secondary consideration.

1 Pictet, supra note 25, at 367. In your view, can this interpretation be reconciled with the plain language of the treaty?

4. By the same token, nothing in international law prevents states from adding violations of common Article 3 to their domestic-law list of war crimes. This has been the approach of the United States, which defines a category of "grave breaches of common Article 3" and makes them war crimes under 18 U.S.C. §2441.[29] Under 18 U.S.C. §2441(d)(1), violations of some clauses of common Article 3 are grave breaches of common Article 3. Until 2006, violations of all clauses of CA 3 counted as war crimes under §2441. When Congress enacted the Military Commissions Act in 2006, it decriminalized outrages on personal dignity and punishment without fair trials retroactive to 1996. Significantly, U.S. forces had been accused of violating both these provisions of CA 3: U.S. forces had subjected detainees to humiliating and degrading treatment, and—a few weeks before Congress enacted the legislation—the U.S. Supreme Court had declared that the Guantánamo military commissions violate common Article 3. Hamdan v. Rumsfeld, 548 U.S. 557, 631-635 (2006). Congress was responding to the perceived threat that U.S. troops and officials might be labeled war criminals under both international and domestic law. In your opinion, is this a good enough reason to decriminalize these acts? For further discussion, see Section C.2 below, discussing the war crime of humiliating or degrading treatment of captives.

---

29. In addition to this statute, which applies to civilians, the Uniform Code of Military Justice provides for prosecution of war crimes. In past practice, the U.S. military has prosecuted war crimes without labeling them as such—prosecuting them instead as murders, assaults, conduct unbecoming of an officer, or other crimes. As of 2009, nobody has been prosecuted under 18 U.S.C. §2441.

3.   War Crimes in the Rome Statute of the ICC

Both the International Criminal Tribunal for Former Yugoslavia (ICTY) and International Criminal Tribunal for Rwanda (ICTR) Statutes include a category of war crimes (derived from conventional IHL). However, the most comprehensive list of war crimes to date is in Article 8 of the Rome Statute.

The first thing to notice about Article 8 is its chapeau: "The Court shall have jurisdiction in respect of war crimes in particular when committed as part of a plan or policy or as part of a large-scale commission of such crimes." This is potentially an important jurisdictional limit because it excludes "one off" war crimes by individuals or small units of soldiers acting spontaneously. In line with its complementarity regime, the restriction implies that such individual war crimes should be left to the justice systems of states — presumably the criminal's own state, or else the adversary's state. Of course, this does not mean that individual killings of civilians (for example) are not war crimes, only that the ICC may have no jurisdiction over them.

The second thing to notice about Article 8 is the large number of crimes it itemizes: 34 crimes in international armed conflicts, plus 16 crimes in noninternational armed conflicts. These include all the grave breaches of the GCs and AP I.[30] They also include all violations of common Article 3, in IAC as well as noninternational armed conflict. Some of the Article 8 crimes are based on the 1907 Hague Conventions — arguably expanding war crimes doctrine beyond existing treaty law because the Hague rules were not backed by criminal sanctions; at Nuremberg, however, they were treated as customary war crimes.

The Rome Statute also adds some crimes that were not previously recognized in Hague or Geneva law. For example, Article 8(2)(b)(iii) makes it a crime to attack UN humanitarian personnel or peacekeepers. Most noticeably, Article 8(e) substantially broadens the list of war crimes in noninternational armed conflict beyond common Article 3.[31]

B.   INTERNATIONAL AND NONINTERNATIONAL ARMED CONFLICTS

1.   When Is an Armed Conflict "International"?

It may not always be obvious when an armed conflict is international, and therefore when violations of JIB count as grave breaches and thus as war crimes. This was a central issue before the ICTY in its first case, that of Duško Tadić. Recall from Chapter 3 that after Bosnia declared independence from Yugoslavia, the Yugoslav national army engaged with Bosnian forces — a clear case of an international armed conflict between the two states. In 1992, however, the Yugoslav national army officially withdrew from Bosnia, and the struggle took the form of a civil war between Bosnian Serbs and Bosnian Croats and Muslims — an "internal" armed conflict to which the

---

30. At first glance it appears that AP I's grave breach of apartheid or outrages on personal dignity based on racial discrimination is absent from Article 8; however, ICC Article 8(2)(b)(xxi) forbids all outrages on personal dignity and is therefore even broader than the apartheid clause of AP I.

31. For a crime-by-crime review of Article 8, discussing the origins of each crime in treaty law, see Commentary on the Rome Statute, supra note 9, at 173-288.

Article 2 Geneva regime of grave breaches seemed on the surface not to apply. Internal armed conflicts, remember, are governed only by common Article 3. What complicated matters, however, was that in fact Yugoslavia was deeply involved in the "civil war" on the side of the Bosnian Serb militias. In this sense, the "internal" armed conflict in Bosnia was internal in name only. The ICTY Appeals Chamber analyzed the legal consequences of this fact in the following path-breaking decision. It discussed the question "when, in an armed conflict which is prima facie internal, armed forces may be regarded as acting on behalf of a foreign power, thereby rendering the conflict international."

PROSECUTOR v. TADIĆ

Case No. IT-94-1-A, Judgment (July 15, 1999)

91. The Appeals Chamber will . . . discuss the question at issue first from the viewpoint of international humanitarian law. In particular, the Appeals Chamber will consider the conditions under which armed forces fighting against the central authorities *of the same State* in which they live and operate may be deemed to act on behalf of another State. In other words, the Appeals Chamber will identify the conditions under which those forces may be assimilated to organs of a State other than that on whose territory they live and operate.

92. A starting point for this discussion is provided by the criteria for lawful combatants laid down in the Third Geneva Convention of 1949. Under this Convention, militias or paramilitary groups or units may be regarded as legitimate combatants if they form "part of [the] armed forces" of a Party to the conflict (Article 4A(1)) or "belong [. . .]" to a "Party to the conflict" (Article 4A(2)) and satisfy the other four requirements provided for in Article 4A(2). It is clear that this provision is primarily directed toward establishing the requirements for the status of lawful combatants. Nevertheless, one of its logical consequences is that if, in an armed conflict, paramilitary units "belong" to a State other than the one against which they are fighting, the conflict is international and therefore serious violations of the Geneva Conventions may be classified as "grave breaches."

94. . . . In order for irregulars to qualify as lawful combatants, it appears that international rules and State practice therefore require control over them by a Party to an international armed conflict and, by the same token, a relationship of dependence and allegiance of these irregulars *vis-à-vis* that Party to the conflict. These then may be regarded as the ingredients of the term "belonging to a Party to the conflict."

95. The Appeals Chamber thus considers that the Third Geneva Convention, by providing in Article 4 the requirement of "belonging to a Party to the conflict," implicitly refers to a test of control.

96. This conclusion, based on the letter and the spirit of the Geneva Conventions, is borne out by the entire logic of international humanitarian law. This body of law is not grounded on formalistic postulates. It is not based on the notion that only those who have the formal status of State organs, i.e., are members of the armed forces of a State, are duty bound both to refrain from engaging in violations of humanitarian law as well as — if they are in a position of authority — to prevent or punish the commission of such crimes. Rather, it is a realistic body of law, grounded on the notion of effectiveness and inspired by the aim of deterring deviation from its standards to the maximum extent possible. It follows, amongst other things, that humanitarian law holds accountable not only those having formal positions of authority but also those

who wield *de facto* power as well as those who exercise control over perpetrators of serious violations of international humanitarian law. Hence, in cases such as that currently under discussion, what is required for criminal responsibility to arise is some measure of control by a Party to the conflict over the perpetrators.

97. It is nevertheless imperative to *specify* what *degree of authority or control* must be wielded by a foreign State over armed forces fighting on its behalf in order to render international an armed conflict which is *prima facie* internal. Indeed, the legal consequences of the characterisation of the conflict as either internal or international are extremely important. Should the conflict eventually be classified as international, it would *inter alia* follow that a foreign State may in certain circumstances be held responsible for violations of international law perpetrated by the armed groups acting on its behalf. . . .

99. In dealing with the question of the legal conditions required for individuals to be considered as acting on behalf of a State, i.e., as *de facto* State officials, a high degree of control has been authoritatively suggested by the International Court of Justice in *Nicaragua*.[32]

100. The issue brought before the International Court of Justice was whether a foreign State, the United States, because of its financing, organising, training, equipping and planning of the operations of organised military and paramilitary groups of Nicaraguan rebels (the so-called *contras*) in Nicaragua, was responsible for violations of international humanitarian law committed by those rebels. The Court held that a high degree of control was necessary for this to be the case. It required that (i) a Party not only be in effective control of a military or paramilitary group, but that (ii) the control be exercised with respect to the specific operation in the course of which breaches may have been committed. The Court went so far as to state that in order to establish that the United States was responsible for "acts contrary to human rights and humanitarian law" allegedly perpetrated by the Nicaraguan *contras*, it was necessary to prove that the United States had specifically "directed or enforced" the perpetration of those acts. . . .

115. The "effective control" test enunciated by the International Court of Justice was regarded as correct and upheld by Trial Chamber II in the Judgement. The Appeals Chamber, with respect, does not hold the *Nicaragua* test to be persuasive. . . .

116. A first ground on which the *Nicaragua* test as such may be held to be unconvincing is based on the very logic of the entire system of international law on State responsibility.

117. The principles of international law concerning the attribution to States of acts performed by private individuals are not based on rigid and uniform criteria. . . . The requirement of international law for the attribution to States of acts performed by private individuals is that the State exercises control over the individuals. The *degree of control* may, however, vary according to the factual circumstances of each case. The Appeals Chamber fails to see why in each and every circumstance international law should require a high threshold for the test of control. Rather, various situations may be distinguished.

118. One situation is the case of a private individual who is engaged by a State to perform some specific illegal acts in the territory of another State (for instance, kidnapping a State official, murdering a dignitary or a high-ranking State official, blowing up a power station or, especially in times of war, carrying out acts of sabotage). In such a case, it would be necessary to show that the State issued specific

---

32. This refers to the International Court of Justice case between Nicaragua and the United States. Military and Paramilitary Activities (Nicar. v. U.S.), 1986 I.C.J. 14 (June 27). — EDS.

instructions concerning the commission of the breach in order to prove — if only by necessary implication — that the individual acted as a *de facto* State agent. Alternatively it would be necessary to show that the State has publicly given retroactive approval to the action of that individual. A generic authority over the individual would not be sufficient to engage the international responsibility of the State. A similar situation may come about when an unorganised group of individuals commits acts contrary to international law. For these acts to be attributed to the State it would seem necessary to prove not only that the State exercised some measure of authority over those individuals but also that it issued specific instructions to them concerning the performance of the acts at issue, or that it *ex post facto* publicly endorsed those acts. . . .

120. One should distinguish the situation of individuals acting on behalf of a State without specific instructions, from that of individuals making up *an organised and hierarchically structured group*, such as a military unit or, in case of war or civil strife, armed bands of irregulars or rebels. Plainly, an organised group differs from an individual in that the former normally has a structure, a chain of command and a set of rules as well as the outward symbols of authority. Normally a member of the group does not act on his own but conforms to the standards prevailing in the group and is subject to the authority of the head of the group. Consequently, for the attribution to a State of acts of these groups it is sufficient to require that the group as a whole be under the overall control of the State.

121. This kind of State control over a military group and the fact that the State is held responsible for acts performed by a group independently of any State instructions, or even contrary to instructions, to some extent equates the group with State organs proper. . . . Generally speaking, it can be maintained that the whole body of international law on State responsibility is based on a realistic concept of accountability, which disregards legal formalities and aims at ensuring that States entrusting some functions to individuals or groups of individuals must answer for their actions, even when they act contrary to their directives.

123. . . . [I]nternational law renders any State responsible for acts in breach of international law performed (i) by individuals having the formal status of organs of a State (and this occurs even when these organs act *ultra vires* or *contra legem*), or (ii) by individuals who make up organised groups subject to the State's control. International law does so regardless of whether or not the State has issued *specific instructions* to those individuals. Clearly, the rationale behind this legal regulation is that otherwise, States might easily shelter behind, or use as a pretext, their internal legal system or the lack of any specific instructions in order to disclaim international responsibility. . . .

125. In cases dealing with members of *military or paramilitary groups*, courts have clearly departed from the notion of "effective control" set out by the International Court of Justice (i.e., control that extends to the issuance of specific instructions concerning the various activities of the individuals in question). . . .

130. Precisely what measure of State control does international law require for organised military groups? Judging from international case law and State practice, it would seem that for such control to come about, it is not sufficient for the group to be financially or even militarily assisted by a State. . . .

131. In order to attribute the acts of a military or paramilitary group to a State, it must be proved that the State wields overall control over the group, not only by equipping and financing the group, but also by coordinating or helping in the general planning of its military activity. Only then can the State be held internationally accountable for any misconduct of the group. However, it is not necessary that, in

addition, the State should also issue, either to the head or to members of the group, instructions for the commission of specific acts contrary to international law. . . .

137. In sum, the Appeals Chamber holds the view that international rules do not always require the same degree of control over armed groups or private individuals for the purpose of determining whether an individual not having the status of a State official under internal legislation can be regarded as a *de facto* organ of the State. The extent of the requisite State control varies. Where the question at issue is whether a *single* private individual or a *group that is not militarily organised* has acted as a *de facto* State organ when performing a specific act, it is necessary to ascertain whether specific instructions concerning the commission of that particular act had been issued by that State to the individual or group in question; alternatively, it must be established whether the unlawful act had been publicly endorsed or approved *ex post facto* by the State at issue. By contrast, control by a State over subordinate *armed forces or militias or paramilitary units* may be of an overall character (and must comprise more than the mere provision of financial assistance or military equipment or training). This requirement, however, does not go so far as to include the issuing of specific orders by the State, or its direction of each individual operation. Under international law it is by no means necessary that the controlling authorities should plan all the operations of the units dependent on them, choose their targets, or give specific instructions concerning the conduct of military operations and any alleged violations of international humanitarian law. The control required by international law may be deemed to exist when a State (or, in the context of an armed conflict, the Party to the conflict) *has a role in organising, coordinating or planning the military actions* of the military group, in addition to financing, training and equipping or providing operational support to that group. Acts performed by the group or members thereof may be regarded as acts of *de facto* State organs regardless of any specific instruction by the controlling State concerning the commission of each of those acts. . . .

141. It should be added that international law does not provide only for a *test of overall control* applying to armed groups and that of *specific instructions* (or subsequent public approval), applying to single individuals or militarily unorganised groups. The Appeals Chamber holds the view that international law also embraces a *third test*. This test is the assimilation of individuals to State organs *on account of their actual behaviour within the structure of a State (and regardless of any possible requirement of State instructions).* Such a test is best illustrated by reference to certain cases that deserve to be mentioned, if only briefly.

142. The first case is *Joseph Kramer et al.* (also called the *Belsen* case), brought before a British military court sitting at Luneburg (Germany). The Defendants comprised not only some German staff members of the Belsen and Auschwitz concentration camps but also a number of camp inmates of Polish nationality and an Austrian Jew "elevated by the camp administrators to positions of authority over the other internees." They were *inter alia* accused of murder and other offences against the camp inmates. According to the official report on this case:

> In meeting the argument that no war crime could be committed by Poles against other Allied nationals, the Prosecutor said that by identifying themselves with the authorities the Polish accused had made themselves as much responsible as the S.S. themselves. Perhaps it could be claimed that by the same process *they could be regarded as having approximated to membership of the armed forces of Germany.*

. . . 144. Other cases also prove that private individuals acting within the framework of, or in connection with, armed forces, or in collusion with State authorities may be regarded as *de facto* State organs. In these cases it follows that the acts of such individuals are attributed to the State, as far as State responsibility is concerned, and may also generate individual criminal responsibility.

145. In the light of the above discussion, the following conclusion may be safely reached. In the case at issue, given that the Bosnian Serb armed forces constituted a "military organization," the control of the FRY authorities over these armed forces required by international law for considering the armed conflict to be international was *overall control* going beyond the mere financing and equipping of such forces and involving also participation in the planning and supervision of military operations. By contrast, international rules do not require that such control should extend to the issuance of specific orders or instructions relating to single military actions, whether or not such actions were contrary to international humanitarian law.

[The Appeals Chamber concludes that Yugoslavia did in fact exercise "overall control" over the Bosnian Serb militias, so that the Bosnian civil war qualifies as an international armed conflict, and crimes committed in it were grave breaches. It also finds that civilians are protected by the Geneva Conventions regardless of nationality.]

C. Conclusion

171. The Appeals Chamber accordingly finds that the Appellant was guilty of grave breaches of the Geneva Conventions. . . .

NOTES AND QUESTIONS

1. This decision broke new ground in international humanitarian law. The Trial Chamber had used the *Nicaragua* test (which it interpreted to mean that Yugoslavia was responsible for the Serb militias only if the militias were Yugoslavia's agents). Prosecutor v. Tadić, Case No. IT-94-1-T, Judgment, ¶¶585, 588 (May 7, 1997). It concluded that Yugoslavia did not exercise that level of control, and therefore the Bosnian civil war was not an international armed conflict. Id. ¶605. By lowering the threshold from "effective control" to "overall control" and reversing the Trial Chamber, the Appeals Chamber expanded the scope of the Geneva Conventions "grave breaches" regime.

2. Of particular importance is the interpretive principle set out by the Appeals Chamber in ¶96, discussing the "entire logic of international humanitarian law." It writes: "This body of law is not grounded on formalistic postulates. . . . Rather, it is a realistic body of law, grounded on the notion of effectiveness and inspired by the aim of deterring deviation from its standards to the maximum extent possible." This principle suggests that, in the Chamber's view, IHL must be read expansively. This principle is reminiscent of a well-known dictum from the European Court of Human Rights' decision in Soering v. United Kingdom, 161 Eur. Ct. H.R. 87 (1989), reprinted in 28 I.L.M. 1066, 1091-1092 (1989): "In interpreting the Convention regard must be had to its special character as a treaty for the collective enforcement of human rights and fundamental freedoms. Thus, the object and purpose of the Convention as an instrument for the protection of individual human beings require that its provisions be interpreted and applied so as to make its safeguards practical and effective." Id. ¶87. Both these dicta suggest that when a body of law aims at safeguarding human rights, it must be interpreted broadly in behalf of the victims.

Is this approach to treaty interpretation consistent with the Principle of Legality and its corollary, the Principle of Lenity? Recall from Chapter 1 that the Principle of Lenity requires interpreters to construe criminal law strictly in favor of the defendant. Consider the rules laid down by the Vienna Convention on the Law of Treaties (VCLT) and our discussion in Chapter 10 of the approaches that various international and national courts have taken to treaty interpretation. How does the ICTY's approach stack up?

2. When Is Noninternational Violence an "Armed Conflict"?

As we saw earlier, any use of military force by one state against another is an "armed conflict" for purposes of common Article 2, whether or not war is declared or one of the states does not recognize the violence as a war. This is true even if the use of force is a one-shot affair, and no matter how slight the force is.[33]

However, such a definition would be far too broad for violence internal to a single state. An assassination, an attack on police, or a riot does not amount to a civil war (an internal armed conflict). When is an internal or (more generally) noninternational use of force an "armed conflict" for purposes of common Article 3? An early ICTY Appeals Chamber decision in the *Tadić* case addresses this important question.

PROSECUTOR v. TADIĆ

Case No. IT-94-1-I, Decision on the Defence Motion for Interlocutory Appeal on Jurisdiction (Oct. 2, 1995)

A. Preliminary Issue: The Existence of an Armed Conflict

66. Appellant now asserts the new position that there did not exist a legally cognizable armed conflict — either internal or international — at the time and place that the alleged offences were committed. Appellant's argument is based on a concept of armed conflict covering only the precise time and place of actual hostilities. Appellant claims that the conflict in the Prijedor region (where the alleged crimes are said to have taken place) was limited to a political assumption of power by the Bosnian Serbs and did not involve armed combat (though movements of tanks are admitted). This argument presents a preliminary issue to which we turn first.

67. International humanitarian law governs the conduct of both internal and international armed conflicts. Appellant correctly points out that for there to be a violation of this body of law, there must be an armed conflict. The definition of "armed conflict" varies depending on whether the hostilities are international or internal but, contrary to Appellant's contention, the temporal and geographical scope of both internal and international armed conflicts extends beyond the exact time and place of hostilities. With respect to the temporal frame of reference of international armed conflicts, each of the four Geneva Conventions contains language intimating that their application may extend beyond the cessation of fighting. For example, both Conventions I and III apply until protected persons who have fallen into the power of the enemy have been released and repatriated.

---

33. 3 Pictet, supra note 25, at 19.

68. Although the Geneva Conventions are silent as to the geographical scope of international "armed conflicts," the provisions suggest that at least some of the provisions of the Conventions apply to the entire territory of the Parties to the conflict, not just to the vicinity of actual hostilities. Certainly, some of the provisions are clearly bound up with the hostilities and the geographical scope of those provisions should be so limited. Others, particularly those relating to the protection of prisoners of war and civilians, are not so limited. With respect to prisoners of war, the Convention applies to combatants in the power of the enemy; it makes no difference whether they are kept in the vicinity of hostilities. In the same vein, Geneva Convention IV protects civilians anywhere in the territory of the Parties. This construction is implicit in Article 6, paragraph 2, of the Convention, which stipulates that:

> "[i]n the territory of Parties to the conflict, the application of the present Convention shall cease on the general close of military operations."

Article 3(b) of Protocol I to the Geneva Conventions contains similar language. In addition to these textual references, the very nature of the Conventions—particularly Conventions III and IV—dictates their application throughout the territories of the parties to the conflict; any other construction would substantially defeat their purpose.

69. The geographical and temporal frame of reference for internal armed conflicts is similarly broad. This conception is reflected in the fact that beneficiaries of common Article 3 of the Geneva Conventions are those taking no active part (or no longer taking active part) in the hostilities. This indicates that the rules contained in Article 3 also apply outside the narrow geographical context of the actual theatre of combat operations. . . .

70. On the basis of the foregoing, we find that an armed conflict exists whenever there is a resort to armed force between States or protracted armed violence between governmental authorities and organized armed groups or between such groups within a State. International humanitarian law applies from the initiation of such armed conflicts and extends beyond the cessation of hostilities until a general conclusion of peace is reached; or, in the case of internal conflicts, a peaceful settlement is achieved. Until that moment, international humanitarian law continues to apply in the whole territory of the warring States or, in the case of internal conflicts, the whole territory under the control of a party, whether or not actual combat takes place there.

Applying the foregoing concept of armed conflicts to this case, we hold that the alleged crimes were committed in the context of an armed conflict.

NOTES AND QUESTIONS

1. Within treaty law, the distinction between internal armed conflict and other violence internal to a state is given in AP II, art. 1(2): "This Protocol shall not apply to situations of internal disturbances and tensions, such as riots, isolated and sporadic acts of violence and other acts of a similar nature, as not being armed conflicts." The same test, in the same words, appears in the Rome Statute, art. 8(2)(d). Is this test different from that in ¶70 of *Tadić*?

2. Under IHL, is the conflict between the United States and al Qaeda an armed conflict? Does it matter that al Qaeda's attacks against U.S. forces were few and far between until the Iraq insurgency (and perhaps even later, because reportedly the group styling itself "al Qaeda in Mesopotamia" was not actually part of Osama bin

Laden's al Qaeda network)? If the conflict does not qualify as an armed conflict, what legal consequences follow?

3. What Is "Armed Conflict Not of an International Character"?

Common Article 3 applies to "armed conflict not of an international character occurring in the territory of one of the High Contracting Parties." What does this phrase refer to? On one interpretation, it refers only to "internal" armed conflicts, that is, civil wars or insurgencies. On another interpretation, it refers more broadly to any armed conflict that is not between two states.

Within the so-called global war on terrorism — sometimes abbreviated GWOT — this seemingly arcane legal question turns out to carry enormous significance. The U.S. conflict with al Qaeda is not an international armed conflict because al Qaeda is not a state. Thus, the Geneva rules under the common Article 2 regime do not govern the GWOT. But neither is the GWOT an internal armed conflict: It occurs in the territories of multiple countries. If common Article 3 applies only to internal armed conflicts, it would follow that *none* of the protections of the GCs, neither the extensive protections in the Article 2 regime nor the protection of basic human rights in Article 3, apply. That is the conclusion drawn in 2002 by officials of the George W. Bush administration. Their analysis is laid out in the following excerpt. Immediately following that analysis is the treatment of the issue by the U.S. Supreme Court.

APPLICATION OF TREATIES AND LAWS TO TALIBAN AND AL QAEDA DETAINEES

Memorandum for William J. Haynes II, General Counsel, Dept. of Defense, from John Yoo, Deputy Assistant Attorney General, & Robert J. Delahunty, Special Counsel (Jan. 9, 2002)

You have asked for our Office's views concerning the effect of international treaties and federal laws on the treatment of individuals detained by the U.S. Armed Forces during the conflict in Afghanistan. In particular, you have asked whether the laws of armed conflict apply to the conditions of detention and the procedures for trial of members of al Qaeda and the Taliban militia. We conclude that these treaties do not protect members of the al Qaeda organization, which as a non-State actor cannot be a party to the international agreements governing war. We further conclude that these treaties do not apply to the Taliban militia. This memorandum expresses no view as to whether the President should decide, as a matter of policy, that the U.S. Armed Forces should adhere to the standards of conduct in those treaties with respect to the treatment of prisoners. . . .

To begin with, Article 3's text strongly supports the interpretation that it applies to large-scale conflicts between a State and an insurgent group. First, the language at the end of Article 3 states that "[t]he application of the preceding provisions shall not affect the legal status of the Parties to the conflict." This provision was designed to ensure that a Party that observed Article 3 during a civil war would not be understood to have granted the "recognition of the insurgents as an adverse party." . . . Second, Article 3 is in terms limited to "armed conflict . . . occurring *in the territory of one of the High Contracting Parties*" (emphasis added). This limitation makes perfect sense if the Article applies to civil wars, which are fought primarily or solely within the territory of a single state. The limitation makes little sense, however, as applied to a conflict between a State and a transnational terrorist group, which may operate from different territorial bases, some of which might be located in States that are parties to the Conventions and some of which might not be. In such a case, the Conventions would apply to a single armed conflict in some scenes of action but not in others — which seems inexplicable.

This interpretation is supported by commentators. . . .

Analysis of the background to the adoption of the Geneva Conventions in 1949 confirms our understanding of common Article 3. It appears that the drafters of the Conventions had in mind only the two forms of armed conflict that were regarded as matters of general *international* concern at the time: armed conflict between Nation States (subject to Article 2), and large-scale civil war within a Nation State (subject to Article 3). To understand the context in which the Geneva Conventions were drafted, it will be helpful to identify three distinct phases in the development of the laws of war.

First, the traditional law of war was based on a stark dichotomy between "belligerency" and "insurgency." The category of "belligerency" applied to armed conflicts between sovereign States (unless there was recognition of belligerency in a civil war), while the category of "insurgency" applied to armed violence breaking out within the territory of a sovereign State. Correspondingly, international law treated the two classes of conflict in different ways. Interstate wars were regulated by a body of international legal rules governing both the conduct of hostilities and the protection of noncombatants. By contrast, there were very few international rules governing civil unrest, for States preferred to regard internal strife as rebellion, mutiny and treason coming within the purview of national criminal law, which precluded any possible intrusion by other States. This was a "clearly sovereignty-oriented" phase of international law.

The second phase began as early as the Spanish Civil War (1936-39) and extended through the time of the drafting of the Geneva Conventions until relatively recently. During this period, State practice began to apply certain general principles of humanitarian law beyond the traditional field of State-to-State conflict to "those internal conflicts that constituted large-scale civil wars." In addition to the Spanish Civil War, events in 1947 during the Civil War between the Communists and the Nationalist regime in China illustrated this new tendency. Common Article 3, which was prepared during this second phase, was apparently addressed to armed conflicts akin to the Chinese and Spanish civil wars. As one commentator has described it, Article 3 was designed to restrain governments "in the handling of armed violence directed against them for the express purpose of secession or at securing a change in the government of a State," but even after the adoption of the Conventions it remained "uncertain whether [Article 3] applied to full-scale civil war."

The third phase represents a more complete break than the second with the traditional "State-sovereignty-oriented approach" of international law. This approach gives central place to individual human rights. As a consequence, it blurs the distinction between international and internal armed conflicts, and even between civil wars and other forms of internal armed conflict. This approach was well illustrated by the ICTY's decision in *Tadić,* which appears to take the view that common Article 3 applies to non-international armed conflicts of *any* description, and is not limited to civil wars between a State and an insurgent group. In this conception, common Article 3 is not just a complement to common Article 2; rather, it is a catch-all that establishes standards for any and all armed conflicts not included in common Article 2.

Nonetheless, despite this recent trend, we think that such an interpretation of common Article 3 fails to take into account, not only the language of the provision, but also its historic context. First, as we have described above, such a reading is inconsistent with the text of Article 3 itself, which applies only to "armed conflict not of an international character occurring in the territory of one of the High Contracting Parties." In conjunction with common Article 2, the text of Article 3 simply does not reach international conflicts where one of the parties is not a Nation State. If we were to read the Geneva Conventions as applying to all forms of armed conflict, we would expect the High Contracting Parties to have used broader language, which they easily could have done. To interpret common Article 3 by expanding its scope well beyond the meaning borne by the text is effectively to amend the Geneva Conventions without the approval of the State Parties to the agreements.

Second, as we have discussed, Article 3 was prepared during a period in which the traditional, State-centered view of international law was still dominant and was only just beginning to give way to a human-rights-based approach. Giving due weight to the State practice and doctrinal understanding of the time, it seems to us overwhelmingly likely that an armed conflict between a Nation State and a transnational terrorist organization, or between a Nation State and a failed State harboring or supporting a transnational terrorist organization, could not have been within the contemplation of the drafters of common Article 3. These would have been simply unforeseen and, therefore, not provided for. . . .

HAMDAN v. RUMSFELD
548 U.S. 567, 630-631 (2006)

The Court of Appeals thought, and the Government asserts, that Common Article 3 does not apply to Hamdan because the conflict with al Qaeda, being " 'international in scope,' " does not qualify as a " 'conflict not of an international character.' " That reasoning is erroneous. The term "conflict not of an international character" is used here in contradistinction to a conflict between nations. So much is demonstrated by the "fundamental logic [of] the Convention's provisions on its application." Common Article 2 provides that "the present Convention shall apply to all cases of declared war or of any other armed conflict which may arise between two or more of the High Contracting Parties." High Contracting Parties (signatories) also must abide by all terms of the Conventions vis-a-vis one another even if one party to the conflict is a nonsignatory "Power," and must so abide vis-a-vis the nonsignatory if "the latter accepts and applies" those terms. Common Article 3, by contrast, affords some minimal protection, falling short of full protection under the Conventions, to individuals associated with neither a signatory nor even a nonsignatory "Power" who are involved in a conflict "in the territory of" a signatory. The latter kind of conflict is distinguishable from the conflict described in Common Article 2 chiefly because it does not involve a clash between nations (whether signatories or not). In context, then, the phrase "not of an international character" bears its literal meaning. See, e.g., J. Bentham, Introduction to the Principles of Morals and Legislation 6, 296 (J. Burns & H. Hart eds. 1970) (using the term "international law" as a "new though not inexpressive appellation" meaning "betwixt nation and nation"; defining "international" to include "mutual transactions between sovereigns as such"); Int'l Comm. of Red Cross Commentary on the Additional Protocols to the Geneva Conventions of 12 August 1949, p. 1351 (1987) ("[A] non-international armed conflict is distinct from an international armed conflict because of the legal status of the entities opposing each other").

Although the official commentaries accompanying Common Article 3 indicate that an important purpose of the provision was to furnish minimal protection to rebels involved in one kind of "conflict not of an international character," i.e., a civil war, see GC III Commentary 36-37, the commentaries also make clear "that the scope of application of the Article must be as wide as possible," id., at 36. In fact, limiting language that would have rendered Common Article 3 applicable "especially [to] cases of civil war, colonial conflicts, or wars of religion" was omitted from the final version of the Article, which coupled broader scope of application with a narrower range of rights than did earlier proposed iterations. See id. at 42-43.

NOTES AND QUESTIONS

1. The issue in the *Hamdan* case was whether Salim Hamdan, Osama bin Laden's driver, could be tried before a military commission in Guantánamo. Hamdan asserted that such a trial would violate his rights under common Article 3, and the Supreme Court ultimately agreed. First, however, he had to show that common Article 3 applied to the GWOT, in the face of government assertions that it does not. Hamdan prevailed on this issue in the district court. He lost in the D.C. Court of Appeals and ultimately prevailed, once again, in the Supreme Court. In the wake of the *Hamdan* decision, Congress amended the military commission rules in response to the Supreme Court's holding that as constituted the commissions violated CA 3. Hamdan was eventually convicted by a military commission, but given a far shorter sentence than the prosecution had requested — time served plus a few months. Hamdan was returned to Yemen to serve out the few remaining months of his sentence. He had been imprisoned at Guantánamo for six years.

2. The Supreme Court sides with Hamdan in determining that an "armed conflict not of an international character" is simply any armed conflict that is not between states, whether or not it is internal. The Supreme Court follows the usage of Jeremy Bentham, the British jurist and philosopher who coined the expression *international law* and used *international* as a synonym for *among nations*, that is, *states*. How does the Supreme Court handle the other half of CA 3's condition: "armed conflict not of an international character *occurring in the territory of one of the High Contracting Parties*" (emphasis added)? The court of appeals had reasoned that this clause restricts CA 3 to armed conflicts within a single country. That would exclude the GWOT, which involves conflicts in multiple countries.

One possible interpretation of "occurring in the territory of one of the High Contracting Parties" is that the drafters included this clause for jurisdictional reasons. Treaties cannot bind nonparties, and the phrase indicates that the GCs do not purport to do so. On this interpretation, the phrase means "occurring in the territory of *at least* one of the High Contracting Parties," which the court of appeals had read to mean ". . . *exactly* one. . . ." In your view, which interpretation makes better sense of the language of CA 3?

3. During the negotiations over the Geneva Conventions, Australia proposed an amendment (submitted to the Special Committee on what would eventually become CA 3) to replace the "not of an international character" formulation with "civil wars." Special Committee, Seventh Report, vol. II B, at 121. The amendment was rejected. Does this show that the "framers' intent" of CA 3 was that it should apply more broadly than merely to civil wars? Is "intent" relevant to treaty interpretation, at least under the VCLT? See, e.g., Chapter 10.

Professor Derek Jinks has pointed out one reason to suppose that Geneva's drafters did intend CA 3 to apply more broadly than in civil wars. International rules on how a state should deal with internal violence (such as a civil war or revolution) represent a maximum invasion of traditional state sovereignty. It seems unlikely that CA 3 imposed this maximum invasion — by requiring states to honor certain human rights even in a purely internal matter — but did not intend the same human rights guarantees to apply in transterritorial conflicts with non-state actors. Private communication with Derek Jinks, Mar. 25, 2006; see Jinks, The Rules of War: The Geneva Conventions in the Age of Terror (forthcoming 2009).

The Yoo/Delahunty memorandum objects that applying CA 3 in conflicts other than civil wars would amount, in effect, to amending the GCs without going through the received procedure of consulting the states parties to Geneva. In effect, Yoo and Delahunty treat the Convention as akin to a contract, the terms of which cannot be modified without the consent of the parties. Compare this way of reading the Conventions with the ICTY's method as explained in ¶96 of the *Tadić* decision (July 15, 1999), excerpted above. "This body of law is not grounded on formalistic postulates. . . . Rather, it is a realistic body of law, grounded on the notion of effectiveness and inspired by the aim of deterring deviation from its standards to the maximum extent possible." As noted above, this dictum implies reading IHL provisions in a gap-filling way, so that even in novel forms of armed conflict qualifying persons retain Geneva protections. Which method of treaty interpretation makes the most sense to you? Which method best conforms to the rule of treaty interpretation set out in VCLT art. 31(1): "A treaty shall be interpreted in good faith in accordance with the ordinary meaning to be given to the terms of the treaty in their context and in the light of its object and purpose"?

C. SPECIFIC WAR CRIMES

The array of war crimes is large, and this chapter does not survey them all. Instead, we focus on two significant examples that have made headlines in recent years — in part because not everyone agrees that they are war crimes. First, we examine targeted killings of terrorists, and second, we examine humiliating treatment of captives.

1. Targeted Killings

One of the most controversial tactics in governments' efforts to defeat terrorist groups is the "targeted killing" of militants and terrorist leaders in their hiding places, often by missiles or aerial attack. Arguably, at least from one point of view, the targets are civilians; arguably, then, by definition, the attacks are war crimes. Yet many reject that conclusion. It is hard to believe, after all, that Osama bin Laden is not a legitimate target of the U.S. military — and bin Laden's own tactics are themselves war crimes or crimes against humanity.

Further complicating the issue is the fact that targeted killings sometimes miss their targets and kill innocent civilians. For that matter, even successful targeted killings kill bystanders as well; militants often hide in heavily populated areas, essentially using civilians as a shield against detection and attack. To take an example, a U.S. missile strike in Pakistan against Ayman al Zawahiri, the number two commander of al Qaeda, missed Zawahiri, but "reportedly killed as many as 18 civilians, many of them women and children, and triggered protests in Pakistan."[34] According to the same article, "Several U.S. officials confirmed at least 19 occasions since Sept. 11 on which Predators successfully fired Hellfire missiles on terrorist suspects overseas, including 10 in Iraq in one month last year [2005]. The Predator strikes have killed at least four senior Al Qaeda leaders, but also many civilians."[35] As the reading that follows indicates, the Israeli targeted killing campaign against Palestinian militants has also caused substantial deaths of innocent civilians. See infra, ¶¶2 and 8 of *Public Committee Against Torture in Israel v. Israel.*

These, then, are the questions: Are targeted killings lawful under IHL? If so, under what conditions?

When targeted killings occur in peacetime, they are usually labeled assassinations (or murder). Although the term *assassination* has no fixed, agreed-on legal meaning, it generally refers to "an intentional killing of a targeted individual committed for political purposes."[36] The term also suggests a covert or "surprise" operation.[37]

Peacetime assassinations violate the domestic law against murder in the states in which they occur (even if the state has secretly cooperated with the assassination, as is sometimes alleged). Peacetime assassinations by a state, either in its own territory or abroad, also violate international human rights norms against extrajudicial killings, although to date no tribunal has ever prosecuted an assassination for violating international human rights law.

What if the targeted killing occurs during an armed conflict? Commentators in the early centuries of international law frowned on assassinating enemy leaders, even during a war. Their skepticism "generally involved perceptions of what constituted honorable warfare, together with a desire to protect kings and generals . . . from unpredictable assaults against which they would find it difficult to defend themselves. Implicit in the latter was the premise that making war was a proper activity of sovereigns for which they ought not be required to sacrifice their personal safety."[38]

Under the UN Charter, war is no longer "a proper activity of sovereigns" except in self-defense; but intentionally targeting the leaders of enemy states may still be a war crime, provided the leader is a civilian not directly involved in military decision making. That is because intentionally targeting *any* civilian during an international armed conflict is a war crime. On the other hand, nothing in contemporary IHL prohibits intentionally targeting enemy military leaders. The hard cases are those in between, where the civilian leader plays a military role. Some civilian leaders hold a position in the military chain of command; the president of the United States, for example, is the commander in chief of the military. Other civilian leaders may be de facto military decision makers. The implications are unclear. GC IV (civilians) draws no distinction between a civilian involved in hostilities against a state and any other civilian; however, AP I art. 51(3) makes a civilian who takes part in hostilities a legitimate target.[39]

---

34. Josh Meyer, CIA Expands Use of Drones in Terror War, L.A. Times, Jan. 29, 2006, at A1.

35. Id.

36. Elizabeth B. Bazan, Assassination Ban and E.O. 12333: A Brief Summary, Congressional Research Service RS21037 (Jan. 2002), at 2.

37. W. Hays Parks, Memorandum of Law: Executive Order 12333 and Assassination, DAJA-IA (27-1a), The Army Lawyer 4 (Dec. 1989).

38. Lt. Com. Patricia Zengel, Assassination and the Law of Armed Conflict, 134 Military L. Rev. 123, 130 (1991).

39. The United Kingdom's law of war manual suggests in a footnote that a civilian head of state who serves as commander in chief may be treated as a POW if captured, but would be a legitimate target only if "actively serving in the armed forces." UK Ministry of Defence, The Manual of the Law of Armed Conflict 148 n.52, §8.15 (2004).

Matters are murkier still in a noninternational armed conflict against a terrorist organization. The following decision by the Israeli Supreme Court examines this issue.

HCJ 769/02 PUBLIC COMMITTEE AGAINST TORTURE IN ISRAEL v. ISRAEL

46 I.L.M. 375 (Isr. 2007)[40]

JUDGMENT

President (Emeritus) A. Barak:

The Government of Israel employs a policy of preventative strikes which cause the death of terrorists in Judea, Samaria, or the Gaza Strip.[41] It fatally strikes these terrorists, who plan, launch, or commit terrorist attacks in Israel and in the area of Judea, Samaria, and the Gaza Strip, against both civilians and soldiers. These strikes at times also harm innocent civilians. Does the State thus act illegally? That is the question posed before us.

1. FACTUAL BACKGROUND

In February 2000, the second *intifada* began. A massive assault of terrorism was directed against the State of Israel, and against Israelis, merely because they are Israelis. This assault of terrorism differentiates neither between combatants and civilians, nor between women, men, and children. The terrorist attacks take place both in the territory of Judea, Samaria, and the Gaza Strip, and within the borders of the State of Israel. They are directed against civilian centers, shopping centers and markets, coffee houses and restaurants. Over the last five years, thousands of acts of terrorism have been committed against Israel. In the attacks, more than one thousand Israeli citizens have been killed. Thousands of Israeli citizens have been wounded. Thousands of Palestinians have been killed and wounded during this period as well.

2. In its war against terrorism, the State of Israel employs various means. As part of the security activity intended to confront the terrorist attacks, the State employs what it calls "the policy of targeted frustration" of terrorism. Under this policy, the security forces act in order to kill members of terrorist organizations involved in the planning, launching, or execution of terrorist attacks against Israel. During the second *intifada*, such preventative strikes have been performed across Judea, Samaria, and the Gaza Strip. According to the data relayed by petitioners, since the commencement of these acts, and up until the end of 2005, close to three hundred members of terrorist organizations have been killed by them. More than thirty targeted killing attempts have failed. Approximately one hundred and fifty civilians who were proximate to the location of the targeted persons have been killed during those acts. Hundreds of others have been wounded. The policy of targeted killings is the focus of this petition.

2. THE PETITIONERS' ARGUMENTS

3. Petitioners' position is that the targeted killings policy is totally illegal, and contradictory to international law, Israeli law, and basic principles of human morality. It violates the human rights recognized in Israeli and international law, both the

---

40. Full text is available in English on the Israel Supreme Court's Web site, http://elyon1.court.gov.il/files_eng/02/690/007/A34/02007690.a34.pdf (last visited July 16, 2009).

41. Judea and Samaria are the biblical names used by the Israeli government to designate the West Bank — territories captured by Israel in the 1967 Six Days' War, inhabited primarily by Palestinians, as well as (today) Jewish settlers. — EDS.

rights of those targeted, and the rights of innocent passersby caught in the targeted killing zone.

4. Petitioners' position is that the legal system applicable to the armed conflict between Israel and the terrorist organizations is not the laws of war, rather the legal system dealing with law enforcement in occupied territory. . . .

5. Alternatively, petitioners claim that the targeted killings policy violates the rules of international law even if the laws applicable to the armed conflict between Israel and the Palestinians are the laws of war. These laws recognize only two statuses of people: combatants and civilians. . . . There is no intermediate status, and there is no third category of "unlawful combatants." . . . Petitioners note that the State itself refuses to grant those members [of terrorist organizations] the rights and protections granted in international law to combatants, such as the right to the status as prisoners of war. The result is that the State wishes to treat them according to the worst of the two worlds: as combatants, regarding the justification for killing them, and as civilians, regarding the need to arrest them and try them. That result is unacceptable. . . .

8. Petitioners' stance is that the targeted killings policy, as employed in practice, violates the proportionality requirements which are part of Israeli law and customary international law. . . . Thus, for example, on July 22, 2002 a 1000 kg bomb was dropped on the house of wanted terrorist Salah Shehade, in a densely populated civilian neighborhood in the city of Gaza. The bomb and its shock waves caused the death of the wanted terrorist, his wife, his family, and the deaths of twelve neighbors. Scores were wounded. . . .

3. THE RESPONDENTS' RESPONSE

10. On the merits, respondents point out the security background which led to the targeted killings policy. Since late September 2000, acts of combat and terrorism are being committed against Israel. As a result of those acts, more than one thousand Israeli citizens have been killed during the period from 2000-2005. Thousands more have been wounded. . . . Respondents' stance is that the argument that Israel is permitted to defend herself against terrorism only via means of law enforcement is to be rejected. . . .

11. . . . These laws [of war] allow striking at persons who are party to the armed conflict and take an active part in it, whether it is an international or non-international armed conflict. . . . Respondents' position is that the members of terrorist organizations are party to the armed conflict between Israel and the terrorist organizations, and they take an active part in the fighting. Thus, they are legal targets for attack for as long as the armed conflict continues. . . . However, they are not entitled to all the rights granted to legal combatants, as they themselves do not fulfill the requirements of the laws of war. . . .

12. Alternatively, respondents' position is that the targeted killings policy is legal even if the Court should reject the argument that terrorist organization members are combatants and party to the armed conflict, and even if they are to be seen as having the status of civilians. That is because the laws of armed conflict allow harming civilians taking a direct part in hostilities. . . . Respondents' stance is that the simultaneity requirement determined in article 51(3) of The First Protocol,[42] pursuant to which a civilian who takes a direct part in hostilities can be harmed only during such time that he is taking that direct part, does not obligate Israel, as it does not reflect a rule of customary international law. On this point respondents note that Israel, like

---

42. "The First Protocol" refers to AP I to the Geneva Conventions. — EDS.

other states, has not joined The First Protocol. Thus, harming civilians who take a direct part in hostilities is permitted even when they are not participating in the hostilities. There is no prohibition on striking at the terrorist at any time and place, as long as he has not laid down his arms and exited the circle of violence. . . .

5. THE GENERAL NORMATIVE FRAMEWORK

A. *International Armed Conflict*

16. The general, principled starting point is that between Israel and the various terrorist organizations active in Judea, Samaria, and the Gaza Strip (hereinafter "the area") a continuous situation of armed conflict has existed since the first *intifada*. . . .

18. The normative system which applies to the armed conflict between Israel and the terrorist organizations in the area is complex. In its center stands the international law regarding international armed conflict. . . . This law includes the laws of belligerent occupation. However, it is not restricted only to them. This law applies in any case of an armed conflict of international character — in other words, one that crosses the borders of the state — whether or not the place in which the armed conflict occurs is subject to belligerent occupation. This law constitutes a part of *jus in bello*. From the humanitarian perspective, it is part of international humanitarian law. That humanitarian law is the *lex specialis* which applies in the case of an armed conflict. When there is a gap (*lacuna*) in that law, it can be supplemented by human rights law. . . . Alongside the international law dealing with armed conflicts, fundamental principles of Israeli public law, which every Israeli soldier "carries in his pack" and which go along with him wherever he may turn, may apply.

19. Substantial parts of international law dealing with armed conflicts are of customary character. That customary law is part of Israeli law, "by force of the State of Israel's existence as a sovereign and independent state." . . . The international law entrenched in international conventions which is not part of customary international law (whether Israel is party to them or not), is not enacted in domestic law of the State of Israel.

20. . . . [Although Israel is not a party to AP I,] the customary provisions of The First Protocol are part of Israeli law.

21. Our starting point is that the law that applies to the armed conflict between Israel and the terrorist organizations in the area is the international law dealing with armed conflicts. . . . [T]hat armed conflict should be categorized as a conflict which is not of purely internal national character, but also not of international character, rather is of a mixed character, to which both international human rights law and international humanitarian law apply. . . .

22. The international law dealing with armed conflicts is based upon a delicate balance between two contradictory considerations. One consists of the humanitarian considerations regarding those harmed as a result of an armed conflict. These considerations are based upon the rights of the individual, and his dignity. The other consists of military need and success. . . . The result of that balancing is that human rights are protected by the law of armed conflict, but not to their full scope. The same is so regarding the military needs. They are given an opportunity to be fulfilled, but not to their full scope. . . .

23. A central consideration affecting the balancing point is the identity of the person harmed, or the objective compromised in armed conflict. That is the central principle of the distinction. . . . According to the basic principle of the distinction, the balancing point between the State's military need and the other side's combatants and military objectives is not the same as the balancing point between the state's military need and the other side's civilians and civilian objectives. . . . Are terrorist

organizations and their members combatants, in regards to their rights in the armed conflict? Are they civilians taking an active part in the armed conflict? Are they possibly neither combatants nor civilians? What, then, is the status of those terrorists?

B. Combatants

24. . . . [T]he terrorist organizations from the area, and their members, do not fulfill the conditions for combatants. It will suffice to say that they have no fixed emblem recognizable at a distance, and they do not conduct their operations in accordance with the laws and customs of war. . . .

25. . . . Needless to say, unlawful combatants are not beyond the law. They are not "outlaws." God created them as well in his image; their human dignity as well is to be honored; they as well enjoy and are entitled to protection, even if most minimal, by customary international law. . . .

C. Civilians

26. . . . The approach of customary international law is that "civilians" are those who are not "combatants" (see §50(1) of The First Protocol . . .) . . . . That definition is "negative" in nature. It defines the concept of "civilian" as the opposite of "combatant." It thus views unlawful combatants—who, as we have seen, are not "combatants"—as civilians. Does that mean that the unlawful combatants are entitled to the same protection to which civilians who are not unlawful combatants are entitled? The answer is, no. Customary international law regarding armed conflicts determines that a civilian taking a direct part in the hostilities does not, at such time, enjoy the protection granted to a civilian who is not taking a direct part in the hostilities (see §51(3) of The First Protocol). The result is that an unlawful combatant is not a combatant, rather a "civilian." However, he is a civilian who is not protected from attack as long as he is taking a direct part in the hostilities. . . .

D. A Third Category: Unlawful Combatants?

27. In the oral and written arguments before us, the State asked us to recognize a third category of persons, that of unlawful combatants. These are people who take active and continuous part in an armed conflict, and therefore should be treated as combatants, in the sense that they are legitimate targets of attack, and they do not enjoy the protections granted to civilians. However, they are not entitled to the rights and privileges of combatants, since they do not differentiate themselves from the civilian population, and since they do not obey the laws of war. . . .

28. The literature on this subject is comprehensive. . . . In our opinion, as far as existing law goes, the data before us are not sufficient to recognize this third category. . . . However, new reality at times requires new interpretation. Rules developed against the background of a reality which has changed must take on a dynamic interpretation which adapts them, in the framework of accepted interpretational rules, to the new reality. . . . In the spirit of such interpretation, we shall now proceed to the customary international law dealing with the status of civilians who constitute unlawful combatants.

6. CIVILIANS WHO ARE UNLAWFUL COMBATANTS . . .

B. The Source of the Basic Principle and Its Customary Character

30. The basic principle is that the civilians taking a direct part in hostilities are not protected from attack upon them at such time as they are doing so. . . . Does the basic principle express customary international law? The position of The Red Cross is that it is a principle of customary international law. That position is acceptable to us. . . .

C. The Essence of the Basic Principle . . .

32. We have seen that the basic principle is that the civilian population, and single civilians, are protected from the dangers of military activity and are not targets for attack. That protection is granted to civilians "unless and for such time as they take a direct part in hostilities" (§51(3) of The First Protocol). That provision is composed of three main parts. The first part is the requirement that civilians take part in "hostilities"; the second part is the requirement that civilians take a "direct" part in hostilities; the third part is the provision by which civilians are not protected from attack "for such time" as they take a direct part in hostilities. We shall discuss each of those parts separately.

D. The First Part: "Taking . . . Part in Hostilities"

33. Civilians lose the protection of customary international law dealing with hostilities of international character if they "take . . . part in hostilities." What is the meaning of that provision? The accepted view is that "hostilities" are acts which by nature and objective are intended to cause damage to the army. . . . It seems that acts which by nature and objective are intended to cause damage to civilians should be added to that definition. According to the accepted definition, a civilian is taking part in hostilities when using weapons in an armed conflict, while gathering intelligence, or while preparing himself for the hostilities. Regarding taking part in hostilities, there is no condition that the civilian use his weapon, nor is there a condition that he bear arms (openly or concealed). It is possible to take part in hostilities without using weapons at all. . . .

E. Second Part: "Takes a Direct Part"

34. Civilians lose the protection against military attack, granted to them by customary international law dealing with international armed conflict (as adopted in The First Protocol, §51(3)), if "they take a direct part in hostilities." That provision differentiates between civilians taking a direct part in hostilities (from whom the protection from attack is removed) and civilians taking an indirect part in hostilities (who continue to enjoy protection from attack). What is that differentiation? . . . It seems accepted in the international literature that an agreed upon definition of the term "direct" in the context under discussion does not exist. In that state of affairs, and without a comprehensive and agreed upon customary standard, there is no escaping going case by case, while narrowing the area of disagreement. . . . Indeed, a civilian bearing arms (openly or concealed) who is on his way to the place where he will use them against the army, at such place, or on his way back from it, is a civilian taking "an active part" in the hostilities. However, a civilian who generally supports the hostilities against the army is not taking a direct part in the hostilities. Similarly, a civilian who sells food or medicine to unlawful combatants is also taking an indirect part in the hostilities. . . . And what is the law in the space between these two extremes? On the one hand, the desire to protect innocent civilians leads, in the hard cases, to a narrow interpretation of the term "direct" part in hostilities. . . . On the other hand, it can be said that the desire to protect combatants and the desire to protect innocent civilians leads, in the hard cases, to a wide interpretation of the "direct" character of the hostilities, as thus civilians are encouraged to stay away from the hostilities to the extent possible. . . .

35. Against the background of these considerations, the following cases should also be included in the definition of taking a "direct part" in hostilities: a person who collects intelligence on the army, whether on issues regarding the hostilities, or beyond those issues; a person who transports unlawful combatants to or from the

place where the hostilities are taking place; a person who operates weapons which unlawful combatants use, or supervises their operation, or provides service to them, be the distance from the battlefield as it may. All those persons are performing the function of combatants. The function determines the directness of the part taken in the hostilities. However, a person who sells food or medicine to an unlawful combatant is not taking a direct part, rather an indirect part in the hostilities. The same is the case regarding a person who aids the unlawful combatants by general strategic analysis, and grants them logistical, general support, including monetary aid. . . . In the international literature there is a debate surrounding the following case: a person driving a truck carrying ammunition. Some are of the opinion that such a person is taking a direct part in the hostilities (and thus he can be attacked), and some are of the opinion that he is not taking a direct part (and thus he cannot be attacked). Both opinions are in agreement that the ammunition in the truck can be attacked. The disagreement regards the attack upon the civilian driver. . . . In our opinion, if the civilian is driving the ammunition to the place from which it will be used for the purposes of hostilities, he should be seen as taking a direct part in the hostilities.

36. What is the law regarding civilians serving as a "human shield" for terrorists taking a direct part in the hostilities? Certainly, if they are doing so because they were forced to do so by terrorists, those innocent civilians are not to be seen as taking a direct part in the hostilities. They themselves are victims of terrorism. However, if they do so of their own free will, out of support for the terrorist organization, they should be seen as persons taking a direct part in the hostilities.

37. . . . In our opinion, the "direct" character of the part taken should not be narrowed merely to the person committing the physical act of attack. Those who have sent him, as well, take "a direct part." The same goes for the person who decided upon the act, and the person who planned it. It is not to be said about them that they are taking an indirect part in the hostilities. Their contribution is direct (and active).

F. The Third Part: "For Such Time"

38. Article 51(3) of The First Protocol states that civilians enjoy protection from the dangers stemming from military acts, and that they are not targets for attack, unless "and for such time" as they are taking a direct part in hostilities. The provisions of article 51(3) of The First Protocol present a time requirement. . . . The key question is: how is that provision to be interpreted, and what is its scope?

39. As regarding the scope of the wording "takes a direct part" in hostilities, so too regarding the scope of the wording "and for such time" there is no consensus in the international literature. . . . With no consensus regarding the interpretation of the wording "for such time," there is no choice but to proceed from case to case. Again, it is helpful to examine the extreme cases. On the one hand, a civilian taking a direct part in hostilities one single time, or sporadically, who later detaches himself from that activity, is a civilian who, starting from the time he detached himself from that activity, is entitled to protection from attack. He is not to be attacked for the hostilities which he committed in the past. On the other hand, a civilian who has joined a terrorist organization which has become his "home," and in the framework of his role in that organization he commits a chain of hostilities, with short periods of rest between them, loses his immunity from attack "for such time" as he is committing the chain of acts. Indeed, regarding such a civilian, the rest between hostilities is nothing other than preparation for the next hostility.

40. . . . In the wide area between those two possibilities, one finds the "gray" cases, about which customary international law has not yet crystallized. There is thus no

escaping examination of each and every case. In that context, the following four things should be said: first, well based information is needed before categorizing a civilian as falling into one of the discussed categories. . . . The burden of proof on the attacking army is heavy. . . . Second, a civilian taking a direct part in hostilities cannot be attacked at such time as he is doing so, if a less harmful means can be employed. . . . Thus, if a terrorist taking a direct part in hostilities can be arrested, interrogated, and tried, those are the means which should be employed. . . . Arrest, investigation, and trial are not means which can always be used. At times the possibility does not exist whatsoever; at times it involves a risk so great to the lives of the soldiers, that it is not required. However, it is a possibility which should always be considered. It might actually be particularly practical under the conditions of belligerent occupation, in which the army controls the area in which the operation takes place, and in which arrest, investigation, and trial are at times realizable possibilities. . . . Third, after an attack on a civilian suspected of taking an active part, at such time, in hostilities, a thorough investigation regarding the precision of the identification of the target and the circumstances of the attack upon him is to be performed (retroactively). That investigation must be independent. In appropriate cases it is appropriate to pay compensation as a result of harm caused to an innocent civilian. Last, if the harm is not only to a civilian directly participating in the hostilities, rather also to innocent civilians nearby, the harm to them is collateral damage. That damage must withstand the proportionality test. We shall now proceed to the examination of that question.

7. PROPORTIONALITY . . .

Proper Proportion Between Benefit and Damage

45. The proportionality test determines that attack upon innocent civilians is not permitted if the collateral damage caused to them is not proportionate to the military advantage (in protecting combatants and civilians). In other words, attack is proportionate if the benefit stemming from the attainment of the proper military objective is proportionate to the damage caused to innocent civilians harmed by it. That is a values based test. . . .

46. . . . Performing that balance is difficult. Here as well, one must proceed case by case, while narrowing the area of disagreement. Take the usual case of a combatant, or of a terrorist sniper shooting at soldiers or civilians from his porch. Shooting at him is proportionate even if as a result, an innocent civilian neighbor or passerby is harmed. That is not the case if the building is bombed from the air and scores of its residents and passersby are harmed. The hard cases are those which are in the space between the extreme examples. There, a meticulous examination of every case is required. . . . That balancing is difficult when it regards human life. It raises moral and ethical problems. Despite the difficulty of that balancing, there's no choice but to perform it. . . .

CONCLUSION

61. . . . Every struggle of the state — against terrorism or any other enemy — is conducted according to rules and law. There is always law which the state must comply with. There are no "black holes." In this case, the law was determined by customary international law regarding conflicts of an international character. Indeed, the State's struggle against terrorism is not conducted "outside" of the law. It is conducted "inside" the law, with tools that the law places at the disposal of democratic states. . . .

64. In one case we decided the question whether the State is permitted to order its interrogators to employ special methods of interrogation which involve the use of

force against terrorists, in a "ticking bomb" situation. We answered that question in the negative. In my judgment, I described the difficult security situation in which Israel finds itself, and added:

> We are aware that this judgment of ours does not make confronting that reality any easier. That is the fate of democracy, in whose eyes not all means are permitted, and to whom not all the methods used by her enemies are open. At times democracy fights with one hand tied behind her back. Despite that, democracy has the upper hand, since preserving the rule of law and recognition of individual liberties constitute an important component of her security stance. At the end of the day, they strengthen her and her spirit, and allow her to overcome her difficulties (HCJ 5100/94 The Public Committee Against Torture in Israel v. The State of Israel, 53(4) PD 817, 845).

Let it be so.

NOTES AND QUESTIONS

1. Justice Barak's opinion nominally leaves open the question whether terrorists constitute a category of "unlawful enemy combatants" who are neither lawful combatants nor civilians. See ¶18. Has he in fact rejected this category? Two commentators write that "the judgment, while denying that there is a third status of 'unlawful combatants,' nevertheless de facto recognizes such status, equating it with civilians who take a direct part in the hostilities. Such 'civilians/unlawful combatants' are bereft of either immunity (of civilians) or privileges (of combatants)." Orna Ben-Naftali & Keren Michaeli, International Decisions: *Public Committee Against Torture in Israel v. Government of Israel*, 101 Am. J. Intl. L. 459, 462 (2007). Is this correct?

2. During the 1972 Munich Olympics, Palestinian terrorists from the Black September group attacked the Israeli wrestling team, killing 11 Israeli athletes and coaches and a German policeman. In response, Israel launched a "battle of Europe"—a covert killing campaign against Palestinian militants in Europe (depicted in Steven Spielberg's 2005 film *Munich*). The campaign included one botched operation that killed an Algerian waiter in Norway, in a case of mistaken identity. Norwegian authorities captured the Israeli agents and convicted them of murder; Israel did not protest. Was the "battle of Europe" an armed conflict under IHL? Israel did not claim at the time that it was engaged in an "armed conflict" with Black September in the legal sense pertinent to IHL. Would it have been legitimate to do so?

3. Compare this with the well-publicized (but not officially acknowledged) campaign by the United States to kill al Qaeda leaders through the use of unmanned, remote-controlled Predator drones that launch Hellfire missiles. Josh Meyer, supra note 34. One such launch killed an al Qaeda planner while he was driving in Yemen; it also killed five passengers. Amnesty International "stated that if the attack was a deliberate killing, in lieu of arrest, in circumstances in which the men did not pose an immediate threat, the killings would amount to extrajudicial executions in violation of international human rights law." Yemen: The Rule of Law Sidelined in the Name of Security 21 (2003), available at http://www.amnesty.org/en/library/asset/ MDE31/006/2003/en/dom-MDE310062003en.pdf. A UN report likewise described the strike as "a clear case of extrajudicial killing," and called it "an alarming precedent." Report of the Special Rapporteur, Asma Jahangir, §39, U.N. Doc. E/CN.4/

2003/3 (Jan. 13, 2003). Both Amnesty and the Special Rapporteur viewed the killings through the lens of international human rights law rather than IHL.

Shortly after 9/11, the U.S. Congress authorized the president "to use all necessary and appropriate force against those nations, organizations, or persons he determines planned, authorized, committed, or aided the terrorist attacks that occurred on September 11, 2001, or harbored such organizations or persons, in order to prevent any future acts of international terrorism against the United States by such nations, organizations or persons." Authorization for the Use of Military Force (AUMF), S.J. Res. 23, 107th Cong. (2001). Under U.S. domestic law, the Predator strikes were arguably acts of war, not simply assassinations carried out in another state's sovereign territory.

The United States government's use of Predator drones to conduct targeted killings represents a change in official policy. In July 2001, Martin Indyk, the U.S. ambassador to Israel, stated that "[t]he United States government is very clearly on record as against targeted assassinations. . . . They are extrajudicial killings, and we do not support that." Quoted in Jane Mayer, The Predator War, The New Yorker, Oct. 26, 2009, at 40.

Which viewpoint — that of IHL or that of international human rights law — is appropriate? Notice that in ¶18, the Israeli court describes IHL as the *lex specialis* for armed conflicts, while human rights law can only "supplement" it.

4. The Predator drones are remotely controlled from the United States. Reportedly, their "pilots" are not uniformed military personnel but CIA agents, who are civilians. Does their civilian status make them unlawful combatants under IHL?

5. In 1981, President Reagan issued Executive Order 12,333, 46 Fed. Reg. 59,941 (Dec. 4, 1981), on intelligence activities. Section 2.11 states, "No person employed by or acting on behalf of the United States Government shall engage in, or conspire to engage in, assassination." Id. Unless a subsequent president has revoked this order with a secret executive order, the assassination ban (which followed similar bans by Presidents Carter and Ford) remains on the books. For discussion of the assassination ban, including the question of whether the AUMF supersedes it, see Bazan, supra note 36.

The Israeli court's opinion cites extensively to a large scholarly literature on targeted killings and the laws of war; we have omitted these citations for reasons of space. For additional reading on targeted killings and the Israeli decision, consult the works cited in the full text of the judgment. For useful analysis, see Orna Ben-Naftali & Keren R. Michaeli, "We Must Not Make a Scarecrow of the Law": A Legal Analysis of the Israeli Policy of Targeted Killings, 36 Cornell Intl. L.J. 233 (2003); Daniel Statman, Targeted Killing, 5 Theoretical Inquiries in Law 179 (2004); and, for critique of the court's decision, see the Ben-Naftali & Michaeli article cited in Note 1 above, and Kristen Eichensehr, On Target? The Israeli Supreme Court and the Expansion of Targeted Killings, 116 Yale L.J. 1873 (2007).

6. In May 2009, the ICRC issued an 85-page report, Interpretive Guidance on the Notion of Direct Participation in Hostilities (2009). According to the ICRC,

> For a specific act to qualify as "direct" rather than "indirect" participation in hostilities there must be a sufficiently close causal relation between the act and the resulting harm. . .
> In the present context, direct causation should be understood as meaning that the harm in question must be brought about in one causal step. Therefore, individual conduct that merely builds up or maintains the capacity of a party to harm its adversary, or which otherwise only indirectly causes harm, is excluded from the concept of direct participation in hostilities.

Id. at 52-53. How, if at all, does this criterion differ from the Israeli Supreme Court's?

7. The ICRC also addressed the issue of whether voluntary human shields are direct participants in hostilities. It concluded that voluntary human shields are indeed direct participants if they "create a physical obstacle to military operations." But if they merely place themselves next to a military target, without physically blocking the attackers, they retain their protection. The ICRC acknowledges that such human shields "voluntarily and deliberately abuse their legal entitlement to protection against direct attack." But doing so poses only "a *legal* — rather than a *physical* — obstacle to military operations"; thus, even if "the presence of voluntary human shields may eventually lead to the cancellation or suspension of an operation by the attacker, the causal relation between their conduct and the resulting harm remains indirect." Id. at 56-57. Compare this analysis with that of the Israeli Supreme Court. Which is better?

2.   *Humiliating Captives*

TRIAL OF LIEUTENANT GENERAL KURT MAELZER

U.S. Military Commn., Florence, Italy (Sept. 9-14, 1946)

1. THE CHARGE

The accused was charged with "... exposing prisoners of war ... in his custody ... to acts of violence, insults and public curiosity."

2. THE EVIDENCE

Some time in January, 1944, Field Marshal Kesselring, commander-in-chief of the German forces in Italy, ordered the accused who was commander of Rome garrison to hold a parade of several hundreds of British and American prisoners of war in the streets of the Italian capital. This parade, emulating the tradition of triumphal marches of ancient Rome, was to be staged to bolster the morale of the Italian population in view of the recent allied landings, not very far from the capital. The accused ordered the parade which took place on 2nd February, 1944. 200 American prisoners of war were marched from the Coliseum, through the main streets of Rome under armed German escort. The streets were lined by forces under the control of the accused. The accused and his staff officers attended the parade. According to the Prosecution witnesses (some of whom were American ex-prisoners of war who had taken part in the march), the population threw stones and sticks at the prisoners, but, according to the defence witnesses, they threw cigarettes and flowers. The prosecution also alleged that when some of the prisoners were giving the "victory sign" with their fingers the accused ordered the guards to fire. This order, however, was not carried out. A film was made of the parade and a great number of photographs taken which appeared in the Italian press under the caption "Anglo-Americans enter Rome after all ... flanked by German bayonets." The accused pleaded in the main that the march was planned and ordered by his superiors and that his only function as commander of Rome garrison was to guarantee the safe conduct and security of the prisoners during the march, which he did. He stated that the march was to quell rumours of the German defeat and to quieten the population of Rome, not to scorn or ridicule the prisoners.

3. FINDINGS AND SENTENCE

The accused was found guilty and sentenced to 10 years' imprisonment. The sentence was reduced to three years' imprisonment by higher military authority.

NOTES AND QUESTIONS

1. Article 13 of GC-POW states that "prisoners of war must at all times be protected, particularly against acts of violence or intimidation and against insults and public curiosity." The same prohibition, in almost the same words, appears in Article 2 of the 1929 Geneva Conventions, which were in force at the time General Maelzer staged his parade.

2. During the 2003 invasion of Iraq, images of captured U.S. military personnel were broadcast on Iraqi television. Then-Secretary of Defense Donald Rumsfeld criticized these broadcasts as violations of the Geneva Conventions. Some military law experts disagreed, pointing to the difference between putting prisoners on display and putting their photographs on display. Should Article 13 be read to prohibit the latter as well as the former?

3. As we have seen, a broader prohibition may be found in common Article 3, part 1(c) of which prohibits "outrages upon personal dignity, in particular, humiliating and degrading treatment." In this connection, consider the following.

ARMY REGULATION 15-6: FINAL REPORT INVESTIGATION INTO FBI ALLEGATIONS OF DETAINEE ABUSE AT GUANTÁNAMO BAY, CUBA DETENTION FACILITY

(April 1, 2005; amended June 9, 2005)

[FBI agents at Guantánamo complained to their superiors that they were witnessing abusive treatment of detainees. Air Force General Randall M. Schmidt was appointed to investigate. He found "only three interrogation acts in violation of interrogation techniques authorized by Army Field Manual 34-52 and DoD guidance." Field Manual 34-52 is the army's manual for interrogators (subsequently revised). In addition, Schmidt found that one high-value detainee had been exposed to "degrading and abusive treatment [that] did not rise to the level of inhumane treatment." This detainee, not identified by name in the report, was later determined to be Mohammed Al Qahtani.]

. . . **Finding #2b:** During the month of March 2003, a female interrogator approached a detainee from behind, rubbed against his back, leaned over the detainee touching him on his knee and shoulder and whispered in his ear that his situation was futile, and ran her fingers through his hair.

Technique: Authorized: FM 34-52 technique — Futility — Act used to highlight futility of the detainee's situation.

. . . **Finding #3:** In March 2003 a female interrogator told a detainee that red ink on her hand was menstrual blood and then wiped her hand on the detainee's arm.

Technique: Authorized: FM 34-52 technique — Futility — Act used to highlight futility of the detainee's situation.

Discussion: The female interrogator is no longer in military service and declined to be interviewed. According to a former ICE [Intelligence Control Element] Deputy the incident occurred when a detainee spat in the interrogator's face. According to the former ICE Deputy, the interrogator left the interrogation room and was crying outside the booth. She developed a plan to psychologically get back at him. She touched the detainee on the shoulder, showed him the red ink on her hand and said; by the way, I am menstruating. The detainee threw himself on the floor and started banging his head. The technique was not in an approved interrogation plan.

Organizational response: The ICE Deputy verbally reprimanded the interrogator for this incident. No formal disciplinary action was taken. There is no evidence that this happened again.

. . . **Eight Techniques Below: Authorized:** FM 34-52 technique—Ego down and Futility.

Finding #16b: On 06 Dec 02, the subject of the first Special Interrogation Plan was forced to wear a woman's bra and had a thong placed on his head during the course of the interrogation.

Finding #16c: On 17 Dec 02, the subject of the first Special Interrogation Plan was told that his mother and sister were whores.

Finding #16d: On 17 Dec 02, the subject of the first Special Interrogation Plan was told that he was a homosexual, had homosexual tendencies, and that other detainees had found out about these tendencies.

Finding #16e: On 20 Dec 02, an interrogator tied a leash to the subject of the first Special Interrogation Plan's chains, led him around the room, and forced him to perform a series of dog tricks.

Finding #16f: On 20 Dec 02, an interrogator forced the subject of the first Special Interrogation Plan to dance with a male interrogator.

Finding #16h: On one occasion in Dec 02, the subject of the First Special Interrogation Plan was forced to stand naked for five minutes with females present. This incident occurred in the course of a strip search.

. . . **Discussion:** The subject of the first Special Interrogation Plan was a high value detainee that ultimately provided extremely valuable intelligence. His ability to resist months of standard interrogation in the summer of 2002 was the genesis for the request to have authority to employ additional counter resistance interrogation techniques. . . . Despite the fact that the AR 15-6 concluded that every technique employed against the subject of the first Special Interrogation Plan was legally permissible under the existing guidance, the AR 15-6 finds that the creative, aggressive, and persistent interrogation of the subject of the first Special Interrogation Plan resulted in the cumulative effect [of] being degrading and abusive treatment. . . . Requiring the subject of the first Special Interrogation Plan to be led around by a leash tied to his chains, placing a thong on his head, insulting his mother and sister, being forced to stand naked in front of a female interrogator for five minutes, and using strip searches as an interrogation technique the AR 15-6 found to be abusive and degrading, particularly when done in the context of the 48 days of intense and long interrogations. While this treatment did not rise to the level of prohibited inhumane treatment the JTF-GTMO CDR was responsible for the interrogation of the subject of the first Special Interrogation Plan and had a responsibility to provide strategic guidance to the interrogation team. He failed to monitor the interrogation and exercise commander discretion by placing limits on the application of otherwise authorized techniques. . . .

Recommendation #16: The Commander JTF-GTMO should be held accountable for failing to supervise the interrogation of the subject of the first Special Interrogation Plan and should be admonished for that failure.

NOTES AND QUESTIONS

1. Do these interrogation techniques rise to the level prohibited by common Article 3? How do they compare with the public exposure to which Maelzer subjected U.S. and British soldiers in the preceding case? Is humiliation a serious enough form of wrongdoing to be made a war crime? Notice that General Maelzer received a three-year sentence, reduced from an initial ten years. Do you consider that sentence appropriate?

2. In pushing to decriminalize portions of common Article 3, President George W. Bush stated:

> This article includes provisions that prohibit "outrages upon personal dignity" and "humiliating and degrading treatment." The problem is that these and other provisions of Common Article Three are vague and undefined, and each could be interpreted in different ways by American or foreign judges. And some believe our military and intelligence personnel involved in capturing and questioning terrorists could now be at risk of prosecution under the War Crimes Act — simply for doing their jobs in a thorough and professional way. This is unacceptable.

White House Office of the Press Secretary, President Discusses Creation of Military Commissions to Try Suspected Terrorists (Sept. 6, 2006), available at http://georgewbush-whitehouse.archives.gov/news/releases/2006/09/20060906-3.html.

In your view, are the CA 3 standards too vague or undefined to leave interrogators in doubt about whether the tactics described above are humiliating or degrading?

These interrogations took place after February 7, 2002, when President Bush declared that the Geneva Conventions do not apply to al Qaeda captives, and well before June 2005, when the Supreme Court concluded in *Hamdan* that al Qaeda captives are indeed protected by CA 3. At the time, then, interrogators believed that the detainees were unprotected by the Geneva Conventions, including CA 3. Should that by itself have relieved the concern that interrogators might be prosecuted?

3. General Schmidt describes all the techniques as authorized by FM 34-52, the army's interrogation manual. All of them fall under the categories of "Futility" and "Ego Down." In the version of FM 34-52 in force at the time, Futility techniques are described as follows. "In this approach, the interrogator convinces the source that resistance to questioning is futile. When employing this technique, the interrogator must have factual information. These facts are presented by the interrogator in a persuasive, logical manner." Ego Down is described as "based on attacking the source's sense of personal worth . . . by attacking his loyalty, intelligence, abilities, leadership qualities, slovenly appearance, or any other perceived weakness. This will usually goad the source into becoming defensive, and he will try to convince the interrogator he is wrong. In his attempt to redeem his pride, the source will usually involuntarily provide pertinent information in attempting to vindicate himself." FM 34-52 (1992), at 3-18. Under these descriptions, are the humiliations recited here authorized by the Field Manual?

4. According to journalist Jane Mayer,

> [T]he notion that Arabs were particularly vulnerable to . . . [sexual humiliation] became an article of faith among many conservatives in Washington who were influenced by a book that obtained something of a cult status, *The Arab Mind* by Raphael Patai, a study of Arab culture and psychology first published in 1973. A cultural anthropologist, Patai included a twenty-five-page chapter on Arabs and sex, depicting the

culture as crippled by shame and repression. . . . Bush Administration foreign-policy intellectuals soon held two articles of faith about Arabs, as a source put it, "one, that Arabs only understand force, and two, that the biggest weakness of Arabs is shame and humiliation." Both ideas became mainstays of the interrogation program.

The Dark Side: The Inside Story of How the War on Terror Turned into a War on American Ideals 167-168 (2008).

CHAPTER

22

Torture and Cruel, Inhuman, and Degrading Treatment or Punishment

The practice of torture is universally rejected by states throughout the world and unequivocally banned under international law. Yet torture remains widespread. The organization Human Rights Watch asserted in 2005, for example, that its research revealed that torture was "common" in China's criminal justice system and was "systematic" among Nigeria's police; in Pakistan, civilian law enforcement agents, military personnel, and intelligence agencies "routinely" used torture to elicit confessions and frighten government critics into changing their political stances or halting their criticisms; North Korea subjected uncounted numbers of its people to forced labor, torture, and other mistreatment; Russian federal forces, apparently in part in response to "unspeakable acts of terrorism in Chechnya," detained, tortured, and "disappeared" thousands of Chechens; Indonesian security forces in the Aceh province systematically tortured detainees suspected of supporting the separatist Free Aceh Movement; the use of torture "featured prominently in escalating human rights violations by Ugandan security and military forces since 2001"; and torture claimed to be part of the global campaign against terrorism led to the death of many prisoners in Uzbekistan and in Egypt.[1]

Rather than devote this chapter to exploring this gruesome global catalog of horrors, we choose instead to focus on the issue of torture in the context of the United States' recent "global war on terror," or GWOT as it is sometimes abbreviated. This case study is appropriate because since September 11, 2001, the United States has been the site of the world's most vigorous and public legal, ethical, and policy debates about torture. The United States' expressed commitment to the ban on torture has been unequivocal, and its human rights record has at least until recently been among the best in the world. After the terrorist atrocities of September 11, however, the United States' commitment to the ban on both torture and lesser forms of "cruel, inhuman, or degrading treatment or punishment" (CIDTP, often further abbreviated as CID) eroded, both as a factual and a legal matter. Tracing this evolution permits us to explore the legal questions of the applicability and enforceability of international bars on torture and CIDTP, the larger question of how deep public abhorrence of torture is, or should be, and the ethical obligations of government lawyers responsible for interpreting legal obligations to prevent certain types of

---

1. Human Rights Watch, Torture Worldwide, Apr. 27, 2005, http://www.hrw.org/english/docs/2005/04/27/china10549.hytm; see also, e.g., U.N. Special Rapporteur's Report to the U.N. General Assembly, available at http://www2.ohchr.org/english/bodies/hrcouncil/7session/reports.htm.

internationally condemned behavior in times of national crisis. Although the number of captives subjected to so-called enhanced interrogation techniques (EITs) remains small—and nowhere near the numbers of torture victims in many other countries—the legal and moral debate in the United States has been exceptionally vigorous.

Nine years before September 11, the U.S. Court of Appeals for the Ninth Circuit, after tracing the "extraordinary consensus" regarding the status of torture in international law, concluded that

> the right to be free of official torture is fundamental and universal, a right deserving of the highest status under international law, a norm of jus cogens. The crack of the whip, the clamp of the thumb screw, the crush of the iron maiden, and, in these more efficient modern times, the shock of the electric cattle prod are forms of torture that the international order will not tolerate. To subject a person to such horrors is to commit one of the most egregious violations of the personal security and dignity of a human being. That states engage in official torture cannot be doubted, but all states believe it is wrong, all that engage in torture deny it, and no state claims a sovereign right to torture its own citizens.[2]

The United States ratified the Convention Against Torture and Other Cruel, Inhuman or Degrading Treatment or Punishment (CAT) in 1994, seven years after it went into effect. It has enacted federal legislation to implement CAT, and has long read its Constitution to bar official torture. In October 1999, the U.S. State Department filed its Initial Report to the UN Committee Against Torture, which was established under CAT to monitor compliance with the Convention. In that report, the State Department emphasized the absolute and unconditional nature of the bar on torture:

> Torture is prohibited by law throughout the United States. It is categorically denounced as a matter of policy and as a tool of state authority. Every act constituting torture under the [CAT] constitutes a criminal offense under the law of the United States. No official of the government, federal, state or local, civilian or military, is authorized to commit or to instruct anyone else to commit torture. Nor may any official condone or tolerate torture in any form. No exceptional circumstances may be invoked as a justification of torture. U.S. law contains no provision permitting otherwise prohibited acts of torture or other cruel, inhuman or degrading treatment or punishment to be employed on grounds of exigent circumstances (for example, during a "state of public emergency") or on orders from a superior officer or public authority, and the protective mechanisms of an independent judiciary are not subject to suspension. The United States is committed to the full and effective implementation of its obligations under the Convention throughout its territory.[3]

Then came September 11, 2001. By 2009, the Pew Research Center reported that seven out of ten Americans believe torture of terror suspects is justified often,

---

2. Siderman de Blake v. Republic of Arg., 965 F.2d 699, 717 (9th Cir. 1992); see also Filartiga v. Pena-Irala, 630 F.2d 876 (2d Cir. 1980). In *Filartiga*, the Second Circuit noted the "universal condemnation of torture in numerous international agreements[] and the renunciation of torture as an instrument of official policy by virtually all of the nations of the world (in principle if not in practice)," and ruled that "an act of torture committed by a state official against one held in detention violates established norms of the international law of human rights, and hence the law of nations." 630 F.2d at 880.

3. U.S. Dept. of State, Initial Report of the United States of America to the UN Comm. Against Torture, Introduction, at 2 (Oct. 15, 1999), available at http://www.state.gov/www/global/human_rights/torture_toc99.html.

sometimes, or rarely; only one out of four answered "never."[4] And in 2007 "a survey of 1,767 U.S. soldiers and marines deployed to Iraq found that over one-third of those questioned believed torture should be permitted if it helps gather important information about insurgents" and "[f]orty percent said they approved of such abuse if it would save the life of a fellow soldier."[5]

One might expect that the institutional (that is, U.S. governmental) commitment to the ban on torture would outstrip that of individual citizens responding to the passions of the moment, if for no other reason than to serve the U.S. government's interest in inducing reciprocal compliance by those nations that come into custody of U.S. service persons or other nationals.[6] And indeed, the president and other officials continued to condemn torture vigorously. Yet the George W. Bush administration, at various points in the war on terror, promoted exceedingly narrow constructions of the U.S. crime of torture, fought congressional efforts explicitly to recognize that U.S. actors abroad have an obligation to avoid CIDTP, and subjected detainees within its custody to methods of interrogation long considered to constitute torture or CIDTP.[7]

For example, "[o]n December 2nd, [2002], former Secretary of Defense Rumsfeld gave formal approval for the use of 'hooding,' 'exploitation of phobias,' 'stress positions,' 'deprivation of light and auditory stimuli,' and other coercive tactics ordinarily forbidden by the [United States' own] Army Field Manual"[8] and categorized as CIDTP by various courts around the world. These interrogation techniques were used at places such as Guantánamo and Abu Ghraib despite the vehement objections of some military and law enforcement officials (including, for example, the general counsel of the U.S. navy[9] and FBI agents posted to Guantánamo).[10] The Senate Armed Services Committee concluded in December 2008 that

> [t]he abuse of detainees at Abu Ghraib in late 2003 was not simply the result of a few soldiers acting on their own. Interrogation techniques such as stripping detainees of

---

4. See Pew Forum on Religion and Public Life, The Religious Dimensions of the Torture Debate, May 7, 2009, available at http://pewforum.org/docs/?DocID=156 (15% of Americans believe torture of terror suspects is "often" justified; 34% believe it is "sometimes" justified; 22% said that it was "rarely" justified; 25% said it was "never" justified; and 4% didn't know or refused to answer the question).

5. David A. Wallace, Torture v. the Basic Principles of the US Military, 6 J. Intl. Crim. J. 309, 310 (2008) (referencing Brian Murphy, Petraeus "Concerned" by Ethics Report, Wash. Post, May 7, 2007). General David Petraeus, commanding general of the U.S. troops in Iraq, reportedly responded to the survey results by arguing that "we can never sink to the level of the enemy" and lamenting that " '[w]e have done that at times in theater and it has cost us enormously,' referring to the torture and ill-treatment of prisoners at the Abu Ghraib prison." Murphy, supra.

6. See, e.g., Hendrik Hertzberg, Talk of the Town: Comment, New Yorker, Mar. 24, 2003, at 29 ("When the Senate ratified the Torture Convention in 1990, it did so at the urging of the first President Bush, who, with war looming in the Persian Gulf, wanted to deny Saddam Hussein the slightest cover for mistreating any American soldiers his forces might capture.").

7. See, e.g., Senate Armed Services Comm. Inquiry into the Treatment of Detainees in U.S. Custody, Executive Summary, at xii(U) (Dec. 11, 2008) ("The abuse of detainees in U.S. custody cannot simply be attributed to the actions of 'a few bad apples' acting on their own. The fact is that senior officials in the United States government solicited information on how to use aggressive techniques, redefined the law to create the appearance of their legality, and authorized their use against detainees.").

8. Jane Mayer, Annals of the Pentagon, The Memo: How an Internal Effort to Ban Abuse and Torture of Detainees Was Thwarted, New Yorker, Feb. 27, 2006, at 82 [hereinafter The Memo]; see also Jane Mayer, The Experiment: The Military Trains People to Withstand Interrogation. Are Those Methods Being Misused at Guantanamo?, New Yorker, July 11, 2005, at 60.

9. See Philippe Sands, The Torture Team: Rumsfeld's Memo and the Betrayal of American Values 131-144 (2008); see also Alberto Mora & John Shattuck, Self-Inflicted Wounds, Wash. Post, Nov. 6, 2007, at 19. On May 10, 2007, General David Petraeus stated, "What sets us apart from our enemies in this fight . . . is how we behave. In everything we do, we must observe the standards and values that dictate that we treat noncombatants and detainees with dignity and respect. While we are warriors, we are also all human beings." Senate Armed Services Comm. Inquiry into the Treatment of Detainees in U.S. Custody, Executive Summary, at xii (Dec. 11, 2008).

10. Mayer, The Memo, supra note 8, at 4-5.

their clothes, placing them in stress positions, and using military dogs to intimidate them appeared in Iraq only after they had been approved for use in Afghanistan and GTMO. [Rumsfeld's December 2, 2002,] authorization of aggressive interrogation techniques and subsequent interrogation policies and plans approved by senior military and civilian officials conveyed the message that physical pressures and degradation were appropriate treatment for detainees in U.S. military custody. What followed was an erosion in standards dictating that detainees be treated humanely.[11]

The CIA used even harsher tactics against so-called high-value detainees — tactics that included sleep deprivation for up to 180 hours and waterboarding, in which the victim is strapped to a board, his feet are placed higher than his head, a cloth is placed over his mouth, and water is poured over the cloth. Within seconds, the victim experiences the physical sensations of drowning.[12]

As interrogation techniques pressed beyond previously recognized legal boundaries, those asked to engage in such interrogations and their bosses looked for legal reassurances. Post–September 11, a dozen legal memoranda were shuttled among the Department of Defense, the State Department, the Justice Department, and the White House.[13] The most controversial, though, emerged from a single office: the Office of Legal Counsel (OLC) in the Justice Department. OLC is tasked with providing legal advice and analysis for the entire executive branch of government. OLC memos are normally maintained in confidence.[14] Some memos came to light after being leaked; others the government chose to make public well after the fact.

The first memo, written by OLC's Deputy Assistant Attorney General John Yoo, is dated two weeks after 9/11. In it, OLC concluded for the first time that the president's authority as commander in chief overrides federal criminal statutes.[15] Two subsequent OLC memos argued that the Geneva Conventions do not protect either al Qaeda members or members of the Taliban. (One of these memos is discussed in Chapter 21.B.3.) These set the stage for President Bush's February 7, 2002 finding affirming that conclusion[16] and asserting that prisoners would be treated consistently with Geneva "to the extent appropriate and consistent with military necessity" — a large loophole for intelligence gathering.[17] This presidential determination regarding the coverage of Geneva proved crucial because it meant that, under U.S. government

---

11. Senate Armed Services Comm. Inquiry into the Treatment of Detainees in U.S. Custody, Executive Summary, at xxix; Conclusion, at 19 (Dec. 11, 2008).

12. U.S. Dept. of Justice, Office of Legal Counsel, Memorandum for John A. Rizzo, Senior Deputy General Counsel of the CIA, from Steven G. Bradbury, Office of Legal Counsel, re: Application of 18 U.S.C. §§2340-2340A to Certain Techniques That May Be Used in the Interrogation of a High Value al Qaeda Detainee (May 10, 2005), available at http://luxmedia.vo.llnwd.net/o10/clients/aclu/olc_05102005_bradbury46pg.pdf [hereinafter Bradbury "Techniques" Memo] (describing 13 EITs used by the CIA).

13. See Natl. Security Archive, The Interrogation Documents: Debating U.S. Policy and Methods, July 14, 2004, available at http://www.gwu.edu/~nsarchiv/NSAEBB/NSAEBB127/index.htm.

14. For a discussion of the OLC memo process and its implications, see Daniel L. Pines, Are Even Torturers Immune from Suit? How Attorney General Opinions Shield Government Employees from Civil Litigation and Criminal Prosecution, 43 Wake Forest L. Rev. 93, passim (2008).

15. Memorandum Opinion for the Deputy Counsel to the President, The President's Constitutional Authority to Conduct Military Operations Against Terrorists and Nations Supporting Them (Sept. 25, 2001), available at http://www.usdoj.gov/olc/warpowers925.htm.

16. The OLC memos and President Bush's order are reproduced in The Torture Papers: The Road to Abu Ghraib 38-79, 81-117, 134-135 (Karen J. Greenberg & Joshua L. Dratel eds., 2005). Others are collected in The Torture Memos (David Cole, ed., 2009).

17. Id. at 134-135, Memorandum from President Bush (Feb. 7, 2002).

policy, neither al Qaeda nor Taliban members could claim the Geneva Conventions' prohibitions on torture, cruel treatment, and "outrages against personal dignity, including humiliating and degrading treatment" of captives. This decision was also not without detractors: The State Department's legal adviser strongly criticized the OLC's reasoning,[18] and some U.S. military officers and military lawyers argued that for the United States to deny Geneva Convention protections to captives would jeopardize U.S. prisoners of war in the future.[19] In the end, the Supreme Court determined that the OLC—and the president—were wrong as a matter of law and that common Article 3 of the Geneva Conventions applied to al Qaeda.[20]

The OLC wrote at least seven opinions interpreting the legal prohibitions on torture and CIDTP in interrogations, and all of them reached the same conclusion: None of the CIA's "Enhanced Interrogation Techniques" (EITs) were illegal. The best known was dated August 1, 2002, authored by John Yoo, signed by former OLC head (now Ninth Circuit judge) Jay S. Bybee, and addressed to the president's then counsel (and later attorney general) Alberto Gonzales. The memo discussed whether harsh interrogation tactics violate U.S. obligations under CAT and the U.S. statute prohibiting torture. This memo has become known variously as the "Bybee Memo," which is the usage employed in these materials, or simply the "Torture Memo." It became public in June 2004, just months after the revelation of prisoner abuse by U.S. forces at Abu Ghraib prison in Iraq. A second Bybee/Yoo memo from the same day (the "Bybee techniques memo") discussed in detail the legality of specific techniques proposed by the CIA for the interrogation of a high-value al Qaeda detainee, Abu Zubaydah. These included tactics such as prolonged nudity, replacement of solid food with a commercial liquid nutrient, and face slapping; "walling" (slamming a detainee into a wall); prolonged sleep deprivation accomplished by chaining a detainee loosely in an upright position using ankle and wrist shackles; waterboarding; hosing him with cold water; confining him in a small box and placing a harmless insect in the box with him (because it was believed that Abu Zubaydah had an insect phobia). The "techniques memo" remained secret until the Obama Justice Department released it in April 2009.

The Bybee Memo addressed more general legal questions about the interpretation of the torture statutes. In so doing, it reached a series of significant conclusions: that the infliction of pain rises to the level of torture only if the pain is as severe as that accompanying "death, organ failure, or the permanent impairment of a significant body function"; that the infliction of psychological pain rises to the level of torture only if the interrogator specifically intended it to cause "lasting . . . damage" such as posttraumatic stress disorder; that it would be unconstitutional to apply anti-torture laws to interrogations authorized by the president in the war on terror; and that, "under current circumstances, necessity or self-defense may justify interrogation methods that violate" the criminal prohibition on torture.[21] As we shall see in this chapter's readings (as well as later in Chapter 23 (defenses)), some of these conclusions are supported by conventional, if debatable, legal arguments; others are more problematic.

The Bybee Memo proved to be very influential. In January 2003, former defense secretary Donald Rumsfeld formed a working group on interrogation techniques,

---

18. The State Department's critique is Memorandum from William Howard Taft IV to John Yoo (Jan. 11, 2002), available at http://www.cartoonbank.com/newyorker/slideshows/01TaftMemo.pdf.
19. See, e.g., Wallace, supra note 5, passim.
20. See Hamdan v. Rumsfeld, 548 U.S. 557, 628-632 (2006). *Hamdan* is excerpted in Chapter 21.B.3.
21. U.S. Dept. of Justice, Office of Legal Counsel, Memorandum for Alberto R. Gonzales, Counsel to the President, re: Standards of Conduct for Interrogation under 18 U.S.C. §§2340-2340A, at 2, 6-8 (Aug. 1, 2002) [hereinafter Bybee Memo].

which produced its own report in April. Significantly, the working group report relied substantially on the Bybee Memo, and in fact incorporated large chunks of it verbatim.[22] Rumsfeld subsequently approved a list of "aggressive" procedures for Guantánamo Bay interrogations that eventually migrated to Iraq. "When stories of systematic abuse, mistreatment, and torture at U.S. detention facilities came to light, many saw a direct connection between the [Bybee Memo] and these crimes."[23] The CIA subjected at least three of its captives, including Khalid Sheikh Mohammed (KSM), to techniques approved by OLC, including waterboarding.[24] A 2005 OLC memo reveals that EITs were used in interrogating 28 of 92 CIA captives.[25] Abu Zubaydah was waterboarded 83 times in a month, while KSM was waterboarded 183 times in a month.[26] According to the CIA's inspector general, "the CIA, at least initially, could not always distinguish detainees who had information but were successfully resisting interrogation from those who did not actually have the information. On at least one occasion, this may have resulted in what might be deemed in retrospect to have been the unnecessary use of enhanced techniques."[27] A highly confidential Red Cross report based on interviews with detainees who had not had a chance to coordinate their stories concluded that EITs were used in excess of guidelines established in the OLC memos.[28]

The George W. Bush administration's principal response to concerns about maltreatment of detainees was to assert that the United States does not "torture," while recrafting the legal parameters of that term.[29] Indeed, as recently as January 2008, former attorney general Mukasey refused during his confirmation process to describe waterboarding as illegal torture in all circumstances, stating that in some circumstances the legality of this interrogation device could be a "close[] question" about which "[r]easonable people can disagree."[30] This has not been the historical position of U.S. legal authorities. The U.S. military court-martialed troops who waterboarded Philippine rebels in the early twentieth century and condemned a Japanese general who used "the water cure" on Allied POWs in World War II.[31] During the Reagan administration, a U.S. court of appeals referred to the technique several times as "torture" in an opinion upholding lengthy sentences for sheriff's deputies who

---

22. See David Luban, Liberalism, Torture, and the Ticking Time Bomb, 91 Va. L. Rev. 1425, 1454 (2005); see also Final Report of Independent Panel to Review DoD Detention Operations (Aug. 2004) [hereinafter Schlesinger Report], in The Torture Papers, supra note 16, at 911.

23. Milan Markovic, Can Lawyers Be War Criminals?, 20 Geo. J. Legal Ethics 347, 348 & n.16 (2007) (listing sources).

24. Memorandum for John A. Rizzo, Senior Deputy General Counsel, CIA, re: Application of United States Obligations Under Article 16 of the United Nations Convention Against Torture to Certain Techniques that May Be Used in the Interrogation of High Value al Qaeda Detainees, at 6 (May 30, 2005), available at http://luxmedia.vo.llnwd.net/o10/clients/aclu/olc_05302005_bradbury.pdf [hereinafter OLC Article 16 Memo] (reporting that KSM, Abu Zubaydah, and Abd al-Rahim al-Nashiri were waterboarded).

25. Id. at 5.

26. Id. at 37. For a classic discussion of the art of interrogation, see Mark Bowden, The Dark Art of Interrogation, Atl. Monthly, Oct. 2003, at 51.

27. OLC Article 16 Memo, supra note 24, at 31.

28. ICRC Report on the Treatment of Fourteen "High Value Detainees" in CIA Custody, (Feb. 2007), available at http://www.nybooks.com/icrc-report.pdf.

29. Dan Eggen, White House Pushes Waterboarding Rationale, Wash. Post, Feb. 13, 2008, at A03.

30. See, e.g., Letter from Attorney General Michael B. Mukasey to Senator Patrick Leahy, at 2 (Jan. 29, 2008), available at http://i.a.cnn.net/cnn/2008/images/01/29/letter.to.senator.leahy.pdf; see also Marty Lederman, How Can the Legality of Waterboarding Depend on the Circumstances? (Jan. 30, 2008), http://balkin.blogspot.com/2008/01/how-can-legality-of-waterboarding.html.

31. Evan Wallach, Drop by Drop: Forgetting the History of Water Torture in U.S. Courts, 45 Colum. Transnatl. L. Rev. 468 (2007).

used it to extract confessions from prisoners in Texas.[32] The U.S. military forbids waterboarding captives.[33]

Once they were leaked, the OLC memos triggered great controversy. For example, Harold H. Koh, a dean and professor of law at Yale Law School and a former official in both Republican and Democratic administrations, testified before the Senate Judiciary Committee that "in my professional opinion, the [Bybee Memo] is perhaps the most clearly erroneous legal opinion I have ever read."[34] Harvard professor Jack Goldsmith, who replaced Judge Bybee as head of the OLC, criticized its "cursory and one-sided legal arguments" that "lacked the tenor of detachment and caution that usually characterizes OLC work."[35] Other prominent experts defended the memo.[36] So great was the pressure that the Department of Justice, in December 2004, took the very unusual step of retracting and replacing the Bybee Memo. In its stead, an OLC memo signed by the acting chief, Daniel Levin, was released (the "Levin Memo").[37] In 2005, then-OLC head Steven Bradbury authored three additional memos on the legality of the CIA techniques. One memo examined the legality of each technique individually; the second examined all of them used cumulatively; and the third analyzed whether the EITs constitute CIDTP. All three memos concluded that, with appropriate safeguards of the detainee's health, the techniques are not torture or CIDTP. These memos were made public by the Obama administration in 2009.

Promptly upon taking office, President Obama issued a series of executive orders repudiating many of the policies and practices of the prior administration that allegedly led to torture or cruel, inhuman, or degrading treatment or punishment. Thus, he ordered the closure within one year of the detention facilities at Guantánamo Bay, a review of the status of all individuals held there to effect their prompt and appropriate disposition, and treatment of detainees in conformity with Article 3 of the Geneva Conventions.[38] He created a special interagency task force on detainee disposition that must "identify lawful options for the disposition of individuals captured or apprehended in connection with armed conflicts and counterterrorism

---

32. United States v. Lee, 744 F.2d 1124 (5th Cir. 1984); Ex-Sheriff Given 10-Year Sentence, N.Y. Times, Oct. 27, 1983, at A11 (describing 2-, 4-, and 10-year sentences); Wallach, supra note 31, at 502-503. The technique "included the placement of a towel over the nose and mouth of the prisoner and the pouring of water in the towel until the prisoner began to move, jerk, or otherwise indicate that he was suffocating and/or drowning." Brief of Petitioner-Appellee, United States v. Lee, No. 83-2675 (5th Cir. Nov. 9, 1984).

33. Oral Statements by the U.S. Delegation to the Comm. Against Torture, at 6 (May 8, 2006), available at http://www.state.gov/documents/organization/66174.pdf (Charles Stimson, Dept. of Defense, stating that "waterboarding . . . is not permitted for detainees under DoD control. . . . [W]aterboarding is specifically prohibited in the revised Army Field Manual.").

34. Nomination of the Hon. Alberto R. Gonzales as Attorney General of the United States: Hearing Before the S. Judiciary Comm., 109th Cong. (Jan. 6, 2005) (statement of Harold Hongju Koh, Dean, Yale Law School), available at http://judiciary.senate.gov/hearings/testimony.cfm?id=1345&wit_id=3938; see also Ruth Wedgwood & R. James Woolsey, Law and Torture, Wall St. J., June 28, 2004.

35. Jack Goldsmith, The Terror Presidency: Law and Judgment Inside the Bush Administration 149 (2007).

36. Eric Posner & Adrian Vermeule, A "Torture" Memo and Its Tortuous Critics, Wall St. J., July 6, 2004.

37. U.S. Dept. of Justice, Memorandum for James B. Comey, Deputy Attorney General, re: Legal Standards Applicable Under 18 U.S.C. §§2340-2340A (Dec. 30, 2004), available at http://www.humanrightsfirst.org/us_law/etn/pdf/levin-memo-123004.pdf [hereinafter the "Levin Memo"].

38. Exec. Order No. 13,492, Review and Disposition of Individuals Detained at the Guantánamo Bay Naval Base and Closure of Detention Facilities, 74 Fed. Reg. 4897 (Jan. 22, 2009); see also Office of the President, Memorandum for the Attorney General et al., re: Review of the Detention of Ali Saleh Kahlah al-Marri (Jan. 22, 2009), available at http://www.whitehouse.gov/the_press_office/ReviewoftheDetentionofAliSalehKahlah/ (ordering a review of the status of al-Marri, the only individual currently being held as an enemy combatant within the United States).

operations."[39] Finally, President Obama issued an executive order that revoked prior executive orders pertaining to CIA interrogation practices and requires in the future that interrogation of all individuals in the custody or control of the United States in armed conflicts conform, as a "minimum baseline," with Common Article 3 of the Geneva Conventions.[40] The order goes on to state:

> Effective immediately, an individual in the custody or under the effective control of an officer, employee, or other agent of the United States Government, or detained within a facility owned, operated, or controlled by a department or agency of the United States, in any armed conflict, shall not be subjected to any interrogation technique or approach, or any treatment related to interrogation, that is not authorized by and listed in the Army Field Manual 2-22.3 [Human Intelligence Collector Operations].[41]

This executive order also orders the "expeditious[]" closure of CIA detention facilities and creates a special interagency task force to review interrogation and "transfer" (rendition) policies.[42]

The George W. Bush administration policies and practices, then, have been altered, but the lessons they impart continue to have relevance. To understand the importance of this episode, one must realize that the OLC is one of the most elite groups of lawyers in the federal government. Its two dozen lawyers serve as primary legal advisors to the entire executive branch, and its alumni include Supreme Court justices, solicitors general, attorneys general, and distinguished lawyers and academics. The Bybee Memo also reportedly passed muster with many lawyers and other officials in the White House, the vice president's office, and the National Security Council.[43] In short, those who put together and approved the Bybee Memo are widely perceived to be among the best and the brightest in the U.S. legal profession.

The following exploration of the international and U.S. crime of torture begins with a problem designed to help you work through the definitional issues posed in Section A. Although much of the recent debate assumes that "torture" has one invariable meaning, it in fact does not — either legally or in public discourse. The translation of words such as *torture* into a concrete set of interrogation guidelines is a daunting task, as we shall see. We challenge you to examine the interpretations provided by the OLC — including the most controversial definitional paragraphs from the Bybee and Levin Memos — to reach your own conclusions regarding the legal viability of the conclusions they reached.

In Section B, we explore the distinction between "torture" and other "cruel, inhuman, and degrading treatment or punishment," and the important legal and practical implications of this distinction. In this section, we also discuss the "McCain Amendment," through which Congress extended the obligation of U.S. actors to avoid CIDTP beyond U.S. borders, and the legality of the U.S. "irregular rendition" program. Section C contains a brief analysis of the application of the ban on torture and CIDTP in armed conflict. And in Section D, we examine whether, if U.S. actors relied on legal memoranda such as the Bybee Memo in engaging in torture and CIDTP, they would have a valid defense in a criminal prosecution.

---

39. Exec. Order No. 13,493, Review of Detention Policy Options, at §1(a), 74 Fed. Reg. 4901 (Jan. 22, 2009).

40. Exec. Order 13,491, Ensuring Lawful Interrogations, at §3(a), 74 Fed. Reg. 4893-4894 (Jan. 22, 2009).

41. Id. §3(b).

42. Id. §§4, 5.

43. Dana Priest, CIA Puts Harsh Tactics on Hold; Memo on Methods of Interrogation Had Wide Review, Wash. Post, June 27, 2004, at A1.

After surveying this landscape, we turn in Section E to the question raised by this legal debate (which seemed unthinkable in the United States prior to September 11): whether torture is ever acceptable. This discussion leads to another problem in Section F through which we explore the role — and ethical obligations — of the government lawyers who drafted the Bybee Memo.

A. TORTURE

1. Problem

An OLC "techniques" memo of May 10, 2005, describes 13 EITs used by the CIA on high-value detainees. Which, if any, of these procedures do you consider to be torture? Cruel, inhuman, or degrading treatment that falls short of torture? Do the legal definitions in the materials following help settle these questions?

1. *Dietary manipulation.* This technique involves the substitution of commercial liquid meal replacements for normal food, presenting detainees with a bland, unappetizing but nutritionally complete diet. . . .
2. *Nudity.* . . .
3. *Attention grasp.* This technique consists of grasping the individual with both hands, one hand on each side of the collar opening, in a controlled and quick motion. In the same motion as the grasp, the individual is drawn toward the interrogator.
4. *Walling.* This technique involves the use of a flexible, false wall. The individual is placed with his heels touching the flexible wall. The interrogator pulls the individual forward and then quickly and firmly pushes the individual into the wall. It is the individual's shoulder blades that hit the wall. During this motion, the head and neck are supported with a rolled hood or towel that provides a C-collar effect to help prevent whiplash. . . .
5. *Facial hold.* This technique is used to hold the head immobile during interrogation. . . .
6. *Facial slap or insult slap.* With this technique, the interrogator slaps the individual's face with fingers slightly spread. . . .
7. *Abdominal slap.* In this technique, the interrogator strikes the abdomen of the detainee with the back of his open hand. . . .
8. *Cramped confinement.* This technique involves placing the individual in a confined space, the dimensions of which restrict the individual's movements. The confined space is usually dark. . . . For the larger confined space, the individual can stand up or sit down; the smaller space is large enough for the subject to sit down. Confinement in the larger space may last no more than 8 hours at a time for no more than 18 hours a day; for the smaller space, confinement may last no more than two hours. . . .
9. *Wall standing.* . . . The individual stands about four to five feet from a wall, with his feet spread approximately to shoulder width. His arms are stretched out in front of him, with his fingers resting on the wall and supporting his body weight. The individual is not permitted to move or reposition his hands or feet.
10. *Stress positions.* . . . The three stress positions are (1) sitting on the floor with legs extended straight out in front and arms raised above the head, (2) kneeling on the floor while leaning back at a 45 degree angle, and

      (3) leaning against a wall generally about three feet away from the detainee's feet, with only the detainee's head touching the wall, while his wrists are handcuffed in front of him or behind his back. . . .

11. *Water dousing.* Cold water is poured on the detainee either from a container or from a hose without a nozzle. . . . To ensure an adequate margin of safety, the maximum period of time that a detainee may be permitted to remain wet has been set at two-thirds the time at which . . . hypothermia could be expected to develop in healthy individuals. . . .

12. *Sleep deprivation (more than 48 hours).* . . . The primary method of sleep deprivation involves the use of shackling to keep the detainee awake. In this method, the detainee is standing and is handcuffed, and the handcuffs are attached by a length of chain to the ceiling. The detainee's hands are shackled in front of his body. . . . The detainee's feet are shackled to a bolt in the floor. . . . All of the detainee's weight is borne by his legs and feet during standing sleep deprivation. You have informed us that the detainee is not allowed to hang from or support his body weight with the shackles. . . . If the detainee is clothed, he wears an adult diaper under his pants. Detainees subject to sleep deprivation who are also subject to nudity as a separate interrogation technique will at times be nude and wearing a diaper. . . . You have informed us that to date no detainee has experienced any skin problems resulting from use of diapers. The maximum allowable duration for sleep deprivation authorized by the CIA is 180 hours, after which the detainee must be permitted to sleep for at least eight hours. You have informed us that to date, more than a dozen detainees have been subjected to sleep deprivation of more than 48 hours, and three detainees have been subjected to sleep deprivation of more than 96 hours; the longest period of time for which any detainee has been deprived of sleep by the CIA is 180 hours.

13. *The "waterboard."* . . . [44]

2.   Definitions: Convention and Statutes

What is torture? Certainly, as Judge Richard Posner of the U.S. Court of Appeals for the Seventh Circuit explains, "[t]he word 'torture' lacks a stable definition."[45] But is it also true, as he argues, that "what is involved in using the word is picking out the point along a continuum at which the observer's queasiness turns to revulsion"?[46] Prior to CAT, torture had been outlawed in a variety of international conventions, but a definition had not been attempted.[47] Consider CAT's definition of torture and other definitions that have followed it. In so doing, compare the types, severity, and length of pain and suffering required to meet the torture threshold. Consider, too, the difference among the definitions relating to the intent, articulated motive, and government instigation or custody requirements.

---

44. Bradbury "Techniques" Memo, supra note 12, at 10-13.

45. Richard A. Posner, Torture, Terrorism, and Interrogation, in Torture: A Collection 291 (S. Levinson ed., 2004).

46. Id.

47. See, e.g., Statute of the ICTY arts. 2 and 5; Statute of the ICTR arts. 3 and 4; International Covenant on Civil and Political Rights (ICCPR) art. 7; European Convention on Human Rights art. 3; Geneva Convention Relative to the Treatment of Prisoners of War art. 3; Geneva Convention Relative to the Protection of Civilian Persons in Time of War art. 3; Charter of the International Military Tribunal at Nuremberg art. 6; Tokyo Charter for the International Military Tribunal for the Far East art. 5; Allied Control Council Law No. 10 art. II.

CONVENTION AGAINST TORTURE AND OTHER CRUEL, INHUMAN OR DEGRADING TREATMENT OR PUNISHMENT (CAT)

1465 U.N.T.S. 85

ARTICLE 1

1. For the purposes of this Convention, the term "torture" means any act by which severe pain or suffering, whether physical or mental, is intentionally inflicted on a person for such purposes as obtaining from him or a third person information or a confession, punishing him for an act he or a third person has committed or is suspected of having committed, or intimidating or coercing him or a third person, or for any reason based on discrimination of any kind, when such pain or suffering is inflicted by or at the instigation of or with the consent or acquiescence of a public official or other person acting in an official capacity. It does not include pain or suffering arising only from, inherent in or incidental to lawful sanctions.

U.S. RESERVATIONS, DECLARATIONS, AND UNDERSTANDINGS (RUDs) TO THE CONVENTION AGAINST TORTURE

1830 U.N.T.S. 320

. . . II. The Senate's advice and consent is subject to the following understandings, which shall apply to the obligations of the United States under this Convention:

(1) (a) That with reference to Article 1, the United States understands that, in order to constitute torture, an act must be specifically intended to inflict severe physical or mental pain or suffering and that mental pain or suffering refers to prolonged mental harm caused by or resulting from (1) the intentional infliction or threatened infliction of severe physical pain or suffering; (2) the administration or application, or threatened administration or application, of mind altering substances or other procedures calculated to disrupt profoundly the senses or the personality; (3) the threat of imminent death; or (4) the threat that another person will imminently be subjected to death, severe physical pain or suffering, or the administration or application of mind altering substances or other procedures calculated to disrupt profoundly the senses or personality;

(b) That the United States understands that the definition of torture in Article 1 is intended to apply only to acts directed against persons in the offender's custody or physical control.

(c) That with reference to Article 1 of the Convention, the United States understands that "sanctions" includes judicially-imposed sanctions and other enforcement actions authorized by United States law or by judicial interpretation of such law. Nonetheless, the United States understands that a State Party could not through its domestic sanctions defeat the object and purpose of the Convention to prohibit torture.

(d) That with reference to Article 1 of the Convention, the United States understands that the term "acquiescence" requires that the public official, prior to the activity constituting torture, have awareness of such activity and thereafter breach his legal responsibility to intervene to prevent such activity.

(e) That with reference to Article 1 of the Convention, the United States understands that noncompliance with applicable legal procedural standards does not per se constitute torture.

(2) That the United States understands the phrase "where there is substantial grounds for believing that he would be in danger of being subjected to torture," as used in Article 3 of the Convention, to mean "if it is more likely than not that he would be tortured." . . .

(4) That the United States understands that international law does not prohibit the death penalty, and does not consider this Convention to restrict or prohibit the United States from applying the death penalty consistent with the Fifth, Eighth and/or Fourteenth Amendments to the Constitution of the United States, including any constitutional period of confinement prior to the imposition of the death penalty. . . .

III. The Senate's advice and consent is subject to the following declaration[]:

(1) That the United States declares that the provisions of Articles 1 through 16 of the Convention are not self-executing. . . .

UNITED STATES CODE
Title 18, Chapter 113C — Torture

§2340. DEFINITIONS

As used in this chapter—

(1) "torture" means an act committed by a person acting under the color of law specifically intended to inflict severe physical or mental pain or suffering (other than pain or suffering incidental to lawful sanctions) upon another person within his custody or physical control;

(2) "severe mental pain or suffering" means the prolonged mental harm caused by or resulting from—

(A) the intentional infliction or threatened infliction of severe physical pain or suffering;

(B) the administration or application, or threatened administration or application, of mind-altering substances or other procedures calculated to disrupt profoundly the senses or the personality;

(C) the threat of imminent death; or

(D) the threat that another person will imminently be subjected to death, severe physical pain or suffering, or the administration or application of mind-altering substances or other procedures calculated to disrupt profoundly the senses or personality.

(3) "United States" means the several States of the United States, the District of Columbia, and the commonwealths, territories, and possessions of the United States.

§2340A. TORTURE

(a) **Offense.** — Whoever outside the United States commits or attempts to commit torture shall be fined under this title or imprisoned not more than 20 years, or both, and if death results to any person from conduct prohibited by this subsection, shall be punished by death or imprisoned for any term of years or for life.

(b) **Jurisdiction.** — There is jurisdiction over the activity prohibited in subsection (a) if —

(1) the alleged offender is a national of the United States; or

(2) the alleged offender is present in the United States, irrespective of the nationality of the victim or alleged offender.

(c) **Conspiracy.** — A person who conspires to commit an offense under this section shall be subject to the same penalties (other than the penalty of death) as the penalties prescribed for the offense, the commission of which was the object of the conspiracy.

ICC ELEMENTS OF CRIMES
ICC-ASP/1/3 (part II-B)

ARTICLE 7(1)(f) CRIME AGAINST HUMANITY OF TORTURE[48]

ELEMENTS

1. The perpetrator inflicted severe physical or mental pain or suffering upon one or more persons.
2. Such person or persons were in the custody or under the control of the perpetrator.
3. Such pain or suffering did not arise only from, and was not inherent in or incidental to, lawful sanctions.
4. The conduct was committed as part of a widespread or systematic attack directed against a civilian population.
5. The perpetrator knew that the conduct was part of or intended the conduct to be part of a widespread or systematic attack directed against a civilian population.

NOTES AND QUESTIONS

1. Why is a precise definition of torture necessary? For example, Michael Kozak, formerly the acting assistant secretary of state for democracy, human rights, and labor, stated, in connection with the release of the department's annual human rights report in 2005, that President Bush "has been very clear on the issue of torture, which is we are against it — and torture by anyone's common-sense definition of it, not some fancy definition." On-the-Record Briefing on the Release of the 2004 Annual Report on Human Rights, Paula Dobriansky & Michael Kozak, in Washington, D.C. (Feb. 28, 2005).

Recall that our subject contemplates *criminal* prosecution of those responsible for official abuse, and the principle of legality requires that some effort be made to give official actors fair notice of that which is proscribed. Absent a sufficiently specific definition, criminal prosecutions may be dismissed based on due process vagueness objections. With this in mind, recall that former attorney general Mukasey relied on the fact-specific and seemingly indeterminate nature of the torture definition to resist congressional invitations to call waterboarding "torture" in all circumstances during his confirmation hearings.

---

48. [Elements' footnote 17:] It is understood that no specific purpose need be proved for this crime.

On December 2006, the U.S. Justice Department brought the first ever criminal charges under 18 U.S.C. §2340A charging that, while in Liberia, the defendant — Roy M. Belfast, Jr., aka Charles "Chuckie" Taylor, Jr., son of a former Liberian president and at the time of the operative events the commander of the Liberian armed forces' Antiterrorism Unit — conspired to torture and did torture a Liberian victim to obtain information about opponents of the Taylor presidency. See United States v. Roy M. Belfast, Jr., Superceding Indictment, Case No. 06-20758-Cr-Altonaga(s), Count 2 (S.D. Fla. 2007). Could the Justice Department's own difficulties arriving at a definitive criterion of torture have given Taylor an argument that the torture statute is unconstitutional? Note in this regard that Taylor moved to dismiss his indictment on the ground that the statutory definition of "torture" was "impermissibly vague and overbroad," relying explicitly on the series of OLC memos struggling with the definition of that term. Taylor asserted that, in view of the difficulties the department faced in deciding what constituted torture, it was incongruous that the "government now insists that the statute is clear enough to put laymen on notice as to what conduct is prohibited." Id., Defendant's Reply to Government's Response to Motion to Dismiss Indictment Based on Facial and As-Applied Unconstitutionality, at 16 (May 7, 2007). Taylor's motion was denied, he was convicted, and, in January 2009, he was sentenced to 97 years' imprisonment.

Some specificity is also important from a policy standpoint. The government interest in information gathering is extremely strong during armed conflicts and in the present war on terror. Interrogators working to serve this interest cannot fairly be asked to operate at their own peril. A workable definition, then, should accommodate the need for information, while promoting lawful practices and deterring abuses by providing guidance to those official actors who detain and interrogate others; it should also make possible accountability when interrogators step over the line. Finally, defining torture to include almost anything that involves the infliction of "any level of physical or emotional pain" arguably undermines the ultimate power of the norm:

> Some commentators define torture incredibly broadly to include the infliction of virtually any level of physical or emotional pain. . . . The problem with such a definition is that it knows no real limits; if virtually anything can constitute torture, the concept loses some of its ability to shock and disgust. [U]niversal condemnation may evaporate when the definition is so all encompassing. . . .
>
> Moreover, to condemn everything equally as torture may lead to the unintended result of creating a sliding scale of torture — a "rating" of torture methods. For example, one commentator suggested that "medium" or "moderate" torture might be acceptable to prevent future terrorist attacks. What exactly is that, and how do we set limits?

Marcy Strauss, Torture, 48 N.Y.L. Sch. L. Rev. 201, 215-216 (2003-2004).

2. The first requisite of torture under CAT and under §2340(1) is an "act." The law in the United Kingdom, by contrast, provides that "it is immaterial whether the pain or suffering . . . is caused by an act or omission." Canada, too, provides that "any act or omission by which severe pain or suffering" is imposed constitutes torture. Gail H. Miller, Defining Torture 7 (Floersheimer Center for Constitutional Democracy, Cardozo Law School, Yeshiva University 2005). Does a failure to refer in the text to intentional omissions — such as the failure to provide food, water, or pain medication — mean that such practices are not prohibited? Is an intentional omission an "act"?

3. Under any definition, it appears that the heart of the crime of torture is conduct that inflicts *severe* physical or mental pain or suffering. But just how does one calibrate

"severe" pain? The heart of the OLC torture and techniques memos is, quite simply, the assertion that while the EITs inflict pain and suffering, it does not rise to the level of *severe* pain and suffering. Notice that the U.S. RUDs to the Convention Against Torture (reprinted above) define and limit the meaning of severe *mental* pain or suffering, and the U.S. torture statutes mirror that limitation: Severe mental pain or suffering is the prolonged mental harm resulting from physical torture or threatened physical torture, mind-altering substances, or death threats. But there is no corresponding definition of severe physical pain or suffering.

The European Convention, in Article 3, provides for a nonderogable ban on torture: "No one shall be subject to torture or to inhuman or degrading treatment or punishment." The European Court for Human Rights (ECHR) "is generally lauded for its extensive and detailed jurisprudence interpreting Article 3 of the Convention, with the predictable caveat of academic and policy quibbles around individual decisions." Fionnuala Ní Aoláin, The European Convention on Human Rights and Its Prohibition on Torture, in Torture: A Collection 213, 213 (S. Levinson ed., 2004).

Note that there is not an exact correspondence between Article 3 of the European Convention and CAT: CAT contains an explicit ban on "cruel" treatment or punishment, but that word is not mentioned in Article 3. That said, the ECHR's jurisprudence provides an excellent source for attempting to isolate how persons and governments outside the United States (and some persons within it) define torture, and how they distinguish that concept from lesser forms of abuse, including cruel (for purposes of CAT) and "inhuman or degrading treatment or punishment." See also Assn. for the Prevention of Torture & Center for Justice & Intl. Law, Torture in International Law: A Guide to Jurisprudence (2008) (summarizing, inter alia, torture jurisprudence of UN bodies and European, Inter-American, and African regional tribunals).

The ECHR, in deciding cases under Article 3, has drawn an explicit hierarchy, differentiating between (1) "torture"; (2) "deliberate inhuman treatment causing very serious and cruel suffering"; and (3) inhuman or degrading treatment. Askoy v. Turkey, 23 Eur. H.R. Rep. 553, ¶63 (1996). This hierarchy is not absolute; that is, the categories to some extent meld into each other and the ECHR's categorization of practices seems to evolve with time. See, e.g., Yutaka Arai-Yokoi, Grading Scale of Degradation: Identifying the Threshold of Degrading Treatment or Punishment Under Article 3 ECHR, 21 Netherlands Q. Hum. Rts. 385, 387 (2003). The ECHR does not need to draw as sharp a distinction as may be required under CAT because the European Convention imposes a single, uniform ban on torture and CIDTP, while CAT, as we shall see, treats torture and CIDTP very differently.

That said, the ECHR reasons that "[t]he distinction between torture and inhuman or degrading treatment derived principally from a difference in the intensity of the suffering inflicted. . . . The term 'torture' attached a special stigma to deliberate inhuman treatment causing very serious and cruel suffering." Republic of Ireland v. United Kingdom, 2 Eur. H.R. Rep. (ser. A) 25, 36 (1978). Does this standard get one much beyond a "we know it when we see it" definition?

4. CAT does not attempt to define the word *severe*, although the first draft of the Convention defined torture as an "aggravated and deliberate form of cruel, inhuman or degrading treatment or punishment." Miller, supra, at 9. This definition seems to focus on the "aggravated and deliberate" methods employed. Should the torture definition focus on objective consideration of methods or should (in addition or instead) consideration be given to the subjective ("deliberate") intention of the torturer?

What about the subjective experience of the victim? Different people may experience pain differently; ultimately, what may impose "severe" suffering on me may be more tolerable for you. Should the definition of torture depend on the victim's pain threshold? The ECHR does expressly refer, among other more objective factors, to the *subjective* experience of the victim to assess the severity of the pain inflicted for purposes of deciding whether given conduct constituted "torture." As Gail Miller explains, "The ECHR approaches the severity of the act within the context of the particular case, considering factors such as the physical and mental effects on the person experiencing the harm, the duration of the act, and the age, sex, and culture of the person experiencing the harm." Miller, supra, at 10. What might be the drawbacks of relying on such a subjective inquiry?

5. Should lawyers, instead of attempting to ascertain the subjective severity of pain inflicted, attempt to evaluate the permissibility of specific types of pain-inducing conduct? One might question the usefulness of this seemingly more "objective" approach after reviewing two of the most famous decisions in which courts focused on the permissibility of the methods used.

In the first, Republic of Ireland v. United Kingdom, 2 Eur. H.R. Rep. (ser. A) 25, 36 (1978), the ECHR concluded that wall standing (forcing detainees to remain for hours spread-eagled against a wall, with their fingers placed high above their head against the wall, their legs spread apart and feet back, causing them to stand on their toes with the weight of their bodies mainly on their fingers), hooding for extended periods of time, subjection to continuous loud noise, and deprivation of sleep, food, and drink all constituted inhuman and degrading treatment or punishment but "did not occasion suffering of the particular intensity and cruelty implied by the word torture." Id. at 36.

This opinion, however, is of questionable future assistance, for two reasons. First, as Fionnuala Ní Aoláin notes, were the ECHR to decide this case using the standards it employs today, "the outcome might well be a very different one." Fionnuala Ní Aoláin, supra, at 216. For example, in Selmouni v. France, App. No. 25803/94, 29 Eur. H.R. Rep. 403, ¶101 (1999), the ECHR held that severe beatings, sexual abuse, and threats amounted to torture:

> [C]ertain acts which were classified in the past as "inhuman and degrading" as opposed to "torture" could be classified differently in the future. . . . [T]he increasingly high standard being required in the area of the protection of human rights and fundamental liberties correspondingly and inevitably requires greater firmness in assessing breaches of the fundamental values of democratic societies.

See also Aksoy v. Turkey, App. No. 21987/93, 23 Eur. H.R. Rep. 553 (1996) (holding that suspension by arms tied behind the back, which was deliberately inflicted on the detainee, was of "such a serious and cruel nature that it could only be described as torture"); Aydin v. Turkey, App. No. 23178/94, 25 Eur. H.R. Rep. 251 (1997) (concluding that the accumulation of acts of violence such as isolation, blindfolding, nudity, hosing with pressurized water, and rape of a detainee by security forces amounted to torture); İlhan v. Turkey, App. No. 22277/93, 34 Eur. H.R. Rep. 869 (2000) (beating with sticks and rifle butts while in police custody and delayed medical treatment constituted torture); Akkoç v. Turkey, App. Nos. 22947/93 and 22948/93 (2000) (electric shocks, hot and cold water treatment, blows to the head, and psychological pressures constituted torture).

Second, Professor Ní Aoláin tells us that the Ireland case "needs to be read in the context of its time as a highly sensitive political case — a leading Western democracy being accused of systematic torture, in the context of a fraught internal conflict in Northern Ireland to which the British government had committed its military forces. In such a context, the decision should be read as much in terms of its political weight as the practices being examined." Fionnuala Ní Aoláin, supra, at 216.

In the second important case, HCJ 5100/94 Public Committee Against Torture in Israel v. Israel [1999] IsrSC 43(4) 817, the Israeli Supreme Court held unlawful (while avoiding specifically labeling them "torture") the following tactics described at length in the opinion: violent shaking, excessive tightening of handcuffs, sleep deprivation, hooding for long periods, playing loud music for prolonged periods, the "Shabach" or "frog" position (placing a detainee in a low chair with a downward-tilting seat and his arms in an uncomfortable position), and a combination of the above. In deciding that these were prohibited means, however, the court provided its conclusion but little analysis, stating, for example, that shaking "harms the suspect's body," "violates his dignity," and "surpasses that which is necessary," id. ¶24, without specifying whether each finding was necessary, or sufficient, to its ruling that shaking is unlawful.

6. One of the difficulties of focusing on particular techniques is deciding whether to evaluate them alone or together. There is also a temporal dimension to be dealt with: Often, various interrogation methods are used over a period of time. For example, a prisoner may be subjected to sleep deprivation, a practice augmented over time with other means — use of loud music, forced stress positions, and the like. To evaluate whether the victim's experience rises to the level of torture, should one evaluate the coercive methods brought to bear on him singly, or attempt to judge what combination, and over what time period, may constitute "torture"? The former is obviously artificial, but the latter provides little guidance for those seeking to locate a firm border between that which is permitted and that which is not. Should those who draft these definitions — particularly those to be employed in criminal cases — provide greater guidance on these types of application questions? For example, should torture definitions generally include, as does Greece, a requirement that "infliction" of severe pain be "systematic," or, as does Latvia, a requirement that the torturer inflict "multiple or prolonged acts" upon the victim? Miller, supra, at 7; see also Bati v. Turkey, App. Nos. 3097/96 and 57834/00 (2005) (ECHR making explicit that the accumulation over time of acts that may not be sufficiently "severe" individually may add up to torture).

In May 2005, the OLC issued a companion opinion to the one discussing the 13 individual CIA techniques enumerated in the problem above. The companion opinion concluded that combining the techniques does not push them over the threshold to torture. OLC found the use of sleep deprivation in combination with other techniques the most problematic because "sleep deprivation might lower a detainee's tolerance for pain," which "might be more likely . . . to place the detainee in a state of severe physical distress and, therefore, that the detainee might be more likely to experience severe physical suffering." U.S. Dept. of Justice, Office of Legal Counsel, Memorandum for John A. Rizzo, Senior Deputy General Counsel, CIA, from Steven G. Bradbury, re: Application of 18 U.S.C. §§2340-2340A to the Combined Use of Certain Techniques in the Interrogation of High Value al Qaeda Detainees, at 16 (May 10, 2005), available at http://luxmedia.vo.llnwd.net/o10/clients/aclu/olc_05102005_bradbury_20pg.pdf. The OLC memo responded to the worry as follows:

> However, you have informed us that the interrogation techniques at issue would not
> be used during a course of extended sleep deprivation with such frequency and inten-
> sity as to induce in the detainee a persistent condition of extreme physical distress

such as may constitute "severe physical suffering" within the meaning of Sections 2340-2340A. . . . Based on these assumptions, . . . we conclude that the combination of techniques . . . would not be expected by the interrogators to cause "severe physical . . . suffering." . . .

Id. at 16-17. Do you find this analysis plausible? Or is it circular?

7. When thinking "torture," many people immediately imagine *physical* acts that make them cringe. There are also, however, various techniques that are designed to inflict intense psychological suffering. It is sometimes difficult to separate the two because physical harm can also cause psychic injury, and psychological suffering may manifest itself in physical injury. For example, some forms of waterboarding can result in physical effects, including pain and damage to the lungs and brain damage caused by oxygen deprivation. At the same time, according to Dr. Allen Keller, the director of the Bellevue/N.Y.U. Program for Survivors of Torture, victims of water-boarding also experience significant psychological pain: in a *New Yorker* interview, Keller is quoted as saying that "[s]ome victims were still traumatized years later. . . . One patient couldn't take showers, and panicked when it rained. 'The fear of being killed is a terrifying experience.'" Jane Mayer, Outsourcing Torture: The Secret History of America's "Extraordinary Rendition" Program, New Yorker, Feb. 14, 2005, available at http://www.newyorker.com/archive/2005/02/14/050214fa_fact6.

That said, commonly cited examples of psychological techniques include sleep deprivation, playing loud music constantly, keeping the lights on or off for extended periods, and hooding suspects. Credible threats to, for example, harm members of the victim's family may also constitute torture, even if the threats are not fulfilled.

The U.S. RUDs and 18 U.S.C. §2340, reproduced above, attempt to narrow the scope of *mental* pain or suffering, in part by defining the qualifying anguish by reference to its source. Also, the mental pain or suffering, under U.S. definitions, must be "prolonged." Does this mean that the pain be constant and endure over a lengthy period of time? Would "periodic yet debilitating flashbacks suffice"? Miller, supra, at 12. Note that the UN Committee Against Torture, in its most recent country review of the United States, requested that the United States "ensure that acts of psychological torture, prohibited by the Convention, were not limited to 'prolonged mental harm,' but constituted a wider category of acts, which caused severe mental suffering, irrespective of their prolongation or duration." Committee Against Torture Concludes Thirty-Sixth Session (May 19, 2006), available at http://www.unog .ch/80256EDD006B9C2E/(httpNewsByYear_en)/5FBB9C351B9E70EBC1257173004 EB4CE?OpenDocument. How *should* mental torture be defined?

8. Notice that CAT requires that the severe pain and suffering be inflicted for a particular purpose, such as information gathering, to qualify as torture, but §2340 has no such requirement. What function does this purpose requirement serve? Gail H. Miller notes that

> [i]t is unclear why some countries have decided to refer to specific purposes and others have not. Perhaps the purpose requirement is intended to be a means of contextualizing the crime to distinguish torture from other forms of abuse. On the other hand, lack of a purpose requirement may be an attempt to capture all potential forms of extreme violence by public officials.

Miller, supra, at 17. As far is CAT is concerned, Miller explains that "it is evident from the text that not just any purpose will do; otherwise the reference to purpose would be meaningless." Id. at 15-16. But according to CAT's Senate Report, "[t]he purposes given are not exhaustive, as is indicated by the phrasing 'for such purposes as.' Rather, they indicate the type of motivation that typically underlies torture, and emphasize the requirement for deliberate intention and malice." Sen. Exec. Rep. No. 101-30, at 14 (Aug. 30, 1990). The last purpose identified in CAT, "for any reason based on discrimination of any kind," is different from the other purposes. "Discrimination is more akin to a reason or motivation as opposed to a goal such as interrogation or punishment." Miller, supra, at 16.

9. Section 2340 requires that the tortuous act be done with the *specific intent* to inflict severe physical or mental pain or suffering. Under CAT, the act by which such pain or suffering is caused must be "*intentionally* inflicted on a person." (Emphasis added.) Is this a meaningful difference? Does the ICC Statute require a showing of specific intent?

If one is attempting to place the term *specific intent* in the landscape of the Model Penal Code (MPC), the Supreme Court has said that *specific intent* corresponds generally with "purposely." United States v. Bailey, 444 U.S. 394, 405 (1980). Under the MPC §2.02, a person who causes a particular result is said to act "purposely" if "it is his conscious object to . . . cause such a result." But what must be the *object* of this specific intent or purpose in the torture crime context? That is, must an actor (1) specifically intend (act with the purpose) to perform a painful act; (2) specifically intend by that act (act with the purpose) to inflict severe pain and suffering on the victim; (3) specifically intend (act with the purpose) to torture the victim; and/or (4) specifically intend (act with the purpose) to get information for an identified purpose such as intelligence gathering? The answer appears to be that (1) and (2) are required, while (3) and (4) are not. Intuitively, this analysis implies that "I wasn't trying to make him hurt, I was trying to get him to talk" is not a defense against charges of torture, but "I was trying to make him hurt, but not severely" may be a defense.

The Third Circuit explored this question in an immigration case, Auguste v. Ridge, 395 F.3d 123 (3d Cir. 2005). It ruled that "in the context of the Convention, for an act to constitute torture, there must be a showing that the actor had the intent to commit the act as well as the intent to achieve the consequences of the act, namely the infliction of the severe pain and suffering." Id. at 145-146. The court noted that "if the actor intended the act but did not intend the consequences of the act, i.e., the infliction of the severe pain and suffering, although such pain and suffering may have been a foreseeable consequence, the specific intent standard would not be satisfied." Id. at 146. The Third Circuit then made clear that an intent to torture "is not required under the specific intent standard." Id. It clarified that "the act be specifically intended to inflict severe pain and suffering, not that the actor intended to commit torture"; in the court's view, these "two are distinct and separate inquiries." Id.

Finally, the government need not prove that the severe pain and suffering were inflicted with the specific intent to achieve a given purpose, such as gathering information or punishment. Generally speaking, the motive behind an act, which this last level of intent would require, is irrelevant to criminal liability.

Clear? Sorting this out may require reference to the presumed purpose underlying this specific intent requirement. Without the specific intent requirement of §2340, a government-employed dentist performing oral surgery in Germany or a cardiologist performing a bypass on a U.S. military base in Japan might be guilty of torture because they intentionally performed actions *knowing* they would be severely painful. Specific intent is essential to guarantee that innocents do not get convicted of torture by making it clear that the torturer must act for the *purpose* of causing severe pain. This intent requirement, however, is *not* designed to give a pass to persons whose *motives* may be patriotic but who nonetheless are acting with the intention and purpose of inflicting pain. Perhaps the clearest way to express the difference is to note that the dentist or cardiologist would perform the surgery even if it were not painful (and indeed would probably prefer that it not be), but the interrogator would not torture if it did not hurt. He may not specifically intend to *torture*, he may regret that torture is necessary to serve his noble ends, but he certainly knowingly and purposefully intends to inflict severe pain and thus has the mental state required to be found guilty of torture.

10. An important limitation included in CAT is its requirement that the abusive activity, to constitute "torture," must be done "by or at the instigation or with the consent or acquiescence of a public official or other person acting in an official capacity." CAT art. 1(1). Is there a meaningful difference between this requirement and the requisite "acting under color of law" used in §2340's prohibition on torture?

The United States, in its RUDs to CAT, noted that the term *acquiescence,* as used in Article 1, requires that the public official, prior to the activity constituting torture, have an awareness of such activity and thereafter breach her legal responsibility to intervene to prevent such activity. In the report accompanying Senate consent to CAT, as well as subsequent case law decided in the immigration context, *acquiescence* is read to include both actual knowledge *and* "willful blindness." Sen. Exec. Rep. No. 101-30, supra, at 9; see also, e.g., Zheng v. Ashcroft, 332 F.3d 1186 (9th Cir. 2003) (rejecting standard that would require showing that governmental actors were "willfully accepting" of private torture under 8 C.F.R. §208.18(a)(7)). Does §2340A permit the imposition of criminal liability on this basis?

It is clear that "the Convention applies only to torture that occurs in the context of governmental authority, excluding torture that occurs as a wholly private act." Sen. Exec. Rep. No. 101-30, supra, at 14. *Should* torture be confined to *official* torture? Does CAT's inclusion of those official actors who "acquiesce" in torture potentially expand its proscription to private torture to which the government remains willfully blind?

11. The exception in CAT's definition for pain and suffering resulting from lawful sanctions was controversial. The reason the United States favored this exception was to clarify the continuing legitimacy of capital punishment. But if national law authorizes beatings, stoning to death, flogging, or amputation for certain crimes, should such sanctions be exempted from the limitations of CAT?

"In the view of the United States, the term 'sanctions' also embraces law enforcement actions other than judicially imposed sanctions," including penalties imposed in order to induce compliance. Sen. Exec. Rep. No. 101-30, supra, at 14. Although CAT does not specify whether the "lawfulness" of sanctions is determined by domestic or international law, the U.S. Senate embraced the view that the former should provide the relevant standard. "Although law enforcement actions authorized by U.S. law are not performed with the specific intent to cause excruciating and agonizing pain or suffering and therefore do not meet the definition of torture contained in Article 1, we believe it is desirable to express the understanding that the 'lawfulness' of such actions would be determined by U.S. law or by judicial interpretation of the law, in order to guard against illegitimate claims that such law enforcement actions constitute torture." Id. at 14.

12. The U.S. Senate declared that the provisions of Articles 1 through 16 of CAT are non-self-executing, "by which it meant they do not establish rights enforceable in United States courts unless and until Congress has approved implementing legislation." David Stewart, The Torture Convention and the Reception of International Criminal Law Within the United States, 15 Nova L. Rev. 449, 467-468 (1991). As we know, this proviso limits the domestic effect of CAT but does not limit or alter the

extent of the United States' obligations under international law. CAT provides in Article 2(2) that "[n]o exceptional circumstances whatsoever, whether a state of war or a threat of war, internal political instability or any other public emergency, may be a justification for torture." Yet Article 2(2) is not incorporated into either §2340 or §2340A. What, then, is its status or effect under U.S. law? Review the discussion of self-execution and the *Medellín* decision in Chapter 2.

Could one argue that Article 2(2) should be read into the torture statutes as a matter of *statutory* interpretation — that is, that Congress's failure, in implementing the torture ban, to negate Article 2(2) indicates a congressional intent to implement CAT's non derogable prohibition? According to the State Department's analysis of CAT when submitting it to Congress, this blanket prohibition was viewed by CAT's drafters as "necessary if the Convention is to have significant effect, as public emergencies are commonly invoked as a source of extraordinary powers or as a justification for limiting fundamental rights and freedoms." President's Message to Congress Transmitting the Convention Against Torture and Other Cruel, Inhuman, or Degrading Treatment or Punishment (CAT), Summary and Analysis of CAT, May 23, 1988, S. Treaty Doc. No. 100-20, reprinted in 13857 U.S. Cong. Serial Set at 5 (1990) [hereinafter S. Treaty Doc. No. 100-20]. Because the executive and the Senate evidently believed that U.S. law, at both the federal and state levels, was in compliance with the Convention, little action was deemed necessary to implement the treaty. Stewart, supra, 15 Nova L. Rev. at n.67. In such circumstances, what inference should be drawn from Congress's failure to disclaim any "emergency exception" to the scope of §2340A?

The total ban on torture was U.S. policy in 1999, when the State Department filed its Initial Report with the Committee Against Torture quoted in the introduction to this chapter, but, more recently, the OLC argued in the Bybee Memo that self-defense or necessity might justify torture, at least in the context of the war on terror. Does this change the statutory analysis?

13. It is critical to understand that §2340A applies only to torture or attempted torture "outside the United States." This restriction apparently stemmed from the belief that torture committed within the United States was already criminalized under a variety of state and federal laws that, although not specifically addressed to torture per se, were thought to cover the conduct subject to the torture proscription (for example, under state law, crimes such as assault and murder; under federal law crimes ranging from assault, maiming, murder, and kidnapping to civil rights offenses). See S. Exec. Rep. No. 101-30, supra, at 18-20. Human rights activists object that the "problems with these standard felony crimes are that they may not be applicable in many abuse cases and often carry lower sentences than the Torture and War Crimes Statutes." John Sifton, United States Military and Central Intelligence Agency Personnel Abroad: Plugging the Prosecutorial Gaps, 43 Harv. J. Legis. 487, 503 (2006). The UN Committee Against Torture in May 2006 expressed a concern that §2340A does not, by its terms, apply to acts of torture inside the United States. Committee Against Torture, Convention Against Torture and Other Cruel, Inhuman, or Degrading Treatment or Punishment, ¶13, U.N. Doc. CAT/C/USA/CO/2 (July 25, 2006).

Might one use the conspiracy prohibition in §2340A to skirt this issue? That is, could one argue that even if a particular official's own actions were taken in the United States, if he conspired with others to torture someone abroad, he can be liable for their conduct? Consider, in this respect, Chapter 7.C, discussing Harbury v. Deutch, 233 F.3d 596 (D.C. Cir. 2000), *rev'd on other grounds*, 536 U.S. 403 (2002), *aff'g dismissal after remand on other grounds*, 522 F.3d 413 (D.C. 2008).

14. There was a significant hole in coverage of torture abroad under §2340A as originally enacted. Until 2004, the term *United States* referred to all areas under the

jurisdiction of the United States, including those falling within its special maritime and territorial jurisdiction (SMTJ), such as embassies, military bases, and other buildings abroad when the crime was committed by a U.S. national. See 18 U.S.C. §2340(3) (2003). Thus, because the torture statute by its terms applied only *outside* the United States, it did not apply to SMTJ jurisdiction, including such places as Guantánamo Bay, Abu Ghraib, bases in Iraq and Afghanistan where detainees were abused, and the "secret" CIA detention facilities. It appears, then, that under the technical terms of the statute, torture committed between 2002 and 2004 in those locations could not be prosecuted under §2340A. In response to Abu Ghraib, Congress amended the statute in 2004 to define *United States* without reference to the SMTJ; oddly, by narrowing the definition of *United States*, this amendment had the effect of expanding the coverage of the torture prohibition.

3.   *Application: The Bybee and Levin Memos*

BYBEE MEMO

Memorandum from Jay S. Bybee to Alberto Gonzales
(Aug. 1, 2002)

You have asked for our Office's views regarding the standards of conduct under [CAT] as implemented by Sections 2340-2340A of title 18 of the United States Code. As we understand it, this question has arisen in the context of the conduct of interrogations outside of the United States. . . .

We conclude that for an act to constitute torture as defined in Section 2340, it must inflict pain that is difficult to endure. Physical pain amounting to torture must be equivalent in intensity to the pain accompanying serious physical injury, such as organ failure, impairment of bodily function, or even death. For purely mental pain or suffering to amount to torture under Section 2340, it must result in significant psychological harm of significant duration, e.g., lasting for months or even years. . . . We conclude that the statute, taken as a whole, makes plain that it prohibits only extreme acts. . . .

B. "SEVERE PAIN OR SUFFERING"

The key statutory phrase in the definition of torture is the statement that acts amount to torture if they cause "severe physical or mental pain or suffering." In examining the meaning of a statute, its text must be the starting point. . . . Section 2340 makes plain that the infliction of pain or suffering per se, whether it is physical or mental, is insufficient to amount to torture. Instead, the text provides that pain or suffering must be "severe." The statute does not, however, define the term "severe." "In the absence of such a definition, we construe a statutory term in accordance with its ordinary or natural meaning." FDIC v. Meyer, 510 U.S. 471, 476 (1994). [The memo then sets out several dictionary definitions of "severe."] Thus, the adjective "severe" conveys that the pain or suffering must be of such a high level of intensity that the pain is difficult for the subject to endure.

Congress' use of the phrase "severe pain" elsewhere in the United States Code can shed more light on its meaning. See, e.g., West Va. Univ. Hosps., Inc. v. Casey, 499 U.S. 83, 100 (1991) ("[W]e construe [a statutory term] to contain that permissible meaning which fits most logically and comfortably into the body of both previously and subsequently enacted law."). Significantly, the phrase "severe pain" appears in statutes defining an emergency medical condition for the purpose of providing health benefits. See, e.g., 8 U.S.C. §1369 (2000); 42 U.S.C. §1395w-22 (2000); id. §1395x (2000); id. §1395dd (2000); id. §1396b (2000); id. §1396u-2 (2000). These statutes define an emergency medical condition as one "manifesting itself by acute symptoms of sufficient severity (including *severe pain*) such that a prudent lay person, who possesses an average knowledge of health and medicine, could reasonably expect the absence of immediate medical attention to result in — placing the health of the individual . . . (i) in serious jeopardy; (ii) serious impairment to bodily functions, or (iii) serious dysfunction of any bodily organ or part." Id. §1395w-22(d)(3)(B) (emphasis added). Although these statutes address a substantially different subject from Section 2340, they are nonetheless helpful for understanding what constitutes severe physical pain. They treat severe pain as an indicator of ailments that are likely to result in permanent and serious physical damage in the absence of immediate medical treatment. Such damage must rise to the level of death, organ failure, or the permanent impairment of a significant bodily function. These statutes suggest that "severe pain," as used in Section 2340, must rise to a similarly high level — the level that would ordinarily be associated with a sufficiently serious physical condition or injury such as death, organ failure, or serious impairment of body functions — in order to constitute torture. . . .

"*Prolonged Mental Harm.*" As an initial matter, Section 2340(2) requires that the severe mental pain must be evidenced by "prolonged mental harm." To prolong is to "lengthen in time" or to "extend the duration of, to draw out." Webster's Third New International Dictionary 1815 (1988); Webster's New International Dictionary 1980 (2d ed. 1935). Accordingly, . . . the acts giving rise to the harm must cause some lasting, though not necessarily permanent, damage. For example the mental strain experienced by an individual during a lengthy and intense interrogation — such as one that state or local police might conduct upon a criminal suspect — would not violate Section 2340(2). On the other hand, the development of a mental disorder such as post-traumatic stress disorder, which can last months or even years, or even chronic depression, which also can last for a considerable period of time if untreated, might satisfy the prolonged harm requirement. . . .

A defendant must specifically intend to cause prolonged mental harm for the defendant to have committed torture. It could be argued that a defendant needs to have specific intent only to commit the predicate acts that give rise to prolonged mental harm. Under that view, so long as the defendant specifically intended to, for example, threaten a victim with imminent death, he would have had sufficient mens rea for a conviction. . . . We believe that this approach is contrary to the text of the statute. . . .

V. The President's Commander-in-Chief Power

Even if an interrogation method arguably were to violate Section 2340A, the statute would be unconstitutional if it impermissibly encroached on the President's constitutional power to conduct a military campaign. As Commander-in-Chief, the President has the constitutional authority to order interrogations of enemy combatants to gain intelligence information concerning the military plans of the enemy. . . . Any effort to apply Section 2340A in a manner that interferes with the President's direction of such core war matters as the detention and interrogation of enemy combatants thus would be unconstitutional.

LEVIN MEMO

Memorandum from Daniel Levin to James B. Comey
(Dec. 24, 2004)

. . . This memorandum supersedes the August 2002 Memorandum in its entirety. Because the discussion in that memorandum concerning the President's Commander-in-Chief power and the potential defenses to liability was—and remains—unnecessary, it has been eliminated from the analysis that follows. Consideration of the bounds of any such authority would be inconsistent with the President's unequivocal directive that United States personnel not engage in torture.

We have also modified in some important respects our analysis of the legal standards applicable under 18 U.S.C. §§2340-2340A. For example, we disagree with statements in the August 2002 Memorandum limiting "severe" pain under the statute to "excruciating and agonizing" pain, or to pain "equivalent in intensity to the pain accompanying serious physical injury, such as organ failure, impairment of bodily function, or even death. . . ." There are additional areas where we disagree with or modify the analysis in the August 2002 Memorandum, as identified in the discussion below.[49] . . .

Although Congress defined "torture" under sections 2340-2340A to require conduct specifically intended to cause "severe" pain or suffering, we do not believe Congress intended to reach only conduct involving "excruciating or agonizing" pain or suffering. Although there is some support for this formulation in the ratification history of CAT, a proposed express understanding to that effect was "criticized for setting too high a threshold of pain," S. Exec. Rep. No. 101-30 at 9, and was not adopted. . . .[50]

Drawing distinctions among gradations of pain (for example, severe, mild, moderate, substantial, extreme, intense, excruciating, or agonizing) is obviously not an easy task, especially given the lack of any precise, objective scientific criteria for measuring pain. We are, however, aided in this task by judicial interpretations of the Torture Victims Protection Act ("TVPA"). . . . The TVPA . . . provides a civil remedy to victims of torture. . . .

---

49. [Levin's footnote 8:] While we have identified various disagreements with the August 2002 Memorandum, we have reviewed this Office's prior opinions addressing issues involving treatment of detainees and do not believe that any of their conclusions would be different under the standards set forth in this memorandum.

50. [Levin's footnote 17:] . . . The August 2002 Memorandum also looked to the use of "severe pain" in certain other statutes, and concluded that to satisfy the definition in section 2340, pain "must be equivalent in intensity to the pain accompanying serious physical injury, such as organ failure, impairment of bodily function, or even death." We do not agree with those statements. Those other statutes define an "emergency medical condition," for purposes of providing health benefits. . . . They do not define "severe pain" even in that very different context (rather, they use it as an indication of an "emergency medical condition"), and they do not state that death, organ failure, or impairment of bodily function cause "severe pain," but rather that "severe pain" may indicate a condition that, if untreated, could cause one of those results. We do not believe that they provide a proper guide for interpreting "severe pain" in the very different context of the prohibition against torture in sections 2340-2340A. Cf. United States v. Cleveland Indians Baseball Co., 532 U.S. 200, 213 (2001) (phrase "wages paid" has different meaning in different parts of Title 26); Robinson v. Shell Oil Co., 519 U.S. 337, 343-44 (1997) (term "employee" has different meanings in different parts of Title VII).

. . . Cases in which courts have found torture suggest the nature of the extreme conduct that falls within the statutory definition. [The memo then summarizes the conduct constituting torture in four TVPA decisions:] a course of conduct that included, among other things, severe beatings of the plaintiff, repeated threats of death and electric shock, sleep deprivation, extended shackling to a cot (at times with a towel over his nose and mouth and water poured down his nostrils), seven months of confinement in a "suffocatingly hot" and cramped cell, and eight years of solitary or near-solitary confinement . . . ; severe beatings to the genitals, head and other parts of the body with metal pipes, brass knuckles, batons, a baseball bat, and various other items; removal of teeth with pliers; kicking in the face and ribs; breaking of bones and ribs and dislocation of fingers; cutting a figure into the victim's forehead; hanging the victim and beating him; extreme limitations of food and water; and subjection to games of "Russian roulette" . . . ; "cutting off . . . fingers, pulling out . . . fingernails," and electric shocks to the testicles . . . ; frequent beatings, pistol whipping, threats of imminent death, electric shocks, and attempts to force confessions by playing Russian roulette and pulling the trigger at each denial, constituted torture. . . .

. . . The inclusion of the words "or suffering" in the phrase "severe physical pain or suffering" suggests that the statutory category of physical torture is not limited to "severe physical pain." . . . Exactly what is included in the concept of "severe physical suffering," however, is difficult to ascertain. . . . We conclude that under some circumstances "physical suffering" may be of sufficient intensity and duration to meet the statutory definition of torture even if it does not involve "severe physical pain." To constitute such torture, "severe physical suffering" would have to be a condition of some extended duration or persistence as well as intensity. . . .

Turning to the question of what constitutes "prolonged mental harm caused by or resulting from" a predicate act, we believe that . . . [the harm] has some lasting duration. . . .[51]

NOTES AND QUESTIONS

1. The Bybee Memo attracted a great deal of attention. Among its defenders were Professors Eric Posner (an OLC alumnus) and Adrian Vermeule, who asserted that "the memorandum's arguments are standard lawyerly fare, routine stuff." Eric Posner & Adrian Vermeule, A "Torture" Memo and Its Tortuous Critics," Wall St. J., July 6, 2004. They explain:

> The Justice Department memorandum came out of the OLC, whose jurisprudence has traditionally been highly pro-executive. . . . Not everyone likes OLC's traditional jurisprudence, or its awkward role as both defender and adviser of the executive branch; but former officials who claim that the OLC's function is solely to supply "disinterested" advice, or that it serves as a "conscience" for the government, are providing a sentimental, distorted and self-serving picture of a complex reality.

Id. John Yoo, they add, belongs to "a dynamic generation of younger scholars . . . who argue for an expansive conception of presidential power over foreign affairs." Id.

---

51. [Levin's footnote 24:] . . . Although we believe that the mental harm must be of some lasting duration to be "prolonged," to the extent that formulation was intended to suggest that the mental harm would have to last for at least "months or even years," we do not agree.

Other commentators were less flattering. Focusing particularly on the interpretation of "severe pain" in the criminal law of torture by drawing on Medicare statutes, Peter Brooks labeled the memo "textual interpretation run amok — less 'lawyering as usual' than the work of some bizarre literary deconstructionist." Peter Brooks, The Plain Meaning of Torture?, Slate, Feb. 9, 2005, http://www.slate.com/id/2113314. The voluminous academic commentary was almost entirely negative. See, e.g., David Luban, The Torture Lawyers of Washington, in Legal Ethics and Human Dignity (2007); H.H. Koh, Can the President Be Torturer in Chief?, 81 Indiana L.J. 1145 (2006); Julie Angell, Ethics, Torture, and Marginal Memoranda at the DOJ Office of Legal Counsel, 18 Geo. J. Legal Ethics 557 (2005); Kathleen Clark, Ethical Issues Raised by the OLC Torture Memorandum, 1 J. Natl. Sec. L. & Poly. 455 (2005); Ruth Wedgwood & R. James Woolsey, Law and Torture, Wall St. J., June 28, 2004; Richard B. Bilder & Detlev A. Vagts, Speaking Law to Power: Lawyers and Torture, 98 Am. J. Intl. L. 689 (2004).

Was the Bybee Memo's "organ failure or death" interpretation of the phrase "severe pain," derived from Medicare statutes, legally frivolous? Was it, as Brooks put it, "textual interpretation run amok," or was it (in Posner and Vermeule's words) "standard lawyerly fare, routine stuff"? Is there any objective way to tell?

2. Perhaps the strongest criticism came from an unexpected source: Jack Goldsmith, who describes himself as John Yoo's "friend and fellow legal academic," adding that he and Yoo "were part of a group of conservative intellectuals . . . who were skeptical about the creeping influence of international law on American law." Jack Goldsmith, The Terror Presidency: Law and Judgment Inside the Bush Administration 21 (2007). At Yoo's recommendation, Goldsmith was named to head OLC in 2003 after Jay Bybee's departure. Id. at 25. However, after reviewing the Bybee Memo and others, Goldsmith became alarmed and warned the Pentagon not to rely on the memos. In his memoirs, he writes that the Bybee Memo's "extreme conclusion [about executive power] has no foundation in prior OLC opinions, or in judicial decisions, or in any other source of law," and describes the opinion as a whole as "more an exercise of sheer power than reasoned analysis." Id. at 149, 150. In his own memoirs, Yoo insists that replacing his memo with the Levin Memo was a political rather than a legal decision. He points out that the Levin Memo states in a footnote (included in the excerpt above) that "we have reviewed this Office's prior opinions addressing issues involving treatment of detainees and do not believe that any of their conclusions would be different under the standards set forth in this memorandum." John Yoo, War by Other Means: An Insider's Account of the War on Terror 182-183 (2006).

3. Participants in formulating U.S. interrogation policy emphasize that at the time the torture memos were written, there was a great deal of fear within the government about a possible al Qaeda attack on or around the anniversary of 9/11. According to General Richard Myers, who chaired the Joint Chiefs of Staff at the time: "There was a sense of urgency that in my forty years of military experience hadn't existed in other contingencies." Philippe Sands, The Torture Team: Rumsfeld's Memo and the Betrayal of American Values 88 (2008). He explained that there was "the real fear that one of the detainees might know when the next attack would happen, and that they would miss vital information." Id. Should this influence what an executive branch lawyer puts in a legal opinion? Or is the decision to minimize relevant legal prohibitions one for policymakers, not lawyers?

In January 2009, five days before President Obama was sworn in, Steven Bradbury, the OLC's principal deputy assistant attorney general, issued a memorandum summarizing the status of certain OLC opinions issued in the aftermath of 9/11 and identifying nine memos that had been repudiated in whole or in part, including the Bybee Memo. Consider his explanation:

> The opinions addressed herein were issued in the wake of the atrocities of 9/11, when policy makers, fearing that additional catastrophic terrorist attacks were imminent, strived to employ all lawful means to protect the Nation. In the months following 9/11, attorneys in the Office of Legal Counsel and in the Intelligence Community confronted novel and complex legal questions in a time of great danger and under extraordinary time pressure. Perhaps reflecting this context, several of the opinions identified do not address specific and concrete policy proposals, but rather address in general terms the broad contours of legal issues potentially raised in the uncertain aftermath of the 9/11 attacks. Thus, several of these opinions represent a departure from this Office's preferred practice of rendering formal opinions addressed to particular policy proposals and not undertaking a general survey of a broad area of the law or addressing general or amorphous hypothetical scenarios involving difficult areas of law.

Steven G. Bradbury, Principal Deputy Assistant Attorney General, U.S. Dept. of Justice, Office of Legal Counsel, Memorandum for the Files 1 (Jan. 15, 2009).

4. Notice that the statute requires that severe *mental* pain or suffering must be prolonged, but has no parallel requirement for severe physical pain or suffering. The Levin Memo, however, also states that, to be torture under §2340, "severe *physical* suffering" would "have to be a condition of some extended duration or persistence as well as intensity" (emphasis added). Can the statute be read to support this requirement? The "duration or persistence" requirement turned out to be crucial in several subsequent OLC opinions determining that waterboarding is not torture because "[t]he physical distress of the waterboard . . . lasts only during the relatively short periods during a session when the technique is actually being used." Memorandum for John A. Rizzo, Senior Deputy General Counsel, CIA, from Steven G. Bradbury, re: Application of 18 U.S.C. §§2340-2340A to the Combined Use of Certain Techniques in the Interrogation of High Value al Qaeda Detainees (May 10, 2005), at 16, available at http://luxmedia.vo.llnwd.net/o10/clients/aclu/olc_05102005_bradbury_20pg.pdf. Reportedly, virtually everyone who is waterboarded "breaks" within a few seconds because the sensation is so unbearable. OLC reasoned that the physical distress caused by waterboarding would be "suffering" rather than "pain"; and if each waterboarding session lasts only a few seconds — the legal opinion approves waterboarding for at most 40 seconds per pour — the suffering, while intense, would not be prolonged, and therefore could not, as a matter of law, be "severe."

5. Daniel Levin, the author of the second Memo, reportedly had himself waterboarded while he was preparing it, in order to experience the technique firsthand. Jan Crawford Greenburg & Ariane deVogue, Bush Administration Blocked Waterboarding Critic, ABC News, Nov. 2, 2007, available at http://abcnews.go.com/WN/DOJ/story?id=3814076&page=1. Was Levin's action an instance of heroic conscientiousness or a misunderstanding of the lawyer's job? How could his experience be relevant to the interpretation of the torture statute? Alternatively, how else could he determine whether the pain or suffering of waterboarding rises to the statutory level of *severe*?

6. What guidance does the Levin Memo offer to interrogators trying to determine whether aggressive tactics are prohibited by the torture statutes? Would it lead them to steer clear of aggressive techniques such as manipulating room temperature, forcing detainees to stand for long periods of time, placing detainees in stress positions,

or waterboarding? Or would it encourage them because these are not as bad as the atrocities canvassed in the case law?

7. Did the Levin Memo truly change anything? Note that in May 2006, the U.S. government informed the Committee Against Torture that the Bybee Memo was withdrawn and replaced by another memo because it addressed matters "unnecessary" to its subject—the definition of *torture* for purposes of the U.S. criminal statute—and not because the definition it adopted was wrong. See Response of the United States of America, List of Issues to Be Considered During the Examination of the Second Periodic Report of the United States of America, Questions 1-2, at 1-3, http://www.state.gov/documents/organization/66172.pdf (last visited July 20, 2009).

Recall that the Levin Memo states in a footnote that "we have reviewed this Office's prior opinions addressing issues involving treatment of detainees and do not believe that any of their conclusions would be different under the standards set forth in this memorandum." However, Daniel Levin stated in testimony to the House Judiciary Committee that he "did *not* mean, as some have interpreted—and . . . this is my fault, no doubt, in drafting—that we had concluded that we would have reached the same conclusions as those earlier opinions did. We were in fact analyzing that at the time and we never completed that analysis." From the Department of Justice to Guantanamo Bay: Administration Lawyers and Administration Interrogation Rules (Part II), Hearing Before the S. Comm. on the Constitution, Civil Rights, and Civil Liberties of the H. Comm. on the Judiciary, 110th Cong., 42 (2008) (statement of Daniel Levin, White, & Case LLP). By May 2005, Levin's successor Steven Bradbury had completed three memoranda on the techniques and approved them all.

8. Some have argued that lawyers who participated in the approval of the EITs should be criminally prosecuted for aiding and abetting war crimes. See, e.g., Milan Markovic, Can Lawyers Be War Criminals?, 20 Geo. J. Legal Ethics 347 (2007). Markovic argues that "lawyers are potentially complicit in war crimes when they 'materially contribute' to the commission of crimes like torture. Writing a memorandum can qualify as a 'material contribution,' and precedents before the [International Criminal Tribunal for Former Yugoslavia] . . . and the Nuremberg Tribunals suggest that lawyers can be held liable as accomplices if their legal advice facilitated or encouraged the commission of illegal acts." Id. at 349. Others, including George Terwilliger, a former deputy solicitor general, have opined to the contrary, arguing essentially that "legal opinions have [n]ever caused anyone any injury." See Vanessa Blum, Culture of Yes: Signing Off on a Strategy, Legal Times, June 14, 2004, at 1.

Others have criticized efforts to go after the lawyers as a "witch hunt" and "the criminalization of policy differences." Even if potential criminal sanction were advisable, where would such a prosecution proceed? Could any of the states parties to CAT prosecute individuals responsible for U.S. policy? Efforts by human rights organizations to obtain criminal investigations in Europe under universal jurisdiction statutes were rebuffed by prosecutors in Germany and France. However, in 2009 a Spanish magistrate approved such an investigation of Bush administration lawyers. As this book goes to press, the question of whether to launch an investigation is still under consideration by the Spanish courts.

9. Some have suggested that the authors of the interrogation memos committed ethical violations by misstating the law. In 2004, the Justice Department's internal ethics office, the Office of Professional Responsibility (OPR), launched an investigation of lawyers involved in writing the Bybee Memo. As of November 2009, the OPR report has not been released.

B. CRUEL, INHUMAN, OR DEGRADING TREATMENT OR PUNISHMENT

1. *Definition and Consequences*

CAT requires each state party to:

(1) prevent acts of torture in "any territory under its jurisdiction," CAT art. 2(1);

(2) ensure that torture (including attempts to commit and complicity in torture) are criminal offenses under its domestic law, CAT art. 4(1); and

(3) cooperate with all other states parties to ensure that torturers will be criminally prosecuted by relying on "universal jurisdiction" and the duty to extradite or prosecute alleged torturers, CAT Arts. 5-9.

CAT requires that victims of torture committed within the state party's jurisdiction be provided enforceable rights of redress, compensation, and rehabilitation.[52] Under CAT Article 3, no state party is permitted to "expel, return (*"refouler"*) or extradite a person to another state where substantial grounds exist for believing that he or she would be in danger of being subject to torture."[53] (The U.S. RUDs specify that Article 3's non-refoulement provision applies where it is "more likely than not" that the individual in question would be tortured.) Finally, the prohibition on torture is nonderogable, even in times of war or national emergency, under Article 2.

The border between torture and CIDTP is an important one because Article 16 of the Convention, dealing with CIDTP, imposes far fewer obligations on states parties. Article 16(1) provides as follows:

> Each State Party shall undertake to prevent in any territory under its jurisdiction other acts of cruel, inhuman or degrading treatment or punishment which do not amount to torture as defined in article 1, when such acts are committed by or at the instigation of or with the consent or acquiescence of a public official or other person acting in an official capacity. . . .

Thus, CAT Article 16 requires states parties to *undertake to prevent* in any territory under its jurisdiction, *but not to prohibit or criminalize*, acts of cruel, inhuman or degrading treatment or punishment (CIDTP) not amounting to torture. The only other portions of CAT that, by their explicit terms, apply to both torture *and* CIDTP are those provisions that mandate that the states parties take certain educational and remedial measures to prevent such abuses.[54] The non-refoulement provision embodied in Article 3 does not on its face apply to the expulsion, return, or extradition of a person in danger of CIDTP.

Perhaps the most fundamental distinction between torture and CIDTP in CAT is that the nonderogation provision of Article 2 does not apply to CIDTP. By negative implication, the states parties to CAT have retained the ability (at least under CAT) to

---

52. See CAT art. 14; Torture Victims Protection Act of 1991, 28 U.S.C. §1350 et seq.

53. CAT art. 3(1) (emphasis added); see generally David Weissbrodt & Isabel Hortreiter, The Principle of Non-refoulement, 5 Buff. Hum. Rts. L. Rev. 1 (1999).

54. See CAT art. 16(1); CAT arts. 10-13 (requiring training of law enforcement personnel, review of interrogation techniques and detention rules and practices, investigation of violations by state authorities, and ensuring the right to bring a complaint for investigation).

employ, or at least the freedom to not prevent, cruel, inhuman, or degrading treatment or punishment during times of war or national emergency.

In short, CAT treats CIDTP very differently than torture — thus making this distinction critical. Unfortunately, CAT does not *define* CIDTP. Once again, reference may be made to the jurisprudence of the ECHR, which under Article 3 of the European Convention has struggled to make a similar distinction, treating torture as the apex of a three-tiered hierarchy of abuse, with "inhuman" treatment in the intermediate position and "degrading" treatment at the bottom. (Recall that Article 3, unlike CAT, does not contain a bar on "cruel" treatment or punishment, and so the two prohibitions are not textually identical.) To the extent one can generalize from the ECHR's voluminous and wide-ranging CIDTP jurisprudence, the difference between "torture" and "inhuman" treatment or punishment under the European Convention is one of degree, measured in both subjective and objective terms. The distinction appears to rest primarily on the intensity of the victim's felt suffering, the type of mistreatment involved (the application of electric shocks versus short period of sleep deprivation, for example), and the degree of deliberation and intention displayed by the torturer.[55] "Degrading" treatment, by contrast, appears to relate to a somewhat distinct category of abuses. Ní Aoláin explains that "[g]enerally, degrading treatment encompasses treatment or punishment that humiliates or demeans a person in a way that shows a lack of respect for his or her dignity and personhood. It is also characterized by the feelings it arouses in the victim, including inferiority, fear, anguish, and physical and mental suffering. The inflicted and experienced aspects of this come together when they operate to break an individual's moral and physical resistance."[56]

The ECHR's interpretation of the phrase "inhuman or degrading treatment or punishment" has, at times, varied from decisions on equivalent conduct under U.S. law. Recall our discussion of *Soering v. United Kingdom* in Chapter 10. In *Soering*, the ECHR decreed that the "death row phenomenon," which consists of the agony of waiting for years on death row pending the execution of a capital sentence, at least in some circumstances constitutes torture or inhuman or degrading treatment or punishment under Article 3 of the European Convention. U.S. courts, however, do not recognize the "death row phenomenon" as a valid claim under the Eighth Amendment's ban on "cruel and unusual" punishment.

At the time of ratification, the United States, concerned about decisions like *Soering* and uncertain how the CAT's "cruel, inhumane or degrading" phrase would be interpreted in future, conditioned its ratification of CAT on a formal reservation:

> [T]he United States considers itself bound by the obligation under Article 16 to prevent "cruel, inhuman or degrading treatment or punishment," only insofar as the term "cruel, inhuman or degrading treatment or punishment" means the cruel, unusual and inhumane treatment or punishment prohibited by the Fifth, Eighth, and/or Fourteenth Amendment to the Constitution of the United States.[57]

---

55. Fionnuala Ní Aoláin, The European Convention on Human Rights and Its Prohibition on Torture, in Torture: A Collection 213, 216-217 (S. Levinson ed., 2004).

56. Id. at 215; see also Yutaka Arai-Yokoi, Grading Scale of Degradation: Identifying the Threshold of Degrading Treatment or Punishment Under Article 3 ECHR, 21 Netherlands Q. Hum. Rts. 385, 389-391 (2003).

57. CAT, U.S. Reservations I(1) (emphasis added); see also David Stewart, The Torture Convention and the Reception of International Criminal Law Within the United States, 15 Nova L. Rev. 449, 460-612 (1991).

The State Department has suggested that the requirements of Article 16 concerning "degrading" treatment or punishment potentially include treatment that "probably would not be prohibited by the U.S. Constitution," citing, for example, the ECHR's conclusion that German officials' refusal to give formal recognition to an individual's sex change might constitute "degrading" treatment.[58] Thus, in May 2006, the United States informed the UN Committee Against Torture that this reservation meant that "the United States did not accept the obligation to prohibit 'cruel, unusual or *degrading* treatment or punishment' but to prevent 'cruel and unusual treatment or punishment' as proscribed by the U.S. Constitution."[59]

What does it mean to say that the scope of CIDTP, at least under U.S. law, is defined by reference to the Fifth, Eighth, and Fourteenth Amendments? No statutory definition is available to shed light on this question. The United States has no generally applicable federal statute that specifically criminalizes CIDTP and defines CIDTP for that purpose. (However, as we shall see, the federal war crimes statute outlaws torture and "cruel and inhuman" treatment in the context of certain armed conflicts.) The McCain Amendment, enacted to ensure that U.S. actors do not engage in CIDTP outside the borders of the United States, and examined at greater length below, specifically defines CIDTP in 42 U.S.C. §2000dd. But that section does not criminalize CIDTP and, in any case, defines it identically with the CAT reservation — that is, by reference to the Fifth, Eighth, and Fourteenth Amendments.

The case law, then, must control our analysis. Recall our discussion of the various lines of precedent, and confusing doctrinal tangle, governing due process standards in Chapter 7. What standard applies? The George W. Bush administration chose the position expressly adopted by only three Justices in *Chavez v. Martinez*.[60] Thus, Assistant Attorney General William E. Moschella advised Senator Patrick Leahy on January 25, 2005, in connection with former attorney general Alberto Gonzales's confirmation hearings, as follows:

> With respect to treatment of detainees by the United States Government, as opposed to punishment for crimes (which is governed by the Eighth Amendment) or treatment by state governments (which is governed by the Fourteenth Amendment), the pertinent Amendment is the Fifth Amendment. As relevant here, that Amendment protects against treatment that, in the words of the Supreme Court, "shocks the conscience," meaning (again in the words of the Court) "only the most egregious conduct," such as "conduct intended to injure in some way unjustifiable by any government interest." County of Sacramento v. Lewis, 523 U.S. 833, 845, 849 (1998).[61]

The OLC used the same analysis in its opinion on U.S. obligations under Article 16 of CAT. Pointing to cases such as *Chavez* where the Court found that police conduct did not "shock the conscience," OLC argued that "[t]he CIA program is considerably less invasive. . . . In addition, the government interest at issue in each of these cases was

58. President's Message to Congress Transmitting the Convention Against Torture and Other Cruel, Inhuman, or Degrading Treatment or Punishment, Summary and Analysis of the Convention Against Torture and Other Cruel, Inhuman, or Degrading Treatment or Punishment, May 23, 1988, S. Treaty Doc. No. 100-20 (1988), reprinted in 13857 U.S. Cong. Serial Set at 15 (1990).

59. Response of the United States of America, List of Issues to Be Considered During the Examination of the Second Periodic Report of the United States of America, Question 44, at 87, available at http://www.state.gov/documents/organization/66172.pdf (emphasis added).

60. 538 U.S. 760 (2003).

61. William E. Moschella, Asst. Atty. Gen., Letter to Hon. Patrick J. Leahy (April 4, 2005), available at http://www.scotusblog.com/movabletype/archives/CAT%20Article%2016.Leahy-Feinstein-Feingold%20Letters.pdf.

the general interest in ordinary law enforcement. . . . That government interest is strikingly different from what is at stake here: the national security—in particular, the protection of the United States against attacks that may result in massive civilian casualties."[62]

What are the implications of a standard that appears to define CIDTP by reference to both the nature of the abusive conduct *and* the government interest at stake?[63] According to OLC, "We do not conclude that any conduct, no matter how extreme, could be justified by a sufficiently weighty government interest coupled with appropriate tailoring."[64] But OLC does employ a balancing test weighing the abusiveness of the CIA techniques against national security—and concludes that all 13 techniques pass that test. None of them "shocks the conscience."

Is this balancing test a fair summary of the state of Supreme Court precedents on what does or does not shock the conscience? Recall the context of the excerpted quotation from *Lewis*: The Court was rejecting a proposed *negligence* standard for due process civil rights suits for damages in a case where the parents of a motorcycle passenger killed in a high-speed police chase sought damages based on an alleged deprivation of the passenger's substantive due process right to life. What the passage quoted by the Department of Justice says, *in context*, is that a *deliberate* act—an act *intended* to injure—was required before damages could be claimed.[65] The passage, which was, in any case, dicta, does not obviously support a claim that the "shocks the conscience" standard requires balancing the type of intentional harm inflicted and the governmental interest served.

Note too that the Supreme Court did not "balance" in *Rochin v. California*,[66] the case that gave birth to the due process "shocks the conscience" standard. In *Rochin*, three deputy sheriffs, acting on suspicion that Rochin was selling narcotics,

> forced open the door of [his] room . . . Inside they found [Rochin] sitting partly dressed on the side of the bed, upon which his wife was lying. On a "night stand" beside the bed the deputies spied two capsules. When asked "Whose stuff is this?" Rochin seized the capsules and put them in his mouth. A struggle ensued, in the course of which the three officers "jumped upon him" and attempted to extract the capsules. The force they

---

62. OLC Article 16 Memo, supra note 24, at 33-34.

63. Note that the protections of the Eighth Amendment apply only to cruel and unusual "punishments," that is, to the treatment of individuals who have been convicted of crimes and are therefore in custody of the government.

Whether treatment by public officials constitutes "cruel and unusual" treatment that is prohibited by the Constitution is assessed using a two-prong test. First, it must be determined whether the individual who has been mistreated was denied "the minimal civilized measures of life's necessities." This standard may change over time to reflect evolving societal standards of decency. Secondly, the offending individual must have a "sufficiently culpable state of mind," indicating that the infliction of pain was "wanton" or, in the context of general prison conditions, reflected "deliberate indifference to inmate health or safety."

Michael John Garcia, CRS Report No. RL32438, U.N. Convention Against Torture (CAT): Overview and Application to Interrogation Techniques CRS-8 n.35 (Jan. 25, 2008).

64. OLC Article 16 Memo, supra note 24, at 30.

65. County of Sacramento v. Lewis, 523 U.S. 833, 848-849 (1998) ("We have . . . rejected the lowest common denominator of customary tort liability as a mark of sufficiently shocking conduct, and have held that the Constitution does not guarantee due care on the part of state officials; liability for negligently inflicted harm is categorically beneath the threshold of constitutional due process. It is, on the contrary, behavior at the other end of the culpability spectrum that would most probably support a due process claim; *conduct intended to injure in some way unjustifiable by any government interest is the sort of official action most likely to rise to the conscience-shocking level*.") (emphasis added).

66. 342 U.S. 165 (1952).

applied proved unavailing against Rochin's resistance. He was handcuffed and taken to a hospital. At the direction of one of the officers a doctor forced an emetic solution through a tube into Rochin's stomach against his will. This "stomach pumping" produced vomiting. In the vomited matter were found two capsules which proved to contain morphine.[67]

Without considering the state's interest in the evidence so seized, the Court concluded that these "brutal" tactics violated due process, reasoning as follows:

> [W]e are compelled to conclude that the proceedings by which this conviction was obtained do more than offend some fastidious squeamishness or private sentimentalism about combating crime too energetically. This is conduct that shocks the conscience. Illegally breaking into the privacy of the petitioner, the struggle to open his mouth and remove what was there, the forcible extraction of his stomach's contents — this course of proceeding by agents of government to obtain evidence is bound to offend even hardened sensibilities. They are methods too close to the rack and the screw to permit of constitutional differentiation.[68]

Was OLC wise to argue that waterboarding may survive *Rochin* review? If CAT had been in effect in 1952, would the conduct in *Rochin* have qualified as CIDTP? Would it today? Do relevant standards change?

Finally, an even more serious question is whether the emphasis on *Rochin* and its "shocks the conscience" test for when a tactic violates the Due Process Clause is misplaced, and perhaps even irrelevant. As discussed in Chapter 7, another line of Supreme Court Fifth and Fourteenth Amendment Due Process precedent applies in these types of cases: the Court's "due process voluntariness" cases. This line of cases does not permit balancing between the government interest and the intentionality of the harm inflicted; instead, the due process voluntariness precedents simply bar the admission of confessions deemed to be involuntary because secured through abusive interrogation techniques. Why are these cases — which focus specifically on interrogations and on the methods by which confessions may and may not be obtained from suspects — not the focus rather than the *Rochin* line of cases?

2. Applications Abroad

a. The McCain Amendment

The Bush administration had argued that because CIDTP is defined in U.S. law as violations of Fifth, Eighth, or Fourteenth Amendment rights, and these amendments do not apply outside U.S. territory, the legal obligation to prevent CIDTP does not apply outside U.S. territory.[69] In response to the assertion that CAT's Article 16 obligation to prevent CIDTP did not apply extraterritorially, Congress passed in the Detainee Treatment Act of 2005 (DTA) a statute sometimes referred to as the "McCain Amendment" and codified at 42 U.S.C. §2000dd. Section 2000dd(a) makes clear the extraterritorial obligations of the U.S. government with respect to CIDTP: "No individual in the custody or under the physical control of the United States Government, regardless of nationality or physical location, shall be subject to

---

67. Id. at 166.
68. Id. at 172.
69. OLC Article 16 Memo, supra note 24, at 23-25.

cruel, inhuman, or degrading treatment or punishment."[70] Congress also included a similar provision, with an identical prohibition, in the Military Commissions Act of 2006 (MCA), which is codified at 42 U.S.C. §2000dd-0(1). (The McCain Amendment also provided for a defense to prosecution for abuses committed in certain circumstances; this defense is considered below). The McCain Amendment passed six months after the OLC memo on CIDTP. However, because the memo declared that none of the CIA's techniques is cruel, inhuman, or degrading, it is unclear what effect the Amendment had on the conclusions of that opinion.

Section 2000dd-0(3) also authorizes the president, through executive order, to take action to ensure compliance with the McCain Amendment. In July 2007, President Bush signed an executive order entitled "Interpretation of the Geneva Conventions Common Article 3 as Applied to a Program of Detention and Interrogation Operated by the [CIA]."[71] President Obama revoked this executive order upon taking office and issued in its stead Executive Order 13,491. This order requires that interrogation of all individuals in the custody or control of the United States in armed conflicts conform, as a "minimum baseline," with common Article 3 of the Geneva Conventions.[72] The order goes on to state:

> Effective immediately, an individual in the custody or under the effective control of an officer, employee, or other agent of the United States Government, or detained within a facility owned, operated, or controlled by a department or agency of the United States, in any armed conflict, shall not be subjected to any interrogation technique or approach, or any treatment related to interrogation, that is not authorized by and listed in the Army Field Manual 2-22.3 [Human Intelligence Collector Operations].[73]

Although the decision to measure CIA conduct by reference to the Army Field Manual pleased many in the human rights community, some continue to express concerns about potential interrogation abuses. They point in particular to Appendix M to the Army Field Manual—added in 2006 and applicable only to "unlawful combatants"—which continues to authorize techniques such as sleep and sensory deprivation that may, in combination, constitute cruel, inhuman, and degrading treatment or punishment.[74] The story is not yet over. On January 22, 2009, President Obama ordered a Special Interagency Task Force chaired by Attorney General Eric Holder

> to study and evaluate whether the interrogation practices and techniques in Army Field Manual 2-22.3, when employed by departments or agencies outside the military, provide an appropriate means of acquiring the intelligence necessary to protect the Nation, and, if warranted, to recommend any additional or different guidance for other departments or agencies.[75]

---

70. See also id. §2000dd(b).

71. Exec. Order No. 13,440, 72 Fed. Reg. 40707 (July 20, 2007).

72. Exec. Order No. 13,491, Ensuring Lawful Interrogations, at §3(a) 74 Fed. Reg. 4893 (Jan. 22, 2009).

73. Id. §3(b).

74. See, e.g., Center for Constitutional Rights, Close Torture Loopholes in the Army Field Manual, http://ccrjustice.org/get-involved/action/close-torture-loopholes-army-field-manual (last visited July 21, 2009).

75. Exec. Order No. 13,491, Ensuring Lawful Interrogations, at §5(3)(i), 74 Fed. Reg. 4893 (Jan. 22, 2009).

b. Irregular Rendition[76]

Numerous sources have now documented the CIA's "top secret" program for sending ("rendering") suspected terrorists captured outside the United States to countries where allegations of official torture are common.[77] Although reliable numbers are hard to come by, some estimated in 2005 that the CIA has flown "100 to 150 suspected terrorists to countries like Egypt, Syria, Saudi Arabia, Jordan and Pakistan — each a habitual offender when it comes to torture."[78] These stories also detail instances in which innocent persons may have been "rendered" and allegations that many of those seized have been tortured in the states to which they were rendered.

It is important to recognize that this activity differs fundamentally from the extradition (and even the abduction and luring) practices discussed in Chapter 9. First, many of these persons apparently were neither found in the United States nor held at its borders. If press accounts are to be believed, many of the persons seized were swept off the streets of foreign nations and into CIA custody (with or without the consent of the state on whose territory they were found). In such circumstances, the deportation option is obviously not relevant. Second, the object of these kidnappings, in many cases, apparently is *not* (at least for present) to bring these persons back to U.S. territory for criminal (or even military) trial. Rather, again according to press accounts, the persons seized have been transferred to the custody of *other* states whose records for torture have been documented in the U.S. State Department's own reports on human rights abuses. Therefore, extradition — which presupposes that the person is being sent to the requesting state to stand trial — is also not a viable alternative.

The use of "irregular rendition" has been vigorously attacked by human rights advocates who contend that, despite official assurances from the receiving countries that no abuse will occur, the United States knows that torture or CIDTP will occur and is essentially letting other countries do the United States' "dirty work" to avoid the jurisdiction of U.S. courts.[79] Officials defended the policy on a variety of grounds, including the need for intelligence, and asserted that the official assurances it received from those countries to which the individuals were removed were credible and sufficient to satisfy U.S. obligations.[80] The question for present purposes,

---

76. By irregular renditions, what is meant is the transfer of an individual with the involvement of the United States or its agents from one foreign state to another, in circumstances that suggest that the person transferred may be tortured. For detailed analyses of the legality of "extraordinary" renditions (a broader category of transfers), see NYU Center for Human Rights & Global Justice (June 2005); NYU Center for Human Rights & Global Justice & The Assn. of the Bar of New York City, Torture by Proxy: International and Domestic Law Applicable to "Extraordinary Renditions" (Oct. 2004) (using the term *extraordinary rendition*), *available at* http://www.chrgj.org/docs/TortureByProxy.pdf.

77. See, e.g., Torture by Proxy, Editorial, N.Y. Times, Mar. 8, 2005, at A22.

78. Id.; see also Jane Mayer, Outsourcing Torture: The Secret History of America's "Extraordinary Rendition Program," New Yorker, Feb. 14, 2005, at 106; M. Hirsh et al., Aboard Air CIA, Newsweek, Feb. 28, 2005.

79. See, e.g., Torture by Proxy, supra note 78; Douglas Jehl, Pentagon Seeks to Transfer More Detainees from Base in Cuba, N.Y. Times, Mar. 11, 2005, at A1; Extraordinary Rendition in U.S. Counterterrorism Policy: The Impact on Transatlantic Relations, Hearing Before the H. Subcomm. on Intl. Organizations, Human Rights, and Oversight, and the Subcomm. on Europe, 110th Cong. (April 17, 2007).

80. See, e.g, John Yoo, Transferring Terrorist, 79 Notre Dame L. Rev. 1183, 1187-1188 (2004); R. Jeffrey Smith, Gonzalez Defends Transfer of Defendants, Wash. Post, Mar. 8, 2005, at A03; Michael Scheuer, A Fine Rendition, N.Y. Times, Mar. 11, 2005. For an analysis of assurances, see Human Rights Watch, "Diplomatic Assurances" Against Torture: Questions and Answers (Nov. 2006), available at http://www.hrw.org/legacy/backgrounder/eca/ecaqna1106/ecaqna1106web.pdf.

however, is not whether these renditions are wise policy. Our inquiry is whether this irregular rendition was lawful under CAT.[81]

Does CAT's Article 3 bar the United States from rendering persons seized outside U.S. territory to other states where torture or CIDTP may well be inflicted upon the detainees? If so (or if not), can a criminal case be made against those who order such renditions, if such officials are aware of, or willfully blind to, the likelihood that those transferred will be subjected to torture? Would official "assurances" by countries regularly cited for human rights abuses of detainees by the U.S. State Department provide shelter to persons ordering irregular renditions? Consider the following arguments provided by the U.S. government to the Committee Against Torture in May 2006.

RESPONSE OF THE UNITED STATES OF AMERICA, LIST OF ISSUES TO BE CONSIDERED DURING THE EXAMINATION OF THE SECOND PERIODIC REPORT OF THE UNITED STATES OF AMERICA, QUESTION 13, at 32-37[82]

. . . Regarding the Committee's question concerning the implementation of Article 3 to persons outside of U.S. territory, the United States, while recognizing that some members of the Committee may disagree, believes that Article 3 of the CAT does not impose obligations on the United States with respect to an individual who is outside the territory of the United States.

. . . Neither the text of the Convention, its negotiating history, nor the U.S. record of ratification supports a view that Article 3 of CAT applies to persons outside the territory of the United States.

On its face, the text of Article 3 speaks of actions taken with respect to persons already present in the territory of a State. Both in the cases of expulsion, the deportation of an individual, and extradition, the transfer of a person pursuant to an extradition treaty to another country for the purpose of prosecution, there is no question that such terms describe conduct taken against individuals within a State Party's territory. Accordingly, if there is any debate at all as to whether Article 3 applies outside the territory of a State Party, it turns on whether the term "return ('*refouler*')" prohibits the return of persons by a State Party in those circumstances covered by Article 3, regardless of where the officials and the individual benefiting from the protection are located.

In the view of the United States, the meaning of the term "return ('*refouler*')" contained in Article 3 of CAT is limited to actions occurring within the territory of a State Party. Construing the same term, "return ('*refouler*')," as employed in Article 33 of the Refugee Convention, the U.S. Supreme Court [in Sale v. Haitian Centers Council, Inc., 509 U.S. 155 (1993),] found that the legal meaning of the term "return," as modified by reference to the French "*refouler*" (the English translations of which included "repulse," "repel," "drive back," and "expel"), implied that "'return' means a defensive act of resistance or exclusion at a border rather than an act of transporting someone to a particular destination." The Supreme Court thereby concluded in *Sale* that the non-refoulement protection contained in the Refugee Convention and Protocol was not intended to govern the conduct of States Parties outside of their national borders. . . .

---

81. A number of international legal instruments contain nonrefoulement provisions. For now, however, we will focus on the most frequently cited legal constraint on irregular renditions for the purposes of torture — the CAT.

82. Available at http://www.state.gov/documents/organization/66172.pdf (last visited July 21, 2009).

The negotiating history of Article 3 of the CAT confirms the view that the provision was intended to apply to the territory of a State Party, and not to persons who had not yet entered the country. . . .

Finally, the record of proceedings related to U.S. ratification of the CAT demonstrates that at the time of ratification, the United States did not interpret Article 3 to impose obligations with respect to individuals located outside of U.S. territory. . . .

Although as a legal matter Article 3 does not impose obligations on the United States . . . with respect to an individual who is outside the territory of the United States, as a matter of policy, the United States . . . does not transfer persons to countries where it believes it is "more likely than not" that they will be tortured. . . . The essential question in evaluating government assurances is whether the competent U.S. government officials believe it is more likely than not that the individual will be tortured in the country to which he is being transferred. If a case were to arise in which the assurances obtained from the receiving government are not sufficient when balanced against treatment concerns, the United States . . . would not transfer an individual to the control of another government unless the treatment concerns were satisfactorily resolved.

Finally, in those exceptional cases where the United States conducts renditions of individuals, the United States does not transport anyone to a country if the United States believes he or she will be tortured. Where appropriate, the United States seeks assurances it considers to be credible that transferred persons will not be tortured.

NOTES AND QUESTIONS

1. Recall that CAT Article 3, by its terms, applies only where a state seeks to "expel, return ('*refouler*') or extradite a person to another state where there are substantial grounds for believing that he would be in danger of being subject to *torture*" (emphasis added). Article 3 does not apply where there are substantial grounds for believing (or, under the U.S. RUDs to the CAT, it is "more likely than not") that detainees will be subjected to lesser abuses (that is, "only" to CIDTP). Does the McCain Amendment change this by statute?

2. President Obama ordered a Special Interagency Task Force chaired by Attorney General Eric Holder

> to study and evaluate the practices of transferring individuals to other nations in order to ensure that such practices comply with the domestic laws, international obligations, and policies of the United States and do not result in the transfer of individuals to other nations to face torture or otherwise for the purpose, or with the effect, of undermining or circumventing the commitments or obligations of the United States to ensure the humane treatment of individuals in its custody or control.

Exec. Order No. 13,491, Ensuring Lawful Interrogations, at §5(3)(ii), 74 Fed. Reg. 4893 (Jan. 22, 2009).

C. TORTURE AND CIDTP IN WARTIME

We covered war crimes in greater depth in Chapter 21, but some mention of torture and CIDTP in the context of armed conflict is appropriate here. The four 1949

Geneva Conventions Relative to the Treatment of Victims of War protect specified categories of vulnerable persons during war. The Conventions share several common provisions, the most important of which for present purposes is an identically phrased Article 3. "Common Article 3" has been interpreted to provide certain baseline protections to persons caught up in armed conflicts. Thus, common Article 3 provides, in pertinent part:

> Persons taking no part in the hostilities, including members of armed forces who have laid down their arms and those placed hors de combat . . . shall in all circumstances be treated humanely. . . . To this end, the following acts are and shall remain prohibited at any time and in any place whatsoever with respect to the above-mentioned persons: (a) violence to life and person, in particular murder of all kinds, mutilation, cruel treatment and torture; . . . (c) outrages upon personal dignity, in particular, humiliating and degrading treatment.[83]

The Bush administration consistently took the position, after 9/11, that common Article 3 was inapplicable to the United States' armed conflict with al Qaeda. The Supreme Court, in its 2006 decision in *Hamdan v. Rumsfeld*, rejected this position, ruling that common Article 3 provides "some minimal protection, falling short of full protection under the Conventions, to [any] individuals . . . who are involved in a conflict in the territory of a signatory."[84]

1.   Lex Specialis

The rule of *lex specialis* provides that when two different legal standards can control in a given circumstance, the more specific standard controls. As the Congressional Research Service has reported:

> There is some debate whether the rule of *lex specialis* means that the laws of war are the singular international standard governing the treatment of persons during armed conflict or whether human rights treaties such as CAT may impose complementary duties. . . . In a 2006 hearing before the Committee Against Torture, representatives of the U.S. State Department argued that CAT did not apply to detainee operations in Afghanistan, Iraq, and Guantánamo, which were controlled by the laws of armed conflict. In support of this position, the U.S. argued that CAT's negotiating history revealed an understanding by the negotiating parties that the treaty was intended to cover domestic obligations owed by parties and was not meant to overlap with different treaties governing the standard owed in armed conflicts. The Committee Against Torture disagreed with this view and recommended that the United States "should recognize and ensure that the Convention applies at all times, whether in peace, war or armed conflict, in any territory under its jurisdiction."[85]

2.   The War Crimes Act

The Geneva Conventions have been implemented in U.S. law through the War Crime Act, codified at 18 U.S.C. §2441. The War Crimes Act imposes criminal penalties on

---

83. Geneva Convention Relative to the Treatment of Prisoners of War art. 3.
84. 548 U.S. 557, 562 (2006).
85. Michael John Garcia, CRS Rep. No. RL 33662, The War Crimes Act: Current Issues CRS-18 (July 23, 2007) (footnotes omitted).

"[w]hoever, whether inside or outside the United States," commits a covered war crime when those offenses are committed by or against a U.S. national or member of the U.S. armed forces. Those convicted under the act are subject to life imprisonment or any term of years and can receive the death penalty if their offense results in the victim's death.[86]

Until 2006, the War Crimes Act made it a criminal offense, inter alia, to commit an act that constituted a "grave breach" of the Geneva Conventions or their protocols, under 18 U.S.C. §2441(c)(1), *or* "a violation of common Article 3," under 18 U.S.C. §2441(c)(3). The statute did not, however, further define what specific conduct might constitute a "grave breach" or a violation of common Article 3.

After *Hamdan*, President Bush suggested that some provisions of common Article 3 provided U.S. actors with inadequate notice as to what interrogation methods were lawful and requested legislation that provided greater specificity in the War Crimes Act. Congress passed the Military Commission Act of 2006 (MCA), which, among other things, amended the War Crimes Act to substantially curtail the scope of actionable war crimes founded on common Article 3.

In particular, while the statute previously classified *any* violation of common Article 3 as a war crime, the post-MCA statute covers only conduct that "constitutes a *grave breach* of common Article 3 (as defined in subsection (d)) *when committed in the context of and in association with an armed conflict not of an international character.*"[87] The statute then goes on to define with specificity what is meant by "grave breaches of common Article 3" for these purposes in §2441(d)(1) ("Prohibited Conduct"). The specified prohibited conduct is restricted to (A) torture, (B) cruel or inhuman treatment, (C) performing biological experiments, (D) murder, (E) mutilation or maiming, (F) intentionally causing serious bodily injury, (G) rape, (H) sexual assault or abuse, and (I) taking of hostages. The definitions of torture and cruel treatment are provided below.

18 U.S.C. §2441(D)

(1)(A) Torture. — The action of a person who commits, or conspires or attempts to commit, an act specifically intended to inflict severe physical or mental pain or suffering (other than pain or suffering incidental to lawful sanctions) upon another person within his custody or physical control for the purpose of obtaining information or a confession, punishment, intimidation, coercion, or any reason based on discrimination of any kind.

(B) Cruel or inhuman treatment. — The act of a person who commits, or conspires or attempts to commit, an act intended to inflict severe or serious physical or mental pain or suffering (other than the pain or suffering incident to lawful

---

86. The means by which soldiers may be held accountable for war crimes was discussed at length in Chapter 21. Recall that U.S. military personnel are directly subject to the laws of war and may be tried by international or national tribunals with jurisdiction over the violations. Where stationed overseas, they may be subject to the domestic law of the country in which they are stationed, normally under the terms of a Status of Forces Agreement (SOFA) between the United States and the host country. The most likely site of accountability for military personnel, however, is a court-martial conducted under the Uniform Code of Military Justice. See, e.g., 10 U.S.C. §§893 (cruelty or maltreatment), 928 (assault and battery), 924 (maiming); see generally Garcia, supra note 65; Jennifer K. Elsea, CRS Rep. No. RL32395, U.S. Treatment of Prisoners in Iraq: Selected Legal Issues (May 19, 2005); John Sifton, United States Military and Central Intelligence Agency Personnel Abroad: Plugging the Prosecutorial Gaps, 43 Harv. J. Legis. 487 (2006).

87. 18 U.S.C. §2441(c)(3) (emphasis added).

sanctions), including serious physical abuse, on another in his custody or control. . . .

(2)(D) The term "serious physical pain or suffering" shall be applied for purposes of paragraph (1)(B) as meaning bodily injury that involves—

(i) a substantial risk of death;

(ii) extreme physical pain;

(iii) a burn or physical disfigurement of a serious nature (other than cuts, abrasions, or bruises); or

(iv) significant loss or impairment of the function of a bodily member, organ, or mental faculty; and

(E) the term "serious mental pain or suffering" shall be applied for purposes of paragraph (1)(B) in accordance with the meaning given the term "severe mental pain or suffering" (as defined in section 2340(2) of this title), except that—

(i) the term "serious" shall replace the term "severe" where it appears; and

(ii) as to conduct occurring after the date of enactment [of this amendment], the term "serious and non-transitory mental harm (which need not be prolonged)" shall replace the term "prolonged mental harm" where it appears.

NOTES AND QUESTIONS

1. Does the War Crimes Act cover all of the prohibitions found in common Article 3? How do these crimes stack up against 18 U.S.C. §2340A?

2. Both the U.S. definitions (18 U.S.C. §§2340A and 2441), like the ICC definition but unlike CAT, contain a requirement that the acts be directed against a person in the torturer's custody or physical control. According to the Senate Report on CAT, "[t]his understanding is designed to clarify the relationship of the Convention to normal military and law enforcement operations." Sen. Exec. Rep. No. 101-30, at 9 (Aug. 30, 1990). What problem might this understanding have been designed to address? Why would this qualification be necessary if CAT does not, as the United States contends, apply to armed conflicts?

3. As though it is not confusing enough to have two crimes involving torture in two different chapters of Title 18—one outlawing torture per se (§2340A) and another criminalizing the war crimes of torture and cruel and inhuman treatment (§2441)— recall yet another provision of the code that is relevant to our definitional odyssey: the McCain Amendment, 42 U.S.C. §2000dd, examined in Section B.2.a above. That statute defines cruel, inhuman, and degrading treatment in the same way that U.S. reservations to CAT do: that is, by reference to the Fifth, Eighth, and Fourteenth Amendments to the U.S. Constitution. Id. §2000dd(d). Note that §2000dd, unlike §2441, prohibits but does *not* criminalize CIDTP.

4. On September 6, 2006, the Department of Defense implemented the requirements of the McCain Amendment by amending the Army Field Manual to prohibit the "cruel, inhuman, or degrading treatment" of any person in the custody or control of the U.S. military. This document identifies specific techniques that may not be used in intelligence interrogations. Among the techniques prohibited are forcing the detainee to be naked, perform sexual poses, or pose in a sexual manner; placing hoods or sacks over the head of a detainee; using duct tape over the eyes; using beatings, electric shocks, burns, or other forms of physical pain; waterboarding;

using military working dogs to scare or threaten a detainee; inducing hypothermia or heat injury; conducting mock executions; and depriving the detainee of necessary food, water, or medical care. See Dept. of the Army Field Manual 34-52, Human Intelligence Collector Operations, at 5-75 (2006), available at http://www.army .mil/institution/armypublicaffairs/pdf/fm2-22-3.pdf.

D.   RELIANCE OR ESTOPPEL DEFENSES

Recall that the Bybee Memo (and perhaps the Bradbury Memo) was written to give CIA interrogators some assurance that their "aggressive" interrogation techniques would not land them in prison. Indeed, some assert that the Bybee Memo "was written as an immunity, a blank check," on the theory that anyone who relied on it had a defense, whether or not the OLC's analysis was correct.[88] Is this true? Consider the following questions as you read the following excerpted article: If it could be proven that senior officials, relying on the Bybee Memo, either approved of abusive interrogation tactics or did nothing to remedy abuses when they came to their attention, would they be subject to criminal sanction?[89] What about military personnel, CIA officers, or civilian contractors who violate the ban on torture or subject detainees to CIDTP, overseas or in facilities under the control of the United States?

JOHN SIFTON, UNITED STATES MILITARY AND CENTRAL INTELLIGENCE AGENCY PERSONNEL ABROAD: PLUGGING THE PROSECUTORIAL GAPS
43 Harv. J. Legis. 487, 509-514 (2006)

. . . FEDERAL LAW: THE McCAIN AMENDMENT DEFENSE

The McCain Amendment extended a legal defense to U.S. personnel, both military and non-military, involved in interrogations of terrorism suspects overseas.[90] The Amendment defined the defense by borrowing language from the same rule in military law, despite the notable fact that the military's strict obligation to follow orders generally is not found in non-military contexts. The McCain Amendment, providing for "protection of United States Government Personnel," states that in any criminal prosecution arising out of the detention or interrogation of non-citizen terrorist suspects, defendants can escape conviction if they show that first, the

---

88. Jane Mayer, A Deadly Interrogation: Can the C.I.A. Legally Kill a Prisoner?, New Yorker, Nov. 14, 2005, at 44, 46 (quoting anonymous source).

89. The question of the availability of civil sanctions is beyond the scope of this chapter. A very general survey of possibly relevant statutes and causes of action can be found in Michael John Garcia, CRS Rep. No. RL32438, U.N. Convention Against Torture (CAT): Overview and Application to Interrogation Techniques (Nov. 7, 2005). For recent decisions discussing the application of the Torture Victim Protection Act (TVPA), 28 U.S.C. §1350, and constitutional tort remedies to government actors, see In re Iraq & Afg. Detainees Litig., 2007 U.S. Dist. LEXIS 21853 (D.D.C. Mar. 27, 2007); Rasul v. Rumsfeld, 414 F. Supp. 2d 26 (D.D.C. 2006); Arar v. Ashcroft, 414 F. Supp. 2d 250, 264-266 (E.D.N.Y. 2006); Schneider v. Kissinger, 310 F. Supp. 2d 251 (D.D.C. 2004), aff'd, 412 F.3d 190 (D.C. Cir. 2005). For cases against private contractors, see Saleh v. Titan Corp., 436 F. Supp. 2d 55 (D.D.C. 2006); and Ibrahim v. Titan Corp., 391 F. Supp. 2d 10 (D.D.C. 2005).

90. [Sifton's footnote 167:] Detainee Treatment Act of 2005, Pub. L. No. 109-163, Div. A, §1404, 119 Stat. 3136, 3475 (codified at 42 U.S.C.A. §2000dd-1 (West 2006)).

practices for which they are being prosecuted were "*authorized* and *determined to be lawful* at the time that they were conducted"; second, they did not know the practices were unlawful; and third, a "person of ordinary sense and understanding would not know the practices were unlawful."[91]

The Act adds that "[g]ood faith reliance on advice of counsel should be an important factor, among others, to consider in assessing whether a person of ordinary sense and understanding would have known the practices to be unlawful."[92] Presumably, this means that when defendants can show that they relied on legal advice (perhaps from CIA or OLC attorneys), the likelihood increases that a jury will find that a reasonable person would not have deemed the conduct to be unlawful.

In cases where such an authorization is shown, juries can still convict if they find either that an official knew the techniques were illegal or that a "person of ordinary sense and understanding" would have known the practices to be unlawful. The defense may therefore be viewed skeptically in cases of outright torture, since it is less likely that official authorization was actually given and more likely that a "person of ordinary sense and understanding" would have known that such techniques were illegal.

The defense could meet greater success in cases where the applicable law is unclear. For example, . . . where CIA lawyers have told CIA officials that certain techniques were legal because of jurisdictional or definitional issues, both agents and officials may have a viable defense even if the attorneys' interpretation of the law is ultimately shown to be incorrect.[93]

. . . PREVIOUSLY AVAILABLE DEFENSES UNDER FEDERAL LAW[94]

The defenses of "innocent intent," "public authority," and "entrapment by estoppel" typically are raised by federal defendants in cases where they claim to have been misled to believe that their actions were part of government-sanctioned operations. The defenses are also frequently raised when the defendants claim to have been told by government officials that their conduct was lawful, when in fact it was not.[95] Those accused of detainee abuse may use one or more of these defenses either alone or to supplement the McCain Amendment defense.

First, a defendant may invoke an "innocent intent" defense by claiming to have acted in cooperation with the government under the sincere belief that the conduct in question was legal. Second, a defendant may invoke a "public authority" defense by admitting to having knowingly committed a criminal act but claiming that the act was done in reasonable reliance upon a grant of authority from a government official. Third, a defendant may invoke a defense of "entrapment by estoppel" by claiming that a government official with legal authority in a certain area told him that the proscribed conduct was permissible and that he reasonably relied on that official statement.

---

91. [Sifton's footnote 168:] Id. §2000dd-1(a).

92. [Sifton's footnote 169:] Id.

93. [Sifton's footnote 175:] The defense applies where "good faith reliance" on legal counsel has been shown, seemingly regardless of that counsel's ultimate accuracy.

94. With respect to defenses available to U.S. servicepersons, see Chapter 18; Garcia, supra note 90, at CRS-5 n.5. — EDS.

95. [Sifton's footnote 177:] See, e.g., Cox v. Louisiana, 379 U.S. 559, 570-571 (1965) (stating that protestors claimed that they were told by a local police chief that they could lawfully protest across the street from the courthouse).

1. THE "INNOCENT INTENT" DEFENSE

The "innocent intent" defense requires that "(1) the defendant honestly believed that he was acting in cooperation with the government, and [that] (2) the government official or officials upon whose authority the defendant relied possessed actual authority to authorize his otherwise criminal acts." The strategy has typically been invoked only in cases where the defendant has been charged with a crime that a law enforcement agency might actually authorize as part of its operations. Thus, its application is rare: when authorities use an FBI informant to make an initial drug buy from a suspected drug dealer (in order to gain the dealer's trust), the involved U.S. attorney typically will grant immunity in return for the informant's testimony regarding his role in the operation.

The innocent intent defense is probably not directly applicable to most cases of detainee abuse, since the government, as a general matter, has agreed to forgo authorization of torture. However, in cases involving conduct that takes advantage of the definitional ambiguities currently surrounding "torture" under U.S. law, one can imagine the defense at least being raised, if not successful. For example, in cases where the authorized acts toe the line between a violation of the Torture Statute and a simple assault under Title 18, the likelihood of the defense's success is uncertain.

2. THE "PUBLIC AUTHORITY" DEFENSE

The "public authority" defense, also known as the "CIA defense," can be invoked only when a government official authorized the criminal conduct in question, and, in fact, possessed *actual* and not merely *apparent* authority to sanction such illegal activity. Thus, the defense cannot be raised in most cases involving CIA personnel because, as a baseline rule, CIA officials do not have *actual* authority to allow lower-level personnel or contractors to engage in illegal activities. Accordingly, a defendant's mistaken assumption that CIA officials or agents can authorize commission of illegal acts does not constitute a valid defense.

Notably, an apparent public authority defense was allowed in one of the Watergate break-in cases in the 1970s, where the defendants mistakenly believed they had been recruited for a CIA operation. However, the clear weight of subsequent case law has disfavored such a defense when based on mistake of law. As such, an "apparent public authority" defense is likely applicable only where the mistake was actually one of fact, for example, where a defendant mistakenly believed that the person who authorized his criminal conduct was a public official. . . .

3. THE "ENTRAPMENT BY ESTOPPEL" DEFENSE

The third defense, "entrapment by estoppel," may be useful to CIA agents or officials and civilian contractors charged with detainee abuse. Similar to the McCain Amendment defense, entrapment by estoppel applies in cases where the defendant reasonably relied on a government official's statement that proscribed conduct is permissible, if the government official actually had legal authority in that area. A defendant's reliance on the government official is "reasonable" if "a person sincerely desirous of obeying the law would have accepted the information as true, and would not have been put on notice to make further inquiries."

This defense is most plausible in the context of reliance by agents, officials, or civilian contractors on legal opinions issued by the OLC or DOJ. For instance, if the OLC were to issue an opinion stating that waterboarding does not constitute torture, it might prompt U.S. personnel to utilize the technique during interrogations. Depending on the circumstances, reliance on that opinion might be considered reasonable and thus grounds for an entrapment by estoppel defense. While the waterboarding opinion is almost certainly legally incorrect, that alone would not prevent the use of the opinion as the source of a potentially successful entrapment by estoppel defense.

The likelihood of success of these defenses in future detainee abuse cases is difficult to predict. The defenses have caused some confusion in the courts, fueled at least in part by the difficulty in distinguishing between defenses based on mistake of fact and defenses based on mistake of law. The overlap between some of these defenses and the McCain Amendment defense will likely only exacerbate the confusion over the correct applicable standards and elements. . . .

E. THE TORTURE DEBATE

Much of the preceding discussion concerned determining what is prohibited torture (and CIDTP) and what is not. There are those who argue, however, that instead of attempting to determine whether abusive techniques are or are not torture through lawyerly legerdemain, we ought to debate the more fundamental question: whether in some circumstances torturing is justified. Note that part of this debate centers on two factors that are very difficult to test — at least in current circumstances. First, defenders of the CIA techniques, in addition to attempting to move the legal boundaries surrounding what constitutes torture, have also justified these aggressive techniques as effective in preventing further terrorist attacks. Given that the basis for administration assertions remains classified, it is impossible to verify this rationale; indeed, OLC notes that "it is difficult to determine conclusively whether interrogations have provided information critical to interdicting specific imminent attacks."[96] Moreover, as former Bush administration advisor Philip Zelikow observes, "In such an analysis, the elementary question would not be: Did you get information that proved useful? Instead it would be: Did you get information that could have been usefully gained only from these methods?"[97] This, too, is unverifiable, in part because the CIA's interrogation protocol gave detainees only one chance to "provide information on actionable threats and location information on High-Value Targets at large" before beginning "enhanced" interrogation as early as the first day.[98]

Second, opponents of these tactics argue that they don't work — that what they produce is unreliable and of questionable accuracy.[99] Critics, including many in the military, also argue that the United States' use of these tactics legitimates their reciprocal use on U.S. soldiers (or at least dampens the force of U.S. protests in response to such actions) and, once publicized, may further radicalize opponents of U.S. foreign and military policy.[100] These assertions, too, are difficult to empirically verify.

---

96. OLC Article 16 Memo, supra note 24, at 10.

97. Philip Zelikow, Legal Policy for a Twilight War, 30 Hous. J. Intl. L. 89, 105 (2007).

98. OLC Article 16 Memo, supra note 24, at 7, 8.

99. See, e.g., Stuart Herrington, Two Problems with Torture: It's Wrong and It Doesn't Work, Pittsburgh Post-Gazette, Oct. 21, 2007, available at http://www.post-gazette.com/pg/07294/826876 -35.stm# (authored by 30-year veteran intelligence officer in U.S. army); Press Release, Human Rights First, Top Interrogators Declare Torture Ineffective in Intelligence Gathering (June 24, 2008), available at http://www.humanrightsfirst.org/media/etn/2008/alert/313/index.htm.

100. See, e.g., Wallace, supra note 5; Mora & Shattuck, supra note 9, at 19 (former Secretary of the Navy noting that "[s]ome military officials today believe that the proximate causes of Abu Ghraib were the

Consider the following in evaluating for yourself whether official torture is ever justified and, if so, in what circumstances.

CHARLES KRAUTHAMMER, IT'S TIME TO BE HONEST ABOUT DOING TERRIBLE THINGS

Wkly. Standard, Dec. 5, 2006

During the last few weeks in Washington the pieties about torture have lain so thick in the air that it has been impossible to have a reasoned discussion. The McCain amendment that would ban "cruel, inhuman, or degrading" treatment of any prisoner by any agent of the United States sailed through the Senate by a vote of 90-9. [The McCain Amendment is codified at 18 U.S.C. §2000dd and is discussed in Section B.2.a above.] . . . Now, John McCain has great moral authority on this issue, having heroically borne torture at the hands of the North Vietnamese. . . . And McCain is acting out of the deep and honorable conviction that what he is proposing is not only right but is in the best interest of the United States. His position deserves respect. But that does not mean, as seems to be the assumption in Washington today, that a critical analysis of his "no torture, ever" policy is beyond the pale.

Let's begin with a few analytic distinctions. For the purpose of torture and prisoner maltreatment, there are three kinds of war prisoners: First, there is the ordinary soldier caught on the field of battle. There is no question that he is entitled to humane treatment. Indeed, we have no right to disturb a hair on his head. His detention has but a single purpose: to keep him hors de combat. The proof of that proposition is that if there were a better way to keep him off the battlefield that did not require his detention, we would let him go. . . . Because the only purpose of detention in these circumstances is to prevent the prisoner from becoming a combatant again, he is entitled to all the protections and dignity of an ordinary domestic prisoner — indeed, more privileges, because, unlike the domestic prisoner, he has committed no crime. He merely had the misfortune to enlist on the other side of a legitimate war. He is therefore entitled to many of the privileges enjoyed by an ordinary citizen — the right to send correspondence, to engage in athletic activity and intellectual pursuits, to receive allowances from relatives — except, of course, for the freedom to leave the prison.

Second, there is the captured terrorist. A terrorist is by profession, indeed by definition, an unlawful combatant: He lives outside the laws of war because he does not wear a uniform, he hides among civilians, and he deliberately targets innocents. He is entitled to no protections whatsoever. People seem to think that the postwar Geneva Conventions were written only to protect detainees. In fact, their deeper purpose was

---

legal opinions issued by the Justice Department that sanctioned abusive interrogations. There are other serving military officials who maintain that the leading causes of U.S. combat deaths in Iraq are, respectively, Abu Ghraib and Guantanamo, as gauged by their effectiveness in stimulating the recruitment and fielding of jihadists on the battlefield."); Sen. Lindsey Graham & Rep. Jane Harman, Clearing the Fog on Interrogations, Op-Ed, Wash. Post, Feb. 19, 2005, at A31 ("It is clear to us that the events at Abu Ghraib prison in Iraq, as well as the allegations of abuse at the U.S. military prison in Guantanamo Bay, Cuba, must be thoroughly addressed, and reforms enacted. Any attempt to 'play cute' with international, domestic or military laws inevitably puts our own troops at risk, leaving our armed services personnel vulnerable to the same type of treatment if captured. It has been proved that torture or other inhuman conduct as a technique of information-gathering is flawed and often produces unreliable information."); cf. American Civil Liberties Union, Closing Argument of Air Force Major David J.R. Frakt in Favor of Dismissal of the Case Against Mohammad Jawad (June 19, 2008), available at http://www.aclu.org/safefree/detention/35753res20080619.html.

to provide a deterrent to the kind of barbaric treatment of civilians that had become so horribly apparent during the first half of the 20th century, and in particular, during the Second World War. The idea was to deter the abuse of civilians by promising combatants who treated noncombatants well that they themselves would be treated according to a code of dignity if captured — and, crucially, that they would be denied the protections of that code if they broke the laws of war and abused civilians themselves.

Breaking the laws of war and abusing civilians are what, to understate the matter vastly, terrorists do for a living. They are entitled, therefore, to nothing. Anyone who blows up a car bomb in a market deserves to spend the rest of his life roasting on a spit over an open fire. But we don't do that because we do not descend to the level of our enemy. We don't do that because, unlike him, we are civilized. Even though terrorists are entitled to no humane treatment, we give it to them because it is in our nature as a moral and humane people. And when on rare occasions we fail to do that, as has occurred in several of the fronts of the war on terror, we are duly disgraced.

The norm, however, is how the majority of prisoners at Guantánamo have been treated. We give them three meals a day, superior medical care, and provision to pray five times a day. Our scrupulousness extends even to providing them with their own Korans, which is the only reason alleged abuses of the Koran at Guantánamo ever became an issue. That we should have provided those who kill innocents in the name of Islam with precisely the document that inspires their barbarism is a sign of the absurd lengths to which we often go in extending undeserved humanity to terrorist prisoners.

Third, there is the terrorist with information. Here the issue of torture gets complicated and the easy pieties don't so easily apply. Let's take the textbook case. Ethics 101: A terrorist has planted a nuclear bomb in New York City. It will go off in one hour. A million people will die. You capture the terrorist. He knows where it is. He's not talking.

Question: If you have the slightest belief that hanging this man by his thumbs will get you the information to save a million people, are you permitted to do it? Now, on most issues regarding torture, I confess tentativeness and uncertainty. But on this issue, there can be no uncertainty: Not only is it permissible to hang this miscreant by his thumbs. It is a moral duty.

Yes, you say, but that's an extreme and very hypothetical case. Well, not as hypothetical as you think. Sure, the (nuclear) scale is hypothetical, but in the age of the car- and suicide-bomber, terrorists are often captured who have just set a car bomb to go off or sent a suicide bomber out to a coffee shop, and you only have minutes to find out where the attack is to take place. . . .

And even if the example I gave were entirely hypothetical, the conclusion — yes, in this case even torture is permissible — is telling because it establishes the principle: Torture is not always impermissible. However rare the cases, there are circumstances in which, by any rational moral calculus, torture not only would be permissible but would be required (to acquire life-saving information). And once you've established the principle, to paraphrase George Bernard Shaw, all that's left to haggle about is the price. In the case of torture, that means that the argument is not whether torture is ever permissible, but when — i.e., under what obviously stringent circumstances: how big, how imminent, how preventable the ticking time bomb. That is why the McCain amendment, which by mandating "torture never" refuses even to recognize the legitimacy of any moral calculus, cannot be right. There must be exceptions. The real argument should be over what constitutes a legitimate exception.

Let's take an example that is far from hypothetical. You capture Khalid Sheikh Mohammed in Pakistan. He not only has already killed innocents, he is deeply involved in the planning for the present and future killing of innocents. He not only was the architect of the 9/11 attack that killed nearly three thousand people in one day, most of them dying a terrible, agonizing, indeed tortured death. But as the top al Qaeda planner and logistical expert he also knows a lot about terror attacks to come. He knows plans, identities, contacts, materials, cell locations, safe houses, cased targets, etc. What do you do with him?

We have recently learned that since 9/11 the United States has maintained a series of "black sites" around the world, secret detention centers where presumably high-level terrorists like Khalid Sheikh Mohammed have been imprisoned. The world is scandalized. Black sites? Secret detention? Jimmy Carter calls this "a profound and radical change in the . . . moral values of our country." The Council of Europe demands an investigation, calling the claims "extremely worrying." Its human rights commissioner declares "such practices" to constitute "a serious human rights violation, and further proof of the crisis of values" that has engulfed the war on terror. The gnashing of teeth and rending of garments has been considerable.

I myself have not gnashed a single tooth. My garments remain entirely unrent. Indeed, I feel reassured. It would be a gross dereliction of duty for any government not to keep Khalid Sheikh Mohammed isolated, disoriented, alone, despairing, cold and sleepless, in some godforsaken hidden location in order to find out what he knew about plans for future mass murder. What are we supposed to do? Give him a nice cell in a warm Manhattan prison, complete with *Miranda* rights, a mellifluent lawyer, and his own website? Are not those the kinds of courtesies we extended to the 1993 World Trade Center bombers, then congratulated ourselves on how we "brought to justice" those responsible for an attack that barely failed to kill tens of thousands of Americans, only to discover a decade later that we had accomplished nothing — indeed, that some of the disclosures at the trial had helped Osama bin Laden avoid U.S. surveillance?

Have we learned nothing from 9/11? Are we prepared to go back with complete amnesia to the domestic-crime model of dealing with terrorists, which allowed us to sleepwalk through the nineties while al Qaeda incubated and grew and metastasized unmolested until on 9/11 it finished what the first World Trade Center bombers had begun? . . .

. . . [Consider] waterboarding, a terrifying and deeply shocking torture technique in which the prisoner has his face exposed to water in a way that gives the feeling of drowning. According to CIA sources cited by ABC News, Khalid Sheikh Mohammed [was waterboarded]. . . . Should we regret having done that? Should we abolish by law that practice, so that it could never be used on the next Khalid Sheikh Mohammed having thus gotten his confession? And what if he possessed information with less imminent implications? Say we had information about a cell that he had helped found or direct, and that cell was planning some major attack and we needed information about the identity and location of its members. A rational moral calculus might not permit measures as extreme as the nuke-in-Manhattan scenario, but would surely permit measures beyond mere psychological pressure.

Such a determination would not be made with an untroubled conscience. I would be troubled because there is no denying the monstrous evil that is any form of torture. And there is no denying how corrupting it can be to the individuals and society that practice it. But elected leaders, responsible above all for the protection of their citizens, have the obligation to tolerate their own sleepless nights by doing what is necessary — and only what is necessary, nothing more — to get information that could prevent mass murder.

Given the gravity of the decision, if we indeed cross the Rubicon — as we must — we need rules. The problem with the McCain amendment is that once you have gone public with a blanket ban on all forms of coercion, it is going to be very difficult to publicly carve out exceptions. The Bush administration is to be faulted for having attempted such a codification with the kind of secrecy, lack of coherence, and lack of strict enforcement that led us to the McCain reaction.

What to do at this late date? Begin, as McCain does, by banning all forms of coercion or inhuman treatment by anyone serving in the military—an absolute ban on torture by all military personnel everywhere. We do not want a private somewhere making these fine distinctions about ticking and slow-fuse time bombs. We don't even want colonels or generals making them. It would be best for the morale, discipline, and honor of the Armed Forces for the United States to maintain an absolute prohibition, both to simplify their task in making decisions and to offer them whatever reciprocal treatment they might receive from those who capture them—although I have no illusion that any anti-torture provision will soften the heart of a single jihadist holding a knife to the throat of a captured American soldier. We would impose this restriction on ourselves for our own reasons of military discipline and military honor.

Outside the military, however, I would propose, contra McCain, a ban against all forms of torture, coercive interrogation, and inhuman treatment, except in two contingencies: (1) the ticking time bomb and (2) the slower-fuse high-level terrorist (such as KSM). Each contingency would have its own set of rules. In the case of the ticking time bomb, the rules would be relatively simple: Nothing rationally related to getting accurate information would be ruled out. The case of the high-value suspect with slow-fuse information is more complicated. The principle would be that the level of inhumanity of the measures used (moral honesty is essential here—we would be using measures that are by definition inhumane) would be proportional to the need and value of the information. Interrogators would be constrained to use the least inhumane treatment necessary relative to the magnitude and imminence of the evil being prevented and the importance of the knowledge being obtained.

These exceptions to the no-torture rule would not be granted to just any non-military interrogators, or anyone with CIA credentials. They would be reserved for highly specialized agents who are experts and experienced in interrogation, and who are known not to abuse it for the satisfaction of a kind of sick sadomasochism Lynndie England and her cohorts indulged in at Abu Ghraib. Nor would they be acting on their own. They would be required to obtain written permission for such interrogations from the highest political authorities in the country (cabinet level) or from a quasi-judicial body modeled on the Foreign Intelligence Surveillance Court (which permits what would ordinarily be illegal searches and seizures in the war on terror). Or, if the bomb was truly ticking and there was no time, the interrogators would be allowed to act on their own, but would require post facto authorization within, say, 24 hours of their interrogation, so that they knew that whatever they did would be subject to review by others and be justified only under the most stringent terms.

One of the purposes of these justifications would be to establish that whatever extreme measures are used are for reasons of nothing but information. Historically, the torture of prisoners has been done for a variety of reasons apart from information, most prominently reasons of justice or revenge. We do not do that. We should not do that. Ever. Khalid Sheikh Mohammed, murderer of 2,973 innocents, is surely deserving of the most extreme suffering day and night for the rest of his life. But it is neither our role nor our right to be the agents of that suffering. Vengeance is mine, sayeth the Lord. His, not ours. Torture is a terrible and monstrous thing, as degrading and morally corrupting to those who practice it as any conceivable human activity including its moral twin, capital punishment.

If Khalid Sheikh Mohammed knew nothing, or if we had reached the point where his knowledge had been exhausted, I'd be perfectly prepared to throw him into a nice, comfortable Manhattan cell and give him a trial to determine what would be fit and just punishment. But as long as he had useful information, things would be different. Very different. And it simply will not do to take refuge in the claim that all of the above discussion is superfluous because torture never works anyway. Would that this were true. Unfortunately, on its face, this is nonsense. Is one to believe that in the entire history of human warfare, no combatant has ever received useful information by the use of pressure, torture, or any other kind of inhuman treatment? It may indeed be true that torture is not a reliable tool. But that is very different from saying that it is never useful. . . .

The monstrous thing about torture is that sometimes it does work. . . .

According to *Newsweek*, in the ticking time bomb case McCain says that the president should disobey the very law that McCain seeks to pass — under the justification that "you do what you have to do. But you take responsibility for it." But if torturing the ticking time bomb suspect is "what you have to do," then why has McCain been going around arguing that such things must never be done? As for exception number two, the high-level terrorist with slow-fuse information, Stuart Taylor, the superb legal correspondent for *National Journal*, argues that with appropriate legal interpretation, the "cruel, inhuman, or degrading" standard, "though vague, is said by experts to codify . . . the commonsense principle that the toughness of interrogation techniques should be calibrated to the importance and urgency of the information likely to be obtained." That would permit "some very aggressive techniques . . . on that small percentage of detainees who seem especially likely to have potentially life-saving information." Or as Evan Thomas and Michael Hirsh put it in the *Newsweek* report on McCain and torture, the McCain standard would "presumably allow for a sliding scale" of torture or torture-lite or other coercive techniques, thus permitting "for a very small percentage — those High Value Targets like Khalid Sheikh Mohammed — some pretty rough treatment." But if that is the case, then McCain embraces the same exceptions I do, but prefers to pretend he does not. If that is the case, then his much-touted and endlessly repeated absolutism on inhumane treatment is merely for show. If that is the case, then the moral preening and the phony arguments can stop now, and we can all agree that in this real world of astonishingly murderous enemies, in two very circumscribed circumstances, we must all be prepared to torture. Having established that, we can then begin to work together to codify rules of interrogation for the two very unpleasant but very real cases in which we are morally permitted — indeed morally compelled — to do terrible things.

DAVID LUBAN, LIBERALISM, TORTURE, AND THE TICKING TIME BOMB[101]

Harper's, Mar. 2006

Torture used to be thought incompatible with American values. This was true across the political divide, because for the most part, American conservatives belong no less than progressives to liberal culture in the broad sense of "liberalism" that began with John Stuart Mill, a culture that stresses limited government, human dignity, and

---

101. Adapted from an essay of the same name by David Luban, published in the Virginia Law Review. — EDS.

individual rights. Liberalism incorporates a vision of engaged, active human beings possessing an inherent dignity regardless of their social station. The victim of torture is in every respect the opposite of this vision. The torture victim is isolated instead of engaged, terrified instead of active, humiliated instead of dignified.

. . . What makes torture, the deliberate infliction of suffering and pain, especially abhorrent to liberals? This may seem like a bizarre question, because the answer seems self-evident: making people suffer is a horrible thing. But let me pose the question in different terms. Realistically, the abuses of detainees at Abu Ghraib, Baghram, and Guantánamo pale by comparison with the death, maiming, and suffering in collateral damage during the Afghan and Iraq wars. Bombs crush limbs and burn people's faces off; nothing even remotely as horrifying has been reported in American prisoner-abuse cases. Yet as much as we may regret or in some cases decry the wartime suffering of innocents, we do not regard it with the special abhorrence with which we regard torture. This seems hypocritical and irrational, almost fetishistic — why should torture be more illiberal than bombing and killing?

The answer lies in the relationship between torturer and victim. Torture aims to strip away from its victim all the qualities of human dignity that liberalism prizes. Torture is a microcosm, raised to the highest level of intensity, of the tyrannical political relationships that liberalism hates most. In both ancient Greece and Rome, for example, slaves were permitted to testify in a court of law only under torture, which, according to classicist Moses Finley, served to mark off the absolute difference in status between slaves and even the lowliest freemen. . . .

. . . [There are] four illiberal motives for torture: victor's pleasure, terror, punishment, and extracting confessions. That leaves only one rationale for torture that might conceivably be acceptable to a liberal: torture as a technique of intelligence gathering from captives who will not talk. This may seem indistinguishable from torture to extract confessions, but there is a crucial difference in the fact that confession aims to document and ratify the past for purposes of retribution, whereas intelligence gathering aims to forestall future evils. In a somewhat perverse and paradoxical way, liberalism's insistence on limited government that exercises its power only for pragmatic purposes creates the possibility of seeing torture as a civilized, not an atavistic, practice, provided that its sole aim is preventing future harm. Now, for the first time, it becomes possible to think of the torturer as a conscientious public servant, heroic in the way that the New York firefighters were heroic, willing to do desperate things only because so many innocent lives weigh in the balance. Even though prohibition remains liberalism's primary position regarding torture, and the basic liberal stance is empathy for the torture victim, a more permissive stance remains a possibility, and in response to a catastrophe like 9/11, liberals may cautiously conclude that, in the words of a well-known *Newsweek* article, it is "Time to Think About Torture."

But the pressure of liberalism will compel them to think about torture in a highly stylized and artificial way, creating what I call the "liberal ideology of torture." This ideology insists that the sole purpose of torture must be intelligence gathering to prevent a catastrophe; that torture is necessary to prevent the catastrophe; that torture is the exception, not the rule, so that it has nothing to do with state tyranny; that those who inflict the torture are motivated solely by the looming catastrophe, with no tincture of cruelty; that torture in such circumstances is, in fact, little more than self-defense; and that, because of the associations of torture with the horrors of yesteryear, perhaps one should not even call harsh interrogation "torture." And the liberal ideology will crystallize all of these ideas in a single, mesmerizing example: the ticking bomb. . . .

But look at the example one more time. The authorities know there may be a bomb plot in the offing, and they have captured a man who may know something about it but may not. Torture him? How much? For how long? How likely does it have to be that he knows something important? Fifty-fifty? A one percent chance of saving a thousand lives yields ten statistical lives. Does that mean that you can torture up to nine people? If suspects will not break under torture, why not torture their loved ones in front of them? Of course, you won't know until you try whether torturing his child will break the suspect. But that just changes the odds; it does not alter the argument. Once you accept that only the numbers count, then anything, no matter how gruesome, becomes possible. As philosopher Bernard Williams points out, "There are certain situations so monstrous that the idea that the processes of moral rationality could yield an answer in them is insane" and "to spend time thinking what one would decide if one were in such a situation is also insane, if not merely frivolous."

A second, insidious, error built into the ticking-bomb hypothesis is that it assumes a single, ad hoc decision about whether to torture, by officials who ordinarily would only do so in a desperate emergency. But the real world is a world of policies, guidelines, and directives, not of ad hoc emergency measures. We would much rather talk about the ticking bomb than about torture as an organized social practice, which would mean asking questions like these: Should we create a professional cadre of trained torturers? Do we want federal grants for research to devise new and better techniques? Patents issued on high-tech torture devices? Trade conventions in Las Vegas? Should there be a medical sub-specialty of torture doctors, who ensure that captives do not die before they talk? The fiction must also presume that the interrogator operates only under the strictest supervision, in a chain of command where his every move is vetted and controlled by superiors who are actually doing the deliberating. This assumption flies in the face of everything that we know about how organizations work. The basic rule in every bureaucratic organization is that operational details and the guilty knowledge that goes with them get pushed down the chain of command as far as possible. We saw this phenomenon at Abu Ghraib, where military-intelligence officers gave military police vague orders like: "Loosen this guy up for us"; "Make sure he has a bad night"; "Make sure he gets the treatment."

Who guarantees that case-hardened torturers, inured to levels of violence and pain that would make ordinary people vomit at the sight, will know where to draw the line on when torture should be used? They rarely have in the past. They didn't in Algeria. They didn't in Israel, where, in 1999, the Supreme Court backpedaled from an earlier consent to harsh interrogation practices because the interrogators were . . . torturing two thirds of their Palestinian captives. Mark Osiel, who studied the Argentine military in the Dirty War, reports that many of the torturers had qualms about what they were doing until priests reassured them that they were fighting God's fight. By the end of the Dirty War, the qualms were gone, and, as John Simpson and Jana Bennett report, officers were placing bets on who could kidnap the prettiest girl to rape and torture. Escalation is the rule, not the aberration. Abu Ghraib is the fully predictable image of what a torture culture looks like. You cannot reasonably expect that interrogators in a torture culture will be the fastidious and well-meaning torturers that the liberal ideology fantasizes.

For all these reasons, the ticking-bomb scenario is an intellectual fraud. In its place, we must address the real questions about torture — questions about uncertainty, questions about the morality of consequences, and questions about what it does to a culture and the torturers themselves to introduce the practice. Once we do so, I suspect that few Americans will be willing to accept the ticking-bomb scenario as a serious argument. . . .

The liberal ideology of torture, which assumes that torture can be neatly confined to exceptional ticking-bomb cases and surgically severed from cruelty and tyranny, represents a dangerous delusion. It becomes more dangerous still coupled with an endless war on terror, a permanent emergency in which the White House insists that its emergency powers rise above the limiting power of statutes and treaties. Claims to long-term emergency powers that entail the power to torture should send chills through liberals of the right as well as the left, and no one should still think that liberal torture has nothing to do with tyranny.

MICHAEL IGNATIEFF, THE TORTURE WARS
The New Republic, Apr. 22, 2002

. . . Torture is fundamentally a political strategy. Generally, it is not used . . . to save lives, but to break the will of political opponents. Whenever a state is locked in an ongoing battle of wills with a terrorist group, the purpose of torture soon ceases to be the extraction of information alone. Its objective becomes to spread fear, to reduce the number of people willing to work for terror organizations. That is the basic reason why torture metastasizes so rapidly from the exception to the rule. And the natural strategy of terrorists is to respond in kind. If you want to make more terrorists, one sure way to do so — the French in Algeria would be the example here — is to torture more suspects.

Thinking that torture will help us in a war against terror also falsifies what our problem is. We think that our problem is information, and so we need torture to get the truth. In reality, before September 11 there was plenty of information in the possession of the American authorities (noise, but no signal). No, our problem is not a problem of knowledge. It is a problem of belief. It is not what terrorists know that makes them dangerous; it is what they believe. And beliefs cannot be changed by physical duress. Indeed, they may be reinforced. Those who survive torture become living monuments to the brutality that has been inflicted upon them. If they die under torture, they become martyrs to their cause.

Any counter-terror campaign is a battle to persuade as well as to dissuade. Terrorists do need to know that what they believe about us is false. They believe that we are weak and will not fight; and so we should prove them wrong. They believe that we are hypocrites; and so they need to know that we actually believe in the constitutional prohibition against cruel and unusual punishment. They need to know all this if we are to win. Winning is about not losing our nerve, about not losing control in the face of provocation. The military logic of terror is to provoke us into reciprocal atrocity that will lose us the war for legitimacy and the war for opinion.

The barbarians who kidnapped Daniel Pearl undoubtedly tortured him. He was subjected to indecent abuse, followed by horrifying death, because he was an American and a Jew. It is hard not to want to do the same in return, but it would be a mistake. Torturing his captors would set in motion an escalation of reprisals that would probably end up jeopardizing the life of every American in Pakistan. The people who killed Pearl may have violated all humane norms, but we have strong prudential reasons for holding on to these norms, even when our enemies do not. . . .

If we can kill warrior terrorists in combat, why can't we torture sleeper terrorists when we capture them in our midst? But the situation is not so simple. If we are at war, then the ethics of war apply. The basic principle of those ethics is: kill if you have to kill, but do not inflict unnecessary suffering. A warrior kills his enemy as efficiently as possible. A barbarian seeks to inflict suffering. This moral distinction is not just a warrior's code of honor, dependent on reciprocity among fellow warriors. It is meant to apply also in the conduct of warriors toward civilians, and even toward barbarians. A soldier who would not hesitate to kill an enemy has good reason to have additional scruples about torturing him.

There is something about inflicting suffering, even for the extraction of useful information, that exposes those who act in our name to unnecessary moral harm. We may not feel any tenderness toward terrorist suspects, but we should feel special concern for our own agents. Torture is a face-to-face activity. As Wislawa Szymborska has written, it is highly dependent on the human capacity for empathy:

> *The body is painful,*
> *it must eat, breathe air, and sleep,*
> *it has thin skin, with blood right beneath,*
> *it has a goodly supply of teeth and nails,*
> *its bones are brittle, its joints extensible.*
> *In torture, all this is taken into account.*

If a good torturer must be able to imagine, with some precision, what pain must be like for another human being, then we can only imagine what inner violence the torturer must do to deafen his own instincts to the screams that he causes. Over time, when torture becomes routine, it creates dead souls. To the degree that we care about causing moral hazard, we should be concerned about exposing our own citizens to the face-to-face infliction of pain. To advocate torture, in other words, we must be willing to ask another person to do it in our name and to be scarred by it. This is the deontological ditch — not just the harm done to the victim, but the harm done to the perpetrator — that I, for one, would prefer not to cross.

All of these preliminary thoughts about torture, it might be said, do not escape the frame of the thought experiment. They, too, remain abstract and unreal and high-minded. We need the test of relevant historical contexts, which might offer credible examples where, despite what liberals may think, torture actually works. The central case here is Algeria.

Although successive French governments from the 1950s right up to the present administration have denied that torture was anything but an exceptional and sadistic abuse by particular individuals, the evidence is overwhelming that torture was a systemic and central tool in the French struggle against Algerian independence. One obvious reason for this practice was racism, linked to fear. The belief that those whom you torture do not quite belong to the same human race certainly helps when you are applying the electrodes. It is a general rule that torture anchors itself in situations — apartheid South Africa, for example — in which one race or ethnic group is trying to keep another group down by force.

From a strategic point of view, the rationale for torture in these racially charged situations is rather the same as the rationale for terror. It becomes rational to torture when the group that you are trying to control outnumbers your forces and when that group appears to have you on the run, just as it can seem rational to resort to terror when the state you are opposing has such a preponderant advantage of force that only asymmetrical assault will make a difference. Both torture and terror are the weapons of the weak.

The French might have decided that a better response to Algerian demands for self-determination would be to win Algerians over to some continuing association with

France, just as the Algerian FLN movement might have decided that non-violent public demonstrations, strikes, and sit-ins would build a better case for freedom than the random butchery of settlers. There was nothing inevitable about the descent into the inferno. As Alistair Horne's exemplary history of the Algerian war, *A Savage War of Peace*, makes clear, even as late as 1958 thousands of Muslim Algerians greeted Charles de Gaulle's historic visit to Algiers with joy, believing that some kind of association between France and a free Algeria could be achieved without more violence. Indeed, one of the key lessons of the Algerian war is that the state counter-terror actions have to maintain control of the escalation gradient. Terrorists deliberately seek to provoke ever more extreme reactions in order to foreclose peaceful alternatives. The state party that succumbs to this provocation rapidly loses control of the capacity to control its own violence or the violence of the other side.

By launching attacks on French settlers on May 9, 1945, the Algerian independence movement set in motion the brutal reprisals of Setif that confirmed the FLN in its determination to resort to terror. Reprisal, torture, and killing by both sides became the inexorable consequences of the initial choice of violence. The violence that the FLN used in its freedom struggle provoked French retaliation, and the French response provoked violence from the Algerians. In the end, the side that prevailed was the one that had the capacity to absorb the most punishment. This turned out to be (as could have been predicted from the beginning) the side that was fighting for its freedom on its own native soil.

In the years since Algerian independence in 1962, it has become conventional in the center of French public opinion to believe that torture helped to lose Algeria. It disgraced the country, hardened Algerian hatreds, and did not stop the independence movement. This view was always contested at the margins by Jean-Marie Le Pen's right-wing political followers, and by the Algerian pieds noirs who went into exile in France after 1962. They have always believed that France lost Algeria not because it was too brutal, but because it was not brutal enough.

This view found a recent champion in the person of a retired French general named Paul Aussaresses, who had been a captain in the French special services attached to the French army in Algeria between 1955 and 1957. In a memoir published in France last year and now translated into English, Aussaresses wrote that he routinely tortured suspects and killed them afterwards, and also ordered and supervised reprisals of civilians after FLN terrorist attacks. His military and police superiors in Algiers explicitly approved all of these actions, and the French government — including François Mitterrand, the French minister of the interior at the time and later president of France — knew what he was doing.

It was not the revelations themselves that caused the scandal. The use of torture was widely denounced by many French intellectuals. What was distinctive about Aussaresses was his jaunty impudence about the whole issue, his insistence that he had no regrets and that he would do it again in the context of the contemporary war on terrorism. When his American publisher got him onto *60 Minutes* and Mike Wallace asked the inevitable question — should the United States torture Zacarias Moussaoui and other suspected terrorist detainees to force them to disclose future plots? — Aussaresses replied: "It seems to me that it's obvious." . . .

Torture divided and weakened the French determination to keep Algeria. Aussaresses's memoir confirms that it was opposed not only by intellectuals. Prefects and policemen and military leaders asked to be transferred. A few military doctors moved tortured prisoners into civilian hospitals to save their lives. Journalists wrote against it: the means corrupted the end itself, destroyed the very justification for staying. Aussaresses regards all these forms of dissent and moral scruple as hypocritical weakness.

In fact they were a strength that saved France. It had granted independence to Tunisia and Morocco and thereafter to its other French colonies. It was impossible, over the longer term, to keep Algeria, whether by torture or by any other means. De Gaulle's moral realism — that no amount of repression could succeed against a people bent on independence — displayed a far greater grasp on reality than the hard-boiled Aussaresses.

The real picture of torture in Algeria comes not from Aussaresses's smug and disagreeable memoir, but from Frantz Fanon's recollections of the asylum in Blida, Algeria, where until his flight in 1956 he cared for both victims and perpetrators of torture. Fanon was wrong about many things, especially the fatuous idea, expressed in *The Wretched of the Earth,* that violence in the service of liberation actually heals and transforms the oppressed; but he was not wrong about the special horror into which societies sink when they meet terror with torture. In his psychiatric clinic at Blida, Fanon treated a twenty-eight-year-old French policeman who was so disturbed by memories of the screams of the men whom he had tortured that he stopped up his windows, put cotton in his ears, and still could not stop the screaming inside his head.

At the same time, Fanon was treating a "patriot" (an Algerian militant) who had been tortured and was still recovering from the use of electric shock. One day the tormented policeman, while waiting to see Fanon, happened to spot the "patriot" in the hospital garden. When Fanon came upon the policeman shortly afterwards, he was "leaning against a tree, looking overcome, trembling and drenched with sweat." Fanon took him home, where the policeman, lying on the sofa, confessed that he had just met one of his victims. After Fanon had sedated the policeman, he went back to the hospital and found that the policeman's victim, the patriot, had tried to hang himself in a toilet. The staff of the clinic could only calm him down by lying: they persuaded him that he had never actually seen his torturer. As for the torturer, he secured a sick-leave transfer back to France.

Torture in Algeria was not only a crime. It was also a mistake. It corrupted victim and perpetrator, French and Algerian alike. Paul Aussaresses's memoir is written in a style of rugged tough-mindedness, which calls itself realism, and which likes to mock liberal scruple for its sentimentality and inability to face hard choices. But this supposed realism and tough-mindedness is nothing of the sort. It is the kind of realism that wins battles and loses wars, a nihilistic cynicism that betrays and eventually destroys the causes it claims to defend. Americans, sorely tried by terror, should take note.

F.   THE ROLE AND ETHICAL OBLIGATIONS OF GOVERNMENT LAWYERS: THE BYBEE MEMORANDUM

1.   Problem

The following excerpt comes from the minutes of a 2002 meeting at Guantánamo Bay Naval Base to discuss interrogation techniques. It was released by the Senate Judiciary Committee. Two of the ten participants were lawyers: One was staff judge advocate to the task force commander at Guantánamo; the other was assistant general counsel to the CIA and chief counsel to the CIA's counterterrorism center. The other participants were military and intelligence officers. Nine days after this meeting, the JAG provided a legal memorandum that approved more than a dozen aggressive interrogation techniques, including stress positions, sleep deprivation, intimidation through the use of military working dogs, forced nudity and forced grooming, isolation, and the "wet towel" technique (a technique similar to waterboarding).[102] Many of these techniques were used on Guantánamo detainees.

1. As you read this excerpt, consider the nature of the lawyers' comments. To what extent are the lawyers providing legal advice? Moral or other advice? Policy recommendations? Do any of their comments exceed the role of a legal advisor?
2. After reading the materials following the excerpt, determine the soundness of the legal advice offered by the lawyers.
3. Consider an e-mail from Mark Fallon, deputy commander of the Department of Defense's Criminal Investigation Task Force, reproduced below directly following the minutes of the meeting. Do you agree or disagree with the concerns Fallon presents there?

In a letter written six years after this meeting, the CIA counsel strongly protested that the minutes distorted his actual comments, and that he did not say that whether something is torture "is basically subject to perception." Rather, he recalls emphasizing "that all interrogation practices . . . must be based upon definitive and binding analysis from the Department of Justice."[103] No other participants have disputed the accuracy of the minutes. In considering this problem, keep in mind that the reality may have been different from what the minutes portray.

For purposes of this problem, we do not use the names of the participants in the meeting. Instead, we identify the staff judge advocate as *JAG* and the CIA lawyer as *CIA counsel*. An officer is identified as *Colonel*, and a representative of the Defense Intelligence Agency is identified as *DIA rep*. Ten persons were present at the meeting.

COUNTER RESISTANCE STRATEGY MEETING MINUTES[104]

The following notes were taken during the aforementioned meeting at 1340 on October 2, 2002. All questions and comments have been paraphrased: . . .

Colonel: We can't do sleep deprivation.

JAG: Yes we can — with approval. . . .

JAG: We may need to curb the harsher operations while ICRC [the International Committee of the Red Cross] is around. It is better not to expose them to any controversial techniques. We must have the support of the DOD.

DIA rep: We have had many reports from Bagram [a U.S. base in Afghanistan] about sleep deprivation being used.

---

102. Legal Brief on Proposed Counter-Resistance Strategies from Diane Beaver to Gen. James T. Hill, Oct. 11, 2002, in The Torture Papers, supra note 16, at 229. The techniques are catalogued in id. at 227-228.

103. Statement from Jonathan Fredman to Sen. Carl Levin, Chair of the Senate Armed Forces Committee, and Sen. John McCain, Ranking Member of the Committee (Nov. 7, 2008), available at http://s3.amazonaws.com/propublica/assets/docs/05aFredman_Statement.pdf.

104. This document was released during Senate hearings on detainee abuse in June 2008, and is available at http://levin.senate.gov/newsroom/supporting/2008/Documents.SASC.061708.pdf, Tab 7.

JAG: True, but officially it is not happening. It is not being reported officially. The ICRC is a serious concern. They will be in and out, scrutinizing our operations, unless they are displeased and decide to protest and leave. This would draw a lot of negative attention. . . .

CIA counsel: The DOJ has provided much guidance on this issue. The CIA is not held to the same rules as the military. In the past when the ICRC has made a big deal about certain detainees, the DOD has "moved" them away from the attention of ICRC. Upon questioning from the ICRC about their whereabouts, the DOD's response has repeatedly been that the detainee merited no status under the Geneva Convention. The CIA has employed aggressive techniques against less than a handful of suspects since 9/11.

Under the Torture Convention, torture has been prohibited under international law, but the language of the statutes is written vaguely. Severe mental and physical pain is prohibited. The mental part is explained as poorly as the physical. Severe physical pain described as anything causing permanent physical damage to major organs or body parts. Mental torture described as anything leading to permanent, profound damage to the senses or personality. It is basically subject to perception. If the detainee dies you're doing it wrong. . . . Any of the techniques that lie on the harshest end of the spectrum must be performed by a highly trained individual. Medical personnel should be present to treat any possible accidents. The CIA operates without military intervention. When the CIA has wanted to use more aggressive techniques in the past, the FBI has pulled their personnel from theatre. In those rare instances, aggressive techniques have proven very helpful.

JAG: We will need documentation to protect us.

CIA counsel: Yes, if someone dies while aggressive techniques are being used, regardless of cause of death, the backlash of attention would be severely detrimental. Everything must be approved and documented.

DIA rep: LEA [law enforcement agency] personnel will not participate in harsh techniques.

JAG: There is no legal reason why LEA personnel cannot participate in these operations. . . . LEA choice not participate in these types of interrogations is more ethical and moral as opposed to legal.

CIA counsel: The videotaping of even totally legal techniques will look "ugly." . . . The Torture Convention prohibits torture and cruel, inhumane and degrading treatment. The US did not sign up on the second part, because of the 8th amendment (cruel and unusual punishment), but we did sign the part about torture. This gives us more license to use more controversial techniques.

JAG: Does SERE employ the "wet towel" technique?[105]

CIA counsel: If a well-trained individual is used to perform this technique it can feel like you're drowning. The lymphatic system will react as if you're suffocating, but your body will not cease to function. It is very effective to identify phobias and use them (i.e, insects, snakes, claustrophobia). . . .

JAG: In the BSCT [Behavioral Science Consultation Team] paper it says something about "imminent threat of death." . . .

CIA counsel: The threat of death is also subject to scrutiny, and should be handled on a case by case basis. Mock executions don't work as well as friendly approaches, like letting someone write a letter home, or providing them with an extra book.

DIA rep: I like the part about ambient noise. . . .

Meeting ended at 1450.

———————————————

105. *SERE* stands for "Survival, Evasion, Resistance, Escape." SERE training is given by the United States to its own special forces to teach resistance to torture and abuse. Several SERE tactics, including waterboarding, were "reverse engineered" to be used by U.S. interrogators against uncooperative detainees. See Jane Mayer, The Dark Side 158 (2008). — Eps.

The approval of the harsh techniques drew some internal criticism at the Department of Defense. Noteworthy is the following e-mail from Mark Fallon, the deputy commander of DOD's Criminal Investigation Task Force.

> **From:** Fallon Mark
> **Sent:** Monday, October 28, 2002
> **To:** McCahon Sam
>
> Sam:
>   . . . This looks like the kinds of stuff Congressional hearings are made of. Quotes from [the JAG] regarding things that are not being reported give the appearance of impropriety. Other comments like "It is basically subject to perception. If the detainee dies you're doing it wrong" and "Any of the techniques that lie on the harshest end of the spectrum must be performed by a highly trained individual. Medical personnel should be present to treat any possible accidents" seem to stretch beyond the bounds of legal propriety. Talk of "wet towel treatment" which results in the lymphatic gland reacting as if you are suffocating, would in my opinion shock the conscience of any legal body looking at using the results of the interrogations or possibly even the interrogators. Someone needs to be considering how history will look back at this.
>
> R/Mark Fallon
> Deputy Commander
> Criminal Investigation Task Force [Department of Defense]

2. Reading

DAVID LUBAN, LIBERALISM, TORTURE, AND THE TICKING TIME BOMB

in The Torture Debate in America 34, 56
(Karen J. Greenberg ed., 2005)

. . . What makes the Bybee Memo jarring by conventional legal standards is that in its most controversial sections, it barely goes through the motions of standard legal argument. Instead of addressing and rebutting the obvious arguments against its conclusions, it elects not to mention them; in several of its crucial sections it cites no statutes, regulations, or judicial decisions to support its most controversial conclusions (presumably because there are none); and when it does cite conventional sources of law, it employs them in utterly unconventional ways.

[Other memos produced by the OLC] are less transparent about it, but they too simply discard the project of providing an impartial analysis of the law as mainstream lawyers and judges understand it. Instead, they provide aggressive advocacy briefs to give those who order or engage in torture legal cover.

Lawyers have a word for a legal opinion that does this. It is called a CYA memorandum—Cover Your Ass. Without the memorandum, the client who wants to push the legal envelope is on his own. But with a CYA memo in hand, he can insist that he cleared it with the lawyers first, and that way he can duck responsibility.

Notice that my diagnosis here differs from Anthony Lewis's oft-quoted judgment that the torture memos "read like the advice of a mob lawyer to a mafia don on how to skirt the law and stay out of prison." They are not advice about how to stay out of prison; they advise their clients that they are not going to prison. They are opinion letters blessing or koshering conduct for the twin purposes of all CYA memos: reassuring cautious lower level employees that they can follow orders without getting into trouble, and allowing wrongdoers to duck responsibility.

At this point, I wish to examine the torture memos from the standpoint of legal ethics. Is there anything wrong with writing a CYA memo for a client? Aren't lawyers supposed to spin the law to their clients' advantage? The traditional answer for courtroom advocates is obviously yes. A criminal defender is stuck with the case she is stuck with, and her legal briefs will make the best purse she can out of the sow's ear before her. The only constraint on legal argument in the adversary system is the weak and vague requirement of non-frivolity.

But the torture memos are not trial briefs. They are legal advice, and in traditional legal ethics they answer to a different standard: not non-frivolity but candor.

The distinction between the roles of advocate and advisor is fundamental. The ABA's former Code of Professional Responsibility states that "the two roles are essentially different. . . . While serving as advocate, a lawyer should resolve in favor of his client doubts as to the bounds of the law. In serving a client as adviser, a lawyer . . . should give his professional opinion as to . . . the applicable law." The current Model Rules of Professional Conduct likewise distinguish the roles of advocate and advisor, and the rule for advisors calls for "independent professional judgment" and "candid advice." A comment to this rule explains that the lawyer should provide independent and candid advice even if "the advice will be unpalatable to the client."

That's the doctrine. What's the theory? Perhaps the clearest explanation of this conception of the legal advisor's role appears in a classic report on professional responsibility issued by a joint conference of the ABA and the Association of American Law Schools nearly half a century ago. Co-authored by Lon Fuller and John Randall, the report argues that the two roles of advocate and counselor

> must be sharply distinguished. The man who has been called into court to answer for his own actions is entitled to a fair hearing. Partisan advocacy plays its essential part in such a hearing, and the lawyer pleading his client's case may properly present it in the most favorable light. A similar resolution of doubts in one direction becomes inappropriate when the lawyer acts as counselor. The reasons that justify and even require partisan advocacy in the trial of a cause do not grant any license to the lawyer to participate as legal adviser in a line of conduct that is immoral, unfair, or of doubtful legality.

Notice the argument here. The Joint Conference Report begins with the assumption that it is one-sided partisan advocacy, not impartial advising, that stands in need of special justification. This point is fundamental. Legal ethics is at its most troubling when a lawyer adopts a wholly partisan point of view on behalf of a client, because that viewpoint discounts to zero the interests of everyone but the client, and no real-life system of ethical thought, secular or religious, countenances writing off all interests but one. Legal ethicists usually go on to provide a special justification of partisan advocacy, often based on the requirements of the adversary system. I myself am skeptical of those arguments; but even granting the legitimacy of partisanship in its best-justified context, the formal give-and-take of appellate argument, legal spin-doctoring with no adversary to counter it and no impartial decision-maker to evaluate it is, quite simply, dishonest. That is the theory behind Rule 2.1.

Furthermore, without the "independent and candid advice" standard, the theoretical basis of lawyer-client confidentiality crumbles. Confidentiality has always been one of the major puzzles in legal ethics. After all, on utilitarian grounds it's a bad bet for society because it allows crooked clients to hide the evidence so frequently—as witness the 40-year history of Big Tobacco stonewalling the facts via their lawyers. Given this embarrassing fact, how does the profession justify its sacred norm of confidentiality? It does so by arguing that the lawyer needs confidential information

> to advise the client to refrain from wrongful conduct. . . . Based upon experience, lawyers know that almost all clients follow the advice given, and the law is upheld.

In other words: confidentiality is a good bet for society *only* because we can count on lawyers to give sound advice on compliance (and clients to take that advice). If the lawyer doesn't give independent, candid advice, this entire argument, and with it the whole edifice of confidentiality, comes tumbling down.

But what happens when the client doesn't want candid advice? When the client comes to the lawyer and says, in effect, "Give me an opinion that lets me do what I want to do"? The answer is that the lawyer cannot do this—or rather, that if the lawyer does it, she has crossed the fatal line from legal advisor to moral or legal accomplice. . . .

Giving the client skewed advice because the client wants it is a different role from either advocate or advisor. I call it the Lawyer As Absolver, or, less nicely, the Lawyer As Indulgence Seller. . . .

The important thing to notice is that the role of Absolver, unlike the roles of Advocate and Advisor, is totally illegitimate. The courtroom advocate's biased presentation will get countered by the adversary in a public hearing. The advisor's presentation will not. In the courtroom, the adversary is supposed to check the advocate's excesses. In the lawyer's office, advising the client, the lawyer is supposed to check the client's excesses. Conflating the two roles moves the lawyer out of the limited role-based immunity that advocates enjoy into the world of the indulgence seller.

NOTES AND QUESTIONS

1. Shortly after the release of the Bybee Memorandum in 2004, its critics began to question the legal ethics of writing memoranda that seemingly gave the green light to torture. It was often unclear whether the critics objected to the conclusions of the Bybee Memo on moral grounds, because they are opponents of torture, or whether they objected on the ground that writing the opinion violated formal ethics rules. Obviously, these are not mutually exclusive. But the two criticisms are fundamentally different. The former criticism would be the same no matter what the law said. Even if the plain language of the law approved torture, moralists might argue that lawyers should refuse to put their imprimatur on torture.

The latter criticism is that the lawyers did not interpret the law honestly. That could violate several rules of legal ethics. In the American Bar Association's Model Rules of Professional Conduct—the model for almost all U.S. jurisdictions—these are:

> Rule 2.1 (discussed in the reading above): "In representing a client, a lawyer shall exercise independent professional judgment and render candid advice."
> Rule 1.2(d): "A lawyer shall not counsel a client to engage, or assist a client, in conduct that the lawyer knows is criminal or fraudulent. . . ."
> Rule 1.4(b): "A lawyer shall explain a matter to the extent reasonably necessary to permit the client to make informed decisions regarding the representation."
> Rule 8.4(c): "It is professional misconduct for a lawyer to engage in conduct involving dishonesty, fraud, deceit or misrepresentation."

For the interrogation memos to violate these rules, it seems that the lawyers must know that the advice in the opinions is a misrepresentation of the law — or at least have written them believing that they do not faithfully represent the law. How would one know that, or prove it? What if the lawyer responds, "I believe what I wrote"?

2. Is the critique that the legal analysis is so frivolous that intelligent, capable lawyers could not have written it in good faith? How do you tell when a legal argument is frivolous (as opposed to merely being an argument you disagree with)? What if other scholars disagree that the opinions are frivolous? In testimony to the Senate Judiciary Committee, Professor Michael Stokes Paulsen, a noted scholar and former OLC lawyer, strongly defends the memoranda:

> I have studied the legal memoranda in question, drawing on my expertise as a legal scholar whose work over much of the past decade has embraced these types of issues as a major area of research and writing, and on my experience as a government attorney in OLC in the late 1980s and early 1990s. The analysis contained in the memoranda in question is analysis with which, in certain respects, persons of good will can reasonably disagree, but it is well within the range of customary, legitimate, proper, and entirely ethical legal advice that may be provided by confidential legal advisors to the president and his administration.

What Went Wrong: Torture and the Office of Legal Counsel in the Bush Administration: Hearing Before the S. Subcomm. on Administrative Oversight and the Courts of the S. Comm. on the Judiciary (May 13, 2009) (testimony of Michael Stokes Paulsen, Prof. of Law, Univ. of St. Thomas), available at http://www.stthomas.edu/law/academics/curriculum/PaulsenSenateTestimony.pdf.

3. Beginning in 2004, the Justice Department's internal ethics unit, the Office of Professional Responsibility, launched an investigation of the Bybee Memo, examining e-mail traffic and earlier drafts. OPR completed a lengthy report in 2008, but as of November 2009 the report has not been released. It is reportedly critical of the OLC lawyers.

4. If a client asks a lawyer to make the strongest argument possible for the legality of what the client wants to do, can the lawyer do so, or must the lawyer provide a candid and independent opinion? (This does not appear to be what the OLC lawyers claimed to be doing, however. The August 1, 2002, "techniques" memo states, "We wish to emphasize that this is our best reading of the law," while Bradbury describes his May 10, 2005, "techniques" memo in similar terms: "the legal standards we apply in this memorandum . . . constitute our authoritative view of the legal standards applicable under [the torture statutes]." U.S. Dept. of Justice, Office of Legal Counsel, Memorandum for John Rizzo, Acting General Counsel CIA, Interrogation of al Qaeda Operative, at 18 (Aug. 1, 2002), available at http://luxmedia.vo.llnwd.net/o10/clients/aclu/olc_08012002_bybee.pdf.; Bradbury "Techniques" Memo, supra note 12, at 1.

CHAPTER
23

Sexual Violence

This chapter concerns the treatment under international law of rape and other forms of sexually violent, abusive, or degrading conduct. We have thus far examined a range of crimes applicable to the murder of innocents and the senseless torture, violence, and suffering inflicted on others. Even in this horrific landscape, the crimes of sexual violence inflicted on men[1] as well as women, but primarily on women, challenge credulity because of the degree of barbarism, depraved imagination, and sheer cruelty they reflect. Our first reading in Section A is intended to bring home this reality.

In Section B, we examine the legal treatment of various forms of sexual violence and abuse. Although a variety of charges may be appropriate depending upon the circumstances of the individual case — including sexual slavery, persecution, forced pregnancy, enforced sterilization, and forced marriage[2] — we will largely focus on rape. In international tribunals, rape, like torture, cannot be charged as a stand-alone crime. Rather, it must be charged as a species of war crime, genocide, or crime against humanity. We isolate rape and other forms of sexual violence for special consideration for two reasons.

First, as is explored in Section B, this topic provides the best example of evolving international criminal norms being translated first into legal proscriptions and ultimately into accountability. Historically, "the incidence of rape in armed conflict has been widely ignored, underplayed or tolerated. Rape is too frequently regarded as an unfortunate but inevitable side-effect of conflict or as an anticipated bonus for

---

1. For example, in the case of Prosecutor v. Tadić, Case No. IT-94-1-T, Opinion and Judgment, ¶206 (May 7, 1997), the following finding was made regarding the treatment of concentration camp inmates (including witnesses G and H):

> ... [Witness] G and Witness H ... were ordered to jump down into the inspection pit, then Fikret Harambasic, who was naked and bloody from beating, was made to jump into the pit with them and Witness H was ordered to lick his naked bottom and G to suck his penis and then to bite his testicles. Meanwhile a group of men in uniform stood around the inspection pit watching and shouting to bite harder. All three were then made to get out of the pit onto the hangar floor and Witness H was threatened with a knife that both his eyes would be cut out if he did not hold Fikret Harambasic's mouth closed to prevent him from screaming; G was then made to lie between the naked Fikret Harambasic's legs and, while the latter struggled, hit and bite his genitals. G then bit off one of Fikret Harambasic's testicles and spat it out and was told he was free to leave. ... Fikret Harambasic has not been seen or heard of since.

2. For a useful survey of these and other crimes, see Kelly D. Askin, The Jurisprudence of International War Crimes Tribunals: Securing Gender Justice for Some Survivors, in Listening to the Silences: Women and War 125 (Helen Durham & Tracey Gurd eds., 2005).

soldiers on all sides."[3] For example, as Kelly Dawn Askin reports, throughout the European theater in World War II "sexual assault was committed with a vengeance, and reports of these crimes were submitted to the Nuremberg Tribunal. The transcripts contain evidence of vile and torturous rape, forced prostitution, forced sterilization, forced abortion, pornography, sexual mutilation, and sexual sadism."[4] Yet a "major deficiency of the Nuremberg Trial was its absolute neglect of crimes against women."[5] No crimes of sexual violence — not even rape — were expressly included within the jurisdiction of the Nuremberg Tribunals,[6] and no such cases were pursued under more general prohibitions.

Victims of sexual violence fared better in the Tokyo Tribunal. Although rape was not, again, specifically identified in the Tokyo Charter, it was successfully charged in that tribunal as a war crime under "inhumane treatment," "ill-treatment," and "failure to respect family honour and rights."[7] The Tribunal documented evidence of widespread rapes and heard evidence regarding the approximately 20,000 rapes that occurred in the Chinese city of Nanking during the first six weeks of its occupation by Japanese forces.[8] Yet even in this tribunal, rape was prosecuted as a secondary offense, and the Tribunal ignored other types of extreme criminal abuses since recognized as international crimes, notably the sexual slavery of between 80,000 and 200,000 "comfort women" by Japanese troops.[9]

Since the 1990s sexual predation in conflict situations has been a focus of a great deal of attention — among women's groups and other nongovernmental organizations (NGOs), in feminist[10] and academic circles,[11] in international legal instruments,[12] and finally in the prosecution of those who commit sexualized crimes. The heightened focus on sex and gender crimes flows from a number of

---

3. Christine Chinkin, Rape and Sexual Abuse of Women in International Law, in Humanitarian Law 365, 373 (Judith Gardam ed., 1999).

4. See Kelly Dawn Askin, War Crimes Against Women: Prosecution in International War Crimes Tribunals 97 (1997). Thus, for example, there was evidence that in some European towns and villages every woman and girl was sexually assaulted, sometimes in exceedingly brutal fashion, often by gangs of soldiers. Id. at 57. Approximately 100,000 rapes took place in Berlin alone in the last two weeks of the war. Id. at 52.

5. Id. at 97.

6. See Charter of the Intl. Military Tribunal [IMT] at Nuremberg, Annex to the London Agreement, Aug. 8, 1945, 82 U.N.T.S. 279; Tokyo Charter for the Intl. Military Tribunal for the Far East, as amended by General Orders No. 20, Apr. 26, 1946, T.I.A.S. No. 1589. However, Article II(1)(c) of Control Council Law No. 10 (CC10), put in place in December 20, 1945, to prosecute war criminals not dealt with by the IMT, did explicitly list rape as a crime against humanity. See Control Council for Germany, Official Gazette 50 (Jan. 31, 1946).

7. Askin, supra note 4, at 202.

8. See id. at 180.

9. See id. at 74.

10. See, e.g., Karen Engle, Feminism and Its (Dis)contents: Criminalizing Wartime Rape in Bosnia and Herzegovina, 99 Am. J. Intl. L. 778 (2005); Janet Halley, Rape at Rome: Feminist Interventions in the Criminalization of Sex-Related Violence in Positive International Criminal Law, 30 Mich. J. Intl. L. 1 (2008).

11. See, e.g., Annette Demers, Women and War: A Bibliography of Recent Works, 34 Intl. J. Legal Info. 98 (2006); David S. Mitchell, The Prohibition of Rape in International Humanitarian Law as a Norm of *Jus Cogens*: Clarifying the Doctrine, 15 Duke J. Comp. & Intl. L. 219, 220 n.5 (2005) (gathering sources).

12. Discussed passim in this chapter. It is worth noting, however, that while the instruments constituting international *criminal* tribunals have increasingly recognized crimes of sexual violence, abuse, and degradation, international human rights conventions have largely neglected this subject. See, e.g., Mitchell, supra note 11, at 245 ("Regrettably, the Inter-American Convention on the Prevention, Punishment and Eradication of Violence Against Women is the only major human rights treaty that expressly lists rape as a violation or even mentions the word 'rape.'"); Patricia Viseur Sellers, Sexual Violence and Peremptory Norms: The Legal Value of Rape, 34 Case W. Res. J. Intl. L. 287, 301 (2002); see generally Bibliography and Resource List: Human Rights for Women — Human Rights for All (2008), http://www.cwgl.rutgers.edu/16days/kit08/biblio.pdf. This is important in part because the focus of transitional justice mechanisms — and particularly the truth and reconciliation commissions examined further in Chapter 24 — is often limited by such conventions. "Frequently, what constitutes human rights abuse for the purposes of the

circumstances, including the global women's movement and increased attention in domestic legal regimes to rape and related crimes. Certainly, media coverage of the sexual atrocities committed in the former Yugoslavia played a role.[13] Changes in the nature of recent conflicts and thus the potential magnitude of sex crimes has lent a new urgency to the subject. According to Amnesty International, "[o]nly five per cent of the casualties in the First World War were civilians. By the mid-1990's, about 80 per cent of the casualties in conflicts were civilians — most of them women and children. . . . Women who have taken no part in conflicts are being murdered, raped[,] and mutilated."[14]

Perhaps most striking, however, is the increasing use of sexual violence and abuse in conflict situations in a premeditated and organized way as a tool of war. "Rape, when used as a weapon of war, is systematically employed for a variety of purposes, including intimidation, humiliation, political terror, extracting information, rewarding soldiers, and 'ethnic cleansing.' "[15] This type of organized sexual violence was pronounced in the conflict in the former Yugoslavia, where an estimated 30,000 to 60,000 women were raped.[16] It is estimated that 80 percent of the rapes occurred in detention or "rape camps."[17]

Although rape was committed by men in every warring faction in that conflict against women of every ethnicity and religion, it is reported that the majority of rape victims in the Yugoslav conflict were Muslim women. They were apparently targeted in part because it was felt that, given their cultural and religious traditions, rape would be an effective instrument of ethnic cleansing. Rape is always traumatic, of course, but commentators assert that its consequences may be "*particularly severe* in traditional, patriarchal societies, where the rape survivor is often perceived as soiled and unmarriageable, thus, becoming a target of societal ostracism."[18] With this understanding, Serbian forces used sexual violence to achieve their policy goals. As Catharine MacKinnon notes, "[i]t is rape as an instrument of forced exile, to make you leave your home and never come back. It is rape to be seen and heard by others,

---

truth commission is limited to violations of civil and political rights, particularly that narrow core of rights which are defined as non-derogable under international human rights treaties. . . . The effect of these definitional limitations is to leave out a range of harms, which coincidently overlap with those rights violations most often experienced by women." Fionnuala Ní Aoláin & Catherine Turner, Gender, Truth, and Transition, 16 UCLA Women's L.J. 229, 250-251 (2007).

13. See, e.g., Peggy Kuo, Prosecuting Crimes of Sexual Violence in an International Tribunal, 34 Case W. Res. J. Intl. L. 305, 308 (2002) ("Certainly, the attention paid to what happened to women in the Balkans was a direct consequence of the outrage by the international community, non-governmental organizations, women's groups, the media, and individual journalists who had the courage to go into the war zones, talk to women, record their testimony, and bring the information to the world."); but see Rhonda Copelon, Gender Crimes as War Crimes: Integrating Crimes Against Women into International Criminal Law, 46 McGill L.J. 217, 224 (2000) ("[T]he media and other observers of the genocide in Rwanda did not report the massive and notorious rape of women during the Rwandan genocide. Rape was essentially invisible until nine months later, when a Belgian doctor publicized that women were presenting themselves in unusual numbers to bear the children of rape. Nor was it, thereafter, officially documented. That was left to the initiatives of two NGOs, African Rights and the Women's Project of Human Rights Watch."); Binaifer Nowrojee, Making the Invisible War Crime Visible: Post-conflict Justice for Sierra Leone's Rape Victims, 18 Harv. Hum. Rts. J. 85, 86-87 (2005) (noting same with respect to Sierra Leone).

14. The International Criminal Court: Ensuring Justice for Women, Amnesty International 1 (1998). For example, it is estimated that 72 percent of Sierra Leonean women and girls "experienced human rights abuses . . . [and] over 50% were victims of sexual violence." Nowrojee, supra note 13, at 86.

15. Amnesty International, Violence Against Women, Rape as a Tool of War, http://www.amnestyusa.org/women/violence/rapeinwartime.html (last visited Aug. 19, 2009).

16. See Human Rights Watch, Women and Global Human Rights, Rape: A Weapon of War, http://www.webster.edu/~woolflm/warrape.html (last visited Aug. 19, 2009).

17. Engle, supra note 10, at 785.

18. Askin, supra note 4, at 267-268; see also Adrien Katherine Wing & Sylke Merchán, Rape, Ethnicity, and Culture: Spirit Injury from Bosnia to Black America, 25 Colum. Hum. Rts. L. Rev. 1, 20-25 (1993).

rape as spectacle. It is rape to shatter a people, to drive a wedge through a community."[19] And it is also rape as genocide. According to Islamic law and culture, the ethnicity of the child is determined by the ethnicity of its father.[20] "[T]he children of non-Muslim Serbian rapists are not considered to be Muslims."[21] "There are reports on all sides that 'women are held hostages until they become pregnant; and that once confirmed as pregnant, they are held by their captors until they are past the point of abortion.' "[22] In this way, Serbs attempted to destroy the Muslim population of portions of Bosnia, "replacing" that population with "Serbian" children born of rape. Professor Kelly Dawn Askin, a leading expert on war crimes against women, concluded after surveying the horrific crimes visited on women through centuries of warfare that the organized sexual violence in the former Yugoslavia distinguished that conflict from others. While World War II is remembered for the Holocaust, the Balkan war will be remembered for its "manipulation and abuse of the female gender to commit ethnic cleansing and genocide."[23]

In 1994, during the Rwandan genocide, an estimated 250,000 to 500,000 women were raped[24] and otherwise subjected to sexualized crimes. The UN Special Rapporteur on human rights in Rwanda concluded that, as in the former Yugoslavia, "[r]ape was systemic and was used as a 'weapon' by the perpetrators of the massacres . . . [and a]ccording to consistent and reliable testimony, . . . rape was the rule and its absence the exception."[25]

The chart that follows is designed to illustrate how the international tribunals' charters have evolved to respond to the sexual predation in the former Yugoslavia, Rwanda, and other armed conflicts. The chart shows that it was only in the International Criminal Tribunal for Rwanda (ICTR) Statute that the international community's willingness to explicitly outlaw rape and other forms of sexual violence as both war crimes and crimes against humanity was demonstrated. After 1994 and the ICTR Statute, the regulations for the East Timor Special Panels ("ETimor"), the statute of the Special Court for Sierra Leone ("SCSL"), and the ICC Statute ("ICC") reflect international recognition of additional crimes against humanity and war crimes based on sexual violence. (The law establishing the Cambodian Extraordinary Chambers ("Cambodia"), however, is a throw-back in terms of its recognition of crimes of sexual violence.)

	IMT 1945	CC10 1945	Tokyo 1946	GCs 1949	ICTY 1993	ICTR 1994	ETimor 2000	SCSL 2002	ICC 2002	Cambodia 2004
Crimes Against Humanity										
Rape		x			x	x	x	x	x	x

---

19. Catharine A. MacKinnon, Crimes of War, Crimes of Peace, in on Human Rights: The Oxford Amnesty Lectures 83, 89 (Stephen Shute & Susan Hurley eds., 1993).

20. See, e.g., Askin, supra note 4, at 268; Wing & Merchán, supra note 18, at 18; Jocelyn Campanaro, Women, War, and International Law: The Historical Treatment of Gender-Based War Crimes, 89 Geo. L.J. 2557, 2571 (2001).

21. Wing & Merchán, supra note 18, at 18.

22. Askin, supra note 4, at 273.

23. Id. at 295-296.

24. See Human Rights Watch, Rape: A Weapon of War, supra note 16; see also Human Rights Watch, Struggling to Survive: Barriers to Justice for Rape Victims in Rwanda (Sept. 2004).

25. Special Rapporteur of the Commn. on Human Rights, Report on the Situation of Human Rights in Rwanda, U.N. Doc. E/CN.4/1996/68 (Jan. 29, 1996).

	IMT 1945	CC10 1945	Tokyo 1946	GCs 1949	ICTY 1993	ICTR 1994	ETimor 2000	SCSL 2002	ICC 2002	Cambodia 2004
Enforced prostitution							x	x	x	
Sexual slavery							x	x	x	
Forced pregnancy							x	x	x	
Enforced sterilization							x		x	
Any other form of indecent assault (ICTR)/ sexual violence (SCSL) of a comparable gravity (ETimor/ ICC)							x	x	x	
Persecution based on gender							x		x	
War Crimes										
Rape						x	x	x	x	
Enforced prostitution						x	x	x	x	
Sexual slavery							x		x	
Forced pregnancy							x		x	
Enforced sterilization							x		x	
Any other form of indecent assault (ICTR/ SCSL)/sex- ual violence also constitut- ing a grave breach of the Geneva Conven- tions (ETi- mor/ICC)						x	x	x	x	

Most recently, in February 2009, after a four-year trial, the Trial Chambers of the Special Court for Sierra Leone convicted three former leaders of the Revolutionary United Front (RUF) of, inter alia, "forced marriage." This constitutes the first time that an international court entered a conviction for the crime of "forced marriage" — although that crime has not yet been explicitly recognized in any international charter and instead was charged in Sierra Leone under the "other inhumane acts" category of crimes against humanity.[26] The prosecution argued that forced marriage was a crime different than other forms of sexual violence, such as sexual slavery, because the abducted women forced to become the sexual partners of their captors were subjected to lengthy associations of a domestic nature. After the verdicts, the lead prosecutor explained: " 'Our position is that sexual slavery is a horrendous crime. . . . Victims would be held for days or weeks and forced into sex acts. Forced marriage is all of that plus essentially being consorts to the rebels.' The result . . . is stigma, with the women being seen as responsible for the crimes of their 'husbands.' "[27]

The evolution in the explicit legal recognition of crimes of sexual violence, abuse, and degradation provides cold comfort to survivors absent active enforcement. Perhaps most significant, then, is the increasing willingness of international prosecutors to seek convictions based on sexualized criminal conduct. Successful prosecutions in the ICTY and ICTR were founded, at least in part, on the widespread sexual violence visited primarily upon women in the Yugoslav and Rwandan conflicts. These prosecutions led to greater attention to procedural matters of critical importance to rape survivors, including witness protection, victim services, and protective evidentiary rules. Although many commentators wish that more could have been done in investigating and sanctioning rapists in these and other ongoing conflicts where widespread and systematic rapes are endemic,[28] most concede that much progress has been made in the last few decades.

A second reason to isolate crimes of sexual violence and degradation for separate consideration, explored in Section C, is that the subject permits us to focus on the critical discretionary choices that face prosecutors when choosing how to charge a case. Sexual violence can be, and has been, prosecuted under offense categories that are not explicitly identified as sexual crimes. Thus, for example, defendants in the ICTY were convicted not only of the crime against humanity of rape,[29] but also were convicted of torture[30] and persecution[31] based on rape and other sexual abuses. And as we shall see, in *Prosecutor v. Jean-Paul Akayesu*,[32] the ICTR entered a judgment of conviction for genocide based in part on numerous rapes.

Because rape and other sexual abuses could be charged under a number of different provisions, prosecutors must decide how a given crime ought to be characterized. Such decisions may be driven by legal factors, such as double jeopardy and the elements of crimes; practical considerations, such as the available evidence or potentially applicable penalties; the effect of certain charges on survivors and other

---

26. See Prosecutor v. Brima, Kamara & Kanu, Case No. SCSL-04-16-PT, Decision on Prosecution Request for Leave to Amend the Indictment (May 6, 2004); Nowrojee, supra note 13, at 101.

27. Sierra Leone: "Forced Marriage" Conviction a First, http://www.irinnews.org/Report.aspx?ReportId=83160 (last visited Aug. 19, 2009).

28. For example, Amnesty International had documented the existence of such sexual violence in the Democratic Republic of Congo and Sudan. See Amnesty International Report 2009, The State of the World's Human Rights, available at http://www.thereport.amnesty.org.

29. See Prosecutor v. Kunarac, Case No. IT-96-23 & IT-96-23/1-A, Judgment, ¶133 (June 12, 2002).

30. See id. & ¶156.

31. See, e.g., Prosecutor v. Kvočka, Case No. IT-98-30/1-A, Judgment, ¶¶340-347 (Feb. 28, 2005).

32. Case No. IT-96-4-T, Judgment (Sept. 2, 1998).

witnesses; and more abstract issues, such as the message sent, for example, by charging rape as genocide as opposed to rape as a crime against humanity or a war crime.

A. SEXUAL VIOLENCE IN RWANDA AND WOMEN'S ROLES IN CONFLICTS

PETER LANDESMAN, A WOMAN'S WORK
N.Y. Times Magazine, Sept. 15, 2002

Slaughter, and then worse, came to Butare, a sleepy, sun-bleached Rwandan town, in the spring of 1994. Hutu death squads armed with machetes and nail-studded clubs had deployed throughout the countryside, killing, looting and burning. Roadblocks had been set up to cull fleeing Tutsis. By the third week of April, as the Rwanda genocide was reaching its peak intensity, tens of thousands of corpses were rotting in the streets of Kigali, the country's capital. Butare, a stronghold of Tutsis and politically moderate Hutus that had resisted the government's orders for genocide, was the next target. Its residents could hear gunfire from the hills in the west; at night they watched the firelight of torched nearby villages. Armed Hutus soon gathered on the edges of town, but Butare's panicked citizens defended its borders.

Enraged by Butare's revolt, Rwanda's interim government dispatched Pauline Nyiramasuhuko, the national minister of family and women's affairs, from Kigali on a mission. Before becoming one of the most powerful women in Rwanda's government, Pauline — as everyone, enemy and ally alike, called her — had grown up on a small farming commune just outside Butare. She was a local success story, known to some as Butare's favorite daughter. Her return would have a persuasive resonance there.

Soon after Pauline's arrival in town, cars mounted with loudspeakers crisscrossed Butare's back roads, announcing that the Red Cross had arrived at a nearby stadium to provide food and guarantee sanctuary. By April 25, thousands of desperate Tutsis had gathered at the stadium.

It was a trap. Instead of receiving food and shelter, the refugees were surrounded by men wearing bandoleers and headdresses made of spiky banana leaves. These men were Interahamwe, thuggish Hutu marauders whose name means "those who attack together." According to an eyewitness I spoke with this summer in Butare, supervising from the sidelines was Pauline, then 48, a portly woman of medium height in a colorful African wrap and spectacles.

Before becoming Rwanda's chief official for women's affairs, Pauline was a social worker, roaming the countryside, offering lectures on female empowerment and instruction on child care and AIDS prevention. Her days as minister were similarly devoted to improving the lives of women and children. But at the stadium, a 30-year-old farmer named Foster Mivumbi told me, Pauline assumed a different responsibility. Mivumbi, who has confessed to taking part in the slaughter, told me that Pauline goaded the Interahamwe, commanding, "Before you kill the women, you need to rape them."

Tutsi women were then selected from the stadium crowd and dragged away to a forested area to be raped, Mivumbi recalled. Back at the stadium, he told me, Pauline waved her arms and then observed in silence as Interahamwe rained machine-gun fire and hand grenades down upon the remaining refugees. The Hutus finished off survivors with machetes. It took about an hour, ending at noon. Pauline stayed on, Mivumbi told me, until a bulldozer began piling bodies for burial in a nearby pit. (When questioned about this incident, Pauline's lawyers denied that she took part in atrocities in Butare.)

Shortly afterward, according to another witness, Pauline arrived at a compound where a group of Interahamwe was guarding 70 Tutsi women and girls. One Interahamwe, a young man named Emmanuel Nsabimana, told me through a translator that Pauline ordered him and the others to burn the women. Nsabimana recalled that one Interahamwe complained that they lacked sufficient gasoline. "Pauline said, 'Don't worry, I have jerrycans of gasoline in my car,'" Nsabimana recalled. "She said, 'Go take that gasoline and kill them.' I went to the car and took the jerrycans. Then Pauline said, 'Why don't you rape them before you kill them?' But we had been killing all day, and we were tired. We just put the gasoline in bottles and scattered it among the women, then started burning."

Around the same time, some Interahamwe arrived at the local hospital, where a unit of Doctors Without Borders was in residence. Rose, a young Tutsi woman who had sought refuge at the hospital, watched in terror as soldiers stormed the complex. (Rose, who is now under military protection, requested that her last name not be printed.) "They said that Pauline had given them permission to go after the Tutsi girls, who were too proud of themselves," Rose told me. "She was the minister, so they said they were free to do it." Pauline had led the soldiers to see rape as a reward.

Chief among the Interahamwe at the hospital was Pauline's only son, a 24-year-old student named Arsène Shalom Ntahobali. Shalom, as he was known, was over six feet tall, slightly overweight and clean-shaven. He wore a track suit and sneakers; grenades dangled from his waist. Rose said that Shalom, who repeatedly announced that he had "permission" from his mother to rape Tutsis, found her cowering in the maternity ward. He yanked her to her feet and raped her against the wall. Before leaving Rose to chase after some students who had been hiding nearby, he promised that he'd return to kill her. But before Shalom could do so, she fled the hospital and ran home to her family.

A few days later, Rose recalled, a local official knocked on her door. Rose told me that the official informed her that even though all Tutsis would be exterminated, one Tutsi would be left alive — one who could deliver a progress report to God. Rose was to be that witness. And her instruction on her new role began that moment. "Hutu soldiers took my mother outside," Rose told me, "stripped off her clothes and raped her with a machete." On that first day, 20 family members were slaughtered before her eyes.

Rose told me that until early July, when the genocide ended, she was led by Interahamwe to witness atrocity after atrocity. She said that even though the Interahamwe's overarching objective was to kill, the men seemed particularly obsessed by what they did to women's bodies. "I saw them rape two girls with spears then burn their pubic hair," she said. "Then they took me to another spot where a lady was giving birth. The baby was halfway out. They speared it." All the while, Rose repeatedly heard the soldiers say, "We are doing what was ordered by Pauline Nyiramasuhuko."

I met Rose in Butare this summer. She is 32 now. . . . She explained that since the genocide she has suffered from stomach ulcers, and occasionally slips into semiconsciousness, racked with delirium and pain. "People think I'm possessed," she said. These fits, she said, frighten her children — her two born before 1994 and the four genocide orphans she adopted afterward. As we spoke, it was clear that Rose was telling her horrific story as carefully as possible, to finally fulfill, in a way much different from intended, her role as witness.

Rose said that during the months the genocide was carried out, she saw Pauline Nyiramasuhuko three times. The minister was an unforgettable sight. She'd exchanged her colorful civilian wraps for brand-new military fatigues and boots. She was seen carrying a machine gun over her shoulder. Other survivors told me they heard the minister for women and family affairs spit invectives at Tutsi women, calling them "cockroaches" and "dirt." She advised the men to choose the young women for sex and kill off the old. By one account, women were forced to raise their shirts to separate the mothers from the "virgins." Sometimes, I was told, Pauline handed soldiers packets of condoms.

Much of the violence took place in the scrubby yard in front of Butare's local government offices, or prefecture, where at one point hundreds of Tutsis were kept under guard. Witnesses recalled that Pauline showed up at night in a white Toyota pickup truck, often driven by Shalom, and supervised as Interahamwe loaded the truck with women who were driven off and never seen again. Often, when a woman at the prefecture saw Pauline, she appealed to her, as a fellow woman and mother, for mercy. But this, claimed survivors, only enraged Pauline. When one woman wouldn't stop crying out, a survivor recalled, the minister told the Interahamwe to shut her up. They stabbed the pleading woman and then slit her throat.

There will never be a precise accounting of how many Rwandans were massacred between April and July 1994. Human Rights Watch calculates the number to be at least 500,000, while the United Nations estimates that between 800,000 and one million Rwandans died during that period. Whatever the total, the rate of carnage and the concentration of the killing (Rwanda is roughly the size of New Jersey) give it the distinction of being the most ferocious mass slaughter in recorded history. Three-quarters of the Tutsi population was exterminated. Today, Rwanda's common greeting, the Kinyarwanda expression *mwaramutse*—which translates as "did you wake?"—is less an expression of "good morning" than it is of relief that one is breathing at all.

Understandably, the world's attention subsequently focused on the sheer volume of the Rwandan slaughter. But the prosecutors and judges of the International Criminal Tribunal for Rwanda in Arusha, Tanzania, are now coming to recognize the equally alarming and cynical story of what was left behind. Though most women were killed before they could tell their stories, a U.N. report has concluded that at least 250,000 women were raped during the genocide. Some were penetrated with spears, gun barrels, bottles or the stamens of banana trees. Sexual organs were mutilated with machetes, boiling water and acid; women's breasts were cut off. According to one study, Butare province alone has more than 30,000 rape survivors. Many more women were killed after they were raped.

These facts are harrowing. More shocking still is that so many of these crimes were supposedly inspired and orchestrated by Pauline Nyiramasuhuko, whose very job was the preservation, education and empowerment of Rwanda's women. . . .

At the tribunal, Pauline faces 11 charges, including genocide, crimes against humanity and war crimes. She is the first woman ever to be charged with these crimes in an international court. And she is the first woman ever to be charged with rape as a crime against humanity. (Her son, Shalom, faces 10 charges, to which he has pled innocence.)

[Beginning in 1997, when Pauline and Shalom were apprehended in Nairobi, Kenya,] mother and son have spent their days at the U.N. Detention Facility in Arusha in nearby 16-by-19 cells. They have access to a gym and a nurse. Pauline often spends time tending flowers and singing to herself in a common open-air courtyard.

Since June 2001, when their trials began, Pauline and Shalom have spent most of their weekdays in a courtroom inside Arusha's dilapidated conference center. . . . [As of May 2009, the trial is still ongoing.]

This summer, I attended sessions of Pauline's trial. In court, her appearance suggested a schoolteacher. . . . The courtroom is typically crowded with three judges, 12 defense attorneys and prosecutors, clerks, interpreters and other staff. Most days there are only a handful of spectators watching all this in a narrow gallery behind bulletproof glass — and frequently there are none at all.

Pauline and Shalom are being tried together with four other Hutu leaders from Butare who are also accused of genocide. Fourteen witnesses for the prosecution have testified so far, with 73 more still to go, most of whom will have something to say against Pauline, who faces life imprisonment. In most cases, she is accused of inciting crimes rather than carrying them out herself. However, according to a document prepared by tribunal investigators in preparation for the trial, one witness, code-named Q.C., saw a Tutsi community leader die "at the hands of Nyiramasuhuko." (The report does not specify what weapon Pauline used.) Attorneys for each of the six accused will most likely open their defenses in 2004 and will probably call more than 100 witnesses of their own as the trial creeps along for at least another two years. Justice at the tribunal has moved at a glacial pace, with only eight convictions and one acquittal handed down in seven years.

Pauline has consistently denied the charges against her. In 1995, before she was arrested, she gave an interview to the BBC in a squalid Hutu refugee camp across the Congo border, where she had been leading the camp's social services; her job duties included the reuniting of separated parents and children. When asked what she did during the war, Pauline replied: "We moved around the region to pacify. We wrote a pacification document saying people shouldn't kill each other. Saying it's genocide, that's not true. It was the Tutsi who massacred the Hutu." Told that witnesses had accused her of murder, Pauline shot back: "I cannot even kill a chicken. If there is a person who says that a woman — a mother — killed, then I'll confront that person." . . .

Pauline Nyiramasuhuko was born in 1946 amid lush banana groves and green, misty valleys. Her parents were subsistence farmers in Ndora, a small, neat roadside settlement six miles east of Butare. Her family and friends remember her as more ambitious and disciplined than bright. . . .

In 1968 Pauline married Maurice Ntahobari, who later became president of the Rwanda National Assembly, then minister of higher education and later rector of National University in Butare. . . . [Pauline had a son, Shalom, and three daughters. She] eventually enrolled in law school, one of the few women in Rwanda to do so. . . . Already a local MRND party boss, in 1992 she was appointed minister of family and women's affairs. . . .

A woman eager to prove herself in a party structure built around men and Rwanda's patriarchal society, Pauline soon found that the road to political success led her back to her birthplace. Butare had become the government's biggest headache. . . . The town had been largely immune to Hutu extremism[,] . . . [b]ut Pauline tried to change all that through a program of intimidation. She would convoy through town with party thugs, setting up barricades in the streets, paralyzing traffic and disrupting town life. Pauline's periodic invasions of the town became known as Ghost Days, days when Butare stood still.

Pauline was soon caught up in the anti-Tutsi ideology of her party. "Before 1994 there was no racism in Butare," said Leoncie Mukamisha, an old schoolmate of Pauline's who worked under her at the ministry. "Then Pauline came and organized demonstrations in town. The local papers described her as a frenzied madwoman." Leoncie said that Pauline's actions won the favor of the president, who recognized her obedience and anti-Tutsi virulence, and assigned to her a number of extremist Hutu ideologues as advisers. . . .

In his confession to genocide and crimes against humanity, former Hutu Prime Minister Jean Kambanda identifies the members of his inner sanctum, where the blueprint of the genocide was first drawn up. The confession names only five names. Pauline Nyiramasuhuko's is one of them.

During my visit to Butare this summer, two young women, Mary Mukangoga, 24, and Chantal Kantarama, 28, led me into the center of Butare to the prefecture, where they first met and became friends. "I went to the prefecture because other refugees were there," Mary said in a near whisper. "I preferred to be killed when we were all together."

In the first weeks of the genocide, Chantal said, she had been abducted and raped by two Hutu men. She escaped and took refuge at a school near the prefecture. One day, Chantal recalled, she heard Pauline announcing through a microphone: "I have a problem. The cockroaches are now near my house. Tomorrow come and help me. Help me get rid of them." Chantal fled to the prefecture. The next day, Chantal said, Pauline visited the prefecture with Shalom. Mother and son came with the young men of the Interahamwe and selected girls to rape.

In silence, Mary and Chantal led me to the ruins of what was once a plastics factory, in a shady grove of trees 200 yards from the prefecture office. They explained that the Interahamwe used to store their ammunition in the factory, and that many evenings they were taken from the prefecture, led there and raped. "Pauline would come and say, 'I don't want this dirt here, get rid of this *dirt*,'" Chantal recalled.

The two young women became part of a group of five sex slaves who were kept at the prefecture and raped, repeatedly and together, every night for weeks. Then one day, the women were thrown into a nearby pit that was full of corpses. The pit, about 400 feet square, is now half-filled in with rubble and weeds. Chantal took me there, stepping to the edge; at that point she turned aside, refusing to look in. "They used machetes to kill the ones who resisted and dumped them into the hole," she explained. She began to weep. She remained inside the pit for a night and a day, she said; then, on the second night, she climbed the jumbled corpses to pull herself out.

I took Chantal back to her home, a neat mud hut in a bustling, dusty neighborhood of shops and wandering livestock. Chantal is married with two children; she was the only genocidal-rape survivor I met who was married. Her husband knows what happened to her. But for thousands of Rwandan survivors, one of the most insidious legacies of the rapes is the stigma — and the inevitable isolation. In Rwandan society, it is almost impossible for a woman who is known to have been raped to marry. One witness who testified against Pauline in Arusha had been engaged to be married a month later. When her fiancé heard about the testimony, he broke off the engagement.

Then there is the generation of children born of the rapes. As many as 5,000 such children have been documented and, most likely, there are many more than that who haven't. These children will most likely never know their fathers — in most cases, the mother was raped so many times that the issue of paternity was not only pointless but emotionally perilous: in effect, all of her attackers had fathered that child.

Compounding the dishonor, the mere sight of these children — those who aren't abandoned — can bring on savage memories to survivors. Two women I met who gave birth to their rapists' children named the children with words that translate as "Blessing From God" as a way to ease the pain. But others in the community gave them names that put them in the same category as their fathers: "Children of Shame," "Gifts of the Enemy," "Little Interahamwe."

"Did you ever see the look in a woman's eyes when she sees a child of rape?" asked Sydia Nduna, an adviser at the International Rescue Committee Rwanda who works for a program in Kigali aimed at reducing gender violence. "It's a depth of sadness you cannot imagine." The impact of the mass rapes in Rwanda, she said, will be felt for generations. "Mass rape forces the victims to live with the consequences, the damage, the children," Nduna explained.

Making matters worse, the rapes, most of them committed by many men in succession, were frequently accompanied by other forms of physical torture and often staged as public performances to multiply the terror and degradation. So many women feared them that they often begged to be killed instead. Often the rapes were in fact a prelude to murder. But sometimes the victim was not killed but instead repeatedly violated and then left alive; the humiliation would then affect not only the victim but also those closest to her. Other times, women were used as a different kind of tool: half-dead, or even already a corpse, a woman would be publicly raped as a way for Interahamwe mobs to bond together.

But the exposure — and the destruction — did not stop with the act of rape itself. Many women were purposely left alive to die later, and slowly. Two women I met outside Butare, Francina Mukamazina and Liberata Munganyinka, are dying of AIDS they contracted through rape. "My biggest worry is what will happen to my children when I'm gone," Francina told me. These children are as fragile as Francina fears: a U.N. survey of Rwandan children of war concluded that 31 percent witnessed a rape or sexual assault, and 70 percent witnessed murder. Francina's and Liberata's daughters survived but watched their siblings slaughtered and their mothers violated. They will grow up beside children born of rape, all of them together forced to navigate different but commingling resentments.

During my visit to Chantal's home, I asked her how she coped with her savage memories. She replied: "I just want to forget. My children are my consolation. Most rape survivors have nothing. We're poor, but I have my family. It's all I want."

I found Mary later that afternoon a few miles of dirt track away. She was sitting alone in her home, a stifling mud hut about 20 feet square with one small window. Mary told me that the rapes were her first and only sexual experience. Then, eyes averted, twisting her hands, she told me that five months ago she discovered she had AIDS. She said that two of the other young women she and Chantal were kept with are already dead. Their fate is not the exception but the rule. According to one estimate, 70 percent of women raped during the Rwanda genocide have H.I.V.; most will eventually die from it. . . .

The most cynical purpose of the rapes in Butare was to transmit a slower, more agonizing form of death. "By using a disease, a plague, as an apocalyptic terror, as biological warfare, you're annihilating the procreators, perpetuating the death unto the generations," said Charles B. Strozier, a psychoanalyst and professor of history at John Jay College of Criminal Justice in New York. "The killing continues and endures."

The use of AIDS as a tool of warfare against Tutsi women helped prosecutors in Arusha focus on rape as a driving force of the genocide. "H.I.V. infection is murder," said Silvana Arbia, the Rwanda Tribunal's acting chief of prosecutions. "Sexual aggression is as much an act of genocide as murder is."

During my visit with Mary, I learned that she had been "murdered" in just this way. This young woman has only one relative who lived through the genocide, a younger brother who lives in Kigali. "All of my friends have AIDS," she told me in June. "But I'll die of loneliness before I die of AIDS," she whispered, choking on her tears. "All I wanted was to marry and have a family." Today, she lies gravely ill in her hut, cared for by Chantal, withering away. . . .

"The intention in Rwanda was an abstraction: to kill without killing," said Arbia, the tribunal prosecutor. She described the case of a 45-year-old Rwandan woman who was raped by her 12-year-old son — with Interahamwe holding a hatchet to his throat — in front of her husband, while their five other young children were forced to hold open her thighs. "The offense against an individual woman becomes an offense against the family," Arbia said, "which becomes an offense against the country, and so, by deduction, against humanity."

On Aug. 10, 1999, a year after Akayesu's conviction, Pauline Nyiramasuhuko's indictment was amended to include rape as a crime against humanity. According to prosecutors and witnesses, her frequent instructions to Interahamwe at the prefecture to rape before they killed, or to rape women instead of killing them, had triggered a collective sadism in Butare — one that had even inspired violence in the local peasants.

One Tutsi rape survivor I met in Butare, a farmer named Suzanne Bukabangwa [had been kept by] neighbors, uneducated farmers, . . . as a sex slave during the genocide, she said, torturing her nightly. She remembered two things most of all: the stamens from the banana trees they used to violate her, leaving her body mutilated, and the single sentence one of the men used: "We're going to kill all the Tutsis, and one day Hutu children will have to ask what did a Tutsi child look like."

In Butare, I spoke to a local peasant, Lucien Simbayobewe, who was caught up in this cycle of humiliation. Now 40, he was being held prisoner in the local prison. (Only leaders of the genocide have been sent to Arusha.) He wore the pink shorts and matching pink shirt of the Rwandan inmate's uniform. Wringing his hands in his lap, he told me about one woman he killed who still comes to him every night in his dreams. He couldn't remember this apparition's name, but he said he'd killed her when Pauline first organized the Butare Interahamwe. Choking on emotion, he said, "She comes in the night dancing and gesturing with her hands invitingly, like a lover." My translator gyrated her arms to show me the motion. "The woman smiles, and says, 'How are you?' But before I can answer, she says, 'Goodbye,' and then she vanishes — and I wake up." Lucien then told me in detail about killing her. But when I asked Lucien if he'd raped the woman, he fell silent and fought back tears. Every prisoner I spoke with described explicitly whom he killed and how. Not a single one admitted to raping a Tutsi woman.

Perhaps this is because after the war, Rwanda's Legislature declared that rapes committed during the genocide were the highest category of crime; those convicted are sentenced to death. Or maybe these men could somehow justify to themselves having murdered but not raped. In any event, the weight of that level of confession was obviously too much to bear, and if there could be any tangible proof that rape was considered the more shameful crime, it was this.

Some scholars are beginning to share this opinion. "Rape sets in motion continuous suffering and extreme humiliation that affects not just the individual victim but everyone around her," said the philosopher and historian Robert Jay Lifton, who in books like "The Nazi Doctors" has explored the psychology of genocide. . . .

The case against Pauline further cements the precedent . . . that inciting mass rape is a crime against humanity. But Pauline's case transcends jurisprudence. She presents to the world a new kind of criminal. "There is a shared concept across cultures that women don't do this kind of thing," said Carolyn Nordstrom, an anthropologist at the University of Notre Dame. "Society doesn't yet have a way to talk about it, because it violates all our concepts of what women are."

I found Pauline's mother, Theresa Nyirakabue, on the same plot of land in Ndora where Pauline was born and reared. . . .

I asked her if she thought her daughter was innocent of the charges against her. . . . "It is unimaginable that she did these things," she said. "She wouldn't order people to rape and kill. After all, Pauline is a mother." Then Theresa leaned forward, her hands outstretched. "Before the war, Hutu and Tutsi were the same," she said. She told me that Pauline had many Tutsi friends. Theresa added that during the genocide, she herself had hidden a Tutsi boy in her home.

At first, Theresa's story took me by surprise. But then, Rwanda's lethal racialism could never be as starkly delineated as, say, Nazi Germany's. Whether Hutus and Tutsis are separate ethnic groups is a subject of debate, but it was only after European colonists arrived in Rwanda that any political distinction was made between them. Intermarriage had long been common, and both groups spoke the same language and practiced the same religion. Around the turn of the 20th century, however, German and Belgian colonists used dubious racialist logic — namely, that Tutsis had a more "Caucasian" appearance — to designate the minority Tutsi the ruling class, empowering them as their social and governing proxy.

In the 1930's, the Belgians, deciding to limit administrative posts and higher education to the Tutsi, needed to decide exactly who was who in Rwanda. The most efficient procedure was simply to register everyone and require them to carry cards identifying them as one or the other. Eighty-four percent of the population declared themselves Hutu and 15 percent Tutsi. Considering the degree of intermarriage in Rwandan history, this accounting was hardly scientific. What's more, Rwandans sometimes switched ethnic identities, the wealthy relabeling themselves as Tutsis and the poor as Hutus.

"Identity became based on what you could get away with," said Alison Des Forges, a senior adviser to the African Division of Human Rights Watch who has studied Rwanda for 30 years. "Half of the people are not clearly distinguishable. There was significant intermarriage. Women who fit the Tutsi stereotype — taller, lighter, with more Caucasian-like features — became desirable. But it didn't necessarily mean that the women were one or the other."

. . . A revolution in 1959 brought the majority Hutus to power. As tensions increased around 1990, politicians began disseminating propaganda denouncing Tutsi females as temptresses, whores and sexual deviants. Before the 1994 genocide began, Hutu newspapers ran cartoon after cartoon depicting Tutsi women as lascivious seducers.

. . . "The propaganda made Tutsi women powerful, desirable — and therefore something to be destroyed," Rhonda Copelon[, a law professor at CUNY,] told me. "When you make the woman the threat, you enhance the idea that violence against them is permitted." . . .

This explanation conformed with my sense of Pauline's view of the Tutsis; like many of her countrymen, she seemed able to view individual Tutsis as abstractions. But in my conversations with Pauline's mother, things became even more complicated. After Theresa told me about the Tutsi boy she had hidden, she paused, looked at me intently and told me, matter-of-factly, that Pauline's great-grandfather was a Tutsi. The great-grandfather had been redesignated a Hutu, Theresa explained, because he became poor. Stunned, and knowing that in Rwanda kinship is defined patrilineally — through the blood of fathers — I asked Theresa if that didn't mean that Pauline was a Tutsi. "Yes, of course," she said eagerly. And would Pauline have known that she came from Tutsi lineage? Theresa pursed her lips and gave a firm, affirmative nod.

The young man Theresa hid was not difficult to find. His name is Dutera Agide, 36, a jobless handyman in Ndora. He told me that he is Pauline's second cousin, and that he is a Tutsi. He said he had spent one week hiding in Theresa's house, listening to the slaughter going on outside. Then he said something even more surprising. At one point, he said, he was hidden in Pauline's house. "I saw Pauline twice a week during the genocide," Dutera told me. "One day she came home, and she said: 'The war is not ending. I'm starting to get afraid. I don't know what will happen.' Then she came back again with her husband, loaded things from the house into a car and left. She looked scared."

After my conversation with Dutera, I went back to Theresa's home one more time. . . . "People killed people because of fear to be also killed by the perpetrators of the genocide," she said. "My daughter, who was also a minister in the government, could have participated in the killing not because she wanted to kill but because of fear." Theresa then used the Kinyarwanda expression *Mpemuke ndamuke:* "to be dishonest in order to escape death."

I spoke . . . with Pauline's sister, Vineranda. "In 1959, when the Tutsi regime changed, our family changed with the situation," Vineranda explained. "Because she was a Tutsi, Pauline was afraid that maybe the government would find out. And she was among many men in the government. And she had money and a position. She didn't want to lose that." . . .

The crimes Pauline Nyiramasuhuko [is] accused of are monstrous. Her capacity for pity and compassion, and her professional duty to shield the powerless, deserted her, or collapsed under the irresistible urge for power. But in seeking a reasonable explanation for Pauline's barbarity, I remembered something that Alison Des Forges of Human Rights Watch told me.

"This behavior lies just under the surface of any of us," Des Forges said. "The simplified accounts of genocide allow distance between us and the perpetrators of genocide. They are so evil we couldn't ever see ourselves doing the same thing. But if you consider the terrible pressure under which people were operating, then you automatically reassert their humanity—and that becomes alarming. You are forced to look at these situations and say, 'What would I have done?' Sometimes the answer is not encouraging." . . .

B. DEFINING THE CRIMES

PROSECUTOR V. AKAYESU

Case No. IT-96-4-T, Judgment (Sept. 2, 1998)

. . . THE INDICTMENT

6. The Indictment against Jean-Paul Akayesu . . . is here set out . . . :

"The Prosecutor of the International Criminal Tribunal for Rwanda, pursuant to his authority under Article 17 of the Statute of the Tribunal, charges:

JEAN PAUL AKAYESU

with GENOCIDE [and] CRIMES AGAINST HUMANITY . . . as set forth below:[33]

---

33. We have omitted from the Indictment the war crimes counts. The counts identified in the text, with the exception of Count 2, are those for which Akayesu was eventually convicted. He was acquitted of Count 2 (Complicity in Genocide), for the reasons explained in the opinion below, ¶¶525-532, 723-734. Counts 6, 8, 10, 12, and 15 charged violations of the laws of war under common Article 3 of the Geneva Conventions and Additional Protocol II. The Trial Chamber found Akayesu not guilty of those charges,

Background . . .

2. Rwanda is divided into 11 prefectures, each of which is governed by a prefect. The prefectures are further subdivided into communes which are placed under the authority of bourgmestres. The bourgmestre of each commune is appointed by the President of the Republic, upon the recommendation of the Minister of the Interior. In Rwanda, the bourgmestre is the most powerful figure in the commune. His de facto authority in the area is significantly greater than that which is conferred upon him de jure.

The Accused

3. Jean Paul AKAYESU, born in 1953 in Murehe sector, Taba commune, served as bourgmestre of that commune from April 1993 until June 1994. Prior to his appointment as bourgmestre, he was a teacher and school inspector in Taba.

4. As bourgmestre, Jean Paul AKAYESU was charged with the performance of executive functions and the maintenance of public order within his commune, subject to the authority of the prefect. He had exclusive control over the communal police, as well as any gendarmes put at the disposition of the commune. He was responsible for the execution of laws and regulations and the administration of justice, also subject only to the prefect's authority. . . .

Charges

12. As bourgmestre, Jean Paul AKAYESU was responsible for maintaining law and public order in his commune. At least 2000 Tutsis were killed in Taba between April 7 and the end of June, 1994, while he was still in power. The killings in Taba were openly committed and so widespread that, as bourgmestre, Jean Paul AKAYESU must have known about them. Although he had the authority and responsibility to do so, Jean Paul AKAYESU never attempted to prevent the killing of Tutsis in the commune in any way or called for assistance from regional or national authorities to quell the violence.

12A. Between April 7 and the end of June, 1994, hundreds of civilians (hereinafter "displaced civilians") sought refuge at the bureau communal. The majority of these displaced civilians were Tutsi. While seeking refuge at the bureau communal, female displaced civilians were regularly taken by armed local militia and/or communal police and subjected to sexual violence, and/or beaten on or near the bureau communal premises. Displaced civilians were also murdered frequently on or near the bureau communal premises. Many women were forced to endure multiple acts of sexual violence which were at times committed by more than one assailant. These acts of sexual violence were generally accompanied by explicit threats of death or bodily harm. The female displaced civilians lived in constant fear and their physical and

---

id. ¶644, because it was not proved that the acts perpetrated by him "were committed in conjunction with the armed conflict." Id. ¶643. The Chamber further found that it was not proved that "Akayesu was a member of the armed forces, or that he was legitimately mandated and expected, as a public official or agent or person otherwise holding public authority or de facto representing the Government, to support or fulfill the war efforts." — EDs.

psychological health deteriorated as a result of the sexual violence and beatings and killings.

12B. Jean Paul AKAYESU knew that the acts of sexual violence, beatings and murders were being committed and was at times present during their commission. Jean Paul AKAYESU facilitated the commission of the sexual violence, beatings and murders by allowing the sexual violence and beatings and murders to occur on or near the bureau communal premises. By virtue of his presence during the commission of the sexual violence, beatings and murders and by failing to prevent the sexual violence, beatings and murders, Jean Paul AKAYESU encouraged these activities.

13. On or about 19 April 1994, before dawn, in Gishyeshye sector, Taba commune, a group of men, one of whom was named Francois Ndimubanzi, killed a local teacher, Sylvere Karera, because he was accused of associating with the Rwandan Patriotic Front ("RPF") and plotting to kill Hutus. Even though at least one of the perpetrators was turned over to Jean Paul AKAYESU, he failed to take measures to have him arrested.

14. The morning of April 19, 1994, following the murder of Sylvere Karera, Jean Paul AKAYESU led a meeting in Gishyeshye sector at which he sanctioned the death of Sylvere Karera and urged the population to eliminate accomplices of the RPF, which was understood by those present to mean Tutsis. Over 100 people were present at the meeting. The killing of Tutsis in Taba began shortly after the meeting.

15. At the same meeting in Gishyeshye sector on April 19, 1994, Jean Paul AKAYESU named at least three prominent Tutsis — Ephrem Karangwa, Juvénal Rukundakuvuga and Emmanuel Sempabwa — who had to be killed because of their alleged relationships with the RPF. Later that day, Juvénal Rukundakuvuga was killed in Kanyinya. Within the next few days, Emmanuel Sempabwa was clubbed to death in front of the Taba bureau communal.

16. Jean Paul AKAYESU, on or about April 19, 1994, conducted house-to-house searches in Taba. During these searches, residents, including Victim V, were interrogated and beaten with rifles and sticks in the presence of Jean Paul AKAYESU. Jean Paul AKAYESU personally threatened to kill the husband and child of Victim U if she did not provide him with information about the activities of the Tutsis he was seeking.

17. On or about April 19, 1994, Jean Paul AKAYESU ordered the interrogation and beating of Victim X in an effort to learn the whereabouts of Ephrem Karangwa. During the beating, Victim X's fingers were broken as he tried to shield himself from blows with a metal stick.

18. On or about April 19, 1994, the men who, on Jean Paul AKAYESU's instructions, were searching for Ephrem Karangwa destroyed Ephrem Karangwa's house and burned down his mother's house. They then went to search the house of Ephrem Karangwa's brother-in-law in Musambira commune and found Ephrem Karangwa's three brothers there. The three brothers — Simon Mutijima, Thaddée Uwanyiligira and Jean Chrysostome Gakuba — tried to escape, but Jean Paul AKAYESU blew his whistle to alert local residents to the attempted escape and ordered the people to capture the brothers. After the brothers were captured, Jean Paul AKAYESU ordered and participated in the killings of the three brothers.

19. On or about April 19, 1994, Jean Paul AKAYESU took 8 detained men from the Taba bureau communal and ordered militia members to kill them. The militia killed them with clubs, machetes, small axes and sticks. The victims had fled from Runda commune and had been held by Jean Paul AKAYESU.

20. On or about April 19, 1994, Jean Paul AKAYESU ordered the local people and militia to kill intellectual and influential people. Five teachers from the secondary school of Taba were killed on his instructions. The victims were Theogene, Phoebe

Uwineze and her fiance (whose name is unknown), Tharcisse Twizeyumuremye and Samuel. The local people and militia killed them with machetes and agricultural tools in front of the Taba bureau communal.

21. On or about April 20, 1994, Jean Paul AKAYESU and some communal police went to the house of Victim Y, a 68 year old woman. Jean Paul AKAYESU interrogated her about the whereabouts of the wife of a university teacher. During the questioning, under Jean Paul AKAYESU's supervision, the communal police hit Victim Y with a gun and sticks. They bound her arms and legs and repeatedly kicked her in the chest. Jean Paul AKAYESU threatened to kill her if she failed to provide the information he sought.

22. Later that night, on or about April 20, 1994, Jean Paul AKAYESU picked up Victim W in Taba and interrogated her also about the whereabouts of the wife of the university teacher. When she stated she did not know, he forced her to lay on the road in front of his car and threatened to drive over her.

23. Thereafter, on or about April 20, 1994, Jean Paul AKAYESU picked up Victim Z in Taba and interrogated him. During the interrogation, men under Jean Paul AKAYESU's authority forced Victims Z and Y to beat each other and used a piece of Victim Y's dress to strangle Victim Z. . . .

By his acts in relation to the events described in paragraphs 12-23, Jean Paul AKAYESU is criminally responsible for:

COUNT 1: GENOCIDE, punishable by Article 2(3)(a) of the Statute of the Tribunal;

COUNT 2: Complicity in GENOCIDE, punishable under Article 2(3)(e) of the Statute of the Tribunal;

COUNT 3: CRIMES AGAINST HUMANITY (extermination), punishable by Article 3(b) of the Statute of the Tribunal. . . .

By his acts in relation to the events described in paragraphs 14 and 15, Jean Paul AKAYESU is criminally responsible for:

COUNT 4: Direct and Public Incitement to Commit GENOCIDE, punishable by Article 2(3)(c) of the Statute of the Tribunal. . . .

By his acts in relation [to] the murders of Juvénal Rukundakuvuga, Emmanuel Sempabwa, Simon Mutijima, Thaddée Uwanyiligira and Jean Chrysostome Gakuba, as described in paragraphs 15 and 18, Jean Paul AKAYESU committed:

COUNT 5: CRIMES AGAINST HUMANITY (murder) punishable by Article 3(a) of the Statute of the Tribunal; . . .

By his acts in relation [to] the murders of 8 detained men in front of the bureau communal as described in paragraph 19, Jean Paul AKAYESU committed:

COUNT 7: CRIMES AGAINST HUMANITY (murder) punishable by Article 3(a) of the Statute of the Tribunal; . . .

By his acts in relation to the murders of 5 teachers in front of the bureau communal as described in paragraph 20, Jean Paul AKAYESU committed:

COUNT 9: CRIMES AGAINST HUMANITY (murder) punishable by Article 3(a) of the Statute of the Tribunal; . . .

By his acts in relation to the beatings of U, V, W, X, Y and Z as described in paragraphs 16, 17, 21, 22 and 23, Jean Paul AKAYESU committed:

COUNT 11: CRIMES AGAINST HUMANITY (torture), punishable by Article 3(f) of the Statute of the Tribunal; . . .

By his acts in relation to the events at the bureau communal, as described in paragraphs 12(A) and 12(B), Jean Paul AKAYESU committed:

COUNT 13: CRIMES AGAINST HUMANITY (rape), punishable by Article 3(g) of the Statute of the Tribunal; and

COUNT 14: CRIMES AGAINST HUMANITY, (other inhumane acts), punishable by Article 3(i) of the Statute of the Tribunal. . . .

. . . THE ACCUSED'S LINE OF DEFENCE

29. The Accused has pleaded not guilty to all counts of the Indictment. . . .

30. In essence, the Defence case — insofar as the Chamber has been able to establish it — is that the Accused did not commit, order or participate in any of the killings, beatings or acts of sexual violence alleged in the Indictment. The Defence concedes that a genocide occurred in Rwanda and that massacres of Tutsi took place in Taba Commune, but it argues that the Accused was helpless to prevent them, being outnumbered and overpowered by one Silas Kubwimana and the Interahamwe. The Defence pointed out that, according to prosecution witness R, Akayesu had been so harassed by the Interahamwe that at one point he had had to flee Taba commune. Once the massacres had become widespread, the Accused was denuded of all authority and lacked the means to stop the killings.

31. The Defence claims that the Chamber should not require the Accused to be a hero, to have laid down his life — as, for example, did the bourgmestre of Mugina — in a futile attempt to prevent killings and beatings. The Defence alluded to the fact that General Dallaire, in charge of UNAMIR and 2,500 troops, was unable to prevent the genocide. How, then, was Akayesu, with 10 communal policemen at his disposal, to fare any better? Moreover, the Defence argue, no bourgmestre in the whole of Rwanda was able to prevent the massacres in his Commune, no matter how willing he was to do so.

32. As for acts of sexual violence, the Defence case is somewhat different from that for killings and beatings, in that, whereas for the latter the Defence does not contest that there were killings and beatings, it does deny that there were acts of sexual violence committed, at least at the Bureau Communal. During his testimony the Accused emphatically denied that any rapes had taken place at the Bureau Communal, even when he was not there. The Chamber notes the Accused's emphatic denial of facts which are not entirely within his knowledge. . . .

6. THE LAW

6.1. CUMULATIVE CHARGES

461. In the amended Indictment, the accused is charged cumulatively with more than one crime in relation to the same sets of facts, in all but count 4. For example the events described in paragraphs 12 to 23 of the Indictment are the subject of three counts of the Indictment — genocide (count 1), complicity in genocide (count 2) and crimes against humanity/extermination (count 3). Likewise, . . . counts 13 (crime against humanity/rape) [and] 14 (crimes against humanity/other inhumane acts) . . . [also relate to the same set of facts].

462. The question which arises at this stage is whether, if the Chamber is convinced beyond a reasonable doubt that a given factual allegation set out in the Indictment has been established, it may find the accused guilty of all of the crimes charged in relation to those facts or only one. The reason for posing this question is that it might be argued that the accumulation of criminal charges offends against the principle of double jeopardy or a substantive *non bis in idem* principle in criminal law. Thus an accused who is found guilty of both genocide and crimes against humanity in relation

to the same set of facts may argue that he has been twice judged for the same offence, which is generally considered impermissible in criminal law.

463. The Chamber notes that this question has been posed, and answered, by the Trial Chamber of the ICTY in the first case before that Tribunal, *The Prosecutor v. Duško Tadić.* Trial Chamber II, confronted with this issue, stated:

> "In any event, since this is a matter that will only be relevant insofar as it might affect penalty, it can best be dealt with if and when matters of penalty fall for consideration. What can, however, be said with certainty is that penalty cannot be made to depend upon whether offences arising from the same conduct are alleged cumulatively or in the alternative. What is to be punished by penalty is proven criminal conduct and that will not depend upon technicalities of pleading."

464. In that case, when the matter reached the sentencing stage, the Trial Chamber dealt with the matter of cumulative criminal charges by imposing *concurrent* sentences for each cumulative charge. Thus, for example, in relation to one particular beating, the accused received 7 years' imprisonment for the beating as a crime against humanity, and a 6 year concurrent sentence for the same beating as a violation of the laws or customs of war. . . .

466. It is clear that the practice of concurrent sentencing ensures that the accused is not twice punished for the same acts. Notwithstanding this absence of prejudice to the accused, it is still necessary to justify the prosecutorial practice of accumulating criminal charges. . . .

468. On the basis of national and international law and jurisprudence, the Chamber concludes that it is acceptable to convict the accused of two offences in relation to the same set of facts in the following circumstances: (1) where the offences have different elements; or (2) where the provisions creating the offences protect different interests; or (3) where it is necessary to record a conviction for both offences in order fully to describe what the accused did. However, the Chamber finds that it is not justifiable to convict an accused of two offences in relation to the same set of facts where (a) one offence is a lesser included offence of the other, for example, murder and grievous bodily harm, robbery and theft, or rape and indecent assault; or (b) where one offence charges accomplice liability and the other offence charges liability as a principal, e.g. genocide and complicity in genocide.

469. Having regard to its Statute, the Chamber believes that the offences under the Statute — genocide, crimes against humanity, and violations of article 3 common to the Geneva Conventions and of Additional Protocol II — have different elements and, moreover, are intended to protect different interests. The crime of genocide exists to protect certain groups from extermination or attempted extermination. The concept of crimes against humanity exists to protect civilian populations from persecution. The idea of violations of article 3 common to the Geneva Conventions and of Additional Protocol II is to protect non-combatants from war crimes in civil war. These crimes have different purposes and are, therefore, never co-extensive. Thus it is legitimate to charge these crimes in relation to the same set of facts. It may, additionally, depending on the case, be necessary to record a conviction for more than one of these offences in order to reflect what crimes an accused committed. If, for example, a general ordered that all prisoners of war belonging to a particular ethnic group should be killed, with the intent thereby to eliminate the group, this would be both genocide and a violation of common article 3, although not necessarily a crime against humanity. Convictions for genocide and violations of common article 3 would accurately reflect the accused general's course of conduct.

470. Conversely, the Chamber does not consider that any of genocide, crimes against humanity, and violations of article 3 common to the Geneva Conventions and of Additional Protocol II are lesser included forms of each other. The ICTR Statute does not establish a hierarchy of norms, but rather all three offences are presented on an equal footing. While genocide may be considered the gravest crime, there is no justification in the Statute for finding that crimes against humanity or violations of common article 3 and additional protocol II are in all circumstances alternative charges to genocide and thus lesser included offences. As stated, and it is a related point, these offences have different constituent elements. Again, this consideration renders multiple convictions for these offences in relation to the same set of facts permissible. . . .

6.3.1. GENOCIDE . . .

Imposing Measures Intended to Prevent Births Within the Group (Paragraph d):

507. For purposes of interpreting Article 2(2)(d) of the Statute, the Chamber holds that the measures intended to prevent births within the group, should be construed as sexual mutilation, the practice of sterilization, forced birth control, separation of the sexes and prohibition of marriages. In patriarchal societies, where membership of a group is determined by the identity of the father, an example of a measure intended to prevent births within a group is the case where, during rape, a woman of the said group is deliberately impregnated by a man of another group, with the intent to have her give birth to a child who will consequently not belong to its mother's group.

508. Furthermore, the Chamber notes that measures intended to prevent births within the group may be physical, but can also be mental. For instance, rape can be a measure intended to prevent births when the person raped refuses subsequently to procreate, in the same way that members of a group can be led, through threats or trauma, not to procreate. . . .

6.3.2. COMPLICITY IN GENOCIDE

The Crime of Complicity in Genocide, Punishable Under Article 2(3)(e) of the Statute. . . .

529. . . . The Chamber notes that, as stated above, complicity can only exist when there is a punishable, principal act, in the commission of which the accomplice has associated himself. Complicity, therefore, implies a predicate offence committed by someone other than the accomplice. . . .

532. The Chamber notes that the logical inference from the foregoing is that an individual cannot thus be both the principal perpetrator of a particular act and the accomplice thereto. An act with which an accused is being charged cannot, therefore, be characterized both as an act of genocide and an act of complicity in genocide as pertains to this accused. Consequently, since the two are mutually exclusive, the same individual cannot be convicted of both crimes for the same act. . . .

7. LEGAL FINDINGS . . .

7.7. COUNT 13 (RAPE) AND COUNT 14 (OTHER INHUMANE ACTS) — CRIMES AGAINST HUMANITY . . .

686. In considering the extent to which acts of sexual violence constitute crimes against humanity under Article 3(g) of its Statute, the Tribunal must define rape, as there is no commonly accepted definition of the term in international law. The Tribunal notes that many of the witnesses have used the term "rape" in their testimony. At times, the Prosecution and the Defence have also tried to elicit an explicit

description of what happened in physical terms, to document what the witnesses mean by the term "rape." The Tribunal notes that while rape has been historically defined in national jurisdictions as non-consensual sexual intercourse, variations on the form of rape may include acts which involve the insertion of objects and/or the use of bodily orifices not considered to be intrinsically sexual. An act such as that described by Witness KK in her testimony—the Interahamwes thrusting a piece of wood into the sexual organs of a woman as she lay dying—constitutes rape in the Tribunal's view.

687. The Tribunal considers that rape is a form of aggression and that the central elements of the crime of rape cannot be captured in a mechanical description of objects and body parts. The Tribunal also notes the cultural sensitivities involved in public discussion of intimate matters and recalls the painful reluctance and inability of witnesses to disclose graphic anatomical details of sexual violence they endured. The United Nations Convention Against Torture and Other Cruel, Inhuman and Degrading Treatment or Punishment does not catalogue specific acts in its definition of torture, focusing rather on the conceptual framework of state-sanctioned violence. The Tribunal finds this approach more useful in the context of international law. Like torture, rape is used for such purposes as intimidation, degradation, humiliation, discrimination, punishment, control or destruction of a person. Like torture, rape is a violation of personal dignity, and rape in fact constitutes torture when it is inflicted by or at the instigation of or with the consent or acquiescence of a public official or other person acting in an official capacity.

688. The Tribunal defines rape as a physical invasion of a sexual nature, committed on a person under circumstances which are coercive. The Tribunal considers sexual violence, which includes rape, as any act of a sexual nature which is committed on a person under circumstances which are coercive. Sexual violence is not limited to physical invasion of the human body and may include acts which do not involve penetration or even physical contact. The incident described by Witness KK in which the Accused ordered the Interahamwe to undress a student and force her to do gymnastics naked in the public courtyard of the bureau communal, in front of a crowd, constitutes sexual violence. The Tribunal notes in this context that coercive circumstances need not be evidenced by a show of physical force. Threats, intimidation, extortion and other forms of duress which prey on fear or desperation may constitute coercion, and coercion may be inherent in certain circumstances, such as armed conflict or the military presence of Interahamwe among refugee Tutsi women at the bureau communal. Sexual violence falls within the scope of "other inhumane acts", set forth Article 3(i) of the Tribunal's Statute, "outrages upon personal dignity," set forth in Article 4(e) of the Statute, and "serious bodily or mental harm," set forth in Article 2(2)(b) of the Statute. . . .

690. The Tribunal also notes that on the basis of acts described in paragraphs 12(A) and 12(B), the Accused is charged only pursuant to Article 3(g) (rape) and 3(i) (other inhumane acts) of its Statute, but not Article 3(a)(murder) or Article 3(f) (torture). . . . The Tribunal notes, however, that paragraphs 12(A) and 12(B) are referenced in Counts 1-3, Genocide and it considers the beatings and killings, as well as sexual violence, in connection with those counts. . . .

692. The Tribunal finds, under Article 6(1) of its Statute, that the Accused, by his own words, specifically ordered, instigated, aided and abetted the following acts of sexual violence:

(i) the multiple acts of rape of ten girls and women, including Witness JJ, by numerous Interahamwe in the cultural center of the bureau communal;

(ii) the rape of Witness OO by an Interahamwe named Antoine in a field near the bureau communal;

(iii) the forced undressing and public marching of Chantal naked at the bureau communal.

693. The Tribunal finds, under Article 6(1) of its Statute, that the Accused aided and abetted the following acts of sexual violence, by allowing them to take place on or near the premises of the bureau communal, while he was present on the premises in respect of (i) and in his presence in respect of (ii) and (iii), and by facilitating the commission of these acts through his words of encouragement in other acts of sexual violence, which, by virtue of his authority, sent a clear signal of official tolerance for sexual violence, without which these acts would not have taken place:

(i) the multiple acts of rape of fifteen girls and women, including Witness JJ, by numerous Interahamwe in the cultural center of the bureau communal;

(ii) the rape of a woman by Interahamwe in between two buildings of the bureau communal, witnessed by Witness NN;

(iii) the forced undressing of the wife of Tharcisse after making her sit in the mud outside the bureau communal, as witnessed by Witness KK;

694. The Tribunal finds, under Article 6(1) of its Statute, that the Accused, having had reason to know that sexual violence was occurring, aided and abetted the following acts of sexual violence, by allowing them to take place on or near the premises of the bureau communal and by facilitating the commission of such sexual violence through his words of encouragement in other acts of sexual violence which, by virtue of his authority, sent a clear signal of official tolerance for sexual violence, without which these acts would not have taken place:

(i) the rape of Witness JJ by an Interahamwe who took her from outside the bureau communal and raped her in a nearby forest;

(ii) the rape of the younger sister of Witness NN by an Interahamwe at the bureau communal;

(iii) the multiple rapes of Alexia, wife of Ntereye, and her two nieces Louise and Nishimwe by Interahamwe near the bureau communal;

(iv) the forced undressing of Alexia, wife of Ntereye, and her two nieces Louise and Nishimwe, and the forcing of the women to perform exercises naked in public near the bureau communal.

695. The Tribunal has established that a widespread and systematic attack against the civilian ethnic population of Tutsis took place in Taba, and more generally in Rwanda, between April 7 and the end of June, 1994. The Tribunal finds that the rape and other inhumane acts which took place on or near the bureau communal premises of Taba were committed as part of this attack. . . .

7.8. COUNT 1 — GENOCIDE, COUNT 2 — COMPLICITY IN GENOCIDE . . .

706. With regard to the acts alleged in paragraphs 12(A) and 12(B) of the Indictment, the Prosecutor has shown beyond a reasonable doubt that between 7 April and the end of June 1994, numerous Tutsi who sought refuge at the Taba Bureau communal were frequently beaten by members of the Interahamwe on or near the premises of the Bureau communal. Some of them were killed. Numerous Tutsi women were forced to endure acts of sexual violence, mutilations and rape, often repeatedly,

often publicly and often by more than one assailant. Tutsi women were systematically raped, as one female victim testified to by saying that "each time that you met assailants, they raped you." Numerous incidents of such rape and sexual violence against Tutsi women occurred inside or near the Bureau communal. It has been proven that some communal policemen armed with guns and the accused himself were present while some of these rapes and sexual violence were being committed. Furthermore, it is proven that on several occasions, by his presence, his attitude and his utterances, Akayesu encouraged such acts, one particular witness testifying that Akayesu, addressed the Interahamwe who were committing the rapes and said that "never ask me again what a Tutsi woman tastes like." In the opinion of the Chamber, this constitutes tacit encouragement to the rapes that were being committed.

707. In the opinion of the Chamber, the above-mentioned acts with which Akayesu is charged indeed render him individually criminally responsible for having abetted in the preparation or execution of the killings of members of the Tutsi group and the infliction of serious bodily and mental harm on members of said group. . . . [The Chambers then found that the prosecution had proved beyond a reasonable doubt the allegations in paragraphs 14-16, 18-23 of the indictment, but not the allegations of paragraphs 13 and 17 — EDS.]

723. The Chamber holds that by virtue of the above-mentioned acts Akayesu is individually criminally responsible for having ordered, committed, aided and abetted in the preparation or infliction of serious bodily or mental harm on members of the Tutsi group. . . .

725. Since the Prosecutor charged both genocide and complicity in genocide with respect to each of the above-mentioned acts, and since, as indicated supra, the Chamber is of the opinion that these charges are mutually exclusive, it must rule whether each of such acts constitutes genocide or complicity in genocide. . . .

729. First of all, regarding Akayesu's acts and utterances during the period relating to the acts alleged in the Indictment, the Chamber is satisfied beyond reasonable doubt, on the basis of all evidence brought to its attention during the trial, that on several occasions the accused made speeches calling, more or less explicitly, for the commission of genocide. . . .

730. . . . [G]enocide was committed against the Tutsi group in Rwanda in 1994, throughout the period covering the events alleged in the Indictment. Owing to the very high number of atrocities committed against the Tutsi, their widespread nature not only in the commune of Taba, but also throughout Rwanda, and to the fact that the victims were systematically and deliberately selected because they belonged to the Tutsi group, with persons belonging to other groups being excluded, the Chamber is also able to infer, beyond reasonable doubt, the genocidal intent of the accused in the commission of the above-mentioned crimes.

731. With regard, particularly, to the acts described in paragraphs 12(A) and 12(B) of the Indictment, that is, rape and sexual violence, the Chamber wishes to underscore the fact that in its opinion, they constitute genocide in the same way as any other act as long as they were committed with the specific intent to destroy, in whole or in part, a particular group, targeted as such. Indeed, rape and sexual violence certainly constitute infliction of serious bodily and mental harm on the victims and are even, according to the Chamber, one of the worst ways [to] inflict harm on the victim as he or she suffers both bodily and mental harm. In light of all the evidence before it, the Chamber is satisfied that the acts of rape and sexual violence described above, were committed solely against Tutsi women, many of whom were subjected to the worst public humiliation, mutilated, and raped several times, often in public, in the Bureau Communal premises or in other public places, and often by more than

one assailant. These rapes resulted in physical and psychological destruction of Tutsi women, their families and their communities. Sexual violence was an integral part of the process of destruction, specifically targeting Tutsi women and specifically contributing to their destruction and to the destruction of the Tutsi group as a whole.

732. The rape of Tutsi women was systematic and was perpetrated against all Tutsi women and solely against them. A Tutsi woman, married to a Hutu, testified before the Chamber that she was not raped because her ethnic background was unknown. As part of the propaganda campaign geared to mobilizing the Hutu against the Tutsi, the Tutsi women were presented as sexual objects. Indeed, the Chamber was told, for an example, that before being raped and killed, Alexia, who was the wife of the Professor, Ntereye, and her two nieces, were forced by the Interahamwe to undress and ordered to run and do exercises "in order to display the thighs of Tutsi women." The Interahamwe who raped Alexia said, as he threw her on the ground and got on top of her, "let us now see what the vagina of a Tutsi woman tastes like." As stated above, Akayesu himself, speaking to the Interahamwe who were committing the rapes, said to them: "don't ever ask again what a Tutsi woman tastes like." This sexualized representation of ethnic identity graphically illustrates that Tutsi women were subjected to sexual violence because they were Tutsi. Sexual violence was a step in the process of destruction of the Tutsi group — destruction of the spirit, of the will to live, and of life itself.

733. On the basis of the substantial testimonies brought before it, the Chamber finds that in most cases, the rapes of Tutsi women in Taba, were accompanied with the intent to kill those women. Many rapes were perpetrated near mass graves where the women were taken to be killed. A victim testified that Tutsi women caught could be taken away by peasants and men with the promise that they would be collected later to be executed. Following an act of gang rape, a witness heard Akayesu say "tomorrow they will be killed" and they were actually killed. In this respect, it appears clearly to the Chamber that the acts of rape and sexual violence, as other acts of serious bodily and mental harm committed against the Tutsi, reflected the determination to make Tutsi women suffer and to mutilate them even before killing them, the intent being to destroy the Tutsi group while inflicting acute suffering on its members in the process.

734. In light of the foregoing, the Chamber finds firstly that the acts described supra are indeed acts as enumerated in Article 2(2) of the Statute, which constitute the factual elements of the crime of genocide, namely the killings of Tutsi or the serious bodily and mental harm inflicted on the Tutsi. The Chamber is further satisfied beyond reasonable doubt that these various acts were committed by Akayesu with the specific intent to destroy the Tutsi group, as such. Consequently, the Chamber is of the opinion that the acts alleged in paragraphs 12, 12A, 12B, 16, 18, 19, 20, 22 and 23 of the Indictment and proven above, constitute the crime of genocide, but not the crime of complicity; hence, the Chamber finds Akayesu individually criminally responsible for genocide. . . .

NOTES AND QUESTIONS

1. *Rape as genocide.* Jean-Paul Akayesu was convicted for the crimes against humanity of rape and genocide founded on rape; both were firsts in international criminal law. With respect to the genocide conviction, the *Akayesu* Trial Chamber concluded that the rapes visited serious bodily and mental harm on those violated and in many cases ended in the killing of the victims, thus satisfying the "act" element of the crime of genocide. Relying on evidence that Tutsi women were systematically targeted for

rape, the Chamber further ruled that these rapes were encouraged by Akayesu with the specific intent to destroy the Tutsi group, as such. Yet some wonder whether the *Akayesu* Court made a leap — unsupported in hard evidence — from proof of discriminatory intent combined with systematic rape to a conclusion that the rapists evidenced an intent to *destroy* the targeted group. "That the rapes were systematic might make for a convincing argument that they constituted crimes against humanity, but what exactly made them genocidal? Perhaps some advocates would be satisfied with the equation of systematic rape, or perhaps even systematic sexual violence, and genocide. But if genocide requires an intent to destroy a group, more would seem to be required." Karen Engle, Feminism and Its (Dis)contents: Criminalizing Wartime Rape in Bosnia and Herzegovina, 99 Am. J. Intl. L. 778, 791 (2005).

Concentrating on the question of whether the systematic rape of Bosnian Muslim women could constitute genocide, Karen Engle outlines the following theories that may provide a link between discriminatory and systematic rape and a genocidal intent to *destroy* a group.

> *Rape as ethnic cleansing as genocide.* Part of the aim of the Serbs during the war was to rid certain areas of Bosnian Muslims. To the extent that rape was used to make women's lives so miserable that they would leave the territory, the violations were considered by some to constitute ethnic cleansing, which they then equated — with little explanation — to genocide. . . . [The equation of ethnic cleansing and genocide] views rape as a tool of genocide because it is a tool of ethnic cleansing — used, together with other tools, in attempts to force movement with the intent of destroying the group. . . .
>
> *Rape as social ostracism that destroys "in whole or in part."* Some advocates argued that the effect of the rapes on Bosnian Muslim women was social ostracism, which advocates then linked to the intended destruction of the Bosnian Muslim group. Those who pointed to this link between rape and genocide discerned something unique in the rapes of Bosnian Muslim women that would distinguish them from the rapes of women on other sides of the war. The sense of uniqueness relied on problematic beliefs about the special trauma caused by the rape of a Muslim woman because of the likely response of her Muslim family and community. Presumably, Orthodox and Catholic families would respond differently. . . .
>
> . . . The rapes become genocidal, under this interpretation, because they are aimed at destroying the group by splitting it — by turning Muslim communities against the women who are raped. Pinning the effects on Muslim culture and religion, the argument relies on the assumption both that such effects are *intended* by the Serbian rapists *and* that they have occurred and will continue to occur. . . . [T]he argument often uses presumed effects to impute intent. That the Muslim communities might respond differently from the ways suggested by the stereotype, even with acceptance, is not considered. . . .
>
> *Rape as forced impregnation.* Charli Carpenter considers the treatment of rape as genocide as "fundamentally hinged on the existence of forced impregnation." . . . [T]he arguments of many advocates rely on such a claim. . . .
>
> . . . At first, the forced impregnation argument seems counterintuitive. If children resulted from the rapes, there would be more, not fewer, Bosnian Muslims. But the argument assumes that any children born as a result of such a union would be Serbian, not Muslim. Of course, given that women might have additional children, this alone would not ensure the destruction of a people. Even were the intended effect to produce more Serbian children, it would not necessarily be to destroy all Muslim children. . . .
>
> In this narrative, forced impregnation would function to create Serbian babies who, by populating otherwise Muslim territory, would effectively take it over. Rather than forcibly removing the population, Serbs would *change* the Muslim population by ensuring that the next generation was composed of Serbs. . . . Because genocide depends on the intent of the perpetrators, imputing the above intent to Serbian policy (and those with command responsibility) would be crucial to any such prosecution.

In fact, little evidence of such intent has ever surfaced. Thus, many advocates accepted that the offspring would be Serbian to buttress their arguments for inferring intent. . . .

Forced impregnation as a means to prevent birth. Another way that forced impregnation was seen to constitute genocide was by evidencing intent to prevent births within a group. . . .

Advocates using this definition of genocide argued that, when a Muslim woman was forced to carry a child (or fetus) that resulted from a Serbian rape, her womb was "occupied" by the enemy, making her "incapable of conceiving and bearing a child of *her own ethnicity.*"

Id. at 789-794; see also generally Susana Sàcouto, Advances and Missed Opportunities in the International Prosecution of Gender-Based Crimes, 10 Gonz. J. Intl. L. 49 (2006-2007). Which, if any, of the above theories underpinned the genocide conviction in *Akayesu*? How would one, as a prosecutor, seek to prove allegedly widespread cultural or religious assumptions — such as critical allegations that "Serbian children would emerge from a Muslim egg impregnated by Serbian sperm" or that rape would lead to social ostracism? Engle, supra, 99 Am. J. Intl. L. at 793.

Note that a debate has been ongoing in the literature about whether an emphasis on the genocidal nature of many rapes in Rwanda or Yugoslavia was wise. Some argue, for example, that a genocide charge — which focuses on the offense done to the ethnic or religious group sought to be destroyed — obscures the essence of rape: violence to the body and a violation of the personal sexual autonomy of the individual rape victim involved. Consider the following critique:

When the international legal discourse on rape accepts that a woman's body represents her nation, that her ability to bear children marks her as the locus of biology and culture for her group, that her rape is a shame and a breach of her entire community, it reinforces the stereotypes and symbolisms that make women the target of war time violence in the first place. This attempt to articulate the outrage of the international community misses the mark when choosing to elevate violations of groups over the violation of individual women. Even if the perpetrators selected the victim because of her membership in a specific group with the purpose of impregnating her, "the fact that genocidal rape has a political aim does not change the rape victim's traumatic experience." To fully protect the human rights of women, international law should focus on the rape as a violation of and violence to a woman's body and autonomy.

Katie C. Richey, Note, Several Steps Sideways: International Legal Developments Concerning War Rape and the Human Rights of Women, 17 Tex. J. Women & L. 109, 125 (2007). How *should* one charge rape so as to recognize the injury done to the victim, as well as to the group with which she is identified?

2. *Evolution of the concept of rape in humanitarian law.* The crime of rape in peacetime originated as a crime against the property of men — the harm accrued to the husband or father to whom the woman "belonged." See Susan Brownmiller, Against Our Will: Men, Women and Rape 18 (1975). This view of rape carried over into the wartime context:

Societal attitudes toward rape in war start from the premise that women who "belong" to the enemy are legitimate targets. The phrase "rape and pillage" captures the concept that women are a form of "property," available for appropriation along with the enemy's other possessions. The often prevailing belief has been that such abuse of women is the right of the victorious warrior.

Beth Stephens, Humanitarian Law and Gender Violence: An End to Centuries of Neglect?, 3 Hofstra L. & Poly. Symp. 87, 89 (1999).

Modern humanitarian law did not codify rape as a property crime. However, until recently, it largely failed to recognize rape as a serious crime of violence, tending instead to categorize rape as a crime of "troop discipline" or as an offense against the chastity and honor of the woman or the honor of her family. The first international indictment to charge rape reflected this latter view. Thus, the Tokyo Tribunal charged rape as a war crime under "inhumane treatment," "ill-treatment," and "failure to respect family honour and rights." See Kelly Dawn Askin, War Crimes Against Women: Prosecution in International War Crimes Tribunals 202 (1997). Allied Control Council Law No. 10, Art. II (1)(c), adopted in 1946, marked a (brief) move away from an "honor" approach by listing rape alongside other violent crimes against humanity such as murder, extermination, and torture. However, the Geneva Conventions, adopted three years later, reverted back to a focus on the woman's honor. Professor Copelon writes:

> The *Leiber Code*, drafted to regulate the Union army during the American Civil War, identified rape as a capital offence [but classified it under "troop discipline" offenses]. Otherwise, if condemned, as rape was in the *Hague Convention* of 1907 and the *Geneva Conventions*, it was implicitly so, categorized as an offence against "family honour and rights" or as "outrages against personal dignity" or "humiliating and degrading treatment." The *Fourth Geneva Convention* called for "protect[ion] against [rape as an] . . . attack on their honour," but rape was not treated as violence, and was therefore not named in the list of "grave breaches" subject to the universal obligation to prosecute. In 1977 the *Protocols to the Geneva Conventions* mentioned "rape, forced prostitution and any other form of indecent assault," but only as "humiliating and degrading treatment," a characterization that reinforced the secondary importance as well as the shame and stigma of the victimized women. The offence was against male dignity and honour, or national or ethnic honour. In this scenario, women were the object of a shaming attack, the property or objects of others, needing protection perhaps, but not the subjects of rights.

Rhonda Copelon, Gender Crimes as War Crimes: Integrating Crimes Against Women into International Criminal Law, 46 McGill L.J. 217, 220-221 (2000); see generally Sàcouto, supra, 10 Gonz. J. Intl. L. at 49.

The ICTY Statute did not explicitly reference rape as a grave breach of the Geneva Conventions or other war crime but it listed rape among other violent crimes against humanity, such as murder and extermination. Viewed in terms of its categorization of rape, the ICTR Statute is more of a mixed bag. The ICTR Statute did explicitly recognize rape as a war crime, but its jurisdiction over violations of common Article 3 of the Geneva Conventions echoes the language describing rape as an "outrage on personal dignity." Like the ICTY Statute, however, the ICTR Statute identified rape as a crime against humanity of a kind with torture and other violent offenses.

The Rome Statute for the International Criminal Court embodies a complete abandonment of the notion of rape as a crime against honor. Thus, Article 7 explicitly names rape as an act of violence; it states that the crimes against humanity within the jurisdiction of the Court include "rape, sexual slavery, enforced prostitution, forced pregnancy, enforced sterilization, or any other form of sexual violence of comparable gravity." See Rome Statute of the International Criminal Court, adopted by the U.N. Diplomatic Conference of Plenipotentiaries on the Establishment of an International Criminal Court on 12 July 1998, art. 7, U.N. Doc. A/CONF. 183/9 (1998), 37 I.L.M. 999 (hereinafter ICC Statute). Further, in setting out the ICC's jurisdiction over war crimes, the ICC Statute lists rape and other forms of sexual violence *separately* from outrages upon personal dignity. Compare id. art. 8.2(b)(xxi) (Committing outrages upon personal dignity, in particular humiliating and degrading treatment), with id. art. 8.2(b)(xxii) (Committing rape, sexual slavery, enforced prostitution, forced pregnancy, enforced sterilization, or any other form of sexual violence also constituting a grave breach of the Geneva Conventions).

Rhonda Copelon stresses the importance of this development: "It makes a difference, to the elements that must be proved, to the penalty imposed, and to the larger cultural understanding of violence against women, to treat rape as torture rather than humiliation." Copelon, supra, 46 McGill L.J. at 234.

3. *Definition of rape.* Although rape has long been implicitly if not explicitly prohibited under the laws of war, no definition of the crime existed in the international criminal law context when the Ad Hoc Tribunals for Rwanda and Yugoslavia began hearing cases in the 1990s. Because rape was a central feature of both conflicts, these tribunals were forced to address this gap in international criminal law.

Surveying the accounts of survivors and eyewitnesses immediately illustrates one of the challenges in coming up with a workable definition of rape for international criminal tribunals: The accounts provide a litany of the horrifically imaginative and brutal ways rapists attack their victims in the context of armed conflict. See, e.g., Kelly Dawn Askin, War Crimes Against Women: Prosecution in International War Crimes Tribunals 261-297 (1997); Human Rights Watch, Shattered Lives: Sexual Violence During the Rwandan Genocide and Its Aftermath (1996); Human Rights Watch, "We'll Kill You if You Cry": Sexual Violence in the Sierra Leone Conflict 25-48 (Jan. 2003).

The ICTR recognized this problem when it took the first step in defining rape internationally. Review the discussion of the definition of rape in the *Akayesu* judgment, ¶¶686-688, above. Acknowledging that "variations on the form of rape may include acts which involve the insertion of objects and/or the use of bodily orifices not considered to be intrinsically sexual," the Trial Chamber went on in ¶688 to adopt a broad definition of rape: "a physical invasion of a sexual nature, committed on a person under circumstances which are coercive."

Later the same year, however, the ICTY seemingly adopted the explicit "body-parts" approach rejected in *Akayesu*. See Catharine MacKinnon, Defining Rape Internationally: A Comment on *Akayesu*, 44 Colum. J. Transnatl. L. 940, 945 (2006). In the *Furundžija* Judgment, an ICTY Trial Chamber stressed the need for specificity in the law and defined rape as:

> (i) the sexual penetration, however slight:
> (a) of the vagina or anus of the victim by the penis of the perpetrator or any other object used by the perpetrator; or
> (b) of the mouth of the victim by the penis of the perpetrator;
> (ii) by coercion or force or threat of force against the victim or a third person.

Prosecutor v. Furundžija, Case No. IT-95-17/1-T, Judgment, ¶¶178, 185 (Dec. 10, 1998). A number of subsequent cases in both Ad Hoc Tribunals relied on the *Furundžija* definition. See MacKinnon, supra, 44 Colum. J. Transnatl. L. at 945-946.

In 2005, the ICTR tried to reconcile the two definitions in the case of Mikaeli Muhimana. Muhimana was charged with genocide, murder, and rape for his actions between April and June 1994 in Rwanda's Kibuye prefecture. In one incident, Muhimana disemboweled a woman with a machete, cutting her open from her breasts to her vagina. The prosecutor charged this "physical invasion of a sexual nature" as rape, testing the scope of the *Akayesu* definition. The Trial Chamber endorsed the *Akayesu* definition of rape but held that the *Furundžija* approach "provide[s] additional details on the constituent elements of acts considered to be rape." Prosecutor v. Muhimana, Case No. ICTR-95-1B-T, Judgment and Sentence, ¶549 (Apr. 28, 2005). The Chamber asserted that the two approaches were "not incompatible or substantially different in their application," reasoning that the ICTY approach merely "articulate[s] the parameters of what would constitute a physical invasion of a sexual nature amounting to rape." Id. ¶550.

For the disembowelment, the Trial Chamber convicted Muhimana for murder, not rape. It reasoned that "[a]lthough the act interferes with the sexual organs, in the Chamber's opinion, it does not constitute a physical invasion of a sexual nature." Id. ¶557. Do you agree? Does this conviction adequately capture the nature of the crime? How else could this act have been charged? Do you agree that the *Akayesu* and the *Furundžija* approaches are not "substantially different in their application"?

4. *Hearsay and circumstantial evidence.* Daniel Franklin argues that the differences in the *Akayesu* and the *Furundžija* approaches generally made little difference to the outcome of prosecutions. Daniel J. Franklin, Note, Failed Rape Prosecutions at the International Criminal Tribunal for Rwanda, 9 Geo. J. Gender & L. 181 (2008). He notes that, as of 2008, the success rate for ICTR prosecutions of the crime against humanity of rape stood at 30 percent. In examining the reasons for the high failure rate of such charges, Franklin concluded that the legal definition of rape did not play a role. Rather, the prosecutions failed either because the indictments were overly vague or because, the Trial Chamber concluded, the evidence was insufficient. The latter ground is worth exploring further because such evidentiary issues are common in rape cases.

In many of the failed rape cases, the victims were dead, and the rapes were done in private, or at least outside the view of eyewitnesses. Accordingly, the charges relied on hearsay or circumstantial evidence, which was found wanting. Consider whether the following proof would have satisfied you:

[Alfred Musema-Uwimana, a lifetime civil servant, was director of Rwanda's state-owned Gisovu Tea Factory during the genocide. . . . Musema was alleged to have been] involved in the rape of Annunciata Mujawayezu. According to a witness, Annunciata had been hiding in a field near a guest house when a child began to cry. To prevent those with whom she was hiding from being found, Annunciata abandoned her hiding area and was spotted by Musema. Musema, who was with the Twas, told them to rape Annunciata. The witness stated that this command was followed by shouting and crying, after which she overheard "you slept with the Tutsi and now you have slept with the Twa." Though nobody else presented evidence specifically addressing this rape, a second witness testified to having seen Musema in the place where the first witness said Musema had called for Annunciata to be raped. . . . A majority of the Chamber found that Musema had indeed ordered Annunciata to be raped. It also found that, due to his high position in the community, Musema's orders would almost assuredly be followed. Even so, because none of the witnesses had actually *seen* the rape take place (the primary witness had been hiding with her head to the ground) and no other direct evidence was presented, the Chamber found there to be no conclusive evidence that Annunciata had been raped.

Id. at 199.

[Eliezer Niyitegeka, a journalist, worked for Radio Rwanda and then as Rwanda's Minister of Information.] The prosecution's rape charge rested primarily on the account of one witness. This witness testified that he was hiding in a bush near Niyitegeka's car at the time of the alleged rape. He further testified that from his hiding spot, he saw Interahamwe catch a young girl and force her into the car with Niyitegeka. The witness stated that Niyitegeka then slammed the door shut. According to the witness, Niyitegeka opened the door approximately thirty minutes later, pushed the girl out and shot her dead. Although the witness acknowledged that he did not see Niyitegeka rape the girl, he testified to overhearing the Interahamwe talk about Niyitegeka's having raped her.

The Trial Chamber found the witness to be "credible" and accepted his testimony regarding what he had seen at the scene of the alleged rape. . . . Rejecting the allegation of rape, [however,] the Trial Chamber pointed out that not only had the witness not seen the rape with his own eyes, but also that the Interahamwe whose statements he overheard could not have seen the rape either. The Chamber suggested that the witness had merely "surmised" the rape based on the circumstances [and acquitted Niyitegeka on the charge of the crime against humanity of rape].

Id. at 203-204.

5. *Coercion and consent.* In the *Furundžija* judgment, the Trial Chamber required proof that the act occurred "by coercion or force or threat of force against the victim or a third person." How does this compare to the *Akayesu* approach: "a physical invasion of a sexual nature, committed on a person under circumstances which are coercive"?

In a later ICTY case, *Prosecutor v. Kunarac,* the Appeals Chamber expanded on what was meant by the requirement that the act occur "by coercion or force or threat of force against the victim or a third person." Case No. IT-96-23 & IT-96-23/1-A, Judgment, ¶¶125-133 (June 12, 2002). The Chamber noted with approval the Trial Chamber's statement that an act is rape when it occurs "without the consent of the victim. Consent for this purpose must be consent given voluntarily, as a result of the victim's free will, assessed in the context of the surrounding circumstances." Id. ¶127. Thus,

[f]orce or threat of force provides clear evidence of non-consent, but force is not an element *per se* of rape. . . . [T]here are "factors—other than force—which would render an act of sexual penetration *non-consensual or non-voluntary* on the part of the victim." A narrow focus on force or threat of force could permit perpetrators to evade liability for sexual activity to which the other party had not consented by taking advantage of coercive circumstances without relying on physical force. . . .

Id. ¶129. The *Kunarac* Appeals Chamber also made clear that there is no "resistance" requirement. Id. ¶128.

Note that the circumstances of the case — whether the rape(s) occurred in a camp, by armed fighters, or involved multiple persons — will bear on the question of implied nonconsent. As the Appeals Chamber held in *Kunarac*:

For the most part, the [defendants] in this case were convicted of raping women held in de facto military headquarters, detention centres and apartments maintained as soldiers' residences. As the most egregious aspect of the conditions, the victims were considered the legitimate sexual prey of their captors. Typically, the women were raped by more than one perpetrator and with a regularity that is nearly inconceivable. (Those who initially sought help or resisted were treated with an extra level of brutality). Such detentions amount to circumstances that were so coercive as to negate any possibility of consent.

Id. ¶132. Defendants continue to claim "consent" in such circumstances, however. One ICTY defendant, Radomir Kovač, who held four girls captive, delivered them up to be raped by soldiers under his command, and finally sold them off to other soldiers, "claimed that the girls were actually in love with him." Peggy Kuo, Prosecuting Crimes of Sexual Violence in an International Tribunal, 34 Case W. Res. J. Intl L. 305, 318 (2002). The Tribunal rejected the defense, sentencing him to 28 years. Id.

The Appeals Chamber, though willing to focus on consent rather than force, refused the prosecution's invitation to further liberalize the definition. In an ICTR case before the Appeals Chamber in 2006, the prosecutor argued that

> the crime of rape only comes within the Tribunal's jurisdiction when it occurs in the context of genocide, armed conflict, or a widespread or systematic attack against a civilian population — circumstances in which genuine consent is impossible . . . [and] that rape should be viewed in the same way as other violations of international criminal law, such as torture or enslavement, for which the Prosecution is not required to establish absence of consent.

Prosecutor v. Gacumbitsi, Case No. ICTR-2001-64-A, Judgment, ¶¶148-149 (July 7, 2006). The prosecutor explicitly requested the Appeals Chamber to consider whether the absence of consent is an element of the crime of rape, for which the prosecutor has the burden of proof, or whether consent to rape is an affirmative defense, and therefore the defendant bears the burden of proof. The Appeals Chamber held that nonconsent is an element of the crime of rape that the prosecutor must prove beyond a reasonable doubt. However, it reiterated that such nonconsent may be proved by "the existence of coercive circumstances under which meaningful consent is not possible." Id. ¶155.

6. *ICC definition.* Consider the definition of the crime against humanity of rape (art. 7(1)(g)-1) set forth in the ICC Elements of Crimes:

> (1) The perpetrator invaded[15] the body of a person by conduct resulting in penetration, however slight, of any part of the body of the victim or of the perpetrator with a sexual organ, or of the anal or genital opening of the victim with any object or any other part of the body.
> (2) The invasion was committed by force, or by threat of force or coercion, such as that caused by fear of violence, duress, detention, psychological oppression or abuse of power, against such person or another person, or by taking advantage of a coercive environment, or the invasion was committed against a person incapable of giving genuine consent.[16]
> (3) The conduct was committed as part of a widespread or systematic attack directed against a civilian population.
> (4) The perpetrator knew that the conduct was part of or intended the conduct to be part of a widespread or systematic attack directed against a civilian population.

> 15. The concept of "invasion" is intended to be broad enough to be gender-neutral.
> 16. It is understood that a person may be incapable of giving genuine consent if affected by natural, induced or age-related incapacity.

See also ICC Elements of Crimes, art. 8(2)(b)(xxii)-1 (war crime of rape in international armed conflict); art. 8(2)(e)(vi)-1 (war crime of rape in noninternational armed conflict). How does this definition differ from the ICTR and ICTY approaches? Commentators note that Element 1

defines precisely the type of invasion which amounts to the crime of rape. Rape consists of the invasion of the body of a person resulting in penetration. This expression reflects the compromise reached by delegations between defining rape as an invasion or as a penetration. The majority of delegations supported the concept of an invasion and took especially into account the views expressed by the ICTR in *Akayesu*. . . . Others, however, recalled that most national legislation defines the *actus reus* as forced physical penetration.

The International Criminal Court Elements of Crimes and Rules of Procedure and Evidence 188 (Roy S. Lee ed., 2001). Element 2 requires proof that the rape was committed by force, threat of force, or coercion. But

> it is sufficient to prove that the perpetrator took advantage of the coercive environment surrounding the armed conflict, or the widespread or systematic attack against a civilian population in cases of rape as a crime against humanity. The intention of the drafters here is clearly to point out that coercive circumstances are not restricted to the use of physical force. Furthermore, non-consent is not an element of the crime of rape when coercive circumstances are involved.

Id. at 189. Finally, Rule 70 of the ICC's Rules of Procedure and Evidence provides that "[c]onsent cannot be inferred by reason of any words or conduct of a victim where force, threat of force, coercion or taking advantage of a coercive environment undermined the victim's ability to give voluntary and genuine consent . . . [or where] the victim is incapable of giving genuine consent . . . [or] by reason of the silence of, or lack of resistance by, a victim to the alleged sexual violence."

7. *Rape as torture (as war crime/crime against humanity).* *Akayesu* recognizes that rape can constitute torture as well as genocide. Prosecutors in the ICTY secured a number of convictions for rape as torture. See Prosecutor v. Kunarac, Case No. IT-96-23 & IT 96-23/1-A, Judgment, ¶¶142-156 (June 12, 2002); Prosecutor v. Furundžija, Case No. IT-95-17/1-A, Judgment, ¶¶109-114 (July 21, 2000). In *Kunarac*, the Appeals Chamber identified the elements of torture as (1) the intentional (2) infliction of severe pain or suffering, whether physical or mental; (3) for the purpose of obtaining information or a confession, or of punishing, intimidating or coercing the victim or a third person, or of discriminating, on any ground, against the victim or a third person. Case No. IT-96-23 & IT 96-23/1-A, Judgment, ¶142. To constitute a crime against humanity, the rape/torture would have be committed as part of a widespread or systematic attack against a civilian population. One element of torture as defined in the Convention Against Torture (CAT) — the official actor element — was ruled inapplicable to cases in the ICTY. In *Kunarac*, the Appeals Chamber explained that CAT's requirement that the torturer act in an official capacity or with official sanction was relevant to judging the culpability of states parties to that treaty, but it is not an element of the international crime of torture. Id. ¶¶145-148.

In response to defenses that sought to challenge whether the rapes alleged actually inflicted severe pain and suffering, the ICTY Appeals Chamber appeared to adopt a per se rule that rape presumptively inflicts torturous suffering. Thus, the *Kunarac* Appeals Chambers noted that "[s]evere pain or suffering, as required by the definition of torture, can . . . be said to be established once rape has been proved, since the act of rape necessarily implies such pain or suffering." Id. ¶151. Additionally, being forced to witness a rape can result in severe pain or suffering. See, e.g., Prosecutor v. Furundžija, Case No. IT-95-17/1-T, Judgment, ¶267 (Dec. 10, 1998).

With respect to defenses aimed at the "purpose" requirement of torture, the *Kunarac* Appeals Chamber was not persuaded by assertions that the defendants sought "only" sexual gratification and did not act for the purpose of obtaining information or punishing the victim. The Chamber distinguished between motivation (for example, sexual desire) and intention, noting that a defendant can harbor a number of motives and purposes; so long as he intends to act in a way that will cause severe pain or suffering and has at least one of the purposes prohibited by international law, he is guilty of rape as torture. In the ICTY, the list provided in CAT is not exhaustive; thus, for example, the *Furundžija* Trial Chamber added "humiliation" to the list of qualifying prohibited purposes. Id. ¶162.

8. *Participation and protection of victims in cases of sexual violence.* Recall one of the concerns of the *Akayesu* Trial Chamber (¶687): "The Tribunal also notes the cultural sensitivities involved in public discussion of intimate matters and recalls the painful reluctance and inability of witnesses to disclose graphic anatomical details of sexual violence they endured."

Cultural sensitivity, shame, and fear contribute to survivors' reluctance or even unwillingness to testify before international tribunals prosecuting crimes of sexual violence. For example, the case of Duško Tadić, who was charged with the rape of women prisoners at the Omarska camp in Bosnia, "was expected to be the first international war crimes trial in history to prosecute rape separately as a war crime and not solely in conjunction with other crimes. In trial proceedings, however, the [prosecutor] was compelled to withdraw [certain] rape charges . . . because witness 'F' was too frightened to testify." Kelly Dawn Askin, Sexual Violence in Decisions and Indictments of the Yugoslav and Rwandan Tribunals: Current Status, 93 Am. J. Intl. L. 97, 101 (1999). ICTY prosecutor Peggy Kuo outlined some of the difficulties the ICTY encountered in securing the testimony of witnesses:

> [Over the course of two years, several lawyers and investigators] used the statements gathered by NGOs and refugee organizations and found the witnesses and talked personally with them. The women were scattered all over the world as refugees — Germany, Sweden, Turkey, the United States — so it entailed a great deal of travel to talk to them. We had to bring interpreters so that we could communicate, and most of the time, although not always, we used female staff members to make the women feel more comfortable and able to open up. We also had to convince them to trust us even though we were an untested and new institution. . . . The only thing we could promise them was that their contribution would be important to our work and essential for justice. . . .
>
> [The lawyers faced many problems with the witnesses.] First, many of the witnesses . . . were reluctant to testify. They were reluctant to talk to anybody. It had been eight years since the incidents, and many of them wanted to put what had happened behind them. Many also downplayed what had happened to them. They would talk about what happened to their fathers or their brothers or other relatives who were killed and add, "Oh, by the way, I was raped." It was instructive . . . and also shocking to see that in their list of horrors, what happened to them was something they placed at the bottom. We had to convince potential witnesses that what they had to say, what they had to tell the world, was actually important. . . .
>
> Shame was also involved. One girl told us finally at trial about an incident of oral rape which she had never told anybody, including the investigators who had interviewed her several times over three or four years. When we asked her, "Why didn't you tell anyone?" she said, "I was just too ashamed. I felt so dirty; I didn't know how to explain it. But now that I'm here at the Tribunal and I know that this is my one chance to tell the truth and the whole truth, I'm going to say it," which she did.
>
> There were many, many more victims than we were able to convince to come in to testify. There were many, many more victims whom we were not able to identify and there were many, many perpetrators whom no one could identify — people who came and went at night, whose faces the girls were not able to see or whom they knew only by a

nickname or a vague description. We were not able to call those victims as witnesses. This highlights one of the limitations of using criminal law and trials to address mass atrocities. You can only handle a few at a time and the cases are only as good as the witnesses' ability to remember, describe, and testify honestly.

Kuo, supra, 34 Case W. Res. J. Inl. L. at 311-312, 316-317.

9. *Participation of women in the investigation and adjudication of cases.* Many commentators have concluded that the participation of women as investigators, prosecutors, and judges has been a critical factor in raising the visibility of gendered violence and increasing the prosecutorial resources devoted to it. Indeed, as the ICTR's Chief Prosecutor at the time, Justice Richard Goldstone, later noted:

> . . . The initial indictment against Akayesu did not charge him with gender crimes. When the trial commenced, however, witnesses began to make repeated reference in their testimony to widespread rape and sexual violence in the Taba Commune in Rwanda. They also referred to Akeyesu's tacit support for the commission of those gender crimes. The only woman judge in the Rwanda Tribunal, Navantham Pillay, . . . was astute in eliciting from witnesses evidence of sexual violence, taking initiative from the bench to do so. Her actions, combined with the amicus brief of the Coalition for Women's Human Rights in Conflict Situations urging the Tribunal to request an amendment of the indictments to include sexual violence, resulted in a postponement of the trial during which the indictment was amended to include charges of sexual violence against displaced women who sought refuge at the Taba Commune.

Richard J. Goldstone, Prosecuting Rape as a War Crime, 34 Case W. Res. J. Intl. L. 277, 282 (2002).

10. *Rules of procedure in rape cases.* Through various rules of evidence and procedure, the tribunals have sought to address the needs of those testifying about crimes of sexual violence. Peggy Kuo describes some of the methods used to protect witnesses and victims in the Foča rape camp case:

> We gave them all pseudonyms, and they were assigned numbers. Almost all of them also had digitized distortion of their faces, with squares that blocked their faces, when our proceedings were broadcast over video. Many of them had the voices electronically masked as well so their voices could not be recognized. A few witnesses testified in closed session, an exceptional measure whereby the courtroom is closed off to the public. . . . In an extreme circumstance, one witness had to be relocated to a secret country where she is permitted limited contact with her family because of security concerns.

Kuo, supra, 34 Case W. Res. J. Intl. L. at 317-318. The ICC has incorporated and built on the Ad Hoc Tribunals' protections for witnesses and victims, particularly in cases of sexual violence. Article 68 of the ICC Statute governs protection of victims and witnesses. The Rules of Procedure and Evidence expand on the general principles of Article 68: Rules 16-19 establish and set out the role of the Victims and Witnesses Unit. Rule 63 bars a requirement of corroboration of testimony, particularly in cases of sexual violence. Rule 71 bars admission of "evidence of the prior or subsequent sexual conduct of a victim or witness." Rule 72 provides for *in camera* determination of admissibility of evidence of consent in sexual violence cases. Finally, Rules 87-88 provide for protections for victims and witnesses, including anonymity measures, nondisclosure of victims' and witnesses' identities, and *in camera* proceedings.

C. CHARGING CONSIDERATIONS

Given that rape and other acts of sexual violence and degradation often can be charged in many different ways — for example, as genocide or as different types of crimes against humanity or war crimes — how do prosecutors decide what the indictment ought to look like? Obviously, prosecutors will consider what constellation of charges are appropriate given the facts of a case. We explore some additional considerations — in these types of cases as well as others — that influence prosecutorial charging choices.

1. Victims' Views

Kelly Dawn Askin argues that "[w]henever possible in the prosecution of sex crimes — particularly when there are multiple viable options for prosecuting a particular crime — the victim-survivor should be informed of the alternatives and consulted as to which charge is preferable" because the charge chosen may have significant consequences for the victim.[34] For example, "sexual slavery and enforced prostitution cover largely the same acts and, especially taking into account the survivor's views, sexual slavery is the preferred and more appropriate term to use" because victim-survivors find the term "enforced prostitution" offensive.[35] Similarly, "[f]or many women, it may be easier to marry or continue in a relationship if the crime committed against them is legally classified as, for example, torture instead of rape."[36] Other survivors may insist that their sexual violation be publicly identified as rape and the offender bear the stigma of a sex crime.

2. Purposes of Punishment: Expressive Function

Prosecutors will consider what charges they believe will best serve the goals of punishment (retribution, deterrence, and the like). They will certainly consider, in this regard, the expressive function of an indictment. Prosecutors at the ICTY, many of them women, who wished to focus on sex crimes often had to combat the lingering belief that such crimes were simply less important than others. Justice Goldstone has noted that he was "amazed at the gender bias that emerged in our international office," explaining his belief that the bias was due to the predominance of male police and army officers in the investigatory staff: "Their culture was not such as to make them concerned about gender-related crime."[37] One of Justice Goldstone's prosecutors, Peggy Kuo, confirmed these difficulties:

> Those lawyers and investigators who worked in the early days on the sex crimes cases had full support from [ICTY Prosecutor] Justice Goldstone and the top management, but among their colleagues, they often faced resistance. There were comments made by

---

34. Kelly D. Askin, The Jurisprudence of International War Crimes Tribunals: Securing Gender Justice for Some Survivors, in Listening to the Silences: Women and War 125, 129 (Helen Durham & Tracey Gurd eds., 2005).

35. Id.

36. Id.

37. Richard J. Goldstone, Prosecuting Rape as a War Crime, 34 Case W. Res. Intl. L. Rev. 277, 280 (2002).

investigators, who were admittedly overworked at the time, saying things like, "I've got ten dead bodies, how do I have time for rape? That's not as important," or, "So a bunch of guys got riled up after a day of war, what's the big deal?" But they persisted and my American colleagues, Nancy Paterson and Brenda Hollis, both prosecutors who left their jobs in the United States to work at the Tribunal, along with [the ICTY's Legal Advisor on Gender,] Patricia Sellers, made significant contributions in pushing these cases and making sure that those investigations did not completely fade away or disappear.[38]

By simply bringing the cases, then, prosecutors sent a clear message about the serious nature of these offenses.

The choice of which charge to bring — for example, a charge of genocide as opposed to a crime against humanity or war crime charge based on rape — also carries with it a message. As indicated in the notes following *Akayesu*, there is an ongoing dispute about the degree of emphasis that ought to be placed on the "special" nature of systematic and discriminatory rapes of the kind that occurred in the Balkans. The issue is whether charging choices ought to emphasize these rapes as an extraordinary, genocidal species of rape or whether they ought to be treated as "everyday" wartime rape, with the emphasis on gender victimization rather than ethnicity.[39]

Similarly, some object that a crime against humanity charge, like a genocide charge, does not recognize the victimization of the individual violated. Rape is only a crime against humanity when that rape is part of a broader widespread or systematic attack on a civilian population. One rape will not sustain such a count. Thus, some contend that relying only on a crime against humanity charge implies that there is some "normal" level of spontaneous, "recreational" rape that occurs in wartime; and it is only when many rapes reveal a pattern of victimization against a population that prosecution is appropriate. Accordingly, the "humanity" that is the focus of the charge, it is argued, is not the victim's humanity, but rather "the neutral, unsexed, social body of humanity" or the "body politic."[40] As Katie Richey argues, "[t]he wrong of rape must be identified first and foremost as a crime against the raped woman's bodily integrity and sexual autonomy. It should not be subordinated to the harm done to the body politic."[41]

Charging multiple counts may be responsive to the concerns underlying this debate (but may, as we will see below, create other legal and practical issues). Prosecutors, then, may wish to charge genocide where they have proof that discriminatory and systematic rapes were used to destroy a particular group. Where they can prove a widespread or systematic attack on a civilian population, a crimes against humanity-rape count may also be appropriate. Recognizing, however, the fact that some believe that such charges emphasize the group's victimhood (genocide) or the harm done to the body politic (crimes against humanity) rather than the violation of the individual victim's body and autonomy, prosecutors may also wish to bring a war crimes charge. A war crimes charge of rape would focus on the individual victimized. It also recognizes that "everyday" rape — not only the rapes that are part of a larger attack on a civilian population or that are accompanied by a genocidal intent — is an international crime. However, such charges obviously can be brought only when the rape occurred during a period of armed conflict.

---

38. Kuo, supra note 13, at 310-311.

39. Engle, supra note 10, at 786-787; Katie C. Richey, Note, Several Steps Sideways: International Legal Developments Concerning War Rape and the Human Rights of Women, 17 Tex. J. Women & L. 109 (2007).

40. Richey, supra note 39, at 116, 117.

41. Id. at 117.

The "expressive function" of an indictment must be weighed against practical concerns, such as difficulties in finding a legal theory to correspond with the conduct alleged[42] or in proof. Most obviously, the failure to secure a conviction will also send a message. For example, August 2006 brought the beginning of Saddam Hussein's second trial on charges of genocide, crimes against humanity, and war crimes related to his systematic attempts to annihilate Iraq's Kurdish population in 1987 and 1988.

> Legal experts say it is notoriously difficult to prove genocide. . . . "Genocide being the crime of all crimes, if he is convicted of it, then it proves that he is one of the worst of the worst that mankind has ever seen," said Michael P. Scharf, a professor . . . and an adviser to the Iraqi Special Tribunal. "But the risks are high, because if he is acquitted, then people will say that he is just a minor thug."[43]

3. Resources and Trial

We touched earlier on some significant practical concerns that bear on charging: whether survivors can be found and induced to cooperate, whether cooperating survivors and witnesses can be protected, and whether hearsay and circumstantial evidence will be sufficient to secure a guilty verdict. Another critical practical issue concerns resource constraints. ICTY Prosecutor Peggy Kuo noted that in the Foča "rape camp" case, the initial indictment included 300 counts and 25 defendants, a "completely unwieldy" result.[44] "As a result of discussion, the case was whittled down to about fifty counts and eight defendants who were at least commanders and sub-commanders and had committed multiple crimes. The other targeted defendants were cut out simply because we lack the resources to charge everybody against whom we have even overwhelming evidence."[45]

Carla Del Ponte, one of the Chief Prosecutors for the ICTY, echoed the importance of resource constraints, and provided the following nonexhaustive list of factors that she considered in preparing and issuing indictments:

> (1) the seriousness of the crime including its severity, magnitude, nature and impact decided after comprehensive investigation and analysis including reviewing open source material, NGO reports, identifying and conducting interviews of victims throughout the former Yugoslavia and in countries where victims have sought refugee status, forensic evidence, demographic evidence, expert evidence and exhumation and autopsy reports; (2) the leadership level and position in the military and political hierarchical structures as well as information about the military formations, the political organizations, the *de facto* as well as the *de jure* command structures, the relationship between political, military, paramilitary and police organizations at the time of the conflict; (3) the responsibility quotient among the senior leaders assessing their involvement, manner of participation, contribution to the crime and importance of their role.[46]

---

42. See, e.g., Patricia Viseur Sellers & Kaoru Okuizumi, Intentional Prosecution of Sexual Assaults, 7 Transnatl. L. & Contemp. Probs. 45 (1997) (discussing legal difficulties encountered in the ICTY's prosecutions of sexual assaults).

43. Amit R. Paley, As Genocide Trial Begins, Hussein Is Again Defiant, Wash. Post, Aug. 22, 2006, at A10-11.

44. Kuo, supra note 13, at 312.

45. Id.

46. Carla Del Ponte, Investigation and Prosecution of Large-Scale Crimes at the International Level: The Experience of the ICTY, 4 J. Intl. Crim. Just. 539, 543 (2006).

Del Ponte further notes that prioritizing cases against the most senior leaders of a criminal regime will affect investigative methods and, ultimately, related charging choices. "Building a case against the most senior persons responsible may involve a series of cases which 'work up the ladder,' prosecuting lower-level perpetrators in the collection of evidence against higher-level perpetrators, or in obtaining the substantive cooperation of 'insiders.' "[47]

Another pragmatic consideration is what a trial will look like — and how judges will respond to an overly prolix set of charges. Dermot M. Groome, an experienced U.S. prosecutor who served as one of the principal prosecutors in the ICTY's trial of Slobodan Milošević, asked his staff of lawyers and investigators to identify which charges they considered essential. Groome explained:

> We had evidence of so many crimes I decided to limit the indictment to the crimes which occurred in only a small number of the multitude of municipalities in which crimes occurred. Before I implemented this admittedly arbitrary criterion, I gave my staff an opportunity to convince me why a particular crime simply had to be in the indictment. I will never forget the looks of disgust as I dropped the horrific crimes they had labored to investigate. My goal at that stage was to draft the smallest, most efficient indictment possible that reflected the different crimes Milošević was responsible for — crimes like murder, rape and destruction of religious property and also reflected the ways in which crimes were committed — for example through political structures, the army, the police and paramilitaries.
>
> So the large body of crimes was dispassionately whittled down to what I believed to be the absolute minimum number. When the indictment was made public there was a loud outcry from victims' groups criticizing us for having omitted many notorious crimes. [Yet during] the trial the court continually challenged us to reduce the size of our case and each day we held a meeting reviewing the previous day's gains and considering how we might further prune our indictment. . . .
>
> . . . As we proceeded through the prosecution case, constantly beset by Milošević's illness and other delays that are simply an inherent part of large international criminal trials — those of us involved with the case came to see that despite our best efforts at designing an efficient prosecution we were still left with a case that exceeded the international community's patience.[48]

One way to respond to these issues is to attempt to winnow cases based on "themes" rather than particular defendants or crimes. Recall the discussion in Chapter 3 of the second round of Nuremberg trials, where prosecutors consciously pursued "theme" cases, such as the doctors (or medical) case, the justice (or judges) case, the ministries case, and the industrialist (Krupp) case. According to Mina Schrag, at the ICTY:

> A decision was made at the outset not to pursue theme cases, and, in other ways, not to give priority to the didactic purposes of prosecution. (The only theme case tried so far, about sexual assault at Foča [(the *Kunarac* case)], has received more press attention than any other than the Milošević trial.) The refusal to pursue theme cases reflects a misapprehension about Nuremberg. The antipathy to theme cases was usually explained as not wanting to be perceived as "political" or to present "show" trials. However, if prosecutions are based on solid evidence, and trials are conducted fairly, that criticism cannot stand. And theme cases, properly presented, might have demonstrated the over-arching fact that the particular crimes at issue in each separate case were part of a pattern, and

---

47. Id.
48. Dermot M. Groome, Re-evaluating the Theoretical Basis and Methodology of International Criminal Trials, 25 Penn. St. Intl. L. Rev. 791, 792 (2007).

not isolated, separate events. Indeed, the very reasons why international tribunals have been established — perceptions that extraordinary crimes have been committed — call for didactic and theme cases.[49]

4. Concursus Delictorum

Consider the following chart that matches the facts alleged with the charges brought in *Akayesu*. You will see that some facts — such as the rapes alleged in ¶¶12A and 12B of the indictment — are the basis for multiple specific charges addressed to that conduct (the two crimes against humanity (CAH) charged in counts 13 and 14). These same factual allegations, with others, serve as the basis for additional counts (the genocide, complicity in genocide, and crime against humanity charged in counts 1 through 3). In other words, multiple charges were brought based on a single course of conduct. Additionally, this chart demonstrates that, upon conviction, Akayesu received four different sentences (two life sentences and sentences of 10 and 15 years) for the same acts or transactions alleged in ¶¶12A and 12B, although all such sentences were to be served concurrently.

Charting the Akeyesu *Indictment*
(War Crimes Omitted)

Facts	*Specific Charge*	*Component of Charge*
All the facts described in ¶¶12-23	**Count 1**-Life (Genocide) **Count 2**-Acquitted (Complicity in Genocide) **Count 3**-Life (CAH-Extermination)	
Rape and abuse discussed in ¶¶12A, 12B	**Count 13**-Fifteen years (CAH-Rape) **Count 14**-Ten years (CAH-Other Inhumane Acts)	**Count 1**-Life (Genocide) **Count 2**-Acquitted (Complicity in Genocide) **Count 3**-Life (CAH-Extermination)
Speeches and directions to kill Tutsis described in ¶¶14-15	**Count 4**-Life (Incitement to Genocide)	**Count 1**-Life (Genocide) **Count 2**-Acquitted (Complicity in Genocide) **Count 3**-Life (CAH-Extermination)
Murder of six people identified in ¶¶15-18	**Count 5**-Fifteen years (CAH-Murder)	**Count 1**-Life (Genocide) **Count 2**-Acquitted (Complicity in Genocide) **Count 3**-Life (CAH-Extermination)

---

49. Minna Schrag, Lessons Learned from ICTY Experience, 2 J. Intl. Crim. Just. 427, 431 (2004).

Facts	Specific Charge	Component of Charge
Murder of eight people described in ¶19	**Count 7**-Fifteen years (CAH-Murder)	**Count 1**-Life (Genocide) **Count 2**-Acquitted (Complicity in Genocide) **Count 3**-Life (CAH-Extermination)
Murder of five teachers described in ¶20	**Count 9**-Fifteen years (CAH-Murder)	**Count 1**-Life (Genocide) **Count 2**-Acquitted (Complicity in Genocide) **Count 3**-Life (CAH-Extermination)
Beatings and other nonsexual abuse described in ¶¶16, 17, 21, 22, and 23	**Count 11**-Ten years (CAH-Torture)	**Count 1**-Life (Genocide) **Count 2**-Acquitted (Complicity in Genocide) **Count 3**-Life (CAH-Extermination)

Akeyesu, then, raises a difficult question common to almost every case: When is charging for, and conviction of, multiple charges predicated on one act or transaction impermissible?

The rules regulating this question—referred to as *concursus delictorum* (roughly, "concurrent offenses"), *concurrence,* or *multiplicity of offenses*—sit in a no-man's land between substantive criminal law (elements of crimes and modes of participation) and sentencing rules. It is "one of the least developed branches of international criminal law."[50] Yet the subject is critical because of its implications for procedural issues such as the form of indictments and trial issues (cumulative charging), and the application of double jeopardy principles (cumulative convictions).

Cumulative Charging. With respect to the form of indictments, prosecutors must decide early on what charges to bring, forecasting the proof that will be available at trial. If there is one truism about trial work, it is that a case rarely "comes in" as anticipated. Witness testimony, in particular, can diverge from its expected course, especially in contexts (like ICC prosecutions) where witnesses cannot be prepared ("proofed") by the prosecution before taking the stand. Judges may also disagree with the prosecutor's proposed application of the law to the facts, deciding, for example, that what the prosecutor viewed as an internal armed conflict is actually of international scope. Prosecutors, then, would like to bring a variety of charges in order to guard against these perils. For example, in *Akayesu*, the defendant was charged both as a principal and as an accomplice to genocide. As the court correctly pointed out, one cannot be both, but by bringing both charges the prosecution hedged its bets, ensuring that the court could convict no matter which characterization it adopted of Akayesu's role.

---

50. See Carl-Friedrich Stuckenberg, Multiplicity of Offences: *Concursus Delictorum*, in International and National Prosecution of Crimes Under International Law, Current Developments 559 (Horst Fisher, Claus Kress, & Sascha Rolf Lüder eds., 2003).

Cumulative charging, while advantageous to the prosecution, is a problem for the defense. Some believe that overcharging implicates the legality principle. If the prosecutor throws into the indictment everything but the kitchen sink, the defendant, who will not have access to all the prosecution's evidence, will not truly know which are the serious charges likely to be proved and which are filler that will likely fall by the wayside. In such circumstances, this will not feel like effective "notice" of the charges the defendant will be forced to defend. Multiple charges will require greater preparation and complicate defense counsel's efforts to make appropriate strategic choices. A defendant faced with cumulative charges will certainly need to prepare to confront a wider range of factual and legal issues. For example, bringing a crimes against humanity charge as well as a war crimes charge for murder requires the defense to address the question of whether the alleged killing happened in the context of a widespread attack on a civilian population.

In the United States, some judges have expressed a concern that overcharging may prejudice a defendant before juries. Thus, "[t]he very fact that a defendant has been arrested, charged, and brought to trial on several charges may suggest to the jury that he must be guilty of at least one of those crimes."[51] Further, "where the prosecution's evidence is weak, its ability to bring multiple charges may substantially enhance the possibility that, even though innocent, the defendant may be found guilty on one or more charges as a result of a compromise verdict."[52] That is, a " 'doubtful jury' " is given the option " 'to find the defendant guilty of the less serious offense rather than to continue the debate as to his innocence.' "[53] These defense concerns will not be present to the same degree where, as in international tribunals, the fact finding is conducted by judges rather than juries, but the potential for prejudice of this sort cannot be completely discounted.

Finally, if prosecutors are allowed to lodge every conceivable charge relating to a discrete set of facts, they will have much greater leverage in pressuring the defendant to plead out. The fear is that innocent but risk averse defendants may well accept a plea deal to a crime that generally carries less sentencing punch and stigma (e.g., a war crimes count) if it means that cumulative counts carrying more severe consequences (e.g., genocide or crimes against humanity counts) will be dismissed.

In sum, as the ICTY Trial Chamber in *Prosecutor v. Kupreskic* explained, what is needed are rules governing cumulative charging that simultaneously ensure "that the rights of the accused be fully safeguarded" while granting the prosecutor "all powers consistent with the Statute to enable her to fulfil her mission efficiently and in the interests of justice."[54] The outcome of this balancing is different in civil and common law systems; civil law systems are generally stricter in their pleading rules, often "precluding cumulative charging or charging in the alternative as part of prosecutorial strategy."[55] How the ICC will approach these issues is, as yet, unclear. The ICTY Appeals Chamber adopted the more permissive charging approach that prevails in common law countries like the United States. Thus, in the *Celebici* judgment, the Appeals Chamber concluded:

> Cumulative charging is to be allowed in light of the fact that, prior to the presentation of all of the evidence, it is not possible to determine to a certainty which of the charges

---

51. Missouri v. Hunter, 459 U.S. 359, 372 (1983) (Marshall, J., dissenting).
52. Id.
53. Id. (quoting Cichos v. Indiana, 385 U.S. 76, 81 (1966) (Fortas, J., dissenting from denial of certiorari)).
54. Case No. IT-95-16-T, Judgment, ¶724 (Jan. 14, 2000).
55. See, e.g., Attila Bogdan, Cumulative Charges, Convictions and Sentencing at the Ad Hoc International Tribunals for the Former Yugoslavia and Rwanda, 3 Melb. J. Intl. L. 1, 3 (2002).

brought against an accused will be proven. The Trial Chamber is better poised, after the parties' presentation of the evidence, to evaluate which of the charges may be retained, based upon the sufficiency of the evidence. In addition, cumulative charging constitutes the usual practice of both this Tribunal and the ICTR.[56]

The Ad Hoc Tribunals generally addressed issues arising from the improper accumulation of counts at the sentencing stage.[57]

Cumulative Convictions. In the United States, the Double Jeopardy Clause precludes a defendant from being "subject for the same offence to be twice put in jeopardy of life or limb."[58] A defendant who is improperly charged with two offenses when one is appropriate obviously faces the potential for much greater sentencing exposure.[59] Inappropriately cumulative convictions also create " 'a very real risk of . . . prejudice to the accused,' " in that "such persons suffer the stigma inherent in being convicted of an additional crime for the same conduct. In a more tangible sense there may be such consequences as losing eligibility for early release under the law of the state enforcing the sentence."[60] These last two types of prejudice cannot be cured simply by concurrent sentencing, a fact recognized in the *Akayesu* opinion, supra, ¶466.

The "Values" Test: Akayesu Trial Court. Initially, the "values" test articulated by the *Akayesu* Trial Court (¶468) was favored by the Ad Hoc Tribunals' trial chambers. It provides that

> it is acceptable to convict the accused of two offences in relation to the same set of facts in the following circumstances: (1) where the offences have different elements; or (2) where the provisions creating the offences protect different interests; or (3) where it is necessary to record a conviction for both offences in order fully to describe what the accused did. However, the Chamber finds that it is not justifiable to convict an accused of two offences in relation to the same set of facts where (a) one offence is a lesser included offence of the other, for example, murder and grievous bodily harm, robbery and theft, or rape and indecent assault; or (b) where one offence charges accomplice liability and the other offence charges liability as a principal, e.g. genocide and complicity in genocide.[61]

This is not, however, the test eventually adopted by the ICTY and ICTR Appeals Chamber. Why not? Does step (2) of this test invite the Chambers to inject its own judgment regarding the "interests" or values served by different crimes into the equation — and in so doing to unduly impinge on the prosecution's charging discretion? Does the second part of this test (under (a), above) require Chambers to construct a hierarchy of crimes so as to determine what constitutes a greater or lesser offense?[62]

---

56. Prosecutor v. Delalic, Case No. IT-96-21-A, Judgment, ¶400 (Feb. 20, 2001) (the *Čelibići* case); Musema v. Prosecutor, Case. No. ICTR-96-13-A, Judgment, ¶369 (Nov. 16, 2001).

57. See, e.g., Musema v. Prosecutor, Case. No. ICTR-96-13-A, Judgment, ¶360 (Nov. 16, 2001).

58. U.S. Const. amend. V.

59. In theory, the double jeopardy guarantee precludes trial on duplicative charges. See Witte v. United States, 515 U.S. 389, 396 (1995) ("Significantly, the language of the Double Jeopardy Clause protects against more than the actual imposition of two punishments for the same offense; by its terms, it protects a criminal defendant from being *twice put in* jeopardy for such punishment."). Yet the general focus of double jeopardy inquiries is whether duplicative charges will result in duplicative convictions and sentences.

60. Prosecutor v. Kunarac, Case No. IT-96-23 & IT-96-23/1-A, Judgment, ¶169 (June 12, 2002).

61. Prosecutor v. Akayesu, Case No. IT-96-4-T, Judgment, ¶468 (Sept. 2, 1998).

62. See, e.g., Prosecutor v. Kunarac, IT-96-23 & IT-96-23/1-A, Judgment, ¶171 (June 12, 2002); see also Bogdan, supra note 55; Andrea Carcano, Sentencing and the Gravity of the Offence in International Criminal Law, 51 Intl. & Comp. L.Q. 583 (2002); Allison Marston Danner, Constructing a Hierarchy of Crimes in International Criminal Law Sentencing, 87 Va. L. Rev. 415 (2001).

The "Elements" Test: The Appeals Chambers. The ICTY and ICTR Appeals Chambers ultimately rejected the *Akayesu* "values" test and instead adopted an "elements" test that is derived from U.S. constitutional law. The U.S. Supreme Court has held that

> "[w]here consecutive sentences are imposed *at a single criminal trial*, the role of the constitutional [double jeopardy] guarantee is limited to assuring that the court does not exceed its legislative authorization by imposing multiple punishments for the same offense." Thus, the question of what punishments are constitutionally permissible is not different from the question of what punishments the Legislative Branch intended to be imposed. Where Congress intended . . . to impose multiple punishments, imposition of such sentences does not violate the Constitution.[63]

Where legislative intent is clear regarding whether Congress sought to authorize multiple punishments, that is the end of the analysis. Where, however, the legislative design is not clear, the courts must apply a rule of construction, referred to as the *Blockburger* test:

> [W]here the same act or transaction constitutes a violation of two distinct statutory provisions, the test to be applied to determine whether there are two offenses or only one, is whether each provision requires proof of a fact the other does not.[64]

Essentially, then, in the absence of clear legislative intent to the contrary, the Supreme Court applies the *Blockburger* rule as a default "means of discerning congressional purpose" with respect to cumulative convictions.[65]

Critical to the correct application of the *Blockburger* standard is an understanding that it is truly an "elements" test and not one that depends on the facts of any given case. As the D.C. Circuit has explained:

> . . . The Supreme Court has consistently indicated that *Blockburger* calls for comparison of the *statutorily-prescribed elements* of the offenses, *not* the *constituent facts either as alleged or proven.* The Court has stated unqualifiedly that "application of the [*Blockburger*] test focuses on the statutory elements of the offense"; it has emphatically disavowed an attempt to apply the test "to the facts alleged in a particular indictment"; and it has declared that "[i]f each [offense] requires proof of a fact that the other does not, the *Blockburger* test is satisfied, notwithstanding a substantial overlap in the proof offered to establish the crimes." . . .[66]

The ICTY Appeals Chamber adopted "an approach heavily indebted to the *Block-burger* decision," ruling that a two-step analysis is appropriate:

> . . . [First, f]airness to the accused and the consideration that only distinct crimes may justify multiple convictions, lead to the conclusion that multiple criminal convictions entered under different statutory provisions but based on the same conduct are permissible only if each statutory provision involved has a materially distinct element not contained in the other. An element is materially distinct from another if it requires proof of a fact not required by the other.

---

63. Albernaz v. United States, 450 U.S. 333, 344 (1981) (emphasis added).

64. Blockburger v. United States, 284 U.S. 299, 304 (1932).

65. *Albernaz,* 450 U.S. at 340. Consequently, it does not override "a clear indication of contrary legislative intent," Missouri v. Hunter, 459 U.S. 359, 367 (1983), and may not come into play at all if that intent otherwise appears obvious.

66. United States v. Coachman, 727 F.2d 1293, 1301 (D.C. Cir. 1984).

. . . [Second, w]here this test is not met, the Chamber must decide in relation to which offence it will enter a conviction. This should be done on the basis of the principle that the conviction under the more specific provision should be upheld. Thus, if a set of facts is regulated by two provisions, one of which contains an additional materially distinct element, then a conviction should be entered only under that provision.[67]

An ICTR Appeals Chamber later endorsed the same test in all its particulars.[68] Does it make sense for the Ad Hoc Tribunals to adopt the *Blockburger* rule, which in the United States is a tool of statutory construction? The U.S. rule is built on the assumption that where Congress does not make its intention with respect to cumulative charging clear, it knows that the Court will resolve the issue by applying *Blockburger*; thus, the Court in so doing is implicitly following congressional intent. The ICTY Appeals Chamber appears to believe that the *Blockburger* test plays a similar role in international law:

The Appeals Chamber notes that the permissibility of multiple convictions ultimately turns on the intentions of the lawmakers. The Appeals Chamber believes that the Security Council intended that convictions for the same conduct constituting distinct offences under several of the Articles of the Statute be entered. Surely the Security Council, in promulgating the Statute and listing in it the principal offences against International Humanitarian Law, did not intend these offences to be exclusive. Rather, the *chapeau* elements disclose the animating desire that all species of such crimes be adequately described and punished.[69]

The first prong of the Tribunals' two-part test involves application of the *Blockburger* standard. The second prong tells us how to decide which charge should be dismissed and which saved when two charges failed the *Blockburger* test — that is, when they are considered the "same offence" for double jeopardy purposes. Choosing what the Appeals Chamber labels the more "specific" charge appears to be consistent with both civil and common law rules, as well as the latter part of the *Akayesu* test. In civil law jurisdictions, choosing the more specific crime is dictated by what is called the "rule of specialty." In the United States and some other common law jurisdictions, this exercise falls under the rubric of greater and lesser offenses. Where two offenses fail the *Blockburger* test because one "lesser" offense is congruent in its elements with a "greater" offense that requires the additional proof of one or more elements, the "lesser included offense" would be dismissed upon a conviction for the greater offense.

The issues that have arisen in applying the *Blockburger* standard in the Ad Hoc Tribunals could be classified according to whether one is attempting to compare one of the great crimes (war crimes, crimes against humanity, genocide, or aggression) with another one of those crimes (inter-article convictions) or whether one is attempting to decide whether charging two subsets of the greater crime, such as the crime against humanity of rape and the crime against humanity of torture, are jeopardy-barred (intra-article convictions).

---

67. Prosecutor v. Delalic, Case No. IT-96-21-A, Judgment, ¶¶412-413 (Feb. 20, 2001); see also Prosecutor v. Krstić, Case No. IT-98-33-A, Judgment, ¶218 (Apr. 14, 2004) (describing the elements test as the "established jurisprudence" of the tribunal); Prosecutor v. Kunarac, Case No. IT-96-23 & IT-96-23/1-A, Judgment, ¶179 (June 12, 2002).

68. Musema v. Prosecutor, Case. No. ICTR-96-13-A, Judgment, ¶¶346-369 (Nov. 16, 2001).

69. Prosecutor v. Kunarac, Case No. IT-96-23 & IT-96-23/1-A, Judgment, ¶178 (June 12, 2002).

Inter-Article Convictions. The most critical question with respect to inter-article convictions is whether the court ought to consider the crimes' *chapeau* when comparing the elements of two of the great crimes. The ICTY and ICTR Appeals Chamber, over a dissent, concluded that *chapeau* elements ought to be including in the *Blockburger* analysis.[70] This opens the door for multiple charges based on the same act or transaction. Crimes against humanity will always require proof of the *chapeau* element of a widespread or systematic attack on a civilian population, while genocide and war crimes will not; and genocide will always require proof of the *chapeau* element of an intent to destroy a qualifying group as such, while crimes against humanity and war crimes will not.[71] War crimes, of course, will require a war nexus, while the other two will not.[72]

Intra-Article Convictions. The critical determinant in intra-article comparisons is whether the court sticks to a comparison strictly of statutory elements, or whether it is willing to consider the facts as well. When a strictly elements-based comparison is made, prosecutors will have greater leeway in bringing, for example, multiple crimes against humanity charges based on the same course of conduct.

Illustrative is *Prosecutor v. Kunarac,* sometimes referred to as the "rape camp" or "Foča" case. While the Bosnian Serb Army and paramilitary groups were trying to "cleanse" the Foča area of non-Serbs, they targeted Muslim women. Many of these women were detained in "intolerably unhygienic conditions" in public buildings "where they were mistreated in many ways, including being raped repeatedly."[73] The prosecution charged the three defendants with violations of the law or customs of war (torture and rape) and crimes against humanity (rape, torture, and enslavement).

The *Kunarac* Appeals Chamber held that the defendants could be convicted of two crimes against humanity—torture and rape—for the same offense conduct (that is, the same rapes). It reasoned that each offense contained "one materially distinct element not contained in the other, making convictions under both crimes permissible."[74] "[A]n element of the crime of rape is penetration, whereas an element for

---

70. Id. ¶177; Musema v. Prosecutor, Case. No. ICTR-96-13-A, Judgment, ¶363 (Nov. 16, 2001); see also Prosecutor v. Jelisić, Case No. IT-95-10-A, Judgment, ¶82 (July 5, 2001). In the Appeals Chambers' judgment in *Prosecutor v. Delalic,* Judges David Hunt and Mohamed Bennouna filed a separate and dissenting opinion arguing that the *chapeau* elements ought not be considered in the *Blockburger* analysis. Case No. IT-96-21-A, ¶26 (Feb. 20, 2001) (dissenting opinion). They argued that

> . . . the fundamental consideration arising from charges relating to the same conduct is that an accused should not be penalised more than once for the same *conduct.* The purpose of applying this test is therefore to determine whether the *conduct* of the accused genuinely encompasses more than one crime. For that reason, we believe that it is not meaningful to consider for this purpose legal prerequisites or contextual elements which do not have a bearing on the accused's conduct, and that the focus of the test should therefore be on the substantive elements which relate to the accused's conduct [including the *actus reus* and *mens rea* of the crime].

Id.

71. See, e.g., Prosecutor v. Krstić, Case No. IT-98-33-A, Judgment, ¶¶218-227 (April 19, 2004) (overturning Trial Chamber's conclusion that genocide and CAH-extermination charges were improperly cumulative); Musema v. Prosecutor, Case No. ICTR-96-13-A, Judgment, ¶¶366-367 (Nov. 16, 2001) (upholding that convictions for genocide and CAH-extermination based on the same conduct).

72. Prosecutor v. Kunarac, Case No. IT-96-23 & IT-96-23/1-A, Judgment, ¶176 (June 12, 2002) (holding that convictions for crimes against humanity and war crimes permissible even where based on the same conduct); Prosecutor v. Jelisić, Case No. IT-95-10-A, Judgment, ¶¶78-83 (July 5, 2001) (same). Under the ICTY Statute, due to the way the statute is drawn, it is only when charges are brought as both war crimes and grave breaches that one will have inter-article problems. See, e.g., Prosecutor v. Delalic, Case No. IT-96-21-A, Judgment, ¶423 (Feb. 20, 2001).

73. Case No. IT-96-23 & IT-96-23/1-A, Judgment, ¶3 (June 12, 2002).

74. Id. ¶179.

the crime of torture is a prohibited purpose, neither element being found in the other crime."[75] Similarly, the war crimes of torture and rape each include an element that the other does not and thus charging both crimes was appropriate.[76] Finally, the Appeals Chamber also found meritless the contention that the crimes against humanity convictions for enslavement and rape were impermissibly cumulative.[77] "That the Appellants also forced their captives to endure rape as an especially odious form of their domestic servitude does not merge the two convictions. . . . [E]nslavement, even if based on sexual exploitation, is a distinct offence from that of rape" under the *Blockburger* test.[78]

---

75. Id.
76. Id. ¶¶188, 196.
77. Id. ¶186.
78. Id.

CHAPTER
24

Alternatives to Prosecution After Atrocity: A Survey of Other Transitional Justice Mechanisms

In the preceding chapters our focus has been on transborder and international crimes and the procedures used to investigate and prosecute such crimes. In particular, we have explored the use of international criminal tribunals to prosecute those responsible for the most egregious crimes and have touched upon the use of national and hybrid tribunals. At several points, we have alluded to the inherent limitations of criminal trials and the ways in which such trials may be viewed as an imperfect mechanism for holding individuals accountable for their roles in mass atrocities. In post-conflict situations, after the killing and maiming have ended, national and international actors may be unable to summon the resources or the political will to launch criminal prosecutions. Where the violence has not ceased, even victims may argue that if a trade-off must be made between a politically brokered resolution to an ongoing conflict and "justice" in the form of criminal prosecution, they choose peace over accountability. All too often, practical obstacles — such as finding competent proof or securing the presence of the defendant — complicate accountability efforts. Legal issues — such as the difficulty of proving a specific type of intent or isolating a qualifying mode of responsibility — can preclude conviction.

If these and other challenges limit or even preclude the use of criminal trials as a means of holding perpetrators responsible for the most serious international crimes, one has to ask: Are there any alternatives? To conclude our analysis of international criminal prosecutions, we now turn to a discussion of what mechanisms might be employed instead of, or in addition to, criminal trials. Necessarily, we approach this topic at a general or systemic level, since every situation is unique and fraught with "particularities" that distinguish it from all other situations, at least in the eyes of those most directly involved. Our aim is to provide an overview.

The first questions one must confront before exploring the viability of alternatives to criminal prosecutions are: What are one's goals in light of the needs of a particular conflict or population? If, as is usually the case, there are multiple goals, how should one prioritize them? Commentators have claimed a very ambitious range of aims for criminal sanctions in the context of atrocity. Minna Schrag itemizes the following benefits that are sometimes said to flow from international criminal accountability:

> bringing a sense of justice to war-torn places;
> re-establishing the rule of law;

providing a sound foundation for lasting peace;

enforcing international law, ending impunity for violations, especially for senior political and military leaders;

bringing repose to victims and providing an outlet to end cycles of violence and revenge;

demonstrating that culpability is individual and not the responsibility of entire groups;

providing a safe forum for victims to tell their stories;

demonstrating fairness and the highest standards of due process;

providing exemplary procedures to serve as a model for rebuilding a legal system devastated by war crimes and human rights violations;

creating an accurate historical record to forestall those who might later try to deny that wide-scale violations of international law occurred;

explaining what caused the violations and illustrating particular patterns of violations;

developing and expanding the application and interpretation of international law and norms; and

providing a forum for considering restitution and reparations.[1]

These worthy aims may not always be achieved; indeed, sometimes criminal trials may do as much harm as good. While they may satisfy a fundamental sense of justice, they may also be perceived as "victors' justice" and serve to exacerbate rather than resolve the underlying tensions and conflicts. At a more individual level, a "focus on prosecution can entrench an adversarial thirst for revenge. That kind of thirst is seldom satisfied even by successful prosecutions, and failure in the prosecutorial structure can seem another betrayal."[2] Not prosecuting the perpetrators, on the other hand, offends basic notions of morality and fairness, and may leave the underlying tensions to reignite in the future. The experiences of those traumatized by atrocities "defy description and perhaps even memory; yet refusing to remember . . . can risk insulting the victimized and leaving the victim to fester. To seek a path between vengeance and forgiveness is also to seek a route between too much memory and too much forgetting."[3]

Consideration of whether criminal trials (domestic, hybrid, or international), or any other accountability mechanisms, can achieve identified goals has lately been the subject of a voluminous literature, much of it falling under the rubric "transitional justice." This is a relatively new term of art. "Many analysts and advocates use the term 'transitional justice' to refer to societal responses to severe repression, societal violence, and systemic human rights violations that seek to establish the truth about the past, determine accountability, and offer some form of redress, at least of a symbolic nature."[4] Jon Elster succinctly defines "transitional justice" as "the processes of trials, purges, and reparations that take place after the transition from one political regime to another."[5]

---

1. Minna Schrag, Lessons Learned for ICTY Experience, 2 J. Intl. Crim. Just. 427, 428-429 (2004); see also Jose E. Alvarez, Rush to Closure: Lessons of the Tadić Judgment, 96 Mich. L. Rev. 2031, 2031 (1998).

2. Martha Minow, Between Vengeance and Forgiveness: Facing History After Genocide and Mass Violence 8 (1998).

3. Id. at 118.

4. Assessing the Impact of Transitional Justice: Challenges for Empirical Research 1-2 (Hugo van der Merwe, Victoria Baxter, & Audrey R. Chapman eds., 2009) [hereinafter Challenges].

5. Jon Elster, Closing the Books: Transitional Justice in Historical Perspective 1 (2004). Although many if not most of the conflicts that spawned atrocity over the last few decades arose out of internal power struggles and accompanying violence, this is not invariably the case. Aggression by one state against another, rather than a population's desire for a domestic "transition" from one regime to another, has

The various issues that arise in such transitional contexts include not only punishment for criminal oppressors but also questions about how to compensate those whose property was expropriated under the prior regime, whether compromised persons with useful skills or knowledge should retain their official positions, and how to balance often competing demands for accountability and reconciliation. "Beyond these initiatives, there is also the need to find ways to overcome or at least manage the conflicts among contending groups, rebuild the institutional and social infrastructure, and promote a sense of shared commitment to the new political system. Many of the societies moving away from repressive political systems and dictatorial rule also have the goal of establishing more democratic forms of government."[6] Thus, "[t]ransitional justice evokes many aspirations: rule of law, legitimacy, liberalization, nation-building, reconciliation, and conflict resolution."[7]

To the extent that the term *transitional* is understood to imply a movement from chaos and autocratic rule to peaceful democratic functioning, its use may be misleading because by no means all of the societies faced with these challenges have managed (yet) to achieve this goal.[8] Similarly, although much of the literature focuses on "post-conflict" situations, that is not always what traumatized populations experience. "[T]he political settlements that end . . . internal conflicts or bring about the resignation of repressive regimes are not necessarily stable and enduring. In many instances the problems that gave rise to the strife persist, and efforts to deal with the past can give rise to new tensions."[9] Enduring instability may stymie efforts to effect the reforms that will preclude further abuses, to say nothing of compromising attempts to provide justice, truth, or compensation to victims of the prior regime. Finally, "[w]hile the transitions literature appears to presume a goal of 'transitions to democracy' . . . , the democratization goal is often in tension with other aspirations identified . . . , such as the new focus on conflict resolution and reconciliation."[10]

This "transitional" process — if it happens at all — is a highly complex one in which a variety of mechanisms may be employed in tandem or sequentially to achieve different aims. We have explored some of these mechanisms in preceding chapters, including both formal criminal prosecutions and alternative dispute resolution mechanisms such as Rwanda's *gacaca* process. In the following readings, we first focus on the primary alternative to criminal proceedings that many nations have employed to bring some measure of accountability and reconciliation in the wake of atrocity: namely, commissions of inquiry, also known as truth and reconciliation commissions (TRCs). We then excerpt a piece by Tina Rosenberg that talks about another transitional justice technique — lustration — as well as trials and TRCs.[11]

---

been responsible for many of the international crimes this book explores. That said, where there have been widespread human rights abuses in a conflict arising out of aggression, many of the same remedial and "justice" issues examined in the transitional justice literature will be raised.

6. Challenges, supra note 4, at 1-2.

7. Ruti Teitel, The Law and Politics of Contemporary Transitional Justice, 38 Cornell Intl. L.J. 837, 838 (2005); see also generally Jane Stromseth, David Wippman, & Rosa Brooks, Can Might Make Rights? Building the Rule of Law After Military Inteventions ch. 7 (2006); Ruti G. Teitel, Transitional Justice (2000).

8. Challenges, supra note 4, at 2; see also Thomas Carothers, The End of the Transition Paradigm, 13 J. Democracy 5 (2002).

9. Challenges, supra note 4, at 2.

10. Teitel, supra note 7, 38 Cornell Intl. L.J. at 838.

11. An underdiscussed aspect of transitional justice has lately received greater attention: processes that flow from the "bottom up" through local indigenous efforts as opposed to "top down" mechanisms such as internationalized courts. *Gacaca* could, at one point, have been deemed one such effort at "justice from below," but it has been transformed in nature and may be deemed to have been co-opted by those at the top. See, e.g., Phil Clark, Hybridity, Holism, and "Traditional" Justice: The Case of the Gacaca Courts in Post-genocide Rwanda, 39 Geo. Wash. Intl. L. Rev. 765 (2007); Lars Waldorf, Mass Justice for Mass

It is exceedingly difficult to test empirically what "works" and what does not in societies facing transitional justice issues.[12] This is due in part to the complexity of the project and in part to the reality that there is simply no one-size-fits-all solution. What each society requires will depend on the way in which it orders the goals of transitional justice as well as its unique history, culture, resource base, and security situation. The Rosenberg piece below illustrates this fact by contrasting the transitional justice issues recently faced in some South American nations with those present in many parts of Eastern Europe. The final excerpt, by Miriam Aukerman, allows us to pursue the question of what mechanisms — trials, TRCs, or the like — will most effectively further the goals of punishment introduced in Chapter 1.

A. TRUTH AND RECONCILIATION COMMISSIONS

More than 30 truth commissions or TRCs have been used to address past human rights violations. Many people associate a truth commission with the South African model, but in fact these commissions vary significantly in their origins, mandates, and attributes. A TRC may be the product of political negotiations that resolved a conflict, as in South Africa, or may be instituted after a transition has been effected in lieu of, or in addition to, national prosecutions of wrongdoers. TRCs may be authorized or supported by domestic authorities (for example, South Africa, Argentina, and Chile), the international community (for example, the United Nations Truth Commission for El Salvador), or some combination thereof (for example, the Guatemalan Historical Clarification Commission).[13] There is, in short, no single model or paradigm.

However, TRCs do share some common characteristics. Patricia Hayner has identified the fundamental features of this transition mechanism: A commission that (1) focuses on the past; (2) investigates a pattern of abuses over a period of time, rather than a specific event; (3) is a temporary body, typically operating between six months and two years; (4) completes its work with a report; and (5) is officially sanctioned, authorized, or empowered by the state and sometimes by the armed opposition.[14] Hayner further explains that "[t]hough presented with varying degrees of emphasis, a truth commission may have any or all of the following five basic aims: to discover, clarify, and formally acknowledge past abuses; to respond to specific needs of victims; to contribute to justice and accountability; to outline institutional responsibility and recommend reforms; and to promote reconciliation and reduce conflict over the past."[15]

Relationship to Criminal Trials. TRCs have been used to achieve some measure of "justice" for victims, generally when criminal proceedings are not feasible. Where the crimes committed in a given atrocity implicate more persons than could ever be ztried, a truth commission may be the best way of providing some accountability.

Atrocity: Rethinking Local Justice as Transitional Justice, 79 Temp. L. Rev. 1 (2006). For additional discussion of "bottom up" mechanisms, see Transitional Justice from Below: Grassroots Activism and the Struggle for Change (Kiernan McEvoy & Lorna McGregor eds., 2008) and Kieran McEvoy & Harry Mika, Restorative Justice and the Critique of Informalism in Northern Ireland, 42 Brit. J. Criminology 534 (2002).

12. See generally Challenges, supra note 4.

13. See U.N. Secretary-General Report to the U.N. Security Council, The Rule of Law and Transitional Justice in Conflict and Post-conflict Societies, S/2004/616, ¶¶50-51, at 17 (Aug. 23, 2004).

14. Priscilla B. Hayner, Unspeakable Truths: Confronting State Terror and Atrocity 14 (2001).

15. Id. at 24.

For example, in Rwanda, it is believed that approximately 100,000 individuals took part in the genocide. No court system — international, hybrid, or national — could try that many cases in a reasonable period of time. Thus, former International Criminal Tribunal for Former Yugoslovia (ICTY) judge Patricia Wald has opined that where it is impossible to bring lower-level defendants to trial, a TRC presents a viable alternative.[16]

Although "justice" may be one aim of TRCs, these commissions differ from criminal proceedings in a number of important respects. Most significantly, they do not have the power to adjudicate criminal guilt, nor can they impose criminal punishment. Accordingly, use of a TRC does not foreclose criminal proceedings and, indeed, TRCs are often used in tandem with other transitional justice mechanisms such as trials. TRCs also generally have fewer coercive powers. Most could not compel individuals or institutions to cooperate with their inquiry or with the implementation of whatever recommendations they made. In some ways, however, commissions have greater powers to address the suffering of victims and the overall needs of a given society than do criminal proceedings. By their nature, TRCs have a broader perspective: Rather than focusing on whether this particular defendant wronged this particular person, they are potentially capable of addressing the causes of, and wrongs committed during, an extended conflict, and they can identify the responsibility of the state in criminal wrongs. Many commissions are empowered to recommend programs or reforms necessary to prevent future abuses. By arriving at a comprehensive overview of the events in question, they can "promote national reconciliation by settling long-festering disagreements about disputed charges and countercharges. [Finally, t]hey can recommend the payment of compensation to various categories of victims, public trials of alleged perpetrators, and amnesties."[17]

TRCs are often described as more victim-centered than criminal proceedings, in two respects. First, victims are often more active participants in a truth commission's investigative and hearing process — as opposed to criminal proceedings in which the defendant, not the victim, is the primary focus, and the victim often plays a limited role. As a result, commissions have the potential to offer individual victims some concrete acknowledgment of their suffering, as well as to identify the fate of loved ones. Participation in TRCs is claimed to be cathartic, healing, and empowering for at least some victims. Second, truth commissions may provide for victim services and reparation, which up until now have not been a big part of the criminal process.

The particular attributes and jurisdiction of a TRC depend on a variety of circumstances, including the historical and political context. Some significant variables include the following.

Identifying the Perpetrators. One very controversial issue surrounding the use of TRCs is whether, or when, commissions should publicly "name names," by identifying the individuals most responsible for the atrocities in question, as opposed to providing only a general description of the human rights abuses at issue. Most TRCs' mandates have not spoken to the question, leaving the decision to the commissioners; most commissions have declined to name names. Patricia Hayner explains:

> [The controversy surrounding this question is due to the fact that it implicates] two contradictory principles, both of which can be strongly argued by rights advocates. The

---

16. Patricia M. Wald, Accountability for War Crimes: What Roles for National, International and Hybrid Tribunals?, 98 Am. Socy. Intl. L. Proc. 192, 195 (2004).

17. Thomas Buergenthal, Truth Commissions: Between Impunity and Prosecution, 38 Case W. Res. J. Intl. L. 217, 222 (2006-2007).

first of these is that due process requires that individuals accused of crimes be allowed to defend themselves before being pronounced guilty. . . . The second principle is that telling the full truth requires naming persons responsible for human rights crimes when there is clear evidence of their culpability. Naming names is part of the truth-telling process, and is especially important when the judicial system does not function well enough to expect trials. . . .

[Ultimately] . . . the decision whether to name names has been affected by a number of factors far beyond concerns for due process. . . . In some cases there are explicit or implicit political pressures on a commission to keep names out of the report. Some commissions have been especially concerned about the security risks in naming perpetrators: concerned either for the safety of witnesses who provided the names, for the security of commission members or staff, or about the possibility of revenge (in the form of street justice) taken against those named, especially where there is no chance that justice will be found in the courts. Commissioners must also gauge the quality of their information, the depth of their investigations and the sources on which they have based their conclusions, and whether there is any risk that their conclusions could be wrong. Those truth commissions that have identified perpetrators in their reports have tried to state clearly that the commission report is not a legal judgment and does not determine the persons' criminal liability. Yet regardless of such a caveat, those named in a truth commission's report are popularly understood to be guilty, period. . . .[18]

Amnesties. Perhaps the most difficult and controversial aspect of TRCs' functioning is whether they should have the power to grant amnesties to those who have been identified as most responsible for the atrocities at issue. As Alexander K.A. Greenawalt explains:

> . . . Many states facing atrocities committed by a past regime have chosen not to prosecute the wrongdoers, but have either ignored past crimes or employed alternate mechanisms to expose and acknowledge those crimes without subjecting individual perpetrators to prosecution. The paradigmatic and most celebrated example of this approach is South Africa's Truth and Reconciliation Commission (TRC), which addressed political crimes committed by both the government and its opponents during decades of apartheid. Operating during the country's transition to a constitutional democracy rooted in equal rights, the TRC offered amnesty to individual perpetrators of politically motivated crimes who offered a full confession — many of them testifying in televised public proceedings at which victims and family members were free to confront their tormentors. Other states have adopted similar mechanisms, with varying methods of truth-seeking and degrees of individual accountability. In Chile, for example, a truth commission arose after the legislature passed a blanket amnesty precluding prosecution of crimes committed by the Pinochet regime, whereas in El Salvador, a blanket amnesty followed the release of a truth commission report that named specific high-level government perpetrators of notorious crimes.
>
> The rationales invoked to defend amnesty tend to assume one of two standard forms. One argument allows that prosecutions may be preferable under ideal circumstances, but maintains that nonprosecutorial alternatives may be justified as a compromise necessary to facilitate political transition to a more just society that rebukes the evils of the past. As Rajeev Bhargava has observed:
>
> > [N]ormally such transitional moments emerge out of a settlement in which former oppressors refuse to share power unless guaranteed that they will escape the criminal justice system characteristic of a minimally decent society. . . .

18. Hayner, supra note 14, at 107-108.

The danger [of insisting upon criminal justice] is obvious: victims may forever remain victims and their society may never cease to be barbaric.[19]

TRC Chair Archbishop Desmond Tutu invoked this rationale in the Commission's final report, arguing that "[h]ad the miracle of the negotiated settlement not occurred, we would have been overwhelmed by the bloodbath that virtually everyone predicted as the inevitable ending for South Africa."[20] Although rooted in compromise, the justification is ultimately a moral one: Justice is sacrificed, but only for the sake of greater future justice or other equivalent moral goods.

This line of reasoning is, of course, highly contingent. The mechanism that best maximizes goals of justice or moral goods in one context does not necessarily apply in another. To the extent, for example, that the international community chooses to engage in Kosovo- and Iraq-style military interventions aimed at regime change and proves willing to commit itself financially and militarily to the future stability of such societies through peacekeeping operations and the like, the political compromise argument is less compelling. Thus, W. Michael Reisman has urged a diverse approach to transitional justice, arguing that where the international community is unwilling to make the military commitment to defeat wrongdoers, "it is preferable to emphasize techniques that reestablish public order as quickly as possible and fulfill feasible sanctioning goals of public order."[21] At the extreme, considerations of this sort could also be invoked to justify ever more diluted forms of accountability, such as less-thorough or less-public truth commissions, blanket rather than individualized amnesties, or simply inaction.

A second line of argument maintains that truth commissions paired with amnesty can supply an intrinsically superior form of transitional justice to prosecution, irrespective of political compromises. Martha Minow has argued that truth commissions "are not a second best alternative to prosecutions. . . . When the societal goals include restoring dignity to victims, offering a basis for individual healing, and also promoting reconciliation across a divided nation, a truth commission may be as or more powerful than prosecutions."[22] In the South African context, Tutu has similarly advocated a form of "restorative justice" rooted in forgiveness and has argued that "the route of trials would have stretched an already hard-pressed judicial system beyond reasonable limits. It would also have been counterproductive to devote years to hearing about events that, by their nature, arouse very strong feelings. It would have rocked the boat massively and for too long." To accept this line of logic, one need not agree that the justice provided by a nonprosecutorial alternative is qualitatively equivalent or superior to conventional forms of criminal justice. As with the political compromise rationale, one may allow that nonprosecutorial solutions require some sacrifice of justice but nevertheless defend them in contexts where they may be expected to achieve an aggregate amount of justice greater than that which would otherwise be realized.[23]

Composition. Frequently, the perceived legitimacy, and thus success, of a TRC depends on its composition. A "national" commission — that is, one that is composed of persons drawn from the local population — "established by consensus among all

---

19. [Greenawalt's footnote 99:] Rajeev Bhargava, Restoring Decency to Barbaric Societies, in [Truth v. Justice: the Morality of Truth Commissions 48 (Robert I. Rotberg & Dennis Thompson eds., 2000)].

20. [Greenawalt's footnote 100:] [1 The Truth and Reconciliation Commission, The Truth and Reconciliation Commission of South Africa Report 5 (1998).]

21. [Greenawalt's footnote 102:] W. Michael Reisman, Institutions and Practices for Restoring and Maintaining Public Order, 6 Duke J. Comp. & Intl. L. 175, 186 (1995).

22. [Greenawalt's footnote 104:] [Martha Minow, Between Vengeance and Forgiveness: Facing History After Genocide and Mass Violence 88-89 (1999).]

23. Alexander K.A. Greenawalt, Justice Without Politics? Prosecutorial Discretion and the International Criminal Court, 39 N.Y.U. J. Intl. L. & Pol. 583, 614-616 (2007).

major political groups will, as a rule, enjoy national legitimacy and be able to count on broad support for its findings and recommendations. But when such a consensus is lacking and the composition of the commission is controversial, it will lack the credibility it needs to make a difference."[24] A commission composed entirely of international investigators will make sense where the population of a small country is politically polarized, and it would therefore be difficult to find even a few nationals who would be trusted by all to be impartial. In such circumstances, international commissions ensure that the affected population views the commission as independent and impartial, thus avoiding charges of scapegoating. International participation may also bring with it expertise, additional resources, and visibility. Where remnants of the old regime remain — either in the government or security forces — and create security concerns for nationals on the commission and for victims and witnesses, international participation may be essential. A wholly international commission, however, may be hampered by its lack of a deep understanding of the political and social context in which the crimes occurred. Investigators who are nationals may also have a greater stake in the success of the enterprise and be in a better position to ensure that any commission recommendations are effectively implemented.

Procedures. The length and limits of TRCs' investigative mandates are negotiated, as are the rules of evidence, the participation of counsel, and the like. The proceedings generally are far less formal and rigorous in terms of evidentiary requirements than are criminal trials. If the commission determines to identify perpetrators by name, the process accorded them becomes particularly critical, but fair procedures will increase the credibility of the result whether or not this is the case.

An important procedural issue confronting commissions is how much of the inquiry, if any, ought to be conducted in public. Obviously, the preliminary fact finding and investigative work will normally be done in private, in order to increase the willingness of frightened victims and witnesses to cooperate and to mitigate the security concerns of the investigators themselves. But conducting all its work, including any formal hearings, in closed session may well undermine the credibility of a commission's final conclusions. Again, political and security considerations will dictate how the public-private balance is struck.

Most commissions have lacked the power to compel the production or seizure of evidence (with the notable exception of the South African TRC). Lacking such process, commissions are often hampered by the intransigence of those under investigation. The "carrot" of amnesty — especially when accompanied by a credible "stick" of criminal prosecution if cooperation is lacking — is sometimes viewed as necessary to secure the "truth." Another critical question facing commissioners is whether they may share their results with criminal investigators. Many commissions have passed the evidence they have gathered on to prosecutors, and (where prosecutors have the requisite political support, evidence, and resources) this has sometimes resulted in criminal convictions.[25]

Truth commissions, like criminal prosecutions, are not a magic bullet. Commentators have concluded that many commissions have failed to achieve much "in part because the expectations for truth commissions are almost always greater than what these

---

24. Buergenthal, supra note 17, at 221.
25. See Hayner, supra note 14, at 29, 34.

bodies can ever reasonably hope to achieve."[26] Commissions, like trials, have been freighted with a variety of hopes: that they will establish a historic record, which prevents the truth from being lost or rewritten and allows the victimized society a basis upon which to find ways to prevent a repetition of violence; that they will visit condemnation on the people and institutions that deserve it, perhaps laying an evidentiary foundation for future criminal prosecutions as well as institutional reforms; that, by achieving some measure of justice through condemnation, they will ensure continuing peace by deterring future abuses and removing the need for vigilante justice; that they will give victims a voice and thus catharsis; that they will, as they foster victim forgiveness, allow perpetrators to be reintegrated into society; that they will promote societal reconciliation, permitting former adversaries to interact without violence on a national level; and that they will, by revealing the toxic past, allow the country to move on to a progressive and democratic future. Even if a commission is able to achieve some or even all of these aims effectively, it will always be second-best to criminal proceedings in the view of victims who demand retribution — in the form of criminal sanctions — following atrocity.

Whether a truth commission can fulfill its goals depends very much on context. As one UN report concluded:

> Factors that can limit the[] potential benefits [of a TRC] include a weak civil society, political instability, victim and witness fears about testifying, a weak or corrupt justice system, insufficient time to carry out investigations, lack of public support and inadequate funding. Truth commissions are invariably compromised if appointed through a rushed or politicized process. . . . To be successful, they must enjoy meaningful independence and have credible commissioner selection criteria and processes. Strong public information and communication strategies are essential to manage public and victim expectations and to advance credibility and transparency. Their gender sensitivity and responsiveness to victims and victims of discrimination must be assured. Finally, many such commissions will require strong international support to function, as well as respect by international partners for their operational independence.[27]

The context that must be considered also includes the timing of the TRC and its relation to articulated political goals. For example, the South African TRC is widely viewed as one of the more successful commissions.[28] Its success is attributable not only to the people who led the enterprise — including Archbishop Desmond Tutu — and the conduct of the proceedings, but also to the unique circumstances of the South African transition from apartheid to constitutional democracy. In South Africa, the TRC was presented as the solution to a political stalemate; without it, a peaceful transition to a post-apartheid world was exceedingly unlikely. Further, the

---

26. Id. at 8.

27. U.N. Secretary-General Report to the Security Council, supra note 13, ¶51, at 17. As Patricia Hayner points out:

> Truth commissions are difficult and controversial entities; they are given a mammoth, almost impossible task and usually insufficient time and resources to complete it; they must struggle with rampant lies, denials, and deceit, and the painful, almost unspeakable memories of victims to uncover still-dangerous truths that many in power may well continue to resist. At the end of a commission's work, a country may well find the past still unsettled and some key questions still unresolved.

Hayner, supra note 14, at 23.

28. But see Mahmood Mamdani, Amnesty or Impunity? A Preliminary Critique of the Report of the Truth and Reconciliation Commission of South Africa (TRC), 32 Diacritics 33 (Fall-Winter 2002).

overarching narrative or storyline was evident: that the apartheid system was a crime against humanity and that it had many victims. Also, the South Africans knew what they wanted to achieve through the TRC process. As Professor James Gibson notes, the South African conception was that amnesty would lead to truth, which would lead to reconciliation, which would end in democratization.[29] It was this ultimate political goal that made the journey worthwhile.

By contrast, those who have experienced "the troubles" in Northern Ireland have been considering for some time whether to adopt the truth commission model.[30] There seems to be good reason for hesitancy. The political movement from civil war to political compromise and civic peace has been successfully negotiated and appears to be enduring (even if there have been bumps in the road along the way). A commission, then, is not necessary to the political solution already achieved. The story line is not nearly as clear; indeed, some fear that the blame game that will inevitably erupt in the course of commission proceedings would fuel discord rather than reconciling hostile populations. Perhaps most important, the end of Northern Ireland's political journey—whether it be in continued union with Britain or consolidation into the Republic of Ireland—is still subject to dispute. And these are the types of disputes that cannot be resolved through a historical truth-revealing process. Indeed, to the extent that such a process causes people to revisit past harms, it may actually inhibit the type of forward-looking political discussions necessary to true peace.

B. CONTEXT IS KEY

TINA ROSENBERG, OVERCOMING THE LEGACIES OF DICTATORSHIP
74 Foreign Aff. 134 (1995)

. . . After World War II, the notion of human rights and civil liberties—previously believed to be out of reach for the citizens of most countries—was increasingly accepted by a growing number of nations. In addition, since the mid-1970s, a staggering number of countries have turned from dictatorship to elected civilian government. First came southern Europe—Portugal, Greece, and Spain. In the 1980s, the wave hit Latin America—Argentina, Bolivia, Brazil, Chile, Ecuador, Honduras, Nicaragua, Panama, Paraguay, Peru, and Uruguay. In 1992, El Salvador ended a war that took the lives of 75,000 civilians. In the 1980s and early 1990s, at least 15 African nations moved away from repressive one-party rule and held multiparty elections. After 1989, the Soviet bloc completed the avalanche. All are now wrestling with their repressive pasts.

There are two main reasons to confront a grim past: to heal tyranny's victims and to alter the conditions that nurtured dictatorship in order to prevent its return. The new democracies have dreamed up a plethora of creative and often contradictory methods

---

29. James L. Gibson, Overcoming Apartheid: Can Truth Reconcile a Divided Nation? (2004).

30. See, e.g., Christine Bell, Dealing with the Past in Northern Ireland, 26 Fordham Intl. L.J. 1095 (2002-2003); Adrian Guelke, Commentary: Truth, Reconciliation and Political Accommodation, 22 Irish Pol. Stud. 363 (2007); Angela Hegarty, The Government of Memory: Public Inquiries and the Limits of Justice in Northern Ireland, 26 Fordham Intl. L.J. 1148 (2002-2003); Patricia Lundy & Mark McGovern, Attitudes Towards a Truth Commission for Northern Ireland in Relation to Party Political Affiliation, 22 Irish Pol. Stud. 321 (2007).

for fulfilling these broad obligations to past and future. They include choosing to leave the past behind and start afresh, an official apology by the new head of state, monetary reparations to the victims or their families, employment bans and purges that keep abusers from positions of public trust, truth commissions, and trials of political leaders or those who carried out torture and murder.

The instruments chosen depend on the type of dictatorial system, the types of crimes it committed, the level of citizen participation in the dictatorship, the nation's political culture and history, the abruptness of the transition to democracy, and the new civilian government's resources and political power. As these factors vary widely, so do the choices countries have made. While it is early to judge these choices, some general guidelines can be drawn up by comparing two large groups of new democracies: the former military dictatorships of Latin America and the former communist dictatorships of Eastern Europe.

In the two regions, both the type of the past victim and the nature of the future threat are almost diametrically opposed. Roughly put, repression in Eastern Europe was wide, while in Latin America it was deep. And in Latin America the challenge to democracy comes from military dominance of a weak civilian government, while in Eastern Europe the danger is repression by capricious government officials unchecked by law. The challenge to both continents is to deal with past abuses of power in ways that do not replicate them.

Some nations have met the challenge. Most, although they could still change course, have merely reinforced old antidemocratic habits. The lessons of Latin America and Eastern Europe might help other countries to choose their paths: nations recently emerging from dictatorship or restricted democracy, such as South Africa, Haiti, and Malawi, and nations that are ending long and brutal wars, such as Ethiopia, Mozambique, Guatemala, and Angola. Sadly, for many countries, democracy will be only a temporary phenomenon. If they do not successfully deal with a repressive past today, future opportunities may await.

THE BAD OLD DAYS

The new democracies' strategies for confronting the past depend largely on the nature of the former authoritarian regime. While comparisons between such different regions must be flawed by overgeneralization — Latin American countries can differ almost as sharply from one another as from the countries of Eastern Europe — the differences between the two areas shed much light on the problems of confronting the past.

Ideology. Communist leaders pronounced themselves the instrument of the working class, the standard-bearers of a beautiful ideal. They aimed for nothing less than the transformation of their citizens, the building of a "new socialist man." The good socialist citizen attended May Day parades, joined Marxist-Leninist scientific study groups, voted for the party slate, and hung peace slogans in his window. In the harsher police states, he denounced suspicious activity by his neighbors or colleagues. Latin leaders, by and large, indulged in no such nonsense. They ruled because they possessed more guns. Military leaders held a highly developed anticommunist ideology, but they did not seek to impose it on the public. In Pinochet's Chile, for example, the regime's good citizen was apolitical — he went to work, came home to play with his children, and kept his head down. If his neighbor returned from a long absence with a shuffling gait and dead eyes, the good citizen noticed nothing.

The nature of repression. The nature of the typical state crime in the two regions also differed. In Latin America, the generals crushed dissent with murder, torture, and forced disappearance. This intense repression was focused on a small percentage of the population. Even the 9,000-plus Argentines who disappeared in the "dirty war" against the left were a small slice of the nation. These crimes, while sponsored by the state, had clear authors. In tiny Uruguay, former political prisoners sometimes ran into their torturers on the street. Mothers in Argentina often knew the names and whereabouts of their disappeared children's military kidnappers. And torture and murder were illegal according to then-extant laws.

While Stalinism in the U.S.S.R. itself was violent and sustained on a scale unimaginable in Latin America — 7 million executed, 5 million dead of government-induced famine, 15 million sent to the gulag — communist violence was much reduced in Eastern Europe. After Stalin's death in 1953, communist regimes kept power mainly through corruption and coercion. Citizens and apparatchiks who behaved correctly won privileges, and those who did not lost them. Violence was seldom necessary. (The great exception was Albania, which was still shooting its poets in the late 1970s and was staunchly Stalinist until 1990.) In Eastern Europe, state repression was far more diffuse than in Latin America — few people suffered physical harm, but almost everyone suffered some deprivation. While the outspoken went to jail, one did not need to be politically active to suffer the regime's wrath. Millions who exhibited insufficient communist enthusiasm lost their jobs, their children's schooling, their weekend cottages, or their passports. All except the most privileged endured travel restrictions, lack of privacy, shoddy goods, shortages, and constant lies. All lived smaller lives in nations where all things were measured by political loyalty. This repression was not illegal, but the very foundation of the system. It was perpetrated not by an individual, but a whole government. Tapping a telephone or sending a family into internal exile can only be done with the support of an entire bureaucratic apparatus. Indeed, it required the collaboration of virtually the whole populace.

Cooperating with tyranny. Another difference between the two types of dictatorship is that Eastern Europe's communist dictatorships sought public participation, while Latin America's right-wing military dictatorships sought public silence. In Latin America, although many influential people endorsed the ideologies that gave rise to murder and torture, one can point to a few hundred men who committed the actual crimes. The Eastern bloc dictatorships were conspiracies of all of society. Just as almost everyone was a victim of communism by virtue of living under it, almost everyone also participated in repression. Inside a communist regime, lines of complicity ran like veins and arteries inside the human body. Even the most natural responses of self-preservation were also, in a sense, acts of collaboration. The eighth-grade history teacher who taught students of the glorious march of the proletariat and its vanguard, the Communist Party; the journalist who wrote positive articles because she knew she would be fired for writing negative ones; the millions who fooled their leaders into thinking they were beloved by granting them their votes and cheering at party rallies — all were complicit. Their complicity was hidden, even from themselves, by that fact that every ordinary citizen behaved the same way. It seemed normal. But such "normal" collaboration kept the regime alive. "The question we must ask isn't what some 'they' did," said Jan Urban, a Czech journalist and dissident. "It's what we did." The horror of communism was in the sum of the parts. In short, the East European dictatorships were criminal regimes, while the Latin American dictatorships were regimes of criminals.

LEGACIES OF INJUSTICE

Besides differing in nature, the Latin American and East European dictatorships also differ in the troubling legacies they have left behind — legacies that threaten democracy in contrasting ways. In Latin America, the old dictatorships gave way to newly democratic states that are too weak to guarantee that the juntas will not return to power. In Eastern Europe, it is the state that is too strong, prone to abuses reminiscent of the dictatorial past.

The East Europeans lived on ideology, and that ideology is now discredited. In the former Soviet Union, there are several regimes as repressive, centralized, and personalist as their communist predecessors, but they manage to achieve all of communism's oppressiveness without its ideology. Although post-communist socialist political parties thrive today and have even regained power in Lithuania, Poland, Bulgaria, and Hungary, they differ startlingly little from their current political adversaries. The 1993 elections in Poland, for instance, saw a dispute between the socialists and a center-right party over an economic plan they both advocated. . . . [C]ommunism in Eastern Europe was shot through the heart and will not rise from the grave.

But communism has left behind a poisonous residue. The people of Eastern Europe had 45 years to accustom themselves to governments endowed with arbitrary and absolute power. (In many parts of Eastern Europe, they began getting used to this centuries ago.) They saw law twisted daily for political ends. No institutions existed that could check the power of the party — no independent judiciary or stubborn legislature inside the government, no opposition parties or independent press outside. In Albania, the very practice of law was banned. With a few notable exceptions, there was no civil society. The word "rights" meant nothing to the average citizen.

This legacy poses a triple threat to the future of democracy. It has left citizens unaccustomed to searching for their own values and morals, and more comfortable simply accepting those supplied ready-made by the state. Today most people still do not acknowledge this lack of responsibility for their own actions, nor that this acquiescence was crucial to perpetuating the repressive regime. Such people can be easily persuaded to let demagogues do their thinking for them. . . .

Today many East Europeans want new devils to blame for their troubles. They seek harsh measures to restore order to a complex and insecure world. The trend grows toward Europe's historic pathology, intolerant nationalism. . . .

Communism's second poisonous legacy is a state unsure of its role. The states of Eastern Europe do not suffer the existential crises of the former Soviet republics, which are building governments from scratch. But they have no experience in checking the whims of their leaders through laws and constitutions. While most East European leaders are not budding tyrants, the point is to limit personalist rule with laws that can stop those who are.

The third piece of the grim communist heritage is that Eastern Europe's democracies lack the judicial and civil institutions that could rein in unscrupulous leaders. In most East European countries, judges are accustomed to the phone call from a party boss suggesting the disposition of a case. Recently there has been a spurt of laws — some of them revivals of communist-era statutes — punishing criticism of government officials and the publication of state secrets. These laws are so vague they can be turned against any critic of government policy. Political control of the judiciary and media and restrictions on free expression and assembly are most widespread in the former Yugoslavia and the East European countries where civil society always lagged behind: Romania, Slovakia, and Albania. Here, leaders' new "nationalist" or "democratic" labels seem to matter little; many still behave like old communists. And a lack of democratic experience encourages the average East European to accept laws like these as normal.

The legacy of the Latin American dictatorships is very different. While the East European dictatorships lived on an ideology that is now discredited, the Latins lived on guns, which never go out of fashion. Even after a transition to democracy, powerful militaries still have those guns, the support of the influential upper class, and the arrogance that justified their abuses.

Civilian governments have proven unable to keep repressive security forces from carrying out torture and murder in many countries, notably Peru, Brazil, Venezuela, Colombia, El Salvador, and Guatemala. Even under democracy, police and soldiers remain secure in the knowledge that their crimes will be judged in friendly military courts or not at all. The number of security officers who served or are serving significant terms for murder or torture in all of Latin America's former dictatorships probably does not reach double digits.

The militaries are more than a day-to-day threat to civilians: they have put elected governments on notice that democracy exists at the military's pleasure. Latin America has seen two previous waves of democratization in this century. At the crest of the second wave, in 1960, Paraguay was the only military dictatorship in South America. But by 1976, Colombia, Venezuela, Suriname, and Costa Rica were the only non-dictatorships in Central and South America. And monsters lurk below the glassy surface of today's elected Latin American governments. . . . In 1992 Peru's president, Alberto Fujimori, assumed dictatorial powers with the backing of the military. . . . In most Latin nations, civilian presidents face the threat of overthrow if they attempt to cut military budgets or pensions, investigate military corruption, or try officers for human rights violations. Dictatorship falls periodically to democracy in most Latin nations, but it never stays dead.

The challenges to democracy in Latin America and Eastern Europe, then, come from opposite directions. In Latin America, state power is too limited to discipline a rogue military. In Eastern Europe, state power needs more limits to keep abusive officials from violating civil and human rights, and such abuses are tolerated by citizens who have been taught to accept the ready-made values provided by the state. This is a situation ripe for exploitation by the next demagogue to come along.

THE URGE TO PURGE

The contrast between Latin America, with its dangerously weak governments, and Eastern Europe, with its dangerously strong ones, becomes starker as the fledgling republics consider bold methods for dealing with the past. One such measure is the purge. Victims everywhere deserve to feel confidence in their new democratic governments, to know that the torturers and repressors are now outcasts who neither represent the state nor are able to continue their old practices. Spain's remarkable transformation after General Franco's death shows that this is not necessarily an absolute — people can break their old habits and forgive their enemies for events long past without purges. But in Latin America, such purges are crucial for democracy. There, the victims' blood is fresh, and the vicious cycle of repression and impunity that has plagued Latin America for centuries cannot be broken unless the military accepts civilian rule. Spain may have experienced real reconciliation, but most Latin countries have only an uneasy truce in which both sides are acutely aware of the distribution of power. True reconciliation cannot take place at gunpoint.

But guns limit the purges that have occurred. After El Salvador's civil war, the United Nations sponsored a groundbreaking ad hoc commission — a panel of Salvadorans chosen to name military officers who actively participated in or covered up human rights abuses. The government promised to purge, or in some cases transfer, the officers named. The commission interviewed witnesses, invited officers to present a defense, and finally named 102 men. Few in El Salvador were surprised when the most powerful of them refused to resign. The top 15 officers named, including General Rene Emilio Ponce, then defense minister, served out their 30 years in the armed forces and retired with full honors and pensions.

Eastern Europe is attempting purges as well. In the fall of 1991, President Vaclav Havel submitted a bill to the Czechoslovak Federal Assembly calling for a ban on top government jobs for everyone the state could prove did concrete harm. This commendable bill failed to pass. Instead, the assembly passed a law that came to be known as "lustration," which bans from top public-sector jobs for five years all those who were members of the People's Militia, held high-ranking government or party positions under communism, or appear in the secret police registry as collaborators. Those so found are considered guilty and must sue in court to prove their innocence.

Lustration shows that the trouble with purges in Eastern Europe is the reverse of the Latin American problem. The biggest danger is not that the guilty will stay in power, but that the innocent will be removed. Lustration's supporters maintain not that the secret police registry is largely correct, which is indisputable, but that it is perfect, and that no innocent person could possibly be considered guilty. The secret police, however, were no more perfect than any other large bureaucracy in communist Czechoslovakia. Some secret police officers wrote down names to meet a quota or win more expense money. The lustration law has ruined the careers and reputations of many who were listed by mistake or whose collaboration harmed no one. Indeed, one of those listed as a candidate for collaboration in the secret police files from 1965 was a youthful absurdist playwright who thanked his interrogator for "giving him inspiration for further literary endeavors." On this basis, a secret police official wrote that the young Václav Havel had a "positive" attitude toward the secret police and should be actively recruited as an agent.

Czechoslovakia's lustration has been the most publicized, but other countries have comparable laws. Bulgaria's law, which applies only to people in academic posts, is being challenged by a new socialist government. In Germany, lustration for high-level officials is fairer than the Czechoslovak version — firings are based on information from the subject's file, rather than just appearance on a list. But the average worker does not benefit from such subtleties. . . . The bans last 15 years. While the cabinet minister from Prague can surely find a new job in private industry, where can the third-grade teacher from Dresden go? Many former East Germans perceive the firings as a massacre. They have produced the least auspicious emotion for working through the past: victimization.

Poland and Hungary have abstained from the lustration boom. In part this is because their communist regimes — and particularly their secret police — were far less Stalinist. These were also places where the transition to democracy was negotiated, a process that encourages people to see each other in shades of gray rather than in black and white. Enemies become political adversaries, with whom it is possible to work. In Poland, the Solidarity government emerged from the transition negotiations with a policy of walling off the past with what leaders called a "thick line." . . .

. . . Lustration smells like communism. The accused do not enjoy due process rights or the presumption of innocence. It can be a powerful political tool used against those who inconvenience new governments. Lustration punishes people not for their individual actions but for their appearance on a list. "I do not protect communists," said former Czech Premier Petr Pithart, a lustration opponent. "I protest against lists of any kind. Today it is communists who are on the list. It could be wealthy people tomorrow, perhaps macrobiotics the day after, and certainly the Jews. The logic of lists is implacable."

TRUTH COMMISSIONS

In both Eastern Europe and Latin America, high-profile official commissions to investigate a former dictatorship's crimes can help restore integrity to a country's political life. Truth commissions are especially necessary after dictatorships or wars marked by widespread torture and disappearance — crimes whose hideousness hinges in part on secrecy. Unveiling the full scope of tyranny lets its victims come to terms with their suffering and starts replacing the legacies of dictatorship with the habits of democracy.

It is not enough that the regime's crimes are widely known, or even that they are discussed on the state-sponsored TV news. The state must acknowledge and apologize for what it has done. On March 4, 1991 Patricio Aylwin, who succeeded General Pinochet as president of Chile, went on television and, voice breaking, apologized to the families of those killed by the previous government in the name of the entire nation. This was a moving statement, but more important, he presented a study of the junta's murders and disappearances, carried out by an eight-person Commission on Truth and Reconciliation whose members ranged from a human rights lawyer to former members of Pinochet's cabinet.

Aylwin took the idea from Argentina. When the junta's "dirty war" ended in 1983, Argentina's new democratic president, Raul Alfonsin, named a panel of distinguished citizens to a National Commission on the Disappeared. When they were finished taking testimony in all corners of Argentina and in exile, they found the military junta had produced — or rather, not produced — at least 9,000 disappearances. "We have reason to believe the true figure is much higher," wrote the commission's chairman. Its report, called *Nunca Mas* (Never again), described the torture and killing inside secret detention centers, discussed the collaboration of judges and other groups, and told the stories of the victims where it could.

The value of such commissions is evident even before their reports are published. "We had just opened an office in a city in the south," said Alejandro Salinas, a commission staffer in Chile. "A woman came in to talk about her husband, who had disappeared. We invited her to take a seat. The Chilean flag was very prominently displayed, and she started to cry. To have the government of Chile invite her into this office to talk about her husband — it was overwhelming to her."

Truth commissions would be just as beneficial in Eastern Europe, although for different reasons. For the victims of communism, the workings of the repressive state remain veiled in secrecy, especially the great hydra-headed monster of the secret police. Victims deserve to understand the hidden structures that judged and punished them. In addition, democracy in Eastern Europe demands a society-wide self-examination to explain how dictatorship won the complicity of ordinary people. . . .

CRIME AND PUNISHMENT

The most sweeping mechanism for dealing with past repression is trial in a court of law. Here, too, the contrasts between the Latin and East European dictatorships dictate very different paths for the two continents. External support and U.S. encouragement would embolden Latin America's weak new democracies, who fear that trying to bring junta veterans to justice might prompt a military coup. By contrast, in Eastern Europe, the danger is not that the new democracy might fall, but that it might go so far in its pursuit of the cogs in a communist state's wheels that it mimics its dictatorial predecessor's contempt for the rule of law.

In both regions, victims of torture and the relatives of the murdered and disappeared deserve justice. Trials can help restore victims' dignity and prevent private acts of revenge by those who, in the absence of justice, would take it into their own hands. Some lawyers also view them as an obligation under international law.

In Latin America, torture and murder were typical of a regime's repression, illegal at the time of commission, and committed by clearly identifiable perpetrators. Trials for such crimes are crucial for democracy's long-term prospects in Latin America. They are the only way to establish civilian control of the military and the primacy of law over force. They warn would-be murderers and torturers that crime carries a price. And, of course, convictions deter the specific individuals on trial, many of whom still pose a threat to democracy, from future offenses. Trials demonstrate to polarized nations accustomed to solving disputes through killing that other ways exist, express society's condemnation of violence, and show that democratic governments do indeed differ from dictatorships.

The few trials of past human rights violators that the new Latin American democracies have managed to hold have given defendants no cause to claim abuse. The 1985 trials in Argentina of nine members of the "dirty war" junta were models of due process. When injustice has occurred, it has worked to the advantage of powerful defendants; those accused of death squad murders in El Salvador have usually been acquitted for "lack of evidence." Indeed, the truth commission in El Salvador recommended against trials, concluding that the courts were so weak that trials would not be a meaningful exercise.

Trials are crucial for democracy's long-term health, but they are seldom attempted. Most new civilian governments view trials as the equivalent of throwing democracy out a 20-story window. Three military uprisings in Argentina were enough to convince Alfonsin to end the trials; his successor as president, Carlos Sául Menem, even pardoned the junta leaders already convicted. The newly elected government of Paraguay was able to try some of its human rights abusers only because they came from the police, not the army, which was more of a threat.

There are, however, ways to strengthen democracy in the long term without committing suicide in the short term. More pressure for justice from the United States, the Organization of American States, human rights groups, and others could help balance military pressure for impunity. Civilian governments might privately welcome such pressure. . . . While a country's own courts are the preferred forum, the Inter-American Court of Human Rights is now providing a court of last resort. In 1988 it decided its first case, ordering the government of Honduras to pay reparations to the families of two disappeared men. Since then it has heard 16 cases against seven countries and has become a regular forum for human rights trials when national courts have proven impotent.

As in Latin America, victims of torture and the relatives of the murdered and disappeared of Eastern Europe should demand full justice. But most of the criminals of the Stalinist regimes are now dead or very old, and since that time, acts of physical violence have been few. They should, however, be prosecuted. By the end of 1993, 198 officials of the former Czechoslovakia had been prosecuted—some for corruption, others for beating demonstrators and other acts of violence. Twenty-nine have been convicted. Polish General Wojciech Jaruzelski may be tried for his role in the shootings of protesters in Gdansk in 1970, when he was defense minister.

These trials serve justice, but as the crimes involved were not the typical communist abuses suffered by the general public, they do not satisfy the thirst for justice among communism's victims. People want to try the men and women who opened their letters, taught them lies in the guise of history, designed their pitiful Trabant automobiles, and took their passports. But it cannot be done. Complicity was so widely shared that trials would add literally millions of new cases to already overburdened and understaffed courts. Such trials would be impossible without violating individuals' rights to due process. East Germans hated Erich Mielke, the head of the Stasi, and Margo Honecker, who was minister of education, but it is hard to find a legally indictable reason to try them: tapping telephones and teaching Marxist-Leninist social studies were both legal at the time. And who tapped the telephones? Who barred students from college? Trials by their very nature judge the actions of individuals, and these were acts of the great repressive machine as a whole.

Some of the new democracies, however, are determined to try their old leaders — with the charges to be filled in later. They are like the marksman who shoots first and then chooses his target. The worst offender is Germany. Markus Wolf, the head of foreign espionage for the Stasi, was sentenced to six years for bribery and treason. Treason, however, is usually defined as an offense against one's own country, and West Germany was decidedly not Wolf's. . . . Germany has . . . tried border guards for killing fleeing citizens at the Berlin Wall. Their superiors, who gave the orders to shoot, often come to testify at the trials. If they are government employees, they receive a day's pay for their time. Then they walk out free men.

Such travesties of justice are unnecessary. Eastern Europe's new democracies need not struggle to convince the old dictators to submit to the law. Their surrender was unconditional. And surely the last place in Europe that needs to worry about the resurgence of its old communists is Germany, which simply engulfed them. . . .

Even worse, ersatz justice resorts to the communist habits of twisting law to fit political needs. In some places this means criminalizing decisions that were clearly political judgment calls. Bulgaria, for example, is trying several former officials for giving away government funds to Third World communist movements. Trials are also used to solve current political problems. In Albania, former Prime Minister Fatos Nano — the most attractive leader of the socialist party opposing the current government — was sentenced to 12 years in jail for embezzlement. Many Albanians suspect that the government simply wanted to lock up its most charismatic critic. Such trials undermine the rule of law.

Unchecked power was necessary to maintain a communist regime. But the reverse is not true; one does not need to be a communist to seek unchecked power. Such power in the service of anticommunism is just as dangerous. Unfortunately, many of the measures East European governments have taken to deal with the past abuse their power. Citizens do not enjoy full due process rights to defend themselves from lustration. Decisions that affect lives, careers, and reputations are made in secret. The legal system is placed at the service of political goals. This behavior is the legacy of the past that is hardest to change. The real threat to democracy in Eastern Europe today is not communism but the state's unchecked power.

How can a nation deal with its history in ways that do not repeat it? Despite their great differences, the new democracies of Latin America and Eastern Europe have essentially the same task: to go as far as they can to bring past repressors to accountability without crossing the line into new injustice. The Latins must struggle to go further, while the East Europeans must resist the impulse to go too far. But Latin

America and Eastern Europe share a newfound belief in tolerance, accountability, and the rule of law. For both, the best way to deal with the past is to treat it according to the democratic standards they have now supposedly embraced.

NOTES AND QUESTIONS

1. How does one evaluate the efficacy of domestic criminal prosecutions in achieving post-atrocity accountability? Which type of tribunal — an international forum like the International Criminal Court (ICC) or a hybrid or domestic court — is most likely to deter other wrongdoers, either in the same society or outside it? Where is retribution most likely to be effectively achieved? How about national reconciliation — when would domestic trials promote reconciliation and when might they not? In particular cases, these theoretical issues may well ultimately be less important than some very practical ones: What is the security situation in the country (that is, might the abusive regime still have sufficient sway to threaten judges, prosecutors, and witnesses)? What types of due process guarantees are in place to ensure that trials are not viewed as witch hunts? Does the government involved have the infrastructure, trained personnel, and resources necessary to try those responsible for atrocity while maintaining peace and order in an unstable post-conflict society? As you ponder these issues, consider the following.

A domestic prosecution, or a hybrid international-national tribunal, may have significant practical advantages over a purely international tribunal. Assuming local authorities are cooperating, investigators and prosecutors who are nationals may have an easier time locating evidence and witnesses. Those involved in the prosecution and adjudication of the domestic/hybrid case likely will be much more familiar with the country's political history, culture, and the nature of the conflict that gave rise to the alleged international crimes than will those staffing an international tribunal. Those victimized are likely to have more access to the proceedings and more knowledge regarding what is being done in their names, hopefully promoting a greater sense that justice has been done and reconstruction is appropriate. "[P]roceedings can be conducted in the local language and the local population may be more aware of the proceedings, thereby getting a better moral education and awareness of international law." Milena Sterio, Seeking the Best Forum to Prosecute International War Crimes: Proposed Paradigms and Solutions, 18 Fla. J. Intl. L. 887, 900 (2006). In sum, as former ICTY Judge Patricia Wald explains:

> There appears to be widespread agreement, after a decade of trial and error, that courts conducted inside the country where the atrocities took place are most likely to satisfy the involved populace's desire for justice, if . . . There are many big "ifs" here. Physical security of judges, prosecutors, defense counsel, and witnesses is a primary concern. These same players must be immune from overwhelming pressures from other parts of the national government if the trial is to be and to look impartial to the rest of the world as well as the home audience. In several nationally held trials, prosecutors have displayed inexplicable docility, witnesses have not been protected from intimidation, courtrooms have been filled with noisy and uncontrollable demonstrators for one side, and adequate resources have been withheld from the judges or court administrators.

Patricia M. Wald, Accountability for War Crimes: What Roles for National, International, and Hybrid Tribunals?, 98 Am. Socy. Intl. L. Proc. 192, 193-194 (2004). Additional "ifs" include whether the domestic system has in place sufficient procedural safeguards to ensure fair and reliable verdicts and whether prosecutions are being brought to settle scores or sideline political opponents.

International tribunals serve, of course, as a last resort where political, security, or resource constraints preclude domestic prosecutions. We have previously explored some of the downsides of international prosecutions: They are expensive, time-consuming, and can only deal with a small fraction of those potentially implicated in a given situation. The Ad Hoc Tribunals were criticized as well for being geographically too remote from the traumatized populations. See, e.g., Patricia M. Wald, Punishment of War Crimes by International Tribunals, 69 Soc. Res. 1119, 1122 (Winter 2002). Patricia Wald has concluded that a recent trend "bringing international courts closer to home both geographically and operationally comes from an increasing sense that to the maximum extent possible individual national court systems should handle such cases. That way the populations most affected — including victims — will feel closer to the process and it will be more transparent to them; it is also more likely to be less expensive and will have the additional benefit of catalyzing the judicial and organizational reforms necessary to create such a capacity in other parts of underdeveloped national court systems." Id. at 1123. Wald goes on to say:

> But there are counterindications to the national or even the hybrid solution in some instances. The crux of the matter is that often the relevant states are not capable of pursuing their own war criminals during or immediately after wars or internal conflicts. Their own judicial infrastructure has frequently been so damaged in terms of resources, personnel, and facilities that there is no possibility they can prosecute major war crimes in the immediate future. . . . War crime prosecutions, especially against top leaders who have planned or executed countrywide strategies of abuse, are enormously complex, expensive, and lengthy. Many of the ICTY prosecutions, such as that of the Srebrenica genocide, followed five-year field investigations in which hundreds of witnesses were interviewed, thousands of documents seized or accessed, and exhumations of mass burial sites conducted and scattered body parts of thousands of victims collected and analyzed, and their identification attempted. It would have been impossible for Bosnian authorities in the mid-1990s — or even now — to have conducted anything on this scale. And yet if these investigations had to wait until the recuperating war-torn countries had the facilities to undertake them, potential witnesses and documents would likely have been lost and graves vandalized or robbed.
>
> In the case of other Balkan countries, most exhibited no desire to pursue war crimes until their internal politics changed, which was only several years after the ICTY began operations. In many of those countries, war criminals indicted at The Hague were still "homeland heroes." . . . Bosnia as well as other countries in the region have to pass new laws to define war crimes in their national codes and to provide for the protection of victim-witnesses; they have to train prosecutors and defense counsel to perform new functions in investigating and prosecuting novel theories of criminal responsibility. . . .
>
> . . . I am satisfied [that the situation in the former Yugoslavia was one in which the countries involved could not pursue accountability for war crimes through their own systems] . . . when the ICTY was set up. After listening to hundreds of witnesses who suffered hideous assaults on their bodies, minds, and souls yet found the courage to come to The Hague to testify against their accused violators, I cannot imagine that the majority of them would have testified willingly in their local courts, which in many cases were located in villages and towns still populated and in some areas dominated by forces sympathetic to the alleged wrongdoers. . . .

Id. at 1123-1125.

One final consideration concerns the viability — and perhaps ultimately the perceived legitimacy — of the entire project of international criminal law. See id.

at 1126-1127. Commentators have become concerned about a possible "fragmentation" of international criminal law because of the variety of tribunals presently interpreting and applying it—in international criminal and human rights tribunals, as well as hybrid and national courts. Might the fact that the variety of tribunals now passing, for example, on issues like the definition of crimes against humanity or the *mens rea* that ought to apply to command responsibility cases create the possibility of disuniform results? Would the fact that different courts may arrive at different resolutions to such issues threaten the perceived uniformity and universality, and thus the legitimacy, of international criminal law?

2. *Lustration and "vetting."* "Lustration" mechanisms have been used in Lithuania, Bulgaria, the Czech and Slovak Republics, Haiti, and Ethiopia. These mechanisms aim to remove from office those who supported or participated in the prior regime's abuses; in some cases, lustration legislation will bar such persons from future participation in government or the armed forces for a specified time. Lustration is intended to prevent continuing abuses, promote trust in the new government, lend the new regime credibility as one concerned with human rights, and deter these and other persons from again using their positions to perpetrate human rights abuses.

Lustration remedies have, however, been the subject of widespread criticism because they are punitive in nature but have not been accompanied by even the rudiments of due process in many cases. They tend to target classes of people without regard to personal guilt and so may punish the innocent. The stigmatizing effect of such "purges" tend to spill over to family members and other blameless third parties, generating resentment that is not conducive to future peace and reconciliation. That said, the lack of process is not inherent in the remedy; additional process could be provided, but it would be expensive and time-consuming.

Vetting appears to be a term that describes "purging" or "lustration" done right. A UN report had the following to say about this mechanism:

> Vetting the public service to screen out individuals associated with past abuses is [an] . . . important component of transitional justice for which the assistance of the United Nations has frequently been sought. Vetting processes help to facilitate a stable rule of law in post-conflict societies. In Bosnia and Herzegovina, Kosovo, Timor-Leste, Liberia and now in Haiti, our operations have been called upon to support vetting processes in various ways. We have helped, variously, to develop professional standards, set up oversight mechanisms and identify objective and lawful criteria. Vetting usually entails a formal process for the identification and removal of individuals responsible for abuses, especially from police, prison services, the army and the judiciary. Parties under investigation are notified of the allegations against them and given an opportunity to respond before a body administering the vetting process. Those charged are usually entitled to reasonable notice of the case against them, the right to contest the case and the right to appeal an adverse decision to a court or other independent body. The inclusion of such due process elements distinguishes formal vetting processes from wholesale purges practiced in some countries, involving wide-scale dismissal and disqualification based not on individual records, but rather on party affiliation, political opinion, or association with a prior State institution.
>
> We have learned many lessons through our work in these areas. First, whether established as administrative or quasi-judicial bodies, legitimate vetting mechanisms should function in a manner respectful both of the sensitivities of victims and of the human rights of those suspected of abuses. Secondly, civil society should be consulted early and the public must be kept informed. Thirdly, vetting processes should include attention to the technical skills, objective qualifications and integrity of candidates. Fourthly, procedural protections should be afforded to all those subject to vetting processes,

whether current employees or new applicants. Finally, where such mechanisms exist and are seen to function fairly, effectively and in accordance with international human rights standards, they can play an important role in enhancing the legitimacy of official structures, restoring the confidence of the public and building the rule of law. . . .

U.N. Secretary-General Report to the Security Council, The Rule of Law and Transitional Justice in Conflict and Post-conflict Societies, S/2004/616, ¶¶52-53, at 17-18 (Aug. 23, 2004).

C. GOALS AND MEANS

MIRIAM J. AUKERMAN, EXTRAORDINARY EVIL, ORDINARY CRIME: A FRAMEWORK FOR UNDERSTANDING TRANSITIONAL JUSTICE
15 Harv. Hum. Rts. J. 39 (2002)

. . . The social and political realities of a particular transitional context will affect the kind of justice that can be pursued. Before one determines whether or not prosecution is feasible, however, one must ask if it is even desirable. Prosecutions are better designed to achieve some goals than others. Non-prosecution alternatives are indeed a second-rate option when prosecution, though politically difficult, would best serve the goals of transitional justice. But one cannot presume the inferiority of non-prosecution alternatives without first articulating the desired goals of transitional justice. Some goals can be best achieved through non-prosecution alternatives, regardless of whether prosecutions are politically feasible. As Argentinian philosopher and human rights activist Carlos Nino has suggested, "the extent of the duty of a government . . . to prosecute past human rights abuses depends . . . on the theory that underlies the justification of punishment." In other words, we must decide what we want from transitional justice before we can decide if prosecutions are the best way to achieve it.

B. THE GOALS OF CRIMINAL JUSTICE: AN OVERVIEW

In the context of domestic crime, penologists have provided a variety of theoretical frameworks for justifying punishment and for dealing with offenders and the crimes they commit. These approaches may be classified generally as: desert/retribution/ vengeance, deterrence, rehabilitation, [and] restorative justice. . . . [A]lthough each of these themes is relevant to transitional justice, none can blindly be transposed from the domestic context. . . .

If the appropriate mechanism for confronting grave human rights violations depends upon specified goals, who has the authority to set these goals? If transitional societies themselves have the right to decide, then we must recognize that different societies will have differing goals. Some societies emerging from mass trauma will demand retribution, while others will focus on compensation. Still others may concentrate on rebuilding a shattered economy or on strengthening democratic institutions. If different societies want different things, and if prosecution is a more effective tool for achieving some goals than others, we cannot presuppose that all societies in transition should choose prosecution.

If, on the other hand, the international community has the right to set goals for transitional justice, we must ask whether or not the international community even agrees about what the most important goals should be. An indiscriminate duty to prosecute assumes that the international community shares a fixed hierarchy of goals, agrees that these goals are best served by prosecution, and feels comfortable imposing such a vision on the society in question. Certainly there is at least superficial agreement that human rights atrocities should be prevented and condemned. But this limited consensus provides little aid in deciding how to prioritize these two goals as against others, nor does it signify complete agreement that prosecution is the best way to prevent future atrocities or communicate shared outrage. Moreover, even if the international community could make a clear choice as to its goals and the means of achieving them, it is not obvious that such an international strategy should trump the wishes of the local society. Those who have not suffered cannot presume to determine for those who have what should be attempted through transitional justice. . . .

Of course, the international community does have both a role and an interest in transitional justice. Just as ordinary crime is not simply an offense against the individual victim but against the entire society, so extraordinary evil is not merely an assault on the particular traumatized society but on humanity as a whole. As a result, the choice of retribution or deterrence, reconciliation or condemnation cannot be left solely to either the international community or the local society. Transitional justice must reflect the needs, desires, and political realities of the victimized society, while at the same time recognizing the international community's right and responsibility to intervene. In practice, the balance between domestic and international control over transitional justice will likely be determined in large part by the political realities of a particular transition. Nonetheless, we must think more carefully about the extent to which transitional justice should reflect local rather than international choices. . . .

C. ASSUMPTIONS

Before moving to a discussion of each of the different approaches, it is necessary to identify three [implicit] assumptions. . . . First, forgetting is unacceptable. In part this is because victims of horrible atrocities are simply unable to forget. Without some form of accounting, past atrocities inevitably fuel future ones. . . .

Second, if prosecutions are undertaken, they must comport with accepted standards of due process. While this may seem obvious, in fact procedural abnormalities are common in trials undertaken in transitional contexts. . . .

The third assumption . . . is that prosecutions are necessarily selective. . . . Because mass atrocities are generally perpetrated by a large number of people, "[p]rosecution of every single participant in the planning, ordering, or implementation of the atrocities in question — not to mention all those who collaborated with them — would be politically destabilizing, socially divisive, and logistically and economically untenable." . . .

II. CRIMINAL JUSTICE AS TRANSITIONAL JUSTICE

A. DESERT/RETRIBUTION/VENGEANCE

. . . How effective is prosecution in achieving the goal of retribution against those who commit massive human rights abuses? Because it provides a legitimate way in which to impose severe punishment, prosecution is better suited to retribution than other forms of transitional justice. In the face of atrocity, both individuals and societies have a powerful need to call those who caused the suffering to account. It is difficult to accept that the worst perpetrators of genocide and war crimes should escape responsibility.

In fact, advocates of prosecution emphasize its retributive qualities. Some openly use the image of "getting even." . . . Generally, however, retribution is more politely described in terms of combating impunity or bringing perpetrators to justice. For example, Diane Orentlicher writes that the world community "has resolved emphatically that it will not countenance impunity for massive atrocities against persecuted groups." . . .

Prosecution is not, of course, the only way to exact retribution. Lustration can strip perpetrators of their jobs or remove them from elective office. Through civil suits, victims and their heirs can exact financial penalties from those who committed abuses. National truth commissions can "generate social opprobrium," turning perpetrators into social outcasts and forcing them to face victims on television. However, the sanctions imposed through alternative mechanisms—sanctions such as social opprobrium, ostracism, money judgments, or loss of jobs and privileges—simply are not proportional to the crimes committed by human rights violators. . . . [B]ecause courts afford defendants far more due process protections than truth commissions or lustration committees, prosecutions can legitimately sanction behavior more severely. As a result, "[t]he greater the felt need for punishment, the more seriously the prosecution option must be considered." In other words, if one adopts a retributive theory of transitional justice, prosecutions have significant advantages over other accountability mechanisms.

While prosecutions may be more effective than other approaches in achieving retributive goals, true retributive justice is almost always unachievable in the wake of radical evil. This is true for several reasons. First, it is often impossible even in prosecutions to impose a punishment that is proportional to the crime. As [Martha] Minow argues, massive human rights atrocities "call for more severe responses than would any ordinary criminal conduct, even the murder of an individual. . . . And yet, there is no punishment that could express the proper scale of outrage." . . .

. . . In the final analysis, however, the ultimate futility of retribution should not be a reason to discount the utility of prosecution. Even if human rights violators can never be punished enough, they can still be punished severely. And if the desired goal for transitional justice is retribution, inadequate penal sanctions imposed after trial are still preferable to grossly inadequate civil liability or public shaming.

The second and more fundamental critique of a retributive approach to transitional justice is that it depends on the concept of blame, which requires character evaluation. As [Carlos] Nino has argued, the viability of character evaluation in the context of radical evil is unclear. . . . Radical evil . . . is often committed by average people who would never commit ordinary crime. How can one understand intent in such circumstances? Perhaps, as Nino suggests, the proper response is to suspend reactive judgments (much as one might do with the insane), because the perpetrators of mass atrocity "have gone beyond the pale of humanity by rejecting the framework of interactions that blame presupposes."

Character evaluation in the aftermath of mass human rights violations is further complicated by the difficulty of assigning individual responsibility, especially in the case of lower-level participants. Minow argues that

> [t]he central premise of individual responsibility portrays defendants as separate people capable of autonomous choice—when the phenomena of mass atrocities render that assumption at best problematic. Those who make the propaganda but wield no physical

weapons influence those with the weapons who in turn claim to have been swept up, threatened, fearful, mobilized.

Of course, individuals always have choices. . . . But individual autonomy in the context of dictatorship or mass violence may not be the same in the context of ordinary crime. Unlike ordinary criminals, who violate social norms by committing crimes, individuals who are swept up in mass violence do not step outside the prevailing moral framework. Rather, they succumb to intense social pressure. While this does not relieve such individuals of moral agency or responsibility, it does make them more difficult to judge. Former German President Richard von Weizsäcker has noted a widespread and unfortunate tendency among young Germans "to believe that then people were evil but today they are good." As Reinhold Neibuhr has quipped, the universality of sin is the only concept in the Judeo-Christian tradition that is empirically verifiable. Those who have never faced such choices should not be too quick to assume that they would have acted differently.

In addition to the conceptual obstacles to a retributive understanding of transitional justice, prosecutions themselves complicate the retributive framework. The first difficulty lies in the relationship between retribution and vengeance. Ethnic conflicts around the world, in which each side justifies the atrocities it inflicts by referring to the wrongs it has suffered, demonstrate the tendency of vengeance to lead to a downward spiral of violence. Prosecutions are designed to channel these demands for vengeance and to break the cycle of personal revenge. As Minow explains, in order

> to avoid such escalating violence . . . [one must] transfer the responsibilities for apportioning blame and punishment from victims to public bodies acting according to the rule of law. This is an attempt to remove personal animus, though not necessarily to excise vengeance. Tame it, balance it, recast it as the retributive dimension of public punishment.

Whether or not we equate retribution and vengeance, it is clear that in the context of transitional justice prosecutions founded on a desire for retribution will have many of the drawbacks of vengeance. Where prosecutions are publicly perceived as a form of victor's justice, they will be unlikely to break the cycle of violence. As José Alvarez notes, "[t]he majority of the thousands detained in Rwanda's jails today report, and perhaps genuinely feel, that 'they have done nothing wrong' and are being victimized merely because they were on the 'wrong side of the war.'" Even if prosecutions satisfy demands for revenge from Tutsis, they may stoke the desire for vengeance by Hutus. Nino describes a related problem in Argentina, where human rights groups, by adopting an "all-out retributive" approach and demanding that all the guilty be punished, ended up undermining their own credibility, fanning a backlash by military and government forces against the trials, and ultimately weakening the impact of those trials that did take place. Nino suggests that although

> many people approach the issue of human rights violations with a strong retributive impulse, almost all who think momentarily about the issue are not prepared to defend a policy of punishing those abuses once it becomes clear that such a policy would probably provoke, by a causal chain, similar or even worse abuses.

The second difficulty is that prosecutions . . . are necessarily limited and selective. Retribution theory, by contrast, is predicated on the notion that everyone should get their just deserts. In the wake of genocide or other mass violence, many people in society will "deserve" to be punished. Yet prosecutions, even at their most extensive, will only reach a few of the culpable. . . . [A] deterrence-based rationale for prosecutions can account for exemplary prosecutions of genocidaires. A retributive one, by contrast, cannot.

Selective prosecution further undermines retributive goals because prosecutors rarely succeed in targeting only the most culpable. "[T]he actual set of individuals who face prosecution," notes Minow, "is likely to reflect factors far removed from considered judgments about who deserves prosecution and punishment." The failure to prosecute all equally culpable individuals, however, violates the principle of proportionality, which dictates that like crimes should be treated alike. Proportionality is further undermined when prosecutions target lower-level offenders while ignoring more blameworthy ones, since such decisions do not reflect the relative level of social disapproval accorded to different crimes. Yet accepted legal principles may make it extremely difficult to convict those who orchestrated abuses rather than simply carrying them out. For example, reunified Germany found it difficult to hold East German leaders adequately accountable for ordering that fleeing citizens be shot, and decided instead to prosecute several young East German border guards. Such selective, limited prosecutions—the only kind possible in transitional justice—fail to meet the basic requirements of retributive justice. . . .

B. DETERRENCE

. . . Scholars and human rights activists have trumpeted deterrence as perhaps the most important justification for prosecution in transitional justice. Orentlicher, for example, writes that "[t]he fulcrum of the case for criminal punishment is that it is the most effective insurance against future repression." . . .

If deterrence is the justification for prosecution, one must determine if prosecutions actually prevent human rights abuses. . . . [I]t is virtually impossible to assess whether or not the threat of prosecution has ever prevented genocide and war crimes. . . . Given the unyielding stream of atrocities the world has witnessed since Nuremberg, it is difficult to argue that these trials had any discernable effect. Similarly, many of the worst atrocities in the former Yugoslavia took place after the ICTY was established. It could be that in the absence of these prosecutions, many more such atrocities would have taken place. But those who point to the deterrent effect of prosecutions bear a heavy burden of proof indeed.

Any deterrent effect that prosecutions might have will depend on context, including the risk of "getting caught," the severity of penalties, the extent of public knowledge about such sanctions, and the degree to which the crime and the offender are deterrable. . . . In the transitional justice context . . . "getting caught" usually has little to do with the risk of detection; indeed, many atrocities are committed in plain view. Rather, "getting caught" primarily concerns the chance of being punished. Thus, the fact that in the wake of mass atrocities only a small number of those implicated will ever be prosecuted undermines the logic of the deterrence argument. Those who "merely" kill, rape, and plunder, but do not mastermind the carnage, have little to fear from prosecution. Even for those who orchestrate human rights abuses, the risk of "getting caught" is low. . . . Of course, in the rare cases where perpetrators do "get caught," the sanctions may be considerable. However, it seems doubtful that severe penalties for massive human rights violations will have much deterrent value when they are so heavily discounted by the negligible likelihood of prosecution. Nor is it clear that the foot soldiers of atrocity will even be aware of the heavy sanctions imposed on a few high-level perpetrators in some far-off land.

[Further,] it is not clear how much of a deterrent effect . . . prosecutions . . . have on genocidaires. Potential war criminals may underestimate the actual risks. Robert Jackson, the lead prosecutor at Nuremberg, questioned the degree to which that tribunal could serve as a deterrent, given that wars are almost always started in anticipation that they will be won. "Personal punishment, to be suffered only in the event the war is lost," he argued, "is probably not [enough] to be a sufficient deterrent to prevent a war where the war-makers feel the chances of defeat to be negligible." Moreover, as Jon Elster notes, "even if violations are harshly punished now, how can future would-be violators know that they, if overthrown, will be treated in the same way? Incentive effects presuppose stable institutions, which almost by assumption do not exist."

Scholars have also debated whether or not massive human rights violations involve crimes or criminals that are deterrable. Are such crimes subject to a rational assessment of costs and benefits? One former prosecutor of the ICTY has claimed that "deterrence has a better chance of working with these kinds of crimes [war crimes, genocide, crimes against humanity] than it does with ordinary domestic crimes because the people who commit these acts are not hardened criminals; they're politicians or leaders of the community that have up until now been law abiding people." Such analysis seems fundamentally misguided. When "ordinary" people commit horrible crimes, it suggests that the normal restraints of law and deterrence are not working, or that these people are no longer functioning rationally. At the same time, some individuals do make rational choices when committing horrific crimes, and would therefore potentially be deterrable. As Douglass Cassel notes, certain dictators like former Yugoslav President Slobodan Milošević are manipulators, not fanatics, and might be restrained by credible threats. Other perpetrators, such as Hitler, however, are probably undeterrable. Moreover, some atrocities are carefully planned and staged, while others are "crimes of passion" or crimes of hate. Just as in the domestic context, deterrence, if it works at all, will only work against some offenders and some crimes. . . .

Given that prosecution is not a particularly effective deterrent against gross human rights violations, are alternative mechanisms any better? In comparing prosecutions and other sanctions — such as civil liability, lustration, or public shaming — we must examine their relative effectiveness in terms of marginal deterrence. . . . If deterrence depends on "intimidation or terror of the law," it is likely that a potential human rights violator will fear incarceration more than a money judgment, the loss of his job, or the shame of a public confession. Moreover, even dictators who never expect to stand trial may fear the consequences of an indictment. Once an international warrant of arrest has been issued against a suspected war criminal, that person is liable to arrest in virtually every country in the world, making it difficult for her to hold high public office in her own country and virtually impossible for her to participate in international negotiations. But even though trials threaten more severe punishment than alternative mechanisms, it is not clear what effect this increased potential sanction has on deterrence. Deterrence depends not only on the severity of the sanction but also the certainty of punishment. While the likelihood that human rights violators will face any sort of sanction remains small, some accountability mechanisms are better equipped than others to handle large numbers of offenders. Prosecutions may yield severe punishments, but they are rare. Will a highly uncertain but severe punishment have a greater deterrent effect than a lesser but more likely sanction? Perhaps the deterrent effect differs depending on the person being deterred; would-be dictators might be dissuaded by the fear of prosecution, while low-level functionaries, well-aware that they are unlikely ever to be tried, might regard lustration or truth commissions as a more credible threat.

Prosecutions may deter some future human rights abusers, and prosecutions may even have a greater deterrent value than alternative post-transition mechanisms. However, it is unlikely that post-atrocity prosecution is the most effective way to prevent future atrocities. . . . An individual's actions are often affected to a greater degree by moral norms than by fear of punishment. The reason most people do not murder is not because they are afraid of getting caught, but because they believe that murder is wrong. Similarly, the constraints a society imposes on itself may have more to do with its political culture and form of government than with concern about the possible consequences of misbehavior. Even where a person does refrain from taking a desired action out of fear of the possible consequences, legal sanctions may play only a minimal role. . . . An individual's decision not to assault someone after an insult in a bar may have more to do with a fear of being beaten up than with any worry about what the police might do. Similarly, while the threat of prosecution may deter some leaders contemplating atrocities, such persons are probably more likely to hold back out of fear of vigorous public criticism, political pressure, diplomatic isolation, economic sanctions, or even military intervention. . . .

C. REHABILITATION

. . . Advocates for prosecutions as the optimal form of transitional justice frequently use the language of rehabilitation, but their focus is on societal, not individual, rehabilitation. Few indeed would think of prosecution and punishment as a way to redeem despots like Pol Pot and Pinochet. By contrast, support for societal rehabilitation — the idea that prosecutions can change a society's moral values by "foster[ing] respect for democratic institutions and thereby deepen[ing] a society's democratic culture" — is widespread.

Prosecutions are believed to have at least three curative powers. First, prosecutions help to establish the truth. Most scholars of transitional justice agree that exposure and acknowledgement of the past is a prerequisite for future social stability. Prosecutions educate the public about the nature and extent of prior wrongdoing and contribute to a shared historical understanding. Through this educational process, writes Stephan Landsman, prosecutions "may serve both to inoculate the populace against lapses into oppressive behavior and as a means of establishing an accurate account of what actually transpired before the democratic regime came to power." Second, prosecutions help to establish the rule of law. "Holding violators accountable for their misdeeds," explains Landsman, demonstrates to "all members of society that the law's authority is superior to that of individuals." By contrast, failure to enforce the law undermines its authority. Third, prosecutions reinforce moral norms and contribute to a shared understanding that certain behavior is wrong. In order to prevent future atrocities, one must establish not only the truth about past abuses, but also a national and international consensus that such acts are unacceptable. One important way to communicate such a moral consensus is through the criminal law. Punishment thus not only reflects but also shapes moral values.

The fact that prosecutions can promote societal rehabilitation does not necessarily mean, however, that trials are more effective than non-prosecution alternatives at curing societies of their evil tendencies. The superiority of prosecution as a means of accomplishing the first goal—establishing the truth, educating the public, and forming a shared historical understanding—is dubious. Some scholars have suggested that trials provide a "higher quality" truth than alternative mechanisms because they are more narrative and dramatic. While trials may have moments of high drama, their formalism and rigidity can also make them excruciatingly boring. This is particularly true if due process standards are respected, since "[w]hat makes for a good 'morality play' tends not to make for a fair trial." Other forms of dramatic truth-telling, such as the televised confrontations between victims and perpetrators before the South African Truth and Reconciliation Commission, may be as good or better at capturing the public imagination.

Some scholars have suggested that, because of the higher evidentiary standards imposed on trials, the truth produced through prosecution is more accurate than that established through alternative mechanisms. In fact, prosecution is at best an imperfect means to develop a complete record of the past. First, rules of evidence typically reflect not only a desire to ascertain the truth, but also competing public policy or constitutional concerns. For example, in the United States relevant and probative evidence is routinely excluded from criminal prosecutions when it is considered excessively prejudicial, denies the defendant her right of confrontation, or forces a defendant to incriminate herself. Yet in the wake of gross human rights violations, gruesome photographs, flagrant hearsay and perpetrator confessions are essential to developing an accurate picture of the past. Moreover, while the threat of prosecution can be an important tool in forcing perpetrators to participate in other truth-seeking mechanisms, prosecutions themselves are ill-suited to eliciting testimony from perpetrators, the very people who know the most about the atrocities. "The primary sources of information concerning those infamies, the perpetrators themselves," notes the late South African Constitutional Court Justice John Didcott, "would hardly be willing to divulge it voluntarily, honestly, and candidly without the protection of exemptions from liability."

The most serious deficiency of prosecutions when it comes to truth-seeking is that trials focus on select individuals and thus do not account, in Minow's words, for "the complex connections among people that make massacres and genocides possible." The history produced by judges is "the by-product of particular moments of examining and cross-examining witnesses and reviewing evidence about the responsibility of particular individuals." Moreover, international tribunals are often located far from the affected society in transition, making the process less accessible to victims, witnesses, and the public. In sum, "if the goal to be served is establishing consensus and memorializing controversial, complex events, trials are not ideal."

Alternative mechanisms may be better suited than prosecution to developing full records of the past. Some have argued that due to the lower standard of proof and evidentiary and discovery advantages of civil proceedings, civil liability is better than criminal prosecution at establishing "a definitive, historically accurate account of the atrocities." This may be true, but civil trials, just like criminal trials, focus on individual responsibility and shift public focus away from systemic, shared culpability. By contrast, truth commissions are not limited to the facts of individual cases, but highlight the vast scope of and widespread complicity in the human rights violations. In addition, the history produced through truth commissions focuses not just on perpetrators but also "on victims, including forgotten victims in forgotten places."

The merits of prosecution in achieving the second goal of rehabilitation, establishing the rule of law, are also unclear. Trials conducted before impartial courts that scrupulously observe due process requirements may showcase the benefits of the rule of law and contrast favorably with the lawless behavior of the defendants. Yet when those same due process protections free those who are perceived to be guilty, fair trials may well inspire contempt for the rule of law. On the other hand, trials which are conducted unfairly or which offend legal principles will undermine the "spirit of legality" that such trials are supposed to inculcate. . . . A similar problem arises when the "small fry" are prosecuted instead of high level officials, fostering a perception that prosecutions are a form of scapegoating, not a means of achieving justice.

Perhaps the most distinctive contribution prosecution can make to societal rehabilitation is in establishing the wrongfulness of past atrocities. The prosecution and punishment of atrocities is a forceful way to disavow such conduct. A process of censure not only expresses disapproval of those who violate international human rights norms, but also serves to define and strengthen the norms themselves. While prosecutions help to establish moral norms, one cannot assume that in every case "once accusations are leveled and indictments and judgments are issued, all will come to acknowledge the barbarous evils committed by genocidaires." Rather, one must identify those situations in which prosecutions will help to forge common moral values. While prosecutions can produce moral consensus, they can also create scapegoats and feelings of bitterness, particularly where the selection of defendants appears to be politically motivated or where there is a perception that the trial represents victor's justice. One must be wary of a vicious circle: where prosecution is not grounded in moral consensus it will be seen as victor's justice. And if it is seen as victor's justice, it will lose its effectiveness as a tool for creating moral consensus. A society cannot be cured of a condition it does not regard as a disease.

Finally, is prosecution the most effective way to foster societal rehabilitation? Certainly prosecutions shape norms by condemning undesirable conduct. But trials also express the belief that "specific individuals — not entire ethnic or religious or political groups — committed atrocities." While individual crime is a component of mass atrocity, "radical evil," as Carlos Nino notes, also requires an evil political and legal framework in which to flourish. Without that framework, it is unlikely that massive, state-sponsored human rights violations will ensue regardless of whether punishment for previous violations takes place. With that framework in place and given certain antecedent circumstances, however, violations are highly likely even with previous convictions and punishment for human rights violations.

Perhaps funds spent on prosecutions would have a stronger rehabilitative effect if spent on reforming a society's political and legal framework. Prosecutions may well be less successful in rehabilitating a society than a concerted effort to reduce inequalities in wealth, provide basic public education, create functioning courts, establish civilian control over the military, ensure the independence of the press, or hold free and fair elections.

D.   RESTORATIVE JUSTICE

. . . Two major paradigms fall within the rubric of restorative justice. The first focuses on compensating victims and views crime as a harm that criminal justice should seek to undo. Under this view, the purpose of punishment is to repair injuries to victims, and thus the goal of criminal justice is for the offender to provide restitution to the victim. The second paradigm envisions crime as conflict and criminal justice as a form of conflict resolution. The basic assumptions of this approach are:

(1) Crime is primarily a conflict among individuals resulting in injuries to victims, communities and the offenders themselves; only secondarily is it lawbreaking.

(2) The overarching aim of the criminal justice process should be to reconcile parties while repairing the injuries caused by crime.
(3) The criminal justice process should facilitate active participation by victims, offenders and their communities. It should not be dominated by the government to the exclusion of others.

Under this view, the goal of criminal justice is the reconciliation of the offender, victim, and community.

These two paradigms, compensation and conflict resolution, are often linked. An apology without restitution may mean little; if a friend apologizes for taking a pen but does not return it, her statement is worthless. . . . Yet conflict resolution cannot rest on compensation alone, particularly since it is often impossible to restore to the victim what she has lost or repair the harm that she has suffered. While a stolen pen can be replaced, a murdered child cannot.

Restorative justice differs from retribution, deterrence and rehabilitation in its focus on the victim. Restorative justice raises questions about the identities of the parties to the conflict. In other words, it asks whose interests are relevant to the case. In the West, crimes are defined as offenses against the state; in this way, as Nils Christie argues, the state has stolen conflicts from victims, communities and offenders. "Virtually every facet of the criminal justice system works to reduce victims, offenders and communities to passive participants," notes Daniel Van Ness. Restorative justice aims to return conflicts to the parties to the conflict. Yet the idea that crimes are offenses against society at large should not be ignored, for offenders harm not only specific victims but also entire societies. Thus, restorative justice must consider the interests of both the individual victim and the wider community.

Theoretically, the compensatory paradigm of restorative justice is somewhat disconnected from culpability, since the degree of harm caused may not reflect the blameworthiness of the offender. Proportionality in this context is based on the amount of harm inflicted on the victim, not the maliciousness of the offender's intent. The conflict resolution paradigm, on the other hand, is more likely adequately to address culpability; a victim will be angrier at someone who hits her intentionally than at someone who does so accidentally, and will require more of the offender in order to resolve the conflict. . . .

In the context of transitional justice, reparations can be seen as a form of compensation, while approaches seeking to heal society's wounds can be understood within a conflict resolution paradigm. In both cases, as in the domestic context, victims claim a central role. [The following] . . . will first look at reparations as a form of transitional justice, and then assess the capacity of prosecutions to reconcile victims, offenders, and society as a whole.

Reparations in the wake of massive human rights violations are designed to provide at least partial restitution to victims. While compensation typically involves monetary payments to individuals, other types of restitution, like building memorials or naming streets for victims, are less tangible and less directly focused on individuals. The truth itself can also be understood as a form of reparation. When the silence is broken, and families learn where the bodies are buried or victims discover the identities of their torturers, the injury caused by past abuse may begin to be repaired.

Reparations should not only acknowledge the survivor's loss, but also repair the harm caused. While this is a valuable goal, it is often difficult to achieve in practice. Where former regimes have harmed both individuals and entire communities, should scarce resources be used to pay compensation to individual victims, or to rebuild a society victimized by poverty, appalling health care and lack of education? Moreover, monetary measures cannot remedy non-monetary harms, like the loss of a child or the agony of remembered torture. "[N]o market measures exist," writes Minow, "for the value of living an ordinary life, without nightmares or survivor guilt." Reparations are likely to be grossly disproportionate to the damage caused, and many thus trivialize suffering. In fact, victims frequently express only modest demands for reparations, such as a tombstone or death certificate for their loved ones or the removal of bullets from their own bodies. Often, their most significant demand is for the truth. Thus while restitution can never fully compensate victims, it can serve an important symbolic function.

Proponents of prosecution sometimes argue that trials are useful as a basis for reparations. This justification seems dubious, at least insofar as it is used to support the primacy of prosecutions. Since prosecution focuses on establishing the guilt of a few individual perpetrators, it is not an ideal tool for identifying victims who deserve compensation. Moreover, because prosecutions are adversarial, defendants may never reveal those facts about the past which victims most want to know. Arguably, alternative mechanisms are better able to identify victims, as well as to provide them with a more comprehensive, and more personal, account of the past. Truth commissions and civil suits offer at least the possibility that victims will be compensated. Reparations may even take the form of governmental or international aid programs providing medical treatment, scholarships for victims' children, or preferential access to government services such as public housing or transportation. Any of these approaches is more likely to provide real restitution to victims than prosecutions. Thus the reparative paradigm of restorative justice offers little justification for prosecution.

How do prosecutions hold up under the conflict resolution paradigm of restorative justice? First, we must ask if reconciliation or forgiveness are even possible after massive human rights violations. In the domestic context, restorative justice programs are usually restricted to minor offenses. Yet conflict resolution in the context of transitional justice requires interaction between those who carried out and those who suffered from horrific atrocities. "Healing," worries Minow, may be "an absurd or even obscene notion for those who have died," as well as for the survivors, who often feel as if they "have died or live among the dead." Susan Dwyer expresses a similar concern that "[r]econciliation is being urged upon people who have been bitter and murderous enemies, upon victims and perpetrators of terrible human rights abuses, upon groups of individuals whose very self-conceptions have been structured in terms of historical and often state-sanctioned relations of dominance and submission." Absent a clear explanation of reconciliation and what it requires, she continues, "proposing reconciliation will seem like a political sop aimed at masking moral defeat."

So, what is reconciliation? Scholars of transitional justice distinguish between the repair of relationships that will suffice for a society to move forward and unrealistic expectations of transformative interactions between victims and perpetrators. Dwyer, for example, believes apologies and forgiveness are not absolutely required for future interaction. She contrasts personal reconciliation between victims and perpetrators, which may be too much to ask, with national reconciliation, which she argues is more possible. What is necessary if perpetrators and victims are to live together in the future, she claims, is the development of a common national historical narrative, based on agreed-upon facts and a shared interpretation of them. Shriver, in contrast, prefers the concept of "forgiveness." Believing victims must have more courage than Dwyer requires, Shriver asks victims "to face still-rankling past evils with first regard for the truth of what actually happened; with resistance to the lures of revenge; with empathy—and no excusing—for all the agents and sufferers of the evil; and with real intent on the part of the sufferers to resume life alongside the evildoers or their political successors."

Whatever words we use to describe it, the concept of restorative justice is certainly relevant to transitional justice. The horrors of the past can be seen as a form of conflict, and the goal of transitional justice as conflict resolution. Transitional justice can be organized so as to give victims a central role and repair relationships between them, perpetrators, and society at large. In this way, transitional justice can strive for at least enough forgiveness, reconciliation, or healing to make coexistence possible.

A reconciliation-based argument for prosecution is premised on the notion that retribution is a precondition for societal healing. There has been considerable debate about the tension between "justice," the requirement that those who violate human rights be punished, and "peace," the desire for both social cohesion and an end to human rights violations. Historically, the concern has been that pushing for justice would jeopardize peace. Increasingly, however, diplomats involved in settling violent disputes and politicians seeking to move their countries forward recognize that a focus on past atrocities is not an obstacle to stability and conflict resolution, but is, in Kritz's words, "an integral and unavoidable element of the peace process."

Proponents of prosecution have equated this new framework, in which justice is a precondition for peace, to an argument that retributive punishment must precede social healing. Accordingly, before there can be reconciliation in places like Bosnia and Rwanda, there must be retribution, at least as far as the most serious offenders are concerned. To achieve closure, "individuals emerging from massive abuse and trauma [must] develop appropriate mechanisms to confront and process that past experience." But the need to face one's past does not adequately explain why such a confrontation must be retributive. Forgiving, after all, is not actually the same as forgetting. . . .

Truth commissions might be better suited to a restorative model of transitional justice than prosecutions. Truth commissions can focus on the victims, craft a shared narrative about the past as the basis for a shared future, and facilitate the active involvement of victims, perpetrators, and the larger community. In essence, truth commissions return the conflict to those who participated in it. The more open, discursive nature of truth commissions better addresses the problem of widespread complicity in massive human rights violations. Moreover, the informality of the process brings other benefits such as the ability of officials to grieve publicly with victims. . . . Furthermore, restorative justice is multi-directional. Prosecutions may be appropriate where individuals can be clearly classified as either victims or perpetrators. Truth commissions, on the other hand, recognize that this distinction is not always clear. During periods of mass atrocity or repression, individuals usually assume different roles over the course of the conflict. As a result, apologies must be both given and received.

Of course, truth commissions will not always work as a form of restorative justice. Repairing relationships through discussion and confrontation requires not only that all parties be engaged in the process, but also that perpetrators recognize their blameworthiness and accept responsibility for past actions. Amnesty can be understood as an annulment of the appropriate retributive penalty in return for truthtelling. But offenders may be unwilling to tell the truth or to express contrition. Moreover, to be meaningful, apologies must be linked to restitution. Reconciliation in the wake of atrocity requires "the credibility that can be established only by implementation of social and economic programs that concretely address the substantive injustices" of the past. Even those who acknowledge their own culpability or complicity through a national truth-telling process may recoil at the loss of privileges and power that true accountability demands. How much reconciliation can be achieved if in post-apartheid South Africa, for example, whites admit that their economic, social, and political status was based on a morally bankrupt system, but then refuse to accept sharply redistributive taxation?

The fundamental difficulty with restorative justice is that it cannot adequately address demands for retribution. This is not really a problem with restorative justice itself, but rather with the difficulty of reconciling two competing goals of transitional justice. . . .

NOTES AND QUESTIONS

1. Providing some form of monetary compensation to victims is viewed by many as a cornerstone of "restorative justice." One noted scholar has observed that "[n]otwithstanding the widespread abuses of recent history, few efforts have been undertaken [on the national level] to provide redress to either the victims or their families. This often results from the reality that the provision of remedies and reparations are undertaken by either the violator regime or a successor government that has treated post-conflict justice as a bargaining chip rather than an affirmative duty." M. Cherif Bassiouni, Introduction to International Criminal Law 721 (2003). As Michael P. Scharf explains:

> The Universal Declaration of Human Rights, the International Covenant on Civil and Political Rights, the European Convention on Human Rights, the American Convention on Human Rights, and the Torture Convention all recognize the right of victims of human rights abuses to receive compensation for their injury. Compensable injuries include loss of life, physical or psychological injury, loss of liberty, loss of or damage to property, loss of opportunity, and other injuries proximately caused by the abuses. Compensation can either be monetary or in the form of non-monetary reparation such as provision of new employment, pension rights, medical and educational services, social security, and housing. A truth commission can play an important role in the provision of such compensation.
>
> The most obvious method of obtaining victim compensation is for the injured party, or their next of kin, to bring suit in the courts of the state involved. However, victims of human rights abuses often do not know the identity of those who perpetrated the abuses against them. Even when the identity of the persecutors is known, the victims frequently lack evidence of the persecutors' participation, as there are rarely written records of abuses and witnesses are generally reluctant to come forward. A truth commission could assist in the attainment of compensation through the judicial process by transmitting to the competent judicial authorities the commission's findings that a victim has suffered injury due to the acts of a specific individual or governmental entity. Yet, even with the findings of a truth commission, there are likely to be other obstacles to obtaining victim compensation through domestic courts: The individuals directly responsible frequently lack sufficient resources for adequate compensation; amnesties often extinguish

the possibility of civil compensation; and the limitations of national law often deprive victims of any cause of action.

Some countries, such as the United States, have opened their courts to foreign citizens wishing to bring suit for human rights abuses committed in a foreign country. The Alien Tort Claims Act provides the U.S. courts with jurisdiction over "any civil action by an alien for a tort only, committed in violation of the law of nations or a treaty of the United States," and the . . . Torture Victim Protection Act provides a private right of action against "an individual who, under actual or apparent authority, or color of law, of any foreign nation," subjects another individual to "torture" or to "extrajudicial killing." If hurdles such as Foreign Sovereign Immunity, the Act of State Doctrine, and the Political Question Doctrine can be overcome, a plaintiff armed with the findings of an international truth commission that the defendant is responsible for the plaintiff's injuries is likely to achieve success on the merits. Unfortunately, such suits ordinarily represent little more than symbolic justice, as few of the defendants would have assets in the United States that could be attached in execution of the judgment.

Another scheme for victim compensation would involve the payment of compensation by the government, rather than by the individual perpetrators. When, as is usually the case, the offender is a government authority or a private person acting as the agent of a government, it should be the duty of the state itself to redress the injury. Under the broad international law principles of state responsibility, the state is also responsible for failing to prevent or respond adequately to human rights violations in its territory committed by purely private parties or agents of a foreign government. In accordance with the "principle of the continuity of the State in international law," the duty of the state to pay compensation applies even to a new government that has replaced the government responsible for the abuses. Recognizing this principle, after World War II the Federal Republic of Germany provided individual compensation amounting to over $10 billion to over three million victims of Nazi persecution. More recently, Albania, Bulgaria, Czechoslovakia, and Russia have enacted laws providing compensation and other relief to the victims of political repression under their former totalitarian governments.

Unfortunately, very few other states have ever voluntarily agreed to pay compensation to the victims of a prior regime. There is precedent, however, for an outside entity to compel a government to pay victim compensation. For example, the European Court of Human Rights has ordered governments to pay compensation to victims of violations in well over one hundred cases. A few of the established domestic truth commissions have put pressure on the national government to provide appropriate victim compensation. For example, the Chile Commission for Truth and Reconciliation recommended that the government award victims various social benefits, such as health care (both physical and psychological), and financial support for the education of children of persons killed or missing. The El Salvador truth commission concluded that "justice does not stop at punishment; it also demands reparation. The victims and, in most cases, their families, are entitled to moral and material compensation." Its report called for a special fund to be established for this purpose, to be funded by the government, and urged foreign governments to allocate one percent of their aid to El Salvador to the fund as well.

Michael P. Scharf, The Case for a Permanent International Truth Commission, 7 Duke J. Comp. & Intl. L. 375, 388-392 (1997).

2. Consider the following chart. What "grades" would you give each accountability mechanism in light of the goals identified? Would those grades depend, for example, on whether one found oneself in Northern Ireland as opposed to South Africa? Would this chart look different for South American countries as opposed to the former communist countries of Eastern Europe?

	Retribution	Deterrence	Making a record	Social healing	Individual healing for victims	Due process	Building rule of law in affected society
International tribunals							
Hybrid tribunals							
National courts							
Informal/ local justice							
Lustration/ Vetting							
Civil litigation							
Suit in human rights tribunals							
TRCs							

TABLE OF CASES

Principal cases are in italics.

TABLE OF AUTHORITIES

INDEX